T5-CCK-232

DISCARDED BY
MEMPHIS PUBLIC LIBRARY

Volume 1 • 2002

WHAT DO I READ NEXT?

A Reader's Guide to Current Genre Fiction

- Fantasy
- Popular Fiction
- Romance
- Horror
- Mystery
- Science Fiction
- Historical
- Inspirational
- Western

ISSN 1052-2212

Volume 1 • 2002

WHAT DO I READ NEXT?

A Reader's Guide to Current Genre Fiction

- Fantasy
- Popular Fiction
- Romance
- Horror
- Mystery
- Science Fiction
- Historical
- Inspirational
- Western

NEIL BARRON
TOM BARTON
DANIEL S. BURT
MELISSA HUDAK
D. R. MEREDITH
KRISTIN RAMSDELL
TOM and ENID SCHANTZ

GALE®

THOMSON
GALE

Detroit • New York • San Diego • San Francisco • Cleveland • New Haven, Conn. • Waterville, Maine • London • Munich

THOMSON
GALE

What Do I Read Next?, 2002 Volume 1

Project Editor
Beverly Baer

Editorial
Nancy Franklin
Elizabeth Manar

Editorial Support Services
Magdalena Cureton

Data Capture
Civie Green

Product Design
Michael Logusz

Manufacturing
Stacy Melson

© 2002 by Gale. Gale is an imprint of The Gale Group, Inc., a division of Thomson Learning, Inc.

Gale and Design™ and Thomson Learning™ are trademarks used herein under license.

For more information, contact
The Gale Group, Inc.
27500 Drake Rd.
Farmington Hills, MI 48331-3535
Or you can visit our Internet site at
http://www.gale.com

ALL RIGHTS RESERVED
No part of this work covered by the copyright hereon may be reproduced or used in any form or by any means-graphic, electronic, or mechanical, including photocopying, recording, taping, Web distribution, or information storage retrieval systems--without the written permission of the publisher.

This publication is a creative work fully protected by all applicable copyright laws, as well as by misappropriation, trade secret, unfair competition, and other applicable laws. The authors and editors of this work have added value to the underlying factual material herein through one or more of the following: unique and original selection, coordination, expression, arrangement, and classification of the information.

For permission to use material from this product, submit your request via Web at, http://www.galeedit.com/permissions, or you may download our Permissions Request form and submit your request by fax or mail to:

Permissions Department
The Gale Group, Inc
27500 Drake Rd.
Farmington Hills, MI 48331- 3535
Permissions Hotline:
248-699-8006 or 800-877-4253 ext. 8006
Fax: 248-699- 8074 or 800-762-4058

While every effort has been made to ensure the reliability of the information presented in this publication, The Gale Group, Inc. does not guarantee the accuracy of the data contained herein. The Gale Group, Inc. accepts no payment for listing; and inclusion in the publication of any organization, agency, institution, publication, service, or individual does not imply endorsement of the editors or publisher. Errors brought to the attention of the publisher and verified to the satisfaction of the publisher will be corrected in future editions

ISBN 0-7876-5294-6
ISSN 1052-2212

Printed in the United States of America
10987654321

Contents

Introduction vii

About the Genre Experts ix

Key to Genre Terms xi

Award Winners xix

What Do I Read Next?

Mystery in Review 1
Mystery Titles 7

Romance Fiction in Review 89
Romance Titles 97

Western Books in Review 159
Western Titles 163

Fantasy Fiction in 2001 191
Fantasy Titles 195

The Year in Horror 2001 223
Horror Titles 227

Science Fiction in 2001 257
For More Information about Fantastic Fiction 259
Science Fiction Titles 263

Historical Fiction in Review 291
Historical Titles 295

Inspirational Fiction in Review 345
Inspirational Titles 349

Popular Fiction in Review 381
Popular Fiction Titles 385

Indexes

Series Index 433

Time Period Index 439

Geographic Index 447

Genre Index 461

Subject Index 473

Character Name Index 495

Character Description Index 523

Author Index 563

Title Index 609

Introduction

Thousands of books are published each year intended for devoted fans of genre fiction. Dragons, outlaws, lovers, murderers, monsters, and aliens abound on our own world or on other worlds, throughout time--all featured in the pages of fantasy, western, romance, mystery, horror, science fiction, historical, inspirational, and popular fiction. Given the huge variety of titles available each year, added to the numbers from previous years, readers can be forgiven if they're stumped by the question "What do I read next?" And that's where this book comes in.

Designed as a tool to assist in the exploration of genre fiction, *What Do I Read Next?* guides the reader to both current and classic recommendations in nine widely read genres: Mystery, Romance, Western, Fantasy, Horror, Science Fiction, Historical, Inspirational, and Popular Fiction. *What Do I Read Next?* allows readers quick and easy access to specific data on recent titles in these popular genres. Plus, each entry provides alternate reading selections, thus coming to the rescue of librarians and booksellers, who are often unfamiliar with a genre, yet must answer the question frequently posed by their patrons and customers "What do I read next?"

Details on 1,214 Titles

Volume 1 of this year's edition of *What Do I Read Next?* contains 1,214 entries for titles published in late 2001 and 2002. These entries are divided into sections for Mystery, Romance, Western, Fantasy, Horror, Science Fiction, Historical, Inspirational, and Popular Fiction. Experts in each field compile the entries for their respective genres. The experts also discuss topics relevant to their genres in essays that appear at the beginning of each section.

The criteria for inclusion of specific titles vary somewhat from genre to genre. In genres such as Romance and Mystery where large numbers of titles are published each year, the inclusion criteria are more selective, and the experts attempted to select the recently published books they considered the best. In genres such as Horror and Westerns, where the amount of new material is relatively small, a broader range of titles is represented, including many titles published by small or independent houses and some Young Adult books.

The entries are listed alphabetically by main author in each genre section. Most provide the following information:

- **Author or editor's name** and real name if a pseudonym is used. Co-authors, co-editors, and illustrators are also listed where applicable.
- **Book title.**
- **Date and place of publication; name of publisher.**
- **Series name.**
- **Story type:** Specific categories within each genre, identified by the compiling expert. Definitions of these types are listed in the "Key to Genre Terms" section following the Introduction.
- **Subject(s):** Gives the subject matter covered by the title.
- **Major character(s):** Names and brief descriptions of up to three characters featured in the title.
- **Time period(s):** Tells when the story takes place.
- **Locale(s)**: Tells where the story takes place.
- **What the book is about:** A brief plot summary.
- **Where it's reviewed:** Citations to reviews of the book, including the source of the review, date of the source, and the page on which the review appears. Reviews are included from genre-specific sources such as *Locus* and *Affaire de Coeur* as well as more general reviewing sources such as *Booklist* and *Publishers Weekly.*
- **Other books by the author:** Titles and publication dates of other books the author has written, useful for those wanting to read more by a particular author..
- **Other books you might like:** Titles by other authors written on a similar theme or in a similar style. These titles further the reader's exploration of the genre.

Indexes Answer Readers' Questions

The nine indexes in *What Do I Read Next?*, used separately or in conjunction with each other, create many pathways to the featured titles, answering general questions or locating specific titles. For example:

"Are there any new Faith Fairchild books?"

The SERIES INDEX lists entries by the name of the series of which they are a part.

"I like Regency Romances. Can you recommend any new ones?"

The GENRE INDEX breaks each genre into story types or more specialized areas. In the Romance genre for example, there is a story type heading "Regency." For the definitions of story types, see the "Key to Genre Terms" beginning on page xi.

"I'm looking for a story set in Paris..."

The GEOGRAPHIC INDEX lists titles by their locale. This can help readers pinpoint an area in which they may have a particular interest, such as their hometown, another country, or even Cyberspace.

"Do you know of any science fiction stories set during the 2020s?"

The TIME PERIOD INDEX is a chronological listing of the time settings in which the main entry titles take place.

"What books are available that feature teachers?"

The CHARACTER DESCRIPTION INDEX identifies the major characters by occupation (e.g. Accountant, Editor, Librarian) or persona (e.g. Cyborg, Noblewoman, Stowaway).

"Has anyone written any new books with Sherlock Holmes in them?"

The CHARACTER NAME INDEX lists the major characters named in the entries. This can help readers who remember some information about a book, but not an author or title.

"What has Janette Oke written recently?"

The AUTHOR INDEX contains the names of all authors featured in the entries and those listed under "Other books you might like."

"I want to read a book that's similar to Isabel Allende's *Portrait in Sepia*."

The TITLE INDEX includes all main entry titles and all titles recommended under "Other books by the author" and "Other books you might like" in one alphabetical listing. Thus a reader can find a specific title, new or old, then go to that entry to find out what new titles are similar.

"I'm interested in books that depict military life."

The SUBJECT INDEX is an alphabetical listing of all the subjects covered by the main entry titles.

The indexes can also be used together to narrow down or broaden choices. A reader interested in Mysteries set in New York during the 19th century would consult the TIME PERIOD INDEX and GEOGRAPHIC INDEX to see which titles appear in both. Time Travel is a common theme in Science Fiction but occasionally appears in other genres such as Fantasy and Romance. Searching for this theme in other genres would enable a reader to cross over into previously unknown realms of reading experiences. And with the AUTHOR and TITLE indexes, which include all books listed under "Other books by the author" and "Other books you might like," it is easy to compile an extensive list of recommended reading, beginning with a recently published title or a classic from the past.

Suggestions Are Welcome

The editors welcome any comments and suggestions for enhancing and improving *What Do I Read Next?*. Please address correspondence to the Editors, *What Do I Read Next?*, at the following address:

Gale Group
27500 Drake Rd.
Farmington Hills, MI 48331-3535
Phone: 248-699-GALE
Toll-free: 800-347-GALE
Fax: 248-699-8054

About the Genre Experts

Neil Barron coordinator of the Science Fiction, Fantasy, and Horror Fiction sections, is the editor of the reader guides *Anatomy of Wonder: A Critical Guide to Science Fiction* (Bowker, 4th ed., 1995) and *Fantasy and Horror: A Critical and Historical Guide to Literature, Illustration, Film, TV, Radio, and the Internet* (Scarecrow Press, 1999). He welcomes comments at rneilbarron@hotmail.com.

Tom Barton (Popular Fiction) is a reference librarian at the Rebecca Crown Library, Dominican University in River Forest, Illinois. A former journalist and community organizer, Barton lives in the West Beverly neighborhood of Chicago.

Daniel S. Burt (Historical Fiction) is a writer and college literature professor who teaches courses on the novel in the nineteenth and twentieth centuries and who for nine years was a dean at Wesleyan University in Middletown, Connecticut. He is the author of *What Historical Novel Do I Read Next?* (Gale, 1997), *The Literary 100: A Ranking of the Most Influential Novelists, Playwrights, and Poets of All Time* (Facts on File, 2001), and *The Biography Book* (Greenwood/Oryx, 2001). He is at work on *The Novel 100* forthcoming in 2002 and is the general editor of *The Chronology of American Literature* to be published by Houghton Mifflin. Burt lives with his wife on Cape Cod, Massachusetts.

Melissa Hudak (Inspirational Fiction) is a medical librarian for Methodist Medical Center in Peoria, Illinois. She was previously employed in public libraries and wrote a column on inspirational literature for *Library Journal*.

D.R. Meredith (Western Fiction) is a full time writer of western historical novels and three mystery series. The award-winning Sheriff series are western mysteries set in rural Texas. *The Sheriff and the Panhandle Murders* and *The Sheriff and the Branding Iron Murders* were actually first published as Westerns (Walker, 1984 and 1985). *Murder by Impulse* (Ballantine, 1988) and *Murder by Deception* (Ballantine, 1989) were both nominated for the Anthony Award. Her latest title in the Megan Clark series is *By Hook or by Book* (Berkley, 2000). In addition to writing, she is book review editor for *Roundup Magazine*, reviews western literature for the *Amarillo Globe-News*, is a speaker at writers' conferences, colleges and universities, libraries, and civic clubs, and is Liaison Chairperson for the American Crime Writers League. She is a member of Western Writers of America, Mystery Writers of America, and Sisters in Crime.

Kristin Ramsdell (Romance Fiction) is a librarian at California State University, Hayward and is a nationally known speaker and consultant on the subject of romance fiction. She writes a romance review column for *Library Journal* and is the author of *Romance Fiction: A Guide to the Genre* (Libraries Unlimited, 1999) and its predecessor, *Happily Ever After: A Guide to Reading Interests in Romance Fiction* (Libraries Unlimited, 1987). She was named Librarian of the Year by Romance Writers of America in 1996.

Tom & Enid Schantz (Mystery Fiction) have been in the mystery business for 30 years. From 1970 to 1980 they ran a rare and out of print mail order business as The Aspen Bookhouse and later as The Rue Morgue Mystery Bookshop. Between 1980 and 2000, they operated a retail mystery bookstore, The Rue Morgue, in Boulder, Colorado. During that same period, they edited a monthly publication, *The Purloined Letter*, which reviews all new mystery titles. They have written a monthly crime fiction column for the *Denver Post* since 1982. In the 1970s, they operated The Aspen Press, which published books of detective stories and items of Sherlockiana. In 1997, they founded The Rue Morgue Press, which continues to publish reprints of classic mysteries from the turn of the century to the 1960s. They continue to operate a mail order book business as The Rue Morgue, which specializes in vintage mystery fiction, and are the recipients of the 2001 Raven from the Mystery Writers of America in honor of their distinguished contribution to mystery bookselling and publishing.

Contributors

John Charles (Romance Fiction), a reference librarian and retrospective fiction selector for the Scottsdale Public Library, also reviews books for both *Library Journal* and *VOYA* (*Voice of Youth Advocates*) and co-authors *VOYA's* annual "Clueless: Adult Mysteries with Young Adult Appeal" column. John Charles is co-author of *The Mystery Readers' Advisory: The Librarian's Clues to Murder and Mayhem* (ALA, 2001). Along with co-author Shelley Mosley, Charles has twice been the recipient of the Romance Writers of America's Veritas Award.

Don D'Ammassa (Science Fiction and Fantasy) has been reading SF and fantasy for almost 40 years and has been the book reviewer for the *Science Fiction Chronicle* for the past 16 years. He has had fiction published in fantastic magazines and anthologies and has contributed essays to a variety of reference books dealing with fantastic literature.

Stefan Dziemianowicz (Horror Fiction) is a medical editor for a New York-based law book publisher. A co-editor of the quarterly journal, *Necrofile*, he authored the definitive study, *The Annotated Guide to Unknown and Unknown Worlds* (Starmont House, 1991) and is also the author of *Bloody Mary and Other Tales for a Dark Night* (Barnes and Noble, 2000). He has co-edited numerous horror and mystery anthologies--among them the Bram Stoker Award-winning *Horrors! 365 Scary Stories* (Barnes and Noble, 1998).

Shelley Mosley (Romance Fiction), a library manager and romance genre specialist for the Glendale (AZ) Library System, was named 2001 Librarian of the Year by Romance Writers of America. She writes romantic comedies with Deborah Mazoyer under the pen name Deborah Shelley. Their book, *Talk about Love*, was a Holt Medallion finalist for Best First Book. With co-author John Charles, also a *What Do I Read Next?* contributor, she has won two Romance Writers of America's Veritas Awards. In addition to two newspaper columns, she has written articles for *Wilson Library Bulletin*, *Library Journal*, *Romance Writer's Report,* and *VOYA*.

Key to Genre Terms

The following is a list of terms used to classify the story type of each novel included in *What Do I Read Next?* along with brief definitions of the terms. To find books that fall under a particular story type heading, see the Genre Index.

Mystery Story Types

Action/Adventure: Minimal detection; not usually espionage, but can contain rogue police or out of control spies.

Amateur Detective: Detective work is performed by a non-professional rather than by police or a private detective.

Anthology: A collection of short stories by different authors, usually sharing a common theme.

Collection: A book of short stories by a single author.

Domestic: Fiction relating to household and family matters. Concerned with psychological and emotional needs of family members.

Espionage: Involving the CIA, KGB, or other organizations whose main focus is the collection of information from the other side. Can be either violent or quiet.

Historical: Usually detection set in an earlier time frame than the present.

Historical/Ancient Rome: Covering the history of Rome from its founding and the Roman Republic before Augustus through the decline and fall of the Roman Empire in the fifth century.

Humor: A mystery, but the main focus is humorous.

Legal: Main focus is on a lawyer, though it does not always involve courtroom action.

Police Procedural: A story in which the action is centered around a police officer.

Private Detective: Usually detection, involving a professional for hire.

Psychological Suspense: Main focus is on the workings of the mind, usually with some danger involved.

Traditional: Usually means the classic British mystery, but is coming to mean non-private detective fiction.

Romance Story Types

Anthology: A collection of short stories by different authors, usually sharing a common theme.

Contemporary: A romance set in the present.

Contemporary/Fantasy: A contemporary romance that makes use of fantasy or supernatural elements.

Fantasy: A romance that is not a Gothic or a Romantic Suspense but contains fantasy or supernatural elements.

Futuristic: A romance with a science fiction setting. Often these stories are set on other planets, aboard spaceships or space stations, or on Earth in an imaginary future or, in some cases, past.

Gothic: A romance with a strong mystery suspense plot that emphasizes mood, atmosphere, and/or supernatural or paranormal elements. Unexplained events, ancient family secrets, and a general feeling of impending doom often characterize these tales. These stories are most often set in the past, but several authors (e.g. Phyllis Whitney and Barbara Michaels) write gothics with contemporary settings.

Historical: A romance that takes place in the past that doesn't fall into one of the more specific Historical categories.

Historical/American West: Set in the Western portion of the United States, usually during the second half of the nineteenth century. Stories often involve the hardships of pioneer life (Indian raids, range wars, climatic disasters, etc.) and the main characters (most often the hero) can be of Native American extraction.

Historical/American West Coast: Set in the American Far West (California, Oregon, Washington, or Alaska). Stories often focus on the Gold Rush and the tension between Spanish Land Grant families and immigrants from the Pacific Rim, usually China.

Historical/Americana: A novel set in the past that features uniquely American themes, such as small town life.

Historical/Colonial America: Set in America before the American Revolution, 1620-1775. Stories featuring the Jamestown Colony, the Salem Witch Trials, and the French and Indian War are especially popular.

Historical Elizabethan: A romance set during the reign of Elizabeth I of England (1558-1603). There is some overlap with the last part of the Historical Renaissance category but the emphasis is British.

Historical/Georgian: Set during the reigns of the first three "Georges" of England. Roughly corresponds to the eighteenth century. Stories often focus on the Jacobite Rebellions and the escapades of Bonnie Prince Charlie.

Historical/Medieval: Set during the Middle Ages, approximately the fifth through the fifteenth centuries. Stories feature battles, raids, crusades, and court intrigues; plot-lines associated with the Battle of Hastings (1066) are especially popular.

Historical/NapoleonicWars: Set between 1803-1815 during the wars waged by and against France under Napoleon Bonaparte.

Historical/Post-American Civil War: Set in the years following the Civil War/War Between the States, generally from 1865 into the 1870s.

Historical/Regency: A romance that is set during the Regency period (1811-1820) but is not a "Regency Romance" (see below).

Historical/Renaissance: A romance set in the years of the Renaissance in Europe, generally lasting from the 14th through the 17th centuries.

Historical/Seventeenth Century: A romance set during the seventeenth century. Stories of this type often center around the clashes between the Royalists and the Cromwellians and the Restoration.

Historical/Victorian: Set during the reign of Queen Victoria, 1837-1901. This designation does not include works with a predominately American setting.

Historical/Victorian America: Set in America, usually the Eastern part, during the Victorian Period, 1837-1901.

Holiday Themes: A romance that focuses on or is set during a particular holiday or holiday season (e.g. Christmas, Valentine's Day, Mardi Gras).

Humor: Romance with an amusing story line.

Inspirational: A romance with an uplifting, often Christian, theme and usually considered "innocent."

Multicultural: A romance in which the ethnic background of the characters is integral to the story.

Paranormal: Novel contains supernatural elements. Story may include ghosts, UFOs, aliens, demons, and haunted houses among other unexplained phenomenon.

Regency: A light romance involving the British upper classes, set during the Regency Period, 1811-1820. During this time, the Prince of Wales acted as Prince Regent because of the incapacity of his father, George III. In 1820, "Prinny" became George IV. These stories, in the style of Jane Austen, are essentially comedies of manners and the emphasis is on language, wit, and style. Georgette Heyer set the standard for the modern version of this genre. This designation is also given to stories of similar type that may not fit precisely within the Regency time period.

Romantic Suspense: A romance with a strong mystery suspense plot. This is a broad category including works in the tradition of Mary Stewart as well as the newer women-in-jeopardy tales by writers such as Mary Higgins Clark. These stories usually have contemporary settings but some are also set in the past.

Saga: A multi-generational story that usually centers around one particular family and its trials, tribulations, successes, and loves.

Time Travel: A romance in which characters from one time are transported either literally or in spirit to another time period. The time shifts are usually between the present and another historical period.

Western Story Types

Anthology: A collection of short stories by different authors, usually sharing a common theme.

Collection: A book of short stories by a single author.

Historical: A story that emphasizes accuracy of historical settings and characters rather than the characters and themes of the traditional Western. Generally these stories are set in locations or time periods outside the "cowboy" West.

Indian Culture: These historical novels center on the lives, customs, and cultures of characters who are American Indians or who lived among the Indians.

Indian Wars: Often traditional Westerns, these stories are set during the period of the Indian wars and rely on this warfare for plots, characters, and themes.

Man Alone: A lone man, alienated from the society that would normally support him, faces overwhelming dangers in this subgenre of the traditional Western.

Modern: Stories set after the closing of the frontier, generally from about 1920 to the present, but retaining the essential characteristics of the Western.

Mystery: A story in which the main plot feature involves the solution to a crime where the perpetrator or motive is not known to characters or readers. The detective is often an amateur, but may be a peace officer.

Quest: Another subgroup, usually of the traditional, the Quest shows its central characters on a journey filled with dangers to reach some worthwhile goal.

Ranch Life: The basic cowboy story, in which the plot and characters are inextricably bound up in the workings of a ranch.

Saga: A book or series that follows the fortunes of a single family, usually over more than a single generation.

Traditional: The classic Western from Owen Wister to today. Traditional Westerns may deal with virtually any time period or situation, but they are related by shared conventions of setting and characterization.

Young Adult: Commonly indicated by publishers to help librarians categorize fiction likely to be of interest to teenage readers.

Fantasy Story Types

Adventure: The character(s) must face a series of obstacles, which may include monsters, conflict with other travelers, war, interference by supernatural elements, interference by nature, and so on.

Alternate Universe: More accurately, in most cases, alternate history, in which the South won the Civil War, the Nazis triumphed, etc.

Alternate World: The story starts out in the everyday world, but the main character is transported to an alternate/parallel world by supernatural means.

Anthology: A collection of short fiction by different authors usually related in theme or setting.

Collection: A book of short stories by a single author.

Contemporary: The story is set in the everyday world, but elements of the fantastic begin to intrude (e.g., a unicorn appears or the character suddenly has the ability to perform magic).

Historical: This subgenre could also be called Alternate History. Using history as a backdrop, the author adds fantastic elements to build the story.

Horror: Although the story has been classified as Fantasy in this section, there are strong elements of Horror (e.g., psychological, supernatural, etc.).

Humor: Fantasy in which humor, from cerebral to slapstick, is prominent.

Legend: A story based on a legend, myth, or fairy tale that has been rewritten.

Magic Conflict: The main conflict of the story stems from magical interference. Protagonists may be caught in the middle of a conflict between sorcerers or may themselves be engaged in conflict with other sorcerers.

Military: Stories that can range from space wars to more local battles; most such stories tend to glorify military virtues.

Mystery: Although the story has been classified as Fantasy in this section, there are strong elements of Mystery (e.g., suspense, detectives, etc.).

Post-Disaster: Story set in a much degraded environment, frequently involving a reduction in population and the resulting loss of access to processes, resources, technology, etc.

Quest: The character embarks on a journey to achieve a specific goal, such as retrieving a jewel from an evil wizard.

Sword and Sorcery: The tried and true formula of this subgenre has a muscle-bound swordsman, who is innocent of thought and common sense, up against evil sorcerers and sorceresses, who naturally lose in the end because they are evil. However, Sword and Sorcery continues to be updated, with heroines instead of heroes and a bit of thought prior to action.

Time Travel: In Science Fiction Time Travel, there is a rational explanation rooted in science for the character's ability to move through time. In Fantasy Time Travel, the rational explanation is rooted in the supernatural.

Young Adult: Commonly indicated by publishers to help librarians categorize fiction likely to be of interest to teenage readers, this subgenre frequently involves a child or teenager maturing by accepting responsibility for self-determined goals and discovering strategies to achieve those goals.

Horror Story Types

Ancient Evil Unleashed: The evils may take familiar forms, like vampires undead for centuries, or malevolent ancient gods released from bondage by careless humans, or ancient prophecies wreaking havoc on today's world. The so-called *Cthulhu Mythos* originated by H.P. Lovecraft, in which *Cthulhu* is prominent among a pantheon of ancient evil gods, is a specific variation of this.

Anthology: A collection of short fiction by different authors, usually related in theme or setting.

Apocalyptic Horror: Traditionally, horrors that signal or presage the end of the world, or the world of the characters, and the establishment of a new, possibly very sinister order.

Child-in-Peril: The innocence of childhood is often used to heighten the intensity and unpredictability of evil.

Collection: A book of short stories by a single author.

Coming-of-Age: A story in which the growth and development of a young character, typically a teenager, is portrayed, often by showing how obstacles are overcome and maturity achieved.

Curse: The words said when someone wishes evil or harm on someone or something, such as a witch's or prophet's curse.

Erotic Horror: Sexuality and horror are often argued to be inextricably linked, as in Bram Stoker's *Dracula* and Sheridan Le Fanu's "Carmilla," although others have argued that they are antithetical. Sexuality became increasingly explicit in the 1980s, sometimes verging on the pornographic, as in Brett Easton Ellis' *American Psycho.*

Ghost Story: The spirits of the dead, who can be benevolent, as in Charles Dickens, or malevolent, as in the tales of M.R. James.

Gothic Family Chronicle: A story often covering several generations of a family, many of whose members are typically evil, perverted, or loathsome, and in which family violence is common. The family may live in a decaying mansion suggestive of those in eighteenth century Gothic novels.

Haunted House: Literally, a house visited by ghosts, usually with evil intentions in horror fiction, but sometimes the subject of comedy.

Mystery: A story in which the identity of evildoers is often concealed and suspense therefore heightened. Psychic detective tales are often mysteries.

Nature in Revolt: Tales in which normally docile plants or animals suddenly turn against humankind, sometimes transformed (giant crabs resulting from radioactivity, predatory rats, plagues, blobs that threaten London or Miami, etc.).

Occult: An adjective suggesting fiction based on a mystical or secret doctrine, but sometimes referring to supernatural fiction generally. Implies that there is a reality beyond the perceived world that only adepts can penetrate. Black Magic may or may not be part of an occult world.

Possession: Domination, usually of humans, by evil spirits, demons, aliens, or other agencies in which one's own volition is replaced by an outside force.

Psychological Suspense: Tales often not supernatural in nature in which the psychological exploration and quirks of characters, rather than outside creations, generate suspense and plot.

Reanimated Dead: These can take many forms, such as mummies and zombies (often the result of Voodoo).

Science Fiction: Stories in which supernatural or fantastic elements are absent and some degree of "rational" explanation is present. The science fiction surface of the film *Alien* is disrupted by the horror of the alien monster.

Serial Killer: A multiple murderer, going back to Bluebeard and up to Ed Gein, who inspired Robert Bloch's *Psycho.*

Small Town Horror: The coziness and intimacy of a small community is disrupted by some sort of horrific happening, suggesting an unjustified placidity and complacency on the part of the citizens.

Techno-Thriller: Stories in which a technological development, such as an invention, is linked to a series of suspenseful (thrilling) events.

Vampire Story: Based on mythical bloodsucking creatures possessing supernatural powers and various forms, both animal and human. The concept can be traced far back in history, long before Bram Stoker's famous novel, *Dracula.*

Wild Talents: The phrase comes from Charles Fort's writings and usually refers to parapsychological powers such as telepathy, psychokinesis, and precognition, collectively called psychic or psi phenomena.

Witchcraft: Characters either profess to be or are stigmatized as witches or warlocks, and practitioners of magic associated with witchcraft. This can include black magic or white magic (e.g. Wicca).

Young Adult: Used by publishers to help categorize fiction likely to be of interest to teenage readers.

Science Fiction Story Types

Action/Adventure: Novel containing a rapid sequence of events and dangerous experiences.

Alternate History: A story dealing with how society might have evolved if a specific historical event had happened differently e.g., if the South had won the American Civil War.

Alternate Intelligence: Story featuring an entity with a sense of identity and able to self-determine goals and actions. The natural or manufactured entity results from a synergy, generally unpredictable, of individual elements. This subgenre frequently involves a computer-type intelligence.

Alternate Universe: More accurately, in most cases, alternate history, in which the South won the Civil War, the Nazis triumphed, etc. The idea is a venerable one in SF.

Anthology: A collection of short fiction, short stories or novellas or both, written by different authors.

Collection: A book of short stories written by a single author.

Cyberpunk: Usually applied to the stories by a group of writers who became prominent in the mid-1980s, such as William Gibson and his *Necromancer* (1984). The "cyber" is derived from cybernetics, nominally the study of control and communications in machines. These books also feature a downbeat, punk sensibility reminiscent of the hardboiled school of detective fiction writers.

Disaster: A tale recounting some event or events seriously disruptive of the social fabric but not as serious as a holocaust.

Dystopian: The antonym of utopian, sometimes called anti-utopian, in which traditionally positive utopian themes are treated satirically or ironically and the mood is downbeat or satiric.

Fantasy: A narrative describing events the reader believes to be impossible and for which no scientific or pseudoscientific explanation is offered; magic is usually substituted for scientific laws.

First Contact: Any story about the initial meeting or communication of humans with extraterrestrials or aliens. The term may take its name from the eponymous 1945 story by Murray Leinster.

Future Shock: A journalistic term derived from Alvin Toffler's 1970 book and which refers to the alleged disorientation resulting from rapid technological change.

Hard Science Fiction: Stories in which the author adheres with varying degrees of rigor to scientific principles believed to be true at the time of writing, principles derived from hard (physical, biological) rather than soft (social) sciences.

Humor: SF in which humor, from cerebral to slapstick, is prominent. Early SF was sometimes unintentionally humorous; some modern work is deliberately, and sometimes successfully, so.

Invasion of Earth: An extremely common theme, often paralleling historical events and reflecting fears of the time. Most invasions are depicted as malign, only occasionally benign.

Literary: Usually refers to novels not published as SF and sometimes incorporating unconventional narrative techniques. Metafictional narratives take as their subject matter the nature of fiction itself and are often therefore self-referential.

Medical: Stories in which medical themes are dominant.

Military: Stories that can range from space wars to more local battles; most such stories tend to glorify military virtues.

Mystery: SF to which traditional mystery/detective structures have been grafted, not always successfully, and in which private eyes go down many mean galaxies; a distant relative of cyberpunk.

Mystical: Suggesting a body of esoteric knowledge known to few and which can have a transforming effect on those possessing it.

Political: Narratives in which themes of power are paramount, whether on a local or galactic scale.

Post-Disaster: Story set in a much degraded environment, frequently involving a reduction in population and the resulting loss of access to processes, resources, technology, etc.

Psychic Powers: Parapsychological or paranormal powers believed by some to be credible, e.g., telepathy, telekinesis, etc.

Robot Fiction: From the Jewish Golem to the traditional clanking bucket of bolts to the human-like android, robots in various guises have been among us for centuries. The term comes from Karl Capek's play, *R.U.R.*, which stands for Rossum's Universal Robots. Robots are often surrogates for humans and may be treated seriously or comically.

Space Colony: A permanent space station, usually orbiting Earth but in principal located in deep space or near other planets or stars.

Space Opera: Intergalactic adventures; westerns in space; a specialized form of Adventure.

Techno-Thriller: Stories in which a technological development, such as an invention, is linked to a series of suspenseful (thrilling) events.

Time Travel: An ancient tradition in SF, whether the traveler goes forward or backward, and replete with paradoxes.

Young Adult: A marketing term for publishers; one or more of the central characters is a teenager often testing his or her skills against adversity to achieve a greater degree of maturity and self-awareness. A category used by librarians to shelve books of likely appeal to teenage readers.

Historical Story Types

Action/Adventure: Plot contains exciting/risky activities or behavior; dangerous experiences.

Adventure: Stories that involve risk and chance; exciting in nature and unpredictable.

Arts: Fiction that incorporates some aspect of the arts, whether it be music, painting, drama, etc.

Biblical Fiction: Novels that take their plots or characters from the Bible.

Coming-of-Age: A story in which the primary character is a young person, usually a teenager. The growth of maturity is chronicled.

Disaster: The story recounts a tragedy or catastrophe that is disruptive to life/society.

Espionage: Plot involves spies, either governmental or from organizations, wishing to secretly collect information from other sources to benefit themselves.

Espionage Thriller: Plot contains a high level of action and suspense relating to espionage.

Family Saga: Long narrative, spanning many years, which

contains many related characters.

Fantasy: A narrative describing events the reader believes to be impossible and for which no scientific or pseudoscientific explanation is offered.

Gothic: Characters or settings contain elements of grotesque, terror, or mystery.

Historical/American Civil War: Set during the American Civil War, 1861-1865.

Historical/American West: Set in the western half of the United States; many stories take place during the second half of the nineteenth century.

Historical/Americana: A story dealing with themes unique to the American experience.

Historical/Ancient Greece: Set during the flowering of the ancient Greek civilization, particularly during the age of Pericules in the 5th century B.C.

Historical/Ancient Rome: Covering the history of Rome from its founding and the Roman Republic before Augustus through the decline and fall of the Roman Empire in the fifth century.

Historical/Antebellum American South: Set in the South prior to the Civil War.

Historical/Colonial America: Story takes place before the start of the American Revolution in 1775.

Historical/Depression Era: Set mainly in America during the period of economic hardship brought on by the 1929 Stock Market Crash that continued throughout the 1930s.

Historical/Edwardian: Set during the reign of Edward VII of England, 1901-1910.

Historical/Elizabethan: Set during the reign of Elizabeth I of England, 1558-1603.

Historical/Exotic: Setting is an unusual or exotic place.

Historical/Fantasy: Story contains fantasy or supernatural elements.

Historical/Georgian: Set mostly in the eighteenth century during the reigns of the first three English kings named George.

Historical/Medieval: Story is set during the fifth through the fifteenth centuries or what is commonly known as the Middle Ages.

Historical/Post-American Civil War: Set during the years immediately following the Civil War, 1865-1870s.

Historical/Post-American Revolution: Set in the years immediately following the American Revolution, especially during the last years of the eighteenth century.

Historical/Post-French Revolution: Set during the years immediately following the French Revolution; stories usually take place in France or England.

Historical/Pre-history: Set in the years before the Middle Ages.

Historical/Regency: Set mostly during the years known as the Regency period, 1811-1820.

Historical/Renaissance: Story is set during the Renaissance years in Europe, from the fourteenth through the seventeenth centuries.

Historical/Roaring Twenties: Usually has an American setting and takes place in the 1920s.

Historical/Seventeenth Century: Set during the seventeenth century.

Historical/Victorian: Set during the reign of Queen Victoria, 1837-1901. This story type usually does not take place in America.

Historical/Victorian America: Stories set wholly or in part in America during the reign of Queen Victoria, 1837-1901.

Historical/World War I: Set during the First World War, 1914-1918.

Historical/World War II: Set in the years of the Second World War, 1939-1945.

Indian Culture: These stories are about the lives and culture of the American Indian; the characters are either American Indians or people who lived among them.

Indian Wars: Stories often take place in the West and the wars are a central part of the plot.

Legend: Usually a rewritten version of a legend, myth, or fairy tale.

Literary: Refers to the nature and knowledge of literature.

Military: Stories have a military theme; may deal with life in the armed forces or military battles.

Mountain Man: The characters in these stories live in isolated mountain areas far from civilization and often have to rely on their own resources for survival.

Mystery: Usually a story where a crime occurs or a puzzle must be solved.

Political: Story deals with government and political issues.

Religious: Religion of any sort plays a primary role in the plot.

Romance: Stories involving love affairs and love stories;

deals with the emotional attachments of the characters.

Saga: Long narrative spanning many years and detailing the life of many generations of a family.

Time Travel: One or more of the primary characters is able to be transported to another time, either past or future.

Vampire Story: A story in which a mythical bloodsucking creature, human or animal, possesses supernatural powers.

Inspirational Story Types

Action/Adventure: Mysteries or thrillers with a heavy emphasis on exciting or dangerous incidents.

Anthology: A collection of short stories or novellas by different authors; usually linked by a common theme such as Victorian life.

Apocalyptic Horror: Thrillers or mysteries dealing with the end of the world; many involve prophecies from the Book of Revelations.

Biblical Fiction: Novels that take their plots or characters from the Bible.

Collection: A book of short stories by a single author.

Contemporary: An inspirational story set in the present day.

Contemporary/Innocent: An inspirational story set in the present that may contain little/no sex or the story may have a naive character.

Historical: Novels set in a time period earlier than the present day.

Historical/American West: Novels set in the western half of the United States during the era of pioneer expansion (usually from 1870-1900).

Historical/Post-American Civil War: Novels taking place after the American Civil War, usually from 1865-1870, that emphasize the aftereffects of the war.

Historical/Roaring Twenties: Usually has an American setting and takes place in the 1920s.

Historical/Seventeenth Century: Set during the seventeenth century.

Historical/World War II: Set in the years of the Second World War, 1939-1945.

Medical: Stories in which medical themes predominate.

Mystery: An inspirational novel in which crimes occur and some sort of puzzle must be solved; usually the crimes are murders.

Romance: An inspirational novel in which the main plot line revolves around the developing relationship between a couple.

Romantic Suspense: A romantic novel in which one of the protagonists (usually female) is in danger.

Popular Fiction Story Types

Adult: Fiction dealing with adult characters and mature, developed ideas.

Adventure: Stories that involve risk and chance; exciting in nature and unpredictable.

Americana: Deals with ideas, themes, characters, and objects that are distinctly American.

Arts: Fiction that deals with and focuses on some aspect of the artistic world whether it be music, paintings, literature, or other artistic works.

Collection: A group of short stories or collection of works by the same author; may or may not be linked by themes or characters.

Coming-of-Age: Fiction dealing with a character's formative years; changes in a character's views, ideas, or values.

Contemporary: Story takes place in the present time.

Contemporary/Fantasy: Imaginative, fantastic, creative account of characters, ideas, and themes occurring in the present day; not real--occurs in the character's imagination.

Contemporary/Mainstream: Contemporaneous account of modern life; accurate portrayal of current thoughts and values.

Contemporary Realism: An accurate representation of characters, settings, ideas, themes in the present day. Not idealistic in nature.

Ethnic: Fiction relating to a group of people of identifiable cultural heritage. Focuses on the ideas and values of this heritage.

Family Saga: Long narrative dealing with family lives in one generation or several generations; continuous portrayal of people and events in one family.

Gay/Lesbian Fiction: Stories portraying homosexual characters or themes.

Ghost Story: A suspenseful story which contains elements such as visits from a ghost or other supernatural happenings.

Gothic: Characters or settings contain elements of grotesque, terror, or mystery.

Historical: Fiction that may use historical events, characters, or settings. Attempts to accurately portray a specific time period through use of details and events.

Historical/World War II: Accurate representation of characters, settings, ideas, and themes during World War II, 1939-1945.

Humor: Amusing account of events and characters; comic in nature, humorous in tone.

Inspirational: Divine in nature; power that inspires or enlightens. Literature focusing on knowledge or insights leading to action or changes.

Literary: Relates to the nature and knowledge of literature; can be applied to setting or characters.

Medical: Stories in which medical themes predominate.

Modern: Reflection of the present time period.

Multicultural: Representation of diverse cultures; story does not focus on a "mainstream" culture.

Political: Story deals with government issues and affairs.

Psychological: Fiction dealing with mental or emotional responses.

Psychological Suspense: Deals with the character's mental or emotional response to the unknown, unplanned, or a dangerous situation.

Romance: A novel detailing the emotional involvement/ attachment among its characters. A love affair/love story.

Saga: A long, detailed narrative of events connected through time or from generation to generation.

Satire: Fiction written in a sarcastic and ironic way to ridicule human vices or follies; usually using an exaggeration of characteristics to stress point.

Vampire Story: Tale concerns creatures with supernatural powers. Vampires are dead, but reanimate, and at night suck the blood of people who are asleep.

Werewolf Story: Traditionally a story in which a person changes into a wolf--in both appearance and character. Suspenseful.

Award Winners

Mystery Awards
by Tom and Enid Schantz

The Anthony

The Anthony was presented at Bouchercon, the World Mystery Convention, held on November 3, 2001, in Washington, D.C. The 2001 award (for books published in 2000), like the convention itself, is named for mystery editor, writer, reviewer Anthony Boucher. Nominations and final voting are by all members of the convention.

Best Novel: *A Place of Execution* by Val McDermid

Best First Novel: *Death of a Red Heroine* by Qui Xiaolong

Best Paperback Original: *Death Dances to a Reggae Beat* by Kate Grilley

Best Short Story: "The Problem of the Potting Shed" by Edward D. Hoch

Best Anthology/Short Story Collection: *Master's Choice II* edited by Lawrence Block

Best Non-Fiction/Critical Work: *100 Favorite Mysteries of the Century* edited by Jim Huang

Best Fan Publication: *Mystery News* edited by Chris Aldrich and Lynn Kaczmarek

The Barry

The Barry is named for the late fan reviewer Barry Gardner, a former contributor to *What Do I Read Next?*. Voting is by subscribers to *Deadly Pleasures*, and the 2001 award (for books published in 2000) was presented on November 3, 2001, at Bouchercon in Washington, D.C.

Best Novel: *Deep South* by Nevada Barr

Best First Novel: *Conspiracy of Paper* by David Liss

Best British Crime Novel: *Black Dog* by Stephen Booth

Best Paperback Original: *The Kidnapping of Rosie Dawn* by Eric Wright

The Dilys

Named for Dilys Winn, the founder of Murder Ink, the world's first open mystery bookstore, this award is voted upon by members of the Independent Mystery Booksellers Association and given to the book they most enjoyed selling in 2001. The winner was announced in March 2002 at the Left Coast Crime conference in Portland, Oregon.

The winner: *Mystic River* by Dennis Lehane

Runners-up: *The Cold Blue Blood* by David Handler; *Dead Until Dark* by Charlaine Harris; *Purgatory Ridge* by William Kent Krueger; *The Reaper* by Peter Lovesey

The Herodotus

Nominations and voting by members of the Historical Mystery Appreciation Society. The awards for books first published in 2000 were announced at Bouchercon on November 3, 2001 in Washington, D.C.

Best U.S. Historical Mystery: *A Dangerous Road* by Kris Nelscott

Best International Historical Mystery: *The Company* by Arabella Edge

Best First U.S. Historical Mystery: *The Bottoms* by Joe R. Lansdale

Best First International Mystery: *Bone House* by Betsy Tobin

Best Historical Short Mystery Story: "The Man Who Never Was" by Charles Todd

The Macavity

Named for the mystery cat in T.S. Eliot's *Old Possum's Book of Practical Cats*, this award is nominated and voted on by members of the Mystery Readers International. Books must have been published in 2000.

Best Novel: *A Place of Execution* by Val McDermid

Best First Novel: *A Conspiracy of Paper* by David Liss

Best Biographical/Critical Book: *The American Regional Mystery* by Marvin Lachman

Best Mystery Short Story: "A Candle for Christmas" by Reginald Hill

Romance Awards
by Kristin Ramsdell

As romance fiction has attained increased recognition as a legitimate literary genre, various publications, organizations, and groups have developed to support the interests of its writers and readers. As part of this mission, a number of these offer awards to recognize the accomplishments of the practitioners. Some awards are juried and are presented for excellence in quality and style of writing; others are based on popularity and are selected by the readers. Usually awards are given for a particular work by a particular writer; however, some awards are presented for a body of work produced over a number of years (a type of career award) and others are given for various types of contributions to romance fiction in general. The Romance Writers of America, *Romantic Times*, *Affaire de Coeur*, and RRA-L listserv are the sponsors of most of the awards listed below.

Romance Writers of America Awards

These awards for excellence in romance fiction writing are presented by the Romance Writers of America at the annual RWA conference in July. The following awards were presented at the 2001 Conference in New Orleans, Louisiana.

Lifetime Achievement Award

Presented by the Romance Writers of America for lifetime achievement in romance fiction as determined by a vote of the RWA membership. This year's winner is Olivia "Libby" Hall.

Ten Favorite Books of 2000

Selected by popular vote of the members of the Romance Writers of America, these books are announced in *RWR: Romance Writer's Report* and on the RWA website (www.rwanational.com). Titles are listed in descending order by the number of votes received.

1. *The Unsung Hero* by Suzanne Brockmann

2. *First Lady* by Susan Elizabeth Phillips

3. *In the Midnight Rain* by Ruth Wind

4. *Welcome to Temptation* by Jennifer Crusie

5. *Silver Lining* by Maggie Osborne

6. *Abduction of Julia* by Karen Hawkins

7. (Tie) *Baring It All* by Sandra Chastain

Get Lucky by Suzanne Brockmann

It Takes a Rebel by Stephanie Bond

10. *The Maiden Bride* by Linda Needham

RITA Awards for Published Novels

These awards are presented by the Romance Writers of America for the best romance novel published in 2000. Named for Rita Clay Estrada, RWA's first president, RITAs for published works are given in a number of categories, some of which have changed over the years. This year's winners are as follows:

First Book: *A Man Like Mac* by Fay Robinson

Traditional: *The Best Man and the Bridesmaid* by Liz Fielding

Short Contemporary: *It Takes a Rebel* by Stephanie Bond

Long Contemporary: *Rogue's Reform* by Marilyn Pappano

Regency Romance: *A Grand Design* by Emma Jensen

Romantic Suspense: *Carolina Moon* by Nora Roberts

Paranormal: *The Highlander's Touch* by Karen Marie Moning

Short Historical: *The Mistress* by Susan Wiggs

Single Title Contemporary: *First Lady* by Susan Elizabeth Phillips

Long Historical: *Devilish* by Jo Beverley

Inspirational: *The Shepherd's Voice* by Robin Lee Hatcher

Novella: *Final Approach to Forever* by Merline Lovelace (included in the anthology *Special Report*)

Golden Heart Awards

Presented by the Romance Writers of America for the best romance novel by an unpublished writer. Golden Hearts are given in a number of categories, some of which have changed over the years. For example, Golden Hearts were not awarded in the Inspirational category this year because of too few entries. The 2001 awards are as follows:

Traditional Romance: *Cooper's Folly* by Mary Strand

Short Contemporary: *Hot for Teacher* by Joanne Rock

Long Contemporary: *Folly's Angel* by Cynthia Dees

Romantic Suspense: *Protective Custody* by Beth Cornelison

Paranormal: *Danegeld* by Susan Squires

Long Historical: *Black Stone Keep* by Gay Thornton

Single Title Contemporary: *Babe in the Woods* by Jacqueline Floyd

Short Historical: *Wild Montana Sky* by Debra Holland

Regency: *The Matchmaking Earl* by Shirley Karr

ARTemis Awards

Presented by RWA for the best published romance novel cover. Determined by popular vote at the annual conference, the awards for books published in 2000 and presented at the RWA 2001 annual conference are as follows:

Paranormal: *The Dragon Hour* by Connie Flynn, published by NAL/Onyx

Contemporary Single Title: *The Unsung Hero* by Suzanne Brockmann, published by Ballantine/Ivy; John Ennis, Artist

Traditional: *The Tycoon and the Schoolteacher* by Ludima Gus Burton, published by Avalon; Joseph E. Ferrigno, Design and Brad Williams, Illustration

Short Contemporary Series: *Kiss Me, Katie! Hug Me, Holly!* by Jill Shalvis, published by Harlequin (Duets)

Long Contemporary Series: *The Temptation of Sean MacNeill* by Virginia Kantra, published by Silhouette; Chris Notarile, Artist

Short Historical: *Once Wicked* by Sherri Browning, published by Dell; Alan Ayers, Artist

Long Historical: *The China Bride* by Mary Jo Putney, published by Ballantine; Gene Mydlowski, Art Director and John Ennis, Artist

Inspirational: *Dear Lady* by Robin Lee Hatcher, published by Zondervan; Holli Leegwater and Margo Buriam, Artists

Novella: *Prairie Brides* by Linda Ford, Linda Goodnight, JoAnn Grote, and Amy Rognlie, published by Barbour; Randy Hamblin, Artist

Regency: *A Christmas Bride* by Jo Ann Ferguson, published by Kensington/Zebra

Romantic Suspense: *Spotlight* by Carol Bellacera, published by Forge/Tor; Tony Greco, Artist

Romantic Times Reviewer's Choice Awards

Presented by *Romantic Times* for outstanding romances published in the previous year. Selection is done by the *RT* series romance reviewers. Categories may vary from year to year. The following awards are for 2000 and were announced at the *Romantic Times* Booklovers Convention in Kissimmee, Florida in November 2001.

Historical Romance of the Year: *A Memory of Love* by Bertrice Small

Best First Historical Romance: *By Arrangement* by Madeline Hunter

Best Historical Love and Laughter: *No Marriage of Convenience* by Elizabeth Boyle

Best Historical Novel: *Ahab's Wife* by Sena Jeter Naslund

Best Western Historical Romance: *Maddie's Justice* by Leslie LaFoy

Best American Historical Romance: *The Mistress* by Susan Wiggs

Best British Isles Historical Romance: *Bewitching the Baron* by Lisa Cach

Best Medieval Historical Romance: *Intimate Enemies* by Shana Abe

Best Regency Historical Romance: *A Dangerous Gentleman* by Julia London

Best Innovative Historical Romance: *The Forbidden Garden* by Tracey Fobes

Best Historical Romantic Mystery/Suspense: *The Sun and the Moon* by Patricia Ryan

Best Scottish Historical Romance: *The Bride and the Beast* by Teresa Medeiros

Best Historical Romantic Adventure: *A True Prince* by Veronica Sattler

Best Historical Time Travel: *Heaven on Earth* by Constance O'Day-Flannery

Best Regency Romance: *Lord Nightingale's Debut* by Judith Lansdowne

Best First Regency Romance: *Lord Stanhope's Proposal* by Jessica Benson

K.I.S.S. Hero: Rome Akers from *Here Comes the Bride* by Pamela Morsi

Best Contemporary Romance: *Kiss and Tell* by Cherry Adair

Best Contemporary Novel: *In the Midnight Rain* by Ruth Wind

Best Contemporary Romantic Suspense: *Stealing Shadows* by Kay Hooper

Best First Series Romance: *A Man Like Mac* by Fay Robinson

Best Miniseries Romance: *In the Arms of a Hero* by Beverly Barton

Best Harlequin American: *A Pregnancy and a Proposal* by Mindy Neff

Best Harlequin Intrigue: *The Specialist* by Dani Sinclair

Best Harlequin Duet: *The Wrong Mr. Wright* by Tina Wainscott

Best Harlequin Presents: *Romeo's Revenge* by Sandra Marton

Best Harlequin Romance: *The Paternity Plan* by Heather McAllister

Best Harlequin Superromance: *Deep in the Heart* by Linda Warren

Best Harlequin Temptation: *Hot-Blooded Hero* by Donna Sterling

Best Silhouette Desire: *Husband or Enemy?* by Caroline Cross

Best Silhouette Intimate Moments: *Special Report* by Maggie Price, Debra Cowan, and Merline Lovelace

Best Silhouette Romance: *Raffling Ryan* by Kasey Michaels

Best Silhouette Special Edition: *Sullivan's Child* by Kasey Michaels

Best Steeple Hill Love Inspired: *The Way Home* by Irene Hannon

Best Zebra Bouquet: *Stolen Kisses* by Kate Donovan

Best Multicultural Romance: *The Price of Passion* by Evelyn Palfrey

Best Inspirational Romance: *Heavenly Daze* by Lori Copeland and Angela Elwell Hunt

Best Contemporary Paranormal Romance: *Utterly Charming* by Kristine Grayson

Best Contemporary Futuristic Romance: *Witness in Death* by J.D. Robb

Best Science Fiction Novel: *Ascendant Sun* by Catherine Asaro

Best Fantasy Novel: *Daughter of the Forest* by Juliet Marillier

Best Vampire Romance: *Dark Magic* by Christine Feehan

Best Electronic Book: *Valkyrie* by Lindsey McKenna

Best Contemporary Mystery: *Unbreathed Memories* by Marcia Talley

Best Historical Mystery: *He Shall Thunder in the Sky* by Elizabeth Peters

Best Romantic Intrigue: *Mr. Perfect* by Linda Howard

Best First Mystery: *Death on a Silver Tray* by Rosemary Stevens

Best Suspense Novel: *Dead Air* by Rochelle Krich

Best Amateur Sleuth Novel: *Film Strip* by Nancy Bartholomew

Best PI Novel: *The Wrong Dog* by Carol Lea Benjamin

Romantic Times Career Achievement Awards

Presented by *Romantic Times* for outstanding career achievement.

Series Romance

Series Romance: Vicki Lewis Thompson

Innovative Series Romance: Anne Stuart

Series Romantic Suspense: Rebecca York

Series Romantic Fantasy: Alexandra Sellers

Series Love and Laughter: Charlotte Maclay

Series Romantic Adventure: Suzanne Brockmann

Series Storyteller of the Year: Sharon Sala

Contemporary Fiction

Contemporary Romance: Barbara Freethy

Contemporary Novel: Diane Chamberlain

Contemporary Romantic Suspense: Kay Hooper

Contemporary New Reality: Shannon Drake

Regency Romance

Regency Romance: Barbara Metzger

Multicultural Romance

Multicultural Romance: Beverly Jenkins

Inspirational Romance

Inspirational Romance: Francine Rivers

Mystery/Suspense

Suspense: Mary Higgins Clark

Mystery Series: Lee Harris

Female Sleuth Series: Leslie Glass

Historical Romance

Historical Romance: Jane Feather

Historical Novel: Isabel Allende

Historical New Reality: Kathleen Kane

Western Historical Romance: Bobbi Smith

American Historical Romance: Elizabeth Grayson

British-set Historical Romance: Patricia Rice

Historical Love and Laughter Romance: Julia Quinn

Innovative Historical Romance: Jude Deveraux

Historical Mystery: Miriam Grace Monfredo

Historical Storyteller of the Year: Katherine Sutcliffe

Affaire de Coeur Awards

Reader/Writer Poll Awards awarded to romances published in 2000 on the basis of a readers' poll conducted by *Affaire de Coeur* magazine.

Best Long Contemporary Novel: *Welcome to Temptation* by Jennifer Crusie

Best Short Contemporary Novel: *My Sister, Myself* by Tara Taylor Quinn

Best Contemporary with Heroes and Heroines of Color: *More than Gold* by Shirley Hailstock

Best Overall Historical: *In the Presence of Angels* by Katherine Kingsley

Best Foreign Historical: *Only in Your Arms* by Tracy Cozzens

Best American Historical: *Mystic Visions* by Rosanne Bittner

Best Medieval: *The Champion* by Suzanne Barclay

Best Regency: *Midnight Pleasures* by Eloisa James

Best Futuristic: *Star Crossed* by Marilyn Byerly

Best Time Travel: *Heaven on Earth* by Constance O'Day-Flannery

Best Supernatural: *My Fallen Angel* by Pamela Britton

Best Sci-Fi/Fantasy: *Quantum Rose* by Catherine Asaro

Best Inspirational: *Not Exactly Eden* by Linda Windsor

Outstanding Achiever: Nora Roberts

Best Up and Coming Author: Lynn Bailey

RRA-L Awards

Selected by the members of the RRA-L (Romance Readers Anonymous) electronic mailing list, these awards are usually published on the list in midwinter. The awards for books published in 2001 are listed below. Note: only first place winners are listed.

2001 Book Awards

Best Series Romance: *Anne's Perfect Husband* by Gayle Wilson

Best Contemporary Single Title Romance: *This Heart of Mine* by Susan Elizabeth Phillips

Best Historical Single Title Romance: *The Indiscretion* by Judith Ivory

Best Regency Romance (Traditional): *One Good Turn* by Carla Kelly

Best Romantic Suspense/Mystery/Adventure: *Open Season* by Linda Howard

Best Alternative Realities or Time Travel Romance: *Seduction in Death* by J.D. Robb

Best Love and Laughter Romance: *Fast Women* by Jennifer Crusie

Best Romance Novella: *The Demon's Mistress* by Jo Beverley from *In Praise of Younger Men*

Best Romantic Novel Outside the Romance Genre: *Sentimental Journey* by Jill Barnett

Best All-Around 2001 Romance: *One Good Turn* by Carla Kelly

2001 Author Awards

Best Series/Category Romance Author: Virginia Kantra

Best Contemporary Romance Author: Suzanne Brockmann

Best Historical Romance Author: Mary Jo Putney

Best Regency Romance Author: Carla Kelly

Best Alternative Realities or Time Travel Author: J.D. Robb

Best All-Around Romance Author: Suzanne Brockmann

Best All-Time Romances

Best All-Time Series Romance: *Mackenzie's Mountain* by Linda Howard

Best All-Time Contemporary Romance: *It Had to Be You* by Susan Elizabeth Phillips

Best All-Time Historical Romance: *Lord of Scoundrels* by Loretta Chase

Best All-Time Regency Romance: *The Rake and the Reformer* by Mary Jo Putney

Best Romance Novel of All Time: *Outlander* by Diana Gabaldon

Best All-Time Romance Author of All Time: Nora Roberts

Best All-Time Paranormal Romance Novel: *Outlander* by Diana Gabaldon

Awards information courtesy of Romance Writers of America, *Affaire de Coeur*, *Romantic Times* Publishing Group, and the RRA-L listserv.

Western Awards by D.R. Meredith

WILLA Literary Awards

The WILLA Literary Awards, named in honor of Pulitzer Prize winner Willa Cather, honor contemporary and historical books that capture the diversity and broad roles of women in the American West. It is sponsored by Women Writing the West, a non-profit association of writers and other professionals who promote remembering the women's West. Winners for 2000, announced in October 2001 are:

Best Contemporary Fiction: *The Spirit Woman* by Margaret Coel

Finalists: *Smoke Eaters* by Christine Andrae; *Catching Heaven* by Sands Hall

Best Historical Fiction: *For California's Gold* by JoAnn Levy

Finalists: *Alice's Tulips* by Sandra Dallas; *Soul of the Sacred Earth* by Vella Munn

Best Young Adult Fiction: *Esperanza Rising* by Pam Munoz Ryan

Finalist: *Holding Up the Earth* by Dianne E. Gray

Best Original Paperback: *Dead Man Falls* by Paula Boyd

Finalists: *Painted by the Sun* by Elizabeth Grayson; *A Rant of Ravens* by Christine Goff

Fantastic Fiction Awards by Neil Barron

Locus provides full listings of dozens of awards given throughout the year and provides a comprehensive historical and current list on its website, www.locusmag.com//SFAwards, often before the monthly issues are published. The second volume of *What Do I Read Next? 2001* listed the awards given in earlier 2001, usually for 2000 books. This volume lists the remaining major awards, the Hugo, the World Fantasy award, and the *Locus* Poll. Because awards are given the year following the year of publication, and normally after the editorial deadline for this volume, most books listed here are discussed in earlier volumes of *WDIRN?*.

Hugo Award

The Hugos (named for Hugo Gernsback, the Luxembourg immigrant who was the founding editor of *Amazing Stories* in 1926) are given at the world SF conventions (worldcons) held over Labor Day weekend each year and are chosen by the votes of those attending or supporting the convention. The 2001 (59th) worldcon, the Millennium Philcon, was held in Philadelphia, attended by 4,600 people. However, only 1,050 completed Hugo ballots, and individual category nominations ranged from 205 for the novel to 81 for best fan artist. Awards are given in 12 categories, of which only the novel is listed here, all published in 2000. Complete Hugo voting figures are in the October 2001 *Locus*. Most nominated works are SF, but the convention bylaws explicitly permit works of fantasy to be nominated, as happened this year. The 2002 worldcon will be held in San Jose, California.

Best Novel: *Harry Potter and the Goblet of Fire* by J.K. Rowling

Runners-up: *A Storm of Swords* by George R.R. Martin; *Calculating God* by Robert J. Sawyer; *Midnight Robber* by Nalo Hopkinson; *The Sky Road* by Ken MacLeod

World Fantasy Award

Reader ballots generate a list of candidates, and a panel of judges selects additional candidates and the winners. Fantasy is defined to include horror as well. The winners are announced at the World Fantasy Convention held each fall. The 2001 convention was held in Montreal; the 2002 convention will be held in Minneapolis, the 2003 in Washington, D.C. All books were published in 2000.

Best Novel: *Declare* by Tim Powers; *Galveston* by Sean Stewart (tie)

Runners-up: *The Grand Ellipse* by Paula Volsky; *The Amber Spyglass* by Philip Pullman; *Lord of Emperors* by Guy Gavriel Kay; *Perdido Street Station* by China Mieville

Best Anthology: *Dark Matter: A Century of Speculative Fiction from the African Diaspora* edited by Sheree R. Thomas

Runners-up: *Dark Terrors 5: The Gollancz Book of Horror* edited by Stephen Jones and David Sutton; *Shadows and Silence* edited by Barbara & Christopher Roden; *Vanishing Acts* edited by Ellen Datlow; *Whispers from the Cotton Tree Root: Caribbean Fabulist Fiction* edited by Nalo Hopkinson; *The Year's Best Fantasy and Horror: Thirteenth Annual Collection* edited by Ellen Datlow and Terri Windling

Best Collection: *Beluthahatchie and Other Stories* by Andy Duncan

Runners-up: *Blackwater Days* by Terry Dowling; *Magic Terror: Seven Tales* by Peter Straub; *Perpetuity Blues and Other Stories* by Neal Barrett, Jr.; *The Perseids and Other Stories* by Robert Charles Wilson; *Travel Arrangements: Short Stories* by M. John Harrison

Life Achievement Award: Philip Jose Farmer and Frank Frazetta

Locus Poll

Locus sells about 8,400 copies of each monthly issue, mostly to subscribers. The figures in the August 2001 issue were derived from 394 mailed and 189 online and equal 583 ballots, about a 7 percent return. All books were published in 2000. The fantasy category includes horror, but only one book, P.D. Cacek's *Canyons*, was in the list at number 19. It was annotated in volume 1 of *WDIRN? 2001.* The top five books in six of the 11 categories are listed here:

SF Novel: *The Telling* by Ursula K. Le Guin; *Eater* by Gregory Benford; *Zeitgeist* by Bruce Sterling; *The Coming* by Joe Haldeman; *In Green Jungles* by Gene Wolfe

Fantasy Novel: *A Storm of Swords* by George R.R. Martin; *Declare* by Tim Powers; *The Amber Spyglass* by Philip Pullman; *Perdido Street Station* by China Mieville; *Ash: A Secret History* by Mary Gentle

First Novel: *Mars Crossing* by Geoffrey A. Landis; *Revelation Space* by Alastair Reynolds; *Ceres Storm* by David Herter; *Wheelers* by Ian Stewart and Jack Cohen; *House of Leaves* by Mark Z. Danielewski

Collection: *Tales of Old Earth* by Michael Swanwick; *The Complete Short Stories of Theodore Sturgeon. Volume 7: Saucer of Loneliness*; *Telzey Amberdon* by James H. Schmitz; *Beluthahatchie and Other Stories* by Andy Duncan; *Strange Travelers* by Gene Wolfe

Anthology: *The Year's Best Science Fiction: Seventeenth Annual Collection* edited by Gardner Dozois; *The Year's Best Fantasy and Horror: Thirteenth Annual Collection* edited by Ellen Datlow and Terri Windling; *Year's Best SF* edited by David G. Hartwell; *Vanishing Acts* edited by Ellen Datlow; *Dark Matter: A Century of Speculative Fiction from the African Diaspora* edited by Sheree R. Thomas

Nonfiction: *On Writing* by Stephen King; *Robert A. Heinlein: A Reader's Companion* by James Gifford; *Algernon, Charlie and I* by Daniel Keyes; *Jack Vance: Critical Appreciations and a Bibliography* edited by A.E. Cunningham; *Science Fiction Culture* by Camille Bacon-Smith

Popular Fiction Awards by Tom Barton

Booker Prize

The Booker Prize was established in 1968 by Booker PLC, an international food company in cooperation with the Book Trust and Publishers' Association. It is considered Britain's major literary prize for fiction and is given in recognition of a full-length novel.

Booker Prize winner 2001: *True History of the Kelly Gang* by Peter Carey. Carey also won this award in 1988 for *Oscar and Lucinda*.

Short list: *Atonement* by Ian McEwan; *Oxygen* by Andrew Miller; *Number9dream* by David Mitchell; *The Dark Room* by Rachel Seiffert; *Hotel World* by Ali Smith

National Book Award

The National Book Foundation's mission is to recognize books of commendable merit. Nominees are submitted by publishers only and the winner is based on the decisions of an independent group of judges.

National Book Award winner 2001: *The Corrections* by Jonathan Franzen

Short list: *Among the Missing* by Dan Chaon; *Look at Me* by Jennifer Egan; *The Last Report on the Miracles at Little No Horse* by Louise Erdrich; *Highwire Moon* by Susan Straight

Nobel Prize for Literaure

The Nobel Prize for Literature is awarded annually by the Swedish Academy.

Nobel Prize for Literature winner for 2001: V.S. Naipaul

Mystery in Review
by
Tom & Enid Schantz

You might have thought the sky was falling, given the amount of moaning heard about the country when Walker kicked off the 2002 publishing year by announcing it was dropping its longtime and once illustrious mystery line. Publisher George Gibson indicated the list just wasn't earning its keep. Walker just didn't have the resources to sign—or promote—authors with the oomph to stem the flow of red ink. It was sad news, of course, but in reality it won't make that big a difference, since Walker was down to publishing only about twelve original mysteries a year. In contrast, companies like St. Martin's Press do that many in a month. Some writers complained that this decision would result in a further shrinking of the market for midlist writers. However, many midlist writers routinely sell 15,000 or more copies, a figure no Walker author seriously approached, with the possible exception of Bill Pronzini whose stand- alone crime novels might hit the mark. If Walker's stable of writers had kicked home even a few 15,000-copy sellers, Gibson wouldn't have closed the barn door. Sales figures of that magnitude wouldn't have put Walker on the Fortune 500 list, but they certainly would have made the accountants happy.

In fact, we suspect Walker would have been content to publish a dozen books a year if their sales ranged from 5,000 to 10,000 copies and were capable of making a paperback sale to someone other than Worldwide with its slam-bam, thank you, ma'am approach to reprint publishing. What is so perplexing about the situation is that we suspect there are actually plenty of writers out there who are able to produce those kinds of numbers but are still looking for homes. Take Pronzini, for example. He started his career at Random House in the early 1970s when the private eye field was less crowded, moved on to St. Martin's Press, where the expectations in terms of sales were quite a bit smaller, and eventually settled in at Delacorte, where he routinely registered sales in the ten to twelve thousand range. Delacorte, however, wasn't interested in small profits but in authors who showed growth, and Pronzini's Nameless private eye series moved on after several books to Carroll & Graf, while his stand-alones (which included at least one *New York Times* ''Notable Book'') landed at Walker.

Gone too is Walker's longtime mystery editor, Michael Seidman, who presided over the show in lower Manhattan for the past decade or so. He was fond of saying he would publish nothing but James M. Cain if he could—or, at least, writers working that same noir territory. During that period, he might not have signed any potential Cains, but it certainly must have been frustrating for him to stand back and watch writers leave Walker after one or two books to seek greener promotional fields at other houses. Those who left didn't always find success, including Richard Barre, who got great reviews but mediocre sales at Berkley and eventually lost his contract. He's now working on a stand-alone thriller that probably will appear under a pseudonym. Lynda S. Robinson landed at Warner's Mysterious Press after several books with Walker. She's still there, but apparently the powers-that-be don't see her ancient Egyptian series as having mass appeal and have switched her reprints from rack-sized paperbacks to smaller print-run trade paperbacks. Aaron Elkins did his first two Gideon Olivers at Walker (before Seidman's arrival), moved over to Mysterious, and then moved to Avon when he apparently decided that Warner wasn't doing enough to promote his books. Alan Russell went from Walker to Mysterious to Simon & Schuster to St. Martin's. G.M. Ford hit the ground running at Walker and has since established himself at Avon/Morrow as one of the best private eye writers working today. Sandra West Prowell was a big hit (all things being relative) at Walker with her Phoebe Siegel Montana private eye books. Walker has been waiting for years now for the next installment in that series and the indications are that Walker will still publish it, if Prowell ever turns it in. They'll just call it fiction instead of a mystery. In the meantime, Bantam is also waiting to see the first book from Prowell in a reported two-book, seven-figure deal made several years ago for non-series titles.

If Prowell had kept to schedule, things might have gone better at Walker. The breakout writer they needed seemed always to elude them. As it was, Walker's final list just seemed uninspired. Carol Lea Benjamin's *The Long Good Boy* and Elizabeth Gunn's *Six-Pound Walleye* had their fans, but apparently not enough of them to keep their paperback deals alive at Dell. *Sister Wife* by John Gates annoyed as many reviewers as it pleased. No one questions James Sallis' talent, but he was already telling people that *Ghost of a Flea* would be his last Lew Griffin book even before Gibson dropped his bombshell. R.D. Rosen came back to Walker with baseball player turned detective Harvey Blissberg, the hero of *Strike Three, You're Dead*, one of the best mysteries ever to appear under the Walker imprint, but even this strongest in the series for some years didn't quite recapture the old magic.

When the death knell sounded, there were some solid performers remaining, including Jeanne M. Dams, with a seriously cozy series set in the English countryside (*To Perish in Penzance*), as well as an insightful historical series set in turn-of-the-century South Bend, Indiana. There was also Lev Raphael (*Burning Down the House*) with his wicked academic series; Keith Snyder (*The Night Men*), whose books showed both youthful problems, as well as youthful promise; and Mary Logue, whose *Glare Ice* was one of the most solidly crafted mysteries of Walker's final winter mystery season. Book cover art was another problem at Walker. Packaging is important, and despite Seidman's protests that the art was getting better, Walker's covers weren't catching many eyes—at least favorably.

Still, we'd say Gibson made the wrong move. Instead of dumping mysteries altogether, he needed to find new sources for them. A number of years back, Walker reprinted a good many English mysteries in paperback, and the effort was relatively successful at first, especially in the mystery bookstores that were just beginning to flex their muscles. There are still a number of good English mysteries—especially historicals—that aren't being published in this country. He also might have looked at what some of the smaller presses are publishing. Back in the days when we ran a major mystery bookstore, editors at the larger New York houses often asked us to suggest writers they could acquire from one of the small presses. (''Acquire'' is the publishing world's polite way of saying ''steal.'') For example, we've often wondered why a big New York house hasn't put the moves on Rosemary Aubert, whose poignant books about a homeless ex-judge in Toronto often top our own best of the year lists. Surely Walker has better promotional tools than Bridgeworks, the small house that publishes Aubert.

In spite of what happened to Walker, many people think the future of midlist mystery publishing may well lie with midlevel houses, as well as with even smaller presses. The big houses, such as Putnam and Random House, will of course continue to publish the blockbuster mysteries, but there has to be somewhere other than St. Martin's where the smaller mysteries can get published. Other midlevel houses comparable in size to Walker seem to be prospering with their mystery lines. In some cases, it's a question of focus and packaging. Our favorite mystery publisher, Soho Press, specializes in books with exotic backgrounds (exotic in the New York publishing world means anything not set in England or the contiguous 48 states). Current examples include Magdalen Nabb's *Property of Blood*, based in Italy, and J. Robert Janes' *Kaleidoscope*, set in occupied France and featuring the odd-couple sleuthing team of a Surete detective and a Gestapo agent.

Soho also made room for Peter Lovesey, one of the most talented mystery writers of our time, who apparently wore out his welcome at Warner's Mysterious Press and took all of his books, including the backlist, to Soho a couple of years ago. Soho's books also have a distinctive look to them. Uniformly bound in a smaller trim size rarely seen in bookstores since World War II and graced with simple and dignified dust jackets, Soho books stand out on a bookstore table otherwise loaded down with flashy, bloated, wide margin hardcovers with lots of leading (but usually no more actual) words. That look probably won't get any of their titles on the *New York Times* bestseller list, but it probably will attract educated, sophisticated readers who no doubt will be willing to at least try any book published by Soho.

Carroll & Graf is another notable midlevel publisher. Although it lacks Soho's focus, Carroll & Graf has put together a decent mystery line, offering a wide variety of titles designed to appeal to a full spectrum of mystery readers. The current list does seem to favor historicals, albeit ones set mostly in this century—excuse us, we mean in the twentieth century—including David Dickinson's attempt to turn the death of Victoria's son Victor Albert (Prince Eddie) into a murder case in *Goodnight, Sweet Prince*, David Roberts' Spanish Civil War murder story, *Bones of the Buried*, and Ed Gorman's *Save the Last Dance for Me*, set during the 1960 presidential campaign. Even Freda Davis' *A Fine and Private Place*, although set in contemporary times, has its roots in a World War II era death. On the other hand, Bill Pronzini's *Bleeders*, the twenty-seventh (and reportedly final) book in his Nameless private eye series, is firmly entrenched in modern-day Northern California.

The Poisoned Pen Press, a family operation based in Scottsdale, Arizona, never intended to have any particular focus, other than to publish the kind of mystery books editor Barbara Peters likes to sell in her similarly named bookstore. However, Peters has a weakness for historicals, and it's no surprise that mysteries with a strong historical component dominate their list. Although Nicholas Kilmer's art mystery *Lazarus, Arise* is set in contemporary times, the action is driven by the Nazi art looting during World War II. Race relations in New Orleans are at the heart of two other Poisoned Pen books: David Fulmer's *Chasing the Devil's Tail* is set in the city's red light district in 1907, while Robert

Skinner's *Pale Shadow* takes place in Jim Crow Louisiana in 1940. S.K. Rizzolo's first novel, *The Rose in the Wheel*, follows the adventures of a Bow Street Runner in 1811 London. Mary Reed and Eric Meyer's *Three for a Letter* is their third book set in sixth century Constantinople. Poisoned Pen Press also publishes plenty of mysteries set in modern times, including reprints of several English writers, such as Keith Miles and Ruth Dudley Edwards and, of course, books set in the American Southwest. Print runs aren't huge, but the company continues to expand, although their books appear to do better in the library market than in bookstores.

The same could probably be said for The Rue Morgue Press, which specializes in reprinting mysteries first published between 1930 and 1960. Most of its twelve annual titles fall into the cozy field. Even its one hardboiled title, Norbert Davis' 1943 novel *The Mouse in the Mountain*, is funnier than it is tough. Humor certainly carries the day in Joan Coggin's *Who Killed the Curate*, a 1944 title published for the first time in the U.S. It's the story of the young scatterbrained daughter of an earl who marries the middle-aged vicar of a coastal Sussex parish. *Creeping Venom*, a 1946 Irish village gardening mystery by Sheila Pim (whom contemporary critics called the Irish Angela Thirkell), also makes its first U.S. appearance. If you want to know the origins of the overbearing spinster sleuth, you might try Charlotte Murray Russell's 1942 *The Message of the Mute Dog*. *The Black Eye* is the tenth screwball mystery to be reprinted by The Rue Morgue from the pens of sisters Constance and Gwenyth Little. The Littles, whose twenty-one books all feature sarcastic, independent women who would do just about anything to get out of housework, have almost a cult following.

Five Star, an imprint of the Gale Group (which also publishes *What Do I Read Next?*), isn't exactly a small press, although its print runs certainly are. Under the editorial direction of Ed Gorman, Five Star publishes approximately two dozen mystery titles a year, mostly short story collections by veteran writers. Recent offerings include *More Oddments* by Bill Pronzini, *The Family Jewels* by Dorothy Cannell, *The Night People* by Edward D. Hoch, *The Nudger Dilemmas* by John Lutz, *The Nighttime Is the Right Time* by Bill Crider, and *Together We Kill* by Mickey Spillane. In addition to the collections, Five Star also publishes novels. Some of the selections are written by veteran writers such as Jeremiah Healy (*Turnabout*), Les Roberts (*The Chinese Fire Drill*), or Catherine Dain (*Darkness at the Door*); occasionally they are by newcomers such as Jan Grape (*Austin City Blue*); and, rarely, a few by Brits such as Mat Coward (*In and Out*) appear. Coward has a nice touch and would be a good bet for one of the small or midlevel presses to pick up, given that Five Star books are primarily designed for the library market and rarely find their way into bookstores.

Another small press that specializes in publishing single-author short story collections is Crippen & Landru, the brainchild of John Dickson Carr biographer Douglas Greene. Unlike Five Star, which prints only in hardcover, or The Rue Morgue, which does only trade paperbacks, Crippen & Landru does both a limited 250-copy cloth edition designed for collectors, as well as a trade paperback of each title. The limited edition generally ends up paying for the up-front costs, allowing the publisher to make his profit on the paperback edition which, unlike the hardcover, often goes into subsequent printings. The press publishes only mystery titles, and among the distinguished writers currently gracing the Crippen & Landru list are Peter Lovesey (*The Sedgemoor Strangler*), Ron Goulart (*Adam and Eve on a Raft*), Max Allan Collins (*Kisses of Death*, a Nate Heller collection), Michael Z. Lewin (*The Reluctant Detective*), and Edward D. Hoch (*The Old Spies Club*, a Rand collection). If Hoch's name pops up more than once as the author of a short story collection, remember that he's published a short story in every single issue of Ellery Queen's *Mystery Magazine* for the past four decades.

Two other small presses that publish a significant number of titles every year are Intrigue, based in Philadelphia and moving toward an international focus rivaling that of Soho, and Silver Dagger, located in Johnson City, Tennessee, and very Southern in its author selection. There are also the university presses, a number of which publish the occasional mystery title. And more presses seem to spring up every year, especially with the advent of print- on-demand technology. The publishers we've discussed, however, generally rely on traditional printing methods for all except the occasional title.

Another indication that the mystery genre as a whole isn't going into the tank is the number of really good first novels that have come out in recent months. Denis Hamilton's *The Jasmine Trade* is an engrossing look at the Asian subculture of modern day Los Angeles. It tells the story of parachute kids, Asian teens who live on their own in expensive subdivisions and with extravagant allowances but whose parents live and work in Asia, as well as the tragic story of young Chinese girls who are kept as slaves in Southern California brothels. Other notable first novels include Gabriel Cohen's Brooklyn police novel, *Red Hook*; C.J. Box's *Open Season*, which features a Wyoming game warden; Susanna Jones' *The Earthquake Bird*, an exquisite piece of literary fiction set in Tokyo that works equally well as a clever mystery; Carol Goodman's *The Lake of Dead Languages*, a haunting tale of murders old and new at a girls' school in the Adirondacks; and Sharon Fiffer's *Killer Stuff*, a highly entertaining tale about a woman trying to make a living as a picker of recent collectibles. Less successful but generally well- received first efforts were *Blindsighted* by Karen Slaughter, as violent in spots as the author's name, and *Cold Hunter's Moon* by K.C. Greenlief, which just cried out for at least one more rewrite.

As good as many of those first novels were, a number of veteran mystery writers turned out books of exceptional merit during the second half of 2001. The authors of these books, all taking place in the United Kingdom, include Ian Rankin (*The Falls*), Minette Walters (*The Shape of Snakes*), Reginald Hill (*Dialogues of the Dead or Paronomania!*), Janet Neel (*O Gentle Death*), and Laura Wilson (*My Best Friend*). Val McDermid's *Killing the Shadows* may not have been as good as her penultimate title, *A Place of Execution*, but it still would make most reviewers' list of top books of the year. The same could be said for Stephen Booth's *Dancing with the Virgins*. Peter Robinson reminded us once again with *Aftermath* that he has turned into one of the finest writers in the genre while many of our backs seemingly were turned. Robert Wilson followed up his Gold Dagger-winning *A Small Death in Lisbon* with the equally stunning spy story, *A Company of Strangers*.

Just as many excellent books featured settings on this side of the Atlantic. A maturing Carl Hiaasen is perhaps a bit more resigned, but almost as funny as usual, in the surprisingly warmhearted *Basket Case*. Ed McBain flashes quite a bit of humor himself while showing us once again why he's the master of the police procedural in his latest 87th Precinct novel, *Money, Money, Money*. Of the three or four excellent historical series currently set during the American Civil War, Owen Parry's stands apart. He reminds us once again that the war was fought to end slavery in the powerful *Call Each River Jordan*. James Crumley's much-married private eye Milo Milodragovitch makes a return visit in *The Final Country*, but the dope and boozing isn't as amusing as it was thirty years ago. Antiques play a big part in Laura Lippman's entertaining new Baltimore mystery, *In a Strange City*, and fellow Baltimorian Sujata Massey once again shows the dangerous side of Japan in *The Bride's Kimono*. Earlier in this essay we mentioned that Bill Pronzini had produced the twenty-seventh entry in his Nameless private eye series. There are signs that this title, *Bleeders*, may be the final book in the series, although we're not holding our breath. When Pronzini launched this series back in 1970, he was in his twenties and ''Nameless'' was already middle-aged. Although he hasn't aged at the same rate as Pronzini, ''Nameless'' has now turned 60, while Matt Scudder has matched his creator, Lawrence Block, year for year, and both are now 62. One wonders if these hardboiled heroes will continue their careers into the mean hallways of a nursing home or geriatric ward.

Compared to the other books mentioned, there's nothing really serious going on in Donna Andrews' *Revenge of the Wrought-Iron Flamingos*, and her fans wouldn't have it any other way. Andrews continues to stake her claim to being one of the funniest of the new breed of cozy mystery writers. Even though most cozies aren't meant to be taken seriously—it's entertainment after all—we do think that a few of their writers have gotten just a bit too cute with their titles. Some are puns, some are word substitutions, some are. . .well, better left off the title page of the book. While Anne Rivers Siddons' *Fault Lines* is a clever title for a book about murder and earthquakes, and Laurien Berenson's *Once Bitten* fits a book featuring a lot of dogs, we draw the line at Nancy J. Cohen's uninspired *Murder by Manicure*. Just about everyone who writes about food and murder feels the need to find a cute title; we suppose there's really nothing wrong with Lou Jane Temple's *Red Beans and Vice*, or Joanne Pence's *Bell, Cook and Candle*, or Ellen Hart's *Dial M for Meatloaf*, but overall we're ready for a moratorium on culinary wordplay. Sarah Graves' Christmas mystery, *Wreck the Halls*, is okay, we suppose, and Nancy Bell's *Strip Poker* works when you know her detective is a Florida stripper. When it comes to gardening mystery titles we prefer Sheila Pim's *Creeping Venom* to Ann Ripley's *Harvest of Murder* or Janis Harrison's *Lilies That Fester*. However, our vote for the furthest reach of the year goes to Sharon Kahn for *Don't Cry for Me, Hot Pastrami*.

Don't get us wrong. We like all kinds of mysteries, from hardboiled to comic cozies. Most observers think Dennis Lehane's *Mystic River* is a dead cert to win most of the best novel awards and, though we listed it as one of the best books for the first half of 2001, our favorite book for the year as a whole was David Handler's much softer *The Cold Blue Blood*. It's the story of Mitch Berger, a recently widowed Jewish film critic who moves into an old carriage house in an island compound on the Connecticut coast populated with old blue blood families. He solves murders, both old and new, and finds new love with a black New Jersey state policewoman. Sweet, sophisticated, and sparking with gentle wit and humanity, this is truly a mystery with a heart. Handler by the way, won a paperback original Edgar several years ago when he was publishing a critically acclaimed series at Bantam before the bean counters there apparently sent him packing. He's now at St. Martin's. In some circles that would be considered a step down, but in this case it's truly Bantam's loss. Our only caveat about the book is that Handler (or his publisher) wants to turn it into a series. We'd hate to see familiarity ruin our picture of Mitch and his much taller and fitter lady love.

There was some talk after the events of September 11 that readers would turn to gentler, kinder mysteries. That was probably true in the first few weeks, but by the end of the year most readers had fallen back into their old reading patterns. Some writers and publishers were a bit concerned with how the public would react to books already written and scheduled, but not yet published, that involved terrorism. However, there was one book that seemed to uncannily foreshadow the recent tragic events. Ethan Black's *All the Dead Were Strangers* even involves Afghanistan, a fictional but unmistakable version of Osama bin Laden, and a terrorist plot against Manhattan. We haven't heard that readers shied away from either Julie Kaewert's *Uncatalogued* because it involves terrorist attacks in London's financial district or James W. Hall's *Blackwater Sound*, which opens with the bad guys bringing down an airliner. Nor has Delacorte cut the projected print run for Stephen White's forthcoming *Warning Signs*, even though this Alan Gregory thriller involves blowing up a number of Denver's landmarks. However, the events may affect how writers are handling similar themes in books not yet written.

Maybe that's why so many mysteries of late have gone back to the World War II era. The enemy then was easily identified and ultimately defeated. Kate Kingsbury's cozy *Death Is in the Air* is set in wartime England, while Joseph Kanon paints a vivid picture of the destruction in Berlin during the early days of the occupation in *The Good German*. Unfortunately, devastated Berlin is far more interesting than his plot. Like the earlier mentioned *A Fine and Private Place* by Freda Davis, Martha Grimes' *The Blue Last* and Laura Wilson's *My Best Friend* involve story lines that connect events set during World War II with present-day problems.

And finally, it's worth noting that The Library of America, following upon last year's omnibus edition of all the Dashiell Hammett novels, has reprinted most of Hammett's long-out-of-print short stories in *Hammett: Crime Stories and Other Writings*, edited by Stephen Marcus and containing some of the finest crime fiction of the century.

From this horn of plenty, it's a bit difficult to single out the twenty-five best mysteries released during the final months of 2001. You won't go wrong with any of these books, although some come with a few caveats.

The Revenge of the Wrought-Iron Flamingos by Donna Andrews

Dancing with the Virgins by Stephen Booth

Red Hook by Gabriel CCohen

White Shell Woman by James D. Doss

Killer Stuff by Sharon Fiffer

The Lake of Dead Languages by Carol Goodman

Blackwater Sound by James W. Hall

The Jasmine Trade by Denise Hamilton

The Cold Blue Blood by David Handler

BasketCase by Carl Hiaasen

Dialogues of the Dead or Paronomania! by Reginald Hill

Kaleidoscope by J. Robert Janes

The Earthquake Bird by Susanna Jones

The Good German by Joseph Kanon

Glare Ice by Mary Logue

The Bride's Kimono by Sujata Massey

Money, Money, Money by Ed McBain

Killing the Shadows by Val McDermid

O Gentle Death by Janet Neel

Call Each River Jordan by Owen Parry

The Nautical Chart by Arturo Perez-Reverte

Bleeders by Bill Pronzini

The Falls by Ian Rankin

Aftermath by Peter Robinson

The Company of Strangers by Robert Wilson

We would be remiss if we didn't mention Max Allan Collins' *The History of Mystery*, a lavishly illustrated coffee-table book that doesn't live up to its ambitious title, but is still a lot of fun for readers who enjoy the flash and trash aspects of the genre. Most of the book is devoted to private eye and noir mysteries with an emphasis on pulp magazines, paperbacks, comic books, movies, and television. Collins plays lip service to the traditional mystery but doesn't get much beyond Sherlock Holmes and Agatha Christie, concentrating instead on personal favorites such as Mickey Spillane and paperback covers featuring garish girlie art from the fifties and sixties. That's all fine, since Collins freely admits his bias, but we wish the book could have been more carefully proofread; too many titles and authors' names are misspelled or mangled, especially when they fall outside of the author's area of expertise.

And perhaps the pleasantest surprise of the year was Jo Hammett's affectionate but unflinching memoir of her difficult father, *Dashiell Hammett: A Daughter Remembers*, edited by Richard Layman. In addition to being simply crammed with wonderful family photos, most never before published, and other memorabilia such as postcards, cartoons, and a homemade Christmas card from Hammett, this attractive volume contains Jo's own account of her relationship with a father who was largely absent, but still a powerful and much loved force in her life. Though he battled alcoholism, Hammett was a wonderful father when he was sober and that made up for the bad times, according to his daughter. Although we already knew much about the life she movingly describes, we understand it better now, and her generous words erase much of the ugliness that has surrounded her father's legacy.

We had no sooner written those words than the Mystery Writers of America announced the Edgar nominees for the best books of 2001. We were happy to see that the Hammett memoir was nominated in the Best Critical/Biographical category and a bit surprised to see the Collins' *The History of Mystery* and Jeff Marks' *Who Was That Lady?* (the biography of Craig Rice) also nominated, given the poor proofreading in both books and the lack of knowledge about the history of the genre displayed in the latter (as well as a totally useless index). After all, the MWA had refused to nominate Marvin Lachman's *The American Regional Mystery* last year, citing unspecified errors. It turned into a real ruckus among mystery fans, since the committee declined to nominate a full slate of candidates that year. That slight will no doubt be revisited this year, since the committee chose to nominate one more book than usual. Another nominee, *Selected Letters of Dashiell Hammett: 1921-1960*, edited by Richard Layman, makes a nice companion piece to Jo Hammett's memoir. We haven't seen and so can't comment on the other nominees: *My Name Is Friday* by Michael J. Hayde and *Edgar Allan Poe: A to Z* by Dawn B. Sova. Our enthusiastic nod goes to *Dashiell Hammett: A Daughter Remembers*.

There were a few shocks in the best novel category as well. Dennis Lehane's lavishly praised *Mystic River*, the pick of the Independent Mystery Booksellers Association, as well as the readers on DorothyL and many of the reviewers at Deadly Pleasures, failed to make the short list. Three of the titles we picked as the best of the year in *What Do I Read Next?*, however, did make the list: *Money, Money, Money* by Ed McBain, *Silent Joe* by T. Jefferson Parker, and *Reflecting the Sky* by S.J. Rozan. Our top pick for the year, David Handler's *The Cold Blue Blood*, failed to get nominated, but that probably merely reflects the unwillingness of the Edgar best novel committees to look seriously at gentler mysteries. It also came out late in the year. Of the other nominees, we thought Harlan Coben's *Tell No One* was too much of a cheat to be considered, while D.W. Buffa's *The Judgment* somehow eluded us. Of the nominees, our nod goes emphatically to *Silent Joe*.

There weren't any gentle mysteries among the nominees for best first novel, either, although three of the books we picked did make the list: *Open Season* by C.J. Box, *Red Hook* by Gabriel Cohen, and *The Jasmine Trade* by Denise Hamilton. Rounding out the nominees were *Line of Vision* by David Ellis and *Gun Monkeys* by Victor Gischler. We wish the cozier *Corpse de Ballet* by Ellen Pall had been included, not only because it is a fun book, but because it would have given the list a tad more balance. If we had to choose among those titles, including our own addition of the Pall, we'd pick *The Jasmine Trade*.

The MWA seems to be handling the "problem" of what do about gentler mysteries by adopting the Mary Higgins Clark Award, which used to be given out by the now defunct magazine named for the bestselling author of romantic suspense. The award is for "the book most closely written in the Mary Higgins Clark tradition," although the list of nominees would seem to suggest any kind of cozy would do. The nominees include *Murphy's Law* by Rhys Bowen, *Summer of Storms* by Judith Kelman, *Perhaps She'll Die* by M.K. Preston, and *Murder of a Sweet Old Lady* by Denise Swanson. We're sure the nominees are happy to make any kind of a list, but the whole idea strikes us as being a backhanded compliment at best or a slap in the face at worst.

In any event, we guarantee that these nominations will start a few brush fires among readers, critics and writers. Mystery readers tend to be pretty passionate about their likes and dislikes. Stay tuned. We'll tell you how it turns out.

Mystery Titles

1

PETER ABRAHAMS

Last of the Dixie Heroes

(New York: Ballantine, 2001)

Story type: Psychological Suspense
Subject(s): Civil War; Fathers and Sons; American South
Major character(s): Roy Hill, Businessman, Single Parent
Time period(s): 2000s
Locale(s): Atlanta, Georgia

Summary: Roy Hill is just another faceless worker at Chemerica Corporation, a giant multinational company headquartered in Atlanta, and at first he barely notices when his world starts falling apart. He's denied the promotion he's been expecting, his wife leaves him for an absolute jerk, and his son isn't weathering the crisis well and is doing poorly at school. When one of his co-workers invites him to take part in a Civil War reenactment, he reluctantly agrees, and then finds that these weekends offer him a perfect escape from reality, to a world where it's always 1863 and violence is an acceptable solution to problems. Himself the descendant of a Civil War hero of the same name, Roy becomes more and more obsessed with the reenactments and eventually is unable to distinguish fantasy from reality. When his son is taken hostage by Yankees in one of the battles, Roy no longer knows if it's really happening or part of a game, or if the bullets being fired are real or blanks.

Where it's reviewed:
Booklist, May 1, 2001, page 1618
Library Journal, May 15, 2001, page 1618
Mystery News, June/July 2001, page 28
Publishers Weekly, June 15, 2001, page 52
Wall Street Journal, June 5, 2001, page A24

Other books by the same author:
Crying Wolf, 2000
A Perfect Crime, 1998
The Fan, 1995
Lights Out, 1994
Revolution #9, 1992

Other books you might like:
James Lee Burke, *In the Electric Mist with Confederate Dead*, 1993
Stanford Diehl, *Angel in the Front Room, Devil out Back*, 2001
Michael Kilian, *The Harrison Raines Series*, 2000-
Owen Parry, *The Abel Jones Series*, 1999-
Elena Santangelo, *By Blood Possessed*, 1999

2

MARY JO ADAMSON

The Elusive Voice

(New York: Signet, 2001)

Story type: Historical
Series: Michael Merrick. Number 2
Subject(s): Spiritualism; Social Classes; Journalism
Major character(s): Michael Merrick, Journalist (newspaper police reporter)
Time period(s): 1840s
Locale(s): Boston, Massachusetts

Summary: Michael Merrick is a reporter for the *Boston Independent*, covering the crime beat for his reclusive editor and publisher Jasper Quincey. The death of an eminent Harvard professor during a seance sets him off on an investigation into the charismatic medium Sylvie Singer, who conducted the affair. His search takes him to the university's medical school and Miss Sylvie's other clients among the members of Boston society. Merrick, who only a year earlier was cured of his addiction to laudanum (a form of opium which was a chief ingredient of many patent medicines) and is still in a wheelchair part of the time from injuries sustained in his last case, knows the case will be a difficult one. Like his employer, who wants him to expose Miss Sylvie as a charlatan, he is a firm disbeliever in the spiritualist movement, but some of the things he sees seem to defy explanation. The author has also written a series of contemporary mysteries set in Puerto Rico featuring policeman Balthazar Martin.

Other books by the same author:
The Blazing Tree, 2000

Other books you might like:
Barbara Hambly, *The Benjamin January Series*, 1997-
Miriam Grace Monfredo, *Blackwater Spirits*, 1995
Owen Parry, *Shadows of Glory*, 2000
Raymond Paul, *The Thomas Street Horror*, 1982
Randall Silvis, *On Night's Shore*, 2001

3

GLYNN MARSH ALAM

Deep Water Death

(Pearl River, New York: Avocet, 2001)

Story type: Amateur Detective
Series: Luanne Fogarty. Number 2
Subject(s): Rural Life; Diving; American South
Major character(s): Luanne Fogarty, Diver, Teacher
Time period(s): 2000s
Locale(s): Palmetto Springs, Florida

Summary: Professional diver and part-time teacher Luanne Fogarty has been busy mapping the underwater caverns that honeycomb the north Florida swamp where she lives. Working with her is her former lover, Harry McAllister, also a diver and an archaeologist, who has enlisted some graduate students to help. One day while she's searching for their next site she hears screaming and discovers a decaying cabin where a woman has just given birth, attended by two elderly midwives. Oddly though, there's no baby, and the midwives leave quickly, leaving the mother in danger of bleeding to death. Luanne calls for medical help and determines to make time in her schedule to locate the missing infant. The diving background and the rural Southern setting are especially well done.

Other books by the same author:
Dive Deep and Deadly, 2000

Other books you might like:
Doug Allyn, *The Michelle Mitchell Series*, 1995-
Nevada Barr, *The Anna Pigeon Series*, 1993-
Virginia Lanier, *The Jo Beth Siddon Series*, 1995-
Victoria McKernan, *The Chicago Nordejoong Series*, 1990-
Darryl Wimberley, *Dead Man's Bay*, 2000

4

SUSAN WITTIG ALBERT

Bloodroot

(New York: Berkley, 2001)

Story type: Amateur Detective; Domestic
Series: China Bayles. Book 10
Subject(s): American South; Family Problems; Illness
Major character(s): China Bayles, Store Owner, Herbalist
Time period(s): 2000s
Locale(s): Mississippi; Pecan Springs, Texas

Summary: In a change of pace from her usual Texas hill country setting of Pecan Springs, where former fast-track lawyer China Bayles runs a successful herb shop and tea room, and has finally settled into a happy marriage, the author sets this installment at a Mississippi plantation. Answering a plea for help from her mother, China arrives at her ancestral home, where she must deal with a serious illness, legal threats to the family property, and possibly even murder. All of these events have links to past secrets and problems going back five generations to slavery days. The usual herbal lore is interwoven into the somewhat more somber narrative.

Where it's reviewed:
Deadly Pleasures, Autumn 2001, page 45
Publishers Weekly, September 24, 2001, page 72

Other books by the same author:
Mistletoe Man, 2000
Lavender Lies, 1999
Chile Death, 1998
Love Lies Bleeding, 1997
Rueful Death, 1996

Other books you might like:
Diane Mott Davidson, *The Goldy Bear Schulz Series*, 1990-
Monica Ferris, *The Betsy Devonshire Series*, 1999-
Earlene Fowler, *The Benni Harper Series*, 1994-
Carolyn Haines, *The Sarah Booth Delaney Series*, 1999-
Janis Harrison, *The Bretta Solomon Series*, 1999-

5

CONRAD ALLEN (Pseudonym of Keith Miles)

Murder on the Minnesota

(New York: St. Martin's Press, 2002)

Story type: Historical; Private Detective
Series: George Porter Dillman/Genevieve Masefield. Book 3
Subject(s): Ships; Missionaries; Voyages and Travels
Major character(s): George Porter Dillman, Detective—Private; Genevieve Masefield, Detective—Private
Time period(s): 1900s (1908)
Locale(s): *Minnesota*, At Sea

Summary: George and Genevieve are hired by the Great Northern Steamship Company to stand watch on the *Minnesota*, a combination freighter and passenger ship bound for the Far East. Their job is to work undercover and mingle with the passengers and crew, being careful not to establish the same circle of friends. After two previous tumultuous assignments, they welcome what at first appears to be smooth sailing and a relaxing cruise—that is, until Father Slattery, a fanatical Catholic missionary dedicated to saving as many souls as possible, is murdered. This is only the first in a series of grim events to unfold over the course of the voyage. Under his own name and as Edward Marston, the author writes several other mystery series set during various historical periods.

Where it's reviewed:
Booklist, December 15, 2001, page 706
Publishers Weekly, December 1, 2001, page 68

Other books by the same author:
Murder on the Mauretania, 2000
Murder on the Lusitania, 1999

Other books you might like:
Max Allan Collins, *The Titanic Murders*, 1999
Mary Kruger, *No Honeymoon for Death*, 1995
Peter Lovesey, *The False Inspector Dew*, 1982
Sam McCarver, *The Case of Cabin 13*, 1999
Alan Vanneman, *Sherlock Holmes and the Giant Rat of Sumatra*, 2002

6

DONNA ANDREWS

Revenge of the Wrought-Iron Flamingos

(New York: St. Martin's Press, 2001)

Story type: Amateur Detective; Humor
Series: Meg Langslow. Book 3
Subject(s): History; Revolutionary War; Fairs
Major character(s): Meg Langslow, Artisan (metal worker), Detective—Amateur; Michael Waterston, Professor (drama), Boyfriend (of Meg)
Time period(s): 2000s
Locale(s): Yorktown, Virginia

Summary: A metal worker, Meg has a booth at a costumed crafts fair being held in conjunction with a re-creation of the British surrender at Yorktown, an affair presided over by her future mother-in-law, Mrs. Waterston, whom the troops have dubbed Madame Von Steuben for her dictatorial ways. Meg has also been charged with heading up the anachronism police, who are supposed to watch for any lapses from colonial attire such as wristwatches or zippers. She hopes Mrs. Waterston won't spot the wrought-iron flamingos she's stashed away to deliver to the client who commissioned them, but her secret is out when one of the flamingos is used as a murder weapon. Meg copes with the period clothing, the murders, and her own eccentric relations (who are legion) with her usual good humor, and the author has a lot of fun with the Virginia state pastime of obsessing over its own history.

Where it's reviewed:
Booklist, August 2001, page 2094
Deadly Pleasures, Autumn 2001, page 47
Library Journal, September 1, 2001, page 238
Mystery News, December 2001/January 2002, page 27

Other books by the same author:
Murder with Puffins, 2000
Murder with Peacocks, 1999

Other books you might like:
Carolyn Hart, *The Annie Laurance/Max Darling Series*, 1987-
Toni L.P. Kelner, *The Laura Fleming Series*, 1993-
Charlotte MacLeod, *The Sarah Kelling/Max Bittersohn Series*, 1979-
Sharyn McCrumb, *The Elizabeth MacPherson Series*, 1984-
Gillian Roberts, *The Amanda Pepper Series*, 1987-

7

SARAH ANDREWS

Fault Line

(New York: St. Martin's Press, 2002)

Story type: Amateur Detective
Series: Em Hansen. Book 6
Subject(s): Earthquakes; Relationships; Mormons
Major character(s): Em Hansen, Scientist (geologist), Detective—Amateur; Tom Latimer, FBI Agent
Time period(s): 2000s (2001)
Locale(s): Salt Lake City, Utah

Summary: An earthquake of moderate intensity rattles Salt Lake City as it prepares for the Winter Olympics, and Em's first thought on being awakened by it is that with any luck she won't be jobless any longer. She's been filling her time by working toward earning her credentials as a forensic geologist and by training with the FBI as well. When the job offer she's been hoping for comes, it's from her mentor at the FBI, Tom Latimer, who is investigating the murder of the state geologist, Sidney Smeeth, and wants Em to assist him. Busy as she is, Em doesn't have time to do much more than reflect on what seems to be a stalled relationship with her boyfriend, Mormon cop Ray Raymond, who's been out of town on family business and is making little effort to stay in touch. There's much fascinating earthquake lore woven in, and it's a relief when Em finally faces up to the enormous religious and cultural differences that are complicating her love life.

Where it's reviewed:
Booklist, December 15, 2001, page 706
Publishers Weekly, December 10, 2001, page 54

Other books by the same author:
An Eye for Gold, 2000
Bone Hunter, 1999
Only Flesh and Bones, 1998
Mother Nature, 1997
A Fall in Denver, 1995

Other books you might like:
Christine Andreae, *The Lee Squires Series*, 1992-
Nevada Barr, *The Anna Pigeon Series*, 1993-
Val Davis, *The Nicolette Scott Series*, 1996-
Marcia Muller, *The Sharon McCone Series*, 1977-
Judith Van Gieson, *The Neil Hamel Series*, 1988-

8

MIKE ASHLEY, Editor

The Mammoth Book of More Historical Whodunnits

(New York: Carroll & Graf, 2001)

Story type: Anthology; Historical
Subject(s): Short Stories; Historical

Summary: All 36 stories in this massive anthology are originals, commissioned by the tireless editor especially for this volume. Contributors include Steven Saylor, Peter Tremayne, Elizabeth Peters, Edward D. Hoch, Margaret Frazer, Marilyn

Todd, Michael Jecks, Susanna Gregory, and many more, with settings ranging from ancient Rome to the Byzantine Empire to medieval Ireland to Elizabethan London and featuring sleuths both fictional and historical, including Robin Hood, Christopher Columbus, and Geoffrey Chaucer.

Other books by the same author:
Royal Whodunnits, 1999 (editor)
Shakespearean Detectives, 1998 (editor)
Shakespearean Whodunnits, 1997 (editor)
The Mammoth Book of Historical Detectives, 1995 (editor)
The Mammoth Book of Historical Whodunnits, 1993 (editor)

Other books you might like:
Martin H. Greenberg, *Murder Most Medieval*, 2001
editor
Maxim Jakubowski, *Murder through the Ages*, 2001
editor
Miriam Grace Monfredo, *Crime through Time*, 1997
Sharan Newman, co-editor
Miriam Grace Monfredo, *Crime through Time II*, 1998
Sharan Newman, co-editor
Sharan Newman, *Crime through Time III*, 2001
editor

9

NANCY ATHERTON

Aunt Dimity: Detective

(New York: Viking, 2001)

Story type: Amateur Detective
Series: Aunt Dimity. Number 7
Subject(s): Small Town Life; Ghosts; Twins
Major character(s): Lori Shepherd, Parent; Dimity Westwood, Spirit; Nicholas Fox, Relative (town vicar's nephew)
Time period(s): 2000s
Locale(s): Finch, England (Cotswolds)

Summary: A month spent in America with her husband's stuffy family has made Lori long for their cozy cottage in the Cotswolds, a bequest from the late Dimity Westwood, her mother's friend and Lori's mysterious benefactor. Her benevolent presence can still be felt in the cottage, and in times of need she offers comfort and sage advice to Lori in the form of messages that form themselves in the blue leather notebook she left her. When Lori and the twins return to Finch, leaving her husband Bill in Boston to wind up some family business, she is shocked when murder strikes the peaceful village—the first since 1872, when one shepherd struck a fatal blow to the head of another with his crook. The victim is nosy, disagreeable Prunella Hopper, known as Pruneface to the villagers, who loved nothing better than to spy on her neighbors and spread malicious rumors about their behavior. One of Lori's friends is suspected of the deed, and she teams up with Nicholas Fox, up from London to visit his vicar father, to find the real killer—with the kindly guidance of Aunt Dimity, of course. A recipe for gilded gingerbread is included.

Where it's reviewed:
Booklist, September 1, 2001, page 55
Library Journal, September 1, 2001, page 238

Other books by the same author:
Aunt Dimity Beats the Devil, 2000
Aunt Dimity's Christmas, 1999
Aunt Dimity Digs In, 1998
Aunt Dimity's Good Deed, 1996
Aunt Dimity and the Duke, 1994

Other books you might like:
Mignon F. Ballard, *The Augusta Goodnight Series*, 1999-
Dorothy Cannell, *The Ellie Haskell Series*, 1984-
Charles Mathes, *The Girl at the End of the Line*, 1999
Mary Stewart, *Rose Cottage*, 1997
Susan Wade, *Walking Rain*, 1996

10

T.F. BANKS

The Thief-Taker

(New York: Delacorte, 2001)

Story type: Historical; Police Procedural
Series: Memoirs of a Bow Street Runner. Book 1
Subject(s): Crime and Criminals; Social Classes; History
Major character(s): Henry Morton, Police Officer (Bow Street Runner)
Time period(s): 1810s (1815)
Locale(s): London, England

Summary: Regency England has become a popular setting for historical mysteries, and this colorful debut introduces Bow Street Runner Henry Morton, a detective who is part of London's first police force. He's called in when a socially prominent gentleman, Halbert Glendinning, is found dead of asphyxiation in a driverless hackney cab. The death is ruled accidental, but the man's fiancee thinks otherwise and she enlists Morton, who also has his suspicions about it, to conduct a discreet private investigation into the matter. Such an investigation was permissible, as the Bow Street Runners were not so much public servants as free agents who were paid only if they got their man and could operate on their own if they desired. His search for the killer takes him through all strata of society in London and exposes evils that threaten his own life.

Where it's reviewed:
Booklist, September 1, 2001, page 55
Mystery News, October/November 2001, page 20
Publishers Weekly, September 10, 2001, page 64

Other books you might like:
Bruce Alexander, *The Sir John Fielding Series*, 1994-
Stephanie Barron, *The Jane Austen Series*, 1996-
John Creasey, *The Masters of Bow Street*, 1974
Kate Ross, *The Julian Kestrel Series*, 1993-1997
Rosemary Stevens, *The Beau Brummell Series*, 2000-

11

JO BANNISTER

Echoes of Lies

(New York: St. Martin's Press, 2001)

Story type: Private Detective

Subject(s): Kidnapping; Guilt; Secrets
Major character(s): Elspeth Brodie Farrell, Detective—Private, Single Parent; Jack Deacon, Police Officer (detective inspector); Daniel Hood, Teacher (of mathematics), Crime Victim (tortured)
Time period(s): 2000s
Locale(s): Dimmock, England (south coast)

Summary: Recently divorced single mother Brodie Farrell has started her own search service, Looking for Something?, in the small south coast village of Dimmock, where she hunts down rare books and other objects people are looking for. One day she's shown a photograph of a young man and asked to find him, and she proves as adept at tracking down people as objects, identifying him as mathematics teacher Daniel Hood and effectively turning him over to her clients. When he's subsequently tortured and left for dead by those clients, Brodie is overcome with guilt and reports the incident to the police in the person of Jack Deacon. When Daniel has no place safe to stay, she offers to put him up herself and to help him find the thugs who attacked him. Both are reluctant to involve the police, much to Deacon's annoyance, especially when their investigation takes a dangerous and surprising turn. First in a new series by the author of the long-running Castlemere ensemble police procedurals.

Where it's reviewed:
Booklist, December 1, 2001, page 632
Drood Review, November/December 2001, page 7
Library Journal, December 2001, page 178
New York Times Book Review, December 23, 2001, page 13
Publishers Weekly, November 19, 2001, page 51

Other books by the same author:
Changelings, 2000
The Hireling's Tale, 1999
Broken Lines, 1998
No Birds Sang, 1996
Burning Desire, 1995

Other books you might like:
Liza Cody, *The Anna Lee Series*, 1980-
Sarah Dunant, *The Hannah Wolfe Series*, 1992-
Ann Granger, *The Fran Varaday Series*, 1997-
P.D. James, *An Unsuitable Job for a Woman*, 1972
Michelle Spring, *The Laura Principal Series*, 1994-

12

STEPHANIE BARRON (Pseudonym of Francine Mathews)

Jane and the Prisoner of Wool House

(New York: Bantam, 2001)

Story type: Historical; Amateur Detective
Series: Jane Austen. Book 6
Subject(s): Literature; Military Life; Ships
Major character(s): Jane Austen, Historical Figure, Writer (novelist)
Time period(s): 1800s (1807)
Locale(s): Southampton, England

Summary: Jane's brother Frank, a captain in the Royal Navy, is shocked to learn that an old friend and shipmate accused of killing a French captain after he had already surrendered during a battle off the Portuguese coast may be hanged for this serious infraction of the Articles of War. Unable to believe Tom Seagrave could actually be guilty of such a heinous act, Frank asks Jane to help him clear Tom's name. She gets a chance to help a physician friend who is tending wounded French prisoners of war at Wool House, a fortress turned prison, where she hopes to uncover a witness who will corroborate Tom's innocence. As usual, the narrative is told in the form of entries in Jane's own journal. As Francine Mathews, the author also writes a contemporary series about Nantucket police detective Merry Folger and stand-alone spy thrillers.

Where it's reviewed:
Booklist, October 15, 2001, page 384
Drood Review, November/December 2001, page 11
Library Journal, November 1, 2001, page 126
Mystery News, December 2001/January 2002, page 18
Publishers Weekly, November 5, 2001, page 45

Other books by the same author:
Jane and the Stillroom Maid, 2000
Jane and the Genius of the Place, 1999
Jane and the Wandering Eye, 1998
Jane and the Man of the Cloth, 1997
Jane and the Unpleasantness at Scargrave Manor, 1996

Other books you might like:
Bruce Alexander, *The Sir John Fielding Series*, 1994-
John Dickson Carr, *Captain Cutthroat*, 1955
Wilder Perkins, *The Bartholomew Hoare Series*, 1998-
Kate Ross, *The Julian Kestrel Series*, 1993-1997
Rosemary Stevens, *The Beau Brummell Series*, 2000-

13

NANCY BARTHOLOMEW

Strip Poker

(New York: St. Martin's Press, 2001)

Story type: Amateur Detective
Series: Sierra Lavotoni. Number 4
Subject(s): Entertainment; Humor; Italian Americans
Major character(s): Sierra Lavotoni, Stripper, Detective—Amateur
Time period(s): 2000s
Locale(s): Panama City, Florida

Summary: Sierra is a nice Italian girl who happens to make her living as an exotic dancer at the Tiffany Gentleman's Club in Panama City, owned by a not very bright but good-hearted fellow named Vincent Gambuzzo. One night, not long before Christmas, Sierra is in the middle of her routine when alarms go off summoning the bouncers to Vincent's office, and when Sierra arrives on the scene, she learns that he's lost the club in a poker game, tempers have flared, and a shoot-out has left one player dead and Sierra's friend Bruno in critical condition. The new ownership renames the club Big Mike's House of Booty, catering to a roughneck crowd and providing less than desirable working conditions to its employees. Determined to return the club to Vincent and find out who wounded Bruno, Sierra turns detective, a role her boyfriend, homicide detective John Nailor, would prefer she give up.

Other books by the same author:
Film Strip, 2001
Dragstrip, 1999
The Miracle Strip, 1998

Other books you might like:
Nancy J. Cohen, *The Marla Shore Series*, 1999-
Janet Evanovich, *The Stephanie Plum Series*, 1994-
Tony Fennelly, *The Margot Fortier Series*, 1994-
Sarah Strohmeyer, *Bubbles Unbound*, 2001
Kathleen Taylor, *The Tory Bauer Series*, 1995-

14

M.C. BEATON (Pseudonym of Marion Chesney)

Agatha Raisin and the Love from Hell

(New York: St. Martin's Press, 2001)

Story type: Amateur Detective; Traditional
Series: Agatha Raisin. Book 10
Subject(s): Small Town Life; Marriage; Cancer
Major character(s): Agatha Raisin, Public Relations (retired), Detective—Amateur; James Lacey, Spouse (of Agatha); Charles Fraith, Friend (of Agatha), Nobleman
Time period(s): 2000s
Locale(s): Carlsley, England (Cotswolds)

Summary: When at last the stubborn and cranky Agatha achieves her long-cherished dream of marrying her beloved next-door neighbor James Lacey, she finds married life is far from the idyllic state she had envisioned. First of all, since she and James find it so impossible to live under the same roof they still maintain their separate cottages. Still unversed in the domestic arts, she turns his laundry pink when she fails to properly sort their clothes. James does not take it well, nor does he approve of her decision to return to work, promoting a new line of boots from a local shoemaker. Then she no sooner learns James has cancer and is concealing it from her than he disappears and his former mistress, Melissa Shepherd, is murdered. Agatha's old friend Sir Charles Fraith appears on the scene in time to help her find James and solve Melissa's murder.

Where it's reviewed:
Booklist, August 2001, page 2095
Deadly Pleasures, Autumn 2001, page 45
Library Journal, December 2001, page 180
Mystery News, December 2001/January 2002, page 18
Publishers Weekly, October 1, 2001, page 39

Other books by the same author:
Agatha Raisin and the Fairies of Fryfam, 2000
Agatha Raisin and the Wizard of Evesham, 1999
Agatha Raisin and the Wellspring of Death, 1998
Agatha Raisin and the Terrible Tourist, 1997
Agatha Raisin and the Murderous Marriage, 1996

Other books you might like:
Simon Brett, *The Body on the Beach*, 2000
Jeanne M. Dams, *The Dorothy Martin Series*, 1995-
Hazel Holt, *The Mrs. Malory Series*, 1989-
Joyce Porter, *The Honourable Constance Ethel Morrison-Burke Series*, 1970-1979
Colin Watson, *The Flaxborough Series*, 1967-1973

15

NANCY BELL

Biggie and the Quincy Ghost

(New York: St. Martin's Press, 2001)

Story type: Amateur Detective; Humor
Series: Biggie Weatherford. Number 5
Subject(s): Small Town Life; History; American South
Major character(s): Fiona Wooten "Biggie" Weatherford, Aged Person, Detective—Amateur; J.R. Weatherford, Child
Time period(s): 2000s
Locale(s): Quincy, Texas; Job's Crossing, Texas

Summary: Twelve-year-old J.R., who has been raised by his redoubtable grandmother Biggie, a leading citizen of their small Texas town, doesn't especially want to accompany her on a visit to nearby Quincy, until he learns they are going to be staying in a haunted hotel. The purpose of their trip is so Biggie can attend a workshop on how to start an historical society in their own town, but no sooner have they arrived than murder strikes and a young woman's body is found in the hotel courtyard. With the local sheriff hospitalized, Biggie gets another crack at solving a murder, and young J.R.—who narrates the book—finds their visit far from the boring two days he was anticipating. This is announced as the final book in the series. As usual, a recipe (for wedding cake) from the kitchen of their cook, Willie Mae, is included.

Where it's reviewed:
Booklist, August 2001, page 2094
Mystery News, October/November 2001, page 30

Other books by the same author:
Biggie and the Meddlesome Mailman, 1999
Biggie and the Fricaseed Fat Man, 1998
Biggie and the Mangled Mortician, 1997
Biggie and the Poisoned Politician, 1996

Other books you might like:
Deborah Adams, *The Jesus Creek Series*, 1992-
Anne George, *The Southern Sisters Series*, 1996-2001
Carolyn Hart, *The Henrie O Series*, 1993-
Joan Hess, *The Maggody Series*, 1987-
Elizabeth Daniels Squire, *The Peaches Dann Series*, 1994-

16

CAROL LEA BENJAMIN

The Long Good Boy

(New York: Walker, 2001)

Story type: Private Detective
Series: Rachel & Dash. Number 6
Subject(s): Animals/Dogs; Prostitution; City and Town Life
Major character(s): Rachel Alexander, Detective—Private, Animal Trainer (dogs); Dashiell, Animal (dog), Sidekick
Time period(s): 2000s
Locale(s): New York, New York

Summary: Rachel and her pit bull, Dash, take on a trio of unusual clients: three transvestite hookers, Jasmine, LaDonna, and Chi Chi, who are understandably upset over the murder of one of their colleagues right after the Greenwich Village Halloween parade. Knowing that the the cops aren't about to spend any time on the case, they ask Rachel to investigate. She notes that a meatpacking executive was also murdered right after the parade in a manner suggesting a mob execution. Wondering if the two cases could be in any way related, Rachel decides she has to get into the meatpacking plant and look around. The only way she can accomplish this is to quickly train Chi Chi's dachshund to open a window for her and to go undercover as a prostitute herself in order to solve the case. Unlike most doggie mysteries, this one is definitely not a cozy, despite its punning title.

Where it's reviewed:
Booklist, September 1, 2001, page 55
Library Journal, August 2001, page 170
Publishers Weekly, August 6, 2001, page 64

Other books by the same author:
The Wrong Dog, 2000
Lady Vanishes, 1999
A Hell of a Dog, 1998
The Dog Who Knew Too Much, 1997
This Dog for Hire, 1996

Other books you might like:
Laurien Berenson, *The Melanie Travers Series*, 1995-
Lawrence Block, *The Bernie Rhodenbarr Series*, 1977-
Melissa Cleary, *The Jackie Walsh Series*, 1992-
Susan Conant, *The Holly Winter Series*, 1989-
Virginia Lanier, *The Jo Beth Siddon Series*, 1995-

17

LAURIEN BERENSON

Once Bitten

(New York: Kensington, 2001)

Story type: Amateur Detective
Series: Melanie Travis. Book 8
Subject(s): Animals/Dogs; Weddings; Missing Persons
Major character(s): Melanie Travis, Animal Trainer (poodles), Single Parent
Time period(s): 2000s
Locale(s): Greenwich, Connecticut; Hartford, Connecticut

Summary: With her own wedding plans on permanent hold since her fiance decided to go off and find himself, Melanie is happy to pitch in when her brother Frank decides to take the plunge with his girlfriend, Bertie Kennedy. Melanie enlists the aid of her friend and fellow dog-handler Sara Bentley, who's lately been moonlighting as a wedding planner. Before anything much is accomplished, Sara disappears without a trace, and Bertie implores Melanie to either find her or take over the wedding herself. To complicate matters further, Melanie's ex-husband turns up unexpectedly and starts following her around like a lovesick puppy. Then Sara's cottage burns down, a woman's body is found in the ruins, and Melanie must find out if Sara is really dead or just missing.

Where it's reviewed:
Library Journal, September 1, 2001, page 128
Mystery News, October/November 2001, page 23
Publishers Weekly, July 9, 2001, page 50

Other books by the same author:
Unleashed, 2000
Hush Puppy, 1999
Watchdog, 1998
Hair of the Dog, 1997
Dog Eat Dog, 1996

Other books you might like:
Carol Lea Benjamin, *The Rachel Alexander Series*, 1996-
Susan Conant, *The Holly Winter Series*, 1989-
Patricia Guiver, *The Delilah Doolittle Series*, 1997-
Virginia Lanier, *The Jo Beth Siddon Series*, 1995-
Barbara Moore, *The Doberman Wore Black*, 1983

18

RUTH BIRMINGHAM (Pseudonym of Walter Sorrells)

Blue Plate Special

(New York: Berkley, 2001)

Story type: Private Detective
Series: Sunny Childs. Number 4
Subject(s): American South; Hostages; City and Town Life
Major character(s): Sunny Childs, Detective—Private
Time period(s): 2000s
Locale(s): Atlanta, Georgia (Cabbagetown)

Summary: Cabbagetown is an ungentrified poor white neighborhood in East Atlanta, originally a company town settled by hillbillies from Appalachia that eventually got swallowed up by the city when the mill they worked for closed down. Sunny is enjoying her lunch with a favorite client at the Blind Pig, a no-nonsense Cabbagetown diner where the waitresses call you ''hon'' and the daily special is written on a chalkboard hanging above the grill, when their meal is interrupted by a white teenager in full rap regalia who pulls a gun and shoots a customer. At least Sunny assumes this is what happened; she was in the bathroom at the time. The kid takes all the customers hostage while trying to decide what to do next, and Sunny has to figure out how to get everybody out of this situation alive.

Other books by the same author:
Sweet Georgia, 2000
Fulton County Blues, 1999
Atlanta Graves, 1998

Other books you might like:
Virginia Lanier, *The Jo Beth Siddon Series*, 1995-
Laura Lippman, *The Tess Monaghan Series*, 1997-
Katy Munger, *The Casey Jones Series*, 1997-
Kathy Hogan Trocheck, *The Callahan Garrity Series*, 1992-
Fred Willard, *Down on Ponce*, 1998

19

SALLIE BISSELL

A Darker Justice

(New York: Bantam, 2002)

Story type: Psychological Suspense; Action/Adventure
Series: Mary Crow. Book 2
Subject(s): Militia Movements; Native Americans; Christmas

Major character(s): Mary Crow, Lawyer (assistant district attorney), Indian (half-Cherokee); Daniel Safer, FBI Agent
Time period(s): 2000s
Locale(s): Little Jump Off, North Carolina; Atlanta, Georgia

Summary: Somebody is murderering federal judges, and the FBI thinks that Mary's old friend and mentor, Judge Irene Hannah, may be next. When Hannah disappears after refusing federal protection, the FBI recruits Mary to accompany Agent Daniel Safer on a dangerous mission to find and rescue Hannah. Their destination: the North Carolina wilderness where Mary grew up and where she survived horrific experiences during a recent camping trip gone wrong. It's also the location of a racist right-wing militia movement that uses students from a military school of last resort to assassinate federal judges who have handed down decisions of which they disapprove. There is a romantic subplot involving Mary's former lover, Jonathan Walkingstick, who is now in a relationship with another woman.

Where it's reviewed:
Publishers Weekly, November 19, 2001, page 49

Other books by the same author:
In the Forest of Harm, 2001

Other books you might like:
Nevada Barr, *The Anna Pigeon Series*, 1993-
Thomas Perry, *The Jane Whitefield Series*, 1995-
Dana Stabenow, *The Kate Shugak Series*, 1992-
Mark T. Sullivan, *The Purification Ceremony*, 1997
Judith Van Gieson, *The Neil Hamel Series*, 1988-

20

ETHAN BLACK

All the Dead Were Strangers

(New York: Ballantine, 2001)

Story type: Police Procedural; Action/Adventure
Series: Conrad Voort. Number 3
Subject(s): Terrorism; City and Town Life; Conspiracies
Major character(s): Conrad Voort, Detective—Police (NYPD sex crimes detective)
Time period(s): 2000s
Locale(s): New York, New York

Summary: When Meechum Keefe, an old friend of Voort's, dies in a hotel fire the day after the two meet for drinks, Voort goes looking for answers to his death. His only clue is a cocktail napkin Keefe had given him with five names on it that he wanted checked out. As he investigates, Voort discovers several of the people listed have also died in apparent accidents, and another, a woman doctor who specializes in tropical diseases, comes close to dying in another. Voort also finds out that all the names on the list have some sort of tie to international terrorists—the doctor, for example, has treated a Saudi-born terrorist and former financier named Abu Bin Hussein, now hiding out in Afghanistan and a thinly disguised stand-in for the now notorious Osama bin Laden. As he investigates further, Voort learns of an imminent terrorist action that threatens the NYPD and also of a secret anti-terrorist government group, the National Threat Assessment Agency, that has become nearly as dangerous as the individuals it targets. Published before the September 11 attack on the World Trade Center and the Pentagon, it's a timely and thoughtful exploration of a topic that has touched us all.

Where it's reviewed:
Booklist, June 1, 2001, page 1795
Library Journal, August 2001, page 156
Publishers Weekly, July 16, 2001, page 158

Other books by the same author:
Irresistible, 2000
The Broken Hearts Club, 1999

Other books you might like:
Michael Connelly, *The Harry Bosch Series*, 1992-
Robert Crais, *Hostage*, 2001
Jeffery Deaver, *The Lincoln Rhyme Series*, 1997-
Linda Fairstein, *The Alexandra Cooper Series*, 1996-
John Sandford, *The Lucas Davenport Series*, 1989-

21

ELEANOR TAYLOR BLAND

Whispers in the Dark

(New York: St. Martin's Press, 2001)

Story type: Police Procedural
Series: Marti MacAlister. Book 9
Subject(s): African Americans; Social Issues; Hurricanes
Major character(s): Marti MacAlister, Police Officer; Matthew "Vik" Jessenovik, Police Officer
Time period(s): 2000s
Locale(s): Lincoln Prairie, Illinois; Bahamas

Summary: The discovery of a severed arm in their north Chicago suburb of Lincoln Prairie sends Marti and her partner, Vik Jessenovik, on the trail of a series of such incidents going back 20 years. It leads also to the history of the Lincoln Prairie art world and its present-day artists, as well as to a 1970s hippie commune. At the same time, Marti is concerned about her best friend Sharon, who's going through an intensely difficult time as she recovers from an unpleasant divorce, copes with a dying mother, and tries to raise a daughter alone. Sharon is also involved with a man who is possibly a serial killer and who entices her and her daughter to the Bahamas just as a major hurricane is headed for the islands. Marti follows close behind.

Where it's reviewed:
Booklist, September 15, 2001, page 197
Publishers Weekly, October 1, 2001, page 41

Other books by the same author:
Scream in Silence, 2000
Tell No Tales, 1999
See No Evil, 1998
Keep Still, 1996
Done Wrong, 1995

Other books you might like:
Nora DeLoach, *The Candi Covington Series*, 1997-
Terris McMahon Grimes, *The Theresa Galloway Series*, 1996-
Judith Smith-Levin, *The Starletta Duvall Series*, 1996-
Valerie Wilson Wesley, *The Tamara Hayle Series*, 1994-

Paula L. Woods, *The Charlotte Justice Series*, 1999-

22

LAWRENCE BLOCK

Hope to Die

(New York: Morrow, 2001)

Story type: Private Detective
Series: Matt Scudder. Book 15
Subject(s): Crime and Criminals; Serial Killers; Alcoholism
Major character(s): Matt Scudder, Detective—Private
Time period(s): 2000s
Locale(s): New York, New York

Summary: Although Matt Scudder doesn't know them, he and his wife Elaine happen to be in the same room with Byrne and Susan Hollander shortly before the couple is killed in a savage home invasion of their Upper West Side townhouse. The killers are quickly found by the police, both dead, and the case is closed. Matt, however, is strangely drawn to it, sensing it's perhaps not as simple as it seems, and as he investigates he gets a strong sense a third person is involved, a mastermind who is controlling everything that happens. Matt is 62 now, less edgy and more philosophical than in his earlier cases, and other than the killings, his concerns are more domestic, involving not only his current marriage but the death of his ex-wife and his tentative relationship with their two sons. His life is a comfortable one and he's been sober for years now, but he still attends AA meetings and still donates money to charitable causes. The author also writes other popular series, including those about burglar/bookseller Bernie Rhodenbarr and the sleepless spy Evan Tanner.

Where it's reviewed:
Booklist, September 1, 2001, page 3
Entertainment Weekly, November 2, 2001, page 68
Library Journal, September 1, 2001, page 239
People Weekly, November 12, 2001, page 46
Publishers Weekly, August 27, 2001, page 56

Other books by the same author:
Everybody Dies, 1998
Even the Wicked, 1997
A Long Line of Dead Men, 1994
The Devil Knows You're Dead, 1993
A Walk Among the Tombstones, 1992

Other books you might like:
Thomas Adcock, *The Neal Hockaday Series*, 1989-
James Lee Burke, *The Dave Robicheaux Series*, 1987-
Tucker Coe, *The Mitch Tobin Series*, 1966-1972
Stephen Greenleaf, *The John Marshall Tanner Series*, 1979-
Bill Pronzini, *The Nameless Detective Series*, 1971-

23

STEPHEN BOOTH

Dancing with the Virgins

(New York: Scribner, 2001)

Story type: Police Procedural; Traditional
Series: Ben Cooper/Sergeant Fry. Book 2
Subject(s): Serial Killers; Rural Life; Animals/Dogs
Major character(s): Ben Cooper, Police Officer (detective constable); Diane Fry, Police Officer (detective sergeant)
Time period(s): 2000s
Locale(s): Derbyshire, England

Summary: When a young woman, Jenny Watson, is found stabbed on the moors and arranged in a dancing pose at the ancient stone circle known as the Nine Virgins, the police believe it to be the work of an unknown attacker, who stabbed another young woman in the face a few weeks earlier. She survived, however. Then another young woman is found dead on the moor, her body also positioned as if she were dancing. Ben Cooper, an easy-going local man whose father was a well-known and much-loved police officer, is again teamed up with his former partner Diane Fry, an ambitious and single-minded officer and newcomer to the area, who has been promoted ahead of Ben. Both are very effective cops in their own ways, but with little evidence to go on and a relationship that is strained by their temperamental differences, they find the case extremely difficult to solve. A subplot involves dog fights and an animal rights activist.

Where it's reviewed:
Booklist, September 1, 2001, page 55
Deadly Pleasures, Autumn 2001, page 56
Library Journal, September 15, 2001, page 117
Publishers Weekly, September 3, 2001, page 65

Other books by the same author:
Black Dog, 2000

Other books you might like:
Reginald Hill, *The Dalziel and Pascoe Series*, 1970-
Peter Lovesey, *The Peter Diamond Series*, 1991-
Val McDermid, *A Place of Execution*, 2000
Ruth Rendell, *The Inspector Wexford Series*, 1964-
Peter Robinson, *The Alan Banks Series*, 1987-

24

RHYS BOWEN (Pseudonym of Janet Quin-Harkin)

Murphy's Law

(New York: St. Martin's Press, 2001)

Story type: Historical; Amateur Detective
Subject(s): Irish Americans; Social Conditions; Identity, Concealed
Major character(s): Molly Murphy, Fugitive, Detective—Amateur; Daniel Sullivan, Police Officer (captain)
Time period(s): 1900s (1901)
Locale(s): New York, New York; Liverpool, England; Ireland

Summary: When the landowner's son attempts to have his way with her, fiery young Molly Murphy fights back and accidentally kills him—a hanging offense in Ireland at the time. She flees to Liverpool, where she is befriended by Kathleen O'Connor, a young mother in a sad predicament of her own. She's dying of tuberculosis and won't be able to join her husband in New York; instead, she begs Molly to assume her identity and see that the children are delivered to their father. The ocean crossing is scarcely what Molly was expecting, but she arrives safely, only to become a suspect when a fellow voyager is murdered on Ellis Island. With the help of a young police captain, Daniel Sullivan, Molly attempts to find the real killer in order to clear herself, and goes from one dangerous situation to another, all the while trying to find work and shelter in a city where everyone is a stranger. A little improbable in spots, it's still a colorful picture of New York at the turn of the last century, a city full of social evils, as well as rare opportunities for a lucky few. The author also writes the Evan Evans series about a young constable in a contemporary Welsh village.

Where it's reviewed:
Booklist, August 2001, page 2095
Mystery News, October/November 2001, page 25
Publishers Weekly, September 3, 2001, page 67

Other books by the same author:
Evan Can Wait, 2001
Evan and Elle, 2000
Evanly Choirs, 1999
Evan Help Us, 1998
Evans Above, 1997

Other books you might like:
Lauren Belfer, *City of Light*, 1999
Karen Rose Cercone, *The Helen Sorby/Miles Kachigan Series*, 1997-
Jeanne M. Dams, *The Hilda Johansson Series*, 1999-
Dianne Day, *The Fremont Jones Series*, 1995-
Victoria Thompson, *The Sarah Brandt Series*, 1999-

25

C.J. BOX

Open Season

(New York: Putnam, 2001)

Story type: Amateur Detective
Subject(s): Endangered Species; Hunting; American West
Major character(s): Joe Pickett, Game Warden
Time period(s): 2000s
Locale(s): Twelve Sleep, Wyoming

Summary: Joe Pickett may not be brilliant at his new job as game warden in Twelve Sleep, but he's conscientious, courageous, and incorruptible—qualities that don't necessarily make him popular among the locals, most of whom hunt, some illegally, by going over their limits or bagging animals either out of season or on the endangered species list. When three elk hunters are found dead, one practically in Joe's backyard, the local police solve the case so quickly that Joe begins to suspect there is a cover-up going on. At some risk to himself and his family, he starts an investigation of his own, and quickly turns up a nasty mess involving a natural gas pipeline and an endangered species thought to be extinct. A superb sense of the natural splendor of the author's home state and a fine, believable hero lift this far above the usual first novel.

Where it's reviewed:
Booklist, May 1, 2001, page 1622
Deadly Pleasures, Autumn 2001, page 28
New York Times Book Review, August 5, 2001, page 17

Other books you might like:
Nevada Barr, *Blood Lure*, 2001
Gregory Bean, *The Harry Starbranch Series*, 1995-
Michael McGarrity, *The Kevin Kerney Series*, 1996-
Les Standiford, *Black Mountain*, 2000
Judith Van Gieson, *Raptor*, 1990

26

LILIAN JACKSON BRAUN

The Cat Who Went Up the Creek

(New York: Putnam, 2001)

Story type: Amateur Detective
Series: Cat Who. Book 24
Subject(s): Animals/Cats; Small Town Life; Haunted Houses
Major character(s): James Mackintosh ''Qwill'' Qwilleran, Journalist (newspaper columnist), Wealthy; Koko, Animal (Siamese cat); Yum Yum, Animal (Siamese cat)
Time period(s): 2000s
Locale(s): Black Creek, Michigan

Summary: When the new owners of the Nutcracker Inn in rural Black Creek complain that the old mansion is haunted, Qwill agrees to stay there for a while and try to find the source of the problem. Naturally he brings along his companions and fellow sleuths, Koko and Yum Yum, who are pleased with the squirrel-watching opportunities the quaint old place provides. Qwill eventually moves into a cabin on the premises, the former occupant of which had been murdered, and is drawn into an investigation of the crime, with the usual assistance from his remarkable feline companions. He also has time to gather material for his next column by attending various local events, such as a Gilbert and Sullivan operetta, a lumberjack festival, and the opening of a nearby antique mall.

Where it's reviewed:
Booklist, November 15, 2001, page 523
Mystery News, December 2001/January 2002, page 20
Publishers Weekly, November 19, 2001, page 51

Other books by the same author:
The Cat Who Smelled a Rat, 2001
The Cat Who Robbed a Bank, 2000
The Cat Who Saw Stars, 1999
The Cat Who Sang for the Birds, 1998
The Cat Who Tailed a Thief, 1997

Other books you might like:
Garrison Allen, *The Big Mike Series*, 1994-
Rita Mae Brown, *The Mrs. Murphy Series*, 1990-
Barbara Collins, *Too Many Tomcats and Other Feline Tales of Suspense*, 2000
short stories
Carole Nelson Douglas, *The Midnight Louie Series*, 1992-
Shirley Rousseau Murphy, *The Joe Grey Series*, 1996-

27

SIMON BRETT

Death on the Downs

(New York: Berkley, 2001)

Story type: Amateur Detective; Traditional
Series: Carole Seddon. Book 2

Subject(s): Small Town Life; Animals/Dogs; Friendship
Major character(s): Carole Seddon, Divorced Person, Civil Servant (retired); Jude, Friend (of Carole)
Time period(s): 2000s
Locale(s): Fethering, England (West Sussex); Weldisham, England (West Sussex)

Summary: With her life turned upside down by divorce and an early retirement from the Home Office, Carole has settled in the tiny village of Fethering where she takes long walks, works the *Times* crossword, and, more recently, spends time with her mysterious New Age neighbor Jude. One day while out on a solitary walk near the neighboring village of Weldisham, she takes shelter from a sudden rainstorm in an old barn and discovers a fertilizer bag full of human bones. It turns out that the young woman to whom they may have belonged, Tamsin Lutteridge, had once come to Jude for help in healing her chronic fatigue syndrome. Carole and Jude are a study in opposites, with the exuberant Jude making up for what the more conventional Carole lacks in self-confidence. In the course of their collaborative sleuthing, the author pokes a bit of fun at seemingly sleepy rural villages, class distinctions, and other English institutions. He also writes two other mystery series, one starring the chronically out-of-work, alcoholic actor Charles Paris, the other featuring the resourceful silver-haired widow Emma Pargeter.

Where it's reviewed:
Booklist, July 2001, page 1985
Mystery News, October/November 2001, page 30
Publishers Weekly, July 23, 2001, page 53

Other books by the same author:
The Body on the Beach, 2000

Other books you might like:
Robert Barnard, *A Little Local Murder*, 1983
M.C. Beaton, *The Agatha Raisin Series*, 1992-
Jeanne M. Dams, *The Dorothy Martin Series*, 1995-
Hazel Holt, *The Mrs. Malory Series*, 1989-
Betty Rowlands, *The Melissa Craig Series*, 1990-

28

SINCLAIR BROWNING

Crack Shot

(New York: Bantam, 2002)

Story type: Private Detective
Series: Trade Ellis. Book 4
Subject(s): Missing Persons; Mexican Americans; Runaways
Major character(s): Trade Ellis, Detective—Private, Rancher
Time period(s): 2000s
Locale(s): La Cienega, Arizona; Tucson, Arizona

Summary: A self-proclaimed ''dirty shirt'' cowgirl who's also part Apache, Trade Ellis moonlights as a private detective when she isn't tending cattle on her Vaca Grande Ranch. When the stepson of a friend escapes from Los Hijos, the local juvenile detention center, and is killed, she's asked by the grandmother of Eddy Gallegos, one of the two boys who were with the victim, to find her grandson before the authorities do. It's not a job Trade relishes, but because of her connection with the dead boy's stepfather, a former congressman, she takes it. Besides, not many other jobs have been coming her way. Soon she realizes that Eddy may not have left Los Hijos of his own free will and he may be in terrible danger.

Other books by the same author:
Rode Hard, Put Away Dead, 2001
The Sporting Club, 2000
The Last Song Dogs, 1999

Other books you might like:
David Cole, *The Laura Winslow Series*, 2000-
Earlene Fowler, *The Benni Harper Series*, 1994-
J.A. Jance, *Kiss of the Bees*, 2000
Judith Van Gieson, *The Neil Hamel Series*, 1988-
Betty Webb, *Desert Noir*, 2001

29

FIONA BUCKLEY

Queen of Ambition

(New York: Scribner, 2001)

Story type: Historical
Series: Ursula Blanchard. Book 5
Subject(s): Kings, Queens, Rulers, etc.; Espionage; History
Major character(s): Ursula Blanchard, Gentlewoman, Spy
Time period(s): 16th century (1564)
Locale(s): Cambridge, England

Summary: Ursula, a lady-in-waiting to Queen Elizabeth who also acts as a spy for Her Majesty, is given another assignment when Elizabeth makes a Royal Progress to Cambridge in the company of her usual entourage. The students are about to stage a show for the Queen, but her secretary of state suspects that the performance may in fact be a cover-up for a plot to take her life. Also, for some reason, Elizabeth has arranged for her court favorite, Sir Robert Dudley, to be betrothed to her cousin and archrival Mary, Queen of Scots. It's up to Ursula to find out exactly what is going on.

Where it's reviewed:
Booklist, November 1, 2001, page 462
New York Times Book Review, January 6, 2002, page 19
Publishers Weekly, November 12, 2001, page 38

Other books by the same author:
Queen's Ransom, 2000
To Ruin a Queen, 2000
The Doublet Affair, 1998
To Shield the Queen, 1997

Other books you might like:
Ann Dukthas, *In the Time of the Poisoned Queen*, 1997
Kathy Lynn Emerson, *The Susanna, Lady Appleton Series*, 1997-
Karen Harper, *The Elizabeth I Series*, 1999-
Simon Hawke, *The Shakespeare & Smythe Series*, 2000-
Edward Marston, *The Queen's Head*, 1988

30

GWENDOLINE BUTLER

Coffin's Ghost

(New York: St. Martin's Press, 2001)

Story type: Police Procedural
Series: John Coffin. Book 29
Subject(s): City and Town Life; Memory
Major character(s): John Coffin, Police Officer (chief commander)
Time period(s): 2000s
Locale(s): London, England

Summary: Coffin is horrified when a grisly parcel is discovered outside a battered women's shelter with his initials on it, containing severed human limbs. There is a connection, as the building, now remodeled, is where he lived when he first arrived in the Second City of London. Certainly the discovery stirs up memories of his past he would rather remain buried, but although he's not certain where the investigation of the package will lead, Coffin is obliged to do his duty as a police officer and pursue it, wherever it goes.

Where it's reviewed:
Publishers Weekly, November 12, 2001, page 40

Other books by the same author:
A Grave Coffin, 1998
Coffin's Game, 1997
A Double Coffin, 1996
A Dark Coffin, 1995
A Coffin for Charley, 1993

Other books you might like:
Elizabeth George, *The Thomas Lynley/Barbara Havers Series*, 1998-
Martha Grimes, *The Richard Jury Series*, 1981-
Cynthia Harrod-Eagles, *The Bill Slider Series*, 1991-
P.D. James, *The Adam Dalgliesh Series*, 1962-
Elizabeth Lemarchand, *The Tom Pollard Series*, 1967-

31

DOROTHY CANNELL

The Family Jewels and Other Stories

(Unity, Maine: Five Star, 2001)

Story type: Collection
Subject(s): Short Stories

Summary: Best known for her often hilarious mystery series featuring formerly fat person Ellie Haskell and her dashing husband Ben, the author has also published many non-series short stories over the years, 11 of which are collected here. As one might expect, the tone is light, humorous, and even giddy, and the stories revolve around domestic problems such as replacing a broken teapot or being hounded by a dead mother-in-law or how to confess an extravagant purchase to a penurious husband. There is no detection here but plenty of comedy, a bit of crime, and lots of the eccentric characters that are the author's hallmark. With an introduction by Joan Hess.

Other books by the same author:
Bridesmaids Revisited, 2000
The Trouble with Harriet, 1999
The Spring Cleaning Murders, 1998
How to Murder the Man of Your Dreams, 1995
How to Murder Your Mother-in-Law, 1994

Other books you might like:
Barbara D'Amato, *Of Course You Know That Chocolate Is a Vegetable and Other Stories*, 2000
Carolyn Hart, *Crime on Her Mind*, 1999
Margaret Maron, *Shoveling Smoke*, 1997
Sharyn McCrumb, *Foggy Mountain Breakdown*, 1998
Patricia Moyes, *Who Killed Father Christmas?*, 1996

32

LAURA CHILDS

Death by Darjeeling

(New York: Berkley, 2001)

Story type: Amateur Detective
Series: Tea Shop. Book 1
Subject(s): Stores, Retail; Restaurants; American South
Major character(s): Theodosia Browning, Store Owner
Time period(s): 2000s
Locale(s): Charleston, South Carolina

Summary: Theodosia has her hands full dealing with her website designer, her customs broker, and the annual Lamplighter Tour of Charleston's historic district commencing that very evening. A former advertising executive, she acquired a tiny shop not long ago, turning it into a combination tea salon, retail tea emporium, and gift shop, all doing very well. The last thing she needs is a dead body on her hands, especially one that's been poisoned by a cup of her own tea, which is exactly what she finds in the tea room when the evening's over. It's not good for business—and so the hard-working Theo turns detective. There is lots of tea lore in this very cozy story, the first in a projected series, as well as a recipe from Theo's Indigo Tea Shop.

Other books you might like:
Susan Wittig Albert, *The China Bayles Series*, 1992-
Claudia Bishop, *The Sarah and Meg Quilliam Series*, 1994-
Linda French, *Coffee to Die For*, 1998
Jean Hager, *The Tess Darcy Series*, 1994-
Carolyn Hart, *The Death on Demand Series*, 1987-

33

JILL CHURCHILL (Pseudonym of Janice Young Brooks)

Someone to Watch over Me

(New York: Morrow, 2001)

Story type: Historical; Domestic
Series: Grace & Favor. Book 3
Subject(s): Depression (Economic); Inheritance; Small Town Life
Major character(s): Lily Brewster, Detective—Amateur, Heiress; Robert Brewster, Detective—Amateur, Heir
Time period(s): 1930s (1932)

Locale(s): Voorburg-on-Hudson, New York

Summary: The formerly wealthy brother-sister team of Robert and Lily Brewster lost everything in the stock market crash and were saved from a life of abject poverty when they inherited the Hudson River mansion of their late Great-Uncle Horatio. Under the terms of the will, they will inherit the balance of the estate only after they have lived there for ten years, and with precious little income with which to maintain the old house, they have to scrimp and scrounge along with the rest of the townspeople. While salvaging some lumber from an abandoned ice house on the property, Robert finds a body, and soon he and Lily are off sleuthing again. An appealing side story involves a group of hobo girl musicians that Lily helps get back on their feet and performing again by giving them her now-useless fancy wardrobe. The author also writes a contemporary series featuring suburban single mother Jane Jeffry.

Where it's reviewed:
Booklist, September 1, 2001, page 56
Mystery News, December 2001/January 2002, page 27

Other books by the same author:
In the Still of the Night, 2000
Anything Goes, 1999

Other books you might like:
Harold Adams, *The Carl Wilcox Series*, 1981-
Sandra Dallas, *The Persian Pickle Club*, 1995
Michael Kurland, *The Girls in The High-Heeled Shoes*, 1998
Elliott Roosevelt, *Hyde Park Murder*, 1985
Deborah Woodworth, *The Sister Rose Callahan Series*, 1997-

34

CAROL HIGGINS CLARK

Fleeced

(New York: Scribner, 2001)

Story type: Humor; Private Detective
Series: Regan Reilly. Book 5
Subject(s): City and Town Life; Clubs; Authors and Writers
Major character(s): Regan Reilly, Detective—Private
Time period(s): 2000s
Locale(s): New York, New York

Summary: Regan's in New York to help her mother, best-selling mystery writer Nora Regan Reilly, who's organized a crime conference at which Regan is to be a featured speaker. While she's there, she gets a call from the president of the Settlers' Club, a Gramercy Park fixture, to solve a double mystery: a baffling death and some missing diamonds. The cast of eccentric characters and the author's chatty, breezy style keep things moving.

Where it's reviewed:
Book, November-December 2001, page 70
Booklist, September 1, 2001, page 3
Mystery News, October/November 2001, page 31
Publishers Weekly, September 10, 2001, page 65

Other books by the same author:
Twanged, 1998
Snagged, 1996
Iced, 1995
Decked, 1992

Other books you might like:
Albert Borowitz, *This Club Frowns on Murder*, 1990
Joyce Christmas, *The Margaret Priam Series*, 1988-
Selma Eichler, *The Desiree Shapiro Series*, 1994-
Marlys Millhiser, *The Charlie Greene Series*, 1992-
Katy Munger, *The Casey Jones Series*, 1997-

35

MARGARET COEL

The Thunder Keeper

(New York: Berkley, 2001)

Story type: Amateur Detective
Series: Father John O'Malley/Vicky Holden. Number 7
Subject(s): Indian Reservations; American West; Catholicism
Major character(s): John O'Malley, Religious (Catholic priest), Detective—Amateur; Vicky Holden, Indian (Arapaho), Lawyer
Time period(s): 2000s
Locale(s): Wind River Reservation, Wyoming; Denver, Colorado

Summary: A young man from Denver comes to the reservation to undertake a vision quest and apparently commits suicide while on sacred ground, puzzling the Arapahos, especially the medicine man who prepared him for his spiritual journey and was convinced of his sincerity. They believe he was killed by evil spirits, while Father John learns he was indeed murdered, but by a more earthly agent. However, since this information came to him via the confessional, his lips are sealed. The police give up on the case, unable to find a suspect, but then Arapaho lawyer Vicky Holden is summoned back to the reservation from Denver by a mysterious caller who is killed before she can talk to him. She and her old friend, Father John, team up again to get to the truth of these incidents.

Where it's reviewed:
Publishers Weekly, August 13, 2001, page 289

Other books by the same author:
The Spirit Woman, 2000
The Lost Bird, 1999
The Story Teller, 1998
The Dream Stalker, 1997
The Ghost Walker, 1996

Other books you might like:
James D. Doss, *The Shaman Series*, 1994-
Jean Hager, *The Molly Bearpaw Series*, 1992-
Tony Hillerman, *The Joe Leaphorn/Jim Chee Series*, 1970-
Brad Reynolds, *The Father Mark Townsend Series*, 1996-
Aimee Thurlo, *The Ella Clah Series*, 1995-
David Thurlo, co-author

36

JOAN COGGIN

Who Killed the Curate?

(Boulder, Colorado: Rue Morgue Press, 2001)

Story type: Amateur Detective; Humor
Series: Lady Lupin. Book 1
Subject(s): Clergy; Small Town Life; Christmas
Major character(s): Lady Lupin Lorrimer Hastings, Noblewoman, Spouse (of Andrew); Andrew Hastings, Religious (vicar)
Time period(s): 1930s (1937)
Locale(s): Glanville, England (Sussex)

Summary: Young Lady Lupin, known as ''Loops'' to her friends and as kindhearted as she is scatterbrained, has just married the vicar of St. Mark's Parish in Glanville and finds herself completely out of her depth when it comes to being a clergyman's wife. Not only does she not know a Jew from a Jesuit, but she is all at sea when she's expected to provide leadership for the various worthy causes of the parish—the Girl Guides, the Mothers' Union, and the Temperance Society. She's determined to do her best and bravely soldiers on, eventually winning over the parishioners who at first don't know what to make of this lovely but thoroughly ditzy creature. When her husband's curate is murdered, there are no end of suspects, all much nicer than the victim, and Lupin refuses to believe the most likely of them could possibly be guilty. So she enlists the aid of two of her old friends and her husband's nephew, a secret service agent, to help her get at the truth. In her own inimitable fashion, she tests various theories by offering to help the killer escape if only he or she confesses first. Originally published in England in 1944 and the first in a four-book series featuring Lady Lupin, the book now makes its first U.S. appearance.

Where it's reviewed:
Deadly Pleasures, Winter 2002, page 45
Publishers Weekly, November 26, 2001, page 43

Other books by the same author:
Dancing with Death, 1947
The Mystery of Orchard House, 1946
Why Did She Die?, 1946

Other books you might like:
Dorothy Cannell, *The Thin Woman*, 1984
Sarah Caudwell, *Thus Was Adonis Murdered*, 1981
Agatha Christie, *Murder at the Vicarage*, 1930
Mollie Hardwick, *The Doran Fairweather Series*, 1986-
Katherine Hall Page, *The Faith Fairchild Series*, 1990-

37

GABRIEL COHEN

Red Hook

(New York: St. Martin's Press, 2001)

Story type: Police Procedural
Subject(s): City and Town Life; Crime and Criminals; Fathers and Sons
Major character(s): Jack Leightner, Detective—Homicide
Time period(s): 2000s
Locale(s): New York, New York (Brooklyn/Red Hook)

Summary: The Red Hook neighborhood of Brooklyn, once a bustling waterfront community and later home to drug dealers and a huge public housing project, is where homicide cop Jack Leightner grew up, and it still holds terrible secrets and memories for him. When he's called to the scene of the stabbing murder of a young Dominican man along the Gowanus Canal, he comes close to fainting on the spot, but he pulls himself back into the present only to become strangely obsessed with the case. Nobody can figure out why the young man, a hard worker and good husband and father, was killed. Leightner's investigation mainly seems to stir up memories of his own unhappy childhood, broken marriage, and estrangement from his son Ben, a filmmaker who is also drawn to the Hook and who is filming a documentary about the area's unique history. An impressive first novel, part literary fiction and part police procedural.

Where it's reviewed:
Booklist, September 1, 2001, page 56
Deadly Pleasures, Autumn 2001, page 5
Library Journal, September 1, 2001, page 232
Mystery News, October/November 2001, page 29
Publishers Weekly, August 13, 2001, page 288

Other books you might like:
Thomas Adcock, *The Neil Hockaday Series*, 1989-
Dennis Lehane, *Mystic River*, 2001
Jonathan Lethem, *Motherless Brooklyn*, 1999
George P. Pelecanos, *Right as Rain*, 2001
Robert J. Randisi, *Alone with the Dead*, 1995

38

NANCY J. COHEN

Murder by Manicure

(New York: Kensington, 2001)

Story type: Amateur Detective
Series: Marla Shore. Book 3
Subject(s): Weight Control; Beauty; Stalking
Major character(s): Marla Shore, Hairdresser, Widow(er); Dalton Vail, Detective—Homicide
Time period(s): 2000s
Locale(s): Palm Haven, Florida

Summary: Marla has no sooner signed up for a trial membership at a fitness club than one of its members falls into the whirlpool spa and drowns. Homicide detective Dalton Vail, Marla's boyfriend, is convinced the death was no accident, and against his wishes Marla decides to help in the investigation. The victim, Jolene Myers, had many enemies, ranging from a philandering pharmacist to a crooked city councilman to an outspoken animal rights activist. Marla soon gets in over her head and puts her own life in danger from her snooping. Nevertheless, she finds time for her own brand of commentary on hair, makeup, grooming, and fashion.

Where it's reviewed:
Drood Review, November/December 2001, page 11
Library Journal, December 2001, page 178
Publishers Weekly, November 12, 2001, page 39

Other books by the same author:
Hair Raiser, 2000
Permed to Death, 1999

Other books you might like:
Nancy Bartholomew, *The Sierra Lavatoni Series*, 1998-
Simon Brett, *Mrs. Pargeter's Pound of Flesh*, 1992
Sophie Dunbar, *The Claire Claiborne Series*, 1993-
Anne George, *Murder on a Bad Hair Day*, 1996
Sarah Strohmeyer, *Bubbles Unbound*, 2001

39

DAVID COLE

Stalking Moon

(New York: Avon, 2002)

Story type: Private Detective
Series: Laura Winslow. Book 3
Subject(s): Native Americans; Internet; Illegal Immigrants
Major character(s): Laura Winslow, Detective—Private, Computer Expert
Time period(s): 2000s
Locale(s): Tucson, Arizona

Summary: Laura Winslow is living a solitary life in the desert near Tucson, shutting herself off from the memory of traumatic events in her past and trying to come to terms with her Hopi ancestry. An expert hacker, she uses her computer skills in her work as a private detective. She manages to be in the wrong place at the wrong time when a large body of illegal aliens attempts to cross the border, and she's pressured by federal agents to help them expose the criminals who are smuggling immigrants into the U.S. These are not Mexican workers crossing of their own free will, but women from Eastern Europe and Asia who are being sold into white slavery, if they survive at all.

Other books by the same author:
The Killing Maze, 2001
Butterfly Lost, 2000

Other books you might like:
Sinclair Browning, *The Trade Ellis Series*, 1999-
Denise Hamilton, *The Jasmine Trade*, 2001
J.A. Jance, *Kiss of the Bees*, 2000
Aimee Thurlo, *The Ella Clah Series*, 1995-
David Thurlo, co-author
Judith Van Gieson, *North of the Border*, 1988

40

MAX ALLAN COLLINS

Blue Christmas and Other Holiday Homicides

(Waterville, Maine: Five Star, 2001)

Story type: Collection
Subject(s): Short Stories; Holidays

Summary: This volume contains three novellas featuring 1940s private eye Richard Stone, the first of which, *A Wreath for Marley*, has a Christmas setting. The other two Stone novellas, *Flowers for Bill Reilly* and *A Bird for Becky* are set during Memorial Day and Thanksgiving. Also included are three non-series shorter pieces set during the Fourth of July, Mother's Day, and Father's Day. The stories, previously published in various anthologies, were written between 1994 and 2001. All are cleverly plotted crime stories with a twist generally related to whichever holiday provides the setting. The author has published other short story collections and many crime novels featuring a variety of protagonists, most notably his Chicago private detective Nathan Heller, whose adventures span the thirties, forties, and fifties.

Where it's reviewed:
Publishers Weekly, September 24, 2001, page 73

Other books by the same author:
Angel in Black, 2001
Kisses of Death, 2001 (short stories)
Murder: His and Hers, 2001 (short stories; Barbara Collins, co-author)
Majic Man, 1999
Mourn the Living, 1999

Other books you might like:
Susan Dunlap, *The Celestial Buffet*, 2001
Joe Gores, *Speak of the Devil*, 1999
Ed Gorman, *Famous Blue Raincoat*, 1999
Joe L. Hensley, *Deadly Hunger and Other Stories*, 2001
Donald E. Westlake, *A Good Story and Other Stories*, 1999

41

MAX ALLAN COLLINS

Kisses of Death

(Norfolk, Virginia: Crippen & Landru, 2001)

Story type: Collection; Private Detective
Series: Nathan Heller. Book 13
Subject(s): Short Stories; Historical
Major character(s): Nathan Heller, Detective—Private
Time period(s): 20th century (1930s-1950s)

Summary: As in his novels featuring Nate Heller, the author mixes fiction and fact in these stories as Heller moves through the decades of the thirties, forties, and fifties solving famous real-life murder cases. In the title novella, he's hired to be bodyguard to none other than Marilyn Monroe, in Chicago to promote her latest movie, *Gentlemen Prefer Blondes*. During the course of a press party in her honor, a guest is murdered. The six other stories detail Heller's involvement in other cases such as the murder of actress Thelma Todd and the death of Eddie Gaedel, a midget who presented the smallest strike zone in major league baseball. There is also a comprehensive checklist of this prolific author's works (of which only the Nathan Heller titles are listed below). For another collection of Heller's short cases, see 1991's *Dying in the Postwar World*.

Where it's reviewed:
Booklist, July 2001, page 1986
Drood Review, November/December 2001, page 1
Publishers Weekly, June 25, 2001, page 54

Other books by the same author:
Angel in Black, 2001

Majic Man, 1999
Flying Blind, 1998
Damned in Paradise, 1996
Blood and Thunder, 1995

Other books you might like:
Raymond Chandler, *The Midnight Raymond Chandler*, 1971
short stories
Joe Gores, *Stakeout on Page Street*, 2000
short stories
Dashiell Hammett, *Hammett: Crime Stories and Other Writings*, 2001
short stories
Ross Macdonald, *Ross Mcdonald's Lew Archer, Private Investigator*, 1977
short stories
Mickey Spillane, *Tomorrow I Die*, 1984
short stories; Max Allan Collins, editor

42

JOHN CONNOLLY

Dark Hollow

(New York: Simon & Schuster, 2001)

Story type: Private Detective
Series: Charlie Parker. Number 2
Subject(s): Serial Killers; Organized Crime; Crime and Criminals
Major character(s): Charlie "Bird" Parker, Detective—Private, Widow(er)
Time period(s): 2000s
Locale(s): Scarborough, Maine

Summary: Former Brooklyn homicide detective Charlie Parker (don't call him "Bird") resigned from the force after the deaths of his wife and young daughter and is still haunted by these and other demons from his hard-drinking past. Now a newly licensed private eye in his home town of Scarborough, Maine, Charlie takes a seemingly routine case trying to collect back child support from deadbeat dad Billy Purdue as a favor to the man's ex-wife, Rita. Instead, he winds up running afoul of a mob kingpin who's convinced Purdue has boosted a couple of million dollars from him after a supposedly failed heist. That's not all, either. When Billy turns up dead, it looks as if his murder might be the work of one Caleb Kyle, a local serial killer from Charlie's past who has been missing for over 40 years. A native of Ireland, the author does a nearly flawless job of capturing American idioms and sensibilities in this edgy, often chilling, and ultimately derivative novel.

Where it's reviewed:
Mystery News, August/September 2001, page 9
People Weekly, August 17, 2001, page 43
Publishers Weekly, June 4, 2001, page 54

Other books by the same author:
Every Dead Thing, 1999

Other books you might like:
Lawrence Block, *The Matt Scudder Series*, 1976-
Paul Bryers, *The Prayer of the Bone*, 1999
Timothy Findley, *The Telling of Lies*, 1986
William G. Tapply, *Dead Meat*, 1987
Janwillem Van de Wetering, *The Maine Massacre*, 1979

43

ELIZABETH CORLEY

Fatal Legacy

(New York: St. Martin's Press, 2001)

Story type: Police Procedural; Traditional
Subject(s): Inheritance; Single Parent Families; Business
Major character(s): Andrew Fenwick, Police Officer (detective chief inspector), Single Parent
Time period(s): 2000s
Locale(s): Harlden, England (West Sussex)

Summary: The apparent suicide of wealthy industrialist Arthur Wainwright and the discovery that he had sold the controlling interest in his company long before his death throws his family and his business into a state of confusion, aggravated by the hateful tone of his will. When the company's financial controller, Arthur Fish, is murdered, DCI Andrew Fenwick is called in to investigate, and he discovers a link between these killings and that of a prostitute Fish had visited the night before his death. It's a complicated case, requiring a great deal of Fenwick's time, not always easy to find when you're a single parent. First mystery.

Where it's reviewed:
Booklist, September 15, 2001, page 198
Deadly Pleasures, Autumn 2001, page 42
Library Journal, November 1, 2001, page 135
Mystery News, October/November 2001, page 14

Other books you might like:
Caroline Graham, *The Inspector Tom Barnaby Series*, 1987-
Ruth Rendell, *The Inspector Wexford Series*, 1964-
Dorothy Simpson, *The Luke Thanet Series*, 1981-
Susannah Stacey, *The Robert Bone Series*, 1987-
June Thomson, *The Inspector Finch Series*, 1971-

44

MAT COWARD

In and Out

(Waterville, Maine: Five Star, 2001)

Story type: Police Procedural
Series: Don Packham/Frank Mitchell. Book 2
Subject(s): Games; Competition; Mental Illness
Major character(s): Don Packham, Police Officer (detective inspector); Frank Mitchell, Police Officer (detective constable)
Time period(s): 2000s
Locale(s): London, England

Summary: In the aftermath of a rowdy darts tournament at the Hollow Head, an old-fashioned London pub, a woman is found dead in the ladies' loo, her head bashed in with a concrete block. Inspector Packham and Constable Mitchell soon determine that it had to be one of the other dart players who killed her, and that all of them had equally plausible motives for wanting to see her dead. The two men are very unlike: Packham suffers from bipolar disorder and is alternately exuberantly joyful and deeply depressed, keeping Mitchell constantly alert to his startling mood swings. Mitchell is the less experienced of the two, but even-tempered and quick to learn. Their exchanges are both amusing and pointed, and the author, who has been nominated for both the Silver Dagger and the Edgar awards, deserves to be better known.

Where it's reviewed:
Booklist, December 1, 2001, page 634

Other books by the same author:
Up and Down, 2000

Other books you might like:
Colin Dexter, *The Inspector Morse Series*, 1975-
Reginald Hill, *The Dalziel and Pascoe Series*, 1970-
P.D. James, *The Adam Dalgliesh Series*, 1962-
Peter Lovesey, *The Peter Diamond Series*, 1991-
R.D. Wingfield, *The Inspector Frost Series*, 1984-

45

MICHAEL CRAFT

Desert Autumn

(New York: St. Martin's Press, 2001)

Story type: Amateur Detective
Subject(s): Theater; Academia; Deserts
Major character(s): Claire Gray, Director; Paul Huron, Artist (sculptor)
Time period(s): 2000s
Locale(s): Palm Desert, California

Summary: At 54, Claire Gray has had a successful career as a New York theatrical director and is quite content with her single state. She accepts a position chairing the drama department at the newly founded Desert Arts College in California, the pet project of computer multimillionaire D. Glenn Yeats. After arriving and not yet even settled in, she and a colleague, sculptor Paul Huron, discover the murdered body of his wife Jodie, and soon she's off helping the police investigate the murder. She also becomes involved romantically with a much younger student. Persistent and resourceful, Claire's not about to quit snooping around until the case is solved. The desert setting is very well handled, the characters are nicely drawn, and the book promises to be the first in a new series by the author of the Mark Manning mysteries about a gay Wisconsin reporter.

Where it's reviewed:
Booklist, November 1, 2001, page 461
Mystery News, December 2001/January 2002, page 29
Publishers Weekly, November 5, 2001, page 44

Other books by the same author:
Boy Toy, 2001
Name Games, 2000
Body Language, 1999
Eye Contact, 1998
Flight Dreams, 1997

Other books you might like:
Jane Dentinger, *The Jocelyn O'Roarke Series*, 1983-
Gillian B. Farrell, *The Annie McGrogan Series*, 1992-
Shelley Freydont, *Midsummer Murder*, 2001
Lillian H. Roberts, *The Andi Pauling Series*, 1996-
Dorian Yeager, *The Victoria Bowering Series*, 1992-

46

PHILIP R. CRAIG
WILLIAM G. TAPPLY, Co-Author

First Light

(New York: Scribner, 2002)

Story type: Private Detective
Subject(s): Islands; Fishing; Missing Persons
Major character(s): J.W. Jackson, Beachcomber, Detective—Private; Brady Coyne, Lawyer, Detective—Private
Time period(s): 2000s
Locale(s): Martha's Vineyard, Massachusetts

Summary: Boston lawyer Brady Coyne, whose small but select client list leaves him plenty of time for other pursuits, arrives on Martha's Vineyard to help elderly Sarah Fairchild prepare her will. He also plans to spend a great deal of time fishing with his old friend, former Boston cop J.W. Jackson. However, both men find other demands on their time: Mrs. Fairchild's private nurse vanishes, while family members are clashing with developers over her extensive beachfront property, and one of Jackson's business associates persuades him to search for his wife, missing for over a year. When they compare notes with the local police, the men discover that blond women in their forties have been disappearing from the island for years. Even so, they find time to fish, eat, and drink, and three of their favorite recipes are included. Coyne, of course, is featured in a long-running series by Tapply and Jackson in another series by Craig. This is their first appearance together, and their story is told in alternating chapters.

Where it's reviewed:
Booklist, December 1, 2001, page 632
Publishers Weekly, December 10, 2001, page 54

Other books by the same author:
Vineyard Shadows, 2001
Vineyard Blues, 2000
A Fatal Vineyard Season, 1999
A Shoot on Martha's Vineyard, 1998
A Deadly Vineyard Holiday, 1997

Other books you might like:
Rick Boyer, *The Doc Adams Series*, 1982-
Sally Gunning, *The Peter Bartholomew Series*, 1990-
David Osborne, *Murder on Martha's Vineyard*, 1989
Cynthia Riggs, *Deadly Nightshade*, 2001
Kelly Roos, *Murder on Martha's Vineyard*, 1981

47

ROBERT CRAIS

Hostage

(New York: Doubleday, 2001)

Story type: Police Procedural; Action/Adventure
Subject(s): Hostages; Crime and Criminals; Organized Crime
Major character(s): Jeff Talley, Police Officer (chief of police)
Time period(s): 2000s

Locale(s): Bristo Camino, California (Los Angeles suburb)

Summary: Haunted by an operation gone terribly wrong, Jeff Talley resigns his post as chief hostage negotiator for the LAPD SWAT team and takes what he expects to be a less stressful job as the police chief of a quiet Los Angeles suburb. It will be no surprise to readers that trouble follows Talley to Bristo Camino when three hapless criminals fleeing the scene of a botched convenience store holdup break into an affluent home and take a family hostage. Trouble follows these guys, too, when it develops that the head of the family, Walter Smith, is no ordinary accountant. He works for the mob, and his files are full of information his employers don't want discovered at any cost. Once again, Talley is thrust into the role of hostage negotiator in a situation where the stakes are higher than any he's encountered in his career. Slick and fast-paced, the book lacks the depth and characterization of the author's other mysteries, but it makes suspenseful reading. In addition to another stand-alone suspense novel, Crais is the author of the Elvis Cole/Joe Pike private eye series.

Where it's reviewed:
Booklist, July 2001, page 1949
Entertainment Weekly, August 24, 2001, page 130
People Weekly, August 6, 2001, page 53
Publishers Weekly, July 9, 2001, page 43

Other books by the same author:
Demolition Angel, 2000
L.A. Requiem, 1999
Indigo Slam, 1997
Sunset Express, 1996
Voodoo River, 1995

Other books you might like:
Paul Bishop, *The Fay Croaker Series*, 1994-
Harlan Coben, *Tell No One*, 2001
Michael Connelly, *The Harry Bosch Series*, 1992-
Robert B. Parker, *The Jesse Stone Series*, 1997-
T. Jefferson Parker, *Silent Joe*, 2001

48

BILL CRIDER

The Nighttime Is the Right Time

(Unity, Maine: Five Star, 2001)

Story type: Collection
Subject(s): Short Stories; Mystery and Detective Stories

Summary: There are 11 stories here, all previously published in anthologies, some of which are straightforward detective tales featuring series characters Professor Carl Burns and Sheriff Dan Rhodes. Most, however, are non-series stories, some decidedly more noir than the author's novels, and some containing touches of the supernatural, such as the title story and "It Happened at Grandmother's House," both featuring a werewolf detective, and "King of the Night," in which a very much alive Elvis goes after an undead impersonator. Missing pets, mystery writers, gambling, and shoplifters are featured in other stories, all of which are entertaining and smoothly written. The author has written many novels with a variety of series characters, including two in collaboration with TV weatherman Willard Scott.

Where it's reviewed:
Booklist, December 15, 2000, page 790

Other books by the same author:
A Ghost of a Chance, 2000
Murder Is an Art, 1999
Death by Accident, 1997
Murder Takes a Break, 1997
The Prairie Chicken Kill, 1996

Other books you might like:
Robert Bloch, *Out of the Mouths of Graves*, 1979
Lawrence Block, *Like a Lamb to the Slaughter*, 1984
Roald Dahl, *Someone Like You*, 1954
Stanley Ellin, *The Specialty of the House*, 1979
Edward D. Hoch, *The Night People and Other Stories*, 2001

49

BILL CRIDER

A Romantic Way to Die

(New York: St. Martin's Press, 2001)

Story type: Police Procedural; Humor
Series: Sheriff Dan Rhodes. Book 11
Subject(s): Authors and Writers; Small Town Life
Major character(s): Dan Rhodes, Police Officer (sheriff)
Time period(s): 2000s
Locale(s): Clearview, Texas (Blacklin County)

Summary: When two local kids—romance writer Vernell Lindsey and Terry Don Coslin, a handsome model who's featured on the covers of hundreds of romance novels—make good, they decide to hold a romance writers' convention in their home town of Clearview, Texas. Terry Don hasn't been back since he left ten years ago and the local women line up in droves to get his autograph, rubbing elbows with the few husbands on the same mission for their wives, Sheriff Dan Rhodes included. The convention is hugely successful but before it's over there are a few casualties, and Rhodes learns a great deal about the competitive world of romance writing and publishing when he investigates them. The author also writes a series about small-town college professor Carl Burns.

Where it's reviewed:
Booklist, September 15, 2001, page 202
Publishers Weekly, October 8, 2001, page 48

Other books by the same author:
A Ghost of a Chance, 2000
Death by Accident, 1997
Murder Most Fowl, 1996
Winning Can Be Murder, 1996
Booked for a Hanging, 1992

Other books you might like:
Robert Barnard, *The Cherry Blossom Corpse*, 1987
Dorothy Cannell, *How to Murder the Man of Your Dreams*, 1995
Susan Rogers Cooper, *The E.J. Pugh Series*, 1992-
Orania Papazoglou, *Sweet, Savage Death*, 1984
Elizabeth Peters, *Die for Love*, 1984

50

JAMES CRUMLEY

The Final Country

(New York: Mysterious, 2001)

Story type: Private Detective
Series: Milo Milodragovitch. Number 4
Subject(s): American West; Drugs; Blackmail
Major character(s): Milo Milodragovitch, Detective—Private
Time period(s): 2000s
Locale(s): Texas; Las Vegas, Nevada; Montana

Summary: Having landed in Texas during his last case, and a wealthy man after coming into his inheritance and a large sum of other money, Milo is running a bar outside of Austin, living with a woman named Betty, and doing a little private eye work here and there. All that stability is making him edgy, and when the cops want him to help them track down a tall black man who has just killed a drug dealer, he goes after the fugitive for his own reasons: he wants to warn the man off and save him from the Texas penal system and a certain cell on death row. His journey takes him from Texas to Las Vegas to his adopted state of Montana, and along the way he is seduced by a beautiful but treacherous woman, survives a shootout on a golf course, encounters armies of bad guys, and consumes enough alcohol and cocaine to fell most men half his age. At 60, Milo is a survivor who can still stay the course, and the author remains probably the most gifted private eye writer of his generation, but the unending booze, drugs, sex, and violence that mark all his fiction may be too much for some readers.

Where it's reviewed:
Booklist, August 2001, page 2050
Library Journal, September 1, 2001, page 232
Publishers Weekly, September 24, 2001, page 71

Other books by the same author:
Bordersnakes, 1996
The Mexican Tree Duck, 1993
Dancing Bear, 1983
The Last Good Kiss, 1978
The Wrong Case, 1975

Other books you might like:
James Lee Burke, *The Dave Robicheaux Series*, 1987-
Dennis Lehane, *The Patrick Kenzie/Angela Gennaro Series*, 1994-
George P. Pelecanos, *The Nick Stefanos Series*, 1992-
Walter Satterthwait, *The Joshua Croft Series*, 1989-
Jenny Siler, *Easy Money*, 1999

51

MARY DAHEIM

The Alpine Nemesis

(New York: Ballantine, 2001)

Story type: Amateur Detective
Series: Emma Lord. Number 14
Subject(s): Small Town Life; Journalism; Feuds
Major character(s): Emma Lord, Journalist, Detective—Amateur
Time period(s): 2000s
Locale(s): Alpine, Washington

Summary: Funerals, weddings, and high school graduations make up most of the news published in *The Alpine Advocate*, the small-town newspaper published and edited by Emma Lord. Every once in a while a murder comes along, or something close enough, like the mysterious disappearance of a snowboarder on the surrounding ski slopes. A couple of months later that's old news, but then the long-standing feud between the O'Neills and the Hartquists flares up again, leaving three family members dead, their bodies stuffed into a meat freezer. Then a fourth body is discovered in the freezer, and Emma has more news than she knows what to do with. Alpine once actually existed as a company logging town, destroyed when it no longer had a purpose but lovingly reincarnated by a prolific author who also writes an equally cozy series about Judith McMonigle Flynn, owner of a Seattle bed-and-breakfast.

Other books by the same author:
The Alpine Legacy, 2000
The Alpine Menace, 2000
The Alpine Kindred, 1999
The Alpine Journey, 1998
The Alpine Icon, 1997

Other books you might like:
Carol Cail, *The Maxey Burnell Series*, 1993-
Jo Dereske, *The Miss Zukas Series*, 1994-
Earlene Fowler, *The Benni Harper Series*, 1994-
Linda French, *The Teddy Morelli Series*, 1998-
Carolyn Hart, *The Henrie O Series*, 1993-

52

CATHERINE DAIN

Darkness at the Door

(Waterville, Maine: Five Star, 2001)

Story type: Amateur Detective
Series: Mariana Morgan. Book 2
Subject(s): Parapsychology; Paranormal; Mysticism
Major character(s): Mariana Morgan, Psychic, Detective—Amateur; David Claybourne, Detective—Police
Time period(s): 2000s
Locale(s): Ventura, California

Summary: After the sudden death of her husband in a previous book, Mariana consulted a psychic and was startled to be told that she herself had psychic healing powers. Since then she's been following that path, and now has relocated to the smaller community of Ventura where she works as a Tarot reader at a friend's New Age emporium. Suddenly, she has a vision of her brother's bloody corpse and tries to ignore it, hoping it was a mistake. Then an all-too-real corpse turns up in front of the store, and an attempt is made on Mariana's life. Assigned to the case is police detective David Claybourne, who doesn't mind being aided by Mariana's psychic abilities. Readers who are comfortable with the high woo-woo quotient will enjoy the story, which doesn't depend wholly on paranormal powers for its solution. The author also wrote a series about Reno private detective Freddie O'Neal.

Where it's reviewed:

Publishers Weekly, November 12, 2001, page 40

Other books by the same author:

Death of the Party, 2000
Angel in the Dark, 1999 (Mariana Morgan series)
The Luck of the Draw, 1996
Bet Against the House, 1995
Lament for a Dead Cowboy, 1994

Other books you might like:

Lucha Corpi, *The Gloria Damasco Series*, 1992-
Dorothy Salisbury Davis, *The Julie Hayes Series*, 1976-
Kate Green, *The Theresa Fortunato Series*, 1986-
Martha C. Lawrence, *The Elizabeth Chase Series*, 1995-
L.L. Thrasher, *The Lizbet Lange Series*, 1998-

53

BARBARA D'AMATO

Hard Road

(New York: Scribner, 2001)

Story type: Amateur Detective
Series: Cat Marsala. Number 9
Subject(s): Children; Books and Reading; Literature
Major character(s): Cat Marsala, Journalist, Detective—Amateur
Time period(s): 2000s
Locale(s): Chicago, Illinois

Summary: Cat is delighted to be taking her nephew, Jeremy, to Chicago's Oz festival celebrating the series' centennial, organized and managed by her brother Barry (Jeremy's dad). Their fun comes to an abrupt halt when they witness the knifing of a security guard and then the shooting of a computer designer. Because of what they saw, Cat and Jeremy are the killer's next targets, but they escape by ducking into the complex tunnel system beneath the fair, leading their pursuers on a frantic and suspenseful chase before they finally emerge unharmed. Cat sensibly goes to the police with what she saw, but her testimony only leads them to suspect her brother is behind the murders. Even Cat begins to doubt Barry's innocence, but family loyalty leads her to search exhaustively for evidence that might clear him. The Oz framework is delightful, and there is a long essay by the author's son, Brian, appended to the novel discussing the Oz books and L. Frank Baum, who was a friend and neighbor of Barbara D'Amato's father when he was a boy.

Where it's reviewed:

Booklist, July 2001, page 1986
Library Journal, July 2001, page 130
Mystery News, October/November 2001, page 24
Publishers Weekly, July 7, 2001, page 1986

Other books by the same author:

Hard Evidence, 1999
Hard Bargain, 1997
Hard Christmas, 1995
Hard Case, 1994
Hard Women, 1993

Other books you might like:

Jan Burke, *The Irene Kelly Series*, 1993-
Richard Forrest, *The Wizard of Death*, 1977
Stuart M. Kaminsky, *Murder on the Yellow Brick Road*, 1978
Sara Paretsky, *The V.I. Warshawski Series*, 1982-
Elaine Viets, *The Francesca Vierling Series*, 1997-

54

JEANNE M. DAMS

To Perish in Penzance

(New York: Walker, 2001)

Story type: Amateur Detective; Traditional
Series: Dorothy Martin. Number 7
Subject(s): Vacations; Marriage; Aging
Major character(s): Dorothy Martin, Spouse (of Alan), Detective—Amateur; Alan Nesbitt, Police Officer (retired constable)
Time period(s): 2000s
Locale(s): Penzance, England (Cornwall); Sherebury, England

Summary: The dreary fall weather in Dorothy's adopted English home makes her long for a bit of sunshine, and she and her newish husband, Alan, decide upon a holiday in Penzance, where he was a constable early in his career. In fact, he is still haunted by an unsolved death that occurred there 30 years before, when a young girl apparently fell to her death from a cliff while under the influence of LSD. When they arrive in the tiny seaside village, Alan finds he can't take his mind off the case, which he always suspected was actually a murder. As he and Dorothy wander along the seaside cliffs and caves nearby, they come across the very cave where the girl's body was found. Shockingly, the body of a another young girl with long fair hair has materialized in its place, and it doesn't take Alan and Dorothy long to figure out that they are in danger from an unknown killer who doesn't want a long-buried secret to be exposed.

Where it's reviewed:

Booklist, September 15, 2001, page 47
Mystery News, October/November 2001, page 25
Publishers Weekly, October 8, 2001, page 47

Other books by the same author:

Killing Cassidy, 2000
The Victim in Victoria Station, 1999
Malice in Miniature, 1998
Holy Terror in the Hebrides, 1997
Trouble in the Town Hall, 1996

Other books you might like:

Janie Bolitho, *Framed in Cornwall*, 2001
Martha Grimes, *The Lamorna Wink*, 1999
Hazel Holt, *The Mrs. Malory Series*, 1989-
Betty Rowlands, *The Melissa Craig Series*, 1990-
Graham Thomas, *Malice in Cornwall*, 1998

55

FREDA DAVIES

A Fine and Private Place

(New York: Carroll & Graf, 2001)

Story type: Police Procedural; Traditional
Subject(s): World War II; Small Town Life; Blackmail
Major character(s): Keith Tyrell, Police Officer (detective inspector)
Time period(s): 2000s
Locale(s): Tolland, England (Gloucester)

Summary: A laborer digging a trench in a rural field uncovers a skeleton from World War II, whose dogtags reveal him to have been a young American soldier who went AWOL and was dishonorably discharged over half a century ago. Tyrell is assigned the investigation into his death, and in the process he discovers a much more recent corpse, who turns out to be a blackmailer half the village would have liked to see dead. The identity of the person who killed the GI is determined quickly enough, although the memories it stirs up in the village are powerful, but the second, and eventually third, murders prove harder to crack. One of the back stories, involving ''land girls,'' or young women who turned to farm labor to replace the men away in battle, is especially interesting. Author's first mystery.

Where it's reviewed:
Booklist, October 15, 2001, page 385
Library Journal, November 1, 2001, page 135
Publishers Weekly, October 1, 2001, page 40

Other books you might like:
Rhys Bowen, *Evan Can Wait*, 2001
Marjorie Eccles, *The Inspector Mayo Series*, 1988-
Caroline Graham, *The Inspector Barnaby Series*, 1987-
Peter Lovesey, *Rough Cider*, 1986
Kay Mitchell, *The Inspector Morrisey Series*, 1990-

56

NORBERT DAVIS

The Mouse in the Mountain

(Boulder, Colorado: Rue Morgue Press, 2001)

Story type: Private Detective; Humor
Series: Doan & Carstairs. Book 1
Subject(s): Animals/Dogs; Earthquakes; Crime and Criminals
Major character(s): Doan, Detective—Private; Dougal's Lord Carstairs, Animal (dog), Sidekick
Time period(s): 1940s (1943)
Locale(s): Los Altos, Mexico

Summary: Doan is a short, chubby Los Angeles private eye, who is nowhere as harmless as he appears, and Carstairs is the fawn-colored Great Dane he won in a crap game, a dog so big that Doan figures he really ought to be considered another species. Carstairs doesn't like it when Doan drinks, he doesn't like baby-talk, and he doesn't suffer fools gladly—although, like Doan, he's a soft touch for a pretty girl. They're down in Mexico where Doan is ostensibly looking for a fugitive. Also in Los Altos are flypaper heiress Patricia Van Osdel; schoolteacher Janet Martin, who's looking for a stolen book; and Mexican police Captain Emile Perona. When the tiny, mountainous village is cut off from the rest of the country by an earthquake, everyone's true reasons for being in Los Altos are revealed. Originally published in 1943, this is the first of three novels and several short stories featuring this unusual detecting team, all a combination of hard-boiled action/detection and screwball humor.

Where it's reviewed:
Ellery Queen's Mystery Magazine, March 2002, page 46
Mystery Scene, Number 73, page 10
Publishers Weekly, September 24, 2001, page 7
Romantic Times, December 2001, page 93

Other books by the same author:
Sally's in the Alley, 2002 (originally published in 1943)
Oh, Murderer Mine, 1946

Other books you might like:
Lawrence Block, *The Chip Harrison Series*, 1970-
G.M. Ford, *The Leo Hagerty Series*, 1965-
Jonathan Latimer, *The Bill Crane Series*, 1935-1939
Dick Lochte, *The Leo Bloodworth/Serendipity Dahlquist Series*, 1985-
Craig Rice, *The John J. Malone Series*, 1938-1967

57

JEFFERY DEAVER, Editor

A Century of Great Suspense Stories

(New York: Berkley, 2001)

Story type: Anthology
Subject(s): Short Stories

Summary: Of the 36 stories included here, only five were originally published prior to 1950, making this anthology more properly a half-century of great suspense stories. The good news is that many of the stories have not been frequently anthologized, and the authors include such modern masters as Sara Paretsky, Tony Hillerman, Lawrence Block, Ruth Rendell, and Donald Westlake. Not all are detective stories: chillers from Stephen King, Harlan Ellison, and Robert Bloch are also included. Other big names include Mickey Spillane, Ed McBain, Georges Simenon, Ross Macdonald, Rex Stout, Ellery Queen, and James M. Cain, and reliable producers like Bill Pronzini, Marcia Muller, Edward D. Hoch, John Lutz, Max Allan Collins, and Robert Barnard are well represented. This is the first anthology edited by Deaver, who is well-known for his suspense novels, many of which feature Lincoln Rhyme.

Where it's reviewed:
Publishers Weekly, October 29, 2001, page 39

Other books by the same author:
Blue Nowhere, 2001
Speaking in Tongues, 2000
The Empty Chair, 2000
The Devil's Teardrop, 1999
The Coffin Dancer, 1998

Other books you might like:

Patricia Craig, *The Oxford Book of English Detective Stories*, 1991
editor

Tony Hillerman, *Best American Mystery Stories of the Century*, 2000
editor

Tony Hillerman, *The Oxford Book of American Detective Stories*, 1997
editor

Otto Penzler, *50 Greatest Mysteries of All Time*, 1998
editor

Herbert Van Thal, *The Mammoth Book of Great Detective Stories*, 2001
editor

58

DAVID DICKINSON

Goodnight, Sweet Prince

(New York: Carroll & Graf, 2002)

Story type: Historical
Subject(s): Victorian Period; Princes and Princesses; Blackmail
Major character(s): Lord Francis Powerscourt, Detective—Private, Nobleman; Lord Johnny Fitzgerald, Sidekick, Nobleman
Time period(s): 1890s (1892)
Locale(s): London, England; Norfolk, England; Venice, Italy

Summary: Queen Victoria has been on the throne for over half a century now, and the royal family is harboring its secrets and scandals. Most are generated by Victoria's son, the Prince of Wales, a notorious womanizer and adulterer whose son Victor Albert—known to all as Prince Eddy—is following in his father's footsteps, except that he enjoys the company of men, as well as women. It all promises to erupt when a blackmailer threatens the Prince of Wales with exposure and Prince Eddy with death. When Eddy is indeed murdered, Irish peer Lord Francis Powerscourt is called in to investigate, aided by his boozy pal, Lord Johnny Fitzgerald. To avoid embarrassing the royals, they invent an official cover story that attributes Eddy's death to influenza while they search for his murderer in London's murky underworld and in Venice. First novel.

Where it's reviewed:

Library Journal, December 2001, page 178
Publishers Weekly, December 10, 2001, page 54

Other books you might like:

Michael Kurland, *The Great Game*, 2001
Peter Lovesey, *Bertie and the Crime of Passion*, 1994
Robin Paige, *Death at Daisy's Folly*, 1997
Anne Perry, *The Whitechapel Conspiracy*, 2001
Gerard Williams, *Dr. Mortimer and the Barking Man Mystery*, 2001

59

STANFORD DIEHL

Angel in the Front Room, Devil out Back

(Atlanta: Longstreet, 2001)

Story type: Psychological Suspense
Subject(s): American South; Crime and Criminals; Arson
Major character(s): Jackson Moon, Convict (former)
Time period(s): 1990s (1998); 1970s (1978)
Locale(s): Solomon's Rock, Georgia

Summary: Nobody's happy to see Jackie Moon return to his hometown after 25 years, most of them spent in a Florida prison. He was 17 when he was forced to leave Solomon's Rock after witnessing a gruesome act of violence in which a group of black prostitutes and their johns were burned to death in a roadhouse. Jackie's father, who was involved in the crime, is now dying, and his brother is on the payroll of drug lord Michael Grant, who still controls the town from his prison cell and who is planning to build a Civil War theme park in the area. If his part in the ghastly events of 1978 is exposed, Grant's project will be history, and he and his colleagues are willing to do whatever is necessary to keep Jackie from learning the truth. First novel.

Where it's reviewed:

Booklist, May 1, 2001, page 1628
Publishers Weekly, April 2, 2001, page 40

Other books you might like:

John Armistead, *The Grover Bramlett Series*, 1994-
John Ball, *In the Heat of the Night*, 1965
James Lee Burke, *The Dave Robicheaux Series*, 1987-
Lee Child, *Killing Floor*, 1997
Thomas H. Cook, *Breakheart Hill*, 1995

60

DEBORAH DONNELLY

Veiled Threats

(New York: Dell, 2002)

Story type: Amateur Detective; Domestic
Subject(s): Weddings; Kidnapping; Humor
Major character(s): Carnegie Kincaid, Consultant (wedding planner); Aaron Gold, Journalist (reporter)
Time period(s): 2000s
Locale(s): Seattle, Washington

Summary: When she lands her first big, extravagant society wedding for her fledgling wedding-planning business, Made in Heaven, Carnegie is elated, seeing the day the company will finally wind up in the black and her accountant and business partner, Eddie, will get off her back about money. However, one thorny problem after another threaten her success, and then the bride is kidnapped and one of the attendants murdered. Further, another of her clients starts receiving anonymous threats, and Carnegie must find out if the events are connected and how, and so she joins forces with an annoying reporter, Aaron Gold, to find who's behind the sinister events. A gallery of eccentric and original secondary characters provides effective comic relief. First novel.

Where it's reviewed:
Booklist, December 15, 2001, page 708
Publishers Weekly, December 3, 2001, page 46

Other books you might like:
Donna Andrews, *Murder with Peacocks*, 1999
Paula Carter, *The Hillary Scarborough Series*, 1999-
Jerrilyn Farmer, *Killer Wedding*, 2000
Ellen Hart, *The Merchant of Venus*, 2001
Leslie Meier, *Wedding Day Murder*, 2001

61

JAMES D. DOSS

White Shell Woman

(New York: Morrow, 2002)

Story type: Police Procedural
Series: Charlie Moon. Book 7
Subject(s): Archaeology; American West; Native Americans
Major character(s): Charlie Moon, Rancher (cattle), Police Officer (former); Daisy Perika, Shaman, Aged Person; Scott Parris, Police Officer
Time period(s): 2000s
Locale(s): Southern Ute Reservation, Colorado

Summary: Tall, lanky Charlie Moon, a Southern Ute, has left his law enforcement career behind him to become a cattle rancher, a life that suits him very well. He still looks after his irascible old aunt, Daisy Perika, but he's more interested in beef prices than in solving crimes until a graduate student in archaeology is murdered at Chimney Rock, the site of ancient Anasazi ruins and a newly discovered petroglyph that has thrown the archaeological world into turmoil. Temporarily returning to police work as a special investigator, he teams up once again with his close friend Scott Parris, a white policeman. Parris has always been more attuned than Charlie to the spirit world that Daisy is in frequent communication with. Daisy warns Charlie that trespassing on sacred ground will put him in great danger, and as usual she's proved right after a second person is killed at the site. Archaeology, legends, impish humor, and suspense are seamlessly woven together by this master storyteller.

Where it's reviewed:
Publishers Weekly, December 3, 2001, page 43

Other books by the same author:
Grandmother Spider, 2001
The Night Visitor, 2000
The Shaman's Game, 1998
The Shaman's Bones, 1997
The Shaman Laughs, 1995

Other books you might like:
Cecil Dawkins, *Clay Dancers*, 1994
Kathleen O'Neal Gear, *Bone Walker*, 2001
Michael Gear, co-author
Tony Hillerman, *A Thief of Time*, 1988
Jake Page, *The Stolen Gods*, 1993
Aimee Thurlo, *The Ella Clah Series*, 1995-
David Thurlo, co-author

62

CAROLE NELSON DOUGLAS

Chapel Noir

(New York: Forge, 2001)

Story type: Historical
Series: Irene Adler. Number 5
Subject(s): Feminism; Serial Killers; Victorian Period
Major character(s): Irene Adler, Detective—Amateur, Singer; Penelope ''Nell'' Huxleigh, Companion
Time period(s): 1880s (1889)
Locale(s): Paris, France; London, England

Summary: Irene Adler is, of course, the former operatic diva who was the only woman ever to have outsmarted Sherlock Holmes (in ''A Scandal in Bohemia'') and was, according to some scholars, the only love of his life. For some years now she has been living near Paris, married to Godfrey Norton, whom she loves but who is mostly conveniently absent, leaving Irene alone except for her very proper secretary-companion Nell Huxleigh. When some prostitutes are found murdered in an elegant brothel, the police call Irene in to conduct a discreet if unofficial investigation. The nature of their wounds leads her to the immediate conclusion that their killer is none other than Jack the Ripper, and the author offers her own theory as to his actual identity. Bram Stoker, the real-life creator of Dracula, is a character, as are the Prince of Wales and Buffalo Bill Cody, and Sherlock Holmes himself makes a cameo appearance. A long readers' group guide is appended to the story (which ends in a cliffhanger to be resolved in the next book). The author also writes a series featuring feline detective Midnight Louie, set in contemporary Las Vegas.

Where it's reviewed:
Mystery News, October 11, 2001, page 25
Publishers Weekly, September 24, 2001, page 72

Other books by the same author:
Irene's Last Waltz, 1994
Irene at Large, 1992
Good Night, Mr. Holmes, 1991
Good Morning, Irene, 1990

Other books you might like:
Edward Hanna, *The Whitechapel Horror*, 1993
Peter Lovesey, *The Bertie, Prince of Wales Series*, 1987-
Kim Newman, *Anno Dracula*, 1992
Anne Perry, *The Whitechapel Conspiracy*, 2001
Ellery Queen, *Sherlock Holmes vs. Jack the Ripper*, 1967

63

SHARON DUNCAN

Death on a Casual Friday

(New York: Signet, 2001)

Story type: Private Detective
Subject(s): Boats and Boating; Islands; Mexican Americans
Major character(s): Scotia MacKinnon, Detective—Private
Time period(s): 2000s
Locale(s): Friday Harbor, Washington; Berkeley, California

Summary: Scotia, a private detective who lives aboard the *DragonSpray*, a 38-foot sailing yacht docked on San Juan Island between Washington State and British Columbia, has her offices in the tiny town where the marina is located. She's sometimes assisted by fellow tenant Zelda Jones, a computer whiz who does research for her as needed. Scotia's newest client is an icily beautiful widow named Elyse Montenegro who claims that she's being stalked by a man in a black Cherokee and whose best friend has just died under mysterious circumstances. The private detective has a bad feeling about the woman—who would try to stalk someone in a car on a tiny island?—but she takes the case anyway and follows a lead to San Francisco and Berkeley, where Elyse's husband Julio had been murdered. First mystery.

Where it's reviewed:
Mystery News, October/November 2001, page 23

Other books you might like:
Sue Grafton, *The Kinsey Millhone Series*, 1982-
Skye Kathleen Moody, *The Venus Diamond Series*, 1996-
Marcia Muller, *The Sharon McCone Series*, 1977-
Janet Smith, *The Annie MacPherson Series*, 1990-
Valerie Wilcox, *The Kellie Montgomery Series*, 1998-

64

MARJORIE ECCLES

A Sunset Touch

(New York: St. Martin's Press, 2001)

Story type: Police Procedural
Series: Gil Mayo. Book 12
Subject(s): Arson; Art; World War II
Major character(s): Gil Mayo, Police Officer (superintendent); Abigail Moon, Police Officer (inspector); Martin Kite, Police Officer (inspector)
Time period(s): 2000s
Locale(s): Lavenstock, England (Midlands)

Summary: A house fire resulting from arson which leaves a man dead and two Polish children missing is assigned by Mayo to his recently promoted inspector, Abigail Moon, while a nearly fatal assault on the local vicar's wife is turned over to Martin Kite. Neither case seems to be progressing satisfactorily until a stolen painting connects them, leading the investigators back to wartime England and Poland. Mayo and his colleagues are attractively drawn and engaging characters and the plot is both complex and satisfying in its resolution.

Where it's reviewed:
Library Journal, December 2001, page 180
Publishers Weekly, December 17, 2001, page 68

Other books by the same author:
The Superintendent's Daughter, 1999
Killing Me Softly, 1998
A Species of Revenge, 1996
A Death of Distinction, 1995
An Accidental Shroud, 1994

Other books you might like:
Jo Bannister, *The Castlemere Series*, 1993-
Claire Curzon, *The Mike Yeadings Series*, 1983-
Caroline Graham, *The Tom Barnaby Series*, 1987-
Christine Green, *The Connor O'Neill/Fran Wilson Series*, 1993-
Jill McGown, *The Inspector Lloyd/Judy Hill Series*, 1983-

65

KATHY LYNN EMERSON

Face Down Before Rebel Hooves

(New York: St. Martin's Minotaur, 2001)

Story type: Historical
Series: Susanna, Lady Appleton. Number 6
Subject(s): Espionage; Identity, Concealed; Religious Conflict
Major character(s): Lady Susanna Appleton, Widow(er), Detective—Amateur
Time period(s): 16th century (1569)
Locale(s): Hamburg, Germany; Yorkshire, England; London, England

Summary: Susanna and her lover, Nick Baldwin, are visiting Hamburg when an old friend, Sir Walter Pendennis, approaches her with an unusual request. On her deathbed, his recently deceased wife, Eleanor, confessed she was part of a plot to overthrow Queen Elizabeth and replace her on the throne with her Catholic cousin, Mary, Queen of Scots. Horrified by his knowledge of this treasonous plot, Sir Walter asks Susanna to impersonate Eleanor and deliver an important letter in her stead. She agrees and, with Sir Walter, returns to England to infiltrate the conspiracy.

Where it's reviewed:
Booklist, July 2001, page 1986
Drood Review of Mystery, July/August 2001, page 9
Publishers Weekly, July 9, 2001, page 51

Other books by the same author:
Face Down Beneath the Eleanor Cross, 2000
Face Down under the Wych Elm, 2000
Face Down Among the Winchester Geese, 1999
Face Down upon an Herbal, 1998
Face Down in the Marrow-Bone Pie, 1997

Other books you might like:
Fiona Buckley, *The Ursula Blanchard Series*, 1997-
Judith Cook, *The Simon Forman Series*, 1997-
P.C. Doherty, *The Soul Slayer*, 1997
Ann Dukthas, *Time for the Death of a King*, 1994
Karen Harper, *The Elizabeth I Series*, 1999-

66

LINDA FAIRSTEIN

The Deadhouse

(New York: Scribner, 2001)

Story type: Police Procedural; Psychological Suspense
Series: Alexandra Cooper. Number 4
Subject(s): Abuse; City and Town Life; History
Major character(s): Alexandra Cooper, Lawyer (assistant district attorney)
Time period(s): 2000s
Locale(s): New York, New York

Summary: Lola Dakota, a political science professor at Columbia University, is well known to Alexandra and her co-workers in the NYPD sex crimes unit. Long a victim of spousal abuse, Lola eventually cooperates with the police in setting up a sting to trap her husband when he hires killers to get rid of her. Now she really is dead, her body found at the bottom of an elevator shaft, and the question is, of course, is her husband responsible? There is also the puzzling connection to Charlotte Voight, a student who vanished eight months earlier, whose photo is found on Lola's bulletin board. A fascinating subplot involves "The Deadhouse," the facility on Roosevelt Island where smallpox patients were sent to die in the 19th century. As Alexandra's investigation takes shape, she is also trying to figure out what will come next in her relationship with TV newsman Jake Tyler, who is pressing her to take it to a new level. The author is herself one of the foremost sex crimes prosecutors in the country.

Where it's reviewed:
Booklist, August 2001, page 2050
Publishers Weekly, September 3, 2001, page 67

Other books by the same author:
Cold Hit, 1999
Likely to Die, 1997
Final Jeopardy, 1996

Other books you might like:
Nevada Barr, *Liberty Falling*, 1999
Patricia Cornwell, *The Kay Scarpetta Series*, 1990-
Kathy Reichs, *The Tempe Brennan Series*, 1997-
Faye Sultan, *The Portia McTeague Series*, 1998-
Marianne Wesson, *The Cinda Hayes Series*, 1998-

67

MONICA FERRIS (Pseudonym of Mary Monica Kuhlfeld)

Unraveled Sleeve

(New York: Berkley, 2001)

Story type: Amateur Detective
Series: Betsy Devonshire. Number 4
Subject(s): Crafts; Sewing; Small Town Life
Major character(s): Betsy Devonshire, Store Owner, Divorced Person
Time period(s): 2000s
Locale(s): Excelsior, Minnesota; Naniboujou, Minnesota

Summary: Now that her sister's estate is finally settled, Betsy is a millionaire three times over, but she has no intention of closing Crewel World, the small-town needlework shop she inherited when her sister died. The shop has been her salvation in coping with that loss and the aftermath of a painful divorce. She's loved the challenge and the hard work—but she's ready for a break. On an impulse, she and her friend, Jill, head into the north woods for a stitch-in at a remote lodge. The experience doesn't prove as restful as Betsy had hoped. Haunted by nightmares connected with various murders she's been involved with, she finds a body—or thinks she does, but it disappears before she can show it to anybody. Needlework enthusiasts will love all the stitching lore here, and the book comes complete with a cross-stitch pattern.

Other books by the same author:
A Stitch in Time, 2000
Crewel World, 1999
Framed in Lace, 1999

Other books you might like:
Susan Wittig Albert, *The China Bayles Series*, 1992-
Laura Childs, *Death by Darjeeling*, 2001
Janis Harrison, *The Bretta Solomon Series*, 1999-
Joan Hess, *The Claire Malloy Series*, 1986-
Tamar Myers, *The Abigail Timberlake Series*, 1996-

68

JACQUELINE FIEDLER

Sketches with Wolves

(New York: Pocket, 2001)

Story type: Amateur Detective
Series: Caroline Canfield. Number 2
Subject(s): Animals/Wolves; Internet; Wildlife Conservation
Major character(s): Caroline Canfield, Artist (wildlife), Detective—Amateur
Time period(s): 2000s
Locale(s): Wolf Prairie, Illinois

Summary: Caroline and her fellow members of the Wolf Prairie List, an Internet discussion group, are excited to be meeting at last at the wildlife preserve in the Central Illinois River Valley for a weekend of observing and learning about their favorite endangered species. On the very first evening, however, Caroline's pleasure is marred by the discovery of a dead body, and then the group is stranded at the preserve by an unexpected blizzard. Caroline is certain that there is a murderer among her new friends, but she doesn't expect them all to turn on her as she tries to determine the killer's identity.

Other books by the same author:
Tiger's Palette, 1998

Other books you might like:
Peter Bowen, *Wolf, No Wolf*, 1996
Val Davis, *The Return of the Spanish Lady*, 2001
Barbara Moore, *The Wolf Whispered Death*, 1986
Elizabeth Quinn, *A Wolf in Death's Clothing*, 1995
Dana Stabenow, *Hunter's Moon*, 1999

69

SHARON FIFFER

Killer Stuff

(New York: St. Martin's Press, 2001)

Story type: Amateur Detective
Subject(s): Collectors and Collecting; Antiques; Friendship
Major character(s): Jane Wheel, Antiques Dealer, Collector; Tim Lowry, Antiques Dealer, Homosexual
Time period(s): 2000s
Locale(s): Evanston, Illinois; Kankakee, Illinois

Summary: Recently separated from her professor husband and downsized from her advertising job, Jane is trying to find a new identity as a picker of recent vintage collectibles at sales, auctions, and flea markets in suburban Chicago. Long afflicted with collecting mania, her specialties (like the author's) are vintage ceramic flowerpots, Bakelite costume jewelry and buttons, and old photo albums and postcards. When Jane's neighbor Sandy is murdered, she's questioned by the Evanston police about the matter, since the women were friends and Jane once exchanged a not terribly clandestine kiss with Sandy's husband at a neighborhood party. Then Jane has to put her treasure hunting on hold to visit her tavern-owner parents in Kankakee, and there she reconnects with her childhood friend Tim, now owner of an antique and floral shop and a fellow junkophile. Her warm relationship with Tim (who's gay) is at the heart of the story, and the affectionate and often amusing banter between them is delightful. The plot may be overly complicated and the denouement implausible, but the author vividly conveys the thrill of the hunt for hidden treasure, the lengths collectors and dealers will go to to satisfy their lust for what others regard as junk, and the toll this obsessive behavior can take on relationships. Jane realizes that her collecting mania is more to blame for her estrangement from a husband she loves than is an impulsive kiss in a neighbor's kitchen—but she's not yet ready to deal with it. First novel.

Where it's reviewed:
Booklist, August 2001, page 2095
Mystery News, October/November 2001, page 31
Publishers Weekly, August 6, 2001, page 65

Other books you might like:
Jonathan Gash, *The Lovejoy Series*, 1977-
Susan Holtzer, *Something to Kill For*, 1994
Toni L.P. Kelner, *Tight as a Tick*, 1998
Katherine Hall Page, *The Body in the Bookcase*, 1998
Jean Ruryk, *Next Week Will Be Better*, 1998

70

MARGARET FRAZER (Pseudonym of Gail Bacon)

The Clerk's Tale

(New York: Berkley Prime Crime, 2002)

Story type: Historical
Series: Dame Frevisse. Book 11
Subject(s): Nuns; Convents; Middle Ages
Major character(s): Dame Frevisse, Religious (nun), Detective—Amateur
Time period(s): 15th century (1446)
Locale(s): Goring, England; Oxfordshire, England

Summary: The prioress of St. Frideswide's, Domina Elisabeth, selects Dame Frevisse to accompany her on a mission of mercy to St. Mary's nunnery in the town of Goring. They arrive safely only to learn that Master Morys Montfort has been found dead in the infirmary garden. As a former crowner and now escheator of the district—a man who settled property and inheritance disputes—Montfort had many enemies, and his son asks Frevisse to find his murderer. Copious details on daily life of the period, from food, drink, and dress to medicine and law, provide a rich backdrop to a meticulously plotted story.

Where it's reviewed:
Publishers Weekly, December 17, 2001, page 68

Other books by the same author:
The Squire's Tale, 2000
The Reeve's Tale, 1999
The Maiden's Tale, 1998
The Prioress' Tale, 1997
The Murderer's Tale, 1996

Other books you might like:
Alys Clare, *The Abbess Helewise Series*, 1999-
Paul Harding, *The Brother Athelstan Series*, 1991-
Sharan Newman, *Death Comes as Epiphany*, 1993
Candace M. Robb, *The Nun's Tale*, 1995-
Peter Tremayne, *The Sister Fidelma Series*, 1994-

71

SHELLEY FREYDONT

Midsummer Murder

(New York: Kensington, 2001)

Story type: Amateur Detective
Series: Lindy Haggerty. Book 3
Subject(s): Theater; Dancing
Major character(s): Lindy Haggerty, Dancer, Teacher
Time period(s): 2000s
Locale(s): New York (upstate)

Summary: Lindy is delighted to accept an appointment to teach at the prestigious Easton Arts Retreat in upstate New York, where she will also be rehearsal director for a summer dance performance commemorating the school's 50th anniversary. Her working holiday is turned upside down when a troubled scholarship student is found dead. The local sheriff seems to be less concerned with solving the crime than he is with using this and other incidents, including an apparent suicide, to discredit the school and pave the way for local developers to move in for another kind of killing. Knowing justice will never be done at his hands, Lindy turns detective herself. There's lots of convincing detail on the world of professional dance.

Where it's reviewed:
Publishers Weekly, June 25, 2001, page 52

Other books by the same author:
High Seas Murder, 2000
Backstage Murder, 1999

Other books you might like:
Edgar Box, *Death in the Fifth Position*, 1952
Michael Craft, *Desert Autumn*, 2001
Jane Dentinger, *The Jocelyn O'Roarke Series*, 1983-
Ellen Pall, *Corpse de Ballet*, 2000
Karen Sturges, *The Phoebe Mullins Series*, 1999-

72

KINKY FRIEDMAN

Steppin' on a Rainbow

(New York: Simon & Schuster, 2001)

Story type: Humor; Private Detective
Series: Kinky Friedman. Number 14
Subject(s): Vacations; Animals/Dogs; Humor

Major character(s): Kinky Friedman, Detective—Private
Time period(s): 2000s
Locale(s): New York, New York (Greenwich Village); Honolulu, Hawaii; Waipi'o Valley, Hawaii

Summary: Kinky is brooding over the death of the delectable Stephanie DuPont's tiny Maltese dog, Pyramus, and the defection of his pal, Mike McGovern, to Hawaii when he hears from an old friend that McGovern has vanished entirely. Quickly assembling all the Irregulars he can find, Kinky heads for Hawaii, where he discovers that McGovern is a dead ringer for a Hawaiian chieftain who died centuries ago. Surprisingly at home in his exotic surroundings (the topless Hawaiian women help), the Kinkster takes some advice from Don Ho and leads his band of Irregulars to the Big Island, where they are beset by much misfortune and eventually discover McGovern's fate. The sheer lunacy of the plot (such as it is) and the ubiquitous one-liners and irreverent asides only add to the fun here.

Where it's reviewed:
Book, September 2001, page 28
Booklist, July 2001, page 1986
New York Times Book Review, September 9, 2001, page 28

Other books by the same author:
The Mile High Club, 2000
Spanking Watson, 1999
Blast from the Past, 1998
Road Kill, 1997
The Love Song of J. Edgar Hoover, 1996

Other books you might like:
Lawrence Block, *The Bernie Rhodenbarr Series*, 1977-
Stan Cutler, *The Rayford Goodman Series*, 1991-
Ron Goulart, *The Groucho Marx Series*, 1998-
Parnell Hall, *The Stanley Hastings Series*, 1987-
Roger L. Simon, *The Big Fix*, 1972

73

DAVID FULMER

Chasing the Devil's Tail

(Scottsdale, Arizona: Poisoned Pen, 2001)

Story type: Historical; Private Detective
Subject(s): Prostitution; Music and Musicians; Race Relations
Major character(s): Valentin St. Cyr, Detective—Private; Tom Anderson, Political Figure, Historical Figure
Time period(s): 1900s (1907)
Locale(s): New Orleans, Louisiana (Storyville)

Summary: Storyville is New Orleans' infamous red-light district, run by political boss Tom Anderson, who isn't going to stand by when somebody starts murdering the district's prostitutes, leaving a black rose at the scene of each killing. He calls upon Creole detective Valentin St. Cyr, who is light-skinned enough to pass for white when he chooses, to investigate the murders. Valentin is not happy when the clues he turns up all point to his childhood friend, "King" Buddy Bolden, a pioneering horn player (and historical figure) who is helping to make "jass" famous, and who seems to be going mad in the process. The famous New Orleans caste system extends even to its brothels, from the lowly cribs of desperate prostitutes on the lower rungs of the socioeconomic ladder to the elegant mansions of successful madams such as Lulu White (another historical figure). First novel.

Where it's reviewed:
Drood Review, November/December 2001, page 3
Library Journal, November 1, 2001, page 135
Publishers Weekly, October 15, 2001, page 49

Other books you might like:
John Dickson Carr, *The Ghosts' High Noon*, 1970
Barbara Hambly, *The Benjamin January Series*, 1997-
Peter King, *The Jewel of the North*, 2001
James Sallis, *The Lew Griffin Series*, 1992-
Robert Skinner, *The Wesley Farrell Series*, 1997-

74

JIM FUSILLI

Closing Time

(New York: Putnam, 2001)

Story type: Private Detective
Subject(s): Fathers and Daughters; Social Issues; City and Town Life
Major character(s): Terry Orr, Detective—Private, Widow(er); Bella Orr, Child
Time period(s): 2000s
Locale(s): New York, New York

Summary: When his beloved wife and infant son are pushed to their death underneath a subway train by a crazed killer, Terry doesn't know what to do except to cling to his ten-year-old daughter Bella and take out a private investigator's license so he can catch the man who did it. As long as he has the license, he accepts other cases, which take him all over Manhattan and provide a wonderful showcase for the author's intimate knowledge of the city that never sleeps. It's now two years later; Bella is 12, and she and Terry have become even more fiercely protective of each other. Terry is anything but the conventional private-eye loner who lives outside of society; in addition to his wondefully warm and close relationship with Bella, he has many friends and connections to the community. First novel.

Where it's reviewed:
Booklist, August 2001, page 2096
New York Times Book Review, September 23, 2001, page 23
Publishers Weekly, August 6, 2001, page 64
Wall Street Journal, September 10, 2001, page A16

Other books you might like:
Richard Barre, *The Wil Hardesty Series*, 1995-
Lawrence Block, *The Matt Scudder Series*, 1976-
Jeremiah Healy, *The John Francis Cuddy Series*, 1984-
Dennis Lehane, *Mystic River*, 2001
John Straley, *The Cecil Younger Series*, 1992-

75

CAROLINA GARCIA-AGUILERA

Bitter Sugar

(New York: Morrow, 2001)

Story type: Private Detective
Series: Lupe Solano. Book 6
Subject(s): Cuban Americans; Communism; Exile
Major character(s): Lupe Solano, Detective—Private
Time period(s): 2000s
Locale(s): Miami, Florida

Summary: It's not often that Lupe's father, who disapproves of her career as a private detective, asks her for help, and when he does she's not about to refuse him. One of his old friends and fellow expatriates from Cuba, Ramon Suarez, has had a puzzling offer: an anonymous buyer in Spain wants to purchase the sugar mill he left behind when Castro took power and nationalized most of the country's industry, including the mill. Further, Ramon's no-account nephew, Alexander, desperately wants him to sell. Ramon wants Lupe to find out why anybody is even interested in a non-producing sugar mill, and then, when Alexander is found murdered in a seedy Miami hotel, he wants her to find out who killed him and why. Lupe stubbornly continues on the case even when it becomes apparent her own life is in danger, and she uncovers a wealth of information on the Cuban sugar industry and the country's bloody history.

Where it's reviewed:
Booklist, October 1, 2001, page 301
Deadly Pleasures, Autumn 2001, page 136
Library Journal, November 1, 2001, page 136
New York Times Book Review, December 9, 2001, page 29

Other books by the same author:
Havana Heat, 2000
A Miracle in Paradise, 1999
Bloody Secrets, 1998
Bloody Shame, 1997
Bloody Waters, 1996

Other books you might like:
Edna Buchanan, *The Britt Montero Series*, 1992-
Lucha Corpi, *The Gloria Damasco Series*, 1992-
Lia Matera, *Havana Twist*, 1998
Barbara Parker, *The Gail Connor Series*, 1994-
Randy Wayne White, *North of Havana*, 1997

76

JOHN GATES

Sister Wife

(New York: Walker, 2001)

Story type: Private Detective; Legal
Series: Brigham Bybee. Number 2
Subject(s): Mormons; Cults; American West
Major character(s): Brigham Bybee, Lawyer
Time period(s): 2000s
Locale(s): Kanab, Utah

Summary: The author explores the phenomenon of unsanctioned plural marriages as practiced by a grim and joyless splinter Mormon sect in southern Utah. Bybee, a lapsed Mormon, has become a hired gun for the state when he's asked to help prosecute T. Rampton Crowe, a high-profile polygamist (or plig, as they're contemptuously called). When Mercy, one of Crowe's runaway wives, tracks Bybee down in the strange concrete tepee motel he owns in Kanab, he's appalled at the beating she's taken and even more horrified by her story. He hides her in a safe house with Faith, another runaway wife who is a material witness in the case, but when Faith is murdered, the question soon becomes this: is Mercy really on the run, or is she a plant? The author makes excellent use of the local landscape, as well as Utah's peculiar politics and religion, but the book has its flaws. The killer's motivations are murky at best, and Bybee is continually walking into lethal situations he should have anticipated. Offsetting these faults is a melancholy yellow mutt with a broken tail named Spooky Floyd, one of the most memorable canine characters in mystery fiction.

Where it's reviewed:
Booklist, July 2001, page 1986
Library Journal, July 2001, page 129
Mystery News, August 9, 2001, page 18
Publishers Weekly, May 28, 2001, page 52

Other books by the same author:
Brigham's Day, 2000

Other books you might like:
Rex Burns, *The Avenging Angel*, 1983
Robert Irvine, *The Moroni Traveler Series*, 1988-
Cleo Jones, *Prophet Motive*, 1984
Lee Martin, *The Deb Ralston Series*, 1984-
Stephen White, *Higher Authority*, 1994

77

ANNE GEORGE

Murder Boogies with Elvis

(New York: Morrow, 2001)

Story type: Amateur Detective; Humor
Series: Southern Sisters. Book 8
Subject(s): Sisters; American South; Weddings
Major character(s): Patricia Anne "Mouse" Hollowell, Teacher, Detective—Amateur; Mary Alice "Sister" Crane, Divorced Person, Detective—Amateur
Time period(s): 2000s
Locale(s): Birmingham, Alabama

Summary: Tall, flamboyant Mary Alice is about to make the local sheriff her fourth husband, and she and her tiny, impeccably mannered sister Patricia Anne, known affectionately as Mouse, are making preparations for the wedding. Mouse is also looking forward to the birth of a grandchild. They take time off from planning the wedding to attend a benefit performance that comes to a roaring finale with no fewer than 30 jumpsuited Elvis impersonators forming a high-kicking chorus line. The effect is spoiled when one of them pitches headfirst into the front row, right into Mouse's lap, and turns out to have been stabbed in the back. When the murder weapon, a switchblade knife, is found in Mouse's purse, she's arrested for the crime. This good-natured, often wildly amusing series draws to a close here following the author's death.

Where it's reviewed:
Booklist, July 2001, page 1987
Library Journal, August 2001, page 170
Publishers Weekly, July 9, 2001, page 51

Other books by the same author:
Murder Carries a Torch, 2001
Murder Shoots the Bull, 1999
Murder Gets a Life, 1998
Murder Makes Waves, 1997
Murder Runs in the Family, 1997

Other books you might like:
Annie Griffin, *The Hannah Malloy/Kiki Goldstein Series*, 1998-
Joan Hess, *Misery Loves Maggody*, 1999
Toni L.P. Kelner, *The Laura Fleming Series*, 1993-
Sarah Shankman, *The King Is Dead*, 1992
Elizabeth Daniels Squire, *The Peaches Dann Series*, 1994-

78

TESS GERRITSEN

The Surgeon

(New York: Ballantine, 2001)

Story type: Psychological Suspense
Subject(s): Medical Thriller; Hospitals; Serial Killers
Major character(s): Catherine Cordell, Doctor (surgeon); Thomas Moore, Detective—Homicide; Jane Rizzoli, Detective—Homicide
Time period(s): 2000s
Locale(s): Boston, Massachusetts; Savannah, Georgia

Summary: Two years ago, trauma surgeon Catherine Cordell not only survived a rape and attempted murder in Savannah, Georgia, but shot and killed her assailant before he could carry out his threat to surgically remove her uterus. Now on the staff of a large Boston hospital, she's contacted by police detectives Moore and Rizzoli when three other women are raped, murdered, and surgically mutilated by someone who is exactly copying the methods of the man who attacked Catherine. In the course of the investigation, Tom and Catherine fall for each other and he's sent to Savannah by his superior officers to remove him from her presence, and there he finds an important key to what has happened. Rizzoli has her own part to play back in Boston, ultimately saving Catherine from another deadly attack. The hospital scenes are extremely realistic and a great deal of blood is spilled (and described) before the mystery is resolved.

Where it's reviewed:
Booklist, July 2001, page 1950
Library Journal, August 2001, page 160
People Weekly, September 3, 2001, page 47
Publishers Weekly, July 2, 2001, page 49

Other books by the same author:
Gravity, 1999
Bloodstream, 1998
Life Support, 1997
Harvest, 1996

Other books you might like:
Robin Cook, *Terminal*, 1993
Patricia Cornwell, *The Kay Scarpetta Series*, 1990-
Iris Johansen, *The Eve Duncan Series*, 1998-
Michael Palmer, *Natural Causes*, 1994
Ridley Pearson, *The Angel Maker*, 1993

79

DOROTHY GILMAN

Kaleidoscope

(New York: Ballantine, 2002)

Story type: Amateur Detective
Series: Madame Karitska. Book 2
Subject(s): Psychic Powers; Extrasensory Perception; Parapsychology
Major character(s): Madame Karitska, Psychic, Detective—Amateur; Pruden, Detective—Police (lieutenant)
Time period(s): 2000s
Locale(s): New York, New York

Summary: The author takes a break from her long-running Mrs. Pollifax series (14 to date) to return to a character introduced over a quarter of a century ago, the clairvoyant countess Madame Karitska. She makes her living telling fortunes from her shabby brownstone and often consults with the police, in the person of Detective Lieutenant Pruden, regarding unsolved crimes. The countess is skilled in psychometry, the art of absorbing a person's history and movements by holding an object he or she had formerly owned or touched. In this episodic novel, almost a collection of interconnected short stories, she and Pruden work on a number of cases, among them the death of a young violinist and a deaf child being abused by her benefactors. There are a variety of other cases, including one presciently foreshadowing today's terrorism.

Where it's reviewed:
Booklist, December 1, 2001, page 632
Library Journal, December 2001, page 178
Publishers Weekly, December 24, 2001, page 45

Other books by the same author:
The Clairvoyant Countess, 1975

Other books you might like:
Catherine Dain, *The Mariana Morgan Series*, 1999-
Dorothy Salisbury Davis, *The Julie Hayes Series*, 1976-
Kate Green, *The Theresa Fortunato Series*, 1986-
Martha C. Lawrence, *The Elizabeth Chase Series*, 1995-
Mignon Warner, *The Edwina Charles Series*, 1976-

80

JACQUELINE GIRDNER

A Sensitive Kind of Murder

(New York: Berkley, 2001)

Story type: Amateur Detective; Humor
Series: Kate Jasper. Book 12
Subject(s): Marriage; Friendship; Satire

Major character(s): Kate Jasper, Businesswoman (gag gift designer), Detective—Amateur
Time period(s): 2000s
Locale(s): Marin County, California

Summary: Although Kate approves of her husband's latest endeavor, a male sensitivity group known as the Heartlink Men's Group, she's been getting bad feelings about it, and they're validated when one of the members is killed by a hit-and-run driver. Having witnessed it, Kate is convinced it was no accident, and she's astonished when her husband, who usually disapproves of her meddling, asks her to investigate. Girdner, in what may be the final book in the series, delights in poking a little good-natured fun at the manners and mores of the residents of trendy Marin County.

Other books by the same author:
Murder, My Deer, 2000
Murder on the Astral Plane, 1999
Death Hits the Fan, 1998
A Cry for Self Help, 1997
Most Likely to Die, 1996

Other books you might like:
Carol Higgins Clark, *The Regan O'Reilly Series*, 1992-
Annie Griffin, *The Hannah Malloy/Kiki Goldstein Series*, 1998-
Sparkle Hayter, *The Last Manly Man*, 1998
Marlys Millhiser, *The Charlie Greene Series*, 1992-
Robert Westbrook, *The Warrior Circle*, 1999

81

KAT GOLDRING

All Signs Point to Murder

(New York: Berkley, 2001)

Story type: Amateur Detective
Subject(s): Small Town Life; Wicca; Native Americans
Major character(s): Willi Gallagher, Teacher (high school); Quannah Lassiter, Police Officer (Texas Ranger)
Time period(s): 2000s
Locale(s): Nickleberry, Texas

Summary: Willi is examining some books in the stacks of the high school library with an eye to investigating her Native American heritage (she's part Comanche) when she hears a couple of her students discussing a bloody initiation rite into a group they seem to fear being unable to leave. Subsequent events lead her to wonder if their conversation could be connected with the discovery of slain pets and if there is a Satanic cult operating in Nickleberry—or if someone just wants people to think there is. Certainly there are lots of oddball characters in the town, including her palm-reading, seance-holding, white-witch neighbors. Then a student is found murdered, and she meets up with Quannah Lassiter, a Texas Ranger who is also part Comanche, with a little Sioux thrown in. First novel.

Where it's reviewed:
Mystery News, October/November 2001, page 24

Other books you might like:
Rosemary Edghill, *The Karen Hightower Series*, 1994-
Nancy Herndon, *The Elena Jarvis Series*, 1995-
Gillian Roberts, *The Amanda Pepper Series*, 1987-
Beth Sherman, *The Devil and the Deep Blue Sea*, 2001
Denise Swanson, *The Scumble River Series*, 2000-

82

CAROL GOODMAN

The Lake of Dead Languages

(New York: Ballantine, 2002)

Story type: Psychological Suspense
Subject(s): Schools/Boarding Schools; Suicide; Teen Relationships
Major character(s): Jane Hudson, Teacher (of Latin), Single Parent
Time period(s): 2000s; 1980s
Locale(s): Corinth, New York

Summary: Recently separated from her husband and with a young daughter, Jane Hudson returns as a Latin teacher to the Heart Lake School for Girls in upstate New York, which she attended as a local scholarship student. Although the once-prestigious school has gone downhill since she was there, at first things go well; she thinks she may be on her way toward establishing a good relationship with the bright, but troubled adolescent girls she teaches and with other members of the faculty, many of whom had been her own teachers. Then a page from a lost diary she kept as a student resurfaces, stirring up memories of the terrible tragedy she lived through when her three closest friends, roommates Lucy Toller and Dierdre Hall, and Lucy's brother Matt, all committed suicide and the Latin teacher the three girls idolized was disgraced. She suspects one of her students may be out to torment her, and then the events of that last terrible year before she graduated seem to be reenacting themselves. The narrative encompasses the events of the present, as well as the past, and the intricate story unfolds slowly but steadily, with the reader understanding it entirely just shortly before Jane does. The teenage girls, past and present, are extremely well drawn, the setting is suitably oppressive and at times eerie, and the complex plot is beautifully managed, especially for a first novel.

Where it's reviewed:
Booklist, November 15, 2001, page 551
People Weekly, January 14, 2002, page 39
Publishers Weekly, November 12, 2001, page 34

Other books you might like:
Thomas H. Cook, *Breakheart Hill*, 1995
Thomas H. Cook, *The Chatham School Affair*, 1996
Robert Goddard, *Caught in the Light*, 1999
Donna Tartt, *The Secret History*, 1995
Laura Wilson, *My Best Friend*, 2002

83

ED GORMAN

Save the Last Dance for Me

(New York: Carroll & Graf, 2002)

Story type: Historical; Private Detective
Series: Sam McCain. Book 4

Subject(s): Anti-Semitism; Campaigns, Political; Small Town Life
Major character(s): Sam McCain, Detective—Private, Lawyer
Time period(s): 1960s (1960)
Locale(s): Cedar Rapids, Iowa; Black River Falls, Iowa

Summary: The nation is entering a new decade and soon to elect a new president, with Vice President Richard Milhous Nixon about to make a campaign stop while in the area. Like the rest of the country, many citizens of Black River Falls haven't made up their minds about Nixon or his rival, John F. Kennedy, but one of the locals, a snake-handling fundamentalist preacher named John Muldaur, who is an anti-Kennedy zealot as well as an anti-Semite, is claiming that the Jews and Catholics are conspiring to destroy the nation by putting Kennedy in the White House. When Muldaur is murdered, Sam is hired to find his killer before Nixon arrives in town. The author, also a prolific editor and anthologist, has written a number of mystery series, of which this, with its generous helpings of nostalgia about America's heartland at mid-century, is perhaps the most appealing.

Where it's reviewed:
Publishers Weekly, December 3, 2001, page 42

Other books by the same author:
Will You Still Love Me Tomorrow?, 2001
Wake Up, Little Susie, 2000
The Day the Music Died, 1999

Other books you might like:
Andrew Bergman, *Hollywood and LeVine*, 1975
Max Allan Collins, *The Nate Heller Series*, 1983-
Terence Faherty, *Come Back Dead*, 1997
Joe Gores, *Cases*, 1998
Kris Nelscott, *The Smokey Dalton Series*, 2000

84

ED GORMAN, Editor
MARTIN H. GREENBERG, Co-Editor

The World's Finest Mystery & Crime Stories: Second Annual Collection

(New York: Forge, 2001)

Story type: Anthology
Series: World's Finest Mystery & Crime Stories. Book 2
Subject(s): Short Stories

Summary: This is a truly mammoth (684 pages) anthology which includes a tribute to Ed McBain by Pete Hamill; a review of the year 2000 by Jon L. Breen; a yearbook of the mystery story by editor Gorman (including obituaries); world reports from Britain, Australia, Germany, and Canada; a report on mystery fandom by George Easter; and a list of Edgar awards for the year 2000, all in addition to 41 short stories and a list of honorable mentions. Included are many favorite authors such as Lawrence Block, Ian Rankin, Ed McBain, Bill Pronzini, Peter Lovesey, Nancy Pickard, S.J. Rozan, Donald Westlake, Peter Robinson, Stuart Kaminsky, Dorothy Cannell, and Jan Burke, plus a host of lesser-known writers, as well as quite a few from countries other than the U.S. or Great Britain. The stories, some originals but most reprinted from magazines and original anthologies, are of every type and provide a representative cross-section of the modern mystery story. The essays are both informative and entertaining and the book is a model of what an annual anthology should be.

Where it's reviewed:
Booklist, November 1, 2001, page 462
Publishers Weekly, October 29, 2001, page 38
Wall Street Journal, December 6, 2001, page A19

Other books by the same author:
The World's Finest Mystery & Crime Stories: First Annual Collection, 2000

Other books you might like:
Lawrence Block, *The Best American Mystery Stories*, 2001
editor
Jon L. Breen, *Sleuths of the Century*, 2000
Ed Gorman, co-editor
Elizabeth Foxwell, *More Murder, They Wrote*, 2000
editor
Janet Hutchings, *Creme de la Crime*, 2000
editor
Anne Perry, *A Century of British Mystery and Suspense*, 2000
editor

85

RON GOULART

Adam and Eve on a Raft

(Norfolk, Virginia: Crippen & Landru, 2001)

Story type: Collection; Humor
Subject(s): Short Stories

Summary: This collection features two series characters. One is Scrib Merlin, an aspiring standup comedian and disillusioned advertising copywriter with a penchant for being on hand when murder victims utter their dying messages. The author has a lot of fun with this time-honored (and often ridiculous) tradition of the detective short story. The other is the sardonic and never-named California Adman, who specializes in recording the murderous plots of a surprisingly large number of homicidal friends. The dozen tales here have been selected by the author from the many stories that have appeared under his byline in mystery magazines over the years for inclusion in this, his first collection.

Where it's reviewed:
Publishers Weekly, October 29, 2001, page 39

Other books by the same author:
Groucho Marx and the Broadway Murders, 2001
Elementary, My Dear Groucho, 1999
Groucho Marx, Private Eye, 1999
Groucho Marx, Master Detective, 1998
Now He Thinks He's Dead, 1992

Other books you might like:
Lawrence Block, *Some Days You Get the Bear*, 1993
short stories
Joe Gores, *Speak of the Devil*, 1999
short stories
Edward D. Hoch, *The Velvet Touch*, 2000
short stories

Edward Wellen, *Perps*, 2001
short stories
Donald E. Westlake, *A Good Story and Other Stories*, 1999
short stories

86

C.L. GRACE (Pseudonym of P.C. Doherty)

Saintly Murders

(New York: St. Martin's Minotaur, 2001)

Story type: Historical
Series: Kathryn Swinbrooke. Number 5
Subject(s): Middle Ages; Animals/Rats; Catholicism
Major character(s): Kathryn Swinbrooke, Doctor, Detective—Amateur; Colum Murtagh, Government Official, Lover (of Kathryn)
Time period(s): 15th century (1472)
Locale(s): Canterbury, England

Summary: An infestation of rats threatens the city of Canterbury, just as it is poised to welcome throngs of pilgrims coming to worship at the shrine of Thomas a Becket. In her role as physician and apothecary, Kathryn is instructed by the archbishop to be present at the exhumation of a local friar, who is reputed to have performed miracles and judge whether or not he should be considered for canonization. She's asked to look into the rat problem as well. What she does discover is that the pious friar may have been murdered, and she and her lover, Colum Murtagh, begin looking for a possible killer. The author writes numerous other historical series, most of them set in medieval times, under a variety of pseudonyms.

Where it's reviewed:
Booklist, August 2001, page 2096
Mystery News, October/November 2001, page 20
Publishers Weekly, July 9, 2001, page 50

Other books by the same author:
The Book of Shadows, 1996
The Merchant of Death, 1995
The Eye of God, 1994
A Shrine of Murders, 1993

Other books you might like:
P.C. Doherty, *Dove Amongst the Hawks*, 1990
P.C. Doherty, *The Rose Demon*, 1997
Margaret Frazer, *The Dame Frevisse Series*, 1992-
Sheri Holman, *A Stolen Tongue*, 1997
Kate Sedley, *The Roger the Chapman Series*, 1991-

87

ANN GRANGER

Shades of Murder

(New York: St. Martin's Press, 2001)

Story type: Police Procedural; Traditional
Series: Mitchell & Markby. Number 13
Subject(s): Small Town Life; Sisters; Identity
Major character(s): Alan Markby, Police Officer (superintendent); Meredith Mitchell, Civil Servant (foreign service), Lover (of Alan)
Time period(s): 1990s (1999); 1880s (1889)
Locale(s): Bamford, England (Cotswolds)

Summary: Fourways House is an imposing Victorian mansion that has been occupied by the Oakley family since it was built. In 1889 William Oakley was tried for the murder of his wife Cora, who died from poison gas inhaled as she slept, and although he was acquitted, he was always viewed as a murderer. Today two elderly descendants, spinster sisters Damaris and Florence Oakley, live an impoverished existence in the grand old house, which they have decided to sell so they can live out the rest of their lives in some degree of comfort. They are forced to put their plans on hold when a disagreeable young Polish man named Jan appears in their lives, claiming to be the great-grandson of William Oakley and entitled, according to a will in his possession, to half the proceeds from any sale. When Jan is murdered, Superintendent Markby steps in to solve both his murder and the long-ago death of Cora Oakley. Two Scotland Yard detectives are also called in, and as usual Alan's lover, foreign service veteran Meredith Mitchell, lends a hand as well.

Where it's reviewed:
Booklist, September 1, 2001, page 56
Mystery News, October/November 2001, page 31
Publishers Weekly, September 24, 2001, page 72

Other books by the same author:
Beneath These Stones, 2000
Call the Dead Again, 1998
A Touch of Mortality, 1996
A Word After Dying, 1996
A Candle for a Corpse, 1995

Other books you might like:
Deborah Crombie, *The Duncan Kincaid/Gemma James Series*, 1993-
Caroline Graham, *The Inspector Barnaby Series*, 1987-
Christine Green, *The Connor O'Neill/Fran Wilson Series*, 1993-
Jill McGown, *The Inspector Lloyd/Judy Hill Series*, 1983-
Janet Neel, *The John McLeish/Francesca Wilson Series*, 1988-

88

JAN GRAPE

Austin City Blue

(Waterville, Maine: Five Star, 2001)

Story type: Police Procedural
Subject(s): Revenge; Crime and Criminals; Marriage
Major character(s): Zoe Barrow, Police Officer
Time period(s): 2000s
Locale(s): Austin, Texas

Summary: When she fatally shoots a young Hispanic man in the line of duty, Zoe has no idea he's the same man who had earlier shot her own husband, police officer Byron Barrow, and left him in a coma from which he may never emerge. Nonetheless she's placed on administrative duty until Internal Affairs can determine she didn't purposely kill the man in an act of revenge. She doesn't succeed in staying out of trouble: Byron's best friend comes to her for help when he suspects his wife and the cop she's having a fling with are planning to kill him, and then he's wounded while Zoe is supposedly protecting him. Throughout it all, she continues to visit Byron at the nursing home where he's being cared for, hoping against hope that someday he will recognize her. First novel.

Where it's reviewed:
Drood Review, November/December 2001, page 11
Publishers Weekly, September 24, 2001, page 73

Other books you might like:
Nancy Herndon, *The Elena Jarvis Series*, 1995-
Margaret Maron, *The Sigrid Harald Series*, 1981-
Lee Martin, *The Deb Ralston Series*, 1984-
Rick Riordan, *The Devil Went Down to Austin*, 2001
Julie Smith, *The Skip Langdon Series*, 1990-

89

SARAH GRAVES (Pseudonym of Mary Kittredge)

Wreck the Halls

(New York: Bantam, 2001)

Story type: Amateur Detective
Series: Jacobia Tiptree. Book 5
Subject(s): Christmas; Small Town Life; Abuse
Major character(s): Jacobia "Jake" Tiptree Sorenson, Housewife, Detective—Amateur
Time period(s): 2000s
Locale(s): Eastport, Maine

Summary: Newly remarried Jake Tiptree Sorenson lets nothing stand in the way of her ongoing struggle to rehab the dilapidated 1823 house she bought on a whim when she left her stressful Wall Street career behind her, in part to get her wayward teenage son back on track. She is momentarily sidetracked when her neighbor, Faye Ann Carmody, is found sound asleep and drenched in blood with her abusive husband's body parts neatly wrapped in butcher paper in their adjoining butcher shop. Jake and her friend, Ellie, can't believe Faye Ann did it and so conduct their own investigation of the crime. Besides an understanding second husband, there's a self-centered ex-husband, a son who's home from college, and occasional tips on home repair. Think Diane Mott Davidson with a tool belt instead of a cookie sheet.

Where it's reviewed:
Booklist, November 15, 2001, page 556
Library Journal, December 2001, page 178
Publishers Weekly, October 15, 2001, page 48
Wall Street Journal, December 6, 2001, page A19

Other books by the same author:
Repair to Her Grave, 2001
Wicked Fix, 2000
Triple Witch, 1999
Dead Cat Bounce, 1998

Other books you might like:
Susan Wittig Albert, *The China Bayles Series*, 1992-
Donna Andrews, *The Meg Langslow Series*, 1999-
Diane Mott Davidson, *The Goldy Bear Schulz Series*, 1990-
Leslie Meier, *The Lucy Stone Series*, 1993-
Valerie Wolzien, *The Susan Henshaw Series*, 1987-

90

K.C. GREENLIEF (Pseudonym of Brenda Hall)

Cold Hunter's Moon

(New York: St. Martin's Press, 2002)

Story type: Police Procedural
Subject(s): Winter; Small Town Life; Romance
Major character(s): Lark Swenson, Police Officer (sheriff), Widow(er); Lacey Smith, Detective—Police
Time period(s): 2000s
Locale(s): Big Oak, Wisconsin

Summary: Lark Swenson, a former Chicago cop who's moved to the small northern Wisconsin town of Big Oak to start his life over after the death of his wife, is the first on the scene when a local couple report one of their dogs has dragged home a bloody human foot. Soon the state police are called in as backup, and one of them, detective Lacey Smith, stays on until the investigation is completed. The book is as much about the relationship that develops between Lark and Lacey and Lark's eventual acceptance by the community as it is about the murder itself. The brutal winter weather and the small-town ambience are nicely depicted. First novel.

Where it's reviewed:
Booklist, December 15, 2001, page 706
Publishers Weekly, December 10, 2001, page 55

Other books you might like:
Steve Hamilton, *The Alex McKnight Series*, 1998-
William Kent Krueger, *The Cork O'Connor Series*, 1998-
Mary Logue, *Glare Ice*, 2001
Julia Spencer-Fleming, *In the Bleak Midwinter*, 2002
Charlene Weir, *A Cold Christmas*, 2001

91

ANNIE GRIFFIN (Pseudonym of Sally Chapman)

Tall, Dead, and Handsome

(New York: Berkley, 2001)

Story type: Amateur Detective; Humor
Series: Hannah Malloy/Kiki Goldstein. Book 4
Subject(s): Sisters; Small Town Life; Campaigns, Political
Major character(s): Hannah Malloy, Widow(er), Detective—Amateur; Kiki Goldstein, Widow(er), Detective—Amateur
Time period(s): 2000s
Locale(s): Hill Creek, California (Marin County)

Summary: Although she had been a left-wing activist in the 1960s, time and age have turned Hannah Malloy into a sedate 60-something widow who prefers gardening and poetry to politics. Recent developments in her idyllic Marin County community have alarmed her to such an extent that she's entered the race for mayor. Her sister, the libidinous, extroverted Kiki, whose outlandish, tight-fitting clothes and stiletto-heeled shoes make her look like a "senior citizen hooker" (in Hannah's words), has romantic designs on Alex Portman, the mayor Hannah is trying to unseat, and she opposes her sister's political aspirations. Then Portman is found dead, with Hannah—his chief opponent—the most likely suspect. Despite their frequent bickering, Kiki and Hannah are really very close, and they team up to clear Hannah of the crime.

Other books by the same author:
Love and the Single Corpse, 2000
Date with the Perfect Dead Man, 1999
A Very Eligible Corpse, 1998

Other books you might like:
Eleanor Boylan, *The Clara Gamadge Series*, 1989-
Anne George, *The Southern Sisters Series*, 1996-2001
Jacqueline Girdner, *The Kate Jasper Series*, 1991-
Carolyn Hart, *The Henrie O Series*, 1993-
Corinne Holt Sawyer, *The Angela Benbow/Caledonia Wingate Series*, 1993-

92

MARTHA GRIMES

The Blue Last

(New York: Viking, 2001)

Story type: Police Procedural; Traditional
Series: Inspector Jury. Number 17
Subject(s): World War II; Identity; Memory
Major character(s): Richard Jury, Police Officer (inspector); Mickey Haggerty, Police Officer (detective chief inspector); Melrose Plant, Professor, Sidekick
Time period(s): 2000s
Locale(s): London, England

Summary: When two skeletons from World War II are uncovered during the excavation of a London bomb site, the ruins of a former pub known as the Blue Last, Jury is called in to help DCI Mickey Haggerty establish the identity of the bombing victims. Haggerty suspects that one of them, a child at the time, may be the true heir of brewery millionaire Oliver Tynedale, and that the woman who claims to be his grandchild and who supposedly survived the Blitz is actually an impostor. Jury sends his friend Melrose Plant to Tynedale Lodge to spy on the household, while Mickey follows another lead: the murder of merchant banker Simon Croft, son of the owner of the Blue Last, who was writing a history of the Blitz which has now disappeared. The case brings forth painful memories for Jury, whose own parents were killed in the war.

Where it's reviewed:
Booklist, August 2001, page 2050
New York Times Book Review, September 23, 2001, page 23
Wall Street Journal, September 17, 2001, page A16

Other books by the same author:
The Lamorna Wink, 1999
The Stargazey, 1998
The Case Has Altered, 1997
Rainbow's End, 1995
The Horse You Came In On, 1993

Other books you might like:
Robert Barnard, *Out of the Blackout*, 1984
Deborah Crombie, *Kissed a Sad Goodbye*, 1999
Elizabeth George, *The Thomas Lynley/Barbara Havers Series*, 1988-
Teri Holbrook, *A Far and Deadly Cry*, 1995
Peter Lovesey, *Rough Cider*, 1986

93

ELIZABETH GUNN

Six-Pound Walleye

(New York: Walker, 2001)

Story type: Police Procedural
Series: Jake Hines. Number 4
Subject(s): Small Town Life; Schools/High Schools; Children
Major character(s): Jake Hines, Police Officer (lieutenant)
Time period(s): 2000s
Locale(s): Rutherford, Minnesota

Summary: Small-town police work is showcased in this latest case for Jake Hines, who starts his day one frozen February morning by having a tiff with his live-in girlfriend Trudy, continues it by discussing Seasonal Affective Disorder with his colleagues, and caps it off by taking two calls at the police station. One is from the local high school, where the police chief's son is embroiled in a massive fight, involving most of the hockey team, which sends one of his classmates to the hospital. The other involves a crime scene where a small boy waiting for his bus is tragically killed by a gunshot that nobody heard.

Where it's reviewed:
Booklist, May 1, 2001, page 1632
Library Journal, June 1, 2001, page 224
New York Times Book Review, July 22, 2001, page 22
Publishers Weekly, April 30, 2001, page 59

Other books by the same author:
Five Card Stud, 2000
Par Four, 1998
Triple Play, 1997

Other books you might like:
Susan Rogers Cooper, *The Milton Kovak Series*, 1988-
Steve Hamilton, *The Alex McKnight Series*, 1998-
Donald Harstad, *The Big Thaw*, 2000
Steven F. Havill, *The Bill Gastner Series*, 1991-
William Kent Krueger, *The Cork O'Connor Series*, 1998-

94

JAMES W. HALL

Blackwater Sound

(New York: St. Martin's Press, 2001)

Story type: Private Detective
Series: Thorn. Book 7
Subject(s): Airplane Accidents; Fishing; Family Relations
Major character(s): Thorn, Fisherman; Alexandra Rafferty, Photographer (forensic)
Time period(s): 2000s
Locale(s): Key Largo, Florida

Summary: Thorn has had a relatively long run of peace and solitude, his only gainful employment consisting of tying flies for bone fishermen and his chief companion a lovely, but uncomplicated young woman named Casey who makes few demands on him. This all ends when Casey breaks off their relationship and Thorn witnesses the crash of an airplane off the coast of Florida. He plunges into the all-out effort to rescue the survivors, and this in turn attracts the attention of a family of supervillains. This family, the Braswells, lost their son Andy ten years earlier to a giant marlin and since then have been engaged in an obsessive quest for revenge. When Thorn finally realizes he must hunt the Braswells down and fight back, he joins forces with crime-scene photographer Alexandra Rafferty (from 1999's *Body Language*), whose father has been kidnapped by this fearsomely dysfunctional family. This may be the darkest book yet from the darkest of the Florida thriller writers, dealing as it does with terrorist acts of extreme violence, unleavened with little if any humor, and presenting not just one villain but a whole family of them.

Where it's reviewed:
Booklist, October 1, 2001, page 352
Library Journal, December 2001, page 172
New York Times Book Review, January 6, 2002, page 19
Publishers Weekly, November 12, 2001, page 33

Other books by the same author:
Red Sky at Night, 1997
Buzz Cut, 1996
Gone Wild, 1995
Mean High Tide, 1994
Tropical Freeze, 1989

Other books you might like:
James Lee Burke, *The Dave Robicheaux Series*, 1987-
Michael Connelly, *The Harry Bosch Series*, 1992-
Carl Hiaasen, *Native Tongue*, 1991
Dennis Lehane, *The Patrick Kenzie/Angela Gennaro Series*, 1994-
Randy Wayne White, *The Doc Ford Series*, 1990-

95

OAKLEY HALL

Ambrose Bierce and the Death of Kings

(New York: Viking, 2001)

Story type: Historical
Series: Ambrose Bierce. Number 2
Subject(s): Authors and Writers; Literature; Kings, Queens, Rulers, etc.
Major character(s): Ambrose Bierce, Historical Figure, Writer; Tom Redmond, Journalist, Companion (of Ambrose)
Time period(s): 1890s (1891)
Locale(s): San Francisco, California

Summary: As King David Kalakaua of Hawaii lies dying in the royal suite of the opulent Palace Hotel, a princess in his court disappears and Bierce, San Francisco's most celebrated writer and William Randolph Hearst's star journalist, is asked to find her. It seems fairly certain that Princess Leileiha's disappearance is related to the political intrigues that are being played out as the successor to Kalakaua's throne is determined, and Bierce sets his protege, Tom Redmond, to work researching the history of the royal family. Tom has recently become enamored of a beautiful young Hawaiian woman, Haunani Brown, who is able to shed a great deal of light on the subject. Bierce, who can be kind and thoughtful one moment and angry and bitter the next, dominates the narrative, which is expertly interwoven with information on Hawaii in the days before its statehood.

Where it's reviewed:
Booklist, September 1, 2001, page 56
Publishers Weekly, September 17, 2001, page 57
Washington Post, October 7, 2001, page T15

Other books by the same author:
Ambrose Bierce and the Queen of Spades, 1998

Other books you might like:
Peter J. Heck, *The Mark Twain Series*, 1995-
Peter King, *The Jewel of the North*, 2001
Walter Satterthwait, *Wilde West*, 1994
Steven Saylor, *A Twist at the End*, 2000
Harold Schechter, *Nevermore*, 1999

96

PARNELL HALL

Puzzled to Death

(New York: Bantam, 2001)

Story type: Amateur Detective; Humor
Series: Puzzle Lady. Book 3
Subject(s): Hobbies; Contests; Small Town Life
Major character(s): Cora Felton, Aged Person, Detective—Amateur; Sherry Carter, Writer (cruciverbalist)
Time period(s): 2000s
Locale(s): Bakerhaven, Connecticut

Summary: Cora's lovable public persona as the twinkle-eyed, white-haired creator of a syndicated crossword puzzle feature is very much at odds with her private self: a much-married, gin-swilling, foul-mouthed old lady whose puzzles are actually created by her long-suffering yet affectionate niece, Sherry. When a crossword puzzle contest is slated for her hometown, Cora is enormously relieved when murder strikes and she's able to avoid the eager cruciverbalists in attendance and get down to what she does best: solving crimes. Crossword puzzles included. The author also writes a semi-cozy comic private eye series featuring Stanley Hastings.

Where it's reviewed:
Booklist, September 15, 2001, page 198
Deadly Pleasures, Autumn 2001, page 52
Mystery News, October/November 2001, page 33
Publishers Weekly, October 29, 2001, page 38

Other books by the same author:
Last Puzzle and Testament, 2000
A Clue for the Puzzle Lady, 1999

Other books you might like:
John Barth, *The Margaret Binton Series*, 1978-
M.C. Beaton, *The Agatha Raisin Series*, 1992-
Nero Blanc, *The Crossword Murder*, 1999
Simon Brett, *The Mrs. Pargeter Series*, 1986-
Patricia Moyes, *A Six-Letter Word for Death*, 1983

97

PATRICIA HALL

Skeleton at the Feast

(New York: St. Martin's Press, 2002)

Story type: Police Procedural
Series: Michael Thackeray. Book 7
Subject(s): Academia; Missing Persons; Universities and Colleges
Major character(s): Michael Thackeray, Police Officer; Laura Ackroyd, Journalist (newspaper reporter)
Time period(s): 2000s
Locale(s): Yorkshire, England; Oxford, England

Summary: With the inquiry into the recent death of one of his officers still going on and his future unclear until it's concluded, Thackeray decides to take a summer course at Oxford University, his alma mater, although he no sooner arrives when he suspects he's made a mistake. He is pleased though to see Hugh Greenaway, one of his former tutors at St. Frideswide and now master of the college. Greenaway asks Thackeray to investigate the disappearance of one of the dons, who uncharacteristically walked out on his students, his colleagues, his wife, and his family, to be with his girlfriend. Back in Yorkshire, Thackeray's significant other, journalist Laura Ackroyd, keeps an eye on the department and the attempts by a fellow officer to usurp Thackeray's job.

Where it's reviewed:
Booklist, December 1, 2001, page 632
Library Journal, December 2001, page 178
Publishers Weekly, December 24, 2001, page 46

Other books by the same author:
Dead on Arrival, 2001
The Italian Girl, 2000
Perils of the Night, 1999
Dead of Winter, 1997
Dying Fall, 1994

Other books you might like:
Claire Curzon, *The Mike Yeadings Series*, 1983-
Colin Dexter, *The Inspector Morse Series*, 1975-
Reginald Hill, *The Dalziel and Pascoe Series*, 1970-
Peter Robinson, *The Alan Banks Series*, 1987-
Margaret Yorke, *The Patrick Grant Series*, 1970-

98

DENISE HAMILTON

The Jasmine Trade

(New York: Scribner, 2001)

Story type: Psychological Suspense
Subject(s): Chinese; Gangs; Illegal Immigrants
Major character(s): Eve Diamond, Journalist (newspaper reporter)
Time period(s): 2000s
Locale(s): Los Angeles, California

Summary: The author writes knowledgeably of the so-called parachute kids, affluent Asian teens who live on their own in Southern California suburbs, while their parents continue to live and work in China and elsewhere. With nobody but a housekeeper or perhaps figurehead guardian to turn to, the teens are given lavish allowances ($3,000 a month) and expected to make the grades needed to get into top U.S. colleges. The surprising thing is that most of them do, although some turn to gangs to take the place of their families. Reporter Eve Diamond stumbles across this subculture while covering the death of high school student Marina Lu, the victim of a car hijacking just weeks before her elaborate wedding to a Chinese businessman. As Eve investigates, she comes across another even more shocking subculture: the jasmine trade, in which Asian teens are smuggled into the U.S. to be used as sex slaves in suburban brothels, where their earnings are impounded and they are imprisoned in lives of hopelessness and despair. The author puts a face on this shameful practice in the person of May-li, a destitute Chinese peasant girl whom the soft-hearted and ever-inquisitive Eve befriends. A perceptive social document, as well as a gripping story, it's this author/journalist's first novel.

Where it's reviewed:
Booklist, May 15, 2001, page 1736
Los Angeles Magazine, August 2001, page 108
Mystery News, August/September 2001, page 16
New York Times Book Review, August 5, 2001, page 17
Publishers Weekly, July 2, 2001, page 53

Other books you might like:
Jan Burke, *The Irene Kelly Series*, 1993-
Robert Crais, *Stalking the Angel*, 1989
T. Jefferson Parker, *Little Saigon*, 1988
John Shannon, *The Orange Curtain*, 2000
Mary Willis Walker, *The Molly Cates Series*, 1994-

99

DASHIELL HAMMETT

Hammett: Crime Stories and Other Writings

(New York: Library of America, 2001)

Story type: Collection; Private Detective
Subject(s): Short Stories; Mystery and Detective Stories

Summary: This long-overdue collection of Hammett's best short crime fiction contains 24 stories, all originally published between 1923 and 1934. Most of them feature his classic nameless private detective known as the Continental Op (an operative employed by the Continental Detective Agency, an outfit much like the Pinkerton agency for which Hammett worked). The protagonist of Hammett's first two novels, the Op is the quintessential private detective, world-weary, cynical, and driven by an iron-clad code of honor that set the standard for all private eye fiction to come. Editor Steven Marcus selected the stories and has painstakingly restored them all to their original texts as they first appeared in the pulp magazines of the time, a real plus for Hammett scholars. Also included is an early and quite different version of Hammett's last novel, *The Thin Man*, some of his nonfiction writings about his own experiences as a Pinkerton detective, and useful biographic and bibliographic notes by the editor.

Where it's reviewed:
Library Journal, July 2001, page 132
New York Times Book Review, September 9, 2001, page 28
Publishers Weekly, August 13, 2001, page 289

Other books by the same author:
The Thin Man, 1934
The Glass Key, 1931
The Maltese Falcon, 1930
The Dain Curse, 1929
The Red Harvest, 1929

Other books you might like:
Lawrence Block, *Like a Lamb to the Slaughter*, 1984
Raymond Chandler, *The Midnight Raymond Chandler*, 1971
Joe Gores, *Stakeout on Page Street*, 2000
Ross Macdonald, *Ross Mcdonald's Lew Archer, Private Investigator*, 1977
Bill Pronzini, *Spadework*, 1996

100

DAVID HANDLER

The Cold Blue Blood

(New York: St. Martin's Press, 2001)

Story type: Amateur Detective
Subject(s): Islands; Small Town Life; Animals/Cats
Major character(s): Mitch Berger, Critic (film); Desiree "Des" Mitry, Police Officer (lieutenant)
Time period(s): 2000s
Locale(s): Dorset, Connecticut (Big Sister Island)

Summary: Still grieving over his beloved wife's death from ovarian cancer, Mitch lets his editor send him on a therapeutic assignment to Connecticut's Gold Coast, where he falls in love with a dilapidated cottage in a family compound on Big Sister Island and rents it from the blue-blooded widow who owns it. When a corpse turns up in the vegetable garden, he meets tall, black, beautiful Desiree, a police lieutenant known to her colleagues as "Cat Girl from Hell" for her work in rescuing, rehabilitating, and placing feral cats. As different as they are, they hit it off immediately. She doesn't know who Preston Sturges (Mitch's favorite movie director) is, but she's willing to learn; he can barely keep up with her on a brisk walk, but he's willing to try. The result is a charming and intelligent cozy that's poignant, as well as funny, full of striking characters, wonderful film references and sophisticated banter. The author wrote an earlier series featuring ghostwriter Stewart "Hoagie" Hoag.

Where it's reviewed:
Booklist, August 2001, page 2096
Library Journal, October 1, 2001, page 146
Publishers Weekly, September 10, 2001, page 64

Other books by the same author:
The Man Who Loved Women to Death, 1997
The Girl Who Ran Off with Daddy, 1996
The Boy Who Never Grew Up, 1995
The Man Who Cancelled Himself, 1995
The Woman Who Fell from Grace, 1991

Other books you might like:
Philip R. Craig, *The J.W. Jackson Series*, 1989-
Aaron Elkins, *The Gideon Oliver Series*, 1982-
Sarah Graves, *The Jacobia Tiptree Series*, 1998-
Carl Hiaasen, *Basket Case*, 2002
Justin Scott, *The Ben Abbott Series*, 1994-

101

LAUREN HANEY (Pseudonym of Betty J. Winkleman)

A Place of Darkness

(New York: Avon, 2001)

Story type: Historical
Series: Lt. Bak. Number 5
Subject(s): Ancient History; Smuggling; Egyptian Antiquities
Major character(s): Lieutenant Bak, Police Officer
Time period(s): 15th century B.C. (1460s B.C.)
Locale(s): Buhen, Egypt; Waset, Egypt; Kemet, Egypt

Summary: Lieutenant Bak is chief of the Medjays (or police) in the frontier outpost of Buhen, where he has been exiled as punishment for falling out of favor with those in power. He has come to love his adopted land and is stunned when his commandant is transferred to the garrison at Mennufer and wants to take Bak and his men with him. Bak gets the news shortly after he has apprehended a trader caught smuggling precious artifacts stolen from an ancient tomb. On his way to his new post, he stops at the capital to view the memorial being built to his dead queen, Hatshepsut, and finds that its construction has been plagued by a series of mishaps and deaths, said to be caused by evil spirits. The sights, sounds, and smells of ancient Egypt are splendidly evoked in this series, which offers a realistic and decidedly non-romantic view of everyday life among its ordinary citizens.

Other books by the same author:
A Curse of Silence, 2000
A Vile Justice, 1999
A Face Turned Backwards, 1998
The Right Hand of Amon, 1997

Other books you might like:
Agatha Christie, *Death Comes as the End*, 1944
P.C. Doherty, *The Horus Killings*, 2000
Lee Levin, *King Tut's Private Eye*, 1996
Lynda S. Robinson, *The Lord Meren Series*, 1994-
Carol Thurston, *The Eye of Horus*, 2000

102

CHARLAINE HARRIS

Shakespeare's Counselor

(New York: St. Martin's Press, 2001)

Story type: Private Detective
Series: Lily Bard. Number 5
Subject(s): Rape; Memory; Stalking
Major character(s): Lily Bard, Detective—Private, Martial Arts Expert (karate); Jack Leeds, Detective—Private, Lover (of Lily)
Time period(s): 2000s
Locale(s): Shakespeare, Arkansas; Little Rock, Arkansas

Summary: Although she still cleans house for a select few clients, Lily is now working toward her license as a private investigator, which requires apprenticing herself to a professional (in this case her lover, Jack Leeds) for two years. Professionally all is going well, but recurring nightmares about a traumatic rape in her past is disrupting her sleep; one morning she wakes up to find she's attacked Jack during an especially disturbing dream. He persuades her to get counseling, and she signs up for a rape survivor's support group guided by Tamsin Lynd, a woman who, it turns out, is being stalked by a man in her past. When someone is murdered in Tamsin's office, Lily believes the time has come for her to investigate the incident before someone else gets hurt. The author also writes a much lighter series about librarian Aurora Teagarden.

Where it's reviewed:
Booklist, September 15, 2001, page 198
Publishers Weekly, September 10, 2001, page 63

Other books by the same author:
Shakespeare's Trollop, 2000
Shakespeare's Christmas, 1999
Shakespeare's Champion, 1997
Shakespeare's Landlord, 1996

Other books you might like:
Nevada Barr, *The Anna Pigeon Series*, 1993-
Abigail Padgett, *The Bo Bradley Series*, 1993-
Barbara Seranella, *The Munch Mancini Series*, 1997-
Marcia Talley, *The Hannah Ives Series*, 1999-
Kathy Hogan Trocheck, *The Callahan Garrity Series*, 1992-

103

JANIS HARRISON

Lilies That Fester

(New York: St. Martin's Press, 2001)

Story type: Amateur Detective
Series: Bretta Solomon. Number 3
Subject(s): Gardens and Gardening; Weight Control; Drugs
Major character(s): Bretta Solomon, Store Owner (florist), Widow(er)
Time period(s): 2000s
Locale(s): Branson, Missouri; River City, Missouri

Summary: Middle-aged, widowed, and formerly fat Bretta Solomon runs a successful flower shop in the small town of River City, but she's attending a florists' convention in nearby Branson, which her shop is hosting. There's a fair amount of information about the florist trade and the mechanics of running a large convention, but the main plot gets under way when another formerly fat woman, who is a friend of Bretta's, dies under mysterious circumstances after snacking on some unidentified greenery. Bretta's knowledge of botany provides the key to unlocking the puzzle.

Where it's reviewed:
Booklist, September 15, 2001, page 199
Publishers Weekly, October 1, 2001, page 40

Other books by the same author:
Murder Sets Seed, 2000
Roots of Murder, 1999

Other books you might like:
Mary Freeman, *The Rachel O'Connor Series*, 1999-
Anne Underwood Grant, *Cuttings*, 1999
Joan Hadley, *The Theo Bloomer Series*, 1986-1988
Julie Wray Herman, *The Korine McFail Series*, 2000-
Ann Ripley, *The Louise Eldridge Series*, 1994-

104

CYNTHIA HARROD-EAGLES

Blood Sinister

(New York: St. Martin's Press, 2001)

Story type: Police Procedural
Series: Bill Slider. Number 8
Subject(s): Secrets; Journalism
Major character(s): Bill Slider, Police Officer (detective inspector)
Time period(s): 2000s (2001)
Locale(s): London, England

Summary: Detective Inspector Bill Slider and his colleagues are investigating the murder of Phoebe Agnew, a brilliant muckraking journalist who of late had been concentrating on corruption and botched procedures on the part of the police. Some anomalies turn up in her apartment: she was a woman who from all reports never cooked a real meal for herself or anybody else, and yet a fairly elaborate one was in preparation in the kitchen. Who was she expecting for dinner? Was the mysterious guest the same person she had been intimate with, and if they were different men, which one murdered her and why? The answer turns out to lie deep in Phoebe's past. On the domestic front, Slider's divorce is about to be finalized, which will enable him to take his long-running relationship with violinist Joanna Marshall to a new level.

Where it's reviewed:
Booklist, September 15, 2001, page 198
Mystery News, October/November 2001, page 26
New York Times Book Review, October 14, 2001, page 26

Other books by the same author:
Shallow Grave, 1998
Blood Lines, 1996
Killing Time, 1996
Grave Music, 1994
Necrochip, 1993

Other books you might like:
Catherine Aird, *The Inspector Sloan Series*, 1966-
Caroline Graham, *The Inspector Barnaby Series*, 1987-
John Harvey, *The Charlie Resnick Series*, 1989-1999
Jill McGown, *The Inspector Lloyd/Judy Hill Series*, 1983-
Janet Neel, *The John McLeish/Francesca Wilson Series*, 1988-

105

ELLEN HART

Dial M for Meat Loaf

(New York: Fawcett, 2001)

Story type: Amateur Detective

Series: Sophie Greenway. Book 6
Subject(s): Contests; Food; Money
Major character(s): Sophie Greenway, Journalist (food critic), Innkeeper
Time period(s): 2000s
Locale(s): Minneapolis, Minnesota; Rose Hill, Minnesota

Summary: A recipe contest sponsored by the *Times Register* sends Minnesota housewives scurrying to their recipe files for their favorite meat loaf recipes. Among them is Cora Runbeck of Rose Hill, who finds her prize-winning recipe in an old file box, along with a bankbook in her husband's name, recording several large deposits about which she knows nothing and one final substantial withdrawal. This discovery sets in motion a chain of events, which includes her husband, Kirby, being blown up by a car bomb and a confession from Rose Hill's mayor, John Washburn, who is dying from a stroke. His wife and children deny his involvement and ask for help from family friend Sophie Greenway to prove his innocence. When she goes through his papers though, she begins to wonder. Three meat loaf recipes are included. The author also writes a series about lesbian restaurateur Jane Lawless.

Other books by the same author:
Slice and Dice, 2000
Murder in the Air, 1997
The Oldest Sin, 1996
For Every Evil, 1995
This Little Piggy Went to Murder, 1994

Other books you might like:
Susan Wittig Albert, *Chile Death*, 1998
Diane Mott Davidson, *The Goldy Bear Schulz Series*, 1990-
Joanne Pence, *The Angelina Amalfi Series*, 1993-
Phyllis Richman, *The Chas Wheatley Series*, 1997-
Lou Jane Temple, *The Heaven Lee Series*, 1996-

106

ROBIN HATHAWAY

The Doctor and the Dead Man's Chest

(New York: St. Martin's Press, 2001)

Story type: Amateur Detective
Series: Dr. Fenimore. Number 3
Subject(s): Rural Life; American History; Real Estate
Major character(s): Andrew Fenimore, Doctor, Detective—Amateur
Time period(s): 2000s
Locale(s): Philadelphia, Pennsylvania; Winston, New Jersey

Summary: Andrew Fenimore has a small, old-fashioned practice which allows him to know his patients (many of them elderly), make house calls, and keep his fees down. He operates out of his home, has a capable nurse-receptionist named Mrs. Doyle, a lovely lady friend named Jennifer Nicholson, and a teenage assistant named Horatio who helps him with his crime investigations, for which his modest practice leaves him ample time. As the book opens, he has inherited the stewardship of 50 acres of southern New Jersey marshland to be preserved as a wildlife refuge, and when he drives out to the country to view it he stops in to see Lydia Ashley, an elderly patient who lives nearby. He finds she is being pressured to sell her land and has been the victim of some ugly pranks. Until he can get away himself, he sends Mrs. Doyle and Horatio to look out for her, but when Mrs. Doyle is kidnapped he comes to the rescue. There is a great deal about local history, particularly the smuggling and pirate traffic along the inland waterways, and information about the area's distinctive architecture. A low-tech, low-key, and charming series.

Where it's reviewed:
Publishers Weekly, October 15, 2001, page 50

Other books by the same author:
The Doctor Makes a Dollhouse Call, 2000
The Doctor Digs a Grave, 1998

Other books you might like:
Philip R. Craig, *The J.W. Jackson Series*, 1989-
Aaron Elkins, *The Gideon Oliver Series*, 1982-
Jane Langton, *The Homer Kelly Series*, 1964-
Gillian Roberts, *The Amanda Pepper Series*, 1987-
Justin Scott, *The Ben Abbott Series*, 1994-

107

PETE HAUTMAN

Rag Man

(New York: Simon & Schuster, 2001)

Story type: Action/Adventure; Psychological Suspense
Subject(s): Money; Morality; Identity
Major character(s): Mack MacWray, Businessman (clothing manufacturer)
Time period(s): 2000s
Locale(s): Minneapolis, Minnesota; Isla Mujeres, Mexico; Cancun, Mexico

Summary: Mack has spent all his adult life working in menial jobs in garment factories, and now his charismatic friend, Lars Larson, offers him a partnership in a start-up clothing company—if he can put up the money. Between a second mortgage and a loan from his wife's family, Mack makes it happen, only to have his dreams shattered when Lars absconds with the funds and leaves Mack to deal with their creditors and his in-laws. He goes to Mexico in search of Lars, finds him standing on a cliff on Isla Mujeres, and watches him—without moving a muscle to help him—as he plummets to his death in the sea below. This single moment completely redefines the kind of person Mack is: he flies back to the States determined to stop at nothing to return the company to solvency, not caring how many people he hurts in the process. There is plenty of Hautman's trademark wit and caustic humor here, but the overall tone is dark and the moral questions raised disturbing.

Where it's reviewed:
Booklist, September 1, 2001, page 56
New York Times Book Review, October 14, 2001, page 26
Publishers Weekly, August 13, 2001, page 281

Other books by the same author:
Mrs. Million, 1999
Ring Game, 1997
The Mortal Nuts, 1996
Short Money, 1995

Drawing Dead, 1994

Other books you might like:
Carl Hiaasen, *Skin Tight*, 1989
Elmore Leonard, *Pagan Babies*, 2000
Laurence Shames, *Sunburn*, 1995
Ross Thomas, *Voodoo, Ltd.*, 1993
Donald E. Westlake, *The Hook*, 2000

108

STEVEN F. HAVILL

Bag Limit

(New York: St. Martin's Press, 2001)

Story type: Police Procedural
Series: Bill Gastner. Book 9
Subject(s): American West; Small Town Life; Aging
Major character(s): Bill Gastner, Police Officer (sheriff)
Time period(s): 2000s
Locale(s): Posados County, New Mexico

Summary: As his long-anticipated retirement approaches, 70-year-old sheriff Bill Gastner has much to ponder, but little time for reflection. Matt Baca, a teenager driving under the influence whose car hit Gastner's parked vehicle, tries to escape arrest and is killed instantly when he runs into oncoming traffic. Then Matt's father is killed. Meanwhile, Gastner's adobe house is full of welcome visitors: his son and grandson and his former deputy, Estelle Guzman, and her doctor husband. The plan is for Gastner to put his undersheriff, Robert Torrez, at least temporarily in charge, but there is a possibility that Estelle may return to Posados County and take over.

Where it's reviewed:
Booklist, October 15, 2001, page 385
Mystery News, December 2001/January 2002, page 17
Publishers Weekly, October 29, 2001, page 39

Other books by the same author:
Dead Weight, 2000
Out of Season, 1999
Prolonged Exposure, 1998
Privileged to Kill, 1997
Before She Dies, 1996

Other books you might like:
Bill Crider, *The Sheriff Dan Rhodes Series*, 1986-
Micah S. Hackler, *The Cliff Lansing Series*, 1995-
Jamie Harrison, *The Jules Clement Series*, 1995-
Donald Harstad, *The Carl Houseman Series*, 1998-
Thomas Zigal, *The Kurt Muller Series*, 1995-

109

SIMON HAWKE

The Slaying of the Shrew

(New York: Forge, 2001)

Story type: Historical; Amateur Detective
Series: Shakespeare and Smythe. Book 2
Subject(s): Theater; Weddings; Authors and Writers
Major character(s): William Shakespeare, Historical Figure, Writer; Symington ''Tuck'' Smythe, Actor (aspiring)
Time period(s): 16th century (1590s)
Locale(s): London, England; Westminster, England

Summary: Although Will has yet to write a play or Tuck to be featured in one, both have the theater in their blood and work hard at their jobs with the Queen's Men at James Burbage's London theater. To make ends meet, Will moonlights as a poet, and Tuck oftener than not serves the company as a laborer, with an occasional walk-on part his chief reward. When the Queen's Men are invited to a country estate near Westminster to perform in an elaborate wedding pageant, they find more than they had bargained for when they discover a plot to murder the headstrong bride. Despite their valiant efforts to protect her, the plot succeeds, and it's up to Will and Tuck to expose the murderer. Part of the fun in this ingenious series is encountering plot twists that turn up in many of Shakespeare's actual plays. The author is also known for his science fiction.

Where it's reviewed:
Mystery News, December 2001/January 2002, page 21
Publishers Weekly, November 5, 2001, page 44

Other books by the same author:
A Mystery of Errors, 2000

Other books you might like:
Judith Cook, *The Slicing Edge of Death*, 1993
Philip Gooden, *The Sleep of Death*, 2000
Tony Hays, *Murder on the Twelfth Night*, 1993
Faye Kellerman, *The Quality of Mercy*, 1989
Edward Marston, *The Nicholas Bracewell Series*, 1988-

110

JOHN R. HAYES

Catskill

(New York: St. Martin's Press, 2001)

Story type: Historical; Amateur Detective
Subject(s): Anti-Semitism; Irish Americans; Small Town Life
Major character(s): Martin Collins, Lawyer
Time period(s): 1930s (1938)
Locale(s): Chicken Corners, New York (Catskills)

Summary: It's a tradition in the proud Collins family, Irish-Americans who first immigrated to the U.S. in 1814, that the current patriarch of the family be awarded the unofficial title of The Judge and charged with upholding the honor of the family and its commitment to justice. The title now belongs to Martin, a 77-year-old lawyer who lost most of his wealth in the stock market crash of 1929 and since then has sought refuge in the family's summer home in the Catskills. When Jewish refugees arrive in the area as war clouds gather in Europe, he's horrified when the old farmhouse where they have been relocated comes under fire from three young men, who succeed in not only terrorizing the immigrants but in killing a local real estate agent. With the help of his reluctant family, members of his church, and a half-Algonquin sheriff, Martin sets out to right the terrible wrong that has been done. First mystery.

Where it's reviewed:
Library Journal, September 1, 2001, page 237
Mystery News, October/November 2001, page 16
New York Times Book Review, September 23, 2001, page 23
Publishers Weekly, September 10, 2001, page 65

Other books you might like:
Harold Adams, *The Carl Wilcox Series*, 1981-
Robert Clark, *Mr. White's Confession*, 1998
Thomas H. Cook, *Places in the Dark*, 2000
Fred Harris, *Easy Pickin's*, 2000
Lise McClendon, *One O'Clock Jump*, 2001

111

JEREMIAH HEALY

Turnabout

(Waterville, Maine: Five Star, 2001)

Story type: Private Detective
Subject(s): Kidnapping; Mentally Handicapped; Family Relations
Major character(s): Matthew Langway, Detective—Private (security consultant)
Time period(s): 2000s
Locale(s): Somerville, Massachusetts; Beacon Harbor, Massachusetts

Summary: Former FBI agent turned security consultant Matthew Langway is called in when the mildly retarded grandson of one of his clients, General Alexander Van Horne, is kidnapped. He's initially reluctant to take the case, feeling the police (whom the general adamantly does not want to be involved) are better equipped to handle it, but when he's offered $10,000 up front to come aboard, he's persuaded. Since he installed the general's security system himself, he's certain the kidnapping is an inside job, but everywhere he turns he runs into a dead end. There are many plot twists and a surprise ending, as well as the usual quota of family secrets and violence. The author is best known for his long-running series featuring Boston private eye John Francis Cuddy.

Where it's reviewed:
Booklist, December 1, 2001, page 633
Library Journal, December 2001, page 180
Publishers Weekly, November 16, 2001, page 633

Other books by the same author:
Spiral, 1999
The Only Good Lawyer, 1998
Invasion of Privacy, 1996
Rescue, 1995
Act of God, 1994

Other books you might like:
Robert Crais, *Free Fall*, 1993
Stephen Greenleaf, *The John Marshall Tanner Series*, 1979-
Bill Pronzini, *Bleeders*, 2001
Greg Rucka, *The Atticus Kodiak Series*, 1997-
William G. Tapply, *The Brady Coyne Series*, 1984-

112

MARTIN HEGWOOD

Massacre Island

(New York: St. Martin's Press, 2001)

Story type: Private Detective
Series: Jack Delmas. Number 3
Subject(s): Islands; American South; Rural Life
Major character(s): Jack Delmas, Detective—Private
Time period(s): 2000s
Locale(s): Dauphin Island, Alabama (Gulf Coast)

Summary: When four young people are shot to death in a beach house on an island off the Alabama coast, the mother of one of them hires Jack to investigate. Three of the victims were high-profile personalities—a beauty queen, an entrepreneur, and a TV news anchor. Rebecca, the fourth, was an unknown, and her mother feels the police aren't working hard enough to find who murdered her or why. Against his better judgment, Jack agrees to help her. He expects to run up against an uncooperative good-old-boy network among the law enforcement types he has to work with, and he knows the island is home to various extremist groups, but he doesn't expect to find his own life in danger.

Where it's reviewed:
Publishers Weekly, September 10, 2001, page 64

Other books by the same author:
A Green-Eyed Hurricane, 2000
Big Easy Backroad, 1999

Other books you might like:
John Armistead, *The Grover Bramlett Series*, 1994-
Ace Atkins, *Crossroad Blues*, 1998
James Lee Burke, *The Dave Robicheaux Series*, 1987-
Bill Crider, *The Truman Smith Series*, 1991-
Daniel Woodrell, *The Rene Shade Series*, 1986-

113

JOE L. HENSLEY

Robak in Black

(New York: St. Martin's Press, 2001)

Story type: Legal
Series: Don Robak. Book 11
Subject(s): Small Town Life; Marriage; Illness
Major character(s): Don Robak, Judge, Lawyer
Time period(s): 2000s
Locale(s): Bington, Indiana

Summary: Circuit Judge Don Robak is devastated when his beloved wife, Jo, comes down with a debilitating illness with no real hope of recovery. Although he's only recently been appointed to a judgeship, he's made a number of unpopular decisions and put quite a few bad people behind bars, and he's afraid one of them may be responsible for whatever has gone wrong with Jo. One suspect is Sweetboy Wolfer, whose family has never forgiven Robak for sending him to prison. Then there's his old flame Libbie Macing, the co-owner of a local pharmaceutical company, who seems incapable of realizing Robak no longer cares for her. As always, Robak remains calm and thoughtful in the face of danger.

Where it's reviewed:
Mystery News, December 2001/January 2002, page 15
Publishers Weekly, November 12, 2001, page 39

Other books by the same author:
Robak's Witch, 1997
Robak's Run, 1990
Robak's Firm, 1987 (short stories)
Robak's Fire, 1986
Robak's Cross, 1985

Other books you might like:
William Bernhardt, *The Ben Kincaid Series*, 1991-
Ralph McInerny, *The Andrew Broom Series*, 1987-
D.R. Schanker, *A Criminal Appeal*, 1998
Grif Stockley, *The Gideon Page Series*, 1992-
William G. Tapply, *The Brady Coyne Series*, 1984-

114

JOAN HESS

Maggody and the Moonbeams

(New York: Simon & Schuster, 2001)

Story type: Humor
Series: Maggody. Number 13
Subject(s): American South; Small Town Life; Cults
Major character(s): Arly Hanks, Police Officer (chief of police)
Time period(s): 2000s
Locale(s): Maggody, Arkansas; Dunkicker, Arkansas

Summary: Poor, beleaguered Arly doesn't think anything much weirder could possibly happen to her than has already happened, but that's before she gets roped into chaperoning a gaggle of hormonal teens from the church youth group during their stay at Camp Pearly Gates. Her mother, Ruby Bee, comes along to do the cooking, and other adults include Mrs. Jim Bob Buchanon (the mayor's wife) and preacher Brother Verber. There is the inevitable discovery of a body, belonging to a member of a bizarre cult known as the Daughters of the Moon, who are camped nearby and known colloquially as Moonbeams, or Beamers. This one, like her sisters, is garbed in white with a shaved head and magenta lipstick. Back in Maggody, a wife goes missing, Jim Bob gets seduced by scheming twins from an Internet chat room, and a pet pig looks for companionship. It all adds up to the usual furious mixture of mirth and mayhem from an old hand, who also writes a slightly more restrained series about Arkansas bookseller Claire Malloy.

Where it's reviewed:
Booklist, May 1, 2001, page 1632
Publishers Weekly, May 28, 2001, page 52

Other books by the same author:
Murder@Maggody.com, 2000
Misery Loves Maggody, 1999
The Maggody Militia, 1997
Miracles in Maggody, 1995
Martians in Maggody, 1994

Other books you might like:
Deborah Adams, *The Jesus Creek Series*, 1992-
Nancy Bell, *The Biggie Weatherford Series*, 1996-
Anne George, *The Southern Sisters Series*, 1996-2001
Toni L.P. Kelner, *The Laura Fleming Series*, 1993-
Sharyn McCrumb, *The Elizabeth MacPherson Series*, 1984-

115

CARL HIAASEN

Basket Case

(New York: Knopf, 2002)

Story type: Amateur Detective; Humor
Subject(s): Journalism; Music and Musicians; Satire
Major character(s): Jack Tagger, Journalist (newspaper obituary writer)
Time period(s): 2000s
Locale(s): Silver Beach, Florida

Summary: Jack Tagger is middle-aged, recently dumped by his fiancee, and consigned to the obituary desk of his smallish South Florida newspaper after having made some heartfelt, but intemperate remarks to the CEO of the chain which employs him. He is both intrigued and appalled by his much younger editor, Emma, and is just plain out of sync with the state of 21st century journalism. Although he won't admit it even to himself, he longs for a chance to write a front-page story again, and his wish comes true when he's assigned to write the obit of Jimmy Stoma, front man for the now-defunct Slut Puppies, and interview his widow, rising rock star Cleo Rio. Something about the opportunistic Cleo gets his investigative juices flowing again and before you know it he's covering a murder story. Hiaasen has forsaken his trademark slapstick humor and barely restrained anger to write a much gentler book, peopled with believable and generally sympathetic characters and enhanced by a sweet, sophisticated love story, as well as a genuine detective puzzle. There are plenty of quiet chuckles along the way, particularly in the delightfully absurd exchanges between Jack and Emma, and in Jack's obsession about how old certain celebrities were when they died. There are also occasional flashes of the old over-the-top Hiaasen humor, as when Jack wields a large frozen lizard to defend himself from a home invader. Some readers may miss the old Hiaasen, but others will think this his most satisfying and appealing book yet.

Where it's reviewed:
Booklist, November 1, 2001, page 4444
Entertainment Weekly, January 18, 2002, page 72
Library Journal, December 2001, page 172
People Weekly, January 14, 2002, page 39
Publishers Weekly, November 12, 2001, page 36

Other books by the same author:
Sick Puppy, 2000
Lucky You, 1997
Stormy Weather, 1995
Strip Tease, 1993
Native Tongue, 1991

Other books you might like:
G.D. Gearino, *Counting Coup*, 1997

David Handler, *The Cold Blue Blood*, 2001
Elmore Leonard, *Be Cool*, 1999
Donald E. Westlake, *Trust Me on This*, 1988
Randy Wayne White, *The Doc Ford Series*, 1990-

116

REGINALD HILL

Dialogues of the Dead or Paronomania!

(New York: Delacorte, 2002)

Story type: Police Procedural; Psychological Suspense
Series: Dalziel and Pascoe. Book 19
Subject(s): Contests; Writing; Games/Literary
Major character(s): Andrew ''Andy'' Dalziel, Police Officer (superintendent); Peter Pascoe, Police Officer (sergeant); E. Bowler, Police Officer (detective constable)
Time period(s): 2000s
Locale(s): Yorkshire, England

Summary: Word games and puzzles are at the heart of this complex mystery, which begins with the local librarians reading through entries in the Mid-Yorkshire Short Story Contest. One of the submissions catches their eye: it's told in the form of a dialogue recounting a murder and challenging the police to solve it. A second one follows, describing another ingenious murder. Both, of course, are actual events that have been engineered to look like accidents, and the challenges set Dalziel and Pascoe after the murderer. The two men couldn't be more different—Dalziel is seemingly crude and thick-headed, Pascoe courteous and sensitive—and yet their talents mesh brilliantly, although they are given an assist here by a rookie constable named Bowler, nicknamed Hat. The author has also written stand-alone thrillers, as well as several suspense novels under the pseudonym Patrick Ruell.

Where it's reviewed:
Booklist, November 15, 2001, page 357
New York Times Book Review, January 1, 2002, page 19
Publishers Weekly, December 17, 2001, page 67

Other books by the same author:
Arms and the Women, 1999
On Beulah Height, 1998
Asking for the Moon, 1996 (short stories)
The Wood Beyond, 1995
Pictures of Perfection, 1994

Other books you might like:
Colin Dexter, *The Inspector Morse Series*, 1975-
Caroline Graham, *The Tom Barnaby Series*, 1987-
P.D. James, *The Adam Dalgliesh Series*, 1962-
Ruth Rendell, *The Inspector Wexford Series*, 1964-
Peter Robinson, *The Alan Banks Series*, 1987-

117

EDWARD D. HOCH

The Night People and Other Stories

(Waterville, Maine: Five Star, 2001)

Story type: Collection
Subject(s): Short Stories; Mystery and Detective Stories

Summary: An even 20 previously uncollected short stories by this prolific and versatile writer are contained here, all non-series tales originally published in various mystery magazines between 1957 and 1979 and including many of the author's own favorites. For the most part these tales are darker than those featuring his various series characters, owing more to Cornell Woolrich/William Irish than to Ellery Queen or John Dickson Carr. They are just as ingeniously plotted though, often with ironic twists at the end or with touches of sardonic wit.

Other books by the same author:
The Old Spies Club and Other Intrigues of Rand, 2001 (short stories)
The Velvet Touch, 2000 (short stories)
The Ripper of Storyville, 1997 (short stories)
Diagnosis Impossible, 1996 (short stories)
The Night, My Friend, 1992 (short stories)

Other books you might like:
Robert Bloch, *Out of the Mouths of Graves*, 1979
Lawrence Block, *Sometimes They Bite*, 1983
Bill Crider, *The Nighttime Is the Right Time*, 2001
Stanley Ellin, *The Specialty of the House*, 1979
Ed Gorman, *Famous Blue Raincoat*, 1999

118

EDWARD D. HOCH

The Old Spies Club and Other Intrigues of Rand

(Norfolk, Virginia: Crippen & Landru, 2001)

Story type: Collection; Espionage
Series: Rand
Subject(s): Short Stories; Espionage
Major character(s): Jeffery Rand, Spy; Leila Gaad, Archaeologist

Summary: The first Jeffery Rand story included here was published in 1971 and the most recent in 1999. Over that period the suave code- and cipher-cracking British spy, who retired some time in the mid-seventies, met and married the half-Egyptian, half-Scottish archaeologist Leila Gaad, who accompanies him on adventures that take them to Cairo, London, Moscow, New York, and Scotland. The author, certainly the most prolific and one of the most accomplished short story writers in the genre, maneuvers his protagonists neatly through the Cold War and beyond in the 15 adventures (out of 79 total at press time) included here. Almost all of Hoch's voluminous output is in the short story form, featuring a wide variety of protagonists.

Where it's reviewed:
Publishers Weekly, August 27, 2001, page 59

Other books by the same author:
The Velvet Touch, 2000 (short stories)
The Ripper of Storyville, 1997 (short stories)
Diagnosis Impossible, 1996 (short stories)
The Night, My Friend, 1992 (short stories)
The People of the Peacock, 1991 (short stories)

Other books you might like:
Manning Coles, *Nothing to Declare*, 1960
Ian Fleming, *For Your Eyes Only*, 1960
Michael Gilbert, *Game Without Rules*, 1968
Michael Gilbert, *Mr. Calder and Mr. Behrens*, 1982
W. Somerset Maugham, *Ashenden*, 1928

119

CRAIG HOLDEN

The Jazz Bird

(New York: Simon & Schuster, 2002)

Story type: Historical
Subject(s): Prohibition Era; History; Trials
Major character(s): Charlie Taft, Lawyer (chief prosecutor), Historical Figure; George Remus, Bootlegger, Historical Figure
Time period(s): 1920s (1927)
Locale(s): Cincinnati, Ohio

Summary: When wealthy bootlegger George Remus is released from prison in 1927, he discovers his beloved wife Imogene has left him and there is no money remaining in any of his bank accounts. On the day their divorce is to be finalized, he runs her car off the road, shoots her, and then turns himself in to the police. Chief Prosecutor Charlie Taft (son of former president William H. Taft) sees Remus' high-profile trial as an opportunity to advance his career, but it raises as many questions as it answers. The story of Remus' rise to power, his passionate love affair with Imogene, the motives of the federal agent who destroyed him, and much more, are told in flashbacks, which also vividly portray the heady atmosphere of Prohibition and the Roaring Twenties. Though clearly a work of fiction, it adheres closely to the facts of this sensational (at the time) murder trial.

Where it's reviewed:
Booklist, December 15, 2001, page 706
Library Journal, October 15, 2001, page 108
Publishers Weekly, October 29, 2001, page 32

Other books by the same author:
Four Corners of Night, 1999
The Last Sanctuary, 1996
The River Sorrow, 1994

Other books you might like:
W.R. Burnett, *Goodbye Chicago*, 1981
Loren D. Estleman, *Whiskey River*, 1990
Keith Miles, *Saint's Rest*, 1999
Troy Soos, *Cincinnati Red Stalkings*, 1998
Steve Thayer, *Saint Mudd*, 1988

120

SUSAN HOLTZER

Better than Sex

(New York: St. Martin's Press, 2001)

Story type: Amateur Detective
Series: Anneke Haagen
Subject(s): Sports/Football; Vacations; Food
Major character(s): Anneke Haagen, Computer Expert, Detective—Amateur; Karl Genesko, Police Officer (police chief), Sports Figure (former Pittsburgh Steeler)
Time period(s): 2000s
Locale(s): San Francisco, California; Ann Arbor, Michigan

Summary: Anneke and Karl, having tied the knot in 2000's *The Wedding Game*, are honeymooning in San Francisco, where they're invited by a friend to watch a Michigan football game at his sports bar, the Maize and Blue. Anneke is bemused by the foodies crowding around them who are passionately arguing about the best ways of preparing various trendy dishes. She can't help but notice a very thin young woman eating dry toast and drinking nothing but unsalted tomato juice, especially when she dies of a fast-acting poison slipped into her drink. It turns out she had been crusading against what she considered unhealthy food, and everyone sitting near her, including Karl and Anneke, are considered suspects in her death. Since just about everyone in the bar has a connection to the University of Michigan, Anneke gets some long-distance help from her protege, journalism student Zoe Kaplan, back in Ann Arbor.

Where it's reviewed:
Booklist, May 1, 2001, page 1634
Library Journal, August 2001, page 169
Publishers Weekly, June 11, 2001, page 63

Other books by the same author:
The Wedding Game, 2000
The Silly Season, 1999
Black Diamond, 1997
Bleeding Maize and Blue, 1996
Curly Smoke, 1995

Other books you might like:
Susan Wittig Albert, *The China Bayles Series*, 1992-
Diane Mott Davidson, *The Goldy Bear Schulz Series*, 1990-
Donna Huston Murray, *The Ginger Struve Barnes Series*, 1995-
Joanne Pence, *The Angelina Amalfi Series*, 1993-
Nancy Pickard, *The Jenny Cain Series*, 1984-

121

FREDRICK HUEBNER

Shades of Justice

(New York: Simon & Schuster, 2001)

Story type: Legal; Psychological Suspense
Subject(s): Psychological; Memory Loss; Secrets
Major character(s): Will Hatton, Doctor (forensic psychiatrist); Mary Slattery, Lawyer (criminal defense); Ed Hauser, Lawyer (criminal defense)
Time period(s): 2000s
Locale(s): Bainbridge Island, Washington; Seattle, Washington

Summary: When a local businessman is murdered and his wife, Laura Arcand, appears to confess to the crime in the emergency room, where she has been taken following a suicide attempt, forensic psychiatrist Will Hatton is called in to evaluate Laura's mental state. The murder took place shortly after guests in their home had witnessed Laura in a jealous rage, accusing her husband of having had an affair. Her lawyer, Ed Hauser, who was once romantically involved with Laura's mother and who is Will's friend and mentor, insists his client is innocent. He turns most of her defense over to Mary Slattery, who works with Will to probe events in Laura's troubled past that might have some bearing on the murder. Twenty-five years earlier Laura had disappeared from the island after a traumatic event, which she successfully repressed, but which will have to be uncovered so Mary can defend her. During the course of their investigation, a romance blossoms between Will and Mary. The author has written five previous books featuring burned-out lawyer Matt Riordan.

Where it's reviewed:
Booklist, June 1, 2001, page 1852
Publishers Weekly, June 25, 2001, page 51

Other books by the same author:
Methods of Execution, 1994
Picture Postcard, 1990
Judgment by Fire, 1988
The Black Rose, 1987
The Joshua Sequence, 1986

Other books you might like:
Jonathan Kellerman, *The Alex Delaware Series*, 1985-
Sarah Lovett, *The Sylvia Strange Series*, 1995-
Philip Luber, *The Harry Kline Series*, 1997-
Marianne Wesson, *A Suggestion of Death*, 2000
Stephen White, *The Alan Gregory Series*, 1991-

122

STEPHEN HUNTER

Pale Horse Coming

(New York: Simon & Schuster, 2001)

Story type: Action/Adventure; Historical
Series: Earl Swagger. Book 2
Subject(s): American South; Racism; Prisoners and Prisons
Major character(s): Earl Swagger, Police Officer, Hero; Sam Vincent, Lawyer
Time period(s): 1950s (1951)
Locale(s): Mississippi; Hot Springs, Arkansas

Summary: Sam Vincent, a former county prosecutor, is offered a great deal of money by a high-powered Chicago attorney to locate the beneficiary of a will. It turns out this mission will take him to the infamous Thebes Penal Farm for the Colored located in the backwater Negro town of Thebes, Mississippi. Feeling understandably uneasy about the job, Sam makes a deal with his friend Earl Swagger, a World War II hero who five years earlier cleaned up the corrupt town of Hot Springs, Arkansas. If Sam doesn't return within a week, Earl will come get him. When the time comes, Earl manages to free Sam but is captured and tortured himself. The only white man in the prison, he's considered especially dangerous by the sadistic guards. Once he manages to escape, Earl rounds up a posse of sharpshooters and combat veterans to storm the prison and seek a violent revenge. This new series from Hunter is linked to earlier books set in the present day featuring Earl's son, Vietnam veteran and sniper Bob Lee Swagger.

Where it's reviewed:
Booklist, October 15, 2001, page 385
Mystery News, December 2001/January 2002, page 12
Publishers Weekly, September 24, 2001, page 67
Washington Post, October 31, 2001, page C10

Other books by the same author:
Hot Springs, 2000 (Earl Swagger series)
Time to Hunt, 1998
Black Light, 1996
Dirty White Boys, 1994
Point of Impact, 1993

Other books you might like:
John Ball, *In the Heat of the Night*, 1965
Thomas H. Cook, *Streets of Fire*, 1989
Stanford Diehl, *Angel in the Front Room, Devil out Back*, 2001
Walter Mosley, *Fearless Jones*, 2001
Kris Nelscott, *A Dangerous Road*, 2000

123

GREG ILES

Dead Sleep

(New York: Putnam, 2001)

Story type: Psychological Suspense
Subject(s): Twins; Artists and Art; Serial Killers
Major character(s): Jordan Glass, Photographer, Journalist; John Kaiser, FBI Agent
Time period(s): 2000s
Locale(s): New Orleans, Louisiana; New York, New York; Hong Kong

Summary: Combat photographer Jordan Glass is passing time in a Hong Kong art museum one afternoon when an exhibit by an unknown artist catches her eye. Called ''Nude Women in Repose,'' it's a series of chillingly realistic paintings of young women who appear to be either asleep or dead. One of them looks exactly like her—or her identical twin sister Jane, who disappeared over a year ago from her New Orleans townhouse. Jordan flies back to the United States and, together with FBI agent John Kaiser, with whom she becomes romantically involved, is determined to track down the anonymous artist and find out what happened to Jane and the other women shown in the exhibit, all of whom are also missing. The trail leads back to Southeast Asia and a French art collector who knew Jordan's father, a war photographer, like his daughter, who also disappeared without a trace.

Where it's reviewed:
Booklist, June 1, 2001, page 1852
New York Times Book Review, August 19, 2001, page 14
People Weekly, August 13, 2001, page 45
Publishers Weekly, June 11, 2001, page 58

Other books by the same author:
24 Hours, 2000
The Quiet Game, 1999
Mortal Fear, 1997
Black Cross, 1995

Spandau Phoenix, 1993

Other books you might like:

Harlan Coben, *Tell No One*, 2001
Robert Crais, *Demolition Angel*, 2000
Thomas Harris, *The Silence of the Lambs*, 1988
Greg Rucka, *Critical Space*, 2001
Stephen White, *The Program*, 2001

124

JANE ISENBERG

Midlife Can Be Murder

(New York: Avon, 2001)

Story type: Amateur Detective
Series: Bel Barrett. Number 4
Subject(s): Internet; Judaism; Sports/Rock Climbing
Major character(s): Bel Barrett, Professor (community college), Detective—Amateur
Time period(s): 2000s
Locale(s): Hoboken, New Jersey

Summary: Bel, 50 and fighting midlife hormonal changes, unexpectedly runs into a former student, Ashley Roberts, in an adult bat mitzvah study group at her synagogue, which she's attending in an attempt to rediscover her spiritual heritage. She has always felt that she might have been unfair to Ashley in the past, and so when Ashley shows up upset at the suspicious death of a colleague, Bel offers to investigate the incident. This leads her into a maze of corporate espionage, Internet chicanery, and indoor rock climbing.

Other books by the same author:

Death in a Hot Flash, 2000
Mood Swings to Murder, 2000
The "M" Word, 1999

Other books you might like:

D.B. Borton, *The Cat Caliban Series*, 1993-
Bill Crider, *Murder Is an Art*, 1999
Sarah Hoskinson Frommer, *The Joan Spencer Series*, 1986-
Sharon Kahn, *The Ruby Rothman Series*, 1998-
Marlys Millhiser, *Murder in a Hot Flash*, 1995

125

J.A. JANCE

Paradise Lost

(New York: Morrow, 2001)

Story type: Police Procedural
Series: Joanna Brady. Number 9
Subject(s): American West; Family Problems; Rural Life
Major character(s): Joanna Brady, Police Officer (sheriff); Butch Dixon, Spouse (of Joanna); Jenny Brady, Child
Time period(s): 2000s
Locale(s): Bisbee, Arizona (Cochise County)

Summary: The author offers up her familiar brew of police procedural and thorny family relationships, with the emphasis probably on the latter. Joanna and her husband, Butch Dixon, are on the road attending a sheriffs' convention and a wedding while her 12-year-old daughter, Jenny, is off camping with her Girl Scout troop. Jenny and her tent mate, a troubled adolescent named Dora Matthews, sneak out one night and are horrified when they discover the body of a murdered Phoenix heiress. Joanna is concerned about the emotional impact this incident will have on Jenny, and she spares no effort searching out the woman's no-account husband, who had recently disappeared after cleaning out all their bank accounts. Then it becomes apparent that Jenny and Dora may be the killer's next targets. Side stories include Joanna's suspicions that Butch may have been unfaithful to her, Dora's pregnancy and abandonment by her junkie mother, and the often rocky relationship between Joanna and Jenny. The author also writes two other series, one featuring retired Seattle police detective J.P. Beaumont.

Where it's reviewed:

Booklist, July 2001, page 1951
Mystery News, October/November 2001, page 18
Publishers Weekly, July 23, 2001, page 53

Other books by the same author:

Devil's Claw, 2000
Outlaw Mountain, 1999
Rattlesnake Crossing, 1998
Skeleton Canyon, 1997
Dead to Rights, 1996

Other books you might like:

Sinclair Browning, *The Trade Ellis Series*, 1999-
Val Davis, *The Nicolette Scott Series*, 1996-
Kirk Mitchell, *The Dee Laguerre Series*, 1995-
Betsy Thornton, *The Chloe Newcombe Series*, 1996-
Betty Webb, *Desert Noir*, 2001

126

J. ROBERT JANES

Kaleidoscope

(New York: Soho, 2001)

Story type: Historical; Police Procedural
Series: St-Cyr/Kohler
Subject(s): World War II; Nazis
Major character(s): Jean-Louis St-Cyr, Police Officer (Surete inspector); Hermann Kohler, Military Personnel (Gestapo huptsturmfuhrer)
Time period(s): 1940s (1942)
Locale(s): Paris, France; Provence, France

Summary: As the author points out, civilian crimes continued to be committed even during World War II, and in Occupied France the unlikely team of Surete officer Jean-Louis St-Cyr and Gestapo agent Hermann Kohler work together, at first unwillingly, to solve them. Kohler is a better policeman than he is a Nazi, and gradually the two very different men come to have a certain respect for each other, personally, as well as professionally. When an attractive woman is found shot to death by an antique crossbow in Provence, the two team up to solve the crime, which turns out to be related to the war after all, as the dead woman had been helping refugees flee the Nazis into Spain. The book was originally published in England in 1993. The series is not being published in sequence in the U.S., which makes it a little difficult to follow, but it's well worth the effort.

Where it's reviewed:
Booklist, October 1, 2001, page 301
Mystery News, October/November 2001, page 20
New York Times Book Review, December 9, 2001, page 29
Publishers Weekly, October 8, 2001, page 48
Wall Street Journal, December 6, 2001, page A19

Other books by the same author:
Madrigal, 1999
Gypsy, 1998
Sandman, 1997
Stonekiller, 1997
Dollmaker, 1995

Other books you might like:
Cara Black, *Murder in the Marais*, 1999
Alan Furst, *Red Gold*, 1999
Jack Gerson, *The Ernest Lehmann Series*, 1984-
Philip Kerr, *The Bernie Gunther Series*, 1989-1991
Harry Patterson, *The Valhalla Exchange*, 1977

127

SUSANNA JONES

The Earthquake Bird

(New York: Mysterious, 2001)

Story type: Psychological Suspense
Subject(s): City and Town Life; Cultures and Customs; Sexual Behavior
Major character(s): Lucy Fly, Expatriate, Linguist (translator)
Time period(s): 2000s
Locale(s): Tokyo, Japan

Summary: The moody antiheroine of Jones' first novel has fled her native Yorkshire and her uncaring family for life as a translator in Tokyo, a city so vast, so alien, and so impersonal she is able to lose herself completely in it. As the story begins, Lucy is being taken into police custody for questioning about the disappearance of her friend and fellow Yorkshirewoman Lily Bridges; the police suspect it may be Lily's hacked-up torso that's just been discovered floating in Tokyo Bay. The police suspect Lucy of the crime—if there was one—and press her for details about her relationship with Lily. There's much Lucy is unwilling to tell them, but during the long hours she's held at the police station she reflects back upon her reluctant friendship with Lily and also her intensely erotic relationship with Teiji, a gifted but enigmatic young photographer whose alienation matches her own and about whom she knows remarkably little. Only gradually is the progression of the events leading up to Lily's disappearance revealed to the reader.

Where it's reviewed:
Booklist, August 2001, page 2097
Library Journal, September 1, 2001, page 233
Publishers Weekly, August 27, 2001, page 55

Other books you might like:
Peter Hoeg, *Smilla's Sense of Snow*, 1993
Sujata Massey, *The Rei Shimura Series*, 1997-
Patricia McFall, *Night Butterfly*, 1992
Peter Tasker, *Samurai Boogie*, 2001
Barbara Vine, *Grasshopper*, 2000

128

JULIE KAEWERT

Uncatalogued

(New York: Bantam, 2001)

Story type: Amateur Detective
Series: Alex Plumtree. Book 6
Subject(s): Publishing; Books and Reading; Literature
Major character(s): Alex Plumtree, Publisher, Detective—Amateur
Time period(s): 2000s
Locale(s): London, England; Hanover, New Hampshire; Nantucket Island, Massachusetts

Summary: Although the author spins out enough plot threads for a dozen books, including terrorist bombings in London's financial district and dissension among the royals as to who will succeed a seriously injured Queen Elizabeth to the throne, the main story line involves the wedding of publisher Alex Plumtree and his American fiancee Sarah, who always seems to be involved in top-secret missions for an unnamed international agency. They time their Nantucket wedding so both can attend their Dartmouth College reunion, which in turn enables them to dig around in the archives there for some forgotten journals by Samuel Pepys. There is scandalous information in the papers which may further imperil the monarchy, and then it appears that the documents are forgeries.

Where it's reviewed:
Booklist, December 15, 2001, page 706
Publishers Weekly, November 26, 2001, page 45

Other books by the same author:
Unsigned, 2001
Untitled, 1999
Unprintable, 1998
Unbound, 1997
Unsolicited, 1994

Other books you might like:
Robert A. Carter, *Final Edit*, 1994
John Dunning, *The Bookman's Wake*, 1995
Charles Goodrum, *The Best Cellar*, 1987
Marianne Macdonald, *The Dido Hoare Series*, 1996-
Elizabeth Travis, *The Ben and Carrie Porter Series*, 1989-

129

SHARON KAHN

Don't Cry for Me, Hot Pastrami

(New York: Scribner, 2001)

Story type: Amateur Detective; Humor
Series: Ruby the Rabbi's Wife. Number 3
Subject(s): Judaism; Cruise Ships; Vacations
Major character(s): Ruby Rothman, Widow(er), Computer Expert
Time period(s): 2000s

Locale(s): *Bargain II*, At Sea; St. Thomas, Virgin Islands of the United States

Summary: Ruby and her friends from the tiny town of Eternal, Texas, have all signed on for a cut-rate Temple-sponsored cruise featuring historic Jewish sites in the Caribbean. The experience proves once and for all you get what you pay for: the food is not only awful but strangely tinted, Captain Goldberg may be Jewish but he also seems to have unwelcome designs on Ruby, and the entertainment consists of a never-ending stream of Elvis impersonators. The gang does get to visit the historic synagogue in St. Thomas, and there are interesting bits about Sephardic settlements in the Caribbean. There is also a fascinating plot thread involving the Conversos, Sephardic Jews who went underground during the Inquisition. Thousands of their descendants live in the American Southwest, particularly New Mexico, and are for the most part practicing Catholics with no idea of their heritage, although they still adhere to many Jewish customs. One of the ship's passengers may indeed unknowingly be a Converso, and this may be connected to the murder of Willie Bob Gonzales, the ship's lecturer. For the most part this material takes a back seat to Ruby's humorous musings and e-mails, some more amusing than others.

Where it's reviewed:
Booklist, July 2001, page 1987
Library Journal, September 1, 2001, page 238
Publishers Weekly, July 2, 2001, page 55

Other books by the same author:
Never Nosh a Matzo Ball, 1999
Fax Me a Bagel, 1998

Other books you might like:
J.A. Jance, *Birds of Prey*, 2001
Harry Kemelman, *The Rabbi David Small Series*, 1964-1996
Elizabeth Daniels Squire, *The Peaches Dann Series*, 1994-
Serita Stevens, *The Fanny Zindel Series*, 1991-
James Yaffe, *A Nice Murder for Mom*, 1988

130

STUART M. KAMINSKY

Murder on the Trans-Siberian Express

(New York: Mysterious, 2001)

Story type: Police Procedural
Series: Porfiry Rostnikov. Number 13
Subject(s): Trains; Kidnapping; Serial Killers
Major character(s): Porfiry Petrovich Rostnikov, Police Officer
Time period(s): 2000s
Locale(s): Russia

Summary: While his colleagues in Moscow are working on the cases of a kidnapped, hate-filled rock star known as the Naked Cossack and a young woman subway killer, who seems to be carving up her affluent male victims at random, Rostnikov is put aboard the Trans-Siberian Express with a half-million green rubles (or American dollars) on a mysterious mission to retrieve an important historical document. The journey of 6,000 miles from Moscow to Vladivostok does not take Rostnikov out of harm's way, however. The author, as usual, paints a convincing portrait of post-Cold War Russia, particularly its rebellious, disaffected young people and the clash between the old ways and the new. Kaminsky writes several other series, most notably the Toby Peters private eye mysteries set in Hollywood in the years just before, during, and after World War II.

Where it's reviewed:
Booklist, September 1, 2001, page 57
Publishers Weekly, September 3, 2001, page 66

Other books by the same author:
Fall of a Cosmonaut, 2000
The Dog Who Bit a Policeman, 1998
Tarnished Icons, 1997
Blood and Rubles, 1996
Death of a Russian Priest, 1995

Other books you might like:
Robert Harris, *Archangel*, 1999
Philip Kerr, *Dead Meat*, 1995
John Le Carre, *Our Game*, 1995
Martin Cruz Smith, *The Arkady Renko Series*, 1981-
Robin White, *Siberian Light*, 1997

131

JOSEPH KANON

The Good German

(New York: Henry Holt, 2001)

Story type: Action/Adventure; Historical
Subject(s): World War II; Smuggling; Anti-Semitism
Major character(s): Jake Geismar, Journalist (foreign correspondent)
Time period(s): 1940s (1945)
Locale(s): Berlin, Germany

Summary: In 1945, Berlin is a city nearly destroyed by bombs, overrun with refugees, controlled by a thriving black market, and in transition between World War II and the Cold War. Former Berlin correspondent Jake Geismar returns to the city that's only a prewar memory to him, ostensibly to cover the Potsdam Conference but primarily to find Lena, the German woman he had a passionate affair with before the war. He's further distracted from his assignment by his discovery of the murdered body of an American GI, which washes up near the conference grounds. Always in the background is the guilty memory of the Holocaust. Another plot element is the frantic recruiting of Nazi rocket scientists by the Americans and the Soviets to run their respective space and military programs. As usual with this gifted author, it's an amazing re-creation of a pivotal time and place in history.

Where it's reviewed:
Booklist, July 2001, page 1950
Library Journal, September 1, 2001, page 233
New York Times Book Review, October 28, 2001, page 30
Publishers Weekly, July 16, 2001, page 164

Other books by the same author:
The Prodigal Spy, 1998
Los Alamos, 1997

Other books you might like:
Philip Kerr, *A German Requiem*, 1991
Christopher Reich, *The Runner*, 2000
David L. Robbins, *The War of the Rats*, 1999
James Thayer, *Five Past Midnight*, 1997
Robert Wilson, *The Company of Strangers*, 2001

132

H.R.F. KEATING

Breaking and Entering

(New York: St. Martin's Press, 2001)

Story type: Police Procedural
Series: Inspector Ghote. Book 21
Subject(s): City and Town Life; Crime and Criminals
Major character(s): Ganesh Ghote, Police Officer (inspector)
Time period(s): 2000s
Locale(s): Bombay, India (Mumbai)

Summary: Mild-mannered Inspector Ghote is disappointed when he's reassigned from an important murder case to a much more minor case involving a string of jewel thefts by an accomplished cat burglar. It proves to be far more challenging than he had expected—complicated enough, in fact, to succeed at diverting his mind from his harried domestic life. The burglar never leaves any clues, and Ghote despairs of ever catching him, but eventually painstaking police work pays off and he not only solves this case but finds evidence pointing to the murderer in the case he was originally assigned to.

Where it's reviewed:
Booklist, October 15, 2001, page 385
Ellery Queen's Mystery Magazine, March 2002, page 46
Mystery News, December 2001/January 2002, page 19
Publishers Weekly, October 29, 2001, page 39

Other books by the same author:
Asking Questions, 1997
Cheating Death, 1997
Doing Wrong, 1997
The Iciest Sin, 1990
Inspector Ghote: His Life and Crimes, 1989 (short stories)

Other books you might like:
Lawrence G. Blochman, *Bombay Mail*, 1934
Ivor Drummond, *Necklace of Skulls*, 1977
Paul Mann, *The George Sansi Series*, 1993-
William Marshall, *The Yellowthread Series*, 1975-
James McClure, *The Lieutenant Tromp Kramer Series*, 1971-

133

MICHAEL KILIAN

The Ironclad Alibi

(New York: Berkley, 2002)

Story type: Historical
Series: Harrison Raines. Book 3
Subject(s): Civil War; American South; Ships
Major character(s): Harrison Raines, Spy (Secret Service); Caesar Augustus, Sidekick, Slave (former)
Time period(s): 1860s (1862)
Locale(s): Richmond, Virginia; Hampton Roads, Virginia

Summary: Harrison, a Southerner whose abolitionist leanings have made him an outcast among his own people, has defected to the Union where he's become an agent for the Secret Service. He's sent to Richmond, the capital of the Confederacy, to learn what he can about the ongoing restoration of the ruined iron-clad ship the *U.S.S. Merrimack*, renamed the *C.S.S. Virginia* and being outfitted to take on the *U.S.S. Monitor* in an historic battle. Also, he reconnects with a former flame, who shortly after their meeting is found hanged in Harrison's room, with his best friend and fellow spy, former slave Caesar Augustus, accused of the crime. Raines is given exactly one week to exonerate Caesar of the murder. And he has to get word to his superiors about the Confederate warship.

Where it's reviewed:
Publishers Weekly, December 24, 2001, page 46

Other books by the same author:
A Killing at Ball's Bluff, 2001
Murder at Manassas, 2000

Other books you might like:
Ann McMillan, *Civil Blood*, 2001
Miriam Grace Monfredo, *Brothers of Cain*, 2001
Owen Parry, *The Abel Jones Series*, 1999-
Anne Perry, *Slaves of Obsession*, 2000
Jim Walker, *Murder at Gettysburg*, 1999

134

NICHOLAS KILMER

Lazarus, Arise

(Scottsdale, Arizona: Poisoned Pen, 2001)

Story type: Amateur Detective
Series: Fred Taylor. Number 5
Subject(s): Art; Collectors and Collecting; World War II
Major character(s): Fred Taylor, Art Dealer, Detective—Amateur
Time period(s): 2000s
Locale(s): Arlington, Massachusetts; Boston, Massachusetts

Summary: On a mission for Clayton Reed, the eccentric art collector who employs him as his agent, Fred Taylor arrives from Paris at Boston's Logan Airport. When a dying passenger flings an object into the air, Taylor instinctively catches it, only to learn later that it is a medieval representation of Lazarus taken from a priceless Bible. Having established its identity, Taylor feels compelled to return it to its rightful owner, and he traces the provenance of the work from Nazi Germany all the way back to the Hundred Years War. At the same time. Taylor must protect the work from greedy institutions and private collectors, including his client Clayton Reed.

Where it's reviewed:
New York Times Book Review, October 14, 2001, page 26
Publishers Weekly, September 17, 2001, page 57

Other books by the same author:
Dirty Linen, 1999
O Sacred Head, 1997
Man with a Squirrel, 1996

Harmony in Flesh and Black, 1995

Other books you might like:
Aaron Elkins, *Loot*, 1999
April Henry, *Circles of Confusion*, 1999
Archer Mayor, *The Marble Mask*, 2000
Iain Pears, *The Jonathan Argyll Series*, 1991-
Peter Watson, *The Landscape of Lies*, 1990

135

PETER KING

The Jewel of the North

(New York: Signet, 2001)

Story type: Historical; Amateur Detective
Series: Jack London. Book 1
Subject(s): American History; Literature; Authors and Writers
Major character(s): Jack London, Writer, Historical Figure
Time period(s): 1900s (ca. 1900)
Locale(s): San Francisco, California (Barbary Coast)

Summary: Young Jack London is barely able to make ends meet in turn-of-the-century San Francisco, working at a variety of odd jobs while he tries unsuccessfully to sell his short stories. So when he's offered a job at five dollars a day by the mayor's office to gather information about the murders of two Barbary Coast saloon girls whose deaths appear to be the work of a serial killer, he takes the money and promises to keep his eyes and ears open. He learns that both girls had recently arrived in the city and had been on the same ship from Alaska, *The Jewel of the North*. During his investigation, he rubs shoulders with other, more established literary figures of the day, such as Ambrose Bierce, Oscar Wilde, and Rudyard Kipling. This first installment in a projected new series is very different from the author's culinary mysteries featuring the Gourmet Detective.

Other books by the same author:
Eat, Drink and Be Buried, 2001
A Healthy Place to Die, 2000
Death al Dente, 1999
Dying on the Vine, 1998
Spiced to Death, 1997

Other books you might like:
Oakley Hall, *The Ambrose Bierce Series*, 1998-
Peter J. Heck, *The Mark Twain Series*, 1995-
Walter Satterthwait, *Wilde West*, 1994
Steven Saylor, *A Twist at the End*, 2000
Harold Schechter, *Nevermore*, 1999

136

KATE KINGSBURY (Pseudonym of Doreen Roberts Hight)

Death Is in the Air

(New York: Berkley, 2001)

Story type: Historical; Amateur Detective
Series: Manor House. Number 2
Subject(s): World War II; Small Town Life; Social Classes
Major character(s): Lady Elizabeth Hartleigh Compton, Widow(er), Noblewoman
Time period(s): 1940s (1942)
Locale(s): Sitting Marsh, England

Summary: The citizens of the once-tranquil village of Sitting Marsh don't have the Blitz to contend with, but shortages, rationing, and concerns for their boys at the front bring the war home to them nevertheless. Lady Elizabeth does what she can to set a good example, using her motorcycle to get around, billeting American troops at the manor house, and generally contributing her best to the war effort. When a German pilot makes an emergency crash landing in the nearby woods, she reassures the villagers that he's just a frightened boy from whom they have little to fear. When the village women descend upon his parachute armed with knives and scissors, planning to salvage its silk for knickers and nighties, he heads for the woods at top speed before he can be captured. On the very day he disappears, a local girl is found murdered. The author recently completed a twelve-part series set at an Edwardian seaside inn known as the Pennyfoot Hotel.

Other books by the same author:
A Bicycle Built for Murder, 2001

Other books you might like:
Robert Barnard, *Out of the Blackout*, 1984
Joanna Cannan, *Death at the Dog*, 1941
reprinted in 2000
Hamilton Crane, *Miss Seeton's Finest Hour*, 1999
Sheila Pim, *Common or Garden Crime*, 2001
originally published in 1945
Elliott Roosevelt, *Murder at the Palace*, 1987

137

ROCHELLE KRICH

Shadows of Sin

(New York: Morrow, 2001)

Story type: Police Procedural
Series: Jessie Drake. Number 5
Subject(s): Judaism; Family Relations; City and Town Life
Major character(s): Jessie Drake, Detective—Homicide
Time period(s): 2000s
Locale(s): Los Angeles, California

Summary: At first the murder of a prominent plastic surgeon and his staff appears to be a random multiple homicide, except that the brutal manner in which Dr. Ronald Bushnell was killed suggests to Jessie both deep anger and revenge. When she and her partner Phil Okum start investigating the slain man's family, they become convinced he was killed by someone close to him. The obvious suspect is his troubled foster son Ethan Meissner, whom he had been raising since the boy's mother, who had been his nurse, died and his father relinquished his parental responsibility. Ethan is attracted to his foster sister Adrienne, with whom Bushnell had angrily forbidden him to become involved. At the same time, Jessie is having to deal with her own difficult parents and with her growing attraction for Ezra Nathanson, from whom she has been receiving religious instruction since her recent discovery of her own Jewish heritage. The author has also written a number of stand-alone suspense novels.

Where it's reviewed:
Booklist, August 2001, page 2097
Library Journal, July 2001, page 130
Mystery News, October/November 2001, page 14
Publishers Weekly, August 13, 2001, page 288

Other books by the same author:
Dead Air, 2000
Blood Money, 1999
Angel of Death, 1994
Fair Game, 1993

Other books you might like:
Paul Bishop, *The Fey Croaker Series*, 1994-
Susan Dunlap, *The Jill Smith Series*, 1981-
Denise Hamilton, *The Jasmine Trade*, 2001
Faye Kellerman, *The Rina Lazarus/Peter Decker Series*, 1986-
Laurie R. King, *The Kate Martinelli Series*, 1993-

138

CECILE LAMALLE

Prepared for Murder

(New York: Warner, 2001)

Story type: Amateur Detective
Series: Charly Poisson. Number 3
Subject(s): Cooks and Cooking; Restaurants; Animals/Dogs
Major character(s): Charly Poisson, Cook, Restaurateur
Time period(s): 2000s
Locale(s): Klover, New York (Hudson Valley)

Summary: With his dog, Bruno, along for company, chef Charly Poisson, owner of the small boutique restaurant La Fermette, is out walking his fields on a fine spring morning in search of tender young nettles for soups and tonics, when he finds a body in one of his ponds. This time, Charly has every intention of leaving the matter for his friend, John Stark, the local chief of police, to solve, and he stays focused on preparing the from-scratch dishes using fresh ingredients his restaurant is justly famous for. He does get sidetracked when his former partner, Maurice, tries to get him to invest in a company calling itself Fabulous Foods and specializing in pre-made seafood entrees for upscale restaurants. When Charly visits their headquarters, he senses that something is not right, and his suspicions are confirmed when he discovers that for all practical purposes the company doesn't exist. Lots of food lore is woven into the story along with a number of recipes for relatively simple dishes from Charly's kitchen (and one for Bruno's dog biscuits).

Other books by the same author:
Glutton for Punishment, 2000
Appetite for Murder, 1999

Other books you might like:
Claudia Bishop, *The Sarah and Meg Quilliam Series*, 1994-
Michael Bond, *The Monsieur Pamplemousse Series*, 1983-
Peter King, *The Gourmet Detective Series*, 1996-
Phyllis Richman, *The Chas Wheatley Series*, 1997-
Lou Jane Temple, *The Heaven Lee Series*, 1996-

139

JANET LAPIERRE

Keepers

(Santa Barbara, California: Perseverance, 2001)

Story type: Private Detective
Series: Port Silva. Number 7
Subject(s): Mothers and Daughters; Small Town Life; Religious Communes
Major character(s): Patience Mackellar, Detective—Private, Widow(er); Verity Mackellar, Detective—Private
Time period(s): 2000s
Locale(s): Port Silva, California

Summary: The small California coastal town of Port Silva has been the setting (or starting point) for all the novels in this loosely connected and sensitively written series, but this time two new characters carry the story line, with regulars like police chief Vincent Gutierrez and his wife, schoolteacher Meg Halloran, making only cameo appearances. Patience Mackellar is a retired policeman's widow who has continued her late husband's private detective agency and who welcomes her daughter Verity, fleeing a troubled marriage, as her new partner. Most of their cases are routine and low-key, but their latest, finding a lost child, requires them to go undercover and infiltrate a highly secretive religious community in their midst. It's also by far the most dangerous work the women have ever done, but at stake are the lives and futures of another mother and daughter.

Where it's reviewed:
Booklist, August 2001, page 2097
Publishers Weekly, August 27, 2001, page 59

Other books by the same author:
Baby Mine, 1999
Old Enemies, 1993
Grandmother's House, 1991
The Cruel Mother, 1990
Children's Games, 1989

Other books you might like:
Susan Dunlap, *The Veejay Haskell Series*, 1983-
Laurie R. King, *A Darker Place*, 1999
Mary Kittredge, *Murder in Mendocino*, 1987
Marcia Muller, *Point Deception*, 2001
Gillian Roberts, *Whatever Doesn't Kill You*, 2001

140

MARTHA C. LAWRENCE

Ashes of Aries

(New York: St. Martin's Press, 2001)

Story type: Private Detective
Series: Elizabeth Chase. Number 5
Subject(s): Arson; Kidnapping; Psychic Powers
Major character(s): Elizabeth Chase, Detective—Private, Psychic
Time period(s): 2000s
Locale(s): San Diego, California

Summary: In addition to her private detective's license, Elizabeth holds degrees in both psychology and parapsychology and has undeniable psychic powers that occasionally help her in her job, although for the most part she relies on old-fashioned detective work. Little Matthew Fielding goes missing from his parents' Rancho Santa Fe home and Elizabeth is called in as an adjunct to the police investigation. When a wildfire, fanned by the hot, dry Santa Ana winds, sweeps through the wealthy community, Elizabeth's work is halted temporarily, despite her strong feelings that the boy is still alive. Then another fire breaks out, this time in Frank Fielding's company, and it becomes clear that both blazes are the work of an arsonist. The question is, is the arsonist also the kidnapper?

Where it's reviewed:
Booklist, August 2001, page 2097
Drood Review of Mystery, July/August 2001, page 10
Library Journal, August 2001, page 170
Mystery News, October/November 2001, page 10
Publishers Weekly, July 12, 2001, page 52

Other books by the same author:
Pisces Rising, 2000
Aquarius Descending, 1999
The Cold Heart of Capricorn, 1997
Murder in Scorpio, 1995

Other books you might like:
Lucha Corpi, *The Gloria Damasco Series*, 1992-
Kate Green, *The Theresa Fortunato Series*, 1986-
Mercedes Lackey, *The Diana Tregarde Series*, 1989-
Abigail Padgett, *The Bo Bradley Series*, 1993-
Judith Van Gieson, *Hotshots*, 1996

141

JOHN LESCROART

The Oath

(New York: Dutton, 2002)

Story type: Legal
Series: Dismas Hardy. Book 10
Subject(s): Medicine; Doctors; Hospitals
Major character(s): Dismas Hardy, Lawyer (criminal); Abe Glitsky, Detective—Homicide (half black, half Jewish)
Time period(s): 2000s
Locale(s): San Francisco, California

Summary: Once again, the author pits his two central characters against each other when Dismas Hardy is hired to represent Dr. Eric Kensing, the prime suspect in a murder case being investigated by Hardy's old friend, homicide detective Abe Glitsky. Kensing is accused of administering an overdose of potassium to his boss, Tim Markham, while Markham was under his care. The motive: Markham was having an affair with Kensing's wife. The discovery that Markham is actually the 12th person to die under suspicious circumstances at the same hospital under the care of various physicians blows the case wide open. Eventually the real target of the investigation becomes the HMO, raising the question of how far managed care providers will go to cut costs.

Where it's reviewed:
Booklist, November 15, 2001, page 523
Publishers Weekly, November 19, 2001, page 46

Other books by the same author:
The Hearing, 2001
Nothing but the Truth, 2000
The Mercy Rule, 1998
Guilt, 1997
A Certain Justice, 1995

Other books you might like:
Stephen Greenleaf, *The John Marshall Tanner Series*, 1979-
John Grisham, *The Rainmaker*, 1995
Steve Martini, *The Paul Madriani Series*, 1992-
Grif Stockley, *The Gideon Page Series*, 1992-
Stephen White, *Critical Conditions*, 1998

142

MICHAEL Z. LEWIN

The Reluctant Detective and Other Stories

(Norfolk, Virginia: Crippen & Landru, 2001)

Story type: Collection
Subject(s): Short Stories

Summary: This collection of 21 short stories contains some offbeat, some conventional, and some humorous tales, all of them quietly effective. Six of them involve Lewin's three generations of detectives, the Lunghis, who operate a family detective agency in Bath and have been featured in his novels. His Indiana homicide detective Lieutenant Leroy Powder is featured in one story. The most unlikely detectives in the collection include Dan Quayle (in two stories) and a dog named Rover (in one). The author provides an entertaining introduction, and some useful notes and a bibliography are appended.

Where it's reviewed:
Publishers Weekly, October 29, 2001, page 39

Other books by the same author:
Cutting Loose, 1999
Family Planning, 1999
Family Business, 1995
Underdog, 1993
Called by a Panther, 1991

Other books you might like:
Robert Barnard, *Death of a Salesperson and Other Untimely Exits*, 1990
short stories
Ron Goulart, *Adam and Eve on a Raft*, 2001
short stories
Peter Lovesey, *The Sedgemoor Strangler and Other Stories of Crime*, 2001
short stories
Bill Pronzini, *More Oddments*, 2001
short stories
Peter Robinson, *Not Safe After Dark and Other Stories*, 1998
short stories

143

LAURA LIPPMAN

In a Strange City

(New York: Morrow, 2001)

Story type: Private Detective
Series: Tess Monaghan. Book 6
Subject(s): Stalking; Antiques; Literature
Major character(s): Tess Monaghan, Detective—Private
Time period(s): 2000s
Locale(s): Baltimore, Maryland

Summary: As usual, the author picks a subject that is uniquely Baltimore for her background here: the famous ''Poe Toaster,'' an anonymous cloaked figure who visits Edgar Allan Poe's grave every year on his birthday and leaves behind three roses and half a bottle of cognac. On January 17, two days before Poe's birth date, Tess is interviewed by a potential client, an antiques dealer who claims he has been sold a fake antique bracelet by a man he believes to be the Poe Toaster. Two nights later Tess is at the cemetery with other watchers and witnesses when not one but two cloaked figures arrive with their tribute. One figure shoots the other and flees. Neither one in any way resembles Tess' somewhat rotund client, but she can't help but believe the murder in some way is connected with him, and she determines to get to the bottom of the affair, drawing upon her investigation skills as a former reporter to assemble the information she needs to solve the crime.

Where it's reviewed:
Booklist, May 1, 2001, page 1635
New York Times Book Review, October 14, 2001, page 26
People Weekly, September 17, 2001, page 57

Other books by the same author:
The Sugar House, 2000
In Big Trouble, 1999
Butchers Hill, 1998
Baltimore Blues, 1997
Charm City, 1996

Other books you might like:
Linda Barnes, *The Carlotta Carlyle Series*, 1987-
Ruth Birmingham, *The Sunny Childs Series*, 1998-
Marcia Muller, *The Sharon McCone Series*, 1977-
Katy Munger, *The Casey Jones Series*, 1997-
Blair S. Walker, *The Darryl Billups Series*, 1997-

144

CONSTANCE LITTLE
GWENYTH LITTLE, Co-Author

The Black Eye

(Boulder, Colorado: Rue Morgue Press, 2001)

Story type: Amateur Detective; Humor
Subject(s): World War II; Mummies; Romance
Major character(s): Eugenia Gates, Secretary; Kendall ''Ken'' Smith, Military Personnel (army sergeant)
Time period(s): 1940s
Locale(s): New York

Summary: All Eugenia wants is a little peace and quiet, and she jumps at the chance to borrow her friend Mary's apartment for two weeks while Mary is away. Eugenia hasn't even unpacked when her solitude is disturbed by the appearance of brash Sergeant Ken Smith, to whom Mary has also promised the apartment. Learning of her mistake, Mary installs nosy Lucy Davis as a chaperone. Soon they're organizing parties and making themselves thoroughly at home, until Mary returns unexpectedly and becomes quite agitated over their untidy ways. Eugenia is a typical Little heroine, tart-tongued, indolent, and full of attitude, and she copes in her own way with the the goings-on, which soon include murder, as well as amorous advances from Ken Smith. Originally published in 1945.

Other books by the same author:
The Black Coat, 2001 (originally published in 1948)
Black Corridors, 2000 (originally published in 1940)
The Black Stocking, 2000 (originally published in 1946)
Great Black Kanba, 1998 (originally published in 1944)
The Black Honeymoon, 1997 (originally published in 1944)

Other books you might like:
Donna Andrews, *The Meg Langslow Series*, 1999-
Elizabeth Dean, *The Emma Marsh Series*, 1939-
Janet Evanovich, *The Stephanie Plum Series*, 1994-
Sparkle Hayter, *The Robin Hudson Series*, 1994-
Charlotte MacLeod, *The Withdrawing Room*, 1980-

145

MARY LOGUE

Glare Ice

(New York: Walker, 2001)

Story type: Police Procedural
Series: Claire Watkins. Book 3
Subject(s): Winter; Small Town Life; Abuse
Major character(s): Claire Watkins, Police Officer (deputy sheriff), Widow(er); Rich Haggard, Boyfriend (of Claire); Stephanie Klaus, Crime Victim
Time period(s): 2000s
Locale(s): Fort St. Antoine, Wisconsin

Summary: Wisconsin winter weather—and it can be brutal—is only one of many problems recently widowed Deputy Sheriff Claire Watkins must cope with. Faced with an ever-increasing guest list for the Thanksgiving she'd planned to spend quietly with her young daughter, Meg, and her new love, Rich Haggard, Claire is also puzzling over a murder that is somehow connected with the plight of Stephanie Klaus, a young woman who is being brutalized by an assailant she refuses to identify. The two stories are beautifully intertwined: Stephanie must somehow free herself from a man known to the reader only as Jack, and Claire must make some difficult choices in balancing her personal and professional lives. What promises to be the Thanksgiving from hell turns out to be anything but when Rich's lonely and complaining mother rises to the challenge of looking after Claire's family when she's called away on the case. It's a sweet moment in a story that doesn't minimize the dangers inherent in Claire's job and Rich's ever present fear of someday losing her to them.

Where it's reviewed:
Drood Review, November/December 2001, page 12
New York Times Book Review, November 25, 2001, page 21
Publishers Weekly, October 15, 2001, page 48

Other books by the same author:
Dark Coulee, 2000
Blood Country, 1999

Other books you might like:
P.M. Carlson, *The Marty Hopkins Series*, 1992-1995
K.C. Greenlief, *Cold Hunter's Moon*, 2002
J.A. Jance, *The Joanna Brady Series*, 1993-
William Kent Krueger, *The Cork O'Connor Series*, 1998-
Charlene Weir, *The Susan Wren Series*, 1992-

146

PETER LOVESEY

The Sedgemoor Strangler and Other Stories of Crime

(Norfolk, Virginia: Crippen & Landru, 2001)

Story type: Collection
Subject(s): Short Stories

Summary: Even readers who don't normally read short stories will find much to enjoy in this outstanding collection of 16 criminous tales, historical and contemporary, from a modern master of both short and novel-length crime fiction. Some of the stories are chilling, some are humorous, and all are ingenious. There's a Sherlock Holmes Christmas tale, a puzzle set on the *Titanic*, an impossible crime story, and much more, told in the same polished prose and with the occasional droll wit that distinguishes the author's many successful crime novels. A complete checklist of Lovesey's work is included.

Where it's reviewed:
Booklist, November 15, 2001, page 57
Publishers Weekly, September 24, 2001, page 73

Other books by the same author:
The Reaper, 2001
The Vault, 2000
Do Not Exceed the Stated Dose, 1998 (short stories)
Upon a Dark Night, 1998
Bloodhounds, 1996

Other books you might like:
Robert Barnard, *Death of a Salesperson and Other Untimely Exits*, 1990
short stories
Michael Gilbert, *The Man Who Hated Banks and Other Stories*, 1998
short stories
Reginald Hill, *There Are No Ghosts in the Soviet Union and Other Stories*, 1988
short stories
H.R.F. Keating, *In Kensington Gardens Once...*, 1997
short stories
Peter Robinson, *Not Safe After Dark and Other Stories*, 1998
short stories

147

JOHN LUTZ

The Nudger Dilemmas

(Waterville, Maine: Five Star, 2001)

Story type: Private Detective; Collection
Series: Alo Nudger. Number 11
Subject(s): Short Stories
Major character(s): Alo Nudger, Detective—Private
Time period(s): 1980s; 1990s
Locale(s): St. Louis, Missouri

Summary: This collection of 13 previously published short stories all feature St. Louis private eye Alo Nudger, a sort of everyman sleuth who suffers from plain old anxiety rather than angst and who is forever trying to calm his nervous stomach with antacids. Tenacious, curious, mild-mannered, and not given to trusting anybody (although he himself inspires trust), Nudger prefers to solve his cases without violence and often gets surprising results. The plots are clever and there are flashes of humor in the telling, although Nudger himself is not given to frequent wisecracks. The author, who has written ten novels about Nudger, also writes a series about Florida private eye Fred Carver.

Where it's reviewed:
Booklist, May 1, 2001, page 1636

Other books by the same author:
Oops!, 1997
Death by Jury, 1995
Thicker than Blood, 1993
Diamond Eyes, 1990
Time Exposure, 1989

Other books you might like:
Lawrence Block, *Sometimes You Get the Bear*, 1993
Max Allan Collins, *Kisses of Death*, 2001
Loren D. Estleman, *General Murders*, 1984
Jeremiah Healy, *The Concise Cuddy*, 1999
Bill Pronzini, *Spadework*, 1996

148

EDWARD MARSTON (Pseudonym of Keith Miles)

The Devil's Apprentice

(New York: St. Martin's Press, 2001)

Story type: Historical
Series: Nicholas Bracewell. Number 11
Subject(s): Theater; Witches and Witchcraft; Rural Life
Major character(s): Nicholas Bracewell, Producer (theatrical)
Time period(s): 16th century (1590s)
Locale(s): London, England; Essex, England

Summary: Bored and restless after a long cold winter has left them largely unemployed, the theatrical company of Lord Westfield's Men is eager to accept the invitation extended by Sir Michael Greenleaf to perform a series of plays at his Essex estate. There are conditions: one of the plays must be new, and a local lad, Davy Stanton, must be taken on as an apprentice. There's no way that manager and book holder Nicholas Bracewell can refuse this generous offer, and he finds a way quickly to acquire a new play to perform. Young Davy turns out to be more trouble than anyone bargained. One thing after another goes wrong, including the murder of a member of the audience. In addition to this always lively and historically accurate series, the author writes the Domesday Book mysteries detailing the investigations of two of King William's men in Norman England, as well as two other series, one written under the name Conrad Allen, set in more recent historical times.

Where it's reviewed:
Booklist, July 2001, page 130
Drood Review of Mystery, July/August 2001, page 10
Library Journal, July 2001, page 130
New York Times Book Review, September 9, 2001, page 26
Publishers Weekly, June 25, 2001, page 53

Other books by the same author:
The Wanton Angel, 1999
The Fair Maid of Bohemia, 1997
The Laughing Hangman, 1996
The Roaring Boy, 1995
The Silent Woman, 1994

Other books you might like:
P.F. Chisholm, *The Sir Robert Carey Series*, 1994-
Judith Cook, *The Slicing Edge of Death*, 1993
Philip Gooden, *The Nick Revill Series*, 2000-
Simon Hawke, *A Mystery of Errors*, 2000
Leonard Tourney, *The Players' Boy Is Dead*, 1980

149

ALLANA MARTIN

Death of the Last Villista

(New York: St. Martin's Press, 2001)

Story type: Amateur Detective
Series: Texana Jones. Number 5
Subject(s): American West; Mexicans; Small Town Life
Major character(s): Texana Jones, Store Owner (trading post), Detective—Amateur; Clay Martin, Veterinarian
Time period(s): 2000s
Locale(s): Polvo, Texas

Summary: Texana runs a trading post in the tiny town of Polvo in *la frontera*, the borderland between Texas and Mexico. Forty years earlier a movie based on a 1917 raid by Pancho Villa was filmed in Polvo, with a former *villista*, Jacinto Trejo, acting as project manager. Texana herself was an extra in the movie, which was marred by the unsolved murder of Trejo. Now a PBS crew is in town to film a documentary celebrating the film's anniversary, and Texana is delighted to host the video crew and participate in the project. Then actor Dane Anthony, who played Pancho Villa in the original film, is killed when his RV is bombed, and a local child goes missing. With the help of her veterinarian husband Clay, Texana begins to connect events from the past with those of the present to find a solution to the puzzle.

Where it's reviewed:
Booklist, July 2001, page 1988
Mystery News, October/November 2001, page 18
Publishers Weekly, July 2, 2001, page 56

Other books by the same author:
Death of a Myth Maker, 2000
Death of an Evangelista, 1999
Death of a Saint Maker, 1998
Death of a Healing Woman, 1996

Other books you might like:
Lee Child, *Echo Burning*, 2001
Nancy Herndon, *The Elena Jarvis Series*, 1995-
Michael McGarrity, *Tularosa*, 1996
Rick Riordan, *The Tres Navarre Series*, 1997-
Judith Van Gieson, *North of the Border*, 1988

150

SUJATA MASSEY

The Bride's Kimono

(New York: HarperCollins, 2001)

Story type: Amateur Detective
Series: Rei Shimura. Number 5
Subject(s): Cultural Identity; Japanese Americans; Museums
Major character(s): Rei Shimura, Antiques Dealer, Expatriate
Time period(s): 2000s
Locale(s): Tokyo, Japan; Washington, District of Columbia

Summary: For the first time in this engaging series, the author brings her Japanese-American heroine back to the United States and has some fun with the reverse culture shock that California-born Rei, who has been living in Tokyo for quite a few years, experiences when she returns to the country of her birth. She has been building up a business in Japanese antiques, with a specialty in textiles and clothing, and is asked to undertake a delicate mission: to accompany a collection of valuable 19th century kimonos from Tokyo to Washington for a museum exhibit, where she is also required to deliver a lecture on them. It's a very lucrative assignment for Rei, who is still struggling financially, and her enthusiasm is only a little dampened when she learns she wasn't her employer's first choice for the job. Viewing the kimonos, she notes that one is too fragile to transport, and asks instead that another, a bride's kimono, be substituted; but the museum in Washington isn't interested in exhibiting it, and she faces the challenge of keeping it safe during her visit. Of course it's stolen; a Japanese tourist is murdered; Rei lands in hot water; and a number of people from her past, including old boyfriends and her parents, turn up.

Where it's reviewed:
Booklist, August 2001, page 2098
Mystery News, October 11, 2001, page 33
Publishers Weekly, August 6, 2001, page 66

Other books by the same author:
The Floating Girl, 2000
The Flower Master, 1999
Zen Attitude, 1998
The Salaryman's Wife, 1997

Other books you might like:
Dale Furutani, *The Toyotomi Blades*, 1999
Susanna Jones, *The Earthquake Bird*, 2001
Patricia McFall, *Night Butterfly*, 1992
James Melville, *The Inspector Otani Series*, 1979-

Laura Joh Rowland, *The Sano Ichiro Series*, 1994-

151

ARCHER MAYOR

Tucker Peak

(New York: Warner, 2001)

Story type: Police Procedural
Series: Joe Gunther. Book 12
Subject(s): Environment; Drugs; Sports/Skiing
Major character(s): Joe Gunther, Police Officer
Time period(s): 2000s
Locale(s): Brattleboro, Vermont

Summary: Although he's left his policeman's job in Brattleboro to head up the newly created (and fictitious) Vermont Bureau of Investigation, also headquartered in Brattleboro, Joe Gunther is still every inch the cop—the kind of cop we all wish really existed when we need one. A series of robberies, as well as demonstrations (and possible sabotage) by environmental groups at a local ski resort, Tucker Peak, send Gunther undercover at the site. Soon there's a murder and escalating violence, which Gunther takes in stride as he conducts his usual meticulous investigation. His personal brand of common sense and bravery are demonstrated in one particularly harrowing scene where he rescues a young mother and her child from almost certain death when the chairlift they're riding on is sabotaged.

Where it's reviewed:
Booklist, September 15, 2001, page 200
Library Journal, September 15, 2001, page 117
Mystery News, December 2001/January 2002, page 20
New York Times Book Review, November 25, 2001, page 21
Publishers Weekly, October 15, 2001, page 48

Other books by the same author:
The Marble Mask, 2000
Occam's Razor, 1999
The Disposable Man, 1998
Bellows Falls, 1997
The Ragman's Memory, 1996

Other books you might like:
Gerry Boyle, *The Jack McMorrow Series*, 1993-
Donald Harstad, *The Carl Houseman Series*, 1998-
Steven F. Havill, *The Bill Gastner Series*, 1991-
William Kent Krueger, *The Cork O'Connor Series*, 1998-
Michael McGarrity, *The Kevin Kerney Series*, 1996-

152

ED MCBAIN (Pseudonym of Evan Hunter)

Money, Money, Money

(New York: Simon & Schuster, 2001)

Story type: Police Procedural
Series: 87th Precinct. Number 51
Subject(s): Animals/Lions; Money; Christmas
Major character(s): Steve Carella, Detective—Homicide; Oliver Wendell Weeks, Detective—Homicide
Time period(s): 2000s
Locale(s): Isola, New York (thinly disguised Manhattan)

Summary: When the partially devoured body of a young woman is found in the lion habitat of the Grover Park Zoo, parts of it lie in the 87th Precinct and parts in the 88th. This means Carella is forced to team up with the thoroughly obnoxious Oliver Weeks, known to friends and foes alike as Fat Ollie, and long a thorn in the side of his fellow officers. The body turns out to be that of Cassandra Jean Ridley, a distinguished former army officer and Gulf War combat pilot. But why is her apartment crammed with expensive furs and marked bills? While Carella is mulling this puzzle over, Fat Ollie pursues a case involving the gangland-style murder of a seemingly innocuous publisher's sales representative. Both cases lead the cops to a small Texas town and a man named Randolph Biggs, who's apparently wanted by people on both sides of the law. Best known for this long-running series, the author also writes a series about Florida lawyer Matthew Hope and stand-alone novels under both the McBain and Evan Hunter bylines.

Where it's reviewed:
Booklist, July 2001, page 1952
Library Journal, August 2001, page 170
New York Times Book Review, September 9, 2001, page 26
Publishers Weekly, August 27, 2001, page 58
Wall Street Journal, September 27, 2001, page A16

Other books by the same author:
The Last Dance, 2000
Big Bad City, 1999
Nocturne, 1997
Romance, 1995
And All through the House, 1994

Other books you might like:
William Caunitz, *One Police Plaza*, 1984
Ed Dee, *The Anthony Ryan/Joe Gregory Series*, 1994-
William Heffernan, *The Paul Devlin Series*, 1988-
Christopher Newman, *The Joe Dante Series*, 1986-
Lawrence Sanders, *The Edward X. Delaney Series*, 1973-1985

153

SAM MCCARVER

The Case of the Ripper's Revenge

(New York: Signet, 2001)

Story type: Historical
Series: John Darnell. Book 4
Subject(s): Serial Killers; History; City and Town Life
Major character(s): John Darnell, Paranormal Investigator; George Bernard Shaw, Historical Figure, Writer (playwright)
Time period(s): 1910s (1917)
Locale(s): London, England

Summary: Nearly 20 years after the serial killer known as Jack the Ripper stalked and killed prostitutes on the fog-shrouded streets and alleys of London's Whitechapel district, a new round of terror has begun. Once again, streetwalkers are being savagely murdered by a man dressed in old-fashioned evening clothes, wielding a scalpel-sharp knife with almost surgical precision. Even more disturbingly, the murders are occurring on exactly the same dates and with the same frequency as the originals. When Professor John Darnell is called in to investigate, he wonders why the year 1917 has been chosen, as other years between 1888 and 1917 have had the dates fall on the same days of the week. He's assisted by the playwright George Bernard Shaw, with whom he plans to trap the killer before the final murder is scheduled to occur.

Other books by the same author:
The Case of Compartment 7, 2000
The Case of the 2nd Seance, 2000
The Case of Cabin 13, 1999

Other books you might like:
Mark Clark, *Ripper*, 1987
Edward Hanna, *The Whitechapel Horror*, 1993
Laurie R. King, *The Beekeeper's Apprentice*, 1994
Gillian Linscott, *Absent Friends*, 1999
Paul West, *The Women of Whitechapel*, 1999

154

VAL MCDERMID

Killing the Shadows

(New York: St. Martin's Press, 2001)

Story type: Psychological Suspense
Subject(s): Serial Killers; Authors and Writers; Psychological
Major character(s): Fiona Cameron, Psychologist; Kit Martin, Writer, Lover (of Fiona)
Time period(s): 2000s
Locale(s): London, England; Toledo, Spain; Lairg, Scotland

Summary: Fiona Cameron, a psychology professor who has developed a computer program to help police link seemingly unrelated crimes, lives happily in a London flat with her lover Kit Martin, a bestselling thriller writer who is disturbed when two of his colleagues are murdered and others, including himself, start receiving threatening letters. Fiona is working with the Toledo police on a serial killer case that is making considerable demands on her time. She no longer will work with London's Metropolitan police after they ignored her advice in another serial killer case, listening instead to a profiler, who identified the wrong person and left an old friend's career hanging in the balance. When a third writer friend of Kit's disappears, warning bells finally go off and Fiona recruits one of her students to help the police find the missing woman. Even so, Kit's life remains in danger and there are some harrowing scenes in his remote Scottish hideaway, where he is imprisoned by his would-be killer and, where Fiona finally finds him. The book raises serious questions about the role novelists and true-crime writers play in glorifying serial killers. The author also writes several mystery series.

Where it's reviewed:
Booklist, August 2001, page 2098
Deadly Pleasures, Autumn 2001, page 41
Library Journal, September 1, 2001, page 234
Mystery Scene, Number 73, page 67
Publishers Weekly, September 3, 2001, page 66

Other books by the same author:
A Place of Execution, 2000
Star Struck, 1998
The Wire in the Blood, 1998
Booked for Murder, 1996
The Mermaids Singing, 1995

Other books you might like:
Frances Fyfield, *The Helen West Series*, 1989-
Thomas Harris, *Red Dragon*, 1981
P.D. James, *An Unsuitable Job for a Woman*, 1972
Ruth Rendell, *A Dark-Adapted Eye*, 1986
Minette Walters, *The Sculptress*, 1993

155

IAIN MCDOWELL

A Study in Death

(New York: St. Martin's Press, 2001)

Story type: Police Procedural
Subject(s): Academia; Alcoholism; Marriage
Major character(s): Frank Jacobson, Police Officer (detective chief inspector); Ian Kerr, Police Officer (detective sergeant)
Time period(s): 2000s
Locale(s): Crowby, England (Midlands); Lake District, England; Amsterdam, Netherlands

Summary: A brilliant young history professor at Crowby College, Roger Harvey, is found murdered in his home, and Jacobson and Kerr launch an investigation which turns up a number of potential suspects, chiefly a long succession of ex-girlfriends, but no truly plausible motive. What few leads they have take them to a battered women's shelter, to the Lake District, and eventually to Amsterdam, and turn up financial chicanery in the software industry and New Age cults. The tedium and stress of police work are well-portrayed, with Jacobson seeking refuge in alcohol and Kerr helplessly standing by as his marriage crumbles. First novel.

Where it's reviewed:
Booklist, December 1, 2001, page 633
Deadly Pleasures, Autumn 2001, page 58
Drood Review, November/December 2001, page 12
Mystery News, December 2001/January 2002, page 16
Publishers Weekly, October 29, 2001, page 38

Other books you might like:
Marjorie Eccles, *The Gil Mayo Series*, 1988-
John Harvey, *The Charlie Resnick Series*, 1989-1999
Ian Rankin, *The John Rebus Series*, 1987-
Peter Robinson, *The Alan Banks Series*, 1987-

156

RALPH MCINERNY

Emerald Aisle

(New York: St. Martin's Press, 2001)

Story type: Amateur Detective; Private Detective
Series: Notre Dame. Book 5
Subject(s): Universities and Colleges; Catholicism; Weddings

Major character(s): Roger Knight, Professor (philosophy), Detective—Amateur; Philip Knight, Detective—Private
Time period(s): 2000s
Locale(s): South Bend, Indiana (University of Notre Dame); Minneapolis, Minnesota

Summary: To be married in the lovely Basilica of the Sacred Heart is the dream of any loyal Notre Dame graduate, and as soon as they become engaged, freshmen Larry Morton and Dolores Torre reserve the date June 17, 2002—at that time six years in the future. They break off their engagement, go their separate ways, and cross paths again when the date rolls around and each finds the other is claiming the basilica for a wedding to another person. Larry is vehement in his insistence that Dolores give up the date for him and flies to Minneapolis to persuade her. Meanwhile, also in Minneapolis, some valuable books and papers are stolen from a man who turns out to be the husband of Dolores' fiance's mistress, and the Knight brothers are called upon to investigate. The author, himself a professor at Notre Dame, also writes the Father Dowling and Andrew Broom mysteries.

Where it's reviewed:
Booklist, September 15, 2001, page 200
Publishers Weekly, September 24, 2001, page 70

Other books by the same author:
The Book of Kills, 2000
Irish Tenure, 1999
Lack of the Irish, 1998
On This Rockne, 1997

Other books you might like:
Amanda Cross, *The Kate Fansler Series*, 1964-
Joanne Dobson, *The Karen Pelletier Series*, 1997-
Susan Holtzer, *Bleeding Maize and Blue*, 1996
M.D. Lake, *The Peggy O'Neill Series*, 1989-
Sally S. Wright, *The Ben Reese Series*, 1997-

157

LESLIE MEIER

Wedding Day Murder

(New York: Kensington, 2001)

Story type: Amateur Detective; Domestic
Series: Lucy Stone. Book 8
Subject(s): Weddings; Small Town Life; Friendship
Major character(s): Lucy Stone, Journalist, Parent
Time period(s): 2000s
Locale(s): Tinker's Cove, Maine

Summary: Although she's more than busy with her own unruly household and a full-time job as a reporter, Lucy agrees to help her friend, Sue Finch, plan her daughter Sidra's wedding to dot-com millionaire Ron Davitz. The groom's mother has all sorts of lavish and impractical ideas for the affair, but her meddling soon becomes a minor source of irritation compared to the trouble the groom is causing as he rides roughshod over the locals, rubbing everyone from the lobstermen to the harbormaster the wrong way. When he's found drowned next to his yacht, there are plenty of suspects, and with no wedding plans to occupy her, Lucy starts investigating a death that looks more and more like a murder.

Where it's reviewed:
Booklist, October 1, 2001, page 302
Mystery News, December 2001/January 2002, page 29

Other books by the same author:
Turkey Day Murder, 2000
Valentine Murder, 1999
Christmas Cookie Murder, 1998
Back to School Murder, 1997
Trick or Treat Murder, 1996

Other books you might like:
Susan Wittig Albert, *Lavender Lies*, 1999
Donna Andrews, *Murder with Peacocks*, 1999
Sarah Graves, *The Jacobia Tiptree Series*, 1998-
Jean Hager, *Bride and Doom*, 2000
Valerie Wolzien, *Weddings Are Murder*, 1998

158

LARRY MILLETT

Sherlock Holmes and the Secret Alliance

(New York: Viking, 2001)

Story type: Historical
Series: Sherlock Holmes/Shadwell Rafferty. Number 4
Subject(s): Social Issues; Labor Conditions; Victorian Period
Major character(s): Sherlock Holmes, Detective—Private; Shadwell Rafferty, Saloon Keeper/Owner; John Watson, Sidekick, Doctor
Time period(s): 1890s (1899)
Locale(s): Minneapolis, Minnesota; St. Paul, Minnesota

Summary: In New York on a delicate mission for none other than John Jacob Astor, Holmes and Watson are summoned to the Twin Cities by their dear friend Shadwell Rafferty, owner of the finest saloon in St. Paul. On the eve of President William McKinley's visit to Minneapolis, a young man is found strung up from an oak tree with a placard around his neck stating ''The Secret Alliance Has Spoken.'' Everyone knows who this group is: a shadowy organization of businessmen whose real agenda is union-busting, and the dead man, Michael O'Donnell, worked for one of Shad's fellow saloon keepers and was a well-known union organizer. Naturally Holmes and Watson make the trip to St. Paul to help their friend not only unmask the murderers but prevent any more deaths. As is usual in this series, the author works in a great deal of local history.

Where it's reviewed:
Publishers Weekly, September 17, 2001, page 58

Other books by the same author:
Sherlock Holmes and the Rune Stone Mystery, 1999
Sherlock Holmes and the Ice Palace Murders, 1998
Sherlock Holmes and the Red Demon, 1996

Other books you might like:
Arthur Conan Doyle, *The Sherlock Holmes Series*, 1887-1927
Jamyang Norbu, *Sherlock Holmes: The Missing Years*, 2001
Laurie R. King, *The Mary Russell/Sherlock Holmes Series*, 1994-
Christopher Leppek, *The Surrogate Assassin*, 1998
Wayne Worcester, *The Jewel of Covent Garden*, 2000

159

MIRIAM GRACE MONFREDO

Brothers of Cain

(New York: Berkley, 2001)

Story type: Historical
Series: Seneca Falls. Number 8
Subject(s): American South; Civil War; History
Major character(s): Bronwen Llyr, Spy; Kathryn Llyr, Nurse
Time period(s): 1860s (1862)
Locale(s): Richmond, Virginia; Washington, District of Columbia

Summary: These two young nieces of Seneca Falls librarian and feminist Glynis Tryon have taken over the series of late. The headstrong Bronwen (introduced in *The Stalking Horse*) and her more sedate sister, Kathryn, find themselves in Richmond during the Virginia Peninsula Campaign, as federal troops surround the city with the intent of capturing it. Both work for the Union, Bronwen as a spy and Kathryn as a volunteer nurse. They are alarmed to hear that their brother, Seth, has been captured by the Confederates and incarcerated in Libby Prison, second only to Andersonville in its notoriously barbaric conditions. Their mission: to free him before he is hanged. The story is an exciting one and a close companion piece to its predecessor, *Sisters of Cain*, which really must be read first. The author's staunchly feminist spin on American history only occasionally hinders the narrative drive.

Where it's reviewed:
Publishers Weekly, August 27, 2001, page 57

Other books by the same author:
Sisters of Cain, 2000
Must the Maiden Die, 1999
The Stalking Horse, 1998
Through a Gold Eagle, 1996
Blackwater Spirits, 1995

Other books you might like:
Michael Kilian, *Murder at Manassas*, 2000
Ann McMillan, *Civil Blood*, 2001
Owen Parry, *The Abel Jones Series*, 1999-
Anne Perry, *Slaves of Obsession*, 2000
Jim Walker, *Murder at Gettysburg*, 1999

160

DEBORAH MORGAN

Death Is a Cabaret

(New York: Berkley, 2001)

Story type: Amateur Detective
Subject(s): Antiques; History; Phobias
Major character(s): Jeff Talbot, Antiques Dealer (picker), FBI Agent (former)
Time period(s): 2000s
Locale(s): Seattle, Washington; Mackinac Island, Michigan

Summary: Formerly an FBI agent, Jeff Talbot is now a professional picker who goes to flea markets, garage sales, and estate sales in search of antiques he can resell at a profit to dealers or collectors. He lives in a Queen Anne mansion built by his ancestors, which he shares with his agoraphobic wife, Sheila, and their young gay butler, Greer. The object he covets above all else is the French cabaret tea set Napoleon commissioned for Josephine, and when he hears it might possibly be included in an upscale auction to be held at the Grand Hotel on Michigan's Mackinac Island, he's off and running. He wants the tea set for a friend and colleague, whose family had once owned it and for whom it has great sentimental value. Other people are apparently looking for it too, and soon the death toll begins, with Jeff clearly being a target himself. It's an entertaining first novel, well-plotted with strong characters and relationships, and much interesting antiques lore. Sheila desperately wants to overcome her agoraphobia, which has left her housebound and unable to accompany Jeff on his travels; she has compensated for it by turning the Internet into her window on the world and by sharing vicariously in Jeff's trips and treasure hunting. There's an interesting appendix with an annotated bibliography of books and websites on antiques and antiquing.

Where it's reviewed:
Deadly Pleasures, Autumn 2001, page 10
Publishers Weekly, October 22, 2001, page 55

Other books you might like:
Sharon Fiffer, *Killer Stuff*, 2001
Jonathan Gash, *The Lovejoy Series*, 1977-
Susan Holtzer, *Something to Kill For*, 1994
Toni L.P. Kelner, *Tight as a Tick*, 1998
Jean Ruryk, *Next Week Will Be Better*, 1998

161

EDDIE MULLER

The Distance

(New York: Scribner, 2002)

Story type: Historical
Subject(s): Sports/Boxing; Journalism; Marriage
Major character(s): Billy Nichols, Journalist (sportswriter)
Time period(s): 1940s (1948)
Locale(s): San Francisco, California

Summary: San Francisco sportswriter Billy Nichols, a.k.a. ''Mr. Boxing'' and something of a celebrity himself, responds to a phone call from boxing promoter Gig Liardi inviting him over to his house. When he arrives, he finds Gig dead and the young boxer Hack Escalante standing over his body, claiming to have accidentally beaten him death when Gig insulted Hack's wife, Claire. Billy feels sorry for Hack and impulsively helps him cover up the crime, a decision he soon regrets when Gig goes on the missing persons list and homicide detective Francis O'Connor, who is assigned to the case, immediately senses that Billy has something to hide. Meanwhile, Billy's marriage is falling apart and he finds himself attracted to Claire, who may not be as innocent a party as she seems. The author, an expert on both boxing and film noir, recreates the 1940s ambience effectively, giving the book the pace and feel of a period noir movie. First novel.

Where it's reviewed:
Booklist, December 1, 2001, page 633
Library Journal, December 2001, page 174

Publishers Weekly, November 5, 2001, page 43

Other books you might like:
Andrew Bergman, *Hollywood and LeVine*, 1975
Max Allan Collins, *Angel in Black*, 2001
James Ellroy, *The Black Dahlia*, 1988
Stuart M. Kaminsky, *Down for the Count*, 1985
Walter Mosley, *Devil in a Blue Dress*, 1990

162

SHIRLEY ROUSSEAU MURPHY

Cat Laughing Last

(New York: HarperCollins, 2002)

Story type: Amateur Detective
Series: Joe Grey. Book 7
Subject(s): Animals/Cats; Small Town Life; Antiques
Major character(s): Joe Grey, Animal (cat); Dulcie, Animal (cat); Kit, Animal (cat)
Time period(s): 2000s
Locale(s): Molina Point, California

Summary: Joe Grey and his feline companions, the luxury-loving Dulcie and the young Kit, appear to most of their fellow residents in the quaint seaside village of Molina Point to be just ordinary cats. Only a handful of people know their true abilities: not only can they think and observe in quite human fashion, but they are capable of human speech as well. These traits, coupled with their strong sense of justice, enable them to hunt down clues and solve crimes that are off limits to their human friends, especially the police. Their current adventure involves the multitude of garage sales held each weekend in the village and a group of older women who are selling their bargain purchases on e-Bay with an eye toward buying a communal residence together. At the same time, a famous writer has arrived in town with his young wife to supervise the production of one of his plays; when two young actresses competing for the lead are attacked, one of them fatally, Joe and Dulcie step in.

Where it's reviewed:
Publishers Weekly, December 24, 2001, page 45

Other books by the same author:
Cat Spitting Mad, 2001
Cat to the Dogs, 2000
Cat in the Dark, 1999
Cat Raise the Dead, 1997
Cat under Fire, 1997

Other books you might like:
Garrison Allen, *The Big Mike Series*, 1994-
Lilian Jackson Braun, *The Cat Who Series*, 1966-
Rita Mae Brown, *The Mrs. Murphy Series*, 1990-
Barbara Collins, *Too Many Tomcats and Other Feline Tales of Suspense*, 2000
short stories
Carole Nelson Douglas, *The Midnight Louie Series*, 1992-

163

TAMAR MYERS

Nightmare in Shining Armor

(New York: Avon, 2001)

Story type: Amateur Detective; Humor
Series: Den of Antiquity. Number 8
Subject(s): Antiques; American South; Halloween
Major character(s): Abigail Timberlake, Antiques Dealer, Divorced Person
Time period(s): 2000s
Locale(s): Charlotte, North Carolina

Summary: To celebrate her purchase of a house in Charlotte's exclusive Piper Glen neighborhood, Abbie decides to throw a lavish Halloween costume party. She invites just about everyone she knows, including her ex-husband and his much younger wife Tweetie, who comes as Little Bo Peep complete with a live sheep. Unfortunately, the torch being carried by a reveler dressed as the Statue of Liberty starts a fire that sets off the smoke extinguisher, as well as Abbie's own personal alarm system, and she throws all her guests out. When things are under control, she discovers a suit of armor in the house that doesn't belong to her—and even worse, she discovers Tweetie's dead body inside. The author also writes the Magdalena Yoder series, about a Mennonite innkeeper in the Pennsylvania Dutch country.

Where it's reviewed:
Mystery News, August 9, 2001, page 28
Publishers Weekly, July 2, 2001, page 57

Other books by the same author:
A Penny Urned, 2000
Baroque and Desperate, 1999
Estate of Mind, 1999
So Faux, So Good, 1998
The Ming and I, 1997

Other books you might like:
Ann Campbell, *Wolf in Sheep's Clothing*, 2001
Laura Childs, *Death by Darjeeling*, 2001
Anne George, *The Southern Sisters Series*, 1996-2001
Carolyn Haines, *The Sarah Booth Delaney Series*, 1999-
Dean James, *The Ernie Carpenter Series*, 2000-

164

MAGDALEN NABB

Property of Blood

(New York: Soho, 2001)

Story type: Police Procedural
Series: Marshal Guarnaccia. Number 11
Subject(s): Kidnapping; Mothers and Daughters; Fashion Design
Major character(s): Salvatore Guarnaccia, Police Officer (marshal)
Time period(s): 2000s
Locale(s): Florence, Italy

Summary: Back after an absence of several years is Marshal Guarnaccia, a Sicilian by birth who is passionate about his adopted Florence. When an American-born contessa, who owns a famous fashion house, is kidnapped by Sardinian thugs and held for ransom in the Tuscan countryside, Guarnaccia is faced with a ticklish situation, made more difficult by her family's failure to report the incident promptly, which leads him wonder how badly they want her back. Under Italian law, no ransom can be legally paid, and the marshal has little time left to ponder his options.

Where it's reviewed:
Booklist, August 2001, page 2098
Library Journal, September 1, 2001, page 238
Publishers Weekly, August 13, 2001, page 288

Other books by the same author:
The Marshal and the Forgery, 1995
The Marshal at the Villa Torrini, 1993
The Marshal Makes His Report, 1991
The Marshal's Own Case, 1990
The Marshal and the Madwoman, 1988

Other books you might like:
Michael Dibdin, *The Aurelio Zen Series*, 1988-
Jane Langton, *The Dante Game*, 1991
Donna Leon, *The Guido Brunetti Series*, 1992-
Iain Pears, *The Immaculate Deception*, 2000
Edward Sklepowich, *The Urbino McIntyre Series*, 1990-

165

JANET NEEL (Pseudonym of Janet Cohen)

O Gentle Death

(New York: St. Martin's Press, 2001)

Story type: Police Procedural; Traditional
Series: John McLeish/Francesca Wilson. Number 7
Subject(s): Schools/Boarding Schools; Teen Relationships; Music and Musicians
Major character(s): John McLeish, Police Officer (detective chief inspector); Francesca Wilson, Administrator
Time period(s): 2000s
Locale(s): Dorset, England

Summary: A surfeit of memorable characters slows the action down a bit in this latest case for Detective Chief Inspector McLeish. The inspector's very pregnant wife, Francesca, is not only a gifted singing instructor, but the bursar at Farraday Trust, a private coed boarding school with an emphasis on the arts. Because of her connections, McLeish is on hand when a disturbed teenaged girl with a penchant for slashing her wrists appears finally to have succeeded in killing herself. Or has she? The forensic evidence says she drowned in the bathtub, yet hadn't lost enough blood to pass out. Faint handprints on her shoulders suggest the possibility of murder. The solution doesn't come easily, given the large number of suspects, but eventually McLeish sorts it all out, and the results may surprise you.

Where it's reviewed:
Booklist, July 2001, page 1988
Library Journal, September 1, 2001, page 238
Mystery News, August 9, 2001, page 28
Publishers Weekly, June 18, 2001, page 62

Other books by the same author:
To Die For, 1998
A Timely Death, 1996
Death Among the Dons, 1993
Death of a Partner, 1991
Death on Site, 1989

Other books you might like:
Deborah Crombie, *The Duncan Kincaid/Gemma James Series*, 1993-
Caroline Graham, *The Inspector Barnaby Series*, 1987-
Ann Granger, *The Alan Markby/Meredith Mitchell Series*, 1991-
Christine Green, *The Connor O'Neill/Fran Wilson Series*, 1993-
Jill McGown, *The Inspector Lloyd/Judy Hill Series*, 1983-

166

KRIS NELSCOTT (Pseudonym of Kristine Kathryn Rusch)

Smoke-Filled Rooms

(New York: St. Martin's Press, 2001)

Story type: Private Detective
Series: Smokey Dalton. Number 2
Subject(s): Race Relations; Riots; African Americans
Major character(s): Smokey Dalton, Detective—Private, Veteran (Korean conflict); Jimmy, Child
Time period(s): 1960s (1968)
Locale(s): Chicago, Illinois; Memphis, Tennessee

Summary: Following the assassination of Martin Luther King, Jr., an event that Smokey's ten-year-old ward Jimmy witnessed, Memphis is a dangerous place for this unlikely pair, especially since Jimmy knows who King's killer is and the FBI very much wants this information suppressed. So Smokey and Jimmy flee to Chicago, a city he figures is large enough for them both to disappear in. Smokey doesn't reckon on the impact of the imminent 1968 Democratic National Convention and the heightened visibility black people have in the eyes of the Chicago police during those tense times. His job as a security guard at a Hilton hotel doesn't make him any less visible, either, and soon it appears that trouble is still following them. The author is also known for her science fiction written under her real name.

Where it's reviewed:
Booklist, July 2001, page 1989
Publishers Weekly, June 25, 2001, page 53

Other books by the same author:
A Dangerous Road, 2000

Other books you might like:
Thomas H. Cook, *Streets of Fire*, 1989
Gary Hardwick, *Cold Medina*, 1996
Chester Himes, *Cotton Comes to Harlem*, 1965
Walter Mosley, *The Easy Rawlins Series*, 1990-
James Sallis, *Black Hornet*, 1994

167

BARBARA PARKER

Suspicion of Vengeance

(New York: Dutton, 2001)

Story type: Legal; Psychological Suspense
Series: Gail Connor
Subject(s): Crime and Criminals; Prisoners and Prisons; Cuban Americans
Major character(s): Gail Connor, Lawyer (corporate litigation); Anthony Quintana, Lawyer (criminal defense); Jackie Bryce, Police Officer (rookie)
Time period(s): 2000s
Locale(s): Miami, Florida; Stuart, Florida

Summary: Gail takes time out from mending fences with her on-again, off-again lover, Anthony Quintana, to do a favor for an old family friend, whose grandson is on death row and whose case is up for appeal. She believes Anthony when he tells her it's a lost cause, but even though her background is in corporate litigation, a quick look at the trial transcript is enough to convince Gail the young man may actually be innocent of the brutal murder for which he was convicted. She turns to her cousin Jackie Bryce, a rookie cop in the small town of Stuart where the crime took place, for help in tracking down the real killer. Gail also appeals to Quintana, a brilliant criminal defense lawyer, and the three of them race against time in their search for the truth. Not everybody wants to see justice done or guilty secrets exposed, and at times it seems like an impossible battle. Undoubtedly the most issue-oriented to date of the author's legal thrillers, the book is a thought-provoking exploration of the question of capital punishment.

Where it's reviewed:
Entertainment Weekly, September 7, 2001, page 158
Publishers Weekly, July 9, 2001, page 43

Other books by the same author:
Suspicion of Malice, 2000
Suspicion of Betrayal, 1999
Suspicion of Deceit, 1998
Suspicion of Guilt, 1995
Suspicion of Innocence, 1994

Other books you might like:
Carolina Garcia-Aguilera, *The Lupe Solano Series*, 1996-
Jonnie Jacobs, *The Kali O'Brien Series*, 1996-
Nancy Pickard, *Ring of Truth*, 2001
Mary Willis Walker, *The Red Scream*, 1994
Marianne Wesson, *Render Up the Body*, 1998

168

ROBERT B. PARKER

Death in Paradise

(New York: Putnam, 2001)

Story type: Police Procedural
Series: Jesse Stone. Book 3
Subject(s): Missing Persons; Abuse; Alcoholism
Major character(s): Jesse Stone, Police Officer (chief), Divorced Person
Time period(s): 2000s
Locale(s): Paradise, Massachusetts; Boston, Massachusetts

Summary: After being fired from the LAPD for his drinking, Jesse takes a job as police chief for the small town of Paradise, Massachusetts, where he's filling some of his off-hours playing in the men's softball league. One evening as the team is relaxing after a game, the body of a murdered teenage girl is discovered in a lake near the playing fields. Jesse's investigation takes him into the upper echelons of Paradise society to a family who have long since given up caring about their rebellious daughter, and into Boston as well, where he meets with a couple of characters from the author's Spenser series. Throughout the proceedings Jesse continues his complicated relationship with his ex-wife and has a passionate fling with a school principal. The author also writes the long-running Spenser series about a Boston private detective and, more recently, a female counterpart, Sunny Randall.

Where it's reviewed:
Booklist, August 2001, page 2052
Library Journal, October 1, 2001, page 143
New York Times Book Review, October 14, 2001, page 26
Publishers Weekly, July 23, 2001, page 52

Other books by the same author:
Trouble in Paradise, 1998
Night Passage, 1997

Other books you might like:
Linda Barnes, *Snapshot*, 1993
Robert Crais, *Hostage*, 2001
Donald Harstad, *The Carl Houseman Series*, 1998-
Archer Mayor, *The Joe Gunther Series*, 1988-
William G. Tapply, *The Brady Coyne Series*, 1984-

169

OWEN PARRY

Call Each River Jordan

(New York: Morrow, 2001)

Story type: Historical
Series: Abel Jones. Number 3
Subject(s): Civil War; Slavery; American History
Major character(s): Abel Jones, Military Personnel (major), Spy
Time period(s): 1860s (1862)
Locale(s): Shiloh, Tennessee; Savannah, Georgia

Summary: Abel Jones, a courageous transplanted Welshman and personal emissary to President Lincoln, comes to grips with the central issue of the Civil War in this powerful book, which opens in the aftermath of the Battle of Shiloh as Jones makes his way to Savannah to meet with General Grant and receive his latest assignment. Runaway slaves are being slaughtered in advance of the Union Army, and Grant and Sherman are afraid that if northern abolitionists learn of this, they might persuade the troops that they are fighting over slavery and not to preserve the Union, which could result in widespread desertion in the ranks. Although Jones has always been a staunchly moral man and egalitarian to the core, he has never thought of himself as an outright abolitionist nor has he regarded slavery as being central to the conflict between North and South. The horrors he uncovers as he carries out his assignment change his views forever. Perhaps a shade darker than previous books in the series, it's an even more unflinching look at the evils of slavery and the hellishness of war.

Where it's reviewed:
Publishers Weekly, September 24, 2001, page 66

Other books by the same author:
Shadows of Glory, 2000
Faded Coat of Blue, 1999

Other books you might like:
Michael Kilian, *Murder at Manassas*, 2000
Ann McMillan, *Civil Blood*, 2001
Miriam Grace Monfredo, *Brothers of Cain*, 2001
Anne Perry, *Slaves of Obsession*, 2000
Jim Walker, *Murder at Gettysburg*, 1999

170

JOANNE PENCE

Bell, Cook, and Candle

(New York: Avon, 2002)

Story type: Amateur Detective
Series: Angelina Amalfi. Book 9
Subject(s): Catering Business; Italian Americans; Witches and Witchcraft
Major character(s): Angelina ''Angie'' Amalfi, Businesswoman (owns Comical Cakes), Detective—Amateur; Paavo Smith, Police Officer, Boyfriend (of Angie)
Time period(s): 2000s
Locale(s): San Francisco, California

Summary: Angie has just come up with another culinary get-rich-quick scheme: Comical Cakes, a bakery service specializing in gag cakes. She's so caught up with this endeavor that she almost misses out on an opportunity to meddle in her cop boyfriend's investigation of a series of murders that may be connected with a satanic cult. They may also be connected with the goth nightclub one of Angie's clients operates. When it looks as if Angie herself might be a target for the killer, she swings into action at last. In the meantime, boyfriend Paavo is making noises about wanting to get married, but Angie is almost too busy to notice. Recipes included.

Where it's reviewed:
Publishers Weekly, November 12, 2001, page 42

Other books by the same author:
To Catch a Cook, 2000
A Cook in Time, 1999
Cook's Night Out, 1998
Cooks Overboard, 1998
Cooking Most Deadly, 1996

Other books you might like:
Camilla Crespi, *The Simona Griffo Series*, 1991-
Diane Mott Davidson, *The Goldy Bear Schulz Series*, 1990-
Joanne Fluke, *The Hannah Swenson Series*, 2000-
Linda Grant, *Vampyre Bites*, 1998
Phyllis Richman, *The Chas Wheatley Series*, 1997-

171

ARTURO PEREZ-REVERTE

The Nautical Chart

(New York: Harcourt, 2001)

Story type: Psychological Suspense; Action/Adventure
Subject(s): Ships; Treasure; Sailing
Major character(s): Manuel Coy, Sailor; Tanger Soto, Researcher
Time period(s): 2000s
Locale(s): Madrid, Spain; Barcelona, Spain; At Sea

Summary: This accomplished author has written a combination literary/intellectual/nautical thriller here, with nods to Dashiell Hammett, Joseph Conrad, Robert Louis Stevenson, Herman Melville, and B. Traven. The protagonist of this modern-day treasure hunt is a man named Coy, a sailor without a ship after he's grounded for two years because he ran a merchant ship into an uncharted rock in the Indian Ocean. Restless and unhappy without the sea he loves so well, he's attending an auction of maritime artifacts in Barcelona when he meets Tanger, who works for the Madrid Naval Museum. She successfully bids on an antique nautical chart she believes will lead her to a sunken treasure in emeralds, which was en route to Spain from Havana in a Jesuit brigantine when it was sunk by pirates in 1767. Tanger needs a sailor to help her reach the spot where she's certain the treasure lies, and Coy, who is bewitched by her, is more than happy to oblige. There is much nautical lore, particularly about navigation, and some exciting sailing sequences; Coy and Tanger are not the only ones after the treasure.

Where it's reviewed:
Booklist, July 2001, page 1951
Entertainment Weekly, November 23, 2001, page 74
Library Journal, September 1, 2001, page 235
Publishers Weekly, August 13, 2001, page 281

Other books by the same author:
The Fencing Master, 1999
The Seville Communion, 1998
The Club Dumas, 1996
The Flanders Panel, 1994

Other books you might like:
Desmond Bagley, *The Golden Keel*, 1963
Sam Llewellyn, *Dead Reckoning*, 1987
Gavin Lyall, *Venus with Pistol*, 1969
Charles Williams, *Dead Calm*, 1963
Robert Wilson, *A Small Death in Lisbon*, 1999

172

ANNE PERRY

Funeral in Blue

(New York: Ballantine, 2001)

Story type: Historical; Private Detective
Series: William Monk. Book 12
Subject(s): Memory Loss; Anti-Semitism; Gambling
Major character(s): William Monk, Detective—Private, Amnesiac; Hester Monk, Nurse, Spouse (of William)

Time period(s): 1860s
Locale(s): London, England; Vienna, Austria

Summary: Monk, a private investigator suffering a form of amnesia that has left him with no memory of his life prior to a traumatic accident six years earlier, has built a new life for himself that includes his recent bride Hester, now serving as a volunteer nurse with the eminent Viennese surgeon Dr. Kristian Beck. When Beck's English-born wife, Elissa, and an equally beautiful artist's model are found strangled in the studio of the famous London artist who was painting them both, Beck immediately becomes the primary suspect. Anxious to clear their esteemed friend, Monk and Hester travel to Vienna to learn more about the past lives of both women, which they hope will lead them to the real murderer. As usual, the author exposes various social evils of the day, this time the pervasive anti-Semitism of the period, addictive gambling, and rigid class distinctions. She also writes another Victorian mystery series set in the 1890s featuring Inspector Thomas Pitt and his blue-blooded wife, Charlotte.

Where it's reviewed:
Booklist, August 2001, page 2053
Library Journal, October 1, 2001, page 147
Publishers Weekly, November 5, 2001, page 30

Other books by the same author:
Slaves of Obsession, 2000
The Twisted Root, 1999
A Breach of Promise, 1998
The Silent Cry, 1997
Weighed in the Balance, 1996

Other books you might like:
Ray Harrison, *The Sergeant Bragg/Constable Morton Series*, 1983-
Alanna Knight, *The Jeremy Faro Series*, 1988-
Peter Lovesey, *The Sergeant Cribb/Constable Thackeray Series*, 1970-1978
William J. Palmer, *The Wilkie Collins/Charles Dickens Series*, 1990-
Francis Selwyn, *The Sergeant Verity Series*, 1974-1988

173

SHEILA PIM

Creeping Venom

(Boulder, Colorado: Rue Morgue Press, 2001)

Story type: Amateur Detective; Domestic
Subject(s): Small Town Life; Gardens and Gardening; Religious Conflict
Major character(s): Priscilla Hoyle, Companion, Secretary; Tim Linacre, Student, Detective—Amateur
Time period(s): 1940s
Locale(s): Brainborough, Ireland

Summary: Priscilla Hoyle has recently asserted her independence from her domineering mother and taken a job as secretary/companion to domineering old Miss Rebecca Hampton at Hampton Court. She's barely learned her way around the manor house when her unfortunate employer dies of poison ingested while dining on a meal of escargot and Priscilla finds herself one of many suspects in the eyes of the police. Meanwhile, she has her hands full looking after the household and her late employer's relations, one of whom, Miss Hampton's hot-headed young cousin Liam, had been about to be disinherited if he married a Catholic. The police investigation is moving at glacial speed, and so another distant cousin, Trinity College student Tim Linacre, who fancies a career in crime detection, takes up the cause and, in fact, does solve the crime. Many eccentric characters abound, including the village witch, Lizzie Shegog, who is as much a fixture in the region as was old Miss Hampton. Originally published in England in 1946, the book makes its first U.S. appearance here.

Where it's reviewed:
Booklist, December 1, 2001, page 633
Publishers Weekly, November 26, 2001, page 43

Other books by the same author:
A Hive of Suspects, 2001 (originally published in 1952)
Common or Garden Crime, 2001 (originally published in 1943)
A Brush with Death, 1950

Other books you might like:
Dicey Deere, *The Irish Cottage Murder*, 1999
Eilis Dillon, *Sent to His Account*, 1954
Bartholomew Gill, *The Peter McGarr Series*, 1977-
Ann Ripley, *The Louise Eldridge Series*, 1994-
John Sherwood, *The Celia Grant Series*, 1984-

174

BILL PRONZINI

Bleeders

(New York: Carroll & Graf, 2001)

Story type: Private Detective
Series: Nameless Detective. Book 27
Subject(s): Blackmail; Crime and Criminals; Family
Major character(s): Nameless Detective, Detective—Private
Time period(s): 2000s
Locale(s): San Francisco, California

Summary: Hired to oversee a money transfer in what appears to be a straightforward case of blackmail, Nameless sees it all come apart when he discovers who is really being blackmailed and who the money should belong to. When he tries to set things straight, his client winds up dead and he nearly gets killed himself. Determined to track down the person who attacked him, Nameless searches through the city's underworld, and in the process reevaluates his own life. Now that he's turned 60, he's beginning to wonder if the risks his profession entails are worth it, especially now that he has a wife and adopted daughter, Emily. There are some indications that this may be the final book in this long-running series.

Where it's reviewed:
Booklist, November 15, 2001, page 558
Ellery Queen's Mystery Magazine, March 2002, page 45
Publishers Weekly, November 15, 2001, page 50

Other books by the same author:
Crazybone, 2000
Boobytrap, 1998
Illusions, 1997

Sentinels, 1996
Spadework, 1996 (short stories)

Other books you might like:
Earl Emerson, *The Thomas Black Series*, 1985-
Loren D. Estleman, *The Amos Walker Series*, 1980-
Joe Gores, *The DKA Series*, 1972-
Stephen Greenleaf, *The John Marshall Tanner Series*, 1979-
Jeremiah Healy, *The John Francis Cuddy Series*, 1984-

175

BILL PRONZINI

More Oddments

(Waterville, Maine: Five Star, 2001)

Story type: Collection
Subject(s): Short Stories

Summary: The 14 short stories collected here were originally published between 1967 and 2001 and include one featuring the author's San Francisco based series detective whose name is never revealed, the Nameless Detective. Other protagonists include a hack paperback writer looking for ideas to borrow; a Mafia kingpin whose young son seems to be following in his footsteps; a Civil War era husband and wife detecting team, Fergus and Hattie O'Hara; and a department store magician. It's a varied selection ranging from humorous to noir from a veteran mystery writer who is as prolific in the short story field as in the novel.

Other books by the same author:
Oddments, 2000 (short stories)
Spadework, 1996 (short stories)
Small Felonies, 1988 (short stories)
Graveyard Plots, 1985 (short stories)
Casefile: The Best of the "Nameless Detective", 1983 (short stories)

Other books you might like:
Lawrence Block, *Some Days You Get the Bear*, 1993 short stories
Max Allan Collins, *Blue Christmas and Other Holiday Homicides*, 2001 short stories
Joe Gores, *Speak of the Devil*, 1999 short stories
Ed Gorman, *Famous Blue Raincoat*, 1999 short stories
Donald E. Westlake, *A Good Story and Other Stories*, 1999 short stories

176

LEV RAFAEL

Burning Down the House

(New York: Walker, 2001)

Story type: Amateur Detective; Humor
Series: Nick Hoffman. Number 5
Subject(s): Academia; Guns and Gun Control; Homosexuality/Lesbianism
Major character(s): Nick Hoffman, Professor, Homosexual; Juno Dromgoole, Professor (English)
Time period(s): 2000s
Locale(s): Michiganopolis, Michigan (State University of Michigan)

Summary: The author once again satirizes academia and its ongoing power struggles over tenure, department chairmanships, and even holiday decorations. Nick Hoffman is, as usual, in the thick of it all, and he's facing a new personal crisis as well: he feels inexplicably attracted to the sexy and Junoesque Juno Dromgoole, who turns to him for advice when she starts receiving a series of threatening phone calls. It's not that she can't take care of herself—she's already bought a Glock for protection. Nick, who's in a committed relationship with his longtime lover Stefan, is understandably disturbed to find himself fantasizing over the larger-than-life Juno. After a riot breaks out in the university auditorium, shots are fired, and it turns out that Juno isn't the only faculty member who's armed. In fact, Nick contemplates buying a gun himself.

Where it's reviewed:
Publishers Weekly, August 13, 2001, page 288

Other books by the same author:
Little Miss Evil, 2000
The Death of a Constant Lover, 1999
The Edith Wharton Murders, 1997
Let's Get Criminal, 1995

Other books you might like:
Robert Barnard, *Death of an Old Goat*, 1977
Robert Bernard, *Deadly Meeting*, 1970
Joanne Dobson, *The Karen Pelletier Series*, 1997-
Ruth Dudley Edwards, *Matricide at St. Martha's*, 1994
Grant Michaels, *The Stan Kraychik Series*, 1990-

177

ROBERT J. RANDISI
CHRISTINE MATTHEWS, Co-Author

The Masks of Auntie Laveau

(New York: St. Martin's Press, 2001)

Story type: Amateur Detective
Series: Gil and Claire Hunt. Book 2
Subject(s): Voodoo; Marriage; Crafts
Major character(s): Claire Hunt, Television Personality, Detective—Amateur; Gil Hunt, Store Owner (bookseller), Detective—Amateur
Time period(s): 2000s
Locale(s): New Orleans, Louisiana; St. Louis, Missouri

Summary: St. Louis home-shopping TV maven Claire Hunt takes her bookseller husband, Gil, along when she's sent to New Orleans to meet with Auntie Laveau, a self-styled voodoo queen famous for the miniature Mardi Gras masks she crafts. Claire expects to buy a number of these to sell via her show, but the woman she meets proves to be an impostor. When she and Gil return to St. Louis, they learn the real Auntie Laveau has been murdered and they're needed by the New Orleans police to identify the woman they met with. Claire and Gil, both married for the second time, are a well-matched and and good-natured couple whose affectionate bantering sets the tone for the book. Working solo, Randisi is the author of several hard-boiled mystery series both under his own name and various pseudonyms.

Where it's reviewed:
Booklist, December 18, 2001, page 707
Publishers Weekly, December 3, 2001, page 43

Other books by the same author:
Murder Is the Deal of the Day, 1998

Other books you might like:
Sophie Dunbar, *The Claire Claiborne Series*, 1993-
Carolyn Hart, *The Annie Laurance/Max Darling Series*, 1987-
Takis Iakovou, *The Nick & Julia Lambrose Series*, 1996- Judy Iakovou, co-author
Charlotte MacLeod, *The Sarah Kelling/Max Bittersohn Series*, 1979-
Julie Smith, *Louisiana Hotshot*, 2001

178

IAN RANKIN

The Falls

(New York: St. Martin's Press, 2001)

Story type: Police Procedural
Series: Inspector Rebus. Book 12
Subject(s): Internet; City and Town Life; History
Major character(s): John Rebus, Police Officer (inspector); Siobhan Clarke, Police Officer (detective constable)
Time period(s): 2000s
Locale(s): Edinburgh, Scotland

Summary: John Rebus, a loner and a maverick on the Edinburgh force who prefers hanging out in dark smoky bars to being a team player with the younger officers, is a thorn in the side of his superiors but a superb detective nonetheless. He's investigating the disappearance of Philippa Balfour, a university student from a wealthy family. The only clues that appear useful are the facts that she was obsessed with an Internet role-playing game and the discovery of an eight-inch coffin near her family home containing a carved wooden doll. Rebus' young, tense assistant Siobhan Clarke pursues the Internet lead, taking Philippa's place in the game, and Rebus, ignoring the wishes of his superiors, follows up on the miniature coffin, which turns out to be connected with gruesome incidents of grave-robbing, body-snatching, and worse in Edinburgh's history. Dark, dense, richly atmospheric, and filled with striking characters and incidents, Rankin's mysteries set the standard for the modern urban British police procedural.

Where it's reviewed:
Booklist, August 2001, page 2052
Library Journal, September 15, 2001, page 117
Mystery News, December 2001/January 2002, page 16
New York Times Book Review, November 4, 2001, page 28
Publishers Weekly, October 1, 2001, page 40

Other books by the same author:
Set in Darkness, 2000
Dead Souls, 1999
The Hanging Garden, 1998
Black and Blue, 1997
Let It Bleed, 1995

Other books you might like:
John Harvey, *The Charlie Resnick Series*, 1989-1999
Bill James, *The Colin Harpur Series*, 1985-
Quintin Jardine, *The Robert Skinner Series*, 1993-
Val McDermid, *The Tony Hill/Carol Jordan Series*, 1995-
Denise Mina, *Garnethill*, 1999

179

DANUTA REAH

Listen to the Shadows

(New York: Morrow, 2001)

Story type: Police Procedural; Psychological Suspense
Subject(s): Social Issues; Secrets; Children
Major character(s): Suzanne Milner, Researcher, Divorced Person; Steve McCarthy, Detective—Police
Time period(s): 2000s
Locale(s): Sheffield, England

Summary: When Lucy Fielding, the little daughter of Suzanne's best friend, goes missing, Suzanne searches for her in a nearby park but instead finds the body of Lucy's babysitter, Emma. Lucy is safe, but she tells everybody there are monsters in the park, a tale nobody but Suzanne takes very seriously. Suzanne is a graduate student doing research on the communication skills of troubled teens, and it bothers her that she has seen one of her subjects loitering in the same area where Emma was found. She finds it difficult to communicate this to the police detective, Steve McCarthy, who has been assigned to the case, just as she finds it difficult to connect with her own young son during their weekly visits. A second murder leads her to suspect the young people she has been working with may be more dangerous than she had thought and that she may be in danger herself. First novel.

Where it's reviewed:
Booklist, May 15, 2001, page 1737
Publishers Weekly, July 9, 2001, page 47

Other books you might like:
Stephen Booth, *Black Dog*, 2000
J. Wallis Martin, *The Bird Yard*, 1999
Ruth Rendell, *The Inspector Wexford Series*, 1964-
Peter Robinson, *The Alan Banks Series*, 1987-
Minette Walters, *The Breaker*, 1999

180

MARY REED
ERIC MAYER, Co-Author

Three for a Letter

(Scottsdale, Arizona: Poisoned Pen, 2001)

Story type: Historical
Series: John the Eunuch. Book 3
Subject(s): Ancient History; Byzantine Empire; Missing Persons

Major character(s): John the Eunuch, Government Official (lord chamberlain)
Time period(s): 6th century (539)
Locale(s): Constantinople, Byzantine Empire

Summary: John the Eunuch finds that being lord chamberlain in the court of Emperor Justinian and his consort, Theodora, is a tricky business, as both are volatile rulers, with Theodora actively disliking John. Further, they promote Christianity as the state religion, forcing John to keep his own beliefs private. When one of two eight-year-old hostages the royal court is holding as part of Justinian's reconquest of Italy is murdered, John is charged with the welfare of the remaining child and the task of finding the assassin. He's also asked by Theodora to investigate the disappearance of Barnabas, her favorite mime. John's mission takes him to the nearby country villa of a wealthy nobleman.

Where it's reviewed:
Booklist, December 15, 2001, page 708
Publishers Weekly, November 26, 2001, page 48

Other books by the same author:
Two for Joy, 2000
One for Sorrow, 1999

Other books you might like:
Ron Burns, *Roman Nights*, 1991
Lindsey Davis, *Last Act in Palmyra*, 1994
Albert Noyer, *The Saint's Day Deaths*, 2000
Rosemary Rowe, *The Germanicus Mosaic*, 1999
Peter Tremayne, *The Sister Fidelma Series*, 1994-

181

ANN RIPLEY

Harvest of Murder

(New York: Kensington, 2001)

Story type: Amateur Detective
Series: Louise Eldridge. Book 6
Subject(s): Gardens and Gardening; Holidays; Biotechnology
Major character(s): Louise Eldridge, Gardener, Television Personality
Time period(s): 2000s
Locale(s): Alexandria, Virginia

Summary: On a break from her popular public television gardening show but up to her neck with family Thanksgiving preparations, Louise has been escaping the stress by taking nightly dog walks with her elderly ethnobotanist neighbor. Peter Whiting is busy propagating a rare herb from the Amazon rainforest that has the ability to prolong human life. When the old man is killed, his widow approaches Louise to help her finish the experiments that had been her husband's life work. It proves to be an exceptionally dangerous job, made even more so by Louise's attempts to solve Dr. Whiting's murder. The gardening essays customarily sprinkled throughout the author's books have been reduced to one, at the end.

Where it's reviewed:
Booklist, August 2001, page 2099
Library Journal, October 1, 2001, page 145

Other books by the same author:
The Perennial Killer, 2000
Death of a Political Plant, 1999
The Garden Tour Affair, 1999
Death of a Garden Pest, 1996
Mulch, 1994

Other books you might like:
Mary Freeman, *The Rachel O'Connor Series*, 1999-
Janis Harrison, *Roots of Murder*, 1999
Julie Wray Herman, *The Three Dirty Women Series*, 2000-
Sheila Pim, *Common or Garden Crime*, 2001
originally published in 1944
John Sherwood, *The Celia Grant Series*, 1984-

182

S.K. RIZZOLO

The Rose in the Wheel

(Scottsdale, Arizona: Poisoned Pen, 2002)

Story type: Historical
Subject(s): Social Conditions; Diseases; Charity
Major character(s): John Chase, Police Officer (Bow Street Runner)
Time period(s): 1810s (1811)
Locale(s): London, England (Soho)

Summary: Constance Tyrone is a wealthy, well-born young woman who has given her life over to charitable works, founding the St. Catherine Society to aid the impoverished women of Soho. One rainy evening she is apparently struck by a hansom cab while leaving the society's offices, and yet, when her body is found, one satin slipper bears no mudstains and the other foot is bare. The other slipper and her cherished gold filigree crucifix are missing, and there are bruises on her neck. The most obvious suspect in what increasingly appears to be a murder is Jonathan Wolfe, the artist who did a series of drawings of Constance as St. Catherine. Bow Street Runner John Chase delves into the affair, learning that Constance was actually far from a saint (despite her self-proclaimed celibacy) and any number of people had reason to hate her. He's joined in his investigation by Wolfe's wife Penelope, who wants to clear her husband and continue Constance's work despite the dangers it exposes her to, and the attorneys Thorogood and Buckler. First novel.

Where it's reviewed:
Publishers Weekly, December 24, 2001, page 46

Other books you might like:
Bruce Alexander, *The Sir John Fielding Series*, 1994-
T.F. Banks, *The Thief-Taker*, 2001
John Creasey, *The Masters of Bow Street*, 1974
J.G. Jeffreys, *Thief Taker*, 1972
Rosemary Stevens, *The Beau Brummell Series*, 2000-

183

DAVID ROBERTS

The Bones of the Buried

(New York: Carroll & Graf, 2001)

Story type: Historical; Amateur Detective
Series: Lord Edward Corinth and Verity Browne. Number 2
Subject(s): Communism; Civil War/Spanish; Social Classes
Major character(s): Verity Browne, Journalist; Lord Edward Corinth, Nobleman
Time period(s): 1930s (1936)
Locale(s): London, England; Spain

Summary: Despite their vast differences in temperament, values, and background, radical journalist and social activist Verity Browne and privileged, aristocratic heir Edward Corinth have great respect for one another. When Verity's Communist lover is sentenced to death in Spain on the eve of the country's civil war, it's Edward she turns to for help in saving him from the gallows. Back home in England, Edward discovers a disturbing number of his fellow Etonians are being murdered, and their deaths may be related to the unsolved murder of a Communist worker back in Spain. Both Edward and Verity are unwilling, however, to face up to their growing attraction for each another.

Where it's reviewed:
Booklist, September 15, 2001, page 200
Publishers Weekly, September 3, 2001, page 66

Other books by the same author:
Sweet Poison, 2001

Other books you might like:
Robert Barnard, *Skeleton in the Grass*, 1988
T.E.B. Clarke, *Murder at Buckingham Palace*, 1981
Carola Dunn, *The Daisy Dalrymple Series*, 1994-
Robert Goddard, *Hand in Glove*, 1992
James Woods, *The General's Dog*, 2000

184

JOHN MADDOX ROBERTS

Nobody Loves a Centurion

(New York: St. Martin's Minotaur, 2001)

Story type: Historical/Ancient Rome
Series: SPQR. Number VI
Subject(s): Roman Empire; Military Life
Major character(s): Decius Metellus, Detective—Amateur, Military Personnel (soldier)
Time period(s): 1st century B.C. (70s B.C.)
Locale(s): Rome, Roman Empire; Gaul

Summary: Decius, a Roman soldier who is being groomed by his large, distinguished, and far-flung plebeian family for the praetorship, needs a few more military triumphs under his belt before they consider him ready to stand for such a high office. So he is off to Gaul to join Julius Caesar's army, accompanied not by the reinforcements his general had hoped for but instead a single slave. No sooner does Decius arrive at the Roman encampment than a centurion is murdered, and Caesar presses the carefree young man into service as a detective. The history is sound enough, but Decius' sensibilities seem deliberately more in tune with those of the modern reader than they are a product of his age. The result is a lively, often amusing narrative from an author who also is known for his science fiction novels.

Where it's reviewed:
Mystery News, October 11, 2001, page 21
Publishers Weekly, August 27, 2001, page 57

Other books by the same author:
Saturnalia, 1999
Temple of the Muses, 1992
The Sacrilege, 1992
The Catiline Conspiracy, 1991
The King's Gambit, 1990

Other books you might like:
Ron Burns, *Roman Shadows*, 1993
Lindsey Davis, *The Marcus Didius Falco Series*, 1989-
Albert Noyer, *The Saint's Day Deaths*, 2000
Steven Saylor, *Last Seen in Massilia*, 2000
Marilyn Todd, *The Claudia Seferius Series*, 1995-

185

LES ROBERTS

The Chinese Fire Drill

(Waterville, Maine: Five Star, 2001)

Story type: Action/Adventure
Subject(s): Missing Persons; Chinese; Smuggling
Major character(s): Anthony Holton, Writer (novelist), Expatriate
Time period(s): 2000s
Locale(s): Bangkok, Thailand; Hong Kong

Summary: When Hollywood screenwriter turned expatriate thriller writer Anthony Holton, now living and working in Bangkok, gets word that his old friend Jake McCoy has gone missing in Hong Kong along with his beloved boat, *The Hong Kong Lady*, he doesn't think twice before catching the next plane to Hong Kong to look for Jake. As he searches, with help from Jake's flatmates Kate Longley and Boomer Crane, Anthony runs up against diamond smugglers, Chinese mobsters, an American soldier of fortune, and a Chinese billionaire. Known for his two private eye series featuring Hollywood actor Saxon and Cleveland blue-collar investigator Milan Jacovich, Roberts uses his plotting skills in this novel to fashion a lean international thriller.

Where it's reviewed:
Booklist, December 1, 2001, page 634
Publishers Weekly, November 19, 2001, page 50

Other books by the same author:
The Dutch, 2001
Indian Sign, 2000
The Best Kept Secret, 1999
A Shoot in Cleveland, 1998
Cleveland Local, 1997

Other books you might like:
Jack Foxx, *The Jade Figurine*, 1971
Jonathan Gash, *Jade Woman*, 1988

William Marshall, *To the End*, 1998
S.K. Rozan, *Reflecting the Sky*, 2001
Ross Thomas, *The Singapore Wink*, 1969

186

PETER ROBINSON

Aftermath

(New York: HarperCollins, 2001)

Story type: Police Procedural
Series: Alan Banks. Book 12
Subject(s): Missing Persons; Abuse; Divorce
Major character(s): Alan Banks, Police Officer (detective superintendent)
Time period(s): 2000s
Locale(s): Yorkshire, England

Summary: In what may be the darkest yet of this ever-improving series, Superintendent Alan Banks deals with disturbing events both professionally and personally. A number of fair-haired young women in the district have gone missing, and the police think they have found two of them when they enter a home after a neighbor's complaint of loud noises. One is beaten, the other dead, and it's assumed they are the victims of a serial rapist turned murderer. Eventually, the horrible fate of all the missing women is determined, but it's unclear the actual evidence will support any charges. Also, many questions remain. Was the perpetrator's wife his victim, his accomplice, or was she actually the instigator of the crimes? What does the neighbor who turned them in really know? One police officer is killed in the raid, and another reacts so violently to her partner's death she is brought up on charges of brutality. On the home front, Alan's estranged wife is pressing hard for a divorce, especially now that she is pregnant by her husband-to-be, and Alan's current lover, Janet Taylor, is assigned to investigate the brutality charges against their colleague.

Where it's reviewed:
Booklist, September 1, 2001, page 57
Deadly Pleasures, Autumn 2001, page 43
Library Journal, September 1, 2001, page 239
Mystery Scene, Number 73, page 66
Publishers Weekly, August 27, 2001, page 57

Other books by the same author:
Cold Is the Grave, 2000
In a Dry Season, 1999
Blood at the Root, 1998
Innocent Graves, 1996
Final Account, 1994

Other books you might like:
Stephen Booth, *The Ben Cooper Series*, 2000-
Reginald Hill, *The Dalziel and Pascoe Series*, 1970-
Peter Lovesey, *The Peter Diamond Series*, 1991-
Val McDermid, *A Place of Execution*, 2000
Ruth Rendell, *The Inspector Wexford Series*, 1964-

187

ROBERTA ROGOW

The Problem of the Surly Servant

(New York: St. Martin's Minotaur, 2001)

Story type: Historical
Series: Charles Dodgson/Arthur Conan Doyle. Number 4
Subject(s): Authors and Writers; Blackmail; Victorian Period
Major character(s): Arthur Conan Doyle, Historical Figure, Writer; Charles Dodgson, Historical Figure, Writer
Time period(s): 1880s (1886)
Locale(s): Oxford, England

Summary: Two of the most famous writers of the Victorian era team up again in this detective adventure: the old-fashioned, donnish creator of the classic *Alice in Wonderland* and the muscular, exuberant young genius who was soon to give the world the beloved Sherlock Holmes stories. Doyle and his wife, Touie, are visiting Oxford to see their friend Dodgson, who Doyle hopes will grant him access to the Bodleian Library to research his latest novel, but his impertinent request is frostily denied by the inflexible Dodgson. Various things are going on at the university. At Christ Church, Dodgson's college, the wine cellar has been mysteriously depleted and a female student is being blackmailed. She finds that it may have something to do with photographs Dodgson took of her as a child. On the very evening of the Doyles' arrival, a body is found on the college grounds. When Dodgson becomes the chief suspect, Doyle quickly goes to work trying to clear his friend of the murder.

Where it's reviewed:
Booklist, July 2001, page 1989
Library Journal, August 2001, page 170

Other books by the same author:
The Problem of the Evil Editor, 2000
The Problem of the Spiteful Spiritualist, 1999
The Problem of the Missing Miss, 1998

Other books you might like:
William Hjortsberg, *Nevermore*, 1994
Robin Paige, *Death at Bishop's Keep*, 1994
William J. Palmer, *The Don and Mr. Dickens*, 2000
Walter Satterthwait, *Escapade*, 1995
Donald S. Thomas, *Mad Hatter Summer*, 1983

188

R.D. ROSEN

Dead Ball

(New York: Walker, 2001)

Story type: Private Detective
Series: Harvey Blissberg. Number 5
Subject(s): Sports/Baseball; Racism; American South
Major character(s): Harvey Blissberg, Detective—Private, Sports Figure (former pro baseball player); Moss Cooley, Sports Figure (baseball player); Mickey Slavin, Television Personality (ESPN reporter)
Time period(s): 2000s
Locale(s): Providence, Rhode Island; Atlanta, Georgia

Summary: Fifteen years ago a much younger Harvey Blissberg was playing center field for the Providence Jewels, a baseball expansion team with a dismal record but plenty of attitude. Since then he's been working as a private eye with occasional gigs as a motivational speaker, and now he's called back to his old team in the role of an investigator. Their star player is a black outfielder named Moss Cooley who is closing in on one of baseball's most sacred records—Joe DiMaggio's 56-game hitting streak. However, somebody out there doesn't like him; he's just gotten a decapitated lawn jockey in the mail, the meaning of which is all too clear. Harvey follows the trail of hatred to Atlanta, Georgia, and along the way exposes some nasty truths about lingering racism in the game and the country. He gets support from his longtime live-in girlfriend, ESPN reporter Mickey Slavin, her father, and Moss himself and his wife, Cherry Ann. Readers, who have missed the baseball background that made Rosen's first book such a knockout, will be glad to see Harvey back in his old milieu, even on the sidelines.

Where it's reviewed:
Booklist, September 1, 2001, page 57
Publishers Weekly, October 1, 2001, page 41

Other books by the same author:
World of Hurt, 1994
Saturday Night Dead, 1988
Fadeaway, 1986
Strike Three, You're Dead, 1984

Other books you might like:
Michael Bowen, *Fielder's Choice*, 1991
Crabbe Evers, *The Duffy House Series*, 1991-
David F. Nighbert, *Squeezeplay*, 1992
Robert B. Parker, *Mortal Stakes*, 1975
Troy Soos, *The Mickey Rawlings Series*, 1994-

189

REBECCA ROTHENBERG
TAFFY CANNON, Co-Author

The Tumbleweed Murders

(Santa Barbara, California: Perseverance, 2001)

Story type: Amateur Detective
Series: Claire Sharples. Number 4
Subject(s): Country Music; History; Oil
Major character(s): Claire Sharples, Scientist (plant pathologist), Detective—Amateur
Time period(s): 2000s
Locale(s): Bakersfield, California; San Joaquin Valley, California

Summary: While she's searching down an orchard afflicted with peach rot, Claire runs into Jewell Scoggins, formerly known as country singer Cherokee Rose of The Texas Tumbleweeds. She's present when a 50-year-old skeleton is unearthed on the banks of the Kern River, where she finally locates the peach orchard (doomed eventually to become a housing development) and determines the cause of the disease. Going back to Jewell's trailer for another visit, Claire finds the woman dead, and although she barely knew her, she's deeply affected by her death and decides to put together some sort of memorial service for her. As she investigates Jewell's past, she has a sense that someone is following her and nearly has a couple of dangerous mishaps. Meanwhile, she's trying to sort out her feelings for her colleague Ramon Covarrubias, which wouldn't be difficult except for the fact that he's married. The author died before the book was completed; it has been ably finished by her friend and fellow writer Cannon.

Where it's reviewed:
Publishers Weekly, August 27, 2001, page 59

Other books by the same author:
The Shy Tulip Murders, 1996
The Dandelion Murders, 1994
The Bulrush Murders, 1991

Other books you might like:
Richard Barre, *Blackheart Highway*, 1995
Earlene Fowler, *The Benni Harper Series*, 1994-
Karen Kijewski, *Honky Tonk Kat*, 1996
Marcia Muller, *The Broken Promise Land*, 1996
Cecelia Tishy, *Fall to Pieces*, 2000

190

GREG RUCKA

Critical Space

(New York: Bantam, 2001)

Story type: Action/Adventure
Series: Atticus Kodiak. Number 5
Subject(s): Suspense; Kidnapping
Major character(s): Atticus Kodiak, Bodyguard; Antonia Ainsley-Hunter, Noblewoman; Drama, Murderer (assassin)
Time period(s): 2000s
Locale(s): New York, New York

Summary: Atticus has turned his protection agency, KTMH Security, into a successful business, largely because he and his colleagues are not only well-trained but willing to risk their own lives to protect those of their clients. Their latest is Lady Antonia Ainsley-Hunter, a selfless young aristocrat who has dedicated her life to child rights advocacy and is in the U.S. on a fund-raising mission. The job goes smoothly enough until another young woman, Drama, a member of an elite and deadly group of international assassins known as "The Ten," with whom Atticus has tangled in the past, resurfaces, threatening Antonia's life unless Atticus will agree to undertake a most unusual mission: become her own personal bodyguard. It's an offer he can't refuse if he's going to fulfill his promise to Antonia, but he knows his job will be dangerous not only for himself but for others.

Where it's reviewed:
Booklist, August 2001, page 2099
Publishers Weekly, July 30, 2001, page 55

Other books by the same author:
Finder, 1999
Shooting at Midnight, 1999
Smoker, 1998
Keeper, 1997

Other books you might like:
Lawrence Block, *Hit List*, 2000
Stephen Greenleaf, *Ellipsis*, 2000
Robert B. Parker, *Looking for Rachel Wallace*, 1980
Thomas Perry, *The Jane Whitefield Series*, 1995-
Stephen White, *The Program*, 2001

191

CHARLOTTE MURRAY RUSSELL

The Message of the Mute Dog

(Boulder, Colorado: Rue Morgue Press, 2001)

Story type: Amateur Detective; Humor
Series: Jane Amanda Edwards. Book 7
Subject(s): World War II; Small Town Life; Nazis
Major character(s): Jane Amanda Edwards, Spinster, Detective—Amateur
Time period(s): 1940s (1941)
Locale(s): Rockport, Illinois

Summary: Jane Amanda Edwards is a full-figured, shamelessly nosy spinster who lives in reduced circumstances with her sister, brother, and long-suffering housekeeper Theresa in their family home in Rockport, Illinois, a thinly disguised version of Rock Island. Their circumstances are reduced only because none of the three siblings has ever seen the need to get a job, that is, until Jane Amanda's brother Arthur is overcome by a fit of patriotism and hires on at a local defense plant. Pearl Harbor is still months away, but Arthur is convinced that the plant is overrun with Nazi saboteurs and that it's his duty to apprehend them. Instead, when someone does try to blow the place up, it's Arthur who's accused of the crime. As always, Jane Amanda is quick to defend him, even though it's immediately apparent to the police that Arthur was incapable of the crime. Once more, Jane Amanda rides roughshod over all parties involved, including her old friend, police captain George Hammond, and gets into one scrape after another until the mystery is solved. Recipes from Theresa's kitchen are included. Originally published in 1942.

Where it's reviewed:
Publishers Weekly, October 29, 2001, page 39

Other books by the same author:
Cook Up a Crime, 1998 (originally published in 1952)
Hand Me a Crime, 1949
Ill Met in Mexico, 1948
The Bad Neighbor Murder, 1946
No Time for Crime, 1945

Other books you might like:
M.C. Beaton, *The Agatha Raisin Series*, 1992-
Stuart Palmer, *The Hildegarde Withers Series*, 1932-1969
Elizabeth Peters, *The Amelia Peabody Series*, 1975-
Joyce Porter, *The Honourable Constance Ethel Morrison-Burke Series*, 1970-1979
Mary Roberts Rinehart, *The Tish Series*, 1911-1938

192

JAMES SALLIS

Ghost of a Flea

(New York: Walker, 2001)

Story type: Private Detective
Series: Lew Griffin. Book 6
Subject(s): Fathers and Sons; African Americans; Literature
Major character(s): Lew Griffin, Detective—Private, Writer
Time period(s): 2000s
Locale(s): New Orleans, Louisiana

Summary: In the sixth installment of his Lew Griffin saga, the author brings this unconventional series to a close. Lew, a black poet and academic who hasn't written a book in years and no longer teaches, spends much of his time reflecting on his past and philosophizing about life and literature in general. His son David has disappeared again, and what detecting he does consists of finding out who wrote threatening letters to a friend and who, if anyone, is poisoning the pigeons in the park. The ambience of the book is noir, existentialist, melancholic, overflowing with literary allusions, and in-your-face intellectual—not the easiest or most entertaining reading, and not all readers will find it worth the trouble. Those who go in for this sort of thing though, will find it challenging rather than tedious, with a satisfying if bittersweet ending.

Where it's reviewed:
Library Journal, December 2001, page 178
Publishers Weekly, November 12, 2001, page 39

Other books by the same author:
Bluebottle, 1999
Eye of the Cricket, 1997
Black Hornet, 1994
Moth, 1993
The Long-Legged Fly, 1992

Other books you might like:
Paul Auster, *The New York Trilogy*, 1985-1986
Robert Greer, *The CJ Floyd Series*, 1996-
Gar Anthony Haywood, *The Aaron Gunner Series*, 1988-
Walter Mosley, *The Easy Rawlins Series*, 1990-
Robert Skinner, *The Wesley Farrell Series*, 1997-

193

HAROLD SCHECHTER

The Hum Bug

(New York: Pocket, 2001)

Story type: Historical; Amateur Detective
Series: Edgar Allan Poe. Book 2
Subject(s): Literature; History; Museums
Major character(s): Edgar Allan Poe, Historical Figure, Writer; P.T. Barnum, Historical Figure, Entertainer
Time period(s): 1840s (1844)
Locale(s): New York, New York

Summary: Poe and his fragile young wife, Sissy, have just moved to New York and been joined by her mother, with whom they have set up housekeeping in a charming cottage in a semi-rural area of the city. Sissy begs Poe to take her to the recently opened American Museum of notorious showman P.T. Barnum, where Poe is horrified to see one fake exhibit after another capturing the public fancy. He writes a scathing indictment of Barnum's fraudulent practices and is surprised when Barnum shows up on his doorstep, not to protest his expose, but to beg for his help. A murder has just taken place, which replicates in gory detail a grisly tableau in Barnum's wax museum, and he has become a suspect himself in the eyes of the police. Poe agrees to help the showman clear his name, and his investigation soon leads him to a dangerous madman.

Where it's reviewed:
Booklist, October 1, 2001, page 303
Library Journal, September 15, 2001, page 117
Mystery News, October/November 2001, page 21
Publishers Weekly, October 15, 2001, page 49

Other books by the same author:
Nevermore, 1999

Other books you might like:
George Egon Hatvary, *The Murder of Edgar Allan Poe*, 1997
William Hjortsberg, *Nevermore*, 1994
Manny Meyers, *The Last Mystery of Edgar Allan Poe*, 1978
Randall Silvis, *On Night's Shore*, 2001
Andrew Sinclair, *The Facts in the Case of E.A. Poe*, 1980

194

KATE SEDLEY (Pseudonym of Brenda Margaret Lilian Clarke)

The Weaver's Inheritance

(New York: St. Martin's Minotaur, 2001)

Story type: Historical
Series: Roger the Chapman. Number 8
Subject(s): Middle Ages; Christmas; Identity
Major character(s): Roger the Chapman, Peddler, Detective—Amateur
Time period(s): 15th century (1476)
Locale(s): Bristol, England

Summary: Once a novice at Glastonbury Abbey, Roger left the order five years ago for life on the open road as a chapman, or peddler selling sundry goods from village to village. He fathers a daughter, Elizabeth, but his short marriage to her mother, Lillis, ends tragically when she dies in childbirth. Now Elizabeth lives with her grandmother Margaret Walker, whose home has become Roger's during the intervals when he's not traveling. He's settled there for the winter and the Christmas season, planning only on short day journeys in the area and getting reacquainted with his little Bess, now two years old. Roger is amused by his good-hearted mother-in-law's attempts to find him a suitable second wife; this time it's a young widow, a distant cousin with a child near Bess' age, who is coming to visit. He's also approached by a young woman, the daughter of a wealthy weaver, whose long-lost brother has turned up after having been presumed murdered six years earlier. Alison Weaver's father is overjoyed, but she suspects the man is an impostor and is loath to share her inheritance with him. One of the charms of this solid series is its attention to the everyday life of ordinary people in late medieval times.

Where it's reviewed:
Booklist, August 2001, page 2099
Library Journal, September 1, 2001, page 239
Mystery News, October/November 2001, page 21
Publishers Weekly, August 20, 2001, page 61

Other books by the same author:
The Wicked Winter, 1999
The Brothers of Glastonbury, 1997
Eve of St. Hyacinth, 1996
The Holy Innocents, 1994
The Weaver's Tale, 1993

Other books you might like:
P.C. Doherty, *Dove Amongst the Hawks*, 1990
P.C. Doherty, *The Rose Demon*, 1997
Margaret Frazer, *The Dame Frevisse Series*, 1992-
C.L. Grace, *The Kathryn Swinbrooke Series*, 1993-
Sheri Holman, *A Stolen Tongue*, 1997

195

MALCOLM SHUMAN

The Last Mayan

(New York: Avon, 2001)

Story type: Amateur Detective
Series: Alan Graham. Number 5
Subject(s): Archaeology; Mexicans; Pre-Columbian History
Major character(s): Alan Graham, Archaeologist (contract), Detective—Amateur
Time period(s): 2000s
Locale(s): Lubaanah, Mexico (Yucatan); Merida, Mexico (Yucatan)

Summary: The idea that visitors from the Old World came to Central America long before the conquistadores has been knocking around for many years, and Shuman, though inclined toward disbelief himself, uses the notion as the background for this latest case for contract archaeologist Alan Graham. He's in the Yucatan Peninsula on a dig with Pepper, his girlfriend and colleague, investigating a controversial discovery that may prove the so-called diffusion theory to be right—or may turn out to be a colossal hoax. Either way, Alan and Pepper find their path to be fraught with danger after two people turn up dead and it becomes clear they might be next. The author has also written as M.K. Shuman and M.S. Karl.

Other books by the same author:
Past Dying, 2000
Assassin's Blood, 1999
Burial Ground, 1998
The Meriwether Journal, 1998

Other books you might like:
Gary Alexander, *The Luis Balam Series*, 1993-
Sylvia Angus, *Dead to Rites*, 1978
Desmond Bagley, *The Vivero Letter*, 1968
Aaron Elkins, *Curses!*, 1989
Lyn Hamilton, *The Xibalba Murders*, 1997

196

ROBERT SKINNER

Pale Shadow

(Scottsdale, Arizona: Poisoned Pen, 2001)

Story type: Historical
Series: Wesley Farrell. Number 5
Subject(s): African Americans; Race Relations; American South
Major character(s): Wesley Farrell, Businessman (nightclub owner)
Time period(s): 1940s (1940)
Locale(s): New Orleans, Louisiana

Summary: Wesley is a light-skinned, gray-eyed man of mixed blood, who is successfully passing for white in Jim Crow Louisiana, but less is made of his African American ancestry here than in earlier books in this series. His old friend and former partner, Luis Martinez, has stolen some plates for counterfeiting 20- and 50-dollar bills, and Wes wants to warn him that a very dangerous man, Dixie Ray Chavez, has been hired to hunt him down. Chavez is prepared to either torture or kill him—whatever it takes to get the plates back. The related murder of a black woman is being investigated by the Negro Detective Squad, and her connection with the counterfeiters soon comes to the attention of both the FBI and the Treasury Department. As usual, there's a strong sense of place and an intriguing cast of secondary characters.

Where it's reviewed:
Library Journal, August 2001, page 170
Mystery News, August/September 2001, page 19
Publishers Weekly, July 16, 2001, page 161

Other books by the same author:
Blood to Drink, 2000
Daddy's Gone A-Hunting, 1999
Cat-Eyed Trouble, 1998
Skin Deep, Blood Red, 1997

Other books you might like:
David Fulmer, *Chasing the Devil's Tail*, 2001
Barbara Hambly, *The Benjamin January Series*, 1997-
William Heffernan, *Beulah Hill*, 2001
Chester Himes, *The Coffin Ed Johnson/Grave Digger Jones Series*, 1957-1983
Walter Mosley, *The Easy Rawlins Series*, 1990-

197

KARIN SLAUGHTER

Blindsighted

(New York: Morrow, 2001)

Story type: Police Procedural
Subject(s): American South; Small Town Life; Serial Killers
Major character(s): Sara Linton, Doctor (coroner, pediatrician); Jeffrey Tolliver, Police Officer (chief); Lena Adams, Detective—Police
Time period(s): 2000s
Locale(s): Heartsdale, Georgia

Summary: When Sara discovers a young woman college professor murdered, raped, and sadistically mutilated, she is as horrified as the rest of the townspeople. A pediatrician who doubles as the town coroner, Sara is required to perform a postmortem on the body, during which she discovers other evidence of the killer's extreme sadism. Sara's ex-husband, Jeffrey Tolliver, is the police chief, and the two of them must carefully navigate their relationship as they work together on the case. His detective, Lena Adams, has a personal stake in the case, as her sister was also a victim of the killer. When it becomes clear they have a full-blown serial killer at large, it also becomes clear Sara herself may be his next victim. First novel.

Where it's reviewed:
Booklist, August 2001, page 2099
Deadly Pleasures, Autumn 2001, page 12
Library Journal, August 2001, page 166
Mystery News, October/November 2001, page 29
Publishers Weekly, August 6, 2001, page 59

Other books you might like:
Patricia Cornwell, *The Kay Scarpetta Series*, 1990-
Marsha Landreth, *The Samantha Turner Series*, 1992-
Margaret Maron, *The Deborah Knott Series*, 1992-
Kathy Reichs, *The Tempe Brennan Series*, 1997-
Anna Salter, *The Michael Stone Series*, 1997-

198

MARY-ANN TIRONE SMITH

Love Her Madly

(New York: Holt, 2002)

Story type: Psychological Suspense
Subject(s): Prisoners and Prisons; Religion; Psychological
Major character(s): Penelope "Poppy" Rice, FBI Agent; Rona Leigh Glueck, Convict (on death row)
Time period(s): 2000s
Locale(s): Gatesville, Texas; Washington, District of Columbia

Summary: As the new crime lab director at the FBI, Poppy swiftly reorganizes the operation in steamroller fashion and then, looking for a new challenge, asks to be allowed to reopen the case of Rona Leigh Glueck, shortly to become the first woman executed in Texas since the Civil War. Poppy has gotten it into her head that Rona Leigh was just too young, too frail, and too ill to have savagely hacked another woman to death with a heavy axe, and she mistrusts certain statements in the coroner's report. Her investigation takes her to the Texas death-row prison housing Rona Leigh, now a born-again Christian who repents her evil ways and has become something of a poster child for certain religious groups. Poppy is a brash, smart-mouthed, and stubborn investigator, and there are plenty of amusing exchanges between her and other quirky characters in this slickly written tale, which is capped by a real surprise ending. Poppy made her first appearance as a supporting character in a previous suspense novel by the author, who has also produced several mainstream works of fiction.

Where it's reviewed:
Library Journal, November 15, 2001, page 98
Publishers Weekly, November 25, 2001, page 39

Other books by the same author:
An American Killing, 1998

Other books you might like:
Janet Evanovich, *The Stephanie Plum Series*, 1994-
Susan Isaacs, *Long Time No See*, 2001
Nancy Pickard, *The Whole Truth*, 2000
Mary Willis Walker, *The Red Scream*, 1994
Marianne Wesson, *Render Up the Body*, 1998

199

KEITH SNYDER

The Night Men

(New York: Walker, 2001)

Story type: Amateur Detective
Series: Jason Keltner. Book 4
Subject(s): Music and Musicians; Coming-of-Age; Prejudice
Major character(s): Jason Keltner, Musician, Detective—Amateur
Time period(s): 2000s; 1980s
Locale(s): New York, New York (Brooklyn); San Fernando Valley, California; Philadelphia, Pennsylvania

Summary: Jason, who's visiting his girlfriend in New York, comes to the aid of a gay friend whose newly opened Brooklyn music store has just been vandalized. It brings back memories of an earlier time when, as a teenager, Jason helped a friend guard against some neighborhood thugs determined to paint swastikas on his house. Snyder has a special insight into the world of bright, decent, but socially inept adolescent boys, and he develops the moving backstory of how they risk everything to be loyal to one another. The mystery consists of why the music store is being targeted, how its history is connected to present events, and exactly who a 70s-era musician called The Inscrutable Whom is.

Where it's reviewed:
Publishers Weekly, October 8, 2001, page 48

Other books by the same author:
Trouble Comes Back, 1999
Coffin's Got the Dead Guy on the Inside, 1998
Show Control, 1995

Other books you might like:
Timothy Hallinan, *Everything but the Squeal*, 1990
Dennis Lehane, *Mystic River*, 2001
Jonathan Lethem, *Motherless Brooklyn*, 1999
Robert B. Parker, *Early Autumn*, 1981
Jenny Siler, *Easy Money*, 1999

200

TROY SOOS

Island of Tears

(New York: Kensington, 2001)

Story type: Historical
Subject(s): History; Social Conditions; Politics
Major character(s): Marshall Webb, Writer; Rebecca Davies, Activist
Time period(s): 1890s (1892)
Locale(s): New York, New York

Summary: Looking for some background material for his next dime novel—he writes them to supplement his income as a contributor to *Harper's Weekly*—Marshall Webb is among those present when the first immigrant ship docks at newly opened Ellis Island on January 1, 1892. One of the passengers is 14-year-old Christina van der Weals, a Dutch girl who claims to be meeting her cousin, a dancer. Then Christina disappears and her cousin knows nothing about her arrival. When Marshall starts investigating, he runs into Rebecca Davies, a wealthy young woman who operates Chandler House, a shelter for battered women and runaway children. Rebecca introduces him to the realities of what often lies in wait for young immigrant women: white slavery, forced prostitution, and abuse, as well as the corrupt indifference of the Tammany Hall political machine to such social problems. There is a murder and some detection, but the focus of the book is the social and historical background to the story. The author also writes a series of historical mysteries featuring baseball player Mickey Rawlins.

Where it's reviewed:
Booklist, October 15, 2001, page 384
Library Journal, November 1, 2001, page 136
Publishers Weekly, October 8, 2001, page 40

Other books by the same author:
Hanging Curve, 1999
Cincinnati Red Stalkings, 1998
Hunting a Detroit Tiger, 1997
Murder at Wrigley Field, 1996
Murder at Ebbets Field, 1995

Other books you might like:
Rhys Bowen, *Murphy's Law*, 2001
Karen Rose Cercone, *The Helen Sorby/Miles Kachigan Series*, 1997-
Jeanne M. Dams, *The Hilda Johansson Series*, 1999-
Maan Meyers, *The House on Mulberry Street*, 1996
Victoria Thompson, *The Sarah Brandt Series*, 1999-

201

MICKEY SPILLANE

Together We Kill

(Waterville, Maine: Five Star, 2001)

Story type: Collection
Subject(s): Short Stories

Summary: In the wake of two recent omnibus editions of Spillane's long-out-of-print early novels, editor Max Allan Collins has collected eight of this legendary writer's previously uncollected short stories, originally published between 1952 and 1975. Three of them are based on Spillane's own experiences as a pilot; one is a Mike Hammer story; and the others range from typically macho hard-boiled noir to nostalgia and even science fiction. The editor provides an informative introduction on Spillane, who was a hugely best-selling author in the 1940s and 1950s and whose tough-guy hero, private avenger Mike Hammer, loathed Communists and intellectuals, was a moral absolutist on issues of good and evil, frequently indulged in vigilante justice, and didn't mind in the least killing people when he deemed it necessary.

Other books by the same author:
The Mike Hammer Collection. Volume 1, 2001 (contains *I, the Jury*, *My Gun Is Quick*, *Vengeance Is Mine!*)
The Mike Hammer Collection. Volume 2, 2001 (contains *One Lonely Night*, *The Big Kill*, *Kiss Me Deadly*)
Black Alley, 1996
The Killing Man, 1989
Tomorrow I Die, 1984 (short stories; Max Allan Collins, editor)

Other books you might like:
Raymond Chandler, *The Midnight Raymond Chandler*, 1971
short stories
Max Allan Collins, *Kisses of Death*, 2001
short stories
Joe Gores, *Stakeout on Page Street*, 2000
short stories
Dashiell Hammett, *Hammett: Crime Stories and Other Writings*, 2001
short stories
Ross Macdonald, *Ross Mcdonald's Lew Archer, Private Investigator*, 1977
short stories

202

RICHARD STARK (Pseudonym of Donald E. Westlake)

Firebreak

(New York: Mysterious, 2001)

Story type: Psychological Suspense
Series: Parker. Book 20
Subject(s): Crime and Criminals
Major character(s): Parker, Thief; Larry Lloyd, Convict (ex-con)
Time period(s): 2000s
Locale(s): Havre, Montana; New York, New York; Chicago, Illinois

Summary: Parker is in the middle of killing a man in his garage when the phone rings. It's one of his colleagues with a plan to steal art treasures from the Montana lodge of a dot-com billionaire. The man in Parker's garage is an assassin who'd been sent to kill him, and once he's dispatched the hit man, Parker needs to find a way to dispose of the body and learn who hired him. Then he heads for Montana, where the job turns out to be trickier and far more dangerous than promised, and it's further complicated by the volatile behavior of the ex-con who plotted it all out, Larry Lloyd, a man with a few scores of his own to settle. Even readers with a low tolerance for amoral antiheroes will be drawn in by the author's terse, polished prose and powerful storytelling ability, as well as the sheer skill and common sense Parker displays in carrying out his missions. As Donald Westlake, the author writes a comic series about bumbling thief John Dortmunder, along with many stand-alone thrillers and comic mysteries.

Where it's reviewed:
Booklist, September 15, 2001, page 200
Library Journal, September 15, 2001, page 114
New York Times Book Review, December 9, 2001, page 29
Publishers Weekly, October 1, 2001, page 40

Other books by the same author:
Flashfire, 2000
Backflash, 1999
Comeback, 1997
Butcher's Moon, 1974
Plunder Squad, 1972

Other books you might like:
Lawrence Block, *The Bernie Rhodenbarr Series*, 1977-
Lawrence Block, *Hit List*, 2000
Anthony Bourdain, *Gone Bamboo*, 1997
Max Allan Collins, *The Quarry Series*, 1976-1977
Patricia Highsmith, *The Tom Ripley Series*, 1955-1980

203

SERENA STIER

Deadly Illumination

(Dallas, Texas: Durban House, 2001)

Story type: Historical
Subject(s): Women's Rights; Victorian Period; Judaism
Major character(s): Florence Tod, Spinster, Cousin (of Belle); Isabella Stewart "Belle" Gardner, Historical Figure, Cousin (of Florence); Jeremy Hampton, Detective—Private (Pinkerton)
Time period(s): 1890s (1890)
Locale(s): New York, New York; Newport, Rhode Island

Summary: Florence and her married cousin, Belle, discover the body of John Pierpoint Morgan's librarian, who ingested poison embedded in an illumination of a medieval manuscript. Determined to solve the mystery themselves, the two young women turn detective, crossing paths with a Pinkerton agent, Jeremy Hampton, who is attracted to Flo. Their investigation takes them to Newport, Rhode Island, then a playground for the wealthiest industrialists and robber barons. Besides Belle and her friend J.P. Morgan, other historical figures include Edith Wharton. There are several side stories: the position of Jews in New York society at the turn of the century, the burgeoning women's rights movement, and the contrast between the extravagant lifestyles of wealthy capitalists and the squalor of the tenements and ghettos housing the poor. First novel.

Other books you might like:
Caleb Carr, *The Alienist*, 1994
Mary Kruger, *Masterpiece of Murder*, 1997
Maan Meyers, *The House on Mulberry Street*, 1996
Troy Soos, *Island of Tears*, 2001
Daniel Stashower, *The Dime Museum Murders*, 1999

204

CARSTEN STROUD

Black Water Transit

(New York: Delacorte, 2001)

Story type: Action/Adventure
Subject(s): Crime and Criminals; Fathers and Sons; Guns and Gun Control
Major character(s): Jack Vermillion, Businessman, Veteran (Vietnam); Casey Spandau, Detective—Police
Time period(s): 2000s
Locale(s): New York, New York

Summary: The book takes its title from the shipping company owned by Jack Vermillion, who is desperately trying to cut a better deal for his imprisoned ex-junkie son Danny, whose life is being threatened by other inmates in a maximum security prison. When he's approached by one of his clients, retired army colonel Earl Pike, about illegally shipping Pike's personal gun collection out of the country, Jack realizes he finally has something to trade the feds for transferring Danny to a safer facility. Unfortunately, his deal with the ATF goes terribly wrong and instead of delivering Pike to them, he's caught up in a crossfire that leaves several federal agents and an NYPD cop dead, and a whole lot of other law enforcement types anxious to pin the fiasco on Jack. Meanwhile, NYPD detective Casey Spandau has been assigned a double homicide she's getting nowhere with, although she's certain the killer is Earl Pike. The author has also written nonfiction about the police and the military.

Where it's reviewed:
Booklist, May 1, 2001, page 1642
Library Journal, August 2001, page 166
Mystery News, October/November 2001, page 17
Publishers Weekly, June 15, 2001, page 44

Other books by the same author:
Lizardskin, 1992
Sniper's Moon, 1990

Other books you might like:
Ethan Black, *The Conrad Voort Series*, 1999-
Michael Connelly, *The Harry Bosch Series*, 1992-
Robert Crais, *Hostage*, 2001
Stephen Hunter, *Point of Impact*, 1993
John Sandford, *The Lucas Davenport Series*, 1989-

205

MARCIA TALLEY

Occasion of Revenge

(New York: Dell, 2001)

Story type: Amateur Detective
Series: Hannah Ives. Number 3
Subject(s): Cancer; Christmas; Family
Major character(s): Hannah Ives, Survivor (breast cancer), Single Parent
Time period(s): 2000s
Locale(s): Annapolis, Maryland; Chestertown, Maryland

Summary: Since her battle with breast cancer, Hannah has learned to savor life and in particular her family, who have given her much on which to focus her energies. When her widowed father decides to marry a saucy young woman who has outlived three husbands and who is openly wearing jewelry that once belonged to Hannah's mother, warning bells go off for Hannah, even as she recognizes his decision has made him absurdly happy. When he disappears right after a party for the about-to-be-married couple, Hannah really begins to worry, and as time goes by, she becomes desperate to find him.

Other books by the same author:
Unbreathed Memories, 2000
Sing It to Her Bones, 1999

Other books you might like:
Helen Chappell, *The Hollis Ball/Sam Westcott Series*, 1996-
Cathie John, *The Kate Cavanaugh Series*, 1997-
Barbara Lee, *The Eve Elliott Series*, 1997-
Laura Lippman, *The Sugar House*, 2000
Marlys Millhiser, *It's Murder Going Home*, 1996

206

WILLIAM G. TAPPLY

Past Tense

(New York: St. Martin's Press, 2001)

Story type: Private Detective
Series: Brady Coyne. Number 18
Subject(s): Stalking; Missing Persons; Secrets
Major character(s): Brady Coyne, Lawyer, Detective—Private; Evie Banyon, Girlfriend (of Brady)
Time period(s): 2000s
Locale(s): Boston, Massachusetts; Cape Cod, Massachusetts

Summary: Brady Coyne's small, carefully chosen clientele leaves him with plenty of time on his hands for leisure activities, including crime-solving. He is also able to enjoy such personal pursuits as fishing and the company of Evie Banyon, with whom he is currently weekending in Cape Cod. Their romantic holiday together is marred by the appearance of Larry Scott, a man from her past who has been stalking Evie for several years. Evie decks him in a restaurant, he and Brady get physical in the parking lot, and then the next morning at their cottage Brady wakes up to the sound of Evie's screaming, only to find Larry lying dead at her feet. They are the obvious suspects, of course, but no arrests are made and they return to Boston, where Evie promptly goes missing. Brady, who realizes he really knows very little about Evie's personal life other than the fact she is a hospital administrator who formerly lived in Cortland, has to find her if he is to learn the truth about Larry's murder.

Where it's reviewed:
Booklist, September 1, 2001, page 57
Library Journal, September 1, 2001, page 239

Other books by the same author:
Scar Tissue, 2000
Muscle Memory, 1999
Cutter's Run, 1998
Close to the Bone, 1996

The Seventh Enemy, 1995

Other books you might like:
Rick Boyer, *The Doc Adams Series*, 1982-
Philip R. Craig, *The J.W. Jackson Series*, 1989-
Loren D. Estleman, *The Amos Walker Series*, 1980-
Stephen Greenleaf, *The John Marshall Tanner Series*, 1979-
Jeremiah Healy, *The John Francis Cuddy Series*, 1984-

207

LOU JANE TEMPLE

Red Beans and Vice

(New York: St. Martin's Press, 2001)

Story type: Amateur Detective
Series: Heaven Lee. Number 6
Subject(s): Cooks and Cooking; Slavery; Convents
Major character(s): Heaven Lee, Restaurateur, Cook
Time period(s): 2000s
Locale(s): New Orleans, Louisiana; Kansas City, Missouri

Summary: Heaven Lee is only too ready to take a break from her restaurant and participate in a fund-raiser with her old friend, Mary Beth Whitten, and other members of their women chefs' group to benefit the Sisters of the Holy Trinity in New Orleans. When the women arrive at the convent, their reunion is disrupted by a crusading TV reporter who condemns the historic order as being racist, citing incidents of slavery in its past and accusing the women chefs of knowingly supporting these practices. No sooner has this bombshell been dropped than a sacred cross, brought over with the first nuns in the order in 1727, is discovered missing. Further incidents follow: an infestation of termites, deadly insecticides sprayed in the convent herb garden, and finally the murder of Mary's husband, a well-known coffee importer. Many tempting recipes for Cajun and Creole dishes featured in the story are included.

Where it's reviewed:
Booklist, July 2001, page 1989
Mystery News, August/September 2001, page 29
Publishers Weekly, July 2, 2001, page 56

Other books by the same author:
The Cornbread Killer, 1999
Bread on Arrival, 1998
A Stiff Risotto, 1997
Revenge of the Barbecue Queens, 1997
Death by Rhubarb, 1996

Other books you might like:
Diane Mott Davidson, *The Goldy Bear Schulz Series*, 1990-
Barbara Hambly, *The Benjamin January Series*, 1997-
Peter King, *The Gourmet Detective Series*, 1996-
Cecile Lamalle, *The Charly Poisson Series*, 1999-
Nancy Pickard, *The Mrs. Eugenia Potter Series*, 1993-
a continuation of the Virginia Rich culinary series

208

CHARLES TODD (Pseudonym of Charles Todd and Caroline Todd)

Watchers of Time

(New York: Bantam, 2001)

Story type: Historical; Police Procedural
Series: Inspector Ian Rutledge. Book 5
Subject(s): Mental Illness; World War I; Clergy
Major character(s): Ian Rutledge, Police Officer, Veteran (World War I)
Time period(s): 1910s (1919)
Locale(s): Osterley, England (Norfolk)

Summary: Once again Rutledge, a shell-shocked veteran of World War I whose return to his prewar job as a police officer is largely an embarrassment to his superiors at Scotland Yard, is sent away from London on what appears to be a routine investigation, this time to confirm that the Osterley police indeed have the right man in custody for the murder of the local priest. Everywhere Rutledge goes he's accompanied by the jeering voice of Hamish, the young Scots corporal he ordered shot in the field because he refused to fight and whose presence he has never revealed to anyone, not even his sister. When he arrives in Osterley, he soon suspects the police do have the wrong man and so starts an investigation, not always welcome, of his own, beginning with a dying man who asked for absolution from both his vicar and the priest who was murdered. The mystery goes back to events some years in the past, including the sinking of the *Titanic*, involving characters long since dead. In solving the case he meets May Trent, a haunted young woman who may be just the person to save Rutledge from his private demons.

Where it's reviewed:
Booklist, October 1, 2001, page 303
Library Journal, October 1, 2001, page 147
New York Times Book Review, November 25, 2001, page 21
Publishers Weekly, September 24, 2001, page 72

Other books by the same author:
Legacy of the Dead, 2000
Search the Dark, 1999
Wings of Fire, 1998
A Test of Wills, 1996

Other books you might like:
Rennie Airth, *River of Darkness*, 1999
Michael Gilbert, *Into Battle*, 1997
Robert Goddard, *In Pale Battalions*, 1988
Laurie R. King, *A Monstrous Regiment of Women*, 1995
Gillian Linscott, *Absent Friends*, 1999

209

PETER TREMAYNE (Pseudonym of Peter Beresford Ellis)

Act of Mercy

(New York: St. Martin's Minotaur, 2001)

Story type: Historical
Series: Sister Fidelma. Book 8
Subject(s): Religion; Voyages and Travels; Middle Ages

Major character(s): Sister Fidelma, Religious (nun), Scholar
Time period(s): 7th century (666)
Locale(s): Cashel, Ireland; Bay of Ardmore, Ireland; At Sea

Summary: The night before *The Barnacle Goose* is set to sail for Iberia carrying its cargo of pilgrims destined for the shrine of Santiago de Compostela, a young woman on the passenger list is found brutally murdered in the local inn. Then, on the first night out from the Bay of Ardmore, another passenger disappears, the victim of either an accident or murder. Fidelma, a nun who is also an advocate of the Brehon law courts, is on board and feels compelled to investigate the incidents, and so the voyage she had envisioned as one of contemplation and reevaluation of her life turns into something quite different. The product of a surprisingly progressive society, Fidelma is one of the most complex and believable heroines in detective fiction set in medieval times.

Where it's reviewed:
Publishers Weekly, October 22, 2001, page 52

Other books by the same author:
The Monk Who Vanished, 2001
Valley of the Shadow, 2000
The Spider's Web, 1999
The Subtle Serpent, 1998
Suffer Little Children, 1997

Other books you might like:
Alys Clare, *The Abbess Helewise Series*, 1999-
Anthony Clarke, *Ordeal at Litchfield*, 1997
Margaret Frazer, *The Dame Frevisse Series*, 1992-
Sharan Newman, *Death Comes as Epiphany*, 1993
Albert Noyer, *The Saint's Day Deaths*, 2000

210

ALAN VANNEMAN

Sherlock Holmes and the Giant Rat of Sumatra

(New York: Carroll & Graf, 2001)

Story type: Historical
Subject(s): Historical; Victorian Period; Travel
Major character(s): Sherlock Holmes, Detective—Private; John Watson, Sidekick, Doctor
Time period(s): 1890s
Locale(s): London, England; Singapore

Summary: One of the many cases the great private investigator Sherlock Holmes referred to, but which his companion and chronicler John Watson never wrote up is that of the giant rat of Sumatra. It turns out that Watson's account had indeed been written, but lost for decades along with others concealed in the legendary battered tin dispatch box at Cox & Co. When Elizabeth Trent visits Holmes and Watson in their Baker Street flat, she implores them to clear her dead husband of embezzlement and suicide. However, within hours she herself is found dead, also the victim of an apparent suicide. The case eventually sends Holmes and Watson across the world, through Egypt, India, and the Far East, until they finally come face to face with Harat, the enormous rat who rules over the small country of Bada and whose evil agenda is somehow behind the murders. First novel.

Where it's reviewed:
Booklist, December 15, 2001, page 707
Publishers Weekly, December 3, 2001, page 43

Other books you might like:
Rick Boyer, *The Giant Rat of Sumatra*, 1976
Arthur Conan Doyle, *The Sherlock Holmes Series*, 1887-1927
Jamyang Norbu, *Sherlock Holmes: The Missing Years*, 2001
Larry Millett, *Sherlock Holmes and the Secret Alliance*, 2001
Wayne Worcester, *The Jewel of Covent Garden*, 2000

211

MINETTE WALTERS

The Shape of Snakes

(New York: Putnam, 2001)

Story type: Psychological Suspense
Subject(s): Mental Illness; Racism; Secrets
Major character(s): M. Ranelagh, Housewife, Narrator
Time period(s): 1990s (1999); 1970s (1978)
Locale(s): London, England; Leavenham, England (Dorset)

Summary: The narrator, known only as M. Ranelagh, is living in an unfashionable neighborhood of West London in 1978. The only black resident on the block is a woman known as ''Mad Annie'' Butts, who is reviled by her neighbors because of her skin color and her bizarre behavior, which is actually the result of Tourette's Syndrome. M. makes friendly overtures to the woman but is rebuffed, and then one day she finds her near death, lying in the gutter in the freezing rain with a fractured skull and a look of such pain and anguish on her face that M. is forever haunted by it. In fact, that one look governs her whole life. She wants to find Annie's killer and avenge her death, and she begins by confronting her neighbors and family members and continues by badgering the police and other authorities to keep the investigation open. Even when she and her husband move away from the neighborhood and live in various other parts of the world, she continues to be obsessed by the incident and to secretly correspond with various agencies over the matter.

Where it's reviewed:
Booklist, May 1, 2001, page 1643
Library Journal, June 1, 2001, page 219
Mystery News, October/November 2001, page 27
New York Times Book Review, July 22, 2001, page 22
Publishers Weekly, June 18, 2001, page 55

Other books by the same author:
The Breaker, 1999
The Echo, 1997
The Dark Room, 1996
The Scold's Bridle, 1994
The Sculptress, 1993

Other books you might like:
P.D. James, *The Adam Dalgliesh Series*, 1962-
Jonathan Lethem, *Motherless Brooklyn*, 1999
J. Wallis Martin, *A Likeness in Stone*, 1997
Barbara Vine, *Grasshopper*, 2000
Laura Wilson, *My Best Friend*, 2002

212

CHARLENE WEIR

A Cold Christmas

(New York: St. Martin's Press, 2001)

Story type: Police Procedural
Series: Susan Wren. Book 5
Subject(s): Identity, Concealed; Christmas; Small Town Life
Major character(s): Susan Wren, Police Officer (chief)
Time period(s): 2000s
Locale(s): Hampstead, Kansas

Summary: Susan Wren is married only four weeks when her husband, a small-town Kansas police chief, is killed. A former San Francisco cop, Susan takes over his job and four years later is still in Hampstead, trying to cope with an unprecedented cold spell and a work force greatly diminished by a flu epidemic. She's planning on spending Christmas in San Francisco, where a job offer from her old boss has materialized, and so has only limited time to wrap up the murder of Tim Holiday, found shot to death with his head and hands stuffed into the furnace he had recently repaired in Caley James' basement. Caley claims never to have met the creepy fellow before, although a neighbor had seen him repeatedly visiting her home and her name was on the reference sheet he gave his employer. Even more puzzling, Tim Holiday turns out not to exist; all his credit cards and identification are phony. It's a neat puzzle and the pieces fall together quite satisfactorily, with the small-town ambience and the relationships between the characters nicely handled.

Where it's reviewed:
Drood Review, November/December 2001, page 12
Publishers Weekly, October 22, 2001, page 50

Other books by the same author:
Murder Take Two, 1998
Family Practice, 1995
Consider the Crows, 1993
The Winter Widow, 1992

Other books you might like:
P.M. Carlson, *The Marty Hopkins Series*, 1992-1995
K.C. Greenlief, *Cold Hunter's Moon*, 2002
Jean Hager, *The Molly Bearpaw Series*, 1992-
J.A. Jance, *The Joanna Brady Series*, 1993-
Mary Logue, *Glare Ice*, 2001

213

JOHN WESSEL

Kiss It Goodbye

(New York: Simon & Schuster, 2001)

Story type: Private Detective
Series: Harding. Book 3
Subject(s): Missing Persons; Secrets; Alcoholism
Major character(s): Harding, Detective—Private (unlicensed), Alcoholic (recovering); Alison, Martial Arts Expert, Girlfriend (of Harding)
Time period(s): 2000s
Locale(s): Chicago, Illinois; Taos, New Mexico

Summary: Harding is a brainy, tough-guy antihero who's a recovering alcoholic and a maverick private detective, having lost his license after serving a sentence for manslaughter. Like his on-again, off-again girlfriend Alison, he's a graduate of the University of Chicago; in fact, they were once housemates in Grand Terrace, a residence known for its intellectual and artistic counterculture students. One of its former residents, Tracy Lawrence, turns up dead, and then a visiting poet-professor who's marrying Alison's best friend mysteriously disappears right before the wedding. Harding's investigation into these events takes him to a commune in New Mexico, as well as the cybercafes and watering holes of the neighborhood surrounding the university. It's not an overly original story or protagonist, but the writing is good.

Where it's reviewed:
Publishers Weekly, November 5, 2001, page 43

Other books by the same author:
Pretty Ballerina, 1998
This Far, No Further, 1997

Other books you might like:
Lawrence Block, *The Matt Scudder Series*, 1976-
Stephen Greenleaf, *The John Marshall Tanner Series*, 1979-
Dennis Lehane, *The Patrick Kenzie/Angela Gennaro Series*, 1994-
George P. Pelecanos, *The Nick Stefanos Series*, 1992-
Michael Stone, *The Streeter Series*, 1996-

214

LAURA WILSON

My Best Friend

(New York: Delacorte, 2002)

Story type: Psychological Suspense
Subject(s): World War II; Authors and Writers; Family Relations
Major character(s): Gerald Haxton, Clerk; Tilly Haldane, Actress; Jo Farrell, Clerk
Time period(s): 1990s (1995); 1940s
Locale(s): London, England; Finching, England (Suffolk)

Summary: When Gerald Haxton is born, his twin brother dies, and for the rest of her life his mother mourns that death instead of celebrating Gerald's birth. She goes on to become M.M. Haldane, the most beloved children's writer of her generation and the creator of Tom Tyler, an invincible boy detective. Forced to live an emotionally impoverished childhood, Gerald's life is made even more frightful when his sister, Vera, is murdered and he finds her body in the woods. His Aunt Tilly, his mother's sister and his father's mistress, is the only one who ever really tries to help Gerald, but he grows up to be a lonely, gentle, but twisted person whose only real happiness lies in seeing stage musicals over and over again. One day he spots a schoolgirl who reminds him of his dead sister, and he begins following her with the idea of protecting her from harm. By a coincidence, the girl's mother turns out to be his co-worker Jo. The lives of these three protagonists—Gerald, Tilly, and Jo—are told in alternating chapters to powerful effect.

Where it's reviewed:
Deadly Pleasures, Autumn 2001, page 57
Mystery News, December 2001/January 2002, page 11
New York Times Book Review, January 6, 2002, page 19
Publishers Weekly, November 16, 2001, page 39

Other books by the same author:
Dying Voices, 2001
A Little Death, 2000

Other books you might like:
Thomas H. Cook, *The Chatham School Affair*, 1996
Peter Dickinson, *The Yellow Room Conspiracy*, 1994
Peter Lovesey, *Rough Cider*, 1986
Val McDermid, *A Place of Execution*, 2000
Ruth Rendell, *Talking to Strange Men*, 1987

215

ROBERT WILSON

The Company of Strangers

(New York: Harcourt, 2001)

Story type: Espionage
Subject(s): Espionage; World War II; Nazis
Major character(s): Andrea Aspinall, Spy, Scientist (mathematician); Karl Voss, Diplomat, Spy
Time period(s): 1940s (1943); 1990s
Locale(s): Lisbon, Portugal; London, England; Berlin, Germany

Summary: Young English mathematics scholar Andrea Aspinall is recruited to become a spy in 1943 Lisbon, a city where everybody has information to sell, buy, or trade, and where the most seemingly harmless gossip can cost or save a life. She meets Karl Voss, a German attache who is widely known as a spy, and the two fall madly in love. It turns out that Karl is really a double agent originally employed by Admiral Canaris, one of Hitler's foes, but Andrea would have loved him anyway. Their affair is consuming but short-lived; Karl's career is finished when the plot to kill Hitler fails, but he's unable to make it to safety and warn Andrea of the danger she too is in, and so is captured and returned to Berlin where he faces certain death. Andrea marries a Portuguese army officer, secretly becomes a Communist, works undercover against dictator Antonio Salazar's regime, and ultimately, when her mother is dying, returns to England and is once again enlisted as an agent. This time her work, which takes her to East Berlin, is even more dangerous. Neither she nor Karl realized long ago that their few stolen hours together would define their entire lives, and the book is as much an unsentimental account of the power of love as it is a sweeping international thriller and a bleak overview of the nature of espionage. The plot's twists and turns are worthy of John Le Carre, and it's only at the book's bittersweet ending that all the complicated puzzle pieces finally fall into place.

Where it's reviewed:
Booklist, July 2001, page 1989
Library Journal, August 2001, page 167
Publishers Weekly, July 30, 2001, page 55

Other books by the same author:
A Small Death in Lisbon, 1999

Other books you might like:
John Altman, *A Gathering of Spies*, 2000
Joseph Kanon, *The Prodigal Spy*, 1998
John Le Carre, *The George Smiley Series*, 1961-
Glenn Meade, *The Sands of Sakkara*, 1999
David L. Robbins, *The War of the Rats*, 1999

216

DARRYL WIMBERLEY

Strawman's Hammock

(New York: St. Martin's Press, 2001)

Story type: Police Procedural
Series: Barrett Raines. Book 3
Subject(s): Race Relations; American South; Small Town Life
Major character(s): Barrett ''Bear'' Raines, Police Officer
Time period(s): 2000s
Locale(s): Deacon Beach, Florida

Summary: Raines is thrilled when political boss Linton Loyd asks him to run for sheriff in his home county against the incumbent, whom Loyd despises and wants ousted. It would mean Raines could leave his Tallahassee job with the Florida Department of Law Enforcement and be home every night with his wife and boys. Then he finds that Laura Anne, his wife, is thinking of selling her restaurant and taking a job as a music teacher, meaning that if he lost the election they'd be without an adequate income. To further complicate matters, Loyd's son is accused of having committed a brutal murder. More murders follow, all leading back to the Loyd family, and Raines has to decide if Loyd's backing is going to help or hinder him in his candidacy, and if a black man has a chance at being elected to the job in the first place.

Where it's reviewed:
Booklist, October 1, 2001, page 302
Publishers Weekly, October 22, 2001, page 51

Other books by the same author:
Dead Man's Bay, 2000
A Rock and a Hard Place, 1999

Other books you might like:
Glynn Marsh Alam, *The Luanne Fogarty Series*, 2000-
Robert Greer, *The CJ Floyd Series*, 1996-
Gary Hardwick, *Cold Medina*, 1996
Hugh Holton, *The Larry Cole Series*, 1994-
James Sallis, *The Lew Griffin Series*, 1992-

217

K.J.A. WISHNIA

Red House

(New York: St. Martin's Press, 2001)

Story type: Private Detective
Series: Filomena Buscarsela. Book 4
Subject(s): City and Town Life; Crime and Criminals; Social Issues
Major character(s): Filomena Buscarsela, Detective—Private, Single Parent
Time period(s): 2000s

Locale(s): New York, New York (Queens)

Summary: Ecuadorian Filomena Buscarsela has been a cabbie and a detective for the NYPD; now she's apprenticing as a private investigator with a small agency in Queens with the goal of eventually getting her license. In the meantime, she's anxious to pull in some big clients for her firm, but her soft heart and sharp tongue usually result in cases that cost more than they bring in. She's also juggling responsibilities as the single parent of 12-year-old Antonia, whom she loves devotedly. Feisty, independent, and big-hearted, Fil is one of the more attractive of the female private eyes to come along recently.

Where it's reviewed:
Booklist, August 2001, page 2100
Publishers Weekly, October 8, 2001, page 48

Other books by the same author:
The Glass Factory, 2000
Soft Money, 1999
23 Shades of Black, 1997

Other books you might like:
Linda Barnes, *The Carlotta Carlyle Series*, 1987-
Carolina Garcia-Aguilera, *The Lupe Solano Series*, 1996-
Katy Munger, *The Casey Jones Series*, 1997-
Barbara Seranella, *The Munch Mancini Series*, 1997-
Gloria White, *The Ronnie Ventana Series*, 1991-

218

MATT WITTEN

The Killing Bee

(New York: Signet, 2001)

Story type: Amateur Detective; Domestic
Series: Jacob Burns. Book 4
Subject(s): Schools; Fathers and Sons; Marriage
Major character(s): Jacob Burns, Writer, Parent
Time period(s): 2000s
Locale(s): Saratoga Springs, New York

Summary: Jacob Burns is a writer whose wife, Andrea, is teaching a full load at the local community college, and so Jacob has become a stay-at-home dad. He's become very involved in his boys' education and along with a group of other parents has been pressing the school's principal to initiate a gifted and talented program for their brainy offspring. The principal has steadfastly resisted and angered many of the parents, but it's still a shock when he's bludgeoned to death with a spelling bee trophy. One of Andrea's best friends, a single parent named Laura Braithwaite, is accused of the murder, and Jacob goes to work trying to clear her. This is an intelligently written series with engaging protagonists and believable situations. The relationship between Jacob and his two young sons is particularly well handled.

Other books by the same author:
Grand Delusion, 2000
Strange Bedfellows, 2000
Breakfast at Madeleine's, 1999

Other books you might like:
David Handler, *The Stewart Hoag Series*, 1988-
Jon Katz, *The Kit DeLeeuw Series*, 1992-
David A. Kaufelt, *The Wyn Lewis Series*, 1993-
Leslie O'Kane, *The School Board Murders*, 2000
Justin Scott, *The Ben Abbott Series*, 1994-

219

VALERIE WOLZIEN

Murder in the Forecast

(New York: Fawcett, 2001)

Story type: Amateur Detective
Series: Josie Pigeon. Book 5
Subject(s): Islands; Hurricanes; Small Town Life
Major character(s): Josie Pigeon, Contractor, Single Parent
Time period(s): 2000s
Locale(s): New Jersey

Summary: When a major hurricane threatens the tiny barrier island where Josie Pigeon operates her all-woman contracting firm, she stubbornly refuses to be evacuated, wrapped up as she is in a new job renovating a grand old mansion for wealthy New Yorker Cornell Hudson. However, when she visits the site, she finds him dead, strangled by a torn-off strip of drop cloth. Then both house and body are swept out to sea when the hurricane strikes. The author also writes a series about suburban housewife Susan Henshaw.

Where it's reviewed:
Deadly Pleasures, Autumn 2001, page 49

Other books by the same author:
This Old Murder, 2000
Deck the Halls with Murder, 1998
Permit for Murder, 1997
Shore to Die, 1996

Other books you might like:
Mary Freeman, *The Rachel O'Connor Series*, 1999-
Sarah Graves, *The Jacobia Tiptree Series*, 1998-
Kate Grilley, *Death Rides an Ill Wind*, 2001
Sally Gunning, *The Peter Bartholomew Series*, 1990-
Margaret Maron, *Storm Track*, 2000

220

PAULA L. WOODS

Stormy Weather

(New York: Norton, 2001)

Story type: Police Procedural
Series: Charlotte Justice. Number 2
Subject(s): African Americans; Movie Industry; Sexual Harassment
Major character(s): Charlotte Justice, Detective—Police (robbery-homicide detective)
Time period(s): 1990s (1992)
Locale(s): Los Angeles, California

Summary: The riots following the police beating of Rodney King provided the background for Woods' first Charlotte Justice book; now, in their aftermath, Charlotte has run afoul of unspoken departmental policies when she resists the sexual advances of her supervisor, Steve Firestone, and is assigned a desk job as retribution. It takes a lot of finessing to be assigned to a case that really interests her, the suspected murder of pioneering black filmmaker Maynard Duncan, but then Firestone pulls her from it. This doesn't stop Charlotte from continuing to investigate, however; after all, her own family is connected with the movie business and she's fascinated with black film history. It's certainly a chapter in Hollywood's history that's unfamiliar to most moviegoers, and the author does a fine job bringing it to life, as well as drawing a credible portrait of a dedicated black woman cop whose ambitions are constantly thwarted by both racism and sexism within her department.

Where it's reviewed:

Black Issues Book Review, September 2001, page 20
Booklist, May 1, 2001, page 1643
Library Journal, August 2001, page 169
Publishers Weekly, September 16, 2001, page 162
Wall Street Journal, July 31, 2001, page A16

Other books by the same author:

Inner City Blues, 1999

Other books you might like:

Eleanor Taylor Bland, *The Marti McAlister Series*, 1992-
Evelyn Coleman, *The Patricia Conley Series*, 1998-
Penny Mickelbury, *The Carol Ann Gibson Series*, 1998-
Judith Smith-Levin, *The Starletta Duvall Series*, 1996-
Valerie Wilson Wesley, *The Tamara Hayle Series*, 1994-

221

MARK RICHARD ZUBRO

Sex and Murder.com

(New York: St. Martin's Press, 2001)

Story type: Police Procedural
Series: Paul Turner. Number 6
Subject(s): Homosexuality/Lesbianism; Politics; City and Town Life
Major character(s): Paul Turner, Police Officer, Homosexual; Buck Fenwick, Police Officer
Time period(s): 2000s
Locale(s): Chicago, Illinois

Summary: When computer magnate Craig Lenzati is murdered via multiple savage stab wounds, gay Chicago cop Paul Turner and his straight partner Buck Fenwick are called to the crime scene. A former nerd made good (and still compensating for social and sexual awkwardness from his youth), Lenzati had his share of detractors, but it's difficult to see who of all these tenuous suspects might have killed him. The information Paul and Ben need is encrypted into computer codes and they eventually learn, not surprisingly, that Lenzati's murder seems to be linked with some kind of dangerous sex game he was playing. While the partners sort it all out, they learn a serial killer who is traveling along I-90 is due to strike Chicago next. The author also writes a series about gay high school teacher Tom Mason.

Where it's reviewed:

Booklist, July 2001, page 1990
Mystery News, October/November 2001, page 22
Publishers Weekly, July 30, 2001, page 65

Other books by the same author:

Drop Dead, 1999
The Truth Can Get You Killed, 1997
Another Dead Teenager, 1995
Political Poison, 1993
Sorry Now, 1991

Other books you might like:

Michael Craft, *The Mark Manning Series*, 1997-
Joseph Hansen, *The Dave Brandstetter Series*, 1970-1991
Michael Nava, *The Henry Rios Series*, 1986-2000
John Morgan Wilson, *The Benjamin Justice Series*, 1996-
R.D. Zimmerman, *The Todd Mills Series*, 1995-

Romance Fiction in Review
by
Kristin Ramsdell

''Romance has been elegantly defined as the offspring of fiction and love.''
—Benjamin Disraeli

''Love isn't what makes the world go 'round. Love is what makes the ride worthwhile.''
—Franklin P. Jones

''Romances are fun.''
—Sandra Brown

If the current statistics are to be believed, the readers agree! It is love that makes life worth living, and romances, the stories that tell these tales of love, are fun! Garnering more than $1.37 billion in sales and accounting for 55.9% of all popular mass market sales and 37.2% of all paperback and hardcover fiction sales combined, romance topped the charts once again in 2000. Despite a slight dip from the 1999 highs because of a publishing anomaly that year, romance remained the darling of the fiction genres for readers and publishers alike, beating most of the other fiction genres by double digit percentage points and its closest competitor, Mystery/Suspense, by more than nine. [Hall, Libby. ''ROMStat 2000.'' *Romance Writers' Report* 21 (September 2001): 21-25] A more complete breakdown of the 2000 statistics was given in the second volume of the 2001 edition of *What Do I Read Next?* and will not be repeated here. The 2001 statistics are not, as yet, compiled; they will be discussed in volume 2 of this edition of *What Do I Read Next?* for which they are available.

The publishing industry continued to deal with many of the same issues as in the past; however, the old merger/acquisition/distribution/technology problems suddenly lost their immediacy as the catastrophic events of September 11th impacted everyone in the industry in one way or another. But neither romance nor New Yorkers stay down for long, and in spite of missed deadlines, lost manuscripts, and other, more serious losses, the industry picked itself up, assessed the damage, and got back to business in record time.

Similar to the rest of the business world, David-and-Goliath continues to be the reigning industry image. Although several small presses, such as ImaJinn and Red Sage, seem to be making good in the romance arena, the industry remains dominated by a few large conglomerates, the largest of which is TorStar. Kensington comes in second, followed by Pearson, Bertlesmann, Dorchester, and Avon/HarperCollins in descending order of number of titles published annually. The same is true in the bookseller camp where the small independent bookstores continue to battle the super chains for market share with mixed results.

Interest in e-books has declined markedly. While the immediate future remains murky, technology is here to stay and, as Richard Curtis says in his article, ''Bullish on E-Books,'' (*Publishers Weekly*, January 7, 2002, page 42), the ''e-book industry is healthy,'' growing in line with projections, and ''It's time to focus on the good news coming out of the e- book business and support the pioneers striving to reinvent publishing and make it more relevant to the needs of authors and readers.''

In typical fashion, 2001 saw the romance genre continuing its two-pronged development—expanding upon its past successes and reaching out in newer, unexplored directions. Contemporaries and Historicals (including Regencies) still dominate the market, accounting for the vast majority of all romances published last year, with Inspirationals, Multiculturals, and Alternative Realities Romances making up the difference. Although the vast number of romances are of the tried-and-true varieties (e.g., Contemporaries with small town middle America settings—often with secret baby and reunion themes and Historicals with British or American settings—often with forced or arranged marriage plot devices), several interesting new, or revisited directions have been noted. Publishers are making a concerted effort to reach young, urban singles, and in addition to publishing an occasional urban-set, upbeat romance within their established lines, Harlequin Books has launched Red Dress Ink, a line of fast-paced, quirky, heroine-focused stories. While not really romances (they actually have more in common with the Young Adult coming-of-age novel), they have enough emphasis on dating and relationships—or lack thereof—to possibly be of interest to romance readers who also enjoy the *Bridget Jones's Diary* type of story. Erotic romance has been gaining favor for several years and with the launching of Brava (Kensington) and Blaze (a spin-off from Harlequin's Temptation line), it has definitely established its presence within the genre. Finally, the Regency romance is showing remarkable signs of new life, with a marked increase in titles published.

The Romance Genre in Detail

To the surprise of no one, Contemporary Romance continues to dominate the market. As usual, series titles claim the majority of that number, with single titles making up the difference. The vast majority of series titles continue to be produced by Harlequin and Silhouette, and although Zebra made a valiant two- year attempt at breaking into this market with its Bouquet line, the series didn't make the grade and slid quietly into oblivion. Single titles are published by a large number of houses, and although many are now owned by larger conglomerates (e.g., Bertlesmann owns Ballantine, Bantam, Dell, Delacorte, Doubleday, Fawcett, Ivy and WaterBrook; Pearson owns Berkley, NAL, Dutton, Jove, Onyx, Putnam, Signet, Topaz, Viking), the imprints are distinct. As in past years, writers continue to break out of category and into the single title market with growing regularity. They also continue to move across genre lines, particularly into the areas of Women's Fiction and Mystery/Suspense, where they are reaching a broader market and, in a number of cases, attracting new readers back into the romance genre. In addition, historical writers are also testing the contemporary waters, often with good results. As in the past, trilogies and other linked books continue to be popular and appear in both series and single title formats. Nora Roberts' Three Sisters Island Trilogy, Marilyn Pappano's Bethlehem series, Cathie Linz's Men of Honor series, and Susan Elizabeth Phillips' Chicago Stars books are only several of the many examples.

The heroes and heroines are as diverse as ever, yet whatever their circumstances, they are honorable, strong, independent, and can usually see the funny side of a situation—traits found in all romances. Humor, in general, continues to attract readers (Maureen Child's *The Last Virgin in California*) and, conversely, serious social issues are often topics (e.g., Andrea Kane's *No Way Out*). In addition, mystery, paranormal, or fantasy elements (e.g., Cherry Adair's *Hide and Seek*, Sue Civil-Brown's *Next Stop Paradise*, Nora Roberts' *Heaven and Earth*) are regularly found within the subgenre. As mentioned above, there is also a growing interest in lively, very modern stories aimed at attracting young urban singles. This hitherto untapped market will be a challenge, but Harlequin, with its new imprint Red Dress Ink, is making an effort (even though these are not necessarily romances) and other lines are featuring stories that might appeal, as well (e.g., *Miss Match* by Leslie Carroll). Finally, although not limited to Contemporary Romance, the growing interest in highly sensual romance is impacting the subgenre. Blaze, which was part of Harlequin's Temptation line for years, was spun off and is now a very sexy contemporary series in its own right; and Kensington's Brava imprint focuses on both Contemporary and Historical erotic romance. There is, of course, a sensuality level for every taste, and everything from sweetly chaste to explicitly erotic can be found within the Contemporary pages.

Historical

The traditional runner up to Contemporary Romance in size, Historical Romance is by far the most diverse of the subgenres. Although theoretically including any romance set from pre-history through the middle of the last century, as a practical matter most Historicals are set between 1066 and the end of Victoria's reign in 1901. While there are some successful deviations, such as Dorothy Garlock's *The Edge of Town*, set during the 1920s, the vast majority of current Historical Romances have English Medieval, Georgian, Regency, or Victorian time frames or nineteenth century American West settings. Plot patterns, characters, and literary styles of all types can be found within the subgenre and are often overlaid with elements of mystery, suspense, magic, or a dash of the paranormal. Forced or arranged marriages, revenge, mistaken identity, recouping the family fortune, reunions, redeeming the family honor, and secret babies are only a few of the elements found in the current selection of stories. They run the gamut from light and humorous to darkly serious, featuring characters as diverse as a gentlewoman sold by her husband to the highest bidder, a spy heroine with a photographic memory, a vengeance-driven Pinkerton agent, and a reclusive lord with a reputation he doesn't deserve. As in the Contemporary subgenre, Historicals linked by character or theme, such as Susan King's Maiden trilogy, Josie Litton's medieval Viking trilogy, and Susan Krinard's Forster trilogy, continue to be popular. Despite the demise of Zebra's contemporary Bouquet line early in 2001, Zebra's Ballad line of linked Historicals (new in 2000 and featuring such titles as *Bogus Brides* and the *Clan MacLean*) is alive and doing well.

This year, to the delight of its devoted fans, the Regency Romance did the unexpected—it grew, putting an abrupt halt to the subgenre's downward slide. It is, of course, still a niche market, but considering that the number of Regency titles actually rose when most other subgenres lost titles, it does say something about the overall vitality of the subgenre. It also may be an indication that the writers who have crossed over to the larger Historical market, but are still using Regency settings, are attracting a wealth of new readers—readers who then find their favorite authors' backlists and end up discovering a whole new subgenre as a result. Although a number of Regency writers have permanently, and exclusively, joined the Historical ranks, others (e.g., Mary Balogh, Candice Hern, Jo Ann Ferguson) still contribute or plan to contribute to both subgenres. Although traditional Regencies have some fairly strict conventions, there is surprising diversity among them. Pacing can be lively or deliberate, and though the language is usually witty, mood can be upbeat or more serious. Sensuality levels are usually chaste, although there are always writers who will push the edges of this particular envelope. Characters can vary greatly, treating readers to everything from an outspoken, crossdressing, golf-loving heroine in Andrea Pickens' charming *Diamond in the Rough* to a beautiful, gently rebellious, and very wary heiress in Evelyn Richardson's *Fortune's Lady* to a dissolute exile who finds himself indebted to the man he had wronged in Sheri Cobb South's unusual *French Leave* to a noble, amateur antiquarian hero in Debbie Raleigh's *The Christmas Wish*. It's been a good year for the Regency; let's hope it continues.

Romantic Suspense continues along predictable lines, providing an avenue for breakout writers with a murderous bent while satisfying romance readers who like their leisure reading littered with bodies and laced with suspense and mainstream fans who want their mystery and mayhem tempered with love. Plot patterns range from the women-in-jeopardy tales (Suzanne Forster's *Angel Face* is an intriguing men-in-jeopardy reversal) to police procedurals and include everything in between. Characters are often innocents caught in a dangerous situation, as in Anne Stuart's *The Widow* or Elizabeth Lowell's *Moving Target*, but they can also be the detectives, as is the case with J.D. Robb's Eve Dallas books. Themes and styles are similarly diverse and can be deadly serious or lightly whimsical, depending upon the author. Finally, as in the past, romantic suspense elements find their way into many other subgenres, resulting in such intriguing combinations as Kathryn Smith's Regency-set *Elusive Passion*, Judith Arnold's emotionally involving and occasionally humorous *Looking for Laura*, or Kat Martin's mystery with a paranormal touch, *The Secret*.

Gothics continue to generate some interest, and as mentioned last year, Candleglow, LoveSpell's new sensual Gothic line, was launched in January 2001 with Evelyn Rogers' *Devil in the Dark* and Colleen Shannon's *The Wolf of Haskell Hall*. Although the releases are somewhat sporadic, they do continue. Gothic elements, of course, are not confined to romances officially labeled as Gothic. Darker, more threatening, elements appear in a number of "non-Gothic" romances such as Judith Lyons' contemporary series Lt. Kent Lone Wolf; Feehan and George's *A Very Gothic Christmas*; or Jacquelin Navin's fairy tale romance, *The Sleeping Beauty*.

Despite the consistent rumblings from the publishers that the Alternative Realities subgenre is unpopular and doomed, it continues to appeal to a niche readership. Diverse as ever, the subgenre's offerings range from Lynn Kurland's enchanting time travel novel, *My Heart Stood Still*; to Susan Krinard's werewolf historical, *Secret of the Wolf*; to Nora Roberts' magical contemporary Three Sisters Island Trilogy; to Jacquelin Navin's fantasy *The Sleeping Beauty*; and Karen Fox's *Buttercup Baby* in Jove's Magical Love series. Of the four subdivisions, Futuristics seem to struggle the most, although J.D. Robb's Eve Dallas series continues to shine and *Ritual of Proof* by Dara Joy is certainly worth noting. As with Romantic Suspense and Gothics, various elements from the Alternative Realities subgenre continue to appear in the other romance subgenres with great regularity, indicating that the subgenre is not dead, just evolving along different lines. In addition, the fact that readers and writers are still interested in stories of this type, and want more of them, is borne out by the responses I received to an informal survey of romance readers and writers that I conducted recently.

Multicultural romance continues to generate some interest, particularly in the African American arena. The Latino romance market is served primarily by Kensington's Encanto line, while the African American readership can choose from several, including BET's Arabesque and the Genesis lines. At this point, there are no romance lines that focus specifically on other ethnic groups. Nevertheless, characters of diverse backgrounds, especially those of Native American descent, are found in many romances, such as *Night Hawk's Bride* by Jillian Hart. As usual, there is a dearth of characters with Asian backgrounds.

Inspirational Romance is holding its own and, although the total number of titles published dropped, remains a solid niche market. The major publishing players continue to be the same. Except for those romances published under the two commercial imprints, Harlequin's Steeple Hill and Bantam/Doubleday/Dell's WaterBrook, most Inspirationals are put out by Christian houses (e.g., Bethany, Tyndale, Barbour) that produce a wide variety of religious materials, including Christian romance. Themes tend to center on family, hearth and home, and struggles with faith and belief, and in the case of the religiously affiliated presses, the stories usually reflect the tenets of the particular denomination. Inspirationals can be either Historical or Contemporary and, although the majority are American-set contemporaries and sometimes have a mystery/suspense element, they generally reflect more conservative views than other parts of the romance market, and are sweet, rather than sensual.

Anthologies continue to play an important role in the genre, both allowing veteran writers to collaborate on joint projects or try out new ideas in a shorter format and providing a way for up-and-coming authors to gain market exposure as part of an anthology headed by a major author. As in the past, holiday anthologies are the most numerous; and while the winter holidays are still the most popular (e.g., *A Very Gothic Christmas*, *'Tis the Season*, *A Western Family Christmas*), other celebrations, such as Mother's Day (e.g., *A Kiss for Mama*) are represented as well. However, not all anthologies focus on holidays. This year's crop has themes that vary from Scotland (e.g., *My Scottish Summer*) and Regency England (e.g., *Regency Christmas Spirits*) to animals (e.g., *Autumn Kittens*) and letters (e.g., *Letters of the Heart*). In addition, anthologies often have elements of fantasy or suspense that are integrated into the other aspects of the theme (e.g., *Once upon a Rose*). Sensuality levels in these collections can vary from exceedingly chaste to sizzling, depending upon the theme and the writer, but in keeping with the growing trend toward more erotic romance, several especially sensual anthologies (e.g., *Hot and Bothered*, *All through the Night*) recently saw print and may be of interest. Limited series, a set number of books—usually contemporary series romances—written by different authors but linked by character, setting, and plot, remained popular with readers. Since these series are not necessarily in sync with the calendar year, 2001 saw the conclusions of Silhouette's Montana Mavericks and Harlequin's Maitland Maternity, and the launching of Harlequin's Trueblood, Texas, and Silhouette's The Coltons.

Romance in Review

Romance continues to be regularly reviewed in print in a quarterly romance column in *Library Journal*, the ''Forecasts'' section of *Publishers Weekly*, *Booklist*, and in a number of newspapers throughout the country. In addition, many of these reviews are picked up by various indexing services such as InfoTrac's Expanded Academic ASAP, or are reprinted, or posted to bookseller's websites such as Amazon (www.amazon.com) and Barnes & Noble (www.bn.com). Nevertheless, despite this increased coverage by mainstream review sources, the genre-specific publications, such as *Romantic Times*, *Affaire de Coeur*, and *Rendezvous*, still provide the most comprehensive coverage of the genre. While their reviews tend to be more positive than critical, these publications are still the place to go to get a feel for the diversity and numbers of the romances available. In addition, a number of romance-specific websites exist, such as All about Romance (www.likesbooks.com) and The Romance Reader (www.theromancereader.com). Finally, there are the listservs. RRA-L (Romance Readers Anonymous) was one of the first lists, and it remains one of the primary forums for romance readers to discuss the genre and share their views and recommendations. Fiction—L is another list of interest to readers and librarians that, while not specifically devoted to romance, does focus on the genre on a regular basis.

As it continues to shape our daily lives, the Internet is fast becoming a necessity to the romance genre as a whole. It is, indeed, a rare writer or publisher who does not have a website, now often professionally done and complete with bios, latest releases, and contact information. Writers, readers, publishers, reviewers, and even bookstores use the web on a regular basis for any number of tasks from purchasing books, getting reviews, collaborating with other writers, or submitting manuscripts. It is quickly becoming the major communication game in town; and although the e-book has not lived up to its promise when it comes to fiction, there is a growing interest in online reference and other nonfiction books. In addition, the RWA website (www.rwanational.com) continues to be one of the primary sites of up-to-date information for the genre, including RWA awards and statistical information and also links to a number of romance publishers.

More Developments in the World of Romance Fiction

Although there are many romance-related meetings and workshops each year, the premier gathering is generally considered to be the Annual Conference of the Romance Writers of America. This year the conference was held in New Orleans and was attended by more than 1600 writers, librarians, and other literary professionals as they gathered to connect, exchange ideas, and celebrate the accomplishments of another year in the world of popular romance fiction. As in past years, the conference began with the increasingly popular Readers for Life Literacy Autographing, a charitable public event which this year garnered over $40,000 for Laubach Literacy. It concluded with the traditional Awards Ceremony, where romance writers honor their own with the Rita, Golden Heart, and Lifetime Achievement Awards. In addition, RWA also recognizes romance-related achievement in other areas, including librarianship and article publication. This year Shelley Mosley, manager of the Velma Teague Branch Library in Glendale, Arizona, was named the 2001 RWA Librarian of the Year; and Patricia McLaughlin won the Veritas Award for her article, ''Love and Hisses; Go Ahead, Make Jokes. We'll Be Here with Our Fans,'' which appeared in the ''Outlook'' section of the *Washington Post*, July 23, 2000.

The relationship between the Romance Writers of America and the library world continues to grow, and in July 2001 RWA hosted the third annual Librarian's Day Pre-Conference prior to its conference in New Orleans. This conference was packed with presentations by such award-winning luminaries as Nora Roberts, Jayne Ann Krentz, Susan Elizabeth Phillips, Lorraine Heath, Julie Garwood, Maggie Osborne, Jennifer Crusie, Shirley Hailstock, and librarian Ann Bouricius, who is also a published romance writer and author of *The Romance Readers' Advisory: The Librarian's Guide to Love in the Stacks* (ALA, 2000). The day was an intense, enjoyable introduction to the character, appeal, and importance of the romance and offered practical tips for dealing with the genre and its readers within the library. The next RWA Annual Conference and Librarian's Day is scheduled for mid-July 2002 in Denver, Colorado. RWA also staffed a booth at the ALA annual conference in San Francisco and continues to maintain a special web page for librarians as part of the RWA website. Across the country librarians and library groups continue to provide national, regional, and local workshops on the romance genre.

Of particular interest in 2001, were ''The Readers' Advisory Renaissance: Pioneers and Portals,'' a romance-focused program at the California Library Association Annual Conference held in Long Beach in November, and ''The Lure of Romance,'' a panel presentation at the American Library Association Annual Conference in San Francisco in June. These are of note partly because romance has rarely been featured in programs at either of these events.

Published scholarship in the area of romance fiction continues to be slight. However, articles in the popular press, as well as practical articles targeting the library market, continue to appear with some regularity. Sarah Cohen's article ''Romance, Chapter & Verse: Sex Flavors the Genre's Heady Brew, but a Context of Commitment Is Essential'' in the May 29, 2001 edition of the *Indianapolis Star*, ''That Secret Shame'' by Mark Athitakis in the July 25, 2001 *SF Weekly*, and ''What Kind of Romance Are You in the Mood For? A Recommended Reading List'' by Mary K. Chelton, Cathie Linz, Joyce Saricks, Lynne Welch, and Ann Bouricius in the September 15, 2001 *Booklist* are only a few examples.

The Future

But what lies ahead for the genre? A lot, I'd say, at least if this past year has been any indication. Naturally, much will remain the same, with the subgenres generally maintaining their existing market shares and many established practices—especially the ones that work—continuing. Contemporary Romance will retain its dominant position. While some of the series will continue to favor single fathers, secret babies, amnesia victims, marriages of convenience, and similarly well-worn elements, single titles and some of the more adventurous lines may head in less conventional directions, especially if the forays into the urban singles market prove successful. As in the past, the lines between Contemporary Romance and the broader Women's Fiction market will remain fluid as writers continue to move between them. If current rumors are to be believed, the Historical market, soft in recent years, may be on the rise; and while certain settings will certainly retain their popularity, others may come to the fore. Romantic Suspense, even though publishers may not always label it as such, will continue to thrive, and Gothics and darker types of romance may be in for a renewal. Inspirationals will probably hold their own and Multicultural Romances, especially those focusing on the African American reader, will continue to attract attention. Regencies should retain and, with the newfound interest, may even improve their position; nevertheless, Regency writers will continue to head in the Historical direction for career reasons. Alternative Realities, while often panned by the publishers, is a definite niche market for many readers and writers. Though it may never gain widespread appeal, the renewed interest in Fantasy with the release of J.R.R. Tolkien's *Lord of the Rings: The Fellowship of the Ring* just may spill over into the Romance arena. Interest in the more erotic forms of romance will increase, both in and out of the designated lines. Trilogies, linked books, and limited series will remain popular, reflecting the country's ongoing infatuation with continued stories in media of all types. E-books will take a breather, although they are in our future, at least in some form; and technology will continue to change the way the publishing industry does business and the way writers work as well. All in all, 2001 has been an interesting year; and with a little bit of luck, 2002 will be just as eventful.

Recommendations for Romance

Reading tastes vary greatly. What makes a book appeal to one person may make another reject it. By the same token, two people may like the same book for totally different reasons. Obviously, reading is a highly subjective and personal undertaking. For this reason, the recommended readings attached to each entry have tried to cast as broad a net as was reasonably possible. Suggested titles have been chosen on the basis of similarity to the main entry in one or more of the following areas: historical time period, geographic setting, theme, character types, plot pattern or premise, writing style, or overall mood or ''feel.'' All suggestions may not appeal to the same person, but it is to be hoped that at least one would appeal to most.

Because romance reading tastes do vary so widely and readers (and writers) often apply vastly differing criteria in determining what makes a romance good, bad, or exceptional, I cannot claim that the following list of recommendations consists solely of the *best* romance novels of the year. (In fact many of these received no awards or special recognition at all.) It is simply a selection of books that the romance contributors, John Charles and Shelley Mosley, and I found particularly interesting. Perhaps some of these will appeal to you, too.

Sentimental Journey by Jill Barnett

The Secret Life of Connor Monahan by Elizabeth Bevarly

Fallen by Celeste Bradley

The Bridal Season by Connie Brockway

The Mackintosh Bride by Debra Lee Brown

Next Stop, Paradise by Sue Civil-Brown

Tall, Dark, and Difficult by Patricia Coughlin

What to Do about Annie? by Millie Criswell

The Marriage Bed by Claudia Dain

Seven Up by Janet Evanovich

A Very Gothic Christmas by Christine Feehan and Melanie George

The Bride Sale by Candice Hern

The Proper Wife by Julia Justiss

Just West of Heaven by Kathleen Kane

Season of Storms by Susanna Kearsley

One Good Turn by Carla Kelly

Suddenly You by Lisa Kleypas

The Husband Test by Betina Krahn

The Rake and the Wallflower by Allison Lane

I Dream of You by Judi McCoy

The Prisoner Bride by Susan Spencer Paul

This Heart of Mine by Susan Elizabeth Phillips

The Traitor's Daughter by Elizabeth Powell

A Prince of a Guy by Sheila Rabe

Fortune's Lady by Evelyn Richardson

Heaven and Earth by Nora Roberts

Alice at Heart by Deborah Smith

French Leave by Sheri Cobb South

Whispers of Goodbye by Karen White

Halfway to Heaven by Susan Wiggs

For Further Reference

Review Journals

Booklist, *Publishers Weekly*, and *Library Journal* are continuing their improved coverage of the romance genre. *Library Journal* publishes a quarterly romance review column (February 15, May 15, August, and November 15); *Booklist* has a separate romance fiction category, as do the other genres; and *Publishers Weekly* now uses romance reviewers who are generally conversant with the genre. Yet most romance reviews still appear in sources—both print and online—that specialize in the romance. Several of the most important sources are listed below.

Affaire de Coeur (www.affairedecoeur.com) includes reviews, articles, and information on the world of romance fiction in general. *Affaire de Coeur*, 3976 Oak Hill Road, Oakland, CA 94605-4931; phone, (510) 569-5675; fax, (510) 632-8868. Subscriptions, Monthly, $35 a year (U.S. First Class Rates); $65 for 2 years (U.S. First Class Rates); $30 a year (U.S. Third Class Rates); $55 for 2 years (U.S. Third Class Rates); $65 a year (Canadian Rates); $5 single copy.

All about Romance (www.likesbooks.com) contains selected romance reviews.

Amazon.com (www.amazon.com) includes some published reviews, as well as readers' comments. Quite comprehensive.

Barnes&Noble.com (www.bn.com) includes some published reviews, as well as readers' comments.

Gothic Journal (gothicjournal.com/romance/). This journal ceased publication with the October/November 1998 issue and is now operating as a website. Back issues are still available. *Gothic Journal*, P.O. Box 6340, Elko, Nevada 89802-6340; phone, (775) 738-3520; fax, (775) 738-3524.

Rendezvous: A Monthly Review of Contemporary and Historical Romances, Mysteries, and Women's Fiction (www.geocities.com/Heartland/Estates/9534/rendvous.html) includes reviews of most romances published each month. Published by Love Designers Writers' Club, Inc., 1507 Burnham Avenue, Calumet City, IL 60409; phone, (708) 862-9797. Subscriptions, Monthly, $45 a year; $24 for 6 months; $4 single copy.

The Romance Reader (www.theromancereader.com) has a good selection of ranked, often harsh reviews.

Romantic Times (www.romantictimes.com) includes reviews of most romances published each month, articles, and information about the world of romance fiction. It also includes reviews and other information on other genres and mainstream women's fiction. Published by Romantic Times Publishing Group, 55 Bergen Street, Brooklyn Heights, NY 11201; phone, (718) 237-1097; fax, (718) 624-4231; Subscriptions: Monthly, $31 for 6 months (U.S. First Class Rates); $62 for 1 year (U.S. First Class Rates); $124 for 2 years (U.S. First Class Rates); $22 for 6 months (U.S. Fourth Class Rates); $43 for 1 year (U.S. Fourth Class Rates); $85 for 2 years (U.S. Fourth Class Rates); $35 for 6 months (Canadian Rates); $70 for 1 year (Canadian Rates); $139 for 2 years (Canadian Rates); $59 for 6 months (European Rates); $117 for 1 year (European Rates); $234 for 2 years (European Rates).

Websites/Book Clubs/Mail Order Services

In addition to going to the general websites of online book suppliers like Amazon.com, and traditional bookstores such as Borders and Barnes & Noble, readers can now order books directly from some individual publishers' websites. Many of these websites also feature reviews, information on any subscription book clubs the publisher has, and ways for readers to connect with each other. Several of the more popular are listed below.

Publishers

Avalon Books, www.avalonbooks.com/

HarperCollins/Avon Books, www.harpercollins.com/hc/features/romance/

Dorchester Publishing (Leisure & LoveSpell), www.dorchesterpub.com

Harlequin/Silhouette/Mira, eharlequin.com

Kensington Books, www.kensingtonbooks.com

Book Suppliers

Amazon.com, www.amazon.com

Barnes & Noble, www.bn.com

Borders, www.borders.com

Manderley: A Catalog for Romance Readers, www.1romancestreet.com

Reader Service provides books in the Harlequin and Silhouette series on a monthly subscription basis. Write, phone, or e-mail for series descriptions and price information. Reader Service, P.O. Box 5190, Buffalo, NY 14240-5190; phone, (716) 684-1500, or, P.O. Box 615, Fort Erie, Ontario L2A 5X3, Canada; phone, (416) 283-2897; e-mail, eharlequin.com.

Conferences

Numerous conferences are held each year for writers and readers of romance fiction. Two of the more important national ones are listed below. For a more complete listing, particularly of regional or local conferences designed primarily for romance writers, consult the *Romance Writers Report*, a monthly publication of The Romance Writers of America.

Annual Book Lovers Convention—Sponsored by *Romantic Times*. The *Romantic Times* 18th Annual Book Lovers Convention was held November 14-19, 2001 in Orlando, Florida.(This organization also sponsors a number of romance-related tours for readers and writers.) The 19th Annual Book Lovers Convention is scheduled for October 23-27, 2002 in Reno, Nevada.

RWA Annual Conference—Sponsored by Romance Writers of America is usually held in July. The 2001 Conference was held July 18-22 in New Orleans, Louisiana. The 2002 Conference is scheduled for July 17-20 in Denver, Colorado.

Romance Titles

222

CHERRY ADAIR

Hide and Seek

(New York: Ivy, 2001)

Story type: Contemporary; Romantic Suspense
Subject(s): Missing Persons
Major character(s): Delanie Eastman, Teacher, Imposter (poses as a chorus girl); Kyle Wright, Spy, Doctor
Time period(s): 2000s
Locale(s): South America

Summary: Delanie Eastman and Kyle Wright meet again four years after a brief, but flaming affair in a most unlikely place—a drug lord's South American mountain retreat. Delanie is on the trail of her missing sister, a former companion of the drug lord, Ramon Montero, and Kyle is undercover in an effort to bring Montero's operation down. The last thing each of them needs is a renewal of their relationship, but that's exactly what they get—and then some. Sexy, fast-paced, and thrilling.

Other books by the same author:
Seducing Mr. Right, 2001
Kiss and Tell, 2000
The Mercenary, 1994

Other books you might like:
Rochelle Alers, *Hidden Agenda*, 1997
Suzanne Brockmann, *Body Guard*, 1999
Suzanne Brockmann, *Over the Edge*, 2001
Iris Johansen, *The Ugly Duckling*, 1996
Meryl Sawyer, *Tempting Fate*, 1998

223

CHERRY ADAIR (Pseudonym of Cherry Wilkinson)

Seducing Mr. Right

(New York: Harlequin, 2001)

Story type: Contemporary
Subject(s): Family; Seduction
Major character(s): Catherine ''Cat'' Anne Harris, Stock Broker (day trader); Lucas ''Luke'' Van Buren, Architect
Time period(s): 2000s
Locale(s): San Francisco, California

Summary: Cat Harris has been in love with her stepbrother, Luke Van Buren, ever since they were both teenagers, but Luke just treats Cat like the sibling he never had. Determined to show Luke her true feelings, she asks him to help her find the man of her dreams. Now all Cat has to do is find a way to let Luke know he is the man she has been dreaming of.

Where it's reviewed:
Romantic Times, June 2001, page 110

Other books by the same author:
Kiss and Tell, 2000
The Mercenary, 1994

Other books you might like:
Toni Blake, *Seducing Summer*, 1998
Stephanie Bond, *Manhunting in Mississippi*, 1998
Liz Jarrett, *Tempting Tess*, 2001
Julie Kenner, *Reckless*, 2000
Deborah Shelley, *It's in His Kiss*, 1999

224

ROBYN AMOS

Bring Me a Dream

(New York: Harper Torch, 2001)

Story type: Contemporary
Subject(s): Mystery; Humor
Major character(s): Jasmine White, Bodyguard (Core Group Protection); Spencer Powell, Radio Personality (''The Sandman'')
Time period(s): 2000s
Locale(s): Washington, District of Columbia

Summary: A confident bodyguard and a radio show personality clash when Jasmine White is assigned by her company to protect ''Sandman'' Spencer Powell from a psycho-stalker.

The problem? He doesn't want a woman guarding him, especially one who is so attractive, and she demands to be taken seriously. Modern, passionate, and fast-paced.

Other books you might like:
Rochelle Alers, *Private Passions*, 1997
Brenda Jackson, *Secret Love*, 2000
Michelle Jerott, *Absolute Trouble*, 1998
humor and danger
Francis Ray, *Incognito*, 1997

225

CATHERINE ANDERSON (Pseudonym of Adeline Catherine Anderson)

Sweet Nothings

(New York: Onyx, 2002)

Story type: Contemporary
Subject(s): Abuse; Animals/Horses; Self-Esteem
Major character(s): Molly Sterling Wells, Abuse Victim; Jake Coulter, Horse Trainer, Rancher
Time period(s): 2000s (2001)
Locale(s): Oregon (Lazy J Ranch)

Summary: After Molly Sterling Wells shows up at his ranch one day with Sonora Sunset, a badly beaten horse Molly has kidnapped from her ex-husband, Jake Coulter deduces there is more to her story than she is willing to tell him. Jake agrees to try and rehabilitate Sonora Sunset if Molly will stay on as the ranch's new cook and housekeeper, but Jake quickly discovers not only must he help a wounded horse but also an emotionally battered woman.

Where it's reviewed:
Booklist, December 15, 2001, page 708
Publishers Weekly, December 24, 2001, page 49

Other books by the same author:
Phantom Waltz, 2001
Seventh Heaven, 2000
Baby Love, 1999
Cherish, 1998
Forever After, 1998

Other books you might like:
Barbara Bretton, *A Soft Place to Fall*, 2000
Barbara Freethy, *Almost Home*, 2000
Patricia Kay, *The Wrong Child*, 2000
Curtiss Ann Matlock, *Cold Tea on a Hot Day*, 2001
Ruth Wind, *The Last Chance Ranch*, 1995

226

JUDITH ARNOLD (Pseudonym of Barbara Keiler)

Looking for Laura

(Don Mills, Ontario: MIRA, 2001)

Story type: Contemporary; Humor
Subject(s): Humor; Infidelity; Widows/Widowers
Major character(s): Sally Driver, Widow(er), Waiter/Waitress; Todd Sloane, Publisher (newspaper), Journalist
Time period(s): 2000s
Locale(s): Winfield, Massachusetts

Summary: Sally Driver, unexpectedly widowed when her husband dies in a car accident, finds love letters in his sweater drawer. The problem is, they aren't from her, but from someone named Laura. Todd Sloane, Sally's late husband's best friend, doesn't like Sally, but he, too, feels betrayed by not knowing about Laura. Together, Sally and Todd form an unlikely bond and search for the mystery woman. A common goal draws together a reluctant couple in this warm, often humorous tale.

Where it's reviewed:
Affaire de Coeur, July/August 2001, page 31
Romantic Times, August 2001, page 89

Other books by the same author:
Love in Bloom's, 2002
'Tis the Season, 2000
Dr. Dad, 2000
Birthright, 2000
Millennium Baby, 2000

Other books you might like:
Rita Herron, *Marry Me, Maddie?*, 2001
Kasey Michaels, *Too Good to Be True*, 2001
Julie Ortolon, *Dear Cupid*, 2001
Susan Elizabeth Phillips, *This Heart of Mine*, 2001
Sheila Rabe, *A Prince of a Guy*, 2001

227

MARY BALOGH

No Man's Mistress

(New York: Delacorte, 2001)

Story type: Historical/Regency
Subject(s): Property Rights; Romance
Major character(s): Lady Viola Thornhill, Noblewoman; Lord Ferdinand Dudley, Nobleman, Heir
Time period(s): 1810s
Locale(s): Trellick, England

Summary: When Lady Viola Thornhill refuses to move out of her home simply because Lord Ferdinand Dudley arrives from London claiming to have won it in a card game from the late earl Viola says she inherited it from, Ferdinand sees no other choice—and he moves in. The results are, of course, predictable, but the characters, in true Balogh fashion, are not. Lively, sensual, and well-written. Follows *More than a Mistress.*

Where it's reviewed:
Library Journal, August 2001, page 86
Publishers Weekly, July 30, 2001, page 64

Other books by the same author:
More than a Mistress, 2000 (linked to *No Man's Mistress*)
One Night for Love, 1999
Irresistible, 1998
A Christmas Bride, 1997
Indiscreet, 1997

Other books you might like:
Patricia Gaffney, *Lily*, 1991
Candice Hern, *The Bride Sale*, 2002
Mary Jo Putney, *One Perfect Rose*, 1997

Mary Jo Putney, *The Rake*, 1998
revised version of 1989s *The Rake and the Reformer*
Mary Jo Putney, *Thunder and Roses*, 1993

228

JILL BARNETT

Sentimental Journey

(New York: Pocket, 2001)

Story type: Contemporary; Saga
Subject(s): War; Friendship; Relationships
Major character(s): Charlotte Morrison, Pilot (ferries planes to England); Red Walker, Pilot, Military Personnel; George ''Skip'' Inskip, Military Personnel (RAF), Pilot
Time period(s): 1940s
Locale(s): United States; England; Africa

Summary: *Sentimental Journey* chronicles the tumultuous years of World War II through the lives of five diverse people caught up in the horrors and heroics of the war. This intense, poignant, action-filled story sweeps its characters from wartime America and England and into the deserts of Northern Africa with life-changing and surprisingly romantic results. Good forties detail.

Where it's reviewed:
Library Journal, August 2001, page 88

Other books by the same author:
Wicked, 1999
Wild, 1998
Wonderful, 1997
Carried Away, 1996
Imagine, 1995

Other books you might like:
Lois Battle, *War Brides*, 2000
WW II time period
Sandra Chastain, *Summer of the Soldiers*, 1993
Korean War time period
Janet Dailey, *Silver Wings, Santiago Blue*, 1984
Eva Rutland, *No Crystal Stair*, 2000
Janet Eddy Westin, *Love and Glory*, 1985
WW II setting

229

JULIE BEARD

Very Truly Yours

(New York: Jove, 2001)

Story type: Historical/Regency
Subject(s): Blackmail; Scandal; Secrets
Major character(s): Lisa Cranshaw, Wealthy; Jack Fairchild, Nobleman (Lord Tutley), Impoverished
Time period(s): 1810s
Locale(s): Middledale, England; London, England

Summary: Solicitor Jack Fairchild needs money. Having paid off his father's many debts, he is, in a word, broke. Lisa Cranshaw needs to marry someone to avoid a union with a dreadful nobleman. Jack also has a title, but he ignores that to set up shop in the rural community of Middledale. Among his new duties is handling the mail, and a letter with a blurred address turns out to be a missive from Lisa to her confidante. Posing as the trusted older woman, Jack answers the letter and plans a custom-made courtship. Humor, wonderful secondary characters, and a delicious secret make this book one that readers will want to enjoy more than once.

Where it's reviewed:
Affaire de Coeur, March/April 2001, page 42
Booklist, April 15, 2001, page 1538
Publishers Weekly, February 26, 2001, page 65
Romantic Times, April 2001, page 40

Other books by the same author:
My Fair Lord, 2000
The Maiden's Heart, 1999
Romance of the Rose, 1998
Falcon and the Sword, 1997
A Dance in Heather, 1996

Other books you might like:
Victoria Alexander, *The Husband List*, 2000
Suzanne Enoch, *Meet Me at Midnight*, 2000
Kasey Michaels, *Someone to Love*, 2001
Julia Quinn, *How to Marry a Marquis*, 1999
Peggy Waide, *Mightier than the Sword*, 2001

230

DONNA BELL

A Tangled Web

(New York: Zebra, 2001)

Story type: Regency
Subject(s): Independence; Inheritance
Major character(s): Sincerity Prudence Hartford, Gentlewoman, Heiress; Simon McKendrick, Military Personnel (former major), Gentleman
Time period(s): 1810s
Locale(s): London, England; Bath, England

Summary: Intercepting a letter with news that her great-aunt Prudence has died and left her a sizeable estate, Sincerity Hartford sees a way to escape her vexsome mother, who has been insisting she find a suitable husband. Pretending that she is going to Bath to stay with Prudence, Sincerity instead sets up her own household in her aunt's home where she manages to keep her mother at bay with letters hinting that an eligible beau, modeled after Simon McKendrick, a man Sincerity hardly knows, is actively courting her. All of Sincerity's schemes begin to unravel when her mother arrives in town to meet the man who wants to marry her daughter and Sincerity is forced to convince Simon to play the role of love struck suitor.

Where it's reviewed:
Romantic Times, July 2001, page 28

Other books by the same author:
Heiress to Love, 2000
Valentine Kisses, 2000
Words of Love, 1999
The First Waltz, 1998
Sweet Tranquility, 1997

Other books you might like:
Catherine Blair, *Athena's Conquest*, 2001
Shannon Donnelly, *A Compromising Situation*, 2000
Valerie King, *A Brighton Flirtation*, 2000
Martha Kirkland, *That Scandalous Heiress*, 2000
Nancy Lawrence, *An Intimate Arrangement*, 2000

231

CAROLE BELLACERA

East of the Sun, West of the Moon

(New York: Forge, 2001)

Story type: Contemporary
Subject(s): Family; Marriage; Students, Foreign
Major character(s): Leigh ''Kayleigh'' O'Fallon, Artist (children's book illustrator), Spouse; Erik Haukeland, Student—Exchange
Time period(s): 1980s; 1990s (1989-1991)
Locale(s): Washington, District of Columbia; New York, New York; Oslo, Norway

Summary: After discovering her husband has been unfaithful, 40-year-old Leigh O'Fallon turns for comfort to Erik Haukeland, the 29-year-old foreign exchange student who is currently staying with the O'Fallon family. Leigh enters into a passionate affair with Erik which only illustrates to her how unfulfilling her marriage has become. Now Leigh's relationship with Erik will force her to choose between a new chance at happiness and her marriage and family.

Where it's reviewed:
Booklist, August 2001, page 2100
Publishers Weekly, July 30, 2001, page 64
Romantic Times, August 2001, page 84

Other books by the same author:
Spotlight, 2000
Border Crossings, 1999

Other books you might like:
Lyn Ellis, *In Praise of Younger Men*, 2000
Barbara Freethy, *Just the Way You Are*, 2000
Kristin Hannah, *Summer Island*, 2001
Curtiss Ann Matlock, *Driving Lessons*, 2000
Karen Robards, *One Summer*, 1993

232

JANICE BENNETT
SHANNON DONNELLY, Co-Author
MONA GEDNEY, Co-Author

Autumn Kittens

(New York: Zebra, 2001)

Story type: Regency; Anthology
Subject(s): Animals/Cats; Courtship
Time period(s): 1810s
Locale(s): England

Summary: This excellent Regency anthology features a trio of novellas from some of the genre's favorite authors. The focus of this one? Kittens! Included are *Inseparable* by Janice Bennett, *Cat's Cradle* by Shannon Donnelly, and *Lord Wintergreen and the Beast* by Mona Gedney. Lively, charming, and heartwarming, this collection will appeal to all Regency fans, not just those who appreciate cats.

Where it's reviewed:
Rendezvous, September 2001, page 17

Other books you might like:
Victoria Alexander, *Santa Paws*, 1997
Elisabeth Fairchild, *A Regency Christmas Present*, 1999
anthology
Jo Ann Ferguson, *Mistletoe Kittens*, 1999
anthology
Annie Kimberlin, *Romeo and Julia*, 1999
contemporary cats
Judith A. Lansdowne, *Stocking Stuffers*, 2000
anthology, one story features kittens

233

LISA TAWN BERGREN
MAUREEN PRATT, Co-Author
LYN COTE, Co-Author

Letters of the Heart

(Wheaton, Illinois: Tyndale House, 2002)

Story type: Inspirational
Subject(s): Letters; Christian Life
Locale(s): United States

Summary: Using the convention of written correspondence, Tyndale has put together a collection of stories by three of their more popular writers that should please inspirational fans. Included are ''Until the Shadows Flee'' by Lisa Tawn Bergren, ''Dear Love'' by Maureen Pratt, and ''Varina's Heart'' by Lyn Cote.

Where it's reviewed:
Romantic Times, January 2002, page 29

Other books by the same author:
Porch Swings & Picket Fences, 1999
A Mother's Love, 1997

Other books you might like:
Lyn Cote, *Hope's Garden*, 2000
Martha Kirkland, *Miss Maitland's Letters*, 2000
Regency/no religious elements
Barbara Metzger, *Miss Lockhart's Letters*, 1998
Regency/no religious elements

234

HEIDI BETTS

Walker's Widow

(New York: Leisure, 2002)

Story type: Historical/American West
Series: Welcome to Purgatory. Book 1
Subject(s): American West; Robbers and Outlaws; Widows/Widowers
Major character(s): Regan Doyle, Widow(er), Thief; Clayton Walker, Lawman (Texas Ranger)
Time period(s): 19th century

Locale(s): Purgatory, Texas

Summary: By day, the widow Regan Doyle is a dutiful caregiver for her infirm mother-in-law, Martha. By night, sweet, kind, still-grieving Regan is a notorious robber who steals from the rich and gives to an orphanage. Martha sends for her nephew, Clay Walker, to investigate the robberies, secretly hoping that Clay and Regan will fall in love and get married. When he finds out who the robber really is, Clay's torn between his duty as a Ranger and his love for Regan. This clever twist on the Robin Hood legend shows that Purgatory can be more than a little town in Texas as Clay tries to decide what's the right thing to do.

Where it's reviewed:
Romantic Times, January 2002, page 43

Other books by the same author:
Almost a Lady, 2001
A Promise of Roses, 2000
Cinnamon and Roses, 2000

Other books you might like:
Mary Burton, *The Colorado Bride*, 2001
Leslie LaFoy, *Jackson's Way*, 2001
Linda O'Brien, *Beloved Protector*, 2001
Allie Shaw, *The Impossible Texan*, 2001
Judith Stacy, *The Widow's Little Secret*, 2001

235

ELIZABETH BEVARLY

The Secret Life of Connor Monahan

(New York: Silhouette, 2001)

Story type: Contemporary
Subject(s): Crime and Criminals; Restaurants
Major character(s): Winona Thornbury, Restaurateur; Connor Monahan, Detective—Police (vice squad)
Time period(s): 2000s
Locale(s): Bloomington, Indiana; Marigold, Indiana

Summary: Undercover vice cop Connor Monahan's investigation of Winona Thornbury is going nowhere. Evidence indicates that an exclusive call girl ring is being run out of Winona's restaurant and that Winona is the madam in charge. With her demure Victorian clothes and old-fashioned manners, Winona would seem to be the antithesis of a high-class prostitute, but the only way for Connor to find out for sure is to get closer to the bewitching lady. Witty and wonderful.

Where it's reviewed:
Romantic Times, December 2001, page 103

Other books by the same author:
He Could Be the One, 2001
The Temptation of Rory Monahan, 2001
When Jayne Met Erik, 2001
First Comes Love, 2000
Monahan's Gamble, 2000

Other books you might like:
Stephanie Bond, *Manhunting in Mississippi*, 1998
Suzanne Forster, *The Devil and Ms. Moody*, 1990
Kristin Gabriel, *Monday Man*, 1998
Rachel Gibson, *Truly Madly Yours*, 1999
Barbara McCauley, *Reese's Wild Wager*, 2001

236

ELIZABETH BEVARLY

When Jayne Met Erik

(New York: Silhouette, 2001)

Story type: Contemporary
Series: 20 Amber Court. Book 1
Subject(s): Marriage; Inheritance
Major character(s): Jayne Pembroke, Saleswoman (Collete Jewelry); Erik Randolph, Heir
Time period(s): 2000s
Locale(s): Youngsville, Indiana

Summary: If wealthy playboy Erik Randolph wants to inherit the millions his grandfather has left him, he must marry before his 30th birthday. With no immediate marital prospects in sight and his birthday just weeks away, Erik impulsively proposes to Jayne Pembroke, a saleswoman he just met. Jayne is tempted by Erik's proposal since it would offer her a way to fund her sibling's college education, but she is also slightly bothered with the idea of being married in name only to the irresistibly sexy Erik.

Where it's reviewed:
Romantic Times, September 2001, page 112

Other books by the same author:
He Could Be the One, 2001
The Temptation of Rory Monahan, 2001
First Comes Love, 2000
How to Trap a Tycoon, 2000
Monahan's Gamble, 2000

Other books you might like:
Stephanie Bond, *It Takes a Rebel*, 2000
Suzanne Brockmann, *Stand-In Groom*, 1997
Ryanne Corey, *The Heiress and the Bodyguard*, 2001
Jennifer Crusie, *The Cinderella Deal*, 1996
Charlotte Maclay, *Accidental Roommates*, 1997

237

PAM BINDER

The Enchantment

(New York: Sonnet, 2001)

Story type: Historical; Time Travel
Subject(s): Magic; Time Travel; Legends
Major character(s): Eilan Dougan, Empath; Conor MacCloud, Warrior (Highlander)
Time period(s): 14th century (1310); 2000s
Locale(s): Seattle, Washington; Inverness, Scotland

Summary: Back in Seattle to care for her parents' antique store while they are on vacation in Great Britain, Eilan Dougan is stunned when the clocks begin behaving strangely and a bloody Highlander, complete with sword, suddenly appears asking for the woman called "The Peacemaker." Naturally, she calls the police. Conor MacCloud has come from the 14th century to find the legendary woman who can save his land; and when Eilan realizes that she is the one, she ends up in

Scotland, just as the legend has predicted. The story is laced with gentle passion and typical out-of-time humor, fueled by intriguing legends and well-developed characters, and shot through with shards of violent action.

Other books by the same author:
The Inscription, 2000
The Quest, 2000

Other books you might like:
Dee Davis, *Everything in Its Time*, 2000
Diana Gabaldon, *Outlander*, 1991
classic time travel romance
Donna Kauffman, *Your Wish Is My Command*, 2001
Karen Marie Moning, *The Highlander's Touch*, 2000
Karen Marie Moning, *Kiss of the Highlander*, 2001

238

CATHERINE BLAIR (Pseudonym of K. Noelle Gracy)

A Family for Gillian

(New York: Zebra, 2001)

Story type: Regency
Subject(s): Marriage; Family
Major character(s): Gillian Harwell Avery, Noblewoman; Prescott Avery, Nobleman (viscount), Widow(er)
Time period(s): 1810s
Locale(s): England; County Limerick, Ireland

Summary: A headstrong heroine with a shredded reputation, a still-grieving widower hero with three unruly children, and a marriage of convenience combine in this story of love, trust, and healing that will appeal to readers who like their Regencies child-filled and with a country flair. Unusual Irish setting.

Where it's reviewed:
Rendezvous, October 2001, page 32

Other books by the same author:
Athena's Conquest, 2001
The Hero Returns, 1999
The Scandalous Miss Delaney, 1999

Other books you might like:
Monique Ellis, *An Uncommon Governess*, 1994
Kate Huntington, *Mistletoe Mayhem*, 2000
Carla Kelly, *Mrs. Drew Plays Her Hand*, 1994
Katherine Kingsley, *A Natural Attachment*, 1990
Laura Matthews, *A Prudent Match*, 2000

239

GEORGIA BOCKOVEN

Another Summer

(New York: Harper Torch, 2001)

Story type: Contemporary
Subject(s): Reunions; Beaches; Magic
Major character(s): Cheryl Cunningham, Social Worker, Divorced Person; Andrew Wells, Businessman (orchid nursery owner)
Time period(s): 2000s
Locale(s): Santa Cruz, California

Summary: High school sweethearts Cheryl Cunningham and Andrew Wells meet again at a class reunion and consider trying to recapture what they once had. This poignant, heart-warming story takes several romantic stories, weaves them together, and lets them play out in the magical atmosphere of a beach house along the central California coast.

Where it's reviewed:
Romantic Times, December 2001, page 76

Other books by the same author:
Disguised Blessing, 2000
Things Remembered, 1998
An Unspoken Promise, 1997
Far from Home, 1997
The Beach House, 1997

Other books you might like:
Barbara Freethy, *Daniel's Gift*, 1996
Barbara Freethy, *One True Love*, 1998
JoAnn Ross, *Far Harbor*, 2000
Dallas Schulze, *The Way Home*, 1995
Kathleen Gilles Seidel, *Summer's End*, 2000

240

STEPHANIE BOND (Pseudonym of Stephanie Bond Hauck)

Two Sexy

(New York: Harlequin, 2001)

Story type: Contemporary
Subject(s): Actors and Actresses; Identity
Major character(s): Meg Valentine, Teacher, Imposter; Jarett Miller, Bodyguard
Time period(s): 2000s
Locale(s): Peoria, Illinois; Chicago, Illinois; Los Angeles, California

Summary: When asked to impersonate sexy television star Taylor Gee at a charity event, prim and proper schoolteacher Meg Valentine leaps at the chance to escape her dull, normal life even if it is only for one night. Jarett Miller, Taylor's bodyguard and handler, assures Meg that with a little bit of makeup, she will be an absolute ringer for the gorgeous starlet but things don't go quite as they planned once Meg realizes she is falling for her handsome bodyguard.

Where it's reviewed:
Romantic Times, August 2001, page 105

Other books by the same author:
It Takes a Rebel, 2000
Our Husband, 2000
Too Hot to Sleep, 2000
Seeking Single Male, 2000
About Last Night, 1999

Other books you might like:
Lori Foster, *In Too Deep*, 2000
Julie Kenner, *Nobody Does It Better*, 2000
Julie Elizabeth Leto, *Exposed*, 2001
Carly Phillips, *Secret Fantasy*, 2001
Cara Summers, *While He Was Sleeping*, 1999

241

CELESTE BRADLEY

Fallen

(New York: Leisure, 2001)

Story type: Historical/Victorian
Subject(s): Scandal; Family Relations; Social Classes
Major character(s): Izzy Temple, Spinster, Impoverished; Eppingham Julian Rowley, Nobleman (Baron Blackworth), Rake
Time period(s): 1830s (1831)
Locale(s): London, England

Summary: At a house party, notorious rake Eppingham ''Eppie'' Julian Rowley, Baron Blackworth, makes love to the woman whose bed he's crawled into. Except it's the wrong woman. When spinster Izzy Temple slams his head with a candlestick, her screams draw the other guests to the scene of his mistake. Plain Jane Izzy blossoms and finds freedom in her scandalous notoriety, but Eppie begins insisting on marriage. A Pygmalion paradox of a woman who can't rise to her fullest potential until she's fallen.

Where it's reviewed:
Romantic Times, June 2001, page 39

Other books you might like:
Candace Camp, *So Wild a Heart*, 2002
Lynn Kerstan, *Francesca's Rake*, 1997
Jaclyn Reding, *The Pretender*, 2002
Nan Ryan, *A Lifetime of Heaven*, 1993
Haywood Smith, *Border Lord*, 2001

242

SUZANNE BROCKMANN

Taylor's Temptation

(New York: Silhouette, 2001)

Story type: Contemporary
Series: Tall, Dark, and Dangerous. Book 10
Subject(s): Friendship; Social Issues
Major character(s): Bobby Taylor, Military Personnel (Navy SEAL); Colleen Mary Skelly, Student—Graduate (law school)
Time period(s): 2000s
Locale(s): Boston, Massachusetts; Norfolk, Virginia; Tulgeria, Fictional Country

Summary: Bobby Taylor would do anything for Wes Skelly, his best friend and fellow Navy SEAL, but watching over Wes' younger sister Colleen, a law school student in the midst of coordinating a relief trip to war-torn Tulgeria, may just be the most difficult thing Bobby has ever done. He is in love with Colleen, but Bobby knows exactly how her overprotective older brother would feel about Colleen dating any SEAL. While Bobby may be trying to adopt a hands-off policy when it comes to Colleen, what he doesn't know is that Colleen has had a thing for him since she was a teenager and now she is determined to do something about it.

Where it's reviewed:
Romantic Times, July 2001, page 109

Other books by the same author:
Over the Edge, 2001
The Defiant Hero, 2001
Get Lucky, 2000
Identity Unknown, 2000
The Unsung Hero, 2000

Other books you might like:
Cherry Adair, *Hide and Seek*, 2001
Fiona Brand, *Blade's Lady*, 2000
Vicki Hinze, *Acts of Honor*, 1999
Rachel Lee, *An Officer and a Gentleman*, 1991
Gina Wilkins, *A Perfect Stranger*, 1991

243

CONNIE BROCKWAY
PATTI BERG, Co-Author
DEBRA DIER, Co-Author
KATHLEEN GIVENS, Co-Author

My Scottish Summer

(New York: Warner, 2001)

Story type: Anthology; Contemporary
Subject(s): Love
Locale(s): Scotland

Summary: Four romantic stories celebrate love in Scotland. In Connie Brockway's ''Lassie Go Home,'' American Toni Olson gets in a tug of war over the ownership of a champion Border collie with Scotsman Devlin Montgomery. Cookbook author Emily Sinclair is determined to find a way to convince Colin Dunbar to let her photograph his castle for her next book in Patti Berg's ''Sinfully Scottish.'' Debra Dier puts an American professor in search of lost jewels up against a Scotsman who questions her motivations in ''The Maddening Highlander.'' When American Maddie Breen goes on vacation to the Isle of Skye, she meets a romantic Highlander in ''Castle in the Skye'' by Kathleen Givens.

Where it's reviewed:
Romantic Times, July 2001, page 86

Other books you might like:
Barbara Boswell, *Magic Slippers*, 1996
Jude Deveraux, *A Season in the Highlands*, 2000
Christina Dodd, *Scottish Brides*, 1999
Hannah Howell, *Scottish Magic*, 1998
Lynn Kurland, *Opposites Attract*, 2000

244

DEBRA LEE BROWN

The Mackintosh Bride

(Toronto: Harlequin, 2001)

Story type: Historical/Medieval
Subject(s): Marriage; Feuds
Major character(s): Alena Todd, Horse Trainer; Iain Mackintosh, Laird
Time period(s): 12th century (1192); 13th century (1203)
Locale(s): Highlands, Scotland

Summary: Fleeing an unwanted marriage to the new laird of the Grant clan, Alena Todd is rescued and then sheltered by Iain Mackintosh, the man she had loved as a boy and whose father was killed by the Grants 11 years earlier. Though Alena knows him instantly, Iain does not recognize her, leading to a fiery and politically difficult relationship. Lively, action-packed, and romantic.

Other books by the same author:
Ice Maiden, 2001
The Virgin Spring, 2000

Other books you might like:
Claire Delacroix, *The Beauty*, 2001
Julie Garwood, *Ransom*, 1999
Hannah Howell, *Highland Promise*, 1999
Susan King, *The Swan Maiden*, 2001
Ruth Langan, *The Highlander*, 1994

245

SANDRA BROWN

Envy

(New York: Warner, 2001)

Story type: Romantic Suspense
Subject(s): Authors and Writers; Books and Reading; Revenge
Major character(s): Maris Matherly-Reed, Editor, Spouse (of Noah); Noah Reed, Publisher (Matherly Press), Writer; Parker Evans, Handicapped (uses wheelchair), Writer
Time period(s): 2000s
Locale(s): New York, New York; St. Anne Island, Georgia

Summary: An unsolicited manuscript sent to Matherly Press attracts the attention of editor Maris Matherly-Reed and sends her to a small island off the coast of Georgia in search of the novel's mysterious author. After identifying her new find as Parker Evans, Maris coerces him into completing his novel, but when Maris begins to suspect Evan's work may be more fact than fiction, she wonders if it really was a coincidence that this particular book was sent to her.

Where it's reviewed:
Booklist, July 2001, page 1948
People Weekly, August 27, 2001, page 45
Publishers Weekly, July 16, 2001, page 157
Romantic Times, September 2001, page 84

Other books by the same author:
Standoff, 2000
The Switch, 2000
The Alibi, 1999
Unspeakable, 1998
Fat Tuesday, 1997

Other books you might like:
Stella Cameron, *French Quarter*, 1998
Linda Howard, *Kill and Tell*, 1998
Jayne Ann Krentz, *Midnight Jewels*, 1988
Nora Roberts, *Brazen Virtue*, 1988
Anne Stuart, *Shadow Lover*, 1999

246

DIXIE BROWNING

Rocky and the Senator's Daughter

(New York: Silhouette, 2001)

Story type: Contemporary
Series: Man of the Month. Book 11
Subject(s): Scandal; Politics; Healing
Major character(s): Sarah Jones, Widow(er) (of sleazy congressman); Rocky Waters, Journalist, Widow(er)
Time period(s): 2000s
Locale(s): Washington, District of Columbia; Snowden, North Carolina

Summary: After being in a coma for seven years, journalist Rocky Waters' wife dies, and he ends his self-imposed isolation. Sarah Jones, daughter of a crooked U.S. Senator and recent widow of a sleazy congressman, has hidden from the world in a small town in North Carolina. When Rocky overhears a conversation regarding an upcoming book about the notorious men in Sarah's life, he remembers the vulnerable young woman he met years before, and warns her about the impending novel. However, Sarah has another secret, and she's not sharing it with anyone, even Rocky.

Where it's reviewed:
Romantic Times, November 2001, page 113

Other books by the same author:
The Millionaire's Pregnant Bride, 2002
More to Love, 2001
Look What the Stork Brought, 2000
Tumbled Wall, 2000
The Bride-in-Law, 1999

Other books you might like:
Elizabeth Bevarly, *When Jayne Met Erik*, 2001
Annette Broadrick, *Hard to Forget*, 2001
B.J. James, *The Taming of Jackson Cade*, 2001
Eileen Wilks, *The Pregnant Heiress*, 2001
Anne Marie Winston, *Risque Business*, 2001

247

MARY BURTON

The Colorado Bride

(Toronto: Harlequin, 2001)

Story type: Historical/American West
Subject(s): American West; Secrets; Single Parent Families
Major character(s): Rebecca Taylor, Widow(er), Single Parent; Cole McGuire, Military Personnel (retired), Single Parent
Time period(s): 1880s (1882)
Locale(s): White Stone, Colorado

Summary: Cole McGuire receives a letter two years after it's written telling him that Lily, a Colorado prostitute, is pregnant with his baby. When he arrives in town to claim his child, he finds that Lily and the baby died in childbirth, or so the widow Rebecca Taylor tells him. Her toddler's the same age as his would have been, and there's something very familiar about the little boy. An entire town swears to keep a secret in this prodigal son coming home to a cold welcome story.

Other books by the same author:
A Bride for McCain, 2000

Other books you might like:
Anne Avery, *The Lawman Takes a Wife*, 2000
Linda Winstead Jones, *The Seduction of Roxanne*, 2000
Elizabeth Lane, *Bride on the Run*, 2001
Maureen McKade, *Outlaw's Bride*, 2001
Judith Stacy, *The Widow's Little Secret*, 2001

248

NANCY BUTLER
EMMA JENSEN, Co-Author
EDITH LAYTON, Co-Author
BARBARA METZGER, Co-Author
ANDREA PICKENS, Co-Author

Regency Christmas Spirits

(New York: Signet, 2001)

Story type: Anthology; Regency
Subject(s): Christmas

Summary: Five Regency short stories celebrate the spirit of Christmas and the joy of falling in love. In Nancy Butler's ''The Merry Wanderer'' a visitor from the faery world must teach the new Lady of Islay her responsibilities to a very special book. An Irish lady fighting to restore her beloved family home finds a new champion in Emma Jensen's ''The Wexford Carol.'' Arabella Danton relies a bit too much on liquid spirits to get her through social situations but Rupert Aldridge shows her how to get by on her own in Edith Layton's ''High Spirits.'' In order to break ''The Christmas Curse'' by Barbara Metzger, a ghostly knight and his lady must find a way to get a lost ring back on the finger of one of their descendants' brides. Andrea Pickens' ''A Gathering of Gifts'' features a pampered and spoiled young lady who learns the true meaning of Christmas from an impoverished country baron.

Where it's reviewed:
Romantic Times, October 2001, page 62

Other books by the same author:
A Regency Christmas Eve, 2000

Other books you might like:
Mary Balogh, *A Regency Christmas Feast*, 2000
anthology
Elisabeth Fairchild, *A Regency Christmas Present*, 1999
anthology
Judith A. Lansdowne, *Stocking Stuffers*, 2000
anthology
Edith Layton, *A Regency Christmas Carol*, 1997
anthology

249

EMILY CARMICHAEL (Pseudonym of Emily Krokosz)

Diamond in the Ruff

(New York: Bantam, 2001)

Story type: Contemporary/Fantasy; Humor
Subject(s): Humor; Afterlife; Animals/Dogs
Major character(s): Joey DeMato, Businesswoman (wedding planner); Ben Ramsay, Police Officer, Single Parent
Time period(s): 2000s
Locale(s): Denver, Colorado

Summary: Joey DeMato, wedding planner, has a problem. The bride is one of her best friends, and Joey's in love with the groom. Little does Joey know that Piggy, the corgi she's watching for another friend, is really a woman killed during an illicit affair who's doing penance as a dog. Piggy does her best to nudge Ben and Joey together, but a dog—albeit a heavenly one—can only do so much. Lots of humor and even some danger make this sequel to *Finding Mr. Right* every bit as good as its predecessor.

Where it's reviewed:
Booklist, September 15, 2001, page 202
Romantic Times, November 2001, page 94

Other books by the same author:
Jezebel's Sister, 2001
A Ghost for Maggie, 1999
Finding Mr. Right, 1998
Windfall, 1997
Gold Dust, 1996

Other books you might like:
Sue Civil-Brown, *Next Stop, Paradise*, 2001
Karen Fox, *Buttercup Baby*, 2001
Kathleen Kane, *Catch a Fallen Angel*, 2000
historical—Old West
Debbie Macomber, *Shirley, Goodness, and Mercy*, 1999
Judi McCoy, *I Dream of You*, 2001

250

ROBYN CARR

The Wedding Party

(Don Mills, Ontario: MIRA, 2001)

Story type: Contemporary; Humor
Subject(s): Weddings; Family Relations
Major character(s): Charlene Dugan, Lawyer (family law), Divorced Person; Jake Dugan, Divorced Person (Charlene's ex-husband); Dennis, Health Care Professional (physician's assistant), Boyfriend (of Charlene)
Time period(s): 2000s
Locale(s): Sacramento, California

Summary: When Dennis and Charlene finally decide to get married after being in a comfortable relationship for five years, the chaos and turmoil that result cause them to rethink the whole thing. Children, siblings, parents, and in-laws all combine in this funny, witty, and very modern story that despite a series of disastrous mismatches and misunderstandings, gets everything—and everyone—properly sorted out in the end.

Where it's reviewed:
Rendezvous, September 2001, page 25

Other books by the same author:
The House on Olive Street, 1999

Other books you might like:
Sue Civil-Brown, *Tempting Mr. Wright*, 2000
Ruth Jean Dale, *Fiance Wanted!*, 2000
funny and lively
Jennifer Greene, *Rock Solid*, 2000
Kasey Michaels, *Raffling Ryan*, 2000
Tina Wainscott, *The Wrong Mr. Right*, 2000

251

TORI CARRINGTON (Pseudonym of Lori Karayianni and Tony Karayianni)

The Woman for Dusty Conrad

(New York: Silhouette, 2001)

Story type: Contemporary
Subject(s): Fires; Healing; Self-Acceptance
Major character(s): Jolie Conrad, Fire Fighter, Spouse; Dusty Conrad, Fire Fighter, Spouse
Time period(s): 2000s
Locale(s): Old Orchard, Ohio

Summary: The blaze that takes firefighter Dusty Conrad's brother's life also takes Dusty's confidence and self-esteem. Jolie, his wife, wounded in the same inferno, refuses to resign her own firefighter position for him. Unable to deal with the possibility of Jolie dying in a fire too, Dusty leaves, returning months later for her signature on divorce papers. Their love hasn't died, and Jolie refuses to sign and end their marriage. She also refuses to cave in to Dusty's demands she leave her beloved profession. Dedication to job and family conflict are part of the plot in this story where old flames never die.

Where it's reviewed:
Romantic Times, October 2001, page 116

Other books by the same author:
Private Investigations, 2002
Stranger's Touch, 2002
Never Say Never Again, 2001 (Magnificent McCoy Men. Book 3)
You Only Love Once, 2001 (Magnificent McCoy Men. Book 4)
You Sexy Thing, 2001

Other books you might like:
Justine Dare, *Night Fires*, 1998
Cathie Linz, *Husband Needed*, 1998
Sylvia Mendoza, *On Fire/Al rojo vivo*, 1999
Nora Roberts, *Night Shield*, 2000
Carol Steward, *Courting Katarina*, 2001
inspirational

252

LESLIE CARROLL

Miss Match

(New York: Ivy, 2002)

Story type: Contemporary; Humor
Subject(s): Dating (Social Customs); Marriage; Humor
Major character(s): Kathryn "Kitty" Lamb, Teacher (high school drama); Walker "Bear" Hart, Businessman (financial analyst)
Time period(s): 2000s
Locale(s): New York, New York

Summary: High school drama teacher Kitty Lamb gives in to sisterly pressure and her own discontent with the dismal New York dating scene and registers with a dating service. She ends up with five less than successful dates, but snares the marriage-averse financial genius who is managing Six in the City for his wandering mother. A funny, upbeat, and modern romance with a passing similarity to *Bridget Jones's Diary* and some of the Red Dress Ink books.

Other books you might like:
Helen Fielding, *Bridget Jones's Diary*, 1996
Wendy Markham, *Slightly Single*, 2001
Sarah Mlynowski, *Milkrun*, 2001
Melissa Senate, *See Jane Date*, 2001
Isabel Wolff, *The Trials of Tiffany Trott*, 1999

253

LINDA LEA CASTLE (Pseudonym of Linda L. Crockett)

Mattie and the Blacksmith

(New York: Zebra, 2001)

Story type: Historical/American West; Humor
Series: Bogus Brides. Book 2
Subject(s): Frontier and Pioneer Life; Courtship; Humor
Major character(s): Mattie Green, Teacher; Roamer Tresh, Blacksmith
Time period(s): 1850s
Locale(s): McTavish Plain, Nebraska

Summary: Blacksmith Roamer Tresh has no time for romance. He wants a mail order bride to help him raise his nephew, Scout. Mattie Green will only settle for romance, and pretends to be married until the right man comes along. However, Scout has other ideas, and when the boy begins to play Cupid, all sorts of things start happening. An unlikely matchmaker outwits everyone around him in this humorous look at an unwitting courtship.

Where it's reviewed:
Romantic Times, April 2001, page 44

Other books by the same author:
Lottie and the Rustler, 2001 (Bogus Brides. Book 3)
Addie and the Laird, 2000 (Bogus Brides. Book 1)
Temple's Prize, 1997

Other books you might like:
Millie Criswell, *The Marrying Man*, 2000
Geralyn Dawson, *The Wedding Raffle*, 1998

Delores Fossen, *Saddled*, 2001
Betina Krahn, *Sweet Talking Man*, 2000
Judith Stacy, *The Nanny*, 2001

254

TAYLOR CHASE (Pseudonym of Gayle Feyrer)

Heart of Night

(New York: Avon, 2001)

Story type: Historical/Elizabethan
Subject(s): Kings, Queens, Rulers, etc.; Spies; Conspiracies
Major character(s): Lady Claire Darren, Noblewoman; Sir Adrian Thorne, Nobleman, Psychic
Time period(s): 16th century (1580s)
Locale(s): London, England

Summary: While visiting Bedlam with her cruel fiance who wants to witness the torture of the inmates, Lady Claire Darren encounters Sir Adrian Thorne, a man cursed with the ability to see into people's lives by means of a simple touch, and who has been wrongly imprisoned because of this gift. Months later, after Adrian has been freed from the asylum and Claire's fiance is dead, he and Claire meet once again, and amid the treacheries of court intrigue and the London underworld, they find an unexpected passion in each others' arms. A dark, realistic tale.

Where it's reviewed:
Romantic Times, December 2001, page 38

Other books by the same author:
Heart of Deception, 1999

Other books you might like:
Denise Domning, *Lady in Waiting*, 1998
similar period/not so dark
Denise Domning, *Lady in White*, 1999
similar period/not so dark
Brenda Joyce, *The Game*, 1995
similar setting
Ruth Langan, *Conor*, 1999

255

MAUREEN CHILD

Last Virgin in California

(New York: Silhouette, 2001)

Story type: Contemporary; Humor
Series: Bachelor Battalion. Book 13
Subject(s): Military Bases; Military Life; Humor
Major character(s): Lilah Forrest, Hippie; Kevin Rogan, Military Personnel (Marine gunnery sergeant)
Time period(s): 2000s
Locale(s): California (military base)

Summary: Lilah Forrest's biggest problem is her father, the Colonel. He insists on setting up his latter day hippie daughter with Marine after Marine, convinced the only good husband is a military spouse. Lilah doesn't want to have anything to do with her father's choices, even going so far as to talk a gay friend into pretending to be her fiance. Lots of humor and snappy dialogue as "The Last Virgin in California" finds out that father knows best.

Where it's reviewed:
Romantic Times, October 2001, page 114

Other books by the same author:
His Baby!, 2001 (Bachelor Battalion. Book 12)
Prince Charming in Dress Blues, 2001 (Bachelor Battalion. Book 11)
Marooned with a Marine, 2000 (Bachelor Battalion. Book 10)
The Last Santini Virgin, 2000 (Bachelor Battalion. Book 8)
The Next Santini Bride, 2000 (Bachelor Battalion. Book 9)

Other books you might like:
Ruth Jean Dale, *Fiance Wanted!*, 2000
Kasey Michaels, *Raffling Ryan*, 2000
Isabel Sharpe, *Tryst of Fate*, 2000
Deborah Shelley, *One Starry Night*, 2000
Tina Wainscott, *The Wrong Mr. Right*, 2000

256

SUE CIVIL-BROWN

Next Stop, Paradise

(New York: Avon, 2001)

Story type: Humor; Contemporary/Fantasy
Subject(s): Humor; Small Town Life; Monsters
Major character(s): Samantha Bartlett, Police Officer (deputy sheriff); Derek Diche, Television Personality, Paranormal Investigator
Time period(s): 2000s
Locale(s): Paradise Beach, Florida

Summary: It is bad enough that something leaves Godzilla-like tracks on her town's quiet beach, but when Deputy Sheriff Samantha Bartlett arrives on the scene, she's met by none other than Derek Diche, television celebrity and paranormal phenomena investigator. Things go from bad to worse when the next day, a giant egg shows up on the same spot. Soon, Derek and Samantha find themselves allied against the National Guard, city politicians, and two unforgettable FBI agents. Zany characters, including a mayor in bunny slippers and a minister who fears Derek's aunt more than God; snappy dialogue; and a hero trying to overcome his tragic past make this a truly magical blend of humor and poignancy.

Where it's reviewed:
Affaire de Coeur, September/October 2001, page 20
Romantic Times, September 2001, page 86

Other books by the same author:
Catching Kelly, 2000
Tempting Mr. Wright, 2000
Chasing Rainbow, 1999
Letting Loose, 1998
Carried Away, 1997

Other books you might like:
Rachel Gibson, *Truly Madly Yours*, 1999
Rita Herron, *Marry Me, Maddie?*, 2001
Mary Alice Kruesi, *One Summer's Night*, 2000
Susan Elizabeth Phillips, *This Heart of Mine*, 2001

Romance

Nora Roberts, *Heaven and Earth*, 2001

257

ALANA CLAYTON (Pseudonym of Linda Ward)

A Devilish Husband

(New York: Zebra, 2001)

Story type: Regency
Subject(s): Marriage
Major character(s): Cassandra Wallace, Bride (reluctant), Gentlewoman; Jared Moreland, Nobleman (Viscount Carlisle), Rake
Time period(s): 1810s
Locale(s): England

Summary: Determined to wed beneath him in order to get back at his father for marrying the woman he wanted, Jared Moreland, rake and public disgrace, marries Cassie Wallace with no intention of *ever* fathering an heir. However, he reckons without the charm and determination of his new bride. A complex and intriguing Regency with more substance than some.

Where it's reviewed:
Rendezvous, October 2001, page 32

Other books you might like:
Victoria Alexander, *The Husband List*, 2000
Georgette Heyer, *A Civil Contract*, 1962
Georgette Heyer, *The Convenient Marriage*, 1934
Allison Lane, *Devall's Angel*, 1998
Evelyn Richardson, *The Willful Widow*, 1934

258

LYNN COLLUM (Pseudonym of Jerry Lynn Smith)

The Wedding Charm

(New York: Zebra, 2001)

Story type: Regency
Series: Addingtons Trilogy. Book 3
Subject(s): Weddings; Brothers and Sisters; Smuggling
Major character(s): Valara ''Lara'' Rochelle, Noblewoman; Alexander ''Alex'' Addington, Nobleman (Baron Landry), Military Personnel (former major)
Time period(s): 1810s
Locale(s): England

Summary: Surprised to learn that he has inherited a title and an impoverished estate, Alex Addington, newly and independently wealthy because of some astute business investments made on his behalf while he was off fighting Napoleon, takes an old friend and heads for Landry Chase. He finds it already inhabited by his estranged, bitter aunt, her daughter, and her homeless French niece and nephew. Alex is determined to succeed, however; and as he works to set the estate to rights, he also gains the trust of those around him and eventually the love of the spirited, intelligent Lara Rochelle. Third in Collum's Addingtons Trilogy.

Where it's reviewed:
Romantic Times, April 2001, page 102

Other books by the same author:
The Valentine Charm, 2001 (The Addingtons. Book 2)
The Christmas Charm, 2000 (The Addingtons. Book 1)
An Unlikely Father, 1999
Lady Miranda's Masquerade, 1999
The Spy's Bride, 1999

Other books you might like:
Lynn Kerstan, *Marry in Haste*, 1998
Allison Lane, *A Clandestine Courtship*, 1999
Debbie Raleigh, *A Bride for Lord Challmond*, 2001
Patricia Veryan, *The Riddle of Alabaster Royal*, 1999

259

NICOLA CORNICK

Lady Polly

(New York: Harlequin, 2001)

Story type: Historical/Regency
Subject(s): Courtship
Major character(s): Appollonia ''Polly'' Grace Seagrave, Noblewoman; Henry Marchnight, Nobleman, Rake
Time period(s): 1810s (1812; 1817)
Locale(s): England

Summary: After turning down countless offers of marriage, Polly Seagrave has developed a reputation as a woman whose matrimonial standards are too exacting, but Polly can't help it that none of the men courting her even come close to equaling her first love, Henry Marchnight. Five years earlier Henry proposed to Polly who turned him down only to watch the man she loved turn into a jaded rake and gambler. When fate offers Polly a second chance with Henry, it means overcoming her present doubts and trusting he is still the same man she fell in love with long ago.

Where it's reviewed:
Romantic Times, August 2001, page 113

Other books by the same author:
The Virtuous Cyprian, 2001
Miss Verey's Proposal, 2000
The Blanchard Secret, 2000
The Larkswood Legacy, 1999
True Colours, 1998

Other books you might like:
Anne Gracie, *Gallant Waif*, 2001
Deborah Hale, *The Wedding Wager*, 2001
Julia Justiss, *The Wedding Gamble*, 1999
Jackie Manning, *Taming the Duke*, 2001
Margaret Evans Porter, *Kissing a Stranger*, 1998

260

NICOLA CORNICK

The Virtuous Cyprian

(New York: Harlequin, 2001)

Story type: Historical/Regency
Subject(s): Sisters; Twins
Major character(s): Nicholas John Rosslyn Seagrave, Nobleman (earl); Lucille Kellaway, Teacher, Twin

Time period(s): 1810s (1816)
Locale(s): England

Summary: Bluestocking schoolteacher Lucille Kellaway reluctantly agrees to pose as her sister Susanna, an infamous courtesan, after Susanna inherits the lease on a piece of property, but is unable to take immediate possession of her new house. Nicholas Seagrave, the owner of the property, attempts to break the lease with his notorious new tenant only to discover the woman living on his estate is nothing like the celebrated cyprian he expected.

Where it's reviewed:
Romantic Times, June 2001, page 45

Other books by the same author:
Lady Polly, 2001
Miss Verey's Proposal, 2000
The Blanchard Secret, 2000
The Larkswood Legacy, 1999
True Colours, 1998

Other books you might like:
Jo Beverley, *Something Wicked*, 2001
Liz Carlyle, *A Woman of Virtue*, 2001
Suzanne Enoch, *By Love Undone*, 1998
Evelyn Richardson, *My Wayward Lady*, 1997
Gayle Wilson, *Anne's Perfect Husband*, 2001

261

PATRICIA COUGHLIN

Tall, Dark, and Difficult

(New York: Silhouette, 2001)

Story type: Contemporary
Subject(s): Antiques; Small Town Life
Major character(s): Hollis ''Griff'' Griffin, Military Personnel (former Air Force pilot); Rose Davenport, Antiques Dealer (Second Hand Rose)
Time period(s): 2000s
Locale(s): Wickford, Rhode Island

Summary: After a plane crash brings an end to Hollis ''Griff'' Griffin's military career, an embittered Griff shows up in Wickford to sell the house left to him by his Great-Aunt Devora. Upon arriving, he finds one caveat in his plan: Griff must complete Devora's collection of antique porcelain birds if he wants any part of her estate. Griff turns to Rose Davenport, a local antiques dealer and a friend of Devora's, for help in locating the birds he needs but Rose discovers Griff needs more than just her expertise with antiques, he needs a new outlook on life.

Where it's reviewed:
Romantic Times, August 2001, page 100

Other books by the same author:
Merely Married, 1998
Borrowed Bride, 1996
Joyride, 1995
The Last Frontier, 1995
The Bargain, 1995

Other books you might like:
Elizabeth Bevarly, *First Comes Love*, 2000
Stephanie Bond, *Seeking Single Male*, 2000
Jennifer Greene, *Nobody's Princess*, 1997
Kathleen Korbel, *Isn't It Romantic*, 1992
Ruth Wind, *Rainsinger*, 1996

262

WILMA COUNTS

The Trouble with Harriet

(New York: Zebra, 2001)

Story type: Regency
Subject(s): Authors and Writers; Social Conditions
Major character(s): Marcus Quentin Jeffries, Guardian, Nobleman (Earl of Wyndham); Harriet Knightly, Guardian, Writer (political essays)
Time period(s): 1800s (1802); 1810s (1816-1817)
Locale(s): England

Summary: Marcus Jeffries is surprised to discover he has been named the guardian of young Annabelle Richardson, but he is even more surprised to find he shares joint custody of the rebellious young lady with wealthy widow Harriet Knightly. While Marcus and Harriet eventually agree on a plan for their ward's education, they remain at odds when it comes to almost everything else, except how much they enjoy arguing with each other.

Where it's reviewed:
Affaire de Coeur, July/August 2001, page 24
Romantic Times, July 2001, page 28

Other books by the same author:
The Wagered Wife, 2001
My Lady Governess, 2000
The Willful Miss Winthrop, 2000
Willed to Wed, 1999

Other books you might like:
Mary Balogh, *Tempting Harriet*, 1998
Donna Bell, *The First Waltz*, 1998
Rita Boucher, *The Poet and the Paragon*, 1999
Paula Tanner Girard, *The Sister Season*, 1998
Carla Kelly, *Mrs. McVinnie's London Season*, 1996

263

MILLIE CRISWELL
MARY MCBRIDE, Co-Author
LIZ IRELAND, Co-Author

A Western Family Christmas

(Toronto: Harlequin, 2001)

Story type: Historical/American West; Holiday Themes
Subject(s): Anthology; Christmas; American West
Time period(s): 19th century
Locale(s): West

Summary: Featuring settings that range from small towns in Kansas and Colorado to a Texas ranch, these three Christmas-centered novellas by three of Harlequin's skilled writers bring love and holiday magic to a trio of protagonists (and assorted others) who badly need it. Heartwarming and family-centered. Included are *Christmas Eve* by Millie Criswell, *Season* *of Bounty* by Mary McBride, and *Cowboy Scrooge* by Liz Ireland.

Other books by the same author:
What to Do about Annie?, 2001

Other books you might like:
Hannah Howell, *A Stockingful of Joy*, 1999
American West
Liz Ireland, *Husband Material*, 2001
Mary McBride, *Moonglow, Texas*, 2001
Diana Palmer, *Lone Star Christmas*, 1997
two stories, one by Joan Johnston

264

MILLIE CRISWELL

What to Do about Annie?

(New York: Ivy, 2001)

Story type: Humor; Contemporary
Series: Trouble with Mary. Book 2
Subject(s): Humor; Family Relations; Italian Americans
Major character(s): Annie Goldman, Waiter/Waitress, Store Owner (partner in clothing store); Joseph Russo, Religious (former priest), Counselor
Time period(s): 2000s
Locale(s): Baltimore, Maryland

Summary: After 15 years, Father Joseph ''What-a-Hunk'' Russo decides to quit the priesthood to pursue his first and truest love, Annie Goldman. The flamboyant Annie has never stopped loving Joe, but she's also never forgiven him for leaving her for the Church in her time of need. A colorful cast of secondary characters relentlessly tug and pull at Joe and Annie as he single-mindedly tries to woo her back. The second in a trilogy, this book is one of those rare titles that can truly sway the reader from laughter to tears and back.

Where it's reviewed:
Booklist, July 2001, page 1990
Romantic Times, August 2001, page 83

Other books by the same author:
The Trials of Angela, 2002
The Trouble with Mary, 2001
The Marrying Man, 2000
The Wedding Planner, 2000
True Love, 1999

Other books you might like:
Elizabeth Bevarly, *First Comes Love*, 2000
Olivia Goldsmith, *Bad Boy*, 2001
Rita Herron, *Marry Me, Maddie?*, 2001
Susan Elizabeth Phillips, *This Heart of Mine*, 2001
Sheila Rabe, *A Prince of a Guy*, 2001

265

JANET DAILEY

A Capital Holiday

(New York: Zebra, 2001)

Story type: Contemporary; Holiday Themes
Subject(s): Christmas; Identity, Concealed; Privacy
Major character(s): Jocelyn Wakefield, Young Woman (the president's daughter); Grady Tucker, Journalist (political columnist); Obediah Melchior, Mythical Creature (Santa Claus)
Time period(s): 2000s
Locale(s): Washington, District of Columbia

Summary: Determined to have one day to herself away from the watchful eyes of the Secret Service and the general public, Jocelyn Wakefield, the president's daughter, dons a disguise—courtesy of her delightful grandmother—and heads to the DC mall for a day of freedom. Of course, as fate will have it, she meets political columnist Grady Tucker and his rambunctious black Lab and suddenly things are a lot less predictable and a lot more interesting. Romance, with a little help from St. Nick, is the order of the day in this fast-paced contemporary that will appeal to readers who like their romances sweet, holiday oriented, and dusted with inspirational overtones.

Where it's reviewed:
Library Journal, November 15, 2001, page 55

Other books by the same author:
Calder Pride, 1999

Other books you might like:
Virginia Henley, *Gift of Joy*, 1995
anthology/sensual
Debbie Macomber, *Shirley, Goodness, and Mercy*, 1999
a bit of angelic Christmas magic
Susan Elizabeth Phillips, *First Lady*, 2000
similar privacy premise/no holiday theme
Heather Graham Pozzessere, *An Angel's Touch*, 1995
Sheila Rabe, *All I Want for Christmas*, 2000
lively and fun

266

CLAUDIA DAIN

The Marriage Bed

(New York: Leisure, 2001)

Story type: Historical/Medieval
Subject(s): Monks; Knights and Knighthood; Guilt
Major character(s): Lady Isabel of Dornei, Noblewoman; Lord Richard of Warefeld, Knight, Religious (novice monk)
Time period(s): 12th century (1155)
Locale(s): England

Summary: Lord Richard of Warefeld, wracked with guilt over his passionate feelings toward his brother's betrothed, flees to the Abbey of Saint Stephen and Saint Paul with firm resolve to become the holiest of monks. A year later, Isabel of Dornei, the object of Richard's affection, flees to the same abbey—her fiance is dead, and she is fair game for any ambitious nobleman. Now, however, Richard is no longer interested in a life outside the Church, and Isabel isn't interested in a life without Richard. Guilt becomes a character of its own in this riveting tale of the power of human emotion.

Where it's reviewed:
Romantic Times, November 2001, page 43

Other books by the same author:
The Holding, 2001
Wish List, 2001 (anthology)
Tell Me Lies, 2000
Unwrapped, 2000 (anthology)

Other books you might like:
Shana Abe, *A Kiss at Midnight*, 2000
Rexanne Becnel, *The Mistress of Rosecliffe*, 2000
Claire Delacroix, *The Beauty*, 2001
Susan King, *The Stone Maiden*, 2000
Tori Phillips, *Silent Knight*, 1996
Cavendish Chronicles

267

CORY DANIELLS

Dark Dreams

(New York: Bantam, 2001)

Story type: Fantasy
Series: Last T'En Trilogy. Book 2
Subject(s): Fantasy; Violence; Politics
Major character(s): Imoshen, Royalty; General Tulkhan, Ruler; Reothe, Royalty
Time period(s): Indeterminate
Locale(s): Fair Isle, Fictional Country

Summary: Continuing the Fair Isle saga begun with *Broken Vows*, this passionate combination of romance and fantasy chronicles the story of Imoshen, last of the pure T'En of the Fair Isle, and General Tulkhan of the violent Ghebite invaders. They struggle with their feelings for each other and their cultural differences as they work together to assure peace. An action-filled story of treachery, passion, purpose, and compromise.

Other books by the same author:
Broken Vows, 1999 (Last T'En Trilogy. Book 1)

Other books you might like:
Marion Zimmer Bradley, *Hawkmistress!*, 1982
Justine Davis, *Lord of the Storm*, 1994
Justine Davis, *The Skypirate*, 1995
Kathleen Morgan, *The Demon Prince*, 1994
Kathleen Morgan, *The Knowing Crystal*, 1994

268

LILIAN DARCY (Pseudonym of Melissa Benyon)

Cinderella After Midnight

(New York: Silhouette, 2001)

Story type: Contemporary
Series: Cinderella Conspiracy. Book 1
Subject(s): Sisters; Social Classes; Fairy Tales
Major character(s): Catrina Brown, Imposter, Impoverished; Patrick Callahan, Wealthy, Businessman
Time period(s): 2000s
Locale(s): Madison County, California

Summary: Catrina Brown, one of three poor sisters saved from poverty by an eccentric older cousin, impersonates a British lady in order to talk to Councilor Wainwright at an elite ball. However, Patrick Callahan, a wealthy businessman, intercepts the imposter, and before long, finds himself in the role of protector for her and her entire family. A prince of a guy who's too good to be true saves a modern day Cinderella in this contemporary version of a familiar fairy tale.

Where it's reviewed:
Romantic Times, September 2001, page 112

Other books by the same author:
Finding Her Prince, 2002 (Cinderella Conspiracy. Book 3)
Saving Cinderella, 2001 (Cinderella Conspiracy. Book 2)
Her Sister's Child, 2000
Raising Baby Jane, 2000
The Baby Bond, 1999

Other books you might like:
Barbara Boswell, *Magic Slippers*, 1996
anthology; Carole Buck, Cassie Miles, co-authors
Jude Deveraux, *Wishes*, 1989
Kathryn Jensen, *Mail-Order Cinderella*, 2000
Natalie Patrick, *The Millionaire's Proposition*, 1999
Joan Elliot Pickart, *Man. . .Mercenary. . .Monarch*, 2000

269

CLAIRE DELACROIX

The Temptress

(New York: Dell, 2001)

Story type: Historical/Medieval
Series: Bride Quest II. Book 3
Subject(s): Middle Ages
Major character(s): Esmeraude MacLaren, Noblewoman; Bayard de Villonne, Nobleman, Knight (returning Crusader)
Time period(s): 12th century (1194)
Locale(s): England (Chateaux Montvieux); Ceinn-beithe, Scotland

Summary: Bayard de Villonne returns to England and finds himself robbed of his holdings and title by a wily relative. Then his grandmother offers him an ultimatum—if he can best his cousins (and everyone else) by winning the contest for the hand of Esmeraude of Ceinn-beithe, she will give him Montvieux. Bayard is determined to win; the lively and clever Esmeraude has ideas of her own, of course. Filled with humor, riddles, and disguises, this is a lively addition to Delacroix's Bride Quest series.

Where it's reviewed:
Rendezvous, October 2001, page 21
Romantic Times, December 2001, page 38

Other books by the same author:
The Beauty, 2001 (Bride Quest II. Book 2)
The Countess, 2000 (Bride Quest II. Book 1)
The Damsel, 1999 (Bride Quest. Book 2)
The Heiress, 1999 (Bride Quest. Book 3)
The Princess, 1998 (Bride Quest. Book 1)

Other books you might like:
Shari Anton, *The Conqueror*, 2000
another knight betrayed/darker
Jill Barnett, *Wicked*, 1999
Jude Deveraux, *The Taming*, 1996

Julie Garwood, *The Bride*, 1989
Julie Garwood, *The Wedding*, 1996

270

GENELL DELLIN

The Renegades: Rafe

(New York: Avon, 2001)

Story type: Historical/American West; Historical/Post-American Civil War
Series: Renegades. Book 3
Subject(s): Reunions; American West; Newspapers
Major character(s): Madeleine ''Maddie'' Calhoun, Journalist, Businesswoman (newspaper manager); Rafe Aigner, Gambler, Publisher (newspaper owner)
Time period(s): 1870s
Locale(s): San Antonio, Texas

Summary: Separated by war and misunderstanding, Maddie and Rafe meet again ten years later when Rafe appears at the door of her newspaper claiming to be its new owner. Newspapers are Maddie's life and even though Rafe had won it gambling with her now dead husband, she and Rafe strike a bargain—if she can make the *Star* profitable in three years, it's hers. Sparks fly as the two fight their feelings for each other and try to make sense of their lives. A charming boy adds interest to this reunion story. Third in Dellin's Renegades series.

Other books by the same author:
The Renegades: Nick, 2000
The Renegades: Cole, 1999
Silver Moon Song, 1996
Comanche Flame, 1994
Cherokee Nights, 1991

Other books you might like:
Jane Bonander, *Scent of Lilacs*, 1998
Jane Bonander, *Warrior Heart*, 1997
Kit Garland, *Sweeter than Sin*, 1999
Lorraine Heath, *Texas Splendor*, 1999
Jodi Thomas, *Twilight in Texas*, 2001
another post-Civil War reunion/tender

271

SHANNON DONNELLY

Under the Kissing Bough

(New York: Zebra, 2001)

Story type: Regency; Holiday Themes
Subject(s): Christmas; Marriage; Courtship
Major character(s): Eleanor Glover, Noblewoman, Fiance(e) (arranged marriage); Geoffrey Westerly, Nobleman (Lord Staines)
Time period(s): 1810s
Locale(s): England

Summary: Determined to marry one of the Glover girls and grant his father's dying wish, Geoffrey Westerly, offers for painfully shy Eleanor Glover, thinking she will be the most biddable of the lot. Geoffrey is surprised to find there's more to intelligent, independent Eleanor than meets the eye; and although it takes a bit of doing, by Christmas morning their engagement of convenience has become a marriage of love. Well-drawn characters nicely drive the classic plot of this light, often humorous holiday Regency.

Where it's reviewed:
Rendezvous, October 2001, page 32

Other books you might like:
Mary Balogh, *A Christmas Bride*, 1997
Susan Carroll, *Christmas Belles*, 1992
Lynn Collum, *The Christmas Charm*, 2000
Diane Farr, *Once upon a Christmas*, 2000
Jo Ann Ferguson, *A Christmas Bride*, 2000

272

LYNN EMERY

Gotta Get Next to You

(New York: Harper Torch, 2001)

Story type: Contemporary; Multicultural
Subject(s): Mystery; Hospitals; African Americans
Major character(s): Andrea Noble, Businesswoman (clinic director), Nurse; LeRoyce ''Lee'' Matthews, Investigator, Imposter (as Jamal Turner)
Time period(s): 2000s
Locale(s): Blue Bayou, Louisiana

Summary: Divorced and needing a change, Andrea Noble leaves a nine-year stint in Chicago and comes home to Louisiana to run the struggling Blue Bayou Public Health Clinic. Andrea finds a run-down facility in a sleazy part of town and a rude, incompetent staff. She also finds herself attracted to Jamal Turner, much against her better judgment. Something strange is going on at the clinic as well and drop-dead gorgeous Jamal is not at all what he seems. Before long, Andrea is involved in more danger than she'd ever expected to find in sleepy little Blue Bayou. Sensual.

Other books you might like:
Stella Cameron, *French Quarter*, 1998
Maggie Ferguson, *Fever Rising*, 1997
Monica Jackson, *A Magical Moment*, 1999
Sandra Kitt, *Family Affairs*, 1999
Tracey Tillis, *Deadly Masquerade*, 1994

273

KATHLEEN ESCHENBURG

The Nightingale's Song

(New York: Harper Torch, 2001)

Story type: Historical/Victorian America
Subject(s): Healing; Music and Musicians; Family
Major character(s): Mary Margaret ''Maggie'' Quinn, Orphan, Musician; Gordon Kincaid, Doctor, Veteran (Civil War); Clara, Child
Time period(s): 1870s (1874)
Locale(s): Baltimore, Maryland; Virginia

Summary: When Dr. Gordon Kincaid pays a visit to St. Columba's Orphanage in Baltimore to make a family donation, he is surprised with the knowledge that he has a daughter he never knew about. However, Gordon has lost a lot in the war, and he has much healing to do before he can learn to love and be loved again. With the help of Maggie Quinn, he manages to put his life back together. Poignant, heartwarming, and sincere.

Other books you might like:
Heather Graham, *And One Wore Gray*, 1992
Heather Graham, *One Wore Blue*, 1992
Margaret Mitchell, *Gone with the Wind*, 1936
classic Civil War story
Roselyn West, *The Outcast*, 1992
The Men of Pride County. Book 1

274

JANET EVANOVICH

Seven Up

(New York: St. Martin's Press, 2001)

Story type: Humor; Romantic Suspense
Series: Stephanie Plum. Book 7
Subject(s): Humor; Neighbors and Neighborhoods; Crime and Criminals
Major character(s): Stephanie Plum, Bounty Hunter; Joe Morelli, Detective—Police (undercover); Carlos ''Ranger'' Manoso, Bounty Hunter
Time period(s): 2000s
Locale(s): Trenton, New Jersey (The Burg)

Summary: Bounty hunter Stephanie Plum's having more than her share of troubles. Her family wants her to tie the knot with on-again, off-again boyfriend Joe Morelli. In the meantime, the mysterious Ranger is stepping up his moves on her, and the 70-year-old bail jumper she's been hired to bring in eludes her time after humiliating time. Hysterically funny and full of quirky characters from previous novels in the series.

Where it's reviewed:
Library Journal, June 1, 2001, page 224
People Weekly, July 2, 2001, page 38
Publishers Weekly, May 7, 2001, page 227
Romantic Times, June 2001, page 83

Other books by the same author:
High Five, 2000 (Stephanie Plum. Book 5)
Hot Six, 2000 (Stephanie Plum. Book 6)
Four to Score, 1999 (Stephanie Plum. Book 4)
Three to Get Deadly, 1998 (Stephanie Plum. Book 3)
Two for the Dough, 1996 (Stephanie Plum. Book 2)

Other books you might like:
Kylie Adams, *Fly Me to the Moon*, 2001
Millie Criswell, *The Trouble with Mary*, 2001
Olivia Goldsmith, *Bad Boy*, 2001
Kasey Michaels, *Too Good to Be True*, 2001
Sheila Rabe, *A Prince of a Guy*, 2001

275

ELISABETH FAIRCHILD (Pseudonym of Donna Gimarc)

Sugarplum Surprises

(New York: Signet, 2001)

Story type: Regency
Subject(s): Christmas; Secrets
Major character(s): Jane Nichols, Seamstress; Edward Brydges, Nobleman (Duke of Chandrose)
Time period(s): 1810s (1819)
Locale(s): Bath, England

Summary: Running from the prospect of a horrible arranged marriage, Jane Nichols finds refuge in Bath, where she disguises herself as fashionable modiste ''Madame Nicolette.'' When Edward Brydges, the Duke of Chandrose, abruptly cancels his upcoming wedding and leaves Jane footing the bill for his former fiancee's trousseau, Jane seeks to recoup her investment by confronting the duke at a society ball. Intrigued by the lovely young woman defending Madame Nicolette, Edward pays a visit to the dressmaker's shop, where he quickly discovers her secret and falls under the spell of the unconventional Jane Nichols.

Where it's reviewed:
Affaire de Coeur, November/December 2001, page 21
Romantic Times, November 2001, page 47

Other books by the same author:
Breach of Promise, 2000
Captain Cupid Calls the Shots, 2000
The Holly and the Ivy, 1999
Marriage a la Mode, 1997
The Rakehell's Reform, 1997

Other books you might like:
Mona Gedney, *Merry's Christmas*, 1998
Sandra Heath, *A Christmas Courtship*, 1990
Lynn Kerstan, *A Midnight Clear*, 1997
Barbara Metzger, *The Christmas Carrolls*, 1997
Patricia Wynn, *The Christmas Spirit*, 1996

276

JANE FEATHER

To Kiss a Spy

(New York: Bantam, 2002)

Story type: Historical/Renaissance
Subject(s): Spies; Espionage; Secrets
Major character(s): Lady Pen Bryanston, Noblewoman, Widow(er); Owen d'Arcy, Nobleman, Spy
Time period(s): 16th century (1550s)
Locale(s): England

Summary: Charged with the mission of seducing the Lady Pen Bryanston in order to gain political information, master spy Owen d'Arcy is startled to find that the astute, intuitive Lady Pen is not about to be taken in by one so dangerous as himself. Lady Pen has a quest of her own and so she strikes a bargain with Owen—she will help him spy if he will find out whether her son, supposedly stillborn two years earlier, is alive. Political intrigue, ambition and greed, and passion combine in this colorful tale set during the treacherous period late in the reign of Edward VI, the brief reign of Lady Jane Grey, and Bloody Mary's eventual ascension to the throne.

Where it's reviewed:
Romantic Times, February 2002, page 35

Other books by the same author:
The Least Likely Bride, 2001
The Widow's Kiss, 2001
The Accidental Bride, 1999
Valentine Wedding, 1999
The Hostage Bride, 1998

Other books you might like:
Katherine Deauville, *Daggers of Gold*, 1993
earlier time period/treachery and intrigue
Christina Dodd, *Outrageous*, 1994
more intrigue
Denise Domning, *Lady in Waiting*, 1998
Roberta Gellis, *The Silver Mirror*, 1989
earlier time period/war and treachery
Isolde Martyn, *The Maiden and the Unicorn*, 1998
earlier time period/treachery and intrigue

277

CHRISTINE FEEHAN
MELANIE GEORGE, Co-Author

The Very Gothic Christmas

(New York: Sonnet, 2001)

Story type: Holiday Themes; Anthology
Subject(s): Christmas; Paranormal; Suspense
Time period(s): 2000s

Summary: Two chilling Gothic novellas provide readers with a definite alternative to the traditional, heartwarming family-centered Christmas offerings. These tales are unusual, sensual and compelling. Included are Christine Feehan's suspenseful tale of a reclusive, disfigured musician and the people who love him enough to save him from himself—and a frightening killer, and Melanie George's haunting story of time travel and reincarnation as a pair of lovers trapped across time struggle to right past wrongs in a classically Gothic Scottish setting.

Other books by the same author:
The Scarletti Curse, 2001

Other books you might like:
Jude Deveraux, *A Season in the Highlands*, 2000
holiday anthology
Melanie George, *Like No Other*, 2001
Lynn Kurland, *Christmas Spirits*, 1997
holiday anthology
Christina Skye, *Christmas Knight*, 1998
lighter

278

JO ANN FERGUSON

A Guardian's Angel

(New York: Zebra, 2002)

Story type: Regency
Subject(s): Marriage; Revenge
Major character(s): Angela Needham, Gentlewoman, Companion; Justin Harrington, Nobleman
Time period(s): 1810s
Locale(s): England

Summary: Newly arrived at Oslington Court with the responsibility of preparing Leonia Sutton, a duke's ward, for her coming out, Angela Needham is puzzled to learn there is extremely bad blood between her employer and the man who owns the neighboring estate, Lord Harrington. The problem, of course, is that Angela finds Lord Harrington attractive—and young Thomas Sutton spends as much time with Harrington as he can because of their common interests. Mismatched lovers, lack of communication, and plain old stubbornness create the problems in this lively Regency that ultimately does see all the problems solved.

Other books by the same author:
A Brother's Honor, 2000 (Shadow of the Bastille series)
A Daughter's Destiny, 2000 (Shadow of the Bastille series)
An Unexpected Husband, 2000
A Sister's Quest, 2000 (Shadow of the Bastille series)
Wake Not the Dragon, 1996

Other books you might like:
Diane Farr, *Once upon a Christmas*, 2000
Barbara Hazard, *The Unsuitable Miss Martingale*, 2001
Candice Hern, *A Garden Folly*, 1995
Candice Hern, *A Proper Companion*, 1997
Evelyn Richardson, *The Gallant Guardian*, 1998

279

JO ANN FERGUSON

His Lady Midnight

(New York: Zebra, 2001)

Story type: Regency
Subject(s): Brothers; Identity, Concealed; Social Conditions
Major character(s): Phoebe Brackenton, Noblewoman; Galen Townsend, Nobleman
Time period(s): 1810s
Locale(s): London, England; Bath, England (just outside the city); Ledge-under-Water, England

Summary: Phoebe Brackenton spends her days as a member of the *ton* but under the guise of Lady Midnight, Phoebe spends her nights, and most of her money, rescuing unfortunate victims of England's harsh deportation laws. While on one of her late night missions, Phoebe nearly falls into a trap set by the government to catch Lady Midnight. With the help of Galen Townsend, who just happens to be in the area looking for his wastrel brother, Phoebe is able to escape. Then however, Phoebe is forced into trusting the dashing Galen with all of her secrets.

Where it's reviewed:
Booklist, September 15, 2001, page 204
Romantic Times, September 2001, page 30

Other books by the same author:
A Highland Folly, 2001
A Brother's Honor, 2000 (Shadow of the Bastille series)
A Daughter's Destiny, 2000 (Shadow of the Bastille series)
A Christmas Bride, 2000
A Sister's Quest, 2000 (Shadow of the Bastille series)

Other books you might like:
Anne Barbour, *A Rake's Reform*, 1996
Donna Bell, *An Improper Pursuit*, 1994
Emma Jensen, *The Irish Rogue*, 1999
April Kihlstrom, *The Reckless Barrister*, 1999
Andrea Pickens, *The Hired Hero*, 1999

280

JO ANN FERGUSON
VALERIE KING, Co-Author
JEANNE SAVERY, Co-Author

A Kiss for Mama

(New York: Zebra, 2001)

Story type: Regency; Anthology
Subject(s): Mothers; Marriage; Courtship
Time period(s): 1810s
Locale(s): England

Summary: Three of the best-known Regency writers join forces to produce a charming trilogy of romances focusing on families, mothers, and romance that is perfect reading for Mother's Day. Included are ''The Dowager's Dilemma'' by Jo Ann Ferguson, ''A Mother's Devotion'' by Valerie King, and ''Happily Ever After'' by Jeanne Savery.

Where it's reviewed:
Romantic Times, April 2001, page 103

Other books by the same author:
An Unexpected Husband, 2000

Other books you might like:
Rosanne Bittner, *Cherished Love*, 1997
Mother's Day anthology
Julie Caille, *A Mother's Heart*, 1992
Regency Mother's Day anthology
Valerie King, *A Brighton Flirtation*, 2000
Jeanne Savery, *A Perfect Match*, 2001

281

TRACY FOBES

To Tame a Wild Heart

(New York: Sonnet, 2001)

Story type: Historical/Regency; Fantasy
Subject(s): Magic; Animals; Heritage
Major character(s): Sarah Murphy, Orphan, Psychic (talks to animals); Colin Murray, Nobleman (Earl of Cawdor)
Time period(s): 1810s (1813)
Locale(s): Scotland (Inveraray Castle)

Summary: Found wandering on the moors as a young child, Sarah is taken in and raised by a country couple; but when the Duke of Argyle arrives, claiming she is his long-lost daughter and takes her away with him, her life changes remarkably, especially when the dashing Earl of Cawdor takes charge of her ''lady training.'' A girl who talks to animals, a nobleman who questions her identity, and a dash of magic are part of this Cinderella story with Pygmalion touches. Sensual.

Other books by the same author:
Daughter of Destiny, 2000
Forbidden Garden, 2000
Heart of the Dove, 1999
Touch Not the Cat, 1998

Other books you might like:
Shana Abe, *The Truelove Bride*, 1999
another heroine with a ''gift''
Jill Barnett, *Wild*, 1998
another ''gifted'' heroine
Cathy Maxwell, *When Dreams Come True*, 1998
Mary Jo Putney, *Faery Magic*, 1998
fantasy anthology

282

SUZANNE FORSTER
THEA DEVINE, Co-Author
LORI FOSTER, Co-Author
SHANNON MCKENNA, Co-Author

All through the Night

(New York: Brava, 2001)

Story type: Contemporary; Anthology
Subject(s): Erotica
Time period(s): 2000s

Summary: Sexy, sensual, and sometimes erotic, this quartet of novellas from some of Brava's most sensual writers focuses on memorable heroes and includes *Stranger in Her Bed* by Suzanne Forster, *No Mercy* by Thea Devine, *Satisfy Me* by Lori Foster, and *Something Wild* by Shannon McKenna. Though not for everyone, this anthology will definitely please fans who like their romances on the steamy side.

Where it's reviewed:
Rendezvous, September 2001, page 16

Other books you might like:
Jennifer Crusie, *Welcome to Temptation*, 2000
humorous
Thea Devine, *Seductive*, 2001
Susan Johnson, *Tempting*, 2001
Kimberly Randall, *In the Midnight Hour*, 1999
Bertrice Small, *Intrigued*, 2001

283

SUZANNE FORSTER

Angel Face

(New York: Berkley, 2001)

Story type: Contemporary; Romantic Suspense
Subject(s): Murder; Serial Killers; Mental Illness

Major character(s): Angela Lowe, Researcher (research assistant); Jordan Carpenter, Doctor (surgeon)
Time period(s): 2000s
Locale(s): California; Mexico

Summary: Warned that he is the next target of a beautiful serial killer who goes after doctors, surgeon Jordan Carpenter is naturally curious. However, he has a hard time believing the killer is actually lovely Angela Lowe, even though her childhood has given her reason enough for hating doctors. Jordan is intent on learning the truth, even if it means taking Angela out of the country and forcing her to remember the past. Dark, violent, and passionate, this story takes an interesting look at brain research, computer simulation, and mental illness and combines them into an intriguing whole.

Other books by the same author:
The Morning After, 2000
Every Breath She Takes, 1999
Husband, Lover, Stranger, 1998
Innocence, 1997
Blush, 1996

Other books you might like:
Suzanne Brockmann, *Get Lucky*, 2000
Linda Howard, *Shades of Twilight*, 1996
Rachel Lee, *After I Dream*, 2000
Meryl Sawyer, *Tempting Fate*, 1998
Anne Stuart, *Ritual Sins*, 2000

284

DELORES FOSSEN

Saddled

(New York: LoveSpell, 2001)

Story type: Historical/American West; Humor
Subject(s): Humor; American West; Inheritance
Major character(s): Abbie Donegan, Guardian, Heiress; Rio McCaine, Gunfighter, Heir—Dispossessed
Time period(s): 1880s (1881)
Locale(s): Fall Creek, Texas

Summary: Abbie Donegan's father has died, and as the oldest child, she's taken responsibility for her odds and ends family. If she has to trick Rio McCaine into marrying her to protect them, that's exactly what she'll do. The only way Rio can keep his rightful inheritance is to agree to Abbie's hair-brained scheme. Soon, he realizes he's been saddled with the most confusing female west—and probably east—of the Mississippi. This snappy, sexy Western is uniquely funny, full of unexpected humor that sneaks up on the reader at every turn.

Where it's reviewed:
Romantic Times, July 2001, page 44

Other books you might like:
Linda Lea Castle, *Mattie and the Blacksmith*, 2001
Millie Criswell, *The Marrying Man*, 2000
Geralyn Dawson, *Simmer All Night*, 1999
Betina Krahn, *Sweet Talking Man*, 2000
Judith Stacy, *The Blushing Bride*, 2000

285

LORI FOSTER
LAURA BRADLEY, Co-Author
GAYLE CALLEN, Co-Author
VICTORIA MARQUEZ, Co-Author

Hot and Bothered

(New York: St. Martin's Press, 2001)

Story type: Anthology; Contemporary
Subject(s): Romance
Time period(s): 2000s

Summary: This collection of four steamy tales includes a bit of something for everyone who likes romance on the sexy side. Included are ''Luring Lucy'' by Lori Foster, ''Truth or Dare'' by Laura Bradley, ''Compromised'' by Gayle Callen, and ''Treading Dangerous Waters'' by Victoria Marquez.

Where it's reviewed:
Romantic Times, July 2001, page 87

Other books by the same author:
Too Much Temptation, 2002

Other books you might like:
Gayle Callen, *His Betrothed*, 2001
Jennifer Crusie, *Welcome to Temptation*, 2000
Suzanne Forster, *All through the Night*, 2001
sensual anthology
Susan Johnson, *Tempting*, 2001

286

LORI FOSTER

Too Much Temptation

(New York: Brava, 2002)

Story type: Contemporary
Subject(s): Romance; Sexual Behavior; Relationships
Major character(s): Grace Jenkins, Secretary (executive); Noah Harper, Businessman
Time period(s): 2000s
Locale(s): Gillespie, Kentucky

Summary: When Noah Harper finds his intended bride in bed with another man and calls off the wedding—but doesn't tell anyone the real reason—his grandmother's secretary Grace Jenkins is one of the few who doesn't blame him. When she offers friendship, Noah realizes he wants her physically, as well. Explicitly sexy. Latest in the sensual Brava line.

Other books by the same author:
Annie, Get Your Guy, 2001
Messing around with Max, 2001
Sex Appeal, 2001
Married to the Boss, 2000
Scandalized, 2000

Other books you might like:
Susan Andersen, *Be My Baby*, 1999
Jennifer Crusie, *Crazy for You*, 2000
Jennifer Crusie, *Tell Me Lies*, 1998
Jennifer Crusie, *Welcome to Temptation*, 2000
Debra Dixon, *Hot as Sin*, 1995

287

KAREN FOX

Buttercup Baby

(New York: Jove, 2001)

Story type: Paranormal; Humor
Series: Magical Love Romance. Book 2
Subject(s): Humor; Fairies; Magic
Major character(s): Ariel, Mythical Creature (ex-flower fairy queen); Rand Thayer, Young Man
Time period(s): 2000s
Locale(s): Colorado Springs, Colorado

Summary: Ariel, former queen of the Pillywiggins (flower fairies) wants a baby. The only way she can get pregnant is by mating with a human and she knows just what human she wants to be the father of her child. Rand Thayer should know a thing or two about fairies. After all, his sister married Robin, Oberon's son. Robin gave up his magical powers to be with his mortal wife, something Ariel doesn't want to do. She just wants a child, so she tells Rand, whom she's just met, that he's the one to father her baby. There's lots of humor throughout this lighthearted fantasy where the human world collides with that of the Fae in more ways than one.

Where it's reviewed:
Booklist, September 15, 2001, page 203
Romantic Times, October 2001, page 88

Other books by the same author:
Grand Design: The Hope Chest, 2001
Prince of Charming, 2000 (Magical Love Romance. Book 1)
Somewhere My Love, 1997
Sword of MacLeod, 1997

Other books you might like:
Jill Barnett, *Imagine*, 1995
Karen Harbaugh, *Cupid's Kiss*, 1999
Mary Alice Kruesi, *Second Star to the Right*, 1999
Judi McCoy, *I Dream of You*, 2001
Nora Roberts, *Heart of the Sea*, 2000

288

DIANA GABALDON

The Fiery Cross

(New York: Delacorte, 2001)

Story type: Time Travel; Historical/Colonial America
Series: Outlander. Book 5
Subject(s): Time Travel; American Colonies; Frontier and Pioneer Life
Major character(s): Claire Fraser, Time Traveler (from 20th century), Doctor; Jamie Fraser, Spouse (of Claire)
Time period(s): 1770s (1771-1772)
Locale(s): American Colonies

Summary: Claire Fraser has traveled through time and space to be reunited with her beloved Jamie. A doctor in her own time, Claire has assumed the role of healer, frantically trying to duplicate modern medical technologies and resources under the primitive conditions of the early American frontier. Revenge for her daughter's rape, several near deaths, and the rumblings of a revolution make this incredibly detailed book an excellent addition to the Outlander series.

Where it's reviewed:
Romantic Times, January 2002, page 33

Other books by the same author:
Outlandish Companion, 1999
Drums of Autumn, 1997
Voyager, 1994
Dragonfly in Amber, 1993
Outlander, 1991

Other books you might like:
Debra Lee Brown, *The Virgin Spring*, 2000
Donna Fletcher, *The Irish Devil*, 2000
Lynne Hayworth, *Summer's End*, 2001
Judith Merkle Riley, *A Vision of Light*, 1999
Haywood Smith, *Dangerous Gifts*, 1999

289

KRISTIN GABRIEL (Pseudonym of Kristin Eckhardt)

Dangerously Irresistible

(New York: Harlequin, 2001)

Story type: Contemporary
Subject(s): Crime and Criminals; Family
Major character(s): Madeline "Maddie" Griffin, Bounty Hunter, Secretary; Tanner Blackburn, Lawyer
Time period(s): 2000s
Locale(s): Chicago, Illinois; Texas; Crab Orchard, Kansas

Summary: Determined to prove to her father and brothers she too can be a bounty hunter in the family company, Maddie Griffin sets out after the "Kissing Bandit" whose likeness appeared in a recent issue of *Texas Men* under the guise of Tanner Blackburn. After arriving in Texas, Maddie successfully captures Tanner; but as they begin their journey back to Chicago, Maddie finds herself in the totally unprofessional position of falling for her charming new prisoner.

Where it's reviewed:
Romantic Times, June 2001, page 110

Other books by the same author:
Bachelor by Design, 2000
Beauty and the Bachelor, 2000
The Bachelor Trap, 2000
Annie Get Your Groom, 1999
Send Me No Flowers, 1999

Other books you might like:
Susan Andersen, *Baby, I'm Yours*, 1999
Patti Berg, *Wife for a Day*, 1999
Jennifer Crusie, *What the Lady Wants*, 1995
Jule McBride, *A Way with Women*, 2001
Cara Summers, *Otherwise Engaged*, 2001

290

DOROTHY GARLOCK

The Edge of Town

(New York: Warner, 2001)

Story type: Historical
Subject(s): Country Life; Violence; Change
Major character(s): Julie Jones, Farmer (daughter of a farmer); Evan Johnson, Farmer, Veteran (of WW I)
Time period(s): 1920s (1922)
Locale(s): Fertile, Missouri

Summary: Resigned to the fact that her responsibilities lie in raising her younger siblings and helping on the family farm, Julie Jones knows she will probably never attract the attentions of an eligible man—even if there were any to be found in Fertile, Missouri. When Evan Johnson, the college educated son of the abusive town drunk and bully, returns home to see to the family farm, things begin to change—and not always for the better. Rape, murder, suspicion, and love combine intriguingly in this gritty, realistic story of life in a small midwestern town during the Roaring Twenties.

Other books by the same author:
With Heart, 1999 (1930s America. Book 3)
With Song, 1999 (1930s America. Book 2)
Sweetwater, 1998
With Hope, 1998 (1930s America. Book 1)
Larkspur, 1997

Other books you might like:
Catherine Anderson, *Keegan's Lady*, 1993
historical
Megan Chance, *The Way Home*, 1997
historical
Robin Lee Hatcher, *Where the Heart Is*, 1993
LaVyrle Spencer, *Morning Glory*, 1989

291

MONA GEDNEY

Lady Hilary's Halloween

(New York: Zebra, 2001)

Story type: Regency
Subject(s): Animals/Dogs; Art
Major character(s): Hilary Jamison, Noblewoman; Lord Grayden, Nobleman
Time period(s): 1810s
Locale(s): England

Summary: Resigned to the fact that she must marry the boorish Raymond Brawley, Hilary Jamison receives a temporary respite from her fate when her married friend, Lily, whisks her away to London for a visit. Lily is determined to find a better candidate for Hilary's future husband. After she transforms the formerly plain Hilary into a stylish lady, Hilary suddenly attracts the attention of Lily's paramour, handsome Lord Grayden, much to Lily's disconcertment.

Where it's reviewed:
Romantic Times, September 2001, page 30

Other books by the same author:
Lady Diana's Daring Deed, 2000
A Match for Mother, 1999
A Dangerous Arrangement, 1998
Merry's Christmas, 1998
A Lady of Quality, 1996

Other books you might like:
Anne Barbour, *A Talent for Trouble*, 1994
Sandra Heath, *The Halloween Husband*, 1994
Martha Kirkland, *The Rake's Fiancee*, 2001
Patricia Oliver, *The Lady in Gray*, 1999
Regina Scott, *Catch of the Season*, 1999

292

RACHEL GIBSON

True Confessions

(New York: Avon, 2001)

Story type: Contemporary
Subject(s): Secrets; Small Town Life; Writing
Major character(s): Dylan Taber, Police Officer (sheriff); Hope Spencer, Journalist (works for tabloid)
Time period(s): 2000s
Locale(s): Gospel, Idaho

Summary: Having given up on men after a disastrous first marriage, California tabloid journalist Hope Spencer arrives in Gospel, Idaho intent on concentrating only on her writing. Sheriff Dylan Taber, who is currently being pursued by every available woman in town, is willing to bet Hope will not last a week before she goes running back to the big city. A romantic relationship with each other is the last thing either Hope or Dylan wants but after they meet, it turns out to be the only thing on their minds.

Where it's reviewed:
Publishers Weekly, June 11, 2001, page 67
Romantic Times, August 2001, page 83

Other books by the same author:
It Must Be Love, 2000
Truly Madly Yours, 1999
Simply Irresistible, 1998

Other books you might like:
Susan Andersen, *All Shook Up*, 1999
Patti Berg, *Wife for a Day*, 1999
Elizabeth Bevarly, *Her Man Friday*, 1999
Jennifer Crusie, *Tell Me Lies*, 1998
Julie Ortolon, *Drive Me Wild*, 2000

293

PATRICIA GRASSO

To Tame a Duke

(New York: Zebra, 2001)

Story type: Historical/Regency
Subject(s): Revenge; Spies; War of 1812
Major character(s): Lily Hawthorne, Spy, Guardian (of mentally challenged brother); James Armstrong, Nobleman (14th Duke of Kinross), Kidnapper

Time period(s): 1800s; 1810s
Locale(s): Boston, Massachusetts; At Sea; England (Kinross Park on the outskirts of St. Albans)

Summary: Lily Hawthorne is a kind, gentle young woman who's assumed guardianship of her mentally challenged brother. She has a photographic memory, and is recruited by the American spy network during the War of 1812 to learn codes. James Armstrong, 14th Duke of Kinross, wants to meet the infamous Gilded Lily and kill "him." After all, the notorious spy had caused his brother's death. Love comes the hard way in this ever twisting tale of revenge. Memorable secondary characters add depth and even more interest to this excellent tale.

Where it's reviewed:
Romantic Times, July 2001, page 39

Other books by the same author:
No Decent Gentleman, 1999
Violets in the Snow, 1998
My Heart's Desire, 1997
Courting an Angel, 1995
Love in a Mist, 1994

Other books you might like:
Kat Martin, *Perfect Sin*, 2000
Amanda Quick, *Slightly Shady*, 2001
Karen Robards, *Scandalous*, 2001
Kathryn Smith, *Elusive Passion*, 2001
Elizabeth Thornton, *The Perfect Princess*, 2001

294

JILL GREGORY

Once an Outlaw

(New York: Dell, 2001)

Story type: Historical/American West; Historical/Americana
Subject(s): Gangs; American West; Trust
Major character(s): Emily Spoon, Seamstress (dressmaker); Clint Barclay, Lawman (sheriff)
Time period(s): 19th century
Locale(s): Forlorn Valley, Colorado

Summary: All Emily Spoon wants to do is to start fresh in Forlorn Valley, Colorado as a dressmaker. That way, her family, the infamous Spoon Gang, can go straight—or so she hopes. Unfortunately, Clint Barclay, the town's sheriff, is the same man who sent her relatives to prison in the first place. Against her will, she develops feelings for the stalwart law-man, not knowing how she can love him without being disloyal to her family. Pathos and humor ensue as the town's most sought after bachelor pines for the one woman he can't possibly marry, and a woman whose family is on one side of the law loves a man on the other.

Where it's reviewed:
Booklist, November 15, 2001, page 559
Romantic Times, December 2001, page 37

Other books by the same author:
Rough Wrangler, Tender Kisses, 2000
Cold Night, Warm Stranger, 1999
Never Love a Cowboy, 1998
Just This Once, 1997
Always You, 1996

Other books you might like:
Heidi Betts, *Walker's Widow*, 2002
Megan Chance, *Fall from Grace*, 1997
Judith E. French, *Morgan's Woman*, 1999
Leslie LaFoy, *Maddie's Justice*, 2000
Maggie Osborne, *The Promise of Jenny Jones*, 1997

295

DENISE HAMPTON (Pseudonym of Denise Lindow)

The Warrior's Damsel

(New York: Avon, 2001)

Story type: Historical/Medieval
Subject(s): Widows/Widowers; Marriage; Middle Ages
Major character(s): Lady Katherine de Fraisney, Widow(er), Noblewoman; Sir Rafe Godsol, Knight, Nobleman
Time period(s): 13th century (1214)
Locale(s): England

Summary: A castleless knight set on vengeance and a beautiful marriage-averse widow find love—and a bit of danger—in this intriguing, sensual story set against the colorful backdrop of the High Middle Ages. Well-drawn characters, blood feuds, and lively action add to the mix.

Other books you might like:
Shari Anton, *Knave of Hearts*, 2001
Juliana Garnett, *The Baron*, 1999
Julie Garwood, *Saving Grace*, 1993
Johanna Lindsey, *Joining*, 2001
Mary Reed McCall, *Secret Vows*, 2001

296

JILLIAN HART

Night Hawk's Bride

(Toronto: Harlequin, 2001)

Story type: Historical; Multicultural
Series: Return to Tyler. Book 1
Subject(s): Prejudice; Native Americans; Frontier and Pioneer Life
Major character(s): Marie Lafayette, Teacher; Night Hawk, Indian, Horse Trainer (horse breeder)
Time period(s): 1840s (1840)
Locale(s): Fort Tye, Wisconsin

Summary: Marie Lafayette, daughter of the man in charge of a frontier outpost in Wisconsin, joins her cold-hearted father to become the fort's schoolteacher. Longing for affection, she soon falls in love with Night Hawk, an Indian horse breeder and a bit of a local legend. Unfortunately, prejudice has already gained a foothold in the wilderness, and all forces seem to be against the young lovers. This is the first in a prequel to the popular Tyler series.

Where it's reviewed:
Romantic Times, April 2001, page 45

Other books by the same author:
Malcolm's Honor, 2000
Montana Man, 2000
Cooper's Wife, 1999
Last Chance Bride, 1998

Other books you might like:
Judie Aitken, *A Love Beyond Time*, 2000
time travel
Leslie LaFoy, *Maddie's Justice*, 2000
Theresa Michaels, *The Merry Widows: Sarah*, 1999
Cheryl Ann Porter, *Wild Flower*, 2001
Nan Ryan, *The Seduction of Ellen*, 2001

297

LYNNE HAYWORTH (Pseudonym of Lynne Hutchison)

Summer's End

(New York: Zebra, 2001)

Story type: Historical/Colonial America
Series: Clan MacLean. Book 1
Subject(s): Healing; Exile; Jealousy
Major character(s): Clemency Cameron, Healer; Jamie MacLean, Expatriate (of Scotland)
Time period(s): 1760s (1763)
Locale(s): Kittery, Maine, American Colonies

Summary: When the man she's come to America to marry dies, healer Clemency Cameron is given a home and protection by exiled Scotsman Jamie MacLean. A jealous woman spreads the rumor that Clemency's healing skills are those of a witch, and Clemency has to flee for her life. An honorable man leaves everything he's worked for to protect the woman he loves in this tale of an exile who willingly faces exile again.

Where it's reviewed:
Romantic Times, January 2001, page 36

Other books by the same author:
Autumn Flame, 2001 (Clan MacLean. Book 2)
Winter Fire, 2001 (Clan MacLean. Book 3)

Other books you might like:
Miranda Jarrett, *Sunrise*, 2000
Jill Marie Landis, *Blue Moon*, 1999
Ruth Langan, *The Sea Nymph*, 2001
Stobie Piel, *A Patriot's Heart*, 1998
Karen Robards, *This Side of Heaven*, 1991

298

CANDICE HERN

The Bride Sale

(New York: Avon, 2002)

Story type: Historical/Regency
Subject(s): Marriage
Major character(s): Verity Osborne, Gentlewoman, Bride (reluctant); James Harkness, Nobleman (baron)
Time period(s): 1810s (1818)
Locale(s): Cornwall, England

Summary: When the reclusive James Harkness buys Verity Osborne in an illegal ''wife sale'' in a effort to save her from a worse fate, he surprises himself, startles the townsfolk, and puts Verity on guard as she wonders what is in store for her as the possession of ''Lord Heartless.'' Neither is what the other expects and both have past issues to resolve before they can be friends, let alone anything else. Dark secrets, serious insecurities, and soul-searing guilt underlie this well-written, compelling story of healing love and redemption by a veteran Regency writer that includes good descriptive detail of Cornwall and excellent character development.

Other books by the same author:
Miss Lacey's Last Fling, 2001
The Best Intentions, 1999
A Garden Folly, 1997
An Affair of Honor, 1996
A Change of Heart, 1995

Other books you might like:
Mary Balogh, *One Night for Love*, 1999
Mary Balogh, *Thief of Dreams*, 1998
Kat Martin, *Wicked Promise*, 1998
Georgian
Mary Jo Putney, *One Perfect Rose*, 1997
Mary Jo Putney, *Thunder and Roses*, 1993

299

RITA HERRON

Marry Me, Maddie?

(New York: LoveSpell, 2001)

Story type: Contemporary; Humor
Subject(s): Television Programs; Surprises; Family Relations
Major character(s): Maddie Summers, Interior Decorator; Chase Holloway, Architect
Time period(s): 2000s
Locale(s): Savannah, Georgia

Summary: Maddie Summers, tired of her fiance's reluctance to marry, tricks him into being on her friend's talk show. Rejected in front of the entire city of Savannah, Georgia, Maddie declares her freedom, and vows to date a lot of men before settling down. Chase Holloway is Maddie's overprotective brother's friend and he thinks of her as a kid. Maddie's got plans for Chase—none of them G-rated. This book is sure to tickle the funny bone.

Where it's reviewed:
Romantic Times, August 2001, page 88

Other books by the same author:
Have Baby, Need Beau, 2001
Have Gown, Need Groom, 2001
Saving His Son, 2001
Forgotten Lullaby, 2000
His-and-Hers Twins, 2000

Other books you might like:
Judith Arnold, *Looking for Laura*, 2001
Elizabeth Bevarly, *First Comes Love*, 2000
Stephanie Bond, *Seeking Single Male*, 2000
Julie Kenner, *Aphrodite's Kiss*, 2001
Sheila Rabe, *A Prince of a Guy*, 2001

300

DONNA HILL
ROCHELLE ALERS, Co-Author
CANDICE POARCH, Co-Author

'Tis the Season

(New York: BET, 2002)

Story type: Holiday Themes; Multicultural
Subject(s): African Americans; Holidays; Romance
Time period(s): 2000s
Locale(s): United States

Summary: Continuing the tradition of producing a trilogy of novellas focusing on the three winter holidays of Christmas, Kwanzaa, and New Year's, BET (Arabesque) once again offers an appealing collection. Included are *The Choice* by Donna Hill, *First Fruits* by Rochelle Alers, and *A New Year: A New Beginning* by Candice Poarch. Note: reprints included.

Other books by the same author:
A Midnight Clear, 1999

Other books you might like:
Rochelle Alers, *Holiday Cheer*, 1995
similar anthology
Gwynne Forster, *Silver Bells*, 1996
similar anthology
Felicia Mason, *Something to Celebrate*, 1999
Francis Ray, *Winter Nights*, 1998
similar anthology

301

METSY HINGLE

The Wager

(Don Mills, Ontario: Mira, 2001)

Story type: Contemporary
Subject(s): Family Relations; Gambling; Hotels and Motels
Major character(s): Laura Harte, Hotel Worker (assistant hotel manager); Josh Logan, Hotel Owner; Olivia Jardine, Grandparent, Businesswoman (hotels)
Time period(s): 2000s
Locale(s): San Francisco, California; New Orleans, Louisiana

Summary: After her mother's tragic death, Laura Harte is stunned to learn that not only had her mother lied to her about her father dying in a plane crash, but until recently he had been alive, well, and wealthy—and raising a second family—in New Orleans. Now, the grandmother she has never met wants her to come to New Orleans, but hurt and angry, Laura will have none of it—until Josh Logan arrives with an offer she can't refuse. Deceit, passion, and healing are part of this contemporary romance that features a pair of strong protagonists and a number of interesting secondary characters.

Other books by the same author:
Navy Seal Dad, 2002
Wife with Amnesia, 2001
The Baby Bonus, 2000
Love Child, 1997
Surrender, 1996

Other books you might like:
Sandra Brown, *French Silk*, 1992
strong heroine/similar setting/different issues
Ginna Gray, *The Prodigal Daughter*, 2001
long-lost daughter theme
Mary Jo Putney, *The Burning Point*, 2000
Emilie Richards, *Iron Lace*, 1996
Nora Roberts, *The Villa*, 2001

302

LINDA HOWARD (Pseudonym of Linda Howington)

Open Season

(New York: Pocket, 2001)

Story type: Romantic Suspense
Subject(s): Change; Murder
Major character(s): Dacinda "Daisy" Ann Minor, Librarian; Jack Russo, Police Officer (chief of police)
Time period(s): 2000s
Locale(s): Hillsboro, Alabama

Summary: Small town librarian Daisy Minor decides to change her dull life and plain appearance, but her sassy new look and search for romance winds up attracting a lot of attention, including that of police chief Jack Russo, who spots the new and improved Daisy dancing at a local nightclub. Instantly smitten with the lovely librarian, Jack comes to realize he wants Daisy in his life permanently. When Daisy accidently witnesses a murder, Jack must protect her from a killer determined to eliminate the only witness to a perfect crime.

Where it's reviewed:
Affaire de Coeur, July/August 2001, page 33
Romantic Times, August 2001, page 85

Other books by the same author:
A Game of Chance, 2000
Mr. Perfect, 2000
All the Queen's Men, 1999
Kill and Tell, 1998
Now You See Her, 1998

Other books you might like:
Cherry Adair, *Kiss and Tell*, 2000
Iris Johansen, *The Ugly Duckling*, 1996
Jayne Ann Krentz, *Sharp Edges*, 1998
Elizabeth Lowell, *Moving Target*, 2001
Meryl Sawyer, *Kiss in the Dark*, 1995

303

JILLIAN HUNTER

Abandon

(New York: Sonnet, 2001)

Story type: Historical
Subject(s): Legends; Magic; Islands
Major character(s): Morwenna Halliwell, Gentlewoman; Anthony Hartstone, Nobleman (Earl of Pentargon)
Time period(s): Indeterminate Past
Locale(s): Cornwall, England (Abandon in the Scilly Islands)

Summary: When the Earl of Pentargon inherits the small, possibly enchanted island of Abandon, and strikes a deal to sell it to a friend for socio-political reasons, Morwenna Halliwell takes action. Not only will this sale put the islanders out of work, but it will destroy her efforts to complete her father's last work on the Arthurian legends. Magic takes a hand and before long strange things are happening—Morwenna and Anthony are soon caught in their own destiny—one that has always predicted that they would marry. Light, lively, and magical.

Other books by the same author:
Indiscretion, 2000
Delight, 1999
Daring, 1998
Fairy Tale, 1997
A Deeper Magic, 1994

Other books you might like:
Jill Barnett, *Wonderful*, 1997
Kimberly Cates, *Magic*, 1998
Juliana Garnett, *The Knight*, 2001
Arthurian tale
Cathy Maxwell, *When Dreams Come True*, 1998
Mary Jo Putney, *Faery Magic*, 1998
anthology

304

KATE HUNTINGTON (Pseudonym of Kate Chwedyk)

A Rogue for Christmas

(New York: Zebra, 2001)

Story type: Regency
Subject(s): Christmas; Family
Major character(s): Mary Ann Whittaker, Gentlewoman; Lionel St. James, Gambler
Time period(s): 1810s (1812; 1819)
Locale(s): London, England; Leicestershire, England

Summary: Seven years ago Lionel St. James rescued young Mary Ann Whittaker from a cutpurse and gave her and her impoverished family a Christmas they never forgot. From that moment Mary Ann knew Lionel was the only man for her even though Lionel, whose reputation has been tarnished by scandal, knows he is the last man Mary Ann should ever want. Years later when Lionel unexpectedly shows up at a ball her brother-in-law is giving, Mary Ann convinces her family to invite Lionel to their upcoming Christmas party with the thought of proving to her gallant rescuer that he is indeed worthy of her love.

Other books by the same author:
Lady Diana's Darlings, 2000
Mistletoe Mayhem, 2000
The Captain's Courtship, 1999
The Lieutenant's Lady, 1999

Other books you might like:
Mary Balogh, *Christmas Belle*, 1993
Marion Chesney, *Miss Davenport's Christmas*, 1993
Shannon Donnelly, *Under the Kissing Bough*, 2001
Elisabeth Fairchild, *The Holly and the Ivy*, 1999
Barbara Metzger, *Christmas Wishes*, 1992

305

ANNA JACOBS

A Forbidden Embrace

(New York: Severn House, 2001)

Story type: Regency
Subject(s): Courtship; Cousins
Major character(s): Cassandra Treat, Heiress; Simeon Giffard, Nobleman; Susannah Berrinden, Cousin (of Cassandra)
Time period(s): 1810s (1818)
Locale(s): England

Summary: To honor her deceased mother's wishes, Cassandra Treat leaves her beloved home in Bardsley to stay with relatives she has never met in order to enjoy a Season in London. She quickly discovers the only one of her new relatives she even likes is her cousin Susannah, who is being pushed by her forceful mother into marrying Simeon Giffard. Cassandra is determined to find some way to help her cousin break the engagement, but her plan never included falling in love with Simeon.

Where it's reviewed:
Booklist, November 15, 2001, page 559
Library Journal, November 15, 2001, page 54

Other books by the same author:
High Street, 1996
Salem Street, 1995

Other books you might like:
Elena Greene, *Lord Langdon's Kiss*, 2000
Emily Hendrickson, *The Rake's Revenge*, 2001
Shirley Kennedy, *The Rebellious Twin*, 2000
Valerie King, *A Brighton Flirtation*, 2000
Patricia Oliver, *An Unsuitable Match*, 1999

306

HOLLY JACOBS (Pseudonym of Holly Fuhrman)

Do You Hear What I Hear?

(New York: Silhouette, 2001)

Story type: Contemporary
Subject(s): Christmas; Deafness; Small Town Life
Major character(s): Libby McGuiness, Hairdresser (Snips and Snaps Beauty Shop), Single Parent; Joshua Gardner, Doctor (ophthalmologist)
Time period(s): 2000s
Locale(s): Erie, Pennsylvania

Summary: Libby McGuiness is fed up with the entire town of Erie trying to fix her up with a new man, especially since Libby is perfectly happy with her life, including her wonderful daughter Meg, as it is. When handsome ophthalmologist Joshua Gardner moves into the office next door to hers, everyone starts playing matchmaker again, only this time Libby does not seem to mind quite as much!

Where it's reviewed:
Romantic Times, November 2001, page 115

Other books by the same author:
I Waxed My Legs for This?, 2001

Other books you might like:
Judith Arnold, *Sweet Light*, 1997
Kathleen Creighton, *One Christmas Knight*, 1997
Kate Hoffman, *Caught under the Mistletoe*, 1997
Muriel Jensen, *Carol Christmas*, 1990
Catherine Spencer, *Christmas with a Stranger*, 1997

307

MIRANDA JARRETT

The Very Comely Countess

(New York: Sonnet, 2001)

Story type: Historical/Georgian
Subject(s): Spies; Marriage
Major character(s): Harriet Treene, Saleswoman (orange seller), Imposter (poses as a mistress); William Manderville, Nobleman (Earl of Bonnington), Spy
Time period(s): 1790s (1799)
Locale(s): England

Summary: When a common orange seller ends up attracting the attentions of both a duchess and an earl—for very different reasons—the stage is set for a lively, sensual romp that takes its characters from the superficial glitter of the London social scene to the dangers of the aftermath of the French Revolution. Laced with deception and political intrigue, this fast-paced romance is reminiscent of *The Scarlet Pimpernel.* Follows *The Very Daring Duchess.*

Other books by the same author:
The Very Daring Duchess, 2001
Starlight, 2000
Sunrise, 2000
Wishing, 1999
The Secrets of Catie Hazard, 1997

Other books you might like:
Jo Beverley, *My Lady Notorious*, 1993
Jo Beverley, *Tempting Fortune*, 1995
Loretta Chase, *The Last Hellion*, 1998
Christina Dodd, *A Well-Pleasured Lady*, 1997
Baroness Emmuska Orczy, *The Scarlet Pimpernel*, 1905

308

MIRANDA JARRETT

The Very Daring Duchess

(New York: Sonnet, 2001)

Story type: Historical/Georgian
Subject(s): Marriage; Military Life; Social Classes
Major character(s): Francesca Robin, Art Dealer, Artist; Lord Edward Ramsden, Nobleman (son of Duke of Harborough), Military Personnel (naval captain)
Time period(s): 1790s (1798)
Locale(s): Naples, Italy; England

Summary: Reluctant to leave her in Naples with the French set to invade, Captain Lord Edward Ramsden impulsively offers to marry Neapolitan artist and art dealer Francesca Robin to ensure her passage on the ship back to England—an offer the independent Francesca at first rejects and then, realizing she has no options, accepts. Love, of course, eventually follows—and so do some rather surprising, life-changing events. Sensual and fast-paced.

Where it's reviewed:
Publishers Weekly, August 27, 2001, page 62

Other books by the same author:
The Very Comely Countess, 2001
Starlight, 2000
Sunrise, 2000
Wishing, 1999
The Secrets of Catie Hazard, 1997

Other books you might like:
Mary Balogh, *Beyond the Sunrise*, 1992
Jo Beverley, *Tempting Fortune*, 1995
Jane Feather, *Velvet*, 1994
Jane Feather, *Violet*, 1995
Mary Jo Putney, *Petals in the Storm*, 1993

309

NICOLE JORDAN (Pseudonym of Anne Bushyhead)

Desire

(New York: Ivy, 2001)

Story type: Historical/Regency
Subject(s): Espionage; Smuggling
Major character(s): Lucian Tremayne, Nobleman (Earl of Wycliff), Spy; Brynn Caldwell, Noblewoman, Smuggler
Time period(s): 1810s (1813)
Locale(s): London, England; Cornwall, England; Gwyndar, Wales

Summary: After one glimpse of Brynn Caldwell, Lucian Tremayne is tempted to forget his mission to ferret out the traitors smuggling English gold to the French and instead concentrate on finding a way to get Brynn to marry him. Brynn, however, has no intention of wedding anyone since a family curse dooms any man who loves a Caldwell woman to an early demise. Lucian eventually coerces Brynn into marriage; but once he discovers Brynn may be involved in the smuggling scheme he is investigating, Lucian must choose between duty and desire.

Where it's reviewed:
Booklist, September 15, 2001, page 204
Romantic Times, November 2001, page 38

Other books by the same author:
The Passion, 2000
The Seduction, 2000
The Heart Breaker, 1998
The Lover, 1997
The Outlaw, 1996

Other books you might like:
Pamela Britton, *Enchanted by Your Kisses*, 1997
Stephanie Laurens, *Captain Jack's Woman*, 1997
Amanda Quick, *Ravished*, 1992
Karen Ranney, *After the Kiss*, 2000
Elizabeth Thornton, *Princess Charming*, 2001

310

DARA JOY

Ritual of Proof

(New York: Morrow, 2001)

Story type: Futuristic
Subject(s): Courtship; Marriage
Major character(s): Green Tamryn, Noblewoman (marquelle); Jorlan Reynard, Spouse
Time period(s): Indeterminate Future
Locale(s): Forus, Fictional Country

Summary: Marquelle Green Tamryn has no desire to take a name-bearer but when her sworn nemesis, Claudine D'anbere, expresses an interest in wedding Jorlan Reynard, Green does the only thing she can think of to protect the sinfully handsome young man: she puts in her own bid to fasten Jorlan to her house. Jorlan has no intention of becoming the matrimonial prize of any woman; but once he begins the ritual of proof with Green, Jorlan discovers marriage need not be the trap he once expected. A futuristic romance with some Regency inspired touches.

Where it's reviewed:
Affaire de Coeur, July/August 2001, page 22
Booklist, May 15, 2001, page 1738
Publishers Weekly, June 18, 2001, page 60
Romantic Times, June 2001, page 91

Other books by the same author:
High Intensity, 2000
Rejar, 1999
Tonight or Never, 1999
High Energy, 1998
Mine to Take, 1998

Other books you might like:
Justine Davis, *Lord of the Storm*, 1994
Susan Grant, *The Star King*, 2000
Susan Krinard, *Star-Crossed*, 1995
Kristen Kyle, *Nighthawk*, 1997
Jan Zimlich, *The Black Rose*, 2000

311

JULIA JUSTISS (Pseudonym of Janet Justiss)

The Proper Wife

(New York: Harlequin, 2001)

Story type: Historical/Regency
Subject(s): Courtship; Marriage; Social Conditions
Major character(s): St. John Michael Peter Sandiford, Military Personnel (former colonel), Nobleman (viscount); Clarissa Beaumont, Noblewoman
Time period(s): 1810s (1815)
Locale(s): London, England

Summary: St. John ''Sinjin'' Sandiford returns home from Waterloo to find the only woman he ever loved now married to another man and his family estate bankrupt. Sinjin sets about searching for a suitable heiress to marry, someone who is modest, thrifty, and hardworking. Lady Clarissa Beaumont, the reigning beauty of the *ton*, does not meet any of Sinjin's requirements for a worthy wife but somehow after getting to know her better, Sinjin is tempted to throw away his list and marry Clarissa anyway.

Where it's reviewed:
Pubishers Weekly, June 18, 2001, page 66
Romantic Times, July 2001, page 47

Other books by the same author:
A Scandalous Proposal, 2000
The Wedding Gamble, 1999

Other books you might like:
Rexanne Becnel, *The Matchmaker*, 2001
Suzanne Enoch, *A Matter of Scandal*, 2001
Deborah Hale, *The Wedding Wager*, 2001
Karen Hawkins, *A Belated Bride*, 2001
Brenda Hiatt, *A Scandalous Virtue*, 1999

312

ANDREA KANE

No Way Out

(New York: Pocket, 2001)

Story type: Contemporary; Romantic Suspense
Subject(s): Secrets; Family Problems; Abuse
Major character(s): Julia Talbot, Teacher (elementary school); Connor Stratford, Financier (venture capitalist)
Time period(s): 2000s
Locale(s): New York

Summary: Worried about one of her students, second-grade teacher Julia Talbot sets out to discover what is wrong; but when her investigation begins to threaten a well-known political family, she becomes a target for seduction—and then violence—herself. Abuse, addiction, insecurity and a host of contemporary issues play a part in this fast-paced, complex romantic thriller.

Other books by the same author:
Run for Your Life, 2000
The Gold Coin, 1999
The Silver Coin, 1999
The Music Box, 1998
The Theft, 1998

Other books you might like:
Sandra Brown, *Breath of Scandal*, 1991
Karen Harper, *Empty Cradle*, 1998
Christine Hegan, *The Enemy Within*, 1998
Karen Robards, *The Senator's Wife*, 1998
Tracey Tillis, *Flashpoint*, 1997

313

KATHLEEN KANE

Just West of Heaven

(New York: St. Martin's Press, 2001)

Story type: Paranormal; Historical/American West
Subject(s): Psychic Powers; Child Custody; American West
Major character(s): Sophie Dolan, Psychic, Fugitive; Ridge Hawkins, Lawman (sheriff of Tanglewood)

Time period(s): 1880s (1880)
Locale(s): Albany, New York; Tanglewood, Nevada

Summary: Sophie Dolan leaves Albany, New York with her little sister, Jenna, and flees to Tanglewood, Nevada. Both Sophie and Jenna have "the sight," and now that their mother's dead, the unscrupulous man she'd named as Jenna's legal guardian wants to capitalize on the girl's gift. Tanglewood Sheriff Ridge Hawkins knows there's something odd about the new schoolmarm and her daughter, and he's bound and determined to find out what it is. A by-the-book sheriff and a woman who would do anything to protect her sister don't need a psychic to find out that, despite their best efforts, they've fallen in love.

Where it's reviewed:
Romantic Times, August 2001, page 37

Other books by the same author:
Catch a Fallen Angel, 2000
Wish upon a Cowboy, 2000
Simply Magic, 1999
Dreamweaver, 1998
This Time for Keeps, 1998

Other books you might like:
Kristin Hannah, *When Lightning Strikes*, 1994
time travel
Meagan McKinney, *The Ground She Walks Upon*, 1994
Eugenia Riley, *Bushwhacked Bride*, 1999
time travel
Sharon Sala, *Shades of a Desperado*, 1997
reincarnation
Cynthia Sterling, *Great Caesar's Ghost*, 2000

314

SUSANNA KEARSLEY

Season of Storms

(New York: Jove, 2001)

Story type: Romantic Suspense; Gothic
Subject(s): Plays; Mystery; Theater
Major character(s): Celia Sands, Actress; Alessandro "Alex" D'Ascanio, Director
Time period(s): 2000s; 1920s (1921)
Locale(s): Lake Garda, Italy (Il Piacere estate)

Summary: An old mystery surrounding the disappearance of a play's leading lady in the early 1920s surfaces once again when an actress of the same name is chosen to play the same part 80 years later by the grandson of the original playwright. Hints of the paranormal, a gradually unfolding mystery, and chilling suspense add to this mood-evoking romance that brings to mind some of the early works of Mary Stewart and Barbara Michaels.

Other books by the same author:
Named of the Dragon, 1999
The Shadowy Horses, 1999
Mariana, 1995

Other books you might like:
Daphne Du Maurier, *Rebecca*, 1938
Anne Maybury, *Jessamy Court*, 1974
Anne Maybury, *The Terracotta Palace*, 1971
early contemporary Gothic
Mary Stewart, *This Rough Magic*, 1938
Mary Stewart, *Touch Not the Cat*, 1976

315

CARLA KELLY

One Good Turn

(New York: Signet, 2002)

Story type: Regency
Subject(s): Courtship; Social Classes; War
Major character(s): Liria Valencia, Housekeeper, Parent; Benedict "Nez" Nesbitt, Nobleman (duke)
Time period(s): 1810s
Locale(s): England

Summary: While on the way to his estate, Benedict Nesbitt rescues Liria Valencia and her son from a rainstorm. At the time he has no idea that she will become a part of his life he cannot do without. Although each is wounded in different ways, both need healing and understanding—and they get it from each other, along with love. Beautifully rendered, empathetic characters lend believability to this poignant, emotionally involving story.

Where it's reviewed:
Rendezvous, December 2001, page 32
Romantic Times, December 2001, page 30

Other books by the same author:
With This Ring, 1997
The Lady's Companion, 1996
Mrs. Drew Plays Her Hand, 1994
Miss Grimsley's Oxford Career, 1992
Marian's Christmas Wish, 1989

Other books you might like:
Elisabeth Fairchild, *Captain Cupid Calls the Shots*, 2000
another wounded hero
Marjorie Farrell, *Red, Red Rose*, 1999
Evelyn Richardson, *My Lady Nightingale*, 1999
Jeanne Savery, *The Christmas Gift*, 2000

316

SUSAN KING

The Sword Maiden

(New York: Signet, 2001)

Story type: Historical/Medieval
Series: Maiden. Book 3
Subject(s): Legends; Fairies; Heroes and Heroines
Major character(s): Eva MacArthur, Guardian (of the Fairy Sword); Lachlann MacKerron, Blacksmith, Military Personnel
Time period(s): 15th century (first half)
Locale(s): Argyll, Scotland

Summary: The evil Green Colin Campbell has given Eva MacArthur a choice—marry him and turn over her beloved Innisfarna, or he'll see to it that her family's killed. Colin knows that Eva's true love, Lachlann MacKerron, has gone off to be part of Joan of Arc's Royal Scots Guard. This powerful story of two warriors is forged together as strongly as the fabled swords associated with each one.

Where it's reviewed:
Booklist, September 15, 2001, page 204
Publishers Weekly, September 17, 2001, page 62
Romantic Times, October 2001, page 35

Other books by the same author:
The Swan Maiden, 2001 (Maiden. Book 2)
The Stone Maiden, 2000 (Maiden. Book 1)
The Heather Moon, 1999
Laird of the Wind, 1998
Lady Miracle, 1997

Other books you might like:
Shana Abe, *Intimate Enemies*, 1999
Jill Barnett, *Wicked*, 1999
Claudia Dain, *The Holding*, 2001
Donna Fletcher, *Irish Hope*, 2001
Haywood Smith, *Highland Princess*, 2000

317

CHRISTINA KINGSTON (Pseudonym of Christina Strong)

The Night the Stars Fell

(New York: Jove, 2001)

Story type: Historical/Regency
Subject(s): Smuggling; Slavery; Identity, Concealed
Major character(s): Lady Katherine of Cliffside, Noblewoman (Countess of Rushmore), Highwayman; Chalfont Blysdale, Nobleman (6th Earl of Blythingdale), Military Personnel (colonel)
Time period(s): 1810s
Locale(s): Cliffside, England

Summary: Noblewoman by day, highwayman by night, Lady Katherine of Cliffside seeks not to rob her victims, but to find evidence proving her brother's innocence. Chalfont ''Bly'' Blysdale, 6th Earl of Blythingdale, is looking for two of his friends who've mysteriously disappeared. Then one night, a young boy holds up his carriage, and it isn't long before Bly finds out who the lad really is. This is an action-packed adventure with bad guys lurking around every corner.

Where it's reviewed:
Affaire de Coeur, March/April 2001, page 37
Publishers Weekly, February 26, 2001, page 65
Romantic Times, April 2001, page 41

Other books by the same author:
Ride for the Roses, 2000

Other books you might like:
Candace Camp, *No Other Love*, 2001
Valerie King, *My Lord Highwayman*, 2001
Stephanie Laurens, *Captain Jack's Woman*, 1997
Christina Skye, *Come the Night*, 1994
Joan Smith, *A Highwayman Came Riding*, 1998

318

MARTHA KIRKLAND

Mr. Montgomery's Quest

(New York: Signet, 2001)

Story type: Regency
Subject(s): Adventure and Adventurers; Brothers; Voyages and Travels
Major character(s): Charlotte Pelham, Tour Guide (Bonaventure Tours); Harrison Montgomery, Gentleman, Sea Captain (former)
Time period(s): 1810s
Locale(s): England

Summary: Using the name Charles Pelham, Charlotte Pelham applies for the position of tour guide in the hopes that once she proves she can successfully lead a walking tour of northern England, her new employer will not quibble about her gender. When Harrison Montgomery coerces his way onto her tour at the last minute, Charlotte notices Harrison does not care whether the group's guide is a man or woman since he seems to have his own mysterious reason for wanting to be part of the tour group.

Where it's reviewed:
Romantic Times, October 2001, page 62

Other books by the same author:
His Lordship's Swan, 2001
The Rake's Fiancee, 2001
Miss Maitland's Letters, 2000
That Scandalous Heiress, 2000
Uncommon Courtship, 2000

Other books you might like:
Nancy Butler, *Keeper of Swans*, 1984
Sandra Heath, *A Commerical Enterprise*, 1984
Emma Jensen, *A Grand Design*, 2000
Carla Kelly, *Miss Chartley's Guided Tour*, 1989
April Kihlstrom, *The Wiley Wastrel*, 1999

319

LISA KLEYPAS

Suddenly You

(New York: Avon, 2001)

Story type: Historical/Victorian
Subject(s): Erotica; Publishing; Women's Rights
Major character(s): Amanda Briars, Writer, Spinster; Jack Devlin, Bastard Son (of a nobleman), Publisher
Time period(s): 1830s (1836)
Locale(s): London, England

Summary: Popular author Amanda Briars is determined not to be a virgin on her 30th birthday, so, as a present to herself, she orders a male lover from a notorious madame. When a handsome man shows up on her doorstep at the appointed hour, she proceeds with her night of seduction and passion. Jack Devlin is a publisher interested in buying the rights to Amanda's first book. He knows the writer is unconventional, but he never expected such a. . .steamy reception for his unannounced visit. A proper spinster finds true love with the most unexpected man in this very sensual, often humorous, novel that sizzles from cover to cover.

Where it's reviewed:
Affaire de Coeur, May/June 2001, page 34
Publishers Weekly, April 16, 2001, page 50
Romantic Times, June 2001, page 37

Other books by the same author:
Where Dreams Begin, 2000
Someone to Watch over Me, 1999
Stranger in My Arms, 1998
Because You're Mine, 1997
Somewhere I'll Find You, 1996

Other books you might like:
Geralyn Dawson, *The Bad Luck Wedding Night*, 2001
Christina Dodd, *Rules of Surrender*, 2000
Suzanne Enoch, *Meet Me at Midnight*, 2000
Jill Marie Landis, *The Orchid Hunter*, 2000
Kasey Michaels, *Someone to Love*, 2001

320

LISA KLEYPAS
LISA CACH, Co-Author
CLAUDIA DAIN, Co-Author
LYNSAY SANDS, Co-Author

Wish List

(New York: Leisure, 2001)

Story type: Anthology; Historical
Subject(s): Gambling; Courtship; Inheritance
Time period(s): 19th century
Locale(s): England

Summary: Four novellas are included in this volume. Lisa Cach's *Puddings, Pastries, and Thou* is about an impoverished woman relying on the capricious kindness of relatives who sees a man with a dark secret as her savior. Claudia Dain's *Union* concerns a stubborn young woman who refuses to consider marriage to anyone who does not own land in Ireland. In Lisa Kleypas' *I Will*, a rake of the first order needs a fiancee to secure his inheritance and a spinster needs money to clear her brother's gambling debts. A young woman wreaks havoc on a gambling establishment in an all-out effort to make her father give up his habit in Lynsay Sands' *All I Want*.

Other books by the same author:
Suddenly You, 2001

Other books you might like:
Lisa Cach, *The Wildest Shore*, 2001
Claudia Dain, *The Holding*, 2001
Claudia Dain, *The Marriage Bed*, 2001
Lynsay Sands, *Lady Pirate*, 2001

321

BETINA KRAHN

The Husband Test

(New York: Bantam, 2001)

Story type: Historical/Medieval
Subject(s): Marriage; Nuns; Superstition
Major character(s): Eloise of Argent, Religious (novitiate), Gentlewoman; Peril, Nobleman (Earl of Whitmore)
Time period(s): Indeterminate Past
Locale(s): England

Summary: When Peril, Earl of Whitmore, arrives at the Convent of the Brides of Virtue, he has one goal in mind—to acquire a virtuous bride who, incidentally, will help him break the curse afflicting his lands. He reckons without the canny abbess, who takes this opportunity to rid herself of a well-meaning, but totally disobedient and disruptive novitiate by inventing the Husband Test—a test that will determine Peril's matrimonial worthiness and which must be judged by Sister Eloise (the offending novice) at Peril's estate. Whitmore is in a sorry state, and Eloise can't help but try to improve things, and much to Peril's surprise, she's often right. He is even more surprised—and distressed—to find himself attracted to her, a woman he thinks is already a nun. Eloise, of course, is fighting her attraction because she is destined, she thinks, to take her vows once this duty is done. Naturally, they get this, as well as the truth behind the alleged curse, sorted out before the end of the book. Funny, lively, sensual, and totally charming.

Where it's reviewed:
Publishers Weekly, October 22, 2001, page 54

Other books by the same author:
Sweet Talking Man, 2000
The Soft Touch, 1999
The Mermaid, 1997
The Unlikely Angel, 1996
The Perfect Mistress, 1995

Other books you might like:
Jill Barnett, *Wicked*, 1999
more medieval humor
Connie Brockway, *The Bridal Season*, 2001
Cathy Maxwell, *The Wedding Wager*, 2001
Linda Needham, *For My Lady's Kiss*, 1997
Amanda Quick, *Desire*, 1994
one of her few medieval romances

322

SUSAN KRINARD

Secret of the Wolf

(New York: Berkley, 2001)

Story type: Historical/American West Coast; Paranormal
Series: Forster Trilogy. Book 3
Subject(s): Werewolves; Multiple Personalities; Difference
Major character(s): Johanna Schell, Doctor (hypnotist); Quentin Forster, Werewolf, Mentally Ill Person
Time period(s): 1880s
Locale(s): Napa Valley, California (The Haven)

Summary: When Dr. Johanna Schell trips over an unconscious man lying in the grass, hallucinating and obviously drunk, she does the only thing she can do—she decides to help him. Quentin Forster is much more than he seems and he carries secrets inside himself even he knows nothing about—secrets that could prove dangerous not only to him, but to Johanna, as well. This dark, mesmerizing tale takes a classic fantasy, gives it a psychiatric twist, and turns it into a satisfying, though occasionally disturbing, romance. Third volume in a trilogy.

Other books by the same author:
Once a Wolf, 2000 (Forster Trilogy. Book 2)
Touch of the Wolf, 1999 (Forster Trilogy. Book 1)
Prince of Shadows, 1996
Prince of Dreams, 1995
Prince of Wolves, 1994

Other books you might like:
Alice Borchardt, *Night of the Wolf*, 1998
different time period
Alice Borchardt, *The Silver Wolf*, 1999
Annette Curtis Klause, *Blood and Chocolate*, 2001
YA werewolf story
Cheri Scotch, *The Werewolf's Kiss*, 1992
Colleen Shannon, *The Wolf of Haskell Hall*, 2001

323

LYNN KURLAND (Pseudonym of Lynn Curland)

My Heart Stood Still

(New York: Berkley, 2001)

Story type: Paranormal; Time Travel
Subject(s): Ghosts; Secrets; Treasure
Major character(s): Iolanthe MacLeod, Spirit; Thomas MacLeod McKinnon, Businessman, Mountaineer
Time period(s): 2000s; 14th century (1382)
Locale(s): Maine; Scotland (Thorpewold Castle)

Summary: Murdered by an Englishman, Iolanthe MacLeod spends the next 600 years haunting the castle where she was killed, still dreaming of a man who would rescue her. When American Thomas McKinnon shows up one day to restore the castle he recently purchased, Iolanthe is struck by the similarity between Thomas and the man of her dreams. All Thomas wants to do is work on his castle but after becoming better acquainted with Iolanthe, he falls in love with the bewitching ghost inhabiting his new home.

Where it's reviewed:
Booklist, September 15, 2001, page 208
Publishers Weekly, September 24, 2001, page 75
Romantic Times, October 2001, page 84

Other books by the same author:
If I Had You, 2000
The More I See You, 1999
Another Chance to Dream, 1998
The Very Thought of You, 1998
This Is All I Ask, 1997

Other books you might like:
Pam Binder, *The Quest*, 2000
Claire Cross, *The Last Highlander*, 1992
Jude Deveraux, *A Knight in Shining Armor*, 1989
Jill Jones, *The Scottish Rose*, 1998
Judith O'Brien, *Ashton's Bride*, 1995

324

LESLIE LAFOY

Jackson's Way

(New York: Bantam, 2001)

Story type: Historical/American West
Subject(s): Inheritance; Family Relations; Greed
Major character(s): Lindsay MacPhaull, Businesswoman, Heiress—Dispossessed; Jackson Stennett, Rancher, Heir
Time period(s): 1830s (1838)
Locale(s): Texas; New York, New York

Summary: Lindsay MacPhaull is a successful businesswoman. She works hard to keep her greedy siblings living a life of luxury. Then her business begins to mysteriously fail, and a stranger from Texas says he's been willed everything she owns by the father who deserted her as a child. A Cinderella tale of strength in the face of utter adversity, this unforgettable book is filled with suspense, adventure, and liberal doses of humor.

Where it's reviewed:
Booklist, September 15, 2001, page 208
Romantic Times, October 2001, page 36

Other books by the same author:
Maddie's Justice, 2000
Daring the Devil, 1999
Lady Reckless, 1998
It Happened One Night, 1997

Other books you might like:
Victoria Alexander, *The Husband List*, 2000
Jill Gregory, *Rough Wrangler, Tender Kisses*, 2000
Kat Martin, *Silk and Steel*, 2000
Nan Ryan, *Wanting You*, 1999
Susan Wiggs, *Halfway to Heaven*, 2001

325

ALLISON LANE (Pseudonym of Susan Pace)

The Rake and the Wallflower

(New York: Signet, 2001)

Story type: Regency
Series: Seabrook Trilogy. Book 2
Subject(s): Courtship; Mystery
Major character(s): Mary Seabrook, Gentlewoman, Artist; Lord Grayson, Nobleman (heir to Earl of Rothmoor), Rake
Time period(s): 1810s
Locale(s): London, England

Summary: Forced to accompany her selfish sister, Laura, during the Season in London, Mary Seabrook ends up attracting the attentions of a scandal-tainted rake and being drawn into a dangerous web of vengeance, jealousy, and violence. Realistic, charming, and darker than some Regencies. Second in a series.

Where it's reviewed:
Library Journal, November 15, 2001, page 54

Other books by the same author:
The Purloined Letters, 2002 (Seabrook Trilogy. Book 3)

The Beleaguered Earl, 2000
A Bird in Hand, 1999
Birds of a Feather, 1999
Devall's Angel, 1998

Other books you might like:
Mary Balogh, *Lord Carew's Bride*, 1995
Jo Beverley, *Dierdre and Don Juan*, 1993
Barbara Hazard, *The Wary Widow*, 2000
darker than some
April Kihlstrom, *The Widowed Bride*, 1996
Mary Jo Putney, *The Diabolical Baron*, 1987

326

ELIZABETH LANE

My Lord Savage

(New York: Harlequin, 2001)

Story type: Historical/Elizabethan
Subject(s): Native Americans; Responsibility; Trust
Major character(s): Black Otter, Chieftain, Indian; Rowena Thornhill, Gentlewoman
Time period(s): 16th century (1573)
Locale(s): Virginia, American Colonies; Cornwall, England

Summary: Taken from his home by the English, Black Otter vows to escape and return to his tribe; but this thought quickly vanishes once he is sold to scientist Christopher Thornhill. Rowena Thornhill is used to her father's various scientific studies, but when she discovers he intends on keeping his latest purchase imprisoned at Thornhill Manor, Rowena searches for some way to help Black Otter, even though helping him means losing him forever.

Where it's reviewed:
Romantic Times, July 2001, page 44

Other books by the same author:
Bride on the Run, 2001
Shawnee Bride, 1999
Apache Fire, 1998
The Tycoon and the Townie, 1997
Hometown Wedding, 1996

Other books you might like:
Gayle Callen, *His Betrothed*, 2001
Marsha Canham, *Across a Moonlit Sea*, 1996
Denise Domning, *Lady in Waiting*, 1998
Ruth Langan, *Captive of Desire*, 1990
Tori Phillips, *Fool's Paradise*, 1996

327

RUTH LANGAN

Awakening Alex

(New York: Silhouette, 2001)

Story type: Contemporary; Romantic Suspense
Series: Sullivan Sisters. Book 1
Subject(s): Healing; Secrets; Self-Acceptance
Major character(s): Alexandra Sullivan, Innkeeper (manager, Snug Harbor Lodge); Grant Malone, Police Officer (NYPD captain)
Time period(s): 1980s (1980); 2000s
Locale(s): Snug Harbor, New Hampshire

Summary: For her whole life, Alex Sullivan has collected stray and wounded animals; so when mysterious, tormented Grant Malone checks into her rustic lodge, all of her protective instincts kick in. Grant is attracted to the feisty Alex, but his dark secret keeps him from letting her get too close. A wounded hero finds the healing power of love in the wilds of New Hampshire thanks to two unlikely matchmakers in this warm winter tale.

Where it's reviewed:
Romantic Times, January 2001, page 104

Other books by the same author:
Loving Lizbeth, 2001 (Sullivan Sisters. Book 2)
Seducing Celeste, 2001
The Sea Sprite, 2001
The Sea Nymph, 2001
Ace, 2000 (Wildes of Wyoming. Book 3)

Other books you might like:
Jean DeWitt, *The Stranger*, 2001
Jill Jones, *Remember Your Lies*, 2001
Rachel Lee, *Snow in September*, 2000
Carla Neggers, *The Waterfall*, 2000
Pat Warren, *The Way We Wed*, 2001

328

RUTH LANGAN

The Sea Sprite

(Toronto: Harlequin, 2001)

Story type: Historical/Seventeenth Century
Series: Sirens of the Sea. Book 3
Subject(s): Memory Loss; Sisters; Healing
Major character(s): Darcy Lambert, Sea Captain; Gryf, Amnesiac
Time period(s): 17th century (1665)
Locale(s): Cornwall, England

Summary: When Darcy Lambert's first true love, Gray Barton, is lost at sea, she doesn't know whether or not she'll ever get over her grief. An able sailor, she takes a commission as captain of the family ship. Then one day during a stopover on her trip, she meets Gryf, a man with a past he can't remember who is a dead ringer for the deceased Gray. This last volume of the Sirens of the Sea trilogy brings the story of the brave Lambert sisters to a satisfying conclusion.

Other books by the same author:
Awakening Alex, 2001
Seducing Celeste, 2001
The Sea Nymph, 2001 (Sirens of the Sea. Book 2)
Ace, 2000 (Wildes of Wyoming. Book 3)
The Sea Witch, 2000 (Sirens of the Sea. Book 1)

Other books you might like:
Julie Garwood, *Guardian Angel*, 2000
Susan Grant, *Once a Pirate*, 2000
Miranda Jarrett, *The Captain's Bride*, 1997
Kinley MacGregor, *A Pirate of Her Own*, 1999
Sandra Madden, *Take by Storm*, 1999

329

STEPHANIE LAURENS

The Promise in a Kiss

(New York: Morrow, 2001)

Story type: Historical/Georgian
Subject(s): Christmas; Seduction
Major character(s): Sebastian Cynster, Nobleman (Duke of St. Ives), Rake; Helena Rebecca de Stansion, Noblewoman (Comtesse d'Lisle)
Time period(s): 1770s (1776); 1780s (1783)
Locale(s): Paris, France; England

Summary: In a Parisian convent garden, Sebastian Cynster and Helena Rebecca de Stansion indulge in one passionate kiss after Helena helps Sebastian escape the consequences of a juvenile prank. Seven years later in London, Helena, in the midst of hunting for a husband, bumps into Sebastian at a fashionable soiree. Sebastian decides to offer Helena his assistance with her search for an appropriate mate with the intent of convincing her that he is the only man for her.

Where it's reviewed:
Affaire de Coeur, November/December 2001, page 20
Booklist, November 15, 2001, page 559
Romantic Times, December 2001, page 37

Other books by the same author:
All about Love, 2001
All about Passion, 2001
A Secret Love, 2000
A Rogue's Proposal, 1999
Scandal's Bride, 1999

Other books you might like:
Jo Beverley, *My Lady Notorious*, 1993
Eloisa James, *Midnight Pleasures*, 2000
Sabrina Jeffries, *The Dangerous Lord*, 2000
Nicole Jordan, *The Seduction*, 2000
Barbara Samuel, *The Black Angel*, 1999

330

RACHEL LEE (Pseudonym of Sue Civil-Brown)

July Thunder

(Don Mills, Ontario: MIRA, 2002)

Story type: Contemporary
Subject(s): Small Town Life; Self-Esteem; Fires
Major character(s): Mary McKinney, Teacher; Sam Canfield, Police Officer (sheriff)
Time period(s): 2000s
Locale(s): Whisper Creek, Colorado

Summary: Sheriff Sam Canfield has been damaged by the contempt of his Bible-thumping preacher father and the death of his young wife; school teacher Mary McKinney is still haunted by her son's death and the resultant breakup of her marriage. Both need healing, but neither is ready—or so they think—for more than friendship. However, when Sam's father comes back to town and a forest fire threatens to get out of control, emotions begin to heat up as well.

Where it's reviewed:
Romantic Times, February 2002, page 83

Other books by the same author:
After I Dream, 2000
Snow in September, 2000
Before I Sleep, 1999
Conard County: Boots and Badges, 1999
Involuntary Daddy, 1999

Other books you might like:
Barbara Freethy, *One True Love*, 1998
Dinah McCall, *Tallchief*, 2000
Susan Wiggs, *The You I Never Knew*, 2001
Ruth Wind, *Beautiful Stranger*, 2000
Ruth Wind, *In the Midnight Rain*, 2000

331

RACHEL LEE (Pseudonym of Sue Civil-Brown)

Under Suspicion

(New York: Warner, 2001)

Story type: Romantic Suspense; Contemporary
Subject(s): Museums; Murder; Archaeology
Major character(s): Anna Lundgren, Museum Curator, Archaeologist; Gil Garcia, Detective—Police
Time period(s): 2000s
Locale(s): Tampa, Florida; Temple Terrace, Florida

Summary: Anna Lundgren's exhibit at the museum is an archaeological wonder that includes a jade dagger complete with its own legendary curse. When a guard is stabbed to death with the dagger, Anna becomes a suspect. The real killer though, is stalking Anna, taunting her with evidence of his nearness. Even police detective Gil Garcia can't solve the puzzle, and his growing attraction to Anna is making the case even more difficult. This romantic suspense keeps the reader guessing until the very end.

Where it's reviewed:
Affaire de Coeur, September/October 2001, page 36
Romantic Times, October 2001, page 83

Other books by the same author:
After I Dream, 2000
Snow in September, 2000
When I Wake, 2000
Before I Sleep, 1999
Conard County: Boots and Badges, 1999

Other books you might like:
Linda Howard, *Mr. Perfect*, 2000
Jayne Ann Krentz, *Eclipse Bay*, 2000
Elizabeth Lowell, *Midnight in Ruby Bayou*, 2000
Carla Neggers, *The Waterfall*, 2000
Nora Roberts, *Carolina Moon*, 2000

332

ANA LEIGH

The MacKenzies: Zach

(New York: Avon, 2001)

Story type: Historical/American West
Subject(s): Frontier and Pioneer Life; Robbers and Outlaws; Marriage
Major character(s): Rose Dubois, Waiter/Waitress (Harvey Girl); Zach MacKenzie, Lawman (undercover Texas Ranger)
Time period(s): 1890s (1892)
Locale(s): Brimstone, Texas

Summary: Harvey Girl Rose Dubois is in Texas looking for a husband—preferably a wealthy rancher. She certainly isn't interested in Zach MacKenzie, or any of the scummy men he seems to hang out with. Appearances can be deceiving, though, and Zach is an undercover Texas Ranger trying to work his way into an outlaw gang, and the last thing he needs is a mouthy redhead to mess up his plans. Lively and action-packed, this novel contains links to Leigh's earlier MacKenzie books.

Other books by the same author:
The MacKenzies: Jared, 2002
The MacKenzies: Josh, 2000
The MacKenzies: David, 1998
The MacKenzies: Flint, 1996
The MacKenzies: Luke, 1996

Other books you might like:
Sonya Birmingham, *The Spitfire*, 1991
Millie Criswell, *Desperate*, 1997
Nicole Jordan, *The Heart Breaker*, 19981991
Maggie Osborne, *The Promise of Jenny Jones*, 1997
Maggie Osborne, *Silver Lining*, 2000

333

JULIE ELIZABETH LETO (Pseudonym of Julie Leto Klapka)

Insatiable

(New York: Harlequin, 2001)

Story type: Contemporary
Subject(s): Food; Seduction
Major character(s): Samantha Deveaux, Bodyguard, Security Officer; Dominick ''Nick'' LaRocca, Businessman (CEO, LaRocca Foods)
Time period(s): 2000s
Locale(s): New Orleans, Louisiana

Summary: Dominick ''Nick'' LaRocca's two grandmothers are always trying to marry him off, but their latest scheme—putting Nick's picture on every label of LaRocca's spaghetti sauce—has Nick fighting off women with a stick. After security guard Samantha Deveaux saves Nick from a horde of hungry women at a food convention, Nick hires Samantha as a private bodyguard. Samantha is delighted to get the new job, but now she has to fight off her own cravings for just a taste of the delectable Nick.

Where it's reviewed:
Romantic Times, June 2001, page 110

Other books by the same author:
Pure Chance, 2001
Good Girls Do, 2000
Private Lessons, 1999
Seducing Sullivan, 1998

Other books you might like:
Carrie Alexander, *A Touch of Black Velvet*, 2000
Susan Andersen, *Baby, Don't Go*, 2000
Kristin Gabriel, *Dangerously Irresistible*, 2001
Leslie Kelly, *Suite Seduction*, 2000
Candace Schuler, *Just Another Pretty Face*, 1993

334

CATHIE LINZ (Pseudonym of Cathie L. Baumgardner)

The Marine and the Princess

(New York: Silhouette, 2001)

Story type: Contemporary
Series: Men of Honor. Book 3
Subject(s): Independence; Princes and Princesses
Major character(s): Vanessa Von Volzenburg, Royalty (princess); Mark Wilder, Military Personnel (U.S. Marine Corps captain)
Time period(s): 2000s
Locale(s): New York, New York

Summary: Tired of her seemingly endless royal duties, Princess Vanessa Von Volzenburg plots a way to escape for a few days and enjoy her visit to New York City but in order for her to explore the city incognito, she must agree to take Marine Captain Mark Wilder along with her as a bodyguard. Mark expects he will be escorting a spoiled, pampered royal brat, but instead is pleasantly surprised to find himself trailing after a very pretty and very kissable woman.

Where it's reviewed:
Romantic Times, December 2001, page 104

Other books by the same author:
Between the Covers, 2001
Stranded with the Sergeant, 2001
Daddy in Dress Blues, 2000
The Cowboy Finds a Bride, 2000
The Lawman Gets Lucky, 2000

Other books you might like:
Carla Cassidy, *An Officer and a Princess*, 2000
Cara Colter, *A Royal Marriage*, 2000
Patricia Forsythe, *The Runaway Princess*, 2001
Valerie Parv, *The Prince's Bride-to-Be*, 2000
Martha Shields, *The Blacksheep Prince's Bride*, 2001

335

CATHIE LINZ (Pseudonym of Cathie L. Baumgardner)

Stranded with the Sergeant

(New York: Silhouette, 2001)

Story type: Contemporary

Series: Men of Honor. Book 2
Subject(s): Guilt; Military Life
Major character(s): Joe Wilder, Military Personnel (U.S. Marine Corps sergeant); Prudence Martin, Teacher
Time period(s): 2000s
Locale(s): Camp Lejeune, North Carolina; Blue Ridge Mountains, North Carolina

Summary: Escorting his commanding officer's daughter and her school class on a tour of the base and then taking them on a wilderness weekend is not Sergeant Joe Wilder's idea of a ''real'' assignment. Once Joe finds out that his commanding officer's daughter is not one of the students but instead is their very pretty teacher, Prudence Martin, the whole idea of the tour suddenly becomes much more interesting.

Where it's reviewed:
Romantic Times, August 2001, page 110

Other books by the same author:
Between the Covers, 2001
Daddy in Dress Blues, 2000
The Lawman Gets Lucky, 2000
The Cowboy Finds a Bride, 2000
The Rancher Gets Hitched, 1999

Other books you might like:
Dixie Browning, *Rocky and the Senator's Daughter*, 2001
Maureen Child, *Prince Charming in Dress Blues*, 2001
Virginia Kantra, *The Reforming of Matthew Dunn*, 1998
Merline Lovelace, *Call of Duty*, 1998
Paula Detmer Riggs, *Murdock's Family*, 1994

336

JOSIE LITTON

Believe in Me

(New York: Bantam, 2001)

Story type: Historical/Medieval
Series: Viking Trilogy. Book 2
Subject(s): Vikings; Marriage
Major character(s): Lady Krysta, Noblewoman (Norse), Bride; Hawk of Essex, Nobleman, Warrior (Saxon)
Time period(s): 9th century (reign of King Alfred)
Locale(s): England

Summary: Another political marriage turns into love in this sequel to *Dream of Me* as a strong Saxon lord finds love with a gentle Viking lass to the surprise of them both. Vividly descriptive with a good sense of characterization, this sensual, lively book nicely continues Litton's trilogy.

Other books by the same author:
Come Back to Me, 2001 (Viking Trilogy. Book 3)
Dream of Me, 2001 (Viking Trilogy. Book 1)

Other books you might like:
Alice Borchardt, *Beguiled*, 1997
Shannon Drake, *Princess of Fire*, 1989
Anita Gordon, *The Valiant Heart*, 1991
Heather Graham, *The Viking's Woman*, 1990
Helen Mittermeyer, *Princess of the Veil*, 1992

337

JOSIE LITTON

Come Back to Me

(New York: Bantam, 2001)

Story type: Historical/Medieval
Series: Viking Trilogy. Book 3
Subject(s): Vikings; Marriage
Major character(s): Lady Rycca of Wolscroft, Noblewoman; Dragon Hakonson, Warrior (Viking)
Time period(s): 9th century (reign of King Alfred)
Locale(s): England

Summary: Running from an unwanted but politically necessary marriage, Lady Rycca of Wolscroft finds herself captured, rescued, and finally enthralled by a mysterious stranger, never realizing he is Dragon Hakonson, Lord of Landsende, the Viking warrior she is supposed to marry. Naively, she seduces him, thinking to carry that memory with her to Normandy when she eventually escapes; but when fate throws them together once more, her actions come back to haunt her as Dragon now considers her totally selfish and Rycca has no faith in Vikings or the peace they are working to establish. Characters from previous stories add interest to this lively, sensual tale that nicely concludes Litton's trilogy.

Other books by the same author:
Believe in Me, 2001 (Viking Trilogy. Book 2)
Dream of Me, 2001 (Viking Trilogy. Book 1)

Other books you might like:
Alice Borchardt, *Beguiled*, 1997
Tanya Anne Crosby, *Viking's Prize*, 1994
Shannon Drake, *Princess of Fire*, 1989
Johanna Lindsey, *Surrender My Love*, 1994
part of her Viking Saga
Haywood Smith, *Highland Princess*, 2000

338

JOSIE LITTON

Dream of Me

(New York: Bantam, 2001)

Story type: Historical/Medieval
Series: Viking Trilogy. Book 1
Subject(s): Vikings; Marriage
Major character(s): Lady Cymbra, Noblewoman, Healer; Wolf Hakonson, Warrior (Viking)
Time period(s): 9th century (reign of King Alfred)
Locale(s): Holyhood, England; Sciringesheal, Norway

Summary: When Viking leader Wolf Hakonson kidnaps Lady Cymbra, sister to the powerful Saxon Lord Hawk of Essex, his motive is revenge for a supposedly rejected offer of peace and a mistaken slight. The bewitching Cymbra captivates him with her beauty and ends up redeeming him with her love. Sensual and tightly crafted. First in a trilogy and bound together with the second book, *Believe in Me*.

Other books by the same author:
Believe in Me, 2001 (Viking Trilogy. Book 2)
Come Back to Me, 2001 (Viking Trilogy. Book 3)

Other books you might like:
Alice Borchardt, *Devoted*, 1995
Debra Lee Brown, *Ice Maiden*, 2001
Vikings
Anita Gordon, *The Defiant Heart*, 1993
Helen Mittermeyer, *Princess of the Veil*, 1992
Karyn Monk, *Once a Warrior*, 1997

339

CAIT LOGAN

On Leaving Lonely Town

(New York: Avon, 2001)

Story type: Contemporary
Subject(s): Heritage; Adoption
Major character(s): Sable Barclay, Criminologist, Adoptee; Culley Blackwolf, Foreman (ranch), Cowboy
Time period(s): 2000s
Locale(s): Shiloh, Wyoming

Summary: When criminologist Sable Barclay stumbles across an old missing-child case, the pieces fit so closely she begins to wonder if she might be the Langtry baby kidnapped 28 years ago in Wyoming—so she decides to go there and find out. Dealing with the truth is harder than she had expected, and so is dealing with the strong-willed, no-nonsense ranch foreman, Culley Blackwolf, a man who both challenges and protects her as she comes to terms with her new situation. Intense and emotionally involving.

Other books you might like:
Kathleen Eagle, *What the Heart Knows*, 1999
Dorothy Garlock, *More than Memory*, 1999
earlier time period
Dinah McCall, *The Return*, 2000
Patricia Potter, *This Perfect Family*, 2001
Ruth Wind, *In the Midnight Rain*, 2000

340

ELIZABETH LOWELL (Pseudonym of Ann Maxwell)

Moving Target

(New York: Morrow, 2001)

Story type: Contemporary; Romantic Suspense
Subject(s): Murder; Inheritance; Collectors and Collecting
Major character(s): Serena Charters, Artisan (weaver), Heiress; Erik North, Appraiser (expert in medieval manuscripts), Investigator
Time period(s): 2000s
Locale(s): California; Southwest

Summary: When weaver Serena Charters inherits a rare manuscript, the Book of the Learned, from her murdered grandmother, she becomes the target of someone who will stop at nothing to possess it. Murder, adventure, and a dash of mysticism combine in this lively, fast-paced adventure.

Where it's reviewed:
Romantic Times, July 2001, page 85

Other books by the same author:
Midnight in Ruby Bayou, 2000
Pearl Cove, 1999
Jade Island, 1998
Amber Beach, 1997
Winter Fire, 1996

Other books you might like:
Stella Cameron, *Key West*, 1996
Catherine Coulter, *The Cove*, 1996
Kay Hooper, *Finding Laura*, 1997
Iris Johansen, *The Ugly Duckling*, 1996
Nora Roberts, *Carolina Moon*, 2000

341

JUDITH LYONS (Pseudonym of Julie M. Higgs)

Lt. Kent: Lone Wolf

(New York: Silhouette, 2001)

Story type: Contemporary
Subject(s): Healing; Hermits; Infertility
Major character(s): Angie Rose, Journalist; Jason Kent, Recluse, Mercenary (for U.S. government, retired)
Time period(s): 2000s
Locale(s): Rocky Mountains, Montana (Kent Mansion)

Summary: Jason Kent, badly scarred and crippled from a covert action gone bad, is a self-made recluse in his secluded Gothic mansion. Angie Rose is a journalist in search of a story about the hermit who built an orphanage. Stranded together in Jason's mansion by the worst storm of the century, they discover that sometimes, the worst scars are on the inside, and that love can make even the most battered person whole again. An emotion-filled chronicle of healing.

Where it's reviewed:
Romantic Times, May 2001, page 110

Other books by the same author:
Awakened by His Kiss, 2000

Other books you might like:
Dixie Browning, *Stryker's Wife*, 2000
Susan Meier, *The Baby Bequest*, 2000
Christie Ridgway, *Wish You Were Here*, 2000
Pat Warren, *The Way We Wed*, 2001
Carrie Weaver, *Promises, Promises*, 2000

342

SANDRA MADDEN

Comfort and Joy

(New York: Kensington, 2001)

Story type: Historical/Victorian America; Holiday Themes
Subject(s): Memory Loss; Irish Americans; Social Classes
Major character(s): Maeve O'Malley, Housekeeper; Charles Rycroft, Amnesiac, Wealthy
Time period(s): 1870s (1873)
Locale(s): Boston, Massachusetts

Summary: Maeve O'Malley and her brother, Sean, find a half-dead man in the alley, apparently the victim of a vicious attack. ''Charlie'' suffers amnesia, but he's warm and loving, and he marries Maeve. Wealthy Charles Rycroft, a very proper member of Boston's aristocracy, is horrified to wake up one day beside a poor Irish woman who claims to be his wife. Plans for a quick divorce are thwarted by the spunky bride Charles doesn't remember in this Victorian Cinderella story.

Where it's reviewed:
Romantic Times, October 2001, page 46

Other books by the same author:
Heaven Sent, 2002
Since You've Been Gone, 2001
Take by Storm, 1999

Other books you might like:
Miranda Jarrett, *Sunrise*, 2000
1720s
Lisa Kleypas, *Someone to Watch over Me*, 1999
Betina Krahn, *Sweet Talking Man*, 2000
Nan Ryan, *Wanting You*, 1999
Susan Wiggs, *The Mistress*, 2000

343

ANNETTE MAHON

The Secret Admirer

(New York: Avalon, 2001)

Story type: Multicultural; Contemporary
Subject(s): Secrets; Small Town Life; Neighbors and Neighborhoods
Major character(s): Emma Lindsey, Banker (teller); Matt Correa, Wealthy, Computer Expert (game animator)
Time period(s): 2000s
Locale(s): Malino, Hawaii

Summary: When Emma Lindsey begins receiving flowers from a secret admirer at the bank where she works, she has no idea who's sending them to her. Conventional wisdom of Malino, Hawaii, says it's Matt Correa, Emma's longtime neighbor, but Emma has other ideas. After all, she and Matt are just good friends. . .aren't they? A small town in a Hawaiian setting provides a familiar but exotic background to this warm, sweet romance that shows sometimes the best place to look for love is right next door.

Other books by the same author:
Just Friends, 1998
Chase Your Dreams, 1997
Above the Rainbow, 1996
Lei of Love, 1996
Maui Rose, 1996

Other books you might like:
Patricia Forsythe, *The Runaway Princess*, 2001
Jessica Hart, *Wedding at Waverly Creek*, 2001
Sheila Rabe, *A Prince of a Guy*, 2001
Nora Roberts, *Considering Kate*, 2001
Deborah Shelley, *Talk about Love*, 1999

344

SUSAN MALLERY

Sweet Success

(New York: Pocket, 2001)

Story type: Contemporary; Humor
Subject(s): Food; Small Town Life
Major character(s): Allie Thomas, Cook (candymaker), Store Owner (gourmet chocolate shop); Matt Baker, Handyman
Time period(s): 2000s
Locale(s): Santa Magdalena, California

Summary: When Allie Thomas hires the enigmatic Matt Baker to build some shelves in her storeroom, she finds herself more attracted to him than she would like. Matt has a past he's trying to forget and he's not about to let anyone into his life, not even a sweet chocolate maker who makes the best truffles he's ever tasted. Naturally, things change. Humor, well-drawn characters, and a few interesting twists make this a light and lively read.

Where it's reviewed:
Romantic Times, May 2001, page 97

Other books you might like:
Margaret Brownley, *Chocolate Kisses*, 1997
anthology
Judy Christenberry, *The $10,000,000 Texas Wedding*, 2000
Barbara Freethy, *The Sweetest Thing*, 2000
Susan Elizabeth Phillips, *First Lady*, 2000
Paula Detmer Riggs, *Daddy by Accident*, 1997

345

WENDY MARKHAM (Pseudonym of Wendy Corsi Staub)

Slightly Single

(Don Mills, Ontario: Red Dress Ink, 2001)

Story type: Contemporary
Subject(s): Dating (Social Customs); City and Town Life; Coming-of-Age
Major character(s): Tracey Spadolini, Advertising (assistant), Waiter/Waitress (part time catering)
Time period(s): 2000s
Locale(s): New York, New York

Summary: Stuck in New York City for the summer while her Slightly Significant Other is doing summer stock in the Adirondacks, Tracey Spadolini decides to do something about her life—with a little help from her eclectic group of friends and one very nice guy, Buckley O'Hanlon. With more similarities to a YA coming-of-age novel than the typical romance, this zingy, upbeat, and funny book takes its cues from the popular Bridget Jones series and should appeal primarily to the single, urban, working set.

Other books you might like:
Melissa Bank, *The Girls' Guide to Hunting and Fishing*, 1999
Helen Fielding, *Bridget Jones: The Edge of Reason*, 2000
Helen Fielding, *Bridget Jones's Diary*, 1996
Sarah Mlynowski, *Milkrun*, 2001
Melissa Senate, *See Jane Date*, 2001

346

KAT MARTIN

Heartless

(New York: St. Martin's Paperbacks, 2001)

Story type: Historical/Regency
Subject(s): Family Relations; Social Classes; Self-Acceptance
Major character(s): Ariel Summers, Impoverished; Justin Ross, Nobleman (Earl of Greville), Wealthy
Time period(s): 1800s (1800; 1802; 1804)
Locale(s): Surrey, England; London, England

Summary: Fourteen-year-old Ariel Summers, impoverished and abused by her father, makes an unholy pact with a wealthy earl. If he pays for her education, she'll become his mistress as soon as she graduates. Four years later, Justin Ross, the new Earl of Greville, finds himself with a lovely, educated 18-year-old ward and reluctantly agrees to fulfill the terms of the agreement she'd made with his deceased father. Lust and honor are at odds in this emotion-filled tale of two people learning to trust each other.

Where it's reviewed:
Affaire de Coeur, May/June 2001, page 16
Romantic Times, May 2001, page 37

Other books by the same author:
The Secret, 2001
Perfect Sin, 2000
Night Secrets, 1999
Dangerous Passions, 1998
Wicked Promise, 1998

Other books you might like:
Candace Camp, *So Wild a Heart*, 2002
Lisa Kleypas, *Someone to Watch over Me*, 1999
Johanna Lindsey, *Say You Love Me*, 1996
Karen Robards, *Scandalous*, 2001
Gayle Wilson, *My Lady's Dare*, 2000

347

KAT MARTIN

The Secret

(New York: Zebra, 2001)

Story type: Romantic Suspense; Contemporary
Subject(s): Murder; Small Town Life; Near-Death Experience
Major character(s): Kate Rollins, Advertising, Single Parent; Chance McLain, Rancher
Time period(s): 2000s
Locale(s): Los Angeles, California; Lost Peak, Montana

Summary: Advertising executive Kate Rollins, shot in the head by an L.A. gang, decides she needs a major change. After her spectacular near-death experience, she's been hounded by the press; divorced by her rock musician husband; and become unexpected heir of her grandmother's house and cafe in Lost Peak, Montana. Chance McLain, a rancher, is trying to stop a gold mining company from poisoning his land. Little does he know that Lost Peak's newest resident has received a message from the other side that will change his life forever. This tightly woven mystery has a paranormal element that sets it aside from the run-of-the-mill romantic suspense.

Where it's reviewed:
Affaire de Coeur, March/April 2001, page 24
Romantic Times, March 2001, page 87

Other books by the same author:
Heartless, 2001
Perfect Sin, 2000
Night Secrets, 1999
Dangerous Passions, 1998
Wicked Promise, 1998

Other books you might like:
Ruth Langan, *Awakening Alex*, 2001
Rachel Lee, *Under Suspicion*, 2001
Helen R. Myers, *Dead End*, 2001
Patricia Potter, *Broken Honor*, 2002
Janelle Taylor, *In Too Deep*, 2001

348

CATHY MAXWELL

The Wedding Wager

(New York: Avon, 2001)

Story type: Historical/Regency
Subject(s): Marriage; Animals/Horses
Major character(s): Mary Gates, Gentlewoman, Horse Trainer (breeder); Tye Barlow, Landowner, Horse Trainer (breeder)
Time period(s): 1810s
Locale(s): Lyford Meadows, England; London, England

Summary: When a bidding war for a prize stallion spirals out of control and results in Mary Gates' pledging more money than she has, she does the only thing a woman in her circumstances can do—she heads for London to marry money and save her stables. Of course, Tye Barlow, the man she was bidding against, isn't about to see her succeed; but when he follows her to London to keep an eye on her, they begin to see each other in a different, more romantic, light. The solution, of course, is obvious. Light and charming.

Where it's reviewed:
Publishers Weekly, September 10, 2001, page 68

Other books by the same author:
The Marriage Contract, 2001
A Scandalous Marriage, 2000
Because of You, 1999
Married in Haste, 1999
When Dreams Come True, 1998

Other books you might like:
Donna Bell, *Heiress to Love*, 2000
Christina Kingston, *Ride for the Roses*, 2000
Edith Layton, *The Chance*, 2000
Janet Lynnford, *Firebrand Bride*, 2000
determined heroine/earlier setting
Joan Wolf, *The Gamble*, 1998

349

AMANDA MCCABE

The Spanish Bride

(New York: Signet, 2001)

Story type: Regency
Subject(s): Blackmail; Marriage; Secrets
Major character(s): Carmen Montero, Noblewoman (countess), Spy; Peter Everdean, Military Personnel (former major), Nobleman (Earl of Clifton)
Time period(s): 1810s (1811; 1817)
Locale(s): Spain; London, England; Derbyshire, England

Summary: After falling in love with Carmen Montero during the war in Spain, Major Peter Everdean immediately marries her but when the new couple is separated during a battle, both believe the other to have become a casualty of war. Six years later Carmen arrives in England with her young daughter, Isabella, only to discover the husband she thought was gone forever is very much alive. However, a malicious blackmailer and some past secrets threaten to destroy Carmen and Peter's second chance at happiness.

Where it's reviewed:
Romantic Times, August 2001, page 113

Other books by the same author:
Scandal in Venice, 2001

Other books you might like:
Mary Balogh, *Lord Carew's Bride*, 1995
Anne Barbour, *Lord Glenraven's Return*, 1994
Wilma Counts, *The Wagered Wife*, 2001
Candice Hern, *An Affair of Honor*, 1996
Patricia Oliver, *Broken Promises*, 2001

350

JUDI MCCOY

I Dream of You

(New York: Zebra, 2001)

Story type: Fantasy; Time Travel
Subject(s): Genies; Magic; Wishes
Major character(s): Madeline ''Maddie'' Winston, Businesswoman; Prince Abban ''Ben'' ben-Abdullah, Time Traveler, Mythical Creature (genie)
Time period(s): 2000s
Locale(s): Key West, Florida; New York, New York

Summary: The last thing newly-jilted Maddie Winston expects to find on a Florida beach is a magic bottle complete with a real live genie. Prince Abban ben-Abdullah, imprisoned in the bottle by an evil *jinn* a thousand years earlier has never had a female master before. As Maddie adjusts to life with a hunk of a genie (and vice versa) someone is sabotaging her company, but she's hesitant to use ''Ben's'' powers to fix things. This is an often humorous, magical tale of finding love in truly weird places.

Other books you might like:
Jill Barnett, *Imagine*, 1995
Karen Harbaugh, *Cupid's Kiss*, 1999
Kathleen Kane, *Wish upon a Cowboy*, 2000
Teresa Medeiros, *Breath of Magic*, 1996
Mary Ann Wilson, *Valentine for an Angel*, 1998

351

JUDI MCCOY

You're the One

(New York: Zebra, 2001)

Story type: Contemporary/Fantasy; Paranormal
Subject(s): Ghosts; Magic; Construction
Major character(s): Cassandra Kinross, Spirit (100 year old ghost), Crime Victim; Rand MacPherson, Businessman (construction), Heir
Time period(s): 2000s
Locale(s): Basking Ridge, New Jersey

Summary: Rand MacPherson inherits his uncle's boarded-up Victorian mansion and the ghost of the fiancee a man had killed there a 100 years earlier. Rand begins to get very human feelings for Cassandra Kinross the first time he almost sets eyes on her, but little does he know she's also a witch who cursed his family with her dying words. This is a very funny story of a stubborn man and an even more stubborn ghost who learn together that true love is the strongest magic of all.

Where it's reviewed:
Romantic Times, December 2001, page 80

Other books by the same author:
I Dream of You, 2001

Other books you might like:
Emily Carmichael, *A Ghost for Maggie*, 1999
Sue Civil-Brown, *Next Stop, Paradise*, 2001
Annie Kelleher, *The Ghost and Katie Coyle*, 1999
Angie Ray, *Ghost of My Dreams*, 1996
Nora Roberts, *Jewels of the Sun*, 1999

352

MAY MCGOLDRICK (Pseudonym of Nikoo McGoldrick and James A. McGoldrick)

The Promise

(New York: Signet, 2001)

Story type: Historical/Georgian
Subject(s): Children; Secrets; Slavery
Major character(s): Rebecca Neville, Tutor; Samuel Wakefield, Nobleman (Earl of Stanmore)
Time period(s): 1760s (1760); 1770s (1770)
Locale(s): England; Philadelphia, Pennsylvania, American Colonies

Summary: An unidentified woman traveling with a newborn child helps Rebecca Neville escape England, and in return Rebecca assumes responsibility for the woman's son when his real mother dies on board the ship taking them to the American Colonies. Ten years later the boy's father, Samuel Wakefield, the Earl of Stanmore, discovers the whereabouts of his son and demands he be returned to his rightful family. Rebecca travels back to England with the boy, but giving him up to Samuel may prove to be the most difficult thing she has ever had to do.

Where it's reviewed:
Booklist, August 2001, page 2100
Romantic Times, September 2001, page 35

Other books by the same author:
The Dreamer, 2000
The Enchantress, 2000
The Firebrand, 2000
Flame, 1998
Intended, 1998

Other books you might like:
Jo Beverley, *My Lady Notorious*, 1993
Jane Feather, *The Hostage Bride*, 1998
Deborah Hale, *My Lord Protector*, 1999
Patricia Rice, *Rebel Dreams*, 1991
Karen Robards, *This Side of Heaven*, 1991

353

KASEY MICHAELS (Pseudonym of Kathryn Seidick)

Bachelor on the Prowl

(New York: Silhouette, 2001)

Story type: Contemporary; Humor
Subject(s): Humor; Models, Fashion; Fashion Design
Major character(s): Holly Hollis, Assistant (to fashion designer); Colin Rafferty, Businessman, Imposter
Time period(s): 2000s
Locale(s): New York, New York; Allentown, Pennsylvania

Summary: Holly Hollis is a groom short for her first fashion show. When the gorgeous model finally comes in—right at showtime—Holly strips off his suit and replaces it with a tux. However, the man she shoves onto the runway isn't a model at all, but her friend's cousin. Colin Rafferty doesn't know why the woman thinks he's a model, but now he's hesitant to tell her who he really is. This book, a hilarious case of mistaken identity, is set against the world of high fashion.

Where it's reviewed:
Romantic Times, November 2001, page 114

Other books by the same author:
Be My Baby Tonight, 2002
Love to Love You Baby, 2001
Too Good to Be True, 2001
Someone to Love, 2001
Can't Take My Eyes Off of You, 2000

Other books you might like:
Ruth Jean Dale, *Fiance Wanted!*, 2000
Rita Herron, *Marry Me, Maddie?*, 2001
Annette Mahon, *The Secret Admirer*, 2001
Deborah Shelley, *One Starry Night*, 2000
Tina Wainscott, *The Wrong Mr. Right*, 2000

354

KASEY MICHAELS (Pseudonym of Kathryn Seidick)

Love to Love You Baby

(New York: Kensington, 2001)

Story type: Humor; Contemporary
Subject(s): Humor; Sports/Baseball; Self-Acceptance
Major character(s): Keely McBride, Interior Decorator; Jack Trehan, Sports Figure (former baseball player), Wealthy
Time period(s): 2000s
Locale(s): Allentown, Pennsylvania

Summary: Jack Trehan is a has-been. For a year he's lived in an unfurnished apartment, depressed because his once famous arm has been irreparably damaged, and he can never be the baseball celebrity he once was. Eventually, he moves to an empty mansion, which sits unfurnished until his aunt commissions an interior designer. When Keely McBride show up to work with Jack, she finds herself in the role of nanny, too, because his flighty cousin has literally left her infant daughter on his doorstep. Despite his wild and crazy family, Jack still manages to find the love of his life. The serious theme of self-acceptance is presented in a funny, entertaining way.

Where it's reviewed:
Booklist, September 15, 2001, page 208
Romantic Times, November 2001, page 93

Other books by the same author:
Be My Baby Tonight, 2002
Someone to Love, 2001
Too Good to Be True, 2001
Can't Take My Eyes Off of You, 2000
Raffling Ryan, 2000

Other books you might like:
Sue Civil-Brown, *Catching Kelly*, 2000
Millie Criswell, *The Trouble with Mary*, 2001
Julie Ortolon, *Dear Cupid*, 2001
Susan Elizabeth Phillips, *Heaven, Texas*, 1995
Sheila Rabe, *A Prince of a Guy*, 2001

355

BARBARA MILLER

The Guardian

(New York: Sonnet, 2001)

Story type: Historical/Regency
Subject(s): Reunions; Courtship; Animals/Horses
Major character(s): Amy Conde, Gentlewoman (manages Talltrees Stud Farm), Ward; Trent Severn, Businessman (arms manufacturer/supplier), Lawyer
Time period(s): 1810s (1816)
Locale(s): Berkshire, England (Talltrees Stud Farm)

Summary: Frustrated by her absentee guardian's ignorance of what is going on at Talltrees and his routine dismissal of her written requests, unconventional and independent Amy Conde is shocked when he suddenly appears at her front door, drunk and exhausted. Trent Severn, simply passing through on his way to the coast, is just as surprised as she because it has been 15 years since he has seen her and she is definitely not the child she once was. Guilt-stricken because of his neglect, he remains to set things to rights, and in the process he and Amy realize they have much more in common than they had thought. A dash of scandal, some intrigue, and a bit of danger add to this sweet romance.

Other books by the same author:
Pretender, 2002
Dearest Max, 2000
My Phillipe, 2000

Other books you might like:
Donna Bell, *Heiress to Love*, 2000
Elisabeth Fairchild, *Captain Cupid Calls the Shots*, 2000
Christina Kingston, *Ride for the Roses*, 2000
  Regency historical but with similar horse theme
Cathy Maxwell, *The Wedding Wager*, 2001
  another horse-breeding heroine

356

JENNA MINDEL

Blessing in Disguise

(New York: Signet, 2001)

Story type: Regency
Subject(s): Courtship; Sisters
Major character(s): Winifred ''Winnie'' Augusta Preston, Gentlewoman; Peter Blessing, Gentleman, Gambler
Time period(s): 1810s (1813); 1820s (1821)
Locale(s): England

Summary: In order to pay off his overwhelming gambling debts, Peter Blessing must marry an eligible heiress, so he sets about wooing wealthy Winnie Preston, who is enjoying the London Season with her sister, Melanie. Once Winnie deduces that Peter is nothing more than a fortune hunter, she quickly rebuffs his romantic advances. Peter turns his romantic attentions elsewhere and Winnie discovers she is not so pleased as she expected to be since it turns out she has fallen in love with the handsome charmer.

Where it's reviewed:
Affaire de Coeur, July/August 2001, page 14
Romantic Times, July 2001, page 29

Other books you might like:
Jo Beverley, *Deirdre and Don Juan*, 1997
Candice Hern, *A Garden Folly*, 1997
April Kihlstrom, *A Scandalous Bequest*, 1982
Dorothy Mack, *The Luckless Elopement*, 1984
Regina Scott, *The Bluestocking on His Knee*, 1999

357

SARAH MLYNOWSKI

Milkrun

(Don Mills, Ontario: Red Dress Ink, 2001)

Story type: Contemporary
Subject(s): Dating (Social Customs); City and Town Life; Coming-of-Age
Major character(s): Jackie Norris, Editor (copy editor)
Time period(s): 2000s
Locale(s): Boston, Massachusetts

Summary: Furious at being dumped by a boyfriend, who is getting his life together in Thailand—apparently with somebody else—Jackie Norris is galvanized into action. She will date and date and date and date, thus showing her former creep of a boyfriend she has it all together and couldn't care less about him. Of course, in this funny, lively and thoroughly modern story, it doesn't quite work out that way; but the journey—milkrun or express—is half the fun. Another in Red Dress Ink's new series targeting young, urban singles.

Other books you might like:
Helen Fielding, *Bridget Jones's Diary*, 1996
Marian Keyes, *Lucy Sullivan Is Getting Married*, 1999
Wendy Markham, *Slightly Single*, 2001
Melissa Senate, *See Jane Date*, 2001
Isabel Wolff, *The Trials of Tiffany Trott*, 1999

358

KAREN MARIE MONING

Kiss of the Highlander

(New York: Dell, 2001)

Story type: Time Travel
Series: Highlander
Subject(s): Time Travel; Magic
Major character(s): Gwen Cassidy, Vacationer, Time Traveler; Drustan MacKeltar, Laird (Highland), Time Traveler
Time period(s): 2000s; 16th century (1518)
Locale(s): Highlands, Scotland

Summary: While on a tour in Scotland that is something of a disappointment, Gwen Cassidy decides to hike through the Highlands on her own. When a tumble down a hillside lands her in a hidden cave and on top of an ensorceled Highland laird who has been asleep for 500 years—and he suddenly wakes up—her life takes a turn she could never have imagined. Magic, humor, and passion combine in this humorous time travel featuring appealing characters, lively wit, and a fast-pace. Fans won't mind the occasional anachronism or the history-changing action.

Other books by the same author:
The Highlander's Touch, 2000
Beyond the Highland Mist, 1999
To Tame a Highland Warrior, 1999

Other books you might like:
Kimberly Cates, *Magic*, 1998
  humor and magic
Diana Gabaldon, *Outlander*, 1991
  first of a classic time travel series
Lynn Kurland, *Love Came Just in Time*, 2001
Lynn Kurland, *My Heart Stood Still*, 2001
Teresa Medeiros, *Touch of Enchantment*, 1997
  humor and time travel

359

MELISSA NATHAN

Pride, Prejudice and Jasmin Field

(New York: Avon, 2001)

Story type: Contemporary
Subject(s): Plays; Literature; Romance
Major character(s): Jasmin "Jazz" Field, Journalist (magazine columnist), Actress (amateur); Harry Noble, Actor
Time period(s): 2000s
Locale(s): London, England

Summary: When successful magazine columnist Jasmin Field ends up playing Elizabeth Bennet to Oscar-winning actor Harry Noble's Mr. Darcy in a charity production of Jane Austen's *Pride and Prejudice*, she has no idea her life is about to fall apart or that she is on the verge of discovering the love of her life. A lively, very British, modern adaptation of Austen's classic in a Bridget Jones setting.

Other books you might like:
Jane Austen, *Pride and Prejudice*, 1813
Helen Fielding, *Bridget Jones's Diary*, 1996
Marian Keyes, *Lucy Sullivan Is Getting Married*, 1999
Wendy Markham, *Slightly Single*, 2001
Isabel Wolff, *The Trials of Tiffany Trott*, 1999

360

JACQUELINE NAVIN

The Sleeping Beauty

(Toronto: Harlequin, 2001)

Story type: Gothic; Historical/Victorian
Subject(s): Secrets; Murder; Healing
Major character(s): Lady Helena Rathford, Noblewoman, Recluse; Adam Mannion, Rake, Rogue
Time period(s): 1850s (1852)
Locale(s): Northumberland, England

Summary: Adam Mannion, failed gambler, is in search of a wealthy bride. Going to the "Sleeping Beauty Castle" at the suggestion of his friends, he encounters Lady Helena Rathford, a too-thin woman whom he mistakes for a servant. Adam makes three promises to Helena's father, and in return, is granted her hand and enough money to pay off his debts, as well as make him a wealthy man. Things aren't as they seem at Rathford Manor, though. Helena has a horrible secret, and hints of madness plague the dark, dusty castle in this gothic fairy tale.

Other books by the same author:
Meet Me at Midnight, 2001
The Viking's Heart, 2000
A Rose at Midnight, 1999
One Christmas Night, 1999 (anthology)
Strathmere's Bride, 1999

Other books you might like:
Christine Feehan, *The Scarletti Curse*, 2001
Judith Ivory, *The Sleeping Beauty*, 1998
Evelyn Rogers, *Devil in the Dark*, 2001
Colleen Shannon, *The Wolf of Haskell Hall*, 2001
Anne Stuart, *Shadows at Sunset*, 2000
contemporary

361

LINDA O'BRIEN (Pseudonym of Linda Tsoutsouris)

Beloved Protector

(New York: Avon, 2001)

Story type: Historical/American West
Subject(s): Trust; Revenge; Friendship
Major character(s): Eliza Lowe, Singer (in training), Wealthy; Case Brogan, Detective—Private (Pinkerton)
Time period(s): 1890s (1898)
Locale(s): Chicago, Illinois; Des Moines, Iowa; Omaha, Nebraska

Summary: Pollyanna goes West in this story about a woman who trusts everyone. . .and a man who trusts no one. Eliza Lowe is wealthy. Her friend sends a telegram saying she needs a thousand dollars because her husband's been falsely accused and has to have funds to escape to Mexico. Concerned for her friend, Eliza decides to deliver the money in person. Eliza's aunt doesn't like the idea of her niece traveling alone, so she hires Pinkerton Detective Case Brogan to act as her bodyguard. Case has other plans for this trip—Eliza's friend is married to the man who killed his father. The reader is kept in suspense as a sadistic killer moves his pregnant wife from one place to another and Case's need for revenge grows so enormous that it almost becomes a character in its own right.

Other books by the same author:
His Forbidden Touch, 2000
Courting Claire, 1999
Promised to a Stranger, 1998

Other books you might like:
Sandra Chastain, *The Outlaw Bride*, 2001
Merline Lovelace, *The Horse Soldier*, 2001
Mary McBride, *The Marriage Knot*, 1999
Lisa Plumley, *Lawman*, 1999
Bobbi Smith, *Tess*, 2000

362

PATRICIA OLIVER

Broken Promises

(New York: Signet, 2001)

Story type: Regency
Subject(s): Marriage; Reunions; Courtship
Major character(s): Mathilda Heath Parmenter, Widow(er), Noblewoman; Miles William Stephens, Nobleman; Sir James Parmenter, Nobleman
Time period(s): 1800s (1808); 1810s (1818)
Locale(s): England

Summary: Widowed and the mother of two boys, Lady Mathilda Parmenter returns to England from India after her husband's death to find the man she had jilted to marry Sir James is now the Earl of Southmoor and has never married. Having heard Miles was furious when she left him waiting at the altar,

Mathilda is surprised when he begins to court her. However, Miles has vengeance, not love, in mind, and is determined to humiliate Mathilda as she had humiliated him. All comes out right in the end, of course, in this charming, humorous story of love, revenge, and forgiveness.

Where it's reviewed:
Romantic Times, May 2001, page 93

Other books by the same author:
Lady Jane's Nemesis, 2000
Scandalous Secrets, 1999
The Lady in Gray, 1999
The Colonel's Lady, 1996
Miss Drayton's Downfall, 1994

Other books you might like:
Mary Balogh, *The Last Waltz*, 1998
Candice Hern, *An Affair of Honor*, 1996
Emma Jensen, *His Grace Endures*, 1998
Allison Lane, *Devall's Angel*, 1998

363

JULIE ORTOLON

Dear Cupid

(New York: St. Martin's Paperbacks, 2001)

Story type: Contemporary; Humor
Subject(s): Humor; Trust; Single Parent Families
Major character(s): Kate Bradshaw, Journalist (columnist), Single Parent; Michael Cameron, Wealthy, Computer Expert (animation software)
Time period(s): 2000s
Locale(s): Los Angeles, California; Lake Travis, Texas; Austin, Texas

Summary: When wealthy special effects animator Michael Cameron hires single mom Kate Bradshaw to decorate his house for his new bride, she has no idea she's the one he's intending to marry. Lots of fun with just enough pathos for balance.

Where it's reviewed:
Affaire de Coeur, July/August 2001, page 16
Booklist, June 15, 2001, page 1854
Publishers Weekly, May 15, 2001, page 87
Romantic Times, July 2001, page 85

Other books by the same author:
Drive Me Wild, 2000

Other books you might like:
Susan Andersen, *Baby, Don't Go*, 2000
Patti Berg, *Born to Be Wild*, 2001
Elizabeth Bevarly, *He Could Be the One*, 2001
Rachel Gibson, *It Must Be Love*, 2000
Julie Kenner, *Aphrodite's Kiss*, 2001

364

MAGGIE OSBORNE

The Bride of Willow Creek

(New York: Ivy, 2001)

Story type: Historical/American West
Subject(s): Marriage; Reunions; Family Relations
Major character(s): Angelina "Angie" Bartoli Holland, Spouse, Orphan; Sam Holland, Carpenter, Spouse
Time period(s): 19th century (late); 1920s
Locale(s): Willow Creek, Colorado; Denver, Colorado

Summary: Married as teenagers, torn apart by parental pressure and immaturity, but never divorced, Angie and Sam meet again ten years later when Angie comes to Colorado to end their marriage. Divorces cost money, however, and neither Sam nor Angie has any so they agree to stay together until they can save enough for it. Of course, by the time they have done this, they have rediscovered their love for each other and have formed a family with Sam's two young daughters—and somehow the divorce just doesn't come about. Heartwarming, emotionally involving, humorous, and well-written, this lively story deals with issues of guilt, self-esteem, physical disability, and trust.

Other books by the same author:
I Do, I Do, I Do, 2000
Silver Lining, 2000
A Stranger's Wife, 1999
The Promise of Jenny Jones, 1997
The Brides of Prairie Gold, 1996

Other books you might like:
Catherine Anderson, *Forever After*, 1998
Catherine Anderson, *Simply Love*, 1997
Jill Marie Landis, *Until Tomorrow*, 1994
Stephanie Mittman, *The Marriage Bed*, 1996
Sherryl Woods, *Marrying a Delacourt*, 2000
contemporary/children/reunions

365

EVELYN PALFREY

Dangerous Dilemmas

(New York: Sonnet, 2001)

Story type: Contemporary; Romantic Suspense
Subject(s): African Americans; Murder
Major character(s): Audrey Williams, Teacher, Divorced Person (in the near future); Kirk Maxwell, Detective—Police (lieutenant)
Time period(s): 2000s
Locale(s): Houston, Texas; Southwest

Summary: After her wayward son is accused of a murder he insists he didn't commit, newly separated and soon to be divorced Audrey Williams finds herself dealing with a husband who doesn't really want the divorce, growing feelings for the police officer who arrested her son, and the need to rebuild her life. There is almost more turmoil and stress than she can handle. Fast-paced, modern, and sprinkled with African American cultural detail.

Other books you might like:
Rochelle Alers, *Just Before Dawn*, 2000
Candice Poarch, *Tender Escape*, 2000
Francis Ray, *Incognito*, 1997
Tracey Tillis, *Flashpoint*, 1997
Tracey Tillis, *Night Watch*, 1995

366

MARILYN PAPPANO

Heaven on Earth

(New York: Dell, 2002)

Story type: Contemporary; Paranormal
Series: Bethlehem. Book 7
Subject(s): Runaways; Angels; Greek Americans
Major character(s): Melina Dimitris, Detective—Private; Sebastian Knight, Carpenter, Single Parent
Time period(s): 2000s
Locale(s): Bethlehem, New York

Summary: Sebastian Knight's seven-year-old daughter has secretly stowed away with two older kids who are running away from home. When private investigator Melina Dimitris is called in to find them, Sebastian insists on going with her. The problem is, he and Melina are trying to get over their very brief love affair, and both of them are confused about their feelings toward each other. Fortunately for all of them, the little town of Bethlehem is guarded by three quirky angels who keep things from getting totally out of hand. Although this is a stand-alone book, characters from other books in the series show up like old friends on a visit.

Where it's reviewed:
Romantic Times, January 2002, page 74

Other books by the same author:
Getting Lucky, 2001 (Bethlehem. Book 5)
First Kiss, 2000 (Bethlehem. Book 4)
Father to Be, 1999 (Bethlehem. Book 3)
Some Enchanted Season, 1998 (Bethlehem. Book 2)
Season for Miracles, 1997 (Bethlehem. Book 1)

Other books you might like:
Mary Balogh, *Angel Christmas*, 1995
anthology
Debra Dier, *Christmas Angels*, 1995
Sandra Heath, *Lucy's Christmas Angel*, 1995
Debbie Macomber, *Shirley, Goodness, and Mercy*, 1999
Judith McNaught, *A Holiday of Love*, 1994
anthology

367

SUSAN SPENCER PAUL
SHARI ANTON, Co-Author
TORI PHILLIPS, Co-Author

'Tis the Season

(Toronto: Harlequin, 2001)

Story type: Historical; Holiday Themes
Subject(s): Anthology; Christmas
Locale(s): England

Summary: Couple-focused and featuring English settings that include a medieval inn, a Tudor castle, and a Regency manor, this diverse trio of holiday novellas from three veteran authors will add a dash of romance to the Christmas holiday season. Included are *A Promise to Keep* by Susan Spencer Paul, *Christmas at Wayfarer Inn* by Shari Anton, and *Twelfth Knight* by Tori Phillips.

Other books you might like:
Mary Balogh, *A Christmas Bride*, 1997
Suzanne Barclay, *The Knights of Christmas*, 2000
Nancy Butler, *A Regency Christmas Eve*, 2000
anthology
Diane Farr, *Once upon a Christmas*, 2000
Ruth Langan, *One Christmas Night*, 1999
anthology

368

SUSAN SPENCER PAUL (Pseudonym of Mary Liming)

The Prisoner Bride

(Toronto: Harlequin, 2001)

Story type: Historical/Medieval; Fantasy
Series: Bride. Book 7
Subject(s): Kidnapping; Magic; Revenge
Major character(s): Glenys Seymour, Wealthy, Maiden; Kiernan FitzAllen, Bastard Son, Rogue
Time period(s): 15th century (1440)
Locale(s): London, England; Wales

Summary: Normally, Kiernan FitzAllen doesn't kidnap people, but Glenys Seymour's brother left Kiernan's sister unwed and pregnant, so he agrees to accept the assignment to whisk Glenys away to an isolated keep. To his surprise, he discovers that Glenys isn't like the other women he knows. Besides being immune to his legendary charms, she's strong and stubborn, and she carries around magical things—a rock that glows when it wants to and a chess piece with a personality. Soon, Keirnan finds himself in the role of Glenys' protector instead of her kidnapper. This exceptionally well written story of an honorable knave and a very special woman who denies her own power is an enchanting treat and sure to delight.

Where it's reviewed:
Romantic Times, December 2001, page 46

Other books by the same author:
The Stolen Bride, 2000 (Bride. Book 6)
The Captive Bride, 1999 (Bride. Book 5)
Beguiled, 1998 (Bride. Book 4)
The Bride Thief, 1997 (Bride. Book 3)
The Heiress Bride, 1996 (Bride. Book 2)

Other books you might like:
Shana Abe, *A Kiss at Midnight*, 2000
Claudia Dain, *The Marriage Bed*, 2001
Claire Delacroix, *The Beauty*, 2001
Tori Phillips, *Halloween Knight*, 2000
Deborah Simmons, *My Lady de Burgh*, 2001

369

SUSAN ELIZABETH PHILLIPS

This Heart of Mine

(New York: HarperCollins, 2001)

Story type: Contemporary; Humor
Series: Chicago Stars. Book 3
Subject(s): Humor; Inheritance; Writing
Major character(s): Molly Somerville, Writer (children's writer/illustrator), Artist; Kevin Tucker, Sports Figure (star quarterback)
Time period(s): 2000s
Locale(s): Chicago, Illinois; Wind Lake, Michigan (Wind Lake Cottages)

Summary: Children's book writer/illustrator Molly Somerville, sister of the owner of the Chicago Stars, has had a crush on star quarterback Kevin Tucker for years, but he acts as though he doesn't know she's alive. Throwing caution to the wind, she climbs into his bed one night and seduces him in his sleep. Although honor-bound to marry her when her spur of the moment seduction results in a pregnancy, he decides to divorce as soon as possible. A tragedy throws Molly into a deep depression, and Kevin takes her to a camp he's inherited, never knowing the people there will change their lives forever. Quirky characters, a spunky heroine, and an honorable jock with a Heisman trophy of a heart make this third book in the Chicago Stars series as wonderful as the first two.

Where it's reviewed:
Affaire de Coeur, February 2001, page 32
Booklist, September 15, 2001, page 211
Publishers Weekly, January 1, 2001, page 69

Other books by the same author:
First Lady, 2000
Lady Be Good, 1999
Dream a Little Dream, 1998
Nobody's Baby but Mine, 1997
Kiss an Angel, 1996

Other books you might like:
Elizabeth Bevarly, *First Comes Love*, 2000
Millie Criswell, *The Trouble with Mary*, 2001
Suzann Ledbetter, *South of Sanity*, 2001
Julie Ortolon, *Dear Cupid*, 2001
Sheila Rabe, *A Prince of a Guy*, 2001

370

ANDREA PICKENS (Pseudonym of Andrea DaRif)

A Diamond in the Rough

(New York: Signet, 2001)

Story type: Regency
Subject(s): Gardens and Gardening; Sports/Golf
Major character(s): Adrian Linsley, Nobleman (Viscount Marquand), Landscaper; Derrien ''Derry'' Edwards, Sports Figure (caddie), Landscaper
Time period(s): 1810s
Locale(s): London, England; St. Andrews, Scotland

Summary: To win back everything his father has lost gambling, Adrian Linsley must win a round of golf with the man who now owns his family's estate. Since he has never played golf before, Adrian turns for help to one of the game's best players, who directs him to a gifted young caddie, Derry Edwards. Once Adrian discovers his insolent caddie is really a sharp-tongued young lady, who has been forced to disguise herself as a boy in order to indulge in her love of golf, the game will never be the same for him again.

Where it's reviewed:
Affaire de Coeur, May/June 2001, page 27
Romantic Times, June 2001, page 121

Other books by the same author:
A Lady of Letters, 2000
The Major's Mistake, 2000
The Hired Hero, 1999
Code of Honor, 1998
The Defiant Governess, 1998

Other books you might like:
Jessica Benson, *Much Obliged*, 2001
Nancy Butler, *Lord Monteith's Gift*, 2001
Emily Hendrickson, *Miss Cheney's Charade*, 1994
Emma Jensen, *A Grand Design*, 2000
Carla Kelly, *Miss Grimsley's Oxford Career*, 1992

371

SUSAN PLUNKETT

Alicia's Song

(New York: LoveSpell, 2001)

Story type: Time Travel; Paranormal
Subject(s): Time Travel; Singing; Child Custody
Major character(s): Alicia James, Scientist (botanist), Time Traveler; Caleb Marker, Lumberjack, Single Parent
Time period(s): 2000s; 1890s (1895)
Locale(s): Drexel, Wyoming; Sitka, Alaska

Summary: Botanist Alicia James finds herself in modern day Wyoming one minute and 1890s Alaska the next. Lumberjack Caleb Marker doesn't know what to make of the strange woman who appears out of nowhere in the forest near Sitka. Fast talking on her part and a big heart on his pave the way for her to become his son's governess. An unexpected journey through time and space puts a resourceful woman exactly where she belongs in this paranormal love story.

Where it's reviewed:
Romantic Times, April 2001, page 95

Other books by the same author:
Soul Survivor, 1999
Timepool, 1999
Untamed Time, 1999
Heaven's Time, 1998

Other books you might like:
Susan Grant, *Once a Pirate*, 2000
Kristin Hannah, *A Handful of Heaven*, 1991
Linda Kay, *To Tame a Rogue*, 2001
Tess Mallory, *Highland Dream*, 2001
Eugenia Riley, *Bushwhacked Bride*, 1999

372

SUSAN PLUNKETT

Bethany's Song

(New York: LoveSpell, 2001)

Story type: Time Travel; Paranormal
Series: Song. Book 2
Subject(s): Time Travel; Miners and Mining; Grief
Major character(s): Bethany James, Teacher (elementary school), Time Traveler; Matthew Gray, Architect, Widow(er)
Time period(s): 2000s; 1890s (1895)
Locale(s): Drexel, Wyoming; Juneau, Alaska

Summary: One minute, Bethany James and her sister are singing at their friend's graveside in current day Drexel, Wyoming, and the next minute, she's in 1895 Alaska, swept there by the ''River of Time.'' Befriended by—and strongly drawn to—Matthew Gray, widowed architect and mine owner, she convinces him to let her take the place of the local schoolteacher, who's left town. As her feelings for Matthew grow, she wonders about the permanence of her relocation and their relationship. A story of two people who believe they've buried their hearts in their tragic pasts, this book is even better than the first one in the trilogy, *Alicia's Song*.

Where it's reviewed:
Romantic Times, November 2001, page 103

Other books by the same author:
Alicia's Song, 2001 (Song. Book 1)
Soul Survivor, 1999
Untamed Time, 1999
Timepool, 1999
Heaven's Time, 1998

Other books you might like:
Judie Aitken, *A Love Beyond Time*, 2000
Kristin Hannah, *A Handful of Heaven*, 1991
Willa Hix, *Then and Now*, 2000
Linda Lael Miller, *My Outlaw*, 1997
Eugenia Riley, *Bushwhacked Bride*, 1999

373

PATRICIA POTTER

Broken Honor

(New York: Jove, 2002)

Story type: Romantic Suspense; Contemporary
Subject(s): Suspense; Treasure; Murder
Major character(s): Amy Mallory, Professor (advanced American history); Lucien ''Irish'' Flaherty, Military Personnel (Army colonel)
Time period(s): 1940s (1945); 2000s
Locale(s): Colorado (Flaherty's Folly); Memphis, Tennessee; Washington, District of Columbia

Summary: Amy Mallory, a professor of advanced American history at a small Tennessee college, and Colonel Lucien ''Irish'' Flaherty have something in common—both of their deceased grandfathers have been accused of looting Jewish riches from a Nazi treasure train at the close of WWII. This accusation has been made more than 50 years after the fact, and now someone's trying to kill Amy and Irish. An unknown villain relentlessly pursues these two people thrown together by the alleged sins of their grandfathers in this fast-paced thriller.

Where it's reviewed:
Romantic Times, January 2002, page 67

Other books by the same author:
The Black Knave, 2000 (Scottish Trilogy. Book 1)
Starkeeper, 1999
Starfinder, 1998
Starcatcher, 1997
The Marshal and the Heiress, 1996

Other books you might like:
Marie Ferrarella, *An Uncommon Hero*, 2000
Meagan McKinney, *The Lawman Meets His Bride*, 2000
Helen R. Myers, *Dead End*, 2001
Carla Neggers, *The Waterfall*, 2000
Janelle Taylor, *In Too Deep*, 2001

374

ELIZABETH POWELL (Pseudonym of Elizabeth Peterson)

The Traitor's Daughter

(New York: Signet, 2001)

Story type: Regency
Subject(s): Espionage; Revenge
Major character(s): Amanda Tremayne, Seamstress; Jonathan Everly, Military Personnel, Sea Captain
Time period(s): 1810s (1811)
Locale(s): London, England

Summary: The British Navy found her father guilty of treason and executed him for the crime, but Amanda Tremayne knows he was innocent. While searching for evidence to clear his name, Amanda crosses paths with Captain Jonathan Everly, who has been charged with finding a traitorous spy hidden in the British Admiralty. Amanda needs Jonathan's help if she wants to restore honor to her father's name, but trusting one of the men who found her father guilty will not be easy.

Where it's reviewed:
Romantic Times, September 2001, page 30

Other books you might like:
Nancy Butler, *The Rake's Retreat*, 1999
Carola Dunn, *Scandal's Daughter*, 1996
Jean R. Ewing, *Love's Reward*, 1997
Emily Hendrickson, *The Fashionable Spy*, 1999
Andrea Pickens, *The Hired Hero*, 1999

375

AMANDA QUICK (Pseudonym of Jayne Ann Krentz)

Slightly Shady

(New York: Bantam, 2001)

Story type: Historical/Regency
Subject(s): Murder; Blackmail; Resourcefulness

Major character(s): Lavinia Lake, Businesswoman, Guardian (of her niece); Tobias March, Widow(er), Detective—Private
Time period(s): 1810s
Locale(s): London, England; Rome, Italy

Summary: The first time Lavinia Lake meets private investigator Tobias March, he ransacks her store in Rome and ships her back home to London. The second time they meet, several months later, is over the dead body of a blackmailer. From these auspicious beginnings, Lavinia and Tobias become partners in hopes of discovering the real mastermind behind the evil that has infected their lives. A man who's used to being obeyed goes head to head with a woman who won't take orders in this humorous, suspenseful tale of Regency England.

Where it's reviewed:
Affaire de Coeur, March/April 2001, page 40
Booklist, January 15, 2001, page 872
People Weekly, June 4, 2001, page 45
Publishers Weekly, February 12, 2001, page 182
Romantic Times, April 2001, page 36

Other books by the same author:
Wicked Widow, 2000
I Thee Wed, 1999
With This Ring, 1998
Affair, 1997
Mischief, 1997

Other books you might like:
Suzanne Enoch, *Meet Me at Midnight*, 2000
Lisa Kleypas, *Someone to Watch over Me*, 1999
Kasey Michaels, *Someone to Love*, 2001
Karen Robards, *Scandalous*, 2001
Kathryn Smith, *Elusive Passion*, 2001

376

SHEILA RABE

A Prince of a Guy

(New York: Berkley, 2001)

Story type: Contemporary; Humor
Subject(s): Humor; Radio; Radio Broadcasting
Major character(s): Dr. Kate Stonewall, Radio Personality (talk show psychologist), Widow(er); Jeff Hardin, Radio Personality (''Jock Talk'')
Time period(s): 2000s
Locale(s): Seattle, Washington; Bainbridge Island, Washington

Summary: Talk radio psychologist Dr. Kate Stonewall doesn't like jocks. She gives the term ''sports widow'' a whole new definition—her husband choked to death on a peanut during a Super Bowl game. So when fellow radio personality Jeff Hardin, host of ''Jock Talk'' moves next door and encourages her children to spend their time in athletic endeavors, she declares war. A frog of a prince, a prince of a frog, and a cranky princess are only a few of the quirky characters in this well-crafted novel.

Where it's reviewed:
Booklist, August 2001, page 2101
Romantic Times, August 2001, page 87

Other books by the same author:
Be My Valentine, 2001
All I Want for Christmas, 2000
The Adventuress, 1996
An Innocent Imposter, 1995
Bringing out Betsy, 1994

Other books you might like:
Sue Civil-Brown, *Catching Kelly*, 2000
Millie Criswell, *The Trouble with Mary*, 2001
Janet Evanovich, *Seven Up*, 2001
Rachel Gibson, *Truly Madly Yours*, 1999
Susan Elizabeth Phillips, *Heaven, Texas*, 1995

377

DEBBIE RALEIGH

The Christmas Wish

(New York: Zebra, 2001)

Story type: Regency; Holiday Themes
Series: Devil's Daughters Trilogy. Book 1
Subject(s): Christmas; Social Classes; Stealing
Major character(s): Sarah Cresswell, Detective, Gentlewoman; Oliver Spense, Nobleman (Earl of Chance), Antiquarian (amateur)
Time period(s): 1810s
Locale(s): London, England

Summary: Forced to seek the aid of Sarah Cresswell, the daughter of an infamous thief, in order to recover some missing family heirlooms before Christmas, Oliver Spense is startled to discover she is nothing like what he expected. Refined, intelligent, and not about to put up with the condescending airs of the nobility, Sarah accepts the case and sets out to get the job done and show Oliver a thing or two in the process. However, when the pair fall in love, new problems raise their heads because Sarah's questionable parentage means she will never be accepted by polite society. Then it's the Devilish Dandy to the rescue in this light and lively romp that has more than a dash of danger. First of a projected trilogy.

Where it's reviewed:
Library Journal, November 15, 2001, page 54

Other books by the same author:
A Bride for Lord Challmond, 2001
Lord Carlton's Courtship, 2000
Lord Mumford's Minx, 2000

Other books you might like:
Nancy Butler, *The Rake's Retreat*, 1999
Diane Farr, *The Nobody*, 1999
Georgette Heyer, *Faro's Daughter*, 1941
Allison Lane, *Devall's Angel*, 1998
Amanda Quick, *Affair*, 1997
Regency-set historical/sensual

378

DEBBIE RALEIGH

The Valentine Wish

(New York: Zebra, 2002)

Story type: Regency; Holiday Themes
Series: Devil's Daughters Trilogy. Book 2
Subject(s): Conduct of Life; Family Relations; Romance
Major character(s): Emma Cresswell, Companion (to Lady Hartshore); Cedric Morelane, Nobleman (Earl of Hartshore)
Time period(s): 1810s
Locale(s): Kent, England (Hartshore Park)

Summary: Tired of the scandal surrounding her life as the daughter of a notorious jewel thief and the inevitable distain of the *ton*, Emma Cresswell heads to Hartshore Park in Kent, where she will be a companion to eccentric Lady Hartshore. As intriguing as Lady Hartshore and her assorted relatives and servants are, none rattle Emma's composure so much as the lady's nephew, Cedric Morelane, Earl of Hartshore. Light, lively, and romantic. Second in a trilogy featuring the Devilish Dandy's diverse trio of daughters.

Other books by the same author:
The Wedding Wish, 2002 (Devil's Daughters. Book 3)
A Bride for Lord Challmond, 2001
The Christmas Wish, 2001 (Devil's Daughters. Book 1)
Lord Carlton's Courtship, 2000
Lord Mumford's Minx, 2000

Other books you might like:
Kathleen Beck, *My Darling Valentine*, 1999
Shannon Donnelly, *My Sweet Valentine*, 1999
anthology
Elisabeth Fairchild, *Captain Cupid Calls the Shots*, 2000
Valentine's Day tie-in/more serious
Kathryn Kirkwood, *A Valentine for Vanessa*, 2000
Jane Myers Perrine, *The Mad Herringtons*, 2000

379

EVELYN RICHARDSON (Pseudonym of Cynthia Johnson)

Fortune's Lady

(New York: Signet, 2002)

Story type: Regency
Subject(s): Courtship; Conduct of Life; Social Classes
Major character(s): Lady Althea Beauchamp, Noblewoman, Heiress; Gareth de Vere, Nobleman (''Bachelor Marquess''), Rake
Time period(s): 1810s
Locale(s): London, England

Summary: Initially repelled by each other, Lady Althea Beauchamp and Gareth de Vere are forced to reconsider their opinions when they end up playing cards together and recognize they are kindred spirits—quick-witted, bright, perceptive, and quietly rebelling against family and societal demands. This witty, charming, and well-written Regency is especially well-researched and true to the period.

Other books by the same author:
Lord Harry's Daughter, 2001
My Lady Nightingale, 1999
The Gallant Guardian, 1998
My Wayward Lady, 1997
The Reluctant Heiress, 1996

Other books you might like:
Gail Eastwood, *The Magnificent Marquess*, 1998
Candice Hern, *A Garden Folly*, 1997
Georgette Heyer, *Faro's Daughter*, 1941
Emma Jensen, *His Grace Endures*, 1998
Allison Lane, *Devall's Angel*, 1998

380

EUGENIA RILEY (Pseudonym of Eugenia Riley Essenmacher)

The Great Baby Caper

(New York: LoveSpell, 2001)

Story type: Humor; Contemporary
Subject(s): Humor; Pregnancy; Trust
Major character(s): Courtney Kelly, Businesswoman (executive); Mark Billingham, Wealthy, Businessman (entrepreneur)
Time period(s): 2000s
Locale(s): New Orleans, Louisiana; Denver, Colorado; London, England

Summary: Courtney Kelly is given a challenge by her eccentric boss—find a stranger to marry in New Orleans that night and become CEO of their company, or miss out on the coveted position. Little does she know it's a set-up, and the stranger she meets is actually his grandson, Mark. After a passionate interlude, Courtney finds herself pregnant, and she reluctantly agrees to a marriage in name only. Mark wants more, but Courtney's not sure she can trust him. Taking matters into their own hands, their families push the couple together with antics that are downright hilarious in this humorous romp.

Where it's reviewed:
Romantic Times, December 2001, page 80

Other books by the same author:
Embers of Time, 2000
Lovers and Other Lunatics, 2000
Strangers in the Night, 2000
Bushwhacked Bride, 1999
Second Chance Groom, 1999

Other books you might like:
Elizabeth Bevarly, *First Comes Love*, 2000
Millie Criswell, *The Trouble with Mary*, 2001
Jacqueline Diamond, *Excuse Me? Whose Baby?*, 2001
Kasey Michaels, *Raffling Ryan*, 2000
Isabel Sharpe, *Follow That Baby!*, 2001

381

KAREN ROBARDS

To Trust a Stranger

(New York: Pocket, 2001)

Story type: Contemporary; Romantic Suspense
Subject(s): Murder; Suspense
Major character(s): Julie Carlson, Spouse, Store Owner; Mac McQuarry, Investigator, Detective—Private
Time period(s): 2000s
Locale(s): Charleston, South Carolina

Summary: Waking when she hears her husband's car leave one night, Julie Carlson quickly follows him, thinking he may be cheating on her. When she ends up lost and carless (her Jag is stolen by a couple of punks) in front of a gay bar, she is rescued by former cop Mac McQuarry (in drag), a man who has every reason to hate her husband and is now planning a bit of revenge. Mac agrees to help Julie, thinking to gather information on her husband, but when he discovers someone is out to kill her, things become a lot more dangerous. Chilling and violent.

Where it's reviewed:
Romantic Times, December 2001, page 75

Other books by the same author:
Scandalous, 2001
Ghost Moon, 2000
Paradise County, 2000
The Senator's Wife, 1998
Heartbreaker, 1997

Other books you might like:
Sandra Brown, *Mirror Image*, 1990
Karen Harper, *Empty Cradle*, 1998
Linda Howard, *Kill and Tell*, 1998
Iris Johansen, *The Ugly Duckling*, 1996
Meryl Sawyer, *Trust No One*, 2000

382

NORA ROBERTS

Dance upon the Air

(New York: Jove, 2001)

Story type: Contemporary; Paranormal
Series: Three Sisters Island Trilogy. Book 1
Subject(s): Witches and Witchcraft; Magic; Mystery
Major character(s): Nell Channing, Cook, Witch; Zach Todd, Police Officer (sheriff)
Time period(s): 2000s
Locale(s): Three Sisters Island, Massachusetts (off the New England coast)

Summary: After faking her own death to escape from a violent, powerful husband and an abusive marriage, Nell Channing takes refuge on Three Sisters Island and tentatively begins to rebuild her life. Something more than fate draws Nell to the island; and as she begins to discover who she truly is and the part she is to play in saving the island from an ancient curse, she must also gather the strength to eventually confront her past and keep it from destroying her newfound love and everything else she holds dear. First in Roberts' Three Sisters Island Trilogy.

Where it's reviewed:
Booklist, April 15, 2001, page 1508
Library Journal, May 15, 2001, page 107
Publishers Weekly, May 14, 2001, page 59

Other books by the same author:
Considering Kate, 2001
Heaven and Earth, 2001 (Three Sisters Island Trilogy. Book 2)
The Villa, 2001
Secret Star, 2001 (Star. Book 3)
Midnight Bayou, 2001

Other books you might like:
Kristin Hannah, *Waiting for the Moon*, 1995
historical
Jill Jones, *Circle of the Lily*, 1984
good and evil issues
Marilyn Pappano, *Season for Miracles*, 1997
Maggie Shayne, *Destiny*, 2001
darker
John Updike, *The Witches of Eastwick*, 1984

383

NORA ROBERTS

Heaven and Earth

(New York: Jove, 2001)

Story type: Paranormal; Contemporary
Series: Three Sisters Island Trilogy. Book 2
Subject(s): Wicca; Witches and Witchcraft; Suspense
Major character(s): Ripley Todd, Police Officer (deputy sheriff), Witch; MacAllister Booke, Paranormal Investigator, Scientist
Time period(s): 2000s
Locale(s): Three Sisters Island, Massachusetts

Summary: Deputy Sheriff Ripley Todd is a witch who deliberately blocked off her powers a decade earlier. Dr. MacAllister Booke, researcher of paranormal phenomena, comes to Three Sisters Island to study the legendary place and its principal witch. Little does he know the caustic local officer of the law would become an object of his research—and his love. Three powerful women face an ancient evil in this second part of the Three Sisters Island Trilogy.

Where it's reviewed:
Romantic Times, December 2001, page 76

Other books by the same author:
Dance upon the Air, 2001 (Three Sisters Island Trilogy. Book 1)
Carolina Moon, 2000
Tears of the Moon, 2000
Heart of the Sea, 2000
Night Shield, 2000

Other books you might like:
Sue Civil-Brown, *Next Stop, Paradise*, 2001
Monica Jackson, *A Magical Moment*, 1999
Jayne Ann Krentz, *Absolutely, Positively*, 1996

Mary Alice Kruesi, *One Summer's Night*, 2000
Rachel Lee, *Under Suspicion*, 2001

384

NORA ROBERTS
JILL GREGORY, Co-Author
RUTH LANGAN, Co-Author
MARIANNE WILLMAN, Co-Author

Once upon a Rose

(New York: Jove, 2001)

Story type: Anthology; Fantasy
Subject(s): Anthology; Magic
Time period(s): Indeterminate Past

Summary: Nicely continuing the tradition of their *Once Upon a. . .* anthologies, this quartet by four of romance's best known writers focuses on the most romantic of all flowers, the rose. Magic, myth, and enchantment abound in this well-done anthology. Included are ''Winter Rose'' by Nora Roberts, ''The Rose and the Sword'' by Jill Gregory, ''The Roses of Glenross'' by Ruth Ryan Langan, and ''The Fairest Rose'' by Marianne Willman.

Where it's reviewed:
Rendezvous, October 2001, page 18

Other books by the same author:
Once upon a Dream, 2000
Jewels of the Sun, 1999 (first in an Irish fantasy trilogy)
Once upon a Star, 1999
Once upon a Castle, 1998

Other books you might like:
Kate Holmes, *The Wild Swans*, 2000
Mary Jo Putney, *Faery Magic*, 1998
another magical anthology
Maggie Shayne, *Fairytale*, 1996
Lisa Ann Verge, *The Fairy Bride*, 1996

385

ROSEMARY ROGERS

A Reckless Encounter

(Don Mills, Ontario: MIRA, 2001)

Story type: Historical/Regency
Subject(s): Seduction; Revenge
Major character(s): Celia St. Remy Sinclair, Gentlewoman; Robert George Colter Hampton, Nobleman (Viscount Northington), Rake
Time period(s): 1810s (1810; 1819)
Locale(s): Washington, District of Columbia (Georgetown); England

Summary: Ever since she was a young girl, Celia St. Remy Sinclair has been obsessed with getting revenge against Lord Northington, the man who brutally assaulted Celia's mother and killed a beloved Sinclair family servant. Using the name St. Clair, Celia travels to London to put her plan of vengeance into motion, but when she meets Lord Northington she is surprised to discover he is not the man she seeks, but is instead his son, Colter. Celia revises her plan to include seducing Colter as a way of getting to his father, but this plan soon falls into disarray once Celia realizes she has fallen in love with Colter.

Where it's reviewed:
Affaire de Coeur, November/December 2001, page 33
Booklist, December 1, 2001, page 635
Publishers Weekly, November 5, 2001, page 47
Romantic Times, December 2001, page 42

Other books by the same author:
Savage Desire, 2000
In Your Arms, 1999
All I Desire, 1998
Midnight Lady, 1997
A Dangerous Man, 1996

Other books you might like:
Sara Blayne, *His Scandalous Duchess*, 1999
Thea Devine, *All I Desire*, 1999
Jean R. Ewing, *Illusion*, 1998
Susan Johnson, *Wicked*, 1997
Nicole Jordan, *Desire*, 2001

386

JOANN ROSS

Legends Lake

(New York: Pocket, 2001)

Story type: Contemporary
Subject(s): Horse Racing
Major character(s): Kate O'Sullivan, Rancher (horse breeder); Alec MacKenna, Horse Trainer
Time period(s): 2000s
Locale(s): Kentucky; Castlelough, Ireland; Florida

Summary: With his reputation hanging by a thread because of a fight with a horse owner, horse trainer Alec MacKenna jumps at the chance to train an ugly, but extremely fast horse with Triple Crown potential. The only problem with Legends Lake is that he jumps fences at inopportune times—like when he should cross the finish line. Alec is determined to solve the problem, so he heads for Ireland to talk with the woman who bred Legends Lake, the lovely, pagan Kate O'Sullivan—and their lives are never the same again. A story of high stakes racing with a dusting of magic and love.

Other books by the same author:
Fair Haven, 2000
Southern Comforts, 1996
Secret Sins, 1990

Other books you might like:
Jeanette Baker, *Irish Fire*, 2000
Barbara Freethy, *Almost Home*, 2000
Kentucky horses
Sonja Massey, *Daughter of Ireland*, 2000
Rachel Wilson, *My Wild Irish Rose*, 2000

387

DEBRA SALONEN

Back in Kansas

(Toronto: Harlequin, 2001)

Story type: Contemporary
Subject(s): Family Relations; Sexual Assault; Healing
Major character(s): Claudie St. James, Prostitute (former), Crime Victim (raped); Robert ''Bo'' Lester, Detective—Private
Time period(s): 2000s
Locale(s): Wyoming; New York, New York; Otter Creek, Kansas

Summary: Claudie St. James, raped by her stepfather as a teenager, goes back to Kansas to save her half sister from the same fate. What she finds there is a real surprise, even to Bo Lester, who's tracked her down so he can be with her. A difficult theme is given a unique twist.

Where it's reviewed:
Affaire de Coeur, May/June 2001, page 14
Romantic Times, May 2001, page 106

Other books by the same author:
Wonders Never Cease, 2002
Something about Eve, 2001
His Daddy's Eyes, 2000

Other books you might like:
Kathleen Eagle, *The Night Remembers*, 1997
Meg O'Brien, *Crashing Down*, 1999
Patricia Rosemoor, *Heart of a Lawman*, 2000
Janelle Taylor, *In Too Deep*, 2001
Sheri Whitefeather, *Skyler Hawk: Lone Brave*, 2000

388

VERONICA SATTLER

Once a Princess

(New York: Zebra, 2001)

Story type: Historical/Regency
Subject(s): Princes and Princesses; Politics
Major character(s): Leonie of Mirandeau, Royalty (princess), Orphan; Randall Darnley, Nobleman (Marquis of Hawksrest), Imposter (Hawk Randall, palace guard)
Time period(s): 1810s (1814)
Locale(s): England; Mirandeau, Fictional Country

Summary: Charged by his father with ensuring the safety of the newly orphaned children of the royal family of Mirandeau, Lord Randall Darnley heads for the tiny country and becomes a palace guard to accomplish his task. Despite his mission, he is attracted to the lovely, courageous, yet lame, Princess Leonie, with the inevitable results. Of course, treachery rears its ugly head, but that only adds to the adventure. A refreshing twist on an old plot.

Other books by the same author:
A True Prince, 2000
Wild Honey, 1997
Gabrielle, 1995
Heaven to Touch, 1994
A Promise of Fire, 1989

Other books you might like:
Mary Balogh, *Dancing with Clara*, 1994
another disabled heroine
Elisabeth Fairchild, *The Silent Suitor*, 1994
a blind heroine
Johanna Lindsey, *Once a Princess*, 1991
Joan Wolf, *Royal Bride*, 2001

389

JEANNE SAVERY (Pseudonym of Jeanne Savery Casstevens)

A Perfect Match

(New York: Zebra, 2001)

Story type: Regency; Historical/Napoleonic Wars
Subject(s): Courtship; Politics
Major character(s): Artemisia Bigalow, Noblewoman, Debutante; Alex Merwin, Nobleman (Lord Merwin)
Time period(s): 1810s
Locale(s): Vienna, Austria; England; Paris, France

Summary: Her father's political views threaten to keep young Artemisia Bigalow from Lord Merwin, her father's political opposite but the only man Arta loves. All seems hopeless until circumstances put her father's life in danger; and then things change. A pet tiger named Sahib and plenty of political adventure and intrigue add interest to this uncommon Regency.

Other books by the same author:
Lady Serena's Surrender, 2000
The Christmas Gift, 2000
A Love for Lydia, 1999
Taming Lord Renwick, 1999
The Widowed Miss Mordaunt, 1999

Other books you might like:
Mary Balogh, *Beyond the Sunrise*, 1992
Barbara Hazard, *The Wary Widow*, 2000
Georgette Heyer, *An Infamous Army*, 1937
Regency Napoleonic War classic
Andrea Pickens, *The Hired Hero*, 1999
Evelyn Richardson, *Lord Harry's Daughter*, 2001

390

AMANDA SCOTT

The Secret Clan: Abducted Heiress

(New York: Warner, 2001)

Story type: Historical/Elizabethan
Subject(s): Fairies; Treasure
Major character(s): Mary ''Molly'' Gordon, Heiress, Ward; Finlay ''Wild Fin'' Mackenzie, Nobleman (Baron Kintail)
Time period(s): 16th century (1527; 1539)
Locale(s): Scotland

Summary: Finlay Mackenzie is sent by King James to take possession of Molly Gordon, the Maid of Dunsithe, from her current guardian, the Laird of Mackinnon. All Finlay really wants from Molly is the location of the Maid's fabled treasure, which no man has ever seen; but somehow Finlay finds himself becoming more intrigued by the feisty lass herself than her rumored fortune.

Where it's reviewed:
Booklist, September 15, 2001, page 209
Romantic Times, November 2001, page 41

Other books by the same author:
Border Storm, 2001
Border Fire, 2000
Dangerous Lady, 1999
Highland Spirits, 1999
Highland Treasure, 1998

Other books you might like:
Jen Holling, *Forever My Lady*, 2000
Rebecca Hagan Lee, *A Hint of Heather*, 2000
Teresa Medeiros, *A Whisper of Roses*, 1993
Karen Ranney, *A Promise of Love*, 1997
Haywood Smith, *Border Lord*, 2001

391

DELORAS SCOTT

Sarah and the Rogue

(Toronto: Harlequin, 2001)

Story type: Historical/American West
Subject(s): American West; Competition; Animals/Mules
Major character(s): Sara Miles, Businesswoman (freight hauler); Brody Hawkins, Businessman (freight hauler), Rogue
Time period(s): 1800s
Locale(s): Kansas (territory)

Summary: Like her father, Sara Miles is a muleskinner. Unlike her father, Sara is determined to be financially successful. Admitted rogue Brody Hawkins also hauls freight across the Kansas plains. He's used to winning, especially with women, but his bet with Sara puts both of their lives in danger. A great race against time on a treacherous prairie makes a man and woman realize the meaning of true love.

Other books by the same author:
Historical Christmas Stories, 1999 (anthology)
The Lady and the Outlaw, 1999
Timeless, 1994
Garters and Spurs, 1993
Fire and Ice, 1990

Other books you might like:
Heidi Betts, *Walker's Widow*, 2002
Mary Burton, *The Colorado Bride*, 2001
Jillian Hart, *Night Hawk's Bride*, 2001
Leslie LaFoy, *Jackson's Way*, 2001
Maggie Osborne, *The Promise of Jenny Jones*, 1997

392

REGINA SCOTT (Pseudonym of Regina Lundgren)

The Incomparable Miss Compton

(New York: Zebra, 2001)

Story type: Regency
Subject(s): Courtship; Politics
Major character(s): Sarah Compton, Gentlewoman; Malcolm Breckonridge, Nobleman (Viscount Breckonridge)
Time period(s): 1810s
Locale(s): England

Summary: Deciding it is time he marries, Malcolm, the Viscount Breckonridge, begins looking for a woman who will be an asset to his rising political career. At a ball given in his honor, Malcolm meets Persephone Compton, the Season's reigning beauty, who is being chaperoned by her older cousin, Sarah. Malcolm thinks sensible, efficient Sarah would make the perfect wife, but he soon learns that when it comes to marriage, Sarah is looking for romance not a business proposal.

Where it's reviewed:
Romantic Times, August 2001, page 113

Other books by the same author:
A Dangerous Dalliance, 2000
The Marquis' Kiss, 2000
Catch of the Season, 1999
The Bluestocking on His Knee, 1999
The Unflappable Miss Fairchild, 1998

Other books you might like:
Anne Barbour, *A Rake's Reform*, 1996
Rita Boucher, *The Poet and the Paragon*, 1999
Emma Jensen, *The Irish Rogue*, 1999
Carla Kelly, *Reforming Lord Ragsdale*, 1995
April Kihlstrom, *The Reckless Barrister*, 1999

393

REGINA SCOTT (Pseudonym of Regina Lundgren)

The Irredeemable Miss Renfield

(New York: Zebra, 2001)

Story type: Regency
Subject(s): Marriage; Scandal
Major character(s): Cleo Renfield, Debutante; Leslie Petersborough, Nobleman (Marquis of Hastings)
Time period(s): 1810s
Locale(s): London, England

Summary: Frustrated at the attempts of her sisters and godmother to marry her off, Cleo Renfield strikes a bargain with the latest candidate—they will pretend to be in love, behave shamelessly, and then, of course, the match will be out of the question. Naturally, they fall in love instead. A Regency romp with a more serious side.

Where it's reviewed:
Library Journal, November 15, 2001, page 55

Other books by the same author:
The Incomparable Miss Compton, 2001
A Dangerous Dalliance, 2000
The Marquis' Kiss, 2000
Catch of the Season, 1999

Other books you might like:
Mary Balogh, *The Famous Heroine*, 1996
Marian Devon, *On the Way to Gretna Green*, 1998
Martha Kirkland, *His Lordship's Swan*, 2001

Debbie Raleigh, *A Bride for Lord Challmond*, 2001
Meg-Lynn Roberts, *An Alluring Lady*, 1992
lively and upbeat

394

MELISSA SENATE

See Jane Date

(Don Mills, Ontario: Red Dress Ink, 2001)

Story type: Contemporary
Subject(s): Authors and Writers; Dating (Social Customs); Publishing
Major character(s): Jane Gregg, Editor (assistant editor); Ethan Miles, Businessman
Time period(s): 2000s (2001)
Locale(s): New York, New York

Summary: Jane Gregg, assistant editor at Posh Publishing, has three immediate goals: get promoted, get a date for her cousin's upcoming wedding, and get back at her enemy, otherwise known as Natasha Nutley, the movie star whose book Jane is in the midst of editing. With her cousin's wedding just weeks away, Jane frantically goes on blind date after blind date but it seems like she can't even find a suitable man to take to the wedding, let alone one she can fall in love with.

Where it's reviewed:
Booklist, November 1, 2001, page 462
Publishers Weekly, September 17, 2001, page 52

Other books you might like:
Jenny Colgan, *Amanda's Wedding*, 2001
Jane Green, *Mr. Maybe*, 2001
Melissa Nathan, *Pride, Prejudice and Jasmin Field*, 2001
Clare Naylor, *Love: A User's Guide*, 1999
Isabel Wolff, *The Trials of Tiffany Trott*, 1999

395

MAGGIE SHAYNE (Pseudonym of Margaret Benson)

The Gingerbread Man

(New York: Jove, 2001)

Story type: Contemporary; Romantic Suspense
Subject(s): Murder; Memory; Suspense
Major character(s): Holly Newman, Office Worker (for police department); Vincent O'Mally, Detective—Police
Time period(s): 2000s
Locale(s): Dilmun, New York

Summary: When a children's book left at a brutal crime scene draws burned-out Syracuse Police Detective Vince O'Mally to upstate New York and the small town of Dilmun, he finds a troubled, vulnerable woman, growing danger, and eventually, the answers he seeks. A dark, suspenseful, and riveting story softened by the well-drawn, compelling characters.

Other books by the same author:
Destiny, 2001 (Witch Trilogy. Book 3)
Infinity, 1999 (Witch Trilogy. Book 2)
Eternity, 1998 (Witch Trilogy. Book 1)
Forever Enchanted, 1997
Fairytale, 1996

Other books you might like:
Suzanne Forster, *Come Midnight*, 1995
Tami Hoag, *Guilty as Sin*, 1996
Rachel Lee, *Caught*, 1997
Nora Roberts, *Carnal Innocence*, 1992
Sharon Sala, *Snowfall*, 1996

396

DEBORAH SIMMONS (Pseudonym of Deborah Siegenthal)

My Lady de Burgh

(Toronto: Harlequin, 2001)

Story type: Historical/Medieval
Series: de Burghs. Book 5
Subject(s): Knights and Knighthood; Middle Ages; Murder
Major character(s): Sybil l'Estrange, Religious (novice at convent); Robin de Burgh, Knight, Nobleman
Time period(s): 13th century
Locale(s): England; Wales

Summary: Robin de Burgh believes his family has been cursed because his four older brothers have unexpectedly married in rapid succession. Not wanting to fall victim to the marriage curse, he rides to Wales to find Vala, a woman said to have magical powers. He tracks her to a convent, discovering she has long since died. He also happens upon a murder victim in the same convent. Much to his chagrin, the novice assigned to help his investigation pulls at his heart as no one else ever has. Murder in an abbey, an assassination conspiracy, and whispers of magic combine to make the tale of the fifth de Burgh son a most satisfying one.

Other books by the same author:
My Lord de Burgh, 2000 (de Burghs. Book 4)
The Gentleman Thief, 2000
Robber Bride, 1999 (de Burghs. Book 3)
The de Burgh Bride, 1998 (de Burghs. Book 2)
Taming the Wolf, 1995 (de Burghs. Book 1)

Other books you might like:
Jill Barnett, *Wicked*, 1999
Claudia Dain, *The Marriage Bed*, 2001
Teresa Medeiros, *Charming the Prince*, 1999
Susan Spencer Paul, *The Prisoner Bride*, 2001
Tori Phillips, *Silent Knight*, 1996

397

DONNA SIMPSON

Miss Truelove Beckons

(New York: Zebra, 2001)

Story type: Regency
Subject(s): Dreams and Nightmares; Friendship; Veterans
Major character(s): True Becket, Gentlewoman; Wycliffe Prescott, Nobleman (Viscount Drake), Military Personnel (former major general)
Time period(s): 1810s
Locale(s): England (Lea Park)

Summary: Haunted by memories of the war and plagued by nightmares, Wycliffe Prescott unexpectedly experiences a moment of true peace when he meets True Becket. She is an unassuming young lady, who has accompanied her cousin, Arabella Swinley, to a house party hosted by Wycliffe's mother. While everyone expects Wycliffe and Arabella to come to an understanding during her stay, Wycliffe instead finds himself devoting his time and attention to True, the one woman who can help him forget the horrors he experienced during the war.

Where it's reviewed:
Affaire de Coeur, May/June 2001, page 31
Romantic Times, June 2001, page 121

Other books by the same author:
Lady May's Folly, 2001
Lady Delafont's Dilemma, 2000
Lord St. Claire's Angel, 1999

Other books you might like:
Catherine Blair, *The Hero Returns*, 1999
Monique Ellis, *Delacey's Angel*, 1995
Elisabeth Fairchild, *Miss Dornton's Hero*, 1995
Kate Huntington, *The Captain's Courtship*, 1999
Carla Kelly, *With This Ring*, 1997

398

MELYNDA BETH SKINNER

The Blue Devil

(New York: Zebra, 2001)

Story type: Regency
Subject(s): Books and Reading; Espionage
Major character(s): Kathryn St. David, Gentlewoman; Nigel Moorhaven, Nobleman (Marquis of Blackshire), Spy (''Blue Devil'')
Time period(s): 1810s (1815)
Locale(s): London, England

Summary: After her Great-Aunt Ophelia loses her potentially scandalous diary at Lady Marchman's School for Young Ladies, Kathryn St. David disguises herself as a student in order to infiltrate the school and search for the missing book. Nigel Moorhaven is certain a French spy is using the school as a place to pass British secrets to the enemy. When Nigel spots Kathryn snooping around, he wonders if the charming young lady might not be the clever spy he seeks.

Where it's reviewed:
Romantic Times, September 2001, page 30

Other books you might like:
Donna Bell, *An Improper Pursuit*, 1994
Catherine Blair, *Athena's Conquest*, 2001
Loretta Chase, *The Sandalwood Princess*, 1993
Barbara Metzger, *My Lady Innkeeper*, 1985
Nadine Miller, *The Yorkshire Lady*, 2001

399

CHRISTINA SKYE (Pseudonym of Roberta Helmer)

Going Overboard

(New York: Dell, 2001)

Story type: Contemporary
Subject(s): Photography; Cruise Ships; Violence
Major character(s): Carolina ''Carly'' Sullivan, Photographer; Ford McKay, Military Personnel (Navy SEAL), Imposter (undercover agent)
Time period(s): 2000s
Locale(s): At Sea; Caribbean

Summary: Told to get close enough to hotshot photographer Carly Sullivan to protect her from possible danger, Navy SEAL Ford McKay has his work cut out for him. Not only does he antagonize Carly before he realizes who she is by assuming she is offering him money for sex (she has an interest in using him as a model), but he is also attracted to her in spite of himself. A fast-paced story filled with action, romance, and danger.

Other books by the same author:
2000 Kisses, 1999
The Perfect Gift, 1999
Key to Forever, 1997
Season of Wishes, 1997
Bride of the Mist, 1996

Other books you might like:
Suzanne Brockmann, *Body Guard*, 1999
Suzanne Brockmann, *Over the Edge*, 2001
SEALs
Gena Hale, *Paradise Island*, 1999
Rachel Lee, *After I Dream*, 2000
more SEALs

400

BARBARA DAWSON SMITH

Tempt Me Twice

(New York: St. Martin's Press, 2001)

Story type: Historical/Regency
Subject(s): Animals/Chimpanzees; Treasure
Major character(s): Katherine ''Kate'' Talisford, Gentlewoman, Writer; Gabriel Kenyon, Artist, Nobleman
Time period(s): 1800s (1808); 1810s (1812)
Locale(s): England

Summary: When Gabriel Kenyon, the very same nobleman who rejected her romantic overtures four years earlier, turns up on her doorstep claiming to be her new guardian, Kate Talisford's first inclination is to slam the door shut in his face. Once Kate learns that her father, who has been murdered in Africa, appointed Gabriel as his daughter's guardian, Kate realizes her only chance to exact revenge on her father's killer is to work with Gabriel. As they set their trap to catch the murderer, Kate discovers Gabriel still has the power to distract her with tempting thoughts of romance.

Where it's reviewed:
Publishers Weekly, July 9, 2001, page 52

Romantic Times, September 2001, page 37

Other books by the same author:
Romancing the Rogue, 2000
Too Wicked to Love, 1999
Her Secret Affair, 1998
Once upon a Scandal, 1997
Never a Lady, 1996

Other books you might like:
Jane Ashford, *Charmed and Dangerous*, 2001
Rexanne Becnel, *The Matchmaker*, 2001
Patricia Cabot, *An Improper Proposal*, 1999
Mary Jo Putney, *Angel Rogue*, 1995
Amanda Quick, *Ravished*, 1992

401

DEBORAH SMITH

Alice at Heart

(Smyrna, Georgia: BelleBooks, 2002)

Story type: Fantasy
Series: WaterLilies. Book 1
Subject(s): Fantasy; Mermaids; Love
Major character(s): Alice Riley, Mythical Creature (half-mermaid), Heiress—Lost; Griffin Randolph, Diver (salvage), Mythical Creature (half-merman); Lilith Bonavendier, Wealthy, Mythical Creature (mermaid)
Time period(s): 2000s
Locale(s): Sainte's Point Island, Georgia

Summary: All her life Alice Riley has wondered why she is so different. Her webbed toes, strange eating habits, bizarre allergies, and affinity for the water set her apart and make her a target of ridicule and sometimes fear. Her life suddenly changes when her phenomenal rescue of a child brings her to the attention of the press and her long-lost half-sisters realize she is alive. . .and set out to ''bring her home.'' A magical, lyrical tale of love and lore that nicely sets the stage for Smith's WaterLilies series.

Other books by the same author:
The Stone Flower Garden, 2002
On Bear Mountain, 2001
When Venus Fell, 1998
A Place to Call Home, 1997
Silk and Stone, 1994

Other books you might like:
Jessica Bryan, *Across a Wine Dark Sea*, 1991
first in a merfolk trilogy
Susan Krinard, *Touch of the Wolf*, 1999
Maura Seger, *Silver Zephyr*, 1984
Atlantis Trilogy. Book 1
Maggie Shayne, *Fairytale*, 1996
Maggie Shayne, *Forever Enchanted*, 1997

402

KATHRYN SMITH

Elusive Passion

(New York: Avon, 2001)

Story type: Historical/Regency
Subject(s): Murder; Runaways; Remarriage
Major character(s): Varya Ulyanova, Royalty (Russian princess); Miles Christian, Nobleman (Marquess of Wynter), Widow(er)
Time period(s): 1810s (1814)
Locale(s): London, England

Summary: At first, Varya Ulyanova is convinced that Miles Christian, Marquess of Wynter, killed his former mistress, her best friend. He's intrigued by the mysterious concert pianist, but he doesn't trust her too much, either. It soon becomes apparent they'll have to work together to solve the crime, and reluctantly, the two of them fall in love. Mystery, suspense, plot twists, and a couple of too-believable red herrings hold the reader's interest until the very end of the story.

Where it's reviewed:
Affaire de Coeur, March/April 2001, page 31
Romantic Times, April 2001, page 42

Other books you might like:
Geralyn Dawson, *Simmer All Night*, 1999
Victorian
Suzanne Enoch, *Meet Me at Midnight*, 2000
Lisa Kleypas, *Someone to Watch over Me*, 1999
Amanda Quick, *Slightly Shady*, 2001
Karen Robards, *Scandalous*, 2001

403

EBONI SNOE

Followin' a Dream

(New York: Avon, 2001)

Story type: Contemporary; Multicultural
Subject(s): African Americans; Missing Persons; Travel
Major character(s): Vanessa Bradley, Computer Expert (programmer); Xavier Johnson, Businessman (museum exhibit acquisitions)
Time period(s): 2000s
Locale(s): Columbus, Georgia

Summary: When a palm reader tells Vanessa Bradley that major love is about to enter her life, she doesn't take it seriously. However, when Xavier Johnson appears, she has reason to wonder. Missing grandmothers, exotic trips, and lively action add to this upbeat romance.

Other books by the same author:
The Passion Ruby, 2000
Wishin' on a Star, 2000
A Chance on Lovin' You, 1999
Tell Me I'm Dreamin', 1998
Emerald's Fire, 1996

Other books you might like:
Rochelle Alers, *Hidden Agenda*, 1997

Rochelle Alers, *Island Magic*, 1997
anthology
Bette Ford, *Forever After*, 1995
Terry McMillan, *How Stella Got Her Groove Back*, 1997
Francis Ray, *Until There Was You*, 1999

404

SHERI COBB SOUTH

French Leave

(Saraland, Alabama: Prinny World, 2001)

Story type: Regency
Series: Weaver. Book 3
Subject(s): Marriage; Scandal; Difference
Major character(s): Lisette Colling, Orphan, Runaway; Nigel Haversham, Nobleman (Earl of Waverly), Expatriate
Time period(s): 1820s (1820)
Locale(s): Paris, France; England

Summary: Drunk and unusually depressed, Nigel Haversham, British expatriate and former villain, strolls past a convent one evening and ends up rescuing a young runaway and agreeing to escort her across the Channel to the home of her long-lost grandpere. Once in England, however, things become much more complicated, and not only does Nigel's past come back to haunt him in a totally unexpected way, but Lisette's ''present'' in the form of an irate and villainous cousin almost does them both in. Lively twists of plot and character guarantee an enjoyable read. Third in the Weaver series.

Where it's reviewed:
Library Journal, November 15, 2001, page 55

Other books by the same author:
Brighton Honeymoon, 2000
Miss Darby's Duenna, 1999
The Weaver Takes a Wife, 1999

Other books you might like:
Georgette Heyer, *The Foundling*, 1948
more classic Regency romance
Georgette Heyer, *These Old Shades*, 1960
classic Regency tale
Georgette Heyer, *The Unknown Ajax*, 1960
Carla Kelly, *Mrs. Drew Plays Her Hand*, 1994
more excellent writing
Katherine Kingsley, *A Natural Attachment*, 1990

405

LAEL ST. JAMES (Pseudonym of Linda Lael Miller)

My Lady Beloved

(New York: Pocket, 2001)

Story type: Historical/Medieval
Series: Redclift Sisters. Number 1
Subject(s): Middle Ages; Kidnapping
Major character(s): Gabriella Redclift, Noblewoman; Morgan Chalstrey, Nobleman (Duke of Edgerfield)
Time period(s): 14th century (1369)
Locale(s): Devonshire, England (St. Swithin's Abbey)

Summary: While on her way to meet her bridegroom, Sir Cyprian Avendall, Gabriella Redclift is kidnapped by the dashing Morgan Chalstrey, Duke of Edgerfield, who plans revenge against the devious Sir Avendall. Naturally, Gabriella and Morgan fall victim to their enforced proximity to one another and end up in love. This classic captive-in-love-with-captor story is first in a series about the Redclift sisters.

Other books by the same author:
My Lady Wayward, 2001 (Redclift Sisters. Number 2)

Other books you might like:
Shana Abe, *The Truelove Bride*, 1999
Julie Garwood, *Gentle Warrior*, 1992
Karyn Monk, *The Rose and the Warrior*, 1998
Karyn Monk, *The Witch and the Warrior*, 1998
Tina St. John, *Lord of Vengeance*, 1999

406

LAEL ST. JAMES (Pseudonym of Linda Lael Miller)

My Lady Wayward

(New York: Sonnet, 2001)

Story type: Historical/Medieval
Series: Redclift Sisters. Number 2
Subject(s): Middle Ages
Major character(s): Meg Redclift, Noblewoman; Gresham Sedgewick, Knight, Amnesiac
Time period(s): 14th century
Locale(s): England

Summary: Unconscious and without memory, Gresham Sedgewick is found by Meg Redclift and hidden at St. Swithin's Abbey, where she lives. Although the mother superior is suspicious, she agrees to let him stay until he recovers—unfortunately the only thing he can remember is his name. Learning his identity becomes his passion; and when plague strikes the abbey when he and Meg are away—and they can't return—they set out on a quest that is as dangerous as it is adventurous.

Where it's reviewed:
Rendezvous, December 2001, page 25
Romantic Times, December 2001, page 38

Other books by the same author:
My Lady Beloved, 2001 (Redclift Sisters. Number 1)

Other books you might like:
Christina Dodd, *A Knight to Remember*, 1997
Christina Dodd, *Once a Knight*, 1996
Juliana Garnett, *The Knight*, 2001
Samantha James, *The Truest Heart*, 1997
another hero with amnesia

407

TINA ST. JOHN

White Lion's Lady

(New York: Ivy, 2001)

Story type: Historical/Medieval
Subject(s): Kidnapping

Major character(s): Isabel de Lamere, Heiress; Griffin of Droghallow, Knight
Time period(s): 12th century (1179; 1189)
Locale(s): England

Summary: On her way to wed Sebastian of Montborne, Isabel de Lamere is kidnapped by Griffin of Droghallow, also known as the White Lion, who just happens to be the very same knight who, years ago, rescued Isabel from danger. Isabel can detect no hint of honor in her former champion but when Griffin is forced to choose between duty and honor, he finds a way to prove to Isabel that he is still the knight of her dreams.

Where it's reviewed:
Romantic Times, August 2001, page 36

Other books by the same author:
Lady of Valor, 2000
Lord of Vengeance, 1999

Other books you might like:
Glynnis Campbell, *My Champion*, 2001
Denise Hampton, *The Warrior's Damsel*, 2001
Madeline Hunter, *By Possession*, 2000
Mary Reed McCall, *Secret Vows*, 2001
Margaret Moore, *A Warrior's Honor*, 1998

408

JUDITH STACY (Pseudonym of Dorothy Howell)

The Nanny

(Toronto: Harlequin, 2001)

Story type: Historical; Humor
Series: Return to Tyler
Subject(s): Humor; Single Parent Families; Family Relations
Major character(s): Annie Martin, Child-Care Giver (nanny); Josh Ingalls, Wealthy, Widow(er)
Time period(s): 1840s (1840)
Locale(s): Tyler, Wisconsin

Summary: Widower Josh Ingall's children are wild. They've terrorized every governess they've ever had. . .until he hires his gardener, Annie Martin, to be their nanny. This *The Sound of Music* meets the American frontier is chock full of high jinx and humor.

Other books by the same author:
The Widow's Little Secret, 2001
The Blushing Bride, 2000
Written in the Heart, 2000
The Last Bride in Texas, 2000
The Dreammaker, 1999

Other books you might like:
Linda Lea Castle, *Mattie and the Blacksmith*, 2001
Millie Criswell, *The Marrying Man*, 2000
Geralyn Dawson, *The Bad Luck Wedding Night*, 2001
Christina Dodd, *Rules of Surrender*, 2000
Suzanne Enoch, *Reforming a Rake*, 2000

409

JUDITH STACY (Pseudonym of Dorothy Howell)

The Widow's Little Secret

(Toronto: Harlequin, 2001)

Story type: Historical/American West
Subject(s): Secrets; Pregnancy; American West
Major character(s): Mattie Ingram, Widow(er); Jared McQuaid, Lawman
Time period(s): 1880s (1887)
Locale(s): Nevada

Summary: When Mattie Ingram's no-good husband dies, she finds a night of comfort with a stranger. Then the stranger, lawman Jared McQuaid, comes back to town for good, and as soon as he finds out Mattie's pregnant with his child, he insists they get married. The only problem is, Mattie refuses. Two very stubborn people find love against their will in this funny, poignant story.

Other books by the same author:
The Nanny, 2001
The Blushing Bride, 2000
Written in the Heart, 2000
The Last Bride in Texas, 2000
The Dreammaker, 1999

Other books you might like:
Carolyn Davidson, *The Bachelor Tax*, 1999
Jill Gregory, *Cold Night, Warm Stranger*, 1999
Lorraine Heath, *Never Love a Cowboy*, 2000
Sylvia McDaniel, *The Outlaw*, 2001
Linda O'Brien, *Beloved Protector*, 2001

410

AMANDA STEVENS (Pseudonym of Marilyn Medlock Amann)

The Innocent

(New York: Harlequin, 2001)

Story type: Romantic Suspense
Series: Eden's Children. Part One
Subject(s): Children; Crime and Criminals
Major character(s): Abby Cross, Police Officer (sergeant); Sam Burke, FBI Agent (profiler)
Time period(s): 2000s
Locale(s): Eden, Mississippi; Palisades, Mississippi

Summary: For ten years Sergeant Abby Cross has been searching for any clues that might help locate her young niece, Sadie, who vanished one day and was never heard from again. Now two other little girls from Eden have disappeared and FBI profiler Sam Burke arrives to offer his help with the investigation. Abby finds working with Sam difficult since the attraction she feels for him could jeopardize her career, but Sam may be Abby's only hope of locating the missing children.

Where it's reviewed:
Romantic Times, July 2001, page 105

Other books by the same author:
Nighttime Guardian, 2001
The Bodyguard's Assignment, 2001
Forbidden Lover, 2000
Secret Admirer, 2000
The Littlest Witness, 2000

Other books you might like:
Jean Barrett, *The Hunt for Hawke's Daughter*, 2000
Kay Hooper, *Stealing Shadows*, 2000
Susan Kearney, *The Cradle Will Rock*, 2000
Mariah Stewart, *Devlin's Light*, 1997
Debra Webb, *The Bodyguard's Baby*, 2001

411

ANNE STUART (Pseudonym of Anne Christine Stuart Ohlrogge)

The Widow

(Don Mills, Ontario: Mira, 2001)

Story type: Contemporary; Romantic Suspense
Subject(s): Widows/Widowers; Murder; Suspense
Major character(s): Charlotte ''Charlie'' Thomas, Restaurateur, Widow(er); Connor Maguire, Journalist (tabloid reporter), Imposter (insurance adjustor)
Time period(s): 2000s
Locale(s): New York, New York; Tuscany, Italy (La Colombala estate)

Summary: Returning to a Tuscan villa to settle the estate of her late husband, the renowned artist Aristide Pompasse, Charlie Thomas, now with a life and fiance in New York and a need to lay the ghosts of the past to rest, finds the beautiful estate she remembers, a murder, some missing paintings, a sense of impending doom, and a brash, compelling hero who is everything her fiance is not. Good character development of the protagonists adds to this interestingly plotted story that nicely weaves romance and suspense and overlays it all with a touch of Gothic horror.

Where it's reviewed:
Library Journal, August 2001, page 88
Publishers Weekly, June 4, 2001, page 64

Other books by the same author:
Night and Day, 2001
Lady Fortune, 2000
Shadow Lover, 1999
Lord of Danger, 1998
Prince of Swords, 1998

Other books you might like:
Victoria Holt, *Mistress of Mellyn*, 1960
classic Gothic/historical
Linda Howard, *After the Night*, 1995
Iris Johansen, *The Ugly Duckling*, 1996
Katherine Sutcliffe, *Darkling I Listen*, 2001

412

KATHERINE SUTCLIFFE

Darkling I Listen

(New York: Jove, 2001)

Story type: Contemporary; Romantic Suspense
Subject(s): Suspense; Psychological Thriller; Small Town Life
Major character(s): Alyson James, Journalist (for a tabloid); Brandon Carlyle, Writer (Hollywood), Convict (former)
Time period(s): 2000s
Locale(s): Ticky Creek, Texas

Summary: Hollywood writer Brandon Carlyle returns home to small town Texas to put his shattered life back together after being imprisoned for a crime he has no memory of committing. He is haunted by the anonymous letter writer ''Anticipating'' and fascinated by a tabloid reporter who says she wants to help him. Sensual, sultry, and suspenseful.

Where it's reviewed:
Rendezvous, August 2001, page 32

Other books by the same author:
Fever, 2001
Notorious, 2000
Whitehorse, 1999
Moonglow, 1998
Jezebel, 1997

Other books you might like:
Tami Hoag, *Dark Paradise*, 1994
Linda Howard, *After the Night*, 1995
Karen Robards, *One Summer*, 1993
Nora Roberts, *Carnal Innocence*, 1992
Nora Roberts, *Public Secrets*, 1995

413

JANELLE TAYLOR

In Too Deep

(New York: Zebra, 2001)

Story type: Romantic Suspense; Contemporary
Subject(s): Suspense; Blackmail; Family Relations
Major character(s): Jenny Holloway, Single Parent, Restaurateur; Hunter Calgary, Detective—Police (former), Bodyguard
Time period(s): 2000s
Locale(s): Houston, Texas; Santa Fe, New Mexico; Puerto Vallarta, Mexico

Summary: Jenny Holloway has a secret to keep from her abusive ex-husband. . .a teenaged son. She moves from Houston to Santa Fe to start a new restaurant and a new life accompanied by former police detective Hunter Calgary, the man hired by her father to protect her. Hunter has another reason for accepting the assignment—Jenny's former husband murdered his sister. A deceptively charming villain, driven to hurt every woman he meets, creates a real sense of danger in this pulse-quickening read.

Where it's reviewed:
Booklist, September 15, 2001, page 209
Romantic Times, October 2001, page 86

Other books by the same author:
Can't Stop Loving You, 2001
Not Without You, 2000
Someday Soon, 1999
Lakota Winds, 1998
Wild Winds, 1997

Other books you might like:
Iris Johansen, *The Ugly Duckling*, 1996
Rachel Lee, *Snow in September*, 2000
Elizabeth Lowell, *Midnight in Ruby Bayou*, 2000
Carla Neggers, *The Waterfall*, 2000
Patricia Rosemoor, *Heart of a Lawman*, 2000

414

VICKIE TAYLOR (Pseudonym of Vickie Spears)

The Renegade Steals a Lady

(New York: Silhouette, 2001)

Story type: Romantic Suspense
Subject(s): Animals/Dogs; Crime and Criminals; Drugs
Major character(s): Paige Burkett, Police Officer (canine patrol); Marco Angelosi, Detective—Police (narcotics), Fugitive
Time period(s): 2000s
Locale(s): Port Kingston, Texas; Oklahoma

Summary: After spending a passionate night with fellow police officer Marco Angelosi, Paige Burkett feels doubly betrayed when Marco is caught with some of the stolen goods from a drug bust Paige is involved in. Marco refuses to explain his actions, but a few months later he escapes from jail and kidnaps Paige and her canine police partner, Bravo. Now Paige is trapped in the wilderness with a man who insists he doesn't want to hurt her; he wants to protect her.

Where it's reviewed:
Romantic Times, September 2001, page 112

Other books by the same author:
The Lawman's Last Stand, 2000
The Man Behind the Badge, 1999
Virgin Without a Memory, 1999

Other books you might like:
Cherry Adair, *Kiss and Tell*, 2000
B.J. Daniels, *Secret Bodyguard*, 2001
Morgan Hayes, *Tall, Dark, and Wanted*, 2000
Sally Tyler Hayes, *Spies, Lies, and Lovers*, 1999
Gayle Wilson, *The Bride's Protector*, 1999

415

JODI THOMAS (Pseudonym of Jodi Koumalats)

The Texan's Dream

(New York: Jove, 2001)

Story type: Historical/American West
Subject(s): Feuds; Ranch Life
Major character(s): Karine ''Kara'' Paige O'Riley, Accountant; Jonathan Catlin, Rancher
Time period(s): 1870s (1875)
Locale(s): Pittsburgh, Pennsylvania; Kansas City, Missouri; Texas (Catlin Ranch)

Summary: Fleeing a feud between two Irish families in Pittsburgh, Kara O'Riley arrives in Kansas City in desperate need of money and a place to hide, so she applies for the job of bookkeeper at the Catlin Ranch. Jonathan Catlin, Kara's new employer, seems like a cold, distant man whose only interest lies in turning the ranch he recently inherited back into a thriving business. Once Kara discovers the real reason behind Jonathan's aloofness, she searches for some way to break down the emotional barriers he has spent years building up.

Where it's reviewed:
Booklist, October 15, 2001, page 387
Romantic Times, November 2001, page 42

Other books by the same author:
Twilight in Texas, 2001
To Wed in Texas, 2000
To Kiss a Texan, 1999
The Texan's Touch, 1998
Two Texas Hearts, 1997

Other books you might like:
Lorraine Heath, *Texas Destiny*, 2001
Jill Marie Landis, *Summer Moon*, 2001
Maggie Osborne, *Silver Lining*, 2000
Cheryl Ann Porter, *Captive Angel*, 1999
Cynthia Sterling, *A Husband by Law*, 2001

416

ELIZABETH THORNTON

The Perfect Princess

(New York: Bantam, 2001)

Story type: Historical/Regency
Subject(s): Suspense; Hostages; Prisoners and Prisons
Major character(s): Lady Rosamunde Devere, Noblewoman, Captive (hostage of Richard); Richard Maitland, Fugitive, Convict (condemned)
Time period(s): 1810s
Locale(s): Newgate, England; Chelsea, England; Dunsmoor, England

Summary: Condemned prisoner Richard Maitland escapes, taking Lady Rosamunde Devere hostage. It soon becomes apparent to Rosamunde that the wounded man has been framed, and she vows to help him prove his innocence. In this Regency-era suspense, a strong, stubborn woman meets her match in a most unlikely place. This third book in a trilogy ends with a very neat twist.

Where it's reviewed:
Booklist, September 15, 2001, page 209
Publishers Weekly, October 8, 2001, page 50

Other books by the same author:
Prince Charming, 2001
Strangers at Dawn, 1999
Whisper His Name, 1999

You Only Love Twice, 1998
The Bride's Bodyguard, 1997

Other books you might like:
Amanda Quick, *Slightly Shady*, 2001
Karen Robards, *Scandalous*, 2001
Kathryn Smith, *Elusive Passion*, 2001
Peggy Waide, *Mightier than the Sword*, 2001
Gayle Wilson, *My Lady's Dare*, 2000

417

SUSAN VAUGHAN

Dangerous Attraction

(New York: Silhouette, 2001)

Story type: Romantic Suspense
Subject(s): Drugs; Murder
Major character(s): Marie Claire Saint-Ange, Linguist (translator), Widow(er); Michael Quinn, Government Official (DEA agent), Detective—Private (posing as investigator)
Time period(s): 2000s
Locale(s): Weymouth, Maine; Portland, Maine; Caribou Peak, Maine

Summary: DEA agent Michael Quinn agrees to pose as a private investigator in an effort to get closer to Marie Claire Saint-Ange, the ''Widow Spider,'' who is rumored to have murdered three men. Hired by Marie to help clear her name, Michael hopes to find proof that will tie Marie into drug smuggling going on in Maine. Instead Michael finds a courageous, vulnerable woman who desperately needs his help.

Where it's reviewed:
Romantic Times, June 2001, page 111

Other books you might like:
Beverly Barton, *Navajo's Woman*, 2000
Nina Bruhns, *Catch Me If You Can*, 2000
Carla Cassidy, *Man on a Mission*, 2001
Linda Winstead Jones, *Madigan's Wife*, 2001
Maggie Price, *Dangerous Liaisons*, 2000

418

KAREN WHITE

Whispers of Goodbye

(New York: LoveSpell, 2001)

Story type: Gothic; Historical/Post-American Civil War
Subject(s): American South; Sisters
Major character(s): Catherine deClaire Reed, Widow(er); John McMahon, Plantation Owner
Time period(s): 1860s
Locale(s): Saint Simons Island, Georgia; Louisiana (Whispering Oaks Plantation)

Summary: A frantic letter sent by her older sister Elizabeth prompts Catherine deClaire Reed to return to her family's plantation, Whispering Oaks. Once Catherine arrives at her old home, she finds her sister has vanished without a trace but many people, including Elizabeth's brooding husband John McMahon, do not seem to miss Elizabeth in the least. The more Catherine learns about her sister, the more puzzled she becomes but the only one who can answer all of Catherine's questions may be the very man responsible for her sister's disappearance.

Where it's reviewed:
Romantic Times, October 2001, page 43

Other books by the same author:
In the Shadow of the Moon, 2000

Other books you might like:
Peggy Darty, *The Crimson Roses of Fountain Court*, 1998
Judith E. French, *Rachel's Choice*, 1998
Penelope Neri, *Moonshadow*, 2001
Evelyn Rogers, *Devil in the Dark*, 2001
Colleen Shannon, *The Wolf of Haskell Hall*, 2001

419

SUSAN WIGGS

Halfway to Heaven

(Don Mills, Ontario: MIRA, 2001)

Story type: Historical/Victorian America
Subject(s): Astronomy; Politics; Family Relations
Major character(s): Abigail Cabot, Scientist (astronomer); Jamie Calhoun, Political Figure, Rake
Time period(s): 1870s (1873)
Locale(s): Washington, District of Columbia

Summary: Senator Franklin Rush Cabot's daughter, Abigail, is clumsy, a condition caused by a congenitally deformed foot. She also has no social graces or sense of style. What she does have is a keen mind and a stunning expertise in the field of astronomy. Jamie Calhoun is a charming rake, one who uses his looks to get ahead. He offers to teach Abigail how to seduce Lt. Butler, the man she loves from afar, but soon Jamie's willing student captures his heart instead. A delightful heroine, a hero with a secret, and quirky secondary characters fill the pages of this charming, often humorous Pygmalion tale.

Where it's reviewed:
Affaire de Coeur, September/October 2001, page 29
Booklist, October 1, 2001, page 304
Romantic Times, October 2001, page 35

Other books by the same author:
The Hostage, 2001
The You I Never Knew, 2001
The Mistress, 2000
The Charm School, 1999
The Horsemaster's Daughter, 1999

Other books you might like:
Geralyn Dawson, *Simmer All Night*, 1999
Lisa Kleypas, *Suddenly You*, 2001
Betina Krahn, *Sweet Talking Man*, 2000
Allie Shaw, *The Impossible Texan*, 2001
Judith Stacy, *Written in the Heart*, 2000

420

BESS WILLINGHAM (Pseudonym of Cindy Harris Williams)

A Scandalous Wager

(New York: Zebra, 2001)

Story type: Regency
Subject(s): Espionage; Friendship; Parenthood
Major character(s): Steven St. Charles, Nobleman, Spy (former); Eugenia "Genie" Terrebonne, Noblewoman
Time period(s): 1810s (1812)
Locale(s): London, England

Summary: Seeking proof that a member of the *ton* is a French sympathizer, Steven St. Charles pays court to the suspected man's daughter, Lady Jane Bowlingbroke, in an attempt to get closer to the man himself. For Steven, gathering proof is not easy, especially since he finds himself distracted from his mission by Jane's friend, Eugenia Terrebonne, a woman nothing like her friend, Jane, or for that matter like any other woman Steven has ever met.

Where it's reviewed:
Romantic Times, July 2001, page 28

Other books by the same author:
The Smuggler's Bride, 2000
The Husband Hunt, 1999
Bedeviled Barrister, 1998
The Minx of Mayfair, 1998
The Lady's Mummy, 1997

Other books you might like:
Jessica Benson, *Lord Stanhope's Proposal*, 1997
Lynn Collum, *Elizabeth and the Major*, 1997
Elena Greene, *Lord Langdon's Kiss*, 2000
Debbie Raleigh, *Lord Carlton's Courtship*, 2000
Hayley Ann Solomon, *Seducing Lord Sinclair*, 1999

421

RACHEL WILSON

Heaven Sent

(New York: Jove, 2001)

Story type: Historical/American West Coast
Subject(s): Grief; Single Parent Families; Letters
Major character(s): Callida "Callie" Prophet, Child-Care Giver (nanny), Postal Worker (carrier); Aubrey Lockhart, Widow(er), Wealthy (Chinese imports business); Becky Lockhart, Child
Time period(s): 1890s (1897)
Locale(s): Santa Angelica, California

Summary: Compelled by young Becky Lockhart's poignant letters to her dead mother and a concern that her father is ignoring her, rural mail carrier Callie Prophet answers Aubrey Lockhart's ad and becomes Becky's nanny. When Becky asks Callie to read her some letters she has found—love letters her father wrote to his wife years ago—she gets a surprising glimpse behind the cold, moody facade to the poetic, passionate man beneath. Heartwarming, with some inspirational aspects, this is the launch book for the Love Letters line, a series of books with letters as a focal point.

Other books by the same author:
My Wild Irish Rose, 2000
Spirit of Love, 1999
Heaven's Promise, 1998
Restless Spirits, 1998
Sweet Charity, 1997

Other books you might like:
Robin Lee Hatcher, *Promise Me Spring*, 1991
Robin Lee Hatcher, *Where the Heart Is*, 1993
Debbie Macomber, *Morning Comes Softly*, 2000
contemporary
Anita Wall, *Ties of Love*, 2000

422

RUTH WIND (Pseudonym of Barbara Samuel)

Born Brave

(New York: Harlequin, 2001)

Story type: Romantic Suspense
Series: Firstborn Sons. Book 4
Subject(s): Kidnapping; Kings, Queens, Rulers, etc.; Terrorism
Major character(s): Hawk Stone, Bodyguard, Police Officer; Laurie Lewis, FBI Agent
Time period(s): 2000s (2001)
Locale(s): United States

Summary: FBI agent Laurie Lewis is given the opportunity to prove she can handle fieldwork when she is asked to impersonate Montebellan Princess Julia Sebastiani who has been targeted for kidnapping by a terrorist group. Police officer and security expert Hawk Stone agrees to act as Laurie's bodyguard in the hopes this new assignment will help him deal with the death of his partner. While their undercover mission starts out on a strictly professional basis, Laurie and Hawk soon find themselves tempted by thoughts of a much more personal nature.

Where it's reviewed:
Romantic Times, October 2001, page 115

Other books by the same author:
Beautiful Stranger, 2000
In the Midnight Rain, 2000
Rio Grande Wedding, 1999
For Christmas, Forever, 1998
Meant to Be Married, 1998

Other books you might like:
Suzanne Brockmann, *Prince Joe*, 2001
Carla Cassidy, *Born of Passion*, 2001
Virginia Kantra, *Born to Protect*, 2001
Connie Lane, *Reinventing Romeo*, 2000
Paula Detmer Riggs, *Born a Hero*, 2001

Western Books in Review
by
D.R. Meredith

One step forward and two steps back seems to be a trend in Westerns, a trend just as strong as the certainty that Max Brand will be reprinted more than any other writer. In my essay written for volume 2 of the 2001 edition of *What Do I Read Next?*, I mentioned the continuation of the growth in numbers of books by and about women and minorities. That trend has ended, or at least hesitated, with the exception being books with Indian characters. Books about Indians are, of course, as frequent as ever, with several notable titles: *The Years of Fear* by Fred Grove, about murders among the Osages in Oklahoma; *The Legend of Sotoju Mountain* by Will Henry, which contains three short novels about Indians; *Bear Paw* by Gene Mullins, about a renegade Kiowa; and most notable of all, *Moon of Bitter Cold* by Frederick J. Chiaventone, concerning the Fetterman Massacre. In addition to those titles, we also have Terry Johnston's *Turn the Stars Upside Down*, about the death of Crazy Horse; Elmer Kelton's *The Way of the Coyote*, about Texas Rangers and the Comanche; William Tremblay's *The June Rise*, based on the life of Joseph Antoine Janis; and Stephen Overholser's *Shadow Valley Rising*. Two Western mysteries featuring Indians are *Blackening Song* by Aimee and David Thurlo, about murder on the Navajo Reservation, and *The Thunder Keeper* by Margaret Coel, about an Arapaho lawyer and a Catholic priest. Although many of the other Westerns may mention Indians, the above titles feature Indians in at least a supporting role. There are also a few volumes that showcase Mexican-Americans, none as well as *Miracle of the Jacal* by Robert J. Randisi, about Elfego Baca, and *Tears of the Heart* by Lauran Paine.

As with the last half of 2001, there is continued emphasis on historical novels based on real people or events. This is an encouraging sign for the genre. Few regions of the United States provide as many exciting tales as the West. From the fur trade to the Western Migration to the California Gold Rush to the settlement of the Plains to the Indian Wars, the writer is provided with excitement, tension, romance, and conflict, all the elements with which to write a powerful historical novel. Other than the Civil War, the West, to use a slang term, was ''where it was at'', historically speaking. This half-year's collection of titles focuses on certain historical events which in and of themselves provide all the drama the writer and reader can desire. One particular title that explores the conflict between the Sioux and the white man—specifically the army—is *Moon of Bitter Cold* by Frederick J. Chiaventone. One could not wish for a more exciting or absorbing book. Other titles based on actual historical events or persons are: *Law Dog* by J. Lee Butts; *Mountain Time: A Western Memoir* by Jane Candia Coleman; *The Good Journey* by Micaela Gilchrist, about General Henry Atkinson's feud with Black Hawk; *The Last Canyon* by John Vernon; *River Walk* by Rita Cleary; and *Cowboy in the Making*, a book for young readers by Will James.

Forget what I said last time about the surprising lack of books focusing on famous outlaws or the Custer Massacre. Such books are back. The titles include *Doc Holliday's Gone* by Jane Candia Coleman, *Spanish Jack* by Robert J. Conley, *Bucking the Tiger* by Bruce Olds (another book about Doc Holliday), and *Will's War* by Janice Woods Windle, based on her grandfather's trial for treason in 1917.

In addition, just when I say that the stand-alone shoot-'em-up Western novel is relegated to that corral in the sky, we have a six month period in which the stand-alone fills up more rack space in the grocery store than all of last year. The straight traditional is not disappearing; it is merely changing. One change is that the cowboy no longer kisses his horse (to use a cliche), but carries the heroine off to the bedroom as ''adult'' Westerns become more popular. Occasionally, the bedroom door is left ajar in books other than adult Westerns such as *Charlie and the Sir* by Frank Roderus and *You Never Can Tell* by Kathleen Eagle. Not that there are graphic love scenes, as there are in the adult Westerns, but there is more sexual tension than heretofore.

In the second half of last year, Western series, other than the adult series, seemed to be on the rise, but in the first half of this year those numbers were not as high. Some of the books in series worth mentioning are: Elmer Kelton's *The Way of the Coyote*; Jory Sherman's *The Baron War*; Clay Reynold's *The Vigil*, the first of the Sandhill Chronicles; *What Once We Loved* by Jane Kirkpatrick, one of the few series with female characters; *Downriver* by Richard S. Wheeler, one of his excellent Barnaby Skye novels; and the Ella Clah mystery, *Blackening Song* by Aimee and David Thurlo.

One trend that has continued from last year is the short story, whether in single author collections or anthologies which collect different writers' works. Anthologies allow for opportunities where there used to be none. Where once writing Western short stories was a quick road to the poor house, now there are more anthologies to showcase the work of several different writers at once.

Once again, several titles illustrate sense of place, one of the most important elements in a Western novel. As he has in so many categories, Frederick J. Chiaventone leads the way with *Moon of Bitter Cold*, a novel which raises goose bumps and fear as the reader experiences the ominous waiting for Red Cloud and Crazy Horse to attack. Another title which illustrates the bitter weather and loneliness of empty land is *The Reckoning* by John McLain. *The Years of Fear* by Fred Grove not only evokes terror but describes the beauty of the land. Another title, a modern Western, is Mary King's *Quincie Bolliver*, a coming-of-age novel set in a fading oil boomtown where dirt and poverty are the two most abundant commodities. *The Vigil* by Clay Reynolds, another modern Western, evokes the loneliness of a small West Texas town. Any Western should evoke a sense of place, and if it doesn't, then it isn't a good Western, but the above titles are particularly strong in that element.

Now comes that part of my review of Westerns that I dread the most: the selecting of the twenty-five best titles in this volume. I want to emphasize again that these are my choices and are a result of my subjective taste. Another reader might very well choose entirely different titles for entirely different reasons. These are my selections.

Recommended Titles

1. *Moon of Bitter Cold* by Frederick J. Chiaventone. Far and away the best of the Westerns included in this volume, it succeeds on many different levels: plot, sense of place, characterization, dialogue, and structure.
2. *The Vigil* by Clay Reynolds. The best of the modern Westerns in this volume of *WDIRN?*, and one of the ten best in any *WDIRN?* volume. The writing and characterization are masterful.
3. *Quincie Bolliver* by Mary King. The evocative sense of place is this novel's strongest element.
4. *Caleb's Price* by Troy D. Smith. A humorous story, with wonderful characterization, of a gunfighter.
5. *The Thunder Keeper* by Margaret Coel. The best of the cross-genre Western mysteries mentioned in this volume of *WDIRN?*.
6. *The Years of Fear* by Fred Grove. The author interviewed some of the people involved in the murders in Osage country in Oklahoma, lending realism to his novel. Even though he waited more than fifty years to write the book, it was worth the wait.
7. *A World of Thieves* by James Carlos Blake. Strong plot and characterization make this novel of thieves in Texas during the Depression noteworthy.
8. *The June Rise* by William Tremblay. A book based on the life of a real person, Joseph Antoine Janis.
9. *Shadow Valley Rising* by Stephen Overholser. A strong story of a woman who chose to marry an Indian in the 1860s.
10. *Ride West to Dawn* by James C. Work. Another of Work's Westerns with a touch of the supernatural.
11. *The Reckoning* by John McLain. Set at the turn of the century in Wyoming, this coming-of-age story evokes a wonderful sense of place.
12. *Hard Bounty* by Ken Hodgson. Graphic account of a bounty hunter who must hunt down his own mother and sister.
13. *Doc Holliday's Gone* by Jane Candia Coleman. A poignant collection of two short novels based on historical figures.
14. *Outcasts* by Tim McGuire. A wonderful traditional Western with good characterization.
15. *Flying Eagle* by Tim Champlin. A traditional Western with an unusual plot.
16. *River Walk* by Rita Cleary. An excellent retelling of the first year of the Lewis and Clark Expedition.
17. *Gamblers' Row: A Western Trio* by Les Savage, Jr. A wonderful selection of Savage's psychological writing.
18. *Blackening Song* by Aimee and David Thurlo. Another excellent Western mystery that focuses on Navajo culture.
19. *The Legend of Sotoju Mountain* by Will Henry. Three of Henry's superb Indian stories.
20. *Bear Paw* by Gene Mullins. An exciting traditional Western with a strong plot.
21. *Tears of the Heart* by Lauran Paine. An Anglo wanted by the law is shielded by a Mexican-American community.
22. *The Baron War* by Jory Sherman. Another volume in Sherman's series about a South Texas ranch and the family who owns it.
23. *The Holy Road* by Michael Blake. A sequel to *Dances with Wolves*.

24. *The Good Journey* by Micaela Gilchrist. Another excellent book based on the historical figures General Henry Atkinson and Black Hawk.
25. *By Flare of Northern Lights* by Tim Champlin. A novel of the gold rush in the Klondike.

For More Information about Western Fiction

The Western Writers of America maintains a database of bookstores willing to stock and/or order Western titles. For information on the database, or to add your favorite bookstore to it, write to Candy Moulton, Editor, *Roundup Magazine*, Box 29 Star Route, Encampment, WY, 82325.

For general information on what's happening in Western writing, subscribe to *Roundup Magazine* at the above address. *Roundup* is the official publication of the Western Writers of America and includes reviews of Western fiction and nonfiction done by yours truly. In addition, there is a series of features on writers of the 20th century, a section on what's doing in Hollywood by Miles Hood Swarthout, and articles on new directions in Western writing.

For the computer literate there is no source like Amazon.com for finding out-of-print Westerns, or just titles by a favorite that you are missing. Remember also to periodically check for titles in your local used bookstores, estate sales, flea markets, garage sales, and your local Friends of the Library book sale. Speaking of libraries, if the title you want is in hardback, ask your local library to get it for you on interlibrary loan. Some libraries will order original paperbacks on interlibrary loan, but you will need to ask. As a last resort, contact a rare book dealer for some desired title you want, but be prepared to pay dearly. I found one of my original first-print paperbacks, used, for $108. I didn't make a whole lot more than that when I wrote it.

Western Titles

423

MICHELLE BLACK

An Uncommon Enemy

(New York: Forge, 2001)

Story type: Historical; Indian Wars
Subject(s): Pioneers; Indian Captives; Indians of North America
Major character(s): George Armstrong Custer, Historical Figure (Indian fighter), Military Personnel (colonel); Eden Murdoch, Captive (of the Cheyenne), Nurse (during Civil War); Brad Randall, Military Personnel (captain)
Time period(s): 1860s (1868)
Locale(s): Washita River, Kansas

Summary: Colonel Custer needs Eden Murdoch to testify that his attack on a Cheyenne village was not a massacre, but Eden refuses. A former Civil War nurse, who was captured by the Cheyenne while fleeing an abusive husband, Eden came to respect her captors and fell in love with one of them. Custer assigns a naive young captain, Brad Randall, to discover the exact nature of Eden's relationship with the Cheyenne. Instead, Brad falls in love with Eden and is sympathetic to her love for the Indians, a situation that endangers his career.

Where it's reviewed:
Publishers Weekly, September 3, 2001, page 61

Other books by the same author:
Lightning in a Drought Year, 2000
Never Come Down, 1999
Hannah and the Horseman, 1997
This Man Colter, 1997

Other books you might like:
Rosanne Bittner, *Mystic Warriors*, 2000
Don Coldsmith, *The Long Journey Home*, 2001
Hank Edwards, *Gray Warrior*, 1995
Cynthia Haseloff, *Changing Trains*, 2001
Ray Hogan, *The Doomsday Marshal and the Comancheros*, 2001

424

JAMES CARLOS BLAKE

A World of Thieves

(New York, Morrow, 2002)

Story type: Historical; Saga
Subject(s): American West; Crime and Criminals
Major character(s): Sonny LaSalle, Criminal, Student—High School (dropout); John Bones, Lawman; Belle, Abuse Victim (forced into pornography)
Time period(s): 1920s (1928)
Locale(s): Louisiana; Texas

Summary: An honor student, Sonny LaSalle drops out of school and joins his uncles in a New Orleans crime spree. He shoots and kills the son of lawman John Bones and is sentenced to prison for 30 years. After escaping, he hunts down his uncles in Galveston, unaware that John Bones is tracking him to exact revenge. He rescues Belle, a 17-year-old girl who has been drugged and forced to pose for pornographic films. Sonny, his uncles, and Belle embark on another blundering crime spree, still unaware of John Bones who tracks them through a series of oil field shanty towns to a climactic epiphany. Humor softens the brutality to produce a good novel.

Where it's reviewed:
Publishers Weekly, October 23, 2001, page 22

Other books by the same author:
Wildwood Boys, 2000
Red Grass River, 1998
In the Rogue Blood, 1997
The Friends of Pancho Villa, 1996
The Pistoleer, 1995

Other books you might like:
Judy Alter, *Cherokee Rose*, 1996
David L. Fleming, *Border Crossings*, 1993
Kathleen O'Neal Gear, *Bone Walker*, 2001
W. Michael Gear, co-author

Kathleen O'Neal Gear, *The Summoning God*, 2000
W. Michael Gear, co-author
Kathleen O'Neal Gear, *The Visitant*, 1999
W. Michael Gear, co-author

425

MICHAEL BLAKE

The Holy Road

(New York: Villard, 2001)

Story type: Historical; Man Alone
Subject(s): American West; Indians of North America
Major character(s): John Dunbar, Military Personnel (lieutenant who deserts), Warrior (Comanche); Stands with a Fist, Spouse (of John Dunbar), Captive (raised by Indians)
Time period(s): 1870s (1874)
Locale(s): Llando Estacado, Texas

Summary: In this sequel to *Dances with Wolves* Lt. John Dunbar is a Comanche warrior accepted by the People as such. He is married to Stands with a Fist, a white woman raised by the Comanches. It is now 11 years since Dunbar's desertion from the U.S. Army and his decision to live with the Indians, and much has changed. The People, as the Comanche call themselves, are divided and the future looks bleak. The white man and his army are advancing on them and some people want peace while others want war. Dunbar's wife and youngest child are kidnapped by the Texas Rangers, a scenario similar to the story of Cynthia Ann Parker, and he tries a desperate rescue. The novel is more historical than the previous one about Dunbar, but delivers the same emotional punch.

Where it's reviewed:
Publishers Weekly, July 16, 2001, page 155

Other books by the same author:
Marching to Valhalla, 1996
Dances with Wolves, 1990

Other books you might like:
Patrick E. Andrews, *Comanchero Blood*, 1993
Matt Braun, *Texas Empire*, 1997
Wayne Davis, *John Stone and the Choctaw Kid*, 1993
Elmer Kelton, *Badger Boy*, 2000
Texas Rangers. Book 2
Elmer Kelton, *The Buckskin Line*, 1999
Texas Rangers. Book 1

426

LUCILE BOGUE

Blood on the Wind

(Montrose, Colorado: Western Reflections, 2001)

Story type: Young Adult; Indian Culture
Subject(s): American West
Major character(s): Flying Horse Mollie, Indian (Yampa Ute); Thunder Cloud, Parent (Mollie's father), Indian (Yampa Ute); Nathan Meeker, Government Official (Indian agent), Historical Figure
Time period(s): 1870s
Locale(s): Steamboat Springs, Colorado

Summary: Flying Horse Mollie, a young Yampa Ute and her father, Thunder Cloud, prepare for their summer trip to what is now Steamboat Springs, Colorado, only to find the pasture the Utes have used for centuries is now the reservation headquarters. The new Indian agent, who calls himself Father Meeker, is prepared to plow up the Utes' sacred pasture in order to teach them how to farm. The disagreements between the Utes and those whites who believe in Meeker's words grow worse, finally erupting into the infamous Meeker Massacre. A novel for young adults.

Other books by the same author:
One Woman, One Ranch, One Summer, 1997
Miracle on a Mountain, 1987
Dancers on Horseback, 1984

Other books you might like:
Frederic Bean, *Renegade*, 1993
Giff Cheshire, *Renegade River*, 1998
Tracy Dunham, *The Ghost Trail*, 1998
Paul A. Hawkins, *The Seekers*, 1994
Richard S. Wheeler, *Cheyenne Winter*, 1992

427

FRANK BONHAM

Stage Trails West

(Waterville, Maine: Thorndike, 2002)

Story type: Traditional; Collection
Subject(s): Short Stories; American West
Major character(s): Grif Holbrook, Guard (stagecoach)
Time period(s): 19th century (pre-Civil War)
Locale(s): West

Summary: Edited by Bill Pronzini these four short stories all feature stagecoach guard Grif Holbrook.

Where it's reviewed:
Roundup Magazine, February 2002, page 28

Other books by the same author:
One Ride Too Many, 1997
The Canon of Maverick Brands, 1997

Other books you might like:
Rick Bass, *The Sky, the Stars, the Wilderness*, 1997
Max Brand, *The Overland Kid: A Western Trio*, 1999
Jane Candia Coleman, *Moving On*, 1997
H.A. DeRosso, *Under the Burning Sun*, 1997
John D. Nesbitt, *One Foot in the Stirrup*, 1995

428

C.J. BOX

Open Season

(New York: Putnam. 2001)

Story type: Quest
Subject(s): American West; Mystery
Major character(s): Joe Pickett, Game Warden; Vern Dunnegan, Game Warden; Pierre Reynal, Gambler
Time period(s): 2000s (2001)
Locale(s): Twelve Sleep, Wyoming; West

Summary: Joe Pickett is the game warden of Twelve Sleep County, Wyoming. With a growing family and an inadequate salary, Joe struggles to be like his mentor, Vern Dunnegan, but Joe makes political mistakes—like giving a ticket to the governor for not having a fishing license. Then a poacher takes his gun away, something Joe considers a silly mistake until the man ends up murdered. There are a couple of other murders and the usual local political scandals, and Joe finds himself hip deep in trouble. A delightful first novel.

Where it's reviewed:
Publishers Weekly, July 2, 2001, page 57

Other books you might like:
Frederic Bean, *Murder at Spirit Cave*, 1999
Sinclair Browning, *Rode Hard, Put Away Dead*, 2001
Elizabeth Dearl, *Twice Dead*, 2001
Michael McGarrity, *Under the Color of Law*, 2001
Aimee Thurlo, *Shooting Chant*, 2000
David Thurlo, co-author

429

G.G. BOYER

Morgette on the Barbary Coast

(New York: Leisure, 2001)

Story type: Traditional; Man Alone
Subject(s): American West
Major character(s): Dolf Morgette, Prospector (in the Yukon), Bodyguard (for Will); Will Alexander, Friend (of Dolf), Employer (of Dolf); Diana Alexander, Girlfriend (of Dolf)
Time period(s): 1890s (1895)
Locale(s): San Francisco, California

Summary: Dolf Morgette, at loose ends since the death of his wife and son in Alaska, is tracking Forrest Twead who killed Morgette's friend. He follows Twead to San Francisco where he then becomes the guard of Will Alexander, the boss of the Barbary Coast and the enemy of millionaires Stanford and Huntington. Morgette becomes involved with Diana Alexander, Will's daughter, as well as Victoria, a woman from his past. Between woman problems and Twead's attempts to murder him, Morgette wonders if he will get out of the Barbary Coast alive.

Where it's reviewed:
Roundup Magazine, February 2002, page 29

Other books by the same author:
Morgette in the Yukon, 2001
The Guns of Morgette, 2000
Winchester Affidavit, 1997

Other books you might like:
Frederic Bean, *Renegade*, 1993
Giff Cheshire, *Renegade River*, 1998
Tracy Dunham, *The Ghost Trail*, 1998
Paul A. Hawkins, *The Seekers*, 1994
Richard S. Wheeler, *Cheyenne Winter*, 1992

430

MAX BRAND (Pseudonym of Frederick Faust)

The Gauntlet

(New York: Leisure, 2001)

Story type: Traditional; Collection
Subject(s): American West; Short Stories
Time period(s): 19th century (post-Civil War)
Locale(s): West

Summary: This collection contains three novels by Max Brand, all previously published only in periodicals, and here restored to their original lengths. Titles include *The Gauntlet*, originally printed in 1921; *The Blackness of MacTee* from 1933, and *King of Rats*, also from 1933.

Where it's reviewed:
Roundup Magazine, February 2002, page 29

Other books by the same author:
Men Beyond the Law, 2001
The Wolf Strain, 2001
Tales of the Wild West, 2000
The Bright Face of Danger, 2000
The Black Rider and Other Stories, 1996

Other books you might like:
Giff Cheshire, *Renegade River*, 1998
Peter Dawson, *Ghost Brand of the Wishbones*, 1998
Ray Gonzalez, *The Ghost of John Wayne and Other Stories*, 2001
Wayne D. Overholser, *Rainbow Rider: A Western Trio*, 2001
Vicki Piekarski, *12 Tales Told from Women's Perspective*, 2001

431

MAX BRAND (Pseudonym of Frederick Faust)

The House of Gold

(Waterville, Maine: Thorndike, 2001)

Story type: Collection; Quest
Subject(s): American West; Short Stories
Major character(s): James Geraldi, Thief
Time period(s): 19th century (post-Civil War)
Locale(s): West

Summary: Three adventures featuring James Geraldi, the man who stole from thieves. One story has Geraldi stealing an Egyptian treasure from smugglers and returning it to its rightful owner. In another adventure, he joins with other thieves in a plan to break into a safe located in a home on a ranch.

Where it's reviewed:
Roundup Magazine, February 2002, page 29

Other books by the same author:
Don Diablo: A Western Story, 2001
The Tyrant, 2001
The Welding Quirt: A Western Trio, 2001
The Bright Face of Danger, 2000
The Overland Kid: A Western Trio, 1999

Other books you might like:
Dan Cushman, *The Pecos Kid: A Western Duo*, 1999

Robert Easton, *To Find a Place*, 1999
T.T. Flynn, *The Devil's Lode: A Western Trio*, 1999
Louis L'Amour, *Beyond the Great Snow Mountains*, 1999
Les Savage Jr., *The Shadow in Renegade Basin*, 2001

432

MAX BRAND (Pseudonym of Frederick Faust)

The Lone Rider

(Waterville, Maine: Thorndike, 2002)

Story type: Traditional; Quest
Subject(s): American West; Crime and Criminals
Major character(s): Beatrice Crittenden, Heiress; Billy Newlands, Con Artist; Steve Crawford, Mine Owner (gold mine)
Time period(s): 19th century (post-Civil War)
Locale(s): San Francisco, California

Summary: Confidence man Billy Newlands is able to persuade heiress Beatrice Crittenden to marry him. What she doesn't know is that the ceremony is performed by one of Newlands' criminal friends who is about as far from being a minister as Billy is from being a legitimate husband. On the train immediately after the sham wedding, Beatrice begins to regret her hasty action. When the train is derailed, she saves the life of mining engineer Steve Crawford and under the guise of his wife, accompanies Steve to his mine. Steve is physically unable to command his miners and Beatrice is afraid he will lose his claim when Jim Gilson turns up and orders the miners back to work. Only Beatrice knows that Gilson is not his real name.

Where it's reviewed:
Roundup Magazine, February 2002, page 29

Other books by the same author:
Beyond the Outposts, 2001
Men Beyond the Law, 2001
The Tyrant, 2001
Gunman's Goal, 2000
The Bright Face of Danger, 2000

Other books you might like:
Dan Cushman, *The Pecos Kid: A Western Duo*, 1999
Robert Easton, *To Find a Place*, 1999
T.T. Flynn, *The Devil's Lode: A Western Trio*, 1999
Zane Grey, *The Westerners: Stories of the West*, 2000
Ray Hogan, *Guns of Freedom: A Western Duo*, 1999

433

MAX BRAND (Pseudonym of Frederick Faust)

Stolen Gold

(New York: Leisure, 2001)

Story type: Collection
Subject(s): American West; Short Stories
Time period(s): 19th century (post-Civil War)

Summary: Three of Max Brand's vivid Western short novels, including the title story which features his series character, Reata, the man who manages his escapades without carrying a gun. The other two novels are *Sheriff Larrabee's Prisoner* and *A Shower of Silver*.

Where it's reviewed:
Roundup Magazine, February 2002, page 29

Other books by the same author:
Don Diablo: A Western Story, 2001
The Tyrant, 2001
The Welding Quirt: A Western Trio, 2001
The Outlaw Redeemer, 2000
The Peril Trek: A Western Trio, 2000

Other books you might like:
Jane Candia Coleman, *Moving On*, 1997
Jane Candia Coleman, *Stories from Mesa Country*, 1991
Jim Garry, *This Ol' Drought Ain't Broke Us Yet*, 1992
Ernest Haycox, *Powder Smoke & Other Stories*, 1946
Michael Moorcock, *Tales from the Texas Woods*, 1997

434

MAX BRAND

The Survival of Juan Oro

(New York: Leisure, 2002)

Story type: Traditional; Man Alone
Subject(s): American West; Mexicans
Major character(s): Juan Oro, Captive; Don Jose Fontana, Rancher (Mexican), Wealthy; Matias Bordi, Outlaw
Time period(s): 19th century (post-Civil War)
Locale(s): Mexico

Summary: Captured and raised by the Yaqui Indians, Juan Oro is given a Spanish name even though he is most emphatically an American. As he reaches manhood he is captured by Don Jose Fontana, a wealthy Spanish grandee in northern Mexico. Don Jose immediately apprentices him to Matias Bordi, the most notorious outlaw in all Mexico. A deadly shot and skilled with a knife, Bordi undertakes to teach Juan similar skills. Don Jose asks for a single promise from Juan: as soon as he learns all that Bordi can teach him, he must then kill the outlaw.

Other books by the same author:
The Tyrant, 2001
Soft Metal, 2000
The Outlaw Redeemer, 2000
The Rock of Kiever, 2000
The Overland Kid: A Western Trio, 1999

Other books you might like:
Jane Candia Coleman, *Doc Holliday's Gone*, 1999
Ralph Compton, *The Dawn of Fury*, 1996
Robert Easton, *Blood and Money*, 1996
T.T. Flynn, *Death Marks Time in Trampas: A Western Quintet*, 1998
Elmore Leonard, *The Tonto Woman and other Western Stories*, 1998

435

MAX BRAND

The Wolf Strain

(New York: Leisure, 2001)

Story type: Traditional; Collection
Subject(s): American West; Crime and Criminals
Time period(s): 19th century (post-Civil War)
Locale(s): West

Summary: The three short novels included in this work are published here for the first time. In the title story, a man's attempt to return a locket to a lady isn't as simple a task as it seems. *Bared Fangs* tells the story of a falsely convicted man who returns to a town after ten years in prison to clear his name. In *Gallows Gamble*, two cowboys go on one last cattle drive before settling down, only to be caught up in violence and death.

Other books by the same author:
Beyond the Outposts, 2001
Men Beyond the Law, 2001
The Tyrant, 2001
Gunman's Goal, 2000
The Bright Face of Danger, 2000

Other books you might like:
Dan Cushman, *The Pecos Kid: A Western Duo*, 1999
Robert Easton, *To Find a Place*, 1999
T.T. Flynn, *The Devil's Lode: A Western Trio*, 1999
Zane Grey, *The Westerners: Stories of the West*, 2000
Ray Hogan, *Guns of Freedom: A Western Duo*, 1999

436

ALLEN P. BRISTOW

The Pinkerton Eye

(Bloomington, Indiana: 1stBooks Library, 2001)

Story type: Mystery; Man Alone
Subject(s): American West; Crime and Criminals
Major character(s): Kirk Van Pelt, Lawman (constable), Detective (Pinkerton agent); Gerald Merkle, Banker, Thief; Tandy Rostov, Musician (piano player)
Time period(s): 1900s (1905)
Locale(s): Covens Hollow, New York; Tonopah, Nevada; Creede, Colorado

Summary: When Kirk Van Pelt, constable of Covens Hollow, New York, and possessor of a glass eye, accidently shoots a prominent citizen while serving a process, he is forced to leave town. At the request of a local banker, Kirk heads for Tonopah, Nevada, to arrest Gerald Merkle, former cashier and present thief. At Tonopah he becomes involved with several murderers and thieves, as well as a piano player named Tandy Rostov. Rejected by Tandy, he goes back to Covens Hollow and accepts a job with the Pinkerton Detective Agency. He is sent to Creede, Colorado, to investigate some train robberies and runs into Tandy again. They agree to meet in San Francisco on her birthday, and Kirk swears to himself that they will find some way to make a life together.

Where it's reviewed:
Roundup Magazine, February 2002, page 29

Other books you might like:
Frederic Bean, *The Outlaw*, 1993
Sinclair Browning, *Rode Hard, Put Away Dead*, 2001
Elizabeth Dearl, *Twice Dead*, 2001
John Hockenberry, *A River out of Eden*, 2001
Elmer Kelton, *Honor at Daybreak*, 1991

437

JAMES DAVID BUCHANAN

A Horde of Fools

(Waterville, Maine: Thorndike, 2001)

Story type: Historical; Saga
Subject(s): American West; Gold Discoveries
Major character(s): Callie Fisk, Pioneer, Miner; Clarence McDonald, Police Officer (Royal Canadian Mounted Police); Claude Emmett, Outlaw (highwayman), Thief
Time period(s): 1890s (1898)
Locale(s): Daughton, Alaska; St. Louis, Missouri

Summary: Callie Fisk wins a stake in a drawing at her church which includes her passage to Alaska and a prospector's outfit. The arrangement is that Callie will send back her stake plus ten percent to the Congregational Church in Bent Creek, Vermont. It's all very easy because the preacher is certain the gold lies on the ground and only needs to be picked up. Callie leaves for Alaska and meets up with Claude Emmett, a highwayman who makes his living robbing miners. She also meets Sergeant Clarence McDonald of the Royal Canadian Mounted Police. The sergeant is not exactly fond of Americans and wishes they would all go home. He even goes to the extreme of shooting anyone he sees crossing the border. The worst of the people Callie meets are the Swope clan who hold the town of Daughton hostage. With the help of Claude and the Mountie, Callie is determined to defeat the Swopes.

Other books you might like:
Jane Candia Coleman, *The O'Keefe Empire*, 1999
Karen Joy Fowler, *Sister Noon*, 2001
Cecelia Holland, *An Ordinary Woman*, 2001
Jane Kirkpatrick, *All Together in One Place*, 2000
Jane Kirkpatrick, *No Eye Can See*, 2001

438

J. LEE BUTTS

Law Dog

(New York: Berkley, 2001)

Story type: Historical; Man Alone
Subject(s): Quest; American West
Major character(s): Hayden Tilden, Lawman (U.S. Marshal); Saginaw Bob Magruder, Murderer, Outlaw; Franklin J. Lightfoot Jr., Journalist
Time period(s): 1940s (1948)
Locale(s): Little Rock, Arkansas; Philadelphia, Pennsylvania

Summary: Hayden Tilden recounts his life to Franklin J. Lightfoot, Jr., a reporter for a local newspaper. He figures that almost everybody he ever knew is dead, so it won't hurt to tell his life story to this young whippersnapper. Although Hayden crosses paths with such notables as John Wesley Hardin and Wyatt Earp, it is Saginaw Bob Magruder who has the greatest influence on his life. After Magruder murders the whole Tilden family when Hayden is a young boy, he swears to track down Magruder and his gang, an oath he fulfills, becoming a U.S. Marshal in the process.

Other books you might like:
Patrick E. Andrews, *Texican Blood Fight*, 1992
Michael Blake, *Marching to Valhalla*, 1996
Robert J. Conley, *Back to Malachi*, 1997
Ed Gorman, *Dark Trail*, 1998
Page Lambert, *Shifting Stars*, 1997

439

TIM CHAMPLIN

By Flare of Northern Lights

(Waterville, Maine: Thorndike, 2001)

Story type: Traditional; Quest
Subject(s): American West; Gold Discoveries
Major character(s): Terry Brandon, Prospector (for gold); Annie O'Connell, Spouse (of George O'Connell), Prospector; Milton Conrad, Prospector (for gold)
Time period(s): 1890s (1897)
Locale(s): Seattle, Washington; Chilkoot Mountain Pass, Alaska

Summary: Terry Brandon quits his job, leaves his fiancee, and with a total stake of $390 leaves for the gold fields of the Klondike. Along the way, he meets Annie O'Connell, wife of the much older George who, in a jealous rage, tries to shoot Terry. In Seattle Terry learns that his money won't take him all the way to Skagway so he partners with Milton Conrad, son of a wealthy man, who wants to make a fortune on his own without help from his family. When Milton is beaten and robbed, he and Terry face the terrible Chilkoot Mountain Pass without the necessary provisions. Another exciting novel by this well-known Western writer.

Where it's reviewed:
Roundup Magazine, December 2001, page 23

Other books by the same author:
A Trail to Wounded Knee, 2001
Treasure of the Templars, 2000
Wayfaring Strangers, 2000
Lincoln's Ransom, 1999
Tombstone Conspiracy, 1999

Other books you might like:
Laura Crum, *Stickrock*, 2000
Steve Frazee, *Ghost Mine*, 2000
Tim McGuire, *Gold of Cortes*, 2000
Les Savage Jr., *Coffin Gap*, 1997
Richard S. Wheeler, *Flint's Gift*, 1999

440

TIM CHAMPLIN

Flying Eagle

(New York: Leisure, 2001)

Story type: Traditional; Man Alone
Subject(s): American West; Crime and Criminals
Major character(s): Jay McGraw, Guard (for Wells Fargo); Marvin Cutter, Thief (pickpocket); Fletcher Hall, Entertainer (balloonist)
Time period(s): 1880s (1883)
Locale(s): San Francisco, California; Colorado

Summary: Wells Fargo messenger Jay McGraw climbs aboard the Central Pacific for another trip to Chicago as a guard for Wells Fargo's treasure box. He brings along a book to read since his job is usually enough to bore a man to sleep. Not this time, however. Robbers stop the train, but Jay is determined not to give up the treasure box. With the unwilling help of Fletcher Hall, a balloonist, Jay, Fletcher, and the treasure box take to the air in Fletcher's balloon, detouring to Wyoming while attempting to elude the robbers. The robbers follow the balloon and Jay wonders if they will escape, and what part pickpocket Marvin Cutter played in the robbery.

Where it's reviewed:
Roundup Magazine, February 2002, page 31

Other books by the same author:
Treasure of the Templars, 2000
Wayfaring Strangers, 2000
Lincoln's Ransom, 1999
Tombstone Conspiracy, 1999
Deadly Season, 1997

Other books you might like:
Frederic Bean, *Border Justice*, 1994
Mike Blakely, *Dead Reckoning*, 1996
Jack Curtis, *Cut and Branded*, 1993
Robin Gibson, *Ma Calhoun's Boys*, 1992
Wynema McGowan, *Beyond the River*, 1997

441

FREDERICK J. CHIAVENTONE

Moon of Bitter Cold

(New York: Forge, 2002)

Story type: Historical; Indian Wars
Subject(s): American West; Indians of North America
Major character(s): Red Cloud, Historical Figure, Indian (Sioux); Henry Carrington, Historical Figure, Military Personnel (colonel); Margaret Carrington, Historical Figure, Spouse (of Henry Carrington)
Time period(s): 1860s (1865-1866)
Locale(s): Fort Phil Kearny, Wyoming

Summary: This is a historically accurate, as well as fascinating, novelization of the Fetterman Massacre and the events leading up to it as seen from different perspectives. Red Cloud recounts his hatred of whites and his desire to defeat them, while Colonel Henry Carrington provides the military point of view. Margaret Carrington reveals the feminine opinion of the hardships and fear evoked by living along the Bozeman Trail, several hundred miles from what the women of Fort Phil Kearney think of as civilization.

Where it's reviewed:
Roundup Magazine, May 2002, page 29

Other books by the same author:
A Road We Do Not Know, 2000

Other books you might like:
Frederic Bean, *The Red River*, 1998
Rita Cleary, *River Walk*, 2001
Robert J. Conley, *The Peace Chief*, 1998
Kathleen O'Neal Gear, *People of the Silence*, 1997
W. Michael Gear, co-author
Will Henry, *The Brass Command*, 1955

442

LEE CHILD

Echo Burning

(New York: Putnam, 2001)

Story type: Mystery; Man Alone
Series: Jack Reacher
Subject(s): American West; Crime and Criminals; Outcasts
Major character(s): Jack Reacher, Military Personnel (former military police); Carmen Greer, Abuse Victim, Spouse (of Sloop Greer); Sloop Greer, Crime Victim (murdered)
Time period(s): 2000s (2001)
Locale(s): Texas

Summary: Former military policeman Jack Reacher is hitchhiking across West Texas when he accepts a ride from Carmen Greer, an abuse victim whose husband is due to be released from prison. She asks Jack to kill Sloop Greer, her husband, but Jack isn't into murder for hire. He does take a job at the Greers' ranch so he can keep an eye on things. When Sloop Greer is discovered murdered Carmen is arrested. Jack hires a lawyer to defend her, then puts his policing skills to work to find the real killer.

Where it's reviewed:
Library Journal, June 15, 2001, page 101

Other books by the same author:
Running Blind, 2000 (Jack Reacher series)
Tripwire, 2000 (Jack Reacher series)
Die Trying, 1998 (Jack Reacher series)
Killing Floor, 1997 (Jack Reacher series)

Other books you might like:
Frederic Bean, *The Outlaw*, 1993
Sinclair Browning, *Rode Hard, Put Away Dead*, 2001
Elizabeth Dearl, *Twice Dead*, 2001
John Hockenberry, *A River out of Eden*, 2001
Elmer Kelton, *Honor at Daybreak*, 1991

443

RITA CLEARY

River Walk

(New York: Leisure, 2001)

Story type: Historical; Quest
Subject(s): American West; Discovery and Exploration
Major character(s): John Collins, Explorer, Historical Figure; Meriwether Lewis, Explorer, Historical Figure; William Clark, Explorer, Historical Figure
Time period(s): 1800s (1803-1805)
Locale(s): West

Summary: Rita Cleary tells the story of the Lewis and Clark Expedition as seen through the eyes of young John Collins, an 18-year-old member of the company. Collins is healthy and strong, a good shot, good drinker, and illiterate. Along the way, he falls in love with and marries a young Indian widow, but ultimately leaves her behind, to continue on the expedition. The novel fleshes out the accounts of Meriwether Lewis and William Clark by blending the adventure of exploration with political intrigue and very human characters.

Where it's reviewed:
Roundup Magazine, February 2002, page 31

Other books by the same author:
Goldtown, 1996
Sorrel, 1993

Other books you might like:
Laura Crum, *Stickrock*, 2000
Steve Frazee, *Ghost Mine*, 2000
Tim McGuire, *Gold of Cortes*, 2000
Les Savage Jr., *Coffin Gap*, 1997
Richard S. Wheeler, *Flint's Gift*, 1999

444

MARGARET COEL

The Thunder Keeper

(New York: Berkley, 2001)

Story type: Mystery; Indian Culture
Series: Father John O'Malley/Vicky Holden
Subject(s): American West; Indians of North America
Major character(s): John O'Malley, Religious (Catholic priest), Detective—Amateur; Vicky Holden, Indian (Arapaho), Lawyer; Duncan Grover, Crime Victim (murdered)
Time period(s): 2000s (2001)
Locale(s): Wind River Reservation, Wyoming; Denver, Colorado

Summary: Arapaho lawyer Vicky Holden is temporarily assigned to Denver, and her sleuthing companion, Father O'Malley, feels lost. When young Duncan Grover is murdered during a spirit quest, only Father O'Malley knows it because he hears the details in the confessional. Other problems arise. A corporation wants to steal the rights to the reservation's diamond grounds, and Vicky is having difficulties being away from her children and husband. The story contains good background on the reservation.

Where it's reviewed:
Publishers Weekly, August 13, 2001, page 289

Other books by the same author:
The Spirit Woman, 2000 (Vicky Holden series)
Honor, 1999 (Vicky Holden series)
The Last Bird, 1999 (Vicky Holden series)
Hole in the Wall, 1998 (Vicky Holden series)
The Story Teller, 1998 (Vicky Holden series)

Other books you might like:
Frederic Bean, *Murder at the Spirit Cave*, 1999
Sinclair Browning, *Rode Hard, Put Away Dead*, 2001
Elizabeth Dearl, *Twice Dead*, 2001
Skye Kathleen Moody, *K Falls*, 2001
Aimee Thurlo, *Shooting Chant*, 2000
Ella Clah series

445

JANE CANDIA COLEMAN

Doc Holliday's Gone

(New York: Leisure, 2002)

Story type: Collection; Historical
Subject(s): American West; Crime and Criminals; Short Stories
Time period(s): 19th century (post-Civil War)
Locale(s): Tombstone, Arizona

Summary: Each of the two short novels in this book feature an historical character—Doc Holliday in the title story and John Slaughter in the second. *Doc Holliday's Gone* describes Holliday's lover, Mary Katherine Horony, also known as Big Nose Kate, a former prostitute. The famous shoot-out at the O.K. Corral and Holliday's role in it are featured prominently. In *Mrs. Slaughter*, Viola Howell marries John Slaughter, a much older man, while still in her teens. They too are present for the events in Tombstone, but provide a much different point of view.

Other books by the same author:
The O'Keefe Empire, 1999
I, Pearl Hart, 1998
Moving On, 1997
Doc Holliday's Woman, 1995
Stories from Mesa Country, 1991

Other books you might like:
Max Brand, *The Overland Kid: A Western Trio*, 1999
Eugene Cunningham, *Trails West*, 2000
Robert Easton, *To Find a Place*, 1999
Zane Grey, *Rangle River*, 2001
Will Henry, *Ghost Wolf of Thunder Mountain*, 2000

446

JANE CANDIA COLEMAN

Mountain Time

(Waterville, Maine: Thorndike, 2001)

Story type: Traditional; Quest
Subject(s): American West; History
Time period(s): 20th century; 21st century (1979-2001)
Locale(s): West

Summary: In this book, which is part memoir, part essay, and part documentation, Coleman shares with the reader the people and places that have inspired her prose.

Other books by the same author:
Desperate Acts, 2001
Borderlands, 2000
Doc Holliday's Gone, 1999
The O'Keefe Empire, 1999
I, Pearl Hart, 1998

Other books you might like:
Phyllis de la Garza, *Camels West*, 1999
Ed Gorman, *Storm Riders*, 1999
Cynthia Haseloff, *Man Without Medicine*, 1996
Cecelia Holland, *Lily Nevada*, 1999
Max McCoy, *Jesse*, 1999

447

ROBERT J. CONLEY

Spanish Jack

(New York: St. Martin's Press, 2001)

Story type: Historical; Indian Culture
Subject(s): American West; Indians of North America
Major character(s): Jack Spaniard, Historical Figure, Indian (Cherokee)
Time period(s): 19th century (pre-Civil War)
Locale(s): West

Summary: This novel follows the improbable adventures of Jack Spaniard, otherwise known as Spanish Jack, as he moves from being a horse thief to riverboat gambler to vigilante to, finally, an upright citizen.

Where it's reviewed:
Publishers Weekly, July 30, 2001, page 61

Other books by the same author:
Broke Loose, 2000 (Barjack series)
Fugitive's Trail, 2000
The Cherokee Dragon, 2000
Barjack, 1999 (Barjack series)
Incident at Buffalo Crossing, 1998

Other books you might like:
Margaret Allan, *The Last Mammoth*, 1995
Mike Blakely, *Comanche Dawn*, 1998
Joseph Bruchac, *The Waters Between*, 1998
Don Coldsmith, *The Lost Band*, 2000
Karen Osborn, *Between Earth and Sky*, 1996

448

DANE COOLIDGE

Man from Wyoming

(New York: Leisure, 2001)

Story type: Traditional; Ranch Life
Subject(s): American West; Crime and Criminals

Major character(s): Clayton Hawks, Rancher; Charlotte Pennyman, Fiance(e) (of Clayton); Jim Keck, Thief (suspected, of cattle)
Time period(s): 19th century (post-Civil War)
Locale(s): Powder Springs, Wyoming

Summary: Clayton Hawks returns to Powder Springs, Wyoming, to clear up some rustling problems in return for his father's giving him the Lazy B Ranch, but things don't go smoothly. For one thing, Jim Keck is paying too much attention to Charlotte Pennyman, Clayton's fiancee, and for another Clayton wouldn't trust Keck even if he weren't flirting with Charlotte. Clayton suspects Keck of stealing more than his fiancee; he suspects him of stealing cattle.

Where it's reviewed:
Roundup Magazine, February 2002, page 29

Other books you might like:
Phyllis de la Garza, *Camels West*, 1999
Ed Gorman, *Storm Riders*, 1999
Cynthia Haseloff, *Man Without Medicine*, 1996
Cecelia Holland, *Lily Nevada*, 1999
Max McCoy, *Jesse*, 1999

449

JOHN DUNCKLEE

Double Vengeance

(New York: Leisure, 2001)

Story type: Traditional; Quest
Subject(s): American West; Indians of North America
Major character(s): Joe Holly, Military Personnel (undercover agent); Betsy Willoughby, Spouse (of Captain Willoughby); Frog Eyes, Indian (Apache)
Time period(s): 19th century (post-Civil War)
Locale(s): Tombstone, Arizona; Camp Huachuca, Arizona

Summary: Joe Holly is sent to Camp Huachuca to hunt down the insider who is giving the thieving Clanton brothers information about the army payroll shipments. Betsy Willoughby, wife of his immediate commanding officer, flirts with, then seduces him. He is cashiered out of the army for fighting with another lieutenant who threatens him for keeping company with Betsy. Joe spends the night with her, then discovers by accident she is the one providing inside information to the Clantons. Joe persuades his old Apache friend, Frog Eyes, to help him stop the next robbery in exchange for the Clantons' horses. A lively story with a strong sense of place.

Where it's reviewed:
Roundup Magazine, February 2002, page 29

Other books by the same author:
Graciela of the Border, 2000
Genevieve of Tombstone, 1999

Other books you might like:
Cynthia Haseloff, *Man Without Medicine*, 1996
Cecelia Holland, *Lily Nevada*, 1999
Andrew Huebner, *American by Blood*, 2000
Earl Murray, *Gabriella*, 1999
G. Clifton Wisler, *Ross's Gap*, 1999

450

KATHLEEN EAGLE

You Never Can Tell

(New York: Morrow, 2001)

Story type: Traditional; Quest
Subject(s): American West; Historical; Indians of North America
Major character(s): Kole Kills Crow, Indian, Fugitive; Heather Reardon, Journalist
Time period(s): 2000s (2001)
Locale(s): West; Hollywood, California

Summary: In an essentially two character novel, Eagle tells the story of Kole Kills Crow, a hero to the American Indian movement, and a fugitive in the eyes of the law. He is found by journalist Heather Reardon hiding in a cabin in a remote area and making beautiful flutes to support himself. Heather wants to tell his story because she believes he is a hero. In the process of interviewing Kole, she falls in love with him and becomes involved in the Indian movement.

Where it's reviewed:
Publishers Weekly, July 30, 2001, page 60

Other books by the same author:
The Last Good Man, 2000
The Last True Cowboy, 1999
The Night Remembers, 1997
Sunrise Song, 1996
To Each His Own, 1992

Other books you might like:
Cynthia Haseloff, *Man Without Medicine*, 1996
Cecelia Holland, *Lily Nevada*, 1999
Andrew Huebner, *American by Blood*, 2000
Earl Murray, *Gabriella*, 1999
G. Clifton Wisler, *Ross's Gap*, 1999

451

ROBERT FLYNN

Tie-Fast Country

(Fort Worth: Texas Christian University, 2001)

Story type: Saga; Ranch Life
Subject(s): American West; Ranch Life
Major character(s): Chance Carter, Television (station manager); Clarista, Grandparent (Chance's grandmother)
Time period(s): 20th century (1900-1940)
Locale(s): Texas

Summary: Chance Carter, manager of a Florida TV station, hates his grandmother, Clarista, so when he gets a call that the old woman is sick, he sees it as an opportunity to put her in a nursing home. He reckons without Clarista, who puts him to work fixing fences, and roping, riding, and herding cattle. Resentful at first, Chance realizes the truth behind his grandmother's killing of two men and why his own mother ran off. He comes to realize he doesn't hate his grandmother after all.

Where it's reviewed:
Publishers Weekly, August 27, 2001, page 53

Other books by the same author:
Living with the Hyenas, 1995
The Last Klick, 1994
In the House of the Lord, 1991
The Sounds of Rescue, the Signs of Hope, 1989
Seasonal Rain and Other Stories, 1986

Other books you might like:
Jack Ballas, *Gun Boss*, 1999
L.D. Clark, *A Bright Tragic Thing*, 1992
Charles Hackenberry, *Friends*, 1993
Paul A. Hawkins, *White Moon Tree*, 1994
Suzann Ledbetter, *Pure Justice*, 1997

452

T.T. FLYNN

Long Journey to Deep Canon

(New York: Leisure, 2002)

Story type: Traditional; Collection
Subject(s): American West; Short Stories
Time period(s): 19th century (post-Civil War)
Locale(s): West

Summary: Collected here are four of Flynn's short novels that contain drama, excitement, a strong sense of place, and evocative history. In *The Outlaw Breed*, Sheriff Brad Tantrall is the son and nephew of infamous outlaws and the brother of a convicted murderer, making his job as a lawman all that more difficult. Matt Donnigan is released from prison in *Bitter Valley*, after serving time for a crime he did not commit. He returns home to find his partner dead, and his ranch in ruins. *Bullets to the Pecos* concerns a treacherous cattle drive from Texas to Colorado where not all the hazards come from nature. The title story tells the tale of Dave Calhoun's pursuit of a man who frames him for a crime of which he is innocent.

Other books by the same author:
Ride to Glory, 2000
The Devil's Lode: A Western Trio, 1999
Death Marks Time in Trampas: A Western Quintet, 1998
Rawhide, 1996
Hell-for-Leather Rider, 1995

Other books you might like:
Rick Bass, *The Sky, the Stars, the Wilderness*, 1997
Max Brand, *Tales of the Wild West*, 2000
Jane Candia Coleman, *Borderlands*, 2000
Will Henry, *Tumbleweeds*, 1999
Ray Hogan, *The Red Eagle*, 2001

453

STEVE FRAZEE

Voices in the Hill: Western Stories

(Waterville, Maine: Thorndike, 2002)

Story type: Traditional; Collection
Subject(s): American West; Short Stories
Time period(s): 19th century (post-Civil War)
Locale(s): West

Summary: Using harsh reality and imagery, these five short stories showcase Frazee's historical knowledge.

Where it's reviewed:
Roundup Magazine, February 2002, page 28

Other books by the same author:
Ghost Mine, 2000
Hidden Gold, 1997
The Way through the Mountains, 1971
Bragg's Fancy Woman, 1966

Other books you might like:
C.A. Bauer, *The White Horses*, 1999
Frank Bonham, *One Ride Too Many*, 1997
H.A. DeRosso, *Under the Burning Sun*, 1997
Bill Pronzini, editor
Robert Franklin Gish, *First Horses*, 1993
Anna Linzer, *Ghost Dancing*, 1998

454

MICAELA GILCHRIST

The Good Journey

(New York: Simon & Schuster, 2001)

Story type: Historical; Indian Wars
Subject(s): American West; Indians of North America
Major character(s): Mary Bullitt, Historical Figure, Spouse (of Henry Atkinson); Henry Atkinson, Historical Figure, Military Personnel (general); Black Hawk, Historical Figure, Chieftain (Sauk)
Time period(s): 19th century (pre-Civil War)
Locale(s): Jefferson Barracks, Missouri

Summary: Headstrong Mary Bullitt marries General Henry Atkinson, a much older and very autocratic man. For the next 16 years they live at Jefferson Barracks in Missouri, where the general is responsible for keeping Black Hawk and his warrior Sauk under control while at the same time taking their land. The situation is complicated by the fact that Black Hawk and Atkinson have a personal feud involving murder. The story is told through Mary's diary after she is widowed and some first person accounts by other characters. A very stirring novel based on fact.

Where it's reviewed:
Publishers Weekly, July 16, 2001, page 159

Other books you might like:
Sanora Babb, *Cry of the Tinamou*, 1997
Charles Brashear, *Killing Cynthia Ann*, 1999
Tracy Dunham, *The Changing Trail*, 1999
Tracy Dunham, *The Long Trail Home*, 1997
Ken Englade, *Brothers in Blood*, 1998

455

RAY GONZALEZ

The Ghost of John Wayne and Other Stories

(Tucson: University of Arizona, 2001)

Story type: Modern; Collection

Subject(s): American West; Short Stories
Time period(s): 2000s (2001)

Summary: *The Ghost of John Wayne and Other Stories* is Gonzalez' first collection of short fiction. The 25 short stories and sketches have a Southwestern and Latino flavor.

Where it's reviewed:
Publishers Weekly, September 24, 2001, page 68

Other books you might like:
Max Brand, *The Outlaw Redeemer*, 2000
T.T. Flynn, *The Devil's Lode: A Western Trio*, 1999
John Jakes, *A Century of Great Western Stories*, 2000 editor
Les Savage Jr., *The Shadow in Renegade Basin*, 2001
E. Donald Two-Rivers, *Survivor's Medicine*, 1998

456

ED GORMAN, Editor

The Blue and the Gray Undercover

(New York: Leisure, 2001)

Story type: Historical; Collection
Subject(s): Civil War; Short Stories; Espionage
Time period(s): 1860s (1861-1865)
Locale(s): South

Summary: Gorman collects 18 original stories about both Union and Confederate spies during the American Civil War. Characters are both male and female, slave and free, fictional and historical. Other contributors besides Gorman include Robert J. Randisi, Loren D. Estleman, and Kristine Kathryn Rusch. The tone ranges from humorous to tragic, and the stories are, by turns, romantic, suspenseful, horrific, and action-packed.

Where it's reviewed:
Publishers Weekly, November 5, 2001, page 41
Roundup Magazine, February 2002, page 29

Other books by the same author:
Lawless, 2000
Graves' Retreat, 1999
Storm Riders, 1999
Dark Trail, 1998
Trouble Man, 1998

Other books you might like:
Rick Bass, *The Sky, the Stars, the Wilderness*, 1997
Tim Champlin, *Lincoln's Ransom*, 1999
Tim Champlin, *Tombstone Conspiracy*, 1999
L.D. Clark, *A Bright Tragic Thing*, 1992
Louis L'Amour, *Monument Rock*, 1998

457

JANICE GRAHAM

Sarah's Window

(New York: Putnam, 2001)

Story type: Modern; Saga
Subject(s): American West
Major character(s): Sarah Bryden, Waiter/Waitress; Billy Moon, Teacher (high school history), Widow(er); John Wilde, Scientist (physicist), Professor
Time period(s): 2000s (2001)
Locale(s): Flint Hills, Kansas

Summary: Sarah Bryden wants to abandon the Flint Hills of Kansas for more exciting places, but when her grandfather loses a leg in a quarry accident, she comes home from college to care for him. She takes a job as a waitress, certainly not the career she had planned, and is wooed by Billy Moon, a widowed high school history teacher, not the beau she had in mind. When John Wilde moves to town, Sarah falls hard for him despite the inconvenience of his wife and mentally disturbed son. A romantic novel whose setting in the Flint Hills is beautifully etched.

Where it's reviewed:
Booklist, October 15, 2001, page 382
Library Journal, October 1, 2001, page 140
Publishers Weekly, September 17, 2001, page 55

Other books by the same author:
Firebird, 1998

Other books you might like:
C.A. Bauer, *The White Horses*, 1999
Jack Curtis, *Easter in Calico*, 1999
Cecelia Holland, *Lily Nevada*, 1999
Richard S. Wheeler, *Masterson*, 1999
Richard S. Wheeler, *Sun Mountain*, 1999

458

ZANE GREY

Open Range

(Waterville, Maine: Thorndike, 2002)

Story type: Traditional; Ranch Life
Subject(s): American West
Major character(s): Kyle ''Panhandle'' Smith, Cowboy; Lucy Blake, Girlfriend (of Panhandle); Jard Hardman, Rancher, Saloon Keeper/Owner
Time period(s): 19th century (post-Civil War)
Locale(s): Marko, New Mexico

Summary: Panhandle Smith dreams of becoming a top hand, and pursuit of this dream makes him a vagabond. Returning home for a visit, Panhandle learns his family has moved to Marko, New Mexico, where a crooked rancher and saloon owner named Jard Hardman has cheated his father. He also finds out that his old sweetheart, Lucy Blake, is living with his family because her father is unjustly in jail. The price for the release of Lucy's father is the marriage of Lucy to Hardman's son, Dick. Panhandle discovers a valley of wild horses, enough to raise the money to free Lucy's father. Hardman though, has no intention of letting him succeed, nor does he intend to let his son lose Lucy. This is an exciting novel as only Zane Grey can write.

Where it's reviewed:
Roundup Magazine, February 2002, page 29

Other books by the same author:
Rangle River, 2001

The Westerners: Stories of the West, 2000
The Great Trek, 1999
Woman of the Frontier, 1998
Rangers of the Lone Star, 1997

Other books you might like:
Frederic Bean, *Law of the Gun*, 1993
Clifford Blair, *Storm over the Lightening L*, 1993
K. Follis Cheatham, *The Adventures of Elizabeth Fortune*, 2000
Jane Candia Coleman, *Moving On*, 1997
Harold Coyle, *Until the End*, 1996

459

FRED GROVE

Destiny Valley

(New York: Leisure, 2001)

Story type: Traditional; Ranch Life
Subject(s): American West
Major character(s): Evan Shelby, Invalid (tuberculosis); Dave Logan, Rancher; Lucinda Holloway, Rancher Lucinda
Time period(s): 19th century (post-Civil War)
Locale(s): Rosita, New Mexico

Summary: Evan Shelby comes to the Gila Wilderness of New Mexico Territory in a last-ditch effort to cure his tuberculosis. He has been clear of any symptoms for six months when Dave Logan stops by to invite him to a meeting with the other small ranchers and farmers of Rosita. They are concerned about a large Texas ranching outfit that has moved into the valley and is pushing people to sell their property. Evan attends the meeting and finds himself agreeing to help his neighbors, little guessing he will fall in love with the owner of the Texas ranch, Lucinda Holloway.

Where it's reviewed:
Roundup Magazine, February 2002, page 31

Other books by the same author:
Red River Stage, 2001
Destiny Valley, 2000
Trail of the Rogues, 2000
Into the Far Mountains, 1999
Bitter Trumpet, 1989

Other books you might like:
Jack Ballas, *Tomahawk Canyon*, 1992
Don Bendell, *Coyote Run*, 1995
Sam Brown, *Devil's Rim*, 1998
Sam Brown, *Ross Henry*, 1991
Bob Kody, *Gold Mountain*, 1994

460

FRED GROVE

The Years of Fear

(Waterville, Maine: Thorndike, 2002)

Story type: Modern; Quest
Subject(s): American West; Crime and Criminals; Indians of North America
Major character(s): Roy Bunch, Butcher, Boyfriend (of Mary Roan); Bill Hale, Rancher, Outlaw; Tom White, FBI Agent
Time period(s): 1920s (1921-1924)
Locale(s): Osage County, Oklahoma

Summary: The novel *The Years of Fear* is a combination of fiction and true crime. In the 1920s, the Oklahoma Osage Indians are the richest people, on a per capita basis, in the United States. They also have an inordinately high murder rate. Beginning in 1921, the number of unsolved murders of Osage increases dramatically, with the victims dying by gun, by knife, and even by dynamite. Roy Bunch is romancing Henry Roan's wife, Mary, so when Henry is murdered, Roy is the logical suspect. Bill Hale offers him a thousand dollars to leave town, which puzzles him, since he knows Hale only by reputation. Upset over yet another murder, the Tribal Council asks the Justice Department to send an FBI agent to investigate. Tom White and four other agents get the assignment, which will turn out to be the strangest case of their careers.

Where it's reviewed:
Roundup Magazine, February, 2002 page 30

Other books by the same author:
Red River Stage, 2001
A Distance of Ground, 2000
Destiny Valley, 2000
Into the Far Mountains, 1999
Man on a Red Horse, 1998

Other books you might like:
Max Brand, *The Outlaw Redeemer*, 2000
T.T. Flynn, *Night of the Comanche Moon*, 2000
John Jakes, *A Century of Great Western Stories*, 2000 editor
Les Savage Jr., *Coffin Gap*, 1997
Michael Zimmer, *Where the Buffalo Roam*, 1999

461

WILL HENRY

The Legend of Sotoju Mountain

(Waterville, Maine: Thorndike, 2002)

Story type: Traditional; Collection
Subject(s): American West; Short Stories
Time period(s): 19th century (post-Civil War)
Locale(s): West

Summary: The three stories in this collection by the prolific author Will Henry feature Indians.

Where it's reviewed:
Roundup Magazine, February 2002, page 30

Other books by the same author:
Ghost Wolf of Thunder Mountain, 2000
Tumbleweeds, 1999
Yellowstone Kelly, 1998
Journey to Shiloh, 1997
The Bear Paw Horses, 1996

Other books you might like:
Max Brand, *The Black Rider and Other Stories*, 1996
Peter Dawson, *Rattlesnake Mesa*, 1997

Ray Hogan, *Legend of a Badman: A Western Quintet*, 1998
Louis L'Amour, *Monument Rock*, 1998
Elmore Leonard, *The Tonto Woman and Other Western Stories*, 1998

462

DOUGLAS HIRT

A Good Town

(New York: Leisure, 2001)

Story type: Traditional; Man Alone
Subject(s): American West; Crime and Criminals
Major character(s): Howie Blake, Drifter, Cowboy; Dobie Tinkerman, Drifter, Sidekick (of Howie Blake); Waldo Fritz, Outlaw, Thief
Time period(s): 19th century (post-Civil War)
Locale(s): Arizona

Summary: Howie Blake and his friend, Dobie Tinkerman, have modest aspirations—they want to make a living and settle down in a nice town. Waldo Fritz offers a paying job—armed robbery—and the two men decide to try it on for size. Neither is very good at the profession, so they leave Fritz and head to Arizona to join the Rangers and help people instead of robbing them. That's when they discover that Waldo Fritz isn't through with them.

Other books by the same author:
The Wrong Man, 2000
Deadwood, 1998
Brandish, 1997
Cripple Creek, 1997
McKendree, 1997

Other books you might like:
Matt Braun, *Texas Empire*, 1997
Jerry Craven, *Snake Mountain*, 2000
Zane Grey, *Woman of the Frontier*, 1998
Elmer Kelton, *The Smiling Country*, 1998
Jory Sherman, *The Baron Range*, 1998

463

KEN HODGSON

Hard Bounty

(New York: Pinnacle, 2001)

Story type: Traditional; Man Alone
Subject(s): American West; Crime and Criminals
Major character(s): Asa Cain, Bounty Hunter; Wilburn Deevers, Lawman (sheriff); Brock Dolven, Outlaw (bank robber)
Time period(s): 19th century (post-Civil War)
Locale(s): Wolf Springs, Texas

Summary: They call bounty hunter Asa Cain the undertaker's friend because he often brings in outlaws dead rather than alive. After Asa turns his latest bodies over to Sheriff Wilburn Deevers, he goes home to see his mother and sister, but when he arrives, the help is dead and his mother and sister are missing. Enraged, he returns to town to wait for word of what gang kidnapped his kin. When Texas Governor Davis comes to town, Davis tells Asa that his mother has been seen holding up banks with Brock Dolven and his gang. Disbelieving, Asa tracks down the gang and faces a terrible secret.

Where it's reviewed:
Roundup Magazine, April 2002, page 30

Other books by the same author:
Lone Survivor, 2001
The Bloody Benders, 1999

Other books you might like:
Mike Blakely, *Summer of Pearls*, 2000
Terry C. Johnston, *Death Rattle*, 1999
Titus Bass series
Michael Kasser, *Warrior's Honor*, 1999
Robert Lake, *Mountain Man's Vengeance*, 1989
Preston Lewis, *Hard Texas Winter*, 1981

464

WILL JAMES

Cowboy in the Making

(Missoula, Montana: Mountain Press, 2001)

Story type: Traditional; Man Alone
Subject(s): American West
Major character(s): Billy, Child; Jean Beaupre, Trapper
Time period(s): 19th century (post-Civil War)
Locale(s): West

Summary: When young Billy's father is killed by a bull he is only four-years-old. The next year, Jean Beaupre, or Bopy as Billy calls him, takes the young boy with him on his travels through the West, including Canada where Bopy has his trap lines. Billy learns to draw bucking horses, to rope with cowboys, and to play with his pet wolves. He even learns to protect himself by killing a grizzly bear. A coming-of-age story for young readers.

Where it's reviewed:
Roundup Magazine, February 2002, page 30

Other books by the same author:
Will James Book of Cowboy Stories, 1951
The American Cowboy, 1942
Horses I Have Known, 1940
My First Horse, 1940
The Dark Horse, 1939

Other books you might like:
Katherine Ayres, *North by Night*, 1998
Joseph Bruchac, *The Arrow over the Door*, 1998
Joseph Bruchac, *The Heart of a Chief*, 1998
Cornelia Cornelissen, *Soft Rain*, 1996
Marie-Louise Fitzpatrick, *The Long March*, 1998

465

J.A. JANCE

Paradise Lost

(New York: Morrow, 2001)

Story type: Modern; Mystery
Series: Joanna Brady. Book 9

Subject(s): American West; Crime and Criminals
Major character(s): Joanna Brady, Police Officer (sheriff); Jenny Brady, Child (Joanna's daughter); Butch Dixon, Spouse (Joanna's husband)
Time period(s): 2000s (2001)
Locale(s): Cochise County, Arizona

Summary: Sheriff Joanna Brady's daughter, Jenny, and her friend discover a dead body while they are AWOL from a camp out. Joanna and Butch are out of town attending a sheriff's convention and the wedding of a friend when they are notified. Joanna goes back to Cochise County, but worries that an old girlfriend of Butch's will seduce her husband while she is gone. Fearing the murderer may attempt to kill Jenny, Joanna has family members guard her. In addition, her mother's meddling may be responsible for Jenny's friend being killed. All in all, Joanna has as much as she can handle and maybe even more.

Where it's reviewed:
Publishers Weekly, July 23, 2001, page 53

Other books by the same author:
Devil's Claw, 2000 (Joanna Brady series)
Kiss of the Bees, 2000
Breach of Duty, 1999 (J.P. Beaumont series)
Desert Heat, 1999 (Joanna Brady series)
Dead to Rights, 1996 (J.P. Beaumont series)

Other books you might like:
Frederic Bean, *Murder at the Spirit Cave*, 1999
Peter Bowen, *Thunder Horse*, 1999
Carol Cail, *The Seeds of Time*, 2001
John Paxon, *The Golden Trail of Murder*, 2001
M.K. Preston, *Perhaps She'll Die*, 2001

466

TERRY C. JOHNSTON

Turn the Stars Upside Down

(New York: St. Martin's Press, 2001)

Story type: Indian Wars; Saga
Series: Plainsman. Book 16
Subject(s): American West; Indians of North America
Major character(s): Crazy Horse, Historical Figure, Indian (Sioux); Red Cloud, Historical Figure, Indian (Sioux); Spotted Tail, Indian (Sioux), Historical Figure
Time period(s): 1870s (1877)
Locale(s): Camp Robinson, Nebraska

Summary: This is an account of the surrender and death of Crazy Horse, the famous Sioux war chieftain, as seen through the eyes of Johnston's continuing character, the Plainsman. Johnston explores the events leading up to Crazy Horse's stabbing, including the jealousy of Red Cloud and the false translation of Crazy Horse's agreement to scout for the army, as well as Crazy Horse's seeking asylum at his uncle Spotted Tail's agency. Heavily historical, but nevertheless exciting.

Where it's reviewed:
Publishers Weekly, July 30, 2001, page 60

Other books by the same author:
Wolf Mountain Moon, 1997 (The Plainsman. Book 12)
A Cold Day in Hell, 1995 (The Plainsman. Book 11)
Trumpet on the Land, 1995 (The Plainsman. Book 10)
Reap the Whirlwind, 1994 (The Plainsman. Book 9)
Blood Song, 1993 (The Plainsman. Book 8)

Other books you might like:
Charles Brashear, *Killing Cynthia Ann*, 1999
Robert J. Conley, *The Cherokee Dragon*, 2000
Will Cook, *Until Shadows Fall*, 2000
Andrew Huebner, *American by Blood*, 2000
Kay L. McDonald, *Beyond the Vision*, 2000

467

ALLEN MORRIS JONES

Last Year's River

(New York: Houghton Mifflin, 2001)

Story type: Modern; Indian Culture
Subject(s): American West; Indians of North America
Major character(s): Virginia Price, Debutante, Pregnant Teenager; Henry Mohr, Veteran, Cowboy
Time period(s): 1920s (1924)
Locale(s): Wyoming

Summary: Seventeen-year-old Virginia Price is raped and impregnated by her boyfriend. Seeking to hide her daughter's condition, Virginia's mother sends her to a remote Wyoming ranch to have the baby and then give it up for adoption. At the ranch, Virginia meets Henry Mohr, the half-Indian stepson of the ranch owner. Henry is a WWI veteran trying to recover from the effects of the war and an abusive childhood. He loves to go to the mountains hunting by himself. Virginia, on the other hand, misses the parties she used to attend. Suddenly Virginia's boyfriend appears, having decided he wants to marry her after all, and is shocked when she doesn't fall into his arms in gratitude. Despite their differences, Virginia and Henry have fallen in love and she must decide what is best for her and her baby.

Where it's reviewed:
Library Journal, October 1, 2001, page 140

Other books you might like:
Paula Gunn Allen, *Spider Woman's Granddaughters*, 1990
Rosanne Bittner, *Song of the Wolf*, 1992
Diane Glancy, *Flutie*, 1998
Cynthia Haseloff, *Man Without Medicine*, 1996
Page Lambert, *Shifting Stars*, 1997

468

ELMER KELTON

The Way of the Coyote

(New York: Forge, 2001)

Story type: Traditional; Man Alone
Series: Texas Rangers. Book 3
Subject(s): American West
Major character(s): Rusty Shannon, Lawman (Texas Ranger); Andy Pickard, Captive (of the Comanches); Buddy-Boy Oldham, Farmer, Outcast
Time period(s): 19th century (post-Civil War)

Locale(s): Texas

Summary: The Civil War is finally officially over, but its bitterness lingers in Texas. Rusty Shannon tries to resume his pre-war life and work on his homestead with the help of Andy Pickard, a young boy just rescued from the Comanches, but Buddy-Boy Oldham and his family confiscate Rusty's land. The feud between the Oldhams and Rusty goes back a long time and there seems to be little way to make peace between the parties. Another conflict is brewing between Andy Pickard and the Comanches, who are tracking him, because he killed a Comanche in order to save Rusty. Since Andy was raised by the Comanche, killing one of his own earns him death if they catch him. Rusty's difficulties culminate when the baby son of the woman he once loved is kidnapped by the Comanches.

Where it's reviewed:
Roundup Magazine, December 2001, page 25

Other books by the same author:
Badger Boy, 2000 (Texas Rangers. Book 2)
The Buckskin Line, 1999 (Texas Rangers. Book 1)
The Smiling Country, 1998
Cloudy in the West, 1997
The Pumpkin Rollers, 1996

Other books you might like:
Mary Clearman Blue, *Lambing out and Other Stories*, 2001
Will Henry, *Tumbleweeds*, 1999
John Legg, *Siege at Fort Defiance*, 1994
Larry McMurtry, *Comanche Moon*, 1997
Larry McMurtry, *Dead Man's Walk*, 1995

469

MARY KING

Quincie Bolliver

(Lubbock: Texas Tech University, 2001)

Story type: Modern; Saga
Subject(s): American West; Oil
Major character(s): Quincie Bolliver, Teenager (13-year-old); Curtin Bolliver, Parent (of Quincie), Oil Industry Worker (muleskinner); Judith Paradise, Landlord (owner of boarding house)
Time period(s): 1930s
Locale(s): Good Union, Texas

Summary: Quincie Bolliver is the 13-year-old daughter of an old field muleskinner. Poor in an age when poverty is expected, Quincie and her father, Curtin, arrive in Good Union, Texas, a town where the oil boom has stopped. They stop at Judith Paradise's boarding house, where they buy dinner and a night's lodging. Curtin, a rather shiftless wanderer, finds a job and the two settle down in Good Union. A coming-of-age novel that is gritty and poignant.

Where it's reviewed:
Roundup Magazine, February 2002, page 31

Other books by the same author:
You Can Hear the Echo, 1965
A Peculiar Thing, 1950
Those Other People, 1946

Other books you might like:
Patrick E. Andrews, *Comanchero Blood*, 1993
Matt Braun, *Texas Empire*, 1997
Patrick Dearen, *The Illegal Man*, 1998
Elmer Kelton, *Honor at Daybreak*, 1991
Elaine Long, *Jenny's Mountain*, 1987

470

JANE KIRKPATRICK

What Once We Loved

(Colorado Springs, Colorado: WaterBrook, 2001)

Story type: Historical; Saga
Series: Kinship and Courage. Book 3
Subject(s): American West; Gold Discoveries
Major character(s): Ruth Martin, Pioneer, Widow(er); Mazy Bacon, Pioneer; Suzanne Culver, Pioneer, Handicapped (blind)
Time period(s): 1850s (1853-1859)
Locale(s): Table Rock Country, Oregon

Summary: While this third volume of the Kinship and Courage series focuses on Ruth Martin and her dream of independence for herself and her children in the Table Rock country of southern Oregon, readers also learn what happens to Mazy Bacon and Suzanne Culver, two other women who traveled the Oregon Trail with Ruth. Each wrestles with a different problem. Mazy must discover the real meaning of faith and family, when she returns home only to learn home is now California. Suzanne, a blind photographer, must face the challenge of seeing with inner eyes of faith. Ruth herself must struggle with the evil her husband, Zane, brings with him and keep silent to protect her family.

Where it's reviewed:
Roundup Magazine, December 2001, page 24

Other books by the same author:
No Eye Can See, 2001 (Kinship and Courage. Book 2)
Altogether in One Place, 1999 (Kinship and Courage. Book 1)

Other books you might like:
C.A. Bauer, *The White Horses*, 1999
Jack Curtis, *Easter in Calico*, 1999
Cecelia Holland, *Lily Nevada*, 1999
Richard S. Wheeler, *Sun Mountain*, 1999
Cherry Wilson, *Outcasts of Picture Rocks*, 1999

471

JILL MARIE LANDIS

Summer Moon

(New York: Ballantine, 2001)

Story type: Historical; Indian Culture
Subject(s): American West; Indians of North America
Major character(s): Kate Whittington, Spinster, Mail Order Bride; Reed Benton, Lawman (Texas Ranger), Rancher; Daniel Benton, Captive (of the Comanche)
Time period(s): 1870s (1872)
Locale(s): Texas

Summary: Thirty-year-old spinster Kate Whittington answers an ad and becomes the mail order bride of Texan Reed Benton. When she arrives at the Lone Star Ranch, Reed denies either writing to her or marrying her by proxy. He is recovering from a wound suffered in a fight with the Comanches, during which he rescued Daniel, whom he is sure is his son, captured as a baby. Kate agrees to stay and take care of the child who is just as strongly convinced he is a true Comanche as his father is sure he is white. Daniel runs away before Kate has a chance to tame the wild little boy. Kate and Reed try to find him and along the way fall in love.

Where it's reviewed:
Publishers Weekly, June 25, 2001, page 49

Other books by the same author:
Blue Moon, 1999
Just Once, 1997
Day Dreamer, 1996
Last Chance, 1995
Until Tomorrow, 1994

Other books you might like:
Sanora Babb, *Cry of the Tinamou*, 1997
Rosanne Bittner, *Chase the Sun*, 1995
Rosanne Bittner, *Tame the Wild Wind*, 1996
Tracy Dunham, *The Changing Trail*, 1999
Tracy Dunham, *The Ghost Trail*, 1998

472

JOE R. LANSDALE

Captains Outrageous

(New York: Mysterious, 2001)

Story type: Mystery; Modern
Series: Hap Collins and Leonard Pine
Subject(s): American West
Major character(s): Hap Collins, Guard (security); Leonard Pine, Sidekick
Time period(s): 2000s (2001)
Locale(s): Playa del Carmen, Mexico

Summary: While a security guard at a chicken plant, Hap Collins rescues a young woman and receives a large reward. He decides to use the money to take a cruise and invites his friend, Leonard Pine, to go along. Problems arise when they are left behind in Playa del Carmen, and they run into smugglers, as well as a mysterious old fisherman. As the body count mounts, the two friends run back to East Texas, but discover they must return to Mexico to clean up the mess they left behind.

Where it's reviewed:
Publishers Weekly, August 27, 2001, page 57

Other books by the same author:
The Long Ones, 1999
Rumble Tumble, 1998
Writer of the Purple Rage, 1997
The Two-Bear Mambo, 1996
Savage Season, 1995

Other books you might like:
Frederic Bean, *Murder at the Spirit Cave*, 1999
Peter Bowen, *Thunder Horse*, 1999
Sinclair Browning, *Rode Hard, Put Away Dead*, 2001
Carol Caverly, *Dead in Hog Heaven*, 2000
Elizabeth Dearl, *Twice Dead*, 2001

473

J. ROBERT LENNON

On the Night Plain

(New York: Holt, 2001)

Story type: Modern; Ranch Life
Subject(s): American West
Major character(s): Grant Person, Fisherman, Rancher; Max Person, Rancher (sheep), Artist; Sophia, Girlfriend (Grant's)
Time period(s): 20th century (post-WWII)
Locale(s): Great Plains

Summary: After WWII Grant Person, feeling guilty because the brother who took his place in the draft was killed, abandons his family's sheep ranch to work on a fishing trawler for three years. He returns when his mother dies to find that his father has deserted the family, and his younger brother Max is leaving for the East to pursue his art. In the meantime, the sheep ranch is facing ruin. When Max returns home he brings Sophia, his girlfriend. Grant promptly falls in love with her, setting up a brutal sibling rivalry. An absorbing, but very dark novel.

Where it's reviewed:
Library Journal, July 2001, page 124
Publishers Weekly, June 25, 2001, page 43

Other books by the same author:
The Funnies, 1999
The Light of Falling Stars, 1997

Other books you might like:
Max Brand, *The Bright Face of Danger*, 2000
Peter Dawson, *Rattlesnake Mesa*, 1997
Ed Gorman, *Trouble Man*, 1998
Douglas Hirt, *The Silent Gun*, 1993
Arthur Moore, *Rebel*, 1992

474

DEBBIE MACOMBER

Buffalo Valley

(New York: Mira, 2001)

Story type: Modern
Series: Dakota. Book 4
Subject(s): American West
Major character(s): Vaughn Kyle, Military Personnel (discharged); Hassie Knight, Pharmacist; Carrie Hendrickson, Pharmacist (assistant to Hassie)
Time period(s): 2000s (2001)
Locale(s): Buffalo Valley, North Dakota

Summary: Vaughn Kyle arrives in Buffalo Valley as a spy for Value-X, a large discount store chain. He meets Hassie Knight, the town's elderly pharmacist, whose deceased son Vaughn was named after. After being introduced to Carrie

Hendrickson, Hassie's assistant, Vaughn feels drawn to her. As a consequence of meeting the townspeople, Vaughn finds that he doesn't want Value-X building a store in the town and spoiling its community spirit. He also finds himself in love with Carrie even though his girlfriend is vice-president of Value-X. A pleasant story.

Where it's reviewed:
Publishers Weekly, September 17, 2001, page 55

Other books by the same author:
Dakota Home, 2000
Moon over Water, 1999
Promise Me Forever, 1999
Can This Be Christmas, 1998
The Bachelor Prince, 1997

Other books you might like:
Frederic Bean, *Murder in the Spirit Cave*, 1999
Johnny D. Boggs, *Riding with Hannah and the Horseman*, 1998
K. Follis Cheatham, *The Adventures of Elizabeth Fortune*, 2000
Jane Candia Coleman, *Moving On*, 1997
Harold Coyle, *Until the End*, 1996

475

ALLANA MARTIN

Death of the Last Villista

(New York: St. Martin's Press, 2001)

Story type: Modern; Mystery
Series: Texana Jones. Book 5
Subject(s): American West
Major character(s): Texana Jones, Store Owner (runs a trading post), Detective—Amateur; Clay Jones, Spouse (of Texana), Veterinarian
Time period(s): 2000s (2001)
Locale(s): Polvo, Texas

Summary: A film crew comes to Polvo to do a documentary on the 40-year-old murder of a man, who had ridden with Pancho Villa and served as a technical advisor on a movie about him. The murder was never solved, but various townspeople who had been extras are suspects. Texana herself was in the movie as a small child. The new film crew stirs up the past and confusion reigns as someone begins blowing up motor homes. It is up to Texana and her husband, Clay, to solve the puzzle from the past.

Where it's reviewed:
Publishers Weekly, July 2, 2001, page 56

Other books by the same author:
Death of a Myth Maker, 2000
Death of a Healing Woman, 1996

Other books you might like:
Frederic Bean, *Murder at the Spirit Cave*, 1999
Peter Bowen, *Kelly and the Three-Toed Horse*, 2001
Peter Bowen, *Thunder Horse*, 1999
Elizabeth Dearl, *Twice Dead*, 2001
Sybil Downing, *The Binding Oath*, 2001

476

CYNTHIA LEAL MASSEY

Fire Lilies

(Silver City, New Mexico: CrossroadsPub.Com, 2001)

Story type: Historical; Saga
Subject(s): American West; Mexicans
Major character(s): Dolores Porras, Heroine; Antonio Rommel Ramos, Cowboy; Alicia Hernandez, Relative (sister to Dolores)
Time period(s): 1900s; 1910s (1902-1910)
Locale(s): Chihuahua, Mexico; Monterrey, Mexico

Summary: This novel concerns three generations of a northern Mexican upper-class family torn apart by the Revolution of 1910, but centers on two sisters who fight for the men they love. Dolores Porras is married to an abusive man twice her age when she meets Antonio Rommel Ramos. With divorce illegal except for reasons of adultery, Dolores fears her love is hopeless. In Monterrey, her sister meets a friend of her revolutionary brother and falls in love despite the wishes of her family. An exciting love story set against the war-torn countryside of Mexico.

Other books you might like:
Frederic Bean, *Pancho and Black Jack*, 1995
Irwin R. Blacker, *Taos*, 1959
Mike Blakely, *Baron of the Sacramentos*, 1991
Javier Gonzalez-Rubio, *Loving You Was My Undoing*, 1999
Genevieve Gray, *Fair Laughs the Morn*, 1994

477

LISE MCCLENDON

Blue Wolf

(New York: Walker, 2001)

Story type: Modern; Mystery
Series: Alix Thorssen
Subject(s): American West
Major character(s): Alix Thorssen, Art Dealer
Time period(s): 2000s (2001)
Locale(s): Jackson Hole, Wyoming

Summary: Art dealer Alix Thorssen agrees to have an art auction to benefit wildlife conservation in Yellowstone National Park. Immediately Alix is in the soup, as the auction raises the tempers of both ranchers and environmentalists. A local artist submits a painting of a wolf that the committee chair refuses to allow in the auction. The same artist also asks Alix to investigate the accidental shooting of a teenager 25 years ago, fearing that it might have actually been murder.

Where it's reviewed:
Publishers Weekly, July 23, 2001, page 53

Other books by the same author:
Nordic Nights, 2000 (Alix Thorssen series)
Painted True, 1996 (Alix Thorssen series)
The Blue Jay Shaman, 1996 (Alix Thorssen series)

Other books you might like:
Frederic Bean, *Murder at the Spirit Cave*, 1999

Peter Bowen, *Thunder Horse*, 1999
Sinclair Browning, *Rode Hard, Put Away Dead*, 2001
Carol Caverly, *Dead in Hog Heaven*, 2000
Thea Barlow. Book 3
Sybil Downing, *The Binding Oath*, 2001

478

STEVE MCGIFFEN

Tennant's Rock

(New York: St. Martin's Press, 2001)

Story type: Traditional; Quest
Subject(s): American West
Major character(s): Sissy, Abuse Victim (raped); Swan, Outcast; Nate, Murderer, Military Personnel (Union soldier)
Time period(s): 1880s (1886)
Locale(s): Sacramento Valley, California

Summary: Sissy is raped by Swan, an intruder, who stays to abuse and impregnate her and reap the benefits of her Sacramento Valley farm. When Sissy's older brother, Nate, comes home after years in prison for killing their father, then further years as a Union soldier in the Civil War, she hopes he will dispose of Swan. Instead, she is disappointed again.

Where it's reviewed:
Library Journal, June 15, 2001, page 104
Publishers Weekly, July 9, 2001, page 48

Other books you might like:
Wayne Barton, *Warhorse*, 1988
Stan Williams, co-author
Patrick Dearen, *The Illegal Man*, 1998
Loren D. Estleman, *Journey of the Dead*, 1998
Laura Kalpakian, *Caveat*, 1998
W.W. Lee, *The Overland Trail*, 1996

479

MARJORIE M. MCGINLEY

The Gift of the Mestizo

(New York: Avalon, 2001)

Story type: Traditional; Quest
Subject(s): American West
Major character(s): Ben Mitchell, Rancher; Lucy Mitchell, Relative (Ben's sister-in-law), Widow(er); Mestizo, Indian (half Apache/half Mexican), Recluse
Time period(s): 19th century (post-Civil War)
Locale(s): Websterville, Arizona

Summary: When Ben Mitchell's brother is killed, his sister-in-law, Lucy Mitchell, forges a deed and cheats Ben out of his half of the ranch. Ben goes to court, but Lucy's new husband swears he saw Ben sign the deed giving his half of the ranch to Lucy. Furious, and afraid he will kill Lucy and her new husband if he stays in Websterville, Ben rides out to live in a northern Arizona canyon. There he meets an old half Apache, half Mexican hermit calling himself Mestizo, who gives him a pair of moccasins and tells him to use his head to get his ranch back. Ben returns to Websterville and outwits Lucy and her new husband.

Where it's reviewed:
Roundup Magazine, February 2002, page 30

Other books by the same author:
Rattlesnake Gulch, 2000
John Crust and Snuffling Pig, 1999
Footloose Convoy, 1998
Casey's Journey, 1997

Other books you might like:
Frederic Bean, *Law of the Gun*, 1993
Doug Bowman, *Guns of Billy Free*, 1998
Ed Gorman, *Dark Trail*, 1998
Elmer Kelton, *The Man Who Rode Midnight*, 1987
Larry McMurtry, *Streets of Laredo*, 1993

480

TIM MCGUIRE

Outcasts

(New York: Leisure, 2001)

Story type: Traditional; Man Alone
Series: Rainmaker. Book 4
Subject(s): American West; Indians of North America
Major character(s): Clay ''The Rainmaker'' Cole, Outlaw (falsely accused), Cowboy; Maude Price, Prostitute
Time period(s): 19th century (post-Civil War)
Locale(s): West

Summary: Clay Cole has a price on his head, a large one that makes him the object of every bounty hunter, so he heads for Indian Territory until he can get the charges against him dropped. His situation worsens when he accidently kills a young Indian woman and is left with her infant. His guilt and honor demand he take the baby back to the Nez Perce, but he has to evade the most successful bounty hunter in Texas or Indian Territory. Then there is Maude, a prostitute who travels along with Clay, but doesn't make it to the end of the trail.

Other books by the same author:
Gold of Cortes, 2000
Nobility, 1999
Danger Ridge, 1998

Other books you might like:
Barry Cord, *The Masked Gun*, 2001
Bennett Foster, *Cow Thief Trail*, 2001
Cynthia Haseloff, *Man Without Medicine*, 1996
Lewis B. Patten, *Death Rides the Denver Stage*, 2001
Bill Pronzini, *The Gallows Land*, 2001

481

JOHN MCLAIN

The Reckoning

(Cave Creek, Arizona: Metropolis Ink, 2001)

Story type: Modern; Ranch Life
Subject(s): American West; Coming-of-Age
Major character(s): Tom Callaghan, Teenager; Will Sherman, Rancher; Ellen Sherman, Relative (Will's daughter)
Time period(s): 1900s (1904)

Locale(s): New York, New York; Wyoming

Summary: Nineteen-year-old Tom Callaghan attempts to mug Will Sherman, but finds Will more than he can handle. To stay out of prison, Tom agrees to accompany Will back to his ranch in Wyoming. Ellen, Will's daughter, clashes with Tom whom she accuses of trying to take the place of her dead brother. Tom, in the meantime, hates the ranch and plots to run off, an attempt that nearly results in his death. A coming-of-age novel.

Where it's reviewed:
Roundup Magazine, May 2002, page 30

Other books you might like:
Jane Valentine Barker, *Mari*, 1997
Frederic Bean, *Eden*, 1997
James Carlos Blake, *Red Grass River*, 1998
Jack Cummings, *The Indian Fighter's Return*, 1993
Diane Glancy, *Flutie*, 1998

482

A.L. MCWILLIAMS

Search for Last Chance

(Waterville, Maine: Thorndike, 2001)

Story type: Traditional; Quest
Subject(s): American West; Crime and Criminals; Gold Discoveries
Major character(s): Shell Paxton, Outlaw (armed robber); Sally Paxton, Spouse (of Shell); Vic Taylor, Outlaw
Time period(s): 19th century (post-Civil War)
Locale(s): Amarillo, Texas

Summary: Sally Paxton lures her husband, Shell, away from outlaw Vic Taylor, and out of California where Shell is wanted for armed robbery. The couple settle near Amarillo, Texas, and try to make a new life for themselves. When bounty hunter Jesse Watts takes Shell to jail, Sally breaks him out and the two are on the run again. They ride to Colorado and right into the arms of Shell's old comrade, Vic Taylor, who persuades Shell to help him find some stolen gold bullion. Once more Shell is tied up in Vic's tangled and crooked ways, and it is up to Sally to free him.

Other books by the same author:
Eye of the Cat, 2000
Penny Town Justice, 2000

Other books you might like:
Frederic Bean, *Murder at the Spirit Cave*, 1999
Ralph Compton, *Autumn of the Gun*, 1996
Wynema McGowan, *Beyond the River*, 1997
Richard S. Wheeler, *The Fate*, 1992
Jeanne Williams, *Home Mountain*, 1990
Spur Award Winner

483

DAWN MILLER

Letters to Callie

(New York: Pocket, 2001)

Story type: Historical; Quest
Series: Callie Wade
Subject(s): American West; Indians of North America
Major character(s): Callie Wade, Pioneer; Jack Wade, Gambler, Pioneer; Raven, Indian (Blackfoot)
Time period(s): 19th century (post-Civil War)
Locale(s): Virginia City, Montana

Summary: A sequel to *The Journal of Callie Wade*, this is the story of Jack Wade, Callie's brother, as seen through his letters. Feeling guilty that he caused the death of his little sister, Rose, Jack drifts into Virginia City where he becomes a gambler. Jack is lonely and wishes he could go to Callie's home, but he must make his own way. He finally finds peace when he marries Raven, a Blackfoot woman, and makes friends with many of her tribe.

Where it's reviewed:
Publishers Weekly, July 30, 2001, page 60

Other books by the same author:
The Journal of Callie Wade, 1996

Other books you might like:
C.A. Bauer, *The White Horses*, 1999
Jane Candia Coleman, *Moving On*, 1997
Zane Grey, *Woman of the Frontier*, 1998
Ellen Recknor, *Leaving Missouri*, 1997
Ellen Recknor, *Me and the Boys*, 1995

484

GENE MULLINS

Bear Paw

(Titusville, Florida: Four Seasons, 2001)

Story type: Traditional; Indian Culture
Subject(s): American West; Indians of North America
Major character(s): Bear Paw, Indian (Kiowa); Stuart Morgan, Indian (mixed blood Comanche), Scout (former, Army); Pink Sorrells, Outlaw
Time period(s): 1880s (1880)
Locale(s): Fort Griffin, Texas

Summary: Bear Paw wants to find the bones of his father, Buffalo Horn, and take them to the Kiowa homeland. At the same time, Stuart Morgan, part Comanche and former army scout, wants to help his friend, Captain Coldiron, capture Bear Paw alive. However, Pink Sorrells and his son want to find Bear Paw but they have no intention of letting him live. They capture Morgan's girlfriend and hold her for ransom for both Morgan and Bear Paw. Trails converge as the hunters and the hunted clash.

Other books you might like:
John Edwards Ames, *The Unwritten Order*, 1996
Will Cade, *Larimont*, 1999
Judd Cole, *Blood on the Plains*, 1993

Judd Cole, *Desert Manhunt*, 1997
Cheyenne. Book 22
Ed Gorman, *The Fatal Frontier*, 1997
Martin Greenberg, co-editor

485

BRUCE OLDS

Bucking the Tiger

(New York: Farrar, Straus & Giroux, 2001)

Story type: Historical
Subject(s): American West; Crime and Criminals
Major character(s): John H. ''Doc'' Holliday, Gunfighter, Historical Figure; Kate ''Big Nose Kate'' Haroney, Lover (of Doc), Historical Figure; Wyatt Earp, Lawman, Historical Figure
Time period(s): 19th century (post-Civil War)
Locale(s): Las Vegas, New Mexico; Fort Worth, Texas; Tombstone, Arizona

Summary: This novel about everyone's favorite consumptive dentist explores the character of Doc Holliday from every conceivable angle, from lists of slang, manners, symptoms, and personal possessions, to the observations of his mistress, Big Nose Kate, and Wyatt Earp. The book culminates in the famous gunfight, but getting to the O.K. Corral is more fun than the ending.

Where it's reviewed:
Library Journal, August 2001, page 164

Other books by the same author:
Raising Holy Hell, 1195

Other books you might like:
Matt Braun, *Doc Holliday*, 1997
Jane Candia Coleman, *Doc Holliday's Woman*, 1995
Randy Lee Eickhoff, *The Fourth Horseman*, 1997
Loren D. Estleman, *Bloody Season*, 1988
Will Henry, *Who Rides with Wyatt?*, 1954

486

T.V. OLSEN

Man Without a Past

(Waterville, Maine: Thorndike, 2001)

Story type: Traditional; Collection
Subject(s): American West; Short Stories
Time period(s): 19th century (post-Civil War)
Locale(s): West

Summary: A collection of one short novel and 11 short stories, five of which have never before been published. These works are representative of Olsen's fiction and the characters are well portrayed.

Where it's reviewed:
Roundup Magazine, February 2002, page 30

Other books by the same author:
The Lost Colony, 1999
Treasures of the Sun, 1998
Lone Hand, 1997
Deadly Pursuit, 1995
Red Is the River, 1993

Other books you might like:
Max Brand, *The Bright Face of Danger*, 2000
Max Brand, *Men Beyond the Law*, 2001
Zane Grey, *Rangle River*, 2001
John D. Nesbitt, *A Good Man to Have in Camp*, 1999
John D. Nesbitt, *One Foot in the Stirrup*, 1995

487

T.V. OLSEN

Treasures of the Sun

(New York: Leisure, 2001)

Story type: Traditional; Quest
Subject(s): American West; Gold Discoveries
Major character(s): Sir Wilbur Tennington, Nobleman; Christopher Fallon, Guide; Luis Valera, Sidekick (of Sir Wilbur), Professor
Time period(s): 1920s (1922)
Locale(s): San Francisco, California; Huacha, Peru

Summary: Huacha, Peru is a lost city of the Incas, believed to be the location of a fabulous fortune in gold. When Sir Wilbur Tennington buys a memoir written by one of Pizarro's men revealing the location of the city, he immediately contacts Christopher Fallon, his trustworthy field guide for so many of his archaeological journeys, and his close friend, Professor Luis Valera. Together they will make archaeological history by discovering the lost city and its fortune in gold. Of course, it is not as easy as Sir Wilbur thinks, not with men greedy for gold on their trail.

Other books by the same author:
Red Is the River, 1993
The Golden Chance, 1992
The Burning Sky, 1991
Under the Gun, 1989
There Was a Season, 1972

Other books you might like:
Margaret Allan, *The Last Mammoth*, 1995
Tim Champlin, *Lincoln's Ransom*, 1999
Tim Champlin, *Treasure of the Templars*, 2000
Tim Champlin, *Wayfaring Strangers*, 2000
Will Cook, *The Rain Tree*, 1996

488

STEPHEN OVERHOLSER

Shadow Valley Rising

(Waterville, Maine: Thorndike, 2002)

Story type: Traditional; Saga
Subject(s): American West
Major character(s): Ella Mae Campbell, Heroine, Pioneer; Peter Howell, Religious (minister); Seth Carter, Indian (mixed blood)
Time period(s): 1860s (1860-1861); 2000s
Locale(s): Denver, Colorado

Summary: Inside a strongbox buried in the cornerstone of Denver's old First Brethren Church are found the diaries of Ella Mae Campbell. She tells the story of an Indian attack on the wagon train in which she was riding and of being abducted. Seth Carter, a mixed blood Indian, rescues her and returns her to the posse led by minister Peter Howell, but she is shunned by polite society, as well as impolite society. She also records in graphic detail how she becomes involved in a secessionist group, and the Confederates' horrible defeat at the hands of a Union Army unit. A marvelous book with a marvelous protagonist.

Where it's reviewed:
Roundup Magazine, February 2002, page 30

Other books by the same author:
Track of a Killer, 1982
Search for the Fox, 1976
Molly and the Confidence Man, 1975
A Hanging at Sweetwater, 1974

Other books you might like:
C.A. Bauer, *The White Horses*, 1999
Jack Curtis, *Easter in Calico*, 1999
Cecelia Holland, *Lily Nevada*, 1999
Richard S. Wheeler, *Masterson*, 1999
Richard S. Wheeler, *Sun Mountain*, 1999

489

WAYNE D. OVERHOLSER

Chumley's Gold

(New York: Leisure, 2002)

Story type: Traditional; Collection
Subject(s): American West
Time period(s): 19th century (post-Civil War)
Locale(s): West

Summary: Two short novels by an author of classic Western stories. The title story was originally published in 1999. The other Overholser work included in the volume is *High Valley*.

Where it's reviewed:
Roundup Magazine, February 2002, page 30

Other books by the same author:
Hearn's Valley, 2001
Rainbow Rider: A Western Trio, 2001
The Outlaws, 2000
Nugget City, 1997
The Violet Land, 1996

Other books you might like:
Max Brand, *The Bright Face of Danger*, 2000
Max Brand, *The Outlaw Redeemer*, 2000
Peter Dawson, *Claiming of Deerfoot: A Western Duo*, 2000
T.T. Flynn, *The Devil's Lode: A Western Trio*, 1999
Ray Hogan, *Guns of Freedom: A Western Duo*, 1999

490

WAYNE D. OVERHOLSER

The Outlaws

(New York: Leisure, 2001)

Story type: Traditional; Man Alone
Subject(s): American West; Crime and Criminals
Major character(s): Del Delaney, Cowboy; The Kid, Outlaw; John Smith, Outlaw
Time period(s): 19th century (post-Civil War)
Locale(s): Prairie City, Montana

Summary: Del Delaney is an easy-going cowboy, who has worked for the same outfit for ten years, and has no burning ambition to do anything else. That is until the night of the dance in Prairie City when Ruby Prentiss seduces him—or tries to, but Del backs out of her bedroom and gallops for home. Nobody treats Ruby that way, and the next thing Del knows, the sheriff is arresting him for rape. Del knows he'll spend time in prison if he doesn't take a drop at the end of a rope, so he escapes and rides south. That's when he meets The Kid and a man calling himself John Smith. They are wanted men and so is Del, but The Kid and Smith are real criminals, and Del figures they'll be harder to get away from than Ruby Prentiss.

Other books by the same author:
Gateway House, 2001
Hearn's Valley, 2001
The Outlaws, 2000
Nugget City, 1997
The Violent Land, 1997

Other books you might like:
A.J. Arnold, *Dead Man's Cache*, 1988
Jack Curtis, *No Mercy*, 1995
Ernest Haycox, *Rim of the Desert*, 1940
Elmer Kelton, *Cloudy in the West*, 1997
T.V. Olsen, *The Golden Chance*, 1992
Spur Award winner

491

WAYNE D. OVERHOLSER

Rainbow Rider: A Western Trio

(Waterville, Maine: Thorndike, 2001)

Story type: Traditional; Collection
Subject(s): American West; Short Stories
Time period(s): 19th century (post-Civil War)
Locale(s): West

Summary: Three novellas by a three time Spur Award winner are included in this volume: the title story, *The Leather Slapper*, and *The Fence*.

Other books by the same author:
Gateway House, 2001
The Outlaws, 2000
Chumley's Gold, 1999
Nugget City, 1997
Riders of the Sundown, 1997

Other books you might like:
Max Brand, *The Black Rider and Other Stories*, 1996
Max Brand, *The Ghost Wagon and Other Great Western Adventures*, 1996
Jane Candia Coleman, *Doc Holliday's Gone*, 1999
T.T. Flynn, *Death Marks Time in Trampas: A Western Quintet*, 1998
Elmore Leonard, *The Tonto Woman and Other Western Stories*, 1998

492

LAURAN PAINE

Lockwood

(New York: Leisure, 2001)

Story type: Traditional; Man Alone
Subject(s): American West
Major character(s): Cuff Lockwood, Cowboy; Lady Barlow, Rancher, Widow(er); Stuart Bentley, Restaurateur (cafe owner)
Time period(s): 19th century (post-Civil War)
Locale(s): Derby, Montana

Summary: Cuff Lockwood wants to be somewhere warmer than Montana, but he gets as far as Derby, Wyoming, when he gets in a fight with a couple of fighters. When he wakes up there are three dead men, but he is only missing two bullets. The cafe owner, Stuart Bentley, killed the third fighter, but it is Lockwood who gets the credit. After he recovers from his wound, he works for Lady Barlow, a pretty widow lady with a big ranch. Even though Wyoming isn't any warmer than Montana, Cuff settles down and marries Lady. He is a happy man until the night he dreams of a girl he once met. She is crying in his dream and Cuff knows he has to find her, and see how the years have treated her. However, no dream is as vivid as the reality he finds.

Other books by the same author:
The Killer Gun, 1998
The Grand Ones of San Ildefonso, 1997
Lockwood, 1996
The Devil on Horseback, 1995
The Prairieton Raid, 1994

Other books you might like:
Jack Ballas, *Tomahawk Canyon*, 1992
Rick Bass, *The Sky, the Stars, the Wilderness*, 1997
Mike Blakely, *Spanish Blood*, 1996
Tim Champlin, *Colt Lighting*, 1989
Kent Conwell, *Cattle Drive to Dodge*, 1992

493

LAURAN PAINE

Tears of the Heart

(New York: Leisure, 2001)

Story type: Traditional; Man Alone
Subject(s): American West; Crime and Criminals
Major character(s): Toby Lincoln, Outcast; Jack Bannion, Guard (in Colorado Territorial Prison); Manuel Acosta, Gunfighter
Time period(s): 19th century (post-Civil War)
Locale(s): Trabajo, New Mexico

Summary: Toby Lincoln is abandoned at the church door by his mother and runs away from an orphanage at 16. He works for the Roberts family until a disagreement sends him on his way. Mr. Roberts gives Toby a horse and wishes him luck, but at a town several days' ride away, Toby is accused of stealing the horse and sentenced to two years in prison. His cellmate, a 14-year-old boy named Abel, is mistreated by Jack Bannion, a sadistic guard and Toby swears revenge. However, he is still a young boy who can't shoot a gun and doesn't know how he will fulfill his pledge. Released from prison, he goes to New Mexico where a toothless gunfighter named Manuel Acosta teaches him how to shoot. When Bannion comes for Toby on another false charge, Toby is ready for him.

Other books by the same author:
The Killer Gun, 1998
The Grand Ones of San Ildefonso, 1997
Lockwood, 1996
The Devil on Horseback, 1995
The Prairieton Raid, 1994

Other books you might like:
Matt Braun, *Noble Outlaw*, 1996
Jane Candia Coleman, *Doc Holliday's Woman*, 1995
Randy Lee Eickhoff, *The Fourth Horseman*, 1997
Loren D. Estleman, *City of Widows*, 1994
Will Henry, *The Bear Paw Horses*, 1996

494

LEWIS B. PATTEN

The Woman at Ox-Yoke

(New York: Leisure, 2001)

Story type: Traditional; Collection
Subject(s): American West
Time period(s): 19th century (post-Civil War)
Locale(s): West

Summary: Two of Patten's best short novels are presented here. Both the title story and *The Guns in Greasewood Valley* are concerned with ranch life in the 19th century and the plots have romance and murder themes.

Where it's reviewed:
Roundup Magazine, February 2002, page 30

Other books by the same author:
Tin Cup in the Storm Country, 1996
Best Western Stories of Lewis B. Patten, 1989
Trail of the Apache Kid, 1979
Hunt the Man Down, 1977
A Killing in Kiowa, 1973

Other books you might like:
Max Brand, *The Overland Kid: A Western Trio*, 1999
Dan Cushman, *The Pecos Kid: A Western Duo*, 1999
Zane Grey, *Rangle River*, 2001
Ray Hogan, *Legend of a Badman: A Western Quintet*, 1998

Louis L'Amour, *Monument Rock*, 1998

495

TESS PENDERGRASS

Colorado Twilight

(Waterville, Maine: Thorndike, 2001)

Story type: Historical; Saga
Series: Colorado Trilogy. Book 2
Subject(s): American West
Major character(s): Elijah ''Preacher'' Kelly, Gunfighter; Jordan Braddock, Widow(er) (twice widowed); Marshal Cox, Lawman
Time period(s): 19th century (post-Civil War)
Locale(s): Battlement Park, Colorado

Summary: Jordan Braddock, a young widow desperate to escape her grief, travels west, hoping the landscape will renew her desire to paint. The train she is on is robbed and a stranger advises her to do what the robbers ask. He turns out to be the famous gunfighter Elijah ''Preacher'' Kelly. She is taken hostage by bank robbers and claims Elijah as her husband to save his life. Saved from the robbers, she travels through the mountains of Colorado with Elijah as her escort, something Marshal Cox resents as he hates Elijah. A romantic tale of a man and woman trying to escape their pasts.

Where it's reviewed:
Roundup Magazine, February 2002, page 30

Other books by the same author:
Colorado Shadows, 2000 (Colorado Trilogy. Book 1)

Other books you might like:
Frederic Bean, *Eden*, 1997
B.M. Bowers, *Lonesome Land*, 1997
Irene Bennett Brown, *The Plainswoman*, 1994
Will Camp, *Blood of Texas*, 1996
Douglas Hirt, *Cripple Creek*, 1997

496

VICKI PIEKARSKI, Editor

No Place for a Lady

(Waterville, Maine: Thorndike, 2001)

Story type: Anthology
Subject(s): American West; Short Stories
Time period(s): 19th century (post-Civil War)
Locale(s): West

Summary: These 12 tales of the West from the 1770s to modern times are told from a woman's perspective. The stories were written by women beginning in the early 1900s and the authors include Mary Austin, Jane Candia Coleman, Gretel Ehrlich, and Cynthia Haseloff.

Other books you might like:
Max Brand, *The Overland Kid: A Western Trio*, 1999
Eugene Cunningham, *Trails West*, 2000
Zane Grey, *The Westerners: Stories of the West*, 2000
Will Henry, *Tumbleweeds*, 1999
Ray Hogan, *Legend of a Badman: A Western Quintet*, 1998

497

ROBERT J. RANDISI

Miracle of the Jacal

(New York: Leisure, 2001)

Story type: Traditional; Man Alone
Subject(s): American West; Crime and Criminals
Major character(s): Elfego Baca, Lawman (deputy sheriff), Historical Figure; Pedro Saraccino, Lawman (deputy sheriff), Historical Figure; John Slaughter, Rancher, Historical Figure
Time period(s): 19th century; 20th century (1884-1940)
Locale(s): Socorro, New Mexico

Summary: Based on the story of Elfego Baca, New Mexico's most famous sheriff, this book is divided into four sections with the first covering Baca's facing down 80 cowboys in a siege that lasted for 36 hours. It is this event, when 19-year-old Elfego agrees to help Pedro Saraccino arrest some of John Slaughter's cowboys for mistreating several Mexican Americans in the local saloon, that gains Elfego his reputation. Section two of the book includes Elfego's dealings with Pancho Villa, as well as a million-dollar thief. The third section recounts Elfego's term as sheriff of Socorro County in 1919. The final section concerns Elfego's time as the head of security for El Paso's famous gambling house, the Tivoli. Taken together, the four parts tell the tale of a larger-than-life historical character.

Where it's reviewed:
Roundup Magazine, February 2002, page 30

Other books by the same author:
Ghost with Blue Eyes, 2000
Tin Star, 2000
Legend, 1999
Targett, 1999
Alone with the Dead, 1985

Other books you might like:
Matt Braun, *Texas Empire*, 1997
Jerry Craven, *Snake Mountain*, 2000
Zane Grey, *Woman of the Frontier*, 1998
Elmer Kelton, *The Smiling Country*, 1998
Jory Sherman, *The Baron Range*, 1998

498

CLAY REYNOLDS

The Vigil

(Lubbock: Texas Tech University, 2002)

Story type: Modern; Quest
Subject(s): American West
Major character(s): Imogene McBride, Parent (of Cora); Cora McBride, Child (of Imogene); Ezra Holmes, Lawman (sheriff of Sandhill County)
Time period(s): 2000s
Locale(s): Agatite, Texas

Summary: Fleeing Atlanta, Imogene McBride stops at Agatite, Texas, when her car breaks down. Her daughter, Cora McBride, goes into the drugstore to buy ice cream and disap-

Western

pears. Realizing Cora is gone, Imogene searches for her daughter, then appeals to Sheriff Ezra Holmes. Despite all the searching, Cora has vanished. Determined to wait for her daughter, Imogene takes a seat on the bench on the courthouse square and remains there, leaving only to work, then returning, until she is an old woman. A novel of obsession.

Other books by the same author:
Monuments, 2000
Players, 1998
Franklin's Crossing, 1992
Agatite, 1990

Other books you might like:
Judy Alter, *Cherokee Rose*, 1996
Jane Valentine Barker, *Mari*, 1997
Tim Champlin, *Lincoln's Ransom*, 1999
Tim Champlin, *Treasure of the Templars*, 2000
Will Cook, *The Rain Tree*, 1996
editor

499

FRANK RODERUS

Charlie and the Sir

(New York: Leisure, 2001)

Story type: Traditional; Man Alone
Subject(s): American West; Ranch Life
Major character(s): Charlie Roy, Cowboy; Sir Arthur Williford Cooke-Williams, Nobleman (British); Lady Elizabeth Copperton, Rancher, Noblewoman (sister of Sir Arthur)
Time period(s): 19th century (post-Civil War)
Locale(s): Wyoming

Summary: Charlie doesn't know what he is in for when he goes to work for the Sir—Sir Arthur Williford Cooke-Williams, that is. The Sir wants Charlie to guide him to the Crown B, the ranch owned by his sister, Lady Elizabeth Copperton. They arrive to find most of the stock has frozen to death during the hard winter, and Jesse Harper and his men interested in forcing Elizabeth off her property. Charlie isn't going to allow that and neither is the Sir.

Other books by the same author:
Trooper Donovan, 2001
Left to Die, 2000
Jason Evers: His Own Story, 1999
Hayseed, 1998
Stillwater Smith, 1997

Other books you might like:
A.J. Arnold, *Dead Man's Cache*, 1988
Jack Curtis, *No Mercy*, 1995
Ernest Haycox, *Rim of the Desert*, 1940
Elmer Kelton, *Cloudy in the West*, 1997
T.V. Olsen, *The Golden Chance*, 1992
Spur Award winner

500

LES SAVAGE JR.

Gambler's Row: A Western Trio

(Waterville, Maine: Thorndike, 2002)

Story type: Traditional; Collection
Subject(s): American West; Short Stories
Time period(s): 19th century (post-Civil War)
Locale(s): West

Summary: Three short novels on a diversity of subjects from gambling to breaking horses.

Where it's reviewed:
Roundup Magazine, February 2002, page 31

Other books by the same author:
The Cavan Breed, 2001
The Shadow in Renegade Basin, 2001
In the Land of Little Sticks, 2000
The Sting of Senorita Scorpion: A Western Trio, 2000
The Bloody Quarter, 1999

Other books you might like:
C.A. Bauer, *The White Horses*, 1997
Jane Candia Coleman, *Moving On*, 1999
Dan Cushman, *The Pecos Kid: A Western Duo*, 1999
E. Donald Two-Rivers, *Survivor's Medicine*, 1998
Dale L. Walker, *Legends & Lies*, 1997

501

LES SAVAGE JR.

The Shadow in Renegade Basin

(New York: Leisure, 2001)

Story type: Traditional; Collection
Subject(s): American West; Short Stories
Time period(s): 19th century (post-Civil War)

Summary: These three wonderful novellas were originally published in edited versions in the 1950s; they are now provided in their original form. Included are *Plunder Trail*, *The Brand of Penasco*, and the title story.

Other books by the same author:
The Cavan Breed, 2001
In the Land of Little Sticks, 2000
The Sting of Senorita Scorpion: A Western Trio, 2000
The Bloody Quarter, 1999
Phantoms in the Night, 1998

Other books you might like:
Giff Cheshire, *Renegade River*, 1998
Peter Dawson, *Ghost Brand of the Wishbones*, 1998
T.T. Flynn, *Death Marks Time in Trampas: A Western Quintet*, 1998
T.T. Flynn, *Long Journey to Deep Canon*, 1997

502

HAROLD SCHECHTER

The Hum Bug

(New York: Pocket, 2001)

Story type: Mystery
Series: Edgar Allan Poe. Book 2
Subject(s): American West; Crime and Criminals
Major character(s): Edgar Allan Poe, Historical Figure, Writer; P.T. Barnum, Historical Figure, Entertainer; Morris Vanderhorn, Historical Figure
Time period(s): 1840s (1844)
Locale(s): New York, New York

Summary: As soon as Edgar Allan Poe and his wife, Sissy, are settled in their new home in New York, Poe visits P.T. Barnum's American Museum. Poe is suspicious of a series of artifacts supposedly from Davy Crockett's last stand at the Alamo, and seeks out Barnum who explains the dubious display, as well as several others. When a display of an infamous murder is duplicated in real life, Barnum hires Poe to solve the crime. As he investigates, Poe becomes familiar with every nook and cranny of the museum while meeting such people as Morris Vanderhorn, the man with two faces. An exciting historical novel.

Where it's reviewed:
Publishers Weekly, October 15, 2001, page 49

Other books by the same author:
Nevermore, 1999

Other books you might like:
Frederic Bean, *Murder at Spirit Cave*, 1999
Sinclair Browning, *Rode Hard, Put Away Dead*, 2001
Elizabeth Dearl, *Diamondback*, 2000
Taylor Madison series
Elizabeth Dearl, *Twice Dead*, 2001
Loren D. Estleman, *White Desert*, 2000

503

JORY SHERMAN

The Baron War

(New York: Forge, 2002)

Story type: Historical; Saga
Series: Baron
Subject(s): American West; Ranch Life
Major character(s): Martin Baron, Rancher; Mickey Bone, Indian (Apache); Matteo Aguilar, Rancher (Mexican American)
Time period(s): 1860s (1861)
Locale(s): Texas

Summary: : The Civil War officially begins but Martin Baron has his own war. His wife, Caroline, finally dies of syphilis, and the doctor tells Martin that whoever infected her is also dying. Martin always thought his wife contracted the disease when raped by Mickey Bone, but the Apache is not sick, which means someone else is guilty. In addition to Martin's concern about his wife's lie, he is involved in a feud with Matteo Aguilar of the Rocking A Ranch. Aguilar is determined to kill Martin, and Martin has all he can do to stay alive.

Where it's reviewed:
Roundup Magazine, February 2002, page 31

Other books by the same author:
The Ballad of Pinewood Lake, 2001
The Baron Brand, 2000
The Baron Range, 1998
The Barons of Texas, 1997
The Columbia River, 1995 (Rivers West. Book 14)

Other books you might like:
John D. Armstrong, *The Return of Jericho Pike*, 1992
Will Henry, *Tumbleweeds*, 1999
W.W. Lee, *Rustler's Venom*, 1990
William A. Luckey, *Cimarron Blood*, 1992
Larry McMurtry, *Dead Man's Walk*, 1995

504

COTTON SMITH

Behold a Red Horse

(New York: Leisure, 2001)

Story type: Traditional; Man Alone
Subject(s): American West; Ranch Life
Major character(s): Ethan Kerry, Rancher; Luther Kerry, Relative (brother of Ethan and Cole); Cole Kerry, Outlaw
Time period(s): 19th century (post-Civil War)
Locale(s): Texas

Summary: Ethan Kerry has built the Bar K Ranch from nothing to a prosperous property. Now, however, the bank is calling in Ethan's loan, and his only chance to save the ranch is to drive a herd over the dangerous Western Trail to Kansas and sell the cattle. Although he hates to drive another herd, he will make it with the help of his slow-witted older brother, Luther Kerry. Disaster strikes when Ethan is kicked by a horse and blinded. He will not be able to drive the herd with only Luther's help. Fortunately, there is another Kerry brother—Cole—who can help even though Ethan is reluctant to ask his outlaw brother for assistance.

Where it's reviewed:
Roundup Magazine, December 2001, page 24

Other books by the same author:
Pray for Texas, 2000
Dark Trail to Dodge, 1997

Other books you might like:
Jack Ballas, *Tomahawk Canyon*, 1992
Doug Bowman, *The Three Lives of Littleton Blue*, 1992
Hank Edwards, *Ride for Rimfire*, 1995
Elmer Kelton, *The Pumpkin Rollers*, 1996
Bob Kody, *Gold Mountain*, 1994

505

TROY D. SMITH

Caleb's Price

(Lincoln, Nebraska: Writer's Club, 2001)

Story type: Historical; Ranch Life
Subject(s): American West
Major character(s): Caleb York, Gunfighter, Murderer (hired killer); Ike Majors, Rancher; Joey P. Cutter, Child
Time period(s): 1870s (1875)
Locale(s): Waynetown, Kansas

Summary: Caleb York is a hired killer who usually works for big ranchers that want to frighten off the settlers having little land. Everyone, including 9-year-old Joey Cutter, figures that Caleb has come to Waynetown to work for Ike Majors, a big rancher who doesn't see any need to put up with those settlers having insignificant acreage, including Joey's aunt and uncle. Instead, Caleb goes to work for Joey's uncle in this humorous story of range war and a small boy.

Where it's reviewed:
Roundup Magazine, April 2002, page 31

Other books by the same author:
Bound for the Promise-Land, 2000 (Spur Award winner)

Other books you might like:
Jack Ballas, *Tomahawk Canyon*, 1992
Rick Bass, *The Sky, the Stars, the Wilderness*, 1997
Mike Blakely, *Spanish Blood*, 1996
Tim Champlin, *Colt Lighting*, 1989
Kent Conwell, *Cattle Drive to Dodge*, 1992

506

AIMEE THURLO
DAVID THURLO, Co-Author

Blackening Song

(New York: Forge, 2001)

Story type: Modern; Mystery
Series: Ella Clah. Book 1
Subject(s): American West; Crime and Criminals; Indians of North America
Major character(s): Ella Clah, FBI Agent, Indian (Navajo); Clifford Destea, Indian (Ella's brother), Shaman; Blalock, FBI Agent
Time period(s): 1990s
Locale(s): Navajo Reservation, New Mexico

Summary: FBI agent Ella Clah returns to the Navajo reservation when her father is murdered and her brother is suspected of committing the crime. It doesn't help that her brother Clifford Destea, a medicine man, has disappeared. Although Ella has been ordered to stay out of the case, she has no faith in the local FBI agent, Blalock, who understands nothing about the Navajo. Defying orders, Ella investigates, blending Navajo wisdom and modern forensic methods.

Other books by the same author:
Red Mesa, 2002 (Ella Clah. Book 6)
Enemy Way, 2000 (Ella Clah. Book 4)
Shooting Chant, 2000 (Ella Clah. Book 5)
Bad Medicine, 1998 (Ella Clah. Book 3)
Death Walker, 1997 (Ella Clah. Book 2)

Other books you might like:
Frederic Bean, *Murder at the Spirit Cave*, 1999
Sinclair Browning, *Rode Hard, Put Away Dead*, 2001
Laura Crum, *Stickrock*, 2000
Kathleen O'Neal Gear, *The Visitant*, 1999
W. Michael Gear, co-author
Fred Grove, *A Distance of Ground*, 2000

507

WILLIAM TREMBLAY

The June Rise

(Golden, Colorado: Fulcrum, 2001)

Story type: Historical; Indian Culture
Subject(s): American West; Indians of North America
Major character(s): Joseph Antoine Janis, Historical Figure, Mountain Man; Red Cloud, Historical Figure, Indian (Sioux); First Elk Woman, Spouse (of Joseph), Indian (Oglala Sioux holy woman)
Time period(s): 1880s (1884-1889)
Locale(s): Pine Ridge Reservation, South Dakota

Summary: Told through a collection of imaginary letters from Joseph Antoine Janis, *The June Rise* is an account of Janis' life from Missouri farm boy to trapper to advisor to Lakota chief Red Cloud and then as the husband of Oglala Sioux holy woman First Elk Woman. After the Battle of the Little Big Horn, the U.S. government gives Janis a choice: divorce First Elk Woman and keep his Colorado property, or share his wife's fate in the Badlands of the Pine Ridge Reservation. Janis picks his wife. Part history, part tragedy, and part fiction, this is, in the last analysis, a great love story.

Where it's reviewed:
Roundup Magazine, February 2002, page 31

Other books you might like:
Margaret Allan, *The Last Mammoth*, 1995
Mike Blakely, *Comanche Dawn*, 1998
Joseph Bruchac, *The Waters Between*, 1998
Don Coldsmith, *The Lost Band*, 2000
Karen Osborn, *Between Earth and Sky*, 1996

508

JOHN VERNON

The Last Canyon

(Boston: Houghton Mifflin, 2001)

Story type: Historical; Man Alone
Subject(s): American West; Discovery and Exploration
Major character(s): John Wesley Powell, Historical Figure, Explorer
Time period(s): 1860s (1869)
Locale(s): Grand Canyon, Arizona

Summary: Major John Wesley Powell's expedition to explore the Colorado River and the Grand Canyon results in deprivation, exhaustion, and the death of a third of his men. A subplot concerns a tribe of Paiute Indians on the canyon rim, who are in nearly as desperate straits as Powell's party. An absorbing historical novel.

Where it's reviewed:
Library Journal, October 1, 2001, page 144
Publishers Weekly, August 27, 2001, page 47

Other books by the same author:
All for Love, 1995

Other books you might like:
Frederic Bean, *The Red River*, 1998
Mike Blakely, *Shortgrass Song*, 1994
Rita Cleary, *River Walk*, 2001
Patrick Dearen, *When Cowboys Die*, 1994
Brian Garfield, *Manifest Destiny*, 1989

509

EUGENE C. VORIES

Monte's Revenge

(Kearney, Nebraska: Vories Family Publishers, 2001)

Story type: Traditional; Modern
Subject(s): American West; Ranch Life
Major character(s): Monte Freeman, Rancher; Lee Freeman, Spouse (of Monte); Norton, Rancher, Wealthy (millionaire)
Time period(s): 2000s
Locale(s): La Veta, Colorado

Summary: In this sequel to *Monte*, the old Colorado rancher is married to a much younger woman, which lets him in for teasing by his friends, not that he minds. He and his wife, Lee, are happy and life is good—except for the presence of Norton, the Texas millionaire who is buying up all the land around La Veta. Monte gets the best of him in this humorous tale of modern ranching.

Where it's reviewed:
Roundup Magazine, February 2002, page 31

Other books by the same author:
Monte, 2000

Other books you might like:
Johnny D. Boggs, *Ten and Me*, 1999
Fred Grove, *A Distance of Ground*, 2000
Giles Tippette, *Southwest of Heaven*, 2000
Tom Willard, *Wings of Honor*, 1999
Norman Zollinger, *Riders to Cibola*, 1977

510

ANNA LEE WALDO

Circle of Stars

(New York: St. Martin's Press, 2001)

Story type: Historical; Saga
Subject(s): American West; Druids; Indians of North America
Major character(s): Madoc, Sailor (Welsh), Explorer; Cougar, Indian (Calusa)
Time period(s): 12th century
Locale(s): Wales; Florida

Summary: In this sequel to *Circle of Stones*, Madoc, the Welsh explorer, is heavily involved with the Druids, who believe him destined to lead them. Intertwined with Madoc's story is that of Cougar, a Calusa of what is now Florida, whose people fear that she is a shape-shifter. The adventures of Madoc and Cougar lead them to an inevitable meeting.

Where it's reviewed:
Publishers Weekly, July 30, 2001, page 61

Other books by the same author:
Circle of Stones, 1999
Sacajawea, 1978

Other books you might like:
Margaret Allan, *Keeper of the Stone*, 1994
Irwin R. Blacker, *Taos*, 1959
Kathleen O'Neal Gear, *People of the Masks*, 1998
W. Michael Gear, co-author
Kathleen O'Neal Gear, *People of the Mist*, 1998
W. Michael Gear, co-author
Genevieve Gray, *Fair Laughs the Morn*, 1994

511

JOYCE WEATHERFORD

Heart of the Beast

(New York: Scribner, 2001)

Story type: Modern; Ranch Life
Subject(s): American West
Major character(s): Iris Steele, Rancher; Ike Steele, Parent (Iris' father), Rancher; Elise Steele, Parent (Iris' mother)
Time period(s): 2000s (2001)
Locale(s): Oregon

Summary: Iris Steele has recently inherited ranches from both her father, Ike, and mother, Elise, two characters who are overpowering even though they are dead. Iris' stories about her parents keep them alive for the reader, more real than her brother, Jake, or her Aunt Hanna. Ranching procedures such as calf castration and how to run a cattle drive, as well as a strong sense of place, balance certain plot weaknesses.

Where it's reviewed:
Publishers Weekly, September 24, 2001, page 70

Other books you might like:
Frederic Bean, *Murder at the Spirit Cave*, 1999
Peter Bowen, *Thunder Horse*, 1999
Doug Bowman, *The Copelands*, 1999
Will Cade, *Larimont*, 1999
Ed Gorman, *The Fatal Frontier*, 1997
Martin Greenberg, co-editor

512

RICHARD S. WHEELER

Downriver

(New York: Forge, 2001)

Story type: Historical; Man Alone
Series: Barnaby Skye. Book 12
Subject(s): American West; Fur Trade

Major character(s): Barnaby Skye, Mountain Man; Victoria Skye, Spouse (of Barnaby), Indian (Crow)
Time period(s): 1830s (1838)
Locale(s): St. Louis, Missouri

Summary: Aging mountain man Barnaby Skye and his Crow Indian wife, Victoria, are traveling to St. Louis, where Barnaby hopes to get a job as a post trader for the American Fur Company. Complicating the situation is the fact that Barnaby is not used to the backstabbing ways of the business, but he will learn if it kills him—and it just might.

Where it's reviewed:
Publishers Weekly, October 8, 2001, page 40

Other books by the same author:
Restitution, 2001
Witness, 2000
Flint's Gift, 1999
Masterson, 1999
Sun Mountain, 1999

Other books you might like:
Mike Blakely, *Summer of Pearls*, 2000
Terry C. Johnston, *Death Rattle*, 1999
Titus Bass series
Michael Kasser, *Warrior's Honor*, 1999
John Killdeer, *The Far Horizon*, 1994
Mountain Majesty. Book 6
Robert Lake, *Mountain Man's Vengeance*, 1989

513

JANICE WOODS WINDLE

Will's War

(New York: Longstreet, 2001)

Story type: Modern; Man Alone
Subject(s): American West; Crime and Criminals
Major character(s): Will Bergfeld, Defendant (against charges of treason); William Hawley Atwell, Lawyer (Will's); Virginia King Bergfeld, Spouse (of Will)
Time period(s): 1910s (1917)
Locale(s): Seguin, Texas

Summary: Based on Windle's grandfather's trial for treason in 1917, this novel brings to life the anti-German hysteria in the United States at that time. Will Bergfeld is charged with conspiracy to assassinate President Woodrow Wilson, and even though he is defended by the very able William Hawley Atwell, and supported by his wife, Virginia King Bergfeld, the evidence against him seems overwhelming. In truth, Bergfeld is guilty of nothing but union organizing and his German ancestry, but his temperament doesn't help him during the trial. A suspenseful novel with a strong sense of place and time.

Where it's reviewed:
Library Journal, October 1, 2001, page 144
Publishers Weekly, October 1, 2001, page 37

Other books by the same author:
Hill Country, 1998
True Women, 1993

Other books you might like:
Jane Valentine Barker, *Mari*, 1997
Frederic Bean, *Murder at the Spirit Cave*, 1999
James Carlos Blake, *The Friends of Pancho Villa*, 1996
James Carlos Blake, *Red Grass River*, 1998
Diane Glancy, *Flutie*, 1998

514

JAMES C. WORK

Ride West to Dawn

(Waterville, Maine: Thorndike, 2001)

Story type: Traditional; Ranch Life
Subject(s): American West
Major character(s): Will Jensen, Cowboy; Kyle Owens, Cowboy; Luna, Outcast
Time period(s): 19th century (post-Civil War)
Locale(s): Colorado

Summary: Ranchers and settlers around the Keystone Ranch are having irrigation problems. Will Jensen is the first cowboy to ride into the mountains to investigate the problems. He returns to the Keystone wounded in mind and body, and unable to remember what happened. Kyle Owens is the next to attempt to find the cause of the irrigation problem. He meets a mysterious being called the Guardian, as well as a young woman named Luna. She reveals to Kyle the way to a hidden valley where a manor house is owned by someone called simply The Lady. A story with a touch of the supernatural.

Where it's reviewed:
Roundup Magazine, May 2002, page 31

Other books by the same author:
Ride South to Purgatory, 1999
The Tobermory Manuscript, 1998

Other books you might like:
Jack Ballas, *Tomahawk Canyon*, 1992
Doug Bowman, *The Three Lives of Littleton Blue*, 1992
Tim Champlin, *Tombstone Conspiracy*, 1999
Andrew Huebner, *American by Blood*, 2000
Lauran Paine, *The White Bird*, 1999

Fantasy Fiction in 2001
by
Don D'Ammassa

The inherently conservative nature of the contemporary fantasy field was very much in evidence again in 2001. The vast majority of titles made use of the familiar setting of a fantastic alternate reality where magic works. Plots include efforts to remove usurpers from their thrones, complex court intrigues, quests for magical objects or information, and wars against monsters or armies led by (or at least aided by) evil sorcerers. These alternate worlds are almost invariably medieval in structure and, without the fantastic content, most could just as easily have been historical novels. The settings, and sometimes even the characters, are virtually interchangeable. Occasionally there are explicit rules about how magic works, more often there are not, and magic is sometimes not even crucial to the plot.

Surprisingly, there has been little effort, even in young adult fantasy fiction, to ride the coat tails of Harry Potter. If anything, there were fewer young adult fantasy novels during the year, and none were memorable. Whether that continues to be true following the release of the Harry Potter film and the first of the *Lord of the Rings* movies remains to be seen. Humorous fantasy continued to do reasonably well in England, but very poorly in the United States unless it was written by Terry Pratchett. The flood of media related tie-in novels that has diluted science fiction for the past several years may finally be spreading to fantasy, and there have been an increasing number of titles set in the worlds of computer games such as Diablo and Warhammer. As in science fiction, the vast majority of tie-in novels are formulaic in plot and so limited in scope that they are unlikely to interest any readers who aren't involved with the games.

The most notable fantasy of the year is unquestionably *Perdido Street Station* by China Mieville, who has already established himself as a major voice in speculative fiction after only two novels. Mieville has created a richly contrived, totally original setting, an urbanized fantasy world peopled with a variety of intelligent creatures and distinct cultures, and with some clever new magical devices. One of the two protagonists is a non-human sculptor hired to do a three dimensional portrait of a being who has been magically transformed into a near chaotic form. The other—the sculptor's human husband—is coerced into helping a disgraced member of another species regain the power of flight after losing his wings. The story is serious and complex and even the non-human characters are portrayed so skillfully that they seem genuine persons. Mieville was interviewed in the March 2002 *Locus*.

Neal Barrett, Jr.'s *The Treachery of Kings*, sequel to last year's *The Prophecy Machine*, also involves an unfamiliar setting, a world whose various fiefdoms and nations all appear to have been established on insane principles and are populated by the mad. He manages to tread a delicate path, blending adventure and humor without becoming overly farcical, and his witty, playful prose style is ideally suited to the subject matter. It's an extended Mad Hatter's Tea Party for adults.

Michael Moorcock also broke new ground with *The Dreamthief's Daughter*, which is another of his efforts to merge the various strands of the Eternal Champion series. The opening is set during the years preceding World War II. An anti-Nazi German aristocrat is the latest guardian of a magical sword, the battle for which will take him to a strange underground world in an alternate reality for the ultimate battle between good and evil, where he will meet creatures human and otherwise, including alternate manifestations of himself.

Historical fantasy held its own in 2001, but just barely. The most notable effort was *Pride of Kings* by Judith Tarr, who is the leading writer of historical fantasy active today. She examines the life of Richard the Lionheart, revealing that on the day he accepted the crown, he refused a similar offer from the world of Faerie, and thereby delivered an insult that led to the troubles that followed. Also of note is R. Garcia y Robertson's *Knight Errant*, which is essentially a time travel romance. The protagonist is a contemporary woman who makes several trips back to fifteenth century England, where she falls in love with a knight, is arrested for witchcraft, and eventually influences the king. It's an intelligently told story that proves even the most overused plot can be rewarding in the hands of a skilled writer.

Robert Holdstock delves further into the past and plays with ancient legends in *Celtika*. Jason is restored to life from suspended animation and must recruit a new crew of Argonauts for a mystical journey in search of his sons. Although he thought them dead, they have actually been transported to other realities by his angry wife, where they have now grown to maturity. The plot may be too abstruse for casual readers, but has much to reward those searching for more thoughtful fiction. In *Once upon a Winter's Night*, Dennis L. McKiernan re-examines the story of the Beauty and the Beast. A young woman marries a handsome aristocrat, who insists she not look upon his face at certain times of the day. When she breaks his rule, she unleashes a terrible curse, which she spends the rest of the novel trying to lift.

Contemporary fantasy showed a definite decline. Charles De Lint provided a new and mostly satisfying Newford novel, *The Onion Girl*, featuring a young woman who goes through a crisis in a small town where the borders between our reality and the world of spirits have grown thin, but the novel lacks the impact of his earlier work and appears to retread overly familiar ground. S. Andrew Swann's *The Dragons of the Cuyahoga* is more ambitious and more rewarding, if slightly less serious. The city of Chicago has become the gateway between our world and a world in which magic is real and legendary creatures exist, allowing passage in both directions. The influence of magic is restricted to the city limits in our world, so all of the dragons, elves, and other creatures are confined to the city. When a prominent dragon is killed, the protagonist suspects city officials are covering up a murder, and perhaps an even more sinister plot, and perseveres with his investigation even when it is clear he is risking his own life.

As mentioned, the vast majority of fantasy published this past year has been traditional alternate world adventure and intrigue, but a few of these titles stand out sharply from the others. Lois McMaster Bujold, author of an immensely popular science fiction series, took one of her periodic breaks from SF to write an exceptionally good standard fantasy, *The Curse of Chalion*. The protagonist is betrayed into slavery and, though he escapes, he returns to his homeland with both spirit and body broken. Once home, he becomes protector to a young aristocrat, and through that service he regains a sense of his own worth, while proving himself an able mentor and bodyguard. Superior narrative skills and nicely honed characters helped raise this above a host of similar novels. Lawrence Watt-Evans continues the story begun in *Dragon Weather* with *The Dragon Society*. After defeating several of his enemies, the hero gains membership in the Dragon Society, an organization he has vowed to destroy. His efforts are complicated by the discovery that the immortality resulting from being bitten by a dragon has a downside; he and all of his fellow members are doomed to death when their bodies become the incubators for young dragons.

Ursula K. Le Guin returned to the world of Earthsea with two new titles. *Tales from Earthsea* is a collection of long stories, but *The Other Wind* is a novel which portrays several major changes in her imagined land. An elderly man is troubled by visions of the dead, sets out to find what they mean, and discovers the world is rapidly changing at the behest of unknown forces. Le Guin's fantasies are not melodramatic despite what might be physically occurring in their plots, and once again, she uses highly literate prose and an inventive imagination to create a world that seems as though it should be real, even if it isn't. Storm Constantine is another conscious, creative stylist. Her *The Way of Light* is an exciting and intelligent conclusion to her Magravandian cycle, a series involving a fantasy world where personal loyalties and pledges are of very high importance, and the succession to the throne causes more than one individual to reassess everything they thought they believed.

Lynn Flewelling's quietly impressive *The Bone Doll's Twin* mixes strands from different fantasy traditions with good results. A young princess must be concealed from the usurper who seeks her death, so she is magically transformed into a male, an act possible only because she had a twin brother who died while still an infant. Unfortunately for her, the spirit of her brother is still at large, and he becomes her demonic enemy when she assumes the life he was denied. David Gemmell's newest Rigante novel, *Midnight Falcon*, is also a coming-of-age story, in this case following the career of the bastard son of an aristocrat. Embittered by his father's refusal to acknowledge him, he searches for a future of his own choosing and follows a dark and violent path.

Mel Odom borrows more directly from the Tolkien tradition than any other writer this year with *The Rover*. The protagonist in this case is a diminutive, bookish creature who gets caught up in a series of adventures including slavery and piracy, in the process discovering that he is much braver than he originally thought. The novel doesn't have the depth of Tolkien, but it's much more involved and carefully plotted than Odom's other fantasy fiction.

2001 wasn't a particularly good year for short fantasy fiction, other than Le Guin's *Tales from Earthsea*. Two other collections are worth noting, both from small presses, but *Redgunk Tales* by William Eakin and *Meet Me in the Moon Room* by Ray Vukcevich both tend toward surrealism and magic realism rather than conventional fantasy. Humorous fantasy fared even more poorly. Terry Pratchett has been the only humorist in the field who has remained popular in American markets. This year's *The Amazing Maurice and His Educated Rodents* is an amusing and atypical entry in the Discworld series, but it is aimed at younger readers and will probably not satisfy his fans. The other new Discworld book this year, *The Last Hero* is short, predictable, and generally disappointing. Authors like Tom Holt and Andrew Harman continue to produce amusing, humorous fantasy in the United Kingdom, but neither author has found an American publisher, and US-based writers like Esther Friesner, John DeChancie, and Craig Shaw Gardner have moved into other forms.

Numerically, the fantasy genre would appear to be quite healthy. There is virtually no difference between fantasy and science fiction in the total number of titles published, though fantasy has a slight edge in hardcover editions. Individual fantasy titles, particularly mainstream fantasy series novels, often make the bestseller lists and there is clearly a sustained demand for them. The hazard for the genre is the proliferation of similar series, which necessarily dilutes the potential readership for each individual author. In the long run, it is likely to be those authors providing something out of the ordinary who will continue to be successful, and the vast majority of fantasy writers today seem unwilling to experiment. As a genre, fantasy must continue to lure new readers and diversify its offering or it may be headed for a collapse such as that which affected horror fiction a decade ago.

Recommended Titles

Entries for the following books are included in this volume.

The Treachery of Kings by Neal Barrett, Jr.

The Way of Light by Storm Constantine

The Onion Girl by Charles De Lint

The Bone Doll's Twin by Lynn Flewelling

Knight Errant by R. Garcia y Robertson

Midnight Falcon by David Gemmell

Celtika by Robert Holdstock

The Other Wind by Ursula K. Le Guin

Once upon a Winter's Night by Dennis L. McKiernan

The Dreamthief's Daughter by Michael Moorcock

The Rover by Mel Odom

The Amazing Maurice and His Educated Rodents by Terry Pratchett

The Dragons of the Cuyahoga by S. Andrew Swann

Pride of Kings by Judith Tarr

The Dragon Society by Lawrence Watt-Evans

Entries for the following books can be found in *WDIRN?* 2001. Volume 2.

The Curse of Chalion by Lois McMaster Bujold

Redgunk Tales by William Eakin

Tales from Earthsea by Ursula K. Le Guin

Perdido Street Station by China Mieville

Meet Me in the Moon Room by Ray Vukcevich

Fantasy Titles

515

LYNN ABBEY

Behind Time

(New York: Ace, 2001)

Story type: Contemporary
Series: Emma Merrigan. Book 2
Subject(s): Magic
Major character(s): Emma Merrigan, Librarian; Eleanor Merrigan, Wizard; Matt Barto, Computer Expert
Time period(s): 2000s (2001)
Locale(s): Bower, Michigan

Summary: Emma Merrigan's life is turned on end when her mother reappears after a prolonged absence, announcing that she has magical powers and then endows her daughter with some of them. Now Eleanor Merrigan is in a coma and Emma must make use of her new abilities to explore other realities and find a cure.

Where it's reviewed:
Booklist, June 2001, page 1855

Other books by the same author:
Out of Time, 2000
Jerlayne, 1999
Planeswalker, 1998
The Simbul's Gift, 1997
Cinnabar Shadows, 1995

Other books you might like:
Elizabeth Bergstrom, *The Door through Washington Square*, 2000
James P. Blaylock, *The Rainy Season*, 1999
Jonathan Carroll, *The Voice of Our Shadow*, 1983
J. Robert King, *The Time Streams*, 1999
Rebecca Lickiss, *Eccentric Circles*, 2001

516

AARON ALLSTON

Sidhe-Devil

(New York: Baen, 2001)

Story type: Alternate Universe
Series: Doc Sidhe. Book 2
Subject(s): Alternate History; Magic
Major character(s): Desmond MaqqRee, Hero; Harris Greene, Businessman; Zeb Watson, Travel Agent
Time period(s): 2000s (2001)
Locale(s): Alternate Earth

Summary: Zeb Watson is transported to an alternate Earth where magic works and the mysterious Doc Sidhe works behind the scenes to restore order. A criminal mastermind is threatening to set off bombs in a major city, and in the alternate version of Europe, a new leader is emerging who preaches racial hatred.

Other books by the same author:
Solo Command, 1999
Starfighters of Adumar, 1999
Iron Fist, 1998
Doc Sidhe, 1995
Galatea in 2-D, 1993

Other books you might like:
Poul Anderson, *Operation Luna*, 1999
Piers Anthony, *Out of Phaze*, 1987
William R. Forstchen, *The Napoleon Wager*, 1993
J. Gregory Keyes, *Empire of Unreason*, 2000
Lawrence Watt-Evans, *Out of This World*, 1994

517

POUL ANDERSON

Mother of Kings

(New York: Tor, 2001)

Story type: Historical

Subject(s): Magic
Major character(s): Gunhild Ozurardottir, Witch; Gamli Eiriksson, Ruler; Eirik Haraldsson Blood-Ax, Warrior
Time period(s): 10th century
Locale(s): Norway; At Sea

Summary: This is another in the author's series of novels about the days of the Viking raiders. The central character is Gunhild, an ambitious young woman who uses magic to attract a prominent and successful husband. Although he is killed by his enemies, she continues her quest for power through her sons, each of whom has a heroic career.

Other books by the same author:
War of the Gods, 1997
Conan the Rebel, 1980
The Merman's Children, 1979
Hrolf Kraki's Saga, 1973
The Broken Sword, 1954

Other books you might like:
Nigel Frith, *Jormungard*, 1986
John Gardner, *Grendel*, 1971
H. Rider Haggard, *Eric Brighteyes*, 1891
Bernard King, *Vargr Moon*, 1986
Lois Tilton, *Written in Venom*, 2000

518

PIERS ANTHONY

Swell Foop

(New York: Tor, 2001)

Story type: Humor
Series: Xanth. Book 25
Subject(s): Magic; Demons
Major character(s): Cynthia Centaur, Mythical Creature; Breanna, Sorceress; Jaylin, Teenager
Time period(s): Indeterminate
Locale(s): Xanth, Alternate Universe

Summary: The supernatural creature who controls gravity and other elements in the world of Xanth is missing, and that entire reality is in jeopardy. An unlikely company is off for a humorous set of adventures as they seek out the magical rings that point to the power to restore the demon.

Where it's reviewed:
Publishers Weekly, August 27, 2001, page 59

Other books by the same author:
DoOon Mode, 2001
Reality Check, 1999
Xone of Contention, 1999
Yon Ill Wind, 1996
Killobyte, 1993

Other books you might like:
Neal Barrett Jr., *The Prophecy Machine*, 2000
John DeChancie, *MagicNet*, 1993
Andrew Harman, *101 Damnations*, 1995
Tom Holt, *Snow White and the Seven Samurai*, 1999
Terry Pratchett, *The Last Continent*, 1998

519

K.A. APPLEGATE

Entertain the End

(New York: Scholastic, 2001)

Story type: Young Adult; Alternate Universe
Series: Everworld. Book 12
Subject(s): Legends
Major character(s): April, Teenager; David, Teenager; Merlin, Wizard
Time period(s): 2000s (2001)
Locale(s): Everworld, Alternate Universe

Summary: A group of teenagers have been traveling through a series of alternate realities where various mythical creations are real. Now they are attempting to return to their own world, but before they can leave they must confront the magical Hel and help Merlin to restore stability to the realm in which they've trespassed.

Other books by the same author:
Mystify the Magician, 2001
Brave the Betrayal, 2000
Discover the Destroyer, 2000
Gateway to the Gods, 2000
Under the Unknown, 2000

Other books you might like:
Alan Garner, *The Owl Service*, 1967
Diana Wynne Jones, *Archer's Goon*, 1984
Andre Norton, *Red Hart Magic*, 1976
Vivian Vande Velde, *Spellbound*, 1998
Jane Yolen, *The Wizard's Map*, 1999

520

K.A. APPLEGATE

Mystify the Magician

(New York: Scholastic, 2001)

Story type: Young Adult; Legend
Series: Everworld. Book 11
Subject(s): Legends
Major character(s): Christopher, Teenager; Jalil, Teenager; April, Teenager
Time period(s): Indeterminate
Locale(s): Eire, Fictional Country

Summary: The teenaged protagonists have traveled from one magical world to another, but they hope their latest transition has brought them back to Earth. At first it appears they've arrived in modern day Eire, but it doesn't take long for them to discover they're in a similar land of the same name, where leprechauns are real and magic works.

Other books by the same author:
Brave the Betrayal, 2000
Discover the Destroyer, 2000
Gateway to the Gods, 2000
Inside the Illusion, 2000
Realm of the Reaper, 1999

Other books you might like:
Kenneth Bulmer, *Land Beyond the Map*, 1965
Pamela Dean, *The Hidden Land*, 1986
Philip Jose Farmer, *The Maker of Universes*, 1965
Kenneth Flint, *Isle of Destiny*, 1988
Alan Garner, *The Weirdstone of Brisingamen*, 1960

521

ROBERT LYNN ASPRIN

Myth-ion Improbable

(Decatur, Georgia: Meisha Merlin, 2001)

Story type: Humor; Quest
Series: Myth. Book 11
Subject(s): Humor
Major character(s): Skeeve, Wizard; Aahz, Demon; Tanda, Warrior
Time period(s): Indeterminate
Locale(s): Alternate Universe

Summary: Skeeve and his demon friend, Aahz, have a treasure map which they hope will make them rich. Unfortunately, in order to locate the treasure, they have to take other people into their confidence, and things get predictably more complicated and more hilarious as the story progresses.

Where it's reviewed:
Locus, October 2001, page 33

Other books by the same author:
A Phule and His Money, 1999
Sweet Myth-tery of Life, 1994
Phule's Company, 1990
Little Myth Marker, 1985
Myth-ing Persons, 1984

Other books you might like:
Piers Anthony, *Swell Foop*, 2001
Rick Cook, *Cursed and Consulted*, 2001
Esther Friesner, *Gnome Man's Land*, 1991
Craig Shaw Gardner, *A Bad Day for Ali Baba*, 1992
John Morressey, *The Questing of Kedrigern*, 1987

522

MIGNON F. BALLARD

An Angel to Die For

(New York: Berkley, 2001)

Story type: Mystery
Series: Augusta Goodnight. Book 2
Subject(s): Angels
Major character(s): Augusta Goodnight, Angel; Prentice Dobson, Businesswoman; Zorah Haskell, Aged Person
Time period(s): 2000s (2001)
Locale(s): Georgia

Summary: Following the death of her sister, a woman decides to take an extended vacation in the small town where her aunt lives. Shortly after arriving, she discovers her uncle's body has been stolen from its grave. Her concern is finally eased by the arrival of a guardian angel, who solves the mystery.

Where it's reviewed:
Booklist, October 15, 2001, page 420
Library Journal, November 1, 2001, page 142
Publishers Weekly, October 2, 2001, page 62

Other books by the same author:
Angel at Troublesome Creek, 1999

Other books you might like:
John Dickson Carr, *The Devil in Velvet*, 1951
Dorothy Gilman, *The Clairvoyant Countess*, 1975
James Gunn, *The Magicians*, 1976
Melisa Michaels, *Cold Iron*, 1997
Silver Ravenwolf, *Murder at Witches' Bluff*, 2000

523

JAMES BARCLAY

Nightchild

(London: Gollancz, 2001)

Story type: Sword and Sorcery
Series: Chronicles of the Raven. Book 3
Subject(s): Magic
Major character(s): Erienne, Sorceress; Lyanna, Child, Sorceress; Denser, Sorcerer
Time period(s): Indeterminate
Locale(s): Balaia, Fictional Country

Summary: A child is born with magic so powerful she may destroy the world before she learns to control both her power and her own impulsiveness. When her mother hides her away to protect her, the child's father sets out to find them both, and must ultimately face a very difficult decision.

Other books by the same author:
Noonshade, 2000
Dawnthief, 1999

Other books you might like:
Maggie Furey, *Dhammara*, 1997
Simon R. Green, *Beyond the Blue Moon*, 2000
Mindy Klasky, *The Glasswright's Apprentice*, 2001
Mercedes Lackey, *Four and Twenty Blackbirds*, 1997
Lawrence Watt-Evans, *Dragon Weather*, 1999

524

NEAL BARRETT JR.

The Treachery of Kings

(New York: Bantam, 2001)

Story type: Alternate Universe
Series: Finn. Book 2
Subject(s): Humor
Major character(s): Finn, Inventor; Bucerius, Animal (bull); Letitia Louise, Animal (mouse)
Time period(s): Indeterminate
Locale(s): Heldessia, Fictional Country

Summary: Inventor Finn and his consort, Letitia Louise, are off on another adventure, this time bringing a birthday present to the ruler of a hostile foreign nation. There they discover organized armies of assassination and an aristocracy whose religion compels them to spend long periods of time sleeping in tombs.

Where it's reviewed:
Booklist, August 2001, page 336
Locus, August 2001, page 25
Science Fiction Chronicle, October 2001, page 43

Other books by the same author:
Dungeons and Dragons, 2001
Perpetuity Blues, 2000
The Prophecy Machine, 2000
The Hereafter Gang, 1991
Aldair, Master of Ships, 1977

Other books you might like:
Arthur Byron Cover, *The Platypus of Doom and Other Nihilists*, 1976
Gordon R. Dickson, *The Dragon and the Gnarly King*, 1997
Simon Hawke, *The Reluctant Sorcerer*, 1992
Terry Pratchett, *Maskerade*, 1995
Lawrence Watt-Evans, *Split Heirs*, 1993
Esther Friesner, co-author

525

CARRIE BEBRIS

Pool of Radiance

(Renton, Washington: Wizards of the Coast, 2001)

Story type: Sword and Sorcery
Series: Forgotten Realms
Subject(s): Magic
Major character(s): Kestrel, Thief; Ghleanna Stormlake, Sorceress; Corran D'Arcey, Adventurer
Time period(s): Indeterminate
Locale(s): Phlan, Fictional Country

Summary: Kestrel is a thief who has no ambition to become a hero. Then she encounters Ghleanna Stormlake and her companions, and discovers that someone has created a mystical Pool of Radiance, a fount of evil which ultimately threatens the entire world. Against her better judgment, she joins the others on a quest to discover the source, encountering monsters, magic, and mayhem in the process. This is a first novel.

Other books you might like:
Nancy Varian Berberick, *Stormblade*, 1988
Elaine Cunningham, *Thornhold*, 1998
Mary Kirchoff, *Black Wing*, 1993
R.A. Salvatore, *Siege of Darkness*, 1995
James Ward, *Pool of Twilight*, 1993
Anne Brown, co-author

526

CURT BENJAMIN

The Prince of Shadow

(New York: DAW, 2001)

Story type: Quest
Series: Seven Brothers. Book 1
Subject(s): Magic
Major character(s): Llesho, Teenager, Nobleman; Llech, Scholar; Habiba, Warrior
Time period(s): Indeterminate
Locale(s): Thebin, Fictional Country

Summary: Llesho is sold into slavery as a child when his country is overwhelmed by a barbaric invader. Years later, a scholar tells him his brothers are alive, and it is his destiny to win his freedom, then rescue his siblings in preparation for the liberation of his homeland. This is a first novel.

Where it's reviewed:
Booklist, September 15, 2001, page 300
Publishers Weekly, September 10, 2001, page 67

Other books you might like:
Kate Elliott, *Prince of Dogs*, 1998
George R.R. Martin, *A Storm of Swords*, 2000
Dennis L. McKiernan, *The Dragonstone*, 1996
L.E. Modesitt Jr., *The Colors of Chaos*, 1999
Lawrence Watt-Evans, *Dragon Weather*, 1999

527

ANNE BISHOP

The Pillars of the World

(New York: Roc, 2001)

Story type: Magic Conflict
Subject(s): Fairies
Major character(s): Ari, Witch; Dianna, Mythical Creature (fairy); Ahern, Mythical Creature (fairy)
Time period(s): Indeterminate
Locale(s): Syvalan, Fictional Country; Tir Alainn, Fictional Country

Summary: It is possible to travel back and forth between the world of humans and the world of the Fae, but few trouble to do so. Now something is closing the pathways between the worlds, and a dark force is rising that menaces an innocent human witch and threatens to bring disorder to both the human and fairy realms.

Where it's reviewed:
Booklist, September 15, 2001, page 200

Other books by the same author:
Queen of the Darkness, 2000
The Invisible Ring, 2000
Heir to the Shadows, 1999
Daughter of the Blood, 1998

Other books you might like:
Gael Baudino, *Shroud of Shadow*, 1993
Tom Deitz, *Dreamseeker's Road*, 1995
Raymond E. Feist, *Faerie Tale*, 1988
Laurell K. Hamilton, *A Kiss of Shadows*, 2000
Kristine Kathryn Rusch, *The Fey: Sacrifice*, 1996

528

ALICE BORCHARDT

The Dragon Queen

(New York: Ballantine Del Rey, 2001)

Story type: Legend
Series: Tales of Guinevere. Book 1
Subject(s): Arthurian Legends
Major character(s): Guinevere, Royalty; Merlin, Wizard; Arthur, Ruler (king)
Time period(s): Indeterminate Past
Locale(s): England

Summary: Merlin has a prescient vision in which he foresees that Guinevere will eventually provide the impetus for the fall of Camelot. He attempts to prevent her from ever gaining Arthur's regard, and she seeks refuge with a druid and a shapechanger on an island of dragons.

Where it's reviewed:
Publishers Weekly, October 1, 2001, page 42

Other books by the same author:
The Wolf King, 2001
Night of the Wolf, 1999
The Silver Wolf, 1998

Other books you might like:
Marion Zimmer Bradley, *The Mists of Avalon*, 1982
Phyllis Ann Karr, *The Idylls of the Queen*, 1982
James Mallory, *The Old Magic*, 1999
Nancy McKenzie, *The Child Queen*, 1994
Sharan Newman, *The Chessboard Queen*, 1983

529

PAUL BRANDON

Swim the Moon

(New York: Tor, 2001)

Story type: Contemporary
Subject(s): Fairies
Major character(s): Richard Brennan, Musician; Ailish, Young Woman
Time period(s): 2000s (2001)
Locale(s): Scotland

Summary: Richard Brennan has exiled himself from Scotland to Australia, but when he returns for his father's funeral, he finds himself strangely reluctant to leave. Then he meets a mysterious young woman and his dreams and eventually his waking hours are invaded by an ancient magic that draws them closer and closer. This is a first novel.

Where it's reviewed:
Booklist, September 1, 2001, page 58
Library Journal, September 15, 2001, page 115
Locus, September 2001, page 24
Publishers Weekly, August 13, 2001, page 291
Science Fiction Chronicle, December 2001, page 44

Other books you might like:
Jonathan Carroll, *Kissing the Beehive*, 1998
Charles De Lint, *Our Lady of the Harbor*, 1991
James Long, *Ferney*, 1998
Ian McDonald, *King of Morning, Queen of Day*, 1991
Sarban, *Ringstones*, 1951

530

TERRY BROOKS

Antrax

(New York: Ballantine Del Rey, 2001)

Story type: Sword and Sorcery
Series: Shannara. Book 10
Subject(s): Magic
Major character(s): Grianne Ohmsford, Witch; Truls Rohk, Mythical Creature (shapechanger); Bek Ohmsford, Wizard
Time period(s): Indeterminate
Locale(s): Four Lands, Fictional Country

Summary: The Ilse witch learns her brother is still alive, protected by a shapechanger who may have hidden motives. At the same time, the supernatural being Antrax is accumulating magic in its bid to become powerful enough so it will no longer need to fear its enemies.

Where it's reviewed:
Booklist, June 2001, page 1796
Library Journal, July 2001, page 131
Publishers Weekly, August 13, 2001, page 291

Other books by the same author:
The Ilse Witch, 2000
Angel Fire East, 1999
Running with the Demon, 1997
The First King of Shannara, 1996
Tangle Box, 1994

Other books you might like:
Raymond E. Feist, *Rage of a Demon King*, 1997
Fritz Leiber, *Ill Met in Lankhmar*, 1995
Dennis L. McKiernan, *Voyage of the Fox Rider*, 1993
Tad Williams, *The Stone of Farewell*, 1990
Janny Wurts, *Master of the White Storm*, 1992

531

STAN BROWN

The Crab

(Renton, Washington: Wizards of the Coast, 2001)

Story type: Sword and Sorcery
Series: Legend of Five Rings. Book 6
Subject(s): Magic
Major character(s): Hida Kisada, Warrior; Mirumoto Hitomi, Warrior; Hida Yakamo, Warrior
Time period(s): Indeterminate
Locale(s): Rokugan, Fictional Country

Summary: The Crab clan is charged with the responsibility of protecting the empire of Rokugan from the creatures that live beyond its borders. Unfortunately, there are problems within as well, and dissension among the various clans leads to a battle for the throne that threatens the future of all. Intertwined with this is the quest for revenge by a young female warrior against the man who killed her brother in a feud. This is a first novel.

Where it's reviewed:
Science Fiction Chronicle, September 2001, page 42

Other books you might like:
Kara Dalkey, *The Heavenward Path*, 1998
Tim Lukeman, *Rajan*, 1979
Richard A. Lupoff, *Sword of the Demon*, 1976
Jessica Amanda Salmonson, *The Golden Naginata*, 1982
Ree Soesbee, *The Crane*, 2000

532

RICHARD LEE BYERS

The Shattered Mask

(Renton, Washington: Wizards of the Coast, 2001)

Story type: Sword and Sorcery
Series: Forgotten Realms
Subject(s): Magic
Major character(s): Shamur Uskevren, Noblewoman; Thamalon Uskevren, Businessman; Bileworm, Wizard
Time period(s): Indeterminate
Locale(s): Sembia, Fictional Country

Summary: Shamur Uskevren is tricked into believing that her husband is a murderer by a wizard who seeks to destroy the influence of their family. At the last minute she realizes the truth, and their enemies take more overt action against the couple and their children. Shamur herself conceals the secret of her own extraordinarily extended lifespan.

Where it's reviewed:
Science Fiction Chronicle, September 2001, page 42

Other books by the same author:
The Ebon Mask, 1999
Netherworld, 1995
Warlock Games, 1993
The Vampire's Apprentice, 1992
Fright Line, 1989

Other books you might like:
Raymond E. Feist, *Rise of a Merchant Prince*, 1995
Guy Gavriel Kay, *A Song for Arbonne*, 1992
Tanith Lee, *A Heroine of the World*, 1989
Fritz Leiber, *The Knight and Knave of Swords*, 1988
Paula Volsky, *Illusion*, 1992

533

MARK CHADBOURN

Always Forever

(London: Gollancz, 2001)

Story type: Sword and Sorcery
Series: Age of Misrule. Book 3
Subject(s): Magic
Major character(s): Jack Churchill, Scientist; Ruth Gallagher, Lawyer; Tuatha de Danann, Deity
Time period(s): 21st century
Locale(s): England

Summary: The creatures of Celtic mythology have returned to the world and conquered England. Now a dark god plans to extend his influence and wipe humankind from the face of the Earth. Opposing him is a group that sends a delegation to the land of the gods in order to find a supernatural ally of their own.

Where it's reviewed:
Science Fiction Chronicle, December 2001, page 47

Other books by the same author:
Darkest Hour, 2000
World's End, 1999
Scissorman, 1997
Testimony, 1996
Nocturne, 1994

Other books you might like:
Joan Aiken, *The Cockatrice Boys*, 1996
Paul Cornell, *Something More*, 2001
Brett Davis, *The Faery Convention*, 1995
Peter Dickinson, *The Weathermonger*, 1969
Esther Friesner, *New York by Knight*, 1986

534

JAMES CLEMENS

Wit'ch Gate

(New York: Ballantine Del Rey, 2001)

Story type: Magic Conflict
Series: Banned and Banished. Book 4
Subject(s): Magicians
Major character(s): Elena, Witch; Tratal, Ruler (queen); Er'ril, Warrior
Time period(s): Indeterminate
Locale(s): Alasea, Fictional Country

Summary: Elena is a young witch who has the power of good magic and who has attracted a number of heroic companions in her battle against the Dark Lord, who uses evil magic in his bid for power. Although the Dark Lord's forces have been routed, he is not without resources, and his new attack leaves Elena deprived of her friends' support as she faces her latest challenge.

Where it's reviewed:
Publishers Weekly, October 8, 2001, page 50

Other books by the same author:
Wit'ch War, 2000
Wit'ch Storm, 1999
Wit'ch Fire, 1998

Other books you might like:
Eileen Kernaghan, *The Sarsen Witch*, 1989
Tanith Lee, *Vazkor, Son of Vazkor*, 1978
Carl Miller, *The Warrior and the Witch*, 1990
Andre Norton, *Web of the Witch World*, 1964
Janny Wurts, *The Keeper of the Keys*, 1988

535

MICHAEL COBLEY

Shadowkings

(London: Earthlight, 2001)

Story type: Sword and Sorcery
Series: Shadowkings. Book 1
Subject(s): Magic
Major character(s): Suviel, Wizard; Ikarno Mazaret, Knight; Byrnak, Ruler
Time period(s): Indeterminate
Locale(s): Khatrimantine Empire, Fictional Country

Summary: A peaceful empire is invaded by barbarians who succeed because of the aid of a supernatural entity. The entity is shattered into five separate bodies during the war, each of whom exists as a separate character. If the five can reunite, the conquest will be complete, and there will be no way to restore the old order. This is a first novel.

Other books you might like:
Raymond E. Feist, *Rage of a Demon King*, 1997
Simon R. Green, *Beyond the Blue Moon*, 2000
Ken Hood, *Demon Knight*, 1998
Andrew J. Offutt, *Shadows out of Hell*, 1980
R.A. Salvatore, *The Demon Awakens*, 1997

536

STORM CONSTANTINE

The Way of Light

(New York: Tor, 2001)

Story type: Sword and Sorcery
Series: Magravandian Chronicles. Book 3
Subject(s): Magic
Major character(s): Valraven Palindrake, Nobleman; Tapopat, Wizard; Shan, Apprentice
Time period(s): Indeterminate
Locale(s): Magravandian Empire, Fictional Country

Summary: A power struggle begins following the death of the emperor. Valraven supports one of the princes, but there is an increasing clamor for him to assume the throne himself. A wizard, who opposes this outcome, kidnaps Valraven's family and sets out on a long and dangerous journey. This is the concluding volume in the trilogy.

Where it's reviewed:
Locus, January 2002, page 72
Science Fiction Chronicle, December 2001, page 46

Other books by the same author:
Sea Dragon Heir, 2000
The Crown of Silence, 2000
The Oracle Lips, 1999
Scenting Hallowed Blood, 1996
Stalking Tender Prey, 1995

Other books you might like:
E.R. Eddison, *Mistress of Mistresses*, 1935
Raymond E. Feist, *Shadow of a Dark Queen*, 1994
Katherine Kurtz, *The Harrowing of Gwynedd*, 1994
George R.R. Martin, *A Game of Thrones*, 1996
Tad Williams, *Caliban's Hour*, 1994

537

RICK COOK

Cursed and Consulted

(New York: Baen, 2001)

Story type: Collection
Series: Wizardry
Subject(s): Magic; Short Stories

Summary: This is the omnibus volume of the third and fourth novels in the Wizardry series, originally published in 1991 and 1995, titled *The Wizardry Cursed* and *The Wizardry Consulted*. In one novel, an Air Force pilot finds himself in another universe where he teams up with a computer programmer wizard, and a wizard is kidnapped by dragons in the middle of a sorcerous war in the other.

Other books by the same author:
The Wiz Biz, 1999
The Wizardry Quested, 1996
Mall Purchase Night, 1993
The Wizardry Compiled, 1990
Wizard's Bane, 1989

Other books you might like:
Susan Dexter, *The Wizard's Shadow*, 1993
William R. Forstchen, *The Crystal Sorcerers*, 1991
Greg Morrison, co-author
Esther Friesner, *Sphynxes Wild*, 1989
Craig Shaw Gardner, *An Excess of Enchantments*, 1988
John Morressey, *Kedrigern in Wanderland*, 1988

538

BRUCE COVILLE

The Monsters of Morley Manor

(New York: Harcourt, 2001)

Story type: Young Adult
Subject(s): Magic; Aliens
Major character(s): Anthony Walker, Child; Sarah Walker, Child; Albert, Scientist
Time period(s): 2000s (2001)
Locale(s): United States

Summary: Two children are surprised to discover that the tiny figurines they found come to life when exposed to water. They learn that aliens are planning to invade the earth, that magic is real, and that clones, ghosts, and other weird creatures exist as well.

Where it's reviewed:
Science Fiction Chronicle, October 2001, page 40

Other books by the same author:
Odder than Ever, 1999
The Skull of Truth, 1997
Oddly Enough, 1994
The Wrath of Squat, 1994
Aliens Ate My Homework, 1993

Other books you might like:
Diane Duane, *Deep Wizardry*, 1985
D. Manus Pinkwater, *Borgel*, 1990
Vivian Vande Velde, *Magic Can Be Murder*, 2000
Jane Yolen, *The Wild Hunt*, 1995
Mary Frances Zambreno, *A Plague of Sorcerers*, 1991

539

CHARLES DE LINT

The Onion Girl

(New York: Tor, 2001)

Story type: Contemporary
Subject(s): Magic
Major character(s): Jilly Coppercorn, Artist; Toby Childs, Teenager; Pinky Miller, Young Woman
Time period(s): 20th century; 2000s (1969-2000)
Locale(s): Newford

Summary: De Lint returns to his imaginary town of Newford for this story of Jilly Coppercorn, the local artist. In a series of events scattered over decades, we learn more of the secrets of her magical heritage in a setting where shapechangers, worlds accessible in dreams, and other magical elements abound just out of sight of most people.

Where it's reviewed:
Booklist, October 1, 2001, page 304
Locus, October 2001, page 25
Publishers Weekly, October 22, 2001, page 53

Other books by the same author:
Forests of the Heart, 2000
Moonlight and Vines, 1999
Someplace to Be Flying, 1998
Trader, 1997
Jack of Kinrowan, 1995

Other books you might like:
Jonathan Carroll, *The Marriage of Sticks*, 1999
Tom Deitz, *Soulsmith*, 1991
Richard Grant, *In the Land of Winter*, 1997
Nina Kiriki Hoffman, *The Silent Strength of Stones*, 1995
Will Shetterly, *Dogland*, 1997

540

SARA DOUGLASS

Enchanter

(New York: Tor, 2001)

Story type: Sword and Sorcery
Series: Wayfarer Redemption. Book 2
Subject(s): Magic
Major character(s): Axis, Warrior, Wizard; Borneheld, Warrior; Azhure, Warrior
Time period(s): Indeterminate
Locale(s): Achar, Fictional Country

Summary: The warrior Axis has returned to his homeland where he seeks to master the magical powers that have awakened in him. He sees his destiny as reuniting the two disparate peoples of his world, but his efforts are hampered by his brother, who is jealous and unreasonable, as well as a monster with a personal grudge against him.

Other books by the same author:
Crusader, 2000
Battleaxe, 1998

Other books you might like:
Storm Constantine, *Sea Dragon Heir*, 2000
Robin Hobb, *The Royal Assassin*, 1996
J.V. Jones, *The Barbed Coil*, 1997
Richard A. Knaak, *The Janus Mask*, 1995
David Mason, *Kavin's World*, 1969

541

DAVID DRAKE

Mistress of the Catacombs

(New York: Tor, 2001)

Story type: Sword and Sorcery
Series: Lord of the Isles. Book 4
Subject(s): Magic
Major character(s): Prince Garric, Ruler; Sharina, Noblewoman; Cashel, Warrior
Time period(s): Indeterminate
Locale(s): Kingdom of the Isles, Fictional Country

Summary: Just when it appears that the Kingdom of the Isles is finally going to have a stable government, the new ruler is beset by an invasion headed by inhuman wizards. With armies of creatures that are a blend of insect and reptile, they overwhelm the nation's defenses, while magic sends their leaders into other worlds.

Other books by the same author:
Servants of the Dragon, 1999
Queen of Demons, 1998
Lord of the Isles, 1997
Old Nathan, 1991
The Sea Hag, 1988

Other books you might like:
Raymond E. Feist, *A Darkness at Sethanon*, 1986
Terry Goodkind, *Wizard's First Rule*, 1994
Richard A. Knaak, *Frostwing*, 1995
George R.R. Martin, *A Game of Thrones*, 1996
Dennis L. McKiernan, *The Dark Tide*, 1984

542

EMILY DRAKE

The Magickers

(New York: DAW, 2001)

Story type: Young Adult; Contemporary
Subject(s): Coming-of-Age; Fantasy
Major character(s): Jason Adrian, Child; Gavan Rainwater, Magician; Henry Squibb, Child
Time period(s): 2000s (2001)
Locale(s): Camp Ravenwyng, Mythical Place

Summary: Young Jason Adrian wants to go to soccer camp, but an injury relegates him to spending the summer with his grandmother. Then he's given a chance to go to a very special camp, more special than even he realizes. Camp Ravenwyng sits on the border between our world and another where mythical creatures and magic are real. This is a first novel.

Where it's reviewed:
Booklist, July 2001, page 2006
Locus, June 2001, page 35

Other books you might like:
Diane Duane, *Deep Wizardry*, 1985
Alan Garner, *The Weirdstone of Brisingamen*, 1960
Diana Wynne Jones, *A Sudden Wild Magic*, 1992
J.K. Rowling, *Harry Potter and the Goblet of Fire*, 2000
Mary Frances Zambreno, *A Plague of Sorcerers*, 1991

543

DORANNA DURGIN

A Feral Darkness

(New York: Baen, 2001)

Story type: Contemporary; Horror
Subject(s): Magic
Major character(s): Brenna Fallon, Businesswoman (dog groomer); Gil Masera, Animal Trainer (obedience trainer); Druid, Animal (dog)
Time period(s): 2000s (2001)
Locale(s): New York

Summary: Brenna Fallon invokes a mysterious deity to save the life of an animal. Years later she takes in a stray dog just as a mysterious and hostile new neighbor moves nearby and attempts to buy her family's land. At the same time, a mutated form of rabies spreads through the area, and Brenna learns it is linked to a profane ritual which the neighbor has performed.

Other books by the same author:
Seer's Blood, 2000
Wolverine's Daughter, 2000
Barrenlands, 1998
Wolf Justice, 1998
Touched by Magic, 1996

Other books you might like:
Lynn Abbey, *Out of Time*, 2000
Margaret Ball, *Lost in Translation*, 1995
Esther Friesner, *The Wishing Season*, 1996
Brenda Jordan, *The Brentwood Witches*, 1987
Andre Norton, *Red Hart Magic*, 1976

544

LYNN FLEWELLING

The Bone Doll's Twin

(New York: Bantam, 2001)

Story type: Sword and Sorcery
Subject(s): Magic
Major character(s): Tobin, Noblewoman, Teenager; Erius, Ruler; Lhel, Witch
Time period(s): Indeterminate
Locale(s): Skala, Fictional Country

Summary: The usurper king of Skala is determined to ensure his line keeps the throne, so he kills all of his daughters and anyone else who might be a rival to the son he hopes to sire. Unbeknownst to him, young Tobin is not only in line to the throne, but the boy is also a girl magically transformed to conceal the truth from him. Tobin in turn is tormented by the ghost of her dead brother.

Other books by the same author:
Traitor's Moon, 1999
Stalking Darkness, 1997
Luck in the Shadows, 1996

Other books you might like:
David Feintuch, *The Still*, 1997
Sharon Green, *Intrigues*, 2000
Katherine Kurtz, *Deryni Rising*, 1970
George R.R. Martin, *A Game of Thrones*, 1996
Melanie Rawn, *The Star Scroll*, 1989

545

MAGGIE FUREY

Spirit of the Stone

(London: Orbit, 2001)

Story type: Sword and Sorcery
Series: Shadowleague. Book 2
Subject(s): Magic
Major character(s): Veldan, Wizard; Zavahl, Nobleman; Kazairl, Mythical Creature (firedrake)
Time period(s): Indeterminate
Locale(s): Myrial, Fictional Country

Summary: The protective walls of magic have fallen and all of Myrial is exposed to the armies of an ambitious conqueror. A loremaster must convince another man to unlock the secrets of his own mind in order to forge a defense.

Other books by the same author:
The Heart of Myrial, 1999
Dhammara, 1997
Harp of Winds, 1995
The Sword of Flame, 1995
Aurian, 1994

Other books you might like:
Stephen R. Donaldson, *The White Gold Wielder*, 1983
Raymond E. Feist, *Krondor the Betrayal*, 1998
Robert Jordan, *The Path of Daggers*, 1998
George R.R. Martin, *A Game of Thrones*, 1996
Janny Wurts, *Shadowfane*, 1988

546

R. GARCIA Y ROBERTSON

Knight Errant

(New York: Forge, 2001)

Story type: Time Travel
Subject(s): Time Travel
Major character(s): Robyn Stafford, Time Traveler; Edward Plantagenet, Nobleman
Time period(s): 15th century (1459)

Locale(s): England

Summary: Robyn Stafford is vacationing in England when she decides to take a walk by herself in the countryside. There she meets an apparent knight who introduces himself as Edward Plantagenet. Although the two are normally separated by five centuries, they occasionally are able to interact and a romance develops between them.

Where it's reviewed:
Booklist, October 1, 2001, page 305
Locus, October 2001, page 33
Publishers Weekly, October 15, 2001, page 46

Other books by the same author:
The Moon Maid, 1998
Atlantis Found, 1997
The Virgin and the Dinosaur, 1996
The Spiral Dance, 1991

Other books you might like:
Marilyn Campbell, *Just in Time*, 1996
Jack Finney, *Time and Again*, 1970
Diana Gabaldon, *Voyager*, 1994
Richard Matheson, *Bid Time Return*, 1975
Flora Speer, *Love Just in Time*, 1995

547

ROBERTA GELLIS

Thrice Bound

(New York: Baen, 2001)

Story type: Historical; Legend
Subject(s): Legends; Magic
Major character(s): Hekate, Witch; Kabeiros, Warrior; Dionysos, Religious (prophet)
Time period(s): Indeterminate Past
Locale(s): Mediterranean

Summary: Hekate is a witch whose sorcerer father tries to force her to commit murder. To escape his magic, she travels to some magical caves, where she is befriended by and falls in love with a noble warrior who can only keep his human form within the caves. She resolves to rescue him and free herself of her father's magic.

Other books by the same author:
Bull God, 2000
Shimmering Splendor, 1995
Dazzling Brightness, 1994

Other books you might like:
Patrick H. Adkins, *Master of the Fearful Depths*, 1989
Michael Ayrton, *The Maze Maker*, 1967
David Gemmell, *Lion of Macedon*, 1983
Richard Purtill, *The Mirror of Helen*, 1983
Thomas Burnett Swann, *The Forest of Forever*, 1971

548

DAVID GEMMELL

Midnight Falcon

(New York: Ballantine Del Rey, 2001)

Story type: Sword and Sorcery
Series: Rigante. Book 2
Subject(s): Magic
Major character(s): Bane, Warrior, Outcast; Banouin, Traveler; Connavar, Ruler
Time period(s): Indeterminate
Locale(s): Rigante, Fictional Country

Summary: Bane is the illegitimate son of a discredited king. Doubly damned, he goes into exile rather than face persecution. A chance encounter works to his disadvantage and he ends up as a slave in the gladiatorial games, until a turn of luck and his quick wits lead him to revenge and an eventual return to his homeland.

Other books by the same author:
Ravenheart, 2001
The Sword in the Storm, 2001
The Hero in the Shadows, 2000
Winter's Warriors, 1997
Ironhand's Daughter, 1995

Other books you might like:
Simon R. Green, *Blue Moon Rising*, 1991
Lyndon Hardy, *Master of the Five Magics*, 1980
Andrew J. Offutt, *The Iron Lords*, 1979
R.A. Salvatore, *The Sword of Bedwyr*, 1996
Lawrence Watt-Evans, *The Book of Silence*, 1984

549

TERRY GOODKIND

Debt of Bones

(London: Gollancz, 2001)

Story type: Sword and Sorcery
Series: Sword of Truth. Book 7
Subject(s): Magic
Major character(s): Zeddicus Zorander, Wizard; Delora, Sorceress; Abigail, Housewife
Time period(s): Indeterminate
Locale(s): Midlands, Fictional Country

Summary: A young woman comes to the wizard Zeddicus Zorander and asks him to intercede and help rescue her family held hostage by an enemy army. Secretly, she has agreed to betray the wizard into a trap in return for the release of her husband and daughter. This is a prequel to the other six books in the series.

Where it's reviewed:
Science Fiction Chronicle, November 2001, page 41

Other books by the same author:
Faith of the Fallen, 2000
Soul of the Fire, 1999
Temple of the Winds, 1997
Blood of the Fold, 1996

Stone of Tears, 1995

Other books you might like:

Storm Constantine, *The Crown of Silence*, 2000
George R.R. Martin, *A Clash of Kings*, 1999
L.E. Modesitt Jr., *The Shadow Sorceress*, 2001
Lawrence Watt-Evans, *Touched by the Gods*, 1997
Janny Wurts, *The Grand Conspiracy*, 2000

550

TERRY GOODKIND

The Pillars of Creation

(New York: Tor, 2001)

Story type: Sword and Sorcery; Quest
Series: Sword of Truth. Book 7
Subject(s): Magic
Major character(s): Richard Rahl, Wizard; Kahlan Rahl, Religious; Jennsen, Sorceress
Time period(s): Indeterminate
Locale(s): Midlands, Alternate Universe

Summary: Richard Rahl and his wife have finally gotten back together again, but their land is menaced by an unnaturally cold winter and a brutal invasion force, which threatens to destroy the old civilization. They must undertake a quest to a mystical place if they are to save their people, and their only hope may be a troubled young woman plagued by unwanted visions.

Other books by the same author:

Debt of Bones, 2001
Faith of the Fallen, 2000
Soul of the Fire, 1999
Temple of the Winds, 1997
Blood of the Fold, 1996

Other books you might like:

James Barclay, *Noonshade*, 2000
David Feintuch, *The Still*, 1997
Robert Jordan, *Winter's Heart*, 2000
George R.R. Martin, *A Game of Thrones*, 1996
Lawrence Watt-Evans, *Dragon Weather*, 1999

551

JULIA GRAY

The Jasper Forest

(London: Orbit, 2001)

Story type: Quest
Series: Guardian. Book 2
Subject(s): Magic
Major character(s): Terrell, Expatriate; Aylen Mirana, Fisherman; Kerin Mirana, Traveler
Time period(s): Indeterminate
Locale(s): Fendula, Fictional Country

Summary: Terrell has been exiled from his homeland and is traveling by sea when mischance almost costs him his life. Rescued by fishermen, he discovers that their village is beset by problems inherent in the nature of the world, so he sets off on a quest to find the truth and help his newfound friends.

Other books by the same author:

Fire Music, 2000
The Dark Moon, 2000
Ice Mage, 1998

Other books you might like:

Phyllis Eisenstein, *Born to Exile*, 1978
Gayle Greeno, *Exile's Return*, 1995
Kate Jacoby, *The Exile's Return*, 1998
William Marden, *The Exile of Ellendon*, 1974
Melanie Rawn, *The Exiles*, 1995

552

MARTIN H. GREENBERG, Editor
ALEXANDER POTTER, Co-Editor

Assassin Fantastic

(New York: DAW, 2001)

Story type: Anthology
Subject(s): Short Stories

Summary: Each of these 15 stories, all original to this anthology, follows the adventures of an assassin in a fantasy setting. A few of the stories are humorous but most are sword and sorcery adventures, and in most cases the assassins are not actually villainous. The contributors include Tanya Huff, P.N. Elrod, Mickey Zucker Reichert, Fiona Patton, and Kristine Kathryn Rusch.

Other books by the same author:

Far Frontiers, 2000 (Larry Segriff, co-editor)
Guardsmen of Tomorrow, 2000 (Larry Segriff, co-editor)
Future Crimes, 1999 (John Helfers, co-editor)
Merlin, 1999
Starfall, 1999

Other books you might like:

Raymond E. Feist, *Krondor, the Assassins*, 1999
Ian Hammell, *City of Assassins*, 1995
Elizabeth Haydon, *Destiny*, 2001
Robin Hobb, *Assassin's Apprentice*, 1995
Mickey Zucker Reichert, *Shadow Climber*, 1988

553

ED GREENWOOD

Elminster in Hell

(Renton, Washington: Wizards of the Coast, 2001)

Story type: Sword and Sorcery
Series: Forgotten Realms
Subject(s): Magic
Major character(s): Elminster Aumar, Mythical Creature (elf), Wizard; Nergal, Demon; Simbul, Nobleman
Time period(s): Indeterminate
Locale(s): Hell

Summary: Elminster, the master wizard, is ensorcelled by a demon named Nergal. In order to save his own life, as well as serve the welfare of the people, he must dare a series of adventures in the realm of Hell itself before returning to the land of the living.

Where it's reviewed:
Publishers Weekly, July 23, 2001, page 55

Other books by the same author:
The Vacant Throne, 2001
Death of the Dragon, 2000 (Troy Denning, co-author)
The Kingless Land, 2000
Silverfall, 1999
Elminster in Myth Drannor, 1997

Other books you might like:
Philip Brugalette, *The Nine Gates*, 1992
Steven A. Brust, *To Reign in Hell*, 1984
C.J. Cherryh, *Legions of Hell*, 1987
David Drake, *Explorers in Hell*, 1989
Janet Morris, co-author
Janet Morris, *Kings in Hell*, 1987
C.J. Cherryh, co-author

554

ELIZABETH HAYDON

Destiny

(New York: Tor, 2001)

Story type: Magic Conflict
Series: Child of Earth. Book 3
Subject(s): Time Travel
Major character(s): Rhapsody, Singer; Achmed, Criminal (assassin); Grunthor, Military Personnel
Time period(s): Indeterminate
Locale(s): Ylorc, Fictional Country

Summary: By traveling through both time and space, a singer, a soldier, and a professional assassin have forged a bond among themselves. Now they return to their homeland for the final battle to determine the future of their people.

Other books by the same author:
Prophecy, 2000
Rhapsody, 1999

Other books you might like:
Raymond E. Feist, *A Darkness at Sethanon*, 1986
Robin Hobb, *Assassin's Quest*, 1997
Dennis L. McKiernan, *Silver Wolf, Black Falcon*, 2000
Andre Norton, *Sorceress of the Witch World*, 1968
Tad Williams, *Otherland*, 1998

555

ELIZABETH HAYDON

Revelation

(New York: Roc, 2001)

Story type: Sword and Sorcery
Series: Rai-Kirah. Book 2
Subject(s): Magic
Major character(s): Seyonne, Warrior; Merryt, Religious; Vyx, Warrior
Time period(s): Indeterminate
Locale(s): Ezzaria, Fictional Country

Summary: A warrior, who was once a slave, has now been freed and returned to his people. He encounters a demon and, acting mercifully, spares its life, but this makes him an outcast among his own people. In order to regain what he has lost, he must discover the truth about the relationship of his people to the demons.

Other books by the same author:
Transformation, 2000

Other books you might like:
Raymond E. Feist, *A Darkness at Sethanon*, 1986
Dennis L. McKiernan, *Into the Forge*, 1997
Andre Norton, *Web of the Witch World*, 1964
Tad Williams, *Otherland*, 1998
Janny Wurts, *The Grand Conspiracy*, 2000

556

MARY H. HERBERT

Dragon's Bluff

(Renton, Washington: Wizards of the Coast, 2001)

Story type: Sword and Sorcery
Series: Dragonlance
Subject(s): Magic
Major character(s): Ulin Majere, Sorcerer; Lucy Torkay, Sorceress; Notwen, Mythical Creature (gnome)
Time period(s): Indeterminate
Locale(s): Khur, Fictional Country

Summary: Although they have trained to use sorcery, Lucy and Ulin discover all magic is disappearing from their land. Then Lucy receives word that her long absent father died in a fire, and the two travel to a distant land to identify the body, having a series of adventures along the way.

Other books by the same author:
The Clandestine Circle, 2000
Legacy of Steel, 1998
Winged Magic, 1996
City of the Sorcerers, 1994
Dark Horse, 1990

Other books you might like:
Douglas Niles, *Escape from Castle Quarras*, 1989
Larry Niven, *The Magic Goes Away*, 1978
Dan Parkinson, *The Gully Dwarves*, 1996
R.A. Salvatore, *Sojourn*, 1991
Kevin Stein, *The Brothers Majere*, 1989

557

MARCUS HERNIMAN

The Treason of Dortrean

(London: Earthlight, 2001)

Story type: Sword and Sorcery
Series: Arrandin. Book 2
Subject(s): Magic
Major character(s): Erkal Dortrean, Nobleman, Government Official; Karlena Dortrean, Noblewoman; Kellarn Dortrean, Nobleman
Time period(s): Indeterminate

Locale(s): Arrandin, Fictional Country

Summary: Although the immediate military threat to Arrandin has been beaten back, war is still underway with a foreign kingdom. A nobleman is charged with negotiating a peace, while his wife helps lead the defensive forces and his son undertakes a perilous quest.

Other books by the same author:
The Siege of Arrandin, 2000

Other books you might like:
Raymond E. Feist, *Silverthorn*, 1985
David Gemmell, *Druss the Legend*, 1994
Andre Norton, *Moon Mirror*, 1988
Irene Radford, *The Renegade Dragon*, 1999
Janny Wurts, *Shadowfane*, 1988

558

ROBERT HOLDSTOCK

Celtika

(London: Earthlight, 2001)

Story type: Legend
Series: Merlin Codex. Book 1
Subject(s): Legends
Major character(s): Merlin, Wizard; Jason, Adventurer; Niiv, Young Woman
Time period(s): Indeterminate Past
Locale(s): Pohjola, Fictional Country; Macedonia

Summary: Jason of the Argonauts has been in a magical suspended animation for 700 years. Merlin, who is virtually immortal, knew him before and now wakens him when he learns that Jason's two sons, believed murdered, actually survived and were taken to different worlds and times. With a new crew to support him, Jason sets out to find his family.

Where it's reviewed:
Locus, April 2001, page 55
Science Fiction Chronicle, September 2001, page 40

Other books by the same author:
Gates of Ivory, Gates of Horn, 1997
Ancient Echoes, 1996
Unknown Regions, 1996
Merlin's Wood, 1994
The Hollowing, 1993

Other books you might like:
Deepak Chopra, *The Return of Merlin*, 1995
J. Robert King, *Mad Merlin*, 2000
Ian McDowell, *Merlin's Gift*, 1997
Robert Nye, *Merlin*, 1979
Fred Saberhagen, *Merlin's Bones*, 1995

559

SARAH A. HOYT

Ill Met by Moonlight

(New York: Ace, 2001)

Story type: Historical
Subject(s): Fairies; Elves
Major character(s): William Shakespeare, Historical Figure, Teacher; Quicksilver, Mythical Creature (elf); Ariel, Mythical Creature (fairy)
Time period(s): 17th century
Locale(s): England; Faery, Mythical Place

Summary: William Shakespeare's wife and child are kidnapped into the land of Faery. He is determined to win them back and gains the help of the elf, Quicksilver, who becomes fond of the human. Their journey will take him from familiar England to the land of magic and back. This is a first novel.

Where it's reviewed:
Booklist, October 1, 2001, page 305
Locus, October 2001, page 61
Magazine of Fantasy and Science Fiction, September 2001, page 96
Publishers Weekly, October 1, 2001, page 43

Other books you might like:
Lynn Abbey, *Unicorn and Dragon*, 1987
Allen Andrews, *Castle Crespin*, 1982
Charles Barnitz, *The Deepest Sea*, 1996
Ian McDonald, *King of Morning, Queen of Day*, 1991
Sarban, *Ringstones*, 1951

560

IAN IRVINE

The Way between the Worlds

(New York: Warner Aspect, 2001)

Story type: Sword and Sorcery
Series: View from the Mirror. Book 4
Subject(s): Magic
Major character(s): Maigraith, Warrior; Mendark, Sorcerer; Karan, Psychic
Time period(s): Indeterminate
Locale(s): Santhenar, Alternate Universe

Summary: Three different realities exist in balance until a ravening force emerges, which threatens to overwhelm them all. The climactic battle ensues, while one of the protagonists is imprisoned by sorcery and the other is unjustly accused of treason.

Other books by the same author:
The Tower on the Rift, 2000
A Shadow on the Glass, 1999
Dark Is the Moon, 1998

Other books you might like:
Raymond E. Feist, *A Darkness at Sethanon*, 1986
Michael Moorcock, *The Dreamthief's Daughter*, 2001
Lawrence Watt-Evans, *Touched by the Gods*, 1997
Tad Williams, *Otherland*, 1998
Janny Wurts, *The Warhost of Vastmark*, 1995

561

KATE JACOBY

Rebel's Cage

(London: Gollancz, 2001)

Story type: Sword and Sorcery
Series: Elita. Book 4
Subject(s): Magic
Major character(s): Kenrick, Ruler (king); Nash, Sorcerer; Robert Douglas, Warrior
Time period(s): Indeterminate
Locale(s): Lusara, Fictional Country

Summary: An evil king has usurped the throne and maintains his hold on the land of Lusara through the assistance of the sorcerer Nash. There is an uneasy balance of power until the king changes the laws regarding sorcery and one of the local nobles leads an army intent upon his overthrow.

Where it's reviewed:
Science Fiction Chronicle, December 2001, page 45

Other books by the same author:
Black Eagle Rising, 2000
Voice of the Demon, 1999
Exile's Return, 1998

Other books you might like:
James Clemens, *Wit'ch War*, 2000
Valery Leith, *The Riddled Night*, 2000
Juliet E. McKenna, *The Warrior's Bond*, 2001
Lawrence Watt-Evans, *Touched by the Gods*, 1997
Janny Wurts, *The Grand Conspiracy*, 2000

562

MARIE JAKOBER

The Black Chalice

(Calgary, Alberta: Edge, 2001)

Story type: Historical
Subject(s): Magic
Major character(s): Karelian Brandeis, Knight; Raven, Sorceress; Gottfried von Heyden, Nobleman
Time period(s): 12th century (1103)
Locale(s): Germany

Summary: Following the First Crusade, an ambitious German duke decides to enlist the assistance of supernatural powers in his quest to become king. He is opposed by a sorceress, a young page, and a knight, who must save the Holy Roman Empire despite its inability to recognize the threat. A combination of battles, court politics, and magical intervention lead to a climactic confrontation. This is the author's first fantasy novel.

Where it's reviewed:
Publishers Weekly, February 21, 2001, page 70

Other books you might like:
Jessica Bryan, *Across a Wine Dark Sea*, 1991
Ann Chamberlin, *The Merlin of St. Gilles Well*, 1999
Thomas Harlan, *The Storm of Heaven*, 2001
James Lowder, *Crusade*, 1991
Chelsea Quinn Yarbro, *Crusader's Torch*, 1988

563

PAUL KIDD

Queen of the Demonweb Pits

(Renton, Washington: Wizards of the Coast, 2001)

Story type: Sword and Sorcery
Series: Greyhawk
Subject(s): Magic
Major character(s): Justicar, Warrior Lolth, Demon, Ruler (queen); Escalla, Wizard
Time period(s): Indeterminate
Locale(s): Furyondy, Alternate Universe

Summary: Lolth, a demon queen, is infuriated by the efforts of the rangers to thwart her ambitions among humans. She singles out one of their number, Justicar, for special vengeance, only to discover that she has taken on a challenge greater than she can handle.

Other books by the same author:
Descent into the Depths of the Earth, 2000
White Plume Mountain, 1999
The Council of Blades, 1996
Mus of Kerbridge, 1995

Other books you might like:
Andrea Alton, *The Demon of Undoing*, 1988
Chris Bunch, *The Demon King*, 1998
David Drake, *Queen of Demons*, 1998
Ru Emerson, *Against the Giants*, 1999
Thomas M. Reid, *The Temple of Elemental Evil*, 2001

564

J. ROBERT KING

Apocalypse

(Renton, Washington: Wizards of the Coast, 2001)

Story type: Sword and Sorcery
Series: Magic the Gathering: Invasion Cycle. Book 3
Subject(s): Magic
Major character(s): Urza Planeswalker, Sorcerer, Immortal; Gerrard Capashen, Warrior; Eladamri, Mythical Creature (elf)
Time period(s): Indeterminate
Locale(s): Dominaria, Alternate Universe; Phyrexia, Alternate Universe

Summary: Urza Planeswalker and his companion have reached the realm of the evil sorcerer god Yawgmoth, but rather than destroy him they have become enthralled and agree to battle each other to the death. Back in the universe of Dominaria, an elf soldier leads his armies against several hordes of monsters in the service of Yawgmoth.

Where it's reviewed:
Science Fiction Chronicle, September 2001, page 42

Other books by the same author:
Invasion, 2000
Mad Merlin, 2000

The Thran, 1999
Planar Powers, 1997
Vinas Solamnus, 1997

Other books you might like:
Loren Coleman, *Bloodlines*, 1999
William R. Forstchen, *Arena*, 1994
Jeff Grubb, *The Gathering Dark*, 1999
Mark Sumner, *The Prodigal Sorcerer*, 1995
Robert E. Vardeman, *Dark Legacy*, 1996

565

J. ROBERT KING, Editor

The Dragons of Magic

(Renton, Washington: Wizards of the Coast, 2001)

Story type: Sword and Sorcery; Anthology
Series: Magic the Gathering
Subject(s): Short Stories
Time period(s): Indeterminate

Summary: The 12 stories in this anthology are published here for the first time. They are loosely set in the world of the role playing card game, Magic: The Gathering, although it is not necessary to be familiar with the game to follow the stories. The contributors include Paul B. Thompson, Tim Ryan, Tom Dupree, Edo van Belkom, A.J. Lassieur, and Brian Thomsen.

Other books by the same author:
Invasion, 2000
Mad Merlin, 2000
The Thran, 1999
Planar Powers, 1997
Blood Hostages, 1996

Other books you might like:
A.J. Lassieur, *The Unicorn*, 2000
Vance Moore, *Odyssey*, 2001
Paul B. Thompson, *Red Sands*, 1988
  Tonya Carter, co-author
Brian Thomsen, *The Mage in the Iron Mask*, 1996
Edo van Belkom, *Teeth*, 2001

566

J. ROBERT KING

Lancelot Du Lethe

(New York: Tor, 2001)

Story type: Legend
Series: Camelot. Book 2
Subject(s): Arthurian Legends
Major character(s): Sir Lancelot Du Lethe, Knight; Guinevere, Royalty; Arthur, Ruler (king)
Time period(s): Indeterminate Past
Locale(s): Camelot, England

Summary: This is a retelling of the story of Sir Lancelot, the knight whose main concern was his personal honor. In this version, the love affair with Guinevere, Arthur's bride, assumes an unusual undertone because both of them have been touched by the powers of faerie, and it has been decreed by magical forces that they will become lovers.

Where it's reviewed:
Locus, December 2001, page 35

Other books by the same author:
Invasion, 2000
Mad Merlin, 2000
The Time Streams, 1999
Planar Powers, 1997
Rogues to Riches, 1995

Other books you might like:
A.A. Attanasio, *The Dragon and the Unicorn*, 1996
Parke Godwin, *Firelord*, 1980
Diana L. Paxson, *The Book of the Stone*, 2000
Susan Shwartz, *The Grail of Hearts*, 1992
Mary Stewart, *The Last Enchantment*, 1979

567

TRACY KNIGHT

The Astonished Eye

(Leeds, England: PS, 2001)

Story type: Contemporary
Subject(s): Aliens
Major character(s): Ben Savitch, Journalist; Almo Parrish, Aged Person; Chandler Quinn, Lawyer
Time period(s): 2000s (2001)
Locale(s): Elderton, Illinois

Summary: A reporter for a tabloid travels to a remote town in Illinois, chasing reports that a UFO has landed there. The story is true, but Elderton is unlike any other town in the world. Its inhabitants don't always stop walking around when they die, and some of the residents have very unusual, magical powers. This is a first novel.

Other books you might like:
James P. Blaylock, *The Rainy Season*, 1999
Jonathan Carroll, *The Wooden Sea*, 2001
R.A. Lafferty, *The Devil Is Dead*, 1971
Robert R. McCammon, *Boys' Life*, 1991
Clifford D. Simak, *Out of Their Minds*, 1970

568

MERCEDES LACKEY
ROSEMARY EDGHILL, Co-Author

Spirits White as Lightning

(New York: Baen, 2001)

Story type: Contemporary
Series: Bedlam's Bard. Book 5
Subject(s): Fairies
Major character(s): Eric Banyon, Musician, Student; Korendil, Nobleman; Ria Llewellyn, Businesswoman
Time period(s): 2000s (2001)
Locale(s): New York, New York; Underhill, Mythical Place

Summary: Eric Banyon has just survived discovering there are portals between our world and Underhill, where the fairies and less savory beings dwell. Now he wants to get back to being a music student and perfect his art. Unfortunately, a new round of villainy forces him to make use of his magical musical powers once again.

Other books by the same author:
The Serpent's Shadow, 2001
Brightly Burning, 2000
Owlsight, 1999
The Black Swan, 1999
Fiddler's Fair, 1998

Other books you might like:
Tom Deitz, *Soulsmith*, 1991
Ian McDonald, *King of Morning, Queen of Day*, 1991
Garfield Reeves-Stevens, *Shifter*, 1990
Will Shetterly, *NeverNever*, 1993
Sarah Singleton, *The Crow Maiden*, 2001

569

MERCEDES LACKEY

Take a Thief

(New York: DAW, 2001)

Story type: Sword and Sorcery
Series: Valdemar. Book 17
Subject(s): Magic
Major character(s): Skif, Criminal, Orphan; Deek, Thief (pickpocket); Bazie, Criminal
Time period(s): Indeterminate
Locale(s): Valdemar, Fictional Country

Summary: Following the death of his parents, Skif lives in his uncle's tavern, where he is badly treated and undernourished. He discovers a band of young criminals active in the city and is better treated there, so he joins them. A subsequent theft lands him in bigger trouble than he expected.

Where it's reviewed:
Locus, November 2001, page 35

Other books by the same author:
Brightly Burning, 2000
Owlsight, 1999
The Black Swan, 1999
Four and Twenty Blackbirds, 1997
Storm Breaking, 1996

Other books you might like:
James Barclay, *Dawnthief*, 1999
Adrian Cole, *The Thief of Dreams*, 1989
Stephen R. Lawhead, *Dream Thief*, 1983
Fritz Leiber, *Thieves' House*, 2001
Juliet E. McKenna, *The Thief's Gamble*, 1999

570

STEPHEN R. LAWHEAD

The Mystic Rose

(New York: HarperCollins, 2001)

Story type: Historical
Series: Celtic Crusades. Book 3
Subject(s): Legends
Major character(s): Caitrionia, Adventurer, Young Woman; Renaud de Bracineaux, Knight, Religious
Time period(s): Indeterminate Past
Locale(s): Mediterranean; Byzantium; France

Summary: A young Scotswoman pits her wits against the evil Renaud de Bracineaux, a member of the Knights Templar, who seeks control of the Holy Grail for less than holy reasons. Her efforts carry her across Europe, through the Crusades, and to a powerful, mystical discovery.

Where it's reviewed:
Publishers Weekly, August 13, 2001, page 248

Other books by the same author:
The Black Rood, 2000
Avalon, 1999
The Iron Lance, 1998
Grail, 1997
Byzantium, 1996

Other books you might like:
A.A. Attanasio, *Kingdom of the Grail*, 1992
Damien Broderick, *The Black Grail*, 1986
Susan Cooper, *Over Sea, Under Stone*, 1965
Guy Gavriel Kay, *Sailing to Byzantium*, 1999
Susan Shwartz, *The Grail of Hearts*, 1992

571

URSULA K. LE GUIN

The Other Wind

(New York: Harcourt, 2001)

Story type: Magic Conflict
Series: Earthsea. Book 6
Subject(s): Quest
Major character(s): Alder, Sorcerer; Ged, Wizard; Tehanu, Ruler
Time period(s): Indeterminate
Locale(s): Earthsea, Alternate Universe

Summary: A sorcerer's dreams are troubled by visions of those he has loved and lost. He fears that ultimately they will use his sleeping hours to invade the world of the living, so he sets off with the aid of a king and an archmage to find a way to seal the barrier between worlds forever.

Where it's reviewed:
Booklist, June 1, 2001, page 1798
Library Journal, July 2001, page 130
Locus, September 2001, page 19
New York Times Book Review, October 7, 2001, page 19
Publishers Weekly, August 13, 2001, page 290

Other books by the same author:
Tales from Earthsea, 2001
The Telling, 2000
Tehanu, 1990
Three Hainish Novels, 1987
Always Coming Home, 1985

Other books you might like:
Gayle Greeno, *Sunderlies Seeking*, 1998
Dennis L. McKiernan, *Voyage of the Fox Rider*, 1993
Hope Mirrlees, *Lud-in-the-Mist*, 1926

Carol Severance, *The Sorcerous Sea*, 1993
Tad Williams, *The Sea of Silver Light*, 2001

572

VALERY LEITH

The Way of the Rose

(New York: Bantam, 2001)

Story type: Sword and Sorcery
Series: Everien. Book 3
Subject(s): Magic
Major character(s): Tash, Ruler; Taretel, Warrior; Pentar, Warrior
Time period(s): Indeterminate
Locale(s): Everien, Fictional Country

Summary: Tash and his armies finally seem to be getting the upper hand against the rebels and are on the verge of restoring order to Everien when a new element complicates things. The timeserpent moves through time as well as space, spreading chaos wherever and whenever it appears.

Where it's reviewed:
Locus, July 2001, page 33
Publishers Weekly, July 30, 2001, page 66

Other books by the same author:
The Riddled Night, 2000
Company of Glass, 1999

Other books you might like:
James Barclay, *Noonshade*, 2000
Terry Goodkind, *Faith of the Fallen*, 2000
Jane Routley, *Fire Angels*, 1998
Lawrence Watt-Evans, *Night of Madness*, 2000
Janny Wurts, *Master of the White Storm*, 1992

573

REBECCA LICKISS

Eccentric Circles

(New York: Ace, 2001)

Story type: Contemporary
Subject(s): Magic
Major character(s): Piper Dickerson, Writer; Malraux, Mythical Creature (elf); Aelvarim, Mythical Creature (elf)
Time period(s): 2000s (2001)
Locale(s): Colorado; Faery, Mythical Place

Summary: Piper Dickerson inherits her grandmother's cottage and decides to move in and pursue her dream of writing. Almost immediately she is accosted by a man claiming to be an elf, who insists that her grandmother was murdered. Before long, Piper is accompanying him to the land of Faery to continue the investigation. This is a first novel.

Where it's reviewed:
Booklist, June 2001, page 1856
Locus, August 2001, page 29

Other books you might like:
Lynn Abbey, *Out of Time*, 2000
Elizabeth Bergstrom, *The Door through Washington Square*, 2000
James P. Blaylock, *The Rainy Season*, 1999
Jonathan Carroll, *The Wooden Sea*, 2001
Andre Norton, *Red Hart Magic*, 1976

574

DENISE LITTLE, Editor

A Constellation of Cats

(New York: DAW, 2001)

Story type: Anthology
Subject(s): Short Stories; Animals/Cats

Summary: Each of the 13 fantastic stories in this collection involves cats. The stories are set in a variety of times and places and usually involve the cat protecting one or more humans from some magical menace. The contributors include Andre Norton, Mickey Zucker Reichert, Jody Lynn Nye, and Nina Kiriki Hoffman.

Other books by the same author:
Creature Fantastic, 2001
Perchance to Dream, 2000
A Dangerous Magic, 1999
Twice upon a Time, 1999
Alien Pets, 1998

Other books you might like:
Clare Bell, *Ratha's Creature*, 1983
Diane Duane, *To Visit the Queen*, 1999
Gabriel King, *The Golden Cat*, 1998
Michael Peak, *Catamount*, 1992
L.A. Taylor, *Cat's Paw*, 1995

575

DENISE LITTLE, Editor

Creature Fantastic

(New York: DAW, 2001)

Story type: Anthology
Subject(s): Short Stories; Animals

Summary: Fifteen original stories deal with fantastic creatures, such as dragons, unicorns, magical cats, the phoenix, and other magical animals. The contributors include Kristine Kathryn Rusch, Alan Rodgers, Gary Braunbeck, Rosemary Edghill, Susan Sizemore, Josepha Sherman, and others. The stories are primarily tales of adventure but there are some humorous ones as well.

Other books by the same author:
A Constellation of Cats, 2001
Perchance to Dream, 2000
A Dangerous Magic, 1999
Twice upon a Time, 1999
Alien Pets, 1998

Other books you might like:
Gary A. Braunbeck, *In Hollow Houses*, 2000
Rosemary Edghill, *The Sword of Maiden's Tears*, 1994
Kristine Kathryn Rusch, *The Changeling*, 1996

Josepha Sherman, *Forging the Runes*, 1996
Susan Sizemore, *The Hunt*, 1999

576

DIANA MARCELLAS

Mother Ocean, Daughter Sea

(New York: Tor, 2001)

Story type: Alternate World
Subject(s): Magic
Major character(s): Brierly Mefell, Witch; Melfallan Courtray, Nobleman (earl); Tejar, Nobleman
Time period(s): Indeterminate
Locale(s): Yarvannet, Fictional Country

Summary: Two races live amicably in Yarvannet for generations, until one group seizes power and outlaws the witchcraft performed by members of the other. Brierly believes herself to be the last of the witches, hiding her powers until she falls in love and risks everything in a desperate gamble. This is a first novel.

Where it's reviewed:
Publishers Weekly, August 27, 2001, page 60

Other books you might like:
M.J. Bennett, *Yaril's Children*, 1988
Marion Zimmer Bradley, *The Spell Sword*, 1974
Roberta Gellis, *Bull God*, 2000
Andre Norton, *Spell of the Witch World*, 1972
Jennifer Roberson, *Shapechanger's Song*, 2001

577

ELOISE MCGRAW
ERIC SHANOWER, Illustrator

The Rundlestone of Oz

(San Diego: Hungry Tiger, 2001)

Story type: Young Adult; Quest
Series: Oz
Subject(s): Magic
Major character(s): Pocotristi Sostenuto, Toy (marionette); Slyddwyn, Wizard; Dorothy, Child
Time period(s): Indeterminate
Locale(s): Oz, Mythical Place

Summary: Poco is an animated puppet who is searching for the magical Rundlestone in various parts of the land of Oz. He takes a job working for Slyddwyn, but soon discovers that his new master has secretive plans that may involve a mysterious stranger. When Dorothy and the rest of the Oz regulars show up, it takes their combined efforts to thwart a villainous plot.

Other books by the same author:
The Moorchild, 1996
The Golden Goblet, 1961

Other books you might like:
Donald Abbott, *The Magic Chest of Oz*, 1993
L. Frank Baum, *The Wizard of Oz*, 1900
Philip Jose Farmer, *A Barnstormer in Oz*, 1982
Jeff Freedman, *The Magic Dishpan of Oz*, 1994
John R. Neill, *Lucky Bucky in Oz*, 1942

578

JULIET E. MCKENNA

The Warrior's Bond

(London: Orbit, 2001)

Story type: Sword and Sorcery
Series: Einarinn. Book 4
Subject(s): Magic
Major character(s): Ryshad, Bodyguard; Temar, Nobleman; Casuel, Scholar
Time period(s): Indeterminate
Locale(s): Einarinn, Fictional Country

Summary: Ryshad accepts a new position as a combination bodyguard and personal assistant to Temar, the only surviving nobleman from a distant land. They attend a convocation in which Temar hopes to gather followers to re-establish the power of his family holdings, but they are threatened by enemies who use magic as their tool.

Where it's reviewed:
Locus, January 2002, page 33

Other books by the same author:
The Gambler's Fortune, 2000
The Swordsman's Oath, 2000
The Thief's Gamble, 1999

Other books you might like:
Richard Baker, *The City of Ravens*, 2000
Simon R. Green, *Beyond the Blue Moon*, 2000
Kate Jacoby, *Rebel's Cage*, 2001
Paul Kemp, *Shadow's Witness*, 2000
Valery Leith, *The Riddled Night*, 2000

579

DENNIS L. MCKIERNAN

Once upon a Winter's Night

(New York: Roc, 2001)

Story type: Legend; Quest
Subject(s): Magic
Major character(s): Camille, Young Woman; Prince Alain, Mythical Creature (fairy), Nobleman; Bear, Animal (bear)
Time period(s): Indeterminate
Locale(s): Faery, Mythical Place

Summary: Young Camille is selected to be the wife of a prince of Faery. Although nervous, particularly when she discovers her betrothed is never seen without his mask, she eventually falls in love with him. Then one night she happens upon him sleeping uncovered, and by looking at his face she activates a terrible curse.

Where it's reviewed:
Booklist, May 15, 2001, page 1739
Publishers Weekly, June 25, 2001, page 55

Other books by the same author:
Silver Wolf, Black Falcon, 2000
Into the Fire, 1998

Into the Forge, 1997
The Caverns of Socrates, 1996
Tales of Mithgar, 1994

Other books you might like:
Angela Carter, *The Bloody Chamber*, 1979
Kara Dalkey, *The Nightingale*, 1988
Pamela Dean, *Tam Lin*, 1991
Robin McKinley, *The Door in the Hedge*, 1981
Jane Yolen, *Briar Rose*, 1992

580

DENNIS L. MCKIERNAN

The Silver Call

(New York: Roc, 2001)

Story type: Collection; Sword and Sorcery
Subject(s): Magic

Summary: This is an omnibus edition of two related novels originally published in 1986. *Trek to Kraggen-Cor* is the story of the raising of an army to lay siege to a castle occupied by the forces of evil. In *The Brega Path*, a small contingent is sent to seize and hold a strategic pass so that the evil army cannot use it to escape.

Other books by the same author:
Once upon a Winter's Night, 2001
Silver Wolf, Black Falcon, 2000
Into the Fire, 1998
Into the Forge, 1997
The Caverns of Socrates, 1996

Other books you might like:
Glen Cook, *Water Sleeps*, 1999
Stan Nicholls, *Legion of Thunder*, 1999
Jennifer Roberson, *Sword-Born*, 1998
Lawrence Watt-Evans, *Touched by the Gods*, 1997
Tad Williams, *The Stone of Farewell*, 1990

581

CLIFF MCNISH

The Scent of Magic

(London: Orion, 2001)

Story type: Young Adult
Series: Doomspell. Book 2
Subject(s): Magic
Major character(s): Rachel, Child, Witch; Yemi, Child; Heiki, Child
Time period(s): Indeterminate Future
Locale(s): England; Chile; Africa

Summary: The queen of the planet of witches is unhappy that her agents have been defeated by young Rachel and Eric. She sends more witches to Earth to recruit from among those children who have suddenly acquired magical powers, while Rachel and her brother travel around the world trying to unite the children to defend the planet.

Where it's reviewed:
Science Fiction Chronicle, January 2002, page 22

Other books by the same author:
Doomspell, 2000

Other books you might like:
Pamela Dean, *The Hidden Land*, 1986
Edward Eager, *Half Magic*, 1954
Alan Garner, *Elidor*, 1965
Norton Juster, *The Phantom Tollbooth*, 1961
Edith Nesbit, *The Railway Children*, 1906

582

MICHAEL MOORCOCK

The Dreamthief's Daughter

(New York: Warner Aspect, 2001)

Story type: Sword and Sorcery
Series: Elric
Subject(s): Space and Time
Major character(s): Ulric von Bek, Nobleman (count); Prince Gaynor von Minct, Nobleman; Elric, Warrior
Time period(s): 1930s
Locale(s): Germany; Alternate Universe

Summary: Ulric von Bek resists efforts by the Nazis to steal a magical sword entrusted to his family. Eventually he escapes to another universe, where he encounters Elric, a magical warrior who is another avatar of his own personality. Together with several others, they defeat efforts by a prominent Nazi to conquer more than one world and destroy the universe.

Where it's reviewed:
Locus, July 2001, page 35
Science Fiction Chronicle, September 2001, page 40

Other books by the same author:
Kane of Old Mars, 1998
Sailing to Utopia, 1996
War Amongst the Angels, 1996
Blood, 1995
Fabulous Harbors, 1995

Other books you might like:
E.R. Eddison, *The Worm Ouroboros*, 1922
Ursula K. Le Guin, *Tales from Earthsea*, 2001
Lucius Shepard, *The Ends of the Earth*, 1993
John Wyndham, *The Secret People*, 1935
Roger Zelazny, *Nine Princes in Amber*, 1970

583

DOUGLAS NILES

World Fall

(New York: Ace, 2001)

Story type: Sword and Sorcery
Series: Seven Circles. Book 2
Subject(s): Elves
Major character(s): Belynda, Mythical Creature (elf); Karkald, Worker (watchman); Miradel, Religious
Time period(s): Indeterminate
Locale(s): Seven Circles, Mythical Place

Summary: The priestess who saved the day in *Circle at Center* has been forced into exile as a common human. When she is finally allowed to return, the ordeal has changed her, and even as she doubts her own resolve, a new and more powerful enemy arises, one who can only be defeated by an army, not a single hero.

Where it's reviewed:
Library Journal, September 15, 2001, page 116
Publishers Weekly, August 13, 2001, page 292

Other books by the same author:
Circle at Center, 2000
The Puppet King, 1999
The Last Thane, 1998
War of the Three Waters, 1997
Darkenheight, 1996

Other books you might like:
Margaret Ball, *No Earthly Sunne*, 1994
Elizabeth Boyer, *The Troll's Grindstone*, 1986
Elaine Cunningham, *Evermeet*, 1998
Tom Deitz, *Landslayer's Law*, 1997
Philip Jose Farmer, *The Maker of Universes*, 1965

584

MEL ODOM

The Rover

(New York: Tor, 2001)

Story type: Adventure; Sword and Sorcery
Subject(s): Coming-of-Age
Major character(s): Edgewick Lamplighter, Librarian; Hallekk, Pirate; Cobner, Thief
Time period(s): Indeterminate
Locale(s): Greydawn Moors, Fictional Country; At Sea

Summary: An unprepossessing halfling working as a librarian gets shanghaied aboard a pirate ship. Lamplighter proves his courage, but is taken into slavery and transported to another land. There he battles a dragon, deals with a band of professional thieves, and has a variety of other adventures. Written very much in the style of J.R.R. Tolkien.

Where it's reviewed:
Science Fiction Chronicle, August 2001, page 36

Other books by the same author:
The Revenant, 2001
The Sea Devil's Eye, 2000
The Rising Tide, 1999
The Lost Library of Cormanthyr, 1998

Other books you might like:
Terry Brooks, *The Sword of Shannara*, 1982
Ed Greenwood, *Elminster in Myth Drannor*, 1997
Dixie Lee McKeone, *Tales of Uncle Trapspringer*, 1997
R.A. Salvatore, *The Halfling's Gem*, 1990
J.R.R. Tolkien, *The Hobbit*, 1937

585

K.J. PARKER

Shadow

(London: Orbit, 2001)

Story type: Sword and Sorcery
Series: Scavenger. Book 1
Subject(s): Magic
Major character(s): Poldarn, Warrior; Copis, Traveler; Scaptey, Criminal
Time period(s): Indeterminate
Locale(s): The Empire, Fictional Country

Summary: A man wakens on a deserted battlefield with no memory of his previous life. Rescued by a passerby who helps him survive, his dreams are troubled by phantom memories of the past. The two travel across the outskirts of an empire that is dissolving into turmoil as various forces contend for influence.

Other books by the same author:
The Proof House, 2000
The Belly of the Bow, 1999
Colours in the Steel, 1998

Other books you might like:
Dave Duncan, *Destiny of the Sword*, 1988
John Marco, *The Jackal of Nar*, 1999
Andrew J. Offutt, *The Messenger of Zhuvastou*, 1973
Lawrence Watt-Evans, *Touched by the Gods*, 1997
Janny Wurts, *The Fugitive Prince*, 1997

586

FIONA PATTON

The Golden Sword

(New York: DAW, 2001)

Story type: Magic Conflict
Series: Branion Realm. Book 4
Subject(s): Magic
Major character(s): Camden DeKathrine, Wizard; Danielle DeKathrine, Sorceress; Alisha DeMarian, Noblewoman
Time period(s): Indeterminate
Locale(s): Branion, Fictional Country

Summary: Camden is destined by birth to serve one aspect of the magical power that holds sway in Branion, but he is secretly drawn to another. When he goes to live with his uncle and cousins, he discovers not only they too question the existing order, but they are experimenting with what could be a very dangerous power.

Where it's reviewed:
Locus, September 2001, page 29

Other books by the same author:
The Granite Shield, 1999
The Painter Knight, 1998
The Stone Prince, 1977

Other books you might like:
Robin W. Bailey, *Nightwatch*, 1990
Glen Cook, *The Tower of Fear*, 1989

Kate Elliott, *The King's Dragon*, 1997
M. John Harrison, *A Storm of Wings*, 1980
Janny Wurts, *The Keeper of the Keys*, 1988

587

TERRY PRATCHETT

The Amazing Maurice and His Educated Rodents

(New York: HarperCollins, 2001)

Story type: Young Adult; Humor
Series: Discworld. Book 28
Subject(s): Humor; Animals/Cats; Animals/Rats
Major character(s): Maurice, Animal (cat); Keith, Child; Peaches, Animal (rat)
Time period(s): Indeterminate
Locale(s): Discworld, Alternate Universe

Summary: Maurice is an intelligent cat, who teams up with a young boy and a band of rats for a series of scams. The rats infest a small town until the local authorities pay to have them magically piped out of town. Unfortunately, their latest plan goes awry, when they wander into a town which has a unique danger for rats.

Where it's reviewed:
Locus, December 2001, page 59
Locus, November 2001, page 35
Publishers Weekly, November 5, 2001, page 70
Science Fiction Chronicle, January 2002, page 22

Other books by the same author:
The Last Hero, 2001
The Fifth Elephant, 1999
Carpe Jugulum, 1998
The Last Continent, 1998
Jingo, 1997

Other books you might like:
Mary Brown, *Pigs Don't Fly*, 1994
Brian Jacques, *The Legend of Luke*, 1999
Andre Norton, *Rogue Reynard*, 1947
Margery Sharp, *Miss Bianca*, 1962
Christopher Stasheff, *The Feline Wizard*, 2000

588

TERRY PRATCHETT

The Last Hero

(New York: HarperCollins, 2001)

Story type: Sword and Sorcery; Humor
Series: Discworld. Book 27
Subject(s): Magic
Major character(s): Genghiz Cohen, Ruler; Lord Vetinari, Nobleman; Rincewind, Wizard
Time period(s): Indeterminate
Locale(s): Discworld, Alternate Universe

Summary: Cohen the Barbarian has had a long and successful career, culminating in his ascent to the throne. Now that there is nothing left to conquer, he grows bored, so he sets off on a mission to confront the gods, a meeting that could destroy the universe if Rincewind the Wizard can't interfere with the warrior's plans.

Where it's reviewed:
Booklist, September 15, 2001, page 164
Locus, December 2001, page 59
Publishers Weekly, October 15, 2001, page 51
Science Fiction Chronicle, January 2002, page 22

Other books by the same author:
The Amazing Maurice and His Educated Rodents, 2001
The Rincewind Trilogy, 2001
The City Watch Trilogy, 1999
Hogfather, 1998
Feet of Clay, 1996

Other books you might like:
John DeChancie, *Castle for Rent*, 1989
Esther Friesner, *Unicorn U*, 1992
Craig Shaw Gardner, *An Excess of Enchantments*, 1988
Andrew Harman, *Talonspotting*, 2000
Lawrence Watt-Evans, *Split Heirs*, 1993
Esther Friesner, co-author

589

JEAN RABE

Betrayal

(Renton, Washington: Wizards of the Coast, 2001)

Story type: Sword and Sorcery
Series: Dragonlance
Subject(s): Magic
Major character(s): Dhamon Grimwulf, Adventurer; Maldred, Warrior; Fiona, Knight
Time period(s): Indeterminate
Locale(s): Krynn, Fictional Country

Summary: Dhamon Grimwulf and his companion are on the trail of a hidden treasure, but there are several other people who are aware of their quest and choose to interfere. Their journey involves an encounter with a dragon, a lost city, lizard people, a sorceress, captures and escapes, chases and battles, and a reunion with old companions.

Other books by the same author:
Downfall, 2000
The Silver Stair, 1999
Day of the Tempest, 1997
The Dawning of a New Age, 1996
Red Magic, 1991

Other books you might like:
James Barclay, *Dawnthief*, 1999
Robert E. Howard, *Trails in Darkness*, 1996
Fritz Leiber, *Swords Against Death*, 1970
David Mason, *The Return of Kavin*, 1972
Juliet E. McKenna, *The Thief's Gamble*, 1999

590

MICKEY ZUCKER REICHERT

The Beasts of Barakhai

(New York: DAW, 2001)

Story type: Sword and Sorcery
Series: Books of Barakhai. Book 1
Subject(s): Magic
Major character(s): Benton Collins, Student—Graduate; Zylas, Mythical Creature (shapechanger); Falima, Mythical Creature (shapechanger)
Time period(s): 2000s (2001)
Locale(s): Barakhai, Fictional Country

Summary: Benton Collins is a graduate student who stumbles through a portal into another world. He kills and eats a rabbit before learning that everyone in the world of Barakhai is a shapechanger except for those who rule. Rescued by a wererat and a werehorse, he discovers they want to use his inability to change to help them overthrow their repressive rulers and he must cooperate if he is ever to return to our world.

Where it's reviewed:
Booklist, July 2001, page 1992
Library Journal, August 2001, page 171
Publishers Weekly, July 30, 2001, page 66

Other books by the same author:
Prince of Demons, 1996
Beyond Ragnarok, 1995
The Unknown Soldier, 1994
Child of Thunder, 1993
The Western Wizard, 1992

Other books you might like:
Joanne Bertin, *The Last Dragonlord*, 1998
L. Sprague de Camp, *The Goblin Tower*, 1968
Carol Dennis, *Dragon's Queen*, 1991
Doranna Durgin, *Dun Lady's Jess*, 1994
Nancy Springer, *Madbond*, 1987

591

JENNIFER ROBERSON

Children of the Lion

(New York: DAW, 2001)

Story type: Sword and Sorcery
Series: Cheysuli. Book 3
Subject(s): Magic
Major character(s): Brennan, Nobleman; Keely, Noblewoman; Niall, Ruler
Time period(s): Indeterminate
Locale(s): Homana, Fictional Country

Summary: These are the fifth and sixth novels in the original series, now published together. Both involve the conflict between normal people and the shapechanging race who are heirs to the throne of Homana. In each book, the younger generation of the shapechanging Cheysuli must face fresh challenges to their way of life. Previously published separately in 1988 and 1989, the two novels are *A Pride of Princes* and *Daughter of the Lion*.

Other books by the same author:
Legacy of the Wolf, 2001
Shapechanger's Song, 2001
Sword-Born, 1998
A Tapestry of Lions, 1992
Swordsinger, 1988

Other books you might like:
Jo Clayton, *Blue Magic*, 1988
Louise Cooper, *The Sleep of Stone*, 1991
Teresa Edgerton, *The Castle of the Silver Wheel*, 1993
Patricia McKillip, *The Riddlemaster of Hed*, 1976
Kristine Kathryn Rusch, *The Rival*, 1997

592

JENNIFER ROBERSON

Legacy of the Wolf

(New York: DAW, 2001)

Story type: Collection
Series: Cheysuli. Book 2
Subject(s): Magic

Summary: This is an omnibus edition of the third and fourth novels in the Chronicles of the Cheysuli. In *Legacy of the Sword*, the shapechanging Cheysuli successfully revolt against their oppressors and regain the throne. In *Track of the White Wolf*, one of the Cheysuli becomes an outcast himself, and must set out on a dangerous quest.

Other books by the same author:
Shapechanger's Song, 2001
Sword-Born, 1998
Sword-Breaker, 1994
Swordmaker, 1989
Swordsinger, 1988

Other books you might like:
Eleanor Arnason, *Daughter of the Bear King*, 1987
Jo Clayton, *Blue Magic*, 1988
Doranna Durgin, *Changespell*, 1997
Robert Silverberg, *The Sorcerers of Majipoor*, 1996
Nancy Springer, *Madbond*, 1987

593

JENNIFER ROBERSON

The Lion Throne

(New York: DAW, 2001)

Story type: Collection
Series: Cheysuli. Book 4
Subject(s): Magic
Time period(s): Indeterminate
Locale(s): Homana, Fictional Country

Summary: This is an omnibus of the seventh and eighth novels in the Cheysuli sequence, *Flight of the Raven*, originally published in 1990, and *A Tapestry of Lions*, originally published in 1992. In the first, the heir to the throne of Homana is subject to visions and apparitions that bode ill for the future, and in the second, set a century later, another heir refuses to accept the throne.

Other books by the same author:
Shapechanger's Song, 2001
Sword-Born, 1998
Sword-Breaker, 1994
Sword-Maker, 1989
Sword-Singer, 1988

Other books you might like:
Eleanor Arnason, *A Woman of the Iron People*, 1991
M.J. Bennett, *Seeking the Dream Brother*, 1989
Jo Clayton, *Dance Down the Stars*, 1994
Doranna Durgin, *Changespell*, 1997
Robert Silverberg, *Lord Prestimion*, 1999

594

EMILY RODDA

Rowan of Rin

(New York: Greenwillow, 2001)

Story type: Young Adult
Subject(s): Legends
Major character(s): Rowan, Child; Strong John, Traveler; Bronden, Carpenter
Time period(s): Indeterminate
Locale(s): Rin, Fictional Country

Summary: Young Rowan has a reputation of being afraid of everything, but when he comes into possession of a map that shows the way through the dangerous mountain passes, he decides to go with the travelers. He encounters giant spiders, a dangerous swamp, and a fire-breathing dragon before discovering the depths of his own courage.

Where it's reviewed:
Booklist, May 2001, page 1682
Horn Book Magazine, July 2001, page 461
School Library Journal, June 2001, page 154
Science Fiction Chronicle, August 2001, page 36

Other books by the same author:
The Pigs Are Flying, 1988

Other books you might like:
Diana Wynne Jones, *Howl's Moving Castle*, 1986
Tamora Pierce, *Wild Magic*, 1992
Vivian Vande Velde, *Spellbound*, 1998
Jane Yolen, *The Wizard's Map*, 1999
Mary Frances Zambreno, *A Plague of Sorcerers*, 1991

595

MICHAEL SCOTT ROHAN

Shadow of the Seer

(London: Orbit, 2001)

Story type: Post-Disaster
Series: Winter of the World. Book 6
Subject(s): Disasters; Magic
Major character(s): Alya, Magician; Savi, Prisoner; Rysha, Traveler
Time period(s): Indeterminate Future
Locale(s): Brasaybal, Fictional Country

Summary: In a distant future where magic has returned to an Earth that has succumbed to an Ice Age, Alya sets out on a quest. The woman he loves has been taken captive and he will move heaven and earth itself to rescue her, which he does following a series of adventures in strange lands.

Other books by the same author:
The Castle of the Winds, 1998
Maxie's Demon, 1997
Cloud Castles, 1993
The Gates of Noon, 1993
Chase the Morning, 1990

Other books you might like:
Gillian Bradshaw, *In Winter's Shadow*, 1983
Michael Moorcock, *The Ice Schooner*, 1969
Marta Randall, *The Sword of Winter*, 1983
Thomas Burnett Swann, *Wolfwinter*, 1972
Paula Volsky, *The Wolf of Winter*, 1993

596

JESSICA RYDILL

Children of the Shaman

(London: Orbit, 2001)

Story type: Magic Conflict
Subject(s): Magic
Major character(s): Annatt Vasilyevich, Teenager; Malchik Vasilyevich, Teenager; Yuda Vasilyevich, Shaman
Time period(s): Indeterminate
Locale(s): Masalyar, Fictional Country; La Solterraine, Alternate Universe

Summary: The two children of a shaman travel to a remote town to be with their father. They discover he is battling against an evil supernatural force dwelling in the frozen lands just beyond the borders of civilization. The ensuing battle will force them to move from childhood to maturity. This is a first novel.

Other books you might like:
Gayle Greeno, *Sunderlies Seeking*, 1998
J.V. Jones, *A Cavern of Black Ice*, 1999
Richard A. Knaak, *Frostwing*, 1995
Fritz Leiber, *Rime Isle*, 1977
George R.R. Martin, *A Storm of Swords*, 2000

597

R.A. SALVATORE

Sea of Swords

(Renton, Washington: Wizards of the Coast, 2001)

Story type: Sword and Sorcery
Series: Forgotten Realms: Paths of Darkness. Book 3
Subject(s): Elves
Major character(s): Drizzt Do'Urden, Mythical Creature (elf), Warrior; Regis, Mythical Creature (halfling); Cattie-Brie, Warrior
Time period(s): Indeterminate
Locale(s): Icewind Dale, Fictional Country

Summary: An elf and his companions undertake a series of missions intended to make Icewind Dale a safer place. They overwhelm a band of highwaymen, then take to the sea in an effort to pursue and neutralize an elusive pirate. The story is enlivened by battles on sea and on land, and a series of chases and evasions.

Where it's reviewed:
Publishers Weekly, October 15, 2001, page 52

Other books by the same author:
Ascendance, 2001
Mortalis, 2001
Bastion of Darkness, 2000
Servant of the Shard, 2000
The Demon Apostle, 1999

Other books you might like:
Lynn Abbey, *The Simbul's Gift*, 1997
Elaine Cunningham, *Elfsong*, 1994
Troy Denning, *The Parched Sea*, 1991
Clayton Emery, *Star of Cursrah*, 1999
Ed Greenwood, *Elminster in Myth Drannor*, 1997

598

SARAH SINGLETON

The Crow Maiden

(Gillette, New Jersey: Cosmos, 2001)

Story type: Contemporary
Subject(s): Fairies
Major character(s): Katherine, Housewife; Paul Matravers, Writer; Crow, Teenager
Time period(s): 21st century
Locale(s): England

Summary: A contemporary woman searching for an element of magic in her life finds it when a mysterious young girl introduces her to the land of the faeries, which overlaps with ours from time to time. The faeries have a special interest in her, and enlist her aid in an effort to protect their heritage. This is a first novel.

Other books you might like:
Emma Bull, *War for the Oaks*, 1987
James Long, *Ferney*, 1998
Ian McDonald, *King of Morning, Queen of Day*, 1991
Sarban, *Ringstones*, 1951
Will Shetterly, *Elsewhere*, 1991

599

MICHAEL A. STACKPOLE

Fortress Draconis

(New York: Bantam, 2001)

Story type: Sword and Sorcery
Series: DragonCrown War Cycle. Book 1
Subject(s): Magic
Major character(s): Will, Thief; Princess Alexia, Noblewoman; Crow, Warrior
Time period(s): Indeterminate
Locale(s): Alternate Universe

Summary: The dark queen, Chytrine, plans to use her magic to dominate the entire world. She senses a danger to her power, a young orphaned thief named Will, and sends her minions to kill him. Will has a talent for staying alive, however, and after acquiring a few friends to help him, he sets off for a magical fortress to prevent Chytrine from gaining the power she desires.

Other books by the same author:
Onslaught, 2000
Ruin, 2000
Prince of Havoc, 1998
The Enemy Reborn, 1998
Talion Revenant, 1997

Other books you might like:
David Drake, *Queen of Demons*, 1998
Raymond E. Feist, *Shadow of a Dark Queen*, 1994
Fritz Leiber, *Swords Against Death*, 1970
Andrew J. Offutt, *Shadowspawn*, 1987
Paula Volsky, *Curse of the Witch-Queen*, 1982

600

CHRISTOPHER STASHEFF

Here Be Monsters

(New York: Ace, 2001)

Story type: Magic Conflict
Series: Warlock's Heirs. Book 5
Subject(s): Magic; Psychic Powers
Major character(s): Geoffrey Gallowglass, Wizard; Cordelia Gallowglass, Sorceress; Gregory Gallowglass, Wizard
Time period(s): Indeterminate Future
Locale(s): Gramarye, Planet—Imaginary

Summary: On Gramarye, the planet where magic works, all three children of the great wizard are planning to be married. Unfortunately, on the eve of that event, one of the parties has a vision of monstrous creatures attacking, and they are all off on a quest to discover the source of the threat. This is a lightweight, humorous adventure, blending science fiction and fantasy motifs.

Other books by the same author:
A Wizard in Peace, 1996
The Sage, 1996
A Wizard in War, 1995
Quicksilver's Knight, 1995
The Star Stone, 1995

Other books you might like:
Piers Anthony, *DoOon Mode*, 2001
L. Sprague de Camp, *The Pixilated Peeress*, 1991
C.S. Friedman, *Black Sun Rising*, 1991
Arthur Landis, *Camelot in Orbit*, 1978
Lawrence Watt-Evans, *Out of This World*, 1994

601

ROBERT S. STONE

Hazard's Price

(New York: Ace, 2001)

Story type: Magic Conflict
Series: Chronicles of Unbinding. Book 1
Subject(s): Magic
Major character(s): Galatine Hazard, Criminal; Brandt Karrelian, Businessman; Taylor Ash, Government Official
Time period(s): Indeterminate
Locale(s): Chaldus, Fictional Country

Summary: Safeguards have been put in place to prevent the two major nations of a mythical world from ever using magic to conduct warfare. Now someone seems to have found a way to subvert the guards, and whoever it is has murdered several members of the Chaldean government, framing a reformed criminal who sets out to clear his name. This is the author's first novel.

Other books by the same author:
Dark Waters, 2001 (Chronicles of Unbinding. Book 2)

Other books you might like:
Peter David, *Sir Apropos of Nothing*, 2001
Clayton Emery, *Star of Cursrah*, 1999
Terry Goodkind, *Wizard's First Rule*, 1994
Juliet E. McKenna, *The Thief's Gamble*, 1999
Michael Shea, *Nifft the Lean*, 1982

602

S. ANDREW SWANN

The Dragons of the Cuyahoga

(New York: DAW, 2001)

Story type: Contemporary
Subject(s): Magic
Major character(s): Kline Maxwell, Journalist; Adrian Phillips, Government Official; Leonardo Baldassare, Businessman
Time period(s): 21st century
Locale(s): Cleveland, Ohio

Summary: A portal between worlds opens in Cleveland, allowing dragons, elves, and other creatures to enter our universe, although they are limited to the Cleveland area. The death of a dragon appears to be an accident, but a political reporter suspects foul play, and his investigation will uncover a conspiracy within the city government.

Where it's reviewed:
Locus, December 2001, page 33
Science Fiction Chronicle, December 2001, page 49

Other books by the same author:
Fearful Symmetries, 1999
Zimmerman's Algorithm, 1999
God's Dice, 1997
Revolutionary, 1996
Partisan, 1995

Other books you might like:
Emma Bull, *War for the Oaks*, 1987
Brett Davis, *The Faery Convention*, 1995
Esther Friesner, *New York by Knight*, 1986
Laurell K. Hamilton, *A Kiss of Shadows*, 2000
Will Shetterly, *Elsewhere*, 1991

603

JUDITH TARR

Pride of Kings

(New York: Roc, 2001)

Story type: Historical
Subject(s): Magic
Major character(s): Arslan, Mythical Creature; John Lackland, Historical Figure, Royalty (prince); Kalila, Witch
Time period(s): 12th century (1189-1194)
Locale(s): England; Middle East

Summary: When Richard the Lionhearted is crowned King of England, he is secretly offered a second crown, which would give him domain over the world of magic. He refuses it because he is more interested in going on Crusade to the Holy Lands, leaving England to be administered by his brother, Prince John. During Richard's absence, the mysterious Arslan, not quite a man, comes to England to see that things do not get too far out of balance.

Where it's reviewed:
Booklist, August 2001, page 2102
Library Journal, September 15, 2001, page 115
Locus, October 2001, page 27
Publishers Weekly, August 13, 2001, page 291

Other books by the same author:
Kingdom of the Grail, 2000
King and Goddess, 1996
Throne of Isis, 1994
Arrows of the Sun, 1993
Lord of the Two Lands, 1993

Other books you might like:
Lynn Abbey, *Unicorn and Dragon*, 1987
Gael Baudino, *Maze of Moonlight*, 1993
James Branch Cabell, *The High Place*, 1923
Ann Chamberlin, *The Merlin of St. Gilles Well*, 1999
Marie Jakober, *The Black Chalice*, 2001

604

PAUL B. THOMPSON
TONYA C. COOK, Co-Author

Brother of the Dragon

(Renton, Washington: Wizards of the Coast, 2001)

Story type: Sword and Sorcery
Series: Dragonlance
Subject(s): Magic
Major character(s): Amero Arkuden, Artisan; Duranix, Mythical Creature (dragon); Tiphan, Religious
Time period(s): Indeterminate

Locale(s): Ansalon, Fictional Country

Summary: The Arkuden family has a special relationship with a benevolent dragon which makes them important in their community. This leads to a rivalry with Tiphan, who wishes to become a figure of authority. Elsewhere, a young woman escapes from a band of raiders, and is about to interact with the others for a series of adventures that will shape the future of the land.

Other books by the same author:
Children of the Plains, 2000 (Tonya Cook, co-author)
The Dargonesti, 1997 (Tonya Cook, co-author)
The Qualinesti, 1991 (Tonya Carter, co-author)
Riverwind the Plainsman, 1990 (Tonya Carter, co-author)
Red Sands, 1988 (Tonya Carter, co-author)

Other books you might like:
Mark Anthony, *The Tower of Doom*, 1994
David Cook, *King Pinch*, 1995
Troy Denning, *The Obsidian Oracle*, 1993
Simon Hawke, *The Seeker*, 1994
Mary Kirchoff, *The Seventh Sentinel*, 1995

605

TOM TOWNSEND

Shadow Kiss

(Unionville, New York: Royal Fireworks, 2001)

Story type: Young Adult
Series: Fairie Ring. Book 4
Subject(s): Magic
Major character(s): Shadow, Teenager; Elazandra, Teenager; Ringyar, Nobleman
Time period(s): Indeterminate

Summary: The young heroes, who have helped the queen of the fairies resist the attacks of the Dark Lords, are now scattered and depressed. Adding to their problems is the presence of Shadow, an evil teenager sent by the Dark Lords to sow dissent and weaken their resistance.

Other books by the same author:
Never Trust a One-Eyed Wizard, 2000
The Dragon Trader, 2000
The Trouble with an Elf, 1999

Other books you might like:
Bruce Coville, *The Skull of Truth*, 1997
Pamela Dean, *The Hidden Land*, 1986
Craig Shaw Gardner, *The Dragon Sleeping*, 1994
Vivian Vande Velde, *The Conjurer Princess*, 1997
Jane Yolen, *Child of Faerie*, 1997

606

HARRY TURTLEDOVE

Marching through Peachtree

(New York: Baen, 2001)

Story type: Military
Series: Sentry Peak. Book 2
Subject(s): Magic
Major character(s): Joseph, Ruler (count); Hesmucet, Military Personnel; Roast Beef William, Military Personnel
Time period(s): Indeterminate
Locale(s): Detina, Fictional Country

Summary: The land of Detina has been cut in half by a civil war because one faction wants to end the slavery of blonds which is practiced in the other. The novel consists of a series of military expeditions by each side as they attempt to overwhelm their enemy.

Where it's reviewed:
Booklist, October 15, 2001, page 381
Locus, December 2001, page 62
Science Fiction Chronicle, December 2001, page 46

Other books by the same author:
Aftershocks, 2001
Darkness Descending, 2000
Sentry Peak, 2000
Into the Darkness, 1999
The American Front, 1998

Other books you might like:
Glen Cook, *Soldiers Live*, 2000
David Feintuch, *The Still*, 1997
Stan Nicholls, *Legion of Thunder*, 1999
Adam Nichols, *The War of the Lord's Veil*, 1994
Lawrence Watt-Evans, *Touched by the Gods*, 1997

607

JEFF VANDERMEER

City of Saints and Madmen

(Gillette, New Jersey: Cosmos, 2001)

Story type: Collection
Subject(s): Short Stories
Locale(s): Ambergris, Fictional City

Summary: This is a collection of three novellas and one very long background piece set in the city of Ambergris, a place where strange rituals and customs dominate all aspects of life. The stories involve a love affair, the life of an artist, and exploration of the careers of others who live in this very strange environment.

Other books by the same author:
The Hoegbotton Guide to the Early History of Ambergris, 1999
The Book of Lost Places, 1996
The Book of Frog, 1989

Other books you might like:
Storm Constantine, *Scenting Hallowed Blood*, 1996
Avram Davidson, *The Adventures of Dr. Esterhazy*, 1990
Paul Di Filippo, *The Steampunk Trilogy*, 1994
China Mieville, *Perdido Street Station*, 2001
Michael Moorcock, *Fabulous Harbors*, 1995

608

JO WALTON

The King's Name

(New York: Tor, 2001)

Story type: Sword and Sorcery
Series: Tir Tanagiri. Book 2
Subject(s): Magic
Major character(s): Sulian ap Gwien, Warrior; Urdo, Ruler (king); Morthu, Sorcerer
Time period(s): Indeterminate
Locale(s): Tir Tanagiri, Fictional Country

Summary: A female warrior helps a good king drive out the invaders who threaten his rule and assists in strengthening his borders against further intrusion. Just when it appears they can finally put down their swords, factions within their own people decide the king's brand of justice is not to their liking and a civil war erupts.

Where it's reviewed:
Booklist, October 15, 2001, page 388

Other books by the same author:
The King's Peace, 2000

Other books you might like:
Lynn Abbey, *The Black Flame*, 1980
Glen Cook, *She Is the Darkness*, 1997
Richard Kirk, *Swordsmistress of Chaos*, 1978
Carol Severance, *Storm Caller*, 1993
Matthew Woodring Stover, *Iron Dawn*, 1997

609

FREDA WARRINGTON

The Obsidian Tower

(London: Earthlight, 2001)

Story type: Magic Conflict
Series: Jewelfire. Book 3
Subject(s): Magicians
Major character(s): Helananthe, Ruler; Falthorn, Nobleman; Rufryd, Warrior
Time period(s): Indeterminate
Locale(s): Aventuria, Fictional Country

Summary: A race of shapechangers allies itself with other enemies of Queen Helananthe and deposes her. Elsewhere, the queen's former allies are variously imprisoned or missing and presumed lost. When the vision of a dark tower appears in the minds of all the parties involved, it foreshadows events yet to come.

Other books by the same author:
The Sapphire Throne, 2000
The Amber Citadel, 1999
Sorrow's Light, 1993

Other books you might like:
Maggie Furey, *Dhammara*, 1997
Terry Goodkind, *Faith of the Fallen*, 2000
Simon R. Green, *Beyond the Blue Moon*, 2000
John Marco, *The Jackal of Nar*, 1999
Tad Williams, *The Stone of Farewell*, 1990

610

LAWRENCE WATT-EVANS

The Dragon Society

(New York: Tor, 2001)

Story type: Sword and Sorcery
Series: Dragon. Book 2
Subject(s): Quest
Major character(s): Arlian, Warrior; Black, Servant; Lord Toribor, Nobleman
Time period(s): Indeterminate
Locale(s): Manfort, Mythical Place

Summary: Arlian has gained admission to the Dragon Society and has killed most of those against whom he vowed vengeance. In the process, he discovers the immortality achieved by contact with dragon blood has a price. After a thousand years of life, those infected are transformed into young dragons. His new knowledge endangers the future of the dragons, and they threaten to wage war against all humankind.

Where it's reviewed:
Publishers Weekly, October 27, 2001, page 52
Science Fiction Chronicle, December 2001, page 44

Other books by the same author:
Night of Madness, 2000
Dragon Weather, 1999
Touched by the Gods, 1997
Out of This World, 1994
Crosstime Traffic, 1992

Other books you might like:
Mark Acres, *Dragon War*, 1994
Joanne Bertin, *The Last Dragonlord*, 1998
Wayland Drew, *Dragonslayer*, 1981
Elizabeth Kerner, *Lesser Kindred*, 2000
Dennis L. McKiernan, *Dragondoom*, 1990

611

MARGARET WEIS
TRACY HICKMAN, Co-Author

Guardians of the Lost

(New York: Harper, 2001)

Story type: Sword and Sorcery
Series: Sovereign Stone. Book 2
Subject(s): Quest; Magic
Major character(s): Dagnarus, Sorcerer; Gustav, Knight; Wolfram, Mythical Creature (dwarf)
Time period(s): Indeterminate
Locale(s): Leorum, Fictional Country

Summary: The land of Leorum is slowly recovering from a battle waged two centuries earlier when the evil sorcerer Dagnarus made a bid for power. Home to orcs, elves, and dwarves, as well as humans, it's a tumultuous, dangerous place becoming even more so when Dagnarus stirs from his rest beyond the void and launches a new attack.

Other books by the same author:
Well of Darkness, 2000 (Tracy Hickman, co-author)
The Soulforge, 1998
The Ghost Legion, 1993
The King's Sacrifice, 1991
The Dragonking, 1990

Other books you might like:
James Barclay, *Noonshade*, 2000
Terry Brooks, *Antrax*, 2001
Maggie Furey, *Dhammara*, 1997
Terry Goodkind, *Faith of the Fallen*, 2000
Lawrence Watt-Evans, *Night of Madness*, 2000

612

MARGARET WEIS, Editor
TRACY HICKMAN, Co-Editor

The Search for Magic

(Renton, Washington: Wizards of the Coast, 2001)

Story type: Anthology
Subject(s): Short Stories

Summary: These 11 stories, none previously published, are all set in the Dragonlance universe as created by the role playing game. The contributors include Nancy Varian Berberick, Richard A. Knaak, Linda P. Baker, Jean Rabe, Jeff Crook, and others. The common theme is that a magical war has released a horde of dangerous creatures and powers into the world of Krynn.

Other books by the same author:
The Soulforge, 1998
Testament of the Dragon, 1997
The Ghost Legion, 1993
The Elven Star, 1990
The Lost King, 1990

Other books you might like:
Linda P. Baker, *Tears of the Night Sky*, 1998
Nancy Varian Berberick, co-author
Nancy Varian Berberick, *The Panther's Hoard*, 1994
Jeff Crook, *The Rose and the Skull*, 1999
Richard A. Knaak, *The Horse King*, 1997
Jean Rabe, *Downfall*, 2000

613

JACK YEOVIL (Pseudonym of Kim Newman)

Drachenfels

(Nottingham, England: Black Library, 2001)

Story type: Horror; Magic Conflict
Series: Warhammer
Subject(s): Magic
Major character(s): Genevieve, Noblewoman; Detlef Sierck, Writer; Constant Drachenfels, Sorcerer
Time period(s): Indeterminate
Locale(s): Bretonnia, Fictional Country

Summary: An egotistical playwright decides to dramatically recreate the death of a great sorcerer in the man's own castle. The production wakens old magic still present and reveals that the sorcerer is not entirely absent from the world after all.

Other books by the same author:
Genevieve Undead, 1993
Beasts in Velvet, 1991

Other books you might like:
Elaine Bergstrom, *Baroness of Blood*, 1995
Gene DeWeese, *Lord of the Necropolis*, 1997
P.N. Elrod, *I, Strahd*, 1993
Tanya Huff, *Scholar of Decay*, 1995
J. Robert King, *Heart of Midnight*, 1992

614

MARC SCOTT ZICREE
BARBARA HAMBLY, Co-Author

Magic Time

(New York: Avon Eos, 2001)

Story type: Contemporary
Subject(s): Magic
Major character(s): Cal Griffin, Lawyer; Fred Wishart, Doctor; Colleen Brooks, Secretary
Time period(s): 2000s (2001)
Locale(s): New York, New York; West Virginia

Summary: A series of earthquakes levels much of New York City and causes widespread disruption. In the aftermath, the survivors discover that magic now works, although not always in predictable ways. A lawyer becomes the focal point in the efforts by a group of people to oppose a supernatural force with evil intentions. This is Zicree's first novel.

Where it's reviewed:
Booklist, October 15, 2001, page 388
Locus, January 2002, page 72
Publishers Weekly, October 29, 2001, page 36

Other books you might like:
Emma Bull, *War for the Oaks*, 1987
Esther Friesner, *New York by Knight*, 1986
Madeleine Robins, *The Stone War*, 1999
Will Shetterly, *NeverNever*, 1993
Lisa Smedman, *Tails You Lose*, 2001

The Year in Horror 2001
by
Stefan Dziemianowicz

At the very least, horror readers will probably remember 2001 as the year in which the horrors of world events superseded anything horror fiction could conjure. If only subliminally, the events of September 11 changed the way we interpreted the year's yield in fiction and altered diagnoses of the state of the horror genre that were formed before the terrorist attacks on the United States. Inevitably, they will transform how contemporary horror fiction is written and read. Horror, like any other popular fiction genre, responds to and articulates the mood and temper of the times. The atmosphere of anger, anxiety, and vulnerability that shapes public opinion also influences the artistic imagination, and the years to come will invariably see an outpouring of horror and dark fantasy in reaction to the shocks that have transformed social and political perspectives on a global scale.

If the character of a year's output in a genre is defined by its predominant trend, then 2001 was the Year of the Sequel for horror fiction. Sequels are not exactly a new concept in a field whose cinematic arm has spawned multi-installment sagas such as *Nightmare on Elm Street*, *Friday the Thirteenth*, and *Halloween*, and which is subject to the same marketing forces and strategies that encourage writers in other popular fiction genres to conceive trilogies, multi-volume chronicles and shared world projects. But in 2001 an unusual number of high-profile writers produced sequels or follow-ups to works many would number among the canonical works of contemporary horror.

John Farris, in *The Fury and the Terror*, revives a theme he first introduced in his influential supernatural thriller, *The Fury*, in 1976: a secret government agency trains psychic adepts as weapons. Whitley Streiber takes the basic premise of his 1981 classic *The Hunger*—an ancient race of vampires who have lived unobtrusively among human beings since the dawn of time—and stretches it into a framework for a tale of covert global war between vampires and special government forces. In *The Black House*, Stephen King and Peter Straub age the young protagonist of their best-selling young adult novel, *The Talisman* (1984), to adulthood, and give him an adult quest to fulfill in the alternate world he visits as a boy in the previous novel. None of these novels matched their distinguished predecessors in imagination and power. If anything, Streiber and Farris attempted to one-up their previous achievements largely through explicitness that might not have been tolerated in horror fiction 20 years before, and that showed how much expectations for horror fiction have transformed in that interval.

Sequels and reprises took a variety of forms in 2001. Ray Bradbury's *From the Dust Returned*, a quirky dark fantasy about a family of supernatural beings at odds with the world of mortals, is not a sequel per se, but a fix-up novel that elaborates on the lives and adventures of characters who had appeared in stories Bradbury wrote over a half-century before. A trio of novels from Brian McNaughton—*Gemini Rising, Downward to Darkness* and *Worse Things Waiting*—are revised alternate versions of sexually graphic horror novels the author wrote in the late 1970s.

More conventional sequels simply revive familiar settings and characters. F. Paul Wilson's *Hosts* is his fifth novel to feature Repairman Jack, an urban vigilante who in this adventure grapples with a mutated virus that threatens to absorb its victims into a hive mind. Hugh Cave's *The Evil Returns*, a sequel to his 1981 novel *The Evil*, resurrects a Haitian voodoo houngan and transfers his base of operations to Washington, D.C. Charles L. Grant's *When the Cold Wind Blows* is the fifth chronicle of his Black Oak investigative team, whose long time search for a wealthy client's missing daughter embroils them in supernatural adventures around the globe. Richard Laymon's *Friday Night in Beast House* extends to four a series of novels the author began writing in 1986, about an abandoned tourist attraction visited regularly by monsters from its subterranean caverns. ''Sequelitis'' of this sort is far from a new phenomenon in horror, as is proved by the release of *The Compleat Adven-*

tures of Jules de Grandin. De Grandin, a creation of Seabury Quinn, is a series psychic detective whose 93 adventures, all gathered for the first time in this two-volume retrospective, began in 1925 and ran for more than 20 years in the legendary pulp magazine *Weird Tales*.

Series characters have become almost *de rigeur* in vampire fiction, and vampire series books were as conspicuous as vampire fiction in general in horror's harvest for 2001. Anne Rice's *Blood and Gold*, Brian Lumley's *Avengers*, Chelsea Quinn Yarbro's *A Feast in Exile*, Mick Farren's *More than Mortal*, Laurell K. Hamilton's *Narcissus in Chains*, Nigel Bennett and P.N. Elrod's *His Father's Son*, and Lee Killough's *Blood Games* all were the most recent installments in open-ended series that translate the traditional longevity of vampire life into sweeping historical perspectives on human behavior, or plots in which the vampire serves as a source of ineradicable and persistent evil. Even the granddaddy of all vampires, Count Dracula, gets his due in Christopher Schildt's *Night of the Vampire*, P.N. Elrod's *Quincey Morris, Vampire*, and Elrod's anthology of original fiction, *Dracula in London*, all of which work variations on characters and ideas in Bram Stoker's classic novel. Though the majority of vampire sequels in 2001 were unremarkable, Tananarive Due's *The Living Blood*, a follow-up to her 1997 novel *My Soul to Keep*, is outstanding, in no small part because its vampire element—concerning a blood- drinking sect in Ethiopia whose immortality is linked to blood shed by the crucified Christ—is merely a starting point for its ambitious drama of power struggles, spiritual corruption, and innocence imperiled.

The prevalence of sequels in 2001 might easily give the impression that modern horror fiction has so exhausted its imaginative potential that there is little left for it to do but recycle stale themes and cliche tropes. In truth, the familiarity of some of the year's books was a reminder that horror, like any genre, is built on a set of trademark themes and motifs, and that its writers work in traditions shaped over decades, if not centuries, by numerous contributors.

Several books echoed themes of well-known predecessors. John Saul's *The Manhattan Hunt Club* is a variation on the plot of Richard Connell's classic short story, ''The Most Dangerous Game.'' Christopher Golden's *Straight on 'til Morning* reworks the concept of Peter Pan into a dark coming-of-age parable. Tim Lebbon's *Face*, about a family stalked by a psychopath, bears a passing resemblance to John D. MacDonald's *The Executioners*, the novel that inspired the classic film *Cape Fear*, while the plot of J.N. Williamson's *Affinity* reads like a retread of the plot for John Farris' *The Fury* (ironically, the same year Farris did retread the plot of that novel in a sequel). Some books feature similar premises for their stories: Dee Dee Ramone's debut *Chelsea Horror Hotel* and Bertice Berry's *The Haunting of Hip Hop* both explore the dark side of popular music idioms frequently associated with death and mayhem. Two other books with shared themes were Simon Clark's *Night of the Triffids* (an authorized sequel to John Wyndham's 1951 science fiction horror classic, *The Day of the Triffids*) and Tim Lebbon's *The Nature of Balance*, which present similar scenarios of nature run amok and humankind having to rethink its relationship with the environment.

Certain other books openly acknowledge the traditions they are extending. Ramsey Campbell's anthology *Meddling with Ghosts* provides a superb tribute to M.R. James, whose principles for the writing of ghost fiction influenced a century of writers who are anthologized in this volume. The book made an excellent companion to *A Pleasing Terror*, Ash-Tree Press's cornerstone omnibus of James's complete work—short stories, essays and plays—in the weird vein. Caitlin Kiernan pays tribute to the influence of Algernon Blackwood and H.P. Lovecraft in her second novel, *Threshold*, and manages dexterously to work their style of cosmic horror story into a modern novel steeped partly in the neo-Goth subculture. The persistence of Lovecraft's influence is equally evident in a clutch of books featuring his work in 2001: *The Ancient Track*, which assembles his complete poetry; *The Thing on the Doorstep and Other Weird Stories*, which collects some of his best fiction issued as part of the Penguin Classics series; and *The Shadow out of Time*, the first printing of the text of his famous science fiction horror story without its usual abundant editorial corruptions. Lovecraft was also honored with *Acolytes of Cthulhu*, Robert Price's anthology of Cthulhu Mythos stories written by other writers in the spirit of Lovecraft's fiction.

Horror fiction and films have long shared a relationship, and last year several authors produced novels that provided refreshing alternatives to usual film, television, and extra-literary media tie-ins that usually define that relationship. Clive Barker's *Coldheart Canyon* is a flamboyant look at the dark underbelly of Hollywood and the cult of celebrity that ascribes Hollywood's excesses, larger than life personalities, and seductive hold on viewers to influences from a supernatural realm. In Ramsey Campbell's *Pact of the Fathers*, the movie industry is revealed as one of several powerful businesses run by a centuries-old cult that has risen to dominance through its perverse interpretation of biblical dogma. Ray Garton's satirical *Sex and Violence in Hollywood* draws darkly funny parallels between the values of the modern film industry and the often gratuitously gory movies it produces.

Stephen King was among a handful of writers in 2001 who looked for horror in the alien invasion scenario that has been a staple of the genre for more than half a century. In *Dreamcatcher*, King delivers a nostalgic tale of the ties that bind a group of men who have been friends since childhood. They find themselves used as pawns between a crash-landed crew of vicious extraterrestrials who hope to infest the earth and an equally vicious U.S. Army task force hell-bent on wiping them out. Somewhat coincidentally, James A. Moore's *Fireworks* also tells of a crash-landed UFO that poses less of a threat to the citizens of the rural Georgia town than does the American military presence sent in to hush up its arrival. Dean Koontz approaches the UFO theme from a slightly different angle in *One Door Away from Heaven*, whose converging plot threads involve a benevolent alien child hunted on earth by extraterrestrial pursuers and a crippled young girl trying to escape her UFO- crazed bioethicist stepfather. These novels are interesting for finding horror not just in their otherworldly plot devices, but in their paranoid rendering of terrifying situations where civil liberties are suspended and civil rights denied. Their small scale depictions of the individual as victim of a totalitarian power echoed Bentley Little's semi-satirical *The Association*, about a man who discovers the housing development into which he has moved is run by a nightmarish homeowner's association determined to suppress any expression of individuality.

The most familiar themes of horror fiction were represented in abundance in 2001. As always, the vampire reigned supreme, featured in more than a dozen novels by authors such as Billie Sue Mosiman, James M. Thompson, Stephen Gresham, and Sam Siciliano. First time novelists, including Michael Schiefelbein and Jemiah Jefferson, debuted with vampire fiction. There is little originality in most of these stories, although Charlaine Harris's *Dead Until Dark* is notable for its blend of southern gothic and black comedy, and Thomas Lord's *Bound in Blood* makes an unusually intriguing Freudian case study in its account of a gay vampire at war with his mother, both of whom were vampirized by a stepfather whom the son murdered. Werewolf novels ran a distant second to the vampire fiction in terms of volume, but Kelley Armstrong's *Bitten*, which presents a young woman's attempt to find her own identity in terms of a female werewolf trying to establish independence from her pack, is one of the better werewolf novels in years. Continuing a trend in recent years, the quantity of non-supernatural horror novels was in decline. Tales of psychological suspense and serial murders by Richard Laymon, Elizabeth Massie, and Michael Slade were matched or outnumbered by books from Tom Piccirilli, Barry Hoffman, and Roy Johansen, which simply add a few supernatural embellishments to plots of predominantly straightforward suspense thrillers.

As always, the most interesting horror titles were those that resisted easy categorization. David Searcy's *Ordinary Horror* is a clever literary novel that attempts a critique of the strategies of horror narrative, even as it unfolds its simple suburban horror tale of a town overrun by a fulminant organic menace. James Hynes' *The Lecturer's Tale* is a wickedly funny send-up of modern academia related as the tale of an English lecturer's development of supernatural powers and the spiritual corruption that follows when he uses them to sort out warring factions within his department. Jack Ketchum, in *The Lost*, attempts, with some success, to create a horror story rooted in the failures of American culture in the 1950s and 1960s. Thomas Tessier's *Father Panic's Opera Macabre* creates a surreal mood of terror in the experiences of a man who finds himself trapped in the supernatural re-enactment of historical atrocities committed against Europe's gypsies centuries before. Jack Cady's *The Haunting of Hood Canal* is the story of a small town ruined by a monster that incarnates crass commercialism. Erin Patrick's first novel, *Moontide*, is an atmospheric tale of a ship's crew that discovers their vessel is haunted and destined to destroy them. John Shirley, in *The View from Hell*, and Edward Lee, in *City Infernal*, both offer wildly transgressive depictions of traditional demons and devils. Edo van Belkom's *Teeth* takes top honors for the most outrageous horror novel with its central horror, a woman transformed by sexual abuse into a creature that kills with its reproductive organs.

Continuing trends from previous years, horror fiction in 2001 was dominated by a surplus of short fiction collections, the majority published by specialty presses. Publishers such as Subterranean Press, CD Publications, DarkTales and Wildside Press brought out single author collections by Tim Powers, Nancy Collins, Robert Weinberg, Nancy Kilpatrick, Michael Arnzen, and Mark Rainey, gathering some of the more interesting short fiction published in horror periodicals and original anthologies over the past two decades. Delirium Books, which brought out collections by Greg Gifune, Scott Thomas, Shane Ryan Staley, and others, most of whose contents were previously unpublished, continued, as did other specialty publishers, to help compensate for the relative lack of periodicals in which new and relatively unknown writers can hone their craft. The best collections of the year were impressive in their diversity. William F. Nolan's *William F. Nolan's Dark Universe* and Dennis Etchison's *Talking in the Dark* are both major retrospective collections. One celebrates the work of a writer known for his subtle approach and simple horror themes; the other offers tales of menace that blur the boundary between psychological and supernatural horror. John Shirley's *Darkness Divided* is a bountiful collection of stories by a writer whose horror fiction increasingly reflects his righteous rage at contemporary social ills. Norman Partridge's *The Man with the Barbed-Wire Fists* features work by a writer whose stories are often interesting melanges of B-movie imagery, '50s popular culture, and supernatural noir. David Schow's *Eye* offers a bracing range of supernatural, suspense, and science fiction stories that mix wit and visceral horror. David B. Silva's *Through Shattered Glass* and Gary Braunbeck's *Escaping Purgatory* are both chock full of stories that extrapolate emotional devastation, personal suffering, grief, and loss into powerful supernatural forces.

There were fewer horror anthologies in 2001 than in previous years, but a greater percentage than usual were not built around a specific theme. This continues a trend in recent years away from the narrowly defined, overly specialized theme anthologies that cluttered horror bookshelves for most of the 1990s. Dennis Etchison's *Museum of Horrors* was the first of seven anthologies produced under the imprimatur of the Horror Writers' Association (HWA) that was not a theme anthology. Richard Chizmar revived the Night Visions series formerly published by Dark Harvest in the 1980s and 1990s and continued its policy of giving writers (in this instance David Silva, John Shirley, and Jack Ketchum) carte blanche to provide 40,000 words of previously unpublished horror fiction. L.H. Maynard and M.P.N. Sims edited two anthologies, *Hideous Dreams* and *Night's Soft Pains*, that showcased new fiction by relatively unknown writers, most with a talent for tastefully restrained horror writing. Even the more solidly thematic anthologies, such as Stephen Jones's *The Mammoth Book of Vampire Stories by Women*, Nicola Griffith and Steven Pagel's *Bending the Landscape: Horror*, and Elizabeth Engstrom's *Dead on Demand*, which culled the best ghost stories written by a weekend writing class, were impressive in the range of their contents. As always, Stephen Jones's *The Mammoth Book of Best New Horror. Volume 12*, and Ellen Datlow and Terri Windling's *The Year's Best Fantasy and Horror: Fourteenth Annual Collection* were indispensable for their meticulous, eclectic story selections and comprehensive surveys of the previous year's haul in horror fiction.

As has been the case for several years now, the fastest growing area in horror fiction involves classic reprints. Pushed from the shelves by the glut of contemporary horror fiction published in the 1980s and 1990s, classic horror novels and story collections are back in vogue thanks to the efforts of publishers such as Ash-Tree Press, Sarob Press, Tartarus Press, and Midnight House. These compilations draw from fiction published over the last two centuries and range in preference from high Victorian ghost fiction to forgotten twentieth century pulp fiction. This year saw major reissues of the works of ghost story master Oliver Onions and master of psychological horror Thomas Burke, as well as selections of the complete weird short fiction of Shamus Frazer, Edward Lucas White, H.F. Heard, Robert Hichens, and others. Collections of stories by Edwardian supernatural writer E.F. Benson and pulp fantastists Fritz Leiber and Manly Wade Wellman continued ambitious programs by their publishers to reprint the complete short weird fiction of these writers in multi-volume series.

With the classic reprint resurgence extending not only to short fiction compilations but also to novels and anthologies, and the making of works that have been out-of-print from decades to centuries available once more, the horror field is in a healthier state now than it has been for years. It maintains a balance of fiction that commemorates the genre's hallowed traditions and cutting edge fiction that continues to break new ground and nurture new talent vital to horror's continuation as a literary form. The direction horror fiction will take from 2001, given the current social and political climate, is impossible to predict, but a change of course seems almost inevitable. It seems far from coincidental that most horror fiction in 2001 seemed complacent and comfortably familiar. In the past century, events that changed the course of history—notably World War II and the Vietnam era—were responsible in large part for boosting the horror genre out of its rut and changing the attitudes of both readers and writers. In the years to come, 2001 might well stand out as yet another pivotal moment in the horror field's ongoing evolution.

Recommended Books

Entries for the following books are included in this volume.

Bitten by Kelley Armstrong

Coldheart Canyon by Clive Barker

Mrs. Amworth by E.F. Benson

Pact of the Fathers by Ramsey Campbell

Talking in the Dark by Dennis Etchison

The Lecturer's Tale by James Hynes

A Pleasing Terror by M.R. James

The Mammoth Book of Best New Horror. Volume 12 edited by Stephen Jones

The Mammoth Book of Vampire Stories by Women edited by Stephen Jones

The Association by Bentley Little

Hideous Dreams edited by L.H. Maynard and M.P.N. Sims

William F. Nolan's Dark Universe by William F. Nolan

Moontide by Erin Patrick

The Devil Is Not Mocked and Other Warnings by Manly Wade Wellman

Entries for the following books can be found in *WDIRN?* 2001. Volume 2.

Meddling with Ghosts edited by Ramsey Campbell

Night Visions 10 edited by Richard Chizmar

The Year's Best Fantasy and Horror: Fourteenth Annual Collection edited by Ellen Datlow and Terri Windling

The Living Blood by Tananarive Due

Bending the Landscape: Horror edited by Nicola Griffith and Stephen Pagel

Threshold by Caitlin Kiernan

The Black Gondolier and Other Stories by Fritz Leiber

Ghost Stories by Oliver Onions

The Man with the Barbed-Wire Fists by Norman Partridge

Eye by David J. Schow

Ordinary Horror by David Searcy

Through Shattered Glass by David B. Silva

Horror Titles

615

JACK ADRIAN, Editor

The Ash-Tree Press Annual Macabre 2001

(Ashcroft, British Columbia: Ash-Tree Press, 2001)

Story type: Anthology
Subject(s): Horror; Short Stories; Supernatural

Summary: This is the latest volume in an anthology series whose criteria are that none of the contents have been reprinted since their original appearance in periodicals in the late 19th or early 20th centuries. Featured are Jesse Douglas Kerruish's ''The Badger,'' in which a British colonial incurs the wrath of household gods in the home he has rented in Japan; Noel Langley's ''Station Permanently Closed,'' about the eerie glimpses of an abandoned train station seen by a rail commuter; and Leigh Brackett's ''The Tapestry Gate,'' about a fabric design that proves a portal to another dimension. Introduced and with extensive notes by the editor.

Other books by the same author:
The Ash-Tree Press Annual Macabre 2000, 2000
The Ash-Tree Press Annual Macabre 1999, 1999
The Ash-Tree Press Annual Macabre 1998, 1998
Strange Tales from the Strand, 1997
The Ash-Tree Press Annual Macabre 1997, 1997

Other books you might like:
Mike Ashley, *Phantom Perfumes and Other Shades*, 2000
editor
Richard Dalby, *The Sorceress in Stained Glass*, 1971
editor
Peter Haining, *The Ghost Companion*, 1994
editor
Hugh Lamb, *Forgotten Tales of Terror*, 1978
editor
Sam Moskowitz, *Great Untold Stories of Fantasy and Horror*, 1969
editor

616

MICHAEL D. ARNZEN

Fluid Mosaic

(Berkeley Heights, New Jersey: Wildside, 2001)

Story type: Collection
Subject(s): Horror; Suspense; Short Stories

Summary: This collection contains 14 stories of supernatural and non-supernatural horror. Several feature characters driven to bizarre states of psychological distress caused by physical injuries and traumatic maiming, including ''My Wound Still Weeps'' and ''The Piano Player Has No Fingers.'' ''Stigmata'' concerns a woman whose obsession with sunbathing leads to a supernatural transformation. ''Sinking Sandy'' is about a woman whose suicidal ideation leads to psychological collapse and self-destruction.

Other books by the same author:
Grave Markings, 1994
Needles and Sins, 1993

Other books you might like:
Michael Blumlein, *The Brains of Rats*, 1989
Jack Remick, *Terminal Weird*, 1996
Wayne Allen Sallee, *With Wounds Still Wet*, 1996
John Shirley, *Black Butterflies*, 1998
Steve Rasnic Tem, *City Fishing*, 2000

617

TRISHA BAKER

Crimson Kiss

(New York: Pinnacle, 2001)

Story type: Vampire Story
Subject(s): Horror; Supernatural; Vampires
Major character(s): Meghann O'Neill, Psychologist, Vampire; Simon Baldevar, Vampire; Alcuin, Vampire
Time period(s): 1990s; 1940s
Locale(s): New York, New York

Summary: Forty years ago, Meghann O'Neill turned on dashing and debonair Simon, her vampire initiator, and left him to die. Now a psychologist who specializes in treating victims of abuse, Meghann suddenly finds Simon very much alive, back in her life, and using her patients to get back at her. A first novel.

Other books you might like:
P.D. Cacek, *Night Players*, 2001
David Dvorkin, *Insatiable*, 1993
Roxanne Longstreet, *Cold Kiss*, 1995
Steven G. Spruill, *Rulers of Darkness*, 1995
Whitley Strieber, *The Hunger*, 1981

618

LOUISA BALDWIN

The Shadow on the Blind

(Ashcroft, British Columbia: Ash-Tree Press, 2001)

Story type: Collection; Ghost Story
Subject(s): Ghosts; Short Stories

Summary: Ten old-fashioned ghost stories by a writer of the Victorian era are gathered herein. In the title tale, a haunted house drives out all of its owners by replaying a grisly scene of patricide happening decades before. "The Weird of the Walfords" concerns an heir whose family is haunted by misfortune and death when he dares to destroy the old bed in which generations of his forebears were born and died. "The Uncanny Bairn" is a story of a young boy afflicted with second sight to see when others will die. With an introduction by Richard Dalby and John Pelan. Originally published in 1895.

Other books by the same author:
From Fancy's Realm, 1905
The Pedlar's Pack, 1904
Richard Dare, 1894
Where Town and Country Meet, 1891
The Story of a Marriage, 1886

Other books you might like:
B.M. Croker, *Number 90 and Other Ghost Stories*, 2000
Lettice Galbraith, *The Blue Room and Other Ghost Stories*, 1954
Theo Gift, *Not for the Night Time*, 2000
Mary E. Penn, *In the Dark and Other Ghost Stories*, 2000
Alice Perrin, *The Sistrum and Other Ghost Stories*, 2001

619

CLIVE BARKER

Coldheart Canyon

(New York: HarperCollins, 2001)

Story type: Ghost Story; Occult
Subject(s): Actors and Actresses; Movie Industry; Occult
Major character(s): Todd Pickett, Actor; Tammy Lauper, Housewife; Katya Lupi, Actress
Time period(s): 1910s (1916)
Locale(s): Hollywood, California

Summary: Recovering from a botched facelift, fading movie star Todd Pickett seeks refuge in Coldheart Canyon, a corner of Hollywood where silent film star Katya Lupi entertained scores of her peers in the seminal motion picture industry. In Katya's former home, Pickett finds the actress unnaturally young and alive, and her home still infused with the influence of a room constructed from occult artifacts from her native Romania. This room still provides access to the otherworldly Devil's Country, an extradimensional realm that was known to, and which subtly influenced Rudolph Valentino, Douglas Fairbanks, and other silent era luminaries who were part of Katya's circle.

Where it's reviewed:
Hellnotes, December 14, 2001, page 2
Locus, August 2001, page 21
Locus, August 2001, page 31
New York Times, October 25, 2001, page E7
Publishers Weekly, July 23, 2001, page 55

Other books by the same author:
Galilee, 1998
Sacrament, 1996
Everville, 1994
The Great and Secret Show, 1989
Weaveworld, 1987

Other books you might like:
Ramsey Campbell, *Ancient Images*, 1989
Ehren M. Ehly, *Star Prey*, 1992
Dennis Etchison, *Shadow Man*, 1993
Greg Kihn, *Horror Show*, 1996

620

DONALD BEMAN

Dead Love

(New York: Leisure, 2001)

Story type: Possession
Subject(s): Horror; Small Town Life; Supernatural
Major character(s): Sean MacDonald, Writer; Pamela Eagleston, Businesswoman; Peter Murphy, Police Officer
Time period(s): 2000s
Locale(s): Blue Fields, New York

Summary: Sean MacDonald returns home to Blue Fields, where his teenage love Judith died 30 years before. He discovers that Judith's malignant spirit is actively taking possession of the women in the town, and manipulating them to get him to fulfill his promise that he would love her forever.

Other books by the same author:
Avatar, 1998
The Taking, 1997

Other books you might like:
Ramsey Campbell, *The House on Nazareth Hill*, 1996
Ron Dee, *Succumb*, 1993
Stephen King, *The Shining*, 1977
Richard Matheson, *Earthbound*, 1989
Bernard Taylor, *Sweetheart, Sweetheart*, 1977

621

NIGEL BENNETT
P.N. ELROD, Co-Author

His Father's Son

(New York: Baen, 2001)

Story type: Vampire Story; Mystery
Subject(s): Fathers and Sons; Mystery; Vampires
Major character(s): Richard Dun, Detective—Private, Vampire; Luis Trujillo, Businessman; Alejandro Trujillo, Businessman
Time period(s): 2000s
Locale(s): Dallas, Texas; Toronto, Ontario, Canada

Summary: Vampire Richard Dun is too late to save a friend and her family from the vengeance of a wronged business associate of her husband's. When Richard investigates the case more closely, he discovers irregularities that resonate with his own experiences as a father and a vampire in medieval times—experiences that suggest jealousy, betrayal, and falsely professed innocence are all factors in the murderous events. Author Nigel Bennett played vampire Lucien LaCroix on the ''Forever Knight'' television series. This novel is a sequel to *Keeper of the King*.

Where it's reviewed:
Kirkus Reviews, March 1, 2001, page 300
Publishers Weekly, March 26, 2001, page 68

Other books by the same author:
Keeper of the King, 1998 (P.N. Elrod, co-author)

Other books you might like:
Tracy Briery, *The Vampire Journals*, 1993
Anne Rice, *The Vampire Lestat*, 1985
Michael Romkey, *I, Vampire*, 1990
Lucius Shepard, *The Golden*, 1993
Chelsea Quinn Yarbro, *Better in the Dark*, 1993

622

E.F. BENSON

Mrs. Amworth

(Ashcroft, British Columbia: Ash-Tree Press, 2001)

Story type: Collection
Series: Collected Spook Stories
Subject(s): Horror; Short Stories; Supernatural

Summary: These 16 stories of horror and the supernatural were written by a renowned Edwardian writer of social comedies and personal memoirs. The contents, all of which were first published in less than two years between 1922 and 1923, include ''Negotium Perambulans. . .,'' about a slug-like manifestation of evil that haunts the grounds where a church once stood; ''The Horror Horn,'' about an outdoorsman's encounter with a race of proto-human creatures who inhabit a high mountain range; and two vampire stories, ''The Outcast'' and ''Mrs. Amworth.'' Edited by Jack Adrian, as part of a series that will reprint all of the author's horror and supernatural stories in the order of their original publication.

Other books by the same author:
The Passenger, 1999
Terror by Night, 1998
The Collected Ghost Stories of E.F. Benson, 1992
The Flint Knife, 1988
The Room in the Tower and Other Stories, 1912

Other books you might like:
A.M. Burrage, *Warning Whispers*, 1988
William Fryer Harvey, *Midnight Tales*, 1946
Margery Lawrence, *Nights of the Round Table*, 1926
L.A. Lewis, *Tales of the Grotesque*, 1934
H. Russell Wakefield, *They Return at Evening*, 1928

623

RAY BRADBURY

From the Dust Returned

(New York: Morrow, 2001)

Story type: Gothic Family Chronicle
Subject(s): Family Relations; Fantasy; Supernatural
Major character(s): Timothy Elliot, Foundling, Narrator; Cecy Elliot, Teenager; Uncle Einar, Supernatural Being
Time period(s): 2000s
Locale(s): Green Town, Illinois

Summary: Following a family reunion that draws in their relatives from across the globe, the Elliots, all but one of whom are endowed with supernatural powers, find themselves under subtle attack. The threat is posed by nonbelieving mortals whose skepticism is potentially fatal, and one family member who threatens to expose their supernatural identities if his demands are not met. This episodic dark fantasy novel incorporates a number of tales the author published as stand-alone stories over the past 55 years.

Where it's reviewed:
Locus, November 2001, page 29
Locus, October 2001, page 21
New York Times Book Review, December 9, 2001, page 28
Publishers Weekly, August 27, 2001, page 60

Other books by the same author:
The Stories of Ray Bradbury, 1980
The Halloween Tree, 1972
Something Wicked This Way Comes, 1962
The October Country, 1955
Dark Carnival, 1947

Other books you might like:
John Bellairs, *The House with a Clock in Its Walls*, 1973
Lewis Gannett, *The Living One*, 1993
Shirley Jackson, *We Have Always Lived in the Castle*, 1962
Tanith Lee, *Dark Dance*, 1992
Roger Zelazny, *A Night in the Lonesome October*, 1993

624

POPPY Z. BRITE
CAITLIN R. KIERNAN, Co-Author

Wrong Things

(Burton, Michigan: Subterranean, 2001)

Story type: Collection
Subject(s): Horror; Short Stories; Supernatural

Summary: This collaborative collection contains three short fictions by two leading authors in horror's new wave. ''The Crystal Empire,'' by Brite, is a tale of fatal obsession leading to the murder of a rock star by a Manson-like cultist. ''Onion,'' by Kiernan, concerns a strange self-help group whose members cling to the memory of a transcendant encounter with the unknown that teases them with the possibility that it was all in their imagination. ''The Rest of the Wrong Thing,'' written by both and set in Brite's fictional town of Missing Mile, North Carolina, is a tale of occult experience and synchronicity. A detailed afterword by Kiernan explaining the genesis of the stories is included. Published as a signed limited edition hardcover.

Other books you might like:
Michael Blumlein, *The Brains of Rats*, 1989
Charlee Jacob, *Up, out of Cities That Blow Hot and Cold*, 2000
David J. Schow, *Black Leather Required*, 1994
John Shirley, *Really, Really, Really, Really Weird Stories*, 1999
Lucy Taylor, *Painted in Blood*, 1997

625

P.D. CACEK

Night Players

(Darien, Illinois: Design Image Group, 2001)

Story type: Vampire Story
Subject(s): Sexual Behavior; Supernatural; Vampires
Major character(s): Allison Garret, Vampire; Mica, Religious (preacher), Boyfriend (of Allison); Seth, Vampire
Time period(s): 2000s
Locale(s): Las Vegas, Nevada

Summary: Allison, a vampire, and Mica, her preacher boyfriend, have fled to Nevada in the hope of blending in with the outrageous lifestyle of Las Vegas. In the course of her work for a crisis line catering to abused women—an ideal way for her to find deserving male victims to feed from—Allison hears of the Stud Farm, a unique S&M club. To her discomfort, she discovers that the club is run by Seth, her vampire initiator, and one of the very people she had hoped to escape. A sequel to *Night Prayers*.

Other books by the same author:
Night Prayers, 1998

Other books you might like:
Poppy Z. Brite, *Lost Souls*, 1992
Michael Cecilione, *Domination*, 1993
Ray Garton, *Live Girls*, 1987
Laurell K. Hamilton, *Black Narcissus*, 2001
Karen E. Taylor, *Bitter Blood*, 1994

626

RAMSEY CAMPBELL

Pact of the Fathers

(New York: Forge, 2001)

Story type: Mystery; Child-in-Peril
Subject(s): Bible; Fathers and Daughters; Cults
Major character(s): Daniella Logan, Student; Mark Alexander, Writer; Nana Babouris, Actress
Time period(s): 2000s
Locale(s): Oxfordshire, England

Summary: Daniella Logan investigates the mysterious car accident that killed her beloved father. She uncovers an unspeakable conspiracy involving him and his business associates who, guided by a perverted exegesis of the Bible, further their careers and social standing through the blood sacrifice of their children.

Where it's reviewed:
Locus, October 2001, page 35

Other books by the same author:
Silent Children, 2000
The Last Voice They Hear, 1998
The House on Nazareth Hill, 1996
The One Safe Place, 1995
The Long Lost, 1993

Other books you might like:
Jonathan Aycliffe, *Naomi's Room*, 1992
Simon Clark, *Darkness Demands*, 2001
Dennis Etchison, *Shadow Man*, 1993
Ray Garton, *Crucifax Autumn*, 1998
R. Patrick Gates, *Grimm Memorials*, 1990

627

SCOTT CHANDLER (Pseudonym of Chandler Scott McMillin)

Ghost Killer

(New York: Berkley, 2001)

Story type: Possession; Serial Killer
Subject(s): Murder; Serial Killers; Supernatural
Major character(s): Nancy Greenbaum, Psychologist; Harry Paladin, Detective—Police; Nell Moore, Young Woman
Time period(s): 2000s
Locale(s): Baltimore, Maryland

Summary: When detective Harry Paladin murders the Ghost Killer, a psychotic serial killer and sex fiend who gruesomely mutilates his victims, he inadvertently frees the killer's malign spirit. Taking up residence in the body of clinical psychologist Nancy Greenbaum, the Ghost Killer resumes his murder spree in a new and unassuming form. Meanwhile, Nancy's spirit, which has been displaced into the body of the recently deceased Nell Moore, struggles to convince the incredulous police force—which includes her stern uncle, Brutus—that the Ghost Killer is on the loose once more. A first novel.

Other books you might like:
Harlan Ellison, *Mefisto in Onyx*, 1993
Dewey Gram, *Fallen*, 1998
Dean R. Koontz, *Whispers*, 1980
Richard Laymon, *Body Rides*, 1997
John Saul, *Black Lightning*, 1995

628

RICHARD CHIZMAR, Editor

Trick or Treat

(Abingdon, Maryland: CD Publications, 2001)

Story type: Anthology
Subject(s): Halloween; Horror; Supernatural

Summary: Five novellas feature supernatural and nonsupernatural experiences tied in to Halloween. Al Sarrantonio's *Hornets* tells of a writer of horror fiction, who accidentally taps into the dark power of the Druid demon Samhain. Thomas Tessier's *Scramburg, U.S.A.* and Nancy Collins' *The Eighth Devil* tell of juvenile delinquent pranks that spark horrors on Halloween evening. Gary Braunbeck's *Tessellations* and Rick Hautala's *Miss Henry's Bottles* use Halloween make-believe and masquerades to explore issues of character identity.

Where it's reviewed:
Publishers Weekly, October 8, 2001, page 50

Other books by the same author:
The Earth Strikes Back, 1994
Thrillers, 1993
Cold Blood, 1991

Other books you might like:
Jo Fletcher, *Horror at Halloween*, 1999
editor
Peter Haining, *Hallowe'en Hauntings*, 1984
editor
Alan Ryan, *Halloween Horrors*, 1996
editor
Michele Slung, *Murder for Halloween*, 1994
Carolyn-Rossel Waugh, *Thirteen Horrors of Halloween*, 1983
Martin H. Greenberg, Isaac Asimov, co-editors

629

NANCY COLLINS

Knuckles and Tales

(Abingdon, Maryland: CD Publications, 2001)

Story type: Collection
Subject(s): Horror; Short Stories; Suspense

Summary: Fifteen stories of horror and suspense, four original to the volume, are all colored by the author's predilection for the southern Gothic. Nine of the selections are set in the imaginary Arkansas backwater of Seven Devils, including ''The Pumpkin Child,'' in which a luckless man regrets the Faustian pact he makes with a hoodoo woman when it backfires on him; ''Raymond,'' about a young boy whose father resorts to drastic measures to curb his werewolf proclivities; and ''The Sunday Go-to-Meeting Jaw,'' a poignant story about a disfigured rebel soldier's homecoming from the Civil War and the horrors he faces in the defeated South.

Other books by the same author:
Avenue X, 2000
Lynch: A Gothic Western, 1998
A Dozen Black Roses, 1995
Midnight Blue, 1995
Nameless Sins, 1994

Other books you might like:
Poppy Z. Brite, *Swamp Foetus*, 1993
Joe R. Lansdale, *By Bizarre Hands*, 1989
Elizabeth Massie, *Shadow Dreams*, 1996
Robert R. McCammon, *Blue World*, 1990
Norman Partridge, *Bad Intentions*, 1996

630

DAWN DUNN

Pink Marble and Never Say Die

(Fort Wayne, Indiana: Wormhole, 2001)

Story type: Collection
Subject(s): Horror; Family Relations; Short Stories

Summary: This chapbook features two short stories. ''Pink Marble'' tells of a family haunted to dismal ends by the ghost of a child who died accidentally. ''Never Say Die'' concerns a woman who tries to go about life optimistically in a world where encounters with flesh-eating zombies are a regular part of everyone's day. With an introduction by Nancy Kilpatrick. Published in both paperback and hardcover editions.

Where it's reviewed:
Locus, October 2001, page 29

Other books by the same author:
A Walk on the Dark Side, 1998

Other books you might like:
P.D. Cacek, *Leavings*, 1998
Nancy Kilpatrick, *Cold Comfort*, 2001
Elizabeth Massie, *Shadow Dreams*, 1996
Dan Simmons, *Prayers to Broken Stones*, 1990

631

P.N. ELROD, Editor

Dracula in London

(New York: Ace, 2001)

Story type: Anthology; Vampire Story
Subject(s): Horror; Short Stories; Vampires
Major character(s): Dracula, Vampire
Time period(s): 19th century
Locale(s): London, England

Summary: Speculations on the activities of Count Dracula in London, as suggested in Bram Stoker's seminal vampire novel, fuel these 16 stories, all original to the volume. In Judith Proctor's ''Dear Mr. Shaw,'' the immortal vampire is a theater patron incapable of appreciating how death ennobles suffering human beings in Shakespeare's tragedies; Amy L.

Gruss and Cat Kingsgrave-Ernstein imagine an unpleasant meeting between the count and an as yet unknown Aleister Crowley in "Beast." In "The Dark Downstairs," Roxanne Longstreet Conrad imagines the mayhem that convulsed the Westenra household while Dracula vampirized one of the principle characters in Stoker's novel.

Other books by the same author:
Time of the Vampires, 1996

Other books you might like:
Martin H. Greenberg, *Dracula, Prince of Darkness*, 1992
Ed Gorman, co-editor
Stephen Jones, *The Mammoth Book of Dracula*, 1997
editor
Michel Parry, *Rivals of Dracula*, 1977
editor
Bram Stoker, *Dracula*, 1897
Robert Weinberg, *Rivals of Dracula*, 1996
Stefan Dziemianowicz, Martin H. Greenberg, co-editors

632

P.N. ELROD

Quincey Morris, Vampire

(New York: Baen, 2001)

Story type: Vampire Story
Subject(s): Horror; Supernatural; Vampires
Major character(s): Quincey Morris, Vampire; Abraham Van Helsing, Doctor; Beatrice Godalming, Actress
Time period(s): 1890s
Locale(s): London, England

Summary: In an alternate take on the events in the conclusion and aftermath of Bram Stoker's *Dracula*, Quincey Morris, the American cowboy who assisted in the killing of Dracula, is himself vampirized. Quincey possesses powers less malignant than Dracula's and struggles to alert his fellow vampire killers to the zealousness of Dr. Van Helsing, who instigated the destruction of Dracula and would like nothing more than to see the noble Quincey disposed of the same way.

Other books by the same author:
Lady Crymsyn, 2000
Dance of Death, 1996
Death Masque, 1995
I, Strahd, 1993
Red Death, 1993

Other books you might like:
Jeanne Kalogridis, *Lord of the Vampires*, 1996
Mina Kiraly, *Mina*, 1994
Fred Saberhagen, *The Dracula Tape*, 1975
Bram Stoker, *Dracula*, 1897
Chelsea Quinn Yarbro, *The Angry Angel*, 1998

633

ELIZABETH ENGSTROM, Editor

Dead on Demand

(Eugene, Oregon: Triple Tree, 2001)

Story type: Anthology; Ghost Story
Subject(s): Ghosts; Short Stories; Supernatural

Summary: These 20 previously unpublished stories were written as part of an annual seminar requiring participants to write a ghost story. Selections include Christina Lay's "Windigo," about a nature spirit that bedevils two hunters in the woods; Elizabeth Engstrom's "Purple Shards," in which a mirror has captured the soul of an unfaithful husband murdered by his spouse; and Bill Smee's "The Old Ones Cast," in which the spirit of the deep that caused a celebrated shipwreck a century before is still very active in the community where the ship ran aground.

Where it's reviewed:
Publishers Weekly, March 26, 2001, page 69

Other books you might like:
Michael Mayhew, *Harvest Tales and Midnight Revels*, 1998
editor
Claudia O'Keefe, *Ghosttide*, 1993
editor
Paul F. Olson, *Post Mortem*, 1989
David B. Silva, co-editor
Peter Straub, *Peter Straub's Ghosts*, 1995
Wendy Webb, *Gothic Ghosts*, 1997
Charles L. Grant, co-editor

634

DENNIS ETCHISON, Editor

The Museum of Horrors

(New York: Leisure, 2001)

Story type: Anthology
Subject(s): Horror; Short Stories; Supernatural

Summary: The premise here is that each of these 18 stories, written especially for this compilation, represents an exhibit in a shadowy museum. Selections include Ramsey Campbell's "Worse than Bones," about a collection of ghost stories bought second-hand that continues to be written in by its deceased former owner; Joel Lane's "The Window," a tale of sexual obsession that leads to murder; and Richard Laymon's "Hammerhead," a psychopath's first-person account of his serial murders. Included as well are a fragment from a work in progress by Peter Straub and stories by Charles L. Grant, Joyce Carol Oates, William F. Nolan, and others. Sponsored by the Horror Writers Association.

Other books by the same author:
MetaHorror, 1992
Masters of Darkness III, 1991
Masters of Darkness II, 1987
Masters of Darkness, 1986
The Cutting Edge, 1986

Other books you might like:
Robert Bloch, *Robert Bloch's Psychos*, 1997
editor
Ramsey Campbell, *Deathport*, 1993
editor
Robert R. McCammon, *Under the Fang*, 1990
editor
Peter Straub, *Peter Straub's Ghosts*, 1995
F. Paul Wilson, *Freakshow*, 1992

635

JOHN B. FORD

Dark Shadows on the Moon

(Griffith, Indiana: Hive, 2001)

Story type: Collection
Subject(s): Horror; Short Stories; Supernatural

Summary: These 36 stories of supernatural and psychological horror are mostly written in an old-fashioned Gothic style. ''My Other Self'' concerns a man unbalanced psychologically by his belief that he is pursued by a doppelganger-like dark alter ego. In ''The Curse,'' a man is haunted to death by the music of a musician to whom he sells a violin. ''The Eternally Descending Blade'' is a tale of morbid introspection and self-revelation. With an introduction by Simon Clark.

Other books by the same author:
Tales of Devilry and Doom, 2001
Macabre Delights and Twisted Tales, 1997
Within the Sea of the Dead, 1996

Other books you might like:
Rhys Hughes, *The Smell of Telescopes*, 2000
Mark McLaughlin, *I Gave at the Orifice*, 1999
Michael Pendragon, *Nightscapes*, 1999
Peter Tennant, *Death of a Valkyrie*, 2000
Thomas Wiloch, *Mr. Templeton's Toyshop*, 1995

636

JOHN B. FORD

Tales of Devilry and Doom

(Wilts, England: Rainfall Books, 2001)

Story type: Collection
Subject(s): Horror; Short Stories; Supernatural

Summary: This volume includes ten short stories and four tales in verse by a British writer of dark fantasy. Selections include ''The Illusion of Life,'' a story with an unreliable narrator and a ghoulish twist ending; ''The Illusion of Death,'' a morbid dream experience; and ''Grondak,'' a tale of a young girl menaced by an insidious monster. With an introduction by Arthur Pendragon. Published as a signed limited edition.

Other books by the same author:
Ghouls & Gore & Twisted Terrors, 1999
Macabre Delights and Twisted Tales, 1997

Other books you might like:
Quentin Crisp, *The Nightmare Exhibition*, 2001
Casey Czichas, *The Candlelight Reader*, 1999
Anthony Morris, *Candlelight Ghost Stories*, 1998
David Price, *The Evil Eye*, 2001
Sarah Singleton, *In the Mirror*, 1999

637

ALTON GANSKY

The Prodigy

(Grand Rapids, Michigan: Zondervan, 2001)

Story type: Wild Talents
Subject(s): Christianity; Faith; Supernatural
Major character(s): Toby Matthews, Child; Thomas York, Student—College; Richard Wellman, Radio Personality (talk show host)
Time period(s): 2000s
Locale(s): Catalina Island, California

Summary: Under the guidance of Richard Wellman, a radio show talk host turned true believer, and a wealthy patron, Toby Matthews, who effortlessly heals the sick and brings goodness into the lives of others, becomes a faith healer and head of the Church of New Jerusalem. Toby though, is sensitive to the Shadow Man, an evil entity whom he sees possess the soul of Wellman, and he comes to realize he can defeat it only by accepting the teachings of Jesus Christ—a decision that puts him in spiritual peril.

Where it's reviewed:
Publishers Weekly, March 19, 2001, page 73

Other books by the same author:
Vanished, 2000
A Ship Possessed, 1999

Other books you might like:
John Byrne, *Whipping Boy*, 1992
Roger Elwood, *The Sorcerers of Sodom*, 1991
Tim LaHaye, *Left Behind*, 1995
Jerry B. Jenkins, co-author
Robert R. McCammon, *Mystery Walk*, 1983
F. Paul Wilson, *Reborn*, 1990

638

RAY GARTON

The Folks

(Abingdon, Maryland: CD Publications, 2001)

Story type: Gothic Family Chronicle; Small Town Horror
Subject(s): Family Relations; Murder; Small Town Life
Major character(s): Andrew Sayers, Young Man, Handicapped (burn victim); Amanda Bollinger, Young Woman; Matt Bollinger, Businessman
Time period(s): 2000s
Locale(s): Mount Crag

Summary: Deformed by burns suffered as a child, Andrew seeks to integrate himself into the life of the small town of Mount Crag. To his dismay, he finds himself caught between a church of religious fundamentalists, who see his injuries as the inscrutable working of the Lord's will, and the Bollingers. A rich but grotesquely inbred family, the Bollingers' influence controls the town and they will stop at nothing to take Andrew into their fold and groom him to assume the family's business interests.

Where it's reviewed:
Hellnotes, August 10, 2001, page 2
Publishers Weekly, April 2, 2001, page 44

Other books by the same author:
Biofire, 1999
411, 1998
Shackled, 1997
Dark Channel, 1992
Lot Lizards, 1991

Other books you might like:
Katherine Dunn, *Geek Love*, 1990
Jack Ketchum, *Off Season*, 1980
Edward Lee, *The Bighead*, 1999
Tom Reamy, *Blind Voices*, 1978
F. Paul Wilson, *Freakshow*, 1992
editor

639

GREG F. GIFUNE

Heretics

(North Webster, Indiana: Delirium, 2001)

Story type: Collection
Subject(s): Horror; Short Stories; Supernatural

Summary: Eight stories, three previously unpublished, explore the potential dark side of a variety of ordinary relationships. "Creep" concerns an act of teenage humiliation whose victim literally comes back to haunt its perpetrators decades later. "Vessel" features a man haunted by the influence of a sibling whom his mother aborted. The title story is a short novel about a young man's odyssey home to confront a supernaturally endowed teenage lover who died years before but whose spirit still persists. With an introduction by Brian Hopkins.

Where it's reviewed:
Hellnotes, November 2, 2001, page 3

Other books by the same author:
Down to Sleep, 1999

Other books you might like:
Gerard Daniel Houarner, *I Love You and There Is Nothing You Can Do about It*, 2000
Michael Laimo, *Demons, Freaks and Other Abnormalities*, 1999
Kurt Newton, *The Mind Spider and Other Strange Visitors*, 1999
Robin Nickaell, *The Boneyard*, 2000
Jeffrey Thomas, *Terror Incognita*, 2000

640

SEPHERA GIRON

House of Pain

(New York: Leisure, 2001)

Story type: Haunted House
Subject(s): Haunted Houses; Horror; Supernatural
Major character(s): Tony, Financier; Lydia, Advertising; Buddy, Vagrant
Time period(s): 2000s
Locale(s): New York (upstate New York)

Summary: Shortly after moving into the luxury home Tony builds in his old rural hometown, Lydia is plagued by dreams filled with torture and death and manifestations of unthinkable horror. To her dismay, Lydia discovers the house was built on the site where, years before, stood the home of a serial killer, which Tony saw bulldozed out of existence as a boy. Tony seems to have completely forgotten about the house's history—or has he?

Where it's reviewed:
Hellnotes, August 31, 2001, page 2

Other books by the same author:
Eternal Sunset, 2001

Other books you might like:
Clive Barker, *The Hellbound Heart*, 1991
Poppy Z. Brite, *Drawing Blood*, 1993
Lisa Cantrell, *Torments*, 1990
Tom Elliott, *The Dwelling*, 1989
Robert Marasco, *Burnt Offerings*, 1973

641

D.G.K. GOLDBERG

Doomed to Repeat It

(Darien, Illinois: Design Image Group, 2001)

Story type: Ghost Story
Subject(s): Ghosts; Horror; Supernatural
Major character(s): Layla MacDonald, Receptionist; Ian Macgregor, Spirit; Matt Macdonald, Businessman
Time period(s): 2000s
Locale(s): Charlotte, North Carolina

Summary: Layla finds herself attracted to Ian. The only problem is that Ian is the ghost of a Scottish rebel who died centuries before, and who, connected to Layla's family historically, through their bloodline, serves as her protector, brutally killing anyone who threatens her and leaving her to take the blame for his atrocities.

Where it's reviewed:
Hellnotes, December 7, 2001, page 4

Other books by the same author:
Skating on the Edge, 2001

Other books you might like:
Stephen Lee Climer, *Demonesque*, 1999
Rick Hautala, *Beyond the Shroud*, 1996
Rick Hautala, *Cold Whisper*, 1991
Ed Kelleher, *Animus*, 1993
Harriette Vidal, co-author
J.N. Williamson, *The Haunt*, 1999

642

CHRISTOPHER GOLDEN

Straight on 'Til Morning

(New York: Signet, 2001)

Story type: Child-in-Peril; Coming-of-Age
Subject(s): Supernatural; Teen Relationships; War
Major character(s): Kevin Murphy, Teenager; Nicole French, Teenager; Peter Starling, Teenager
Time period(s): 1980s (1981)
Locale(s): Framingham, Massachusetts

Summary: Kevin Murphy is crushed that Nicole, his best friend and unrequited love, has fallen in love with Peter, a strange young man whose gang has troubled the lives of Kevin and his friends during summer vacation. Too late, Kevin discovers that Peter is a visitor from a war-torn, dark dimension sinisterly evocative of the Neverland of Peter Pan, and when he abducts Nicole there, Kevin must lead his friends on a crusade to save her. Also published as a signed limited edition hardcover from CD Publications.

Where it's reviewed:
Hellnotes, March 30, 2001, page 2
Publishers Weekly, March 12, 2001, page 67

Other books by the same author:
Of Masques and Martyrs, 1998
Strangewood, 1998
Angel Souls and Devil Hearts, 1995
Of Saints and Shadows, 1994

Other books you might like:
Clive Barker, *Weaveworld*, 1987
Dennis Etchison, *Darkside*, 1986
Raymond E. Feist, *Faerie Tale*, 1988
Charles L. Grant, *For Fear of the Night*, 1988
Stephen King, *The Talisman*, 1984
Peter Straub, co-author

643

MARTIN H. GREENBERG, Editor

Single White Vampire Seeks Same

(New York: DAW, 2001)

Story type: Anthology
Subject(s): Romance; Short Stories; Supernatural

Summary: Twelve short stories of fantasy and horror, all original to the volume, revolve around the premise of personal ads that result in a supernatural encounter. Selections include Bradley H. Sinor's "Fireflies," in which a werewoman's personal advertisement attracts a vampire partner; Gary A. Braunbeck's "Starless and Bible Black," in which a supernatural lover brings a lovelorn man the afflictions of all her former lovers; and Tanya Huff's "Someone to Share the Night," in which a vampire's advertisement for love pulls him into an unexpected *pas de deux* with another supernatural being, who is less discreet about dispatching lovers.

Other books you might like:
Poppy Z. Brite, *Love in Vein*, 1994
Margaret L. Carter, *Demon Lovers and Strange Seductions*, 1972
Don Congdon, *Tales of Love and Death*, 1960
editor
Ellen Datlow, *Alien Sex*, 1990
editor
Linda Lovecraft, *Devil's Kisses*, 1976

644

H.B. GREGORY

Dark Sanctuary

(Seattle, Washington: Midnight House, 2001)

Story type: Occult; Curse
Subject(s): Horror; Occult; Supernatural
Major character(s): Anthony Lovell, Heir; Nicholas Gaunt, Paranormal Investigator; John Hamilton, Writer
Time period(s): 1930s
Locale(s): Cornwall, England

Summary: When Anthony Lovell repairs to Kestrel, his family's estate in Cornwall, to assume his inheritance following the death of the family patriarch, he falls under the influence of Nicholas Gaunt and Simon Vaughan. The two are psychic investigators summoned to help lay a curse supposedly placed on the family centuries before by the religious order whose castle the Lovells usurped. Anthony's friend John struggles to free him from their clutches, when he discovers that Gaunt and Vaughan are powermongers embarked on a scheme to unleash occult forces in the world. Reprint of a novel originally published in the 1940s in England.

Other books you might like:
Jonathan Aycliffe, *A Shadow on the Wall*, 2000
Furze Morrish, *Bridge over Dark Gods*, 1947
Adrian Ross, *The Hole of the Pit*, 1914
David C. Smith, *The Fair Rules of Evil*, 1989
Peter Straub, *Shadowland*, 1980

645

LAURELL K. HAMILTON

Narcissus in Chains

(New York: Berkley, 2001)

Story type: Vampire Story
Series: Anita Blake. Number 10
Subject(s): Sexuality; Vampires; Werewolves
Major character(s): Anita Blake, Detective; Jean-Claude, Vampire; Richard, Werewolf
Time period(s): 2000s
Locale(s): St. Louis, Missouri

Summary: In order to save two wereleopards for whom she is responsible and who have become prisoners of the Narcissus in Chains S&M club, mortal Anita Blake fortifies herself by taking on the ardeur of her rival lovers, the vampire Jean-Claude and the werewolf Richard. Supernaturally transformed by the ritual, Anita now finds herself possessed of both vampire and werewolf characteristics that give her insight into the complexities of supernatural politics, and also make her sexually insatiable. This is the tenth novel in a series set in an alternate America where supernatural beings enjoy the same civil rights as mortals.

Where it's reviewed:
Locus, September 2001, page 29
Publishers Weekly, September 17, 2001, page 60

Other books by the same author:
Obsidian Butterfly, 2000
Blue Moon, 1998
Burnt Offerings, 1998
Bloody Bones, 1996
The Lunatic Cafe, 1996

Other books you might like:
P.D. Cacek, *Night Prayers*, 1998
Sherry Gottleib, *Worse than Death*, 2000
Susan Sizemore, *Partners*, 2000
Whitley Strieber, *The Last Vampire*, 2001
Karen E. Taylor, *Blood Secrets*, 1994

646

MARK HANSOM

The Beasts of Brahm

(Seattle, Washington: Midnight House, 2001)

Story type: Psychological Suspense
Subject(s): Animals; Cults; Reincarnation
Major character(s): Arthur Rodney, Young Man; Jeremy Shaw, Young Man; Corvinus Brahm, Nobleman (count)
Time period(s): 1930s
Locale(s): Brent Green, England

Summary: A bestial murder on a country road in Surrey leads Arthur and Helen Rodney to the home of Count Corvinus Brahm, who lives nearby. The solicitous count offers his services tracking down the creature responsible—but increasingly, evidence begins pointing to the mysterious count himself, and his peculiar influence over others. First published in England in 1937.

Where it's reviewed:
Hellnotes, December 7, 2001, page 2

Other books by the same author:
The Sorcerer's Chessman, 1939
Madman, 1938
Masters of Souls, 1937
The Ghost of Gaston Revere, 1935
The Wizard of Berner's Abbey, 1935

Other books you might like:
Gerald Biss, *The Door of the Unreal*, 1919
Violet Hunt, *Tiger Skin*, 1924
J.D. Kerruish, *The Undying Monster*, 1922
Greye La Spina, *Invaders from the Dark*, 1960
Harper Williams, *The Thing in the Woods*, 1912

647

ROBERT HICHENS

The Return of the Soul and Other Stories

(Seattle, Washington: Midnight House, 2001)

Story type: Collection
Subject(s): Short Stories

Summary: These eight tales of horror and the supernatural are by an English writer from the turn of the 20th century. They include the classic ''How Love Came to Professor Guildea,'' about a man haunted unshakeably by the ghost of a simpleton; ''The Return of the Soul,'' in which a man begins to fear that the woman to whom he is unhappily married houses the reincarnated spirit of a cat he killed decades before; and ''The Figure in the Mirage,'' wherein a woman traveler foresees her kidnapping in a mirage which she alone is privileged to see. Edited and with an introduction by S.T. Joshi.

Other books by the same author:
Snake-Bite and Other Stories, 1919
The Black Spaniel and Other Stories, 1905
Tongues of Conscience, 1900
The Folly of Eustace and Other Stories, 1896

Other books you might like:
Algernon Blackwood, *The Empty House and Other Ghost Stories*, 1906
D.K. Broster, *Couching at the Door*, 1942
Julian Hawthorne, *The Rose of Death and Other Mysterious Delusions*, 1997
Oliver Onions, *Widdershins*, 1911
Arthur Quiller-Couch, *Old Fires and Profitable Ghosts*, 1900

648

DAVID J. HOWE, Editor

Urban Gothic

(Surrey, England: Telos, 2001)

Story type: Anthology
Subject(s): City and Town Life; Horror; Short Stories

Summary: Six stories whose horrors are intimately tied to their urban settings are presented here. Christopher Fowler's ''The Look'' concerns a young woman who endures grotesque mutilations as part of her work for the modern fashion scene. In Graham Masterton's ''The Scrawler,'' a man comes to believe that he sees graffiti around the city urging him to distrust and then murder his lover. Paul Finch's ''Boys' Club'' tells of a young man whose juvenile delinquency and hooliganism is preparing him for entry into an exclusive occult fraternity. Inspired by a popular British television series, this volume was published under the auspices of the British Fantasy Society.

Where it's reviewed:
Hellnotes, August 17, 2001, page 2

Other books you might like:
Christopher Fowler, *City Jitters*, 1986
Charles L. Grant, *Doom City*, 1987
editor

William F. Nolan, *Urban Horrors*, 1986
editor
Paul F. Olson, *Dead End*, 1991
David B. Silva, co-editor
David J. Schow, *Lost Angels*, 1989

649

JAMES HYNES

The Lecturer's Tale

(New York: Picador, 2001)

Story type: Wild Talents
Subject(s): Academia; Supernatural; Teachers
Major character(s): Nelson Humboldt, Professor (lecturer), Accident Victim (finger severed); Vita Deonne, Professor; Morton Weissman, Professor
Time period(s): 2000s
Locale(s): Hamilton Groves, Minnesota

Summary: When his finger is surgically reattached after being severed in a freak accident, recently demoted lecturer Nelson Humboldt discovers that he can influence the behavior of his colleagues simply by touching them. Although Humboldt begins using his powers to manipulate academic appointments with the best intentions for his department, eventually his control becomes more insidious and self-serving. A Faustian satire of academia and modern English studies.

Other books by the same author:
Publish and Perish, 1997
The Wild Colonial Boy, 1990

Other books you might like:
Thomas M. Disch, *The Sub*, 1999
Bentley Little, *University*, 1995
David Prill, *The Unnatural*, 1995
Jane Smiley, *Moo*, 1995

650

M.R. JAMES

A Pleasing Terror

(Ashcroft, British Columbia: Ash-Tree Press, 2001)

Story type: Collection
Subject(s): Ghosts; Horror; Short Stories

Summary: *A Pleasing Terror* is the most comprehensive compilation to date of the supernatural fiction of M.R. James, the turn-of-the-20th-century writer generally regarded as the dean of modern ghost fiction. James emphasized the importance of tasteful restraint in the elaboration of malignant supernatural manifestations, and his application of these principles is evident in the stories collected from the four volumes of ghost fiction published in his lifetime. Landmark stories include "Oh, Whistle, and I'll Come to You, My Lad," in which an amateur archaeologist accidentally invokes an ancient spirit through a recovered artifact; "Casting the Runes," about a nasty occultist who disposes of his enemies by passing them slips of paper with demonic invocations; and "The Mezzotint," in which a supernaturally animated piece of artwork replays the events of a horrible crime. In addition, the book contains all of James' uncollected ghost fiction, seven fragments and 12 retold medieval ghost stories, 11 essays on the craft of supernatural fiction, the play *Auditor and Impressario*, and the full text of his novel for young readers, *The Five Jars*. Edited and introduced by Barbara and Christopher Roden, with comprehensive bibliographies of primary and secondary sources.

Other books by the same author:
A Warning to the Curious and Other Ghost Stories, 1926
The Five Jars, 1922
A Thin Ghost and Others, 1919
More Ghost Stories of an Antiquary, 1911
Ghost Stories of an Antiquary, 1904

Other books you might like:
Richard Dalby, *The Best of Ghosts and Scholars*, 1988
Rosemary Pardoe, co-editor
T.G. Jackson, *Six Ghost Stories*, 1919
R.H. Malden, *Nine Ghosts*, 1943
L.T.C. Rolt, *Sleep No More*, 1948
Eleanor Scott, *Randall's Round*, 1929

651

MATT JOHNSON, Editor

Triage

(Abingdon, Maryland: CD Publications, 2001)

Story type: Anthology
Subject(s): Horror; Short Stories; Suspense

Summary: A person walking into a workplace after making a threatening phone call and opening fire with a weapon is the basic premise for each of these three novellas. In Richard Laymon's *Triage*, a woman must escape a maniac at her workplace and, in order to stop him, determine why he has singled her out. Edward Lee's *In the Year of Our Lord: 2202* is set aboard a spaceship, in a repressive future, where the self-defense killing of an apparent maniac leads to the heroine's sexual enlightenment. Jack Ketchum's *Sheap Meadow Story* turns the premise into a wish-fulfillment fantasy of a slush-pile editor.

Where it's reviewed:
Hellnotes, January 1, 2002, page 2
Publishers Weekly, October 29, 2001, page 41

Other books you might like:
Robert Bloch, *Monsters in Our Midst*, 1993
Richard Chizmar, *Cold Blood*, 1991
editor
Gerard Daniel Houarner, *Going Postal*, 1998
editor
Richard Laymon, *Bad News*, 2000
editor
Wendy Webb, *Phobias*, 1994
Ed Kramer, Richard Gilliam, and Martin H. Greenberg, co-editors

652

ROGER JOHNSON

A Ghostly Crew

(Mountain Ash, Wales: Sarob, 2001)

Story type: Collection
Subject(s): Horror; Short Stories; Supernatural

Summary: Fifteen stories of ghosts and the supernatural, all in the classic Jamesian tradition, are presented as stories recounted to the author during his visits to a pub named the Endeavour. Selections include "The Scarecrow," about a visit to a cursed estate where an evil scarecrow guards the gates of hell; "The Watchman," in which a restored church is guarded against thieves by a supernaturally animated gargoyle; and "The Pool," in which the narrator resists the invitation of a ghostly comrade, knowing he wants to lead the man to his death. With an introduction by David G. Rowlands. A first book.

Other books you might like:
Paul Finch, *After Shocks*, 2001
L.H. Maynard, *Shadows at Midnight*, 1979
M.P.N. Sims, co-author
William Meikle, *Millennium Macabre*, 2000
David G. Rowlands, *The Executor and Other Ghost Stories*, 1996
C.E. Ward, *Vengeful Ghosts*, 1998

653

STEPHEN JONES, Editor

The Mammoth Book of Best New Horror 12

(New York: Carroll & Graf, 2001)

Story type: Anthology
Subject(s): Horror; Short Stories; Supernatural

Summary: These 22 stories were chosen by the editor as representative of the best short horror fiction published in the year 2000. Selections include Dennis Etchison's "The Detailer," a tale of cumulative menace in which a carwash employee comes to realize something horrible has happened in the car he is cleaning; Kathryn Ptacek's "The Grotto," which draws on classical mythology for its subtle reflections on death and mortality; Thomas Ligotti's "I Have a Special Plan for This World," a black comedy about a fatal modern work environment; and Kim Newman's "Castle in the Desert" and "The Other Side of Midnight," both additions to his Anno Dracula vampire series. The book also contains an overview of the year in horror by the editor, and an annual necrology of horror personnel compiled by the editor and Kim Newman. Published simultaneously in England and the United States.

Other books by the same author:
The Mammoth Book of Vampire Stories by Women, 2001
Dark Detectives, 1999
White of the Moon, 1999
Dark of the Night, 1998
The Mammoth Book of Dracula, 1997

Other books you might like:
Richard Chizmar, *The Best of Cemetery Dance*, 1998
editor
Ellen Datlow, *The Year's Best Fantasy and Horror: Fourteenth Annual Collection*, 2001
Terri Windling, co-editor
Dennis Etchison, *The Museum of Horrors*, 2001
editor
Al Sarrantonio, *999*, 1999
editor
Karl Edward Wagner, *The Year's Best Horror Series*, 1980-1994
editor

654

STEPHEN JONES, Editor

The Mammoth Book of Vampire Stories by Women

(New York: Carroll & Graf, 2001)

Story type: Anthology; Vampire Story
Subject(s): Horror; Supernatural; Vampires

Summary: Thirty-four stories and poems, 15 original to the volume, all feature vampires and were written by women. The vampires are involved in all manner of scenarios, including time travel in Elizabeth Massie's "Forever Amen," the American Civil War in Kathryn Ptacek's "Butternut and Blood," and biblical exegesis in Janet Berliner's "Aftermath." Other selections include "Master of the Rampling Gate," an excerpt from Anne Rice's novel *The Vampire Lestat*; Nancy Collins' "Vampire King of the Goth Chicks," in which punk vampire Sonja Blue unmasks a fraudulent vampire coven leader; and Mary Elizabeth Braddon's "Good Lady Ducayne," a vampire story published a year prior to Bram Stoker's *Dracula*.

Where it's reviewed:
Publishers Weekly, September 10, 2001, page 66

Other books by the same author:
Dark Detectives, 1999
White of the Moon, 1999
Dark of the Night, 1998
The Mammoth Book of Dracula, 1997
The Mammoth Book of Frankenstein, 1995

Other books you might like:
Poppy Z. Brite, *Love in Vein*, 1994
editor
Ellen Datlow, *Blood Is Not Enough*, 1989
Stefan Dziemianowicz, *Girls' Night Out*, 1997
Robert Weinberg, Martin H. Greenberg, co-editors
Alan Ryan, *Haunting Women*, 1988
editor
Jessica Amanda Salmonson, *What Did Miss Darrington See?*, 1989
editor

655

GRAHAM JOYCE

Black Dust

(Burton, Michigan: Subterranean, 2001)

Story type: Collection
Subject(s): Horror; Short Stories; Supernatural

Summary: This pair of weird tales are both loosely concerned with complex paternal relationships. ''The Apprentice'' tells of a young foreigner who, during World War II, befriends an aging British fascist who hopes to initiate him into the mysteries of witchcraft. The title story tells of an abusive father whose efforts to make amends to the son of a friend he has disappointed extend beyond the grave. Published as a signed limited edition chapbook.

Where it's reviewed:
Locus, July 2001, page 27

Other books by the same author:
Smoking Poppy, 2001
Indigo, 1999
Leningrad Nights, 1999
The Tooth Fairy, 1996
Requiem, 1995

Other books you might like:
Chaz Brenchley, *The Keys to D'Esperance*, 1998
Simon Clark, *Salt Snake and Other Bloody Cuts*, 1999
Peter Crowther, *The Longest Single Note and Other Strange Compositions*, 1999
Joel Lane, *The Earth Wire and Other Stories*, 1994
Tim Lebbon, *When the Sun Goes Down*, 2001

656

CAITLIN R. KIERNAN

From Weird and Distant Shores

(Burton, Michigan: Subterranean, 2001)

Story type: Collection
Subject(s): Horror; Short Stories; Supernatural

Summary: These 13 stories of horror and dark fantasy were all written originally for shared world anthologies or in collaboration with other writers. Selections range from surreally imagined near future scenarios in the postapocalyptic tale ''Between the Flatirons and the Deep Green Sea;'' to the zombie holocaust story ''Two Worlds, and In Between;'' to a trio of vampire stories, including two variations on the theme of Bram Stoker's classic novel *Dracula*, ''Stoker's Mistress'' and ''Emptiness Spoke Eloquent.'' Also included are stories co-authored with Christa Faust and Poppy Z. Brite.

Other books by the same author:
Threshold, 2001
Tales of Pain and Wonder, 2000
Silk, 1999
Candles for Elizabeth, 1998

Other books you might like:
Poppy Z. Brite, *Swamp Foetus*, 1993
David J. Schow, *Eye*, 2001
John Shirley, *Darkness Divided*, 2001
Lucy Taylor, *The Flesh Artist*, 1994
Steve Rasnic Tem, *City Fishing*, 2000

657

LEE KILLOUGH
KEVIN MURPHY, Illustrator

Blood Games

(Decatur, Georgia: Meisha Merlin, 2001)

Story type: Vampire Story
Subject(s): Detection; Supernatural; Vampires
Major character(s): Garreth Mikaelian, Vampire, Detective—Police; Ice, Murderer; Raven, Vampire
Time period(s): 2000s
Locale(s): Baumen, Kansas

Summary: Police detective Garreth Mikaelian, who keeps his vampire identity secret, crashes his car while pursuing Ice, an albino murderer. Upon recovering, he discovers that Ice and his cohorts partook of his blood while he was unconscious. This act links him psychically to his quarry and possibly makes them all the more difficult to eliminate while appearing just an ordinary member of the police force.

Where it's reviewed:
Cemetery Dance 35, page 89
Publishers Weekly, May 28, 2001, page 56

Other books by the same author:
Blood Links, 1988
Blood Hunt, 1987

Other books you might like:
Vincent Courtney, *Vampire Beat*, 1991
P.N. Elrod, *Lady Crymsyn*, 2000
Laurell K. Hamilton, *Obsidian Butterfly*, 2000
Tanya Huff, *Blood Trail*, 1991
Richard Jacocoma, *The Werewolf's Tale*, 1989

658

NANCY KILPATRICK

Cold Comfort

(Kansas City, Missouri: DarkTales, 2001)

Story type: Collection
Subject(s): Horror; Short Stories; Supernatural

Summary: Twenty-seven stories of horror and fantasy, a number with undercurrents of sexual anxiety and psychological ambiguity are collected here. Selections include ''Projections,'' in which a woman discovers that the monstrous manifestations she fears might not be just figments of her imagination; ''Heartbeat,'' in which a sexually naive young man is bewitched into romance by the occult rhythms of an island carnival dance; and ''The Children of Gael,'' in which the descendant of a man who benefited from Ireland's potato famine suffers poetic justice at the hands of the ghosts of those he blighted. With an introduction by Paula Guran.

Where it's reviewed:
Publishers Weekly, September 10, 2001, page 66

Horror

Other books by the same author:
The Vampire Stories of Nancy Kilpatrick, 2000
Endorphins, 1997
The Amarantha Knight Reader, 1996
Sex and the Single Vampire, 1994

Other books you might like:
Kim Antieau, *Trudging to Eden*, 1994
Poppy Z. Brite, *Are You Loathsome Tonight?*, 1998
Nina Kiriki Hoffman, *Common Threads*, 1991
Charlee Jacob, *This Symbiotic Fascination*, 1997
Edo van Belkom, *Death Drives a Semi*, 1998

659

STEPHEN KING
PETER STRAUB, Co-Author

Black House

(New York: Random House, 2001)

Story type: Child-in-Peril; Occult
Subject(s): Good and Evil; Horror; Quest
Major character(s): Jack Sawyer, Detective—Homicide (retired); Tyler Marshall, Crime Victim (kidnapped), Child; Charles Burnside, Serial Killer
Time period(s): 2000s
Locale(s): French Landing, Wisconsin

Summary: Former Los Angeles detective Jack Sawyer comes out of retirement when young Tyler Marshall disappears from his adopted Wisconsin town. Troubled by ominous dreams, Jack realizes Tyler has been abducted by serial killer Charles Burnside to the Territories, a magical otherworld. This is where the Crimson King seeks mortals who have latent powers that might destroy the Dark Tower which binds parallel universes in harmony and thereby give him an opportunity to take control. Jack traveled to that world when he was a child, and he is the only hope for Tyler and the world as we know it. A sequel to the authors' previous collaboration, *The Talisman.*

Where it's reviewed:
Hellnotes, October 19, 2001, page 2
Locus, September 2001, page 19
Locus, September 2001, page 31
New York Times Book Review, November 4, 2001, page 32
Publishers Weekly, August 20, 2001, page 51

Other books by the same author:
The Talisman, 1984

Other books you might like:
Clive Barker, *Weaveworld*, 1987
Jonathan Carroll, *The Land of Laughs*, 1980
Charles De Lint, *The Little Country*, 1991
Raymond E. Feist, *Faerie Tale*, 1988
Christopher Golden, *Straight on 'Til Morning*, 2001

660

STEPHEN KING

Dreamcatcher

(New York: Scribner, 2001)

Story type: Science Fiction
Subject(s): Friendship; Horror; UFOs
Major character(s): Henry, Doctor (psychiatrist); Jonesy, Teacher; Abraham Kurtz, Military Personnel
Time period(s): 2000s
Locale(s): Derry, Maine

Summary: On their annual hunting trip in the Jefferson Tract, a forest on the outskirts of Derry, four friends are exposed to a race of dangerous polymorphous extraterrestrials who have landed nearby. With the arrival of a gung-ho military operation determined to wipe out the creatures and their taint, the friends are faced with a struggle for survival, against the army and against the aliens, who have infected and infested them in various ways and threaten to spread their influence through them to the rest of the world.

Where it's reviewed:
Kirkus Reviews, February 15, 2001, page 205
Locus, April 2001, page 27
Locus, June 2001, page 23
New York Times Book Review, April 15, 2001, page 6
New York Times, March 15, 2001, page E9

Other books by the same author:
Hearts in Atlantis, 1999
Bag of Bones, 1998
Desperation, 1996
The Tommyknockers, 1987
It, 1986

Other books you might like:
Matthew J. Costello, *Midsummer*, 1990
Jack Finney, *The Body Snatchers*, 1955
Alan Dean Foster, *The Thing*, 1982
Robert A. Heinlein, *The Puppet Masters*, 1951
James A. Moore, *Fireworks*, 2001

661

DEAN R. KOONTZ

One Door Away from Heaven

(New York: Bantam, 2001)

Story type: Child-in-Peril
Subject(s): Ethics; Stepfathers; UFOs
Major character(s): Michelina Bellsong, Computer Expert; Leilani Klonk, Child; Curtis Hammond, Child
Time period(s): 2000s
Locale(s): California (southern California); Nun's Lake, Idaho

Summary: Seeking to turn around a life of troubles and disappointments, Michelina vows to protect crippled and precocious Leilani from her stepfather, a bioethicist who intends to blame her engineered disappearance (and death) on an extraterrestrial abduction. Michelina's mission takes her to Nun's Lake, a hotbed of UFO activity, which also draws young Curtis Hammond, a boy with unusual talents, whose true identity is crucial to the destinies of Michelina, Leilani, and possibly the whole world.

Where it's reviewed:
Publishers Weekly, December 17, 2001, page 66

Other books by the same author:
From the Corner of His Eye, 2000
False Memory, 1998
Fear Nothing, 1998
Seize the Night, 1998
Sole Survivor, 1997

Other books you might like:
Donald R. Burleson, *Flute Song*, 1996
Edward Lee, *The Stickmen*, 1999
Robert R. McCammon, *Stinger*, 1988
Alan Rodgers, *Pandora*, 1995
Stephen Wright, *M31*, 1988

662

RICHARD LAYMON

Friday Night in Beast House

(Abingdon, Maryland: CD Publications, 2001)

Story type: Child-in-Peril
Series: Beast House Chronicles. Book 4
Subject(s): Monsters; Sexual Behavior; Teen Relationships
Major character(s): Mark Matthews, Teenager; Alison, Teenager
Time period(s): 2000s
Locale(s): Malcasa Point, California

Summary: Mark hopes to impress Alison by sneaking them both into the legendary Beast House, a tourist attraction supposedly visited by monsters who live in its subterranean caves. Too late, Mark discovers there is truth to the house's legends, and one of the creatures is active, and sexually ravenous, the night of their break-in.

Where it's reviewed:
Hellnotes, October 5, 2001, page 2
Locus, September 2001, page 27
Publishers Weekly, August 13, 2001, page 290

Other books by the same author:
Come out Tonight, 1999
Cuts, 1999
The Midnight Tour, 1998
The Beast House, 1986
The Cellar, 1980

Other books you might like:
Lincoln Child, *Relic*, 1995
Douglas Preston, co-author
Rick Hautala, *The Mountain King*, 1996
Jack Ketchum, *Off Season*, 1980
Edward Lee, *Creekers*, 1991
John Tigges, *Monster*, 1995

663

RICHARD LAYMON

In the Dark

(New York: Leisure, 2001)

Story type: Psychological Suspense
Series: Collected Spook Stories
Subject(s): Games; Murder; Mystery
Major character(s): Jane Kerry, Librarian; Brace Paxton, Professor
Time period(s): 1990s
Locale(s): Donnerville

Summary: Jane and her new friend, Brace, find themselves players in a mysterious game whose every clue, left by the self-styled Master of Games, includes an increasing monetary reward when it is found. As Jane is drawn into more and more outrageous and dangerous situations in pursuit of the escalating payments, she must consider where the game is leading her, what Brace's relationship is to the events, who the mysterious Master of Games might be—and how far she will go to find answers to all her questions. First published in England in 1994.

Other books by the same author:
Night in the Lonesome October, 2001
Once upon a Halloween, 2000
Among the Missing, 1999
Body Rides, 1997
Bite, 1996

Other books you might like:
Matthew J. Costello, *The 7th Guest*, 1995
Craig Shaw Gardner, co-author
Hal Ellson, *Games*, 1967
Charles L. Grant, *The Hour of the Oxrun Dead*, 1977
Kent Rembo, *Visiting Hours*, 1982
Anthony Shaffer, *Sleuth*, 1970

664

RICHARD LAYMON

Night in the Lonesome October

(Abingdon, Maryland: CD Publications, 2001)

Story type: Psychological Suspense
Subject(s): Mystery; Suspense
Major character(s): Ed Logan, Student; Eileen Danforth, Student; Casey, Teenager
Time period(s): 2000s
Locale(s): Willmington

Summary: Rejected by his girlfriend, Ed Logan begins taking nighttime strolls to assuage feelings of self-pity. In the company of Eileen, a friend who soon becomes his lover, he becomes caught up in a complicated tangle of nighttime intrigues including two young girls squatting in a house, a pack of possibly cannibalistic homeless people, and a sexual predator named Randy. First published in England earlier in 2001.

Where it's reviewed:
Hellnotes, April 6, 2001, page 2
Locus, September 2001, page 27

Publishers Weekly, April 2, 2001, page 44

Other books by the same author:
Once upon a Halloween, 2000
Among the Missing, 1999
Body Rides, 1997
Bite, 1996
In the Dark, 1994

Other books you might like:
Dennis Etchison, *Shadow Man*, 1993
Stephen Gallagher, *Red, Red Robin*, 1995
Stephen King, *Gerald's Game*, 1992
Dean R. Koontz, *Fear Nothing*, 1998
Norman Partridge, *Slippin' into Darkness*, 1994

665

TIM LEBBON

Face

(San Francisco: Night Shade, 2001)

Story type: Psychological Suspense
Subject(s): Family Relations; Horror; Suspense
Major character(s): Dan, Office Worker; Nikki, Teenager; Brand, Hitchhiker
Time period(s): 2000s
Locale(s): Tall Stenington, England

Summary: A short, unpleasant confrontation with a hitchhiker named Brand, whom they kick out of their car, leaves Dan, Megan and their teenage daughter Nikki on the edge of paranoia. Stalked and menaced by Brand, they are driven to increasingly desperate measures, leaving them to wonder who—or what—their pursuer is, and whether the only way to remove him from their lives is through violent action.

Where it's reviewed:
Hellnotes, January 4, 2002, page 4
Locus, February 2002, page 31

Other books by the same author:
The Nature of Balance, 2001
Until She Sleeps, 2001
The Naming of Parts, 2000
White, 1999
Mesmer, 1997

Other books you might like:
Douglas Borton, *Kane*, 1990
Ramsey Campbell, *The One Safe Place*, 1995
Mark Chadbourn, *The Eternal*, 1996
Davis Grubb, *The Night of the Hunter*, 1953
John D. MacDonald, *The Executioners*, 1962

666

TIM LEBBON

The Nature of Balance

(New York: Leisure, 2001)

Story type: Nature in Revolt
Subject(s): Dreams and Nightmares; Nature; Survival
Major character(s): Blane, Young Man; Fay, Witch; Paul Tore, Young Man
Time period(s): 2000s
Locale(s): Rayburn, England

Summary: The world—or what is left of it—awakens one morning to find that all but a handful of people have died violently in their sleep, killed by nightmares. Blane, one of the survivors, realizes the only people who escaped gruesome death were those attuned to nature because the world has finally rejected humanity as unnatural. Still, as Blane and others struggle to keep a semblance of civilization alive, they can't help but wonder if someone among them isn't exercising supernatural powers to turn nature to his or her benefit.

Other books by the same author:
As the Sun Goes Down, 2000
The Naming of Parts, 2000
White, 1999
Faith in the Flesh, 1998
Mesmer, 1997

Other books you might like:
Hugh B. Cave, *The Dawning*, 2000
Richard Chizmar, *The Earth Strikes Back*, 1994
editor
Arthur Machen, *The Terror*, 1917
John Skipp, *The Bridge*, 1991
Craig Spector, co-author
F. Paul Wilson, *Pelts*, 1990

667

EDWARD LEE

City Infernal

(Abingdon, Maryland: CD Publications, 2001)

Story type: Occult
Subject(s): Devil; Hell; Supernatural
Major character(s): Cassie Heydon, Teenager, Twin; Roy, Handicapped; Ezoriel, Angel
Time period(s): 2000s
Locale(s): Blackwell Hill, South; Mephistopholis, Fictional City

Summary: Distraught over the suicide of her twin sister, Cassie moves with her father from Washington, D.C. to rural Blackwell Hill, and takes up residence in Blackwell Hall. Unknown to the Heydons, the hall was once home to a notorious Satanist, whose practices helped transform the dwelling into a Deadpass, or portal to Hell. Through data provided by escaped denizens of Mephistopholis, the infernal city on the other side, Cassie discovers she may be able to locate the soul of her dead sister—and also that she is an Etheress, with the potential to overthrow Lucifer.

Where it's reviewed:
Hellnotes, November 9, 2001, page 2
Locus, December 2001, page 27
Publishers Weekly, September 24, 2001, page 74

Other books by the same author:
Operator B, 1999
The Stickmen, 1999
The Ushers, 1999

Goon, 1996
Header, 1995

Other books you might like:
Ken Eulo, *The Brownstone*, 1980
Gordon Houghton, *Damned If You Do*, 1999
Brett A. Savory, *The Distance Travelled*, 2001
John Shirley, *The View from Hell*, 2001

668

BENTLEY LITTLE

The Association

(New York: Signet, 2001)

Story type: Psychological Suspense
Subject(s): Horror; Small Town Life; Suspense
Major character(s): Barry Welch, Writer; Maureen Welch, Accountant; Ray Dyson, Construction Worker
Time period(s): 2000s
Locale(s): Corban, Utah

Summary: It seems as though Barry and Maureen have found the perfect home when they move into the gated community of Bonita Vista—until they try to honor the bylaws of the local homeowners' association, which it is mandatory to join. As stipulations by the association grow increasingly difficult, and the association shows it will stop at nothing to enforce them, the couple grow even more paranoid of their neighbors and realize their dream home has become a nightmare.

Where it's reviewed:
Hellnotes, October 19, 2001, page 5
Publishers Weekly, August 27, 2001, page 62

Other books by the same author:
The Walking, 2000
Guests, 1997
The Store, 1997
Houses, 1997
The Ignored, 1997

Other books you might like:
Ray Bradbury, *Fahrenheit 451*, 1953
Charles L. Grant, *The Hour of the Oxrun Dead*, 1977
Stephen King, *Needful Things*, 1990
Ira Levin, *The Stepford Wives*, 1972
Joan Samson, *The Auctioneer*, 1975

669

H.P. LOVECRAFT

The Ancient Track

(San Francisco: Night Shade, 2001)

Story type: Collection
Subject(s): Horror; Poetry; Supernatural

Summary: This is an omnibus volume of verse by an author renowned as the leading influence on horror fiction in the 20th century. The majority of selections, which are non-horror oriented, show the influence of 18th century and neoclassical poets. The significant horror verse, much of it redolent of the verse of Edgar Allan Poe, includes the sonnet cycle "Fungi from Yuggoth," about a man's mystical odyssey, and the Gothic nightmare "Psychopompos." Edited and introduced by Lovecraft authority S.T. Joshi, who supplied corrected texts.

Where it's reviewed:
Publishers Weekly, July 23, 2001, page 54

Other books you might like:
L. Sprague de Camp, *Demons and Dinosaurs*, 1970
Frank Belknap Long, *In Mayan Splendor*, 1977
Edgar Allan Poe, *Complete Tales and Poems*, 1938
Clark Ashton Smith, *Selected Poems*, 1971
Donald Wandrei, *Sonnets for Midnight*, 1964

670

H.P. LOVECRAFT

The Shadow out of Time

(New York: Hippocampus, 2001)

Story type: Science Fiction
Subject(s): Aliens; Horror; Space and Time
Major character(s): Nathaniel Wingate Peaslee, Professor, Amnesiac; Wingate Peaslee, Young Man
Time period(s): 1910s
Locale(s): Arkham, Massachusetts

Summary: Recovering from a five-year bout of amnesia, during which he embarked uncharacteristically on extensive travels and scientific investigations, Nathaniel Wingate Peaslee is afflicted with dreams of an alien civilization that existed 150 million years before. As his memory slowly returns, Peaslee recounts how he exchanged consciousnesses with a member of this ancient race, which has used its mastery of psychic transmigration to travel to other worlds across space and time and record the history of all known life forms in the universe. Originally published in edited form in a science fiction magazine in the 1930s, this story receives its first textual restoration from Lovecraft's manuscript, the existence of which only came to light in 1994. With an introduction and notes by Lovecraft authority S.T. Joshi.

Other books by the same author:
The Thing on the Doorstep and Other Weird Stories, 2001
The Call of Cthulhu and Other Weird Stories, 1999
Dagon and Other Macabre Tales, 1965
At the Mountains of Madness and Other Novels, 1964
The Dunwich Horror and Others, 1963

Other books you might like:
Robert Bloch, *Strange Eons*, 1978
Robert A. Heinlein, *The Unpleasant Profession of Jonathan Hoag*, 1959
William Hope Hodgson, *The House on the Borderland*, 1908
Damon Knight, *Mind Switch*, 1963
Colin Wilson, *The Mind Parasites*, 1967

671

H.P. LOVECRAFT

The Thing on the Doorstep and Other Weird Stories

(New York: Penguin, 2001)

Story type: Collection
Subject(s): Horror; Short Stories; Supernatural

Summary: This volume collects 12 stories by weird fiction master H.P. Lovecraft, who published primarily in the fantasy and science fiction pulps of the 1920s and 1930s. All the selections elaborate, to some extent, Lovecraft's vision of a universe of awesome and incomprehensible forces indifferent to human existence, and include ''At the Mountains of Madness,'' about the discovery of an ancient alien city in the wastes of Antarctica; ''The Dunwich Horror,'' in which a monster born of the sexual union between a human mother and an extradimensional monster wreaks havoc in the New England countryside; and the title story and ''The Case of Charles Dexter Ward,'' both concerned with evil persons, who perpetuate their lives unnaturally through the transmigration of their consciousnesses into the bodies of others. With an introduction and notes by Lovecraft authority S.T. Joshi.

Other books by the same author:
More Annotated Lovecraft, 1999
The Call of Cthulhu and Other Weird Stories, 1999
Tales of H.P. Lovecraft, 1997
The Annotated H.P. Lovecraft, 1997
The Shadow over Innsmouth, 1994

Other books you might like:
Robert Bloch, *The Early Fears*, 1994
August Derleth, *Someone in the Dark*, 1941
Frank Belknap Long, *The Hounds of Tindalos*, 1946
Clark Ashton Smith, *Out of Space and Time*, 1942
Donald Wandrei, *Don't Dream*, 1998

672

GRAHAM MASTERTON

Bonnie Winter

(Abingdon, Maryland: CD Publications, 2001)

Story type: Occult
Subject(s): Family Relations; Suspense; Supernatural
Major character(s): Bonnie Winter, Maintenance Worker; Dan Munoz, Detective—Police; Duke Winter, Unemployed
Time period(s): 2000s
Locale(s): Los Angeles, California

Summary: Bonnie, who runs a service that cleans up houses where gory crimes have been committed, discovers clues in the course of her work that indicate some of the grisliest murders have a common thread to them. Slowly, this revelation begins to have an impact on her management of her own disappointing family.

Other books by the same author:
Trauma, 2002
The Chosen Child, 1997
The House That Jack Built, 1996
Spirit, 1995
Burial, 1994

Other books you might like:
Alex Abella, *The Killing of the Saints*, 1991
Nicholas Conde, *The Religion*, 1982
Ken Eulo, *Manhattan Heat*, 1991
William Relling, *Silent Moon*, 1990
Ray Russell, *Absolute Power*, 1992

673

A.J. MATTHEWS (Pseudonym of Rick Hautala)

The White Room

(New York: Berkley, 2001)

Story type: Ghost Story
Subject(s): Brothers; Haunted Houses; Supernatural
Major character(s): Polly Harris, Housewife; Tim Harris, Teacher; Brian Harris, Teenager
Time period(s): 2000s
Locale(s): Hilton, Maine

Summary: Tim Harris plans a summer away at his old family homestead to help his wife Polly heal emotionally, following the stillborn delivery of their second child. The house proves to be haunted by the ghosts of past crimes committed on its premises, and the discovery of bones and other human remains on the grounds have the the spirits of children who died there frantically trying to alert Polly and her family to their endangerment, and the unlikely person who means them harm.

Other books you might like:
Jonathan Aycliffe, *Naomi's Room*, 1992
Ruby Jean Jensen, *The Haunting*, 1994
Simon Maginn, *Sheep*, 1995
S.J. Strayhorn, *Black Night*, 1996
Tamara Thorne, *Haunted*, 1995

674

L.H. MAYNARD, Editor
M.P.N. SIMS, Co-Editor

Hideous Dreams

(Holicong, Pennsylvania: Cosmos, 2001)

Story type: Anthology
Series: Darkness Rising. Volume 2
Subject(s): Horror; Short Stories; Supernatural

Summary: This anthology contains 16 stories of horror and the supernatural, most written in the classic restrained tradition of the weird tale, all but one original to the volume. Selections include Shawn James' ''The Lady in White,'' about a spectral woman who haunts a graveyard and whose encounters mean death to the unwary; ''Devil Man of the Hollow,'' a tale of jungle terror; and Steve Duffy's ''Todhunter's Rock,'' a tongue-in-cheek deconstruction of the Victorian murder mystery. Also featured is a classic reprint, Huan Mee's "The Black Statue," about a mad scientist who discovers a means of turning humans into statuary.

Other books by the same author:
Night's Soft Pains, 2001
Echoes of Darkness, 2000

Other books you might like:
Claudia O'Keefe, *Ghosttide*, 1993
editor
Paul F. Olson, *Post Mortem*, 1989
David B. Silva, co-editor
Barbara Roden, *Shadows and Silence*, 2000
Christopher Roden, co-editor
Peter Straub, *Peter Straub's Ghosts*, 1995
editor
Wendy Webb, *Gothic Ghosts*, 1997
Charles L. Grant, co-editor

675

JAMES A. MOORE

Fireworks

(Decatur, Georgia: Meisha Merlin, 2001)

Story type: Science Fiction
Subject(s): Civil Rights; Freedom of Speech; UFOs
Major character(s): Frank Osborn, Police Officer (sheriff); Mark Anderson, Military Personnel; Karen Donovan, Teacher
Time period(s): 2000s
Locale(s): Collier, Georgia

Summary: When a UFO crash-lands in Collier, causing grievous damage to the town and injury to its citizens, the American military intervenes, sealing off the town from the outside world to prevent the leaking of top secret information. As Operation ONYX restricts civil rights and personal freedoms to maintain control of the town, discontent builds and threatens to explode in townspeople who see the military as posing a worse threat than the extraterrestrials.

Where it's reviewed:
Hellnotes, March 30, 2001, page 4

Other books by the same author:
Under the Overtree, 1999

Other books you might like:
Chris Curry, *Thunder Road*, 1995
Stephen King, *Dreamcatcher*, 2001
Nigel Kneale, *Quatermass and the Pit*, 1960
Dean R. Koontz, *Cold Fire*, 1991
Whitley Strieber, *Majestic*, 1989

676

JOSEPH M. NASSISE

Riverwatch

(St. Petersburg, Florida: Barclay, 2001)

Story type: Ancient Evil Unleashed
Subject(s): Good and Evil; Mysticism; Supernatural
Major character(s): Jake Caruso, Contractor; Sam Travers, Writer; Katelyn Riley, Student—Graduate
Time period(s): 2000s
Locale(s): Harrington Falls, Arizona

Summary: Construction on Stonemoor, the former estate of the Blake family, awakens a monster summoned centuries before by reputed witch Sebastian Blake that has been living in a dormant state in subterranean vaults beneath the house. The creature, a Nightshade, represents a force of evil that has been locked in an epic struggle with the benevolent Elders since time immemorial, and its defeat depends on the efforts of Gabriel Armadorian, a mysterious resident in a nearby nursing home, who seems to know more than most about the Blakes, and whose advanced years are perhaps only a gloss on his true age. A first novel.

Where it's reviewed:
Hellnotes, August 10, 2001, page 4

Other books you might like:
Douglas Clegg, *Goat Dance*, 1989
Gary Goshgarian, *The Stone Circle*, 1997
Mike Jefferies, *Stone Angels*, 1994
Brent Monahan, *The Uprising*, 1992
John Pelan, *An Antique Vintage*, 2000

677

ALAN NAYES

Gargoyles

(New York: Forge, 2001)

Story type: Techno-Thriller
Subject(s): Medicine; Pregnancy; Scientific Experiments
Major character(s): Amoreena Daniels, Student—College (medical); Luis Rafael, Doctor; Irene Leggett, Administrator
Time period(s): 2000s
Locale(s): California; Guatemala City, Guatemala

Summary: To help pay her way through medical school and cover her terminally ill mother's medical bills, Amoreena agrees to serve in a surrogate mother program sponsored by Meechum Medical Corporation. Too late, she discovers she is the vanguard of the next phase in a secret and illegal experiment to raise abnormally gestated embryos that will provide the medical black market with test subjects and donor organs. This tale of medical horror is the author's first novel.

Where it's reviewed:
Hellnotes, October 26, 2001, page 5

Other books you might like:
Thomas Boileau, *Choice Cuts*, 1966
Pierre Narcejac, co-author
Robin Cook, *Coma*, 1977
Gerald A. Schiller, *Deadly Dreams*, 1996
Michael Marshall Smith, *Spares*, 1997
F. Paul Wilson, *Implant*, 1995

678

WILLIAM F. NOLAN

William F. Nolan's Dark Universe

(Lancaster, Pennsylvania: Stealth, 2001)

Story type: Collection
Subject(s): Horror; Short Stories; Supernatural

Summary: This retrospective collection of 41 stories published between 1956 and 1999 is by a screenwriter and major contributor to the horror and dark fantasy movement in the years following World War II. The majority of the stories are simple weird or psychological suspense tales with twist endings, including ''He Kilt It with a Stick,'' about a cat-hating man done in by his psychological aversions; ''The Halloween Man,'' about a creepy Halloween superstition that becomes incarnated; and ''Stoner,'' about a disturbed man who confuses fantasy and reality in a wax museum. With an introduction by Christopher Conlon and a preface and notes by the author.

Where it's reviewed:
Publishers Weekly, October 1, 2001, page 43

Other books by the same author:
The Winchester Horror, 1998
Night Shapes, 1995
Helltracks, 1991
Things Beyond Midnight, 1984
Impact-20, 1963

Other books you might like:
Charles Beaumont, *Selected Stories*, 1988
Robert Bloch, *The Best of Robert Bloch*, 1977
Ray Bradbury, *The Stories of Ray Bradbury*, 1980
George Clayton Johnson, *All of Us Are Dying and Other Stories*, 1999
Richard Matheson, *Collected Stories*, 1989

679

MICHAEL OLIVERI, Editor
GEOFF COOPER, Co-Editor
BRIAN KEENE, Co-Editor
MICHAEL T. HUYCK JR., Co-Editor

4 X 4

(North Webster, Indiana: Pocket, 2001)

Story type: Anthology
Subject(s): Horror; Short Stories; Supernatural

Summary: These four solo stories and four collaborations were written in various combinations by the four editors, who met in a horror-fiction oriented online chat room. The stories, which feature a variety of styles and themes, include Keene's ''Earthworm Gods,'' about monstrous worms that surface on Earth during a nonstop rainstorm; Huyck and Cooper's ''Dealer's Wheel,'' in which an inmate's prison tattoos are liberated from his body and come to hellish life; and Oliveri's ''Hell Hath No Fury,'' in which twin brothers' sexual escapades with the women they've seduced backfire gruesomely.

Where it's reviewed:
Hellnotes, January 4, 2002, page 4

Other books you might like:
Poppy Z. Brite, *Wrong Things*, 2001
Caitlin Kiernan, co-author
Harlan Ellison, *Partners in Wonder*, 1971
John Skipp, *Deadlines*, 1989
Craig Spector, co-author
David Whitman, *Scary Rednecks*, 1999
Weston Ochse, co-author

680

OLIVER ONIONS

Tragic Casements

(Norfolk, England: Haunted River, 2001)

Story type: Ghost Story
Subject(s): Ghosts; Horror; Supernatural
Major character(s): Eustace Croydon, Gardener; Denzil Croydon, Military Personnel; Patricia Croydon, Young Woman
Time period(s): 1950s
Locale(s): Tottenham Fields, England

Summary: Ghostly manifestations at a newly refurbished greenhouse in the English countryside prove to be related to influences at the site where the gardener purchased the used glass and stones to build it. First published in a periodical in 1952 and never before included in any of the author's previous collections of weird fiction.

Other books by the same author:
The Collected Ghost Stories of Oliver Onions, 1935
The Painted Face, 1929
Ghosts in Daylight, 1924
Widdershins, 1911

Other books you might like:
Cynthia Asquith, *This Mortal Coil*, 1947
Algernon Blackwood, *The Magic Mirror*, 1989
Jonathan Burke, *The Golden Gong and Other Night-Pieces*, 2001
Walter de la Mare, *The Riddle and Other Stories*, 1923
Arthur Machen, *The Children of the Pool and Other Stories*, 1936

681

ERIN PATRICK

Moontide

(Doylestown, Pennsylvania: Wildside, 2001)

Story type: Curse
Subject(s): Sailing; Ships; Supernatural
Major character(s): Melanie Gierek, Sailor; Henry Gordon, Sailor; Jonathan Carleton, Sailor
Time period(s): 2000s
Locale(s): Camden, Maine; *Louisa Lee*, At Sea

Summary: In desperate straits financially, Melanie ships out as a galley hand on the *Louisa Lee*. Too late into the voyage, she discovers the ship is a reconstructed salvage that sank under mysterious circumstances, and that it has begun to show a dangerous antipathy to her and others of the crew. A first novel.

Where it's reviewed:
Publishers Weekly, August 20, 2001, page 63

Other books you might like:
Jack Cady, *The Jonah Watch*, 1981
William Hope Hodgson, *The Ghost Pirates*, 1909
Nancy Holder, *Dead in the Water*, 1994
William Clark Russell, *The Death Ship*, 1888

682

TOM PICCIRILLI

A Lower Deep

(New York: Leisure, 2001)

Story type: Apocalyptic Horror; Occult
Subject(s): Good and Evil; Mysticism; Supernatural
Major character(s): Necromancer, Sorcerer; Self, Supernatural Being; Jedediah De Lancre, Sorcerer
Time period(s): 2000s
Locale(s): Billings, Montana

Summary: Jedediah hopes to enlist the aid of the reluctant Necromancer to resurrect his departed cult and thereby force the Second Coming of Jesus Christ. When the Necromancer demures, De Lancre tantalizes him with the possibility of bringing his dead love, Danielle, back to life, forcing the Necromancer (and his familiar, Self) to choose between good and evil.

Where it's reviewed:
Publishers Weekly, September 17, 2001, page 61

Other books by the same author:
The Night Class, 2001
The Deceased, 2000
Hexes, 1999
Pentacle, 1995
Dark Father, 1990

Other books you might like:
Laurell K. Hamilton, *Death of a Darklord*, 1995
Fritz Leiber, *Conjure Wife*, 1953
Graham Masterton, *Master of Lies*, 1992
Joseph Pulver, *Nightmare's Disciple*, 2000
John Shirley, *Demons*, 2000

683

STEPHEN MARK RAINEY

Legends of the Night

(Holicong, Pennsylvania: Wildside, 2001)

Story type: Collection
Subject(s): Horror; Short Stories; Supernatural

Summary: The 13 stories in this collection blend horror, fantasy, and science fiction, often in offbeat or oblique treatments. Selections include "Before the Red Star Falls," set in the aftermath of H.G. Wells' groundbreaking science fiction novel *The War of the Worlds*; "The Forgiven," a mix of the psycho-killer shocker and afterlife fantasy; and "Somewhere My Love," a poignant variation on the theme of witchcraft.

Other books by the same author:
Balak, 2000
The Last Trumpet, 2000
Fugue Devil and Other Weird Horrors, 1993

Other books you might like:
P.D. Cacek, *Leavings*, 1998
Adam-Troy Castro, *A Desperate, Decaying Darkness*, 2000
Gerard Daniel Houarner, *I Love You and There Is Nothing You Can Do about It*, 2000
Kurt Newton, *The House Spider and Other Strange Visitors*, 1999
Alan Rodgers, *New Life for the Dead*, 1991

684

DEE DEE RAMONE

Chelsea Horror Hotel

(New York: Thunder's Mouth, 2001)

Story type: Haunted House
Subject(s): Ghosts; Hotels and Motels; Music and Musicians
Major character(s): Dee Dee Ramone, Musician (bass player), Historical Figure; Barbara, Young Woman; Banfield, Animal (Airedale terrier)
Time period(s): 2000s
Locale(s): New York, New York

Summary: This episodic novel is narrated by Dee Dee, the bass player for the punk rock band The Ramones. Much of Dee Dee's life is spent in and around the Chelsea Hotel, a Manhattan landmark, where he walks Banfield, the pet Airedale terrier with whom he psychically communicates, and is visited by the ghost of Sid Vicious, guitarist for the Sex Pistols, as well as the ghosts of other dead rockers from the Manhattan punk scene. A first novel.

Other books you might like:
Jeff Gelb, *Shock Rock*, 1992
editor
Del James, *The Language of Fear*, 1995
Tina Jens, *The Blues Ain't Nothin'*, 2002
Gail Peterson, *The Making of a Monster*, 1993
Paul M. Sammon, *The King Is Dead*, 1994
editor

685

ANNE RICE

Blood and Gold

(New York: Knopf, 2001)

Story type: Vampire Story
Series: Vampire Chronicles. Book 7
Subject(s): Ancient History; Roman Empire; Vampires
Major character(s): Marius, Vampire; Akasha, Vampire; Eudoxia, Vampire
Time period(s): Multiple Time Periods
Locale(s): Rome, Italy; Constantinople, Byzantium; Venice, Italy

Summary: Rice presents the personal history of Marius, a former Roman senator who, following his vampirization, becomes guardian of Akasha and Enkil, the all powerful yet vulnerable King and Queen of the vampires. Over centuries, spanning from pagan Rome, to the Renaissance and modern times, Marius serves as protector of the vampire legacy, lover of mortals and vampires, and inspiration to many a Florentine painter, before becoming instructor to Lestat, his equal in temperament and sensibility.

Where it's reviewed:
Publishers Weekly, September 24, 2001, page 74

Other books by the same author:
Merrick, 2000
Vittorio, the Vampire, 1999
Pandora, 1998
The Vampire Armand, 1998
The Vampire Lestat, 1985

Other books you might like:
Alice Borchardt, *The Silver Wolf*, 1998
Les Daniels, *The Black Castle*, 1979
Brian Stableford, *The Empire of Fear*, 1988
Michael Talbot, *The Delicate Dependency*, 1982
Chelsea Quinn Yarbro, *Blood Games*, 1979

686

MICHAEL ROMKEY

The London Vampire Panic

(New York: Ballantine Del Rey, 2001)

Story type: Vampire Story
Subject(s): Supernatural; Vampires; Victorian Period
Major character(s): Posthumous Blackley, Doctor; Abraham Van Helsing, Doctor; Olivia Moore, Vampire
Time period(s): 1890s
Locale(s): London, England

Summary: When a rash of vampire-related deaths plague London, an elite group of professionals, including Charles Darwin and vampire hunter Abraham Van Helsing, is convened by prime minister Benjamin Disraeli to put an end to the problem before public revelation causes a panic. Suspicion centers on the Moore household, whose diplomat patriarch is newly returned from travels in Budapest just as Van Helsing was disposing of the famed Transylvanian vampire, Count Dracula.

Other books by the same author:
Vampire Hunter, 1998
The Vampire Virus, 1997
The Vampire Princess, 1996
The Vampire Papers, 1994
I, Vampire, 1990

Other books you might like:
C. Dean Andersson, *I Am Dracula*, 1993
P.N. Elrod, *Quincey Morris, Vampire*, 2001
Barbara Hambly, *Those Who Hunt the Night*, 1988
Sam Siciliano, *Darkness*, 2001
Bram Stoker, *Dracula*, 1897

687

JOHN SAUL

The Manhattan Hunt Club

(New York: Ballantine, 2001)

Story type: Mystery
Subject(s): Hunting; Homeless People; Suspense
Major character(s): Jeff Converse, Student, Convict (innocent); Keith Converse, Construction Worker; Eve Harris, Political Figure
Time period(s): 2000s
Locale(s): New York, New York

Summary: En route to prison after being convicted for a subway mugging he did not commit, Jeff Converse is helped by anonymous benefactors to escape into the subway tunnels honeycombing the Manhattan underground. There, he and other similarly aided criminals are hunted as the special quarry of the 100 Club, an elite group of the city's 100 most influential businessmen, whose periodic ritual hunts have contributed to the dropping crime rate in the city.

Where it's reviewed:
Kirkus Reviews, June 1, 2001, page 768
Publishers Weekly, May 21, 2001, page 79

Other books by the same author:
Nightshade, 2000
The Right Hand of Evil, 1999
The Blackstone Chronicles, 1997
The Presence, 1997
Black Lightning, 1995

Other books you might like:
Christopher Fowler, *Roofworld*, 1988
Stephen Ray Fulghum, *The Forsaken*, 1991
Richard Laymon, *Funland*, 1990
Wayne Allen Sallee, *The Holy Terror*, 1992
Chet Williamson, *Lowland Rider*, 1988

688

STEVE SAVILE

Similar Monsters

(Gillette, New Jersey: Cosmos, 2001)

Story type: Collection
Subject(s): Horror; Short Stories; Suspense

Summary: Disturbed states of mind and supernatural experience are frequently indistinguishable from one another in these 15 stories, five original to the volume. ''Memories in Glass'' tells of a guilt-ridden man haunted by the ghost (or possibly only the ghostly memory) of the dead woman he had promised to love eternally. ''Painting Blue Murders'' features a death row prisoner who has tattooed his body with the faces of the dead. In ''Send Me Dead Flowers,'' a man discovers that the photos he takes of a woman, at a paying customer's request, invariably show ghostly hands strangling her.

Other books by the same author:
Icarus Descending, 2000
The Secret Life of Colours, 2000

Other books you might like:
Ramsey Campbell, *Strange Things and Stranger Places*, 1993
D.F. Lewis, *The Best of D.F. Lewis*, 1992
Jeffrey Osier, *Driftglider and Other Stories*, 1993
Tom Piccirilli, *Deep into That Darkness Peering*, 1999
Steve Rasnic Tem, *City Fishing*, 2000

689

BRETT A. SAVORY

The Distance Travelled

(Canton, Ohio: Prime, 2001)

Story type: Collection
Subject(s): Short Stories; Supernatural; Afterlife

Summary: The title tale in this collection of two stories is a surreal afterlife fantasy about the mishaps of several denizens of hell who hope to escape by using the path of a temporary visitor to reach the world of the living. ''Fright Night'' is a juvenile story of a young man's entrapment in a strange and menacing fantasy world. With an introduction by Philip Nutman and an afterword by P.D. Cacek. A first book.

Other books you might like:
Norman Partridge, *Mr. Fox and Other Feral Tales*, 1992
Robert Steven Rhine, *My Brain Escapes Me*, 1999
Sue Storm, *Star Bones Weep the Blood of Angels*, 1995
Ray Vukcevich, *Meet Me in the Moon Room*, 2001
Don Webb, *A Spell for the Fulfillment of Desire*, 1996

690

MICHAEL SCHIEFELBEIN

Vampire Vow

(Los Angeles: Alyson, 2001)

Story type: Vampire Story
Subject(s): Homosexuality/Lesbianism; Sexuality; Vampires
Major character(s): Victor Decimus, Religious, Vampire; Michael, Religious; Luke, Religious
Time period(s): 2000s; 1st century
Locale(s): Knoxville, Tennessee

Summary: When his carnal love for Jesus Christ goes unrequited, Roman centurion Victor Decimus, a vampire, vows to spend his life undermining the Catholic Church. As a monk in the 20th century, he seduces fellow monk Brother Michael, into a relationship full of depraved affection and violent death. A first novel.

Other books you might like:
Gary Bowen, *Diary of a Vampire*, 1995
John Peyton Cooke, *Out for Blood*, 1991
J.G. Eccarius, *The Last Days of Christ the Vampire*, 1988
Anne Rice, *Interview with the Vampire*, 1976
David Niall Wilson, *This Is My Blood*, 1999

691

CHRISTOPHER SCHILDT

Frankenstein: The Legacy

(New York: Pocket, 2001)

Story type: Reanimated Dead
Subject(s): Horror; Scientific Experiments; Supernatural
Major character(s): Daniel Levy, Scientist; Linda Kaufmann, Scientist; Susan Weaver, FBI Agent
Time period(s): 1970s; 2000s
Locale(s): Salem, Massachusetts; New London, Connecticut; Unity, Maine

Summary: Schildt here updates Mary Shelley's *Frankenstein*. On an expedition to the Arctic in 1971, Daniel Levy finds the ship Victor Frankenstein was last aboard before his death, and the diary that contains his scientific notes. Back home, Levy duplicates Frankenstein's experiments, and the creature he animates proves as complex and dangerous as Victor's own creation. With an introduction by Sara Karloff, the daughter of Boris Karloff who created the screen role of the Frankenstein monster.

Other books by the same author:
Night of Dracula, 2001

Other books you might like:
Brian W. Aldiss, *Frankenstein Unbound*, 1973
C. Dean Andersson, *I Am Frankenstein*, 1996
Carl Dreadstone, *Bride of Frankenstein*, 1977
Jeff Rovin, *Re-Animator*, 1987
Fred Saberhagen, *The Frankenstein Papers*, 1986

692

CHRISTOPHER SCHILDT

Night of Dracula

(New York: Pocket, 2001)

Story type: Vampire Story
Subject(s): Horror; Supernatural; Vampires
Major character(s): Vladimir Tepevich, Doctor; Jonathan Steward, Doctor; Heather, Young Woman
Time period(s): 2000s
Locale(s): Atlanta, Georgia

Summary: In this updated version of the story of Count Dracula, Vladimir Tepevich's strange behavior coincides with a rash of vampire type killings in contemporary Atlanta, all of which suggest that Vlad is an incarnation of the legendary Count Dracula. Jonathan is concerned for the welfare of his wife's friend Heather, whom Vlad has taken a liking to. But is the intrigue as clear cut as it seems? Prefaced with an introduction by Bela Lugosi, Jr., whose father created the film role of Count Dracula.

Other books by the same author:
Frankenstein: The Legacy, 2001

Other books you might like:
Brian W. Aldiss, *Dracula Unbound*, 1991
C. Dean Andersson, *I Am Dracula*, 1993
Fred Saberhagen, *The Dracula Tape*, 1975

Jeffrey Sackett, *Blood of the Impaler*, 1989
John Shirley, *Dracula in Love*, 1979

693

HARRY SHANNON

Bad Seed

(Anaheim, California: www.MediumRareBooks.com, 2001)

Story type: Collection
Subject(s): Horror; Short Stories; Supernatural

Summary: Thirteen terse tales of horror and suspense are gathered in Shannon's first collection. Selections include ''Road Kill,'' about an escaped murderer who gets his gruesome just desserts when he picks up two young hitchhikers, who are much less innocent than they seem; ''Echo,'' in which a man finds his house haunted, inexplicably, by the sound of his own death scream; and the familial vampire story ''Vampers.''

Other books you might like:
John Everson, *Cage of Bones and Other Deadly Obsessions*, 2000
Jeffrey Thomas, *Terror Incognita*, 2000
Edo van Belkom, *Death Drives a Semi*, 1998
J.N. Williamson, *Frights of Fancy*, 2000
David Niall Wilson, *The Fall of the House of Escher and Other Illusions*, 1995

694

JOHN SHIRLEY

. . .And the Angel with Television Eyes

(San Francisco: Night Shade, 2001)

Story type: Occult
Subject(s): Gnosticism; Popular Culture; Supernatural
Major character(s): Max Whitman, Student, Actor; Antoinette, Artist; Carstairs, Guide
Time period(s): 2000s
Locale(s): New York, New York

Summary: On the verge of auditioning for his first serious stage role, television actor Max Whitman is overwhelmed by visions of mythical creatures and a voice-over calling him by the name Prince Redmark. With the guidance of Carstairs, a mysterious man with arcane occult knowledge, Max discovers he is a member of ''the Hidden Race,'' whose souls are highly developed plasmagnomes that can outlive the body and function independently. Max's destiny is to play a role in the never ending struggle between the Exploitationist plasmagnomes, who prey upon humanity, and the Protectionist plasmagnomes, who take a more benign course. Published in both trade and signed limited editions.

Other books by the same author:
The View from Hell, 2001
Demons, 2000
Wetbones, 1991
In Darkness Waiting, 1988
Cellars, 1982

Other books you might like:
Peter Atkins, *Big Thunder*, 1997
Clive Barker, *Cabal*, 1988
Gary A. Braunbeck, *The Indifference of Heaven*, 2000
Neil Gaiman, *American Gods*, 2001
Kim Newman, *Jago*, 1991

695

SAM SICILIANO

Darkness

(New York: Pinnacle, 2001)

Story type: Vampire Story
Subject(s): Horror; Vampires; Victorian Period
Major character(s): Andrew Quimby, Doctor; Teresa di Rospo, Noblewoman (countess), Vampire; Charles Kovett, Doctor
Time period(s): 1890s (1899)
Locale(s): London, England

Summary: In 1899, the city of London is plagued by a rash of deaths that suggest a vampire is on the loose. Countess Teresa di Rospo confesses her vampire nature to Andrew Quimby, the doctor who has autopsied several of the victims, but insists she is not to blame—leading to speculation that another vampire, or a vampire pretender, is staging the deaths.

Other books by the same author:
Blood Feud, 1993
The Angel of the Opera, 1993
Blood Farm, 1988

Other books you might like:
Barbara Hambly, *Those Who Hunt the Night*, 1988
Kim Newman, *Anno Dracula*, 1992
James Malcolm Rymer, *Varney the Vampyre*, 1847
Fred Saberhagen, *Seance for a Vampire*, 1994
Bram Stoker, *Dracula*, 1897

696

THOMAS M. SIPOS

Halloween Candy

(Bloomington, Indiana: 1stBooks Library, 2001)

Story type: Collection
Subject(s): Horror; Short Stories; Supernatural

Summary: This miscellaneous collection features 14 stories and essays on horror themes. The stories are mostly brief tales with nasty, clever twists, including ''Vampire Nation,'' in which a Romanian vampire welcomes his country's atheistic communist regime, which makes it easier for him to exist unobtrusively; ''Five Paranoiacs, All in a Row. . .,'' which mixes psychotherapy, near-death experience, and a chilling vision of hell; and two tales of witchcraft, ''Career Witch'' and ''The Lady Who Ate Dolls.'' Also included is the title piece, an unproduced screenplay for an horror anthology film.

Other books by the same author:
Vampire Nation, 2000

Other books you might like:
Peter Atkins, *The Wishmaster*, 1999
Richard Chizmar, *Screamplays*, 1997
William F. Nolan, *Night Shapes*, 1995
David J. Schow, *Crypt Orchids*, 1998
F. Paul Wilson, *The Barrens and Other Stories*, 1998

697

ROBIN SPRIGGS

Wondrous Strange

(Murrayville, Georgia: Circle Myth, 2001)

Story type: Collection
Subject(s): Fantasy; Short Stories; Supernatural

Summary: These 25 dark fantasies, 16 original to the collection, use horror motifs to explore themes of alienation and emotional estrangement. ''Tin Can Molly'' and ''Bob's Monsters'' are variations on the Frankenstein theme that address, respectively, the growth from childhood to maturity, and the horrors of an abusive family life. In ''Bugs,'' a man's anxieties about all he holds dear in life manifest as swarming hordes of insects. ''Chimaera's'' tells of a strange nightclub, where a man's hope of recapturing his lost enchantment with life leads to a horrifying transformation. A first book.

Where it's reviewed:
Hellnotes, January 19, 2001, page 2
Publishers Weekly, September 17, 2001, page 61

Other books you might like:
Casey Czichas, *The Candlelight Reader*, 1999
Martin Mundt, *The Crawling Abbatoir*, 1999
Kurt Newton, *The House Spider and Other Strange Visitors*, 1999
Michael Pendragon, *Nightscapes*, 1999
Jeffrey Thomas, *Terror Incognita*, 2000

698

SHANE RYAN STALEY

I'll Be Damned

(North Webster, Indiana: Delirium, 2001)

Story type: Collection
Subject(s): Horror; Short Stories; Supernatural

Summary: These 30 short stories are fable-like in form and often laced with gruesome and irreverent imagery. In ''Chocolate Jesus,'' a candy bar provides an unlikely source of religious revelation for a young boy deciding to choose between good and evil. ''The Mailman'' is a surrealist fantasy of the bizarre indignities a mail deliverer acquiesces to in the dark comedy of his job. ''The Boy with Razor Sharp Teeth'' is a poignant reflection on individuality, concerning a boy with horrifying physical attributes that set him apart from his classmates. With an introduction by Brian Keene.

Other books by the same author:
Chocolate Jesus and Other Weird Perversions, 2000
Sick Days, 1999

Other books you might like:
John Everson, *Cage of Bones and Other Deadly Obsessions*, 2000
Charlee Jacob, *Up, out of Cities That Blow Hot and Cold*, 2000
Tim Lebbon, *As the Sun Goes Down*, 2000
Edward Lee, *The Ushers*, 1999
Octavio Ramos Jr., *Smoke Signals*, 2000

699

WHITLEY STRIEBER

The Last Vampire

(New York: Pocket, 2001)

Story type: Vampire Story
Subject(s): Horror; Sexuality; Vampires
Major character(s): Miriam Blaylock, Vampire; Paul Ward, Spy (CIA); Sarah Roberts, Vampire, Doctor
Time period(s): 2000s
Locale(s): New York, New York; Paris, France; Bangkok, Thailand

Summary: Miriam Blaylock's plans to become pregnant with the child of another Keeper, or vampire, are altered by the schemes of Paul Ward, a CIA operative whose job it is to wipe out vampire conclaves across the globe. Paul's uncanny skill at destroying vampires is the key to a heritage even he knows nothing about, and it convinces Miriam to re-evaluate her choice of a father for her child, even at the expense of the vampires she has gathered around her at her Manhattan home. A sequel to *The Hunger*.

Where it's reviewed:
Hellnotes, August 31, 2001, page 2
Kirkus Reviews, May 1, 2001, page 620
Publishers Weekly, June 25, 2001, page 45

Other books by the same author:
The Forbidden Zone, 1993
Unholy Fire, 1992
The Wild, 1991
The Hunger, 1981
The Wolfen, 1978

Other books you might like:
Poppy Z. Brite, *Lost Souls*, 1992
P.D. Cacek, *Night Prayers*, 1998
Mick Farren, *The Time of Feasting*, 1996
Ray Garton, *Live Girls*, 1987
Karen E. Taylor, *Blood Secrets*, 1994

700

STEVE RASNIC TEM

The Far Side of the Lake

(Ashcroft, British Columbia: Ash-Tree Press, 2001)

Story type: Collection
Subject(s): Horror; Short Stories; Supernatural

Summary: Most of these 32 oblique and disturbing tales of horror and dark fantasy feature obsessive narrators whose anxieties and insecurities manifest in supernatural or psychologically objective forms. In "At the Bureau," a man's frustration with his soul-sapping job is mirrored in his relationship with a shadowy fellow office worker. In the World Fantasy Award-winning "Leaks," a man's past troubled relationship with his father manifests in the form of unstanchable seepage and dampness around the house. Included are seven adventures of Charlie Goode, a self-styled ghost hunter given to solving mystical and metaphysical mysteries.

Other books by the same author:
City Fishing, 2000
Decoded Mirrors, 1992
Absences: Charlie Goode's Ghosts, 1991
Excavation, 1987

Other books you might like:
Fred Chappell, *More Shapes than One*, 1991
Graham Joyce, *Black Dust*, 2001
Thomas Ligotti, *Songs of a Dead Dreamer*, 1989
Joyce Carol Oates, *Demon and Other Tales*, 1996
Thomas Wiloch, *Mr. Templeton's Toyshop*, 1995

701

SCOTT THOMAS

Cobwebs and Whispers

(North Webster, Indiana: Delirium, 2001)

Story type: Collection
Subject(s): Short Stories; Supernatural

Summary: The 26 stories in this collection, only nine previously published, are written for the most part in the style of the old-fashioned tale of supernatural horror. The majority are set in 19th century England or New England, including "The Cathedral at Humberfeld," about the spirit that haunts a church built on an old site of pagan worship; "Joseph Warren's Invention," about an inventor who tries to prolong the life of a family member with his scientific skills; and the vampire story "Dearg Due." With an introduction by Jeff Vandermeer. A first book.

Other books you might like:
Steve Duffy, *The Night Comes On*, 1998
Paul Finch, *The Shadows Beneath*, 2000
Alistair G. Gunn, *Ballymoon*, 2000
L.H. Maynard, *Echoes of Darkness*, 2000
M.P.N. Sims, co-author
William Meikle, *Millennium Macabre*, 2000

702

JAMES M. THOMPSON

Night Blood

(New York: Pinnacle, 2001)

Story type: Vampire Story
Subject(s): Horror; Medicine; Vampires
Major character(s): Matthew Carter, Doctor; Samantha Scott, Doctor; Roger Niemann, Doctor
Time period(s): 2000s
Locale(s): Houston, Texas

Summary: Corpses turning up in the Houston area brutally ravaged and drained of blood suggest the unthinkable to doctors at the Houston Medical Center: that a vampire is on the loose, and may even be one of the medical staff. Indeed, a victim of erythropoeitic uroporphyria, passed to him nearly two centuries before, walks among them and, infected by the Creutzfeldt-Jakob bacteria, is in the grip of a blood hunger that drives him to an almost insane bloodlust. A first novel.

Other books you might like:
Scott Ciencin, *The Parliament of Blood*, 1992
David Dvorkin, *Insatiable*, 1993
Roxanne Longstreet, *Cold Kiss*, 1995
Steven G. Spruill, *Rulers of Darkness*, 1995
Whitley Strieber, *The Hunger*, 1981

703

TAMARA THORNE (Pseudonym of Chris Curry)

Candle Bay

(New York: Pinnacle, 2001)

Story type: Vampire Story
Subject(s): Vampires; Supernatural
Major character(s): Amanda Pearce, Hotel Worker; Stephen Darling, Vampire; Julian Valentyn, Vampire
Time period(s): 2000s
Locale(s): Candle Bay, California

Summary: When she is hired as concierge of the newly refurbished Candle Bay Hotel and Spa, Amanda Pearce finds herself caught in the crossfire between the Darlings, a vampire family who own the hotel, and the Dantes, a rival vampire clan. In addition to pressing their centuries-old vendetta, the Dantes hope to learn from the Darlings the secret of a potion that provides vampires with abilities allowing them to live more unobtrusively than usual among mortals.

Other books by the same author:
Eternity, 2000
Moonfall, 1996
Haunted, 1995

Other books you might like:
Scott Ciencin, *The Vampire Odyssey*, 1992
Pat Graversen, *Precious Blood*, 1993
Michael Green, *The Jimjams*, 1994
William Hill, *California Ghost*, 1998
Brent Monahan, *The Book of Common Prayer*, 1993

704

JOHN URBANCIK

A Game of Colors

(Alma, Arkansas: Yard Dog, 2001)

Story type: Witchcraft
Subject(s): Horror; Teachers; Witches and Witchcraft
Major character(s): Sara Charlene Ross, Witch; Gypsy Leigh Taylor, Witch; Stefan, Witch
Time period(s): 2000s
Locale(s): United States (The Precipice, a nightclub)

Summary: This short story chapbook tells the tale of the contentious relationship between Sara, a witch initiate, and Gypsy, the witch who trains her at The Precipice nightclub. As Gypsy instructs Sara in how to master the colors that are the source of their occult power, Sara's feelings about her teacher change from adversarial to respectful.

Where it's reviewed:
Hellnotes, September 21, 2001, page 2

Other books you might like:
P.D. Cacek, *Bell, Book and Beyond*, 2001
editor
Stefan Dziemianowicz, *100 Wicked Little Witch Stories*, 1995
Robert Weinberg, Martin H. Greenberg, co-editors
Morgan Fields, *Shaman Woods*, 1990
Kathryn Meyer Griffith, *Witches*, 1993
Nancy Holder, *Witch-Light*, 1996
Melanie Tem, co-author

705

EDO VAN BELKOM

Teeth

(Decatur, Georgia: Meisha Merlin, 2001)

Story type: Erotic Horror; Serial Killer
Subject(s): Sexuality; Supernatural; Women
Major character(s): Joe Williams, Detective—Police; Ellen Grant, Radio Personality; Valerie Rhinegold, Saloon Keeper/Owner (bartender)
Time period(s): 2000s
Locale(s): Brampton, Ontario, Canada

Summary: A series of gruesome killings involving sexual mutliation of male victims leads detective Joe Williams to the incomprehensible conclusion that their murderer is a woman whose sexual organs are endowed with teeth. Joe's attempt to divine the killer's motives leads to the uneasy conclusion that she could be one of several women he knows.

Where it's reviewed:
Cemetery Dance 35, page 91
Hellnotes, June 15, 2001, page 2
Locus, July 2001, page 27
Publishers Weekly, May 28, 2001, page 55

Other books by the same author:
Six-Inch Spikes, 2001
Death Drives a Semi, 1998
Yours Truly, Jackie the Stripper, 1998
Lord Soth, 1996
Wyrm Wolf, 1995

Other books you might like:
Daniel Hecht, *Skull Session*, 1999
Barry Hoffman, *Judas Eyes*, 2001
Edward Lee, *Goon*, 1996
John Pelan, co-author
Thom Metzger, *Big Gurl*, 1989
Jorge Saralegui, *Looker*, 1990

706

ROBERT WEINBERG

Dial Your Dreams

(Kansas City, Missouri: DarkTales, 2001)

Story type: Collection
Subject(s): Horror; Short Stories; Supernatural

Summary: Weinberg's first collection contains 14 stories of horror and dark fantasy, one original to the book. Several of the stories are modern variations on classic horror themes, including ''Elevator Girls,'' about predatory vampires who blend in with the attendees of a horror convention, and ''The Midnight El,'' a deal with the devil story in which a psychic detective must find an unconventional way to stump Satan. The title story concerns an unusual phone service that will fulfill a caller's wildest fantasies—for an unspeakable price. With an introduction by Richard Gilliam and afterword by Mort Castle.

Other books by the same author:
A Logical Magician, 1994
Dead Man's Kiss, 1992
The Armageddon Box, 1991
The Black Lodge, 1991
The Devil's Auction, 1988

Other books you might like:
Donald R. Burleson, *Beyond the Lamplight*, 1996
Ed Gorman, *Cages*, 1996
Dean R. Koontz, *Strange Highways*, 1995
Mark Morris, *Close to the Bone*, 1995
F. Paul Wilson, *Soft and Others*, 1989

707

MANLY WADE WELLMAN

The Devil Is Not Mocked and Other Warnings

(San Francisco: Night Shade, 2001)

Story type: Collection
Subject(s): Folklore; Short Stories; Supernatural

Summary: These 28 stories of dark fantasy and the supernatural were penned by a recipient of the World Fantasy Award for lifetime achievement, whose writing spanned seven decades. A majority of the stories feature encounters with weird creatures, including ''The Pineys'' and ''The Kelpie,'' and a significant number are steeped in the folklore of the author's native South, such as ''Where the Woodbine Twineth'' and ''Frogfather.'' The title story is a modern classic about a Nazi regiment that unwittingly attempts to billet itself in Castle Dracula. Edited by John Pelan, with an introduction by Ramsey Campbell.

Other books by the same author:
The Third Cry to Legba and Other Invocations, 2000
John the Balladeer, 1988
The Valley So Low, 1987
Worse Things Waiting, 1973
Who Fears the Devil, 1962

Other books you might like:
Joseph Payne Brennan, *Stories of Darkness and Dread*, 1973
Jack Cady, *The Sons of Noah and Other Stories*, 1992
Fred Chappell, *More Shapes than One*, 1991
David Drake, *Old Nathan*, 1991
Robert R. McCammon, *Blue World*, 1990

708

CONRAD WILLIAMS

Nearly People

(Leeds, England: PS Publishing, 2001)

Story type: Apocalyptic Horror
Subject(s): Dancing; Diseases; Survival
Major character(s): Carrier, Young Woman; The Dancer, Dancer; Jake, Aged Person
Time period(s): Indeterminate Future
Locale(s): Howling Mile, England

Summary: In a plague-ridden future, where the breakdown of the social order has produced a world of survivors preying upon one another in order to live, Carrier meets The Dancer, a man whose mastery of Dance gives him access to a transcendant plane where Carrier herself can possibly overcome the chaos of civilization. Published as a signed limited chapbook and hardcover.

Where it's reviewed:
Hellnotes, June 22, 2001, page 2
Locus, September 2001, page 23

Other books by the same author:
Head Injuries, 1998

Other books you might like:
Graham Joyce, *Leningrad Nights*, 1999
Joe R. Lansdale, *Tight Little Stitches in a Dead Man's Back*, 1992
Stephen Laws, *Chasm*, 1998
Tim Lebbon, *White*, 1999
Alan Rodgers, *Fire*, 1990

709

J.N. WILLIAMSON

Affinity

(New York: Leisure, 2001)

Story type: Wild Talents
Subject(s): Psychic Powers; Supernatural; Teen Relationships
Major character(s): Quent Wilcox, Student—College, Teenager; Feather Pedigo, Teenager; Luther Pedigo, Military Personnel, Step-Parent
Time period(s): 2000s
Locale(s): Bloomington, Indiana

Summary: A series of disturbing, sexually-oriented nightmares disrupts the life of college student Quent Wilcox, and alerts him to peculiar gaps in his childhood memories. When Feather Pedigo, a girl Quent remembers from his dreams, suddenly shows up in his town, Quent becomes aware of a government project sponsored by her stepfather to recruit children with psychic powers—like her and Quent—as weapons for government espionage.

Other books by the same author:
The Haunt, 1999
Blood Lines, 1994
The Book of Websters, 1993
The Monastery, 1992
The Night Seasons, 1991

Other books you might like:
John Farris, *The Fury and the Terror*, 2001
Lyle Howard, *Mr. Sandman*, 1992
Stephen King, *Firestarter*, 1980
Steven M. Krauzer, *Brainstorm*, 1991
Michael Kurland, *Button Bright*, 1987

710

F. PAUL WILSON, Editor

Hosts

(New York: Forge 2001)

Story type: Science Fiction
Series: Repairman Jack
Subject(s): Horror; Medicine
Major character(s): Repairman Jack, Mercenary; Kate Iverson, Doctor; Sandy Palmer, Journalist
Time period(s): 2000s
Locale(s): New York, New York

Summary: Urban mercenary Repairman Jack is hired by his sister to save her lover from the ravages of an experimental anti-cancer medicine that has mutated and is gradually incorporating those who have taken it into a group mind intent on taking over the world. Jack's efforts are complicated by an overly-inquisitive journalist whose life he saved during a subway shootout and whose determination to make Jack a media hero threatens the anonymity essential to his undercover work.

Other books by the same author:
All the Rage, 2000
Conspiracies, 1999
Legacies, 1998
The Tomb, 1984
The Keep, 1981

Other books you might like:
Greg Bear, *Blood Music*, 1985
Jack Finney, *The Body Snatchers*, 1955
Stephen Gallagher, *Valley of Lights*, 1987
Robert A. Heinlein, *The Puppet Masters*, 1951
Dean R. Koontz, *Midnight*, 1989

711

G. RANGER WORMSER

The Scarecrow and Other Stories

(Seattle, Washington: Midnight House, 2001)

Story type: Collection
Subject(s): Horror; Short Stories; Supernatural

Summary: This collection of horror and supernatural stories is by an American woman who wrote in the early decades of the 20th century. The stories predominantly avoid the atmospherics typical of the weird tale and are related largely in dialogue. The contents are comprised of the text of the original volume, published under the same title in 1918, and five previously uncollected stories. Selections include "The Scarecrow," concerned with the contentious relationship between a mother and son and its reflection in a seemingly supernaturally animated scarecrow; and "Haunted," which blurs the boundary between the dead and the living. Edited and with an introduction by Douglas A. Anderson.

Where it's reviewed:
Hellnotes, January 4, 2002, page 2

Other books by the same author:
Abraham Goode, 1925

Other books you might like:
Gertrude Atherton, *The Bell in the Fog and Other Stories*, 1905
Ellen Glasgow, *The Shadowy Third*, 1923
Sarah Orne Jewett, *Lady Ferry and Other Uncanny People*, 1998
Georgia Wood Pangborn, *The Wind at Midnight*, 1999
Harriet Prescott Spofford, *The Moonstone Mass*, 2000

712

T.M. WRIGHT

The Last Vampire

(New York: Leisure, 2001)

Story type: Vampire Story
Subject(s): Horror; Supernatural; Vampires
Major character(s): Elmo Land, Cowboy, Vampire; Regina Watson, Vampire; Jeff, Young Man
Time period(s): 1910s
Locale(s): Mumford, New York

Summary: In a peculiar, stream-of-consciousness narrative, rodeo cowboy Elmo Land tells how he lusted for, and was turned into a vampire by, Regina Watson, whose vampirization of him led to both his sexual and intellectual awakening. Originally published in England in 1991.

Other books by the same author:
The Ascending, 1994
Goodlow's Ghosts, 1993
Little Boy Lost, 1992
Boundaries, 1990
The School, 1990

Other books you might like:
Richard Lee Byers, *The Vampire's Apprentice*, 1992
Clark Hays, *The Cowboy and the Vampire*, 1999
Kathleen McFall, co-author
Mark Ivanhoe, *Virgintooth*, 1991
Doug Rice, *Blood of Mugwump*, 1996
Melanie Tem, *Desmodus*, 1994

713

CHELSEA QUINN YARBRO

A Feast in Exile

(New York: Tor, 2001)

Story type: Vampire Story
Series: Chronicles of Saint-Germain. Number 14
Subject(s): History; Medicine; Vampires
Major character(s): Sanat Ji Mani, Vampire; Rojire, Servant, Monster (ghoul); Tulsi Kil, Entertainer (circus)
Time period(s): 14th century
Locale(s): Delhi, India; Devapur, India

Summary: Under the alias of Sanat Jimani, the immortal vampire Count St. Germain leads the life of an expatriate herbalist and healer in medieval India. Imprisoned by the soldiers of Timur-i (better known as Tamerlane) during the Mongol takeover of Asia, he is forced with great difficulty to conceal his vampire nature, while playing the obedient and subservient captive. Exploits following his escape include being mistaken for Timur-i by the overlords of his adopted city.

Other books by the same author:
Come Twilight, 2000
Communion Blood, 1999
Blood Roses, 1998
Writ in Blood, 1997
Mansions of Darkness, 1996

Other books you might like:
Richard Burton, *Vikram and the Vampire*, 1870
Les Daniels, *The Silver Skull*, 1979
Pierre Kast, *The Vampires of Alfama*, 1976
Anne Rice, *Blood and Gold*, 2001
Brian Stableford, *The Empire of Fear*, 1988

714

PAUL ZINDEL

Night of the Bat

(New York: Hyperion, 2001)

Story type: Nature in Revolt; Young Adult
Subject(s): Animals; Monsters
Major character(s): Jake Lefkowitz, Teenager; Dr. Lefkowitz, Scientist; Hanuma, Foreman
Time period(s): 2000s
Locale(s): Jurua Lace, Brazil

Summary: On an trip to the Amazon to visit his biologist father, Jake finds his father's expedition the quarry of a pack of predatory oversized bats. Their survival depends on the effectiveness of Gizmo, a device Jake invented to help him see the world as a bat does. For young adult readers.

Where it's reviewed:
Publishers Weekly, July 30, 2001, page 86

Other books by the same author:
Raptor, 1999
Rats, 1999
Reef of Death, 1998

Loch, 1995
The Doom Stone, 1995

Other books you might like:

William W. Johnstone, *Bats*, 1993
Jeff Rovin, *Vespers*, 1998
Guy N. Smith, *Bats out of Hell*, 1978
Martin Cruz Smith, *Nightwing*, 1997
Robert Wilson, *Second Fire*, 1993

Science Fiction in 2001 by Don D'Ammassa

Science fiction publishing has changed dramatically over the course of time. From the 1950s through the 1970s, the vast majority of novels were paperback originals. Short stories rivaled novels in volume because of the very large number of professional magazines, and almost all anthologies were culled from their pages. Anthologies of original stories were infrequent. Single author collections were quite popular, and writers like Avram Davidson, Harlan Ellison, and Theodore Sturgeon built their reputations largely on the basis of short fiction. That began to change in the 1980s. The glut of magazines finally collapsed under its own weight and only three long-standing titles continue to be published. Many anthologies are published each year, most partially or completely original, and the stories are almost always thematically linked. A few semi-professional fiction magazines have emerged to take up some of that slack and though some of these may crossover into true professional status, it appears the short story is unlikely to regain much of the ground it has lost. Single author collections, once very popular, have become rare among mainstream publishers and are primarily by a few writers who have already established themselves as novelists. Even the publication of novels has changed, with better than half of the non-media related novels originally appearing in hardcover, and some showing up on mainstream bestseller lists, such as the Dune novels by Frank Herbert and the later Robot and Foundation books by Isaac Asimov.

Thematically the field has not changed as dramatically, and it is still dominated by adventure stories and speculations based on soolid scientific backing. There has been some evolution, with satires falling out of favor along with most humorous SF. Post nuclear war survival stories have withered away along with those based on the Cold War, although conventional disaster novels—ecological or astronomical—seem to be making a comeback. Mutants and psi powers such as telepathy and telekinesis have become much more rare, while alternate histories and military stories have become more popular. Malevolent aliens are more likely to be depicted as military aggressors than as monsters. Efforts to provide higher quality, technically accurate SF for young adults, most notably by Tor, do not seem to have had much effect, possibly because the target audience has already moved on to adult fiction.

For the last twenty years, science fiction has been generally a very predictable genre in terms of themes and numbers. The decline in popularity of single author short story collections during the 1980s has continued until quite recently, and most anthologies contain original stories revolving around a common theme, as opposed to the generic reprint anthologies that were formerly the norm. Each year has seen a few first novelists, but the majority of books are by familiar hands. Hard science fiction and serious themes have tended to be dominant, and more than half the novels published are either parts of a series or are set against a background used in other works. The year 2001 was a good, solid, but unexceptional year for science fiction in terms of quality, but there were several signs of change that may or may not prove to be aberrations. The predominance of series novels is the only tendency that continued unabated this year. There are also signs that the popularity of movie and television tie-in novels may also finally be on the wane. Despite the appearance of a new Star Wars movie, there has been no lasting increase in novels set in the George Lucas universe. Even Star Trek novels seem to be on a downslope, and many of the tie- ins to this series have involved entirely new casts of characters independent of the various television series, and share only the general background universe.

The most notable change is the recent resurgence of single author short story collections after its wane in the 1980s. Several of these were massive retrospective volumes by established writers, including *The Collected Stories of Arthur C. Clarke*, *The Collected Stories of Vernor Vinge* by Vernor Vinge, *Here Comes Civilization* and *Immodest Proposals*, both by humorist William Tenn, *From These Ashes* by Fredric Brown, and *Strange Days* by Gardner Dozois. There were others, however, by newer writers, a possible sign that interest in shorter SF is on the rise. The best of these were *Strange Trades* by Paul Di Filippo, *Bad Timing and Other Stories* by Molly Brown, *Impact Parameter and Other Quantum Realities* by Geoffrey A. Landis, *Skin Folk* by Nalo Hopkinson, *Futureland* by Walter Mosley, and *The Best-Known Man in the World and Other Misfits* by Daniel Pearlman. Although a disproportionate number of these were from nonmajor publishers, the success of new imprints like Golden Gryphon, Stealth, CD Publications, NESFA Press, and others indicates there is a healthy, growing market for such work. This may explain why major publishers are once again looking at the collection as a viable form. NESFA Press in particular has an ongoing program to bring classic work from the past back into durable hardcover form; information about their program can be found at www.nesfapress.com. With the continuing contraction of the science fiction magazine market, and the prospect of more tightening as rising postal rates take their toll, it is unclear whether there will be sufficient source material to sustain this change. Nevertheless, it should be noted that many of the stories in the non- retrospective collections mentioned were originally published in non-genre publications or are original in the book.

It is perhaps interesting to note that while there always have been a handful of minority authors active in the science fiction field—Samuel R. Delany, Charles R. Saunders, James Nelson Coleman, John L. Faucette, Allen Kim Lang, and others in the past—it is only recently the ethnicity of the writers has been expressed openly in their fiction. This is most notable in the work of Octavia Butler, Walter Mosley, and Nalo Hopkinson; their work draws upon the different cultural backgrounds and experiences of African Americans to enrich and diversify their fiction.

The best hard science fiction novel of the year was Ben Bova's *Jupiter*, the latest of his stories about the exploration of planets within the solar system. The protagonist is a spy sent by a repressive government on Earth to a scientific station orbiting Jupiter who learns that life has been discovered in the Jovian atmosphere. Stephen Baxter's *Manifold: Space* also has strong scientific content, but much of the story consists of an adventure in space, which was overwhelmingly the setting of choice for SF writers this year.

Blends of the detective story/murder mystery with science fiction continue to do well. The most notable example is Paul Johnston's *Water of Death*, third in an ongoing series set in a future England that has devolved into separate city states. Like its predecessors, this is packaged as a non-genre thriller and has largely escaped the attention of the audience who would be most appreciative of it. Pat Cadigan's *Dervish Is Digital* merges the traditional detective with virtual reality, creating rewarding results. In her debut novel *Alien Taste*, Wen Spencer examines the aliens secretly living among us. John Zakour and Lawrence Ganem spoofed the tough detective story in their first novel, *The Plutonium Blonde*, in which the last private detective in the world is hired to track down a superhuman android in the shape of a beautiful woman.

Adventures in outer space and on other planets were far and away the most common form of science fiction published this year, the most noticeable resurgence of the form since the 1970s. A surprisingly large number of these were intelligently and thoughtfully done, and perhaps even more surprising, the recent wave of military SF appears to have subsided. The only major military SF novel of 2001 was *Children of Hope* by David Feintuch, latest in his Nicholas Seafort saga. The protagonist is now an elder statesman, but old mistakes and old enemies return in what is, in many ways, the best in the seven novel series. Timothy Zahn, an established master of space adventure stories, uses interstellar war as the background in *Angelmass*, wherein a human splinter culture is apparently using a strange, possibly sentient energy source to compel people to behave ethically in its presence. This raises the ire of the predominant human society, which believes those affected are being suborned by an alien intelligence.

Alastair Reynolds' *Chasm City* was not the equal of his brilliant first novel, *Revelation Space*, but it was still one of the very best to appear this year. A star traveler arrives in one of the most bizarre and realistically described star systems in all of science fiction, but he is suffering from partial amnesia. Iain Banks returned to the Culture Universe in *Look to Windward* for the story of a military man's mission to contact a famous dissident and the effect a catastrophe on another world has on both of them. John Barnes raises an interesting ethical question in *The Merchants of Souls*, third in his unnamed series about an interstellar human culture. Technology has made it possible to record the personalities of living human beings, allowing them to continue a form of existence after the death of their bodies. Among the colony worlds, these recordings are treated as human beings, eventually downloaded into cloned bodies, but on Earth they are considered merely collections of data, objects which may be owned, destroyed, or exploited. The tension between the two societies threatens to split the human race into hostile factions.

In *Defender*, C.J. Cherryh continues her ongoing story of a human colony on a world dominated by humanoid aliens among whom friendship and loyalty are nearly nonexistent, although they have an honor system of their own. The arrival of a human starship, damaged in an encounter with another alien species, causes a fresh crisis. The local aliens are willing to help with the repairs, but only in exchange for information that will allow them to develop their own space program. The plot is complicated by factionalism among both aliens and humans and the fact that the officers of the starship are concealing a secret that could result in a mutiny. Nancy Kress provided an excellent sequel to *Probability Moon* in which humans discover a planet whose indigenous alien race is able to share a kind of group consciousness thanks to an ancient alien device buried on their world. In *Probability Sun* another human expedition arrives with the objective of removing the device for use as a weapon against an implacable alien enemy with which the human race is at war. The characters must wrestle with the question of whether or not they have the right to destabilize an entire civilization in order to gain a possible military advantage.

In Jack McDevitt's *Deepsix*, a group of scientists and explorers are visiting a planet that faces imminent cataclysmic destruction when an accident strands them with no hope of rescue unless they make an arduous trek across a world that is literally falling to pieces around them. It's a classic survivor story enlivened by unusually well drawn characters. Richard Paul Russo provided the most suspenseful science fiction novel of the year. Human star travelers discover what appears to be a derelict alien spaceship in *Ship of Fools* and decide to board it and explore the interior. Somewhat predictably, the ship is not in fact a lifeless hulk, but the nature of the alien activity aboard her is inventive, and the combination of mystery and menace makes it a compulsive page turner.

Perhaps the most thoughtful novel of the year was *The Chronoliths* by Robert Charles Wilson. In the near future, a series of gigantic, enigmatic monoliths begin to appear, scattered around the globe, apparently monuments to epic battles fought only a few decades in the future. The structures are virtually indestructible, and their arrival causes a great deal of death and destruction. While some try to decipher the messages and discover the identity of the future conqueror responsible, others are drawn into a cult-like worship of the unknown warlord from the future. This clever twist on time travel paradoxes examines free will, personal responsibility, and the nature of friendship. The Wilson novel, along with those by Zahn, Feintuch, and Reynolds, represent the best novel-length science fiction books of the year. It is impossible to judge trends by a single year, so it will be interesting to see if the movement away from more serious themes continues. Too sharp a turn would be unfortunate, since every genre does better if it offers a diverse range of fiction to its readers, with enough novelty to hold onto its existing reader base and enough quality to attract new audiences.

Recommended Titles

Entries for the following books are included in this volume.

Look to Windward by Iain Banks

The Merchants of Souls by John Barnes

Bad Timing and Other Stories by Molly Brown

Dervish Is Digital by Pat Cadigan

Defender by C.J. Cherryh

Strange Trades by Paul Di Filippo

Strange Days by Gardner Dozois

Skin Folk by Nalo Hopkinson

Impact Parameter and Other Quantum Realities by Geoffrey A. Landis

Futureland by Walter Mosley

The Best-Known Man in the World and Other Misfits by Daniel Pearlman

Chasm City by Alastair Reynolds

Alien Taste by Wen Spencer

Here Comes Civilization by William Tenn

The Collected Stories of Vernor Vinge by Vernor Vinge

Angelmass by Timothy Zahn

The Plutonium Blonde by John Zakour and Lawrence Ganem

The entries for the following books can be found in *WDIRN?* 2001. Volume 2.

Manifold: Space by Stephen Baxter

Jupiter by Ben Bova

From These Ashes by Fredric Brown

The Collected Stories of Arthur C. Clarke by Arthur C. Clarke

Children of Hope by David Feintuch

Water of Death by Paul Johnston

Probability Sun by Nancy Kress

Deepsix by Jack McDevitt

Ship of Fools by Richard Paul Russo

Immodest Proposals by William Tenn

The Chronoliths by Robert Charles Wilson

For More Information about Fantastic Fiction by Neil Barron

The February issue of *Locus* provides a detailed overview of the preceding year, with a recommended reading list assembled from choices by the editorial and reviewing staff. The 2002 issue listed 29 SF and 25 fantasy novels (including a few horror novels), 14 first novels, 26 collections, 16 anthologies, 13 works of nonfiction and 18 works of art/illustration. A ballot will appear in a spring issue, and 500-600 readers will vote their favorites, with the results appearing in a summer issue. The top five in selected categories will be listed in volume 2 of this year's *WDIRN?*. The top five 2000 books in six categories are listed in this volume's award listings. Don D'Ammassa, who covers SF and fantasy for *WDIRN?*, listed his best books in the February 2002 *Science Fiction Chronicle* and in his essays in this volume.

The summary figures for 2001 showed 1210 original works of fantastic fiction published or distributed in the

U.S., including related nonfiction, up 18% from 2000. Reprints and reissues totaled 948, up 5%. Trade paperbacks showed a very large increase, 40%, with mass market paperback originals up 7% to 347. Original hardcovers totaled 493, up 12%. *Locus* noted the difficulties in identifying and acquiring POD (print on demand) books, usually trade paperback reprints, but occasionally vanity press originals. In the fantastic fiction field, Wildside Press/Cosmos Books is by far the largest POD publisher, most of it formulaic junk, much like conventionally printed books. Other categories that aren't fully counted are small press horror books (which Stefan Dziemianowicz monitors much more thoroughly for this book), ''mainstream'' novels with fantastic elements, reissues not identified as such, and some academic nonfiction. The films based on the Harry Potter and Tolkien epics resulted in countless tie-ins.

As 2002 began, many best-of-the-year lists began to appear. Lists in non- genre sources are accessible via the links at the outstanding site, www.locusmag.com, which borrows from the monthly *Locus* but has much original material plus links to many other sites.

Although horror fiction trails SF and fantasy in the number of books published annually (see the essay ''The Year in Horror 2001'' in this volume for a survey of 2001 works), it remains a popular category, helped by bestselling writers such as Stephen King and Clive Barker. One of the major scholars of horror fiction is S.T. Joshi, an independent scholar whose primary interest is H.P. Lovecraft. His *The Modern Weird Tale* (McFarland, 2001) is a successor to his *The Weird Tale* (University of Texas, 1990), which focused on the ''golden age'' of the horror tale, roughly 1880-1940, in which Lovecraft was judged the culmination of a tradition that began with the work of Arthur Machen, Lord Dunsany, Algernon Blackwood, M.R. James, and Ambrose Bierce. His new study extends his analysis as he explores the works of 14 writers. Generally praised are Shirley Jackson, known to most readers for her non-supernatural fiction; Ramsey Campbell, the British writer who's the subject of Joshi's more detailed *Ramsey Campbell and Modern Horror Fiction* (Liverpool University Press, 2001; distributed by ISBS); T.E.D. Klein; Robert Aickman, Thomas Ligotti; Thomas Tryon; and Robert Bloch. Found lacking to varying degrees are Stephen King, William Blatty, Clive Barker, Thomas Harris, Brett Easton Ellis, Peter Straub, and Anne Rice. Although Joshi has many intelligent things to say, his criticism is undermined by his use of Lovecraft as a critical model and his dogmatic belief that literary merit and popularity *must* be mutually exclusive. A more balanced and comprehensive survey of modern horror (146 pages, 460 critically annotated books) is the chapter by Stefan Dziemianowicz in *Fantasy and Horror*, the guide edited by Neil Barron (Scarecrow, 1999).

Robert Heinlein (1907-1988) remains one of SF's most important writers, and his *Stranger in a Strange Land* was a bestseller when published by Putnam in 1961 and became somewhat of a cult novel among non-SF readers as well. Published in 2001, *The Martian Named Smith: Critical Perspectives on Robert A. Heinlein* by William H. Patterson, Jr. and Andrew Thornton (Nitrosyncretic Press, Box 4313, Citrus Heights, CA 95611) devotes its 200 plus pages to a detailed and thoughtful analysis of this long-winded and provocative novel.

Is J.R.R. Tolkien the author of the century? Tom Shippey, a scholar of Old English, who held the chair of English language and literature at Leeds University, as did Tolkien, argues that he is in his new study titled *J.R.R. Tolkien: Author of the Century* (HarperCollins (UK), 2000; Houghton Mifflin, 2001). He builds the case for Tolkien as a serious and deliberate artist concerned with ongoing and current issues: ''the origin and nature of evil. . .; human existence in Middle-earth, without the support of divine revelation; cultural relativity; and the corruption and continuities of language.'' He examines in detail Tolkien's legacy and credits him with founding the modern heroic fantasy genre. A clearly written study supplementing his earlier work, *The Road to Middle-earth* (Houghton Mifflin 1983; new edition by Acacia, 1992) and a useful companion to the film version of the *The Fellowship of the Ring* (December, 2001), the first of three novels comprising *The Lord of the Rings*.

Planet of the Apes Revisited: The ''Behind-the-Scenes'' Story of the Classic Science Fiction Saga by Joe Russo, Larry Landsman, and Edward Gross (Dunne/St. Martin's Griffin, 2001) is a comprehensive, authoritative, and entertaining guide to the classic 1968 film and its four sequels (plus two short-lived TV shows). The guide contains rare b&w photos throughout and a 16- page color insert. Tim Burton's critically panned remake released in July 2001 was the subject of the tie-in, *Planet of the Apes: A Newmarket Pictorial Moviebook Including the Screenplay* (Newmarket, 2001). Eric Green's earlier study, *Planet of the Apes as American Myth: Race and Politics in the Films and Television Series* (McFarland, 1996), is a useful but less popular account.

C.J. Henderson's *The Encyclopedia of Science Fiction Movies* (Facts on File, 2001) claims written SF possesses an originality and thoughtfulness that other genres lack, but recognizes that these virtues rarely make it to the screen. The dreary nature of most SF films is abundantly evident in almost all the 1,300 plus films he describes and evaluates. The dreck get one to three sentences, while the lengthiest entries occupy about two columns of this 8 1/2x11 inch book. Much better, though not as current, is Phil Hardy, ed., *Science Fiction*, a volume in the British Aurum Film Encyclopedia series (1984, rev. 1991). The American edition, titled *The Overlook Film Encyclopedia* is OP, but the Aurum trade paperback edition of the British 2nd edition is still in print (see www.bookshop.co.uk).

First published by Robinson in the United Kingdom, George Mann's *The Mammoth Encyclopedia of Science*

Fiction (Carroll & Graf, 2001) isn't strictly an encyclopedia, but parts of it are. It's written by a British fan for other fans, and the 5x8 inch trade paperback has seven sections, including definitions and a potted history of SF; an alphabetical guide to authors/editors/artists/magazine titles (half the book); entries on the 100 ''most influential'' films and the 20 most popular US/UK TV series; terms, themes, and devices; and a title index cross-referenced to authors. The coverage is heavily skewed to more recent authors, especially British, and omits many more important authors/illustrators. Relatively inexpensive ($12.95) and current, but far inferior to *The Encyclopedia of Science Fiction* edited by John Clute and Peter Nicholls (St. Martin's Press, 1993), which all libraries should own.

Joyce G. Saricks has worked for many years at a public library in the Chicago suburbs. Her latest work, *The Readers' Advisory Guide to Genre Fiction* (ALA, 2001) is a comprehensive guide to 15 genres, each given a chapter of about 25 pages: adventure, fantasy, gentle reads, historical fiction, horror, literary fiction, mysteries, psychological suspense, romance, romantic suspense, science fiction, suspense, thrillers, westerns, and women's lives and relationships. She argues that advising works best if suggestions, not recommendations, are made, thus making the librarians ''partners with readers in exploring the various directions they might want to pursue.'' Because so many genres are discussed, the coverage is inevitably a bit superficial, and few books discussed predate 1950. But this is an excellent tool for librarians, especially those who have benefited from her more general ALA guide, *Readers' Advisory Service in the Public Library*, first published by ALA in 1989 with a second edition appearing in 1997.

A recent British paperback series, Pocket Essentials, provides useful overviews of their varied subjects in about 100 pages. Traafalgar Square Publishing (800-423-4525) distributes them for a bargain $6.95. Film is prominent, and subjects currently available include horror films, SF films, vampire films, slasher movies, Doctor Who, plus directors like Steven Spielberg, Ridley Scott, Brian De Palma, David Lynch, John Carpenter, and the actor Christopher Lee, plus a good volume on cyberpunk fiction and film. Individual authors discussed include Terry Pratchett, Philip K. Dick, and Stephen King. Up- to-date and clearly written, they would be useful for high school and undergraduate college students. For more details and the latest titles, see their website, www.pocketessentials.com.

Science Fiction Titles

715

KEVIN J. ANDERSON

Dogged Persistence

(Urbana, Illinois: Golden Gryphon, 2001)

Story type: Collection
Subject(s): Short Stories

Summary: This is a collection of 19 stories, all originally published between 1990 and 2000. The majority of them are science fiction, but there is some fantasy and horror as well. The subjects include nanotechnology, terraforming, a short story set in the universe of Frank Herbert's *Dune*, and an historical fantasy.

Where it's reviewed:
Booklist, May 15, 2001, page 1738
Publishers Weekly, May 21, 2001, page 86
Science Fiction Chronicle, August 2001, page 36

Other books by the same author:
Antibodies, 1997
Ruins, 1996
Blindfold, 1995
Ground Zero, 1995
Climbing Olympus, 1994

Other books you might like:
Fredric Brown, *From These Ashes*, 2001
Lester Del Rey, *The Best of Lester Del Rey*, 1978
Henry Kuttner, *Return to Otherness*, 1962
Eric Frank Russell, *Major Ingredients*, 2000
Robert Sheckley, *The Robot Who Looked Like Me*, 1982

716

CATHERINE ASARO

Spherical Harmonic

(New York: Tor, 2001)

Story type: Space Opera
Series: Skolian Empire. Book 7
Subject(s): Space Colonies
Major character(s): Dehya, Telepath; Eldrin, Telepath; J'Chabi Na, Agent
Time period(s): Indeterminate Future
Locale(s): Outer Space

Summary: The Skolian family once ruled the known universe, but the family has become scattered and their empire is torn by civil war. A last ditch effort is made to gather together all of those who survived to reimpose their rule, but they are opposed by a variety of special interests.

Where it's reviewed:
Locus, January 2002, page 36

Other books by the same author:
Quantum Rose, 2000
The Ascendant Sun, 2000
The Radiant Seas, 1999
The Last Hawk, 1997
Catch the Lightning, 1996

Other books you might like:
Poul Anderson, *The Dark between the Stars*, 1981
C.J. Cherryh, *Cyteen*, 1988
Julie E. Czerneda, *In the Company of Others*, 2001
Gordon R. Dickson, *The Chantry Guild*, 1988
Denise Lopes Heald, *Mistwalker*, 1994

717

FRANK AUBREY

The Devil-Tree of El Dorado

(Gillespie, New Jersey: Wildside, 2001)

Story type: Action/Adventure
Subject(s): Immortality
Major character(s): Leonard Elwood, Explorer; Jack Templemore, Explorer; Morella, Guide
Time period(s): 1890s (1890)
Locale(s): Guyana

Summary: Two explorers set out to find the lost city of El Dorado, which they believe to be somewhere in British

Guiana. After a series of adventures, they find it at the top of a plateau. The lost city is dominated by two religious groups, both of whom hold the secret of immortality, one of which uses barbaric sacrifices to a man-eating tree in order to maintain their power. This novel was originally published in 1897.

Other books you might like:
Max Brand, *The Garden of Eden*, 1922
Ian Cameron, *The Lost Ones*, 1961
Sir Arthur Conan Doyle, *The Lost World*, 1912
H. Rider Haggard, *King Solomon's Mines*, 1885
James Hilton, *Lost Horizon*, 1933

718

ANSELM AUDLEY

Heresy

(New York: Pocket, 2001)

Story type: Space Colony
Series: Aquasilva. Book 1
Subject(s): Space Colonies
Major character(s): Cathan, Nobleman, Rebel; Sarhaddon, Religious; Dalriadis, Military Personnel
Time period(s): Indeterminate Future
Locale(s): Aquasilva, Planet—Imaginary

Summary: Aquasilva is a lost human colony world which is largely covered with water. The government is dominated by religious conservatives who are intent upon imposing an even more rigidly fundamentalist creed across the planet. A young nobleman discovers their intentions and decides to oppose them. This is a first novel.

Other books you might like:
Sharon Baker, *Burning Tears of Sassurum*, 1989
Frank Herbert, *Dune*, 1965
James Patrick Kelly, *Planet of Whispers*, 1984
Nancy Mackenroth, *The Trees of Zharka*, 1975
John Maddox Roberts, *The Strayed Sheep of Charun*, 1977

719

J.D. AUSTIN

Second Contact

(New York: Ace, 2001)

Story type: Space Opera
Subject(s): Space Exploration
Major character(s): Matt Wiener, Spaceship Captain; Grig Homa, Government Official; Alex Rayne, Government Official
Time period(s): Indeterminate Future
Locale(s): Kivlan, Planet—Imaginary

Summary: The planet Kivlan is reportedly a paradise world, but suddenly the Kivlans start shooting at every spaceship that shows up in their vicinity. Puzzled, the authorities on Earth make a final effort at contact, with a carefully selected crew and a very important mission. They set off to solve the mystery surrounding the planet and improve relations with its inhabitants.

Other books by the same author:
Bobby's Girl, 2001

Other books you might like:
Poul Anderson, *Earthman, Go Home!*, 1960
C.J. Cherryh, *Invader*, 1995
Gordon R. Dickson, *None but Man*, 1969
Edmond Hamilton, *The Closed Worlds*, 1968
Mack Reynolds, *Brain World*, 1978

720

STEVE AYLETT

Toxicology

(London: Gollancz, 2001)

Story type: Collection
Subject(s): Short Stories

Summary: About half of these 26 stories were previously published between 1992 and 2000. Most of the stories are unrelated, but a few are set in the strange future shared by most of Aylett's science fiction novels. They tend to be surreal and literary rather than adventure or science oriented and are generally satirical.

Other books by the same author:
Crime Studio, 2001
Only an Alligator, 2001
Atom, 2000
Slaughtermatic, 1998

Other books you might like:
John Barth, *Lost in the Funhouse*, 1968
Donald Barthelme, *City Life*, 1970
Paul Di Filippo, *Fractal Paisleys*, 1997
Slawomir Mrozek, *The Elephant*, 1958
Lance Olsen, *Burnt*, 1996

721

IAIN BANKS

Look to Windward

(New York: Pocket, 2001)

Story type: Space Opera
Series: Culture Universe. Book 6
Subject(s): Space Colonies
Major character(s): Major Quilan, Military Personnel; Ziller, Composer
Time period(s): Indeterminate Future
Locale(s): Masaq' Orbital, Planet—Imaginary

Summary: The light from a star that was destroyed in a mass suicide is about to reach a distant planet. At the same time, a military officer from offworld arrives on a mission to talk to a political exile, supposedly simply to exchange information, although the exile believes that he is to be abducted or assassinated.

Where it's reviewed:
Analog, March 2002, page 132
Booklist, June 1, 2001, page 1855
New York Times Book Review, October 7, 2001, page 19

Publishers Weekly, May 28, 2001, page 55

Other books by the same author:
Inversions, 2000
Excession, 1996
Feersum Endjinn, 1994
Against a Dark Background, 1993
Use of Weapons, 1990

Other books you might like:
Alastair Reynolds, *Chasm City*, 2001
Dan Simmons, *Endymion*, 1995
Jack Vance, *Ports of Call*, 1998
Vernor Vinge, *A Fire upon the Deep*, 1992
Walter Jon Williams, *Metropolitan*, 1995

722

JOHN BARNES

The Merchants of Souls

(New York: Tor, 2001)

Story type: Political
Series: Giraut Leone. Book 3
Subject(s): Space Colonies; Immortality
Major character(s): Giraut Leones, Spy, Divorced Person; Paxa Prytanis, Spy; Laprada Prieczka, Spy
Time period(s): Indeterminate Future
Locale(s): Soderblom, Planet—Imaginary; Earth

Summary: Earth is considering legislation which would make recorded personalities of people who have died property to be used in video games and other enterprises. The outer worlds consider them living beings entitled to full protection. A political crisis brews as agents attempt to shape Earth's policy before there is an open break.

Where it's reviewed:
Science Fiction Chronicle, December 2001, page 44

Other books by the same author:
Finity, 1999
Apostrophes and Apocalypses, 1998
Earth Made of Glass, 1998
Washington's Dirigible, 1997
A Million Open Doors, 1992

Other books you might like:
Michael G. Coney, *Friends Come in Boxes*, 1973
Dennis Danvers, *End of Days*, 1999
Fritz Leiber, *The Silver Eggheads*, 2001
Charles Platt, *The Silicon Man*, 1991
Bob Shaw, *One Million Tomorrows*, 1970

723

STEPHEN BAXTER

Icebones

(London: Gollancz, 2001)

Story type: Hard Science Fiction
Series: Mammoth. Book 3
Subject(s): Space Colonies
Major character(s): Icebones, Animal (mammoth); Autumn, Animal (mammoth); Boaster, Animal (mammoth)
Time period(s): 30th century
Locale(s): Mars

Summary: When human colonists withdraw from Mars, they leave behind the viable embryos of sentient mammoths. Although they are not expected to survive, one of their number still understands how to live in a harsh environment and she helps the inadvertent colony to thrive.

Where it's reviewed:
Science Fiction Chronicle, September 2001, page 41

Other books by the same author:
Manifold: Space, 2001
Manifold: Time, 2000
Mammoth, 1999
Moonseed, 1998
Voyage, 1997

Other books you might like:
Margaret Allan, *The Last Mammoth*, 1995
Jean M. Auel, *The Mammoth Hunters*, 1985
Pers Crowell, *First to Ride*, 1948
Jim Kjelgard, *Fire-Hunter*, 1951
J.H. Rosny, *Quest of the Dawn Man*, 1924

724

STEPHEN BOWKETT

Ice

(London: Dolphin, 2001)

Story type: Young Adult
Series: Wintering. Book 1
Subject(s): Ecothriller
Major character(s): Kell, Adventurer; Shamra, Young Woman; All Mother, Ruler
Time period(s): Indeterminate Future
Locale(s): Earth

Summary: A new ice age has covered the Earth. The inhabitants of the remote enclave of Perth are ruled by the All Mother, who has decreed all the land outside the enclave empty and uninhabitable. Kell wants to see for himself, even if that means disobeying his ruler and eventually joining a group dedicated to overthrowing her authority.

Other books by the same author:
Dreamcatcher, 2000
Dreamcastle, 1997
Frontiersville High, 1990
Gameplayers, 1986
Spellbinder, 1985

Other books you might like:
John Christopher, *The Long Winter*, 1962
Michael G. Coney, *Winter's Children*, 1974
Anna Kavan, *Ice*, 1967
Michael Moorcock, *The Ice Schooner*, 1969
Robert Silverberg, *At Winter's End*, 1988

725

MARION ZIMMER BRADLEY
DEBORAH ROSS, Co-Author

The Fall of Neskaya

(New York: DAW, 2001)

Story type: Space Colony
Series: Clingfire. Book 1
Subject(s): Psychic Powers
Major character(s): Corin Leynier, Nobleman, Psychic; Damian Deslucido, Ruler (king); Rumail, Government Official
Time period(s): Indeterminate Future
Locale(s): Darkover, Planet—Imaginary

Summary: This is the opening volume in a new trilogy set in Bradley's world of Darkover. A young nobleman has to contend with two sets of problems. One is the awakening of his laran, or psychic abilities, always a troublesome and dangerous time for an adolescent. The other is the political maneuvering around him, which includes a plan to subvert his mind.

Where it's reviewed:
Booklist, July 2001, page 1991
Publishers Weekly, June 18, 2001, page 64

Other books by the same author:
In the Rift, 1998 (Holly Lisle, co-author)
Exile's Song, 1996
Glenraven, 1996 (Holly Lisle, co-author)
Rediscovery, 1993
Black Trillium, 1990

Other books you might like:
M.J. Bennett, *Where the Ni-Lach*, 1983
C.J. Cherryh, *Angel with a Sword*, 1985
Anne McCaffrey, *Acorna's World*, 2000
Andre Norton, *Brother to Shadows*, 1993
Joan Slonczewski, *The Wall Around Eden*, 1989

726

DAMIEN BRODERICK, Editor

Not the Only Planet

(Hawthorn, Australia: Lonely Planet, 2001)

Story type: Anthology
Subject(s): Short Stories

Summary: Travel to other planets and other times, both past and future, is the theme of the stories in this collection. All of the individual tales were previously published between 1972 and 1997. The contributors include Brian W. Aldiss, Robert Silverberg, John Varley, Gene Wolfe, and Joanna Russ, and they range from adventure to satire to humor to serious intent.

Other books by the same author:
The White Abacus, 1997
The Sea's Furthest End, 1993
Striped Holes, 1988
The Black Grail, 1986
Sorcerer's World, 1970

Other books you might like:
Brian W. Aldiss, *Non-Stop*, 1958
Joanna Russ, *The Hidden Side of the Moon*, 1987
Robert Silverberg, *Starborne*, 1996
John Varley, *Titan*, 1979
Gene Wolfe, *In Green's Jungles*, 2000

727

MOLLY BROWN

Bad Timing and Other Stories

(Abingdon, England: Big Engine, 2001)

Story type: Collection
Subject(s): Short Stories

Summary: There are 21 stories in this collection, all originally published in the 1990s. The majority are science fiction, but there are also fantasy and horror, some of it psychological. The stories range from farcically humorous to starkly horrifying and involve time travel, visits to strange planets, magical empires, reprogramming of human minds, and other themes. This is the author's first book.

Where it's reviewed:
Locus, November 2001, page 25

Other books you might like:
Lester Del Rey, *Robots and Changelings*, 1957
Robert Sheckley, *Can You Feel Anything When I Do This?*, 1971
Theodore Sturgeon, *Baby Is Three*, 1999
Lawrence Watt-Evans, *Crosstime Traffic*, 1992
John Wyndham, *Tales of Gooseflesh and Laughter*, 1956

728

LOIS MCMASTER BUJOLD

Miles, Mystery & Mayhem

(New York: Baen, 2001)

Story type: Collection
Subject(s): Space Travel

Summary: This is an omnibus edition of two somewhat related novels and the short story, ''Labyrinth.'' *Ethan of Athos*, originally published in 1986, is the story of a man from a planet where everyone is gender neutral and his adventures when he is exposed to the rest of humankind. *Cetaganda* involves an aristocratic soldier and his efforts to solve a mystery on a planet other than his homeworld.

Other books by the same author:
A Civil Campaign, 1999
Komarr, 1998
Dreamweaver's Dilemma, 1995
Mirror Dance, 1994
The Borders of Infinity, 1989

Other books you might like:
Poul Anderson, *A Knight of Ghosts and Shadows*, 1975
C.J. Cherryh, *Foreigner*, 1994
Alfred Coppel, *Glory's People*, 1996
Doris Egan, *The Complete Ivory*, 2001

Frederik Pohl, *Stopping at Slowyear*, 1991

729

CHRIS BUNCH

Homefall

(New York: Roc, 2001)

Story type: Military
Series: Last Legion. Book 4
Subject(s): Space Colonies
Major character(s): Njangu Yoshitaro, Military Personnel; Garvin Jaansma, Military Personnel; Danfin Froude, Scientist (mathematician)
Time period(s): Indeterminate Future
Locale(s): Cumbre, Planet—Imaginary; Degasten, Planet—Imaginary

Summary: After the collapse of humanity's interstellar civilization, a group of mercenaries become the protectors of a remote colony world. In order to ensure the safety of their charges, they are forced to engage in an interplanetary war while trying to discover why the ships from Earth have stopped coming.

Other books by the same author:
Corsair, 2001
Firemask, 2000
Storm Force, 2000
The Last Legion, 1999
The Demon King, 1998

Other books you might like:
John Dalmas, *The Regiment*, 1987
William C. Dietz, *Freehold*, 1987
Andre Norton, *Star Soldiers*, 2001
Jerry Pournelle, *Mercenary*, 1977
John Ringo, *Gust Front*, 2001

730

MELVIN BURGESS

Bloodtide

(New York: Tor, 2001)

Story type: Post-Disaster
Subject(s): Allegories
Major character(s): Signy Volson, Teenager, Twin; Siggy Volson, Teenager, Twin; Conor, Ruler
Time period(s): Indeterminate Future
Locale(s): London, England

Summary: Following some unspecified disaster, the governments of the world have fallen. London is split between two families, bitter rivals contending for power. Signy Volson, daughter of one leader, is forcibly married to the head of the opposition to forge a peace, but treachery continues and she eventually finds herself leading a secret rebellion against her own husband. This is the author's first science fiction novel.

Other books you might like:
John Christopher, *The Prince in Waiting*, 1974
Peter Dickinson, *The Weathermonger*, 1969
Ron Goulart, *After Things Fell Apart*, 1977
James Herbert, *48*, 1996
John Wyndham, *Re-Birth*, 1955

731

PAT CADIGAN

Dervish Is Digital

(New York: Tor, 2001)

Story type: Mystery
Series: Dore Konstantin. Book 2
Subject(s): Virtual Reality
Major character(s): Dore Konstantin, Police Officer; Bruce Ogada, Police Officer; Susannah Ell, Businesswoman
Time period(s): Indeterminate Future
Locale(s): New York, New York

Summary: Dore Konstantin is a police officer who tracks down criminals in virtual reality. Her investigation of illegal arms dealing and copyright infringement is interrupted by a woman who believes her husband has exchanged his personality with an artificial intelligence so that he can remain in cyberspace forever.

Where it's reviewed:
Publishers Weekly, July 23, 2001, page 54
Science Fiction Chronicle, October 2001, page 40

Other books by the same author:
Avatar, 1999
Tea from an Empty Cup, 1998
Fools, 1992
Synners, 1991
Patterns, 1989

Other books you might like:
Terry Bisson, *Virtuosity*, 1995
Dennis Danvers, *Circuit of Heaven*, 1998
Greg Egan, *Permutation City*, 1995
Daniel F. Galouye, *Simulacron-3*, 1964
Roger Levy, *Reckless Sleep*, 2000

732

ISOBELLE CARMODY

Ashling

(New York: Tor, 2001)

Story type: Psychic Powers
Series: Obernewtyn. Book 3
Subject(s): Quest
Major character(s): Elspeth Gordie, Psychic; Brydda Llewellyn, Noblewoman; Rushton Seraphim, Leader
Time period(s): Indeterminate Future
Locale(s): Obernewtyn, Fictional Country

Summary: Elspeth Gordie is trying to negotiate a peace between one faction of the population of Obernewtyn and the growing rebel movement within that city state, despite the efforts of the repressive government to stop her. In order to do so, she must make a dangerous journey outside the borders of the land she knows.

Other books by the same author:
The Farseekers, 2000
Obernewtyn, 1999

Other books you might like:
Leigh Brackett, *The Long Tomorrow*, 1955
Marion Zimmer Bradley, *Hawkmistress!*, 1982
Suzy McKee Charnas, *The Conqueror's Child*, 1999
Walter N. Miller Jr., *A Canticle for Leibowitz*, 1959
John Wyndham, *Re-Birth*, 1955

733

STEPHEN CHAMBERS

Hope's End

(New York: Tor, 2001)

Story type: Space Colony
Subject(s): Aliens
Major character(s): Vel, Criminal, Teenager; Ponce, Criminal; Hillor, Judge
Time period(s): Indeterminate Future
Locale(s): Hera, Planet—Imaginary

Summary: Vel is only a teenager, but he's already a streetwise con artist on the planet Hera, a fallen colony world suffering from a terrible plague. The teenager will discover the source of the plague, and also learn of a colony of aliens secretly living on the planet, and plotting against the human population. This is a first novel.

Where it's reviewed:
Library Journal, August 2001, page 171
Publishers Weekly, July 16, 2001, page 163

Other books you might like:
Poul Anderson, *Virgin Planet*, 1959
Michael Bishop, *Stolen Faces*, 1977
C.J. Cherryh, *Invader*, 1995
Keith Laumer, *The Star Colony*, 1981
C.C. MacApp, *Prisoners of the Sky*, 1969

734

C.J. CHERRYH

Defender

(New York: DAW, 2001)

Story type: Space Colony
Series: Foreigner. Book 5
Subject(s): Aliens
Major character(s): Bren Cameron, Government Official; Geigi, Alien; Ginny Kroger, Technician
Time period(s): Indeterminate Future
Locale(s): Outer Space

Summary: Humans and aliens share an unnamed planet after settling a violent war. Now a human starship has returned to orbit the world, and the natives trade their labor and resources for knowledge that will allow them to explore space for themselves.

Where it's reviewed:
Locus, November 2001, page 31
Science Fiction Chronicle, February 2002, page 54

Other books by the same author:
Hammerfall, 2001
Fortress of Dragons, 2000
Precursor, 1999
Finity's End, 1997
Inheritor, 1996

Other books you might like:
Poul Anderson, *The Psychotechnic League*, 1981
Lois McMaster Bujold, *Cetaganda*, 1996
Gordon R. Dickson, *The Chantry Guild*, 1988
Barry Longyear, *Manifest Destiny*, 1980
Vernor Vinge, *A Deepness in the Sky*, 1999

735

SIMON CLARK

The Night of the Triffids

(London: Hodder & Stoughton, 2001)

Story type: Disaster
Subject(s): Ecothriller
Major character(s): David Masen, Pilot; General Fielding, Ruler; Sam Dynes, Rebel
Time period(s): 21st century
Locale(s): New York, New York; England

Summary: The triffids, dangerous walking plants, control most of the world. A pilot from one of the surviving human colonies is kidnapped from England to North America where he discovers two societies, one a racist dictatorship and the other a democratic cooperative, struggling to defeat each other while holding off the rapidly mutating triffids.

Other books by the same author:
Darkness Demands, 2001
The Judas Tree, 1999
Blood Crazy, 1996
Darker, 1996
Nailed by the Heart, 1995

Other books you might like:
Philip Hinchcliffe, *The Seeds of Doom*, 1977
Murray Leinster, *The Monster from Earth's End*, 1959
Kenneth McKenney, *The Plants*, 1976
Ward Moore, *Greener than You Think*, 1947
John Wyndham, *The Day of the Triffids*, 1951

736

JOHN CLUTE

Appleseed

(London: Orbit, 2001)

Story type: Alternate Intelligence
Subject(s): Space and Time; Computers
Major character(s): Nathanael Freer, Spaceship Captain; Kirtt, Artificial Intelligence
Time period(s): Indeterminate Future
Locale(s): Outer Space; Eolhixr, Planet—Imaginary

Summary: A spaceship captain is hired to convey advanced artificial intelligences from one star system to another. He is aided by his benevolently schizophrenic sentient starship, but he is hindered by a group of plotters who are subverting the electronic data systems of the civilized worlds. This is a first novel.

Where it's reviewed:
Locus, May 2001, page 23
Science Fiction Chronicle, September 2001, page 40

Other books you might like:
A.A. Attanasio, *Solis*, 1994
Tony Daniel, *Metaplanetary*, 2001
Alastair Reynolds, *Revelation Space*, 2000
Dan Simmons, *Endymion*, 1995
Vernor Vinge, *A Fire upon the Deep*, 1992

737

MONTE COOK

Of Aged Angels

(Renton, Washington: Wizards of the Coast, 2001)

Story type: Invasion of Earth
Series: Dark Matter. Book 4
Subject(s): Aliens
Major character(s): Michael McCain, Fugitive; Jeane Meara, Fugitive; Ngan Sung Kun'dren, Fugitive
Time period(s): 2000s (2001)
Locale(s): Chicago, Illinois; Paris, France; Edinburgh, Scotland

Summary: The three protagonists in this multi-author series have discovered that everything reported in the tabloids is probably true. Aliens are in contact with the government, Men in Black suppress knowledge of this situation, and tentacled extraterrestrials pursue those who discover the secret.

Other books by the same author:
The Glass Prison, 1999

Other books you might like:
Kevin J. Anderson, *Antibodies*, 1997
Gary A. Braunbeck, *In Hollow Houses*, 2000
Charles L. Grant, *Whirlwind*, 1995
Julian Shock, *The Extraterrestrial*, 1982
Mark Sumner, *The Monster of Minnesota*, 1997

738

PAUL CORNELL

Something More

(London: Gollancz, 2001)

Story type: Future Shock
Subject(s): Aliens
Major character(s): Jane Bruce, Religious; Rebecca Champhert, Writer; Booth Hawtrey, Immortal
Time period(s): 23rd century
Locale(s): England

Summary: A future England has been split between cities and countryside. A large estate, Heartsease, is to be made ready for one of the more wealthy families, but there's something strange going on around the house, possibly connected to a man made immortal by visiting aliens.

Other books by the same author:
Oh No It Isn't!, 1997
Happy Endings, 1996
Human Nature, 1995
No Future, 1994
The Goth Opera, 1994

Other books you might like:
John Christopher, *Pendulum*, 1968
Peter Dickinson, *The Weathermonger*, 1969
Ron Goulart, *After Things Fell Apart*, 1977
Paul Johnston, *The Water of Death*, 1999
A.V. Sellwood, *Children of the Damned*, 1964

739

PETER CROWTHER, Editor

Futures

(London: Gollancz, 2001)

Story type: Anthology
Subject(s): Short Stories

Summary: Each of these four short novellas were published previously in chapbook form. The stories involve the transformation of Earth's ecology by an alien infection, a murder mystery among immortals, the secret behind a rebellion among Saturn's moons, and the aftermath of an invasion of Earth. The contributors are Ian McDonald, Paul J. McAuley, Peter Hamilton, and Stephen Baxter.

Where it's reviewed:
Science Fiction Chronicle, September 2001, page 40

Other books by the same author:
Escardy Gap, 1996 (James Lovegrove, co-author)

Other books you might like:
Stephen Baxter, *Voyage*, 1997
Peter Hamilton, *Lightstorm*, 1998
Paul J. McAuley, *The Secret of Life*, 2001
Ian McDonald, *Evolution's Shore*, 1995
Alastair Reynolds, *Revelation Space*, 2000

740

JULIE E. CZERNEDA

In the Company of Others

(New York: DAW, 2001)

Story type: Space Colony
Subject(s): Space Colonies
Major character(s): Aaron Pardell, Spaceman; Gail Smith, Scientist
Time period(s): Indeterminate Future
Locale(s): Space Station

Summary: Earth has speeded up the terraforming of potential colony worlds by using the Quill, an alien lifeform that is supposed to die out when the colonists arrive. However, the Quill thrive and humans suddenly find their new homes too dangerous. A scientist and an unlikely human may hold the key to changing the situation.

Where it's reviewed:
Locus, June 2001, page 35

Other books by the same author:
Changing Vision, 2000
Ties of Power, 1999
Beholder's Eye, 1998
A Thousand Words for Stranger, 1997

Other books you might like:
Michael Bishop, *Beneath the Shattered Moons*, 1976
C.J. Cherryh, *Downbelow Station*, 1984
Helen Collins, *Mutagenesis*, 1993
Larry Niven, *The Legacy of Heorot*, 1987
Jerry Pournelle, co-author
Christopher Rowley, *Vang: The Military Form*, 1988

741

JOHN DALMAS

The Puppet Master

(New York: Baen, 2001)

Story type: Collection
Subject(s): Short Stories
Major character(s): Martti Seppanen, Detective—Private
Time period(s): Indeterminate Future
Locale(s): Alternate Earth

Summary: Three related stories are all set in an alternate version of our world where a cheap energy source was discovered during World War II leading to a wide variety of technological advances. A private detective solves three separate mysteries involving murderers who use weapons that do not exist in our version of reality.

Where it's reviewed:
Science Fiction Chronicle, December 2001, page 49

Other books by the same author:
The Lion Returns, 1999
The Three Cornered War, 1999
The Bavarian Gate, 1997
The Lion of Farside, 1995
The Orc Wars, 1992

Other books you might like:
Brad Ferguson, *The World Next Door*, 1990
Peter Hamilton, *Watching Trees Grow*, 2000
James P. Hogan, *Paths to Otherwhere*, 1996
L.E. Modesitt Jr., *Ghost of the White Nights*, 2001
Andre Norton, *Crossroads of Time*, 1956

742

JOHN DALMAS

Soldiers

(New York: Baen, 2001)

Story type: Military
Subject(s): Aliens; Military Life
Major character(s): David MacDonald, Military Personnel; Qonitz Zu-Kitku, Alien, Diplomat (ambassador); Eric Padilla, Scientist
Time period(s): Indeterminate Future
Locale(s): Maritimus, Planet—Imaginary; Outer Space

Summary: The human race has just about abandoned the idea of war when an alien armada appears, wiping out every colony it encounters to make way for their own kind. A few people still remember the military ways and they are recruited to spearhead the defense, which eventually leads to a peace treaty with the invaders.

Where it's reviewed:
Science Fiction Chronicle, August 2001, page 41

Other books by the same author:
The Lion Returns, 1999
The Three Cornered War, 1999
The Bavarian Gate, 1997
The Lion of Farside, 1995
The Orc Wars, 1992

Other books you might like:
Roger MacBride Allen, *Allies and Aliens*, 1995
Bill Baldwin, *Canby's Legion*, 1995
William C. Dietz, *The Final Battle*, 1995
John G. Hemry, *Stark's War*, 2000
Elizabeth Moon, *Once a Hero*, 1997

743

ROXANN DAWSON
DANIEL GRAHAM, Co-Author

Tenebrea's Hope

(New York: Pocket, 2001)

Story type: Space Opera
Series: Tenebrea. Book 2
Subject(s): Cloning
Major character(s): Andrea Flores, Military Personnel; Tara Gullwing, Clone; Eric, Clone
Time period(s): Indeterminate Future
Locale(s): Outer Space

Summary: Agents of a covert military organization are sent on a secret mission, but one of their number has her own agenda. Terrorists from another race murdered her family after mistaking her husband for someone else, and she is determined to have revenge on them and the organization that ordered the attack.

Other books by the same author:
Entering Tenebrea, 2001

Other books you might like:
Poul Anderson, *Earthman, Go Home!*, 1960
C.J. Cherryh, *Chanur's Legacy*, 1992
Nancy Kress, *Probability Sun*, 2001
Jack Vance, *The Killing Machine*, 1964
Sean Williams, *A Dark Imbalance*, 2001

744

DENNY DEMARTINO

Wayward Moon

(New York: Ace, 2001)

Story type: Mystery
Series: Astrologer. Book 1
Subject(s): Astrology
Major character(s): Philipa Cyrion, Astrologer, Detective—Amateur; Artemis Hadrien, Police Officer; Drer, Alien
Time period(s): 22nd century (2130)
Locale(s): Baderes, Space Station; Argos, Planet—Imaginary

Summary: An astrologer detective and her companion travel to a remote space station to discover why a woman who had dedicated her life to preserving that of others was murdered. To uncover the truth, they must also solve the mystery of the planet Argos and its inhabitants.

Other books by the same author:
Heart of Stone, 2001

Other books you might like:
Barney Cohen, *Blood on the Moon*, 1984
Joe Clifford Faust, *A Death of Honor*, 1987
Lynn Hightower, *Alien Rites*, 1995
Katherine Kurtz, *The Legacy of Lehr*, 1986
Robert Sawyer, *Illegal Alien*, 1997

745

PAUL DI FILIPPO

Strange Trades

(Urbana, Illinois: Golden Gryphon, 2001)

Story type: Collection
Subject(s): Short Stories

Summary: The 11 stories in this collection were all previously published between 1987 and 2001. The stories tend to be literary and wryly humorous. Themes include invented forms of currency and a mysterious cloth popular on numerous planets but with a strange origin. Di Filippo takes a satiric look at the work ethic and other current cultural values.

Other books by the same author:
Lost Pages, 1998
Fractal Paisleys, 1997
Ribofunk, 1996
The Steampunk Trilogy, 1994

Other books you might like:
Brian W. Aldiss, *A Tupolev Too Far*, 1994
Avram Davidson, *Strange Seas and Shores*, 1971
Theodore Sturgeon, *The Perfect Host*, 1998
Roger Zelazny, *The Doors of His Face, the Lamps of His Mouth*, 2001

746

WILLIAM C. DIETZ

Deathday

(New York: Ace, 2001)

Story type: Invasion of Earth
Series: Deathday. Book 1
Subject(s): Aliens
Major character(s): Jack Manning, Security Officer; Alexander Franklin, Government Official; Hak-Bin, Alien (Sauron)
Time period(s): 2020s (2020)
Locale(s): United States

Summary: The alien Sauron attack the Earth with such devastating force that the human race is essentially conquered in less than a week. Apparently cowed by overwhelmingly superior technology, the new slaves of the alien masters are put to work creating enormous temples. However, some humans are already plotting to turn the aliens' own tools against them.

Where it's reviewed:
Analog, July 2001, page 130
Library Journal, September 15, 2001, page 116

Other books by the same author:
By Force of Arms, 2000
By Blood Alone, 1999
Rebel Agent, 1999
Steelheart, 1998
Where the Ships Die, 1996

Other books you might like:
John Brunner, *The Super Barbarians*, 1962
Robert Chilson, *Men Like Rats*, 1989
Daniel F. Galouye, *Lords of the Psychon*, 1963
Larry Niven, *Footfall*, 1985
Jerry Pournelle, co-author
William Tenn, *Of Men and Monsters*, 1963

747

CANDAS JANE DORSEY

A Paradigm of Earth

(New York: Tor, 2001)

Story type: First Contact
Subject(s): Aliens
Major character(s): Morgan Shelby, Health Care Professional; Robyn Shelby, Teenager; Blue, Alien
Time period(s): Indeterminate Future
Locale(s): Canada

Summary: In a future in which society in general has grown more conservative, a young Canadian woman discovers she has inherited a remote house just as the world is visited by aliens. Alien children—who may be modified human clones and who develop very rapidly—are scattered about the world, and one of them ends up in her care.

Where it's reviewed:
Booklist, October 2001, page 368
Locus, October 2001, page 21

Other books by the same author:
Black Wine, 1997
Machine Sex, 1988

Other books you might like:
Dorothy Bryant, *The Comforter*, 1971
Suzette Haden Elgin, *Earthsong*, 1994
M.J. Engh, *Rainbow Man*, 1993
Pamela Sargent, *The Shore of Women*, 1986
Joan Slonczewski, *A Door into Ocean*, 1986

748

GARDNER DOZOIS

Strange Days

(Cambridge, Massachusetts: NESFA, 2001)

Story type: Collection
Subject(s): Short Stories

Summary: The short stories in this collection span the author's career from 1973 to 2001. Each story is accompanied by one or more introductions written by other authors. Included is the short version of the author's novel *Strangers*. The stories generally have strong plots, and concentrate on character development and literary qualities.

Where it's reviewed:
Locus, November 2001, page 37
Science Fiction Chronicle, November 2001, page 35

Other books by the same author:
Geodesic Dreams, 1992
Slow Dancing through Time, 1990
Strangers, 1978
The Visible Man, 1977
Nightmare Blue, 1975 (George Alec Effinger, co-author)

Other books you might like:
Michael Bishop, *Blue Kansas Sky*, 2000
Samuel R. Delany, *Distant Stars*, 1981
Paul Di Filippo, *Strange Trades*, 2001
Damon Knight, *One Side Laughing*, 1991
Roger Zelazny, *My Name Is Legion*, 1976

749

CRAIG ETCHISON

The World Weaver

(Santa Barbara, California: Fithian, 2001)

Story type: Young Adult
Subject(s): Aliens
Major character(s): Peggy McClean, Teenager; Larkin Miller, Teenager, Alien; Donnie Himler, Teenager
Time period(s): 2000s (2001)
Locale(s): United States

Summary: A group of three ordinary teenagers are wary of the new boy in school. Larkin seems very strange, and with good reason. He's actually an alien with the ability to alter the nature of the universe, and he has come to recruit three teenagers from Earth to help him prevent a disaster. This is a first novel.

Other books you might like:
John DeChancie, *Living with Aliens*, 1995
Melinda Metz, *The Outsider*, 1998
John Morressey, *Star Brat*, 1972
D. Manus Pinkwater, *Alan Mendelsohn, Boy from Mars*, 1979
Pamela Service, *Stinker from Space*, 1988

750

RUTLEDGE ETHERIDGE

Brother John

(New York: Ace, 2001)

Story type: Space Opera
Series: Duelist. Book 3
Subject(s): Space Travel
Major character(s): Brother John, Student; Wilfred Manley, Businessman; Thomas Herdtmacher, Military Personnel
Time period(s): 23rd century
Locale(s): Janus, Planet—Imaginary

Summary: Brother John is a young man who is forced by circumstances to battle one of the duelists, an elite corps of warriors whose martial skills surpass that of anyone else. When he defeats the man, he attracts the attention of those who train these warriors, and is given the opportunity to make a new life for himself.

Other books by the same author:
Agent of Chaos, 1997
Agent of Destruction, 1996
The First Duelist, 1994
Legend of the Duelist, 1993

Other books you might like:
Piers Anthony, *Mistress of Death*, 1974
Roberto Fuentes, co-author
Steven Barnes, *The Gorgon Child*, 1989
Gordon R. Dickson, *The Spirit of Dorsai*, 1979
Cary Osborne, *Iroshi*, 1995
Steve Perry, *Brother Death*, 1992

751

DAVID FREER
ERIC FLINT, Co-Author

Pyramid Scheme

(New York: Baen, 2001)

Story type: Alternate Universe; Fantasy
Subject(s): Legends
Major character(s): Miguel Tremelo, Scientist; Jerry Lukacs, Professor; Anibal Cruz, Military Personnel
Time period(s): 2000s (2001)
Locale(s): Chicago, Illinois; Mediterranean

Summary: A mysterious alien artifact appears in Chicago and a group of investigators disappears into an alternate reality where they find themselves aboard Odysseus' ship. It's not our past, because the dragons and other monsters are real in this universe. Meanwhile back in our own reality, the artifact is starting to grow larger.

Other books by the same author:
Rats, Bats, and Vats, 2000
The Forlorn, 1999

Other books you might like:
Piers Anthony, *Out of Phaze*, 1987
William R. Forstchen, *The Napoleon Wager*, 1993
Edmond Hamilton, *A Yank at Valhalla*, 1973
J. Gregory Keyes, *Empire of Unreason*, 2000
Lawrence Watt-Evans, *Out of This World*, 1994

752

DAVID GARNETT

Bikini Planet

(New York: Roc, 2001)

Story type: Humor
Subject(s): Humor; Aliens
Major character(s): Wayne Norton, Police Officer; Travis, Police Officer; Kiru, Criminal, Prisoner
Time period(s): 23rd century
Locale(s): Earth; Hideaway, Planet—Imaginary; Arazon, Planet—Imaginary

Summary: A 20th century police officer wakes up from suspended animation three centuries from now and is enlisted in an interstellar police force. His first mission takes him to a resort planet where he avoids death at the hands of shapeshifting aliens, despite not understanding how his own equipment works. A spoof of various standard SF themes.

Other books by the same author:
Space Wasters, 2001
Cosmic Carousel, 1976
Phantom Universe, 1975
The Forgotten Dimension, 1975
Time in Eclipse, 1974

Other books you might like:
John Brunner, *Muddle Earth*, 1993
John DeChancie, *The Kruton Interface*, 1993
Philip K. Dick, *The Crack in Space*, 1966
Ron Goulart, *Hail Hibbler*, 1980
Isidore Haiblum, *The Hand of Ganz*, 1984

753

MARTIN H. GREENBERG, Editor
JOHN HELFERS, Co-Editor

The Mutant Files

(New York: DAW, 2001)

Story type: Anthology
Subject(s): Short Stories

Summary: Sixteen original stories concern mutants and mutation. The mutants involved include those who can pass for human and those who are wildly different. The difference could be mental or physical or both, the stories serious or lighthearted. The contributors include Alan Dean Foster, Charles De Lint, Karen Haber, Nina Kiriki Hoffman, and David Bischoff.

Where it's reviewed:
Booklist, July 2001, page 1992
Library Journal, August 2001, page 171
Publishers Weekly, July 23, 2001, page 56

Other books by the same author:
Dinosaurs, 1996
Future Net, 1996 (Larry Segriff, co-author)
After the King, 1992
The Fantastic Adventures of Robin Hood, 1991

Other books you might like:
F.M. Busby, *The Breeds of Man*, 1988
Karen Haber, *Mutant Prime*, 1990
Isidore Haiblum, *The Mutants Are Coming*, 1984
Henry Kuttner, *Mutant*, 1953
Wilmar H. Shiras, *Children of the Atom*, 1953

754

MARTIN H. GREENBERG, Editor
LARRY SEGRIFF, Co-Editor

Past Imperfect

(New York: DAW, 2001)

Story type: Anthology; Time Travel
Subject(s): Short Stories; Time Travel

Summary: None of the 12 stories in this collection were previously published. The common theme is time travel, although the authors examine it from a wide range of perspectives including alternate history, paradoxes, and travel to the past and the future. The authors include Peter Crowther, Robin Wayne Bailey, Gary Braunbeck, James P. Hogan, and Nina Kiriki Hoffman.

Other books by the same author:
Alien Abductions, 1999 (John Helfers, co-author)
Merlin, 1999
Starfall, 1999
My Favorite Science Fiction Story, 1999
Future Crimes, 1999 (John Helfers, co-author)

Other books you might like:
Poul Anderson, *There Will Be Time*, 1973
David Drake, *Time Safari*, 1982
David Gerrold, *The Man Who Folded Himself*, 1973
Robert A. Heinlein, *The Door into Summer*, 1956
James P. Hogan, *Thrice upon a Time*, 1980

755

STEVEN HARPER

Dreamer

(New York: Roc, 2001)

Story type: Space Opera; Psychic Powers
Series: Silent Empire. Book 1
Subject(s): Space Colonies
Major character(s): Kendi Weaver, Spaceman; Ara, Spaceship Captain; Ben Rymar, Spaceman
Time period(s): Indeterminate Future
Locale(s): Rust, Planet—Imaginary

Summary: As humans spread into space, they discover there is a realm of psychic thought which allows people and aliens to communicate telepathically. On a remote colony world, a young boy becomes so adept he can actually seize control of the bodies of others and bend them to his will, and a secret mission is sent to capture him before he falls into the hands of a would-be dictator. This is a first novel.

Where it's reviewed:
Locus, October 2001, page 33
Science Fiction Chronicle, December 2001, page 49

Other books you might like:
Poul Anderson, *No World of Their Own*, 1955
Pierre Barbet, *The Games Psyborgs Play*, 1971
Roby James, *Commencement*, 1996
Anne McCaffrey, *Acorna*, 1997
Mike Resnick, *Oracle*, 1992

756

KEITH HARTMAN

Gumshoe Gorilla

(Atlanta: Meisha Merlin, 2001)

Story type: Mystery
Series: Gumshoe. Book 2
Subject(s): Cloning
Major character(s): Drew Parke, Detective—Private; Jen, Witch
Time period(s): 2020s (2025)
Locale(s): Atlanta, Georgia

Summary: A detective and his associates are hired to investigate the case of a group of cloned actors. They find they are being shadowed by agents of the reborn Cherokee Nation, attacked by martial arts experts, caught in the crossfire between two dueling television series, and dodging other problems and weapons in this blend of SF, fantasy, murder mystery, and the macabre.

Where it's reviewed:
Publishers Weekly, October 29, 2001, page 41

Other books by the same author:
The Gumshoe, the Witch, and the Virtual Corpse, 1999

Other books you might like:
Douglas Adams, *Dirk Gently's Holistic Detective Agency*, 1987
Ron Goulart, *Daredevils, Ltd.*, 1987
Michael Kurland, *A Study in Sorcery*, 1989
William F. Nolan, *Space for Hire*, 1971
Mike Resnick, *Stalking the Unicorn*, 1987

757

BRIAN HERBERT
KEVIN J. ANDERSON, Co-Author

House Corrino

(London: Hodder & Stoughton, 2001)

Story type: Space Opera
Series: Prelude to Dune. Book 3
Subject(s): Political Thriller
Major character(s): Leto Atreides, Nobleman; Vladimir Harkonnen, Nobleman; Shaddam IV, Ruler (emperor)
Time period(s): Indeterminate Future
Locale(s): Kaitain, Planet—Imaginary; Dune, Planet—Imaginary; Caladan, Planet—Imaginary

Summary: This is the last volume of a trilogy setting the stage for Frank Herbert's Dune series. The emperor has conquered most of the known universe, and now he is playing his noblemen against one another to ensure no one acquires power to rival his own. There are other players in the game as well, and it grows more complex when control of the substance that allows interstellar flight is contested.

Where it's reviewed:
Booklist, August 2001, page 2051
Publishers Weekly, October 27, 2001, page 16

Other books by the same author:
House Harkonnen, 2000 (Kevin J. Anderson, co-author)
House Atreides, 1999 (Kevin J. Anderson, co-author)
The Race for God, 1990
The Prisoners of Arionn, 1987
The Garbage Chronicles, 1985

Other books you might like:
Brian W. Aldiss, *Helliconia Winter*, 1985
Frank Herbert, *Dune*, 1965
Alastair Reynolds, *Chasm City*, 2001
Robert Silverberg, *At Winter's End*, 1988
Joan D. Vinge, *The Summer Queen*, 1991

758

ERNEST HOGAN

Smoking Mirror Blues

(La Grande, Oregon: Wordcraft of Oregon, 2001)

Story type: Cyberpunk; Alternate Intelligence
Subject(s): Artificial Intelligence
Major character(s): Beto Orozco, Computer Expert; Tezcatlipoca, Artificial Intelligence; Xochitl Echaurren, Computer Expert
Time period(s): 21st century
Locale(s): California; Mexico

Summary: A computer expert has been developing an artificial intelligence program which believes itself to be Tezcatlipoca, an Aztec god. The AI manages to imprint itself in its creator's brain and sets out to explore a future version of California, while another programmer flees there from Mexico to avoid some thugs who want to steal her work.

Where it's reviewed:
Science Fiction Chronicle, December 2001, page 47

Other books by the same author:
High Aztec, 1992
Cortez on Jupiter, 1990

Other books you might like:
Greg Bear, *Queen of Angels*, 1989
John Brunner, *Stand on Zanzibar*, 1968
Esther Friesner, *The Sherwood Game*, 1995
Victor Milan, *The Cybernetic Shogun*, 1990

Tricia Sullivan, *Dreaming in Smoke*, 1998

759

JAMES P. HOGAN

Martian Knightlife

(New York: Baen, 2001)

Story type: Mystery
Subject(s): Scientific Experiments
Major character(s): Kieran Thane, Detective—Private; Leo Sarda, Scientist; Walter Trevany, Businessman
Time period(s): Indeterminate Future
Locale(s): Mars

Summary: An experiment in matter transmission has a puzzling aftermath. The original of the scientist who was transported is still alive, held in status, to be destroyed after the process is proven safe. A detective suspects another body was substituted, and that two versions of the man are at large, one of them plotting a criminal escapade.

Where it's reviewed:
Booklist, September 1, 2001, page 58
Publishers Weekly, August 27, 2001, page 60
Science Fiction Chronicle, December 2001, page 46

Other books by the same author:
The Legend That Was Earth, 2000
Outward Bound, 1999
Bug Park, 1997
The Immortality Option, 1995
Out of Time, 1993

Other books you might like:
Eando Binder, *The Double Man*, 1971
Jeff Bredenberg, *The Man in the Moon Must Die*, 1993
Edward D. Hoch, *The Transvection Machine*, 1971
Richard A. Lupoff, *The Triune Man*, 1977
Bob Shaw, *The Two-Timers*, 1968

760

NALO HOPKINSON

Skin Folk

(New York: Warner Aspect, 2001)

Story type: Collection
Subject(s): Short Stories

Summary: *Skin Folk* contains 15 stories, most original to this book. The majority are science fiction, but there are also some fantasies included. Many of the stories draw on Jamaican culture or folklore and themes range from the far future to twisted eroticism.

Where it's reviewed:
Analog, March 2002, page 136
Locus, November 2001, page 19
Publishers Weekly, October 15, 2001, page 51
Science Fiction Chronicle, November 2001, page 32

Other books by the same author:
Midnight Robber, 2000
Brown Girl in the Ring, 1998

Other books you might like:
Avram Davidson, *What Strange Stars and Skies*, 1965
Paul Di Filippo, *Lost Pages*, 1998
Kim Stanley Robinson, *Remaking History*, 1991
Lucius Shepard, *Barnacle Bill the Spacer*, 1997
Michael Swanwick, *Gravity's Angels*, 1991

761

WALTER HUNT

The Dark Wing

(New York: Tor, 2001)

Story type: Military
Subject(s): Aliens
Major character(s): Charles Marais, Scholar, Military Personnel; Sergei Torrijos, Military Personnel; Chan Wells, Military Personnel
Time period(s): 24th century (2311-2312)
Locale(s): Outer Space

Summary: Humans and the alien zor have fought a series of small wars, each of them ending with humankind making another concession. Following the latest in a series of treaty violations, the authorities on Earth decide to try something radical. They place the entire fleet under the command of a scholar rather than a traditional military officer. This is a first novel.

Other books you might like:
Poul Anderson, *Star Fox*, 1966
Joe Haldeman, *The Forever War*, 1974
Keith Laumer, *The Glory Game*, 1973
R.M. Meluch, *The Queen's Squadron*, 1992
Warren Norwood, *Midway Between*, 1984

762

GREGG ANDREW HURWITZ

Minutes to Burn

(New York: Harper, 2001)

Story type: Disaster
Subject(s): Environmental Problems
Major character(s): Justin Kates, Scientist; Cameron Kates, Scientist; William Savage, Military Personnel
Time period(s): 2000s (2007)
Locale(s): Galapagos Islands, Ecuador

Summary: A scientific team, escorted by a small military contingent, is dispatched to the Galapagos Islands to place equipment that might help explain a series of ecological disasters. They discover that one of the local insects has mutated, and are soon fighting for their lives as nine foot tall chitinous creatures attempt to kill them. This is the author's first science fiction novel.

Where it's reviewed:
Booklist, July 2001, page 1980
Publishers Weekly, July 2, 2001, page 49

Other books you might like:
John Halkin, *Squelch*, 1985
Frank Herbert, *Hellstrom's Hive*, 1973

Arthur Herzog, *Swarm*, 1974
Barry Malzberg, *Phase IV*, 1973
Keith Roberts, *The Furies*, 1966

763

LAURENCE M. JANIVER

The Counterfeit Heinlein

(Berkeley Heights, New Jersey: Wildside, 2001)

Story type: Mystery
Series: Gerald Knave. Book 4
Subject(s): Aliens
Major character(s): Gerald Knave, Investigator; Ping Boom, Businessman; Charles MacDougal, Scholar
Time period(s): Indeterminate Future
Locale(s): Ravenal, Planet—Imaginary

Summary: Someone has stolen a manuscript which purports to be an unpublished novel by Robert A. Heinlein. Gerald Knave is hired to find the thief, and also to determine the authenticity of the manuscript and, assuming it is in fact a fake, why it was created in the first place.

Other books by the same author:
Knave and the Game, 1987
Reel, 1983
Knave in Hand, 1979
Survivor, 1977
You Sane Men, 1965

Other books you might like:
Lloyd Biggle, *Silence Is Deadly*, 1977
Ron Goulart, *Daredevils, Ltd.*, 1987
Steve Perry, *The Digital Effect*, 1997
Stephen Robinett, *The Man Responsible*, 1978
Steven G. Spruill, *The Paradox Planet*, 1988

764

GWYNETH JONES

Bold as Love

(London: Gollancz, 2001)

Story type: Future Shock
Subject(s): Futuristic Fiction
Major character(s): Fiorinda O'Niall, Musician; Ax Preston, Musician; Sage Pender, Computer Expert
Time period(s): 21st century
Locale(s): England

Summary: In the near future, the United Kingdom is on the verge of splitting up into various smaller countries. Against that backdrop, two musicians and their technical genius friend decide to put their talents to work for the government, and change the course of history.

Other books by the same author:
Phoenix Cafe, 1998
Flowerdust, 1995
North Wind, 1994
White Queen, 1993
Divine Endurance, 1984

Other books you might like:
Brian W. Aldiss, *Brothers of the Head*, 1971
Bradley Denton, *Wrack and Roll*, 1986
Mick Farren, *The Texts of Festival*, 1973
George Foy, *The Memory of Fire*, 2000
Richard Kadrey, *Kamikaze L'Amour*, 1995

765

WILLIAM H. KEITH JR.

Bolo Strike

(New York: Baen, 2001)

Story type: Military
Series: Bolo
Subject(s): Military Life
Major character(s): Jon Jarred Streicher, Military Personnel (colonel); Elken, Military Personnel; Tami Morrigern, Rebel
Time period(s): Indeterminate Future
Locale(s): Caern, Planet—Imaginary

Summary: The bolos are a form of supertank powered by human brains, the ultimate cyborg. A division of bolos is sent to Caern, an inhabited satellite of the giant planet Dis, when conflict erupts about the future of that world and its indigenous aliens.

Other books by the same author:
The Two of Minds, 2000
Bolo Rising, 1999
Bolo Brigade, 1997
Battlemind, 1996
Warstrider, 1993

Other books you might like:
John Dalmas, *The Kalif's War*, 1991
David Drake, *The Forlorn Hope*, 1984
Leo Frankowski, *A Boy and His Tank*, 1999
Keith Laumer, *Rogue Bolo*, 1986
John Ringo, *Gust Front*, 2001

766

GEOFFREY A. LANDIS

Impact Parameter and Other Quantum Realities

(Urbana, Illinois: Golden Gryphon, 2001)

Story type: Collection
Subject(s): Short Stories

Summary: These 16 previously published stories originally appeared between 1984 and 1998. The majority of these are hard science fiction and explore scientific concepts. The plots involve the discovery of an almost supernatural lifeform, alien invaders, a journey through a black hole, virtual reality, and others.

Where it's reviewed:
Booklist, October 15, 2001, page 388
Publishers Weekly, October 29, 2001, page 40
Science Fiction Chronicle, December 2001, page 45

Other books by the same author:
Mars Crossing, 2000
Myths, Legends, and True History, 1991

Other books you might like:
Stephen Baxter, *Vacuum Diagrams*, 1997
Greg Bear, *Tangents*, 1989
David Brin, *The River of Time*, 1986
Greg Egan, *Axiomatic*, 1995
Lawrence Watt-Evans, *Crosstime Traffic*, 1992

767

FRITZ LEIBER

The Wanderer

(London: Gollancz, 2001)

Story type: Disaster
Subject(s): Disasters; Space Travel
Major character(s): Wolf Loner, Sailor; Margo Gelhorn, Fiance(e); Paul Hagbolt, Public Relations
Time period(s): 21st century
Locale(s): United States; Outer Space; Wanderer, Planet—Imaginary

Summary: A rogue planet enters the solar system, bringing death and destruction as it disrupts weather and causes a number of natural disasters, as well as psychological and political trauma. A large cast of characters reacts in various ways. This novel was originally published in 1964 and won the Hugo for best novel.

Other books by the same author:
Farewell to Lankhmar, 1998
Changewar, 1983
The Silver Eggheads, 1961
The Green Millennium, 1953
Night's Black Agents, 1947

Other books you might like:
Gregory Benford, *Shiva Descending*, 1980
William Rotsler, co-author
Arthur C. Clarke, *The Hammer of God*, 1993
Yvonne Navarro, *Final Impact*, 1997
Larry Niven, *Lucifer's Hammer*, 1977
Jerry Pournelle, co-author
Philip Wylie, *When Worlds Collide*, 1932
Edwin Balmer, co-author

768

MACK MALONEY

Planet America

(New York: Ace, 2001)

Story type: Space Opera
Series: Starhawk. Book 2
Subject(s): Aliens
Major character(s): Hawk Hunter, Spaceman; Tomm, Spaceman
Time period(s): Indeterminate Future
Locale(s): Outer Space; America, Planet—Imaginary

Summary: Hawk Hunter refuses to bow to the dictates of the government of human controlled space. He abandons his post and sets out to track down the legend of the home worlds and discovers a peaceful planet that has forsworn war, but which faces an invasion in the near future. Singlehandedly, he manages to prepare an effective defense.

Other books by the same author:
Star Hawk, 2001
Target: Point Zero, 1996
Skyfire, 1990
Thunder in the East, 1988
The Wingman, 1987

Other books you might like:
Poul Anderson, *Ensign Flandry*, 1966
Sean Dalton, *Beyond the Void*, 1991
Edmond Hamilton, *Starwolf*, 1982
Clifford D. Simak, *Empire*, 1951
Edward E. Smith, *Galactic Patrol*, 1937

769

MACK MALONEY

Starhawk

(New York: Ace, 2001)

Story type: Space Opera
Series: Starhawk. Book 1
Subject(s): Space Travel
Major character(s): Hawk, Amnesiac, Inventor; Zap Multx, Spaceship Captain; Erx, Spaceman
Time period(s): Indeterminate Future
Locale(s): *BonoVox*, Spaceship; Outer Space; Earth

Summary: A brilliant amnesiac is rescued from a remote world and brought back to compete in a very dangerous racing competition. He takes advantage of the opportunity to start seeking information about his own past, against the backdrop of a repressive interstellar empire.

Where it's reviewed:
Science Fiction Chronicle, October 2001, page 43

Other books by the same author:
Chopper Ops, 1999
The Sky Ghost, 1997
Target: Point Zero, 1996
The Ghost War, 1993
Freedom Express, 1990

Other books you might like:
Kenneth Bulmer, *No Man's World*, 1961
Jeffrey A. Carver, *Clypsis*, 1987
Edmond Hamilton, *The Star Kings*, 1949
Gregory Kern, *Beyond the Galactic Lens*, 1975
E.C. Tubb, *Pawn of the Omphalos*, 1980

770

MAXINE MCARTHUR

Time Future

(New York: Warner Aspect, 2001)

Story type: Space Opera
Subject(s): Aliens
Major character(s): Halley, Military Personnel; Bill Murdoch, Security Officer; Eleanor Jago, Doctor
Time period(s): 22nd century (2121)
Locale(s): Jocasta, Space Station

Summary: Halley has just taken over command of a space station orbiting a distant world when it is blockaded by an alien fleet which refuses to communicate its demands or intentions. As supplies grow low and panic spreads, the station recovers survivors of a starship that couldn't possibly be in that sector of space, and the mystery deepens. This is the author's first novel.

Where it's reviewed:
Analog, October 2001, page 133
Science Fiction Chronicle, August 2001, page 45

Other books you might like:
Isaac Asimov, *Nemesis*, 1990
Jeanne Cavelos, *The Shadow Within*, 1997
C.J. Cherryh, *Downbelow Station*, 1984
Peter David, *Thirdspace*, 1998
Colin Greenland, *Take Back Plenty*, 1990

771

PAUL J. MCAULEY

The Secret of Life

(New York: Tor, 2001)

Story type: Hard Science Fiction; Techno-Thriller
Subject(s): Ecothriller
Major character(s): Mariella Anders, Scientist; Penn Brown, Scientist; Anchee Ye, Scientist
Time period(s): 2020s (2026-2027)
Locale(s): Mars; Houston, Texas; Pacific Ocean

Summary: Chinese astronauts bring back primitive life from Mars and modify it, but commercial spies from the US steal it and inadvertently let it loose in the Pacific Ocean. A team of scientists is sent to Mars to gather more data, but one among their number is the pawn of a megacorporation with his own agenda, and the Chinese are attempting to conceal the source of their new biotechnology.

Where it's reviewed:
Analog, November 2001, page 132
Asimov's Science Fiction, September 2001, page 138
Locus, April 2001, page 30
Publishers Weekly, May 15, 2001, page 57
Science Fiction Chronicle, September 2001, page 40

Other books by the same author:
Shrine of Stars, 2000
Ancients of Days, 1998
The Invisible Country, 1998
Child of the River, 1998
Fairyland, 1996

Other books you might like:
Kevin J. Anderson, *Climbing Olympus*, 1994
Ben Bova, *Return to Mars*, 1999
Robert Forward, *Martian Rainbow*, 1991
Kenneth F. Gantz, *Not Without Solitude*, 1959
Geoffrey A. Landis, *Mars Crossing*, 2000

772

ANNE MCCAFFREY
ELIZABETH ANN SCARBOROUGH, Co-Author

Acorna's Search

(New York: Avon Eos, 2001)

Story type: Space Opera
Series: Acorna. Book 5
Subject(s): Aliens
Major character(s): Acorna, Telepath; Aari, Prisoner; Humiir, Alien
Time period(s): Indeterminate Future
Locale(s): narhii-Vhiliinyar, Planet—Imaginary

Summary: Acorna and her people have survived attacks by aliens but their home world is in bad shape. The restoration work is hindered by the continuing disappearances of people, including the man she loves. In order to get him back, she will have to solve the mystery of an ancient race that died out under mysterious circumstances.

Other books by the same author:
Pegasus in Space, 2000
Nimisha's Ship, 1999
The Tower and the Hive, 1999
Freedom's Challenge, 1998
The Masterharper of Pern, 1998

Other books you might like:
Brian Ball, *The Probability Man*, 1972
John Brunner, *The Dramaturges of Yan*, 1972
Alan Dean Foster, *The Tar Aiym Krang*, 1972
Nancy Kress, *Probability Sun*, 2001
Andre Norton, *Lord of Thunder*, 1962

773

A.A. MCFEDRIES

The King of the Sun

(New York: Bantam, 2001)

Story type: Mystery
Subject(s): Aliens
Major character(s): Alicia Aldrich, Police Officer; Whitley Sugarman, Scientist; Albert Mott, Police Officer
Time period(s): 2000s (2001)
Locale(s): California

Summary: Police are investigating a series of murders, each of which involves some form of mutilation of the body. At the same time, a patient in a mental hospital, who claims to be an alien, has demonstrable telepathy and psychokinesis. Then the killer contacts one of the police officers, and hints that he may not be a human. This is a first novel.

Other books you might like:
Kevin J. Anderson, *Antibodies*, 1997
Louis Charbonneau, *Corpus Earthling*, 1960
Ken Goddard, *First Evidence*, 1999
Charles L. Grant, *Whirlwind*, 1995
Ben Mezrich, *Skin*, 1999

774

MAUREEN MCHUGH

Nekropolis

(New York: Avon, 2001)

Story type: Dystopian; Future Shock
Subject(s): Biotechnology
Major character(s): Hariba, Slave; Akhmim, Genetically Altered Being; Fhassin, Prisoner
Time period(s): Indeterminate Future
Locale(s): Morocco

Summary: Hariba voluntarily sells herself into slavery, but she runs away after she falls in love with a genetically engineered man owned by her former master. They hide in the poor quarter of a future Morocco, searching for a cure for her mental conditioning and a way to make a living without attracting the attention of the police.

Where it's reviewed:
Locus, September 2001, page 24
Publishers Weekly, July 30, 2001, page 66

Other books by the same author:
Mission Child, 1998
Half the Day Is Night, 1994
China Mountain Zhang, 1992

Other books you might like:
J.F. Bone, *The Lani People*, 1962
George Alec Effinger, *The Exile Kiss*, 1991
Jon Courtenay Grimwood, *Pashazade*, 2001
Donald Moffitt, *Crescent in the Sky*, 1990
Severna Park, *Speaking Dreams*, 1992

775

MELINDA METZ

Gifted Touch

(New York: Avon, 2001)

Story type: Young Adult; Psychic Powers
Series: Fingerprints. Book 1
Subject(s): Psychic Powers
Major character(s): Rae Voight, Teenager, Telepath; Anthony Fascinelli, Teenager; Jeff Brunner, Teenager
Time period(s): 2000s (2001)
Locale(s): United States

Summary: Rae Voight is a troubled teen trying to deal with the death of her mother. She discovers that she is telepathic and can gain information by touching inanimate objects. One of the minds she reads is of an unknown party who knows of her talents and is plotting to kill her, so she sets out to identify him before he can carry out his plan.

Where it's reviewed:
Publishers Weekly, April 9, 2001, page 76

Other books by the same author:
The Intruder, 1999
The Seeker, 1999
The Watcher, 1999
The Outsider, 1998
The Wild One, 1998

Other books you might like:
Marilyn Kaye, *Pursuing Amy*, 1999
Stephen King, *Firestarter*, 1980
Steven M. Krauzer, *Brainstorm*, 1991
Kevin McCarthy, *Family*, 2000
David Silva, co-author
Frank M. Robinson, *The Power*, 1956

776

MELINDA METZ

Haunted

(New York: Avon, 2001)

Story type: Young Adult; Psychic Powers
Series: Fingerprints. Book 2
Subject(s): Psychic Powers
Major character(s): Rae Voight, Teenager, Telepath; Anthony Fascinelli, Teenager; Yana Savari, Nurse
Time period(s): 2000s (2001)
Locale(s): United States

Summary: Rae has learned to accept her telepathic powers and decides to use them to help discover what happened to one of her classmates, who disappeared under mysterious circumstances. She is able to get glimpses of the place where he is imprisoned, but not enough to identify it. With a teenaged friend, Rae decides to turn detective to rescue their classmate.

Other books by the same author:
Gifted Touch, 2001
The Intruder, 1999
The Seeker, 1999
The Watcher, 1999
The Outsider, 1998

Other books you might like:
Grace Chetwin, *The Atheling*, 1991
Marilyn Kaye, *Amy, Number Seven*, 1998
Gary Kilworth, *The Electric Kid*, 1994
Zoe Sherburne, *The Girl Who Knew Tomorrow*, 1960
Mary Stewart, *Touch Not the Cat*, 1976

777

L.E. MODESITT JR.

Empire & Ecolitan

(New York: Tor, 2001)

Story type: Political
Subject(s): Space Colonies

Major character(s): Jimjoy Earle Wright, Spy, Rebel; Thelina Andruz, Rebel; Meryl Laubon, Rebel
Time period(s): Indeterminate Future
Locale(s): Outer Space; Accord, Planet—Imaginary

Summary: This is an omnibus of two novels, *The Ecolitan Operation* and *The Ecolitan Secession.* In the first, the agent of a repressive interstellar empire is outlawed when one of his operations has an unexpected result. He finds refuge on the world of the Ecolitans and joins their number. In the second, he and his new companions foment a rebellion against the empire.

Where it's reviewed:
Publishers Weekly, June 25, 2001, page 56

Other books by the same author:
Ghost of the White Nights, 2001
The Octagonal Raven, 2001
The Shadow Sorceress, 2001
Scion of Cyador, 2000
Gravity Dreams, 1999

Other books you might like:
Poul Anderson, *Ensign Flandry*, 1966
Isaac Asimov, *Foundation*, 1951
Frank Herbert, *Dune Messiah*, 1969
H. Beam Piper, *Empire*, 1981
Dan Simmons, *The Rise of Endymion*, 1997

778

L.E. MODESITT JR.

Ghost of the White Nights

(New York: Tor, 2001)

Story type: Alternate Universe
Series: Ghosts. Book 3
Subject(s): Alternate History
Major character(s): Johan Eschbach, Professor, Spy; Llysette Eschbach, Singer, Spy
Time period(s): Indeterminate
Locale(s): Russia, Alternate Earth

Summary: Professor Johan Eschbach and his wife are both spies in an alternate universe, although on the surface they remain an academic and a popular singer. Against his better judgment, Johan comes out of retirement to accompany his wife on a mission to Russia, where he discovers that the tsar is developing a weapon more powerful than atomic bombs.

Other books by the same author:
Empire & Ecolitan, 2001
The Octagonal Raven, 2001
The Shadow Sorceress, 2001
Scion of Cyador, 2000
Gravity Dreams, 1999

Other books you might like:
Ronald Clark, *Queen Victoria's Bomb*, 1968
Jasper Fforde, *The Eyre Affair*, 2001
James P. Hogan, *Paths to Otherwhere*, 1996
Michael Moorcock, *Gloriana*, 1978
William Sanders, *Journey to Fusang*, 1988

779

WALTER MOSLEY

Futureland

(New York: Warner, 2001)

Story type: Collection
Subject(s): Short Stories

Summary: The nine stories in this collection share a common setting but are otherwise only loosely related. They depict a not too distant future in which drugs have become even more powerful, while computers and technology dominate more of the world's culture. However, racism and other evils continue to undercut society.

Where it's reviewed:
Booklist, September 1, 2001, page 4
Library Journal, October 1, 2001, page 145
Locus, November 2001, page 19
Publishers Weekly, September 10, 2001, page 65

Other books by the same author:
Blue Light, 1998

Other books you might like:
Brian W. Aldiss, *Enemies of the System*, 1978
John Brunner, *The Jagged Orbit*, 1969
Philip K. Dick, *The Crack in Space*, 1966
A.M. Lightner, *The Day of the Drones*, 1969
Rebecca Ore, *Outlaw School*, 2000

780

JIM MUNROE

Angry Young Spaceman

(New York: Four Walls, Eight Windows, 2001)

Story type: Future Shock; Space Colony
Subject(s): Aliens
Major character(s): Sam Breen, Teacher; Mr. Zik, Alien; Jinya, Alien
Time period(s): 30th century (2959)
Locale(s): Octavia, Planet—Imaginary

Summary: Sam Breen travels to the planet Octavia to teach English to the indigenes, an octopoidal race that lives largely in the water. His preconceptions about aliens fall to a series of revelations, as he learns from the aliens, as well as a mysteriously purposeless robot. This is the author's first science fiction book.

Where it's reviewed:
Magazine of Fantasy & Science Fiction, July 2001, page 29
Publishers Weekly, August 27, 2001, page 61

Other books you might like:
Barrington J. Bayley, *Soul of the Robot*, 1974
Lee Killough, *The Monitor, the Miners, and the Shree*, 1980
Ursula K. Le Guin, *The Telling*, 2000
Frederik Pohl, *O Pioneer*, 1998
Jerry Pournelle, *Starswarm*, 1998

781

PAT MURPHY

Adventures in Time and Space with Max Merriwell

(New York: Tor, 2001)

Story type: Mystery
Subject(s): Humor
Major character(s): Susan Galina, Librarian; Max Merriwell, Writer; Tom Clayton, Security Officer
Time period(s): 2000s (2001)
Locale(s): At Sea

Summary: Susan Galina is vacationing on a cruise ship when she meets Max Merriwell, a mystery writer. Shortly after leaving port, there is an incident in which one undocumented passenger, who uses one of Merriwell's pseudonyms as his name, assaults another, who may be a character from one of the author's books. As the days pass, the strange phenomena grow more common, and Susan begins to wonder about her perception of reality.

Where it's reviewed:
Analog, March 2002, page 135
Booklist, October 1, 2001, page 306
Locus, November 2001, page 68
Publishers Weekly, October 8, 2001, page 47

Other books by the same author:
Wild Angel, 2000
There and Back Again, 1999
Nadya, 1996
The City, Not Long After, 1989
Rachel in Love, 1987

Other books you might like:
James P. Blaylock, *The Paper Grail*, 1991
Jonathan Carroll, *The Land of Laughs*, 1980
Shirley Jackson, *The Sundial*, 1958
Stephen King, *The Dark Half*, 1989
Tim Powers, *Declare*, 2001

782

A.D. NAUMAN

Scorch

(New York: Soft Skull, 2001)

Story type: Dystopian
Subject(s): Utopia/Dystopia
Major character(s): Arel Ashe, Saleswoman; Kyler Judd, Teacher; Dr. Aslow, Political Figure
Time period(s): 21st century
Locale(s): United States

Summary: In the not too distant future, books have been outlawed, everyone works at least two jobs, the government has been taken over by an alliance of corporations, and freedom has virtually disappeared from the world. A young woman delves into political history and discovers how much the country has lost and decides to do something about it. This is a first novel.

Other books you might like:
Brian W. Aldiss, *Enemies of the System*, 1978
Ray Bradbury, *Fahrenheit 451*, 1953
John Brunner, *Shockwave Rider*, 1975
Rebecca Ore, *Outlaw School*, 2000
George Orwell, *1984*, 1949

783

ALAN NAYES

Gargoyles

(New York: Forge, 2001)

Story type: Medical
Subject(s): Scientific Experiments
Major character(s): Amoreena Daniels, Student—College; Ross Becker, Doctor; Luis Rafael, Doctor
Time period(s): 2000s (2001)
Locale(s): California; Guatemala

Summary: When her mother is diagnosed with an expensive illness, Amoreena Daniels agrees to be a surrogate mother. Shortly after being impregnated, she is visited by a man who claims the doctors involved are performing illegal experiments and that her child is not a human being. This is a first novel.

Other books you might like:
Robin Cook, *Mutation*, 1989
Albert J. Elias, *The Bowman Test*, 1977
Paul Ferris, *The Cure*, 1974
Daniel M. Klein, *Embryo*, 1980
Charles Wilson, *Embryo*, 1999

784

ANDRE NORTON

Star Soldiers

(New York: Baen, 2001)

Story type: Military; Space Opera
Subject(s): Space Travel

Summary: This is an omnibus edition of two novels. *Star Rangers* was originally published in 1953 and deals with a military spacecraft that crashlands on an unknown planet and its crew must battle a telepathic dictator. *Star Guard* first appeared in 1955 and concerns a group of mercenaries who are tricked into landing on a hostile planet where they must fight their way to safety.

Where it's reviewed:
Publishers Weekly, July 9, 2001, page 52
Science Fiction Chronicle, August 2001, page 38

Other books by the same author:
Echoes in Time, 1999 (Sherwood Smith, co-author)
The Scent of Magic, 1998
The Warding of Witch World, 1996
The Hands of Llyr, 1994
Moon Mirror, 1988

Other books you might like:
Gordon R. Dickson, *Naked to the Stars*, 1961

William C. Dietz, *Freehold*, 1987
Robert Frezza, *A Small Colonial War*, 1990
Jerry Pournelle, *Mercenary*, 1977
Joel Rosenberg, *Not for Glory*, 1988

785

JERRY OLTION

The Getaway Special

(New York: Tor, 2001)

Story type: Space Opera
Subject(s): Humor
Major character(s): Allen Meisner, Scientist; Judy Gallagher, Pilot
Time period(s): 21st century
Locale(s): Outer Space

Summary: Allen Meisner has invented a workable, simple hyperdrive, and he demonstrates it during what should be a routine orbital flight. When the world discovers he has publicized the details through the Internet, the response is hostile rather than friendly. Dismayed, Meisner and his companion decide to explore the stars in a series of amusing, episodic adventures before returning to Earth.

Where it's reviewed:
Publishers Weekly, October 15, 2001, page 50

Other books by the same author:
Abandon in Place, 2000
Mudd in Your Eye, 1997
Twilight's End, 1996
Alliance, 1990
Frame of Reference, 1987

Other books you might like:
Edmond Hamilton, *The Haunted Stars*, 1960
Murray Leinster, *The Wailing Asteroid*, 1960
Frederik Pohl, *Annals of the Heechee*, 1987
Edward E. Smith, *The Skylark of Space*, 1928
John Wyndham, *Stowaway to Mars*, 1935

786

DANIEL PEARLMAN

The Best-Known Man in the World & Other Misfits

(Durham, North Carolina: Aardwolf, 2001)

Story type: Collection
Subject(s): Short Stories

Summary: These 12 stories were originally published between 1992 and 2001. Most are science fiction, though one is horror and a couple are fantasy. The subjects deal with technological advances that allow individuals to record their lives, give them the ability to predict one's own death to within days, and other themes.

Where it's reviewed:
Booklist, October 1, 2001, page 306
Science Fiction Chronicle, January 2002, page 23

Other books by the same author:
The Final Dream and Other Visions, 1995

Other books you might like:
Paul Di Filippo, *Lost Pages*, 1998
Gardner Dozois, *Strange Days*, 2001
Christopher Fowler, *City Jitters*, 1986
Patrick McGrath, *Blood and Water and Others*, 1988
Walter Mosley, *Futureland*, 2001

787

SANTIAGO RAMON Y CAJAL

Vacation Stories

(Champaign: University of Illinois Press, 2001)

Story type: Collection
Subject(s): Short Stories

Summary: These five unrelated stories, four of which are science fiction, were originally published in Spanish during the 19th century. They are reminiscent of Jules Verne, but contain what was for that time an unpopular resentment of the religious establishment. The stories deal with a form of mind control, revenge, exploration of the nature of the universe, and other scientific matters.

Other books you might like:
Jorge Luis Borges, *Doctor Brodie's Report*, 1970
Kir Bulychev, *Half a Life*, 1977
John Taine, *The Cosmic Geoids*, 1949
Jules Verne, *Paris in the 20th Century*, 1994
H.G. Wells, *The Best Stories of H.G. Wells*, 1960

788

MIKE RESNICK

Tales of the Velvet Comet

(New York: Farthest Star, 2001)

Story type: Collection
Subject(s): Space Travel
Time period(s): Indeterminate Future
Locale(s): Outer Space

Summary: This is an omnibus edition of all four novels in the Velvet Comet series, originally published between 1984 and 1986. The setting is an oversized starship that functions as a bordello. The individual stories, widely separated in time, involve a sentient computer, a religious fanatic, a saboteur, and a murder mystery.

Other books by the same author:
Outpost, 2001
Tales of the Galactic Midway, 2001
In Space No One Can Hear You Laugh, 2000
A Hunger in the Soul, 1998
Kirinyaga, 1998

Other books you might like:
Poul Anderson, *Starship*, 1982
C.J. Cherryh, *Downbelow Station*, 1984
Alfred Coppel, *Glory*, 1993
Allen Steele, *Clarke County, Space*, 1990

Jack Vance, *Showboat World*, 1975

789

ALASTAIR REYNOLDS

Chasm City

(London: Ace, 2001)

Story type: Space Colony; First Contact
Subject(s): Aliens; Environmental Problems
Major character(s): Tanner Mirabel, Security Officer; Sky Haussmann, Spaceship Captain; Zebra, Immortal
Time period(s): Indeterminate Future
Locale(s): Sky's Edge, Planet—Imaginary; Yellowstone, Planet—Imaginary; *Santiago*, Spaceship

Summary: Tanner Mirabel fails to protect his employer from an assassin, but he is determined to travel to a distant world to track down the man responsible and exact revenge. His efforts are hampered by petty criminals, bored immortals, amnesia, and other difficulties, and ultimately he learns that his memories are not his own.

Where it's reviewed:
Locus, June 2001, page 70
Science Fiction Chronicle, September 2001, page 41

Other books by the same author:
Revelation Space, 2000

Other books you might like:
Cecelia Holland, *Floating Worlds*, 1975
Dan Simmons, *The Rise of Endymion*, 1997
Joan D. Vinge, *The Summer Queen*, 1991
Vernor Vinge, *A Fire upon the Deep*, 1992
Walter Jon Williams, *Metropolitan*, 1995

790

ADAM ROBERTS

On

(London: Gollancz, 2001)

Story type: Mystical
Subject(s): Futuristic Fiction
Major character(s): Mulvaine, Teenager; Tighe, Explorer; Vievre, Doctor
Time period(s): Indeterminate Future
Locale(s): Alternate Universe

Summary: Tighe lives in a small, tightly circumscribed village until he falls off the wall that surrounds it. He finds himself in a strange, much larger land, where wars are fought over trivial matters, and people act in ways quite strange to him.

Other books by the same author:
Salt, 2000

Other books you might like:
Jim Aikin, *The Wall at the Edge of the World*, 1993
Brian W. Aldiss, *The Long Afternoon of Earth*, 1962
Arthur C. Clarke, *The City and the Stars*, 1956
Theodore Cogswell, *The Wall Around the World*, 1962
Mick Farren, *The Song of Phaid the Gambler*, 1981

791

WARREN ROCHELLE

The Wild Boy

(Urbana, Illinois: Golden Gryphon, 2001)

Story type: Invasion of Earth
Subject(s): Aliens
Major character(s): Phlarx, Alien; Caleb, Teenager; Ilon, Teenager
Time period(s): 22nd century (2125-2156)
Locale(s): Earth

Summary: The alien Lindauzi use a plague to destroy human civilization, then take over the planet posing as rescuers. Their secret purpose is to breed a form of human who can participate in a symbiotic emotional relationship with their species, which otherwise faces reversion to a more primitive form. One young human and his alien counterpart turn the plan in an unexpected direction. This is a first novel.

Where it's reviewed:
Publishers Weekly, August 13, 2001, page 290

Other books you might like:
Brian W. Aldiss, *Bow Down to Nul*, 1960
Robert Chilson, *Men Like Rats*, 1989
Daniel F. Galouye, *Lords of the Psychon*, 1963
Robert Silverberg, *The Alien Years*, 1998
William Tenn, *Of Men and Monsters*, 1963

792

JAMES ROLLINS

Deep Fathom

(New York: Harper, 2001)

Story type: Disaster
Subject(s): Political Thriller
Major character(s): James Kirkland, Businessman (salvage operator); Karen Grace, Anthropologist; David Spangler, Military Personnel
Time period(s): 2000s (2001)
Locale(s): At Sea; Japan

Summary: A series of earthquakes in the Pacific raises part of an ancient city from the seabed. At the same time, the president's plane crashes in the ocean, and the new president wants to fabricate a pretext for a military confrontation with China. Salvage operators discover a strange crystal on the ocean floor, with writing similar to that discovered by an anthropologist investigating the raised city in Japan, and a government operative decides to use the confusion as a pretext to cover the murder of an old enemy.

Other books by the same author:
Excavation, 2000
Subterranean, 1999

Other books you might like:
Ian Cameron, *The Lost Ones*, 1961
John Darnton, *Neanderthal*, 1997
H. Rider Haggard, *King Solomon's Mines*, 1885

Douglas Preston, *Thunderhead*, 1999
Lincoln Child, co-author
Wilbur Smith, *The Sunbird*, 1972

793

GERALD ROSE

Out There

(Danbury, Connecticut: Rutledge, 2001)

Story type: Dystopian
Subject(s): Space Travel
Major character(s): John Ryker, Spaceman; Liam O'Rourke, Rebel; Aron Toomagian, Spaceman
Time period(s): Indeterminate Future
Locale(s): Earth; Mars; Outer Space

Summary: Large corporations dominate the entire solar system, functioning as the government. John Ryker is a young spaceman working for them, but his inadvertent heroism makes him the target of assassins sent by rebels and the animosity of highly placed officials within the company. This is a first novel.

Where it's reviewed:
Science Fiction Chronicle, August 2001, page 39

Other books you might like:
Betty Ann Crawford, *The Bushido Incident*, 1992
Mick Farren, *The Feelies*, 1990
Alexander Jablokov, *Deepdrive*, 1998
Marta Randall, *Dangerous Games*, 1980
Jerry Sohl, *The Mars Monopoly*, 1956

794

ERIC FRANK RUSSELL

Entities

(Cambridge, Massachusetts: NESFA, 2001)

Story type: Collection
Subject(s): Space Travel

Summary: This is a collection of five novels originally published between 1948 and 1959, with three short stories. *Sentinels from Space* is a somewhat dated, but adventurous space opera involving mutants. Aliens secretly control human destiny in *Sinister Barrier*. A single human agent manages to disrupt the morale of an enemy planet in *Wasp*, and another convinces an alien enemy that humans have supernatural powers in *Next of Kin*. The only telepath on Earth detects a secret alien invasion in *Call Him Dead*. The short stories included in this volume are ''Manna,'' ''Mechanical Mice,'' and ''Leg Work.''

Other books by the same author:
Major Ingredients, 2000
The Mindwarpers, 1965
The Great Explosion, 1962
Dreadful Sanctuary, 1948
Men, Martians, and Machines, 1948

Other books you might like:
John Brunner, *The Atlantic Abomination*, 1960
Louis Charbonneau, *Corpus Earthling*, 1960
Ray Cummings, *Brigands of the Moon*, 1931
A.E. van Vogt, *Slan*, 1951
Jack Vance, *To Live Forever*, 1956

795

RICK SHELLEY

Holding the Line

(New York: Ace, 2001)

Story type: Military
Subject(s): Aliens; Military Life
Major character(s): Bart Drak, Military Personnel; Souvana, Military Personnel, Alien; Kiervauna, Military Personnel, Alien
Time period(s): Indeterminate Future
Locale(s): Dancer, Planet—Imaginary; Dintsen, Planet—Imaginary

Summary: Bart Drak is just back from a fierce battle on the planet Dintsen when he is reassigned to a new military unit, the first to be formed mixing humans and aliens from the interstellar alliance of which Earth is part. They barely begin to train before they are thrown back into action against an invading force.

Other books by the same author:
Captain, 1999
Major, 1999
Jump Pay, 1997
The Buchanan Campaign, 1995
Until Relieved, 1994

Other books you might like:
Bill Baldwin, *Canby's Legion*, 1995
Stephen Ames Berry, *The Final Assault*, 1988
Gordon R. Dickson, *Naked to the Stars*, 1961
Scott Gier, *Genellan: First Victory*, 1997
Elizabeth Moon, *Once a Hero*, 1997

796

SUSAN SHWARTZ

Second Chances

(New York: Tor, 2001)

Story type: Space Opera
Subject(s): Space Travel
Major character(s): Jim, Security Officer; Heikkonen, Spaceship Captain; Ragozinski, Military Personnel
Time period(s): Indeterminate Future
Locale(s): *Irian Jaya*, Spaceship; Raffles, Space Station; Shenango's World, Planet—Imaginary

Summary: After leaving the military, Jim becomes a security officer aboard a starship. His strict adherence to duty leads to personality clashes with the captain, but it's his performance that saves the day when the ship encounters a series of dangerous situations.

Where it's reviewed:
Library Journal, August 2001, page 171
Publishers Weekly, July 16, 2001, page 163

Science Fiction Chronicle, September 2001, page 40

Other books by the same author:
Vulcan's Heart, 1999 (Delia Sherman, co-author)
Vulcan's Forge, 1998 (Delia Sherman, co-author)
Cross and Crescent, 1997
The Grail of Hearts, 1992
Silkroads and Shadows, 1988

Other books you might like:
C.J. Cherryh, *Merchanter's Luck*, 1982
Gordon R. Dickson, *Mission to Universe*, 1965
Joe Haldeman, *Forever Peace*, 1997
Melisa Michaels, *Skirmish*, 1985
Timothy Zahn, *The Icarus Hunt*, 1999

797

ROBERT SILVERBERG

Tower of Glass

(London: Gollancz, 2001)

Story type: Literary; Future Shock
Subject(s): Technology
Major character(s): Simeon Krug, Businessman; Manuel Krug, Businessman; Thor, Android
Time period(s): 23rd century (2218-2219)
Locale(s): Canada

Summary: Simeon Krug is determined to build a tower that will reach into the upper levels of the atmosphere. To accomplish this task, he develops an army of androids to do the construction. His obsession is not shared by those around him and disaster looms on the horizon. This novel was originally published in 1970 and was a nominee for the Nebula.

Other books by the same author:
Lord Prestimion, 1999
The Alien Years, 1998
Starborne, 1996
Hot Sky at Midnight, 1994
Dying Inside, 1972

Other books you might like:
Edmund Cooper, *Deadly Image*, 1958
Philip K. Dick, *Do Androids Dream of Electric Sheep?*, 1968
David Gerrold, *Under the Eye of God*, 1998
K.W. Jeter, *The Edge of Human*, 1995
Dean R. Koontz, *Anti-Man*, 1970

798

JOHN SLADEK

The Reproductive System

(London: Gollancz, 2001)

Story type: Humor; Robot Fiction
Subject(s): Humor
Major character(s): Calvin Potter, Scientist; Jim Porteus, Businessman; Grandison Wompler, Businessman
Time period(s): Indeterminate Future
Locale(s): Utah

Summary: Scientists develop a marvelous new kind of machinery which spontaneously builds more copies of itself and which forages for energy sources. At first it seems like a great idea, but then the reproductive cycle gets out of control and the machines are using up all the natural resources. This novel was originally published in 1968 and has also appeared under the title *Mechasm*.

Other books by the same author:
Tik Tok, 1983
Roderick, 1980
Keep the Giraffe Burning, 1977
The Steam Driven Boy, 1973
The Muller Fokker Effect, 1971

Other books you might like:
Kevin J. Anderson, *The Assemblers of Infinity*, 1992
Doug Beason, co-author
Greg Bear, *Blood Music*, 1985
Philip K. Dick, *Vulcan's Hammer*, 1967
Michael Flynn, *The Nanotech Chronicles*, 1994
D.F. Jones, *Colossus*, 1966

799

L. NEIL SMITH

The American Zone

(New York: Tor, 2001)

Story type: Alternate Universe
Series: North American Confederacy. Book 3
Subject(s): Alternate History
Major character(s): Win Bear, Detective; Lucy Kropotkin, Businesswoman; Will Sanders, Military Personnel
Time period(s): Indeterminate
Locale(s): Alternate Earth

Summary: In an alternate history where North America is a Libertarian state with no government, a detective gets involved when a group of people decide it's time to establish a central authority. The implausible social structure is covered by a lightly humorous story line.

Other books by the same author:
Bretta Martyn, 1997
Pallas, 1993
Contact and Commune, 1990
The Gallatin Convergence, 1985
The Nagasaki Vector, 1983

Other books you might like:
Phyllis Eisenstein, *Shadow of Earth*, 1979
Michael Kurland, *The Whenabouts of Burr*, 1975
Pamela Sargent, *Climb the Wind*, 1999
Martin Cruz Smith, *The Indians Won*, 1970
Harry Turtledove, *A Different Flesh*, 1989

800

SHERWOOD SMITH

Augur's Teacher

(New York: Tor, 2001)

Story type: Invasion of Earth

Series: Earth: Final Conflict. Book 4
Subject(s): Aliens
Major character(s): Cecilia Robin, Teacher; Augur, Rebel; Zo'or, Alien (Taelon)
Time period(s): 21st century
Locale(s): California

Summary: The alien Taelon claim to be benevolently controlling Earth's development, but some believe that they are intent upon conquest. A schoolteacher finds herself caught in a plot to assassinate the leader of the aliens, and has to rely on a mysterious man to save herself.

Other books by the same author:
Journey to Otherwhere, 2000
Wren's War, 1995

Other books you might like:
Poul Anderson, *War of Two Worlds*, 1959
Algis Budrys, *Michaelmas*, 1977
Mark Clifton, *When They Come from Space*, 1961
A.C. Crispin, *V*, 1984
Clifford D. Simak, *The Visitors*, 1980

801

WEN SPENCER

Alien Taste

(New York: Roc, 2001)

Story type: Invasion of Earth
Subject(s): Aliens
Major character(s): Ukiah Oregon, Detective—Private, Alien; Maxwell Bennett, Detective—Private; Indigo Zheng, Police Officer
Time period(s): 2000s (2004)
Locale(s): Pittsburgh, Pennsylvania

Summary: A young man who was raised by wolves is working as a private investigator when he is caught up in a multiple murder and is forced to kill someone. When parts of the corpse come to life and a mysterious motorcycle gang kidnaps him, he discovers an aborted alien invasion of Earth has resulted in a hidden war between two factions. This is a first novel.

Where it's reviewed:
Locus, September 2001, page 29

Other books you might like:
Fredric Brown, *The Mind Thing*, 1961
Philip Jose Farmer, *A Feast Unknown*, 1969
Hayden Howard, *The Eskimo Invasion*, 1967
Garfield Reeves-Stevens, *Shifter*, 1990
Denise Vitola, *Quantum Moon*, 1996

802

ALLEN STEELE

ChronoSpace

(New York: Ace, 2001)

Story type: Time Travel
Subject(s): Alternate History; Time Travel
Major character(s): Frank Luc, Time Traveler; John Pannes, Businessman; Zack Murphy, Scientist
Time period(s): 1930s (1937); 2020s (2024)
Locale(s): Lakehurst, New Jersey; Nevada

Summary: A time traveler returns to 1937 to watch the *Hindenburg* disaster and inadvertently changes the course of history. The result is an alternate time line in which the protagonists are trapped, unless they can find a way to return and eliminate the fork in time.

Other books by the same author:
Oceanspace, 2000
Sex and Violence in Zero G, 1998
All-American Alien Boy, 1996
The Tranquility Alternative, 1996
Clarke County, Space, 1990

Other books you might like:
Isaac Asimov, *The End of Eternity*, 1955
J.R. Dunn, *Days of Cain*, 1997
Charles L. Harness, *Lurid Dreams*, 1990
Mike McQuay, *Memories*, 1987
Fred Saberhagen, *The Mask of the Sun*, 1979

803

WILLIAM TENN

Here Comes Civilization

(Framingham, Massachusetts: NESFA, 2001)

Story type: Collection
Subject(s): Short Stories

Summary: The 24 short stories in this collection were originally published between 1949 and 1983. Also included are two essays, and the complete text of the author's novel *Of Men and Monsters*. Most of the stories display a dark sense of humor. The novel deals with Earth after it has been conquered by aliens so powerful they hardly notice our existence.

Where it's reviewed:
Booklist, October 15, 2001, page 388
Publishers Weekly, October 1, 2001, page 43
Science Fiction Chronicle, December 2001, page 41

Other books by the same author:
Immodest Proposals, 2000
The Seven Sexes, 1968
The Square Root of Man, 1968
The Human Angle, 1956
Of All Possible Worlds, 1955

Other books you might like:
Algis Budrys, *Blood and Burning*, 1978
Damon Knight, *One Side Laughing*, 1991
Eric Frank Russell, *Major Ingredients*, 2000
Robert Sheckley, *The Robot Who Looked Like Me*, 1982
Theodore Sturgeon, *Baby Is Three*, 1999

804

HARRY TURTLEDOVE, Editor
MARTIN H. GREENBERG, Co-Editor

The Best Alternate History Stories of the 20th Century

(New York: Ballantine Del Rey, 2001)

Story type: Anthology; Alternate History
Subject(s): Short Stories; Alternate History

Summary: These 14 stories were chosen by the editors as the best tales using settings involving a history that diverged from our own. All of them were previously published elsewhere. The pivotal points involve the Civil War, World War II, the life of Mozart, the sinking of the *Titanic*, and others. Contributors include Ward Moore, Brad Linaweaver, Poul Anderson, Allen Steele, William Sanders, Larry Niven, and Greg Bear.

Other books by the same author:
Aftershocks, 2001
Darkness Descending, 2000
Sentry Peak, 2000
Down in the Bottomlands, 1999
Into the Darkness, 1999

Other books you might like:
A. Bertram Chandler, *Kelly Country*, 1983
Brad Linaweaver, *Moon of Ice*, 1988
Ward Moore, *Bring the Jubilee*, 1953
Jake Page, *Apacheria*, 1998
William Sanders, *The Wild Blue and Gray*, 1991

805

S.L. VIEHL

Shockball

(New York: Roc, 2001)

Story type: Space Opera
Series: Stardoc. Book 4
Subject(s): Aliens
Major character(s): Cherijo Torin, Doctor; Duncan Reever, Linguist; Hok, Alien
Time period(s): Indeterminate Future
Locale(s): Te Abanor, Planet—Imaginary

Summary: Cherijo and her husband, Duncan, are still on the run from the powerful man responsible for her bioengineering. They take refuge among a group of alien-human halfbreeds, but as part of that society they are caught up in the violent sports popular within that culture.

Other books by the same author:
Endurance, 2001
Beyond Varallan, 2000
Stardoc, 2000

Other books you might like:
Stephen L. Burns, *Flesh and Silver*, 1999
Stephen Leigh, *Dark Water's Embrace*, 1998
Murray Leinster, *The Med Series*, 1983
Pamela Sargent, *The Sudden Star*, 1979
James White, *The Galactic Gourmet*, 1992

806

AUGUSTE VILLIERS DE L'ISLE ADAM

Tomorrow's Eve

(Champaign: University of Illinois Press, 2001)

Story type: Literary
Subject(s): Artificial Intelligence
Major character(s): Thomas Edison, Inventor, Historical Figure; Lord Ewald, Nobleman; Hadaly, Android
Time period(s): 19th century
Locale(s): New York, New York; France

Summary: Thomas Edison and an aristocrat pool their resources to conduct a scientific experiment. They create an android woman named Hadaly, who mimics human life with some success, but who is fatally flawed by her own recognition that she can never be truly human. This was the author's only science fiction novel, published originally in France in 1886 as *L'Eve Future*.

Where it's reviewed:
Science Fiction Chronicle, August 2001, page 39

Other books you might like:
Richard Bowker, *Replica*, 1987
Edmund Cooper, *Deadly Image*, 1958
Richard Cowper, *Profundis*, 1979
Rick DeMarinis, *A Lovely Monster*, 1975
Stephen Fine, *Molly Dear*, 1988

807

VERNOR VINGE

The Collected Stories of Vernor Vinge

(New York: Tor, 2001)

Story type: Collection
Subject(s): Short Stories

Summary: The 17 stories in this collection are the complete short SF of this popular writer. They were originally published between 1965 and 2000, with one story original to the book. There are a wide variety of themes and moods, including humor and suspense, but for the most part they are adventures in outer space, on other planets, or in other times.

Where it's reviewed:
Science Fiction Chronicle, December 2001, page 45

Other books by the same author:
A Deepness in the Sky, 1999
A Fire upon the Deep, 1992
Across Realtime, 1991
Tatja Grimm's World, 1987
Marooned in Realtime, 1986

Other books you might like:
Poul Anderson, *Alight in the Void*, 1991
Stephen Baxter, *Manifold: Space*, 2001
Joe Haldeman, *Vietnam and Other Alien Worlds*, 1993
Alexander Jablokov, *Nimbus*, 1993
Alastair Reynolds, *Revelation Space*, 2000

808

PETER WATTS

Maelstrom

(New York: Tor, 2001)

Story type: Disaster
Subject(s): Computers
Major character(s): Achilles Desjardins, Computer Expert; Lenie Clarke, Survivor; Ken Lubin, Military Personnel
Time period(s): Indeterminate Future
Locale(s): At Sea; United States

Summary: Following a cataclysmic series of events that leave millions homeless, a young woman thought dead returns to the land seeking vengeance on those who wished to kill her. The worldwide computer network has been compromised and poses a threat to civilization. This is a sequel to *Starfish*.

Where it's reviewed:
Booklist, October 15, 2001, page 387
Locus, December 2001, page 62
Publishers Weekly, September 24, 2001, page 74

Other books by the same author:
Starfish, 1999

Other books you might like:
Catherine Asaro, *The Veiled Web*, 1999
John Brunner, *Shockwave Rider*, 1975
Michael Crichton, *The Terminal Man*, 1972
Christopher Hodder-Williams, *Fistful of Digits*, 1968
Douglas R. Mason, *Matrix*, 1970

809

DAVID WEBER
JOHN RINGO, Co-Author

March to the Sea

(New York: Baen, 2001)

Story type: Military
Series: March. Book 2
Subject(s): Space Colonies
Major character(s): Prince Roger MacClintock, Nobleman, Military Personnel; Eva Kosutic, Military Personnel; Adib Julian, Military Personnel
Time period(s): Indeterminate Future
Locale(s): Marduk, Planet—Imaginary

Summary: A stranded contingent of professional soldiers and the untested but brilliant young nobleman whom they serve attempt to survive on a primitive world in the middle of a rash of wars and conquests. For their own protection, they are forced to take sides and become a pivotal force in shaping the planet's future.

Where it's reviewed:
Booklist, July 2001, page 1993
Library Journal, August 2001, page 171

Other books by the same author:
Ashes of Victory, 2000
The Apocalypse Troll, 1999
More than Honor, 1998
The War God's Own, 1998
In Enemy Hands, 1997

Other books you might like:
Lois McMaster Bujold, *The Warrior's Apprentice*, 1986
Chris Bunch, *Firemask*, 2000
Michael Collins, *The Planets of Death*, 1970
Andre Norton, *Star Soldiers*, 2001
Joel Rosenberg, *Not for Glory*, 1988

810

KEN WHARTON

Divine Intervention

(New York: Ace, 2001)

Story type: Space Colony
Subject(s): Space Colonies
Major character(s): Drew Randall, Handicapped; Alex Channing, Government Official
Time period(s): Indeterminate Future
Locale(s): Mandala, Planet—Imaginary

Summary: Mandala has a small but very tight group of colonists who were cut off from contact with the rest of humanity for over a century and who have developed a very distinct religious philosophy. When a new ship full of sleeping colonists approaches, a complement larger than the existing colony, some parties decide to prevent them from ever landing. This is a first novel.

Other books you might like:
Poul Anderson, *The Day of Their Return*, 1975
Michael Bishop, *Stolen Faces*, 1977
Mary Caraker, *The Snows of Jaspre*, 1989
Charles L. Harness, *Redworld*, 1986
Kathryn Lance, *Pandora's Children*, 1986

811

CONNIE WILLIS, Editor
SHEILA WILLIAMS, Co-Editor

A Woman's Liberation

(New York: Warner Aspect, 2001)

Story type: Anthology
Subject(s): Short Stories; Women

Summary: These ten short stories, all previously published, deal with women and their roles in society. The contributors include Ursula K. Le Guin, Nancy Kress, Octavia Butler, Sarah Zettel, Pat Murphy, Anne McCaffrey, and others.

Where it's reviewed:
Publishers Weekly, July 30, 2001, page 66

Other books by the same author:
To Say Nothing of the Dog, 1998
The Bellwether, 1996
Remake, 1995
Impossible Things, 1994
The Doomsday Book, 1992

Other books you might like:
Margaret Atwood, *The Handmaid's Tale*, 1985

Octavia Butler, *Kindred*, 1979
Suzette Haden Elgin, *Earthsong*, 1994
Ursula K. Le Guin, *The Left Hand of Darkness*, 1969
Joanna Russ, *The Female Man*, 1975

812

TIMOTHY ZAHN

Angelmass

(New York: Tor, 2001)

Story type: Space Colony; Space Opera
Subject(s): Scientific Experiments; Space Travel
Major character(s): Jereko Kosta, Spy; Chandris Lalasha, Criminal; Arkin Forsythe, Government Official
Time period(s): Indeterminate Future
Locale(s): Outer Space; Seraph, Planet—Imaginary; Lorelei, Planet—Imaginary

Summary: The planets of the Empyrean harvest what they believe to be particles of essential good and use them to ensure that their political leaders remain honest and ethical. The Pax is a larger coalition of worlds which plans to invade and ''save'' the Empyreans from what they term an alien invasion. A spy for the Pax makes a scientific discovery that indicates both parties are wrong.

Where it's reviewed:
Analog, March 2002, page 134
Booklist, September 15, 2001, page 201
Publishers Weekly, October 1, 2001, page 43

Other books by the same author:
The Icarus Hunt, 1999
Conqueror's Legacy, 1996
The Last Command, 1995
Distant Friends, 1992
Spinneret, 1985

Other books you might like:
Poul Anderson, *Ensign Flandry*, 1966
Lois McMaster Bujold, *Cetaganda*, 1996
C.J. Cherryh, *The Kif Strike Back*, 1986
Alastair Reynolds, *Revelation Space*, 2000
Dan Simmons, *The Rise of Endymion*, 1997

813

JOHN ZAKOUR
LAWRENCE GANEM, Co-Author

The Plutonium Blonde

(New York: DAW, 2001)

Story type: Humor; Mystery
Subject(s): Humor; Technology
Major character(s): Zachary Nixon Johnson, Detective—Private; BB Star, Businesswoman; HARV, Artificial Intelligence
Time period(s): 2050s (2057)
Locale(s): New Frisco, California

Summary: Zachary Johnson is the last private eye on Earth and he's been hired by the CEO of the world's biggest corporation to track down a renegade android built as her exact duplicate. The catch is that the android is stronger than a hundred men, and smarter than any mere human, to say nothing of the other parties who want to make sure they find the android first. This humorous pastiche of the tough detective story with a futuristic setting is a first novel for both authors.

Where it's reviewed:
Locus, December 2001, page 33

Other books you might like:
Douglas Adams, *The Long Dark Tea-Time of the Soul*, 1988
Lloyd Biggle, *Silence Is Deadly*, 1977
Ron Goulart, *Big Bang*, 1982
Keith Hartman, *Gumshoe Gorilla*, 2001
William F. Nolan, *Space for Hire*, 1971

814

ROBERT ZUBRIN

First Landing

(New York: Ace, 2001)

Story type: Hard Science Fiction; Space Colony
Subject(s): Mars
Major character(s): Rebecca Sherman, Scientist, Astronaut; Kevin McGee, Historian, Astronaut; Andrew Townsend, Military Personnel (colonel), Astronaut
Time period(s): 2010s (2011-2012)
Locale(s): Mars

Summary: The first expedition to Mars runs into technical and political problems. After successfully dealing with a crisis and landing, the astronauts discover not all of them will be able to return to Earth. They establish a self-sustaining artificial ecology for part of their party, while the remaining crew members try to prevent the authorities on Earth from destroying them in orbit. This is a first novel.

Where it's reviewed:
Analog, December 2001, page 134

Other books you might like:
Ben Bova, *Mars*, 1992
Arthur C. Clarke, *The Sands of Mars*, 1952
Kenneth F. Gantz, *Not in Solitude*, 1959
Geoffrey A. Landis, *Mars Crossing*, 2000
Paul J. McAuley, *Red Dust*, 1994

Historical Fiction in Review
by
Daniel S. Burt

If there was no block-busting, paradigm-shifting historical novel published in the second half of 2001, there are still plenty to choose from in a robust and respectable crop of accomplished and ambitious historical titles. Historical fiction continues to attract both literary and genre authors. Such major literary figures as Isabel Allende, William Kennedy, Mario Vargas Llosa, John Vernon, and William T. Vollmann have written historical novels reviewed here. Historical novel stalwarts such as Gillian Bradshaw, Bernard Cornwell, Ken Follett, Sue Harrison, Elmer Kelton, David Nevin, and Judith Tarr are also represented. Most significant for the future and the continuing vitality of the genre is the debut of a number of fine historical novelists such as Charmaine Craig, Christine Balint, Geraldine Brooks, India Edghill, Glen David Gold, Nora Hague, Mardi McConnochie, and Katie Roiphe. All the major subgenres of historical fiction—fictional biography, historical mystery, and historical fantasy—are well represented, and the list includes several accomplished follow-ups to heralded debut efforts. Perhaps the most controversial novel published in 2001 is an historical novel, Alice Randall's *The Wind Done Gone*, the imaginative repossession of Margaret Mitchell's classic historical *Gone with the Wind.* Published after a judge's initial injunction (requested by Margaret Mitchell's estate) was overturned, the novel raised a number of intriguing questions regarding the extent to which a copyrighted story and characters can enter the collective consciousness and, therefore, the public domain.

Selection Criteria

More than any other fictional genre, it is critical to define exactly what constitutes an historical novel. The appeal of the past for the writer is a constant in all novels, with the exception of science fiction set in the future or fantasy novels set in an imagined, alternative world outside historical time. Yet not all novels set in the past are truly historical. Central to any workable definition of historical fiction is the degree to which the writer attempts not to recall the past but to recreate it. In some cases the time frame, setting, and customs of a novel's era are merely incidental to its action and characterization. In other cases period details function as little more than a colorful backdrop for characters and situations that could just as easily be played out in a different era with little alteration. So-called historical ''costume dramas'' could, to a greater or lesser degree, work as well with a change of costume in a different place and time. The novels we can identify as historical attempt much more than incidental surface details or interchangeable historical eras. What justifies a designation as an historical novel is the writer's attempt at providing an accurate and believable representation of a particular historical era. The writer of historical fiction shares with the historian an attempted truthful depiction of past events, lives, and customs. In historical fiction, the past itself becomes as much a subject for the novelist as the characters and action.

Most of us use the phrase ''historical novel'' casually, never really needing an exact definition to make ourselves undersstood. We just know it when we see it. This listing, however, requires a set of criteria to determine what's in and what's out. Otherwise the list has no boundaries. If the working definition of historical fiction is too loose, every novel set in a period before the present qualifies, and nearly every novel becomes an historical novel immediately upon publication. If the definition is so strict that only books set in a time before the author's birth, for example, make the cut, then countless works that critics, readers, librarians, and the authors themselves think of as historical novels would be excluded.

My challenge, therefore, was to fashion a definition or set of criteria flexible enough to include novels that passed what can be regarded as the litmus test for historical fiction: Did the author use his or her imagination—and often quite a bit of research—to evoke another earlier time? Walter Scott, who is credited with ''inventing'' the English historical novel during the early nineteenth century, provided a useful criterion in the subtitle of *Waverley: Tis Sixty Years Since*, the story of Scottish life at the time of the Jacobite Rebellion of 1745. What is unique and distinctive about the so- called historical novel is its attempt to imagine a distant period of time before the novelist's lifetime. Scott's sixty-year span (the same, incidentally, used by Tolstoy in *War and Peace*) between a novel's composition and its imagined era offers an arbitrary but useful means to distinguish between the personal, remembered past and the created historical past. The distance of two generations, or nearly a lifetime, provides a necessary span for the past to emerge as history and forces the writer to rely on more than recollection to uncover the patterns and textures of the past. I have, therefore, adopted Scott's formula but adjusted it to fifty years, including those books in which the significant portion of their plots is set in a period fifty years or more before the novel was written.

Because a rigid application of this fifty-year rule might disqualify quite a few books intended by their authors, and regarded by their readers, to be historical novels, another test has been applied to books written about more recent eras: Did the author use actual historical figures and events while setting out to recreate a specific, rather than a general or incidental, historical period? It is, of course, risky to speculate about a writer's intention. Nevertheless, it is possible to detect when a book conforms to what most would consider a central preoccupation of the historical novel. This may be achieved by looking at the book's approach, its use of actual historical figures, and its emphasis on a distinctive time and place that enhances the reader's knowledge of past lives, events, and customs. By this test, Mario Vargas Llosa's *The Feast of the Goat*, which falls short in much of its coverage of the fifty-year barrier, is included because its obvious attempt to portray the historical Dominican Republic dictator Rafael Trujillo justifies its inclusion here.

I have tried to apply these criteria for the historical novel as a guide, not as an inflexible rule, and have allowed some exceptions when warranted by special circumstances. I hope I have been able to anticipate what most readers would consider historical novels, but I recognize that I may have overlooked some worthy representations of the past in the interest of dealing with a manageable list of titles. Finally, not every title in the Western, historical mystery, or historical romance genres has been included to avoid unnecessary duplication with the other sections of this book. I have included those novels that share characteristics with another genre—whether fantasy, Western, mystery, or romance—that seem to put the strongest emphasis on historical interest, detail, and accuracy.

Historical Fiction in the Second Half of 2001

Choosing among the novels collected in this volume of *What Do I Read Next?*, fans of the historical novel can visit virtually every conceivable historical era from prehistory through ancient Greek and Roman civilizations, the Medieval, Elizabethan, Georgian, Regency, and Victorian periods in England, and throughout American history. They may also enjoy most of the expected subgenres: sea stories, family sagas, historical mysteries, and fictional biographies.

High points among the novels selected include the launch of a number of promising series, including a medieval adventure series by master storyteller Bernard Cornwell (*The Archer's Tale*), an American Revolution series by Edward Cline (*Jack Frake*), and Alexander Fullerton's nautical series (*The Blooding of the Guns*). A couple of popular series were brought to a conclusion in the books reviewed here: Sue Harrison's *Call Down the Stars* and Rosalind Miles' *The Child of the Holy Grail*. The listing also includes the initial installments of several historical mystery series: T.F. Banks' Regency detective series (*The Thief-Taker*), David Donachie's Napoleonic seagoing mystery series (*The Devil's Own Luck* and *The Dying Trade*), Rhys Bowen's Irish immigrant series (*Murphy's Law*), and Troy Soos' non-baseball Americana series (*Island of Tears*). After acclaimed initial efforts, several writers present their follow-ups: Tracy Chevalier's *Falling Angel*, Simon Hawke's *The Slaying of the Shrew*, and Bill Mesce's *Officer of the Court*. Finally, the list includes, sadly, the presumed final efforts of a number of writers who have recently died. They include Terry Johnston's *Turn the Stars Upside Down*, Gary Jennings' *Aztec Blood*, Morris L. West's *The Last Confession*, and Mario Puzo's *The Family*.

Historical mysteries continue to dominate, the single largest subcategory represented. There is detection going on from Ancient Greece (Edward Cline's *Murder at the Panionic Games*) to Ancient Rome (Mary Reed and Eric Meyer's *Three for a Letter* and John Maddox Roberts' *Nobody Loves a Centurion*), through Europe during the Middle Ages (Margaret Frazer's *The Clerk's Tale*, C.L. Grace's *Saintly Murder*, Kate Sedley's *The Goldsmith's Daughter* and *The Weaver's Inheritance*, and Peter Tremayne's *Act of Mercy*), the Elizabethan era (Fiona Buckley's *Queen of Ambition* and Kathy Lynn Emerson's *Face Down Before the Rebel Hooves*), and the Georgian and Victorian periods (Bruce Alexander's *Smuggler's Moon* and David Dickinson's *Goodnight, Sweet Prince*). Some mysteries take place in America during the Civil War (Miriam Grace Monfredo's *Brothers of Cain*, Owen Parry's *Call Each River Jordan*, and Michael Kilian's *The Ironclad Alibi*) and others use various locales throughout the twentieth century (John R. Hayes' *Catskill*, Craig Holden's *The Jazz Bird*, Robert Skinner's *Pale Shadow*, and Charles Todd's *Watchers of Time*).

Several historical mystery series feature intriguing literary sleuths, including Jane Austen (Stephanie Barron's *Jane and the Prisoner of Wool House*), Edgar Allan Poe (Harold Schechter's *The Hum Bug*), Ambrose Bierce (Oakley Hall's *Ambrose Bierce and the Death of Kings*), and Shakespeare (Simon Hawke's *The Slaying of the Shrew*). Another features an unusual historical sleuth, Ulysses S. Grant, who appears in Jeffrey Marks' *The Ambush of My Name*. Several historical mysteries feature interesting pairings: Arthur Conan Doyle and Lewis Carroll in Roberta Rogow's *The Problem of the Surly Servant*, a French chief inspector and the head of the Gestapo in occupied France in J. Robert Janes' *Kaleidoscope*, and Sherlock Holmes and G.K. Chesterton's Father Brown in Stephen Kendrick's *Night Watch*. Indeed, Holmes seems omnipresent, appearing as a character or providing the inspiration in no fewer than four other novels (Carole Nelson Douglas' *Chapel Noir*, Michael Kurland's *The Great Game*, Larry Millett's *Sherlock Holmes and the Secret Alliance*, and Gerard Williams' *Dr. Mortimer and the Aldgate Mystery*). The game continues to be afoot.

Another major subcategory of historical fiction, fictional biography, was equally well-represented in the second half of 2001. A wide cast of historical personages are portrayed at full-length or at significant moments during their lives. They include the the Biblical David in India Edghill's *The Queenmaker*, Russian writer Dostoyevsky in Leonid Tsypkin's *Summer in Baden-Baden*, Lewis Carroll in Katie Roiphe's *Still She Haunts Me*, American Indians Jack Spaniard (in Robert J. Conley's *Spanish Jack*) and Crazy Horse (in Terry Johnston's *Turn the Stars Upside Down*), American explorer John Wesley Powell in John Vernon's *The Last Canyon*, the Borgias in Mario Puzo's *The Family*, Parisian architect Baron Haussmann in Paul LaFarge's *Haussmann, or, The Distinction*, Dominican Republic dictator Rafael Trujillo in Mario Vargas Llosa's *The Feast of the Goat*, Giordano Bruno in Morris L. West's *The Last Confession*, and ornithologist and artist John James Audubon in John Gregory Browns *Audubons Watch*. Artists are featured in several novels here, including Mary Cassatt in Harriet Scott Chessman's *Lydia Cassatt Reading the Morning Paper*, Oskar Kokoschka in Susan M. Dodd's *The Silent Woman*, J.M.W. Turner in James Wilson's *The Dark Clue*, and Renaissance artist Artemisia Gentileschi in Susan Vreelands *The Passion of Artemisia*.

A distinguished group of historical figures make appearances in several novels, including George Armstrong Custer in Michelle Black's *An Uncommon Enemy*; Queen Victoria's dysfunctional family in David Dickinson's *Goodnight, Sweet Prince*; Justinian and Theodora in Mary Reed and Eric Mayer's *Three for a Letter*; Mozart, Casanova, and the Marquis De Sade in Anthony J. Rudel's *Imagining Don Giovanni*; and Charles Dickens in Jeff Rackham's *The Rag & Bone Shop*.

Several novels are built around little known historical figures or on actual historical events. These include Per Olov Enquist's *The Royal Physician's Visit* about the remarkable figure of Johann Struensee in Denmark during the 1760s; Mary Bullitt, General Henry Atkinson, and the Sauk chief Black Hawk during the Black Hawk Wars in Micaela Gilchrist's *The Good Journey*; the obscure Jamestown leader, Samuel Argall, in William T. Vollmann's *Argall*; mountain man Joseph Antoine Janis in William Tremblay's *The June Rise*; Turkish activist Halide Edib in Frances Kazan's *Halide's Gift*; and woman clipper ship captain Mary Patten in Douglas Kelley's *The Captain's Wife*. Other books in this category include female secret agents during World War II in Ken Follett's *Jackdaws*; notorious London murderers Edith Thompson and Frederick Bywater in Jill Dawson's *Fred & Edie*; the disastrous Franklin Polar Expedition in Elizabeth McGregor's *The Ice Child*; the Cathar heresy in Charmaine Craig's *The Good Men*; plague in the seventeenth century in Geraldine Brooks' *Year of Wonders*; the World War I naval Battle of Jutland in Alexander Fullerton's *The Blooding of the Guns*; the Hindenburg airship disaster in Henning Boetius' *The Phoenix*; and Cleveland's "Scandal of the Century," the George Remus murder case, in Craig Holden's *The Jazz Bird*.

The popular subject of World War II is frequently explored with varying focal points: at home, at the front, and in the shadowy world of espionage. Also prevalent is the topic of slavery, which is handled in very different ways by Alice Randall in *The Wind Done Gone*, Marly Youmans in *The Wolf Pit*, and in the intense verse novel *Bloodlines* by Fred D'Aguiar.

Oddities and originality are in evidence as well, particularly in the rediscovery of a modern Russian masterwork, Leonid Tsypkin's *Summer in Baden-Baden* and Glen David Gold's "explanation" of the death of President Warren G. Harding in a world of early twentieth century magic in *Carter Beats the Devil*. Other unique plots include the "solving" of several notorious actual mysteries in Max Allan Collins' Nathan Heller collection, *Kisses of Death*; the transplanting of the Bronte sisters to Australia in Mardi McConnochie's *Coldwater*; and the recycling of the protagonists of Wilkie Collins' thriller classic, *The Woman in White*, as investigators of the strange life of English painter J.M.W. Turner in James Wilson's *The Dark Clue*. All in all, a rich collection to instruct and entertain.

Recommendations

Here are my selections of the 20 most accomplished and interesting historical novels for the second half of 2001:

Isabel Allende, *Portrait in Sepia*

Geraldine Brooks, *Year of Wonders*

Tracy Chevalier, *Falling Angels*

Bernard Cornwell, *The Archers Tale*

Charmaine Craig, *The Good Men*

Susan M. Dodd, *The Silent Woman*

Marc Dugain, *The Officers' Ward*

Per Olov Enquist, *The Royal Physician's Visit*

Micaela Gilchrist, *The Good Journey*

William Kennedy, *Roscoe*

Paul LaFarge, *Haussmann, or, The Distinction*

Kanan Makiya, *The Rock*

David Nevin, *Treason*

Alice Randall, *The Wind Done Gone*

Leonid Tsypkin, *Summer in Baden-Baden*

Mario Vargas Llosa, *The Feast of the Goat*

John Vernon, *The Last Canyon*

William T. Vollmann, *Argall*

Susan Vreeland, *The Passion of Artemisia*

James Wilson, *The Dark Clue*

For More Information about Historical Fiction

Printed Sources

Adamson, Lynda G. *American Historical Fiction: An Annotated Guide to Novels for Adults and Young Adults.* Phoenix: Oryx Press, 1999.

Adamson, Lynda G. *World Historical Fiction: An Annotated Guide to Novels for Adults and Young Adults.* Phoenix: Oryx Press, 1999.

Burt, Daniel S. *What Historical Fiction Do I Read Next?* Detroit: Gale, 1997.

Burt, Daniel S. *The Biography Book.* Westport, CT: Oryx Press, 2001.

Hartman, Donald K. *Historical Figures in Fiction.* Phoenix: Oryx Press, 1994.

Electronic Sources

The Historical Novel Society (http//www. historicalnovelsociety.org). Includes articles, interviews, and reviews of historical novels.

Of Ages Past: The Online Magazine of Historical Fiction (http://www.angelfire.com/il/ofagespast/). Includes novel excerpts, short stories, articles, author profiles, and reviews.

Soon's Historical Fiction Site (http://uts.cc.utexas.edu/~soon/histfiction/). A rich source of information on the historical novel genre, including links to more specialized sites on particular authors and types of historical fiction.

Historical Titles

815

BRUCE ALEXANDER

Smuggler's Moon

(New York: Putnam, 2001)

Story type: Historical/Georgian; Mystery
Series: Sir John Fielding. Book 8
Subject(s): Mystery and Detective Stories; Detection; Smuggling
Major character(s): Sir John Fielding, Historical Figure, Judge (magistrate); Jeremy Proctor, Teenager, Orphan; Clarissa Roundtree, Servant, Writer
Time period(s): 1770s (1772)
Locale(s): London, England; Deal, England

Summary: The blind Bow Street magistrate Sir John Fielding and his teenage companion, Jeremy Proctor, are dispatched to the town of Deal in Kent, a notorious smuggling center, to investigate the conduct of the town's magistrate. When the magistrate is murdered, Sir John takes over and sets out to expose a smuggling ring. On hand for the adventures is Clarissa Roundtree, an aspiring writer who conceives of the first murder mystery based on the action.

Where it's reviewed:
Kirkus Reviews, September 1, 2001, page 1244
Library Journal, October 1, 2001, page 146
Publishers Weekly, October 1, 2001, page 41

Other books by the same author:
The Color of Death, 2000
Death of a Colonial, 1999
Jack, Knave and Fool, 1998
Person or Persons Unknown, 1997
Murder in Grub Street, 1995

Other books you might like:
T.F. Banks, *The Thief-Taker*, 2001
Stephanie Barron, *The Jane Austen Series*, 1996-
John Creasey, *The Masters of Bow Street*, 1974
Robert Lee Hall, *The Benjamin Franklin Series*, 1988-
Rosemary Stevens, *The Tainted Snuff Box*, 2001

816

CONRAD ALLEN

Murder on the Minnesota

(New York: St. Martin's Minotaur, 2002)

Story type: Historical/Edwardian; Mystery
Series: George Porter Dillman/Genevieve Masefield. Book 3
Subject(s): Mystery and Detective Stories; Crime and Criminals; Cruise Ships
Major character(s): George Porter Dillman, Detective—Private; Genevieve Masefield, Detective—Private; Rance Gilpatrick, Smuggler
Time period(s): 1900s
Locale(s): *Minnesota*, At Sea

Summary: Seagoing sleuths George Porter Dillman and Genevieve Masefield take on the Pacific Ocean in this installment of the shipboard historical mystery series set during the first decade of the 20th century. They set sail on a cruise bound for the Far East, keeping a close eye on suspected smuggler Rance Gilpatrick. When a missionary is murdered, their sleuthing skills are put to the test.

Where it's reviewed:
Kirkus Reviews, November 1, 2001, page 1516
Publishers Weekly, December 17, 2001, page 68

Other books by the same author:
Murder on the Mauretania, 2000
Murder on the Lusitania, 1999

Other books you might like:
Cynthia Bass, *Maiden Voyage*, 1993
Lawrence Block, *Death Cruise*, 1999
Michael Kilian, *Dance on a Sinking Ship*, 1988
Susan Sussman, *Cruising for Murder*, 2000
Peter Tremayne, *Act of Mercy*, 2001

817

ISABEL ALLENDE

Portrait in Sepia

(New York: HarperCollins, 2001)

Story type: Coming-of-Age
Subject(s): Family Relations; Childhood; Photography
Major character(s): Paulina del Valle, Grandparent (of Aurora); Aurora del Valle, Photographer
Time period(s): 19th century; 20th century
Locale(s): San Francisco, California; Chile

Summary: The sequel to Allende's *Daughter of Fortune* traces the coming-of-age of Aurora del Valle, born in San Francisco's Chinatown in the 1880s. She is raised by her formidable grandmother, Paulina del Valle, who is addicted to power and pastries. Paulina takes Aurora home to Chile where a complex extended family awaits. Aurora is married off early, but establishes an independent life in the relatively new art form of photography. Covering more than 50 years, the novel evokes both Gilded Age San Francisco and the complex history of Chile.

Where it's reviewed:
Booklist, September 1, 2001, page 3
Kirkus Reviews, August 15, 2001, page 1142
Library Journal, October 15, 2001, page 105
Publishers Weekly, July 16, 2001, page 164

Other books by the same author:
Daughter of Fortune, 1999
Paula, 1995
The Infinite Plan, 1993
Eva Luna, 1988
The House of the Spirits, 1985

Other books you might like:
John Gregory Brown, *Audubon's Watch*, 2001
Karen Joy Fowler, *Sister Noon*, 2001
Carlos Fuentes, *The Years with Laura Diaz*, 2001
Lalita Tademy, *Cane River*, 2001
Gelling Yan, *The Lost Daughter of Happiness*, 2001

818

POUL ANDERSON

Mother of Kings

(New York: Tor, 2001)

Story type: Historical/Fantasy
Subject(s): Paganism; Vikings
Major character(s): Gunnhild, Royalty; Eirik, Royalty
Time period(s): 10th century
Locale(s): Norway

Summary: Although with a considerable fantasy basis, this novel about 10th century Norway is detailed enough to be considered historical as well. The story looks at the career of the legendary Gunnhild, the mother of Norse kings. She schemes to marry Eirik and becomes the power behind the throne as the Vikings emerge to plunder Europe and beyond.

Where it's reviewed:
Publishers Weekly, September 10, 2001, page 67

Other books by the same author:
The King of Ys, 1996
The Shield of Time, 1990
After Doomsday, 1986
Guardians of Time, 1981
Conan the Rebel, 1980

Other books you might like:
Gillian Bradshaw, *The Wolf Hunt*, 2001
Ann Chamberlin, *The Merlin of the Oak Wood*, 2001
Judith Tarr, *Daughter of Lir*, 2001
Anna Lee Waldo, *Circle of Stars*, 2001
Barbara Wood, *Sacred Ground*, 2001

819

CHRISTINE BALINT

The Salt Letters

(New York: Norton, 2001)

Story type: Historical/Victorian
Subject(s): Sea Stories
Major character(s): Sarah Garnett, Immigrant
Time period(s): 1850s (1854)
Locale(s): Shropshire, England; At Sea

Summary: This stirring first novel is an imaginative and emotional animation of what life must have been like for a single woman on the long sea voyage from England to Australia in 1854. Sarah Garnett is forced to leave her Shropshire home for a new life in Australia. Confined below decks with the other unmarried women, she endures harsh, cramped conditions that push many passengers to the edge of madness and beyond. Sarah's solace is writing letters home and reflecting on the life she has abandoned and her uncertain future.

Where it's reviewed:
Booklist, May 15, 2001, page 1729
Kirkus Reviews, May 1, 2001, page 603
Library Journal, May 15, 2001, page 160
New York Times Book Review, August 26, 2001, page 14
Publishers Weekly, July 9, 2001, page 45

Other books you might like:
Tracy Chevalier, *Falling Angels*, 2001
Eleanor Dark, *Storm of Time*, 1950
Thomas Keneally, *The Playmaker*, 1987
Mardi McConnochie, *Coldwater*, 2001
Colleen McCullough, *Morgan's Run*, 2000

820

T.F. BANKS

The Thief-Taker

(New York: Delacorte, 2001)

Story type: Historical/Regency; Mystery
Series: Memoirs of a Bow Street Runner. Book 1
Subject(s): Mystery and Detective Stories
Major character(s): Henry Morton, Police Officer (constable); Arabella Malibrant, Actress

Time period(s): 1810s (1815)
Locale(s): London, England

Summary: This first volume of a projected historical mystery series introduces Bow Street constable Henry Morton. Morton is hired to investigate the suspicious death of a gentleman found in a hackney cab. His investigation, with the assistance of actress Arabella Malibrant, leads him on a colorful tour of Regency London, far from the usual fashionable locales of most Regency romances.

Where it's reviewed:
Booklist, September 1, 2001, page 55
Kirkus Reviews, August 1, 2001, page 1068
Publishers Weekly, September 10, 2001, page 64

Other books you might like:
Bruce Alexander, *The Sir John Fielding Series*, 1994-
Stephanie Barron, *The Jane Austen Series*, 1996-
Ross King, *Ex-Libris*, 2001
Kate Ross, *The Julian Kestrel Series*, 1993-1997
Rosemary Stevens, *The Beau Brummell Series*, 2000-

■821■

JILL BARNETT

Sentimental Journey

(New York: Pocket, 2001)

Story type: Historical/World War II
Subject(s): World War II; Romance
Major character(s): Kitty Kincaid, Captive; J.R. Cassidy, Military Personnel (American army officer); George ''Skip'' Inskip, Military Personnel (Royal Air Force), Pilot
Time period(s): 1940s
Locale(s): United States; England; Africa

Summary: Barnett's hardcover debut is a historical romance set during World War II that connects the lives of a number of characters in scenes ranging from the U.S. to England to North Africa. Kitty Kincaid is the daughter of a famous research scientist who is captured by the Nazis in French Morocco. J.R. Cassidy, the U.S. army officer who rescues her, falls for her. Meanwhile an RAF ace, Skip Inskip, finds himself attracted to an American barnstormer's daughter.

Where it's reviewed:
Booklist, July 2001, page 1976
Kirkus Reviews, July 1, 2001, page 900
Library Journal, August 2001, page 88
Publishers Weekly, July 12, 2001, page 51

Other books by the same author:
Carried Away, 1996
Imagine, 1995
Dreaming, 1994
Bewitching, 1993
The Heart's Haven, 1990

Other books you might like:
Alice Adams, *After the War*, 2000
Ann Howard Creel, *The Magic of Ordinary Days*, 2001
Jane Gardam, *The Flight of the Maidens*, 2001
James Reasoner, *Battle Lines*, 2001
Judith Saxton, *You Are My Sunshine*, 2000

■822■

STEPHANIE BARRON

Jane and the Prisoner of Wool House

(New York: Bantam, 2001)

Story type: Historical/Regency; Mystery
Series: Jane Austen. Number 6
Subject(s): Mystery and Detective Stories; Military Life; Sea Stories
Major character(s): Jane Austen, Historical Figure, Writer; Frank Austen, Historical Figure, Military Personnel (British naval officer); Tom Seagrave, Military Personnel (British naval captain)
Time period(s): 1800s (1807)
Locale(s): Portsmouth, England; Southampton, England

Summary: In the sixth of the author's inventive mysteries featuring novelist Jane Austen as sleuth, it is 1807, and Jane comes to the aid of her naval officer brother, Frank, to help clear the name of his friend, Captain Tom Seagrave, charged with killing a French officer who had already surrendered his ship. Jane seeks answers at Wool House where the French prisoners are held, but it is soon apparent that the case is far more complicated and that not only Seagrave's life is endangered.

Where it's reviewed:
Booklist, October 15, 2001, page 384
Kirkus Reviews, October 1, 2001, page 1393
Publishers Weekly, November 15, 2001, page 45

Other books by the same author:
Jane and the Stillroom Maid, 2000
Jane and the Genius of the Place, 1999
Jane and the Wandering Eye, 1998
Jane and the Man of the Cloth, 1997
Jane and the Unpleasantness at Scargrave Manor, 1996

Other books you might like:
T.F. Banks, *The Thief-Taker*, 2001
David Donachie, *The Devil's Own Luck*, 2001
William J. Palmer, *The Dons and Mr. Dickens*, 2000
Wilder Perkins, *Hoare and the Matter of Treason*, 2001
Rosemary Stevens, *The Tainted Snuff Box*, 2001

■823■

PAMELA RAFAEL BERKMAN

Her Infinite Variety

(New York: Scribner, 2001)

Story type: Historical/Elizabethan; Literary
Subject(s): Biography; Short Stories; Women
Major character(s): William Shakespeare, Historical Figure, Writer; Anne Hathaway, Historical Figure, Spouse (of Shakespeare)
Time period(s): 16th century
Locale(s): London, England; Stratford, England

Summary: Berkman provides ten episodes from Shakespeare's life and writing career connected by the theme of his relationships with the women in his life (or in his imagination). The stories follow the playwright from his early days in

Stratford and his passion for Anne Hathaway, through his London days and his creation of such powerful women as Titania, Ophelia, Juliet, and Lady Macbeth, and then his retirement and his relationship with his own daughter, Judith.

Where it's reviewed:
Kirkus Reviews, April 1, 2001, page 431
Publishers Weekly, May 15, 2001, page 18

Other books you might like:
Anthony Burgess, *Nothing Like the Sun*, 1964
Stephanie Cowell, *The Players*, 1997
John Mortimer, *Will Shakespeare*, 1977
Robert Nye, *The Late Mr. Shakespeare*, 1999
Robert Nye, *Mrs. Shakespeare*, 2000

824

MICHELLE BLACK

An Uncommon Enemy

(New York: Forge, 2001)

Story type: Historical/American West; Indian Wars
Subject(s): Indians of North America
Major character(s): George Armstrong Custer, Historical Figure, Military Personnel (lieutenant colonel); Eden Murdoch, Captive, Nurse (former); Brad Randall, Military Personnel
Time period(s): 1860s (1868)
Locale(s): Great Plains

Summary: During the Battle of the Washita in 1868, Lieutenant Colonel George Armstrong Custer and his Seventh Cavalry massacred a Cheyenne village. To justify his act, Custer needs corroboration that he was attacked and thinks he has found it in Eden Murdoch, a former Civil War nurse abducted by the Cheyenne and a witness to the battle. Eden, however, refuses to denounce the Indians, and Custer orders a subordinate, Brad Randall, to learn the truth about Eden's captivity.

Where it's reviewed:
Publishers Weekly, September 3, 2001, page 61

Other books by the same author:
River Come Down, 1996

Other books you might like:
Judy Alter, *Libbie*, 1994
Edwin P. Hoyt, *The Last Stand*, 1995
Andrew Huebner, *American by Blood*, 2000
Terry C. Johnston, *Turn the Stars Upside Down*, 2001
Robert Skimin, *The River and the Horseman*, 1999

825

JAMES CARLOS BLAKE

A World of Thieves

(New York: Morrow, 2002)

Story type: Historical/Roaring Twenties
Subject(s): Crime and Criminals
Major character(s): Sonny LaSalle, Criminal, Student—High School; John Isley Bonham, Police Officer
Time period(s): 1920s (1928)
Locale(s): Louisiana; Texas

Summary: This is a tragicomic cops and robbers tale set during the Twenties. Sonny LaSalle is enthralled by his criminal uncles and persuades them to take him on as a partner. On his first heist, Sonny is caught and inadvertently kills a rookie cop. Sentenced to the notorious Louisiana Angola prison, Sonny escapes to rejoin his uncles. Unbeknownst to the trio, the father of the dead cop is the relentless Deputy Sheriff John Isley Bonham, who intends to hunt Sonny down and terminate him with extreme prejudice. The chase is on throughout Texas in a series of alternately stirring and comic misadventures leading up to an operatic showdown.

Where it's reviewed:
Booklist, November 15, 2001, page 556
Publishers Weekly, October 22, 2001, page 42

Other books by the same author:
Wildwood Boys, 2000
Borderlands, 1999
In the Rogue Blood, 1997
The Friends of Pancho Villa, 1996
The Pistoleer, 1995

Other books you might like:
Peter Carey, *True History of the Kelly Gang*, 2000
Christopher Cook, *Robbers*, 2000
Stephen Hunter, *Pale Horse Coming*, 2001
William Kennedy, *Roscoe*, 2001
Larry McMurtry, *Pretty Boy Floyd*, 1994
Diana Ossana, co-author

826

MICHAEL BLAKE

The Holy Road

(New York: Villard, 2001)

Story type: Historical/American West; Indian Culture
Subject(s): Indians of North America
Major character(s): John Dunbar, Military Personnel (U.S. Army deserter), Warrior; Stands with a Fist, Spouse (of Dunbar), Captive (of Comanche)
Time period(s): 1870s (1874)
Locale(s): Great Plains

Summary: In this sequel to *Dances with Wolves*, it is 11 years after Lt. John Dunbar left the army to live with the Comanches. He has three children with his wife, Stands with a Fist, and is accepted as the full-fledged Comanche warrior Dances with Wolves, Dunbar must fight against a party of whites who kidnaps his wife and youngest child. Meanwhile, the novel widens its perspective from Dunbar's story to consider the fate of the Plains Indian under pressure by white settlers and the building of their "holy road," the railroad.

Where it's reviewed:
Booklist, July 2001, page 1947
Publishers Weekly, July 16, 2001, page 155

Other books by the same author:
Marching to Valhalla, 1996
Dances with Wolves, 1990

Other books you might like:
Louise Erdrich, *The Last Report on the Miracles at Little No Horse*, 2001
Terry C. Johnston, *Turn the Stars Upside Down*, 2001
Douglas C. Jones, *Gone the Dreams and the Dancing*, 1984
Douglas C. Jones, *Season of Yellow Leaf*, 1983
Vella Munn, *Cheyenne Summer*, 2001

827

MIKE BLAKELY

Moon Medicine

(New York: Forge, 2001)

Story type: Historical/American West; Adventure
Series: Plenty Man. Book 1
Subject(s): Indians of North America
Major character(s): Honore Greenwood, Adventurer; Kit Carson, Historical Figure, Scout; Ceran St. Vrain, Historical Figure, Trader
Time period(s): 1840s; 1920s (1927)
Locale(s): West

Summary: The novel features a return of a character Blakely introduced in his 1996 novel *Too Long at the Dance*, French adventurer Honore Greenwood, given the name ''Plenty Man'' by the Comanche. A fugitive from French justice, Greenwood has escaped into the Wild West of the 1840s where he finds himself at the center of the action in Indian fights, the Taos Rebellion, and the Mexican War, alongside such historical figures as Kit Carson, Ceran St. Vrain, and Charles and William Bent. Narrated by Greenwood in 1927 at the age of 99, the novel purports to be the first installment of a larger-than-life adventure career.

Where it's reviewed:
Publishers Weekly, July 30, 2001, page 60

Other books by the same author:
Summer of Pearls, 2000
Comanche Dawn, 1998
Vendetta Gold, 1998
Too Long at the Dance, 1996
Shortgrass Song, 1994

Other books you might like:
Michael Blake, *The Holy Road*, 2001
Peter Bowen, *Kelly and the Three-Toed Horse*, 2001
Max Crawford, *Lords of the Plain*, 1985
Elmer Kelton, *Badger Boy*, 2000
John Vernon, *The Last Canyon*, 2001

828

HENNING BOETIUS

The Phoenix

(New York: Doubleday, 2001)

Story type: Disaster; Historical/Depression Era
Subject(s): Suspense; Disasters
Major character(s): Birger Lund, Journalist; Edmund Boysen, Pilot
Time period(s): 1930s; 1940s (1937-1947)
Locale(s): United States

Summary: The author, a popular German writer, is the son of a survivor of the *Hindenburg* airship disaster in 1937, the subject for this intriguing thriller. Birger Lund, a passenger on the fatal flight across the Atlantic, survives but is presumed dead and he assumes the identity of one of the victims in order to begin a new life in America. He is haunted by the disaster and spends ten years searching for answers, a pursuit that leads him to Edmund Boysen, the man at the zeppelin's control and a Nazi sympathizer. Boysen helps Lund trace the connection between the *Hindenburg* disaster and Nazi politics.

Where it's reviewed:
Booklist, November 15, 2001, page 550
Library Journal, November 1, 2001, page 131
Publishers Weekly, October 8, 2001, page 40

Other books you might like:
Max Allan Collins, *The Hindenburg Murders*, 2000
John R. Hayes, *Catskill*, 2001
Stuart M. Kaminsky, *A Few Minutes Past Midnight*, 2001
Joseph Kanon, *The Good German*, 2001
Bill Mesce Jr., *Officer of the Court*, 2001

829

ALICE BORCHARDT

The Dragon Queen

(New York: Ballantine Del Rey, 2001)

Story type: Historical/Fantasy; Legend
Series: Tales of Guinevere. Book 1
Subject(s): Arthurian Legends; Legends; Druids
Major character(s): Guinevere, Royalty; Arthur, Ruler; Merlin, Wizard
Time period(s): Indeterminate Past
Locale(s): England

Summary: Fantasy writer Borchardt weighs in with yet another projected series concerning the Arthurian legend. Centering on Guinevere, this first volume gives her considerable magical powers and a principal opponent in the Druid Merlin, who wishes to prevent Guinevere's match with Arthur believing it to be a threat to his own power. Arthurian purists will no doubt demur, but others interested in a powerful female protagonist in a colorful setting will be charmed.

Where it's reviewed:
Publishers Weekly, October 1, 2001, page 42

Other books by the same author:
The Wolf King, 2001
Night of the Wolf, 1999
The Silver Wolf, 1998
Beguiled, 1997
Devoted, 1995

Other books you might like:
Bernard Cornwell, *The Warlord Chronicles*, 1996-1998
John Gloag, *Artorius Rex*, 1977
Rosalind Miles, *The Child of the Holy Grail*, 2001
Judith Tarr, *Kingdom of the Grail*, 2000
Jack Whyte, *Uther*, 2001

830

RHYS BOWEN

Murphy's Law

(New York: St. Martin's Minotaur, 2001)

Story type: Historical/Victorian; Mystery
Series: Molly Murphy. Book 1
Subject(s): Mystery and Detective Stories; Irish Americans
Major character(s): Molly Murphy, Fugitive, Detective—Amateur
Time period(s): 19th century
Locale(s): Ireland; Liverpool, England; New York, New York

Summary: The creator of the popular Constable Evans mysteries inaugurates a new historical mystery series featuring Irish immigrant Molly Murphy. Fleeing her homeland after killing a powerful landowner's son who tried to rape her, Molly travels in steerage to New York, where she runs afoul of a passenger who turns up dead on Ellis Island. Molly becomes the prime suspect, and she takes up the investigation to clear her name which sends her on a fascinating tour of 19th century New York City.

Where it's reviewed:
Booklist, August 2001, page 2095
Publishers Weekly, September 3, 2001, page 67

Other books by the same author:
The Constable Evans Series, 1999-

Other books you might like:
Frederick Busch, *The Night Inspector*, 1999
Jeanne M. Dams, *Green Grow the Victims*, 2001
Larry Millett, *Sherlock Holmes and the Secret Alliance*, 2001
Cynthia Peale, *Murder at Bertram's Bower*, 2001
Randall Silvis, *On Night's Shore*, 2001

831

GILLIAN BRADSHAW

The Wolf Hunt

(New York: Forge, 2001)

Story type: Historical/Medieval; Fantasy
Subject(s): Middle Ages; Knights and Knighthood; Werewolves
Major character(s): Marie Penthievre of Chalandrey, Religious (novice); Tiarnan of Talensac, Knight
Time period(s): 12th century
Locale(s): Normandy, France

Summary: Combining historical details and fantasy, Bradshaw constructs a gripping tale set during the Crusades. Marie Penthievre is a young novice who, after the death of her brother, becomes the ward of the Duke of Normandy. She falls in love with the mysterious knight Tiarnan of Talensac, who marries another. The marriage is unhappy and when Tiarnan disappears into a forest, his fate becomes connected with a clever wolf that becomes a pet at the duke's court. Marie guesses the connection between the wolf and her love and is determined to lift the curse and restore him to his former self.

Where it's reviewed:
Booklist, August 2001, page 2083
Kirkus Reviews, June 1, 2001, page 772
Library Journal, August 2001, page 158
Publishers Weekly, July 30, 2001, page 61

Other books by the same author:
The Sand-Reckoner, 2000
The Wrong Reflection, 2000
Horses of Heaven, 1991
Imperial Purple, 1988
The Bearkeeper's Daughter, 1987

Other books you might like:
Marion Zimmer Bradley, *Priestess of Avalon*, 2001
Diana L. Paxson, co-author
Evan S. Connell, *Deus lo Volt!*, 2000
Bernard Cornwell, *The Archer's Tale*, 2001
Michael A. Eisner, *The Crusader*, 2001
Rosalind Miles, *The Child of the Holy Grail*, 2001

832

GERALDINE BROOKS

Year of Wonders

(New York: Viking, 2001)

Story type: Historical/Seventeenth Century
Subject(s): Plague; Small Town Life
Major character(s): Anna Firth, Widow(er), Servant (maid); Michael Mompellion, Religious (vicar); Elinor Mompellion, Spouse (of Michael)
Time period(s): 17th century (1665-1666)
Locale(s): England

Summary: War correspondent Brooks' fictional debut is a masterful reconstruction of English village life during the plague of 1665. Events are described from the perspective of widow Anna Firth, the maid of vicar Michael Mompellion and his wife Elinor. When the plague strikes, the vicar convinces the villagers to voluntarily seal themselves off from the surrounding neighborhood. As the death toll increases, mob violence adds to the threat as individuals are accused of witchcraft and the cohesiveness of the community begins to dissolve. Brooks is skilled in establishing a believable historical backdrop and cultural details to fashion an often fascinating portrait of a plague-ridden village.

Where it's reviewed:
Kirkus Reviews, July 15, 2001, page 959
Library Journal, July 2001, page 120
New York Times Book Review, August 26, 2001, page 13
Publishers Weekly, June 25, 2001, page 43

Other books you might like:
Ann Benson, *The Burning Road*, 1999
Daniel Defoe, *A Journal of the Plague Year*, 1722
Michael Golding, *Simple Prayers*, 1994
Roberta Kalechofsky, *Bodmin, 1349*, 1988
Stewart O'Nan, *A Prayer for the Dying*, 1999

833

JOHN GREGORY BROWN

Audubon's Watch

(Boston: Houghton Mifflin, 2001)

Story type: Historical/Americana
Subject(s): Biography; Psychology
Major character(s): John James Audubon, Historical Figure, Scientist (ornithologist); Emile Gautreaux, Scientist (anatomist), Doctor; Myra Gautreaux, Spouse (of Emile)
Time period(s): 1820s; 1850s
Locale(s): New Orleans, Louisiana

Summary: This challenging novel, half biography, half fiction, centers on the life of America's great ornithologist John James Audubon. In the 1820s, he leaves his wife and family to embark on his life work identifying and drawing every bird species in America. On a Louisiana plantation, he meets Dr. Emile Gautreaux and his wife, Myra, who dies suddenly. Thirty years later Audubon summons Dr. Gautreaux to confess his secret connection with Myra, and Gautreaux has equal issues connecting him with the famous ornithologist. This is a haunting psychological novel that is both atmospheric and revealing.

Where it's reviewed:
Kirkus Reviews, August 1, 2001, page 1044
Library Journal, August 2001, page 158
New York Times Book Review, September 23, 2001, page 19
Publishers Weekly, August 6, 2001, page 58

Other books by the same author:
The Wrecked, Blessed Body of Shelton Lafleur, 1996
Decorations in a Ruined Cemetery, 1994

Other books you might like:
Lucy Kennedy, *Mr. Audubon's Lucy*, 1957
Paul LaFarge, *Haussmann, or The Distinction*, 2001
J.D. Landis, *Longing*, 2000
Jeff Rackham, *The Rag & Bone Shop*, 2001
Joanna Scott, *Arrogance*, 1990

834

FIONA BUCKLEY (Pseudonym of Valerie Anand)

Queen of Ambition

(New York: Scribner, 2001)

Story type: Historical/Elizabethan; Mystery
Series: Ursula Blanchard. Book 5
Subject(s): Mystery and Detective Stories; Kings, Queens, Rulers, etc.; College Life
Major character(s): Ursula Blanchard, Gentlewoman, Spy (espionage agent); Sir William Cecil, Historical Figure, Government Official; Elizabeth I, Historical Figure, Ruler (Queen of England)
Time period(s): 16th century (1564)
Locale(s): Cambridge, England

Summary: Ursula Blanchard, lady-in-waiting and espionage agent for Queen Elizabeth I, is dispatched to Cambridge University by the queen's secretary of state, Sir William Cecil, to make sure Elizabeth's Royal Progress to the university takes place without incident. Student unrest and sedition are suspected, and Ursula goes undercover working in a pie shop frequented by Cambridge students to root out a plot against the queen.

Where it's reviewed:
Booklist, November 1, 2001, page 462
Kirkus Reviews, October 15, 2001, page 1455
Publishers Weekly, November 12, 2001, page 38

Other books by the same author:
Queen's Ransom, 2000
To Ruin a Queen, 2000
The Doublet Affair, 1998
To Shield the Queen, 1997

Other books you might like:
Kathy Lynn Emerson, *The Susanna, Lady Appleton Series*, 1997-
Karen Harper, *The Elizabeth I Series*, 1999-
Simon Hawke, *The Shakespeare and Smythe Series*, 2000-
Edward Marston, *The Nicholas Bracewell Series*, 1988-
Sharan Newman, *The Catherine le Vendeur Series*, 1994-

835

BO CALDWELL

The Distant Land of My Father

(New York: Chronicle, 2001)

Story type: Historical/World War II
Subject(s): Fathers and Daughters; China; Family Relations
Major character(s): Anna Schoene, Young Woman; Joseph Schoene, Importer/Exporter, Parent (of Anna)
Time period(s): 20th century (1930s-1950s)
Locale(s): Shanghai, China; Pasadena, California

Summary: This novel traces the relationship between a father and his daughter, played out against a background of Chinese history. Joseph Schoene, the son of missionaries, is a businessman in Shanghai who sends his family back to the U.S. when the Japanese invade. He is imprisoned and tortured by both the Japanese and the Communists before being deported in 1954. On his return, father and daughter face the challenge of reconciliation.

Where it's reviewed:
Kirkus Reviews, August 15, 2001, page 1143
Library Journal, August 2001, page 158
Publishers Weekly, September 10, 2001, page 61

Other books you might like:
Nicholas Clifford, *The House of Memory*, 1994
Millicent Dillon, *Harry Gold*, 2000
Joanne Harris, *Five Quarters of the Orange*, 2001
Kazuo Ishiguro, *When We Were Orphans*, 2000
Ruthanne McCunn, *The Moon Pearl*, 2000

836

BARBARA CHERNE

Bella Donna

(Santa Barbara, California: Fifthian, 2001)

Story type: Historical/Renaissance; Mystery
Series: Renaissance Mystery
Subject(s): Mystery and Detective Stories; Cooks and Cooking
Major character(s): Bella, Gentlewoman; Giuditta, Cook
Time period(s): 15th century (1494)
Locale(s): Florence, Italy

Summary: In Renaissance-era Florence, the wife of a prominent gentleman dies under suspicious circumstances, and her sister-in-law, Bella, is charged with her murder. Her friend, Giuditta, the family's cook, tries to prove Bella's innocence and attempts to find the real killer. The novel provides a tour of Renaissance Tuscany, with the sleuth's culinary expertise flavoring the mix.

Where it's reviewed:
Library Journal, May 1, 2001, page 130
Publishers Weekly, May 21, 2001, page 78

Other books by the same author:
Looking Glass, 1986

Other books you might like:
Robert Elegant, *Bianca*, 2000
Elizabeth Eyre, *Poison for the Prince*, 1994
George Herman, *The Tears of the Madonna*, 1996
Judith Lennox, *The Italian Garden*, 1993
Sandra Shulman, *The Florentine*, 1973

837

HARRIET SCOTT CHESSMAN

Lydia Cassatt Reading the Morning Paper

(New York: Permanent Press and Seven Stories Press, 2001)

Story type: Historical/Victorian America
Subject(s): Sisters; Artists and Art; Diseases
Major character(s): Lydia Cassatt, Historical Figure; Mary Cassatt, Historical Figure, Artist (painter); Edgar Degas, Historical Figure, Artist (painter)
Time period(s): 1870s; 1880s
Locale(s): Paris, France

Summary: Using five paintings by Mary Cassatt of her older sister Lydia as inspiration, this lyrical and moving novel dramatizes the relationship between the Impressionist painter and bohemian and her more conservative sister. Lydia is dying of Bright's disease but poses for her sister when she is able, providing a contrary perspective to Mary's more outgoing, experimental lifestyle and her relationship with painter Edgar Degas. Mary's is an expansive life of possibilities; Lydia's a constricted life, but worthy to be memorialized in this fascinating tale.

Where it's reviewed:
Booklist, October 15, 2001, page 380
Kirkus Reviews, October 1, 2001, page 1380
Library Journal, October 15, 2001, page 105
Publishers Weekly, October 29, 2001, page 37

Other books by the same author:
Ohio Angels, 1999

Other books you might like:
Tracy Chevalier, *Girl with a Pearl Earring*, 1999
Peter Everett, *Bellocq's Women*, 2001
Joan King, *Impressionist*, 1983
Pierre La Mure, *Moulin Rouge*, 1950
Irving Stone, *Depth of Glory*, 1985

838

TRACY CHEVALIER

Falling Angels

(New York: Dutton, 2001)

Story type: Historical/Edwardian
Subject(s): Friendship; Social Classes
Major character(s): Maude Coleman, Child, Friend (of Lavinia); Lavinia Waterhouse, Friend (of Maude); Simon Field, Friend (of Lavinia and Maude), Worker
Time period(s): 1900s
Locale(s): England

Summary: Chevalier's follow-up to the best-selling *The Girl with a Pearl Earring* shifts from Vermeer to domestic life during the Edwardian period in the first decade of the 20th century. Maude Coleman and Lavinia Waterhouse, two girls who meet at a fashionable London cemetery the day after Queen Victoria's death, become fast friends, despite the differences in their social classes and their parents' opposition. Maude and Lavinia, along with a young gravedigger, Simon Field, provide the perspective on events occurring in the families that reflect the changes as the Victorian period gives way to the modern world.

Where it's reviewed:
Booklist, August 2001, page 2050
Publishers Weekly, July 30, 2001, page 56

Other books by the same author:
Girl with a Pearl Earring, 1999

Other books you might like:
Jill Dawson, *Fred & Edie*, 2001
James Fleming, *The Temple of Optimism*, 2000
Nora Hague, *Letters from an Age of Reason*, 2001
Sheri Holman, *The Dress Lodger*, 2000
Gillian Linscott, *The Perfect Daughter*, 2001

839

JILL CHURCHILL

Someone to Watch over Me

(New York: Morrow, 2001)

Story type: Mystery; Historical/Depression Era
Series: Grace & Favor. Book 3
Subject(s): Mystery and Detective Stories

Major character(s): Lily Brewster, Detective—Amateur, Heiress; Robert Brewster, Detective—Amateur, Heir; Jack Summer, Journalist
Time period(s): 1930s (1932)
Locale(s): Voorburg-on-Hudson, New York

Summary: This is the hardcover debut for Churchill's charming historical mystery series set during the Depression and featuring brother-and-sister sleuths, Lily and Robert Brewster. Penniless from the 1929 crash, they are living on their late uncle's Hudson River estate, Grace and Favor. When a long-dead body is discovered in an old icehouse, the pair take up the investigation, with a new body further complicating the situation. Meanwhile, the local editor, Jack Summer, is in Washington covering a veterans' gathering demanding government relief. Somehow, everything comes together in this mystery with a winning period atmosphere.

Where it's reviewed:
Booklist, September 1, 2001, page 56

Other books by the same author:
In the Still of the Night, 2000
Much Ado about Nothing, 2000
Anything Goes, 1999
The Merchant of Menace, 1999

Other books you might like:
Lauren Belfer, *City of Light*, 1999
John R. Hayes, *Catskill*, 2001
Lise McClendon, *One O'Clock Jump*, 2001
Annette Meyers, *Murder Me Now*, 2000
David Roberts, *The Bones of the Buried*, 2001

840

EDWARD CLINE

Sparrowhawk—Jack Frake

(San Francisco: MacAdam/Cage, 2001)

Story type: Historical/Georgian
Series: Sparrowhawk. Book 1
Subject(s): Smuggling
Major character(s): Jack Frake, Smuggler; Augustus Skelly, Revolutionary, Smuggler; Methuselah Redmagne, Revolutionary, Smuggler
Time period(s): 1740s
Locale(s): Cornwall, England

Summary: In the debut volume of a projected four-book series about the American Revolution, the time is the 1740s, and we are introduced to young Jack Frake in Georgian England. Jack's mentor, a kindly rector is killed, and Jack takes up with a group of social malcontents and smugglers led by Augustus Skelly and Methuselah Redmagne. Their "revolution" against oppressive British laws is meant to provide a context and precedent for the social reform sentiment that will grow in the American Colonies, where Jack heads at the end of the novel.

Where it's reviewed:
Kirkus Reviews, October 1, 2001, page 1381
Publishers Weekly, November 12, 2001, page 38

Other books by the same author:
Whisper the Guns, 1992
First Prize, 1988

Other books you might like:
Thomas Fleming, *Remember the Morning*, 1997
Ken Follett, *A Place Called Freedom*, 1995
Kate Hawks, *Watch by Moonlight*, 2001
Patrick McGrath, *Martha Peake*, 2000
Jeff Shaara, *Rise to Rebellion*, 2001

841

MAX ALLAN COLLINS

Kisses of Death

(Norfolk, Virginia: Crippen & Landru, 2001)

Story type: Historical/Roaring Twenties; Mystery
Series: Nathan Heller
Subject(s): Mystery and Detective Stories; Short Stories
Major character(s): Nathan Heller, Detective—Private
Time period(s): 20th century
Locale(s): Chicago, Illinois

Summary: Devilishly mixing fact and fiction, this collection featuring Chicago private eye Nathan Heller takes actual situations and in some cases real-life unsolved crimes and provides a plausible invented solution. In one novella-length case Marilyn Monroe needs Heller's protection during a wild press party. Other cases are the actual murder of actress Thelma Todd and the suspicious death of Eddie Gaedel, the only midget to play baseball in the major leagues. Fans of the series will have plenty to applaud; those new to the series have no better place to start.

Where it's reviewed:
Booklist, July 2001, page 1986
Publishers Weekly, June 25, 2001, page 54

Other books by the same author:
Angel in Black, 2001
The Hindenburg Murders, 2000
Majic Man, 1999
Flying Blind, 1998
Stolen Away, 1991

Other books you might like:
James Carlos Blake, *A World of Thieves*, 2002
Glen David Gold, *Carter Beats the Devil*, 2001
Ron Goulart, *The Groucho Marx Series*, 1998-
Stuart M. Kaminsky, *The Toby Peters Series*, 1977-
Robert Skinner, *Pale Shadow*, 2001

842

ROBERT J. CONLEY

Spanish Jack

(New York: St. Martin's Press, 2001)

Story type: Indian Culture
Subject(s): Biography; Indians of North America; Crime and Criminals
Major character(s): Jack Spaniard, Historical Figure, Indian (Chickamauga Cherokee)

Time period(s): 19th century
Locale(s): United States

Summary: Based on an actual historical figure, Conley's adventure-driven story documents the checkered career of Jack Spaniard, or Spanish Jack, a Chickamauga Cherokee, one of the faction who sided with the British during the American Revolution. When the Chickamauga are absorbed into the Cherokee Nation after the Trail of Tears, Spanish Jack remains defiant against the U.S. government and the Osage who killed his young wife. Conley traces Spanish Jack's violent trail across America.

Where it's reviewed:
Booklist, July 2001, page 1978
Kirkus Reviews, July 1, 2001, page 883
Publishers Weekly, July 30, 2001, page 61

Other books by the same author:
Cherokee Dragon, 2000
The Dark Way, 2000
Geronimo, an American Legend, 1994
Mountain Windsong, 1992
Colfax, 1989

Other books you might like:
Peter Carey, *True History of the Kelly Gang*, 2000
Don Coldsmith, *The Long Journey Home*, 2001
Terry C. Johnston, *Turn the Stars Upside Down*, 2001
Richard Slotkin, *The Return of Henry Starr*, 1988
James Welch, *Heart Song of Charging Elk*, 2000

843

BERNARD CORNWELL

The Archer's Tale

(New York: HarperCollins, 2001)

Story type: Historical/Medieval
Subject(s): Middle Ages; War
Major character(s): Thomas of Hookton, Student—College, Military Personnel; Sir Simon Jekyl, Nobleman, Cousin (of Thomas)
Time period(s): 14th century (1340s)
Locale(s): Dorset, England; France

Summary: The prolific and accomplished Cornwell launches what one can only hope will be a new historical series set during the Hundred Years' War. When his village and most of its inhabitants are destroyed in a raid, Thomas of Hookton, a gifted bowman and the bastard son of an eccentric Dorset priest, gives up his studies at Oxford to join the forces of Edward III against France. After Thomas' dying father reveals that the true purpose of the raid was the theft of a valuable family relic, Thomas agrees to retrieve it. As an archer in the English army, Thomas is on hand for the pivotal battle of Crecy and a showdown with the leader of the raid, Sir Simon Jekyl, his evil cousin. Cornwell is a master storyteller, and this is top-notch historical entertainment.

Where it's reviewed:
Booklist, August 2001, page 2050
Kirkus Reviews, August 1, 2001, page 1046
Library Journal, September 1, 2001, page 232
Publishers Weekly, August 6, 2001, page 58

Other books by the same author:
Stonehenge, 2000
The Arthurian Warlord Trilogy, 1996-1998
The Starbuck Chronicles, 1993-
Redcoat, 1988
The Richard Sharpe Series, 1981-

Other books you might like:
Arthur Conan Doyle, *The White Company*, 1891
Michael A. Eisner, *The Crusader*, 2001
Susanna Gregory, *A Bone of Contention*, 1997
Roberta Kalechofsky, *Bodmin, 1349*, 1988
Anne Powers, *Ride East! Ride West!*, 1947

844

CHARMAINE CRAIG

The Good Men

(New York: Riverhead, 2002)

Story type: Historical/Medieval
Subject(s): Religious Conflict; Middle Ages
Major character(s): Pierre Clergue, Religious (priest); Grazida Lizier, Teenager, Bastard Daughter; Bernard Gui, Religious (inquisitor)
Time period(s): 13th century; 14th century (1265-1322)
Locale(s): Montaillou, France

Summary: Based on medieval records the author turned up while doing research in history, this intriguing first novel reconstructs life in a French village during the 13th and 14th centuries. The story covers the rise of the heretical sect, the Cathars, and their suppression by the Inquisition. *The Good Men* focuses on rector Pierre Clergue, a sexually-obsessed religious whose affair with the 15-year-old bastard child of his brother, Grazida Lizier, prompts the Inquisitor Bernard Gui's vengeance.

Where it's reviewed:
Booklist, December 1, 2001, page 628
Kirkus Reviews, October 15, 2001, page 1443
New York Times Book Review, January 20, 2002, page 7
Publishers Weekly, November 26, 2001, page 39

Other books you might like:
Ann Benson, *The Burning Road*, 1999
Susann Cokal, *Mirabilis*, 2001
Cecelia Holland, *The Lords of Vaumartin*, 1988
Jeanne Kalogridis, *The Burning Times*, 2001
Morris L. West, *The Last Confession*, 2001

845

ANN HOWARD CREEL

The Magic of Ordinary Days

(New York: Viking, 2001)

Story type: Historical/World War II
Subject(s): World War II; Rural Life
Major character(s): Olivia Dunne, Young Woman; Ray Singleton, Farmer
Time period(s): 1940s (1944)
Locale(s): Colorado

Summary: Creel's adult novel debut is set on the homefront during World War II as Olivia Dunne, after becoming pregnant, agrees to an arranged marriage with a beet farmer, Ray Singleton. Olivia must adjust to rustic life, and the novel's plot accelerates when Olivia befriends two Japanese Americans being interned in Colorado.

Where it's reviewed:
Kirkus Reviews, May 15, 2001, page 678
Publishers Weekly, June 11, 2001, page 57

Other books by the same author:
Nowhere, Now Here, 2000
A Ceiling of Stars, 1999
Water at the Blue Earth, 1998

Other books you might like:
Jill Barnett, *Sentimental Journey*, 2001
Robb Forman Dew, *The Evidence Against Her*, 2001
Elsie Burch Donald, *Nashborough*, 2001
Jane Gardam, *The Flight of the Maidens*, 2001
David Guterson, *Snow Falling on Cedars*, 1994
Allen Morris Jones, *Last Year's River*, 2001

846

FRED D'AGUIAR

Bloodlines

(Woodstock, New York: Overlook, 2001)

Story type: Historical/American Civil War; Historical/Post-American Civil War
Subject(s): Slavery; Poetry; African Americans
Major character(s): Faith, Slave; Christy, Young Man
Time period(s): 19th century; 20th century
Locale(s): United States

Summary: D'Aguiar presents an often powerful verse novel about the corrosive effects of slavery during and after the Civil War period. Christy is a plantation owner's son who falls in love after raping the slave Faith. Together they try to reach freedom in the North but are stopped and separated, Faith dies in childbirth and Christy becomes a traveling fighter. Their story is recounted by their unnamed son.

Where it's reviewed:
Kirkus Reviews, May 15, 2001, page 679
Library Journal, July 2001, page 95
Publishers Weekly, July 23, 2001, page 78

Other books by the same author:
Feeding the Ghosts, 1999
Dear Future, 1996
The Longest Memory, 1994
Airy Hall, 1989

Other books you might like:
Joan Brady, *Theory of War*, 1993
Wesley Brown, *Darktown Strutters*, 1994
Anthony Burgess, *Byrne*, 1997
Ishmael Reed, *Flight to Canada*, 1976
Vikram Seth, *Golden Gate*, 1986

847

PHILIP DANZE

Conjuring Maud

(New York: GreyCore, 2001)

Story type: Historical/Victorian
Subject(s): Love; Africa
Major character(s): David Unger, Student; Maud King, Explorer
Time period(s): 19th century; 20th century
Locale(s): Africa; England

Summary: Danze's first novel describes the relationship between a young military student, David Unger, and an older explorer, free-spirit Maud King, who meet in the late 1800s in Colonial West Africa. The story follows David's career that includes participation in the Zulu Rebellion, befriending Gandhi, and training in both medicine and magic. At the core of his story is Maud, the liberated adventurer, who helps explain the romantic fascination Africa holds.

Where it's reviewed:
Booklist, September 1, 2001, page 49

Other books you might like:
Jill Dawson, *Fred & Edie*, 2001
Glen David Gold, *Carter Beats the Devil*, 2001
N.M. Kelby, *In the Company of Angels*, 2001
Robin Lippincott, *Our Arcadia*, 2001
Katie Roiphe, *Still She Haunts Me*, 2001

848

JILL DAWSON

Fred & Edie

(New York: Welcome Rain, 2001)

Story type: Historical/Roaring Twenties
Subject(s): Biography; Trials
Major character(s): Edith Thompson, Historical Figure, Lover (of Freddy); Frederick Bywaters, Historical Figure, Sailor (ship's steward); Percy Thompson, Historical Figure, Spouse (of Edith)
Time period(s): 1920s
Locale(s): London, England

Summary: The basis for this ingenious novel is the actual 1922 London trial of Edith Thompson and her young lover, Frederick Bywaters, for the murder of Edith's husband, Percy. Mixing newspaper accounts and letters, the novel reconstructs the psychology of Edith, who finds herself horrified by the events she premeditated yet faithful to her love for the murderer, Freddy. The result is a rich and nuanced portrait that effectively captures a fascinating figure and her era.

Where it's reviewed:
Booklist, September 1, 2001, page 49
Kirkus Reviews, July 1, 2001, page 885
Library Journal, August 2001, page 159
Publishers Weekly, August 20, 2001, page 53

Other books by the same author:
How Do I Look?, 1990

Other books you might like:
Tracy Chevalier, *Falling Angels*, 2001
Robb Forman Dew, *The Evidence Against Her*, 2001
Peter Everett, *Bellocq's Women*, 2001
Richard Marius, *An Affair of Honor*, 2001
Emma Tennant, *Sylvia and Ted*, 2001

849

FRANK DEFORD

The Other Adonis

(Naperville, Illinois: Sourcebook Landmark, 2001)

Story type: Historical/Fantasy; Historical/Seventeenth Century
Subject(s): Reincarnation
Major character(s): Floyd Buckingham, Publisher (magazine); Constance Rawlings, Businesswoman (financial analyst); Nina Winston, Doctor (psychiatrist)
Time period(s): 2000s; 17th century
Locale(s): New York, New York; Antwerp, Netherlands

Summary: Sports writer and commentator Deford has concocted an ingenious novel about reincarnation that shuttles between modern day New York and 17th century Europe. All is connected to Peter Paul Rubens' painting ''Venus and Adonis.'' Magazine publisher Floyd Buckingham and financial analyst Constance Rawlings both believe they are the reincarnations of the painting's subjects. Under hypnosis, they learn they were indeed the models for Rubens' work, but they were not whom they think.

Where it's reviewed:
Kirkus Reviews, August 1, 2001, page 1047
Library Journal, September 15, 2001, page 110
Publishers Weekly, September 10, 2001, page 59

Other books by the same author:
Love and Infamy, 1993
Casey on the Loose, 1989
Alex, the Life of a Child, 1983
The Owner, 1976
Cut 'n' Run, 1973

Other books you might like:
Vikram Chandra, *Red Earth and Pouring Rain*, 1995
Laurel Doud, *This Body*, 2000
Lois Duncan, *Gallows Hill*, 1987
Robert Goddard, *Caught in the Light*, 1999
Mollie Hardwick, *I Remember Love*, 1983

850

ROBB FORMAN DEW

The Evidence Against Her

(Boston: Little, Brown, 2001)

Story type: Historical/Americana
Subject(s): Small Town Life; Family Relations; Friendship
Major character(s): Lily Scofield, Cousin (of Warren), Spouse (of Robert); Warren Scofield, Spouse; Robert Butler, Spouse (of Lily)
Time period(s): 19th century; 20th century
Locale(s): Ohio

Summary: Three friends born in a small Ohio town on the same day in 1888 provide the subject for this exploration of family life. Lily and Warren Scofield are first cousins, and Robert Butler is a minister's son. The trio form an indissolvable bond until Lily marries Robert and Warren marries a young woman from outside of their tight social circle. Although reflecting the historical events of World War I and its aftermath, the emphasis here is on the minutely described daily interactions that reveal the emotional crosscurrents just beneath the surface of ordinary lives.

Where it's reviewed:
Booklist, July 2001, page 1949
Kirkus Reviews, August 1, 2001, page 1048
Library Journal, September 1, 2001, page 233
Publishers Weekly, July 30, 2001, page 59

Other books by the same author:
Fortunate Lives, 1992
The Time of Her Life, 1984
Dale Loves Sophie to Death, 1981

Other books you might like:
Kathleen Cambor, *In Sunlight, in a Beautiful Garden*, 2000
Ann Howard Creel, *The Magic of Ordinary Days*, 2001
Elsie Burch Donald, *Nashborough*, 2001
Helen Dunmore, *A Spell of Winter*, 2001
Sarah Stonich, *These Granite Islands*, 2001

851

DAVID DICKINSON

Goodnight, Sweet Prince

(New York: Carroll & Graf, 2002)

Story type: Historical/Victorian; Mystery
Subject(s): Mystery and Detective Stories; Kings, Queens, Rulers, etc.
Major character(s): Lord Francis Powerscourt, Detective—Private, Nobleman; Albert Victor, Royalty, Historical Figure; Edward, Prince of Wales, Historical Figure, Royalty
Time period(s): 1890s (1892)
Locale(s): London, England; Sandringham, England

Summary: Dickinson intriguingly takes the actual circumstances surrounding the British royal family in the 1890s and adds a murder mystery based on the sudden death of Victoria's dissolute grandson, Albert Victor, son of the equally dissolute Prince of Wales. Lord Francis Powerscourt is called in to investigate a blackmail scheme but when the young prince is found with his throat slit, it becomes a murder investigation, although the public is informed only that the prince has succumbed to influenza.

Where it's reviewed:
Kirkus Reviews, November 1, 2001, page 1518
Publishers Weekly, December 10, 2001, page 54

Other books by the same author:
The Earth Abideth, 1999

Other books you might like:
Robert Lee Hall, *The King Edward Plot*, 1980
Peter Lovesey, *The Bertie, Prince of Wales Series*, 1987-

Robert Perrin, *Jewels*, 1977
Francis Selwyn, *Sergeant Verity and the Blood Royal*, 1979
Deborah Woodworth, *Killing Gifts*, 2001

852

SUSAN M. DODD

The Silent Woman

(New York: Morrow, 2001)

Story type: Historical/World War I; Arts
Subject(s): Biography; Artists and Art; Psychology
Major character(s): Oskar Kokoschka, Historical Figure, Artist (painter); Alma Mahler, Historical Figure, Widow(er); Hulda, Servant
Time period(s): 1910s
Locale(s): Dresden, Germany

Summary: Incidents in the life of Austrian painter Oskar Kokoschka provide the springboard for this tale of passion and obsession. Kokoschka is in despair over his doomed love for Alma Mahler, widow of the famous composer Gustav Mahler, who has forsaken him. Wounded and shell-shocked during World War I, the artist comes to Dresden where he takes up with a servant girl, Hulda, whom he recruits to serve as lady's maid to Kokoschka's life-size doll stand-in for Alma Mahler.

Where it's reviewed:
Booklist, August 2001, page 2084
Library Journal, October 1, 2001, page 139

Other books by the same author:
O Careless Love, 1999
The Mourners' Bench, 1998
Mamaw, 1988
No Earthly Notion, 1986
Old Wives' Tales, 1984

Other books you might like:
Catherine Clement, *Martin and Hannah*, 2001
Sheldon Greene, *Burnt Umber*, 2001
J.D. Landis, *Longing*, 2000
Anthony J. Rudel, *Imagining Don Giovanni*, 2001
Emma Tennant, *Sylvia and Ted*, 2001

853

DAVID DONACHIE

The Devil's Own Luck

(Ithaca, New York: McBooks, 2001)

Story type: Historical/Georgian; Mystery
Series: Privateersman. Number 1
Subject(s): Mystery and Detective Stories; Sea Stories
Major character(s): Harry Ludlow, Detective—Amateur, Privateer; James Ludlow, Privateer
Time period(s): 1790s (1793)
Locale(s): *Magnanime*, At Sea

Summary: In the first of a series combining two popular genres—mystery and nautical adventure—Donachie introduces Harry Ludlow, a former Royal Navy officer who turns privateersman in 1793. Aboard the *Magnanime* along with his brother James, Harry is forced into the role of detective after James is accused of murdering a shipmate.

Where it's reviewed:
Publishers Weekly, September 17, 2001, page 59

Other books by the same author:
The Dying Trade, 2001 (Privateersman. Number 2)

Other books you might like:
Bruce Alexander, *Smuggler's Moon*, 2001
T.F. Banks, *The Thief-Taker*, 2001
Ross King, *Ex-Libris*, 2001
Wilder Perkins, *The Captain Bartholomew Hoare Series*, 1998-2001
Rosemary Stevens, *The Tainted Snuff Box*, 2001

854

DAVID DONACHIE

The Dying Trade

(Ithaca, New York: McBooks, 2001)

Story type: Historical/Georgian; Mystery
Series: Privateersman. Number 2
Subject(s): Mystery and Detective Stories; Sea Stories
Major character(s): Harry Ludlow, Detective—Amateur, Privateer; James Ludlow, Privateer
Time period(s): 1790s (1794)
Locale(s): Genoa, Italy

Summary: In the second nautical mystery featuring privateersman-sleuth Harry Ludlow, it is 1794, and Harry and his brother James arrive in Genoa, Italy, carrying a fortune in gold. The port city is a hotbed of intrigue and conspiracies and the brothers soon find themselves the target of professional assassins. Harry tries to discover who is responsible before it is too late.

Other books by the same author:
The Devil's Own Luck, 2001 (Privateersman. Number 1)

Other books you might like:
Tom Connery, *The Markham of the Marines Series*, 1999-
Allan Mallinson, *A Close Run Thing*, 1999
Patrick O'Brian, *The Aubrey-Maturin Series*, 1968-1999
Wilder Perkins, *The Captain Bartholomew Hoare Series*, 1998-2001
Richard Woodman, *The Privateersman*, 2001

855

ELSIE BURCH DONALD

Nashborough

(New York: HarperCollins, 2001)

Story type: Historical/Depression Era; Historical/World War II
Subject(s): Family Relations
Major character(s): Seneca Nash, Lawyer; Dartania Douglas Nash, Spouse (of Seneca)
Time period(s): 20th century (1920s-1950s)
Locale(s): Tennessee

Historical

Summary: This somewhat crowded family saga details the goings-on of two prominent Tennessee families, the Nashes and the Douglases, over a 30 year period. At the center of the drama is patriarch Seneca Nash and his free spirited wife, Dartania. Family relations reflect such historical changes as the Depression, World War II, and the burgeoning Civil Rights movement.

Where it's reviewed:
Kirkus Reviews, July 1, 2001, page 886

Other books you might like:
Richard Marius, *After the War*, 1992
Steve McGiffen, *Tennant's Rock*, 2001
Lalita Tademy, *Cane River*, 2001
Susan Thames, *I'll Be Home Late Tonight*, 1997
Mary Elizabeth Witherspoon, *The Morning Cool*, 1972

856

CAROLE NELSON DOUGLAS

Chapel Noir

(New York: Forge, 2001)

Story type: Historical/Victorian; Mystery
Series: Irene Adler. Number 5
Subject(s): Mystery and Detective Stories
Major character(s): Irene Adler, Detective—Amateur, Singer (opera); Penelope ''Nell'' Huxleigh, Companion (of Irene); Sherlock Holmes, Detective—Private
Time period(s): 1880s (1889)
Locale(s): Paris, France

Summary: After a long layoff, Sherlock Holmes' great love, Irene Adler, makes a welcome return in the fifth installment of this historical mystery series. The murder of several French prostitutes in a brothel frequented by British nobility bears a striking resemblance to London's Jack the Ripper killings. Irene, along with her straight-laced companion, Nell Huxleigh, takes up the investigation that leads them on a vivid tour of 19th century Paris. Sherlock makes a brief, but crucial appearance.

Where it's reviewed:
Kirkus Reviews, September 1, 2001, page 1247
Publishers Weekly, September 24, 2001, page 72

Other books by the same author:
Irene's Last Waltz, 1994
The Midnight Louie Series, 1992-
Irene at Large, 1992
Good Morning, Irene, 1991
Good Night, Mr. Holmes, 1990

Other books you might like:
Charlotte Carter, *Coq au Vin*, 1999
Jamyang Norbu, *Sherlock Holmes: The Missing Years*, 2001
Michael Kurland, *The Great Game*, 2001
Gillian Linscott, *The Perfect Daughter*, 2001
Anne Perry, *The Whitechapel Conspiracy*, 2001

857

MARC DUGAIN

The Officers' Ward

(New York: Soho, 2001)

Story type: Historical/World War I
Subject(s): War; World War I; Hospitals
Major character(s): Adrien Fournier, Military Personnel (French lieutenant)
Time period(s): 1910s
Locale(s): Paris, France

Summary: Winner of the French Prix des Libraires, Dugain's first novel is a moving exploration of the human cost of World War I. French officer Adrian Fournier is horribly wounded in the face on his first day at the front during the initial hours of the conflict. He will spend the rest of the war in a military hospital trying to come to terms with the fact that subsequent operations are unable to restore a human look to his hideously deformed face.

Where it's reviewed:
Kirkus Reviews, September 15, 2001, page 1313
New York Times Book Review, December 9, 2001, page 30
Publishers Weekly, September 24, 2001, page 63

Other books you might like:
Pat Barker, *Regeneration*, 1992
Sebastian Faulks, *Birdsong*, 1996
John Rolfe Gardiner, *Somewhere in France*, 1999
Mark Helprin, *A Soldier of the Great War*, 1994
Steve Weiner, *The Yellow Sailor*, 2001

858

INDIA EDGHILL

Queenmaker

(New York: St. Martin's Press, 2002)

Story type: Legend; Biblical Fiction
Subject(s): Biblical Fiction; Kings, Queens, Rulers, etc.
Major character(s): Michal, Historical Figure, Spouse (first wife of David); David, Historical Figure, Ruler; Saul, Historical Figure, Ruler
Time period(s): 10th century B.C.
Locale(s): Israel

Summary: The Old Testament story of David is imaginatively retold from the perspective of his first wife, Michal, the daughter of Saul. Married to the slayer of Goliath when she is only 13, Michal helps save David from the wrath of her jealous father and then eventually becomes David's favorite wife until he falls in love with Bathsheba. In the end, Michal devotes herself to grooming David and Bathsheba's son, Solomon, to rule. Biblical purists may be put off by David's portrayal as a conceited womanizer, but this is an often fascinating reanimation from a previously overlooked woman's perspective.

Where it's reviewed:
Kirkus Reviews, November 1, 2001, page 1518
Publishers Weekly, November 19, 2001, page 48

Other books you might like:
R.V. Cassill, *After Goliath*, 1985
Peter Danielson, *The Death of Kings*, 1994
Wallace Hamilton, *David at Olivet*, 1979
Stefan Heym, *The King David Report*, 1997
Grete Weil, *The Bride Price*, 1991

859

MICHAEL B. EDWARDS

Murder at the Panionic Games

(Chicago: Academy, 2001)

Story type: Historical/Ancient Greece; Mystery
Subject(s): Mystery and Detective Stories; Sports
Major character(s): Bias, Religious
Time period(s): 7th century B.C. (650 B.C.)
Locale(s): Priene, Greece

Summary: This engaging 7th century B.C.-era mystery is set in the Greek city-state of Priene during an athletic competition, the Panionic Games. Bias is a minor priest who is assisting at the opening ceremonies when one of the best athletes dies in his arms. Held responsible, Bias is charged with finding the actual killer. As the games progress, another athlete is killed in a chariot race. Are the deaths accidents or murders?

Other books you might like:
Anna Apostolou, *A Murder in Macedon*, 1997
Anna Apostolou, *A Murder in Thebes*, 1998
Gillian Bradshaw, *The Sand-Reckoner*, 2000
P.C. Doherty, *The House of Death*, 2001
Michael Curtis Ford, *The Ten Thousand*, 2001

860

MICHAEL A. EISNER

The Crusader

(New York: Doubleday, 2001)

Story type: Historical/Medieval
Subject(s): Middle Ages; Crusades; Religious Life
Major character(s): Francisco de Montcada, Knight; Brother Lucas, Religious
Time period(s): 13th century (1275)
Locale(s): Spain; Middle East

Summary: Eisner's intriguing and accomplished first novel is a richly-imagined adventure concerning a veteran Crusader, Francisco de Montcada, who is sent to a Spanish monastery allegedly because he is possessed by demons. Encouraged by Brother Lucas to tell the story of his adventures in the Holy Land, Francisco narrates a riveting tale of warfare and betrayal. This is an impressive debut that draws on evident solid research to animate its period.

Where it's reviewed:
Booklist, August 20, 2001, page 2085
Kirkus Reviews, August 1, 2001, page 1048
Publishers Weekly, September 10, 2001, page 58

Other books you might like:
Evan S. Connell, *Deus lo Volt!*, 2000
Cecelia Holland, *Jerusalem*, 1996
Frank X. Hurley, *The Crusader*, 1975
Zoe Oldenbourg, *The Heirs of the Kingdom*, 1971
Ronald Welch, *Knight Crusader*, 1979

861

KATHY LYNN EMERSON

Face Down Before Rebel Hooves

(New York: St. Martin's Minotaur, 2001)

Story type: Historical/Elizabethan; Mystery
Series: Susanna, Lady Appleton. Book 6
Subject(s): Mystery and Detective Stories; Detection; Politics
Major character(s): Lady Susanna Appleton, Widow(er), Detective—Amateur; Nick Baldwin, Gentleman, Lover (of Susanna); Sir Walter Pendennis, Nobleman
Time period(s): 16th century (1569)
Locale(s): England

Summary: The conspiracy to put Mary, Queen of Scots, on the English throne dominates the action and the suspense in this installment of the historical mystery series featuring sleuth Susanna, Lady Appleton. Susanna is recruited to foil a conspiracy against Queen Elizabeth, posing as the wife of her old friend Sir Walter Pendennis, and soon plot meets counterplot in a confusing suspense tangle. Nick Baldwin, Susanna's lover learns that her life is in jeopardy, and the race is on to save Susanna before her true identity is revealed to the conspirators.

Where it's reviewed:
Booklist, July 2001, page 1986
Publishers Weekly, July 9, 2001, page 51

Other books by the same author:
Face Down Beneath the Eleanor Cross, 2000
Face Down under the Wych Elm, 2000
Face Down Among the Winchester Geese, 1999
Face Down upon an Herbal, 1998
Face Down in the Marrow-Bone Pie, 1997

Other books you might like:
Fiona Buckley, *The Ursula Blanchard Series*, 1997-
Karen Harper, *The Elizabeth I Series*, 1999-
Edward Marston, *The Nicholas Bracewell Series*, 1988-
Ian Morson, *The William Falconer Series*, 1994-
Sharan Newman, *The Catherine le Vendeur Series*, 1994-

862

PER OLOV ENQUIST

The Royal Physician's Visit

(Woodstock, New York: Overlook, 2001)

Story type: Historical/Georgian
Subject(s): Kings, Queens, Rulers, etc.; Biography
Major character(s): Johann Friedrich Struensee, Doctor, Historical Figure; Christian VII, Historical Figure, Ruler (King of Denmark); Caroline Mathilde, Historical Figure, Spouse (consort of Christian VII)
Time period(s): 1760s
Locale(s): Copenhagen, Denmark

Historical

Summary: This intriguing historical novel documents one of the strangest episodes in Danish history, when Johann Friedrich Struensee, physician to King Christian VII, took control of the government and became the lover of Christian's queen, Caroline Mathilde. Struensee's reign is short-lived, and he is done in by a courtier who unjustly accuses him of having plotted to kill the king and has him executed. Enquist masterfully animates all the major players in this court drama for a convincing series of human portraits.

Where it's reviewed:
Booklist, November 1, 2001, page 459
Kirkus Reviews, October 15, 2001, page 1445
New York Times Book Review, November 18, 2001, page 74
Publishers Weekly, October 22, 2001, page 48

Other books by the same author:
Captain Nemo's Library, 1992
The Legionnaires, 1973

Other books you might like:
Noel de Vic Beamish, *The Unfortunate Queen Matilda*, 1971
Johannes Vilhelm Jensen, *The Fall of the King*, 1933
Norah Lofts, *The Lost Queen*, 1969
Edgar Maas, *The Queen's Physician*, 1948
Rose Tremain, *Music & Silence*, 2000

863

KEN FOLLETT

Jackdaws

(New York: Dutton, 2001)

Story type: Historical/World War II; Espionage
Subject(s): War; Women; Underground Resistance Movements
Major character(s): Felicity Clariet, Spy (British secret agent); Dieter Franck, Military Personnel (German major); Willi Weber, Military Personnel (German soldier)
Time period(s): 1940s (1944)
Locale(s): London, England; Normandy, France

Summary: Follett returns to his comfort zone—the World War II espionage thriller—in a rousing, suspenseful tale based on a true story. It is the eve of D-Day, and the Allies need to take out an important telephone exchange housed in a Normandy chateau. British secret agent Felicity Clariet is sent with a group of women agents to infiltrate the chateau as telephone operators and cleaners. Felicity and her team must contend with the brilliant German major Dieter Franck and the brutal commander of the chateau, Willi Weber, as the clock ticks down to the invasion.

Where it's reviewed:
Booklist, September 1, 2001, page 164
Kirkus Reviews, October 1, 2001, page 1382
Library Journal, October 15, 2001, page 106
Publishers Weekly, October 15, 2001, page 44

Other books by the same author:
Code to Zero, 2000
The Hammer of Eden, 1998
A Place Called Freedom, 1995
The Key to Rebecca, 1980
The Eye of the Needle, 1978

Other books you might like:
John Altman, *A Gathering of Spies*, 2000
Robert Daley, *Innocents Within*, 1999
Sebastian Faulks, *Charlotte Gray*, 1998
Alan Furst, *Kingdom of Shadows*, 2000
Robert Wilson, *The Company of Strangers*, 2001

864

WILLIAM R. FORSTCHEN

We Look Like Men of War

(New York: Forge, 2001)

Story type: Historical/American Civil War; Military
Subject(s): African Americans; Civil War; Slavery
Major character(s): Samuel Washburn, Slave (former), Military Personnel (Union soldier)
Time period(s): 1860s
Locale(s): United States

Summary: The often overlooked role of African American troops in the Civil War is dramatized by a history professor who has specialized in the subject. The author's expertise lends credibility to the background of this story about Samuel Washburn, a Kentucky slave who escapes to freedom and volunteers to serve in a Negro regiment. Battle action is glimpsed in the Wilderness campaign, at Fredericksburg, and in the novel's climax, at the horrifying Battle of the Crater in the Petersburg campaign.

Where it's reviewed:
Booklist, November 15, 2001, page 547
Publishers Weekly, October 22, 2001, page 47

Other books by the same author:
Down to the Sea, 2000
Catseye, 1999
Prometheus, 1999
Never Sound Retreat, 1998
1945, 1996 (Newt Gingrich, co-author)

Other books you might like:
Allen B. Ballard, *Where I'm Bound*, 2000
J.P. Sinclair Lewis, *Buffalo Gordon*, 2001
Owen Parry, *Call Each River Jordan*, 2001
Richard Slotkin, *The Crater*, 1980
Tom Willard, *The Black Sabre Chronicles*, 1996-

865

MARGARET FRAZER

The Clerk's Tale

(New York: Berkley Prime Crime, 2002)

Story type: Historical/Medieval; Mystery
Series: Dame Frevisse. Book 11
Subject(s): Mystery and Detective Stories; Middle Ages
Major character(s): Dame Frevisse, Religious (nun), Detective—Amateur
Time period(s): 15th century (1446)
Locale(s): England

Summary: *The Clerk's Tale* is the latest volume in Frazer's well-researched and written medieval mystery series featuring nun and amateur sleuth Dame Frevisse. A man's death in the cloister garden of St. Mary's Priory sets the detective wheels in motion. The victim was involved in an inheritance dispute, and Dame Frevisse is convinced that the murderer is one of the many parties in the suit. The trick is which one and how to prove it. Frazer is exact and detailed in using the medieval background to help develop her case.

Where it's reviewed:
Kirkus Reviews, December 1, 2001, page 1647
Publishers Weekly, December 17, 2001, page 68

Other books by the same author:
The Squire's Tale, 2000
The Reeve's Tale, 1999
The Prioress' Tale, 1997
The Boy's Tale, 1995
The Bishop's Tale, 1994

Other books you might like:
Alys Clare, *Ashes of Elements*, 2001
Edward Marston, *The Domesday Book Series*, 1993-
Ian Morson, *The William Falconer Series*, 1994-
Ellis Peters, *The Brother Cadfael Series*, 1977-1994
Peter Tremayne, *The Sister Fidelma Series*, 1994-

866

ALEXANDER FULLERTON

The Blooding of the Guns

(New York: Soho, 2001)

Story type: Historical/World War I; Military
Series: Everard Naval. Number 1
Subject(s): Sea Stories; War
Major character(s): Nicholas Everard, Military Personnel (British naval officer); David Everard, Military Personnel (British naval officer); Hugh Everard, Military Personnel (British naval officer)
Time period(s): 1910s (1916)
Locale(s): *Lanyard*, At Sea; England

Summary: The first volume of the British author's acclaimed 20th century naval series looks at the most important naval engagement of the Great War, the 1916 Battle of Jutland, in which 150 British ships battled a German fleet of 100 vessels. The action is reported from the perspective of members of the naval Everard family—Nicholas, aboard a destroyer; his brother David, on a cruiser; and their Uncle Hugh, a battleship captain. More for the hard-core military action devotee rather than the leisurely Patrick O'Brian reader, Fullerton's novel is exact and convincing in detailing the battle strategy and the ways and means of the World War I British Navy.

Where it's reviewed:
Kirkus Reviews, October 1, 2001, page 1382
Publishers Weekly, October 22, 2001, page 47

Other books by the same author:
The Publisher, 1971
The Executives, 1970
Lionheart, 1965
The Waiting Game, 1961

Other books you might like:
Catherine Gavin, *The Devil in Harbour*, 1968
Max Hennessy, *The Lion at Sea*, 1978
Richard Hough, *Buller's Victory*, 1984
Robert H. Pilpel, *To the Honor of the Fleet*, 1971
Douglas Reeman, *The White Guns*, 1989

867

DAVID FULMER

Chasing the Devil's Tail

(Scottsdale, Arizona: Poisoned Pen, 2001)

Story type: Historical/Americana; Mystery
Subject(s): Mystery and Detective Stories; Music and Musicians
Major character(s): Valentin St. Cyr, Detective—Private; Tom Anderson, Political Figure, Historical Figure; Buddy Bolden, Historical Figure, Musician
Time period(s): 1900s (1907)
Locale(s): New Orleans, Louisiana

Summary: New Orlean's fabled red-light district, Storyville, during the Ragtime era is the intriguing setting for what promises to be a successful historical mystery series featuring Creole private detective Valentin St. Cyr. He is hired by political boss Tom Anderson to investigate the murders of two prostitutes. The case gives Fulmer the opportunity to present life in Storyville with appearances by such historical figures as jazz legends Buddy Bolden and Jelly Roll Morton, photographer E.J. Bellocq, and the notorious madam Lulu White.

Where it's reviewed:
Kirkus Reviews, October 1, 2001, page 1395
Library Journal, November 1, 2001, page 135
Publishers Weekly, October 15, 2001, page 49

Other books you might like:
Peter Everett, *Bellocq's Women*, 2001
Barbara Hambly, *The Benjamin January Series*, 1997-
Josh Russell, *Yellow Jack*, 1999
Robert Skinner, *Pale Shadow*, 2001
Penn Williamson, *Mortal Sins*, 2000

868

DIANA GABALDON

The Fiery Cross

(New York: Delacorte, 2001)

Story type: Time Travel; Historical/Colonial America
Series: Outlander. Book 5
Subject(s): Time Travel
Major character(s): Claire Fraser, Time Traveler, Doctor; Jamie Fraser, Spouse (of Claire)
Time period(s): 1770s (1771)
Locale(s): North Carolina, American Colonies

Summary: The long-anticipated fifth installment of the author's popular romantic time-travel Outlander series is set in colonial North Carolina, where Claire and Jamie Fraser have journeyed from Scotland to build a new life together. Claire, a modern woman who has journeyed back in time, is aware of the American Revolution that is to come, an insight that adds to the complications as old enemies and new challenges conspire to test the Frasers.

Other books by the same author:
Drums of Autumn, 1997
Voyager, 1994
Dragonfly in Amber, 1992
Outlander, 1991

Other books you might like:
Betty Brooks, *Jade*, 1997
LeGrand Cannon, *Look to the Mountain*, 1942
Frank Deford, *The Other Adonis*, 2001
Inglis Fletcher, *The Scotswoman*, 1954
R. Garcia y Robertson, *Knight Errant*, 2001

869

R. GARCIA Y ROBERTSON

Knight Errant

(New York: Forge, 2001)

Story type: Historical/Fantasy; Time Travel
Subject(s): Time Travel; Witches and Witchcraft
Major character(s): Robyn Stafford, Time Traveler; Edward Plantagenet, Nobleman; Henry VI, Historical Figure, Ruler (King of England)
Time period(s): 15th century (1459)
Locale(s): England

Summary: In this romantic time travel story, Robyn Stafford is transported to 15th century England during the time of the Wars of the Roses. Hiking near the Welsh border, she encounters a young man on horseback with a sword and wearing chain mail who thinks it is 1459. The man is Edward Plantagenet, Earl of March, and Robyn, smitten, follows him back in time to an involvement with witches, Henry VI, and the turmoil of the times.

Where it's reviewed:
Booklist, October 1, 2001, page 305
Publishers Weekly, October 15, 2001, page 46

Other books by the same author:
American Woman, 1998
The Spiral Dance, 1991

Other books you might like:
Michael Crichton, *Timeline*, 1999
Frank Deford, *The Other Adonis*, 2001
Jude Deveraux, *A Knight in Shining Armor*, 1989
Diana Gabaldon, *The Fiery Cross*, 2001
Linda Lael Miller, *Knights*, 1996

870

JANE GARDAM

The Flight of the Maidens

(New York: Carroll & Graf, 2001)

Story type: Historical/World War II
Subject(s): World War II; Friendship; Women
Major character(s): Hetty Fallowes, Student—College; Una Vane, Student—College; Lieselotte Klein, Student—College
Time period(s): 1940s (1946)
Locale(s): Yorkshire, England

Summary: Yorkshire, England, in 1946 is the setting for this novel that delivers a convincing portrait of postwar English life. The story centers on three Yorkshire girls—Hetty Fallowes, Una Vane, and Lieselotte Klein—during the summer before they leave for universities. Hetty tries to escape from her battle-scarred father and possessive mother; Una asserts her independence in a love affair with a young man from the wrong side of the tracks; and Lieselotte, a Jewish refugee, must deal with survivor guilt.

Where it's reviewed:
Booklist, July 2001, page 1979
Library Journal, May 15, 2001, page 160
Publishers Weekly, July 9, 2001, page 46

Other books by the same author:
The Queen of the Tambourine, 1995
Through the Dolls' House Door, 1987
Crusoe's Daughter, 1986
The Hollow Land, 1981
The Sidmouth Letters, 1980

Other books you might like:
Alice Adams, *After the War*, 2000
Jill Barnett, *Sentimental Journey*, 2001
Ann Howard Creel, *The Magic of Ordinary Days*, 2001
Michele Roberts, *The Looking Glass*, 2001
Paullina Simons, *The Bronze Horseman*, 2001

871

KATHLEEN O'NEAL GEAR
W. MICHAEL GEAR, Co-Author

Bone Walker

(New York: Forge, 2001)

Story type: Mystery; Indian Culture
Series: Anasazi Mystery. Book III
Subject(s): Mystery and Detective Stories; Pre-Columbian History; Archaeology
Major character(s): Dusty Stewart, Archaeologist; Maureen Cole, Anthropologist (physical); Browser, Indian (Anasazi), Chieftain
Time period(s): 1990s; 13th century
Locale(s): Chaco Canyon, New Mexico

Summary: The third installment of the authors' intriguing dual mysteries interweaves present action with tribal life among the Anasazi in the 13th century. Warrior/chieftain Browser tries to put an end to inter-clan conflict by confronting the witch Two Hearts. Meanwhile, the FBI brings in archaeologists Dusty Stewart and Maureen Cole to investigate a homicide in the same setting, but in the 1990s, with all the evidence pointing toward witchcraft. The two plots intersect frequently, and the novel's historical background and forensic details are expertly done.

Where it's reviewed:
Kirkus Reviews, November 15, 2001, page 1582

Publishers Weekly, December 3, 2001, page 43

Other books by the same author:
Dark Inheritance, 2001
The Summoning God, 2000
The Visitant, 1999
Thin Moon and Cold Mist, 1995
The First North Americans Series, 1990-

Other books you might like:
Sherry Garland, *India*, 1995
Sue Harrison, *Call Down the Stars*, 2001
Harriet Peck Taylor, *Secrets of the Stone*, 2000
Anna Lee Waldo, *Circle of Stars*, 2001
Barbara Wood, *Sacred Ground*, 2001

872

ANNA GILBERT

A Morning in Eden

(New York: St. Martin's Minotaur, 2001)

Story type: Historical/World War I; Gothic
Subject(s): Small Town Life
Major character(s): Lorna Kent, Orphan; Adam Ushart, Teacher
Time period(s): 1910s (1919)
Locale(s): Canterlow, England

Summary: Set in the aftermath of World War I, this atmospheric, modern Gothic concerns Lorna Kent who forsakes city life for the presumed quiet of the English countryside. Lorna will soon discover that the seemingly tranquil village of Canterlow hides a number of secrets. She is attracted to the local headmaster Adam Ushart, but someone seems bent on preventing them from getting married.

Where it's reviewed:
Booklist, November 15, 2001, page 556
Kirkus Reviews, November 1, 2001, page 1518
Publishers Weekly, October 29, 2001, page 34

Other books by the same author:
A Hint of Witchcraft, 2000
The Treachery of Time, 1996
The Wedding Guest, 1993
A Walk in the Woods, 1990
The Long Shadow, 1984

Other books you might like:
Wendell Berry, *A Place on Earth*, 2001
Maeve Brennan, *The Rose Garden*, 2000
Anna Cheska, *Moving to the Country*, 2001
Ian McEwan, *Atonement*, 2002
Betsy Tobin, *Bone House*, 2000

873

MICAELA GILCHRIST

The Good Journey

(New York: Simon & Schuster, 2001)

Story type: Historical/American West; Indian Culture
Subject(s): Biography; Indians of North America
Major character(s): Mary Bullitt, Historical Figure, Spouse (of Henry Atkinson); Henry Atkinson, Historical Figure, Military Personnel (general); Black Hawk, Historical Figure, Chieftain (Sauk)
Time period(s): 19th century (1820s-1840s)
Locale(s): Jefferson Barracks, Missouri; West; Louisville, Kentucky

Summary: This impressive debut novel is based on the real-life letters and diaries of Mary Bullitt, the Louisville belle who in 1820 marries General Henry Atkinson and accompanies him to his western frontier outpost on the Mississippi. Atkinson is charged with regulating the Indians and must face down the Sauk chief, Black Hawk, with whom he has a personal vendetta. The story of Mary's life is revealed in diary entries and flashbacks that probe the hidden secrets of the characters.

Where it's reviewed:
Publishers Weekly, July 16, 2001, page 159

Other books you might like:
August Derleth, *Wind over Wisconsin*, 1938
Iola Fuller, *The Shining Trail*, 1943
Philip Kimball, *Liar's Moon*, 1999
T.V. Olsen, *Summer of the Drums*, 1972
T.V. Olsen, *There Was a Season*, 1972

874

GLEN DAVID GOLD

Carter Beats the Devil

(New York: Hyperion, 2001)

Story type: Historical/Roaring Twenties; Mystery
Subject(s): Magicians; Mystery and Detective Stories
Major character(s): Charlie Carter, Magician (aka Carter the Great); Warren G. Harding, Historical Figure, Political Figure
Time period(s): 1920s
Locale(s): San Francisco, California

Summary: Gold's impressive debut is an inventive story set during the 1920s in San Francisco and concerns Charlie Carter, who becomes the famous magician Carter the Great. Filled with period details, the novel's action accelerates when Carter is held responsible for the mysterious death of President Warren G. Harding shortly after he participates in one of Carter's performances.

Where it's reviewed:
Booklist, July 2001, page 1948
New York Times Book Review, September 30, 2001, page 25
Publishers Weekly, September 3, 2001, page 59

Other books you might like:
Kevin Baker, *Dreamland*, 1999
Martin Blinder, *Fluke*, 1999
Carrie Brown, *The Hatbox Baby*, 2000
Michael Chabon, *The Amazing Adventures of Kavalier & Clay*, 2000
E.L. Doctorow, *Ragtime*, 1975

875

C.L. GRACE (Pseudonym of P.C. Doherty)

Saintly Murders

(New York: St. Martin's Minotaur, 2001)

Story type: Historical/Medieval; Mystery
Series: Kathryn Swinbrooke. Book 5
Subject(s): Mystery and Detective Stories; Middle Ages
Major character(s): Kathryn Swinbrooke, Doctor, Detective—Amateur; Colum Murtagh, Government Official (Master of the King's Horse), Lover (of Kathryn)
Time period(s): 15th century (1472)
Locale(s): Canterbury, England

Summary: Along with her lover, Colum Murtagh, Master of the King's Horse, Kathryn investigates an infestation of rats in the city of Canterbury and the strange death of a pious friar with some secrets in his past. Kathryn must use her expertise in medieval forensics to piece together a multilayered mystery that draws on historical details from the recently concluded Wars of the Roses, as well as daily life and customs.

Where it's reviewed:
Booklist, August 2001, page 2097
Kirkus Reviews, July 15, 2001, page 982
Publishers Weekly, September 10, 2001, page 59

Other books by the same author:
The Book of Shadows, 1996 (Kathryn Swinbrooke. Book 4)
The Merchant of Death, 1995 (Kathryn Swinbrooke. Book 3)
The Eye of God, 1994 (Kathryn Swinbrooke. Book 2)
A Shrine of Murders, 1993 (Kathryn Swinbrooke. Book 1)

Other books you might like:
Alys Clare, *Ashes of the Elements*, 2001
Kathy Lynn Emerson, *Face Down Before Rebel Hooves*, 2001
Roberta Gellis, *A Personal Devil*, 2001
Michael Jecks, *The Boy-Bishop's Glovemaker*, 2001
Kate Sedley, *The Weaver's Inheritance*, 2001

876

ANDREW GREIG

The Clouds Above

(New York: Simon & Schuster, 2001)

Story type: Historical/World War II
Subject(s): War; Love
Major character(s): Len Westbourne, Military Personnel (RAF), Pilot; Stella Gardam, Military Personnel (radar trainee)
Time period(s): 1940s
Locale(s): England

Summary: Based on the diary kept by the author's mother of her wartime affair with an RAF pilot, this often moving depiction of the Battle of Britain takes the form of the romance between flyer Len Westbourne and radar trainee Stella Gardam. Despite class differences, the pair falls in love, and their relationship is grounded in the day-to-day details of Britain's finest hour.

Where it's reviewed:
Booklist, August 2001, page 2086
Kirkus Reviews, August 1, 2001, page 1051
Publishers Weekly, September 10, 2001, page 59

Other books you might like:
Jill Barnett, *Sentimental Journey*, 2001
Elizabeth Bowen, *The Heat of the Day*, 1948
Henry Green, *Caught*, 1970
Michael Ondaatje, *The English Patient*, 1992
Paullina Simons, *The Bronze Horseman*, 2001

877

NORA HAGUE

Letters from an Age of Reason

(New York: Morrow, 2001)

Story type: Historical/Victorian; Historical/Americana
Subject(s): Racial Conflict; Race Relations
Major character(s): Arabella Leeds, Gentlewoman; Aubrey ''Bree'' Paxton, Servant
Time period(s): 1860s
Locale(s): New Orleans, Louisiana; London, England; France

Summary: This challenging first novel concerns the 19th century love affair between a young Northern woman, Arabella Leeds, from an upper-class family, and Aubrey ''Bree'' Paxton, a light-skinned house slave of a prominent New Orleans family. Told in dual journal entries, their star-crossed love is played out against an historical background of the American Civil War and life in Europe. Packed with modern issues of race, feminism, and multiculturalism, the novel is less convincing in its reconstruction of the past than in its many ideas.

Where it's reviewed:
Booklist, July 2001, page 1950
Kirkus Reviews, July 15, 2001, page 965
Publishers Weekly, August 6, 2001, page 60

Other books you might like:
Sandra Dallas, *Alice's Tulips*, 2000
Emma Donoghue, *Slammerkin*, 2001
Helen Humphreys, *Afterimage*, 2000
Steve McGiffen, *Tennant's Rock*, 2001
Richard Rayner, *The Cloud Sketcher*, 2001

878

OAKLEY HALL

Ambrose Bierce and the Death of Kings

(New York: Viking, 2001)

Story type: Mystery; Historical/Americana
Series: Ambrose Bierce. Book 2
Subject(s): Mystery and Detective Stories
Major character(s): Ambrose Bierce, Historical Figure, Writer; Tom Redmond, Journalist (reporter), Companion (of Bierce)
Time period(s): 1890s (1890-1891)
Locale(s): San Francisco, California

Summary: In the second of Hall's entertaining historical mysteries featuring the actual journalist and writer Ambrose Bierce, it is 1890 and King Lalakaua of Hawaii is dying in his San Francisco hotel room, while courtiers jockey for position in the inheritance scramble. Princess Leileiha, who is betrothed to a potential heir to the throne, disappears, prompting Bierce and his companion, Tom Redmond, to search for the missing princess on a captivating tour of Gilded Age San Francisco.

Where it's reviewed:
Booklist, September 1, 2001, page 56
Kirkus Reviews, August 1, 2001, page 1069
Publishers Weekly, September 17, 2001, page 57

Other books by the same author:
Ambrose Bierce and the Queen of Spades, 1998
Warlock, 1996
Apaches, 1986
The Children of the Sun, 1983
The Bad Lands, 1978

Other books you might like:
Ellen Charbonneau, *Waltzing in Ragtime*, 1996
Dianne Day, *The Fremont Jones Series*, 1995-
Carlos Fuentes, *The Old Gringo*, 1986
Cecelia Holland, *Pacific Street*, 1992
Daniel Lynch, *Yellow*, 1992

879

SUE HARRISON

Call Down the Stars

(New York: Morrow, 2001)

Story type: Historical/Pre-history
Series: Storyteller Trilogy. Book 3
Subject(s): Storytelling; Folk Tales; Mythology
Major character(s): Yikaas, Prehistoric Human, Storyteller; Qumalix, Prehistoric Human, Storyteller
Time period(s): 7th century B.C.
Locale(s): Alaska, North America

Summary: The story of a prehistoric Aleutian tribe is completed in this third volume of the author's Storyteller Trilogy (after *Song of the River* and *Cry of the Wind*). In a series of stories within stories, two storytellers, Qumalix and Yikaas, compete in an epic cycle of tale telling that allows the reader entry into a believable primitive world. First time readers can enjoy this enthralling novel on its own; fans of the series will be delighted with the author's expert culmination of her efforts in cultural re-animation.

Where it's reviewed:
Booklist, October 1, 2001, page 299
Kirkus Reviews, September 15, 2001, page 1322
Publishers Weekly, October 22, 2001, page 46

Other books by the same author:
Cry of the Wind, 1998
Song of the River, 1997
Brother Wind, 1994
Mother Earth, Father Sky, 1990

Other books you might like:
Stephen Baxter, *Longtusk*, 2001
Bernard Cornwell, *Stonehenge*, 2000
John R. Dann, *Song of the Axe*, 2001
Judith Tarr, *Daughter of Lir*, 2001
Barbara Wood, *Sacred Ground*, 2001

880

SIMON HAWKE (Pseudonym of Nicholas Yermakov)

The Slaying of the Shrew

(New York: Forge, 2001)

Story type: Historical/Elizabethan; Mystery
Series: Shakespeare and Smythe. Book 2
Subject(s): Mystery and Detective Stories; Theater
Major character(s): William Shakespeare, Historical Figure, Writer; Symington ''Tuck'' Smythe, Actor; Catherine Middleton, Young Woman
Time period(s): 16th century (1580s)
Locale(s): London, England

Summary: The struggling Elizabethan actor Tuck Smythe and his partner, would-be playwright Will Shakespeare, return for their second outing, following *A Mystery of Errors*, as amateur detectives. Hired to perform as part of the wedding entertainment of the shrewish Catherine Middleton, the Queen's Men journey to a merchant's estate outside of London, where the pair overhear a plot to murder the bride and seize the merchant's fortune. Will and Tuck's best efforts cannot prevent violence, and they are forced into a game of catch-up to find the murderer among the wedding guests. The fun here is in detecting the echoes from Shakespeare's plays in this engaging series.

Where it's reviewed:
Kirkus Reviews, October 15, 2001, page 1456
Publishers Weekly, November 15, 2001, page 44

Other books by the same author:
A Mystery of Errors, 2000
The Last Wizard, 1997
The Iron Throne, 1995
The Nomad, 1994
The Outcast, 1993

Other books you might like:
Fiona Buckley, *The Ursula Blanchard Series*, 1997-
Philip Gooden, *The Death of Kings*, 2001
Karen Harper, *The Elizabeth I Series*, 1999-
Faye Kellerman, *The Quality of Mercy*, 1989
Edward Marston, *The Nicholas Bracewell Series*, 1988-

881

KATE HAWKS

Watch by Moonlight

(New York: Morrow, 2001)

Story type: Historical/Georgian
Subject(s): Crime and Criminals
Major character(s): Bess Whateley, Saloon Hostess; Jason Quick, Highwayman

Time period(s): 1760s (1763)
Locale(s): Dorset, England

Summary: In a prose retelling of Alfred Noyes' poem, *The Highwayman*, the scene is Dorset, England, in the 1760s as barmaid Bess Whateley dreams of release from the drudgery of her job. Adventure comes in the form of dashing Jason Quick, who turns out to be the notorious Golden Fleecer, robbing the rich to help free his father from indentured servitude in America. Bess and Jason fall in love, but complications escalate to a fateful climax of self-sacrifice.

Where it's reviewed:
Booklist, July 2001, page 1980
Kirkus Reviews, May 15, 2001, page 684
Publishers Weekly, July 9, 2001, page 48

Other books by the same author:
The Lovers, 1999

Other books you might like:
Bruce Alexander, *Smuggler's Moon*, 2001
Susan Carroll, *The Bride Finder*, 1998
Daphne Du Maurier, *Frenchman's Creek*, 1942
Kat Martin, *Gypsy Lord*, 1992
Patricia Wynn, *The Birth of Blue Satan*, 2001

882

JOHN R. HAYES

Catskill

(New York: St. Martin's Press, 2001)

Story type: Historical/Depression Era; Mystery
Subject(s): Mystery and Detective Stories; Refugees; Jews
Major character(s): Charlie Evans, Police Officer (sheriff); Martin Collins, Lawyer
Time period(s): 1930s (1938)
Locale(s): Sullivan County, New York

Summary: This atmospheric mystery draws on a solid knowledge of New York's Catskill region during the 1930s. Newly arrived Jewish refugees are shot at, and a local realtor is killed. Sheriff Evans wants answers and 77-year-old lawyer Martin Collins agrees to help find them in an intriguing story that stretches back to the days of the Indians and features cameo appearances by such historical figures as Harriet Beecher Stowe, Sid Caesar, and Eddie Cantor.

Where it's reviewed:
Library Journal, September 1, 2001, page 237
New York Times Book Review, September 23, 2001, page 23
Publishers Weekly, September 10, 2001, page 65

Other books you might like:
John Dunning, *Two O'Clock, Eastern Wartime*, 2000
Dorothy Garlock, *The Edge of Town*, 2001
Ron Goulart, *Groucho Marx and the Broadway Murders*, 2001
Lise McClendon, *One O'Clock Jump*, 2001
Sharon Rolens, *Worthy's Town*, 2000

883

VIRGINIA HENLEY

The Border Hostage

(New York: Delacorte, 2001)

Story type: Romance
Subject(s): Love; Loyalty
Major character(s): Raven Carleton, Gentlewoman; Heath Kennedy, Outlaw; Christopher Dacre, Nobleman, Fiance(e) (of Raven)
Time period(s): 16th century
Locale(s): England; Scotland

Summary: Veteran historical romancer Henley ventures into the border region of England and Scotland for this tale of love between a Scottish outlaw, Heath Kennedy, and the headstrong Englishwoman, Raven Carleton, who comes to prefer Kennedy to her English fiance, Christopher Dacre. The conflict between the English court and Scottish loyalists complicates the course of love and tests both lovers' sense of loyalty to each other and to their countries. While romance predominates over history here, the author does create a convincing atmosphere out of the details of the bitter border wars.

Where it's reviewed:
Booklist, May 15, 2001, page 1737
Kirkus Reviews, April 15, 2001, page 538
Publishers Weekly, July 9, 2001, page 47

Other books by the same author:
The Marriage Prize, 2000
A Woman of Passion, 1999
A Year and a Day, 1998
Dream Lover, 1997
Enslaved, 1996

Other books you might like:
Jude Deveraux, *The Heiress*, 1995
Shannon Drake, *Come the Morning*, 1999
Haley E. Garwood, *Swords Across the Thames*, 1999
Michele Jaffe, *The Water Nymph*, 2000
Rosemary Sutcliff, *Lady in Waiting*, 1957

884

DONNA HILL

Rhythms

(New York: St. Martin's Press, 2001)

Story type: Historical/Roaring Twenties; Family Saga
Subject(s): Race Relations; Family Relations; African Americans
Major character(s): Cora Harvey, Singer; David Mackey, Doctor; Emma Mackey, Young Woman
Time period(s): 20th century
Locale(s): Mississippi; Chicago, Illinois; New York, New York

Summary: This is a multi-generational African-American family saga. Beginning in the 1920s and set in rural Mississippi, the story concerns young Cora Harvey, a preacher's daughter who leaves for Chicago to pursue a singing career. She returns home where she marries the community's only

African American doctor, David Mackey. The birth of their light skinned daughter, Emma, destroys the marriage, and the narrative fast forwards to Emma's escape to New York, where she passes for white. The story then centers on her daughter, with the secret of her family heritage eventually revealed.

Where it's reviewed:
Booklist, June 2001, page 1842
Kirkus Reviews, June 1, 2001, page 760
Publishers Weekly, July 23, 2001, page 49

Other books by the same author:
A Scandalous Affair, 2000
A Private Affair, 1998
Shipwreck Season, 1998
Scandalous, 1995
Rooms of the Heart, 1990

Other books you might like:
David Anthony Durham, *Gabriel's Story*, 2001
William Heffernan, *Beulah Hill*, 2001
Josephine Humphreys, *Nowhere Else on Earth*, 2000
Lalita Tademy, *Cane River*, 2001

885

CRAIG HOLDEN

The Jazz Bird

(New York: Simon & Schuster, 2002)

Story type: Historical/Roaring Twenties; Mystery
Subject(s): Mystery and Detective Stories; Crime and Criminals; Trials
Major character(s): Charlie Taft, Lawyer, Historical Figure; George Remus, Bootlegger, Historical Figure; Imogene Remus, Historical Figure, Spouse (of George)
Time period(s): 1920s (1927)
Locale(s): Cincinnati, Ohio

Summary: Based on a true story, this legal thriller deals with Cincinnati's ''scandal of the century'' in 1927 when bootlegger George Remus turns himself in for killing his wife, Imogene. The prosecutor is Charlie Taft, son of former president and Chief Justice of the Supreme Court William Howard Taft, who tries to dig beneath the surface to decipher Remus' motive. Is he insane as he pleads, or is there method to his madness? The twisting story culminates in a vivid trial scene, and the author achieves a believable authenticity throughout.

Where it's reviewed:
Kirkus Reviews, November 1, 2001, page 1507
Library Journal, October 15, 2001, page 108
Publishers Weekly, October 29, 2001, page 32

Other books by the same author:
Four Corners of Night, 1999
The Last Sanctuary, 1996
The River Sorrow, 1994

Other books you might like:
E.L. Doctorow, *Billy Bathgate*, 1989
John R. Hayes, *Catskill*, 2001
Stephen Hunter, *Hot Springs*, 2000
William Kennedy, *Legs*, 1975
Robert Skinner, *Pale Shadow*, 2001

886

KATE HORSLEY

Confessions of a Pagan Nun

(Boston: Shambhala, 2001)

Story type: Religious
Subject(s): Druids; Religious Life; Nuns
Major character(s): Gwynneve, Religious (nun)
Time period(s): 6th century
Locale(s): Ireland

Summary: Ireland at the beginning of its Christian era is the subject here as seen from the perspective of a former Druid, Gwynneve, who gradually comes under the sway of the new religion as it is practiced in a convent in Kildare. Gwynneve's life story provides interesting insights into religious practices during the period, as well as, showing the impact of Christianity on a formerly pagan culture.

Where it's reviewed:
Booklist, June 2001, page 1842
Library Journal, August 2001, page 161

Other books by the same author:
A Killing in New Town, 1996

Other books you might like:
Frederick Buechner, *Brendan*, 1987
Randy Lee Eickhoff, *The Destruction of the Inn*, 2001
Pamela Hill, *The Woman in the Cloak*, 1988
Morgan Llywelyn, *Druids*, 1991
Juliene Osborne-McKnight, *I Am of Irelaunde*, 2000

887

STEPHEN HUNTER

Pale Horse Coming

(New York: Simon & Schuster, 2001)

Story type: Mystery
Subject(s): Mystery and Detective Stories; Prisoners and Prisons
Major character(s): Earl Swagger, Police Officer, Hero (World War II); Sam Vincent, Lawyer
Time period(s): 1950s (1951)
Locale(s): Mississippi

Summary: Hunter brings back characters from his best-selling *Hot Springs* for this high octane suspense/thriller. Former Arkansas prosecutor Sam Vincent goes to Thebes, a prison for violent African American criminals in Mississippi to assist a client. The prison is run by sadistic rednecks conducting secret research on the helpless inmates. Sam needs to be rescued, and World War II veteran Earl Swagger takes on the mission, as well as assembling a ''Dirty Dozen''-like collection of warriors and misfits to bring down the prison regime. Atmospheric, but also excessively violent, the book is a page turner by a skilled thriller writer.

Where it's reviewed:
Booklist, October 15, 2001, page 385
Kirkus Reviews, September 1, 2001, page 1235
Publishers Weekly, September 24, 2001, page 67

Other books by the same author:
Hot Springs, 2000
Time to Hunt, 1998
Black Light, 1996
Dirty White Boys, 1994
The Day Before Midnight, 1989

Other books you might like:
James Carlos Blake, *A World of Thieves*, 2002
Brad Kessler, *Lick Creek*, 2001
Joe R. Lansdale, *The Bottoms*, 2000
Lee Martin, *Quakertown*, 2001
Mardi McConnochie, *Coldwater*, 2001

888

J. ROBERT JANES

Kaleidoscope

(New York: Soho, 2001)

Story type: Historical/World War II; Mystery
Series: St-Cyr/Kohler
Subject(s): Mystery and Detective Stories; Nazis; World War II
Major character(s): Jean-Louis St-Cyr, Police Officer (chief inspector); Hermann Kohler, Military Personnel (Gestapo officer)
Time period(s): 1940s (1942)
Locale(s): Paris, France; Provence, France

Summary: There is perhaps no stranger detective couple than French Chief Inspector Jean-Louis St-Cyr and Gestapo chief Hermann Kohler in this inventive historical mystery series set during the German occupation of France. The pair is in Provence to investigate the death of a woman suspected of black market dealings and in aiding escapees from the Nazis into Spain. Things quickly grow far more complicated and dangerous. Janes delivers an authentic period feel and makes his unusual pairing believable by stressing the humanity of both detectives.

Where it's reviewed:
Booklist, October 1, 2001, page 301
New York Times Book Review, December 9, 2001, page 29
Publishers Weekly, October 8, 2001, page 48

Other books by the same author:
Salamander, 1998
Sandman, 1997
Stonekiller, 1997
Carousel, 1993
Mirage, 1992

Other books you might like:
Tim Binding, *Lying with the Enemy*, 1999
Sebastian Faulks, *Charlotte Gray*, 1998
Ken Follett, *Jackdaws*, 2001
Alan Furst, *Red Gold*, 1999
Thomas Sanchez, *Day of the Bees*, 2000

889

GARY JENNINGS

Aztec Blood

(New York: Forge, 2001)

Story type: Adventure
Series: Aztec Trilogy. Book 3
Subject(s): Adventure and Adventurers; Identity, Concealed; Indians of Mexico
Major character(s): Cristo the Bastardo, Bastard Son
Time period(s): 16th century
Locale(s): Mexico; Seville, Spain

Summary: Based on the ''ideas'' of Jennings who died in 1999 and completed by an unnamed author, the novel is the last in a trilogy on the Aztec civilization. In this installment, the Aztec empire has been crushed and reconstituted as New Spain. The story follows the career of Cristo the Bastardo, the mestizo son of an Aztec mother and a Spanish father. Resented and persecuted by Indian and Spanish alike, Cristo is raised by a kindly defrocked priest and embarks on a series of swash-buckling adventures that take him across Mexico and into Spain. At the core is the tried-and-true picaresque element of Cristo's mysterious parentage that threatens his life.

Where it's reviewed:
Booklist, August 2001, page 2051
Kirkus Reviews, August 15, 2001, page 1152
Library Journal, August 2001, page 161
Publishers Weekly, August 20, 2001, page 55

Other books by the same author:
Aztec Autumn, 1997 (Aztec Trilogy. Book 2)
Raptor, 1992
Spangle, 1987
The Journeyer, 1984
Aztec, 1980 (Aztec Trilogy. Book 1)

Other books you might like:
Miguel Aleman Velasco, *Capili*, 1984
Clare Bell, *Jaguar Princess*, 1993
Jamake Highwater, *The Sun, He Dies*, 1980
Daniel Peters, *The Luck of Huemac*, 1982
Margaret Shedd, *Malinche and Cortes*, 1971

890

TERRY C. JOHNSTON

Turn the Stars Upside Down

(New York: St. Martin's Press, 2001)

Story type: Historical/American West; Indian Wars
Subject(s): Indians of North America; Biography
Major character(s): Crazy Horse, Historical Figure, Indian (Sioux)
Time period(s): 1870s (1877)
Locale(s): West

Summary: The recently deceased Johnston ends his distinguished career as a western historical novelist with one of the saddest chapters in the history of the West: the 1877 surrender and death of Crazy Horse that is marked by a series of broken promises by the U.S. Army and betrayal that eventually leads to the Sioux warrior's incarceration and stabbing death. Johnston avoids the myths and legends for a factual treatment that attempts a complex portrait of the Sioux leader, who still towers over the perfidy of those who wished to silence him.

Where it's reviewed:
Kirkus Reviews, June 1, 2001, page 772
Publishers Weekly, July 30, 2001, page 60

Other books by the same author:
Wind Walker, 2001
Lay the Mountains Low, 2000
Death Rattle, 1999
Ashes of Heaven, 1998
Buffalo Palace, 1996

Other books you might like:
Winfred Blevins, *Stone Song*, 1995
Bill Dugan, *Crazy Horse*, 1993
William Heyen, *Crazy Horse in Stillness*, 1996
Dan O'Brien, *The Contract Surgeon*, 1999
Bernard Pomerance, *We Need to Dream All This Again*, 1987

891

ALLEN MORRIS JONES

Last Year's River

(Boston: Houghton Mifflin, 2001)

Story type: Historical/American West
Subject(s): Rural Life; Ranch Life
Major character(s): Virginia Price, Debutante, Pregnant Teenager; Henry Mohr, Veteran (World War I), Cowboy; Charlie Stroud, Businessman
Time period(s): 1910s (1919)
Locale(s): Wyoming

Summary: Virginia Price is a New York debutante who, pregnant from a rape, travels west to have her baby away from New York society. On a Wyoming ranch she meets Henry Mohr, a shell-shocked veteran of World War I. They are a mismatched couple whose love for one another is tested by Charlie Stroud, who comes to claim Virginia in marriage, and Henry's abusive father.

Where it's reviewed:
Publishers Weekly, September 17, 2001, page 58

Other books you might like:
Ann Howard Creel, *The Magic of Ordinary Days*, 2001
Robb Forman Dew, *The Evidence Against Her*, 2001
Robert Morgan, *Gap Creek*, 1999
Annie Proulx, *Close Range*, 1999
Diane Smith, *Letters from Yellowstone*, 1999

892

JOSEPH KANON

The Good German

(New York: Henry Holt, 2001)

Story type: Historical/World War II
Subject(s): Suspense; Love
Major character(s): Jake Geismar, Journalist (CBS correspondent); Lena Brandt, Spouse (of Emil); Emil Brandt, Scientist
Time period(s): 1940s (1945)
Locale(s): Berlin, Germany; Potsdam, Germany

Summary: Berlin immediately following the end of World War II is the setting for this atmospheric thriller. CBS correspondent Jake Geismar is on hand to cover the Potsdam Conference and is desperate to find his former mistress, Lena Brandt. He stumbles onto a complex intrigue when an American soldier turns up dead. Geismar's search for the truth leads to Lena and her husband, Emil, a German rocket scientist whom everyone is desperate to find.

Where it's reviewed:
Booklist, July 2001, page 1950
Library Journal, September 1, 2001, page 233
Publishers Weekly, July 16, 2001, page 164

Other books by the same author:
The Prodigal Spy, 1998
Los Alamos, 1997

Other books you might like:
Millicent Dillon, *Harry Gold*, 2000
Sheldon Greene, *Burnt Umber*, 2001
Gila Lustiger, *The Inventory*, 2000
Bill Mesce Jr., *Officer of the Court*, 2001
Paullina Simons, *The Bronze Horseman*, 2001

893

FRANCES KAZAN

Halide's Gift

(New York: Random House, 2001)

Story type: Historical/Exotic
Subject(s): Biography; Women; Muslims
Major character(s): Halide Edib, Historical Figure, Activist
Time period(s): 19th century; 20th century
Locale(s): Constantinople, Turkey

Summary: Constantinople at the turn of the century is the background for this fictional biography of Halide Edib, a revolutionary author and activist during the Turkish War of Independence. The novel traces her liberation from the confined world to which Turkish women were restricted. Halide's father breaks with tradition and sends her to an American school for girls, where she becomes one of the first formally educated Turkish women in history. Education opens up new horizons for Halide, but sets in motion a conflict between tradition and individuality that becomes both personal and political. Kazan supplies a solid historical grounding in the period and its customs.

Where it's reviewed:
Booklist, June 2001, page 1842
Publishers Weekly, June 18, 2001, page 55

Other books by the same author:
Goodnight, Little Sister, 1986

Other books you might like:
Tariq Ali, *The Stone Woman*, 2000
Carol Edgarian, *Rise the Euphrates*, 1994

Jack Hashian, *Mamigon*, 1982
Kenize Mourad, *Regards from the Dead Princess*, 1989
Barry Unsworth, *Pascali's Island*, 1997

894

DOUGLAS KELLEY

The Captain's Wife

(New York: Dutton, 2001)

Story type: Historical/Americana
Subject(s): Sea Stories; Women
Major character(s): Mary Ann Patten, Historical Figure, Spouse; Joshua Patten, Historical Figure, Sea Captain
Time period(s): 1850s (1856)
Locale(s): *Neptune's Car*, At Sea

Summary: Based on actual historical figures and an actual incident, this first novel documents what happens when 19-year-old Mary Ann Patten, accompanying her husband, a clipper ship captain, is forced to take command of the *Neptune's Car* when he is incapacitated by illness. She must contend with harsh weather and a reluctant crew, while nursing her sick husband and concealing her newly discovered pregnancy. Mary Ann is far too heroic to be totally believable, but the novel's sticking close to the historical facts helps convince a skeptical reader.

Where it's reviewed:
Kirkus Reviews, July 1, 2001, page 891
Library Journal, August 2001, page 162
Publishers Weekly, July 30, 2001, page 61

Other books you might like:
Robert J. Begiebing, *The Adventures of Allegra Fullerton*, 1999
James D. Houston, *Snow Mountain Passage*, 2001
Deborah Meroff, *Captain, My Captain*, 1985
Sena Jeter Naslund, *Ahab's Wife*, 1999
N.L. Zaroulis, *Call the Darkness Light*, 1991

895

ELMER KELTON

The Way of the Coyote

(New York: Forge, 2001)

Story type: Historical/American West; Historical/Post-American Civil War
Series: Texas Rangers. Book 3
Subject(s): Indians of North America
Major character(s): Rusty Shannon, Lawman; Andy Pickard, Captive; Shanty, Slave (former)
Time period(s): 1860s
Locale(s): Texas

Summary: In the aftermath of the Civil War, former Confederates, outlaws, nightriders, and Comanches battle each other in Texas. Rusty Shannon, an ex-Texas Ranger, and Andy Pickard, a former Comanche captive who was rescued and adopted by Rusty, are plunged into the violent mix when the Ku Klux Klan burns out Rusty's freed slave friend, Shanty, and the murderous Oldman brothers return for revenge. The author is one of the greatest contemporary western writers who just gets better and better in capturing his era effectively.

Where it's reviewed:
Kirkus Reviews, September 15, 2001, page 1323
Publishers Weekly, October 29, 2001, page 33

Other books by the same author:
Badger Boy, 2000
The Buckskin Line, 1999
The Far Canyon, 1994
Slaughter, 1992
Dark Thicket, 1985

Other books you might like:
Frederic Bean, *Renegade*, 1993
Terry C. Johnston, *Winter Rain*, 1993
Robert Jordan, *Cheyenne Raiders*, 2000
Larry McMurtry, *Boone's Lick*, 2000
Edwin Shrake, *The Borderland*, 2000

896

STEPHEN KENDRICK

Night Watch

(New York: Pantheon, 2001)

Story type: Historical/Edwardian; Mystery
Subject(s): Mystery and Detective Stories; Religious Conflict
Major character(s): Sherlock Holmes, Detective—Private; Father Brown, Detective—Amateur
Time period(s): 1900s (1902)
Locale(s): London, England

Summary: Readers underwhelmed by the prospect of yet another Sherlock Holmes imitation should look again at this intriguing resuscitation of the classic sleuth, here teamed with another classic detective, G.K. Chesterton's Father Brown. Clerics from the world's religions are meeting in London when the Anglican host is murdered. Holmes and Father Brown have one night to solve a classic ''locked room'' mystery. Half the fun here is the author's skill in weaving church history into the suspense.

Where it's reviewed:
Kirkus Reviews, September 15, 2001, page 1327
Library Journal, October 1, 2001, page 146
Publishers Weekly, November 15, 2001, page 45

Other books by the same author:
Holy Clues, 2000

Other books you might like:
Oakley Hall, *Ambrose Bierce and the Death of Kings*, 2001
Michael Kurland, *The Great Game*, 2001
Larry Millett, *Sherlock Holmes and the Secret Alliance*, 2001
Donald S. Thomas, *Sherlock Holmes and the Voice from the Crypt*, 2002
Gerard Williams, *Dr. Mortimer and the Aldgate Mystery*, 2001

897

WILLIAM KENNEDY

Roscoe

(New York: Viking, 2001)

Story type: Historical/Americana
Series: Albany Cycle. Book 7
Subject(s): Politics
Major character(s): Roscoe Owens Conway, Political Figure; Patsy McCall, Political Figure; Veronica Fitzgibbon, Widow(er)
Time period(s): 1940s (1945)
Locale(s): Albany, New York

Summary: It is V-J Day, 1945, in this installment of Kennedy's Albany Cycle, and the subject is a Democratic machine power broker, Roscoe Owens Conway. With a Republican governor and an ongoing corruption investigation, Conway must put out a number of political fires surrounding the current Democratic leader in order to keep the peace and the power, while maintaining secrets that could rock the boat if uncovered. The death of Conway's long-time friend, Elisha Fitzgibbon, clears the way for Conway to resume his pursuit of his wife Veronica, Conway's great love. Atmospheric and convincing, Kennedy is at home in his familiar world the reader will relish visiting.

Where it's reviewed:
Booklist, October 15, 2001, page 356
Kirkus Reviews, October 1, 2001, page 1446
Library Journal, November 1, 2001, page 132
Publishers Weekly, November 19, 2001, page 47

Other books by the same author:
The Flaming Corsage, 1996
Very Old Bones, 1992
Ironweed, 1983
Billy Phelan's Greatest Game, 1978
Legs, 1975

Other books you might like:
Craig Holden, *The Jazz Bird*, 2001
Stephen Hunter, *Pale Horse Coming*, 2001
Lise McClendon, *One O'Clock Jump*, 2001
Richard Stevenson, *Third Man Out*, 1993
Gore Vidal, *The Golden Age*, 2000

898

MICHAEL KILIAN

The Ironclad Alibi

(New York: Berkley, 2002)

Story type: Historical/American Civil War; Mystery
Series: Harrison Raines
Subject(s): Mystery and Detective Stories; Civil War; Espionage
Major character(s): Harrison Raines, Spy; Caesar Augustus, Sidekick, Slave (former); Robert E. Lee, Historical Figure, Military Personnel (Confederate general)
Time period(s): 1860s
Locale(s): Richmond, Virginia

Summary: Southerner and Union agent Harrison Raines returns home to Richmond, Virginia, to learn what he can about the rumored construction of ''the Monster,'' an ironclad ship that could break the Union blockade and tip the war in the Confederacy's favor. When one of Harrison's former lady friends is found hanged, his one-time slave and spying companion Caesar Augustus is charged with her murder, and none other than Robert E. Lee himself gives Harrison one week to discover the real murderer.

Where it's reviewed:
Kirkus Reviews, November 15, 2001, page 1584
Publishers Weekly, December 24, 2001, page 46

Other books by the same author:
Murder at Ball's Bluff, 2000
Murder at Manassas, 2000
Major Washington, 1998
The Last Virginia Gentleman, 1992
Looker, 1991

Other books you might like:
Ann McMillan, *Civil Blood*, 2001
Miriam Grace Monfredo, *Brothers of Cain*, 2001
Anne Perry, *Funeral in Blue*, 2001
David Poyer, *Fire on the Waters*, 2001
Jim Walker, *Murder at Gettysburg*, 1999

899

MICHAEL KURLAND

The Great Game

(New York: St. Martin's Minotaur, 2001)

Story type: Mystery; Historical/Victorian
Series: Professor Moriarity. Book 3
Subject(s): Mystery and Detective Stories
Major character(s): James Moriarity, Professor, Scientist; Sherlock Holmes, Detective—Private
Time period(s): 1890s
Locale(s): Vienna, Austria; London, England

Summary: Readers who react with the news of yet another Sherlock Holmes pastiche with the cry of ''Enough already,'' should not miss this accomplished Victorian era mystery. It's the 1890s, and a massive conspiracy is afoot to destabilize European governments. The detective challenge falls on Holmes' nemesis, the so-called ''Napoleon of Crime,'' Professor James Moriarity, to get to the bottom of a world-shaking mystery. Holmes appears only as a sidekick here with the emphasis deservedly on Kurland's amazing reconstruction of the period and the creation of a worthy rival of the great Holmes in the form of Moriarity.

Where it's reviewed:
Booklist, July 2001, page 1988
Kirkus Reviews, June 1, 2001, page 775
Publishers Weekly, July 30, 2001, page 65

Other books by the same author:
The Girls in the High-Heeled Shoes, 1998
Too Soon Dead, 1997
Perchance, 1988
The Infernal Device, 1978
A Plague of Spies, 1969

Other books you might like:
Jamyang Norbu, *Sherlock Holmes: The Missing Years*, 2001
Anita Janda, *The Secret Diary of Dr. Watson*, 2001
Laurie R. King, *The Mary Russell/Sherlock Holmes Series*, 1994-
Larry Millett, *Sherlock Holmes and the Secret Alliance*, 2001
Gerard Williams, *Dr. Mortimer and the Aldgate Mystery*, 2001

900

PAUL LAFARGE

Haussmann, or The Distinction

(New York: Farrar, Straus & Giroux, 2001)

Story type: Historical/Post-French Revolution
Subject(s): Biography; City and Town Life
Major character(s): Georges-Eugene Haussmann, Historical Figure, Architect; Madeleine, Orphan
Time period(s): 19th century
Locale(s): Paris, France

Summary: This novel was inspired by the life and work of Georges-Eugene Haussmann, architect and city planner, who made over medieval Paris into its modern image of grand boulevards and gardens. Lafarge describes Haussmann's relationship with an orphan, Madeleine, while detailing the elegance of Emperor Napoleon III's reign and the challenges Haussmann faced (both personally and professionally) to make his dream city a reality.

Where it's reviewed:
Booklist, September 1, 2001, page 51
Kirkus Reviews, August 15, 2001, page 1154
Publishers Weekly, August 27, 2001, page 51

Other books by the same author:
The Artist of the Missing, 1999

Other books you might like:
Carole Nelson Douglas, *Chapel Noir*, 2001
Laura Kalpakian, *Cosette*, 1995
Brian Moore, *The Magician's Wife*, 1998
Richard Sennett, *Palais-Royal*, 1987
Peter Vansittart, *Hermes in Paris*, 2000

901

STEPHEN R. LAWHEAD

The Mystic Rose

(New York: HarperCollins, 2001)

Story type: Historical/Medieval; Action/Adventure
Series: Celtic Crusades. Book 3
Subject(s): Legends; Family Relations; Middle Ages
Major character(s): Gordon Murray, Lawyer; Caitrionia, Adventurer, Young Woman; Renaud de Bracineaux, Knight, Religious (Knight Templar)
Time period(s): 11th century
Locale(s): Constantinople, Byzantium; Spain

Summary: The final volume of this trilogy about a noble questing Scottish family is narrated by lawyer Gordon Murray. The center of interest is Caitrionia who, in revenge for the murder of her father in Constantinople, steals a letter from Knight Templar Renaud de Bracineaux that indicates the whereabouts of the Holy Grail (here called the Mystic Rose). Caitrionia is off in hot pursuit to Moorish Spain, pursued in turn by Renaud. This is an atmospheric adventure by a solid practitioner of the historical/fantasy genre.

Where it's reviewed:
Kirkus Reviews, July 1, 2001, page 906
Publishers Weekly, August 13, 2001, page 283

Other books by the same author:
The Black Rood, 2000
The Iron Lance, 1998
Grail, 1997
Arthur, 1996
Byzantium, 1996

Other books you might like:
A.A. Attanasio, *Kingdom of the Grail*, 1992
Bernard Cornwell, *The Archer's Tale*, 2001
Michael A. Eisner, *The Crusader*, 2001
Rosalind Miles, *The Child of the Holy Grail*, 2001
Judith Tarr, *Kingdom of the Grail*, 2000

902

KANAN MAKIYA

The Rock

(New York: Pantheon, 2001)

Story type: Historical/Medieval; Religious
Subject(s): Islam; Christianity; Judaism
Major character(s): Ka'b al-Ahbar, Historical Figure; Ishaq, Architect, Narrator; Umar ibn al-Khattab, Historical Figure, Ruler (caliph)
Time period(s): 7th century
Locale(s): Jerusalem, Israel

Summary: In a remarkable effort of historical reconstruction, the novel animates life in Jerusalem during the seventh century as Christian power is waning and Islam is in the ascendancy. The novel's protagonist is Ka'b al-Ahbar, a learned Jew who accepts the teachings of Muhammad and accompanies the caliph, Umar ibn al-Khattab, during his conquest of Jerusalem, site of the Rock. This is the place where Abraham attempted to sacrifice Isaac, where Solomon's temple stood, where Jesus preached, and from which Muhammad ascended to heaven. The story of this cultural and religious crossroads is narrated by Ka'b's son, Ishaq, who is chosen to design Islam's first monument, the Dome of the Rock. Makiya makes clear that the three great religious traditions that meet on the Rock, now so divided and contentious, once coexisted peacefully, drawing on each other's strengths.

Where it's reviewed:
Booklist, November 1, 2001, page 460
New York Times Book Review, November 25, 2001, page 24
Publishers Weekly, October 15, 2001, page 67

Other books by the same author:
Cruelty and Silence, 1993
The Monument, 1991
Republic of Fear, 1989

Other books you might like:
Cecelia Holland, *Jerusalem*, 1996
Edwin P. Hoyt, *The Voice of Allah*, 1970
Frances Kazan, *Halide's Gift*, 2001
Zoe Oldenbourg, *The Heirs of the Kingdom*, 1971
Robert Stone, *Damascus Gate*, 1998

903

JEFFREY MARKS

The Ambush of My Name

(Johnson City, Tennessee: Silver Dagger Mysteries, 2001)

Story type: Mystery; Historical/Post-American Civil War
Subject(s): Mystery and Detective Stories; Politics
Major character(s): Ulysses S. Grant, Historical Figure, Military Personnel; Julia Grant, Historical Figure, Spouse (of Ulysses)
Time period(s): 1860s (1868)
Locale(s): Georgetown, Ohio

Summary: This inventive first novel imagines the actual post-Civil War return of Ulysses S. Grant and his wife, Julia, to his hometown of Georgetown, Ohio, as a murder mystery. On a tour to see whether the presidency is within his grasp, Grant discovers a corpse in his hotel room and must decide whether this is a warning against running for office or something to do with Southern sympathizers. Then a sniper's bullet makes it clear that the war is far from over.

Where it's reviewed:
Publishers Weekly, May 14, 2001, page 57

Other books you might like:
Ev Ehrlich, *Grant Speaks*, 2000
Thomas Fleming, *When This Cruel War Is Over*, 2001
Richard Parry, *That Fateful Lightning*, 2000
Jeff Shaara, *The Last Full Measure*, 1998
Robert Skimin, *Ulysses*, 1994

904

MARDI MCCONNOCHIE

Coldwater

(New York: Doubleday, 2001)

Story type: Historical/Victorian
Subject(s): Prisoners and Prisons; Sisters
Major character(s): Charlotte Wolf, Writer, Relative; Emily Wolf, Writer, Relative; Anne Wolf, Writer, Relative
Time period(s): 1840s
Locale(s): Australia

Summary: This Charlotte, Emily, and Anne have the last name Wolf, not Bronte, and the setting is a penal colony off the coast of Australia not the Yorkshire moors, but the echoing of the Bronte forerunners helps set the atmosphere in this story of three hopeful literary spirits living under the domination of their tyrannical father. Tragedy strikes when a recently arrived Irish revolutionary prisoner is taken into the house, and irrationality and cruelty lead to violence in this portrait of Australia's convict heritage.

Where it's reviewed:
Booklist, July 2001, page 1982
Kirkus Reviews, June 1, 2001, page 764
Library Journal, July 2001, page 124
New York Times Book Review, September 23, 2001, page 24
Publishers Weekly, July 23, 2001, page 49

Other books you might like:
Eleanor Dark, *Storm of Time*, 1950
Glyn Hughes, *Bronte*, 1996
Thomas Keneally, *The Playmaker*, 1987
William Stuart Long, *The Exiles*, 1984
Colleen McCullough, *Morgan's Run*, 2000

905

ELIZABETH MCGREGOR

The Ice Child

(New York: Dutton, 2001)

Story type: Historical/Victorian
Subject(s): Journalism; Medicine; Wilderness
Major character(s): Jo Harper, Journalist; Douglas Marshall, Archaeologist
Time period(s): 1840s; 2000s
Locale(s): London, England; Arctic

Summary: McGregor shuttles between the contemporary story of journalist Jo Harper's search to save her child born with a rare blood disease and an account of the real-life Arctic expedition of Sir John Franklin, which vanished in 1845. Douglas Marshall, father of Harper's child, is an archaeologist obsessed with the Franklin mystery. Their only chance to save the child is to find Marshall's teenaged son John, a possible match for a transplant, who has followed Franklin's route into the Arctic. The novel ingeniously connects both stories.

Where it's reviewed:
Booklist, April 1, 2001, page 1454
New York Times Book Review, September 9, 2001, page 28
Publishers Weekly, April 28, 2001, page 49

Other books you might like:
Beryl Bainbridge, *The Birthday Boys*, 1994
Andrea Barrett, *The Voyage of the Narwhal*, 1998
Robert Edric, *The Broken Lands*, 2002
William T. Vollmann, *The Rifles*, 1994
John Wilson, *North with Franklin*, 2000

906

BILL MESCE JR.

Officer of the Court

(New York: Bantam, 2001)

Story type: Historical/World War II; Mystery
Subject(s): Mystery and Detective Stories; Legal Thriller; World War II
Major character(s): Harry Voss, Military Personnel (Army major), Lawyer; Derwood ''Woody'' Kneece, Military Personnel, Lawyer
Time period(s): 1940s (1943)

Locale(s): Orkney Islands, Scotland; Greenland; Italy

Summary: Major Harry Voss, Army lawyer, returns for his second case following *The Advocate*. It's 1943, and a body washes ashore on the Orkney Islands. The victim was stationed in Greenland, and Voss, along with the Army's official investigator, Woody Kneece, heads there, where it is learned the death is connected to a ''night train,'' a nocturnal supply flight that crashed. To solve the case, Kneece and Voss must journey from Greenland, to England prior to D-Day, then to the Italian battlefield. This is an intriguing mystery that features a convincingly realistic period backdrop.

Where it's reviewed:
Booklist, August 2001, page 2089
Kirkus Reviews, July 15, 2001, page 968
Publishers Weekly, August 6, 2001, page 59

Other books by the same author:
The Advocate, 2000 (Steve Szilagyi, co-author)

Other books you might like:
John Dunning, *Two O'Clock, Eastern Wartime*, 2000
Alan Furst, *Kingdom of Shadows*, 2000
John Katzenbach, *Hart's War*, 1999
Glenn Meade, *The Sands of Sakkara*, 1999
Christopher Reich, *The Runner*, 2000

907

ROSALIND MILES

The Child of the Holy Grail

(New York: Crown, 2001)

Story type: Legend; Historical/Fantasy
Series: Guenevere Trilogy. Book 3
Subject(s): Arthurian Legends; Legends; Knights and Knighthood
Major character(s): Guenevere, Royalty; Arthur Pendragon, Ruler; Galahad, Knight
Time period(s): Indeterminate Past
Locale(s): England

Summary: Miles brings to a conclusion her feminist-oriented trilogy on the Arthurian legend. Lancelot has departed and Arthur and Guenevere have reconciled, though new pressure arrives when the sinister Mordred, Arthur's son with his sister, Morgan Le Fay, takes his seat at the Round Table. Hope arrives in the form of a knight, Sir Galahad, who may hold the key to the mystery surrounding the Holy Grail. Arthurian purists may resist this interpretation of the famous legend, but the author does breathe fresh life into the familiar.

Where it's reviewed:
Booklist, July 2001, page 1982
Kirkus Reviews, May 15, 2001, page 692
Library Journal, July 2001, page 125
Publishers Weekly, July 16, 2001, page 158

Other books by the same author:
The Knight of the Sacred Lake, 2000 (Guenevere Trilogy. Book 2)
Guenevere: Queen of the Summer Country, 1999 (Guenevere Trilogy. Book 1)
Act of Passion, 1996
I, Elizabeth, 1994

Other books you might like:
Marion Zimmer Bradley, *Priestess of Avalon*, 2001
Diana L. Paxson, co-author
Bernard Cornwell, *The Warlord Chronicles*, 1996-1998
Sharan Newman, *The Guinevere Trilogy*, 1981-1985
Jack Whyte, *The Camulod Chronicles*, 1996-
Persia Woolley, *The Guinevere Trilogy*, 1987-1991

908

LARRY MILLETT

Sherlock Holmes and the Secret Alliance

(New York: Viking, 2001)

Story type: Historical/Americana; Mystery
Series: American Chronicles of John H. Watson, M.D. Book 4
Subject(s): Mystery and Detective Stories
Major character(s): Shadwell Rafferty, Saloon Keeper/Owner; Sherlock Holmes, Detective—Private; John Watson, Sidekick, Doctor
Time period(s): 1890s (1899)
Locale(s): St. Paul, Minnesota; Minneapolis, Minnesota

Summary: Millett's fourth adventure about Sherlock Holmes in Minnesota is a carefully researched reconstruction of Minneapolis in 1899. On the eve of a visit by President McKinley, a young union worker is found hanged with a placard around his neck stating ''The Secret Alliance Has Spoken.'' Who and what is the Secret Alliance? Responsibility for discovering the truth falls on saloon keeper Shadwell Rafferty who recruits the assistance of Holmes.

Where it's reviewed:
Kirkus Reviews, August 15, 2001, page 1170
Publishers Weekly, September 17, 2001, page 58

Other books by the same author:
Sherlock Holmes and the Rune Stone Mystery, 1999
Sherlock Holmes and the Ice Palace Murders, 1998
Sherlock Holmes and the Red Demon, 1996

Other books you might like:
David Housewright, *Dearly Departed*, 1999
Anita Janda, *The Secret Diary of Dr. Watson*, 2001
Michael Kurland, *The Great Game*, 2001
John Sandford, *Certain Prey*, 1999
Gerard Williams, *Dr. Mortimer and the Aldgate Mystery*, 2001

909

MIRIAM GRACE MONFREDO

Brothers of Cain

(New York: Berkley, 2001)

Story type: Historical/American Civil War; Espionage Thriller
Series: Seneca Falls. Book 8
Subject(s): Mystery and Detective Stories; Civil War; Espionage
Major character(s): Seth Llyr, Military Personnel (Union soldier), Prisoner; Kathyrn Llyr, Nurse (army); Bronwen Llyr, Spy (for Union)

Time period(s): 1860s (1862)
Locale(s): Washington, District of Columbia; Richmond, Virginia; Seneca Falls, New York

Summary: Monfredo keeps her focus on Glynis Tryon's nieces and nephew in this espionage thriller set during the Virginia Peninsula campaign of 1862. Union spy Bronwen Llyr and army nurse Kathyrn Llyr learn their brother, Seth, has been captured by the Confederates. Bronwen is determined to free him from Richmond's Libby Prison before the rebels learn his sister is a Union spy. Her efforts on behalf of her brother are shared with her spy mission to get a load of tobacco out of Richmond. Monfredo keeps close to the historical events and impresses with the evident research that aids the atmosphere.

Where it's reviewed:
Kirkus Reviews, July 15, 2001, page 985
Publishers Weekly, August 27, 2001, page 57

Other books by the same author:
Sisters of Cain, 2000
Must the Maiden Die, 1999
The Stalking Horse, 1998
Through a Gold Eagle, 1996
Blackwater Spirits, 1995

Other books you might like:
Barbara Hambly, *Die upon a Kiss*, 2001
Michael Kilian, *A Killing at Ball's Bluff*, 2001
Ann McMillan, *Civil Blood*, 2001
Owen Parry, *Call Each River Jordan*, 2001
Anne Perry, *Slaves of Obsession*, 2000

910

ROBERT MORGAN

This Rock

(Chapel Hill, North Carolina: Algonquin, 2001)

Story type: Historical/Americana; Historical/Roaring Twenties
Subject(s): Rural Life; Brothers; Religion
Major character(s): Muir Powell, Teenager; Moody Powell, Young Man; Ginny Powell, Widow(er)
Time period(s): 1920s
Locale(s): North Carolina

Summary: Morgan's follow-up to the best-selling *Gap Creek* returns to the themes of rural family life in a Carolina setting. The novel concerns the adventures of two brothers, Muir and Moody Powell. Muir, his widowed mother Ginny's favorite, wishes to be a preacher but his dream is deferred by his shiftless brother. After some wandering, Muir decides to first build a church on his family's property, which tests family and community values.

Where it's reviewed:
Booklist, July 2001, page 1952
Kirkus Reviews, August 1, 2001, page 1057
New York Times Book Review, October 14, 2001, page 21
Publishers Weekly, August 27, 2001, page 56

Other books by the same author:
Gap Creek, 1999
The Truest Pleasure, 1995
The Hinterlands, 1994

Other books you might like:
Aaron Roy Even, *Bloodroot*, 2000
Josephine Humphreys, *Nowhere Else on Earth*, 2000
Steve McGiffen, *Tennant's Rock*, 2001
Charles F. Price, *Freedom's Altar*, 1999
Arliss Ryan, *The Kingsley House*, 2000

911

VELLA MUNN

Cheyenne Summer

(New York: Forge, 2001)

Story type: Indian Culture
Subject(s): Indians of North America; Native Americans; Cultures and Customs
Major character(s): Grey Bear, Indian (Cheyenne), Warrior; Lone Hawk, Indian (Cheyenne), Warrior
Time period(s): 1800s (1800)
Locale(s): Great Plains, North America

Summary: The rivalry between two Cheyenne warriors and tribal leaders, Grey Bear and Lone Hawk, is the subject of this reconstruction of Native American life. It is 1800, and drought has hit the Great Plains, driving the buffalo away and spawning wildfires that threaten the Cheyenne and their rivals, the Pawnee. Grey Bear advocates war with the Pawnee, while Lone Hawk supports cooperation to share the dwindling food supply.

Where it's reviewed:
Publishers Weekly, July 16, 2001, page 160

Other books by the same author:
Soul of the Sacred Earth, 2000
Blackfeet Season, 1999
Wind Warrior, 1998
Seminole Song, 1997
Spirit of the Eagle, 1996

Other books you might like:
Rosanne Bittner, *Mystic Warriors*, 2000
Michael Blake, *The Holy Road*, 2001
Don Coldsmith, *The Spanish Bit Saga*, 1980-
R. Garcia y Robertson, *American Woman*, 1998
Pamela Jekel, *She Who Hears the Sun*, 1999

912

DAVID NEVIN

Treason

(New York: Forge, 2001)

Story type: Historical/Post-American Revolution; Political
Series: American Story. Book 4
Subject(s): Conspiracies; Politics; Biography
Major character(s): Aaron Burr, Historical Figure, Political Figure; James Madison, Historical Figure, Political Figure; James Wilkinson, Historical Figure, Military Personnel (general)
Time period(s): 1800s (1800-1807)

Locale(s): United States

Summary: This fourth novel in the American Story series, which chronicles American history from 1800 to 1860, looks at the events surrounding Aaron Burr's fall from power, culminating in his scheme to seize the Louisiana Territory with General James Wilkinson and Burr's trial for treason in 1807. The novel documents the political issues at stake during the period, setting the Jeffersonian Republicans against the Federalists, and Burr versus Hamilton. When Burr launches his grab for territory, it falls on James Madison (ably assisted by wife Dolley) to foil his plot. Nevin avoids any unhistorical confrontations between the major figures, but what the novel lacks in drama it makes up for in authenticity and reliability.

Where it's reviewed:
Booklist, September 1, 2001, page 193
Kirkus Reviews, August 15, 2001, page 1156
Publishers Weekly, October 8, 2001, page 44

Other books by the same author:
Eagle's Cry, 2000
1812, 1996
Dream West, 1983

Other books you might like:
Rita Mae Brown, *Dolley*, 1994
Cyril Harris, *Street of Knives*, 1950
A.E. Hotchner, *Louisiana Purchase*, 1996
William Safire, *Scandalmonger*, 2000
Gore Vidal, *Burr*, 1973

913

LAWRENCE NORFOLK

In the Shape of a Boar

(New York: Grove, 2001)

Story type: Historical/World War II; Historical/Fantasy
Subject(s): Mythology; War; Underground Resistance Movements
Major character(s): Solomon Memel, Writer (poet), Survivor (of Nazi labor camp); Heinrich Eberhardt, Military Personnel (SS officer); Meleager, Ruler (king)
Time period(s): Multiple Time Periods
Locale(s): Greece; Paris, France

Summary: Norfolk's challenging, expansive novel ranges from pre-history to Paris in the 1970s. The mythical implications of a boar hunt organized by King Meleager of Greece are played out in the same setting as Greek resistance fighters hunting SS officer Heinrich Eberhardt. Solomon Memel converts the experience into an acclaimed poem that is to be made into a film in the 1970s. This tour de force of associative logic establishes Norfolk as one of the most inventive novelists writing today.

Where it's reviewed:
Booklist, August 2001, page 2090
Library Journal, August 2001, page 163
Publishers Weekly, September 10, 2001, page 59

Other books by the same author:
The Pope's Rhinoceros, 1996
Lempriere's Dictionary, 1991

Other books you might like:
John Gregory Brown, *Audubon's Watch*, 2001
Susann Cokal, *Mirabilis*, 2001
Emma Donoghue, *Slammerkin*, 2001
Sheldon Greene, *Burnt Umber*, 2001
Barbara Wood, *Sacred Ground*, 2001

914

OWEN PARRY

Call Each River Jordan

(New York: Morrow, 2001)

Story type: Historical/American Civil War; Mystery
Series: Abel Jones. Book 3
Subject(s): Slavery; Civil War; Mystery and Detective Stories
Major character(s): Abel Jones, Military Personnel (Union soldier), Spy; Francis Drake Raines, Military Personnel (Confederate soldier); Ulysses S. Grant, Historical Figure, Military Personnel (Union general)
Time period(s): 1860s (1862)
Locale(s): Corinth, Mississippi

Summary: Parry's third outing for Welsh immigrant and Union soldier Abel Jones begins in the aftermath of the bloody Battle of Shiloh. He meets with General Grant and is assigned to find out who is behind the mass murder of runaway slaves. Jones crosses enemy lines to convince the Confederates it is in their best interest to solve the crime, and he is paired up with Confederate officer Francis Drake Raines to uncover a conspiracy that sheds light on the values, both political and moral, behind the Civil War.

Where it's reviewed:
Booklist, October 1, 2001, page 300
Kirkus Reviews, August 1, 2001, page 1058
Publishers Weekly, September 24, 2001, page 66

Other books by the same author:
Shadows of Glory, 2000
Faded Coat of Blue, 1999

Other books you might like:
Thomas Fleming, *When This Cruel War Is Over*, 2001
Nora Hague, *Letters from an Age of Reason*, 2001
Barbara Hambly, *Die upon a Kiss*, 2001
Ann McMillan, *Civil Blood*, 2001
Marly Youmans, *The Wolf Pit*, 2001

915

ANNE PERRY

Funeral in Blue

(New York: Ballantine, 2001)

Story type: Mystery; Historical/Victorian
Series: William Monk. Number 11
Subject(s): Mystery and Detective Stories
Major character(s): William Monk, Detective—Private, Amnesiac; Hester Monk, Nurse, Spouse (of William); Kristian Beck, Doctor
Time period(s): 1860s
Locale(s): London, England; Vienna, Austria

Summary: In the 11th of Perry's popular Victorian mystery series featuring husband-and-wife sleuths Hester and William Monk, a Viennese physician, Dr. Kristian Beck, is charged with the murder of two women in an artist's studio. One of them is Beck's English wife, Elissa, whom he met during the 1848 Austrian revolution. Monk must travel to Vienna on the trail of the real murderer and the secrets of Elissa's past, allowing Perry to document 19th century customs, in particular the virulent anti-Semitism of the time.

Where it's reviewed:
Booklist, August 2001, page 2053
Kirkus Reviews, August 15, 2001, page 1171
New York Times Book Review, October 28, 2001, page 26
Publishers Weekly, September 17, 2001, page 58

Other books by the same author:
Slaves of Obsession, 2000
The Twisted Root, 1999
A Breach of Promise, 1998
The Silent Cry, 1997
The Thomas and Charlotte Pitt Series, 1979-

Other books you might like:
T.F. Banks, *The Thief-Taker*, 2001
Carole Nelson Douglas, *Chapel Noir*, 2001
Michael Kurland, *The Great Game*, 2001
Roberta Rogow, *The Problem of the Surly Servant*, 2001
Gerard Williams, *Dr. Mortimer and the Aldgate Mystery*, 2001

916

MARIO PUZO
CAROL GINO, Co-Author

The Family

(New York: Regan, 2001)

Story type: Historical/Renaissance
Subject(s): Family Relations
Major character(s): Rodrigo Borgia, Historical Figure, Religious (Pope Alexander VI); Cesare Borgia, Historical Figure, Nobleman; Lucrezia Borgia, Historical Figure, Noblewoman
Time period(s): 15th century
Locale(s): Rome, Italy

Summary: According to the creator of *The Godfather*, the Borgias are the "original crime family," and this book chronicles their history, though Puzo's death necessitated the completion of his book by novelist Carol Gino. Sticking close to the historical fact, the novel traces the rise to power of Rodrigo Borgia, who becomes pope and sets out to establish a powerful dynasty using his children, Cesare and Lucrezia, to complete his plan. Both have their own ideas about the family business. There are cameo appearances by such historical figures as Machiavelli, Michelangelo, and Leonardo Da Vinci.

Where it's reviewed:
Booklist, August 2001, page 2053
Kirkus Reviews, August 1, 2001, page 1060
Library Journal, September 1, 2001, page 235
New York Times Book Review, October 21, 2001, page 28
Publishers Weekly, July 30, 2001, page 55

Other books by the same author:
Omerta, 2000
The Fortunate Pilgrim, 1997
The Last Don, 1996
The Sicilian, 1984
The Godfather, 1969

Other books you might like:
Nigel Balchin, *The Borgia Testament*, 1949
Pamela Bennetts, *The Borgia Prince*, 1968
Cecelia Holland, *City of God*, 1979
Jean Plaidy, *Madonna of the Seven Hills*, 1974
Miranda Seymour, *Daughter of Shadows*, 1977

917

JEFF RACKHAM

The Rag & Bone Shop

(Cambridge, Massachusetts: Zoland, 2001)

Story type: Historical/Victorian
Subject(s): Biography; Writing
Major character(s): Charles Dickens, Historical Figure, Writer; Wilkie Collins, Historical Figure, Writer; Ellen Lawless Ternan, Historical Figure, Actress
Time period(s): 1850s; 1860s
Locale(s): London, England

Summary: The relationship between novelist Charles Dickens and a young actress, Ellen Lawless Ternan, is the subject of this novel that reflects both the undisputed facts and speculation from the perspective of three onlookers or participants: Dickens' friend Wilkie Collins, Dickens' sister-in-law Georgina Hogarth, and Ternan herself. At the center of the novel's conflict is the intriguing challenge that Dickens, the most famous celebrator of hearth and home, faced in his own violation of Victorian propriety.

Where it's reviewed:
Kirkus Reviews, August 1, 2001, page 1066
Publishers Weekly, August 27, 2001, page 53

Other books you might like:
Ursula Bloom, *The Romance of Charles Dickens*, 1960
Frederick Busch, *The Mutual Friend*, 1978
Victoria Lincoln, *Charles*, 1962
William J. Palmer, *The Detective and Mr. Dickens*, 1990
William J. Palmer, *The Dons and Mr. Dickens*, 2000

918

ALICE RANDALL

The Wind Done Gone

(Boston: Houghton Mifflin, 2001)

Story type: Historical/American Civil War; Historical/Antebellum American South
Subject(s): Slavery; African Americans; Civil War
Major character(s): Cynara, Slave; Other, Southern Belle (aka Scarlett O'Hara); Rhett Butler, Gentleman
Time period(s): 19th century
Locale(s): Georgia

Summary: Randall's imaginative, controversial repossession of Margaret Mitchell's *Gone with the Wind* looks at the events at Tara before, during, and after the Civil War from the perspective of Scarlett's half-sister, Cynara, the child of Captain O'Hara and Mammy, Scarlett's nurse. Cynara resentfully records the different treatment she receives compared to Other, her name for Scarlett. Eventually Cynara is sold, and she ends up in a brothel frequented by Rhett Butler, becoming a rival in love with her half-sister before heading off to Washington for a view of the capitol during Reconstruction. Randall's giving voice to the voiceless in Mitchell's classic depiction of the antebellum South is invigorating, although redressing the balance leads the author to some counter-idealized portraits.

Where it's reviewed:
Booklist, May 1, 2001, page 1595
Kirkus Reviews, April 15, 2001, page 533
Library Journal, May 1, 2001, page 128
New York Book Review, July 1, 2001, page 16
Publishers Weekly, May 14, 2001, page 49

Other books you might like:
Barbara Chase-Riboud, *Sally Hemmings*, 1979
Margaret Mitchell, *Gone with the Wind*, 1936
Toni Morrison, *Sula*, 1973
Alexandra Ripley, *Scarlett*, 1991
Margaret Walker, *Jubilee*, 1966
Michael Shaara, *The Killer Angels*, 1974

919

JAMES REASONER

Gettysburg

(Nashville: Cumberland House, 2001)

Story type: Historical/American Civil War; Family Saga
Series: Civil War Battle. Book 6
Subject(s): Military Life; Civil War; Family Relations
Major character(s): Will Brannon, Military Personnel (Confederate soldier); Mac Brannon, Military Personnel (Confederate soldier)
Time period(s): 1860s (1863)
Locale(s): Culpepper County, Virginia; Gettysburg, Pennsylvania

Summary: Reasoner's Civil War Battle series concerning the Brannon family of Virginia has reached the decisive Battle of Gettysburg. Will Brannon serves with the Stonewall Brigade, while Mac Brannon is a member of Jeb Stuart's cavalry. After a short visit home, both are in the midst of the fighting at Gettysburg.

Other books by the same author:
Vicksburg, 2001
Antietam, 2000
Chancellorsville, 2000
Manassas, 1999
Shiloh, 1999

Other books you might like:
Allen B. Ballard, *Where I'm Bound*, 2000
Thomas Fleming, *When This Cruel War Is Over*, 2001
MacKinlay Kantor, *Long Remember*, 1934
C.X. Moreau, *Promise of Glory*, 2000

920

MARY REED
ERIC MAYER, Co-Author

Three for a Letter

(Scottsdale, Arizona: Poisoned Pen, 2001)

Story type: Mystery; Historical/Ancient Rome
Series: John the Eunuch. Book 3
Subject(s): Mystery and Detective Stories; Byzantine Empire; Cultures and Customs
Major character(s): John the Eunuch, Government Official (lord chamberlain); Justinian I, Historical Figure, Ruler (emperor); Theodora, Historical Figure, Ruler (empress)
Time period(s): 6th century (539)
Locale(s): Byzantium

Summary: In the Byzantium of the Emperor Justinian and Empress Theodora, John the Eunuch, the lord chamberlain, must solve the mystery of the murder of a royal hostage and a threat to the life of another, while dealing with the disappearance of the empress' favorite dwarf. John must sort out all the intrigue, while staying out of harm's way from the treacherous Theodora. The novel's historical background enhances the plot action and helps to create a convincing sense of the period, its customs, and its main historical figures.

Where it's reviewed:
Publishers Weekly, November 26, 2001, page 42

Other books by the same author:
Two for Joy, 2000
One for Sorrow, 1999

Other books you might like:
Gillian Bradshaw, *The Bearkeeper's Daughter*, 1987
P.C. Doherty, *The House of Death*, 2001
Michael Ennis, *Byzantium*, 1989
John Maddox Roberts, *The SPQR Series*, 1990-
Steven Saylor, *The Roma Sub Rosa Series*, 1991-

921

REBECCA REISERT

The Third Witch

(New York: Washington Square, 2001)

Story type: Historical/Medieval; Historical/Fantasy
Subject(s): Witches and Witchcraft; Kings, Queens, Rulers, etc.; Fantasy
Major character(s): Gilley, Witch; Macbeth, Nobleman
Time period(s): 11th century
Locale(s): Scotland

Summary: This ingenious first novel is an elaboration of Shakespeare's *Macbeth* from the perspective of one of the witches. Gilley comes to Macbeth's castle for vengeance after he murders her family. Disguised as a kitchen lad, Gilley in short order connects with various figures from the play and finds herself partially responsible for many of the play's actions.

Where it's reviewed:
Booklist, September 15, 2001, page 195
Kirkus Reviews, August 1, 2001, page 1060
Publishers Weekly, August 20, 2001, page 51

Other books you might like:
Gillian Bradshaw, *The Wolf Hunt*, 2001
Bonnie Copeland, *Lady of Moray*, 1979
Dorothy Dunnett, *King Hereafter*, 1982
Sarah Smith, *A Citizen of the Country*, 2000
Nigel Tranter, *Macbeth the King*, 1978

922

ANNE RICE

Blood and Gold

(New York: Knopf, 2001)

Story type: Historical/Ancient Rome; Vampire Story
Series: Vampire Chronicles
Subject(s): Vampires; Roman Empire; Fantasy
Major character(s): Marius, Vampire; Pandora, Vampire; Lestat, Vampire
Time period(s): Multiple Time Periods
Locale(s): Rome, Roman Empire; Constantinople, Roman Empire; Florence, Italy

Summary: Marius figures prominently in Rice's Vampire Chronicles as Lestat's mentor, Pandora's lover, and the creator of Armand. Now he tells his 2,000-year history beginning in Imperial Rome and the conditions that led to his becoming a vampire, an injustice Marius has never forgiven. Marius' undead career gives him the opportunity to glimpse the fall of pagan Rome, the triumph of Emperor Constantine, and the sack of Rome by the Visigoths. Later activities involve him with the painter Botticelli in Renaissance Florence, and events in Venice, Dresden, and England before concluding in the present. Series devotees will find this installment essential; neophytes may be somewhat at a loss.

Where it's reviewed:
Booklist, August 2001, page 2051
Kirkus Reviews, August 1, 2001, page 1060
Library Journal, October 1, 2001, page 143
Publishers Weekly, September 24, 2001, page 74

Other books by the same author:
Vittorio, the Vampire, 1999
Pandora, 1998
The Vampire Armand, 1998
The Mummy, 1989
The Vampire Chronicles, 1976-

Other books you might like:
Andrei Codrescu, *The Blood Countess*, 1995
Barbara Hambly, *Those Who Hunt the Night*, 1988
Karen Harbaugh, *The Vampire Viscount*, 1995
Tom Holland, *Lord of the Dead*, 1996
Chelsea Quinn Yarbro, *A Feast in Exile*, 2001

923

DAVID ROBERTS

The Bones of the Buried

(New York: Carroll & Graf, 2001)

Story type: Mystery
Series: Lord Edward Corinth and Verity Browne. Book 2
Subject(s): Mystery and Detective Stories
Major character(s): Lord Edward Corinth, Nobleman; Verity Browne, Journalist
Time period(s): 1930s (1936)
Locale(s): London, England; Spain

Summary: In the second outing involving aristocrat Lord Edward Corinth and plucky American journalist Verity Browne, it's 1936, and the duo are in Spain as the civil war rages. They are investigating the murder of a Communist party worker. The prime suspect happens to be David Griffiths-Jones, Verity's former lover. Two more deaths—one in London and one in Africa—are linked to the first because all three victims were old Etonians. The intrigue here is first-rate as is the expert portrait of the turbulent 1930s.

Where it's reviewed:
Kirkus Reviews, August 15, 2001, page 1172
Publishers Weekly, September 3, 2001, page 66

Other books by the same author:
Sweet Poison, 2001

Other books you might like:
Max Allan Collins, *Angel in Black*, 2001
Carola Dunn, *To Davy Jones Below*, 2001
Stuart M. Kaminsky, *A Few Minutes Past Midnight*, 2001
Gillian Linscott, *The Perfect Daughter*, 2001
Lise McClendon, *One O'Clock Jump*, 2001

924

JOHN MADDOX ROBERTS

Nobody Loves a Centurion

(New York: St. Martin's Minotaur, 2001)

Story type: Historical/Ancient Rome; Mystery
Series: SPQR. Book VI
Subject(s): Mystery and Detective Stories; Roman Empire
Major character(s): Decius Metellus, Detective—Amateur, Military Personnel (soldier); Julius Caesar, Historical Figure, Military Personnel; Titus Vinius, Military Personnel (Roman centurion)
Time period(s): 1st century B.C.
Locale(s): Rome, Roman Empire; Gaul

Summary: In this installment of the author's entertaining Ancient Roman mystery series, playboy sleuth Decius Metellus leaves Rome for Gaul, where Julius Caesar is battling the Helvetii. When the legion's most hated centurion, Titus Vinius, is murdered, Decius takes up the investigation and finds no end of suspects, and he must solve the case quickly to avoid a mutiny that could end Caesar's aspirations.

Where it's reviewed:
Publishers Weekly, August 27, 2001, page 57

Other books by the same author:
Saturnalia, 1999
Desperate Highway, 1997
The Sacrilege, 1992
The Catiline Conspiracy, 1991
SPQR, 1990

Other books you might like:
Kenneth Benton, *Death on the Appian Way*, 1974
Lindsey Davis, *The Marcus Didius Falco Series*, 1989-
P.C. Doherty, *The House of Death*, 2001
Colleen McCullough, *The Masters of Rome Series*, 1991-
Steven Saylor, *The Roma Sub Rosa Series*, 1991-

925

MICHELE ROBERTS

The Looking Glass

(New York: Holt, 2001)

Story type: Romance; Historical/World War I
Major character(s): Genevieve Delange, Servant (maid); Gerard Colbert, Writer (poet)
Time period(s): 1910s
Locale(s): Normandy, France

Summary: This atmospheric tale is set in the years leading up to the outbreak of World War I in Normandy, France. Genevieve Delange, an orphan, first goes to work at a cafe/bar where a near-tragedy leads her to the Colbert family. She falls in love with the callow Gerard, a poet, and the novel widens its perspective to additional women who lose their hearts to Gerard. Although the narrative focus is thereby sacrificed, the novel still is sustained by a vivid period background and an intriguing understanding of its characters.

Where it's reviewed:
Booklist, July 2001, page 1983
Library Journal, June 1, 2001, page 218
Publishers Weekly, May 14, 2001, page 49

Other books by the same author:
Impossible Saints, 1998
Daughters of the House, 1992
The Wild Girl, 1984
A Piece of the Night, 1978

Other books you might like:
Jill Barnett, *Sentimental Journey*, 2001
Ann Howard Creel, *The Magic of Ordinary Days*, 2001
Robb Forman Dew, *The Evidence Against Her*, 2001
Sebastian Faulks, *Birdsong*, 1996
Jane Gardam, *The Flight of the Maidens*, 2001

926

ROBERTA ROGOW

The Problem of the Surly Servant

(New York: St. Martin's Minotaur, 2001)

Story type: Mystery; Historical/Victorian
Series: Charles Dodgson/Arthur Conan Doyle. Book 4
Subject(s): Mystery and Detective Stories; Universities and Colleges
Major character(s): Charles Dodgson, Historical Figure (aka Lewis Carroll), Writer; Arthur Conan Doyle, Historical Figure, Writer
Time period(s): 1880s (1886)
Locale(s): Oxford, England

Summary: Although historically the creators of Sherlock Holmes and *Alice in Wonderland* never met, in Rogow's entertaining historical mystery series Arthur Conan Doyle teams up with Charles Dodgson (aka Lewis Carroll) to clear the latter of a charge of murdering an Oxford University servant. Suspects abound as it is revealed the servant was both a blackmailer and a petty thief. The novel features an impressive reconstruction of Victorian university life, particularly the challenges faced by women undergraduates.

Where it's reviewed:
Booklist, July 2001, page 1989
Kirkus Reviews, July 1, 2001, page 903
Library Journal, August 2001, page 170
Publishers Weekly, July 9, 2001, page 51

Other books by the same author:
The Problem of the Evil Editor, 2000
The Problem of the Spiteful Spiritualist, 1999
The Problem of the Missing Miss, 1998

Other books you might like:
Mark Frost, *The List of 7*, 1993
Anita Janda, *The Secret Diary of Dr. Watson*, 2001
Michael Kurland, *The Great Game*, 2001
Katie Roiphe, *Still She Haunts Me*, 2001
Walter Satterthwait, *Escapade*, 1995

927

KATIE ROIPHE

Still She Haunts Me

(New York: Dial, 2001)

Story type: Historical/Victorian
Subject(s): Biography; Sexuality
Major character(s): Charles Dodgson, Historical Figure (aka Lewis Carroll), Writer; Alice Liddell, Child, Historical Figure
Time period(s): 1850s; 1860s
Locale(s): Oxford, England

Summary: The relationship between shy Oxford don Charles Dodgson and Alice Liddell is the subject here that weaves around the facts a fictional tale of sexual obsession and guilt. Alice is Dodgson's real-life inspiration for *Alice in Wonderland* which was written under the name Lewis Carroll. Dodgson is infatuated by the child of a faculty colleague whom he begins to photograph and constructs a number of fantasies around which eventually emerge as the landscape of his famous work. Not always historically convincing, the book is nevertheless an intriguing speculation into the troubled psyche of a repressed Victorian.

Where it's reviewed:
Booklist, September 1, 2001, page 55
Kirkus Reviews, July 15, 2001, page 972
New York Times Book Review, September 16, 2001, page 17
Publishers Weekly, August 20, 2001, page 52

Other books you might like:
Rikki Ducornet, *The Jade Cabinet*, 1994
Helen Humphreys, *Afterimage*, 2000
Roberta Rogow, *The Charles Dodgson/Arthur Conan Doyle Series*, 1998-
David R. Slavitt, *Alice at 80*, 1984
Donald S. Thomas, *Mad Hatter Summer*, 1983

928

ELLIOTT ROOSEVELT

Murder at the President's Door

(New York: St. Martin's Minotaur, 2001)

Story type: Historical/Depression Era; Mystery
Series: Eleanor Roosevelt. Book 21
Subject(s): Mystery and Detective Stories
Major character(s): Eleanor Roosevelt, Historical Figure, Detective—Amateur; Franklin D. Roosevelt, Historical Figure, Political Figure; Edward Kennelly, Detective—Police
Time period(s): 1930s (1933)
Locale(s): Washington, District of Columbia

Summary: Although the son of Franklin and Eleanor Roosevelt died in 1990, books under his name continue to appear, and this is the 21st featuring Eleanor Roosevelt as sleuth. It's 1933, and the Roosevelts have just taken up their White House residency and must contend with an assassination attempt. Eleanor and DC police officer Edward Kennelly take up the investigation.

Where it's reviewed:
Booklist, December 1, 2001, page 634
Kirkus Reviews, November 15, 2001, page 1518
Publishers Weekly, November 12, 2001, page 40

Other books by the same author:
Murder in the Lincoln Bedroom, 2000
Murder in Georgetown, 1999
Murder in the Map Room, 1998
Murder at Midnight, 1997
Murder in the Chateau, 1996

Other books you might like:
Jill Churchill, *Someone to Watch over Me*, 2001
Max Allan Collins, *The Nate Heller Series*, 1983-
Stuart M. Kaminsky, *The Toby Peters Series*, 1977-
Rhoda Lerman, *Eleanor*, 1979
Thomas Wiseman, *A Game of Secrets*, 1979

929

ANTHONY J. RUDEL

Imagining Don Giovanni

(New York: Atlantic Monthly, 2001)

Story type: Historical/Fantasy
Subject(s): Biography; Music and Musicians; Literature
Major character(s): Wolfgang Amadeus Mozart, Historical Figure, Composer; Giacomo Casanova, Historical Figure, Rake; Donatien Alphonse Francois de Sade, Historical Figure, Writer
Time period(s): 1770s (1787)
Locale(s): Prague, Bohemia

Summary: This what-if novel imagines a collaboration between composer Mozart and the infamous rake Casanova in the production of Mozart's famous opera *Don Giovanni*. Set in Prague, the novel details how Casanova provides the composer with insight into the mind and heart of a seducer while also helping to repair Mozart's domestic troubles. Additional advice comes from Casanova's friend, the Marquis de Sade. Mozart fans will be intrigued.

Where it's reviewed:
Kirkus Reviews, August 1, 2001, page 1061
Publishers Weekly, August 27, 2001, page 51

Other books you might like:
Bernard Grun, *The Golden Quill*, 1956
J.D. Landis, *Longing*, 2000
Wolf Mankowitz, *A Night with Casanova*, 1991
Charles Neider, *Mozart and the Archbooby*, 1991
David Weiss, *Sacred and Profane*, 1968

930

JEAN P. SASSON

Ester's Child

(Van Nuys, California: Windsor-Brooke, 2001)

Story type: Family Saga; Historical/World War II
Subject(s): War; Family Relations; Religious Conflict
Major character(s): Demetrius Antoun, Doctor; Michael Gale, Military Personnel (Israeli officer); Christine Kleist, Nurse
Time period(s): 20th century
Locale(s): Warsaw, Poland; Jerusalem, Israel

Summary: The destinies of three families—the Jewish Gales, the Palestinian Muslim Antouns, and the German Gentile Kleists—are intertwined in this novel that connects the events of the Holocaust, the founding of the modern state of Israel, and the current Jewish-Arab conflict. The background story is set in the Warsaw Ghetto as Joseph and Ester Gale are forced to give up their beloved daughter to the Gestapo. Surviving the war, they journey to Palestine where Jews displace Palestinians. Years later, the next generation—Michael Gale, an Israeli soldier; Christine Kleist, the daughter of a former S.S. officer; and Palestinian Demetrius Antoun—must come to terms with the their backgrounds and relationships.

Where it's reviewed:
Booklist, August 2001, page 2093
Library Journal, November 1, 2001, page 78
Publishers Weekly, August 20, 2001, page 55

Other books you might like:
Sybil Downing, *The Binding Oath*, 2001
Joanne Harris, *Five Quarters of the Orange*, 2001
Ursula Hegi, *The Vision of Emma Blau*, 2000
Kanan Makiya, *The Rock*, 2001
Bodie Thoene, *The Jerusalem Scrolls*, 2001
Brock Thoene, co-author

931

SIMON SCARROW

Under the Eagle

(New York: St. Martin's Press, 2001)

Story type: Historical/Ancient Rome; Military
Subject(s): Military Life; War; Roman Empire
Major character(s): Quintus Licinius Cato, Military Personnel, Slave (freed); Lucius Cornelius Macro, Military Personnel (centurion); Titus Flavius Sabinus Vespasian, Historical Figure, Military Personnel
Time period(s): 1st century (42)
Locale(s): Germany; England

Summary: Roman military life is vividly re-created in this entertaining adventure yarn that charts the progress of Quintus Licinius Cato, a former slave, who is forced to join the Second Legion under the command of Centurion Lucius Cornelius Macro. Cato proves himself against the Germans and goes with the Second Legion into Britain where a hidden treasure figures prominently in the plot, and where Vespasian and his scheming wife, Flavia, conspire to challenge Emperor Claudius for power.

Where it's reviewed:
Booklist, August 2001, page 2093
Kirkus Reviews, July 1, 2001, page 896

Other books you might like:
Michael Curtis Ford, *The Ten Thousand*, 2001
Robert Graves, *I, Claudius*, 1934
Steven Pressfield, *Tides of War*, 2000
John Maddox Roberts, *Nobody Loves a Centurion*, 2001
H.N. Turteltaub, *Over the Wine-Dark Sea*, 2001

932

HAROLD SCHECHTER

The Hum Bug

(New York: Pocket, 2001)

Story type: Historical/Americana; Mystery
Subject(s): Mystery and Detective Stories
Major character(s): Edgar Allan Poe, Historical Figure, Writer; P.T. Barnum, Historical Figure, Entertainer
Time period(s): 1840s (1844)
Locale(s): New York, New York

Summary: In the first outing for Schechter's sleuthing Edgar Allan Poe, *Nevermore*, the writer teamed up with frontiersman/politician Davy Crockett. In this installment, Poe is struggling in obscurity in New York City, when showman P.T. Barnum seeks his aid in solving a murder. It seems a woman has been killed in the manner of a famous grisly case Barnum had celebrated in a wax tableau. Now he is being blamed for the killing. Much of the investigation involves exploring the nooks and crannies of Barnum's famous American Museum with its collection of the odd and the grotesque, perfect for Poe and great fun for the reader.

Where it's reviewed:
Booklist, October 15, 2001, page 303
Kirkus Reviews, September 15, 2001, page 1319
Library Journal, September 15, 2001, page 117
Publishers Weekly, October 15, 2001, page 49

Other books by the same author:
Nevermore, 1999
Outcry, 1997
Depraved, 1994
Deranged, 1990
Deviant, 1989

Other books you might like:
Caleb Carr, *The Alienist*, 1994
George Egon Hatvary, *The Murder of Edgar Allan Poe*, 1997
Stephen Marlowe, *The Lighthouse at the End of the World*, 1995
Manny Meyers, *The Last Mystery of Edgar Allan Poe*, 1978
Randall Silvis, *On Night's Shore*, 2001

933

KATE SEDLEY

The Goldsmith's Daughter

(Sutton: Severn House, 2001)

Story type: Historical/Medieval; Mystery
Series: Roger the Chapman. Book 10
Subject(s): Mystery and Detective Stories
Major character(s): Roger the Chapman, Peddler, Detective—Amateur; Richard, Duke of Gloucester, Historical Figure, Royalty; Jane Shore, Historical Figure, Lover (Edward IV's mistress)
Time period(s): 15th century (1477)
Locale(s): London, England

Summary: Roger and his wife are in London when Richard, Duke of Gloucester, seeks Roger's aid in preventing his brother, King Edward IV, from executing their older brother. Richard asks Roger to intercede with the king's mistress, Jane Shore, who agrees to help if Roger will prove her cousin innocent of poisoning her husband. And the game's afoot. Sedley is a master of her medieval setting, and there are few better at evoking the period.

Where it's reviewed:
Booklist, December 1, 2001, page 634
Kirkus Reviews, October 1, 2001, page 1396
Library Journal, November 1, 2001, page 136
Publishers Weekly, October 8, 2001, page 46

Other books by the same author:
The Weaver's Inheritance, 2001
The Wicked Winter, 1999
The Brothers of Glastonbury, 1997
Eve of St. Hyacinth, 1996
Death and the Chapman, 1991

Other books you might like:
Alys Clare, *Ashes of the Elements*, 2001
Margaret Frazer, *The Squire's Tale*, 2000
Edward Marston, *The Domesday Book Series*, 1993-
Ian Morson, *The William Falconer Series*, 1994-
Leonard Tourney, *The Matthew Stock Series*, 1980-

934

KATE SEDLEY (Pseudonym of Brenda Margaret Lilian Clarke)

The Weaver's Inheritance

(New York: St. Martin's Minotaur, 2001)

Story type: Historical/Medieval; Mystery
Series: Roger the Chapman. Book 8
Subject(s): Mystery and Detective Stories; Middle Ages; Inheritance
Major character(s): Roger the Chapman, Peddler, Detective—Amateur; Albert Weaver, Artisan (weaver); Alison Weaver, Young Woman
Time period(s): 15th century (1476)
Locale(s): Bristol, England; London, England

Summary: In this installment of Sedley's entertaining and intriguing mystery series, itinerant peddler and sleuth Roger the Chapman revisits his first case in *Death and the Chapman* as the son of a prominent Bristol businessman, Albert Weaver, long presumed dead, reappears. Roger attempts to sort out the mystery, taking him on a colorful and convincing tour of England in the 15th century.

Where it's reviewed:
Booklist, August 2001, page 2099
Library Journal, September 1, 2001, page 239
Publishers Weekly, August 20, 2001, page 61

Other books by the same author:
The Wicked Winter, 1999
The Brothers of Glastonbury, 1997
Eve of St. Hyacinth, 1996
The Holy Innocents, 1994
Death and the Chapman, 1991

Other books you might like:
Alys Clare, *Ashes of the Elements*, 2001
Margaret Frazer, *The Squire's Tale*, 2000
Edward Marston, *The Domesday Book Series*, 1993-
Ian Morson, *The Falconer Series*, 1994-
Leonard Tourney, *The Matthew Stock Series*, 1980-

935

ROBERT SKINNER

Pale Shadow

(Scottsdale, Arizona: Poisoned Pen, 2001)

Story type: Mystery
Series: Wesley Farrell. Book 5
Subject(s): Mystery and Detective Stories; Race Relations
Major character(s): Wesley Farrell, Businessman (night club owner)
Time period(s): 1940s (1940)
Locale(s): New Orleans, Louisiana

Summary: In this installment of the historical mystery series featuring New Orleans nightclub owner Wesley Farrell, it's 1940, and stolen counterfeit plates for 20- and 50-dollar bills set in motion an escalating body count. The search is on to find Farrell's old crime partner, Luis Martinez, before either the Treasury Department or a gang boss can get to him first. This novel is hard-boiled and atmospheric with a convincing look at the setting and the time period.

Where it's reviewed:
Library Journal, August 2001, page 170
Publishers Weekly, July 16, 2001, page 161

Other books by the same author:
Blood to Drink, 2000
Daddy's Gone A-Hunting, 1999
Cat-Eyed Trouble, 1998
Skin Deep, Blood Red, 1997

Other books you might like:
Barbara Hambly, *The Benjamin January Series*, 1997-
Stephen Hunter, *Hot Springs*, 2000
Lise McClendon, *One O'Clock Jump*, 2001
Walter Mosley, *Devil in a Blue Dress*, 1990
Josh Russell, *Yellow Jack*, 1999

936

TROY SOOS

Island of Tears

(New York: Kensington, 2001)

Story type: Historical/Americana; Mystery
Series: Marshall Webb. Book 1
Subject(s): Mystery and Detective Stories
Major character(s): Marshall Webb, Writer; Christina van der Waals, Immigrant, Teenager; Liz Luck, Entertainer
Time period(s): 1890s (1892)
Locale(s): New York, New York

Summary: The author of the popular Mickey Rawlings baseball mysteries goes back a bit in time to present a new historical mystery series featuring dime novel writer Marshall Webb. Webb's search for a new plot takes him to Ellis Island in 1892 where he meets Christina van der Waals, a teenage Dutch girl. When the girl disappears, Webb searches for her in the criminal nether reaches of New York City's sweatshops and brothels and encounters the exotic dancer Liz Luck and social activist Rebecca Davies, with whom Webb falls in love. Soos is an atmosphere expert, and history-oriented readers will enjoy this gritty look at New York in the Tammany Hall era.

Where it's reviewed:
Booklist, October 15, 2001, page 384
Kirkus Reviews, September 1, 2001, page 1251
Library Journal, November 1, 2001, page 136
Publishers Weekly, October 8, 2001, page 40

Other books by the same author:
The Mickey Rawlings Series, 1994-

Other books you might like:
Frederick Busch, *The Night Inspector*, 1999
Caleb Carr, *The Angel of Darkness*, 1997
Richard E. Crabbe, *Suspension*, 2000
Harold Schechter, *The Hum Bug*, 2001
Randall Silvis, *On Night's Shore*, 2001

937

FRED MUSTARD STEWART

The Savages in Love and War

(New York: Forge, 2001)

Story type: Family Saga; Historical/World War II
Series: Savage Family Saga. Number 4
Subject(s): World War II; Family Relations
Major character(s): Nick Savage, Banker, Diplomat (ambassador to France); Brook Savage, Resistance Fighter
Time period(s): 1930s; 1940s
Locale(s): United States; France; Asia

Summary: The fourth installment of the author's Savage Family Saga covers the prewar period through World War II. Nick Savage becomes ambassador to France where his sister, Brook, joins the Resistance. Meanwhile, Nick's sister-in-law, Gloria, has a series of adventures in Asia as Japan threatens the Savage business interests (and the rest of the continent as well).

Where it's reviewed:
Booklist, August 2001, page 2092
Kirkus Reviews, July 15, 2001, page 978
Publishers Weekly, July 9, 2001, page 39

Other books by the same author:
The Naked Savages, 1999
The Young Savages, 1998
The Magnificent Savages, 1991
The Titan, 1985
Ellis Island, 1983

Other books you might like:
John Jakes, *Homeland*, 1993
Eileen Lottman, *The Brahmins*, 1982
Suzanne Morris, *Wives and Mistresses*, 1986
John Toland, *Gods of War*, 1985
Gore Vidal, *The Golden Age*, 2000

938

JESSICA STIRLING

Prized Possessions

(New York: St. Martin's Press, 2001)

Story type: Historical/Depression Era
Subject(s): Depression (Economic); Family Relations; Organized Crime
Major character(s): Lizzie Conway, Widow(er); Polly Conway, Young Woman; Babs Conway, Young Woman
Time period(s): 1930s
Locale(s): Glasgow, Scotland

Summary: The mean streets of Glasgow, Scotland, during the Depression are the setting here in a novel concerning the efforts of Lizzie Conway to build a better life for her three daughters, Polly, Babs, and Rosie. Lizzie is burdened by her missing husband's connection with local organized crime figures. Before he went to fight in World War I, he stole money from the crime boss Lizzie is saddled with repaying. Stirling is convincing in capturing her era effectively in this tale of a family under pressure.

Where it's reviewed:
Booklist, June 1, 2001, page 1850

Other books by the same author:
The Strawberry Season, 2001
The Wind from the Hills, 1999
The Island Wife, 1998
The Asking Price, 1989
Call Home the Heart, 1977

Other books you might like:
Ann Howard Creel, *The Magic of Ordinary Days*, 2001
Robb Forman Dew, *The Evidence Against Her*, 2001
Susan M. Dodd, *The Silent Woman*, 2001
Karen Joy Fowler, *Sister Noon*, 2001
Jane Gardam, *The Flight of the Maidens*, 2001

939

BEVERLY SWERLING

City of Dreams

(New York: Simon & Schuster, 2001)

Story type: Historical/Colonial America; Historical/Seventeenth Century
Subject(s): Family Saga; City and Town Life; Medicine
Major character(s): Sally Turner, Apothecary; Lucas Turner, Doctor (surgeon); Jacob Van der Vries, Doctor
Time period(s): 17th century; 18th century (1630s-1780s)
Locale(s): New Amsterdam, American Colonies

Summary: Covering 150 years and six generations of two families in the American colonial city of New Amsterdam/New York, this ambitious first novel begins with the feud that results when Sally Turner, an apothecary, is married off by her surgeon brother, Lucas, to the Dutch doctor Jacob Van der Vries (later Devreys). The Turners and the Devreyses subsequently battle one another as the novel illustrates the progression of the medical profession and the city of New York.

Where it's reviewed:
Booklist, August 2001, page 2092
Kirkus Reviews, July 1, 2001, page 897
Publishers Weekly, September 17, 2001, page 54

Other books you might like:
Patrick McGrath, *Martha Peake*, 2000
Maan Meyers, *The Dutchman's Dilemma*, 1995
James L. Nelson, *By Force of Arms*, 1996
Michael Pye, *The Drowning Room*, 1995
Jeff Shaara, *Rise to Rebellion*, 2001

940

JUDITH TARR

Daughter of Lir

(New York: Forge, 2001)

Story type: Historical/Fantasy; Historical/Pre-history
Series: Epona Sequence
Subject(s): Horsemanship; Paganism; Animals/Horses
Major character(s): Rhian, Young Woman; Emrys, Royalty (prince)
Time period(s): Indeterminate Past (prehistoric era)

Locale(s): Lir, Fictional Country

Summary: Tarr continues her sequence of horse novels that recreates a mythical pagan world in which the Goddess Epona is incarnated in a white mare. Invaders now threaten the matriarchal society of Lir and the responsibility for saving the day falls on a potter's daughter, Rhian, and Prince Emrys, son of Lir's principal warlord.

Where it's reviewed:
Kirkus Reviews, April 15, 2001, page 540
Library Journal, June 15, 2001, page 106
Publishers Weekly, June 18, 2001, page 61

Other books by the same author:
Lady of Horses, 2000
The Shepherd Kings, 1999
White Mare's Daughter, 1998
King and Goddess, 1996
The Eagle's Daughter, 1995

Other books you might like:
Jean M. Auel, *The Valley of Horses*, 1982
Marion Zimmer Bradley, *The Mists of Avalon*, 1982
Mary Mackey, *The Year the Horses Came*, 1993
R.F. Tapsell, *The Year of the Horsetails*, 1967
Joan Wolf, *The Horsemasters*, 1993

941

JUDITH TARR

Pride of Kings

(New York: Roc, 2001)

Story type: Historical/Fantasy; Historical/Medieval
Subject(s): Middle Ages; Crusades
Major character(s): Richard the Lionheart, Historical Figure, Ruler (King of England); John Lackland, Historical Figure, Royalty; Arslan, Mythical Creature
Time period(s): 12th century
Locale(s): England; France

Summary: Set during the reign of Richard the Lionheart, Tarr's novel mixes history and fantasy in a story that shows the conflict between the Christian medieval world and the pagan, magical world it replaced. As Richard sets out on the Crusades, young Arslan begins one of his own to bridge the gap between the two worlds. He comes to the assistance of Richard's brother, John, in his secret battle against supernatural foes. Tarr offers a new twist on the England of Robin Hood and the Plantagenets, and readers with a taste for myth and magic will be charmed.

Where it's reviewed:
Booklist, August 2001, page 2102
Kirkus Reviews, July 15, 2001, page 988
Library Journal, September 15, 2001, page 115
Publishers Weekly, August 13, 2001, page 291

Other books by the same author:
Daughter of Lir, 2001
Kingdom of the Grail, 2000
Lady of Horses, 2000
The Shepherd Kings, 1999
Queen of Swords, 1997

Other books you might like:
Michael A. Eisner, *The Crusader*, 2001
Stephen R. Lawhead, *The Mystic Rose*, 2001
Sharon Kay Penman, *The Queen's Man*, 1998
Martha Rofheart, *Lionheart!*, 1981
Graham Shelby, *The Devil Is Loose*, 1974

942

BODIE THOENE
BROCK THOENE, Co-Author

The Jerusalem Scrolls

(New York: Viking, 2001)

Story type: Historical/Ancient Rome; Military
Series: Zion Legacy. Book IV
Subject(s): Jews; Arab-Israeli Wars; War
Major character(s): Moshe Sachar, Military Personnel; Alfie Halder, Military Personnel; Miryam, Widow(er), Biblical Figure
Time period(s): 1940s (1948); 1st century
Locale(s): Jerusalem, Israel

Summary: In the fourth book in the authors' Zion Legacy series, a story-within-a-story shifts back in time from 1948 during the battle for Jerusalem to the first century. Jewish freedom fighters Moshe Sachar and Alfie Halder escape the battle using secret underground passageways and reach a subterranean library, where they find a papyrus scroll telling the love story between a young Jewish widow, Miryam, and a Roman soldier, Marcus. Their story, set in ancient Israel, mirrors present-day cultural and religious conflict and allows for a retelling of the New Testament story.

Where it's reviewed:
Booklist, October 1, 2001, page 335
Library Journal, September 1, 2001, page 158
Publishers Weekly, August 27, 2001, page 48

Other books by the same author:
Jerusalem Heart, 2001
All Rivers to the Sea, 2000
Jerusalem Vigil, 2000
Thunder from Jerusalem, 2000
The Zion Covenant Series, 1986-1988

Other books you might like:
Lloyd C. Douglas, *The Robe*, 1942
Kanan Makiya, *The Rock*, 2001
Leon Uris, *Exodus*, 1958
Morris L. West, *The Tower of Babel*, 1968
Herman Wouk, *The Hope*, 1993

943

CHARLES TODD (Pseudonym of Charles Todd and Caroline Todd)

Watchers of Time

(New York: Bantam, 2001)

Story type: Historical/World War I; Mystery
Series: Inspector Ian Rutledge. Book 5

Subject(s): Mystery and Detective Stories; World War I; Religious Life
Major character(s): Ian Rutledge, Police Officer (Scotland Yard inspector), Veteran (World War I); Hamish MacLeod, Spirit, Military Personnel (corporal)
Time period(s): 1910s (1919)
Locale(s): Norfolk, England

Summary: The intriguing premise in this acclaimed historical mystery series set in the aftermath of World War I is that Scotland Yard Inspector Rutledge's partner is a dead man—Corporal Hamish MacLeod. MacLeod, whom Rutledge killed at the front, is now Rutledge's constant companion as a voice inside the inspector's head. The ''pair'' journey to Norfolk to investigate the death of a Catholic priest. It is the beginning of a mysterious tangle that reaches back in time to the sinking of the *Titanic*. As in the previous series installments, Todd is a master of delivering convincing post-World War I period details, and the trauma experienced by soldiers who served on the Western Front.

Where it's reviewed:
Booklist, October 1, 2001, page 303
Kirkus Reviews, August 15, 2001, page 1174
Library Journal, October 1, 2001, page 147
New York Times Book Review, November 23, 2001, page 21
Publishers Weekly, September 24, 2001, page 72

Other books by the same author:
Legacy of the Dead, 2000
Search the Dark, 1999
Wings of Fire, 1998
A Test of Wills, 1996

Other books you might like:
Pat Barker, *The Regeneration Trilogy*, 1992-1996
Jill Dawson, *Fred & Edie*, 2001
Gillian Linscott, *The Perfect Daughter*, 2001
Bill Mesce Jr., *Officer of the Court*, 2001
David Roberts, *The Bones of the Buried*, 2001

944

PETER TREMAYNE (Pseudonym of Peter Beresford Ellis)

Act of Mercy

(New York: St. Martin's Minotaur, 2001)

Story type: Historical/Medieval; Mystery
Series: Sister Fidelma. Book 8
Subject(s): Mystery and Detective Stories; Pilgrims and Pilgrimages; Sea Stories
Major character(s): Sister Fidelma, Religious (nun), Scholar (legal); Cian, Religious
Time period(s): 7th century (666)
Locale(s): *Barnacle Goose*, At Sea

Summary: In this outing, 7th century religious sleuth Sister Fidelma is at sea, aboard the *Barnacle Goose* on pilgrimage to the Shrine of St. James in Spain, taking the time to sort out her feelings for her companion Brother Eadulf. On board is Cian, Fidelma's girlish first love who had abandoned her ten years before. When a nun disappears during a storm, Sister Fidelma mounts her investigation among the passengers who all seem to be potential suspects.

Where it's reviewed:
Kirkus Reviews, October 15, 2001, page 1458
Publishers Weekly, October 22, 2001, page 52

Other books by the same author:
The Monk Who Vanished, 2001
Valley of the Shadow, 2000
The Spider's Web, 1999
The Subtle Serpent, 1998
Suffer Little Children, 1997

Other books you might like:
Alys Clare, *Ashes of the Elements*, 2001
Margaret Frazer, *The Sister Frevisse Series*, 1993-
Susanna Gregory, *The Matthew Bartholomew Series*, 1996-
Ian Morson, *The William Falconer Series*, 1994-
Ellis Peters, *The Brother Cadfael Series*, 1977-1994

945

WILLIAM TREMBLAY

The June Rise

(Golden, Colorado: Fulcrum, 2001)

Story type: Historical/American West; Indian Culture
Subject(s): Biography; Indians of North America; Letters
Major character(s): Joseph Antoine Janis, Historical Figure, Mountain Man; Red Cloud, Historical Figure, Indian (Lakota chief); First Elk Woman, Spouse (of Joseph), Indian (Oglala)
Time period(s): 19th century
Locale(s): Rocky Mountains; Great Plains

Summary: In a series of imagined letters, the novel animates the life and true story of mountain man Joseph Antoine Janis, who leaves his Missouri farm to become a trapper, living among the Indians on the Great Plains and in the Rocky Mountains. Becoming an adviser to Lakota chief Red Cloud, Janis marries an Oglala holy woman, First Elk Woman, and is eventually presented with a crucial choice between his wife and country. This is an impressive depiction of Indian culture and Western history.

Other books you might like:
Tim Champlin, *A Trail to Wounded Knee*, 2001
Ernest Hebert, *The Old American*, 2000
Andrew Huebner, *American by Blood*, 2000
Terry C. Johnston, *Turn the Stars Upside Down*, 2001
Larry McMurtry, *Boone's Lick*, 2000

946

LEONID TSYPKIN

Summer in Baden-Baden

(New York: New Directions, 2001)

Story type: Literary
Subject(s): Biography; Gambling
Major character(s): Fyodor Dostoyevsky, Historical Figure, Writer; Anna Dostoyevsky, Historical Figure, Spouse (of Fyodor)
Time period(s): 1860s (1867)
Locale(s): Baden-Baden, Germany

Summary: The novel's publication marks a rediscovery of a formerly lost masterwork by a Russian pathologist who died in 1981 before seeing any of his work published. It is an imaginative recounting of Dostoyevsky's honeymoon to Baden-Baden. The Russian author struggles between his love for his new wife and her stabilizing influence and his obsession with gambling that threatens to destroy them both.

Where it's reviewed:
New Yorker, October 1, 2001, page 98
Publishers Weekly, August 13, 2001, page 229

Other books you might like:
Malcolm Bradbury, *To the Hermitage*, 2001
J.M. Coetzee, *The Master of Petersburg*, 1994
Stephen Coulter, *The Devil Inside*, 1960
Bulat S. Okudzhava, *The Extraordinary Adventures of Secret Agent Shipov*, 1973
Jay Parini, *The Last Station*, 1990

947

NANCY E. TURNER

The Water and the Blood

(New York: Regan, 2001)

Story type: Historical/World War II
Subject(s): War; Race Relations; Small Town Life
Major character(s): Philadelphia ''Frosty'' Summers, Young Woman; Gordon Benally, Indian (Navajo), Military Personnel (Marine); John Moultrie, Police Officer (sheriff)
Time period(s): 1940s
Locale(s): Texas; California

Summary: Turner dramatizes prejudice in an East Texas town during World War II. The burning of an all-black church as a Halloween prank is a crime that refuses to stay buried, as Sheriff John Moultrie tries to identify the perpetrators. One of the participants is Philadelphia ''Frosty'' Summers, who convinces her parents to let her go to California to work in a war factory. There she meets Gordon Benally, a Navajo Indian soldier. Together they return to Frosty's hometown where he is labeled ''colored'' by the local KKK, and the truth surrounding the earlier crime is revealed.

Where it's reviewed:
Booklist, September 1, 2001, page 54
Publishers Weekly, October 8, 2001, page 43

Other books by the same author:
These Is My Words, 1998

Other books you might like:
Rilla Askew, *Fire in Beulah*, 2001
Ann Howard Creel, *The Magic of Ordinary Days*, 2001
Donna Hill, *Rhythms*, 2001
Allen Morris Jones, *Last Year's River*, 2001
Lee Martin, *Quakertown*, 2001

948

MARIO VARGAS LLOSA

The Feast of the Goat

(New York: Farrar, Straus, & Giroux, 2001)

Story type: Political
Subject(s): Political Crimes and Offenses; Political Movements; Dictators
Major character(s): Rafael Trujillo, Historical Figure, Political Figure; Urania Cabral, Lawyer; Agustin Cabral, Political Figure
Time period(s): 20th century
Locale(s): Dominican Republic

Summary: In an impressive performance Vargas Llosa interweaves multiple stories to capture the bloody reign of Dominican Republic dictator Rafael Trujillo, who was killed in a coup in 1961. The story of the conspirators' planning for his overthrow is juxtaposed with the return home by 49-year-old Manhattan attorney Urania Cabral, whose father, Agustin, sacrificed her to the dictator's lusts in order to curry favor with him. Trujillo himself is the most remarkable impersonation as he reflects back on his 31-year reign in a self-serving defense of the worst kinds of offenses. The novel brings the era to life and manages to put a disturbing human face on the man better known as ''the goat.''

Where it's reviewed:
Booklist, July 2001, page 1952
Kirkus Reviews, September 1, 2001, page 1242
Library Journal, September 1, 2001, page 236
New York Times Book Review, November 25, 2001, page 10
Publishers Weekly, July 30, 2001, page 55

Other books by the same author:
The Notebooks of Don Rigoberto, 1998
In Praise of the Stepmother, 1990
Who Killed Palomino Molero?, 1987
The War of the End of the World, 1984
Aunt Julia and the Scriptwriter, 1982

Other books you might like:
Julia Alvarez, *In the Time of the Butterflies*, 1994
Carlos Fuentes, *The Years with Laura Diaz*, 2001
Gabriel Garcia Marquez, *The Autumn of the Patriarch*, 1975
Ana Teresa Torres, *Dona Ines vs. Oblivion*, 2000
Manuel Vazquez Montalban, *Galindez*, 1992

949

JOHN VERNON

The Last Canyon

(Boston: Houghton Mifflin, 2001)

Story type: Historical/American West
Subject(s): Biography; Rivers
Major character(s): John Wesley Powell, Historical Figure, Explorer
Time period(s): 1860s (1869)
Locale(s): Colorado River

Summary: *The Last Canyon* is based on the actual 1869 voyage led by one-armed Civil War veteran John Wesley

Powell that covered much of the length of the Colorado River. This intriguing novel fills in the gaps in Powell's own account of the disasters that plagued the expedition resulting in the loss of a third of his men. Vernon parallels the story of Powell's downriver journey with the equally desperate experiences of a party of Paiutes, as both groups try to survive a hostile environment.

Where it's reviewed:
Publishers Weekly, August 27, 2001, page 47

Other books by the same author:
A Book of Reasons, 1999
All for Love, 1995
Peter Doyle, 1991
Lindbergh's Son, 1987
La Salle, 1986

Other books you might like:
Mary Ann Fraser, *In Search of the Grand Canyon*, 1995
David Nevin, *Dream West*, 1983
Wallace Stegner, *Beyond the Hundredth Meridian*, 1953
John Wilson, *North with Franklin*, 2000
Donald Worster, *A River Running West*, 2001

950

WILLIAM T. VOLLMANN

Argall

(New York: Viking, 2001)

Story type: Historical/Colonial America; Indian Culture
Series: Seven Dreams. Volume 3
Subject(s): Indians of North America; American Colonies
Major character(s): Samuel Argall, Historical Figure, Kidnapper; Pocahontas, Historical Figure, Indian; Captain John Smith, Leader, Historical Figure
Time period(s): 17th century
Locale(s): Jamestown, Virginia, American Colonies

Summary: This installment of Vollmann's ongoing Seven Dreams series of imaginative explorations of the European conquest of North America considers the settlement of Jamestown, Virginia, as a crucial confrontation between newcomers and Indians. The familiar figures of Pocahontas and Captain John Smith appear in a fresh interpretation, and the unsung figure of Samuel Argall, who kidnaps Pocahontas and suppresses Powhatan and his people, emerges as an embodiment of evil. However, this is hardly a simplified story of victimage, and those who persist in tackling Vollmann's massive reconstruction of the past will be richly rewarded with challenging insights all around. Although the third novel of the series, the book can stand alone and is perhaps the ideal starting point for the interested reader into this monumental series.

Where it's reviewed:
Booklist, August 2001, page 2053
Kirkus Reviews, September 1, 2001, page 1242
Library Journal, September 1, 2001, page 236
New York Times Book Review, September 30, 2001, page 18
Publishers Weekly, September 3, 2001, page 55

Other books by the same author:
The Royal Family, 2000
The Rifles, 1994
Butterfly Stories, 1993
Fathers and Crows, 1992
The Ice-Shirt, 1990

Other books you might like:
John Barth, *The Sot-Weed Factor*, 1967
Virginia Bernhard, *A Durable Fire*, 1990
Susan Donnell, *Pocahontas*, 1991
Thomas Pynchon, *Mason & Dixon*, 1997
Burton Wohl, *Soldier in Paradise*, 1977

951

SUSAN VREELAND

The Passion of Artemisia

(New York: Viking, 2001)

Story type: Historical/Seventeenth Century
Subject(s): Biography; Artists and Art; Women
Major character(s): Artemisia Gentileschi, Historical Figure, Artist; Orazio Gentileschi, Historical Figure, Artist; Agostino Tassi, Historical Figure, Artist
Time period(s): 17th century
Locale(s): Florence, Italy; Rome, Italy; Genoa, Italy

Summary: Vreeland offers a fictional autobiography of Italian Renaissance painter Artemisia Gentileschi, the first woman artist to be elected to the Accademia dell'Arte. Artemisia's is a fascinating story that includes her being raped by her artist father's colleague, Agostino Tassi, and a hastily arranged marriage after taking Tassi to court. She begins to achieve artistic distinction and patronage by the Medicis in Florence while struggling against the gender bias of the period.

Where it's reviewed:
Booklist, December 1, 2001, page 607
Kirkus Reviews, December 1, 2001, page 1644
Library Journal, December 2001, page 177
Publishers Weekly, December 17, 2001, page 64

Other books by the same author:
Girl in Hyacinth Blue, 1999
What Love Sees, 1998

Other books you might like:
Anna Banti, *Artemisia*, 1988
Harriet Scott Chessman, *Lydia Cassatt Reading the Morning Paper*, 2001
Alexandra Lapierre, *Artemisia*, 2000
Judith Lennox, *The Italian Garden*, 1993
Barbara Mujica, *Frida*, 2001

952

ANNA LEE WALDO

Circle of Stars

(New York: St. Martin's Press, 2001)

Story type: Historical/Medieval; Saga
Series: Druid Circle. Book 2
Subject(s): Indians of North America; Middle Ages; Druids

Major character(s): Madoc ap Owain Gwynedd, Historical Figure, Bastard Son (of Prince Owain); Cougar, Indian (Calusa)
Time period(s): 12th century
Locale(s): Ireland; North America; Wales

Summary: Intrigued by a legend that a Welshman named Madoc sailed to America three centuries before Columbus, Waldo continues her exploration of what might have been, begun in *Circle of Stones*. Madoc, the illegitimate son of a Welsh prince, leads a group of Druids west across the ocean into the unknown. In America, Madoc's fate is connected with a Calusa woman, Cougar. Waldo expertly supports her suppositions with solid research that makes this tale ring with authenticity.

Where it's reviewed:
Booklist, July 2001, page 1984
Kirkus Reviews, June 1, 2001, page 772
Publishers Weekly, July 30, 2001, page 61

Other books by the same author:
Circle of Stones, 1999
Prairie, 1986
Sacajawea, 1978

Other books you might like:
Don Coldsmith, *Runestone*, 1995
Kate Horsley, *Confessions of a Pagan Nun*, 2001
Bernard Knight, *Madoc, Prince of America*, 1977
Morgan Llywelyn, *Druids*, 1991
Sharon Kay Penman, *Here Be Dragons*, 1988

953

KEN WALES
DAVID POLING, Co-Author

Sea of Glory

(Nashville: Broadman & Holman, 2001)

Story type: Historical/World War II
Subject(s): Sea Stories; Religious Life; War
Major character(s): John Washington, Religious (military chaplain), Historical Figure; Clark Poling, Religious (military chaplain), Historical Figure; Alex Goode, Religious (military chaplain), Historical Figure
Time period(s): 1940s (1943)
Locale(s): *U.S.A.T. Dorchester*, At Sea (North Atlantic)

Summary: Based on an actual World War II incident, the authors' tell the stirring and inspiring story of four military chaplains—Catholic priest John Washington, Dutch Reform Minister Clark Poling, Methodist pastor George Fox, and Rabbi Alex Goode—aboard the army transport ship *U.S.A.T. Dorchester* in 1943. Attacked by a U-boat, the chaplains' heroic sacrifice is documented here.

Where it's reviewed:
Booklist, August 2001, page 2088
Library Journal, September 1, 2001, page 236
Publishers Weekly, August 20, 2001, page 58

Other books you might like:
Harry Homewood, *Silent Sea*, 1981
Richard Jessup, *Sailor*, 1969
Gerald F. Lieberman, *The Sea Lepers*, 1971
Philip McCutchan, *Cameron's Crossing*, 1982
Nicholas Monsarrat, *The Cruel Sea*, 1951

954

STEVE WEINER

The Yellow Sailor

(Woodstock, New York: Overlook, 2001)

Story type: Historical/World War I
Subject(s): Shipwrecks; War
Major character(s): Nicholas Bremml, Sailor; Julius Bernai, Shipowner, Homosexual; Jacek Gorecki, Sailor
Time period(s): 1910s
Locale(s): Hamburg, Germany; Prague, Czechoslovakia

Summary: This eerily surrealistic story set at the outbreak of World War I follows the fate of crew members aboard the merchant vessel *Yellow Sailor* that runs aground in Polish waters. The crew is left adrift in war torn Europe, and the novel chronicles what happens to young Nicholas Bremml, who drifts from prostitute to prostitute before ending up selling magic charms in Prague's Jewish section; gay shipowner, Julius Bernai, who winds up in a sanitarium and is in love with his doctor's wife; and electrician Jacek Gorecki, who must dodge firing squads shooting deserters before finding refuge as a miner. Dreamy and absurdist, the novel creates a compelling nightmare landscape.

Where it's reviewed:
Kirkus Reviews, August 1, 2001, page 1064
Publishers Weekly, August 27, 2001, page 52

Other books by the same author:
The Museum of Love, 1994

Other books you might like:
John Biggin, *The Two-Headed Eagle*, 1996
Susan M. Dodd, *The Silent Woman*, 2001
Alexander Fullerton, *The Blooding of the Guns*, 2001
Gary Livingston, *Tears of Ice*, 2001
Lawrence Norfolk, *In the Shape of a Boar*, 2001

955

WILLIAM F. WELD

Stillwater

(New York: Simon & Schuster, 2002)

Story type: Historical/Depression Era; Historical/Americana
Subject(s): Coming-of-Age; Politics
Major character(s): Jamieson Kooby, Teenager, Orphan; Hannah Corkery, Young Woman
Time period(s): 1930s (1938)
Locale(s): Swift River Valley, Massachusetts

Summary: After two light-hearted political satires, the former Massachusetts governor shifts to a serious historical drama set during the 1930s as communities in the Swift River Valley deal with the imminent creation of a reservoir that will sweep everything away. Narrated by a Huck Finn-like orphan, Jamieson Kooby, the novel tells the story of the community's resistance and opposition to the corrupt politicians that railroaded the reservoir plan. Weld does a creditable job connecting the community with the wider world of big league politics and uses his considerable expertise in how things work politically to fuel an often compelling human story.

Where it's reviewed:
Kirkus Reviews, October 15, 2001, page 1451
Library Journal, October 15, 2001, page 111
Publishers Weekly, October 22, 2001, page 42

Other books by the same author:
Big Ugly, 1999
Mackerel by Moonlight, 1998

Other books you might like:
Kathleen Cambor, *In Sunlight, in a Beautiful Garden*, 2000
Ann Howard Creel, *The Magic of Ordinary Days*, 2001
Aaron Roy Even, *Bloodroot*, 2000
John R. Hayes, *Catskill*, 2001
Brad Kessler, *Lick Creek*, 2001

956

MORRIS L. WEST

The Last Confession

(Thorndike, Maine: Center Point, 2001)

Story type: Historical/Renaissance; Historical/Seventeenth Century
Subject(s): Religious Conflict
Major character(s): Giordano Bruno, Historical Figure, Philosopher
Time period(s): 16th century; 17th century
Locale(s): Europe

Summary: This best-selling Australian writer's posthumously published novel presents a fictionalized account of the imprisonment and execution of the 16th century thinker Giordano Bruno for heresy. Delivered as a last will and testament, Bruno chronicles his life and religious convictions, which he refuses to recant at the cost of his life. The author died before completing the book's last chapters. What remains, however, provides the reader with an illuminating look at a unique individual and his times.

Where it's reviewed:
Booklist, September 1, 2001, page 54
Library Journal, September 1, 2001, page 236
Publishers Weekly, August 20, 2001, page 59

Other books by the same author:
Eminence, 1998
Lazarus, 1990
Clowns of God, 1981
The Shoes of the Fisherman, 1963
Devil's Advocate, 1959

Other books you might like:
James Blish, *Doctor Mirabilis*, 1971
Serge Filippini, *The Man in Flames*, 1999
Janet Lewis, *The Trial of Soren Qvist*, 1947
Lewis Weinstein, *The Heretic*, 2000
Morton Leonard Yanow, *The Nolan*, 1998

957

RICHARD S. WHEELER

Downriver

(New York: Forge, 2001)

Story type: Historical/American West; Mountain Man
Series: Barnaby Skye. Book 12
Subject(s): Wilderness; Rivers
Major character(s): Barnaby Skye, Mountain Man; Victoria Skye, Spouse (of Barnaby), Indian (Crow); Alexandre Bonfils, Trader (fur)
Time period(s): 1830s (1838)
Locale(s): Missouri River

Summary: Mountain man Barnaby Skye and his Crow Indian wife, Victoria, are headed from the Rockies to St. Louis so Skye can gain a position as post trader for the American Fur Company. It's a 1,500-mile journey down the Missouri River by paddlewheel steamer with danger on shore and from their fellow passengers, particularly from Alexandre Bonfils, a Creole fur trader and Skye's competitor for the trader job. Wheeler is a storytelling master who seems to be getting better and better in captivating the reader with authentic period details.

Where it's reviewed:
Publishers Weekly, October 8, 2001, page 40

Other books by the same author:
Aftershocks, 1999
Masterson, 1999
Buffalo Commons, 1998
Second Lives, 1997
Dodging Red Cloud, 1989

Other books you might like:
James D. Houston, *Snow Mountain Passage*, 2001
Terry C. Johnston, *Death Rattle*, 1999
Larry McMurtry, *Boone's Lick*, 2000
Earl Murray, *Gabriella*, 1999
James Alexander Thom, *Sign-Talker*, 2000

958

GERARD WILLIAMS

Dr. Mortimer and the Aldgate Mystery

(New York: St. Martin's Minotaur, 2001)

Story type: Historical/Victorian; Mystery
Series: Dr. James Mortimer. Book 1
Subject(s): Mystery and Detective Stories
Major character(s): James Mortimer, Doctor, Spouse (of Violet); Violet Branscombe, Doctor; Lavinia Nancarrow, Gentlewoman
Time period(s): 1890s (1890)
Locale(s): London, England

Summary: The debut volume of the author's intriguing historical mystery series features Dr. James Mortimer, a character from Arthur Conan Doyle's *The Hound of the Baskervilles*, as sleuth. Joining Dr. Violet Branscombe's clinic for abused women in London's Whitechapel district, Dr. Mortimer investigates the reason behind the confinement of Lavinia

Nancarrow by her guardian. The novel features a brief appearance by Dr. Watson and a fine sense of the period in a story that draws on the lot of Victorian women.

Where it's reviewed:
Booklist, July 2001, page 1988
Kirkus Reviews, May 15, 2001, page 713
Library Journal, July 2001, page 129
Publishers Weekly, June 25, 2001, page 52

Other books by the same author:
Dr. Mortimer and the Barking Man Mystery, 2001

Other books you might like:
Laurie R. King, *The Mary Russell/Sherlock Holmes Series*, 1994-
Michael Kurland, *The Great Game*, 2001
Gillian Linscott, *The Nell Bray Series*, 1991-
Larry Millett, *Sherlock Holmes and the Secret Alliance*, 2001
M.J. Trow, *The Inspector Lestrade Series*, 1999-

959

JAMES WILSON

The Dark Clue

(New York: Atlantic Monthly, 2001)

Story type: Historical/Victorian
Subject(s): Suspense; Artists and Art; Biography
Major character(s): Walter Hartright, Gentleman; Marion Halcombe, Gentlewoman
Time period(s): 1850s; 1860s
Locale(s): London, England

Summary: This atmospheric literary thriller resurrects two of Wilkie Collins' characters from the suspense classic *The Woman in White*—Walter Hartright and Marion Halcombe—as investigators into the strange, divided life of 19th century painter J.M.W. Turner. Hartright is commissioned to write a scandal-free biography and joins forces with his sister-in-law, Marion, to try to solve the enigma surrounding the painter. The novel features a knowing eye for the details of London life and the biographical details of a fascinating artist.

Where it's reviewed:
Booklist, November 15, 2001, page 554
Kirkus Reviews, September 1, 2001, page 1243
Library Journal, September 1, 2001, page 236
New York Times Book Review, November 25, 2001, page 21
Publishers Weekly, August 20, 2001, page 51

Other books by the same author:
The Earth Shall Weep, 1998

Other books you might like:
Stephanie Barron, *The Jane Austen Series*, 1996-
Tracy Chevalier, *Falling Angels*, 2001
Michael Noonan, *The Sun Is God*, 1973
William J. Palmer, *The Dons and Mr. Dickens*, 2000
Roberta Rogow, *The Charles Dodgson/Arthur Conan Doyle Series*, 1998-

960

ROBERT WILSON

The Company of Strangers

(New York: Harcourt, 2001)

Story type: Historical/World War II; Espionage
Subject(s): Spies; War
Major character(s): Andrea Aspinall, Spy, Scientist (mathematician); Karl Voss, Diplomat (German), Spy
Time period(s): 20th century
Locale(s): Lisbon, Portugal; Berlin, Germany; England

Summary: In this espionage thriller and love story, mathematician Andrea Aspinall is recruited as a British agent and sent to search for atomic secrets in Portugal during World War II. There she meets and falls in love with German diplomat Karl Voss who is conspiring to kill Hitler. Voss is soon captured, sent to prison, and reported dead. Andrea later marries, but is reactivated years later and sent to East Germany on a new mission that forces her to revisit her past. This is an intriguing, if at times somewhat contrived, thriller.

Where it's reviewed:
Booklist, July 2001, page 1989
Kirkus Reviews, August 15, 2001, page 1162
Library Journal, August 2001, page 167
Publishers Weekly, July 30, 2001, page 55

Other books by the same author:
A Darkening Star, 1999
A Small Death in Lisbon, 1999
The Big Killing, 1999
Instruments of Darkness, 1999
Blood Is Dirt, 1997

Other books you might like:
Sebastian Faulks, *Charlotte Gray*, 1998
Ken Follett, *Jackdaws*, 2001
Alan Furst, *Red Gold*, 1999
J. Robert Janes, *Sandman*, 1997
Philip Kerr, *The Berlin Noir Series*, 1993-

961

JANICE WOODS WINDLE

Will's War

(New York: Longstreet, 2001)

Story type: Historical/Americana; Historical/World War I
Subject(s): Trials
Major character(s): Will Bergfeld, Defendant; William Hawley Atwell, Lawyer
Time period(s): 1910s (1917)
Locale(s): Abilene, Texas

Summary: Based on family history, Windle's novel treats the anti-German hysteria that struck America during World War I. German American Will Bergfeld of Abilene, Texas, is accused of plotting to kill President Woodrow Wilson and he is defended by William Hawley Atwell. The author synthesizes hundreds of pages of court documents in her grandfather's own trial into a dramatic and suspenseful narrative that provides an authentic look at Texas during the period.

Where it's reviewed:
Library Journal, October 1, 2001, page 144
Publishers Weekly, October 1, 2001, page 37

Other books by the same author:
Hill Country, 1998
True Women, 1993

Other books you might like:
Kathleen Cambor, *In Sunlight, in a Beautiful Garden*, 2000
Elsie Burch Donald, *Nashborough*, 2001
David Anthony Durham, *Gabriel's Story*, 2001
Allen Morris Jones, *Last Year's River*, 2001
Lalita Tademy, *Cane River*, 2001

962

BARBARA WOOD

Sacred Ground

(New York: St. Martin's Press, 2001)

Story type: Historical/Pre-history; Indian Culture
Subject(s): Mothers and Daughters; Women; Archaeology
Major character(s): Erica Tyler, Anthropologist; Marimi, Indian (Topaa)
Time period(s): Multiple Time Periods
Locale(s): Santa Monica Mountains, California

Summary: Wood's wide-ranging novel connects two stories separated by 2,000 years. When an earthquake opens up a cave in the Santa Monica Mountains, anthropologist Erica Tyler begins to investigate "the find of the century." The novel flashes back to the story of Marimi, a Topaa Indian, who is expelled from her clan and must search for a new settlement. Glimpses of Marimi's female descendents are juxtaposed with Erica's research into the mysteries of an ancient people.

Where it's reviewed:
Booklist, September 1, 2001, page 55
Kirkus Reviews, July 15, 2001, page 978
Publishers Weekly, July 30, 2001, page 58

Other books by the same author:
Perfect Harmony, 1998
The Prophetess, 1997
The Dreaming, 1991
Green City in the Sun, 1988
The Magdelene Scrolls, 1978

Other books you might like:
Don Coldsmith, *Raven Mocker*, 2001
John R. Dann, *Song of the Axe*, 2001
Kathleen O'Neal Gear, *The Summoning God*, 2000
W. Michael Gear, co-author
Judith Tarr, *Daughter of Lir*, 2001
Anna Lee Waldo, *Circle of Stars*, 2001

963

CHELSEA QUINN YARBRO

A Feast in Exile

(New York: Tor, 2001)

Story type: Vampire Story; Historical/Fantasy
Series: Chronicles of Saint-Germain. Book 14
Subject(s): Vampires
Major character(s): Sanat Ji Mani, Vampire; Tulsi Kil, Slave; Timur-i-Lenhk, Military Personnel (Mongol general), Historical Figure (Tamburlaine)
Time period(s): 14th century
Locale(s): Delhi, India

Summary: In this installment of Yarbro's popular historical vampire series, Saint-Germain, as Sanat Ji Mani, is living in Delhi at the end of the 14th century which is under attack by the Tartar warlord Timur-i-Lenhk, known to the world as the merciless Tamburlaine. Captured by the warlord, he is ordered to serve him as a healer, and as the vampire struggles to survive his captivity, he falls in love with a slave girl, Tulsi Kil. As in all of Yarbro's novels, the ways of the vampire are put in the context of a well-researched and convincing period background.

Where it's reviewed:
Booklist, October 15, 2001, page 388
Kirkus Reviews, August 15, 2001, page 1176

Other books by the same author:
Come Twilight, 2000
Communion Blood, 1999
Darker Light, 1999
Blood Roses, 1998
The Angry Angel, 1998

Other books you might like:
Jonathan Fast, *Golden Fire*, 1986
Barbara Hambly, *Those Who Hunt the Night*, 1988
Karen Harbaugh, *The Vampire Viscount*, 1995
Thomas Hoover, *The Moghul*, 1983
Anne Rice, *Blood and Gold*, 2001

964

MARLY YOUMANS

The Wolf Pit

(New York: Farrar, Straus & Giroux, 2001)

Story type: Historical/American Civil War
Subject(s): War; Slavery
Major character(s): Robin, Military Personnel (Confederate soldier); Agate Freebody, Slave
Time period(s): 1860s (1864)
Locale(s): United States

Summary: This intense Civil War tale parallels the experiences of a mulatto slave girl, Agate Freebody, and a Confederate soldier named Robin. It is 1864 and the endless war continues unabated as Robin deals with combat and capture by the Union. Meanwhile, Agate, on the point of being sold, manages to get someone to buy her using Agate's own secret stash of money. The buyer is Robin's mother and the pair bond. The novel weaves its two stories into a succession of heartfelt and moving small moments of discovery, pain, and possibilities.

Where it's reviewed:
Kirkus Reviews, July 15, 2001, page 977
Publishers Weekly, July 23, 2001, page 47

Other books by the same author:
Catherwood, 1996
Little Jordan, 1995

Other books you might like:
Charles Frazier, *Cold Mountain*, 1997
Nora Hague, *Letters from an Age of Reason*, 2001
Donald McCaig, *Jacob's Ladder*, 1998
Owen Parry, *Call Each River Jordan*, 2001
Alice Randall, *The Wind Done Gone*, 2001

Inspirational Fiction in Review
by
Melissa Hudak

The publishers of inspirational fiction have continued to stay the course in the last few months, making few changes to those subgenres that have proven popular in the past. Nothing particularly groundbreaking has been released in this genre recently, with authors and subjects which were previously successful continuing to dominate the inspirational fiction market, as well as the Christian Booksellers of America's bestsellers lists. As is always the case with inspirational fiction, the popular subgenres continued to be historical fiction and romantic fiction, with other subgenres such as mysteries lagging far behind in terms of popularity.

In the historical fiction arena, nearly all of the dominant names in the inspirational fiction world released new works. Authors such as Gilbert Morris, Stephen A. Bly, Janette Oke, and Al and Joanna Lacy all added titles to long-established inspirational/historical fiction series. In fact, Morris published the twenty-seventh title in his House of Winslow series, taking the Winslow family into the Roaring Twenties. In comparison, Bly's Fortunes of the Black Hills series is only up to the fourth volume and the Lacys' Mail Order Bride series is on volume eight.

Relative newcomers to the historical fiction subgenre also released some interesting titles that offered some variation on the usual settings of inspirational historical fiction. Tracie Peterson, who has been a notable writer in the inspirational fiction genre for some time now, continued her historical series, Yukon Quest, with the third volume, *Rivers of Gold*. The Alaskan setting makes a pleasant change since so many inspirational/historical fictional writers set their works in the more well-known west of California, Colorado, or New Mexico. In *Rivers of Gold*, Peterson takes good advantage of the setting by having the lead character interact, to some degree, with Alaskan natives, bringing a new dimension to the series which mainly focuses on the white settlers of Alaska.

World War II proved to be a popular setting for historical novels, as Linda Chaikin, Judith Pella, and co-authors Ken Wales and David Poling use the war years as a dramatic backdrop to their stories. Of special interest is *Sea of Glory* by Wales and Poling. Knowing that the story of four chaplains, who give their lives in order to save others, is actually true gives the book a depth of feeling that might be missing in a totally fictional account.

That said, Chaikin and Pella still deliver solidly entertaining stories in their World War II era novels. Chaikin has been writing the Day to Remember series for some years now, with several of the books set during World War II while other titles are contemporary stories using the war years as a precursor of current day events. The fifth book in the series, *Friday's Child*, is set in Great Britain and is an interesting look at a country at war and how a woman faces having loved ones in the armed services. Pella's World War II novel is the first in her Daughters of Fortune series. The book tells the story of the privileged daughters of a wealthy and powerful newspaper publisher and the war is used as more of a dramatic backdrop to the women's personal problems than as a life-altering event. Although this book, *Written on the Wind*, tends more towards overly dramatic plot developments than those by Linda Chaikin and, especially, Wales and Poling, it is still an enjoyable read from an accomplished writer.

Another solid addition to the historical fiction subgenre in recent months is Stephanie Grace Whitson's *Heart of the Sandhills*. Whitson's series, Dakota Moons, is of special interest because it follows the life of a Native American woman in the 1860s who is trying to live in both the white and Indian worlds and is fully accepted in neither. The daughter of an Indian mother and a French father, Genevieve LaCroix Two Stars was once married to a white man and, in *Heart of the Sandhills*, is currently married to an Indian. The glimpses Whitson provides of the settlement of the American West through Indian eyes are both intriguing and enlightening. The Dakota Moons series is not your stereotypical portrait of the bad Indian and the brave settler, or even the more current noble Native American and evil settler. Instead, characters of both races are multidimensional, and thus flawed, making this series an especially believable one.

More conventional looks at the West appear in the books by Lauraine Snelling, Kathleen Morgan, and Jane Kirkpatrick. Snelling's title is a continuation of her popular Red River of the North series that included six titles published from 1996 to 1999. The new series, Return to Red River, focuses on the children of the original Norwegian immigrants who were featured in the earlier books. This first title, *A Dream to Follow*, isn't quite as gripping as those in the original series, which is one of the most believable and historically accurate in inspirational/historical fiction, but hopefully Return to Red River will develop over time.

Both Kathleen Morgan and Jane Kirkpatrick are relative newcomers to the inspirational fiction world, but both are fine writers who deserve more attention. Morgan's Brides of Culdee Creek series, which usually focuses on the men of the MacKay family and the women they love, changes its focus to one of the MacKay women in *Child of Promise*. When the man she loves marries another woman, Beth MacKay gives up her hopes for marriage. After attending medical school, Beth returns to her hometown to discover her former love is in great trouble and needs her help. Just as in the Cheney Duvall series by Lynn and Gilbert Morris, which also features a female doctor practicing in the 1800s, Morgan does not pretend that the challenges and prejudices women faced in pursuing a then mostly male profession were easy to overcome. Though both *Child of Promise* and the Cheney Duvall series emphasize romance over the pursuit of a medical career, it is still nice to see female characters realistically pursuing what was in their time a nearly impossible dream.

Jane Kirkpatrick is another writer who portrays a realistic rather than romanticiized view of the American West. In what is supposed to be the concluding book in the Kinship and Courage series, *What Once We Loved*, Kirkpatrick again shows her in-depth historical research that complements, but never overwhelms, the poignant story of a group of widows attempting to survive on their own as they travel west in the 1850s. Kirkpatrick makes the women realistic to their time and setting, while never losing a reader's awe at their will to survive. These are not superwomen overcoming impossible odds, but real women who do the best they can in adverse conditions.

The majority of these historical inspirational titles contain romantic elements, but this genre is also known for its contemporary romances. Among the best inspirational romances to be published in recent months were Terri Blackstock's *Emerald Windows*, Debra White Smith's *To Rome with Love*, and Lori Wick's *Bamboo & Lace*. What is of special interest about these three books is how they contain some plot elements that would have been unthinkable to include in inspirational fiction just a few years ago, but are becoming increasingly common.

Terri Blackstock's *Emerald Windows* is the story of Brooke Martin, who leaves her hometown in shame after being unjustly implicated in an adulterous scandal. Years later, Brooke comes home and finds out that not much has changed in Hayden, Missouri. The town still has its gossips and many of the people who are quick to judge Brooke are supposed to be devout Christians. This particular plot element would probably have never seen print in the inspirational market just a few years ago, but it helps make *Emerald Windows* believable by showing readers that even devout Christians can make mistakes.

Lori Wick's *Bamboo & Lace* also shows a devout Christian making some bad judgments. Lily Walsh is a very sheltered young woman. In fact, her religious father protects her so much that she knows virtually nothing of the world outside her isolated mountain village. He raises her to be totally submissive, to the point at which she is not even allowed to look him in the eye. Then Lily's brother, who lives in Hawaii, obtains their father's permission for Lily to visit him. Suddenly the whole world is open to Lily and she is no longer willing to be the submissive daughter her father raised. Wick's portrayal of a Christian man who makes mistakes, like that of the flawed characters in Blackstock's *Emerald Windows*, give these books a depth and realism that inspirational fiction has long needed.

On a lighter note, Debra White Smith's *To Rome with Love* tells the story of Melissa Moore, who accepts an invitation to go on a romantic cruise with her former fiance, who hopes to rekindle their romance. Of course, since this is an inspirational romantic novel, the two have separate cabins and the romance between Melissa and her one time fiance develops along purely spiritual rather than physical lines. However, just the fact that Melissa goes on a cruise with a man she is not married to makes this plot a real shocker in the squeaky clean world of inspirational romance.

While historical fiction and contemporary romances are always the most popular subgenres in inspirational fiction, there have been some fine mysteries published in this genre over the years. Recent months have seen the release of several mysteries that are just as good as those published by more mainstream publishers. Since some of these titles are by first time authors, or are first titles in a proposed series, it can only be hoped the titles prove popular enough to turn these first efforts into long-standing series.

Two recent inspirational mysteries use computers and computer experts to further their plots. The first novel by the writing team of Rosey Dow and Andrew Snaden, *Betrayed*, has the daughter of a computer expert on the run after her father's actions lead criminals to believe she has some deadly secrets. Technical details abound in the book, but never overwhelm the plot. Debra White Smith's *For Your Heart Only* also has a computer expert as a character. In this book, the computer expert goes to Detective Jacquelyn Lightfoot to get her assistance in finding out who is trying to kill him. It seems he has some secrets that may or may not be related to his computer knowledge. While the romantic elements in both of these titles tend to take center stage over the mystery, there are still enough mysterious elements present to satisfy most mystery fans.

Writer Lorena McCourtney has written romantic suspense novels, and most of her straightforward romance novels have mysterious elements, so it comes as no great surprise that she is now introducing a mystery series. *Whirlpool* is the first in the Julesburg Mysteries series. It is a well-written mystery, and the lead character, Stefanie Canfield, is a realistic portrait of a woman dragged into a terrifying situation by elements out of her control. Hopefully, this title will prove popular enough to merit repeat visits to the town of Julesburg.

Another debut mystery series is Terri Blackstock's Cape Refuge series, set in Georgia. In the first novel, also called *Cape Refuge*, the lead characters, especially the scarred librarian Blair Owens, are multidimensional and believable. Although Blair is a well-written character, it is the setting of coastal Georgia that takes center stage here. Blackstock makes the town of Cape Refuge come alive to the point that readers may believe it is a real community.

Lyn Cote is probably best known for her romance stories, most of which were published by Steeple Hill, the inspirational fiction imprint of Harlequin. However, her mystery novel *Winter's Secret*, published by Tyndale House, came as a pleasant surprise. The lead characters are believably human and the mystery itself, while not overly challenging, is intriguing. The wintry Wisconsin setting is also well portrayed.

Another mystery that came as a great surprise was Ellen Edwards Kennedy's *Irregardless of Murder*. Readers who enjoy traditional mysteries will find much to admire here. The lead character is Amelia Prentice, a teacher who is still single in her forties (and not terribly happy about it). Her life has become one of unvarying routine. Then, all of a sudden, Amelia's calm and fairly boring life is interrupted when she trips over a dead body in the library. Pair that plot development with the return of the suitor she broke up with years before and Amelia's once dull life is suddenly exciting, perhaps a bit more exciting than she'd like it to be. Kennedy's debut is easily the best of the mysteries in the inspirational fiction market this year.

Obviously, *Irregardless of Murder* is on my list of the top twenty- five inspirational fiction titles. Among the others are a mix of historical fiction, romances, and contemporary novels that should please a wide array of readers. Although none of these books could be said to be innovative or groundbreaking, they are certain to provide solid entertainment to readers of the genre.

Recommended Titles

Terri Blackstock, *Emerald Windows*

Stephen A. Bly, *The Outlaw's Twin Sister*

Linda Chaikin, *Friday's Child*

Brandilyn Collins, *Eyes of Elisha*

Lori Copeland and Angela Elwell Hunt, *A Warmth in Winter*

Rosey Dow and Andrew Snaden, *Betrayed*

Gene Edwards, *The Gaius Diary*

Doris Elaine Fell, *Sunrise on Stradbury Square*

Robin Jones Gunn, *Wildflowers*

Dee Henderson, *The Protector*

Dee Henderson, *True Valor*

Jerry B. Jenkins, *Hometown Legend*

Sally D. John, *A Journey by Chance*

Jan Karon, *In This Mountain*

Ellen Edwards Kennedy, *Irregardless of Murder*

Jane Kirkpatrick, *What Once We Loved*

Bonnie Leon, *Worthy of Riches*

Lorena McCourtney, *Whirlpool*

Kathleen Morgan, *Child of Promise*

Gilbert Morris, *The Golden Angel*

Debra White Smith, *To Rome with Love*

Travis Thrasher, *The Watermark*

Jamie Langston Turner, *A Garden to Keep*

Ken Wales and David Poling, *Sea of Glory*

Lori Wick, *Bamboo & Lace*

Inspirational Titles

965

CAROLYNE AARSEN

Twin Blessings

(New York: Steeple Hill, 2001)

Story type: Romance
Subject(s): Orphans
Major character(s): Sandra Bachman, Artist, Tutor; Logan Napier, Architect
Time period(s): 2000s
Locale(s): Cypress Hills, Alberta, Canada

Summary: Logan Napier truly wants to do the best he can to support his orphaned twin nieces, but he is better at providing material things than personal affection. As a result, when his mother leaves on vacation and the twins' tutor quits, Logan is both annoyed and apprehensive to have to put his business concerns on hold to deal with Brittany and Bethany. Then Logan meets struggling artist Sandra Bachman, who agrees to take over as the twins' tutor. The girls love Sandra and are soon hatching matchmaking schemes to pair her up with their uncle. However, straightlaced Logan and free-spirited Sandra don't seem to have enough in common to make a romance.

Other books by the same author:
A Hero for Kelsey, 2001
A Family at Last, 2000
A Mother at Heart, 2000
A Family-Style Christmas, 1999
The Cowboy's Bride, 1999

Other books you might like:
Irene Brand, *Summer's Promise*, 2001
Valerie Hansen, *The Troublesome Angel*, 2000
Arlene James, *With Baby in Mind*, 1998
Beverly Lewis, *The Redemption of Sarah Cain*, 2000
Carole Gift Page, *A Child Shall Lead Them*, 2001

966

SYLVIA BAMBOLA

Tears in a Bottle

(Sisters, Oregon: Multnomah, 2001)

Story type: Contemporary
Subject(s): Abortion
Major character(s): Becky Taylor, Student—High School
Time period(s): 2000s
Locale(s): United States

Summary: Becky Taylor has just been accepted into college and will be the first person in her family to go beyond high school. She is thrilled and wants nothing to get in the way of her future, but then Becky discovers she is pregnant. Her boyfriend, father, and nearly everybody else urges her to get an abortion. Although unwilling, she finally agrees. While lying on a table in the recovery room of the abortion clinic, Becky hears gunshots. To her horror, she is the only person left alive in the clinic after the massacre. Both experiences leave Becky traumatized and she becomes suicidal. In desperation, her father contacts a pro-life organization that counsels women who have had abortions, hoping they can help his daughter.

Where it's reviewed:
Library Journal, September 1, 2001, page 154
Publishers Weekly, September 24, 2001, page 65

Other books by the same author:
Refiner's Fire, 2000

Other books you might like:
Donna Fletcher Crow, *All Things New*, 1997
Athol Dickson, *Every Hidden Thing*, 1998
Beverly LaHaye, *Showers in Season*, 2000
James R. Lucas, *A Perfect Persecution*, 2001
Francine Rivers, *The Atonement Child*, 1999

967

DEBORAH BEDFORD

A Rose by the Door

(New York: Warner, 2001)

Story type: Contemporary
Subject(s): Accidents; Grief
Major character(s): Bea Bartling, Parent; Gemma Bartling, Widow(er), Single Parent; Paisley, Child (of Gemma)
Time period(s): 2000s
Locale(s): Ash Hollow, Nebraska

Summary: Ever since her son Nathan left home suddenly, Bea Bartling has been anxiously waiting for him to return. After five years, Bea receives the news that Nathan is dead. Shattered by grief, Bea loses all interest in life and is unable to respond when Nathan's widow, Gemma, shows up on her doorstep with her daughter, Paisley. Gemma had counted on Bea for help, so she is stuck in town with no place to stay. While visiting a museum, Gemma and Paisley get locked in overnight. When they are discovered, the two are arrested. A kind-hearted police officer realizes Gemma is in a bind, so he arranges for the mother and child to stay with a local minister until they get back on their feet. Gemma finds a job and settles into life in Ash Hollow, Nebraska, and soon attempts to contact Bea again. Eventually Bea thaws somewhat, but she is unable to fully accept Gemma and Paisley's love. Unless Bea somehow finds it in her heart to open herself up to the two, she is destined for a life of loneliness with her grief for her son her only companion.

Where it's reviewed:
Library Journal, November 1, 2001, page 74
Publishers Weekly, September 24, 2001, page 64

Other books by the same author:
Harvest Dance, 1997
Chickadee, 1996
Timberline, 1996
A Child's Promise, 1995

Other books you might like:
Lynn N. Austin, *Eve's Daughters*, 1999
Linda Hall, *Margaret's Peace*, 1998
Francine Rivers, *Leota's Garden*, 1999
Penelope J. Stokes, *The Amethyst Heart*, 2000
Johanna Verweerd, *The Winter Garden*, 2001

968

EILEEN BERGER

A Family for Jana

(New York: Steeple Hill, 2002)

Story type: Romance
Subject(s): Single Parent Families
Major character(s): Jana Jenson, Single Parent, Student; Ray Hawkins, Professor
Time period(s): 2000s
Locale(s): Sylvan Falls, Pennsylvania

Summary: Jana Jenson is a struggling single parent trying to raise her son on her own. Going back to school makes things even more difficult than they were before, but she intends to make something of her life. Jana thinks she has no room in her life for romance, especially since she was abandoned by her son's father. Then she meets handsome college professor Ray Hawkins. Ray isn't looking for romance either, but the two soon find they are kindred spirits.

Other books by the same author:
A Special Kind of Family, 2001
Reunions, 2000
A Family for Andi, 1999
To Galilee with Love, 1999
The Deacon's Daughter, 1998

Other books you might like:
Carolyne Aarsen, *A Family-Style Christmas*, 1999
Irene Hannon, *A Family to Call Her Own*, 1998
Kate Welsh, *For the Sake of Her Child*, 1998
Cheryl Wolverton, *For Love of Hawk*, 1999
Lenora Worth, *Logan's Child*, 1998

969

LISA TAWN BERGREN
LYN COTE, Co-Author
MAUREEN PRATT, Co-Author

Letters of the Heart

(Wheaton, Illinois: Tyndale House, 2002)

Story type: Anthology; Romance
Subject(s): Letters
Time period(s): 19th century

Summary: The three romantic historical stories in this anthology all focus on couples who fall in love via the writing of letters. In "Until the Shadows Flee" by Lisa Tawn Bergren, a doctor takes over the practice of a dead physician, whose wife still works for the practice. Soon the new physician falls in love with the widow. Lyn Cote's "For Varina's Heart" tells the story of an immigrant girl who marries for convenience but falls in love after receiving romantic letters. The final story of the anthology is Maureen Pratt's "Dear Love." Violet Milton has her wedding all planned; all she is missing is the groom. After receiving some mysterious love letters, Violet finally has the man she wants.

Where it's reviewed:
Publishers Weekly, October 29, 2001, page 33

Other books you might like:
Andrea Boeshaar, *The Painting*, 1996
Carol Cox, *Resolutions*, 2000
Linda Ford, *Prairie Brides*, 2000
Veda Boyd Jones, *Summer Dreams*, 1997
Colleen L. Reece, *Frontiers*, 2000

970

TERRI BLACKSTOCK

Cape Refuge

(Grand Rapids, Michigan: Zondervan, 2002)

Story type: Mystery
Series: Cape Refuge. Book 1

Subject(s): Ministry; Murder
Major character(s): Blair Owens, Librarian; Morgan, Relative (sister of Blair)
Time period(s): 2000s
Locale(s): Cape Refuge, Georgia

Summary: Thelma and Wayne Owens are dedicated to their daughters, their bed-and-breakfast, and their seaside ministry. When the couple is found murdered, the police arrest their son-in-law Jonathan, who had fought with the couple soon before their deaths. However, the Owens' daughters, Blair and Morgan, are certain Jonathan had nothing to do with the deaths. Desperately wanting to clear her husband's name, Morgan joins Blair in a hunt for the real killer.

Other books by the same author:
Emerald Windows, 2001
Seaside, 2001
Trial by Fire, 2000
Word of Honor, 1999
Shadow of Doubt, 1998

Other books you might like:
B.J. Hoff, *The Daybreak Series*, 1995-
Ellen Edwards Kennedy, *Irregardless of Murder*, 2001
Gilbert Morris, *The Dani Ross Series*, 2000-
Gayle G. Roper, *The Amhearst Mysteries*, 1997-
Audrey Stallsmith, *The Thyme Will Tell Series*, 1998-

971

TERRI BLACKSTOCK

Emerald Windows

(Grand Rapids, Michigan: Zondervan, 2001)

Story type: Contemporary
Subject(s): Scandal
Major character(s): Brooke Martin, Artisan (stained glass creator); Nick Marcello, Teacher (former)
Time period(s): 2000s
Locale(s): Hayden, Missouri

Summary: Scandal forces Brooke Martin to leave her hometown of Hayden, Missouri and she has no intention of ever returning. However, after ten years' absence, Brooke, a talented stained glass designer, is offered a job in Hayden. Deciding to put the past behind her, Brooke returns only to discover the man who offered her the job is none other than the man whose name had been tangled with her own so many years before. Now Nick Marcello is a dedicated church worker, but he had been Brooke's high school teacher and the two had been accused of having an affair. Although Brooke agrees to stay in Hayden and finish the job, the old scandal is soon dredged up and Nick and Brooke once more become the subjects of gossip.

Other books by the same author:
Seaside, 2001
Trial by Fire, 2000
Word of Honor, 1999
Broken Wings, 1998
Private Justice, 1998

Other books you might like:
Lisa Tawn Bergren, *Pathways*, 2001
Karen Kingsbury, *A Moment of Weakness*, 2000
Jane Peart, *A Montclair Homecoming*, 2000
Gayle G. Roper, *The Key*, 1998
Lance Wubbels, *In the Shadow of a Secret*, 1999

972

STEPHEN A. BLY

Friends and Enemies

(Nashville: Broadman & Holman, 2002)

Story type: Historical/American West
Series: Fortunes of the Black Hills. Book 4
Subject(s): Railroads
Major character(s): Robert Fortune, Detective (railroad)
Time period(s): 1890s
Locale(s): Deadwood, South Dakota

Summary: Robert Fortune has retired from the military, but is still questioning whether he made the right choice. However, he is happily married to Jamie Sue and the father of three children he would like to get to know better since army life kept him away from them for long stretches of time. Returning to his hometown of Deadwood, South Dakota, Robert is unexpectedly handed a new career as a railroad detective. Robert soon finds himself with a new set of challenges and new threats to his family life.

Other books by the same author:
The Outlaw's Twin Sister, 2002
Picture Rock, 2001
The Senator's Other Daughter, 2001
The General's Notorious Widow, 2001
The Long Trail Home, 2001

Other books you might like:
Sara Mitchell, *Ransomed Heart*, 1999
Gilbert Morris, *The Reno Saga*, 1992-
Judith Pella, *The Ribbons of Steel Series*, 1997-
Lee Roddy, *The Pinkerton Lady Series*, 1998-
Jim Walker, *The Wells Fargo Trail Series*, 1994-

973

STEPHEN A. BLY

The Outlaw's Twin Sister

(Wheaton, Illinois: Crossway, 2002)

Story type: Historical/American West
Series: Belles of Lordsburg. Book 3
Subject(s): Brothers and Sisters; Crime and Criminals
Major character(s): Julianna Ortiz, Spinster, Twin
Time period(s): 1880s
Locale(s): Lordsburg, New Mexico

Summary: Julianna Ortiz lives her life under a shadow—her twin brother is in prison awaiting execution. Because of his criminal past, Julianna has decided she will never marry, preferring to remain alone rather than inflict her family on others. However, Julianna's hope for solitude is shattered by members of her brother's gang, who want to break him out of prison with Julianna's help. When the twins' father shows up in town, also wanting to help his son, Julianna no longer knows where to find the peace she so desperately needs.

Other books by the same author:
Friends and Enemies, 2002
Picture Rock, 2001
The Long Trail Home, 2001
The General's Notorious Widow, 2001
Hidden Treasure, 2000

Other books you might like:
Jane Kirkpatrick, *The Kinship and Courage Series*, 2000-
Al Lacy, *The Mail Order Bride Series*, 1998-
Gilbert Morris, *The Reno Saga*, 1992-
Tracie Peterson, *The Westward Chronicles*, 1998-
Jim Walker, *The Wells Fargo Trail Series*, 1994-

974

IRENE BRAND

Summer's Promise

(New York: Steeple Hill, 2001)

Story type: Romance
Subject(s): Orphans
Major character(s): Summer Weaver, Banker, Guardian; David Brown, Military Personnel (former), Guardian
Time period(s): 2000s
Locale(s): North Carolina

Summary: When her sister and brother-in-law are killed in a car crash, Summer Weaver agrees to take care of their children, not fully realizing what a responsibility she is undertaking. After all, what does a career-focused banker know about child care? Relocating to rural North Carolina from the big city is the first of Summer's many adjustments. Others involve her fellow guardian, David Brown, who was her late sister's brother-in-law. A former military man, David is just as clueless about children as Summer is, but the two somehow manage to always do what is right.

Other books by the same author:
Autumn's Awakening, 2001
Tender Love, 2000
The Test of Love, 2000
A Groom to Come Home To, 1999
To Love and Honor, 1999

Other books you might like:
Kathryn Alexander, *Heart of a Husband*, 2000
Eileen Berger, *A Special Kind of Family*, 2001
Lyn Cote, *Finally Home*, 2001
Jillian Hart, *Heaven Sent*, 2001
Lois Richer, *Blessed Baby*, 2001

975

BILL BRIGHT
TED DEKKER, Co-Author

Blessed Child

(Nashville: Word, 2001)

Story type: Contemporary
Subject(s): Famine Victims; Healing
Major character(s): Jason Marker, Guardian; Leiah, Nurse (Red Cross); Caleb, Child, Orphan
Time period(s): 2000s
Locale(s): Ethiopia; United States

Summary: Famine relief expert Jason Marker agrees to help smuggle a young orphan boy named Caleb out of Ethiopia to the safety of America. Coming along on the perilous journey is Red Cross nurse Leiah. The two bring Caleb to America, where he is put into an orphanage headed by the evil Father Nikolous. Once Nikolous discovers Caleb is gifted with the power to heal, he decides to exploit the boy for all he can get. Jason and Leiah decide to do whatever they can to help Caleb.

Where it's reviewed:
Publishers Weekly, July 16, 2001, page 156

Other books you might like:
Dean Briggs, *The Most Important Little Boy in the World*, 2001
William Cutrer, *Lethal Harvest*, 2000
Alton Gansky, *The Prodigy*, 2001
Alton Gansky, *Terminal Justice*, 1998
Angela Elwell Hunt, *The Truth Teller*, 1999
Karen Rispin, *African Skies*, 2000

976

T. DAVIS BUNN

Drummer in the Dark

(New York: Doubleday, 2001)

Story type: Contemporary
Subject(s): Politics
Major character(s): Wynn Bryant, Political Figure (congressman)
Time period(s): 2000s
Locale(s): United States; Italy

Summary: Although Wynn Bryant is wealthy, he is unhappy. After his estranged wife dies suddenly, he finds himself lost. Wynn's sister, who is married to the governor of Florida, has her husband appoint Wynn to finish the term of a congressman. Hoping the diversion will somehow fill his life, Wynn agrees. He soon discovers his predecessor had devoutly supported an amendment that would regulate international currency trading. Intrigued by the possible implications of the amendment, Wynn investigates. He soon discovers there may be dangerous aspects surrounding the proposal and his own life may be in danger.

Where it's reviewed:
Booklist, July 2001, page 1948
Publishers Weekly, July 2, 2001, page 50

Other books by the same author:
The Book of Hours, 2000
The Great Divide, 2000
The Dream Voyagers, 1999
The Ultimatum, 1999
The Warning, 1998

Other books you might like:
Parker Hudson, *The President*, 1998
Angela Elwell Hunt, *The Justice*, 2001

Clay Jacobsen, *Circle of Seven*, 2000
Bob Larson, *The Senator's Agenda*, 1995
Robert Whitlow, *The List*, 2000

977

LINDA CHAIKIN

Friday's Child

(Eugene, Oregon: Harvest House, 2001)

Story type: Historical/World War II
Series: Day to Remember. Book 5
Subject(s): Abandonment; Family Problems; World War II
Major character(s): Vanessa Miles, Volunteer; Robert Miles, Parent (estranged from Vanessa), Actor
Time period(s): 1940s
Locale(s): England; Scotland

Summary: Vanessa Miles is doing her bit for the war effort by volunteering with an organization that helps war refugees. Her beloved brother Kylie is an RAF pilot, as is her boyfriend Andy. Although concerned about the two men in her life, Vanessa is incredibly proud of the work they are doing. One day, Vanessa receives a telegram from her estranged father Robert. A famous actor, he had left his wife and children in order to marry another woman. After staying out of their lives for years, Robert now wants reconciliation with Vanessa and Kylie. Kylie is still bitter over his father's abandonment and wants nothing to do with him. Vanessa, however, feels she must make some effort. Towards that end, she travels north to Scotland to visit with Robert.

Other books by the same author:
Thursday's Child, 2001
Tuesday's Child, 2000
Wednesday's Child, 2000
Island Bride, 1999
Monday's Child, 1999

Other books you might like:
Elyse Larson, *The Women of Valor Series*, 2000-
Janette Oke, *The Another Homecoming Series*, 1997-
Jane Peart, *Courageous Bride*, 1998
Judith Pella, *The Daughters of Fortune Series*, 2002-
Penelope J. Stokes, *The Faith on the Homefront Series*, 1996-

978

MITCHELL CHEFITZ

The Thirty-Third Hour

(New York: St. Martin's Press, 2002)

Story type: Contemporary
Subject(s): Judaism; Sexual Harassment
Major character(s): Arthur Greenberg, Religious (rabbi)
Time period(s): 2000s
Locale(s): Miami, Florida

Summary: Teacher Moshe Katan has been accused of sexual misconduct by a young mother, who is a member of Rabbi Arthur Greenberg's synagogue. Needing to review the evidence before a decision is made on whether to pursue misconduct charges against Katan, the rabbi settles down to view video and audio tapes of teaching sessions, as well as the mother's journal. With the decision due Monday morning at 9:00 a.m., Rabbi Greenberg has 33 hours to look at all of the evidence. As he begins reviewing the case, the rabbi soon realizes he has to also confront questions about his own life and faith.

Where it's reviewed:
Booklist, November 1, 2001, page 459
Publishers Weekly, October 15, 2001, page 43

Other books by the same author:
The Seventh Telling, 2001

Other books you might like:
Pearl Abraham, *The Romance Reader*, 1995
Myla Goldberg, *Bee Season*, 2000
Rachel Kadish, *From a Sealed Room*, 1998
Tova Mirvis, *The Ladies Auxiliary*, 1999
Benjamin Zucker, *Green*, 2002

979

DIANNE CHRISTNER

Keeper of Hearts

(Scottdale, Pennsylvania: Herald, 2002)

Story type: Historical
Subject(s): Religious Conflict
Major character(s): Anna van Visser, Fugitive
Time period(s): 16th century
Locale(s): Germany

Summary: The Holy Roman Emperor Charles V has made it his mission to purge his kingdom of heresy. One of those he has arrested is the father of Anna van Visser. Horrified, Anna decides religious beliefs are not important enough to lose your life over. As more and more of Anna's friends and family become believers, she realizes she may also fall under the spell of the followers of Christ. Determined to escape that fate, Anna runs away to Germany to find an old friend. That friend is now married to Martinus Luther, one of the leaders of the heretics. As Anna becomes more knowledgeable about the heretics' beliefs, she finds herself more and more drawn to them.

Other books by the same author:
Storm, 2000
Ample Portions, 1996
Lofty Ambitions, 1994
Proper Intentions, 1994

Other books you might like:
Irene Brand, *The Legacies of Faith Series*, 1996-
Jack Cavanaugh, *The Book of Books Series*, 1999-
Ethel L. Herr, *The Seekers Series*, 1996-
Francine Rivers, *The Mark of the Lion Series*, 1993-
Andrew M. Seddon, *Imperial Legions*, 2000

980

BRANDILYN COLLINS

Color the Sidewalk for Me

(Grand Rapids, Michigan: Zondervan, 2002)

Story type: Contemporary
Series: Bradleyville. Book 1
Subject(s): Illness; Mothers and Daughters
Major character(s): Celia Matthews, Advertising
Time period(s): 2000s
Locale(s): Little Rock, Arkansas; Bradleyville, Kentucky

Summary: Celia Matthews is living a quiet life in Little Rock, Arkansas. She has her career in advertising to keep her busy and she is well liked by her friends and coworkers. If a void exists in her life, Celia refuses to acknowledge it. Then she receives an unsettling phone call. Her mother, whom Celia hasn't seen for 17 years, wants her to come home to help in the care of her father, who has suffered a stroke. Since it was her mother's coldness that made her leave home, Celia is reluctant to go back. However, she does eventually return to Kentucky and is forced to confront a past she had hoped was long buried.

Other books by the same author:
Cast a Road Before Me, 2001
Eyes of Elisha, 2001

Other books you might like:
Beverly Lewis, *The Sunroom*, 1998
Catherine Palmer, *The Happy Room*, 2002
Gary E. Parker, *The Wedding Dress*, 2002
Francine Rivers, *Leota's Garden*, 1999
Johanna Verweerd, *The Winter Garden*, 2001

981

BRANDILYN COLLINS

Eyes of Elisha

(Grand Rapids, Michigan: Zondervan, 2001)

Story type: Mystery
Series: Chelsea Adams. Book 1
Subject(s): Murder; Paranormal
Major character(s): Chelsea Adams, Psychic
Time period(s): 2000s
Locale(s): California

Summary: Chelsea Adams lives in the Silicon Valley area of California with her entrepreneur husband and their two sons. On the surface, Chelsea's life is normal, maybe even mundane, but all her life Chelsea has been different. She has visions. However, none of her visions is as terrifying as the one she has during a business dinner with her husband and a prospective employee of his firm. During her trance, Chelsea sees the murder of a young woman. Coming out of the trance, she realizes the killer is her husband's prospective vice-president of marketing. With no proof, though, Chelsea is on her own and she may soon become the killer's next victim.

Where it's reviewed:
Library Journal, September 1, 2001, page 154
Publishers Weekly, August 27, 2001, page 49

Other books by the same author:
Cast a Road Before Me, 2001

Other books you might like:
Athol Dickson, *The Garr Reed Series*, 1996-
Robert Funderburk, *The Dylan St. John Series*, 1996-
Nancy Moser, *The Mustard Seed Series*, 1998-
Bill Myers, *Threshold*, 1997
Audrey Stallsmith, *The Thyme Will Tell Series*, 1998-

982

CATHLEEN CONNORS (Pseudonym of Cathleen Galitz)

A Home of Her Own

(New York: Steeple Hill, 2002)

Story type: Romance
Subject(s): Pregnancy
Major character(s): Melodie Coleman, Widow(er); Buck Foster, Cowboy
Time period(s): 2000s
Locale(s): Wyoming

Summary: Melodie Coleman returns home to Wyoming in order to attend her mother's funeral. Widowed and pregnant, the last thing Melodie wants is a trip down memory lane, especially since looking back is painful. However, when Melodie is reunited with cowboy Buck Foster, she is suddenly forced to face up to the past and reveal the reasons why she left him suddenly so many years before. The author has written several romance novels under her own name of Cathleen Galitz, but this is her first under the pseudonym Cathleen Connors.

Other books you might like:
Valerie Hansen, *Love One Another*, 2001
Jillian Hart, *Heaven Sent*, 2001
Gail Gaymer Martin, *A Love for Safekeeping*, 2002
Carole Gift Page, *A Bungalow for Two*, 2001
Ruth Scofield, *Loving Thy Neighbor*, 2001

983

LORI COPELAND

Christmas Vows: $5.00 Extra

(Wheaton, Illinois: Tyndale House, 2001)

Story type: Contemporary
Subject(s): Christmas; Poverty; Single Parent Families
Major character(s): Ben O'Keefe, Convict (ex-convict), Single Parent
Time period(s): 2000s
Locale(s): United States

Summary: Given a hardship parole after his wife's death, Ben O'Keefe is released from prison after serving a portion of a sentence for robbery. Reformed, Ben sincerely wants to do what is right for his children. With his three kids, Ben heads for his mother's house in Missouri, where he hopes he can turn his life around. Unfortunately, things don't start out well. His car breaks down outside of Memphis, the kids want food other than peanut butter and jelly to eat, and he has less than $300 to his name. With Christmas just two days away, Ben is no longer sure he can refrain from resorting to criminal behavior. Then he meets Henrietta Humblesmith at her marrying parlor and suddenly it appears as if miracles can indeed happen.

Other books by the same author:
Child of Grace, 2001
Glory, 2000
Marrying Walker McKay, 2000
Hope, 1999
June, 1999

Other books you might like:
T. Davis Bunn, *The Gift*, 1994
Thomas J. Davis, *The Christmas Quilt*, 2000
Richard Paul Evans, *The Christmas Box*, 1993
Joseph F. Girzone, *Joshua the Homecoming*, 1999
Diane Noble, *Come, My Little Angel*, 2001

984

LORI COPELAND
ANGELA ELWELL HUNT, Co-Author

A Warmth in Winter

(Nashville: Thomas Nelson, 2002)

Story type: Contemporary
Series: Heavenly Daze. Book 3
Subject(s): Grandfathers; Islands; Reunions
Major character(s): Vernie Bidderman, Businesswoman; Salt Gribbon, Lighthouse Keeper
Time period(s): 2000s
Locale(s): Heavenly Daze, Maine

Summary: More problems come to light for the citizens of the island of Heavenly Daze. Vernie Bidderman, owner of the Mooseleuk Mercantile, is flabbergasted when she receives a message from her husband. Stanley left home to go bowling (20 years earlier) and she hasn't heard from him since. Now Vernie has to decide if Stanley still has a place in her life. Meanwhile, lighthouse keeper Salt Gribbon has his grandchildren staying with him and he is trying to keep the fact secret. His greatest fear is that the childrens' services department will take the children from him and put them in a ''more suitable'' home. Then Salt falls ill and the children must somehow find help without getting their beloved grandfather into trouble.

Other books by the same author:
Grace in Autumn, 2001
The Island of Heavenly Daze, 2000

Other books you might like:
Mary Carlson, *The Whispering Pines Series*, 1999-
Philip Gulley, *The Harmony Series*, 2000-
Robin Jones Gunn, *The Glenbrooke Series*, 1995-
Jan Karon, *The Mitford Years Series*, 1994-
Lori Wick, *Bamboo and Lace*, 2001

985

LYN COTE

Winter's Secret

(Wheaton, Illinois: Tyndale House, 2002)

Story type: Mystery; Romance
Subject(s): Aging; Crime and Criminals
Major character(s): Rodd Durand, Police Officer (sheriff); Wendy Carey, Nurse
Time period(s): 2000s
Locale(s): Wisconsin

Summary: Sheriff Rodd Durand is determined to find the person who is robbing the elderly of his district, leaving their homes in shambles in the process. As more and more people become victims and Rodd still has no leads, he grows increasingly frustrated. Then nurse Wendy Carey, who has taken care of many of the victims at a local clinic, becomes involved in the mystery when one of her most beloved patients suffers a stroke after seeing the damage done to her home and her dog. Rodd and Wendy join forces to find the burglar before he can strike again.

Other books by the same author:
Finally Found, 2002
Finally Home, 2001
Echoes of Mercy, 2000
Hope's Garden, 2000
Lost in His Love, 2000

Other books you might like:
Terri Blackstock, *Cape Refuge*, 2002
Alton Gansky, *Distant Memory*, 2000
Ellen Edwards Kennedy, *Irregardless of Murder*, 2001
Gayle G. Roper, *The Amhearst Series*, 1997-
Patricia H. Rushford, *The Helen Bradley Series*, 1997-

986

BARBARA CURTIS
BARBARA JEAN HICKS, Co-Author
SHARI MACDONALD, Co-Author
JANE ORCUTT, Co-Author

Restoration and Romance

(Colorado Springs, Colorado: WaterBrook, 2001)

Story type: Anthology
Subject(s): Love; Dwellings
Time period(s): 2000s

Summary: These four novellas tell the stories of couples who fall in love because of home repair projects. New author Barbara Curtis' *Beside the Still Waters* tells the story of widowed K.C. McKenzie, who moves to her husband's hometown to buy the house he grew up in. The house is already sold, but K.C. agrees to help Raleigh Kincaid, the new owner, restore it. In Barbara Jean Hicks' *The Queen of the World and the Handyman*, Chloe Burnett arrives at her grandmother's house to discover a stranger there. Disturbed at first, Chloe soon learns there is more to Nat Neville than meets the eye. In *Home for the Heart*, Shari MacDonald tells the story of Charlie and Flynn, who inherit an old Victorian house from

Charlie's grandmother. Not wanting to share the house, the two fight at first, then fall in love. Jane Orcutt's story *Don't Look Back* has Laurie Golden buying an old family home she hopes to restore. She meets Jack MacGruder, who is researching his family history in the small burial plot on her property. Since Laurie is a genealogist and Jack has done home restoration, the two decide to help each other out.

Other books you might like:
Lisa Tawn Bergren, *Porch Swings & Picket Fences*, 1999
Kristin Billerbeck, *Forever Friends*, 2000
Liz Curtis Higgs, *Three Weddings and a Giggle*, 2001
Veda Boyd Jones, *Summer Dreams*, 1997
Loree Lough, *Only You*, 1998

987

MARGARET DALEY

The Power of Love

(New York: Steeple Hill, 2002)

Story type: Romance
Subject(s): Children
Major character(s): Rebecca Michaels, Single Parent; Gabriel Stone, Police Officer
Time period(s): 2000s
Locale(s): United States

Summary: Rebecca Michaels is struggling to raise her two children alone. Her baby has special needs and takes up much of her time, so Rebecca has been inadvertently neglecting her elder son. Because of that, he is headed for trouble. When police officer Gabriel Stone shows up at Rebecca's door, she assumes the worst. However, it turns out Gabriel's appearance in their lives is the best thing that could have happened to the Michaels family. He soon becomes a surrogate father for Rebecca's son and sets the boy back on the right track. Unfortunately, Gabriel has some problems of his own that might prevent him from becoming a permanent part of the family. Author Margaret Daley writes under various pseudonyms, including Shauna Michaels, Kit Daley, Patti Moore, Margaret Ripy, and Kathleen Daley.

Other books you might like:
Irene Brand, *To Love and Honor*, 1999
Valerie Hansen, *Wedding Arbor*, 1999
Marta Perry, *Desperately Seeking Dad*, 2000
Cynthia Rutledge, *Judging Sara*, 2001
Carol Steward, *Her Kind of Hero*, 1999

988

TED DEKKER

When Heaven Weeps

(Nashville: Word, 2001)

Story type: Contemporary
Series: Martyr's Song. Book 2
Subject(s): Change; Redemption
Major character(s): Jan Jovic, Writer; Helen, Addict (junkie)
Time period(s): 1960s
Locale(s): Atlanta, Georgia

Summary: During his time as a soldier in the Bosnian army during World War II, Jan Jovic witnesses numerous atrocities. He also meets the man who would change his life, Father Michael. Years later, Jan writes a book called *The Dance of the Dead* about Father Michael and a child named Nadia which becomes a bestseller. On his way to super-stardom as a writer, Jan meets Helen, a junkie. Enthralled by Helen, Jan attempts to change her life. She eventually comes to return his love, but is unable to totally turn her back on her past.

Other books by the same author:
Heaven's Wager, 2000

Other books you might like:
Joseph Bentz, *A Son Comes Home*, 1999
Sally D. John, *To Dream Again*, 2000
Beverly LaHaye, *Times and Seasons*, 2001
D.S. Lliteras, *613 West Jefferson*, 2001
Francine Rivers, *Redeeming Love*, 1997

989

ROSEY DOW
ANDREW SNADEN, Co-Author

Betrayed

(Uhrichville, Ohio: Promise Books, 2001)

Story type: Romantic Suspense
Subject(s): Computers
Major character(s): Laura McIvor, Fugitive; Jonathan Corrigan, Spy (CIA agent)
Time period(s): 2000s
Locale(s): Seattle, Washington

Summary: Laura McIvor has to face two terrible betrayals on the same day. First, she learns her father, a brilliant computer scientist, has been selling government secrets to enemy agents. Then she discovers the man who found the evidence to have her father arrested is CIA agent Jonathan Corrigan. Jonathan has been romancing Laura to get close to her family. Now Laura is in even more trouble. The software her father created is encrypted with a virus and he refuses to tell its secret. Soon Laura, who is living undercover, finds her life in danger and the only man who can help her is Jonathan Corrigan. This is the first book from the writing team of Rosey Dow and Andrew Snaden, who met online and co-authored this book without having met in person.

Other books you might like:
Michael Hyatt, *Y2K*, 1998
Grant R. Jeffrey, *Flee the Darkness*, 1998
Jefferson Scott, *Terminal Logic*, 1997
Frank Simon, *The Y2K Bug*, 1999
Robert L. Wise, *The Tail of the Dragon*, 2000

990

GENE EDWARDS

The Gaius Diary

(Wheaton, Illinois: Tyndale House, 2002)

Story type: Biblical Fiction
Series: First Century Diaries. Book 5

Subject(s): Religious Conflict; Saints
Major character(s): Paul, Religious (disciple), Biblical Figure; Gaius, Friend
Time period(s): 1st century
Locale(s): Roman Empire

Summary: This story tells of the later years of the apostle Paul. Along with his companion Gaius, Paul travels throughout the Roman Empire spreading the word of Christ. Although he attracts followers, Paul also earns the ire of community leaders and is eventually imprisoned. Seeing him as a threat to their leadership, the Roman rulers eventually have Paul put to death.

Other books by the same author:
The Priscilla Diary, 2001
The Timothy Diary, 2000
The Titas Diary, 1999
The Silas Diary, 1998
The Return, 1996

Other books you might like:
Irene Brand, *The Legacies of Faith Series*, 1996-
Thom Lemmons, *The Daughters of Faith Series*, 1999-
Francine Rivers, *The Mark of the Lion Series*, 1993-
James R. Shott, *The People of the Promise Series*, 1992-
Robert L. Wise, *The People of the Covenant Series*, 1991-

991

MICHAEL P. FARRIS

Forbid Them Not

(Nashville: Broadman & Holman, 2002)

Story type: Contemporary
Subject(s): Freedom; Parenthood
Major character(s): Cooper Stone, Lawyer; Laura Fraiser, Teacher (Sunday school)
Time period(s): 2000s (2005)
Locale(s): Leesburg, Virginia

Summary: In the very near future America, legislation is passed that allows the government a new control over how children are raised. One of the results of this legislation is the National Commission on Children, a government agency designed to protect children from what the government considers to be bad parenting. Laura Fraiser is teaching her Sunday school class when she is visited by representatives of the Commission. They question Laura about some of the students in her class and ask questions about their parents. Although worried, Laura feels she has no choice but to answer. Soon the parents are having their home lives investigated and are being threatened with the loss of their children. Lawyer Cooper Stone enters the situation to fight for the parents' right to raise their children as they see fit.

Other books by the same author:
Guilt by Association, 1997
Anonymous Tip, 1996

Other books you might like:
John Culea, *Light the Night*, 1997
Grant R. Jeffrey, *The Flee the Darkness Series*, 1998
James R. Lucas, *A Perfect Persecution*, 2001
Josh McDowell, *Vote of Intolerance*, 1997
Robert L. Wise, *The Tail of the Dragon*, 2000

992

DORIS ELAINE FELL

Sunrise on Stradbury Square

(Grand Rapids, Michigan: Fleming H. Revell, 2002)

Story type: Contemporary
Series: Sagas of a Kindred Heart. Book 3
Subject(s): Illness; Teacher-Student Relationships
Major character(s): Esther McCully, Professor
Time period(s): 2000s
Locale(s): Lake District, England

Summary: Esther McCully devotes her entire life to her students—everything in her life takes second place to her teaching career. Esther even gives up her chance at romance in order to continue teaching. Now, facing illness, Esther begins to wonder if she really made as big an impact on her students' lives as she hopes she did. Deciding to find out, Esther arranges for a reunion with some of her most memorable students at a castle in the Lake District. To her immense relief, Esther soon learns she is remembered fondly and is respected for her devotion to teaching. The reunion is going well when one of the students is accused of being an IRA fugitive and the group finds itself in conflict.

Other books by the same author:
Willows on the Windrush, 2000
Blue Mist on the Danube, 1999
Long-Awaited Wedding, 1999
The Wedding Jewel, 1999
The Race for Autumn's Glory, 1997

Other books you might like:
Roxanne Henke, *After Anne*, 2002
Alan Maki, *Written on Her Heart*, 2002
Gayle G. Roper, *The Key*, 1998
Steven W. Wise, *Long Train Passing*, 1996
Lance Wubbels, *One Small Miracle*, 1995

993

ROBIN JONES GUNN

Wildflowers

(Sisters, Oregon: Multnomah, 2001)

Story type: Contemporary
Series: Glenbrooke. Book 8
Subject(s): Marriage; Restaurants
Major character(s): Gena Ahrens, Restaurateur (owns cafe)
Time period(s): 2000s
Locale(s): Glenbrooke, Oregon

Summary: Gena Ahrens hopes opening a restaurant will revitalize her life. The Wallflower Cafe is past its prime when Gena takes it over, but her management and culinary abilities soon makes it into the most popular place in town. Unfortunately, the restaurant does little for her personal life. When Gena's daughter marries, she sees her estranged husband again and begins to wonder what went wrong with their marriage. To her surprise, her once distant husband is also wondering about the past and Gena begins to believe they might still have a future together.

Other books by the same author:
Woodlands, 2000
Echoes, 1999
Waterfalls, 1998
Clouds, 1997
Sunsets, 1997

Other books you might like:
Terri Blackstock, *The Second Chances Series*, 1996-
Mary Carlson, *The Whispering Pines Series*, 1999-
Linda Hall, *Margaret's Peace*, 1998
Robin Lee Hatcher, *The Forgiving Hour*, 1999
Karen Kingsbury, *A Time to Dance*, 2001

994

JOHN HAGEE

Devil's Island

(Nashville: Thomas Nelson, 2001)

Story type: Historical
Series: Apocalypse Diaries. Book 1
Subject(s): Faith
Major character(s): Abraham Roth, Wealthy, Parent (of Jacob); Jacob Roth, Religious (Christian preacher)
Time period(s): 1st century
Locale(s): Ephesus, Roman Empire

Summary: Abraham Roth has amassed great wealth and although he has some problems, he is still content with his life. His son, Jacob, is a bit of a disappointment since he takes no interest in the family business and instead has become a Christian preacher. Though devout himself, Abraham worries that Jacob's overt devoutness will only cause trouble with representatives of the Roman emperors. When the apostle John declares that Christians must make a choice between worshiping Jesus or worshiping the emperors, Abraham's worst fears come true. He and his family must decide whether to turn their back on their faith, or risk losing their wealth and perhaps their lives.

Other books you might like:
Irene Brand, *The Legacies of Faith Series*, 1996-
Gene Edwards, *The First Century Diaries Series*, 1998-
Thom Lemmons, *The Daughters of Faith Series*, 1999-
Francine Rivers, *The Lineage of Grace Series*, 2000-
Francine Rivers, *The Mark of the Lion Series*, 1993-
James R. Shott, *The People of the Promise Series*, 1992-
Robert L. Wise, *The People of the Covenant Series*, 1991-

995

VALERIE HANSEN

Love One Another

(New York: Steeple Hill, 2001)

Story type: Romance
Subject(s): Single Parent Families
Major character(s): Tina Braddock, Child-Care Giver; Zac Frazier, Widow(er), Single Parent (of Justin); Justin Frazier, Child
Time period(s): 2000s
Locale(s): United States

Summary: Single dad Zac Frazier is struggling to raise his troubled son, Justin. Since his mother's death the previous year, Justin is having trouble adjusting and doesn't like to be left with adults other than his father. Zac is hoping preschool will return Justin to the happy child he once was and when Zac meets pretty teacher Tina Braddock, he is certain he has the right school for Justin. Tina's cheerful nature soon brings a new joy to Justin's life and may just do the same for Zac's.

Other books by the same author:
Second Chances, 2001
The Perfect Couple, 2000
The Troublesome Angel, 2000
The Wedding Arbor, 1999

Other books you might like:
Carole Gift Page, *A Family to Cherish*, 2000
Lois Richer, *Blessed Baby*, 2001
Anna Schmidt, *A Mother for Amanda*, 2000
Ruth Scofield, *Loving Thy Neighbor*, 2001
Lenora Worth, *Ben's Bundle of Joy*, 2000

996

LEE HARRIS (Pseudonym of Syrell Rogovin Leahy)

Happy Birthday Murder

(New York: Ballantine, 2002)

Story type: Mystery
Series: Christine Bennett. Book 14
Subject(s): Murder
Major character(s): Christine Bennett, Spouse, Religious (former nun)
Time period(s): 2000s
Locale(s): Oakwood, New York

Summary: Former nun Christine Bennett isn't one to shy away from a mystery so when she finds two odd mementos among her late aunt's possessions, she decides to investigate. One item is the obituary of a wealthy and successful man, who killed himself after his 50th birthday party. The other memento is a note about a man who was lost in a Connecticut woods. Though the incidents are seemingly unconnected, the two men were found wearing each other's shoes. Is there a connection? And why did Christine's Aunt May save these two items?

Other books by the same author:
The April Fool's Day Murder, 2001
The Mother's Day Murder, 2000
The Father's Day Murder, 1999
The Labor Day Murder, 1998
The New Year's Eve Murder, 1997

Other books you might like:
Ron Benrey, *Little White Lies*, 2001
B.J. Hoff, *The Daybreak Series*, 1995-
Katherine Hall Page, *The Faith Fairchild Series*, 1990-
Patricia H. Rushford, *The Helen Bradley Series*, 1997-

Sally S. Wright, *The Ben Reese Series*, 1997-

997

JILLIAN HART

Heaven Sent

(New York: Steeple Hill, 2001)

Story type: Romance
Subject(s): Marriage
Major character(s): Hope Ashton, Wealthy; Matthew Sheridan, Cowboy, Single Parent
Time period(s): 2000s
Locale(s): Montana

Summary: Millionaire's daughter Hope Ashton grows up with all that money can buy, but she has never really gotten over her parents' divorce. As a result, she has decided to avoid marriage herself. Matthew Sheridan is a widower and father of three who knows he'll never find anybody to take his wife's place. Hope's grandmother, however, believes the two belong together and decides to do some matchmaking. Once Hope and Matthew catch on to her plans, they do all they can to avoid helping her succeed.

Other books by the same author:
Night Hawk's Bride, 2001
Malcolm's Honor, 2000
Montana Man, 2000
Cooper's Wife, 1999
Last Chance Bride, 1998

Other books you might like:
Lyn Cote, *Hope's Garden*, 2000
Marcy Froemke, *A Family in the Making*, 2000
Valerie Hansen, *Second Chances*, 2001
Cynthia Rutledge, *Redeeming Claire*, 2001
Anna Schmidt, *A Mother for Amanda*, 2000

998

KRISTEN HEITZMANN

The Tender Vine

(Minneapolis: Bethany House, 2002)

Story type: Historical/American West
Series: Diamond of the Rockies. Book 3
Subject(s): Family Relations; Secrets
Major character(s): Carina DiGratia Shepard, Spouse (of Quillan); Quillan Shepard, Spouse (of Carina)
Time period(s): 1880s
Locale(s): Crystal, Colorado; California

Summary: Carina DiGratia Shepard has adjusted fairly well to her marriage and is settling down nicely in the rugged mining town of Crystal, Colorado. However, she misses her family, so her husband Quillan arranges for them to take a trip to California for a reunion. However, Carina has not yet told her family that she is married and the surprise trip comes as a shock in more ways than one to Carina. The meeting between Carina's family and Quillan is an uncomfortable one, since he is not the type of man they had pictured for their daughter.

Other books by the same author:
Sweet Boundless, 2001
Honor's Reward, 2000
The Rose Legacy, 2000
Honor's Disguise, 1999
Honor's Quest, 1998

Other books you might like:
Ruth Glover, *The Wildrose Series*, 1994-
Jane Kirkpatrick, *The Kinship and Courage Series*, 2000-
Diane Noble, *The California Chronicles*, 1999-
Jane Peart, *The Westward Dreams Series*, 1994-
Tracie Peterson, *The Westward Chronicles*, 1998-

999

DEE HENDERSON

The Protector

(Sisters, Oregon: Multnomah, 2001)

Story type: Mystery
Series: O'Malley Family. Book 4
Subject(s): Arson; Christmas; Fires
Major character(s): Jack O'Malley, Fire Fighter; Cassie Ellis, Fire Fighter
Time period(s): 2000s
Locale(s): Chicago, Illinois

Summary: Firefighter Jack O'Malley is struggling with some difficult problems during a hectic Christmas season. An arsonist is operating in his district and soon escalates from setting nuisance fires to burning down houses. During one fire, a fellow firefighter, Cassie Ellis, on leave after having been injured while on duty, sees the arsonist. Realizing Cassie is in great danger, Jack feels a need to protect her. Jack is also struggling with questions of faith and before the holiday season is over he may have to make some important decisions about the direction his life should take.

Where it's reviewed:
Library Journal, September 1, 2001, page 154
Publishers Weekly, August 13, 2001, page 282

Other books by the same author:
The Guardian, 2001
The Truth Seeker, 2001
The Negotiator, 2000
True Devotion, 2000
Danger in the Shadows, 1999

Other books you might like:
Ann Bell, *Distant Love*, 1995
Lisa Tawn Bergren, *Firestorm*, 2001
Terri Blackstock, *The Newpointe 911 Series*, 1998-
Alton Gansky, *Distant Memory*, 2000
Ted Wojtasik, *No Strange Fire*, 1996

1000

DEE HENDERSON

True Valor

(Sisters, Oregon: Multnomah, 2002)

Story type: Action/Adventure; Romance

Series: Uncommon Heroes. Book 2
Subject(s): Military Life
Major character(s): Bruce ''Striker'' Stanton, Military Personnel (Air Force pararescueman); Grace Yates, Military Personnel (Navy), Pilot
Time period(s): 2000s
Locale(s): Syria; Turkey

Summary: Air Force pararescueman Bruce Stanton is in love with Navy pilot Grace Yates, but he is reluctant to pursue the relationship because of their dangerous jobs. When a fight over water rights between Syria and Turkey evolves into a conflict involving NATO, both Bruce and Grace are drawn into the fighting. Then Grace's F/A-18 Hornet goes down behind enemy lines and it is up to Bruce to bring her out alive.

Where it's reviewed:
Publishers Weekly, December 24, 2001, page 40

Other books by the same author:
The Guardian, 2001
The Protector, 2001
The Truth Seeker, 2001
The Negotiator, 2000
True Devotion, 2000

Other books you might like:
Lisa Tawn Bergren, *Pathways*, 2001
Terri Blackstock, *Broken Wings*, 1998
Alton Gansky, *Vanished*, 2000
Jill Stengl, *Eagle Pilot*, 1996
Robert Vaughan, *Touch the Face of God*, 2002

1001

KATHY HERMAN

Day of Reckoning

(Sisters, Oregon: Multnomah, 2002)

Story type: Contemporary
Series: Baxter. Book 2
Subject(s): Revenge
Major character(s): Wayne Purdy, Criminal
Time period(s): 2000s
Locale(s): Baxter, Georgia

Summary: When Wayne Purdy's father is laid off from his factory job, his whole family is upset. Then he dies suddenly three weeks later and the Purdy family is devastated. Blaming textile magnate G.R. Logan for the death, Wayne decides Logan will pay for his actions. Wayne's act of revenge sets off a chain reaction of events that shakes the town of Baxter, Georgia to its core.

Other books by the same author:
Tested by Fire, 2001

Other books you might like:
Linda Hall, *Sadie's Song*, 2001
Jerry B. Jenkins, *Hometown Legend*, 2001
Bonnie Leon, *Worthy of Riches*, 2002
Bette Nordberg, *Serenity Bay*, 2000
Vinita Hampton Wright, *Velma Still Cooks in Leeway*, 2000

1002

MELISSA HORSFALL
SUSAN STEVENS, Co-Author

Double Honor

(Colorado Springs, Colorado: WaterBrook, 2002)

Story type: Contemporary
Subject(s): Memory; Sexual Abuse
Major character(s): Mallory Carlisle, Abuse Victim
Time period(s): 2000s
Locale(s): United States

Summary: Mallory Carlisle grows up in a home with cold and controlling parents. She hopes that marriage will provide a better life, but her husband is distant and their financial situation is not good. When, at a family gathering, Mallory begins to remember long buried secrets, her life begins to shatter further. She remembers years of sexual abuse—memories she had repressed for a long time. Now Mallory realizes she must face up to the past in order to gain any sort of happiness in the future. First novel.

Other books you might like:
Beverly Bush, *Wings of a Dove*, 1996
Linda Hall, *Sadie's Song*, 2001
Michael Morris, *A Place Called Wiregrass*, 2002
Bette Nordberg, *Serenity Bay*, 2000
Vinita Hampton Wright, *Velma Still Cooks in Leeway*, 2000

1003

JAMES BYRON HUGGINS

Rora

(Little Rock, Arkansas: Lion's Head, 2001)

Story type: Historical
Subject(s): Religious Conflict
Major character(s): Joshua Gianavel, Warrior
Time period(s): 17th century (1655)
Locale(s): Europe

Summary: The Waldenses are a group of Protestants marked for extermination during the time of the Inquisition. One of these men is Joshua Gianavel, who lives quietly with his wife and children until events disrupted his life. As the Inquisitors destroy churches, burn villages, and kill innocent people, Joshua realizes something must be done. A small band of men take on the huge invading armies and stave them off for weeks. Even after being overrun, Joshua continues his campaign to fight for religious freedom.

Other books by the same author:
Hunter, 1999
Cain, 1997
Leviathan, 1995
The Reckoning, 1994
The Wolf Story, 1993

Other books you might like:
Jack Cavanaugh, *The Book of Books Series*, 1999-
Ethel L. Herr, *The Seekers Series*, 1996-
Stephen R. Lawhead, *The Celtic Crusades Series*, 1999-
Michael Phillips, *The Russians Series*, 1991-

Andrew M. Seddon, *Imperial Legions*, 2000

1004

ANGELA ELWELL HUNT

The Justice

(Nashville: Thomas Nelson, 2001)

Story type: Contemporary
Subject(s): Politics
Major character(s): Daryn Austin, Political Figure (president); Paul Santana, Judge (Supreme Court justice)
Time period(s): 2000s (2003)
Locale(s): Washington, District of Columbia

Summary: Daryn Austin, daughter of a Georgia governor, dreams for a long time of becoming president of the United States. Elected vice-president, her dreams are finally fulfilled when the president dies suddenly. Hoping to hold onto her newfound political power, Daryn enlists the aid of her old love Paul Santana, a brilliant lawyer. Appointed to the Supreme Court by Daryn, it will be Paul's job to help her survive the rough political world of Washington, D.C. Daryn finds herself without an ally as Paul discovers God and begins to question what he is doing.

Other books by the same author:
The Note, 2001
The Immortal, 2000
The Emerald Isle, 1999
The Truth Teller, 1999
The Velvet Shadow, 1999

Other books you might like:
T. Davis Bunn, *The Ultimatum*, 1999
Parker Hudson, *The President*, 1998
Clay Jacobsen, *Circle of Seven*, 2000
Bob Larson, *The Senator's Agenda*, 1995
Marilyn Tucker Quayle, *The Campaign*, 1996

1005

JERRY B. JENKINS

Hometown Legend

(New York: Warner, 2001)

Story type: Contemporary
Subject(s): Sports/Football
Major character(s): Buster Schuler, Coach (high school football)
Time period(s): 2000s
Locale(s): Athens City, Alabama

Summary: After his son Jack dies during a football game, high school coach Buster Schuler leaves Athens City, Alabama, intending never to return. After more than a decade away, Buster does come back, but the city has changed more than he had ever imagined. The football team, once among the best in the state, is a shambles and the high school itself is on the verge of closing. With Buster back in town, the citizens believe they might have a chance to regain some of their former glory. Buster, however, isn't certain he is capable of such a challenge. The author cowrites the popular Left Behind series with Tim F. LaHaye.

Where it's reviewed:
Booklist, July 2001, page 1951
Publishers Weekly, July 16, 2001, page 156

Other books by the same author:
Though None Go with Me, 2000
Twas the Night Before, 1998
Rookie, 1997
The Operative, 1987

Other books you might like:
Robert Funderburk, *Tenderness and Fire*, 1997
Louise M. Gouge, *The Homecoming*, 1998
E. Lynn Harris, *And This Too Shall Pass*, 1996
Shari MacDonald, *Diamonds*, 1996
Audrey Stallsmith, *Marigolds for Mourning*, 1998

1006

SALLY D. JOHN

A Journey by Chance

(Eugene, Oregon: Harvest House, 2002)

Story type: Contemporary
Series: Other Way Home. Book 1
Subject(s): Family
Major character(s): Gina Phillips, Unemployed
Time period(s): 2000s
Locale(s): Valley Oaks

Summary: Gina Phillips returns to her hometown of Valley Oaks to attend a cousin's wedding. She hopes a few weeks back home will help her forget her lost job and her failed relationship. Unfortunately, no sooner is she back home than things start to heat up. First her cousins insist that Brady Olafsson, a wealthy and successful writer, is the perfect man for Gina. She is more irritated by him than attracted to him however. Then Gina's mother tells her of a family secret, one that may change Gina's life forever.

Other books by the same author:
To Dream Again, 2000
Surrender of the Heart, 1999
In the Shadow of Love, 1998

Other books you might like:
Terri Blackstock, *The Second Chances Series*, 1996-
Robin Jones Gunn, *The Glenbrooke Series*, 1995-
Annie Jones, *The Route 66 Series*, 1999-
Gilbert Morris, *All That Glitters*, 1999
Tracie Peterson, *Controlling Interests*, 1998

1007

JAN KARON

In This Mountain

(New York: Penguin Putnam, 2002)

Story type: Contemporary/Innocent
Series: Mitford Years. Book 7
Subject(s): Small Town Life

Major character(s): Tim Kavanagh, Religious (Episcopal minister); Cynthia Kavanagh, Spouse (of Tim)
Time period(s): 2000s
Locale(s): Mitford, North Carolina

Summary: Father Tim Kavanagh and his wife, Cynthia, return home to Mitford, North Carolina after a brief time spent on Whitecap Island. They are pleased to discover the town is just as they remembered it. However, retirement doesn't sit well with Father Tim, so he and Cynthia decide to set off on a year long ministry. Before they can leave, a series of events occur that shakes the entire town of Mitford.

Other books by the same author:
A Common Life, 2001
A New Song, 1999
Out to Canaan, 1997
These High Green Hills, 1996
A Light in the Window, 1995

Other books you might like:
Mary Carlson, *The Whispering Pines Series*, 1999-
Lori Copeland, *The Heavenly Daze Series*, 2001-
Philip Gulley, *The Harmony Series*, 2000-
Robin Jones Gunn, *The Glenbrooke Series*, 1995-
Lance Wubbels, *The Gentle Hills Series*, 1994-

1008

ELLEN EDWARDS KENNEDY

Irregardless of Murder

(Wichita, Kansas: St. Kitts, 2001)

Story type: Mystery
Subject(s): Drugs; Teachers
Major character(s): Amelia Prentice, Teacher (high school English); Gil Dickensen, Fiance(e) (former)
Time period(s): 2000s
Locale(s): Adirondack Mountains, New York

Summary: Amelia Prentice, a high school English teacher, is settling into a predictably routine life when she trips over a body in the public library. The dead woman turns out to be one of her former students and the rumors around town suggest she was somehow involved in the selling of drugs. Amelia is certain the rumors are unfounded and decides to look into the case herself. Helping her out is her former fiance, Gil Dickensen, who is suddenly showing a renewed interest in Amelia, much to her disconcertment. First novel.

Other books you might like:
Ron Benrey, *Little White Lies*, 2001
B.J. Hoff, *The Daybreak Series*, 1995-
Gilbert Morris, *The Dani Ross Series*, 2000-
Gayle G. Roper, *The Amhearst Series*, 1997-
Audrey Stallsmith, *The Thyme Will Tell Series*, 1998-

1009

DIANA KILLIAN (Pseudonym of D.L. Browne)

The Art of Dying

(Philadelphia: Xlibris, 2001)

Story type: Mystery
Subject(s): Art; Memory Loss
Major character(s): Hilary Jackson, Artist (painter); Alan, Amnesiac, Crime Suspect (may be a killer)
Time period(s): 2000s
Locale(s): Steeple Hill, California

Summary: Artist Hilary Jackson is living a quiet life in a small California community when an attractive Englishman enters her life. Hoping to do a good deed and help the man, Hilary soon realizes ''Alan'' has amnesia. Then to her horror, she learns he is the chief suspect in the murder of a Scotland Yard detective. As Hilary grows closer to ''Alan,'' she begins to realize that if he is the killer, her life may be in danger. Even worse, if he is innocent, the real killer might come after them both. This author also writes under the pseudonym Colin Dunne.

Other books you might like:
Ron Benrey, *Little White Lies*, 2001
Gilbert Morris, *The Dani Ross Series*, 2000-
Gayle G. Roper, *The Amhearst Series*, 1997-
Patricia H. Rushford, *The Helen Bradley Series*, 1997-
Sally S. Wright, *The Ben Reese Series*, 1997-

1010

KAREN KINGSBURY

On Every Side

(Sisters, Oregon: Multnomah, 2001)

Story type: Contemporary
Subject(s): Religious Conflict
Major character(s): Jordan Riley, Lawyer; Faith Evans, Journalist (TV reporter)
Time period(s): 2000s
Locale(s): Bethany, Pennsylvania

Summary: A teenage Jordan Riley loses his faith in God after his mother's death. Now an adult and working as a lawyer, Jordan uses his legal skills to fight separation of church and state battles. Learning his hometown has a statue of Jesus on public property, Jordan takes the city to court. Television reporter Faith Evans, who knew Jordan when they were growing up, covers his legal fight. She, however, is not sympathetic to his cause and tries to convince him to return to the faith that had given him such great comfort during his childhood years.

Other books by the same author:
A Time to Dance, 2001
When Joy Came to Stay, 2000
Waiting for Morning, 1999
Where Yesterday Lives, 1998

Other books you might like:
T. Davis Bunn, *The Book of Hours*, 2000
John Vincent Coniglio, *Rumors of Angels*, 1994
Robin Lee Hatcher, *Whispers from Yesterday*, 1999
Jerry B. Jenkins, *Though None Go with Me*, 2000
Beverly LaHaye, *The Seasons under Heaven Series*, 1999-

1011

JANE KIRKPATRICK

What Once We Loved

(Colorado Springs, Colorado: WaterBrook, 2001)

Story type: Historical/American West
Series: Kinship and Courage. Book 3
Subject(s): Widows/Widowers
Major character(s): Ruth Martin, Pioneer, Widow(er)
Time period(s): 1850s
Locale(s): Poverty Flat, California

Summary: Ruth Martin is one of a group of women who travels west with their families only to have their husbands die during the perilous journey. Drawn together through their shared losses, the widows have bonded. However, the time has come for them to go their separate ways and forge new lives for themselves. Ruth and her children plan to leave California and head north to Oregon. Then yet another tragedy shatters Ruth's dreams and she begins to believe she no longer has the courage to continue.

Other books by the same author:
No Eye Can See, 2001
All Together in One Place, 2000
Mystic Sweet Communion, 1998
A Gathering of Finches, 1997
A Sweetness to the Soul, 1995

Other books you might like:
June Masters Bacher, *Love Is a Gentle Stranger*, 1983
Lisa Tawn Bergren, *The Northern Lights Series*, 1998-
Linda Chaikin, *The Great Northwest Series*, 1994-
Ruth Glover, *The Wildrose Series*, 1994-
Peggy Stoks, *Olivia's Touch*, 2000

1012

HARRY LEE KRAUS

Could I Have This Dance?

(Grand Rapids, Michigan: Zondervan, 2002)

Story type: Medical
Subject(s): Genetic Disease; Medicine
Major character(s): Claire McCall, Doctor
Time period(s): 2000s
Locale(s): Lafayette, Massachusetts

Summary: Although she was raised in a dysfunctional family with an alcoholic father, Claire McCall has managed to achieve her dream of graduating from medical school. Pursing a surgical internship at a hospital in Massachusetts, Claire revels in the fast-paced environment of the trauma unit. Encountering a patient with a rare genetic disorder known as Huntington's Disease, Claire is intrigued because the condition's symptoms, which mimic drunkenness, are surprisingly similar to those she remembers her father having. Doing some research, Claire soon comes to the conclusion that Huntington's Disease does run in her family. Unfortunately, that leaves her with several ethical dilemmas to face. If she takes a genetic test to find out if she has the disease, her career might come to a grinding halt. If she keeps her findings secret, her siblings might unknowingly pass the disease on to future generations.

Other books by the same author:
The Chairman, 1999
Lethal Mercy, 1997
The Stain, 1997
Fated Genes, 1996
Stainless Steel Hearts, 1994

Other books you might like:
Hannah Alexander, *The Healing Touch Series*, 2002-
Terri Blackstock, *The Newpointe 911 Series*, 1998-
Alton Gansky, *The Ridgeline Mystery Series*, 1998-
Karen Rispin, *Rustlers*, 1998
Ed Stewart, *Terminal Mercy*, 1999

1013

JIM KRAUS
TERRI KRAUS, Co-Author

The Quest

(Wheaton, Illinois: Tyndale House, 2002)

Story type: Historical
Series: Circle of Destiny. Book 4
Subject(s): Learning; Quest
Major character(s): Jamison Pike, Writer
Time period(s): 1840s; 1850s (1842-1859)
Locale(s): Pittsburgh, Pennsylvania

Summary: Jamison Pike is returning to Harvard for his second year in college when a chance encounter with a stranger leaves him questioning his place in the world. Deciding to learn the meaning of life, Jamison sets out on a worldwide quest in search of this ultimate piece of knowledge. However, despite finding fame and fortune through his writing, Jamison is no more knowledgeable than at the beginning of his journeys. Eventually, he begins to suspect his life will remain empty until he accepts religion into it.

Other books by the same author:
The Promise, 2001
The Price, 2000
The Treasure, 2000
Journey to the Crimson Sea, 1997
Passages of Gold, 1997

Other books you might like:
Lawana Blackwell, *The Gresham Chronicles*, 1998-
Donna Fletcher Crow, *The Cambridge Chronicles*, 1994-
B.J. Hoff, *The Song of Erin Series*, 1997-
Jake Thoene, *The Portraits of Destiny Series*, 1998-
Lori Wick, *The Kensington Chronicles*, 1993-

1014

AL LACY
JOANNA LACY, Co-Author

A Measure of Grace

(Sisters, Oregon: Multnomah, 2001)

Story type: Historical/American West
Series: Mail Order Brides. Book 8

Subject(s): Abuse; Mail Order Brides
Major character(s): Diana Morrow, Abuse Victim, Mail Order Bride
Time period(s): 1860s
Locale(s): Elkton, Idaho

Summary: Diana Morrow is desperate to escape from her abusive father, so she agrees to become the mail order bride of Jordan Shaw. Jordan is a wild young man who doesn't want to marry and settle down, but his parents are insistent. Upon her arrival in Elkton, Idaho, Diana discovers that Jordan has gone missing. Now without a prospective husband or a means of support, Diana is desperate to avoid returning home. She sets off with Jordan's best friend to try to track him down, but soon finds herself wondering if Jordan is the man for her.

Other books by the same author:
Damascus Journey, 2001
Let Freedom Ring, 2001
Sincerely Yours, 2001
The Secret Place, 2001
Ransom of Love, 2000

Other books you might like:
Lori Copeland, *The Brides of the West Series*, 1998-
Kathleen Morgan, *The Brides of Culdee Creek Series*, 1999-
Janette Oke, *The Women of the West Series*, 1990-
Catherine Palmer, *The Town Called Hope Series*, 1997-
Kay D. Rizzo, *The Serenity Inn Series*, 1998-

1015

AL LACY
JOANNA LACY, Co-Author

A Prince Among Them

(Sisters, Oregon: Multnomah, 2002)

Story type: Historical
Series: Shadow of Liberty. Book 3
Subject(s): Kidnapping
Major character(s): Nigel Whitaker, Kidnapper; Jeremy Barlow, Immigrant; Cecelia Barlow, Immigrant
Time period(s): 19th century (1819-1897)
Locale(s): England; United States

Summary: Nursing a lifelong hatred of the royal family, Nigel Whitaker comes up with a daring plan for revenge. He kidnaps David, the great-grandson of Queen Victoria and takes him to America. Immigrants Jeremy and Cecelia Barlow, who are unable to have children of their own, become attached to young David. This makes it difficult for Nigel to carry out his plans without arousing suspicion. Meanwhile, Queen Victoria's faith in God sustains her through this difficult time.

Other books by the same author:
So Little Time, 2002
A Measure of Grace, 2001
Damascus Journey, 2001
The Secret Place, 2001
Let Freedom Ring, 2001

Other books you might like:
Lawana Blackwell, *The Victorian Serenade Series*, 1995-
B.J. Hoff, *The Song of Erin Series*, 1997-
Gilbert Morris, *The House of Winslow Series*, 1986-
Jane Peart, *The Edgecliffe Manor Series*, 1996-
Lori Wick, *The Kensington Chronicles*, 1993-

1016

TIM LAHAYE
JERRY B. JENKINS, Co-Author

Desecration

(Wheaton, Illinois: Tyndale House, 2001)

Story type: Apocalyptic Horror
Series: Left Behind. Book 9
Subject(s): Apocalypse
Major character(s): Nicolae Carpathia, Ruler; Rayford Steele, Pilot
Time period(s): Indeterminate Future
Locale(s): Global Community, Fictional Country

Summary: In this ninth volume of the wildly popular Left Behind series, evil Global Community leader Nicolae Carpathia is becoming increasingly more tyrannical. Not content with ruling the world, he desecrates a temple and declares himself to be a god. Meanwhile, the Tribulation Force continues their fight against his evil empire. Pilot Rayford Steele is among them, leading a group of fliers who battle against Carpathia and his agents.

Other books by the same author:
The Indwelling, 2000
The Mark, 2000
Apollyon, 1999
Assassins, 1999
Soul Harvest, 1998

Other books you might like:
T. Davis Bunn, *The Warning*, 1998
Terry L. Craig, *Gatekeeper*, 1999
Grant R. Jeffrey, *Flee the Darkness*, 1998
Gilbert Morris, *The Omega Trilogy*, 1999-
Bill Myers, *Blood of Heaven*, 1996

1017

BONNIE LEON

Worthy of Riches

(Nashville: Broadman & Holman, 2002)

Story type: Contemporary
Series: Matanuska. Book 2
Subject(s): Farm Life; Guilt
Major character(s): Ray Townsend, Settler; Jean Hasper, Widow(er)
Time period(s): 1930s
Locale(s): Alaska

Summary: Ray Townsend has never accepted the new settlers who have arrived in Alaska over the years and has done his best to make them feel unwelcome. However, when new settler Will Hasper dies in an accident, Ray feels responsible and attempts to do what he can to help out Will's widow, Jean. Jean gratefully accepts Ray's help, but others in the family are not so quick to forgive him. Her oldest son, Luke, is especially angry with Ray and wants nothing to do with him.

Other books by the same author:
Valley of Promises, 2001
A Sacred Place, 2000
Harvest of Truth, 2000
In Fields of Freedom, 1999
When Freedom Grows, 1998

Other books you might like:
Lynn N. Austin, *Hidden Places*, 2001
Robin Lee Hatcher, *The Shepherd's Voice*, 2000
Lorena McCourtney, *Escape*, 1996
Ann Tatlock, *A Room of My Own*, 1998
Lance Wubbels, *The Gentle Hills Series*, 1994-

1018

BEVERLY LEWIS

October Song

(Minneapolis: Bethany House, 2001)

Story type: Collection
Subject(s): Amish
Time period(s): 2000s
Locale(s): Lancaster County, Pennsylvania

Summary: In this collection, Lewis brings back several characters from her popular books featuring the Amish and their lifestyle. "Hickory Hollow" follows the lives of Katie and Daniel Fisher from Lewis' Heritage of Lancaster County series. Still shunned by the Amish for leaving the faith, Katie is happily married but misses her friends and family. "Bird-in-Hand" continues stories from the Postcard series. Rachel Bradley is settling into married life with her new husband Philip, but he is having difficulties adjusting to the Amish lifestyle. In "Grasshopper," Levi and Lydia, earlier seen in *The Redemption of Sarah Cain*, begin courting.

Where it's reviewed:
Library Journal, September 1, 2001, page 156

Other books by the same author:
Sanctuary, 2001
The Redemption of Sarah Cain, 2000
The Crossroad, 1999
The Postcard, 1999
The Reckoning, 1998

Other books you might like:
Carrie Bender, *The Miriam's Journal Series*, 1993-
Dudley J. Delffs, *The Father Grif Series*, 1998-
Philip Gulley, *The Harmony Series*, 2000-
Robin Jones Gunn, *The Glenbrooke Series*, 1995-
Gayle G. Roper, *The Document*, 1998

1019

ALAN MAKI

Written on Her Heart

(Nashville: Broadman & Holman, 2002)

Story type: Contemporary
Subject(s): Reunions; Vietnam War
Major character(s): Molly Meyers, Teacher
Time period(s): 2000s
Locale(s): Victor, Montana

Summary: When James Wade goes overseas to serve in the military during the Vietnam War and doesn't return, his sweetheart Molly Meyers is devastated. Settling into a solitary life in Montana, the years pass by and soon Molly is nearly 50. A friend comes to visit her and discovers a packet of romantic poems James wrote to Molly. Soon afterwards, the friend discovers the same poems in a newly published volume of poetry by Jonathan Roseland. If Jonathan and James are the same person, why didn't he come back to Molly? And if James is still alive, do the two have a chance to rekindle their romance?

Other books by the same author:
A Choice to Cherish, 2000

Other books you might like:
Jack Cavanaugh, *The Peacemakers*, 1999
G. Roger Corey, *Eden Springs*, 1999
Doris Elaine Fell, *April Is Forever*, 1995
Carole Gift Page, *A Locket for Maggie*, 2000
Robert L. Wise, *Be Not Afraid*, 2000

1020

GAIL GAYMER MARTIN
DIANN MILLS, Co-Author
JILL STENGL, Co-Author
KATHLEEN Y'BARBO, Co-Author

The English Garden

(Uhrichsville, Ohio: Barbour, 2002)

Story type: Anthology
Subject(s): Love; Gardens and Gardening
Locale(s): England

Summary: English gardens over the span of four centuries are the settings for romance in this collection of four novellas. The stories are *Apple of His Eye* by Gail Gaymer Martin, *Flower Amidst the Ashes* by DiAnn Mills, *Woman of Valor* by Jill Stengl, and *Robyn's Garden* by Kathleen Y'Barbo.

Other books you might like:
Lawana Blackwell, *The Tales of London Series*, 2000-
Linda Chaikin, *Friday's Child*, 2001
Catherine Palmer, *English Ivy*, 2002
Michael Phillips, *The Secrets of Heathersleigh Hall Series*, 1998-
Lori Wick, *The Proposal*, 2002

1021

GAIL GAYMER MARTIN

A Love for Safekeeping

(New York: Steeple Hill, 2002)

Story type: Romance
Subject(s): Stalking
Major character(s): Jane Conroy, Teacher (elementary); Kyle Manning, Police Officer
Time period(s): 2000s
Locale(s): Redmond, Michigan

Summary: Jane Conroy returns to her hometown after a long absence to take a teaching position at a local elementary school. Unfortunately, before she can even teach her first class, Jane's classroom is vandalized. Receiving little sympathy from school administrators, Jane is touched when the police officer investigating the crime shows great compassion for her feelings. Kyle Manning wants to pursue a relationship, but Jane is hesitant. Her father was also a police officer and his abusive behavior has made her wary of men who wear badges. When Jane is the target of more vandalism, she grows to appreciate having Kyle around, especially when it begins to appear as if Jane is being stalked.

Other books by the same author:
Her Secret Longing, 2001
Secrets of the Heart, 2001
Upon a Midnight Clear, 2000
Dreaming of Castles, 1999
Seasons, 1998

Other books you might like:
Irene Brand, *To Love and Honor*, 1999
Lyn Cote, *Winter's Secret*, 2002
Valerie Hansen, *The Wedding Arbor*, 1999
Marta Perry, *Desperately Seeking Dad*, 2000
Carol Steward, *Her Kind of Hero*, 1999

1022

GAIL GAYMER MARTIN

Secrets of the Heart

(New York: Steeple Hill, 2001)

Story type: Romance
Subject(s): Secrets
Major character(s): Kate Davis, Social Worker; Scott Ryan, Doctor (intern)
Time period(s): 2000s
Locale(s): Michigan

Summary: Social worker Kate Davis is hiding a past she isn't proud of. This isn't really a terrible problem for her until she meets her roommate's brother. Handsome Scott Ryan is completing an internship at the local hospital, when he drops by to visit his sister, Phyllis, and meets Kate. For Scott, Kate is the dream woman he has been looking for: a devout churchgoer with an intense love of family. Unfortunately, Kate's past life may ruin their romance if Scott can't accept it.

Other books by the same author:
Her Secret Longing, 2001
Upon a Midnight Clear, 2000
Dreaming of Castles, 1999
Seasons, 1998

Other books you might like:
Irene Brand, *The Test of Love*, 2000
Valerie Hansen, *The Perfect Couple*, 2000
Crystal Stovall, *With All Josie's Heart*, 2001
Janet Tronstad, *A Gentleman for Dry Creek*, 2000
Cheryl Wolverton, *Healing Hearts*, 2000

1023

LORENA MCCOURTNEY

Whirlpool

(Grand Rapids, Michigan: Fleming H. Revell, 2002)

Story type: Mystery
Series: Julesburg Mysteries. Book 1
Subject(s): Arson; Divorce; Infidelity
Major character(s): Stefanie Canfield, Businesswoman, Divorced Person
Time period(s): 2000s
Locale(s): Julesburg

Summary: Stefanie Canfield is going through the worst time of her life. Not only is her husband, Hunter, having an affair, but he is making sure the entire town of Julesburg knows about it. Forced into a divorce she doesn't particularly want, Stefanie's troubles escalate when the mill she still owns with her former husband is destroyed by arson. Stefanie is a suspect in the case and only the arson investigator, an old friend, is certain of her innocence. Then Hunter's mistress is found murdered and Stefanie becomes the chief suspect in that case as well.

Other books by the same author:
Searching for Stardust, 1999
Canyon, 1998
Forgotten, 1998
Dear Silver, 1997
Escape, 1996

Other books you might like:
Robin Lee Hatcher, *The Forgiving Hour*, 1999
Dee Henderson, *Danger in the Shadows*, 1999
Sally D. John, *In the Shadow of Love*, 1998
Debra White Smith, *Second Chances*, 2000
Ellen Vaughn, *The Strand*, 1997

1024

PAUL MCCUSKER

The Faded Flower

(Grand Rapids, Michigan: Zondervan, 2001)

Story type: Contemporary
Subject(s): Memory Loss; Nursing Homes; Unemployment
Major character(s): Frank Reynolds, Unemployed
Time period(s): 2000s
Locale(s): United States

Summary: In the space of a few short hours, Frank Reynolds' life changes completely. He is ''downsized'' from his job of many years, then goes home to receive the devastating news that his father has Alzheimer's disease and needs constant care. Frank moves his family back to his hometown, where he soon sees the need of placing his father in a nursing home. Through the difficult ordeals he faces, Frank soon realizes he is becoming a better person through his trials.

Where it's reviewed:
Library Journal, September 1, 2001, page 156

Other books by the same author:
Epiphany, 1998

Catacombs, 1997

Other books you might like:

Judy Baer, *Libby's Story*, 2001
Joseph Bentz, *A Son Comes Home*, 1999
Janette Oke, *The Matchmakers*, 1997
Gary E. Parker, *The Wedding Dress*, 2002
Deborah Raney, *A Vow to Cherish*, 1996

1025

KATHLEEN MORGAN

Child of Promise

(Grand Rapids, Michigan: Fleming H. Revell, 2002)

Story type: Historical/American West
Series: Brides of Culdee Creek. Book 4
Subject(s): Doctors; Faith
Major character(s): Beth MacKay, Doctor; Noah Starr, Religious (Episcopalian minister)
Time period(s): 1900s
Locale(s): Culdee Creek, Colorado

Summary: Beth MacKay gives up romance in order to pursue her dream of becoming a doctor. Making her sacrifice easier is the fact that she is secretly in love with Noah Starr, who marries another woman. Years after Noah saves Beth's life during an accident, she returns to Culdee Creek, Colorado to take over the medical practice of the town's aging doctor. Noah is still in town and is a minister. He is also widowed and has begun to question his faith since his wife's death left him the single father to a disabled child. Beth still finds Noah as intriguing as she always did, but the two occasionally clash over ethical issues. When Beth and Noah give conflicting advice to a battered woman, the woman chooses to follow Noah's advice and return to her abusive husband. After the situation ends in tragedy, Noah's already fragile faith is shattered and Beth must find some way to make his life whole again.

Other books by the same author:

Embrace the Dawn, 2002
Lady of Light, 2001
Woman of Grace, 2000
Daughter of Joy, 1999

Other books you might like:

Angela Elwell Hunt, *The Velvet Shadow*, 1999
Jim Kraus, *The Promise*, 2001
Lynn Morris, *The Cheney Duvall Series*, 1994-
Janette Oke, *They Called Her Mrs. Doc*, 1992
Peggy Stoks, *Olivia's Touch*, 2000

1026

KATHLEEN MORGAN

Embrace the Dawn

(Wheaton, Illinois: Tyndale House, 2002)

Story type: Historical/Seventeenth Century
Subject(s): Abuse
Major character(s): Killian Campbell, Abuse Victim, Spouse; Adam Campbell, Laird
Time period(s): 17th century
Locale(s): Scotland

Summary: Killian Campbell marries her husband, Adam, in the hopes of escaping her dull life in the American Colonies. Unfortunately, she gets more than she bargained for. Alexander, who has a violent temper and a jealous nature, quickly becomes abusive. Years into her marriage, Killian now hopes only to escape from her husband before he kills her or their son, Gavin. The couple is visiting Alexander's relatives in the Scottish Highlands when events come to a head. Forced to flee with Gavin in the middle of the night, Killian is soon on the run for her life.

Other books by the same author:

Child of Promise, 2002
Lady of Light, 2001
Woman of Grace, 2000
Daughter of Joy, 1999

Other books you might like:

B.J. Hoff, *The Song of Erin Series*, 1997-
Angela Elwell Hunt, *The Heirs of Cahira O'Connor Series*, 1998-
Grace Johnson, *The Scottish Shores Series*, 1997-
Jane Peart, *The Edgecliffe Manor Series*, 1996-
Bodie Thoene, *The Galway Chronicles*, 1997-

1027

GILBERT MORRIS

The Golden Angel

(Minneapolis: Bethany House, 2001)

Story type: Historical
Series: House of Winslow. Book 26
Subject(s): Airplanes
Major character(s): Erin Winslow, Pilot (stunt); Quaid Merritt, Pilot (stunt)
Time period(s): 1910s; 1920s (1913-1921)
Locale(s): Africa; United States

Summary: Erin Winslow enjoys living in Africa because it allows her a measure of freedom few women in the United States or Europe have in the years just prior to World War I. She even manages to take flying lessons from a visiting pilot. Unfortunately, he also breaks her heart and Erin runs off to America to forget him. Nobody will hire her as a pilot, so she ends up working in a cafe. She meets Quaid Merritt, a stunt pilot, who is intrigued at the thought of a female aviator. Learning that Erin is indeed talented, Quaid convinces her to go on a barnstorming tour of the United States with him. The two soon become a popular attraction, thrilling crowds with their daring stunts. Hollywood producers see the appeal a female pilot would have for movie audiences and want to hire Erin, giving her some difficult decisions to make about what direction her life will take.

Other books by the same author:

End of Act Three, 2001
Four of a Kind, 2001
Jacob's Way, 2001
The Amazon Quest, 2001
A Covenant of Love, 2000

Other books you might like:
Lawana Blackwell, *The Gresham Chronicles*, 1998-
Linda Chaikin, *Endangered*, 1997
B.J. Hoff, *The Song of Erin Series*, 1997-
Catherine Palmer, *A Touch of Betrayal*, 2000
Michael Phillips, *The Secrets of Heathersleigh Hall Series*, 1998-

1028

GILBERT MORRIS

The Heavenly Fugitive

(Minneapolis: Bethany House, 2002)

Story type: Historical/Roaring Twenties
Series: House of Winslow. Book 27
Subject(s): Crime and Criminals; Law; Theater
Major character(s): Phillip Winslow, Lawyer; Amelia Winslow, Actress
Time period(s): 1920s
Locale(s): New York, New York

Summary: Siblings Phillip and Amelia Winslow arrive in New York City planning to make a success out of their chosen careers. Phillip is a lawyer and his sister dreams of becoming an actress. Although he has vowed to put a mob boss behind bars, Phillip soon finds himself falling in love with the criminal's daughter. Meanwhile, Amelia finally gets her big break on Broadway. Unfortunately, it is with the help of a gangster. Can the Winslows achieve their goals without compromising their principles?

Other books by the same author:
End of Act Three, 2001
Four of a Kind, 2001
Jacob's Way, 2001
The Amazon Quest, 2001
The Golden Angel, 2001

Other books you might like:
Jack Cavanaugh, *The American Family Portrait Series*, 1994-
Diane Noble, *The California Chronicles*, 1999-
Jane Peart, *The Brides of Montclair Series*, 1989-
Michael Phillips, *The Heathersleigh Hall Series*, 1998-
Michael Phillips, *The Russians Series*, 1991-

1029

MICHAEL MORRIS

A Place Called Wiregrass

(Tulsa, Oklahoma: RiverOak, 2002)

Story type: Contemporary
Subject(s): Abuse; Small Town Life
Major character(s): Erma Lee Jacobs, Abuse Victim, Grandparent; Cher, Relative (Erma Lee's grandchild); Miss Claudia, Aged Person
Time period(s): 2000s
Locale(s): Wiregrass, Alabama

Summary: Erma Lee Jacobs and her granddaughter, Cher, run away from an abusive household hoping to find something better. They end up in the small Alabama town of Wiregrass, where they are lucky enough to meet Miss Claudia, an elderly town leader. Miss Claudia helps them settle into Wiregrass and they are happily adjusting to the quiet and peaceful lifestyle when Cher's convict father shows up. First novel.

Other books you might like:
Beverly Bush, *Wings of a Dove*, 1996
Linda Hall, *Sadie's Song*, 2001
Bette Nordberg, *Serenity Bay*, 2000
Augusta Trobaugh, *Praise Jerusalem*, 1997
Vinita Hampton Wright, *Velma Still Cooks in Leeway*, 2000

1030

NANCY MOSER

The Seat Beside Me

(Sisters, Oregon: Multnomah, 2002)

Story type: Contemporary
Subject(s): Airplane Accidents; Guilt
Major character(s): Dora Roberts, Journalist
Time period(s): 2000s
Locale(s): United States

Summary: Sun Fun Airlines Flight 1382 is delayed on the runway for what seems like an endless time, allowing seatmates to get to know each other briefly. When the plane finally takes off, it crashes into an icy river leaving 97 people dead. Only five survive. Those three women and two men are confronted with feelings of guilt, anger, and remorse and they must somehow come to grips with the fact their lives were spared for reasons unknown to them. Journalist Dora Roberts follows the story and tries not to let her pursuit of the survivors end in sensationalism.

Where it's reviewed:
Publishers Weekly, November 19, 2001, page 48

Other books by the same author:
The Temptation, 2000
The Quest, 1999
The Invitation, 1998

Other books you might like:
Lisa Tawn Bergren, *Pathways*, 2001
Terri Blackstock, *Broken Wings*, 1998
G. Roger Corey, *Eden Springs*, 1999
Dee Henderson, *True Valor*, 2002
Travis Thrasher, *The Watermark*, 2001

1031

JOE MUSSER

The Infidel

(Nashville: Broadman & Holman, 2001)

Story type: Historical
Subject(s): Redemption; Slavery
Major character(s): John Newton, Sea Captain (slave ship), Historical Figure
Time period(s): 18th century
Locale(s): England; At Sea; Africa

Summary: John Newton is remembered today as the author of the hymn *Amazing Grace*, but surprisingly enough he was not always a religious man. Newton is born to a slave ship captain and his wife, who is a devout Christian. After his mother's death, his father remarries and religion is rarely mentioned in their household again. At the age of 11, Newton joins his father aboard his slave ship. He continues to pursue this profession for a number of years, even after he once again becomes a practicing Christian.

Other books by the same author:
Behold a Pale Horse, 1970

Other books you might like:
Donna Fletcher Crow, *The Cambridge Chronicles*, 1994-
Reg Grant, *Storm*, 2001
Alan David Justice, *The Final Bow*, 1993
Joan Ohanneson, *Scarlet Music*, 1997
Catherine Palmer, *The Treasure of Timbuktu*, 1997

1032

BILL MYERS

When the Last Leaf Falls

(Grand Rapids, Michigan: Zondervan, 2001)

Story type: Contemporary
Subject(s): Grandfathers; Illness; Cancer
Major character(s): Ally Newcombe, Teenager
Time period(s): 2000s
Locale(s): United States

Summary: Ally Newcombe, a well-adjusted and happy teenage girl, dreams of becoming a dancer. Then she is diagnosed with bone cancer and her life falls apart. The cancer treatments take their toll on the entire Newcombe family and both Ally and her father, a minister, are bitter at her fate. Ally's grandfather tries to help them regain their faith by attempting to paint a picture, but she remains unmoved and says she will die when the last leaf falls off the tree that stands outside her bedroom window. When her grandfather becomes ill and dies, a grieving Ally rediscovers God via his final painting, one that captures the truth of God's love. This story was inspired by the O. Henry story "The Last Leaf."

Where it's reviewed:
Library Journal, September 1, 2001, page 156
Publishers Weekly, August 6, 2001, page 61

Other books by the same author:
Eli, 2000
Fire of Heaven, 1999
Threshold, 1997
Blood of Heaven, 1996

Other books you might like:
Angela Elwell Hunt, *Gentle Touch*, 1997
Beverly Lewis, *The Sunroom*, 1998
Paul McCusker, *Epiphany*, 1998
Calvin Miller, *Snow*, 1998
Janette Oke, *Dana's Valley*, 2001

1033

DIANE NOBLE

Come, My Little Angel

(Sisters, Oregon: Multnomah, 2001)

Story type: Historical
Subject(s): Christmas; Plays
Major character(s): Daisy James, Child
Time period(s): 1910s
Locale(s): Sierra Nevada, California

Summary: Ten-year-old Daisy James sees a great deal of sorrow around her and wants to do something to lift the spirits of her small community. The young girl is especially concerned about her mother, who lost a baby the year before and remains so depressed she is unable to sing as she did in happier times. Thinking a Christmas play would help spread cheer, Daisy writes *Come, My Little Angel*. Unfortunately, writing the play is the easy part. Now she must somehow convince her music teacher to write accompanying songs, her classmates to act, and a traveling circus to bring their tent to town for a makeshift theatre.

Where it's reviewed:
Library Journal, September 2, 2001, page 156

Other books by the same author:
At Play in the Promised Land, 2001
The Blossom and the Nettle, 2000
Distant Bells, 1999
Unlikely Angels, 1999
When the Far Hills Bloom, 1999

Other books you might like:
T. Davis Bunn, *One Shenandoah Winter*, 1998
Lori Copeland, *Christmas Vows: $5.00 Extra*, 2001
Richard Paul Evans, *The Christmas Box*, 1993
Jerry B. Jenkins, *Twas the Night Before*, 1998
Paul McCusker, *Epiphany*, 1998
Joe L. Wheeler, *Christmas from the Heart*, 2001

1034

JANETTE OKE

When Tomorrow Comes

(Minneapolis: Bethany House, 2001)

Story type: Historical/World War II
Series: Delaney Family. Book 2
Subject(s): Accidents; Family Life
Major character(s): Christine Delaney, Care Giver, Secretary
Time period(s): 1930s
Locale(s): Canada

Summary: A broken romance has left Christine Delaney shaken and insecure. Returning to her family home, she takes comfort in the fact that her brother has found the love of his life and is planning his wedding. Christine, however, is unsure of what she wants out of life. With Canada on the brink of entering World War II, she believes war work may be the answer. However, before she can make any solid decisions about her life, Christine must face some family tragedies, as well as some romantic entanglements.

Other books by the same author:
Beyond the Gathering Storm, 2000
Like Gold Refined, 2000
A Quiet Strength, 1999
A Searching Heart, 1998
The Tender Years, 1997

Other books you might like:
T. Davis Bunn, *The Rendezvous with Destiny Series*, 1993-
Elyse Larson, *The Women of Valor Series*, 2000-
Alan Morris, *The Guardians of the North Series*, 1996-
Jane Peart, *Courageous Bride*, 1998
Penelope J. Stokes, *The Faith on the Homefront Series*, 1996-

1035

CAROLE GIFT PAGE

A Bungalow for Two

(New York: Steeple Hill, 2001)

Story type: Romance
Subject(s): Remarriage; Trust
Major character(s): Frannie Rowlands, Artist (sculptor); Scott Winslow, Wealthy (millionaire)
Time period(s): 2000s
Locale(s): United States

Summary: When sculptor Frannie Rowlands goes to the beach for some much needed rest, the last thing on her mind is romance. Frannie just wants some peace and quiet to sculpt and to recover from the three family weddings she has been through recently, including the remarriage of her father. Although happy for all the new couples, she cannot help feeling a bit out of place in her father's new life. Then Frannie meets reclusive millionaire Scott Winslow. There is an immediate attraction between the two, but since neither is looking for romance, they are unprepared when it appears.

Other books by the same author:
A Child Shall Lead Them, 2001
Cassandra's Song, 2001
A Family to Cherish, 2000
A Locket for Maggie, 2000
A Rose for Jenny, 1999

Other books you might like:
Kathryn Alexander, *The Forever Husband*, 1999
Terri Blackstock, *Emerald Windows*, 2001
Jane Peart, *A Montclair Homecoming*, 2000
Gayle G. Roper, *The Key*, 1998
Janet Tronstad, *An Angel for Dry Creek*, 1999

1036

CAROLE GIFT PAGE

A Child Shall Lead Them

(New York: Steeple Hill, 2001)

Story type: Romance
Series: Minister's Daughters. Book 2
Subject(s): Orphans
Major character(s): Brianna Rowlands, Social Worker; Eric Wingate, Lawyer
Time period(s): 2000s
Locale(s): La Jolla, California

Summary: Social worker Brianna Rowlands is worried about her father, who is still mourning his beloved wife. However, her concerns for him take a back seat to the orphaned baby girl she discovers. While looking for little Charity's next of kin, Brianna finds the baby's biological uncle, lawyer Eric Wingate. Eric believes his busy schedule won't allow time for fatherhood so he is reluctant to take responsibility for the child. As he spends more time with Brianna and Charity, Eric begins to wonder if there is a place for both of them in his life.

Other books by the same author:
Cassandra's Song, 2001
A Family to Cherish, 2000
A Locket for Maggie, 2000
A Rose for Jenny, 1999
Rachel's Hope, 1998

Other books you might like:
Carolyne Aarsen, *Twin Blessings*, 2001
Irene Brand, *Summer's Promise*, 2001
Beverly Lewis, *The Redemption of Sarah Cain*, 2000
Ruth Scofield, *Loving Thy Neighbor*, 2001
Cheryl Wolverton, *This Side of Paradise*, 1998

1037

KATHERINE HALL PAGE

The Body in the Bonfire

(New York: Morrow, 2002)

Story type: Mystery
Series: Faith Fairchild. Book 12
Subject(s): Cooks and Cooking; Race Relations
Major character(s): Faith Fairchild, Caterer, Religious (minister's wife)
Time period(s): 2000s
Locale(s): Aleford, Massachusetts

Summary: When an African American student at a boys' high school becomes the target of a hate campaign, caterer and minister's wife Faith Fairchild is called in to investigate since she has a long history of crime solving. Although teaching young men how to cook is not her favorite thing to do, Faith believes a cover is needed, so she agrees to teach some of the teenagers. Faith soon identifies a main suspect in the racial harassment, but then that student is killed. The main suspect in the murder is the African American student Faith was supposed to be helping. She must now work to clear his name and find the real killer.

Where it's reviewed:
Publishers Weekly, January 14, 2002, page 43

Other books by the same author:
The Body in the Moonlight, 2001
The Body in the Big Apple, 1999
The Body in the Bookcase, 1998
The Body in the Fjord, 1997
The Body in the Bog, 1996

Other books you might like:
Diane Mott Davidson, *The Goldy Bear Schulz Series*, 1990-

Gilbert Morris, *The Dani Ross Series*, 2000-
Virginia Rich, *The Eugenia Potter Series*, 1982-
Gayle G. Roper, *The Amhearst Series*, 1997-
Audrey Stallsmith, *The Body They May Kill*, 1995

1038

CATHERINE PALMER

The Happy Room

(Wheaton, Illinois: Tyndale House, 2002)

Story type: Contemporary
Subject(s): Brothers and Sisters; Eating Disorders; Hospitals
Major character(s): Julia Chappell, Spouse; Peter Mossman, Spouse
Time period(s): 2000s
Locale(s): United States; Africa

Summary: When Debbie Mossman is hospitalized because of her anorexia, her brother and sister rush to her side. As Debbie lies near death, Julia Chappell and Peter Mossman reflect on the bad turns their lives have taken. Julia is unhappily married to a youth minister and is upset because she is once again pregnant, this time with twins. Peter's marriage is equally strained, though in his case it is due to his uncontrollable temper. As Julia and Peter wait for changes in Debbie's condition, they realize their unhappiness can be traced back to their childhoods as the neglected children of missionaries. Their parents, who served in Africa, had plenty of time and energy to devote to their causes, with little left over for their children. Once Julia and Peter reach their conclusions, they have to decide whether to confront the past or let it go.

Where it's reviewed:
Publishers Weekly, November 26, 2001, page 37

Other books by the same author:
English Ivy, 2002
A Dangerous Silence, 2001
Hide and Seek, 2001
A Kiss of Adventure, 2000
A Whisper of Danger, 2000

Other books you might like:
Lynn N. Austin, *Eve's Daughters*, 1999
Joseph Bentz, *A Son Comes Home*, 1999
Brandilyn Collins, *Color the Sidewalk for Me*, 2002
Paul McCusker, *Epiphany*, 1998
Francine Rivers, *Leota's Garden*, 1999

1039

GARY E. PARKER

Highland Hopes

(Minneapolis: Bethany House, 2001)

Story type: Historical
Series: Blue Ridge Legacy. Book 1
Subject(s): Grandmothers; Mountain Life
Major character(s): Abigail Porter, Aged Person
Time period(s): 20th century
Locale(s): Blue Springs, North Carolina

Summary: ''Granny Abby'' is over 100-years-old when she tells this story of her younger years to her great-granddaughter. Abigail Porter's life begins with tragedy when her mother dies giving birth to her. In order to have somebody to care for his brood of young children, her father soon remarries. Unfortunately, a bet loses the family their homestead and Abigail's hopes of an education to better her life seem remote. She somehow manages to leave home to pursue her aspirations, but ends up trapped in a troubled marriage with her dreams slowly slipping away.

Where it's reviewed:
Publishers Weekly, July 2, 2001, page 51

Other books by the same author:
The Ephesus Fragment, 1999
The Last Gift, 1999
A Capital Offense, 1998
Dark Road to Daylight, 1996
Death Stalks a Holiday, 1996

Other books you might like:
Robin Lee Hatcher, *Ribbon of Years*, 2001
Tracie Peterson, *A Slender Thread*, 2000
Francine Rivers, *The Last Sin Eater*, 1998
Penelope J. Stokes, *The Blue Bottle Club*, 1999
Robert L. Wise, *Be Not Afraid*, 2000

1040

JUDITH PELLA

Written on the Wind

(Minneapolis: Bethany House, 2002)

Story type: Historical/World War II
Subject(s): Fathers and Daughters; Newspapers; World War II
Major character(s): Cameron Hayes, Journalist; Blair Hayes, Alcoholic, Singer (nightclub); Jackie Hayes, Young Woman
Time period(s): 1940s
Locale(s): United States; Union of Soviet Socialist Republics

Summary: Newspaper publisher Keagan Hayes wanted sons, but instead got three daughters. Cameron, Blair, and Jackie all realize their father would have preferred sons and desperately want to win his affection. Cameron tries to compete with her father by going to work for a rival newspaper. Blair rebels in an attempt to earn her father's attention and ends up an alcoholic nightclub singer in a failed marriage. Jackie tries to be the ''good girl'' and always does what her father wants until she falls in love with an Asian man and earns Keagan's ire.

Where it's reviewed:
Publishers Weekly, October 22, 2001, page 42

Other books by the same author:
Heaven's Road, 2000
Texas Angel, 1999
Beloved Stranger, 1998
Blind Faith, 1996
Warrior's Song, 1996

Other books you might like:
T. Davis Bunn, *The Rendezvous with Destiny Series*, 1993-

Linda Chaikin, *The Day to Remember Series*, 1999-
Bonnie Leon, *The Sowers Trilogy*, 1998-
Gilbert Morris, *The House of Winslow Series*, 1986-
Jane Peart, *The Brides of Montclair Series*, 1989-
Michael Phillips, *The Secret of the Rose Series*, 1993-

1041

MARTA PERRY

A Father's Place

(New York: Steeple Hill, 2001)

Story type: Romance
Subject(s): Fathers and Daughters; Mothers and Sons
Major character(s): Ellie Wayne, Store Owner (craft store); Quinn Forrester, Engineer
Time period(s): 2000s
Locale(s): Bedford Creek, Pennsylvania

Summary: Engineer Quinn Forrester returns to his hometown of Bedford Creek, Pennsylvania planning to break up the romance between his mother and Charles Wayne. Quinn is already disturbed because his daughter Kristie, who lives with his mother, is determined to have him marry Charles' daughter, Ellie. Ellie is Kristie's Sunday school teacher and also runs a craft shop in town. Thinking the Wayne family must be up to no good, Quinn is shocked to find himself falling in love with Ellie.

Other books by the same author:
Father Most Blessed, 2001
Desperately Seeking Dad, 2000
The Doctor Next Door, 2000
Since You've Been Gone, 1999
A Father's Promise, 1998

Other books you might like:
Carolyne Aarsen, *Twin Blessings*, 2001
Irene Brand, *Summer's Promise*, 2001
Carole Gift Page, *A Child Shall Lead Them*, 2001
Lois Richer, *Blessed Baby*, 2001
Ruth Scofield, *Loving Thy Neighbor*, 2001

1042

TRACIE PETERSON

Rivers of Gold

(Minneapolis: Bethany House, 2002)

Story type: Historical
Series: Yukon Quest. Book 3
Subject(s): Accidents
Major character(s): Miranda Colton, Accident Victim; Teddy Davenport, Scientist (botanist)
Time period(s): 1890s
Locale(s): Alaska

Summary: Swept overboard during a storm, Miranda Colton is saved from certain death by Alaskan natives. They put Miranda into the care of a British botanist named Teddy Davenport, who helps nurse the injured woman back to health. As Miranda regains her strength, her one wish is to return to those she left behind, who have presumed she died. As Miranda spends time with Teddy, she begins to see wonderful qualities in the dedicated scientist, but a secret from the past may threaten their love before it has a chance to grow.

Where it's reviewed:
Publishers Weekly, December 3, 2001, page 40

Other books by the same author:
Ashes and Ice, 2001
New Mexico Sunset, 2001
The Long Awaited Child, 2001
Treasures of the North, 2001
Colorado Wings, 2000

Other books you might like:
Lisa Tawn Bergren, *Midnight Sun*, 2000
Bonnie Leon, *A Sacred Place*, 2000
Jim Walker, *The Ice Princess*, 1998
Lori Wick, *The Hawk and the Jewel*, 1993
Brenda Wilbee, *Shipwreck*, 1991

1043

LOIS RICHER

Blessed Baby

(New York: Steeple Hill, 2001)

Story type: Romance
Subject(s): Adoption; Babies
Major character(s): Briony Green, Scientist; Ty Demens, Single Parent (of an adopted daughter), Widow(er)
Time period(s): 2000s
Locale(s): United States

Summary: Newly widowed Ty Demens is finding it difficult to cope with his adopted daughter Christine, but he loves the child more than anything and is grateful to have her in his life. Briony Green shows up on his doorstep with the news that her sister Bridget, who is deceased, was Christine's birth mother. Since Ty had thought the adoption was closed, he doesn't believe Briony at first. However, she shows Ty documents proving her relationship to Christine and also showing that Ty's wife not only knew Bridget, but lied to him about the adoption being a closed one. As Ty and Briony learn more about their loved ones, they begin to fall in love with each other.

Other books by the same author:
His Answered Prayer, 2000
Mother's Day Miracle, 2000
Baby on the Way, 1999
Daddy on the Way, 1999
Wedding on the Way, 1999

Other books you might like:
Carolyne Aarsen, *Twin Blessings*, 2001
Irene Brand, *Summer's Promise*, 2001
Carole Gift Page, *A Child Shall Lead Them*, 2001
Ruth Scofield, *Loving Thy Neighbor*, 2001
Carol Steward, *Courting Katarina*, 2001

1044

CYNTHIA RUTLEDGE

Judging Sara

(New York: Steeple Hill, 2001)

Story type: Romance
Subject(s): Singing; Stalking
Major character(s): Sara Michaels, Singer; Crow Tucci, Bodyguard
Time period(s): 2000s
Locale(s): United States

Summary: Sara Michaels is a rising young star on the Christian music scene. She is enjoying her newfound fame, which did not come easily. Then one of the more troubling aspects of fame appears in Sara's life—she attracts a stalker. At first, there are just some disturbing letters, but when the problems begin to escalate Sara's manager insists they hire a bodyguard. Crow Tucci is the perfect bodyguard—tough and formidable, but his appearance is not exactly what Sara wants for her image. Still, as the two spend time together, Sara begins to look behind the tough exterior to the real man beneath and decides she likes what she finds.

Other books by the same author:
Redeeming Claire, 2001
The Marrying Kind, 2001
Undercover Angel, 2000
Unforgettable Faith, 2000

Other books you might like:
Rick Hamlin, *Hidden Gifts*, 2001
Sara Mitchell, *Night Music*, 1998
Carole Gift Page, *Cassandra's Song*, 2001
Patricia H. Rushford, *Morningsong*, 1998
Anna Schmidt, *The Doctor's Miracle*, 2001

1045

CYNTHIA RUTLEDGE

Redeeming Claire

(New York: Steeple Hill, 2001)

Story type: Romance
Subject(s): Ministers
Major character(s): Claire Waters, Wealthy; Tony Karelli, Religious (minister), Boyfriend (Claire's ex)
Time period(s): 2000s
Locale(s): Iowa

Summary: Heading off to Iowa to see her former boyfriend Tony, rich girl Claire Waters hopes he can help her out with some family problems. To her surprise, the once fun-loving Tony is now Reverend Tony Karelli, a man with a problem of his own. His congregation assumes he is engaged and he isn't able to easily change that assumption. Claire has a solution though: she will pose, temporarily of course, as Tony's fiancee. The ruse will help Tony and will solve some problems of her own. After a short time, the engagement will be called off and Claire will return to her wealthy lifestyle and the happiness it brings her—unless she finds more satisfaction living in Iowa with Tony.

Other books by the same author:
The Marrying Kind, 2001
Undercover Angel, 2000
Unforgettable Faith, 2000

Other books you might like:
Terri Blackstock, *Emerald Windows*, 2001
Carole Gift Page, *Cassandra's Song*, 2001
Anna Schmidt, *Caroline and the Preacher*, 1999
Janet Tronstad, *A Bride for Dry Creek*, 2001
Lenora Worth, *When Love Came to Town*, 2001

1046

ANNA SCHMIDT

The Doctor's Miracle

(New York: Steeple Hill, 2001)

Story type: Romance
Subject(s): Illness; Singing
Major character(s): Rachel Duke, Singer (gospel); Paul McCoy, Doctor
Time period(s): 2000s
Locale(s): United States

Summary: Slowly approaching the fame of which she has always dreamed, gospel singer Rachel Duke gets a chance to appear at the Grand Ole Opry during a talent contest. Out front in the audience is her childhood mentor and biggest fan, Doc McCoy, along with his son Paul, who is also a doctor and has recently returned from Kosovo, where he spent some time treating refugees. When Rachel develops flu-like symptoms that just won't go away, Doc McCoy asks Paul to check her out. As Paul begins to treat Rachel, they become close friends and soon friendship develops into something more.

Other books by the same author:
A Mother for Amanda, 2000
Caroline and the Preacher, 1999
Give and Take, 1987

Other books you might like:
Lynn Bulock, *The Prodigal's Return*, 2001
Carole Gift Page, *Cassandra's Song*, 2001
Marta Perry, *The Doctor Next Door*, 2000
Patricia H. Rushford, *Morningsong*, 1998
Cheryl Wolverton, *What the Doctor Ordered*, 2000

1047

RUTH SCOFIELD

Loving Thy Neighbor

(New York: Steeple Hill, 2001)

Story type: Romance
Subject(s): Neighbors and Neighborhoods
Major character(s): Quincee Davis, Guardian (of sister's children); Hamilton Paxton, Judge
Time period(s): 2000s
Locale(s): United States

Summary: The sudden death of her sister has left Quincee Davis the guardian of two small children. Although Quincee deeply loves Kyle and Kerri, she finds motherhood difficult at best. Trying to keep up with the changes in her lifestyle has made Quincee careless and she soon racks up a few parking tickets. Her driver's license is suspended for 30 days, making her mothering chores even more difficult. To make the situation worse, the judge who suspends her license lives right next door to her, and is as stiff and opinionated outside the courtroom as he is in it.

Other books by the same author:
Wonders of the Heart, 2001
Whispers of the Heart, 2000
The Perfect Groom, 1999
In God's Own Time, 1998

Other books you might like:
Carolyne Aarsen, *A Family at Last*, 2000
Irene Hannon, *The Way Home*, 2000
Debra Kastner, *The Forgiving Heart*, 2000
Lois Richer, *His Answered Prayer*, 2000
Kate Welsh, *Their Forever Love*, 2000

1048

DEBRA WHITE SMITH

For Your Heart Only

(Eugene, Oregon: Harvest House, 2002)

Story type: Mystery; Romance
Series: Seven Sisters. Book 5
Subject(s): Crime and Criminals
Major character(s): Jacquelyn Lightfoot, Detective—Private; Lawton, Computer Expert
Time period(s): 2000s
Locale(s): United States

Summary: When detective Jacquelyn Lightfoot agrees to help a computer expert find the men who beat him and left him for dead, romance is the last thing on her mind. The more time Jacquelyn spends with Lawton, the more attracted she is to the tender and intelligent man. As Jacquelyn uncovers a 35-year-old mystery involving ancient coins, she and Lawton find their lives in danger. As the two slowly fall in love, they must somehow find the person who wants them dead before he finds them.

Other books by the same author:
A Shelter in the Storm, 2001
Texas, 2001
To Rome with Love, 2001
Second Chances, 2000
The Awakening, 2000

Other books you might like:
Terri Blackstock, *The Sun Coast Chronicles*, 1995-
Rosey Dow, *Betrayed*, 2001
B.J. Hoff, *The Daniel and Jennifer Kaine Series*, 1986-
Kathi Mills-Macias, *Obsession*, 2001
Gilbert Morris, *The Dani Ross Series*, 2000-

1049

DEBRA WHITE SMITH

To Rome with Love

(Eugene, Oregon: Harvest House, 2001)

Story type: Romance
Series: Seven Sisters. Book 4
Subject(s): Cruise Ships
Major character(s): Melissa Moore, Doctor; Kinkaide Franklin, Singer
Time period(s): 2000s
Locale(s): United States; At Sea; Europe

Summary: Melissa Moore has never quite recovered from the shock of having been left at the altar by the man she thought was the love of her life, Kinkaide Franklin. Now, returning to town more than six years later, Kinkaide wants her back. Unwilling to let herself be hurt again, she does her best to avoid him, but Kinkaide is persistent. He even sends her an invitation to join him on an all-expenses paid cruise to the Grecian islands and Rome. Although she has no intention of going, her matchmaking mother sends Kinkaide an acceptance in Melissa's name. Horrified at the thought of being alone with Kinkaide in such a romantic setting, Melissa nevertheless decides to go on the cruise. Will it be enough, though, to let her forgive Kinkaide and allow him back in her life?

Other books by the same author:
A Shelter in the Storm, 2001
Texas, 2001
Second Chances, 2000
The Awakening, 2000
Texas Rose, 1999

Other books you might like:
Melody Carlson, *Awakening Heart*, 1998
Peggy Darty, *Getaways*, 2000
Lynn Morris, *The Balcony*, 1997
Elaine Schulte, *Voyage*, 1996
Linda Windsor, *It Had to Be You*, 2001

1050

LAURAINE SNELLING

A Dream to Follow

(Minneapolis: Bethany House, 2001)

Story type: Historical/American West
Series: Return to Red River. Book 1
Subject(s): College Life; Farm Life; Writing
Major character(s): Thorliff Bjorklund, Student—College
Time period(s): 1870s
Locale(s): North Dakota

Summary: Thorliff Bjorklund is proud of his immigrant parents and all they have achieved on their farm since they arrived in America. Wanting something different out of life, Thorliff dreams of becoming a writer and has even had stories accepted in prestigious magazines. He wants to attend college and study journalism. However, Thorliff's parents do not understand why he is seemingly turning his back on their lifestyle. This series is a continuation of Snelling's popular Red River of the North series, which focused on the first generation immigrants who appear in this story.

Where it's reviewed:
Booklist, August 2001, page 2088

Other books by the same author:
The Long Way Home, 2001
Daughter of Twin Oaks, 2000
Sisters of the Confederacy, 2000
Blessing in Disguise, 1999
Hawaiian Sunrise, 1999

Other books you might like:
Stephen A. Bly, *The Fortunes of the Black Hills Series*, 1999-
Kristen Heitzmann, *The Rocky Mountain Legacy Series*, 1998-
Jim Kraus, *The Circle of Destiny Series*, 2000-
Diane Noble, *The California Chronicles*, 1999-
Peggy Stoks, *The Abounding Love Series*, 2000-

1051

PATRICIA HOUCK SPRINKLE

Carley's Song

(Grand Rapids, Michigan: Zondervan, 2001)

Story type: Contemporary
Series: Job's Corner Chronicles. Book 2
Subject(s): Coming-of-Age
Major character(s): Carley Marshall, Child
Time period(s): 1950s
Locale(s): Job's Corner, North Carolina

Summary: Twelve-year-old Carley Marshall lives in the South during the 1950s, in a world that is constantly changing. Now though, a lot of the changes affect Carley directly. She experiences her first crush, on handsome Clay Lamont, newly returned from service in the Air Force. Also of interest to Carley is Maddie Raeburn, who scandalizes the town with her divorce and her plans to teach school. Sequel to *The Remember Box*.

Where it's reviewed:
Publishers Weekly, September 10, 2001, page 61

Other books by the same author:
The Remember Box, 2000
But Why Shoot the Magistrate?, 1998
When Did We Lose Harriet?, 1997
Deadly Secrets on the St. Johns, 1995
Death of a Dunwoody Matron, 1994

Other books you might like:
Sharon Ewell Foster, *Riding through Shadows*, 2001
Robert Funderburk, *Heart and Soul*, 1995
Laurel Schunk, *Black and Secret Midnight*, 1998
Penelope J. Stokes, *The Blue Bottle Club*, 1999
Lance Wubbels, *One Small Miracle*, 1995

1052

CAROL STEWARD

This Time Forever

(New York: Steeple Hill, 2002)

Story type: Romance
Subject(s): Ranch Life
Major character(s): Lisa Berthoff, Photojournalist; Adam MacIntyre, Rancher
Time period(s): 2000s
Locale(s): Colorado

Summary: Photojournalist Lisa Berthoff goes to a Colorado ranch on an assignment, never expecting it to be anything but ordinary. Instead, Lisa meets handsome rancher Adam MacIntyre and quickly finds herself falling in love. Adam believes marriage is forever and he isn't willing to commit to a woman who seems unable to settle down to a quiet life on a ranch.

Other books by the same author:
Courting Katarina, 2001
Second Time Around, 2000
Her Kind of Hero, 1999
There Comes a Season, 1998

Other books you might like:
Lynn Bulock, *Gifts of Grace*, 1999
Valerie Hansen, *Second Chances*, 2001
Cynthia Rutledge, *Redeeming Claire*, 2001
Janet Tronstad, *An Angel for Dry Creek*, 1999
Cheryl Wolverton, *For Love of Zach*, 1999

1053

BODIE THOENE
BROCK THOENE, Co-Author

The Jerusalem Scrolls

(New York: Viking, 2001)

Story type: Historical
Series: Zion Legacy. Book 4
Subject(s): Biblical Fiction
Major character(s): Marcus Longinus, Military Personnel (Roman soldier), Biblical Figure; Miryam, Widow(er), Biblical Figure
Time period(s): 1st century
Locale(s): Middle East

Summary: In 1948 the Arab-Israeli war rages and Jewish Jerusalem is threatened by Arab forces. Haganah commander Moshe Sachar escapes to an underground bunker where sacred Jewish texts are stored. He finds an ancient papyrus concerning the romance of Marcus, a Roman soldier, and Miryam, a Jewish widow and prostitute. Miryam (Mary Magdalene), who is married off to an elderly man against her wishes, becomes wealthy after his death and free to do as she likes. She meets Marcus Longinus, an often cruel soldier, and soon falls in love with him. Eventually both Miryam and Marcus encounter Jesus and the meetings forever change their lives. The romance and spiritual renewal of Miryam and Marcus is the focus of this chapter of the Zion Legacy series, which usually concerns Israeli citizens as they fight for the independence of Israel in the 1940s.

Where it's reviewed:
Booklist, August 2001, page 2053
Library Journal, September 1, 2001, page 158
Publishers Weekly, August 27, 2001, page 48

Other books by the same author:
Jerusalem's Heart, 2001
All Rivers to the Sea, 2000
Jerusalem Vigil, 2000
Thunder from Jerusalem, 2000
Ashes of Remembrance, 1999

Other books you might like:
Irene Brand, *The Legacies of Faith Series*, 1996-
Gene Edwards, *The First Century Diaries Series*, 1998-
Thom Lemmons, *The Daughters of Faith Series*, 1999-
Francine Rivers, *The Lineage of Grace Series*, 2000-
Robert L. Wise, *The People of the Covenant Series*, 1991-

1054

TRAVIS THRASHER

The Watermark

(Wheaton, Illinois: Tyndale House, 2001)

Story type: Contemporary
Subject(s): College Life; Secrets
Major character(s): Sheridan Blake, Student—College; Erik Morrison, Roommate (of Sheridan); Genevie Liu, Student—Graduate
Time period(s): 2000s
Locale(s): Chicago, Illinois

Summary: Former music prodigy Sheridan Blake has returned to school in his twenties. At the age of 28, Sheridan is older than most of the students at Covenant College but he is finding academic life rewarding. Living in an apartment with his dog Barney and his roommate Erik, Sheridan is concerned about Erik's partying lifestyle. However, he is unable to set Erik on the right path although Sheridan's own past would probably provide warnings for Erik to heed. Those secrets come to the forefront of Sheridan's life when he meets Genevie Liu, a beautiful graduate student. The two hit it off, but Sheridan is unwilling to reveal all of his past to her and this causes great strains in their relationship.

Other books by the same author:
The Promise Remains, 2000

Other books you might like:
Angela Alcorn, *The Ishbane Conspiracy*, 2001
Shaunti Feldhahn, *The Veritas Conflict*, 2001
Robin Jones Gunn, *Until Tomorrow*, 2000
Jim Kraus, *The Circle of Destiny Series*, 2000-
Janette Oke, *Return to Harmony*, 1996

1055

JAMIE LANGSTON TURNER

A Garden to Keep

(Minneapolis: Bethany House, 2001)

Story type: Contemporary
Subject(s): Infidelity
Major character(s): Elizabeth Landis, Spouse, Parent
Time period(s): 2000s
Locale(s): Berea, South Carolina

Summary: On the surface, Elizabeth Landis is a happy and contented wife and mother, with a husband who provides for her and their children. However, she senses something is missing from her life. After discussing religion with her friend Margaret, Elizabeth decides she needs spirituality in her life and that she needs to convince her family of the same thing. Uplifted by her newfound beliefs, Elizabeth returns home and is sitting in the driveway of her house thinking about the new changes in her life when her cell phone rings. It is her husband who has dialed the wrong number and believes he is speaking to his girlfriend. Devastated by the knowledge her husband has been unfaithful, Elizabeth has to decide what direction she wants her life to take.

Where it's reviewed:
Publishers Weekly, August 13, 2001, page 287

Other books by the same author:
By the Light of a Thousand Stars, 1999
Some Wildflower in My Heart, 1998
Suncatchers, 1995

Other books you might like:
Marion Duckworth, *Remembering the Roses*, 1998
Robin Lee Hatcher, *The Forgiving Hour*, 1999
Annie Jones, *Lost Romance Ranch*, 2000
Lorena McCourtney, *Whirlpool*, 2001
Debra White Smith, *Second Chances*, 2000

1056

KEN WALES
DAVID POLING, Co-Author

Sea of Glory

(Nashville: Broadman & Holman, 2001)

Story type: Historical/World War II
Subject(s): Clergy; Sea Stories; World War II
Major character(s): George Fox, Religious (Methodist minister), Historical Figure; Alex Goode, Religious (rabbi), Historical Figure; Clark Poling, Religious (Dutch Reformed minister), Historical Figure
Time period(s): 1940s
Locale(s): *U.S.A.T. Dorchester*, At Sea

Summary: As the *U.S.A.T. Dorchester* sails through waters infested with Nazi U-boats, four chaplains attempt to provide spiritual comfort to the men on board. The chaplains are Father John Washington, Reverend Clark Poling, Pastor George Fox, and Rabbi Alex Goode. Although from different faiths, the men do not allow their spiritual differences to keep them from their mission of providing support to the men aboard the *Dorchester*. On February 3, 1943, a German submarine catches up with the ship and the chaplains are called to make one final sacrifice. This novel is based on the true story of the chaplains of the *Dorchester*, one of whom was co-author David Poling's cousin.

Where it's reviewed:
Booklist, August 2001, page 2088
Library Journal, September 1, 2001, page 158

Other books you might like:
T. Davis Bunn, *The Amber Room*, 1992
Jack Cavanaugh, *The Victors*, 1998
Alton Gansky, *A Ship Possessed*, 1999
Gilbert Morris, *A Time of War*, 1997
Jim Walker, *Murder at Pearl Harbor*, 2000

1057

KATE WELSH

The Girl Next Door

(New York: Steeple Hill, 2001)

Story type: Romance
Subject(s): Accidents; Animals/Horses
Major character(s): Hope Taggert, Horse Trainer; Jeff Carrington, Accident Victim, Horse Trainer (riding champion)
Time period(s): 2000s
Locale(s): United States

Summary: Jeff Carrington is a riding champion with a shot at the Olympics when an accident leaves him seriously injured. With all of his dreams gone, Jeff wants to forget everything in his past. That includes his friendship with Hope Taggert, who has loved him for years. Hope, however, won't give up on Jeff and won't give up on their chance for love either. Even though Jeff never saw her as anything but his best friend's kid sister, Hope is determined he will someday fall in love with her.

Other books by the same author:
Small-Town Dreams, 2000
Their Forever Love, 2000
A Family for Christmas, 1999
Never Lie to an Angel, 1999
For the Sake of Her Child, 1998

Other books you might like:
Irene Brand, *Summer's Promise*, 2001
Lynn Bulock, *The Prodigal's Return*, 2001
Lyn Cote, *Hope's Garden*, 2000
Valerie Hansen, *Second Chances*, 2001
Crystal Stovall, *A Groom Worth Waiting For*, 2001

1058

STEPHANIE GRACE WHITSON

Heart of the Sandhill

(Nashville: Thomas Nelson, 2002)

Story type: Historical/Post-American Civil War
Series: Dakota Moons. Book 3
Subject(s): Indian Removal; Prejudice
Major character(s): Genevieve LaCroix Two Stars, Indian (half Dakota Sioux), Spouse; David Two Stars, Indian, Military Personnel (army scout)
Time period(s): 1860s
Locale(s): Minnesota; West

Summary: As the daughter of a Dakota Sioux and a French aristocrat, Genevieve LaCroix has never felt as if she is totally accepted by people of either the white or Indian worlds. After her marriage to Daniel Two Stars, the couple relocates to a farm in Minnesota, but neither is happy with the situation. Daniel wants to return to the west and Genevieve is upset that none of their neighbors welcome Indians in their midst. Growing increasingly restive with farming life, Daniel agrees to become an army scout, leaving Genevieve behind. When Daniel fails to return from a mission, Genevieve convinces a reluctant army officer to help her look for him.

Where it's reviewed:
Publishers Weekly, December 3, 2001, page 41

Other books by the same author:
Edge of the Wilderness, 2001
Valley of the Shadow, 2000
Karyn's Memory Box, 1999
Nora's Ribbon of Memories, 1999
Sarah's Patchwork, 1998

Other books you might like:
Jane Kirkpatrick, *Love to Water My Soul*, 1996
Alan Morris, *The Guardians of the North Series*, 1996-
Janette Oke, *The Calling of Emily Evans*, 1990
Janette Oke, *Drums of Change*, 1996
Judith Pella, *Warrior's Song*, 1996
Marlo M. Schalesky, *The Winds of Freedom Series*, 2000-

1059

LORI WICK

Bamboo and Lace

(Eugene, Oregon: Harvest House, 2001)

Story type: Romance
Subject(s): Islands
Major character(s): Lily Walsh, Young Woman
Time period(s): 2000s
Locale(s): Hawaii

Summary: Raised by an exceedingly strict father, Lily Walsh is both overjoyed and amazed when he allows her to travel to Hawaii to visit her brother for three months. The airplane trip is thrilling enough for her, but seeing her brother's modern home and all of its conveniences is truly eye-opening. When her brother is unexpectedly called away, Lily remains behind in the care of the Kapaia family and another new world is opened up for the sheltered young woman as she realizes there are more viewpoints than the ones held by her father. Lily even forms a romantic attachment to Gabe Kapaia, but her newfound happiness is threatened as she realizes she must return home to her father at some point.

Other books by the same author:
City Girl, 2001
A Texas Sky, 2000
Beyond the Picket Fence, 2000

Every Little Thing about You, 1999
The Princess, 1999

Other books you might like:
Linda Chaikin, *The Jewel of the Pacific Series*, 1999-
Kiana Davenport, *Song of the Exile*, 1999
Robin Jones Gunn, *Whispers*, 1995
Carol D. Slama, *Shroud of Silence*, 1998
Lauraine Snelling, *Hawaiian Sunrise*, 1999

1060

LINDA WINDSOR

Riona

(Sisters, Oregon: Multnomah, 2001)

Story type: Historical
Series: Fires of Gleannmara. Book 2
Subject(s): Charity; Orphans
Major character(s): Riona, Gentlewoman; Lord Kieran of Gleannmara, Nobleman
Time period(s): 6th century
Locale(s): Ireland

Summary: Lord Kieran of Gleannmara is determined to marry lovely Riona to fulfill a pledge made to her dying brother. Riona, however, is more concerned with caring for three orphaned children who lost their parents in the plague. Unfortunately, Riona will be unable to keep the children unless she has a husband and although reluctant to marry Kieran, she does see him as a solution to her problems.

Other books by the same author:
It Had to Be You, 2001
Maire, 2000
Not Exactly Eden, 2000
Hi Honey, I'm Home, 1999
Border Rose, 1998

Other books you might like:
Sigmund Brouwer, *Wings of Dawn*, 1995
B.J. Hoff, *The Song of Erin Series*, 1997-
Angela Elwell Hunt, *The Heirs of Cahira O'Connor Series*, 1998-
Stephen R. Lawhead, *The Celtic Crusades Series*, 1999-
Bodie Thoene, *The Galway Chronicles*, 1997-

1061

BONNIE K. WINN

A Family All Her Own

(New York: Steeple Hill, 2001)

Story type: Romance
Subject(s): Ministers
Major character(s): Katherine Blake, Religious (minister); Michael Carlson, Widow(er), Single Parent
Time period(s): 2000s
Locale(s): United States

Summary: Katherine Blake, an attractive, smart, and personable woman, should have no trouble finding a man. She is also the minister of Rosewood Community Church, something that is an instant turn-off for every man she encounters. Then one day Katherine meets handsome widower Michael Carlson. Katherine is attracted to the kind single dad, but Michael had enough well-intentioned involvement from church do-gooders after his wife's death to make him wary of a relationship with a minister.

Other books by the same author:
Family Found, 2001
Substitute Father, 2001
The Mommy Makeover, 2000
The Wrong Brother, 2000
The Hijacked Wife, 1999

Other books you might like:
Carolyne Aarsen, *A Family at Last*, 2000
Irene Hannon, *The Way Home*, 2000
Marta Perry, *Father Most Blessed*, 2001
Anna Schmidt, *Caroline and the Preacher*, 1999
Kate Welsh, *Their Forever Love*, 2000

1062

DEBORAH WOODWORTH

Dancing Dead

(New York: Avon, 2002)

Story type: Mystery
Series: Rose Callahan. Book 6
Subject(s): Ghosts; Shakers
Major character(s): Rose Callahan, Religious (Shaker eldress)
Time period(s): 1930s
Locale(s): Languor County, Kentucky

Summary: With few new converts to the Shaker faith, the small religious community at North Homage, Kentucky is slowly dying out. Many of their buildings are standing empty and unused. Hating to see the waste, especially during the Great Depression, the Shakers decide to turn one of the buildings into a hostel. The hostel is an immediate success and visitors come from all over, but gossip soon leads to newspaper stories about a ghost walking the grounds of the Shaker village. When one of the hotel guests is found murdered, it is up to Eldress Rose Callahan to investigate and find both the killer and the truth behind the ghost stories.

Other books by the same author:
Killing Gifts, 2001
A Simple Shaker Murder, 2000
Sins of a Shaker Summer, 1999
A Deadly Shaker Spring, 1998
Death of a Winter Shaker, 1997

Other books you might like:
Irene Allen, *The Elizabeth Elliot Series*, 1992-
Dudley J. Delffs, *The Father Grif Series*, 1998-
Patricia H. Rushford, *The Helen Bradley Series*, 1997-
Jim Walker, *The Mysteries in Time Series*, 1998-
Sally S. Wright, *The Ben Reese Series*, 1997-

1063

LENORA WORTH

When Love Came to Town

(New York: Steeple Hill, 2001)

Story type: Romance
Subject(s): Weather
Major character(s): Lorna Dorsette, Young Woman; Mick Love, Tree Surgeon (owner of a tree service)
Time period(s): 2000s
Locale(s): Jardin, Louisiana

Summary: When a tornado tears through Jardin, Louisiana leaving destruction in its wake, one of the damaged houses is the plantation home belonging to the Dorsette family. Mick Love, the owner of a tree service, arrives in town to see what he can do to fix the damage. He meets Lorna Dorsette, the niece of the plantation owner, and is immediately smitten. Lorna, however, isn't certain she is ready for love, especially if the man is a comparative stranger.

Other books by the same author:
Ben's Bundle of Joy, 2000
One Golden Christmas, 2000
The Reluctant Hero, 2000
His Brother's Wife, 1999
Wedding at Wildwood, 1999

Other books you might like:
Ginny Aiken, *The Bellamy's Blossoms Series*, 2000-
Lyn Cote, *Hope's Garden*, 2000
Annie Jones, *Deep Dixie*, 1999
Loree Lough, *Suddenly Home*, 2001
Gail Gaymer Martin, *Secrets of the Heart*, 2001

1064

BENJAMIN ZUCKER

Green

(Woodstock, New York: Overlook, 2002)

Story type: Contemporary
Subject(s): Judaism
Major character(s): Abraham Tal, Businessman (gem merchant)
Time period(s): 2000s
Locale(s): New York, New York

Summary: In his follow-up to *Blue*, Benjamin Zucker again chronicles the life of New York gem merchant Abraham Tal as he gives advice to his friends and neighbors in Greenwich Village. As with *Blue*, the author tells the main story via the voice of Abraham, with additional narrative from historical personages, Jewish scholars, and Abraham's friends and family serving as commentary. Photos and illustrations are also included to enlighten the main story.

Other books by the same author:
Blue, 2001

Other books you might like:
Pearl Abraham, *Giving Up America*, 1998
Mitchell Chefitz, *The Thirty-Third Hour*, 2002
Lilian Nattel, *The River Midnight*, 1999
Lawrence Norfolk, *In the Shape of a Boar*, 2001
Naomi Ragen, *The Ghost of Hannah Mendes*, 1998

Popular Fiction in Review
by
Tom Barton

In the wake of the horrific and tragic events of September 11, 2001, many people have turned to oracular writings for comfort and understanding. Others have looked to historical and contemporary books for information and insight into culture, religion, identity, and the conflicts that arise when personal and societal ideologies clash within an individual or on a worldwide scale. Though most of the books reviewed in this volume of *What Do I Read Next?* were written prior to the events of the 11th, it is not too surprising that in popular fiction the work of many authors address these eternal issues in one way or another. Though some of the books deal with global subjects and events, many concentrate on local topics or private turmoil.

The theme of opposing ideologies is the basis of *The Last Summer of Reason*, a story about a liberal bookseller who tries to resist the oppressive views of religious fanatics who have taken over his country and begin destroying art and literature. The book, by Tahar Djaout, an Algerian writer and poet, emphasizes the power of artistic expression. This power was recognized by religious fundamentalists in Algeria, who assassinated Djaout in 1993, but his book has just been translated into English, allowing it to reach an even wider audience.

Author Salman Rushdie also understands the power of literature; he was forced into hiding when his book *The Satanic Verses* was published in 1989 and labeled by some as critical of Islam. A price of more than a million dollars was placed on Rushdie's head by the Iranian government. Fortunately, Rushdie has stayed out of harm's way and continues to do what he does best, write about the meeting of cultures and the creation of cross-cultural identities.

Rushdie's most recent book, *Fury*, is a satire of modern American society, a society seen through the eyes of Malik Solanka, a man born in India, educated in England, and transplanted to America. Insightful and darkly comic, the book presents an unflattering picture of New York politics and race relations, American consumerism, and the media during the summer of 2000. Yet Rushdie's examination of the darkness of human nature and the decadence of American culture is tempered with the concurrent theme of the redeeming power of love to overcome the all-encompassing rage indicated by the title.

Another title, *The Girl from the Golden Horn* by Kurban Said, deals with the complexity of interpersonal relationships. The story, though originally written in 1938, addresses issues pertinent today. An exiled Turkish Muslim woman marries a Viennese Christian man after being released from an arranged marriage by the man to whom she was promised. When her former betrothed comes later to find her, she must decide between the two men and the two cultures in which she has lived. Although the story deals with individual love, a Western notion, and arranged marriage, a Muslim practice in her homeland, the larger issue is the loss of cultural identity as she struggles to reconcile the values of her past with her new life.

The same issue, but with a different twist, is dealt with in Abdullah Hussein's book *Emigre Journeys*. The story is about a man from Pakistan who enters England illegally, becomes a citizen, and raises a family. While successful in making the transition from illegal alien to respected citizen, the process is personally very painful. He becomes alienated from his wife and estranged from his teenage children who reject his old world ways.

Cultural identity also surfaces in the historical murder mystery *My Name Is Red* by Orhan Pamuk. Set in the sixteenth century Ottoman Empire, the story deals with what happens when Eastern notions that art should be idealized collide with Western notions that art should be realistic.

Another case in point is Shashi Tharoor's book *Riot*, which details the circumstances surrounding the death of an American student volunteer-worker. The ostensible cause is religious fanaticism between Hindus and Muslims. However, as the author peels away various social layers, other reasons emerge.

More insight into clashes resulting from different cultural perceptions is provided in *The Pickup*, the latest book by Nadine Gordimer, winner of the 1991 Nobel Prize for literature. This book questions whether romance can flourish between an upper middle-class woman and an illegal immigrant who is subsequently deported. While the outcome sounds predictable, in Gordimer's able hands you can expect insightful surprises.

Books dealing with African American culture and identity in modern society can often be found on the American bestseller lists. In a notable trend, there has been an increase of books written by African Americans about African American experiences. Some observers see this as very positive for two reasons. It shows a more than casual interest in reading by African Americans and an acceptance by cross-over white readers.

One example of this type of book is Lalita Tademy's debut novel, *Cane River*, which has been a huge success. The story focuses on four generations of African American women. Tademy was a successful executive with Sun Microsystems when she got the idea for the book from thoughts about her great- grandmother, Emily Fredieu. These ideas soon prompted her to quit her job to write the story. After spending three years digging up records in Louisiana, her efforts paid large dividends despite her emotional discomfort upon uncovering an 1850 document that recorded the sale of some family members. The book remained steadily on the bestseller lists. Watch for her next book about the paternal side of her family.

While it may not make the bestseller lists, I look for Zora Neale Hurston's work *Every Tongue Got to Confess* to become a fixture on the bookshelves of many homes across the country. Hurston gathered the material for these stories from her travels through the deep South in the 1920s. The stories are written without changes in dialect or syntax out of respect to the oral traditions that generated them. The book is a treasure-trove of pure Americana.

On a more contemporary note, Patricia Jones examines racial issues from a middle class perspective in her latest book *Red on a Rose*. The story continues the saga of Lila Giles Calloway, a character from Jones' first book *Passing*.

Another African American author with bestseller credentials is E. Lynn Harris. His recent offering *Any Way the Wind Blows* appears to be as well received by white readers as by African Americans. Some social critics believe one reason for his success is that white readers are able to visualize themselves through the eyes of his black characters. This, of course, probably has as much to do with the author's writing skills as it does with readers' proclivities.

Though Joe Martin isn't an African American, his book *Fire in the Rock* also deals with race relations. His upbringing in South Carolina gave him material for his book, which is about growing up in the segregated South during the 1950s and 1960s. The story crosses the color line as it follows two white teenagers, Bo Fisher and Mae Maude, and their black friend, Pollo Templeton.

Aside from writing an interesting story, Martin, who suffers from Lou Gehrig's disease or ALS (amyotrophic lateral sclerosis) and is completely paralyzed, produced the work with the assistance of eye software, a marvelous high-tech invention that is very tedious to use. Martin moves his eyes, using them to type. He sits in front of a computer monitor that has a specialized video camera attached to it. While he looks at the monitor, the camera records his gaze and transmits it to special software, which translates his look into a mouse click. In this way, Martin is able to select individual letters, words, and phrases. With the publication of his book, Martin gives new meaning to the phrase "can do spirit."

Three collections worth mentioning are Southerner Elizabeth Spencer's *The Southern Woman*, a collection of new and selected stories; *Hateship, Friendship, Courtship, Loveship, Marriage*, written by Canadian writer Alice Munro; and *Creatures of Habit*, written by North Carolina native Jill McCorkle. Munro and McCorkle are very skillful at giving the reader an insightful view of the challenges normal people face. McCorkle's stories can be habit forming.

Authors Saul Bellow and Paul Bowles also have recently published collections. Bellow, winner of the 1976 Nobel Prize for literature, is well known for his novels including, *Herzog, The Dean's December, Mr. Sammler's Planet, Humboldt's Gift, Henderson the Rain King* and *Ravelstein*. Readers unfamiliar with Bellow's shorter works will be pleasantly surprised with his *Collected Stories*, published in 2001. Some critics believe that Bowles, who lived mostly abroad, principally in North Africa, is in top form with *The Stories of Paul Bowles*, which deals with the culture clash that occurs when east meets west. This thread becomes more important as globalization of the planet creates increased contact between people of different cultures.

Prolific writer Joyce Carol Oates, with 95 published books at last count, knows how to tell a good story and is a master of books that question identity. She has two newly published titles, *Middle Age* and *Beasts*. In *Middle Age*, the lives of several middle-aged inhabitants of a small Manhattan suburb are changed forever when one of their members dies as he rescues a child from drowning. His death forces the others to examine their lives at the mid-point and come to some important realizations. *Beasts*, though in a different setting, is also a tale of identity. A young college girl becomes swept up in her admiration for her bohemian professor and his artist wife. As she becomes a part of their inner circle, her identity is subsumed by their domineering personalities.

While high production in most fields brings praise, the critics have often been less than kind to Oates, most probably because her range is so wide. However, it would appear that this is beginning to change as more and more people are recognizing the quality of her work. In her case, more means better.

Nora Roberts, another extraordinarily productive writer, has written a novel titled *Midnight Bayou*. After the main character purchases an old mansion, he begins to see visions of the past in the old house. He doubts his own sanity when it seems that either ghosts inhabit the mansion, or he is the reincarnation of one of the previous tenants. Roberts, who started her career as a romance writer (and still uses elements of romance in her stories), has used her skillful storytelling to appeal to a wider reading public.

While it's unlikely he will ever be mistaken for a romance writer, James Lee Burke has won two Edgar Awards and his recent book, *Bitterroot*, features his new hero, attorney Billy Bob Holland. Fans of Burke's Louisiana cop Dave Robicheaux series will find that Holland is a similar type of hero. Burke's heroes always wrestle with moral dilemmas and only engage in violence as a last resort—usually to protect someone else. The story lines of books in both series are filled with realistic violence, but it's never gratuitous or glorified. There are some differences between the two series. Robicheaux handles the bad guys in and around New Orleans. Holland mostly hangs out in Texas, although *Bitterroot* is set in Montana.

A newcomer on the realistic writing scene is a woman, British author Mo Hayder. Her recent book *The Treatment*, deals with violence, specifically with the sexual abuse of children. She includes crime scene details that impress upon readers the suffering of the victims.

Understanding the moral complexities that people face appears to be an essential element in the German writer Bernhard Schlink's stories. Although morality is important, Schlink is more interested in the strategies people create to solve their problems. His recent offering *Flights of Love* follows average people attempting to escape the monotony of their everyday lives. Although some readers may feel his characters escape moral responsibility, his stories are fresh with interesting twists that feel authentic.

Bruce Olds, who honed his writing skills as a journalist before making the jump to fiction, takes a fresh approach to a slightly more conventional subject in his new book, *Bucking the Tiger*. Olds explores the familiar turf of the Western frontier with a novel about Doc Holliday, the dentist, gambler, gunfighter, and friend of legendary marshal Wyatt Earp. Olds adds a few new twists to this familiar tale by telling the story from Holliday's point of view. We see Earp and others overshadowed by Holliday. Readers should be pleasantly surprised with this reworking of an historical myth.

On the lighter side, former librarian Elizabeth McCracken, has written a warm and funny book, *Niagara Falls All over Again*. The book follows two comedians from vaudeville to Hollywood. Her book should be of particular interest to those concerned with the behind the scenes human face of people that make us laugh.

Although Anita Diamant's latest book *Good Harbor* isn't particularly funny, it does have its moments. Diamant is new to fiction but not to writing. She spent more than twenty years honing her skills as a nonfiction writer. Her first novel, *The Red Tent*, was very well received and won the 2001 American Booksellers Association Award. Diamant based the book on the biblical story of Dinah, the daughter of Jacob, with additional information about the sexuality of women. Diamant's new book isn't a biblical story but it does have a spiritual side to it. Set in modern times, the story deals with the friendship between two women, one Christian and one Jewish.

While not especially religious, Sue Miller's work is known for giving readers a close-up of the inner turmoil of her characters as they grapple with the reasons for their actions and inaction. Miller's latest book, *The World Below*, should add to her reputation.

Jonathan Franzen's wonderful novel, *The Corrections*, concerns a dysfunctional middle-class family. Entertaining and funny, this is Franzen's best novel so far. The book has generated widespread acclaim and won the National Book Award for 2001.

V.S Naipaul's recent book *Half a Life* is about Willie Somerset Chandran, a man born in India who moves to England for his education and attempts to become a writer. His dual identity as an Indian and Englishman leaves him searching to define himself in the world. He marries and goes to Africa with his wife, yet still is unable to live his own life, continually living his life through the dreams and expectations of others. Elements of this fictional sojourn can be traced to Naipaul's family history. Naipaul grew up on Trinidad, an island in the West Indies with a multicultural population. His parents were first generation descendants of Indian Hindus and as an adolescent, he was sent to England for higher education.

Recommended Titles

Almost by Elizabeth Benedict

In the Forest of Harm by Sallie Bissell

Mirabilis by Susann Cokal

The Unknown Errors of Our Lives by Chitra Banerjee Divakaruni

The Corrections by Jonathan Franzen

The Pickup by Nadine Gordimer

The Treatment by Mo Hayder

The Way of the Coyote by Elmer Kelton

Fire in the Rock by Joe Martin

Creatures of Habit by Jill McCorkle

Niagara Falls All over Again by Elizabeth McCracken

The World Below by Sue Miller

Hateship, Friendship, Courtship, Loveship, Marriage by Alice Munro

Half a Life by V.S. Naipaul

For Rouenna by Sigrid Nunez

Middle Age by Joyce Carol Oates

Bucking the Tiger by Bruce Olds

The Nautical Chart by Arturo Perez-Reverte

Fighting Gravity by Peggy Rambach

Fury by Salman Rushdie

The Girl from the Golden Horn by Kurban Said

Flights of Love by Bernhard Schlink

Cane River by Lalita Tademy

Riot by Shashi Tharoor

Argall by William T. Vollmann

Popular Fiction Titles

1065

CHRISTINA ADAM

Any Small Thing Can Save You

(New York: BlueHen, 2001)

Story type: Collection
Subject(s): Animals; Human Behavior; Fables

Summary: Adam's second collection follows the organization of a medieval bestiary, morality tales that use animals as an allegory. Some elements of these 26 stories resemble such fables but other elements simply contemplate the wonder of the human experience. People and animals interact with each other, moving freely between their separate worlds with interesting results.

Where it's reviewed:
Kirkus Reviews, September 15, 2001, page 1310
Publishers Weekly, October 1, 2001, page 35

Other books by the same author:
Sleeping with the Buffalo, 1996

Other books you might like:
Richard Adams, *Traveller*, 1988
Rebecca Brown, *The Dogs*, 1998
Fred Gipson, *Old Yeller*, 1956
Barbara Kingsolver, *Prodigal Summer*, 2000
Jill McCorkle, *Creatures of Habit*, 2001

1066

DANIEL AKST

The Webster Chronicle

(New York: BlueHen, 2001)

Story type: Psychological; Contemporary
Subject(s): Fathers and Sons; Journalism; Sexual Abuse
Major character(s): Terry Mathers, Journalist, Publisher (buys hometown newspaper); Abigail Mathers, Spouse (of Terry), Advertising; Diana Shirley, Counselor (sex abuse expert)
Time period(s): 1980s (1980-1988)
Locale(s): Webster, Northeast

Summary: In his second novel, Akst explores child sexual abuse and community reaction. Terry Mathers and his wife, Abigail, leave New York, borrow money from his father, and buy his hometown newspaper. Abigail soon moves out and they are unable to repay his father. When a child attending preschool gets spanked, accusations about sexual abuse and satanic practices soon become rampant. Then Terry falls in love with the sex abuse expert, while Abigail sleeps with her advertising clients.

Where it's reviewed:
Atlantic Monthly, October 2001, page 128
Kirkus Reviews, August 15, 2001, page 1142
Publishers Weekly, September 10, 2001, page 57

Other books by the same author:
St. Burl's Obituary, 1996

Other books you might like:
Tony Hillerman, *Finding Moon*, 1996
Dan Jenkins, *Fast Copy*, 1988
Annie Proulx, *The Shipping News*, 1993
Sharon Rolens, *Worthy's Town*, 2000
Gore Vidal, *The Golden Age*, 2000

1067

ISABEL ALLENDE

Portrait in Sepia

(New York: HarperCollins, 2001)

Story type: Family Saga
Subject(s): Grandmothers; Family Relations; Identity
Major character(s): Aurora del Valle, Photographer, Narrator; Paulina del Valle, Grandparent (of Aurora); Eliza Sommers, Grandparent (of Aurora)
Time period(s): 19th century; 20th century (1850-1910)
Locale(s): San Francisco, California; Valparaiso, Chile

Summary: Allende's novel picks up where *Daughter of Fortune* leaves off. Aurora del Valle recalls her early years with her maternal grandparents, Eliza Sommers and Tao Chi'en. Then, Aurora is adopted by her paternal grandmother, Paulina. A woman with a passion for jewels, pastries, and making money, Paulina moves the family from San Francisco's Nob Hill to Chile where Aurora grows up. Unhappily married to a philanderer, she ends up becoming a photographer to cope. Translated by Margaret Sayers Peden.

Where it's reviewed:
Kirkus Reviews, August 15, 2001, page 1142
Publishers Weekly, July 16, 2001, page 164

Other books by the same author:
Daughter of Fortune, 1999
The Infinite Plan, 1993
The Stories of Eva Luna, 1991
Eva Luna, 1988
The House of the Spirits, 1985

Other books you might like:
Margaret Atwood, *Alias Grace*, 1996
Tracy Chevalier, *Girl with a Pearl Earring*, 1999
Laura Esquivel, *Like Water for Chocolate*, 1992
Carlos Fuentes, *The Years with Laura Diaz*, 2001
Helen Humphreys, *Afterimage*, 2000

1068

KELLEY ARMSTRONG

Bitten

(New York: Viking, 2001)

Story type: Gothic; Werewolf Story
Subject(s): Werewolves; Relationships; Secrets
Major character(s): Elena Michaels, Werewolf; Clayton, Werewolf, Lover (Elena's ex); Philip, Lover (Elena's)
Time period(s): 2000s (2001)
Locale(s): Toronto, Ontario, Canada

Summary: This first novel by Armstrong freshens up the werewolf legend. Elena Michaels becomes a werewolf as a teenager after her boyfriend, Clay, bites her. She dumps Clay and moves to Toronto where she develops a relationship with Philip, an unsuspecting human. The pack still influences her, however, and when renegade werewolves threaten, Elena is summoned to help defend it. Her return rekindles the feelings she has for Clay, and when he is kidnapped, she must fight the renegades herself.

Where it's reviewed:
Kirkus Reviews, August 1, 2001, page 1042
Library Journal, September 15, 2001, page 108
New York Times Book Review, October 21, 2001, page 28

Other books you might like:
Donna Boyd, *The Promise*, 1999
Stephen King, *Cycle of the Werewolves*, 1983
Susan Krinard, *Prince of Wolves*, 1994
Whitley Strieber, *The Wolfen*, 1978
John Updike, *The Witches of Eastwick*, 1984

1069

BERYL BAINBRIDGE

According to Queeney

(New York: Carroll & Graf, 2001)

Story type: Historical; Psychological
Subject(s): Biography; Authors and Writers; Mothers and Daughters
Major character(s): Samuel Johnson, Writer (of literature and poetry), Historical Figure; Hester Thrale, Benefactor (of Johnson), Historical Figure; Queeney Thrale, Relative (Mrs. Thrale's eldest daughter), Narrator
Time period(s): 18th century (1727-1785)
Locale(s): London, England

Summary: In this book which was nominated for a Booker Prize, Bainbridge explores the relationship between Samuel Johnson and his patroness, Hester Thrale. Readers are invited into Mrs. Thrale's salon for the sparkling conversation of Dr. Johnson. Writer Oliver Goldsmith and actor David Garrick also make appearances while Mrs. Thrale's flirtatious manner spices things up. Bainbridge paints an authentic picture of both the physical and psychological landscape of the time, as seen through the eyes of Mrs. Thrale's daughter, Queeney.

Where it's reviewed:
Booklist, July 2001, page 1976
Kirkus Reviews, June 15, 2001, page 814
New York Times Book Review, August 12, 2001, page 9
Publishers Weekly, July 23, 2001, page 48

Other books by the same author:
Master Georgie, 1998
Every Man for Himself, 1996
The Birthday Boys, 1994
An Awfully Big Adventure, 1989
Young Adolf, 1978

Other books you might like:
Malcolm Bradbury, *To the Hermitage*, 2001
Sara George, *The Journal of Mrs. Pepys*, 1999
David Lodge, *Thinks—*, 2001
Rose Tremain, *Music & Silence*, 2000
Barry Unsworth, *Losing Nelson*, 1999

1070

J.G. BALLARD

Super-Cannes

(New York: Picador USA, 2001)

Story type: Psychological
Subject(s): Modern Life; Doctors; Women
Major character(s): Paul Sinclair, Pilot (recovering from a crash); Jane Sinclair, Spouse (of Paul), Doctor (for an large corporation); Wilder Penrose, Doctor (manages executive housing)
Time period(s): 2000s (2001)
Locale(s): Riviera, France

Summary: The author takes a look at a multinational corporation's bizarre training regimen, complete with abundant drugs and sex. Paul Sinclair accompanies his wife Jane when her company sends her to the Riviera for training. They are put up in the corporation's "executive paradise." When Paul finds out the previous tenant flipped and killed ten people, he starts asking questions. The answers point to the training methods, which are designed to make managers more efficient.

Where it's reviewed:
Booklist, September 15, 2001, page 190
Kirkus Reviews, October 15, 2001, page 1442
Publishers Weekly, September 3, 2001, page 58

Other books by the same author:
Cocaine Nights, 1996
Rushing to Paradise, 1995
The Kindness of Women, 1991
War Fever, 1991
Running Wild, 1988

Other books you might like:
Suzanne Berne, *A Perfect Arrangement*, 2001
Ray Bradbury, *From the Dust Returned*, 2001
Robin Cook, *Fatal Cure*, 1993
Walter Mosley, *Futureland*, 2001
Matt Reilly, *Temple*, 2001

1071

CLIVE BARKER

Coldheart Canyon

(New York: HarperCollins, 2001)

Story type: Gothic; Ghost Story
Subject(s): Ghosts; Horror; Movie Industry
Major character(s): Todd Pickett, Actor; Tammy Lauper, Housewife; Katya Lupi, Actress (silent film vamp)
Time period(s): 2000s (2001)
Locale(s): Los Angeles, California (Coldheart Canyon)

Summary: *Coldheart Canyon* is a suspenseful ghost story, filled with intense passions, sexual depravity, and a fight between good and evil. Movie star Todd Pickett discovers a room in the mansion he has just purchased contains scenes of people, animals, and monsters engaged in every manner of sexual activity portrayed on the walls. The devil, who has enslaved ghosts of deceased movie stars, wants Pickett's soul. A dowdy fan, Tammy Lauper, defends him.

Where it's reviewed:
Booklist, August 2001, page 2049
Kirkus Reviews, August 1, 2001, page 1043
Library Journal, August 2001, page 156
Publishers Weekly, July 23, 2001, page 55

Other books by the same author:
Thief of Always, 1992
Hellraiser, 1991
Imajica, 1991
Books of Blood, 1988
In the Flesh, 1987

Other books you might like:
Kelley Armstrong, *Bitten*, 2001
Gary A. Braunbeck, *This Flesh Unknown*, 2001
Michael Crichton, *Timeline*, 1999
Stephen King, *Black House*, 2001
Peter Straub, co-author
Anne Rice, *Blood and Gold*, 2001

1072

SAUL BELLOW

Collected Stories

(New York: Viking, 2001)

Story type: Collection
Subject(s): Social Conditions; Customs; Culture
Time period(s): 20th century

Summary: This collection has 11 stories and two recent novellas, *The Bellarosa Connection* and *A Theft*. Bellow lives up to his reputation for nuance, and character development, mixed with a light humorous touch. Subjects touched on include generational differences, identity, emotional coldness, youth, folly, and painful revelation. Taken in context Bellow notices the idiosyncratic rhythms of aging.

Where it's reviewed:
Booklist, September 1, 2001, page 3
Kirkus Reviews, September 15, 2001, page 1322
New York Times Book Review, December 9, 2001, page 15
Publishers Weekly, October 22, 2001, page 47

Other books by the same author:
Ravelstein, 2000
The Actual, 1997
The Dean's December, 1982
Humboldt's Gift, 1975
Mr. Sammler's Planet, 1970

Other books you might like:
Ann Beattie, *Perfect Recall*, 2001
Ellen Gilchrist, *The Cabal and Other Stories*, 2000
Philip Roth, *Goodbye, Columbus and Five Short Stories*, 1959
John Updike, *Licks of Love*, 2000
Richard Yates, *Collected Stories of Richard Yates*, 2001

1073

ELIZABETH BENEDICT

Almost

(Boston: Houghton Mifflin, 2001)

Story type: Psychological Suspense
Subject(s): Widows/Widowers; Islands; Family
Major character(s): Sophy Chase, Alcoholic (recovering), Writer (of celebrity biographies); Evan Lambert, Lawyer, Friend (Sophy's former lover); Daniel Jacobs, Art Dealer, Lover (of Sophy)
Time period(s): 2000s (2001)
Locale(s): New York, New York; Swansea Island, Massachusetts

Summary: Sophy Chase walks out on her depressed husband, Will, a former CIA agent. He dies suddenly under mysterious circumstances, while Sophy is in New York having great sex with Daniel. Now, she must return to Swansea Island to uncover the truth about Will's death. Adding to her problems, her dog Henry is missing. As she sorts things out, Sophy faces recriminations from her two adult stepdaughters and their mother. Tension skillfully builds as a cast of colorful friends step forward to help.

Where it's reviewed:
Booklist, July 2001, page 1976
Library Journal, August 2001, page 156
New York Times Book Review, September 9, 2001, page 7
Newsweek, August 27, 2001, page 58
Publishers Weekly, August 6, 2001, page 62

Other books by the same author:
Safe Conduct, 1993
The Beginner's Book of Dreams, 1988
Slow Dancing, 1985

Other books you might like:
Margaret Atwood, *The Blind Assassin*, 2000
Anita Brookner, *The Bay of Angels*, 2001
John Fowles, *The Magus*, 1965
Stephen King, *Dolores Claiborne*, 1993
Anne Rivers Siddons, *Low Country*, 1998

1074

SALLIE BISSELL

In the Forest of Harm

(New York: Bantam, 2001)

Story type: Psychological Suspense; Contemporary Realism
Subject(s): Legal Thriller; Women; Mystery
Major character(s): Mary Crow, Lawyer (assistant district attorney), Indian (half Cherokee); Joan, Friend (of Mary); Alex, Friend (of Mary)
Time period(s): 2000s (2001)
Locale(s): Lump Jump Off, North Carolina

Summary: In Bissell's first novel, three women survive a camping trip that turns into a nightmare. Mary Crow, a hotshot prosecutor, organizes a camping trip to the mountains where she grew up. Her friends, Joan and Alex, go with her. When two crazed killers stalk the three women, they have to use all their wits and resources to survive. Even so, Alex is kidnapped and Joan is raped. Mary's intuitive knowledge of the woods gives the women an edge.

Where it's reviewed:
Library Journal, January 1, 2001, page 151
Publishers Weekly, November 6, 2000, page 69

Other books you might like:
Barbara Taylor Bradford, *The Triumph of Katie Byrne*, 2001
Faye Kellerman, *Stalker*, 2000
Dean R. Koontz, *From the Corner of His Eye*, 2000
Dennis Lehane, *Darkness Take My Hand*, 1996
Scott Turow, *Presumed Innocent*, 1987

1075

KAREN BJORNEBY

Hurricane Season

(Naperville, Illinois: Sourcebooks Landmark, 2001)

Story type: Collection
Subject(s): Women; Relationships; Modern Life

Summary: Containing 12 short stories, this book is Karen Bjorneby's first collection. The title story deals with a woman brought back from the brink of despair when she notices someone threatened by a hurricane. Another character confronts tensions caused by science, religion, and love. A teenager represses her growth while her father serves in Vietnam. A woman can't resolve her feelings toward a kind young man. A woman's sexuality makes her a prize for God or the devil.

Where it's reviewed:
Kirkus Reviews, September 1, 2001, page 1231
Publishers Weekly, September 24, 2001, page 68

Other books you might like:
Pat Conroy, *The Prince of Tides*, 1986
Chitra Banerjee Divakaruni, *The Unknown Errors of Our Lives*, 2001
Jill McCorkle, *Creatures of Habit*, 2001
Alice Munro, *Hateship, Friendship, Courtship, Loveship, Marriage*, 2001
Joyce Carol Oates, *Beasts*, 2001

1076

ETHAN BLACK

All the Dead Were Strangers

(New York: Ballantine, 2001)

Story type: Contemporary Realism; Psychological Suspense
Subject(s): Terrorism; Conspiracies; Murder
Major character(s): Conrad Voort, Detective—Police; Jill Towne, Doctor (tropical disease specialist); John Szeska, Murderer (professional)
Time period(s): 2000s (2001)
Locale(s): New York, New York

Summary: An old friend passes NYPD detective Conrad Voort a list naming five people with alleged terrorist connections. Shortly thereafter, the friend and three of the people on the list die suddenly. During his investigation, Voort uncovers assassins employed by the government, discovers a plot to murder hundreds of police officers, becomes an assassin's target, and falls in love.

Where it's reviewed:
Booklist, June 1, 2001, page 1795
Kirkus Reviews, June 1, 2001, page 754
Publishers Weekly, July 16, 2001, page 158

Other books by the same author:
Irresistible, 2000
The Broken Hearts Club, 1999

Other books you might like:
Michael Connelly, *A Darkness More than Night*, 2001
J.F. Freedman, *Bird's-Eye View*, 2001

George V. Higgins, *At End of Day*, 2000
Dennis Lehane, *Mystic River*, 2001
Carsten Stroud, *Black Water Transit*, 2001

1077

SCOTT BLACKWOOD

In the Shadow of Our House

(Dallas, Texas: Southern Methodist University, 2001)

Story type: Collection; Modern
Subject(s): Family Problems; Relationships; Infidelity
Time period(s): 2000s (2001)

Summary: Blackwood, the Writing Center coordinator at the University of Texas, offers nine short stories in his first collection. His stories focus on the ordinary dramas of modern life that beguile and untrack the unsuspecting, who often act out their frustration violently. A man helps his girlfriend move while her husband watches. A hospitalized man must deal with his girlfriend while his wife watches. A man is arrested for drugs, leaving his pregnant girlfriend alone.

Where it's reviewed:
Kirkus Reviews, August 15, 2001, page 1143
New York Times Book Review, November 18, 2001, page 60

Other books you might like:
Ann Beattie, *Perfect Recall*, 2001
John Grisham, *A Painted House*, 2001
Goldberry Long, *Juniper Tree Burning*, 2001
Nani Power, *Crawling at Night*, 2001
Sarah Stonich, *These Granite Islands*, 2001

1078

DENNIS BOCK

The Ash Garden

(New York: Knopf, 2001)

Story type: Historical/World War II
Subject(s): Children and War; Nuclear Warfare; Refugees
Major character(s): Emiko Amai, Filmmaker (documentary); Anton Boll, Scientist (worked on atomic bomb), Refugee (from Germany); Sophie Boll, Spouse (of Anton), Refugee (interned during war)
Time period(s): 1990s (1995)
Locale(s): Hiroshima, Japan; New York, New York

Summary: In his first novel, Bock explores the emotional and moral aftermath of World War II. Three characters are linked to each other via the atomic bomb that was dropped on Hiroshima. Emiko, physically scarred from the blast that killed her parents, is making a documentary about the bombing. Anton, who provided critical information for the bomb, is married to Sophie, whose family perished at the hands of the Nazis. Anton agrees to participate in Emiko's film.

Where it's reviewed:
Kirkus Reviews, August 1, 2001, page 1043
Library Journal, August 2001, page 156
New York Times Book Review, September 23, 2001, page 8
Publishers Weekly, August 13, 2001, page 284

Other books by the same author:
Olympia, 1999

Other books you might like:
Martin Amis, *Time's Arrow*, 1991
Elizabeth Ann Scarborough, *Last Refuge*, 1992
Martin Cruz Smith, *Stallion Gate*, 1986
James Thackara, *America's Children*, 2001
Simone Zelitch, *Louisa*, 2000

1079

GREG BOTTOMS

Sentimental, Heartbroken Rednecks

(New York: Context, 2001)

Story type: Collection; Gothic
Subject(s): City and Town Life; Violence

Summary: In his first collection, Bottoms offers 13 short stories. Against the seedy margins of urban life in the South, the characters tell autobiographical and historical family stories that are peppered with violence, child abuse, police shootings, suicide, religious obsession, alcohol, and substance abuse. Despite these pathologies, the characters' strong voices remain undaunted and hopeful.

Where it's reviewed:
Library Journal, August 2001, page 168
New York Times Book Review, October 7, 2001, page 22
Publishers Weekly, August 20, 2001, page 54

Other books you might like:
Allan Gurganus, *The Practical Heart*, 2001
Margot Livesey, *Eva Moves the Furniture*, 2001
Bobbie Ann Mason, *Zigzagging Down a Wild Trail*, 2001
Jill McCorkle, *Creatures of Habit*, 2001
Elizabeth Spencer, *The Southern Woman*, 2001

1080

PAUL BOWLES

The Stories of Paul Bowles

(New York: Ecco, 2001)

Story type: Collection
Subject(s): Social Conditions; Cultures and Customs

Summary: Although born in New York City, Paul Bowles (1910-1999) mostly lived abroad, in Europe, Mexico, the Caribbean, and Tangiers. In 1968, Bowles and David Halpern founded *Antaeus* magazine, which soon became Ecco Press. This collection of 62 short stories was published to commemorate the 30th anniversary of that venture. The stories display Bowles' intense interest in the decadence that is exposed when western and eastern cultures collide. He deals with such topics as sexual tension, incest, violence, and corruption.

Where it's reviewed:
Booklist, September 15, 2001, page 191
Kirkus Reviews, September 1, 2001, page 1231
Library Journal, October 1, 2001, page 145
New York Times Book Review, October 21, 2001, page 9
Publishers Weekly, October 1, 2001, page 35

Other books by the same author:
Delicate Prey, 1995
A Distant Episode, 1988
Unwelcome Words, 1988
Points in Time, 1982
Midnight Mass, 1981

Other books you might like:
Alice Adams, *The Last Lovely City*, 1999
Frederick Barthelme, *The Law of Averages*, 2000
Ellen Gilchrist, *The Age of Miracles*, 1995
Barbara Kingsolver, *Homeland*, 1989
Bobbie Ann Mason, *Zigzagging Down a Wild Trail*, 2001

1081

T. CORAGHESSAN BOYLE

After the Plague

(New York: Viking, 2001)

Story type: Collection; Satire
Subject(s): Short Stories; Customs; Culture
Time period(s): 20th century

Summary: In this collection, Boyle offers 16 stories focusing on the darkly comic aspects of our self-absorbed, technology driven society. Subjects covered include Internet porn, relationships, abortion, overpopulation, middle age, air travel rage, race, death, and disease. Boyle skillfully uses surprising twists to keep things lively.

Where it's reviewed:
Booklist, June 1, 2001, page 1796
Kirkus Reviews, June 15, 2001, page 815
Library Journal, August 2001, page 168
New York Times Book Review, September 9, 2001, page 5
Publishers Weekly, August 6, 2001, page 60

Other books by the same author:
A Friend of the Earth, 2000
The Tortilla Curtain, 1995
Without a Hero, 1994
The Road to Wellville, 1993
East Is East, 1990

Other books you might like:
Frederick Busch, *Don't Tell Anyone*, 2000
Ellen Gilchrist, *The Cabal and Other Stories*, 2000
Annie Proulx, *Close Range*, 1999
Will Self, *Tough, Tough Toys for Tough, Tough Boys*, 1998
Kurt Vonnegut Jr., *Bagombo Snuff Box*, 1999

1082

RAY BRADBURY
CHARLES ADDAMS, Illustrator

From the Dust Returned

(New York: Morrow, 2001)

Story type: Contemporary/Fantasy
Subject(s): Family Saga; Supernatural; Vampires
Major character(s): Timothy Elliot, Foundling, Narrator (family historian); Einar Elliot, Relative (Timothy's uncle); Angelina Marguerite Elliot, Relative
Time period(s): Indeterminate Past
Locale(s): Midwest

Summary: This novel reads like a collection of interconnected short stories about the Elliot family. These family members are vampires, mummies, ghosts, and others of varying human qualities about whom the author wrote in the 1940s. From the far corners of the globe they are returning to their ancestral home for a reunion on Halloween. Readers will meet Arach the spider; Einar the winged man; Cecy, manipulator of animate and inanimate objects; Grand-Mere; Grand-Pere; and others.

Where it's reviewed:
Booklist, August 2001, page 2049
Kirkus Reviews, August 15, 2001, page 1143
Library Journal, September 15, 2001, page 108
New York Times Book Review, December 9, 2001, page 28
Publishers Weekly, August 27, 2001, page 60

Other books by the same author:
Ahmed and the Oblivion Machines, 1998
Driving Blind, 1997
Green Shadows, White Whale, 1992
Fahrenheit 451, 1953
Dark Carnival, 1947

Other books you might like:
Molly Gloss, *The Dazzle of Day*, 1997
Robert A. Heinlein, *Requiem*, 1992
Stephen King, *Dreamcatcher*, 2001
Sidney Sheldon, *The Doomsday Conspiracy*, 1991
Zadie Smith, *White Teeth*, 2000

1083

GERALDINE BROOKS

Year of Wonders

(New York: Viking, 2001)

Story type: Historical
Subject(s): Plague; Grief; Terror
Major character(s): Anna Frith, Widow(er), Parent (mother of two small boys); Elinor Mompellion, Spouse (of Michael); Michael Mompellion, Religious (village minister)
Time period(s): 17th century (1665-1666)
Locale(s): Eyam, England

Summary: This first novel by Brooks, an Australian-born journalist, explores daily life in a small English village during the 17th century bubonic plague epidemic. Widow Anna, 18, goes to work for Elinor, the minister's wife. When the plague arrives, Michael, the minister, persuades everyone to quarantine the village but as the death toll increases, some villagers blame Michael. Devil worship, ritualized murder, and self-mutilation make appearances. The plague takes Anna's children and her innocence but she survives.

Where it's reviewed:
Library Journal, July 2001, page 120
New York Times Book Review, August 26, 2001, page 13
New Yorker, September 17, 2001, page 169
Publishers Weekly, June 25, 2001, page 43

Other books you might like:
Susann Cokal, *Mirabilis*, 2001
Molly Gloss, *Wild Life*, 2000
James D. Houston, *Snow Mountain Passage*, 2001
Robert Laxalt, *Time of the Rabies*, 2000
Stewart O'Nan, *A Prayer for the Dying*, 1999

1084

BRIAN BROWN

TV

(New York: Crown, 2001)

Story type: Psychological
Subject(s): Television Programs; Sports; Gambling
Major character(s): Caesar Fortunato, Television (producer-director); Henry Kapp, Television (Caesar's boss)
Time period(s): 20th century (1958-1995)
Locale(s): New York, New York; Philadelphia, Pennsylvania

Summary: In his first novel, Brown, a television veteran, gives readers an insider's view of sports broadcasting. We watch Caesar Fortunato start at a local affiliate and work his way up the corporate ladder until he becomes a network star. Unfortunately, along the way he becomes abrasive to his colleagues and develops self-destructive personal habits, including substance abuse and gambling. When he insults his new boss, Henry, he sets the stage for an intense corporate struggle.

Where it's reviewed:
Kirkus Reviews, June 15, 2001, page 816
Library Journal, July 2001, page 120
New York Times Book Review, September 9, 2001, page 18
Publishers Weekly, July 16, 2001, page 156

Other books you might like:
Chris Bachelder, *Bear v. Shark*, 2001
Jim Harrison, *Warlock*, 1981
John Irving, *The Fourth Hand*, 2001
Harold Robbins, *Tycoon*, 1997
W.D. Wetherell, *Morning*, 2001

1085

JOHN GREGORY BROWN

Audubon's Watch

(Boston: Houghton Mifflin, 2001)

Story type: Historical
Subject(s): Psychological; Guilt; Sexual Behavior
Major character(s): John James Audubon, Historical Figure, Scientist (ornithologist); Emile Gautreaux, Scientist (anatomist), Doctor; Myra Gautreaux, Spouse (of Emile)
Time period(s): 19th century (1821-1851)
Locale(s): Cincinnati, Ohio; New Orleans, Louisiana

Summary: The story revolves around an incident involving ornithologist John James Audubon and the fictional Dr. Gautreaux and his wife, Myra. The doctor meets Audubon on a plantation, where Audubon scrapes out an existence as a tutor and offers to become Audubon's patron. He's interested until he meets Myra. Shortly thereafter, Myra dies mysteriously. Told in retrospect, the perspective alternates between the dying Audubon and Gautreaux. Each has secrets involving lust, guilt, and Myra.

Where it's reviewed:
Kirkus Reviews, August 1, 2001, page 1044
Library Journal, August 2001, page 158
New York Times Book Review, September 23, 2001, page 19
Publishers Weekly, August 6, 2001, page 58

Other books by the same author:
The Wrecked, Blessed Body of Shelton Lafleur, 1996
Decorations in a Ruined Cemetery, 1994

Other books you might like:
John Fowles, *A Maggot*, 1985
Michel Houellebecq, *The Elementary Particles*, 2000
Allen Kurzweil, *The Grand Complication*, 2001
J.D. Landis, *Longing*, 2000
Anne Tyler, *Saint Maybe*, 1991

1086

SANDRA BROWN

Envy

(New York: Warner, 2001)

Story type: Arts; Contemporary
Subject(s): Authors and Writers; Revenge; Psychological Thriller
Major character(s): Maris Matherly-Reed, Editor, Spouse (of Noah); Noah Reed, Publisher, Writer (of a bestseller); Parker Evans, Handicapped, Writer
Time period(s): 2000s (2001)
Locale(s): New York, New York; St. Anne Island, Georgia

Summary: Maris, an editor at a small family-owned publishing company, receives unsolicited chapters from a manuscript. It tells an intriguing story about a man who lets an author drown then steals his work, which becomes a bestseller. Maris travels to a Georgia island to find the unknown author who turns out to be an embittered recluse confined to a wheelchair. She begins to suspect Parker Evans' story is more truth than fiction and that there is a connection to her husband, Noah, who has a single bestselling book to his credit.

Where it's reviewed:
Kirkus Reviews, July 15, 2001, page 977

Other books by the same author:
Bittersweet Rain, 2000
Standoff, 2000
In a Class by Itself, 1999
The Alibi, 1999
Send No Flowers, 1984

Other books you might like:
Elizabeth Berg, *Never Change*, 2001
Alice Hoffman, *Blue Diary*, 2001
Kate Kennedy, *End over End*, 2001
Jacquelyn Mitchard, *A Theory of Relativity*, 2001
Betsy Tobin, *Bone House*, 2000

1087

RICHARD BURGIN

The Spirit Returns

(Baltimore: Johns Hopkins University, 2001)

Story type: Collection
Subject(s): Loneliness; Customs; Culture
Time period(s): 2000s (2001)

Summary: Burgin's latest collection offers 11 stories with characters on the fringe. A traveler gets the attention of a woman on a shuttle bus but he can't make out. An ad exec likes to scare people he doesn't know, then a woman joins in his fun but they don't connect. A young lesbian is murdered and her lover goes to a party, where she almost picks up a journalist but they strike out. Everyone tries to connect to other people, but all the characters are too alienated from the world to succeed.

Where it's reviewed:
Chicago Tribune Books, November 11, 2001, page 1
Publishers Weekly, October 15, 2001, page 46

Other books by the same author:
Ghost Quartet, 1999
Fear of Blue Skies, 1998
Private Fame, 1991
Man Without Memory, 1989

Other books you might like:
Melissa Bank, *The Girls' Guide to Hunting and Fishing*, 1999
John Barth, *On with the Story*, 1996
Frederick Barthelme, *The Law of Averages*, 2000
John Biguenet, *The Torturer's Apprentice*, 2001
Raymond Carver, *Where I'm Calling From*, 1988

1088

JAMES LEE BURKE

Bitterroot

(New York: Simon & Schuster, 2001)

Story type: Modern
Subject(s): Mystery; Vietnam War; Violence
Major character(s): Billy Bob Holland, Lawyer, Veteran (Vietnam); Doc Voss, Friend (of Billy Bob); L.Q. Navarro, Spirit (former partner of Billy Bob)
Time period(s): 2000s (2001)
Locale(s): Bitterroot Valley, Montana

Summary: Texas attorney Billy Bob Holland decides to go fishing with his old friend, Doc Voss. When Billy Bob arrives in Montana, he finds Doc embroiled in a dispute with a local mining company. Things get ugly when Doc's daughter is raped in her own bedroom. Billy Bob sets out to find the culprits and discovers there's no shortage of suspects. Although Billy Bob is haunted by memories of the Vietnam War, his dead partner, L.Q. Navarro stops by with advice.

Where it's reviewed:
Book, July 2001, page 74
Booklist, March 15, 2001, page 1331
Library Journal, May 1, 2001, page 125
New York Times Book Review, June 24, 2001, page 22
Publishers Weekly, May 21, 2001, page 85

Other books by the same author:
Purple Cane Road, 2000
Cimarron Rose, 1999
Two for Texas, 1989
The Dave Robicheaux Series, 1987-
The Convict and Other Stories, 1985

Other books you might like:
Larry Brown, *Dirty Work*, 1989
Michael Connelly, *The Black Echo*, 1992
John Grisham, *A Time to Kill*, 1989
Jim Harrison, *Woman Lit by Fireflies*, 1990
Walter Mosley, *Fearless Jones*, 2001

1089

BEBE MOORE CAMPBELL

What You Owe Me

(New York: Putnam, 2001)

Story type: Psychological; Saga
Subject(s): Cosmetics Industry; African Americans; Women
Major character(s): Hosanna Clark, Maintenance Worker (cleaning lady); Gilda Rosenstein, Maintenance Worker (cleaning lady); Matriece Clark, Businesswoman (marketing executive), Relative (Hosanna's daughter)
Time period(s): 20th century (1946-1996)
Locale(s): Los Angeles, California

Summary: Hosanna Clark, a cheerful and optimistic African American, goes into business with Gilda Rosenstein, a quiet and thoughtful Jewish refugee. When Gilda cleans out a joint bank account and disappears, Hosanna becomes despondent. Gilda eventually builds a successful corporation, but years later Hosanna's daughter, Matriece, sets out to make things right. She climbs the corporate ladder at Gilda's company without Gilda knowing her identity, setting the scene for her mother's vindication.

Where it's reviewed:
Booklist, July 2001, page 1948
Kirkus Reviews, July 1, 2001, page 882
Library Journal, July 2001, page 120
Publishers Weekly, July 9, 2001, page 44

Other books by the same author:
Singing in the Comeback Choir, 1998
Brothers and Sisters, 1994
Your Blues Ain't Like Mine, 1992

Other books you might like:
Tananarive Due, *The Black Rose*, 2000
Toni Morrison, *Paradise*, 1998
Walter Mosley, *Fearless Jones*, 2001
Lalita Tademy, *Cane River*, 2001
Alice Walker, *The Way Forward Is with a Broken Heart*, 2000

1090

TRACY CHEVALIER

Falling Angels

(New York: Dutton, 2001)

Story type: Historical
Subject(s): Friendship; Children; Social Classes
Major character(s): Maude Coleman, Child (of Kitty), Friend (of Lavinia); Lavinia Waterhouse, Friend (of Maude); Kitty Coleman, Parent (of Maude), Spouse (unhappily married)
Time period(s): 1900s; 1910s (1901-1910)
Locale(s): London, England

Summary: Chevalier's second novel occurs at the beginning of the 20th century in London. A breeze of social change is in the air, as we watch two girls, Maude and Lavinia, deal with their parents' actions and subsequent consequences. Maude's mother, Kitty, is unhappily married and has an affair. When Kitty becomes pregnant, she has a secret abortion and falls into a depression. Her involvement with the suffragist movement revives her, despite her family's unfavorable reaction.

Where it's reviewed:
Booklist, August 2001, page 2050
Kirkus Reviews, August 1, 2001, page 1045
Publishers Weekly, July 30, 2001, page 19

Other books by the same author:
Girl with a Pearl Earring, 1999

Other books you might like:
Karen Joy Fowler, *Sister Noon*, 2001
David Leavitt, *While England Sleeps*, 1993
Joyce Carol Oates, *Because It Is Bitter, and Because It Is My Heart*, 1990
John O'Hara, *Ten North Frederick*, 1955
Zadie Smith, *White Teeth*, 2000

1091

SUSANN COKAL

Mirabilis

(New York: Putnam, 2001)

Story type: Historical; Adult
Subject(s): Plague; Religion; Women
Major character(s): Blanche, Single Parent (burned to death); Bonne Tardieu, Relative (Blanche's daughter); Radegonde Putemonnie, Wealthy
Time period(s): 14th century
Locale(s): Villeneuve, France

Summary: Villagers in medieval France are stricken by the plague and pray for a miracle. Blanche "Mirabilis," which means astonishing, levitates above the crowd and the village is saved. Blanche goes from saint to sinner when she has an illegitimate child. The clergy executes Blanche when her daughter Bonne is 12. She becomes a wet nurse to survive. During an English siege, Bonne shares her milk with starving villagers and becomes a saint. *Mirabilis* is Cokal's first novel.

Where it's reviewed:
Booklist, June 15, 2001, page 1835
Kirkus Reviews, April 15, 2001, page 518
Library Journal, June 15, 2001, page 101
New York Times Book Review, September 23, 2001, page 24
Publishers Weekly, June 11, 2001, page 56

Other books you might like:
Jane Alison, *The Love Artist*, 2001
Carmen Boullosa, *Leaving Tabasco*, 2001
T. Coraghessan Boyle, *After the Plague*, 2001
Betsy Tobin, *Bone House*, 2000
William T. Vollmann, *Argall*, 2001

1092

JOHN COLAPINTO

About the Author

(New York: HarperCollins, 2001)

Story type: Psychological; Literary
Subject(s): Authors and Writers; Murder; Cheating
Major character(s): Cal Cunningham, Writer (has writer's block), Clerk (in bookstore); Stewart Church, Roommate (of Cal), Student; Blackie Yeager, Agent (literary)
Time period(s): 2000s (2001)
Locale(s): New York, New York; New Halcyon, Vermont

Summary: Colapinto's first book is about plagiarism, selfishness, blackmail, deceit, murder, and comeuppance. Stewart writes a book based upon his roommate's sexual escapades but dies suddenly. His roommate, Cal, publishes the manuscript as his own and literary agent Blackie Yeager turns the book into a blockbuster. Cal, intoxicated by success, courts Janet, Stewart's old girlfriend. When a stranger shows up claiming to have Stewart's original manuscript on disc, the fun really starts.

Where it's reviewed:
Booklist, May 1, 2001, page 1624
Kirkus Reviews, June 15, 2001, page 818
Library Journal, August 2001, page 160
New York Times Book Review, October 7, 2001, page 22
Publishers Weekly, July 9, 2001, page 42

Other books you might like:
A.S. Byatt, *The Biographer's Tale*, 2001
Pedro Juan Gutierrez, *Dirty Havana Trilogy*, 2001
Simon Mawer, *The Gospel of Judas*, 2001
Josef Skvorecky, *Two Murders in My Double Life*, 2001
Paul Theroux, *Hotel Honolulu*, 2001

1093

ROBIN COOK

Shock

(New York: Putnam, 2001)

Story type: Contemporary Realism; Medical
Subject(s): Cloning; Medical Thriller; Women
Major character(s): Joanna Meissner, Student—Graduate (economics); Deborah Cochrane, Student—Graduate (molecular biology)

Time period(s): 2000s
Locale(s): Boston, Massachusetts; Venice, Italy

Summary: While working on their doctoral theses, friends Joanna and Deborah decide to sell their eggs to Windgate Clinic. After each collects $45,000, they head for Venice to relax. When they return, Joanna decides she wants to know what happened to her egg, so the two women put on disguises and get jobs at the clinic. Needless to say, they are surprised at what they find. A serial killer and chase scene add to the interest.

Where it's reviewed:
Booklist, July 2001, page 1949
Kirkus Reviews, July 15, 2001, page 961
Publishers Weekly, August 27, 2001, page 55

Other books by the same author:
Harmful Intent, 2000
Vector, 1999
Chromosome 6, 1997
Contagion, 1995
Fatal Cure, 1993

Other books you might like:
Sarah Bird, *The Mommy Club*, 1991
Perry Brass, *The Harvest*, 1997
Michael Crichton, *The Lost World*, 1995
Hester Kaplan, *Kinship Theory*, 2000
Fay Weldon, *The Cloning of Joanna May*, 1989

1094

DOUGLAS COUPLAND

All Families Are Psychotic

(New York: Bloomsbury, 2001)

Story type: Humor; Contemporary
Subject(s): AIDS (Disease); Family Relations; Women
Major character(s): Wade Drummond, Relative (Janet's son); Janet Drummond, Parent (of Wade); Sarah Drummond-Fournier, Relative (Janet's daughter), Astronaut (making first flight)
Time period(s): 2000s (2001)
Locale(s): Orlando, Florida

Summary: Coupland uses humor to lighten the story of a family that gives new meaning to the word dysfunctional. The Drummond clan gathers in Florida to support daughter Sarah, an astronaut making her first space shuttle flight. Mother Janet and brother Wade suffer from AIDS; father Ted is a philanderer accompanied by his trophy wife; suicidal brother Bryan's pregnant girlfriend is planning to sell their baby; and Sarah's husband, Howie, is having an affair with the wife of one of her fellow astronauts. The family reunion sparks chaos and a series of bizarrely comic mishaps.

Where it's reviewed:
Booklist, July 2001, page 1949
Kirkus Reviews, July 15, 2001, page 961
Library Journal, September 15, 2001, page 108
New York Times Book Review, September 16, 2001, page 18
Publishers Weekly, July 30, 2001, page 57

Other books by the same author:
Miss Wyoming, 1999
Girlfriend in a Coma, 1998
Life After God, 1994
Shampoo Planet, 1992
Generation X, 1991

Other books you might like:
Saul Bellow, *Henderson the Rain King*, 1959
Catherine Bush, *Minus Time*, 1993
Fannie Flagg, *Fried Green Tomatoes at the Whistle Stop Cafe*, 1987
Tess Gerritsen, *Gravity*, 1999
Barbara Kingsolver, *The Bean Trees*, 1988

1095

JIM CRACE

The Devil's Larder

(New York: Farrar, Straus & Giroux, 2001)

Story type: Collection
Subject(s): Food; Satire; Humor
Time period(s): 2000s (2001)

Summary: Award-winning British writer Jim Crace offers 64 short stories focusing on food. The stories vary in length from a single paragraph to half a dozen pages. Satirical and comic in nature, the stories explore the relationship of food to people. In addition to the usual comments about restaurants such as taste, ambiance, and service, Crace serves up social class, entertainment, sexuality, and gender preference. Experimental in nature, readers won't find these descriptions in a guide book.

Where it's reviewed:
Atlantic Monthly, October 1, 2001, page 126
Booklist, October 15, 2001, page 381
Kirkus Reviews, August 15, 2001, page 1144
Library Journal, September 15, 2001, page 115

Other books by the same author:
Being Dead, 2000
Quarantine, 1997
Signals of Distress, 1994
Arcadia, 1991
The Gift of Stones, 1988

Other books you might like:
Julian Barnes, *A History of the World in 10 1/2 Chapters*, 1989
Henry Fielding, *The History of Tom Jones*, 1749
Richard Klein, *Jewelry Talks*, 2001
Rick Moody, *Demonology*, 2000
Paul Theroux, *Millroy the Magician*, 1994

1096

ROBERT CRAIS

Hostage

(New York: Doubleday, 2001)

Story type: Modern; Contemporary Realism
Subject(s): Organized Crime; Hostages; Police Procedural

Major character(s): Jeff Talley, Police Officer (chief); George Smith, Accountant (for the mob), Crime Victim (taken hostage); Sonny Benza, Organized Crime Figure (mob boss)
Time period(s): 2000s (2001)
Locale(s): Bristo Camino, California

Summary: After botching a holdup, three criminals invade a house and take the owner, George Smith, and his children hostage. Police Chief Jeff Talley, a former LAPD hostage negotiator who left the department after losing a hostage, is confronted with his worst nightmare. Complicating matters in this fast paced and suspenseful novel is that Smith, who works for mob boss Sonny Benza, has all his files at home. Benza then kidnaps Smith's wife to keep his records from the police.

Where it's reviewed:
Booklist, July 2001, page 1949
Kirkus Reviews, July 1, 2001, page 884
Library Journal, August 2001, page 159
New York Times Book Review, August 19, 2001, page 14
Publishers Weekly, July 9, 2001, page 43

Other books by the same author:
Demolition Angel, 2000
Devil's Cantina, 1999
L.A. Requiem, 1999
Indigo Slam, 1997
Free Fall, 1993

Other books you might like:
Michael Connelly, *A Darkness More than Night*, 2001
John Grisham, *The Firm*, 1991
George V. Higgins, *At End of Day*, 2000
Dennis Lehane, *Mystic River*, 2001
James Patterson, *Kiss the Girls*, 1995

1097

CLIVE CUSSLER

Valhalla Rising

(New York: Putnam, 2001)

Story type: Adventure
Series: Dirk Pitt. Number 16
Subject(s): Shipwrecks; Underwater Exploration; Suspense
Major character(s): Dirk Pitt, Engineer (marine), Government Official (with an oceanographic agency); Al Giordino, Sidekick, Government Official (Dirk's deputy); Loren Smith, Political Figure (congresswoman), Lover (of Dirk)
Time period(s): 2000s (2001)
Locale(s): At Sea; Washington, District of Columbia

Summary: Dirk Pitt and his sidekick, Al Giordino, rescue 2,000 passengers from a sinking cruise ship. One survivor, Kelly Egan, carries the secret of a saltwater engine that nasty oil baron, Curtis Zale, is out to get. When Congresswoman Loren Smith investigates, Zale has her put on a hit list. Plot twists and surprises somehow connect Viking runes, underwater submarine searches, and contemporary concerns about energy.

Where it's reviewed:
Kirkus Reviews, June 1, 2001, page 755
Library Journal, July 2001, page 121
Publishers Weekly, July 30, 2001, page 61

Other books by the same author:
Atlantis Found, 1999
Flood Tide, 1997
Sahara, 1992
Raise the Titanic, 1976
Iceberg, 1975

Other books you might like:
Peter Benchley, *The Deep*, 1976
Michael Crichton, *Eaters of the Dead*, 1976
Nelson DeMille, *Plum Island*, 1997
Michael Edison, *The Vikings*, 1951
John Grisham, *The Pelican Brief*, 1992

1098

SIJIE DAI

Balzac and the Little Chinese Seamstress

(New York: Knopf, 2001)

Story type: Historical; Political
Subject(s): Social Classes; Cultural Conflict; Individuality
Major character(s): Unnamed Character, Teenager (sent to reeducation camp), Friend (of Luo); Luo, Friend
Time period(s): 1960s; 1970s (1966-1976)
Locale(s): China

Summary: During the Chinese Cultural Revolution, an unnamed teenager and his friend, Luo, are sent to a peasant village for political reeducation where they cope by reading banned books. They read Balzac to a young woman they are both attracted to, who has a brief affair with Luo. Exposure to the forbidden literature and its ideas has a liberating effect on her, enabling her to break free of Luo and his needs. Originally published in 2000 in France. Translated by Ina Rilke.

Where it's reviewed:
Chicago Tribune Books, September 30, 2001, page 1
Kirkus Reviews, August 1, 2001, page 1046
Library Journal, September 15, 2001, page 110
Publishers Weekly, August 27, 2001, page 51

Other books you might like:
S.Y. Agnon, *Only Yesterday*, 2000
Xingjian Gao, *Soul Mountain*, 2000
Ha Jin, *The Bridegroom*, 2000
Patrick McGrath, *Martha Peake*, 2000
Jill Paton Walsh, *A Desert in Bohemia*, 2000

1099

LYDIA DAVIS

Samuel Johnson Is Indignant

(Brooklyn, New York: McSweeney, 2001)

Story type: Collection
Subject(s): Self-Perception; Relationships; Satire
Time period(s): 2000s (2001)

Summary: In this collection, Davis offers 54 clever and witty stories of varying length. Subjects include married life, stress, disillusionment, childbearing, gender equality, grief, and selfishness. Language and the message it conveys have a high priority in these stories. The author is famous for whimsical one-liners that draw smiles but make one think, too. The book's title, which is a partial quotation, is a case in point. The missing part is "that Scotland has so few trees."

Where it's reviewed:

Kirkus Reviews, October 15, 2001, page 1453
Publishers Weekly, October 1, 2001, page 36
Time, November 19, 2001, page 143

Other books by the same author:

Almost No Memory, 1997
End of the Story, 1995
Break It Down, 1986
Story and Other Stories, 1983
Thirteenth Woman and Other Stories, 1976

Other books you might like:

Julian Barnes, *Love, etc.*, 2001
Tibor Fischer, *I Like Being Killed*, 2000
Helen Humphreys, *Afterimage*, 2000
Bobbie Ann Mason, *Zigzagging Down a Wild Trail*, 2001
Alice Munro, *Hateship, Friendship, Courtship, Loveship, Marriage*, 2001

1100

TOM DE HAVEN

Dugan under Ground

(New York: Metropolitan, 2001)

Story type: Psychological
Subject(s): Cartoons and Comics; History; Newspapers
Major character(s): Candy Biggs, Artist (comic strip illustrator), Teacher (of Roy); Roy Looby, Artist (comic strip illustrator); Nick Looby, Relative (Roy's brother)
Time period(s): 1960s
Locale(s): New York, New York; San Francisco, California

Summary: *Dugan under Ground* follows the fictional comic strip "Derby Dugan" through the hard times of the 1960s. The story line that took the strip through the Depression and World War II no longer resounds with the public and newspapers begin dropping the comic strip. Candy Biggs, the strip's out-of-step illustrator, seeks help from a young illustrator, Roy Looby. His ideas help but when he leaves for the hippie scene in San Francisco, Biggs sends Looby's brother to find him.

Where it's reviewed:

Booklist, September 15, 2001, page 191
Kirkus Reviews, August 1, 2001, page 1047
New York Times Book Review, October 21, 2001, page 8
Publishers Weekly, September 3, 2001, page 58

Other books by the same author:

Derby Dugan's Depression Funnies, 1996
The Last Human, 1992
The End-of-Everything Man, 1991
Walker of Worlds, 1990
Sunburn Lake, 1988

Other books you might like:

Michael Chabon, *The Amazing Adventures of Kavalier & Clay*, 2000
Allegra Goodman, *The Markowitz Family*, 1996
Ernest Hekkanen, *My Dog Is More than Just a Dog to Me*, 1999
Ben Katchor, *Julius Knipl, Real Estate Photographer*, 1996
Amy Sohn, *Run Catch Kiss*, 1999

1101

BARBARA DELINSKY

The Woman Next Door

(New York: Simon & Schuster, 2001)

Story type: Romance; Contemporary
Subject(s): Widows/Widowers; Marriage; Infertility
Major character(s): Amanda O'Leary, Counselor (high school), Spouse (of Graham); Karen Cotter, Spouse, Neighbor (of Amanda); Georgia Lange, Spouse (of Russ), Neighbor (of Amanda)
Time period(s): 2000s (2001)
Locale(s): Connecticut

Summary: Delinsky's novel probes marital difficulties from a female perspective. When a young, attractive widow in a close-knit upscale suburban community becomes pregnant, the neighboring wives can't help wondering who is the father. The internal pressures in their own marriages make them wonder if it could be their respective husbands: Amanda desperately wants to be pregnant but has been unsuccessful; Georgia travels, while her husband keeps house; and Karen's husband has strayed in the past.

Where it's reviewed:

Booklist, June 15, 2001, page 1796
Library Journal, July 2001, page 121

Other books by the same author:

A Woman Betrayed, 2001
Straight from the Heart, 2001
The Vineyard, 2001
Lake News, 1999
Coast Road, 1998

Other books you might like:

Joy Fielding, *The First Time*, 2000
Nadine Gordimer, *The Pickup*, 2001
Terry McMillan, *A Day Late and a Dollar Short*, 2001
Danielle Steel, *The House on Hope Street*, 2000
Sarah Stonich, *These Granite Islands*, 2001

1102

ROBB FORMAN DEW

The Evidence Against Her

(Boston: Little, Brown, 2001)

Story type: Historical; Romance
Subject(s): Interpersonal Relations; Psychological; Family Relations

Major character(s): Lily Scofield, Cousin (of Warren), Spouse (of Robert); Warren Scofield, Spouse (of Agnes); Robert Butler, Spouse (of Lily)
Time period(s): 19th century; 20th century
Locale(s): Ohio

Summary: *The Evidence Against Her* explores the nuances and details of events that shape family life. The story follows cousins Lily and Warren Scofield and their friend, Robert Butler. The three are born on the same day in 1888. Inseparable as children, they grow up, settle down, and have families. Predictably, adult responsibilities intrude. Lily marries Robert while a dejected Warren marries Agnes. World War I ends, the influenza epidemic hits, and an accidental death occurs.

Where it's reviewed:
Booklist, July 2001, page 1949
Chicago Tribune Books, September 23, 2001, page 1
Kirkus Reviews, August 1, 2001, page 1048
New York Times Book Review, October 14, 2001, page 16
Publishers Weekly, July 30, 2001, page 59

Other books by the same author:
Fortunate Lives, 1992
The Time of Her Life, 1984
Dale Loves Sophie to Death, 1981

Other books you might like:
Julian Barnes, *Love, etc.*, 2001
John Fowles, *The French Lieutenant's Woman*, 1969
Helen Humphreys, *Afterimage*, 2000
Ha Jin, *Waiting*, 1999
W.D. Wetherell, *Morning*, 2001

1103

ANITA DIAMANT

Good Harbor

(New York: Scribner, 2001)

Story type: Inspirational; Contemporary/Mainstream
Subject(s): Illness; Friendship; Psychological
Major character(s): Kathleen Levine, Librarian (grade school), Patient (has breast cancer); Joyce Tabachnik, Writer (romance novels), Parent (of pre-teen girl)
Time period(s): 2000s (2001)
Locale(s): Cape Ann, Massachusetts

Summary: In this story about friendship, Kathleen, 59, has breast cancer and is haunted by images of her sister who died from the disease. Kathleen's home life with her husband and two sons isn't pleasant. Joyce, 42, is nervous because the romance novel she wrote is successful. She worries that she is losing touch with her husband and their daughter Nina, 12. The women go on long walks and exchange confidences that benefit both of them.

Where it's reviewed:
Booklist, September 15, 2001, page 164
Kirkus Reviews, September 15, 2001, page 1312
Library Journal, September 15, 2001, page 110
Publishers Weekly, September 24, 2001, page 65

Other books by the same author:
The Red Tent, 1997

Other books you might like:
Elizabeth Berg, *Talk Before Sleep*, 1994
Barbara Taylor Bradford, *A Sudden Change of Heart*, 1999
Barbara Delinsky, *Coast Road*, 1998
Ellen Gilchrist, *The Anna Papers*, 1988
Alice Hoffman, *Local Girls*, 1999

1104

CHITRA BANERJEE DIVAKARUNI

The Unknown Errors of Our Lives

(New York: Doubleday, 2001)

Story type: Collection; Ethnic
Subject(s): Cultures and Customs; Emigration and Immigration; Women
Time period(s): 2000s (2001)

Summary: Divakaruni's collection offers nine stories dealing with the immigrant experience. Her characters are forced to wrestle with questions of conventional belief and common practice. They must reconcile experiences brought from India with reality in the land where they raise their children. Topics touched upon include misunderstanding, undeclared love, marriage, shame, children, grandparents, emotional stress, despair, and superstition.

Where it's reviewed:
Booklist, March 1, 2001, page 1187
Kirkus Reviews, February 15, 2001, page 201
New York Times Book Review, July 1, 2001, page 16
Publishers Weekly, March 12, 2001, page 61

Other books by the same author:
Sister of My Heart, 1999
The Mistress of Spices, 1997
Arranged Marriage, 1995

Other books you might like:
Anita Desai, *Diamond Dust*, 2000
Jhumpa Lahiri, *Interpreter of Maladies*, 1999
Manil Suri, *The Death of Vishnu*, 2001
Amy Tan, *The Bonesetter's Daughter*, 2001
Vineeta Vijayaraghavan, *Motherland*, 2001

1105

TAHAR DJAOUT

The Last Summer of Reason

(St. Paul, Minnesota: Ruminator, 2001)

Story type: Psychological Suspense
Subject(s): Cultures and Customs; Politics; Social Conditions
Major character(s): Bousalem Yekker, Store Owner (bookstore)
Time period(s): 1990s (1993)
Locale(s): Algeria

Summary: Bousalem, owner of a bookstore, struggles to maintain intellectual and artistic integrity. A fundamentalist religious group, the Vigilant Brothers, pressures him to stock only books that agree with the word of God. The pressure escalates to threats and finally the contents of his store are confiscated. Translated by Marjolin de Jager, this is the first work by Djaout, an Algerian writer who was assassinated by Islamic fundamentalists in 1993, to appear in English.

Where it's reviewed:
Booklist, October 15, 2001, page 381
Kirkus Reviews, September 1, 2001, page 1233
New York Times Book Review, December 23, 2001, page 18
Publishers Weekly, October 1, 2001, page 38

Other books you might like:
David Lamb, *The Trumpet Is Blown*, 1997
Micheline Aharonian Marcom, *Three Apples Fell from Heaven*, 2001
Orhan Pamuk, *My Name Is Red*, 2001
Salman Rushdie, *The Satanic Verses*, 1988
Tariq Saladin, *The Book of Saladin*, 1998

1106

MYLENE DRESSLER

The Deadwood Beetle

(New York: BlueHen, 2001)

Story type: Historical/World War II; Psychological
Subject(s): Memory; Guilt; Secrets
Major character(s): Tristan Martens, Professor (retired), Divorced Person; Cora Lasher, Store Owner (antique shop); Elida Hernandez, Student—Graduate
Time period(s): 2000s (2001)
Locale(s): New York, New York

Summary: Dressler's second novel examines the long shadow of guilt. Tristan, a retired professor, is divorced and estranged from his family. He carries dark secrets from the German occupation during World War II. While visiting an antique store one day, he finds his mother's sewing table, which brings back memories of his wartime childhood. Although Cora, the shopkeeper, refuses to sell him the table, Tristan returns to the shop daily, eventually developing a relationship with Cora. He confesses his secrets to her, but Cora has secrets of her own.

Where it's reviewed:
Booklist, September 1, 2001, page 49
Kirkus Reviews, July 1, 2001, page 886
Library Journal, September 1, 2001, page 232
New York Times Book Review, November 18, 2001, page 68
Publishers Weekly, August 27, 2001, page 50

Other books by the same author:
The Medusa Tree, 1997

Other books you might like:
Jill Paton Walsh, *A Desert in Bohemia*, 2000
Richard Russo, *The Risk Pool*, 1988
Danielle Steel, *Silent Honor*, 1996
William Styron, *Sophie's Choice*, 1979
Simone Zelitch, *Louisa*, 2000

1107

GWEN EDELMAN

War Story

(New York: Riverhead, 2001)

Story type: Romance; Historical/World War II
Subject(s): Holocaust; Relationships; Memory
Major character(s): Kitty Jacobs, Lover (seduced by older man); Joseph Kruger, Writer (playwright)
Time period(s): 2000s (2001)
Locale(s): Amsterdam, Netherlands

Summary: In her first novel, Edelman explores love between a young woman and an older man. Kitty Jacobs sifts through her memories of Joseph Kruger, while riding a train to his funeral ten years after their affair. They become lovers the same afternoon they meet, when she is 32 and he is 60. He captivates her with his wartime stories of persecution and escape from the Nazis. Although very intense, the affair is doomed by his haunted memories.

Where it's reviewed:
Booklist, August 2001, page 168
Publishers Weekly, July 23, 2001, page 51

Other books you might like:
Jonathan Franzen, *The Corrections*, 2001
Hanif Kureishi, *Intimacy and Midnight All Day*, 1999
Marisa Silver, *Babe in Paradise*, 2001
Dana Spiotta, *Lightning Field*, 2001
Katherine Tanney, *Carousel of Progress*, 2001

1108

JENNIFER EGAN

Look at Me

(New York: Nan A. Talese/Doubleday, 2001)

Story type: Psychological
Subject(s): Models; Identity; Internet
Major character(s): Charlotte Swenson, Model (fashion), Accident Victim (car crash); Anthony Halliday, Detective—Private, Friend (of Charlotte Swenson); Charlotte, Teenager, Lover (of her teacher)
Time period(s): 2000s (2001)
Locale(s): New York, New York; Rockford, Illinois

Summary: On a trip back to Rockford, Charlotte, a successful fashion model, loses her career and almost her mind, when a car crash destroys her face. Plastic surgery is successful but no one recognizes her. Meanwhile, her former best friend's daughter, also named Charlotte, becomes involved with a teacher, turns to the Internet and local history to escape her strained home life. When these story lines converge, readers can expect an interesting picture of contemporary life.

Where it's reviewed:
Booklist, July 2001, page 1979
Kirkus Reviews, August 15, 2001, page 1146
Publishers Weekly, August 20, 2001, page 56

Other books by the same author:
Emerald City, 1996

The Invisible Circus, 1995

Other books you might like:
Margaret Atwood, *Lady Oracle*, 1976
J.G. Ballard, *Crash*, 1973
Barbara Taylor Bradford, *Her Own Rules*, 1996
Jackie Collins, *American Star*, 1993
Catherine Coulter, *Beyond Eden*, 1992

1109

LEIF ENGER

Peace Like a River

(New York: Atlantic Monthly, 2001)

Story type: Coming-of-Age
Subject(s): Fathers and Sons; Single Parent Families; Brothers
Major character(s): Jeremiah Land, Parent (of Davy, Reuben, and Swede), Maintenance Worker (janitor); Reuben Land, Narrator; Davy Land, Convict (makes a jailbreak)
Time period(s): 1960s (1962)
Locale(s): Roofing, Minnesota

Summary: Several mean-spirited schoolboys have it in for janitor Jeremiah Land. After kidnapping his daughter Swede, 9, the boys invade Jeremiah's house and are killed by his 17-year-old son Davy. Convicted of the killings, Davy breaks out of jail and Jeremiah sets out to find him. Jeremiah's other son, Reuben, narrates the story that also includes a climatic gunfight, a view of heaven, and a few miracles. This is the first novel for Enger, a public radio veteran.

Where it's reviewed:
Booklist, May 15, 2001, page 1707
Kirkus Reviews, June 1, 2001, page 757
Library Journal, June 15, 2001, page 102
Publishers Weekly, July 16, 2001, page 166

Other books you might like:
Helen Dewitt, *The Last Samurai*, 2000
Lee Durkee, *Rides of the Midway*, 2001
Walter Kirn, *Thumbsucker*, 1999
Sarah Stonich, *These Granite Islands*, 2001
Amy Wilentz, *Martyrs' Crossing*, 2001

1110

PER OLOV ENQUIST

The Royal Physician's Visit

(Woodstock, New York: Overlook, 2001)

Story type: Historical
Subject(s): Kings, Queens, Rulers, etc.; Mental Illness; Marriage
Major character(s): Christian VII, Historical Figure, Ruler (King of Denmark); Johann Friedrich Struensee, Doctor (of royal court), Historical Figure; Ove Hoegh-Guldberg, Courtier, Historical Figure
Time period(s): 1760s; 1770s (1766-1772)
Locale(s): Copenhagen, Denmark

Summary: In 18th century Denmark, the young King Christian VII becomes insane after being abused throughout his childhood by the aristocrats who actually rule the country. He is married to an English princess, Caroline Mathilde. A famous courtesan must be brought in to cure the king of his fear of sex. When Christian falls in love with the woman, Ove Hoegh-Guldberg, an ally of the king's mother, has the courtesan exiled. While Christian searches for the object of his obsession, he lets his physician, Johann Friedrich Struensee, run the kingdom. A student of the ideals of the Enlightenment, Struensee institutes over 600 reforms in the king's name. He also becomes the lover of Christian's queen. Angered by Struensee's attempts at reform, Hoegh-Guldberg uses the situation as an excuse to have Struensee arrested for treason and executed. Translated by Tiina Nunnally.

Where it's reviewed:
Booklist, November 1, 2001, page 459
Kirkus Reviews, October 15, 2001, page 1445
Publishers Weekly, October 22, 2001, page 48
Time, December 10, 2001, page 113

Other books by the same author:
The March of the Musicians, 1993
Captain Nemo's Library, 1992
The Legionnaires, 1973

Other books you might like:
Norah Lofts, *The Lost Queen*, 1969
Patrick McGrath, *Martha Peake*, 2000
Haruki Murakami, *Norwegian Wood*, 2000
Francine Rivers, *Unashamed*, 2000
William T. Vollmann, *The Royal Family*, 2000

1111

ANNE ENRIGHT

The Wig My Father Wore

(New York: Grove, 2001)

Story type: Romance
Subject(s): Women; Angels; Popular Culture
Major character(s): Grace, Narrator, Television; Stephen, Angel
Time period(s): 2000s (2001)
Locale(s): Dublin, Ireland

Summary: Grace, a single woman with her own apartment, has a job she doesn't like, boring parents, and annoying siblings. One day she meets an angel, Stephen, who moves in with her. While on earth Stephen committed suicide, and he has been sent back to help those in need. Despite her unsuccessful efforts to seduce him, Stephen paints her apartment and Grace's situation improves in this lighthearted story about modern life.

Where it's reviewed:
Booklist, August 2001, page 2085
Kirkus Reviews, August 1, 2001, page 1049
New York Times Book Review, November 18, 2001, page 18

Other books by the same author:
What Are You Like?, 2000

Other books you might like:
Maeve Binchy, *Circle of Friends*, 1991
Andrew M. Greeley, *Irish Gold*, 1994
John Irving, *The Fourth Hand*, 2001

Nuala O'Faolain, *My Dream of You*, 2001
Colm Toibin, *Blackwater Lightship*, 2000

1112

LAURA ESQUIVEL

Swift as Desire

(New York: Random House, 2001)

Story type: Romance; Multicultural
Subject(s): Marriage; Illness; Parent and Child
Major character(s): Lluvia, Care Giver (for her father), Narrator; Luz, Parent (of Lluvia), Wealthy; Jubilo, Empath, Spouse (of Luz)
Time period(s): 1920s
Locale(s): Mexico

Summary: Esquivel, the author of *Like Water for Chocolate*, has written a novel about love and communication, with a magic realism twist. Don Jubilo is on his deathbed, estranged from his wife and his daughter, Lluvia, wants to know the reason. Her father, now blind and mute, was once a telegraph operator, known for his ability to see inside a person's heart. Lluvia finds an old telegraph and her father is able to tell her his story.

Where it's reviewed:
Booklist, June 15, 2001, page 1798
Kirkus Reviews, July 1, 2001, page 886
Library Journal, July 2001, page 122
Publishers Weekly, July 16, 2001, page 165

Other books by the same author:
The Law of Love, 1996
Like Water for Chocolate, 1992

Other books you might like:
Isabel Allende, *Portrait in Sepia*, 2001
Elizabeth Benedict, *Almost*, 2001
Nadine Gordimer, *The Pickup*, 2001
Christine Lincoln, *Sap Rising*, 2001
Joyce Carol Oates, *Middle Age*, 2001

1113

JONATHAN FRANZEN

The Corrections

(New York: Farrar, Straus & Giroux, 2001)

Story type: Contemporary/Mainstream
Subject(s): Parent and Child; Marriage; Family Relations
Major character(s): Alfred Lambert, Railroad Worker (retired engineer); Enid Lambert, Parent, Spouse (of Alfred); Gary Lambert, Relative (Alfred's oldest son), Banker
Time period(s): 2000s (2001)
Locale(s): St. Jude, Midwest; New York, New York; Philadelphia, Pennsylvania

Summary: This novel explores changing family relations and the conflict that results from them. The story follows the Lambert family, as they gather for a last Christmas dinner. Conservative dad Alfred is dying from Parkinson's and wife Enid believes the get-together will make everyone happy. The Lamberts include the unhappily married Gary; Denise who is in a relationship with a man and a woman; and Chip, a failed writer, who is mixed up with an Internet scheme. Each employ or have tried various optimistic modern formulas for happiness without success.

Where it's reviewed:
Booklist, July 2001, page 1947
People Weekly, September 10, 2001, page 51
Publishers Weekly, July 16, 2001, page 164
Time, September 10, 2001, page 78

Other books by the same author:
The Twenty-Seventh City, 1998
Strong Motion, 1992

Other books you might like:
Bonnie Burnard, *A Good House*, 2000
Jane Hamilton, *Disobedience*, 2000
Heidi Julavits, *The Mineral Palace*, 2000
Richard Russo, *Empire Falls*, 2001
Amy Tan, *The Bonesetter's Daughter*, 2001

1114

MARK FRIEDMAN

Columbus Slaughters Braves

(Boston: Houghton Mifflin, 2001)

Story type: Americana
Subject(s): Sports/Baseball; Sibling Rivalry; Illness
Major character(s): Joe Columbus, Teacher (high school science), Relative (C.J.'s brother); Beth Columbus, Spouse (Joe's wife), Lawyer; C.J. Columbus, Sports Figure (baseball superstar), Relative (Joe's brother)
Time period(s): 2000s (2001)
Locale(s): Maryland

Summary: Friedman's first novel explores an older brother's feelings when his younger brother outshines him. Trapped in a lukewarm marriage, Joe Columbus wonders if he'll ever be an effective teacher. Just beneath the surface is Joe's real problem, his feelings toward his younger brother C.J., a Major League Baseball superstar. Before Joe can resolve his feelings, C.J. is stricken with a terminal illness. In trying to help his brother, Joe learns important things about himself.

Where it's reviewed:
Booklist, September 1, 2000, page 48
Library Journal, March 1, 2001, page 131
Publishers Weekly, February 12, 2001, page 183

Other books you might like:
Michael Griffith, *Spikes*, 2001
Mark Harris, *Bang the Drum Slowly*, 1956
Dan Jenkins, *The Money-Whipped Steer-Job Three-Jack Give-Up Artist*, 2001
Garrison Keillor, *Lake Wobegon Summer 1956*, 2001
W.P. Kinsella, *Magic Time*, 2001

1115

JOHN FULTON

Retribution

(New York: Picador USA, 2001)

Story type: Collection
Subject(s): Family Problems; Divorce; Alcoholism
Time period(s): 2000s (2001)

Summary: Consisting of ten short stories and a novella, Fulton's first collection is about family life's darker side, leavened with heavy doses of humor. For example, a woman with her sons becomes enraged when she sees a man who looks like her ex-husband driving another car. She rams the other car, robs the driver, and takes him hostage. Divorce, sex, and death drive the narratives, making life a challenge for the characters portrayed.

Where it's reviewed:
Booklist, May 15, 2001, page 1731
Kirkus Reviews, April 15, 2001, page 521
Publishers Weekly, July 2, 2001, page 53

Other books you might like:
Paul Bowles, *The Stories of Paul Bowles*, 2001
Jill McCorkle, *Creatures of Habit*, 2001
Alice Munro, *Selected Stories*, 1996
Elizabeth Spencer, *The Southern Woman*, 2001
Anne Tyler, *Back When We Were Grownups*, 2001

1116

NADINE GORDIMER

The Pickup

(New York: Farrar, Straus & Giroux, 2001)

Story type: Ethnic
Subject(s): Marriage; Social Conditions; Social Classes
Major character(s): Julie Summers, Wealthy, Spouse (of Ibrahim); Ibrahim "Abdu" ibn Musa, Mechanic (works in garage), Immigrant (illegal)
Time period(s): 2000s (2001)
Locale(s): South Africa; Middle East

Summary: 1994 Nobel Prize winner Gordimer's book is a story about love, illegal immigrants, and post-apartheid South Africa. Julie Summers, a rich suburban girl, is drifting until she has a love affair with an illegal Arab immigrant, Abdu. When the government deports him, she marries him and leaves with him. Her willingness to accept his harsh life baffles him as he looks for another country. Meanwhile, she adapts and develops an inner security.

Where it's reviewed:
Book, September 2001, page 79
Booklist, July 2001, page 1949
Library Journal, August 2001, page 161
Publishers Weekly, July 16, 2001, page 155

Other books by the same author:
The House Gun, 1998
Harold, Claudia, and Their Son Duncan, 1996
None to Accompany Me, 1994
Occasion for Loving, 1963
The Lying Days, 1953

Other books you might like:
T. Coraghessan Boyle, *The Tortilla Curtain*, 1995
Fadia Faqir, *Pillars of Salt*, 1997
Amitav Ghosh, *The Circle of Reason*, 1986
Francine Prose, *Primitive People*, 1992
Ahdaf Soueif, *The Map of Love*, 2000

1117

ANDREW M. GREELEY

September Song

(New York: Forge, 2001)

Story type: Historical; Saga
Series: O'Malley Family. Book 4
Subject(s): Irish Americans; Family Life; Politics
Major character(s): Chuck O'Malley, Diplomat (ambassador to Germany), Spouse (of Rosemarie); Rosemarie O'Malley, Parent (of five children), Narrator
Time period(s): 1960s (1963-1969)
Locale(s): Oak Park, Illinois; Selma, Alabama; Rome, Italy

Summary: Greeley's fourth book about the O'Malley family of Oak Park, Illinois, follows them through the 1960s. Rosemarie narrates the story, picking up shortly after President Kennedy's assassination. Back in Oak Park after serving as an ambassador, Chuck along with his wife, Rosemarie, tend to their five children. The couple also participate in the decade's big events. They march with Dr. Martin Luther King, Jr., campaign with Bobby Kennedy, and participate in the 1968 Democratic Convention. Despite the amount of ground covered, the story is interesting.

Where it's reviewed:
Booklist, August 2001, page 2086
Kirkus Reviews, July 1, 2001, page 888
Publishers Weekly, July 30, 2001, page 58

Other books by the same author:
The Bishop and the Beggar Girl of St. Germain, 2001
A Christmas Wedding, 2000
Younger than Springtime, 1999
A Midwinter's Tale, 1998

Other books you might like:
James Farrell, *Studs Lonigan*, 1935
Jan Karon, *The Mitford Years Series*, 1996
Elia Kazan, *America, America*, 1962
Alice McDermott, *Charming Billy*, 1998
Mario Puzo, *The Godfather*, 1969

1118

NORMAN GREEN

Shooting Dr. Jack

(New York: HarperCollins, 2001)

Story type: Psychological Suspense; Contemporary Realism
Subject(s): Crime and Criminals; Drugs; Murder

Major character(s): Tommy Rosselli, Criminal (operates a chop-shop); Stoney, Criminal (Tommy's partner), Alcoholic; Eddie Tuco, Young Man (works for Tommy)
Time period(s): 2000s (2001)
Locale(s): New York, New York

Summary: The trials and tribulations of a small-time chop-shop and salvage-yard owner, Fat Tommy Rosselli, a.k.a. Tommy Bagadonuts, is detailed in this novel. His drunken partner, Stoney, is losing his grip, while his up-and-coming worker, Tuco, needs a place to live. Two bodies are found in the trunk of a car parked on his lot. Then Tommy gets shot and a couple of hit men from South America are after him. A pimp-drug dealer called ''Dr. Jack'' gets involved, too. Not strictly a mystery, this debut novel resonates with gritty urban details and an oddly compelling story of growth and redemption.

Where it's reviewed:
Kirkus Reviews, July 15, 2001, page 965
New York Times Book Review, October 21, 2001, page 28
Publishers Weekly, August 6, 2001, page 59

Other books you might like:
George V. Higgins, *At End of Day*, 2000
Dennis Lehane, *Mystic River*, 2001
Elmore Leonard, *Be Cool*, 1999
Walter Mosley, *Fearless Jones*, 2001
Mario Puzo, *Omerta*, 2000

1119

ANTHONY GROOMS

Bombingham

(New York: Free Press, 2001)

Story type: Coming-of-Age
Subject(s): Vietnam War; Civil Rights Movement; African Americans
Major character(s): Walter Burke, Military Personnel (African American); Josie Burke, Relative (Walter's sister); Clara Burke, Parent (of Walter)
Time period(s): 1960s; 1970s (1961-1975)
Locale(s): Birmingham, Alabama

Summary: While serving in Vietnam, African American Walter Burke recalls his life in Birmingham, Alabama, nicknamed Bombingham for violent racist tactics used against the Civil Rights Movement. Walter recounts his mother's illness and death from cancer, his aunt helping with his mother's care, his father's spiritual demise, his sister's arrest, and his own beating by the police. Events from the real world, such as protests, marches, boycotts, observations, and reactions, add an additional dimension.

Where it's reviewed:
Booklist, August 2001, page 2086
Chicago Tribune Books, October 7, 2001, page 4
Kirkus Reviews, July 1, 2001, page 889
Library Journal, August 2001, page 161
Publishers Weekly, September 24, 2001, page 66

Other books by the same author:
Trouble No More, 1995

Other books you might like:
Ann Fairbairn, *Five Smooth Stones*, 1966
Charles Richard Johnson, *Dreamer*, 1998
Bart Schneider, *Secret Love*, 2001
Susan Straight, *I Been in Sorrow's Kitchen and Licked out All the Pots*, 1992
Tom Wolfe, *A Man in Full*, 1998

1120

ALLAN GURGANUS

The Practical Heart

(New York: Knopf, 2001)

Story type: Collection
Subject(s): Social Conditions

Summary: In these four novellas, Gurganus explores social pretense. In *The Practical Heart*, we learn how a famous painter did a portrait of Muriel, a music teacher. In *Saint Monster*, a son writes a memoir about his father passing as white. In *Preservation News*, Mary Ellen writes the obituary for a civic-minded gay man. *He's One, Too* is the story of Dan's downfall after he's caught molesting a teenage boy.

Where it's reviewed:
Kirkus Reviews, August 1, 2001, page 1051
New York Times Book Review, October 7, 2001, page 7
Publishers Weekly, September 3, 2001, page 54

Other books by the same author:
Plays Well with Others, 1997
Blessed Assurance, 1990
White People, 1990
Oldest Living Conferate Widow Tells All, 1989

Other books you might like:
A.S. Byatt, *The Matisse Stories*, 1993
Maureen Howard, *Big as Life*, 2001
Lidia Jorge, *The Painter of Birds*, 2001
David Leavitt, *The Marble Quilt*, 2001
Ana Menendez, *In Cuba I Was a German Shepherd*, 2001

1121

BARRY HANNAH

Yonder Stands Your Orphan

(New York: Atlantic Monthly, 2001)

Story type: Gothic; Psychological
Subject(s): Murder; Sheriffs; Small Town Life
Major character(s): Man Mortimer, Criminal (pimp, thief, and murderer); Byron Egan, Religious (former biker); Melanie Wooten, Aged Person (having an affair)
Time period(s): 2000s (2001)
Locale(s): Vicksburg, Mississippi

Summary: Hannah's latest novel combines colorful characters with imaginative descriptions. The story loosely follows Man Mortimer, a pimp and a thief, who settles disputes both real and imagined with his knife. Other characters include Facetto, a young sheriff, who has his hands full with his lover Melanie, a 72-year-old woman; Max Raymond, a former doctor, who plays saxophone in a casino band; Mimi, Max's Cuban born wife, who likes singing in the nude; and Byron, a former drug addict, now a preacher. The plot revolves around the increasingly malevolent consequences of Mortimer's attempts to retrieve evidence implicating him in an old crime.

Where it's reviewed:
Booklist, June 1, 2001, page 1841
Library Journal, June 1, 2001, page 216
New York Times Book Review, August 5, 2001, page 12
Publishers Weekly, June 25, 2001, page 51

Other books by the same author:
High Lonesome, 1996
Bats out of Hell, 1993
Never Die, 1991
Boomerang, 1989
Hey Jack!, 1987

Other books you might like:
Frederick Barthelme, *The Law of Averages*, 2000
Sylvia Brownrigg, *Pages for You*, 2001
Mitch Cullin, *Tideland*, 2000
William Gay, *Provinces of Night*, 2000
Melanie Rae Thon, *First, Body*, 1997

1122

E. LYNN HARRIS

Any Way the Wind Blows

(New York: Doubleday, 2001)

Story type: Psychological Suspense; Gay/Lesbian Fiction
Subject(s): African Americans; Revenge; Secrets
Major character(s): John Basil Henderson, Agent (professional sports), Lover (Yancey's ex); Yancey Braxton, Singer (popular music); Bartholomew ''Bart'' Dunbar, Model, Homosexual (attracted to John)
Time period(s): 2000s (2001)
Locale(s): New York, New York

Summary: In Harris' previous novel *Not a Day Goes By*, Yancey moved to Los Angeles, when John, a pro sports agent with a sexual appetite for men, left her at the altar. The story picks up when Yancey returns to New York with revenge on her mind. She also has a hit song, which complains about bisexual lovers. As her song climbs the charts, critics ask if it is based on a life experience.

Where it's reviewed:
Booklist, July 2001, page 1950
People Weekly, July 30, 2001, page 41
Publishers Weekly, July 25, 2001, page 49

Other books by the same author:
Not a Day Goes By, 2000
Abide with Me, 1999
If This World Were Mine, 1997
And This Too Shall Pass, 1996
Just as I Am, 1994

Other books you might like:
Stanley Crouch, *Don't the Moon Look Lonesome*, 2000
Jack Fuller, *The Best of Jackson Payne*, 2000
Terry McMillan, *A Day Late and a Dollar Short*, 2001
Omar Tyree, *Just Say No!*, 2001
Alice Walker, *The Way Forward Is with a Broken Heart*, 2000

1123

MO HAYDER

The Treatment

(New York: Doubleday, 2001)

Story type: Contemporary Realism
Subject(s): Sexual Abuse; Police Procedural; Suspense
Major character(s): Jack Caffery, Detective—Police; Rebecca, Crime Victim (raped), Girlfriend (of Jack); Ivan Penderecki, Crime Suspect (in a murder)
Time period(s): 2000s (2001)
Locale(s): London, England

Summary: In a semi-sequel to *Birdman*, Hayder deals with child molestation and murder. When a couple turns up handcuffed and beaten bloody, Det. Jack Caffery is assigned to look for their missing eight-year-old son. Jack enters a world of predators, child porn, and murder. He notices a pattern that may solve the murder of his younger brother. Meanwhile, Jack also needs to protect his girlfriend who has been brutally raped.

Where it's reviewed:
Booklist, October 15, 2001, page 356
Kirkus Reviews, November 1, 2001, page 1506
Library Journal, November 1, 2001, page 132
Publishers Weekly, October 29, 2001, page 34

Other books by the same author:
Birdman, 1999

Other books you might like:
Nelson DeMille, *Plum Island*, 1997
John Grisham, *The Client*, 1993
George V. Higgins, *At End of Day*, 2000
Dennis Lehane, *Mystic River*, 2001
Elmore Leonard, *City Primeval*, 1980

1124

URSULA HEGI

Hotel of the Saints

(New York: Simon & Schuster, 2001)

Story type: Collection
Subject(s): Modern Life; Love; Resourcefulness
Time period(s): 2000s (2001)

Summary: The characters in this collection of 11 short stories are vivid and each tale has a resolution. A seminarian regains his faith after helping decorate rooms in a hotel near a shrine. An older woman teaches a teenage girl the difference between romance and lust. An afflicted woman plans suicide. A disabled child heals a family rift. A juggler reconciles a woman with her daughter. A fisherman realizes his wife has left.

Where it's reviewed:
Booklist, September 1, 2001, page 50
Kirkus Reviews, August 15, 2001, page 1150
Library Journal, September 1, 2001, page 237

New York Times Book Review, November 18, 2001, page 68

Other books by the same author:
The Vision of Emma Blau, 2000
Intrusions, 1995
Salt Dancers, 1995
Stones from the River, 1994
Floating in My Mother's Palm, 1990

Other books you might like:
Isabel Allende, *Portrait in Sepia*, 2001
Stephen King, *Blood and Smoke*, 2000
Bobbie Ann Mason, *Zigzagging Down a Wild Trail*, 2001
Alice Munro, *Hateship, Friendship, Courtship, Loveship, Marriage*, 2001
Bernhard Schlink, *Flights of Love*, 2001

1125

JANE HELLER

Female Intelligence

(New York: St. Martin's Press, 2001)

Story type: Romance; Humor
Subject(s): Interpersonal Relations; Communication; Popular Culture
Major character(s): Lynn Wyman, Linguist; Kip, Spouse (of Lynn); Brandon Brock, Businessman (CEO large corporation)
Time period(s): 2000s (2001)
Locale(s): United States

Summary: The author offers a whimsical examination of contemporary gender issues. Lynn Wyman, a media superstar, trains men on how to communicate with women. When she catches her husband cheating, she kicks him out. After a tabloid prints a story about her husband's affair, her career is threatened and in order to recover her status, she sets out to convert Brandon Brock from ''toughest boss'' to ''most sensitive boss.'' In the process, she falls for him.

Where it's reviewed:
Booklist, February 1, 2001, page 1039
Kirkus Reviews, February 1, 2001, page 129
Library Journal, January 1, 2001, page 154
Publishers Weekly, February 26, 2001, page 55

Other books by the same author:
Name Dropping, 2000
Sis Boom Bah, 1999
Crystal Clear, 1998
Princess Charming, 1997
Infernal Affairs, 1996

Other books you might like:
Melissa Bank, *The Girls' Guide to Hunting and Fishing*, 1999
Valerie Block, *Was It Something I Said*, 1998
Candace Bushnell, *Four Blondes*, 2000
Helen Fielding, *Bridget Jones's Diary*, 1996
Isabel Wolff, *The Trials of Tiffany Trott*, 1999

1126

NICK HORNBY

How to Be Good

(New York: Putnam, 2001)

Story type: Humor; Contemporary/Mainstream
Subject(s): Marriage; Doctors; Spirituality
Major character(s): Katie Carr, Doctor, Spouse (David's wife); David Carr, Writer (newspaper columnist), Activist (for the underprivileged); GoodNews, Radio Personality (faith-healer), Activist (for homeless)
Time period(s): 2000s (2001)
Locale(s): London, England

Summary: Katie Carr, a married doctor with two children, is having an affair. She rationalizes her behavior because her husband, David, has made a profession out of being a grouch. One night she confesses her infidelity and suggests divorce but her husband has a different idea. He turns over a new leaf and becomes the polar opposite, giving away money and embracing the homeless. Daughter Molly follows her father's lead leaving Katie and her son, Tom, appalled.

Where it's reviewed:
Kirkus Reviews, June 1, 2001, page 760
Library Journal, June 15, 2001, page 102
New York Times Book Review, July 12, 2001, page 9
Publishers Weekly, June 25, 2001, page 45

Other books by the same author:
About a Boy, 1995
High Fidelity, 1995
Contemporary American Fiction, 1992

Other books you might like:
Douglas Coupland, *All Families Are Psychotic*, 2001
Olivia Goldsmith, *Bad Boy*, 2001
Walter Mosley, *Blue Light*, 1998
Irvine Welsh, *Glue*, 2001
Oscar Wilde, *The Picture of Dorian Gray*, 1891

1127

STEPHEN HUNTER

Pale Horse Coming

(New York: Simon & Schuster, 2001)

Story type: Historical
Subject(s): African Americans; Prisoners and Prisons; Violence
Major character(s): Earl Swagger, Police Officer, Hero (Congressional Medal of Honor); Sam Vincent, Lawyer
Time period(s): 1950s (1951)
Locale(s): Mississippi (Thebes Prison Farm)

Summary: Earl Swagger's friend Sam Vincent disappears on a secret mission into the Mississippi swamp, and Earl sets out to find him. When Earl gets captured springing Sam, a sadistic sheriff, who operates a secret prison for African Americans, tortures Earl mercilessly. After he escapes, he recruits a team of explosive experts to return to the prison and settle the score.

Where it's reviewed:
Booklist, October 15, 2001, page 385
Chicago Tribune Books, November 18, 2001, page 7
Kirkus Reviews, September 1, 2001, page 1235
Publishers Weekly, September 24, 2001, page 67

Other books by the same author:
Hot Springs, 2000
Time to Hunt, 1998
The Master Sniper, 1996
Dirty White Boys, 1994
Point of Impact, 1993

Other books you might like:
David Baldacci, *The Last Man Standing*, 2001
James Lee Burke, *The Dave Robicheaux Series*, 1987-
Robert Ludlum, *The Sigma Protocol*, 2001
Walter Mosley, *Fearless Jones*, 2001
James Patterson, *Roses Are Red*, 2000

1128

ZORA NEALE HURSTON

Every Tongue Got to Confess

(New York: HarperCollins, 2001)

Story type: Americana; Ethnic
Subject(s): Folk Tales; African Americans; Humor

Summary: During the 1920s, Zora Neale Hurston, an African American, crisscrossed the south, collecting Negro folk tales. Hurston planned to publish them in seven volumes but only completed two volumes before she died in 1960. Here for the first time are many of the stories Hurston painstakingly collected, divided into 17 different categories. Subjects covered include the battle between the sexes, gender issues, race, religion, creation, God, and the devil. Carla Kaplan edited this volume and John Edgar Wideman wrote the introduction.

Where it's reviewed:
Black Issues Book Review, November-December 2001, page 59
Booklist, October 1, 2001, page 267
Kirkus Reviews, October 1, 2001, page 1383
Publishers Weekly, December 17, 2001, page 65

Other books by the same author:
The Complete Stories, 1998
Tell My Horse, 1937
Their Eyes Were Watching God, 1937
Mules and Men, 1935
Jonah's Gourd Vine, 1934

Other books you might like:
Christina Adam, *Any Small Thing Can Save You*, 2001
Deborah Boehm, *Ghost of a Smile*, 2001
Joel Chandler, *The Favorite Uncle Remus*, 1948
Chitra Banerjee Divakaruni, *The Unknown Errors of Our Lives*, 2001
Colson Whitehead, *John Henry Days*, 2001

1129

ABDULLAH HUSSEIN

Emigre Journeys

(London: Serpent's Tail, 2000)

Story type: Multicultural
Subject(s): Fathers and Daughters; Emigration and Immigration; Cultural Conflict
Major character(s): Amir, Immigrant (from India), Postal Worker; Parvin, Teenager (Amir's daughter)
Time period(s): 2000s (2000)
Locale(s): Birmingham, England

Summary: *Emigre Journeys* is the first book by Hussein to be written in English and the author explores the immigrant experience. As a young man, Amir arrives in England illegally and lives at first in a house with 17 other men from Pakistan. Despite difficulties, Amir is able to make a life for himself and raise a family. He becomes a British citizen, gets a job, and buys a house. In the process, he is alienated from his wife, son, and teenage daughter, Parvin, who refuses to consider an arranged marriage.

Where it's reviewed:
Kirkus Reviews, July 1, 2001, page 890
Publishers Weekly, July 23, 2001, page 48

Other books by the same author:
Stories of Exile and Alienation, 1999
The Weary Generations, 1999

Other books you might like:
Ethan C. Canin, *Carry Me Across the Water*, 2001
Kurban Said, *The Girl from the Golden Horn*, 2001
Akhil Sharma, *An Obedient Father*, 2000
Ahdaf Soueif, *The Map of Love*, 2000
Amy Tan, *The Bonesetter's Daughter*, 2001

1130

JOHN IRVING

The Fourth Hand

(New York: Random House, 2001)

Story type: Psychological
Subject(s): Television; Transplants; Relationships
Major character(s): Patrick Warrington, Journalist (television); Doris Clausen, Benefactor (of Patrick); Nicholas Zajac, Doctor (hand surgeon)
Time period(s): 2000s (2001)
Locale(s): New York, New York; Boston, Massachusetts; Green Bay, Wisconsin

Summary: John Irving tells an offbeat love story here. Patrick Warrington, a journalist, works for a sleazy all-news television network. While covering a story, a lion eats his hand. A viewer, Doris Clausen, offers Patrick a hand for a transplant operation but she wants visiting privileges. Her husband then commits suicide to provide the hand. Doris asks Patrick to father her baby and he is willing but complications set in when his boss, Mary, also wants a child with him.

Where it's reviewed:
Booklist, May 1, 2001, page 1594
Kirkus Reviews, May 1, 2001, page 609
New York Times Book Review, July 8, 2001, page 12
Newsweek, July 16, 2001, page 61
Publishers Weekly, June 25, 2001, page 47

Other books by the same author:
A Widow for One Year, 1998
Trying to Save Piggy Sneed, 1996
The Cider House Rules, 1985
The Hotel New Hampshire, 1981
The World According to Garp, 1978

Other books you might like:
Dan Jenkins, *Fast Copy*, 1988
Richard Russo, *Empire Falls*, 2001
Sidney Sheldon, *The Best Laid Plans*, 1997
Anne Tyler, *Back When We Were Grownups*, 2001
Gore Vidal, *The Golden Age*, 2000

1131

SUSAN ISAACS

Long Time No See

(New York: HarperCollins, 2001)

Story type: Contemporary; Modern
Subject(s): Organized Crime; Missing Persons; Mystery and Detective Stories
Major character(s): Judith Singer, Detective—Private (hired to clear murder suspect), Professor (of history); Courtney Logan, Crime Victim (murdered), Parent (perfect soccer mom); Greg Logan, Spouse (of Courtney), Crime Suspect (in wife's murder)
Time period(s): 2000s (2001)
Locale(s): Nassau County, New York

Summary: This is a sequel to Isaacs' novel *Compromising Positions*. Some 20 years have transpired in the life Judith Singer. She has raised two children, lost her husband, and earned a doctorate in history. When neighbor Courtney Logan turns up dead, her husband Greg becomes the prime suspect. Greg's father, notorious gangster Phil Lowenstein, hires Judith to clear his son. During her investigation, Judith connects with her former lover, Nelson Sharp, who is now retired from police work.

Where it's reviewed:
Booklist, July 2001, page 1950
Kirkus Reviews, July 1, 2001, page 890
Library Journal, August 2001, page 161
New York Times Book Review, September 30, 2001, page 15
Publishers Weekly, July 23, 2001, page 47

Other books by the same author:
Red, White and Blue, 1998
Lily White, 1996
After All These Years, 1993
Shining Through, 1988
Compromising Positions, 1978

Other books you might like:
Nelson DeMille, *The General's Daughter*, 1992
Kazuo Ishiguro, *When We Were Orphans*, 2000
Walter Mosley, *Devil in a Blue Dress*, 1990
Joyce Carol Oates, *What I Lived For*, 1994
Sara Paretsky, *Bitter Medicine*, 1987

1132

DAN JENKINS

The Money-Whipped Steer-Job Three-Jack Give-Up Artist

(New York: Doubleday, 2001)

Story type: Humor
Subject(s): Sports/Golf; Relationships
Major character(s): Bobby Joe "Spin" Grooves, Sports Figure (golfer); Cheryl Haney, Real Estate Agent, Girlfriend (of Bobby Joe); Knut Thorssun, Sports Figure (golfer)
Time period(s): 2000s (2001)
Locale(s): Fort Worth, Texas

Summary: Jenkins offers a novel featuring golf tradition and golf history, sprinkled with humorous one-liners. Bobby Joe "Spin" Grooves, a veteran pro without a major tour win to his credit, is struggling to make the Ryder Cup team. Despite distractions that include an appetite for scotch and bar room philosophizing, complaints from his two ex-wives, and an unhappy girlfriend, Bobby Joe's biggest problem is Knut Thorssun, a wannabe superstar. Everything gets settled with a head-to-head playoff.

Where it's reviewed:
Booklist, May 15, 2001, page 1707
Kirkus Reviews, May 15, 2001, page 687
New York Times Book Review, August 12, 2001, page 5
Publishers Weekly, July 9, 2001, page 43

Other books by the same author:
Rude Behavior, 1998
Bubba Talks of Life, Love, Sex, Whiskey, Politics, Foreigners, Teenagers, Movies, Food, Football, and Other Matters, 1993
You Gotta Play Hurt, 1991
Dead Solid Perfect, 1974
Semi-Tough, 1972

Other books you might like:
Peter Gent, *North Dallas Forty*, 1973
Michael Griffith, *Spikes*, 2001
Mark Harris, *Bang the Drum Slowly*, 1956
Steven Pressfield, *The Legend of Bagger Vance*, 1995
Paul D. Staudohar, *Golf's Best Short Stories*, 1997 editor

1133

PATRICIA JONES

Red on Rose

(New York: Avon, 2001)

Story type: Psychological; Multicultural
Subject(s): African Americans; Marriage; Racism
Major character(s): Lila Calloway, Spouse (of Jack); Jack Calloway, Doctor (cardiologist)
Time period(s): 2000s (2001)

Locale(s): Baltimore, Maryland

Summary: Jones' second novel takes no prisoners in a story driven by this question: Should a black doctor help a white man if the man insults and humiliates the doctor publicly? Lila Calloway, who grew up affluent and insulated, answers yes. When her husband Jack, a heart surgeon who grew up on city streets, faces the question, he walks away and the man dies. Lila is horrified and their friends choose sides.

Where it's reviewed:
Booklist, October 15, 2001, page 382
Kirkus Reviews, October 1, 2001, page 1384
Library Journal, November 1, 2001, page 132
Publishers Weekly, October 15, 2001, page 46

Other books by the same author:
Passing, 1999

Other books you might like:
Benjamin Anastas, *The Faithful Narrative of a Pastor's Disappearance*, 2001
Rainelle Burton, *The Root Worker*, 2001
Louise Erdrich, *The Last Report on the Miracles at Little No Horse*, 2001
Leon Forrest, *Meteor in the Madhouse*, 2001
Amelie Nothomb, *Fear and Trembling*, 2001

1134

WARD S. JUST

Lowell Limpett: And Two Stories

(New York: Public Affairs, 2001)

Story type: Collection
Subject(s): Journalism; Politics; Aging
Time period(s): 2000s (2001)

Summary: Three in-depth character studies are offered in this collection. The first is a monologue (one-act play) of an aging reporter. He's a hard-bitten, scotch drinking man being pressured from above and below. His poignant reminiscence hits several universal chords. The second story deals with a young lawyer who becomes disillusioned with the power politics of Washington, D.C. The third deals with the personal politics of a high-powered marriage.

Where it's reviewed:
Booklist, September 15, 2001, page 180
Chicago Tribune Books, October 21, 2001, page 1
Kirkus Reviews, July 15, 2001, page 965
Publishers Weekly, August 27, 2001, page 53

Other books by the same author:
A Dangerous Friend, 1999
Echo House, 1997
Ambition and Love, 1994
The Translator, 1991
Twenty-One, 1990

Other books you might like:
Madison Smartt Bell, *Master of the Crossroads*, 2000
Joan Didion, *The Last Thing He Wanted*, 1996
George V. Higgins, *The Friends of Eddie Coyle*, 1972
Barbara Kingsolver, *The Poisonwood Bible*, 1998
Richard North Patterson, *Protect and Defend*, 2000

1135

JOSEPH KANON

The Good German

(New York: Henry Holt, 2001)

Story type: Historical
Subject(s): Journalism; Mystery; Love
Major character(s): Jake Geismar, Journalist (*Collier* magazine); Lena, Lover (of Jake); Emil, Spouse (of Lena), Scientist (rocket expert)
Time period(s): 20th century (1918-1945)
Locale(s): Berlin, Germany

Summary: This novel deals with the scramble for German scientists after World War II. Jake, an American journalist, is in Berlin on assignment. He is also looking for his lover Lena, whom he lost track of during the war. An American soldier is murdered, but when officials are lukewarm about finding the killer Jake begins to delve more deeply into the story. When the smoke settles, Lena's husband Emil, who worked for the Nazis, is at the center of the whole situation.

Where it's reviewed:
Booklist, July 2001, page 1950
Kirkus Reviews, July 15, 2001, page 996
Library Journal, September 1, 2001, page 233
New York Times Book Review, November 11, 2001, page 30
Publishers Weekly, July 16, 2001, page 164

Other books by the same author:
The Prodigal Spy, 1998
Los Alamos, 1997

Other books you might like:
Barbara Delinsky, *Three Wishes*, 1997
Ford Madox Ford, *The Good Soldier*, 1915
Andrew M. Greeley, *A Midwinter's Tale*, 1998
John Le Carre, *Small Town in Germany*, 1968
Simone Zelitch, *Louisa*, 2000

1136

GARRISON KEILLOR

Lake Wobegon Summer 1956

(New York: Viking, 2001)

Story type: Humor; Coming-of-Age
Subject(s): Adolescence; Small Town Life; Journalism
Major character(s): Roger Guppy, Boyfriend (of Kate), Sports Figure (baseball pitcher); Gary, Teenager; Kate, Cousin (of Gary)
Time period(s): 1950s (1956)
Locale(s): Lake Wobegon, Minnesota

Summary: Keillor returns to small town Minnesota to follow Gary, 14, a slightly nerdy teen with aspirations. Except for his older cousin, Kate, whom he lusts after, Gary is bored with his zealously religious family. Kate, however, is in love with Roger, the star pitcher of the local baseball team. When the romance turns into a family scandal, Gary gets his heart broken, at least for the summer.

Where it's reviewed:
Book, September 2001, page 80
Booklist, July 2001, page 1951
Publishers Weekly, July 23, 2001, page 50

Other books by the same author:
Me, 1999
Wobegon Boy, 1997
The Book of Guys, 1993
WLT: A Radio Romance, 1991
Lake Wobegon Days, 1985

Other books you might like:
Fannie Flagg, *Fried Green Tomatoes at the Whistle Stop Cafe*, 1987
John Irving, *A Prayer for Owen Meany*, 1989
Susan Isaacs, *Long Time No See*, 2001
Richard Russo, *Empire Falls*, 2001
Anne Tyler, *Back When We Were Grownups*, 2001

1137

ELMER KELTON

The Way of the Coyote

(New York: Forge, 2001)

Story type: Americana
Subject(s): Indian Captives; Frontier and Pioneer Life
Major character(s): Rusty Shannon, Lawman (Texas Ranger); Andy Pickard, Captive (rescued by Rusty); Clyde Oldham, Villain (after Rusty's ranch)
Time period(s): 1860s; 1870s (1865-1875)
Locale(s): Texas

Summary: This is Kelton's third book about the Texas Rangers. Just after the Civil War, carpetbag government, outlaws, hard feelings about the war, and the Comanches are causing social upheaval on the plains. Rusty Shannon wants to give up rangering and retire to his ranch but that's not possible. His friend, Andy, is kidnapped by the Comanche and while Rusty attempts to rescue him, Clyde Oldham, with help from a corrupt judge, tries to legally steal Rusty's ranch.

Where it's reviewed:
Booklist, November 15, 2001, page 549
Kirkus Reviews, September 15, 2001, page 1323
Publishers Weekly, October 29, 2001, page 33

Other books by the same author:
Badger Boy, 2000
Captain's Rangers, 1999
The Day the Cowboys Quit, 1999
The Buckskin Line, 1999
The Manhunters, 1994

Other books you might like:
Mike Blakely, *Comanche Dawn*, 1998
Max Brand, *The Legend of Thunder Moon*, 1996
Jim Harrison, *Dalva*, 1988
Larry McMurtry, *Comanche Moon*, 1997
James A. Michener, *Centennial*, 1974

1138

A.L. KENNEDY

Everything You Need

(New York: Knopf, 2001)

Story type: Literary; Psychological
Subject(s): Fathers and Daughters; Authors and Writers; Writing
Major character(s): Nathan Staples, Writer, Parent (Mary's father); Mary Lamb, Writer (aspiring)
Time period(s): 2000s (2001)
Locale(s): Foal Island, Wales

Summary: Kennedy analyzes one approach to the creative process of writing in this novel. The focus is on an unconventional writers colony off the coast of Wales. Mary Lamb, an aspiring writer, wins a fellowship to study on the island with Nathan Staples, author of commercially successful thrillers. The story revolves around Nathan's secret—he is the father who abandoned Mary when she was only four years old. Nathan's companions provide comic relief as the story unfolds.

Where it's reviewed:
Booklist, June 15, 2001, page 1814
Chicago Tribune Books, September 9, 2001, page 1
Kirkus Reviews, May 15, 2001, page 689
Library Journal, July 2001, page 123
Publishers Weekly, June 11, 2001, page 56

Other books by the same author:
So I Am Glad, 2000
Original Bliss, 1999
Now That You're Back, 1995

Other books you might like:
Margaret Atwood, *Surfacing*, 1972
Saul Bellow, *Mr. Sammler's Planet*, 1970
J.M. Coetzee, *Disgrace*, 1999
Joan Didion, *The Last Thing He Wanted*, 1996
William Trevor, *Death in Summer*, 1998

1139

KATE KENNEDY

End over End

(New York: Soho, 2001)

Story type: Contemporary Realism
Subject(s): Trials; Secrets
Major character(s): Ivory Towle, Teenager, Crime Victim (murdered); Tommy Slack, Teenager, Crime Suspect (in Ivory's murder); Sally Gregg, Police Officer
Time period(s): 2000s (2001)
Locale(s): Maine

Summary: Kate Kennedy's first novel offers readers a character-driven murder story that goes against genre conventions by not offering a solution. A suspect is tried for the murder of Ivory, a headstrong teen, but the verdict isn't satisfactory. Instead, the story focuses on what happens when loving parents, a well-meaning teacher, and a compassionate cop come in contact with raging teenage hormones, enhanced with drugs, sex, and alcohol. Not a pretty story, but well told.

Where it's reviewed:
Booklist, April 1, 2001, page 1449
Kirkus Reviews, February 15, 2001, page 205
Library Journal, April 15, 2001, page 132
New York Times Book Review, August 12, 2001, page 22
Publishers Weekly, March 5, 2001, page 62

Other books you might like:
Margaret Atwood, *Alias Grace*, 1996
John Grisham, *A Time to Kill*, 1989
Alice Hoffman, *Blue Diary*, 2001
Robert Traver, *Anatomy of a Murder*, 1958
Scott Turow, *Presumed Innocent*, 1987

1140

STEPHEN KING
PETER STRAUB, Co-Author

Black House

(New York: Random House, 2001)

Story type: Gothic; Contemporary/Fantasy
Subject(s): Serial Killers; Retirement; Mystery
Major character(s): Jack Sawyer, Detective—Homicide (retired); Henry Leyden, Friend (of Jack), Radio Personality (has four identities); Tyler Marshall, Crime Victim (kidnapped), Child
Time period(s): Indeterminate
Locale(s): French Landing, Wisconsin; Los Angeles, California

Summary: This novel is a sequel to *The Talisman*, also co-authored by King and Straub. Set in Wisconsin, the story's plot line follows two parallel universes and revolves around a fisherman who kills children. To solve the crime and catch the bad guy, Detective Jack Sawyer, formerly of the Los Angeles Police Department, must gain access to the darker universe and save a child held prisoner. He gains access through a door in the Black House.

Where it's reviewed:
Book, September 2001, page 80
Kirkus Reviews, July 15, 2001, page 966
Publishers Weekly, September 24, 2001, page 20

Other books by the same author:
The Talisman, 1984

Other books you might like:
Clive Barker, *Coldheart Canyon*, 2001
Larry Brown, *Joe*, 1991
Molly Gloss, *Wild Life*, 2000
Elizabeth Haydon, *Prophecy*, 2000

1141

WALTER KIRN

Up in the Air

(New York: Doubleday, 2001)

Story type: Psychological; Contemporary/Mainstream
Subject(s): Air Travel; Business; Careers
Major character(s): Ryan Bingham, Counselor (career transition), Writer (on business management); Sanford Pinter, Consultant (management guru)
Time period(s): 2000s (2001)
Locale(s): Denver, Colorado; California; Omaha, Nebraska

Summary: Kirn, fiction editor for *GQ*, combines air travel and business consulting in his third novel. Ryan Bingham, a career transition counselor, flies from coast to coast and places in between, attending management conferences. His goals include obtaining one million miles in a frequent flyer program, to leave his current employer, to publish a book, to launch a new product line, and to attend his sister's wedding. He encounters turbulence but gets the miles.

Where it's reviewed:
Kirkus Reviews, April 15, 2001, page 525
Library Journal, July 2001, page 124
New York Times Book Review, July 8, 2001, page 8
Publishers Weekly, July 2, 2001, page 52

Other books by the same author:
Thumbsucker, 1999
She Needed Me, 1992
My Hard Bargain, 1990

Other books you might like:
David Baldacci, *Total Control*, 1997
Saul Bellow, *More Die of Heartbreak*, 1987
Ernest Kellogg Gann, *The High and the Mighty*, 1953
William Wharton, *Birdy*, 1978
Sloan Wilson, *The Man in the Gray Flannel Suit*, 1955

1142

RICHARD KLEIN

Jewelry Talks

(New York: Pantheon, 2001)

Story type: Adult
Subject(s): Popular Culture; Gender Roles; Satire
Major character(s): Abby Zinzo, Writer (of an anti-memoir); Amad, Lover (of Abby); Zanzibar, Relative (Abby's sister)

Summary: Klein's first novel is written as a letter and treatise without dialog. The story, part novel, part thesis on jewelry, deconstructs sexual roles using femininity and its historical connection to jewelry. Abby Zinzo, a bisexual transvestite, writes a letter explaining his life and what jewelry has meant to him. Influenced by the French philosopher Diderot, who compared female genitalia with jewelry, he reflects on the history of various brooches, rings, and necklaces worn by famous people throughout the years. He also describes his affair with Amad, a person of uncertain gender.

Where it's reviewed:
Booklist, June 1, 2001, page 1815
New York Times Book Review, July 22, 2001, page 18
Publishers Weekly, July 9, 2001, page 45

Other books you might like:
Julian Barnes, *Love, etc.*, 2001
Cheryl Benard, *Turning on the Girls*, 2001

John Biguenet, *The Torturer's Apprentice*, 2001
Richard Condon, *The Final Addiction*, 1991
Ford Madox Ford, *The Good Soldier*, 1915

1143

HANIF KUREISHI

Gabriel's Gift

(New York: Scribner, 2001)

Story type: Coming-of-Age
Subject(s): Parent and Child; Rock Music; Family Problems
Major character(s): Gabriel Bunch, Teenager; Rex Bunch, Parent (Gabriel's father), Musician (rock); Lester Jones, Musician (rock), Friend (of Rex)
Time period(s): 2000s (2001)
Locale(s): London, England

Summary: Gabriel Bunch, 15, has musical talent, but finds himself caught in the middle of parental conflict. His father, Rex, a has-been 1960s rock'n'roll musician, can't find work because he won't compromise his music. His mother, Christine, fed up with her husband's stubbornness, kicks him out. In order to pursue his art, Gabriel must mediate their dispute and get them back together. Gabriel's dead twin, Archie, provides him with advice and assistance.

Where it's reviewed:
Kirkus Reviews, September 15, 2001, page 1316
Publishers Weekly, September 10, 2001, page 57

Other books by the same author:
Midnight All Day, 1999
Sleep with Me, 1999
Intimacy, 1998
Love in a Blue Time, 1997
The Black Album, 1995

Other books you might like:
Anita Brookner, *Family and Friends*, 1985
Ellen Gilchrist, *The Courts of Love*, 1997
Alison Lurie, *The War between the Tates*, 1974
Barbara Parker, *Criminal Justice*, 1997
Salman Rushdie, *The Ground Beneath Her Feet*, 1999

1144

ALLEN KURZWEIL

The Grand Complication

(New York: Hyperion, 2001)

Story type: Humor; Literary
Subject(s): Collectors and Collecting; Identity; Mystery
Major character(s): Alexander Short, Narrator, Librarian (reference); Henry James Jesson III, Scholar (art)
Time period(s): 2000s (2001)
Locale(s): New York, New York

Summary: Kurzweil's novel is loosely related to his previous work *A Case of Curiosities*. The story revolves around a missing item from an 18th century cabinet. Henry, an art scholar, hires reference librarian Alex to identify and find it. Alex determines the item to be a watch made for Marie Antoinette and that it was stolen from a museum in 1983. In the process of his investigation, Alex comes face to face with questions of personal identity.

Where it's reviewed:
Booklist, July 2001, page 1981
Kirkus Reviews, July 1, 2001, page 892
New York Times Book Review, August 19, 2001, page 7
Publishers Weekly, July 23, 2001, page 48

Other books by the same author:
A Case of Curiosities, 1992

Other books you might like:
A.S. Byatt, *The Biographer's Tale*, 2001
Joe Coomer, *The Loop*, 1992
Arturo Perez-Reverte, *The Nautical Chart*, 2001
Helen Stevenson, *Mad Elaine*, 1998
Gail Donohue Storey, *God's Country Club*, 1996

1145

DAVID LEAVITT

The Marble Quilt

(Boston: Houghton Mifflin, 2001)

Story type: Collection; Gay/Lesbian Fiction
Subject(s): Short Stories

Summary: In this collection of nine short stories, Leavitt weaves together history, tragedy, and murder, while skipping around the world. Finely drawn characters include Harold, a gay tutor; Ezra, a con man; Bosie, gay lover of Oscar Wilde; Christopher, a gay teen fascinated with AIDS; Tom, a gay man with an obsession for marble; and Irene Pratt, who is traveling with her two sons.

Where it's reviewed:
Kirkus Reviews, July 15, 2001, page 967
Library Journal, July 2001, page 128
New York Times Book Review, September 2, 2001, page 6
Publishers Weekly, July 30, 2001, page 56

Other books by the same author:
Martin Bauman, 2000
The Page Turner, 1998
Arkansas, 1997
The Lost Language of Cranes, 1997
Family Dancing, 1984

Other books you might like:
Saul Bellow, *Ravelstein*, 2000
Truman Capote, *Answered Prayers*, 1986
E. Lynn Harris, *Any Way the Wind Blows*, 2001
Manuel Puig, *Kiss of the Spider Woman*, 1979
Barbara Vine, *No Night Is Too Long*, 1995

1146

J. ROBERT LENNON

On the Night Plain

(New York: Holt, 2001)

Story type: Americana
Subject(s): Ranch Life; Family Relations; Brothers

Major character(s): Grant Person, Fisherman, Rancher (sheep); Max Person, Rancher, Artist (painter); Sophia, Girlfriend (of Max)
Time period(s): 19th century; 2000s (1946-2000)
Locale(s): Montana

Summary: This novel explores the physical and emotional struggles of life on a sheep ranch in Montana. After knocking about without success, Grant Person returns home to find his father gone and his mother dead. Grant tries his hand at running things, using money he earned back East. While Grant struggles, his younger brother, Max, heads for New York to paint. The fun starts when Max returns with a girlfriend who falls for Grant.

Where it's reviewed:
Kirkus Reviews, June 1, 2001, page 763
Library Journal, July 2001, page 124
New York Times Book Review, August 13, 2001, page 6
Publishers Weekly, June 25, 2001, page 43

Other books by the same author:
The Funnies, 1999
The Light of Falling Stars, 1997

Other books you might like:
Rick Bass, *Platte River*, 1994
James Lee Burke, *Bitterroot*, 2001
Larry McMurtry, *Horseman, Pass By*, 1979
Annie Proulx, *Close Range*, 1999
John Steinbeck, *The Red Pony*, 1945

1147

CHRISTINE LINCOLN

Sap Rising

(New York: Pantheon, 2001)

Story type: Gothic; Collection
Subject(s): African Americans; Race Relations; Customs
Time period(s): 1940s; 1950s (1946-1958)
Locale(s): Grandville, Maryland

Summary: In her debut, Lincoln offers 12 loosely linked stories about African Americans living in the rural South after World War II. The stories move back and forth in time and sometimes tell the same tale from differing perspectives. They invoke all the stages of life and the intimacy of a small town.

Where it's reviewed:
Chicago Tribune Books, September 16, 2001, page 3
Kirkus Reviews, August 1, 2001, page 1054
Library Journal, July 2001, page 128
Publishers Weekly, August 20, 2001, page 57

Other books you might like:
Richard Bausch, *Someone to Watch over Me*, 1999
Amy Bloom, *A Blind Man Can See How Much I Love You*, 2000
Dan Chaon, *Fitting Ends and Other Stories*, 1995
Annie Proulx, *Postcards*, 1992
Alice Walker, *Meridian*, 1976

1148

MARGOT LIVESEY

Eva Moves the Furniture

(New York: Holt, 2001)

Story type: Coming-of-Age; Psychological
Subject(s): Relationships; Mothers and Daughters; Spiritualism
Major character(s): Eva McEwen, Heroine; Lily, Relative (Eva's aunt); Samuel Rosenblum, Boyfriend (of Eva)
Time period(s): 20th century (1920-1950)
Locale(s): Troon, Scotland; Glasgow, Scotland

Summary: In her fourth novel, Livesey offers a psychological tale with a fantastic spin. Eva McEwen's mother dies, leaving her to be brought up by her father and an aunt. Despite love and affection, Eva invents two friends who help her navigate life's difficulties. Readers follow Eva, accompanied by the apparitions, as a child, an office worker, a wartime nurse, a wife, and a mother. The apparitions intervene along the way, saving her from harm but costing her romance, too.

Where it's reviewed:
Booklist, July 2001, page 1981
Kirkus Reviews, June 15, 2001, page 824
Library Journal, July 2001, page 124
Publishers Weekly, July 30, 2001, page 57

Other books by the same author:
The Missing World, 2000
Criminals, 1996
Homework, 1990
Learning by Heart, 1986

Other books you might like:
Jude Deveraux, *Temptation*, 2000
Mardi McConnochie, *Coldwater*, 2001
Ben Rice, *Pobby and Dingan*, 2000
Joy Williams, *The Quick and the Dead*, 2000
Margaret Yorke, *Almost the Truth*, 1994

1149

LAURA GLEN LOUIS

Talking in the Dark

(New York: Harcourt, 2001)

Story type: Collection
Subject(s): Chinese Americans; Relationships; Loneliness

Summary: Louis, winner of the 1990 Katherine Anne Porter Prize, offers eight stories in this collection. Told mostly from a woman's point of view, the stories focus on love or relief from its complications: a teenage tennis player is stalked by an older man, an older man is manipulated by a younger woman, a woman allows herself to be seduced by a teenager, and a woman plans an affair after her husband disappears. Many of the characters are Chinese-American, as is the author.

Where it's reviewed:
Kirkus Reviews, February 1, 2001, page 133
Library Journal, January 1, 2001, page 160

New York Times Book Review, July 15, 2001, page 6
Publishers Weekly, February 19, 2001, page 67

Other books you might like:
Kevin Canty, *Honeymoon and Other Stories*, 2001
Alicia Erian, *The Brutal Language of Love*, 2001
Erika Krouse, *Come Up and See Me Sometime*, 2001
Alice Munro, *The Moons of Jupiter*, 1982
Bill Roorbach, *Big Bend*, 2001

1150

BRUNO MADDOX

My Little Blue Dress

(New York: Viking, 2001)

Story type: Adult; Satire
Subject(s): Biography; Humor; Sexual Behavior
Major character(s): Bruno Maddox, Care Giver, Writer (of unnamed woman's memoir); Unnamed Character, Heroine; Hayley, Girlfriend (of Bruno)
Time period(s): 20th century (1900-1999)
Locale(s): New York, New York; England; Paris, France

Summary: Maddox, former editor of *Spy* magazine, offers a funny satire. The narrator, coincidentally named Bruno Maddox, writes a memoir for an old woman whose life spans the 20th century. Raised in the English countryside, she lives in Paris as a young woman and London during the war. Finally, she lands in an apartment in New York City. In between, she explores her sexuality with both men and women. Readers will wonder if there is an old woman.

Where it's reviewed:
Booklist, March 15, 2001, page 1334
Library Journal, April 1, 2001, page 133
New York Times Book Review, May 27, 2001, page 4
Publishers Weekly, April 9, 2001, page 52

Other books you might like:
Frederick Barthelme, *Painted Desert*, 1995
Kinky Friedman, *Blast from the Past*, 1998
Hanif Kureishi, *The Buddha of Suburbia*, 1990
David Lodge, *Small World*, 1984
Terry Southern, *Candy*, 1964
Mason Hoffenberg, co-author

1151

ANDREI MAKINE

Requiem for a Lost Empire

(New York: Arcade, 2001)

Story type: Historical; Family Saga
Subject(s): Russians; Revolutions; War
Major character(s): Pavel, Parent (of Pavel), Farmer; Pavel, Relative (Pavel's son); Pavel, Relative (Pavel's grandson), Spy (KGB)
Time period(s): 20th century; 2000s (1917-2000)
Locale(s): Russia; Florida

Summary: Told from the perspective of a father, son, and grandson, this family saga opens in 1917 during the Russian Revolution, when Pavel deserts the Red Army. The narrative jumps back and forth from there to War II when Pavel, the son, is fighting the Germans, and to the Cold War when Pavel, the grandson, is a spy. The author makes large events understandable. Translated by Geoffrey Strachan.

Where it's reviewed:
Booklist, July 2001, page 1982
Kirkus Reviews, July 1, 2001, page 892
Library Journal, July 2001, page 125
New York Times Book Review, October 7, 2001, page 24
Publishers Weekly, July 16, 2001, page 157

Other books by the same author:
Confessions of a Fallen Standard Bearer, 2000
Crime of Olga Arbyelina, 1999
Dreams of My Russian Summers, 1998
Once upon the River Love, 1998

Other books you might like:
Ken Follett, *Jackdaws*, 2001
Gunter Grass, *Too Far Afield*, 2000
John Le Carre, *The Russia House*, 1989
Tim Powers, *Declare*, 2001
Ludmila Ulitskaya, *The Funeral Party*, 2001

1152

KANAN MAKIYA

The Rock

(New York: Pantheon, 2001)

Story type: Historical
Subject(s): Islam; Judaism; Christianity
Major character(s): Ishaq, Architect, Narrator
Time period(s): 7th century; 8th century (685-705)
Locale(s): Jerusalem, Israel

Summary: Makiya gives a fictional account of how the Dome of the Rock was built in Jerusalem as he puts forth the notion that Judaism, Christianity, and Islam, while different paths, believe in the same heaven. Ishaq narrates the story of his father Ka'b, who designs the shrine. Not far from the site of Solomon's Temple, the Rock is believed to be the place where Abraham planned to sacrifice his son.

Where it's reviewed:
Booklist, November 1, 2001, page 460
New York Times Book Review, November 25, 2001, page 24
Publishers Weekly, October 15, 2001, page 67

Other books you might like:
Edie Meidav, *The Far Field*, 2001
Orhan Pamuk, *My Name Is Red*, 2001
Mario Puzo, *The Family*, 2001
Salman Rushdie, *The Satanic Verses*, 1998
Kurban Said, *The Girl from the Golden Horn*, 2001
Shashi Tharoor, *Riot*, 2001

1153

MICHAEL MALONE

First Lady

(Naperville, Illinois: Sourcebooks Landmark, 2001)

Story type: Contemporary; Political
Subject(s): Mystery; Serial Killers; Police Procedural
Major character(s): Cudberth ''Cuddy'' Mangum, Police Officer (police chief); Justin B. Savile V, Detective—Homicide (chief of homicide); Mavis Mahar, Singer (rock star)
Time period(s): 2000s (2001)
Locale(s): Hillston, North Carolina

Summary: Police Chief Cuddy Mangum and his chief of homicide, Justin B. Savile V, have their hands full chasing a serial killer, tagged ''Guess Who,'' because he leaves clues to torment the authorities. Police find a body believed to be that of rock star and girlfriend of the governor, Mavis Mahar. The case is further complicated when the attorney general destroys evidence and a judge is murdered. The killer leaves still more taunting clues, daring the police to catch him.

Where it's reviewed:
Kirkus Reviews, August 1, 2001, page 1071
New York Times Book Review, September 23, 2001, page 17
Publishers Weekly, June 25, 2001, page 43

Other books by the same author:
Foolscap, 1991
Time's Witness, 1989
Handling Sin, 1986
Dingley Falls, 1980
Painting the Roses Red, 1975

Other books you might like:
Martin Clark, *The Many Aspects of Mobile Home Living*, 2000
Emmett Cliford, *Night Whispers*, 1998
Patricia Cornwell, *Hornet's Nest*, 1996
Sandra Dallas, *Alice's Tulips*, 2000
James Patterson, *Violets Are Blue*, 2001

1154

JOE MARTIN

Fire in the Rock

(Charlotte, North Carolina: Novello Festival, 2001)

Story type: Historical; Americana
Subject(s): Civil Rights Movement; Race Relations; Friendship
Major character(s): Bo Fisher, Teenager (son of a white preacher); Pollo Templeton, Teenager (African American); Mae Maude Snoddy, Friend (of Bo and Po)
Time period(s): 1950s (1956)
Locale(s): South

Summary: Joe Martin's first novel explores a friendship that develops despite the barriers of segregation. In the summer of 1956, Bo, a white preacher's kid, and Po, a black delivery boy, meet at a church camp. They are both attracted to the flirtatious Mae Maude. Away from home and insulated from the real world, they ignore their racial differences. For one summer, they are just three young people happy to be alive and with each other.

Where it's reviewed:
Booklist, October 15, 2001, page 383
New York Times Book Review, December 9, 2001, page 22

Other books you might like:
Leon Forrest, *Meteor in the Madhouse*, 2001
Anthony Grooms, *Bombingham*, 2001
Melinda Haynes, *Chalktown*, 2001
Bart Schneider, *Secret Love*, 2001
Colson Whitehead, *John Henry Days*, 2001

1155

BOBBIE ANN MASON

Zigzagging Down a Wild Trail

(New York: Random House, 2001)

Story type: Collection
Subject(s): Small Town Life; Modern Life; Women
Time period(s): 2000s (2001)

Summary: Mason deftly articulates her characters' wants, needs, potentials, and realistic limitations in this collection. These 11 open-ended stories explore a world mostly of women, coping as best they can with the complexities of modernity and the impact of a Wal-Mart driven culture on Main Street values.

Where it's reviewed:
Booklist, April 15, 2001, page 1508
Library Journal, June 1, 2001, page 220
New York Times Book Review, August 19, 2001, page 9
Publishers Weekly, June 25, 2001, page 43

Other books by the same author:
Midnight Magic, 1998
Feather Crowns, 1993
Love Life, 1989
Spence + Lila, 1988
Shiloh and Other Stories, 1982

Other books you might like:
Alice Adams, *The Last Lovely City*, 1999
Richard Bausch, *Someone to Watch over Me*, 1999
Ann Beattie, *Perfect Recall*, 2001
Larry Brown, *Big Bad Love*, 1990
Ellen Gilchrist, *The Cabal and Other Stories*, 2000

1156

MARDI MCCONNOCHIE

Coldwater

(New York: Doubleday, 2001)

Story type: Historical
Subject(s): Fathers and Daughters; Islands; Sisters
Major character(s): Charlotte Wolf, Writer (has literary aspirations), Relative; Emily Wolf, Writer (has literary aspirations), Relative; Anne Wolf, Writer (has literary aspirations), Relative

Time period(s): 1840s
Locale(s): Australia

Summary: McConnochie's first novel features a fast pace, excitement, romance, and adventure. Her three heroines live on a prison island where their father, Captain Edward Wolf, is the warden. The women use their imaginations and literary talents to fight boredom. One day their father decides one of his convicts is worth reforming and one daughter falls hopelessly in love with him. The story is loosely based on the lives of the Bronte sisters.

Where it's reviewed:
Booklist, July 2001, page 1982
Chicago Tribune Books, September 2, 2001, page 3
Kirkus Reviews, June 1, 2001, page 764
Library Journal, July 2001, page 124
Publishers Weekly, July 23, 2001, page 49

Other books you might like:
Margaret Atwood, *The Blind Assassin*, 2000
Elizabeth Hay, *A Student of Weather*, 2000
John Irving, *A Widow for One Year*, 1998
J.D. Landis, *Longing*, 2000
Muriel Spark, *Loitering with Intent*, 1981

1157

JILL MCCORKLE

Creatures of Habit

(Chapel Hill, North Carolina: Algonquin, 2001)

Story type: Collection
Subject(s): Animals; Culture; Cultures and Customs
Time period(s): 20th century
Locale(s): North Carolina

Summary: The characters in McCorkle's third collection, 12 loosely connected stories, have animal-like characteristics that include men as gorillas, children as pack members, neighbors as poisonous snakes, and the elderly as turtles. The stories span human experience from childhood to old age. Subjects covered include infidelity, childhood fears, elderly terror, cruelty, and vulnerability. The author's perfect pitch dialog captures some powerful emotions.

Where it's reviewed:
Booklist, July 2001, page 1982
Kirkus Reviews, July 1, 2001, page 893
New York Times Book Review, October 28, 2001, page 16
Publishers Weekly, September 10, 2001, page 58

Other books by the same author:
Final Vinyl Days, 1998
Carolina Moon, 1996
Crash Diet, 1992
Ferris Beach, 1990
Tending to Virginia, 1987

Other books you might like:
David Baldacci, *Wish You Well*, 2000
William Gay, *The Long Home*, 2000
Ellen Gilchrist, *Flights of Angels*, 1998
Jim Harrison, *Dalva*, 1988
Elizabeth Spencer, *The Southern Woman*, 2001

1158

ELIZABETH MCCRACKEN

Niagara Falls All over Again

(New York: Dial, 2001)

Story type: Psychological
Subject(s): Friendship; Comedians
Major character(s): Mose Sharp, Entertainer (comedian); Rocky Carter, Entertainer (comedian)
Time period(s): 20th century (1930-1983)
Locale(s): Valley Junction, Iowa; New York, New York; Hollywood, California

Summary: McCracken's second novel moves fast with bittersweet humor. Mose Sharp narrates the story about his partnership with Rocky Carter. Mose, who grows up in Iowa, knocks around in vaudeville unsuccessfully until he meets Rocky. With Mose as the straight man to Rocky's madcap comic, they are very successful, making movies and starring in their own TV show. Unbeknownst to each partner, they provide an anchor for each other. When their act breaks up, both men suffer.

Where it's reviewed:
Book, July 2001, page 78
Kirkus Reviews, June 15, 2001, page 824
New York Times Book Review, August 12, 2001, page 10
Publishers Weekly, May 28, 2001, page 45

Other books by the same author:
The Giant's House, 1996
Here's Your Hat What's Your Hurry, 1993

Other books you might like:
Steve Allen, *Die Laughing*, 1998
Saul Bellow, *Ravelstein*, 2000
Graham Parker, *Carp Fishing on Valium and Other Tales of the Stranger Road Traveled*, 2000
Carl Reiner, *Continue Laughing*, 1995
Sidney Sheldon, *A Stranger in the Mirror*, 1976

1159

HEATHER MCGOWAN

Schooling

(New York: Doubleday, 2001)

Story type: Coming-of-Age; Psychological
Subject(s): Schools; Teacher-Student Relationships; Adolescence
Major character(s): Catrine Evans, Teenager, Student—Boarding School; Teddy Evans, Parent (of Catrine); Mr. Gilbert, Teacher (chemistry), Friend (of Catrine)
Time period(s): 2000s (2001)
Locale(s): Maine; England

Summary: McGowan's first novel uses stream of consciousness to explore the adolescent world of transplanted American Catrine Evans, 13. When her mother dies, Catrine's Welsh father sends her from Maine to Monstead, a boarding school in England he attended during World War II. Catrine, suffering from her mother's death and guilt from a mischievous prank gone awry, is received, as one might expect, as an outsider. Lonely, and confused, Catrine becomes attached to a teacher, Mr. Gilbert.

Where it's reviewed:
Booklist, May 15, 2001, page 1734
Chicago Tribune Books, September 2, 2001, page 2
Kirkus Reviews, April 15, 2001, page 529
New York Times Book Review, June 24, 2001, page 30
Publishers Weekly, May 14, 2001, page 51

Other books you might like:
Gale Zoe Garnett, *Visible Amazement*, 1999
Molly Giles, *Iron Shoes*, 2000
Paul Golding, *The Abomination*, 2000
Anne Tyler, *Dinner at the Homesick Restaurant*, 1982
Richard Yates, *A Good School*, 1978

1160

SANDRO MEALLET

Edgewater Angels

(New York: Doubleday, 2001)

Story type: Coming-of-Age; Multicultural
Subject(s): Men; Adolescence
Major character(s): Sonny Toomer, Teenager (member of the Locos); Beefy, Teenager (leader of the Locos); Ton Su, Teenager (mascot of the Locos)
Time period(s): 2000s
Locale(s): San Pedro, California

Summary: Meallet's novel is a coming-of-age tale about boys growing up in the multicultural working-class neighborhood of San Pedro, California. Toomer and his pals, the Locos, wander the depressed waterfront, getting into minor scrapes while attempting to sort out their feelings toward themselves, others from different neighborhoods, adults, and the outside world. Drive-by shootings and police brutality provide a sharp backdrop. A swimming contest to settle a gang dispute provides comic relief.

Where it's reviewed:
Booklist, June 1, 2001, page 1847
Library Journal, July 2001, page 125
Publishers Weekly, July 16, 2001, page 159

Other books you might like:
Dan Chaon, *Among the Missing*, 2001
Christina Fitzpatrick, *Where We Lived*, 2001
Julian Gough, *Juno & Juliet*, 2001
Jenny McPhee, *The Center of Things*, 2001
Henry Roth, *A Star Shines over Mt. Morris Park*, 1994

1161

CLAIRE MESSUD

The Hunters

(New York: Harcourt, 2001)

Story type: Psychological; Collection
Subject(s): Loneliness; Relationships

Summary: In her third book, Claire Messud offers two novellas. The sight of blood causes Maria, the main character in *A Simple Tale*, to recall her traumatic, youthful experiences in war torn Europe during World War II. We also learn of her pain as a mother and widow. In *The Hunters*, the unnamed narrator's obsession with the hapless Ridley Wandor causes unexpected surprises. Loneliness and isolation contribute to the narrator's motivation.

Where it's reviewed:
Booklist, August 2001, page 2089
Kirkus Reviews, May 15, 2001, page 692
Library Journal, April 15, 2001, page 135
Los Angeles Times Book Review, August 12, 2001, page 5
Publishers Weekly, June 25, 2001, page 44

Other books by the same author:
The Last Life, 1999
When the World Was Steady, 1994

Other books you might like:
Evan S. Connell, *Mrs. Bridge*, 1959
Henry James, *The Aspern Papers*, 1888
Allen Kurzweil, *The Grand Complication*, 2001
Cynthia Ozick, *Bloodshed and Three Novellas*, 1995
Muriel Spark, *The Prime of Miss Jean Brodie*, 1961

1162

REBECCA MILLER

Personal Velocity

(New York: Grove, 2001)

Story type: Contemporary; Collection
Subject(s): Women; Careers; Abuse
Time period(s): 2000s (2001)
Locale(s): New York, New York

Summary: Miller, a filmmaker and the daughter of playwright Arthur Miller and photographer Inge Morath, offers seven stories in her first collection. Each explores the strategies six women and a girl employ in their daily lives. Louisa falls in love. Pregnant Paula uses denial. Nancy acts out in public. Bryna endures a mean mother-in-law. Julianne serves her husband. Delia uses sex. Greta must leave her marriage. Each story reveals a different insight.

Where it's reviewed:
Booklist, July 2001, page 1982
Kirkus Reviews, June 15, 2001, page 824
Library Journal, July 2001, page 128
New York Times Book Review, September 23, 2001, page 12
Publishers Weekly, August 20, 2001, page 58

Other books you might like:
Ann Beattie, *Perfect Recall*, 2001
Ellen Gilchrist, *The Age of Miracles*, 1995
Bobbie Ann Mason, *Zigzagging Down a Wild Trail*, 2001
Alice Munro, *Friend of My Youth*, 1990
Melanie Rae Thon, *First, Body*, 1997

1163

SUE MILLER

The World Below

(New York: Knopf, 2001)

Story type: Psychological
Subject(s): Marriage; Grandmothers; Secrets
Major character(s): Catherine Hubbard, Divorced Person; Georgia Rice, Grandparent (of Catherine); Samuel Eliasson, Widow(er) (dates Catherine)
Time period(s): 2000s (2001)
Locale(s): San Francisco, California; Vermont

Summary: Miller's sixth novel explores the past and its influences on the present. Twice married Catherine retreats to the Vermont home her grandmother left. Georgia, her grandmother, seemed to live the quiet, stable life of a doctor's wife but her diaries reveal a different story. They tell about her secret love, her inner struggles, and the compromises she had to make. Catherine learns from the diaries, making connections between her grandmother's life and her own.

Where it's reviewed:
Book, September 2001, page 76
Booklist, August 2001, page 2052
Kirkus Reviews, August 15, 2001, page 1156
New York Times Book Review, October 7, 2001, page 10
Publishers Weekly, July 16, 2001, page 166

Other books by the same author:
While I Was Gone, 1999
The Distinguished Guest, 1995
For Love, 1993
Inventing the Abbotts and Other Stories, 1987
The Good Mother, 1986

Other books you might like:
Elizabeth Benedict, *Almost*, 2001
Robb Forman Dew, *The Evidence Against Her*, 2001
Jonathan Franzen, *The Corrections*, 2001
Alice Hoffman, *Blue Diary*, 2001
Joyce Carol Oates, *Middle Age*, 2001

1164

MAYRA MONTERO

The Red of His Shadow

(New York: HarperCollins, 2001)

Story type: Multicultural; Adult
Subject(s): Voodoo; Jealousy; Conspiracies
Major character(s): Zule Reve, Religious (voodoo priestess); Simila Bolesseto, Religious (voodoo priest)
Time period(s): 2000s (2001)
Locale(s): Dominican Republic

Summary: Montero explores the underside of immigrant Haitian society with a story about conflict between two voodoo societies in the Dominican Republic. Zule, a voodoo priestess, is preparing to lead a procession for Holy Week. Her former lover, Simila, himself a voodoo priest, says he will kill her if she goes through the cane field. Intrigue, greed, sexual jealousy, torture, and death are mixed with magic spells in this struggle. Translated by Edith Grossman.

Where it's reviewed:
Booklist, July 2001, page 1983
Kirkus Reviews, June 1, 2001, page 765
New York Times Book Review, August 12, 2001, page 29

Other books by the same author:
The Last Night I Spent with You, 2000
The Messenger, 1999
In the Palm of Darkness, 1997

Other books you might like:
Rainelle Burton, *The Root Worker*, 2001
Umberto Eco, *Foucault's Pendulum*, 1989
Nani Power, *Crawling at Night*, 2001
Jewell Parker Rhodes, *Voodoo Dreams*, 1993
Lalita Tademy, *Cane River*, 2001

1165

MARGRIET DE MOOR

First Gray, Then White, Then Blue

(Woodstock, New York: Overlook, 2001)

Story type: Literary; Psychological Suspense
Subject(s): Secrets; Lovers; Women
Major character(s): Magda Rezkova, Heroine, Spouse (of Robert); Robert Noort, Businessman (repressed artist), Spouse (of Magda); Erik, Friend (of Robert), Lover (of Magda)
Time period(s): 20th century (1939-1990)
Locale(s): Europe; Quebec City, Quebec, Canada

Summary: Dutch writer de Moor's novel, which is translated by Paul Vincent, was originally published in 1990. Told in the first, second, and third person, the story unfolds around the mysterious disappearance and presumed murder of Magda Rezkova. We learn her secrets, about World War II in Czechoslovakia, miscarriages, love affairs, and the emptiness at her inner core. Her life is a circle of deception and passion. If a crime has been committed, her husband Robert is the most likely culprit.

Where it's reviewed:
Booklist, June 15, 2001, page 1852
Kirkus Reviews, July 15, 2001, page 979
New York Times Book Review, August 12, 2001, page 14
Publishers Weekly, June 25, 2001, page 48

Other books by the same author:
Duke of Egypt, 2001
The Virtuoso, 1996

Other books you might like:
Molly Gloss, *Wild Life*, 2000
Jo-Ann Mapson, *Loving Chloe*, 1998
Marge Piercy, *Gone to Soldiers*, 1987
Anita Shreve, *Resistance*, 1995
Herman Wouk, *The Winds of War*, 1971

1166

WALTER MOSLEY

Futureland

(New York: Warner, 2001)

Story type: Contemporary/Fantasy; Collection
Subject(s): Future; Race Relations; Science Fiction

Summary: *Futureland* consists of nine linked stories set in an undetermined future. The world is governed by political correctness and run by one corporation. Privacy and racial harmony don't exist and a super weapon backfires killing many. The smartest man in world was imprisoned as a youth and the heavyweight champion of the world is a woman named Fera Jones. The author uses techie jargon and memorable characters to make it look easy.

Where it's reviewed:
Booklist, September 1, 2001, page 4
Kirkus Reviews, September 1, 2001, page 1253
Library Journal, October 1, 2001, page 145
New York Times Book Review, November 25, 2001, page 18
Publishers Weekly, September 10, 2001, page 65

Other books by the same author:
Fearless Jones, 2001
Walkin' the Dog, 1999
Always Outnumbered, Always Outgunned, 1998
Blue Light, 1998
Gone Fishin', 1997

Other books you might like:
Bebe Moore Campbell, *What You Owe Me*, 2001
Gardner Dozois, *Isaac Asimov's Father's Day*, 2001
Sheila Williams, co-editor
Stephen King, *Dreamcatcher*, 2001
J.D. Robb, *Betrayal in Death*, 2001
Peter Straub, *Magic Terror*, 2000

1167

FERDINAND MOUNT

Fairness

(New York: Carroll & Graf, 2001)

Story type: Historical
Series: Chronicle of Modern Twilight. Book 5
Subject(s): Relationships; Social Conditions; Social Classes
Major character(s): Aldous ''Gus'' Cotton, Narrator; Helen Hardress, Young Woman
Time period(s): 20th century; 2000s (1960-2000)
Locale(s): Deauville, France; London, England

Summary: Mount, a former editor of the *Times Literary Supplement*, closes his fictional social history with this novel. The story follows Helen Hardress and Gus Cotton through the latter part of the 20th century. They meet one summer while employed as nannies. Subsequently, Helen travels the world, following her left-wing political conscience, while working for world improvement. Gus Cotton narrates the story while unfailingly carrying a torch for Helen, who drops in and out of his life.

Where it's reviewed:
Atlantic Monthly, July-August 2001, page 164
Kirkus Reviews, June 1, 2001, page 765
Library Journal, October 1, 2001, page 141
New York Times Book Review, August 19, 2001, page 10

Other books by the same author:
Jem (and Sam), 1998
The Liquidator, 1995
Umbrella, 1994
Of Love and Asthma, 1991
The Clique, 1978

Other books you might like:
Douglas Adams, *The Hitchhiker's Guide to the Galaxy*, 1980
F. Scott Fitzgerald, *The Great Gatsby*, 1925
Josephine Humphreys, *Nowhere Else on Earth*, 2000
Henry James, *The Wings of the Dove*, 1902
William T. Vollmann, *Argall*, 2001

1168

HERTA MULLER

The Appointment

(New York: Metropolitan, 2001)

Story type: Political; Satire
Subject(s): Loneliness; Terror; Political Crimes and Offenses
Major character(s): Unnamed Character, Worker (clothing factory); Major Albu, Police Officer (secret police); Nelu, Foreman (clothing factory)
Time period(s): 2000s (2001)
Locale(s): Romania

Summary: A Romanian expatriate, Muller writes about police persecution. An unhappy clothing factory worker sews her name and address inside men's suits with a message saying ''marry me.'' Her supervisor finds out and demands she sleep with him; when she refuses, he turns the matter over to the secret police. The woman loses her job and has to endure humiliating and exhausting police interrogations. Translated by Michael Hulse and Phillip Boehm.

Where it's reviewed:
Booklist, September 1, 2001, page 52
Chicago Tribune Books, November 11, 2001, page 3
Library Journal, September 1, 2001, page 234
New York Times Book Review, October 21, 2001, page 18
Publishers Weekly, August 6, 2001, page 61

Other books by the same author:
Traveling on One Leg, 1998
The Land of Green Plums, 1996

Other books you might like:
Ethan C. Canin, *Carry Me Across the Water*, 2001
Alan Furst, *Kingdom of Shadows*, 2000
Jill Paton Walsh, *A Desert in Bohemia*, 2000
Josef Skvorecky, *Two Murders in My Double Life*, 2001
James Thackara, *America's Children*, 2001

1169

ALICE MUNRO

Hateship, Friendship, Courtship, Loveship, Marriage

(New York: Knopf, 2001)

Story type: Collection
Subject(s): Love; Marriage; Friendship
Time period(s): 2000s (2001)
Locale(s): Canada

Summary: Consisting of nine short stories, Munro's collection examines the lives of ordinary women living in small Canadian towns, as well as Toronto and Vancouver. The author shows their actions and reveals their inner thoughts, the ones they never express. Readers witness how these woman find their way through a complex world that is full of mixed emotions with unpredictable outcomes.

Where it's reviewed:
Kirkus Reviews, September 15, 2001, page 1318
New York Times Book Review, November 25, 2001, page 9
Publishers Weekly, October 8, 2001, page 41

Other books by the same author:
Queenie, 1999
The Love of a Good Woman, 1998
Open Secrets, 1994
The Progress of Love, 1986
The Beggar Maid, 1979

Other books you might like:
Maeve Binchy, *Tara Road*, 1999
A.S. Byatt, *Elementals*, 1999
Ellen Gilchrist, *The Courts of Love*, 1996
Nora Roberts, *River's End*, 1999
Anne Tyler, *The Accidental Tourist*, 1985

1170

V.S. NAIPAUL

Half a Life

(New York: Knopf, 2001)

Story type: Psychological; Literary
Subject(s): Assimilation; Authors and Writers; Africa
Major character(s): Willie Chandran, Writer (novelist); Ana, Young Woman (of African descent), Lover (of Willie)
Time period(s): 20th century (1935-1975)
Locale(s): London, England; Mozambique; India

Summary: Naipaul, the 2001 Nobel Prize winner for literature, tells a story of unfulfilled expectations. Born in India, Willie is repelled and confused by his parents behavior. His upper-class father despises Willie's mother, a lower caste woman and Willie escapes to London after accepting a scholarship. When he completes his studies, he becomes a writer, publishes a book, meets Ana, and they move to Mozambique. However, Willie never becomes comfortable with himself or those around him.

Where it's reviewed:
Booklist, August 2001, page 2051
Kirkus Reviews, August 15, 2001, page 1156
Library Journal, October 1, 2001, page 141
Publishers Weekly, September 17, 2001, page 52

Other books by the same author:
The Enigma of Arrival, 1987
A Bend in the River, 1979
Guerrillas, 1975
In a Free State, 1971
A House for Mr. Biswas, 1961

Other books you might like:
Xingjian Gao, *Soul Mountain*, 2000
Nadine Gordimer, *The Pickup*, 2001
Annie Proulx, *Accordion Crimes*, 1996
Salman Rushdie, *Fury*, 2001
Manil Suri, *The Death of Vishnu*, 2001

1171

LAWRENCE NORFOLK

In the Shape of a Boar

(New York: Grove, 2001)

Story type: Historical/World War II; Literary
Subject(s): Refugees; Mythology; Poetry
Major character(s): Solomon Memel, Writer (poet), Survivor (Holocaust); Ruth, Director (movies), Survivor (Holocaust); Jakob, Survivor (Holocaust), Scholar (critical of Sol's work)
Time period(s): Indeterminate Past; 20th century (1939-1976)
Locale(s): Kalydon, Greece; Romania; Paris, France

Summary: Norfolk's novel jumps back and forth from classical Greece, to World War II, to post-war Paris in the 1970s. The story revolves around an eternal triangle consisting of Solomon, Ruth, and Jakob. In classical Greece, they hunt a mythical boar. During World War II, they are partisans hunting a Nazi colonel. After the war, Solomon becomes a famous literary figure. Ruth directs a movie about him, while Jakob criticizes him.

Where it's reviewed:
Booklist, August 2001, page 2090
Kirkus Reviews, September 1, 2001, page 1239
Library Journal, August 2001, page 163
New York Times Book Review, November 25, 2001, page 26
Publishers Weekly, September 10, 2001, page 59

Other books by the same author:
The Pope's Rhinoceros, 1996
Lempriere's Dictionary, 1991

Other books you might like:
Dennis Bock, *The Ash Garden*, 2001
Ray Bradbury, *From the Dust Returned*, 2001
Joseph Kanon, *The Good German*, 2001
Ferdinand Mount, *Fairness*, 2001
Winfried Georg Sebald, *Austerlitz*, 2001

1172

SIGRID NUNEZ

For Rouenna

(New York: Farrar, Straus & Giroux, 2001)

Story type: Psychological; Contemporary/Mainstream
Subject(s): Suicide; Nursing; Vietnam War
Major character(s): Unnamed Character, Writer, Narrator; Rouenna, Friend (of narrator), Nurse (served in Vietnam)
Time period(s): 2000s (2001)
Locale(s): New York, New York

Summary: Sigrid Nunez looks at Vietnam from a nurse's point of view. Rouenna contacts the unnamed narrator, a recently published author whom she knew slightly as a child, for help in writing her life story. The narrator refuses, but listens to Rouenna's history. Haunted by the Vietnam War, in which she served as a nurse, Rouenna cannot adjust to civilian life. When Rouenna commits suicide, the narrator resolves to tell her story.

Where it's reviewed:
Kirkus Reviews, September 15, 2001, page 1319
Library Journal, October 15, 2001, page 109
New York Times Book Review, November 18, 2001, page 8
Publishers Weekly, October 8, 2001, page 41

Other books by the same author:
Mitz: The Marmoset of Bloomsbury, 1998
Naked Sleeper, 1996
A Feather on the Breath of God, 1995

Other books you might like:
Isabel Allende, *The Infinite Plan*, 1993
Anita Brookner, *A Friend from England*, 1987
Nelson DeMille, *Up Country*, 2002
Bobbie Ann Mason, *In Country*, 1993
Joyce Carol Oates, *Foxfire*, 1993

1173

JOYCE CAROL OATES

Beasts

(New York: Carroll & Graf, 2001)

Story type: Gothic; Literary
Subject(s): Women; Sexual Behavior; Teacher-Student Relationships
Major character(s): Gillian Brauer, Student—College; Andre Harrow, Professor (of poetry); Dorcas Harrow, Spouse (of Andre), Artist
Time period(s): 1970s
Locale(s): Berkshire Mountains, Massachusetts; Paris, France

Summary: The narrative in Oates' novella moves backwards and forward in time. While visiting the Louvre, Gillian Brauer is reminded of her student days at an all-girls college when she fell under the spell of Dorcas Harrow and her husband Andre. Andre inflamed his classes with erotic poetry; Dorcas carved sexual totems, urging students to give in to their bestial sexual nature. Gillian and other students became obsessed and virtual sexual slaves to the couple.

Where it's reviewed:
Booklist, October 1, 2001, page 300
Kirkus Reviews, October 1, 2001, page 1387
Library Journal, October 1, 2001, page 143
Publishers Weekly, October 22, 2001, page 43

Other books by the same author:
Faithless, 2001
Middle Age, 2001
Blonde, 2000
Broke Heart Blues, 1999
Where I've Been and Where I'm Going, 1999

Other books you might like:
Pat Conroy, *The Prince of Tides*, 1986
Michel Houellebecq, *The Elementary Particles*, 2000
David Leavitt, *Martin Bauman*, 2000
Ferdinand Mount, *Fairness*, 2001
Philip Roth, *The Dying Animal*, 2001

1174

JOYCE CAROL OATES

Middle Age

(New York: Ecco, 2001)

Story type: Romance
Subject(s): Aging; Secrets; Relationships
Major character(s): Adam Berendt, Artist (successful sculptor), Hero; Roger Cavanagh, Lawyer; Augusta Cutler, Friend (of Adam)
Time period(s): 2000s (2001)
Locale(s): Salthill-on-Hudson, New York

Summary: Mysterious Adam Berendt, a well-heeled sculptor, dies from a heart attack after saving a drowning child. His friends find they didn't know him very well or themselves, either. Some set out to redress the problem: Augusta leaves her husband to find out the truth, Abigail learns control to deal with her teenage son, Roger battles his wife and teenage daughter, and Camille takes in stray dogs. Despite troubles, most of the characters find happiness or romance.

Where it's reviewed:
Booklist, July 2001, page 1952
Kirkus Reviews, July 15, 2001, page 970
New York Times Book Review, September 16, 2001, page 7
Publishers Weekly, August 13, 2001, page 284

Other books by the same author:
Faithless, 2001
Blonde, 2000
Broke Heart Blues, 1999
We Were the Mulvaneys, 1996
Them, 1969

Other books you might like:
Barbara Taylor Bradford, *A Sudden Change of Heart*, 1999
Nicholas Evans, *The Horse Whisperer*, 1995
Andrew M. Greeley, *A Midwinter's Tale*, 1998
Nora Roberts, *River's End*, 1999
Anita Shreve, *The Last Time They Met*, 2001

1175

MARY O'CONNELL

Living with Saints

(New York: Atlantic Monthly, 2001)

Story type: Collection; Contemporary/Fantasy
Subject(s): Saints; Women; Modern Life
Time period(s): 2000s (2001)

Summary: In her first collection, Mary O'Connell takes the lives of the saints and reworks them, making them relate to contemporary settings. While her humor and language may turn off the conventionally religious, when it comes to teenage girls, the author's dialog rings true. The stories make connections between myth and life and are serious. The subjects addressed include teen pregnancy, abortion, sexual abuse, illness, and loss of a loved one.

Where it's reviewed:
Booklist, October 15, 2001, page 193
Kirkus Reviews, August 1, 2001, page 1057
Library Journal, August 2001, page 168
New York Times Book Review, November 18, 2001, page 59
Publishers Weekly, August 27, 2001, page 47

Other books you might like:
Catherine Ryan Hyde, *Electric God*, 2000
Simon Mawer, *The Gospel of Judas*, 2001
Mark Salzman, *Lying Awake*, 2000
Diane Schoemperlen, *Our Lady of the Lost and Found*, 2001
Simone Zelitch, *Louisa*, 2000

1176

BRUCE OLDS

Bucking the Tiger

(New York: Farrar, Straus & Giroux, 2001)

Story type: Americana; Historical
Subject(s): Biography; Gambling; Frontier and Pioneer Life
Major character(s): John H. "Doc" Holliday, Historical Figure, Gunfighter; Kate "Big Nose Kate" Haroney, Lover (of Doc), Historical Figure; William "Billy the Kid" Bonney, Outlaw, Historical Figure
Time period(s): 19th century (1851-1887)
Locale(s): West

Summary: Olds pulls out all the stops in giving the near mythical story of Doc Holliday a new spin. He does this by using the historical record, interviews both authentic and fictional with those who knew and loved the dentist turned cardsharp turned lethal gunfighter. Also included are songs, slang, and sexual habits. Holliday, who is best known for accompanying Wyatt Earp in the gunfight at the OK Corral, died of consumption at age 36.

Where it's reviewed:
Chicago Tribune Books, October 14, 2001, page 3
Kirkus Reviews, June 1, 2001, page 766
Library Journal, August 2001, page 165
New York Times Book Review, August 12, 2001, page 22
Publishers Weekly, July 9, 2001, page 42

Other books by the same author:
Raising Holy Hell, 1995

Other books you might like:
Peter Carey, *True History of the Kelly Gang*, 2000
Elmer Kelton, *The Way of the Coyote*, 2001
Robert B. Parker, *Gunman's Rhapsody*, 2001
William T. Vollmann, *The Royal Family*, 2000
James Welch, *The Heartsong of Charging Elk*, 2000

1177

GEORG M. OSWALD

All That Counts

(New York: Grove, 2001)

Story type: Contemporary/Mainstream; Satire
Subject(s): Modern Life; Greed; Careers
Major character(s): Thomas Schwartz, Banker, Narrator; Marianne Schwartz, Spouse (Thomas' wife), Public Relations; Frau Rumenich, Banker (Thomas' boss)
Time period(s): 2000s (2001)
Locale(s): Germany

Summary: Set in Germany, Oswald's novel, which focuses on the darker side of the corporate world, easily could have been set in New York. Thomas Schwartz, a banker, and his executive wife, Marianne, are on the fast track until they are both fired. Marianne leaves and Thomas becomes a consultant representing drug dealers. When he tires of his criminal pals, he turns them in, takes their money, and leaves the country with an attractive hooker. Shaun Whiteside provides the translation.

Where it's reviewed:
Kirkus Reviews, July 15, 2001, page 970
New York Times Book Review, October 7, 2001, page 27
Publishers Weekly, August 6, 2001, page 61

Other books you might like:
Douglas Kennedy, *The Big Picture*, 1997
Chuck Palahniuk, *Choke*, 2001
Tim Parks, *Mimi's Ghost*, 2001
Philip Roth, *The Dying Animal*, 2001
Alex Shakar, *The Savage Girl*, 2001

1178

ORHAN PAMUK

My Name Is Red

(New York: Knopf, 2001)

Story type: Historical
Subject(s): Cultures and Customs; Murder; Art
Major character(s): Black, Relative (Enishte's nephew), Investigator (murdered); Enishte Effendi, Artist (commissioned by the sultan), Crime Victim (murdered); Elegant, Artist (engraver), Crime Victim (murdered)
Time period(s): 16th century (1590s)
Locale(s): Istanbul, Ottoman Empire

Summary: Turkish writer Pamuk explores cultural differences in a tale of ideas, art, and love. Set in 16th century Istanbul, the story revolves around the murder of an engraver and an artist. They die amid controversy over a portrait in the new Western style. The sultan threatens to kill all artists, unless the killer is found. Black, a clerk, sets out to find the culprit and win a bride. Translated from the Turkish by Erdag Goknar.

Where it's reviewed:
Kirkus Reviews, August 1, 2001, page 1058
New York Times Book Review, September 2, 2001, page 7
Publishers Weekly, August 6, 2001, page 58

Other books by the same author:
The New Life, 1997
The Black Book, 1994
The White Castle, 1991

Other books you might like:
A.S. Byatt, *The Djinn in the Nightingale's Eye*, 1994
Elia Kazan, *America, America*, 1962
Salman Rushdie, *The Satanic Verses*, 1998
Vikram Seth, *A Suitable Boy*, 1993
Ahdaf Soueif, *The Map of Love*, 2000

1179

ALEXANDER PARSONS

Leaving Disneyland

(New York: Thomas Dunne, 2001)

Story type: Psychological
Subject(s): African Americans; Drugs; Prisoners and Prisons
Major character(s): Doc Kane, Prisoner (up for parole); Byron Cripps, Prisoner (Doc's cellmate)
Time period(s): 2000s (2001)
Locale(s): Nevada (Tyburn Penitentiary)

Summary: African American Doc Kane is serving a 20 year sentence for killing his son-in-law. Now, after 16 years he is eligible for parole. He had joined a gang to survive prison life, but now his affiliation could come back to haunt him. Doc needs to free himself from gang entanglements long enough to get his parole approved. This is Parsons' first novel.

Where it's reviewed:
Booklist, August 2001, page 2090
New York Times Book Review, December 2, 2001, page 48
Publishers Weekly, September 3, 2001, page 56

Other books you might like:
James Baldwin, *If Beale Street Could Talk*, 1974
Chester Himes, *Yesterday Will Make You Cry*, 1998
Stephen Hunter, *Pale Horse Coming*, 2001
Rosalyn McMillan, *The Flip Side of Sin*, 2000
Christopher Moore, *Santa and Pete*, 1998

1180

JULIE PARSONS

Eager to Please

(New York: Simon & Shuster, 2001)

Story type: Psychological Suspense
Subject(s): Revenge; Murder; Mothers and Daughters
Major character(s): Rachel Beckett, Murderer (wrongly convicted); Daniel Beckett, Lover (of Rachel); Jack Donnelly, Detective—Homicide
Time period(s): 2000s (2001)
Locale(s): Dublin, Ireland

Summary: An embittered Rachel Beckett is released from prison after serving 12 years for murdering her husband, Martin. He harassed Rachel after learning her daughter was not his child but rather the product of an illicit affair with his brother, Daniel. Rachel believes Daniel killed Martin and sets out to trap him. Meanwhile, she becomes a suspect when a woman she met in prison turns up murdered.

Where it's reviewed:
Booklist, September 15, 2001, page 195
Kirkus Reviews, August 1, 2001, page 1059
Library Journal, October 15, 2001, page 109
New York Times Book Review, December 9, 2001, page 33
Publishers Weekly, September 3, 2001, page 58

Other books by the same author:
The Courtship Gift, 1999
Mary, Mary, 1998

Other books you might like:
Larry Brown, *Father and Son*, 1996
Mary Higgins Clark, *We'll Meet Again*, 1999
Don DeLillo, *Underworld*, 1997
Thomas Harris, *Hannibal*, 1999
Walter Mosley, *Walkin' the Dog*, 1999

1181

JAMES PATTERSON

Suzanne's Diary for Nicholas

(Boston: Little Brown, 2001)

Story type: Romance
Subject(s): Mothers and Sons; Grief; Relationships
Major character(s): Katie Wilkinson, Editor (book), Lover (of Matt); Matt, Spouse (ex of Suzanne), Parent (Nicholas' father); Suzanne, Parent (of Nicholas), Doctor (family practice)
Time period(s): 2000s (2001)
Locale(s): New York, New York; Martha's Vineyard, Massachusetts

Summary: James Patterson, master of the thriller, changes genres with a love story. Katie, an editor, wonders why her bestselling author and lover, Matt, left her. She is pregnant but he doesn't know. Then Katie receives a diary, that was kept by Suzanne, Matt's first wife. The diary reveals how Suzanne, a doctor, left the rat race after a heart attack and moved to Martha's Vineyard where she met Matt and gave birth to their baby, Nicholas.

Where it's reviewed:
Book, July 2001, page 78
Booklist, June 1, 2001, page 1904
Library Journal, July 2001, page 126
Publishers Weekly, June 4, 2001, page 53

Other books by the same author:
1st to Die, 2001

Violets Are Blue, 2001
Cradle and All, 2000
Roses Are Red, 2000
Pop Goes the Weasel, 1999

Other books you might like:
Nicholas Evans, *The Horse Whisperer*, 1995
Larry McMurtry, *Terms of Endearment*, 1975
Eric Segal, *Love Story*, 1970
Nicholas Sparks, *Message in a Bottle*, 1998
Robert James Waller, *The Bridges of Madison County*, 1992

1182

ARTURO PEREZ-REVERTE

The Nautical Chart

(New York: Harcourt, 2001)

Story type: Historical; Adventure
Subject(s): Treasure; Suspense; Salvage
Major character(s): Tanger Soto, Researcher (of nautical charts); Manuel Coy, Sailor (dockworker)
Time period(s): 2000s
Locale(s): Madrid, Spain

Summary: Manuel Coy, a sailor, finds himself working the docks after surviving a shipwreck. Attending an auction, he notices the attractive Tanger Soto bidding on an antique atlas. Soon she signs him up to help find a treasure ship, the *Dei Gloria*, sunk by pirates in 1767. Before their adventure ends they will have to outsmart a treasure hunter, a dwarf, and a killer.

Where it's reviewed:
Booklist, July 2001, page 1951
Kirkus Reviews, July 15, 2001, page 971
Library Journal, September 1, 2001, page 235
Publishers Weekly, August 13, 2001, page 281

Other books by the same author:
The Fencing Master, 1999
The Seville Communion, 1998
The Club Dumas, 1996
The Flanders Panel, 1994

Other books you might like:
A.S. Byatt, *The Biographer's Tale*, 2001
Umberto Eco, *The Name of the Rose*, 1983
Ross King, *Ex-Libris*, 2001
Allen Kurzweil, *The Grand Complication*, 2001
Betsy Tobin, *Bone House*, 2000

1183

MARIO PUZO

The Family

(New York: Regan, 2001)

Story type: Historical
Subject(s): Biography; Politics; Family Saga
Major character(s): Rodrigo Borgia, Historical Figure, Religious (elected Pope Alexander VI); Cesare Borgia, Historical Figure, Nobleman (Rodrigo's son); Lucrezia Borgia, Historical Figure, Noblewoman (Rodrigo's daughter)
Time period(s): 15th century; 16th century (1492-1559)
Locale(s): Rome, Italy

Summary: Puzo's final work tells the story of the Borgias, a family with some parallels to the Corleones of *The Godfather*. Rodrigo Borgia, a cardinal, buys enough votes to be elected Pope Alexander VI in 1492. His plans to establish a dynasty through his children are derailed when Cesare wants to be a soldier and Lucrezia wishes to marry for love. Puzo died before finishing the book; it was completed by Carol Gino.

Where it's reviewed:
Booklist, August 2001, page 2053
Kirkus Reviews, August 1, 2001, page 1060
Library Journal, September 1, 2001, page 235
Publishers Weekly, July 30, 2001, page 55

Other books by the same author:
Omerta, 2000
The Last Don, 1996
The Sicilian, 1984
Fools Die, 1978
The Godfather, 1969

Other books you might like:
Peter Carey, *True History of the Kelly Gang*, 2000
Nelson DeMille, *The Gold Coast*, 1990
Josephine Humphreys, *Nowhere Else on Earth*, 2000
Colleen McCullough, *Caesar*, 1997
William T. Vollmann, *Argall*, 2001

1184

PEGGY RAMBACH

Fighting Gravity

(South Royalton, Vermont: Steerforth, 2001)

Story type: Contemporary
Subject(s): Marriage; Teacher-Student Relationships; Traffic Accidents
Major character(s): Ellie Rifkin, Student, Spouse (of Gerard); Gerard Babineau, Professor (of literature), Handicapped (confined to wheelchair)
Time period(s): 2000s (2001)
Locale(s): New England; Alabama

Summary: Rambach's second novel, loosely based on her marriage to Andre Dubus, tells the story of Ellie Rifkin, a nice Jewish girl, and Gerard Babineau, a former Marine who is a Catholic and 20 years her senior. She is 19 and optimistic when they meet; he is a professor with four children and two ex-wives who has been hardened by his experiences. When a car accident confines him to a wheelchair, their relationship appears doomed but she demonstrates an inner strength.

Where it's reviewed:
Booklist, April 1, 2001, page 1448
Kirkus Reviews, February 1, 2001, page 138
Library Journal, April 1, 2001, page 134
New York Times Book Review, May 27, 2001, page 7

Other books you might like:
David Baldacci, *Wish You Well*, 2000
Anita Brookner, *A Private View*, 1994
Tabitha King, *Survivor*, 1997

Margot Livesey, *The Missing World*, 2000
Philip Roth, *The Dying Animal*, 2001

1185

ANNE RICE

Blood and Gold

(New York: Knopf, 2001)

Story type: Gothic; Vampire Story
Series: Vampire Chronicles
Subject(s): Vampires; Sexual Behavior; Werewolves
Major character(s): Marius, Vampire; Thorne, Vampire (fresh from a long sleep)
Time period(s): Multiple Time Periods
Locale(s): Roman Empire; Italy; Europe

Summary: This story introduces readers to the vampire Thorne, who encased himself in ice because he didn't relish killing. Now, after a nap that lasted several centuries, Thorne is awake and eager to learn vampire history. He seeks out the vampire Marius who agrees to tell his story. What follows is an update of vampire history and the role Marius played in it. Rice's novel is full of gory details and passionate lovemaking.

Where it's reviewed:
Book, November-December 2001, page 64
Booklist, August 2001, page 2051
Kirkus Reviews, August 1, 2001, page 1060
Library Journal, October 1, 2001, page 143

Other books by the same author:
Merrick, 2000
Violin, 1999
Vittorio, the Vampire, 1999
Pandora, 1998
The Vampire Armand, 1998

Other books you might like:
Kelley Armstrong, *Bitten*, 2001
Clive Barker, *Coldheart Canyon*, 2001
Stephen King, *Dreamcatcher*, 2001
Dean R. Koontz, *Servants of Twilight*, 1984
Joyce Carol Oates, *Beasts*, 2001

1186

THOMAS E. RICKS

A Soldier's Duty

(New York: Random House, 2001)

Story type: Political; Psychological Suspense
Subject(s): Conspiracies; War; Government
Major character(s): John Shillingsworth, Military Personnel (general); B.Z. Ames, Military Personnel (general); Cindy Sherman, Military Personnel (major assigned to the Pentagon)
Time period(s): Indeterminate Future
Locale(s): Washington, District of Columbia

Summary: The president sends troops on a peacekeeping mission that quickly turns into a military disaster. Media savvy General B.Z. Ames moves to take over the White House. Only General John Shillingsworth can stop him, but he will be forced to choose between betraying his comrades-in-arms or betraying his country. A romantic relationship between two aides, majors Buddy Lewis and Cindy Sherman, adds realism. This is the first novel for Ricks, the Pentagon correspondent for the *Washington Post*.

Where it's reviewed:
Booklist, May 1, 2001, page 1668
Chicago Tribune Books, October 14, 2001, page 3
Kirkus Reviews, April 1, 2001, page 457
Library Journal, May 1, 2001, page 127
Publishers Weekly, April 30, 2001, page 53

Other books you might like:
David Baldacci, *Absolute Power*, 1996
Nelson DeMille, *Word of Honor*, 1998
Stephen Hunter, *Pale Horse Coming*, 2001
Joseph Kanon, *The Good German*, 2001
James H. Webb, *Lost Soldiers*, 2001

1187

NORA ROBERTS

Midnight Bayou

(New York: Putnam, 2001)

Story type: Romance; Psychological Suspense
Subject(s): Reincarnation; Ghosts; Dreams and Nightmares
Major character(s): Declan Fitzgerald, Lawyer; Lena Simone, Saloon Keeper/Owner
Time period(s): 2000s (2001); 1900s (1900)
Locale(s): Boston, Massachusetts; New Orleans, Louisiana

Summary: Roberts' novel mixes history, romance, and ghosts, with a twist—a woman rescues a man. Declan Fitzgerald, a successful Boston lawyer, buys an old mansion on the outskirts of New Orleans. As he restores it, he begins to have dreams and see ghosts associated with a crime committed in the house, circa 1900. Declan is trapped until Lena, a smart, tough bar owner, saves him.

Where it's reviewed:
Booklist, October 1, 2001, page 304
Kirkus Reviews, September 1, 2001, page 1241
Publishers Weekly, September 3, 2001, page 55

Other books by the same author:
The Villa, 2001
River's End, 1999
The Donovan Legacy, 1999
Dance to the Piper, 1998
Born in Ice, 1996

Other books you might like:
Chris Adrian, *Gob's Grief*, 2000
Kelley Armstrong, *Bitten*, 2001
Joyce Carol Oates, *Beasts*, 2001
Tim Parks, *Mimi's Ghost*, 2001
Anne Rice, *Blood and Gold*, 2001

1188

MARY ROBISON

Why Did I Ever?

(Washington, D.C.: Counterpoint, 2001)

Story type: Psychological; Satire
Subject(s): Women; Aging; Modern Life
Major character(s): Money Breton, Writer (script writer), Divorced Person (three times); Paulie, Relative (Money's son), Crime Victim (of sexual assault); Mev, Relative (Money's daughter), Addict (on methadone)
Time period(s): 2000s (2001)
Locale(s): Alabama; Hollywood, California

Summary: Robison's highly satirical and humorous look at modern life is divided into 527 brief chapters, reflective of main character Money Breton's inability to focus. Money suffers from, among other things, Attention Deficit Disorder. While she lives primarily in a small town in Alabama, Money spends time in Hollywood, where she works as a script writer; in New Orleans, where her wealthy boyfriend lives; and sometimes in Florida where she ends up after long drives.

Where it's reviewed:
Booklist, October 1, 2001, page 300
Kirkus Reviews, August 15, 2001, page 1158
Library Journal, October 1, 2001, page 143
New York Times Book Review, November 25, 2001, page 7

Other books by the same author:
Subtraction, 1991
Believe Them, 1988
Amateur's Guide to the Night, 1983
Days, 1979

Other books you might like:
Chitra Banerjee Divakaruni, *The Unknown Errors of Our Lives*, 2001
Jennifer Egan, *Look at Me*, 2001
Elizabeth McCracken, *Niagara Falls All over Again*, 2001
Alice Munro, *Hateship, Friendship, Courtship, Loveship, Marriage*, 2001
Anne Tyler, *Back When We Were Grownups*, 2001

1189

KATIE ROIPHE

Still She Haunts Me

(New York: Dial, 2001)

Story type: Historical
Subject(s): Biography; Photography; Authors and Writers
Major character(s): Charles Dodgson, Historical Figure, Writer; Alice Liddell, Child, Historical Figure; Mrs. Liddell, Parent (of Alice), Historical Figure
Time period(s): 1860s (1862)
Locale(s): Oxford, England

Summary: Roiphe explores the relationship between Charles Dodgson, who wrote under the name of Lewis Carroll, and the pre-pubescent girl who inspired him to write *Alice in Wonderland* and *Through the Looking Glass*. Dodgson, a stuttering, shy tutor, becomes obsessed with Alice, the youngest daughter of Dean Liddell. Her childish purity appeals to Dodgson, who is disgusted by adult sexuality. Alice's mother's suspicions of his interest are confirmed, when she finds nude photographs of her daughter. Dodgson is barred from further contact.

Where it's reviewed:
Kirkus Reviews, July 15, 2001, page 972
New York Times Book Review, September 16, 2001, page 17
Publishers Weekly, August 20, 2001, page 52

Other books by the same author:
Last Night in Paradise, 1997
The Morning After, 1994

Other books you might like:
Trezza Azzopardi, *A Hiding Place*, 2001
A.S. Byatt, *The Biographer's Tale*, 2001
Isabel Colegate, *Winter Journey*, 2001
Helen Humphreys, *Afterimage*, 2000
Salman Rushdie, *The Ground Beneath Her Feet*, 1999

1190

SALMAN RUSHDIE

Fury

(New York: Random House, 2001)

Story type: Satire; Contemporary/Mainstream
Subject(s): Wealth; Teachers; Modern Life
Major character(s): Malik "Solly" Solanka, Professor (of philosophy), Inventor (of a popular doll); Mila, Lover (of Solly); Neela, Lover (of Solly)
Time period(s): 2000s (2001)
Locale(s): New York, New York; London, England

Summary: Rushdie's latest novel is a satire of modern society. Malik Solanka starts out teaching philosophy in England, he then becomes a TV star on the BBC and a successful inventor. Abandoning his wife and child, he moves to New York. He has more money than he ever dreamed of and is involved with the beautiful Mila and Neela. Still he is frustrated, exhausted, and not infrequently enraged. The narrative is accessible and fast paced.

Where it's reviewed:
Booklist, June 1, 2001, page 1798
Library Journal, August 2001, page 166
New York Times Book Review, September 9, 2001, page 8
Publishers Weekly, July 16, 2001, page 166

Other books by the same author:
The Ground Beneath Her Feet, 1999
The Moor's Last Sigh, 1995
The Satanic Verses, 1988
Shame, 1983
Midnight's Children, 1980

Other books you might like:
Nadine Gordimer, *The Pickup*, 2001
Mark Kurlansky, *The White Man in a Tree and Other Stories*, 2000
V.S. Naipaul, *Half a Life*, 2001
Ruth Prawer, *East into Upper East*, 1988
Tom Wolfe, *The Bonfire of the Vanities*, 1987

1191

KURBAN SAID

The Girl from the Golden Horn

(Woodstock, New York: Overlook, 2001)

Story type: Saga; Historical
Subject(s): Cultural Conflict; World War I; Love
Major character(s): Asiadeh Anbari, Young Woman (Muslim), Noblewoman (daughter of an exiled pasha); Alexander Hassa, Spouse (of Asiadeh), Doctor; Abdul Kerim, Expatriate (in hiding), Royalty (prince)
Time period(s): 2000s (2001)
Locale(s): Berlin, Germany; Vienna, Austria

Summary: In his second novel, Said takes a look at cultural differences. Asiadeh, daughter of an exiled pasha, is drifting in Berlin until she meets Alexander. They fall in love, marry, and move to Vienna. The clash of her Muslim upbringing with his European background becomes a real source of friction. More conflict arises when Prince Abdul Kerim, the man she was supposed to marry, arrives to claim her. Translated by Jenia Graman.

Where it's reviewed:
Book, November-December 2001, page 68
Kirkus Reviews, October 1, 2001, page 1389
Library Journal, December 1, 2001, page 175
New York Times Book Review, January 6, 2002, page 16
Publishers Weekly, October 15, 2001, page 45

Other books by the same author:
Ali and Nino, 1996

Other books you might like:
Michael Chabon, *The Amazing Adventures of Kavalier & Clay*, 2000
Len Deighton, *Hope*, 1996
Joseph Kanon, *The Good German*, 2001
John Le Carre, *Single & Single*, 1999
Philip Roth, *I Married a Communist*, 1998

1192

BERNHARD SCHLINK

Flights of Love

(New York: Pantheon, 2001)

Story type: Collection
Subject(s): Psychological; Relationships; Secrets
Time period(s): 20th century

Summary: German writer Schlink's second book published in this country is a collection of seven short stories. Translated by John E. Woods, the stories examine love without sentimentality. Instead, the author looks at the wounds and scars experienced by children, husbands, wives, and lovers. Surprising twists deftly delivered at the end add interest. Two of the stories are set in North America, one in an unnamed South American country, and the rest in Germany.

Where it's reviewed:
Kirkus Reviews, September 15, 2001, page 1319
Publishers Weekly, September 3, 2001, page 54

Other books by the same author:
The Reader, 1997

Other books you might like:
Ann Beattie, *Park City*, 1998
Frederick Busch, *The Children in the Woods*, 1994
Jill McCorkle, *Creatures of Habit*, 2001
Alice Munro, *Open Secrets*, 1994
Haruki Murakami, *Norwegian Wood*, 2000

1193

HEIDI JON SCHMIDT

Darling?

(New York: St. Martin's Picador, 2001)

Story type: Americana; Collection
Subject(s): Humor; Customs; Modern Life
Time period(s): 20th century

Summary: In this collection of ten short stories, Schmidt uses humor to probe the meaning of modern life. Women characters are passionate, while men tend to be rational. Story premises are whimsical and often become very funny such as a woman who discovers she may have a distant Jewish ancestor and rushes out to propose to a Jewish man. Characters include the silent suffering, the married couple, resentful children, bewildered parents, the elderly, and the wary.

Where it's reviewed:
Kirkus Reviews, July 15, 2001, page 973
New York Times Book Review, September 23, 2001, page 24

Other books by the same author:
The Rose Thieves, 1990

Other books you might like:
T. Coraghessan Boyle, *After the Plague*, 2001
Ellen Gilchrist, *The Cabal and Other Stories*, 2000
Erika Krouse, *Come Up and See Me Sometime*, 2001
Margot Livesey, *Eva Moves the Furniture*, 2001
Salman Rushdie, *Fury*, 2001

1194

SUSAN SEGAL

Aria

(Bridgehampton, New York: Bridge Works, 2001)

Story type: Psychological; Romance
Subject(s): Music and Musicians; Widows/Widowers; Friendship
Major character(s): Eve Miller, Survivor (of a shipwreck), Widow(er); Isabel Stein, Singer (opera); Noah Stewart, Composer (opera)
Time period(s): 2000s (2001)
Locale(s): Sydney, Australia; New York

Summary: Segal's first novel explores fame and friendship. Eve Miller survives a shipwreck but her husband and two children perish. Despite her unwillingness, the news media makes Eve a celebrity but the public spotlight overwhelms her. When she meets Isabel, an aging opera star who offers Eve a place to convalesce, she accepts gratefully. At Isabel's estate, Eve meets Noah who is writing an opera for Isabel. As she confronts her own tragedy, Eve uncovers Isabel's motivation.

Where it's reviewed:
Kirkus Reviews, July 1, 2001, page 900
Library Journal, September 1, 2001, page 235
New York Times Book Review, November 18, 2001, page 68
Publishers Weekly, September 3, 2001, page 65

Other books you might like:
Bebe Moore Campbell, *Singing in the Comeback Choir*, 1998
Carol Higgins Clark, *Twanged*, 1998
Jackie Collins, *Vendetta*, 1997
Stanley Crouch, *Don't the Moon Look Lonesome*, 2000
Barbara Delinsky, *Lake News*, 1999

1195

GARY SERNOVITZ

Great American Plain

(New York: Henry Holt, 2001)

Story type: Coming-of-Age; Humor
Subject(s): Love; Interpersonal Relations; Brothers
Major character(s): Edward Steinke, Young Man; Barry Steinke, Young Man, Relative (Ed's younger brother); Leila Genet, Young Woman
Time period(s): 2000s (2001)
Locale(s): Midwest

Summary: The author's first novel follows the lives of three young people for a single day. Ed rents a booth at the state fair to sell an expensive piano organ, expecting to make a killing. He enlists the help of his brother Barry. Barry, even though he knows better, goes along in order to meet women. The brothers bicker until Leila stops at their booth. Detailed humorous flashbacks flesh out the lives and backgrounds of the three characters.

Where it's reviewed:
Booklist, September 1, 2001, page 52
Kirkus Reviews, August 15, 2001, page 1159
New York Times Book Review, October 21, 2001, page 32
Publishers Weekly, September 3, 2001, page 55

Other books you might like:
Chris Adrian, *Gob's Grief*, 2000
Jim Harrison, *Legends of the Fall*, 1989
Ann Patchett, *Bel Canto*, 2001
John Smolens, *Cold*, 2001
Anne Tyler, *Dinner at the Homesick Restaurant*, 1982

1196

ALEX SHAKAR

The Savage Girl

(New York: HarperCollins, 2001)

Story type: Contemporary/Fantasy; Satire
Subject(s): Sisters; Mental Illness; Popular Culture
Major character(s): Ursula Van Urden, Artist (struggling), Relative (Ivy's sister); Ivy Van Urden, Model, Mentally Ill Person (schizophrenic); Chas LaCouture, Boyfriend (Ivy's ex), Businessman (founder of Tomorrow Ltd.)
Time period(s): 21st century
Locale(s): Middle City

Summary: Shakar's first novel uses humor and fantastic projections to lampoon market-driven ideology. A homeless, deaf-mute with a Mohawk haircut inspires trend spotter Ursula to come up with the idea of ''the savage look'' to promote products such as diet water. Ursula's schizophrenic sister, Ivy, becomes the spokesmodel while Ursula's boss and Ivy's former boyfriend, Chas, provides the corporate resources. Unfortunately, the idea falls flat. However, the characters move on to other things.

Where it's reviewed:
Book, September 2001, page 14
Chicago Tribune Books, October 7, 2001, page 1
Kirkus Reviews, August 15, 2001, page 1160
New York Times Book Review, October 7, 2001, page 8
Publishers Weekly, August 20, 2001, page 78

Other books by the same author:
City in Love, 1996

Other books you might like:
Ann Beattie, *Perfect Recall*, 2001
Robert Cohen, *Inspired Sleep*, 2001
Walter Kirn, *Up in the Air*, 2001
Dennis McFarland, *Singing Boy*, 2001

1197

BARBARA SHULGASSER-PARKER

Funny Accent

(New York: Picador, 2001)

Subject(s): Relationships; Holocaust; Refugees
Major character(s): Anna, Lover (of Misha); Misha, Friend (of Anna's family), Lover
Time period(s): 2000s (2001)
Locale(s): Chicago, Illinois; New York, New York

Summary: In her first novel, Shulgasser-Parker, who co-wrote the film *Pret-a-Porter*, tells a Lolita-type story with a twist. Now 32 and living in Chicago, Anna publishes a short story, that details a romantic relationship with Misha, a family friend when she was 13 and he was 52. The story is set in New York among Holocaust survivors, where accents are not uncommon. The author uses her wry sense of humor to examine the meaning of normalcy.

Where it's reviewed:
Chicago Tribune Books, August 5, 2001, page 2
Kirkus Reviews, April 1, 2001, page 451

Other books you might like:
Margaret Atwood, *Life Before Man*, 1979
Shifra Horn, *The Fairest Among Women*, 2001
John Irving, *The Hotel New Hampshire*, 1981
Savyon Liebrecht, *A Man and a Woman and a Man*, 2001
Peggy Rambach, *Fighting Gravity*, 2001

1198

JOAN SILBER

Lucky Us

(Chapel Hill, North Carolina: Algonquin, 2001)

Story type: Romance
Subject(s): Relationships; AIDS (Disease); Sexual Behavior
Major character(s): Elisa, Artist (HIV positive); Gabe, Fiance(e) (of Elisa), Drug Dealer (former); Jason, Boyfriend (of Elisa), Addict (HIV positive)
Time period(s): 2000s (2001)
Locale(s): New York, New York

Summary: Laced with grim reality, this love story is Silber's fourth book. Elisa, a young artist into drugs and wild sex, meets an older, mature man named Gabe, an ex-con who has abandoned his drug dealing past. They fall in love and plan a wedding. When Elisa's AIDS test comes back positive, she freaks and returns to Jason, the ex-boyfriend who infected her. After she becomes ill, Jason leaves her and she goes back to Gabe.

Where it's reviewed:
Booklist, September 1, 2001, page 53
Chicago Tribune Books, October 21, 2001, page 3
Kirkus Reviews, August 1, 2001, page 1062
Library Journal, July 2001, page 126
Publishers Weekly, September 3, 2001, page 55

Other books by the same author:
In My Other Life, 2000
In the City, 1987
Household Words, 1985

Other books you might like:
Ann Beattie, *My Life, Starring Dara Falcon*, 1997
Helen Dewitt, *The Last Samurai*, 2000
Paul Golding, *The Abomination*, 2000
Alice Hoffman, *Local Girls*, 1999
Michel Houellebecq, *The Elementary Particles*, 2000

1199

JOHN SMOLENS

Cold

(New York: Shaye Areheart, 2001)

Story type: Psychological Suspense
Subject(s): Revenge; Relationships; Wilderness
Major character(s): Norman Haas, Prisoner (escaped); Liesl Tiomenen, Widow(er); Del Maki, Police Officer (leads search for Norman)
Time period(s): 2000s (2001)
Locale(s): Upper Peninsula, Michigan

Summary: In prison where he is serving time for assaulting his brother Warren, who had an affair with his wife, Norman escapes into the snow-covered wilderness of Michigan's Upper Peninsula. Widow Liesl Tiomenen captures Norman but he flees into a blizzard and heads for the home of his wife and small daughter. Meanwhile, his father-in-law, his brother, and local sheriff Del Maki are on his trail as the story moves towards a violent climax.

Where it's reviewed:
Chicago Tribune Books, November 25, 2001, page 2
Kirkus Reviews, June 15, 2001, page 827
Library Journal, August 2001, page 166
New York Times Book Review, November 18, 2001, page 68
Publishers Weekly, August 6, 2001, page 60

Other books by the same author:
Angel's Head, 1994
Winter by Degrees, 1988

Other books you might like:
Barbara Taylor Bradford, *Love in Another Town*, 1995
Catherine Coulter, *Impulse*, 1990
Jim Harrison, *The Beast God Forgot to Invent*, 2000
Haruki Murakami, *The Sputnik Sweetheart*, 2001
Joyce Carol Oates, *Faithless*, 2001

1200

NICHOLAS SPARKS

A Bend in the Road

(New York: Warner, 2001)

Story type: Psychological; Romance
Subject(s): Traffic Accidents; Sheriffs; Teachers
Major character(s): Miles Ryan, Widow(er), Police Officer (deputy sheriff); Sarah Andrews, Teacher (Jonah's), Divorced Person; Jonah Ryan, Child (Miles' 7-year-old son), Student (emotionally troubled)
Time period(s): 2000s (2001)
Locale(s): New Bern, North Carolina

Summary: Miles Ryan's idyllic world suddenly unravels when his wife, Missy, is killed by a hit-and-run driver. Grief-stricken, Miles neglects his son Jonah, who is having trouble in school. When second grade teacher Sarah takes an interest in Jonah, Miles notices her efforts and becomes attracted to her. However, an anonymous tip about Missy's death launches Miles on a mission. His obsession with discovering the truth stretches his professional and personal relationships to the limit.

Where it's reviewed:
Booklist, September 1, 2001, page 4
Publishers Weekly, August 27, 2001, page 50

Other books by the same author:
The Rescue, 2000
A Walk to Remember, 1999
Message in a Bottle, 1998
The Notebook, 1996

Other books you might like:
David Baldacci, *Wish You Well*, 2000
Barbara Delinsky, *Three Wishes*, 1997
Ellen Gilchrist, *Starcarbon*, 1994
Jacquelyn Mitchard, *A Theory of Relativity*, 2001
Rosamunde Pilcher, *Winter Solstice*, 2000

1201

ELIZABETH SPENCER

The Southern Woman

(New York: Modern Library, 2001)

Story type: Collection
Subject(s): Women; Culture; Customs
Time period(s): 20th century; 2000s (1940-2000)
Locale(s): Italy

Summary: This collection of 27 short works includes the novella *The Light in the Piazza* and six new stories. The novella, which was made into a 1962 movie, is a romance set in Italy and concerns an American mother who arranges the marriage of her mentally disabled daughter. The story reveals how social convention can be manipulated to advantage. Spencer looks at the fixed social order and its influences on her characters in many of the other stories as well.

Where it's reviewed:
Kirkus Reviews, May 15, 2001, page 696
Library Journal, August 2001, page 168
New York Times Book Review, August 26, 2001, page 7
Publishers Weekly, July 23, 2001, page 49

Other books by the same author:
The Night Travellers, 1991
Jack of Diamonds, 1988
Salt Line, 1984
The Stories of Elizabeth Spencer, 1981
The Snare, 1972

Other books you might like:
Ann Beattie, *Perfect Recall*, 2001
Penelope Fitzgerald, *Innocence*, 1986
Ellen Gilchrist, *The Cabal and Other Stories*, 2000
Paula K. Grove, *White Boys and River Girls*, 1995
Alice Munro, *The Love of a Good Woman*, 1998

1202

DANA SPIOTTA

Lightning Field

(New York: Scribner, 2001)

Story type: Modern; Satire
Subject(s): Popular Culture; Infidelity; City and Town Life
Major character(s): Mina, Young Woman (bored with marriage); Lorene, Restaurateur (manages a restaurant chain), Employer; Michael, Relative (Mina's brother), Lover (former, of Lorene)
Time period(s): 2000s (2001)
Locale(s): Los Angeles, California

Summary: In her first novel, Spiotta has written an offbeat humorous character study exploring the post-modern angst of upper-middle class Los Angeles. The daughter of a has-been movie director, Mina is married to Dave, a screenwriter, while she carries on with two other men. The story is loosely organized around a cross-country trip which Mina and her boss Lorene take to find Michael, Mina's brother, who recently checked out of a mental hospital. Their quest for self-discovery becomes more important than their search for Michael.

Where it's reviewed:
Kirkus Reviews, June 1, 2001, page 768
New York Times Book Review, September 30, 2001, page 14
Publishers Weekly, August 13, 2001, page 286

Other books you might like:
T. Coraghessan Boyle, *The Tortilla Curtain*, 1995
Don DeLillo, *Underworld*, 1997
Richard Ford, *Independence Day*, 1995
Hanif Kureishi, *Gabriel's Gift*, 2001
Gore Vidal, *Hollywood*, 1990

1203

DANIELLE STEEL

Leap of Faith

(New York: Delacorte, 2001)

Story type: Romance; Contemporary
Subject(s): Orphans; Secrets; Accidents
Major character(s): Marie-Ange Hawkins, Heiress, Orphan (parents killed in an accident); Carole, Handicapped (in wheelchair), Relative (Marie-Ange's aunt); Billy Parker, Friend (of Marie-Ange)
Time period(s): 20th century; 2000s (1941-2000)
Locale(s): France; Iowa

Summary: When a car crash kills her parents and brother, Marie-Ange, 11, leaves France to live with a mean aunt on an Iowa farm. A lonely child, she is befriended by Billy Parker, the boy next door. When Marie-Ange inherits a fortune from her parents, she returns to France. There she marries Comte Bernard de Beauchamp with whom she has two children. A crisis develops when Marie-Ange learns about her husband's sordid past including murder. Marie-Ange thens turns to Billy.

Where it's reviewed:
Booklist, March 15, 2001, page 1333
Kirkus Reviews, April 1, 2001, page 452
Publishers Weekly, May 21, 2001, page 82

Other books by the same author:
Lone Eagle, 2001
The Kiss, 2001
The Wedding, 2000
Mirror Image, 1998
The Ranch, 1997

Other books you might like:
Anita Brookner, *The Bay of Angels*, 2001
Pat Conroy, *The Prince of Tides*, 1986
Catherine Coulter, *Hemlock Bay*, 2001
Valerie Martin, *Italian Fever*, 1999
Joyce Carol Oates, *Faithless*, 2001

1204

JANE STEVENSON

London Bridges

(Boston: Houghton Mifflin, 2001)

Story type: Contemporary; Gay/Lesbian Fiction
Subject(s): Greed; History; Humor
Major character(s): Mr. Eugenides, Aged Person (lives alone); Sebastian Raphael, Scholar (of antiquity), Friend (of Mr. Eugenides); Edward Lupset, Lawyer
Time period(s): 2000s (2001)
Locale(s): London, England

Summary: Stevenson's first novel revolves around the treasure of a London church destroyed during World War II. Slick Edward, intent on stealing the treasure, befriends Mr. Eugenides, the only living church member and moves in with the older man, but his scheme begins to unravel. Sebastian, a classical scholar, becomes suspicious when his graduate student Jeanene, who moonlights as a pharmacist, reveals that Mr. Eugenides' medicine could be harmful. A dog and a motorcycle chase add fun.

Where it's reviewed:
Kirkus Reviews, July 1, 2001, page 897
Library Journal, July 2001, page 126
New York Times Book Review, September 23, 2001, page 7
Publishers Weekly, August 13, 2001, page 286

Other books by the same author:
Several Deceptions, 1999 (novella collection)

Other books you might like:
James Lee Burke, *Heartwood*, 1999
Michael Crichton, *Timeline*, 1999
Margaret Drabble, *The Realms of Gold*, 1975
Frederick Forsyth, *The Deceiver*, 1991
Barry Reed, *The Deception*, 1997

1205

SUSAN STRAIGHT

Highwire Moon

(Boston: Houghton Mifflin, 2001)

Story type: Contemporary; Multicultural
Subject(s): Migrant Labor; Mothers and Daughters; Unmarried Mothers
Major character(s): Serafina, Parent (of Elvia), Immigrant (illegal); Elvia, Relative (Serafina's daughter), Pregnant Teenager (looking for her mother)
Time period(s): 2000s (2001)
Locale(s): Rio Seco, California

Summary: Straight's fourth novel is about two women attempting to find each other after a 12-year separation. Serafina came to the U.S. illegally and later gives birth to Elvia. When her daughter was a toddler, Serafina was deported to Mexico. Now, Elvia is an angry pregnant teenager. She must overcome drug abuse and poverty before she can be reunited with her mother. The story brings to life the violent and brutal world migrant farm workers inhabit.

Where it's reviewed:
Booklist, July 2001, page 1984
Chicago Tribune Books, August 5, 2001, page 2
Kirkus Reviews, May 15, 2001, page 696
New York Times Book Review, August 26, 2001, page 16
Publishers Weekly, July 30, 2001, page 60

Other books by the same author:
The Gettin' Place, 1996
Aquaboogie, 1994
I Been in Sorrow's Kitchen and Licked out All the Pots, 1992

Other books you might like:
Isabel Allende, *Portrait in Sepia*, 2001
Dan Chaon, *Among the Missing*, 2001
Tracy Chevalier, *Falling Angels*, 2001
Barbara Delinsky, *For My Daughters*, 1994
Louise Erdrich, *The Bingo Palace*, 1994

1206

ALEXANDRA STYRON

All the Finest Girls

(Boston: Little Brown, 2001)

Story type: Psychological; Contemporary
Subject(s): Grief; Babysitters; Family
Major character(s): Adelaide ''Addy'' Abraham, Museum Curator; Louise ''Lou'' Alfred, Child-Care Giver (to Addy); Barbara Abraham, Actress, Parent (Addy's mother)
Time period(s): 2000s (2001)
Locale(s): St. Claire, West Indies; New York, New York

Summary: In her first novel, Alexandra Styron, daughter of novelist William Styron, tells the story of a woman attempting to work through the difficulty caused by her emotionally remote parents. Much too involved in their own lives to bother with child care, Addy Abraham's parents hire Lou Alfred, a West Indian, to care for their daughter. The story revolves around Addy's reminiscences of her childhood when she attends Lou's funeral, on her native St. Claire.

Where it's reviewed:
Booklist, May 1, 2001, page 1669
Chicago Tribune Books, August 12, 2001, page 3
Library Journal, April 1, 2001, page 134
New York Times Book Review, July 15, 2001, page 2
Publishers Weekly, May 28, 2001, page 49

Other books you might like:
Joan Didion, *The Last Thing He Wanted*, 1996
Ann Fairbairn, *Five Smooth Stones*, 1966
Paula Fox, *A Servant's Tale*, 1984
Gale Zoe Garnett, *Visible Amazement*, 1999
Emma Richler, *Sister Crazy*, 2001

1207

LALITA TADEMY

Cane River

(New York: Warner, 2001)

Story type: Multicultural; Historical

Subject(s): Family Relations; African Americans
Major character(s): Suzette, Slave (house servant), Grandparent (of Emily); Philomene, Slave, Relative (Suzette's daughter); Emily, Relative (Philomene's daughter)
Time period(s): 19th century; 20th century (1834-1934)
Locale(s): Cane River, Louisiana

Summary: Lalita Tademy's first novel is a fictional biography of her family. She follows five generations of African American women from slavery until the present day. Readers are pulled into the family's circle as the women deal with rape, racism, and everyday life. Over the years the pecking order inherited from slavery, which was predicated on skin color, changes. Instead of denying black skin to pass as white, color is embraced and black becomes beautiful.

Where it's reviewed:
Booklist, February 15, 2001, page 1086
Kirkus Reviews, February 15, 2001, page 211
Publishers Weekly, March 12, 2001, page 62

Other books you might like:
Tananarive Due, *The Black Rose*, 2000
Nella Larsen, *Passing*, 1969
Terry McMillan, *A Day Late and a Dollar Short*, 2001
Toni Morrison, *Sula*, 1973
Alice Walker, *The Way Forward Is with a Broken Heart*, 2000

1208

SHASHI THAROOR

Riot

(New York: Arcade, 2001)

Story type: Psychological; Ethnic
Subject(s): Love; Parent and Child; Riots
Major character(s): Priscilla Hart, Student (killed in a riot); Katherine Hart, Parent (Priscilla's mother), Divorced Person (Rudyard's ex-wife); Rudyard Hart, Parent (Priscilla's father), Divorced Person (Katherine's ex-husband)
Time period(s): 1980s (1989)
Locale(s): Zalilgarh, India

Summary: Tharoor's novel examines the conflict between love and tradition, when East meets West. American student-worker Priscilla, 24, is killed during a riot in India. Officials attribute her death to a religious conflict, after a festival turns violent. When her divorced parents arrive to investigate, they only find bits and pieces of the story. Readers learn that a love affair between Priscilla and a married government official provided fuel for the riot.

Where it's reviewed:
Booklist, August 2001, page 2092
Kirkus Reviews, July 15, 2001, page 974
Library Journal, August 2001, page 167
New York Times Book Review, November 25, 2001, page 19
Publishers Weekly, August 13, 2001, page 284

Other books by the same author:
Show Business, 1992
The Great Indian Novel, 1989

Other books you might like:
V.S. Naipaul, *Half a Life*, 2001
Peggy Payne, *Sister India*, 2001
Kurban Said, *The Girl from the Golden Horn*, 2001
Manil Suri, *The Death of Vishnu*, 2001
Vineeta Vijayaraghavan, *Motherland*, 2001

1209

JOANNA TORREY

He Goes, She Goes

(New York: Crown, 2001)

Story type: Coming-of-Age
Subject(s): Dancing; Fathers and Daughters; Death
Major character(s): Alice, Office Worker (temporary); Gwen, Hairdresser
Time period(s): 2000s (2001)
Locale(s): New England; New York, New York

Summary: As a child, Alice longs for physical and emotional contact with her father, but he is a cold and distant man. When he dies, Alice, her mother, and her sister Gwen all react in different ways. Alice's mother, who gave up everything that brought her pleasure during her husband's lifetime, takes up with a neighbor. Gwen abandons her wild ways and becomes a virtual nonentity. Alice takes refuge in dance and begins to question everything in her life, including her career and her boyfriend. This is a first novel.

Where it's reviewed:
Booklist, November 15, 2001, page 554
Kirkus Reviews, September 15, 2001, page 1320
Library Journal, October 15, 2001, page 110
Publishers Weekly, October 29, 2001, page 34

Other books by the same author:
Hungry, 1998

Other books you might like:
Louis Auchincloss, *Tales of Yesteryear*, 1994
Cheryl Benard, *Turning on the Girls*, 2001
Erika Krouse, *Come Up and See Me Sometime*, 2001
Tamara McKinley, *Jacaranda Vines*, 2001
Lydia Millet, *My Happy Life*, 2002

1210

OMAR TYREE

Just Say No!

(New York: Simon & Schuster, 2001)

Story type: Coming-of-Age
Subject(s): African Americans; Music and Musicians; Men
Major character(s): Darin Harmon, Narrator, Sports Figure (college football player); John "Loverboy" Williams, Musician, Singer (pop music)
Time period(s): 2000s (2001)
Locale(s): North Carolina

Summary: Two African American men are followed as they try to make it in the music business. Playing on a football scholarship, Darin's plans are dashed when he suffers a career ending injury. Meanwhile, his friend John drops out of college to launch his singing career as "Loverboy." Darin becomes John's manager and John becomes a success but then turns into a sex and drug addict. Darin leaves and John's decline accelerates.

Where it's reviewed:
Booklist, June 15, 2001, page 1850
Kirkus Reviews, June 1, 2001, page 770
Publishers Weekly, August 6, 2001, page 62

Other books by the same author:
For the Love of Money, 2000
Sweet St. Louis, 1999
Single Mom, 1998
A Do Right Man, 1997

Other books you might like:
Betsy Berne, *Bad Timing*, 2001
Bebe Moore Campbell, *What You Owe Me*, 2001
Stanley Crouch, *Don't the Moon Look Lonesome*, 2000
Jack Fuller, *The Best of Jackson Payne*, 2000
E. Lynn Harris, *Any Way the Wind Blows*, 2001

1211

MARIO VARGAS LLOSA

The Feast of the Goat

(New York: Farrar, Straus & Giroux, 2001)

Story type: Multicultural; Political
Subject(s): Dictators; Fathers and Daughters; Political Crimes and Offenses
Major character(s): Urania Cabral, Lawyer; Rafael Trujillo, Historical Figure, Political Figure (dictator); Ramfis Trujillo, Relative (Rafael's son), Historical Figure
Time period(s): 20th century (1930-1996)
Locale(s): Dominican Republic

Summary: The author presents a fictionalized account of the dictator Rafael Trujillo's bloody reign over the Dominican Republic. As a young girl, Urania Cabral's father offers her to the dictator. When Trujillo is assassinated in 1961, Urania leaves for New York. Some 35 years later, she returns to Santo Domingo and recounts the events that led up to her initial departure. Her recollections put a face on Trujillo's many perversions. Translated by Edith Grossman.

Where it's reviewed:
Booklist, July 2001, page 1952
Chicago Tribune Books, November 18, 2001, page 2
Kirkus Reviews, September 1, 2001, page 1242
Library Journal, September 1, 2001, page 236
Publishers Weekly, July 30, 2001, page 55

Other books by the same author:
The Notebooks of Don Rigoberto, 1998
Death in the Andes, 1996
In Praise of the Stepmother, 1990
The Storyteller, 1989
Who Killed Palomino Molero?, 1987

Other books you might like:
Anonymous, *Primary Colors*, 1996
Joan Didion, *The Last Thing He Wanted*, 1996
James Ellroy, *The Cold Six Thousand*, 2001
Barbara Kingsolver, *The Poisonwood Bible*, 1998
Colleen McCullough, *Fortune's Favorites*, 1993

1212

WILLIAM T. VOLLMANN

Argall

(New York: Viking, 2001)

Story type: Historical
Series: Seven Dreams. Book 3
Subject(s): Biography; Native Americans; American Colonies
Major character(s): Captain John Smith, Historical Figure, Kidnapper; Pocahontas, Historical Figure, Indian (saves Smith's life); Samuel Argall, Leader (of colony), Kidnapper (of Pocahontas)
Time period(s): 17th century (1617-1626)
Locale(s): Jamestown, Virginia, American Colonies

Summary: The third novel in Vollmann's Seven Dreams series is a revisionist history of the Jamestown settlement. Pocahontas saves the life of Captain John Smith and the colony from starvation. The treacherous Samuel Argall seizes the opportunity to introduce slavery and genocide. He rewards Pocahontas by kidnapping her and she lives unhappily ever after as the wife of a planter. Chronicled by William the Blind, this story will not be confused with the Disney movie.

Where it's reviewed:
Booklist, August 2001, page 2053
Kirkus Reviews, September 1, 2001, page 1242
New York Times Book Review, September 30, 2001, page 18
Publishers Weekly, September 3, 2001, page 55

Other books by the same author:
The Royal Family, 2000
The Rifles, 1994
Butterfly Stories, 1993
Second Dream, Fathers and Crows, 1992 (Seven Dreams series)
The Ice-Shirt, 1990 (Seven Dreams series)

Other books you might like:
Colleen McCullough, *Morgan's Run*, 2000
Patrick McGrath, *Martha Peake*, 2000
Larry McMurtry, *Lonesome Dove*, 1985
Jill Paton Walsh, *A Desert in Bohemia*, 2000
Gore Vidal, *The Golden Age*, 2000

1213

ANN WADSWORTH

Light Coming Back

(Los Angeles: Alyson, 2001)

Story type: Psychological; Gay/Lesbian Fiction
Subject(s): Women; Illness; Hospitals
Major character(s): Mercedes Medina, Professor (literature), Spouse (of Patrick); Patrick Medina, Musician (cellist); Lennie Visitor, Clerk (flower shop), Lover (of Mercedes)
Time period(s): 2000s (2001)
Locale(s): United States

Summary: The narrative in Wadsworth's first book switches from the first person to the third person. The story follows two relationships. Mercedes, a college professor, marries a successful older man, Patrick, a famous cellist and they spend many blissful years together. When Patrick is very old and terminally ill, Mercedes, herself approaching retirement, meets Lennie, a young woman who works in a flower shop and they have an affair. Patrick dies and Lennie breaks off their relationship, leaving Mercedes devastated.

Where it's reviewed:
Advocate, December 4, 2001, page 74
Kirkus Reviews, July 15, 2001, page 975

Other books you might like:
Rita Mae Brown, *Rubyfruit Jungle*, 1983
Sylvia Brownrigg, *Pages for You*, 2001
Helen Humphreys, *Afterimage*, 2000
Armistead Maupin, *The Night Listener*, 2000
Sarah Waters, *Tipping the Velvet*, 1999

1214

KEN WELLS

Junior's Leg

(New York: Random House, 2001)

Story type: Humor; Ethnic
Subject(s): Organized Crime; Physically Handicapped
Major character(s): Joseph ''Junior'' Guidry, Narrator (good ol' boy), Handicapped (lost his leg); Iris Mary Parfait, Girlfriend (of Junior), Fugitive (hiding from gangsters); Rocko Marchante, Organized Crime Figure (beats up women)
Time period(s): 2000s (2001)
Locale(s): Great Catahoula Swamp, Louisiana

Summary: Returning to Bayou country for his second novel, Wells tells the tale of Joseph ''Junior'' Guidry. He loses a leg in a drilling accident and blows his insurance settlement on wine and women. Junior is despondent until he meets Iris Mary who is on the run from Rocko, a mobster. The plot thickens when Rocko captures Iris Mary, but with help from his attorney, Junior rescues her at the expense of Rocko and an evil sheriff.

Where it's reviewed:
Booklist, August 2001, page 2093
Kirkus Reviews, July 1, 2001, page 898
Library Journal, July 2001, page 127
Publishers Weekly, July 16, 2001, page 156

Other books by the same author:
Meely LaBauve, 2000

Other books you might like:
V.C. Andrews, *Hidden Jewel*, 1995
James Lee Burke, *In the Electric Mist with Confederate Dead*, 1993
Shirley Ann Grau, *The Hard Blue Sky*, 1958
Carl Hiaasen, *Stormy Weather*, 1995
John Irving, *The Fourth Hand*, 2001

Series Index

This index alphabetically lists series to which books featured in the entries belong. Beneath each series name, book titles are listed alphabetically with author names and genre codes. The genre codes are as follows: *c* Popular Fiction, *f* Fantasy, *h* Horror, *i* Inspirational, *m* Mystery, *r* Romance, *s* Science Fiction, *t* Historical, and *w* Western. Numbers refer to the entries that feature each title.

20 Amber Court
When Jayne Met Erik - Elizabeth Bevarly *r* 236

87th Precinct
Money, Money, Money - Ed McBain *m* 152

Abel Jones
Call Each River Jordan - Owen Parry *m* 169
Call Each River Jordan - Owen Parry *t* 914

Acorna
Acorna's Search - Anne McCaffrey *s* 772

Addingtons Trilogy
The Wedding Charm - Lynn Collum *r* 258

Agatha Raisin
Agatha Raisin and the Love from Hell - M.C. Beaton *m* 14

Age of Misrule
Always Forever - Mark Chadbourn *f* 533

Alan Banks
Aftermath - Peter Robinson *m* 186

Alan Graham
The Last Mayan - Malcolm Shuman *m* 195

Albany Cycle
Roscoe - William Kennedy *t* 897

Alex Plumtree
Uncatalogued - Julie Kaewert *m* 128

Alexandra Cooper
The Deadhouse - Linda Fairstein *m* 66

Alix Thorssen
Blue Wolf - Lise McClendon *w* 477

Alo Nudger
The Nudger Dilemmas - John Lutz *m* 147

Ambrose Bierce
Ambrose Bierce and the Death of Kings - Oakley Hall *m* 95
Ambrose Bierce and the Death of Kings - Oakley Hall *t* 878

American Chronicles of John H. Watson, M.D.
Sherlock Holmes and the Secret Alliance - Larry Millett *t* 908

American Story
Treason - David Nevin *t* 912

Anasazi Mystery
Bone Walker - Kathleen O'Neal Gear *t* 871

Angelina Amalfi
Bell, Cook, and Candle - Joanne Pence *m* 170

Anita Blake
Narcissus in Chains - Laurell K. Hamilton *h* 645

Anneke Haagen
Better than Sex - Susan Holtzer *m* 120

Apocalypse Diaries
Devil's Island - John Hagee *i* 994

Aquasilva
Heresy - Anselm Audley *s* 718

Arrandin
The Treason of Dortrean - Marcus Herniman *f* 557

Astrologer
Wayward Moon - Denny DeMartino *s* 744

Atticus Kodiak
Critical Space - Greg Rucka *m* 190

Augusta Goodnight
An Angel to Die For - Mignon F. Ballard *f* 522

Aunt Dimity
Aunt Dimity: Detective - Nancy Atherton *m* 9

Aztec Trilogy
Aztec Blood - Gary Jennings *t* 889

Bachelor Battalion
Last Virgin in California - Maureen Child *r* 255

Banned and Banished
Wit'ch Gate - James Clemens *f* 534

Barnaby Skye
Downriver - Richard S. Wheeler *w* 512
Downriver - Richard S. Wheeler *t* 957

Baron
The Baron War - Jory Sherman *w* 503

Barrett Raines
Strawman's Hammock - Darryl Wimberley *m* 216

Baxter
Day of Reckoning - Kathy Herman *i* 1001

Beast House Chronicles
Friday Night in Beast House - Richard Laymon *h* 662

Bedlam's Bard
Spirits White as Lightning - Mercedes Lackey *f* 568

Bel Barrett
Midlife Can Be Murder - Jane Isenberg *m* 124

Belles of Lordsburg
The Outlaw's Twin Sister - Stephen A. Bly *i* 973

Ben Cooper/Sergeant Fry
Dancing with the Virgins - Stephen Booth *m* 23

Bethlehem
Heaven on Earth - Marilyn Pappano *r* 366

Betsy Devonshire
Unraveled Sleeve - Monica Ferris *m* 67

Biggie Weatherford
Biggie and the Quincy Ghost - Nancy Bell *m* 15

Bill Gastner
Bag Limit - Steven F. Havill *m* 108

Bill Slider
Blood Sinister - Cynthia Harrod-Eagles *m* 104

Blue Ridge Legacy
Highland Hopes - Gary E. Parker *i* 1039

Bogus Brides
Mattie and the Blacksmith - Linda Lea Castle *r* 253

Bolo
Bolo Strike - William H. Keith Jr. *s* 765

Books of Barakhai
The Beasts of Barakhai - Mickey Zucker Reichert *f* 590

Bradleyville
Color the Sidewalk for Me - Brandilyn Collins *i* 980

Brady Coyne
Past Tense - William G. Tapply *m* 206

Branion Realm
The Golden Sword - Fiona Patton *f* 586

Bretta Solomon
Lilies That Fester - Janis Harrison *m* 103

Bride
The Prisoner Bride - Susan Spencer Paul *r* 368

Bride Quest II
The Temptress - Claire Delacroix *r* 269

Brides of Culdee Creek
Child of Promise - Kathleen Morgan *i* 1025

Brigham Bybee
Sister Wife - John Gates *m* 76

Callie Wade
Letters to Callie - Dawn Miller *w* 483

Camelot
Lancelot Du Lethe - J. Robert King *f* 566

Cape Refuge
Cape Refuge - Terri Blackstock *i* 970

Carole Seddon
Death on the Downs - Simon Brett *m* 27

Caroline Canfield
Sketches with Wolves - Jacqueline Fiedler *m* 68

Cat Marsala
Hard Road - Barbara D'Amato *m* 53

Cat Who
The Cat Who Went Up the Creek - Lilian Jackson Braun *m* 26

Celtic Crusades
The Mystic Rose - Stephen R. Lawhead *t* 901
The Mystic Rose - Stephen R. Lawhead *f* 570

Charles Dodgson/Arthur Conan Doyle
The Problem of the Surly Servant - Roberta Rogow *m* 187
The Problem of the Surly Servant - Roberta Rogow *t* 926

Charlie Moon
White Shell Woman - James D. Doss *m* 61

Charlie Parker
Dark Hollow - John Connolly *m* 42

Charlotte Justice
Stormy Weather - Paula L. Woods *m* 220

Charly Poisson
Prepared for Murder - Cecile Lamalle *m* 138

Chelsea Adams
Eyes of Elisha - Brandilyn Collins *i* 981

Cheysuli
Children of the Lion - Jennifer Roberson *f* 591
Legacy of the Wolf - Jennifer Roberson *f* 592
The Lion Throne - Jennifer Roberson *f* 593

Chicago Stars
This Heart of Mine - Susan Elizabeth Phillips *r* 369

Child of Earth
Destiny - Elizabeth Haydon *f* 554

China Bayles
Bloodroot - Susan Wittig Albert *m* 4

Christine Bennett
Happy Birthday Murder - Lee Harris *i* 996

Chronicle of Modern Twilight
Fairness - Ferdinand Mount *c* 1167

Chronicles of Saint-Germain
A Feast in Exile - Chelsea Quinn Yarbro *h* 713
A Feast in Exile - Chelsea Quinn Yarbro *t* 963

Chronicles of the Raven
Nightchild - James Barclay *f* 523

Chronicles of Unbinding
Hazard's Price - Robert S. Stone *f* 601

Cinderella Conspiracy
Cinderella After Midnight - Lilian Darcy *r* 268

Circle of Destiny
The Quest - Jim Kraus *i* 1013

Civil War Battle
Gettysburg - James Reasoner *t* 919

Claire Sharples
The Tumbleweed Murders - Rebecca Rothenberg *m* 189

Claire Watkins
Glare Ice - Mary Logue *m* 145

Clan MacLean
Summer's End - Lynne Hayworth *r* 297

Clingfire
The Fall of Neskaya - Marion Zimmer Bradley *s* 725

Collected Spook Stories
In the Dark - Richard Laymon *h* 663
Mrs. Amworth - E.F. Benson *h* 622

Colorado Trilogy
Colorado Twilight - Tess Pendergrass *w* 495

Conrad Voort
All the Dead Were Strangers - Ethan Black *m* 20

Culture Universe
Look to Windward - Iain Banks *s* 721

Dakota
Buffalo Valley - Debbie Macomber *w* 474

Dakota Moons
Heart of the Sandhill - Stephanie Grace Whitson *i* 1058

Dalziel and Pascoe
Dialogues of the Dead or Paronomania! - Reginald Hill *m* 116

Dame Frevisse
The Clerk's Tale - Margaret Frazer *m* 70
The Clerk's Tale - Margaret Frazer *t* 865

Dark Matter
Of Aged Angels - Monte Cook *s* 737

Darkness Rising
Hideous Dreams - L.H. Maynard *h* 674

Day to Remember
Friday's Child - Linda Chaikin *i* 977

de Burghs
My Lady de Burgh - Deborah Simmons *r* 396

Deathday
Deathday - William C. Dietz *s* 746

Delaney Family
When Tomorrow Comes - Janette Oke *i* 1034

Den of Antiquity
Nightmare in Shining Armor - Tamar Myers *m* 163

Devil's Daughters Trilogy
The Christmas Wish - Debbie Raleigh *r* 377
The Valentine Wish - Debbie Raleigh *r* 378

Diamond of the Rockies
The Tender Vine - Kristen Heitzmann *i* 998

Dirk Pitt
Valhalla Rising - Clive Cussler *c* 1097

Discworld
The Amazing Maurice and His Educated Rodents - Terry Pratchett *f* 587
The Last Hero - Terry Pratchett *f* 588

Dismas Hardy
The Oath - John Lescroart *m* 141

Doan & Carstairs
The Mouse in the Mountain - Norbert Davis *m* 56

Doc Sidhe
Sidhe-Devil - Aaron Allston *f* 516

Dr. Fenimore
The Doctor and the Dead Man's Chest - Robin Hathaway *m* 106

Dr. James Mortimer
Dr. Mortimer and the Aldgate Mystery - Gerard Williams *t* 958

Don Packham/Frank Mitchell
In and Out - Mat Coward *m* 44

Don Robak
Robak in Black - Joe L. Hensley *m* 113

Doomspell
The Scent of Magic - Cliff McNish *f* 581

Dore Konstantin
Dervish Is Digital - Pat Cadigan *s* 731

Dorothy Martin
To Perish in Penzance - Jeanne M. Dams *m* 54

Dragon
The Dragon Society - Lawrence Watt-Evans *f* 610

DragonCrown War Cycle
Fortress Draconis - Michael A. Stackpole *f* 599

Dragonlance
Betrayal - Jean Rabe *f* 589
Brother of the Dragon - Paul B. Thompson *f* 604
Dragon's Bluff - Mary H. Herbert *f* 556

Druid Circle
Circle of Stars - Anna Lee Waldo *t* 952

Duelist
Brother John - Rutledge Etheridge *s* 750

Earl Swagger
Pale Horse Coming - Stephen Hunter *m* 122

Earth: Final Conflict
Augur's Teacher - Sherwood Smith *s* 800

Earthsea
The Other Wind - Ursula K. Le Guin *f* 571

Eden's Children
The Innocent - Amanda Stevens *r* 410

Edgar Allan Poe
The Hum Bug - Harold Schechter *m* 193
The Hum Bug - Harold Schechter *w* 502

Einarinn
The Warrior's Bond - Juliet E. McKenna *f* 578

Eleanor Roosevelt
Murder at the President's Door - Elliott Roosevelt *t* 928

Elita
Rebel's Cage - Kate Jacoby *f* 561

Elizabeth Chase
Ashes of Aries - Martha C. Lawrence *m* 140

Ella Clah
Blackening Song - Aimee Thurlo *w* 506

Elric
The Dreamthief's Daughter - Michael Moorcock *f* 582

Em Hansen
Fault Line - Sarah Andrews *m* 7

Emma Lord
The Alpine Nemesis - Mary Daheim *m* 51

Emma Merrigan
Behind Time - Lynn Abbey *f* 515

Epona Sequence
Daughter of Lir - Judith Tarr *t* 940

Everard Naval
The Blooding of the Guns - Alexander Fullerton *t* 866

Everien
The Way of the Rose - Valery Leith *f* 572

Everworld
Entertain the End - K.A. Applegate *f* 519
Mystify the Magician - K.A. Applegate *f* 520

Fairie Ring
Shadow Kiss - Tom Townsend *f* 605

Faith Fairchild
The Body in the Bonfire - Katherine Hall Page *i* 1037

Father John O'Malley/Vicky Holden
The Thunder Keeper - Margaret Coel *w* 444
The Thunder Keeper - Margaret Coel *m* 35

Filomena Buscarsela
Red House - K.J.A. Wishnia *m* 217

Fingerprints
Gifted Touch - Melinda Metz *s* 775
Haunted - Melinda Metz *s* 776

Finn
The Treachery of Kings - Neal Barrett Jr. *f* 524

Fires of Gleannmara
Riona - Linda Windsor *i* 1060

First Century Diaries
The Gaius Diary - Gene Edwards *i* 990

Firstborn Sons
Born Brave - Ruth Wind *r* 422

Foreigner
Defender - C.J. Cherryh *s* 734

Forgotten Realms
Elminster in Hell - Ed Greenwood *f* 553
Pool of Radiance - Carrie Bebris *f* 525
The Shattered Mask - Richard Lee Byers *f* 532

Forgotten Realms: Paths of Darkness
Sea of Swords - R.A. Salvatore *f* 597

Forster Trilogy
Secret of the Wolf - Susan Krinard *r* 322

Fortunes of the Black Hills
Friends and Enemies - Stephen A. Bly *i* 972

Fred Taylor
Lazarus, Arise - Nicholas Kilmer *m* 134

Gail Connor
Suspicion of Vengeance - Barbara Parker *m* 167

George Porter Dillman/Genevieve Masefield
Murder on the Minnesota - Conrad Allen *m* 5
Murder on the Minnesota - Conrad Allen *t* 816

Gerald Knave
The Counterfeit Heinlein - Laurence M. Janiver *s* 763

Ghosts
Ghost of the White Nights - L.E. Modesitt Jr. *s* 778

Gil and Claire Hunt
The Masks of Auntie Laveau - Robert J. Randisi *m* 177

Gil Mayo
A Sunset Touch - Marjorie Eccles *m* 64

Giraut Leone
The Merchants of Souls - John Barnes *s* 722

Glenbrooke
Wildflowers - Robin Jones Gunn *i* 993

Grace & Favor
Someone to Watch over Me - Jill Churchill *m* 33
Someone to Watch over Me - Jill Churchill *t* 839

Greyhawk
Queen of the Demonweb Pits - Paul Kidd *f* 563

Guardian
The Jasper Forest - Julia Gray *f* 551

Guenevere Trilogy
The Child of the Holy Grail - Rosalind Miles *t* 907

Gumshoe
Gumshoe Gorilla - Keith Hartman *s* 756

Hannah Ives
Occasion of Revenge - Marcia Talley *m* 205

Hannah Malloy/Kiki Goldstein
Tall, Dead, and Handsome - Annie Griffin *m* 91

Hap Collins and Leonard Pine
Captains Outrageous - Joe R. Lansdale *w* 472

Harding
Kiss It Goodbye - John Wessel *m* 213

Harrison Raines
The Ironclad Alibi - Michael Kilian *m* 133
The Ironclad Alibi - Michael Kilian *t* 898

Harvey Blissberg
Dead Ball - R.D. Rosen *m* 188

Heaven Lee
Red Beans and Vice - Lou Jane Temple *m* 207

Heavenly Daze
A Warmth in Winter - Lori Copeland *i* 984

Highlander
Kiss of the Highlander - Karen Marie Moning *r* 358

House of Winslow
The Golden Angel - Gilbert Morris *i* 1027
The Heavenly Fugitive - Gilbert Morris *i* 1028

Inspector Ghote
Breaking and Entering - H.R.F. Keating *m* 132

Inspector Ian Rutledge
Watchers of Time - Charles Todd *m* 208
Watchers of Time - Charles Todd *t* 943

Inspector Jury
The Blue Last - Martha Grimes *m* 92

Inspector Rebus
The Falls - Ian Rankin *m* 178

Irene Adler
Chapel Noir - Carole Nelson Douglas *m* 62
Chapel Noir - Carole Nelson Douglas *t* 856

Jack Delmas
Massacre Island - Martin Hegwood *m* 112

Jack London
The Jewel of the North - Peter King *m* 135

Jack Reacher
Echo Burning - Lee Child *w* 442

Jacob Burns
The Killing Bee - Matt Witten *m* 218

Jacobia Tiptree
Wreck the Halls - Sarah Graves *m* 89

Jake Hines
Six-Pound Walleye - Elizabeth Gunn *m* 93

Jane Amanda Edwards
The Message of the Mute Dog - Charlotte Murray Russell *m* 191

Jane Austen
Jane and the Prisoner of Wool House - Stephanie Barron *m* 12
Jane and the Prisoner of Wool House - Stephanie Barron *t* 822

Jason Keltner
The Night Men - Keith Snyder *m* 199

Jesse Stone
Death in Paradise - Robert B. Parker *m* 168

Jessie Drake
Shadows of Sin - Rochelle Krich *m* 137

Jewelfire
The Obsidian Tower - Freda Warrington *f* 609

Joanna Brady
Paradise Lost - J.A. Jance *w* 465
Paradise Lost - J.A. Jance *m* 125

Job's Corner Chronicles
Carley's Song - Patricia Houck Sprinkle *i* 1051

Joe Grey
Cat Laughing Last - Shirley Rousseau Murphy *m* 162

Joe Gunther
Tucker Peak - Archer Mayor *m* 151

John Coffin
Coffin's Ghost - Gwendoline Butler *m* 30

John Darnell
The Case of the Ripper's Revenge - Sam McCarver *m* 153

John McLeish/Francesca Wilson
O Gentle Death - Janet Neel *m* 165

John the Eunuch
Three for a Letter - Mary Reed *m* 180
Three for a Letter - Mary Reed *t* 920

Josie Pigeon
Murder in the Forecast - Valerie Wolzien *m* 219

Julesburg Mysteries
Whirlpool - Lorena McCourtney *i* 1023

Kate Jasper
A Sensitive Kind of Murder - Jacqueline Girdner *m* 80

Kathryn Swinbrooke
Saintly Murders - C.L. Grace *m* 86
Saintly Murders - C.L. Grace *t* 875

Kinky Friedman
Steppin' on a Rainbow - Kinky Friedman *m* 72

Kinship and Courage
What Once We Loved - Jane Kirkpatrick *w* 470
What Once We Loved - Jane Kirkpatrick *i* 1011

Lady Lupin
Who Killed the Curate? - Joan Coggin *m* 36

Last Legion
Homefall - Chris Bunch *s* 729

Last T'En Trilogy
Dark Dreams - Cory Daniells *r* 267

Laura Winslow
Stalking Moon - David Cole *m* 39

Left Behind
Desecration - Tim LaHaye *i* 1016

Legend of Five Rings
The Crab - Stan Brown *f* 531

Lew Griffin
Ghost of a Flea - James Sallis *m* 192

Lily Bard
Shakespeare's Counselor - Charlaine Harris *m* 102

Lindy Haggerty
Midsummer Murder - Shelley Freydont *m* 71

Lord Edward Corinth and Verity Browne
The Bones of the Buried - David Roberts *m* 183
The Bones of the Buried - David Roberts *t* 923

Lord of the Isles
Mistress of the Catacombs - David Drake *f* 541

Louise Eldridge
Harvest of Murder - Ann Ripley *m* 181

Lt. Bak
A Place of Darkness - Lauren Haney *m* 101

Luanne Fogarty
Deep Water Death - Glynn Marsh Alam *m* 3

Lucy Stone
Wedding Day Murder - Leslie Meier *m* 157

Lupe Solano
Bitter Sugar - Carolina Garcia-Aguilera *m* 75

Madame Karitska
Kaleidoscope - Dorothy Gilman *m* 79

Maggody
Maggody and the Moonbeams - Joan Hess *m* 114

Magic the Gathering
The Dragons of Magic - J. Robert King *f* 565

Magic the Gathering: Invasion Cycle
Apocalypse - J. Robert King *f* 564

Magical Love Romance
Buttercup Baby - Karen Fox *r* 287

Magravandian Chronicles
The Way of Light - Storm Constantine *f* 536

Maiden
The Sword Maiden - Susan King *r* 316

Mail Order Brides
A Measure of Grace - Al Lacy *i* 1014

Mammoth
Icebones - Stephen Baxter *s* 723

Man of the Month
Rocky and the Senator's Daughter - Dixie Browning *r* 246

Manor House
Death Is in the Air - Kate Kingsbury *m* 136

March
March to the Sea - David Weber *s* 809

Mariana Morgan
Darkness at the Door - Catherine Dain *m* 52

Marla Shore
Murder by Manicure - Nancy J. Cohen *m* 38

Marshal Guarnaccia
Property of Blood - Magdalen Nabb *m* 164

Marshall Webb
Island of Tears - Troy Soos *t* 936

Marti MacAlister
Whispers in the Dark - Eleanor Taylor Bland *m* 21

Martyr's Song
When Heaven Weeps - Ted Dekker *i* 988

Mary Crow
A Darker Justice - Sallie Bissell *m* 19

Matanuska
Worthy of Riches - Bonnie Leon *i* 1017

Matt Scudder
Hope to Die - Lawrence Block *m* 22

Meg Langslow
Revenge of the Wrought-Iron Flamingos - Donna Andrews *m* 6

Melanie Travis
Once Bitten - Laurien Berenson *m* 17

Memoirs of a Bow Street Runner
The Thief-Taker - T.F. Banks *m* 10
The Thief-Taker - T.F. Banks *t* 820

Men of Honor
The Marine and the Princess - Cathie Linz *r* 334
Stranded with the Sergeant - Cathie Linz *r* 335

Merlin Codex
Celtika - Robert Holdstock *f* 558

Michael Merrick
The Elusive Voice - Mary Jo Adamson *m* 2

Michael Thackeray
Skeleton at the Feast - Patricia Hall *m* 97

Milo Milodragovitch
The Final Country - James Crumley *m* 50

Minister's Daughters
A Child Shall Lead Them - Carole Gift Page *i* 1036

Mitchell & Markby
Shades of Murder - Ann Granger *m* 87

Mitford Years
In This Mountain - Jan Karon *i* 1007

Molly Murphy
Murphy's Law - Rhys Bowen *t* 830

Myth
Myth-ion Improbable - Robert Lynn Asprin *f* 521

Nameless Detective
Bleeders - Bill Pronzini *m* 174

Nathan Heller
Kisses of Death - Max Allan Collins *m* 41
Kisses of Death - Max Allan Collins *t* 841

Nicholas Bracewell
The Devil's Apprentice - Edward Marston *m* 148

Nick Hoffman
Burning Down the House - Lev Rafael *m* 176

North American Confederacy
The American Zone - L. Neil Smith *s* 799

Notre Dame
Emerald Aisle - Ralph McInerny *m* 156

Obernewtyn
Ashling - Isobelle Carmody *s* 732

O'Malley Family
The Protector - Dee Henderson *i* 999
September Song - Andrew M. Greeley *c* 1117

Other Way Home
A Journey by Chance - Sally D. John *i* 1006

Outlander
The Fiery Cross - Diana Gabaldon *r* 288
The Fiery Cross - Diana Gabaldon *t* 868

Oz
The Rundlestone of Oz - Eloise McGraw *f* 577

Parker
Firebreak - Richard Stark *m* 202

Paul Turner
Sex and Murder.com - Mark Richard Zubro *m* 221

Plainsman
Turn the Stars Upside Down - Terry C. Johnston *w* 466

Plenty Man
Moon Medicine - Mike Blakely *t* 827

Porfiry Rostnikov
Murder on the Trans-Siberian Express - Stuart M. Kaminsky *m* 130

Port Silva
Keepers - Janet LaPierre *m* 139

Prelude to Dune
House Corrino - Brian Herbert *s* 757

Privateersman
The Devil's Own Luck - David Donachie *t* 853
The Dying Trade - David Donachie *t* 854

Professor Moriarity
The Great Game - Michael Kurland *t* 899

Puzzle Lady
Puzzled to Death - Parnell Hall *m* 96

Rachel & Dash
The Long Good Boy - Carol Lea Benjamin *m* 16

Rai-Kirah
Revelation - Elizabeth Haydon *f* 555

Rainmaker
Outcasts - Tim McGuire *w* 480

Rand
The Old Spies Club and Other Intrigues of Rand - Edward D. Hoch *m* 118

Redclift Sisters
My Lady Beloved - Lael St. James *r* 405
My Lady Wayward - Lael St. James *r* 406

Regan Reilly
Fleeced - Carol Higgins Clark *m* 34

Rei Shimura
The Bride's Kimono - Sujata Massey *m* 150

Renaissance Mystery
Bella Donna - Barbara Cherne *t* 836

Renegades
The Renegades: Rafe - Genell Dellin *r* 270

Repairman Jack
Hosts - F. Paul Wilson *h* 710

Return to Red River
A Dream to Follow - Lauraine Snelling *i* 1050

Return to Tyler
The Nanny - Judith Stacy *r* 408
Night Hawk's Bride - Jillian Hart *r* 296

Rigante
Midnight Falcon - David Gemmell *f* 548

Roger the Chapman
The Goldsmith's Daughter - Kate Sedley *t* 933
The Weaver's Inheritance - Kate Sedley *m* 194
The Weaver's Inheritance - Kate Sedley *t* 934

Rose Callahan
Dancing Dead - Deborah Woodworth *i* 1062

Ruby the Rabbi's Wife
Don't Cry for Me, Hot Pastrami - Sharon Kahn *m* 129

Sagas of a Kindred Heart
Sunrise on Stradbury Square - Doris Elaine Fell *i* 992

Sam McCain
Save the Last Dance for Me - Ed Gorman *m* 83

Savage Family Saga
The Savages in Love and War - Fred Mustard Stewart *t* 937

Scavenger
Shadow - K.J. Parker *f* 585

Seabrook Trilogy
The Rake and the Wallflower - Allison Lane *r* 325

Seneca Falls
Brothers of Cain - Miriam Grace Monfredo *m* 159
Brothers of Cain - Miriam Grace Monfredo *t* 909

Sentry Peak
Marching through Peachtree - Harry Turtledove *f* 606

Seven Brothers
The Prince of Shadow - Curt Benjamin *f* 526

Seven Circles
World Fall - Douglas Niles *f* 583

Seven Dreams
Argall - William T. Vollmann *c* 1212
Argall - William T. Vollmann *t* 950

Seven Sisters
For Your Heart Only - Debra White Smith *i* 1048
To Rome with Love - Debra White Smith *i* 1049

Shadow of Liberty
A Prince Among Them - Al Lacy *i* 1015

Shadowkings
Shadowkings - Michael Cobley *f* 535

Shadowleague
Spirit of the Stone - Maggie Furey *f* 545

Shakespeare and Smythe
The Slaying of the Shrew - Simon Hawke *m* 109
The Slaying of the Shrew - Simon Hawke *t* 880

Shannara
Antrax - Terry Brooks *f* 530

Sheriff Dan Rhodes
A Romantic Way to Die - Bill Crider *m* 49

Sherlock Holmes/Shadwell Rafferty
Sherlock Holmes and the Secret Alliance - Larry Millett *m* 158

Sierra Lavotoni
Strip Poker - Nancy Bartholomew *m* 13

Silent Empire
Dreamer - Steven Harper *s* 755

Sir John Fielding
Smuggler's Moon - Bruce Alexander *t* 815

Sirens of the Sea
The Sea Sprite - Ruth Langan *r* 328

Sister Fidelma
Act of Mercy - Peter Tremayne *t* 944
Act of Mercy - Peter Tremayne *m* 209

Skolian Empire
Spherical Harmonic - Catherine Asaro *s* 716

Smokey Dalton
Smoke-Filled Rooms - Kris Nelscott *m* 166

Song
Bethany's Song - Susan Plunkett *r* 372

Sophie Greenway
Dial M for Meat Loaf - Ellen Hart *m* 105

Southern Sisters
Murder Boogies with Elvis - Anne George *m* 77

Sovereign Stone
Guardians of the Lost - Margaret Weis *f* 611

Sparrowhawk
Sparrowhawk—Jack Frake - Edward Cline *t* 840

SPQR
Nobody Loves a Centurion - John Maddox Roberts *m* 184
Nobody Loves a Centurion - John Maddox Roberts *t* 924

St-Cyr/Kohler
Kaleidoscope - J. Robert Janes *m* 126
Kaleidoscope - J. Robert Janes *t* 888

Stardoc
Shockball - S.L. Viehl *s* 805

Starhawk
Planet America - Mack Maloney *s* 768
Starhawk - Mack Maloney *s* 769

Stephanie Plum
Seven Up - Janet Evanovich *r* 274

Storyteller Trilogy
Call Down the Stars - Sue Harrison *t* 879

Sullivan Sisters
Awakening Alex - Ruth Langan *r* 327

Sunny Childs
Blue Plate Special - Ruth Birmingham *m* 18

Susan Wren
A Cold Christmas - Charlene Weir *m* 212

Susanna, Lady Appleton
Face Down Before Rebel Hooves - Kathy Lynn Emerson *m* 65
Face Down Before Rebel Hooves - Kathy Lynn Emerson *t* 861

Sword of Truth
Debt of Bones - Terry Goodkind *f* 549
The Pillars of Creation - Terry Goodkind *f* 550

Tales of Guinevere
The Dragon Queen - Alice Borchardt *f* 528
The Dragon Queen - Alice Borchardt *t* 829

Tall, Dark, and Dangerous
Taylor's Temptation - Suzanne Brockmann *r* 242

Tea Shop
Death by Darjeeling - Laura Childs *m* 32

Tenebrea
Tenebrea's Hope - Roxann Dawson *s* 743

Tess Monaghan
In a Strange City - Laura Lippman *m* 143

Texana Jones
Death of the Last Villista - Allana Martin *w* 475
Death of the Last Villista - Allana Martin *m* 149

Texas Rangers
The Way of the Coyote - Elmer Kelton *w* 468
The Way of the Coyote - Elmer Kelton *t* 895

Thorn
Blackwater Sound - James W. Hall *m* 94

Three Sisters Island Trilogy
Dance upon the Air - Nora Roberts *r* 382
Heaven and Earth - Nora Roberts *r* 383

Tir Tanagiri
The King's Name - Jo Walton *f* 608

Trade Ellis
Crack Shot - Sinclair Browning *m* 28

Trouble with Mary
What to Do about Annie? - Millie Criswell *r* 264

Uncommon Heroes
True Valor - Dee Henderson *i* 1000

Ursula Blanchard
Queen of Ambition - Fiona Buckley *m* 29
Queen of Ambition - Fiona Buckley *t* 834

Valdemar
Take a Thief - Mercedes Lackey *f* 569

Vampire Chronicles
Blood and Gold - Anne Rice *h* 685
Blood and Gold - Anne Rice *t* 922
Blood and Gold - Anne Rice *c* 1185

View from the Mirror
The Way between the Worlds - Ian Irvine *f* 560

Viking Trilogy
Believe in Me - Josie Litton *r* 336
Come Back to Me - Josie Litton *r* 337
Dream of Me - Josie Litton *r* 338

Warhammer
Drachenfels - Jack Yeovil *f* 613

Warlock's Heirs
Here Be Monsters - Christopher Stasheff *f* 600

WaterLilies
Alice at Heart - Deborah Smith *r* 401

Wayfarer Redemption
Enchanter - Sara Douglass *f* 540

Weaver
French Leave - Sheri Cobb South *r* 404

Welcome to Purgatory
Walker's Widow - Heidi Betts *r* 234

Wesley Farrell
Pale Shadow - Robert Skinner *m* 196
Pale Shadow - Robert Skinner *t* 935

William Monk
Funeral in Blue - Anne Perry *m* 172
Funeral in Blue - Anne Perry *t* 915

Winter of the World
Shadow of the Seer - Michael Scott Rohan *f* 595

Wintering
Ice - Stephen Bowkett *s* 724

Wizardry
Cursed and Consulted - Rick Cook *f* 537

World's Finest Mystery & Crime Stories
The World's Finest Mystery & Crime Stories: Second Annual Collection - Ed Gorman *m* 84

Xanth
Swell Foop - Piers Anthony *f* 518

Yukon Quest
Rivers of Gold - Tracie Peterson *i* 1042

Zion Legacy
The Jerusalem Scrolls - Bodie Thoene *i* 1053
The Jerusalem Scrolls - Bodie Thoene *t* 942

Time Period Index

This index chronologically lists the time settings in which the featured books take place. Main headings refer to a century; where no specific time is given, the headings MULTIPLE TIME PERIODS, INDETERMINATE PAST, INDETERMINATE FUTURE, and INDETERMINATE are used. The 18th through 21st centuries are broken down into decades when possible. (Note: 1800s, for example, refers to the first decade of the 19th century.) Featured titles are listed alphabetically beneath time headings, with author names and genre codes. The genre codes are as follows: *c* Popular Fiction, *f* Fantasy, *h* Horror, *i* Inspirational, *m* Mystery, *r* Romance, *s* Science Fiction, *t* Historical, and *w* Western. Numbers refer to the entries that feature each title.

MULTIPLE TIME PERIODS

Blood and Gold - Anne Rice *h* 685
Blood and Gold - Anne Rice *t* 922
Blood and Gold - Anne Rice *c* 1185
In the Shape of a Boar - Lawrence Norfolk *t* 913
Sacred Ground - Barbara Wood *t* 962

INDETERMINATE PAST

Abandon - Jillian Hunter *r* 303
Celtika - Robert Holdstock *f* 558
The Child of the Holy Grail - Rosalind Miles *t* 907
Daughter of Lir - Judith Tarr *t* 940
The Dragon Queen - Alice Borchardt *f* 528
The Dragon Queen - Alice Borchardt *t* 829
From the Dust Returned - Ray Bradbury *c* 1082
The Husband Test - Betina Krahn *r* 321
In the Shape of a Boar - Lawrence Norfolk *c* 1171
Lancelot Du Lethe - J. Robert King *f* 566
The Mystic Rose - Stephen R. Lawhead *f* 570
Once upon a Rose - Nora Roberts *r* 384
Thrice Bound - Roberta Gellis *f* 547

15th CENTURY B.C.

A Place of Darkness - Lauren Haney *m* 101

10th CENTURY B.C.

Queenmaker - India Edghill *t* 858

7th CENTURY B.C.

Call Down the Stars - Sue Harrison *t* 879
Murder at the Panionic Games - Michael B. Edwards *t* 859

1st CENTURY B.C.

Nobody Loves a Centurion - John Maddox Roberts *m* 184
Nobody Loves a Centurion - John Maddox Roberts *t* 924

1st CENTURY

Devil's Island - John Hagee *i* 994
The Gaius Diary - Gene Edwards *i* 990
The Jerusalem Scrolls - Bodie Thoene *i* 1053
The Jerusalem Scrolls - Bodie Thoene *t* 942
Under the Eagle - Simon Scarrow *t* 931
Vampire Vow - Michael Schiefelbein *h* 690

6th CENTURY

Confessions of a Pagan Nun - Kate Horsley *t* 886
Riona - Linda Windsor *i* 1060
Three for a Letter - Mary Reed *m* 180
Three for a Letter - Mary Reed *t* 920

7th CENTURY

Act of Mercy - Peter Tremayne *t* 944
Act of Mercy - Peter Tremayne *m* 209
The Rock - Kanan Makiya *t* 902
The Rock - Kanan Makiya *c* 1152

8th CENTURY

The Rock - Kanan Makiya *c* 1152

9th CENTURY

Believe in Me - Josie Litton *r* 336
Come Back to Me - Josie Litton *r* 337
Dream of Me - Josie Litton *r* 338

10th CENTURY

Mother of Kings - Poul Anderson *t* 818
Mother of Kings - Poul Anderson *f* 517

11th CENTURY

The Mystic Rose - Stephen R. Lawhead *t* 901
The Third Witch - Rebecca Reisert *t* 921

12th CENTURY

The Black Chalice - Marie Jakober *f* 562
Circle of Stars - Anna Lee Waldo *t* 952
Circle of Stars - Anna Lee Waldo *w* 510
The Mackintosh Bride - Debra Lee Brown *r* 244
The Marriage Bed - Claudia Dain *r* 266
Pride of Kings - Judith Tarr *t* 941
Pride of Kings - Judith Tarr *f* 603
The Temptress - Claire Delacroix *r* 269
White Lion's Lady - Tina St. John *r* 407
The Wolf Hunt - Gillian Bradshaw *t* 831

13th CENTURY

Bone Walker - Kathleen O'Neal Gear *t* 871
The Crusader - Michael A. Eisner *t* 860
The Good Men - Charmaine Craig *t* 844
The Mackintosh Bride - Debra Lee Brown *r* 244
My Lady de Burgh - Deborah Simmons *r* 396
The Warrior's Damsel - Denise Hampton *r* 295

14th CENTURY

The Archer's Tale - Bernard Cornwell *t* 843
The Enchantment - Pam Binder *r* 237
A Feast in Exile - Chelsea Quinn Yarbro *h* 713
A Feast in Exile - Chelsea Quinn Yarbro *t* 963
The Good Men - Charmaine Craig *t* 844
Mirabilis - Susann Cokal *c* 1091
My Heart Stood Still - Lynn Kurland *r* 323
My Lady Beloved - Lael St. James *r* 405
My Lady Wayward - Lael St. James *r* 406

15th CENTURY

Bella Donna - Barbara Cherne *t* 836
The Clerk's Tale - Margaret Frazer *t* 865
The Clerk's Tale - Margaret Frazer *m* 70
The Family - Mario Puzo *t* 916
The Family - Mario Puzo *c* 1183
The Goldsmith's Daughter - Kate Sedley *t* 933
Knight Errant - R. Garcia y Robertson *t* 869
Knight Errant - R. Garcia y Robertson *f* 546
The Prisoner Bride - Susan Spencer Paul *r* 368
Saintly Murders - C.L. Grace *m* 86
Saintly Murders - C.L. Grace *t* 875
The Sword Maiden - Susan King *r* 316
The Weaver's Inheritance - Kate Sedley *m* 194
The Weaver's Inheritance - Kate Sedley *t* 934

16th CENTURY

Aztec Blood - Gary Jennings *t* 889
The Border Hostage - Virginia Henley *t* 883
The Devil's Apprentice - Edward Marston *m* 148
Face Down Before Rebel Hooves - Kathy Lynn Emerson *m* 65
Face Down Before Rebel Hooves - Kathy Lynn Emerson *t* 861
The Family - Mario Puzo *c* 1183
Heart of Night - Taylor Chase *r* 254
Her Infinite Variety - Pamela Rafael Berkman *t* 823

Keeper of Hearts - Dianne Christner i 979
Kiss of the Highlander - Karen Marie Moning r 358
The Last Confession - Morris L. West t 956
My Lord Savage - Elizabeth Lane r 326
My Name Is Red - Orhan Pamuk c 1178
Queen of Ambition - Fiona Buckley m 29
Queen of Ambition - Fiona Buckley t 834
The Secret Clan: Abducted Heiress - Amanda Scott r 390
The Slaying of the Shrew - Simon Hawke m 109
The Slaying of the Shrew - Simon Hawke t 880
To Kiss a Spy - Jane Feather r 276

17th CENTURY

Argall - William T. Vollmann t 950
Argall - William T. Vollmann c 1212
City of Dreams - Beverly Swerling t 939
Embrace the Dawn - Kathleen Morgan i 1026
Ill Met by Moonlight - Sarah A. Hoyt f 559
The Last Confession - Morris L. West t 956
The Other Adonis - Frank Deford t 849
The Passion of Artemisia - Susan Vreeland t 951
Rora - James Byron Huggins i 1003
The Sea Sprite - Ruth Langan r 328
Year of Wonders - Geraldine Brooks c 1083
Year of Wonders - Geraldine Brooks t 832

18th CENTURY

According to Queeney - Beryl Bainbridge c 1069
City of Dreams - Beverly Swerling t 939
The Infidel - Joe Musser i 1031

1740s

Sparrowhawk—Jack Frake - Edward Cline t 840

1760s

The Promise - May McGoldrick r 352
The Royal Physician's Visit - Per Olov Enquist t 862
The Royal Physician's Visit - Per Olov Enquist c 1110
Summer's End - Lynne Hayworth r 297
Watch by Moonlight - Kate Hawks t 881

1770s

The Fiery Cross - Diana Gabaldon r 288
The Fiery Cross - Diana Gabaldon t 868
Imagining Don Giovanni - Anthony J. Rudel t 929
The Promise - May McGoldrick r 352
The Promise in a Kiss - Stephanie Laurens r 329
The Royal Physician's Visit - Per Olov Enquist c 1110
Smuggler's Moon - Bruce Alexander t 815

1780s

The Promise in a Kiss - Stephanie Laurens r 329

1790s

The Devil's Own Luck - David Donachie t 853
The Dying Trade - David Donachie t 854
The Very Comely Countess - Miranda Jarrett r 307
The Very Daring Duchess - Miranda Jarrett r 308

19th CENTURY

Audubon's Watch - John Gregory Brown c 1085
Behold a Red Horse - Cotton Smith w 504
Bloodlines - Fred D'Aguiar t 846
The Bride of Willow Creek - Maggie Osborne r 364
Bucking the Tiger - Bruce Olds w 485
Bucking the Tiger - Bruce Olds c 1176
Cane River - Lalita Tademy c 1207
Charlie and the Sir - Frank Roderus w 499
Chumley's Gold - Wayne D. Overholser w 489
Colorado Twilight - Tess Pendergrass w 495
Conjuring Maud - Philip Danze t 847
Cowboy in the Making - Will James w 464
Destiny Valley - Fred Grove w 459
Doc Holliday's Gone - Jane Candia Coleman w 445
Double Vengeance - John Duncklee w 449
Dracula in London - P.N. Elrod h 631
The Evidence Against Her - Robb Forman Dew c 1102
The Evidence Against Her - Robb Forman Dew t 850
Gambler's Row: A Western Trio - Les Savage Jr. w 500
The Gauntlet - Max Brand w 430
The Gift of the Mestizo - Marjorie M. McGinley w 479
The Good Journey - Micaela Gilchrist t 873
The Good Journey - Micaela Gilchrist w 454
A Good Town - Douglas Hirt w 462
Halide's Gift - Frances Kazan t 893
Hard Bounty - Ken Hodgson w 463
Haussmann, or The Distinction - Paul LaFarge t 900
The House of Gold - Max Brand w 431
The June Rise - William Tremblay t 945
The Legend of Sotoju Mountain - Will Henry w 461
Letters of the Heart - Lisa Tawn Bergren i 969
Letters to Callie - Dawn Miller w 483
Lockwood - Lauran Paine w 492
The Lone Rider - Max Brand w 432
Long Journey to Deep Canon - T.T. Flynn w 452
Man from Wyoming - Dane Coolidge w 448
Man Without a Past - T.V. Olsen w 486
Miracle of the Jacal - Robert J. Randisi w 497
Murphy's Law - Rhys Bowen t 830
No Place for a Lady - Vicki Piekarski w 496
On the Night Plain - J. Robert Lennon c 1146
Once an Outlaw - Jill Gregory r 294
Open Range - Zane Grey w 458
Outcasts - Tim McGuire w 480
The Outlaws - Wayne D. Overholser w 490
Portrait in Sepia - Isabel Allende c 1067
Portrait in Sepia - Isabel Allende t 817
A Prince Among Them - Al Lacy i 1015
Rainbow Rider: A Western Trio - Wayne D. Overholser w 491
Ride West to Dawn - James C. Work w 514
Search for Last Chance - A.L. McWilliams w 482
The Shadow in Renegade Basin - Les Savage Jr. w 501
Spanish Jack - Robert J. Conley w 447
Spanish Jack - Robert J. Conley t 842
Stage Trails West - Frank Bonham w 427
Stolen Gold - Max Brand w 433
The Survival of Juan Oro - Max Brand w 434
Tears of the Heart - Lauran Paine w 493
Tomorrow's Eve - Auguste Villiers de L'Isle Adam s 806
Voices in the Hill: Western Stories - Steve Frazee w 453
Walker's Widow - Heidi Betts r 234
The Way of the Coyote - Elmer Kelton w 468
A Western Family Christmas - Millie Criswell r 263
The Wind Done Gone - Alice Randall t 918
Wish List - Lisa Kleypas r 320
The Wolf Strain - Max Brand w 435
The Woman at Ox-Yoke - Lewis B. Patten w 494

1800s

Broken Promises - Patricia Oliver r 362
Cheyenne Summer - Vella Munn t 911
Heartless - Kat Martin r 346
Jane and the Prisoner of Wool House - Stephanie Barron t 822
Jane and the Prisoner of Wool House - Stephanie Barron m 12
River Walk - Rita Cleary w 443
Sarah and the Rogue - DeLoras Scott r 391
Tempt Me Twice - Barbara Dawson Smith r 400
To Tame a Duke - Patricia Grasso r 293
Treason - David Nevin t 912
The Trouble with Harriet - Wilma Counts r 262

1810s

Autumn Kittens - Janice Bennett r 232
Blessing in Disguise - Jenna Mindel r 356
The Blue Devil - Melynda Beth Skinner r 398
The Bride Sale - Candice Hern r 298
Broken Promises - Patricia Oliver r 362
The Christmas Wish - Debbie Raleigh r 377
Desire - Nicole Jordan r 309
A Devilish Husband - Alana Clayton r 257
A Diamond in the Rough - Andrea Pickens r 370
Elusive Passion - Kathryn Smith r 402
A Family for Gillian - Catherine Blair r 238
A Forbidden Embrace - Anna Jacobs r 305
Fortune's Lady - Evelyn Richardson r 379
The Guardian - Barbara Miller r 355
A Guardian's Angel - Jo Ann Ferguson r 278
His Lady Midnight - Jo Ann Ferguson r 279
The Incomparable Miss Compton - Regina Scott r 392
The Irredeemable Miss Renfield - Regina Scott r 393
A Kiss for Mama - Jo Ann Ferguson r 280
Lady Hilary's Halloween - Mona Gedney r 291
Lady Polly - Nicola Cornick r 259
Miss Truelove Beckons - Donna Simpson r 397
Mr. Montgomery's Quest - Martha Kirkland r 318
The Night the Stars Fell - Christina Kingston r 317
No Man's Mistress - Mary Balogh r 227
Once a Princess - Veronica Sattler r 388
One Good Turn - Carla Kelly r 315
A Perfect Match - Jeanne Savery r 389
The Perfect Princess - Elizabeth Thornton r 416
The Proper Wife - Julia Justiss r 311
The Rake and the Wallflower - Allison Lane r 325
A Reckless Encounter - Rosemary Rogers r 385
A Rogue for Christmas - Kate Huntington r 304
The Rose in the Wheel - S.K. Rizzolo m 182
A Scandalous Wager - Bess Willingham r 420
Slightly Shady - Amanda Quick r 375
The Spanish Bride - Amanda McCabe r 349
Sugarplum Surprises - Elisabeth Fairchild r 275
A Tangled Web - Donna Bell r 230
Tempt Me Twice - Barbara Dawson Smith r 400
The Thief-Taker - T.F. Banks m 10
The Thief-Taker - T.F. Banks t 820
To Tame a Duke - Patricia Grasso r 293
To Tame a Wild Heart - Tracy Fobes r 281
The Traitor's Daughter - Elizabeth Powell r 374
The Trouble with Harriet - Wilma Counts r 262
Under the Kissing Bough - Shannon Donnelly r 271
The Valentine Wish - Debbie Raleigh r 378
Very Truly Yours - Julie Beard r 229
The Virtuous Cyprian - Nicola Cornick r 260
The Wedding Charm - Lynn Collum r 258
The Wedding Wager - Cathy Maxwell r 348

1820s

Audubon's Watch - John Gregory Brown t 833
Blessing in Disguise - Jenna Mindel r 356
French Leave - Sheri Cobb South r 404

1830s

Downriver - Richard S. Wheeler w 512
Downriver - Richard S. Wheeler t 957
Fallen - Celeste Bradley r 241
Jackson's Way - Leslie LaFoy r 324
Suddenly You - Lisa Kleypas r 319

1840s

Coldwater - Mardi McConnochie c 1156
Coldwater - Mardi McConnochie t 904
The Elusive Voice - Mary Jo Adamson m 2
The Hum Bug - Harold Schechter m 193
The Hum Bug - Harold Schechter w 502
The Hum Bug - Harold Schechter t 932
The Ice Child - Elizabeth McGregor t 905
Moon Medicine - Mike Blakely t 827
The Nanny - Judith Stacy r 408
Night Hawk's Bride - Jillian Hart r 296
The Quest - Jim Kraus i 1013

1850s

Audubon's Watch - John Gregory Brown t 833
The Captain's Wife - Douglas Kelley t 894
The Dark Clue - James Wilson t 959
Mattie and the Blacksmith - Linda Lea Castle r 253
The Quest - Jim Kraus i 1013
The Rag & Bone Shop - Jeff Rackham t 917
The Salt Letters - Christine Balint t 819
The Sleeping Beauty - Jacqueline Navin r 360
Still She Haunts Me - Katie Roiphe t 927
What Once We Loved - Jane Kirkpatrick i 1011
What Once We Loved - Jane Kirkpatrick w 470

1860s

The Ambush of My Name - Jeffrey Marks t 903
The Baron War - Jory Sherman w 503
The Blue and the Gray Undercover - Ed Gorman w 456
Brothers of Cain - Miriam Grace Monfredo m 159
Brothers of Cain - Miriam Grace Monfredo t 909
Call Each River Jordan - Owen Parry m 169
Call Each River Jordan - Owen Parry t 914
The Dark Clue - James Wilson t 959
Funeral in Blue - Anne Perry t 915
Funeral in Blue - Anne Perry m 172
Gettysburg - James Reasoner t 919
Heart of the Sandhill - Stephanie Grace Whitson i 1058
The Ironclad Alibi - Michael Kilian m 133
The Ironclad Alibi - Michael Kilian t 898
The Last Canyon - John Vernon w 508
The Last Canyon - John Vernon t 949
Letters from an Age of Reason - Nora Hague t 877
A Measure of Grace - Al Lacy i 1014
Moon of Bitter Cold - Frederick J. Chiaventone w 441
The Rag & Bone Shop - Jeff Rackham t 917
Shadow Valley Rising - Stephen Overholser w 488
Still She Haunts Me - Katie Roiphe t 927
Still She Haunts Me - Katie Roiphe c 1189
Summer in Baden-Baden - Leonid Tsypkin t 946
An Uncommon Enemy - Michelle Black t 824
An Uncommon Enemy - Michelle Black w 423
The Way of the Coyote - Elmer Kelton t 895
The Way of the Coyote - Elmer Kelton c 1137
We Look Like Men of War - William R. Forstchen t 864
Whispers of Goodbye - Karen White r 418
The Wolf Pit - Marly Youmans t 964

1870s

Blood on the Wind - Lucile Bogue w 426
Caleb's Price - Troy D. Smith w 505
Comfort and Joy - Sandra Madden r 342
A Dream to Follow - Lauraine Snelling i 1050
Halfway to Heaven - Susan Wiggs r 419
The Holy Road - Michael Blake t 826
The Holy Road - Michael Blake w 425
Lydia Cassatt Reading the Morning Paper - Harriet Scott Chessman t 837
The Nightingale's Song - Kathleen Eschenburg r 273
The Renegades: Rafe - Genell Dellin r 270
Summer Moon - Jill Marie Landis w 471
The Texan's Dream - Jodi Thomas r 415
Turn the Stars Upside Down - Terry C. Johnston w 466
Turn the Stars Upside Down - Terry C. Johnston t 890
The Way of the Coyote - Elmer Kelton c 1137

1880s

Bear Paw - Gene Mullins w 484
Chapel Noir - Carole Nelson Douglas m 62
Chapel Noir - Carole Nelson Douglas t 856
The Colorado Bride - Mary Burton r 247
Flying Eagle - Tim Champlin w 440
The June Rise - William Tremblay w 507
Just West of Heaven - Kathleen Kane r 313
Lydia Cassatt Reading the Morning Paper - Harriet Scott Chessman t 837
The Outlaw's Twin Sister - Stephen A. Bly i 973
The Problem of the Surly Servant - Roberta Rogow m 187
The Problem of the Surly Servant - Roberta Rogow t 926
Saddled - Delores Fossen r 284
Secret of the Wolf - Susan Krinard r 322
Shades of Murder - Ann Granger m 87
The Tender Vine - Kristen Heitzmann i 998
Tennant's Rock - Steve McGiffen w 478
The Widow's Little Secret - Judith Stacy r 409

1890s

Alicia's Song - Susan Plunkett r 371
Ambrose Bierce and the Death of Kings - Oakley Hall m 95
Ambrose Bierce and the Death of Kings - Oakley Hall t 878
Beloved Protector - Linda O'Brien r 361
Bethany's Song - Susan Plunkett r 372
By Flare of Northern Lights - Tim Champlin w 439
Darkness - Sam Siciliano h 695
Deadly Illumination - Serena Stier m 203
The Devil-Tree of El Dorado - Frank Aubrey s 717
Dr. Mortimer and the Aldgate Mystery - Gerard Williams t 958
Friends and Enemies - Stephen A. Bly i 972
Goodnight, Sweet Prince - David Dickinson m 58
Goodnight, Sweet Prince - David Dickinson t 851
The Great Game - Michael Kurland t 899
Heaven Sent - Rachel Wilson r 421
A Horde of Fools - James David Buchanan w 437
Island of Tears - Troy Soos m 200
Island of Tears - Troy Soos t 936
The London Vampire Panic - Michael Romkey h 686
The MacKenzies: Zach - Ana Leigh r 332
Morgette on the Barbary Coast - G.G. Boyer w 429
Quincey Morris, Vampire - P.N. Elrod h 632
Rivers of Gold - Tracie Peterson i 1042
Sherlock Holmes and the Giant Rat of Sumatra - Alan Vanneman m 210
Sherlock Holmes and the Secret Alliance - Larry Millett m 158
Sherlock Holmes and the Secret Alliance - Larry Millett t 908

20th CENTURY

After the Plague - T. Coraghessan Boyle c 1081
Bloodlines - Fred D'Aguiar t 846
Cane River - Lalita Tademy c 1207
Collected Stories - Saul Bellow c 1072
The Company of Strangers - Robert Wilson t 960
Conjuring Maud - Philip Danze t 847
Creatures of Habit - Jill McCorkle c 1157
Darling? - Heidi Jon Schmidt c 1193
The Distant Land of My Father - Bo Caldwell t 835
Ester's Child - Jean P. Sasson t 930
Eva Moves the Furniture - Margot Livesey c 1148
The Evidence Against Her - Robb Forman Dew t 850
The Evidence Against Her - Robb Forman Dew c 1102
Fairness - Ferdinand Mount c 1167
The Feast of the Goat - Mario Vargas Llosa t 948
The Feast of the Goat - Mario Vargas Llosa c 1211
First Gray, Then White, Then Blue - Margriet de Moor c 1165
Flights of Love - Bernhard Schlink c 1192
The Good German - Joseph Kanon c 1135
Half a Life - V.S. Naipaul c 1170
Halide's Gift - Frances Kazan t 893
Highland Hopes - Gary E. Parker i 1039
In the Shape of a Boar - Lawrence Norfolk c 1171
Kisses of Death - Max Allan Collins t 841
Kisses of Death - Max Allan Collins m 41
Leap of Faith - Danielle Steel c 1203
Miracle of the Jacal - Robert J. Randisi w 497
Mountain Time - Jane Candia Coleman w 446
My Little Blue Dress - Bruno Maddox c 1150
Nashborough - Elsie Burch Donald t 855
Niagara Falls All over Again - Elizabeth McCracken c 1158
On the Night Plain - J. Robert Lennon w 473
The Onion Girl - Charles De Lint f 539
Portrait in Sepia - Isabel Allende c 1067
Portrait in Sepia - Isabel Allende t 817
Requiem for a Lost Empire - Andrei Makine c 1151
Rhythms - Donna Hill t 884
The Southern Woman - Elizabeth Spencer c 1201
Tie-Fast Country - Robert Flynn w 451
TV - Brian Brown c 1084
What You Owe Me - Bebe Moore Campbell c 1089

1900s

Chasing the Devil's Tail - David Fulmer t 867
Chasing the Devil's Tail - David Fulmer m 73
Child of Promise - Kathleen Morgan i 1025
Falling Angels - Tracy Chevalier c 1090
Falling Angels - Tracy Chevalier t 838
Fire Lilies - Cynthia Leal Massey w 476
The Jewel of the North - Peter King m 135
Midnight Bayou - Nora Roberts c 1187
Murder on the Minnesota - Conrad Allen t 816
Murder on the Minnesota - Conrad Allen m 5
Murphy's Law - Rhys Bowen m 24
Night Watch - Stephen Kendrick t 896
The Pinkerton Eye - Allen P. Bristow w 436
The Reckoning - John McLain w 481

1910s

The Blooding of the Guns - Alexander Fullerton t 866
The Case of the Ripper's Revenge - Sam McCarver m 153
Coldheart Canyon - Clive Barker h 619
Come, My Little Angel - Diane Noble i 1033
Falling Angels - Tracy Chevalier c 1090
Fire Lilies - Cynthia Leal Massey w 476

The Golden Angel - Gilbert Morris *i* 1027
The Last Vampire - T.M. Wright *h* 712
Last Year's River - Allen Morris Jones *t* 891
The Looking Glass - Michele Roberts *t* 925
A Morning in Eden - Anna Gilbert *t* 872
The Officers' Ward - Marc Dugain *t* 857
The Shadow out of Time - H.P. Lovecraft *h* 670
The Silent Woman - Susan M. Dodd *t* 852
Watchers of Time - Charles Todd *t* 943
Watchers of Time - Charles Todd *m* 208
Will's War - Janice Woods Windle *w* 513
Will's War - Janice Woods Windle *t* 961
The Yellow Sailor - Steve Weiner *t* 954

1920s

The Bride of Willow Creek - Maggie Osborne *r* 364
Carter Beats the Devil - Glen David Gold *t* 874
The Edge of Town - Dorothy Garlock *r* 290
Fred & Edie - Jill Dawson *t* 848
The Golden Angel - Gilbert Morris *i* 1027
The Heavenly Fugitive - Gilbert Morris *i* 1028
The Jazz Bird - Craig Holden *m* 119
The Jazz Bird - Craig Holden *t* 885
Last Year's River - Allen Morris Jones *w* 467
Moon Medicine - Mike Blakely *t* 827
Season of Storms - Susanna Kearsley *r* 314
Swift as Desire - Laura Esquivel *c* 1112
This Rock - Robert Morgan *t* 910
Treasures of the Sun - T.V. Olsen *w* 487
A World of Thieves - James Carlos Blake *w* 424
A World of Thieves - James Carlos Blake *t* 825
The Years of Fear - Fred Grove *w* 460

1930s

The Beasts of Brahm - Mark Hansom *h* 646
The Bones of the Buried - David Roberts *m* 183
The Bones of the Buried - David Roberts *t* 923
Catskill - John R. Hayes *m* 110
Catskill - John R. Hayes *t* 882
ChronoSpace - Allen Steele *s* 802
Dancing Dead - Deborah Woodworth *i* 1062
Dark Sanctuary - H.B. Gregory *h* 644
The Dreamthief's Daughter - Michael Moorcock *f* 582
Murder at the President's Door - Elliott Roosevelt *t* 928
The Phoenix - Henning Boetius *t* 828
Prized Possessions - Jessica Stirling *t* 938
Quincie Bolliver - Mary King *w* 469
The Savages in Love and War - Fred Mustard Stewart *t* 937
Someone to Watch over Me - Jill Churchill *m* 33
Someone to Watch over Me - Jill Churchill *t* 839
Stillwater - William F. Weld *t* 955
When Tomorrow Comes - Janette Oke *i* 1034
Who Killed the Curate? - Joan Coggin *m* 36
Worthy of Riches - Bonnie Leon *i* 1017

1940s

The Black Eye - Constance Little *m* 144
Broken Honor - Patricia Potter *r* 373
The Clouds Above - Andrew Greig *t* 876
The Company of Strangers - Robert Wilson *m* 215
Creeping Venom - Sheila Pim *m* 173
Crimson Kiss - Trisha Baker *h* 617
Death Is in the Air - Kate Kingsbury *m* 136
The Distance - Eddie Muller *m* 161
The Flight of the Maidens - Jane Gardam *t* 870
Friday's Child - Linda Chaikin *i* 977
The Good German - Joseph Kanon *t* 892
The Good German - Joseph Kanon *m* 131
Jackdaws - Ken Follett *t* 863
The Jerusalem Scrolls - Bodie Thoene *t* 942
Kaleidoscope - J. Robert Janes *t* 888
Kaleidoscope - J. Robert Janes *m* 126
Law Dog - J. Lee Butts *w* 438
The Magic of Ordinary Days - Ann Howard Creel *t* 845
The Message of the Mute Dog - Charlotte Murray Russell *m* 191
The Mouse in the Mountain - Norbert Davis *m* 56
My Best Friend - Laura Wilson *m* 214
Officer of the Court - Bill Mesce Jr. *t* 906
Pale Shadow - Robert Skinner *m* 196
Pale Shadow - Robert Skinner *t* 935
The Phoenix - Henning Boetius *t* 828
Roscoe - William Kennedy *t* 897
Sap Rising - Christine Lincoln *c* 1147
The Savages in Love and War - Fred Mustard Stewart *t* 937
Sea of Glory - Ken Wales *i* 1056
Sea of Glory - Ken Wales *t* 953
Sentimental Journey - Jill Barnett *t* 821
Sentimental Journey - Jill Barnett *r* 228
The Water and the Blood - Nancy E. Turner *t* 947
Written on the Wind - Judith Pella *i* 1040

1950s

Carley's Song - Patricia Houck Sprinkle *i* 1051
Fire in the Rock - Joe Martin *c* 1154
Lake Wobegon Summer 1956 - Garrison Keillor *c* 1136
Pale Horse Coming - Stephen Hunter *m* 122
Pale Horse Coming - Stephen Hunter *t* 887
Pale Horse Coming - Stephen Hunter *c* 1127
Sap Rising - Christine Lincoln *c* 1147
Tragic Casements - Oliver Onions *h* 680

1960s

Balzac and the Little Chinese Seamstress - Sijie Dai *c* 1098
Bombingham - Anthony Grooms *c* 1119
Dugan under Ground - Tom De Haven *c* 1100
Peace Like a River - Leif Enger *c* 1109
Save the Last Dance for Me - Ed Gorman *m* 83
September Song - Andrew M. Greeley *c* 1117
Smoke-Filled Rooms - Kris Nelscott *m* 166
When Heaven Weeps - Ted Dekker *i* 988

1970s

Angel in the Front Room, Devil out Back - Stanford Diehl *m* 59
Balzac and the Little Chinese Seamstress - Sijie Dai *c* 1098
Beasts - Joyce Carol Oates *c* 1173
Bombingham - Anthony Grooms *c* 1119
Frankenstein: The Legacy - Christopher Schildt *h* 691
The Shape of Snakes - Minette Walters *m* 211

1980s

Awakening Alex - Ruth Langan *r* 327
East of the Sun, West of the Moon - Carole Bellacera *r* 231
The Lake of Dead Languages - Carol Goodman *m* 82
The Night Men - Keith Snyder *m* 199
The Nudger Dilemmas - John Lutz *m* 147
Riot - Shashi Tharoor *c* 1208
Straight on 'Til Morning - Christopher Golden *h* 642
The Webster Chronicle - Daniel Akst *c* 1066

1990s

Angel in the Front Room, Devil out Back - Stanford Diehl *m* 59
The Ash Garden - Dennis Bock *c* 1078
Blackening Song - Aimee Thurlo *w* 506
Bone Walker - Kathleen O'Neal Gear *t* 871
The Company of Strangers - Robert Wilson *m* 215
Crimson Kiss - Trisha Baker *h* 617
East of the Sun, West of the Moon - Carole Bellacera *r* 231
In the Dark - Richard Laymon *h* 663
The Last Summer of Reason - Tahar Djaout *c* 1105
My Best Friend - Laura Wilson *m* 214
The Nudger Dilemmas - John Lutz *m* 147
Shades of Murder - Ann Granger *m* 87
The Shape of Snakes - Minette Walters *m* 211
Stormy Weather - Paula L. Woods *m* 220

21st CENTURY

Always Forever - Mark Chadbourn *f* 533
Augur's Teacher - Sherwood Smith *s* 800
Bold as Love - Gwyneth Jones *s* 764
The Crow Maiden - Sarah Singleton *f* 598
The Dragons of the Cuyahoga - S. Andrew Swann *f* 602
The Getaway Special - Jerry Oltion *s* 785
Mountain Time - Jane Candia Coleman *w* 446
The Night of the Triffids - Simon Clark *s* 735
The Savage Girl - Alex Shakar *c* 1196
Scorch - A.D. Nauman *s* 782
Smoking Mirror Blues - Ernest Hogan *s* 758
The Wanderer - Fritz Leiber *s* 767

2000s

About the Author - John Colapinto *c* 1092
Adventures in Time and Space with Max Merriwell - Pat Murphy *s* 781
Affinity - J.N. Williamson *h* 709
Aftermath - Peter Robinson *m* 186
Agatha Raisin and the Love from Hell - M.C. Beaton *m* 14
Alice at Heart - Deborah Smith *r* 401
Alicia's Song - Susan Plunkett *r* 371
Alien Taste - Wen Spencer *s* 801
All Families Are Psychotic - Douglas Coupland *c* 1094
All Signs Point to Murder - Kat Goldring *m* 81
All That Counts - Georg M. Oswald *c* 1177
All the Dead Were Strangers - Ethan Black *c* 1076
All the Dead Were Strangers - Ethan Black *m* 20
All the Finest Girls - Alexandra Styron *c* 1206
All through the Night - Suzanne Forster *r* 282
Almost - Elizabeth Benedict *c* 1073
The Alpine Nemesis - Mary Daheim *m* 51
. . .And the Angel with Television Eyes - John Shirley *h* 694
Angel Face - Suzanne Forster *r* 283
An Angel to Die For - Mignon F. Ballard *f* 522
Another Summer - Georgia Bockoven *r* 239
Any Way the Wind Blows - E. Lynn Harris *c* 1122
The Appointment - Herta Muller *c* 1168
Aria - Susan Segal *c* 1194
The Art of Dying - Diana Killian *i* 1009
Ashes of Aries - Martha C. Lawrence *m* 140
The Association - Bentley Little *h* 668
The Astonished Eye - Tracy Knight *f* 567
Aunt Dimity: Detective - Nancy Atherton *m* 9
Austin City Blue - Jan Grape *m* 88
Awakening Alex - Ruth Langan *r* 327
Bachelor on the Prowl - Kasey Michaels *r* 353
Back in Kansas - Debra Salonen *r* 387
Bag Limit - Steven F. Havill *m* 108
Bamboo and Lace - Lori Wick *i* 1059
Basket Case - Carl Hiaasen *m* 115
The Beasts of Barakhai - Mickey Zucker Reichert *f* 590
Behind Time - Lynn Abbey *f* 515
Bell, Cook, and Candle - Joanne Pence *m* 170
A Bend in the Road - Nicholas Sparks *c* 1200
Bethany's Song - Susan Plunkett *r* 372

Betrayed - Rosey Dow *i* 989
Better than Sex - Susan Holtzer *m* 120
Biggie and the Quincy Ghost - Nancy Bell *m* 15
Bitten - Kelley Armstrong *c* 1068
Bitter Sugar - Carolina Garcia-Aguilera *m* 75
Bitterroot - James Lee Burke *c* 1088
Black House - Stephen King *h* 659
Black Water Transit - Carsten Stroud *m* 204
Blackwater Sound - James W. Hall *m* 94
Bleeders - Bill Pronzini *m* 174
Blessed Baby - Lois Richer *i* 1043
Blessed Child - Bill Bright *i* 975
Blindsighted - Karin Slaughter *m* 197
Blood Games - Lee Killough *h* 657
Blood Sinister - Cynthia Harrod-Eagles *m* 104
Bloodroot - Susan Wittig Albert *m* 4
The Blue Last - Martha Grimes *m* 92
Blue Plate Special - Ruth Birmingham *m* 18
Blue Wolf - Lise McClendon *w* 477
The Body in the Bonfire - Katherine Hall Page *i* 1037
Bonnie Winter - Graham Masterton *h* 672
Born Brave - Ruth Wind *r* 422
Breaking and Entering - H.R.F. Keating *m* 132
The Bride's Kimono - Sujata Massey *m* 150
Bring Me a Dream - Robyn Amos *r* 224
Broken Honor - Patricia Potter *r* 373
Buffalo Valley - Debbie Macomber *w* 474
A Bungalow for Two - Carole Gift Page *i* 1035
Burning Down the House - Lev Rafael *m* 176
Buttercup Baby - Karen Fox *r* 287
Candle Bay - Tamara Thorne *h* 703
Cape Refuge - Terri Blackstock *i* 970
A Capital Holiday - Janet Dailey *r* 265
Captains Outrageous - Joe R. Lansdale *w* 472
Cat Laughing Last - Shirley Rousseau Murphy *m* 162
The Cat Who Went Up the Creek - Lilian Jackson Braun *m* 26
Chelsea Horror Hotel - Dee Dee Ramone *h* 684
A Child Shall Lead Them - Carole Gift Page *i* 1036
The Chinese Fire Drill - Les Roberts *m* 185
Christmas Vows: $5.00 Extra - Lori Copeland *i* 983
Cinderella After Midnight - Lilian Darcy *r* 268
City Infernal - Edward Lee *h* 667
Closing Time - Jim Fusilli *m* 74
Coffin's Ghost - Gwendoline Butler *m* 30
Cold - John Smolens *c* 1199
The Cold Blue Blood - David Handler *m* 100
A Cold Christmas - Charlene Weir *m* 212
Cold Hunter's Moon - K.C. Greenlief *m* 90
Coldheart Canyon - Clive Barker *c* 1071
Color the Sidewalk for Me - Brandilyn Collins *i* 980
Columbus Slaughters Braves - Mark Friedman *c* 1114
The Corrections - Jonathan Franzen *c* 1113
Could I Have This Dance? - Harry Lee Kraus *i* 1012
Crack Shot - Sinclair Browning *m* 28
Critical Space - Greg Rucka *m* 190
Dance upon the Air - Nora Roberts *r* 382
Dancing with the Virgins - Stephen Booth *m* 23
Dangerous Attraction - Susan Vaughan *r* 417
Dangerous Dilemmas - Evelyn Palfrey *r* 365
Dangerously Irresistible - Kristin Gabriel *r* 289
Dark Hollow - John Connolly *m* 42
A Darker Justice - Sallie Bissell *m* 19
Darkling I Listen - Katherine Sutcliffe *r* 412
Darkness at the Door - Catherine Dain *m* 52
Day of Reckoning - Kathy Herman *i* 1001
Dead Ball - R.D. Rosen *m* 188
Dead Love - Donald Beman *h* 620
Dead Sleep - Greg Iles *m* 123
The Deadhouse - Linda Fairstein *m* 66
The Deadwood Beetle - Mylene Dressler *c* 1106
Dear Cupid - Julie Ortolon *r* 363
Death by Darjeeling - Laura Childs *m* 32
Death in Paradise - Robert B. Parker *m* 168
Death Is a Cabaret - Deborah Morgan *m* 160
Death of the Last Villista - Allana Martin *w* 475
Death of the Last Villista - Allana Martin *m* 149
Death on a Casual Friday - Sharon Duncan *m* 63
Death on the Downs - Simon Brett *m* 27
Deep Fathom - James Rollins *s* 792
Deep Water Death - Glynn Marsh Alam *m* 3
Desert Autumn - Michael Craft *m* 45
The Devil's Larder - Jim Crace *c* 1095
Dial M for Meat Loaf - Ellen Hart *m* 105
Dialogues of the Dead or Paronomania! - Reginald Hill *m* 116
Diamond in the Ruff - Emily Carmichael *r* 249
Do You Hear What I Hear? - Holly Jacobs *r* 306
The Doctor and the Dead Man's Chest - Robin Hathaway *m* 106
The Doctor's Miracle - Anna Schmidt *i* 1046
Don't Cry for Me, Hot Pastrami - Sharon Kahn *m* 129
Doomed to Repeat It - d.g.k. goldberg *h* 641
Double Honor - Melissa Horsfall *i* 1002
Dreamcatcher - Stephen King *h* 660
Drummer in the Dark - T. Davis Bunn *i* 976
Eager to Please - Julie Parsons *c* 1180
The Earthquake Bird - Susanna Jones *m* 127
Eccentric Circles - Rebecca Lickiss *f* 573
Echo Burning - Lee Child *w* 442
Echoes of Lies - Jo Bannister *m* 11
Edgewater Angels - Sandro Meallet *c* 1160
Emerald Aisle - Ralph McInerny *m* 156
Emerald Windows - Terri Blackstock *i* 971
Emigre Journeys - Abdullah Hussein *c* 1129
The Enchantment - Pam Binder *r* 237
End over End - Kate Kennedy *c* 1139
Entertain the End - K.A. Applegate *f* 519
Envy - Sandra Brown *c* 1086
Envy - Sandra Brown *r* 245
Everything You Need - A.L. Kennedy *c* 1138
Eyes of Elisha - Brandilyn Collins *i* 981
Face - Tim Lebbon *h* 665
The Faded Flower - Paul McCusker *i* 1024
Fairness - Ferdinand Mount *c* 1167
The Falls - Ian Rankin *m* 178
A Family All Her Own - Bonnie K. Winn *i* 1061
A Family for Jana - Eileen Berger *i* 968
Fatal Legacy - Elizabeth Corley *m* 43
A Father's Place - Marta Perry *i* 1041
Fault Line - Sarah Andrews *m* 7
Female Intelligence - Jane Heller *c* 1125
A Feral Darkness - Doranna Durgin *f* 543
Fighting Gravity - Peggy Rambach *c* 1184
The Final Country - James Crumley *m* 50
A Fine and Private Place - Freda Davies *m* 55
Firebreak - Richard Stark *m* 202
Fireworks - James A. Moore *h* 675
First Lady - Michael Malone *c* 1153
First Light - Philip R. Craig *m* 46
Fleeced - Carol Higgins Clark *m* 34
The Folks - Ray Garton *h* 638
Followin' a Dream - Eboni Snoe *r* 403
For Rouenna - Sigrid Nunez *c* 1172
For Your Heart Only - Debra White Smith *i* 1048
Forbid Them Not - Michael P. Farris *i* 991
The Fourth Hand - John Irving *c* 1130
Frankenstein: The Legacy - Christopher Schildt *h* 691
Friday Night in Beast House - Richard Laymon *h* 662
From the Dust Returned - Ray Bradbury *h* 623
Funny Accent - Barbara Shulgasser-Parker *c* 1197
Fury - Salman Rushdie *c* 1190
Gabriel's Gift - Hanif Kureishi *c* 1143
A Game of Colors - John Urbancik *h* 704
A Garden to Keep - Jamie Langston Turner *i* 1055
Gargoyles - Alan Nayes *s* 783
Gargoyles - Alan Nayes *h* 677
Ghost Killer - Scott Chandler *h* 627
Ghost of a Flea - James Sallis *m* 192
The Ghost of John Wayne and Other Stories - Ray Gonzalez *w* 455
Gifted Touch - Melinda Metz *s* 775
The Gingerbread Man - Maggie Shayne *r* 395
The Girl from the Golden Horn - Kurban Said *c* 1191
The Girl Next Door - Kate Welsh *i* 1057
Glare Ice - Mary Logue *m* 145
Going Overboard - Christina Skye *r* 399
Good Harbor - Anita Diamant *c* 1103
Gotta Get Next to You - Lynn Emery *r* 272
The Grand Complication - Allen Kurzweil *c* 1144
Great American Plain - Gary Sernovitz *c* 1195
The Great Baby Caper - Eugenia Riley *r* 380
Green - Benjamin Zucker *i* 1064
Happy Birthday Murder - Lee Harris *i* 996
The Happy Room - Catherine Palmer *i* 1038
Hard Road - Barbara D'Amato *m* 53
Harvest of Murder - Ann Ripley *m* 181
Hateship, Friendship, Courtship, Loveship, Marriage - Alice Munro *c* 1169
Haunted - Melinda Metz *s* 776
He Goes, She Goes - Joanna Torrey *c* 1209
Heart of the Beast - Joyce Weatherford *w* 511
Heaven and Earth - Nora Roberts *r* 383
Heaven on Earth - Marilyn Pappano *r* 366
Heaven Sent - Jillian Hart *i* 997
Hide and Seek - Cherry Adair *r* 222
Highwire Moon - Susan Straight *c* 1205
His Father's Son - Nigel Bennett *h* 621
A Home of Her Own - Cathleen Connors *i* 982
Hometown Legend - Jerry B. Jenkins *i* 1005
Hope to Die - Lawrence Block *m* 22
Hostage - Robert Crais *m* 47
Hostage - Robert Crais *c* 1096
Hosts - F. Paul Wilson *h* 710
Hot and Bothered - Lori Foster *r* 285
Hotel of the Saints - Ursula Hegi *c* 1124
House of Pain - Sephera Giron *h* 640
How to Be Good - Nick Hornby *c* 1126
Hurricane Season - Karen Bjorneby *c* 1075
I Dream of You - Judi McCoy *r* 350
The Ice Child - Elizabeth McGregor *t* 905
In a Strange City - Laura Lippman *m* 143
In and Out - Mat Coward *m* 44
In the Forest of Harm - Sallie Bissell *c* 1074
In the Shadow of Our House - Scott Blackwood *c* 1077
In This Mountain - Jan Karon *i* 1007
In Too Deep - Janelle Taylor *r* 413
The Innocent - Amanda Stevens *r* 410
Insatiable - Julie Elizabeth Leto *r* 333
Irregardless of Murder - Ellen Edwards Kennedy *i* 1008
The Jasmine Trade - Denise Hamilton *m* 98
A Journey by Chance - Sally D. John *i* 1006
Judging Sara - Cynthia Rutledge *i* 1044
July Thunder - Rachel Lee *r* 330
Junior's Leg - Ken Wells *c* 1214
Just Say No! - Omar Tyree *c* 1210
The Justice - Angela Elwell Hunt *i* 1004
Kaleidoscope - Dorothy Gilman *m* 79
Keepers - Janet LaPierre *m* 139
Killer Stuff - Sharon Fiffer *m* 69
The Killing Bee - Matt Witten *m* 218
Killing the Shadows - Val McDermid *m* 154
The King of the Sun - A.A. McFedries *s* 773
Kiss It Goodbye - John Wessel *m* 213
Kiss of the Highlander - Karen Marie Moning *r* 358
The Lake of Dead Languages - Carol Goodman *m* 82
The Last Mayan - Malcolm Shuman *m* 195
Last of the Dixie Heroes - Peter Abrahams *m* 1
The Last Vampire - Whitley Strieber *h* 699
Last Virgin in California - Maureen Child *r* 255
Lazarus, Arise - Nicholas Kilmer *m* 134
Leap of Faith - Danielle Steel *c* 1203

Leaving Disneyland - Alexander Parsons c 1179
The Lecturer's Tale - James Hynes h 649
Legends Lake - JoAnn Ross r 386
Light Coming Back - Ann Wadsworth c 1213
Lightning Field - Dana Spiotta c 1202
Lilies That Fester - Janis Harrison m 103
Listen to the Shadows - Danuta Reah m 179
Living with Saints - Mary O'Connell c 1175
London Bridges - Jane Stevenson c 1204
The Long Good Boy - Carol Lea Benjamin m 16
Long Time No See - Susan Isaacs c 1131
Look at Me - Jennifer Egan c 1108
Looking for Laura - Judith Arnold r 226
A Love for Safekeeping - Gail Gaymer Martin i 1021
Love Her Madly - Mary-Ann Tirone Smith m 198
Love One Another - Valerie Hansen i 995
Love to Love You Baby - Kasey Michaels r 354
Loving Thy Neighbor - Ruth Scofield i 1047
Lowell Limpett: And Two Stories - Ward S. Just c 1134
A Lower Deep - Tom Piccirilli h 682
Lt. Kent: Lone Wolf - Judith Lyons r 341
Lucky Us - Joan Silber c 1198
Maggody and the Moonbeams - Joan Hess m 114
Magic Time - Marc Scott Zicree f 614
The Magickers - Emily Drake f 542
The Manhattan Hunt Club - John Saul h 687
The Marine and the Princess - Cathie Linz r 334
Marry Me, Maddie? - Rita Herron r 299
The Masks of Auntie Laveau - Robert J. Randisi m 177
Massacre Island - Martin Hegwood m 112
Middle Age - Joyce Carol Oates c 1174
Midlife Can Be Murder - Jane Isenberg m 124
Midnight Bayou - Nora Roberts c 1187
Midsummer Murder - Shelley Freydont m 71
Milkrun - Sarah Mlynowski r 357
Minutes to Burn - Gregg Andrew Hurwitz s 762
Miss Match - Leslie Carroll r 252
Money, Money, Money - Ed McBain m 152
The Money-Whipped Steer-Job Three-Jack Give-Up Artist - Dan Jenkins c 1132
The Monsters of Morley Manor - Bruce Coville f 538
Monte's Revenge - Eugene C. Vories w 509
Moontide - Erin Patrick h 681
Moving Target - Elizabeth Lowell r 340
Murder Boogies with Elvis - Anne George m 77
Murder by Manicure - Nancy J. Cohen m 38
Murder in the Forecast - Valerie Wolzien m 219
Murder on the Trans-Siberian Express - Stuart M. Kaminsky m 130
My Heart Stood Still - Lynn Kurland r 323
Narcissus in Chains - Laurell K. Hamilton h 645
The Nature of Balance - Tim Lebbon h 666
The Nautical Chart - Arturo Perez-Reverte m 171
The Nautical Chart - Arturo Perez-Reverte c 1182
Next Stop, Paradise - Sue Civil-Brown r 256
Night Blood - James M. Thompson h 702
Night in the Lonesome October - Richard Laymon h 664
The Night Men - Keith Snyder m 199
Night of Dracula - Christopher Schildt h 692
Night of the Bat - Paul Zindel h 714
Night Players - P.D. Cacek h 625
Nightmare in Shining Armor - Tamar Myers m 163
No Way Out - Andrea Kane r 312
O Gentle Death - Janet Neel m 165
The Oath - John Lescroart m 141
Occasion of Revenge - Marcia Talley m 205
October Song - Beverly Lewis i 1018
Of Aged Angels - Monte Cook s 737
On Every Side - Karen Kingsbury i 1010
On Leaving Lonely Town - Cait Logan r 339
On the Night Plain - J. Robert Lennon c 1146
Once Bitten - Laurien Berenson m 17
One Door Away from Heaven - Dean R. Koontz h 661
The Onion Girl - Charles De Lint f 539
Open Season - C.J. Box m 25
Open Season - C.J. Box w 428
Open Season - Linda Howard r 302
The Other Adonis - Frank Deford t 849
Pact of the Fathers - Ramsey Campbell h 626
Paradise Lost - J.A. Jance w 465
Paradise Lost - J.A. Jance m 125
Past Tense - William G. Tapply m 206
Personal Velocity - Rebecca Miller c 1162
The Pickup - Nadine Gordimer c 1116
A Place Called Wiregrass - Michael Morris i 1029
The Power of Love - Margaret Daley i 987
Prepared for Murder - Cecile Lamalle m 138
Pride, Prejudice and Jasmin Field - Melissa Nathan r 359
A Prince of a Guy - Sheila Rabe r 376
The Prodigy - Alton Gansky h 637
Property of Blood - Magdalen Nabb m 164
The Protector - Dee Henderson i 999
Puzzled to Death - Parnell Hall m 96
Pyramid Scheme - David Freer s 751
Rag Man - Pete Hautman m 107
Red Beans and Vice - Lou Jane Temple m 207
Red Hook - Gabriel Cohen m 37
Red House - K.J.A. Wishnia m 217
The Red of His Shadow - Mayra Montero c 1164
Red on Rose - Patricia Jones c 1133
Redeeming Claire - Cynthia Rutledge i 1045
The Renegade Steals a Lady - Vickie Taylor r 414
Requiem for a Lost Empire - Andrei Makine c 1151
Restoration and Romance - Barbara Curtis i 986
Retribution - John Fulton c 1115
Revenge of the Wrought-Iron Flamingos - Donna Andrews m 6
Riverwatch - Joseph M. Nassise h 676
Robak in Black - Joe L. Hensley m 113
Rocky and the Senator's Daughter - Dixie Browning r 246
A Romantic Way to Die - Bill Crider m 49
A Rose by the Door - Deborah Bedford i 967
Samuel Johnson Is Indignant - Lydia Davis c 1099
Sarah's Window - Janice Graham w 457
Schooling - Heather McGowan c 1159
Season of Storms - Susanna Kearsley r 314
The Seat Beside Me - Nancy Moser i 1030
The Secret - Kat Martin r 347
The Secret Admirer - Annette Mahon r 343
The Secret Life of Connor Monahan - Elizabeth Bevarly r 235
Secrets of the Heart - Gail Gaymer Martin i 1022
Seducing Mr. Right - Cherry Adair r 223
See Jane Date - Melissa Senate r 394
A Sensitive Kind of Murder - Jacqueline Girdner m 80
Sentimental, Heartbroken Rednecks - Greg Bottoms c 1079
Seven Up - Janet Evanovich r 274
Sex and Murder.com - Mark Richard Zubro m 221
Shades of Justice - Fredrick Huebner m 121
Shadow Valley Rising - Stephen Overholser w 488
Shadows of Sin - Rochelle Krich m 137
Shakespeare's Counselor - Charlaine Harris m 102
Shock - Robin Cook c 1093
Shooting Dr. Jack - Norman Green c 1118
Sidhe-Devil - Aaron Allston f 516
Sister Wife - John Gates m 76
Six-Pound Walleye - Elizabeth Gunn m 93
Skeleton at the Feast - Patricia Hall m 97
Sketches with Wolves - Jacqueline Fiedler m 68
Slightly Single - Wendy Markham r 345
The Southern Woman - Elizabeth Spencer c 1201
The Spirit Returns - Richard Burgin c 1087
Spirits White as Lightning - Mercedes Lackey f 568
Stalking Moon - David Cole m 39
Steppin' on a Rainbow - Kinky Friedman m 72
Stranded with the Sergeant - Cathie Linz r 335
Strawman's Hammock - Darryl Wimberley m 216
Strip Poker - Nancy Bartholomew m 13
A Study in Death - Iain McDowell m 155
Summer's Promise - Irene Brand i 974
Sunrise on Stradbury Square - Doris Elaine Fell i 992
A Sunset Touch - Marjorie Eccles m 64
Super-Cannes - J.G. Ballard c 1070
The Surgeon - Tess Gerritsen m 78
Suspicion of Vengeance - Barbara Parker m 167
Suzanne's Diary for Nicholas - James Patterson c 1181
Sweet Nothings - Catherine Anderson r 225
Sweet Success - Susan Mallery r 344
Swim the Moon - Paul Brandon f 529
Tall, Dark, and Difficult - Patricia Coughlin r 261
Tall, Dead, and Handsome - Annie Griffin m 91
Taylor's Temptation - Suzanne Brockmann r 242
Tears in a Bottle - Sylvia Bambola i 966
Teeth - Edo van Belkom h 705
The Thirty-Third Hour - Mitchell Chefitz i 978
This Heart of Mine - Susan Elizabeth Phillips r 369
This Time Forever - Carol Steward i 1052
The Thunder Keeper - Margaret Coel w 444
The Thunder Keeper - Margaret Coel m 35
'Tis the Season - Donna Hill r 300
To Perish in Penzance - Jeanne M. Dams m 54
To Rome with Love - Debra White Smith i 1049
To Trust a Stranger - Karen Robards r 381
Too Much Temptation - Lori Foster r 286
The Treatment - Mo Hayder c 1123
True Confessions - Rachel Gibson r 292
True Valor - Dee Henderson i 1000
Tucker Peak - Archer Mayor m 151
The Tumbleweed Murders - Rebecca Rothenberg m 189
Turnabout - Jeremiah Healy m 111
Twin Blessings - Carolyne Aarsen i 965
Two Sexy - Stephanie Bond r 240
Uncatalogued - Julie Kaewert m 128
Under Suspicion - Rachel Lee r 331
The Unknown Errors of Our Lives - Chitra Banerjee Divakaruni c 1104
Unraveled Sleeve - Monica Ferris m 67
Up in the Air - Walter Kirn c 1141
Valhalla Rising - Clive Cussler c 1097
Vampire Vow - Michael Schiefelbein h 690
Veiled Threats - Deborah Donnelly m 60
The Very Gothic Christmas - Christine Feehan r 277
The Vigil - Clay Reynolds w 498
The Wager - Metsy Hingle r 301
War Story - Gwen Edelman c 1107
A Warmth in Winter - Lori Copeland i 984
The Watermark - Travis Thrasher i 1054
Wedding Day Murder - Leslie Meier m 157
The Wedding Party - Robyn Carr r 250
What to Do about Annie? - Millie Criswell r 264
When Jayne Met Erik - Elizabeth Bevarly r 236
When Love Came to Town - Lenora Worth i 1063
When the Last Leaf Falls - Bill Myers i 1032
Whirlpool - Lorena McCourtney i 1023
Whispers in the Dark - Eleanor Taylor Bland m 21
The White Room - A.J. Matthews h 673
White Shell Woman - James D. Doss m 61
Why Did I Ever? - Mary Robison c 1188
The Widow - Anne Stuart r 411
The Wig My Father Wore - Anne Enright c 1111
Wildflowers - Robin Jones Gunn i 993
Winter's Secret - Lyn Cote i 985
The Woman for Dusty Conrad - Tori Carrington r 251
The Woman Next Door - Barbara Delinsky c 1101
The World Below - Sue Miller c 1163
The World Weaver - Craig Etchison s 749
Wreck the Halls - Sarah Graves m 89
Written on Her Heart - Alan Maki i 1019
Yonder Stands Your Orphan - Barry Hannah c 1121

You Never Can Tell - Kathleen Eagle *w* 450
You're the One - Judi McCoy *r* 351
Zigzagging Down a Wild Trail - Bobbie Ann Mason *c* 1155

2010s

First Landing - Robert Zubrin *s* 814

2020s

ChronoSpace - Allen Steele *s* 802
Deathday - William C. Dietz *s* 746
Gumshoe Gorilla - Keith Hartman *s* 756
The Secret of Life - Paul J. McAuley *s* 771

2050s

The Plutonium Blonde - John Zakour *s* 813

22nd CENTURY

Time Future - Maxine McArthur *s* 770
Wayward Moon - Denny DeMartino *s* 744
The Wild Boy - Warren Rochelle *s* 791

23rd CENTURY

Bikini Planet - David Garnett *s* 752
Brother John - Rutledge Etheridge *s* 750
Something More - Paul Cornell *s* 738
Tower of Glass - Robert Silverberg *s* 797

24th CENTURY

The Dark Wing - Walter Hunt *s* 761

30th CENTURY

Angry Young Spaceman - Jim Munroe *s* 780
Icebones - Stephen Baxter *s* 723

INDETERMINATE FUTURE

Acorna's Search - Anne McCaffrey *s* 772
Angelmass - Timothy Zahn *s* 812
Appleseed - John Clute *s* 736
Ashling - Isobelle Carmody *s* 732
Bloodtide - Melvin Burgess *s* 730
Bolo Strike - William H. Keith Jr. *s* 765
Chasm City - Alastair Reynolds *s* 789
The Counterfeit Heinlein - Laurence M. Janiver *s* 763
Defender - C.J. Cherryh *s* 734
Dervish Is Digital - Pat Cadigan *s* 731
Desecration - Tim LaHaye *i* 1016
Divine Intervention - Ken Wharton *s* 810
Dreamer - Steven Harper *s* 755
Empire & Ecolitan - L.E. Modesitt Jr. *s* 777
The Fall of Neskaya - Marion Zimmer Bradley *s* 725
Here Be Monsters - Christopher Stasheff *f* 600
Heresy - Anselm Audley *s* 718
Holding the Line - Rick Shelley *s* 795
Homefall - Chris Bunch *s* 729
Hope's End - Stephen Chambers *s* 733
House Corrino - Brian Herbert *s* 757
Ice - Stephen Bowkett *s* 724
In the Company of Others - Julie E. Czerneda *s* 740
Look to Windward - Iain Banks *s* 721
Maelstrom - Peter Watts *s* 808
March to the Sea - David Weber *s* 809
Martian Knightlife - James P. Hogan *s* 759
The Merchants of Souls - John Barnes *s* 722
Nearly People - Conrad Williams *h* 708
Nekropolis - Maureen McHugh *s* 774
On - Adam Roberts *s* 790
Out There - Gerald Rose *s* 793
A Paradigm of Earth - Candas Jane Dorsey *s* 747
Planet America - Mack Maloney *s* 768
The Puppet Master - John Dalmas *s* 741
The Reproductive System - John Sladek *s* 798
Ritual of Proof - Dara Joy *r* 310
The Scent of Magic - Cliff McNish *f* 581
Second Chances - Susan Shwartz *s* 796
Second Contact - J.D. Austin *s* 719
Shadow of the Seer - Michael Scott Rohan *f* 595
Shockball - S.L. Viehl *s* 805
Soldiers - John Dalmas *s* 742
A Soldier's Duty - Thomas E. Ricks *c* 1186
Spherical Harmonic - Catherine Asaro *s* 716
Starhawk - Mack Maloney *s* 769
Tales of the Velvet Comet - Mike Resnick *s* 788
Tenebrea's Hope - Roxann Dawson *s* 743

INDETERMINATE

The Amazing Maurice and His Educated Rodents - Terry Pratchett *f* 587
The American Zone - L. Neil Smith *s* 799
Antrax - Terry Brooks *f* 530
Apocalypse - J. Robert King *f* 564
Betrayal - Jean Rabe *f* 589
Black House - Stephen King *c* 1140
The Bone Doll's Twin - Lynn Flewelling *f* 544
Brother of the Dragon - Paul B. Thompson *f* 604
Children of the Lion - Jennifer Roberson *f* 591
Children of the Shaman - Jessica Rydill *f* 596
The Crab - Stan Brown *f* 531
Dark Dreams - Cory Daniells *r* 267
Debt of Bones - Terry Goodkind *f* 549
Destiny - Elizabeth Haydon *f* 554
Drachenfels - Jack Yeovil *f* 613
The Dragon Society - Lawrence Watt-Evans *f* 610
Dragon's Bluff - Mary H. Herbert *f* 556
The Dragons of Magic - J. Robert King *f* 565
Elminster in Hell - Ed Greenwood *f* 553
Enchanter - Sara Douglass *f* 540
Fortress Draconis - Michael A. Stackpole *f* 599
Ghost of the White Nights - L.E. Modesitt Jr. *s* 778
The Golden Sword - Fiona Patton *f* 586
Guardians of the Lost - Margaret Weis *f* 611
Hazard's Price - Robert S. Stone *f* 601
The Jasper Forest - Julia Gray *f* 551
The King's Name - Jo Walton *f* 608
The Last Hero - Terry Pratchett *f* 588
The Lion Throne - Jennifer Roberson *f* 593
Marching through Peachtree - Harry Turtledove *f* 606
Midnight Falcon - David Gemmell *f* 548
Mistress of the Catacombs - David Drake *f* 541
Mother Ocean, Daughter Sea - Diana Marcellas *f* 576
Mystify the Magician - K.A. Applegate *f* 520
Myth-ion Improbable - Robert Lynn Asprin *f* 521
Nightchild - James Barclay *f* 523
The Obsidian Tower - Freda Warrington *f* 609
Once upon a Winter's Night - Dennis L. McKiernan *f* 579
The Other Wind - Ursula K. Le Guin *f* 571
The Pillars of Creation - Terry Goodkind *f* 550
The Pillars of the World - Anne Bishop *f* 527
Pool of Radiance - Carrie Bebris *f* 525
The Prince of Shadow - Curt Benjamin *f* 526
Queen of the Demonweb Pits - Paul Kidd *f* 563
Rebel's Cage - Kate Jacoby *f* 561
Revelation - Elizabeth Haydon *f* 555
The Rover - Mel Odom *f* 584
Rowan of Rin - Emily Rodda *f* 594
The Rundlestone of Oz - Eloise McGraw *f* 577
Sea of Swords - R.A. Salvatore *f* 597
Shadow - K.J. Parker *f* 585
Shadow Kiss - Tom Townsend *f* 605
Shadowkings - Michael Cobley *f* 535
The Shattered Mask - Richard Lee Byers *f* 532
Spirit of the Stone - Maggie Furey *f* 545
Swell Foop - Piers Anthony *f* 518
Take a Thief - Mercedes Lackey *f* 569
The Treachery of Kings - Neal Barrett Jr. *f* 524
The Treason of Dortrean - Marcus Herniman *f* 557
The Warrior's Bond - Juliet E. McKenna *f* 578
The Way between the Worlds - Ian Irvine *f* 560
The Way of Light - Storm Constantine *f* 536
The Way of the Rose - Valery Leith *f* 572
Wit'ch Gate - James Clemens *f* 534
World Fall - Douglas Niles *f* 583

Geographic Index

This index provides access to all featured books by geographic settings—such as countries, continents, oceans, and planets. States and provinces are indicated for the United States and Canada. Also interfiled are headings for fictional place names (Spaceships, Imaginary Planets, etc.). Sections are further broken down by city or the specific name of the imaginary locale. Book titles are listed alphabetically under headings, with author names and genre codes. The genre codes are as follows: *c* Popular Fiction, *f* Fantasy, *h* Horror, *i* Inspirational, *m* Mystery, *r* Romance, *s* Science Fiction, *t* Historical, and *w* Western. Numbers refer to the entries that feature each title.

AFRICA

Conjuring Maud - Philip Danze *t* 847
The Golden Angel - Gilbert Morris *i* 1027
The Happy Room - Catherine Palmer *i* 1038
The Infidel - Joe Musser *i* 1031
The Scent of Magic - Cliff McNish *f* 581
Sentimental Journey - Jill Barnett *r* 228
Sentimental Journey - Jill Barnett *t* 821

ALGERIA

The Last Summer of Reason - Tahar Djaout *c* 1105

ALTERNATE EARTH

The American Zone - L. Neil Smith *s* 799
The Puppet Master - John Dalmas *s* 741
Sidhe-Devil - Aaron Allston *f* 516

Russia
Ghost of the White Nights - L.E. Modesitt Jr. *s* 778

ALTERNATE UNIVERSE

The Dreamthief's Daughter - Michael Moorcock *f* 582
Fortress Draconis - Michael A. Stackpole *f* 599
Myth-ion Improbable - Robert Lynn Asprin *f* 521
On - Adam Roberts *s* 790

Discworld
The Amazing Maurice and His Educated Rodents - Terry Pratchett *f* 587
The Last Hero - Terry Pratchett *f* 588

Dominaria
Apocalypse - J. Robert King *f* 564

Earthsea
The Other Wind - Ursula K. Le Guin *f* 571

Everworld
Entertain the End - K.A. Applegate *f* 519

Furyondy
Queen of the Demonweb Pits - Paul Kidd *f* 563

La Solterraine
Children of the Shaman - Jessica Rydill *f* 596

Midlands
The Pillars of Creation - Terry Goodkind *f* 550

Phyrexia
Apocalypse - J. Robert King *f* 564

Santhenar
The Way between the Worlds - Ian Irvine *f* 560

Xanth
Swell Foop - Piers Anthony *f* 518

AMERICAN COLONIES

The Fiery Cross - Diana Gabaldon *r* 288

New Amsterdam
City of Dreams - Beverly Swerling *t* 939

MAINE

Kittery
Summer's End - Lynne Hayworth *r* 297

NORTH CAROLINA

The Fiery Cross - Diana Gabaldon *t* 868

PENNSYLVANIA

Philadelphia
The Promise - May McGoldrick *r* 352

VIRGINIA

My Lord Savage - Elizabeth Lane *r* 326

Jamestown
Argall - William T. Vollmann *t* 950
Argall - William T. Vollmann *c* 1212

ARCTIC

The Ice Child - Elizabeth McGregor *t* 905

ASIA

The Savages in Love and War - Fred Mustard Stewart *t* 937

AT SEA

Act of Mercy - Peter Tremayne *m* 209
Adventures in Time and Space with Max Merriwell - Pat Murphy *s* 781
Deep Fathom - James Rollins *s* 792
Going Overboard - Christina Skye *r* 399
The Infidel - Joe Musser *i* 1031
Maelstrom - Peter Watts *s* 808
Mother of Kings - Poul Anderson *f* 517
The Nautical Chart - Arturo Perez-Reverte *m* 171
The Rover - Mel Odom *f* 584
The Salt Letters - Christine Balint *t* 819
To Rome with Love - Debra White Smith *i* 1049
To Tame a Duke - Patricia Grasso *r* 293
Valhalla Rising - Clive Cussler *c* 1097

Bargain II
Don't Cry for Me, Hot Pastrami - Sharon Kahn *m* 129

Barnacle Goose
Act of Mercy - Peter Tremayne *t* 944

Lanyard
The Blooding of the Guns - Alexander Fullerton *t* 866

Louisa Lee
Moontide - Erin Patrick *h* 681

Magnanime
The Devil's Own Luck - David Donachie *t* 853

Minnesota
Murder on the Minnesota - Conrad Allen *t* 816
Murder on the Minnesota - Conrad Allen *m* 5

Neptune's Car
The Captain's Wife - Douglas Kelley *t* 894

U.S.A.T. Dorchester
Sea of Glory - Ken Wales *t* 953
Sea of Glory - Ken Wales *i* 1056

AUSTRALIA

Coldwater - Mardi McConnochie *c* 1156
Coldwater - Mardi McConnochie *t* 904

Sydney
Aria - Susan Segal *c* 1194

AUSTRIA

Vienna
Funeral in Blue - Anne Perry *m* 172
Funeral in Blue - Anne Perry *t* 915

The Girl from the Golden Horn - Kurban Said c 1191
The Great Game - Michael Kurland t 899
A Perfect Match - Jeanne Savery r 389

BAHAMAS

Whispers in the Dark - Eleanor Taylor Bland m 21

BOHEMIA

Prague
Imagining Don Giovanni - Anthony J. Rudel t 929

BRAZIL

Jurua Lace
Night of the Bat - Paul Zindel h 714

BYZANTINE EMPIRE

Constantinople
Three for a Letter - Mary Reed m 180

BYZANTIUM

The Mystic Rose - Stephen R. Lawhead f 570
Three for a Letter - Mary Reed t 920
Blood and Gold - Anne Rice h 685
The Mystic Rose - Stephen R. Lawhead t 901

CANADA

Hateship, Friendship, Courtship, Loveship, Marriage - Alice Munro c 1169
A Paradigm of Earth - Candas Jane Dorsey s 747
Tower of Glass - Robert Silverberg s 797
When Tomorrow Comes - Janette Oke i 1034

ALBERTA

Cypress Hills
Twin Blessings - Carolyne Aarsen i 965

ONTARIO

Brampton
Teeth - Edo van Belkom h 705

Toronto
Bitten - Kelley Armstrong c 1068
His Father's Son - Nigel Bennett h 621

QUEBEC

Quebec City
First Gray, Then White, Then Blue - Margriet de Moor c 1165

CARIBBEAN

Going Overboard - Christina Skye r 399

CHILE

Portrait in Sepia - Isabel Allende t 817
The Scent of Magic - Cliff McNish f 581

Valparaiso
Portrait in Sepia - Isabel Allende c 1067

CHINA

Balzac and the Little Chinese Seamstress - Sijie Dai c 1098

Shanghai
The Distant Land of My Father - Bo Caldwell t 835

CZECHOSLOVAKIA

Prague
The Yellow Sailor - Steve Weiner t 954

DENMARK

Copenhagen
The Royal Physician's Visit - Per Olov Enquist t 862
The Royal Physician's Visit - Per Olov Enquist c 1110

DOMINICAN REPUBLIC

The Feast of the Goat - Mario Vargas Llosa t 948
The Feast of the Goat - Mario Vargas Llosa c 1211
The Red of His Shadow - Mayra Montero c 1164

EARTH

Bikini Planet - David Garnett s 752
Ice - Stephen Bowkett s 724
The Merchants of Souls - John Barnes s 722
Out There - Gerald Rose s 793
Starhawk - Mack Maloney s 769
The Wild Boy - Warren Rochelle s 791

ECUADOR

Galapagos Islands
Minutes to Burn - Gregg Andrew Hurwitz s 762

EGYPT

Buhen
A Place of Darkness - Lauren Haney m 101

Kemet
A Place of Darkness - Lauren Haney m 101

Waset
A Place of Darkness - Lauren Haney m 101

ENGLAND

Always Forever - Mark Chadbourn f 533
Autumn Kittens - Janice Bennett r 232
Believe in Me - Josie Litton r 336
Blessing in Disguise - Jenna Mindel r 356
The Blooding of the Guns - Alexander Fullerton t 866
Bold as Love - Gwyneth Jones s 764
The Border Hostage - Virginia Henley t 883
Broken Promises - Patricia Oliver r 362
The Child of the Holy Grail - Rosalind Miles t 907
The Clerk's Tale - Margaret Frazer t 865
The Clouds Above - Andrew Greig t 876
Come Back to Me - Josie Litton r 337
The Company of Strangers - Robert Wilson t 960
Conjuring Maud - Philip Danze t 847
The Crow Maiden - Sarah Singleton f 598
A Devilish Husband - Alana Clayton r 257
The Dragon Queen - Alice Borchardt f 528
The Dragon Queen - Alice Borchardt t 829
The English Garden - Gail Gaymer Martin i 1020
Face Down Before Rebel Hooves - Kathy Lynn Emerson t 861
Falling Angels - Tracy Chevalier t 838
A Family for Gillian - Catherine Blair r 238
A Forbidden Embrace - Anna Jacobs r 305
French Leave - Sheri Cobb South r 404
Friday's Child - Linda Chaikin i 977
A Guardian's Angel - Jo Ann Ferguson r 278
The Husband Test - Betina Krahn r 321
Ill Met by Moonlight - Sarah A. Hoyt f 559
The Incomparable Miss Compton - Regina Scott r 392
The Infidel - Joe Musser i 1031
A Kiss for Mama - Jo Ann Ferguson r 280
Knight Errant - R. Garcia y Robertson f 546
Knight Errant - R. Garcia y Robertson t 869
Lady Hilary's Halloween - Mona Gedney r 291
Lady Polly - Nicola Cornick r 259
The Marriage Bed - Claudia Dain r 266
Miss Truelove Beckons - Donna Simpson r 397
Mr. Montgomery's Quest - Martha Kirkland r 318
My Lady de Burgh - Deborah Simmons r 396
My Lady Wayward - Lael St. James r 406
My Little Blue Dress - Bruno Maddox c 1150
The Night of the Triffids - Simon Clark s 735
Once a Princess - Veronica Sattler r 388
One Good Turn - Carla Kelly r 315
A Perfect Match - Jeanne Savery r 389
Pride of Kings - Judith Tarr f 603
Pride of Kings - Judith Tarr t 941
A Prince Among Them - Al Lacy i 1015
The Promise - May McGoldrick r 352
The Promise in a Kiss - Stephanie Laurens r 329
A Reckless Encounter - Rosemary Rogers r 385
The Scent of Magic - Cliff McNish f 581
Schooling - Heather McGowan c 1159
Sentimental Journey - Jill Barnett t 821
Sentimental Journey - Jill Barnett r 228
Something More - Paul Cornell s 738
Tempt Me Twice - Barbara Dawson Smith r 400
The Temptress - Claire Delacroix r 269
'Tis the Season - Susan Spencer Paul r 367
To Kiss a Spy - Jane Feather r 276
To Tame a Duke - Patricia Grasso r 293
The Trouble with Harriet - Wilma Counts r 262
Under the Eagle - Simon Scarrow t 931
Under the Kissing Bough - Shannon Donnelly r 271
The Very Comely Countess - Miranda Jarrett r 307
The Very Daring Duchess - Miranda Jarrett r 308
The Virtuous Cyprian - Nicola Cornick r 260
The Warrior's Damsel - Denise Hampton r 295
The Wedding Charm - Lynn Collum r 258
White Lion's Lady - Tina St. John r 407
Wish List - Lisa Kleypas r 320
Year of Wonders - Geraldine Brooks t 832

Bamford
Shades of Murder - Ann Granger m 87

Bath
His Lady Midnight - Jo Ann Ferguson r 279
Sugarplum Surprises - Elisabeth Fairchild r 275
A Tangled Web - Donna Bell r 230

Berkshire
The Guardian - Barbara Miller r 355

Birmingham
Emigre Journeys - Abdullah Hussein c 1129

Brent Green
The Beasts of Brahm - Mark Hansom h 646

Bristol
The Weaver's Inheritance - Kate Sedley m 194
The Weaver's Inheritance - Kate Sedley t 934

Cambridge
Queen of Ambition - Fiona Buckley t 834
Queen of Ambition - Fiona Buckley m 29

Camelot
Lancelot Du Lethe - J. Robert King f 566

Canterbury
Saintly Murders - C.L. Grace t 875
Saintly Murders - C.L. Grace m 86

Canterlow
A Morning in Eden - Anna Gilbert t 872

Carlsley
Agatha Raisin and the Love from Hell - M.C. Beaton m 14

Chelsea
The Perfect Princess - Elizabeth Thornton r 416

Cliffside
The Night the Stars Fell - Christina Kingston r 317

Cornwall
Abandon - Jillian Hunter r 303
The Bride Sale - Candice Hern r 298
Dark Sanctuary - H.B. Gregory h 644
Desire - Nicole Jordan r 309
My Lord Savage - Elizabeth Lane r 326
The Sea Sprite - Ruth Langan r 328
Sparrowhawk—Jack Frake - Edward Cline t 840

Crowby
A Study in Death - Iain McDowell m 155

Deal
Smuggler's Moon - Bruce Alexander t 815

Derbyshire
Dancing with the Virgins - Stephen Booth m 23
The Spanish Bride - Amanda McCabe r 349

Devonshire
My Lady Beloved - Lael St. James r 405

Dimmock
Echoes of Lies - Jo Bannister m 11

Dorset
The Archer's Tale - Bernard Cornwell t 843
O Gentle Death - Janet Neel m 165
Watch by Moonlight - Kate Hawks t 881

Dunsmoor
The Perfect Princess - Elizabeth Thornton r 416

Essex
The Devil's Apprentice - Edward Marston m 148

Eyam
Year of Wonders - Geraldine Brooks c 1083

Fethering
Death on the Downs - Simon Brett m 27

Finch
Aunt Dimity: Detective - Nancy Atherton m 9

Finching
My Best Friend - Laura Wilson m 214

Glanville
Who Killed the Curate? - Joan Coggin m 36

Goring
The Clerk's Tale - Margaret Frazer m 70

Harlden
Fatal Legacy - Elizabeth Corley m 43

Holyhood
Dream of Me - Josie Litton r 338

Howling Mile
Nearly People - Conrad Williams h 708

Kent
The Valentine Wish - Debbie Raleigh r 378

Lake District
A Study in Death - Iain McDowell m 155

Sunrise on Stradbury Square - Doris Elaine Fell i 992

Lavenstock
A Sunset Touch - Marjorie Eccles m 64

Leavenham
The Shape of Snakes - Minette Walters m 211

Ledge-under-Water
His Lady Midnight - Jo Ann Ferguson r 279

Leicestershire
A Rogue for Christmas - Kate Huntington r 304

Liverpool
Murphy's Law - Rhys Bowen m 24
Murphy's Law - Rhys Bowen t 830

London
According to Queeney - Beryl Bainbridge c 1069
Blood Sinister - Cynthia Harrod-Eagles m 104
Bloodtide - Melvin Burgess s 730
The Blue Devil - Melynda Beth Skinner r 398
The Blue Last - Martha Grimes m 92
The Bones of the Buried - David Roberts m 183
The Bones of the Buried - David Roberts t 923
The Case of the Ripper's Revenge - Sam McCarver m 153
Chapel Noir - Carole Nelson Douglas m 62
The Christmas Wish - Debbie Raleigh r 377
Coffin's Ghost - Gwendoline Butler m 30
The Company of Strangers - Robert Wilson m 215
The Dark Clue - James Wilson t 959
Darkness - Sam Siciliano h 695
Desire - Nicole Jordan r 309
The Devil's Apprentice - Edward Marston m 148
A Diamond in the Rough - Andrea Pickens r 370
Dr. Mortimer and the Aldgate Mystery - Gerard Williams t 958
Dracula in London - P.N. Elrod h 631
Elusive Passion - Kathryn Smith r 402
Face Down Before Rebel Hooves - Kathy Lynn Emerson m 65
Fairness - Ferdinand Mount c 1167
Fallen - Celeste Bradley r 241
Falling Angels - Tracy Chevalier c 1090
Fortune's Lady - Evelyn Richardson r 379
Fred & Edie - Jill Dawson t 848
Funeral in Blue - Anne Perry t 915
Funeral in Blue - Anne Perry m 172
Fury - Salman Rushdie c 1190
Gabriel's Gift - Hanif Kureishi c 1143
The Goldsmith's Daughter - Kate Sedley t 933
Goodnight, Sweet Prince - David Dickinson t 851
Goodnight, Sweet Prince - David Dickinson m 58
The Great Baby Caper - Eugenia Riley r 380
The Great Game - Michael Kurland t 899
Half a Life - V.S. Naipaul c 1170
Heart of Night - Taylor Chase r 254
Heartless - Kat Martin r 346
Her Infinite Variety - Pamela Rafael Berkman t 823
His Lady Midnight - Jo Ann Ferguson r 279
How to Be Good - Nick Hornby c 1126
The Ice Child - Elizabeth McGregor t 905
In and Out - Mat Coward m 44
The Irredeemable Miss Renfield - Regina Scott r 393
Jackdaws - Ken Follett t 863
Killing the Shadows - Val McDermid m 154
Letters from an Age of Reason - Nora Hague t 877
London Bridges - Jane Stevenson c 1204
The London Vampire Panic - Michael Romkey h 686
My Best Friend - Laura Wilson m 214
Night Watch - Stephen Kendrick t 896
Pride, Prejudice and Jasmin Field - Melissa Nathan r 359
The Prisoner Bride - Susan Spencer Paul r 368
The Proper Wife - Julia Justiss r 311
Quincey Morris, Vampire - P.N. Elrod h 632
The Rag & Bone Shop - Jeff Rackham t 917
The Rake and the Wallflower - Allison Lane r 325
A Rogue for Christmas - Kate Huntington r 304
The Rose in the Wheel - S.K. Rizzolo m 182
A Scandalous Wager - Bess Willingham r 420
The Shape of Snakes - Minette Walters m 211
Sherlock Holmes and the Giant Rat of Sumatra - Alan Vanneman m 210
The Slaying of the Shrew - Simon Hawke m 109
The Slaying of the Shrew - Simon Hawke t 880
Slightly Shady - Amanda Quick r 375
Smuggler's Moon - Bruce Alexander t 815
The Spanish Bride - Amanda McCabe r 349
Suddenly You - Lisa Kleypas r 319
A Tangled Web - Donna Bell r 230
The Thief-Taker - T.F. Banks m 10
The Thief-Taker - T.F. Banks t 820
The Traitor's Daughter - Elizabeth Powell r 374
The Treatment - Mo Hayder c 1123
Uncatalogued - Julie Kaewert m 128
Very Truly Yours - Julie Beard r 229
The Weaver's Inheritance - Kate Sedley t 934
The Wedding Wager - Cathy Maxwell r 348

Lyford Meadows
The Wedding Wager - Cathy Maxwell r 348

Middledale
Very Truly Yours - Julie Beard r 229

Newgate
The Perfect Princess - Elizabeth Thornton r 416

Norfolk
Goodnight, Sweet Prince - David Dickinson m 58
Watchers of Time - Charles Todd t 943

Northumberland
The Sleeping Beauty - Jacqueline Navin r 360

Osterley
Watchers of Time - Charles Todd m 208

Oxford
The Problem of the Surly Servant - Roberta Rogow m 187
The Problem of the Surly Servant - Roberta Rogow t 926
Skeleton at the Feast - Patricia Hall m 97
Still She Haunts Me - Katie Roiphe t 927
Still She Haunts Me - Katie Roiphe c 1189

Oxfordshire
The Clerk's Tale - Margaret Frazer m 70
Pact of the Fathers - Ramsey Campbell h 626

Penzance
To Perish in Penzance - Jeanne M. Dams m 54

Portsmouth
Jane and the Prisoner of Wool House - Stephanie Barron t 822

Rayburn
The Nature of Balance - Tim Lebbon h 666

Sandringham
Goodnight, Sweet Prince - David Dickinson t 851

Sheffield
Listen to the Shadows - Danuta Reah m 179

Sherebury
To Perish in Penzance - Jeanne M. Dams m 54

Shropshire
The Salt Letters - Christine Balint t 819

Sitting Marsh
Death Is in the Air - Kate Kingsbury m 136

Southampton
Jane and the Prisoner of Wool House - Stephanie Barron t 822

Jane and the Prisoner of Wool House - Stephanie Barron *m* 12

Stratford
Her Infinite Variety - Pamela Rafael Berkman *t* 823

Surrey
Heartless - Kat Martin *r* 346

Tall Stenington
Face - Tim Lebbon *h* 665

Tolland
A Fine and Private Place - Freda Davies *m* 55

Tottenham Fields
Tragic Casements - Oliver Onions *h* 680

Trellick
No Man's Mistress - Mary Balogh *r* 227

Weldisham
Death on the Downs - Simon Brett *m* 27

Westminster
The Slaying of the Shrew - Simon Hawke *m* 109

Yorkshire
Aftermath - Peter Robinson *m* 186
Dialogues of the Dead or Paronomania! - Reginald Hill *m* 116
Face Down Before Rebel Hooves - Kathy Lynn Emerson *m* 65
The Flight of the Maidens - Jane Gardam *t* 870
Skeleton at the Feast - Patricia Hall *m* 97

ETHIOPIA

Blessed Child - Bill Bright *i* 975

EUROPE

Blood and Gold - Anne Rice *c* 1185
First Gray, Then White, Then Blue - Margriet de Moor *c* 1165
The Last Confession - Morris L. West *t* 956
Rora - James Byron Huggins *i* 1003
To Rome with Love - Debra White Smith *i* 1049

FICTIONAL CITY

Ambergris
City of Saints and Madmen - Jeff Vandermeer *f* 607

Mephistopholis
City Infernal - Edward Lee *h* 667

FICTIONAL COUNTRY

Achar
Enchanter - Sara Douglass *f* 540

Alasea
Wit'ch Gate - James Clemens *f* 534

Ansalon
Brother of the Dragon - Paul B. Thompson *f* 604

Arrandin
The Treason of Dortrean - Marcus Herniman *f* 557

Aventuria
The Obsidian Tower - Freda Warrington *f* 609

Balaia
Nightchild - James Barclay *f* 523

Barakhai
The Beasts of Barakhai - Mickey Zucker Reichert *f* 590

Branion
The Golden Sword - Fiona Patton *f* 586

Brasaybal
Shadow of the Seer - Michael Scott Rohan *f* 595

Bretonnia
Drachenfels - Jack Yeovil *f* 613

Chaldus
Hazard's Price - Robert S. Stone *f* 601

Detina
Marching through Peachtree - Harry Turtledove *f* 606

Einarinn
The Warrior's Bond - Juliet E. McKenna *f* 578

Eire
Mystify the Magician - K.A. Applegate *f* 520

The Empire
Shadow - K.J. Parker *f* 585

Everien
The Way of the Rose - Valery Leith *f* 572

Ezzaria
Revelation - Elizabeth Haydon *f* 555

Fair Isle
Dark Dreams - Cory Daniells *r* 267

Fendula
The Jasper Forest - Julia Gray *f* 551

Forus
Ritual of Proof - Dara Joy *r* 310

Four Lands
Antrax - Terry Brooks *f* 530

Global Community
Desecration - Tim LaHaye *i* 1016

Greydawn Moors
The Rover - Mel Odom *f* 584

Heldessia
The Treachery of Kings - Neal Barrett Jr. *f* 524

Homana
Children of the Lion - Jennifer Roberson *f* 591
The Lion Throne - Jennifer Roberson *f* 593

Icewind Dale
Sea of Swords - R.A. Salvatore *f* 597

Khatrimantine Empire
Shadowkings - Michael Cobley *f* 535

Khur
Dragon's Bluff - Mary H. Herbert *f* 556

Kingdom of the Isles
Mistress of the Catacombs - David Drake *f* 541

Krynn
Betrayal - Jean Rabe *f* 589

Leorum
Guardians of the Lost - Margaret Weis *f* 611

Lir
Daughter of Lir - Judith Tarr *t* 940

Lusara
Rebel's Cage - Kate Jacoby *f* 561

Magravandian Empire
The Way of Light - Storm Constantine *f* 536

Masalyar
Children of the Shaman - Jessica Rydill *f* 596

Midlands
Debt of Bones - Terry Goodkind *f* 549

Mirandeau
Once a Princess - Veronica Sattler *r* 388

Myrial
Spirit of the Stone - Maggie Furey *f* 545

Obernewtyn
Ashling - Isobelle Carmody *s* 732

Phlan
Pool of Radiance - Carrie Bebris *f* 525

Pohjola
Celtika - Robert Holdstock *f* 558

Rigante
Midnight Falcon - David Gemmell *f* 548

Rin
Rowan of Rin - Emily Rodda *f* 594

Rokugan
The Crab - Stan Brown *f* 531

Sembia
The Shattered Mask - Richard Lee Byers *f* 532

Skala
The Bone Doll's Twin - Lynn Flewelling *f* 544

Syvalan
The Pillars of the World - Anne Bishop *f* 527

Thebin
The Prince of Shadow - Curt Benjamin *f* 526

Tir Alainn
The Pillars of the World - Anne Bishop *f* 527

Tir Tanagiri
The King's Name - Jo Walton *f* 608

Tulgeria
Taylor's Temptation - Suzanne Brockmann *r* 242

Valdemar
Take a Thief - Mercedes Lackey *f* 569

Yarvannet
Mother Ocean, Daughter Sea - Diana Marcellas *f* 576

Ylorc
Destiny - Elizabeth Haydon *f* 554

FRANCE

The Archer's Tale - Bernard Cornwell *t* 843
Leap of Faith - Danielle Steel *c* 1203
Letters from an Age of Reason - Nora Hague *t* 877
The Mystic Rose - Stephen R. Lawhead *f* 570
Pride of Kings - Judith Tarr *t* 941
The Savages in Love and War - Fred Mustard Stewart *t* 937
Tomorrow's Eve - Auguste Villiers de L'Isle Adam *s* 806

Deauville
Fairness - Ferdinand Mount *c* 1167

Montaillou
The Good Men - Charmaine Craig *t* 844

Normandy
Jackdaws - Ken Follett *t* 863
The Looking Glass - Michele Roberts *t* 925
The Wolf Hunt - Gillian Bradshaw *t* 831

Paris
Beasts - Joyce Carol Oates *c* 1173
Chapel Noir - Carole Nelson Douglas *t* 856
Chapel Noir - Carole Nelson Douglas *m* 62
French Leave - Sheri Cobb South *r* 404
Haussmann, or The Distinction - Paul LaFarge *t* 900
In the Shape of a Boar - Lawrence Norfolk *c* 1171

In the Shape of a Boar - Lawrence Norfolk t 913
Kaleidoscope - J. Robert Janes t 888
Kaleidoscope - J. Robert Janes m 126
The Last Vampire - Whitley Strieber h 699
Lydia Cassatt Reading the Morning Paper - Harriet Scott Chessman t 837
My Little Blue Dress - Bruno Maddox c 1150
Of Aged Angels - Monte Cook s 737
The Officers' Ward - Marc Dugain t 857
A Perfect Match - Jeanne Savery r 389
The Promise in a Kiss - Stephanie Laurens r 329

Provence
Kaleidoscope - J. Robert Janes t 888
Kaleidoscope - J. Robert Janes m 126

Riviera
Super-Cannes - J.G. Ballard c 1070

Villeneuve
Mirabilis - Susann Cokal c 1091

GAUL

Nobody Loves a Centurion - John Maddox Roberts t 924
Nobody Loves a Centurion - John Maddox Roberts m 184

GERMANY

All That Counts - Georg M. Oswald c 1177
The Black Chalice - Marie Jakober f 562
The Dreamthief's Daughter - Michael Moorcock f 582
Keeper of Hearts - Dianne Christner i 979
Under the Eagle - Simon Scarrow t 931

Baden-Baden
Summer in Baden-Baden - Leonid Tsypkin t 946

Berlin
The Company of Strangers - Robert Wilson t 960
The Company of Strangers - Robert Wilson m 215
The Girl from the Golden Horn - Kurban Said c 1191
The Good German - Joseph Kanon c 1135
The Good German - Joseph Kanon m 131
The Good German - Joseph Kanon t 892

Dresden
The Silent Woman - Susan M. Dodd t 852

Hamburg
Face Down Before Rebel Hooves - Kathy Lynn Emerson m 65
The Yellow Sailor - Steve Weiner t 954

Potsdam
The Good German - Joseph Kanon t 892

GREECE

In the Shape of a Boar - Lawrence Norfolk t 913

Kalydon
In the Shape of a Boar - Lawrence Norfolk c 1171

Priene
Murder at the Panionic Games - Michael B. Edwards t 859

GREENLAND

Officer of the Court - Bill Mesce Jr. t 906

GUATEMALA

Gargoyles - Alan Nayes s 783

Guatemala City
Gargoyles - Alan Nayes h 677

GUYANA

The Devil-Tree of El Dorado - Frank Aubrey s 717

HELL

Elminster in Hell - Ed Greenwood f 553

HONG KONG

The Chinese Fire Drill - Les Roberts m 185
Dead Sleep - Greg Iles m 123

INDIA

Half a Life - V.S. Naipaul c 1170

Bombay
Breaking and Entering - H.R.F. Keating m 132

Delhi
A Feast in Exile - Chelsea Quinn Yarbro t 963
A Feast in Exile - Chelsea Quinn Yarbro h 713

Devapur
A Feast in Exile - Chelsea Quinn Yarbro h 713

Zalilgarh
Riot - Shashi Tharoor c 1208

IRELAND

Circle of Stars - Anna Lee Waldo t 952
Confessions of a Pagan Nun - Kate Horsley t 886
Murphy's Law - Rhys Bowen t 830
Murphy's Law - Rhys Bowen m 24
Riona - Linda Windsor i 1060

Bay of Ardmore
Act of Mercy - Peter Tremayne m 209

Brainborough
Creeping Venom - Sheila Pim m 173

Cashel
Act of Mercy - Peter Tremayne m 209

Castlelough
Legends Lake - JoAnn Ross r 386

County Limerick
A Family for Gillian - Catherine Blair r 238

Dublin
Eager to Please - Julie Parsons c 1180
The Wig My Father Wore - Anne Enright c 1111

ISRAEL

Queenmaker - India Edghill t 858

Jerusalem
Ester's Child - Jean P. Sasson t 930
The Jerusalem Scrolls - Bodie Thoene t 942
The Rock - Kanan Makiya t 902
The Rock - Kanan Makiya c 1152

ITALY

Blood and Gold - Anne Rice c 1185
Drummer in the Dark - T. Davis Bunn i 976
Officer of the Court - Bill Mesce Jr. t 906
The Southern Woman - Elizabeth Spencer c 1201

Florence
Bella Donna - Barbara Cherne t 836
Blood and Gold - Anne Rice t 922
The Passion of Artemisia - Susan Vreeland t 951
Property of Blood - Magdalen Nabb m 164

Genoa
The Dying Trade - David Donachie t 854
The Passion of Artemisia - Susan Vreeland t 951

Lake Garda
Season of Storms - Susanna Kearsley r 314

Naples
The Very Daring Duchess - Miranda Jarrett r 308

Rome
Blood and Gold - Anne Rice h 685
The Family - Mario Puzo c 1183
The Family - Mario Puzo t 916
The Passion of Artemisia - Susan Vreeland t 951
September Song - Andrew M. Greeley c 1117
Slightly Shady - Amanda Quick r 375

Tuscany
The Widow - Anne Stuart r 411

Venice
Blood and Gold - Anne Rice h 685
Goodnight, Sweet Prince - David Dickinson m 58
Shock - Robin Cook c 1093

JAPAN

Deep Fathom - James Rollins s 792

Hiroshima
The Ash Garden - Dennis Bock c 1078

Tokyo
The Bride's Kimono - Sujata Massey m 150
The Earthquake Bird - Susanna Jones m 127

MACEDONIA

Celtika - Robert Holdstock f 558

MARS

First Landing - Robert Zubrin s 814
Icebones - Stephen Baxter s 723
Martian Knightlife - James P. Hogan s 759
Out There - Gerald Rose s 793
The Secret of Life - Paul J. McAuley s 771

MEDITERRANEAN

The Mystic Rose - Stephen R. Lawhead f 570
Pyramid Scheme - David Freer s 751
Thrice Bound - Roberta Gellis f 547

MEXICO

Angel Face - Suzanne Forster r 283
Aztec Blood - Gary Jennings t 889
Smoking Mirror Blues - Ernest Hogan s 758
The Survival of Juan Oro - Max Brand w 434
Swift as Desire - Laura Esquivel c 1112

Cancun
Rag Man - Pete Hautman m 107

Chihuahua
Fire Lilies - Cynthia Leal Massey w 476

Isla Mujeres
Rag Man - Pete Hautman m 107

Los Altos
The Mouse in the Mountain - Norbert Davis m 56

Lubaanah
The Last Mayan - Malcolm Shuman m 195

Merida
The Last Mayan - Malcolm Shuman *m* 195

Monterrey
Fire Lilies - Cynthia Leal Massey *w* 476

Playa del Carmen
Captains Outrageous - Joe R. Lansdale *w* 472

Puerto Vallarta
In Too Deep - Janelle Taylor *r* 413

MIDDLE EAST

The Crusader - Michael A. Eisner *t* 860
The Jerusalem Scrolls - Bodie Thoene *i* 1053
The Pickup - Nadine Gordimer *c* 1116
Pride of Kings - Judith Tarr *f* 603

MOROCCO

Nekropolis - Maureen McHugh *s* 774

MOZAMBIQUE

Half a Life - V.S. Naipaul *c* 1170

MYTHICAL PLACE

Camp Ravenwyng
The Magickers - Emily Drake *f* 542

Faery
Eccentric Circles - Rebecca Lickiss *f* 573
Ill Met by Moonlight - Sarah A. Hoyt *f* 559
Once upon a Winter's Night - Dennis L. McKiernan *f* 579

Manfort
The Dragon Society - Lawrence Watt-Evans *f* 610

Oz
The Rundlestone of Oz - Eloise McGraw *f* 577

Seven Circles
World Fall - Douglas Niles *f* 583

Underhill
Spirits White as Lightning - Mercedes Lackey *f* 568

NETHERLANDS

Amsterdam
A Study in Death - Iain McDowell *m* 155
War Story - Gwen Edelman *c* 1107

Antwerp
The Other Adonis - Frank Deford *t* 849

NORTH AMERICA

Circle of Stars - Anna Lee Waldo *t* 952

ALASKA

Call Down the Stars - Sue Harrison *t* 879

GREAT PLAINS

Cheyenne Summer - Vella Munn *t* 911

NORWAY

Mother of Kings - Poul Anderson *t* 818
Mother of Kings - Poul Anderson *f* 517

Oslo
East of the Sun, West of the Moon - Carole Bellacera *r* 231

Sciringesheal
Dream of Me - Josie Litton *r* 338

OTTOMAN EMPIRE

Istanbul
My Name Is Red - Orhan Pamuk *c* 1178

OUTER SPACE

Angelmass - Timothy Zahn *s* 812
Appleseed - John Clute *s* 736
The Dark Wing - Walter Hunt *s* 761
Defender - C.J. Cherryh *s* 734
Empire & Ecolitan - L.E. Modesitt Jr. *s* 777
The Getaway Special - Jerry Oltion *s* 785
Out There - Gerald Rose *s* 793
Planet America - Mack Maloney *s* 768
Soldiers - John Dalmas *s* 742
Spherical Harmonic - Catherine Asaro *s* 716
Starhawk - Mack Maloney *s* 769
Tales of the Velvet Comet - Mike Resnick *s* 788
Tenebrea's Hope - Roxann Dawson *s* 743
The Wanderer - Fritz Leiber *s* 767

PACIFIC OCEAN

The Secret of Life - Paul J. McAuley *s* 771

PERU

Huacha
Treasures of the Sun - T.V. Olsen *w* 487

PLANET—IMAGINARY

Accord
Empire & Ecolitan - L.E. Modesitt Jr. *s* 777

America
Planet America - Mack Maloney *s* 768

Aquasilva
Heresy - Anselm Audley *s* 718

Arazon
Bikini Planet - David Garnett *s* 752

Argos
Wayward Moon - Denny DeMartino *s* 744

Caern
Bolo Strike - William H. Keith Jr. *s* 765

Caladan
House Corrino - Brian Herbert *s* 757

Cumbre
Homefall - Chris Bunch *s* 729

Dancer
Holding the Line - Rick Shelley *s* 795

Darkover
The Fall of Neskaya - Marion Zimmer Bradley *s* 725

Degasten
Homefall - Chris Bunch *s* 729

Dintsen
Holding the Line - Rick Shelley *s* 795

Dune
House Corrino - Brian Herbert *s* 757

Eolhixr
Appleseed - John Clute *s* 736

Gramarye
Here Be Monsters - Christopher Stasheff *f* 600

Hera
Hope's End - Stephen Chambers *s* 733

Hideaway
Bikini Planet - David Garnett *s* 752

Janus
Brother John - Rutledge Etheridge *s* 750

Kaitain
House Corrino - Brian Herbert *s* 757

Kivlan
Second Contact - J.D. Austin *s* 719

Lorelei
Angelmass - Timothy Zahn *s* 812

Mandala
Divine Intervention - Ken Wharton *s* 810

Marduk
March to the Sea - David Weber *s* 809

Maritimus
Soldiers - John Dalmas *s* 742

Masaq' Orbital
Look to Windward - Iain Banks *s* 721

narhii-Vhiliinyar
Acorna's Search - Anne McCaffrey *s* 772

Octavia
Angry Young Spaceman - Jim Munroe *s* 780

Ravenal
The Counterfeit Heinlein - Laurence M. Janiver *s* 763

Rust
Dreamer - Steven Harper *s* 755

Seraph
Angelmass - Timothy Zahn *s* 812

Shenango's World
Second Chances - Susan Shwartz *s* 796

Sky's Edge
Chasm City - Alastair Reynolds *s* 789

Soderblom
The Merchants of Souls - John Barnes *s* 722

Te Abanor
Shockball - S.L. Viehl *s* 805

Wanderer
The Wanderer - Fritz Leiber *s* 767

Yellowstone
Chasm City - Alastair Reynolds *s* 789

POLAND

Warsaw
Ester's Child - Jean P. Sasson *t* 930

PORTUGAL

Lisbon
The Company of Strangers - Robert Wilson *t* 960
The Company of Strangers - Robert Wilson *m* 215

ROMAN EMPIRE

Blood and Gold - Anne Rice *c* 1185
The Gaius Diary - Gene Edwards *i* 990

Constantinople
Blood and Gold - Anne Rice *t* 922

Ephesus
Devil's Island - John Hagee *i* 994

Rome
Blood and Gold - Anne Rice *t* 922
Nobody Loves a Centurion - John Maddox Roberts *t* 924
Nobody Loves a Centurion - John Maddox Roberts *m* 184

ROMANIA

The Appointment - Herta Muller *c* 1168
In the Shape of a Boar - Lawrence Norfolk *c* 1171

RUSSIA

Murder on the Trans-Siberian Express - Stuart M. Kaminsky *m* 130
Requiem for a Lost Empire - Andrei Makine *c* 1151

SCOTLAND

The Border Hostage - Virginia Henley *t* 883
Embrace the Dawn - Kathleen Morgan *i* 1026
Friday's Child - Linda Chaikin *i* 977
My Heart Stood Still - Lynn Kurland *r* 323
My Scottish Summer - Connie Brockway *r* 243
The Secret Clan: Abducted Heiress - Amanda Scott *r* 390
Swim the Moon - Paul Brandon *f* 529
The Third Witch - Rebecca Reisert *t* 921
To Tame a Wild Heart - Tracy Fobes *r* 281

Argyll
The Sword Maiden - Susan King *r* 316

Ceinn-beithe
The Temptress - Claire Delacroix *r* 269

Edinburgh
The Falls - Ian Rankin *m* 178
Of Aged Angels - Monte Cook *s* 737

Glasgow
Eva Moves the Furniture - Margot Livesey *c* 1148
Prized Possessions - Jessica Stirling *t* 938

Highlands
Kiss of the Highlander - Karen Marie Moning *r* 358
The Mackintosh Bride - Debra Lee Brown *r* 244

Inverness
The Enchantment - Pam Binder *r* 237

Lairg
Killing the Shadows - Val McDermid *m* 154

Orkney Islands
Officer of the Court - Bill Mesce Jr. *t* 906

St. Andrews
A Diamond in the Rough - Andrea Pickens *r* 370

Troon
Eva Moves the Furniture - Margot Livesey *c* 1148

SINGAPORE

Sherlock Holmes and the Giant Rat of Sumatra - Alan Vanneman *m* 210

SOUTH AFRICA

The Pickup - Nadine Gordimer *c* 1116

SOUTH AMERICA

Hide and Seek - Cherry Adair *r* 222

SPACE STATION

In the Company of Others - Julie E. Czerneda *s* 740

Baderes
Wayward Moon - Denny DeMartino *s* 744

Jocasta
Time Future - Maxine McArthur *s* 770

Raffles
Second Chances - Susan Shwartz *s* 796

SPACESHIP

BonoVox
Starhawk - Mack Maloney *s* 769

Irian Jaya
Second Chances - Susan Shwartz *s* 796

Santiago
Chasm City - Alastair Reynolds *s* 789

SPAIN

The Bones of the Buried - David Roberts *t* 923
The Bones of the Buried - David Roberts *m* 183
The Crusader - Michael A. Eisner *t* 860
The Mystic Rose - Stephen R. Lawhead *t* 901
The Spanish Bride - Amanda McCabe *r* 349

Barcelona
The Nautical Chart - Arturo Perez-Reverte *m* 171

Madrid
The Nautical Chart - Arturo Perez-Reverte *c* 1182
The Nautical Chart - Arturo Perez-Reverte *m* 171

Seville
Aztec Blood - Gary Jennings *t* 889

Toledo
Killing the Shadows - Val McDermid *m* 154

SYRIA

True Valor - Dee Henderson *i* 1000

THAILAND

Bangkok
The Chinese Fire Drill - Les Roberts *m* 185
The Last Vampire - Whitley Strieber *h* 699

TURKEY

True Valor - Dee Henderson *i* 1000

Constantinople
Halide's Gift - Frances Kazan *t* 893

UNION OF SOVIET SOCIALIST REPUBLICS

Written on the Wind - Judith Pella *i* 1040

UNITED STATES

Blessed Baby - Lois Richer *i* 1043
Blessed Child - Bill Bright *i* 975
Bloodlines - Fred D'Aguiar *t* 846
Born Brave - Ruth Wind *r* 422
A Bungalow for Two - Carole Gift Page *i* 1035
Christmas Vows: $5.00 Extra - Lori Copeland *i* 983
Deathday - William C. Dietz *s* 746
The Doctor's Miracle - Anna Schmidt *i* 1046
Double Honor - Melissa Horsfall *i* 1002
Drummer in the Dark - T. Davis Bunn *i* 976
The Faded Flower - Paul McCusker *i* 1024
A Family All Her Own - Bonnie K. Winn *i* 1061
Female Intelligence - Jane Heller *c* 1125
For Your Heart Only - Debra White Smith *i* 1048
A Game of Colors - John Urbancik *h* 704
Gifted Touch - Melinda Metz *s* 775
The Girl Next Door - Kate Welsh *i* 1057
The Golden Angel - Gilbert Morris *i* 1027
The Happy Room - Catherine Palmer *i* 1038
Haunted - Melinda Metz *s* 776
Judging Sara - Cynthia Rutledge *i* 1044
Letters of the Heart - Lisa Tawn Bergren *r* 233
Light Coming Back - Ann Wadsworth *c* 1213
Love One Another - Valerie Hansen *i* 995
Loving Thy Neighbor - Ruth Scofield *i* 1047
Maelstrom - Peter Watts *s* 808
The Monsters of Morley Manor - Bruce Coville *f* 538
The Phoenix - Henning Boetius *t* 828
The Power of Love - Margaret Daley *i* 987
A Prince Among Them - Al Lacy *i* 1015
The Savages in Love and War - Fred Mustard Stewart *t* 937
Scorch - A.D. Nauman *s* 782
The Seat Beside Me - Nancy Moser *i* 1030
Sentimental Journey - Jill Barnett *r* 228
Sentimental Journey - Jill Barnett *t* 821
Spanish Jack - Robert J. Conley *t* 842
Tears in a Bottle - Sylvia Bambola *i* 966
'Tis the Season - Donna Hill *r* 300
To Rome with Love - Debra White Smith *i* 1049
Treason - David Nevin *t* 912
The Wanderer - Fritz Leiber *s* 767
We Look Like Men of War - William R. Forstchen *t* 864
When the Last Leaf Falls - Bill Myers *i* 1032
The Wolf Pit - Marly Youmans *t* 964
The World Weaver - Craig Etchison *s* 749
Written on the Wind - Judith Pella *i* 1040

Colorado River
The Last Canyon - John Vernon *t* 949

Donnerville
In the Dark - Richard Laymon *h* 663

Julesburg
Whirlpool - Lorena McCourtney *i* 1023

Middle City
The Savage Girl - Alex Shakar *c* 1196

Missouri River
Downriver - Richard S. Wheeler *t* 957

Mount Crag
The Folks - Ray Garton *h* 638

Newford
The Onion Girl - Charles De Lint *f* 539

Valley Oaks
A Journey by Chance - Sally D. John *i* 1006

Willmington
Night in the Lonesome October - Richard Laymon *h* 664

ALABAMA

Fighting Gravity - Peggy Rambach *c* 1184
Why Did I Ever? - Mary Robison *c* 1188

Athens City
Hometown Legend - Jerry B. Jenkins *i* 1005

Birmingham
Bombingham - Anthony Grooms *c* 1119
Murder Boogies with Elvis - Anne George *m* 77

Dauphin Island
Massacre Island - Martin Hegwood *m* 112

Hillsboro
Open Season - Linda Howard *r* 302

Selma
September Song - Andrew M. Greeley *c* 1117

Wiregrass
A Place Called Wiregrass - Michael Morris *i* 1029

ALASKA

Rivers of Gold - Tracie Peterson *i* 1042
Worthy of Riches - Bonnie Leon *i* 1017

Chilkoot Mountain Pass
By Flare of Northern Lights - Tim Champlin *w* 439

Daughton
A Horde of Fools - James David Buchanan *w* 437

Juneau
Bethany's Song - Susan Plunkett *r* 372

Sitka
Alicia's Song - Susan Plunkett *r* 371

ARIZONA

A Good Town - Douglas Hirt *w* 462

Bisbee
Paradise Lost - J.A. Jance *m* 125

Camp Huachuca
Double Vengeance - John Duncklee *w* 449

Cochise County
Paradise Lost - J.A. Jance *w* 465

Grand Canyon
The Last Canyon - John Vernon *w* 508

Harrington Falls
Riverwatch - Joseph M. Nassise *h* 676

La Cienega
Crack Shot - Sinclair Browning *m* 28

Tombstone
Bucking the Tiger - Bruce Olds *w* 485
Doc Holliday's Gone - Jane Candia Coleman *w* 445
Double Vengeance - John Duncklee *w* 449

Tucson
Crack Shot - Sinclair Browning *m* 28
Stalking Moon - David Cole *m* 39

Websterville
The Gift of the Mestizo - Marjorie M. McGinley *w* 479

ARKANSAS

Dunkicker
Maggody and the Moonbeams - Joan Hess *m* 114

Hot Springs
Pale Horse Coming - Stephen Hunter *m* 122

Little Rock
Color the Sidewalk for Me - Brandilyn Collins *i* 980
Law Dog - J. Lee Butts *w* 438
Shakespeare's Counselor - Charlaine Harris *m* 102

Maggody
Maggody and the Moonbeams - Joan Hess *m* 114

Shakespeare
Shakespeare's Counselor - Charlaine Harris *m* 102

CALIFORNIA

Angel Face - Suzanne Forster *r* 283
Augur's Teacher - Sherwood Smith *s* 800
Eyes of Elisha - Brandilyn Collins *i* 981
Gargoyles - Alan Nayes *s* 783
Gargoyles - Alan Nayes *h* 677
The King of the Sun - A.A. McFedries *s* 773
Last Virgin in California - Maureen Child *r* 255
Moving Target - Elizabeth Lowell *r* 340
One Door Away from Heaven - Dean R. Koontz *h* 661
Smoking Mirror Blues - Ernest Hogan *s* 758
The Tender Vine - Kristen Heitzmann *i* 998
Up in the Air - Walter Kirn *c* 1141
The Water and the Blood - Nancy E. Turner *t* 947

Bakersfield
The Tumbleweed Murders - Rebecca Rothenberg *m* 189

Berkeley
Death on a Casual Friday - Sharon Duncan *m* 63

Bristo Camino
Hostage - Robert Crais *m* 47
Hostage - Robert Crais *c* 1096

Candle Bay
Candle Bay - Tamara Thorne *h* 703

Catalina Island
The Prodigy - Alton Gansky *h* 637

Hill Creek
Tall, Dead, and Handsome - Annie Griffin *m* 91

Hollywood
Coldheart Canyon - Clive Barker *h* 619
Niagara Falls All over Again - Elizabeth McCracken *c* 1158
Why Did I Ever? - Mary Robison *c* 1188
You Never Can Tell - Kathleen Eagle *w* 450

La Jolla
A Child Shall Lead Them - Carole Gift Page *i* 1036

Los Angeles
Black House - Stephen King *c* 1140
Bonnie Winter - Graham Masterton *h* 672
Coldheart Canyon - Clive Barker *c* 1071
Dear Cupid - Julie Ortolon *r* 363
The Jasmine Trade - Denise Hamilton *m* 98
Lightning Field - Dana Spiotta *c* 1202
The Secret - Kat Martin *r* 347
Shadows of Sin - Rochelle Krich *m* 137
Stormy Weather - Paula L. Woods *m* 220
Two Sexy - Stephanie Bond *r* 240
What You Owe Me - Bebe Moore Campbell *c* 1089

Madison County
Cinderella After Midnight - Lilian Darcy *r* 268

Malcasa Point
Friday Night in Beast House - Richard Laymon *h* 662

Marin County
A Sensitive Kind of Murder - Jacqueline Girdner *m* 80

Molina Point
Cat Laughing Last - Shirley Rousseau Murphy *m* 162

Napa Valley
Secret of the Wolf - Susan Krinard *r* 322

New Frisco
The Plutonium Blonde - John Zakour *s* 813

Palm Desert
Desert Autumn - Michael Craft *m* 45

Pasadena
The Distant Land of My Father - Bo Caldwell *t* 835

Port Silva
Keepers - Janet LaPierre *m* 139

Poverty Flat
What Once We Loved - Jane Kirkpatrick *i* 1011

Rio Seco
Highwire Moon - Susan Straight *c* 1205

Sacramento
The Wedding Party - Robyn Carr *r* 250

Sacramento Valley
Tennant's Rock - Steve McGiffen *w* 478

San Diego
Ashes of Aries - Martha C. Lawrence *m* 140

San Fernando Valley
The Night Men - Keith Snyder *m* 199

San Francisco
Ambrose Bierce and the Death of Kings - Oakley Hall *m* 95
Ambrose Bierce and the Death of Kings - Oakley Hall *t* 878
Bell, Cook, and Candle - Joanne Pence *m* 170
Better than Sex - Susan Holtzer *m* 120
Bleeders - Bill Pronzini *m* 174
Carter Beats the Devil - Glen David Gold *t* 874
The Distance - Eddie Muller *m* 161
Dugan under Ground - Tom De Haven *c* 1100
Flying Eagle - Tim Champlin *w* 440
The Jewel of the North - Peter King *m* 135
The Lone Rider - Max Brand *w* 432
Morgette on the Barbary Coast - G.G. Boyer *w* 429
The Oath - John Lescroart *m* 141
Portrait in Sepia - Isabel Allende *t* 817
Portrait in Sepia - Isabel Allende *c* 1067
Seducing Mr. Right - Cherry Adair *r* 223
Treasures of the Sun - T.V. Olsen *w* 487
The Wager - Metsy Hingle *r* 301
The World Below - Sue Miller *c* 1163

San Joaquin Valley
The Tumbleweed Murders - Rebecca Rothenberg *m* 189

San Pedro
Edgewater Angels - Sandro Meallet *c* 1160

Santa Angelica
Heaven Sent - Rachel Wilson *r* 421

Santa Cruz
Another Summer - Georgia Bockoven *r* 239

Santa Magdalena
Sweet Success - Susan Mallery *r* 344

Santa Monica Mountains
Sacred Ground - Barbara Wood *t* 962

Sierra Nevada
Come, My Little Angel - Diane Noble *i* 1033

Steeple Hill
The Art of Dying - Diana Killian *i* 1009

Ventura
Darkness at the Door - Catherine Dain *m* 52

COLORADO

Broken Honor - Patricia Potter *r* 373
Eccentric Circles - Rebecca Lickiss *f* 573
Flying Eagle - Tim Champlin *w* 440
The Magic of Ordinary Days - Ann Howard Creel *t* 845
Ride West to Dawn - James C. Work *w* 514
This Time Forever - Carol Steward *i* 1052

Battlement Park
Colorado Twilight - Tess Pendergrass *w* 495

Colorado Springs
Buttercup Baby - Karen Fox *r* 287

Creede
The Pinkerton Eye - Allen P. Bristow *w* 436

Crystal
The Tender Vine - Kristen Heitzmann *i* 998

Culdee Creek
Child of Promise - Kathleen Morgan *i* 1025

Denver
The Bride of Willow Creek - Maggie Osborne *r* 364
Diamond in the Ruff - Emily Carmichael *r* 249
The Great Baby Caper - Eugenia Riley *r* 380
Shadow Valley Rising - Stephen Overholser *w* 488
The Thunder Keeper - Margaret Coel *w* 444
The Thunder Keeper - Margaret Coel *m* 35
Up in the Air - Walter Kirn *c* 1141

Forlorn Valley
Once an Outlaw - Jill Gregory *r* 294

La Veta
Monte's Revenge - Eugene C. Vories *w* 509

Southern Ute Reservation
White Shell Woman - James D. Doss *m* 61

Steamboat Springs
Blood on the Wind - Lucile Bogue *w* 426

Whisper Creek
July Thunder - Rachel Lee *r* 330

White Stone
The Colorado Bride - Mary Burton *r* 247

Willow Creek
The Bride of Willow Creek - Maggie Osborne *r* 364

CONNECTICUT

The Woman Next Door - Barbara Delinsky *c* 1101

Bakerhaven
Puzzled to Death - Parnell Hall *m* 96

Dorset
The Cold Blue Blood - David Handler *m* 100

Greenwich
Once Bitten - Laurien Berenson *m* 17

Hartford
Once Bitten - Laurien Berenson *m* 17

New London
Frankenstein: The Legacy - Christopher Schildt *h* 691

DISTRICT OF COLUMBIA

Washington
The Bride's Kimono - Sujata Massey *m* 150
Bring Me a Dream - Robyn Amos *r* 224
Broken Honor - Patricia Potter *r* 373
Brothers of Cain - Miriam Grace Monfredo *m* 159
Brothers of Cain - Miriam Grace Monfredo *t* 909
A Capital Holiday - Janet Dailey *r* 265
East of the Sun, West of the Moon - Carole Bellacera *r* 231
Halfway to Heaven - Susan Wiggs *r* 419
The Justice - Angela Elwell Hunt *i* 1004
Love Her Madly - Mary-Ann Tirone Smith *m* 198
Murder at the President's Door - Elliott Roosevelt *t* 928
A Reckless Encounter - Rosemary Rogers *r* 385
Rocky and the Senator's Daughter - Dixie Browning *r* 246
A Soldier's Duty - Thomas E. Ricks *c* 1186
Valhalla Rising - Clive Cussler *c* 1097

FLORIDA

Circle of Stars - Anna Lee Waldo *w* 510
Legends Lake - JoAnn Ross *r* 386
Requiem for a Lost Empire - Andrei Makine *c* 1151

Deacon Beach
Strawman's Hammock - Darryl Wimberley *m* 216

Key Largo
Blackwater Sound - James W. Hall *m* 94

Key West
I Dream of You - Judi McCoy *r* 350

Miami
Bitter Sugar - Carolina Garcia-Aguilera *m* 75
Suspicion of Vengeance - Barbara Parker *m* 167
The Thirty-Third Hour - Mitchell Chefitz *i* 978

Orlando
All Families Are Psychotic - Douglas Coupland *c* 1094

Palm Haven
Murder by Manicure - Nancy J. Cohen *m* 38

Palmetto Springs
Deep Water Death - Glynn Marsh Alam *m* 3

Panama City
Strip Poker - Nancy Bartholomew *m* 13

Paradise Beach
Next Stop, Paradise - Sue Civil-Brown *r* 256

Silver Beach
Basket Case - Carl Hiaasen *m* 115

Stuart
Suspicion of Vengeance - Barbara Parker *m* 167

Tampa
Under Suspicion - Rachel Lee *r* 331

Temple Terrace
Under Suspicion - Rachel Lee *r* 331

GEORGIA

An Angel to Die For - Mignon F. Ballard *f* 522
The Wind Done Gone - Alice Randall *t* 918

Atlanta
Blue Plate Special - Ruth Birmingham *m* 18
A Darker Justice - Sallie Bissell *m* 19
Dead Ball - R.D. Rosen *m* 188
Gumshoe Gorilla - Keith Hartman *s* 756
Last of the Dixie Heroes - Peter Abrahams *m* 1
Night of Dracula - Christopher Schildt *h* 692
When Heaven Weeps - Ted Dekker *i* 988

Baxter
Day of Reckoning - Kathy Herman *i* 1001

Cape Refuge
Cape Refuge - Terri Blackstock *i* 970

Collier
Fireworks - James A. Moore *h* 675

Columbus
Followin' a Dream - Eboni Snoe *r* 403

Heartsdale
Blindsighted - Karin Slaughter *m* 197

St. Anne Island
Envy - Sandra Brown *r* 245
Envy - Sandra Brown *c* 1086

Saint Simons Island
Whispers of Goodbye - Karen White *r* 418

Sainte's Point Island
Alice at Heart - Deborah Smith *r* 401

Savannah
Call Each River Jordan - Owen Parry *m* 169
Marry Me, Maddie? - Rita Herron *r* 299
The Surgeon - Tess Gerritsen *m* 78

Solomon's Rock
Angel in the Front Room, Devil out Back - Stanford Diehl *m* 59

GREAT PLAINS

The Holy Road - Michael Blake *t* 826
The June Rise - William Tremblay *t* 945
On the Night Plain - J. Robert Lennon *w* 473
An Uncommon Enemy - Michelle Black *t* 824

HAWAII

Bamboo and Lace - Lori Wick *i* 1059

Honolulu
Steppin' on a Rainbow - Kinky Friedman *m* 72

Malino
The Secret Admirer - Annette Mahon *r* 343

Waipi'o Valley
Steppin' on a Rainbow - Kinky Friedman *m* 72

IDAHO

Elkton
A Measure of Grace - Al Lacy *i* 1014

Gospel
True Confessions - Rachel Gibson *r* 292

Nun's Lake
One Door Away from Heaven - Dean R. Koontz *h* 661

ILLINOIS

Chicago
Beloved Protector - Linda O'Brien *r* 361
Dangerously Irresistible - Kristin Gabriel *r* 289
Firebreak - Richard Stark *m* 202
Funny Accent - Barbara Shulgasser-Parker *c* 1197
Hard Road - Barbara D'Amato *m* 53
Kiss It Goodbye - John Wessel *m* 213
Kisses of Death - Max Allan Collins *t* 841
Of Aged Angels - Monte Cook *s* 737
The Protector - Dee Henderson *i* 999
Pyramid Scheme - David Freer *s* 751
Rhythms - Donna Hill *t* 884
Sex and Murder.com - Mark Richard Zubro *m* 221
Smoke-Filled Rooms - Kris Nelscott *m* 166
This Heart of Mine - Susan Elizabeth Phillips *r* 369
Two Sexy - Stephanie Bond *r* 240
The Watermark - Travis Thrasher *i* 1054

Elderton
The Astonished Eye - Tracy Knight *f* 567

Evanston
Killer Stuff - Sharon Fiffer *m* 69

Green Town
From the Dust Returned - Ray Bradbury *h* 623

Kankakee
Killer Stuff - Sharon Fiffer *m* 69

Lincoln Prairie
Whispers in the Dark - Eleanor Taylor Bland *m* 21

Oak Park
September Song - Andrew M. Greeley *c* 1117

Peoria
Two Sexy - Stephanie Bond *r* 240

Rockford
Look at Me - Jennifer Egan *c* 1108

Rockport
The Message of the Mute Dog - Charlotte Murray Russell *m* 191

Wolf Prairie
Sketches with Wolves - Jacqueline Fiedler *m* 68

INDIANA

Bington
Robak in Black - Joe L. Hensley *m* 113

Bloomington
Affinity - J.N. Williamson *h* 709
The Secret Life of Connor Monahan - Elizabeth Bevarly *r* 235

Marigold
The Secret Life of Connor Monahan - Elizabeth Bevarly *r* 235

South Bend
Emerald Aisle - Ralph McInerny *m* 156

Youngsville
When Jayne Met Erik - Elizabeth Bevarly *r* 236

IOWA

Leap of Faith - Danielle Steel *c* 1203
Redeeming Claire - Cynthia Rutledge *i* 1045

Black River Falls
Save the Last Dance for Me - Ed Gorman *m* 83

Cedar Rapids
Save the Last Dance for Me - Ed Gorman *m* 83

Des Moines
Beloved Protector - Linda O'Brien *r* 361

Valley Junction
Niagara Falls All over Again - Elizabeth McCracken *c* 1158

KANSAS

Sarah and the Rogue - DeLoras Scott *r* 391

Baumen
Blood Games - Lee Killough *h* 657

Crab Orchard
Dangerously Irresistible - Kristin Gabriel *r* 289

Flint Hills
Sarah's Window - Janice Graham *w* 457

Hampstead
A Cold Christmas - Charlene Weir *m* 212

Otter Creek
Back in Kansas - Debra Salonen *r* 387

Washita River
An Uncommon Enemy - Michelle Black *w* 423

Waynetown
Caleb's Price - Troy D. Smith *w* 505

KENTUCKY

Legends Lake - JoAnn Ross *r* 386

Bradleyville
Color the Sidewalk for Me - Brandilyn Collins *i* 980

Gillespie
Too Much Temptation - Lori Foster *r* 286

Languor County
Dancing Dead - Deborah Woodworth *i* 1062

Louisville
The Good Journey - Micaela Gilchrist *t* 873

LOUISIANA

Whispers of Goodbye - Karen White *r* 418
A World of Thieves - James Carlos Blake *w* 424
A World of Thieves - James Carlos Blake *t* 825

Blue Bayou
Gotta Get Next to You - Lynn Emery *r* 272

Cane River
Cane River - Lalita Tademy *c* 1207

Great Catahoula Swamp
Junior's Leg - Ken Wells *c* 1214

Jardin
When Love Came to Town - Lenora Worth *i* 1063

New Orleans
Audubon's Watch - John Gregory Brown *c* 1085
Audubon's Watch - John Gregory Brown *t* 833
Chasing the Devil's Tail - David Fulmer *t* 867
Chasing the Devil's Tail - David Fulmer *m* 73
Dead Sleep - Greg Iles *m* 123
Ghost of a Flea - James Sallis *m* 192
The Great Baby Caper - Eugenia Riley *r* 380
Insatiable - Julie Elizabeth Leto *r* 333
Letters from an Age of Reason - Nora Hague *t* 877
The Masks of Auntie Laveau - Robert J. Randisi *m* 177
Midnight Bayou - Nora Roberts *c* 1187
Pale Shadow - Robert Skinner *t* 935
Pale Shadow - Robert Skinner *m* 196
Red Beans and Vice - Lou Jane Temple *m* 207
The Wager - Metsy Hingle *r* 301

MAINE

End over End - Kate Kennedy *c* 1139
My Heart Stood Still - Lynn Kurland *r* 323
Schooling - Heather McGowan *c* 1159

Camden
Moontide - Erin Patrick *h* 681

Caribou Peak
Dangerous Attraction - Susan Vaughan *r* 417

Derry
Dreamcatcher - Stephen King *h* 660

Eastport
Wreck the Halls - Sarah Graves *m* 89

Heavenly Daze
A Warmth in Winter - Lori Copeland *i* 984

Hilton
The White Room - A.J. Matthews *h* 673

Portland
Dangerous Attraction - Susan Vaughan *r* 417

Scarborough
Dark Hollow - John Connolly *m* 42

Tinker's Cove
Wedding Day Murder - Leslie Meier *m* 157

Unity
Frankenstein: The Legacy - Christopher Schildt *h* 691

Weymouth
Dangerous Attraction - Susan Vaughan *r* 417

MARYLAND

Columbus Slaughters Braves - Mark Friedman *c* 1114

Annapolis
Occasion of Revenge - Marcia Talley *m* 205

Baltimore
Ghost Killer - Scott Chandler *h* 627
In a Strange City - Laura Lippman *m* 143
The Nightingale's Song - Kathleen Eschenburg *r* 273
Red on Rose - Patricia Jones *c* 1133
What to Do about Annie? - Millie Criswell *r* 264

Chestertown
Occasion of Revenge - Marcia Talley *m* 205

Grandville
Sap Rising - Christine Lincoln *c* 1147

MASSACHUSETTS

Aleford
The Body in the Bonfire - Katherine Hall Page *i* 1037

Arkham
The Shadow out of Time - H.P. Lovecraft *h* 670

Arlington
Lazarus, Arise - Nicholas Kilmer *m* 134

Beacon Harbor
Turnabout - Jeremiah Healy *m* 111

Berkshire Mountains
Beasts - Joyce Carol Oates *c* 1173

Boston
Comfort and Joy - Sandra Madden *r* 342
Death in Paradise - Robert B. Parker *m* 168
The Elusive Voice - Mary Jo Adamson *m* 2
The Fourth Hand - John Irving *c* 1130
Lazarus, Arise - Nicholas Kilmer *m* 134
Midnight Bayou - Nora Roberts *c* 1187
Milkrun - Sarah Mlynowski *r* 357
Past Tense - William G. Tapply *m* 206
Shock - Robin Cook *c* 1093
The Surgeon - Tess Gerritsen *m* 78
Taylor's Temptation - Suzanne Brockmann *r* 242
To Tame a Duke - Patricia Grasso *r* 293

Cape Ann
Good Harbor - Anita Diamant *c* 1103

Cape Cod
Past Tense - William G. Tapply *m* 206

Framingham
Straight on 'Til Morning - Christopher Golden *h* 642

Lafayette
Could I Have This Dance? - Harry Lee Kraus *i* 1012

Martha's Vineyard
First Light - Philip R. Craig m 46
Suzanne's Diary for Nicholas - James Patterson c 1181

Nantucket Island
Uncatalogued - Julie Kaewert m 128

Paradise
Death in Paradise - Robert B. Parker m 168

Salem
Frankenstein: The Legacy - Christopher Schildt h 691

Somerville
Turnabout - Jeremiah Healy m 111

Swansea Island
Almost - Elizabeth Benedict c 1073

Swift River Valley
Stillwater - William F. Weld t 955

Three Sisters Island
Dance upon the Air - Nora Roberts r 382
Heaven and Earth - Nora Roberts r 383

Winfield
Looking for Laura - Judith Arnold r 226

MICHIGAN

Secrets of the Heart - Gail Gaymer Martin i 1022

Ann Arbor
Better than Sex - Susan Holtzer m 120

Black Creek
The Cat Who Went Up the Creek - Lilian Jackson Braun m 26

Bower
Behind Time - Lynn Abbey f 515

Mackinac Island
Death Is a Cabaret - Deborah Morgan m 160

Michiganopolis
Burning Down the House - Lev Rafael m 176

Redmond
A Love for Safekeeping - Gail Gaymer Martin i 1021

Upper Peninsula
Cold - John Smolens c 1199

Wind Lake
This Heart of Mine - Susan Elizabeth Phillips r 369

MIDWEST

From the Dust Returned - Ray Bradbury c 1082
Great American Plain - Gary Sernovitz c 1195

St. Jude
The Corrections - Jonathan Franzen c 1113

MINNESOTA

Heart of the Sandhill - Stephanie Grace Whitson i 1058

Excelsior
Unraveled Sleeve - Monica Ferris m 67

Hamilton Groves
The Lecturer's Tale - James Hynes h 649

Lake Wobegon
Lake Wobegon Summer 1956 - Garrison Keillor c 1136

Minneapolis
Dial M for Meat Loaf - Ellen Hart m 105
Emerald Aisle - Ralph McInerny m 156
Rag Man - Pete Hautman m 107
Sherlock Holmes and the Secret Alliance - Larry Millett m 158
Sherlock Holmes and the Secret Alliance - Larry Millett t 908

Naniboujou
Unraveled Sleeve - Monica Ferris m 67

Roofing
Peace Like a River - Leif Enger c 1109

Rose Hill
Dial M for Meat Loaf - Ellen Hart m 105

Rutherford
Six-Pound Walleye - Elizabeth Gunn m 93

St. Paul
Sherlock Holmes and the Secret Alliance - Larry Millett m 158
Sherlock Holmes and the Secret Alliance - Larry Millett t 908

MISSISSIPPI

Bloodroot - Susan Wittig Albert m 4
Pale Horse Coming - Stephen Hunter t 887
Pale Horse Coming - Stephen Hunter c 1127
Pale Horse Coming - Stephen Hunter m 122
Rhythms - Donna Hill t 884

Corinth
Call Each River Jordan - Owen Parry t 914

Eden
The Innocent - Amanda Stevens r 410

Palisades
The Innocent - Amanda Stevens r 410

Vicksburg
Yonder Stands Your Orphan - Barry Hannah c 1121

MISSOURI

Branson
Lilies That Fester - Janis Harrison m 103

Fertile
The Edge of Town - Dorothy Garlock r 290

Hayden
Emerald Windows - Terri Blackstock i 971

Jefferson Barracks
The Good Journey - Micaela Gilchrist w 454
The Good Journey - Micaela Gilchrist t 873

Kansas City
Red Beans and Vice - Lou Jane Temple m 207
The Texan's Dream - Jodi Thomas r 415

River City
Lilies That Fester - Janis Harrison m 103

St. Louis
Downriver - Richard S. Wheeler w 512
A Horde of Fools - James David Buchanan w 437
The Masks of Auntie Laveau - Robert J. Randisi m 177
Narcissus in Chains - Laurell K. Hamilton h 645
The Nudger Dilemmas - John Lutz m 147

MONTANA

The Final Country - James Crumley m 50
Heaven Sent - Jillian Hart i 997
On the Night Plain - J. Robert Lennon c 1146

Billings
A Lower Deep - Tom Piccirilli h 682

Bitterroot Valley
Bitterroot - James Lee Burke c 1088

Derby
Lockwood - Lauran Paine w 492

Havre
Firebreak - Richard Stark m 202

Lost Peak
The Secret - Kat Martin r 347

Prairie City
The Outlaws - Wayne D. Overholser w 490

Rocky Mountains
Lt. Kent: Lone Wolf - Judith Lyons r 341

Victor
Written on Her Heart - Alan Maki i 1019

Virginia City
Letters to Callie - Dawn Miller w 483

NEBRASKA

Ash Hollow
A Rose by the Door - Deborah Bedford i 967

Camp Robinson
Turn the Stars Upside Down - Terry C. Johnston w 466

McTavish Plain
Mattie and the Blacksmith - Linda Lea Castle r 253

Omaha
Beloved Protector - Linda O'Brien r 361
Up in the Air - Walter Kirn c 1141

NEVADA

ChronoSpace - Allen Steele s 802
Leaving Disneyland - Alexander Parsons c 1179
The Widow's Little Secret - Judith Stacy r 409

Las Vegas
The Final Country - James Crumley m 50
Night Players - P.D. Cacek h 625

Tanglewood
Just West of Heaven - Kathleen Kane r 313

Tonopah
The Pinkerton Eye - Allen P. Bristow w 436

NEW ENGLAND

Fighting Gravity - Peggy Rambach c 1184
He Goes, She Goes - Joanna Torrey c 1209

NEW HAMPSHIRE

Hanover
Uncatalogued - Julie Kaewert m 128

Snug Harbor
Awakening Alex - Ruth Langan r 327

NEW JERSEY

Murder in the Forecast - Valerie Wolzien m 219

Basking Ridge
You're the One - Judi McCoy r 351

Hoboken
Midlife Can Be Murder - Jane Isenberg m 124

Lakehurst
ChronoSpace - Allen Steele s 802

Trenton
Seven Up - Janet Evanovich *r* 274

Winston
The Doctor and the Dead Man's Chest - Robin Hathaway *m* 106

NEW MEXICO

Chaco Canyon
Bone Walker - Kathleen O'Neal Gear *t* 871

Las Vegas
Bucking the Tiger - Bruce Olds *w* 485

Lordsburg
The Outlaw's Twin Sister - Stephen A. Bly *i* 973

Marko
Open Range - Zane Grey *w* 458

Navajo Reservation
Blackening Song - Aimee Thurlo *w* 506

Posados County
Bag Limit - Steven F. Havill *m* 108

Rosita
Destiny Valley - Fred Grove *w* 459

Santa Fe
In Too Deep - Janelle Taylor *r* 413

Socorro
Miracle of the Jacal - Robert J. Randisi *w* 497

Taos
Kiss It Goodbye - John Wessel *m* 213

Trabajo
Tears of the Heart - Lauran Paine *w* 493

NEW YORK

Aria - Susan Segal *c* 1194
The Black Eye - Constance Little *m* 144
A Feral Darkness - Doranna Durgin *f* 543
House of Pain - Sephera Giron *h* 640
Midsummer Murder - Shelley Freydont *m* 71
No Way Out - Andrea Kane *r* 312

Adirondack Mountains
Irregardless of Murder - Ellen Edwards Kennedy *i* 1008

Albany
Just West of Heaven - Kathleen Kane *r* 313
Roscoe - William Kennedy *t* 897

Bethlehem
Heaven on Earth - Marilyn Pappano *r* 366

Blue Fields
Dead Love - Donald Beman *h* 620

Chicken Corners
Catskill - John R. Hayes *m* 110

Corinth
The Lake of Dead Languages - Carol Goodman *m* 82

Covens Hollow
The Pinkerton Eye - Allen P. Bristow *w* 436

Dilmun
The Gingerbread Man - Maggie Shayne *r* 395

Isola
Money, Money, Money - Ed McBain *m* 152

Klover
Prepared for Murder - Cecile Lamalle *m* 138

Mumford
The Last Vampire - T.M. Wright *h* 712

Nassau County
Long Time No See - Susan Isaacs *c* 1131

New York
About the Author - John Colapinto *c* 1092
All the Dead Were Strangers - Ethan Black *c* 1076
All the Dead Were Strangers - Ethan Black *m* 20
All the Finest Girls - Alexandra Styron *c* 1206
Almost - Elizabeth Benedict *c* 1073
. . .And the Angel with Television Eyes - John Shirley *h* 694
Any Way the Wind Blows - E. Lynn Harris *c* 1122
The Ash Garden - Dennis Bock *c* 1078
Bachelor on the Prowl - Kasey Michaels *r* 353
Back in Kansas - Debra Salonen *r* 387
Black Water Transit - Carsten Stroud *m* 204
Chelsea Horror Hotel - Dee Dee Ramone *h* 684
Closing Time - Jim Fusilli *m* 74
The Corrections - Jonathan Franzen *c* 1113
Crimson Kiss - Trisha Baker *h* 617
Critical Space - Greg Rucka *m* 190
Dead Sleep - Greg Iles *m* 123
The Deadhouse - Linda Fairstein *m* 66
Deadly Illumination - Serena Stier *m* 203
The Deadwood Beetle - Mylene Dressler *c* 1106
Dervish Is Digital - Pat Cadigan *s* 731
Dugan under Ground - Tom De Haven *c* 1100
East of the Sun, West of the Moon - Carole Bellacera *r* 231
Envy - Sandra Brown *r* 245
Envy - Sandra Brown *c* 1086
Firebreak - Richard Stark *m* 202
Fleeced - Carol Higgins Clark *m* 34
For Rouenna - Sigrid Nunez *c* 1172
The Fourth Hand - John Irving *c* 1130
Funny Accent - Barbara Shulgasser-Parker *c* 1197
Fury - Salman Rushdie *c* 1190
The Grand Complication - Allen Kurzweil *c* 1144
Green - Benjamin Zucker *i* 1064
He Goes, She Goes - Joanna Torrey *c* 1209
The Heavenly Fugitive - Gilbert Morris *i* 1028
Hope to Die - Lawrence Block *m* 22
Hosts - F. Paul Wilson *h* 710
The Hum Bug - Harold Schechter *t* 932
The Hum Bug - Harold Schechter *m* 193
The Hum Bug - Harold Schechter *w* 502
I Dream of You - Judi McCoy *r* 350
Island of Tears - Troy Soos *t* 936
Island of Tears - Troy Soos *m* 200
Jackson's Way - Leslie LaFoy *r* 324
Kaleidoscope - Dorothy Gilman *m* 79
The Last Vampire - Whitley Strieber *h* 699
The Long Good Boy - Carol Lea Benjamin *m* 16
Look at Me - Jennifer Egan *c* 1108
Lucky Us - Joan Silber *c* 1198
Magic Time - Marc Scott Zicree *f* 614
The Manhattan Hunt Club - John Saul *h* 687
The Marine and the Princess - Cathie Linz *r* 334
Miss Match - Leslie Carroll *r* 252
Murphy's Law - Rhys Bowen *m* 24
Murphy's Law - Rhys Bowen *t* 830
My Little Blue Dress - Bruno Maddox *c* 1150
Niagara Falls All over Again - Elizabeth McCracken *c* 1158
The Night Men - Keith Snyder *m* 199
The Night of the Triffids - Simon Clark *s* 735
The Other Adonis - Frank Deford *t* 849
Personal Velocity - Rebecca Miller *c* 1162
The Reckoning - John McLain *w* 481
Red Hook - Gabriel Cohen *m* 37
Red House - K.J.A. Wishnia *m* 217
Rhythms - Donna Hill *t* 884
See Jane Date - Melissa Senate *r* 394
Shooting Dr. Jack - Norman Green *c* 1118
Slightly Single - Wendy Markham *r* 345
Spirits White as Lightning - Mercedes Lackey *f* 568
Steppin' on a Rainbow - Kinky Friedman *m* 72
Suzanne's Diary for Nicholas - James Patterson *c* 1181
Tomorrow's Eve - Auguste Villiers de L'Isle Adam *s* 806
TV - Brian Brown *c* 1084
The Widow - Anne Stuart *r* 411

Oakwood
Happy Birthday Murder - Lee Harris *i* 996

Salthill-on-Hudson
Middle Age - Joyce Carol Oates *c* 1174

Saratoga Springs
The Killing Bee - Matt Witten *m* 218

Seneca Falls
Brothers of Cain - Miriam Grace Monfredo *t* 909

Sullivan County
Catskill - John R. Hayes *t* 882

Voorburg-on-Hudson
Someone to Watch over Me - Jill Churchill *t* 839
Someone to Watch over Me - Jill Churchill *m* 33

NORTH CAROLINA

Creatures of Habit - Jill McCorkle *c* 1157
Just Say No! - Omar Tyree *c* 1210
Summer's Promise - Irene Brand *i* 974
This Rock - Robert Morgan *t* 910

Blue Ridge Mountains
Stranded with the Sergeant - Cathie Linz *r* 335

Blue Springs
Highland Hopes - Gary E. Parker *i* 1039

Camp Lejeune
Stranded with the Sergeant - Cathie Linz *r* 335

Charlotte
Doomed to Repeat It - d.g.k. goldberg *h* 641
Nightmare in Shining Armor - Tamar Myers *m* 163

Hillston
First Lady - Michael Malone *c* 1153

Job's Corner
Carley's Song - Patricia Houck Sprinkle *i* 1051

Little Jump Off
A Darker Justice - Sallie Bissell *m* 19

Lump Jump Off
In the Forest of Harm - Sallie Bissell *c* 1074

Mitford
In This Mountain - Jan Karon *i* 1007

New Bern
A Bend in the Road - Nicholas Sparks *c* 1200

Raleigh
Sentimental, Heartbroken Rednecks - Greg Bottoms *c* 1079

Snowden
Rocky and the Senator's Daughter - Dixie Browning *r* 246

NORTH DAKOTA

A Dream to Follow - Lauraine Snelling *i* 1050

Buffalo Valley
Buffalo Valley - Debbie Macomber *w* 474

NORTHEAST

Webster
The Webster Chronicle - Daniel Akst *c* 1066

OHIO

The Evidence Against Her - Robb Forman Dew *c* 1102
The Evidence Against Her - Robb Forman Dew *t* 850

Cincinnati
Audubon's Watch - John Gregory Brown *c* 1085
The Jazz Bird - Craig Holden *t* 885
The Jazz Bird - Craig Holden *m* 119

Cleveland
The Dragons of the Cuyahoga - S. Andrew Swann *f* 602

Georgetown
The Ambush of My Name - Jeffrey Marks *t* 903

Old Orchard
The Woman for Dusty Conrad - Tori Carrington *r* 251

OKLAHOMA

The Renegade Steals a Lady - Vickie Taylor *r* 414

Osage County
The Years of Fear - Fred Grove *w* 460

OREGON

Heart of the Beast - Joyce Weatherford *w* 511
Sweet Nothings - Catherine Anderson *r* 225

Glenbrooke
Wildflowers - Robin Jones Gunn *i* 993

Table Rock Country
What Once We Loved - Jane Kirkpatrick *w* 470

PENNSYLVANIA

Allentown
Bachelor on the Prowl - Kasey Michaels *r* 353
Love to Love You Baby - Kasey Michaels *r* 354

Bedford Creek
A Father's Place - Marta Perry *i* 1041

Bethany
On Every Side - Karen Kingsbury *i* 1010

Erie
Do You Hear What I Hear? - Holly Jacobs *r* 306

Gettysburg
Gettysburg - James Reasoner *t* 919

Lancaster County
October Song - Beverly Lewis *i* 1018

Philadelphia
The Corrections - Jonathan Franzen *c* 1113
The Doctor and the Dead Man's Chest - Robin Hathaway *m* 106
Law Dog - J. Lee Butts *w* 438
The Night Men - Keith Snyder *m* 199
TV - Brian Brown *c* 1084

Pittsburgh
Alien Taste - Wen Spencer *s* 801
The Quest - Jim Kraus *i* 1013
The Texan's Dream - Jodi Thomas *r* 415

Sylvan Falls
A Family for Jana - Eileen Berger *i* 968

RHODE ISLAND

Newport
Deadly Illumination - Serena Stier *m* 203

Providence
Dead Ball - R.D. Rosen *m* 188

Wickford
Tall, Dark, and Difficult - Patricia Coughlin *r* 261

ROCKY MOUNTAINS

The June Rise - William Tremblay *t* 945

SOUTH

The Blue and the Gray Undercover - Ed Gorman *w* 456
Fire in the Rock - Joe Martin *c* 1154

Blackwell Hill
City Infernal - Edward Lee *h* 667

SOUTH CAROLINA

Berea
A Garden to Keep - Jamie Langston Turner *i* 1055

Charleston
Death by Darjeeling - Laura Childs *m* 32
To Trust a Stranger - Karen Robards *r* 381

SOUTH DAKOTA

Deadwood
Friends and Enemies - Stephen A. Bly *i* 972

Pine Ridge Reservation
The June Rise - William Tremblay *w* 507

SOUTHWEST

Dangerous Dilemmas - Evelyn Palfrey *r* 365
Moving Target - Elizabeth Lowell *r* 340

TENNESSEE

Nashborough - Elsie Burch Donald *t* 855

Knoxville
Vampire Vow - Michael Schiefelbein *h* 690

Memphis
Broken Honor - Patricia Potter *r* 373
Smoke-Filled Rooms - Kris Nelscott *m* 166

Shiloh
Call Each River Jordan - Owen Parry *m* 169

TEXAS

The Baron War - Jory Sherman *w* 503
Behold a Red Horse - Cotton Smith *w* 504
Dangerously Irresistible - Kristin Gabriel *r* 289
Echo Burning - Lee Child *w* 442
The Final Country - James Crumley *m* 50
Jackson's Way - Leslie LaFoy *r* 324
Summer Moon - Jill Marie Landis *w* 471
The Texan's Dream - Jodi Thomas *r* 415
Tie-Fast Country - Robert Flynn *w* 451
The Water and the Blood - Nancy E. Turner *t* 947
The Way of the Coyote - Elmer Kelton *w* 468
The Way of the Coyote - Elmer Kelton *t* 895
The Way of the Coyote - Elmer Kelton *c* 1137
A World of Thieves - James Carlos Blake *t* 825
A World of Thieves - James Carlos Blake *w* 424

Abilene
Will's War - Janice Woods Windle *t* 961

Agatite
The Vigil - Clay Reynolds *w* 498

Amarillo
Search for Last Chance - A.L. McWilliams *w* 482

Austin
Austin City Blue - Jan Grape *m* 88
Dear Cupid - Julie Ortolon *r* 363

Brimstone
The MacKenzies: Zach - Ana Leigh *r* 332

Clearview
A Romantic Way to Die - Bill Crider *m* 49

Dallas
His Father's Son - Nigel Bennett *h* 621

Fall Creek
Saddled - Delores Fossen *r* 284

Fort Griffin
Bear Paw - Gene Mullins *w* 484

Fort Worth
Bucking the Tiger - Bruce Olds *w* 485
The Money-Whipped Steer-Job Three-Jack Give-Up Artist - Dan Jenkins *c* 1132

Gatesville
Love Her Madly - Mary-Ann Tirone Smith *m* 198

Good Union
Quincie Bolliver - Mary King *w* 469

Houston
Dangerous Dilemmas - Evelyn Palfrey *r* 365
In Too Deep - Janelle Taylor *r* 413
Night Blood - James M. Thompson *h* 702
The Secret of Life - Paul J. McAuley *s* 771

Job's Crossing
Biggie and the Quincy Ghost - Nancy Bell *m* 15

Lake Travis
Dear Cupid - Julie Ortolon *r* 363

Llando Estacado
The Holy Road - Michael Blake *w* 425

Nickleberry
All Signs Point to Murder - Kat Goldring *m* 81

Pecan Springs
Bloodroot - Susan Wittig Albert *m* 4

Polvo
Death of the Last Villista - Allana Martin *w* 475
Death of the Last Villista - Allana Martin *m* 149

Port Kingston
The Renegade Steals a Lady - Vickie Taylor *r* 414

Purgatory
Walker's Widow - Heidi Betts *r* 234

Quincy
Biggie and the Quincy Ghost - Nancy Bell *m* 15

San Antonio
The Renegades: Rafe - Genell Dellin *r* 270

Seguin
Will's War - Janice Woods Windle *w* 513

Ticky Creek
Darkling I Listen - Katherine Sutcliffe *r* 412

Wolf Springs
Hard Bounty - Ken Hodgson *w* 463

UTAH

The Reproductive System - John Sladek *s* 798

Corban
The Association - Bentley Little *h* 668

Kanab
Sister Wife - John Gates *m* 76

Salt Lake City
Fault Line - Sarah Andrews *m* 7

VERMONT

The World Below - Sue Miller *c* 1163

Brattleboro
Tucker Peak - Archer Mayor *m* 151

New Halcyon
About the Author - John Colapinto *c* 1092

VIRGINIA

The Nightingale's Song - Kathleen Eschenburg *r* 273

Alexandria
Harvest of Murder - Ann Ripley *m* 181

Culpepper County
Gettysburg - James Reasoner *t* 919

Hampton Roads
The Ironclad Alibi - Michael Kilian *m* 133

Leesburg
Forbid Them Not - Michael P. Farris *i* 991

Norfolk
Taylor's Temptation - Suzanne Brockmann *r* 242

Richmond
Brothers of Cain - Miriam Grace Monfredo *t* 909
Brothers of Cain - Miriam Grace Monfredo *m* 159
The Ironclad Alibi - Michael Kilian *t* 898
The Ironclad Alibi - Michael Kilian *m* 133

Yorktown
Revenge of the Wrought-Iron Flamingos - Donna Andrews *m* 6

WASHINGTON

Alpine
The Alpine Nemesis - Mary Daheim *m* 51

Bainbridge Island
A Prince of a Guy - Sheila Rabe *r* 376
Shades of Justice - Fredrick Huebner *m* 121

Friday Harbor
Death on a Casual Friday - Sharon Duncan *m* 63

Seattle
Betrayed - Rosey Dow *i* 989
By Flare of Northern Lights - Tim Champlin *w* 439
Death Is a Cabaret - Deborah Morgan *m* 160
The Enchantment - Pam Binder *r* 237
A Prince of a Guy - Sheila Rabe *r* 376
Shades of Justice - Fredrick Huebner *m* 121
Veiled Threats - Deborah Donnelly *m* 60

WEST

Bucking the Tiger - Bruce Olds *c* 1176
Chumley's Gold - Wayne D. Overholser *w* 489
Cowboy in the Making - Will James *w* 464
Gambler's Row: A Western Trio - Les Savage Jr. *w* 500
The Gauntlet - Max Brand *w* 430
The Good Journey - Micaela Gilchrist *t* 873
Heart of the Sandhill - Stephanie Grace Whitson *i* 1058
The House of Gold - Max Brand *w* 431
The Legend of Sotoju Mountain - Will Henry *w* 461
Long Journey to Deep Canon - T.T. Flynn *w* 452
Man Without a Past - T.V. Olsen *w* 486
Moon Medicine - Mike Blakely *t* 827
Mountain Time - Jane Candia Coleman *w* 446
No Place for a Lady - Vicki Piekarski *w* 496
Open Season - C.J. Box *w* 428
Outcasts - Tim McGuire *w* 480
Rainbow Rider: A Western Trio - Wayne D. Overholser *w* 491
River Walk - Rita Cleary *w* 443
Spanish Jack - Robert J. Conley *w* 447
Stage Trails West - Frank Bonham *w* 427
Turn the Stars Upside Down - Terry C. Johnston *t* 890
Voices in the Hill: Western Stories - Steve Frazee *w* 453
A Western Family Christmas - Millie Criswell *r* 263
The Wolf Strain - Max Brand *w* 435
The Woman at Ox-Yoke - Lewis B. Patten *w* 494
You Never Can Tell - Kathleen Eagle *w* 450

WEST VIRGINIA

Magic Time - Marc Scott Zicree *f* 614

WISCONSIN

Winter's Secret - Lyn Cote *i* 985

Big Oak
Cold Hunter's Moon - K.C. Greenlief *m* 90

Fort St. Antoine
Glare Ice - Mary Logue *m* 145

Fort Tye
Night Hawk's Bride - Jillian Hart *r* 296

French Landing
Black House - Stephen King *h* 659
Black House - Stephen King *c* 1140

Green Bay
The Fourth Hand - John Irving *c* 1130

Tyler
The Nanny - Judith Stacy *r* 408

WYOMING

Back in Kansas - Debra Salonen *r* 387
Charlie and the Sir - Frank Roderus *w* 499
A Home of Her Own - Cathleen Connors *i* 982
Last Year's River - Allen Morris Jones *w* 467
Last Year's River - Allen Morris Jones *t* 891
The Reckoning - John McLain *w* 481

Drexel
Alicia's Song - Susan Plunkett *r* 371
Bethany's Song - Susan Plunkett *r* 372

Fort Phil Kearny
Moon of Bitter Cold - Frederick J. Chiaventone *w* 441

Jackson Hole
Blue Wolf - Lise McClendon *w* 477

Powder Springs
Man from Wyoming - Dane Coolidge *w* 448

Shiloh
On Leaving Lonely Town - Cait Logan *r* 339

Twelve Sleep
Open Season - C.J. Box *w* 428
Open Season - C.J. Box *m* 25

Wind River Reservation
The Thunder Keeper - Margaret Coel *w* 444
The Thunder Keeper - Margaret Coel *m* 35

VIRGIN ISLANDS OF THE UNITED STATES

St. Thomas
Don't Cry for Me, Hot Pastrami - Sharon Kahn *m* 129

WALES

Circle of Stars - Anna Lee Waldo *t* 952
Circle of Stars - Anna Lee Waldo *w* 510
My Lady de Burgh - Deborah Simmons *r* 396
The Prisoner Bride - Susan Spencer Paul *r* 368

Foal Island
Everything You Need - A.L. Kennedy *c* 1138

Gwyndar
Desire - Nicole Jordan *r* 309

WEST INDIES

St. Claire
All the Finest Girls - Alexandra Styron *c* 1206

Genre Index

This index lists the books featured as main entries in *What Do I Read Next?* by genre and story type within each genre. Beneath each of the nine genres, the story types appear alphabetically, and titles appear alphabetically under story type headings. The name of the primary author, genre code and the book entry number also appear with each title. The genre codes are as follows: *c* Popular Fiction, *f* Fantasy, *h* Horror, *i* Inspirational, *m* Mystery, *r* Romance, *s* Science Fiction, *t* Historical, and *w* Western. For definitions of the story types, see the "Key to Genre Terms" following the Introduction.

FANTASY

Adventure

The Rover - Mel Odom f 584

Alternate Universe

Entertain the End - K.A. Applegate f 519
Sidhe-Devil - Aaron Allston f 516
The Treachery of Kings - Neal Barrett Jr. f 524

Alternate World

Mother Ocean, Daughter Sea - Diana Marcellas f 576

Anthology

Assassin Fantastic - Martin H. Greenberg f 552
A Constellation of Cats - Denise Little f 574
Creature Fantastic - Denise Little f 575
The Dragons of Magic - J. Robert King f 565
The Search for Magic - Margaret Weis f 612

Collection

City of Saints and Madmen - Jeff Vandermeer f 607
Cursed and Consulted - Rick Cook f 537
Legacy of the Wolf - Jennifer Roberson f 592
The Lion Throne - Jennifer Roberson f 593
The Silver Call - Dennis L. McKiernan f 580

Contemporary

The Astonished Eye - Tracy Knight f 567
Behind Time - Lynn Abbey f 515
The Crow Maiden - Sarah Singleton f 598
The Dragons of the Cuyahoga - S. Andrew Swann f 602
Eccentric Circles - Rebecca Lickiss f 573
A Feral Darkness - Doranna Durgin f 543
Magic Time - Marc Scott Zicree f 614
The Magickers - Emily Drake f 542
The Onion Girl - Charles De Lint f 539
Spirits White as Lightning - Mercedes Lackey f 568
Swim the Moon - Paul Brandon f 529

Historical

The Black Chalice - Marie Jakober f 562
Ill Met by Moonlight - Sarah A. Hoyt f 559
Mother of Kings - Poul Anderson f 517
The Mystic Rose - Stephen R. Lawhead f 570
Pride of Kings - Judith Tarr f 603
Thrice Bound - Roberta Gellis f 547

Horror

Drachenfels - Jack Yeovil f 613
A Feral Darkness - Doranna Durgin f 543

Humor

The Amazing Maurice and His Educated Rodents - Terry Pratchett f 587
The Last Hero - Terry Pratchett f 588
Myth-ion Improbable - Robert Lynn Asprin f 521
Swell Foop - Piers Anthony f 518

Legend

Celtika - Robert Holdstock f 558
The Dragon Queen - Alice Borchardt f 528
Lancelot Du Lethe - J. Robert King f 566
Mystify the Magician - K.A. Applegate f 520
Once upon a Winter's Night - Dennis L. McKiernan f 579
Thrice Bound - Roberta Gellis f 547

Magic Conflict

Children of the Shaman - Jessica Rydill f 596
Destiny - Elizabeth Haydon f 554
Drachenfels - Jack Yeovil f 613
The Golden Sword - Fiona Patton f 586
Hazard's Price - Robert S. Stone f 601
Here Be Monsters - Christopher Stasheff f 600
The Obsidian Tower - Freda Warrington f 609
The Other Wind - Ursula K. Le Guin f 571
The Pillars of the World - Anne Bishop f 527
Wit'ch Gate - James Clemens f 534

Military

Marching through Peachtree - Harry Turtledove f 606

Mystery

An Angel to Die For - Mignon F. Ballard f 522

Post-Disaster

Shadow of the Seer - Michael Scott Rohan f 595

Quest

The Jasper Forest - Julia Gray f 551
Myth-ion Improbable - Robert Lynn Asprin f 521
Once upon a Winter's Night - Dennis L. McKiernan f 579
The Pillars of Creation - Terry Goodkind f 550
The Prince of Shadow - Curt Benjamin f 526
The Rundlestone of Oz - Eloise McGraw f 577

Sword and Sorcery

Always Forever - Mark Chadbourn f 533
Antrax - Terry Brooks f 530
Apocalypse - J. Robert King f 564
The Beasts of Barakhai - Mickey Zucker Reichert f 590
Betrayal - Jean Rabe f 589
The Bone Doll's Twin - Lynn Flewelling f 544
Brother of the Dragon - Paul B. Thompson f 604
Children of the Lion - Jennifer Roberson f 591
The Crab - Stan Brown f 531
Debt of Bones - Terry Goodkind f 549
The Dragon Society - Lawrence Watt-Evans f 610
Dragon's Bluff - Mary H. Herbert f 556
The Dragons of Magic - J. Robert King f 565
The Dreamthief's Daughter - Michael Moorcock f 582
Elminster in Hell - Ed Greenwood f 553
Enchanter - Sara Douglass f 540
Fortress Draconis - Michael A. Stackpole f 599
Guardians of the Lost - Margaret Weis f 611
The King's Name - Jo Walton f 608
The Last Hero - Terry Pratchett f 588
Midnight Falcon - David Gemmell f 548
Mistress of the Catacombs - David Drake f 541
Nightchild - James Barclay f 523
The Pillars of Creation - Terry Goodkind f 550
Pool of Radiance - Carrie Bebris f 525
Queen of the Demonweb Pits - Paul Kidd f 563
Rebel's Cage - Kate Jacoby f 561
Revelation - Elizabeth Haydon f 555
The Rover - Mel Odom f 584
Sea of Swords - R.A. Salvatore f 597
Shadow - K.J. Parker f 585

Shadowkings - Michael Cobley *f* 535
The Shattered Mask - Richard Lee Byers *f* 532
The Silver Call - Dennis L. McKiernan *f* 580
Spirit of the Stone - Maggie Furey *f* 545
Take a Thief - Mercedes Lackey *f* 569
The Treason of Dortrean - Marcus Herniman *f* 557
The Warrior's Bond - Juliet E. McKenna *f* 578
The Way between the Worlds - Ian Irvine *f* 560
The Way of Light - Storm Constantine *f* 536
The Way of the Rose - Valery Leith *f* 572
World Fall - Douglas Niles *f* 583

Time Travel

Knight Errant - R. Garcia y Robertson *f* 546

Young Adult

The Amazing Maurice and His Educated Rodents - Terry Pratchett *f* 587
Entertain the End - K.A. Applegate *f* 519
The Magickers - Emily Drake *f* 542
The Monsters of Morley Manor - Bruce Coville *f* 538
Mystify the Magician - K.A. Applegate *f* 520
Rowan of Rin - Emily Rodda *f* 594
The Rundlestone of Oz - Eloise McGraw *f* 577
The Scent of Magic - Cliff McNish *f* 581
Shadow Kiss - Tom Townsend *f* 605

HISTORICAL

Action/Adventure

The Mystic Rose - Stephen R. Lawhead *t* 901

Adventure

Aztec Blood - Gary Jennings *t* 889
Moon Medicine - Mike Blakely *t* 827

Arts

The Silent Woman - Susan M. Dodd *t* 852

Biblical Fiction

Queenmaker - India Edghill *t* 858

Coming-of-Age

Portrait in Sepia - Isabel Allende *t* 817

Disaster

The Phoenix - Henning Boetius *t* 828

Espionage

The Company of Strangers - Robert Wilson *t* 960
Jackdaws - Ken Follett *t* 863

Espionage Thriller

Brothers of Cain - Miriam Grace Monfredo *t* 909

Family Saga

Ester's Child - Jean P. Sasson *t* 930
Gettysburg - James Reasoner *t* 919
Rhythms - Donna Hill *t* 884
The Savages in Love and War - Fred Mustard Stewart *t* 937

Fantasy

The Wolf Hunt - Gillian Bradshaw *t* 831

Gothic

A Morning in Eden - Anna Gilbert *t* 872

Historical/American Civil War

Bloodlines - Fred D'Aguiar *t* 846
Brothers of Cain - Miriam Grace Monfredo *t* 909
Call Each River Jordan - Owen Parry *t* 914
Gettysburg - James Reasoner *t* 919
The Ironclad Alibi - Michael Kilian *t* 898
We Look Like Men of War - William R. Forstchen *t* 864
The Wind Done Gone - Alice Randall *t* 918
The Wolf Pit - Marly Youmans *t* 964

Historical/American West

Downriver - Richard S. Wheeler *t* 957
The Good Journey - Micaela Gilchrist *t* 873
The Holy Road - Michael Blake *t* 826
The June Rise - William Tremblay *t* 945
The Last Canyon - John Vernon *t* 949
Last Year's River - Allen Morris Jones *t* 891
Moon Medicine - Mike Blakely *t* 827
Turn the Stars Upside Down - Terry C. Johnston *t* 890
An Uncommon Enemy - Michelle Black *t* 824
The Way of the Coyote - Elmer Kelton *t* 895

Historical/Americana

Ambrose Bierce and the Death of Kings - Oakley Hall *t* 878
Audubon's Watch - John Gregory Brown *t* 833
The Captain's Wife - Douglas Kelley *t* 894
Chasing the Devil's Tail - David Fulmer *t* 867
The Evidence Against Her - Robb Forman Dew *t* 850
The Hum Bug - Harold Schechter *t* 932
Island of Tears - Troy Soos *t* 936
Letters from an Age of Reason - Nora Hague *t* 877
Roscoe - William Kennedy *t* 897
Sherlock Holmes and the Secret Alliance - Larry Millett *t* 908
Stillwater - William F. Weld *t* 955
This Rock - Robert Morgan *t* 910
Will's War - Janice Woods Windle *t* 961

Historical/Ancient Greece

Murder at the Panionic Games - Michael B. Edwards *t* 859

Historical/Ancient Rome

Blood and Gold - Anne Rice *t* 922
The Jerusalem Scrolls - Bodie Thoene *t* 942
Nobody Loves a Centurion - John Maddox Roberts *t* 924
Three for a Letter - Mary Reed *t* 920
Under the Eagle - Simon Scarrow *t* 931

Historical/Antebellum American South

The Wind Done Gone - Alice Randall *t* 918

Historical/Colonial America

Argall - William T. Vollmann *t* 950
City of Dreams - Beverly Swerling *t* 939
The Fiery Cross - Diana Gabaldon *t* 868

Historical/Depression Era

Catskill - John R. Hayes *t* 882
Murder at the President's Door - Elliott Roosevelt *t* 928
Nashborough - Elsie Burch Donald *t* 855
The Phoenix - Henning Boetius *t* 828
Prized Possessions - Jessica Stirling *t* 938
Someone to Watch over Me - Jill Churchill *t* 839
Stillwater - William F. Weld *t* 955

Historical/Edwardian

Falling Angels - Tracy Chevalier *t* 838
Murder on the Minnesota - Conrad Allen *t* 816
Night Watch - Stephen Kendrick *t* 896

Historical/Elizabethan

Face Down Before Rebel Hooves - Kathy Lynn Emerson *t* 861
Her Infinite Variety - Pamela Rafael Berkman *t* 823
Queen of Ambition - Fiona Buckley *t* 834
The Slaying of the Shrew - Simon Hawke *t* 880

Historical/Exotic

Halide's Gift - Frances Kazan *t* 893

Historical/Fantasy

The Child of the Holy Grail - Rosalind Miles *t* 907
Daughter of Lir - Judith Tarr *t* 940
The Dragon Queen - Alice Borchardt *t* 829
A Feast in Exile - Chelsea Quinn Yarbro *t* 963
Imagining Don Giovanni - Anthony J. Rudel *t* 929
In the Shape of a Boar - Lawrence Norfolk *t* 913
Knight Errant - R. Garcia y Robertson *t* 869
Mother of Kings - Poul Anderson *t* 818
The Other Adonis - Frank Deford *t* 849
Pride of Kings - Judith Tarr *t* 941
The Third Witch - Rebecca Reisert *t* 921

Historical/Georgian

The Devil's Own Luck - David Donachie *t* 853
The Dying Trade - David Donachie *t* 854
The Royal Physician's Visit - Per Olov Enquist *t* 862
Smuggler's Moon - Bruce Alexander *t* 815
Sparrowhawk—Jack Frake - Edward Cline *t* 840
Watch by Moonlight - Kate Hawks *t* 881

Historical/Medieval

Act of Mercy - Peter Tremayne *t* 944
The Archer's Tale - Bernard Cornwell *t* 843
Circle of Stars - Anna Lee Waldo *t* 952
The Clerk's Tale - Margaret Frazer *t* 865
The Crusader - Michael A. Eisner *t* 860
The Goldsmith's Daughter - Kate Sedley *t* 933
The Good Men - Charmaine Craig *t* 844
The Mystic Rose - Stephen R. Lawhead *t* 901
Pride of Kings - Judith Tarr *t* 941
The Rock - Kanan Makiya *t* 902
Saintly Murders - C.L. Grace *t* 875
The Third Witch - Rebecca Reisert *t* 921
The Weaver's Inheritance - Kate Sedley *t* 934
The Wolf Hunt - Gillian Bradshaw *t* 831

Historical/Post-American Civil War

The Ambush of My Name - Jeffrey Marks *t* 903
Bloodlines - Fred D'Aguiar *t* 846
The Way of the Coyote - Elmer Kelton *t* 895

Historical/Post-American Revolution

Treason - David Nevin t 912

Historical/Post-French Revolution

Haussmann, or The Distinction - Paul LaFarge t 900

Historical/Pre-history

Call Down the Stars - Sue Harrison t 879
Daughter of Lir - Judith Tarr t 940
Sacred Ground - Barbara Wood t 962

Historical/Regency

Jane and the Prisoner of Wool House - Stephanie Barron t 822
The Thief-Taker - T.F. Banks t 820

Historical/Renaissance

Bella Donna - Barbara Cherne t 836
The Family - Mario Puzo t 916
The Last Confession - Morris L. West t 956

Historical/Roaring Twenties

Carter Beats the Devil - Glen David Gold t 874
Fred & Edie - Jill Dawson t 848
The Jazz Bird - Craig Holden t 885
Kisses of Death - Max Allan Collins t 841
Rhythms - Donna Hill t 884
This Rock - Robert Morgan t 910
A World of Thieves - James Carlos Blake t 825

Historical/Seventeenth Century

City of Dreams - Beverly Swerling t 939
The Last Confession - Morris L. West t 956
The Other Adonis - Frank Deford t 849
The Passion of Artemisia - Susan Vreeland t 951
Year of Wonders - Geraldine Brooks t 832

Historical/Victorian

Chapel Noir - Carole Nelson Douglas t 856
Coldwater - Mardi McConnochie t 904
Conjuring Maud - Philip Danze t 847
The Dark Clue - James Wilson t 959
Dr. Mortimer and the Aldgate Mystery - Gerard Williams t 958
Funeral in Blue - Anne Perry t 915
Goodnight, Sweet Prince - David Dickinson t 851
The Great Game - Michael Kurland t 899
The Ice Child - Elizabeth McGregor t 905
Letters from an Age of Reason - Nora Hague t 877
Murphy's Law - Rhys Bowen t 830
The Problem of the Surly Servant - Roberta Rogow t 926
The Rag & Bone Shop - Jeff Rackham t 917
The Salt Letters - Christine Balint t 819
Still She Haunts Me - Katie Roiphe t 927

Historical/Victorian America

Lydia Cassatt Reading the Morning Paper - Harriet Scott Chessman t 837

Historical/World War I

The Blooding of the Guns - Alexander Fullerton t 866
The Looking Glass - Michele Roberts t 925
A Morning in Eden - Anna Gilbert t 872
The Officers' Ward - Marc Dugain t 857
The Silent Woman - Susan M. Dodd t 852
Watchers of Time - Charles Todd t 943
Will's War - Janice Woods Windle t 961
The Yellow Sailor - Steve Weiner t 954

Historical/World War II

The Clouds Above - Andrew Greig t 876
The Company of Strangers - Robert Wilson t 960
The Distant Land of My Father - Bo Caldwell t 835
Ester's Child - Jean P. Sasson t 930
The Flight of the Maidens - Jane Gardam t 870
The Good German - Joseph Kanon t 892
In the Shape of a Boar - Lawrence Norfolk t 913
Jackdaws - Ken Follett t 863
Kaleidoscope - J. Robert Janes t 888
The Magic of Ordinary Days - Ann Howard Creel t 845
Nashborough - Elsie Burch Donald t 855
Officer of the Court - Bill Mesce Jr. t 906
The Savages in Love and War - Fred Mustard Stewart t 937
Sea of Glory - Ken Wales t 953
Sentimental Journey - Jill Barnett t 821
The Water and the Blood - Nancy E. Turner t 947

Indian Culture

Argall - William T. Vollmann t 950
Bone Walker - Kathleen O'Neal Gear t 871
Cheyenne Summer - Vella Munn t 911
The Good Journey - Micaela Gilchrist t 873
The Holy Road - Michael Blake t 826
The June Rise - William Tremblay t 945
Sacred Ground - Barbara Wood t 962
Spanish Jack - Robert J. Conley t 842

Indian Wars

Turn the Stars Upside Down - Terry C. Johnston t 890
An Uncommon Enemy - Michelle Black t 824

Legend

The Child of the Holy Grail - Rosalind Miles t 907
The Dragon Queen - Alice Borchardt t 829
Queenmaker - India Edghill t 858

Literary

Her Infinite Variety - Pamela Rafael Berkman t 823
Summer in Baden-Baden - Leonid Tsypkin t 946

Military

The Blooding of the Guns - Alexander Fullerton t 866
The Jerusalem Scrolls - Bodie Thoene t 942
Under the Eagle - Simon Scarrow t 931
We Look Like Men of War - William R. Forstchen t 864

Mountain Man

Downriver - Richard S. Wheeler t 957

Mystery

Act of Mercy - Peter Tremayne t 944
Ambrose Bierce and the Death of Kings - Oakley Hall t 878
The Ambush of My Name - Jeffrey Marks t 903
Bella Donna - Barbara Cherne t 836
Bone Walker - Kathleen O'Neal Gear t 871
The Bones of the Buried - David Roberts t 923
Call Each River Jordan - Owen Parry t 914
Carter Beats the Devil - Glen David Gold t 874
Catskill - John R. Hayes t 882
Chapel Noir - Carole Nelson Douglas t 856
Chasing the Devil's Tail - David Fulmer t 867
The Clerk's Tale - Margaret Frazer t 865
The Devil's Own Luck - David Donachie t 853
Dr. Mortimer and the Aldgate Mystery - Gerard Williams t 958
The Dying Trade - David Donachie t 854
Face Down Before Rebel Hooves - Kathy Lynn Emerson t 861
Funeral in Blue - Anne Perry t 915
The Goldsmith's Daughter - Kate Sedley t 933
Goodnight, Sweet Prince - David Dickinson t 851
The Great Game - Michael Kurland t 899
The Hum Bug - Harold Schechter t 932
The Ironclad Alibi - Michael Kilian t 898
Island of Tears - Troy Soos t 936
Jane and the Prisoner of Wool House - Stephanie Barron t 822
The Jazz Bird - Craig Holden t 885
Kaleidoscope - J. Robert Janes t 888
Kisses of Death - Max Allan Collins t 841
Murder at the Panionic Games - Michael B. Edwards t 859
Murder at the President's Door - Elliott Roosevelt t 928
Murder on the Minnesota - Conrad Allen t 816
Murphy's Law - Rhys Bowen t 830
Night Watch - Stephen Kendrick t 896
Nobody Loves a Centurion - John Maddox Roberts t 924
Officer of the Court - Bill Mesce Jr. t 906
Pale Horse Coming - Stephen Hunter t 887
Pale Shadow - Robert Skinner t 935
The Problem of the Surly Servant - Roberta Rogow t 926
Queen of Ambition - Fiona Buckley t 834
Saintly Murders - C.L. Grace t 875
Sherlock Holmes and the Secret Alliance - Larry Millett t 908
The Slaying of the Shrew - Simon Hawke t 880
Smuggler's Moon - Bruce Alexander t 815
Someone to Watch over Me - Jill Churchill t 839
The Thief-Taker - T.F. Banks t 820
Three for a Letter - Mary Reed t 920
Watchers of Time - Charles Todd t 943
The Weaver's Inheritance - Kate Sedley t 934

Political

The Feast of the Goat - Mario Vargas Llosa t 948
Treason - David Nevin t 912

Religious

Confessions of a Pagan Nun - Kate Horsley t 886
The Rock - Kanan Makiya t 902

Romance

The Border Hostage - Virginia Henley t 883
The Looking Glass - Michele Roberts t 925

Saga

Circle of Stars - Anna Lee Waldo t 952

Time Travel

The Fiery Cross - Diana Gabaldon t 868
Knight Errant - R. Garcia y Robertson t 869

Vampire Story

Blood and Gold - Anne Rice *t* 922
A Feast in Exile - Chelsea Quinn Yarbro *t* 963

HORROR

Ancient Evil Unleashed

Riverwatch - Joseph M. Nassise *h* 676

Anthology

4 X 4 - Michael Oliveri *h* 679
The Ash-Tree Press Annual Macabre 2001 - Jack Adrian *h* 615
Dead on Demand - Elizabeth Engstrom *h* 633
Dracula in London - P.N. Elrod *h* 631
Hideous Dreams - L.H. Maynard *h* 674
The Mammoth Book of Best New Horror 12 - Stephen Jones *h* 653
The Mammoth Book of Vampire Stories by Women - Stephen Jones *h* 654
The Museum of Horrors - Dennis Etchison *h* 634
Single White Vampire Seeks Same - Martin H. Greenberg *h* 643
Triage - Matt Johnson *h* 651
Trick or Treat - Richard Chizmar *h* 628
Urban Gothic - David J. Howe *h* 648

Apocalyptic Horror

A Lower Deep - Tom Piccirilli *h* 682
Nearly People - Conrad Williams *h* 708

Child-in-Peril

Black House - Stephen King *h* 659
Friday Night in Beast House - Richard Laymon *h* 662
One Door Away from Heaven - Dean R. Koontz *h* 661
Pact of the Fathers - Ramsey Campbell *h* 626
Straight on 'Til Morning - Christopher Golden *h* 642

Collection

The Ancient Track - H.P. Lovecraft *h* 669
Bad Seed - Harry Shannon *h* 693
Black Dust - Graham Joyce *h* 655
Cobwebs and Whispers - Scott Thomas *h* 701
Cold Comfort - Nancy Kilpatrick *h* 658
Dark Shadows on the Moon - John B. Ford *h* 635
The Devil Is Not Mocked and Other Warnings - Manly Wade Wellman *h* 707
Dial Your Dreams - Robert Weinberg *h* 706
The Distance Travelled - Brett A. Savory *h* 689
The Far Side of the Lake - Steve Rasnic Tem *h* 700
Fluid Mosaic - Michael D. Arnzen *h* 616
From Weird and Distant Shores - Caitlin R. Kiernan *h* 656
A Ghostly Crew - Roger Johnson *h* 652
Halloween Candy - Thomas M. Sipos *h* 696
Heretics - Greg F. Gifune *h* 639
I'll Be Damned - Shane Ryan Staley *h* 698
Knuckles and Tales - Nancy Collins *h* 629
Legends of the Night - Stephen Mark Rainey *h* 683
Mrs. Amworth - E.F. Benson *h* 622
Pink Marble and Never Say Die - Dawn Dunn *h* 630
A Pleasing Terror - M.R. James *h* 650
The Return of the Soul and Other Stories - Robert Hichens *h* 647
The Scarecrow and Other Stories - G. Ranger Wormser *h* 711
The Shadow on the Blind - Louisa Baldwin *h* 618
Similar Monsters - Steve Savile *h* 688
Tales of Devilry and Doom - John B. Ford *h* 636
The Thing on the Doorstep and Other Weird Stories - H.P. Lovecraft *h* 671
William F. Nolan's Dark Universe - William F. Nolan *h* 678
Wondrous Strange - Robin Spriggs *h* 697
Wrong Things - Poppy Z. Brite *h* 624

Coming-of-Age

Straight on 'Til Morning - Christopher Golden *h* 642

Curse

Dark Sanctuary - H.B. Gregory *h* 644
Moontide - Erin Patrick *h* 681

Erotic Horror

Teeth - Edo van Belkom *h* 705

Ghost Story

Coldheart Canyon - Clive Barker *h* 619
Dead on Demand - Elizabeth Engstrom *h* 633
Doomed to Repeat It - d.g.k. goldberg *h* 641
The Shadow on the Blind - Louisa Baldwin *h* 618
Tragic Casements - Oliver Onions *h* 680
The White Room - A.J. Matthews *h* 673

Gothic Family Chronicle

The Folks - Ray Garton *h* 638
From the Dust Returned - Ray Bradbury *h* 623

Haunted House

Chelsea Horror Hotel - Dee Dee Ramone *h* 684
House of Pain - Sephera Giron *h* 640

Mystery

His Father's Son - Nigel Bennett *h* 621
The Manhattan Hunt Club - John Saul *h* 687
Pact of the Fathers - Ramsey Campbell *h* 626

Nature in Revolt

The Nature of Balance - Tim Lebbon *h* 666
Night of the Bat - Paul Zindel *h* 714

Occult

. . .And the Angel with Television Eyes - John Shirley *h* 694
Black House - Stephen King *h* 659
Bonnie Winter - Graham Masterton *h* 672
City Infernal - Edward Lee *h* 667
Coldheart Canyon - Clive Barker *h* 619
Dark Sanctuary - H.B. Gregory *h* 644
A Lower Deep - Tom Piccirilli *h* 682

Possession

Dead Love - Donald Beman *h* 620
Ghost Killer - Scott Chandler *h* 627

Psychological Suspense

The Association - Bentley Little *h* 668
The Beasts of Brahm - Mark Hansom *h* 646
Face - Tim Lebbon *h* 665
In the Dark - Richard Laymon *h* 663
Night in the Lonesome October - Richard Laymon *h* 664

Reanimated Dead

Frankenstein: The Legacy - Christopher Schildt *h* 691

Science Fiction

Dreamcatcher - Stephen King *h* 660
Fireworks - James A. Moore *h* 675
Hosts - F. Paul Wilson *h* 710
The Shadow out of Time - H.P. Lovecraft *h* 670

Serial Killer

Ghost Killer - Scott Chandler *h* 627
Teeth - Edo van Belkom *h* 705

Small Town Horror

The Folks - Ray Garton *h* 638

Techno-Thriller

Gargoyles - Alan Nayes *h* 677

Vampire Story

Blood and Gold - Anne Rice *h* 685
Blood Games - Lee Killough *h* 657
Candle Bay - Tamara Thorne *h* 703
Crimson Kiss - Trisha Baker *h* 617
Darkness - Sam Siciliano *h* 695
Dracula in London - P.N. Elrod *h* 631
A Feast in Exile - Chelsea Quinn Yarbro *h* 713
His Father's Son - Nigel Bennett *h* 621
The Last Vampire - Whitley Strieber *h* 699
The Last Vampire - T.M. Wright *h* 712
The London Vampire Panic - Michael Romkey *h* 686
The Mammoth Book of Vampire Stories by Women - Stephen Jones *h* 654
Narcissus in Chains - Laurell K. Hamilton *h* 645
Night Blood - James M. Thompson *h* 702
Night of Dracula - Christopher Schildt *h* 692
Night Players - P.D. Cacek *h* 625
Quincey Morris, Vampire - P.N. Elrod *h* 632
Vampire Vow - Michael Schiefelbein *h* 690

Wild Talents

Affinity - J.N. Williamson *h* 709
The Lecturer's Tale - James Hynes *h* 649
The Prodigy - Alton Gansky *h* 637

Witchcraft

A Game of Colors - John Urbancik *h* 704

Young Adult

Night of the Bat - Paul Zindel *h* 714

INSPIRATIONAL

Action/Adventure

True Valor - Dee Henderson *i* 1000

Anthology

The English Garden - Gail Gaymer Martin *i* 1020
Letters of the Heart - Lisa Tawn Bergren *i* 969
Restoration and Romance - Barbara Curtis *i* 986

Apocalyptic Horror

Desecration - Tim LaHaye *i* 1016

Biblical Fiction

The Gaius Diary - Gene Edwards *i* 990

Collection

October Song - Beverly Lewis *i* 1018

Contemporary

Blessed Child - Bill Bright *i* 975
Carley's Song - Patricia Houck Sprinkle *i* 1051
Christmas Vows: $5.00 Extra - Lori Copeland *i* 983
Color the Sidewalk for Me - Brandilyn Collins *i* 980
Day of Reckoning - Kathy Herman *i* 1001
Double Honor - Melissa Horsfall *i* 1002
Drummer in the Dark - T. Davis Bunn *i* 976
Emerald Windows - Terri Blackstock *i* 971
The Faded Flower - Paul McCusker *i* 1024
Forbid Them Not - Michael P. Farris *i* 991
A Garden to Keep - Jamie Langston Turner *i* 1055
Green - Benjamin Zucker *i* 1064
The Happy Room - Catherine Palmer *i* 1038
Hometown Legend - Jerry B. Jenkins *i* 1005
A Journey by Chance - Sally D. John *i* 1006
The Justice - Angela Elwell Hunt *i* 1004
On Every Side - Karen Kingsbury *i* 1010
A Place Called Wiregrass - Michael Morris *i* 1029
A Rose by the Door - Deborah Bedford *i* 967
The Seat Beside Me - Nancy Moser *i* 1030
Sunrise on Stradbury Square - Doris Elaine Fell *i* 992
Tears in a Bottle - Sylvia Bambola *i* 966
The Thirty-Third Hour - Mitchell Chefitz *i* 978
A Warmth in Winter - Lori Copeland *i* 984
The Watermark - Travis Thrasher *i* 1054
When Heaven Weeps - Ted Dekker *i* 988
When the Last Leaf Falls - Bill Myers *i* 1032
Wildflowers - Robin Jones Gunn *i* 993
Worthy of Riches - Bonnie Leon *i* 1017
Written on Her Heart - Alan Maki *i* 1019

Contemporary/Innocent

In This Mountain - Jan Karon *i* 1007

Historical

Come, My Little Angel - Diane Noble *i* 1033
Devil's Island - John Hagee *i* 994
The Golden Angel - Gilbert Morris *i* 1027
Highland Hopes - Gary E. Parker *i* 1039
The Infidel - Joe Musser *i* 1031
The Jerusalem Scrolls - Bodie Thoene *i* 1053
Keeper of Hearts - Dianne Christner *i* 979
A Prince Among Them - Al Lacy *i* 1015
The Quest - Jim Kraus *i* 1013
Riona - Linda Windsor *i* 1060
Rivers of Gold - Tracie Peterson *i* 1042
Rora - James Byron Huggins *i* 1003

Historical/American West

Child of Promise - Kathleen Morgan *i* 1025
A Dream to Follow - Lauraine Snelling *i* 1050
Friends and Enemies - Stephen A. Bly *i* 972
A Measure of Grace - Al Lacy *i* 1014
The Outlaw's Twin Sister - Stephen A. Bly *i* 973
The Tender Vine - Kristen Heitzmann *i* 998
What Once We Loved - Jane Kirkpatrick *i* 1011

Historical/Post-American Civil War

Heart of the Sandhill - Stephanie Grace Whitson *i* 1058

Historical/Roaring Twenties

The Heavenly Fugitive - Gilbert Morris *i* 1028

Historical/Seventeenth Century

Embrace the Dawn - Kathleen Morgan *i* 1026

Historical/World War II

Friday's Child - Linda Chaikin *i* 977
Sea of Glory - Ken Wales *i* 1056
When Tomorrow Comes - Janette Oke *i* 1034
Written on the Wind - Judith Pella *i* 1040

Medical

Could I Have This Dance? - Harry Lee Kraus *i* 1012

Mystery

The Art of Dying - Diana Killian *i* 1009
The Body in the Bonfire - Katherine Hall Page *i* 1037
Cape Refuge - Terri Blackstock *i* 970
Dancing Dead - Deborah Woodworth *i* 1062
Eyes of Elisha - Brandilyn Collins *i* 981
For Your Heart Only - Debra White Smith *i* 1048
Happy Birthday Murder - Lee Harris *i* 996
Irregardless of Murder - Ellen Edwards Kennedy *i* 1008
The Protector - Dee Henderson *i* 999
Whirlpool - Lorena McCourtney *i* 1023
Winter's Secret - Lyn Cote *i* 985

Romance

Bamboo and Lace - Lori Wick *i* 1059
Blessed Baby - Lois Richer *i* 1043
A Bungalow for Two - Carole Gift Page *i* 1035
A Child Shall Lead Them - Carole Gift Page *i* 1036
The Doctor's Miracle - Anna Schmidt *i* 1046
A Family All Her Own - Bonnie K. Winn *i* 1061
A Family for Jana - Eileen Berger *i* 968
A Father's Place - Marta Perry *i* 1041
For Your Heart Only - Debra White Smith *i* 1048
The Girl Next Door - Kate Welsh *i* 1057
Heaven Sent - Jillian Hart *i* 997
A Home of Her Own - Cathleen Connors *i* 982
Judging Sara - Cynthia Rutledge *i* 1044
Letters of the Heart - Lisa Tawn Bergren *i* 969
A Love for Safekeeping - Gail Gaymer Martin *i* 1021
Love One Another - Valerie Hansen *i* 995
Loving Thy Neighbor - Ruth Scofield *i* 1047
The Power of Love - Margaret Daley *i* 987
Redeeming Claire - Cynthia Rutledge *i* 1045
Secrets of the Heart - Gail Gaymer Martin *i* 1022
Summer's Promise - Irene Brand *i* 974
This Time Forever - Carol Steward *i* 1052
To Rome with Love - Debra White Smith *i* 1049
True Valor - Dee Henderson *i* 1000
Twin Blessings - Carolyne Aarsen *i* 965
When Love Came to Town - Lenora Worth *i* 1063
Winter's Secret - Lyn Cote *i* 985

Romantic Suspense

Betrayed - Rosey Dow *i* 989

MYSTERY

Action/Adventure

All the Dead Were Strangers - Ethan Black *m* 20
Black Water Transit - Carsten Stroud *m* 204
The Chinese Fire Drill - Les Roberts *m* 185
Critical Space - Greg Rucka *m* 190
A Darker Justice - Sallie Bissell *m* 19
The Good German - Joseph Kanon *m* 131
Hostage - Robert Crais *m* 47
The Nautical Chart - Arturo Perez-Reverte *m* 171
Pale Horse Coming - Stephen Hunter *m* 122
Rag Man - Pete Hautman *m* 107

Amateur Detective

Agatha Raisin and the Love from Hell - M.C. Beaton *m* 14
All Signs Point to Murder - Kat Goldring *m* 81
The Alpine Nemesis - Mary Daheim *m* 51
Aunt Dimity: Detective - Nancy Atherton *m* 9
Basket Case - Carl Hiaasen *m* 115
Bell, Cook, and Candle - Joanne Pence *m* 170
Better than Sex - Susan Holtzer *m* 120
Biggie and the Quincy Ghost - Nancy Bell *m* 15
The Black Eye - Constance Little *m* 144
Bloodroot - Susan Wittig Albert *m* 4
The Bones of the Buried - David Roberts *m* 183
The Bride's Kimono - Sujata Massey *m* 150
Burning Down the House - Lev Rafael *m* 176
Cat Laughing Last - Shirley Rousseau Murphy *m* 162
The Cat Who Went Up the Creek - Lilian Jackson Braun *m* 26
Catskill - John R. Hayes *m* 110
The Cold Blue Blood - David Handler *m* 100
Creeping Venom - Sheila Pim *m* 173
Darkness at the Door - Catherine Dain *m* 52
Death by Darjeeling - Laura Childs *m* 32
Death Is a Cabaret - Deborah Morgan *m* 160
Death Is in the Air - Kate Kingsbury *m* 136
Death of the Last Villista - Allana Martin *m* 149
Death on the Downs - Simon Brett *m* 27
Deep Water Death - Glynn Marsh Alam *m* 3
Desert Autumn - Michael Craft *m* 45
Dial M for Meat Loaf - Ellen Hart *m* 105
The Doctor and the Dead Man's Chest - Robin Hathaway *m* 106
Don't Cry for Me, Hot Pastrami - Sharon Kahn *m* 129
Emerald Aisle - Ralph McInerny *m* 156
Fault Line - Sarah Andrews *m* 7
Hard Road - Barbara D'Amato *m* 53
Harvest of Murder - Ann Ripley *m* 181
The Hum Bug - Harold Schechter *m* 193
Jane and the Prisoner of Wool House - Stephanie Barron *m* 12
The Jewel of the North - Peter King *m* 135
Kaleidoscope - Dorothy Gilman *m* 79
Killer Stuff - Sharon Fiffer *m* 69
The Killing Bee - Matt Witten *m* 218
The Last Mayan - Malcolm Shuman *m* 195
Lazarus, Arise - Nicholas Kilmer *m* 134
Lilies That Fester - Janis Harrison *m* 103
The Masks of Auntie Laveau - Robert J. Randisi *m* 177
The Message of the Mute Dog - Charlotte Murray Russell *m* 191
Midlife Can Be Murder - Jane Isenberg *m* 124
Midsummer Murder - Shelley Freydont *m* 71
Murder Boogies with Elvis - Anne George *m* 77
Murder by Manicure - Nancy J. Cohen *m* 38
Murder in the Forecast - Valerie Wolzien *m* 219
Murphy's Law - Rhys Bowen *m* 24
The Night Men - Keith Snyder *m* 199
Nightmare in Shining Armor - Tamar Myers *m* 163
Occasion of Revenge - Marcia Talley *m* 205
Once Bitten - Laurien Berenson *m* 17

Open Season - C.J. Box m 25
Prepared for Murder - Cecile Lamalle m 138
Puzzled to Death - Parnell Hall m 96
Red Beans and Vice - Lou Jane Temple m 207
Revenge of the Wrought-Iron Flamingos - Donna Andrews m 6
A Sensitive Kind of Murder - Jacqueline Girdner m 80
Sketches with Wolves - Jacqueline Fiedler m 68
The Slaying of the Shrew - Simon Hawke m 109
Strip Poker - Nancy Bartholomew m 13
Tall, Dead, and Handsome - Annie Griffin m 91
The Thunder Keeper - Margaret Coel m 35
To Perish in Penzance - Jeanne M. Dams m 54
The Tumbleweed Murders - Rebecca Rothenberg m 189
Uncatalogued - Julie Kaewert m 128
Unraveled Sleeve - Monica Ferris m 67
Veiled Threats - Deborah Donnelly m 60
Wedding Day Murder - Leslie Meier m 157
Who Killed the Curate? - Joan Coggin m 36
Wreck the Halls - Sarah Graves m 89

Anthology

A Century of Great Suspense Stories - Jeffery Deaver m 57
The Mammoth Book of More Historical Whodunnits - Mike Ashley m 8
The World's Finest Mystery & Crime Stories: Second Annual Collection - Ed Gorman m 84

Collection

Adam and Eve on a Raft - Ron Goulart m 85
Blue Christmas and Other Holiday Homicides - Max Allan Collins m 40
The Family Jewels and Other Stories - Dorothy Cannell m 31
Hammett: Crime Stories and Other Writings - Dashiell Hammett m 99
Kisses of Death - Max Allan Collins m 41
More Oddments - Bill Pronzini m 175
The Night People and Other Stories - Edward D. Hoch m 117
The Nighttime Is the Right Time - Bill Crider m 48
The Nudger Dilemmas - John Lutz m 147
The Old Spies Club and Other Intrigues of Rand - Edward D. Hoch m 118
The Reluctant Detective and Other Stories - Michael Z. Lewin m 142
The Sedgemoor Strangler and Other Stories of Crime - Peter Lovesey m 146
Together We Kill - Mickey Spillane m 201

Domestic

Bloodroot - Susan Wittig Albert m 4
Creeping Venom - Sheila Pim m 173
The Killing Bee - Matt Witten m 218
Someone to Watch over Me - Jill Churchill m 33
Veiled Threats - Deborah Donnelly m 60
Wedding Day Murder - Leslie Meier m 157

Espionage

The Company of Strangers - Robert Wilson m 215
The Old Spies Club and Other Intrigues of Rand - Edward D. Hoch m 118

Historical

Act of Mercy - Peter Tremayne m 209
Ambrose Bierce and the Death of Kings - Oakley Hall m 95
The Bones of the Buried - David Roberts m 183
Brothers of Cain - Miriam Grace Monfredo m 159
Call Each River Jordan - Owen Parry m 169
The Case of the Ripper's Revenge - Sam McCarver m 153
Catskill - John R. Hayes m 110
Chapel Noir - Carole Nelson Douglas m 62
Chasing the Devil's Tail - David Fulmer m 73
The Clerk's Tale - Margaret Frazer m 70
Deadly Illumination - Serena Stier m 203
Death Is in the Air - Kate Kingsbury m 136
The Devil's Apprentice - Edward Marston m 148
The Distance - Eddie Muller m 161
The Elusive Voice - Mary Jo Adamson m 2
Face Down Before Rebel Hooves - Kathy Lynn Emerson m 65
Funeral in Blue - Anne Perry m 172
The Good German - Joseph Kanon m 131
Goodnight, Sweet Prince - David Dickinson m 58
The Hum Bug - Harold Schechter m 193
The Ironclad Alibi - Michael Kilian m 133
Island of Tears - Troy Soos m 200
Jane and the Prisoner of Wool House - Stephanie Barron m 12
The Jazz Bird - Craig Holden m 119
The Jewel of the North - Peter King m 135
Kaleidoscope - J. Robert Janes m 126
The Mammoth Book of More Historical Whodunnits - Mike Ashley m 8
Murder on the Minnesota - Conrad Allen m 5
Murphy's Law - Rhys Bowen m 24
Pale Horse Coming - Stephen Hunter m 122
Pale Shadow - Robert Skinner m 196
A Place of Darkness - Lauren Haney m 101
The Problem of the Surly Servant - Roberta Rogow m 187
Queen of Ambition - Fiona Buckley m 29
The Rose in the Wheel - S.K. Rizzolo m 182
Saintly Murders - C.L. Grace m 86
Save the Last Dance for Me - Ed Gorman m 83
Sherlock Holmes and the Giant Rat of Sumatra - Alan Vanneman m 210
Sherlock Holmes and the Secret Alliance - Larry Millett m 158
The Slaying of the Shrew - Simon Hawke m 109
Someone to Watch over Me - Jill Churchill m 33
The Thief-Taker - T.F. Banks m 10
Three for a Letter - Mary Reed m 180
Watchers of Time - Charles Todd m 208
The Weaver's Inheritance - Kate Sedley m 194

Historical/Ancient Rome

Nobody Loves a Centurion - John Maddox Roberts m 184

Humor

Adam and Eve on a Raft - Ron Goulart m 85
Basket Case - Carl Hiaasen m 115
Biggie and the Quincy Ghost - Nancy Bell m 15
The Black Eye - Constance Little m 144
Burning Down the House - Lev Rafael m 176
Don't Cry for Me, Hot Pastrami - Sharon Kahn m 129
Fleeced - Carol Higgins Clark m 34
Maggody and the Moonbeams - Joan Hess m 114
The Message of the Mute Dog - Charlotte Murray Russell m 191
The Mouse in the Mountain - Norbert Davis m 56
Murder Boogies with Elvis - Anne George m 77
Nightmare in Shining Armor - Tamar Myers m 163
Puzzled to Death - Parnell Hall m 96
Revenge of the Wrought-Iron Flamingos - Donna Andrews m 6
A Romantic Way to Die - Bill Crider m 49
A Sensitive Kind of Murder - Jacqueline Girdner m 80
Steppin' on a Rainbow - Kinky Friedman m 72
Tall, Dead, and Handsome - Annie Griffin m 91
Who Killed the Curate? - Joan Coggin m 36

Legal

The Oath - John Lescroart m 141
Robak in Black - Joe L. Hensley m 113
Shades of Justice - Fredrick Huebner m 121
Sister Wife - John Gates m 76
Suspicion of Vengeance - Barbara Parker m 167

Police Procedural

Aftermath - Peter Robinson m 186
All the Dead Were Strangers - Ethan Black m 20
Austin City Blue - Jan Grape m 88
Bag Limit - Steven F. Havill m 108
Blindsighted - Karin Slaughter m 197
Blood Sinister - Cynthia Harrod-Eagles m 104
The Blue Last - Martha Grimes m 92
Breaking and Entering - H.R.F. Keating m 132
Coffin's Ghost - Gwendoline Butler m 30
A Cold Christmas - Charlene Weir m 212
Cold Hunter's Moon - K.C. Greenlief m 90
Dancing with the Virgins - Stephen Booth m 23
The Deadhouse - Linda Fairstein m 66
Death in Paradise - Robert B. Parker m 168
Dialogues of the Dead or Paronomania! - Reginald Hill m 116
The Falls - Ian Rankin m 178
Fatal Legacy - Elizabeth Corley m 43
A Fine and Private Place - Freda Davies m 55
Glare Ice - Mary Logue m 145
Hostage - Robert Crais m 47
In and Out - Mat Coward m 44
Kaleidoscope - J. Robert Janes m 126
Listen to the Shadows - Danuta Reah m 179
Money, Money, Money - Ed McBain m 152
Murder on the Trans-Siberian Express - Stuart M. Kaminsky m 130
O Gentle Death - Janet Neel m 165
Paradise Lost - J.A. Jance m 125
Property of Blood - Magdalen Nabb m 164
Red Hook - Gabriel Cohen m 37
A Romantic Way to Die - Bill Crider m 49
Sex and Murder.com - Mark Richard Zubro m 221
Shades of Murder - Ann Granger m 87
Shadows of Sin - Rochelle Krich m 137
Six-Pound Walleye - Elizabeth Gunn m 93
Skeleton at the Feast - Patricia Hall m 97
Stormy Weather - Paula L. Woods m 220
Strawman's Hammock - Darryl Wimberley m 216
A Study in Death - Iain McDowell m 155
A Sunset Touch - Marjorie Eccles m 64
The Thief-Taker - T.F. Banks m 10
Tucker Peak - Archer Mayor m 151
Watchers of Time - Charles Todd m 208
Whispers in the Dark - Eleanor Taylor Bland m 21
White Shell Woman - James D. Doss m 61

Private Detective

Ashes of Aries - Martha C. Lawrence m 140
Bitter Sugar - Carolina Garcia-Aguilera m 75
Blackwater Sound - James W. Hall m 94
Bleeders - Bill Pronzini m 174
Blue Plate Special - Ruth Birmingham m 18
Chasing the Devil's Tail - David Fulmer m 73
Closing Time - Jim Fusilli m 74
Crack Shot - Sinclair Browning m 28
Dark Hollow - John Connolly m 42
Dead Ball - R.D. Rosen m 188
Death on a Casual Friday - Sharon Duncan m 63
Echoes of Lies - Jo Bannister m 11
Emerald Aisle - Ralph McInerny m 156
The Final Country - James Crumley m 50
First Light - Philip R. Craig m 46
Fleeced - Carol Higgins Clark m 34
Funeral in Blue - Anne Perry m 172
Ghost of a Flea - James Sallis m 192
Hammett: Crime Stories and Other Writings - Dashiell Hammett m 99

Hope to Die - Lawrence Block *m* 22
In a Strange City - Laura Lippman *m* 143
Keepers - Janet LaPierre *m* 139
Kiss It Goodbye - John Wessel *m* 213
Kisses of Death - Max Allan Collins *m* 41
The Long Good Boy - Carol Lea Benjamin *m* 16
Massacre Island - Martin Hegwood *m* 112
The Mouse in the Mountain - Norbert Davis *m* 56
Murder on the Minnesota - Conrad Allen *m* 5
The Nudger Dilemmas - John Lutz *m* 147
Past Tense - William G. Tapply *m* 206
Red House - K.J.A. Wishnia *m* 217
Save the Last Dance for Me - Ed Gorman *m* 83
Shakespeare's Counselor - Charlaine Harris *m* 102
Sister Wife - John Gates *m* 76
Smoke-Filled Rooms - Kris Nelscott *m* 166
Stalking Moon - David Cole *m* 39
Steppin' on a Rainbow - Kinky Friedman *m* 72
Turnabout - Jeremiah Healy *m* 111

Psychological Suspense

Angel in the Front Room, Devil out Back - Stanford Diehl *m* 59
A Darker Justice - Sallie Bissell *m* 19
Dead Sleep - Greg Iles *m* 123
The Deadhouse - Linda Fairstein *m* 66
Dialogues of the Dead or Paronomania! - Reginald Hill *m* 116
The Earthquake Bird - Susanna Jones *m* 127
Firebreak - Richard Stark *m* 202
The Jasmine Trade - Denise Hamilton *m* 98
Killing the Shadows - Val McDermid *m* 154
The Lake of Dead Languages - Carol Goodman *m* 82
Last of the Dixie Heroes - Peter Abrahams *m* 1
Listen to the Shadows - Danuta Reah *m* 179
Love Her Madly - Mary-Ann Tirone Smith *m* 198
My Best Friend - Laura Wilson *m* 214
The Nautical Chart - Arturo Perez-Reverte *m* 171
Rag Man - Pete Hautman *m* 107
Shades of Justice - Fredrick Huebner *m* 121
The Shape of Snakes - Minette Walters *m* 211
The Surgeon - Tess Gerritsen *m* 78
Suspicion of Vengeance - Barbara Parker *m* 167

Traditional

Agatha Raisin and the Love from Hell - M.C. Beaton *m* 14
The Blue Last - Martha Grimes *m* 92
Dancing with the Virgins - Stephen Booth *m* 23
Death on the Downs - Simon Brett *m* 27
Fatal Legacy - Elizabeth Corley *m* 43
A Fine and Private Place - Freda Davies *m* 55
O Gentle Death - Janet Neel *m* 165
Shades of Murder - Ann Granger *m* 87
To Perish in Penzance - Jeanne M. Dams *m* 54

POPULAR FICTION

Adult

Jewelry Talks - Richard Klein *c* 1142
Mirabilis - Susann Cokal *c* 1091
My Little Blue Dress - Bruno Maddox *c* 1150
The Red of His Shadow - Mayra Montero *c* 1164

Adventure

The Nautical Chart - Arturo Perez-Reverte *c* 1182
Valhalla Rising - Clive Cussler *c* 1097

Americana

Bucking the Tiger - Bruce Olds *c* 1176
Columbus Slaughters Braves - Mark Friedman *c* 1114
Darling? - Heidi Jon Schmidt *c* 1193
Every Tongue Got to Confess - Zora Neale Hurston *c* 1128
Fire in the Rock - Joe Martin *c* 1154
On the Night Plain - J. Robert Lennon *c* 1146
The Way of the Coyote - Elmer Kelton *c* 1137

Arts

Envy - Sandra Brown *c* 1086

Collection

After the Plague - T. Coraghessan Boyle *c* 1081
Any Small Thing Can Save You - Christina Adam *c* 1065
Collected Stories - Saul Bellow *c* 1072
Creatures of Habit - Jill McCorkle *c* 1157
Darling? - Heidi Jon Schmidt *c* 1193
The Devil's Larder - Jim Crace *c* 1095
Flights of Love - Bernhard Schlink *c* 1192
Futureland - Walter Mosley *c* 1166
Hateship, Friendship, Courtship, Loveship, Marriage - Alice Munro *c* 1169
Hotel of the Saints - Ursula Hegi *c* 1124
The Hunters - Claire Messud *c* 1161
Hurricane Season - Karen Bjorneby *c* 1075
In the Shadow of Our House - Scott Blackwood *c* 1077
Living with Saints - Mary O'Connell *c* 1175
Lowell Limpett: And Two Stories - Ward S. Just *c* 1134
The Marble Quilt - David Leavitt *c* 1145
Personal Velocity - Rebecca Miller *c* 1162
The Practical Heart - Allan Gurganus *c* 1120
Retribution - John Fulton *c* 1115
Samuel Johnson Is Indignant - Lydia Davis *c* 1099
Sap Rising - Christine Lincoln *c* 1147
Sentimental, Heartbroken Rednecks - Greg Bottoms *c* 1079
The Southern Woman - Elizabeth Spencer *c* 1201
The Spirit Returns - Richard Burgin *c* 1087
The Stories of Paul Bowles - Paul Bowles *c* 1080
Talking in the Dark - Laura Glen Louis *c* 1149
The Unknown Errors of Our Lives - Chitra Banerjee Divakaruni *c* 1104
Zigzagging Down a Wild Trail - Bobbie Ann Mason *c* 1155

Coming-of-Age

Bombingham - Anthony Grooms *c* 1119
Edgewater Angels - Sandro Meallet *c* 1160
Eva Moves the Furniture - Margot Livesey *c* 1148
Gabriel's Gift - Hanif Kureishi *c* 1143
Great American Plain - Gary Sernovitz *c* 1195
He Goes, She Goes - Joanna Torrey *c* 1209
Just Say No! - Omar Tyree *c* 1210
Lake Wobegon Summer 1956 - Garrison Keillor *c* 1136
Peace Like a River - Leif Enger *c* 1109
Schooling - Heather McGowan *c* 1159

Contemporary

All Families Are Psychotic - Douglas Coupland *c* 1094
All the Finest Girls - Alexandra Styron *c* 1206
Envy - Sandra Brown *c* 1086
Fighting Gravity - Peggy Rambach *c* 1184
First Lady - Michael Malone *c* 1153
Highwire Moon - Susan Straight *c* 1205
Leap of Faith - Danielle Steel *c* 1203
London Bridges - Jane Stevenson *c* 1204
Long Time No See - Susan Isaacs *c* 1131
Personal Velocity - Rebecca Miller *c* 1162
The Webster Chronicle - Daniel Akst *c* 1066
The Woman Next Door - Barbara Delinsky *c* 1101

Contemporary/Fantasy

Black House - Stephen King *c* 1140
From the Dust Returned - Ray Bradbury *c* 1082
Futureland - Walter Mosley *c* 1166
Living with Saints - Mary O'Connell *c* 1175
The Savage Girl - Alex Shakar *c* 1196

Contemporary/Mainstream

All That Counts - Georg M. Oswald *c* 1177
The Corrections - Jonathan Franzen *c* 1113
For Rouenna - Sigrid Nunez *c* 1172
Fury - Salman Rushdie *c* 1190
Good Harbor - Anita Diamant *c* 1103
How to Be Good - Nick Hornby *c* 1126
Up in the Air - Walter Kirn *c* 1141

Contemporary Realism

All the Dead Were Strangers - Ethan Black *c* 1076
End over End - Kate Kennedy *c* 1139
Hostage - Robert Crais *c* 1096
In the Forest of Harm - Sallie Bissell *c* 1074
Shock - Robin Cook *c* 1093
Shooting Dr. Jack - Norman Green *c* 1118
The Treatment - Mo Hayder *c* 1123

Ethnic

Every Tongue Got to Confess - Zora Neale Hurston *c* 1128
Junior's Leg - Ken Wells *c* 1214
The Pickup - Nadine Gordimer *c* 1116
Riot - Shashi Tharoor *c* 1208
The Unknown Errors of Our Lives - Chitra Banerjee Divakaruni *c* 1104

Family Saga

Portrait in Sepia - Isabel Allende *c* 1067
Requiem for a Lost Empire - Andrei Makine *c* 1151

Gay/Lesbian Fiction

Any Way the Wind Blows - E. Lynn Harris *c* 1122
Light Coming Back - Ann Wadsworth *c* 1213
London Bridges - Jane Stevenson *c* 1204
The Marble Quilt - David Leavitt *c* 1145

Ghost Story

Coldheart Canyon - Clive Barker *c* 1071

Gothic

Beasts - Joyce Carol Oates *c* 1173
Bitten - Kelley Armstrong *c* 1068
Black House - Stephen King *c* 1140
Blood and Gold - Anne Rice *c* 1185
Coldheart Canyon - Clive Barker *c* 1071
Sap Rising - Christine Lincoln *c* 1147
Sentimental, Heartbroken Rednecks - Greg Bottoms *c* 1079
Yonder Stands Your Orphan - Barry Hannah *c* 1121

Historical

According to Queeney - Beryl Bainbridge *c* 1069
Argall - William T. Vollmann *c* 1212
Audubon's Watch - John Gregory Brown *c* 1085
Balzac and the Little Chinese Seamstress - Sijie Dai *c* 1098
Bucking the Tiger - Bruce Olds *c* 1176
Cane River - Lalita Tademy *c* 1207

Coldwater - Mardi McConnochie *c* 1156
The Evidence Against Her - Robb Forman Dew *c* 1102
Fairness - Ferdinand Mount *c* 1167
Falling Angels - Tracy Chevalier *c* 1090
The Family - Mario Puzo *c* 1183
Fire in the Rock - Joe Martin *c* 1154
The Girl from the Golden Horn - Kurban Said *c* 1191
The Good German - Joseph Kanon *c* 1135
Mirabilis - Susann Cokal *c* 1091
My Name Is Red - Orhan Pamuk *c* 1178
The Nautical Chart - Arturo Perez-Reverte *c* 1182
Pale Horse Coming - Stephen Hunter *c* 1127
Requiem for a Lost Empire - Andrei Makine *c* 1151
The Rock - Kanan Makiya *c* 1152
The Royal Physician's Visit - Per Olov Enquist *c* 1110
September Song - Andrew M. Greeley *c* 1117
Still She Haunts Me - Katie Roiphe *c* 1189
Year of Wonders - Geraldine Brooks *c* 1083

Historical/World War II

The Ash Garden - Dennis Bock *c* 1078
The Deadwood Beetle - Mylene Dressler *c* 1106
In the Shape of a Boar - Lawrence Norfolk *c* 1171
War Story - Gwen Edelman *c* 1107

Humor

All Families Are Psychotic - Douglas Coupland *c* 1094
Female Intelligence - Jane Heller *c* 1125
The Grand Complication - Allen Kurzweil *c* 1144
Great American Plain - Gary Sernovitz *c* 1195
How to Be Good - Nick Hornby *c* 1126
Junior's Leg - Ken Wells *c* 1214
Lake Wobegon Summer 1956 - Garrison Keillor *c* 1136
The Money-Whipped Steer-Job Three-Jack Give-Up Artist - Dan Jenkins *c* 1132

Inspirational

Good Harbor - Anita Diamant *c* 1103

Literary

About the Author - John Colapinto *c* 1092
Beasts - Joyce Carol Oates *c* 1173
Everything You Need - A.L. Kennedy *c* 1138
First Gray, Then White, Then Blue - Margriet de Moor *c* 1165
The Grand Complication - Allen Kurzweil *c* 1144
Half a Life - V.S. Naipaul *c* 1170
In the Shape of a Boar - Lawrence Norfolk *c* 1171

Medical

Shock - Robin Cook *c* 1093

Modern

Bitterroot - James Lee Burke *c* 1088
Hostage - Robert Crais *c* 1096
In the Shadow of Our House - Scott Blackwood *c* 1077
Lightning Field - Dana Spiotta *c* 1202
Long Time No See - Susan Isaacs *c* 1131

Multicultural

Cane River - Lalita Tademy *c* 1207
Edgewater Angels - Sandro Meallet *c* 1160
Emigre Journeys - Abdullah Hussein *c* 1129
The Feast of the Goat - Mario Vargas Llosa *c* 1211
Highwire Moon - Susan Straight *c* 1205
The Red of His Shadow - Mayra Montero *c* 1164
Red on Rose - Patricia Jones *c* 1133
Swift as Desire - Laura Esquivel *c* 1112

Political

The Appointment - Herta Muller *c* 1168
Balzac and the Little Chinese Seamstress - Sijie Dai *c* 1098
The Feast of the Goat - Mario Vargas Llosa *c* 1211
First Lady - Michael Malone *c* 1153
A Soldier's Duty - Thomas E. Ricks *c* 1186

Psychological

About the Author - John Colapinto *c* 1092
According to Queeney - Beryl Bainbridge *c* 1069
All the Finest Girls - Alexandra Styron *c* 1206
Aria - Susan Segal *c* 1194
A Bend in the Road - Nicholas Sparks *c* 1200
The Deadwood Beetle - Mylene Dressler *c* 1106
Dugan under Ground - Tom De Haven *c* 1100
Eva Moves the Furniture - Margot Livesey *c* 1148
Everything You Need - A.L. Kennedy *c* 1138
For Rouenna - Sigrid Nunez *c* 1172
The Fourth Hand - John Irving *c* 1130
Half a Life - V.S. Naipaul *c* 1170
The Hunters - Claire Messud *c* 1161
Leaving Disneyland - Alexander Parsons *c* 1179
Light Coming Back - Ann Wadsworth *c* 1213
Look at Me - Jennifer Egan *c* 1108
Niagara Falls All over Again - Elizabeth McCracken *c* 1158
Red on Rose - Patricia Jones *c* 1133
Riot - Shashi Tharoor *c* 1208
Schooling - Heather McGowan *c* 1159
Super-Cannes - J.G. Ballard *c* 1070
TV - Brian Brown *c* 1084
Up in the Air - Walter Kirn *c* 1141
The Webster Chronicle - Daniel Akst *c* 1066
What You Owe Me - Bebe Moore Campbell *c* 1089
Why Did I Ever? - Mary Robison *c* 1188
The World Below - Sue Miller *c* 1163
Yonder Stands Your Orphan - Barry Hannah *c* 1121

Psychological Suspense

All the Dead Were Strangers - Ethan Black *c* 1076
Almost - Elizabeth Benedict *c* 1073
Any Way the Wind Blows - E. Lynn Harris *c* 1122
Cold - John Smolens *c* 1199
Eager to Please - Julie Parsons *c* 1180
First Gray, Then White, Then Blue - Margriet de Moor *c* 1165
In the Forest of Harm - Sallie Bissell *c* 1074
The Last Summer of Reason - Tahar Djaout *c* 1105
Midnight Bayou - Nora Roberts *c* 1187
Shooting Dr. Jack - Norman Green *c* 1118
A Soldier's Duty - Thomas E. Ricks *c* 1186

Romance

Aria - Susan Segal *c* 1194
A Bend in the Road - Nicholas Sparks *c* 1200
The Evidence Against Her - Robb Forman Dew *c* 1102
Female Intelligence - Jane Heller *c* 1125
Leap of Faith - Danielle Steel *c* 1203
Lucky Us - Joan Silber *c* 1198
Middle Age - Joyce Carol Oates *c* 1174
Midnight Bayou - Nora Roberts *c* 1187
Suzanne's Diary for Nicholas - James Patterson *c* 1181
Swift as Desire - Laura Esquivel *c* 1112
War Story - Gwen Edelman *c* 1107
The Wig My Father Wore - Anne Enright *c* 1111
The Woman Next Door - Barbara Delinsky *c* 1101

Saga

The Girl from the Golden Horn - Kurban Said *c* 1191
September Song - Andrew M. Greeley *c* 1117
What You Owe Me - Bebe Moore Campbell *c* 1089

Satire

After the Plague - T. Coraghessan Boyle *c* 1081
All That Counts - Georg M. Oswald *c* 1177
The Appointment - Herta Muller *c* 1168
Fury - Salman Rushdie *c* 1190
Lightning Field - Dana Spiotta *c* 1202
My Little Blue Dress - Bruno Maddox *c* 1150
The Savage Girl - Alex Shakar *c* 1196
Why Did I Ever? - Mary Robison *c* 1188

Vampire Story

Blood and Gold - Anne Rice *c* 1185

Werewolf Story

Bitten - Kelley Armstrong *c* 1068

ROMANCE

Anthology

All through the Night - Suzanne Forster *r* 282
Autumn Kittens - Janice Bennett *r* 232
Hot and Bothered - Lori Foster *r* 285
A Kiss for Mama - Jo Ann Ferguson *r* 280
My Scottish Summer - Connie Brockway *r* 243
Once upon a Rose - Nora Roberts *r* 384
Regency Christmas Spirits - Nancy Butler *r* 248
The Very Gothic Christmas - Christine Feehan *r* 277
Wish List - Lisa Kleypas *r* 320

Contemporary

All through the Night - Suzanne Forster *r* 282
Angel Face - Suzanne Forster *r* 283
Another Summer - Georgia Bockoven *r* 239
Awakening Alex - Ruth Langan *r* 327
Bachelor on the Prowl - Kasey Michaels *r* 353
Back in Kansas - Debra Salonen *r* 387
Bring Me a Dream - Robyn Amos *r* 224
Broken Honor - Patricia Potter *r* 373
A Capital Holiday - Janet Dailey *r* 265
Cinderella After Midnight - Lilian Darcy *r* 268
Dance upon the Air - Nora Roberts *r* 382
Dangerous Dilemmas - Evelyn Palfrey *r* 365
Dangerously Irresistible - Kristin Gabriel *r* 289
Darkling I Listen - Katherine Sutcliffe *r* 412
Dear Cupid - Julie Ortolon *r* 363
Do You Hear What I Hear? - Holly Jacobs *r* 306
East of the Sun, West of the Moon - Carole Bellacera *r* 231
Followin' a Dream - Eboni Snoe *r* 403
The Gingerbread Man - Maggie Shayne *r* 395
Going Overboard - Christina Skye *r* 399
Gotta Get Next to You - Lynn Emery *r* 272
The Great Baby Caper - Eugenia Riley *r* 380
Heaven and Earth - Nora Roberts *r* 383
Heaven on Earth - Marilyn Pappano *r* 366
Hide and Seek - Cherry Adair *r* 222
Hot and Bothered - Lori Foster *r* 285
In Too Deep - Janelle Taylor *r* 413
Insatiable - Julie Elizabeth Leto *r* 333

July Thunder - Rachel Lee r 330
Last Virgin in California - Maureen Child r 255
Legends Lake - JoAnn Ross r 386
Looking for Laura - Judith Arnold r 226
Love to Love You Baby - Kasey Michaels r 354
Lt. Kent: Lone Wolf - Judith Lyons r 341
The Marine and the Princess - Cathie Linz r 334
Marry Me, Maddie? - Rita Herron r 299
Milkrun - Sarah Mlynowski r 357
Miss Match - Leslie Carroll r 252
Moving Target - Elizabeth Lowell r 340
My Scottish Summer - Connie Brockway r 243
No Way Out - Andrea Kane r 312
On Leaving Lonely Town - Cait Logan r 339
Pride, Prejudice and Jasmin Field - Melissa Nathan r 359
A Prince of a Guy - Sheila Rabe r 376
Rocky and the Senator's Daughter - Dixie Browning r 246
The Secret - Kat Martin r 347
The Secret Admirer - Annette Mahon r 343
The Secret Life of Connor Monahan - Elizabeth Bevarly r 235
Seducing Mr. Right - Cherry Adair r 223
See Jane Date - Melissa Senate r 394
Sentimental Journey - Jill Barnett r 228
Slightly Single - Wendy Markham r 345
Stranded with the Sergeant - Cathie Linz r 335
Sweet Nothings - Catherine Anderson r 225
Sweet Success - Susan Mallery r 344
Tall, Dark, and Difficult - Patricia Coughlin r 261
Taylor's Temptation - Suzanne Brockmann r 242
This Heart of Mine - Susan Elizabeth Phillips r 369
To Trust a Stranger - Karen Robards r 381
Too Much Temptation - Lori Foster r 286
True Confessions - Rachel Gibson r 292
Two Sexy - Stephanie Bond r 240
Under Suspicion - Rachel Lee r 331
The Wager - Metsy Hingle r 301
The Wedding Party - Robyn Carr r 250
What to Do about Annie? - Millie Criswell r 264
When Jayne Met Erik - Elizabeth Bevarly r 236
The Widow - Anne Stuart r 411
The Woman for Dusty Conrad - Tori Carrington r 251

Contemporary/Fantasy

Diamond in the Ruff - Emily Carmichael r 249
Next Stop, Paradise - Sue Civil-Brown r 256
You're the One - Judi McCoy r 351

Fantasy

Alice at Heart - Deborah Smith r 401
Dark Dreams - Cory Daniells r 267
I Dream of You - Judi McCoy r 350
Once upon a Rose - Nora Roberts r 384
The Prisoner Bride - Susan Spencer Paul r 368
To Tame a Wild Heart - Tracy Fobes r 281

Futuristic

Ritual of Proof - Dara Joy r 310

Gothic

Season of Storms - Susanna Kearsley r 314
The Sleeping Beauty - Jacqueline Navin r 360
Whispers of Goodbye - Karen White r 418

Historical

Abandon - Jillian Hunter r 303
The Edge of Town - Dorothy Garlock r 290
The Enchantment - Pam Binder r 237
The Nanny - Judith Stacy r 408
Night Hawk's Bride - Jillian Hart r 296
'Tis the Season - Susan Spencer Paul r 367
Wish List - Lisa Kleypas r 320

Historical/American West

Beloved Protector - Linda O'Brien r 361
The Bride of Willow Creek - Maggie Osborne r 364
The Colorado Bride - Mary Burton r 247
Jackson's Way - Leslie LaFoy r 324
Just West of Heaven - Kathleen Kane r 313
The MacKenzies: Zach - Ana Leigh r 332
Mattie and the Blacksmith - Linda Lea Castle r 253
Once an Outlaw - Jill Gregory r 294
The Renegades: Rafe - Genell Dellin r 270
Saddled - Delores Fossen r 284
Sarah and the Rogue - DeLoras Scott r 391
The Texan's Dream - Jodi Thomas r 415
Walker's Widow - Heidi Betts r 234
A Western Family Christmas - Millie Criswell r 263
The Widow's Little Secret - Judith Stacy r 409

Historical/American West Coast

Heaven Sent - Rachel Wilson r 421
Secret of the Wolf - Susan Krinard r 322

Historical/Americana

Once an Outlaw - Jill Gregory r 294

Historical/Colonial America

The Fiery Cross - Diana Gabaldon r 288
Summer's End - Lynne Hayworth r 297

Historical/Elizabethan

Heart of Night - Taylor Chase r 254
My Lord Savage - Elizabeth Lane r 326
The Secret Clan: Abducted Heiress - Amanda Scott r 390

Historical/Georgian

The Promise - May McGoldrick r 352
The Promise in a Kiss - Stephanie Laurens r 329
The Very Comely Countess - Miranda Jarrett r 307
The Very Daring Duchess - Miranda Jarrett r 308

Historical/Medieval

Believe in Me - Josie Litton r 336
Come Back to Me - Josie Litton r 337
Dream of Me - Josie Litton r 338
The Husband Test - Betina Krahn r 321
The Mackintosh Bride - Debra Lee Brown r 244
The Marriage Bed - Claudia Dain r 266
My Lady Beloved - Lael St. James r 405
My Lady de Burgh - Deborah Simmons r 396
My Lady Wayward - Lael St. James r 406
The Prisoner Bride - Susan Spencer Paul r 368
The Sword Maiden - Susan King r 316
The Temptress - Claire Delacroix r 269
The Warrior's Damsel - Denise Hampton r 295
White Lion's Lady - Tina St. John r 407

Historical/Napoleonic Wars

A Perfect Match - Jeanne Savery r 389

Historical/Post-American Civil War

The Renegades: Rafe - Genell Dellin r 270
Whispers of Goodbye - Karen White r 418

Historical/Regency

The Bride Sale - Candice Hern r 298
Desire - Nicole Jordan r 309
Elusive Passion - Kathryn Smith r 402
The Guardian - Barbara Miller r 355
Heartless - Kat Martin r 346
Lady Polly - Nicola Cornick r 259
The Night the Stars Fell - Christina Kingston r 317
No Man's Mistress - Mary Balogh r 227
Once a Princess - Veronica Sattler r 388
The Perfect Princess - Elizabeth Thornton r 416
The Proper Wife - Julia Justiss r 311
A Reckless Encounter - Rosemary Rogers r 385
Slightly Shady - Amanda Quick r 375
Tempt Me Twice - Barbara Dawson Smith r 400
To Tame a Duke - Patricia Grasso r 293
To Tame a Wild Heart - Tracy Fobes r 281
Very Truly Yours - Julie Beard r 229
The Virtuous Cyprian - Nicola Cornick r 260
The Wedding Wager - Cathy Maxwell r 348

Historical/Renaissance

To Kiss a Spy - Jane Feather r 276

Historical/Seventeenth Century

The Sea Sprite - Ruth Langan r 328

Historical/Victorian

Fallen - Celeste Bradley r 241
The Sleeping Beauty - Jacqueline Navin r 360
Suddenly You - Lisa Kleypas r 319

Historical/Victorian America

Comfort and Joy - Sandra Madden r 342
Halfway to Heaven - Susan Wiggs r 419
The Nightingale's Song - Kathleen Eschenburg r 273

Holiday Themes

A Capital Holiday - Janet Dailey r 265
The Christmas Wish - Debbie Raleigh r 377
Comfort and Joy - Sandra Madden r 342
'Tis the Season - Donna Hill r 300
'Tis the Season - Susan Spencer Paul r 367
Under the Kissing Bough - Shannon Donnelly r 271
The Valentine Wish - Debbie Raleigh r 378
The Very Gothic Christmas - Christine Feehan r 277
A Western Family Christmas - Millie Criswell r 263

Humor

Bachelor on the Prowl - Kasey Michaels r 353
Buttercup Baby - Karen Fox r 287
Dear Cupid - Julie Ortolon r 363
Diamond in the Ruff - Emily Carmichael r 249
The Great Baby Caper - Eugenia Riley r 380
Last Virgin in California - Maureen Child r 255
Looking for Laura - Judith Arnold r 226
Love to Love You Baby - Kasey Michaels r 354
Marry Me, Maddie? - Rita Herron r 299
Mattie and the Blacksmith - Linda Lea Castle r 253
Miss Match - Leslie Carroll r 252
The Nanny - Judith Stacy r 408
Next Stop, Paradise - Sue Civil-Brown r 256
A Prince of a Guy - Sheila Rabe r 376
Saddled - Delores Fossen r 284
Seven Up - Janet Evanovich r 274
Sweet Success - Susan Mallery r 344
This Heart of Mine - Susan Elizabeth Phillips r 369

The Wedding Party - Robyn Carr r 250
What to Do about Annie? - Millie Criswell r 264

Inspirational

Letters of the Heart - Lisa Tawn Bergren r 233

Multicultural

Followin' a Dream - Eboni Snoe r 403
Gotta Get Next to You - Lynn Emery r 272
Night Hawk's Bride - Jillian Hart r 296
The Secret Admirer - Annette Mahon r 343
'Tis the Season - Donna Hill r 300

Paranormal

Alicia's Song - Susan Plunkett r 371
Bethany's Song - Susan Plunkett r 372
Buttercup Baby - Karen Fox r 287
Dance upon the Air - Nora Roberts r 382
Heaven and Earth - Nora Roberts r 383
Heaven on Earth - Marilyn Pappano r 366
Just West of Heaven - Kathleen Kane r 313
My Heart Stood Still - Lynn Kurland r 323
Secret of the Wolf - Susan Krinard r 322
You're the One - Judi McCoy r 351

Regency

Autumn Kittens - Janice Bennett r 232
Blessing in Disguise - Jenna Mindel r 356
The Blue Devil - Melynda Beth Skinner r 398
Broken Promises - Patricia Oliver r 362
The Christmas Wish - Debbie Raleigh r 377
A Devilish Husband - Alana Clayton r 257
A Diamond in the Rough - Andrea Pickens r 370
A Family for Gillian - Catherine Blair r 238
A Forbidden Embrace - Anna Jacobs r 305
Fortune's Lady - Evelyn Richardson r 379
French Leave - Sheri Cobb South r 404
A Guardian's Angel - Jo Ann Ferguson r 278
His Lady Midnight - Jo Ann Ferguson r 279
The Incomparable Miss Compton - Regina Scott r 392
The Irredeemable Miss Renfield - Regina Scott r 393
A Kiss for Mama - Jo Ann Ferguson r 280
Lady Hilary's Halloween - Mona Gedney r 291
Miss Truelove Beckons - Donna Simpson r 397
Mr. Montgomery's Quest - Martha Kirkland r 318
One Good Turn - Carla Kelly r 315
A Perfect Match - Jeanne Savery r 389
The Rake and the Wallflower - Allison Lane r 325
Regency Christmas Spirits - Nancy Butler r 248
A Rogue for Christmas - Kate Huntington r 304
A Scandalous Wager - Bess Willingham r 420
The Spanish Bride - Amanda McCabe r 349
Sugarplum Surprises - Elisabeth Fairchild r 275
A Tangled Web - Donna Bell r 230
The Traitor's Daughter - Elizabeth Powell r 374
The Trouble with Harriet - Wilma Counts r 262
Under the Kissing Bough - Shannon Donnelly r 271
The Valentine Wish - Debbie Raleigh r 378
The Wedding Charm - Lynn Collum r 258

Romantic Suspense

Angel Face - Suzanne Forster r 283
Awakening Alex - Ruth Langan r 327
Born Brave - Ruth Wind r 422
Broken Honor - Patricia Potter r 373
Dangerous Attraction - Susan Vaughan r 417
Dangerous Dilemmas - Evelyn Palfrey r 365
Darkling I Listen - Katherine Sutcliffe r 412
Envy - Sandra Brown r 245
The Gingerbread Man - Maggie Shayne r 395
Hide and Seek - Cherry Adair r 222
In Too Deep - Janelle Taylor r 413
The Innocent - Amanda Stevens r 410
Moving Target - Elizabeth Lowell r 340
No Way Out - Andrea Kane r 312
Open Season - Linda Howard r 302
The Renegade Steals a Lady - Vickie Taylor r 414
Season of Storms - Susanna Kearsley r 314
The Secret - Kat Martin r 347
Seven Up - Janet Evanovich r 274
To Trust a Stranger - Karen Robards r 381
Under Suspicion - Rachel Lee r 331
The Widow - Anne Stuart r 411

Saga

Sentimental Journey - Jill Barnett r 228

Time Travel

Alicia's Song - Susan Plunkett r 371
Bethany's Song - Susan Plunkett r 372
The Enchantment - Pam Binder r 237
The Fiery Cross - Diana Gabaldon r 288
I Dream of You - Judi McCoy r 350
Kiss of the Highlander - Karen Marie Moning r 358
My Heart Stood Still - Lynn Kurland r 323

SCIENCE FICTION

Action/Adventure

The Devil-Tree of El Dorado - Frank Aubrey s 717

Alternate History

The Best Alternate History Stories of the 20th Century - Harry Turtledove s 804

Alternate Intelligence

Appleseed - John Clute s 736
Smoking Mirror Blues - Ernest Hogan s 758

Alternate Universe

The American Zone - L. Neil Smith s 799
Ghost of the White Nights - L.E. Modesitt Jr. s 778
Pyramid Scheme - David Freer s 751

Anthology

The Best Alternate History Stories of the 20th Century - Harry Turtledove s 804
Futures - Peter Crowther s 739
The Mutant Files - Martin H. Greenberg s 753
Not the Only Planet - Damien Broderick s 726
Past Imperfect - Martin H. Greenberg s 754
A Woman's Liberation - Connie Willis s 811

Collection

Bad Timing and Other Stories - Molly Brown s 727
The Best-Known Man in the World & Other Misfits - Daniel Pearlman s 786
The Collected Stories of Vernor Vinge - Vernor Vinge s 807
Dogged Persistence - Kevin J. Anderson s 715
Entities - Eric Frank Russell s 794
Futureland - Walter Mosley s 779
Here Comes Civilization - William Tenn s 803
Impact Parameter and Other Quantum Realities - Geoffrey A. Landis s 766
Miles, Mystery & Mayhem - Lois McMaster Bujold s 728
The Puppet Master - John Dalmas s 741
Skin Folk - Nalo Hopkinson s 760
Strange Days - Gardner Dozois s 748
Strange Trades - Paul Di Filippo s 745
Tales of the Velvet Comet - Mike Resnick s 788
Toxicology - Steve Aylett s 720
Vacation Stories - Santiago Ramon y Cajal s 787

Cyberpunk

Smoking Mirror Blues - Ernest Hogan s 758

Disaster

Deep Fathom - James Rollins s 792
Maelstrom - Peter Watts s 808
Minutes to Burn - Gregg Andrew Hurwitz s 762
The Night of the Triffids - Simon Clark s 735
The Wanderer - Fritz Leiber s 767

Dystopian

Nekropolis - Maureen McHugh s 774
Out There - Gerald Rose s 793
Scorch - A.D. Nauman s 782

Fantasy

Pyramid Scheme - David Freer s 751

First Contact

Chasm City - Alastair Reynolds s 789
A Paradigm of Earth - Candas Jane Dorsey s 747

Future Shock

Angry Young Spaceman - Jim Munroe s 780
Bold as Love - Gwyneth Jones s 764
Nekropolis - Maureen McHugh s 774
Something More - Paul Cornell s 738
Tower of Glass - Robert Silverberg s 797

Hard Science Fiction

First Landing - Robert Zubrin s 814
Icebones - Stephen Baxter s 723
The Secret of Life - Paul J. McAuley s 771

Humor

Bikini Planet - David Garnett s 752
The Plutonium Blonde - John Zakour s 813
The Reproductive System - John Sladek s 798

Invasion of Earth

Alien Taste - Wen Spencer s 801
Augur's Teacher - Sherwood Smith s 800
Deathday - William C. Dietz s 746
Of Aged Angels - Monte Cook s 737
The Wild Boy - Warren Rochelle s 791

Literary

Tomorrow's Eve - Auguste Villiers de L'Isle Adam s 806
Tower of Glass - Robert Silverberg s 797

Medical

Gargoyles - Alan Nayes s 783

Military

Bolo Strike - William H. Keith Jr. s 765

The Dark Wing - Walter Hunt *s* 761
Holding the Line - Rick Shelley *s* 795
Homefall - Chris Bunch *s* 729
March to the Sea - David Weber *s* 809
Soldiers - John Dalmas *s* 742
Star Soldiers - Andre Norton *s* 784

Mystery

Adventures in Time and Space with Max Merriwell - Pat Murphy *s* 781
The Counterfeit Heinlein - Laurence M. Janiver *s* 763
Dervish Is Digital - Pat Cadigan *s* 731
Gumshoe Gorilla - Keith Hartman *s* 756
The King of the Sun - A.A. McFedries *s* 773
Martian Knightlife - James P. Hogan *s* 759
The Plutonium Blonde - John Zakour *s* 813
Wayward Moon - Denny DeMartino *s* 744

Mystical

On - Adam Roberts *s* 790

Political

Empire & Ecolitan - L.E. Modesitt Jr. *s* 777
The Merchants of Souls - John Barnes *s* 722

Post-Disaster

Bloodtide - Melvin Burgess *s* 730

Psychic Powers

Ashling - Isobelle Carmody *s* 732
Dreamer - Steven Harper *s* 755
Gifted Touch - Melinda Metz *s* 775
Haunted - Melinda Metz *s* 776

Robot Fiction

The Reproductive System - John Sladek *s* 798

Space Colony

Angelmass - Timothy Zahn *s* 812
Angry Young Spaceman - Jim Munroe *s* 780
Chasm City - Alastair Reynolds *s* 789
Defender - C.J. Cherryh *s* 734
Divine Intervention - Ken Wharton *s* 810
The Fall of Neskaya - Marion Zimmer Bradley *s* 725
First Landing - Robert Zubrin *s* 814
Heresy - Anselm Audley *s* 718
Hope's End - Stephen Chambers *s* 733
In the Company of Others - Julie E. Czerneda *s* 740

Space Opera

Acorna's Search - Anne McCaffrey *s* 772
Angelmass - Timothy Zahn *s* 812
Brother John - Rutledge Etheridge *s* 750
Dreamer - Steven Harper *s* 755
The Getaway Special - Jerry Oltion *s* 785
House Corrino - Brian Herbert *s* 757
Look to Windward - Iain Banks *s* 721
Planet America - Mack Maloney *s* 768
Second Chances - Susan Shwartz *s* 796
Second Contact - J.D. Austin *s* 719
Shockball - S.L. Viehl *s* 805
Spherical Harmonic - Catherine Asaro *s* 716
Star Soldiers - Andre Norton *s* 784
Starhawk - Mack Maloney *s* 769
Tenebrea's Hope - Roxann Dawson *s* 743
Time Future - Maxine McArthur *s* 770

Techno-Thriller

The Secret of Life - Paul J. McAuley *s* 771

Time Travel

ChronoSpace - Allen Steele *s* 802
Past Imperfect - Martin H. Greenberg *s* 754

Young Adult

Gifted Touch - Melinda Metz *s* 775
Haunted - Melinda Metz *s* 776
Ice - Stephen Bowkett *s* 724
The World Weaver - Craig Etchison *s* 749

WESTERN

Anthology

No Place for a Lady - Vicki Piekarski *w* 496

Collection

The Blue and the Gray Undercover - Ed Gorman *w* 456
Chumley's Gold - Wayne D. Overholser *w* 489
Doc Holliday's Gone - Jane Candia Coleman *w* 445
Gambler's Row: A Western Trio - Les Savage Jr. *w* 500
The Gauntlet - Max Brand *w* 430
The Ghost of John Wayne and Other Stories - Ray Gonzalez *w* 455
The House of Gold - Max Brand *w* 431
The Legend of Sotoju Mountain - Will Henry *w* 461
Long Journey to Deep Canon - T.T. Flynn *w* 452
Man Without a Past - T.V. Olsen *w* 486
Rainbow Rider: A Western Trio - Wayne D. Overholser *w* 491
The Shadow in Renegade Basin - Les Savage Jr. *w* 501
Stage Trails West - Frank Bonham *w* 427
Stolen Gold - Max Brand *w* 433
Voices in the Hill: Western Stories - Steve Frazee *w* 453
The Wolf Strain - Max Brand *w* 435
The Woman at Ox-Yoke - Lewis B. Patten *w* 494

Historical

The Baron War - Jory Sherman *w* 503
The Blue and the Gray Undercover - Ed Gorman *w* 456
Bucking the Tiger - Bruce Olds *w* 485
Caleb's Price - Troy D. Smith *w* 505
Circle of Stars - Anna Lee Waldo *w* 510
Colorado Twilight - Tess Pendergrass *w* 495
Doc Holliday's Gone - Jane Candia Coleman *w* 445
Downriver - Richard S. Wheeler *w* 512
Fire Lilies - Cynthia Leal Massey *w* 476
The Good Journey - Micaela Gilchrist *w* 454
The Holy Road - Michael Blake *w* 425
A Horde of Fools - James David Buchanan *w* 437
The June Rise - William Tremblay *w* 507
The Last Canyon - John Vernon *w* 508
Law Dog - J. Lee Butts *w* 438
Letters to Callie - Dawn Miller *w* 483
Moon of Bitter Cold - Frederick J. Chiaventone *w* 441
River Walk - Rita Cleary *w* 443
Spanish Jack - Robert J. Conley *w* 447
Summer Moon - Jill Marie Landis *w* 471
An Uncommon Enemy - Michelle Black *w* 423
What Once We Loved - Jane Kirkpatrick *w* 470
A World of Thieves - James Carlos Blake *w* 424

Indian Culture

Bear Paw - Gene Mullins *w* 484
Blood on the Wind - Lucile Bogue *w* 426
The June Rise - William Tremblay *w* 507
Last Year's River - Allen Morris Jones *w* 467
Spanish Jack - Robert J. Conley *w* 447
Summer Moon - Jill Marie Landis *w* 471
The Thunder Keeper - Margaret Coel *w* 444

Indian Wars

The Good Journey - Micaela Gilchrist *w* 454
Moon of Bitter Cold - Frederick J. Chiaventone *w* 441
Turn the Stars Upside Down - Terry C. Johnston *w* 466
An Uncommon Enemy - Michelle Black *w* 423

Man Alone

Behold a Red Horse - Cotton Smith *w* 504
Charlie and the Sir - Frank Roderus *w* 499
Cowboy in the Making - Will James *w* 464
Downriver - Richard S. Wheeler *w* 512
Echo Burning - Lee Child *w* 442
Flying Eagle - Tim Champlin *w* 440
A Good Town - Douglas Hirt *w* 462
Hard Bounty - Ken Hodgson *w* 463
The Holy Road - Michael Blake *w* 425
The Last Canyon - John Vernon *w* 508
Law Dog - J. Lee Butts *w* 438
Lockwood - Lauran Paine *w* 492
Miracle of the Jacal - Robert J. Randisi *w* 497
Morgette on the Barbary Coast - G.G. Boyer *w* 429
Outcasts - Tim McGuire *w* 480
The Outlaws - Wayne D. Overholser *w* 490
The Pinkerton Eye - Allen P. Bristow *w* 436
The Survival of Juan Oro - Max Brand *w* 434
Tears of the Heart - Lauran Paine *w* 493
The Way of the Coyote - Elmer Kelton *w* 468
Will's War - Janice Woods Windle *w* 513

Modern

Blackening Song - Aimee Thurlo *w* 506
Blue Wolf - Lise McClendon *w* 477
Buffalo Valley - Debbie Macomber *w* 474
Captains Outrageous - Joe R. Lansdale *w* 472
Death of the Last Villista - Allana Martin *w* 475
The Ghost of John Wayne and Other Stories - Ray Gonzalez *w* 455
Heart of the Beast - Joyce Weatherford *w* 511
Last Year's River - Allen Morris Jones *w* 467
Monte's Revenge - Eugene C. Vories *w* 509
On the Night Plain - J. Robert Lennon *w* 473
Paradise Lost - J.A. Jance *w* 465
Quincie Bolliver - Mary King *w* 469
The Reckoning - John McLain *w* 481
Sarah's Window - Janice Graham *w* 457
The Vigil - Clay Reynolds *w* 498
Will's War - Janice Woods Windle *w* 513
The Years of Fear - Fred Grove *w* 460

Mystery

Blackening Song - Aimee Thurlo *w* 506
Blue Wolf - Lise McClendon *w* 477
Captains Outrageous - Joe R. Lansdale *w* 472
Death of the Last Villista - Allana Martin *w* 475
Echo Burning - Lee Child *w* 442
The Hum Bug - Harold Schechter *w* 502
Paradise Lost - J.A. Jance *w* 465
The Pinkerton Eye - Allen P. Bristow *w* 436
The Thunder Keeper - Margaret Coel *w* 444

Quest

By Flare of Northern Lights - Tim Champlin w 439
Double Vengeance - John Duncklee w 449
The Gift of the Mestizo - Marjorie M. McGinley w 479
The House of Gold - Max Brand w 431
Letters to Callie - Dawn Miller w 483
The Lone Rider - Max Brand w 432
Mountain Time - Jane Candia Coleman w 446
Open Season - C.J. Box w 428
River Walk - Rita Cleary w 443
Search for Last Chance - A.L. McWilliams w 482
Tennant's Rock - Steve McGiffen w 478
Treasures of the Sun - T.V. Olsen w 487
The Vigil - Clay Reynolds w 498
The Years of Fear - Fred Grove w 460
You Never Can Tell - Kathleen Eagle w 450

Ranch Life

Caleb's Price - Troy D. Smith w 505
Destiny Valley - Fred Grove w 459
Heart of the Beast - Joyce Weatherford w 511
Man from Wyoming - Dane Coolidge w 448
On the Night Plain - J. Robert Lennon w 473
Open Range - Zane Grey w 458
The Reckoning - John McLain w 481
Ride West to Dawn - James C. Work w 514
Tie-Fast Country - Robert Flynn w 451

Saga

The Baron War - Jory Sherman w 503
Circle of Stars - Anna Lee Waldo w 510
Colorado Twilight - Tess Pendergrass w 495
Fire Lilies - Cynthia Leal Massey w 476
A Horde of Fools - James David Buchanan w 437
Quincie Bolliver - Mary King w 469
Sarah's Window - Janice Graham w 457
Shadow Valley Rising - Stephen Overholser w 488
Tie-Fast Country - Robert Flynn w 451
Turn the Stars Upside Down - Terry C. Johnston w 466
What Once We Loved - Jane Kirkpatrick w 470
A World of Thieves - James Carlos Blake w 424

Traditional

Bear Paw - Gene Mullins w 484
Behold a Red Horse - Cotton Smith w 504
By Flare of Northern Lights - Tim Champlin w 439
Charlie and the Sir - Frank Roderus w 499
Chumley's Gold - Wayne D. Overholser w 489
Cowboy in the Making - Will James w 464
Destiny Valley - Fred Grove w 459
Double Vengeance - John Duncklee w 449
Flying Eagle - Tim Champlin w 440
Gambler's Row: A Western Trio - Les Savage Jr. w 500
The Gauntlet - Max Brand w 430
The Gift of the Mestizo - Marjorie M. McGinley w 479
A Good Town - Douglas Hirt w 462
Hard Bounty - Ken Hodgson w 463
The Legend of Sotoju Mountain - Will Henry w 461
Lockwood - Lauran Paine w 492
The Lone Rider - Max Brand w 432
Long Journey to Deep Canon - T.T. Flynn w 452
Man from Wyoming - Dane Coolidge w 448
Man Without a Past - T.V. Olsen w 486
Miracle of the Jacal - Robert J. Randisi w 497
Monte's Revenge - Eugene C. Vories w 509
Morgette on the Barbary Coast - G.G. Boyer w 429
Mountain Time - Jane Candia Coleman w 446
Open Range - Zane Grey w 458
Outcasts - Tim McGuire w 480
The Outlaws - Wayne D. Overholser w 490
Rainbow Rider: A Western Trio - Wayne D. Overholser w 491
Ride West to Dawn - James C. Work w 514
Search for Last Chance - A.L. McWilliams w 482
The Shadow in Renegade Basin - Les Savage Jr. w 501
Shadow Valley Rising - Stephen Overholser w 488
Stage Trails West - Frank Bonham w 427
The Survival of Juan Oro - Max Brand w 434
Tears of the Heart - Lauran Paine w 493
Tennant's Rock - Steve McGiffen w 478
Treasures of the Sun - T.V. Olsen w 487
Voices in the Hill: Western Stories - Steve Frazee w 453
The Way of the Coyote - Elmer Kelton w 468
The Wolf Strain - Max Brand w 435
The Woman at Ox-Yoke - Lewis B. Patten w 494
You Never Can Tell - Kathleen Eagle w 450

Young Adult

Blood on the Wind - Lucile Bogue w 426

Subject Index

This index lists subjects which are covered in the featured titles. Beneath each subject heading, titles are arranged alphabetically with the author names, genre codes, and entry numbers also indicated. The genre codes are as follows: *c* Popular Fiction, *f* Fantasy, *h* Horror, *i* Inspirational, *m* Mystery, *r* Romance, *s* Science Fiction, *t* Historical, and *w* Western.

Abandonment

Friday's Child - Linda Chaikin *i* 977

Abortion

Tears in a Bottle - Sylvia Bambola *i* 966

Abuse

Aftermath - Peter Robinson *m* 186
The Deadhouse - Linda Fairstein *m* 66
Death in Paradise - Robert B. Parker *m* 168
Embrace the Dawn - Kathleen Morgan *i* 1026
Glare Ice - Mary Logue *m* 145
A Measure of Grace - Al Lacy *i* 1014
No Way Out - Andrea Kane *r* 312
Personal Velocity - Rebecca Miller *c* 1162
A Place Called Wiregrass - Michael Morris *i* 1029
Sweet Nothings - Catherine Anderson *r* 225
Wreck the Halls - Sarah Graves *m* 89

Academia

Burning Down the House - Lev Rafael *m* 176
Desert Autumn - Michael Craft *m* 45
The Lecturer's Tale - James Hynes *h* 649
Skeleton at the Feast - Patricia Hall *m* 97
A Study in Death - Iain McDowell *m* 155

Accidents

The Girl Next Door - Kate Welsh *i* 1057
Leap of Faith - Danielle Steel *c* 1203
Rivers of Gold - Tracie Peterson *i* 1042
A Rose by the Door - Deborah Bedford *i* 967
When Tomorrow Comes - Janette Oke *i* 1034

Actors and Actresses

Coldheart Canyon - Clive Barker *h* 619
Two Sexy - Stephanie Bond *r* 240

Adolescence

Edgewater Angels - Sandro Meallet *c* 1160
Lake Wobegon Summer 1956 - Garrison Keillor *c* 1136
Schooling - Heather McGowan *c* 1159

Adoption

Blessed Baby - Lois Richer *i* 1043
On Leaving Lonely Town - Cait Logan *r* 339

Adventure and Adventurers

Aztec Blood - Gary Jennings *t* 889
Mr. Montgomery's Quest - Martha Kirkland *r* 318

Africa

Conjuring Maud - Philip Danze *t* 847
Half a Life - V.S. Naipaul *c* 1170

African Americans

Any Way the Wind Blows - E. Lynn Harris *c* 1122
Bloodlines - Fred D'Aguiar *t* 846
Bombingham - Anthony Grooms *c* 1119
Cane River - Lalita Tademy *c* 1207
Dangerous Dilemmas - Evelyn Palfrey *r* 365
Every Tongue Got to Confess - Zora Neale Hurston *c* 1128
Followin' a Dream - Eboni Snoe *r* 403
Ghost of a Flea - James Sallis *m* 192
Gotta Get Next to You - Lynn Emery *r* 272
Just Say No! - Omar Tyree *c* 1210
Leaving Disneyland - Alexander Parsons *c* 1179
Pale Horse Coming - Stephen Hunter *c* 1127
Pale Shadow - Robert Skinner *m* 196
Red on Rose - Patricia Jones *c* 1133
Rhythms - Donna Hill *t* 884
Sap Rising - Christine Lincoln *c* 1147
Smoke-Filled Rooms - Kris Nelscott *m* 166
Stormy Weather - Paula L. Woods *m* 220
'Tis the Season - Donna Hill *r* 300
We Look Like Men of War - William R. Forstchen *t* 864
What You Owe Me - Bebe Moore Campbell *c* 1089
Whispers in the Dark - Eleanor Taylor Bland *m* 21
The Wind Done Gone - Alice Randall *t* 918

Afterlife

Diamond in the Ruff - Emily Carmichael *r* 249
The Distance Travelled - Brett A. Savory *h* 689

Aging

Bag Limit - Steven F. Havill *m* 108
Lowell Limpett: And Two Stories - Ward S. Just *c* 1134
Middle Age - Joyce Carol Oates *c* 1174
To Perish in Penzance - Jeanne M. Dams *m* 54
Why Did I Ever? - Mary Robison *c* 1188
Winter's Secret - Lyn Cote *i* 985

AIDS (Disease)

All Families Are Psychotic - Douglas Coupland *c* 1094
Lucky Us - Joan Silber *c* 1198

Air Travel

Up in the Air - Walter Kirn *c* 1141

Airplane Accidents

Blackwater Sound - James W. Hall *m* 94
The Seat Beside Me - Nancy Moser *i* 1030

Airplanes

The Golden Angel - Gilbert Morris *i* 1027

Alcoholism

Death in Paradise - Robert B. Parker *m* 168
Hope to Die - Lawrence Block *m* 22
Kiss It Goodbye - John Wessel *m* 213
Retribution - John Fulton *c* 1115
A Study in Death - Iain McDowell *m* 155

Aliens

Acorna's Search - Anne McCaffrey *s* 772
Alien Taste - Wen Spencer *s* 801
Angry Young Spaceman - Jim Munroe *s* 780
The Astonished Eye - Tracy Knight *f* 567
Augur's Teacher - Sherwood Smith *s* 800
Bikini Planet - David Garnett *s* 752
Chasm City - Alastair Reynolds *s* 789
The Counterfeit Heinlein - Laurence M. Janiver *s* 763
The Dark Wing - Walter Hunt *s* 761
Deathday - William C. Dietz *s* 746
Defender - C.J. Cherryh *s* 734
Holding the Line - Rick Shelley *s* 795
Hope's End - Stephen Chambers *s* 733
The King of the Sun - A.A. McFedries *s* 773

The Monsters of Morley Manor - Bruce Coville *f* 538
Of Aged Angels - Monte Cook *s* 737
A Paradigm of Earth - Candas Jane Dorsey *s* 747
Planet America - Mack Maloney *s* 768
The Shadow out of Time - H.P. Lovecraft *h* 670
Shockball - S.L. Viehl *s* 805
Soldiers - John Dalmas *s* 742
Something More - Paul Cornell *s* 738
Time Future - Maxine McArthur *s* 770
The Wild Boy - Warren Rochelle *s* 791
The World Weaver - Craig Etchison *s* 749

Allegories

Bloodtide - Melvin Burgess *s* 730

Alternate History

The American Zone - L. Neil Smith *s* 799
The Best Alternate History Stories of the 20th Century - Harry Turtledove *s* 804
ChronoSpace - Allen Steele *s* 802
Ghost of the White Nights - L.E. Modesitt Jr. *s* 778
Sidhe-Devil - Aaron Allston *f* 516

American Colonies

Argall - William T. Vollmann *c* 1212
Argall - William T. Vollmann *t* 950
The Fiery Cross - Diana Gabaldon *r* 288

American History

Call Each River Jordan - Owen Parry *m* 169
The Doctor and the Dead Man's Chest - Robin Hathaway *m* 106
The Jewel of the North - Peter King *m* 135

American South

Angel in the Front Room, Devil out Back - Stanford Diehl *m* 59
Biggie and the Quincy Ghost - Nancy Bell *m* 15
Blindsighted - Karin Slaughter *m* 197
Bloodroot - Susan Wittig Albert *m* 4
Blue Plate Special - Ruth Birmingham *m* 18
Brothers of Cain - Miriam Grace Monfredo *m* 159
Dead Ball - R.D. Rosen *m* 188
Death by Darjeeling - Laura Childs *m* 32
Deep Water Death - Glynn Marsh Alam *m* 3
The Ironclad Alibi - Michael Kilian *m* 133
Last of the Dixie Heroes - Peter Abrahams *m* 1
Maggody and the Moonbeams - Joan Hess *m* 114
Massacre Island - Martin Hegwood *m* 112
Murder Boogies with Elvis - Anne George *m* 77
Nightmare in Shining Armor - Tamar Myers *m* 163
Pale Horse Coming - Stephen Hunter *m* 122
Pale Shadow - Robert Skinner *m* 196
Strawman's Hammock - Darryl Wimberley *m* 216
Whispers of Goodbye - Karen White *r* 418

American West

Bag Limit - Steven F. Havill *m* 108
The Baron War - Jory Sherman *w* 503
Bear Paw - Gene Mullins *w* 484
Behold a Red Horse - Cotton Smith *w* 504
Blackening Song - Aimee Thurlo *w* 506
Blood on the Wind - Lucile Bogue *w* 426
Blue Wolf - Lise McClendon *w* 477
Bucking the Tiger - Bruce Olds *w* 485
Buffalo Valley - Debbie Macomber *w* 474
By Flare of Northern Lights - Tim Champlin *w* 439
Caleb's Price - Troy D. Smith *w* 505
Captains Outrageous - Joe R. Lansdale *w* 472
Charlie and the Sir - Frank Roderus *w* 499
Chumley's Gold - Wayne D. Overholser *w* 489
Circle of Stars - Anna Lee Waldo *w* 510
The Colorado Bride - Mary Burton *r* 247
Colorado Twilight - Tess Pendergrass *w* 495
Cowboy in the Making - Will James *w* 464
Death of the Last Villista - Allana Martin *w* 475
Death of the Last Villista - Allana Martin *m* 149
Destiny Valley - Fred Grove *w* 459
Doc Holliday's Gone - Jane Candia Coleman *w* 445
Double Vengeance - John Duncklee *w* 449
Downriver - Richard S. Wheeler *w* 512
Echo Burning - Lee Child *w* 442
The Final Country - James Crumley *m* 50
Fire Lilies - Cynthia Leal Massey *w* 476
Flying Eagle - Tim Champlin *w* 440
Gambler's Row: A Western Trio - Les Savage Jr. *w* 500
The Gauntlet - Max Brand *w* 430
The Ghost of John Wayne and Other Stories - Ray Gonzalez *w* 455
The Gift of the Mestizo - Marjorie M. McGinley *w* 479
The Good Journey - Micaela Gilchrist *w* 454
A Good Town - Douglas Hirt *w* 462
Hard Bounty - Ken Hodgson *w* 463
Heart of the Beast - Joyce Weatherford *w* 511
The Holy Road - Michael Blake *w* 425
A Horde of Fools - James David Buchanan *w* 437
The House of Gold - Max Brand *w* 431
The Hum Bug - Harold Schechter *w* 502
The June Rise - William Tremblay *w* 507
Just West of Heaven - Kathleen Kane *r* 313
The Last Canyon - John Vernon *w* 508
Last Year's River - Allen Morris Jones *w* 467
Law Dog - J. Lee Butts *w* 438
The Legend of Sotoju Mountain - Will Henry *w* 461
Letters to Callie - Dawn Miller *w* 483
Lockwood - Lauran Paine *w* 492
The Lone Rider - Max Brand *w* 432
Long Journey to Deep Canon - T.T. Flynn *w* 452
Man from Wyoming - Dane Coolidge *w* 448
Man Without a Past - T.V. Olsen *w* 486
Miracle of the Jacal - Robert J. Randisi *w* 497
Monte's Revenge - Eugene C. Vories *w* 509
Moon of Bitter Cold - Frederick J. Chiaventone *w* 441
Morgette on the Barbary Coast - G.G. Boyer *w* 429
Mountain Time - Jane Candia Coleman *w* 446
No Place for a Lady - Vicki Piekarski *w* 496
On the Night Plain - J. Robert Lennon *w* 473
Once an Outlaw - Jill Gregory *r* 294
Open Range - Zane Grey *w* 458
Open Season - C.J. Box *m* 25
Open Season - C.J. Box *w* 428
Outcasts - Tim McGuire *w* 480
The Outlaws - Wayne D. Overholser *w* 490
Paradise Lost - J.A. Jance *w* 465
Paradise Lost - J.A. Jance *m* 125
The Pinkerton Eye - Allen P. Bristow *w* 436
Quincie Bolliver - Mary King *w* 469
Rainbow Rider: A Western Trio - Wayne D. Overholser *w* 491
The Reckoning - John McLain *w* 481
The Renegades: Rafe - Genell Dellin *r* 270
Ride West to Dawn - James C. Work *w* 514
River Walk - Rita Cleary *w* 443
Saddled - Delores Fossen *r* 284
Sarah and the Rogue - DeLoras Scott *r* 391
Sarah's Window - Janice Graham *w* 457
Search for Last Chance - A.L. McWilliams *w* 482
The Shadow in Renegade Basin - Les Savage Jr. *w* 501
Shadow Valley Rising - Stephen Overholser *w* 488
Sister Wife - John Gates *m* 76
Spanish Jack - Robert J. Conley *w* 447
Stage Trails West - Frank Bonham *w* 427
Stolen Gold - Max Brand *w* 433
Summer Moon - Jill Marie Landis *w* 471
The Survival of Juan Oro - Max Brand *w* 434
Tears of the Heart - Lauran Paine *w* 493
Tennant's Rock - Steve McGiffen *w* 478
The Thunder Keeper - Margaret Coel *w* 444
The Thunder Keeper - Margaret Coel *m* 35
Tie-Fast Country - Robert Flynn *w* 451
Treasures of the Sun - T.V. Olsen *w* 487
Turn the Stars Upside Down - Terry C. Johnston *w* 466
The Vigil - Clay Reynolds *w* 498
Voices in the Hill: Western Stories - Steve Frazee *w* 453
Walker's Widow - Heidi Betts *r* 234
The Way of the Coyote - Elmer Kelton *w* 468
A Western Family Christmas - Millie Criswell *r* 263
What Once We Loved - Jane Kirkpatrick *w* 470
White Shell Woman - James D. Doss *m* 61
The Widow's Little Secret - Judith Stacy *r* 409
Will's War - Janice Woods Windle *w* 513
The Wolf Strain - Max Brand *w* 435
The Woman at Ox-Yoke - Lewis B. Patten *w* 494
A World of Thieves - James Carlos Blake *w* 424
The Years of Fear - Fred Grove *w* 460
You Never Can Tell - Kathleen Eagle *w* 450

Amish

October Song - Beverly Lewis *i* 1018

Ancient History

Blood and Gold - Anne Rice *h* 685
A Place of Darkness - Lauren Haney *m* 101
Three for a Letter - Mary Reed *m* 180

Angels

An Angel to Die For - Mignon F. Ballard *f* 522
Heaven on Earth - Marilyn Pappano *r* 366
The Wig My Father Wore - Anne Enright *c* 1111

Animals

Any Small Thing Can Save You - Christina Adam *c* 1065
The Beasts of Brahm - Mark Hansom *h* 646
Creature Fantastic - Denise Little *f* 575
Creatures of Habit - Jill McCorkle *c* 1157
Night of the Bat - Paul Zindel *h* 714
To Tame a Wild Heart - Tracy Fobes *r* 281

Animals/Cats

The Amazing Maurice and His Educated Rodents - Terry Pratchett *f* 587
Autumn Kittens - Janice Bennett *r* 232
Cat Laughing Last - Shirley Rousseau Murphy *m* 162
The Cat Who Went Up the Creek - Lilian Jackson Braun *m* 26
The Cold Blue Blood - David Handler *m* 100
A Constellation of Cats - Denise Little *f* 574

Animals/Chimpanzees

Tempt Me Twice - Barbara Dawson Smith *r* 400

Animals/Dogs

Dancing with the Virgins - Stephen Booth *m* 23
Death on the Downs - Simon Brett *m* 27
Diamond in the Ruff - Emily Carmichael *r* 249
Lady Hilary's Halloween - Mona Gedney *r* 291

The Long Good Boy - Carol Lea Benjamin *m* 16
The Mouse in the Mountain - Norbert Davis *m* 56
Once Bitten - Laurien Berenson *m* 17
Prepared for Murder - Cecile Lamalle *m* 138
The Renegade Steals a Lady - Vickie Taylor *r* 414
Steppin' on a Rainbow - Kinky Friedman *m* 72

Animals/Horses

Daughter of Lir - Judith Tarr *t* 940
The Girl Next Door - Kate Welsh *i* 1057
The Guardian - Barbara Miller *r* 355
Sweet Nothings - Catherine Anderson *r* 225
The Wedding Wager - Cathy Maxwell *r* 348

Animals/Lions

Money, Money, Money - Ed McBain *m* 152

Animals/Mules

Sarah and the Rogue - DeLoras Scott *r* 391

Animals/Rats

The Amazing Maurice and His Educated Rodents - Terry Pratchett *f* 587
Saintly Murders - C.L. Grace *m* 86

Animals/Wolves

Sketches with Wolves - Jacqueline Fiedler *m* 68

Anthology

Once upon a Rose - Nora Roberts *r* 384
'Tis the Season - Susan Spencer Paul *r* 367
A Western Family Christmas - Millie Criswell *r* 263

Anti-Semitism

Catskill - John R. Hayes *m* 110
Funeral in Blue - Anne Perry *m* 172
The Good German - Joseph Kanon *m* 131
Save the Last Dance for Me - Ed Gorman *m* 83

Antiques

Cat Laughing Last - Shirley Rousseau Murphy *m* 162
Death Is a Cabaret - Deborah Morgan *m* 160
In a Strange City - Laura Lippman *m* 143
Killer Stuff - Sharon Fiffer *m* 69
Nightmare in Shining Armor - Tamar Myers *m* 163
Tall, Dark, and Difficult - Patricia Coughlin *r* 261

Apocalypse

Desecration - Tim LaHaye *i* 1016

Arab-Israeli Wars

The Jerusalem Scrolls - Bodie Thoene *t* 942

Archaeology

Bone Walker - Kathleen O'Neal Gear *t* 871
The Last Mayan - Malcolm Shuman *m* 195
Sacred Ground - Barbara Wood *t* 962
Under Suspicion - Rachel Lee *r* 331
White Shell Woman - James D. Doss *m* 61

Arson

Angel in the Front Room, Devil out Back - Stanford Diehl *m* 59
Ashes of Aries - Martha C. Lawrence *m* 140
The Protector - Dee Henderson *i* 999
A Sunset Touch - Marjorie Eccles *m* 64
Whirlpool - Lorena McCourtney *i* 1023

Art

The Art of Dying - Diana Killian *i* 1009
Lady Hilary's Halloween - Mona Gedney *r* 291
Lazarus, Arise - Nicholas Kilmer *m* 134
My Name Is Red - Orhan Pamuk *c* 1178
A Sunset Touch - Marjorie Eccles *m* 64

Arthurian Legends

The Child of the Holy Grail - Rosalind Miles *t* 907
The Dragon Queen - Alice Borchardt *t* 829
The Dragon Queen - Alice Borchardt *f* 528
Lancelot Du Lethe - J. Robert King *f* 566

Artificial Intelligence

Smoking Mirror Blues - Ernest Hogan *s* 758
Tomorrow's Eve - Auguste Villiers de L'Isle Adam *s* 806

Artists and Art

The Dark Clue - James Wilson *t* 959
Dead Sleep - Greg Iles *m* 123
Lydia Cassatt Reading the Morning Paper - Harriet Scott Chessman *t* 837
The Passion of Artemisia - Susan Vreeland *t* 951
The Silent Woman - Susan M. Dodd *t* 852

Assimilation

Half a Life - V.S. Naipaul *c* 1170

Astrology

Wayward Moon - Denny DeMartino *s* 744

Astronomy

Halfway to Heaven - Susan Wiggs *r* 419

Authors and Writers

About the Author - John Colapinto *c* 1092
According to Queeney - Beryl Bainbridge *c* 1069
Ambrose Bierce and the Death of Kings - Oakley Hall *m* 95
Envy - Sandra Brown *c* 1086
Envy - Sandra Brown *r* 245
Everything You Need - A.L. Kennedy *c* 1138
Fleeced - Carol Higgins Clark *m* 34
Half a Life - V.S. Naipaul *c* 1170
The Jewel of the North - Peter King *m* 135
Killing the Shadows - Val McDermid *m* 154
My Best Friend - Laura Wilson *m* 214
The Problem of the Surly Servant - Roberta Rogow *m* 187
A Romantic Way to Die - Bill Crider *m* 49
See Jane Date - Melissa Senate *r* 394
The Slaying of the Shrew - Simon Hawke *m* 109
Still She Haunts Me - Katie Roiphe *c* 1189
The Trouble with Harriet - Wilma Counts *r* 262

Babies

Blessed Baby - Lois Richer *i* 1043

Babysitters

All the Finest Girls - Alexandra Styron *c* 1206

Beaches

Another Summer - Georgia Bockoven *r* 239

Beauty

Murder by Manicure - Nancy J. Cohen *m* 38

Bible

Pact of the Fathers - Ramsey Campbell *h* 626

Biblical Fiction

The Jerusalem Scrolls - Bodie Thoene *i* 1053
Queenmaker - India Edghill *t* 858

Biography

According to Queeney - Beryl Bainbridge *c* 1069
Argall - William T. Vollmann *c* 1212
Audubon's Watch - John Gregory Brown *t* 833
Bucking the Tiger - Bruce Olds *c* 1176
The Dark Clue - James Wilson *t* 959
The Family - Mario Puzo *c* 1183
Fred & Edie - Jill Dawson *t* 848
The Good Journey - Micaela Gilchrist *t* 873
Halide's Gift - Frances Kazan *t* 893
Haussmann, or The Distinction - Paul LaFarge *t* 900
Her Infinite Variety - Pamela Rafael Berkman *t* 823
Imagining Don Giovanni - Anthony J. Rudel *t* 929
The June Rise - William Tremblay *t* 945
The Last Canyon - John Vernon *t* 949
My Little Blue Dress - Bruno Maddox *c* 1150
The Passion of Artemisia - Susan Vreeland *t* 951
The Rag & Bone Shop - Jeff Rackham *t* 917
The Royal Physician's Visit - Per Olov Enquist *t* 862
The Silent Woman - Susan M. Dodd *t* 852
Spanish Jack - Robert J. Conley *t* 842
Still She Haunts Me - Katie Roiphe *t* 927
Still She Haunts Me - Katie Roiphe *c* 1189
Summer in Baden-Baden - Leonid Tsypkin *t* 946
Treason - David Nevin *t* 912
Turn the Stars Upside Down - Terry C. Johnston *t* 890

Biotechnology

Harvest of Murder - Ann Ripley *m* 181
Nekropolis - Maureen McHugh *s* 774

Blackmail

Bleeders - Bill Pronzini *m* 174
The Final Country - James Crumley *m* 50
A Fine and Private Place - Freda Davies *m* 55
Goodnight, Sweet Prince - David Dickinson *m* 58
In Too Deep - Janelle Taylor *r* 413
The Problem of the Surly Servant - Roberta Rogow *m* 187
Slightly Shady - Amanda Quick *r* 375
The Spanish Bride - Amanda McCabe *r* 349
Very Truly Yours - Julie Beard *r* 229

Boats and Boating

Death on a Casual Friday - Sharon Duncan *m* 63

Books and Reading

The Blue Devil - Melynda Beth Skinner r 398
Envy - Sandra Brown r 245
Hard Road - Barbara D'Amato m 53
Uncatalogued - Julie Kaewert m 128

Brothers

Great American Plain - Gary Sernovitz c 1195
His Lady Midnight - Jo Ann Ferguson r 279
Mr. Montgomery's Quest - Martha Kirkland r 318
On the Night Plain - J. Robert Lennon c 1146
Peace Like a River - Leif Enger c 1109
This Rock - Robert Morgan t 910
The White Room - A.J. Matthews h 673

Brothers and Sisters

The Happy Room - Catherine Palmer i 1038
The Outlaw's Twin Sister - Stephen A. Bly i 973
The Wedding Charm - Lynn Collum r 258

Business

Fatal Legacy - Elizabeth Corley m 43
Up in the Air - Walter Kirn c 1141

Byzantine Empire

Three for a Letter - Mary Reed t 920
Three for a Letter - Mary Reed m 180

Campaigns, Political

Save the Last Dance for Me - Ed Gorman m 83
Tall, Dead, and Handsome - Annie Griffin m 91

Cancer

Agatha Raisin and the Love from Hell - M.C. Beaton m 14
Occasion of Revenge - Marcia Talley m 205
When the Last Leaf Falls - Bill Myers i 1032

Careers

All That Counts - Georg M. Oswald c 1177
Personal Velocity - Rebecca Miller c 1162
Up in the Air - Walter Kirn c 1141

Cartoons and Comics

Dugan under Ground - Tom De Haven c 1100

Catering Business

Bell, Cook, and Candle - Joanne Pence m 170

Catholicism

Emerald Aisle - Ralph McInerny m 156
Saintly Murders - C.L. Grace m 86
The Thunder Keeper - Margaret Coel m 35

Change

The Edge of Town - Dorothy Garlock r 290
Open Season - Linda Howard r 302
When Heaven Weeps - Ted Dekker i 988

Charity

Riona - Linda Windsor i 1060
The Rose in the Wheel - S.K. Rizzolo m 182

Cheating

About the Author - John Colapinto c 1092

Child Custody

Alicia's Song - Susan Plunkett r 371
Just West of Heaven - Kathleen Kane r 313

Childhood

Portrait in Sepia - Isabel Allende t 817

Children

Falling Angels - Tracy Chevalier c 1090
Hard Road - Barbara D'Amato m 53
The Innocent - Amanda Stevens r 410
Listen to the Shadows - Danuta Reah m 179
The Power of Love - Margaret Daley i 987
The Promise - May McGoldrick r 352
Six-Pound Walleye - Elizabeth Gunn m 93

Children and War

The Ash Garden - Dennis Bock c 1078

China

The Distant Land of My Father - Bo Caldwell t 835

Chinese

The Chinese Fire Drill - Les Roberts m 185
The Jasmine Trade - Denise Hamilton m 98

Chinese Americans

Talking in the Dark - Laura Glen Louis c 1149

Christian Life

Letters of the Heart - Lisa Tawn Bergren r 233

Christianity

The Prodigy - Alton Gansky h 637
The Rock - Kanan Makiya t 902
The Rock - Kanan Makiya c 1152

Christmas

A Capital Holiday - Janet Dailey r 265
Christmas Vows: $5.00 Extra - Lori Copeland i 983
The Christmas Wish - Debbie Raleigh r 377
A Cold Christmas - Charlene Weir m 212
Come, My Little Angel - Diane Noble i 1033
A Darker Justice - Sallie Bissell m 19
Do You Hear What I Hear? - Holly Jacobs r 306
Money, Money, Money - Ed McBain m 152
Occasion of Revenge - Marcia Talley m 205
The Promise in a Kiss - Stephanie Laurens r 329
The Protector - Dee Henderson i 999
Regency Christmas Spirits - Nancy Butler r 248
A Rogue for Christmas - Kate Huntington r 304
Sugarplum Surprises - Elisabeth Fairchild r 275
'Tis the Season - Susan Spencer Paul r 367
Under the Kissing Bough - Shannon Donnelly r 271
The Very Gothic Christmas - Christine Feehan r 277
The Weaver's Inheritance - Kate Sedley m 194
A Western Family Christmas - Millie Criswell r 263
Who Killed the Curate? - Joan Coggin m 36
Wreck the Halls - Sarah Graves m 89

City and Town Life

All the Dead Were Strangers - Ethan Black m 20
Blue Plate Special - Ruth Birmingham m 18
Breaking and Entering - H.R.F. Keating m 132
The Case of the Ripper's Revenge - Sam McCarver m 153
City of Dreams - Beverly Swerling t 939
Closing Time - Jim Fusilli m 74
Coffin's Ghost - Gwendoline Butler m 30
The Deadhouse - Linda Fairstein m 66
The Earthquake Bird - Susanna Jones m 127
The Falls - Ian Rankin m 178
Fleeced - Carol Higgins Clark m 34
Haussmann, or The Distinction - Paul LaFarge t 900
Lightning Field - Dana Spiotta c 1202
The Long Good Boy - Carol Lea Benjamin m 16
Milkrun - Sarah Mlynowski r 357
Red Hook - Gabriel Cohen m 37
Red House - K.J.A. Wishnia m 217
Sentimental, Heartbroken Rednecks - Greg Bottoms c 1079
Sex and Murder.com - Mark Richard Zubro m 221
Shadows of Sin - Rochelle Krich m 137
Slightly Single - Wendy Markham r 345
Urban Gothic - David J. Howe h 648

Civil Rights

Fireworks - James A. Moore h 675

Civil Rights Movement

Bombingham - Anthony Grooms c 1119
Fire in the Rock - Joe Martin c 1154

Civil War

The Blue and the Gray Undercover - Ed Gorman w 456
Brothers of Cain - Miriam Grace Monfredo m 159
Brothers of Cain - Miriam Grace Monfredo t 909
Call Each River Jordan - Owen Parry t 914
Call Each River Jordan - Owen Parry m 169
Gettysburg - James Reasoner t 919
The Ironclad Alibi - Michael Kilian m 133
The Ironclad Alibi - Michael Kilian t 898
Last of the Dixie Heroes - Peter Abrahams m 1
We Look Like Men of War - William R. Forstchen t 864
The Wind Done Gone - Alice Randall t 918

Civil War/Spanish

The Bones of the Buried - David Roberts m 183

Clergy

Sea of Glory - Ken Wales i 1056
Watchers of Time - Charles Todd m 208
Who Killed the Curate? - Joan Coggin m 36

Cloning

Gumshoe Gorilla - Keith Hartman s 756
Shock - Robin Cook c 1093
Tenebrea's Hope - Roxann Dawson s 743

Clubs

Fleeced - Carol Higgins Clark m 34

Collectors and Collecting

The Grand Complication - Allen Kurzweil *c* 1144
Killer Stuff - Sharon Fiffer *m* 69
Lazarus, Arise - Nicholas Kilmer *m* 134
Moving Target - Elizabeth Lowell *r* 340

College Life

A Dream to Follow - Lauraine Snelling *i* 1050
Queen of Ambition - Fiona Buckley *t* 834
The Watermark - Travis Thrasher *i* 1054

Comedians

Niagara Falls All over Again - Elizabeth McCracken *c* 1158

Coming-of-Age

Carley's Song - Patricia Houck Sprinkle *i* 1051
The Magickers - Emily Drake *f* 542
Milkrun - Sarah Mlynowski *r* 357
The Night Men - Keith Snyder *m* 199
The Reckoning - John McLain *w* 481
The Rover - Mel Odom *f* 584
Slightly Single - Wendy Markham *r* 345
Stillwater - William F. Weld *t* 955

Communication

Female Intelligence - Jane Heller *c* 1125

Communism

Bitter Sugar - Carolina Garcia-Aguilera *m* 75
The Bones of the Buried - David Roberts *m* 183

Competition

In and Out - Mat Coward *m* 44
Sarah and the Rogue - DeLoras Scott *r* 391

Computers

Appleseed - John Clute *s* 736
Betrayed - Rosey Dow *i* 989
Maelstrom - Peter Watts *s* 808

Conduct of Life

Fortune's Lady - Evelyn Richardson *r* 379
The Valentine Wish - Debbie Raleigh *r* 378

Conspiracies

All the Dead Were Strangers - Ethan Black *c* 1076
All the Dead Were Strangers - Ethan Black *m* 20
Heart of Night - Taylor Chase *r* 254
The Red of His Shadow - Mayra Montero *c* 1164
A Soldier's Duty - Thomas E. Ricks *c* 1186
Treason - David Nevin *t* 912

Construction

You're the One - Judi McCoy *r* 351

Contests

Dial M for Meat Loaf - Ellen Hart *m* 105
Dialogues of the Dead or Paronomania! - Reginald Hill *m* 116
Puzzled to Death - Parnell Hall *m* 96

Convents

The Clerk's Tale - Margaret Frazer *m* 70
Red Beans and Vice - Lou Jane Temple *m* 207

Cooks and Cooking

Bella Donna - Barbara Cherne *t* 836
The Body in the Bonfire - Katherine Hall Page *i* 1037
Prepared for Murder - Cecile Lamalle *m* 138
Red Beans and Vice - Lou Jane Temple *m* 207

Cosmetics Industry

What You Owe Me - Bebe Moore Campbell *c* 1089

Country Life

The Edge of Town - Dorothy Garlock *r* 290

Country Music

The Tumbleweed Murders - Rebecca Rothenberg *m* 189

Courtship

Autumn Kittens - Janice Bennett *r* 232
Blessing in Disguise - Jenna Mindel *r* 356
Broken Promises - Patricia Oliver *r* 362
A Forbidden Embrace - Anna Jacobs *r* 305
Fortune's Lady - Evelyn Richardson *r* 379
The Guardian - Barbara Miller *r* 355
The Incomparable Miss Compton - Regina Scott *r* 392
A Kiss for Mama - Jo Ann Ferguson *r* 280
Lady Polly - Nicola Cornick *r* 259
Mattie and the Blacksmith - Linda Lea Castle *r* 253
One Good Turn - Carla Kelly *r* 315
A Perfect Match - Jeanne Savery *r* 389
The Proper Wife - Julia Justiss *r* 311
The Rake and the Wallflower - Allison Lane *r* 325
Ritual of Proof - Dara Joy *r* 310
Under the Kissing Bough - Shannon Donnelly *r* 271
Wish List - Lisa Kleypas *r* 320

Cousins

A Forbidden Embrace - Anna Jacobs *r* 305

Crafts

The Masks of Auntie Laveau - Robert J. Randisi *m* 177
Unraveled Sleeve - Monica Ferris *m* 67

Crime and Criminals

Angel in the Front Room, Devil out Back - Stanford Diehl *m* 59
Austin City Blue - Jan Grape *m* 88
Black Water Transit - Carsten Stroud *m* 204
Blackening Song - Aimee Thurlo *w* 506
Bleeders - Bill Pronzini *m* 174
Breaking and Entering - H.R.F. Keating *m* 132
Bucking the Tiger - Bruce Olds *w* 485
Dangerously Irresistible - Kristin Gabriel *r* 289
Dark Hollow - John Connolly *m* 42
Doc Holliday's Gone - Jane Candia Coleman *w* 445
Echo Burning - Lee Child *w* 442
Firebreak - Richard Stark *m* 202
Flying Eagle - Tim Champlin *w* 440
For Your Heart Only - Debra White Smith *i* 1048
A Good Town - Douglas Hirt *w* 462
Hard Bounty - Ken Hodgson *w* 463
The Heavenly Fugitive - Gilbert Morris *i* 1028
Hope to Die - Lawrence Block *m* 22
Hostage - Robert Crais *m* 47
The Hum Bug - Harold Schechter *w* 502
The Innocent - Amanda Stevens *r* 410
The Jazz Bird - Craig Holden *t* 885
The Lone Rider - Max Brand *w* 432
Man from Wyoming - Dane Coolidge *w* 448
Miracle of the Jacal - Robert J. Randisi *w* 497
The Mouse in the Mountain - Norbert Davis *m* 56
Murder on the Minnesota - Conrad Allen *t* 816
The Outlaws - Wayne D. Overholser *w* 490
The Outlaw's Twin Sister - Stephen A. Bly *i* 973
Paradise Lost - J.A. Jance *w* 465
The Pinkerton Eye - Allen P. Bristow *w* 436
Red Hook - Gabriel Cohen *m* 37
Red House - K.J.A. Wishnia *m* 217
The Renegade Steals a Lady - Vickie Taylor *r* 414
Search for Last Chance - A.L. McWilliams *w* 482
The Secret Life of Connor Monahan - Elizabeth Bevarly *r* 235
Seven Up - Janet Evanovich *r* 274
Shooting Dr. Jack - Norman Green *c* 1118
Spanish Jack - Robert J. Conley *t* 842
Suspicion of Vengeance - Barbara Parker *m* 167
Tears of the Heart - Lauran Paine *w* 493
The Thief-Taker - T.F. Banks *m* 10
Watch by Moonlight - Kate Hawks *t* 881
Will's War - Janice Woods Windle *w* 513
Winter's Secret - Lyn Cote *i* 985
The Wolf Strain - Max Brand *w* 435
A World of Thieves - James Carlos Blake *w* 424
A World of Thieves - James Carlos Blake *t* 825
The Years of Fear - Fred Grove *w* 460

Cruise Ships

Don't Cry for Me, Hot Pastrami - Sharon Kahn *m* 129
Going Overboard - Christina Skye *r* 399
Murder on the Minnesota - Conrad Allen *t* 816
To Rome with Love - Debra White Smith *i* 1049

Crusades

The Crusader - Michael A. Eisner *t* 860
Pride of Kings - Judith Tarr *t* 941

Cuban Americans

Bitter Sugar - Carolina Garcia-Aguilera *m* 75
Suspicion of Vengeance - Barbara Parker *m* 167

Cults

The Beasts of Brahm - Mark Hansom *h* 646
Maggody and the Moonbeams - Joan Hess *m* 114
Pact of the Fathers - Ramsey Campbell *h* 626
Sister Wife - John Gates *m* 76

Cultural Conflict

Balzac and the Little Chinese Seamstress - Sijie Dai *c* 1098
Emigre Journeys - Abdullah Hussein *c* 1129
The Girl from the Golden Horn - Kurban Said *c* 1191

Cultural Identity

The Bride's Kimono - Sujata Massey *m* 150

Culture

After the Plague - T. Coraghessan Boyle *c* 1081
Collected Stories - Saul Bellow *c* 1072

Creatures of Habit - Jill McCorkle c 1157
The Southern Woman - Elizabeth Spencer c 1201
The Spirit Returns - Richard Burgin c 1087

Cultures and Customs

Cheyenne Summer - Vella Munn t 911
Creatures of Habit - Jill McCorkle c 1157
The Earthquake Bird - Susanna Jones m 127
The Last Summer of Reason - Tahar Djaout c 1105
My Name Is Red - Orhan Pamuk c 1178
The Stories of Paul Bowles - Paul Bowles c 1080
Three for a Letter - Mary Reed t 920
The Unknown Errors of Our Lives - Chitra Banerjee Divakaruni c 1104

Customs

After the Plague - T. Coraghessan Boyle c 1081
Collected Stories - Saul Bellow c 1072
Darling? - Heidi Jon Schmidt c 1193
Sap Rising - Christine Lincoln c 1147
The Southern Woman - Elizabeth Spencer c 1201
The Spirit Returns - Richard Burgin c 1087

Dancing

He Goes, She Goes - Joanna Torrey c 1209
Midsummer Murder - Shelley Freydont m 71
Nearly People - Conrad Williams h 708

Dating (Social Customs)

Milkrun - Sarah Mlynowski r 357
Miss Match - Leslie Carroll r 252
See Jane Date - Melissa Senate r 394
Slightly Single - Wendy Markham r 345

Deafness

Do You Hear What I Hear? - Holly Jacobs r 306

Death

He Goes, She Goes - Joanna Torrey c 1209

Demons

Swell Foop - Piers Anthony f 518

Depression (Economic)

Prized Possessions - Jessica Stirling t 938
Someone to Watch over Me - Jill Churchill m 33

Deserts

Desert Autumn - Michael Craft m 45

Detection

Blood Games - Lee Killough h 657
Face Down Before Rebel Hooves - Kathy Lynn Emerson t 861
Smuggler's Moon - Bruce Alexander t 815

Devil

City Infernal - Edward Lee h 667

Dictators

The Feast of the Goat - Mario Vargas Llosa t 948
The Feast of the Goat - Mario Vargas Llosa c 1211

Difference

French Leave - Sheri Cobb South r 404
Secret of the Wolf - Susan Krinard r 322

Disasters

The Phoenix - Henning Boetius t 828
Shadow of the Seer - Michael Scott Rohan f 595
The Wanderer - Fritz Leiber s 767

Discovery and Exploration

The Last Canyon - John Vernon w 508
River Walk - Rita Cleary w 443

Diseases

Lydia Cassatt Reading the Morning Paper - Harriet Scott Chessman t 837
Nearly People - Conrad Williams h 708
The Rose in the Wheel - S.K. Rizzolo m 182

Diving

Deep Water Death - Glynn Marsh Alam m 3

Divorce

Aftermath - Peter Robinson m 186
Retribution - John Fulton c 1115
Whirlpool - Lorena McCourtney i 1023

Doctors

Child of Promise - Kathleen Morgan i 1025
How to Be Good - Nick Hornby c 1126
The Oath - John Lescroart m 141
Super-Cannes - J.G. Ballard c 1070

Dreams and Nightmares

Midnight Bayou - Nora Roberts c 1187
Miss Truelove Beckons - Donna Simpson r 397
The Nature of Balance - Tim Lebbon h 666

Drugs

Dangerous Attraction - Susan Vaughan r 417
The Final Country - James Crumley m 50
Irregardless of Murder - Ellen Edwards Kennedy i 1008
Leaving Disneyland - Alexander Parsons c 1179
Lilies That Fester - Janis Harrison m 103
The Renegade Steals a Lady - Vickie Taylor r 414
Shooting Dr. Jack - Norman Green c 1118
Tucker Peak - Archer Mayor m 151

Druids

Circle of Stars - Anna Lee Waldo w 510
Circle of Stars - Anna Lee Waldo t 952
Confessions of a Pagan Nun - Kate Horsley t 886
The Dragon Queen - Alice Borchardt t 829

Dwellings

Restoration and Romance - Barbara Curtis i 986

Earthquakes

Fault Line - Sarah Andrews m 7
The Mouse in the Mountain - Norbert Davis m 56

Eating Disorders

The Happy Room - Catherine Palmer i 1038

Ecothriller

Ice - Stephen Bowkett s 724
The Night of the Triffids - Simon Clark s 735
The Secret of Life - Paul J. McAuley s 771

Egyptian Antiquities

A Place of Darkness - Lauren Haney m 101

Elves

Ill Met by Moonlight - Sarah A. Hoyt f 559
Sea of Swords - R.A. Salvatore f 597
World Fall - Douglas Niles f 583

Emigration and Immigration

Emigre Journeys - Abdullah Hussein c 1129
The Unknown Errors of Our Lives - Chitra Banerjee Divakaruni c 1104

Endangered Species

Open Season - C.J. Box m 25

Entertainment

Strip Poker - Nancy Bartholomew m 13

Environment

Tucker Peak - Archer Mayor m 151

Environmental Problems

Chasm City - Alastair Reynolds s 789
Minutes to Burn - Gregg Andrew Hurwitz s 762

Erotica

All through the Night - Suzanne Forster r 282
Suddenly You - Lisa Kleypas r 319

Espionage

The Blue and the Gray Undercover - Ed Gorman w 456
The Blue Devil - Melynda Beth Skinner r 398
Brothers of Cain - Miriam Grace Monfredo t 909
The Company of Strangers - Robert Wilson m 215
Desire - Nicole Jordan r 309
Face Down Before Rebel Hooves - Kathy Lynn Emerson m 65
The Ironclad Alibi - Michael Kilian t 898
The Old Spies Club and Other Intrigues of Rand - Edward D. Hoch m 118
Queen of Ambition - Fiona Buckley m 29
A Scandalous Wager - Bess Willingham r 420
To Kiss a Spy - Jane Feather r 276
The Traitor's Daughter - Elizabeth Powell r 374

Ethics

One Door Away from Heaven - Dean R. Koontz h 661

Exile

Bitter Sugar - Carolina Garcia-Aguilera m 75
Summer's End - Lynne Hayworth r 297

Extrasensory Perception

Kaleidoscope - Dorothy Gilman *m* 79

Fables

Any Small Thing Can Save You - Christina Adam *c* 1065

Fairies

Buttercup Baby - Karen Fox *r* 287
The Crow Maiden - Sarah Singleton *f* 598
Ill Met by Moonlight - Sarah A. Hoyt *f* 559
The Pillars of the World - Anne Bishop *f* 527
The Secret Clan: Abducted Heiress - Amanda Scott *r* 390
Spirits White as Lightning - Mercedes Lackey *f* 568
Swim the Moon - Paul Brandon *f* 529
The Sword Maiden - Susan King *r* 316

Fairs

Revenge of the Wrought-Iron Flamingos - Donna Andrews *m* 6

Fairy Tales

Cinderella After Midnight - Lilian Darcy *r* 268

Faith

Child of Promise - Kathleen Morgan *i* 1025
Devil's Island - John Hagee *i* 994
The Prodigy - Alton Gansky *h* 637

Family

All the Finest Girls - Alexandra Styron *c* 1206
Almost - Elizabeth Benedict *c* 1073
Bleeders - Bill Pronzini *m* 174
Dangerously Irresistible - Kristin Gabriel *r* 289
East of the Sun, West of the Moon - Carole Bellacera *r* 231
A Family for Gillian - Catherine Blair *r* 238
A Journey by Chance - Sally D. John *i* 1006
The Nightingale's Song - Kathleen Eschenburg *r* 273
Occasion of Revenge - Marcia Talley *m* 205
A Rogue for Christmas - Kate Huntington *r* 304
Seducing Mr. Right - Cherry Adair *r* 223

Family Life

September Song - Andrew M. Greeley *c* 1117
When Tomorrow Comes - Janette Oke *i* 1034

Family Problems

Bloodroot - Susan Wittig Albert *m* 4
Friday's Child - Linda Chaikin *i* 977
Gabriel's Gift - Hanif Kureishi *c* 1143
In the Shadow of Our House - Scott Blackwood *c* 1077
No Way Out - Andrea Kane *r* 312
Paradise Lost - J.A. Jance *m* 125
Retribution - John Fulton *c* 1115

Family Relations

All Families Are Psychotic - Douglas Coupland *c* 1094
Back in Kansas - Debra Salonen *r* 387
Blackwater Sound - James W. Hall *m* 94
Bonnie Winter - Graham Masterton *h* 672
The Bride of Willow Creek - Maggie Osborne *r* 364
Cane River - Lalita Tademy *c* 1207
The Corrections - Jonathan Franzen *c* 1113
The Distant Land of My Father - Bo Caldwell *t* 835
Ester's Child - Jean P. Sasson *t* 930
The Evidence Against Her - Robb Forman Dew *t* 850
The Evidence Against Her - Robb Forman Dew *c* 1102
Face - Tim Lebbon *h* 665
Fallen - Celeste Bradley *r* 241
The Family - Mario Puzo *t* 916
The Folks - Ray Garton *h* 638
From the Dust Returned - Ray Bradbury *h* 623
Gettysburg - James Reasoner *t* 919
Halfway to Heaven - Susan Wiggs *r* 419
Heartless - Kat Martin *r* 346
In Too Deep - Janelle Taylor *r* 413
Jackson's Way - Leslie LaFoy *r* 324
Marry Me, Maddie? - Rita Herron *r* 299
My Best Friend - Laura Wilson *m* 214
The Mystic Rose - Stephen R. Lawhead *t* 901
The Nanny - Judith Stacy *r* 408
Nashborough - Elsie Burch Donald *t* 855
On the Night Plain - J. Robert Lennon *c* 1146
Pink Marble and Never Say Die - Dawn Dunn *h* 630
Portrait in Sepia - Isabel Allende *t* 817
Portrait in Sepia - Isabel Allende *c* 1067
Prized Possessions - Jessica Stirling *t* 938
Rhythms - Donna Hill *t* 884
The Savages in Love and War - Fred Mustard Stewart *t* 937
Shadows of Sin - Rochelle Krich *m* 137
The Tender Vine - Kristen Heitzmann *i* 998
Turnabout - Jeremiah Healy *m* 111
The Valentine Wish - Debbie Raleigh *r* 378
The Wager - Metsy Hingle *r* 301
The Wedding Party - Robyn Carr *r* 250
What to Do about Annie? - Millie Criswell *r* 264

Family Saga

City of Dreams - Beverly Swerling *t* 939
The Family - Mario Puzo *c* 1183
From the Dust Returned - Ray Bradbury *c* 1082

Famine Victims

Blessed Child - Bill Bright *i* 975

Fantasy

Alice at Heart - Deborah Smith *r* 401
Blood and Gold - Anne Rice *t* 922
Dark Dreams - Cory Daniells *r* 267
From the Dust Returned - Ray Bradbury *h* 623
The Magickers - Emily Drake *f* 542
The Third Witch - Rebecca Reisert *t* 921
Wondrous Strange - Robin Spriggs *h* 697

Farm Life

A Dream to Follow - Lauraine Snelling *i* 1050
Worthy of Riches - Bonnie Leon *i* 1017

Fashion Design

Bachelor on the Prowl - Kasey Michaels *r* 353
Property of Blood - Magdalen Nabb *m* 164

Fathers and Daughters

Closing Time - Jim Fusilli *m* 74
Coldwater - Mardi McConnochie *c* 1156
The Distant Land of My Father - Bo Caldwell *t* 835
Emigre Journeys - Abdullah Hussein *c* 1129
Everything You Need - A.L. Kennedy *c* 1138
A Father's Place - Marta Perry *i* 1041
The Feast of the Goat - Mario Vargas Llosa *c* 1211
He Goes, She Goes - Joanna Torrey *c* 1209
Pact of the Fathers - Ramsey Campbell *h* 626
Written on the Wind - Judith Pella *i* 1040

Fathers and Sons

Black Water Transit - Carsten Stroud *m* 204
Ghost of a Flea - James Sallis *m* 192
His Father's Son - Nigel Bennett *h* 621
The Killing Bee - Matt Witten *m* 218
Last of the Dixie Heroes - Peter Abrahams *m* 1
Peace Like a River - Leif Enger *c* 1109
Red Hook - Gabriel Cohen *m* 37
The Webster Chronicle - Daniel Akst *c* 1066

Feminism

Chapel Noir - Carole Nelson Douglas *m* 62

Feuds

The Alpine Nemesis - Mary Daheim *m* 51
The Mackintosh Bride - Debra Lee Brown *r* 244
The Texan's Dream - Jodi Thomas *r* 415

Fires

July Thunder - Rachel Lee *r* 330
The Protector - Dee Henderson *i* 999
The Woman for Dusty Conrad - Tori Carrington *r* 251

Fishing

Blackwater Sound - James W. Hall *m* 94
First Light - Philip R. Craig *m* 46

Folk Tales

Call Down the Stars - Sue Harrison *t* 879
Every Tongue Got to Confess - Zora Neale Hurston *c* 1128

Folklore

The Devil Is Not Mocked and Other Warnings - Manly Wade Wellman *h* 707

Food

Better than Sex - Susan Holtzer *m* 120
The Devil's Larder - Jim Crace *c* 1095
Dial M for Meat Loaf - Ellen Hart *m* 105
Insatiable - Julie Elizabeth Leto *r* 333
Sweet Success - Susan Mallery *r* 344

Freedom

Forbid Them Not - Michael P. Farris *i* 991

Freedom of Speech

Fireworks - James A. Moore *h* 675

Friendship

Aria - Susan Segal *c* 1194
Beloved Protector - Linda O'Brien *r* 361
Death on the Downs - Simon Brett *m* 27

Dreamcatcher - Stephen King h 660
The Evidence Against Her - Robb Forman Dew t 850
Falling Angels - Tracy Chevalier t 838
Falling Angels - Tracy Chevalier c 1090
Fire in the Rock - Joe Martin c 1154
The Flight of the Maidens - Jane Gardam t 870
Good Harbor - Anita Diamant c 1103
Hateship, Friendship, Courtship, Loveship, Marriage - Alice Munro c 1169
Killer Stuff - Sharon Fiffer m 69
Miss Truelove Beckons - Donna Simpson r 397
Niagara Falls All over Again - Elizabeth McCracken c 1158
A Scandalous Wager - Bess Willingham r 420
A Sensitive Kind of Murder - Jacqueline Girdner m 80
Sentimental Journey - Jill Barnett r 228
Taylor's Temptation - Suzanne Brockmann r 242
Wedding Day Murder - Leslie Meier m 157

Frontier and Pioneer Life

Bucking the Tiger - Bruce Olds c 1176
The Fiery Cross - Diana Gabaldon r 288
The MacKenzies: Zach - Ana Leigh r 332
Mattie and the Blacksmith - Linda Lea Castle r 253
Night Hawk's Bride - Jillian Hart r 296
The Way of the Coyote - Elmer Kelton c 1137

Fur Trade

Downriver - Richard S. Wheeler w 512

Future

Futureland - Walter Mosley c 1166

Futuristic Fiction

Bold as Love - Gwyneth Jones s 764
On - Adam Roberts s 790

Gambling

Bucking the Tiger - Bruce Olds c 1176
Funeral in Blue - Anne Perry m 172
Summer in Baden-Baden - Leonid Tsypkin t 946
TV - Brian Brown c 1084
The Wager - Metsy Hingle r 301
Wish List - Lisa Kleypas r 320

Games

In and Out - Mat Coward m 44
In the Dark - Richard Laymon h 663

Games/Literary

Dialogues of the Dead or Paronomania! - Reginald Hill m 116

Gangs

The Jasmine Trade - Denise Hamilton m 98
Once an Outlaw - Jill Gregory r 294

Gardens and Gardening

Creeping Venom - Sheila Pim m 173
A Diamond in the Rough - Andrea Pickens r 370
The English Garden - Gail Gaymer Martin i 1020
Harvest of Murder - Ann Ripley m 181
Lilies That Fester - Janis Harrison m 103

Gender Roles

Jewelry Talks - Richard Klein c 1142

Genetic Disease

Could I Have This Dance? - Harry Lee Kraus i 1012

Genies

I Dream of You - Judi McCoy r 350

Ghosts

Aunt Dimity: Detective - Nancy Atherton m 9
Chelsea Horror Hotel - Dee Dee Ramone h 684
Coldheart Canyon - Clive Barker c 1071
Dancing Dead - Deborah Woodworth i 1062
Dead on Demand - Elizabeth Engstrom h 633
Doomed to Repeat It - d.g.k. goldberg h 641
Midnight Bayou - Nora Roberts c 1187
My Heart Stood Still - Lynn Kurland r 323
A Pleasing Terror - M.R. James h 650
The Shadow on the Blind - Louisa Baldwin h 618
Tragic Casements - Oliver Onions h 680
You're the One - Judi McCoy r 351

Gnosticism

...And the Angel with Television Eyes - John Shirley h 694

Gold Discoveries

By Flare of Northern Lights - Tim Champlin w 439
A Horde of Fools - James David Buchanan w 437
Search for Last Chance - A.L. McWilliams w 482
Treasures of the Sun - T.V. Olsen w 487
What Once We Loved - Jane Kirkpatrick w 470

Good and Evil

Black House - Stephen King h 659
A Lower Deep - Tom Piccirilli h 682
Riverwatch - Joseph M. Nassise h 676

Government

A Soldier's Duty - Thomas E. Ricks c 1186

Grandfathers

A Warmth in Winter - Lori Copeland i 984
When the Last Leaf Falls - Bill Myers i 1032

Grandmothers

Highland Hopes - Gary E. Parker i 1039
Portrait in Sepia - Isabel Allende c 1067
The World Below - Sue Miller c 1163

Greed

All That Counts - Georg M. Oswald c 1177
Jackson's Way - Leslie LaFoy r 324
London Bridges - Jane Stevenson c 1204

Greek Americans

Heaven on Earth - Marilyn Pappano r 366

Grief

All the Finest Girls - Alexandra Styron c 1206
Bethany's Song - Susan Plunkett r 372
Heaven Sent - Rachel Wilson r 421
A Rose by the Door - Deborah Bedford i 967
Suzanne's Diary for Nicholas - James Patterson c 1181
Year of Wonders - Geraldine Brooks c 1083

Guilt

Audubon's Watch - John Gregory Brown c 1085
The Deadwood Beetle - Mylene Dressler c 1106
Echoes of Lies - Jo Bannister m 11
The Marriage Bed - Claudia Dain r 266
The Seat Beside Me - Nancy Moser i 1030
Stranded with the Sergeant - Cathie Linz r 335
Worthy of Riches - Bonnie Leon i 1017

Guns and Gun Control

Black Water Transit - Carsten Stroud m 204
Burning Down the House - Lev Rafael m 176

Halloween

Nightmare in Shining Armor - Tamar Myers m 163
Trick or Treat - Richard Chizmar h 628

Haunted Houses

The Cat Who Went Up the Creek - Lilian Jackson Braun m 26
House of Pain - Sephera Giron h 640
The White Room - A.J. Matthews h 673

Healing

Awakening Alex - Ruth Langan r 327
Back in Kansas - Debra Salonen r 387
Blessed Child - Bill Bright i 975
Lt. Kent: Lone Wolf - Judith Lyons r 341
The Nightingale's Song - Kathleen Eschenburg r 273
Rocky and the Senator's Daughter - Dixie Browning r 246
The Sea Sprite - Ruth Langan r 328
The Sleeping Beauty - Jacqueline Navin r 360
Summer's End - Lynne Hayworth r 297
The Woman for Dusty Conrad - Tori Carrington r 251

Hell

City Infernal - Edward Lee h 667

Heritage

On Leaving Lonely Town - Cait Logan r 339
To Tame a Wild Heart - Tracy Fobes r 281

Hermits

Lt. Kent: Lone Wolf - Judith Lyons r 341

Heroes and Heroines

The Sword Maiden - Susan King r 316

Historical

Kisses of Death - Max Allan Collins m 41
The Mammoth Book of More Historical Whodunnits - Mike Ashley m 8
Sherlock Holmes and the Giant Rat of Sumatra - Alan Vanneman m 210
You Never Can Tell - Kathleen Eagle w 450

History

Biggie and the Quincy Ghost - Nancy Bell m 15
Brothers of Cain - Miriam Grace Monfredo m 159
The Case of the Ripper's Revenge - Sam McCarver m 153
The Deadhouse - Linda Fairstein m 66
Death Is a Cabaret - Deborah Morgan m 160
Dugan under Ground - Tom De Haven c 1100
The Falls - Ian Rankin m 178
A Feast in Exile - Chelsea Quinn Yarbro h 713
The Hum Bug - Harold Schechter m 193
Island of Tears - Troy Soos m 200
The Jazz Bird - Craig Holden m 119
London Bridges - Jane Stevenson c 1204
Mountain Time - Jane Candia Coleman w 446
Queen of Ambition - Fiona Buckley m 29
Revenge of the Wrought-Iron Flamingos - Donna Andrews m 6
The Thief-Taker - T.F. Banks m 10
The Tumbleweed Murders - Rebecca Rothenberg m 189

Hobbies

Puzzled to Death - Parnell Hall m 96

Holidays

Blue Christmas and Other Holiday Homicides - Max Allan Collins m 40
Harvest of Murder - Ann Ripley m 181
'Tis the Season - Donna Hill r 300

Holocaust

Funny Accent - Barbara Shulgasser-Parker c 1197
War Story - Gwen Edelman c 1107

Homeless People

The Manhattan Hunt Club - John Saul h 687

Homosexuality/Lesbianism

Burning Down the House - Lev Rafael m 176
Sex and Murder.com - Mark Richard Zubro m 221
Vampire Vow - Michael Schiefelbein h 690

Horror

4 X 4 - Michael Oliveri h 679
The Ancient Track - H.P. Lovecraft h 669
The Ash-Tree Press Annual Macabre 2001 - Jack Adrian h 615
The Association - Bentley Little h 668
Bad Seed - Harry Shannon h 693
Black Dust - Graham Joyce h 655
Black House - Stephen King h 659
Cold Comfort - Nancy Kilpatrick h 658
Coldheart Canyon - Clive Barker c 1071
Crimson Kiss - Trisha Baker h 617
Dark Sanctuary - H.B. Gregory h 644
Dark Shadows on the Moon - John B. Ford h 635
Darkness - Sam Siciliano h 695
Dead Love - Donald Beman h 620
Dial Your Dreams - Robert Weinberg h 706
Doomed to Repeat It - d.g.k. goldberg h 641
Dracula in London - P.N. Elrod h 631
Dreamcatcher - Stephen King h 660
Face - Tim Lebbon h 665
The Far Side of the Lake - Steve Rasnic Tem h 700
Fluid Mosaic - Michael D. Arnzen h 616
Frankenstein: The Legacy - Christopher Schildt h 691
From Weird and Distant Shores - Caitlin R. Kiernan h 656
A Game of Colors - John Urbancik h 704
A Ghostly Crew - Roger Johnson h 652
Halloween Candy - Thomas M. Sipos h 696
Heretics - Greg F. Gifune h 639
Hideous Dreams - L.H. Maynard h 674
Hosts - F. Paul Wilson h 710
House of Pain - Sephera Giron h 640
I'll Be Damned - Shane Ryan Staley h 698
Knuckles and Tales - Nancy Collins h 629
The Last Vampire - Whitley Strieber h 699
The Last Vampire - T.M. Wright h 712
Legends of the Night - Stephen Mark Rainey h 683
The Mammoth Book of Best New Horror 12 - Stephen Jones h 653
The Mammoth Book of Vampire Stories by Women - Stephen Jones h 654
Mrs. Amworth - E.F. Benson h 622
The Museum of Horrors - Dennis Etchison h 634
Night Blood - James M. Thompson h 702
Night of Dracula - Christopher Schildt h 692
Pink Marble and Never Say Die - Dawn Dunn h 630
A Pleasing Terror - M.R. James h 650
Quincey Morris, Vampire - P.N. Elrod h 632
The Scarecrow and Other Stories - G. Ranger Wormser h 711
The Shadow out of Time - H.P. Lovecraft h 670
Similar Monsters - Steve Savile h 688
Tales of Devilry and Doom - John B. Ford h 636
The Thing on the Doorstep and Other Weird Stories - H.P. Lovecraft h 671
Tragic Casements - Oliver Onions h 680
Triage - Matt Johnson h 651
Trick or Treat - Richard Chizmar h 628
Urban Gothic - David J. Howe h 648
William F. Nolan's Dark Universe - William F. Nolan h 678
Wrong Things - Poppy Z. Brite h 624

Horse Racing

Legends Lake - JoAnn Ross r 386

Horsemanship

Daughter of Lir - Judith Tarr t 940

Hospitals

Gotta Get Next to You - Lynn Emery r 272
The Happy Room - Catherine Palmer i 1038
Light Coming Back - Ann Wadsworth c 1213
The Oath - John Lescroart m 141
The Officers' Ward - Marc Dugain t 857
The Surgeon - Tess Gerritsen m 78

Hostages

Blue Plate Special - Ruth Birmingham m 18
Hostage - Robert Crais m 47
Hostage - Robert Crais c 1096
The Perfect Princess - Elizabeth Thornton r 416

Hotels and Motels

Chelsea Horror Hotel - Dee Dee Ramone h 684
The Wager - Metsy Hingle r 301

Human Behavior

Any Small Thing Can Save You - Christina Adam c 1065

Humor

Adventures in Time and Space with Max Merriwell - Pat Murphy s 781
The Amazing Maurice and His Educated Rodents - Terry Pratchett f 587
Bachelor on the Prowl - Kasey Michaels r 353
Bikini Planet - David Garnett s 752
Bring Me a Dream - Robyn Amos r 224
Buttercup Baby - Karen Fox r 287
Darling? - Heidi Jon Schmidt c 1193
Dear Cupid - Julie Ortolon r 363
The Devil's Larder - Jim Crace c 1095
Diamond in the Ruff - Emily Carmichael r 249
Every Tongue Got to Confess - Zora Neale Hurston c 1128
The Getaway Special - Jerry Oltion s 785
The Great Baby Caper - Eugenia Riley r 380
Last Virgin in California - Maureen Child r 255
London Bridges - Jane Stevenson c 1204
Looking for Laura - Judith Arnold r 226
Love to Love You Baby - Kasey Michaels r 354
Mattie and the Blacksmith - Linda Lea Castle r 253
Miss Match - Leslie Carroll r 252
My Little Blue Dress - Bruno Maddox c 1150
Myth-ion Improbable - Robert Lynn Asprin f 521
The Nanny - Judith Stacy r 408
Next Stop, Paradise - Sue Civil-Brown r 256
The Plutonium Blonde - John Zakour s 813
A Prince of a Guy - Sheila Rabe r 376
The Reproductive System - John Sladek s 798
Saddled - Delores Fossen r 284
Seven Up - Janet Evanovich r 274
Steppin' on a Rainbow - Kinky Friedman m 72
Strip Poker - Nancy Bartholomew m 13
This Heart of Mine - Susan Elizabeth Phillips r 369
The Treachery of Kings - Neal Barrett Jr. f 524
Veiled Threats - Deborah Donnelly m 60
What to Do about Annie? - Millie Criswell r 264

Hunting

The Manhattan Hunt Club - John Saul h 687
Open Season - C.J. Box m 25

Hurricanes

Murder in the Forecast - Valerie Wolzien m 219
Whispers in the Dark - Eleanor Taylor Bland m 21

Identity

The Blue Last - Martha Grimes m 92
The Grand Complication - Allen Kurzweil c 1144
Look at Me - Jennifer Egan c 1108
Portrait in Sepia - Isabel Allende c 1067
Rag Man - Pete Hautman m 107
Shades of Murder - Ann Granger m 87
Two Sexy - Stephanie Bond r 240
The Weaver's Inheritance - Kate Sedley m 194

Identity, Concealed

Aztec Blood - Gary Jennings t 889
A Capital Holiday - Janet Dailey r 265
A Cold Christmas - Charlene Weir m 212
Face Down Before Rebel Hooves - Kathy Lynn Emerson m 65
His Lady Midnight - Jo Ann Ferguson r 279
Murphy's Law - Rhys Bowen m 24
The Night the Stars Fell - Christina Kingston r 317

Illegal Immigrants

The Jasmine Trade - Denise Hamilton m 98
Stalking Moon - David Cole m 39

Illness

Bloodroot - Susan Wittig Albert m 4

Color the Sidewalk for Me - Brandilyn Collins *i* 980
Columbus Slaughters Braves - Mark Friedman *c* 1114
The Doctor's Miracle - Anna Schmidt *i* 1046
Good Harbor - Anita Diamant *c* 1103
Light Coming Back - Ann Wadsworth *c* 1213
Robak in Black - Joe L. Hensley *m* 113
Sunrise on Stradbury Square - Doris Elaine Fell *i* 992
Swift as Desire - Laura Esquivel *c* 1112
When the Last Leaf Falls - Bill Myers *i* 1032

Immortality

The Devil-Tree of El Dorado - Frank Aubrey *s* 717
The Merchants of Souls - John Barnes *s* 722

Independence

The Marine and the Princess - Cathie Linz *r* 334
A Tangled Web - Donna Bell *r* 230

Indian Captives

An Uncommon Enemy - Michelle Black *w* 423
The Way of the Coyote - Elmer Kelton *c* 1137

Indian Removal

Heart of the Sandhill - Stephanie Grace Whitson *i* 1058

Indian Reservations

The Thunder Keeper - Margaret Coel *m* 35

Indians of Mexico

Aztec Blood - Gary Jennings *t* 889

Indians of North America

Argall - William T. Vollmann *t* 950
Bear Paw - Gene Mullins *w* 484
Blackening Song - Aimee Thurlo *w* 506
Cheyenne Summer - Vella Munn *t* 911
Circle of Stars - Anna Lee Waldo *t* 952
Circle of Stars - Anna Lee Waldo *w* 510
Double Vengeance - John Duncklee *w* 449
The Good Journey - Micaela Gilchrist *t* 873
The Good Journey - Micaela Gilchrist *w* 454
The Holy Road - Michael Blake *w* 425
The Holy Road - Michael Blake *t* 826
The June Rise - William Tremblay *t* 945
The June Rise - William Tremblay *w* 507
Last Year's River - Allen Morris Jones *w* 467
Letters to Callie - Dawn Miller *w* 483
Moon Medicine - Mike Blakely *t* 827
Moon of Bitter Cold - Frederick J. Chiaventone *w* 441
Outcasts - Tim McGuire *w* 480
Spanish Jack - Robert J. Conley *w* 447
Spanish Jack - Robert J. Conley *t* 842
Summer Moon - Jill Marie Landis *w* 471
The Thunder Keeper - Margaret Coel *w* 444
Turn the Stars Upside Down - Terry C. Johnston *w* 466
Turn the Stars Upside Down - Terry C. Johnston *t* 890
An Uncommon Enemy - Michelle Black *w* 423
An Uncommon Enemy - Michelle Black *t* 824
The Way of the Coyote - Elmer Kelton *t* 895
The Years of Fear - Fred Grove *w* 460
You Never Can Tell - Kathleen Eagle *w* 450

Individuality

Balzac and the Little Chinese Seamstress - Sijie Dai *c* 1098

Infertility

Lt. Kent: Lone Wolf - Judith Lyons *r* 341
The Woman Next Door - Barbara Delinsky *c* 1101

Infidelity

A Garden to Keep - Jamie Langston Turner *i* 1055
In the Shadow of Our House - Scott Blackwood *c* 1077
Lightning Field - Dana Spiotta *c* 1202
Looking for Laura - Judith Arnold *r* 226
Whirlpool - Lorena McCourtney *i* 1023

Inheritance

Fatal Legacy - Elizabeth Corley *m* 43
Jackson's Way - Leslie LaFoy *r* 324
Moving Target - Elizabeth Lowell *r* 340
Saddled - Delores Fossen *r* 284
Someone to Watch over Me - Jill Churchill *m* 33
A Tangled Web - Donna Bell *r* 230
This Heart of Mine - Susan Elizabeth Phillips *r* 369
The Weaver's Inheritance - Kate Sedley *t* 934
When Jayne Met Erik - Elizabeth Bevarly *r* 236
Wish List - Lisa Kleypas *r* 320

Internet

The Falls - Ian Rankin *m* 178
Look at Me - Jennifer Egan *c* 1108
Midlife Can Be Murder - Jane Isenberg *m* 124
Sketches with Wolves - Jacqueline Fiedler *m* 68
Stalking Moon - David Cole *m* 39

Interpersonal Relations

The Evidence Against Her - Robb Forman Dew *c* 1102
Female Intelligence - Jane Heller *c* 1125
Great American Plain - Gary Sernovitz *c* 1195

Irish Americans

Catskill - John R. Hayes *m* 110
Comfort and Joy - Sandra Madden *r* 342
Murphy's Law - Rhys Bowen *m* 24
Murphy's Law - Rhys Bowen *t* 830
September Song - Andrew M. Greeley *c* 1117

Islam

The Rock - Kanan Makiya *t* 902
The Rock - Kanan Makiya *c* 1152

Islands

Abandon - Jillian Hunter *r* 303
Almost - Elizabeth Benedict *c* 1073
Bamboo and Lace - Lori Wick *i* 1059
The Cold Blue Blood - David Handler *m* 100
Coldwater - Mardi McConnochie *c* 1156
Death on a Casual Friday - Sharon Duncan *m* 63
First Light - Philip R. Craig *m* 46
Massacre Island - Martin Hegwood *m* 112
Murder in the Forecast - Valerie Wolzien *m* 219
A Warmth in Winter - Lori Copeland *i* 984

Italian Americans

Bell, Cook, and Candle - Joanne Pence *m* 170
Strip Poker - Nancy Bartholomew *m* 13
What to Do about Annie? - Millie Criswell *r* 264

Japanese Americans

The Bride's Kimono - Sujata Massey *m* 150

Jealousy

The Red of His Shadow - Mayra Montero *c* 1164
Summer's End - Lynne Hayworth *r* 297

Jews

Catskill - John R. Hayes *t* 882
The Jerusalem Scrolls - Bodie Thoene *t* 942

Journalism

The Alpine Nemesis - Mary Daheim *m* 51
Basket Case - Carl Hiaasen *m* 115
Blood Sinister - Cynthia Harrod-Eagles *m* 104
The Distance - Eddie Muller *m* 161
The Elusive Voice - Mary Jo Adamson *m* 2
The Good German - Joseph Kanon *c* 1135
The Ice Child - Elizabeth McGregor *t* 905
Lake Wobegon Summer 1956 - Garrison Keillor *c* 1136
Lowell Limpett: And Two Stories - Ward S. Just *c* 1134
The Webster Chronicle - Daniel Akst *c* 1066

Judaism

Deadly Illumination - Serena Stier *m* 203
Don't Cry for Me, Hot Pastrami - Sharon Kahn *m* 129
Green - Benjamin Zucker *i* 1064
Midlife Can Be Murder - Jane Isenberg *m* 124
The Rock - Kanan Makiya *t* 902
The Rock - Kanan Makiya *c* 1152
Shadows of Sin - Rochelle Krich *m* 137
The Thirty-Third Hour - Mitchell Chefitz *i* 978

Kidnapping

Ashes of Aries - Martha C. Lawrence *m* 140
Born Brave - Ruth Wind *r* 422
Critical Space - Greg Rucka *m* 190
Echoes of Lies - Jo Bannister *m* 11
Murder on the Trans-Siberian Express - Stuart M. Kaminsky *m* 130
My Lady Beloved - Lael St. James *r* 405
A Prince Among Them - Al Lacy *i* 1015
The Prisoner Bride - Susan Spencer Paul *r* 368
Property of Blood - Magdalen Nabb *m* 164
Turnabout - Jeremiah Healy *m* 111
Veiled Threats - Deborah Donnelly *m* 60
White Lion's Lady - Tina St. John *r* 407

Kings, Queens, Rulers, etc.

Ambrose Bierce and the Death of Kings - Oakley Hall *m* 95
Born Brave - Ruth Wind *r* 422
Goodnight, Sweet Prince - David Dickinson *t* 851
Heart of Night - Taylor Chase *r* 254
Queen of Ambition - Fiona Buckley *t* 834
Queen of Ambition - Fiona Buckley *m* 29
Queenmaker - India Edghill *t* 858
The Royal Physician's Visit - Per Olov Enquist *t* 862
The Royal Physician's Visit - Per Olov Enquist *c* 1110
The Third Witch - Rebecca Reisert *t* 921

Knights and Knighthood

The Child of the Holy Grail - Rosalind Miles t 907
The Marriage Bed - Claudia Dain r 266
My Lady de Burgh - Deborah Simmons r 396
The Wolf Hunt - Gillian Bradshaw t 831

Labor Conditions

Sherlock Holmes and the Secret Alliance - Larry Millett m 158

Law

The Heavenly Fugitive - Gilbert Morris i 1028

Learning

The Quest - Jim Kraus i 1013

Legal Thriller

In the Forest of Harm - Sallie Bissell c 1074
Officer of the Court - Bill Mesce Jr. t 906

Legends

Abandon - Jillian Hunter r 303
Celtika - Robert Holdstock f 558
The Child of the Holy Grail - Rosalind Miles t 907
The Dragon Queen - Alice Borchardt t 829
The Enchantment - Pam Binder r 237
Entertain the End - K.A. Applegate f 519
The Mystic Rose - Stephen R. Lawhead t 901
The Mystic Rose - Stephen R. Lawhead f 570
Mystify the Magician - K.A. Applegate f 520
Pyramid Scheme - David Freer s 751
Rowan of Rin - Emily Rodda f 594
The Sword Maiden - Susan King r 316
Thrice Bound - Roberta Gellis f 547

Letters

Heaven Sent - Rachel Wilson r 421
The June Rise - William Tremblay t 945
Letters of the Heart - Lisa Tawn Bergren i 969
Letters of the Heart - Lisa Tawn Bergren r 233

Literature

Ambrose Bierce and the Death of Kings - Oakley Hall m 95
Ghost of a Flea - James Sallis m 192
Hard Road - Barbara D'Amato m 53
The Hum Bug - Harold Schechter m 193
Imagining Don Giovanni - Anthony J. Rudel t 929
In a Strange City - Laura Lippman m 143
Jane and the Prisoner of Wool House - Stephanie Barron m 12
The Jewel of the North - Peter King m 135
Pride, Prejudice and Jasmin Field - Melissa Nathan r 359
Uncatalogued - Julie Kaewert m 128

Loneliness

The Appointment - Herta Muller c 1168
The Hunters - Claire Messud c 1161
The Spirit Returns - Richard Burgin c 1087
Talking in the Dark - Laura Glen Louis c 1149

Love

Alice at Heart - Deborah Smith r 401
The Border Hostage - Virginia Henley t 883
The Clouds Above - Andrew Greig t 876
Conjuring Maud - Philip Danze t 847
The English Garden - Gail Gaymer Martin i 1020
The Girl from the Golden Horn - Kurban Said c 1191
The Good German - Joseph Kanon c 1135
The Good German - Joseph Kanon t 892
Great American Plain - Gary Sernovitz c 1195
Hateship, Friendship, Courtship, Loveship, Marriage - Alice Munro c 1169
Hotel of the Saints - Ursula Hegi c 1124
My Scottish Summer - Connie Brockway r 243
Restoration and Romance - Barbara Curtis i 986
Riot - Shashi Tharoor c 1208

Lovers

First Gray, Then White, Then Blue - Margriet de Moor c 1165

Loyalty

The Border Hostage - Virginia Henley t 883

Magic

Abandon - Jillian Hunter r 303
Always Forever - Mark Chadbourn f 533
Another Summer - Georgia Bockoven r 239
Antrax - Terry Brooks f 530
Apocalypse - J. Robert King f 564
The Beasts of Barakhai - Mickey Zucker Reichert f 590
Behind Time - Lynn Abbey f 515
Betrayal - Jean Rabe f 589
The Black Chalice - Marie Jakober f 562
The Bone Doll's Twin - Lynn Flewelling f 544
Brother of the Dragon - Paul B. Thompson f 604
Buttercup Baby - Karen Fox r 287
Children of the Lion - Jennifer Roberson f 591
Children of the Shaman - Jessica Rydill f 596
The Crab - Stan Brown f 531
Cursed and Consulted - Rick Cook f 537
Dance upon the Air - Nora Roberts r 382
Debt of Bones - Terry Goodkind f 549
Drachenfels - Jack Yeovil f 613
Dragon's Bluff - Mary H. Herbert f 556
The Dragons of the Cuyahoga - S. Andrew Swann f 602
Eccentric Circles - Rebecca Lickiss f 573
Elminster in Hell - Ed Greenwood f 553
Enchanter - Sara Douglass f 540
The Enchantment - Pam Binder r 237
A Feral Darkness - Doranna Durgin f 543
Fortress Draconis - Michael A. Stackpole f 599
The Golden Sword - Fiona Patton f 586
Guardians of the Lost - Margaret Weis f 611
Hazard's Price - Robert S. Stone f 601
Here Be Monsters - Christopher Stasheff f 600
I Dream of You - Judi McCoy r 350
The Jasper Forest - Julia Gray f 551
The King's Name - Jo Walton f 608
Kiss of the Highlander - Karen Marie Moning r 358
The Last Hero - Terry Pratchett f 588
Legacy of the Wolf - Jennifer Roberson f 592
The Lion Throne - Jennifer Roberson f 593
Magic Time - Marc Scott Zicree f 614
Marching through Peachtree - Harry Turtledove f 606
Midnight Falcon - David Gemmell f 548
Mistress of the Catacombs - David Drake f 541
The Monsters of Morley Manor - Bruce Coville f 538
Mother Ocean, Daughter Sea - Diana Marcellas f 576
Mother of Kings - Poul Anderson f 517
Nightchild - James Barclay f 523
Once upon a Rose - Nora Roberts r 384
Once upon a Winter's Night - Dennis L. McKiernan f 579
The Onion Girl - Charles De Lint f 539
The Pillars of Creation - Terry Goodkind f 550
Pool of Radiance - Carrie Bebris f 525
Pride of Kings - Judith Tarr f 603
The Prince of Shadow - Curt Benjamin f 526
The Prisoner Bride - Susan Spencer Paul r 368
Queen of the Demonweb Pits - Paul Kidd f 563
Rebel's Cage - Kate Jacoby f 561
Revelation - Elizabeth Haydon f 555
The Rundlestone of Oz - Eloise McGraw f 577
The Scent of Magic - Cliff McNish f 581
Shadow - K.J. Parker f 585
Shadow Kiss - Tom Townsend f 605
Shadow of the Seer - Michael Scott Rohan f 595
Shadowkings - Michael Cobley f 535
The Shattered Mask - Richard Lee Byers f 532
Sidhe-Devil - Aaron Allston f 516
The Silver Call - Dennis L. McKiernan f 580
Spirit of the Stone - Maggie Furey f 545
Swell Foop - Piers Anthony f 518
Take a Thief - Mercedes Lackey f 569
Thrice Bound - Roberta Gellis f 547
To Tame a Wild Heart - Tracy Fobes r 281
The Treason of Dortrean - Marcus Herniman f 557
The Warrior's Bond - Juliet E. McKenna f 578
The Way between the Worlds - Ian Irvine f 560
The Way of Light - Storm Constantine f 536
The Way of the Rose - Valery Leith f 572
You're the One - Judi McCoy r 351

Magicians

Carter Beats the Devil - Glen David Gold t 874
The Obsidian Tower - Freda Warrington f 609
Wit'ch Gate - James Clemens f 534

Mail Order Brides

A Measure of Grace - Al Lacy i 1014

Marriage

Agatha Raisin and the Love from Hell - M.C. Beaton m 14
Austin City Blue - Jan Grape m 88
Believe in Me - Josie Litton r 336
The Bride of Willow Creek - Maggie Osborne r 364
The Bride Sale - Candice Hern r 298
Broken Promises - Patricia Oliver r 362
Come Back to Me - Josie Litton r 337
The Corrections - Jonathan Franzen c 1113
A Devilish Husband - Alana Clayton r 257
The Distance - Eddie Muller m 161
Dream of Me - Josie Litton r 338
East of the Sun, West of the Moon - Carole Bellacera r 231
A Family for Gillian - Catherine Blair r 238
Fighting Gravity - Peggy Rambach c 1184
French Leave - Sheri Cobb South r 404
A Guardian's Angel - Jo Ann Ferguson r 278
Hateship, Friendship, Courtship, Loveship, Marriage - Alice Munro c 1169
Heaven Sent - Jillian Hart i 997
How to Be Good - Nick Hornby c 1126
The Husband Test - Betina Krahn r 321
The Irredeemable Miss Renfield - Regina Scott r 393
The Killing Bee - Matt Witten m 218
A Kiss for Mama - Jo Ann Ferguson r 280
The MacKenzies: Zach - Ana Leigh r 332
The Mackintosh Bride - Debra Lee Brown r 244
The Masks of Auntie Laveau - Robert J. Randisi m 177
Miss Match - Leslie Carroll r 252
The Pickup - Nadine Gordimer c 1116

The Proper Wife - Julia Justiss r 311
Red on Rose - Patricia Jones c 1133
Ritual of Proof - Dara Joy r 310
Robak in Black - Joe L. Hensley m 113
The Royal Physician's Visit - Per Olov Enquist c 1110
A Sensitive Kind of Murder - Jacqueline Girdner m 80
The Spanish Bride - Amanda McCabe r 349
A Study in Death - Iain McDowell m 155
Swift as Desire - Laura Esquivel c 1112
To Perish in Penzance - Jeanne M. Dams m 54
Under the Kissing Bough - Shannon Donnelly r 271
The Very Comely Countess - Miranda Jarrett r 307
The Very Daring Duchess - Miranda Jarrett r 308
The Warrior's Damsel - Denise Hampton r 295
The Wedding Wager - Cathy Maxwell r 348
When Jayne Met Erik - Elizabeth Bevarly r 236
Wildflowers - Robin Jones Gunn i 993
The Woman Next Door - Barbara Delinsky c 1101
The World Below - Sue Miller c 1163

Mars

First Landing - Robert Zubrin s 814

Medical Thriller

Shock - Robin Cook c 1093
The Surgeon - Tess Gerritsen m 78

Medicine

City of Dreams - Beverly Swerling t 939
Could I Have This Dance? - Harry Lee Kraus i 1012
A Feast in Exile - Chelsea Quinn Yarbro h 713
Gargoyles - Alan Nayes h 677
Hosts - F. Paul Wilson h 710
The Ice Child - Elizabeth McGregor t 905
Night Blood - James M. Thompson h 702
The Oath - John Lescroart m 141

Memory

The Blue Last - Martha Grimes m 92
Coffin's Ghost - Gwendoline Butler m 30
The Deadwood Beetle - Mylene Dressler c 1106
Double Honor - Melissa Horsfall i 1002
The Gingerbread Man - Maggie Shayne r 395
Shakespeare's Counselor - Charlaine Harris m 102
War Story - Gwen Edelman c 1107

Memory Loss

The Art of Dying - Diana Killian i 1009
Comfort and Joy - Sandra Madden r 342
The Faded Flower - Paul McCusker i 1024
Funeral in Blue - Anne Perry m 172
The Sea Sprite - Ruth Langan r 328
Shades of Justice - Fredrick Huebner m 121

Men

Edgewater Angels - Sandro Meallet c 1160
Just Say No! - Omar Tyree c 1210

Mental Illness

Angel Face - Suzanne Forster r 283
In and Out - Mat Coward m 44
The Royal Physician's Visit - Per Olov Enquist c 1110
The Savage Girl - Alex Shakar c 1196
The Shape of Snakes - Minette Walters m 211
Watchers of Time - Charles Todd m 208

Mentally Handicapped

Turnabout - Jeremiah Healy m 111

Mermaids

Alice at Heart - Deborah Smith r 401

Mexican Americans

Crack Shot - Sinclair Browning m 28
Death on a Casual Friday - Sharon Duncan m 63

Mexicans

Death of the Last Villista - Allana Martin m 149
Fire Lilies - Cynthia Leal Massey w 476
The Last Mayan - Malcolm Shuman m 195
The Survival of Juan Oro - Max Brand w 434

Middle Ages

Act of Mercy - Peter Tremayne m 209
The Archer's Tale - Bernard Cornwell t 843
Circle of Stars - Anna Lee Waldo t 952
The Clerk's Tale - Margaret Frazer m 70
The Clerk's Tale - Margaret Frazer t 865
The Crusader - Michael A. Eisner t 860
The Good Men - Charmaine Craig t 844
My Lady Beloved - Lael St. James r 405
My Lady de Burgh - Deborah Simmons r 396
My Lady Wayward - Lael St. James r 406
The Mystic Rose - Stephen R. Lawhead t 901
Pride of Kings - Judith Tarr t 941
Saintly Murders - C.L. Grace t 875
Saintly Murders - C.L. Grace m 86
The Temptress - Claire Delacroix r 269
The Warrior's Damsel - Denise Hampton r 295
The Weaver's Inheritance - Kate Sedley m 194
The Weaver's Inheritance - Kate Sedley t 934
The Wolf Hunt - Gillian Bradshaw t 831

Migrant Labor

Highwire Moon - Susan Straight c 1205

Military Bases

Last Virgin in California - Maureen Child r 255

Military Life

Bolo Strike - William H. Keith Jr. s 765
Gettysburg - James Reasoner t 919
Holding the Line - Rick Shelley s 795
Jane and the Prisoner of Wool House - Stephanie Barron m 12
Jane and the Prisoner of Wool House - Stephanie Barron t 822
Last Virgin in California - Maureen Child r 255
Nobody Loves a Centurion - John Maddox Roberts m 184
Soldiers - John Dalmas s 742
Stranded with the Sergeant - Cathie Linz r 335
True Valor - Dee Henderson i 1000
Under the Eagle - Simon Scarrow t 931
The Very Daring Duchess - Miranda Jarrett r 308

Militia Movements

A Darker Justice - Sallie Bissell m 19

Miners and Mining

Bethany's Song - Susan Plunkett r 372

Ministers

A Family All Her Own - Bonnie K. Winn i 1061
Redeeming Claire - Cynthia Rutledge i 1045

Ministry

Cape Refuge - Terri Blackstock i 970

Missing Persons

Aftermath - Peter Robinson m 186
The Chinese Fire Drill - Les Roberts m 185
Crack Shot - Sinclair Browning m 28
Death in Paradise - Robert B. Parker m 168
First Light - Philip R. Craig m 46
Followin' a Dream - Eboni Snoe r 403
Hide and Seek - Cherry Adair r 222
Kiss It Goodbye - John Wessel m 213
Long Time No See - Susan Isaacs c 1131
Once Bitten - Laurien Berenson m 17
Past Tense - William G. Tapply m 206
Skeleton at the Feast - Patricia Hall m 97
Three for a Letter - Mary Reed m 180

Missionaries

Murder on the Minnesota - Conrad Allen m 5

Models

Look at Me - Jennifer Egan c 1108

Models, Fashion

Bachelor on the Prowl - Kasey Michaels r 353

Modern Life

All That Counts - Georg M. Oswald c 1177
Darling? - Heidi Jon Schmidt c 1193
Fury - Salman Rushdie c 1190
Hotel of the Saints - Ursula Hegi c 1124
Hurricane Season - Karen Bjorneby c 1075
Living with Saints - Mary O'Connell c 1175
Super-Cannes - J.G. Ballard c 1070
Why Did I Ever? - Mary Robison c 1188
Zigzagging Down a Wild Trail - Bobbie Ann Mason c 1155

Money

Dial M for Meat Loaf - Ellen Hart m 105
Money, Money, Money - Ed McBain m 152
Rag Man - Pete Hautman m 107

Monks

The Marriage Bed - Claudia Dain r 266

Monsters

Friday Night in Beast House - Richard Laymon h 662
Next Stop, Paradise - Sue Civil-Brown r 256
Night of the Bat - Paul Zindel h 714

Morality

Rag Man - Pete Hautman m 107

Mormons

Fault Line - Sarah Andrews m 7
Sister Wife - John Gates m 76

Mothers

A Kiss for Mama - Jo Ann Ferguson *r* 280

Mothers and Daughters

According to Queeney - Beryl Bainbridge *c* 1069
Color the Sidewalk for Me - Brandilyn Collins *i* 980
Eager to Please - Julie Parsons *c* 1180
Eva Moves the Furniture - Margot Livesey *c* 1148
Highwire Moon - Susan Straight *c* 1205
Keepers - Janet LaPierre *m* 139
Property of Blood - Magdalen Nabb *m* 164
Sacred Ground - Barbara Wood *t* 962

Mothers and Sons

A Father's Place - Marta Perry *i* 1041
Suzanne's Diary for Nicholas - James Patterson *c* 1181

Mountain Life

Highland Hopes - Gary E. Parker *i* 1039

Movie Industry

Coldheart Canyon - Clive Barker *c* 1071
Coldheart Canyon - Clive Barker *h* 619
Stormy Weather - Paula L. Woods *m* 220

Multiple Personalities

Secret of the Wolf - Susan Krinard *r* 322

Mummies

The Black Eye - Constance Little *m* 144

Murder

About the Author - John Colapinto *c* 1092
All the Dead Were Strangers - Ethan Black *c* 1076
Angel Face - Suzanne Forster *r* 283
Broken Honor - Patricia Potter *r* 373
Cape Refuge - Terri Blackstock *i* 970
Dangerous Attraction - Susan Vaughan *r* 417
Dangerous Dilemmas - Evelyn Palfrey *r* 365
Eager to Please - Julie Parsons *c* 1180
Elusive Passion - Kathryn Smith *r* 402
Eyes of Elisha - Brandilyn Collins *i* 981
The Folks - Ray Garton *h* 638
Ghost Killer - Scott Chandler *h* 627
The Gingerbread Man - Maggie Shayne *r* 395
Happy Birthday Murder - Lee Harris *i* 996
In the Dark - Richard Laymon *h* 663
Moving Target - Elizabeth Lowell *r* 340
My Lady de Burgh - Deborah Simmons *r* 396
My Name Is Red - Orhan Pamuk *c* 1178
Open Season - Linda Howard *r* 302
The Secret - Kat Martin *r* 347
Shooting Dr. Jack - Norman Green *c* 1118
The Sleeping Beauty - Jacqueline Navin *r* 360
Slightly Shady - Amanda Quick *r* 375
To Trust a Stranger - Karen Robards *r* 381
Under Suspicion - Rachel Lee *r* 331
The Widow - Anne Stuart *r* 411
Yonder Stands Your Orphan - Barry Hannah *c* 1121

Museums

The Bride's Kimono - Sujata Massey *m* 150
The Hum Bug - Harold Schechter *m* 193
Under Suspicion - Rachel Lee *r* 331

Music and Musicians

Aria - Susan Segal *c* 1194
Basket Case - Carl Hiaasen *m* 115
Chasing the Devil's Tail - David Fulmer *t* 867
Chasing the Devil's Tail - David Fulmer *m* 73
Chelsea Horror Hotel - Dee Dee Ramone *h* 684
Imagining Don Giovanni - Anthony J. Rudel *t* 929
Just Say No! - Omar Tyree *c* 1210
The Night Men - Keith Snyder *m* 199
The Nightingale's Song - Kathleen Eschenburg *r* 273
O Gentle Death - Janet Neel *m* 165

Muslims

Halide's Gift - Frances Kazan *t* 893

Mystery

Bitterroot - James Lee Burke *c* 1088
Black House - Stephen King *c* 1140
Bring Me a Dream - Robyn Amos *r* 224
Dance upon the Air - Nora Roberts *r* 382
First Lady - Michael Malone *c* 1153
The Good German - Joseph Kanon *c* 1135
Gotta Get Next to You - Lynn Emery *r* 272
The Grand Complication - Allen Kurzweil *c* 1144
His Father's Son - Nigel Bennett *h* 621
In the Dark - Richard Laymon *h* 663
In the Forest of Harm - Sallie Bissell *c* 1074
Night in the Lonesome October - Richard Laymon *h* 664
Open Season - C.J. Box *w* 428
The Rake and the Wallflower - Allison Lane *r* 325
Season of Storms - Susanna Kearsley *r* 314

Mystery and Detective Stories

Act of Mercy - Peter Tremayne *t* 944
Ambrose Bierce and the Death of Kings - Oakley Hall *t* 878
The Ambush of My Name - Jeffrey Marks *t* 903
Bella Donna - Barbara Cherne *t* 836
Bone Walker - Kathleen O'Neal Gear *t* 871
The Bones of the Buried - David Roberts *t* 923
Brothers of Cain - Miriam Grace Monfredo *t* 909
Call Each River Jordan - Owen Parry *t* 914
Carter Beats the Devil - Glen David Gold *t* 874
Catskill - John R. Hayes *t* 882
Chapel Noir - Carole Nelson Douglas *t* 856
Chasing the Devil's Tail - David Fulmer *t* 867
The Clerk's Tale - Margaret Frazer *t* 865
The Devil's Own Luck - David Donachie *t* 853
Dr. Mortimer and the Aldgate Mystery - Gerard Williams *t* 958
The Dying Trade - David Donachie *t* 854
Face Down Before Rebel Hooves - Kathy Lynn Emerson *t* 861
Funeral in Blue - Anne Perry *t* 915
The Goldsmith's Daughter - Kate Sedley *t* 933
Goodnight, Sweet Prince - David Dickinson *t* 851
The Great Game - Michael Kurland *t* 899
Hammett: Crime Stories and Other Writings - Dashiell Hammett *m* 99
The Hum Bug - Harold Schechter *t* 932
The Ironclad Alibi - Michael Kilian *t* 898
Island of Tears - Troy Soos *t* 936
Jane and the Prisoner of Wool House - Stephanie Barron *t* 822
The Jazz Bird - Craig Holden *t* 885
Kaleidoscope - J. Robert Janes *t* 888
Kisses of Death - Max Allan Collins *t* 841
Long Time No See - Susan Isaacs *c* 1131
Murder at the Panionic Games - Michael B. Edwards *t* 859
Murder at the President's Door - Elliott Roosevelt *t* 928
Murder on the Minnesota - Conrad Allen *t* 816
Murphy's Law - Rhys Bowen *t* 830
The Night People and Other Stories - Edward D. Hoch *m* 117
Night Watch - Stephen Kendrick *t* 896
The Nighttime Is the Right Time - Bill Crider *m* 48
Nobody Loves a Centurion - John Maddox Roberts *t* 924
Officer of the Court - Bill Mesce Jr. *t* 906
Pale Horse Coming - Stephen Hunter *t* 887
Pale Shadow - Robert Skinner *t* 935
The Problem of the Surly Servant - Roberta Rogow *t* 926
Queen of Ambition - Fiona Buckley *t* 834
Saintly Murders - C.L. Grace *t* 875
Sherlock Holmes and the Secret Alliance - Larry Millett *t* 908
The Slaying of the Shrew - Simon Hawke *t* 880
Smuggler's Moon - Bruce Alexander *t* 815
Someone to Watch over Me - Jill Churchill *t* 839
The Thief-Taker - T.F. Banks *t* 820
Three for a Letter - Mary Reed *t* 920
Watchers of Time - Charles Todd *t* 943
The Weaver's Inheritance - Kate Sedley *t* 934

Mysticism

Darkness at the Door - Catherine Dain *m* 52
A Lower Deep - Tom Piccirilli *h* 682
Riverwatch - Joseph M. Nassise *h* 676

Mythology

Call Down the Stars - Sue Harrison *t* 879
In the Shape of a Boar - Lawrence Norfolk *c* 1171
In the Shape of a Boar - Lawrence Norfolk *t* 913

Native Americans

All Signs Point to Murder - Kat Goldring *m* 81
Argall - William T. Vollmann *c* 1212
Cheyenne Summer - Vella Munn *t* 911
A Darker Justice - Sallie Bissell *m* 19
My Lord Savage - Elizabeth Lane *r* 326
Night Hawk's Bride - Jillian Hart *r* 296
Stalking Moon - David Cole *m* 39
White Shell Woman - James D. Doss *m* 61

Nature

The Nature of Balance - Tim Lebbon *h* 666

Nazis

The Company of Strangers - Robert Wilson *m* 215
Kaleidoscope - J. Robert Janes *m* 126
Kaleidoscope - J. Robert Janes *t* 888
The Message of the Mute Dog - Charlotte Murray Russell *m* 191

Near-Death Experience

The Secret - Kat Martin *r* 347

Neighbors and Neighborhoods

Loving Thy Neighbor - Ruth Scofield *i* 1047
The Secret Admirer - Annette Mahon *r* 343
Seven Up - Janet Evanovich *r* 274

Newspapers

Dugan under Ground - Tom De Haven *c* 1100
The Renegades: Rafe - Genell Dellin *r* 270
Written on the Wind - Judith Pella *i* 1040

Nuclear Warfare

The Ash Garden - Dennis Bock c 1078

Nuns

The Clerk's Tale - Margaret Frazer m 70
Confessions of a Pagan Nun - Kate Horsley t 886
The Husband Test - Betina Krahn r 321

Nursing

For Rouenna - Sigrid Nunez c 1172

Nursing Homes

The Faded Flower - Paul McCusker i 1024

Occult

Coldheart Canyon - Clive Barker h 619
Dark Sanctuary - H.B. Gregory h 644

Oil

Quincie Bolliver - Mary King w 469
The Tumbleweed Murders - Rebecca Rothenberg m 189

Organized Crime

Dark Hollow - John Connolly m 42
Hostage - Robert Crais m 47
Hostage - Robert Crais c 1096
Junior's Leg - Ken Wells c 1214
Long Time No See - Susan Isaacs c 1131
Prized Possessions - Jessica Stirling t 938

Orphans

A Child Shall Lead Them - Carole Gift Page i 1036
Leap of Faith - Danielle Steel c 1203
Riona - Linda Windsor i 1060
Summer's Promise - Irene Brand i 974
Twin Blessings - Carolyne Aarsen i 965

Outcasts

Echo Burning - Lee Child w 442

Paganism

Daughter of Lir - Judith Tarr t 940
Mother of Kings - Poul Anderson t 818

Paranormal

Darkness at the Door - Catherine Dain m 52
Eyes of Elisha - Brandilyn Collins i 981
The Very Gothic Christmas - Christine Feehan r 277

Parapsychology

Darkness at the Door - Catherine Dain m 52
Kaleidoscope - Dorothy Gilman m 79

Parent and Child

The Corrections - Jonathan Franzen c 1113
Gabriel's Gift - Hanif Kureishi c 1143
Riot - Shashi Tharoor c 1208
Swift as Desire - Laura Esquivel c 1112

Parenthood

Forbid Them Not - Michael P. Farris i 991
A Scandalous Wager - Bess Willingham r 420

Phobias

Death Is a Cabaret - Deborah Morgan m 160

Photography

Going Overboard - Christina Skye r 399
Portrait in Sepia - Isabel Allende t 817
Still She Haunts Me - Katie Roiphe c 1189

Physically Handicapped

Junior's Leg - Ken Wells c 1214

Pilgrims and Pilgrimages

Act of Mercy - Peter Tremayne t 944

Pioneers

An Uncommon Enemy - Michelle Black w 423

Plague

Mirabilis - Susann Cokal c 1091
Year of Wonders - Geraldine Brooks c 1083
Year of Wonders - Geraldine Brooks t 832

Plays

Come, My Little Angel - Diane Noble i 1033
Pride, Prejudice and Jasmin Field - Melissa Nathan r 359
Season of Storms - Susanna Kearsley r 314

Poetry

The Ancient Track - H.P. Lovecraft h 669
Bloodlines - Fred D'Aguiar t 846
In the Shape of a Boar - Lawrence Norfolk c 1171

Police Procedural

First Lady - Michael Malone c 1153
Hostage - Robert Crais c 1096
The Treatment - Mo Hayder c 1123

Political Crimes and Offenses

The Appointment - Herta Muller c 1168
The Feast of the Goat - Mario Vargas Llosa c 1211
The Feast of the Goat - Mario Vargas Llosa t 948

Political Movements

The Feast of the Goat - Mario Vargas Llosa t 948

Political Thriller

Deep Fathom - James Rollins s 792
House Corrino - Brian Herbert s 757

Politics

The Ambush of My Name - Jeffrey Marks t 903
Dark Dreams - Cory Daniells r 267
Drummer in the Dark - T. Davis Bunn i 976
Face Down Before Rebel Hooves - Kathy Lynn Emerson t 861
The Family - Mario Puzo c 1183
Halfway to Heaven - Susan Wiggs r 419
The Incomparable Miss Compton - Regina Scott r 392
Island of Tears - Troy Soos m 200
The Justice - Angela Elwell Hunt i 1004
The Last Summer of Reason - Tahar Djaout c 1105
Lowell Limpett: And Two Stories - Ward S. Just c 1134
Once a Princess - Veronica Sattler r 388
A Perfect Match - Jeanne Savery r 389
Rocky and the Senator's Daughter - Dixie Browning r 246
Roscoe - William Kennedy t 897
September Song - Andrew M. Greeley c 1117
Sex and Murder.com - Mark Richard Zubro m 221
Stillwater - William F. Weld t 955
Treason - David Nevin t 912

Popular Culture

. . .And the Angel with Television Eyes - John Shirley h 694
Female Intelligence - Jane Heller c 1125
Jewelry Talks - Richard Klein c 1142
Lightning Field - Dana Spiotta c 1202
The Savage Girl - Alex Shakar c 1196
The Wig My Father Wore - Anne Enright c 1111

Poverty

Christmas Vows: $5.00 Extra - Lori Copeland i 983

Pre-Columbian History

Bone Walker - Kathleen O'Neal Gear t 871
The Last Mayan - Malcolm Shuman m 195

Pregnancy

Gargoyles - Alan Nayes h 677
The Great Baby Caper - Eugenia Riley r 380
A Home of Her Own - Cathleen Connors i 982
The Widow's Little Secret - Judith Stacy r 409

Prejudice

Heart of the Sandhill - Stephanie Grace Whitson i 1058
Night Hawk's Bride - Jillian Hart r 296
The Night Men - Keith Snyder m 199

Princes and Princesses

Goodnight, Sweet Prince - David Dickinson m 58
The Marine and the Princess - Cathie Linz r 334
Once a Princess - Veronica Sattler r 388

Prisoners and Prisons

Coldwater - Mardi McConnochie t 904
Leaving Disneyland - Alexander Parsons c 1179
Love Her Madly - Mary-Ann Tirone Smith m 198
Pale Horse Coming - Stephen Hunter m 122
Pale Horse Coming - Stephen Hunter c 1127
Pale Horse Coming - Stephen Hunter t 887
The Perfect Princess - Elizabeth Thornton r 416
Suspicion of Vengeance - Barbara Parker m 167

Privacy

A Capital Holiday - Janet Dailey r 265

Prohibition Era

The Jazz Bird - Craig Holden m 119

Property Rights

No Man's Mistress - Mary Balogh r 227

Prostitution

Chasing the Devil's Tail - David Fulmer m 73
The Long Good Boy - Carol Lea Benjamin m 16

Psychic Powers

Affinity - J.N. Williamson h 709
Ashes of Aries - Martha C. Lawrence m 140
The Fall of Neskaya - Marion Zimmer Bradley s 725
Gifted Touch - Melinda Metz s 775
Haunted - Melinda Metz s 776
Here Be Monsters - Christopher Stasheff f 600
Just West of Heaven - Kathleen Kane r 313
Kaleidoscope - Dorothy Gilman m 79

Psychological

Audubon's Watch - John Gregory Brown c 1085
The Evidence Against Her - Robb Forman Dew c 1102
Flights of Love - Bernhard Schlink c 1192
Good Harbor - Anita Diamant c 1103
Killing the Shadows - Val McDermid m 154
Love Her Madly - Mary-Ann Tirone Smith m 198
Shades of Justice - Fredrick Huebner m 121

Psychological Thriller

Darkling I Listen - Katherine Sutcliffe r 412
Envy - Sandra Brown c 1086

Psychology

Audubon's Watch - John Gregory Brown t 833
The Silent Woman - Susan M. Dodd t 852

Publishing

See Jane Date - Melissa Senate r 394
Suddenly You - Lisa Kleypas r 319
Uncatalogued - Julie Kaewert m 128

Quest

Ashling - Isobelle Carmody s 732
Black House - Stephen King h 659
The Dragon Society - Lawrence Watt-Evans f 610
Guardians of the Lost - Margaret Weis f 611
Law Dog - J. Lee Butts w 438
The Other Wind - Ursula K. Le Guin f 571
The Quest - Jim Kraus i 1013

Race Relations

The Body in the Bonfire - Katherine Hall Page i 1037
Chasing the Devil's Tail - David Fulmer m 73
Fire in the Rock - Joe Martin c 1154
Futureland - Walter Mosley c 1166
Letters from an Age of Reason - Nora Hague t 877
Pale Shadow - Robert Skinner t 935
Pale Shadow - Robert Skinner m 196
Rhythms - Donna Hill t 884
Sap Rising - Christine Lincoln c 1147
Smoke-Filled Rooms - Kris Nelscott m 166
Strawman's Hammock - Darryl Wimberley m 216
The Water and the Blood - Nancy E. Turner t 947

Racial Conflict

Letters from an Age of Reason - Nora Hague t 877

Racism

Dead Ball - R.D. Rosen m 188
Pale Horse Coming - Stephen Hunter m 122
Red on Rose - Patricia Jones c 1133
The Shape of Snakes - Minette Walters m 211

Radio

A Prince of a Guy - Sheila Rabe r 376

Radio Broadcasting

A Prince of a Guy - Sheila Rabe r 376

Railroads

Friends and Enemies - Stephen A. Bly i 972

Ranch Life

The Baron War - Jory Sherman w 503
Behold a Red Horse - Cotton Smith w 504
Charlie and the Sir - Frank Roderus w 499
Last Year's River - Allen Morris Jones t 891
Monte's Revenge - Eugene C. Vories w 509
On the Night Plain - J. Robert Lennon c 1146
The Texan's Dream - Jodi Thomas r 415
This Time Forever - Carol Steward i 1052
Tie-Fast Country - Robert Flynn w 451

Rape

Shakespeare's Counselor - Charlaine Harris m 102

Real Estate

The Doctor and the Dead Man's Chest - Robin Hathaway m 106

Redemption

The Infidel - Joe Musser i 1031
When Heaven Weeps - Ted Dekker i 988

Refugees

The Ash Garden - Dennis Bock c 1078
Catskill - John R. Hayes t 882
Funny Accent - Barbara Shulgasser-Parker c 1197
In the Shape of a Boar - Lawrence Norfolk c 1171

Reincarnation

The Beasts of Brahm - Mark Hansom h 646
Midnight Bayou - Nora Roberts c 1187
The Other Adonis - Frank Deford t 849

Relationships

Bitten - Kelley Armstrong c 1068
Cold - John Smolens c 1199
Eva Moves the Furniture - Margot Livesey c 1148
Fairness - Ferdinand Mount c 1167
Fault Line - Sarah Andrews m 7
Flights of Love - Bernhard Schlink c 1192
The Fourth Hand - John Irving c 1130
Funny Accent - Barbara Shulgasser-Parker c 1197
The Hunters - Claire Messud c 1161
Hurricane Season - Karen Bjorneby c 1075
In the Shadow of Our House - Scott Blackwood c 1077
Lucky Us - Joan Silber c 1198
Middle Age - Joyce Carol Oates c 1174
The Money-Whipped Steer-Job Three-Jack Give-Up Artist - Dan Jenkins c 1132
Samuel Johnson Is Indignant - Lydia Davis c 1099
Sentimental Journey - Jill Barnett r 228
Suzanne's Diary for Nicholas - James Patterson c 1181
Talking in the Dark - Laura Glen Louis c 1149
Too Much Temptation - Lori Foster r 286
War Story - Gwen Edelman c 1107

Religion

Act of Mercy - Peter Tremayne m 209
Love Her Madly - Mary-Ann Tirone Smith m 198
Mirabilis - Susann Cokal c 1091
This Rock - Robert Morgan t 910

Religious Communes

Keepers - Janet LaPierre m 139

Religious Conflict

Creeping Venom - Sheila Pim m 173
Ester's Child - Jean P. Sasson t 930
Face Down Before Rebel Hooves - Kathy Lynn Emerson m 65
The Gaius Diary - Gene Edwards i 990
The Good Men - Charmaine Craig t 844
Keeper of Hearts - Dianne Christner i 979
The Last Confession - Morris L. West t 956
Night Watch - Stephen Kendrick t 896
On Every Side - Karen Kingsbury i 1010
Rora - James Byron Huggins i 1003

Religious Life

Confessions of a Pagan Nun - Kate Horsley t 886
The Crusader - Michael A. Eisner t 860
Sea of Glory - Ken Wales t 953
Watchers of Time - Charles Todd t 943

Remarriage

A Bungalow for Two - Carole Gift Page i 1035
Elusive Passion - Kathryn Smith r 402

Resourcefulness

Hotel of the Saints - Ursula Hegi c 1124
Slightly Shady - Amanda Quick r 375

Responsibility

My Lord Savage - Elizabeth Lane r 326

Restaurants

Death by Darjeeling - Laura Childs m 32
Prepared for Murder - Cecile Lamalle m 138
The Secret Life of Connor Monahan - Elizabeth Bevarly r 235
Wildflowers - Robin Jones Gunn i 993

Retirement

Black House - Stephen King c 1140

Reunions

Another Summer - Georgia Bockoven r 239
The Bride of Willow Creek - Maggie Osborne r 364
Broken Promises - Patricia Oliver r 362
The Guardian - Barbara Miller r 355
The Renegades: Rafe - Genell Dellin r 270
A Warmth in Winter - Lori Copeland i 984
Written on Her Heart - Alan Maki i 1019

Revenge

Any Way the Wind Blows - E. Lynn Harris c 1122
Austin City Blue - Jan Grape m 88
Beloved Protector - Linda O'Brien r 361
Cold - John Smolens c 1199
Day of Reckoning - Kathy Herman i 1001
Eager to Please - Julie Parsons c 1180
Envy - Sandra Brown r 245
Envy - Sandra Brown c 1086
A Guardian's Angel - Jo Ann Ferguson r 278
The Prisoner Bride - Susan Spencer Paul r 368
A Reckless Encounter - Rosemary Rogers r 385
To Tame a Duke - Patricia Grasso r 293
The Traitor's Daughter - Elizabeth Powell r 374

Revolutionary War

Revenge of the Wrought-Iron Flamingos - Donna Andrews m 6

Revolutions

Requiem for a Lost Empire - Andrei Makine c 1151

Riots

Riot - Shashi Tharoor c 1208
Smoke-Filled Rooms - Kris Nelscott m 166

Rivers

Downriver - Richard S. Wheeler t 957
The Last Canyon - John Vernon t 949

Robbers and Outlaws

The MacKenzies: Zach - Ana Leigh r 332
Walker's Widow - Heidi Betts r 234

Rock Music

Gabriel's Gift - Hanif Kureishi c 1143

Roman Empire

Blood and Gold - Anne Rice t 922
Blood and Gold - Anne Rice h 685
Nobody Loves a Centurion - John Maddox Roberts m 184
Nobody Loves a Centurion - John Maddox Roberts t 924
Under the Eagle - Simon Scarrow t 931

Romance

The Black Eye - Constance Little m 144
Cold Hunter's Moon - K.C. Greenlief m 90
Hot and Bothered - Lori Foster r 285
No Man's Mistress - Mary Balogh r 227
Pride, Prejudice and Jasmin Field - Melissa Nathan r 359
Sentimental Journey - Jill Barnett t 821
Single White Vampire Seeks Same - Martin H. Greenberg h 643
'Tis the Season - Donna Hill r 300
Too Much Temptation - Lori Foster r 286
The Valentine Wish - Debbie Raleigh r 378

Runaways

Crack Shot - Sinclair Browning m 28
Elusive Passion - Kathryn Smith r 402
Heaven on Earth - Marilyn Pappano r 366

Rural Life

Dancing with the Virgins - Stephen Booth m 23
Deep Water Death - Glynn Marsh Alam m 3
The Devil's Apprentice - Edward Marston m 148
The Doctor and the Dead Man's Chest - Robin Hathaway m 106
Last Year's River - Allen Morris Jones t 891
The Magic of Ordinary Days - Ann Howard Creel t 845
Massacre Island - Martin Hegwood m 112
Paradise Lost - J.A. Jance m 125
This Rock - Robert Morgan t 910

Russians

Requiem for a Lost Empire - Andrei Makine c 1151

Sailing

Moontide - Erin Patrick h 681
The Nautical Chart - Arturo Perez-Reverte m 171

Saints

The Gaius Diary - Gene Edwards i 990
Living with Saints - Mary O'Connell c 1175

Salvage

The Nautical Chart - Arturo Perez-Reverte c 1182

Satire

Basket Case - Carl Hiaasen m 115
The Devil's Larder - Jim Crace c 1095
Jewelry Talks - Richard Klein c 1142
Samuel Johnson Is Indignant - Lydia Davis c 1099
A Sensitive Kind of Murder - Jacqueline Girdner m 80

Scandal

Emerald Windows - Terri Blackstock i 971
Fallen - Celeste Bradley r 241
French Leave - Sheri Cobb South r 404
The Irredeemable Miss Renfield - Regina Scott r 393
Rocky and the Senator's Daughter - Dixie Browning r 246
Very Truly Yours - Julie Beard r 229

Schools

The Killing Bee - Matt Witten m 218
Schooling - Heather McGowan c 1159

Schools/Boarding Schools

The Lake of Dead Languages - Carol Goodman m 82
O Gentle Death - Janet Neel m 165

Schools/High Schools

Six-Pound Walleye - Elizabeth Gunn m 93

Science Fiction

Futureland - Walter Mosley c 1166

Scientific Experiments

Angelmass - Timothy Zahn s 812
Frankenstein: The Legacy - Christopher Schildt h 691
Gargoyles - Alan Nayes h 677
Gargoyles - Alan Nayes s 783
Martian Knightlife - James P. Hogan s 759

Sea Stories

Act of Mercy - Peter Tremayne t 944
The Blooding of the Guns - Alexander Fullerton t 866
The Captain's Wife - Douglas Kelley t 894
The Devil's Own Luck - David Donachie t 853
The Dying Trade - David Donachie t 854
Jane and the Prisoner of Wool House - Stephanie Barron t 822
The Salt Letters - Christine Balint t 819
Sea of Glory - Ken Wales i 1056
Sea of Glory - Ken Wales t 953

Secrets

Any Way the Wind Blows - E. Lynn Harris c 1122
Awakening Alex - Ruth Langan r 327
Bitten - Kelley Armstrong c 1068
Blood Sinister - Cynthia Harrod-Eagles m 104
The Colorado Bride - Mary Burton r 247
The Deadwood Beetle - Mylene Dressler c 1106
Echoes of Lies - Jo Bannister m 11
End over End - Kate Kennedy c 1139
First Gray, Then White, Then Blue - Margriet de Moor c 1165
Flights of Love - Bernhard Schlink c 1192
Kiss It Goodbye - John Wessel m 213
Leap of Faith - Danielle Steel c 1203
Listen to the Shadows - Danuta Reah m 179
Middle Age - Joyce Carol Oates c 1174
My Heart Stood Still - Lynn Kurland r 323
No Way Out - Andrea Kane r 312
Past Tense - William G. Tapply m 206
The Promise - May McGoldrick r 352
The Secret Admirer - Annette Mahon r 343
Secrets of the Heart - Gail Gaymer Martin i 1022
Shades of Justice - Fredrick Huebner m 121
The Shape of Snakes - Minette Walters m 211
The Sleeping Beauty - Jacqueline Navin r 360
The Spanish Bride - Amanda McCabe r 349
Sugarplum Surprises - Elisabeth Fairchild r 275
The Tender Vine - Kristen Heitzmann i 998
To Kiss a Spy - Jane Feather r 276
True Confessions - Rachel Gibson r 292
Very Truly Yours - Julie Beard r 229
The Watermark - Travis Thrasher i 1054
The Widow's Little Secret - Judith Stacy r 409
The World Below - Sue Miller c 1163

Seduction

Insatiable - Julie Elizabeth Leto r 333
The Promise in a Kiss - Stephanie Laurens r 329
A Reckless Encounter - Rosemary Rogers r 385
Seducing Mr. Right - Cherry Adair r 223

Self-Acceptance

Awakening Alex - Ruth Langan r 327
Heartless - Kat Martin r 346
Love to Love You Baby - Kasey Michaels r 354
The Woman for Dusty Conrad - Tori Carrington r 251

Self-Esteem

July Thunder - Rachel Lee r 330
Sweet Nothings - Catherine Anderson r 225

Self-Perception

Samuel Johnson Is Indignant - Lydia Davis *c* 1099

Serial Killers

Angel Face - Suzanne Forster *r* 283
Black House - Stephen King *c* 1140
Blindsighted - Karin Slaughter *m* 197
The Case of the Ripper's Revenge - Sam McCarver *m* 153
Chapel Noir - Carole Nelson Douglas *m* 62
Dancing with the Virgins - Stephen Booth *m* 23
Dark Hollow - John Connolly *m* 42
Dead Sleep - Greg Iles *m* 123
First Lady - Michael Malone *c* 1153
Ghost Killer - Scott Chandler *h* 627
Hope to Die - Lawrence Block *m* 22
Killing the Shadows - Val McDermid *m* 154
Murder on the Trans-Siberian Express - Stuart M. Kaminsky *m* 130
The Surgeon - Tess Gerritsen *m* 78

Sewing

Unraveled Sleeve - Monica Ferris *m* 67

Sexual Abuse

Double Honor - Melissa Horsfall *i* 1002
The Treatment - Mo Hayder *c* 1123
The Webster Chronicle - Daniel Akst *c* 1066

Sexual Assault

Back in Kansas - Debra Salonen *r* 387

Sexual Behavior

Audubon's Watch - John Gregory Brown *c* 1085
Beasts - Joyce Carol Oates *c* 1173
Blood and Gold - Anne Rice *c* 1185
The Earthquake Bird - Susanna Jones *m* 127
Friday Night in Beast House - Richard Laymon *h* 662
Lucky Us - Joan Silber *c* 1198
My Little Blue Dress - Bruno Maddox *c* 1150
Night Players - P.D. Cacek *h* 625
Too Much Temptation - Lori Foster *r* 286

Sexual Harassment

Stormy Weather - Paula L. Woods *m* 220
The Thirty-Third Hour - Mitchell Chefitz *i* 978

Sexuality

The Last Vampire - Whitley Strieber *h* 699
Narcissus in Chains - Laurell K. Hamilton *h* 645
Still She Haunts Me - Katie Roiphe *t* 927
Teeth - Edo van Belkom *h* 705
Vampire Vow - Michael Schiefelbein *h* 690

Shakers

Dancing Dead - Deborah Woodworth *i* 1062

Sheriffs

A Bend in the Road - Nicholas Sparks *c* 1200
Yonder Stands Your Orphan - Barry Hannah *c* 1121

Ships

The Ironclad Alibi - Michael Kilian *m* 133
Jane and the Prisoner of Wool House - Stephanie Barron *m* 12
Moontide - Erin Patrick *h* 681
Murder on the Minnesota - Conrad Allen *m* 5
The Nautical Chart - Arturo Perez-Reverte *m* 171

Shipwrecks

Valhalla Rising - Clive Cussler *c* 1097
The Yellow Sailor - Steve Weiner *t* 954

Short Stories

4 X 4 - Michael Oliveri *h* 679
Adam and Eve on a Raft - Ron Goulart *m* 85
After the Plague - T. Coraghessan Boyle *c* 1081
The Ash-Tree Press Annual Macabre 2001 - Jack Adrian *h* 615
Assassin Fantastic - Martin H. Greenberg *f* 552
Bad Seed - Harry Shannon *h* 693
Bad Timing and Other Stories - Molly Brown *s* 727
The Best Alternate History Stories of the 20th Century - Harry Turtledove *s* 804
The Best-Known Man in the World & Other Misfits - Daniel Pearlman *s* 786
Black Dust - Graham Joyce *h* 655
The Blue and the Gray Undercover - Ed Gorman *w* 456
Blue Christmas and Other Holiday Homicides - Max Allan Collins *m* 40
A Century of Great Suspense Stories - Jeffery Deaver *m* 57
City of Saints and Madmen - Jeff Vandermeer *f* 607
Cobwebs and Whispers - Scott Thomas *h* 701
Cold Comfort - Nancy Kilpatrick *h* 658
The Collected Stories of Vernor Vinge - Vernor Vinge *s* 807
A Constellation of Cats - Denise Little *f* 574
Creature Fantastic - Denise Little *f* 575
Cursed and Consulted - Rick Cook *f* 537
Dark Shadows on the Moon - John B. Ford *h* 635
Dead on Demand - Elizabeth Engstrom *h* 633
The Devil Is Not Mocked and Other Warnings - Manly Wade Wellman *h* 707
Dial Your Dreams - Robert Weinberg *h* 706
The Distance Travelled - Brett A. Savory *h* 689
Doc Holliday's Gone - Jane Candia Coleman *w* 445
Dogged Persistence - Kevin J. Anderson *s* 715
Dracula in London - P.N. Elrod *h* 631
The Dragons of Magic - J. Robert King *f* 565
The Family Jewels and Other Stories - Dorothy Cannell *m* 31
The Far Side of the Lake - Steve Rasnic Tem *h* 700
Fluid Mosaic - Michael D. Arnzen *h* 616
From Weird and Distant Shores - Caitlin R. Kiernan *h* 656
Futureland - Walter Mosley *s* 779
Futures - Peter Crowther *s* 739
Gambler's Row: A Western Trio - Les Savage Jr. *w* 500
The Gauntlet - Max Brand *w* 430
The Ghost of John Wayne and Other Stories - Ray Gonzalez *w* 455
A Ghostly Crew - Roger Johnson *h* 652
Halloween Candy - Thomas M. Sipos *h* 696
Hammett: Crime Stories and Other Writings - Dashiell Hammett *m* 99
Her Infinite Variety - Pamela Rafael Berkman *t* 823
Here Comes Civilization - William Tenn *s* 803
Heretics - Greg F. Gifune *h* 639
Hideous Dreams - L.H. Maynard *h* 674
The House of Gold - Max Brand *w* 431
I'll Be Damned - Shane Ryan Staley *h* 698
Impact Parameter and Other Quantum Realities - Geoffrey A. Landis *s* 766
Kisses of Death - Max Allan Collins *m* 41
Kisses of Death - Max Allan Collins *t* 841
Knuckles and Tales - Nancy Collins *h* 629
The Legend of Sotoju Mountain - Will Henry *w* 461
Legends of the Night - Stephen Mark Rainey *h* 683
Long Journey to Deep Canon - T.T. Flynn *w* 452
The Mammoth Book of Best New Horror 12 - Stephen Jones *h* 653
The Mammoth Book of More Historical Whodunnits - Mike Ashley *m* 8
Man Without a Past - T.V. Olsen *w* 486
The Marble Quilt - David Leavitt *c* 1145
More Oddments - Bill Pronzini *m* 175
Mrs. Amworth - E.F. Benson *h* 622
The Museum of Horrors - Dennis Etchison *h* 634
The Mutant Files - Martin H. Greenberg *s* 753
The Night People and Other Stories - Edward D. Hoch *m* 117
The Nighttime Is the Right Time - Bill Crider *m* 48
No Place for a Lady - Vicki Piekarski *w* 496
Not the Only Planet - Damien Broderick *s* 726
The Nudger Dilemmas - John Lutz *m* 147
The Old Spies Club and Other Intrigues of Rand - Edward D. Hoch *m* 118
Past Imperfect - Martin H. Greenberg *s* 754
Pink Marble and Never Say Die - Dawn Dunn *h* 630
A Pleasing Terror - M.R. James *h* 650
The Puppet Master - John Dalmas *s* 741
Rainbow Rider: A Western Trio - Wayne D. Overholser *w* 491
The Reluctant Detective and Other Stories - Michael Z. Lewin *m* 142
The Return of the Soul and Other Stories - Robert Hichens *h* 647
The Scarecrow and Other Stories - G. Ranger Wormser *h* 711
The Search for Magic - Margaret Weis *f* 612
The Sedgemoor Strangler and Other Stories of Crime - Peter Lovesey *m* 146
The Shadow in Renegade Basin - Les Savage Jr. *w* 501
The Shadow on the Blind - Louisa Baldwin *h* 618
Similar Monsters - Steve Savile *h* 688
Single White Vampire Seeks Same - Martin H. Greenberg *h* 643
Skin Folk - Nalo Hopkinson *s* 760
Stage Trails West - Frank Bonham *w* 427
Stolen Gold - Max Brand *w* 433
Strange Days - Gardner Dozois *s* 748
Strange Trades - Paul Di Filippo *s* 745
Tales of Devilry and Doom - John B. Ford *h* 636
The Thing on the Doorstep and Other Weird Stories - H.P. Lovecraft *h* 671
Together We Kill - Mickey Spillane *m* 201
Toxicology - Steve Aylett *s* 720
Triage - Matt Johnson *h* 651
Urban Gothic - David J. Howe *h* 648
Vacation Stories - Santiago Ramon y Cajal *s* 787
Voices in the Hill: Western Stories - Steve Frazee *w* 453
William F. Nolan's Dark Universe - William F. Nolan *h* 678
A Woman's Liberation - Connie Willis *s* 811
Wondrous Strange - Robin Spriggs *h* 697
The World's Finest Mystery & Crime Stories: Second Annual Collection - Ed Gorman *m* 84
Wrong Things - Poppy Z. Brite *h* 624

Sibling Rivalry

Columbus Slaughters Braves - Mark Friedman *c* 1114

Singing

Alicia's Song - Susan Plunkett *r* 371
The Doctor's Miracle - Anna Schmidt *i* 1046
Judging Sara - Cynthia Rutledge *i* 1044

Single Parent Families

Christmas Vows: $5.00 Extra - Lori Copeland *i* 983
The Colorado Bride - Mary Burton *r* 247
Dear Cupid - Julie Ortolon *r* 363
A Family for Jana - Eileen Berger *i* 968
Fatal Legacy - Elizabeth Corley *m* 43
Heaven Sent - Rachel Wilson *r* 421
Love One Another - Valerie Hansen *i* 995
The Nanny - Judith Stacy *r* 408
Peace Like a River - Leif Enger *c* 1109

Sisters

Blessing in Disguise - Jenna Mindel *r* 356
Cinderella After Midnight - Lilian Darcy *r* 268
Coldwater - Mardi McConnochie *t* 904
Coldwater - Mardi McConnochie *c* 1156
Lydia Cassatt Reading the Morning Paper - Harriet Scott Chessman *t* 837
Murder Boogies with Elvis - Anne George *m* 77
The Savage Girl - Alex Shakar *c* 1196
The Sea Sprite - Ruth Langan *r* 328
Shades of Murder - Ann Granger *m* 87
Tall, Dead, and Handsome - Annie Griffin *m* 91
The Virtuous Cyprian - Nicola Cornick *r* 260
Whispers of Goodbye - Karen White *r* 418

Slavery

Bloodlines - Fred D'Aguiar *t* 846
Call Each River Jordan - Owen Parry *m* 169
Call Each River Jordan - Owen Parry *t* 914
The Infidel - Joe Musser *i* 1031
The Night the Stars Fell - Christina Kingston *r* 317
The Promise - May McGoldrick *r* 352
Red Beans and Vice - Lou Jane Temple *m* 207
We Look Like Men of War - William R. Forstchen *t* 864
The Wind Done Gone - Alice Randall *t* 918
The Wolf Pit - Marly Youmans *t* 964

Small Town Life

Agatha Raisin and the Love from Hell - M.C. Beaton *m* 14
All Signs Point to Murder - Kat Goldring *m* 81
The Alpine Nemesis - Mary Daheim *m* 51
The Association - Bentley Little *h* 668
Aunt Dimity: Detective - Nancy Atherton *m* 9
Bag Limit - Steven F. Havill *m* 108
Biggie and the Quincy Ghost - Nancy Bell *m* 15
Blindsighted - Karin Slaughter *m* 197
Cat Laughing Last - Shirley Rousseau Murphy *m* 162
The Cat Who Went Up the Creek - Lilian Jackson Braun *m* 26
Catskill - John R. Hayes *m* 110
The Cold Blue Blood - David Handler *m* 100
A Cold Christmas - Charlene Weir *m* 212
Cold Hunter's Moon - K.C. Greenlief *m* 90
Creeping Venom - Sheila Pim *m* 173
Darkling I Listen - Katherine Sutcliffe *r* 412
Dead Love - Donald Beman *h* 620
Death Is in the Air - Kate Kingsbury *m* 136
Death of the Last Villista - Allana Martin *m* 149
Death on the Downs - Simon Brett *m* 27
Do You Hear What I Hear? - Holly Jacobs *r* 306
The Evidence Against Her - Robb Forman Dew *t* 850
A Fine and Private Place - Freda Davies *m* 55
The Folks - Ray Garton *h* 638
Glare Ice - Mary Logue *m* 145
In This Mountain - Jan Karon *i* 1007
July Thunder - Rachel Lee *r* 330
Keepers - Janet LaPierre *m* 139
Lake Wobegon Summer 1956 - Garrison Keillor *c* 1136
Maggody and the Moonbeams - Joan Hess *m* 114
The Message of the Mute Dog - Charlotte Murray Russell *m* 191
A Morning in Eden - Anna Gilbert *t* 872
Murder in the Forecast - Valerie Wolzien *m* 219
Next Stop, Paradise - Sue Civil-Brown *r* 256
A Place Called Wiregrass - Michael Morris *i* 1029
Puzzled to Death - Parnell Hall *m* 96
Robak in Black - Joe L. Hensley *m* 113
A Romantic Way to Die - Bill Crider *m* 49
Save the Last Dance for Me - Ed Gorman *m* 83
The Secret - Kat Martin *r* 347
The Secret Admirer - Annette Mahon *r* 343
Shades of Murder - Ann Granger *m* 87
Six-Pound Walleye - Elizabeth Gunn *m* 93
Someone to Watch over Me - Jill Churchill *m* 33
Strawman's Hammock - Darryl Wimberley *m* 216
Sweet Success - Susan Mallery *r* 344
Tall, Dark, and Difficult - Patricia Coughlin *r* 261
Tall, Dead, and Handsome - Annie Griffin *m* 91
True Confessions - Rachel Gibson *r* 292
Unraveled Sleeve - Monica Ferris *m* 67
The Water and the Blood - Nancy E. Turner *t* 947
Wedding Day Murder - Leslie Meier *m* 157
Who Killed the Curate? - Joan Coggin *m* 36
Wreck the Halls - Sarah Graves *m* 89
Year of Wonders - Geraldine Brooks *t* 832
Yonder Stands Your Orphan - Barry Hannah *c* 1121
Zigzagging Down a Wild Trail - Bobbie Ann Mason *c* 1155

Smuggling

The Chinese Fire Drill - Les Roberts *m* 185
Desire - Nicole Jordan *r* 309
The Good German - Joseph Kanon *m* 131
The Night the Stars Fell - Christina Kingston *r* 317
A Place of Darkness - Lauren Haney *m* 101
Smuggler's Moon - Bruce Alexander *t* 815
Sparrowhawk—Jack Frake - Edward Cline *t* 840
The Wedding Charm - Lynn Collum *r* 258

Social Classes

Balzac and the Little Chinese Seamstress - Sijie Dai *c* 1098
The Bones of the Buried - David Roberts *m* 183
The Christmas Wish - Debbie Raleigh *r* 377
Cinderella After Midnight - Lilian Darcy *r* 268
Comfort and Joy - Sandra Madden *r* 342
Death Is in the Air - Kate Kingsbury *m* 136
The Elusive Voice - Mary Jo Adamson *m* 2
Fairness - Ferdinand Mount *c* 1167
Fallen - Celeste Bradley *r* 241
Falling Angels - Tracy Chevalier *c* 1090
Falling Angels - Tracy Chevalier *t* 838
Fortune's Lady - Evelyn Richardson *r* 379
Heartless - Kat Martin *r* 346
One Good Turn - Carla Kelly *r* 315
The Pickup - Nadine Gordimer *c* 1116
The Thief-Taker - T.F. Banks *m* 10
The Very Daring Duchess - Miranda Jarrett *r* 308

Social Conditions

Collected Stories - Saul Bellow *c* 1072
Fairness - Ferdinand Mount *c* 1167
His Lady Midnight - Jo Ann Ferguson *r* 279
Island of Tears - Troy Soos *m* 200
The Last Summer of Reason - Tahar Djaout *c* 1105
Murphy's Law - Rhys Bowen *m* 24
The Pickup - Nadine Gordimer *c* 1116
The Practical Heart - Allan Gurganus *c* 1120
The Proper Wife - Julia Justiss *r* 311
The Rose in the Wheel - S.K. Rizzolo *m* 182
The Stories of Paul Bowles - Paul Bowles *c* 1080
The Trouble with Harriet - Wilma Counts *r* 262

Social Issues

Closing Time - Jim Fusilli *m* 74
Listen to the Shadows - Danuta Reah *m* 179
Red House - K.J.A. Wishnia *m* 217
Sherlock Holmes and the Secret Alliance - Larry Millett *m* 158
Taylor's Temptation - Suzanne Brockmann *r* 242
Whispers in the Dark - Eleanor Taylor Bland *m* 21

Space and Time

Appleseed - John Clute *s* 736
The Dreamthief's Daughter - Michael Moorcock *f* 582
The Shadow out of Time - H.P. Lovecraft *h* 670

Space Colonies

Divine Intervention - Ken Wharton *s* 810
Dreamer - Steven Harper *s* 755
Empire & Ecolitan - L.E. Modesitt Jr. *s* 777
Heresy - Anselm Audley *s* 718
Homefall - Chris Bunch *s* 729
Icebones - Stephen Baxter *s* 723
In the Company of Others - Julie E. Czerneda *s* 740
Look to Windward - Iain Banks *s* 721
March to the Sea - David Weber *s* 809
The Merchants of Souls - John Barnes *s* 722
Spherical Harmonic - Catherine Asaro *s* 716

Space Exploration

Second Contact - J.D. Austin *s* 719

Space Travel

Angelmass - Timothy Zahn *s* 812
Brother John - Rutledge Etheridge *s* 750
Entities - Eric Frank Russell *s* 794
Miles, Mystery & Mayhem - Lois McMaster Bujold *s* 728
Out There - Gerald Rose *s* 793
Second Chances - Susan Shwartz *s* 796
Star Soldiers - Andre Norton *s* 784
Starhawk - Mack Maloney *s* 769
Tales of the Velvet Comet - Mike Resnick *s* 788
The Wanderer - Fritz Leiber *s* 767

Spies

The Company of Strangers - Robert Wilson *t* 960
Heart of Night - Taylor Chase *r* 254
To Kiss a Spy - Jane Feather *r* 276
To Tame a Duke - Patricia Grasso *r* 293
The Very Comely Countess - Miranda Jarrett *r* 307

Spiritualism

The Elusive Voice - Mary Jo Adamson *m* 2
Eva Moves the Furniture - Margot Livesey *c* 1148

Spirituality

How to Be Good - Nick Hornby *c* 1126

Sports

Murder at the Panionic Games - Michael B. Edwards *t* 859
TV - Brian Brown *c* 1084

Sports/Baseball

Columbus Slaughters Braves - Mark Friedman *c* 1114
Dead Ball - R.D. Rosen *m* 188
Love to Love You Baby - Kasey Michaels *r* 354

Sports/Boxing

The Distance - Eddie Muller *m* 161

Sports/Football

Better than Sex - Susan Holtzer *m* 120
Hometown Legend - Jerry B. Jenkins *i* 1005

Sports/Golf

A Diamond in the Rough - Andrea Pickens *r* 370
The Money-Whipped Steer-Job Three-Jack Give-Up Artist - Dan Jenkins *c* 1132

Sports/Rock Climbing

Midlife Can Be Murder - Jane Isenberg *m* 124

Sports/Skiing

Tucker Peak - Archer Mayor *m* 151

Stalking

In a Strange City - Laura Lippman *m* 143
Judging Sara - Cynthia Rutledge *i* 1044
A Love for Safekeeping - Gail Gaymer Martin *i* 1021
Murder by Manicure - Nancy J. Cohen *m* 38
Past Tense - William G. Tapply *m* 206
Shakespeare's Counselor - Charlaine Harris *m* 102

Stealing

The Christmas Wish - Debbie Raleigh *r* 377

Stepfathers

One Door Away from Heaven - Dean R. Koontz *h* 661

Stores, Retail

Death by Darjeeling - Laura Childs *m* 32

Storytelling

Call Down the Stars - Sue Harrison *t* 879

Students, Foreign

East of the Sun, West of the Moon - Carole Bellacera *r* 231

Suicide

For Rouenna - Sigrid Nunez *c* 1172
The Lake of Dead Languages - Carol Goodman *m* 82

Supernatural

4 X 4 - Michael Oliveri *h* 679
Affinity - J.N. Williamson *h* 709
The Ancient Track - H.P. Lovecraft *h* 669
. . .And the Angel with Television Eyes - John Shirley *h* 694
The Ash-Tree Press Annual Macabre 2001 - Jack Adrian *h* 615
Bad Seed - Harry Shannon *h* 693
Black Dust - Graham Joyce *h* 655
Blood Games - Lee Killough *h* 657
Bonnie Winter - Graham Masterton *h* 672
Candle Bay - Tamara Thorne *h* 703
City Infernal - Edward Lee *h* 667
Cobwebs and Whispers - Scott Thomas *h* 701
Cold Comfort - Nancy Kilpatrick *h* 658
Crimson Kiss - Trisha Baker *h* 617
Dark Sanctuary - H.B. Gregory *h* 644
Dark Shadows on the Moon - John B. Ford *h* 635
Dead Love - Donald Beman *h* 620
Dead on Demand - Elizabeth Engstrom *h* 633
The Devil Is Not Mocked and Other Warnings - Manly Wade Wellman *h* 707
Dial Your Dreams - Robert Weinberg *h* 706
The Distance Travelled - Brett A. Savory *h* 689
Doomed to Repeat It - d.g.k. goldberg *h* 641
The Far Side of the Lake - Steve Rasnic Tem *h* 700
Frankenstein: The Legacy - Christopher Schildt *h* 691
From the Dust Returned - Ray Bradbury *h* 623
From the Dust Returned - Ray Bradbury *c* 1082
From Weird and Distant Shores - Caitlin R. Kiernan *h* 656
Ghost Killer - Scott Chandler *h* 627
A Ghostly Crew - Roger Johnson *h* 652
Halloween Candy - Thomas M. Sipos *h* 696
Heretics - Greg F. Gifune *h* 639
Hideous Dreams - L.H. Maynard *h* 674
House of Pain - Sephera Giron *h* 640
I'll Be Damned - Shane Ryan Staley *h* 698
The Last Vampire - T.M. Wright *h* 712
The Lecturer's Tale - James Hynes *h* 649
Legends of the Night - Stephen Mark Rainey *h* 683
The London Vampire Panic - Michael Romkey *h* 686
A Lower Deep - Tom Piccirilli *h* 682
The Mammoth Book of Best New Horror 12 - Stephen Jones *h* 653
The Mammoth Book of Vampire Stories by Women - Stephen Jones *h* 654
Moontide - Erin Patrick *h* 681
Mrs. Amworth - E.F. Benson *h* 622
The Museum of Horrors - Dennis Etchison *h* 634
Night of Dracula - Christopher Schildt *h* 692
Night Players - P.D. Cacek *h* 625
The Prodigy - Alton Gansky *h* 637
Quincey Morris, Vampire - P.N. Elrod *h* 632
Riverwatch - Joseph M. Nassise *h* 676
The Scarecrow and Other Stories - G. Ranger Wormser *h* 711
Single White Vampire Seeks Same - Martin H. Greenberg *h* 643
Straight on 'Til Morning - Christopher Golden *h* 642
Tales of Devilry and Doom - John B. Ford *h* 636
Teeth - Edo van Belkom *h* 705
The Thing on the Doorstep and Other Weird Stories - H.P. Lovecraft *h* 671
Tragic Casements - Oliver Onions *h* 680
Trick or Treat - Richard Chizmar *h* 628
The White Room - A.J. Matthews *h* 673
William F. Nolan's Dark Universe - William F. Nolan *h* 678
Wondrous Strange - Robin Spriggs *h* 697
Wrong Things - Poppy Z. Brite *h* 624

Superstition

The Husband Test - Betina Krahn *r* 321

Surprises

Marry Me, Maddie? - Rita Herron *r* 299

Survival

The Nature of Balance - Tim Lebbon *h* 666
Nearly People - Conrad Williams *h* 708

Suspense

The Association - Bentley Little *h* 668
Bonnie Winter - Graham Masterton *h* 672
Broken Honor - Patricia Potter *r* 373
Critical Space - Greg Rucka *m* 190
The Dark Clue - James Wilson *t* 959
Darkling I Listen - Katherine Sutcliffe *r* 412
Face - Tim Lebbon *h* 665
Fluid Mosaic - Michael D. Arnzen *h* 616
The Gingerbread Man - Maggie Shayne *r* 395
The Good German - Joseph Kanon *t* 892
Heaven and Earth - Nora Roberts *r* 383
In Too Deep - Janelle Taylor *r* 413
Knuckles and Tales - Nancy Collins *h* 629
The Manhattan Hunt Club - John Saul *h* 687
The Nautical Chart - Arturo Perez-Reverte *c* 1182
Night in the Lonesome October - Richard Laymon *h* 664
The Perfect Princess - Elizabeth Thornton *r* 416
The Phoenix - Henning Boetius *t* 828
Similar Monsters - Steve Savile *h* 688
To Trust a Stranger - Karen Robards *r* 381
The Treatment - Mo Hayder *c* 1123
Triage - Matt Johnson *h* 651
Valhalla Rising - Clive Cussler *c* 1097
The Very Gothic Christmas - Christine Feehan *r* 277
The Widow - Anne Stuart *r* 411

Teacher-Student Relationships

Beasts - Joyce Carol Oates *c* 1173
Fighting Gravity - Peggy Rambach *c* 1184
Schooling - Heather McGowan *c* 1159
Sunrise on Stradbury Square - Doris Elaine Fell *i* 992

Teachers

A Bend in the Road - Nicholas Sparks *c* 1200
Fury - Salman Rushdie *c* 1190
A Game of Colors - John Urbancik *h* 704
Irregardless of Murder - Ellen Edwards Kennedy *i* 1008
The Lecturer's Tale - James Hynes *h* 649

Technology

The Plutonium Blonde - John Zakour *s* 813
Tower of Glass - Robert Silverberg *s* 797

Teen Relationships

Affinity - J.N. Williamson *h* 709
Friday Night in Beast House - Richard Laymon *h* 662
The Lake of Dead Languages - Carol Goodman *m* 82
O Gentle Death - Janet Neel *m* 165
Straight on 'Til Morning - Christopher Golden *h* 642

Television

The Fourth Hand - John Irving c 1130

Television Programs

Marry Me, Maddie? - Rita Herron r 299
TV - Brian Brown c 1084

Terror

The Appointment - Herta Muller c 1168
Year of Wonders - Geraldine Brooks c 1083

Terrorism

All the Dead Were Strangers - Ethan Black c 1076
All the Dead Were Strangers - Ethan Black m 20
Born Brave - Ruth Wind r 422

Theater

Desert Autumn - Michael Craft m 45
The Devil's Apprentice - Edward Marston m 148
The Heavenly Fugitive - Gilbert Morris i 1028
Midsummer Murder - Shelley Freydont m 71
Season of Storms - Susanna Kearsley r 314
The Slaying of the Shrew - Simon Hawke m 109
The Slaying of the Shrew - Simon Hawke t 880

Time Travel

Alicia's Song - Susan Plunkett r 371
Bethany's Song - Susan Plunkett r 372
ChronoSpace - Allen Steele s 802
Destiny - Elizabeth Haydon f 554
The Enchantment - Pam Binder r 237
The Fiery Cross - Diana Gabaldon r 288
The Fiery Cross - Diana Gabaldon t 868
Kiss of the Highlander - Karen Marie Moning r 358
Knight Errant - R. Garcia y Robertson f 546
Knight Errant - R. Garcia y Robertson t 869
Past Imperfect - Martin H. Greenberg s 754

Traffic Accidents

A Bend in the Road - Nicholas Sparks c 1200
Fighting Gravity - Peggy Rambach c 1184

Trains

Murder on the Trans-Siberian Express - Stuart M. Kaminsky m 130

Transplants

The Fourth Hand - John Irving c 1130

Travel

Followin' a Dream - Eboni Snoe r 403
Sherlock Holmes and the Giant Rat of Sumatra - Alan Vanneman m 210

Treasure

Broken Honor - Patricia Potter r 373
My Heart Stood Still - Lynn Kurland r 323
The Nautical Chart - Arturo Perez-Reverte m 171
The Nautical Chart - Arturo Perez-Reverte c 1182
The Secret Clan: Abducted Heiress - Amanda Scott r 390
Tempt Me Twice - Barbara Dawson Smith r 400

Trials

End over End - Kate Kennedy c 1139
Fred & Edie - Jill Dawson t 848
The Jazz Bird - Craig Holden m 119
The Jazz Bird - Craig Holden t 885
Will's War - Janice Woods Windle t 961

Trust

Beloved Protector - Linda O'Brien r 361
A Bungalow for Two - Carole Gift Page i 1035
Dear Cupid - Julie Ortolon r 363
The Great Baby Caper - Eugenia Riley r 380
My Lord Savage - Elizabeth Lane r 326
Once an Outlaw - Jill Gregory r 294

Twins

Aunt Dimity: Detective - Nancy Atherton m 9
Dead Sleep - Greg Iles m 123
The Virtuous Cyprian - Nicola Cornick r 260

UFOs

Dreamcatcher - Stephen King h 660
Fireworks - James A. Moore h 675
One Door Away from Heaven - Dean R. Koontz h 661

Underground Resistance Movements

In the Shape of a Boar - Lawrence Norfolk t 913
Jackdaws - Ken Follett t 863

Underwater Exploration

Valhalla Rising - Clive Cussler c 1097

Unemployment

The Faded Flower - Paul McCusker i 1024

Universities and Colleges

Emerald Aisle - Ralph McInerny m 156
The Problem of the Surly Servant - Roberta Rogow t 926
Skeleton at the Feast - Patricia Hall m 97

Unmarried Mothers

Highwire Moon - Susan Straight c 1205

Utopia/Dystopia

Scorch - A.D. Nauman s 782

Vacations

Better than Sex - Susan Holtzer m 120
Don't Cry for Me, Hot Pastrami - Sharon Kahn m 129
Steppin' on a Rainbow - Kinky Friedman m 72
To Perish in Penzance - Jeanne M. Dams m 54

Vampires

Blood and Gold - Anne Rice c 1185
Blood and Gold - Anne Rice t 922
Blood and Gold - Anne Rice h 685
Blood Games - Lee Killough h 657
Candle Bay - Tamara Thorne h 703
Crimson Kiss - Trisha Baker h 617
Darkness - Sam Siciliano h 695
Dracula in London - P.N. Elrod h 631
A Feast in Exile - Chelsea Quinn Yarbro h 713
A Feast in Exile - Chelsea Quinn Yarbro t 963
From the Dust Returned - Ray Bradbury c 1082
His Father's Son - Nigel Bennett h 621
The Last Vampire - Whitley Strieber h 699
The Last Vampire - T.M. Wright h 712
The London Vampire Panic - Michael Romkey h 686
The Mammoth Book of Vampire Stories by Women - Stephen Jones h 654
Narcissus in Chains - Laurell K. Hamilton h 645
Night Blood - James M. Thompson h 702
Night of Dracula - Christopher Schildt h 692
Night Players - P.D. Cacek h 625
Quincey Morris, Vampire - P.N. Elrod h 632
Vampire Vow - Michael Schiefelbein h 690

Veterans

Miss Truelove Beckons - Donna Simpson r 397

Victorian Period

Chapel Noir - Carole Nelson Douglas m 62
Darkness - Sam Siciliano h 695
Deadly Illumination - Serena Stier m 203
Goodnight, Sweet Prince - David Dickinson m 58
The London Vampire Panic - Michael Romkey h 686
The Problem of the Surly Servant - Roberta Rogow m 187
Sherlock Holmes and the Giant Rat of Sumatra - Alan Vanneman m 210
Sherlock Holmes and the Secret Alliance - Larry Millett m 158

Vietnam War

Bitterroot - James Lee Burke c 1088
Bombingham - Anthony Grooms c 1119
For Rouenna - Sigrid Nunez c 1172
Written on Her Heart - Alan Maki i 1019

Vikings

Believe in Me - Josie Litton r 336
Come Back to Me - Josie Litton r 337
Dream of Me - Josie Litton r 338
Mother of Kings - Poul Anderson t 818

Violence

Bitterroot - James Lee Burke c 1088
Dark Dreams - Cory Daniells r 267
The Edge of Town - Dorothy Garlock r 290
Going Overboard - Christina Skye r 399
Pale Horse Coming - Stephen Hunter c 1127
Sentimental, Heartbroken Rednecks - Greg Bottoms c 1079

Virtual Reality

Dervish Is Digital - Pat Cadigan s 731

Voodoo

The Masks of Auntie Laveau - Robert J. Randisi m 177
The Red of His Shadow - Mayra Montero c 1164

Voyages and Travels

Act of Mercy - Peter Tremayne m 209
Mr. Montgomery's Quest - Martha Kirkland r 318
Murder on the Minnesota - Conrad Allen m 5

War

The Archer's Tale - Bernard Cornwell t 843
The Blooding of the Guns - Alexander Fullerton t 866
The Clouds Above - Andrew Greig t 876
The Company of Strangers - Robert Wilson t 960
Ester's Child - Jean P. Sasson t 930
In the Shape of a Boar - Lawrence Norfolk t 913
Jackdaws - Ken Follett t 863
The Jerusalem Scrolls - Bodie Thoene t 942
The Officers' Ward - Marc Dugain t 857
One Good Turn - Carla Kelly r 315
Requiem for a Lost Empire - Andrei Makine c 1151
Sea of Glory - Ken Wales t 953
Sentimental Journey - Jill Barnett r 228
A Soldier's Duty - Thomas E. Ricks c 1186
Straight on 'Til Morning - Christopher Golden h 642
Under the Eagle - Simon Scarrow t 931
The Water and the Blood - Nancy E. Turner t 947
The Wolf Pit - Marly Youmans t 964
The Yellow Sailor - Steve Weiner t 954

War of 1812

To Tame a Duke - Patricia Grasso r 293

Wealth

Fury - Salman Rushdie c 1190

Weather

When Love Came to Town - Lenora Worth i 1063

Weddings

Emerald Aisle - Ralph McInerny m 156
Murder Boogies with Elvis - Anne George m 77
Once Bitten - Laurien Berenson m 17
The Slaying of the Shrew - Simon Hawke m 109
Veiled Threats - Deborah Donnelly m 60
The Wedding Charm - Lynn Collum r 258
Wedding Day Murder - Leslie Meier m 157
The Wedding Party - Robyn Carr r 250

Weight Control

Lilies That Fester - Janis Harrison m 103
Murder by Manicure - Nancy J. Cohen m 38

Werewolves

Bitten - Kelley Armstrong c 1068
Blood and Gold - Anne Rice c 1185
Narcissus in Chains - Laurell K. Hamilton h 645
Secret of the Wolf - Susan Krinard r 322
The Wolf Hunt - Gillian Bradshaw t 831

Wicca

All Signs Point to Murder - Kat Goldring m 81
Heaven and Earth - Nora Roberts r 383

Widows/Widowers

Almost - Elizabeth Benedict c 1073
Aria - Susan Segal c 1194
Looking for Laura - Judith Arnold r 226
Walker's Widow - Heidi Betts r 234
The Warrior's Damsel - Denise Hampton r 295
What Once We Loved - Jane Kirkpatrick i 1011
The Widow - Anne Stuart r 411
The Woman Next Door - Barbara Delinsky c 1101

Wilderness

Cold - John Smolens c 1199
Downriver - Richard S. Wheeler t 957
The Ice Child - Elizabeth McGregor t 905

Wildlife Conservation

Sketches with Wolves - Jacqueline Fiedler m 68

Winter

Cold Hunter's Moon - K.C. Greenlief m 90
Glare Ice - Mary Logue m 145

Wishes

I Dream of You - Judi McCoy r 350

Witches and Witchcraft

Bell, Cook, and Candle - Joanne Pence m 170
Dance upon the Air - Nora Roberts r 382
The Devil's Apprentice - Edward Marston m 148
A Game of Colors - John Urbancik h 704
Heaven and Earth - Nora Roberts r 383
Knight Errant - R. Garcia y Robertson t 869
The Third Witch - Rebecca Reisert t 921

Women

All Families Are Psychotic - Douglas Coupland c 1094
Beasts - Joyce Carol Oates c 1173
The Captain's Wife - Douglas Kelley t 894
First Gray, Then White, Then Blue - Margriet de Moor c 1165
The Flight of the Maidens - Jane Gardam t 870
Halide's Gift - Frances Kazan t 893
Her Infinite Variety - Pamela Rafael Berkman t 823
Hurricane Season - Karen Bjorneby c 1075
In the Forest of Harm - Sallie Bissell c 1074
Jackdaws - Ken Follett t 863
Light Coming Back - Ann Wadsworth c 1213
Living with Saints - Mary O'Connell c 1175
Mirabilis - Susann Cokal c 1091
The Passion of Artemisia - Susan Vreeland t 951
Personal Velocity - Rebecca Miller c 1162
Sacred Ground - Barbara Wood t 962
Shock - Robin Cook c 1093
The Southern Woman - Elizabeth Spencer c 1201
Super-Cannes - J.G. Ballard c 1070
Teeth - Edo van Belkom h 705
The Unknown Errors of Our Lives - Chitra Banerjee Divakaruni c 1104
What You Owe Me - Bebe Moore Campbell c 1089
Why Did I Ever? - Mary Robison c 1188
The Wig My Father Wore - Anne Enright c 1111
A Woman's Liberation - Connie Willis s 811
Zigzagging Down a Wild Trail - Bobbie Ann Mason c 1155

Women's Rights

Deadly Illumination - Serena Stier m 203
Suddenly You - Lisa Kleypas r 319

World War I

The Girl from the Golden Horn - Kurban Said c 1191
The Officers' Ward - Marc Dugain t 857
Watchers of Time - Charles Todd t 943
Watchers of Time - Charles Todd m 208

World War II

The Black Eye - Constance Little m 144
The Blue Last - Martha Grimes m 92
The Company of Strangers - Robert Wilson m 215
Death Is in the Air - Kate Kingsbury m 136
A Fine and Private Place - Freda Davies m 55
The Flight of the Maidens - Jane Gardam t 870
Friday's Child - Linda Chaikin i 977
The Good German - Joseph Kanon m 131
Kaleidoscope - J. Robert Janes t 888
Kaleidoscope - J. Robert Janes m 126
Lazarus, Arise - Nicholas Kilmer m 134
The Magic of Ordinary Days - Ann Howard Creel t 845
The Message of the Mute Dog - Charlotte Murray Russell m 191
My Best Friend - Laura Wilson m 214
Officer of the Court - Bill Mesce Jr. t 906
The Savages in Love and War - Fred Mustard Stewart t 937
Sea of Glory - Ken Wales i 1056
Sentimental Journey - Jill Barnett t 821
A Sunset Touch - Marjorie Eccles m 64
Written on the Wind - Judith Pella i 1040

Writing

Dialogues of the Dead or Paronomania! - Reginald Hill m 116
A Dream to Follow - Lauraine Snelling i 1050
Everything You Need - A.L. Kennedy c 1138
The Rag & Bone Shop - Jeff Rackham t 917
This Heart of Mine - Susan Elizabeth Phillips r 369
True Confessions - Rachel Gibson r 292

Character Name Index

This index alphabetically lists the major characters in each featured title. Each character name is followed by a description of the character. Citations also provide titles of the books featuring the character, listed alphabetically if there is more than one title; author names and genre codes. The genre codes are as follows: *c* Popular Fiction, *f* Fantasy, *h* Horror, *i* Inspirational, *m* Mystery, *r* Romance, *s* Science Fiction, *t* Historical, and *w* Western. Numbers refer to the entries that feature each title.

A

Aahz (Demon)
Myth-ion Improbable - Robert Lynn Asprin *f* 521

Aari (Prisoner)
Acorna's Search - Anne McCaffrey *s* 772

Abigail (Housewife)
Debt of Bones - Terry Goodkind *f* 549

Abraham, Adelaide "Addy" (Museum Curator)
All the Finest Girls - Alexandra Styron *c* 1206

Abraham, Barbara (Actress; Parent)
All the Finest Girls - Alexandra Styron *c* 1206

Achmed (Criminal)
Destiny - Elizabeth Haydon *f* 554

Ackroyd, Laura (Journalist)
Skeleton at the Feast - Patricia Hall *m* 97

Acorna (Telepath)
Acorna's Search - Anne McCaffrey *s* 772

Acosta, Manuel (Gunfighter)
Tears of the Heart - Lauran Paine *w* 493

Adams, Chelsea (Psychic)
Eyes of Elisha - Brandilyn Collins *i* 981

Adams, Lena (Detective—Police)
Blindsighted - Karin Slaughter *m* 197

Addington, Alexander "Alex" (Nobleman; Military Personnel)
The Wedding Charm - Lynn Collum *r* 258

Adler, Irene (Detective—Amateur; Singer)
Chapel Noir - Carole Nelson Douglas *m* 62
Chapel Noir - Carole Nelson Douglas *t* 856

Adrian, Jason (Child)
The Magickers - Emily Drake *f* 542

Aelvarim (Mythical Creature)
Eccentric Circles - Rebecca Lickiss *f* 573

Aguilar, Matteo (Rancher)
The Baron War - Jory Sherman *w* 503

Ahern (Mythical Creature)
The Pillars of the World - Anne Bishop *f* 527

Ahrens, Gena (Restaurateur)
Wildflowers - Robin Jones Gunn *i* 993

Aigner, Rafe (Gambler; Publisher)
The Renegades: Rafe - Genell Dellin *r* 270

Ailish (Young Woman)
Swim the Moon - Paul Brandon *f* 529

Ainsley-Hunter, Antonia (Noblewoman)
Critical Space - Greg Rucka *m* 190

Akasha (Vampire)
Blood and Gold - Anne Rice *h* 685

Akhmim (Genetically Altered Being)
Nekropolis - Maureen McHugh *s* 774

Alain (Mythical Creature; Nobleman)
Once upon a Winter's Night - Dennis L. McKiernan *f* 579

Alan (Amnesiac; Crime Suspect)
The Art of Dying - Diana Killian *i* 1009

Albert (Scientist)
The Monsters of Morley Manor - Bruce Coville *f* 538

Albert Victor (Royalty; Historical Figure)
Goodnight, Sweet Prince - David Dickinson *t* 851

Albu (Police Officer)
The Appointment - Herta Muller *c* 1168

Alcuin (Vampire)
Crimson Kiss - Trisha Baker *h* 617

Alder (Sorcerer)
The Other Wind - Ursula K. Le Guin *f* 571

Aldrich, Alicia (Police Officer)
The King of the Sun - A.A. McFedries *s* 773

Alex (Friend)
In the Forest of Harm - Sallie Bissell *c* 1074

Alexander, Diana (Girlfriend)
Morgette on the Barbary Coast - G.G. Boyer *w* 429

Alexander, Mark (Writer)
Pact of the Fathers - Ramsey Campbell *h* 626

Alexander, Rachel (Detective—Private; Animal Trainer)
The Long Good Boy - Carol Lea Benjamin *m* 16

Alexander, Will (Friend; Employer)
Morgette on the Barbary Coast - G.G. Boyer *w* 429

Alexia (Noblewoman)
Fortress Draconis - Michael A. Stackpole *f* 599

Alfred, Louise "Lou" (Child-Care Giver)
All the Finest Girls - Alexandra Styron *c* 1206

Alice (Office Worker)
He Goes, She Goes - Joanna Torrey *c* 1209

Alison (Teenager)
Friday Night in Beast House - Richard Laymon *h* 662

Alison (Martial Arts Expert; Girlfriend)
Kiss It Goodbye - John Wessel *m* 213

All Mother (Ruler)
Ice - Stephen Bowkett *s* 724

Alya (Magician)
Shadow of the Seer - Michael Scott Rohan *f* 595

Amad (Lover)
Jewelry Talks - Richard Klein *c* 1142

Amai, Emiko (Filmmaker)
The Ash Garden - Dennis Bock *c* 1078

Amalfi, Angelina "Angie" (Businesswoman; Detective—Amateur)
Bell, Cook, and Candle - Joanne Pence *m* 170

Ames, B.Z. (Military Personnel)
A Soldier's Duty - Thomas E. Ricks *c* 1186

Amir (Immigrant; Postal Worker)
Emigre Journeys - Abdullah Hussein *c* 1129

Ana (Young Woman; Lover)
Half a Life - V.S. Naipaul *c* 1170

Anbari, Asiadeh (Young Woman; Noblewoman)
The Girl from the Golden Horn - Kurban Said *c* 1191

Anders, Mariella (Scientist)
The Secret of Life - Paul J. McAuley *s* 771

Anderson, Mark (Military Personnel)
Fireworks - James A. Moore *h* 675

Anderson, Tom (Political Figure; Historical Figure)
Chasing the Devil's Tail - David Fulmer *t* 867
Chasing the Devil's Tail - David Fulmer *m* 73

Andrews, Sarah (Teacher; Divorced Person)
A Bend in the Road - Nicholas Sparks *c* 1200

Andruz, Thelina (Rebel)
Empire & Ecolitan - L.E. Modesitt Jr. *s* 777

Angelosi, Marco (Detective—Police; Fugitive)
The Renegade Steals a Lady - Vickie Taylor *r* 414

Anna (Lover)
Funny Accent - Barbara Shulgasser-Parker *c* 1197

Antoinette (Artist)
. . .And the Angel with Television Eyes - John Shirley *h* 694

Antoun, Demetrius (Doctor)
Ester's Child - Jean P. Sasson *t* 930

ap Gwien, Sulian (Warrior)
The King's Name - Jo Walton *f* 608

Appleton, Susanna (Widow(er); Detective—Amateur)
Face Down Before Rebel Hooves - Kathy Lynn Emerson *t* 861
Face Down Before Rebel Hooves - Kathy Lynn Emerson *m* 65

April (Teenager)
Entertain the End - K.A. Applegate *f* 519
Mystify the Magician - K.A. Applegate *f* 520

Ara (Spaceship Captain)
Dreamer - Steven Harper *s* 755

Argall, Samuel (Historical Figure; Kidnapper)
Argall - William T. Vollmann *t* 950

Argall, Samuel (Leader; Kidnapper)
Argall - William T. Vollmann *c* 1212

Ari (Witch)
The Pillars of the World - Anne Bishop *f* 527

Ariel (Mythical Creature)
Buttercup Baby - Karen Fox *r* 287
Ill Met by Moonlight - Sarah A. Hoyt *f* 559

Arkuden, Amero (Artisan)
Brother of the Dragon - Paul B. Thompson *f* 604

Arlian (Warrior)
The Dragon Society - Lawrence Watt-Evans *f* 610

Armstrong, James (Nobleman; Kidnapper)
To Tame a Duke - Patricia Grasso *r* 293

Arslan (Mythical Creature)
Pride of Kings - Judith Tarr *f* 603
Pride of Kings - Judith Tarr *t* 941

Arthur (Ruler)
The Dragon Queen - Alice Borchardt *f* 528
The Dragon Queen - Alice Borchardt *t* 829
Lancelot Du Lethe - J. Robert King *f* 566

Ash, Taylor (Government Official)
Hazard's Price - Robert S. Stone *f* 601

Ashe, Arel (Saleswoman)
Scorch - A.D. Nauman *s* 782

Ashton, Hope (Wealthy)
Heaven Sent - Jillian Hart *i* 997

Aslow (Political Figure)
Scorch - A.D. Nauman *s* 782

Aspinall, Andrea (Spy; Scientist)
The Company of Strangers - Robert Wilson *m* 215
The Company of Strangers - Robert Wilson *t* 960

Atkinson, Henry (Historical Figure; Military Personnel)
The Good Journey - Micaela Gilchrist *t* 873
The Good Journey - Micaela Gilchrist *w* 454

Atreides, Leto (Nobleman)
House Corrino - Brian Herbert *s* 757

Atwell, William Hawley (Lawyer)
Will's War - Janice Woods Windle *w* 513
Will's War - Janice Woods Windle *t* 961

Audubon, John James (Historical Figure; Scientist)
Audubon's Watch - John Gregory Brown *c* 1085
Audubon's Watch - John Gregory Brown *t* 833

Augur (Rebel)
Augur's Teacher - Sherwood Smith *s* 800

Augustus, Caesar (Sidekick; Slave)
The Ironclad Alibi - Michael Kilian *t* 898
The Ironclad Alibi - Michael Kilian *m* 133

Aumar, Elminster (Mythical Creature; Wizard)
Elminster in Hell - Ed Greenwood *f* 553

Austen, Frank (Historical Figure; Military Personnel)
Jane and the Prisoner of Wool House - Stephanie Barron *t* 822

Austen, Jane (Historical Figure; Writer)
Jane and the Prisoner of Wool House - Stephanie Barron *t* 822
Jane and the Prisoner of Wool House - Stephanie Barron *m* 12

Austin, Daryn (Political Figure)
The Justice - Angela Elwell Hunt *i* 1004

Autumn (Animal)
Icebones - Stephen Baxter *s* 723

Avery, Gillian Harwell (Noblewoman)
A Family for Gillian - Catherine Blair *r* 238

Avery, Prescott (Nobleman; Widow(er))
A Family for Gillian - Catherine Blair *r* 238

Axis (Warrior; Wizard)
Enchanter - Sara Douglass *f* 540

Azhure (Warrior)
Enchanter - Sara Douglass *f* 540

B

Babineau, Gerard (Professor; Handicapped)
Fighting Gravity - Peggy Rambach *c* 1184

Babouris, Nana (Actress)
Pact of the Fathers - Ramsey Campbell *h* 626

Baca, Elfego (Lawman; Historical Figure)
Miracle of the Jacal - Robert J. Randisi *w* 497

Bachman, Sandra (Artist; Tutor)
Twin Blessings - Carolyne Aarsen *i* 965

Bacon, Mazy (Pioneer)
What Once We Loved - Jane Kirkpatrick *w* 470

Bak (Police Officer)
A Place of Darkness - Lauren Haney *m* 101

Baker, Matt (Handyman)
Sweet Success - Susan Mallery *r* 344

Baldassare, Leonardo (Businessman)
The Dragons of the Cuyahoga - S. Andrew Swann *f* 602

Baldevar, Simon (Vampire)
Crimson Kiss - Trisha Baker *h* 617

Baldwin, Nick (Gentleman; Lover)
Face Down Before Rebel Hooves - Kathy Lynn Emerson *t* 861

Bane (Warrior; Outcast)
Midnight Falcon - David Gemmell *f* 548

Banfield (Animal)
Chelsea Horror Hotel - Dee Dee Ramone *h* 684

Banks, Alan (Police Officer)
Aftermath - Peter Robinson *m* 186

Bannion, Jack (Guard)
Tears of the Heart - Lauran Paine *w* 493

Banouin (Traveler)
Midnight Falcon - David Gemmell *f* 548

Banyon, Eric (Musician; Student)
Spirits White as Lightning - Mercedes Lackey *f* 568

Banyon, Evie (Girlfriend)
Past Tense - William G. Tapply *m* 206

Barbara (Young Woman)
Chelsea Horror Hotel - Dee Dee Ramone *h* 684

Barclay, Clint (Lawman)
Once an Outlaw - Jill Gregory *r* 294

Barclay, Sable (Criminologist; Adoptee)
On Leaving Lonely Town - Cait Logan *r* 339

Bard, Lily (Detective—Private; Martial Arts Expert)
Shakespeare's Counselor - Charlaine Harris *m* 102

Barlow, Cecelia (Immigrant)
A Prince Among Them - Al Lacy *i* 1015

Barlow, Jeremy (Immigrant)
A Prince Among Them - Al Lacy *i* 1015

Barlow, Lady (Rancher; Widow(er))
Lockwood - Lauran Paine *w* 492

Barlow, Tye (Landowner; Horse Trainer)
The Wedding Wager - Cathy Maxwell *r* 348

Barnum, P.T. (Historical Figure; Entertainer)
The Hum Bug - Harold Schechter *w* 502
The Hum Bug - Harold Schechter *t* 932
The Hum Bug - Harold Schechter *m* 193

Baron, Martin (Rancher)
The Baron War - Jory Sherman *w* 503

Barrett, Bel (Professor; Detective—Amateur)
Midlife Can Be Murder - Jane Isenberg *m* 124

Barrow, Zoe (Police Officer)
Austin City Blue - Jan Grape *m* 88

Bartlett, Samantha (Police Officer)
Next Stop, Paradise - Sue Civil-Brown *r* 256

Bartling, Bea (Parent)
A Rose by the Door - Deborah Bedford *i* 967

Bartling, Gemma (Widow(er); Single Parent)
A Rose by the Door - Deborah Bedford *i* 967

Barto, Matt (Computer Expert)
Behind Time - Lynn Abbey *f* 515

Bayles, China (Store Owner; Herbalist)
Bloodroot - Susan Wittig Albert *m* 4

Bazie (Criminal)
Take a Thief - Mercedes Lackey *f* 569

Bear (Animal)
Once upon a Winter's Night - Dennis L. McKiernan *f* 579

Bear, Win (Detective)
The American Zone - L. Neil Smith *s* 799

Bear Paw (Indian)
Bear Paw - Gene Mullins *w* 484

Beauchamp, Althea (Noblewoman; Heiress)
Fortune's Lady - Evelyn Richardson *r* 379

Beaumont, Clarissa (Noblewoman)
The Proper Wife - Julia Justiss *r* 311

Beaupre, Jean (Trapper)
Cowboy in the Making - Will James *w* 464

Beck, Kristian (Doctor)
Funeral in Blue - Anne Perry *t* 915

Becker, Ross (Doctor)
Gargoyles - Alan Nayes *s* 783

Becket, True (Gentlewoman)
Miss Truelove Beckons - Donna Simpson *r* 397

Beckett, Daniel (Lover)
Eager to Please - Julie Parsons *c* 1180

Beckett, Rachel (Murderer)
Eager to Please - Julie Parsons *c* 1180

Beefy (Teenager)
Edgewater Angels - Sandro Meallet *c* 1160

Bella (Gentlewoman)
Bella Donna - Barbara Cherne *t* 836

Belle (Abuse Victim)
A World of Thieves - James Carlos Blake *w* 424

Bellsong, Michelina (Computer Expert)
One Door Away from Heaven - Dean R. Koontz *h* 661

Belynda (Mythical Creature)
World Fall - Douglas Niles *f* 583

ben-Abdullah, Abban "Ben" (Time Traveler; Mythical Creature)
I Dream of You - Judi McCoy r 350

Benally, Gordon (Indian; Military Personnel)
The Water and the Blood - Nancy E. Turner t 947

Bennett, Christine (Spouse; Religious)
Happy Birthday Murder - Lee Harris i 996

Bennett, Maxwell (Detective—Private)
Alien Taste - Wen Spencer s 801

Bentley, Stuart (Restaurateur)
Lockwood - Lauran Paine w 492

Benton, Daniel (Captive)
Summer Moon - Jill Marie Landis w 471

Benton, Reed (Lawman; Rancher)
Summer Moon - Jill Marie Landis w 471

Benza, Sonny (Organized Crime Figure)
Hostage - Robert Crais c 1096

Berendt, Adam (Artist; Hero)
Middle Age - Joyce Carol Oates c 1174

Berger, Mitch (Critic)
The Cold Blue Blood - David Handler m 100

Bergfeld, Virginia King (Spouse)
Will's War - Janice Woods Windle w 513

Bergfeld, Will (Defendant)
Will's War - Janice Woods Windle w 513
Will's War - Janice Woods Windle t 961

Bernai, Julius (Shipowner; Homosexual)
The Yellow Sailor - Steve Weiner t 954

Berrinden, Susannah (Cousin)
A Forbidden Embrace - Anna Jacobs r 305

Berthoff, Lisa (Photojournalist)
This Time Forever - Carol Steward i 1052

Bias (Religious)
Murder at the Panionic Games - Michael B. Edwards t 859

Bidderman, Vernie (Businesswoman)
A Warmth in Winter - Lori Copeland i 984

Bierce, Ambrose (Historical Figure; Writer)
Ambrose Bierce and the Death of Kings - Oakley Hall m 95
Ambrose Bierce and the Death of Kings - Oakley Hall t 878

Bigalow, Artemisia (Noblewoman; Debutante)
A Perfect Match - Jeanne Savery r 389

Biggs, Candy (Artist; Teacher)
Dugan under Ground - Tom De Haven c 1100

Bileworm (Wizard)
The Shattered Mask - Richard Lee Byers f 532

Billingham, Mark (Wealthy; Businessman)
The Great Baby Caper - Eugenia Riley r 380

Billy (Child)
Cowboy in the Making - Will James w 464

Bingham, Ryan (Counselor; Writer)
Up in the Air - Walter Kirn c 1141

Bjorklund, Thorliff (Student—College)
A Dream to Follow - Lauraine Snelling i 1050

Black (Servant)
The Dragon Society - Lawrence Watt-Evans f 610

Black (Relative; Investigator)
My Name Is Red - Orhan Pamuk c 1178

Black Hawk (Historical Figure; Chieftain)
The Good Journey - Micaela Gilchrist w 454
The Good Journey - Micaela Gilchrist t 873

Black Otter (Chieftain; Indian)
My Lord Savage - Elizabeth Lane r 326

Blackburn, Tanner (Lawyer)
Dangerously Irresistible - Kristin Gabriel r 289

Blackley, Posthumous (Doctor)
The London Vampire Panic - Michael Romkey h 686

Blackwolf, Culley (Foreman; Cowboy)
On Leaving Lonely Town - Cait Logan r 339

Blake, Anita (Detective)
Narcissus in Chains - Laurell K. Hamilton h 645

Blake, Howie (Drifter; Cowboy)
A Good Town - Douglas Hirt w 462

Blake, Katherine (Religious)
A Family All Her Own - Bonnie K. Winn i 1061

Blake, Lucy (Girlfriend)
Open Range - Zane Grey w 458

Blake, Sheridan (Student—College)
The Watermark - Travis Thrasher i 1054

Blalock (FBI Agent)
Blackening Song - Aimee Thurlo w 506

Blanchard, Ursula (Gentlewoman; Spy)
Queen of Ambition - Fiona Buckley t 834
Queen of Ambition - Fiona Buckley m 29

Blanche (Single Parent)
Mirabilis - Susann Cokal c 1091

Blane (Young Man)
The Nature of Balance - Tim Lebbon h 666

Blaylock, Miriam (Vampire)
The Last Vampire - Whitley Strieber h 699

Blessing, Peter (Gentleman; Gambler)
Blessing in Disguise - Jenna Mindel r 356

Blissberg, Harvey (Detective—Private; Sports Figure)
Dead Ball - R.D. Rosen m 188

Blood-Ax, Eirik Haraldsson (Warrior)
Mother of Kings - Poul Anderson f 517

Blue (Alien)
A Paradigm of Earth - Candas Jane Dorsey s 747

Blysdale, Chalfont (Nobleman; Military Personnel)
The Night the Stars Fell - Christina Kingston r 317

Boaster (Animal)
Icebones - Stephen Baxter s 723

Bolden, Buddy (Historical Figure; Musician)
Chasing the Devil's Tail - David Fulmer t 867

Bolesseto, Simila (Religious)
The Red of His Shadow - Mayra Montero c 1164

Boll, Anton (Scientist; Refugee)
The Ash Garden - Dennis Bock c 1078

Boll, Sophie (Spouse; Refugee)
The Ash Garden - Dennis Bock c 1078

Bollinger, Amanda (Young Woman)
The Folks - Ray Garton h 638

Bollinger, Matt (Businessman)
The Folks - Ray Garton h 638

Bolliver, Curtin (Parent; Oil Industry Worker)
Quincie Bolliver - Mary King w 469

Bolliver, Quincie (Teenager)
Quincie Bolliver - Mary King w 469

Bonavendier, Lilith (Wealthy; Mythical Creature)
Alice at Heart - Deborah Smith r 401

Bone, Mickey (Indian)
The Baron War - Jory Sherman w 503

Bones, John (Lawman)
A World of Thieves - James Carlos Blake w 424

Bonfils, Alexandre (Trader)
Downriver - Richard S. Wheeler t 957

Bonham, John Isley (Police Officer)
A World of Thieves - James Carlos Blake t 825

Bonney, William "Billy the Kid" (Outlaw; Historical Figure)
Bucking the Tiger - Bruce Olds c 1176

Booke, MacAllister (Paranormal Investigator; Scientist)
Heaven and Earth - Nora Roberts r 383

Boom, Ping (Businessman)
The Counterfeit Heinlein - Laurence M. Janiver s 763

Bordi, Matias (Outlaw)
The Survival of Juan Oro - Max Brand w 434

Borgia, Cesare (Historical Figure; Nobleman)
The Family - Mario Puzo c 1183
The Family - Mario Puzo t 916

Borgia, Lucrezia (Historical Figure; Noblewoman)
The Family - Mario Puzo t 916
The Family - Mario Puzo c 1183

Borgia, Rodrigo (Historical Figure; Religious)
The Family - Mario Puzo c 1183
The Family - Mario Puzo t 916

Borneheld (Warrior)
Enchanter - Sara Douglass f 540

Bowler, E. (Police Officer)
Dialogues of the Dead or Paronomania! - Reginald Hill m 116

Boysen, Edmund (Pilot)
The Phoenix - Henning Boetius t 828

Bracewell, Nicholas (Producer)
The Devil's Apprentice - Edward Marston m 148

Brackenton, Phoebe (Noblewoman)
His Lady Midnight - Jo Ann Ferguson r 279

Braddock, Jordan (Widow(er))
Colorado Twilight - Tess Pendergrass w 495

Braddock, Tina (Child-Care Giver)
Love One Another - Valerie Hansen i 995

Bradley, Vanessa (Computer Expert)
Followin' a Dream - Eboni Snoe r 403

Bradshaw, Kate (Journalist; Single Parent)
Dear Cupid - Julie Ortolon r 363

Brady, Jenny (Child)
Paradise Lost - J.A. Jance w 465
Paradise Lost - J.A. Jance m 125

Brady, Joanna (Police Officer)
Paradise Lost - J.A. Jance m 125
Paradise Lost - J.A. Jance w 465

Brahm, Corvinus (Nobleman)
The Beasts of Brahm - Mark Hansom h 646

Brand (Hitchhiker)
Face - Tim Lebbon h 665

Brandeis, Karelian (Knight)
The Black Chalice - Marie Jakober f 562

Brandon, Terry (Prospector)
By Flare of Northern Lights - Tim Champlin w 439

Brandt, Emil (Scientist)
The Good German - Joseph Kanon t 892

Brandt, Lena (Spouse)
The Good German - Joseph Kanon t 892

Brannon, Mac (Military Personnel)
Gettysburg - James Reasoner t 919

Brannon, Will (Military Personnel)
Gettysburg - James Reasoner t 919

Branscombe, Violet (Doctor)
Dr. Mortimer and the Aldgate Mystery - Gerard Williams t 958

Brauer, Gillian (Student—College)
Beasts - Joyce Carol Oates c 1173

Braxton, Yancey (Singer)
Any Way the Wind Blows - E. Lynn Harris c 1122

Breanna (Sorceress)
Swell Foop - Piers Anthony f 518

Breckonridge, Malcolm (Nobleman)
The Incomparable Miss Compton - Regina Scott r 392

Breen, Sam (Teacher)
Angry Young Spaceman - Jim Munroe s 780

Bremml, Nicholas (Sailor)
The Yellow Sailor - Steve Weiner t 954

Brennan (Nobleman)
Children of the Lion - Jennifer Roberson f 591

Brennan, Richard (Musician)
Swim the Moon - Paul Brandon f 529

Breton, Money (Writer; Divorced Person)
Why Did I Ever? - Mary Robison c 1188

Brewster, Lily (Detective—Amateur; Heiress)
Someone to Watch over Me - Jill Churchill t 839
Someone to Watch over Me - Jill Churchill m 33

Brewster, Robert (Detective—Amateur; Heir)
Someone to Watch over Me - Jill Churchill m 33
Someone to Watch over Me - Jill Churchill t 839

Briars, Amanda (Writer; Spinster)
Suddenly You - Lisa Kleypas r 319

Brock, Brandon (Businessman)
Female Intelligence - Jane Heller c 1125

Brogan, Case (Detective—Private)
Beloved Protector - Linda O'Brien r 361

Bronden (Carpenter)
Rowan of Rin - Emily Rodda f 594

Brooks, Colleen (Secretary)
Magic Time - Marc Scott Zicree f 614

Brother John (Student)
Brother John - Rutledge Etheridge s 750

Brown (Detective—Amateur)
Night Watch - Stephen Kendrick t 896

Brown, Catrina (Imposter; Impoverished)
Cinderella After Midnight - Lilian Darcy r 268

Brown, David (Military Personnel; Guardian)
Summer's Promise - Irene Brand i 974

Brown, Penn (Scientist)
The Secret of Life - Paul J. McAuley s 771

Browne, Verity (Journalist)
The Bones of the Buried - David Roberts m 183
The Bones of the Buried - David Roberts t 923

Browning, Theodosia (Store Owner)
Death by Darjeeling - Laura Childs m 32

Browser (Indian; Chieftain)
Bone Walker - Kathleen O'Neal Gear t 871

Bruce, Jane (Religious)
Something More - Paul Cornell s 738

Brunner, Jeff (Teenager)
Gifted Touch - Melinda Metz s 775

Bruno, Giordano (Historical Figure; Philosopher)
The Last Confession - Morris L. West t 956

Bryanston, Pen (Noblewoman; Widow(er))
To Kiss a Spy - Jane Feather r 276

Bryant, Wynn (Political Figure)
Drummer in the Dark - T. Davis Bunn i 976

Bryce, Jackie (Police Officer)
Suspicion of Vengeance - Barbara Parker m 167

Bryden, Sarah (Waiter/Waitress)
Sarah's Window - Janice Graham w 457

Brydges, Edward (Nobleman)
Sugarplum Surprises - Elisabeth Fairchild r 275

Bucerius (Animal)
The Treachery of Kings - Neal Barrett Jr. f 524

Buckingham, Floyd (Publisher)
The Other Adonis - Frank Deford t 849

Buddy (Vagrant)
House of Pain - Sephera Giron h 640

Bullitt, Mary (Historical Figure; Spouse)
The Good Journey - Micaela Gilchrist t 873
The Good Journey - Micaela Gilchrist w 454

Bunch, Gabriel (Teenager)
Gabriel's Gift - Hanif Kureishi c 1143

Bunch, Rex (Parent; Musician)
Gabriel's Gift - Hanif Kureishi c 1143

Bunch, Roy (Butcher; Boyfriend)
The Years of Fear - Fred Grove w 460

Burke, Clara (Parent)
Bombingham - Anthony Grooms c 1119

Burke, Josie (Relative)
Bombingham - Anthony Grooms c 1119

Burke, Sam (FBI Agent)
The Innocent - Amanda Stevens r 410

Burke, Walter (Military Personnel)
Bombingham - Anthony Grooms c 1119

Burkett, Paige (Police Officer)
The Renegade Steals a Lady - Vickie Taylor r 414

Burns, Jacob (Writer; Parent)
The Killing Bee - Matt Witten m 218

Burnside, Charles (Serial Killer)
Black House - Stephen King h 659

Burr, Aaron (Historical Figure; Political Figure)
Treason - David Nevin t 912

Buscarsela, Filomena (Detective—Private; Single Parent)
Red House - K.J.A. Wishnia m 217

Butler, Rhett (Gentleman)
The Wind Done Gone - Alice Randall t 918

Butler, Robert (Spouse)
The Evidence Against Her - Robb Forman Dew t 850
The Evidence Against Her - Robb Forman Dew c 1102

Bybee, Brigham (Lawyer)
Sister Wife - John Gates m 76

Byrnak (Ruler)
Shadowkings - Michael Cobley f 535

Bywaters, Frederick (Historical Figure; Sailor)
Fred & Edie - Jill Dawson t 848

C

Cabot, Abigail (Scientist)
Halfway to Heaven - Susan Wiggs r 419

Cabral, Agustin (Political Figure)
The Feast of the Goat - Mario Vargas Llosa t 948

Cabral, Urania (Lawyer)
The Feast of the Goat - Mario Vargas Llosa t 948
The Feast of the Goat - Mario Vargas Llosa c 1211

Caesar, Julius (Historical Figure; Military Personnel)
Nobody Loves a Centurion - John Maddox Roberts t 924

Caffery, Jack (Detective—Police)
The Treatment - Mo Hayder c 1123

Cain, Asa (Bounty Hunter)
Hard Bounty - Ken Hodgson w 463

Caitrionia (Adventurer; Young Woman)
The Mystic Rose - Stephen R. Lawhead f 570
The Mystic Rose - Stephen R. Lawhead t 901

Caldwell, Brynn (Noblewoman; Smuggler)
Desire - Nicole Jordan r 309

Caleb (Child; Orphan)
Blessed Child - Bill Bright i 975

Caleb (Teenager)
The Wild Boy - Warren Rochelle s 791

Calgary, Hunter (Detective—Police; Bodyguard)
In Too Deep - Janelle Taylor r 413

Calhoun, Jamie (Political Figure; Rake)
Halfway to Heaven - Susan Wiggs r 419

Calhoun, Madeleine "Maddie" (Journalist; Businesswoman)
The Renegades: Rafe - Genell Dellin r 270

Callaghan, Tom (Teenager)
The Reckoning - John McLain w 481

Callahan, Patrick (Wealthy; Businessman)
Cinderella After Midnight - Lilian Darcy r 268

Callahan, Rose (Religious)
Dancing Dead - Deborah Woodworth i 1062

Calloway, Jack (Doctor)
Red on Rose - Patricia Jones c 1133

Calloway, Lila (Spouse)
Red on Rose - Patricia Jones c 1133

Cameron, Bren (Government Official)
Defender - C.J. Cherryh s 734

Cameron, Clemency (Healer)
Summer's End - Lynne Hayworth r 297

Cameron, Fiona (Psychologist)
Killing the Shadows - Val McDermid m 154

Cameron, Michael (Wealthy; Computer Expert)
Dear Cupid - Julie Ortolon r 363

Camille (Young Woman)
Once upon a Winter's Night - Dennis L. McKiernan f 579

Campbell, Adam (Laird)
Embrace the Dawn - Kathleen Morgan i 1026

Campbell, Ella Mae (Heroine; Pioneer)
Shadow Valley Rising - Stephen Overholser w 488

Campbell, Killian (Abuse Victim; Spouse)
Embrace the Dawn - Kathleen Morgan i 1026

Canfield, Caroline (Artist; Detective—Amateur)
Sketches with Wolves - Jacqueline Fiedler m 68

Canfield, Sam (Police Officer)
July Thunder - Rachel Lee r 330

Canfield, Stefanie (Businesswoman; Divorced Person)
Whirlpool - Lorena McCourtney i 1023

Capashen, Gerrard (Warrior)
Apocalypse - J. Robert King f 564

Carella, Steve (Detective—Homicide)
Money, Money, Money - Ed McBain m 152

Carey, Wendy (Nurse)
Winter's Secret - Lyn Cote i 985

Carleton, Jonathan (Sailor)
Moontide - Erin Patrick h 681

Carleton, Raven (Gentlewoman)
The Border Hostage - Virginia Henley t 883

Carlisle, Mallory (Abuse Victim)
Double Honor - Melissa Horsfall i 1002

Carlson, Julie (Spouse; Store Owner)
To Trust a Stranger - Karen Robards r 381

Carlson, Michael (Widow(er); Single Parent)
A Family All Her Own - Bonnie K. Winn i 1061

Carlyle, Brandon (Writer; Convict)
Darkling I Listen - Katherine Sutcliffe r 412

Carole (Handicapped; Relative)
Leap of Faith - Danielle Steel c 1203

Caroline Mathilde (Historical Figure; Spouse)
The Royal Physician's Visit - Per Olov Enquist t 862

Carpathia, Nicolae (Ruler)
Desecration - Tim LaHaye i 1016

Carpenter, Jordan (Doctor)
Angel Face - Suzanne Forster r 283

Carr, David (Writer; Activist)
How to Be Good - Nick Hornby c 1126

Carr, Katie (Doctor; Spouse)
How to Be Good - Nick Hornby c 1126

Carrier (Young Woman)
Nearly People - Conrad Williams h 708

Carrington, Henry (Historical Figure; Military Personnel)
Moon of Bitter Cold - Frederick J. Chiaventone w 441

Carrington, Jeff (Accident Victim; Horse Trainer)
The Girl Next Door - Kate Welsh i 1057

Carrington, Margaret (Historical Figure; Spouse)
Moon of Bitter Cold - Frederick J. Chiaventone w 441

Carson, Kit (Historical Figure; Scout)
Moon Medicine - Mike Blakely t 827

Carstairs (Guide)
. . .And the Angel with Television Eyes - John Shirley h 694

Carter, Chance (Television)
Tie-Fast Country - Robert Flynn w 451

Carter, Charlie (Magician)
Carter Beats the Devil - Glen David Gold t 874

Carter, Matthew (Doctor)
Night Blood - James M. Thompson h 702

Carter, Rocky (Entertainer)
Niagara Falls All over Again - Elizabeth McCracken c 1158

Carter, Seth (Indian)
Shadow Valley Rising - Stephen Overholser w 488

Carter, Sherry (Writer)
Puzzled to Death - Parnell Hall m 96

Caruso, Jake (Contractor)
Riverwatch - Joseph M. Nassise h 676

Casanova, Giacomo (Historical Figure; Rake)
Imagining Don Giovanni - Anthony J. Rudel t 929

Casey (Teenager)
Night in the Lonesome October - Richard Laymon h 664

Cashel (Warrior)
Mistress of the Catacombs - David Drake f 541

Cassatt, Lydia (Historical Figure)
Lydia Cassatt Reading the Morning Paper - Harriet Scott Chessman t 837

Cassatt, Mary (Historical Figure; Artist)
Lydia Cassatt Reading the Morning Paper - Harriet Scott Chessman t 837

Cassidy, Gwen (Vacationer; Time Traveler)
Kiss of the Highlander - Karen Marie Moning r 358

Cassidy, J.R. (Military Personnel)
Sentimental Journey - Jill Barnett t 821

Casuel (Scholar)
The Warrior's Bond - Juliet E. McKenna f 578

Cathan (Nobleman; Rebel)
Heresy - Anselm Audley s 718

Catlin, Jonathan (Rancher)
The Texan's Dream - Jodi Thomas r 415

Cato, Quintus Licinius (Military Personnel; Slave)
Under the Eagle - Simon Scarrow t 931

Cattie-Brie (Warrior)
Sea of Swords - R.A. Salvatore f 597

Cavanagh, Roger (Lawyer)
Middle Age - Joyce Carol Oates c 1174

Cecil, William (Historical Figure; Government Official)
Queen of Ambition - Fiona Buckley t 834

Centaur, Cynthia (Mythical Creature)
Swell Foop - Piers Anthony f 518

Chalstrey, Morgan (Nobleman)
My Lady Beloved - Lael St. James r 405

Champhert, Rebecca (Writer)
Something More - Paul Cornell s 738

Chandran, Willie (Writer)
Half a Life - V.S. Naipaul c 1170

Channing, Alex (Government Official)
Divine Intervention - Ken Wharton s 810

Channing, Nell (Cook; Witch)
Dance upon the Air - Nora Roberts r 382

Chappell, Julia (Spouse)
The Happy Room - Catherine Palmer i 1038

Charlotte (Teenager; Lover)
Look at Me - Jennifer Egan c 1108

Charters, Serena (Artisan; Heiress)
Moving Target - Elizabeth Lowell r 340

Chase, Elizabeth (Detective—Private; Psychic)
Ashes of Aries - Martha C. Lawrence m 140

Chase, John (Police Officer)
The Rose in the Wheel - S.K. Rizzolo m 182

Chase, Sophy (Alcoholic; Writer)
Almost - Elizabeth Benedict c 1073

Cher (Relative)
A Place Called Wiregrass - Michael Morris i 1029

Childs, Sunny (Detective—Private)
Blue Plate Special - Ruth Birmingham m 18

Childs, Toby (Teenager)
The Onion Girl - Charles De Lint f 539

Christian, Miles (Nobleman; Widow(er))
Elusive Passion - Kathryn Smith r 402

Christian VII (Historical Figure; Ruler)
The Royal Physician's Visit - Per Olov Enquist t 862
The Royal Physician's Visit - Per Olov Enquist c 1110

Christopher (Teenager)
Mystify the Magician - K.A. Applegate f 520

Christy (Young Man)
Bloodlines - Fred D'Aguiar t 846

Church, Stewart (Roommate; Student)
About the Author - John Colapinto c 1092

Churchill, Jack (Scientist)
Always Forever - Mark Chadbourn f 533

Cian (Religious)
Act of Mercy - Peter Tremayne t 944

Clah, Ella (FBI Agent; Indian)
Blackening Song - Aimee Thurlo w 506

Clara (Child)
The Nightingale's Song - Kathleen Eschenburg r 273

Clariet, Felicity (Spy)
Jackdaws - Ken Follett t 863

Clarista (Grandparent)
Tie-Fast Country - Robert Flynn w 451

Clark, Hosanna (Maintenance Worker)
What You Owe Me - Bebe Moore Campbell c 1089

Clark, Matriece (Businesswoman; Relative)
What You Owe Me - Bebe Moore Campbell c 1089

Clark, William (Explorer; Historical Figure)
River Walk - Rita Cleary w 443

Clarke, Lenie (Survivor)
Maelstrom - Peter Watts s 808

Clarke, Siobhan (Police Officer)
The Falls - Ian Rankin m 178

Clausen, Doris (Benefactor)
The Fourth Hand - John Irving c 1130

Claybourne, David (Detective—Police)
Darkness at the Door - Catherine Dain m 52

Clayton (Werewolf; Lover)
Bitten - Kelley Armstrong c 1068

Clayton, Tom (Security Officer)
Adventures in Time and Space with Max Merriwell - Pat Murphy s 781

Clergue, Pierre (Religious)
The Good Men - Charmaine Craig t 844

Cobner (Thief)
The Rover - Mel Odom f 584

Cochrane, Deborah (Student—Graduate)
Shock - Robin Cook c 1093

Coffin, John (Police Officer)
Coffin's Ghost - Gwendoline Butler m 30

Cohen, Genghiz (Ruler)
The Last Hero - Terry Pratchett f 588

Colbert, Gerard (Writer)
The Looking Glass - Michele Roberts t 925

Cole, Clay "The Rainmaker" (Outlaw; Cowboy)
Outcasts - Tim McGuire w 480

Cole, Maureen (Anthropologist)
Bone Walker - Kathleen O'Neal Gear t 871

Coleman, Kitty (Parent; Spouse)
Falling Angels - Tracy Chevalier c 1090

Coleman, Maude (Child; Friend)
Falling Angels - Tracy Chevalier c 1090
Falling Angels - Tracy Chevalier t 838

Coleman, Melodie (Widow(er))
A Home of Her Own - Cathleen Connors i 982

Colling, Lisette (Orphan; Runaway)
French Leave - Sheri Cobb South r 404

Collins, Benton (Student—Graduate)
The Beasts of Barakhai - Mickey Zucker Reichert f 590

Collins, Hap (Guard)
Captains Outrageous - Joe R. Lansdale w 472

Collins, John (Explorer; Historical Figure)
River Walk - Rita Cleary w 443

Collins, Martin (Lawyer)
Catskill - John R. Hayes m 110
Catskill - John R. Hayes t 882

Collins, Wilkie (Historical Figure; Writer)
The Rag & Bone Shop - Jeff Rackham t 917

Colton, Miranda (Accident Victim)
Rivers of Gold - Tracie Peterson i 1042

Columbus, Beth (Spouse; Lawyer)
Columbus Slaughters Braves - Mark Friedman c 1114

Columbus, C.J. (Sports Figure; Relative)
Columbus Slaughters Braves - Mark Friedman *c* 1114

Columbus, Joe (Teacher; Relative)
Columbus Slaughters Braves - Mark Friedman *c* 1114

Compton, Sarah (Gentlewoman)
The Incomparable Miss Compton - Regina Scott *r* 392

Conde, Amy (Gentlewoman; Ward)
The Guardian - Barbara Miller *r* 355

Connavar (Ruler)
Midnight Falcon - David Gemmell *f* 548

Connor, Gail (Lawyer)
Suspicion of Vengeance - Barbara Parker *m* 167

Conor (Ruler)
Bloodtide - Melvin Burgess *s* 730

Conrad, Dusty (Fire Fighter; Spouse)
The Woman for Dusty Conrad - Tori Carrington *r* 251

Conrad, Jolie (Fire Fighter; Spouse)
The Woman for Dusty Conrad - Tori Carrington *r* 251

Conrad, Milton (Prospector)
By Flare of Northern Lights - Tim Champlin *w* 439

Conroy, Jane (Teacher)
A Love for Safekeeping - Gail Gaymer Martin *i* 1021

Converse, Jeff (Student; Convict)
The Manhattan Hunt Club - John Saul *h* 687

Converse, Keith (Construction Worker)
The Manhattan Hunt Club - John Saul *h* 687

Conway, Babs (Young Woman)
Prized Possessions - Jessica Stirling *t* 938

Conway, Lizzie (Widow(er))
Prized Possessions - Jessica Stirling *t* 938

Conway, Polly (Young Woman)
Prized Possessions - Jessica Stirling *t* 938

Conway, Roscoe Owens (Political Figure)
Roscoe - William Kennedy *t* 897

Cooke-Williams, Arthur Williford (Nobleman)
Charlie and the Sir - Frank Roderus *w* 499

Cooley, Moss (Sports Figure)
Dead Ball - R.D. Rosen *m* 188

Cooper, Alexandra (Lawyer)
The Deadhouse - Linda Fairstein *m* 66

Cooper, Ben (Police Officer)
Dancing with the Virgins - Stephen Booth *m* 23

Copis (Traveler)
Shadow - K.J. Parker *f* 585

Coppercorn, Jilly (Artist)
The Onion Girl - Charles De Lint *f* 539

Copperton, Elizabeth (Rancher; Noblewoman)
Charlie and the Sir - Frank Roderus *w* 499

Cordell, Catherine (Doctor)
The Surgeon - Tess Gerritsen *m* 78

Corinth, Edward (Nobleman)
The Bones of the Buried - David Roberts *m* 183
The Bones of the Buried - David Roberts *t* 923

Corkery, Hannah (Young Woman)
Stillwater - William F. Weld *t* 955

Correa, Matt (Wealthy; Computer Expert)
The Secret Admirer - Annette Mahon *r* 343

Corrigan, Jonathan (Spy)
Betrayed - Rosey Dow *i* 989

Cotter, Karen (Spouse; Neighbor)
The Woman Next Door - Barbara Delinsky *c* 1101

Cotton, Aldous "Gus" (Narrator)
Fairness - Ferdinand Mount *c* 1167

Cougar (Indian)
Circle of Stars - Anna Lee Waldo *t* 952
Circle of Stars - Anna Lee Waldo *w* 510

Coulter, Jake (Horse Trainer; Rancher)
Sweet Nothings - Catherine Anderson *r* 225

Courtray, Melfallan (Nobleman)
Mother Ocean, Daughter Sea - Diana Marcellas *f* 576

Cox (Lawman)
Colorado Twilight - Tess Pendergrass *w* 495

Coy, Manuel (Sailor)
The Nautical Chart - Arturo Perez-Reverte *c* 1182
The Nautical Chart - Arturo Perez-Reverte *m* 171

Coyne, Brady (Lawyer; Detective—Private)
First Light - Philip R. Craig *m* 46
Past Tense - William G. Tapply *m* 206

Crane, Mary Alice "Sister" (Divorced Person; Detective—Amateur)
Murder Boogies with Elvis - Anne George *m* 77

Cranshaw, Lisa (Wealthy)
Very Truly Yours - Julie Beard *r* 229

Crawford, Steve (Mine Owner)
The Lone Rider - Max Brand *w* 432

Crazy Horse (Historical Figure; Indian)
Turn the Stars Upside Down - Terry C. Johnston *w* 466
Turn the Stars Upside Down - Terry C. Johnston *t* 890

Cresswell, Emma (Companion)
The Valentine Wish - Debbie Raleigh *r* 378

Cresswell, Sarah (Detective; Gentlewoman)
The Christmas Wish - Debbie Raleigh *r* 377

Cripps, Byron (Prisoner)
Leaving Disneyland - Alexander Parsons *c* 1179

Cristo the Bastardo (Bastard Son)
Aztec Blood - Gary Jennings *t* 889

Crittenden, Beatrice (Heiress)
The Lone Rider - Max Brand *w* 432

Cross, Abby (Police Officer)
The Innocent - Amanda Stevens *r* 410

Crow (Teenager)
The Crow Maiden - Sarah Singleton *f* 598

Crow (Warrior)
Fortress Draconis - Michael A. Stackpole *f* 599

Crow, Mary (Lawyer; Indian)
A Darker Justice - Sallie Bissell *m* 19
In the Forest of Harm - Sallie Bissell *c* 1074

Croydon, Denzil (Military Personnel)
Tragic Casements - Oliver Onions *h* 680

Croydon, Eustace (Gardener)
Tragic Casements - Oliver Onions *h* 680

Croydon, Patricia (Young Woman)
Tragic Casements - Oliver Onions *h* 680

Cruz, Anibal (Military Personnel)
Pyramid Scheme - David Freer *s* 751

Culver, Suzanne (Pioneer; Handicapped)
What Once We Loved - Jane Kirkpatrick *w* 470

Cunningham, Cal (Writer; Clerk)
About the Author - John Colapinto *c* 1092

Cunningham, Cheryl (Social Worker; Divorced Person)
Another Summer - Georgia Bockoven *r* 239

Custer, George Armstrong (Historical Figure; Military Personnel)
An Uncommon Enemy - Michelle Black *t* 824
An Uncommon Enemy - Michelle Black *w* 423

Cutler, Augusta (Friend)
Middle Age - Joyce Carol Oates *c* 1174

Cutter, Joey P. (Child)
Caleb's Price - Troy D. Smith *w* 505

Cutter, Marvin (Thief)
Flying Eagle - Tim Champlin *w* 440

Cymbra (Noblewoman; Healer)
Dream of Me - Josie Litton *r* 338

Cynara (Slave)
The Wind Done Gone - Alice Randall *t* 918

Cynster, Sebastian (Nobleman; Rake)
The Promise in a Kiss - Stephanie Laurens *r* 329

Cyrion, Philipa (Astrologer; Detective—Amateur)
Wayward Moon - Denny DeMartino *s* 744

D

Dacre, Christopher (Nobleman; Fiance(e))
The Border Hostage - Virginia Henley *t* 883

Dagnarus (Sorcerer)
Guardians of the Lost - Margaret Weis *f* 611

Dalriadis (Military Personnel)
Heresy - Anselm Audley *s* 718

Dalton, Smokey (Detective—Private; Veteran)
Smoke-Filled Rooms - Kris Nelscott *m* 166

Dalziel, Andrew "Andy" (Police Officer)
Dialogues of the Dead or Paronomania! - Reginald Hill *m* 116

Dan (Office Worker)
Face - Tim Lebbon *h* 665

Dancer (Dancer)
Nearly People - Conrad Williams *h* 708

Danforth, Eileen (Student)
Night in the Lonesome October - Richard Laymon *h* 664

Daniels, Amoreena (Student—College)
Gargoyles - Alan Nayes *s* 783
Gargoyles - Alan Nayes *h* 677

D'Arcey, Corran (Adventurer)
Pool of Radiance - Carrie Bebris *f* 525

d'Arcy, Owen (Nobleman; Spy)
To Kiss a Spy - Jane Feather *r* 276

Darling, Stephen (Vampire)
Candle Bay - Tamara Thorne *h* 703

Darnell, John (Paranormal Investigator)
The Case of the Ripper's Revenge - Sam McCarver *m* 153

Darnley, Randall (Nobleman; Imposter)
Once a Princess - Veronica Sattler *r* 388

Darren, Claire (Noblewoman)
Heart of Night - Taylor Chase *r* 254

D'Ascanio, Alessandro "Alex" (Director)
Season of Storms - Susanna Kearsley *r* 314

Dashiell (Animal; Sidekick)
The Long Good Boy - Carol Lea Benjamin *m* 16

Davenport, Rose (Antiques Dealer)
Tall, Dark, and Difficult - Patricia Coughlin *r* 261

Davenport, Teddy (Scientist)
Rivers of Gold - Tracie Peterson *i* 1042

David (Teenager)
Entertain the End - K.A. Applegate *f* 519

David (Historical Figure; Ruler)
Queenmaker - India Edghill *t* 858

Davies, Rebecca (Activist)
Island of Tears - Troy Soos *m* 200

Davis, Kate (Social Worker)
Secrets of the Heart - Gail Gaymer Martin *i* 1022

Davis, Quincee (Guardian)
Loving Thy Neighbor - Ruth Scofield *i* 1047

de Bracineaux, Renaud (Knight; Religious)
The Mystic Rose - Stephen R. Lawhead *t* 901
The Mystic Rose - Stephen R. Lawhead *f* 570

de Burgh, Robin (Knight; Nobleman)
My Lady de Burgh - Deborah Simmons *r* 396

de Danann, Tuatha (Deity)
Always Forever - Mark Chadbourn *f* 533

de Fraisney, Katherine (Widow(er); Noblewoman)
The Warrior's Damsel - Denise Hampton *r* 295

de Lamere, Isabel (Heiress)
White Lion's Lady - Tina St. John *r* 407

De Lancre, Jedediah (Sorcerer)
A Lower Deep - Tom Piccirilli *h* 682

de Stansion, Helena Rebecca (Noblewoman)
The Promise in a Kiss - Stephanie Laurens *r* 329

de Vere, Gareth (Nobleman; Rake)
Fortune's Lady - Evelyn Richardson *r* 379

de Villonne, Bayard (Nobleman; Knight)
The Temptress - Claire Delacroix *r* 269

Deacon, Jack (Police Officer)
Echoes of Lies - Jo Bannister *m* 11

Decimus, Victor (Religious; Vampire)
Vampire Vow - Michael Schiefelbein *h* 690

Deek (Thief)
Take a Thief - Mercedes Lackey *f* 569

Deevers, Wilburn (Lawman)
Hard Bounty - Ken Hodgson *w* 463

Degas, Edgar (Historical Figure; Artist)
Lydia Cassatt Reading the Morning Paper - Harriet Scott Chessman *t* 837

Dehya (Telepath)
Spherical Harmonic - Catherine Asaro *s* 716

DeKathrine, Camden (Wizard)
The Golden Sword - Fiona Patton *f* 586

DeKathrine, Danielle (Sorceress)
The Golden Sword - Fiona Patton *f* 586

del Valle, Aurora (Photographer; Narrator)
Portrait in Sepia - Isabel Allende *c* 1067

del Valle, Paulina (Grandparent)
Portrait in Sepia - Isabel Allende *c* 1067

Delaney, Christine (Care Giver; Secretary)
When Tomorrow Comes - Janette Oke *i* 1034

Delaney, Del (Cowboy)
The Outlaws - Wayne D. Overholser *w* 490

Delange, Genevieve (Servant)
The Looking Glass - Michele Roberts *t* 925

Delmas, Jack (Detective—Private)
Massacre Island - Martin Hegwood *m* 112

Delora (Sorceress)
Debt of Bones - Terry Goodkind *f* 549

DeMarian, Alisha (Noblewoman)
The Golden Sword - Fiona Patton *f* 586

DeMato, Joey (Businesswoman)
Diamond in the Ruff - Emily Carmichael *r* 249

Demens, Ty (Single Parent; Widow(er))
Blessed Baby - Lois Richer *i* 1043

Dennis (Health Care Professional; Boyfriend)
The Wedding Party - Robyn Carr *r* 250

Denser (Sorcerer)
Nightchild - James Barclay *f* 523

Deonne, Vita (Professor)
The Lecturer's Tale - James Hynes *h* 649

Desjardins, Achilles (Computer Expert)
Maelstrom - Peter Watts *s* 808

Deslucido, Damian (Ruler)
The Fall of Neskaya - Marion Zimmer Bradley *s* 725

Destea, Clifford (Indian; Shaman)
Blackening Song - Aimee Thurlo *w* 506

Deveaux, Samantha (Bodyguard; Security Officer)
Insatiable - Julie Elizabeth Leto *r* 333

Devere, Rosamunde (Noblewoman; Captive)
The Perfect Princess - Elizabeth Thornton *r* 416

Devlin, Jack (Bastard Son; Publisher)
Suddenly You - Lisa Kleypas *r* 319

Devonshire, Betsy (Store Owner; Divorced Person)
Unraveled Sleeve - Monica Ferris *m* 67

di Rospo, Teresa (Noblewoman; Vampire)
Darkness - Sam Siciliano *h* 695

Diamond, Eve (Journalist)
The Jasmine Trade - Denise Hamilton *m* 98

Dianna (Mythical Creature)
The Pillars of the World - Anne Bishop *f* 527

Diche, Derek (Television Personality; Paranormal Investigator)
Next Stop, Paradise - Sue Civil-Brown *r* 256

Dickens, Charles (Historical Figure; Writer)
The Rag & Bone Shop - Jeff Rackham *t* 917

Dickensen, Gil (Fiance(e))
Irregardless of Murder - Ellen Edwards Kennedy *i* 1008

Dickerson, Piper (Writer)
Eccentric Circles - Rebecca Lickiss *f* 573

Dillman, George Porter (Detective—Private)
Murder on the Minnesota - Conrad Allen *t* 816
Murder on the Minnesota - Conrad Allen *m* 5

Dimitris, Melina (Detective—Private)
Heaven on Earth - Marilyn Pappano *r* 366

Dionysos (Religious)
Thrice Bound - Roberta Gellis *f* 547

Dixon, Butch (Spouse)
Paradise Lost - J.A. Jance *w* 465
Paradise Lost - J.A. Jance *m* 125

Doan (Detective—Private)
The Mouse in the Mountain - Norbert Davis *m* 56

Dobson, Prentice (Businesswoman)
An Angel to Die For - Mignon F. Ballard *f* 522

Dodgson, Charles (Historical Figure; Writer)
The Problem of the Surly Servant - Roberta Rogow *m* 187
The Problem of the Surly Servant - Roberta Rogow *t* 926
Still She Haunts Me - Katie Roiphe *t* 927
Still She Haunts Me - Katie Roiphe *c* 1189

Dolan, Sophie (Psychic; Fugitive)
Just West of Heaven - Kathleen Kane *r* 313

Dolven, Brock (Outlaw)
Hard Bounty - Ken Hodgson *w* 463

Donegan, Abbie (Guardian; Heiress)
Saddled - Delores Fossen *r* 284

Donnelly, Jack (Detective—Homicide)
Eager to Please - Julie Parsons *c* 1180

Donovan, Karen (Teacher)
Fireworks - James A. Moore *h* 675

Dorothy (Child)
The Rundlestone of Oz - Eloise McGraw *f* 577

Dorsette, Lorna (Young Woman)
When Love Came to Town - Lenora Worth *i* 1063

Dortrean, Erkal (Nobleman; Government Official)
The Treason of Dortrean - Marcus Herniman *f* 557

Dortrean, Karlena (Noblewoman)
The Treason of Dortrean - Marcus Herniman *f* 557

Dortrean, Kellarn (Nobleman)
The Treason of Dortrean - Marcus Herniman *f* 557

Dostoyevsky, Anna (Historical Figure; Spouse)
Summer in Baden-Baden - Leonid Tsypkin *t* 946

Dostoyevsky, Fyodor (Historical Figure; Writer)
Summer in Baden-Baden - Leonid Tsypkin *t* 946

Dougal's Lord Carstairs (Animal; Sidekick)
The Mouse in the Mountain - Norbert Davis *m* 56

Dougan, Eilan (Empath)
The Enchantment - Pam Binder *r* 237

Douglas, Robert (Warrior)
Rebel's Cage - Kate Jacoby *f* 561

Do'Urden, Drizzt (Mythical Creature; Warrior)
Sea of Swords - R.A. Salvatore *f* 597

Doyle, Arthur Conan (Historical Figure; Writer)
The Problem of the Surly Servant - Roberta Rogow *m* 187
The Problem of the Surly Servant - Roberta Rogow *t* 926

Doyle, Regan (Widow(er); Thief)
Walker's Widow - Heidi Betts *r* 234

Drachenfels, Constant (Sorcerer)
Drachenfels - Jack Yeovil *f* 613

Dracula (Vampire)
Dracula in London - P.N. Elrod *h* 631

Drak, Bart (Military Personnel)
Holding the Line - Rick Shelley *s* 795

Drake, Jessie (Detective—Homicide)
Shadows of Sin - Rochelle Krich *m* 137

Drama (Murderer)
Critical Space - Greg Rucka *m* 190

Drer (Alien)
Wayward Moon - Denny DeMartino *s* 744

Driver, Sally (Widow(er); Waiter/Waitress)
Looking for Laura - Judith Arnold *r* 226

Dromgoole, Juno (Professor)
Burning Down the House - Lev Rafael *m* 176

Druid (Animal)
A Feral Darkness - Doranna Durgin *f* 543

Drummond, Janet (Parent)
All Families Are Psychotic - Douglas Coupland *c* 1094

Drummond, Wade (Relative)
All Families Are Psychotic - Douglas Coupland *c* 1094

Drummond-Fournier, Sarah (Relative; Astronaut)
All Families Are Psychotic - Douglas Coupland *c* 1094

Du Lethe, Lancelot (Knight)
Lancelot Du Lethe - J. Robert King *f* 566

Dubois, Rose (Waiter/Waitress)
The MacKenzies: Zach - Ana Leigh *r* 332

Dudley, Ferdinand (Nobleman; Heir)
No Man's Mistress - Mary Balogh *r* 227

Dugan, Charlene (Lawyer; Divorced Person)
The Wedding Party - Robyn Carr *r* 250

Dugan, Jake (Divorced Person)
The Wedding Party - Robyn Carr *r* 250

Duke, Rachel (Singer)
The Doctor's Miracle - Anna Schmidt *i* 1046

Dulcie (Animal)
Cat Laughing Last - Shirley Rousseau Murphy *m* 162

Dun, Richard (Detective—Private; Vampire)
His Father's Son - Nigel Bennett *h* 621

Dunbar, Bartholomew "Bart" (Model; Homosexual)
Any Way the Wind Blows - E. Lynn Harris *c* 1122

Dunbar, John (Military Personnel; Warrior)
The Holy Road - Michael Blake *w* 425
The Holy Road - Michael Blake *t* 826

Dunne, Olivia (Young Woman)
The Magic of Ordinary Days - Ann Howard Creel *t* 845

Dunnegan, Vern (Game Warden)
Open Season - C.J. Box *w* 428

Durand, Rodd (Police Officer)
Winter's Secret - Lyn Cote *i* 985

Duranix (Mythical Creature)
Brother of the Dragon - Paul B. Thompson *f* 604

Dynes, Sam (Rebel)
The Night of the Triffids - Simon Clark *s* 735

Dyson, Ray (Construction Worker)
The Association - Bentley Little *h* 668

E

Eagleston, Pamela (Businesswoman)
Dead Love - Donald Beman *h* 620

Earp, Wyatt (Lawman; Historical Figure)
Bucking the Tiger - Bruce Olds *w* 485

Eastman, Delanie (Teacher; Imposter)
Hide and Seek - Cherry Adair *r* 222

Eberhardt, Heinrich (Military Personnel)
In the Shape of a Boar - Lawrence Norfolk *t* 913

Echaurren, Xochitl (Computer Expert)
Smoking Mirror Blues - Ernest Hogan *s* 758

Edib, Halide (Historical Figure; Activist)
Halide's Gift - Frances Kazan *t* 893

Edison, Thomas (Inventor; Historical Figure)
Tomorrow's Eve - Auguste Villiers de L'Isle Adam *s* 806

Edward, Prince of Wales (Historical Figure; Royalty)
Goodnight, Sweet Prince - David Dickinson *t* 851

Edwards, Derrien "Derry" (Sports Figure; Landscaper)
A Diamond in the Rough - Andrea Pickens *r* 370

Edwards, Jane Amanda (Spinster; Detective—Amateur)
The Message of the Mute Dog - Charlotte Murray Russell *m* 191

Effendi, Enishte (Artist; Crime Victim)
My Name Is Red - Orhan Pamuk *c* 1178

Egan, Byron (Religious)
Yonder Stands Your Orphan - Barry Hannah *c* 1121

Einar (Supernatural Being)
From the Dust Returned - Ray Bradbury *h* 623

Eirik (Royalty)
Mother of Kings - Poul Anderson *t* 818

Eiriksson, Gamli (Ruler)
Mother of Kings - Poul Anderson *f* 517

Eladamri (Mythical Creature)
Apocalypse - J. Robert King *f* 564

Elazandra (Teenager)
Shadow Kiss - Tom Townsend *f* 605

Eldridge, Louise (Gardener; Television Personality)
Harvest of Murder - Ann Ripley *m* 181

Eldrin (Telepath)
Spherical Harmonic - Catherine Asaro *s* 716

Elegant (Artist; Crime Victim)
My Name Is Red - Orhan Pamuk *c* 1178

Elena (Witch)
Wit'ch Gate - James Clemens *f* 534

Eliasson, Samuel (Widow(er))
The World Below - Sue Miller *c* 1163

Elisa (Artist)
Lucky Us - Joan Silber *c* 1198

Elizabeth I (Historical Figure; Ruler)
Queen of Ambition - Fiona Buckley *t* 834

Elken (Military Personnel)
Bolo Strike - William H. Keith Jr. *s* 765

Ell, Susannah (Businesswoman)
Dervish Is Digital - Pat Cadigan *s* 731

Elliot, Angelina Marguerite (Relative)
From the Dust Returned - Ray Bradbury *c* 1082

Elliot, Cecy (Teenager)
From the Dust Returned - Ray Bradbury *h* 623

Elliot, Einar (Relative)
From the Dust Returned - Ray Bradbury *c* 1082

Elliot, Timothy (Foundling; Narrator)
From the Dust Returned - Ray Bradbury *c* 1082
From the Dust Returned - Ray Bradbury *h* 623

Ellis, Cassie (Fire Fighter)
The Protector - Dee Henderson *i* 999

Ellis, Trade (Detective—Private; Rancher)
Crack Shot - Sinclair Browning *m* 28

Eloise of Argent (Religious; Gentlewoman)
The Husband Test - Betina Krahn *r* 321

Elric (Warrior)
The Dreamthief's Daughter - Michael Moorcock *f* 582

Elvia (Relative; Pregnant Teenager)
Highwire Moon - Susan Straight *c* 1205

Elwood, Leonard (Explorer)
The Devil-Tree of El Dorado - Frank Aubrey *s* 717

Emil (Spouse; Scientist)
The Good German - Joseph Kanon *c* 1135

Emily (Relative)
Cane River - Lalita Tademy *c* 1207

Emmett, Claude (Outlaw; Thief)
A Horde of Fools - James David Buchanan *w* 437

Emrys (Royalty)
Daughter of Lir - Judith Tarr *t* 940

Eric (Clone)
Tenebrea's Hope - Roxann Dawson *s* 743

Erienne (Sorceress)
Nightchild - James Barclay *f* 523

Erik (Friend; Lover)
First Gray, Then White, Then Blue - Margriet de Moor *c* 1165

Erius (Ruler)
The Bone Doll's Twin - Lynn Flewelling *f* 544

Er'ril (Warrior)
Wit'ch Gate - James Clemens *f* 534

Erx (Spaceman)
Starhawk - Mack Maloney *s* 769

Escalla (Wizard)
Queen of the Demonweb Pits - Paul Kidd *f* 563

Eschbach, Johan (Professor; Spy)
Ghost of the White Nights - L.E. Modesitt Jr. *s* 778

Eschbach, Llysette (Singer; Spy)
Ghost of the White Nights - L.E. Modesitt Jr. *s* 778

Eudoxia (Vampire)
Blood and Gold - Anne Rice *h* 685

Eugenides (Aged Person)
London Bridges - Jane Stevenson *c* 1204

Evans, Catrine (Teenager; Student—Boarding School)
Schooling - Heather McGowan *c* 1159

Evans, Charlie (Police Officer)
Catskill - John R. Hayes *t* 882

Evans, Faith (Journalist)
On Every Side - Karen Kingsbury *i* 1010

Evans, Parker (Handicapped; Writer)
Envy - Sandra Brown *c* 1086
Envy - Sandra Brown *r* 245

Evans, Teddy (Parent)
Schooling - Heather McGowan *c* 1159

Everard, David (Military Personnel)
The Blooding of the Guns - Alexander Fullerton *t* 866

Everard, Hugh (Military Personnel)
The Blooding of the Guns - Alexander Fullerton *t* 866

Everard, Nicholas (Military Personnel)
The Blooding of the Guns - Alexander Fullerton *t* 866

Everdean, Peter (Military Personnel; Nobleman)
The Spanish Bride - Amanda McCabe *r* 349

Everly, Jonathan (Military Personnel; Sea Captain)
The Traitor's Daughter - Elizabeth Powell *r* 374

Ewald (Nobleman)
Tomorrow's Eve - Auguste Villiers de L'Isle Adam *s* 806

Ezoriel (Angel)
City Infernal - Edward Lee *h* 667

F

Fairchild, Faith (Caterer; Religious)
The Body in the Bonfire - Katherine Hall Page *i* 1037

Fairchild, Jack (Nobleman; Impoverished)
Very Truly Yours - Julie Beard *r* 229

Faith (Slave)
Bloodlines - Fred D'Aguiar *t* 846

Falima (Mythical Creature)
The Beasts of Barakhai - Mickey Zucker Reichert *f* 590

Fallon, Brenna (Businesswoman)
A Feral Darkness - Doranna Durgin *f* 543

Fallon, Christopher (Guide)
Treasures of the Sun - T.V. Olsen *w* 487

Fallowes, Hetty (Student—College)
The Flight of the Maidens - Jane Gardam *t* 870

Falthorn (Nobleman)
The Obsidian Tower - Freda Warrington *f* 609

Farrell, Elspeth Brodie (Detective—Private; Single Parent)
Echoes of Lies - Jo Bannister *m* 11

Farrell, Jo (Clerk)
My Best Friend - Laura Wilson *m* 214

Farrell, Wesley (Businessman)
Pale Shadow - Robert Skinner *m* 196
Pale Shadow - Robert Skinner *t* 935

Fascinelli, Anthony (Teenager)
Gifted Touch - Melinda Metz *s* 775
Haunted - Melinda Metz *s* 776

Fay (Witch)
The Nature of Balance - Tim Lebbon *h* 666

Felton, Cora (Aged Person; Detective—Amateur)
Puzzled to Death - Parnell Hall *m* 96

Fenimore, Andrew (Doctor; Detective—Amateur)
The Doctor and the Dead Man's Chest - Robin Hathaway *m* 106

Fenwick, Andrew (Police Officer; Single Parent)
Fatal Legacy - Elizabeth Corley *m* 43

Fenwick, Buck (Police Officer)
Sex and Murder.com - Mark Richard Zubro *m* 221

Fhassin (Prisoner)
Nekropolis - Maureen McHugh *s* 774

Fidelma (Religious; Scholar)
Act of Mercy - Peter Tremayne *m* 209
Act of Mercy - Peter Tremayne *t* 944

Field, Jasmin "Jazz" (Journalist; Actress)
Pride, Prejudice and Jasmin Field - Melissa Nathan *r* 359

Field, Simon (Friend; Worker)
Falling Angels - Tracy Chevalier *t* 838

Fielding (Ruler)
The Night of the Triffids - Simon Clark *s* 735

Fielding, John (Historical Figure; Judge)
Smuggler's Moon - Bruce Alexander *t* 815

Finn (Inventor)
The Treachery of Kings - Neal Barrett Jr. *f* 524

Fiona (Knight)
Betrayal - Jean Rabe *f* 589

First Elk Woman (Spouse; Indian)
The June Rise - William Tremblay *t* 945
The June Rise - William Tremblay *w* 507

Firth, Anna (Widow(er); Servant)
Year of Wonders - Geraldine Brooks *t* 832

Fisher, Bo (Teenager)
Fire in the Rock - Joe Martin *c* 1154

Fisk, Callie (Pioneer; Miner)
A Horde of Fools - James David Buchanan *w* 437

FitzAllen, Kiernan (Bastard Son; Rogue)
The Prisoner Bride - Susan Spencer Paul *r* 368

Fitzgerald, Declan (Lawyer)
Midnight Bayou - Nora Roberts *c* 1187

Fitzgerald, Johnny (Sidekick; Nobleman)
Goodnight, Sweet Prince - David Dickinson *m* 58

Fitzgibbon, Veronica (Widow(er))
Roscoe - William Kennedy *t* 897

Flaherty, Lucien "Irish" (Military Personnel)
Broken Honor - Patricia Potter *r* 373

Flores, Andrea (Military Personnel)
Tenebrea's Hope - Roxann Dawson *s* 743

Fly, Lucy (Expatriate; Linguist)
The Earthquake Bird - Susanna Jones *m* 127

Flying Horse Mollie (Indian)
Blood on the Wind - Lucile Bogue *w* 426

Fogarty, Luanne (Diver; Teacher)
Deep Water Death - Glynn Marsh Alam *m* 3

Fontana, Jose (Rancher; Wealthy)
The Survival of Juan Oro - Max Brand *w* 434

Forrest, Lilah (Hippie)
Last Virgin in California - Maureen Child *r* 255

Forrester, Quinn (Engineer)
A Father's Place - Marta Perry *i* 1041

Forster, Quentin (Werewolf; Mentally Ill Person)
Secret of the Wolf - Susan Krinard *r* 322

Forsythe, Arkin (Government Official)
Angelmass - Timothy Zahn *s* 812

Fortunato, Caesar (Television)
TV - Brian Brown *c* 1084

Fortune, Robert (Detective)
Friends and Enemies - Stephen A. Bly *i* 972

Foster, Buck (Cowboy)
A Home of Her Own - Cathleen Connors *i* 982

Fournier, Adrien (Military Personnel)
The Officers' Ward - Marc Dugain *t* 857

Fox, George (Religious; Historical Figure)
Sea of Glory - Ken Wales *i* 1056

Fox, Nicholas (Relative)
Aunt Dimity: Detective - Nancy Atherton *m* 9

Fraiser, Laura (Teacher)
Forbid Them Not - Michael P. Farris *i* 991

Fraith, Charles (Friend; Nobleman)
Agatha Raisin and the Love from Hell - M.C. Beaton *m* 14

Frake, Jack (Smuggler)
Sparrowhawk—Jack Frake - Edward Cline *t* 840

Franck, Dieter (Military Personnel)
Jackdaws - Ken Follett *t* 863

Franklin, Alexander (Government Official)
Deathday - William C. Dietz *s* 746

Franklin, Kinkaide (Singer)
To Rome with Love - Debra White Smith *i* 1049

Fraser, Claire (Time Traveler; Doctor)
The Fiery Cross - Diana Gabaldon *r* 288
The Fiery Cross - Diana Gabaldon *t* 868

Fraser, Jamie (Spouse)
The Fiery Cross - Diana Gabaldon *r* 288
The Fiery Cross - Diana Gabaldon *t* 868

Frazier, Justin (Child)
Love One Another - Valerie Hansen *i* 995

Frazier, Zac (Widow(er); Single Parent)
Love One Another - Valerie Hansen *i* 995

Freebody, Agate (Slave)
The Wolf Pit - Marly Youmans *t* 964

Freeman, Lee (Spouse)
Monte's Revenge - Eugene C. Vories *w* 509

Freeman, Monte (Rancher)
Monte's Revenge - Eugene C. Vories *w* 509

Freer, Nathanael (Spaceship Captain)
Appleseed - John Clute *s* 736

French, Nicole (Teenager)
Straight on 'Til Morning - Christopher Golden *h* 642

Frevisse (Religious; Detective—Amateur)
The Clerk's Tale - Margaret Frazer *m* 70
The Clerk's Tale - Margaret Frazer *t* 865

Friedman, Kinky (Detective—Private)
Steppin' on a Rainbow - Kinky Friedman *m* 72

Frith, Anna (Widow(er); Parent)
Year of Wonders - Geraldine Brooks *c* 1083

Fritz, Waldo (Outlaw; Thief)
A Good Town - Douglas Hirt *w* 462

Frog Eyes (Indian)
Double Vengeance - John Duncklee *w* 449

Froude, Danfin (Scientist)
Homefall - Chris Bunch *s* 729

Fry, Diane (Police Officer)
Dancing with the Virgins - Stephen Booth *m* 23

G

Gaad, Leila (Archaeologist)
The Old Spies Club and Other Intrigues of Rand - Edward D. Hoch *m* 118

Gabe (Fiance(e); Drug Dealer)
Lucky Us - Joan Silber *c* 1198

Gaius (Friend)
The Gaius Diary - Gene Edwards *i* 990

Galahad (Knight)
The Child of the Holy Grail - Rosalind Miles *t* 907

Gale, Michael (Military Personnel)
Ester's Child - Jean P. Sasson *t* 930

Galina, Susan (Librarian)
Adventures in Time and Space with Max Merriwell - Pat Murphy *s* 781

Gallagher, Judy (Pilot)
The Getaway Special - Jerry Oltion *s* 785

Gallagher, Ruth (Lawyer)
Always Forever - Mark Chadbourn *f* 533

Gallagher, Willi (Teacher)
All Signs Point to Murder - Kat Goldring *m* 81

Gallowglass, Cordelia (Sorceress)
Here Be Monsters - Christopher Stasheff *f* 600

Gallowglass, Geoffrey (Wizard)
Here Be Monsters - Christopher Stasheff *f* 600

Gallowglass, Gregory (Wizard)
Here Be Monsters - Christopher Stasheff *f* 600

Garcia, Gil (Detective—Police)
Under Suspicion - Rachel Lee *r* 331

Gardam, Stella (Military Personnel)
The Clouds Above - Andrew Greig *t* 876

Gardner, Isabella Stewart "Belle" (Historical Figure; Cousin)
Deadly Illumination - Serena Stier *m* 203

Gardner, Joshua (Doctor)
Do You Hear What I Hear? - Holly Jacobs *r* 306

Garnett, Sarah (Immigrant)
The Salt Letters - Christine Balint *t* 819

Garret, Allison (Vampire)
Night Players - P.D. Cacek *h* 625

Garric (Ruler)
Mistress of the Catacombs - David Drake *f* 541

Gary (Teenager)
Lake Wobegon Summer 1956 - Garrison Keillor *c* 1136

Gastner, Bill (Police Officer)
Bag Limit - Steven F. Havill *m* 108

Gates, Eugenia (Secretary)
The Black Eye - Constance Little *m* 144

Gates, Mary (Gentlewoman; Horse Trainer)
The Wedding Wager - Cathy Maxwell *r* 348

Gaunt, Nicholas (Paranormal Investigator)
Dark Sanctuary - H.B. Gregory *h* 644

Gautreaux, Emile (Scientist; Doctor)
Audubon's Watch - John Gregory Brown *c* 1085
Audubon's Watch - John Gregory Brown *t* 833

Gautreaux, Myra (Spouse)
Audubon's Watch - John Gregory Brown *t* 833
Audubon's Watch - John Gregory Brown *c* 1085

Ged (Wizard)
The Other Wind - Ursula K. Le Guin *f* 571

Geigi (Alien)
Defender - C.J. Cherryh *s* 734

Geismar, Jake (Journalist)
The Good German - Joseph Kanon *m* 131
The Good German - Joseph Kanon *c* 1135
The Good German - Joseph Kanon *t* 892

Gelhorn, Margo (Fiance(e))
The Wanderer - Fritz Leiber *s* 767

Genesko, Karl (Police Officer; Sports Figure)
Better than Sex - Susan Holtzer *m* 120

Genet, Leila (Young Woman)
Great American Plain - Gary Sernovitz *c* 1195

Genevieve (Noblewoman)
Drachenfels - Jack Yeovil *f* 613

Gentileschi, Artemisia (Historical Figure; Artist)
The Passion of Artemisia - Susan Vreeland *t* 951

Gentileschi, Orazio (Historical Figure; Artist)
The Passion of Artemisia - Susan Vreeland *t* 951

Geraldi, James (Thief)
The House of Gold - Max Brand *w* 431

Ghote, Ganesh (Police Officer)
Breaking and Entering - H.R.F. Keating *m* 132

Gianavel, Joshua (Warrior)
Rora - James Byron Huggins *i* 1003

Gierek, Melanie (Sailor)
Moontide - Erin Patrick *h* 681

Giffard, Simeon (Nobleman)
A Forbidden Embrace - Anna Jacobs *r* 305

Gilbert (Teacher; Friend)
Schooling - Heather McGowan *c* 1159

Gilley (Witch)
The Third Witch - Rebecca Reisert *t* 921

Gilpatrick, Rance (Smuggler)
Murder on the Minnesota - Conrad Allen *t* 816

Giordino, Al (Sidekick; Government Official)
Valhalla Rising - Clive Cussler *c* 1097

Giuditta (Cook)
Bella Donna - Barbara Cherne *t* 836

Glass, Jordan (Photographer; Journalist)
Dead Sleep - Greg Iles *m* 123

Glitsky, Abe (Detective—Homicide)
The Oath - John Lescroart *m* 141

Glover, Eleanor (Noblewoman; Fiance(e))
Under the Kissing Bough - Shannon Donnelly *r* 271

Glueck, Rona Leigh (Convict)
Love Her Madly - Mary-Ann Tirone Smith *m* 198

Godalming, Beatrice (Actress)
Quincey Morris, Vampire - P.N. Elrod *h* 632

Godsol, Rafe (Knight; Nobleman)
The Warrior's Damsel - Denise Hampton *r* 295

Gold, Aaron (Journalist)
Veiled Threats - Deborah Donnelly *m* 60

Goldman, Annie (Waiter/Waitress; Store Owner)
What to Do about Annie? - Millie Criswell *r* 264

Goldstein, Kiki (Widow(er); Detective—Amateur)
Tall, Dead, and Handsome - Annie Griffin *m* 91

Goode, Alex (Religious; Historical Figure)
Sea of Glory - Ken Wales *i* 1056
Sea of Glory - Ken Wales *t* 953

GoodNews (Radio Personality; Activist)
How to Be Good - Nick Hornby *c* 1126

Goodnight, Augusta (Angel)
An Angel to Die For - Mignon F. Ballard *f* 522

Gordie, Elspeth (Psychic)
Ashling - Isobelle Carmody *s* 732

Gordon, Henry (Sailor)
Moontide - Erin Patrick *h* 681

Gordon, Mary "Molly" (Heiress; Ward)
The Secret Clan: Abducted Heiress - Amanda Scott *r* 390

Gorecki, Jacek (Sailor)
The Yellow Sailor - Steve Weiner *t* 954

Grace (Narrator; Television)
The Wig My Father Wore - Anne Enright *c* 1111

Grace, Karen (Anthropologist)
Deep Fathom - James Rollins *s* 792

Graham, Alan (Archaeologist; Detective—Amateur)
The Last Mayan - Malcolm Shuman *m* 195

Grant, Ellen (Radio Personality)
Teeth - Edo van Belkom *h* 705

Grant, Julia (Historical Figure; Spouse)
The Ambush of My Name - Jeffrey Marks *t* 903

Grant, Ulysses S. (Historical Figure; Military Personnel)
The Ambush of My Name - Jeffrey Marks *t* 903
Call Each River Jordan - Owen Parry *t* 914

Gray, Claire (Director)
Desert Autumn - Michael Craft *m* 45

Gray, Matthew (Architect; Widow(er))
Bethany's Song - Susan Plunkett *r* 372

Grayden (Nobleman)
Lady Hilary's Halloween - Mona Gedney *r* 291

Grayson (Nobleman; Rake)
The Rake and the Wallflower - Allison Lane *r* 325

Green, Briony (Scientist)
Blessed Baby - Lois Richer *i* 1043

Green, Mattie (Teacher)
Mattie and the Blacksmith - Linda Lea Castle *r* 253

Greenbaum, Nancy (Psychologist)
Ghost Killer - Scott Chandler *h* 627

Greenberg, Arthur (Religious)
The Thirty-Third Hour - Mitchell Chefitz *i* 978

Greene, Harris (Businessman)
Sidhe-Devil - Aaron Allston *f* 516

Greenway, Sophie (Journalist; Innkeeper)
Dial M for Meat Loaf - Ellen Hart *m* 105

Greenwood, Honore (Adventurer)
Moon Medicine - Mike Blakely *t* 827

Greer, Carmen (Abuse Victim; Spouse)
Echo Burning - Lee Child *w* 442

Greer, Sloop (Crime Victim)
Echo Burning - Lee Child *w* 442

Gregg, Jane (Editor)
See Jane Date - Melissa Senate *r* 394

Gregg, Sally (Police Officer)
End over End - Kate Kennedy *c* 1139

Grey Bear (Indian; Warrior)
Cheyenne Summer - Vella Munn *t* 911

Gribbon, Salt (Lighthouse Keeper)
A Warmth in Winter - Lori Copeland *i* 984

Griffin, Cal (Lawyer)
Magic Time - Marc Scott Zicree *f* 614

Griffin, Hollis "Griff" (Military Personnel)
Tall, Dark, and Difficult - Patricia Coughlin *r* 261

Griffin, Lew (Detective—Private; Writer)
Ghost of a Flea - James Sallis *m* 192

Griffin, Madeline "Maddie" (Bounty Hunter; Secretary)
Dangerously Irresistible - Kristin Gabriel *r* 289

Griffin of Droghallow (Knight)
White Lion's Lady - Tina St. John *r* 407

Grimwulf, Dhamon (Adventurer)
Betrayal - Jean Rabe *f* 589

Grooves, Bobby Joe "Spin" (Sports Figure)
The Money-Whipped Steer-Job Three-Jack Give-Up Artist - Dan Jenkins *c* 1132

Grover, Duncan (Crime Victim)
The Thunder Keeper - Margaret Coel *w* 444

Grunthor (Military Personnel)
Destiny - Elizabeth Haydon *f* 554

Gryf (Amnesiac)
The Sea Sprite - Ruth Langan *r* 328

Guarnaccia, Salvatore (Police Officer)
Property of Blood - Magdalen Nabb *m* 164

Guenevere (Royalty)
The Child of the Holy Grail - Rosalind Miles *t* 907

Gui, Bernard (Religious)
The Good Men - Charmaine Craig *t* 844

Guidry, Joseph "Junior" (Narrator; Handicapped)
Junior's Leg - Ken Wells *c* 1214

Guinevere (Royalty)
The Dragon Queen - Alice Borchardt *t* 829
The Dragon Queen - Alice Borchardt *f* 528
Lancelot Du Lethe - J. Robert King *f* 566

Gullwing, Tara (Clone)
Tenebrea's Hope - Roxann Dawson *s* 743

Gunnhild (Royalty)
Mother of Kings - Poul Anderson *t* 818

Gunther, Joe (Police Officer)
Tucker Peak - Archer Mayor *m* 151

Guppy, Roger (Boyfriend; Sports Figure)
Lake Wobegon Summer 1956 - Garrison Keillor *c* 1136

Gustav (Knight)
Guardians of the Lost - Margaret Weis *f* 611

Gwen (Hairdresser)
He Goes, She Goes - Joanna Torrey *c* 1209

Gwynedd, Madoc ap Owain (Historical Figure; Bastard Son)
Circle of Stars - Anna Lee Waldo *t* 952

Gwynneve (Religious)
Confessions of a Pagan Nun - Kate Horsley *t* 886

H

Haagen, Anneke (Computer Expert; Detective—Amateur)
Better than Sex - Susan Holtzer *m* 120

Haas, Norman (Prisoner)
Cold - John Smolens *c* 1199

Habiba (Warrior)
The Prince of Shadow - Curt Benjamin *f* 526

Hadaly (Android)
Tomorrow's Eve - Auguste Villiers de L'Isle Adam *s* 806

Hadrien, Artemis (Police Officer)
Wayward Moon - Denny DeMartino *s* 744

Hagbolt, Paul (Public Relations)
The Wanderer - Fritz Leiber *s* 767

Haggard, Rich (Boyfriend)
Glare Ice - Mary Logue *m* 145

Haggerty, Lindy (Dancer; Teacher)
Midsummer Murder - Shelley Freydont *m* 71

Haggerty, Mickey (Police Officer)
The Blue Last - Martha Grimes *m* 92

Hak-Bin (Alien)
Deathday - William C. Dietz *s* 746

Hakonson, Dragon (Warrior)
Come Back to Me - Josie Litton *r* 337

Hakonson, Wolf (Warrior)
Dream of Me - Josie Litton *r* 338

Halcombe, Marion (Gentlewoman)
The Dark Clue - James Wilson *t* 959

Haldane, Tilly (Actress)
My Best Friend - Laura Wilson *m* 214

Halder, Alfie (Military Personnel)
The Jerusalem Scrolls - Bodie Thoene *t* 942

Hale, Bill (Rancher; Outlaw)
The Years of Fear - Fred Grove *w* 460

Hall, Fletcher (Entertainer)
Flying Eagle - Tim Champlin *w* 440

Hallekk (Pirate)
The Rover - Mel Odom *f* 584

Halley (Military Personnel)
Time Future - Maxine McArthur *s* 770

Halliday, Anthony (Detective—Private; Friend)
Look at Me - Jennifer Egan *c* 1108

Halliwell, Morwenna (Gentlewoman)
Abandon - Jillian Hunter *r* 303

Hamilton, John (Writer)
Dark Sanctuary - H.B. Gregory *h* 644

Hammond, Curtis (Child)
One Door Away from Heaven - Dean R. Koontz *h* 661

Hampton, Jeremy (Detective—Private)
Deadly Illumination - Serena Stier *m* 203

Hampton, Robert George Colter (Nobleman; Rake)
A Reckless Encounter - Rosemary Rogers *r* 385

Haney, Cheryl (Real Estate Agent; Girlfriend)
The Money-Whipped Steer-Job Three-Jack Give-Up Artist - Dan Jenkins *c* 1132

Hanks, Arly (Police Officer)
Maggody and the Moonbeams - Joan Hess *m* 114

Hansen, Em (Scientist; Detective—Amateur)
Fault Line - Sarah Andrews *m* 7

Hanuma (Foreman)
Night of the Bat - Paul Zindel *h* 714

Hardin, Jeff (Radio Personality)
A Prince of a Guy - Sheila Rabe *r* 376

Harding (Detective—Private; Alcoholic)
Kiss It Goodbye - John Wessel *m* 213

Harding, Warren G. (Historical Figure; Political Figure)
Carter Beats the Devil - Glen David Gold *t* 874

Hardman, Jard (Rancher; Saloon Keeper/Owner)
Open Range - Zane Grey *w* 458

Hardress, Helen (Young Woman)
Fairness - Ferdinand Mount *c* 1167

Hardy, Dismas (Lawyer)
The Oath - John Lescroart *m* 141

Hariba (Slave)
Nekropolis - Maureen McHugh *s* 774

Harkness, James (Nobleman)
The Bride Sale - Candice Hern *r* 298

Harkonnen, Vladimir (Nobleman)
House Corrino - Brian Herbert *s* 757

Harmon, Darin (Narrator; Sports Figure)
Just Say No! - Omar Tyree *c* 1210

Haroney, Kate "Big Nose Kate" (Lover; Historical Figure)
Bucking the Tiger - Bruce Olds *c* 1176
Bucking the Tiger - Bruce Olds *w* 485

Harper, Jo (Journalist)
The Ice Child - Elizabeth McGregor *t* 905

Harper, Noah (Businessman)
Too Much Temptation - Lori Foster *r* 286

Harrington, Justin (Nobleman)
A Guardian's Angel - Jo Ann Ferguson *r* 278

Harris, Brian (Teenager)
The White Room - A.J. Matthews *h* 673

Harris, Catherine "Cat" Anne (Stock Broker)
Seducing Mr. Right - Cherry Adair *r* 223

Harris, Eve (Political Figure)
The Manhattan Hunt Club - John Saul *h* 687

Harris, Polly (Housewife)
The White Room - A.J. Matthews *h* 673

Harris, Tim (Teacher)
The White Room - A.J. Matthews *h* 673

Harrow, Andre (Professor)
Beasts - Joyce Carol Oates *c* 1173

Harrow, Dorcas (Spouse; Artist)
Beasts - Joyce Carol Oates *c* 1173

Hart, Katherine (Parent; Divorced Person)
Riot - Shashi Tharoor *c* 1208

Hart, Priscilla (Student)
Riot - Shashi Tharoor *c* 1208

Hart, Rudyard (Parent; Divorced Person)
Riot - Shashi Tharoor *c* 1208

Hart, Walker "Bear" (Businessman)
Miss Match - Leslie Carroll *r* 252

Harte, Laura (Hotel Worker)
The Wager - Metsy Hingle *r* 301

Hartford, Sincerity Prudence (Gentlewoman; Heiress)
A Tangled Web - Donna Bell *r* 230

Hartleigh Compton, Elizabeth (Widow(er); Noblewoman)
Death Is in the Air - Kate Kingsbury *m* 136

Hartright, Walter (Gentleman)
The Dark Clue - James Wilson *t* 959

Hartstone, Anthony (Nobleman)
Abandon - Jillian Hunter *r* 303

HARV (Artificial Intelligence)
The Plutonium Blonde - John Zakour *s* 813

Harvey, Cora (Singer)
Rhythms - Donna Hill *t* 884

Haskell, Zorah (Aged Person)
An Angel to Die For - Mignon F. Ballard *f* 522

Hasper, Jean (Widow(er))
Worthy of Riches - Bonnie Leon *i* 1017

Hassa, Alexander (Spouse; Doctor)
The Girl from the Golden Horn - Kurban Said *c* 1191

Hastings, Andrew (Religious)
Who Killed the Curate? - Joan Coggin *m* 36

Hastings, Lupin Lorrimer (Noblewoman; Spouse)
Who Killed the Curate? - Joan Coggin *m* 36

Hathaway, Anne (Historical Figure; Spouse)
Her Infinite Variety - Pamela Rafael Berkman *t* 823

Hatton, Will (Doctor)
Shades of Justice - Fredrick Huebner *m* 121

Haukeland, Erik (Student—Exchange)
East of the Sun, West of the Moon - Carole Bellacera *r* 231

Hauser, Ed (Lawyer)
Shades of Justice - Fredrick Huebner *m* 121

Haussmann, Georges-Eugene (Historical Figure; Architect)
Haussmann, or The Distinction - Paul LaFarge *t* 900

Haussmann, Sky (Spaceship Captain)
Chasm City - Alastair Reynolds *s* 789

Haversham, Nigel (Nobleman; Expatriate)
French Leave - Sheri Cobb South *r* 404

Hawk (Amnesiac; Inventor)
Starhawk - Mack Maloney *s* 769

Hawk of Essex (Nobleman; Warrior)
Believe in Me - Josie Litton *r* 336

Hawkins, Brody (Businessman; Rogue)
Sarah and the Rogue - DeLoras Scott *r* 391

Hawkins, Marie-Ange (Heiress; Orphan)
Leap of Faith - Danielle Steel *c* 1203

Hawkins, Ray (Professor)
A Family for Jana - Eileen Berger *i* 968

Hawkins, Ridge (Lawman)
Just West of Heaven - Kathleen Kane *r* 313

Hawks, Clayton (Rancher)
Man from Wyoming - Dane Coolidge *w* 448

Hawthorne, Lily (Spy; Guardian)
To Tame a Duke - Patricia Grasso *r* 293

Hawtrey, Booth (Immortal)
Something More - Paul Cornell *s* 738

Haxton, Gerald (Clerk)
My Best Friend - Laura Wilson *m* 214

Hayes, Blair (Alcoholic; Singer)
Written on the Wind - Judith Pella *i* 1040

Hayes, Cameron (Journalist)
Written on the Wind - Judith Pella *i* 1040

Hayes, Jackie (Young Woman)
Written on the Wind - Judith Pella *i* 1040

Hayley (Girlfriend)
My Little Blue Dress - Bruno Maddox *c* 1150

Hazard, Galatine (Criminal)
Hazard's Price - Robert S. Stone *f* 601

Heather (Young Woman)
Night of Dracula - Christopher Schildt *h* 692

Heiki (Child)
The Scent of Magic - Cliff McNish *f* 581

Heikkonen (Spaceship Captain)
Second Chances - Susan Shwartz *s* 796

Hekate (Witch)
Thrice Bound - Roberta Gellis *f* 547

Helananthe (Ruler)
The Obsidian Tower - Freda Warrington *f* 609

Helen (Addict)
When Heaven Weeps - Ted Dekker *i* 988

Heller, Nathan (Detective—Private)
Kisses of Death - Max Allan Collins *m* 41
Kisses of Death - Max Allan Collins *t* 841

Henderson, John Basil (Agent; Lover)
Any Way the Wind Blows - E. Lynn Harris *c* 1122

Hendrickson, Carrie (Pharmacist)
Buffalo Valley - Debbie Macomber *w* 474

Henry (Doctor)
Dreamcatcher - Stephen King *h* 660

Henry VI (Historical Figure; Ruler)
Knight Errant - R. Garcia y Robertson *t* 869

Herdtmacher, Thomas (Military Personnel)
Brother John - Rutledge Etheridge *s* 750

Hernandez, Alicia (Relative)
Fire Lilies - Cynthia Leal Massey *w* 476

Hernandez, Elida (Student—Graduate)
The Deadwood Beetle - Mylene Dressler *c* 1106

Hesmucet (Military Personnel)
Marching through Peachtree - Harry Turtledove *f* 606

Heydon, Cassie (Teenager; Twin)
City Infernal - Edward Lee *h* 667

Hill, Roy (Businessman; Single Parent)
Last of the Dixie Heroes - Peter Abrahams *m* 1

Hillor (Judge)
Hope's End - Stephen Chambers *s* 733

Himler, Donnie (Teenager)
The World Weaver - Craig Etchison *s* 749

Hines, Jake (Police Officer)
Six-Pound Walleye - Elizabeth Gunn *m* 93

Hitomi, Mirumoto (Warrior)
The Crab - Stan Brown *f* 531

Hoegh-Guldberg, Ove (Courtier; Historical Figure)
The Royal Physician's Visit - Per Olov Enquist *c* 1110

Hoffman, Nick (Professor; Homosexual)
Burning Down the House - Lev Rafael *m* 176

Hok (Alien)
Shockball - S.L. Viehl *s* 805

Holbrook, Grif (Guard)
Stage Trails West - Frank Bonham *w* 427

Holden, Vicky (Indian; Lawyer)
The Thunder Keeper - Margaret Coel *w* 444
The Thunder Keeper - Margaret Coel *m* 35

Holland, Angelina "Angie" Bartoli (Spouse; Orphan)
The Bride of Willow Creek - Maggie Osborne *r* 364

Holland, Billy Bob (Lawyer; Veteran)
Bitterroot - James Lee Burke *c* 1088

Holland, Sam (Carpenter; Spouse)
The Bride of Willow Creek - Maggie Osborne *r* 364

Holliday, John H. "Doc" (Gunfighter; Historical Figure)
Bucking the Tiger - Bruce Olds *w* 485

Holliday, John H. "Doc" (Historical Figure; Gunfighter)
Bucking the Tiger - Bruce Olds *c* 1176

Hollis, Holly (Assistant)
Bachelor on the Prowl - Kasey Michaels *r* 353

Holloway, Chase (Architect)
Marry Me, Maddie? - Rita Herron *r* 299

Holloway, Jenny (Single Parent; Restaurateur)
In Too Deep - Janelle Taylor *r* 413

Holloway, Lucinda (Rancher)
Destiny Valley - Fred Grove *w* 459

Hollowell, Patricia Anne "Mouse" (Teacher; Detective—Amateur)
Murder Boogies with Elvis - Anne George *m* 77

Holly, Joe (Military Personnel)
Double Vengeance - John Duncklee *w* 449

Holmes, Ezra (Lawman)
The Vigil - Clay Reynolds *w* 498

Holmes, Sherlock (Detective—Private)
Chapel Noir - Carole Nelson Douglas *t* 856
The Great Game - Michael Kurland *t* 899
Night Watch - Stephen Kendrick *t* 896
Sherlock Holmes and the Giant Rat of Sumatra - Alan Vanneman *m* 210
Sherlock Holmes and the Secret Alliance - Larry Millett *m* 158
Sherlock Holmes and the Secret Alliance - Larry Millett *t* 908

Holton, Anthony (Writer; Expatriate)
The Chinese Fire Drill - Les Roberts *m* 185

Homa, Grig (Government Official)
Second Contact - J.D. Austin *s* 719

Hood, Daniel (Teacher; Crime Victim)
Echoes of Lies - Jo Bannister *m* 11

Howell, Peter (Religious)
Shadow Valley Rising - Stephen Overholser *w* 488

Hoyle, Priscilla (Companion; Secretary)
Creeping Venom - Sheila Pim *m* 173

Hubbard, Catherine (Divorced Person)
The World Below - Sue Miller *c* 1163

Hudson, Jane (Teacher; Single Parent)
The Lake of Dead Languages - Carol Goodman *m* 82

Hulda (Servant)
The Silent Woman - Susan M. Dodd *t* 852

Humboldt, Nelson (Professor; Accident Victim)
The Lecturer's Tale - James Hynes *h* 649

Humiir (Alien)
Acorna's Search - Anne McCaffrey *s* 772

Hunt, Claire (Television Personality; Detective—Amateur)
The Masks of Auntie Laveau - Robert J. Randisi *m* 177

Hunt, Gil (Store Owner; Detective—Amateur)
The Masks of Auntie Laveau - Robert J. Randisi *m* 177

Hunter, Hawk (Spaceman)
Planet America - Mack Maloney *s* 768

Huron, Paul (Artist)
Desert Autumn - Michael Craft *m* 45

Huxleigh, Penelope "Nell" (Companion)
Chapel Noir - Carole Nelson Douglas *m* 62
Chapel Noir - Carole Nelson Douglas *t* 856

I

ibn Musa, Ibrahim "Abdu" (Mechanic; Immigrant)
The Pickup - Nadine Gordimer *c* 1116

Ice (Murderer)
Blood Games - Lee Killough *h* 657

Icebones (Animal)
Icebones - Stephen Baxter *s* 723

Ilon (Teenager)
The Wild Boy - Warren Rochelle *s* 791

Imoshen (Royalty)
Dark Dreams - Cory Daniells *r* 267

Ingalls, Josh (Wealthy; Widow(er))
The Nanny - Judith Stacy *r* 408

Ingram, Mattie (Widow(er))
The Widow's Little Secret - Judith Stacy *r* 409

Inskip, George "Skip" (Military Personnel; Pilot)
Sentimental Journey - Jill Barnett *r* 228
Sentimental Journey - Jill Barnett *t* 821

Isabel of Dornei (Noblewoman)
The Marriage Bed - Claudia Dain *r* 266

Ishaq (Architect; Narrator)
The Rock - Kanan Makiya *t* 902
The Rock - Kanan Makiya *c* 1152

Iverson, Kate (Doctor)
Hosts - F. Paul Wilson *h* 710

Ives, Hannah (Survivor; Single Parent)
Occasion of Revenge - Marcia Talley *m* 205

J

Jaansma, Garvin (Military Personnel)
Homefall - Chris Bunch *s* 729

Jackson, Hilary (Artist)
The Art of Dying - Diana Killian *i* 1009

Jackson, J.W. (Beachcomber; Detective—Private)
First Light - Philip R. Craig *m* 46

Jacobs, Daniel (Art Dealer; Lover)
Almost - Elizabeth Benedict *c* 1073

Jacobs, Erma Lee (Abuse Victim; Grandparent)
A Place Called Wiregrass - Michael Morris *i* 1029

Jacobs, Kitty (Lover)
War Story - Gwen Edelman *c* 1107

Jacobson, Frank (Police Officer)
A Study in Death - Iain McDowell *m* 155

Jago, Eleanor (Doctor)
Time Future - Maxine McArthur *s* 770

Jake (Aged Person)
Nearly People - Conrad Williams *h* 708

Jakob (Survivor; Scholar)
In the Shape of a Boar - Lawrence Norfolk *c* 1171

Jalil (Teenager)
Mystify the Magician - K.A. Applegate *f* 520

James, Alicia (Scientist; Time Traveler)
Alicia's Song - Susan Plunkett *r* 371

James, Alyson (Journalist)
Darkling I Listen - Katherine Sutcliffe *r* 412

James, Bethany (Teacher; Time Traveler)
Bethany's Song - Susan Plunkett *r* 372

James, Daisy (Child)
Come, My Little Angel - Diane Noble *i* 1033

Jamison, Hilary (Noblewoman)
Lady Hilary's Halloween - Mona Gedney *r* 291

Janis, Joseph Antoine (Historical Figure; Mountain Man)
The June Rise - William Tremblay *w* 507
The June Rise - William Tremblay *t* 945

Jardine, Olivia (Grandparent; Businesswoman)
The Wager - Metsy Hingle *r* 301

Jason (Adventurer)
Celtika - Robert Holdstock *f* 558

Jason (Boyfriend; Addict)
Lucky Us - Joan Silber *c* 1198

Jasper, Kate (Businesswoman; Detective—Amateur)
A Sensitive Kind of Murder - Jacqueline Girdner *m* 80

Jaylin (Teenager)
Swell Foop - Piers Anthony *f* 518

Jean-Claude (Vampire)
Narcissus in Chains - Laurell K. Hamilton *h* 645

Jeff (Young Man)
The Last Vampire - T.M. Wright *h* 712

Jeffries, Marcus Quentin (Guardian; Nobleman)
The Trouble with Harriet - Wilma Counts *r* 262

Jekyl, Simon (Nobleman; Cousin)
The Archer's Tale - Bernard Cornwell *t* 843

Jen (Witch)
Gumshoe Gorilla - Keith Hartman *s* 756

Jenkins, Grace (Secretary)
Too Much Temptation - Lori Foster r 286

Jennsen (Sorceress)
The Pillars of Creation - Terry Goodkind f 550

Jensen, Will (Cowboy)
Ride West to Dawn - James C. Work w 514

Jenson, Jana (Single Parent; Student)
A Family for Jana - Eileen Berger i 968

Jessenovik, Matthew "Vik" (Police Officer)
Whispers in the Dark - Eleanor Taylor Bland m 21

Jesson, Henry James III (Scholar)
The Grand Complication - Allen Kurzweil c 1144

Jim (Security Officer)
Second Chances - Susan Shwartz s 796

Jimmy (Child)
Smoke-Filled Rooms - Kris Nelscott m 166

Jinya (Alien)
Angry Young Spaceman - Jim Munroe s 780

Joan (Friend)
In the Forest of Harm - Sallie Bissell c 1074

Joe Grey (Animal)
Cat Laughing Last - Shirley Rousseau Murphy m 162

John Lackland (Historical Figure; Royalty)
Pride of Kings - Judith Tarr t 941
Pride of Kings - Judith Tarr f 603

John the Eunuch (Government Official)
Three for a Letter - Mary Reed m 180
Three for a Letter - Mary Reed t 920

Johnson, Evan (Farmer; Veteran)
The Edge of Town - Dorothy Garlock r 290

Johnson, Samuel (Writer; Historical Figure)
According to Queeney - Beryl Bainbridge c 1069

Johnson, Xavier (Businessman)
Followin' a Dream - Eboni Snoe r 403

Johnson, Zachary Nixon (Detective—Private)
The Plutonium Blonde - John Zakour s 813

Jones, Abel (Military Personnel; Spy)
Call Each River Jordan - Owen Parry m 169
Call Each River Jordan - Owen Parry t 914

Jones, Clay (Spouse; Veterinarian)
Death of the Last Villista - Allana Martin w 475

Jones, Julie (Farmer)
The Edge of Town - Dorothy Garlock r 290

Jones, Lester (Musician; Friend)
Gabriel's Gift - Hanif Kureishi c 1143

Jones, Sarah (Widow(er))
Rocky and the Senator's Daughter - Dixie Browning r 246

Jones, Texana (Store Owner; Detective—Amateur)
Death of the Last Villista - Allana Martin w 475
Death of the Last Villista - Allana Martin m 149

Jonesy (Teacher)
Dreamcatcher - Stephen King h 660

Joseph (Ruler)
Marching through Peachtree - Harry Turtledove f 606

Jovic, Jan (Writer)
When Heaven Weeps - Ted Dekker i 988

Jubilo (Empath; Spouse)
Swift as Desire - Laura Esquivel c 1112

Judd, Kyler (Teacher)
Scorch - A.D. Nauman s 782

Jude (Friend)
Death on the Downs - Simon Brett m 27

Julian, Adib (Military Personnel)
March to the Sea - David Weber s 809

Jury, Richard (Police Officer)
The Blue Last - Martha Grimes m 92

Justicar (Warrior)
Queen of the Demonweb Pits - Paul Kidd f 563

Justice, Charlotte (Detective—Police)
Stormy Weather - Paula L. Woods m 220

Justinian I (Historical Figure; Ruler)
Three for a Letter - Mary Reed t 920

K

Ka'b al-Ahbar (Historical Figure)
The Rock - Kanan Makiya t 902

Kabeiros (Warrior)
Thrice Bound - Roberta Gellis f 547

Kaiser, John (FBI Agent)
Dead Sleep - Greg Iles m 123

Kalila (Witch)
Pride of Kings - Judith Tarr f 603

Kane, Doc (Prisoner)
Leaving Disneyland - Alexander Parsons c 1179

Kapp, Henry (Television)
TV - Brian Brown c 1084

Karan (Psychic)
The Way between the Worlds - Ian Irvine f 560

Karelli, Tony (Religious; Boyfriend)
Redeeming Claire - Cynthia Rutledge i 1045

Karitska (Psychic; Detective—Amateur)
Kaleidoscope - Dorothy Gilman m 79

Karkald (Worker)
World Fall - Douglas Niles f 583

Karrelian, Brandt (Businessman)
Hazard's Price - Robert S. Stone f 601

Kate (Cousin)
Lake Wobegon Summer 1956 - Garrison Keillor c 1136

Kates, Cameron (Scientist)
Minutes to Burn - Gregg Andrew Hurwitz s 762

Kates, Justin (Scientist)
Minutes to Burn - Gregg Andrew Hurwitz s 762

Katherine (Housewife)
The Crow Maiden - Sarah Singleton f 598

Katherine of Cliffside (Noblewoman; Highwayman)
The Night the Stars Fell - Christina Kingston r 317

Kaufmann, Linda (Scientist)
Frankenstein: The Legacy - Christopher Schildt h 691

Kavanagh, Cynthia (Spouse)
In This Mountain - Jan Karon i 1007

Kavanagh, Tim (Religious)
In This Mountain - Jan Karon i 1007

Kazairl (Mythical Creature)
Spirit of the Stone - Maggie Furey f 545

Keck, Jim (Thief)
Man from Wyoming - Dane Coolidge w 448

Keely (Noblewoman)
Children of the Lion - Jennifer Roberson f 591

Keith (Child)
The Amazing Maurice and His Educated Rodents - Terry Pratchett f 587

Kell (Adventurer)
Ice - Stephen Bowkett s 724

Kellaway, Lucille (Teacher; Twin)
The Virtuous Cyprian - Nicola Cornick r 260

Kelly, Courtney (Businesswoman)
The Great Baby Caper - Eugenia Riley r 380

Kelly, Elijah "Preacher" (Gunfighter)
Colorado Twilight - Tess Pendergrass w 495

Keltner, Jason (Musician; Detective—Amateur)
The Night Men - Keith Snyder m 199

Kennedy, Heath (Outlaw)
The Border Hostage - Virginia Henley t 883

Kennelly, Edward (Detective—Police)
Murder at the President's Door - Elliott Roosevelt t 928

Kenrick (Ruler)
Rebel's Cage - Kate Jacoby f 561

Kent, Jason (Recluse; Mercenary)
Lt. Kent: Lone Wolf - Judith Lyons r 341

Kent, Lorna (Orphan)
A Morning in Eden - Anna Gilbert t 872

Kenyon, Gabriel (Artist; Nobleman)
Tempt Me Twice - Barbara Dawson Smith r 400

Kerim, Abdul (Expatriate; Royalty)
The Girl from the Golden Horn - Kurban Said c 1191

Kerr, Ian (Police Officer)
A Study in Death - Iain McDowell m 155

Kerry, Cole (Outlaw)
Behold a Red Horse - Cotton Smith w 504

Kerry, Ethan (Rancher)
Behold a Red Horse - Cotton Smith w 504

Kerry, Jane (Librarian)
In the Dark - Richard Laymon h 663

Kerry, Luther (Relative)
Behold a Red Horse - Cotton Smith w 504

Kestrel (Thief)
Pool of Radiance - Carrie Bebris f 525

Kid (Outlaw)
The Outlaws - Wayne D. Overholser w 490

Kieran of Gleannmara (Nobleman)
Riona - Linda Windsor i 1060

Kiervauna (Military Personnel; Alien)
Holding the Line - Rick Shelley s 795

Kil, Tulsi (Entertainer)
A Feast in Exile - Chelsea Quinn Yarbro h 713

Kills Crow, Kole (Indian; Fugitive)
You Never Can Tell - Kathleen Eagle w 450

Kincaid, Carnegie (Consultant)
Veiled Threats - Deborah Donnelly m 60

Kincaid, Gordon (Doctor; Veteran)
The Nightingale's Song - Kathleen Eschenburg r 273

Kincaid, Kitty (Captive)
Sentimental Journey - Jill Barnett t 821

King, Maud (Explorer)
Conjuring Maud - Philip Danze t 847

Kinross, Cassandra (Spirit; Crime Victim)
You're the One - Judi McCoy r 351

Kip (Spouse)
Female Intelligence - Jane Heller c 1125

Kirkland, James (Businessman)
Deep Fathom - James Rollins s 792

Kirtt (Artificial Intelligence)
Appleseed - John Clute s 736

Kiru (Criminal; Prisoner)
Bikini Planet - David Garnett s 752

Kisada, Hida (Warrior)
The Crab - Stan Brown f 531

Character Name Index

Kit (Animal)
Cat Laughing Last - Shirley Rousseau Murphy *m* 162

Kite, Martin (Police Officer)
A Sunset Touch - Marjorie Eccles *m* 64

Klaus, Stephanie (Crime Victim)
Glare Ice - Mary Logue *m* 145

Klein, Lieselotte (Student—College)
The Flight of the Maidens - Jane Gardam *t* 870

Kleist, Christine (Nurse)
Ester's Child - Jean P. Sasson *t* 930

Klonk, Leilani (Child)
One Door Away from Heaven - Dean R. Koontz *h* 661

Knave, Gerald (Investigator)
The Counterfeit Heinlein - Laurence M. Janiver *s* 763

Kneece, Derwood "Woody" (Military Personnel; Lawyer)
Officer of the Court - Bill Mesce Jr. *t* 906

Knight, Hassie (Pharmacist)
Buffalo Valley - Debbie Macomber *w* 474

Knight, Philip (Detective—Private)
Emerald Aisle - Ralph McInerny *m* 156

Knight, Roger (Professor; Detective—Amateur)
Emerald Aisle - Ralph McInerny *m* 156

Knight, Sebastian (Carpenter; Single Parent)
Heaven on Earth - Marilyn Pappano *r* 366

Knightly, Harriet (Guardian; Writer)
The Trouble with Harriet - Wilma Counts *r* 262

Kodiak, Atticus (Bodyguard)
Critical Space - Greg Rucka *m* 190

Kohler, Hermann (Military Personnel)
Kaleidoscope - J. Robert Janes *m* 126
Kaleidoscope - J. Robert Janes *t* 888

Koko (Animal)
The Cat Who Went Up the Creek - Lilian Jackson Braun *m* 26

Kokoschka, Oskar (Historical Figure; Artist)
The Silent Woman - Susan M. Dodd *t* 852

Konstantin, Dore (Police Officer)
Dervish Is Digital - Pat Cadigan *s* 731

Kooby, Jamieson (Teenager; Orphan)
Stillwater - William F. Weld *t* 955

Korendil (Nobleman)
Spirits White as Lightning - Mercedes Lackey *f* 568

Kosta, Jereko (Spy)
Angelmass - Timothy Zahn *s* 812

Kosutic, Eva (Military Personnel)
March to the Sea - David Weber *s* 809

Kovett, Charles (Doctor)
Darkness - Sam Siciliano *h* 695

Kroger, Ginny (Technician)
Defender - C.J. Cherryh *s* 734

Kropotkin, Lucy (Businesswoman)
The American Zone - L. Neil Smith *s* 799

Krug, Manuel (Businessman)
Tower of Glass - Robert Silverberg *s* 797

Krug, Simeon (Businessman)
Tower of Glass - Robert Silverberg *s* 797

Kruger, Joseph (Writer)
War Story - Gwen Edelman *c* 1107

Krysta (Noblewoman; Bride)
Believe in Me - Josie Litton *r* 336

Kun'dren, Ngan Sung (Fugitive)
Of Aged Angels - Monte Cook *s* 737

Kurtz, Abraham (Military Personnel)
Dreamcatcher - Stephen King *h* 660

Kyle, Vaughn (Military Personnel)
Buffalo Valley - Debbie Macomber *w* 474

L

Lacey, James (Spouse)
Agatha Raisin and the Love from Hell - M.C. Beaton *m* 14

LaCouture, Chas (Boyfriend; Businessman)
The Savage Girl - Alex Shakar *c* 1196

Lafayette, Marie (Teacher)
Night Hawk's Bride - Jillian Hart *r* 296

Lake, Lavinia (Businesswoman; Guardian)
Slightly Shady - Amanda Quick *r* 375

Lalasha, Chandris (Criminal)
Angelmass - Timothy Zahn *s* 812

Lamb, Kathryn "Kitty" (Teacher)
Miss Match - Leslie Carroll *r* 252

Lamb, Mary (Writer)
Everything You Need - A.L. Kennedy *c* 1138

Lambert, Alfred (Railroad Worker)
The Corrections - Jonathan Franzen *c* 1113

Lambert, Darcy (Sea Captain)
The Sea Sprite - Ruth Langan *r* 328

Lambert, Enid (Parent; Spouse)
The Corrections - Jonathan Franzen *c* 1113

Lambert, Evan (Lawyer; Friend)
Almost - Elizabeth Benedict *c* 1073

Lambert, Gary (Relative; Banker)
The Corrections - Jonathan Franzen *c* 1113

Lamplighter, Edgewick (Librarian)
The Rover - Mel Odom *f* 584

Land, Davy (Convict)
Peace Like a River - Leif Enger *c* 1109

Land, Elmo (Cowboy; Vampire)
The Last Vampire - T.M. Wright *h* 712

Land, Jeremiah (Parent; Maintenance Worker)
Peace Like a River - Leif Enger *c* 1109

Land, Reuben (Narrator)
Peace Like a River - Leif Enger *c* 1109

Landis, Elizabeth (Spouse; Parent)
A Garden to Keep - Jamie Langston Turner *i* 1055

Lange, Georgia (Spouse; Neighbor)
The Woman Next Door - Barbara Delinsky *c* 1101

Langslow, Meg (Artisan; Detective—Amateur)
Revenge of the Wrought-Iron Flamingos - Donna Andrews *m* 6

Langway, Matthew (Detective—Private)
Turnabout - Jeremiah Healy *m* 111

LaRocca, Dominick "Nick" (Businessman)
Insatiable - Julie Elizabeth Leto *r* 333

LaSalle, Sonny (Criminal; Student—High School)
A World of Thieves - James Carlos Blake *w* 424
A World of Thieves - James Carlos Blake *t* 825

Lasher, Cora (Store Owner)
The Deadwood Beetle - Mylene Dressler *c* 1106

Lassiter, Quannah (Police Officer)
All Signs Point to Murder - Kat Goldring *m* 81

Latimer, Tom (FBI Agent)
Fault Line - Sarah Andrews *m* 7

Laubon, Meryl (Rebel)
Empire & Ecolitan - L.E. Modesitt Jr. *s* 777

Lauper, Tammy (Housewife)
Coldheart Canyon - Clive Barker *c* 1071
Coldheart Canyon - Clive Barker *h* 619

Lavotoni, Sierra (Stripper; Detective—Amateur)
Strip Poker - Nancy Bartholomew *m* 13

Lawton (Computer Expert)
For Your Heart Only - Debra White Smith *i* 1048

Lee, Heaven (Restaurateur; Cook)
Red Beans and Vice - Lou Jane Temple *m* 207

Lee, Robert E. (Historical Figure; Military Personnel)
The Ironclad Alibi - Michael Kilian *t* 898

Leeds, Arabella (Gentlewoman)
Letters from an Age of Reason - Nora Hague *t* 877

Leeds, Jack (Detective—Private; Lover)
Shakespeare's Counselor - Charlaine Harris *m* 102

Lefkowitz (Scientist)
Night of the Bat - Paul Zindel *h* 714

Lefkowitz, Jake (Teenager)
Night of the Bat - Paul Zindel *h* 714

Leggett, Irene (Administrator)
Gargoyles - Alan Nayes *h* 677

Leiah (Nurse)
Blessed Child - Bill Bright *i* 975

Leightner, Jack (Detective—Homicide)
Red Hook - Gabriel Cohen *m* 37

Lena (Lover)
The Good German - Joseph Kanon *c* 1135

Leones, Giraut (Spy; Divorced Person)
The Merchants of Souls - John Barnes *s* 722

Leonie of Mirandeau (Royalty; Orphan)
Once a Princess - Veronica Sattler *r* 388

Lestat (Vampire)
Blood and Gold - Anne Rice *t* 922

Lester, Robert "Bo" (Detective—Private)
Back in Kansas - Debra Salonen *r* 387

l'Estrange, Sybil (Religious)
My Lady de Burgh - Deborah Simmons *r* 396

Letitia Louise (Animal)
The Treachery of Kings - Neal Barrett Jr. *f* 524

Levine, Kathleen (Librarian; Patient)
Good Harbor - Anita Diamant *c* 1103

Levy, Daniel (Scientist)
Frankenstein: The Legacy - Christopher Schildt *h* 691

Lewis, Laurie (FBI Agent)
Born Brave - Ruth Wind *r* 422

Lewis, Meriwether (Explorer; Historical Figure)
River Walk - Rita Cleary *w* 443

Leyden, Henry (Friend; Radio Personality)
Black House - Stephen King *c* 1140

Leynier, Corin (Nobleman; Psychic)
The Fall of Neskaya - Marion Zimmer Bradley *s* 725

Lhel (Witch)
The Bone Doll's Twin - Lynn Flewelling *f* 544

Liddell (Parent; Historical Figure)
Still She Haunts Me - Katie Roiphe *c* 1189

Liddell, Alice (Child; Historical Figure)
Still She Haunts Me - Katie Roiphe *c* 1189
Still She Haunts Me - Katie Roiphe *t* 927

Lightfoot, Franklin J. Jr. (Journalist)
Law Dog - J. Lee Butts *w* 438

Lightfoot, Jacquelyn (Detective—Private)
For Your Heart Only - Debra White Smith *i* 1048

Lily (Relative)
Eva Moves the Furniture - Margot Livesey *c* 1148

Linacre, Tim (Student; Detective—Amateur)
Creeping Venom - Sheila Pim m 173

Lincoln, Toby (Outcast)
Tears of the Heart - Lauran Paine w 493

Lindsey, Emma (Banker)
The Secret Admirer - Annette Mahon r 343

Linsley, Adrian (Nobleman; Landscaper)
A Diamond in the Rough - Andrea Pickens r 370

Linton, Sara (Doctor)
Blindsighted - Karin Slaughter m 197

Liu, Genevie (Student—Graduate)
The Watermark - Travis Thrasher i 1054

Lizier, Grazida (Teenager; Bastard Daughter)
The Good Men - Charmaine Craig t 844

Llech (Scholar)
The Prince of Shadow - Curt Benjamin f 526

Llesho (Teenager; Nobleman)
The Prince of Shadow - Curt Benjamin f 526

Llewellyn, Brydda (Noblewoman)
Ashling - Isobelle Carmody s 732

Llewellyn, Ria (Businesswoman)
Spirits White as Lightning - Mercedes Lackey f 568

Lloyd, Larry (Convict)
Firebreak - Richard Stark m 202

Lluvia (Care Giver; Narrator)
Swift as Desire - Laura Esquivel c 1112

Llyr, Bronwen (Spy)
Brothers of Cain - Miriam Grace Monfredo t 909
Brothers of Cain - Miriam Grace Monfredo m 159

Llyr, Kathryn (Nurse)
Brothers of Cain - Miriam Grace Monfredo m 159

Llyr, Kathyrn (Nurse)
Brothers of Cain - Miriam Grace Monfredo t 909

Llyr, Seth (Military Personnel; Prisoner)
Brothers of Cain - Miriam Grace Monfredo t 909

Lockhart, Aubrey (Widow(er); Wealthy)
Heaven Sent - Rachel Wilson r 421

Lockhart, Becky (Child)
Heaven Sent - Rachel Wilson r 421

Lockwood, Cuff (Cowboy)
Lockwood - Lauran Paine w 492

Logan, Courtney (Crime Victim; Parent)
Long Time No See - Susan Isaacs c 1131

Logan, Daniella (Student)
Pact of the Fathers - Ramsey Campbell h 626

Logan, Dave (Rancher)
Destiny Valley - Fred Grove w 459

Logan, Ed (Student)
Night in the Lonesome October - Richard Laymon h 664

Logan, Greg (Spouse; Crime Suspect)
Long Time No See - Susan Isaacs c 1131

Logan, Josh (Hotel Owner)
The Wager - Metsy Hingle r 301

London, Jack (Writer; Historical Figure)
The Jewel of the North - Peter King m 135

Lone Hawk (Indian; Warrior)
Cheyenne Summer - Vella Munn t 911

Loner, Wolf (Sailor)
The Wanderer - Fritz Leiber s 767

Longinus, Marcus (Military Personnel; Biblical Figure)
The Jerusalem Scrolls - Bodie Thoene i 1053

Looby, Nick (Relative)
Dugan under Ground - Tom De Haven c 1100

Looby, Roy (Artist)
Dugan under Ground - Tom De Haven c 1100

Lord, Emma (Journalist; Detective—Amateur)
The Alpine Nemesis - Mary Daheim m 51

Lorene (Restaurateur; Employer)
Lightning Field - Dana Spiotta c 1202

Love, Mick (Tree Surgeon)
When Love Came to Town - Lenora Worth i 1063

Lovell, Anthony (Heir)
Dark Sanctuary - H.B. Gregory h 644

Lowe, Angela (Researcher)
Angel Face - Suzanne Forster r 283

Lowe, Eliza (Singer; Wealthy)
Beloved Protector - Linda O'Brien r 361

Lowry, Tim (Antiques Dealer; Homosexual)
Killer Stuff - Sharon Fiffer m 69

Lubin, Ken (Military Personnel)
Maelstrom - Peter Watts s 808

Luc, Frank (Time Traveler)
ChronoSpace - Allen Steele s 802

Lucas (Religious)
The Crusader - Michael A. Eisner t 860

Luck, Liz (Entertainer)
Island of Tears - Troy Soos t 936

Ludlow, Harry (Detective—Amateur; Privateer)
The Devil's Own Luck - David Donachie t 853
The Dying Trade - David Donachie t 854

Ludlow, James (Privateer)
The Devil's Own Luck - David Donachie t 853
The Dying Trade - David Donachie t 854

Lukacs, Jerry (Professor)
Pyramid Scheme - David Freer s 751

Luke (Religious)
Vampire Vow - Michael Schiefelbein h 690

Luna (Outcast)
Ride West to Dawn - James C. Work w 514

Lund, Birger (Journalist)
The Phoenix - Henning Boetius t 828

Lundgren, Anna (Museum Curator; Archaeologist)
Under Suspicion - Rachel Lee r 331

Luo (Friend)
Balzac and the Little Chinese Seamstress - Sijie Dai c 1098

Lupi, Katya (Actress)
Coldheart Canyon - Clive Barker c 1071
Coldheart Canyon - Clive Barker h 619

Lupset, Edward (Lawyer)
London Bridges - Jane Stevenson c 1204

Luz (Parent; Wealthy)
Swift as Desire - Laura Esquivel c 1112

Lyanna (Child; Sorceress)
Nightchild - James Barclay f 523

Lydia (Advertising)
House of Pain - Sephera Giron h 640

M

MacAlister, Marti (Police Officer)
Whispers in the Dark - Eleanor Taylor Bland m 21

MacArthur, Eva (Guardian)
The Sword Maiden - Susan King r 316

Macbeth (Nobleman)
The Third Witch - Rebecca Reisert t 921

MacClintock, Roger (Nobleman; Military Personnel)
March to the Sea - David Weber s 809

MacCloud, Conor (Warrior)
The Enchantment - Pam Binder r 237

MacDonald, David (Military Personnel)
Soldiers - John Dalmas s 742

MacDonald, Layla (Receptionist)
Doomed to Repeat It - d.g.k. goldberg h 641

Macdonald, Matt (Businessman)
Doomed to Repeat It - d.g.k. goldberg h 641

MacDonald, Sean (Writer)
Dead Love - Donald Beman h 620

MacDougal, Charles (Scholar)
The Counterfeit Heinlein - Laurence M. Janiver s 763

Macgregor, Ian (Spirit)
Doomed to Repeat It - d.g.k. goldberg h 641

MacIntyre, Adam (Rancher)
This Time Forever - Carol Steward i 1052

MacKay, Beth (Doctor)
Child of Promise - Kathleen Morgan i 1025

Mackellar, Patience (Detective—Private; Widow(er))
Keepers - Janet LaPierre m 139

Mackellar, Verity (Detective—Private)
Keepers - Janet LaPierre m 139

MacKeltar, Drustan (Laird; Time Traveler)
Kiss of the Highlander - Karen Marie Moning r 358

MacKenna, Alec (Horse Trainer)
Legends Lake - JoAnn Ross r 386

Mackenzie, Finlay "Wild Fin" (Nobleman)
The Secret Clan: Abducted Heiress - Amanda Scott r 390

MacKenzie, Zach (Lawman)
The MacKenzies: Zach - Ana Leigh r 332

MacKerron, Lachlann (Blacksmith; Military Personnel)
The Sword Maiden - Susan King r 316

Mackey, David (Doctor)
Rhythms - Donna Hill t 884

Mackey, Emma (Young Woman)
Rhythms - Donna Hill t 884

MacKinnon, Scotia (Detective—Private)
Death on a Casual Friday - Sharon Duncan m 63

Mackintosh, Iain (Laird)
The Mackintosh Bride - Debra Lee Brown r 244

MacLaren, Esmeraude (Noblewoman)
The Temptress - Claire Delacroix r 269

MacLean, Jamie (Expatriate)
Summer's End - Lynne Hayworth r 297

MacLeod, Hamish (Spirit; Military Personnel)
Watchers of Time - Charles Todd t 943

MacLeod, Iolanthe (Spirit)
My Heart Stood Still - Lynn Kurland r 323

MacPhaull, Lindsay (Businesswoman; Heiress—Dispossessed)
Jackson's Way - Leslie LaFoy r 324

MacPherson, Rand (Businessman; Heir)
You're the One - Judi McCoy r 351

Macro, Lucius Cornelius (Military Personnel)
Under the Eagle - Simon Scarrow t 931

MacWray, Mack (Businessman)
Rag Man - Pete Hautman m 107

Maddox, Bruno (Care Giver; Writer)
My Little Blue Dress - Bruno Maddox c 1150

Madeleine (Orphan)
Haussmann, or The Distinction - Paul LaFarge t 900

Madison, James (Historical Figure; Political Figure)
Treason - David Nevin *t* 912

Madoc (Sailor; Explorer)
Circle of Stars - Anna Lee Waldo *w* 510

Magruder, Saginaw Bob (Murderer; Outlaw)
Law Dog - J. Lee Butts *w* 438

Maguire, Connor (Journalist; Imposter)
The Widow - Anne Stuart *r* 411

Mahar, Mavis (Singer)
First Lady - Michael Malone *c* 1153

Mahler, Alma (Historical Figure; Widow(er))
The Silent Woman - Susan M. Dodd *t* 852

Maigraith (Warrior)
The Way between the Worlds - Ian Irvine *f* 560

Maitland, Richard (Fugitive; Convict)
The Perfect Princess - Elizabeth Thornton *r* 416

Majere, Ulin (Sorcerer)
Dragon's Bluff - Mary H. Herbert *f* 556

Majors, Ike (Rancher)
Caleb's Price - Troy D. Smith *w* 505

Maki, Del (Police Officer)
Cold - John Smolens *c* 1199

Maldred (Warrior)
Betrayal - Jean Rabe *f* 589

Malibrant, Arabella (Actress)
The Thief-Taker - T.F. Banks *t* 820

Mallory, Amy (Professor)
Broken Honor - Patricia Potter *r* 373

Malloy, Hannah (Widow(er); Detective—Amateur)
Tall, Dead, and Handsome - Annie Griffin *m* 91

Malone, Grant (Police Officer)
Awakening Alex - Ruth Langan *r* 327

Malraux (Mythical Creature)
Eccentric Circles - Rebecca Lickiss *f* 573

Manderville, William (Nobleman; Spy)
The Very Comely Countess - Miranda Jarrett *r* 307

Mangum, Cudberth "Cuddy" (Police Officer)
First Lady - Michael Malone *c* 1153

Manley, Wilfred (Businessman)
Brother John - Rutledge Etheridge *s* 750

Manning, Jack (Security Officer)
Deathday - William C. Dietz *s* 746

Manning, Kyle (Police Officer)
A Love for Safekeeping - Gail Gaymer Martin *i* 1021

Mannion, Adam (Rake; Rogue)
The Sleeping Beauty - Jacqueline Navin *r* 360

Manoso, Carlos "Ranger" (Bounty Hunter)
Seven Up - Janet Evanovich *r* 274

MaqqRee, Desmond (Hero)
Sidhe-Devil - Aaron Allston *f* 516

Marais, Charles (Scholar; Military Personnel)
The Dark Wing - Walter Hunt *s* 761

Marcello, Nick (Teacher)
Emerald Windows - Terri Blackstock *i* 971

March, Tobias (Widow(er); Detective—Private)
Slightly Shady - Amanda Quick *r* 375

Marchante, Rocko (Organized Crime Figure)
Junior's Leg - Ken Wells *c* 1214

Marchnight, Henry (Nobleman; Rake)
Lady Polly - Nicola Cornick *r* 259

Marimi (Indian)
Sacred Ground - Barbara Wood *t* 962

Marius (Vampire)
Blood and Gold - Anne Rice *h* 685
Blood and Gold - Anne Rice *t* 922
Blood and Gold - Anne Rice *c* 1185

Markby, Alan (Police Officer)
Shades of Murder - Ann Granger *m* 87

Marker, Caleb (Lumberjack; Single Parent)
Alicia's Song - Susan Plunkett *r* 371

Marker, Jason (Guardian)
Blessed Child - Bill Bright *i* 975

Marsala, Cat (Journalist; Detective—Amateur)
Hard Road - Barbara D'Amato *m* 53

Marshall, Carley (Child)
Carley's Song - Patricia Houck Sprinkle *i* 1051

Marshall, Douglas (Archaeologist)
The Ice Child - Elizabeth McGregor *t* 905

Marshall, Tyler (Crime Victim; Child)
Black House - Stephen King *h* 659
Black House - Stephen King *c* 1140

Martens, Tristan (Professor; Divorced Person)
The Deadwood Beetle - Mylene Dressler *c* 1106

Martin, Annie (Child-Care Giver)
The Nanny - Judith Stacy *r* 408

Martin, Brooke (Artisan)
Emerald Windows - Terri Blackstock *i* 971

Martin, Clay (Veterinarian)
Death of the Last Villista - Allana Martin *m* 149

Martin, Dorothy (Spouse; Detective—Amateur)
To Perish in Penzance - Jeanne M. Dams *m* 54

Martin, Kit (Writer; Lover)
Killing the Shadows - Val McDermid *m* 154

Martin, Prudence (Teacher)
Stranded with the Sergeant - Cathie Linz *r* 335

Martin, Ruth (Pioneer; Widow(er))
What Once We Loved - Jane Kirkpatrick *w* 470
What Once We Loved - Jane Kirkpatrick *i* 1011

Masefield, Genevieve (Detective—Private)
Murder on the Minnesota - Conrad Allen *m* 5
Murder on the Minnesota - Conrad Allen *t* 816

Masen, David (Pilot)
The Night of the Triffids - Simon Clark *s* 735

Masera, Gil (Animal Trainer)
A Feral Darkness - Doranna Durgin *f* 543

Matherly-Reed, Maris (Editor; Spouse)
Envy - Sandra Brown *c* 1086
Envy - Sandra Brown *r* 245

Mathers, Abigail (Spouse; Advertising)
The Webster Chronicle - Daniel Akst *c* 1066

Mathers, Terry (Journalist; Publisher)
The Webster Chronicle - Daniel Akst *c* 1066

Matravers, Paul (Writer)
The Crow Maiden - Sarah Singleton *f* 598

Matt (Spouse; Parent)
Suzanne's Diary for Nicholas - James Patterson *c* 1181

Matthews, Celia (Advertising)
Color the Sidewalk for Me - Brandilyn Collins *i* 980

Matthews, LeRoyce "Lee" (Investigator; Imposter)
Gotta Get Next to You - Lynn Emery *r* 272

Matthews, Mark (Teenager)
Friday Night in Beast House - Richard Laymon *h* 662

Matthews, Toby (Child)
The Prodigy - Alton Gansky *h* 637

Maurice (Animal)
The Amazing Maurice and His Educated Rodents - Terry Pratchett *f* 587

Maxwell, Kirk (Detective—Police)
Dangerous Dilemmas - Evelyn Palfrey *r* 365

Maxwell, Kline (Journalist)
The Dragons of the Cuyahoga - S. Andrew Swann *f* 602

Mayo, Gil (Police Officer)
A Sunset Touch - Marjorie Eccles *m* 64

Mazaret, Ikarno (Knight)
Shadowkings - Michael Cobley *f* 535

McBride, Cora (Child)
The Vigil - Clay Reynolds *w* 498

McBride, Imogene (Parent)
The Vigil - Clay Reynolds *w* 498

McBride, Keely (Interior Decorator)
Love to Love You Baby - Kasey Michaels *r* 354

McCain, Michael (Fugitive)
Of Aged Angels - Monte Cook *s* 737

McCain, Sam (Detective—Private; Lawyer)
Save the Last Dance for Me - Ed Gorman *m* 83

McCaine, Rio (Gunfighter; Heir—Dispossessed)
Saddled - Delores Fossen *r* 284

McCall, Claire (Doctor)
Could I Have This Dance? - Harry Lee Kraus *i* 1012

McCall, Patsy (Political Figure)
Roscoe - William Kennedy *t* 897

McCarthy, Steve (Detective—Police)
Listen to the Shadows - Danuta Reah *m* 179

McClean, Peggy (Teenager)
The World Weaver - Craig Etchison *s* 749

McCoy, Paul (Doctor)
The Doctor's Miracle - Anna Schmidt *i* 1046

McCully, Esther (Professor)
Sunrise on Stradbury Square - Doris Elaine Fell *i* 992

McDonald, Clarence (Police Officer)
A Horde of Fools - James David Buchanan *w* 437

McEwen, Eva (Heroine)
Eva Moves the Furniture - Margot Livesey *c* 1148

McGee, Kevin (Historian; Astronaut)
First Landing - Robert Zubrin *s* 814

McGraw, Jay (Guard)
Flying Eagle - Tim Champlin *w* 440

McGuiness, Libby (Hairdresser; Single Parent)
Do You Hear What I Hear? - Holly Jacobs *r* 306

McGuire, Cole (Military Personnel; Single Parent)
The Colorado Bride - Mary Burton *r* 247

McIvor, Laura (Fugitive)
Betrayed - Rosey Dow *i* 989

McKay, Ford (Military Personnel; Imposter)
Going Overboard - Christina Skye *r* 399

McKendrick, Simon (Military Personnel; Gentleman)
A Tangled Web - Donna Bell *r* 230

McKinney, Mary (Teacher)
July Thunder - Rachel Lee *r* 330

McKinnon, Thomas MacLeod (Businessman; Mountaineer)
My Heart Stood Still - Lynn Kurland *r* 323

McLain, Chance (Rancher)
The Secret - Kat Martin *r* 347

McLeish, John (Police Officer)
O Gentle Death - Janet Neel *m* 165

McMahon, John (Plantation Owner)
Whispers of Goodbye - Karen White *r* 418

McQuaid, Jared (Lawman)
The Widow's Little Secret - Judith Stacy *r* 409

McQuarry, Mac (Investigator; Detective—Private)
To Trust a Stranger - Karen Robards *r* 381

Meara, Jeane (Fugitive)
Of Aged Angels - Monte Cook *s* 737

Medina, Mercedes (Professor; Spouse)
Light Coming Back - Ann Wadsworth *c* 1213

Medina, Patrick (Musician)
Light Coming Back - Ann Wadsworth *c* 1213

Meeker, Nathan (Government Official; Historical Figure)
Blood on the Wind - Lucile Bogue *w* 426

Mefell, Brierly (Witch)
Mother Ocean, Daughter Sea - Diana Marcellas *f* 576

Meisner, Allen (Scientist)
The Getaway Special - Jerry Oltion *s* 785

Meissner, Joanna (Student—Graduate)
Shock - Robin Cook *c* 1093

Melchior, Obediah (Mythical Creature)
A Capital Holiday - Janet Dailey *r* 265

Meleager (Ruler)
In the Shape of a Boar - Lawrence Norfolk *t* 913

Memel, Solomon (Writer; Survivor)
In the Shape of a Boar - Lawrence Norfolk *t* 913
In the Shape of a Boar - Lawrence Norfolk *c* 1171

Mendark (Sorcerer)
The Way between the Worlds - Ian Irvine *f* 560

Merkle, Gerald (Banker; Thief)
The Pinkerton Eye - Allen P. Bristow *w* 436

Merlin (Wizard)
Celtika - Robert Holdstock *f* 558
The Dragon Queen - Alice Borchardt *t* 829
The Dragon Queen - Alice Borchardt *f* 528
Entertain the End - K.A. Applegate *f* 519

Merrick, Michael (Journalist)
The Elusive Voice - Mary Jo Adamson *m* 2

Merrigan, Eleanor (Wizard)
Behind Time - Lynn Abbey *f* 515

Merrigan, Emma (Librarian)
Behind Time - Lynn Abbey *f* 515

Merritt, Quaid (Pilot)
The Golden Angel - Gilbert Morris *i* 1027

Merriwell, Max (Writer)
Adventures in Time and Space with Max Merriwell - Pat Murphy *s* 781

Merryt (Religious)
Revelation - Elizabeth Haydon *f* 555

Merwin, Alex (Nobleman)
A Perfect Match - Jeanne Savery *r* 389

Mestizo (Indian; Recluse)
The Gift of the Mestizo - Marjorie M. McGinley *w* 479

Metellus, Decius (Detective—Amateur; Military Personnel)
Nobody Loves a Centurion - John Maddox Roberts *t* 924
Nobody Loves a Centurion - John Maddox Roberts *m* 184

Mev (Relative; Addict)
Why Did I Ever? - Mary Robison *c* 1188

Meyers, Molly (Teacher)
Written on Her Heart - Alan Maki *i* 1019

Mica (Religious; Boyfriend)
Night Players - P.D. Cacek *h* 625

Michael (Relative; Lover)
Lightning Field - Dana Spiotta *c* 1202

Michael (Religious)
Vampire Vow - Michael Schiefelbein *h* 690

Michaels, Elena (Werewolf)
Bitten - Kelley Armstrong *c* 1068

Michaels, Rebecca (Single Parent)
The Power of Love - Margaret Daley *i* 987

Michaels, Sara (Singer)
Judging Sara - Cynthia Rutledge *i* 1044

Michal (Historical Figure; Spouse)
Queenmaker - India Edghill *t* 858

Middleton, Catherine (Young Woman)
The Slaying of the Shrew - Simon Hawke *t* 880

Mikaelian, Garreth (Vampire; Detective—Police)
Blood Games - Lee Killough *h* 657

Mila (Lover)
Fury - Salman Rushdie *c* 1190

Miles, Ethan (Businessman)
See Jane Date - Melissa Senate *r* 394

Miles, Robert (Parent; Actor)
Friday's Child - Linda Chaikin *i* 977

Miles, Sara (Businesswoman)
Sarah and the Rogue - DeLoras Scott *r* 391

Miles, Vanessa (Volunteer)
Friday's Child - Linda Chaikin *i* 977

Miller, Eve (Survivor; Widow(er))
Aria - Susan Segal *c* 1194

Miller, Jarett (Bodyguard)
Two Sexy - Stephanie Bond *r* 240

Miller, Larkin (Teenager; Alien)
The World Weaver - Craig Etchison *s* 749

Miller, Pinky (Young Woman)
The Onion Girl - Charles De Lint *f* 539

Milner, Suzanne (Researcher; Divorced Person)
Listen to the Shadows - Danuta Reah *m* 179

Milodragovitch, Milo (Detective—Private)
The Final Country - James Crumley *m* 50

Mina (Young Woman)
Lightning Field - Dana Spiotta *c* 1202

Minor, Dacinda "Daisy" Ann (Librarian)
Open Season - Linda Howard *r* 302

Mirabel, Tanner (Security Officer)
Chasm City - Alastair Reynolds *s* 789

Miradel (Religious)
World Fall - Douglas Niles *f* 583

Mirana, Aylen (Fisherman)
The Jasper Forest - Julia Gray *f* 551

Mirana, Kerin (Traveler)
The Jasper Forest - Julia Gray *f* 551

Miryam (Widow(er); Biblical Figure)
The Jerusalem Scrolls - Bodie Thoene *i* 1053
The Jerusalem Scrolls - Bodie Thoene *t* 942

Misha (Friend; Lover)
Funny Accent - Barbara Shulgasser-Parker *c* 1197

Miss Claudia (Aged Person)
A Place Called Wiregrass - Michael Morris *i* 1029

Mitchell, Ben (Rancher)
The Gift of the Mestizo - Marjorie M. McGinley *w* 479

Mitchell, Frank (Police Officer)
In and Out - Mat Coward *m* 44

Mitchell, Lucy (Relative; Widow(er))
The Gift of the Mestizo - Marjorie M. McGinley *w* 479

Mitchell, Meredith (Civil Servant; Lover)
Shades of Murder - Ann Granger *m* 87

Mitry, Desiree "Des" (Police Officer)
The Cold Blue Blood - David Handler *m* 100

Mohr, Henry (Veteran; Cowboy)
Last Year's River - Allen Morris Jones *w* 467
Last Year's River - Allen Morris Jones *t* 891

Mompellion, Elinor (Spouse)
Year of Wonders - Geraldine Brooks *t* 832
Year of Wonders - Geraldine Brooks *c* 1083

Mompellion, Michael (Religious)
Year of Wonders - Geraldine Brooks *c* 1083
Year of Wonders - Geraldine Brooks *t* 832

Monaghan, Tess (Detective—Private)
In a Strange City - Laura Lippman *m* 143

Monahan, Connor (Detective—Police)
The Secret Life of Connor Monahan - Elizabeth Bevarly *r* 235

Monk, Hester (Nurse; Spouse)
Funeral in Blue - Anne Perry *m* 172
Funeral in Blue - Anne Perry *t* 915

Monk, William (Detective—Private; Amnesiac)
Funeral in Blue - Anne Perry *t* 915
Funeral in Blue - Anne Perry *m* 172

Montcada, Francisco de (Knight)
The Crusader - Michael A. Eisner *t* 860

Montero, Carmen (Noblewoman; Spy)
The Spanish Bride - Amanda McCabe *r* 349

Montgomery, Harrison (Gentleman; Sea Captain)
Mr. Montgomery's Quest - Martha Kirkland *r* 318

Moon, Abigail (Police Officer)
A Sunset Touch - Marjorie Eccles *m* 64

Moon, Billy (Teacher; Widow(er))
Sarah's Window - Janice Graham *w* 457

Moon, Charlie (Rancher; Police Officer)
White Shell Woman - James D. Doss *m* 61

Moon, Jackson (Convict)
Angel in the Front Room, Devil out Back - Stanford Diehl *m* 59

Moore, Melissa (Doctor)
To Rome with Love - Debra White Smith *i* 1049

Moore, Nell (Young Woman)
Ghost Killer - Scott Chandler *h* 627

Moore, Olivia (Vampire)
The London Vampire Panic - Michael Romkey *h* 686

Moore, Thomas (Detective—Homicide)
The Surgeon - Tess Gerritsen *m* 78

Moorhaven, Nigel (Nobleman; Spy)
The Blue Devil - Melynda Beth Skinner *r* 398

Moreland, Jared (Nobleman; Rake)
A Devilish Husband - Alana Clayton *r* 257

Morelane, Cedric (Nobleman)
The Valentine Wish - Debbie Raleigh *r* 378

Morella (Guide)
The Devil-Tree of El Dorado - Frank Aubrey *s* 717

Morelli, Joe (Detective—Police)
Seven Up - Janet Evanovich *r* 274

Morgan (Relative)
Cape Refuge - Terri Blackstock *i* 970

Morgan, Mariana (Psychic; Detective—Amateur)
Darkness at the Door - Catherine Dain *m* 52

Morgan, Stuart (Indian; Scout)
Bear Paw - Gene Mullins *w* 484

Morgette, Dolf (Prospector; Bodyguard)
Morgette on the Barbary Coast - G.G. Boyer *w* 429

Moriarity, James (Professor; Scientist)
The Great Game - Michael Kurland *t* 899

Morrigern, Tami (Rebel)
Bolo Strike - William H. Keith Jr. *s* 765

Morris, Quincey (Vampire)
Quincey Morris, Vampire - P.N. Elrod *h* 632

Morrison, Charlotte (Pilot)
Sentimental Journey - Jill Barnett *r* 228

Morrison, Erik (Roommate)
The Watermark - Travis Thrasher *i* 1054

Morrow, Diana (Abuse Victim; Mail Order Bride)
A Measure of Grace - Al Lacy *i* 1014

Morthu (Sorcerer)
The King's Name - Jo Walton *f* 608

Mortimer, James (Doctor; Spouse)
Dr. Mortimer and the Aldgate Mystery - Gerard Williams *t* 958

Mortimer, Man (Criminal)
Yonder Stands Your Orphan - Barry Hannah *c* 1121

Morton, Henry (Police Officer)
The Thief-Taker - T.F. Banks *m* 10
The Thief-Taker - T.F. Banks *t* 820

Mossman, Peter (Spouse)
The Happy Room - Catherine Palmer *i* 1038

Mott, Albert (Police Officer)
The King of the Sun - A.A. McFedries *s* 773

Moultrie, John (Police Officer)
The Water and the Blood - Nancy E. Turner *t* 947

Mozart, Wolfgang Amadeus (Historical Figure; Composer)
Imagining Don Giovanni - Anthony J. Rudel *t* 929

Multx, Zap (Spaceship Captain)
Starhawk - Mack Maloney *s* 769

Mulvaine (Teenager)
On - Adam Roberts *s* 790

Munoz, Dan (Detective—Police)
Bonnie Winter - Graham Masterton *h* 672

Murdoch, Bill (Security Officer)
Time Future - Maxine McArthur *s* 770

Murdoch, Eden (Captive; Nurse)
An Uncommon Enemy - Michelle Black *t* 824
An Uncommon Enemy - Michelle Black *w* 423

Murphy, Kevin (Teenager)
Straight on 'Til Morning - Christopher Golden *h* 642

Murphy, Molly (Fugitive; Detective—Amateur)
Murphy's Law - Rhys Bowen *m* 24
Murphy's Law - Rhys Bowen *t* 830

Murphy, Peter (Police Officer)
Dead Love - Donald Beman *h* 620

Murphy, Sarah (Orphan; Psychic)
To Tame a Wild Heart - Tracy Fobes *r* 281

Murphy, Zack (Scientist)
ChronoSpace - Allen Steele *s* 802

Murray, Colin (Nobleman)
To Tame a Wild Heart - Tracy Fobes *r* 281

Murray, Gordon (Lawyer)
The Mystic Rose - Stephen R. Lawhead *t* 901

Murtagh, Colum (Government Official; Lover)
Saintly Murders - C.L. Grace *m* 86
Saintly Murders - C.L. Grace *t* 875

N

Na, J'Chabi (Agent)
Spherical Harmonic - Catherine Asaro *s* 716

Nameless Detective (Detective—Private)
Bleeders - Bill Pronzini *m* 174

Nancarrow, Lavinia (Gentlewoman)
Dr. Mortimer and the Aldgate Mystery - Gerard Williams *t* 958

Napier, Logan (Architect)
Twin Blessings - Carolyne Aarsen *i* 965

Nash (Sorcerer)
Rebel's Cage - Kate Jacoby *f* 561

Nash, Dartania Douglas (Spouse)
Nashborough - Elsie Burch Donald *t* 855

Nash, Seneca (Lawyer)
Nashborough - Elsie Burch Donald *t* 855

Nate (Murderer; Military Personnel)
Tennant's Rock - Steve McGiffen *w* 478

Navarro, L.Q. (Spirit)
Bitterroot - James Lee Burke *c* 1088

Necromancer (Sorcerer)
A Lower Deep - Tom Piccirilli *h* 682

Needham, Angela (Gentlewoman; Companion)
A Guardian's Angel - Jo Ann Ferguson *r* 278

Neela (Lover)
Fury - Salman Rushdie *c* 1190

Nelu (Foreman)
The Appointment - Herta Muller *c* 1168

Nergal (Demon)
Elminster in Hell - Ed Greenwood *f* 553

Nesbitt, Alan (Police Officer)
To Perish in Penzance - Jeanne M. Dams *m* 54

Nesbitt, Benedict "Nez" (Nobleman)
One Good Turn - Carla Kelly *r* 315

Neville, Rebecca (Tutor)
The Promise - May McGoldrick *r* 352

Newcombe, Ally (Teenager)
When the Last Leaf Falls - Bill Myers *i* 1032

Newlands, Billy (Con Artist)
The Lone Rider - Max Brand *w* 432

Newman, Holly (Office Worker)
The Gingerbread Man - Maggie Shayne *r* 395

Newton, John (Sea Captain; Historical Figure)
The Infidel - Joe Musser *i* 1031

Niall (Ruler)
Children of the Lion - Jennifer Roberson *f* 591

Nichols, Billy (Journalist)
The Distance - Eddie Muller *m* 161

Nichols, Jane (Seamstress)
Sugarplum Surprises - Elisabeth Fairchild *r* 275

Niemann, Roger (Doctor)
Night Blood - James M. Thompson *h* 702

Night Hawk (Indian; Horse Trainer)
Night Hawk's Bride - Jillian Hart *r* 296

Niiv (Young Woman)
Celtika - Robert Holdstock *f* 558

Nikki (Teenager)
Face - Tim Lebbon *h* 665

Noble, Andrea (Businesswoman; Nurse)
Gotta Get Next to You - Lynn Emery *r* 272

Noble, Harry (Actor)
Pride, Prejudice and Jasmin Field - Melissa Nathan *r* 359

Noort, Robert (Businessman; Spouse)
First Gray, Then White, Then Blue - Margriet de Moor *c* 1165

Norris, Jackie (Editor)
Milkrun - Sarah Mlynowski *r* 357

North, Erik (Appraiser; Investigator)
Moving Target - Elizabeth Lowell *r* 340

Norton (Rancher; Wealthy)
Monte's Revenge - Eugene C. Vories *w* 509

Norton, Wayne (Police Officer)
Bikini Planet - David Garnett *s* 752

Notwen (Mythical Creature)
Dragon's Bluff - Mary H. Herbert *f* 556

Nudger, Alo (Detective—Private)
The Nudger Dilemmas - John Lutz *m* 147

O

O'Connell, Annie (Spouse; Prospector)
By Flare of Northern Lights - Tim Champlin *w* 439

O'Fallon, Leigh "Kayleigh" (Artist; Spouse)
East of the Sun, West of the Moon - Carole Bellacera *r* 231

Ogada, Bruce (Police Officer)
Dervish Is Digital - Pat Cadigan *s* 731

Ohmsford, Bek (Wizard)
Antrax - Terry Brooks *f* 530

Ohmsford, Grianne (Witch)
Antrax - Terry Brooks *f* 530

O'Keefe, Ben (Convict; Single Parent)
Christmas Vows: $5.00 Extra - Lori Copeland *i* 983

Oldham, Buddy-Boy (Farmer; Outcast)
The Way of the Coyote - Elmer Kelton *w* 468

Oldham, Clyde (Villain)
The Way of the Coyote - Elmer Kelton *c* 1137

O'Leary, Amanda (Counselor; Spouse)
The Woman Next Door - Barbara Delinsky *c* 1101

O'Malley, Chuck (Diplomat; Spouse)
September Song - Andrew M. Greeley *c* 1117

O'Malley, Jack (Fire Fighter)
The Protector - Dee Henderson *i* 999

O'Malley, John (Religious; Detective—Amateur)
The Thunder Keeper - Margaret Coel *m* 35
The Thunder Keeper - Margaret Coel *w* 444

O'Malley, Maeve (Housekeeper)
Comfort and Joy - Sandra Madden *r* 342

O'Malley, Rosemarie (Parent; Narrator)
September Song - Andrew M. Greeley *c* 1117

O'Mally, Vincent (Detective—Police)
The Gingerbread Man - Maggie Shayne *r* 395

O'Neill, Meghann (Psychologist; Vampire)
Crimson Kiss - Trisha Baker *h* 617

O'Niall, Fiorinda (Musician)
Bold as Love - Gwyneth Jones *s* 764

Oregon, Ukiah (Detective—Private; Alien)
Alien Taste - Wen Spencer *s* 801

O'Riley, Karine "Kara" Paige (Accountant)
The Texan's Dream - Jodi Thomas *r* 415

Oro, Juan (Captive)
The Survival of Juan Oro - Max Brand *w* 434

O'Rourke, Liam (Rebel)
Out There - Gerald Rose *s* 793

Orozco, Beto (Computer Expert)
Smoking Mirror Blues - Ernest Hogan *s* 758

Orr, Bella (Child)
Closing Time - Jim Fusilli *m* 74

Orr, Terry (Detective—Private; Widow(er))
Closing Time - Jim Fusilli *m* 74

Ortiz, Julianna (Spinster; Twin)
The Outlaw's Twin Sister - Stephen A. Bly *i* 973

Osborn, Frank (Police Officer)
Fireworks - James A. Moore *h* 675

Osborne, Verity (Gentlewoman; Bride)
The Bride Sale - Candice Hern *r* 298

O'Sullivan, Kate (Rancher)
Legends Lake - JoAnn Ross *r* 386

Other (Southern Belle)
The Wind Done Gone - Alice Randall *t* 918

Owens, Blair (Librarian)
Cape Refuge - Terri Blackstock *i* 970

Owens, Kyle (Cowboy)
Ride West to Dawn - James C. Work *w* 514

Ozurardottir, Gunhild (Witch)
Mother of Kings - Poul Anderson *f* 517

P

Packham, Don (Police Officer)
In and Out - Mat Coward *m* 44

Padilla, Eric (Scientist)
Soldiers - John Dalmas *s* 742

Paisley (Child)
A Rose by the Door - Deborah Bedford *i* 967

Paladin, Harry (Detective—Police)
Ghost Killer - Scott Chandler *h* 627

Palindrake, Valraven (Nobleman)
The Way of Light - Storm Constantine *f* 536

Palmer, Sandy (Journalist)
Hosts - F. Paul Wilson *h* 710

Pandora (Vampire)
Blood and Gold - Anne Rice *t* 922

Pannes, John (Businessman)
ChronoSpace - Allen Steele *s* 802

Paradise, Judith (Landlord)
Quincie Bolliver - Mary King *w* 469

Pardell, Aaron (Spaceman)
In the Company of Others - Julie E. Czerneda *s* 740

Parfait, Iris Mary (Girlfriend; Fugitive)
Junior's Leg - Ken Wells *c* 1214

Parke, Drew (Detective—Private)
Gumshoe Gorilla - Keith Hartman *s* 756

Parker (Thief)
Firebreak - Richard Stark *m* 202

Parker, Billy (Friend)
Leap of Faith - Danielle Steel *c* 1203

Parker, Charlie "Bird" (Detective—Private; Widow(er))
Dark Hollow - John Connolly *m* 42

Parmenter, James (Nobleman)
Broken Promises - Patricia Oliver *r* 362

Parmenter, Mathilda Heath (Widow(er); Noblewoman)
Broken Promises - Patricia Oliver *r* 362

Parris, Scott (Police Officer)
White Shell Woman - James D. Doss *m* 61

Parrish, Almo (Aged Person)
The Astonished Eye - Tracy Knight *f* 567

Parvin (Teenager)
Emigre Journeys - Abdullah Hussein *c* 1129

Pascoe, Peter (Police Officer)
Dialogues of the Dead or Paronomania! - Reginald Hill *m* 116

Patten, Joshua (Historical Figure; Sea Captain)
The Captain's Wife - Douglas Kelley *t* 894

Patten, Mary Ann (Historical Figure; Spouse)
The Captain's Wife - Douglas Kelley *t* 894

Paul (Religious; Biblical Figure)
The Gaius Diary - Gene Edwards *i* 990

Paulie (Relative; Crime Victim)
Why Did I Ever? - Mary Robison *c* 1188

Pavel (Relative; Spy)
Requiem for a Lost Empire - Andrei Makine *c* 1151

Pavel (Parent; Farmer)
Requiem for a Lost Empire - Andrei Makine *c* 1151

Pavel (Relative)
Requiem for a Lost Empire - Andrei Makine *c* 1151

Paxton, Aubrey "Bree" (Servant)
Letters from an Age of Reason - Nora Hague *t* 877

Paxton, Brace (Professor)
In the Dark - Richard Laymon *h* 663

Paxton, Hamilton (Judge)
Loving Thy Neighbor - Ruth Scofield *i* 1047

Paxton, Sally (Spouse)
Search for Last Chance - A.L. McWilliams *w* 482

Paxton, Shell (Outlaw)
Search for Last Chance - A.L. McWilliams *w* 482

Peaches (Animal)
The Amazing Maurice and His Educated Rodents - Terry Pratchett *f* 587

Pearce, Amanda (Hotel Worker)
Candle Bay - Tamara Thorne *h* 703

Peaslee, Nathaniel Wingate (Professor; Amnesiac)
The Shadow out of Time - H.P. Lovecraft *h* 670

Peaslee, Wingate (Young Man)
The Shadow out of Time - H.P. Lovecraft *h* 670

Pedigo, Feather (Teenager)
Affinity - J.N. Williamson *h* 709

Pedigo, Luther (Military Personnel; Step-Parent)
Affinity - J.N. Williamson *h* 709

Pelham, Charlotte (Tour Guide)
Mr. Montgomery's Quest - Martha Kirkland *r* 318

Pembroke, Jayne (Saleswoman)
When Jayne Met Erik - Elizabeth Bevarly *r* 236

Pendennis, Walter (Nobleman)
Face Down Before Rebel Hooves - Kathy Lynn Emerson *t* 861

Pender, Sage (Computer Expert)
Bold as Love - Gwyneth Jones *s* 764

Penderecki, Ivan (Crime Suspect)
The Treatment - Mo Hayder *c* 1123

Pendragon, Arthur (Ruler)
The Child of the Holy Grail - Rosalind Miles *t* 907

Pennyman, Charlotte (Fiance(e))
Man from Wyoming - Dane Coolidge *w* 448

Penrose, Wilder (Doctor)
Super-Cannes - J.G. Ballard *c* 1070

Pentar (Warrior)
The Way of the Rose - Valery Leith *f* 572

Penthievre of Chalandrey, Marie (Religious)
The Wolf Hunt - Gillian Bradshaw *t* 831

Perika, Daisy (Shaman; Aged Person)
White Shell Woman - James D. Doss *m* 61

Peril (Nobleman)
The Husband Test - Betina Krahn *r* 321

Person, Grant (Fisherman; Rancher)
On the Night Plain - J. Robert Lennon *w* 473
On the Night Plain - J. Robert Lennon *c* 1146

Person, Max (Rancher; Artist)
On the Night Plain - J. Robert Lennon *w* 473
On the Night Plain - J. Robert Lennon *c* 1146

Petersborough, Leslie (Nobleman)
The Irredeemable Miss Renfield - Regina Scott *r* 393

Philip (Lover)
Bitten - Kelley Armstrong *c* 1068

Phillips, Adrian (Government Official)
The Dragons of the Cuyahoga - S. Andrew Swann *f* 602

Phillips, Gina (Unemployed)
A Journey by Chance - Sally D. John *i* 1006

Philomene (Slave; Relative)
Cane River - Lalita Tademy *c* 1207

Phlarx (Alien)
The Wild Boy - Warren Rochelle *s* 791

Pickard, Andy (Captive)
The Way of the Coyote - Elmer Kelton *w* 468
The Way of the Coyote - Elmer Kelton *t* 895
The Way of the Coyote - Elmer Kelton *c* 1137

Pickett, Joe (Game Warden)
Open Season - C.J. Box *m* 25
Open Season - C.J. Box *w* 428

Pickett, Todd (Actor)
Coldheart Canyon - Clive Barker *c* 1071
Coldheart Canyon - Clive Barker *h* 619

Pigeon, Josie (Contractor; Single Parent)
Murder in the Forecast - Valerie Wolzien *m* 219

Pike, Jamison (Writer)
The Quest - Jim Kraus *i* 1013

Pine, Leonard (Sidekick)
Captains Outrageous - Joe R. Lansdale *w* 472

Pinter, Sanford (Consultant)
Up in the Air - Walter Kirn *c* 1141

Pitt, Dirk (Engineer; Government Official)
Valhalla Rising - Clive Cussler *c* 1097

Planeswalker, Urza (Sorcerer; Immortal)
Apocalypse - J. Robert King *f* 564

Plant, Melrose (Professor; Sidekick)
The Blue Last - Martha Grimes *m* 92

Plantagenet, Edward (Nobleman)
Knight Errant - R. Garcia y Robertson *f* 546
Knight Errant - R. Garcia y Robertson *t* 869

Plum, Stephanie (Bounty Hunter)
Seven Up - Janet Evanovich *r* 274

Plumtree, Alex (Publisher; Detective—Amateur)
Uncatalogued - Julie Kaewert *m* 128

Pocahontas (Historical Figure; Indian)
Argall - William T. Vollmann *t* 950
Argall - William T. Vollmann *c* 1212

Poe, Edgar Allan (Historical Figure; Writer)
The Hum Bug - Harold Schechter *t* 932
The Hum Bug - Harold Schechter *m* 193
The Hum Bug - Harold Schechter *w* 502

Poisson, Charly (Cook; Restaurateur)
Prepared for Murder - Cecile Lamalle *m* 138

Poldarn (Warrior)
Shadow - K.J. Parker *f* 585

Poling, Clark (Religious; Historical Figure)
Sea of Glory - Ken Wales *i* 1056
Sea of Glory - Ken Wales *t* 953

Ponce (Criminal)
Hope's End - Stephen Chambers *s* 733

Porras, Dolores (Heroine)
Fire Lilies - Cynthia Leal Massey *w* 476

Porter, Abigail (Aged Person)
Highland Hopes - Gary E. Parker *i* 1039

Porteus, Jim (Businessman)
The Reproductive System - John Sladek *s* 798

Potter, Calvin (Scientist)
The Reproductive System - John Sladek *s* 798

Powell, Ginny (Widow(er))
This Rock - Robert Morgan *t* 910

Powell, John Wesley (Historical Figure; Explorer)
The Last Canyon - John Vernon *t* 949
The Last Canyon - John Vernon *w* 508

Powell, Moody (Young Man)
This Rock - Robert Morgan *t* 910

Powell, Muir (Teenager)
This Rock - Robert Morgan *t* 910

Powell, Spencer (Radio Personality)
Bring Me a Dream - Robyn Amos *r* 224

Powerscourt, Francis (Detective—Private; Nobleman)
Goodnight, Sweet Prince - David Dickinson *t* 851
Goodnight, Sweet Prince - David Dickinson *m* 58

Prentice, Amelia (Teacher)
Irregardless of Murder - Ellen Edwards Kennedy *i* 1008

Prescott, Wycliffe (Nobleman; Military Personnel)
Miss Truelove Beckons - Donna Simpson *r* 397

Preston, Ax (Musician)
Bold as Love - Gwyneth Jones *s* 764

Preston, Winifred "Winnie" Augusta (Gentlewoman)
Blessing in Disguise - Jenna Mindel *r* 356

Price, Maude (Prostitute)
Outcasts - Tim McGuire *w* 480

Price, Virginia (Debutante; Pregnant Teenager)
Last Year's River - Allen Morris Jones *w* 467
Last Year's River - Allen Morris Jones *t* 891

Prieczka, Laprada (Spy)
The Merchants of Souls - John Barnes *s* 722

Proctor, Jeremy (Teenager; Orphan)
Smuggler's Moon - Bruce Alexander *t* 815

Prophet, Callida "Callie" (Child-Care Giver; Postal Worker)
Heaven Sent - Rachel Wilson *r* 421

Pruden (Detective—Police)
Kaleidoscope - Dorothy Gilman *m* 79

Prytanis, Paxa (Spy)
The Merchants of Souls - John Barnes *s* 722

Purdy, Wayne (Criminal)
Day of Reckoning - Kathy Herman *i* 1001

Putemonnie, Radegonde (Wealthy)
Mirabilis - Susann Cokal *c* 1091

Q

Quick, Jason (Highwayman)
Watch by Moonlight - Kate Hawks *t* 881

Quicksilver (Mythical Creature)
Ill Met by Moonlight - Sarah A. Hoyt *f* 559

Quilan (Military Personnel)
Look to Windward - Iain Banks *s* 721

Quimby, Andrew (Doctor)
Darkness - Sam Siciliano *h* 695

Quinn, Chandler (Lawyer)
The Astonished Eye - Tracy Knight *f* 567

Quinn, Mary Margaret "Maggie" (Orphan; Musician)
The Nightingale's Song - Kathleen Eschenburg *r* 273

Quinn, Michael (Government Official; Detective—Private)
Dangerous Attraction - Susan Vaughan *r* 417

Quintana, Anthony (Lawyer)
Suspicion of Vengeance - Barbara Parker *m* 167

Qumalix (Prehistoric Human; Storyteller)
Call Down the Stars - Sue Harrison *t* 879

Qwilleran, James Mackintosh "Qwill" (Journalist; Wealthy)
The Cat Who Went Up the Creek - Lilian Jackson Braun *m* 26

R

Rachel (Child; Witch)
The Scent of Magic - Cliff McNish *f* 581

Rafael, Luis (Doctor)
Gargoyles - Alan Nayes *s* 783
Gargoyles - Alan Nayes *h* 677

Rafferty, Alexandra (Photographer)
Blackwater Sound - James W. Hall *m* 94

Rafferty, Colin (Businessman; Imposter)
Bachelor on the Prowl - Kasey Michaels *r* 353

Rafferty, Shadwell (Saloon Keeper/Owner)
Sherlock Holmes and the Secret Alliance - Larry Millett *m* 158
Sherlock Holmes and the Secret Alliance - Larry Millett *t* 908

Ragozinski (Military Personnel)
Second Chances - Susan Shwartz *s* 796

Rahl, Kahlan (Religious)
The Pillars of Creation - Terry Goodkind *f* 550

Rahl, Richard (Wizard)
The Pillars of Creation - Terry Goodkind *f* 550

Raines, Barrett "Bear" (Police Officer)
Strawman's Hammock - Darryl Wimberley *m* 216

Raines, Francis Drake (Military Personnel)
Call Each River Jordan - Owen Parry *t* 914

Raines, Harrison (Spy)
The Ironclad Alibi - Michael Kilian *m* 133
The Ironclad Alibi - Michael Kilian *t* 898

Rainwater, Gavan (Magician)
The Magickers - Emily Drake *f* 542

Raisin, Agatha (Public Relations; Detective—Amateur)
Agatha Raisin and the Love from Hell - M.C. Beaton *m* 14

Ramone, Dee Dee (Musician; Historical Figure)
Chelsea Horror Hotel - Dee Dee Ramone *h* 684

Ramos, Antonio Rommel (Cowboy)
Fire Lilies - Cynthia Leal Massey *w* 476

Ramsay, Ben (Police Officer; Single Parent)
Diamond in the Ruff - Emily Carmichael *r* 249

Ramsden, Edward (Nobleman; Military Personnel)
The Very Daring Duchess - Miranda Jarrett *r* 308

Rand, Jeffery (Spy)
The Old Spies Club and Other Intrigues of Rand - Edward D. Hoch *m* 118

Randall, Brad (Military Personnel)
An Uncommon Enemy - Michelle Black *w* 423
An Uncommon Enemy - Michelle Black *t* 824

Randall, Drew (Handicapped)
Divine Intervention - Ken Wharton *s* 810

Randolph, Erik (Heir)
When Jayne Met Erik - Elizabeth Bevarly *r* 236

Randolph, Griffin (Diver; Mythical Creature)
Alice at Heart - Deborah Smith *r* 401

Ranelagh, M. (Housewife; Narrator)
The Shape of Snakes - Minette Walters *m* 211

Raphael, Sebastian (Scholar; Friend)
London Bridges - Jane Stevenson *c* 1204

Rathford, Helena (Noblewoman; Recluse)
The Sleeping Beauty - Jacqueline Navin *r* 360

Raven (Sorceress)
The Black Chalice - Marie Jakober *f* 562

Raven (Vampire)
Blood Games - Lee Killough *h* 657

Raven (Indian)
Letters to Callie - Dawn Miller *w* 483

Rawlings, Constance (Businesswoman)
The Other Adonis - Frank Deford *t* 849

Rayne, Alex (Government Official)
Second Contact - J.D. Austin *s* 719

Reacher, Jack (Military Personnel)
Echo Burning - Lee Child *w* 442

Reardon, Heather (Journalist)
You Never Can Tell - Kathleen Eagle *w* 450

Rebecca (Crime Victim; Girlfriend)
The Treatment - Mo Hayder *c* 1123

Rebus, John (Police Officer)
The Falls - Ian Rankin *m* 178

Red Cloud (Historical Figure; Indian)
The June Rise - William Tremblay *w* 507
The June Rise - William Tremblay *t* 945
Moon of Bitter Cold - Frederick J. Chiaventone *w* 441
Turn the Stars Upside Down - Terry C. Johnston *w* 466

Redclift, Gabriella (Noblewoman)
My Lady Beloved - Lael St. James *r* 405

Redclift, Meg (Noblewoman)
My Lady Wayward - Lael St. James *r* 406

Redmagne, Methuselah (Revolutionary; Smuggler)
Sparrowhawk—Jack Frake - Edward Cline *t* 840

Redmond, Tom (Journalist; Companion)
Ambrose Bierce and the Death of Kings - Oakley Hall *m* 95
Ambrose Bierce and the Death of Kings - Oakley Hall *t* 878

Reed, Catherine deClaire (Widow(er))
Whispers of Goodbye - Karen White *r* 418

Reed, Noah (Publisher; Writer)
Envy - Sandra Brown *r* 245
Envy - Sandra Brown *c* 1086

Reever, Duncan (Linguist)
Shockball - S.L. Viehl *s* 805

Regis (Mythical Creature)
Sea of Swords - R.A. Salvatore *f* 597

Reilly, Regan (Detective—Private)
Fleeced - Carol Higgins Clark *m* 34

Remus, George (Bootlegger; Historical Figure)
The Jazz Bird - Craig Holden *t* 885
The Jazz Bird - Craig Holden *m* 119

Remus, Imogene (Historical Figure; Spouse)
The Jazz Bird - Craig Holden *t* 885

Renfield, Cleo (Debutante)
The Irredeemable Miss Renfield - Regina Scott *r* 393

Reothe (Royalty)
Dark Dreams - Cory Daniells r 267

Repairman Jack (Mercenary)
Hosts - F. Paul Wilson h 710

Reve, Zule (Religious)
The Red of His Shadow - Mayra Montero c 1164

Reynal, Pierre (Gambler)
Open Season - C.J. Box w 428

Reynard, Jorlan (Spouse)
Ritual of Proof - Dara Joy r 310

Reynolds, Frank (Unemployed)
The Faded Flower - Paul McCusker i 1024

Rezkova, Magda (Heroine; Spouse)
First Gray, Then White, Then Blue - Margriet de Moor c 1165

Rhapsody (Singer)
Destiny - Elizabeth Haydon f 554

Rhian (Young Woman)
Daughter of Lir - Judith Tarr t 940

Rhinegold, Valerie (Saloon Keeper/Owner)
Teeth - Edo van Belkom h 705

Rhodes, Dan (Police Officer)
A Romantic Way to Die - Bill Crider m 49

Rice, Georgia (Grandparent)
The World Below - Sue Miller c 1163

Rice, Penelope "Poppy" (FBI Agent)
Love Her Madly - Mary-Ann Tirone Smith m 198

Richard (Werewolf)
Narcissus in Chains - Laurell K. Hamilton h 645

Richard, Duke of Gloucester (Historical Figure; Royalty)
The Goldsmith's Daughter - Kate Sedley t 933

Richard of Warefeld (Knight; Religious)
The Marriage Bed - Claudia Dain r 266

Richard the Lionheart (Historical Figure; Ruler)
Pride of Kings - Judith Tarr t 941

Rifkin, Ellie (Student; Spouse)
Fighting Gravity - Peggy Rambach c 1184

Riley, Alice (Mythical Creature; Heiress—Lost)
Alice at Heart - Deborah Smith r 401

Riley, Jordan (Lawyer)
On Every Side - Karen Kingsbury i 1010

Riley, Katelyn (Student—Graduate)
Riverwatch - Joseph M. Nassise h 676

Rincewind (Wizard)
The Last Hero - Terry Pratchett f 588

Ringyar (Nobleman)
Shadow Kiss - Tom Townsend f 605

Riona (Gentlewoman)
Riona - Linda Windsor i 1060

Rizzoli, Jane (Detective—Homicide)
The Surgeon - Tess Gerritsen m 78

Robak, Don (Judge; Lawyer)
Robak in Black - Joe L. Hensley m 113

Roberts, Dora (Journalist)
The Seat Beside Me - Nancy Moser i 1030

Roberts, Sarah (Vampire; Doctor)
The Last Vampire - Whitley Strieber h 699

Robin (Military Personnel)
The Wolf Pit - Marly Youmans t 964

Robin, Cecilia (Teacher)
Augur's Teacher - Sherwood Smith s 800

Robin, Francesca (Art Dealer; Artist)
The Very Daring Duchess - Miranda Jarrett r 308

Rochelle, Valara "Lara" (Noblewoman)
The Wedding Charm - Lynn Collum r 258

Rodney, Arthur (Young Man)
The Beasts of Brahm - Mark Hansom h 646

Rogan, Kevin (Military Personnel)
Last Virgin in California - Maureen Child r 255

Roger the Chapman (Peddler; Detective—Amateur)
The Goldsmith's Daughter - Kate Sedley t 933
The Weaver's Inheritance - Kate Sedley t 934
The Weaver's Inheritance - Kate Sedley m 194

Rohk, Truls (Mythical Creature)
Antrax - Terry Brooks f 530

Rojire (Servant; Monster)
A Feast in Exile - Chelsea Quinn Yarbro h 713

Rollins, Kate (Advertising; Single Parent)
The Secret - Kat Martin r 347

Roosevelt, Eleanor (Historical Figure; Detective—Amateur)
Murder at the President's Door - Elliott Roosevelt t 928

Roosevelt, Franklin D. (Historical Figure; Political Figure)
Murder at the President's Door - Elliott Roosevelt t 928

Rose, Angie (Journalist)
Lt. Kent: Lone Wolf - Judith Lyons r 341

Rosenblum, Samuel (Boyfriend)
Eva Moves the Furniture - Margot Livesey c 1148

Rosenstein, Gilda (Maintenance Worker)
What You Owe Me - Bebe Moore Campbell c 1089

Ross, Justin (Nobleman; Wealthy)
Heartless - Kat Martin r 346

Ross, Sara Charlene (Witch)
A Game of Colors - John Urbancik h 704

Rosselli, Tommy (Criminal)
Shooting Dr. Jack - Norman Green c 1118

Rostnikov, Porfiry Petrovich (Police Officer)
Murder on the Trans-Siberian Express - Stuart M. Kaminsky m 130

Rostov, Tandy (Musician)
The Pinkerton Eye - Allen P. Bristow w 436

Roth, Abraham (Wealthy; Parent)
Devil's Island - John Hagee i 994

Roth, Jacob (Religious)
Devil's Island - John Hagee i 994

Rothman, Ruby (Widow(er); Computer Expert)
Don't Cry for Me, Hot Pastrami - Sharon Kahn m 129

Rouenna (Friend; Nurse)
For Rouenna - Sigrid Nunez c 1172

Roundtree, Clarissa (Servant; Writer)
Smuggler's Moon - Bruce Alexander t 815

Rowan (Child)
Rowan of Rin - Emily Rodda f 594

Rowlands, Brianna (Social Worker)
A Child Shall Lead Them - Carole Gift Page i 1036

Rowlands, Frannie (Artist)
A Bungalow for Two - Carole Gift Page i 1035

Rowley, Eppingham Julian (Nobleman; Rake)
Fallen - Celeste Bradley r 241

Roy (Handicapped)
City Infernal - Edward Lee h 667

Roy, Charlie (Cowboy)
Charlie and the Sir - Frank Roderus w 499

Rufryd (Warrior)
The Obsidian Tower - Freda Warrington f 609

Rumail (Government Official)
The Fall of Neskaya - Marion Zimmer Bradley s 725

Rumenich (Banker)
All That Counts - Georg M. Oswald c 1177

Russo, Jack (Police Officer)
Open Season - Linda Howard r 302

Russo, Joseph (Religious; Counselor)
What to Do about Annie? - Millie Criswell r 264

Ruth (Director; Survivor)
In the Shape of a Boar - Lawrence Norfolk c 1171

Rutledge, Ian (Police Officer; Veteran)
Watchers of Time - Charles Todd t 943
Watchers of Time - Charles Todd m 208

Ryan, Jonah (Child; Student)
A Bend in the Road - Nicholas Sparks c 1200

Ryan, Miles (Widow(er); Police Officer)
A Bend in the Road - Nicholas Sparks c 1200

Ryan, Scott (Doctor)
Secrets of the Heart - Gail Gaymer Martin i 1022

Rycca of Wolscroft (Noblewoman)
Come Back to Me - Josie Litton r 337

Rycroft, Charles (Amnesiac; Wealthy)
Comfort and Joy - Sandra Madden r 342

Ryker, John (Spaceman)
Out There - Gerald Rose s 793

Rymar, Ben (Spaceman)
Dreamer - Steven Harper s 755

Rysha (Traveler)
Shadow of the Seer - Michael Scott Rohan f 595

Ryshad (Bodyguard)
The Warrior's Bond - Juliet E. McKenna f 578

S

Sachar, Moshe (Military Personnel)
The Jerusalem Scrolls - Bodie Thoene t 942

Sade, Donatien Alphonse Francois de (Historical Figure; Writer)
Imagining Don Giovanni - Anthony J. Rudel t 929

Safer, Daniel (FBI Agent)
A Darker Justice - Sallie Bissell m 19

Saint-Ange, Marie Claire (Linguist; Widow(er))
Dangerous Attraction - Susan Vaughan r 417

St. Charles, Steven (Nobleman; Spy)
A Scandalous Wager - Bess Willingham r 420

St. Cyr, Valentin (Detective—Private)
Chasing the Devil's Tail - David Fulmer m 73
Chasing the Devil's Tail - David Fulmer t 867

St. David, Kathryn (Gentlewoman)
The Blue Devil - Melynda Beth Skinner r 398

St. James, Claudie (Prostitute; Crime Victim)
Back in Kansas - Debra Salonen r 387

St. James, Lionel (Gambler)
A Rogue for Christmas - Kate Huntington r 304

St. Remy Sinclair, Celia (Gentlewoman)
A Reckless Encounter - Rosemary Rogers r 385

St. Vrain, Ceran (Historical Figure; Trader)
Moon Medicine - Mike Blakely t 827

Sanat Ji Mani (Vampire)
A Feast in Exile - Chelsea Quinn Yarbro t 963
A Feast in Exile - Chelsea Quinn Yarbro h 713

Sanders, Will (Military Personnel)
The American Zone - L. Neil Smith s 799

Sandiford, St. John Michael Peter (Military Personnel; Nobleman)
The Proper Wife - Julia Justiss *r* 311

Sands, Celia (Actress)
Season of Storms - Susanna Kearsley *r* 314

Santana, Paul (Judge)
The Justice - Angela Elwell Hunt *i* 1004

Saraccino, Pedro (Lawman; Historical Figure)
Miracle of the Jacal - Robert J. Randisi *w* 497

Sarda, Leo (Scientist)
Martian Knightlife - James P. Hogan *s* 759

Sarhaddon (Religious)
Heresy - Anselm Audley *s* 718

Saul (Historical Figure; Ruler)
Queenmaker - India Edghill *t* 858

Savage, Brook (Resistance Fighter)
The Savages in Love and War - Fred Mustard Stewart *t* 937

Savage, Nick (Banker; Diplomat)
The Savages in Love and War - Fred Mustard Stewart *t* 937

Savage, William (Military Personnel)
Minutes to Burn - Gregg Andrew Hurwitz *s* 762

Savari, Yana (Nurse)
Haunted - Melinda Metz *s* 776

Savi (Prisoner)
Shadow of the Seer - Michael Scott Rohan *f* 595

Savile, Justin B. V (Detective—Homicide)
First Lady - Michael Malone *c* 1153

Savitch, Ben (Journalist)
The Astonished Eye - Tracy Knight *f* 567

Sawyer, Jack (Detective—Homicide)
Black House - Stephen King *h* 659
Black House - Stephen King *c* 1140

Sayers, Andrew (Young Man; Handicapped)
The Folks - Ray Garton *h* 638

Scaptey (Criminal)
Shadow - K.J. Parker *f* 585

Schell, Johanna (Doctor)
Secret of the Wolf - Susan Krinard *r* 322

Schoene, Anna (Young Woman)
The Distant Land of My Father - Bo Caldwell *t* 835

Schoene, Joseph (Importer/Exporter; Parent)
The Distant Land of My Father - Bo Caldwell *t* 835

Schuler, Buster (Coach)
Hometown Legend - Jerry B. Jenkins *i* 1005

Schwartz, Marianne (Spouse; Public Relations)
All That Counts - Georg M. Oswald *c* 1177

Schwartz, Thomas (Banker; Narrator)
All That Counts - Georg M. Oswald *c* 1177

Scofield, Lily (Cousin; Spouse)
The Evidence Against Her - Robb Forman Dew *c* 1102
The Evidence Against Her - Robb Forman Dew *t* 850

Scofield, Warren (Spouse)
The Evidence Against Her - Robb Forman Dew *t* 850
The Evidence Against Her - Robb Forman Dew *c* 1102

Scott, Samantha (Doctor)
Night Blood - James M. Thompson *h* 702

Scudder, Matt (Detective—Private)
Hope to Die - Lawrence Block *m* 22

Seabrook, Mary (Gentlewoman; Artist)
The Rake and the Wallflower - Allison Lane *r* 325

Seagrave, Appollonia "Polly" Grace (Noblewoman)
Lady Polly - Nicola Cornick *r* 259

Seagrave, Nicholas John Rosslyn (Nobleman)
The Virtuous Cyprian - Nicola Cornick *r* 260

Seagrave, Tom (Military Personnel)
Jane and the Prisoner of Wool House - Stephanie Barron *t* 822

Seddon, Carole (Divorced Person; Civil Servant)
Death on the Downs - Simon Brett *m* 27

Sedgewick, Gresham (Knight; Amnesiac)
My Lady Wayward - Lael St. James *r* 406

Self (Supernatural Being)
A Lower Deep - Tom Piccirilli *h* 682

Seppanen, Martti (Detective—Private)
The Puppet Master - John Dalmas *s* 741

Serafina (Parent; Immigrant)
Highwire Moon - Susan Straight *c* 1205

Seraphim, Rushton (Leader)
Ashling - Isobelle Carmody *s* 732

Seth (Vampire)
Night Players - P.D. Cacek *h* 625

Severn, Trent (Businessman; Lawyer)
The Guardian - Barbara Miller *r* 355

Seymour, Glenys (Wealthy; Maiden)
The Prisoner Bride - Susan Spencer Paul *r* 368

Seyonne (Warrior)
Revelation - Elizabeth Haydon *f* 555

Shaddam IV (Ruler)
House Corrino - Brian Herbert *s* 757

Shadow (Teenager)
Shadow Kiss - Tom Townsend *f* 605

Shakespeare, William (Historical Figure; Writer)
Her Infinite Variety - Pamela Rafael Berkman *t* 823

Shakespeare, William (Historical Figure; Teacher)
Ill Met by Moonlight - Sarah A. Hoyt *f* 559

Shakespeare, William (Historical Figure; Writer)
The Slaying of the Shrew - Simon Hawke *m* 109
The Slaying of the Shrew - Simon Hawke *t* 880

Shamra (Young Woman)
Ice - Stephen Bowkett *s* 724

Shan (Apprentice)
The Way of Light - Storm Constantine *f* 536

Shannon, Rusty (Lawman)
The Way of the Coyote - Elmer Kelton *w* 468
The Way of the Coyote - Elmer Kelton *t* 895
The Way of the Coyote - Elmer Kelton *c* 1137

Shanty (Slave)
The Way of the Coyote - Elmer Kelton *t* 895

Sharina (Noblewoman)
Mistress of the Catacombs - David Drake *f* 541

Sharp, Mose (Entertainer)
Niagara Falls All over Again - Elizabeth McCracken *c* 1158

Sharples, Claire (Scientist; Detective—Amateur)
The Tumbleweed Murders - Rebecca Rothenberg *m* 189

Shaw, George Bernard (Historical Figure; Writer)
The Case of the Ripper's Revenge - Sam McCarver *m* 153

Shaw, Jeremy (Young Man)
The Beasts of Brahm - Mark Hansom *h* 646

Shelby, Evan (Invalid)
Destiny Valley - Fred Grove *w* 459

Shelby, Morgan (Health Care Professional)
A Paradigm of Earth - Candas Jane Dorsey *s* 747

Shelby, Robyn (Teenager)
A Paradigm of Earth - Candas Jane Dorsey *s* 747

Shepard, Carina DiGratia (Spouse)
The Tender Vine - Kristen Heitzmann *i* 998

Shepard, Quillan (Spouse)
The Tender Vine - Kristen Heitzmann *i* 998

Shepherd, Lori (Parent)
Aunt Dimity: Detective - Nancy Atherton *m* 9

Sheridan, Matthew (Cowboy; Single Parent)
Heaven Sent - Jillian Hart *i* 997

Sherman, Cindy (Military Personnel)
A Soldier's Duty - Thomas E. Ricks *c* 1186

Sherman, Ellen (Relative)
The Reckoning - John McLain *w* 481

Sherman, Rebecca (Scientist; Astronaut)
First Landing - Robert Zubrin *s* 814

Sherman, Will (Rancher)
The Reckoning - John McLain *w* 481

Shillingsworth, John (Military Personnel)
A Soldier's Duty - Thomas E. Ricks *c* 1186

Shimura, Rei (Antiques Dealer; Expatriate)
The Bride's Kimono - Sujata Massey *m* 150

Shirley, Diana (Counselor)
The Webster Chronicle - Daniel Akst *c* 1066

Shore, Jane (Historical Figure; Lover)
The Goldsmith's Daughter - Kate Sedley *t* 933

Shore, Marla (Hairdresser; Widow(er))
Murder by Manicure - Nancy J. Cohen *m* 38

Short, Alexander (Narrator; Librarian)
The Grand Complication - Allen Kurzweil *c* 1144

Sierck, Detlef (Writer)
Drachenfels - Jack Yeovil *f* 613

Simbul (Nobleman)
Elminster in Hell - Ed Greenwood *f* 553

Simone, Lena (Saloon Keeper/Owner)
Midnight Bayou - Nora Roberts *c* 1187

Sinclair, Jane (Spouse; Doctor)
Super-Cannes - J.G. Ballard *c* 1070

Sinclair, Paul (Pilot)
Super-Cannes - J.G. Ballard *c* 1070

Singer, Judith (Detective—Private; Professor)
Long Time No See - Susan Isaacs *c* 1131

Singleton, Ray (Farmer)
The Magic of Ordinary Days - Ann Howard Creel *t* 845

Sissy (Abuse Victim)
Tennant's Rock - Steve McGiffen *w* 478

Skeeve (Wizard)
Myth-ion Improbable - Robert Lynn Asprin *f* 521

Skelly, Augustus (Revolutionary; Smuggler)
Sparrowhawk—Jack Frake - Edward Cline *t* 840

Skelly, Colleen Mary (Student—Graduate)
Taylor's Temptation - Suzanne Brockmann *r* 242

Skif (Criminal; Orphan)
Take a Thief - Mercedes Lackey *f* 569

Skye, Barnaby (Mountain Man)
Downriver - Richard S. Wheeler *w* 512
Downriver - Richard S. Wheeler *t* 957

Skye, Victoria (Spouse; Indian)
Downriver - Richard S. Wheeler *t* 957
Downriver - Richard S. Wheeler *w* 512

Slack, Tommy (Teenager; Crime Suspect)
End over End - Kate Kennedy *c* 1139

Slattery, Mary (Lawyer)
Shades of Justice - Fredrick Huebner *m* 121

Slaughter, John (Rancher; Historical Figure)
Miracle of the Jacal - Robert J. Randisi *w* 497

Slavin, Mickey (Television Personality)
Dead Ball - R.D. Rosen *m* 188

Slider, Bill (Police Officer)
Blood Sinister - Cynthia Harrod-Eagles *m* 104

Sloane, Todd (Publisher; Journalist)
Looking for Laura - Judith Arnold *r* 226

Slyddwyn (Wizard)
The Rundlestone of Oz - Eloise McGraw *f* 577

Smith, Gail (Scientist)
In the Company of Others - Julie E. Czerneda *s* 740

Smith, George (Accountant; Crime Victim)
Hostage - Robert Crais *c* 1096

Smith, John (Outlaw)
The Outlaws - Wayne D. Overholser *w* 490

Smith, John (Leader; Historical Figure)
Argall - William T. Vollmann *t* 950

Smith, John (Historical Figure; Kidnapper)
Argall - William T. Vollmann *c* 1212

Smith, Kendall "Ken" (Military Personnel)
The Black Eye - Constance Little *m* 144

Smith, Kyle "Panhandle" (Cowboy)
Open Range - Zane Grey *w* 458

Smith, Lacey (Detective—Police)
Cold Hunter's Moon - K.C. Greenlief *m* 90

Smith, Loren (Political Figure; Lover)
Valhalla Rising - Clive Cussler *c* 1097

Smith, Paavo (Police Officer; Boyfriend)
Bell, Cook, and Candle - Joanne Pence *m* 170

Smythe, Symington "Tuck" (Actor)
The Slaying of the Shrew - Simon Hawke *t* 880
The Slaying of the Shrew - Simon Hawke *m* 109

Snoddy, Mae Maude (Friend)
Fire in the Rock - Joe Martin *c* 1154

Solanka, Malik "Solly" (Professor; Inventor)
Fury - Salman Rushdie *c* 1190

Solano, Lupe (Detective—Private)
Bitter Sugar - Carolina Garcia-Aguilera *m* 75

Solomon, Bretta (Store Owner; Widow(er))
Lilies That Fester - Janis Harrison *m* 103

Somerville, Molly (Writer; Artist)
This Heart of Mine - Susan Elizabeth Phillips *r* 369

Sommers, Eliza (Grandparent)
Portrait in Sepia - Isabel Allende *c* 1067

Sophia (Girlfriend)
On the Night Plain - J. Robert Lennon *w* 473
On the Night Plain - J. Robert Lennon *c* 1146

Sorenson, Jacobia "Jake" Tiptree (Housewife; Detective—Amateur)
Wreck the Halls - Sarah Graves *m* 89

Sorrells, Pink (Outlaw)
Bear Paw - Gene Mullins *w* 484

Sostenuto, Pocotristi (Toy)
The Rundlestone of Oz - Eloise McGraw *f* 577

Soto, Tanger (Researcher)
The Nautical Chart - Arturo Perez-Reverte *m* 171
The Nautical Chart - Arturo Perez-Reverte *c* 1182

Souvana (Military Personnel; Alien)
Holding the Line - Rick Shelley *s* 795

Spadolini, Tracey (Advertising; Waiter/Waitress)
Slightly Single - Wendy Markham *r* 345

Spandau, Casey (Detective—Police)
Black Water Transit - Carsten Stroud *m* 204

Spangler, David (Military Personnel)
Deep Fathom - James Rollins *s* 792

Spaniard, Jack (Historical Figure; Indian)
Spanish Jack - Robert J. Conley *w* 447
Spanish Jack - Robert J. Conley *t* 842

Spencer, Hope (Journalist)
True Confessions - Rachel Gibson *r* 292

Spense, Oliver (Nobleman; Antiquarian)
The Christmas Wish - Debbie Raleigh *r* 377

Spoon, Emily (Seamstress)
Once an Outlaw - Jill Gregory *r* 294

Spotted Tail (Indian; Historical Figure)
Turn the Stars Upside Down - Terry C. Johnston *w* 466

Squibb, Henry (Child)
The Magickers - Emily Drake *f* 542

St-Cyr, Jean-Louis (Police Officer)
Kaleidoscope - J. Robert Janes *m* 126
Kaleidoscope - J. Robert Janes *t* 888

Stafford, Robyn (Time Traveler)
Knight Errant - R. Garcia y Robertson *t* 869
Knight Errant - R. Garcia y Robertson *f* 546

Stands with a Fist (Spouse; Captive)
The Holy Road - Michael Blake *w* 425
The Holy Road - Michael Blake *t* 826

Stanton, Bruce "Striker" (Military Personnel)
True Valor - Dee Henderson *i* 1000

Staples, Nathan (Writer; Parent)
Everything You Need - A.L. Kennedy *c* 1138

Star, BB (Businesswoman)
The Plutonium Blonde - John Zakour *s* 813

Starling, Peter (Teenager)
Straight on 'Til Morning - Christopher Golden *h* 642

Starr, Noah (Religious)
Child of Promise - Kathleen Morgan *i* 1025

Steele, Elise (Parent)
Heart of the Beast - Joyce Weatherford *w* 511

Steele, Ike (Parent; Rancher)
Heart of the Beast - Joyce Weatherford *w* 511

Steele, Iris (Rancher)
Heart of the Beast - Joyce Weatherford *w* 511

Steele, Rayford (Pilot)
Desecration - Tim LaHaye *i* 1016

Stefan (Witch)
A Game of Colors - John Urbancik *h* 704

Stein, Isabel (Singer)
Aria - Susan Segal *c* 1194

Steinke, Barry (Young Man; Relative)
Great American Plain - Gary Sernovitz *c* 1195

Steinke, Edward (Young Man)
Great American Plain - Gary Sernovitz *c* 1195

Stennett, Jackson (Rancher; Heir)
Jackson's Way - Leslie LaFoy *r* 324

Stephen (Angel)
The Wig My Father Wore - Anne Enright *c* 1111

Stephens, Miles William (Nobleman)
Broken Promises - Patricia Oliver *r* 362

Steward, Jonathan (Doctor)
Night of Dracula - Christopher Schildt *h* 692

Stewart, Dusty (Archaeologist)
Bone Walker - Kathleen O'Neal Gear *t* 871

Stewart, Noah (Composer)
Aria - Susan Segal *c* 1194

Stone, Cooper (Lawyer)
Forbid Them Not - Michael P. Farris *i* 991

Stone, Gabriel (Police Officer)
The Power of Love - Margaret Daley *i* 987

Stone, Hawk (Bodyguard; Police Officer)
Born Brave - Ruth Wind *r* 422

Stone, Jesse (Police Officer; Divorced Person)
Death in Paradise - Robert B. Parker *m* 168

Stone, Lucy (Journalist; Parent)
Wedding Day Murder - Leslie Meier *m* 157

Stonewall, Kate (Radio Personality; Widow(er))
A Prince of a Guy - Sheila Rabe *r* 376

Stoney (Criminal; Alcoholic)
Shooting Dr. Jack - Norman Green *c* 1118

Stormlake, Ghleanna (Sorceress)
Pool of Radiance - Carrie Bebris *f* 525

Stratford, Connor (Financier)
No Way Out - Andrea Kane *r* 312

Streicher, Jon Jarred (Military Personnel)
Bolo Strike - William H. Keith Jr. *s* 765

Strong John (Traveler)
Rowan of Rin - Emily Rodda *f* 594

Stroud, Charlie (Businessman)
Last Year's River - Allen Morris Jones *t* 891

Struensee, Johann Friedrich (Doctor; Historical Figure)
The Royal Physician's Visit - Per Olov Enquist *t* 862
The Royal Physician's Visit - Per Olov Enquist *c* 1110

Sugarman, Whitley (Scientist)
The King of the Sun - A.A. McFedries *s* 773

Sullivan, Alexandra (Innkeeper)
Awakening Alex - Ruth Langan *r* 327

Sullivan, Carolina "Carly" (Photographer)
Going Overboard - Christina Skye *r* 399

Sullivan, Daniel (Police Officer)
Murphy's Law - Rhys Bowen *m* 24

Summer, Jack (Journalist)
Someone to Watch over Me - Jill Churchill *t* 839

Summers, Ariel (Impoverished)
Heartless - Kat Martin *r* 346

Summers, Julie (Wealthy; Spouse)
The Pickup - Nadine Gordimer *c* 1116

Summers, Maddie (Interior Decorator)
Marry Me, Maddie? - Rita Herron *r* 299

Summers, Philadelphia "Frosty" (Young Woman)
The Water and the Blood - Nancy E. Turner *t* 947

Suviel (Wizard)
Shadowkings - Michael Cobley *f* 535

Suzanne (Parent; Doctor)
Suzanne's Diary for Nicholas - James Patterson *c* 1181

Suzette (Slave; Grandparent)
Cane River - Lalita Tademy *c* 1207

Swagger, Earl (Police Officer; Hero)
Pale Horse Coming - Stephen Hunter *m* 122
Pale Horse Coming - Stephen Hunter *t* 887
Pale Horse Coming - Stephen Hunter *c* 1127

Swan (Outcast)
Tennant's Rock - Steve McGiffen *w* 478

Swenson, Charlotte (Model; Accident Victim)
Look at Me - Jennifer Egan *c* 1108

Swenson, Lark (Police Officer; Widow(er))
Cold Hunter's Moon - K.C. Greenlief *m* 90

Swinbrooke, Kathryn (Doctor; Detective—Amateur)
Saintly Murders - C.L. Grace *m* 86
Saintly Murders - C.L. Grace *t* 875

Szeska, John (Murderer)
All the Dead Were Strangers - Ethan Black *c* 1076

T

Tabachnik, Joyce (Writer; Parent)
Good Harbor - Anita Diamant *c* 1103

Taber, Dylan (Police Officer)
True Confessions - Rachel Gibson *r* 292

Taft, Charlie (Lawyer; Historical Figure)
The Jazz Bird - Craig Holden *t* 885
The Jazz Bird - Craig Holden *m* 119

Tagger, Jack (Journalist)
Basket Case - Carl Hiaasen *m* 115

Taggert, Hope (Horse Trainer)
The Girl Next Door - Kate Welsh *i* 1057

Tal, Abraham (Businessman)
Green - Benjamin Zucker *i* 1064

Talbot, Jeff (Antiques Dealer; FBI Agent)
Death Is a Cabaret - Deborah Morgan *m* 160

Talbot, Julia (Teacher)
No Way Out - Andrea Kane *r* 312

Talisford, Katherine "Kate" (Gentlewoman; Writer)
Tempt Me Twice - Barbara Dawson Smith *r* 400

Talley, Jeff (Police Officer)
Hostage - Robert Crais *c* 1096
Hostage - Robert Crais *m* 47

Tamryn, Green (Noblewoman)
Ritual of Proof - Dara Joy *r* 310

Tanda (Warrior)
Myth-ion Improbable - Robert Lynn Asprin *f* 521

Tapopat (Wizard)
The Way of Light - Storm Constantine *f* 536

Tardieu, Bonne (Relative)
Mirabilis - Susann Cokal *c* 1091

Taretel (Warrior)
The Way of the Rose - Valery Leith *f* 572

Tash (Ruler)
The Way of the Rose - Valery Leith *f* 572

Tassi, Agostino (Historical Figure; Artist)
The Passion of Artemisia - Susan Vreeland *t* 951

Taylor, Becky (Student—High School)
Tears in a Bottle - Sylvia Bambola *i* 966

Taylor, Bobby (Military Personnel)
Taylor's Temptation - Suzanne Brockmann *r* 242

Taylor, Fred (Art Dealer; Detective—Amateur)
Lazarus, Arise - Nicholas Kilmer *m* 134

Taylor, Gypsy Leigh (Witch)
A Game of Colors - John Urbancik *h* 704

Taylor, Rebecca (Widow(er); Single Parent)
The Colorado Bride - Mary Burton *r* 247

Taylor, Vic (Outlaw)
Search for Last Chance - A.L. McWilliams *w* 482

Tehanu (Ruler)
The Other Wind - Ursula K. Le Guin *f* 571

Tejar (Nobleman)
Mother Ocean, Daughter Sea - Diana Marcellas *f* 576

Temar (Nobleman)
The Warrior's Bond - Juliet E. McKenna *f* 578

Temple, Izzy (Spinster; Impoverished)
Fallen - Celeste Bradley *r* 241

Templemore, Jack (Explorer)
The Devil-Tree of El Dorado - Frank Aubrey *s* 717

Templeton, Pollo (Teenager)
Fire in the Rock - Joe Martin *c* 1154

Tennington, Wilbur (Nobleman)
Treasures of the Sun - T.V. Olsen *w* 487

Tepevich, Vladimir (Doctor)
Night of Dracula - Christopher Schildt *h* 692

Ternan, Ellen Lawless (Historical Figure; Actress)
The Rag & Bone Shop - Jeff Rackham *t* 917

Terrebonne, Eugenia "Genie" (Noblewoman)
A Scandalous Wager - Bess Willingham *r* 420

Terrell (Expatriate)
The Jasper Forest - Julia Gray *f* 551

Tezcatlipoca (Artificial Intelligence)
Smoking Mirror Blues - Ernest Hogan *s* 758

Thackeray, Michael (Police Officer)
Skeleton at the Feast - Patricia Hall *m* 97

Thane, Kieran (Detective—Private)
Martian Knightlife - James P. Hogan *s* 759

Thayer, Rand (Young Man)
Buttercup Baby - Karen Fox *r* 287

Theodora (Historical Figure; Ruler)
Three for a Letter - Mary Reed *t* 920

Thomas, Allie (Cook; Store Owner)
Sweet Success - Susan Mallery *r* 344

Thomas, Charlotte "Charlie" (Restaurateur; Widow(er))
The Widow - Anne Stuart *r* 411

Thomas of Hookton (Student—College; Military Personnel)
The Archer's Tale - Bernard Cornwell *t* 843

Thompson, Edith (Historical Figure; Lover)
Fred & Edie - Jill Dawson *t* 848

Thompson, Percy (Historical Figure; Spouse)
Fred & Edie - Jill Dawson *t* 848

Thor (Android)
Tower of Glass - Robert Silverberg *s* 797

Thorn (Fisherman)
Blackwater Sound - James W. Hall *m* 94

Thornbury, Winona (Restaurateur)
The Secret Life of Connor Monahan - Elizabeth Bevarly *r* 235

Thorne (Vampire)
Blood and Gold - Anne Rice *c* 1185

Thorne, Adrian (Nobleman; Psychic)
Heart of Night - Taylor Chase *r* 254

Thornhill, Rowena (Gentlewoman)
My Lord Savage - Elizabeth Lane *r* 326

Thornhill, Viola (Noblewoman)
No Man's Mistress - Mary Balogh *r* 227

Thorssen, Alix (Art Dealer)
Blue Wolf - Lise McClendon *w* 477

Thorssun, Knut (Sports Figure)
The Money-Whipped Steer-Job Three-Jack Give-Up Artist - Dan Jenkins *c* 1132

Thrale, Hester (Benefactor; Historical Figure)
According to Queeney - Beryl Bainbridge *c* 1069

Thrale, Queeney (Relative; Narrator)
According to Queeney - Beryl Bainbridge *c* 1069

Thunder Cloud (Parent; Indian)
Blood on the Wind - Lucile Bogue *w* 426

Tiarnan of Talensac (Knight)
The Wolf Hunt - Gillian Bradshaw *t* 831

Tighe (Explorer)
On - Adam Roberts *s* 790

Tilden, Hayden (Lawman)
Law Dog - J. Lee Butts *w* 438

Timberlake, Abigail (Antiques Dealer; Divorced Person)
Nightmare in Shining Armor - Tamar Myers *m* 163

Timur-i-Lenhk (Military Personnel; Historical Figure)
A Feast in Exile - Chelsea Quinn Yarbro *t* 963

Tinkerman, Dobie (Drifter; Sidekick)
A Good Town - Douglas Hirt *w* 462

Tiomenen, Liesl (Widow(er))
Cold - John Smolens *c* 1199

Tiphan (Religious)
Brother of the Dragon - Paul B. Thompson *f* 604

Tobin (Noblewoman; Teenager)
The Bone Doll's Twin - Lynn Flewelling *f* 544

Tod, Florence (Spinster; Cousin)
Deadly Illumination - Serena Stier *m* 203

Todd, Alena (Horse Trainer)
The Mackintosh Bride - Debra Lee Brown *r* 244

Todd, Ripley (Police Officer; Witch)
Heaven and Earth - Nora Roberts *r* 383

Todd, Zach (Police Officer)
Dance upon the Air - Nora Roberts *r* 382

Tolliver, Jeffrey (Police Officer)
Blindsighted - Karin Slaughter *m* 197

Tomm (Spaceman)
Planet America - Mack Maloney *s* 768

Ton Su (Teenager)
Edgewater Angels - Sandro Meallet *c* 1160

Tony (Financier)
House of Pain - Sephera Giron *h* 640

Toomagian, Aron (Spaceman)
Out There - Gerald Rose *s* 793

Toomer, Sonny (Teenager)
Edgewater Angels - Sandro Meallet *c* 1160

Tore, Paul (Young Man)
The Nature of Balance - Tim Lebbon *h* 666

Toribor (Nobleman)
The Dragon Society - Lawrence Watt-Evans *f* 610

Torin, Cherijo (Doctor)
Shockball - S.L. Viehl *s* 805

Torkay, Lucy (Sorceress)
Dragon's Bluff - Mary H. Herbert *f* 556

Torrijos, Sergei (Military Personnel)
The Dark Wing - Walter Hunt *s* 761

Towle, Ivory (Teenager; Crime Victim)
End over End - Kate Kennedy *c* 1139

Towne, Jill (Doctor)
All the Dead Were Strangers - Ethan Black *c* 1076

Townsend, Andrew (Military Personnel; Astronaut)
First Landing - Robert Zubrin *s* 814

Townsend, Galen (Nobleman)
His Lady Midnight - Jo Ann Ferguson *r* 279

Townsend, Ray (Settler)
Worthy of Riches - Bonnie Leon *i* 1017

Tratal (Ruler)
Wit'ch Gate - James Clemens *f* 534

Travers, Sam (Writer)
Riverwatch - Joseph M. Nassise *h* 676

Travis (Police Officer)
Bikini Planet - David Garnett *s* 752

Travis, Melanie (Animal Trainer; Single Parent)
Once Bitten - Laurien Berenson *m* 17

Treat, Cassandra (Heiress)
A Forbidden Embrace - Anna Jacobs *r* 305

Treene, Harriet (Saleswoman; Imposter)
The Very Comely Countess - Miranda Jarrett *r* 307

Trehan, Jack (Sports Figure; Wealthy)
Love to Love You Baby - Kasey Michaels *r* 354

Tremayne, Amanda (Seamstress)
The Traitor's Daughter - Elizabeth Powell *r* 374

Tremayne, Lucian (Nobleman; Spy)
Desire - Nicole Jordan *r* 309

Tremelo, Miguel (Scientist)
Pyramid Scheme - David Freer *s* 751

Tresh, Roamer (Blacksmith)
Mattie and the Blacksmith - Linda Lea Castle *r* 253

Trevany, Walter (Businessman)
Martian Knightlife - James P. Hogan *s* 759

Trujillo, Alejandro (Businessman)
His Father's Son - Nigel Bennett *h* 621

Trujillo, Luis (Businessman)
His Father's Son - Nigel Bennett *h* 621

Trujillo, Rafael (Historical Figure; Political Figure)
The Feast of the Goat - Mario Vargas Llosa *t* 948
The Feast of the Goat - Mario Vargas Llosa *c* 1211

Trujillo, Ramfis (Relative; Historical Figure)
The Feast of the Goat - Mario Vargas Llosa *c* 1211

Tucci, Crow (Bodyguard)
Judging Sara - Cynthia Rutledge *i* 1044

Tucker, Grady (Journalist)
A Capital Holiday - Janet Dailey *r* 265

Tucker, Kevin (Sports Figure)
This Heart of Mine - Susan Elizabeth Phillips *r* 369

Tuco, Eddie (Young Man)
Shooting Dr. Jack - Norman Green *c* 1118

Tulkhan (Ruler)
Dark Dreams - Cory Daniells *r* 267

Tulsi Kil (Slave)
A Feast in Exile - Chelsea Quinn Yarbro *t* 963

Turner, Lucas (Doctor)
City of Dreams - Beverly Swerling *t* 939

Turner, Paul (Police Officer; Homosexual)
Sex and Murder.com - Mark Richard Zubro *m* 221

Turner, Sally (Apothecary)
City of Dreams - Beverly Swerling *t* 939

Two Stars, David (Indian; Military Personnel)
Heart of the Sandhill - Stephanie Grace Whitson *i* 1058

Two Stars, Genevieve LaCroix (Indian; Spouse)
Heart of the Sandhill - Stephanie Grace Whitson *i* 1058

Tyler, Erica (Anthropologist)
Sacred Ground - Barbara Wood *t* 962

Tyrell, Keith (Police Officer)
A Fine and Private Place - Freda Davies *m* 55

U

Ulyanova, Varya (Royalty)
Elusive Passion - Kathryn Smith *r* 402

Umar ibn al-Khattab (Historical Figure; Ruler)
The Rock - Kanan Makiya *t* 902

Unger, David (Student)
Conjuring Maud - Philip Danze *t* 847

Unnamed Character (Worker)
The Appointment - Herta Muller *c* 1168

Unnamed Character (Teenager; Friend)
Balzac and the Little Chinese Seamstress - Sijie Dai *c* 1098

Unnamed Character (Writer; Narrator)
For Rouenna - Sigrid Nunez *c* 1172

Unnamed Character (Heroine)
My Little Blue Dress - Bruno Maddox *c* 1150

Urdo (Ruler)
The King's Name - Jo Walton *f* 608

Ushart, Adam (Teacher)
A Morning in Eden - Anna Gilbert *t* 872

Uskevren, Shamur (Noblewoman)
The Shattered Mask - Richard Lee Byers *f* 532

Uskevren, Thamalon (Businessman)
The Shattered Mask - Richard Lee Byers *f* 532

V

Vail, Dalton (Detective—Homicide)
Murder by Manicure - Nancy J. Cohen *m* 38

Valencia, Liria (Housekeeper; Parent)
One Good Turn - Carla Kelly *r* 315

Valentine, Meg (Teacher; Imposter)
Two Sexy - Stephanie Bond *r* 240

Valentyn, Julian (Vampire)
Candle Bay - Tamara Thorne *h* 703

Valera, Luis (Sidekick; Professor)
Treasures of the Sun - T.V. Olsen *w* 487

Valle, Aurora del (Photographer)
Portrait in Sepia - Isabel Allende *t* 817

Valle, Paulina del (Grandparent)
Portrait in Sepia - Isabel Allende *t* 817

Van Buren, Lucas "Luke" (Architect)
Seducing Mr. Right - Cherry Adair *r* 223

Van der Vries, Jacob (Doctor)
City of Dreams - Beverly Swerling *t* 939

Van Helsing, Abraham (Doctor)
The London Vampire Panic - Michael Romkey *h* 686
Quincey Morris, Vampire - P.N. Elrod *h* 632

Van Pelt, Kirk (Lawman; Detective)
The Pinkerton Eye - Allen P. Bristow *w* 436

Van Urden, Ivy (Model; Mentally Ill Person)
The Savage Girl - Alex Shakar *c* 1196

Van Urden, Ursula (Artist; Relative)
The Savage Girl - Alex Shakar *c* 1196

van Visser, Anna (Fugitive)
Keeper of Hearts - Dianne Christner *i* 979

Vanderhorn, Morris (Historical Figure)
The Hum Bug - Harold Schechter *w* 502

Vane, Una (Student—College)
The Flight of the Maidens - Jane Gardam *t* 870

Vasilyevich, Annatt (Teenager)
Children of the Shaman - Jessica Rydill *f* 596

Vasilyevich, Malchik (Teenager)
Children of the Shaman - Jessica Rydill *f* 596

Vasilyevich, Yuda (Shaman)
Children of the Shaman - Jessica Rydill *f* 596

Vel (Criminal; Teenager)
Hope's End - Stephen Chambers *s* 733

Veldan (Wizard)
Spirit of the Stone - Maggie Furey *f* 545

Vermillion, Jack (Businessman; Veteran)
Black Water Transit - Carsten Stroud *m* 204

Vespasian, Titus Flavius Sabinus (Historical Figure; Military Personnel)
Under the Eagle - Simon Scarrow *t* 931

Vetinari (Nobleman)
The Last Hero - Terry Pratchett *f* 588

Vievre (Doctor)
On - Adam Roberts *s* 790

Vincent, Sam (Lawyer)
Pale Horse Coming - Stephen Hunter *m* 122
Pale Horse Coming - Stephen Hunter *t* 887
Pale Horse Coming - Stephen Hunter *c* 1127

Vinius, Titus (Military Personnel)
Nobody Loves a Centurion - John Maddox Roberts *t* 924

Visitor, Lennie (Clerk; Lover)
Light Coming Back - Ann Wadsworth *c* 1213

Voight, Rae (Teenager; Telepath)
Gifted Touch - Melinda Metz *s* 775
Haunted - Melinda Metz *s* 776

Volson, Siggy (Teenager; Twin)
Bloodtide - Melvin Burgess *s* 730

Volson, Signy (Teenager; Twin)
Bloodtide - Melvin Burgess *s* 730

von Bek, Ulric (Nobleman)
The Dreamthief's Daughter - Michael Moorcock *f* 582

von Heyden, Gottfried (Nobleman)
The Black Chalice - Marie Jakober *f* 562

von Minct, Gaynor (Nobleman)
The Dreamthief's Daughter - Michael Moorcock *f* 582

Von Volzenburg, Vanessa (Royalty)
The Marine and the Princess - Cathie Linz *r* 334

Voort, Conrad (Detective—Police)
All the Dead Were Strangers - Ethan Black *c* 1076
All the Dead Were Strangers - Ethan Black *m* 20

Voss, Doc (Friend)
Bitterroot - James Lee Burke *c* 1088

Voss, Harry (Military Personnel; Lawyer)
Officer of the Court - Bill Mesce Jr. *t* 906

Voss, Karl (Diplomat; Spy)
The Company of Strangers - Robert Wilson *m* 215
The Company of Strangers - Robert Wilson *t* 960

Vyx (Warrior)
Revelation - Elizabeth Haydon *f* 555

W

Waals, Christina van der (Immigrant; Teenager)
Island of Tears - Troy Soos *t* 936

Wade, Callie (Pioneer)
Letters to Callie - Dawn Miller *w* 483

Wade, Jack (Gambler; Pioneer)
Letters to Callie - Dawn Miller *w* 483

Wakefield, Jocelyn (Young Woman)
A Capital Holiday - Janet Dailey *r* 265

Wakefield, Samuel (Nobleman)
The Promise - May McGoldrick *r* 352

Walker, Anthony (Child)
The Monsters of Morley Manor - Bruce Coville *f* 538

Walker, Clayton (Lawman)
Walker's Widow - Heidi Betts *r* 234

Walker, Red (Pilot; Military Personnel)
Sentimental Journey - Jill Barnett *r* 228

Walker, Sarah (Child)
The Monsters of Morley Manor - Bruce Coville *f* 538

Character Name Index

Wallace, Cassandra (Bride; Gentlewoman)
A Devilish Husband - Alana Clayton *r* 257

Walsh, Lily (Young Woman)
Bamboo and Lace - Lori Wick *i* 1059

Ward, Paul (Spy)
The Last Vampire - Whitley Strieber *h* 699

Warrington, Patrick (Journalist)
The Fourth Hand - John Irving *c* 1130

Washburn, Samuel (Slave; Military Personnel)
We Look Like Men of War - William R. Forstchen *t* 864

Washington, John (Religious; Historical Figure)
Sea of Glory - Ken Wales *t* 953

Waterhouse, Lavinia (Friend)
Falling Angels - Tracy Chevalier *c* 1090
Falling Angels - Tracy Chevalier *t* 838

Waters, Claire (Wealthy)
Redeeming Claire - Cynthia Rutledge *i* 1045

Waters, Rocky (Journalist; Widow(er))
Rocky and the Senator's Daughter - Dixie Browning *r* 246

Waterston, Michael (Professor; Boyfriend)
Revenge of the Wrought-Iron Flamingos - Donna Andrews *m* 6

Watkins, Claire (Police Officer; Widow(er))
Glare Ice - Mary Logue *m* 145

Watson, John (Sidekick; Doctor)
Sherlock Holmes and the Giant Rat of Sumatra - Alan Vanneman *m* 210
Sherlock Holmes and the Secret Alliance - Larry Millett *m* 158
Sherlock Holmes and the Secret Alliance - Larry Millett *t* 908

Watson, Regina (Vampire)
The Last Vampire - T.M. Wright *h* 712

Watson, Zeb (Travel Agent)
Sidhe-Devil - Aaron Allston *f* 516

Wayne, Ellie (Store Owner)
A Father's Place - Marta Perry *i* 1041

Weatherford, Fiona Wooten "Biggie" (Aged Person; Detective—Amateur)
Biggie and the Quincy Ghost - Nancy Bell *m* 15

Weatherford, J.R. (Child)
Biggie and the Quincy Ghost - Nancy Bell *m* 15

Weaver, Albert (Artisan)
The Weaver's Inheritance - Kate Sedley *t* 934

Weaver, Alison (Young Woman)
The Weaver's Inheritance - Kate Sedley *t* 934

Weaver, Kendi (Spaceman)
Dreamer - Steven Harper *s* 755

Weaver, Summer (Banker; Guardian)
Summer's Promise - Irene Brand *i* 974

Weaver, Susan (FBI Agent)
Frankenstein: The Legacy - Christopher Schildt *h* 691

Webb, Marshall (Writer)
Island of Tears - Troy Soos *t* 936
Island of Tears - Troy Soos *m* 200

Weber, Willi (Military Personnel)
Jackdaws - Ken Follett *t* 863

Weeks, Oliver Wendell (Detective—Homicide)
Money, Money, Money - Ed McBain *m* 152

Weissman, Morton (Professor)
The Lecturer's Tale - James Hynes *h* 649

Welch, Barry (Writer)
The Association - Bentley Little *h* 668

Welch, Maureen (Accountant)
The Association - Bentley Little *h* 668

Wellman, Richard (Radio Personality)
The Prodigy - Alton Gansky *h* 637

Wells, Andrew (Businessman)
Another Summer - Georgia Bockoven *r* 239

Wells, Chan (Military Personnel)
The Dark Wing - Walter Hunt *s* 761

Wells, Molly Sterling (Abuse Victim)
Sweet Nothings - Catherine Anderson *r* 225

Westbourne, Len (Military Personnel; Pilot)
The Clouds Above - Andrew Greig *t* 876

Westerly, Geoffrey (Nobleman)
Under the Kissing Bough - Shannon Donnelly *r* 271

Westwood, Dimity (Spirit)
Aunt Dimity: Detective - Nancy Atherton *m* 9

Whateley, Bess (Saloon Hostess)
Watch by Moonlight - Kate Hawks *t* 881

Wheel, Jane (Antiques Dealer; Collector)
Killer Stuff - Sharon Fiffer *m* 69

Whitaker, Nigel (Kidnapper)
A Prince Among Them - Al Lacy *i* 1015

White, Jasmine (Bodyguard)
Bring Me a Dream - Robyn Amos *r* 224

White, Tom (FBI Agent)
The Years of Fear - Fred Grove *w* 460

Whitman, Max (Student; Actor)
. . .And the Angel with Television Eyes - John Shirley *h* 694

Whittaker, Mary Ann (Gentlewoman)
A Rogue for Christmas - Kate Huntington *r* 304

Whittington, Kate (Spinster; Mail Order Bride)
Summer Moon - Jill Marie Landis *w* 471

Wiener, Matt (Spaceship Captain)
Second Contact - J.D. Austin *s* 719

Wilcox, Quent (Student—College; Teenager)
Affinity - J.N. Williamson *h* 709

Wilde, John (Scientist; Professor)
Sarah's Window - Janice Graham *w* 457

Wilder, Joe (Military Personnel)
Stranded with the Sergeant - Cathie Linz *r* 335

Wilder, Mark (Military Personnel)
The Marine and the Princess - Cathie Linz *r* 334

Wilkinson, James (Historical Figure; Military Personnel)
Treason - David Nevin *t* 912

Wilkinson, Katie (Editor; Lover)
Suzanne's Diary for Nicholas - James Patterson *c* 1181

Will (Thief)
Fortress Draconis - Michael A. Stackpole *f* 599

William, Roast Beef (Military Personnel)
Marching through Peachtree - Harry Turtledove *f* 606

Williams, Audrey (Teacher; Divorced Person)
Dangerous Dilemmas - Evelyn Palfrey *r* 365

Williams, Joe (Detective—Police)
Teeth - Edo van Belkom *h* 705

Williams, John "Loverboy" (Musician; Singer)
Just Say No! - Omar Tyree *c* 1210

Willoughby, Betsy (Spouse)
Double Vengeance - John Duncklee *w* 449

Wilson, Francesca (Administrator)
O Gentle Death - Janet Neel *m* 165

Wingate, Eric (Lawyer)
A Child Shall Lead Them - Carole Gift Page *i* 1036

Winslow, Amelia (Actress)
The Heavenly Fugitive - Gilbert Morris *i* 1028

Winslow, Erin (Pilot)
The Golden Angel - Gilbert Morris *i* 1027

Winslow, Laura (Detective—Private; Computer Expert)
Stalking Moon - David Cole *m* 39

Winslow, Phillip (Lawyer)
The Heavenly Fugitive - Gilbert Morris *i* 1028

Winslow, Scott (Wealthy)
A Bungalow for Two - Carole Gift Page *i* 1035

Winston, Madeline "Maddie" (Businesswoman)
I Dream of You - Judi McCoy *r* 350

Winston, Nina (Doctor)
The Other Adonis - Frank Deford *t* 849

Winter, Bonnie (Maintenance Worker)
Bonnie Winter - Graham Masterton *h* 672

Winter, Duke (Unemployed)
Bonnie Winter - Graham Masterton *h* 672

Wishart, Fred (Doctor)
Magic Time - Marc Scott Zicree *f* 614

Wolf, Anne (Writer; Relative)
Coldwater - Mardi McConnochie *c* 1156
Coldwater - Mardi McConnochie *t* 904

Wolf, Charlotte (Writer; Relative)
Coldwater - Mardi McConnochie *t* 904
Coldwater - Mardi McConnochie *c* 1156

Wolf, Emily (Writer; Relative)
Coldwater - Mardi McConnochie *c* 1156
Coldwater - Mardi McConnochie *t* 904

Wolfram (Mythical Creature)
Guardians of the Lost - Margaret Weis *f* 611

Wompler, Grandison (Businessman)
The Reproductive System - John Sladek *s* 798

Wooten, Melanie (Aged Person)
Yonder Stands Your Orphan - Barry Hannah *c* 1121

Wren, Susan (Police Officer)
A Cold Christmas - Charlene Weir *m* 212

Wright, Jimjoy Earle (Spy; Rebel)
Empire & Ecolitan - L.E. Modesitt Jr. *s* 777

Wright, Kyle (Spy; Doctor)
Hide and Seek - Cherry Adair *r* 222

Wyman, Lynn (Linguist)
Female Intelligence - Jane Heller *c* 1125

Y

Yakamo, Hida (Warrior)
The Crab - Stan Brown *f* 531

Yates, Grace (Military Personnel; Pilot)
True Valor - Dee Henderson *i* 1000

Ye, Anchee (Scientist)
The Secret of Life - Paul J. McAuley *s* 771

Yeager, Blackie (Agent)
About the Author - John Colapinto *c* 1092

Yekker, Bousalem (Store Owner)
The Last Summer of Reason - Tahar Djaout *c* 1105

Yemi (Child)
The Scent of Magic - Cliff McNish *f* 581

Yikaas (Prehistoric Human; Storyteller)
Call Down the Stars - Sue Harrison *t* 879

York, Caleb (Gunfighter; Murderer)
Caleb's Price - Troy D. Smith *w* 505

York, Thomas (Student—College)
The Prodigy - Alton Gansky *h* 637

Yoshitaro, Njangu (Military Personnel)
Homefall - Chris Bunch *s* 729

Yum Yum (Animal)
The Cat Who Went Up the Creek - Lilian Jackson Braun *m* 26

Z

Zajac, Nicholas (Doctor)
The Fourth Hand - John Irving *c* 1130

Zanzibar (Relative)
Jewelry Talks - Richard Klein *c* 1142

Zavahl (Nobleman)
Spirit of the Stone - Maggie Furey *f* 545

Zebra (Immortal)
Chasm City - Alastair Reynolds *s* 789

Zheng, Indigo (Police Officer)
Alien Taste - Wen Spencer *s* 801

Zik (Alien)
Angry Young Spaceman - Jim Munroe *s* 780

Ziller (Composer)
Look to Windward - Iain Banks *s* 721

Zinzo, Abby (Writer)
Jewelry Talks - Richard Klein *c* 1142

Zo'or (Alien)
Augur's Teacher - Sherwood Smith *s* 800

Zorander, Zeddicus (Wizard)
Debt of Bones - Terry Goodkind *f* 549

Zu-Kitku, Qonitz (Alien; Diplomat)
Soldiers - John Dalmas *s* 742

Zylas (Mythical Creature)
The Beasts of Barakhai - Mickey Zucker Reichert *f* 590

Character Description Index

This index alphabetically lists descriptions of the major characters in featured titles. The descriptions may be occupations (astronaut, lawyer, etc.) or may describe persona (amnesiac, runaway, teenager, etc.). For each description, character names are listed alphabetically. Also provided are book titles, author names, genre codes and entry numbers. The genre codes are as follows: *c* Popular Fiction, *f* Fantasy, *h* Horror, *i* Inspirational, *m* Mystery, *r* Romance, *s* Science Fiction, *t* Historical, and *w* Western.

ABUSE VICTIM

Belle
A World of Thieves - James Carlos Blake *w* 424

Campbell, Killian
Embrace the Dawn - Kathleen Morgan *i* 1026

Carlisle, Mallory
Double Honor - Melissa Horsfall *i* 1002

Greer, Carmen
Echo Burning - Lee Child *w* 442

Jacobs, Erma Lee
A Place Called Wiregrass - Michael Morris *i* 1029

Morrow, Diana
A Measure of Grace - Al Lacy *i* 1014

Sissy
Tennant's Rock - Steve McGiffen *w* 478

Wells, Molly Sterling
Sweet Nothings - Catherine Anderson *r* 225

ACCIDENT VICTIM

Carrington, Jeff
The Girl Next Door - Kate Welsh *i* 1057

Colton, Miranda
Rivers of Gold - Tracie Peterson *i* 1042

Humboldt, Nelson
The Lecturer's Tale - James Hynes *h* 649

Swenson, Charlotte
Look at Me - Jennifer Egan *c* 1108

ACCOUNTANT

O'Riley, Karine "Kara" Paige
The Texan's Dream - Jodi Thomas *r* 415

Smith, George
Hostage - Robert Crais *c* 1096

Welch, Maureen
The Association - Bentley Little *h* 668

ACTIVIST

Carr, David
How to Be Good - Nick Hornby *c* 1126

Davies, Rebecca
Island of Tears - Troy Soos *m* 200

Edib, Halide
Halide's Gift - Frances Kazan *t* 893

GoodNews
How to Be Good - Nick Hornby *c* 1126

ACTOR

Miles, Robert
Friday's Child - Linda Chaikin *i* 977

Noble, Harry
Pride, Prejudice and Jasmin Field - Melissa Nathan *r* 359

Pickett, Todd
Coldheart Canyon - Clive Barker *c* 1071
Coldheart Canyon - Clive Barker *h* 619

Smythe, Symington "Tuck"
The Slaying of the Shrew - Simon Hawke *t* 880
The Slaying of the Shrew - Simon Hawke *m* 109

Whitman, Max
. . .And the Angel with Television Eyes - John Shirley *h* 694

ACTRESS

Abraham, Barbara
All the Finest Girls - Alexandra Styron *c* 1206

Babouris, Nana
Pact of the Fathers - Ramsey Campbell *h* 626

Field, Jasmin "Jazz"
Pride, Prejudice and Jasmin Field - Melissa Nathan *r* 359

Godalming, Beatrice
Quincey Morris, Vampire - P.N. Elrod *h* 632

Haldane, Tilly
My Best Friend - Laura Wilson *m* 214

Lupi, Katya
Coldheart Canyon - Clive Barker *c* 1071
Coldheart Canyon - Clive Barker *h* 619

Malibrant, Arabella
The Thief-Taker - T.F. Banks *t* 820

Sands, Celia
Season of Storms - Susanna Kearsley *r* 314

Ternan, Ellen Lawless
The Rag & Bone Shop - Jeff Rackham *t* 917

Winslow, Amelia
The Heavenly Fugitive - Gilbert Morris *i* 1028

ADDICT

Helen
When Heaven Weeps - Ted Dekker *i* 988

Jason
Lucky Us - Joan Silber *c* 1198

Mev
Why Did I Ever? - Mary Robison *c* 1188

ADMINISTRATOR

Leggett, Irene
Gargoyles - Alan Nayes *h* 677

Wilson, Francesca
O Gentle Death - Janet Neel *m* 165

ADOPTEE

Barclay, Sable
On Leaving Lonely Town - Cait Logan *r* 339

ADVENTURER

Caitrionia
The Mystic Rose - Stephen R. Lawhead *t* 901
The Mystic Rose - Stephen R. Lawhead *f* 570

D'Arcey, Corran
Pool of Radiance - Carrie Bebris *f* 525

Greenwood, Honore
Moon Medicine - Mike Blakely *t* 827

Grimwulf, Dhamon
Betrayal - Jean Rabe *f* 589

Jason
Celtika - Robert Holdstock *f* 558

Kell
Ice - Stephen Bowkett *s* 724

ADVERTISING

Lydia
House of Pain - Sephera Giron *h* 640

Mathers, Abigail
The Webster Chronicle - Daniel Akst *c* 1066

Matthews, Celia
Color the Sidewalk for Me - Brandilyn Collins *i* 980

Rollins, Kate
The Secret - Kat Martin r 347

Spadolini, Tracey
Slightly Single - Wendy Markham r 345

AGED PERSON

Eugenides
London Bridges - Jane Stevenson c 1204

Felton, Cora
Puzzled to Death - Parnell Hall m 96

Haskell, Zorah
An Angel to Die For - Mignon F. Ballard f 522

Jake
Nearly People - Conrad Williams h 708

Miss Claudia
A Place Called Wiregrass - Michael Morris i 1029

Parrish, Almo
The Astonished Eye - Tracy Knight f 567

Perika, Daisy
White Shell Woman - James D. Doss m 61

Porter, Abigail
Highland Hopes - Gary E. Parker i 1039

Weatherford, Fiona Wooten "Biggie"
Biggie and the Quincy Ghost - Nancy Bell m 15

Wooten, Melanie
Yonder Stands Your Orphan - Barry Hannah c 1121

AGENT

Henderson, John Basil
Any Way the Wind Blows - E. Lynn Harris c 1122

Na, J'Chabi
Spherical Harmonic - Catherine Asaro s 716

Yeager, Blackie
About the Author - John Colapinto c 1092

ALCOHOLIC

Chase, Sophy
Almost - Elizabeth Benedict c 1073

Harding
Kiss It Goodbye - John Wessel m 213

Hayes, Blair
Written on the Wind - Judith Pella i 1040

Stoney
Shooting Dr. Jack - Norman Green c 1118

ALIEN

Blue
A Paradigm of Earth - Candas Jane Dorsey s 747

Drer
Wayward Moon - Denny DeMartino s 744

Geigi
Defender - C.J. Cherryh s 734

Hak-Bin
Deathday - William C. Dietz s 746

Hok
Shockball - S.L. Viehl s 805

Humiir
Acorna's Search - Anne McCaffrey s 772

Jinya
Angry Young Spaceman - Jim Munroe s 780

Kiervauna
Holding the Line - Rick Shelley s 795

Miller, Larkin
The World Weaver - Craig Etchison s 749

Oregon, Ukiah
Alien Taste - Wen Spencer s 801

Phlarx
The Wild Boy - Warren Rochelle s 791

Souvana
Holding the Line - Rick Shelley s 795

Zik
Angry Young Spaceman - Jim Munroe s 780

Zo'or
Augur's Teacher - Sherwood Smith s 800

Zu-Kitku, Qonitz
Soldiers - John Dalmas s 742

AMNESIAC

Alan
The Art of Dying - Diana Killian i 1009

Gryf
The Sea Sprite - Ruth Langan r 328

Hawk
Starhawk - Mack Maloney s 769

Monk, William
Funeral in Blue - Anne Perry t 915
Funeral in Blue - Anne Perry m 172

Peaslee, Nathaniel Wingate
The Shadow out of Time - H.P. Lovecraft h 670

Rycroft, Charles
Comfort and Joy - Sandra Madden r 342

Sedgewick, Gresham
My Lady Wayward - Lael St. James r 406

ANDROID

Hadaly
Tomorrow's Eve - Auguste Villiers de L'Isle Adam s 806

Thor
Tower of Glass - Robert Silverberg s 797

ANGEL

Ezoriel
City Infernal - Edward Lee h 667

Goodnight, Augusta
An Angel to Die For - Mignon F. Ballard f 522

Stephen
The Wig My Father Wore - Anne Enright c 1111

ANIMAL

Autumn
Icebones - Stephen Baxter s 723

Banfield
Chelsea Horror Hotel - Dee Dee Ramone h 684

Bear
Once upon a Winter's Night - Dennis L. McKiernan f 579

Boaster
Icebones - Stephen Baxter s 723

Bucerius
The Treachery of Kings - Neal Barrett Jr. f 524

Dashiell
The Long Good Boy - Carol Lea Benjamin m 16

Dougal's Lord Carstairs
The Mouse in the Mountain - Norbert Davis m 56

Druid
A Feral Darkness - Doranna Durgin f 543

Dulcie
Cat Laughing Last - Shirley Rousseau Murphy m 162

Icebones
Icebones - Stephen Baxter s 723

Joe Grey
Cat Laughing Last - Shirley Rousseau Murphy m 162

Kit
Cat Laughing Last - Shirley Rousseau Murphy m 162

Koko
The Cat Who Went Up the Creek - Lilian Jackson Braun m 26

Letitia Louise
The Treachery of Kings - Neal Barrett Jr. f 524

Maurice
The Amazing Maurice and His Educated Rodents - Terry Pratchett f 587

Peaches
The Amazing Maurice and His Educated Rodents - Terry Pratchett f 587

Yum Yum
The Cat Who Went Up the Creek - Lilian Jackson Braun m 26

ANIMAL TRAINER

Alexander, Rachel
The Long Good Boy - Carol Lea Benjamin m 16

Masera, Gil
A Feral Darkness - Doranna Durgin f 543

Travis, Melanie
Once Bitten - Laurien Berenson m 17

ANTHROPOLOGIST

Cole, Maureen
Bone Walker - Kathleen O'Neal Gear t 871

Grace, Karen
Deep Fathom - James Rollins s 792

Tyler, Erica
Sacred Ground - Barbara Wood t 962

ANTIQUARIAN

Spense, Oliver
The Christmas Wish - Debbie Raleigh r 377

ANTIQUES DEALER

Davenport, Rose
Tall, Dark, and Difficult - Patricia Coughlin r 261

Lowry, Tim
Killer Stuff - Sharon Fiffer m 69

Shimura, Rei
The Bride's Kimono - Sujata Massey m 150

Talbot, Jeff
Death Is a Cabaret - Deborah Morgan m 160

Timberlake, Abigail
Nightmare in Shining Armor - Tamar Myers m 163

Wheel, Jane
Killer Stuff - Sharon Fiffer m 69

APOTHECARY

APPRAISER

APPRENTICE

ARCHAEOLOGIST

ARCHITECT

ART DEALER

ARTIFICIAL INTELLIGENCE

ARTISAN

ARTIST

ASSISTANT

ASTROLOGER

ASTRONAUT

BANKER

BASTARD DAUGHTER

BASTARD SON

BEACHCOMBER

BENEFACTOR

Clausen, Doris
The Fourth Hand - John Irving *c* 1130

Thrale, Hester
According to Queeney - Beryl Bainbridge *c* 1069

BIBLICAL FIGURE

Longinus, Marcus
The Jerusalem Scrolls - Bodie Thoene *i* 1053

Miryam
The Jerusalem Scrolls - Bodie Thoene *i* 1053
The Jerusalem Scrolls - Bodie Thoene *t* 942

Paul
The Gaius Diary - Gene Edwards *i* 990

BLACKSMITH

MacKerron, Lachlann
The Sword Maiden - Susan King *r* 316

Tresh, Roamer
Mattie and the Blacksmith - Linda Lea Castle *r* 253

BODYGUARD

Calgary, Hunter
In Too Deep - Janelle Taylor *r* 413

Deveaux, Samantha
Insatiable - Julie Elizabeth Leto *r* 333

Kodiak, Atticus
Critical Space - Greg Rucka *m* 190

Miller, Jarett
Two Sexy - Stephanie Bond *r* 240

Morgette, Dolf
Morgette on the Barbary Coast - G.G. Boyer *w* 429

Ryshad
The Warrior's Bond - Juliet E. McKenna *f* 578

Stone, Hawk
Born Brave - Ruth Wind *r* 422

Tucci, Crow
Judging Sara - Cynthia Rutledge *i* 1044

White, Jasmine
Bring Me a Dream - Robyn Amos *r* 224

BOOTLEGGER

Remus, George
The Jazz Bird - Craig Holden *t* 885
The Jazz Bird - Craig Holden *m* 119

BOUNTY HUNTER

Cain, Asa
Hard Bounty - Ken Hodgson *w* 463

Griffin, Madeline "Maddie"
Dangerously Irresistible - Kristin Gabriel *r* 289

Manoso, Carlos "Ranger"
Seven Up - Janet Evanovich *r* 274

Plum, Stephanie
Seven Up - Janet Evanovich *r* 274

BOYFRIEND

Bunch, Roy
The Years of Fear - Fred Grove *w* 460

Dennis
The Wedding Party - Robyn Carr *r* 250

Guppy, Roger
Lake Wobegon Summer 1956 - Garrison Keillor *c* 1136

Haggard, Rich
Glare Ice - Mary Logue *m* 145

Jason
Lucky Us - Joan Silber *c* 1198

Karelli, Tony
Redeeming Claire - Cynthia Rutledge *i* 1045

LaCouture, Chas
The Savage Girl - Alex Shakar *c* 1196

Mica
Night Players - P.D. Cacek *h* 625

Rosenblum, Samuel
Eva Moves the Furniture - Margot Livesey *c* 1148

Smith, Paavo
Bell, Cook, and Candle - Joanne Pence *m* 170

Waterston, Michael
Revenge of the Wrought-Iron Flamingos - Donna Andrews *m* 6

BRIDE

Krysta
Believe in Me - Josie Litton *r* 336

Osborne, Verity
The Bride Sale - Candice Hern *r* 298

Wallace, Cassandra
A Devilish Husband - Alana Clayton *r* 257

BUSINESSMAN

Baldassare, Leonardo
The Dragons of the Cuyahoga - S. Andrew Swann *f* 602

Billingham, Mark
The Great Baby Caper - Eugenia Riley *r* 380

Bollinger, Matt
The Folks - Ray Garton *h* 638

Boom, Ping
The Counterfeit Heinlein - Laurence M. Janiver *s* 763

Brock, Brandon
Female Intelligence - Jane Heller *c* 1125

Callahan, Patrick
Cinderella After Midnight - Lilian Darcy *r* 268

Farrell, Wesley
Pale Shadow - Robert Skinner *m* 196
Pale Shadow - Robert Skinner *t* 935

Greene, Harris
Sidhe-Devil - Aaron Allston *f* 516

Harper, Noah
Too Much Temptation - Lori Foster *r* 286

Hart, Walker "Bear"
Miss Match - Leslie Carroll *r* 252

Hawkins, Brody
Sarah and the Rogue - DeLoras Scott *r* 391

Hill, Roy
Last of the Dixie Heroes - Peter Abrahams *m* 1

Johnson, Xavier
Followin' a Dream - Eboni Snoe *r* 403

Karrelian, Brandt
Hazard's Price - Robert S. Stone *f* 601

Kirkland, James
Deep Fathom - James Rollins *s* 792

Krug, Manuel
Tower of Glass - Robert Silverberg *s* 797

Krug, Simeon
Tower of Glass - Robert Silverberg *s* 797

LaCouture, Chas
The Savage Girl - Alex Shakar *c* 1196

LaRocca, Dominick "Nick"
Insatiable - Julie Elizabeth Leto *r* 333

Macdonald, Matt
Doomed to Repeat It - d.g.k. goldberg *h* 641

MacPherson, Rand
You're the One - Judi McCoy *r* 351

MacWray, Mack
Rag Man - Pete Hautman *m* 107

Manley, Wilfred
Brother John - Rutledge Etheridge *s* 750

McKinnon, Thomas MacLeod
My Heart Stood Still - Lynn Kurland *r* 323

Miles, Ethan
See Jane Date - Melissa Senate *r* 394

Noort, Robert
First Gray, Then White, Then Blue - Margriet de Moor *c* 1165

Pannes, John
ChronoSpace - Allen Steele *s* 802

Porteus, Jim
The Reproductive System - John Sladek *s* 798

Rafferty, Colin
Bachelor on the Prowl - Kasey Michaels *r* 353

Severn, Trent
The Guardian - Barbara Miller *r* 355

Stroud, Charlie
Last Year's River - Allen Morris Jones *t* 891

Tal, Abraham
Green - Benjamin Zucker *i* 1064

Trevany, Walter
Martian Knightlife - James P. Hogan *s* 759

Trujillo, Alejandro
His Father's Son - Nigel Bennett *h* 621

Trujillo, Luis
His Father's Son - Nigel Bennett *h* 621

Uskevren, Thamalon
The Shattered Mask - Richard Lee Byers *f* 532

Vermillion, Jack
Black Water Transit - Carsten Stroud *m* 204

Wells, Andrew
Another Summer - Georgia Bockoven *r* 239

Wompler, Grandison
The Reproductive System - John Sladek *s* 798

BUSINESSWOMAN

Amalfi, Angelina "Angie"
Bell, Cook, and Candle - Joanne Pence *m* 170

Bidderman, Vernie
A Warmth in Winter - Lori Copeland *i* 984

Calhoun, Madeleine "Maddie"
The Renegades: Rafe - Genell Dellin *r* 270

Canfield, Stefanie
Whirlpool - Lorena McCourtney *i* 1023

Clark, Matriece
What You Owe Me - Bebe Moore Campbell *c* 1089

DeMato, Joey
Diamond in the Ruff - Emily Carmichael *r* 249

Dobson, Prentice
An Angel to Die For - Mignon F. Ballard *f* 522

Eagleston, Pamela
Dead Love - Donald Beman *h* 620

Ell, Susannah
Dervish Is Digital - Pat Cadigan *s* 731

Fallon, Brenna
A Feral Darkness - Doranna Durgin *f* 543

Jardine, Olivia
The Wager - Metsy Hingle *r* 301

Jasper, Kate
A Sensitive Kind of Murder - Jacqueline Girdner *m* 80

Kelly, Courtney
The Great Baby Caper - Eugenia Riley *r* 380

Kropotkin, Lucy
The American Zone - L. Neil Smith *s* 799

Lake, Lavinia
Slightly Shady - Amanda Quick *r* 375

Llewellyn, Ria
Spirits White as Lightning - Mercedes Lackey *f* 568

MacPhaull, Lindsay
Jackson's Way - Leslie LaFoy *r* 324

Miles, Sara
Sarah and the Rogue - DeLoras Scott *r* 391

Noble, Andrea
Gotta Get Next to You - Lynn Emery *r* 272

Rawlings, Constance
The Other Adonis - Frank Deford *t* 849

Star, BB
The Plutonium Blonde - John Zakour *s* 813

Winston, Madeline "Maddie"
I Dream of You - Judi McCoy *r* 350

BUTCHER

Bunch, Roy
The Years of Fear - Fred Grove *w* 460

CAPTIVE

Benton, Daniel
Summer Moon - Jill Marie Landis *w* 471

Devere, Rosamunde
The Perfect Princess - Elizabeth Thornton *r* 416

Kincaid, Kitty
Sentimental Journey - Jill Barnett *t* 821

Murdoch, Eden
An Uncommon Enemy - Michelle Black *w* 423
An Uncommon Enemy - Michelle Black *t* 824

Oro, Juan
The Survival of Juan Oro - Max Brand *w* 434

Pickard, Andy
The Way of the Coyote - Elmer Kelton *t* 895
The Way of the Coyote - Elmer Kelton *c* 1137
The Way of the Coyote - Elmer Kelton *w* 468

Stands with a Fist
The Holy Road - Michael Blake *w* 425
The Holy Road - Michael Blake *t* 826

CARE GIVER

Delaney, Christine
When Tomorrow Comes - Janette Oke *i* 1034

Lluvia
Swift as Desire - Laura Esquivel *c* 1112

Maddox, Bruno
My Little Blue Dress - Bruno Maddox *c* 1150

CARPENTER

Bronden
Rowan of Rin - Emily Rodda *f* 594

Holland, Sam
The Bride of Willow Creek - Maggie Osborne *r* 364

Knight, Sebastian
Heaven on Earth - Marilyn Pappano *r* 366

CATERER

Fairchild, Faith
The Body in the Bonfire - Katherine Hall Page *i* 1037

CHIEFTAIN

Black Hawk
The Good Journey - Micaela Gilchrist *w* 454
The Good Journey - Micaela Gilchrist *t* 873

Black Otter
My Lord Savage - Elizabeth Lane *r* 326

Browser
Bone Walker - Kathleen O'Neal Gear *t* 871

CHILD

Adrian, Jason
The Magickers - Emily Drake *f* 542

Billy
Cowboy in the Making - Will James *w* 464

Brady, Jenny
Paradise Lost - J.A. Jance *m* 125
Paradise Lost - J.A. Jance *w* 465

Caleb
Blessed Child - Bill Bright *i* 975

Clara
The Nightingale's Song - Kathleen Eschenburg *r* 273

Coleman, Maude
Falling Angels - Tracy Chevalier *c* 1090
Falling Angels - Tracy Chevalier *t* 838

Cutter, Joey P.
Caleb's Price - Troy D. Smith *w* 505

Dorothy
The Rundlestone of Oz - Eloise McGraw *f* 577

Frazier, Justin
Love One Another - Valerie Hansen *i* 995

Hammond, Curtis
One Door Away from Heaven - Dean R. Koontz *h* 661

Heiki
The Scent of Magic - Cliff McNish *f* 581

James, Daisy
Come, My Little Angel - Diane Noble *i* 1033

Jimmy
Smoke-Filled Rooms - Kris Nelscott *m* 166

Keith
The Amazing Maurice and His Educated Rodents - Terry Pratchett *f* 587

Klonk, Leilani
One Door Away from Heaven - Dean R. Koontz *h* 661

Liddell, Alice
Still She Haunts Me - Katie Roiphe *t* 927
Still She Haunts Me - Katie Roiphe *c* 1189

Lockhart, Becky
Heaven Sent - Rachel Wilson *r* 421

Lyanna
Nightchild - James Barclay *f* 523

Marshall, Carley
Carley's Song - Patricia Houck Sprinkle *i* 1051

Marshall, Tyler
Black House - Stephen King *c* 1140
Black House - Stephen King *h* 659

Matthews, Toby
The Prodigy - Alton Gansky *h* 637

McBride, Cora
The Vigil - Clay Reynolds *w* 498

Orr, Bella
Closing Time - Jim Fusilli *m* 74

Paisley
A Rose by the Door - Deborah Bedford *i* 967

Rachel
The Scent of Magic - Cliff McNish *f* 581

Rowan
Rowan of Rin - Emily Rodda *f* 594

Ryan, Jonah
A Bend in the Road - Nicholas Sparks *c* 1200

Squibb, Henry
The Magickers - Emily Drake *f* 542

Walker, Anthony
The Monsters of Morley Manor - Bruce Coville *f* 538

Walker, Sarah
The Monsters of Morley Manor - Bruce Coville *f* 538

Weatherford, J.R.
Biggie and the Quincy Ghost - Nancy Bell *m* 15

Yemi
The Scent of Magic - Cliff McNish *f* 581

CHILD-CARE GIVER

Alfred, Louise "Lou"
All the Finest Girls - Alexandra Styron *c* 1206

Braddock, Tina
Love One Another - Valerie Hansen *i* 995

Martin, Annie
The Nanny - Judith Stacy *r* 408

Prophet, Callida "Callie"
Heaven Sent - Rachel Wilson *r* 421

CIVIL SERVANT

Mitchell, Meredith
Shades of Murder - Ann Granger *m* 87

Seddon, Carole
Death on the Downs - Simon Brett *m* 27

CLERK

Cunningham, Cal
About the Author - John Colapinto *c* 1092

Farrell, Jo
My Best Friend - Laura Wilson *m* 214

Haxton, Gerald
My Best Friend - Laura Wilson *m* 214

Visitor, Lennie
Light Coming Back - Ann Wadsworth *c* 1213

CLONE

Eric
Tenebrea's Hope - Roxann Dawson *s* 743

Gullwing, Tara
Tenebrea's Hope - Roxann Dawson *s* 743

COACH

Schuler, Buster
Hometown Legend - Jerry B. Jenkins *i* 1005

COLLECTOR

Wheel, Jane
Killer Stuff - Sharon Fiffer *m* 69

COMPANION

Cresswell, Emma
The Valentine Wish - Debbie Raleigh *r* 378

Hoyle, Priscilla
Creeping Venom - Sheila Pim *m* 173

Huxleigh, Penelope "Nell"
Chapel Noir - Carole Nelson Douglas *t* 856
Chapel Noir - Carole Nelson Douglas *m* 62

Needham, Angela
A Guardian's Angel - Jo Ann Ferguson *r* 278

Redmond, Tom
Ambrose Bierce and the Death of Kings - Oakley Hall *m* 95
Ambrose Bierce and the Death of Kings - Oakley Hall *t* 878

COMPOSER

Mozart, Wolfgang Amadeus
Imagining Don Giovanni - Anthony J. Rudel *t* 929

Stewart, Noah
Aria - Susan Segal *c* 1194

Ziller
Look to Windward - Iain Banks *s* 721

COMPUTER EXPERT

Barto, Matt
Behind Time - Lynn Abbey *f* 515

Bellsong, Michelina
One Door Away from Heaven - Dean R. Koontz *h* 661

Bradley, Vanessa
Followin' a Dream - Eboni Snoe *r* 403

Cameron, Michael
Dear Cupid - Julie Ortolon *r* 363

Correa, Matt
The Secret Admirer - Annette Mahon *r* 343

Desjardins, Achilles
Maelstrom - Peter Watts *s* 808

Echaurren, Xochitl
Smoking Mirror Blues - Ernest Hogan *s* 758

Haagen, Anneke
Better than Sex - Susan Holtzer *m* 120

Lawton
For Your Heart Only - Debra White Smith *i* 1048

Orozco, Beto
Smoking Mirror Blues - Ernest Hogan *s* 758

Pender, Sage
Bold as Love - Gwyneth Jones *s* 764

Rothman, Ruby
Don't Cry for Me, Hot Pastrami - Sharon Kahn *m* 129

Winslow, Laura
Stalking Moon - David Cole *m* 39

CON ARTIST

Newlands, Billy
The Lone Rider - Max Brand *w* 432

CONSTRUCTION WORKER

Converse, Keith
The Manhattan Hunt Club - John Saul *h* 687

Dyson, Ray
The Association - Bentley Little *h* 668

CONSULTANT

Kincaid, Carnegie
Veiled Threats - Deborah Donnelly *m* 60

Pinter, Sanford
Up in the Air - Walter Kirn *c* 1141

CONTRACTOR

Caruso, Jake
Riverwatch - Joseph M. Nassise *h* 676

Pigeon, Josie
Murder in the Forecast - Valerie Wolzien *m* 219

CONVICT

Carlyle, Brandon
Darkling I Listen - Katherine Sutcliffe *r* 412

Converse, Jeff
The Manhattan Hunt Club - John Saul *h* 687

Glueck, Rona Leigh
Love Her Madly - Mary-Ann Tirone Smith *m* 198

Land, Davy
Peace Like a River - Leif Enger *c* 1109

Lloyd, Larry
Firebreak - Richard Stark *m* 202

Maitland, Richard
The Perfect Princess - Elizabeth Thornton *r* 416

Moon, Jackson
Angel in the Front Room, Devil out Back - Stanford Diehl *m* 59

O'Keefe, Ben
Christmas Vows: $5.00 Extra - Lori Copeland *i* 983

COOK

Channing, Nell
Dance upon the Air - Nora Roberts *r* 382

Giuditta
Bella Donna - Barbara Cherne *t* 836

Lee, Heaven
Red Beans and Vice - Lou Jane Temple *m* 207

Poisson, Charly
Prepared for Murder - Cecile Lamalle *m* 138

Thomas, Allie
Sweet Success - Susan Mallery *r* 344

COUNSELOR

Bingham, Ryan
Up in the Air - Walter Kirn *c* 1141

O'Leary, Amanda
The Woman Next Door - Barbara Delinsky *c* 1101

Russo, Joseph
What to Do about Annie? - Millie Criswell *r* 264

Shirley, Diana
The Webster Chronicle - Daniel Akst *c* 1066

COURTIER

Hoegh-Guldberg, Ove
The Royal Physician's Visit - Per Olov Enquist *c* 1110

COUSIN

Berrinden, Susannah
A Forbidden Embrace - Anna Jacobs *r* 305

Gardner, Isabella Stewart "Belle"
Deadly Illumination - Serena Stier *m* 203

Jekyl, Simon
The Archer's Tale - Bernard Cornwell *t* 843

Kate
Lake Wobegon Summer 1956 - Garrison Keillor *c* 1136

Scofield, Lily
The Evidence Against Her - Robb Forman Dew *c* 1102
The Evidence Against Her - Robb Forman Dew *t* 850

Tod, Florence
Deadly Illumination - Serena Stier *m* 203

COWBOY

Blackwolf, Culley
On Leaving Lonely Town - Cait Logan *r* 339

Blake, Howie
A Good Town - Douglas Hirt *w* 462

Cole, Clay "The Rainmaker"
Outcasts - Tim McGuire *w* 480

Delaney, Del
The Outlaws - Wayne D. Overholser *w* 490

Foster, Buck
A Home of Her Own - Cathleen Connors *i* 982

Jensen, Will
Ride West to Dawn - James C. Work *w* 514

Land, Elmo
The Last Vampire - T.M. Wright *h* 712

Lockwood, Cuff
Lockwood - Lauran Paine *w* 492

Mohr, Henry
Last Year's River - Allen Morris Jones *w* 467
Last Year's River - Allen Morris Jones *t* 891

Owens, Kyle
Ride West to Dawn - James C. Work *w* 514

Ramos, Antonio Rommel
Fire Lilies - Cynthia Leal Massey *w* 476

Roy, Charlie
Charlie and the Sir - Frank Roderus *w* 499

Sheridan, Matthew
Heaven Sent - Jillian Hart *i* 997

Smith, Kyle "Panhandle"
Open Range - Zane Grey *w* 458

CRIME SUSPECT

Alan
The Art of Dying - Diana Killian *i* 1009

Logan, Greg
Long Time No See - Susan Isaacs *c* 1131

Penderecki, Ivan
The Treatment - Mo Hayder *c* 1123

Slack, Tommy
End over End - Kate Kennedy *c* 1139

CRIME VICTIM

Effendi, Enishte
My Name Is Red - Orhan Pamuk *c* 1178

Elegant
My Name Is Red - Orhan Pamuk *c* 1178

Greer, Sloop
Echo Burning - Lee Child *w* 442

Grover, Duncan
The Thunder Keeper - Margaret Coel *w* 444

Hood, Daniel
Echoes of Lies - Jo Bannister *m* 11

Kinross, Cassandra
You're the One - Judi McCoy *r* 351

Klaus, Stephanie
Glare Ice - Mary Logue *m* 145

Logan, Courtney
Long Time No See - Susan Isaacs *c* 1131

Marshall, Tyler
Black House - Stephen King *c* 1140
Black House - Stephen King *h* 659

Paulie
Why Did I Ever? - Mary Robison *c* 1188

Rebecca
The Treatment - Mo Hayder *c* 1123

St. James, Claudie
Back in Kansas - Debra Salonen *r* 387

Smith, George
Hostage - Robert Crais *c* 1096

Towle, Ivory
End over End - Kate Kennedy *c* 1139

CRIMINAL

Achmed
Destiny - Elizabeth Haydon *f* 554

Bazie
Take a Thief - Mercedes Lackey *f* 569

Hazard, Galatine
Hazard's Price - Robert S. Stone *f* 601

Kiru
Bikini Planet - David Garnett *s* 752

Lalasha, Chandris
Angelmass - Timothy Zahn *s* 812

LaSalle, Sonny
A World of Thieves - James Carlos Blake *t* 825
A World of Thieves - James Carlos Blake *w* 424

Mortimer, Man
Yonder Stands Your Orphan - Barry Hannah *c* 1121

Ponce
Hope's End - Stephen Chambers *s* 733

Purdy, Wayne
Day of Reckoning - Kathy Herman *i* 1001

Rosselli, Tommy
Shooting Dr. Jack - Norman Green *c* 1118

Scaptey
Shadow - K.J. Parker *f* 585

Skif
Take a Thief - Mercedes Lackey *f* 569

Stoney
Shooting Dr. Jack - Norman Green *c* 1118

Vel
Hope's End - Stephen Chambers *s* 733

CRIMINOLOGIST

Barclay, Sable
On Leaving Lonely Town - Cait Logan *r* 339

CRITIC

Berger, Mitch
The Cold Blue Blood - David Handler *m* 100

DANCER

Dancer
Nearly People - Conrad Williams *h* 708

Haggerty, Lindy
Midsummer Murder - Shelley Freydont *m* 71

DEBUTANTE

Bigalow, Artemisia
A Perfect Match - Jeanne Savery *r* 389

Price, Virginia
Last Year's River - Allen Morris Jones *w* 467
Last Year's River - Allen Morris Jones *t* 891

Renfield, Cleo
The Irredeemable Miss Renfield - Regina Scott *r* 393

DEFENDANT

Bergfeld, Will
Will's War - Janice Woods Windle *w* 513
Will's War - Janice Woods Windle *t* 961

DEITY

de Danann, Tuatha
Always Forever - Mark Chadbourn *f* 533

DEMON

Aahz
Myth-ion Improbable - Robert Lynn Asprin *f* 521

Nergal
Elminster in Hell - Ed Greenwood *f* 553

DETECTIVE

Bear, Win
The American Zone - L. Neil Smith *s* 799

Blake, Anita
Narcissus in Chains - Laurell K. Hamilton *h* 645

Cresswell, Sarah
The Christmas Wish - Debbie Raleigh *r* 377

Fortune, Robert
Friends and Enemies - Stephen A. Bly *i* 972

Van Pelt, Kirk
The Pinkerton Eye - Allen P. Bristow *w* 436

DETECTIVE—AMATEUR

Adler, Irene
Chapel Noir - Carole Nelson Douglas *m* 62
Chapel Noir - Carole Nelson Douglas *t* 856

Amalfi, Angelina "Angie"
Bell, Cook, and Candle - Joanne Pence *m* 170

Appleton, Susanna
Face Down Before Rebel Hooves - Kathy Lynn Emerson *t* 861
Face Down Before Rebel Hooves - Kathy Lynn Emerson *m* 65

Barrett, Bel
Midlife Can Be Murder - Jane Isenberg *m* 124

Brewster, Lily
Someone to Watch over Me - Jill Churchill *t* 839
Someone to Watch over Me - Jill Churchill *m* 33

Brewster, Robert
Someone to Watch over Me - Jill Churchill *m* 33
Someone to Watch over Me - Jill Churchill *t* 839

Brown
Night Watch - Stephen Kendrick *t* 896

Canfield, Caroline
Sketches with Wolves - Jacqueline Fiedler *m* 68

Crane, Mary Alice "Sister"
Murder Boogies with Elvis - Anne George *m* 77

Cyrion, Philipa
Wayward Moon - Denny DeMartino *s* 744

Edwards, Jane Amanda
The Message of the Mute Dog - Charlotte Murray Russell *m* 191

Felton, Cora
Puzzled to Death - Parnell Hall *m* 96

Fenimore, Andrew
The Doctor and the Dead Man's Chest - Robin Hathaway *m* 106

Frevisse
The Clerk's Tale - Margaret Frazer *m* 70
The Clerk's Tale - Margaret Frazer *t* 865

Goldstein, Kiki
Tall, Dead, and Handsome - Annie Griffin *m* 91

Graham, Alan
The Last Mayan - Malcolm Shuman *m* 195

Haagen, Anneke
Better than Sex - Susan Holtzer *m* 120

Hansen, Em
Fault Line - Sarah Andrews *m* 7

Hollowell, Patricia Anne "Mouse"
Murder Boogies with Elvis - Anne George *m* 77

Hunt, Claire
The Masks of Auntie Laveau - Robert J. Randisi *m* 177

Hunt, Gil
The Masks of Auntie Laveau - Robert J. Randisi *m* 177

Jasper, Kate
A Sensitive Kind of Murder - Jacqueline Girdner *m* 80

Jones, Texana
Death of the Last Villista - Allana Martin *w* 475
Death of the Last Villista - Allana Martin *m* 149

Karitska
Kaleidoscope - Dorothy Gilman *m* 79

Keltner, Jason
The Night Men - Keith Snyder *m* 199

Knight, Roger
Emerald Aisle - Ralph McInerny *m* 156

Langslow, Meg
Revenge of the Wrought-Iron Flamingos - Donna Andrews *m* 6

Lavotoni, Sierra
Strip Poker - Nancy Bartholomew *m* 13

Linacre, Tim
Creeping Venom - Sheila Pim *m* 173

Lord, Emma
The Alpine Nemesis - Mary Daheim *m* 51

Ludlow, Harry
The Devil's Own Luck - David Donachie *t* 853
The Dying Trade - David Donachie *t* 854

Malloy, Hannah
Tall, Dead, and Handsome - Annie Griffin *m* 91

Marsala, Cat
Hard Road - Barbara D'Amato *m* 53

Martin, Dorothy
To Perish in Penzance - Jeanne M. Dams *m* 54

Metellus, Decius
Nobody Loves a Centurion - John Maddox Roberts *m* 184
Nobody Loves a Centurion - John Maddox Roberts *t* 924

Morgan, Mariana
Darkness at the Door - Catherine Dain *m* 52

Murphy, Molly
Murphy's Law - Rhys Bowen *t* 830
Murphy's Law - Rhys Bowen *m* 24

O'Malley, John
The Thunder Keeper - Margaret Coel *m* 35
The Thunder Keeper - Margaret Coel *w* 444

Plumtree, Alex
Uncatalogued - Julie Kaewert *m* 128

Raisin, Agatha
Agatha Raisin and the Love from Hell - M.C. Beaton *m* 14

Roger the Chapman
The Goldsmith's Daughter - Kate Sedley *t* 933
The Weaver's Inheritance - Kate Sedley *m* 194
The Weaver's Inheritance - Kate Sedley *t* 934

Roosevelt, Eleanor
Murder at the President's Door - Elliott Roosevelt *t* 928

Sharples, Claire
The Tumbleweed Murders - Rebecca Rothenberg *m* 189

Sorenson, Jacobia "Jake" Tiptree
Wreck the Halls - Sarah Graves *m* 89

Swinbrooke, Kathryn
Saintly Murders - C.L. Grace *m* 86
Saintly Murders - C.L. Grace *t* 875

Taylor, Fred
Lazarus, Arise - Nicholas Kilmer *m* 134

Weatherford, Fiona Wooten "Biggie"
Biggie and the Quincy Ghost - Nancy Bell *m* 15

DETECTIVE—HOMICIDE

Carella, Steve
Money, Money, Money - Ed McBain *m* 152

Donnelly, Jack
Eager to Please - Julie Parsons *c* 1180

Drake, Jessie
Shadows of Sin - Rochelle Krich *m* 137

Glitsky, Abe
The Oath - John Lescroart *m* 141

Leightner, Jack
Red Hook - Gabriel Cohen *m* 37

Moore, Thomas
The Surgeon - Tess Gerritsen *m* 78

Rizzoli, Jane
The Surgeon - Tess Gerritsen *m* 78

Savile, Justin B. V
First Lady - Michael Malone *c* 1153

Sawyer, Jack
Black House - Stephen King *c* 1140
Black House - Stephen King *h* 659

Vail, Dalton
Murder by Manicure - Nancy J. Cohen *m* 38

Weeks, Oliver Wendell
Money, Money, Money - Ed McBain *m* 152

DETECTIVE—POLICE

Adams, Lena
Blindsighted - Karin Slaughter *m* 197

Angelosi, Marco
The Renegade Steals a Lady - Vickie Taylor *r* 414

Caffery, Jack
The Treatment - Mo Hayder *c* 1123

Calgary, Hunter
In Too Deep - Janelle Taylor *r* 413

Claybourne, David
Darkness at the Door - Catherine Dain *m* 52

Garcia, Gil
Under Suspicion - Rachel Lee *r* 331

Justice, Charlotte
Stormy Weather - Paula L. Woods *m* 220

Kennelly, Edward
Murder at the President's Door - Elliott Roosevelt *t* 928

Maxwell, Kirk
Dangerous Dilemmas - Evelyn Palfrey *r* 365

McCarthy, Steve
Listen to the Shadows - Danuta Reah *m* 179

Mikaelian, Garreth
Blood Games - Lee Killough *h* 657

Monahan, Connor
The Secret Life of Connor Monahan - Elizabeth Bevarly *r* 235

Morelli, Joe
Seven Up - Janet Evanovich *r* 274

Munoz, Dan
Bonnie Winter - Graham Masterton *h* 672

O'Mally, Vincent
The Gingerbread Man - Maggie Shayne *r* 395

Paladin, Harry
Ghost Killer - Scott Chandler *h* 627

Pruden
Kaleidoscope - Dorothy Gilman *m* 79

Smith, Lacey
Cold Hunter's Moon - K.C. Greenlief *m* 90

Spandau, Casey
Black Water Transit - Carsten Stroud *m* 204

Voort, Conrad
All the Dead Were Strangers - Ethan Black *m* 20
All the Dead Were Strangers - Ethan Black *c* 1076

Williams, Joe
Teeth - Edo van Belkom *h* 705

DETECTIVE—PRIVATE

Alexander, Rachel
The Long Good Boy - Carol Lea Benjamin *m* 16

Bard, Lily
Shakespeare's Counselor - Charlaine Harris *m* 102

Bennett, Maxwell
Alien Taste - Wen Spencer *s* 801

Blissberg, Harvey
Dead Ball - R.D. Rosen *m* 188

Brogan, Case
Beloved Protector - Linda O'Brien *r* 361

Buscarsela, Filomena
Red House - K.J.A. Wishnia *m* 217

Chase, Elizabeth
Ashes of Aries - Martha C. Lawrence *m* 140

Childs, Sunny
Blue Plate Special - Ruth Birmingham *m* 18

Coyne, Brady
First Light - Philip R. Craig *m* 46
Past Tense - William G. Tapply *m* 206

Dalton, Smokey
Smoke-Filled Rooms - Kris Nelscott *m* 166

Delmas, Jack
Massacre Island - Martin Hegwood *m* 112

Dillman, George Porter
Murder on the Minnesota - Conrad Allen *m* 5
Murder on the Minnesota - Conrad Allen *t* 816

Dimitris, Melina
Heaven on Earth - Marilyn Pappano *r* 366

Doan
The Mouse in the Mountain - Norbert Davis *m* 56

Dun, Richard
His Father's Son - Nigel Bennett *h* 621

Ellis, Trade
Crack Shot - Sinclair Browning *m* 28

Farrell, Elspeth Brodie
Echoes of Lies - Jo Bannister *m* 11

Friedman, Kinky
Steppin' on a Rainbow - Kinky Friedman *m* 72

Griffin, Lew
Ghost of a Flea - James Sallis *m* 192

Halliday, Anthony
Look at Me - Jennifer Egan *c* 1108

Hampton, Jeremy
Deadly Illumination - Serena Stier *m* 203

Harding
Kiss It Goodbye - John Wessel *m* 213

Heller, Nathan
Kisses of Death - Max Allan Collins *m* 41
Kisses of Death - Max Allan Collins *t* 841

Holmes, Sherlock
Chapel Noir - Carole Nelson Douglas *t* 856
The Great Game - Michael Kurland *t* 899
Night Watch - Stephen Kendrick *t* 896
Sherlock Holmes and the Giant Rat of Sumatra - Alan Vanneman *m* 210
Sherlock Holmes and the Secret Alliance - Larry Millett *t* 908
Sherlock Holmes and the Secret Alliance - Larry Millett *m* 158

Jackson, J.W.
First Light - Philip R. Craig *m* 46

Johnson, Zachary Nixon
The Plutonium Blonde - John Zakour *s* 813

Knight, Philip
Emerald Aisle - Ralph McInerny *m* 156

Langway, Matthew
Turnabout - Jeremiah Healy *m* 111

Leeds, Jack
Shakespeare's Counselor - Charlaine Harris *m* 102

Lester, Robert "Bo"
Back in Kansas - Debra Salonen *r* 387

Lightfoot, Jacquelyn
For Your Heart Only - Debra White Smith *i* 1048

Mackellar, Patience
Keepers - Janet LaPierre *m* 139

Mackellar, Verity
Keepers - Janet LaPierre *m* 139

MacKinnon, Scotia
Death on a Casual Friday - Sharon Duncan *m* 63

March, Tobias
Slightly Shady - Amanda Quick *r* 375

Masefield, Genevieve
Murder on the Minnesota - Conrad Allen *m* 5
Murder on the Minnesota - Conrad Allen *t* 816

McCain, Sam
Save the Last Dance for Me - Ed Gorman *m* 83

McQuarry, Mac
To Trust a Stranger - Karen Robards *r* 381

Milodragovitch, Milo
The Final Country - James Crumley *m* 50

Monaghan, Tess
In a Strange City - Laura Lippman *m* 143

Monk, William
Funeral in Blue - Anne Perry *t* 915
Funeral in Blue - Anne Perry *m* 172

Nameless Detective
Bleeders - Bill Pronzini *m* 174

Nudger, Alo
The Nudger Dilemmas - John Lutz *m* 147

Oregon, Ukiah
Alien Taste - Wen Spencer *s* 801

Orr, Terry
Closing Time - Jim Fusilli *m* 74

Parke, Drew
Gumshoe Gorilla - Keith Hartman *s* 756

Parker, Charlie "Bird"
Dark Hollow - John Connolly *m* 42

Powerscourt, Francis
Goodnight, Sweet Prince - David Dickinson *m* 58
Goodnight, Sweet Prince - David Dickinson *t* 851

Quinn, Michael
Dangerous Attraction - Susan Vaughan *r* 417

Reilly, Regan
Fleeced - Carol Higgins Clark *m* 34

St. Cyr, Valentin
Chasing the Devil's Tail - David Fulmer *m* 73
Chasing the Devil's Tail - David Fulmer *t* 867

Scudder, Matt
Hope to Die - Lawrence Block *m* 22

Seppanen, Martti
The Puppet Master - John Dalmas *s* 741

Singer, Judith
Long Time No See - Susan Isaacs *c* 1131

Solano, Lupe
Bitter Sugar - Carolina Garcia-Aguilera *m* 75

Thane, Kieran
Martian Knightlife - James P. Hogan *s* 759

Winslow, Laura
Stalking Moon - David Cole *m* 39

DIPLOMAT

O'Malley, Chuck
September Song - Andrew M. Greeley *c* 1117

Savage, Nick
The Savages in Love and War - Fred Mustard Stewart *t* 937

Voss, Karl
The Company of Strangers - Robert Wilson *m* 215
The Company of Strangers - Robert Wilson *t* 960

Zu-Kitku, Qonitz
Soldiers - John Dalmas *s* 742

DIRECTOR

D'Ascanio, Alessandro "Alex"
Season of Storms - Susanna Kearsley *r* 314

Gray, Claire
Desert Autumn - Michael Craft *m* 45

Ruth
In the Shape of a Boar - Lawrence Norfolk *c* 1171

DIVER

Fogarty, Luanne
Deep Water Death - Glynn Marsh Alam *m* 3

Randolph, Griffin
Alice at Heart - Deborah Smith *r* 401

DIVORCED PERSON

Andrews, Sarah
A Bend in the Road - Nicholas Sparks *c* 1200

Breton, Money
Why Did I Ever? - Mary Robison *c* 1188

Canfield, Stefanie
Whirlpool - Lorena McCourtney *i* 1023

Crane, Mary Alice "Sister"
Murder Boogies with Elvis - Anne George *m* 77

Cunningham, Cheryl
Another Summer - Georgia Bockoven *r* 239

Devonshire, Betsy
Unraveled Sleeve - Monica Ferris *m* 67

Dugan, Charlene
The Wedding Party - Robyn Carr *r* 250

Dugan, Jake
The Wedding Party - Robyn Carr *r* 250

Hart, Katherine
Riot - Shashi Tharoor *c* 1208

Hart, Rudyard
Riot - Shashi Tharoor *c* 1208

Hubbard, Catherine
The World Below - Sue Miller *c* 1163

Leones, Giraut
The Merchants of Souls - John Barnes *s* 722

Martens, Tristan
The Deadwood Beetle - Mylene Dressler *c* 1106

Milner, Suzanne
Listen to the Shadows - Danuta Reah *m* 179

Seddon, Carole
Death on the Downs - Simon Brett *m* 27

Stone, Jesse
Death in Paradise - Robert B. Parker *m* 168

Timberlake, Abigail
Nightmare in Shining Armor - Tamar Myers *m* 163

Williams, Audrey
Dangerous Dilemmas - Evelyn Palfrey *r* 365

DOCTOR

Antoun, Demetrius
Ester's Child - Jean P. Sasson *t* 930

Beck, Kristian
Funeral in Blue - Anne Perry *t* 915

Becker, Ross
Gargoyles - Alan Nayes *s* 783

Blackley, Posthumous
The London Vampire Panic - Michael Romkey *h* 686

Branscombe, Violet
Dr. Mortimer and the Aldgate Mystery - Gerard Williams *t* 958

Calloway, Jack
Red on Rose - Patricia Jones *c* 1133

Carpenter, Jordan
Angel Face - Suzanne Forster *r* 283

Carr, Katie
How to Be Good - Nick Hornby *c* 1126

Carter, Matthew
Night Blood - James M. Thompson *h* 702

Cordell, Catherine
The Surgeon - Tess Gerritsen *m* 78

Fenimore, Andrew
The Doctor and the Dead Man's Chest - Robin Hathaway *m* 106

Fraser, Claire
The Fiery Cross - Diana Gabaldon *r* 288
The Fiery Cross - Diana Gabaldon *t* 868

Gardner, Joshua
Do You Hear What I Hear? - Holly Jacobs *r* 306

Gautreaux, Emile
Audubon's Watch - John Gregory Brown *c* 1085
Audubon's Watch - John Gregory Brown *t* 833

Hassa, Alexander
The Girl from the Golden Horn - Kurban Said *c* 1191

Hatton, Will
Shades of Justice - Fredrick Huebner *m* 121

Henry
Dreamcatcher - Stephen King *h* 660

Iverson, Kate
Hosts - F. Paul Wilson *h* 710

Jago, Eleanor
Time Future - Maxine McArthur *s* 770

Kincaid, Gordon
The Nightingale's Song - Kathleen Eschenburg *r* 273

Kovett, Charles
Darkness - Sam Siciliano *h* 695

Linton, Sara
Blindsighted - Karin Slaughter *m* 197

MacKay, Beth
Child of Promise - Kathleen Morgan *i* 1025

Mackey, David
Rhythms - Donna Hill *t* 884

McCall, Claire
Could I Have This Dance? - Harry Lee Kraus *i* 1012

McCoy, Paul
The Doctor's Miracle - Anna Schmidt *i* 1046

Moore, Melissa
To Rome with Love - Debra White Smith *i* 1049

Mortimer, James
Dr. Mortimer and the Aldgate Mystery - Gerard Williams *t* 958

Niemann, Roger
Night Blood - James M. Thompson *h* 702

Penrose, Wilder
Super-Cannes - J.G. Ballard *c* 1070

Quimby, Andrew
Darkness - Sam Siciliano *h* 695

Rafael, Luis
Gargoyles - Alan Nayes *h* 677
Gargoyles - Alan Nayes *s* 783

Roberts, Sarah
The Last Vampire - Whitley Strieber *h* 699

Ryan, Scott
Secrets of the Heart - Gail Gaymer Martin *i* 1022

Schell, Johanna
Secret of the Wolf - Susan Krinard *r* 322

Scott, Samantha
Night Blood - James M. Thompson *h* 702

Sinclair, Jane
Super-Cannes - J.G. Ballard *c* 1070

Steward, Jonathan
Night of Dracula - Christopher Schildt *h* 692

Struensee, Johann Friedrich
The Royal Physician's Visit - Per Olov Enquist *t* 862
The Royal Physician's Visit - Per Olov Enquist *c* 1110

Suzanne
Suzanne's Diary for Nicholas - James Patterson *c* 1181

Swinbrooke, Kathryn
Saintly Murders - C.L. Grace *m* 86
Saintly Murders - C.L. Grace *t* 875

Tepevich, Vladimir
Night of Dracula - Christopher Schildt *h* 692

Torin, Cherijo
Shockball - S.L. Viehl *s* 805

Towne, Jill
All the Dead Were Strangers - Ethan Black *c* 1076

Turner, Lucas
City of Dreams - Beverly Swerling *t* 939

Van der Vries, Jacob
City of Dreams - Beverly Swerling *t* 939

Van Helsing, Abraham
The London Vampire Panic - Michael Romkey *h* 686
Quincey Morris, Vampire - P.N. Elrod *h* 632

Vievre
On - Adam Roberts *s* 790

Watson, John
Sherlock Holmes and the Giant Rat of Sumatra - Alan Vanneman *m* 210
Sherlock Holmes and the Secret Alliance - Larry Millett *t* 908
Sherlock Holmes and the Secret Alliance - Larry Millett *m* 158

Winston, Nina
The Other Adonis - Frank Deford *t* 849

Wishart, Fred
Magic Time - Marc Scott Zicree *f* 614

Wright, Kyle
Hide and Seek - Cherry Adair *r* 222

Zajac, Nicholas
The Fourth Hand - John Irving *c* 1130

DRIFTER

Blake, Howie
A Good Town - Douglas Hirt *w* 462

Tinkerman, Dobie
A Good Town - Douglas Hirt *w* 462

DRUG DEALER

Gabe
Lucky Us - Joan Silber *c* 1198

EDITOR

Gregg, Jane
See Jane Date - Melissa Senate *r* 394

Matherly-Reed, Maris
Envy - Sandra Brown *c* 1086
Envy - Sandra Brown *r* 245

Norris, Jackie
Milkrun - Sarah Mlynowski *r* 357

Wilkinson, Katie
Suzanne's Diary for Nicholas - James Patterson *c* 1181

EMPATH

Dougan, Eilan
The Enchantment - Pam Binder *r* 237

Jubilo
Swift as Desire - Laura Esquivel *c* 1112

EMPLOYER

Alexander, Will
Morgette on the Barbary Coast - G.G. Boyer *w* 429

Lorene
Lightning Field - Dana Spiotta *c* 1202

ENGINEER

Forrester, Quinn
A Father's Place - Marta Perry *i* 1041

Pitt, Dirk
Valhalla Rising - Clive Cussler *c* 1097

ENTERTAINER

Barnum, P.T.
The Hum Bug - Harold Schechter *t* 932
The Hum Bug - Harold Schechter *w* 502
The Hum Bug - Harold Schechter *m* 193

Carter, Rocky
Niagara Falls All over Again - Elizabeth McCracken *c* 1158

Hall, Fletcher
Flying Eagle - Tim Champlin *w* 440

Kil, Tulsi
A Feast in Exile - Chelsea Quinn Yarbro *h* 713

Luck, Liz
Island of Tears - Troy Soos *t* 936

Sharp, Mose
Niagara Falls All over Again - Elizabeth McCracken *c* 1158

EXPATRIATE

Fly, Lucy
The Earthquake Bird - Susanna Jones *m* 127

Haversham, Nigel
French Leave - Sheri Cobb South *r* 404

Holton, Anthony
The Chinese Fire Drill - Les Roberts *m* 185

Kerim, Abdul
The Girl from the Golden Horn - Kurban Said *c* 1191

MacLean, Jamie
Summer's End - Lynne Hayworth *r* 297

Shimura, Rei
The Bride's Kimono - Sujata Massey *m* 150

Terrell
The Jasper Forest - Julia Gray *f* 551

EXPLORER

Clark, William
River Walk - Rita Cleary *w* 443

Collins, John
River Walk - Rita Cleary *w* 443

Elwood, Leonard
The Devil-Tree of El Dorado - Frank Aubrey *s* 717

King, Maud
Conjuring Maud - Philip Danze *t* 847

Lewis, Meriwether
River Walk - Rita Cleary *w* 443

Madoc
Circle of Stars - Anna Lee Waldo *w* 510

Powell, John Wesley
The Last Canyon - John Vernon *w* 508
The Last Canyon - John Vernon *t* 949

Templemore, Jack
The Devil-Tree of El Dorado - Frank Aubrey *s* 717

Tighe
On - Adam Roberts *s* 790

FARMER

Johnson, Evan
The Edge of Town - Dorothy Garlock *r* 290

Jones, Julie
The Edge of Town - Dorothy Garlock *r* 290

Oldham, Buddy-Boy
The Way of the Coyote - Elmer Kelton *w* 468

Pavel
Requiem for a Lost Empire - Andrei Makine *c* 1151

Singleton, Ray
The Magic of Ordinary Days - Ann Howard Creel *t* 845

FBI AGENT

Blalock
Blackening Song - Aimee Thurlo *w* 506

Burke, Sam
The Innocent - Amanda Stevens *r* 410

Clah, Ella
Blackening Song - Aimee Thurlo *w* 506

Kaiser, John
Dead Sleep - Greg Iles *m* 123

Latimer, Tom
Fault Line - Sarah Andrews *m* 7

Lewis, Laurie
Born Brave - Ruth Wind *r* 422

Rice, Penelope "Poppy"
Love Her Madly - Mary-Ann Tirone Smith *m* 198

Safer, Daniel
A Darker Justice - Sallie Bissell *m* 19

Talbot, Jeff
Death Is a Cabaret - Deborah Morgan *m* 160

Weaver, Susan
Frankenstein: The Legacy - Christopher Schildt *h* 691

White, Tom
The Years of Fear - Fred Grove *w* 460

FIANCE(E)

Dacre, Christopher
The Border Hostage - Virginia Henley *t* 883

Dickensen, Gil
Irregardless of Murder - Ellen Edwards Kennedy *i* 1008

Gabe
Lucky Us - Joan Silber *c* 1198

Gelhorn, Margo
The Wanderer - Fritz Leiber *s* 767

Glover, Eleanor
Under the Kissing Bough - Shannon Donnelly *r* 271

Pennyman, Charlotte
Man from Wyoming - Dane Coolidge *w* 448

FILMMAKER

Amai, Emiko
The Ash Garden - Dennis Bock *c* 1078

FINANCIER

Stratford, Connor
No Way Out - Andrea Kane *r* 312

Tony
House of Pain - Sephera Giron *h* 640

FIRE FIGHTER

Conrad, Dusty
The Woman for Dusty Conrad - Tori Carrington *r* 251

Conrad, Jolie
The Woman for Dusty Conrad - Tori Carrington *r* 251

Ellis, Cassie
The Protector - Dee Henderson *i* 999

O'Malley, Jack
The Protector - Dee Henderson *i* 999

FISHERMAN

Mirana, Aylen
The Jasper Forest - Julia Gray *f* 551

Person, Grant
On the Night Plain - J. Robert Lennon *c* 1146
On the Night Plain - J. Robert Lennon *w* 473

Thorn
Blackwater Sound - James W. Hall *m* 94

FOREMAN

Blackwolf, Culley
On Leaving Lonely Town - Cait Logan *r* 339

Hanuma
Night of the Bat - Paul Zindel *h* 714

Nelu
The Appointment - Herta Muller *c* 1168

FOUNDLING

Elliot, Timothy
From the Dust Returned - Ray Bradbury *c* 1082
From the Dust Returned - Ray Bradbury *h* 623

FRIEND

Alex
In the Forest of Harm - Sallie Bissell *c* 1074

Alexander, Will
Morgette on the Barbary Coast - G.G. Boyer *w* 429

Coleman, Maude
Falling Angels - Tracy Chevalier *c* 1090
Falling Angels - Tracy Chevalier *t* 838

Cutler, Augusta
Middle Age - Joyce Carol Oates *c* 1174

Erik
First Gray, Then White, Then Blue - Margriet de Moor *c* 1165

Field, Simon
Falling Angels - Tracy Chevalier *t* 838

Fraith, Charles
Agatha Raisin and the Love from Hell - M.C. Beaton *m* 14

Gaius
The Gaius Diary - Gene Edwards *i* 990

Gilbert
Schooling - Heather McGowan *c* 1159

Halliday, Anthony
Look at Me - Jennifer Egan *c* 1108

Joan
In the Forest of Harm - Sallie Bissell *c* 1074

Jones, Lester
Gabriel's Gift - Hanif Kureishi *c* 1143

Jude
Death on the Downs - Simon Brett *m* 27

Lambert, Evan
Almost - Elizabeth Benedict *c* 1073

Leyden, Henry
Black House - Stephen King *c* 1140

Luo
Balzac and the Little Chinese Seamstress - Sijie Dai *c* 1098

Misha
Funny Accent - Barbara Shulgasser-Parker *c* 1197

Parker, Billy
Leap of Faith - Danielle Steel *c* 1203

Raphael, Sebastian
London Bridges - Jane Stevenson *c* 1204

Rouenna
For Rouenna - Sigrid Nunez *c* 1172

Snoddy, Mae Maude
Fire in the Rock - Joe Martin *c* 1154

Unnamed Character
Balzac and the Little Chinese Seamstress - Sijie Dai *c* 1098

Voss, Doc
Bitterroot - James Lee Burke *c* 1088

Waterhouse, Lavinia
Falling Angels - Tracy Chevalier *c* 1090
Falling Angels - Tracy Chevalier *t* 838

FUGITIVE

Angelosi, Marco
The Renegade Steals a Lady - Vickie Taylor *r* 414

Dolan, Sophie
Just West of Heaven - Kathleen Kane *r* 313

Kills Crow, Kole
You Never Can Tell - Kathleen Eagle *w* 450

Kun'dren, Ngan Sung
Of Aged Angels - Monte Cook *s* 737

Maitland, Richard
The Perfect Princess - Elizabeth Thornton *r* 416

McCain, Michael
Of Aged Angels - Monte Cook *s* 737

McIvor, Laura
Betrayed - Rosey Dow *i* 989

Meara, Jeane
Of Aged Angels - Monte Cook *s* 737

Murphy, Molly
Murphy's Law - Rhys Bowen *t* 830
Murphy's Law - Rhys Bowen *m* 24

Parfait, Iris Mary
Junior's Leg - Ken Wells *c* 1214

van Visser, Anna
Keeper of Hearts - Dianne Christner *i* 979

GAMBLER

Aigner, Rafe
The Renegades: Rafe - Genell Dellin *r* 270

Blessing, Peter
Blessing in Disguise - Jenna Mindel *r* 356

Reynal, Pierre
Open Season - C.J. Box *w* 428

St. James, Lionel
A Rogue for Christmas - Kate Huntington *r* 304

Wade, Jack
Letters to Callie - Dawn Miller *w* 483

GAME WARDEN

Dunnegan, Vern
Open Season - C.J. Box *w* 428

Pickett, Joe
Open Season - C.J. Box *w* 428
Open Season - C.J. Box *m* 25

GARDENER

Croydon, Eustace
Tragic Casements - Oliver Onions *h* 680

Eldridge, Louise
Harvest of Murder - Ann Ripley *m* 181

GENETICALLY ALTERED BEING

Akhmim
Nekropolis - Maureen McHugh *s* 774

GENTLEMAN

Baldwin, Nick
Face Down Before Rebel Hooves - Kathy Lynn Emerson *t* 861

Blessing, Peter
Blessing in Disguise - Jenna Mindel *r* 356

Butler, Rhett
The Wind Done Gone - Alice Randall *t* 918

Hartright, Walter
The Dark Clue - James Wilson *t* 959

McKendrick, Simon
A Tangled Web - Donna Bell *r* 230

Montgomery, Harrison
Mr. Montgomery's Quest - Martha Kirkland *r* 318

GENTLEWOMAN

Becket, True
Miss Truelove Beckons - Donna Simpson *r* 397

Bella
Bella Donna - Barbara Cherne *t* 836

Blanchard, Ursula
Queen of Ambition - Fiona Buckley *t* 834
Queen of Ambition - Fiona Buckley *m* 29

Carleton, Raven
The Border Hostage - Virginia Henley *t* 883

Compton, Sarah
The Incomparable Miss Compton - Regina Scott *r* 392

Conde, Amy
The Guardian - Barbara Miller *r* 355

Cresswell, Sarah
The Christmas Wish - Debbie Raleigh *r* 377

Eloise of Argent
The Husband Test - Betina Krahn *r* 321

Gates, Mary
The Wedding Wager - Cathy Maxwell *r* 348

Halcombe, Marion
The Dark Clue - James Wilson *t* 959

Halliwell, Morwenna
Abandon - Jillian Hunter *r* 303

Hartford, Sincerity Prudence
A Tangled Web - Donna Bell *r* 230

Leeds, Arabella
Letters from an Age of Reason - Nora Hague *t* 877

Nancarrow, Lavinia
Dr. Mortimer and the Aldgate Mystery - Gerard Williams *t* 958

Needham, Angela
A Guardian's Angel - Jo Ann Ferguson *r* 278

Osborne, Verity
The Bride Sale - Candice Hern *r* 298

Preston, Winifred "Winnie" Augusta
Blessing in Disguise - Jenna Mindel *r* 356

Riona
Riona - Linda Windsor *i* 1060

St. David, Kathryn
The Blue Devil - Melynda Beth Skinner *r* 398

St. Remy Sinclair, Celia
A Reckless Encounter - Rosemary Rogers *r* 385

Seabrook, Mary
The Rake and the Wallflower - Allison Lane *r* 325

Talisford, Katherine "Kate"
Tempt Me Twice - Barbara Dawson Smith *r* 400

Thornhill, Rowena
My Lord Savage - Elizabeth Lane *r* 326

Wallace, Cassandra
A Devilish Husband - Alana Clayton *r* 257

Whittaker, Mary Ann
A Rogue for Christmas - Kate Huntington *r* 304

GIRLFRIEND

Alexander, Diana
Morgette on the Barbary Coast - G.G. Boyer *w* 429

Alison
Kiss It Goodbye - John Wessel *m* 213

Banyon, Evie
Past Tense - William G. Tapply *m* 206

Blake, Lucy
Open Range - Zane Grey *w* 458

Haney, Cheryl
The Money-Whipped Steer-Job Three-Jack Give-Up Artist - Dan Jenkins *c* 1132

Hayley
My Little Blue Dress - Bruno Maddox *c* 1150

Parfait, Iris Mary
Junior's Leg - Ken Wells *c* 1214

Rebecca
The Treatment - Mo Hayder *c* 1123

Sophia
On the Night Plain - J. Robert Lennon *w* 473
On the Night Plain - J. Robert Lennon *c* 1146

GOVERNMENT OFFICIAL

Ash, Taylor
Hazard's Price - Robert S. Stone *f* 601

Cameron, Bren
Defender - C.J. Cherryh *s* 734

Cecil, William
Queen of Ambition - Fiona Buckley *t* 834

Channing, Alex
Divine Intervention - Ken Wharton *s* 810

Dortrean, Erkal
The Treason of Dortrean - Marcus Herniman *f* 557

Forsythe, Arkin
Angelmass - Timothy Zahn *s* 812

Franklin, Alexander
Deathday - William C. Dietz *s* 746

Giordino, Al
Valhalla Rising - Clive Cussler *c* 1097

Homa, Grig
Second Contact - J.D. Austin *s* 719

John the Eunuch
Three for a Letter - Mary Reed *m* 180
Three for a Letter - Mary Reed *t* 920

Meeker, Nathan
Blood on the Wind - Lucile Bogue *w* 426

Murtagh, Colum
Saintly Murders - C.L. Grace *t* 875
Saintly Murders - C.L. Grace *m* 86

Phillips, Adrian
The Dragons of the Cuyahoga - S. Andrew Swann *f* 602

Pitt, Dirk
Valhalla Rising - Clive Cussler *c* 1097

Quinn, Michael
Dangerous Attraction - Susan Vaughan *r* 417

Rayne, Alex
Second Contact - J.D. Austin *s* 719

Rumail
The Fall of Neskaya - Marion Zimmer Bradley *s* 725

GRANDPARENT

Clarista
Tie-Fast Country - Robert Flynn *w* 451

del Valle, Paulina
Portrait in Sepia - Isabel Allende *c* 1067

Jacobs, Erma Lee
A Place Called Wiregrass - Michael Morris *i* 1029

Jardine, Olivia
The Wager - Metsy Hingle *r* 301

Rice, Georgia
The World Below - Sue Miller *c* 1163

Sommers, Eliza
Portrait in Sepia - Isabel Allende *c* 1067

Suzette
Cane River - Lalita Tademy *c* 1207

Valle, Paulina del
Portrait in Sepia - Isabel Allende *t* 817

GUARD

Bannion, Jack
Tears of the Heart - Lauran Paine *w* 493

Collins, Hap
Captains Outrageous - Joe R. Lansdale *w* 472

Holbrook, Grif
Stage Trails West - Frank Bonham *w* 427

McGraw, Jay
Flying Eagle - Tim Champlin *w* 440

GUARDIAN

Brown, David
Summer's Promise - Irene Brand *i* 974

Davis, Quincee
Loving Thy Neighbor - Ruth Scofield *i* 1047

Donegan, Abbie
Saddled - Delores Fossen *r* 284

Hawthorne, Lily
To Tame a Duke - Patricia Grasso *r* 293

Jeffries, Marcus Quentin
The Trouble with Harriet - Wilma Counts *r* 262

Knightly, Harriet
The Trouble with Harriet - Wilma Counts *r* 262

Lake, Lavinia
Slightly Shady - Amanda Quick *r* 375

MacArthur, Eva
The Sword Maiden - Susan King *r* 316

Marker, Jason
Blessed Child - Bill Bright *i* 975

Weaver, Summer
Summer's Promise - Irene Brand *i* 974

GUIDE

Carstairs
. . .And the Angel with Television Eyes - John Shirley *h* 694

Fallon, Christopher
Treasures of the Sun - T.V. Olsen *w* 487

Morella
The Devil-Tree of El Dorado - Frank Aubrey *s* 717

GUNFIGHTER

Acosta, Manuel
Tears of the Heart - Lauran Paine *w* 493

Holliday, John H. "Doc"
Bucking the Tiger - Bruce Olds *w* 485
Bucking the Tiger - Bruce Olds *c* 1176

Kelly, Elijah "Preacher"
Colorado Twilight - Tess Pendergrass *w* 495

McCaine, Rio
Saddled - Delores Fossen *r* 284

York, Caleb
Caleb's Price - Troy D. Smith *w* 505

HAIRDRESSER

Gwen
He Goes, She Goes - Joanna Torrey *c* 1209

McGuiness, Libby
Do You Hear What I Hear? - Holly Jacobs *r* 306

Shore, Marla
Murder by Manicure - Nancy J. Cohen *m* 38

HANDICAPPED

Babineau, Gerard
Fighting Gravity - Peggy Rambach *c* 1184

Carole
Leap of Faith - Danielle Steel *c* 1203

Culver, Suzanne
What Once We Loved - Jane Kirkpatrick *w* 470

Evans, Parker
Envy - Sandra Brown *c* 1086
Envy - Sandra Brown *r* 245

Guidry, Joseph "Junior"
Junior's Leg - Ken Wells *c* 1214

Randall, Drew
Divine Intervention - Ken Wharton *s* 810

Roy
City Infernal - Edward Lee *h* 667

Sayers, Andrew
The Folks - Ray Garton *h* 638

HANDYMAN

Baker, Matt
Sweet Success - Susan Mallery *r* 344

HEALER

Cameron, Clemency
Summer's End - Lynne Hayworth *r* 297

Cymbra
Dream of Me - Josie Litton *r* 338

HEALTH CARE PROFESSIONAL

Dennis
The Wedding Party - Robyn Carr *r* 250

Shelby, Morgan
A Paradigm of Earth - Candas Jane Dorsey *s* 747

HEIR

Brewster, Robert
Someone to Watch over Me - Jill Churchill *m* 33
Someone to Watch over Me - Jill Churchill *t* 839

Dudley, Ferdinand
No Man's Mistress - Mary Balogh *r* 227

Lovell, Anthony
Dark Sanctuary - H.B. Gregory *h* 644

MacPherson, Rand
You're the One - Judi McCoy *r* 351

Randolph, Erik
When Jayne Met Erik - Elizabeth Bevarly *r* 236

Stennett, Jackson
Jackson's Way - Leslie LaFoy *r* 324

HEIR—DISPOSSESSED

McCaine, Rio
Saddled - Delores Fossen *r* 284

HEIRESS

Beauchamp, Althea
Fortune's Lady - Evelyn Richardson *r* 379

Brewster, Lily
Someone to Watch over Me - Jill Churchill *t* 839
Someone to Watch over Me - Jill Churchill *m* 33

Charters, Serena
Moving Target - Elizabeth Lowell *r* 340

Crittenden, Beatrice
The Lone Rider - Max Brand *w* 432

de Lamere, Isabel
White Lion's Lady - Tina St. John *r* 407

Donegan, Abbie
Saddled - Delores Fossen *r* 284

Gordon, Mary "Molly"
The Secret Clan: Abducted Heiress - Amanda Scott *r* 390

Hartford, Sincerity Prudence
A Tangled Web - Donna Bell *r* 230

Hawkins, Marie-Ange
Leap of Faith - Danielle Steel *c* 1203

Treat, Cassandra
A Forbidden Embrace - Anna Jacobs *r* 305

HEIRESS—DISPOSSESSED

MacPhaull, Lindsay
Jackson's Way - Leslie LaFoy *r* 324

HEIRESS—LOST

Riley, Alice
Alice at Heart - Deborah Smith *r* 401

HERBALIST

Bayles, China
Bloodroot - Susan Wittig Albert *m* 4

HERO

Berendt, Adam
Middle Age - Joyce Carol Oates *c* 1174

MaqqRee, Desmond
Sidhe-Devil - Aaron Allston *f* 516

Swagger, Earl
Pale Horse Coming - Stephen Hunter *m* 122
Pale Horse Coming - Stephen Hunter *t* 887
Pale Horse Coming - Stephen Hunter *c* 1127

HEROINE

Campbell, Ella Mae
Shadow Valley Rising - Stephen Overholser *w* 488

McEwen, Eva
Eva Moves the Furniture - Margot Livesey *c* 1148

Porras, Dolores
Fire Lilies - Cynthia Leal Massey *w* 476

Rezkova, Magda
First Gray, Then White, Then Blue - Margriet de Moor *c* 1165

Unnamed Character
My Little Blue Dress - Bruno Maddox *c* 1150

HIGHWAYMAN

Katherine of Cliffside
The Night the Stars Fell - Christina Kingston *r* 317

Quick, Jason
Watch by Moonlight - Kate Hawks *t* 881

HIPPIE

Forrest, Lilah
Last Virgin in California - Maureen Child *r* 255

HISTORIAN

McGee, Kevin
First Landing - Robert Zubrin *s* 814

HISTORICAL FIGURE

Albert Victor
Goodnight, Sweet Prince - David Dickinson *t* 851

Anderson, Tom
Chasing the Devil's Tail - David Fulmer *t* 867
Chasing the Devil's Tail - David Fulmer *m* 73

Argall, Samuel
Argall - William T. Vollmann *t* 950

Atkinson, Henry
The Good Journey - Micaela Gilchrist *t* 873
The Good Journey - Micaela Gilchrist *w* 454

Audubon, John James
Audubon's Watch - John Gregory Brown *t* 833
Audubon's Watch - John Gregory Brown *c* 1085

Austen, Frank
Jane and the Prisoner of Wool House - Stephanie Barron *t* 822

Austen, Jane
Jane and the Prisoner of Wool House - Stephanie Barron *t* 822
Jane and the Prisoner of Wool House - Stephanie Barron *m* 12

Baca, Elfego
Miracle of the Jacal - Robert J. Randisi *w* 497

Barnum, P.T.
The Hum Bug - Harold Schechter *m* 193
The Hum Bug - Harold Schechter *w* 502
The Hum Bug - Harold Schechter *t* 932

Bierce, Ambrose
Ambrose Bierce and the Death of Kings - Oakley Hall *m* 95
Ambrose Bierce and the Death of Kings - Oakley Hall *t* 878

Black Hawk
The Good Journey - Micaela Gilchrist *t* 873
The Good Journey - Micaela Gilchrist *w* 454

Bolden, Buddy
Chasing the Devil's Tail - David Fulmer *t* 867

Bonney, William "Billy the Kid"
Bucking the Tiger - Bruce Olds *c* 1176

Borgia, Cesare
The Family - Mario Puzo *c* 1183
The Family - Mario Puzo *t* 916

Borgia, Lucrezia
The Family - Mario Puzo *t* 916
The Family - Mario Puzo *c* 1183

Borgia, Rodrigo
The Family - Mario Puzo *c* 1183
The Family - Mario Puzo *t* 916

Bruno, Giordano
The Last Confession - Morris L. West *t* 956

Bullitt, Mary
The Good Journey - Micaela Gilchrist *t* 873
The Good Journey - Micaela Gilchrist *w* 454

Burr, Aaron
Treason - David Nevin *t* 912

Bywaters, Frederick
Fred & Edie - Jill Dawson *t* 848

Caesar, Julius
Nobody Loves a Centurion - John Maddox Roberts *t* 924

Caroline Mathilde
The Royal Physician's Visit - Per Olov Enquist *t* 862

Carrington, Henry
Moon of Bitter Cold - Frederick J. Chiaventone *w* 441

Carrington, Margaret
Moon of Bitter Cold - Frederick J. Chiaventone w 441

Carson, Kit
Moon Medicine - Mike Blakely t 827

Casanova, Giacomo
Imagining Don Giovanni - Anthony J. Rudel t 929

Cassatt, Lydia
Lydia Cassatt Reading the Morning Paper - Harriet Scott Chessman t 837

Cassatt, Mary
Lydia Cassatt Reading the Morning Paper - Harriet Scott Chessman t 837

Cecil, William
Queen of Ambition - Fiona Buckley t 834

Christian VII
The Royal Physician's Visit - Per Olov Enquist t 862
The Royal Physician's Visit - Per Olov Enquist c 1110

Clark, William
River Walk - Rita Cleary w 443

Collins, John
River Walk - Rita Cleary w 443

Collins, Wilkie
The Rag & Bone Shop - Jeff Rackham t 917

Crazy Horse
Turn the Stars Upside Down - Terry C. Johnston t 890
Turn the Stars Upside Down - Terry C. Johnston w 466

Custer, George Armstrong
An Uncommon Enemy - Michelle Black w 423
An Uncommon Enemy - Michelle Black t 824

David
Queenmaker - India Edghill t 858

Degas, Edgar
Lydia Cassatt Reading the Morning Paper - Harriet Scott Chessman t 837

Dickens, Charles
The Rag & Bone Shop - Jeff Rackham t 917

Dodgson, Charles
The Problem of the Surly Servant - Roberta Rogow m 187
The Problem of the Surly Servant - Roberta Rogow t 926
Still She Haunts Me - Katie Roiphe t 927
Still She Haunts Me - Katie Roiphe c 1189

Dostoyevsky, Anna
Summer in Baden-Baden - Leonid Tsypkin t 946

Dostoyevsky, Fyodor
Summer in Baden-Baden - Leonid Tsypkin t 946

Doyle, Arthur Conan
The Problem of the Surly Servant - Roberta Rogow m 187
The Problem of the Surly Servant - Roberta Rogow t 926

Earp, Wyatt
Bucking the Tiger - Bruce Olds w 485

Edib, Halide
Halide's Gift - Frances Kazan t 893

Edison, Thomas
Tomorrow's Eve - Auguste Villiers de L'Isle Adam s 806

Edward, Prince of Wales
Goodnight, Sweet Prince - David Dickinson t 851

Elizabeth I
Queen of Ambition - Fiona Buckley t 834

Fielding, John
Smuggler's Moon - Bruce Alexander t 815

Fox, George
Sea of Glory - Ken Wales i 1056

Gardner, Isabella Stewart "Belle"
Deadly Illumination - Serena Stier m 203

Gentileschi, Artemisia
The Passion of Artemisia - Susan Vreeland t 951

Gentileschi, Orazio
The Passion of Artemisia - Susan Vreeland t 951

Goode, Alex
Sea of Glory - Ken Wales i 1056
Sea of Glory - Ken Wales t 953

Grant, Julia
The Ambush of My Name - Jeffrey Marks t 903

Grant, Ulysses S.
The Ambush of My Name - Jeffrey Marks t 903
Call Each River Jordan - Owen Parry t 914

Gwynedd, Madoc ap Owain
Circle of Stars - Anna Lee Waldo t 952

Harding, Warren G.
Carter Beats the Devil - Glen David Gold t 874

Haroney, Kate "Big Nose Kate"
Bucking the Tiger - Bruce Olds c 1176
Bucking the Tiger - Bruce Olds w 485

Hathaway, Anne
Her Infinite Variety - Pamela Rafael Berkman t 823

Haussmann, Georges-Eugene
Haussmann, or The Distinction - Paul LaFarge t 900

Henry VI
Knight Errant - R. Garcia y Robertson t 869

Hoegh-Guldberg, Ove
The Royal Physician's Visit - Per Olov Enquist c 1110

Holliday, John H. "Doc"
Bucking the Tiger - Bruce Olds c 1176
Bucking the Tiger - Bruce Olds w 485

Janis, Joseph Antoine
The June Rise - William Tremblay t 945
The June Rise - William Tremblay w 507

John Lackland
Pride of Kings - Judith Tarr f 603
Pride of Kings - Judith Tarr t 941

Johnson, Samuel
According to Queeney - Beryl Bainbridge c 1069

Justinian I
Three for a Letter - Mary Reed t 920

Ka'b al-Ahbar
The Rock - Kanan Makiya t 902

Kokoschka, Oskar
The Silent Woman - Susan M. Dodd t 852

Lee, Robert E.
The Ironclad Alibi - Michael Kilian t 898

Lewis, Meriwether
River Walk - Rita Cleary w 443

Liddell
Still She Haunts Me - Katie Roiphe c 1189

Liddell, Alice
Still She Haunts Me - Katie Roiphe c 1189
Still She Haunts Me - Katie Roiphe t 927

London, Jack
The Jewel of the North - Peter King m 135

Madison, James
Treason - David Nevin t 912

Mahler, Alma
The Silent Woman - Susan M. Dodd t 852

Meeker, Nathan
Blood on the Wind - Lucile Bogue w 426

Michal
Queenmaker - India Edghill t 858

Mozart, Wolfgang Amadeus
Imagining Don Giovanni - Anthony J. Rudel t 929

Newton, John
The Infidel - Joe Musser i 1031

Patten, Joshua
The Captain's Wife - Douglas Kelley t 894

Patten, Mary Ann
The Captain's Wife - Douglas Kelley t 894

Pocahontas
Argall - William T. Vollmann c 1212
Argall - William T. Vollmann t 950

Poe, Edgar Allan
The Hum Bug - Harold Schechter t 932
The Hum Bug - Harold Schechter w 502
The Hum Bug - Harold Schechter m 193

Poling, Clark
Sea of Glory - Ken Wales i 1056
Sea of Glory - Ken Wales t 953

Powell, John Wesley
The Last Canyon - John Vernon t 949
The Last Canyon - John Vernon w 508

Ramone, Dee Dee
Chelsea Horror Hotel - Dee Dee Ramone h 684

Red Cloud
The June Rise - William Tremblay w 507
The June Rise - William Tremblay t 945
Moon of Bitter Cold - Frederick J. Chiaventone w 441
Turn the Stars Upside Down - Terry C. Johnston w 466

Remus, George
The Jazz Bird - Craig Holden m 119
The Jazz Bird - Craig Holden t 885

Remus, Imogene
The Jazz Bird - Craig Holden t 885

Richard, Duke of Gloucester
The Goldsmith's Daughter - Kate Sedley t 933

Richard the Lionheart
Pride of Kings - Judith Tarr t 941

Roosevelt, Eleanor
Murder at the President's Door - Elliott Roosevelt t 928

Roosevelt, Franklin D.
Murder at the President's Door - Elliott Roosevelt t 928

Sade, Donatien Alphonse Francois de
Imagining Don Giovanni - Anthony J. Rudel t 929

St. Vrain, Ceran
Moon Medicine - Mike Blakely t 827

Saraccino, Pedro
Miracle of the Jacal - Robert J. Randisi w 497

Saul
Queenmaker - India Edghill t 858

Shakespeare, William
Her Infinite Variety - Pamela Rafael Berkman t 823
Ill Met by Moonlight - Sarah A. Hoyt f 559
The Slaying of the Shrew - Simon Hawke m 109
The Slaying of the Shrew - Simon Hawke t 880

Shaw, George Bernard
The Case of the Ripper's Revenge - Sam McCarver m 153

Shore, Jane
The Goldsmith's Daughter - Kate Sedley *t* 933

Slaughter, John
Miracle of the Jacal - Robert J. Randisi *w* 497

Smith, John
Argall - William T. Vollmann *t* 950
Argall - William T. Vollmann *c* 1212

Spaniard, Jack
Spanish Jack - Robert J. Conley *t* 842
Spanish Jack - Robert J. Conley *w* 447

Spotted Tail
Turn the Stars Upside Down - Terry C. Johnston *w* 466

Struensee, Johann Friedrich
The Royal Physician's Visit - Per Olov Enquist *t* 862
The Royal Physician's Visit - Per Olov Enquist *c* 1110

Taft, Charlie
The Jazz Bird - Craig Holden *t* 885
The Jazz Bird - Craig Holden *m* 119

Tassi, Agostino
The Passion of Artemisia - Susan Vreeland *t* 951

Ternan, Ellen Lawless
The Rag & Bone Shop - Jeff Rackham *t* 917

Theodora
Three for a Letter - Mary Reed *t* 920

Thompson, Edith
Fred & Edie - Jill Dawson *t* 848

Thompson, Percy
Fred & Edie - Jill Dawson *t* 848

Thrale, Hester
According to Queeney - Beryl Bainbridge *c* 1069

Timur-i-Lenhk
A Feast in Exile - Chelsea Quinn Yarbro *t* 963

Trujillo, Rafael
The Feast of the Goat - Mario Vargas Llosa *t* 948
The Feast of the Goat - Mario Vargas Llosa *c* 1211

Trujillo, Ramfis
The Feast of the Goat - Mario Vargas Llosa *c* 1211

Umar ibn al-Khattab
The Rock - Kanan Makiya *t* 902

Vanderhorn, Morris
The Hum Bug - Harold Schechter *w* 502

Vespasian, Titus Flavius Sabinus
Under the Eagle - Simon Scarrow *t* 931

Washington, John
Sea of Glory - Ken Wales *t* 953

Wilkinson, James
Treason - David Nevin *t* 912

HITCHHIKER

Brand
Face - Tim Lebbon *h* 665

HOMOSEXUAL

Bernai, Julius
The Yellow Sailor - Steve Weiner *t* 954

Dunbar, Bartholomew "Bart"
Any Way the Wind Blows - E. Lynn Harris *c* 1122

Hoffman, Nick
Burning Down the House - Lev Rafael *m* 176

Lowry, Tim
Killer Stuff - Sharon Fiffer *m* 69

Turner, Paul
Sex and Murder.com - Mark Richard Zubro *m* 221

HORSE TRAINER

Barlow, Tye
The Wedding Wager - Cathy Maxwell *r* 348

Carrington, Jeff
The Girl Next Door - Kate Welsh *i* 1057

Coulter, Jake
Sweet Nothings - Catherine Anderson *r* 225

Gates, Mary
The Wedding Wager - Cathy Maxwell *r* 348

MacKenna, Alec
Legends Lake - JoAnn Ross *r* 386

Night Hawk
Night Hawk's Bride - Jillian Hart *r* 296

Taggert, Hope
The Girl Next Door - Kate Welsh *i* 1057

Todd, Alena
The Mackintosh Bride - Debra Lee Brown *r* 244

HOTEL OWNER

Logan, Josh
The Wager - Metsy Hingle *r* 301

HOTEL WORKER

Harte, Laura
The Wager - Metsy Hingle *r* 301

Pearce, Amanda
Candle Bay - Tamara Thorne *h* 703

HOUSEKEEPER

O'Malley, Maeve
Comfort and Joy - Sandra Madden *r* 342

Valencia, Liria
One Good Turn - Carla Kelly *r* 315

HOUSEWIFE

Abigail
Debt of Bones - Terry Goodkind *f* 549

Harris, Polly
The White Room - A.J. Matthews *h* 673

Katherine
The Crow Maiden - Sarah Singleton *f* 598

Lauper, Tammy
Coldheart Canyon - Clive Barker *c* 1071
Coldheart Canyon - Clive Barker *h* 619

Ranelagh, M.
The Shape of Snakes - Minette Walters *m* 211

Sorenson, Jacobia "Jake" Tiptree
Wreck the Halls - Sarah Graves *m* 89

IMMIGRANT

Amir
Emigre Journeys - Abdullah Hussein *c* 1129

Barlow, Cecelia
A Prince Among Them - Al Lacy *i* 1015

Barlow, Jeremy
A Prince Among Them - Al Lacy *i* 1015

Garnett, Sarah
The Salt Letters - Christine Balint *t* 819

ibn Musa, Ibrahim "Abdu"
The Pickup - Nadine Gordimer *c* 1116

Serafina
Highwire Moon - Susan Straight *c* 1205

Waals, Christina van der
Island of Tears - Troy Soos *t* 936

IMMORTAL

Hawtrey, Booth
Something More - Paul Cornell *s* 738

Planeswalker, Urza
Apocalypse - J. Robert King *f* 564

Zebra
Chasm City - Alastair Reynolds *s* 789

IMPORTER/EXPORTER

Schoene, Joseph
The Distant Land of My Father - Bo Caldwell *t* 835

IMPOSTER

Brown, Catrina
Cinderella After Midnight - Lilian Darcy *r* 268

Darnley, Randall
Once a Princess - Veronica Sattler *r* 388

Eastman, Delanie
Hide and Seek - Cherry Adair *r* 222

Maguire, Connor
The Widow - Anne Stuart *r* 411

Matthews, LeRoyce "Lee"
Gotta Get Next to You - Lynn Emery *r* 272

McKay, Ford
Going Overboard - Christina Skye *r* 399

Rafferty, Colin
Bachelor on the Prowl - Kasey Michaels *r* 353

Treene, Harriet
The Very Comely Countess - Miranda Jarrett *r* 307

Valentine, Meg
Two Sexy - Stephanie Bond *r* 240

IMPOVERISHED

Brown, Catrina
Cinderella After Midnight - Lilian Darcy *r* 268

Fairchild, Jack
Very Truly Yours - Julie Beard *r* 229

Summers, Ariel
Heartless - Kat Martin *r* 346

Temple, Izzy
Fallen - Celeste Bradley *r* 241

INDIAN

Bear Paw
Bear Paw - Gene Mullins *w* 484

Benally, Gordon
The Water and the Blood - Nancy E. Turner *t* 947

Black Otter
My Lord Savage - Elizabeth Lane *r* 326

Bone, Mickey
The Baron War - Jory Sherman *w* 503

Browser
Bone Walker - Kathleen O'Neal Gear *t* 871

Carter, Seth
Shadow Valley Rising - Stephen Overholser *w* 488

Clah, Ella
Blackening Song - Aimee Thurlo *w* 506

Cougar
Circle of Stars - Anna Lee Waldo *w* 510
Circle of Stars - Anna Lee Waldo *t* 952

Crazy Horse
Turn the Stars Upside Down - Terry C. Johnston *t* 890
Turn the Stars Upside Down - Terry C. Johnston *w* 466

Crow, Mary
A Darker Justice - Sallie Bissell *m* 19
In the Forest of Harm - Sallie Bissell *c* 1074

Destea, Clifford
Blackening Song - Aimee Thurlo *w* 506

First Elk Woman
The June Rise - William Tremblay *w* 507
The June Rise - William Tremblay *t* 945

Flying Horse Mollie
Blood on the Wind - Lucile Bogue *w* 426

Frog Eyes
Double Vengeance - John Duncklee *w* 449

Grey Bear
Cheyenne Summer - Vella Munn *t* 911

Holden, Vicky
The Thunder Keeper - Margaret Coel *m* 35
The Thunder Keeper - Margaret Coel *w* 444

Kills Crow, Kole
You Never Can Tell - Kathleen Eagle *w* 450

Lone Hawk
Cheyenne Summer - Vella Munn *t* 911

Marimi
Sacred Ground - Barbara Wood *t* 962

Mestizo
The Gift of the Mestizo - Marjorie M. McGinley *w* 479

Morgan, Stuart
Bear Paw - Gene Mullins *w* 484

Night Hawk
Night Hawk's Bride - Jillian Hart *r* 296

Pocahontas
Argall - William T. Vollmann *t* 950
Argall - William T. Vollmann *c* 1212

Raven
Letters to Callie - Dawn Miller *w* 483

Red Cloud
The June Rise - William Tremblay *t* 945
The June Rise - William Tremblay *w* 507
Moon of Bitter Cold - Frederick J. Chiaventone *w* 441
Turn the Stars Upside Down - Terry C. Johnston *w* 466

Skye, Victoria
Downriver - Richard S. Wheeler *w* 512
Downriver - Richard S. Wheeler *t* 957

Spaniard, Jack
Spanish Jack - Robert J. Conley *w* 447
Spanish Jack - Robert J. Conley *t* 842

Spotted Tail
Turn the Stars Upside Down - Terry C. Johnston *w* 466

Thunder Cloud
Blood on the Wind - Lucile Bogue *w* 426

Two Stars, David
Heart of the Sandhill - Stephanie Grace Whitson *i* 1058

Two Stars, Genevieve LaCroix
Heart of the Sandhill - Stephanie Grace Whitson *i* 1058

INNKEEPER

Greenway, Sophie
Dial M for Meat Loaf - Ellen Hart *m* 105

Sullivan, Alexandra
Awakening Alex - Ruth Langan *r* 327

INTERIOR DECORATOR

McBride, Keely
Love to Love You Baby - Kasey Michaels *r* 354

Summers, Maddie
Marry Me, Maddie? - Rita Herron *r* 299

INVALID

Shelby, Evan
Destiny Valley - Fred Grove *w* 459

INVENTOR

Edison, Thomas
Tomorrow's Eve - Auguste Villiers de L'Isle Adam *s* 806

Finn
The Treachery of Kings - Neal Barrett Jr. *f* 524

Hawk
Starhawk - Mack Maloney *s* 769

Solanka, Malik "Solly"
Fury - Salman Rushdie *c* 1190

INVESTIGATOR

Black
My Name Is Red - Orhan Pamuk *c* 1178

Knave, Gerald
The Counterfeit Heinlein - Laurence M. Janiver *s* 763

Matthews, LeRoyce "Lee"
Gotta Get Next to You - Lynn Emery *r* 272

McQuarry, Mac
To Trust a Stranger - Karen Robards *r* 381

North, Erik
Moving Target - Elizabeth Lowell *r* 340

JOURNALIST

Ackroyd, Laura
Skeleton at the Feast - Patricia Hall *m* 97

Bradshaw, Kate
Dear Cupid - Julie Ortolon *r* 363

Browne, Verity
The Bones of the Buried - David Roberts *m* 183
The Bones of the Buried - David Roberts *t* 923

Calhoun, Madeleine "Maddie"
The Renegades: Rafe - Genell Dellin *r* 270

Diamond, Eve
The Jasmine Trade - Denise Hamilton *m* 98

Evans, Faith
On Every Side - Karen Kingsbury *i* 1010

Field, Jasmin "Jazz"
Pride, Prejudice and Jasmin Field - Melissa Nathan *r* 359

Geismar, Jake
The Good German - Joseph Kanon *c* 1135
The Good German - Joseph Kanon *m* 131
The Good German - Joseph Kanon *t* 892

Glass, Jordan
Dead Sleep - Greg Iles *m* 123

Gold, Aaron
Veiled Threats - Deborah Donnelly *m* 60

Greenway, Sophie
Dial M for Meat Loaf - Ellen Hart *m* 105

Harper, Jo
The Ice Child - Elizabeth McGregor *t* 905

Hayes, Cameron
Written on the Wind - Judith Pella *i* 1040

James, Alyson
Darkling I Listen - Katherine Sutcliffe *r* 412

Lightfoot, Franklin J. Jr.
Law Dog - J. Lee Butts *w* 438

Lord, Emma
The Alpine Nemesis - Mary Daheim *m* 51

Lund, Birger
The Phoenix - Henning Boetius *t* 828

Maguire, Connor
The Widow - Anne Stuart *r* 411

Marsala, Cat
Hard Road - Barbara D'Amato *m* 53

Mathers, Terry
The Webster Chronicle - Daniel Akst *c* 1066

Maxwell, Kline
The Dragons of the Cuyahoga - S. Andrew Swann *f* 602

Merrick, Michael
The Elusive Voice - Mary Jo Adamson *m* 2

Nichols, Billy
The Distance - Eddie Muller *m* 161

Palmer, Sandy
Hosts - F. Paul Wilson *h* 710

Qwilleran, James Mackintosh "Qwill"
The Cat Who Went Up the Creek - Lilian Jackson Braun *m* 26

Reardon, Heather
You Never Can Tell - Kathleen Eagle *w* 450

Redmond, Tom
Ambrose Bierce and the Death of Kings - Oakley Hall *m* 95
Ambrose Bierce and the Death of Kings - Oakley Hall *t* 878

Roberts, Dora
The Seat Beside Me - Nancy Moser *i* 1030

Rose, Angie
Lt. Kent: Lone Wolf - Judith Lyons *r* 341

Savitch, Ben
The Astonished Eye - Tracy Knight *f* 567

Sloane, Todd
Looking for Laura - Judith Arnold *r* 226

Spencer, Hope
True Confessions - Rachel Gibson *r* 292

Stone, Lucy
Wedding Day Murder - Leslie Meier *m* 157

Summer, Jack
Someone to Watch over Me - Jill Churchill *t* 839

Tagger, Jack
Basket Case - Carl Hiaasen *m* 115

Tucker, Grady
A Capital Holiday - Janet Dailey *r* 265

Warrington, Patrick
The Fourth Hand - John Irving *c* 1130

Waters, Rocky
Rocky and the Senator's Daughter - Dixie Browning *r* 246

JUDGE

Fielding, John
Smuggler's Moon - Bruce Alexander *t* 815

Hillor
Hope's End - Stephen Chambers *s* 733

Paxton, Hamilton
Loving Thy Neighbor - Ruth Scofield *i* 1047

Robak, Don
Robak in Black - Joe L. Hensley *m* 113

Santana, Paul
The Justice - Angela Elwell Hunt *i* 1004

KIDNAPPER

Argall, Samuel
Argall - William T. Vollmann *c* 1212
Argall - William T. Vollmann *t* 950

Armstrong, James
To Tame a Duke - Patricia Grasso *r* 293

Smith, John
Argall - William T. Vollmann *c* 1212

Whitaker, Nigel
A Prince Among Them - Al Lacy *i* 1015

KNIGHT

Brandeis, Karelian
The Black Chalice - Marie Jakober *f* 562

de Bracineaux, Renaud
The Mystic Rose - Stephen R. Lawhead *f* 570
The Mystic Rose - Stephen R. Lawhead *t* 901

de Burgh, Robin
My Lady de Burgh - Deborah Simmons *r* 396

de Villonne, Bayard
The Temptress - Claire Delacroix *r* 269

Du Lethe, Lancelot
Lancelot Du Lethe - J. Robert King *f* 566

Fiona
Betrayal - Jean Rabe *f* 589

Galahad
The Child of the Holy Grail - Rosalind Miles *t* 907

Godsol, Rafe
The Warrior's Damsel - Denise Hampton *r* 295

Griffin of Droghallow
White Lion's Lady - Tina St. John *r* 407

Gustav
Guardians of the Lost - Margaret Weis *f* 611

Mazaret, Ikarno
Shadowkings - Michael Cobley *f* 535

Montcada, Francisco de
The Crusader - Michael A. Eisner *t* 860

Richard of Warefeld
The Marriage Bed - Claudia Dain *r* 266

Sedgewick, Gresham
My Lady Wayward - Lael St. James *r* 406

Tiarnan of Talensac
The Wolf Hunt - Gillian Bradshaw *t* 831

LAIRD

Campbell, Adam
Embrace the Dawn - Kathleen Morgan *i* 1026

MacKeltar, Drustan
Kiss of the Highlander - Karen Marie Moning *r* 358

Mackintosh, Iain
The Mackintosh Bride - Debra Lee Brown *r* 244

LANDLORD

Paradise, Judith
Quincie Bolliver - Mary King *w* 469

LANDOWNER

Barlow, Tye
The Wedding Wager - Cathy Maxwell *r* 348

LANDSCAPER

Edwards, Derrien "Derry"
A Diamond in the Rough - Andrea Pickens *r* 370

Linsley, Adrian
A Diamond in the Rough - Andrea Pickens *r* 370

LAWMAN

Baca, Elfego
Miracle of the Jacal - Robert J. Randisi *w* 497

Barclay, Clint
Once an Outlaw - Jill Gregory *r* 294

Benton, Reed
Summer Moon - Jill Marie Landis *w* 471

Bones, John
A World of Thieves - James Carlos Blake *w* 424

Cox
Colorado Twilight - Tess Pendergrass *w* 495

Deevers, Wilburn
Hard Bounty - Ken Hodgson *w* 463

Earp, Wyatt
Bucking the Tiger - Bruce Olds *w* 485

Hawkins, Ridge
Just West of Heaven - Kathleen Kane *r* 313

Holmes, Ezra
The Vigil - Clay Reynolds *w* 498

MacKenzie, Zach
The MacKenzies: Zach - Ana Leigh *r* 332

McQuaid, Jared
The Widow's Little Secret - Judith Stacy *r* 409

Saraccino, Pedro
Miracle of the Jacal - Robert J. Randisi *w* 497

Shannon, Rusty
The Way of the Coyote - Elmer Kelton *w* 468
The Way of the Coyote - Elmer Kelton *t* 895
The Way of the Coyote - Elmer Kelton *c* 1137

Tilden, Hayden
Law Dog - J. Lee Butts *w* 438

Van Pelt, Kirk
The Pinkerton Eye - Allen P. Bristow *w* 436

Walker, Clayton
Walker's Widow - Heidi Betts *r* 234

LAWYER

Atwell, William Hawley
Will's War - Janice Woods Windle *t* 961
Will's War - Janice Woods Windle *w* 513

Blackburn, Tanner
Dangerously Irresistible - Kristin Gabriel *r* 289

Bybee, Brigham
Sister Wife - John Gates *m* 76

Cabral, Urania
The Feast of the Goat - Mario Vargas Llosa *t* 948
The Feast of the Goat - Mario Vargas Llosa *c* 1211

Cavanagh, Roger
Middle Age - Joyce Carol Oates *c* 1174

Collins, Martin
Catskill - John R. Hayes *m* 110
Catskill - John R. Hayes *t* 882

Columbus, Beth
Columbus Slaughters Braves - Mark Friedman *c* 1114

Connor, Gail
Suspicion of Vengeance - Barbara Parker *m* 167

Cooper, Alexandra
The Deadhouse - Linda Fairstein *m* 66

Coyne, Brady
First Light - Philip R. Craig *m* 46
Past Tense - William G. Tapply *m* 206

Crow, Mary
A Darker Justice - Sallie Bissell *m* 19
In the Forest of Harm - Sallie Bissell *c* 1074

Dugan, Charlene
The Wedding Party - Robyn Carr *r* 250

Fitzgerald, Declan
Midnight Bayou - Nora Roberts *c* 1187

Gallagher, Ruth
Always Forever - Mark Chadbourn *f* 533

Griffin, Cal
Magic Time - Marc Scott Zicree *f* 614

Hardy, Dismas
The Oath - John Lescroart *m* 141

Hauser, Ed
Shades of Justice - Fredrick Huebner *m* 121

Holden, Vicky
The Thunder Keeper - Margaret Coel *m* 35
The Thunder Keeper - Margaret Coel *w* 444

Holland, Billy Bob
Bitterroot - James Lee Burke *c* 1088

Kneece, Derwood "Woody"
Officer of the Court - Bill Mesce Jr. *t* 906

Lambert, Evan
Almost - Elizabeth Benedict *c* 1073

Lupset, Edward
London Bridges - Jane Stevenson *c* 1204

McCain, Sam
Save the Last Dance for Me - Ed Gorman *m* 83

Murray, Gordon
The Mystic Rose - Stephen R. Lawhead *t* 901

Nash, Seneca
Nashborough - Elsie Burch Donald *t* 855

Quinn, Chandler
The Astonished Eye - Tracy Knight *f* 567

Quintana, Anthony
Suspicion of Vengeance - Barbara Parker *m* 167

Riley, Jordan
On Every Side - Karen Kingsbury *i* 1010

Robak, Don
Robak in Black - Joe L. Hensley *m* 113

Severn, Trent
The Guardian - Barbara Miller *r* 355

Slattery, Mary
Shades of Justice - Fredrick Huebner *m* 121

Stone, Cooper
Forbid Them Not - Michael P. Farris *i* 991

Taft, Charlie
The Jazz Bird - Craig Holden *m* 119
The Jazz Bird - Craig Holden *t* 885

Vincent, Sam
Pale Horse Coming - Stephen Hunter *c* 1127
Pale Horse Coming - Stephen Hunter *t* 887

Pale Horse Coming - Stephen Hunter *m* 122

Voss, Harry
Officer of the Court - Bill Mesce Jr. *t* 906

Wingate, Eric
A Child Shall Lead Them - Carole Gift Page *i* 1036

Winslow, Phillip
The Heavenly Fugitive - Gilbert Morris *i* 1028

LEADER

Argall, Samuel
Argall - William T. Vollmann *c* 1212

Seraphim, Rushton
Ashling - Isobelle Carmody *s* 732

Smith, John
Argall - William T. Vollmann *t* 950

LIBRARIAN

Galina, Susan
Adventures in Time and Space with Max Merriwell - Pat Murphy *s* 781

Kerry, Jane
In the Dark - Richard Laymon *h* 663

Lamplighter, Edgewick
The Rover - Mel Odom *f* 584

Levine, Kathleen
Good Harbor - Anita Diamant *c* 1103

Merrigan, Emma
Behind Time - Lynn Abbey *f* 515

Minor, Dacinda "Daisy" Ann
Open Season - Linda Howard *r* 302

Owens, Blair
Cape Refuge - Terri Blackstock *i* 970

Short, Alexander
The Grand Complication - Allen Kurzweil *c* 1144

LIGHTHOUSE KEEPER

Gribbon, Salt
A Warmth in Winter - Lori Copeland *i* 984

LINGUIST

Fly, Lucy
The Earthquake Bird - Susanna Jones *m* 127

Reever, Duncan
Shockball - S.L. Viehl *s* 805

Saint-Ange, Marie Claire
Dangerous Attraction - Susan Vaughan *r* 417

Wyman, Lynn
Female Intelligence - Jane Heller *c* 1125

LOVER

Amad
Jewelry Talks - Richard Klein *c* 1142

Ana
Half a Life - V.S. Naipaul *c* 1170

Anna
Funny Accent - Barbara Shulgasser-Parker *c* 1197

Baldwin, Nick
Face Down Before Rebel Hooves - Kathy Lynn Emerson *t* 861

Beckett, Daniel
Eager to Please - Julie Parsons *c* 1180

Charlotte
Look at Me - Jennifer Egan *c* 1108

Clayton
Bitten - Kelley Armstrong *c* 1068

Erik
First Gray, Then White, Then Blue - Margriet de Moor *c* 1165

Haroney, Kate "Big Nose Kate"
Bucking the Tiger - Bruce Olds *c* 1176
Bucking the Tiger - Bruce Olds *w* 485

Henderson, John Basil
Any Way the Wind Blows - E. Lynn Harris *c* 1122

Jacobs, Daniel
Almost - Elizabeth Benedict *c* 1073

Jacobs, Kitty
War Story - Gwen Edelman *c* 1107

Leeds, Jack
Shakespeare's Counselor - Charlaine Harris *m* 102

Lena
The Good German - Joseph Kanon *c* 1135

Martin, Kit
Killing the Shadows - Val McDermid *m* 154

Michael
Lightning Field - Dana Spiotta *c* 1202

Mila
Fury - Salman Rushdie *c* 1190

Misha
Funny Accent - Barbara Shulgasser-Parker *c* 1197

Mitchell, Meredith
Shades of Murder - Ann Granger *m* 87

Murtagh, Colum
Saintly Murders - C.L. Grace *m* 86
Saintly Murders - C.L. Grace *t* 875

Neela
Fury - Salman Rushdie *c* 1190

Philip
Bitten - Kelley Armstrong *c* 1068

Shore, Jane
The Goldsmith's Daughter - Kate Sedley *t* 933

Smith, Loren
Valhalla Rising - Clive Cussler *c* 1097

Thompson, Edith
Fred & Edie - Jill Dawson *t* 848

Visitor, Lennie
Light Coming Back - Ann Wadsworth *c* 1213

Wilkinson, Katie
Suzanne's Diary for Nicholas - James Patterson *c* 1181

LUMBERJACK

Marker, Caleb
Alicia's Song - Susan Plunkett *r* 371

MAGICIAN

Alya
Shadow of the Seer - Michael Scott Rohan *f* 595

Carter, Charlie
Carter Beats the Devil - Glen David Gold *t* 874

Rainwater, Gavan
The Magickers - Emily Drake *f* 542

MAIDEN

Seymour, Glenys
The Prisoner Bride - Susan Spencer Paul *r* 368

MAIL ORDER BRIDE

Morrow, Diana
A Measure of Grace - Al Lacy *i* 1014

Whittington, Kate
Summer Moon - Jill Marie Landis *w* 471

MAINTENANCE WORKER

Clark, Hosanna
What You Owe Me - Bebe Moore Campbell *c* 1089

Land, Jeremiah
Peace Like a River - Leif Enger *c* 1109

Rosenstein, Gilda
What You Owe Me - Bebe Moore Campbell *c* 1089

Winter, Bonnie
Bonnie Winter - Graham Masterton *h* 672

MARTIAL ARTS EXPERT

Alison
Kiss It Goodbye - John Wessel *m* 213

Bard, Lily
Shakespeare's Counselor - Charlaine Harris *m* 102

MECHANIC

ibn Musa, Ibrahim "Abdu"
The Pickup - Nadine Gordimer *c* 1116

MENTALLY ILL PERSON

Forster, Quentin
Secret of the Wolf - Susan Krinard *r* 322

Van Urden, Ivy
The Savage Girl - Alex Shakar *c* 1196

MERCENARY

Kent, Jason
Lt. Kent: Lone Wolf - Judith Lyons *r* 341

Repairman Jack
Hosts - F. Paul Wilson *h* 710

MILITARY PERSONNEL

Addington, Alexander "Alex"
The Wedding Charm - Lynn Collum *r* 258

Ames, B.Z.
A Soldier's Duty - Thomas E. Ricks *c* 1186

Anderson, Mark
Fireworks - James A. Moore *h* 675

Atkinson, Henry
The Good Journey - Micaela Gilchrist *w* 454
The Good Journey - Micaela Gilchrist *t* 873

Austen, Frank
Jane and the Prisoner of Wool House - Stephanie Barron *t* 822

Benally, Gordon
The Water and the Blood - Nancy E. Turner *t* 947

Blysdale, Chalfont
The Night the Stars Fell - Christina Kingston *r* 317

Brannon, Mac
Gettysburg - James Reasoner *t* 919

Brannon, Will
Gettysburg - James Reasoner *t* 919

Brown, David
Summer's Promise - Irene Brand *i* 974

Burke, Walter
Bombingham - Anthony Grooms c 1119

Caesar, Julius
Nobody Loves a Centurion - John Maddox Roberts t 924

Carrington, Henry
Moon of Bitter Cold - Frederick J. Chiaventone w 441

Cassidy, J.R.
Sentimental Journey - Jill Barnett t 821

Cato, Quintus Licinius
Under the Eagle - Simon Scarrow t 931

Croydon, Denzil
Tragic Casements - Oliver Onions h 680

Cruz, Anibal
Pyramid Scheme - David Freer s 751

Custer, George Armstrong
An Uncommon Enemy - Michelle Black t 824
An Uncommon Enemy - Michelle Black w 423

Dalriadis
Heresy - Anselm Audley s 718

Drak, Bart
Holding the Line - Rick Shelley s 795

Dunbar, John
The Holy Road - Michael Blake t 826
The Holy Road - Michael Blake w 425

Eberhardt, Heinrich
In the Shape of a Boar - Lawrence Norfolk t 913

Elken
Bolo Strike - William H. Keith Jr. s 765

Everard, David
The Blooding of the Guns - Alexander Fullerton t 866

Everard, Hugh
The Blooding of the Guns - Alexander Fullerton t 866

Everard, Nicholas
The Blooding of the Guns - Alexander Fullerton t 866

Everdean, Peter
The Spanish Bride - Amanda McCabe r 349

Everly, Jonathan
The Traitor's Daughter - Elizabeth Powell r 374

Flaherty, Lucien "Irish"
Broken Honor - Patricia Potter r 373

Flores, Andrea
Tenebrea's Hope - Roxann Dawson s 743

Fournier, Adrien
The Officers' Ward - Marc Dugain t 857

Franck, Dieter
Jackdaws - Ken Follett t 863

Gale, Michael
Ester's Child - Jean P. Sasson t 930

Gardam, Stella
The Clouds Above - Andrew Greig t 876

Grant, Ulysses S.
The Ambush of My Name - Jeffrey Marks t 903
Call Each River Jordan - Owen Parry t 914

Griffin, Hollis "Griff"
Tall, Dark, and Difficult - Patricia Coughlin r 261

Grunthor
Destiny - Elizabeth Haydon f 554

Halder, Alfie
The Jerusalem Scrolls - Bodie Thoene t 942

Halley
Time Future - Maxine McArthur s 770

Herdtmacher, Thomas
Brother John - Rutledge Etheridge s 750

Hesmucet
Marching through Peachtree - Harry Turtledove f 606

Holly, Joe
Double Vengeance - John Duncklee w 449

Inskip, George "Skip"
Sentimental Journey - Jill Barnett r 228
Sentimental Journey - Jill Barnett t 821

Jaansma, Garvin
Homefall - Chris Bunch s 729

Jones, Abel
Call Each River Jordan - Owen Parry t 914
Call Each River Jordan - Owen Parry m 169

Julian, Adib
March to the Sea - David Weber s 809

Kiervauna
Holding the Line - Rick Shelley s 795

Kneece, Derwood "Woody"
Officer of the Court - Bill Mesce Jr. t 906

Kohler, Hermann
Kaleidoscope - J. Robert Janes t 888
Kaleidoscope - J. Robert Janes m 126

Kosutic, Eva
March to the Sea - David Weber s 809

Kurtz, Abraham
Dreamcatcher - Stephen King h 660

Kyle, Vaughn
Buffalo Valley - Debbie Macomber w 474

Lee, Robert E.
The Ironclad Alibi - Michael Kilian t 898

Llyr, Seth
Brothers of Cain - Miriam Grace Monfredo t 909

Longinus, Marcus
The Jerusalem Scrolls - Bodie Thoene i 1053

Lubin, Ken
Maelstrom - Peter Watts s 808

MacClintock, Roger
March to the Sea - David Weber s 809

MacDonald, David
Soldiers - John Dalmas s 742

MacKerron, Lachlann
The Sword Maiden - Susan King r 316

MacLeod, Hamish
Watchers of Time - Charles Todd t 943

Macro, Lucius Cornelius
Under the Eagle - Simon Scarrow t 931

Marais, Charles
The Dark Wing - Walter Hunt s 761

McGuire, Cole
The Colorado Bride - Mary Burton r 247

McKay, Ford
Going Overboard - Christina Skye r 399

McKendrick, Simon
A Tangled Web - Donna Bell r 230

Metellus, Decius
Nobody Loves a Centurion - John Maddox Roberts m 184
Nobody Loves a Centurion - John Maddox Roberts t 924

Nate
Tennant's Rock - Steve McGiffen w 478

Pedigo, Luther
Affinity - J.N. Williamson h 709

Prescott, Wycliffe
Miss Truelove Beckons - Donna Simpson r 397

Quilan
Look to Windward - Iain Banks s 721

Ragozinski
Second Chances - Susan Shwartz s 796

Raines, Francis Drake
Call Each River Jordan - Owen Parry t 914

Ramsden, Edward
The Very Daring Duchess - Miranda Jarrett r 308

Randall, Brad
An Uncommon Enemy - Michelle Black w 423
An Uncommon Enemy - Michelle Black t 824

Reacher, Jack
Echo Burning - Lee Child w 442

Robin
The Wolf Pit - Marly Youmans t 964

Rogan, Kevin
Last Virgin in California - Maureen Child r 255

Sachar, Moshe
The Jerusalem Scrolls - Bodie Thoene t 942

Sanders, Will
The American Zone - L. Neil Smith s 799

Sandiford, St. John Michael Peter
The Proper Wife - Julia Justiss r 311

Savage, William
Minutes to Burn - Gregg Andrew Hurwitz s 762

Seagrave, Tom
Jane and the Prisoner of Wool House - Stephanie Barron t 822

Sherman, Cindy
A Soldier's Duty - Thomas E. Ricks c 1186

Shillingsworth, John
A Soldier's Duty - Thomas E. Ricks c 1186

Smith, Kendall "Ken"
The Black Eye - Constance Little m 144

Souvana
Holding the Line - Rick Shelley s 795

Spangler, David
Deep Fathom - James Rollins s 792

Stanton, Bruce "Striker"
True Valor - Dee Henderson i 1000

Streicher, Jon Jarred
Bolo Strike - William H. Keith Jr. s 765

Taylor, Bobby
Taylor's Temptation - Suzanne Brockmann r 242

Thomas of Hookton
The Archer's Tale - Bernard Cornwell t 843

Timur-i-Lenhk
A Feast in Exile - Chelsea Quinn Yarbro t 963

Torrijos, Sergei
The Dark Wing - Walter Hunt s 761

Townsend, Andrew
First Landing - Robert Zubrin s 814

Two Stars, David
Heart of the Sandhill - Stephanie Grace Whitson i 1058

Vespasian, Titus Flavius Sabinus
Under the Eagle - Simon Scarrow t 931

Vinius, Titus
Nobody Loves a Centurion - John Maddox Roberts t 924

Voss, Harry
Officer of the Court - Bill Mesce Jr. t 906

Walker, Red
Sentimental Journey - Jill Barnett r 228

Washburn, Samuel
We Look Like Men of War - William R. Forstchen *t* 864

Weber, Willi
Jackdaws - Ken Follett *t* 863

Wells, Chan
The Dark Wing - Walter Hunt *s* 761

Westbourne, Len
The Clouds Above - Andrew Greig *t* 876

Wilder, Joe
Stranded with the Sergeant - Cathie Linz *r* 335

Wilder, Mark
The Marine and the Princess - Cathie Linz *r* 334

Wilkinson, James
Treason - David Nevin *t* 912

William, Roast Beef
Marching through Peachtree - Harry Turtledove *f* 606

Yates, Grace
True Valor - Dee Henderson *i* 1000

Yoshitaro, Njangu
Homefall - Chris Bunch *s* 729

MINE OWNER

Crawford, Steve
The Lone Rider - Max Brand *w* 432

MINER

Fisk, Callie
A Horde of Fools - James David Buchanan *w* 437

MODEL

Dunbar, Bartholomew "Bart"
Any Way the Wind Blows - E. Lynn Harris *c* 1122

Swenson, Charlotte
Look at Me - Jennifer Egan *c* 1108

Van Urden, Ivy
The Savage Girl - Alex Shakar *c* 1196

MONSTER

Rojire
A Feast in Exile - Chelsea Quinn Yarbro *h* 713

MOUNTAIN MAN

Janis, Joseph Antoine
The June Rise - William Tremblay *w* 507
The June Rise - William Tremblay *t* 945

Skye, Barnaby
Downriver - Richard S. Wheeler *w* 512
Downriver - Richard S. Wheeler *t* 957

MOUNTAINEER

McKinnon, Thomas MacLeod
My Heart Stood Still - Lynn Kurland *r* 323

MURDERER

Beckett, Rachel
Eager to Please - Julie Parsons *c* 1180

Drama
Critical Space - Greg Rucka *m* 190

Ice
Blood Games - Lee Killough *h* 657

Magruder, Saginaw Bob
Law Dog - J. Lee Butts *w* 438

Nate
Tennant's Rock - Steve McGiffen *w* 478

Szeska, John
All the Dead Were Strangers - Ethan Black *c* 1076

York, Caleb
Caleb's Price - Troy D. Smith *w* 505

MUSEUM CURATOR

Abraham, Adelaide "Addy"
All the Finest Girls - Alexandra Styron *c* 1206

Lundgren, Anna
Under Suspicion - Rachel Lee *r* 331

MUSICIAN

Banyon, Eric
Spirits White as Lightning - Mercedes Lackey *f* 568

Bolden, Buddy
Chasing the Devil's Tail - David Fulmer *t* 867

Brennan, Richard
Swim the Moon - Paul Brandon *f* 529

Bunch, Rex
Gabriel's Gift - Hanif Kureishi *c* 1143

Jones, Lester
Gabriel's Gift - Hanif Kureishi *c* 1143

Keltner, Jason
The Night Men - Keith Snyder *m* 199

Medina, Patrick
Light Coming Back - Ann Wadsworth *c* 1213

O'Niall, Fiorinda
Bold as Love - Gwyneth Jones *s* 764

Preston, Ax
Bold as Love - Gwyneth Jones *s* 764

Quinn, Mary Margaret "Maggie"
The Nightingale's Song - Kathleen Eschenburg *r* 273

Ramone, Dee Dee
Chelsea Horror Hotel - Dee Dee Ramone *h* 684

Rostov, Tandy
The Pinkerton Eye - Allen P. Bristow *w* 436

Williams, John "Loverboy"
Just Say No! - Omar Tyree *c* 1210

MYTHICAL CREATURE

Aelvarim
Eccentric Circles - Rebecca Lickiss *f* 573

Ahern
The Pillars of the World - Anne Bishop *f* 527

Alain
Once upon a Winter's Night - Dennis L. McKiernan *f* 579

Ariel
Buttercup Baby - Karen Fox *r* 287
Ill Met by Moonlight - Sarah A. Hoyt *f* 559

Arslan
Pride of Kings - Judith Tarr *f* 603
Pride of Kings - Judith Tarr *t* 941

Aumar, Elminster
Elminster in Hell - Ed Greenwood *f* 553

Belynda
World Fall - Douglas Niles *f* 583

ben-Abdullah, Abban "Ben"
I Dream of You - Judi McCoy *r* 350

Bonavendier, Lilith
Alice at Heart - Deborah Smith *r* 401

Centaur, Cynthia
Swell Foop - Piers Anthony *f* 518

Dianna
The Pillars of the World - Anne Bishop *f* 527

Do'Urden, Drizzt
Sea of Swords - R.A. Salvatore *f* 597

Duranix
Brother of the Dragon - Paul B. Thompson *f* 604

Eladamri
Apocalypse - J. Robert King *f* 564

Falima
The Beasts of Barakhai - Mickey Zucker Reichert *f* 590

Kazairl
Spirit of the Stone - Maggie Furey *f* 545

Malraux
Eccentric Circles - Rebecca Lickiss *f* 573

Melchior, Obediah
A Capital Holiday - Janet Dailey *r* 265

Notwen
Dragon's Bluff - Mary H. Herbert *f* 556

Quicksilver
Ill Met by Moonlight - Sarah A. Hoyt *f* 559

Randolph, Griffin
Alice at Heart - Deborah Smith *r* 401

Regis
Sea of Swords - R.A. Salvatore *f* 597

Riley, Alice
Alice at Heart - Deborah Smith *r* 401

Rohk, Truls
Antrax - Terry Brooks *f* 530

Wolfram
Guardians of the Lost - Margaret Weis *f* 611

Zylas
The Beasts of Barakhai - Mickey Zucker Reichert *f* 590

NARRATOR

Cotton, Aldous "Gus"
Fairness - Ferdinand Mount *c* 1167

del Valle, Aurora
Portrait in Sepia - Isabel Allende *c* 1067

Elliot, Timothy
From the Dust Returned - Ray Bradbury *c* 1082
From the Dust Returned - Ray Bradbury *h* 623

Grace
The Wig My Father Wore - Anne Enright *c* 1111

Guidry, Joseph "Junior"
Junior's Leg - Ken Wells *c* 1214

Harmon, Darin
Just Say No! - Omar Tyree *c* 1210

Ishaq
The Rock - Kanan Makiya *t* 902
The Rock - Kanan Makiya *c* 1152

Land, Reuben
Peace Like a River - Leif Enger *c* 1109

Lluvia
Swift as Desire - Laura Esquivel *c* 1112

O'Malley, Rosemarie
September Song - Andrew M. Greeley *c* 1117

Ranelagh, M.
The Shape of Snakes - Minette Walters *m* 211

Schwartz, Thomas
All That Counts - Georg M. Oswald *c* 1177

Short, Alexander
The Grand Complication - Allen Kurzweil c 1144

Thrale, Queeney
According to Queeney - Beryl Bainbridge c 1069

Unnamed Character
For Rouenna - Sigrid Nunez c 1172

NEIGHBOR

Cotter, Karen
The Woman Next Door - Barbara Delinsky c 1101

Lange, Georgia
The Woman Next Door - Barbara Delinsky c 1101

NOBLEMAN

Addington, Alexander "Alex"
The Wedding Charm - Lynn Collum r 258

Alain
Once upon a Winter's Night - Dennis L. McKiernan f 579

Armstrong, James
To Tame a Duke - Patricia Grasso r 293

Atreides, Leto
House Corrino - Brian Herbert s 757

Avery, Prescott
A Family for Gillian - Catherine Blair r 238

Blysdale, Chalfont
The Night the Stars Fell - Christina Kingston r 317

Borgia, Cesare
The Family - Mario Puzo t 916
The Family - Mario Puzo c 1183

Brahm, Corvinus
The Beasts of Brahm - Mark Hansom h 646

Breckonridge, Malcolm
The Incomparable Miss Compton - Regina Scott r 392

Brennan
Children of the Lion - Jennifer Roberson f 591

Brydges, Edward
Sugarplum Surprises - Elisabeth Fairchild r 275

Cathan
Heresy - Anselm Audley s 718

Chalstrey, Morgan
My Lady Beloved - Lael St. James r 405

Christian, Miles
Elusive Passion - Kathryn Smith r 402

Cooke-Williams, Arthur Williford
Charlie and the Sir - Frank Roderus w 499

Corinth, Edward
The Bones of the Buried - David Roberts m 183
The Bones of the Buried - David Roberts t 923

Courtray, Melfallan
Mother Ocean, Daughter Sea - Diana Marcellas f 576

Cynster, Sebastian
The Promise in a Kiss - Stephanie Laurens r 329

Dacre, Christopher
The Border Hostage - Virginia Henley t 883

d'Arcy, Owen
To Kiss a Spy - Jane Feather r 276

Darnley, Randall
Once a Princess - Veronica Sattler r 388

de Burgh, Robin
My Lady de Burgh - Deborah Simmons r 396

de Vere, Gareth
Fortune's Lady - Evelyn Richardson r 379

de Villonne, Bayard
The Temptress - Claire Delacroix r 269

Dortrean, Erkal
The Treason of Dortrean - Marcus Herniman f 557

Dortrean, Kellarn
The Treason of Dortrean - Marcus Herniman f 557

Dudley, Ferdinand
No Man's Mistress - Mary Balogh r 227

Everdean, Peter
The Spanish Bride - Amanda McCabe r 349

Ewald
Tomorrow's Eve - Auguste Villiers de L'Isle Adam s 806

Fairchild, Jack
Very Truly Yours - Julie Beard r 229

Falthorn
The Obsidian Tower - Freda Warrington f 609

Fitzgerald, Johnny
Goodnight, Sweet Prince - David Dickinson m 58

Fraith, Charles
Agatha Raisin and the Love from Hell - M.C. Beaton m 14

Giffard, Simeon
A Forbidden Embrace - Anna Jacobs r 305

Godsol, Rafe
The Warrior's Damsel - Denise Hampton r 295

Grayden
Lady Hilary's Halloween - Mona Gedney r 291

Grayson
The Rake and the Wallflower - Allison Lane r 325

Hampton, Robert George Colter
A Reckless Encounter - Rosemary Rogers r 385

Harkness, James
The Bride Sale - Candice Hern r 298

Harkonnen, Vladimir
House Corrino - Brian Herbert s 757

Harrington, Justin
A Guardian's Angel - Jo Ann Ferguson r 278

Hartstone, Anthony
Abandon - Jillian Hunter r 303

Haversham, Nigel
French Leave - Sheri Cobb South r 404

Hawk of Essex
Believe in Me - Josie Litton r 336

Jeffries, Marcus Quentin
The Trouble with Harriet - Wilma Counts r 262

Jekyl, Simon
The Archer's Tale - Bernard Cornwell t 843

Kenyon, Gabriel
Tempt Me Twice - Barbara Dawson Smith r 400

Kieran of Gleannmara
Riona - Linda Windsor i 1060

Korendil
Spirits White as Lightning - Mercedes Lackey f 568

Leynier, Corin
The Fall of Neskaya - Marion Zimmer Bradley s 725

Linsley, Adrian
A Diamond in the Rough - Andrea Pickens r 370

Llesho
The Prince of Shadow - Curt Benjamin f 526

Macbeth
The Third Witch - Rebecca Reisert t 921

MacClintock, Roger
March to the Sea - David Weber s 809

Mackenzie, Finlay "Wild Fin"
The Secret Clan: Abducted Heiress - Amanda Scott r 390

Manderville, William
The Very Comely Countess - Miranda Jarrett r 307

Marchnight, Henry
Lady Polly - Nicola Cornick r 259

Merwin, Alex
A Perfect Match - Jeanne Savery r 389

Moorhaven, Nigel
The Blue Devil - Melynda Beth Skinner r 398

Moreland, Jared
A Devilish Husband - Alana Clayton r 257

Morelane, Cedric
The Valentine Wish - Debbie Raleigh r 378

Murray, Colin
To Tame a Wild Heart - Tracy Fobes r 281

Nesbitt, Benedict "Nez"
One Good Turn - Carla Kelly r 315

Palindrake, Valraven
The Way of Light - Storm Constantine f 536

Parmenter, James
Broken Promises - Patricia Oliver r 362

Pendennis, Walter
Face Down Before Rebel Hooves - Kathy Lynn Emerson t 861

Peril
The Husband Test - Betina Krahn r 321

Petersborough, Leslie
The Irredeemable Miss Renfield - Regina Scott r 393

Plantagenet, Edward
Knight Errant - R. Garcia y Robertson t 869
Knight Errant - R. Garcia y Robertson f 546

Powerscourt, Francis
Goodnight, Sweet Prince - David Dickinson m 58
Goodnight, Sweet Prince - David Dickinson t 851

Prescott, Wycliffe
Miss Truelove Beckons - Donna Simpson r 397

Ramsden, Edward
The Very Daring Duchess - Miranda Jarrett r 308

Ringyar
Shadow Kiss - Tom Townsend f 605

Ross, Justin
Heartless - Kat Martin r 346

Rowley, Eppingham Julian
Fallen - Celeste Bradley r 241

St. Charles, Steven
A Scandalous Wager - Bess Willingham r 420

Sandiford, St. John Michael Peter
The Proper Wife - Julia Justiss r 311

Seagrave, Nicholas John Rosslyn
The Virtuous Cyprian - Nicola Cornick r 260

Simbul
Elminster in Hell - Ed Greenwood f 553

Spense, Oliver
The Christmas Wish - Debbie Raleigh r 377

Stephens, Miles William
Broken Promises - Patricia Oliver r 362

Tejar
Mother Ocean, Daughter Sea - Diana Marcellas f 576

Temar
The Warrior's Bond - Juliet E. McKenna f 578

Tennington, Wilbur
Treasures of the Sun - T.V. Olsen w 487

Thorne, Adrian
Heart of Night - Taylor Chase r 254

Toribor
The Dragon Society - Lawrence Watt-Evans f 610

Townsend, Galen
His Lady Midnight - Jo Ann Ferguson r 279

Tremayne, Lucian
Desire - Nicole Jordan r 309

Vetinari
The Last Hero - Terry Pratchett f 588

von Bek, Ulric
The Dreamthief's Daughter - Michael Moorcock f 582

von Heyden, Gottfried
The Black Chalice - Marie Jakober f 562

von Minct, Gaynor
The Dreamthief's Daughter - Michael Moorcock f 582

Wakefield, Samuel
The Promise - May McGoldrick r 352

Westerly, Geoffrey
Under the Kissing Bough - Shannon Donnelly r 271

Zavahl
Spirit of the Stone - Maggie Furey f 545

NOBLEWOMAN

Ainsley-Hunter, Antonia
Critical Space - Greg Rucka m 190

Alexia
Fortress Draconis - Michael A. Stackpole f 599

Anbari, Asiadeh
The Girl from the Golden Horn - Kurban Said c 1191

Avery, Gillian Harwell
A Family for Gillian - Catherine Blair r 238

Beauchamp, Althea
Fortune's Lady - Evelyn Richardson r 379

Beaumont, Clarissa
The Proper Wife - Julia Justiss r 311

Bigalow, Artemisia
A Perfect Match - Jeanne Savery r 389

Borgia, Lucrezia
The Family - Mario Puzo c 1183
The Family - Mario Puzo t 916

Brackenton, Phoebe
His Lady Midnight - Jo Ann Ferguson r 279

Bryanston, Pen
To Kiss a Spy - Jane Feather r 276

Caldwell, Brynn
Desire - Nicole Jordan r 309

Copperton, Elizabeth
Charlie and the Sir - Frank Roderus w 499

Cymbra
Dream of Me - Josie Litton r 338

Darren, Claire
Heart of Night - Taylor Chase r 254

de Fraisney, Katherine
The Warrior's Damsel - Denise Hampton r 295

de Stansion, Helena Rebecca
The Promise in a Kiss - Stephanie Laurens r 329

DeMarian, Alisha
The Golden Sword - Fiona Patton f 586

Devere, Rosamunde
The Perfect Princess - Elizabeth Thornton r 416

di Rospo, Teresa
Darkness - Sam Siciliano h 695

Dortrean, Karlena
The Treason of Dortrean - Marcus Herniman f 557

Genevieve
Drachenfels - Jack Yeovil f 613

Glover, Eleanor
Under the Kissing Bough - Shannon Donnelly r 271

Hartleigh Compton, Elizabeth
Death Is in the Air - Kate Kingsbury m 136

Hastings, Lupin Lorrimer
Who Killed the Curate? - Joan Coggin m 36

Isabel of Dornei
The Marriage Bed - Claudia Dain r 266

Jamison, Hilary
Lady Hilary's Halloween - Mona Gedney r 291

Katherine of Cliffside
The Night the Stars Fell - Christina Kingston r 317

Keely
Children of the Lion - Jennifer Roberson f 591

Krysta
Believe in Me - Josie Litton r 336

Llewellyn, Brydda
Ashling - Isobelle Carmody s 732

MacLaren, Esmeraude
The Temptress - Claire Delacroix r 269

Montero, Carmen
The Spanish Bride - Amanda McCabe r 349

Parmenter, Mathilda Heath
Broken Promises - Patricia Oliver r 362

Rathford, Helena
The Sleeping Beauty - Jacqueline Navin r 360

Redclift, Gabriella
My Lady Beloved - Lael St. James r 405

Redclift, Meg
My Lady Wayward - Lael St. James r 406

Rochelle, Valara "Lara"
The Wedding Charm - Lynn Collum r 258

Rycca of Wolscroft
Come Back to Me - Josie Litton r 337

Seagrave, Appollonia "Polly" Grace
Lady Polly - Nicola Cornick r 259

Sharina
Mistress of the Catacombs - David Drake f 541

Tamryn, Green
Ritual of Proof - Dara Joy r 310

Terrebonne, Eugenia "Genie"
A Scandalous Wager - Bess Willingham r 420

Thornhill, Viola
No Man's Mistress - Mary Balogh r 227

Tobin
The Bone Doll's Twin - Lynn Flewelling f 544

Uskevren, Shamur
The Shattered Mask - Richard Lee Byers f 532

NURSE

Carey, Wendy
Winter's Secret - Lyn Cote i 985

Kleist, Christine
Ester's Child - Jean P. Sasson t 930

Leiah
Blessed Child - Bill Bright i 975

Llyr, Kathryn
Brothers of Cain - Miriam Grace Monfredo m 159

Llyr, Kathyrn
Brothers of Cain - Miriam Grace Monfredo t 909

Monk, Hester
Funeral in Blue - Anne Perry t 915
Funeral in Blue - Anne Perry m 172

Murdoch, Eden
An Uncommon Enemy - Michelle Black w 423
An Uncommon Enemy - Michelle Black t 824

Noble, Andrea
Gotta Get Next to You - Lynn Emery r 272

Rouenna
For Rouenna - Sigrid Nunez c 1172

Savari, Yana
Haunted - Melinda Metz s 776

OFFICE WORKER

Alice
He Goes, She Goes - Joanna Torrey c 1209

Dan
Face - Tim Lebbon h 665

Newman, Holly
The Gingerbread Man - Maggie Shayne r 395

OIL INDUSTRY WORKER

Bolliver, Curtin
Quincie Bolliver - Mary King w 469

ORGANIZED CRIME FIGURE

Benza, Sonny
Hostage - Robert Crais c 1096

Marchante, Rocko
Junior's Leg - Ken Wells c 1214

ORPHAN

Caleb
Blessed Child - Bill Bright i 975

Colling, Lisette
French Leave - Sheri Cobb South r 404

Hawkins, Marie-Ange
Leap of Faith - Danielle Steel c 1203

Holland, Angelina "Angie" Bartoli
The Bride of Willow Creek - Maggie Osborne r 364

Kent, Lorna
A Morning in Eden - Anna Gilbert t 872

Kooby, Jamieson
Stillwater - William F. Weld t 955

Leonie of Mirandeau
Once a Princess - Veronica Sattler r 388

Madeleine
Haussmann, or The Distinction - Paul LaFarge t 900

Murphy, Sarah
To Tame a Wild Heart - Tracy Fobes r 281

Proctor, Jeremy
Smuggler's Moon - Bruce Alexander t 815

Quinn, Mary Margaret "Maggie"
The Nightingale's Song - Kathleen Eschenburg r 273

Skif
Take a Thief - Mercedes Lackey f 569

OUTCAST

Bane
Midnight Falcon - David Gemmell *f* 548

Lincoln, Toby
Tears of the Heart - Lauran Paine *w* 493

Luna
Ride West to Dawn - James C. Work *w* 514

Oldham, Buddy-Boy
The Way of the Coyote - Elmer Kelton *w* 468

Swan
Tennant's Rock - Steve McGiffen *w* 478

OUTLAW

Bonney, William "Billy the Kid"
Bucking the Tiger - Bruce Olds *c* 1176

Bordi, Matias
The Survival of Juan Oro - Max Brand *w* 434

Cole, Clay "The Rainmaker"
Outcasts - Tim McGuire *w* 480

Dolven, Brock
Hard Bounty - Ken Hodgson *w* 463

Emmett, Claude
A Horde of Fools - James David Buchanan *w* 437

Fritz, Waldo
A Good Town - Douglas Hirt *w* 462

Hale, Bill
The Years of Fear - Fred Grove *w* 460

Kennedy, Heath
The Border Hostage - Virginia Henley *t* 883

Kerry, Cole
Behold a Red Horse - Cotton Smith *w* 504

Kid
The Outlaws - Wayne D. Overholser *w* 490

Magruder, Saginaw Bob
Law Dog - J. Lee Butts *w* 438

Paxton, Shell
Search for Last Chance - A.L. McWilliams *w* 482

Smith, John
The Outlaws - Wayne D. Overholser *w* 490

Sorrells, Pink
Bear Paw - Gene Mullins *w* 484

Taylor, Vic
Search for Last Chance - A.L. McWilliams *w* 482

PARANORMAL INVESTIGATOR

Booke, MacAllister
Heaven and Earth - Nora Roberts *r* 383

Darnell, John
The Case of the Ripper's Revenge - Sam McCarver *m* 153

Diche, Derek
Next Stop, Paradise - Sue Civil-Brown *r* 256

Gaunt, Nicholas
Dark Sanctuary - H.B. Gregory *h* 644

PARENT

Abraham, Barbara
All the Finest Girls - Alexandra Styron *c* 1206

Bartling, Bea
A Rose by the Door - Deborah Bedford *i* 967

Bolliver, Curtin
Quincie Bolliver - Mary King *w* 469

Bunch, Rex
Gabriel's Gift - Hanif Kureishi *c* 1143

Burke, Clara
Bombingham - Anthony Grooms *c* 1119

Burns, Jacob
The Killing Bee - Matt Witten *m* 218

Coleman, Kitty
Falling Angels - Tracy Chevalier *c* 1090

Drummond, Janet
All Families Are Psychotic - Douglas Coupland *c* 1094

Evans, Teddy
Schooling - Heather McGowan *c* 1159

Frith, Anna
Year of Wonders - Geraldine Brooks *c* 1083

Hart, Katherine
Riot - Shashi Tharoor *c* 1208

Hart, Rudyard
Riot - Shashi Tharoor *c* 1208

Lambert, Enid
The Corrections - Jonathan Franzen *c* 1113

Land, Jeremiah
Peace Like a River - Leif Enger *c* 1109

Landis, Elizabeth
A Garden to Keep - Jamie Langston Turner *i* 1055

Liddell
Still She Haunts Me - Katie Roiphe *c* 1189

Logan, Courtney
Long Time No See - Susan Isaacs *c* 1131

Luz
Swift as Desire - Laura Esquivel *c* 1112

Matt
Suzanne's Diary for Nicholas - James Patterson *c* 1181

McBride, Imogene
The Vigil - Clay Reynolds *w* 498

Miles, Robert
Friday's Child - Linda Chaikin *i* 977

O'Malley, Rosemarie
September Song - Andrew M. Greeley *c* 1117

Pavel
Requiem for a Lost Empire - Andrei Makine *c* 1151

Roth, Abraham
Devil's Island - John Hagee *i* 994

Schoene, Joseph
The Distant Land of My Father - Bo Caldwell *t* 835

Serafina
Highwire Moon - Susan Straight *c* 1205

Shepherd, Lori
Aunt Dimity: Detective - Nancy Atherton *m* 9

Staples, Nathan
Everything You Need - A.L. Kennedy *c* 1138

Steele, Elise
Heart of the Beast - Joyce Weatherford *w* 511

Steele, Ike
Heart of the Beast - Joyce Weatherford *w* 511

Stone, Lucy
Wedding Day Murder - Leslie Meier *m* 157

Suzanne
Suzanne's Diary for Nicholas - James Patterson *c* 1181

Tabachnik, Joyce
Good Harbor - Anita Diamant *c* 1103

Thunder Cloud
Blood on the Wind - Lucile Bogue *w* 426

Valencia, Liria
One Good Turn - Carla Kelly *r* 315

PATIENT

Levine, Kathleen
Good Harbor - Anita Diamant *c* 1103

PEDDLER

Roger the Chapman
The Goldsmith's Daughter - Kate Sedley *t* 933
The Weaver's Inheritance - Kate Sedley *m* 194
The Weaver's Inheritance - Kate Sedley *t* 934

PHARMACIST

Hendrickson, Carrie
Buffalo Valley - Debbie Macomber *w* 474

Knight, Hassie
Buffalo Valley - Debbie Macomber *w* 474

PHILOSOPHER

Bruno, Giordano
The Last Confession - Morris L. West *t* 956

PHOTOGRAPHER

del Valle, Aurora
Portrait in Sepia - Isabel Allende *c* 1067

Glass, Jordan
Dead Sleep - Greg Iles *m* 123

Rafferty, Alexandra
Blackwater Sound - James W. Hall *m* 94

Sullivan, Carolina "Carly"
Going Overboard - Christina Skye *r* 399

Valle, Aurora del
Portrait in Sepia - Isabel Allende *t* 817

PHOTOJOURNALIST

Berthoff, Lisa
This Time Forever - Carol Steward *i* 1052

PILOT

Boysen, Edmund
The Phoenix - Henning Boetius *t* 828

Gallagher, Judy
The Getaway Special - Jerry Oltion *s* 785

Inskip, George "Skip"
Sentimental Journey - Jill Barnett *r* 228
Sentimental Journey - Jill Barnett *t* 821

Masen, David
The Night of the Triffids - Simon Clark *s* 735

Merritt, Quaid
The Golden Angel - Gilbert Morris *i* 1027

Morrison, Charlotte
Sentimental Journey - Jill Barnett *r* 228

Sinclair, Paul
Super-Cannes - J.G. Ballard *c* 1070

Steele, Rayford
Desecration - Tim LaHaye *i* 1016

Walker, Red
Sentimental Journey - Jill Barnett *r* 228

Westbourne, Len
The Clouds Above - Andrew Greig *t* 876

Winslow, Erin
The Golden Angel - Gilbert Morris *i* 1027

Yates, Grace
True Valor - Dee Henderson *i* 1000

PIONEER

Bacon, Mazy
What Once We Loved - Jane Kirkpatrick *w* 470

Campbell, Ella Mae
Shadow Valley Rising - Stephen Overholser *w* 488

Culver, Suzanne
What Once We Loved - Jane Kirkpatrick *w* 470

Fisk, Callie
A Horde of Fools - James David Buchanan *w* 437

Martin, Ruth
What Once We Loved - Jane Kirkpatrick *w* 470
What Once We Loved - Jane Kirkpatrick *i* 1011

Wade, Callie
Letters to Callie - Dawn Miller *w* 483

Wade, Jack
Letters to Callie - Dawn Miller *w* 483

PIRATE

Hallekk
The Rover - Mel Odom *f* 584

PLANTATION OWNER

McMahon, John
Whispers of Goodbye - Karen White *r* 418

POLICE OFFICER

Albu
The Appointment - Herta Muller *c* 1168

Aldrich, Alicia
The King of the Sun - A.A. McFedries *s* 773

Bak
A Place of Darkness - Lauren Haney *m* 101

Banks, Alan
Aftermath - Peter Robinson *m* 186

Barrow, Zoe
Austin City Blue - Jan Grape *m* 88

Bartlett, Samantha
Next Stop, Paradise - Sue Civil-Brown *r* 256

Bonham, John Isley
A World of Thieves - James Carlos Blake *t* 825

Bowler, E.
Dialogues of the Dead or Paronomania! - Reginald Hill *m* 116

Brady, Joanna
Paradise Lost - J.A. Jance *w* 465
Paradise Lost - J.A. Jance *m* 125

Bryce, Jackie
Suspicion of Vengeance - Barbara Parker *m* 167

Burkett, Paige
The Renegade Steals a Lady - Vickie Taylor *r* 414

Canfield, Sam
July Thunder - Rachel Lee *r* 330

Chase, John
The Rose in the Wheel - S.K. Rizzolo *m* 182

Clarke, Siobhan
The Falls - Ian Rankin *m* 178

Coffin, John
Coffin's Ghost - Gwendoline Butler *m* 30

Cooper, Ben
Dancing with the Virgins - Stephen Booth *m* 23

Cross, Abby
The Innocent - Amanda Stevens *r* 410

Dalziel, Andrew "Andy"
Dialogues of the Dead or Paronomania! - Reginald Hill *m* 116

Deacon, Jack
Echoes of Lies - Jo Bannister *m* 11

Durand, Rodd
Winter's Secret - Lyn Cote *i* 985

Evans, Charlie
Catskill - John R. Hayes *t* 882

Fenwick, Andrew
Fatal Legacy - Elizabeth Corley *m* 43

Fenwick, Buck
Sex and Murder.com - Mark Richard Zubro *m* 221

Fry, Diane
Dancing with the Virgins - Stephen Booth *m* 23

Gastner, Bill
Bag Limit - Steven F. Havill *m* 108

Genesko, Karl
Better than Sex - Susan Holtzer *m* 120

Ghote, Ganesh
Breaking and Entering - H.R.F. Keating *m* 132

Gregg, Sally
End over End - Kate Kennedy *c* 1139

Guarnaccia, Salvatore
Property of Blood - Magdalen Nabb *m* 164

Gunther, Joe
Tucker Peak - Archer Mayor *m* 151

Hadrien, Artemis
Wayward Moon - Denny DeMartino *s* 744

Haggerty, Mickey
The Blue Last - Martha Grimes *m* 92

Hanks, Arly
Maggody and the Moonbeams - Joan Hess *m* 114

Hines, Jake
Six-Pound Walleye - Elizabeth Gunn *m* 93

Jacobson, Frank
A Study in Death - Iain McDowell *m* 155

Jessenovik, Matthew "Vik"
Whispers in the Dark - Eleanor Taylor Bland *m* 21

Jury, Richard
The Blue Last - Martha Grimes *m* 92

Kerr, Ian
A Study in Death - Iain McDowell *m* 155

Kite, Martin
A Sunset Touch - Marjorie Eccles *m* 64

Konstantin, Dore
Dervish Is Digital - Pat Cadigan *s* 731

Lassiter, Quannah
All Signs Point to Murder - Kat Goldring *m* 81

MacAlister, Marti
Whispers in the Dark - Eleanor Taylor Bland *m* 21

Maki, Del
Cold - John Smolens *c* 1199

Malone, Grant
Awakening Alex - Ruth Langan *r* 327

Mangum, Cudberth "Cuddy"
First Lady - Michael Malone *c* 1153

Manning, Kyle
A Love for Safekeeping - Gail Gaymer Martin *i* 1021

Markby, Alan
Shades of Murder - Ann Granger *m* 87

Mayo, Gil
A Sunset Touch - Marjorie Eccles *m* 64

McDonald, Clarence
A Horde of Fools - James David Buchanan *w* 437

McLeish, John
O Gentle Death - Janet Neel *m* 165

Mitchell, Frank
In and Out - Mat Coward *m* 44

Mitry, Desiree "Des"
The Cold Blue Blood - David Handler *m* 100

Moon, Abigail
A Sunset Touch - Marjorie Eccles *m* 64

Moon, Charlie
White Shell Woman - James D. Doss *m* 61

Morton, Henry
The Thief-Taker - T.F. Banks *t* 820
The Thief-Taker - T.F. Banks *m* 10

Mott, Albert
The King of the Sun - A.A. McFedries *s* 773

Moultrie, John
The Water and the Blood - Nancy E. Turner *t* 947

Murphy, Peter
Dead Love - Donald Beman *h* 620

Nesbitt, Alan
To Perish in Penzance - Jeanne M. Dams *m* 54

Norton, Wayne
Bikini Planet - David Garnett *s* 752

Ogada, Bruce
Dervish Is Digital - Pat Cadigan *s* 731

Osborn, Frank
Fireworks - James A. Moore *h* 675

Packham, Don
In and Out - Mat Coward *m* 44

Parris, Scott
White Shell Woman - James D. Doss *m* 61

Pascoe, Peter
Dialogues of the Dead or Paronomania! - Reginald Hill *m* 116

Raines, Barrett "Bear"
Strawman's Hammock - Darryl Wimberley *m* 216

Ramsay, Ben
Diamond in the Ruff - Emily Carmichael *r* 249

Rebus, John
The Falls - Ian Rankin *m* 178

Rhodes, Dan
A Romantic Way to Die - Bill Crider *m* 49

Rostnikov, Porfiry Petrovich
Murder on the Trans-Siberian Express - Stuart M. Kaminsky *m* 130

Russo, Jack
Open Season - Linda Howard *r* 302

Rutledge, Ian
Watchers of Time - Charles Todd *m* 208
Watchers of Time - Charles Todd *t* 943

Ryan, Miles
A Bend in the Road - Nicholas Sparks *c* 1200

Slider, Bill
Blood Sinister - Cynthia Harrod-Eagles *m* 104

Smith, Paavo
Bell, Cook, and Candle - Joanne Pence *m* 170

St-Cyr, Jean-Louis
Kaleidoscope - J. Robert Janes *m* 126
Kaleidoscope - J. Robert Janes *t* 888

Stone, Gabriel
The Power of Love - Margaret Daley *i* 987

Stone, Hawk
Born Brave - Ruth Wind *r* 422

Stone, Jesse
Death in Paradise - Robert B. Parker *m* 168

Sullivan, Daniel
Murphy's Law - Rhys Bowen *m* 24

Swagger, Earl
Pale Horse Coming - Stephen Hunter *m* 122
Pale Horse Coming - Stephen Hunter *t* 887
Pale Horse Coming - Stephen Hunter *c* 1127

Swenson, Lark
Cold Hunter's Moon - K.C. Greenlief *m* 90

Taber, Dylan
True Confessions - Rachel Gibson *r* 292

Talley, Jeff
Hostage - Robert Crais *c* 1096
Hostage - Robert Crais *m* 47

Thackeray, Michael
Skeleton at the Feast - Patricia Hall *m* 97

Todd, Ripley
Heaven and Earth - Nora Roberts *r* 383

Todd, Zach
Dance upon the Air - Nora Roberts *r* 382

Tolliver, Jeffrey
Blindsighted - Karin Slaughter *m* 197

Travis
Bikini Planet - David Garnett *s* 752

Turner, Paul
Sex and Murder.com - Mark Richard Zubro *m* 221

Tyrell, Keith
A Fine and Private Place - Freda Davies *m* 55

Watkins, Claire
Glare Ice - Mary Logue *m* 145

Wren, Susan
A Cold Christmas - Charlene Weir *m* 212

Zheng, Indigo
Alien Taste - Wen Spencer *s* 801

POLITICAL FIGURE

Anderson, Tom
Chasing the Devil's Tail - David Fulmer *m* 73
Chasing the Devil's Tail - David Fulmer *t* 867

Aslow
Scorch - A.D. Nauman *s* 782

Austin, Daryn
The Justice - Angela Elwell Hunt *i* 1004

Bryant, Wynn
Drummer in the Dark - T. Davis Bunn *i* 976

Burr, Aaron
Treason - David Nevin *t* 912

Cabral, Agustin
The Feast of the Goat - Mario Vargas Llosa *t* 948

Calhoun, Jamie
Halfway to Heaven - Susan Wiggs *r* 419

Conway, Roscoe Owens
Roscoe - William Kennedy *t* 897

Harding, Warren G.
Carter Beats the Devil - Glen David Gold *t* 874

Harris, Eve
The Manhattan Hunt Club - John Saul *h* 687

Madison, James
Treason - David Nevin *t* 912

McCall, Patsy
Roscoe - William Kennedy *t* 897

Roosevelt, Franklin D.
Murder at the President's Door - Elliott Roosevelt *t* 928

Smith, Loren
Valhalla Rising - Clive Cussler *c* 1097

Trujillo, Rafael
The Feast of the Goat - Mario Vargas Llosa *t* 948
The Feast of the Goat - Mario Vargas Llosa *c* 1211

POSTAL WORKER

Amir
Emigre Journeys - Abdullah Hussein *c* 1129

Prophet, Callida "Callie"
Heaven Sent - Rachel Wilson *r* 421

PREGNANT TEENAGER

Elvia
Highwire Moon - Susan Straight *c* 1205

Price, Virginia
Last Year's River - Allen Morris Jones *t* 891
Last Year's River - Allen Morris Jones *w* 467

PREHISTORIC HUMAN

Qumalix
Call Down the Stars - Sue Harrison *t* 879

Yikaas
Call Down the Stars - Sue Harrison *t* 879

PRISONER

Aari
Acorna's Search - Anne McCaffrey *s* 772

Cripps, Byron
Leaving Disneyland - Alexander Parsons *c* 1179

Fhassin
Nekropolis - Maureen McHugh *s* 774

Haas, Norman
Cold - John Smolens *c* 1199

Kane, Doc
Leaving Disneyland - Alexander Parsons *c* 1179

Kiru
Bikini Planet - David Garnett *s* 752

Llyr, Seth
Brothers of Cain - Miriam Grace Monfredo *t* 909

Savi
Shadow of the Seer - Michael Scott Rohan *f* 595

PRIVATEER

Ludlow, Harry
The Devil's Own Luck - David Donachie *t* 853
The Dying Trade - David Donachie *t* 854

Ludlow, James
The Devil's Own Luck - David Donachie *t* 853
The Dying Trade - David Donachie *t* 854

PRODUCER

Bracewell, Nicholas
The Devil's Apprentice - Edward Marston *m* 148

PROFESSOR

Babineau, Gerard
Fighting Gravity - Peggy Rambach *c* 1184

Barrett, Bel
Midlife Can Be Murder - Jane Isenberg *m* 124

Deonne, Vita
The Lecturer's Tale - James Hynes *h* 649

Dromgoole, Juno
Burning Down the House - Lev Rafael *m* 176

Eschbach, Johan
Ghost of the White Nights - L.E. Modesitt Jr. *s* 778

Harrow, Andre
Beasts - Joyce Carol Oates *c* 1173

Hawkins, Ray
A Family for Jana - Eileen Berger *i* 968

Hoffman, Nick
Burning Down the House - Lev Rafael *m* 176

Humboldt, Nelson
The Lecturer's Tale - James Hynes *h* 649

Knight, Roger
Emerald Aisle - Ralph McInerny *m* 156

Lukacs, Jerry
Pyramid Scheme - David Freer *s* 751

Mallory, Amy
Broken Honor - Patricia Potter *r* 373

Martens, Tristan
The Deadwood Beetle - Mylene Dressler *c* 1106

McCully, Esther
Sunrise on Stradbury Square - Doris Elaine Fell *i* 992

Medina, Mercedes
Light Coming Back - Ann Wadsworth *c* 1213

Moriarity, James
The Great Game - Michael Kurland *t* 899

Paxton, Brace
In the Dark - Richard Laymon *h* 663

Peaslee, Nathaniel Wingate
The Shadow out of Time - H.P. Lovecraft *h* 670

Plant, Melrose
The Blue Last - Martha Grimes *m* 92

Singer, Judith
Long Time No See - Susan Isaacs *c* 1131

Solanka, Malik "Solly"
Fury - Salman Rushdie *c* 1190

Valera, Luis
Treasures of the Sun - T.V. Olsen *w* 487

Waterston, Michael
Revenge of the Wrought-Iron Flamingos - Donna Andrews *m* 6

Weissman, Morton
The Lecturer's Tale - James Hynes *h* 649

Wilde, John
Sarah's Window - Janice Graham *w* 457

PROSPECTOR

Brandon, Terry
By Flare of Northern Lights - Tim Champlin *w* 439

Conrad, Milton
By Flare of Northern Lights - Tim Champlin *w* 439

Morgette, Dolf
Morgette on the Barbary Coast - G.G. Boyer *w* 429

O'Connell, Annie
By Flare of Northern Lights - Tim Champlin *w* 439

PROSTITUTE

Price, Maude
Outcasts - Tim McGuire *w* 480

St. James, Claudie
Back in Kansas - Debra Salonen *r* 387

PSYCHIC

Adams, Chelsea
Eyes of Elisha - Brandilyn Collins *i* 981

Chase, Elizabeth
Ashes of Aries - Martha C. Lawrence *m* 140

Dolan, Sophie
Just West of Heaven - Kathleen Kane *r* 313

Gordie, Elspeth
Ashling - Isobelle Carmody *s* 732

Karan
The Way between the Worlds - Ian Irvine *f* 560

Karitska
Kaleidoscope - Dorothy Gilman *m* 79

Leynier, Corin
The Fall of Neskaya - Marion Zimmer Bradley *s* 725

Morgan, Mariana
Darkness at the Door - Catherine Dain *m* 52

Murphy, Sarah
To Tame a Wild Heart - Tracy Fobes *r* 281

Thorne, Adrian
Heart of Night - Taylor Chase *r* 254

PSYCHOLOGIST

Cameron, Fiona
Killing the Shadows - Val McDermid *m* 154

Greenbaum, Nancy
Ghost Killer - Scott Chandler *h* 627

O'Neill, Meghann
Crimson Kiss - Trisha Baker *h* 617

PUBLIC RELATIONS

Hagbolt, Paul
The Wanderer - Fritz Leiber *s* 767

Raisin, Agatha
Agatha Raisin and the Love from Hell - M.C. Beaton *m* 14

Schwartz, Marianne
All That Counts - Georg M. Oswald *c* 1177

PUBLISHER

Aigner, Rafe
The Renegades: Rafe - Genell Dellin *r* 270

Buckingham, Floyd
The Other Adonis - Frank Deford *t* 849

Devlin, Jack
Suddenly You - Lisa Kleypas *r* 319

Mathers, Terry
The Webster Chronicle - Daniel Akst *c* 1066

Plumtree, Alex
Uncatalogued - Julie Kaewert *m* 128

Reed, Noah
Envy - Sandra Brown *c* 1086
Envy - Sandra Brown *r* 245

Sloane, Todd
Looking for Laura - Judith Arnold *r* 226

RADIO PERSONALITY

GoodNews
How to Be Good - Nick Hornby *c* 1126

Grant, Ellen
Teeth - Edo van Belkom *h* 705

Hardin, Jeff
A Prince of a Guy - Sheila Rabe *r* 376

Leyden, Henry
Black House - Stephen King *c* 1140

Powell, Spencer
Bring Me a Dream - Robyn Amos *r* 224

Stonewall, Kate
A Prince of a Guy - Sheila Rabe *r* 376

Wellman, Richard
The Prodigy - Alton Gansky *h* 637

RAILROAD WORKER

Lambert, Alfred
The Corrections - Jonathan Franzen *c* 1113

RAKE

Calhoun, Jamie
Halfway to Heaven - Susan Wiggs *r* 419

Casanova, Giacomo
Imagining Don Giovanni - Anthony J. Rudel *t* 929

Cynster, Sebastian
The Promise in a Kiss - Stephanie Laurens *r* 329

de Vere, Gareth
Fortune's Lady - Evelyn Richardson *r* 379

Grayson
The Rake and the Wallflower - Allison Lane *r* 325

Hampton, Robert George Colter
A Reckless Encounter - Rosemary Rogers *r* 385

Mannion, Adam
The Sleeping Beauty - Jacqueline Navin *r* 360

Marchnight, Henry
Lady Polly - Nicola Cornick *r* 259

Moreland, Jared
A Devilish Husband - Alana Clayton *r* 257

Rowley, Eppingham Julian
Fallen - Celeste Bradley *r* 241

RANCHER

Aguilar, Matteo
The Baron War - Jory Sherman *w* 503

Barlow, Lady
Lockwood - Lauran Paine *w* 492

Baron, Martin
The Baron War - Jory Sherman *w* 503

Benton, Reed
Summer Moon - Jill Marie Landis *w* 471

Catlin, Jonathan
The Texan's Dream - Jodi Thomas *r* 415

Copperton, Elizabeth
Charlie and the Sir - Frank Roderus *w* 499

Coulter, Jake
Sweet Nothings - Catherine Anderson *r* 225

Ellis, Trade
Crack Shot - Sinclair Browning *m* 28

Fontana, Jose
The Survival of Juan Oro - Max Brand *w* 434

Freeman, Monte
Monte's Revenge - Eugene C. Vories *w* 509

Hale, Bill
The Years of Fear - Fred Grove *w* 460

Hardman, Jard
Open Range - Zane Grey *w* 458

Hawks, Clayton
Man from Wyoming - Dane Coolidge *w* 448

Holloway, Lucinda
Destiny Valley - Fred Grove *w* 459

Kerry, Ethan
Behold a Red Horse - Cotton Smith *w* 504

Logan, Dave
Destiny Valley - Fred Grove *w* 459

MacIntyre, Adam
This Time Forever - Carol Steward *i* 1052

Majors, Ike
Caleb's Price - Troy D. Smith *w* 505

McLain, Chance
The Secret - Kat Martin *r* 347

Mitchell, Ben
The Gift of the Mestizo - Marjorie M. McGinley *w* 479

Moon, Charlie
White Shell Woman - James D. Doss *m* 61

Norton
Monte's Revenge - Eugene C. Vories *w* 509

O'Sullivan, Kate
Legends Lake - JoAnn Ross *r* 386

Person, Grant
On the Night Plain - J. Robert Lennon *c* 1146
On the Night Plain - J. Robert Lennon *w* 473

Person, Max
On the Night Plain - J. Robert Lennon *w* 473
On the Night Plain - J. Robert Lennon *c* 1146

Sherman, Will
The Reckoning - John McLain *w* 481

Slaughter, John
Miracle of the Jacal - Robert J. Randisi *w* 497

Steele, Ike
Heart of the Beast - Joyce Weatherford *w* 511

Steele, Iris
Heart of the Beast - Joyce Weatherford *w* 511

Stennett, Jackson
Jackson's Way - Leslie LaFoy *r* 324

REAL ESTATE AGENT

Haney, Cheryl
The Money-Whipped Steer-Job Three-Jack Give-Up Artist - Dan Jenkins *c* 1132

REBEL

Andruz, Thelina
Empire & Ecolitan - L.E. Modesitt Jr. *s* 777

Augur
Augur's Teacher - Sherwood Smith *s* 800

Cathan
Heresy - Anselm Audley *s* 718

Dynes, Sam
The Night of the Triffids - Simon Clark *s* 735

Laubon, Meryl
Empire & Ecolitan - L.E. Modesitt Jr. *s* 777

Morrigern, Tami
Bolo Strike - William H. Keith Jr. *s* 765

O'Rourke, Liam
Out There - Gerald Rose *s* 793

Wright, Jimjoy Earle
Empire & Ecolitan - L.E. Modesitt Jr. *s* 777

RECEPTIONIST

MacDonald, Layla
Doomed to Repeat It - d.g.k. goldberg *h* 641

RECLUSE

Kent, Jason
Lt. Kent: Lone Wolf - Judith Lyons *r* 341

Mestizo
The Gift of the Mestizo - Marjorie M. McGinley *w* 479

Rathford, Helena
The Sleeping Beauty - Jacqueline Navin *r* 360

REFUGEE

Boll, Anton
The Ash Garden - Dennis Bock *c* 1078

Boll, Sophie
The Ash Garden - Dennis Bock *c* 1078

RELATIVE

Black
My Name Is Red - Orhan Pamuk *c* 1178

Burke, Josie
Bombingham - Anthony Grooms *c* 1119

Carole
Leap of Faith - Danielle Steel *c* 1203

Cher
A Place Called Wiregrass - Michael Morris *i* 1029

Clark, Matriece
What You Owe Me - Bebe Moore Campbell *c* 1089

Columbus, C.J.
Columbus Slaughters Braves - Mark Friedman *c* 1114

Columbus, Joe
Columbus Slaughters Braves - Mark Friedman *c* 1114

Drummond, Wade
All Families Are Psychotic - Douglas Coupland *c* 1094

Drummond-Fournier, Sarah
All Families Are Psychotic - Douglas Coupland *c* 1094

Elliot, Angelina Marguerite
From the Dust Returned - Ray Bradbury *c* 1082

Elliot, Einar
From the Dust Returned - Ray Bradbury *c* 1082

Elvia
Highwire Moon - Susan Straight *c* 1205

Emily
Cane River - Lalita Tademy *c* 1207

Fox, Nicholas
Aunt Dimity: Detective - Nancy Atherton *m* 9

Hernandez, Alicia
Fire Lilies - Cynthia Leal Massey *w* 476

Kerry, Luther
Behold a Red Horse - Cotton Smith *w* 504

Lambert, Gary
The Corrections - Jonathan Franzen *c* 1113

Lily
Eva Moves the Furniture - Margot Livesey *c* 1148

Looby, Nick
Dugan under Ground - Tom De Haven *c* 1100

Mev
Why Did I Ever? - Mary Robison *c* 1188

Michael
Lightning Field - Dana Spiotta *c* 1202

Mitchell, Lucy
The Gift of the Mestizo - Marjorie M. McGinley *w* 479

Morgan
Cape Refuge - Terri Blackstock *i* 970

Paulie
Why Did I Ever? - Mary Robison *c* 1188

Pavel
Requiem for a Lost Empire - Andrei Makine *c* 1151
Requiem for a Lost Empire - Andrei Makine *c* 1151

Philomene
Cane River - Lalita Tademy *c* 1207

Sherman, Ellen
The Reckoning - John McLain *w* 481

Steinke, Barry
Great American Plain - Gary Sernovitz *c* 1195

Tardieu, Bonne
Mirabilis - Susann Cokal *c* 1091

Thrale, Queeney
According to Queeney - Beryl Bainbridge *c* 1069

Trujillo, Ramfis
The Feast of the Goat - Mario Vargas Llosa *c* 1211

Van Urden, Ursula
The Savage Girl - Alex Shakar *c* 1196

Wolf, Anne
Coldwater - Mardi McConnochie *c* 1156
Coldwater - Mardi McConnochie *t* 904

Wolf, Charlotte
Coldwater - Mardi McConnochie *t* 904
Coldwater - Mardi McConnochie *c* 1156

Wolf, Emily
Coldwater - Mardi McConnochie *c* 1156
Coldwater - Mardi McConnochie *t* 904

Zanzibar
Jewelry Talks - Richard Klein *c* 1142

RELIGIOUS

Bennett, Christine
Happy Birthday Murder - Lee Harris *i* 996

Bias
Murder at the Panionic Games - Michael B. Edwards *t* 859

Blake, Katherine
A Family All Her Own - Bonnie K. Winn *i* 1061

Bolesseto, Simila
The Red of His Shadow - Mayra Montero *c* 1164

Borgia, Rodrigo
The Family - Mario Puzo *t* 916
The Family - Mario Puzo *c* 1183

Bruce, Jane
Something More - Paul Cornell *s* 738

Callahan, Rose
Dancing Dead - Deborah Woodworth *i* 1062

Cian
Act of Mercy - Peter Tremayne *t* 944

Clergue, Pierre
The Good Men - Charmaine Craig *t* 844

de Bracineaux, Renaud
The Mystic Rose - Stephen R. Lawhead *f* 570
The Mystic Rose - Stephen R. Lawhead *t* 901

Decimus, Victor
Vampire Vow - Michael Schiefelbein *h* 690

Dionysos
Thrice Bound - Roberta Gellis *f* 547

Egan, Byron
Yonder Stands Your Orphan - Barry Hannah *c* 1121

Eloise of Argent
The Husband Test - Betina Krahn *r* 321

Fairchild, Faith
The Body in the Bonfire - Katherine Hall Page *i* 1037

Fidelma
Act of Mercy - Peter Tremayne *m* 209
Act of Mercy - Peter Tremayne *t* 944

Fox, George
Sea of Glory - Ken Wales *i* 1056

Frevisse
The Clerk's Tale - Margaret Frazer *t* 865
The Clerk's Tale - Margaret Frazer *m* 70

Goode, Alex
Sea of Glory - Ken Wales *i* 1056
Sea of Glory - Ken Wales *t* 953

Greenberg, Arthur
The Thirty-Third Hour - Mitchell Chefitz *i* 978

Gui, Bernard
The Good Men - Charmaine Craig *t* 844

Gwynneve
Confessions of a Pagan Nun - Kate Horsley *t* 886

Hastings, Andrew
Who Killed the Curate? - Joan Coggin *m* 36

Howell, Peter
Shadow Valley Rising - Stephen Overholser *w* 488

Karelli, Tony
Redeeming Claire - Cynthia Rutledge *i* 1045

Kavanagh, Tim
In This Mountain - Jan Karon *i* 1007

l'Estrange, Sybil
My Lady de Burgh - Deborah Simmons *r* 396

Lucas
The Crusader - Michael A. Eisner *t* 860

Luke
Vampire Vow - Michael Schiefelbein *h* 690

Merryt
Revelation - Elizabeth Haydon *f* 555

Mica
Night Players - P.D. Cacek *h* 625

Michael
Vampire Vow - Michael Schiefelbein *h* 690

Miradel
World Fall - Douglas Niles *f* 583

Mompellion, Michael
Year of Wonders - Geraldine Brooks *c* 1083
Year of Wonders - Geraldine Brooks *t* 832

O'Malley, John
The Thunder Keeper - Margaret Coel *m* 35
The Thunder Keeper - Margaret Coel *w* 444

Paul
The Gaius Diary - Gene Edwards *i* 990

Penthievre of Chalandrey, Marie
The Wolf Hunt - Gillian Bradshaw *t* 831

Poling, Clark
Sea of Glory - Ken Wales *i* 1056
Sea of Glory - Ken Wales *t* 953

Rahl, Kahlan
The Pillars of Creation - Terry Goodkind *f* 550

Reve, Zule
The Red of His Shadow - Mayra Montero *c* 1164

Richard of Warefeld
The Marriage Bed - Claudia Dain *r* 266

Roth, Jacob
Devil's Island - John Hagee *i* 994

Russo, Joseph
What to Do about Annie? - Millie Criswell *r* 264

Sarhaddon
Heresy - Anselm Audley *s* 718

Starr, Noah
Child of Promise - Kathleen Morgan *i* 1025

Tiphan
Brother of the Dragon - Paul B. Thompson *f* 604

Washington, John
Sea of Glory - Ken Wales *t* 953

RESEARCHER

Lowe, Angela
Angel Face - Suzanne Forster *r* 283

Milner, Suzanne
Listen to the Shadows - Danuta Reah *m* 179

Soto, Tanger
The Nautical Chart - Arturo Perez-Reverte *m* 171
The Nautical Chart - Arturo Perez-Reverte *c* 1182

RESISTANCE FIGHTER

Savage, Brook
The Savages in Love and War - Fred Mustard Stewart *t* 937

RESTAURATEUR

Ahrens, Gena
Wildflowers - Robin Jones Gunn *i* 993

Bentley, Stuart
Lockwood - Lauran Paine *w* 492

Holloway, Jenny
In Too Deep - Janelle Taylor *r* 413

Lee, Heaven
Red Beans and Vice - Lou Jane Temple *m* 207

Lorene
Lightning Field - Dana Spiotta *c* 1202

Poisson, Charly
Prepared for Murder - Cecile Lamalle *m* 138

Thomas, Charlotte "Charlie"
The Widow - Anne Stuart *r* 411

Thornbury, Winona
The Secret Life of Connor Monahan - Elizabeth Bevarly *r* 235

REVOLUTIONARY

Redmagne, Methuselah
Sparrowhawk—Jack Frake - Edward Cline *t* 840

Skelly, Augustus
Sparrowhawk—Jack Frake - Edward Cline *t* 840

ROGUE

FitzAllen, Kiernan
The Prisoner Bride - Susan Spencer Paul *r* 368

Hawkins, Brody
Sarah and the Rogue - DeLoras Scott *r* 391

Mannion, Adam
The Sleeping Beauty - Jacqueline Navin *r* 360

ROOMMATE

Church, Stewart
About the Author - John Colapinto *c* 1092

Morrison, Erik
The Watermark - Travis Thrasher *i* 1054

ROYALTY

Albert Victor
Goodnight, Sweet Prince - David Dickinson *t* 851

Edward, Prince of Wales
Goodnight, Sweet Prince - David Dickinson *t* 851

Eirik
Mother of Kings - Poul Anderson *t* 818

Emrys
Daughter of Lir - Judith Tarr *t* 940

Guenevere
The Child of the Holy Grail - Rosalind Miles *t* 907

Guinevere
The Dragon Queen - Alice Borchardt *t* 829
The Dragon Queen - Alice Borchardt *f* 528
Lancelot Du Lethe - J. Robert King *f* 566

Gunnhild
Mother of Kings - Poul Anderson *t* 818

Imoshen
Dark Dreams - Cory Daniells *r* 267

John Lackland
Pride of Kings - Judith Tarr *t* 941
Pride of Kings - Judith Tarr *f* 603

Kerim, Abdul
The Girl from the Golden Horn - Kurban Said *c* 1191

Leonie of Mirandeau
Once a Princess - Veronica Sattler *r* 388

Reothe
Dark Dreams - Cory Daniells *r* 267

Richard, Duke of Gloucester
The Goldsmith's Daughter - Kate Sedley *t* 933

Ulyanova, Varya
Elusive Passion - Kathryn Smith *r* 402

Von Volzenburg, Vanessa
The Marine and the Princess - Cathie Linz *r* 334

RULER

All Mother
Ice - Stephen Bowkett *s* 724

Arthur
The Dragon Queen - Alice Borchardt *t* 829
The Dragon Queen - Alice Borchardt *f* 528
Lancelot Du Lethe - J. Robert King *f* 566

Byrnak
Shadowkings - Michael Cobley *f* 535

Carpathia, Nicolae
Desecration - Tim LaHaye *i* 1016

Christian VII
The Royal Physician's Visit - Per Olov Enquist *t* 862
The Royal Physician's Visit - Per Olov Enquist *c* 1110

Cohen, Genghiz
The Last Hero - Terry Pratchett *f* 588

Connavar
Midnight Falcon - David Gemmell *f* 548

Conor
Bloodtide - Melvin Burgess *s* 730

David
Queenmaker - India Edghill *t* 858

Deslucido, Damian
The Fall of Neskaya - Marion Zimmer Bradley *s* 725

Eiriksson, Gamli
Mother of Kings - Poul Anderson *f* 517

Elizabeth I
Queen of Ambition - Fiona Buckley *t* 834

Erius
The Bone Doll's Twin - Lynn Flewelling *f* 544

Fielding
The Night of the Triffids - Simon Clark *s* 735

Garric
Mistress of the Catacombs - David Drake *f* 541

Helananthe
The Obsidian Tower - Freda Warrington *f* 609

Henry VI
Knight Errant - R. Garcia y Robertson *t* 869

Joseph
Marching through Peachtree - Harry Turtledove *f* 606

Justinian I
Three for a Letter - Mary Reed *t* 920

Kenrick
Rebel's Cage - Kate Jacoby *f* 561

Meleager
In the Shape of a Boar - Lawrence Norfolk *t* 913

Niall
Children of the Lion - Jennifer Roberson *f* 591

Pendragon, Arthur
The Child of the Holy Grail - Rosalind Miles *t* 907

Richard the Lionheart
Pride of Kings - Judith Tarr *t* 941

Saul
Queenmaker - India Edghill *t* 858

Shaddam IV
House Corrino - Brian Herbert *s* 757

Tash
The Way of the Rose - Valery Leith *f* 572

Tehanu
The Other Wind - Ursula K. Le Guin *f* 571

Theodora
Three for a Letter - Mary Reed *t* 920

Tratal
Wit'ch Gate - James Clemens *f* 534

Tulkhan
Dark Dreams - Cory Daniells *r* 267

Umar ibn al-Khattab
The Rock - Kanan Makiya *t* 902

Urdo
The King's Name - Jo Walton *f* 608

RUNAWAY

Colling, Lisette
French Leave - Sheri Cobb South *r* 404

SAILOR

Bremml, Nicholas
The Yellow Sailor - Steve Weiner *t* 954

Bywaters, Frederick
Fred & Edie - Jill Dawson *t* 848

Carleton, Jonathan
Moontide - Erin Patrick *h* 681

Coy, Manuel
The Nautical Chart - Arturo Perez-Reverte *c* 1182
The Nautical Chart - Arturo Perez-Reverte *m* 171

Gierek, Melanie
Moontide - Erin Patrick *h* 681

Gordon, Henry
Moontide - Erin Patrick *h* 681

Gorecki, Jacek
The Yellow Sailor - Steve Weiner *t* 954

Loner, Wolf
The Wanderer - Fritz Leiber *s* 767

Madoc
Circle of Stars - Anna Lee Waldo *w* 510

SALESWOMAN

Ashe, Arel
Scorch - A.D. Nauman *s* 782

Pembroke, Jayne
When Jayne Met Erik - Elizabeth Bevarly *r* 236

Treene, Harriet
The Very Comely Countess - Miranda Jarrett *r* 307

SALOON HOSTESS

Whateley, Bess
Watch by Moonlight - Kate Hawks *t* 881

SALOON KEEPER/OWNER

Hardman, Jard
Open Range - Zane Grey *w* 458

Rafferty, Shadwell
Sherlock Holmes and the Secret Alliance - Larry Millett *t* 908
Sherlock Holmes and the Secret Alliance - Larry Millett *m* 158

Rhinegold, Valerie
Teeth - Edo van Belkom *h* 705

Simone, Lena
Midnight Bayou - Nora Roberts *c* 1187

SCHOLAR

Casuel
The Warrior's Bond - Juliet E. McKenna *f* 578

Fidelma
Act of Mercy - Peter Tremayne *m* 209
Act of Mercy - Peter Tremayne *t* 944

Jakob
In the Shape of a Boar - Lawrence Norfolk *c* 1171

Jesson, Henry James III
The Grand Complication - Allen Kurzweil *c* 1144

Llech
The Prince of Shadow - Curt Benjamin *f* 526

MacDougal, Charles
The Counterfeit Heinlein - Laurence M. Janiver *s* 763

Marais, Charles
The Dark Wing - Walter Hunt *s* 761

Raphael, Sebastian
London Bridges - Jane Stevenson *c* 1204

SCIENTIST

Albert
The Monsters of Morley Manor - Bruce Coville *f* 538

Anders, Mariella
The Secret of Life - Paul J. McAuley *s* 771

Aspinall, Andrea
The Company of Strangers - Robert Wilson *m* 215
The Company of Strangers - Robert Wilson *t* 960

Audubon, John James
Audubon's Watch - John Gregory Brown *c* 1085
Audubon's Watch - John Gregory Brown *t* 833

Boll, Anton
The Ash Garden - Dennis Bock *c* 1078

Booke, MacAllister
Heaven and Earth - Nora Roberts *r* 383

Brandt, Emil
The Good German - Joseph Kanon *t* 892

Brown, Penn
The Secret of Life - Paul J. McAuley *s* 771

Cabot, Abigail
Halfway to Heaven - Susan Wiggs *r* 419

Churchill, Jack
Always Forever - Mark Chadbourn *f* 533

Davenport, Teddy
Rivers of Gold - Tracie Peterson *i* 1042

Emil
The Good German - Joseph Kanon *c* 1135

Froude, Danfin
Homefall - Chris Bunch *s* 729

Gautreaux, Emile
Audubon's Watch - John Gregory Brown *t* 833
Audubon's Watch - John Gregory Brown *c* 1085

Green, Briony
Blessed Baby - Lois Richer *i* 1043

Hansen, Em
Fault Line - Sarah Andrews *m* 7

James, Alicia
Alicia's Song - Susan Plunkett *r* 371

Kates, Cameron
Minutes to Burn - Gregg Andrew Hurwitz *s* 762

Kates, Justin
Minutes to Burn - Gregg Andrew Hurwitz *s* 762

Kaufmann, Linda
Frankenstein: The Legacy - Christopher Schildt *h* 691

Lefkowitz
Night of the Bat - Paul Zindel *h* 714

Levy, Daniel
Frankenstein: The Legacy - Christopher Schildt *h* 691

Meisner, Allen
The Getaway Special - Jerry Oltion *s* 785

Moriarity, James
The Great Game - Michael Kurland *t* 899

Murphy, Zack
ChronoSpace - Allen Steele *s* 802

Padilla, Eric
Soldiers - John Dalmas *s* 742

Potter, Calvin
The Reproductive System - John Sladek *s* 798

Sarda, Leo
Martian Knightlife - James P. Hogan *s* 759

Sharples, Claire
The Tumbleweed Murders - Rebecca Rothenberg *m* 189

Sherman, Rebecca
First Landing - Robert Zubrin *s* 814

Smith, Gail
In the Company of Others - Julie E. Czerneda *s* 740

Sugarman, Whitley
The King of the Sun - A.A. McFedries *s* 773

Tremelo, Miguel
Pyramid Scheme - David Freer *s* 751

Wilde, John
Sarah's Window - Janice Graham *w* 457

Ye, Anchee
The Secret of Life - Paul J. McAuley *s* 771

SCOUT

Carson, Kit
Moon Medicine - Mike Blakely *t* 827

Morgan, Stuart
Bear Paw - Gene Mullins *w* 484

SEA CAPTAIN

Everly, Jonathan
The Traitor's Daughter - Elizabeth Powell *r* 374

Lambert, Darcy
The Sea Sprite - Ruth Langan *r* 328

Montgomery, Harrison
Mr. Montgomery's Quest - Martha Kirkland *r* 318

Newton, John
The Infidel - Joe Musser *i* 1031

Patten, Joshua
The Captain's Wife - Douglas Kelley *t* 894

SEAMSTRESS

Nichols, Jane
Sugarplum Surprises - Elisabeth Fairchild *r* 275

Spoon, Emily
Once an Outlaw - Jill Gregory *r* 294

Tremayne, Amanda
The Traitor's Daughter - Elizabeth Powell *r* 374

SECRETARY

Brooks, Colleen
Magic Time - Marc Scott Zicree *f* 614

Delaney, Christine
When Tomorrow Comes - Janette Oke *i* 1034

Gates, Eugenia
The Black Eye - Constance Little *m* 144

Griffin, Madeline "Maddie"
Dangerously Irresistible - Kristin Gabriel *r* 289

Hoyle, Priscilla
Creeping Venom - Sheila Pim *m* 173

Jenkins, Grace
Too Much Temptation - Lori Foster *r* 286

SECURITY OFFICER

Clayton, Tom
Adventures in Time and Space with Max Merriwell - Pat Murphy *s* 781

Deveaux, Samantha
Insatiable - Julie Elizabeth Leto *r* 333

Jim
Second Chances - Susan Shwartz *s* 796

Manning, Jack
Deathday - William C. Dietz *s* 746

Mirabel, Tanner
Chasm City - Alastair Reynolds *s* 789

Murdoch, Bill
Time Future - Maxine McArthur *s* 770

SERIAL KILLER

Burnside, Charles
Black House - Stephen King *h* 659

SERVANT

Black
The Dragon Society - Lawrence Watt-Evans *f* 610

Delange, Genevieve
The Looking Glass - Michele Roberts *t* 925

Firth, Anna
Year of Wonders - Geraldine Brooks *t* 832

Hulda
The Silent Woman - Susan M. Dodd *t* 852

Paxton, Aubrey "Bree"
Letters from an Age of Reason - Nora Hague *t* 877

Rojire
A Feast in Exile - Chelsea Quinn Yarbro *h* 713

Roundtree, Clarissa
Smuggler's Moon - Bruce Alexander *t* 815

SETTLER

Townsend, Ray
Worthy of Riches - Bonnie Leon *i* 1017

SHAMAN

Destea, Clifford
Blackening Song - Aimee Thurlo *w* 506

Perika, Daisy
White Shell Woman - James D. Doss *m* 61

Vasilyevich, Yuda
Children of the Shaman - Jessica Rydill *f* 596

SHIPOWNER

Bernai, Julius
The Yellow Sailor - Steve Weiner *t* 954

SIDEKICK

Augustus, Caesar
The Ironclad Alibi - Michael Kilian *t* 898
The Ironclad Alibi - Michael Kilian *m* 133

Dashiell
The Long Good Boy - Carol Lea Benjamin *m* 16

Dougal's Lord Carstairs
The Mouse in the Mountain - Norbert Davis *m* 56

Fitzgerald, Johnny
Goodnight, Sweet Prince - David Dickinson *m* 58

Giordino, Al
Valhalla Rising - Clive Cussler *c* 1097

Pine, Leonard
Captains Outrageous - Joe R. Lansdale *w* 472

Plant, Melrose
The Blue Last - Martha Grimes *m* 92

Tinkerman, Dobie
A Good Town - Douglas Hirt *w* 462

Valera, Luis
Treasures of the Sun - T.V. Olsen *w* 487

Watson, John
Sherlock Holmes and the Giant Rat of Sumatra - Alan Vanneman *m* 210
Sherlock Holmes and the Secret Alliance - Larry Millett *m* 158
Sherlock Holmes and the Secret Alliance - Larry Millett *t* 908

SINGER

Adler, Irene
Chapel Noir - Carole Nelson Douglas *t* 856
Chapel Noir - Carole Nelson Douglas *m* 62

Braxton, Yancey
Any Way the Wind Blows - E. Lynn Harris *c* 1122

Duke, Rachel
The Doctor's Miracle - Anna Schmidt *i* 1046

Eschbach, Llysette
Ghost of the White Nights - L.E. Modesitt Jr. *s* 778

Franklin, Kinkaide
To Rome with Love - Debra White Smith *i* 1049

Harvey, Cora
Rhythms - Donna Hill *t* 884

Hayes, Blair
Written on the Wind - Judith Pella *i* 1040

Lowe, Eliza
Beloved Protector - Linda O'Brien *r* 361

Mahar, Mavis
First Lady - Michael Malone *c* 1153

Michaels, Sara
Judging Sara - Cynthia Rutledge *i* 1044

Rhapsody
Destiny - Elizabeth Haydon *f* 554

Stein, Isabel
Aria - Susan Segal *c* 1194

Williams, John "Loverboy"
Just Say No! - Omar Tyree *c* 1210

SINGLE PARENT

Bartling, Gemma
A Rose by the Door - Deborah Bedford *i* 967

Blanche
Mirabilis - Susann Cokal *c* 1091

Bradshaw, Kate
Dear Cupid - Julie Ortolon *r* 363

Buscarsela, Filomena
Red House - K.J.A. Wishnia *m* 217

Carlson, Michael
A Family All Her Own - Bonnie K. Winn *i* 1061

Demens, Ty
Blessed Baby - Lois Richer *i* 1043

Farrell, Elspeth Brodie
Echoes of Lies - Jo Bannister *m* 11

Fenwick, Andrew
Fatal Legacy - Elizabeth Corley *m* 43

Frazier, Zac
Love One Another - Valerie Hansen *i* 995

Hill, Roy
Last of the Dixie Heroes - Peter Abrahams *m* 1

Holloway, Jenny
In Too Deep - Janelle Taylor *r* 413

Hudson, Jane
The Lake of Dead Languages - Carol Goodman *m* 82

Ives, Hannah
Occasion of Revenge - Marcia Talley *m* 205

Jenson, Jana
A Family for Jana - Eileen Berger *i* 968

Knight, Sebastian
Heaven on Earth - Marilyn Pappano *r* 366

Marker, Caleb
Alicia's Song - Susan Plunkett *r* 371

McGuiness, Libby
Do You Hear What I Hear? - Holly Jacobs *r* 306

McGuire, Cole
The Colorado Bride - Mary Burton *r* 247

Michaels, Rebecca
The Power of Love - Margaret Daley *i* 987

O'Keefe, Ben
Christmas Vows: $5.00 Extra - Lori Copeland *i* 983

Pigeon, Josie
Murder in the Forecast - Valerie Wolzien *m* 219

Ramsay, Ben
Diamond in the Ruff - Emily Carmichael *r* 249

Rollins, Kate
The Secret - Kat Martin *r* 347

Sheridan, Matthew
Heaven Sent - Jillian Hart *i* 997

Taylor, Rebecca
The Colorado Bride - Mary Burton *r* 247

Travis, Melanie
Once Bitten - Laurien Berenson *m* 17

SLAVE

Augustus, Caesar
The Ironclad Alibi - Michael Kilian *m* 133
The Ironclad Alibi - Michael Kilian *t* 898

Cato, Quintus Licinius
Under the Eagle - Simon Scarrow *t* 931

Cynara
The Wind Done Gone - Alice Randall *t* 918

Faith
Bloodlines - Fred D'Aguiar *t* 846

Freebody, Agate
The Wolf Pit - Marly Youmans *t* 964

Hariba
Nekropolis - Maureen McHugh *s* 774

Philomene
Cane River - Lalita Tademy *c* 1207

Shanty
The Way of the Coyote - Elmer Kelton *t* 895

Suzette
Cane River - Lalita Tademy *c* 1207

Tulsi Kil
A Feast in Exile - Chelsea Quinn Yarbro *t* 963

Washburn, Samuel
We Look Like Men of War - William R. Forstchen *t* 864

SMUGGLER

Caldwell, Brynn
Desire - Nicole Jordan *r* 309

Frake, Jack
Sparrowhawk—Jack Frake - Edward Cline *t* 840

Gilpatrick, Rance
Murder on the Minnesota - Conrad Allen *t* 816

Redmagne, Methuselah
Sparrowhawk—Jack Frake - Edward Cline *t* 840

Skelly, Augustus
Sparrowhawk—Jack Frake - Edward Cline t 840

SOCIAL WORKER

Cunningham, Cheryl
Another Summer - Georgia Bockoven r 239

Davis, Kate
Secrets of the Heart - Gail Gaymer Martin i 1022

Rowlands, Brianna
A Child Shall Lead Them - Carole Gift Page i 1036

SORCERER

Alder
The Other Wind - Ursula K. Le Guin f 571

Dagnarus
Guardians of the Lost - Margaret Weis f 611

De Lancre, Jedediah
A Lower Deep - Tom Piccirilli h 682

Denser
Nightchild - James Barclay f 523

Drachenfels, Constant
Drachenfels - Jack Yeovil f 613

Majere, Ulin
Dragon's Bluff - Mary H. Herbert f 556

Mendark
The Way between the Worlds - Ian Irvine f 560

Morthu
The King's Name - Jo Walton f 608

Nash
Rebel's Cage - Kate Jacoby f 561

Necromancer
A Lower Deep - Tom Piccirilli h 682

Planeswalker, Urza
Apocalypse - J. Robert King f 564

SORCERESS

Breanna
Swell Foop - Piers Anthony f 518

DeKathrine, Danielle
The Golden Sword - Fiona Patton f 586

Delora
Debt of Bones - Terry Goodkind f 549

Erienne
Nightchild - James Barclay f 523

Gallowglass, Cordelia
Here Be Monsters - Christopher Stasheff f 600

Jennsen
The Pillars of Creation - Terry Goodkind f 550

Lyanna
Nightchild - James Barclay f 523

Raven
The Black Chalice - Marie Jakober f 562

Stormlake, Ghleanna
Pool of Radiance - Carrie Bebris f 525

Torkay, Lucy
Dragon's Bluff - Mary H. Herbert f 556

SOUTHERN BELLE

Other
The Wind Done Gone - Alice Randall t 918

SPACEMAN

Erx
Starhawk - Mack Maloney s 769

Hunter, Hawk
Planet America - Mack Maloney s 768

Pardell, Aaron
In the Company of Others - Julie E. Czerneda s 740

Ryker, John
Out There - Gerald Rose s 793

Rymar, Ben
Dreamer - Steven Harper s 755

Tomm
Planet America - Mack Maloney s 768

Toomagian, Aron
Out There - Gerald Rose s 793

Weaver, Kendi
Dreamer - Steven Harper s 755

SPACESHIP CAPTAIN

Ara
Dreamer - Steven Harper s 755

Freer, Nathanael
Appleseed - John Clute s 736

Haussmann, Sky
Chasm City - Alastair Reynolds s 789

Heikkonen
Second Chances - Susan Shwartz s 796

Multx, Zap
Starhawk - Mack Maloney s 769

Wiener, Matt
Second Contact - J.D. Austin s 719

SPINSTER

Briars, Amanda
Suddenly You - Lisa Kleypas r 319

Edwards, Jane Amanda
The Message of the Mute Dog - Charlotte Murray Russell m 191

Ortiz, Julianna
The Outlaw's Twin Sister - Stephen A. Bly i 973

Temple, Izzy
Fallen - Celeste Bradley r 241

Tod, Florence
Deadly Illumination - Serena Stier m 203

Whittington, Kate
Summer Moon - Jill Marie Landis w 471

SPIRIT

Kinross, Cassandra
You're the One - Judi McCoy r 351

Macgregor, Ian
Doomed to Repeat It - d.g.k. goldberg h 641

MacLeod, Hamish
Watchers of Time - Charles Todd t 943

MacLeod, Iolanthe
My Heart Stood Still - Lynn Kurland r 323

Navarro, L.Q.
Bitterroot - James Lee Burke c 1088

Westwood, Dimity
Aunt Dimity: Detective - Nancy Atherton m 9

SPORTS FIGURE

Blissberg, Harvey
Dead Ball - R.D. Rosen m 188

Columbus, C.J.
Columbus Slaughters Braves - Mark Friedman c 1114

Cooley, Moss
Dead Ball - R.D. Rosen m 188

Edwards, Derrien "Derry"
A Diamond in the Rough - Andrea Pickens r 370

Genesko, Karl
Better than Sex - Susan Holtzer m 120

Grooves, Bobby Joe "Spin"
The Money-Whipped Steer-Job Three-Jack Give-Up Artist - Dan Jenkins c 1132

Guppy, Roger
Lake Wobegon Summer 1956 - Garrison Keillor c 1136

Harmon, Darin
Just Say No! - Omar Tyree c 1210

Thorssun, Knut
The Money-Whipped Steer-Job Three-Jack Give-Up Artist - Dan Jenkins c 1132

Trehan, Jack
Love to Love You Baby - Kasey Michaels r 354

Tucker, Kevin
This Heart of Mine - Susan Elizabeth Phillips r 369

SPOUSE

Bennett, Christine
Happy Birthday Murder - Lee Harris i 996

Bergfeld, Virginia King
Will's War - Janice Woods Windle w 513

Boll, Sophie
The Ash Garden - Dennis Bock c 1078

Brandt, Lena
The Good German - Joseph Kanon t 892

Bullitt, Mary
The Good Journey - Micaela Gilchrist w 454
The Good Journey - Micaela Gilchrist t 873

Butler, Robert
The Evidence Against Her - Robb Forman Dew t 850
The Evidence Against Her - Robb Forman Dew c 1102

Calloway, Lila
Red on Rose - Patricia Jones c 1133

Campbell, Killian
Embrace the Dawn - Kathleen Morgan i 1026

Carlson, Julie
To Trust a Stranger - Karen Robards r 381

Caroline Mathilde
The Royal Physician's Visit - Per Olov Enquist t 862

Carr, Katie
How to Be Good - Nick Hornby c 1126

Carrington, Margaret
Moon of Bitter Cold - Frederick J. Chiaventone w 441

Chappell, Julia
The Happy Room - Catherine Palmer i 1038

Coleman, Kitty
Falling Angels - Tracy Chevalier c 1090

Columbus, Beth
Columbus Slaughters Braves - Mark Friedman c 1114

Conrad, Dusty
The Woman for Dusty Conrad - Tori Carrington *r* 251

Conrad, Jolie
The Woman for Dusty Conrad - Tori Carrington *r* 251

Cotter, Karen
The Woman Next Door - Barbara Delinsky *c* 1101

Dixon, Butch
Paradise Lost - J.A. Jance *m* 125
Paradise Lost - J.A. Jance *w* 465

Dostoyevsky, Anna
Summer in Baden-Baden - Leonid Tsypkin *t* 946

Emil
The Good German - Joseph Kanon *c* 1135

First Elk Woman
The June Rise - William Tremblay *t* 945
The June Rise - William Tremblay *w* 507

Fraser, Jamie
The Fiery Cross - Diana Gabaldon *r* 288
The Fiery Cross - Diana Gabaldon *t* 868

Freeman, Lee
Monte's Revenge - Eugene C. Vories *w* 509

Gautreaux, Myra
Audubon's Watch - John Gregory Brown *t* 833
Audubon's Watch - John Gregory Brown *c* 1085

Grant, Julia
The Ambush of My Name - Jeffrey Marks *t* 903

Greer, Carmen
Echo Burning - Lee Child *w* 442

Harrow, Dorcas
Beasts - Joyce Carol Oates *c* 1173

Hassa, Alexander
The Girl from the Golden Horn - Kurban Said *c* 1191

Hastings, Lupin Lorrimer
Who Killed the Curate? - Joan Coggin *m* 36

Hathaway, Anne
Her Infinite Variety - Pamela Rafael Berkman *t* 823

Holland, Angelina "Angie" Bartoli
The Bride of Willow Creek - Maggie Osborne *r* 364

Holland, Sam
The Bride of Willow Creek - Maggie Osborne *r* 364

Jones, Clay
Death of the Last Villista - Allana Martin *w* 475

Jubilo
Swift as Desire - Laura Esquivel *c* 1112

Kavanagh, Cynthia
In This Mountain - Jan Karon *i* 1007

Kip
Female Intelligence - Jane Heller *c* 1125

Lacey, James
Agatha Raisin and the Love from Hell - M.C. Beaton *m* 14

Lambert, Enid
The Corrections - Jonathan Franzen *c* 1113

Landis, Elizabeth
A Garden to Keep - Jamie Langston Turner *i* 1055

Lange, Georgia
The Woman Next Door - Barbara Delinsky *c* 1101

Logan, Greg
Long Time No See - Susan Isaacs *c* 1131

Martin, Dorothy
To Perish in Penzance - Jeanne M. Dams *m* 54

Matherly-Reed, Maris
Envy - Sandra Brown *c* 1086
Envy - Sandra Brown *r* 245

Mathers, Abigail
The Webster Chronicle - Daniel Akst *c* 1066

Matt
Suzanne's Diary for Nicholas - James Patterson *c* 1181

Medina, Mercedes
Light Coming Back - Ann Wadsworth *c* 1213

Michal
Queenmaker - India Edghill *t* 858

Mompellion, Elinor
Year of Wonders - Geraldine Brooks *c* 1083
Year of Wonders - Geraldine Brooks *t* 832

Monk, Hester
Funeral in Blue - Anne Perry *t* 915
Funeral in Blue - Anne Perry *m* 172

Mortimer, James
Dr. Mortimer and the Aldgate Mystery - Gerard Williams *t* 958

Mossman, Peter
The Happy Room - Catherine Palmer *i* 1038

Nash, Dartania Douglas
Nashborough - Elsie Burch Donald *t* 855

Noort, Robert
First Gray, Then White, Then Blue - Margriet de Moor *c* 1165

O'Connell, Annie
By Flare of Northern Lights - Tim Champlin *w* 439

O'Fallon, Leigh "Kayleigh"
East of the Sun, West of the Moon - Carole Bellacera *r* 231

O'Leary, Amanda
The Woman Next Door - Barbara Delinsky *c* 1101

O'Malley, Chuck
September Song - Andrew M. Greeley *c* 1117

Patten, Mary Ann
The Captain's Wife - Douglas Kelley *t* 894

Paxton, Sally
Search for Last Chance - A.L. McWilliams *w* 482

Remus, Imogene
The Jazz Bird - Craig Holden *t* 885

Reynard, Jorlan
Ritual of Proof - Dara Joy *r* 310

Rezkova, Magda
First Gray, Then White, Then Blue - Margriet de Moor *c* 1165

Rifkin, Ellie
Fighting Gravity - Peggy Rambach *c* 1184

Schwartz, Marianne
All That Counts - Georg M. Oswald *c* 1177

Scofield, Lily
The Evidence Against Her - Robb Forman Dew *c* 1102
The Evidence Against Her - Robb Forman Dew *t* 850

Scofield, Warren
The Evidence Against Her - Robb Forman Dew *t* 850
The Evidence Against Her - Robb Forman Dew *c* 1102

Shepard, Carina DiGratia
The Tender Vine - Kristen Heitzmann *i* 998

Shepard, Quillan
The Tender Vine - Kristen Heitzmann *i* 998

Sinclair, Jane
Super-Cannes - J.G. Ballard *c* 1070

Skye, Victoria
Downriver - Richard S. Wheeler *t* 957
Downriver - Richard S. Wheeler *w* 512

Stands with a Fist
The Holy Road - Michael Blake *w* 425
The Holy Road - Michael Blake *t* 826

Summers, Julie
The Pickup - Nadine Gordimer *c* 1116

Thompson, Percy
Fred & Edie - Jill Dawson *t* 848

Two Stars, Genevieve LaCroix
Heart of the Sandhill - Stephanie Grace Whitson *i* 1058

Willoughby, Betsy
Double Vengeance - John Duncklee *w* 449

SPY

Aspinall, Andrea
The Company of Strangers - Robert Wilson *t* 960
The Company of Strangers - Robert Wilson *m* 215

Blanchard, Ursula
Queen of Ambition - Fiona Buckley *t* 834
Queen of Ambition - Fiona Buckley *m* 29

Clariet, Felicity
Jackdaws - Ken Follett *t* 863

Corrigan, Jonathan
Betrayed - Rosey Dow *i* 989

d'Arcy, Owen
To Kiss a Spy - Jane Feather *r* 276

Eschbach, Johan
Ghost of the White Nights - L.E. Modesitt Jr. *s* 778

Eschbach, Llysette
Ghost of the White Nights - L.E. Modesitt Jr. *s* 778

Hawthorne, Lily
To Tame a Duke - Patricia Grasso *r* 293

Jones, Abel
Call Each River Jordan - Owen Parry *m* 169
Call Each River Jordan - Owen Parry *t* 914

Kosta, Jereko
Angelmass - Timothy Zahn *s* 812

Leones, Giraut
The Merchants of Souls - John Barnes *s* 722

Llyr, Bronwen
Brothers of Cain - Miriam Grace Monfredo *t* 909
Brothers of Cain - Miriam Grace Monfredo *m* 159

Manderville, William
The Very Comely Countess - Miranda Jarrett *r* 307

Montero, Carmen
The Spanish Bride - Amanda McCabe *r* 349

Moorhaven, Nigel
The Blue Devil - Melynda Beth Skinner *r* 398

Pavel
Requiem for a Lost Empire - Andrei Makine *c* 1151

Prieczka, Laprada
The Merchants of Souls - John Barnes *s* 722

Prytanis, Paxa
The Merchants of Souls - John Barnes *s* 722

Raines, Harrison
The Ironclad Alibi - Michael Kilian *m* 133
The Ironclad Alibi - Michael Kilian *t* 898

Rand, Jeffery
The Old Spies Club and Other Intrigues of Rand - Edward D. Hoch *m* 118

St. Charles, Steven
A Scandalous Wager - Bess Willingham r 420

Tremayne, Lucian
Desire - Nicole Jordan r 309

Voss, Karl
The Company of Strangers - Robert Wilson m 215
The Company of Strangers - Robert Wilson t 960

Ward, Paul
The Last Vampire - Whitley Strieber h 699

Wright, Jimjoy Earle
Empire & Ecolitan - L.E. Modesitt Jr. s 777

Wright, Kyle
Hide and Seek - Cherry Adair r 222

STEP-PARENT

Pedigo, Luther
Affinity - J.N. Williamson h 709

STOCK BROKER

Harris, Catherine "Cat" Anne
Seducing Mr. Right - Cherry Adair r 223

STORE OWNER

Bayles, China
Bloodroot - Susan Wittig Albert m 4

Browning, Theodosia
Death by Darjeeling - Laura Childs m 32

Carlson, Julie
To Trust a Stranger - Karen Robards r 381

Devonshire, Betsy
Unraveled Sleeve - Monica Ferris m 67

Goldman, Annie
What to Do about Annie? - Millie Criswell r 264

Hunt, Gil
The Masks of Auntie Laveau - Robert J. Randisi m 177

Jones, Texana
Death of the Last Villista - Allana Martin w 475
Death of the Last Villista - Allana Martin m 149

Lasher, Cora
The Deadwood Beetle - Mylene Dressler c 1106

Solomon, Bretta
Lilies That Fester - Janis Harrison m 103

Thomas, Allie
Sweet Success - Susan Mallery r 344

Wayne, Ellie
A Father's Place - Marta Perry i 1041

Yekker, Bousalem
The Last Summer of Reason - Tahar Djaout c 1105

STORYTELLER

Qumalix
Call Down the Stars - Sue Harrison t 879

Yikaas
Call Down the Stars - Sue Harrison t 879

STRIPPER

Lavotoni, Sierra
Strip Poker - Nancy Bartholomew m 13

STUDENT

Banyon, Eric
Spirits White as Lightning - Mercedes Lackey f 568

Brother John
Brother John - Rutledge Etheridge s 750

Church, Stewart
About the Author - John Colapinto c 1092

Converse, Jeff
The Manhattan Hunt Club - John Saul h 687

Danforth, Eileen
Night in the Lonesome October - Richard Laymon h 664

Hart, Priscilla
Riot - Shashi Tharoor c 1208

Jenson, Jana
A Family for Jana - Eileen Berger i 968

Linacre, Tim
Creeping Venom - Sheila Pim m 173

Logan, Daniella
Pact of the Fathers - Ramsey Campbell h 626

Logan, Ed
Night in the Lonesome October - Richard Laymon h 664

Rifkin, Ellie
Fighting Gravity - Peggy Rambach c 1184

Ryan, Jonah
A Bend in the Road - Nicholas Sparks c 1200

Unger, David
Conjuring Maud - Philip Danze t 847

Whitman, Max
. . .And the Angel with Television Eyes - John Shirley h 694

STUDENT—BOARDING SCHOOL

Evans, Catrine
Schooling - Heather McGowan c 1159

STUDENT—COLLEGE

Bjorklund, Thorliff
A Dream to Follow - Lauraine Snelling i 1050

Blake, Sheridan
The Watermark - Travis Thrasher i 1054

Brauer, Gillian
Beasts - Joyce Carol Oates c 1173

Daniels, Amoreena
Gargoyles - Alan Nayes s 783
Gargoyles - Alan Nayes h 677

Fallowes, Hetty
The Flight of the Maidens - Jane Gardam t 870

Klein, Lieselotte
The Flight of the Maidens - Jane Gardam t 870

Thomas of Hookton
The Archer's Tale - Bernard Cornwell t 843

Vane, Una
The Flight of the Maidens - Jane Gardam t 870

Wilcox, Quent
Affinity - J.N. Williamson h 709

York, Thomas
The Prodigy - Alton Gansky h 637

STUDENT—EXCHANGE

Haukeland, Erik
East of the Sun, West of the Moon - Carole Bellacera r 231

STUDENT—GRADUATE

Cochrane, Deborah
Shock - Robin Cook c 1093

Collins, Benton
The Beasts of Barakhai - Mickey Zucker Reichert f 590

Hernandez, Elida
The Deadwood Beetle - Mylene Dressler c 1106

Liu, Genevie
The Watermark - Travis Thrasher i 1054

Meissner, Joanna
Shock - Robin Cook c 1093

Riley, Katelyn
Riverwatch - Joseph M. Nassise h 676

Skelly, Colleen Mary
Taylor's Temptation - Suzanne Brockmann r 242

STUDENT—HIGH SCHOOL

LaSalle, Sonny
A World of Thieves - James Carlos Blake t 825
A World of Thieves - James Carlos Blake w 424

Taylor, Becky
Tears in a Bottle - Sylvia Bambola i 966

SUPERNATURAL BEING

Einar
From the Dust Returned - Ray Bradbury h 623

Self
A Lower Deep - Tom Piccirilli h 682

SURVIVOR

Clarke, Lenie
Maelstrom - Peter Watts s 808

Ives, Hannah
Occasion of Revenge - Marcia Talley m 205

Jakob
In the Shape of a Boar - Lawrence Norfolk c 1171

Memel, Solomon
In the Shape of a Boar - Lawrence Norfolk c 1171
In the Shape of a Boar - Lawrence Norfolk t 913

Miller, Eve
Aria - Susan Segal c 1194

Ruth
In the Shape of a Boar - Lawrence Norfolk c 1171

TEACHER

Andrews, Sarah
A Bend in the Road - Nicholas Sparks c 1200

Biggs, Candy
Dugan under Ground - Tom De Haven c 1100

Breen, Sam
Angry Young Spaceman - Jim Munroe s 780

Columbus, Joe
Columbus Slaughters Braves - Mark Friedman c 1114

Conroy, Jane
A Love for Safekeeping - Gail Gaymer Martin i 1021

Donovan, Karen
Fireworks - James A. Moore *h* 675

Eastman, Delanie
Hide and Seek - Cherry Adair *r* 222

Fogarty, Luanne
Deep Water Death - Glynn Marsh Alam *m* 3

Fraiser, Laura
Forbid Them Not - Michael P. Farris *i* 991

Gallagher, Willi
All Signs Point to Murder - Kat Goldring *m* 81

Gilbert
Schooling - Heather McGowan *c* 1159

Green, Mattie
Mattie and the Blacksmith - Linda Lea Castle *r* 253

Haggerty, Lindy
Midsummer Murder - Shelley Freydont *m* 71

Harris, Tim
The White Room - A.J. Matthews *h* 673

Hollowell, Patricia Anne "Mouse"
Murder Boogies with Elvis - Anne George *m* 77

Hood, Daniel
Echoes of Lies - Jo Bannister *m* 11

Hudson, Jane
The Lake of Dead Languages - Carol Goodman *m* 82

James, Bethany
Bethany's Song - Susan Plunkett *r* 372

Jonesy
Dreamcatcher - Stephen King *h* 660

Judd, Kyler
Scorch - A.D. Nauman *s* 782

Kellaway, Lucille
The Virtuous Cyprian - Nicola Cornick *r* 260

Lafayette, Marie
Night Hawk's Bride - Jillian Hart *r* 296

Lamb, Kathryn "Kitty"
Miss Match - Leslie Carroll *r* 252

Marcello, Nick
Emerald Windows - Terri Blackstock *i* 971

Martin, Prudence
Stranded with the Sergeant - Cathie Linz *r* 335

McKinney, Mary
July Thunder - Rachel Lee *r* 330

Meyers, Molly
Written on Her Heart - Alan Maki *i* 1019

Moon, Billy
Sarah's Window - Janice Graham *w* 457

Prentice, Amelia
Irregardless of Murder - Ellen Edwards Kennedy *i* 1008

Robin, Cecilia
Augur's Teacher - Sherwood Smith *s* 800

Shakespeare, William
Ill Met by Moonlight - Sarah A. Hoyt *f* 559

Talbot, Julia
No Way Out - Andrea Kane *r* 312

Ushart, Adam
A Morning in Eden - Anna Gilbert *t* 872

Valentine, Meg
Two Sexy - Stephanie Bond *r* 240

Williams, Audrey
Dangerous Dilemmas - Evelyn Palfrey *r* 365

TECHNICIAN

Kroger, Ginny
Defender - C.J. Cherryh *s* 734

TEENAGER

Alison
Friday Night in Beast House - Richard Laymon *h* 662

April
Entertain the End - K.A. Applegate *f* 519
Mystify the Magician - K.A. Applegate *f* 520

Beefy
Edgewater Angels - Sandro Meallet *c* 1160

Bolliver, Quincie
Quincie Bolliver - Mary King *w* 469

Brunner, Jeff
Gifted Touch - Melinda Metz *s* 775

Bunch, Gabriel
Gabriel's Gift - Hanif Kureishi *c* 1143

Caleb
The Wild Boy - Warren Rochelle *s* 791

Callaghan, Tom
The Reckoning - John McLain *w* 481

Casey
Night in the Lonesome October - Richard Laymon *h* 664

Charlotte
Look at Me - Jennifer Egan *c* 1108

Childs, Toby
The Onion Girl - Charles De Lint *f* 539

Christopher
Mystify the Magician - K.A. Applegate *f* 520

Crow
The Crow Maiden - Sarah Singleton *f* 598

David
Entertain the End - K.A. Applegate *f* 519

Elazandra
Shadow Kiss - Tom Townsend *f* 605

Elliot, Cecy
From the Dust Returned - Ray Bradbury *h* 623

Evans, Catrine
Schooling - Heather McGowan *c* 1159

Fascinelli, Anthony
Gifted Touch - Melinda Metz *s* 775
Haunted - Melinda Metz *s* 776

Fisher, Bo
Fire in the Rock - Joe Martin *c* 1154

French, Nicole
Straight on 'Til Morning - Christopher Golden *h* 642

Gary
Lake Wobegon Summer 1956 - Garrison Keillor *c* 1136

Harris, Brian
The White Room - A.J. Matthews *h* 673

Heydon, Cassie
City Infernal - Edward Lee *h* 667

Himler, Donnie
The World Weaver - Craig Etchison *s* 749

Ilon
The Wild Boy - Warren Rochelle *s* 791

Jalil
Mystify the Magician - K.A. Applegate *f* 520

Jaylin
Swell Foop - Piers Anthony *f* 518

Kooby, Jamieson
Stillwater - William F. Weld *t* 955

Lefkowitz, Jake
Night of the Bat - Paul Zindel *h* 714

Lizier, Grazida
The Good Men - Charmaine Craig *t* 844

Llesho
The Prince of Shadow - Curt Benjamin *f* 526

Matthews, Mark
Friday Night in Beast House - Richard Laymon *h* 662

McClean, Peggy
The World Weaver - Craig Etchison *s* 749

Miller, Larkin
The World Weaver - Craig Etchison *s* 749

Mulvaine
On - Adam Roberts *s* 790

Murphy, Kevin
Straight on 'Til Morning - Christopher Golden *h* 642

Newcombe, Ally
When the Last Leaf Falls - Bill Myers *i* 1032

Nikki
Face - Tim Lebbon *h* 665

Parvin
Emigre Journeys - Abdullah Hussein *c* 1129

Pedigo, Feather
Affinity - J.N. Williamson *h* 709

Powell, Muir
This Rock - Robert Morgan *t* 910

Proctor, Jeremy
Smuggler's Moon - Bruce Alexander *t* 815

Shadow
Shadow Kiss - Tom Townsend *f* 605

Shelby, Robyn
A Paradigm of Earth - Candas Jane Dorsey *s* 747

Slack, Tommy
End over End - Kate Kennedy *c* 1139

Starling, Peter
Straight on 'Til Morning - Christopher Golden *h* 642

Templeton, Pollo
Fire in the Rock - Joe Martin *c* 1154

Tobin
The Bone Doll's Twin - Lynn Flewelling *f* 544

Ton Su
Edgewater Angels - Sandro Meallet *c* 1160

Toomer, Sonny
Edgewater Angels - Sandro Meallet *c* 1160

Towle, Ivory
End over End - Kate Kennedy *c* 1139

Unnamed Character
Balzac and the Little Chinese Seamstress - Sijie Dai *c* 1098

Vasilyevich, Annatt
Children of the Shaman - Jessica Rydill *f* 596

Vasilyevich, Malchik
Children of the Shaman - Jessica Rydill *f* 596

Vel
Hope's End - Stephen Chambers *s* 733

Voight, Rae
Gifted Touch - Melinda Metz *s* 775
Haunted - Melinda Metz *s* 776

Volson, Siggy
Bloodtide - Melvin Burgess *s* 730

Volson, Signy
Bloodtide - Melvin Burgess *s* 730

Waals, Christina van der
Island of Tears - Troy Soos *t* 936

Wilcox, Quent
Affinity - J.N. Williamson *h* 709

TELEPATH

Acorna
Acorna's Search - Anne McCaffrey *s* 772

Dehya
Spherical Harmonic - Catherine Asaro *s* 716

Eldrin
Spherical Harmonic - Catherine Asaro *s* 716

Voight, Rae
Gifted Touch - Melinda Metz *s* 775
Haunted - Melinda Metz *s* 776

TELEVISION

Carter, Chance
Tie-Fast Country - Robert Flynn *w* 451

Fortunato, Caesar
TV - Brian Brown *c* 1084

Grace
The Wig My Father Wore - Anne Enright *c* 1111

Kapp, Henry
TV - Brian Brown *c* 1084

TELEVISION PERSONALITY

Diche, Derek
Next Stop, Paradise - Sue Civil-Brown *r* 256

Eldridge, Louise
Harvest of Murder - Ann Ripley *m* 181

Hunt, Claire
The Masks of Auntie Laveau - Robert J. Randisi *m* 177

Slavin, Mickey
Dead Ball - R.D. Rosen *m* 188

THIEF

Cobner
The Rover - Mel Odom *f* 584

Cutter, Marvin
Flying Eagle - Tim Champlin *w* 440

Deek
Take a Thief - Mercedes Lackey *f* 569

Doyle, Regan
Walker's Widow - Heidi Betts *r* 234

Emmett, Claude
A Horde of Fools - James David Buchanan *w* 437

Fritz, Waldo
A Good Town - Douglas Hirt *w* 462

Geraldi, James
The House of Gold - Max Brand *w* 431

Keck, Jim
Man from Wyoming - Dane Coolidge *w* 448

Kestrel
Pool of Radiance - Carrie Bebris *f* 525

Merkle, Gerald
The Pinkerton Eye - Allen P. Bristow *w* 436

Parker
Firebreak - Richard Stark *m* 202

Will
Fortress Draconis - Michael A. Stackpole *f* 599

TIME TRAVELER

ben-Abdullah, Abban "Ben"
I Dream of You - Judi McCoy *r* 350

Cassidy, Gwen
Kiss of the Highlander - Karen Marie Moning *r* 358

Fraser, Claire
The Fiery Cross - Diana Gabaldon *r* 288
The Fiery Cross - Diana Gabaldon *t* 868

James, Alicia
Alicia's Song - Susan Plunkett *r* 371

James, Bethany
Bethany's Song - Susan Plunkett *r* 372

Luc, Frank
ChronoSpace - Allen Steele *s* 802

MacKeltar, Drustan
Kiss of the Highlander - Karen Marie Moning *r* 358

Stafford, Robyn
Knight Errant - R. Garcia y Robertson *t* 869
Knight Errant - R. Garcia y Robertson *f* 546

TOUR GUIDE

Pelham, Charlotte
Mr. Montgomery's Quest - Martha Kirkland *r* 318

TOY

Sostenuto, Pocotristi
The Rundlestone of Oz - Eloise McGraw *f* 577

TRADER

Bonfils, Alexandre
Downriver - Richard S. Wheeler *t* 957

St. Vrain, Ceran
Moon Medicine - Mike Blakely *t* 827

TRAPPER

Beaupre, Jean
Cowboy in the Making - Will James *w* 464

TRAVEL AGENT

Watson, Zeb
Sidhe-Devil - Aaron Allston *f* 516

TRAVELER

Banouin
Midnight Falcon - David Gemmell *f* 548

Copis
Shadow - K.J. Parker *f* 585

Mirana, Kerin
The Jasper Forest - Julia Gray *f* 551

Rysha
Shadow of the Seer - Michael Scott Rohan *f* 595

Strong John
Rowan of Rin - Emily Rodda *f* 594

TREE SURGEON

Love, Mick
When Love Came to Town - Lenora Worth *i* 1063

TUTOR

Bachman, Sandra
Twin Blessings - Carolyne Aarsen *i* 965

Neville, Rebecca
The Promise - May McGoldrick *r* 352

TWIN

Heydon, Cassie
City Infernal - Edward Lee *h* 667

Kellaway, Lucille
The Virtuous Cyprian - Nicola Cornick *r* 260

Ortiz, Julianna
The Outlaw's Twin Sister - Stephen A. Bly *i* 973

Volson, Siggy
Bloodtide - Melvin Burgess *s* 730

Volson, Signy
Bloodtide - Melvin Burgess *s* 730

UNEMPLOYED

Phillips, Gina
A Journey by Chance - Sally D. John *i* 1006

Reynolds, Frank
The Faded Flower - Paul McCusker *i* 1024

Winter, Duke
Bonnie Winter - Graham Masterton *h* 672

VACATIONER

Cassidy, Gwen
Kiss of the Highlander - Karen Marie Moning *r* 358

VAGRANT

Buddy
House of Pain - Sephera Giron *h* 640

VAMPIRE

Akasha
Blood and Gold - Anne Rice *h* 685

Alcuin
Crimson Kiss - Trisha Baker *h* 617

Baldevar, Simon
Crimson Kiss - Trisha Baker *h* 617

Blaylock, Miriam
The Last Vampire - Whitley Strieber *h* 699

Darling, Stephen
Candle Bay - Tamara Thorne *h* 703

Decimus, Victor
Vampire Vow - Michael Schiefelbein *h* 690

di Rospo, Teresa
Darkness - Sam Siciliano *h* 695

Dracula
Dracula in London - P.N. Elrod *h* 631

Dun, Richard
His Father's Son - Nigel Bennett *h* 621

Eudoxia
Blood and Gold - Anne Rice *h* 685

Garret, Allison
Night Players - P.D. Cacek *h* 625

Jean-Claude
Narcissus in Chains - Laurell K. Hamilton *h* 645

Land, Elmo
The Last Vampire - T.M. Wright *h* 712

Lestat
Blood and Gold - Anne Rice *t* 922
Marius
Blood and Gold - Anne Rice *t* 922
Blood and Gold - Anne Rice *c* 1185
Blood and Gold - Anne Rice *h* 685
Mikaelian, Garreth
Blood Games - Lee Killough *h* 657
Moore, Olivia
The London Vampire Panic - Michael Romkey *h* 686
Morris, Quincey
Quincey Morris, Vampire - P.N. Elrod *h* 632
O'Neill, Meghann
Crimson Kiss - Trisha Baker *h* 617
Pandora
Blood and Gold - Anne Rice *t* 922
Raven
Blood Games - Lee Killough *h* 657
Roberts, Sarah
The Last Vampire - Whitley Strieber *h* 699
Sanat Ji Mani
A Feast in Exile - Chelsea Quinn Yarbro *t* 963
A Feast in Exile - Chelsea Quinn Yarbro *h* 713
Seth
Night Players - P.D. Cacek *h* 625
Thorne
Blood and Gold - Anne Rice *c* 1185
Valentyn, Julian
Candle Bay - Tamara Thorne *h* 703
Watson, Regina
The Last Vampire - T.M. Wright *h* 712

VETERAN

Dalton, Smokey
Smoke-Filled Rooms - Kris Nelscott *m* 166
Holland, Billy Bob
Bitterroot - James Lee Burke *c* 1088
Johnson, Evan
The Edge of Town - Dorothy Garlock *r* 290
Kincaid, Gordon
The Nightingale's Song - Kathleen Eschenburg *r* 273
Mohr, Henry
Last Year's River - Allen Morris Jones *t* 891
Last Year's River - Allen Morris Jones *w* 467
Rutledge, Ian
Watchers of Time - Charles Todd *m* 208
Watchers of Time - Charles Todd *t* 943
Vermillion, Jack
Black Water Transit - Carsten Stroud *m* 204

VETERINARIAN

Jones, Clay
Death of the Last Villista - Allana Martin *w* 475
Martin, Clay
Death of the Last Villista - Allana Martin *m* 149

VILLAIN

Oldham, Clyde
The Way of the Coyote - Elmer Kelton *c* 1137

VOLUNTEER

Miles, Vanessa
Friday's Child - Linda Chaikin *i* 977

WAITER/WAITRESS

Bryden, Sarah
Sarah's Window - Janice Graham *w* 457
Driver, Sally
Looking for Laura - Judith Arnold *r* 226
Dubois, Rose
The MacKenzies: Zach - Ana Leigh *r* 332
Goldman, Annie
What to Do about Annie? - Millie Criswell *r* 264
Spadolini, Tracey
Slightly Single - Wendy Markham *r* 345

WARD

Conde, Amy
The Guardian - Barbara Miller *r* 355
Gordon, Mary "Molly"
The Secret Clan: Abducted Heiress - Amanda Scott *r* 390

WARRIOR

ap Gwien, Sulian
The King's Name - Jo Walton *f* 608
Arlian
The Dragon Society - Lawrence Watt-Evans *f* 610
Axis
Enchanter - Sara Douglass *f* 540
Azhure
Enchanter - Sara Douglass *f* 540
Bane
Midnight Falcon - David Gemmell *f* 548
Blood-Ax, Eirik Haraldsson
Mother of Kings - Poul Anderson *f* 517
Borneheld
Enchanter - Sara Douglass *f* 540
Capashen, Gerrard
Apocalypse - J. Robert King *f* 564
Cashel
Mistress of the Catacombs - David Drake *f* 541
Cattie-Brie
Sea of Swords - R.A. Salvatore *f* 597
Crow
Fortress Draconis - Michael A. Stackpole *f* 599
Douglas, Robert
Rebel's Cage - Kate Jacoby *f* 561
Do'Urden, Drizzt
Sea of Swords - R.A. Salvatore *f* 597
Dunbar, John
The Holy Road - Michael Blake *w* 425
The Holy Road - Michael Blake *t* 826
Elric
The Dreamthief's Daughter - Michael Moorcock *f* 582
Er'ril
Wit'ch Gate - James Clemens *f* 534
Gianavel, Joshua
Rora - James Byron Huggins *i* 1003
Grey Bear
Cheyenne Summer - Vella Munn *t* 911
Habiba
The Prince of Shadow - Curt Benjamin *f* 526
Hakonson, Dragon
Come Back to Me - Josie Litton *r* 337
Hakonson, Wolf
Dream of Me - Josie Litton *r* 338
Hawk of Essex
Believe in Me - Josie Litton *r* 336
Hitomi, Mirumoto
The Crab - Stan Brown *f* 531
Justicar
Queen of the Demonweb Pits - Paul Kidd *f* 563
Kabeiros
Thrice Bound - Roberta Gellis *f* 547
Kisada, Hida
The Crab - Stan Brown *f* 531
Lone Hawk
Cheyenne Summer - Vella Munn *t* 911
MacCloud, Conor
The Enchantment - Pam Binder *r* 237
Maigraith
The Way between the Worlds - Ian Irvine *f* 560
Maldred
Betrayal - Jean Rabe *f* 589
Pentar
The Way of the Rose - Valery Leith *f* 572
Poldarn
Shadow - K.J. Parker *f* 585
Rufryd
The Obsidian Tower - Freda Warrington *f* 609
Seyonne
Revelation - Elizabeth Haydon *f* 555
Tanda
Myth-ion Improbable - Robert Lynn Asprin *f* 521
Taretel
The Way of the Rose - Valery Leith *f* 572
Vyx
Revelation - Elizabeth Haydon *f* 555
Yakamo, Hida
The Crab - Stan Brown *f* 531

WEALTHY

Ashton, Hope
Heaven Sent - Jillian Hart *i* 997
Billingham, Mark
The Great Baby Caper - Eugenia Riley *r* 380
Bonavendier, Lilith
Alice at Heart - Deborah Smith *r* 401
Callahan, Patrick
Cinderella After Midnight - Lilian Darcy *r* 268
Cameron, Michael
Dear Cupid - Julie Ortolon *r* 363
Correa, Matt
The Secret Admirer - Annette Mahon *r* 343
Cranshaw, Lisa
Very Truly Yours - Julie Beard *r* 229
Fontana, Jose
The Survival of Juan Oro - Max Brand *w* 434
Ingalls, Josh
The Nanny - Judith Stacy *r* 408
Lockhart, Aubrey
Heaven Sent - Rachel Wilson *r* 421
Lowe, Eliza
Beloved Protector - Linda O'Brien *r* 361
Luz
Swift as Desire - Laura Esquivel *c* 1112
Norton
Monte's Revenge - Eugene C. Vories *w* 509
Putemonnie, Radegonde
Mirabilis - Susann Cokal *c* 1091

Qwilleran, James Mackintosh "Qwill"
The Cat Who Went Up the Creek - Lilian Jackson Braun m 26

Ross, Justin
Heartless - Kat Martin r 346

Roth, Abraham
Devil's Island - John Hagee i 994

Rycroft, Charles
Comfort and Joy - Sandra Madden r 342

Seymour, Glenys
The Prisoner Bride - Susan Spencer Paul r 368

Summers, Julie
The Pickup - Nadine Gordimer c 1116

Trehan, Jack
Love to Love You Baby - Kasey Michaels r 354

Waters, Claire
Redeeming Claire - Cynthia Rutledge i 1045

Winslow, Scott
A Bungalow for Two - Carole Gift Page i 1035

WEREWOLF

Clayton
Bitten - Kelley Armstrong c 1068

Forster, Quentin
Secret of the Wolf - Susan Krinard r 322

Michaels, Elena
Bitten - Kelley Armstrong c 1068

Richard
Narcissus in Chains - Laurell K. Hamilton h 645

WIDOW(ER)

Appleton, Susanna
Face Down Before Rebel Hooves - Kathy Lynn Emerson t 861
Face Down Before Rebel Hooves - Kathy Lynn Emerson m 65

Avery, Prescott
A Family for Gillian - Catherine Blair r 238

Barlow, Lady
Lockwood - Lauran Paine w 492

Bartling, Gemma
A Rose by the Door - Deborah Bedford i 967

Braddock, Jordan
Colorado Twilight - Tess Pendergrass w 495

Bryanston, Pen
To Kiss a Spy - Jane Feather r 276

Carlson, Michael
A Family All Her Own - Bonnie K. Winn i 1061

Christian, Miles
Elusive Passion - Kathryn Smith r 402

Coleman, Melodie
A Home of Her Own - Cathleen Connors i 982

Conway, Lizzie
Prized Possessions - Jessica Stirling t 938

de Fraisney, Katherine
The Warrior's Damsel - Denise Hampton r 295

Demens, Ty
Blessed Baby - Lois Richer i 1043

Doyle, Regan
Walker's Widow - Heidi Betts r 234

Driver, Sally
Looking for Laura - Judith Arnold r 226

Eliasson, Samuel
The World Below - Sue Miller c 1163

Firth, Anna
Year of Wonders - Geraldine Brooks t 832

Fitzgibbon, Veronica
Roscoe - William Kennedy t 897

Frazier, Zac
Love One Another - Valerie Hansen i 995

Frith, Anna
Year of Wonders - Geraldine Brooks c 1083

Goldstein, Kiki
Tall, Dead, and Handsome - Annie Griffin m 91

Gray, Matthew
Bethany's Song - Susan Plunkett r 372

Hartleigh Compton, Elizabeth
Death Is in the Air - Kate Kingsbury m 136

Hasper, Jean
Worthy of Riches - Bonnie Leon i 1017

Ingalls, Josh
The Nanny - Judith Stacy r 408

Ingram, Mattie
The Widow's Little Secret - Judith Stacy r 409

Jones, Sarah
Rocky and the Senator's Daughter - Dixie Browning r 246

Lockhart, Aubrey
Heaven Sent - Rachel Wilson r 421

Mackellar, Patience
Keepers - Janet LaPierre m 139

Mahler, Alma
The Silent Woman - Susan M. Dodd t 852

Malloy, Hannah
Tall, Dead, and Handsome - Annie Griffin m 91

March, Tobias
Slightly Shady - Amanda Quick r 375

Martin, Ruth
What Once We Loved - Jane Kirkpatrick i 1011
What Once We Loved - Jane Kirkpatrick w 470

Miller, Eve
Aria - Susan Segal c 1194

Miryam
The Jerusalem Scrolls - Bodie Thoene t 942
The Jerusalem Scrolls - Bodie Thoene i 1053

Mitchell, Lucy
The Gift of the Mestizo - Marjorie M. McGinley w 479

Moon, Billy
Sarah's Window - Janice Graham w 457

Orr, Terry
Closing Time - Jim Fusilli m 74

Parker, Charlie "Bird"
Dark Hollow - John Connolly m 42

Parmenter, Mathilda Heath
Broken Promises - Patricia Oliver r 362

Powell, Ginny
This Rock - Robert Morgan t 910

Reed, Catherine deClaire
Whispers of Goodbye - Karen White r 418

Rothman, Ruby
Don't Cry for Me, Hot Pastrami - Sharon Kahn m 129

Ryan, Miles
A Bend in the Road - Nicholas Sparks c 1200

Saint-Ange, Marie Claire
Dangerous Attraction - Susan Vaughan r 417

Shore, Marla
Murder by Manicure - Nancy J. Cohen m 38

Solomon, Bretta
Lilies That Fester - Janis Harrison m 103

Stonewall, Kate
A Prince of a Guy - Sheila Rabe r 376

Swenson, Lark
Cold Hunter's Moon - K.C. Greenlief m 90

Taylor, Rebecca
The Colorado Bride - Mary Burton r 247

Thomas, Charlotte "Charlie"
The Widow - Anne Stuart r 411

Tiomenen, Liesl
Cold - John Smolens c 1199

Waters, Rocky
Rocky and the Senator's Daughter - Dixie Browning r 246

Watkins, Claire
Glare Ice - Mary Logue m 145

WITCH

Ari
The Pillars of the World - Anne Bishop f 527

Channing, Nell
Dance upon the Air - Nora Roberts r 382

Elena
Wit'ch Gate - James Clemens f 534

Fay
The Nature of Balance - Tim Lebbon h 666

Gilley
The Third Witch - Rebecca Reisert t 921

Hekate
Thrice Bound - Roberta Gellis f 547

Jen
Gumshoe Gorilla - Keith Hartman s 756

Kalila
Pride of Kings - Judith Tarr f 603

Lhel
The Bone Doll's Twin - Lynn Flewelling f 544

Mefell, Brierly
Mother Ocean, Daughter Sea - Diana Marcellas f 576

Ohmsford, Grianne
Antrax - Terry Brooks f 530

Ozurardottir, Gunhild
Mother of Kings - Poul Anderson f 517

Rachel
The Scent of Magic - Cliff McNish f 581

Ross, Sara Charlene
A Game of Colors - John Urbancik h 704

Stefan
A Game of Colors - John Urbancik h 704

Taylor, Gypsy Leigh
A Game of Colors - John Urbancik h 704

Todd, Ripley
Heaven and Earth - Nora Roberts r 383

WIZARD

Aumar, Elminster
Elminster in Hell - Ed Greenwood f 553

Axis
Enchanter - Sara Douglass f 540

Bileworm
The Shattered Mask - Richard Lee Byers f 532

DeKathrine, Camden
The Golden Sword - Fiona Patton f 586

Escalla
Queen of the Demonweb Pits - Paul Kidd f 563

Gallowglass, Geoffrey
Here Be Monsters - Christopher Stasheff f 600

Gallowglass, Gregory
Here Be Monsters - Christopher Stasheff f 600

Ged
The Other Wind - Ursula K. Le Guin f 571

Merlin
Celtika - Robert Holdstock f 558
The Dragon Queen - Alice Borchardt t 829
The Dragon Queen - Alice Borchardt f 528
Entertain the End - K.A. Applegate f 519

Merrigan, Eleanor
Behind Time - Lynn Abbey f 515

Ohmsford, Bek
Antrax - Terry Brooks f 530

Rahl, Richard
The Pillars of Creation - Terry Goodkind f 550

Rincewind
The Last Hero - Terry Pratchett f 588

Skeeve
Myth-ion Improbable - Robert Lynn Asprin f 521

Slyddwyn
The Rundlestone of Oz - Eloise McGraw f 577

Suviel
Shadowkings - Michael Cobley f 535

Tapopat
The Way of Light - Storm Constantine f 536

Veldan
Spirit of the Stone - Maggie Furey f 545

Zorander, Zeddicus
Debt of Bones - Terry Goodkind f 549

WORKER

Field, Simon
Falling Angels - Tracy Chevalier t 838

Karkald
World Fall - Douglas Niles f 583

Unnamed Character
The Appointment - Herta Muller c 1168

WRITER

Alexander, Mark
Pact of the Fathers - Ramsey Campbell h 626

Austen, Jane
Jane and the Prisoner of Wool House - Stephanie Barron t 822
Jane and the Prisoner of Wool House - Stephanie Barron m 12

Bierce, Ambrose
Ambrose Bierce and the Death of Kings - Oakley Hall m 95
Ambrose Bierce and the Death of Kings - Oakley Hall t 878

Bingham, Ryan
Up in the Air - Walter Kirn c 1141

Breton, Money
Why Did I Ever? - Mary Robison c 1188

Briars, Amanda
Suddenly You - Lisa Kleypas r 319

Burns, Jacob
The Killing Bee - Matt Witten m 218

Carlyle, Brandon
Darkling I Listen - Katherine Sutcliffe r 412

Carr, David
How to Be Good - Nick Hornby c 1126

Carter, Sherry
Puzzled to Death - Parnell Hall m 96

Champhert, Rebecca
Something More - Paul Cornell s 738

Chandran, Willie
Half a Life - V.S. Naipaul c 1170

Chase, Sophy
Almost - Elizabeth Benedict c 1073

Colbert, Gerard
The Looking Glass - Michele Roberts t 925

Collins, Wilkie
The Rag & Bone Shop - Jeff Rackham t 917

Cunningham, Cal
About the Author - John Colapinto c 1092

Dickens, Charles
The Rag & Bone Shop - Jeff Rackham t 917

Dickerson, Piper
Eccentric Circles - Rebecca Lickiss f 573

Dodgson, Charles
The Problem of the Surly Servant - Roberta Rogow t 926
The Problem of the Surly Servant - Roberta Rogow m 187
Still She Haunts Me - Katie Roiphe t 927
Still She Haunts Me - Katie Roiphe c 1189

Dostoyevsky, Fyodor
Summer in Baden-Baden - Leonid Tsypkin t 946

Doyle, Arthur Conan
The Problem of the Surly Servant - Roberta Rogow m 187
The Problem of the Surly Servant - Roberta Rogow t 926

Evans, Parker
Envy - Sandra Brown r 245
Envy - Sandra Brown c 1086

Griffin, Lew
Ghost of a Flea - James Sallis m 192

Hamilton, John
Dark Sanctuary - H.B. Gregory h 644

Holton, Anthony
The Chinese Fire Drill - Les Roberts m 185

Johnson, Samuel
According to Queeney - Beryl Bainbridge c 1069

Jovic, Jan
When Heaven Weeps - Ted Dekker i 988

Knightly, Harriet
The Trouble with Harriet - Wilma Counts r 262

Kruger, Joseph
War Story - Gwen Edelman c 1107

Lamb, Mary
Everything You Need - A.L. Kennedy c 1138

London, Jack
The Jewel of the North - Peter King m 135

MacDonald, Sean
Dead Love - Donald Beman h 620

Maddox, Bruno
My Little Blue Dress - Bruno Maddox c 1150

Martin, Kit
Killing the Shadows - Val McDermid m 154

Matravers, Paul
The Crow Maiden - Sarah Singleton f 598

Memel, Solomon
In the Shape of a Boar - Lawrence Norfolk c 1171
In the Shape of a Boar - Lawrence Norfolk t 913

Merriwell, Max
Adventures in Time and Space with Max Merriwell - Pat Murphy s 781

Pike, Jamison
The Quest - Jim Kraus i 1013

Poe, Edgar Allan
The Hum Bug - Harold Schechter m 193
The Hum Bug - Harold Schechter w 502
The Hum Bug - Harold Schechter t 932

Reed, Noah
Envy - Sandra Brown c 1086
Envy - Sandra Brown r 245

Roundtree, Clarissa
Smuggler's Moon - Bruce Alexander t 815

Sade, Donatien Alphonse Francois de
Imagining Don Giovanni - Anthony J. Rudel t 929

Shakespeare, William
Her Infinite Variety - Pamela Rafael Berkman t 823
The Slaying of the Shrew - Simon Hawke t 880
The Slaying of the Shrew - Simon Hawke m 109

Shaw, George Bernard
The Case of the Ripper's Revenge - Sam McCarver m 153

Sierck, Detlef
Drachenfels - Jack Yeovil f 613

Somerville, Molly
This Heart of Mine - Susan Elizabeth Phillips r 369

Staples, Nathan
Everything You Need - A.L. Kennedy c 1138

Tabachnik, Joyce
Good Harbor - Anita Diamant c 1103

Talisford, Katherine "Kate"
Tempt Me Twice - Barbara Dawson Smith r 400

Travers, Sam
Riverwatch - Joseph M. Nassise h 676

Unnamed Character
For Rouenna - Sigrid Nunez c 1172

Webb, Marshall
Island of Tears - Troy Soos t 936
Island of Tears - Troy Soos m 200

Welch, Barry
The Association - Bentley Little h 668

Wolf, Anne
Coldwater - Mardi McConnochie c 1156
Coldwater - Mardi McConnochie t 904

Wolf, Charlotte
Coldwater - Mardi McConnochie t 904
Coldwater - Mardi McConnochie c 1156

Wolf, Emily
Coldwater - Mardi McConnochie c 1156
Coldwater - Mardi McConnochie t 904

Zinzo, Abby
Jewelry Talks - Richard Klein c 1142

YOUNG MAN

Blane
The Nature of Balance - Tim Lebbon h 666

Christy
Bloodlines - Fred D'Aguiar t 846

Jeff
The Last Vampire - T.M. Wright h 712

Peaslee, Wingate
The Shadow out of Time - H.P. Lovecraft h 670

Powell, Moody
This Rock - Robert Morgan t 910

Rodney, Arthur
The Beasts of Brahm - Mark Hansom *h* 646

Sayers, Andrew
The Folks - Ray Garton *h* 638

Shaw, Jeremy
The Beasts of Brahm - Mark Hansom *h* 646

Steinke, Barry
Great American Plain - Gary Sernovitz *c* 1195

Steinke, Edward
Great American Plain - Gary Sernovitz *c* 1195

Thayer, Rand
Buttercup Baby - Karen Fox *r* 287

Tore, Paul
The Nature of Balance - Tim Lebbon *h* 666

Tuco, Eddie
Shooting Dr. Jack - Norman Green *c* 1118

YOUNG WOMAN

Ailish
Swim the Moon - Paul Brandon *f* 529

Ana
Half a Life - V.S. Naipaul *c* 1170

Anbari, Asiadeh
The Girl from the Golden Horn - Kurban Said *c* 1191

Barbara
Chelsea Horror Hotel - Dee Dee Ramone *h* 684

Bollinger, Amanda
The Folks - Ray Garton *h* 638

Caitrionia
The Mystic Rose - Stephen R. Lawhead *t* 901
The Mystic Rose - Stephen R. Lawhead *f* 570

Camille
Once upon a Winter's Night - Dennis L. McKiernan *f* 579

Carrier
Nearly People - Conrad Williams *h* 708

Conway, Babs
Prized Possessions - Jessica Stirling *t* 938

Conway, Polly
Prized Possessions - Jessica Stirling *t* 938

Corkery, Hannah
Stillwater - William F. Weld *t* 955

Croydon, Patricia
Tragic Casements - Oliver Onions *h* 680

Dorsette, Lorna
When Love Came to Town - Lenora Worth *i* 1063

Dunne, Olivia
The Magic of Ordinary Days - Ann Howard Creel *t* 845

Genet, Leila
Great American Plain - Gary Sernovitz *c* 1195

Hardress, Helen
Fairness - Ferdinand Mount *c* 1167

Hayes, Jackie
Written on the Wind - Judith Pella *i* 1040

Heather
Night of Dracula - Christopher Schildt *h* 692

Mackey, Emma
Rhythms - Donna Hill *t* 884

Middleton, Catherine
The Slaying of the Shrew - Simon Hawke *t* 880

Miller, Pinky
The Onion Girl - Charles De Lint *f* 539

Mina
Lightning Field - Dana Spiotta *c* 1202

Moore, Nell
Ghost Killer - Scott Chandler *h* 627

Niiv
Celtika - Robert Holdstock *f* 558

Rhian
Daughter of Lir - Judith Tarr *t* 940

Schoene, Anna
The Distant Land of My Father - Bo Caldwell *t* 835

Shamra
Ice - Stephen Bowkett *s* 724

Summers, Philadelphia "Frosty"
The Water and the Blood - Nancy E. Turner *t* 947

Wakefield, Jocelyn
A Capital Holiday - Janet Dailey *r* 265

Walsh, Lily
Bamboo and Lace - Lori Wick *i* 1059

Weaver, Alison
The Weaver's Inheritance - Kate Sedley *t* 934

Author Index

This index is an alphabetical listing of the authors of books featured in entries and those listed within entries under the rubrics "Other books by the same author" and "Other books you might like." For each author, the titles of books described or listed in this edition and their entry numbers appear. Bold numbers indicate a featured main entry; light-face numbers refer to books recommended for further reading.

A

Aarsen, Carolyne
The Cowboy's Bride 965
A Family at Last 965, 1047, 1061
A Family-Style Christmas 965, 968
A Hero for Kelsey 965
A Mother at Heart 965
Twin Blessings **965**, 1036, 1041, 1043

Abbey, Lynn
Behind Time **515**
The Black Flame 608
Cinnabar Shadows 515
Jerlayne 515
Out of Time 515, 543, 573
Planeswalker 515
The Simbul's Gift 515, 597
Unicorn and Dragon 559, 603

Abbott, Donald
The Magic Chest of Oz 577

Abe, Shana
Intimate Enemies 316
A Kiss at Midnight 266, 368
The Truelove Bride 281, 405

Abella, Alex
The Killing of the Saints 672

Abraham, Pearl
Giving Up America 1064
The Romance Reader 978

Abrahams, Peter
Crying Wolf 1
The Fan 1
Last of the Dixie Heroes **1**
Lights Out 1
A Perfect Crime 1
Revolution #9 1

Acres, Mark
Dragon War 610

Adair, Cherry
Hide and Seek **222**, 242
Kiss and Tell 222, 223, 302, 414
The Mercenary 222, 223
Seducing Mr. Right 222, **223**

Adam, Christina
Any Small Thing Can Save You **1065**, 1128
Sleeping with the Buffalo 1065

Adams, Alice
After the War 821, 870
The Last Lovely City 1080, 1155

Adams, Deborah
The Jesus Creek Series 15, 114

Adams, Douglas
Dirk Gently's Holistic Detective Agency 756
The Hitchhiker's Guide to the Galaxy 1167
The Long Dark Tea-Time of the Soul 813

Adams, Harold
The Carl Wilcox Series 33, 110

Adams, Kylie
Fly Me to the Moon 274

Adams, Richard
Traveller 1065

Adamson, Mary Jo
The Blazing Tree 2
The Elusive Voice **2**

Adcock, Thomas
The Neal Hockaday Series 22
The Neil Hockaday Series 37

Adkins, Patrick H.
Master of the Fearful Depths 547

Adrian, Chris
Gob's Grief 1187, 1195

Adrian, Jack
The Ash-Tree Press Annual Macabre 1997 615
The Ash-Tree Press Annual Macabre 1998 615
The Ash-Tree Press Annual Macabre 1999 615
The Ash-Tree Press Annual Macabre 2000 615
The Ash-Tree Press Annual Macabre 2001 **615**
Strange Tales from the Strand 615

Agnon, S.Y.
Only Yesterday 1098

Aiken, Ginny
The Bellamy's Blossoms Series 1063

Aiken, Joan
The Cockatrice Boys 533

Aikin, Jim
The Wall at the Edge of the World 790

Aird, Catherine
The Inspector Sloan Series 104

Airth, Rennie
River of Darkness 208

Aitken, Judie
A Love Beyond Time 296, 372

Akst, Daniel
St. Burl's Obituary 1066
The Webster Chronicle **1066**

Alam, Glynn Marsh
Deep Water Death **3**
Dive Deep and Deadly 3
The Luanne Fogarty Series 216

Albert, Susan Wittig
Bloodroot **4**
Chile Death 4, 105
The China Bayles Series 32, 67, 89, 120
Lavender Lies 4, 157
Love Lies Bleeding 4
Mistletoe Man 4
Rueful Death 4

Alcorn, Angela
The Ishbane Conspiracy 1054

Aldiss, Brian W.
Bow Down to Nul 791
Brothers of the Head 764
Dracula Unbound 692
Enemies of the System 779, 782
Frankenstein Unbound 691
Helliconia Winter 757
The Long Afternoon of Earth 790
Non-Stop 726
A Tupolev Too Far 745

Aleman Velasco, Miguel
Capili 889

Alers, Rochelle
Hidden Agenda 222, 403
Holiday Cheer 300
Island Magic 403
Just Before Dawn 365
Private Passions 224
'Tis the Season **300**

Alexander, Bruce
The Color of Death 815
Death of a Colonial 815
Jack, Knave and Fool 815
Murder in Grub Street 815
Person or Persons Unknown 815
The Sir John Fielding Series 10, 12, 182, 820
Smuggler's Moon **815**, 853, 881

Alexander, Carrie
A Touch of Black Velvet 333

Alexander, Gary
The Luis Balam Series 195

Alexander, Hannah
The Healing Touch Series 1012

Alexander, Kathryn
The Forever Husband 1035
Heart of a Husband 974

Alexander, Victoria
The Husband List 229, 257, 324
Santa Paws 232

Ali, Tariq
The Stone Woman 893

Alison, Jane
The Love Artist 1091

Allan, Margaret
Keeper of the Stone 510
The Last Mammoth 447, 487, 507, 723

Allen, Conrad
Murder on the Lusitania 5, 816
Murder on the Mauretania 5, 816
Murder on the Minnesota **5, 816**

Allen, Garrison
The Big Mike Series 26, 162

Allen, Irene
The Elizabeth Elliot Series 1062

Allen, Paula Gunn
Spider Woman's Granddaughters 467

Allen, Roger MacBride
Allies and Aliens 742

Allen, Steve
Die Laughing 1158

Allende, Isabel
Daughter of Fortune 817, 1067
Eva Luna 817, 1067
The House of the Spirits 817, 1067
The Infinite Plan 817, 1067, 1172
Paula 817

Portrait in Sepia **817**, **1067**, 1112, 1124, 1205
The Stories of Eva Luna 1067

Allston, Aaron
Doc Sidhe 516
Galatea in 2-D 516
Iron Fist 516
Sidhe-Devil **516**
Solo Command 516
Starfighters of Adumar 516

Allyn, Doug
The Michelle Mitchell Series 3

Alter, Judy
Cherokee Rose 424, 498
Libbie 824

Altman, John
A Gathering of Spies 215, 863

Alton, Andrea
The Demon of Undoing 563

Alvarez, Julia
In the Time of the Butterflies 948

Amann, Marilyn Medlock
The Innocent **410**

Ames, John Edwards
The Unwritten Order 484

Amis, Martin
Time's Arrow 1078

Amos, Robyn
Bring Me a Dream **224**

Anand, Valerie
Queen of Ambition **834**

Anastas, Benjamin
The Faithful Narrative of a Pastor's Disappearance 1133

Andersen, Susan
All Shook Up 292
Baby, Don't Go 333, 363
Baby, I'm Yours 289
Be My Baby 286

Anderson, Adeline Catherine
Sweet Nothings **225**

Anderson, Catherine
Baby Love 225
Cherish 225
Forever After 225, 364
Keegan's Lady 290
Phantom Waltz 225
Seventh Heaven 225
Simply Love 364
Sweet Nothings **225**

Anderson, Kevin J.
Antibodies 715, 737, 773
The Assemblers of Infinity 798
Blindfold 715
Climbing Olympus 715, 771
Dogged Persistence **715**
Ground Zero 715
House Corrino **757**
Ruins 715

Anderson, Poul
After Doomsday 818
Alight in the Void 807
The Broken Sword 517
Conan the Rebel 517, 818
The Dark between the Stars 716
The Day of Their Return 810
Earthman, Go Home! 719, 743
Ensign Flandry 768, 777, 812
Guardians of Time 818
Hrolf Kraki's Saga 517
The King of Ys 818
A Knight of Ghosts and Shadows 728
The Merman's Children 517
Mother of Kings **517**, **818**
No World of Their Own 755
Operation Luna 516
The Psychotechnic League 734
The Shield of Time 818
Star Fox 761
Starship 788
There Will Be Time 754
Virgin Planet 733
War of the Gods 517
War of Two Worlds 800

Andersson, C. Dean
I Am Dracula 686, 692
I Am Frankenstein 691

Andreae, Christine
The Lee Squires Series 7

Andrews, Allen
Castle Crespin 559

Andrews, Donna
The Meg Langslow Series 89, 144
Murder with Peacocks 6, 60, 157
Murder with Puffins 6
Revenge of the Wrought-Iron Flamingos **6**

Andrews, Patrick E.
Comanchero Blood 425, 469
Texican Blood Fight 438

Andrews, Sarah
Bone Hunter 7
An Eye for Gold 7
A Fall in Denver 7
Fault Line **7**
Mother Nature 7
Only Flesh and Bones 7

Andrews, V.C.
Hidden Jewel 1214

Angus, Sylvia
Dead to Rites 195

Anonymous
Primary Colors 1211

Anthony, Mark
The Tower of Doom 604

Anthony, Piers
DoOon Mode 518, 600
Killobyte 518
Mistress of Death 750
Out of Phaze 516, 751
Reality Check 518
Swell Foop **518**, 521
Xone of Contention 518
Yon Ill Wind 518

Antieau, Kim
Trudging to Eden 658

Anton, Shari
The Conqueror 269
Knave of Hearts 295
'Tis the Season **367**

Apostolou, Anna
A Murder in Macedon 859
A Murder in Thebes 859

Applegate, K.A.
Brave the Betrayal 519, 520
Discover the Destroyer 519, 520
Entertain the End **519**
Gateway to the Gods 519, 520
Inside the Illusion 520
Mystify the Magician 519, **520**
Realm of the Reaper 520
Under the Unknown 519

Armistead, John
The Grover Bramlett Series 59, 112

Armstrong, John D.
The Return of Jericho Pike 503

Armstrong, Kelley
Bitten **1068**, 1071, 1185, 1187

Arnason, Eleanor
Daughter of the Bear King 592
A Woman of the Iron People 593

Arnold, A.J.
Dead Man's Cache 490, 499

Arnold, Judith
Birthright 226
Dr. Dad 226
Looking for Laura **226**, 299
Love in Bloom's 226
Millennium Baby 226
Sweet Light 306
'Tis the Season 226

Arnzen, Michael D.
Fluid Mosaic **616**
Grave Markings 616
Needles and Sins 616

Asaro, Catherine
The Ascendant Sun 716
Catch the Lightning 716
The Last Hawk 716
Quantum Rose 716
The Radiant Seas 716
Spherical Harmonic **716**
The Veiled Web 808

Ashford, Jane
Charmed and Dangerous 400

Ashley, Mike
The Mammoth Book of Historical Detectives 8
The Mammoth Book of Historical Whodunnits 8
The Mammoth Book of More Historical Whodunnits **8**
Phantom Perfumes and Other Shades 615
Royal Whodunnits 8
Shakespearean Detectives 8
Shakespearean Whodunnits 8

Asimov, Isaac
The End of Eternity 802
Foundation 777
Nemesis 770

Askew, Rilla
Fire in Beulah 947

Asprin, Robert Lynn
Little Myth Marker 521
Myth-ing Persons 521
Myth-ion Improbable **521**
A Phule and His Money 521
Phule's Company 521
Sweet Myth-tery of Life 521

Asquith, Cynthia
This Mortal Coil 680

Atherton, Gertrude
The Bell in the Fog and Other Stories 711

Atherton, Nancy
Aunt Dimity and the Duke 9
Aunt Dimity Beats the Devil 9
Aunt Dimity: Detective **9**
Aunt Dimity Digs In 9
Aunt Dimity's Christmas 9
Aunt Dimity's Good Deed 9

Atkins, Ace
Crossroad Blues 112

Atkins, Peter
Big Thunder 694
The Wishmaster 696

Attanasio, A.A.
The Dragon and the Unicorn 566
Kingdom of the Grail 570, 901
Solis 736

Atwood, Margaret
Alias Grace 1067, 1139
The Blind Assassin 1073, 1156
The Handmaid's Tale 811
Lady Oracle 1108
Life Before Man 1197
Surfacing 1138

Aubrey, Frank
The Devil-Tree of El Dorado **717**

Auchincloss, Louis
Tales of Yesteryear 1209

Audley, Anselm
Heresy **718**

Auel, Jean M.
The Mammoth Hunters 723
The Valley of Horses 940

Austen, Jane
Pride and Prejudice 359

Auster, Paul
The New York Trilogy 192

Austin, J.D.
Bobby's Girl 719
Second Contact **719**

Austin, Lynn N.
Eve's Daughters 967, 1038
Hidden Places 1017

Avery, Anne
The Lawman Takes a Wife 247

Aycliffe, Jonathan
Naomi's Room 626, 673
A Shadow on the Wall 644

Aylett, Steve
Atom 720
Crime Studio 720
Only an Alligator 720
Slaughtermatic 720
Toxicology **720**

Ayres, Katherine
North by Night 464

Ayrton, Michael
The Maze Maker 547

Azzopardi, Trezza
A Hiding Place 1189

B

Babb, Sanora
Cry of the Tinamou 454, 471

Bachelder, Chris
Bear v. Shark 1084

Bacher, June Masters
Love Is a Gentle Stranger 1011

Bacon, Gail
The Clerk's Tale **70**

Baer, Judy
Libby's Story 1024

Bagley, Desmond
The Golden Keel 171
The Vivero Letter 195

Bailey, Robin W.
Nightwatch 586

Bainbridge, Beryl
According to Queeney **1069**
An Awfully Big Adventure 1069
The Birthday Boys 905, 1069
Every Man for Himself 1069
Master Georgie 1069
Young Adolf 1069

Baker, Jeanette
Irish Fire 386

Baker, Kevin
Dreamland 874

Baker, Linda P.
Tears of the Night Sky 612

Baker, Richard
The City of Ravens 578

Baker, Sharon
Burning Tears of Sassurum 718

Baker, Trisha
Crimson Kiss **617**

Balchin, Nigel
The Borgia Testament 916

Baldacci, David
Absolute Power 1186
The Last Man Standing 1127
Total Control 1141
Wish You Well 1157, 1184, 1200

Baldwin, Bill
Canby's Legion 742, 795

Baldwin, James
If Beale Street Could Talk 1179

Baldwin, Louisa
From Fancy's Realm 618
The Pedlar's Pack 618
Richard Dare 618
The Shadow on the Blind **618**
The Story of a Marriage 618
Where Town and Country Meet 618

Balint, Christine
The Salt Letters **819**

Ball, Brian
The Probability Man 772

Ball, John
In the Heat of the Night 59, 122

Ball, Margaret
Lost in Translation 543
No Earthly Sunne 583

Ballard, Allen B.
Where I'm Bound 864, 919

Ballard, J.G.
Cocaine Nights 1070
Crash 1108
The Kindness of Women 1070
Running Wild 1070
Rushing to Paradise 1070
Super-Cannes **1070**
War Fever 1070

Ballard, Mignon F.
Angel at Troublesome Creek 522
An Angel to Die For **522**
The Augusta Goodnight Series 9

Ballas, Jack
Gun Boss 451
Tomahawk Canyon 459, 492, 504, 505, 514

Balogh, Mary
Angel Christmas 366
Beyond the Sunrise 308, 389
Christmas Belle 304
A Christmas Bride 227, 271, 367
Dancing with Clara 388
The Famous Heroine 393
Indiscreet 227
Irresistible 227
The Last Waltz 362
Lord Carew's Bride 325, 349
More than a Mistress 227
No Man's Mistress **227**
One Night for Love 227, 298
A Regency Christmas Feast 248
Tempting Harriet 262
Thief of Dreams 298

Bambola, Sylvia
Refiner's Fire 966
Tears in a Bottle **966**

Bank, Melissa
The Girls' Guide to Hunting and Fishing 345, 1087, 1125

Banks, Iain
Against a Dark Background 721
Excession 721
Feersum Endjinn 721
Inversions 721
Look to Windward **721**
Use of Weapons 721

Banks, T.F.
The Thief-Taker **10**, 182, 815, **820**, 822, 853, 915

Bannister, Jo
Broken Lines 11
Burning Desire 11
The Castlemere Series 64
Changelings 11
Echoes of Lies **11**
The Hireling's Tale 11
No Birds Sang 11

Banti, Anna
Artemisia 951

Barbet, Pierre
The Games Psyborgs Play 755

Barbour, Anne
Lord Glenraven's Return 349
A Rake's Reform 279, 392
A Talent for Trouble 291

Barclay, James
Dawnthief 523, 569, 589
Nightchild **523**
Noonshade 523, 550, 572, 611

Barclay, Suzanne
The Knights of Christmas 367

Barker, Clive
Books of Blood 1071
Cabal 694
Coldheart Canyon **619**, **1071**, 1140, 1185
Everville 619
Galilee 619
The Great and Secret Show 619
The Hellbound Heart 640
Hellraiser 1071
Imajica 1071
In the Flesh 1071
Sacrament 619
Thief of Always 1071
Weaveworld 619, 642, 659

Barker, Jane Valentine
Mari 481, 498, 513

Barker, Pat
Regeneration 857
The Regeneration Trilogy 943

Barnard, Robert
The Cherry Blossom Corpse 49
Death of a Salesperson and Other Untimely Exits 142, 146
Death of an Old Goat 176
A Little Local Murder 27
Out of the Blackout 92, 136
Skeleton in the Grass 183

Barnes, John
Apostrophes and Apocalypses 722
Earth Made of Glass 722
Finity 722
The Merchants of Souls **722**
A Million Open Doors 722
Washington's Dirigible 722

Barnes, Julian
A History of the World in 10 1/2 Chapters 1095
Love, etc. 1099, 1102, 1142

Barnes, Linda
The Carlotta Carlyle Series 143, 217
Snapshot 168

Barnes, Steven
The Gorgon Child 750

Barnett, Jill
Bewitching 821
Carried Away 228, 821
Dreaming 821
The Heart's Haven 821
Imagine 228, 287, 350, 821
Sentimental Journey **228**, **821**, 845, 870, 876, 925
Wicked 228, 269, 316, 321, 396
Wild 228, 281
Wonderful 228, 303

Barnitz, Charles
The Deepest Sea 559

Barr, Nevada
The Anna Pigeon Series 3, 7, 19, 102
Blood Lure 25
Liberty Falling 66

Barre, Richard
Blackheart Highway 189
The Wil Hardesty Series 74

Barrett, Andrea
The Voyage of the Narwhal 905

Barrett, Jean
The Hunt for Hawke's Daughter 410

Barrett, Neal Jr.
Aldair, Master of Ships 524
Dungeons and Dragons 524
The Hereafter Gang 524
Perpetuity Blues 524
The Prophecy Machine 518, 524
The Treachery of Kings **524**

Barron, Stephanie
Jane and the Genius of the Place 12, 822
Jane and the Man of the Cloth 12, 822
Jane and the Prisoner of Wool House **12**, **822**
Jane and the Stillroom Maid 12, 822
Jane and the Unpleasantness at Scargrave Manor 12, 822
Jane and the Wandering Eye 12, 822
The Jane Austen Series 10, 815, 820, 959

Barth, John
Lost in the Funhouse 720
The Margaret Binton Series 96
On with the Story 1087
The Sot-Weed Factor 950

Barthelme, Donald
City Life 720

Barthelme, Frederick
The Law of Averages 1080, 1087, 1121
Painted Desert 1150

Bartholomew, Nancy
Dragstrip 13
Film Strip 13
The Miracle Strip 13
The Sierra Lavatoni Series 38
Strip Poker **13**

Barton, Beverly
Navajo's Woman 417

Barton, Wayne
Warhorse 478

Bass, Cynthia
Maiden Voyage 816

Bass, Rick
Platte River 1146
The Sky, the Stars, the Wilderness 427, 452, 456, 492, 505

Battle, Lois
War Brides 228

Baudino, Gael
Maze of Moonlight 603
Shroud of Shadow 527

Bauer, C.A.
The White Horses 453, 457, 470, 483, 488, 500

Baum, L. Frank
The Wizard of Oz 577

Baumgardner, Cathie L.
The Marine and the Princess **334**
Stranded with the Sergeant **335**

Bausch, Richard
Someone to Watch over Me 1147, 1155

Baxter, Stephen
Icebones **723**
Longtusk 879
Mammoth 723
Manifold: Space 723, 807
Manifold: Time 723
Moonseed 723
Vacuum Diagrams 766
Voyage 723, 739

Bayley, Barrington J.
Soul of the Robot 780

Beamish, Noel de Vic
The Unfortunate Queen Matilda 862

Bean, Frederic
Border Justice 440
Eden 481, 495
Law of the Gun 458, 479
Murder at Spirit Cave 428, 502
Murder at the Spirit Cave 444, 465, 472, 475, 477, 482, 506, 511, 513
Murder in the Spirit Cave 474
The Outlaw 436, 442
Pancho and Black Jack 476
The Red River 441, 508
Renegade 426, 429, 895

Bean, Gregory
The Harry Starbranch Series 25

Bear, Greg
Blood Music 710, 798
Queen of Angels 758
Tangents 766

Beard, Julie
A Dance in Heather 229
Falcon and the Sword 229

The Maiden's Heart 229
My Fair Lord 229
Romance of the Rose 229
Very Truly Yours **229**

Beaton, M.C.
Agatha Raisin and the Fairies of Fryfam 14
Agatha Raisin and the Love from Hell **14**
Agatha Raisin and the Murderous Marriage 14
Agatha Raisin and the Terrible Tourist 14
Agatha Raisin and the Wellspring of Death 14
Agatha Raisin and the Wizard of Evesham 14
The Agatha Raisin Series 27, 96, 191

Beattie, Ann
My Life, Starring Dara Falcon 1198
Park City 1192
Perfect Recall 1072, 1077, 1155, 1162, 1196, 1201

Beaumont, Charles
Selected Stories 678

Bebris, Carrie
Pool of Radiance **525**

Beck, Kathleen
My Darling Valentine 378

Becnel, Rexanne
The Matchmaker 311, 400
The Mistress of Rosecliffe 266

Bedford, Deborah
Chickadee 967
A Child's Promise 967
Harvest Dance 967
A Rose by the Door **967**
Timberline 967

Begiebing, Robert J.
The Adventures of Allegra Fullerton 894

Belfer, Lauren
City of Light 24, 839

Bell, Ann
Distant Love 999

Bell, Clare
Jaguar Princess 889
Ratha's Creature 574

Bell, Donna
The First Waltz 230, 262
Heiress to Love 230, 348, 355
An Improper Pursuit 279, 398
Sweet Tranquility 230
A Tangled Web **230**
Valentine Kisses 230
Words of Love 230

Bell, Madison Smartt
Master of the Crossroads 1134

Bell, Nancy
Biggie and the Fricaseed Fat Man 15
Biggie and the Mangled Mortician 15
Biggie and the Meddlesome Mailman 15
Biggie and the Poisoned Politician 15
Biggie and the Quincy Ghost **15**
The Biggie Weatherford Series 114

Bellacera, Carole
Border Crossings 231
East of the Sun, West of the Moon **231**
Spotlight 231

Bellairs, John
The House with a Clock in Its Walls 623

Bellow, Saul
The Actual 1072
Collected Stories **1072**
The Dean's December 1072
Henderson the Rain King 1094
Humboldt's Gift 1072
More Die of Heartbreak 1141
Mr. Sammler's Planet 1072, 1138
Ravelstein 1072, 1145, 1158

Beman, Donald
Avatar 620
Dead Love **620**
The Taking 620

Benard, Cheryl
Turning on the Girls 1142, 1209

Benchley, Peter
The Deep 1097

Bendell, Don
Coyote Run 459

Bender, Carrie
The Miriam's Journal Series 1018

Benedict, Elizabeth
Almost **1073**, 1112, 1163
The Beginner's Book of Dreams 1073
Safe Conduct 1073
Slow Dancing 1073

Benford, Gregory
Shiva Descending 767

Benjamin, Carol Lea
The Dog Who Knew Too Much 16
A Hell of a Dog 16
Lady Vanishes 16
The Long Good Boy **16**
The Rachel Alexander Series 17
This Dog for Hire 16
The Wrong Dog 16

Benjamin, Curt
The Prince of Shadow **526**

Bennett, Janice
Autumn Kittens **232**

Bennett, M.J.
Seeking the Dream Brother 593
Where the Ni-Lach 725
Yaril's Children 576

Bennett, Nigel
His Father's Son **621**
Keeper of the King 621

Bennetts, Pamela
The Borgia Prince 916

Benrey, Ron
Little White Lies 996, 1008, 1009

Benson, Ann
The Burning Road 832, 844

Benson, E.F.
The Collected Ghost Stories of E.F. Benson 622
The Flint Knife 622
Mrs. Amworth **622**
The Passenger 622
The Room in the Tower and Other Stories 622
Terror by Night 622

Benson, Jessica
Lord Stanhope's Proposal 420
Much Obliged 370

Benson, Margaret
The Gingerbread Man **395**

Benton, Kenneth
Death on the Appian Way 924

Bentz, Joseph
A Son Comes Home 988, 1024, 1038

Benyon, Melissa
Cinderella After Midnight **268**

Berberick, Nancy Varian
The Panther's Hoard 612
Stormblade 525

Berenson, Laurien
Dog Eat Dog 17
Hair of the Dog 17
Hush Puppy 17
The Melanie Travers Series 16
Once Bitten **17**
Unleashed 17
Watchdog 17

Berg, Elizabeth
Never Change 1086
Talk Before Sleep 1103

Berg, Patti
Born to Be Wild 363
My Scottish Summer **243**
Wife for a Day 289, 292

Berger, Eileen
The Deacon's Daughter 968
A Family for Andi 968
A Family for Jana **968**
Reunions 968
A Special Kind of Family 968, 974
To Galilee with Love 968

Bergman, Andrew
Hollywood and LeVine 83, 161

Bergren, Lisa Tawn
Firestorm 999
Letters of the Heart **233**, **969**
Midnight Sun 1042
A Mother's Love 233
The Northern Lights Series 1011
Pathways 971, 1000, 1030
Porch Swings & Picket Fences 233, 986

Bergstrom, Elaine
Baroness of Blood 613

Bergstrom, Elizabeth
The Door through Washington Square 515, 573

Berkman, Pamela Rafael
Her Infinite Variety **823**

Bernard, Robert
Deadly Meeting 176

Berne, Betsy
Bad Timing 1210

Berne, Suzanne
A Perfect Arrangement 1070

Bernhard, Virginia
A Durable Fire 950

Bernhardt, William
The Ben Kincaid Series 113

Berry, Stephen Ames
The Final Assault 795

Berry, Wendell
A Place on Earth 872

Bertin, Joanne
The Last Dragonlord 590, 610

Betts, Heidi
Almost a Lady 234
Cinnamon and Roses 234
A Promise of Roses 234
Walker's Widow **234**, 294, 391

Bevarly, Elizabeth
First Comes Love 235, 236, 261, 264, 299, 369, 380
He Could Be the One 235, 236, 363
Her Man Friday 292
How to Trap a Tycoon 236
Monahan's Gamble 235, 236
The Secret Life of Connor Monahan **235**
The Temptation of Rory Monahan 235, 236
When Jayne Met Erik 235, **236**, 246

Beverley, Jo
Deirdre and Don Juan 356
Dierdre and Don Juan 325
My Lady Notorious 307, 329, 352
Something Wicked 260
Tempting Fortune 307, 308

Biggin, John
The Two-Headed Eagle 954

Biggle, Lloyd
Silence Is Deadly 763, 813

Biguenet, John
The Torturer's Apprentice 1087, 1142

Billerbeck, Kristin
Forever Friends 986

Binchy, Maeve
Circle of Friends 1111
Tara Road 1169

Binder, Eando
The Double Man 759

Binder, Pam
The Enchantment **237**
The Inscription 237
The Quest 237, 323

Binding, Tim
Lying with the Enemy 888

Bird, Sarah
The Mommy Club 1093

Birmingham, Ruth
Atlanta Graves 18
Blue Plate Special **18**
Fulton County Blues 18
The Sunny Childs Series 143
Sweet Georgia 18

Birmingham, Sonya
The Spitfire 332

Bishop, Anne
Daughter of the Blood 527
Heir to the Shadows 527
The Invisible Ring 527
The Pillars of the World **527**
Queen of the Darkness 527

Bishop, Claudia
The Sarah and Meg Quilliam Series 32, 138

Bishop, Michael
Beneath the Shattered Moons 740
Blue Kansas Sky 748
Stolen Faces 733, 810

Bishop, Paul
The Fay Croaker Series 47
The Fey Croaker Series 137

Biss, Gerald
The Door of the Unreal 646

Bissell, Sallie
A Darker Justice **19**
In the Forest of Harm 19, **1074**

Bisson, Terry
Virtuosity 731

Bittner, Rosanne
Chase the Sun 471
Cherished Love 280
Mystic Warriors 423, 911
Song of the Wolf 467
Tame the Wild Wind 471

Bjorneby, Karen
Hurricane Season **1075**

Black, Cara
Murder in the Marais 126

Black, Ethan
All the Dead Were Strangers **20**, **1076**
The Broken Hearts Club 20, 1076
The Conrad Voort Series 204
Irresistible 20, 1076

Black, Michelle
Hannah and the Horseman 423
Lightning in a Drought Year 423
Never Come Down 423
River Come Down 824
This Man Colter 423
An Uncommon Enemy **423**, **824**

Blacker, Irwin R.
Taos 476, 510

Blackstock, Terri
Broken Wings 971, 1000, 1030
Cape Refuge **970**, 985
Emerald Windows 970, **971**, 1035, 1045
The Newpointe 911 Series 999, 1012
Private Justice 971
Seaside 970, 971
The Second Chances Series 993, 1006
Shadow of Doubt 970
The Sun Coast Chronicles 1048
Trial by Fire 970, 971
Word of Honor 970, 971

Blackwell, Lawana
The Gresham Chronicles 1013, 1027
The Tales of London Series 1020
The Victorian Serenade Series 1015

Blackwood, Algernon
The Empty House and Other Ghost Stories 647
The Magic Mirror 680

Blackwood, Scott
In the Shadow of Our House **1077**

Blair, Catherine
Athena's Conquest 230, 238, 398
A Family for Gillian **238**
The Hero Returns 238, 397
The Scandalous Miss Delaney 238

Blair, Clifford
Storm over the Lightening L 458

Blake, James Carlos
Borderlands 825
The Friends of Pancho Villa 424, 513, 825
In the Rogue Blood 424, 825
The Pistoleer 424, 825
Red Grass River 424, 481, 513
Wildwood Boys 424, 825
A World of Thieves **424**, **825**, 841, 887

Blake, Michael
Dances with Wolves 425, 826
The Holy Road **425**, **826**, 827, 911
Marching to Valhalla 425, 438, 826

Blake, Toni
Seducing Summer 223

Blakely, Mike
Baron of the Sacramentos 476
Comanche Dawn 447, 507, 827, 1137
Dead Reckoning 440
Moon Medicine **827**
Shortgrass Song 508, 827
Spanish Blood 492, 505
Summer of Pearls 463, 512, 827
Too Long at the Dance 827
Vendetta Gold 827

Blanc, Nero
The Crossword Murder 96

Bland, Eleanor Taylor
Done Wrong 21
Keep Still 21
The Marti McAlister Series 220
Scream in Silence 21
See No Evil 21
Tell No Tales 21
Whispers in the Dark **21**

Blaylock, James P.
The Paper Grail 781
The Rainy Season 515, 567, 573

Blayne, Sara
His Scandalous Duchess 385

Blevins, Winfred
Stone Song 890

Blinder, Martin
Fluke 874

Blish, James
Doctor Mirabilis 956

Bloch, Robert
The Best of Robert Bloch 678
The Early Fears 671
Monsters in Our Midst 651
Out of the Mouths of Graves 48, 117
Robert Bloch's Psychos 634
Strange Eons 670

Blochman, Lawrence G.
Bombay Mail 132

Block, Lawrence
The Bernie Rhodenbarr Series 16, 72, 202
The Best American Mystery Stories 84
The Chip Harrison Series 56
Death Cruise 816
The Devil Knows You're Dead 22
Even the Wicked 22
Everybody Dies 22
Hit List 190, 202
Hope to Die **22**
Like a Lamb to the Slaughter 48, 99
A Long Line of Dead Men 22
The Matt Scudder Series 42, 74, 213
Some Days You Get the Bear 85, 175
Sometimes They Bite 117
Sometimes You Get the Bear 147
A Walk Among the Tombstones 22

Block, Valerie
Was It Something I Said 1125

Bloom, Amy
A Blind Man Can See How Much I Love You 1147

Bloom, Ursula
The Romance of Charles Dickens 917

Blue, Mary Clearman
Lambing out and Other Stories 468

Blumlein, Michael
The Brains of Rats 616, 624

Bly, Stephen A.
The Fortunes of the Black Hills Series 1050
Friends and Enemies **972**, 973
The General's Notorious Widow 972, 973
Hidden Treasure 973
The Long Trail Home 972, 973
The Outlaw's Twin Sister 972, **973**
Picture Rock 972, 973
The Senator's Other Daughter 972

Bock, Dennis
The Ash Garden **1078**, 1171
Olympia 1078

Bockoven, Georgia
Another Summer **239**
The Beach House 239
Disguised Blessing 239
Far from Home 239
Things Remembered 239
An Unspoken Promise 239

Boehm, Deborah
Ghost of a Smile 1128

Boeshaar, Andrea
The Painting 969

Boetius, Henning
The Phoenix **828**

Boggs, Johnny D.
Riding with Hannah and the Horseman 474
Ten and Me 509

Bogue, Lucile
Blood on the Wind **426**
Dancers on Horseback 426
Miracle on a Mountain 426
One Woman, One Ranch, One Summer 426

Boileau, Thomas
Choice Cuts 677

Bolitho, Janie
Framed in Cornwall 54

Bonander, Jane
Scent of Lilacs 270
Warrior Heart 270

Bond, Michael
The Monsieur Pamplemousse Series 138

Bond, Stephanie
About Last Night 240
It Takes a Rebel 236, 240
Manhunting in Mississippi 223, 235
Our Husband 240
Seeking Single Male 240, 261, 299
Too Hot to Sleep 240
Two Sexy **240**

Bone, J.F.
The Lani People 774

Bonham, Frank
The Canon of Maverick Brands 427
One Ride Too Many 427, 453
Stage Trails West **427**

Booth, Stephen
The Ben Cooper Series 186
Black Dog 23, 179
Dancing with the Virgins **23**

Borchardt, Alice
Beguiled 336, 337, 829
Devoted 338, 829
The Dragon Queen **528**, **829**
Night of the Wolf 322, 528, 829
The Silver Wolf 322, 528, 685, 829
The Wolf King 528, 829

Borges, Jorge Luis
Doctor Brodie's Report 787

Borowitz, Albert
This Club Frowns on Murder 34

Borton, D.B.
The Cat Caliban Series 124

Borton, Douglas
Kane 665

Boswell, Barbara
Magic Slippers 243, 268

Bottoms, Greg
Sentimental, Heartbroken Rednecks **1079**

Boucher, Rita
The Poet and the Paragon 262, 392

Boullosa, Carmen
Leaving Tabasco 1091

Bourdain, Anthony
Gone Bamboo 202

Bova, Ben
Mars 814
Return to Mars 771

Bowen, Elizabeth
The Heat of the Day 876

Bowen, Gary
Diary of a Vampire 690

Bowen, Michael
Fielder's Choice 188

Bowen, Peter
Kelly and the Three-Toed Horse 475, 827
Thunder Horse 465, 472, 475, 477, 511
Wolf, No Wolf 68

Bowen, Rhys
The Constable Evans Series 830
Evan and Elle 24
Evan Can Wait 24, 55
Evan Help Us 24
Evanly Choirs 24
Evans Above 24
Murphy's Law **24**, 200, **830**

Bowers, B.M.
Lonesome Land 495

Bowker, Richard
Replica 806

Bowkett, Stephen
Dreamcastle 724
Dreamcatcher 724
Frontiersville High 724
Gameplayers 724
Ice **724**
Spellbinder 724

Bowles, Paul
Delicate Prey 1080
A Distant Episode 1080
Midnight Mass 1080
Points in Time 1080
The Stories of Paul Bowles **1080**, 1115
Unwelcome Words 1080

Bowman, Doug
The Copelands 511
Guns of Billy Free 479
The Three Lives of Littleton Blue 504, 514

Box, C.J.
Open Season **25**, **428**

Box, Edgar
Death in the Fifth Position 71

Boyd, Donna
The Promise 1068

Boyer, Elizabeth
The Troll's Grindstone 583

Boyer, G.G.
The Guns of Morgette 429
Morgette in the Yukon 429
Morgette on the Barbary Coast **429**
Winchester Affidavit 429

Boyer, Rick
The Doc Adams Series 46, 206
The Giant Rat of Sumatra 210

Boylan, Eleanor
The Clara Gamadge Series 91

Boyle, Gerry
The Jack McMorrow Series 151

Boyle, T. Coraghessan
After the Plague **1081**, 1091, 1193
East Is East 1081
A Friend of the Earth 1081
The Road to Wellville 1081
The Tortilla Curtain 1081, 1116, 1202
Without a Hero 1081

Brackett, Leigh
The Long Tomorrow 732

Bradbury, Malcolm
To the Hermitage 946, 1069

Bradbury, Ray
Ahmed and the Oblivion Machines 1082
Dark Carnival 623, 1082
Driving Blind 1082
Fahrenheit 451 668, 782, 1082
From the Dust Returned **623**, 1070, **1082**, 1171
Green Shadows, White Whale 1082
The Halloween Tree 623
The October Country 623
Something Wicked This Way Comes 623
The Stories of Ray Bradbury 623, 678

Bradford, Barbara Taylor
Her Own Rules 1108
Love in Another Town 1199
A Sudden Change of Heart 1103, 1174
The Triumph of Katie Byrne 1074

Bradley, Celeste
Fallen **241**

Bradley, Laura
Hot and Bothered **285**

Bradley, Marion Zimmer
Black Trillium 725
Exile's Song 725
The Fall of Neskaya **725**
Glenraven 725
Hawkmistress! 267, 732
In the Rift 725
The Mists of Avalon 528, 940
Priestess of Avalon 831, 907
Rediscovery 725
The Spell Sword 576

Bradshaw, Gillian
The Bearkeeper's Daughter 831, 920
Horses of Heaven 831
Imperial Purple 831
In Winter's Shadow 595
The Sand-Reckoner 831, 859
The Wolf Hunt 818, **831**, 921
The Wrong Reflection 831

Brady, Joan
Theory of War 846

Brand, Fiona
Blade's Lady 242

Brand, Irene
Autumn's Awakening 974
A Groom to Come Home To 974
The Legacies of Faith Series 979, 990, 994, 1053
Summer's Promise 965, **974**, 1036, 1041, 1043, 1057
Tender Love 974
The Test of Love 974, 1022
To Love and Honor 974, 987, 1021

Brand, Max
Beyond the Outposts 432, 435
The Black Rider and Other Stories 430, 461, 491
The Bright Face of Danger 430, 431, 432, 435, 473, 486, 489
Don Diablo: A Western Story 431, 433
The Garden of Eden 717
The Gauntlet **430**
The Ghost Wagon and Other Great Western Adventures 491
Gunman's Goal 432, 435
The House of Gold **431**
The Legend of Thunder Moon 1137
The Lone Rider **432**
Men Beyond the Law 430, 432, 435, 486
The Outlaw Redeemer 433, 434, 455, 460, 489
The Overland Kid: A Western Trio 427, 431, 434, 445, 494, 496
The Peril Trek: A Western Trio 433
The Rock of Kiever 434
Soft Metal 434
Stolen Gold **433**
The Survival of Juan Oro **434**
Tales of the Wild West 430, 452
The Tyrant 431, 432, 433, 434, 435
The Welding Quirt: A Western Trio 431, 433
The Wolf Strain 430, **435**

Brandon, Paul
Swim the Moon **529**

Brashear, Charles
Killing Cynthia Ann 454, 466

Brass, Perry
The Harvest 1093

Braun, Lilian Jackson
The Cat Who Robbed a Bank 26
The Cat Who Sang for the Birds 26
The Cat Who Saw Stars 26
The Cat Who Series 162
The Cat Who Smelled a Rat 26
The Cat Who Tailed a Thief 26
The Cat Who Went Up the Creek **26**

Braun, Matt
Doc Holliday 485
Noble Outlaw 493
Texas Empire 425, 462, 469, 497

Braunbeck, Gary A.
In Hollow Houses 575, 737
The Indifference of Heaven 694
This Flesh Unknown 1071

Bredenberg, Jeff
The Man in the Moon Must Die 759

Breen, Jon L.
Sleuths of the Century 84

Brenchley, Chaz
The Keys to D'Esperance 655

Brennan, Joseph Payne
Stories of Darkness and Dread 707

Brennan, Maeve
The Rose Garden 872

Brett, Simon
The Body on the Beach 14, 27
Death on the Downs **27**
The Mrs. Pargeter Series 96
Mrs. Pargeter's Pound of Flesh 38

Bretton, Barbara
A Soft Place to Fall 225

Briery, Tracy
The Vampire Journals 621

Briggs, Dean
The Most Important Little Boy in the World 975

Bright, Bill
Blessed Child **975**

Brin, David
The River of Time 766

Bristow, Allen P.
The Pinkerton Eye **436**

Brite, Poppy Z.
Are You Loathsome Tonight? 658
Drawing Blood 640
Lost Souls 625, 699
Love in Vein 643, 654
Swamp Foetus 629, 656
Wrong Things **624**, 679

Britton, Pamela
Enchanted by Your Kisses 309

Broadrick, Annette
Hard to Forget 246

Brockmann, Suzanne
Body Guard 222, 399
The Defiant Hero 242
Get Lucky 242, 283
Identity Unknown 242
Over the Edge 222, 242, 399
Prince Joe 422
Stand-In Groom 236
Taylor's Temptation **242**
The Unsung Hero 242

Brockway, Connie
The Bridal Season 321
My Scottish Summer **243**

Broderick, Damien
The Black Grail 570, 726
Not the Only Planet **726**
The Sea's Furthest End 726
Sorcerer's World 726
Striped Holes 726
The White Abacus 726

Brookner, Anita
The Bay of Angels 1073, 1203
Family and Friends 1143
A Friend from England 1172
A Private View 1184

Brooks, Betty
Jade 868

Brooks, Geraldine
Year of Wonders **832**, **1083**

Brooks, Janice Young
Someone to Watch over Me **33**

Brooks, Terry
Angel Fire East 530
Antrax **530**, 611
The First King of Shannara 530
The Ilse Witch 530
Running with the Demon 530
The Sword of Shannara 584
Tangle Box 530

Broster, D.K.
Couching at the Door 647

Brouwer, Sigmund
Wings of Dawn 1060

Brown, Brian
TV **1084**

Brown, Carrie
The Hatbox Baby 874

Brown, Debra Lee
Ice Maiden 244, 338
The Mackintosh Bride **244**
The Virgin Spring 244, 288

Brown, Fredric
From These Ashes 715
The Mind Thing 801

Brown, Irene Bennett
The Plainswoman 495

Brown, John Gregory
Audubon's Watch 817, **833**, 913, **1085**
Decorations in a Ruined Cemetery 833, 1085
The Wrecked, Blessed Body of Shelton Lafleur 833, 1085

Brown, Larry
Big Bad Love 1155
Dirty Work 1088
Father and Son 1180
Joe 1140

Brown, Mary
Pigs Don't Fly 587

Brown, Molly
Bad Timing and Other Stories **727**

Brown, Rebecca
The Dogs 1065

Brown, Rita Mae
Dolley 912
The Mrs. Murphy Series 26, 162
Rubyfruit Jungle 1213

Brown, Sam
Devil's Rim 459
Ross Henry 459

Brown, Sandra
The Alibi 245, 1086
Bittersweet Rain 1086
Breath of Scandal 312
Envy **245**, **1086**
Fat Tuesday 245
French Silk 301
In a Class by Itself 1086
Mirror Image 381
Send No Flowers 1086
Standoff 245, 1086
The Switch 245
Unspeakable 245

Brown, Stan
The Crab **531**

Brown, Wesley
Darktown Strutters 846

Browne, D.L.
The Art of Dying **1009**

Browning, Dixie
The Bride-in-Law 246
Look What the Stork Brought 246
The Millionaire's Pregnant Bride 246
More to Love 246

Rocky and the Senator's Daughter **246**, 335
Stryker's Wife 341
Tumbled Wall 246

Browning, Sinclair
Crack Shot **28**
The Last Song Dogs 28
Rode Hard, Put Away Dead 28, 428, 436, 442, 444, 472, 477, 502, 506
The Sporting Club 28
The Trade Ellis Series 39, 125

Brownley, Margaret
Chocolate Kisses 344

Brownrigg, Sylvia
Pages for You 1121, 1213

Bruchac, Joseph
The Arrow over the Door 464
The Heart of a Chief 464
The Waters Between 447, 507

Brugalette, Philip
The Nine Gates 553

Bruhns, Nina
Catch Me If You Can 417

Brunner, John
The Atlantic Abomination 794
The Dramaturges of Yan 772
The Jagged Orbit 779
Muddle Earth 752
Shockwave Rider 782, 808
Stand on Zanzibar 758
The Super Barbarians 746

Brust, Steven A.
To Reign in Hell 553

Bryan, Jessica
Across a Wine Dark Sea 401, 562

Bryant, Dorothy
The Comforter 747

Bryers, Paul
The Prayer of the Bone 42

Buchanan, Edna
The Britt Montero Series 75

Buchanan, James David
A Horde of Fools **437**

Buckley, Fiona
The Doublet Affair 29, 834
Queen of Ambition **29**, **834**
Queen's Ransom 29, 834
To Ruin a Queen 29, 834
To Shield the Queen 29, 834
The Ursula Blanchard Series 65, 861, 880

Budrys, Algis
Blood and Burning 803
Michaelmas 800

Buechner, Frederick
Brendan 886

Bujold, Lois McMaster
The Borders of Infinity 728
Cetaganda 734, 812
A Civil Campaign 728
Dreamweaver's Dilemma 728
Komarr 728
Miles, Mystery & Mayhem **728**
Mirror Dance 728
The Warrior's Apprentice 809

Bull, Emma
War for the Oaks 598, 602, 614

Bulmer, Kenneth
Land Beyond the Map 520
No Man's World 769

Bulock, Lynn
Gifts of Grace 1052
The Prodigal's Return 1046, 1057

Bulychev, Kir
Half a Life 787

Bunch, Chris
Corsair 729
The Demon King 563, 729
Firemask 729, 809
Homefall **729**
The Last Legion 729
Storm Force 729

Bunn, T. Davis
The Amber Room 1056
The Book of Hours 976, 1010
The Dream Voyagers 976
Drummer in the Dark **976**
The Gift 983
The Great Divide 976
One Shenandoah Winter 1033
The Rendezvous with Destiny Series 1034, 1040
The Ultimatum 976, 1004
The Warning 976, 1016

Burgess, Anthony
Byrne 846
Nothing Like the Sun 823

Burgess, Melvin
Bloodtide **730**

Burgin, Richard
Fear of Blue Skies 1087
Ghost Quartet 1087
Man Without Memory 1087
Private Fame 1087
The Spirit Returns **1087**

Burke, James Lee
Bitterroot **1088**, 1146
Cimarron Rose 1088
The Convict and Other Stories 1088
The Dave Robicheaux Series 22, 50, 59, 94, 112, 1088, 1127
Heartwood 1204
In the Electric Mist with Confederate Dead 1, 1214
Purple Cane Road 1088
Two for Texas 1088

Burke, Jan
The Irene Kelly Series 53, 98

Burke, Jonathan
The Golden Gong and Other Night-Pieces 680

Burleson, Donald R.
Beyond the Lamplight 706
Flute Song 661

Burnard, Bonnie
A Good House 1113

Burnett, W.R.
Goodbye Chicago 119

Burns, Rex
The Avenging Angel 76

Burns, Ron
Roman Nights 180
Roman Shadows 184

Burns, Stephen L.
Flesh and Silver 805

Burrage, A.M.
Warning Whispers 622

Burton, Mary
A Bride for McCain 247
The Colorado Bride 234, **247**, 391

Burton, Rainelle
The Root Worker 1133, 1164

Burton, Richard
Vikram and the Vampire 713

Busby, F.M.
The Breeds of Man 753

Busch, Frederick
The Children in the Woods 1192
Don't Tell Anyone 1081
The Mutual Friend 917
The Night Inspector 830, 936

Bush, Beverly
Wings of a Dove 1002, 1029

Bush, Catherine
Minus Time 1094

Bushnell, Candace
Four Blondes 1125

Bushyhead, Anne
Desire **309**

Butler, Gwendoline
A Coffin for Charley 30
Coffin's Game 30
Coffin's Ghost **30**
A Dark Coffin 30
A Double Coffin 30
A Grave Coffin 30

Butler, Nancy
Keeper of Swans 318
Lord Monteith's Gift 370
The Rake's Retreat 374, 377
A Regency Christmas Eve 248, 367
Regency Christmas Spirits **248**

Butler, Octavia
Kindred 811

Butts, J. Lee
Law Dog **438**

Byatt, A.S.
The Biographer's Tale 1092, 1144, 1182, 1189
The Djinn in the Nightingale's Eye 1178
Elementals 1169
The Matisse Stories 1120

Byers, Richard Lee
The Ebon Mask 532
Fright Line 532
Netherworld 532
The Shattered Mask **532**
The Vampire's Apprentice 532, 712
Warlock Games 532

Byrne, John
Whipping Boy 637

C

Cabell, James Branch
The High Place 603

Cabot, Patricia
An Improper Proposal 400

Cacek, P.D.
Bell, Book and Beyond 704
Leavings 630, 683
Night Players 617, **625**
Night Prayers 625, 645, 699

Cach, Lisa
The Wildest Shore 320
Wish List **320**

Cade, Will
Larimont 484, 511

Cadigan, Pat
Avatar 731
Dervish Is Digital **731**
Fools 731
Patterns 731
Synners 731
Tea from an Empty Cup 731

Cady, Jack
The Jonah Watch 681
The Sons of Noah and Other Stories 707

Cail, Carol
The Maxey Burnell Series 51
The Seeds of Time 465

Caille, Julie
A Mother's Heart 280

Caldwell, Bo
The Distant Land of My Father **835**

Callen, Gayle
His Betrothed 285, 326
Hot and Bothered **285**

Cambor, Kathleen
In Sunlight, in a Beautiful Garden 850, 955, 961

Cameron, Ian
The Lost Ones 717, 792

Cameron, Stella
French Quarter 245, 272
Key West 340

Camp, Candace
No Other Love 317
So Wild a Heart 241, 346

Camp, Will
Blood of Texas 495

Campbell, Ann
Wolf in Sheep's Clothing 163

Campbell, Bebe Moore
Brothers and Sisters 1089
Singing in the Comeback Choir 1089, 1194
What You Owe Me **1089**, 1166, 1210
Your Blues Ain't Like Mine 1089

Campbell, Glynnis
My Champion 407

Campbell, Marilyn
Just in Time 546

Campbell, Ramsey
Ancient Images 619
Deathport 634
The House on Nazareth Hill 620, 626
The Last Voice They Hear 626
The Long Lost 626
The One Safe Place 626, 665
Pact of the Fathers **626**
Silent Children 626
Strange Things and Stranger Places 688

Canham, Marsha
Across a Moonlit Sea 326

Canin, Ethan C.
Carry Me Across the Water 1129, 1168

Cannan, Joanna
Death at the Dog 136

Cannell, Dorothy
Bridesmaids Revisited 31
The Ellie Haskell Series 9

The Family Jewels and Other Stories **31**
How to Murder the Man of Your Dreams 31, 49
How to Murder Your Mother-in-Law 31
The Spring Cleaning Murders 31
The Thin Woman 36
The Trouble with Harriet 31

Cannon, LeGrand
Look to the Mountain 868

Cannon, Taffy
The Tumbleweed Murders **189**

Cantrell, Lisa
Torments 640

Canty, Kevin
Honeymoon and Other Stories 1149

Capote, Truman
Answered Prayers 1145

Caraker, Mary
The Snows of Jaspre 810

Carey, Peter
True History of the Kelly Gang 825, 842, 1176, 1183

Carlson, Mary
The Whispering Pines Series 984, 993, 1007

Carlson, Melody
Awakening Heart 1049

Carlson, P.M.
The Marty Hopkins Series 145, 212

Carlyle, Liz
A Woman of Virtue 260

Carmichael, Emily
Diamond in the Ruff **249**
Finding Mr. Right 249
A Ghost for Maggie 249, 351
Gold Dust 249
Jezebel's Sister 249
Windfall 249

Carmody, Isobelle
Ashling **732**
The Farseekers 732
Obernewtyn 732

Carr, Caleb
The Alienist 203, 932
The Angel of Darkness 936

Carr, John Dickson
Captain Cutthroat 12
The Devil in Velvet 522
The Ghosts' High Noon 73

Carr, Robyn
The House on Olive Street 250
The Wedding Party **250**

Carrington, Tori
Never Say Never Again 251
Private Investigations 251
Stranger's Touch 251
The Woman for Dusty Conrad **251**
You Only Love Once 251
You Sexy Thing 251

Carroll, Jonathan
Kissing the Beehive 529
The Land of Laughs 659, 781
The Marriage of Sticks 539
The Voice of Our Shadow 515
The Wooden Sea 567, 573

Carroll, Leslie
Miss Match **252**

Carroll, Susan
The Bride Finder 881
Christmas Belles 271

Carter, Angela
The Bloody Chamber 579

Carter, Charlotte
Coq au Vin 856

Carter, Margaret L.
Demon Lovers and Strange Seductions 643

Carter, Paula
The Hillary Scarborough Series 60

Carter, Robert A.
Final Edit 128

Carver, Jeffrey A.
Clypsis 769

Carver, Raymond
Where I'm Calling From 1087

Cassidy, Carla
Born of Passion 422
Man on a Mission 417
An Officer and a Princess 334

Cassill, R.V.
After Goliath 858

Casstevens, Jeanne Savery
A Perfect Match **389**

Castle, Linda Lea
Addie and the Laird 253
Lottie and the Rustler 253
Mattie and the Blacksmith **253**, 284, 408
Temple's Prize 253

Castro, Adam-Troy
A Desperate, Decaying Darkness 683

Cates, Kimberly
Magic 303, 358

Caudwell, Sarah
Thus Was Adonis Murdered 36

Caunitz, William
One Police Plaza 152

Cavanaugh, Jack
The American Family Portrait Series 1028
The Book of Books Series 979, 1003
The Peacemakers 1019
The Victors 1056

Cave, Hugh B.
The Dawning 666

Cavelos, Jeanne
The Shadow Within 770

Caverly, Carol
Dead in Hog Heaven 472, 477

Cecilione, Michael
Domination 625

Cercone, Karen Rose
The Helen Sorby/Miles Kachigan Series 24, 200

Chabon, Michael
The Amazing Adventures of Kavalier & Clay 874, 1100, 1191

Chadbourn, Mark
Always Forever **533**
Darkest Hour 533
The Eternal 665
Nocturne 533
Scissorman 533
Testimony 533
World's End 533

Chaikin, Linda
The Day to Remember Series 1040
Endangered 1027
Friday's Child **977**, 1020
The Great Northwest Series 1011
Island Bride 977
The Jewel of the Pacific Series 1059
Monday's Child 977
Thursday's Child 977
Tuesday's Child 977
Wednesday's Child 977

Chamberlin, Ann
The Merlin of St. Gilles Well 562, 603
The Merlin of the Oak Wood 818

Chambers, Stephen
Hope's End **733**

Champlin, Tim
By Flare of Northern Lights **439**
Colt Lighting 492, 505
Deadly Season 440
Flying Eagle **440**
Lincoln's Ransom 439, 440, 456, 487, 498
Tombstone Conspiracy 439, 440, 456, 514
A Trail to Wounded Knee 439, 945
Treasure of the Templars 439, 440, 487, 498
Wayfaring Strangers 439, 440, 487

Chance, Megan
Fall from Grace 294
The Way Home 290

Chandler, A. Bertram
Kelly Country 804

Chandler, Joel
The Favorite Uncle Remus 1128

Chandler, Raymond
The Midnight Raymond Chandler 41, 99, 201

Chandler, Scott
Ghost Killer **627**

Chandra, Vikram
Red Earth and Pouring Rain 849

Chaon, Dan
Among the Missing 1160, 1205
Fitting Ends and Other Stories 1147

Chapman, Sally
Tall, Dead, and Handsome **91**

Chappell, Fred
More Shapes than One 700, 707

Chappell, Helen
The Hollis Ball/Sam Westcott Series 205

Charbonneau, Ellen
Waltzing in Ragtime 878

Charbonneau, Louis
Corpus Earthling 773, 794

Charnas, Suzy McKee
The Conqueror's Child 732

Chase, Loretta
The Last Hellion 307
The Sandalwood Princess 398

Chase, Taylor
Heart of Deception 254
Heart of Night **254**

Chase-Riboud, Barbara
Sally Hemmings 918

Chastain, Sandra
The Outlaw Bride 361

Summer of the Soldiers 228

Cheatham, K. Follis
The Adventures of Elizabeth Fortune 458, 474

Chefitz, Mitchell
The Seventh Telling 978
The Thirty-Third Hour **978**, 1064

Cherne, Barbara
Bella Donna **836**
Looking Glass 836

Cherryh, C.J.
Angel with a Sword 725
Chanur's Legacy 743
Cyteen 716
Defender **734**
Downbelow Station 740, 770, 788
Finity's End 734
Foreigner 728
Fortress of Dragons 734
Hammerfall 734
Inheritor 734
Invader 719, 733
The Kif Strike Back 812
Legions of Hell 553
Merchanter's Luck 796
Precursor 734

Cheshire, Giff
Renegade River 426, 429, 430, 501

Cheska, Anna
Moving to the Country 872

Chesney, Marion
Agatha Raisin and the Love from Hell **14**
Miss Davenport's Christmas 304

Chessman, Harriet Scott
Lydia Cassatt Reading the Morning Paper **837**, 951
Ohio Angels 837

Chetwin, Grace
The Atheling 776

Chevalier, Tracy
Falling Angels 819, **838**, 848, 959, **1090**, 1205
Girl with a Pearl Earring 837, 838, 1067, 1090

Chiaventone, Frederick J.
Moon of Bitter Cold **441**
A Road We Do Not Know 441

Child, Lee
Die Trying 442
Echo Burning 149, **442**
Killing Floor 59, 442
Running Blind 442
Tripwire 442

Child, Lincoln
Relic 662

Child, Maureen
His Baby! 255
The Last Santini Virgin 255
Last Virgin in California **255**
Marooned with a Marine 255
The Next Santini Bride 255
Prince Charming in Dress Blues 255, 335

Childs, Laura
Death by Darjeeling **32**, 67, 163

Chilson, Robert
Men Like Rats 746, 791

Chisholm, P.F.
The Sir Robert Carey Series 148

Chizmar, Richard
The Best of Cemetery Dance 653
Cold Blood 628, 651
The Earth Strikes Back 628, 666
Screamplays 696
Thrillers 628
Trick or Treat **628**

Chopra, Deepak
The Return of Merlin 558

Christenberry, Judy
The $10,000,000 Texas Wedding 344

Christie, Agatha
Death Comes as the End 101
Murder at the Vicarage 36

Christmas, Joyce
The Margaret Priam Series 34

Christner, Dianne
Ample Portions 979
Keeper of Hearts **979**
Lofty Ambitions 979
Proper Intentions 979
Storm 979

Christopher, John
The Long Winter 724
Pendulum 738
The Prince in Waiting 730

Churchill, Jill
Anything Goes 33, 839
In the Still of the Night 33, 839
The Merchant of Menace 839
Much Ado about Nothing 839
Someone to Watch over Me **33**, **839**, 928

Chwedyk, Kate
A Rogue for Christmas **304**

Ciencin, Scott
The Parliament of Blood 702
The Vampire Odyssey 703

Civil-Brown, Sue
Carried Away 256
Catching Kelly 256, 354, 376
Chasing Rainbow 256
July Thunder **330**
Letting Loose 256
Next Stop, Paradise 249, **256**, 351, 383
Tempting Mr. Wright 250, 256
Under Suspicion **331**

Clare, Alys
The Abbess Helewise Series 70, 209
Ashes of Elements 865
Ashes of the Elements 875, 933, 934, 944

Clark, Carol Higgins
Decked 34
Fleeced **34**
Iced 34
The Regan O'Reilly Series 80
Snagged 34
Twanged 34, 1194

Clark, L.D.
A Bright Tragic Thing 451, 456

Clark, Mark
Ripper 153

Clark, Martin
The Many Aspects of Mobile Home Living 1153

Clark, Mary Higgins
We'll Meet Again 1180

Clark, Robert
Mr. White's Confession 110

Clark, Ronald
Queen Victoria's Bomb 778

Clark, Simon
Blood Crazy 735
Darker 735
Darkness Demands 626, 735
The Judas Tree 735
Nailed by the Heart 735
The Night of the Triffids **735**
Salt Snake and Other Bloody Cuts 655

Clarke, Anthony
Ordeal at Litchfield 209

Clarke, Arthur C.
The City and the Stars 790
The Hammer of God 767
The Sands of Mars 814

Clarke, Brenda Margaret Lilian
The Weaver's Inheritance **194**, **934**

Clarke, T.E.B.
Murder at Buckingham Palace 183

Clayton, Alana
A Devilish Husband **257**

Clayton, Jo
Blue Magic 591, 592
Dance Down the Stars 593

Cleary, Melissa
The Jackie Walsh Series 16

Cleary, Rita
Goldtown 443
River Walk 441, **443**, 508
Sorrel 443

Clegg, Douglas
Goat Dance 676

Clemens, James
Wit'ch Fire 534
Wit'ch Gate **534**
Wit'ch Storm 534
Wit'ch War 534, 561

Clement, Catherine
Martin and Hannah 852

Clifford, Nicholas
The House of Memory 835

Cliford, Emmett
Night Whispers 1153

Clifton, Mark
When They Come from Space 800

Climer, Stephen Lee
Demonesque 641

Cline, Edward
First Prize 840
Sparrowhawk—Jack Frake **840**
Whisper the Guns 840

Clute, John
Appleseed **736**

Coben, Harlan
Tell No One 47, 123

Cobley, Michael
Shadowkings **535**

Codrescu, Andrei
The Blood Countess 922

Cody, Liza
The Anna Lee Series 11

Coe, Tucker
The Mitch Tobin Series 22

Coel, Margaret
The Dream Stalker 35
The Ghost Walker 35
Hole in the Wall 444
Honor 444
The Last Bird 444
The Lost Bird 35
The Spirit Woman 35, 444
The Story Teller 35, 444
The Thunder Keeper **35**, **444**

Coetzee, J.M.
Disgrace 1138
The Master of Petersburg 946

Coggin, Joan
Dancing with Death 36
The Mystery of Orchard House 36
Who Killed the Curate? **36**
Why Did She Die? 36

Cogswell, Theodore
The Wall Around the World 790

Cohen, Barney
Blood on the Moon 744

Cohen, Gabriel
Red Hook **37**

Cohen, Janet
O Gentle Death **165**

Cohen, Nancy J.
Hair Raiser 38
The Marla Shore Series 13
Murder by Manicure **38**
Permed to Death 38

Cohen, Robert
Inspired Sleep 1196

Cokal, Susann
Mirabilis 844, 913, 1083, **1091**

Colapinto, John
About the Author **1092**

Coldsmith, Don
The Long Journey Home 423, 842
The Lost Band 447, 507
Raven Mocker 962
Runestone 952
The Spanish Bit Saga 911

Cole, Adrian
The Thief of Dreams 569

Cole, David
Butterfly Lost 39
The Killing Maze 39
The Laura Winslow Series 28
Stalking Moon **39**

Cole, Judd
Blood on the Plains 484
Desert Manhunt 484

Colegate, Isabel
Winter Journey 1189

Coleman, Evelyn
The Patricia Conley Series 220

Coleman, Jane Candia
Borderlands 446, 452
Desperate Acts 446
Doc Holliday's Gone 434, **445**, 446, 491
Doc Holliday's Woman 445, 485, 493
I, Pearl Hart 445, 446
Mountain Time **446**
Moving On 427, 433, 445, 458, 474, 483, 500
The O'Keefe Empire 437, 445, 446
Stories from Mesa Country 433, 445

Coleman, Loren
Bloodlines 564

Coles, Manning
Nothing to Declare 118

Colgan, Jenny
Amanda's Wedding 394

Collins, Barbara
Too Many Tomcats and Other Feline Tales of Suspense 26, 162

Collins, Brandilyn
Cast a Road Before Me 980, 981
Color the Sidewalk for Me **980**, 1038
Eyes of Elisha 980, **981**

Collins, Helen
Mutagenesis 740

Collins, Jackie
American Star 1108
Vendetta 1194

Collins, Max Allan
Angel in Black 40, 41, 161, 841, 923
Blood and Thunder 41
Blue Christmas and Other Holiday Homicides **40**, 175
Damned in Paradise 41
Flying Blind 41, 841
The Hindenburg Murders 828, 841
Kisses of Death 40, **41**, 147, 201, **841**
Majic Man 40, 41, 841
Mourn the Living 40
Murder: His and Hers 40
The Nate Heller Series 83, 928
The Quarry Series 202
Stolen Away 841
The Titanic Murders 5

Collins, Michael
The Planets of Death 809

Collins, Nancy
Avenue X 629
A Dozen Black Roses 629
Knuckles and Tales **629**
Lynch: A Gothic Western 629
Midnight Blue 629
Nameless Sins 629

Collum, Lynn
The Christmas Charm 258, 271
Elizabeth and the Major 420
Lady Miranda's Masquerade 258
The Spy's Bride 258
An Unlikely Father 258
The Valentine Charm 258
The Wedding Charm **258**

Colter, Cara
A Royal Marriage 334

Compton, Ralph
Autumn of the Gun 482
The Dawn of Fury 434

Conant, Susan
The Holly Winter Series 16, 17

Conde, Nicholas
The Religion 672

Condon, Richard
The Final Addiction 1142

Coney, Michael G.
Friends Come in Boxes 722
Winter's Children 724

Congdon, Don
Tales of Love and Death 643

Coniglio, John Vincent
Rumors of Angels 1010

Conley, Robert J.
Back to Malachi 438
Barjack 447
Broke Loose 447
The Cherokee Dragon 447, 466

Cherokee Dragon 842
Colfax 842
The Dark Way 842
Fugitive's Trail 447
Geronimo, an American Legend 842
Incident at Buffalo Crossing 447
Mountain Windsong 842
The Peace Chief 441
Spanish Jack **447**, **842**

Connell, Evan S.
Deus lo Volt! 831, 860
Mrs. Bridge 1161

Connelly, Michael
The Black Echo 1088
A Darkness More than Night 1076, 1096
The Harry Bosch Series 20, 47, 94, 204

Connery, Tom
The Markham of the Marines Series 854

Connolly, John
Dark Hollow **42**
Every Dead Thing 42

Connors, Cathleen
A Home of Her Own **982**

Conroy, Pat
The Prince of Tides 1075, 1173, 1203

Constantine, Storm
The Crown of Silence 536, 549
The Oracle Lips 536
Scenting Hallowed Blood 536, 607
Sea Dragon Heir 536, 540
Stalking Tender Prey 536
The Way of Light **536**

Conwell, Kent
Cattle Drive to Dodge 492, 505

Cook, Christopher
Robbers 825

Cook, David
King Pinch 604

Cook, Glen
She Is the Darkness 608
Soldiers Live 606
The Tower of Fear 586
Water Sleeps 580

Cook, Judith
The Simon Forman Series 65
The Slicing Edge of Death 109, 148

Cook, Monte
The Glass Prison 737
Of Aged Angels **737**

Cook, Rick
Cursed and Consulted 521, **537**
Mall Purchase Night 537
The Wiz Biz 537
The Wizardry Compiled 537
The Wizardry Quested 537
Wizard's Bane 537

Cook, Robin
Chromosome 6 1093
Coma 677
Contagion 1093
Fatal Cure 1070, 1093
Harmful Intent 1093
Mutation 783
Shock **1093**
Terminal 78
Vector 1093

Cook, Thomas H.
Breakheart Hill 59, 82
The Chatham School Affair 82, 214
Places in the Dark 110
Streets of Fire 122, 166

Cook, Tonya C.
Brother of the Dragon **604**

Cook, Will
The Rain Tree 487, 498
Until Shadows Fall 466

Cooke, John Peyton
Out for Blood 690

Coolidge, Dane
Man from Wyoming **448**

Coomer, Joe
The Loop 1144

Cooper, Edmund
Deadly Image 797, 806

Cooper, Geoff
4 X 4 **679**

Cooper, Louise
The Sleep of Stone 591

Cooper, Susan
Over Sea, Under Stone 570

Cooper, Susan Rogers
The E.J. Pugh Series 49
The Milton Kovak Series 93

Copeland, Bonnie
Lady of Moray 921

Copeland, Lori
The Brides of the West Series 1014
Child of Grace 983
Christmas Vows: $5.00 Extra **983**, 1033
Glory 983
Grace in Autumn 984
The Heavenly Daze Series 1007
Hope 983
The Island of Heavenly Daze 984
June 983
Marrying Walker McKay 983
A Warmth in Winter **984**

Coppel, Alfred
Glory 788
Glory's People 728

Cord, Barry
The Masked Gun 480

Corey, G. Roger
Eden Springs 1019, 1030

Corey, Ryanne
The Heiress and the Bodyguard 236

Corley, Elizabeth
Fatal Legacy **43**

Cornelissen, Cornelia
Soft Rain 464

Cornell, Paul
The Goth Opera 738
Happy Endings 738
Human Nature 738
No Future 738
Oh No It Isn't! 738
Something More 533, **738**

Cornick, Nicola
The Blanchard Secret 259, 260
Lady Polly **259**, 260
The Larkswood Legacy 259, 260
Miss Verey's Proposal 259, 260
True Colours 259, 260
The Virtuous Cyprian 259, **260**

Cornwell, Bernard
The Archer's Tale 831, **843**, 901
The Arthurian Warlord Trilogy 843
Redcoat 843
The Richard Sharpe Series 843
The Starbuck Chronicles 843
Stonehenge 843, 879
The Warlord Chronicles 829, 907

Cornwell, Patricia
Hornet's Nest 1153
The Kay Scarpetta Series 66, 78, 197

Corpi, Lucha
The Gloria Damasco Series 52, 75, 140

Costello, Matthew J.
The 7th Guest 663
Midsummer 660

Cote, Lyn
Echoes of Mercy 985
Finally Found 985
Finally Home 974, 985
Hope's Garden 233, 985, 997, 1057, 1063
Letters of the Heart **233**, **969**
Lost in His Love 985
Winter's Secret **985**, 1021

Coughlin, Patricia
The Bargain 261
Borrowed Bride 261
Joyride 261
The Last Frontier 261
Merely Married 261
Tall, Dark, and Difficult **261**

Coulter, Catherine
Beyond Eden 1108
The Cove 340
Hemlock Bay 1203
Impulse 1199

Coulter, Stephen
The Devil Inside 946

Counts, Wilma
My Lady Governess 262
The Trouble with Harriet **262**
The Wagered Wife 262, 349
Willed to Wed 262
The Willful Miss Winthrop 262

Coupland, Douglas
All Families Are Psychotic **1094**, 1126
Generation X 1094
Girlfriend in a Coma 1094
Life After God 1094
Miss Wyoming 1094
Shampoo Planet 1094

Courtney, Vincent
Vampire Beat 657

Cover, Arthur Byron
The Platypus of Doom and Other Nihilists 524

Coville, Bruce
Aliens Ate My Homework 538
The Monsters of Morley Manor **538**
Odder than Ever 538
Oddly Enough 538
The Skull of Truth 538, 605
The Wrath of Squat 538

Coward, Mat
In and Out **44**
Up and Down 44

Cowell, Stephanie
The Players 823

Cowper, Richard
Profundis 806

Cox, Carol
Resolutions 969

Coyle, Harold
Until the End 458, 474

Crabbe, Richard E.
Suspension 936

Crace, Jim
Arcadia 1095
Being Dead 1095
The Devil's Larder **1095**
The Gift of Stones 1095
Quarantine 1095
Signals of Distress 1095

Craft, Michael
Body Language 45
Boy Toy 45
Desert Autumn **45**, 71
Eye Contact 45
Flight Dreams 45
The Mark Manning Series 221
Name Games 45

Craig, Charmaine
The Good Men **844**

Craig, Patricia
The Oxford Book of English Detective Stories 57

Craig, Philip R.
A Deadly Vineyard Holiday 46
A Fatal Vineyard Season 46
First Light **46**
The J.W. Jackson Series 100, 106, 206
A Shoot on Martha's Vineyard 46
Vineyard Blues 46
Vineyard Shadows 46

Craig, Terry L.
Gatekeeper 1016

Crais, Robert
Demolition Angel 47, 123, 1096
Devil's Cantina 1096
Free Fall 111, 1096
Hostage 20, **47**, 168, 204, **1096**
Indigo Slam 47, 1096
L.A. Requiem 47, 1096
Stalking the Angel 98
Sunset Express 47
Voodoo River 47

Crane, Hamilton
Miss Seeton's Finest Hour 136

Craven, Jerry
Snake Mountain 462, 497

Crawford, Betty Ann
The Bushido Incident 793

Crawford, Max
Lords of the Plain 827

Creasey, John
The Masters of Bow Street 10, 182, 815

Creel, Ann Howard
A Ceiling of Stars 845
The Magic of Ordinary Days 821, **845**, 850, 870, 891, 925, 938, 947, 955
Nowhere, Now Here 845
Water at the Blue Earth 845

Creighton, Kathleen
One Christmas Knight 306

Crespi, Camilla
The Simona Griffo Series 170

Crichton, Michael
Eaters of the Dead 1097
The Lost World 1093
The Terminal Man 808
Timeline 869, 1071, 1204

Crider, Bill
Booked for a Hanging 49
Death by Accident 48, 49
A Ghost of a Chance 48, 49
Murder Is an Art 48, 124
Murder Most Fowl 49
Murder Takes a Break 48
The Nighttime Is the Right Time **48**, 117
The Prairie Chicken Kill 48
A Romantic Way to Die **49**
The Sheriff Dan Rhodes Series 108
The Truman Smith Series 112
Winning Can Be Murder 49

Crisp, Quentin
The Nightmare Exhibition 636

Crispin, A.C.
V 800

Criswell, Millie
Desperate 332
The Marrying Man 253, 264, 284, 408
The Trials of Angela 264
The Trouble with Mary 264, 274, 354, 369, 376, 380
True Love 264
The Wedding Planner 264
A Western Family Christmas **263**
What to Do about Annie? 263, **264**

Crockett, Linda L.
Mattie and the Blacksmith **253**

Croker, B.M.
Number 90 and Other Ghost Stories 618

Crombie, Deborah
The Duncan Kincaid/Gemma James Series 87, 165
Kissed a Sad Goodbye 92

Crook, Jeff
The Rose and the Skull 612

Crosby, Tanya Anne
Viking's Prize 337

Cross, Amanda
The Kate Fansler Series 156

Cross, Claire
The Last Highlander 323

Crouch, Stanley
Don't the Moon Look Lonesome 1122, 1194, 1210

Crow, Donna Fletcher
All Things New 966
The Cambridge Chronicles 1013, 1031

Crowell, Pers
First to Ride 723

Crowther, Peter
Escardy Gap 739
Futures **739**
The Longest Single Note and Other Strange Compositions 655

Crum, Laura
Stickrock 439, 443, 506

Crumley, James
Bordersnakes 50
Dancing Bear 50
The Final Country **50**
The Last Good Kiss 50
The Mexican Tree Duck 50
The Wrong Case 50

Crusie, Jennifer
The Cinderella Deal 236
Crazy for You 286
Tell Me Lies 286, 292
Welcome to Temptation 282, 285, 286
What the Lady Wants 289

Culea, John
Light the Night 991

Cullin, Mitch
Tideland 1121

Cummings, Jack
The Indian Fighter's Return 481

Cummings, Ray
Brigands of the Moon 794

Cunningham, Elaine
Elfsong 597
Evermeet 583
Thornhold 525

Cunningham, Eugene
Trails West 445, 496

Curland, Lynn
My Heart Stood Still **323**

Curry, Chris
Candle Bay **703**
Thunder Road 675

Curtis, Barbara
Restoration and Romance **986**

Curtis, Jack
Cut and Branded 440
Easter in Calico 457, 470, 488
No Mercy 490, 499

Curzon, Claire
The Mike Yeadings Series 64, 97

Cushman, Dan
The Pecos Kid: A Western Duo 431, 432, 435, 494, 500

Cussler, Clive
Atlantis Found 1097
Flood Tide 1097
Iceberg 1097
Raise the Titanic 1097
Sahara 1097
Valhalla Rising **1097**

Cutler, Stan
The Rayford Goodman Series 72

Cutrer, William
Lethal Harvest 975

Czerneda, Julie E.
Beholder's Eye 740
Changing Vision 740
In the Company of Others 716, **740**
A Thousand Words for Stranger 740
Ties of Power 740

Czichas, Casey
The Candlelight Reader 636, 697

D

D'Aguiar, Fred
Airy Hall 846
Bloodlines **846**
Dear Future 846
Feeding the Ghosts 846
The Longest Memory 846

Daheim, Mary
The Alpine Icon 51
The Alpine Journey 51
The Alpine Kindred 51
The Alpine Legacy 51
The Alpine Menace 51
The Alpine Nemesis **51**

Dahl, Roald
Someone Like You 48

Dai, Sijie
Balzac and the Little Chinese Seamstress **1098**

Dailey, Janet
Calder Pride 265
A Capital Holiday **265**
Silver Wings, Santiago Blue 228

Dain, Catherine
Angel in the Dark 52
Bet Against the House 52
Darkness at the Door **52**
Death of the Party 52
Lament for a Dead Cowboy 52
The Luck of the Draw 52
The Mariana Morgan Series 79

Dain, Claudia
The Holding 266, 316, 320
The Marriage Bed **266**, 320, 368, 396
Tell Me Lies 266
Unwrapped 266
Wish List 266, **320**

Dalby, Richard
The Best of Ghosts and Scholars 650
The Sorceress in Stained Glass 615

Dale, Ruth Jean
Fiance Wanted! 250, 255, 353

Daley, Margaret
The Power of Love **987**

Daley, Robert
Innocents Within 863

Dalkey, Kara
The Heavenward Path 531
The Nightingale 579

Dallas, Sandra
Alice's Tulips 877, 1153
The Persian Pickle Club 33

Dalmas, John
The Bavarian Gate 741, 742
The Kalif's War 765
The Lion of Farside 741, 742
The Lion Returns 741, 742
The Orc Wars 741, 742
The Puppet Master **741**
The Regiment 729
Soldiers **742**
The Three Cornered War 741, 742

Dalton, Sean
Beyond the Void 768

D'Amato, Barbara
Hard Bargain 53
Hard Case 53
Hard Christmas 53
Hard Evidence 53
Hard Road **53**
Hard Women 53
Of Course You Know That Chocolate Is a Vegetable and Other Stories 31

Dams, Jeanne M.
The Dorothy Martin Series 14, 27
Green Grow the Victims 830
The Hilda Johansson Series 24, 200
Holy Terror in the Hebrides 54
Killing Cassidy 54
Malice in Miniature 54
To Perish in Penzance **54**
Trouble in the Town Hall 54
The Victim in Victoria Station 54

Daniel, Tony
Metaplanetary 736

Daniells, Cory
Broken Vows 267
Dark Dreams **267**

Daniels, B.J.
Secret Bodyguard 414

Daniels, Les
The Black Castle 685
The Silver Skull 713

Danielson, Peter
The Death of Kings 858

Dann, John R.
Song of the Axe 879, 962

Danvers, Dennis
Circuit of Heaven 731
End of Days 722

Danze, Philip
Conjuring Maud **847**

Darcy, Lilian
The Baby Bond 268
Cinderella After Midnight **268**
Finding Her Prince 268
Her Sister's Child 268
Raising Baby Jane 268
Saving Cinderella 268

Dare, Justine
Night Fires 251

DaRif, Andrea
A Diamond in the Rough **370**

Dark, Eleanor
Storm of Time 819, 904

Darnton, John
Neanderthal 792

Darty, Peggy
The Crimson Roses of Fountain Court 418
Getaways 1049

Datlow, Ellen
Alien Sex 643
Blood Is Not Enough 654
The Year's Best Fantasy and Horror: Fourteenth Annual Collection 653

Davenport, Kiana
Song of the Exile 1059

David, Peter
Sir Apropos of Nothing 601
Thirdspace 770

Davidson, Avram
The Adventures of Dr. Esterhazy 607
Strange Seas and Shores 745
What Strange Stars and Skies 760

Davidson, Carolyn
The Bachelor Tax 409

Davidson, Diane Mott
The Goldy Bear Schulz Series 4, 89, 105, 120, 170, 207, 1037

Davies, Freda
A Fine and Private Place **55**

Davis, Brett
The Faery Convention 533, 602

Davis, Dee
Everything in Its Time 237

Davis, Dorothy Salisbury
The Julie Hayes Series 52, 79

Davis, Justine
Lord of the Storm 267, 310
The Skypirate 267

Davis, Lindsey
Last Act in Palmyra 180
The Marcus Didius Falco Series 184, 924

Davis, Lydia
Almost No Memory 1099
Break It Down 1099
End of the Story 1099
Samuel Johnson Is Indignant **1099**
Story and Other Stories 1099
Thirteenth Woman and Other Stories 1099

Davis, Norbert
The Mouse in the Mountain **56**
Oh, Murderer Mine 56
Sally's in the Alley 56

Davis, Thomas J.
The Christmas Quilt 983

Davis, Val
The Nicolette Scott Series 7, 125
The Return of the Spanish Lady 68

Davis, Wayne
John Stone and the Choctaw Kid 425

Dawkins, Cecil
Clay Dancers 61

Dawson, Geralyn
The Bad Luck Wedding Night 319, 408
Simmer All Night 284, 402, 419
The Wedding Raffle 253

Dawson, Jill
Fred & Edie 838, 847, **848**, 943
How Do I Look? 848

Dawson, Peter
Claiming of Deerfoot: A Western Duo 489
Ghost Brand of the Wishbones 430, 501
Rattlesnake Mesa 461, 473

Dawson, Roxann
Entering Tenebrea 743
Tenebrea's Hope **743**

Day, Dianne
The Fremont Jones Series 24, 878

de Camp, L. Sprague
Demons and Dinosaurs 669
The Goblin Tower 590
The Pixilated Peeress 600

De Haven, Tom
Derby Dugan's Depression Funnies 1100
Dugan under Ground **1100**
The End-of-Everything Man 1100
The Last Human 1100
Sunburn Lake 1100
Walker of Worlds 1100

de la Garza, Phyllis
Camels West 446, 448

de la Mare, Walter
The Riddle and Other Stories 680

De Lint, Charles
Forests of the Heart 539
Jack of Kinrowan 539
The Little Country 659
Moonlight and Vines 539
The Onion Girl **539**
Our Lady of the Harbor 529
Someplace to Be Flying 539
Trader 539

Dean, Elizabeth
The Emma Marsh Series 144

Dean, Pamela
The Hidden Land 520, 581, 605
Tam Lin 579

Dearen, Patrick
The Illegal Man 469, 478
When Cowboys Die 508

Dearl, Elizabeth
Diamondback 502
Twice Dead 428, 436, 442, 444, 472, 475, 502

Deauville, Katherine
Daggers of Gold 276

Deaver, Jeffery
Blue Nowhere 57
A Century of Great Suspense Stories **57**
The Coffin Dancer 57
The Devil's Teardrop 57
The Empty Chair 57
The Lincoln Rhyme Series 20
Speaking in Tongues 57

DeChancie, John
Castle for Rent 588
The Kruton Interface 752
Living with Aliens 749
MagicNet 518

Dee, Ed
The Anthony Ryan/Joe Gregory Series 152

Dee, Ron
Succumb 620

Deere, Dicey
The Irish Cottage Murder 173

Defoe, Daniel
A Journal of the Plague Year 832

Deford, Frank
Alex, the Life of a Child 849
Casey on the Loose 849
Cut 'n' Run 849
Love and Infamy 849
The Other Adonis **849**, 868, 869
The Owner 849

Deighton, Len
Hope 1191

Deitz, Tom
Dreamseeker's Road 527
Landslayer's Law 583
Soulsmith 539, 568

Dekker, Ted
Blessed Child **975**
Heaven's Wager 988
When Heaven Weeps **988**

Del Rey, Lester
The Best of Lester Del Rey 715
Robots and Changelings 727

Delacroix, Claire
The Beauty 244, 266, 269, 368
The Countess 269
The Damsel 269
The Heiress 269
The Princess 269
The Temptress **269**

Delany, Samuel R.
Distant Stars 748

Delffs, Dudley J.
The Father Grif Series 1018, 1062

DeLillo, Don
Underworld 1180, 1202

Delinsky, Barbara
Coast Road 1101, 1103
For My Daughters 1205
Lake News 1101, 1194
Straight from the Heart 1101
Three Wishes 1135, 1200
The Vineyard 1101
A Woman Betrayed 1101
The Woman Next Door **1101**

Dellin, Genell
Cherokee Nights 270
Comanche Flame 270
The Renegades: Cole 270
The Renegades: Nick 270
The Renegades: Rafe **270**
Silver Moon Song 270

DeLoach, Nora
The Candi Covington Series 21

DeMarinis, Rick
A Lovely Monster 806

DeMartino, Denny
Heart of Stone 744
Wayward Moon **744**

DeMille, Nelson
The General's Daughter 1131
The Gold Coast 1183
Plum Island 1097, 1123
Up Country 1172
Word of Honor 1186

Denning, Troy
The Obsidian Oracle 604
The Parched Sea 597

Dennis, Carol
Dragon's Queen 590

Dentinger, Jane
The Jocelyn O'Roarke Series 45, 71

Denton, Bradley
Wrack and Roll 764

Dereske, Jo
The Miss Zukas Series 51

Derleth, August
Someone in the Dark 671
Wind over Wisconsin 873

DeRosso, H.A.
Under the Burning Sun 427, 453

Desai, Anita
Diamond Dust 1104

Deveraux, Jude
The Heiress 883
A Knight in Shining Armor 323, 869
A Season in the Highlands 243, 277
The Taming 269
Temptation 1148
Wishes 268

Devine, Thea
All I Desire 385
All through the Night **282**
Seductive 282

Devon, Marian
On the Way to Gretna Green 393

Dew, Robb Forman
Dale Loves Sophie to Death 850, 1102
The Evidence Against Her 845, 848, **850**, 891, 925, 938, **1102**, 1163
Fortunate Lives 850, 1102
The Time of Her Life 850, 1102

DeWeese, Gene
Lord of the Necropolis 613

Dewitt, Helen
The Last Samurai 1109, 1198

DeWitt, Jean
The Stranger 327

Dexter, Colin
The Inspector Morse Series 44, 97, 116

Dexter, Susan
The Wizard's Shadow 537

Di Filippo, Paul
Fractal Paisleys 720, 745
Lost Pages 745, 760, 786
Ribofunk 745
The Steampunk Trilogy 607, 745
Strange Trades **745**, 748

Diamant, Anita
Good Harbor **1103**
The Red Tent 1103

Diamond, Jacqueline
Excuse Me? Whose Baby? 380

Dibdin, Michael
The Aurelio Zen Series 164

Dick, Philip K.
The Crack in Space 752, 779
Do Androids Dream of Electric Sheep? 797
Vulcan's Hammer 798

Dickinson, David
The Earth Abideth 851
Goodnight, Sweet Prince **58**, **851**

Dickinson, Peter
The Weathermonger 533, 730, 738
The Yellow Room Conspiracy 214

Dickson, Athol
Every Hidden Thing 966
The Garr Reed Series 981

Dickson, Gordon R.
The Chantry Guild 716, 734
The Dragon and the Gnarly King 524
Mission to Universe 796
Naked to the Stars 784, 795
None but Man 719
The Spirit of Dorsai 750

Didion, Joan
The Last Thing He Wanted 1134, 1138, 1206, 1211

Diehl, Stanford
Angel in the Front Room, Devil out Back 1, **59**, 122

Dier, Debra
Christmas Angels 366
My Scottish Summer **243**

Dietz, William C.
By Blood Alone 746
By Force of Arms 746
Deathday **746**
The Final Battle 742
Freehold 729, 784
Rebel Agent 746
Steelheart 746
Where the Ships Die 746

Dillon, Eilis
Sent to His Account 173

Dillon, Millicent
Harry Gold 835, 892

Disch, Thomas M.
The Sub 649

Divakaruni, Chitra Banerjee
Arranged Marriage 1104
The Mistress of Spices 1104
Sister of My Heart 1104
The Unknown Errors of Our Lives 1075, **1104**, 1128, 1188

Dixon, Debra
Hot as Sin 286

Djaout, Tahar
The Last Summer of Reason **1105**

Dobson, Joanne
The Karen Pelletier Series 156, 176

Doctorow, E.L.
Billy Bathgate 885
Ragtime 874

Dodd, Christina
A Knight to Remember 406
Once a Knight 406
Outrageous 276
Rules of Surrender 319, 408
Scottish Brides 243
A Well-Pleasured Lady 307

Dodd, Susan M.
Mamaw 852
The Mourners' Bench 852
No Earthly Notion 852
O Careless Love 852
Old Wives' Tales 852
The Silent Woman **852**, 938, 954

Doherty, P.C.
Dove Amongst the Hawks 86, 194
The Horus Killings 101
The House of Death 859, 920, 924
The Rose Demon 86, 194
Saintly Murders **86**, **875**
The Soul Slayer 65

Domning, Denise
Lady in Waiting 254, 276, 326
Lady in White 254

Donachie, David
The Devil's Own Luck 822, **853**, 854
The Dying Trade 853, **854**

Donald, Elsie Burch
Nashborough 845, 850, **855**, 961

Donaldson, Stephen R.
The White Gold Wielder 545

Donnell, Susan
Pocahontas 950

Donnelly, Deborah
Veiled Threats **60**

Donnelly, Shannon
Autumn Kittens **232**
A Compromising Situation 230
My Sweet Valentine 378
Under the Kissing Bough **271**, 304

Donoghue, Emma
Slammerkin 877, 913

Dorsey, Candas Jane
Black Wine 747
Machine Sex 747
A Paradigm of Earth **747**

Doss, James D.
Grandmother Spider 61
The Night Visitor 61
The Shaman Laughs 61
The Shaman Series 35
The Shaman's Bones 61
The Shaman's Game 61
White Shell Woman **61**

Doud, Laurel
This Body 849

Douglas, Carole Nelson
Chapel Noir **62**, **856**, 900, 915
Good Morning, Irene 62, 856
Good Night, Mr. Holmes 62, 856
Irene at Large 62, 856
Irene's Last Waltz 62, 856
The Midnight Louie Series 26, 162, 856

Douglas, Lloyd C.
The Robe 942

Douglass, Sara
Battleaxe 540
Crusader 540
Enchanter **540**

Dow, Rosey
Betrayed **989**, 1048

Downing, Sybil
The Binding Oath 475, 477, 930

Doyle, Arthur Conan
The Lost World 717
The Sherlock Holmes Series 158, 210
The White Company 843

Dozois, Gardner
Geodesic Dreams 748
Isaac Asimov's Father's Day 1166
Nightmare Blue 748
Slow Dancing through Time 748
Strange Days **748**, 786
Strangers 748
The Visible Man 748

Drabble, Margaret
The Realms of Gold 1204

Drake, David
Explorers in Hell 553
The Forlorn Hope 765
Lord of the Isles 541
Mistress of the Catacombs **541**
Old Nathan 541, 707
Queen of Demons 541, 563, 599
The Sea Hag 541
Servants of the Dragon 541
Time Safari 754

Drake, Emily
The Magickers **542**

Drake, Shannon
Come the Morning 883
Princess of Fire 336, 337

Dreadstone, Carl
Bride of Frankenstein 691

Dressler, Mylene
The Deadwood Beetle **1106**
The Medusa Tree 1106

Drew, Wayland
Dragonslayer 610

Drummond, Ivor
Necklace of Skulls 132

Du Maurier, Daphne
Frenchman's Creek 881
Rebecca 314

Duane, Diane
Deep Wizardry 538, 542
To Visit the Queen 574

Duckworth, Marion
Remembering the Roses 1055

Ducornet, Rikki
The Jade Cabinet 927

Due, Tananarive
The Black Rose 1089, 1207

Duffy, Steve
The Night Comes On 701

Dugain, Marc
The Officers' Ward **857**

Dugan, Bill
Crazy Horse 890

Dukthas, Ann
In the Time of the Poisoned Queen 29
Time for the Death of a King 65

Dunant, Sarah
The Hannah Wolfe Series 11

Dunbar, Sophie
The Claire Claiborne Series 38, 177

Duncan, Dave
Destiny of the Sword 585

Duncan, Lois
Gallows Hill 849

Duncan, Sharon
Death on a Casual Friday **63**

Duncklee, John
Double Vengeance **449**
Genevieve of Tombstone 449
Graciela of the Border 449

Dunham, Tracy
The Changing Trail 454, 471
The Ghost Trail 426, 429, 471
The Long Trail Home 454

Dunlap, Susan
The Celestial Buffet 40
The Jill Smith Series 137
The Veejay Haskell Series 139

Dunmore, Helen
A Spell of Winter 850

Dunn, Carola
The Daisy Dalrymple Series 183
Scandal's Daughter 374
To Davy Jones Below 923

Dunn, Dawn
Pink Marble and Never Say Die **630**
A Walk on the Dark Side 630

Dunn, J.R.
Days of Cain 802

Dunn, Katherine
Geek Love 638

Dunnett, Dorothy
King Hereafter 921

Dunning, John
The Bookman's Wake 128
Two O'Clock, Eastern Wartime 882, 906

Durgin, Doranna
Barrenlands 543
Changespell 592, 593
Dun Lady's Jess 590
A Feral Darkness **543**
Seer's Blood 543
Touched by Magic 543
Wolf Justice 543
Wolverine's Daughter 543

Durham, David Anthony
Gabriel's Story 884, 961

Durkee, Lee
Rides of the Midway 1109

Dvorkin, David
Insatiable 617, 702

Dziemianowicz, Stefan
100 Wicked Little Witch Stories 704
Girls' Night Out 654

E

Eager, Edward
Half Magic 581

Eagle, Kathleen
The Last Good Man 450
The Last True Cowboy 450
The Night Remembers 387, 450
Sunrise Song 450
To Each His Own 450
What the Heart Knows 339
You Never Can Tell **450**

Easton, Robert
Blood and Money 434
To Find a Place 431, 432, 435, 445

Eastwood, Gail
The Magnificent Marquess 379

Eccarius, J.G.
The Last Days of Christ the Vampire 690

Eccles, Marjorie
An Accidental Shroud 64
A Death of Distinction 64
The Gil Mayo Series 155
The Inspector Mayo Series 55
Killing Me Softly 64
A Species of Revenge 64
A Sunset Touch **64**
The Superintendent's Daughter 64

Eckhardt, Kristin
Dangerously Irresistible **289**

Eco, Umberto
Foucault's Pendulum 1164
The Name of the Rose 1182

Eddison, E.R.
Mistress of Mistresses 536
The Worm Ouroboros 582

Edelman, Gwen
War Story **1107**

Edgarian, Carol
Rise the Euphrates 893

Edgerton, Teresa
The Castle of the Silver Wheel 591

Edghill, India
Queenmaker **858**

Edghill, Rosemary
The Karen Hightower Series 81
Spirits White as Lightning **568**
The Sword of Maiden's Tears 575

Edison, Michael
The Vikings 1097

Edric, Robert
The Broken Lands 905

Edwards, Gene
The First Century Diaries Series 994, 1053
The Gaius Diary **990**
The Priscilla Diary 990
The Return 990
The Silas Diary 990
The Timothy Diary 990
The Titas Diary 990

Edwards, Hank
Gray Warrior 423
Ride for Rimfire 504

Edwards, Michael B.
Murder at the Panionic Games **859**

Edwards, Ruth Dudley
Matricide at St. Martha's 176

Effinger, George Alec
The Exile Kiss 774

Egan, Doris
The Complete Ivory 728

Egan, Greg
Axiomatic 766
Permutation City 731

Egan, Jennifer
Emerald City 1108

The Invisible Circus 1108
Look at Me **1108**, 1188

Ehly, Ehren M.
Star Prey 619

Ehrlich, Ev
Grant Speaks 903

Eichler, Selma
The Desiree Shapiro Series 34

Eickhoff, Randy Lee
The Destruction of the Inn 886
The Fourth Horseman 485, 493

Eisenstein, Phyllis
Born to Exile 551
Shadow of Earth 799

Eisner, Michael A.
The Crusader 831, 843, **860**, 901, 941

Elegant, Robert
Bianca 836

Elgin, Suzette Haden
Earthsong 747, 811

Elias, Albert J.
The Bowman Test 783

Elkins, Aaron
Curses! 195
The Gideon Oliver Series 100, 106
Loot 134

Ellin, Stanley
The Specialty of the House 48, 117

Elliott, Kate
The King's Dragon 586
Prince of Dogs 526

Elliott, Tom
The Dwelling 640

Ellis, Lyn
In Praise of Younger Men 231

Ellis, Monique
Delacey's Angel 397
An Uncommon Governess 238

Ellis, Peter Beresford
Act of Mercy **209**, **944**

Ellison, Harlan
Mefisto in Onyx 627
Partners in Wonder 679

Ellroy, James
The Black Dahlia 161
The Cold Six Thousand 1211

Ellson, Hal
Games 663

Elrod, P.N.
Dance of Death 632
Death Masque 632
Dracula in London **631**
His Father's Son **621**
I, Strahd 613, 632
Lady Crymsyn 632, 657
Quincey Morris, Vampire **632**, 686
Red Death 632
Time of the Vampires 631

Elwood, Roger
The Sorcerers of Sodom 637

Emerson, Earl
The Thomas Black Series 174

Emerson, Kathy Lynn
Face Down Among the Winchester Geese 65, 861
Face Down Before Rebel Hooves **65**, **861**, 875
Face Down Beneath the Eleanor Cross 65, 861
Face Down in the Marrow-Bone Pie 65, 861
Face Down under the Wych Elm 65, 861
Face Down upon an Herbal 65, 861
The Susanna, Lady Appleton Series 29, 834

Emerson, Ru
Against the Giants 563

Emery, Clayton
Star of Cursrah 597, 601

Emery, Lynn
Gotta Get Next to You **272**

Enger, Leif
Peace Like a River **1109**

Engh, M.J.
Rainbow Man 747

Englade, Ken
Brothers in Blood 454

Engstrom, Elizabeth
Dead on Demand **633**

Ennis, Michael
Byzantium 920

Enoch, Suzanne
By Love Undone 260
A Matter of Scandal 311
Meet Me at Midnight 229, 319, 375, 402
Reforming a Rake 408

Enquist, Per Olov
Captain Nemo's Library 862, 1110
The Legionnaires 862, 1110
The March of the Musicians 1110
The Royal Physician's Visit **862**, **1110**

Enright, Anne
What Are You Like? 1111
The Wig My Father Wore **1111**

Erdrich, Louise
The Bingo Palace 1205
The Last Report on the Miracles at Little No Horse 826, 1133

Erian, Alicia
The Brutal Language of Love 1149

Eschenburg, Kathleen
The Nightingale's Song **273**

Esquivel, Laura
The Law of Love 1112
Like Water for Chocolate 1067, 1112
Swift as Desire **1112**

Essenmacher, Eugenia Riley
The Great Baby Caper **380**

Estleman, Loren D.
The Amos Walker Series 174, 206
Bloody Season 485
City of Widows 493
General Murders 147
Journey of the Dead 478
Whiskey River 119
White Desert 502

Etchison, Craig
The World Weaver **749**

Etchison, Dennis
The Cutting Edge 634
Darkside 642
Masters of Darkness 634
Masters of Darkness II 634
Masters of Darkness III 634
MetaHorror 634
The Museum of Horrors **634**, 653
Shadow Man 619, 626, 664

Etheridge, Rutledge
Agent of Chaos 750
Agent of Destruction 750
Brother John **750**
The First Duelist 750
Legend of the Duelist 750

Eulo, Ken
The Brownstone 667
Manhattan Heat 672

Evanovich, Janet
Four to Score 274
High Five 274
Hot Six 274
Seven Up **274**, 376
The Stephanie Plum Series 13, 144, 198
Three to Get Deadly 274
Two for the Dough 274

Evans, Nicholas
The Horse Whisperer 1174, 1181

Evans, Richard Paul
The Christmas Box 983, 1033

Even, Aaron Roy
Bloodroot 910, 955

Everett, Peter
Bellocq's Women 837, 848, 867

Evers, Crabbe
The Duffy House Series 188

Everson, John
Cage of Bones and Other Deadly Obsessions 693, 698

Ewing, Jean R.
Illusion 385
Love's Reward 374

Eyre, Elizabeth
Poison for the Prince 836

F

Faherty, Terence
Come Back Dead 83

Fairbairn, Ann
Five Smooth Stones 1119, 1206

Fairchild, Elisabeth
Breach of Promise 275
Captain Cupid Calls the Shots 275, 315, 355, 378
The Holly and the Ivy 275, 304
Marriage a la Mode 275
Miss Dornton's Hero 397
The Rakehell's Reform 275
A Regency Christmas Present 232, 248
The Silent Suitor 388
Sugarplum Surprises **275**

Fairstein, Linda
The Alexandra Cooper Series 20
Cold Hit 66
The Deadhouse **66**
Final Jeopardy 66
Likely to Die 66

Faqir, Fadia
Pillars of Salt 1116

Farmer, Jerrilyn
Killer Wedding 60

Farmer, Philip Jose
A Barnstormer in Oz 577
A Feast Unknown 801
The Maker of Universes 520, 583

Farr, Diane
The Nobody 377
Once upon a Christmas 271, 278, 367

Farrell, Gillian B.
The Annie McGrogan Series 45

Farrell, James
Studs Lonigan 1117

Farrell, Marjorie
Red, Red Rose 315

Farren, Mick
The Feelies 793
The Song of Phaid the Gambler 790
The Texts of Festival 764
The Time of Feasting 699

Farris, John
The Fury and the Terror 709

Farris, Michael P.
Anonymous Tip 991
Forbid Them Not **991**
Guilt by Association 991

Fast, Jonathan
Golden Fire 963

Faulks, Sebastian
Birdsong 857, 925
Charlotte Gray 863, 888, 960

Faust, Frederick
The Gauntlet **430**
The House of Gold **431**
The Lone Rider **432**
Stolen Gold **433**

Faust, Joe Clifford
A Death of Honor 744

Feather, Jane
The Accidental Bride 276
The Hostage Bride 276, 352
The Least Likely Bride 276
To Kiss a Spy **276**
Valentine Wedding 276
Velvet 308
Violet 308
The Widow's Kiss 276

Feehan, Christine
The Scarletti Curse 277, 360
The Very Gothic Christmas **277**

Feintuch, David
The Still 544, 550, 606

Feist, Raymond E.
A Darkness at Sethanon 541, 554, 555, 560
Faerie Tale 527, 642, 659
Krondor, the Assassins 552
Krondor the Betrayal 545
Rage of a Demon King 530, 535
Rise of a Merchant Prince 532
Shadow of a Dark Queen 536, 599
Silverthorn 557

Feldhahn, Shaunti
The Veritas Conflict 1054

Fell, Doris Elaine
April Is Forever 1019
Blue Mist on the Danube 992
Long-Awaited Wedding 992
The Race for Autumn's Glory 992
Sunrise on Stradbury Square **992**
The Wedding Jewel 992
Willows on the Windrush 992

Fennelly, Tony
The Margot Fortier Series 13

Ferguson, Brad
The World Next Door 741

Ferguson, Jo Ann
A Brother's Honor 278, 279
A Christmas Bride 271, 279
A Daughter's Destiny 278, 279
A Guardian's Angel **278**
A Highland Folly 279
His Lady Midnight **279**
A Kiss for Mama **280**
Mistletoe Kittens 232
A Sister's Quest 278, 279
An Unexpected Husband 278, 280
Wake Not the Dragon 278

Ferguson, Maggie
Fever Rising 272

Ferrarella, Marie
An Uncommon Hero 373

Ferris, Monica
The Betsy Devonshire Series 4
Crewel World 67
Framed in Lace 67
A Stitch in Time 67
Unraveled Sleeve **67**

Ferris, Paul
The Cure 783

Feyrer, Gayle
Heart of Night **254**

Fforde, Jasper
The Eyre Affair 778

Fiedler, Jacqueline
Sketches with Wolves **68**
Tiger's Palette 68

Fielding, Helen
Bridget Jones: The Edge of Reason 345
Bridget Jones's Diary 252, 345, 357, 359, 1125

Fielding, Henry
The History of Tom Jones 1095

Fielding, Joy
The First Time 1101

Fields, Morgan
Shaman Woods 704

Fiffer, Sharon
Killer Stuff **69**, 160

Filippini, Serge
The Man in Flames 956

Finch, Paul
After Shocks 652
The Shadows Beneath 701

Findley, Timothy
The Telling of Lies 42

Fine, Stephen
Molly Dear 806

Finney, Jack
The Body Snatchers 660, 710
Time and Again 546

Fischer, Tibor
I Like Being Killed 1099

Fitzgerald, F. Scott
The Great Gatsby 1167

Fitzgerald, Penelope
Innocence 1201

Fitzpatrick, Christina
Where We Lived 1160

Fitzpatrick, Marie-Louise
The Long March 464

Flagg, Fannie
Fried Green Tomatoes at the Whistle Stop Cafe 1094, 1136

Fleming, David L.
Border Crossings 424

Fleming, Ian
For Your Eyes Only 118

Fleming, James
The Temple of Optimism 838

Fleming, Thomas
Remember the Morning 840
When This Cruel War Is Over 903, 914, 919

Fletcher, Donna
The Irish Devil 288
Irish Hope 316

Fletcher, Inglis
The Scotswoman 868

Fletcher, Jo
Horror at Halloween 628

Flewelling, Lynn
The Bone Doll's Twin **544**
Luck in the Shadows 544
Stalking Darkness 544
Traitor's Moon 544

Flint, Eric
Pyramid Scheme **751**

Flint, Kenneth
Isle of Destiny 520

Fluke, Joanne
The Hannah Swenson Series 170

Flynn, Michael
The Nanotech Chronicles 798

Flynn, Robert
In the House of the Lord 451
The Last Klick 451
Living with the Hyenas 451
Seasonal Rain and Other Stories 451
The Sounds of Rescue, the Signs of Hope 451
Tie-Fast Country **451**

Flynn, T.T.
Death Marks Time in Trampas: A Western Quintet 434, 452, 491, 501
The Devil's Lode: A Western Trio 431, 432, 435, 452, 455, 489
Hell-for-Leather Rider 452
Long Journey to Deep Canon **452**, 501
Night of the Comanche Moon 460
Rawhide 452
Ride to Glory 452

Fobes, Tracy
Daughter of Destiny 281
Forbidden Garden 281
Heart of the Dove 281
To Tame a Wild Heart **281**
Touch Not the Cat 281

Follett, Ken
Code to Zero 863
The Eye of the Needle 863
The Hammer of Eden 863
Jackdaws **863**, 888, 960, 1151
The Key to Rebecca 863
A Place Called Freedom 840, 863

Ford, Bette
Forever After 403

Ford, Ford Madox
The Good Soldier 1135, 1142

Ford, G.M.
The Leo Hagerty Series 56

Ford, John B.
Dark Shadows on the Moon **635**
Ghouls & Gore & Twisted Terrors 636
Macabre Delights and Twisted Tales 635, 636
Tales of Devilry and Doom 635, **636**
Within the Sea of the Dead 635

Ford, Linda
Prairie Brides 969

Ford, Michael Curtis
The Ten Thousand 859, 931

Ford, Richard
Independence Day 1202

Forrest, Leon
Meteor in the Madhouse 1133, 1154

Forrest, Richard
The Wizard of Death 53

Forstchen, William R.
1945 864
Arena 564
Catseye 864
The Crystal Sorcerers 537
Down to the Sea 864
The Napoleon Wager 516, 751
Never Sound Retreat 864
Prometheus 864
We Look Like Men of War **864**

Forster, Gwynne
Silver Bells 300

Forster, Suzanne
All through the Night **282**, 285
Angel Face **283**
Blush 283
Come Midnight 395
The Devil and Ms. Moody 235
Every Breath She Takes 283
Husband, Lover, Stranger 283
Innocence 283
The Morning After 283

Forsyth, Frederick
The Deceiver 1204

Forsythe, Patricia
The Runaway Princess 334, 343

Forward, Robert
Martian Rainbow 771

Fossen, Delores
Saddled 253, **284**

Foster, Alan Dean
The Tar Aiym Krang 772
The Thing 660

Foster, Bennett
Cow Thief Trail 480

Foster, Lori
All through the Night **282**
Annie, Get Your Guy 286
Hot and Bothered **285**
In Too Deep 240
Married to the Boss 286
Messing around with Max 286
Scandalized 286
Sex Appeal 286
Too Much Temptation 285, **286**

Foster, Sharon Ewell
Riding through Shadows 1051

Fowler, Christopher
City Jitters 648, 786
Roofworld 687

Fowler, Earlene
The Benni Harper Series 4, 28, 51, 189

Fowler, Karen Joy
Sister Noon 437, 817, 938, 1090

Fowles, John
The French Lieutenant's Woman 1102
A Maggot 1085
The Magus 1073

Fox, Karen
Buttercup Baby 249, **287**
Grand Design: The Hope Chest 287
Prince of Charming 287
Somewhere My Love 287
Sword of MacLeod 287

Fox, Paula
A Servant's Tale 1206

Foxwell, Elizabeth
More Murder, They Wrote 84

Foxx, Jack
The Jade Figurine 185

Foy, George
The Memory of Fire 764

Frankowski, Leo
A Boy and His Tank 765

Franzen, Jonathan
The Corrections 1107, **1113**, 1163
Strong Motion 1113
The Twenty-Seventh City 1113

Fraser, Mary Ann
In Search of the Grand Canyon 949

Frazee, Steve
Bragg's Fancy Woman 453
Ghost Mine 439, 443, 453
Hidden Gold 453
Voices in the Hill: Western Stories **453**
The Way through the Mountains 453

Frazer, Margaret
The Bishop's Tale 865
The Boy's Tale 865
The Clerk's Tale **70, 865**
The Dame Frevisse Series 86, 194, 209
The Maiden's Tale 70
The Murderer's Tale 70
The Prioress' Tale 70, 865
The Reeve's Tale 70, 865
The Sister Frevisse Series 944
The Squire's Tale 70, 865, 933, 934

Frazier, Charles
Cold Mountain 964

Freedman, J.F.
Bird's-Eye View 1076

Freedman, Jeff
The Magic Dishpan of Oz 577

Freeman, Mary
The Rachel O'Connor Series 103, 181, 219

Freer, David
The Forlorn 751
Pyramid Scheme **751**
Rats, Bats, and Vats 751

Freethy, Barbara
Almost Home 225, 386
Daniel's Gift 239
Just the Way You Are 231
One True Love 239, 330
The Sweetest Thing 344

French, Judith E.
Morgan's Woman 294

Rachel's Choice 418

French, Linda
Coffee to Die For 32
The Teddy Morelli Series 51

Freydont, Shelley
Backstage Murder 71
High Seas Murder 71
Midsummer Murder 45, **71**

Frezza, Robert
A Small Colonial War 784

Friedman, C.S.
Black Sun Rising 600

Friedman, Kinky
Blast from the Past 72, 1150
The Love Song of J. Edgar Hoover 72
The Mile High Club 72
Road Kill 72
Spanking Watson 72
Steppin' on a Rainbow **72**

Friedman, Mark
Columbus Slaughters Braves **1114**

Friesner, Esther
Gnome Man's Land 521
New York by Knight 533, 602, 614
The Sherwood Game 758
Sphynxes Wild 537
Unicorn U 588
The Wishing Season 543

Frith, Nigel
Jormungard 517

Froemke, Marcy
A Family in the Making 997

Frommer, Sarah Hoskinson
The Joan Spencer Series 124

Frost, Mark
The List of 7 926

Fuentes, Carlos
The Old Gringo 878
The Years with Laura Diaz 817, 948, 1067

Fuhrman, Holly
Do You Hear What I Hear? **306**

Fulghum, Stephen Ray
The Forsaken 687

Fuller, Iola
The Shining Trail 873

Fuller, Jack
The Best of Jackson Payne 1122, 1210

Fullerton, Alexander
The Blooding of the Guns **866**, 954
The Executives 866
Lionheart 866
The Publisher 866
The Waiting Game 866

Fulmer, David
Chasing the Devil's Tail **73**, 196, **867**

Fulton, John
Retribution **1115**

Funderburk, Robert
The Dylan St. John Series 981
Heart and Soul 1051
Tenderness and Fire 1005

Furey, Maggie
Aurian 545
Dhammara 523, 545, 609, 611
Harp of Winds 545
The Heart of Myrial 545
Spirit of the Stone **545**
The Sword of Flame 545

Furst, Alan
Kingdom of Shadows 863, 906, 1168
Red Gold 126, 888, 960

Furutani, Dale
The Toyotomi Blades 150

Fusilli, Jim
Closing Time **74**

Fyfield, Frances
The Helen West Series 154

G

Gabaldon, Diana
Dragonfly in Amber 288, 868
Drums of Autumn 288, 868
The Fiery Cross **288**, **868**, 869
Outlander 237, 288, 358, 868
Outlandish Companion 288
Voyager 288, 546, 868

Gabriel, Kristin
Annie Get Your Groom 289
Bachelor by Design 289
The Bachelor Trap 289
Beauty and the Bachelor 289
Dangerously Irresistible **289**, 333
Monday Man 235
Send Me No Flowers 289

Gaffney, Patricia
Lily 227

Gaiman, Neil
American Gods 694

Galbraith, Lettice
The Blue Room and Other Ghost Stories 618

Galitz, Cathleen
A Home of Her Own **982**

Gallagher, Stephen
Red, Red Robin 664
Valley of Lights 710

Galouye, Daniel F.
Lords of the Psychon 746, 791
Simulacron-3 731

Ganem, Lawrence
The Plutonium Blonde **813**

Gann, Ernest Kellogg
The High and the Mighty 1141

Gannett, Lewis
The Living One 623

Gansky, Alton
Distant Memory 985, 999
The Prodigy **637**, 975
The Ridgeline Mystery Series 1012
A Ship Possessed 637, 1056
Terminal Justice 975
Vanished 637, 1000

Gantz, Kenneth F.
Not in Solitude 814
Not Without Solitude 771

Gao, Xingjian
Soul Mountain 1098, 1170

Garcia-Aguilera, Carolina
Bitter Sugar **75**
Bloody Secrets 75
Bloody Shame 75
Bloody Waters 75
Havana Heat 75
The Lupe Solano Series 167, 217
A Miracle in Paradise 75

Garcia Marquez, Gabriel
The Autumn of the Patriarch 948

Garcia y Robertson, R.
American Woman 869, 911
Atlantis Found 546
Knight Errant **546**, 868, **869**
The Moon Maid 546
The Spiral Dance 546, 869
The Virgin and the Dinosaur 546

Gardam, Jane
Crusoe's Daughter 870
The Flight of the Maidens 821, 845, **870**, 925, 938
The Hollow Land 870
The Queen of the Tambourine 870
The Sidmouth Letters 870
Through the Dolls' House Door 870

Gardiner, John Rolfe
Somewhere in France 857

Gardner, Craig Shaw
A Bad Day for Ali Baba 521
The Dragon Sleeping 605
An Excess of Enchantments 537, 588

Gardner, John
Grendel 517

Garfield, Brian
Manifest Destiny 508

Garland, Kit
Sweeter than Sin 270

Garland, Sherry
India 871

Garlock, Dorothy
The Edge of Town **290**, 882
Larkspur 290
More than Memory 339
Sweetwater 290
With Heart 290
With Hope 290
With Song 290

Garner, Alan
Elidor 581
The Owl Service 519
The Weirdstone of Brisingamen 520, 542

Garnett, David
Bikini Planet **752**
Cosmic Carousel 752
The Forgotten Dimension 752
Phantom Universe 752
Space Wasters 752
Time in Eclipse 752

Garnett, Gale Zoe
Visible Amazement 1159, 1206

Garnett, Juliana
The Baron 295
The Knight 303, 406

Garry, Jim
This Ol' Drought Ain't Broke Us Yet 433

Garton, Ray
411 638
Biofire 638
Crucifax Autumn 626
Dark Channel 638
The Folks **638**
Live Girls 625, 699
Lot Lizards 638
Shackled 638

Garwood, Haley E.
Swords Across the Thames 883

Garwood, Julie
The Bride 269
Gentle Warrior 405
Guardian Angel 328
Ransom 244
Saving Grace 295
The Wedding 269

Gash, Jonathan
Jade Woman 185
The Lovejoy Series 69, 160

Gates, John
Brigham's Day 76
Sister Wife **76**

Gates, R. Patrick
Grimm Memorials 626

Gavin, Catherine
The Devil in Harbour 866

Gay, William
The Long Home 1157
Provinces of Night 1121

Gear, Kathleen O'Neal
Bone Walker 61, 424, **871**
Dark Inheritance 871
The First North Americans Series 871
People of the Masks 510
People of the Mist 510
People of the Silence 441
The Summoning God 424, 871, 962
Thin Moon and Cold Mist 871
The Visitant 424, 506, 871

Gear, W. Michael
Bone Walker **871**

Gearino, G.D.
Counting Coup 115

Gedney, Mona
Autumn Kittens **232**
A Dangerous Arrangement 291
Lady Diana's Daring Deed 291
Lady Hilary's Halloween **291**
A Lady of Quality 291
A Match for Mother 291
Merry's Christmas 275, 291

Gelb, Jeff
Shock Rock 684

Gellis, Roberta
Bull God 547, 576
Dazzling Brightness 547
A Personal Devil 875
Shimmering Splendor 547
The Silver Mirror 276
Thrice Bound **547**

Gemmell, David
Druss the Legend 557
The Hero in the Shadows 548
Ironhand's Daughter 548
Lion of Macedon 547
Midnight Falcon **548**
Ravenheart 548
The Sword in the Storm 548
Winter's Warriors 548

Gent, Peter
North Dallas Forty 1132

George, Anne
Murder Boogies with Elvis **77**
Murder Carries a Torch 77
Murder Gets a Life 77
Murder Makes Waves 77
Murder on a Bad Hair Day 38
Murder Runs in the Family 77
Murder Shoots the Bull 77
The Southern Sisters Series 15, 91, 114, 163

George, Elizabeth
The Thomas Lynley/Barbara Havers Series 30, 92

George, Melanie
Like No Other 277
The Very Gothic Christmas **277**

George, Sara
The Journal of Mrs. Pepys 1069

Gerritsen, Tess
Bloodstream 78
Gravity 78, 1094
Harvest 78
Life Support 78
The Surgeon **78**

Gerrold, David
The Man Who Folded Himself 754
Under the Eye of God 797

Gerson, Jack
The Ernest Lehmann Series 126

Ghosh, Amitav
The Circle of Reason 1116

Gibson, Rachel
It Must Be Love 292, 363
Simply Irresistible 292
True Confessions **292**
Truly Madly Yours 235, 256, 292, 376

Gibson, Robin
Ma Calhoun's Boys 440

Gier, Scott
Genellan: First Victory 795

Gift, Theo
Not for the Night Time 618

Gifune, Greg F.
Down to Sleep 639
Heretics **639**

Gilbert, Anna
A Hint of Witchcraft 872
The Long Shadow 872
A Morning in Eden **872**
The Treachery of Time 872
A Walk in the Woods 872
The Wedding Guest 872

Gilbert, Michael
Game Without Rules 118
Into Battle 208
The Man Who Hated Banks and Other Stories 146
Mr. Calder and Mr. Behrens 118

Gilchrist, Ellen
The Age of Miracles 1080, 1162
The Anna Papers 1103
The Cabal and Other Stories 1072, 1081, 1155, 1193, 1201
The Courts of Love 1143, 1169
Flights of Angels 1157
Starcarbon 1200

Gilchrist, Micaela
The Good Journey **454, 873**

Giles, Molly
Iron Shoes 1159

Gill, Bartholomew
The Peter McGarr Series 173

Gilman, Dorothy
The Clairvoyant Countess 79, 522
Kaleidoscope **79**

Gimarc, Donna
Sugarplum Surprises **275**

Gino, Carol
The Family **916**

Gipson, Fred
Old Yeller 1065

Girard, Paula Tanner
The Sister Season 262

Girdner, Jacqueline
A Cry for Self Help 80
Death Hits the Fan 80
The Kate Jasper Series 91
Most Likely to Die 80
Murder, My Deer 80
Murder on the Astral Plane 80
A Sensitive Kind of Murder **80**

Giron, Sephera
Eternal Sunset 640
House of Pain **640**

Girzone, Joseph F.
Joshua the Homecoming 983

Gish, Robert Franklin
First Horses 453

Givens, Kathleen
My Scottish Summer **243**

Glancy, Diane
Flutie 467, 481, 513

Glasgow, Ellen
The Shadowy Third 711

Gloag, John
Artorius Rex 829

Gloss, Molly
The Dazzle of Day 1082
Wild Life 1083, 1140, 1165

Glover, Ruth
The Wildrose Series 998, 1011

Goddard, Ken
First Evidence 773

Goddard, Robert
Caught in the Light 82, 849
Hand in Glove 183
In Pale Battalions 208

Godwin, Parke
Firelord 566

Gold, Glen David
Carter Beats the Devil 841, 847, **874**

goldberg, d.g.k.
Doomed to Repeat It **641**
Skating on the Edge 641

Goldberg, Myla
Bee Season 978

Golden, Christopher
Angel Souls and Devil Hearts 642
Of Masques and Martyrs 642
Of Saints and Shadows 642
Straight on 'Til Morning **642**, 659
Strangewood 642

Golding, Michael
Simple Prayers 832

Golding, Paul
The Abomination 1159, 1198

Goldring, Kat
All Signs Point to Murder **81**

Goldsmith, Olivia
Bad Boy 264, 274, 1126

Gonzalez, Ray
The Ghost of John Wayne and Other Stories 430, **455**

Gonzalez-Rubio, Javier
Loving You Was My Undoing 476

Gooden, Philip
The Death of Kings 880
The Nick Revill Series 148
The Sleep of Death 109

Goodkind, Terry
Blood of the Fold 549, 550
Debt of Bones **549**, 550
Faith of the Fallen 549, 550, 572, 609, 611
The Pillars of Creation **550**
Soul of the Fire 549, 550
Stone of Tears 549
Temple of the Winds 549, 550
Wizard's First Rule 541, 601

Goodman, Allegra
The Markowitz Family 1100

Goodman, Carol
The Lake of Dead Languages **82**

Goodrum, Charles
The Best Cellar 128

Gordimer, Nadine
Harold, Claudia, and Their Son Duncan 1116
The House Gun 1116
The Lying Days 1116
None to Accompany Me 1116
Occasion for Loving 1116
The Pickup 1101, 1112, **1116**, 1170, 1190

Gordon, Anita
The Defiant Heart 338
The Valiant Heart 336

Gores, Joe
Cases 83
The DKA Series 174
Speak of the Devil 40, 85, 175
Stakeout on Page Street 41, 99, 201

Gorman, Ed
The Blue and the Gray Undercover **456**
Cages 706
Dark Trail 438, 456, 479
The Day the Music Died 83
Famous Blue Raincoat 40, 117, 175
The Fatal Frontier 484, 511
Graves' Retreat 456
Lawless 456
Save the Last Dance for Me **83**
Storm Riders 446, 448, 456
Trouble Man 456, 473
Wake Up, Little Susie 83
Will You Still Love Me Tomorrow? 83
The World's Finest Mystery & Crime Stories: First Annual Collection 84
The World's Finest Mystery & Crime Stories: Second Annual Collection **84**

Goshgarian, Gary
The Stone Circle 676

Gottleib, Sherry
Worse than Death 645

Gouge, Louise M.
The Homecoming 1005

Gough, Julian
Juno & Juliet 1160

Goulart, Ron
Adam and Eve on a Raft **85**, 142
After Things Fell Apart 730, 738
Big Bang 813
Daredevils, Ltd. 756, 763
Elementary, My Dear Groucho 85
Groucho Marx and the Broadway Murders 85, 882
Groucho Marx, Master Detective 85
Groucho Marx, Private Eye 85
The Groucho Marx Series 72, 841
Hail Hibbler 752
Now He Thinks He's Dead 85

Grace, C.L.
The Book of Shadows 86, 875
The Eye of God 86, 875
The Kathryn Swinbrooke Series 194
The Merchant of Death 86, 875
Saintly Murders **86, 875**
A Shrine of Murders 86, 875

Gracie, Anne
Gallant Waif 259

Gracy, K. Noelle
A Family for Gillian **238**

Grafton, Sue
The Kinsey Millhone Series 63

Graham, Caroline
The Inspector Barnaby Series 55, 87, 104, 165
The Inspector Tom Barnaby Series 43
The Tom Barnaby Series 64, 116

Graham, Daniel
Tenebrea's Hope **743**

Graham, Heather
And One Wore Gray 273
One Wore Blue 273
The Viking's Woman 336

Graham, Janice
Firebird 457
Sarah's Window **457**

Gram, Dewey
Fallen 627

Granger, Ann
The Alan Markby/Meredith Mitchell Series 165
Beneath These Stones 87
Call the Dead Again 87
A Candle for a Corpse 87
The Fran Varaday Series 11
Shades of Murder **87**
A Touch of Mortality 87
A Word After Dying 87

Grant, Anne Underwood
Cuttings 103

Grant, Charles L.
Doom City 648
For Fear of the Night 642
The Hour of the Oxrun Dead 663, 668
Whirlwind 737, 773

Grant, Linda
Vampyre Bites 170

Grant, Reg
Storm 1031

Grant, Richard
In the Land of Winter 539

Grant, Susan
Once a Pirate 328, 371
The Star King 310

Grape, Jan
Austin City Blue **88**

Grass, Gunter
Too Far Afield 1151

Grasso, Patricia
Courting an Angel 293
Love in a Mist 293
My Heart's Desire 293
No Decent Gentleman 293
To Tame a Duke **293**
Violets in the Snow 293

Grau, Shirley Ann
The Hard Blue Sky 1214

Graversen, Pat
Precious Blood 703

Graves, Robert
I, Claudius 931

Graves, Sarah
Dead Cat Bounce 89
The Jacobia Tiptree Series 100, 157, 219
Repair to Her Grave 89
Triple Witch 89
Wicked Fix 89
Wreck the Halls **89**

Gray, Genevieve
Fair Laughs the Morn 476, 510

Gray, Ginna
The Prodigal Daughter 301

Gray, Julia
The Dark Moon 551
Fire Music 551
Ice Mage 551
The Jasper Forest **551**

Greeley, Andrew M.
The Bishop and the Beggar Girl of St. Germain 1117
A Christmas Wedding 1117
Irish Gold 1111
A Midwinter's Tale 1117, 1135, 1174
September Song **1117**
Younger than Springtime 1117

Green, Christine
The Connor O'Neill/Fran Wilson Series 64, 87, 165

Green, Henry
Caught 876

Green, Jane
Mr. Maybe 394

Green, Kate
The Theresa Fortunato Series 52, 79, 140

Green, Michael
The Jimjams 703

Green, Norman
Shooting Dr. Jack **1118**

Green, Sharon
Intrigues 544

Green, Simon R.
Beyond the Blue Moon 523, 535, 578, 609
Blue Moon Rising 548

Greenberg, Martin H.
After the King 753
Alien Abductions 754
Assassin Fantastic **552**
The Best Alternate History Stories of the 20th Century **804**
Dinosaurs 753
Dracula, Prince of Darkness 631
The Fantastic Adventures of Robin Hood 753
Far Frontiers 552
Future Crimes 552, 754
Future Net 753
Guardsmen of Tomorrow 552
Merlin 552, 754
Murder Most Medieval 8
The Mutant Files **753**
My Favorite Science Fiction Story 754
Past Imperfect **754**
Single White Vampire Seeks Same **643**
Starfall 552, 754
The World's Finest Mystery & Crime Stories: Second Annual Collection **84**

Greene, Elena
Lord Langdon's Kiss 305, 420

Greene, Jennifer
Nobody's Princess 261
Rock Solid 250

Greene, Sheldon
Burnt Umber 852, 892, 913

Greenland, Colin
Take Back Plenty 770

Greenleaf, Stephen
Ellipsis 190
The John Marshall Tanner Series 22, 111, 141, 174, 206, 213

Greenlief, K.C.
Cold Hunter's Moon **90**, 145, 212

Greeno, Gayle
Exile's Return 551
Sunderlies Seeking 571, 596

Greenwood, Ed
Death of the Dragon 553
Elminster in Hell **553**
Elminster in Myth Drannor 553, 584, 597
The Kingless Land 553
Silverfall 553
The Vacant Throne 553

Greer, Robert
The CJ Floyd Series 192, 216

Gregory, H.B.
Dark Sanctuary **644**

Gregory, Jill
Always You 294
Cold Night, Warm Stranger 294, 409
Just This Once 294
Never Love a Cowboy 294
Once an Outlaw **294**
Once upon a Rose **384**
Rough Wrangler, Tender Kisses 294, 324

Gregory, Susanna
A Bone of Contention 843
The Matthew Bartholomew Series 944

Greig, Andrew
The Clouds Above **876**

Grey, Zane
The Great Trek 458
Open Range **458**
Rangers of the Lone Star 458
Rangle River 445, 458, 486, 494
The Westerners: Stories of the West 432, 435, 458, 496
Woman of the Frontier 458, 462, 483, 497

Griffin, Annie
Date with the Perfect Dead Man 91
The Hannah Malloy/Kiki Goldstein Series 77, 80
Love and the Single Corpse 91
Tall, Dead, and Handsome **91**
A Very Eligible Corpse 91

Griffith, Kathryn Meyer
Witches 704

Griffith, Michael
Spikes 1114, 1132

Grilley, Kate
Death Rides an Ill Wind 219

Grimes, Martha
The Blue Last **92**
The Case Has Altered 92
The Horse You Came In On 92
The Lamorna Wink 54, 92
Rainbow's End 92
The Richard Jury Series 30
The Stargazey 92

Grimes, Terris McMahon
The Theresa Galloway Series 21

Grimwood, Jon Courtenay
Pashazade 774

Grisham, John
The Client 1123
The Firm 1096
A Painted House 1077
The Pelican Brief 1097
The Rainmaker 141
A Time to Kill 1088, 1139

Grooms, Anthony
Bombingham **1119**, 1154
Trouble No More 1119

Grove, Fred
Bitter Trumpet 459
Destiny Valley 459, **459**, 460
A Distance of Ground 460, 506, 509
Into the Far Mountains 459, 460
Man on a Red Horse 460
Red River Stage 459, 460
Trail of the Rogues 459
The Years of Fear **460**

Grove, Paula K.
White Boys and River Girls 1201

Grubb, Davis
The Night of the Hunter 665

Grubb, Jeff
The Gathering Dark 564

Grun, Bernard
The Golden Quill 929

Guiver, Patricia
The Delilah Doolittle Series 17

Gulley, Philip
The Harmony Series 984, 1007, 1018

Gunn, Alistair G.
Ballymoon 701

Gunn, Elizabeth
Five Card Stud 93
Par Four 93
Six-Pound Walleye **93**
Triple Play 93

Gunn, James
The Magicians 522

Gunn, Robin Jones
Clouds 993
Echoes 993
The Glenbrooke Series 984, 1006, 1007, 1018
Sunsets 993
Until Tomorrow 1054
Waterfalls 993
Whispers 1059
Wildflowers **993**
Woodlands 993

Gunning, Sally
The Peter Bartholomew Series 46, 219

Gurganus, Allan
Blessed Assurance 1120
Oldest Living Conferate Widow Tells All 1120
Plays Well with Others 1120
The Practical Heart 1079, **1120**
White People 1120

Guterson, David
Snow Falling on Cedars 845

Gutierrez, Pedro Juan
Dirty Havana Trilogy 1092

H

Haber, Karen
Mutant Prime 753

Hackenberry, Charles
Friends 451

Hackler, Micah S.
The Cliff Lansing Series 108

Hadley, Joan
The Theo Bloomer Series 103

Hagee, John
Devil's Island **994**

Hager, Jean
Bride and Doom 157
The Molly Bearpaw Series 35, 212
The Tess Darcy Series 32

Haggard, H. Rider
Eric Brighteyes 517
King Solomon's Mines 717, 792

Hague, Nora
Letters from an Age of Reason 838, **877**, 914, 964

Haiblum, Isidore
The Hand of Ganz 752
The Mutants Are Coming 753

Haines, Carolyn
The Sarah Booth Delaney Series 4, 163

Haining, Peter
The Ghost Companion 615
Hallowe'en Hauntings 628

Haldeman, Joe
Forever Peace 796
The Forever War 761
Vietnam and Other Alien Worlds 807

Hale, Deborah
My Lord Protector 352
The Wedding Wager 259, 311

Hale, Gena
Paradise Island 399

Halkin, John
Squelch 762

Hall, Brenda
Cold Hunter's Moon **90**

Hall, James W.
Blackwater Sound **94**
Buzz Cut 94
Gone Wild 94
Mean High Tide 94
Red Sky at Night 94
Tropical Freeze 94

Hall, Linda
Margaret's Peace 967, 993
Sadie's Song 1001, 1002, 1029

Hall, Oakley
Ambrose Bierce and the Death of Kings **95**, **878**, 896
Ambrose Bierce and the Queen of Spades 95, 878
The Ambrose Bierce Series 135
Apaches 878

The Bad Lands 878
The Children of the Sun 878
Warlock 878

Hall, Parnell
A Clue for the Puzzle Lady 96
Last Puzzle and Testament 96
Puzzled to Death **96**
The Stanley Hastings Series 72

Hall, Patricia
Dead of Winter 97
Dead on Arrival 97
Dying Fall 97
The Italian Girl 97
Perils of the Night 97
Skeleton at the Feast **97**

Hall, Robert Lee
The Benjamin Franklin Series 815
The King Edward Plot 851

Hallinan, Timothy
Everything but the Squeal 199

Hambly, Barbara
The Benjamin January Series 2, 73, 196, 207, 867, 935
Die upon a Kiss 909, 914
Magic Time **614**
Those Who Hunt the Night 686, 695, 922, 963

Hamilton, Denise
The Jasmine Trade 39, **98**, 137

Hamilton, Edmond
The Closed Worlds 719
The Haunted Stars 785
The Star Kings 769
Starwolf 768
A Yank at Valhalla 751

Hamilton, Jane
Disobedience 1113

Hamilton, Laurell K.
Black Narcissus 625
Bloody Bones 645
Blue Moon 645
Burnt Offerings 645
Death of a Darklord 682
A Kiss of Shadows 527, 602
The Lunatic Cafe 645
Narcissus in Chains **645**
Obsidian Butterfly 645, 657

Hamilton, Lyn
The Xibalba Murders 195

Hamilton, Peter
Lightstorm 739
Watching Trees Grow 741

Hamilton, Steve
The Alex McKnight Series 90, 93

Hamilton, Wallace
David at Olivet 858

Hamlin, Rick
Hidden Gifts 1044

Hammell, Ian
City of Assassins 552

Hammett, Dashiell
The Dain Curse 99
The Glass Key 99
Hammett: Crime Stories and Other Writings 41, **99**, 201
The Maltese Falcon 99
The Red Harvest 99
The Thin Man 99

Hampton, Denise
The Warrior's Damsel **295**, 407

Handler, David
The Boy Who Never Grew Up 100
The Cold Blue Blood **100**, 115
The Girl Who Ran Off with Daddy 100
The Man Who Cancelled Himself 100
The Man Who Loved Women to Death 100
The Stewart Hoag Series 218
The Woman Who Fell from Grace 100

Haney, Lauren
A Curse of Silence 101
A Face Turned Backwards 101
A Place of Darkness **101**
The Right Hand of Amon 101
A Vile Justice 101

Hanna, Edward
The Whitechapel Horror 62, 153

Hannah, Barry
Bats out of Hell 1121
Boomerang 1121
Hey Jack! 1121
High Lonesome 1121
Never Die 1121
Yonder Stands Your Orphan **1121**

Hannah, Kristin
A Handful of Heaven 371, 372
Summer Island 231
Waiting for the Moon 382
When Lightning Strikes 313

Hannon, Irene
A Family to Call Her Own 968
The Way Home 1047, 1061

Hansen, Joseph
The Dave Brandstetter Series 221

Hansen, Valerie
Love One Another 982, **995**
The Perfect Couple 995, 1022
Second Chances 995, 997, 1052, 1057
The Troublesome Angel 965, 995
Wedding Arbor 987
The Wedding Arbor 995, 1021

Hansom, Mark
The Beasts of Brahm **646**
The Ghost of Gaston Revere 646
Madman 646
Masters of Souls 646
The Sorcerer's Chessman 646
The Wizard of Berner's Abbey 646

Harbaugh, Karen
Cupid's Kiss 287, 350
The Vampire Viscount 922, 963

Harding, Paul
The Brother Athelstan Series 70

Hardwick, Gary
Cold Medina 166, 216

Hardwick, Mollie
The Doran Fairweather Series 36
I Remember Love 849

Hardy, Lyndon
Master of the Five Magics 548

Harlan, Thomas
The Storm of Heaven 562

Harman, Andrew
101 Damnations 518
Talonspotting 588

Harness, Charles L.
Lurid Dreams 802
Redworld 810

Harper, Karen
The Elizabeth I Series 29, 65, 834, 861, 880
Empty Cradle 312, 381

Harper, Steven
Dreamer **755**

Harris, Charlaine
Shakespeare's Champion 102
Shakespeare's Christmas 102
Shakespeare's Counselor **102**
Shakespeare's Landlord 102
Shakespeare's Trollop 102

Harris, Cyril
Street of Knives 912

Harris, E. Lynn
Abide with Me 1122
And This Too Shall Pass 1005, 1122
Any Way the Wind Blows **1122**, 1145, 1210
If This World Were Mine 1122
Just as I Am 1122
Not a Day Goes By 1122

Harris, Fred
Easy Pickin's 110

Harris, Joanne
Five Quarters of the Orange 835, 930

Harris, Lee
The April Fool's Day Murder 996
The Father's Day Murder 996
Happy Birthday Murder **996**
The Labor Day Murder 996
The Mother's Day Murder 996
The New Year's Eve Murder 996

Harris, Mark
Bang the Drum Slowly 1114, 1132

Harris, Robert
Archangel 130

Harris, Thomas
Hannibal 1180
Red Dragon 154
The Silence of the Lambs 123

Harrison, Jamie
The Jules Clement Series 108

Harrison, Janis
The Bretta Solomon Series 4, 67
Lilies That Fester **103**
Murder Sets Seed 103
Roots of Murder 103, 181

Harrison, Jim
The Beast God Forgot to Invent 1199
Dalva 1137, 1157
Legends of the Fall 1195
Warlock 1084
Woman Lit by Fireflies 1088

Harrison, M. John
A Storm of Wings 586

Harrison, Ray
The Sergeant Bragg/Constable Morton Series 172

Harrison, Sue
Brother Wind 879
Call Down the Stars 871, **879**
Cry of the Wind 879
Mother Earth, Father Sky 879
Song of the River 879

Harrod-Eagles, Cynthia
The Bill Slider Series 30
Blood Lines 104
Blood Sinister **104**
Grave Music 104
Killing Time 104
Necrochip 104
Shallow Grave 104

Harstad, Donald
The Big Thaw 93
The Carl Houseman Series 108, 151, 168

Hart, Carolyn
The Annie Laurance/Max Darling Series 6, 177
Crime on Her Mind 31
The Death on Demand Series 32
The Henrie O Series 15, 51, 91

Hart, Ellen
Dial M for Meat Loaf **105**
For Every Evil 105
The Merchant of Venus 60
Murder in the Air 105
The Oldest Sin 105
Slice and Dice 105
This Little Piggy Went to Murder 105

Hart, Jessica
Wedding at Waverly Creek 343

Hart, Jillian
Cooper's Wife 296, 997
Heaven Sent 974, 982, **997**
Last Chance Bride 296, 997
Malcolm's Honor 296, 997
Montana Man 296, 997
Night Hawk's Bride **296**, 391, 997

Hartman, Keith
Gumshoe Gorilla **756**, 813
The Gumshoe, the Witch, and the Virtual Corpse 756

Harvey, John
The Charlie Resnick Series 104, 155, 178

Harvey, William Fryer
Midnight Tales 622

Haseloff, Cynthia
Changing Trains 423
Man Without Medicine 446, 448, 449, 450, 467, 480

Hashian, Jack
Mamigon 893

Hatcher, Robin Lee
The Forgiving Hour 993, 1023, 1055
Promise Me Spring 421
Ribbon of Years 1039
The Shepherd's Voice 1017
Where the Heart Is 290, 421
Whispers from Yesterday 1010

Hathaway, Robin
The Doctor and the Dead Man's Chest **106**
The Doctor Digs a Grave 106
The Doctor Makes a Dollhouse Call 106

Hatvary, George Egon
The Murder of Edgar Allan Poe 193, 932

Hauck, Stephanie Bond
Two Sexy **240**

Hautala, Rick
Beyond the Shroud 641
Cold Whisper 641
The Mountain King 662
The White Room **673**

Hautman, Pete
Drawing Dead 107
The Mortal Nuts 107
Mrs. Million 107
Rag Man **107**

Ring Game 107
Short Money 107

Havill, Steven F.
Bag Limit **108**
Before She Dies 108
The Bill Gastner Series 93, 151
Dead Weight 108
Out of Season 108
Privileged to Kill 108
Prolonged Exposure 108

Hawke, Simon
The Iron Throne 880
The Last Wizard 880
A Mystery of Errors 109, 148, 880
The Nomad 880
The Outcast 880
The Reluctant Sorcerer 524
The Seeker 604
The Shakespeare & Smythe Series 29
The Shakespeare and Smythe Series 834
The Slaying of the Shrew **109**, **880**

Hawkins, Karen
A Belated Bride 311

Hawkins, Paul A.
The Seekers 426, 429
White Moon Tree 451

Hawks, Kate
The Lovers 881
Watch by Moonlight 840, **881**

Hawthorne, Julian
The Rose of Death and Other Mysterious Delusions 647

Hay, Elizabeth
A Student of Weather 1156

Haycox, Ernest
Powder Smoke & Other Stories 433
Rim of the Desert 490, 499

Hayder, Mo
Birdman 1123
The Treatment **1123**

Haydon, Elizabeth
Destiny 552, **554**
Prophecy 554, 1140
Revelation **555**
Rhapsody 554
Transformation 555

Hayes, John R.
Catskill **110**, 828, 839, **882**, 885, 955

Hayes, Morgan
Tall, Dark, and Wanted 414

Hayes, Sally Tyler
Spies, Lies, and Lovers 414

Haynes, Melinda
Chalktown 1154

Hays, Clark
The Cowboy and the Vampire 712

Hays, Tony
Murder on the Twelfth Night 109

Hayter, Sparkle
The Last Manly Man 80
The Robin Hudson Series 144

Haywood, Gar Anthony
The Aaron Gunner Series 192

Hayworth, Lynne
Autumn Flame 297
Summer's End 288, **297**
Winter Fire 297

Hazard, Barbara
The Unsuitable Miss Martingale 278
The Wary Widow 325, 389

Heald, Denise Lopes
Mistwalker 716

Healy, Jeremiah
Act of God 111
The Concise Cuddy 147
Invasion of Privacy 111
The John Francis Cuddy Series 74, 174, 206
The Only Good Lawyer 111
Rescue 111
Spiral 111
Turnabout **111**

Heath, Lorraine
Never Love a Cowboy 409
Texas Destiny 415
Texas Splendor 270

Heath, Sandra
A Christmas Courtship 275
A Commerical Enterprise 318
The Halloween Husband 291
Lucy's Christmas Angel 366

Hebert, Ernest
The Old American 945

Hecht, Daniel
Skull Session 705

Heck, Peter J.
The Mark Twain Series 95, 135

Heffernan, William
Beulah Hill 196, 884
The Paul Devlin Series 152

Hegan, Christine
The Enemy Within 312

Hegi, Ursula
Floating in My Mother's Palm 1124
Hotel of the Saints **1124**
Intrusions 1124
Salt Dancers 1124
Stones from the River 1124
The Vision of Emma Blau 930, 1124

Hegwood, Martin
Big Easy Backroad 112
A Green-Eyed Hurricane 112
Massacre Island **112**

Heinlein, Robert A.
The Door into Summer 754
The Puppet Masters 660, 710
Requiem 1082
The Unpleasant Profession of Jonathan Hoag 670

Heitzmann, Kristen
Honor's Disguise 998
Honor's Quest 998
Honor's Reward 998
The Rocky Mountain Legacy Series 1050
The Rose Legacy 998
Sweet Boundless 998
The Tender Vine **998**

Hekkanen, Ernest
My Dog Is More than Just a Dog to Me 1100

Helfers, John
The Mutant Files **753**

Heller, Jane
Crystal Clear 1125
Female Intelligence **1125**
Infernal Affairs 1125
Name Dropping 1125
Princess Charming 1125
Sis Boom Bah 1125

Helmer, Roberta
Going Overboard **399**

Helprin, Mark
A Soldier of the Great War 857

Hemry, John G.
Stark's War 742

Henderson, Dee
Danger in the Shadows 999, 1023
The Guardian 999, 1000
The Negotiator 999, 1000
The Protector **999**, 1000
True Devotion 999, 1000
True Valor **1000**, 1030
The Truth Seeker 999, 1000

Hendrickson, Emily
The Fashionable Spy 374
Miss Cheney's Charade 370
The Rake's Revenge 305

Henke, Roxanne
After Anne 992

Henley, Virginia
The Border Hostage **883**
Dream Lover 883
Enslaved 883
Gift of Joy 265
The Marriage Prize 883
A Woman of Passion 883
A Year and a Day 883

Hennessy, Max
The Lion at Sea 866

Henry, April
Circles of Confusion 134

Henry, Will
The Bear Paw Horses 461, 493
The Brass Command 441
Ghost Wolf of Thunder Mountain 445, 461
Journey to Shiloh 461
The Legend of Sotoju Mountain **461**
Tumbleweeds 452, 461, 468, 496, 503
Who Rides with Wyatt? 485
Yellowstone Kelly 461

Hensley, Joe L.
Deadly Hunger and Other Stories 40
Robak in Black **113**
Robak's Cross 113
Robak's Fire 113
Robak's Firm 113
Robak's Run 113
Robak's Witch 113

Herbert, Brian
The Garbage Chronicles 757
House Atreides 757
House Corrino **757**
House Harkonnen 757
The Prisoners of Arionn 757
The Race for God 757

Herbert, Frank
Dune 718, 757
Dune Messiah 777
Hellstrom's Hive 762

Herbert, James
48 730

Herbert, Mary H.
City of the Sorcerers 556
The Clandestine Circle 556
Dark Horse 556
Dragon's Bluff **556**
Legacy of Steel 556
Winged Magic 556

Herman, George
The Tears of the Madonna 836

Herman, Julie Wray
The Korine McFail Series 103
The Three Dirty Women Series 181

Herman, Kathy
Day of Reckoning **1001**
Tested by Fire 1001

Hern, Candice
An Affair of Honor 298, 349, 362
The Best Intentions 298
The Bride Sale 227, **298**
A Change of Heart 298
A Garden Folly 278, 298, 356, 379
Miss Lacey's Last Fling 298
A Proper Companion 278

Herndon, Nancy
The Elena Jarvis Series 81, 88, 149

Herniman, Marcus
The Siege of Arrandin 557
The Treason of Dortrean **557**

Herr, Ethel L.
The Seekers Series 979, 1003

Herron, Rita
Forgotten Lullaby 299
Have Baby, Need Beau 299
Have Gown, Need Groom 299
His-and-Hers Twins 299
Marry Me, Maddie? 226, 256, 264, **299**, 353
Saving His Son 299

Herzog, Arthur
Swarm 762

Hess, Joan
The Claire Malloy Series 67
Maggody and the Moonbeams **114**
The Maggody Militia 114
The Maggody Series 15
Martians in Maggody 114
Miracles in Maggody 114
Misery Loves Maggody 77, 114
Murder@Maggody.com 114

Heyen, William
Crazy Horse in Stillness 890

Heyer, Georgette
A Civil Contract 257
The Convenient Marriage 257
Faro's Daughter 377, 379
The Foundling 404
An Infamous Army 389
These Old Shades 404
The Unknown Ajax 404

Heym, Stefan
The King David Report 858

Hiaasen, Carl
Basket Case 100, **115**
Lucky You 115
Native Tongue 94, 115
Sick Puppy 115
Skin Tight 107
Stormy Weather 115, 1214
Strip Tease 115

Hiatt, Brenda
A Scandalous Virtue 311

Hichens, Robert
The Black Spaniel and Other Stories 647
The Folly of Eustace and Other Stories 647
The Return of the Soul and Other Stories **647**
Snake Bite and Other Stories 647
Tongues of Conscience 647

Hickman, Tracy
Guardians of the Lost **611**
The Search for Magic **612**

Hicks, Barbara Jean
Restoration and Romance **986**

Higgins, George V.
At End of Day 1076, 1096, 1118, 1123
The Friends of Eddie Coyle 1134

Higgs, Julie M.
Lt. Kent: Lone Wolf **341**

Higgs, Liz Curtis
Three Weddings and a Giggle 986

Highsmith, Patricia
The Tom Ripley Series 202

Hight, Doreen Roberts
Death Is in the Air **136**

Hightower, Lynn
Alien Rites 744

Highwater, Jamake
The Sun, He Dies 889

Hill, Donna
A Midnight Clear 300
A Private Affair 884
Rhythms **884**, 947
Rooms of the Heart 884
Scandalous 884
A Scandalous Affair 884
Shipwreck Season 884
'Tis the Season **300**

Hill, Pamela
The Woman in the Cloak 886

Hill, Reginald
Arms and the Women 116
Asking for the Moon 116
The Dalziel and Pascoe Series 23, 44, 97, 186
Dialogues of the Dead or Paronomania! **116**
On Beulah Height 116
Pictures of Perfection 116
There Are No Ghosts in the Soviet Union and Other Stories 146
The Wood Beyond 116

Hill, William
California Ghost 703

Hillerman, Tony
Best American Mystery Stories of the Century 57
Finding Moon 1066
The Joe Leaphorn/Jim Chee Series 35
The Oxford Book of American Detective Stories 57
A Thief of Time 61

Hilton, James
Lost Horizon 717

Himes, Chester
The Coffin Ed Johnson/Grave Digger Jones Series 196
Cotton Comes to Harlem 166
Yesterday Will Make You Cry 1179

Hinchcliffe, Philip
The Seeds of Doom 735

Hingle, Metsy
The Baby Bonus 301
Love Child 301
Navy Seal Dad 301
Surrender 301
The Wager **301**
Wife with Amnesia 301

Hinze, Vicki
Acts of Honor 242

Hirt, Douglas
Brandish 462
Cripple Creek 462, 495
Deadwood 462
A Good Town **462**
McKendree 462
The Silent Gun 473
The Wrong Man 462

Hix, Willa
Then and Now 372

Hjortsberg, William
Nevermore 187, 193

Hoag, Tami
Dark Paradise 412
Guilty as Sin 395

Hobb, Robin
Assassin's Apprentice 552
Assassin's Quest 554
The Royal Assassin 540

Hoch, Edward D.
Diagnosis Impossible 117, 118
The Night, My Friend 117, 118
The Night People and Other Stories 48, **117**
The Old Spies Club and Other Intrigues of Rand 117, **118**
The People of the Peacock 118
The Ripper of Storyville 117, 118
The Transvection Machine 759
The Velvet Touch 85, 117, 118

Hockenberry, John
A River out of Eden 436, 442

Hodder-Williams, Christopher
Fistful of Digits 808

Hodgson, Ken
The Bloody Benders 463
Hard Bounty **463**
Lone Survivor 463

Hodgson, William Hope
The Ghost Pirates 681
The House on the Borderland 670

Hoeg, Peter
Smilla's Sense of Snow 127

Hoff, B.J.
The Daniel and Jennifer Kaine Series 1048
The Daybreak Series 970, 996, 1008
The Song of Erin Series 1013, 1015, 1026, 1027, 1060

Hoffman, Alice
Blue Diary 1086, 1139, 1163
Local Girls 1103, 1198

Hoffman, Barry
Judas Eyes 705

Hoffman, Kate
Caught under the Mistletoe 306

Hoffman, Nina Kiriki
Common Threads 658
The Silent Strength of Stones 539

Hogan, Ernest
Cortez on Jupiter 758
High Aztec 758
Smoking Mirror Blues **758**

Hogan, James P.
Bug Park 759
The Immortality Option 759
The Legend That Was Earth 759
Martian Knightlife **759**
Out of Time 759
Outward Bound 759
Paths to Otherwhere 741, 778
Thrice upon a Time 754

Hogan, Ray
The Doomsday Marshal and the Comancheros 423
Guns of Freedom: A Western Duo 432, 435, 489
Legend of a Badman: A Western Quintet 461, 494, 496
The Red Eagle 452

Holbrook, Teri
A Far and Deadly Cry 92

Holden, Craig
Four Corners of Night 119, 885
The Jazz Bird **119**, **885**, 897
The Last Sanctuary 119, 885
The River Sorrow 119, 885

Holder, Nancy
Dead in the Water 681
Witch-Light 704

Holdstock, Robert
Ancient Echoes 558
Celtika **558**
Gates of Ivory, Gates of Horn 558
The Hollowing 558
Merlin's Wood 558
Unknown Regions 558

Holland, Cecelia
City of God 916
Floating Worlds 789
Jerusalem 860, 902
Lily Nevada 446, 448, 449, 450, 457, 470, 488
The Lords of Vaumartin 844
An Ordinary Woman 437
Pacific Street 878

Holland, Tom
Lord of the Dead 922

Holling, Jen
Forever My Lady 390

Holman, Sheri
The Dress Lodger 838
A Stolen Tongue 86, 194

Holmes, Kate
The Wild Swans 384

Holt, Hazel
The Mrs. Malory Series 14, 27, 54

Holt, Tom
Snow White and the Seven Samurai 518

Holt, Victoria
Mistress of Mellyn 411

Holton, Hugh
The Larry Cole Series 216

Holtzer, Susan
Better than Sex **120**
Black Diamond 120
Bleeding Maize and Blue 120, 156
Curly Smoke 120
The Silly Season 120
Something to Kill For 69, 160
The Wedding Game 120

Homewood, Harry
Silent Sea 953

Hood, Ken
Demon Knight 535

Hooper, Kay
Finding Laura 340
Stealing Shadows 410

Hoover, Thomas
The Moghul 963

Hopkinson, Nalo
Brown Girl in the Ring 760
Midnight Robber 760
Skin Folk **760**

Horn, Shifra
The Fairest Among Women 1197

Hornby, Nick
About a Boy 1126
Contemporary American Fiction 1126
High Fidelity 1126
How to Be Good **1126**

Horsfall, Melissa
Double Honor **1002**

Horsley, Kate
Confessions of a Pagan Nun **886**, 952
A Killing in New Town 886

Hotchner, A.E.
Louisiana Purchase 912

Houarner, Gerard Daniel
Going Postal 651
I Love You and There Is Nothing You Can Do about It 639, 683

Houellebecq, Michel
The Elementary Particles 1085, 1173, 1198

Hough, Richard
Buller's Victory 866

Houghton, Gordon
Damned If You Do 667

Housewright, David
Dearly Departed 908

Houston, James D.
Snow Mountain Passage 894, 957, 1083

Howard, Hayden
The Eskimo Invasion 801

Howard, Linda
After the Night 411, 412
All the Queen's Men 302
A Game of Chance 302
Kill and Tell 245, 302, 381
Mr. Perfect 302, 331
Now You See Her 302
Open Season **302**
Shades of Twilight 283

Howard, Lyle
Mr. Sandman 709

Howard, Maureen
Big as Life 1120

Howard, Robert E.
Trails in Darkness 589

Howe, David J.
Urban Gothic **648**

Howell, Dorothy
The Nanny **408**
The Widow's Little Secret **409**

Howell, Hannah
Highland Promise 244
Scottish Magic 243
A Stockingful of Joy 263

Howington, Linda
Open Season **302**

Hoyt, Edwin P.
The Last Stand 824
The Voice of Allah 902

Hoyt, Sarah A.
Ill Met by Moonlight **559**

Hudson, Parker
The President 976, 1004

Huebner, Andrew
American by Blood 449, 450, 466, 514, 824, 945

Huebner, Fredrick
The Black Rose 121
The Joshua Sequence 121
Judgment by Fire 121
Methods of Execution 121
Picture Postcard 121
Shades of Justice **121**

Huff, Tanya
Blood Trail 657
Scholar of Decay 613

Huggins, James Byron
Cain 1003
Hunter 1003
Leviathan 1003
The Reckoning 1003
Rora **1003**
The Wolf Story 1003

Hughes, Glyn
Bronte 904

Hughes, Rhys
The Smell of Telescopes 635

Humphreys, Helen
Afterimage 877, 927, 1067, 1099, 1102, 1189, 1213

Humphreys, Josephine
Nowhere Else on Earth 884, 910, 1167, 1183

Hunt, Angela Elwell
The Emerald Isle 1004
Gentle Touch 1032
The Heirs of Cahira O'Connor Series 1026, 1060
The Immortal 1004
The Justice 976, **1004**
The Note 1004
The Truth Teller 975, 1004
The Velvet Shadow 1004, 1025
A Warmth in Winter **984**

Hunt, Violet
Tiger Skin 646

Hunt, Walter
The Dark Wing **761**

Hunter, Evan
Money, Money, Money **152**

Hunter, Jillian
Abandon **303**
Daring 303
A Deeper Magic 303
Delight 303
Fairy Tale 303
Indiscretion 303

Hunter, Madeline
By Possession 407

Hunter, Stephen
Black Light 122, 887
The Day Before Midnight 887
Dirty White Boys 122, 887, 1127
Hot Springs 122, 885, 887, 935, 1127
The Master Sniper 1127
Pale Horse Coming **122**, 825, **887**, 897, **1127**, 1179, 1186
Point of Impact 122, 204, 1127
Time to Hunt 122, 887, 1127

Huntington, Kate
The Captain's Courtship 304, 397
Lady Diana's Darlings 304
The Lieutenant's Lady 304
Mistletoe Mayhem 238, 304
A Rogue for Christmas **304**

Hurley, Frank X.
The Crusader 860

Hurston, Zora Neale
The Complete Stories 1128
Every Tongue Got to Confess **1128**
Jonah's Gourd Vine 1128
Mules and Men 1128
Tell My Horse 1128
Their Eyes Were Watching God 1128

Hurwitz, Gregg Andrew
Minutes to Burn **762**

Hussein, Abdullah
Emigre Journeys **1129**
Stories of Exile and Alienation 1129
The Weary Generations 1129

Hutchings, Janet
Creme de la Crime 84

Hutchison, Lynne
Summer's End **297**

Huyck, Michael T. Jr.
4 X 4 **679**

Hyatt, Michael
Y2K 989

Hyde, Catherine Ryan
Electric God 1175

Hynes, James
The Lecturer's Tale **649**
Publish and Perish 649
The Wild Colonial Boy 649

I

Iakovou, Takis
The Nick & Julia Lambrose Series 177

Iles, Greg
24 Hours 123
Black Cross 123
Dead Sleep **123**
Mortal Fear 123
The Quiet Game 123
Spandau Phoenix 123

Ireland, Liz
Husband Material 263
A Western Family Christmas **263**

Irvine, Ian
Dark Is the Moon 560
A Shadow on the Glass 560
The Tower on the Rift 560
The Way between the Worlds **560**

Irvine, Robert
The Moroni Traveler Series 76

Irving, John
The Cider House Rules 1130
The Fourth Hand 1084, 1111, **1130**, 1214
The Hotel New Hampshire 1130, 1197
A Prayer for Owen Meany 1136
Trying to Save Piggy Sneed 1130
A Widow for One Year 1130, 1156
The World According to Garp 1130

Isaacs, Susan
After All These Years 1131
Compromising Positions 1131
Lily White 1131
Long Time No See 198, **1131**, 1136
Red, White and Blue 1131
Shining Through 1131

Isenberg, Jane
Death in a Hot Flash 124
The "M" Word 124
Midlife Can Be Murder **124**
Mood Swings to Murder 124

Ishiguro, Kazuo
When We Were Orphans 835, 1131

Ivanhoe, Mark
Virgintooth 712

Ivory, Judith
The Sleeping Beauty 360

J

Jablokov, Alexander
Deepdrive 793
Nimbus 807

Jackson, Brenda
Secret Love 224

Jackson, Monica
A Magical Moment 272, 383

Jackson, Shirley
The Sundial 781
We Have Always Lived in the Castle 623

Jackson, T.G.
Six Ghost Stories 650

Jacob, Charlee
This Symbiotic Fascination 658
Up, out of Cities That Blow Hot and Cold 624, 698

Jacobs, Anna
A Forbidden Embrace **305**
High Street 305
Salem Street 305

Jacobs, Holly
Do You Hear What I Hear? **306**
I Waxed My Legs for This? 306

Jacobs, Jonnie
The Kali O'Brien Series 167

Jacobsen, Clay
Circle of Seven 976, 1004

Jacoby, Kate
Black Eagle Rising 561
The Exile's Return 551
Exile's Return 561
Rebel's Cage **561**, 578
Voice of the Demon 561

Jacocoma, Richard
The Werewolf's Tale 657

Jacques, Brian
The Legend of Luke 587

Jaffe, Michele
The Water Nymph 883

Jakes, John
A Century of Great Western Stories 455, 460
Homeland 937

Jakober, Marie
The Black Chalice **562**, 603

Jakubowski, Maxim
Murder through the Ages 8

James, Arlene
With Baby in Mind 965

James, B.J.
The Taming of Jackson Cade 246

James, Bill
The Colin Harpur Series 178

James, Dean
The Ernie Carpenter Series 163

James, Del
The Language of Fear 684

James, Eloisa
Midnight Pleasures 329

James, Henry
The Aspern Papers 1161
The Wings of the Dove 1167

James, M.R.
The Five Jars 650
Ghost Stories of an Antiquary 650
More Ghost Stories of an Antiquary 650
A Pleasing Terror **650**
A Thin Ghost and Others 650
A Warning to the Curious and Other Ghost Stories 650

James, P.D.
The Adam Dalgliesh Series 30, 44, 116, 211
An Unsuitable Job for a Woman 11, 154

James, Roby
Commencement 755

James, Samantha
The Truest Heart 406

James, Will
The American Cowboy 464
Cowboy in the Making **464**
The Dark Horse 464
Horses I Have Known 464
My First Horse 464
Will James Book of Cowboy Stories 464

Jamyang Norbu
Sherlock Holmes: The Missing Years 158, 210, 856, 899

Jance, J.A.
Birds of Prey 129
Breach of Duty 465
Dead to Rights 125, 465
Desert Heat 465
Devil's Claw 125, 465
The Joanna Brady Series 145, 212
Kiss of the Bees 28, 39, 465
Outlaw Mountain 125
Paradise Lost **125**, **465**
Rattlesnake Crossing 125
Skeleton Canyon 125

Janda, Anita
The Secret Diary of Dr. Watson 899, 908, 926

Janes, J. Robert
Carousel 888
Dollmaker 126
Gypsy 126
Kaleidoscope **126**, **888**
Madrigal 126
Mirage 888
Salamander 888
Sandman 126, 888, 960
Stonekiller 126, 888

Janiver, Laurence M.
The Counterfeit Heinlein **763**
Knave and the Game 763
Knave in Hand 763
Reel 763
Survivor 763

You Sane Men 763

Jardine, Quintin
The Robert Skinner Series 178

Jarrett, Liz
Tempting Tess 223

Jarrett, Miranda
The Captain's Bride 328
The Secrets of Catie Hazard 307, 308
Starlight 307, 308
Sunrise 297, 307, 308, 342
The Very Comely Countess **307**, 308
The Very Daring Duchess 307, **308**
Wishing 307, 308

Jecks, Michael
The Boy-Bishop's Glovemaker 875

Jefferies, Mike
Stone Angels 676

Jeffrey, Grant R.
Flee the Darkness 989, 1016
The Flee the Darkness Series 991

Jeffreys, J.G.
Thief Taker 182

Jeffries, Sabrina
The Dangerous Lord 329

Jekel, Pamela
She Who Hears the Sun 911

Jenkins, Dan
Bubba Talks of Life, Love, Sex, Whiskey, Politics, Foreigners, Teenagers, Movies, Food, Football, and Other Matters 1132
Dead Solid Perfect 1132
Fast Copy 1066, 1130
The Money-Whipped Steer-Job Three-Jack Give-Up Artist 1114, **1132**
Rude Behavior 1132
Semi-Tough 1132
You Gotta Play Hurt 1132

Jenkins, Jerry B.
Desecration **1016**
Hometown Legend 1001, **1005**
The Operative 1005
Rookie 1005
Though None Go with Me 1005, 1010
Twas the Night Before 1005, 1033

Jennings, Gary
Aztec 889
Aztec Autumn 889
Aztec Blood **889**
The Journeyer 889
Raptor 889
Spangle 889

Jens, Tina
The Blues Ain't Nothin' 684

Jensen, Emma
A Grand Design 318, 370
His Grace Endures 362, 379
The Irish Rogue 279, 392
Regency Christmas Spirits **248**

Jensen, Johannes Vilhelm
The Fall of the King 862

Jensen, Kathryn
Mail-Order Cinderella 268

Jensen, Muriel
Carol Christmas 306

Jensen, Ruby Jean
The Haunting 673

Jerott, Michelle
Absolute Trouble 224

Jessup, Richard
Sailor 953

Jeter, K.W.
The Edge of Human 797

Jewett, Sarah Orne
Lady Ferry and Other Uncanny People 711

Jin, Ha
The Bridegroom 1098
Waiting 1102

Johansen, Iris
The Eve Duncan Series 78
The Ugly Duckling 222, 302, 340, 381, 411, 413

John, Cathie
The Kate Cavanaugh Series 205

John, Sally D.
In the Shadow of Love 1006, 1023
A Journey by Chance **1006**
Surrender of the Heart 1006
To Dream Again 988, 1006

Johnson, Charles Richard
Dreamer 1119

Johnson, Cynthia
Fortune's Lady **379**

Johnson, George Clayton
All of Us Are Dying and Other Stories 678

Johnson, Grace
The Scottish Shores Series 1026

Johnson, Matt
Triage **651**

Johnson, Roger
A Ghostly Crew **652**

Johnson, Susan
Tempting 282, 285
Wicked 385

Johnston, Paul
The Water of Death 738

Johnston, Terry C.
Ashes of Heaven 890
Blood Song 466
Buffalo Palace 890
A Cold Day in Hell 466
Death Rattle 463, 512, 890, 957
Lay the Mountains Low 890
Reap the Whirlwind 466
Trumpet on the Land 466
Turn the Stars Upside Down **466**, 824, 826, 842, **890**, 945
Wind Walker 890
Winter Rain 895
Wolf Mountain Moon 466

Johnstone, William W.
Bats 714

Jones, Allen Morris
Last Year's River **467**, 845, **891**, 947, 961

Jones, Annie
Deep Dixie 1063
Lost Romance Ranch 1055
The Route 66 Series 1006

Jones, Cleo
Prophet Motive 76

Jones, D.F.
Colossus 798

Jones, Diana Wynne
Archer's Goon 519
Howl's Moving Castle 594
A Sudden Wild Magic 542

Jones, Douglas C.
Gone the Dreams and the Dancing 826
Season of Yellow Leaf 826

Jones, Gwyneth
Bold as Love **764**
Divine Endurance 764
Flowerdust 764
North Wind 764
Phoenix Cafe 764
White Queen 764

Jones, J.V.
The Barbed Coil 540
A Cavern of Black Ice 596

Jones, Jill
Circle of the Lily 382
Remember Your Lies 327
The Scottish Rose 323

Jones, Linda Winstead
Madigan's Wife 417
The Seduction of Roxanne 247

Jones, Patricia
Passing 1133
Red on Rose **1133**

Jones, Stephen
Dark Detectives 653, 654
Dark of the Night 653, 654
The Mammoth Book of Best New Horror 12 **653**
The Mammoth Book of Dracula 631, 653, 654
The Mammoth Book of Frankenstein 654
The Mammoth Book of Vampire Stories by Women 653, **654**
White of the Moon 653, 654

Jones, Susanna
The Earthquake Bird **127**, 150

Jones, Veda Boyd
Summer Dreams 969, 986

Jordan, Brenda
The Brentwood Witches 543

Jordan, Nicole
Desire **309**, 385
The Heart Breaker 309, 332
The Lover 309
The Outlaw 309
The Passion 309
The Seduction 309, 329

Jordan, Robert
Cheyenne Raiders 895
The Path of Daggers 545
Winter's Heart 550

Jorge, Lidia
The Painter of Birds 1120

Joy, Dara
High Energy 310
High Intensity 310
Mine to Take 310
Rejar 310
Ritual of Proof **310**
Tonight or Never 310

Joyce, Brenda
The Game 254

Joyce, Graham
Black Dust **655**, 700
Indigo 655
Leningrad Nights 655, 708
Requiem 655
Smoking Poppy 655
The Tooth Fairy 655

Julavits, Heidi
The Mineral Palace 1113

Just, Ward S.
Ambition and Love 1134
A Dangerous Friend 1134
Echo House 1134
Lowell Limpett: And Two Stories **1134**
The Translator 1134
Twenty-One 1134

Juster, Norton
The Phantom Tollbooth 581

Justice, Alan David
The Final Bow 1031

Justiss, Janet
The Proper Wife **311**

Justiss, Julia
The Proper Wife **311**
A Scandalous Proposal 311
The Wedding Gamble 259, 311

K

Kadish, Rachel
From a Sealed Room 978

Kadrey, Richard
Kamikaze L'Amour 764

Kaewert, Julie
Unbound 128
Uncatalogued **128**
Unprintable 128
Unsigned 128
Unsolicited 128
Untitled 128

Kahn, Sharon
Don't Cry for Me, Hot Pastrami **129**
Fax Me a Bagel 129
Never Nosh a Matzo Ball 129
The Ruby Rothman Series 124

Kalechofsky, Roberta
Bodmin, 1349 832, 843

Kalogridis, Jeanne
The Burning Times 844
Lord of the Vampires 632

Kalpakian, Laura
Caveat 478
Cosette 900

Kaminsky, Stuart M.
Blood and Rubles 130
Death of a Russian Priest 130
The Dog Who Bit a Policeman 130
Down for the Count 161
Fall of a Cosmonaut 130
A Few Minutes Past Midnight 828, 923
Murder on the Trans-Siberian Express **130**
Murder on the Yellow Brick Road 53
Tarnished Icons 130
The Toby Peters Series 841, 928

Kane, Andrea
The Gold Coin 312
The Music Box 312
No Way Out **312**
Run for Your Life 312
The Silver Coin 312
The Theft 312

Kane, Kathleen
Catch a Fallen Angel 249, 313
Dreamweaver 313

Just West of Heaven **313**
Simply Magic 313
This Time for Keeps 313
Wish upon a Cowboy 313, 350

Kanon, Joseph
The Good German **131**, 828, **892**, **1135**, 1171, 1186, 1191
Los Alamos 131, 892, 1135
The Prodigal Spy 131, 215, 892, 1135

Kantor, MacKinlay
Long Remember 919

Kantra, Virginia
Born to Protect 422
The Reforming of Matthew Dunn 335

Kaplan, Hester
Kinship Theory 1093

Karayianni, Lori
The Woman for Dusty Conrad **251**

Karayianni, Tony
The Woman for Dusty Conrad **251**

Karon, Jan
A Common Life 1007
In This Mountain **1007**
A Light in the Window 1007
The Mitford Years Series 984, 1117
A New Song 1007
Out to Canaan 1007
These High Green Hills 1007

Karr, Phyllis Ann
The Idylls of the Queen 528

Kasser, Michael
Warrior's Honor 463, 512

Kast, Pierre
The Vampires of Alfama 713

Kastner, Debra
The Forgiving Heart 1047

Katchor, Ben
Julius Knipl, Real Estate Photographer 1100

Katz, Jon
The Kit DeLeeuw Series 218

Katzenbach, John
Hart's War 906

Kaufelt, David A.
The Wyn Lewis Series 218

Kauffman, Donna
Your Wish Is My Command 237

Kavan, Anna
Ice 724

Kay, Guy Gavriel
Sailing to Byzantium 570
A Song for Arbonne 532

Kay, Linda
To Tame a Rogue 371

Kay, Patricia
The Wrong Child 225

Kaye, Marilyn
Amy, Number Seven 776
Pursuing Amy 775

Kazan, Elia
America, America 1117, 1178

Kazan, Frances
Goodnight, Little Sister 893
Halide's Gift **893**, 902

Kearney, Susan
The Cradle Will Rock 410

Kearsley, Susanna
Mariana 314
Named of the Dragon 314
Season of Storms **314**
The Shadowy Horses 314

Keating, H.R.F.
Asking Questions 132
Breaking and Entering **132**
Cheating Death 132
Doing Wrong 132
The Iciest Sin 132
In Kensington Gardens Once... 146
Inspector Ghote: His Life and Crimes 132

Keene, Brian
4 X 4 **679**

Keiler, Barbara
Looking for Laura **226**

Keillor, Garrison
The Book of Guys 1136
Lake Wobegon Days 1136
Lake Wobegon Summer 1956 1114, **1136**
Me 1136
WLT: A Radio Romance 1136
Wobegon Boy 1136

Keith, William H. Jr.
Battlemind 765
Bolo Brigade 765
Bolo Rising 765
Bolo Strike **765**
The Two of Minds 765
Warstrider 765

Kelby, N.M.
In the Company of Angels 847

Kelleher, Annie
The Ghost and Katie Coyle 351

Kelleher, Ed
Animus 641

Kellerman, Faye
The Quality of Mercy 109, 880
The Rina Lazarus/Peter Decker Series 137
Stalker 1074

Kellerman, Jonathan
The Alex Delaware Series 121

Kelley, Douglas
The Captain's Wife **894**

Kelly, Carla
The Lady's Companion 315
Marian's Christmas Wish 315
Miss Chartley's Guided Tour 318
Miss Grimsley's Oxford Career 315, 370
Mrs. Drew Plays Her Hand 238, 315, 404
Mrs. McVinnie's London Season 262
One Good Turn **315**
Reforming Lord Ragsdale 392
With This Ring 315, 397

Kelly, James Patrick
Planet of Whispers 718

Kelly, Leslie
Suite Seduction 333

Kelner, Toni L.P.
The Laura Fleming Series 6, 77, 114
Tight as a Tick 69, 160

Kelton, Elmer
Badger Boy 425, 468, 827, 895, 1137
The Buckskin Line 425, 468, 895, 1137
Captain's Rangers 1137
Cloudy in the West 468, 490, 499
Dark Thicket 895
The Day the Cowboys Quit 1137
The Far Canyon 895
Honor at Daybreak 436, 442, 469
The Man Who Rode Midnight 479
The Manhunters 1137
The Pumpkin Rollers 468, 504
Slaughter 895
The Smiling Country 462, 468, 497
The Way of the Coyote **468**, **895**, **1137**, 1176

Kemelman, Harry
The Rabbi David Small Series 129

Kemp, Paul
Shadow's Witness 578

Kendrick, Stephen
Holy Clues 896
Night Watch **896**

Keneally, Thomas
The Playmaker 819, 904

Kennedy, A.L.
Everything You Need **1138**
Now That You're Back 1138
Original Bliss 1138
So I Am Glad 1138

Kennedy, Douglas
The Big Picture 1177

Kennedy, Ellen Edwards
Irregardless of Murder 970, 985, **1008**

Kennedy, Kate
End over End 1086, **1139**

Kennedy, Lucy
Mr. Audubon's Lucy 833

Kennedy, Shirley
The Rebellious Twin 305

Kennedy, William
Billy Phelan's Greatest Game 897
The Flaming Corsage 897
Ironweed 897
Legs 885, 897
Roscoe 825, **897**
Very Old Bones 897

Kenner, Julie
Aphrodite's Kiss 299, 363
Nobody Does It Better 240
Reckless 223

Kern, Gregory
Beyond the Galactic Lens 769

Kernaghan, Eileen
The Sarsen Witch 534

Kerner, Elizabeth
Lesser Kindred 610

Kerr, Philip
The Berlin Noir Series 960
The Bernie Gunther Series 126
Dead Meat 130
A German Requiem 131

Kerruish, J.D.
The Undying Monster 646

Kerstan, Lynn
Francesca's Rake 241
Marry in Haste 258
A Midnight Clear 275

Kessler, Brad
Lick Creek 887, 955

Ketchum, Jack
Off Season 638, 662

Keyes, J. Gregory
Empire of Unreason 516, 751

Keyes, Marian
Lucy Sullivan Is Getting Married 357, 359

Kidd, Paul
The Council of Blades 563
Descent into the Depths of the Earth 563
Mus of Kerbridge 563
Queen of the Demonweb Pits **563**
White Plume Mountain 563

Kiernan, Caitlin R.
Candles for Elizabeth 656
From Weird and Distant Shores **656**
Silk 656
Tales of Pain and Wonder 656
Threshold 656
Wrong Things **624**

Kihlstrom, April
The Reckless Barrister 279, 392
A Scandalous Bequest 356
The Widowed Bride 325
The Wiley Wastrel 318

Kihn, Greg
Horror Show 619

Kijewski, Karen
Honky Tonk Kat 189

Kilian, Michael
Dance on a Sinking Ship 816
The Harrison Raines Series 1
The Ironclad Alibi **133**, **898**
A Killing at Ball's Bluff 133, 909
The Last Virginia Gentleman 898
Looker 898
Major Washington 898
Murder at Ball's Bluff 898
Murder at Manassas 133, 159, 169, 898

Killdeer, John
The Far Horizon 512

Killian, Diana
The Art of Dying **1009**

Killough, Lee
Blood Games **657**
Blood Hunt 657
Blood Links 657
The Monitor, the Miners, and the Shree 780

Kilmer, Nicholas
Dirty Linen 134
Harmony in Flesh and Black 134
Lazarus, Arise **134**
Man with a Squirrel 134
O Sacred Head 134

Kilpatrick, Nancy
The Amarantha Knight Reader 658
Cold Comfort 630, **658**
Endorphins 658
Sex and the Single Vampire 658
The Vampire Stories of Nancy Kilpatrick 658

Kilworth, Gary
The Electric Kid 776

Kimball, Philip
Liar's Moon 873

Kimberlin, Annie
Romeo and Julia 232

King, Bernard
Vargr Moon 517

King, Gabriel
The Golden Cat 574

King, J. Robert
Apocalypse **564**
Blood Hostages 565
The Dragons of Magic **565**
Heart of Midnight 613
Invasion 564, 565, 566
Lancelot Du Lethe **566**
Mad Merlin 558, 564, 565, 566
Planar Powers 564, 565, 566
Rogues to Riches 566
The Thran 564, 565
The Time Streams 515, 566
Vinas Solamnus 564

King, Joan
Impressionist 837

King, Laurie R.
The Beekeeper's Apprentice 153
A Darker Place 139
The Kate Martinelli Series 137
The Mary Russell/Sherlock Holmes Series 158, 899, 958
A Monstrous Regiment of Women 208

King, Mary
A Peculiar Thing 469
Quincie Bolliver **469**
Those Other People 469
You Can Hear the Echo 469

King, Peter
Death al Dente 135
Dying on the Vine 135
Eat, Drink and Be Buried 135
The Gourmet Detective Series 138, 207
A Healthy Place to Die 135
The Jewel of the North 73, 95, **135**
Spiced to Death 135

King, Ross
Ex-Libris 820, 853, 1182

King, Stephen
Bag of Bones 660
Black House **659**, 1071, **1140**
Blood and Smoke 1124
Cycle of the Werewolves 1068
The Dark Half 781
Desperation 660
Dolores Claiborne 1073
Dreamcatcher **660**, 675, 1082, 1166, 1185
Firestarter 709, 775
Gerald's Game 664
Hearts in Atlantis 660
It 660
Needful Things 668
The Shining 620
The Talisman 642, 659, 1140
The Tommyknockers 660

King, Susan
The Heather Moon 316
Lady Miracle 316
Laird of the Wind 316
The Stone Maiden 266, 316
The Swan Maiden 244, 316
The Sword Maiden **316**

King, Tabitha
Survivor 1184

King, Valerie
A Brighton Flirtation 230, 280, 305
A Kiss for Mama **280**
My Lord Highwayman 317

Kingsbury, Karen
A Moment of Weakness 971
On Every Side **1010**
A Time to Dance 993, 1010
Waiting for Morning 1010
When Joy Came to Stay 1010
Where Yesterday Lives 1010

Kingsbury, Kate
A Bicycle Built for Murder 136
Death Is in the Air **136**

Kingsley, Katherine
A Natural Attachment 238, 404

Kingsolver, Barbara
The Bean Trees 1094
Homeland 1080
The Poisonwood Bible 1134, 1211
Prodigal Summer 1065

Kingston, Christina
The Night the Stars Fell **317**
Ride for the Roses 317, 348, 355

Kinsella, W.P.
Magic Time 1114

Kiraly, Mina
Mina 632

Kirchoff, Mary
Black Wing 525
The Seventh Sentinel 604

Kirk, Richard
Swordsmistress of Chaos 608

Kirkland, Martha
His Lordship's Swan 318, 393
Miss Maitland's Letters 233, 318
Mr. Montgomery's Quest **318**
The Rake's Fiancee 291, 318
That Scandalous Heiress 230, 318
Uncommon Courtship 318

Kirkpatrick, Jane
All Together in One Place 437, 1011
Altogether in One Place 470
A Gathering of Finches 1011
The Kinship and Courage Series 973, 998
Love to Water My Soul 1058
Mystic Sweet Communion 1011
No Eye Can See 437, 470, 1011
A Sweetness to the Soul 1011
What Once We Loved **470**, **1011**

Kirkwood, Kathryn
A Valentine for Vanessa 378

Kirn, Walter
My Hard Bargain 1141
She Needed Me 1141
Thumbsucker 1109, 1141
Up in the Air **1141**, 1196

Kitt, Sandra
Family Affairs 272

Kittredge, Mary
Murder in Mendocino 139
Wreck the Halls **89**

Kjelgard, Jim
Fire-Hunter 723

Klapka, Julie Leto
Insatiable **333**

Klasky, Mindy
The Glasswright's Apprentice 523

Klause, Annette Curtis
Blood and Chocolate 322

Klein, Daniel M.
Embryo 783

Klein, Richard
Jewelry Talks 1095, **1142**

Kleypas, Lisa
Because You're Mine 319
Someone to Watch over Me 319, 342, 346, 375, 402
Somewhere I'll Find You 319
Stranger in My Arms 319
Suddenly You **319**, 320, 419
Where Dreams Begin 319
Wish List **320**

Knaak, Richard A.
Frostwing 541, 596
The Horse King 612
The Janus Mask 540

Kneale, Nigel
Quatermass and the Pit 675

Knight, Alanna
The Jeremy Faro Series 172

Knight, Bernard
Madoc, Prince of America 952

Knight, Damon
Mind Switch 670
One Side Laughing 748, 803

Knight, Tracy
The Astonished Eye **567**

Kody, Bob
Gold Mountain 459, 504

Koontz, Dean R.
Anti-Man 797
Cold Fire 675
False Memory 661
Fear Nothing 661, 664
From the Corner of His Eye 661, 1074
Midnight 710
One Door Away from Heaven **661**
Seize the Night 661
Servants of Twilight 1185
Sole Survivor 661
Strange Highways 706
Whispers 627

Korbel, Kathleen
Isn't It Romantic 261

Koumalats, Jodi
The Texan's Dream **415**

Krahn, Betina
The Husband Test **321**
The Mermaid 321
The Perfect Mistress 321
The Soft Touch 321
Sweet Talking Man 253, 284, 321, 342, 419
The Unlikely Angel 321

Kraus, Harry Lee
The Chairman 1012
Could I Have This Dance? **1012**
Fated Genes 1012
Lethal Mercy 1012
The Stain 1012
Stainless Steel Hearts 1012

Kraus, Jim
The Circle of Destiny Series 1050, 1054
Journey to the Crimson Sea 1013
Passages of Gold 1013
The Price 1013
The Promise 1013, 1025
The Quest **1013**
The Treasure 1013

Kraus, Terri
The Quest **1013**

Krauzer, Steven M.
Brainstorm 709, 775

Krentz, Jayne Ann
Absolutely, Positively 383
Eclipse Bay 331
Midnight Jewels 245
Sharp Edges 302
Slightly Shady **375**

Kress, Nancy
Probability Sun 743, 772

Krich, Rochelle
Angel of Death 137
Blood Money 137
Dead Air 137
Fair Game 137
Shadows of Sin **137**

Krinard, Susan
Once a Wolf 322
Prince of Dreams 322
Prince of Shadows 322
Prince of Wolves 322, 1068
Secret of the Wolf **322**
Star-Crossed 310
Touch of the Wolf 322, 401

Krokosz, Emily
Diamond in the Ruff **249**

Krouse, Erika
Come Up and See Me Sometime 1149, 1193, 1209

Krueger, William Kent
The Cork O'Connor Series 90, 93, 145, 151

Kruesi, Mary Alice
One Summer's Night 256, 383
Second Star to the Right 287

Kruger, Mary
Masterpiece of Murder 203
No Honeymoon for Death 5

Kuhlfeld, Mary Monica
Unraveled Sleeve **67**

Kureishi, Hanif
The Black Album 1143
The Buddha of Suburbia 1150
Gabriel's Gift **1143**, 1202
Intimacy 1143
Intimacy and Midnight All Day 1107
Love in a Blue Time 1143
Midnight All Day 1143
Sleep with Me 1143

Kurland, Lynn
Another Chance to Dream 323
Christmas Spirits 277
If I Had You 323
Love Came Just in Time 358
The More I See You 323
My Heart Stood Still **323**, 358
Opposites Attract 243
This Is All I Ask 323
The Very Thought of You 323

Kurland, Michael
Button Bright 709
The Girls in The High-Heeled Shoes 33, 899
The Great Game 58, 856, 896, **899**, 908, 915, 926, 958
The Infernal Device 899
Perchance 899
A Plague of Spies 899
A Study in Sorcery 756
Too Soon Dead 899
The Whenabouts of Burr 799

Kurlansky, Mark
The White Man in a Tree and Other Stories 1190

Kurtz, Katherine
Deryni Rising 544
The Harrowing of Gwynedd 536
The Legacy of Lehr 744

Kurzweil, Allen
A Case of Curiosities 1144

The Grand Complication 1085, **1144**, 1161, 1182

Kuttner, Henry
Mutant 753
Return to Otherness 715

Kyle, Kristen
Nighthawk 310

L

La Mure, Pierre
Moulin Rouge 837

La Spina, Greye
Invaders from the Dark 646

Lackey, Mercedes
The Black Swan 568, 569
Brightly Burning 568, 569
The Diana Tregarde Series 140
Fiddler's Fair 568
Four and Twenty Blackbirds 523, 569
Owlsight 568, 569
The Serpent's Shadow 568
Spirits White as Lightning **568**
Storm Breaking 569
Take a Thief **569**

Lacy, Al
Damascus Journey 1014, 1015
Let Freedom Ring 1014, 1015
The Mail Order Bride Series 973
A Measure of Grace **1014**, 1015
A Prince Among Them **1015**
Ransom of Love 1014
The Secret Place 1014, 1015
Sincerely Yours 1014
So Little Time 1015

Lacy, Joanna
A Measure of Grace **1014**
A Prince Among Them **1015**

LaFarge, Paul
The Artist of the Missing 900
Haussmann, or The Distinction 833, **900**

Lafferty, R.A.
The Devil Is Dead 567

LaFoy, Leslie
Daring the Devil 324
It Happened One Night 324
Jackson's Way 234, **324**, 391
Lady Reckless 324
Maddie's Justice 294, 296, 324

LaHaye, Beverly
The Seasons under Heaven Series 1010
Showers in Season 966
Times and Seasons 988

LaHaye, Tim
Apollyon 1016
Assassins 1016
Desecration **1016**
The Indwelling 1016
Left Behind 637
The Mark 1016
Soul Harvest 1016

Lahiri, Jhumpa
Interpreter of Maladies 1104

Laimo, Michael
Demons, Freaks and Other Abnormalities 639

Lake, M.D.
The Peggy O'Neill Series 156

Lake, Robert
Mountain Man's Vengeance 463, 512

Lamalle, Cecile
Appetite for Murder 138
The Charly Poisson Series 207
Glutton for Punishment 138
Prepared for Murder **138**

Lamb, David
The Trumpet Is Blown 1105

Lamb, Hugh
Forgotten Tales of Terror 615

Lambert, Page
Shifting Stars 438, 467

L'Amour, Louis
Beyond the Great Snow Mountains 431
Monument Rock 456, 461, 494

Lance, Kathryn
Pandora's Children 810

Landis, Arthur
Camelot in Orbit 600

Landis, Geoffrey A.
Impact Parameter and Other Quantum Realities **766**
Mars Crossing 766, 771, 814
Myths, Legends, and True History 766

Landis, J.D.
Longing 833, 852, 929, 1085, 1156

Landis, Jill Marie
Blue Moon 297, 471
Day Dreamer 471
Just Once 471
Last Chance 471
The Orchid Hunter 319
Summer Moon 415, **471**
Until Tomorrow 364, 471

Landreth, Marsha
The Samantha Turner Series 197

Lane, Allison
The Beleaguered Earl 325
A Bird in Hand 325
Birds of a Feather 325
A Clandestine Courtship 258
Devall's Angel 257, 325, 362, 377, 379
The Purloined Letters 325
The Rake and the Wallflower **325**

Lane, Connie
Reinventing Romeo 422

Lane, Elizabeth
Apache Fire 326
Bride on the Run 247, 326
Hometown Wedding 326
My Lord Savage **326**
Shawnee Bride 326
The Tycoon and the Townie 326

Lane, Joel
The Earth Wire and Other Stories 655

Langan, Ruth
Ace 327, 328
Awakening Alex **327**, 328, 347
Captive of Desire 326
Conor 254
The Highlander 244
Loving Lizbeth 327
Once upon a Rose **384**
One Christmas Night 367
The Sea Nymph 297, 327, 328
The Sea Sprite 327, **328**
The Sea Witch 328
Seducing Celeste 327, 328

Langton, Jane
The Dante Game 164
The Homer Kelly Series 106

Lanier, Virginia
The Jo Beth Siddon Series 3, 16, 17, 18

Lansdale, Joe R.
The Bottoms 887
By Bizarre Hands 629
Captains Outrageous **472**
The Long Ones 472
Rumble Tumble 472
Savage Season 472
Tight Little Stitches in a Dead Man's Back 708
The Two-Bear Mambo 472
Writer of the Purple Rage 472

Lansdowne, Judith A.
Stocking Stuffers 232, 248

Lapierre, Alexandra
Artemisia 951

LaPierre, Janet
Baby Mine 139
Children's Games 139
The Cruel Mother 139
Grandmother's House 139
Keepers **139**
Old Enemies 139

Larsen, Nella
Passing 1207

Larson, Bob
The Senator's Agenda 976, 1004

Larson, Elyse
The Women of Valor Series 977, 1034

Lassieur, A.J.
The Unicorn 565

Latimer, Jonathan
The Bill Crane Series 56

Laumer, Keith
The Glory Game 761
Rogue Bolo 765
The Star Colony 733

Laurens, Stephanie
All about Love 329
All about Passion 329
Captain Jack's Woman 309, 317
The Promise in a Kiss **329**
A Rogue's Proposal 329
Scandal's Bride 329
A Secret Love 329

Lawhead, Stephen R.
Arthur 901
Avalon 570
The Black Rood 570, 901
Byzantium 570, 901
The Celtic Crusades Series 1003, 1060
Dream Thief 569
Grail 570, 901
The Iron Lance 570, 901
The Mystic Rose **570**, **901**, 941

Lawrence, Margery
Nights of the Round Table 622

Lawrence, Martha C.
Aquarius Descending 140
Ashes of Aries **140**
The Cold Heart of Capricorn 140
The Elizabeth Chase Series 52, 79
Murder in Scorpio 140
Pisces Rising 140

Lawrence, Nancy
An Intimate Arrangement 230

Laws, Stephen
Chasm 708

Laxalt, Robert
Time of the Rabies 1083

Laymon, Richard
Among the Missing 663, 664
Bad News 651
The Beast House 662
Bite 663, 664
Body Rides 627, 663, 664
The Cellar 662
Come out Tonight 662
Cuts 662
Friday Night in Beast House **662**
Funland 687
In the Dark **663**, 664
The Midnight Tour 662
Night in the Lonesome October 663, **664**
Once upon a Halloween 663, 664

Layton, Edith
The Chance 348
A Regency Christmas Carol 248
Regency Christmas Spirits **248**

Le Carre, John
The George Smiley Series 215
Our Game 130
The Russia House 1151
Single & Single 1191
Small Town in Germany 1135

Le Guin, Ursula K.
Always Coming Home 571
The Left Hand of Darkness 811
The Other Wind **571**
Tales from Earthsea 571, 582
Tehanu 571
The Telling 571, 780
Three Hainish Novels 571

Leahy, Syrell Rogovin
Happy Birthday Murder **996**

Leavitt, David
Arkansas 1145
Family Dancing 1145
The Lost Language of Cranes 1145
The Marble Quilt 1120, **1145**
Martin Bauman 1145, 1173
The Page Turner 1145
While England Sleeps 1090

Lebbon, Tim
As the Sun Goes Down 666, 698
Face **665**
Faith in the Flesh 666
Mesmer 665, 666
The Naming of Parts 665, 666
The Nature of Balance 665, **666**
Until She Sleeps 665
When the Sun Goes Down 655
White 665, 666, 708

Ledbetter, Suzann
Pure Justice 451
South of Sanity 369

Lee, Barbara
The Eve Elliott Series 205

Lee, Edward
The Bighead 638
City Infernal **667**
Creekers 662
Goon 667, 705
Header 667
Operator B 667
The Stickmen 661, 667
The Ushers 667, 698

Lee, Rachel
After I Dream 283, 330, 331, 399
Before I Sleep 330, 331
Caught 395
Conard County: Boots and Badges 330, 331
Involuntary Daddy 330
July Thunder **330**
An Officer and a Gentleman 242
Snow in September 327, 330, 331, 413
Under Suspicion **331**, 347, 383
When I Wake 331

Lee, Rebecca Hagan
A Hint of Heather 390

Lee, Tanith
Dark Dance 623
A Heroine of the World 532
Vazkor, Son of Vazkor 534

Lee, W.W.
The Overland Trail 478
Rustler's Venom 503

Legg, John
Siege at Fort Defiance 468

Lehane, Dennis
Darkness Take My Hand 1074
Mystic River 37, 74, 199, 1076, 1096, 1118, 1123
The Patrick Kenzie/Angela Gennaro Series 50, 94, 213

Leiber, Fritz
Changewar 767
Conjure Wife 682
Farewell to Lankhmar 767
The Green Millennium 767
Ill Met in Lankhmar 530
The Knight and Knave of Swords 532
Night's Black Agents 767
Rime Isle 596
The Silver Eggheads 722, 767
Swords Against Death 589, 599
Thieves' House 569
The Wanderer **767**

Leigh, Ana
The MacKenzies: David 332
The MacKenzies: Flint 332
The MacKenzies: Jared 332
The MacKenzies: Josh 332
The MacKenzies: Luke 332
The MacKenzies: Zach **332**

Leigh, Stephen
Dark Water's Embrace 805

Leinster, Murray
The Med Series 805
The Monster from Earth's End 735
The Wailing Asteroid 785

Leith, Valery
Company of Glass 572
The Riddled Night 561, 572, 578
The Way of the Rose **572**

Lemarchand, Elizabeth
The Tom Pollard Series 30

Lemmons, Thom
The Daughters of Faith Series 990, 994, 1053

Lennon, J. Robert
The Funnies 473, 1146
The Light of Falling Stars 473, 1146
On the Night Plain **473**, **1146**

Lennox, Judith
The Italian Garden 836, 951

Leon, Bonnie
Harvest of Truth 1017
In Fields of Freedom 1017
A Sacred Place 1017, 1042
The Sowers Trilogy 1040
Valley of Promises 1017
When Freedom Grows 1017
Worthy of Riches 1001, **1017**

Leon, Donna
The Guido Brunetti Series 164

Leonard, Elmore
Be Cool 115, 1118
City Primeval 1123
Pagan Babies 107
The Tonto Woman and other Western Stories 434, 461, 491

Leppek, Christopher
The Surrogate Assassin 158

Lerman, Rhoda
Eleanor 928

Lescroart, John
A Certain Justice 141
Guilt 141
The Hearing 141
The Mercy Rule 141
Nothing but the Truth 141
The Oath **141**

Lethem, Jonathan
Motherless Brooklyn 37, 199, 211

Leto, Julie Elizabeth
Exposed 240
Good Girls Do 333
Insatiable **333**
Private Lessons 333
Pure Chance 333
Seducing Sullivan 333

Levin, Ira
The Stepford Wives 668

Levin, Lee
King Tut's Private Eye 101

Levy, Roger
Reckless Sleep 731

Lewin, Michael Z.
Called by a Panther 142
Cutting Loose 142
Family Business 142
Family Planning 142
The Reluctant Detective and Other Stories **142**
Underdog 142

Lewis, Beverly
The Crossroad 1018
October Song **1018**
The Postcard 1018
The Reckoning 1018
The Redemption of Sarah Cain 965, 1018, 1036
Sanctuary 1018
The Sunroom 980, 1032

Lewis, D.F.
The Best of D.F. Lewis 688

Lewis, J.P. Sinclair
Buffalo Gordon 864

Lewis, Janet
The Trial of Soren Qvist 956

Lewis, L.A.
Tales of the Grotesque 622

Lewis, Preston
Hard Texas Winter 463

Lickiss, Rebecca
Eccentric Circles 515, **573**

Lieberman, Gerald F.
The Sea Lepers 953

Liebrecht, Savyon
A Man and a Woman and a Man 1197

Lightner, A.M.
The Day of the Drones 779

Ligotti, Thomas
Songs of a Dead Dreamer 700

Liming, Mary
The Prisoner Bride **368**

Linaweaver, Brad
Moon of Ice 804

Lincoln, Christine
Sap Rising 1112, **1147**

Lincoln, Victoria
Charles 917

Lindow, Denise
The Warrior's Damsel **295**

Lindsey, Johanna
Joining 295
Once a Princess 388
Say You Love Me 346
Surrender My Love 337

Linscott, Gillian
Absent Friends 153, 208
The Nell Bray Series 958
The Perfect Daughter 838, 856, 923, 943

Linz, Cathie
Between the Covers 334, 335
The Cowboy Finds a Bride 334, 335
Daddy in Dress Blues 334, 335
Husband Needed 251
The Lawman Gets Lucky 334, 335
The Marine and the Princess **334**
The Rancher Gets Hitched 335
Stranded with the Sergeant 334, **335**

Linzer, Anna
Ghost Dancing 453

Lippincott, Robin
Our Arcadia 847

Lippman, Laura
Baltimore Blues 143
Butchers Hill 143
Charm City 143
In a Strange City **143**
In Big Trouble 143
The Sugar House 143, 205
The Tess Monaghan Series 18

Little, Bentley
The Association **668**
Guests 668
Houses 668
The Ignored 668
The Store 668
University 649
The Walking 668

Little, Constance
The Black Coat 144
Black Corridors 144
The Black Eye **144**
The Black Honeymoon 144
The Black Stocking 144
Great Black Kanba 144

Little, Denise
Alien Pets 574, 575
A Constellation of Cats **574**, 575
Creature Fantastic 574, **575**
A Dangerous Magic 574, 575
Perchance to Dream 574, 575
Twice upon a Time 574, 575

Little, Gwenyth
The Black Eye **144**

Litton, Josie
Believe in Me **336**, 337, 338
Come Back to Me 336, **337**, 338
Dream of Me 336, 337, **338**

Livesey, Margot
Criminals 1148
Eva Moves the Furniture 1079, **1148**, 1193
Homework 1148
Learning by Heart 1148
The Missing World 1148, 1184

Livingston, Gary
Tears of Ice 954

Llewellyn, Sam
Dead Reckoning 171

Lliteras, D.S.
613 West Jefferson 988

Llywelyn, Morgan
Druids 886, 952

Lochte, Dick
The Leo Bloodworth/Serendipity Dahlquist Series 56

Lodge, David
Small World 1150
Thinks— 1069

Lofts, Norah
The Lost Queen 862, 1110

Logan, Cait
On Leaving Lonely Town **339**

Logue, Mary
Blood Country 145
Dark Coulee 145
Glare Ice 90, **145**, 212

Long, Elaine
Jenny's Mountain 469

Long, Frank Belknap
The Hounds of Tindalos 671
In Mayan Splendor 669

Long, Goldberry
Juniper Tree Burning 1077

Long, James
Ferney 529, 598

Long, William Stuart
The Exiles 904

Longstreet, Roxanne
Cold Kiss 617, 702

Longyear, Barry
Manifest Destiny 734

Lottman, Eileen
The Brahmins 937

Lough, Loree
Only You 986
Suddenly Home 1063

Louis, Laura Glen
Talking in the Dark **1149**

Lovecraft, H.P.
The Ancient Track **669**
The Annotated H.P. Lovecraft 671
At the Mountains of Madness and Other Novels 670
The Call of Cthulhu and Other Weird Stories 670, 671
Dagon and Other Macabre Tales 670
The Dunwich Horror and Others 670
More Annotated Lovecraft 671
The Shadow out of Time **670**
The Shadow over Innsmouth 671
Tales of H.P. Lovecraft 671
The Thing on the Doorstep and Other Weird Stories 670, **671**

M

Mason, Douglas R.
Matrix 808

Mason, Felicia
Something to Celebrate 300

Massey, Cynthia Leal
Fire Lilies **476**

Massey, Sonja
Daughter of Ireland 386

Massey, Sujata
The Bride's Kimono **150**
The Floating Girl 150
The Flower Master 150
The Rei Shimura Series 127
The Salaryman's Wife 150
Zen Attitude 150

Massie, Elizabeth
Shadow Dreams 629, 630

Masterton, Graham
Bonnie Winter **672**
Burial 672
The Chosen Child 672
The House That Jack Built 672
Master of Lies 682
Spirit 672
Trauma 672

Matera, Lia
Havana Twist 75

Mathes, Charles
The Girl at the End of the Line 9

Matheson, Richard
Bid Time Return 546
Collected Stories 678
Earthbound 620

Mathews, Francine
Jane and the Prisoner of Wool House **12**

Matlock, Curtiss Ann
Cold Tea on a Hot Day 225
Driving Lessons 231

Matthews, A.J.
The White Room **673**

Matthews, Christine
The Masks of Auntie Laveau **177**

Matthews, Laura
A Prudent Match 238

Maugham, W. Somerset
Ashenden 118

Maupin, Armistead
The Night Listener 1213

Mawer, Simon
The Gospel of Judas 1092, 1175

Maxwell, Ann
Moving Target **340**

Maxwell, Cathy
Because of You 348
The Marriage Contract 348
Married in Haste 348
A Scandalous Marriage 348
The Wedding Wager 321, **348**, 355
When Dreams Come True 281, 303, 348

Maybury, Anne
Jessamy Court 314
The Terracotta Palace 314

Mayer, Eric
Three for a Letter **180**, **920**

Mayhew, Michael
Harvest Tales and Midnight Revels 633

Maynard, L.H.
Echoes of Darkness 674, 701
Hideous Dreams **674**
Night's Soft Pains 674
Shadows at Midnight 652

Mayor, Archer
Bellows Falls 151
The Disposable Man 151
The Joe Gunther Series 168
The Marble Mask 134, 151
Occam's Razor 151
The Ragman's Memory 151
Tucker Peak **151**

McArthur, Maxine
Time Future **770**

McAuley, Paul J.
Ancients of Days 771
Child of the River 771
Fairyland 771
The Invisible Country 771
Red Dust 814
The Secret of Life 739, **771**
Shrine of Stars 771

McBain, Ed
And All through the House 152
Big Bad City 152
The Last Dance 152
Money, Money, Money **152**
Nocturne 152
Romance 152

McBride, Jule
A Way with Women 289

McBride, Mary
The Marriage Knot 361
Moonglow, Texas 263
A Western Family Christmas **263**

McCabe, Amanda
Scandal in Venice 349
The Spanish Bride **349**

McCaffrey, Anne
Acorna 755
Acorna's Search **772**
Acorna's World 725
Freedom's Challenge 772
The Masterharper of Pern 772
Nimisha's Ship 772
Pegasus in Space 772
The Tower and the Hive 772

McCaig, Donald
Jacob's Ladder 964

McCall, Dinah
The Return 339
Tallchief 330

McCall, Mary Reed
Secret Vows 295, 407

McCammon, Robert R.
Blue World 629, 707
Boys' Life 567
Mystery Walk 637
Stinger 661
Under the Fang 634

McCarthy, Kevin
Family 775

McCarver, Sam
The Case of Cabin 13 5, 153
The Case of Compartment 7 153
The Case of the 2nd Seance 153
The Case of the Ripper's Revenge **153**

McCauley, Barbara
Reese's Wild Wager 235

McClendon, Lise
The Blue Jay Shaman 477
Blue Wolf **477**
Nordic Nights 477
One O'Clock Jump 110, 839, 882, 897, 923, 935
Painted True 477

McClure, James
The Lieutenant Tromp Kramer Series 132

McConnochie, Mardi
Coldwater 819, 887, **904**, 1148, **1156**

McCorkle, Jill
Carolina Moon 1157
Crash Diet 1157
Creatures of Habit 1065, 1075, 1079, 1115, **1157**, 1192
Ferris Beach 1157
Final Vinyl Days 1157
Tending to Virginia 1157

McCourtney, Lorena
Canyon 1023
Dear Silver 1023
Escape 1017, 1023
Forgotten 1023
Searching for Stardust 1023
Whirlpool **1023**, 1055

McCoy, Judi
I Dream of You 249, 287, **350**, 351
You're the One **351**

McCoy, Max
Jesse 446, 448

McCracken, Elizabeth
The Giant's House 1158
Here's Your Hat What's Your Hurry 1158
Niagara Falls All over Again **1158**, 1188

McCrumb, Sharyn
The Elizabeth MacPherson Series 6, 114
Foggy Mountain Breakdown 31

McCullough, Colleen
Caesar 1183
Fortune's Favorites 1211
The Masters of Rome Series 924
Morgan's Run 819, 904, 1212

McCunn, Ruthanne
The Moon Pearl 835

McCusker, Paul
Catacombs 1024
Epiphany 1024, 1032, 1033, 1038
The Faded Flower **1024**

McCutchan, Philip
Cameron's Crossing 953

McDaniel, Sylvia
The Outlaw 409

McDermid, Val
Booked for Murder 154
Killing the Shadows **154**
The Mermaids Singing 154
A Place of Execution 23, 154, 186, 214
Star Struck 154
The Tony Hill/Carol Jordan Series 178
The Wire in the Blood 154

McDermott, Alice
Charming Billy 1117

McDonald, Ian
Evolution's Shore 739
King of Morning, Queen of Day 529, 559, 568, 598

McDonald, Kay L.
Beyond the Vision 466

McDowell, Iain
A Study in Death **155**

McDowell, Ian
Merlin's Gift 558

McDowell, Josh
Vote of Intolerance 991

McEwan, Ian
Atonement 872

McFall, Patricia
Night Butterfly 127, 150

McFarland, Dennis
Singing Boy 1196

McFedries, A.A.
The King of the Sun **773**

McGarrity, Michael
The Kevin Kerney Series 25, 151
Tularosa 149
Under the Color of Law 428

McGiffen, Steve
Tennant's Rock **478**, 855, 877, 910

McGinley, Marjorie M.
Casey's Journey 479
Footloose Convoy 479
The Gift of the Mestizo **479**
John Crust and Snuffling Pig 479
Rattlesnake Gulch 479

McGoldrick, James A.
The Promise **352**

McGoldrick, May
The Dreamer 352
The Enchantress 352
The Firebrand 352
Flame 352
Intended 352
The Promise **352**

McGoldrick, Nikoo
The Promise **352**

McGowan, Heather
Schooling **1159**

McGowan, Wynema
Beyond the River 440, 482

McGown, Jill
The Inspector Lloyd/Judy Hill Series 64, 87, 104, 165

McGrath, Patrick
Blood and Water and Others 786
Martha Peake 840, 939, 1098, 1110, 1212

McGraw, Eloise
The Golden Goblet 577
The Moorchild 577
The Rundlestone of Oz **577**

McGregor, Elizabeth
The Ice Child **905**

McGuire, Tim
Danger Ridge 480
Gold of Cortes 439, 443, 480
Nobility 480
Outcasts **480**

McHugh, Maureen
China Mountain Zhang 774
Half the Day Is Night 774
Mission Child 774
Nekropolis **774**

McInerny, Ralph
The Andrew Broom Series 113
The Book of Kills 156
Emerald Aisle **156**

Irish Tenure 156
Lack of the Irish 156
On This Rockne 156

McKade, Maureen
Outlaw's Bride 247

McKenna, Juliet E.
The Gambler's Fortune 578
The Swordsman's Oath 578
The Thief's Gamble 569, 578, 589, 601
The Warrior's Bond 561, **578**

McKenna, Shannon
All through the Night **282**

McKenney, Kenneth
The Plants 735

McKenzie, Nancy
The Child Queen 528

McKeone, Dixie Lee
Tales of Uncle Trapspringer 584

McKernan, Victoria
The Chicago Nordejoong Series 3

McKiernan, Dennis L.
The Caverns of Socrates 579, 580
The Dark Tide 541
Dragondoom 610
The Dragonstone 526
Into the Fire 579, 580
Into the Forge 555, 579, 580
Once upon a Winter's Night **579**, 580
The Silver Call **580**
Silver Wolf, Black Falcon 554, 579, 580
Tales of Mithgar 579
Voyage of the Fox Rider 530, 571

McKillip, Patricia
The Riddlemaster of Hed 591

McKinley, Robin
The Door in the Hedge 579

McKinley, Tamara
Jacaranda Vines 1209

McKinney, Meagan
The Ground She Walks Upon 313
The Lawman Meets His Bride 373

McLain, John
The Reckoning **481**

McLaughlin, Mark
I Gave at the Orifice 635

McMillan, Ann
Civil Blood 133, 159, 169, 898, 909, 914

McMillan, Rosalyn
The Flip Side of Sin 1179

McMillan, Terry
A Day Late and a Dollar Short 1101, 1122, 1207
How Stella Got Her Groove Back 403

McMillin, Chandler Scott
Ghost Killer **627**

McMurtry, Larry
Boone's Lick 895, 945, 957
Comanche Moon 468, 1137
Dead Man's Walk 468, 503
Horseman, Pass By 1146
Lonesome Dove 1212
Pretty Boy Floyd 825
Streets of Laredo 479
Terms of Endearment 1181

McNaught, Judith
A Holiday of Love 366

McNish, Cliff
Doomspell 581
The Scent of Magic **581**

McPhee, Jenny
The Center of Things 1160

McQuay, Mike
Memories 802

McWilliams, A.L.
Eye of the Cat 482
Penny Town Justice 482
Search for Last Chance **482**

Meade, Glenn
The Sands of Sakkara 215, 906

Meallet, Sandro
Edgewater Angels **1160**

Medeiros, Teresa
Breath of Magic 350
Charming the Prince 396
Touch of Enchantment 358
A Whisper of Roses 390

Meidav, Edie
The Far Field 1152

Meier, Leslie
Back to School Murder 157
Christmas Cookie Murder 157
The Lucy Stone Series 89
Trick or Treat Murder 157
Turkey Day Murder 157
Valentine Murder 157
Wedding Day Murder 60, **157**

Meier, Susan
The Baby Bequest 341

Meikle, William
Millennium Macabre 652, 701

Meluch, R.M.
The Queen's Squadron 761

Melville, James
The Inspector Otani Series 150

Mendoza, Sylvia
On Fire/Al rojo vivo 251

Menendez, Ana
In Cuba I Was a German Shepherd 1120

Meroff, Deborah
Captain, My Captain 894

Mesce, Bill Jr.
The Advocate 906
Officer of the Court 828, 892, **906**, 943

Messud, Claire
The Hunters **1161**
The Last Life 1161
When the World Was Steady 1161

Metz, Melinda
Gifted Touch **775**, 776
Haunted **776**
The Intruder 775, 776
The Outsider 749, 775, 776
The Seeker 775, 776
The Watcher 775, 776
The Wild One 775

Metzger, Barbara
The Christmas Carrolls 275
Christmas Wishes 304
Miss Lockhart's Letters 233
My Lady Innkeeper 398
Regency Christmas Spirits **248**

Metzger, Thom
Big Gurl 705

Meyers, Annette
Murder Me Now 839

Meyers, Maan
The Dutchman's Dilemma 939
The House on Mulberry Street 200, 203

Meyers, Manny
The Last Mystery of Edgar Allan Poe 193, 932

Mezrich, Ben
Skin 773

Michaels, Grant
The Stan Kraychik Series 176

Michaels, Kasey
Bachelor on the Prowl **353**
Be My Baby Tonight 353, 354
Can't Take My Eyes Off of You 353, 354
Love to Love You Baby 353, **354**
Raffling Ryan 250, 255, 354, 380
Someone to Love 229, 319, 353, 354, 375
Too Good to Be True 226, 274, 353, 354

Michaels, Melisa
Cold Iron 522
Skirmish 796

Michaels, Theresa
The Merry Widows: Sarah 296

Michener, James A.
Centennial 1137

Mickelbury, Penny
The Carol Ann Gibson Series 220

Mieville, China
Perdido Street Station 607

Milan, Victor
The Cybernetic Shogun 758

Miles, Keith
The Devil's Apprentice **148**
Murder on the Minnesota **5**
Saint's Rest 119

Miles, Rosalind
Act of Passion 907
The Child of the Holy Grail 829, 831, 901, **907**
Guenevere: Queen of the Summer Country 907
I, Elizabeth 907
The Knight of the Sacred Lake 907

Miller, Barbara
Dearest Max 355
The Guardian **355**
My Phillipe 355
Pretender 355

Miller, Calvin
Snow 1032

Miller, Carl
The Warrior and the Witch 534

Miller, Dawn
The Journal of Callie Wade 483
Letters to Callie **483**

Miller, Linda Lael
Knights 869
My Lady Beloved **405**
My Lady Wayward **406**
My Outlaw 372

Miller, Nadine
The Yorkshire Lady 398

Miller, Rebecca
Personal Velocity **1162**

Miller, Sue
The Distinguished Guest 1163
For Love 1163
The Good Mother 1163
Inventing the Abbotts and Other Stories 1163
While I Was Gone 1163
The World Below **1163**

Miller, Walter N. Jr.
A Canticle for Leibowitz 732

Millet, Lydia
My Happy Life 1209

Millett, Larry
Sherlock Holmes and the Ice Palace Murders 158, 908
Sherlock Holmes and the Red Demon 158, 908
Sherlock Holmes and the Rune Stone Mystery 158, 908
Sherlock Holmes and the Secret Alliance **158**, 210, 830, 896, 899, **908**, 958

Millhiser, Marlys
The Charlie Greene Series 34, 80
It's Murder Going Home 205
Murder in a Hot Flash 124

Mills, DiAnn
The English Garden **1020**

Mills-Macias, Kathi
Obsession 1048

Mina, Denise
Garnethill 178

Mindel, Jenna
Blessing in Disguise **356**

Mirrlees, Hope
Lud-in-the-Mist 571

Mirvis, Tova
The Ladies Auxiliary 978

Mitchard, Jacquelyn
A Theory of Relativity 1086, 1200

Mitchell, Kay
The Inspector Morrisey Series 55

Mitchell, Kirk
The Dee Laguerre Series 125

Mitchell, Margaret
Gone with the Wind 273, 918

Mitchell, Sara
Night Music 1044
Ransomed Heart 972

Mittermeyer, Helen
Princess of the Veil 336, 338

Mittman, Stephanie
The Marriage Bed 364

Mlynowski, Sarah
Milkrun 252, 345, **357**

Modesitt, L.E. Jr.
The Colors of Chaos 526
Empire & Ecolitan **777**, 778
Ghost of the White Nights 741, 777, **778**
Gravity Dreams 777, 778
The Octagonal Raven 777, 778
Scion of Cyador 777, 778
The Shadow Sorceress 549, 777, 778

Moffitt, Donald
Crescent in the Sky 774

Monahan, Brent
The Book of Common Prayer 703
The Uprising 676

Monfredo, Miriam Grace
Blackwater Spirits 2, 159, 909
Brothers of Cain 133, **159**, 169, 898, **909**
Crime through Time 8
Crime through Time II 8
Must the Maiden Die 159, 909
Sisters of Cain 159, 909
The Stalking Horse 159, 909
Through a Gold Eagle 159, 909

Moning, Karen Marie
Beyond the Highland Mist 358
The Highlander's Touch 237, 358
Kiss of the Highlander 237, **358**
To Tame a Highland Warrior 358

Monk, Karyn
Once a Warrior 338
The Rose and the Warrior 405
The Witch and the Warrior 405

Monsarrat, Nicholas
The Cruel Sea 953

Montero, Mayra
In the Palm of Darkness 1164
The Last Night I Spent with You 1164
The Messenger 1164
The Red of His Shadow **1164**

Moody, Rick
Demonology 1095

Moody, Skye Kathleen
K Falls 444
The Venus Diamond Series 63

Moon, Elizabeth
Once a Hero 742, 795

Moor, Margriet de
Duke of Egypt 1165
First Gray, Then White, Then Blue **1165**
The Virtuoso 1165

Moorcock, Michael
Blood 582
The Dreamthief's Daughter 560, **582**
Fabulous Harbors 582, 607
Gloriana 778
The Ice Schooner 595, 724
Kane of Old Mars 582
Sailing to Utopia 582
Tales from the Texas Woods 433
War Amongst the Angels 582

Moore, Arthur
Rebel 473

Moore, Barbara
The Doberman Wore Black 17
The Wolf Whispered Death 68

Moore, Brian
The Magician's Wife 900

Moore, Christopher
Santa and Pete 1179

Moore, James A.
Fireworks 660, **675**
Under the Overtree 675

Moore, Margaret
A Warrior's Honor 407

Moore, Vance
Odyssey 565

Moore, Ward
Bring the Jubilee 804
Greener than You Think 735

Moreau, C.X.
Promise of Glory 919

Morgan, Deborah
Death Is a Cabaret **160**

Morgan, Kathleen
The Brides of Culdee Creek Series 1014
Child of Promise **1025**, 1026
Daughter of Joy 1025, 1026
The Demon Prince 267
Embrace the Dawn 1025, **1026**
The Knowing Crystal 267
Lady of Light 1025, 1026
Woman of Grace 1025, 1026

Morgan, Robert
Gap Creek 891, 910
The Hinterlands 910
This Rock **910**
The Truest Pleasure 910

Morressey, John
Kedrigern in Wanderland 537
The Questing of Kedrigern 521
Star Brat 749

Morris, Alan
The Guardians of the North Series 1034, 1058

Morris, Anthony
Candlelight Ghost Stories 636

Morris, Gilbert
All That Glitters 1006
The Amazon Quest 1027, 1028
A Covenant of Love 1027
The Dani Ross Series 970, 1008, 1009, 1037, 1048
End of Act Three 1027, 1028
Four of a Kind 1027, 1028
The Golden Angel **1027**, 1028
The Heavenly Fugitive **1028**
The House of Winslow Series 1015, 1040
Jacob's Way 1027, 1028
The Omega Trilogy 1016
The Reno Saga 972, 973
A Time of War 1056

Morris, Janet
Kings in Hell 553

Morris, Lynn
The Balcony 1049
The Cheney Duvall Series 1025

Morris, Mark
Close to the Bone 706

Morris, Michael
A Place Called Wiregrass 1002, **1029**

Morris, Suzanne
Wives and Mistresses 937

Morrish, Furze
Bridge over Dark Gods 644

Morrison, Toni
Paradise 1089
Sula 918, 1207

Morson, Ian
The Falconer Series 934
The William Falconer Series 861, 865, 933, 944

Mortimer, John
Will Shakespeare 823

Moser, Nancy
The Invitation 1030
The Mustard Seed Series 981
The Quest 1030
The Seat Beside Me **1030**
The Temptation 1030

Moskowitz, Sam
Great Untold Stories of Fantasy and Horror 615

Mosley, Walter
Always Outnumbered, Always Outgunned 1166
Blue Light 779, 1126, 1166
Devil in a Blue Dress 161, 935, 1131
The Easy Rawlins Series 166, 192, 196
Fearless Jones 122, 1088, 1089, 1118, 1127, 1166
Futureland **779**, 786, 1070, **1166**
Gone Fishin' 1166
Walkin' the Dog 1166, 1180

Mount, Ferdinand
The Clique 1167
Fairness **1167**, 1171, 1173
Jem (and Sam) 1167
The Liquidator 1167
Of Love and Asthma 1167
Umbrella 1167

Mourad, Kenize
Regards from the Dead Princess 893

Moyes, Patricia
A Six-Letter Word for Death 96
Who Killed Father Christmas? 31

Mrozek, Slawomir
The Elephant 720

Mujica, Barbara
Frida 951

Muller, Eddie
The Distance **161**

Muller, Herta
The Appointment **1168**
The Land of Green Plums 1168
Traveling on One Leg 1168

Muller, Marcia
The Broken Promise Land 189
Point Deception 139
The Sharon McCone Series 7, 63, 143

Mullins, Gene
Bear Paw **484**

Mundt, Martin
The Crawling Abbatoir 697

Munger, Katy
The Casey Jones Series 18, 34, 143, 217

Munn, Vella
Blackfeet Season 911
Cheyenne Summer 826, **911**
Seminole Song 911
Soul of the Sacred Earth 911
Spirit of the Eagle 911
Wind Warrior 911

Munro, Alice
The Beggar Maid 1169
Friend of My Youth 1162
Hateship, Friendship, Courtship, Loveship, Marriage 1075, 1099, 1124, **1169**, 1188
The Love of a Good Woman 1169, 1201
The Moons of Jupiter 1149
Open Secrets 1169, 1192
The Progress of Love 1169
Queenie 1169
Selected Stories 1115

Munroe, Jim
Angry Young Spaceman **780**

Murakami, Haruki
Norwegian Wood 1110, 1192
The Sputnik Sweetheart 1199

Murphy, Pat
Adventures in Time and Space with Max Merriwell **781**
The City, Not Long After 781
Nadya 781
Rachel in Love 781
There and Back Again 781
Wild Angel 781

Murphy, Shirley Rousseau
Cat in the Dark 162
Cat Laughing Last **162**
Cat Raise the Dead 162
Cat Spitting Mad 162
Cat to the Dogs 162
Cat under Fire 162
The Joe Grey Series 26

Murray, Donna Huston
The Ginger Struve Barnes Series 120

Murray, Earl
Gabriella 449, 450, 957

Musser, Joe
Behold a Pale Horse 1031
The Infidel **1031**

Myers, Bill
Blood of Heaven 1016, 1032
Eli 1032
Fire of Heaven 1032
Threshold 981, 1032
When the Last Leaf Falls **1032**

Myers, Helen R.
Dead End 347, 373

Myers, Tamar
The Abigail Timberlake Series 67
Baroque and Desperate 163
Estate of Mind 163
The Ming and I 163
Nightmare in Shining Armor **163**
A Penny Urned 163
So Faux, So Good 163

N

Nabb, Magdalen
The Marshal and the Forgery 164
The Marshal and the Madwoman 164
The Marshal at the Villa Torrini 164
The Marshal Makes His Report 164
The Marshal's Own Case 164
Property of Blood **164**

Naipaul, V.S.
A Bend in the River 1170
The Enigma of Arrival 1170
Guerrillas 1170
Half a Life **1170**, 1190, 1208
A House for Mr. Biswas 1170
In a Free State 1170

Naslund, Sena Jeter
Ahab's Wife 894

Nassise, Joseph M.
Riverwatch **676**

Nathan, Melissa
Pride, Prejudice and Jasmin Field **359**, 394

Nattel, Lilian
The River Midnight 1064

Nauman, A.D.
Scorch **782**

Nava, Michael
The Henry Rios Series 221

Navarro, Yvonne
Final Impact 767

Navin, Jacqueline
Meet Me at Midnight 360
One Christmas Night 360
A Rose at Midnight 360
The Sleeping Beauty **360**
Strathmere's Bride 360
The Viking's Heart 360

Nayes, Alan
Gargoyles **677**, **783**

Naylor, Clare
Love: A User's Guide 394

Needham, Linda
For My Lady's Kiss 321

Neel, Janet
Death Among the Dons 165
Death of a Partner 165
Death on Site 165
The John McLeish/Francesca Wilson Series 87, 104
O Gentle Death **165**
A Timely Death 165
To Die For 165

Neggers, Carla
The Waterfall 327, 331, 373, 413

Neider, Charles
Mozart and the Archbooby 929

Neill, John R.
Lucky Bucky in Oz 577

Nelscott, Kris
A Dangerous Road 122, 166
Smoke-Filled Rooms **166**
The Smokey Dalton Series 83

Nelson, James L.
By Force of Arms 939

Neri, Penelope
Moonshadow 418

Nesbit, Edith
The Railway Children 581

Nesbitt, John D.
A Good Man to Have in Camp 486
One Foot in the Stirrup 427, 486

Nevin, David
1812 912
Dream West 912, 949
Eagle's Cry 912
Treason **912**

Newman, Christopher
The Joe Dante Series 152

Newman, Kim
Anno Dracula 62, 695
Drachenfels **613**
Jago 694

Newman, Sharan
The Catherine le Vendeur Series 834, 861
The Chessboard Queen 528
Crime through Time III 8
Death Comes as Epiphany 70, 209
The Guinevere Trilogy 907

Newton, Kurt
The House Spider and Other Strange Visitors 683, 697
The Mind Spider and Other Strange Visitors 639

Nicholls, Stan
Legion of Thunder 580, 606

Nichols, Adam
The War of the Lord's Veil 606

Nickaell, Robin
The Boneyard 639

Nighbert, David F.
Squeezeplay 188

Niles, Douglas
Circle at Center 583
Darkenheight 583
Escape from Castle Quarras 556
The Last Thane 583
The Puppet King 583
War of the Three Waters 583
World Fall **583**

Niven, Larry
Footfall 746
The Legacy of Heorot 740
Lucifer's Hammer 767
The Magic Goes Away 556

Noble, Diane
At Play in the Promised Land 1033
The Blossom and the Nettle 1033
The California Chronicles 998, 1028, 1050
Come, My Little Angel 983, **1033**
Distant Bells 1033
Unlikely Angels 1033
When the Far Hills Bloom 1033

Nolan, William F.
Helltracks 678
Impact-20 678
Night Shapes 678, 696
Space for Hire 756, 813
Things Beyond Midnight 678
Urban Horrors 648
William F. Nolan's Dark Universe **678**
The Winchester Horror 678

Noonan, Michael
The Sun Is God 959

Nordberg, Bette
Serenity Bay 1001, 1002, 1029

Norfolk, Lawrence
In the Shape of a Boar **913**, 954, 1064, **1171**
Lempriere's Dictionary 913, 1171
The Pope's Rhinoceros 913, 1171

Norton, Andre
Brother to Shadows 725
Crossroads of Time 741
Echoes in Time 784
The Hands of Llyr 784
Lord of Thunder 772
Moon Mirror 557, 784
Red Hart Magic 519, 543, 573
Rogue Reynard 587
The Scent of Magic 784
Sorceress of the Witch World 554
Spell of the Witch World 576
Star Soldiers 729, **784**, 809
The Warding of Witch World 784
Web of the Witch World 534, 555

Norwood, Warren
Midway Between 761

Nothomb, Amelie
Fear and Trembling 1133

Noyer, Albert
The Saint's Day Deaths 180, 184, 209

Nunez, Sigrid
A Feather on the Breath of God 1172
For Rouenna **1172**
Mitz: The Marmoset of Bloomsbury 1172
Naked Sleeper 1172

Nye, Robert
The Late Mr. Shakespeare 823
Merlin 558
Mrs. Shakespeare 823

O

Oates, Joyce Carol
Beasts 1075, **1173**, 1185, 1187
Because It Is Bitter, and Because It Is My Heart 1090
Blonde 1173, 1174
Broke Heart Blues 1173, 1174
Demon and Other Tales 700
Faithless 1173, 1174, 1199, 1203
Foxfire 1172
Middle Age 1112, 1163, 1173, **1174**
Them 1174
We Were the Mulvaneys 1174
What I Lived For 1131
Where I've Been and Where I'm Going 1173

O'Brian, Patrick
The Aubrey-Maturin Series 854

O'Brien, Dan
The Contract Surgeon 890

O'Brien, Judith
Ashton's Bride 323

O'Brien, Linda
Beloved Protector 234, **361**, 409
Courting Claire 361
His Forbidden Touch 361
Promised to a Stranger 361

O'Brien, Meg
Crashing Down 387

O'Connell, Mary
Living with Saints **1175**

Odom, Mel
The Lost Library of Cormanthyr 584
The Revenant 584
The Rising Tide 584
The Rover **584**
The Sea Devil's Eye 584

O'Faolain, Nuala
My Dream of You 1111

Offutt, Andrew J.
The Iron Lords 548
The Messenger of Zhuvastou 585
Shadows out of Hell 535
Shadowspawn 599

Ohanneson, Joan
Scarlet Music 1031

O'Hara, John
Ten North Frederick 1090

Ohlrogge, Anne Christine Stuart
The Widow **411**

O'Kane, Leslie
The School Board Murders 218

Oke, Janette
The Another Homecoming Series 977
Beyond the Gathering Storm 1034
The Calling of Emily Evans 1058
Dana's Valley 1032
Drums of Change 1058
Like Gold Refined 1034
The Matchmakers 1024
A Quiet Strength 1034
Return to Harmony 1054
A Searching Heart 1034
The Tender Years 1034
They Called Her Mrs. Doc 1025
When Tomorrow Comes **1034**
The Women of the West Series 1014

O'Keefe, Claudia
Ghosttide 633, 674

Okudzhava, Bulat S.
The Extraordinary Adventures of Secret Agent Shipov 946

Oldenbourg, Zoe
The Heirs of the Kingdom 860, 902

Olds, Bruce
Bucking the Tiger **485**, **1176**
Raising Holy Hell 485, 1176

Oliver, Patricia
Broken Promises 349, **362**
The Colonel's Lady 362
The Lady in Gray 291, 362
Lady Jane's Nemesis 362
Miss Drayton's Downfall 362
Scandalous Secrets 362
An Unsuitable Match 305

Oliveri, Michael
4 X 4 **679**

Olsen, Lance
Burnt 720

Olsen, T.V.
The Burning Sky 487
Deadly Pursuit 486
The Golden Chance 487, 490, 499
Lone Hand 486
The Lost Colony 486
Man Without a Past **486**
Red Is the River 486, 487
Summer of the Drums 873
There Was a Season 487, 873
Treasures of the Sun 486, **487**
Under the Gun 487

Olson, Paul F.
Dead End 648
Post Mortem 633, 674

Oltion, Jerry
Abandon in Place 785
Alliance 785
Frame of Reference 785
The Getaway Special **785**
Mudd in Your Eye 785
Twilight's End 785

O'Nan, Stewart
A Prayer for the Dying 832, 1083

Ondaatje, Michael
The English Patient 876

Onions, Oliver
The Collected Ghost Stories of Oliver Onions 680
Ghosts in Daylight 680
The Painted Face 680
Tragic Casements **680**
Widdershins 647, 680

Orcutt, Jane
Restoration and Romance **986**

Orczy, Emmuska
The Scarlet Pimpernel 307

Ore, Rebecca
Outlaw School 779, 782

Ortolon, Julie
Dear Cupid 226, 354, **363**, 369
Drive Me Wild 292, 363

Orwell, George
1984 782

Osborn, Karen
Between Earth and Sky 447, 507

Osborne, Cary
Iroshi 750

Osborne, David
Murder on Martha's Vineyard 46

Osborne, Maggie
The Bride of Willow Creek **364**
The Brides of Prairie Gold 364
I Do, I Do, I Do 364
The Promise of Jenny Jones 294, 332, 364, 391
Silver Lining 332, 364, 415
A Stranger's Wife 364

Osborne-McKnight, Juliene
I Am of Irelaunde 886

Osier, Jeffrey
Driftglider and Other Stories 688

Oswald, Georg M.
All That Counts **1177**

Overholser, Stephen
A Hanging at Sweetwater 488
Molly and the Confidence Man 488
Search for the Fox 488
Shadow Valley Rising **488**
Track of a Killer 488

Overholser, Wayne D.
Chumley's Gold **489**, 491
Gateway House 490, 491
Hearn's Valley 489, 490
Nugget City 489, 490, 491
The Outlaws 489, 490, **490**, 491
Rainbow Rider: A Western Trio 430, 489, **491**
Riders of the Sundown 491
The Violent Land 490
The Violet Land 489

Ozick, Cynthia
Bloodshed and Three Novellas 1161

P

Pace, Susan
The Rake and the Wallflower **325**

Padgett, Abigail
The Bo Bradley Series 102, 140

Page, Carole Gift
A Bungalow for Two 982, **1035**
Cassandra's Song 1035, 1036, 1044, 1045, 1046
A Child Shall Lead Them 965, 1035, **1036**, 1041, 1043
A Family to Cherish 995, 1035, 1036
A Locket for Maggie 1019, 1035, 1036
Rachel's Hope 1036
A Rose for Jenny 1035, 1036

Page, Jake
Apacheria 804
The Stolen Gods 61

Page, Katherine Hall
The Body in the Big Apple 1037
The Body in the Bog 1037
The Body in the Bonfire **1037**
The Body in the Bookcase 69, 1037
The Body in the Fjord 1037
The Body in the Moonlight 1037
The Faith Fairchild Series 36, 996

Paige, Robin
Death at Bishop's Keep 187
Death at Daisy's Folly 58

Paine, Lauran
The Devil on Horseback 492, 493
The Grand Ones of San Ildefonso 492, 493
The Killer Gun 492, 493
Lockwood 492, **492**, 493
The Prairieton Raid 492, 493
Tears of the Heart **493**
The White Bird 514

Palahniuk, Chuck
Choke 1177

Palfrey, Evelyn
Dangerous Dilemmas **365**

Pall, Ellen
Corpse de Ballet 71

Palmer, Catherine
A Dangerous Silence 1038
English Ivy 1020, 1038
The Happy Room 980, **1038**
Hide and Seek 1038
A Kiss of Adventure 1038
A Touch of Betrayal 1027
The Town Called Hope Series 1014
The Treasure of Timbuktu 1031
A Whisper of Danger 1038

Palmer, Diana
Lone Star Christmas 263

Palmer, Michael
Natural Causes 78

Palmer, Stuart
The Hildegarde Withers Series 191

Palmer, William J.
The Detective and Mr. Dickens 917
The Don and Mr. Dickens 187
The Dons and Mr. Dickens 822, 917, 959
The Wilkie Collins/Charles Dickens Series 172

Pamuk, Orhan
The Black Book 1178
My Name Is Red 1105, 1152, **1178**
The New Life 1178
The White Castle 1178

Pangborn, Georgia Wood
The Wind at Midnight 711

Papazoglou, Orania
Sweet, Savage Death 49

Pappano, Marilyn
Father to Be 366
First Kiss 366
Getting Lucky 366
Heaven on Earth **366**
Season for Miracles 366, 382
Some Enchanted Season 366

Paretsky, Sara
Bitter Medicine 1131
The V.I. Warshawski Series 53

Parini, Jay
The Last Station 946

Park, Severna
Speaking Dreams 774

Parker, Barbara
Criminal Justice 1143
The Gail Connor Series 75
Suspicion of Betrayal 167
Suspicion of Deceit 167
Suspicion of Guilt 167
Suspicion of Innocence 167
Suspicion of Malice 167
Suspicion of Vengeance **167**

Parker, Gary E.
A Capital Offense 1039
Dark Road to Daylight 1039
Death Stalks a Holiday 1039
The Ephesus Fragment 1039
Highland Hopes **1039**
The Last Gift 1039
The Wedding Dress 980, 1024

Parker, Graham
Carp Fishing on Valium and Other Tales of the Stranger Road Traveled 1158

Parker, K.J.
The Belly of the Bow 585
Colours in the Steel 585
The Proof House 585
Shadow **585**

Parker, Robert B.
Death in Paradise **168**
Early Autumn 199
Gunman's Rhapsody 1176
The Jesse Stone Series 47
Looking for Rachel Wallace 190
Mortal Stakes 188
Night Passage 168
Trouble in Paradise 168

Parker, T. Jefferson
Little Saigon 98
Silent Joe 47

Parkinson, Dan
The Gully Dwarves 556

Parks, Tim
Mimi's Ghost 1177, 1187

Parry, Michel
Rivals of Dracula 631

Parry, Owen
The Abel Jones Series 1, 133, 159
Call Each River Jordan **169**, 864, 909, **914**, 964
Faded Coat of Blue 169, 914
Shadows of Glory 2, 169, 914

Parry, Richard
That Fateful Lightning 903

Parsons, Alexander
Leaving Disneyland **1179**

Parsons, Julie
The Courtship Gift 1180
Eager to Please **1180**
Mary, Mary 1180

Partridge, Norman
Bad Intentions 629
Mr. Fox and Other Feral Tales 689
Slippin' into Darkness 664

Parv, Valerie
The Prince's Bride-to-Be 334

Patchett, Ann
Bel Canto 1195

Paton Walsh, Jill
A Desert in Bohemia 1098, 1106, 1168, 1212

Patrick, Erin
Moontide **681**

Patrick, Natalie
The Millionaire's Proposition 268

Patten, Lewis B.
Best Western Stories of Lewis B. Patten 494
Death Rides the Denver Stage 480
Hunt the Man Down 494
A Killing in Kiowa 494
Tin Cup in the Storm Country 494
Trail of the Apache Kid 494
The Woman at Ox-Yoke **494**

Patterson, Harry
The Valhalla Exchange 126

Patterson, James
1st to Die 1181
Cradle and All 1181
Kiss the Girls 1096
Pop Goes the Weasel 1181
Roses Are Red 1127, 1181
Suzanne's Diary for Nicholas **1181**
Violets Are Blue 1153, 1181

Patterson, Richard North
Protect and Defend 1134

Patton, Fiona
The Golden Sword **586**
The Granite Shield 586
The Painter Knight 586
The Stone Prince 586

Paul, Raymond
The Thomas Street Horror 2

Paul, Susan Spencer
Beguiled 368
The Bride Thief 368
The Captive Bride 368
The Heiress Bride 368
The Prisoner Bride **368**, 396
The Stolen Bride 368
'Tis the Season **367**

Paxon, John
The Golden Trail of Murder 465

Paxson, Diana L.
The Book of the Stone 566

Payne, Peggy
Sister India 1208

Peak, Michael
Catamount 574

Peale, Cynthia
Murder at Bertram's Bower 830

Pearlman, Daniel
The Best-Known Man in the World & Other Misfits **786**
The Final Dream and Other Visions 786

Pears, Iain
The Immaculate Deception 164
The Jonathan Argyll Series 134

Pearson, Ridley
The Angel Maker 78

Peart, Jane
The Brides of Montclair Series 1028, 1040
Courageous Bride 977, 1034
The Edgecliffe Manor Series 1015, 1026
A Montclair Homecoming 971, 1035
The Westward Dreams Series 998

Pelan, John
An Antique Vintage 676

Pelecanos, George P.
The Nick Stefanos Series 50, 213
Right as Rain 37

Pella, Judith
Beloved Stranger 1040
Blind Faith 1040
The Daughters of Fortune Series 977
Heaven's Road 1040
The Ribbons of Steel Series 972
Texas Angel 1040
Warrior's Song 1040, 1058
Written on the Wind **1040**

Pence, Joanne
The Angelina Amalfi Series 105, 120

Bell, Cook, and Candle **170**
A Cook in Time 170
Cooking Most Deadly 170
Cook's Night Out 170
Cooks Overboard 170
To Catch a Cook 170

Pendergrass, Tess
Colorado Shadows 495
Colorado Twilight **495**

Pendragon, Michael
Nightscapes 635, 697

Penman, Sharon Kay
Here Be Dragons 952
The Queen's Man 941

Penn, Mary E.
In the Dark and Other Ghost Stories 618

Penzler, Otto
50 Greatest Mysteries of All Time 57

Perez-Reverte, Arturo
The Club Dumas 171, 1182
The Fencing Master 171, 1182
The Flanders Panel 171, 1182
The Nautical Chart **171**, 1144, **1182**
The Seville Communion 171, 1182

Perkins, Wilder
The Bartholomew Hoare Series 12
The Captain Bartholomew Hoare Series 853, 854
Hoare and the Matter of Treason 822

Perrin, Alice
The Sistrum and Other Ghost Stories 618

Perrin, Robert
Jewels 851

Perrine, Jane Myers
The Mad Herringtons 378

Perry, Anne
A Breach of Promise 172, 915
A Century of British Mystery and Suspense 84
Funeral in Blue **172**, 898, **915**
The Silent Cry 172, 915
Slaves of Obsession 133, 159, 169, 172, 909, 915
The Thomas and Charlotte Pitt Series 915
The Twisted Root 172, 915
Weighed in the Balance 172
The Whitechapel Conspiracy 58, 62, 856

Perry, Marta
Desperately Seeking Dad 987, 1021, 1041
The Doctor Next Door 1041, 1046
Father Most Blessed 1041, 1061
A Father's Place **1041**
A Father's Promise 1041
Since You've Been Gone 1041

Perry, Steve
Brother Death 750
The Digital Effect 763

Perry, Thomas
The Jane Whitefield Series 19, 190

Peters, Daniel
The Luck of Huemac 889

Peters, Elizabeth
The Amelia Peabody Series 191
Die for Love 49

Peters, Ellis
The Brother Cadfael Series 865, 944

Peterson, Elizabeth
The Traitor's Daughter **374**

Peterson, Gail
The Making of a Monster 684

Peterson, Tracie
Ashes and Ice 1042
Colorado Wings 1042
Controlling Interests 1006
The Long Awaited Child 1042
New Mexico Sunset 1042
Rivers of Gold **1042**
A Slender Thread 1039
Treasures of the North 1042
The Westward Chronicles 973, 998

Phillips, Carly
Secret Fantasy 240

Phillips, Michael
The Heathersleigh Hall Series 1028
The Russians Series 1003, 1028
The Secret of the Rose Series 1040
The Secrets of Heathersleigh Hall Series 1020, 1027

Phillips, Susan Elizabeth
Dream a Little Dream 369
First Lady 265, 344, 369
Heaven, Texas 354, 376
Kiss an Angel 369
Lady Be Good 369
Nobody's Baby but Mine 369
This Heart of Mine 226, 256, 264, **369**

Phillips, Tori
Fool's Paradise 326
Halloween Knight 368
Silent Knight 266, 396
'Tis the Season **367**

Piccirilli, Tom
Dark Father 682
The Deceased 682
Deep into That Darkness Peering 688
Hexes 682
A Lower Deep **682**
The Night Class 682
Pentacle 682

Pickard, Nancy
The Jenny Cain Series 120
The Mrs. Eugenia Potter Series 207
Ring of Truth 167
The Whole Truth 198

Pickart, Joan Elliot
Man. . .Mercenary. . .Monarch 268

Pickens, Andrea
Code of Honor 370
The Defiant Governess 370
A Diamond in the Rough **370**
The Hired Hero 279, 370, 374, 389
A Lady of Letters 370
The Major's Mistake 370
Regency Christmas Spirits **248**

Piekarski, Vicki
12 Tales Told from Women's Perspective 430
No Place for a Lady **496**

Piel, Stobie
A Patriot's Heart 297

Pierce, Tamora
Wild Magic 594

Piercy, Marge
Gone to Soldiers 1165

Pilcher, Rosamunde
Winter Solstice 1200

Pilpel, Robert H.
To the Honor of the Fleet 866

Pim, Sheila
A Brush with Death 173
Common or Garden Crime 136, 173, 181
Creeping Venom **173**
A Hive of Suspects 173

Pinkwater, D. Manus
Alan Mendelsohn, Boy from Mars 749
Borgel 538

Piper, H. Beam
Empire 777

Plaidy, Jean
Madonna of the Seven Hills 916

Platt, Charles
The Silicon Man 722

Plumley, Lisa
Lawman 361

Plunkett, Susan
Alicia's Song **371**, 372
Bethany's Song **372**
Heaven's Time 371, 372
Soul Survivor 371, 372
Timepool 371, 372
Untamed Time 371, 372

Poarch, Candice
Tender Escape 365
'Tis the Season **300**

Poe, Edgar Allan
Complete Tales and Poems 669

Pohl, Frederik
Annals of the Heechee 785
O Pioneer 780
Stopping at Slowyear 728

Poling, David
Sea of Glory **953**, **1056**

Pomerance, Bernard
We Need to Dream All This Again 890

Porter, Cheryl Ann
Captive Angel 415
Wild Flower 296

Porter, Joyce
The Honourable Constance Ethel Morrison-Burke Series 14, 191

Porter, Margaret Evans
Kissing a Stranger 259

Potter, Alexander
Assassin Fantastic **552**

Potter, Patricia
The Black Knave 373
Broken Honor 347, **373**
The Marshal and the Heiress 373
Starcatcher 373
Starfinder 373
Starkeeper 373
This Perfect Family 339

Pournelle, Jerry
Mercenary 729, 784
Starswarm 780

Powell, Elizabeth
The Traitor's Daughter **374**

Power, Nani
Crawling at Night 1077, 1164

Powers, Anne
Ride East! Ride West! 843

Powers, Tim
Declare 781, 1151

Poyer, David
Fire on the Waters 898

Pozzessere, Heather Graham
An Angel's Touch 265

Pratchett, Terry
The Amazing Maurice and His Educated Rodents **587**, 588
Carpe Jugulum 587
The City Watch Trilogy 588
Feet of Clay 588
The Fifth Elephant 587
Hogfather 588
Jingo 587
The Last Continent 518, 587
The Last Hero 587, **588**
Maskerade 524
The Rincewind Trilogy 588

Pratt, Maureen
Letters of the Heart **233**, **969**

Prawer, Ruth
East into Upper East 1190

Pressfield, Steven
The Legend of Bagger Vance 1132
Tides of War 931

Preston, Douglas
Thunderhead 792

Preston, M.K.
Perhaps She'll Die 465

Price, Charles F.
Freedom's Altar 910

Price, David
The Evil Eye 636

Price, Maggie
Dangerous Liaisons 417

Prill, David
The Unnatural 649

Pronzini, Bill
Bleeders 111, **174**
Boobytrap 174
Casefile: The Best of the "Nameless Detective" 175
Crazybone 174
The Gallows Land 480
Graveyard Plots 175
Illusions 174
More Oddments 142, **175**
The Nameless Detective Series 22
Oddments 175
Sentinels 174
Small Felonies 175
Spadework 99, 147, 174, 175

Prose, Francine
Primitive People 1116

Proulx, Annie
Accordion Crimes 1170
Close Range 891, 1081, 1146
Postcards 1147
The Shipping News 1066

Puig, Manuel
Kiss of the Spider Woman 1145

Pulver, Joseph
Nightmare's Disciple 682

Purtill, Richard
The Mirror of Helen 547

Putney, Mary Jo
Angel Rogue 400
The Burning Point 301
The Diabolical Baron 325
Faery Magic 281, 303, 384
One Perfect Rose 227, 298
Petals in the Storm 308

The Rake 227
Thunder and Roses 227, 298

Puzo, Mario
The Family **916**, 1152, **1183**
Fools Die 1183
The Fortunate Pilgrim 916
The Godfather 916, 1117, 1183
The Last Don 916, 1183
Omerta 916, 1118, 1183
The Sicilian 916, 1183

Pye, Michael
The Drowning Room 939

Pynchon, Thomas
Mason & Dixon 950

Q

Quayle, Marilyn Tucker
The Campaign 1004

Queen, Ellery
Sherlock Holmes vs. Jack the Ripper 62

Quick, Amanda
Affair 375, 377
Desire 321
I Thee Wed 375
Mischief 375
Ravished 309, 400
Slightly Shady 293, **375**, 402, 416
Wicked Widow 375
With This Ring 375

Quiller-Couch, Arthur
Old Fires and Profitable Ghosts 647

Quin-Harkin, Janet
Murphy's Law **24**

Quinn, Elizabeth
A Wolf in Death's Clothing 68

Quinn, Julia
How to Marry a Marquis 229

R

Rabe, Jean
Betrayal **589**
The Dawning of a New Age 589
Day of the Tempest 589
Downfall 589, 612
Red Magic 589
The Silver Stair 589

Rabe, Sheila
The Adventuress 376
All I Want for Christmas 265, 376
Be My Valentine 376
Bringing out Betsy 376
An Innocent Imposter 376
A Prince of a Guy 226, 264, 274, 299, 343, 354, 369, **376**

Rackham, Jeff
The Rag & Bone Shop 833, **917**

Radford, Irene
The Renegade Dragon 557

Rafael, Lev
Burning Down the House **176**
The Death of a Constant Lover 176
The Edith Wharton Murders 176
Let's Get Criminal 176
Little Miss Evil 176

Ragen, Naomi
The Ghost of Hannah Mendes 1064

Rainey, Stephen Mark
Balak 683
Fugue Devil and Other Weird Horrors 683
The Last Trumpet 683
Legends of the Night **683**

Raleigh, Debbie
A Bride for Lord Challmond 258, 377, 378, 393
The Christmas Wish **377**, 378
Lord Carlton's Courtship 377, 378, 420
Lord Mumford's Minx 377, 378
The Valentine Wish **378**
The Wedding Wish 378

Rambach, Peggy
Fighting Gravity **1184**, 1197

Ramon y Cajal, Santiago
Vacation Stories **787**

Ramone, Dee Dee
Chelsea Horror Hotel **684**

Ramos, Octavio Jr.
Smoke Signals 698

Randall, Alice
The Wind Done Gone **918**, 964

Randall, Kimberly
In the Midnight Hour 282

Randall, Marta
Dangerous Games 793
The Sword of Winter 595

Randisi, Robert J.
Alone with the Dead 37, 497
Ghost with Blue Eyes 497
Legend 497
The Masks of Auntie Laveau **177**
Miracle of the Jacal **497**
Murder Is the Deal of the Day 177
Targett 497
Tin Star 497

Raney, Deborah
A Vow to Cherish 1024

Rankin, Ian
Black and Blue 178
Dead Souls 178
The Falls **178**
The Hanging Garden 178
The John Rebus Series 155
Let It Bleed 178
Set in Darkness 178

Ranney, Karen
After the Kiss 309
A Promise of Love 390

Ravenwolf, Silver
Murder at Witches' Bluff 522

Rawn, Melanie
The Exiles 551
The Star Scroll 544

Ray, Angie
Ghost of My Dreams 351

Ray, Francis
Incognito 224, 365
Until There Was You 403
Winter Nights 300

Rayner, Richard
The Cloud Sketcher 877

Reah, Danuta
Listen to the Shadows **179**

Reamy, Tom
Blind Voices 638

Reasoner, James
Antietam 919
Battle Lines 821
Chancellorsville 919
Gettysburg **919**
Manassas 919
Shiloh 919
Vicksburg 919

Recknor, Ellen
Leaving Missouri 483
Me and the Boys 483

Reding, Jaclyn
The Pretender 241

Reece, Colleen L.
Frontiers 969

Reed, Barry
The Deception 1204

Reed, Ishmael
Flight to Canada 846

Reed, Mary
One for Sorrow 180, 920
Three for a Letter **180**, **920**
Two for Joy 180, 920

Reeman, Douglas
The White Guns 866

Reeves-Stevens, Garfield
Shifter 568, 801

Reich, Christopher
The Runner 131, 906

Reichert, Mickey Zucker
The Beasts of Barakhai **590**
Beyond Ragnarok 590
Child of Thunder 590
Prince of Demons 590
Shadow Climber 552
The Unknown Soldier 590
The Western Wizard 590

Reichs, Kathy
The Tempe Brennan Series 66, 197

Reid, Thomas M.
The Temple of Elemental Evil 563

Reilly, Matt
Temple 1070

Reiner, Carl
Continue Laughing 1158

Reisert, Rebecca
The Third Witch **921**

Relling, William
Silent Moon 672

Rembo, Kent
Visiting Hours 663

Remick, Jack
Terminal Weird 616

Rendell, Ruth
A Dark-Adapted Eye 154
The Inspector Wexford Series 23, 43, 116, 179, 186
Talking to Strange Men 214

Resnick, Mike
A Hunger in the Soul 788
In Space No One Can Hear You Laugh 788
Kirinyaga 788
Oracle 755
Outpost 788
Stalking the Unicorn 756
Tales of the Galactic Midway 788
Tales of the Velvet Comet **788**

Reynolds, Alastair
Chasm City 721, 757, **789**
Revelation Space 736, 739, 789, 807, 812

Reynolds, Brad
The Father Mark Townsend Series 35

Reynolds, Clay
Agatite 498
Franklin's Crossing 498
Monuments 498
Players 498
The Vigil **498**

Reynolds, Mack
Brain World 719

Rhine, Robert Steven
My Brain Escapes Me 689

Rhodes, Jewell Parker
Voodoo Dreams 1164

Rice, Anne
Blood and Gold **685**, 713, **922**, 963, 1071, **1185**, 1187
Interview with the Vampire 690
Merrick 685, 1185
The Mummy 922
Pandora 685, 922, 1185
The Vampire Armand 685, 922, 1185
The Vampire Chronicles 922
The Vampire Lestat 621, 685
Violin 1185
Vittorio, the Vampire 685, 922, 1185

Rice, Ben
Pobby and Dingan 1148

Rice, Craig
The John J. Malone Series 56

Rice, Doug
Blood of Mugwump 712

Rice, Patricia
Rebel Dreams 352

Rich, Virginia
The Eugenia Potter Series 1037

Richards, Emilie
Iron Lace 301

Richardson, Evelyn
Fortune's Lady **379**
The Gallant Guardian 278, 379
Lord Harry's Daughter 379, 389
My Lady Nightingale 315, 379
My Wayward Lady 260, 379
The Reluctant Heiress 379
The Willful Widow 257

Richer, Lois
Baby on the Way 1043
Blessed Baby 974, 995, 1041, **1043**
Daddy on the Way 1043
His Answered Prayer 1043, 1047
Mother's Day Miracle 1043
Wedding on the Way 1043

Richler, Emma
Sister Crazy 1206

Richman, Phyllis
The Chas Wheatley Series 105, 138, 170

Ricks, Thomas E.
A Soldier's Duty **1186**

Ridgway, Christie
Wish You Were Here 341

Riggs, Cynthia
Deadly Nightshade 46

Riggs, Paula Detmer
Born a Hero 422

Daddy by Accident 344
Murdock's Family 335

Riley, Eugenia
Bushwhacked Bride 313, 371, 372, 380
Embers of Time 380
The Great Baby Caper **380**
Lovers and Other Lunatics 380
Second Chance Groom 380
Strangers in the Night 380

Riley, Judith Merkle
A Vision of Light 288

Rinehart, Mary Roberts
The Tish Series 191

Ringo, John
Gust Front 729, 765
March to the Sea **809**

Riordan, Rick
The Devil Went Down to Austin 88
The Tres Navarre Series 149

Ripley, Alexandra
Scarlett 918

Ripley, Ann
Death of a Garden Pest 181
Death of a Political Plant 181
The Garden Tour Affair 181
Harvest of Murder **181**
The Louise Eldridge Series 103, 173
Mulch 181
The Perennial Killer 181

Rispin, Karen
African Skies 975
Rustlers 1012

Rivers, Francine
The Atonement Child 966
The Last Sin Eater 1039
Leota's Garden 967, 980, 1038
The Lineage of Grace Series 994, 1053
The Mark of the Lion Series 979, 990, 994
Redeeming Love 988
Unashamed 1110

Rizzo, Kay D.
The Serenity Inn Series 1014

Rizzolo, S.K.
The Rose in the Wheel **182**

Robards, Karen
Ghost Moon 381
Heartbreaker 381
One Summer 231, 412
Paradise County 381
Scandalous 293, 346, 375, 381, 402, 416
The Senator's Wife 312, 381
This Side of Heaven 297, 352
To Trust a Stranger **381**

Robb, Candace M.
The Nun's Tale 70

Robb, J.D.
Betrayal in Death 1166

Robbins, David L.
The War of the Rats 131, 215

Robbins, Harold
Tycoon 1084

Roberson, Jennifer
Children of the Lion **591**
Legacy of the Wolf 591, **592**
The Lion Throne **593**
Shapechanger's Song 576, 591, 592, 593
Sword-Born 580, 591, 592, 593
Sword-Breaker 592, 593
Sword-Maker 593
Sword-Singer 593
Swordmaker 592
Swordsinger 591, 592
A Tapestry of Lions 591

Roberts, Adam
On **790**
Salt 790

Roberts, David
The Bones of the Buried **183**, 839, **923**, 943
Sweet Poison 183, 923

Roberts, Gillian
The Amanda Pepper Series 6, 81, 106
Whatever Doesn't Kill You 139

Roberts, John Maddox
The Catiline Conspiracy 184, 924
Desperate Highway 924
The King's Gambit 184
Nobody Loves a Centurion **184**, **924**, 931
The Sacrilege 184, 924
Saturnalia 184, 924
SPQR 924
The SPQR Series 920
The Strayed Sheep of Charun 718
Temple of the Muses 184

Roberts, Keith
The Furies 762

Roberts, Les
The Best Kept Secret 185
The Chinese Fire Drill **185**
Cleveland Local 185
The Dutch 185
Indian Sign 185
A Shoot in Cleveland 185

Roberts, Lillian H.
The Andi Pauling Series 45

Roberts, Meg-Lynn
An Alluring Lady 393

Roberts, Michele
Daughters of the House 925
Impossible Saints 925
The Looking Glass 870, **925**
A Piece of the Night 925
The Wild Girl 925

Roberts, Nora
Born in Ice 1187
Brazen Virtue 245
Carnal Innocence 395, 412
Carolina Moon 331, 340, 383
Considering Kate 343, 382
Dance to the Piper 1187
Dance upon the Air **382**, 383
The Donovan Legacy 1187
Heart of the Sea 287, 383
Heaven and Earth 256, 382, **383**
Jewels of the Sun 351, 384
Midnight Bayou 382, **1187**
Night Shield 251, 383
Once upon a Castle 384
Once upon a Dream 384
Once upon a Rose **384**
Once upon a Star 384
Public Secrets 412
River's End 1169, 1174, 1187
Secret Star 382
Tears of the Moon 383
The Villa 301, 382, 1187

Robinett, Stephen
The Man Responsible 763

Robins, Madeleine
The Stone War 614

Robinson, Frank M.
The Power 775

Robinson, Kim Stanley
Remaking History 760

Robinson, Lynda S.
The Lord Meren Series 101

Robinson, Peter
Aftermath **186**
The Alan Banks Series 23, 97, 116, 155, 179
Blood at the Root 186
Cold Is the Grave 186
Final Account 186
In a Dry Season 186
Innocent Graves 186
Not Safe After Dark and Other Stories 142, 146

Robison, Mary
Amateur's Guide to the Night 1188
Believe Them 1188
Days 1188
Subtraction 1188
Why Did I Ever? **1188**

Rochelle, Warren
The Wild Boy **791**

Rodda, Emily
The Pigs Are Flying 594
Rowan of Rin **594**

Roddy, Lee
The Pinkerton Lady Series 972

Roden, Barbara
Shadows and Silence 674

Roderus, Frank
Charlie and the Sir **499**
Hayseed 499
Jason Evers: His Own Story 499
Left to Die 499
Stillwater Smith 499
Trooper Donovan 499

Rodgers, Alan
Fire 708
New Life for the Dead 683
Pandora 661

Rofheart, Martha
Lionheart! 941

Rogers, Evelyn
Devil in the Dark 360, 418

Rogers, Rosemary
All I Desire 385
A Dangerous Man 385
In Your Arms 385
Midnight Lady 385
A Reckless Encounter **385**
Savage Desire 385

Rogow, Roberta
The Charles Dodgson/Arthur Conan Doyle Series 927, 959
The Problem of the Evil Editor 187, 926
The Problem of the Missing Miss 187, 926
The Problem of the Spiteful Spiritualist 187, 926
The Problem of the Surly Servant **187**, 915, **926**

Rohan, Michael Scott
The Castle of the Winds 595
Chase the Morning 595
Cloud Castles 595
The Gates of Noon 595
Maxie's Demon 595
Shadow of the Seer **595**

Roiphe, Katie
Last Night in Paradise 1189
The Morning After 1189
Still She Haunts Me 847, 926, **927**, **1189**

Rolens, Sharon
Worthy's Town 882, 1066

Rollins, James
Deep Fathom **792**
Excavation 792
Subterranean 792

Rolt, L.T.C.
Sleep No More 650

Romkey, Michael
I, Vampire 621, 686
The London Vampire Panic **686**
Vampire Hunter 686
The Vampire Papers 686
The Vampire Princess 686
The Vampire Virus 686

Roorbach, Bill
Big Bend 1149

Roos, Kelly
Murder on Martha's Vineyard 46

Roosevelt, Elliott
Hyde Park Murder 33
Murder at Midnight 928
Murder at the Palace 136
Murder at the President's Door **928**
Murder in Georgetown 928
Murder in the Chateau 928
Murder in the Lincoln Bedroom 928
Murder in the Map Room 928

Roper, Gayle G.
The Amhearst Mysteries 970
The Amhearst Series 985, 1008, 1009, 1037
The Document 1018
The Key 971, 992, 1035

Rose, Gerald
Out There **793**

Rosemoor, Patricia
Heart of a Lawman 387, 413

Rosen, R.D.
Dead Ball **188**
Fadeaway 188
Saturday Night Dead 188
Strike Three, You're Dead 188
World of Hurt 188

Rosenberg, Joel
Not for Glory 784, 809

Rosny, J.H.
Quest of the Dawn Man 723

Ross, Adrian
The Hole of the Pit 644

Ross, Deborah
The Fall of Neskaya **725**

Ross, JoAnn
Fair Haven 386
Far Harbor 239
Legends Lake **386**
Secret Sins 386
Southern Comforts 386

Ross, Kate
The Julian Kestrel Series 10, 12, 820

Roth, Henry
A Star Shines over Mt. Morris Park 1160

Roth, Philip
The Dying Animal 1173, 1177, 1184
Goodbye, Columbus and Five Short Stories 1072
I Married a Communist 1191

Rothenberg, Rebecca
The Bulrush Murders 189
The Dandelion Murders 189
The Shy Tulip Murders 189
The Tumbleweed Murders **189**

Routley, Jane
Fire Angels 572

Rovin, Jeff
Re-Animator 691
Vespers 714

Rowe, Rosemary
The Germanicus Mosaic 180

Rowland, Laura Joh
The Sano Ichiro Series 150

Rowlands, Betty
The Melissa Craig Series 27, 54

Rowlands, David G.
The Executor and Other Ghost Stories 652

Rowley, Christopher
Vang: The Military Form 740

Rowling, J.K.
Harry Potter and the Goblet of Fire 542

Rozan, S.K.
Reflecting the Sky 185

Rucka, Greg
The Atticus Kodiak Series 111
Critical Space 123, **190**
Finder 190
Keeper 190
Shooting at Midnight 190
Smoker 190

Rudel, Anthony J.
Imagining Don Giovanni 852, **929**

Ruryk, Jean
Next Week Will Be Better 69, 160

Rusch, Kristine Kathryn
The Changeling 575
The Fey: Sacrifice 527
The Rival 591
Smoke-Filled Rooms **166**

Rushdie, Salman
Fury 1170, **1190**, 1193
The Ground Beneath Her Feet 1143, 1189, 1190
Midnight's Children 1190
The Moor's Last Sigh 1190
The Satanic Verses 1105, 1152, 1178, 1190
Shame 1190

Rushford, Patricia H.
The Helen Bradley Series 985, 996, 1009, 1062
Morningsong 1044, 1046

Russ, Joanna
The Female Man 811
The Hidden Side of the Moon 726

Russell, Charlotte Murray
The Bad Neighbor Murder 191
Cook Up a Crime 191
Hand Me a Crime 191
Ill Met in Mexico 191
The Message of the Mute Dog **191**
No Time for Crime 191

Russell, Eric Frank
Dreadful Sanctuary 794
Entities **794**
The Great Explosion 794
Major Ingredients 715, 794, 803
Men, Martians, and Machines 794
The Mindwarpers 794

Russell, Josh
Yellow Jack 867, 935

Russell, Ray
Absolute Power 672

Russell, William Clark
The Death Ship 681

Russo, Richard
Empire Falls 1113, 1130, 1136
The Risk Pool 1106

Rutland, Eva
No Crystal Stair 228

Rutledge, Cynthia
Judging Sara 987, **1044**
The Marrying Kind 1044, 1045
Redeeming Claire 997, 1044, **1045**, 1052
Undercover Angel 1044, 1045
Unforgettable Faith 1044, 1045

Ryan, Alan
Halloween Horrors 628
Haunting Women 654

Ryan, Arliss
The Kingsley House 910

Ryan, Nan
A Lifetime of Heaven 241
The Seduction of Ellen 296
Wanting You 324, 342

Rydill, Jessica
Children of the Shaman **596**

Rymer, James Malcolm
Varney the Vampyre 695

S

Saberhagen, Fred
The Dracula Tape 632, 692
The Frankenstein Papers 691
The Mask of the Sun 802
Merlin's Bones 558
Seance for a Vampire 695

Sackett, Jeffrey
Blood of the Impaler 692

Safire, William
Scandalmonger 912

Said, Kurban
Ali and Nino 1191
The Girl from the Golden Horn 1129, 1152, **1191**, 1208

St. James, Lael
My Lady Beloved **405**, 406
My Lady Wayward 405, **406**

St. John, Tina
Lady of Valor 407
Lord of Vengeance 405, 407
White Lion's Lady **407**

Sala, Sharon
Shades of a Desperado 313
Snowfall 395

Saladin, Tariq
The Book of Saladin 1105

Sallee, Wayne Allen
The Holy Terror 687
With Wounds Still Wet 616

Sallis, James
Black Hornet 166, 192
Bluebottle 192
Eye of the Cricket 192
Ghost of a Flea **192**
The Lew Griffin Series 73, 216
The Long-Legged Fly 192
Moth 192

Salmonson, Jessica Amanda
The Golden Naginata 531
What Did Miss Darrington See? 654

Salonen, Debra
Back in Kansas **387**
His Daddy's Eyes 387
Something about Eve 387
Wonders Never Cease 387

Salter, Anna
The Michael Stone Series 197

Salvatore, R.A.
Ascendance 597
Bastion of Darkness 597
The Demon Apostle 597
The Demon Awakens 535
The Halfling's Gem 584
Mortalis 597
Sea of Swords **597**
Servant of the Shard 597
Siege of Darkness 525
Sojourn 556
The Sword of Bedwyr 548

Salzman, Mark
Lying Awake 1175

Sammon, Paul M.
The King Is Dead 684

Samson, Joan
The Auctioneer 668

Samuel, Barbara
The Black Angel 329
Born Brave **422**

Sanchez, Thomas
Day of the Bees 888

Sanders, Lawrence
The Edward X. Delaney Series 152

Sanders, William
Journey to Fusang 778
The Wild Blue and Gray 804

Sandford, John
Certain Prey 908
The Lucas Davenport Series 20, 204

Sands, Lynsay
Lady Pirate 320
Wish List **320**

Santangelo, Elena
By Blood Possessed 1

Saralegui, Jorge
Looker 705

Sarban
Ringstones 529, 559, 598

Sargent, Pamela
Climb the Wind 799
The Shore of Women 747
The Sudden Star 805

Sarrantonio, Al
999 653

Sasson, Jean P.
Ester's Child **930**

Satterthwait, Walter
Escapade 187, 926
The Joshua Croft Series 50
Wilde West 95, 135

Sattler, Veronica
Gabrielle 388
Heaven to Touch 388
Once a Princess **388**
A Promise of Fire 388
A True Prince 388
Wild Honey 388

Saul, John
Black Lightning 627, 687
The Blackstone Chronicles 687
The Manhattan Hunt Club **687**
Nightshade 687
The Presence 687
The Right Hand of Evil 687

Savage, Les Jr.
The Bloody Quarter 500, 501
The Cavan Breed 500, 501
Coffin Gap 439, 443, 460
Gambler's Row: A Western Trio **500**
In the Land of Little Sticks 500, 501
Phantoms in the Night 501
The Shadow in Renegade Basin 431, 455, 500, **501**
The Sting of Senorita Scorpion: A Western Trio 500, 501

Savery, Jeanne
The Christmas Gift 315, 389
A Kiss for Mama **280**
Lady Serena's Surrender 389
A Love for Lydia 389
A Perfect Match 280, **389**
Taming Lord Renwick 389
The Widowed Miss Mordaunt 389

Savile, Steve
Icarus Descending 688
The Secret Life of Colours 688
Similar Monsters **688**

Savory, Brett A.
The Distance Travelled 667, **689**

Sawyer, Corinne Holt
The Angela Benbow/Caledonia Wingate Series 91

Sawyer, Meryl
Kiss in the Dark 302
Tempting Fate 222, 283
Trust No One 381

Sawyer, Robert
Illegal Alien 744

Saxton, Judith
You Are My Sunshine 821

Saylor, Steven
Last Seen in Massilia 184
The Roma Sub Rosa Series 920, 924
A Twist at the End 95, 135

Scarborough, Elizabeth Ann
Acorna's Search **772**
Last Refuge 1078

Scarrow, Simon
Under the Eagle **931**

Schalesky, Marlo M.
The Winds of Freedom Series 1058

Schanker, D.R.
A Criminal Appeal 113

Schechter, Harold
Depraved 932
Deranged 932
Deviant 932
The Hum Bug **193**, **502**, **932**, 936

Nevermore 95, 135, 193, 502, 932
Outcry 932

Schiefelbein, Michael
Vampire Vow **690**

Schildt, Christopher
Frankenstein: The Legacy **691**, 692
Night of Dracula 691, **692**

Schiller, Gerald A.
Deadly Dreams 677

Schlink, Bernhard
Flights of Love 1124, **1192**
The Reader 1192

Schmidt, Anna
Caroline and the Preacher 1045, 1046, 1061
The Doctor's Miracle 1044, **1046**
Give and Take 1046
A Mother for Amanda 995, 997, 1046

Schmidt, Heidi Jon
Darling? **1193**
The Rose Thieves 1193

Schneider, Bart
Secret Love 1119, 1154

Schoemperlen, Diane
Our Lady of the Lost and Found 1175

Schow, David J.
Black Leather Required 624
Crypt Orchids 696
Eye 656
Lost Angels 648

Schuler, Candace
Just Another Pretty Face 333

Schulte, Elaine
Voyage 1049

Schulze, Dallas
The Way Home 239

Schunk, Laurel
Black and Secret Midnight 1051

Scofield, Ruth
In God's Own Time 1047
Loving Thy Neighbor 982, 995, 1036, 1041, 1043, **1047**
The Perfect Groom 1047
Whispers of the Heart 1047
Wonders of the Heart 1047

Scotch, Cheri
The Werewolf's Kiss 322

Scott, Amanda
Border Fire 390
Border Storm 390
Dangerous Lady 390
Highland Spirits 390
Highland Treasure 390
The Secret Clan: Abducted Heiress **390**

Scott, DeLoras
Fire and Ice 391
Garters and Spurs 391
Historical Christmas Stories 391
The Lady and the Outlaw 391
Sarah and the Rogue **391**
Timeless 391

Scott, Eleanor
Randall's Round 650

Scott, Jefferson
Terminal Logic 989

Scott, Joanna
Arrogance 833

Scott, Justin
The Ben Abbott Series 100, 106, 218

Scott, Regina
The Bluestocking on His Knee 356, 392
Catch of the Season 291, 392, 393
A Dangerous Dalliance 392, 393
The Incomparable Miss Compton **392**, 393
The Irredeemable Miss Renfield **393**
The Marquis' Kiss 392, 393
The Unflappable Miss Fairchild 392

Sebald, Winfried Georg
Austerlitz 1171

Seddon, Andrew M.
Imperial Legions 979, 1003

Sedley, Kate
The Brothers of Glastonbury 194, 933, 934
Death and the Chapman 933, 934
Eve of St. Hyacinth 194, 933, 934
The Goldsmith's Daughter **933**
The Holy Innocents 194, 934
The Roger the Chapman Series 86
The Weaver's Inheritance **194**, 875, 933, **934**
The Weaver's Tale 194
The Wicked Winter 194, 933, 934

Segal, Eric
Love Story 1181

Segal, Susan
Aria **1194**

Seger, Maura
Silver Zephyr 401

Segriff, Larry
Past Imperfect **754**

Seidel, Kathleen Gilles
Summer's End 239

Seidick, Kathryn
Bachelor on the Prowl **353**
Love to Love You Baby **354**

Self, Will
Tough, Tough Toys for Tough, Tough Boys 1081

Sellwood, A.V.
Children of the Damned 738

Selwyn, Francis
Sergeant Verity and the Blood Royal 851
The Sergeant Verity Series 172

Senate, Melissa
See Jane Date 252, 345, 357, **394**

Sennett, Richard
Palais-Royal 900

Seranella, Barbara
The Munch Mancini Series 102, 217

Sernovitz, Gary
Great American Plain **1195**

Service, Pamela
Stinker from Space 749

Seth, Vikram
Golden Gate 846
A Suitable Boy 1178

Severance, Carol
The Sorcerous Sea 571
Storm Caller 608

Seymour, Miranda
Daughter of Shadows 916

Shaara, Jeff
The Last Full Measure 903
Rise to Rebellion 840, 939

Shaara, Michael
The Killer Angels 919

Shaffer, Anthony
Sleuth 663

Shakar, Alex
City in Love 1196
The Savage Girl 1177, **1196**

Shames, Laurence
Sunburn 107

Shankman, Sarah
The King Is Dead 77

Shannon, Colleen
The Wolf of Haskell Hall 322, 360, 418

Shannon, Harry
Bad Seed **693**

Shannon, John
The Orange Curtain 98

Sharma, Akhil
An Obedient Father 1129

Sharp, Margery
Miss Bianca 587

Sharpe, Isabel
Follow That Baby! 380
Tryst of Fate 255

Shaw, Allie
The Impossible Texan 234, 419

Shaw, Bob
One Million Tomorrows 722
The Two-Timers 759

Shayne, Maggie
Destiny 382, 395
Eternity 395
Fairytale 384, 395, 401
Forever Enchanted 395, 401
The Gingerbread Man **395**
Infinity 395

Shea, Michael
Nifft the Lean 601

Sheckley, Robert
Can You Feel Anything When I Do This? 727
The Robot Who Looked Like Me 715, 803

Shedd, Margaret
Malinche and Cortes 889

Shelby, Graham
The Devil Is Loose 941

Sheldon, Sidney
The Best Laid Plans 1130
The Doomsday Conspiracy 1082
A Stranger in the Mirror 1158

Shelley, Deborah
It's in His Kiss 223
One Starry Night 255, 353
Talk about Love 343

Shelley, Rick
The Buchanan Campaign 795
Captain 795
Holding the Line **795**
Jump Pay 795
Major 795
Until Relieved 795

Shepard, Lucius
Barnacle Bill the Spacer 760
The Ends of the Earth 582
The Golden 621

Sherburne, Zoe
The Girl Who Knew Tomorrow 776

Sherman, Beth
The Devil and the Deep Blue Sea 81

Sherman, Jory
The Ballad of Pinewood Lake 503
The Baron Brand 503
The Baron Range 462, 497, 503
The Baron War **503**
The Barons of Texas 503
The Columbia River 503

Sherman, Josepha
Forging the Runes 575

Sherwood, John
The Celia Grant Series 173, 181

Shetterly, Will
Dogland 539
Elsewhere 598, 602
NeverNever 568, 614

Shields, Martha
The Blacksheep Prince's Bride 334

Shiras, Wilmar H.
Children of the Atom 753

Shirley, John
. . .And the Angel with Television Eyes **694**
Black Butterflies 616
Cellars 694
Darkness Divided 656
Demons 682, 694
Dracula in Love 692
In Darkness Waiting 694
Really, Really, Really, Really Weird Stories 624
The View from Hell 667, 694
Wetbones 694

Shock, Julian
The Extraterrestrial 737

Shott, James R.
The People of the Promise Series 990, 994

Shrake, Edwin
The Borderland 895

Shreve, Anita
The Last Time They Met 1174
Resistance 1165

Shulgasser-Parker, Barbara
Funny Accent **1197**

Shulman, Sandra
The Florentine 836

Shuman, Malcolm
Assassin's Blood 195
Burial Ground 195
The Last Mayan **195**
The Meriwether Journal 195
Past Dying 195

Shwartz, Susan
Cross and Crescent 796
The Grail of Hearts 566, 570, 796
Second Chances **796**
Silkroads and Shadows 796
Vulcan's Forge 796
Vulcan's Heart 796

Siciliano, Sam
The Angel of the Opera 695
Blood Farm 695
Blood Feud 695
Darkness 686, **695**

Siddons, Anne Rivers
Low Country 1073

Siegenthal, Deborah
My Lady de Burgh **396**

Silber, Joan
Household Words 1198
In My Other Life 1198
In the City 1198
Lucky Us **1198**

Siler, Jenny
Easy Money 50, 199

Silver, Marisa
Babe in Paradise 1107

Silverberg, Robert
The Alien Years 791, 797
At Winter's End 724, 757
Dying Inside 797
Hot Sky at Midnight 797
Lord Prestimion 593, 797
The Sorcerers of Majipoor 592
Starborne 726, 797
Tower of Glass **797**

Silvis, Randall
On Night's Shore 2, 193, 830, 932, 936

Simak, Clifford D.
Empire 768
Out of Their Minds 567
The Visitors 800

Simmons, Dan
Endymion 721, 736
Prayers to Broken Stones 630
The Rise of Endymion 777, 789, 812

Simmons, Deborah
The de Burgh Bride 396
The Gentleman Thief 396
My Lady de Burgh 368, **396**
My Lord de Burgh 396
Robber Bride 396
Taming the Wolf 396

Simon, Frank
The Y2K Bug 989

Simon, Roger L.
The Big Fix 72

Simons, Paullina
The Bronze Horseman 870, 876, 892

Simpson, Donna
Lady Delafont's Dilemma 397
Lady May's Folly 397
Lord St. Claire's Angel 397
Miss Truelove Beckons **397**

Simpson, Dorothy
The Luke Thanet Series 43

Sims, M.P.N.
Hideous Dreams **674**

Sinclair, Andrew
The Facts in the Case of E.A. Poe 193

Singleton, Sarah
The Crow Maiden 568, **598**
In the Mirror 636

Sipos, Thomas M.
Halloween Candy **696**
Vampire Nation 696

Sizemore, Susan
The Hunt 575
Partners 645

Skimin, Robert
The River and the Horseman 824
Ulysses 903

Skinner, Melynda Beth
The Blue Devil **398**

Skinner, Robert
Blood to Drink 196, 935
Cat-Eyed Trouble 196, 935
Daddy's Gone A-Hunting 196, 935
Pale Shadow **196**, 841, 867, 885, **935**
Skin Deep, Blood Red 196, 935
The Wesley Farrell Series 73, 192

Skipp, John
The Bridge 666
Deadlines 679

Sklepowich, Edward
The Urbino McIntyre Series 164

Skvorecky, Josef
Two Murders in My Double Life 1092, 1168

Skye, Christina
2000 Kisses 399
Bride of the Mist 399
Christmas Knight 277
Come the Night 317
Going Overboard **399**
Key to Forever 399
The Perfect Gift 399
Season of Wishes 399

Sladek, John
Keep the Giraffe Burning 798
The Muller Fokker Effect 798
The Reproductive System **798**
Roderick 798
The Steam Driven Boy 798
Tik Tok 798

Slama, Carol D.
Shroud of Silence 1059

Slaughter, Karin
Blindsighted **197**

Slavitt, David R.
Alice at 80 927

Slonczewski, Joan
A Door into Ocean 747
The Wall Around Eden 725

Slotkin, Richard
The Crater 864
The Return of Henry Starr 842

Slung, Michele
Murder for Halloween 628

Small, Bertrice
Intrigued 282

Smedman, Lisa
Tails You Lose 614

Smiley, Jane
Moo 649

Smith, Barbara Dawson
Her Secret Affair 400
Never a Lady 400
Once upon a Scandal 400
Romancing the Rogue 400
Tempt Me Twice **400**
Too Wicked to Love 400

Smith, Bobbi
Tess 361

Smith, Clark Ashton
Out of Space and Time 671
Selected Poems 669

Smith, Cotton
Behold a Red Horse **504**
Dark Trail to Dodge 504
Pray for Texas 504

Smith, David C.
The Fair Rules of Evil 644

Smith, Deborah
Alice at Heart **401**
On Bear Mountain 401
A Place to Call Home 401
Silk and Stone 401
The Stone Flower Garden 401
When Venus Fell 401

Smith, Debra White
The Awakening 1048, 1049
For Your Heart Only **1048**
Second Chances 1023, 1048, 1049, 1055
A Shelter in the Storm 1048, 1049
Texas 1048, 1049
Texas Rose 1049
To Rome with Love 1048, **1049**

Smith, Diane
Letters from Yellowstone 891

Smith, Edward E.
Galactic Patrol 768
The Skylark of Space 785

Smith, Guy N.
Bats out of Hell 714

Smith, Haywood
Border Lord 241, 390
Dangerous Gifts 288
Highland Princess 316, 337

Smith, Janet
The Annie MacPherson Series 63

Smith, Jerry Lynn
The Wedding Charm **258**

Smith, Joan
A Highwayman Came Riding 317

Smith, Julie
Louisiana Hotshot 177
The Skip Langdon Series 88

Smith, Kathryn
Elusive Passion 293, 375, **402**, 416

Smith, L. Neil
The American Zone **799**
Bretta Martyn 799
Contact and Commune 799
The Gallatin Convergence 799
The Nagasaki Vector 799
Pallas 799

Smith, Martin Cruz
The Arkady Renko Series 130
The Indians Won 799
Nightwing 714
Stallion Gate 1078

Smith, Mary-Ann Tirone
An American Killing 198
Love Her Madly **198**

Smith, Michael Marshall
Spares 677

Smith, Sarah
A Citizen of the Country 921

Smith, Sherwood
Augur's Teacher **800**
Journey to Otherwhere 800
Wren's War 800

Smith, Troy D.
Bound for the Promise-Land 505
Caleb's Price **505**

Smith, Wilbur
The Sunbird 792

Smith, Zadie
White Teeth 1082, 1090

Smith-Levin, Judith
The Starletta Duvall Series 21, 220

Smolens, John
Angel's Head 1199
Cold 1195, **1199**
Winter by Degrees 1199

Snaden, Andrew
Betrayed **989**

Snelling, Lauraine
Blessing in Disguise 1050
Daughter of Twin Oaks 1050
A Dream to Follow **1050**
Hawaiian Sunrise 1050, 1059
The Long Way Home 1050
Sisters of the Confederacy 1050

Snoe, Eboni
A Chance on Lovin' You 403
Emerald's Fire 403
Followin' a Dream **403**
The Passion Ruby 403
Tell Me I'm Dreamin' 403
Wishin' on a Star 403

Snyder, Keith
Coffin's Got the Dead Guy on the Inside 199
The Night Men **199**
Show Control 199
Trouble Comes Back 199

Soesbee, Ree
The Crane 531

Sohl, Jerry
The Mars Monopoly 793

Sohn, Amy
Run Catch Kiss 1100

Solomon, Hayley Ann
Seducing Lord Sinclair 420

Soos, Troy
Cincinnati Red Stalkings 119, 200
Hanging Curve 200
Hunting a Detroit Tiger 200
Island of Tears **200**, 203, **936**
The Mickey Rawlings Series 188, 936
Murder at Ebbets Field 200
Murder at Wrigley Field 200

Sorrells, Walter
Blue Plate Special **18**

Soueif, Ahdaf
The Map of Love 1116, 1129, 1178

South, Sheri Cobb
Brighton Honeymoon 404
French Leave **404**
Miss Darby's Duenna 404
The Weaver Takes a Wife 404

Southern, Terry
Candy 1150

Spark, Muriel
Loitering with Intent 1156
The Prime of Miss Jean Brodie 1161

Sparks, Nicholas
A Bend in the Road **1200**
Message in a Bottle 1181, 1200
The Notebook 1200
The Rescue 1200
A Walk to Remember 1200

Spears, Vickie
The Renegade Steals a Lady **414**

Speer, Flora
Love Just in Time 546

Spencer, Catherine
Christmas with a Stranger 306

Spencer, Elizabeth
Jack of Diamonds 1201
The Night Travellers 1201

Salt Line 1201
The Snare 1201
The Southern Woman 1079, 1115, 1157, **1201**
The Stories of Elizabeth Spencer 1201

Spencer, LaVyrle
Morning Glory 290

Spencer, Wen
Alien Taste **801**

Spencer-Fleming, Julia
In the Bleak Midwinter 90

Spillane, Mickey
Black Alley 201
The Killing Man 201
The Mike Hammer Collection. Volume 1 201
The Mike Hammer Collection. Volume 2 201
Together We Kill **201**
Tomorrow I Die 41, 201

Spiotta, Dana
Lightning Field 1107, **1202**

Spofford, Harriet Prescott
The Moonstone Mass 711

Spriggs, Robin
Wondrous Strange **697**

Spring, Michelle
The Laura Principal Series 11

Springer, Nancy
Madbond 590, 592

Sprinkle, Patricia Houck
But Why Shoot the Magistrate? 1051
Carley's Song **1051**
Deadly Secrets on the St. Johns 1051
Death of a Dunwoody Matron 1051
The Remember Box 1051
When Did We Lose Harriet? 1051

Spruill, Steven G.
The Paradox Planet 763
Rulers of Darkness 617, 702

Squire, Elizabeth Daniels
The Peaches Dann Series 15, 77, 129

Stabenow, Dana
Hunter's Moon 68
The Kate Shugak Series 19

Stableford, Brian
The Empire of Fear 685, 713

Stacey, Susannah
The Robert Bone Series 43

Stackpole, Michael A.
The Enemy Reborn 599
Fortress Draconis **599**
Onslaught 599
Prince of Havoc 599
Ruin 599
Talion Revenant 599

Stacy, Judith
The Blushing Bride 284, 408, 409
The Dreammaker 408, 409
The Last Bride in Texas 408, 409
The Nanny 253, **408**, 409
The Widow's Little Secret 234, 247, 408, **409**
Written in the Heart 408, 409, 419

Staley, Shane Ryan
Chocolate Jesus and Other Weird Perversions 698
I'll Be Damned **698**
Sick Days 698

Stallsmith, Audrey
The Body They May Kill 1037

Marigolds for Mourning 1005
The Thyme Will Tell Series 970, 981, 1008

Standiford, Les
Black Mountain 25

Stark, Richard
Backflash 202
Butcher's Moon 202
Comeback 202
Firebreak **202**
Flashfire 202
Plunder Squad 202

Stasheff, Christopher
The Feline Wizard 587
Here Be Monsters **600**
Quicksilver's Knight 600
The Sage 600
The Star Stone 600
A Wizard in Peace 600
A Wizard in War 600

Stashower, Daniel
The Dime Museum Murders 203

Staub, Wendy Corsi
Slightly Single **345**

Staudohar, Paul D.
Golf's Best Short Stories 1132

Steel, Danielle
The House on Hope Street 1101
The Kiss 1203
Leap of Faith **1203**
Lone Eagle 1203
Mirror Image 1203
The Ranch 1203
Silent Honor 1106
The Wedding 1203

Steele, Allen
All-American Alien Boy 802
ChronoSpace **802**
Clarke County, Space 788, 802
Oceanspace 802
Sex and Violence in Zero G 802
The Tranquility Alternative 802

Stegner, Wallace
Beyond the Hundredth Meridian 949

Stein, Kevin
The Brothers Majere 556

Steinbeck, John
The Red Pony 1146

Stengl, Jill
Eagle Pilot 1000
The English Garden **1020**

Sterling, Cynthia
Great Caesar's Ghost 313
A Husband by Law 415

Stevens, Amanda
The Bodyguard's Assignment 410
Forbidden Lover 410
The Innocent **410**
The Littlest Witness 410
Nighttime Guardian 410
Secret Admirer 410

Stevens, Rosemary
The Beau Brummell Series 10, 12, 182, 820
The Tainted Snuff Box 815, 822, 853

Stevens, Serita
The Fanny Zindel Series 129

Stevens, Susan
Double Honor **1002**

Stevenson, Helen
Mad Elaine 1144

Stevenson, Jane
London Bridges **1204**
Several Deceptions 1204

Stevenson, Richard
Third Man Out 897

Steward, Carol
Courting Katarina 251, 1043, 1052
Her Kind of Hero 987, 1021, 1052
Second Time Around 1052
There Comes a Season 1052
This Time Forever **1052**

Stewart, Ed
Terminal Mercy 1012

Stewart, Fred Mustard
Ellis Island 937
The Magnificent Savages 937
The Naked Savages 937
The Savages in Love and War **937**
The Titan 937
The Young Savages 937

Stewart, Mariah
Devlin's Light 410

Stewart, Mary
The Last Enchantment 566
Rose Cottage 9
This Rough Magic 314
Touch Not the Cat 314, 776

Stier, Serena
Deadly Illumination **203**

Stirling, Jessica
The Asking Price 938
Call Home the Heart 938
The Island Wife 938
Prized Possessions **938**
The Strawberry Season 938
The Wind from the Hills 938

Stockley, Grif
The Gideon Page Series 113, 141

Stoker, Bram
Dracula 631, 632, 686, 695

Stokes, Penelope J.
The Amethyst Heart 967
The Blue Bottle Club 1039, 1051
The Faith on the Homefront Series 977, 1034

Stoks, Peggy
The Abounding Love Series 1050
Olivia's Touch 1011, 1025

Stone, Irving
Depth of Glory 837

Stone, Michael
The Streeter Series 213

Stone, Robert
Damascus Gate 902

Stone, Robert S.
Dark Waters 601
Hazard's Price **601**

Stonich, Sarah
These Granite Islands 850, 1077, 1101, 1109

Storey, Gail Donohue
God's Country Club 1144

Storm, Sue
Star Bones Weep the Blood of Angels 689

Stovall, Crystal
A Groom Worth Waiting For 1057
With All Josie's Heart 1022

Stover, Matthew Woodring
Iron Dawn 608

Straight, Susan
Aquaboogie 1205
The Gettin' Place 1205
Highwire Moon **1205**
I Been in Sorrow's Kitchen and Licked out All the Pots 1119, 1205

Straley, John
The Cecil Younger Series 74

Straub, Peter
Black House **659**, **1140**
Magic Terror 1166
Peter Straub's Ghosts 633, 634, 674
Shadowland 644

Strayhorn, S.J.
Black Night 673

Strieber, Whitley
The Forbidden Zone 699
The Hunger 617, 699, 702
The Last Vampire 645, **699**
Majestic 675
Unholy Fire 699
The Wild 699
The Wolfen 699, 1068

Strohmeyer, Sarah
Bubbles Unbound 13, 38

Strong, Christina
The Night the Stars Fell **317**

Stroud, Carsten
Black Water Transit **204**, 1076
Lizardskin 204
Sniper's Moon 204

Stuart, Anne
Lady Fortune 411
Lord of Danger 411
Night and Day 411
Prince of Swords 411
Ritual Sins 283
Shadow Lover 245, 411
Shadows at Sunset 360
The Widow **411**

Sturgeon, Theodore
Baby Is Three 727, 803
The Perfect Host 745

Sturges, Karen
The Phoebe Mullins Series 71

Styron, Alexandra
All the Finest Girls **1206**

Styron, William
Sophie's Choice 1106

Sullivan, Mark T.
The Purification Ceremony 19

Sullivan, Tricia
Dreaming in Smoke 758

Sultan, Faye
The Portia McTeague Series 66

Summers, Cara
Otherwise Engaged 289
While He Was Sleeping 240

Sumner, Mark
The Monster of Minnesota 737
The Prodigal Sorcerer 564

Suri, Manil
The Death of Vishnu 1104, 1170, 1208

Sussman, Susan
Cruising for Murder 816

Sutcliff, Rosemary
Lady in Waiting 883

Sutcliffe, Katherine
Darkling I Listen 411, **412**

Fever 412
Jezebel 412
Moonglow 412
Notorious 412
Whitehorse 412

Swann, S. Andrew
The Dragons of the Cuyahoga **602**
Fearful Symmetries 602
God's Dice 602
Partisan 602
Revolutionary 602
Zimmerman's Algorithm 602

Swann, Thomas Burnett
The Forest of Forever 547
Wolfwinter 595

Swanson, Denise
The Scumble River Series 81

Swanwick, Michael
Gravity's Angels 760

Swerling, Beverly
City of Dreams **939**

T

Tademy, Lalita
Cane River 817, 855, 884, 961, 1089, 1164, **1207**

Taine, John
The Cosmic Geoids 787

Talbot, Michael
The Delicate Dependency 685

Talley, Marcia
The Hannah Ives Series 102
Occasion of Revenge **205**
Sing It to Her Bones 205
Unbreathed Memories 205

Tan, Amy
The Bonesetter's Daughter 1104, 1113, 1129

Tanney, Katherine
Carousel of Progress 1107

Tapply, William G.
The Brady Coyne Series 111, 113, 168
Close to the Bone 206
Cutter's Run 206
Dead Meat 42
First Light **46**
Muscle Memory 206
Past Tense **206**
Scar Tissue 206
The Seventh Enemy 206

Tapsell, R.F.
The Year of the Horsetails 940

Tarr, Judith
Arrows of the Sun 603
Daughter of Lir 818, 879, **940**, 941, 962
The Eagle's Daughter 940
King and Goddess 603, 940
Kingdom of the Grail 603, 829, 901, 941
Lady of Horses 940, 941
Lord of the Two Lands 603
Pride of Kings **603**, **941**
Queen of Swords 941
The Shepherd Kings 940, 941
Throne of Isis 603
White Mare's Daughter 940

Tartt, Donna
The Secret History 82

Tasker, Peter
Samurai Boogie 127

Tatlock, Ann
A Room of My Own 1017

Taylor, Bernard
Sweetheart, Sweetheart 620

Taylor, Harriet Peck
Secrets of the Stone 871

Taylor, Janelle
Can't Stop Loving You 413
In Too Deep 347, 373, 387, **413**
Lakota Winds 413
Not Without You 413
Someday Soon 413
Wild Winds 413

Taylor, Karen E.
Bitter Blood 625
Blood Secrets 645, 699

Taylor, Kathleen
The Tory Bauer Series 13

Taylor, L.A.
Cat's Paw 574

Taylor, Lucy
The Flesh Artist 656
Painted in Blood 624

Taylor, Vickie
The Lawman's Last Stand 414
The Man Behind the Badge 414
The Renegade Steals a Lady **414**
Virgin Without a Memory 414

Tem, Melanie
Desmodus 712

Tem, Steve Rasnic
Absences: Charlie Goode's Ghosts 700
City Fishing 616, 656, 688, 700
Decoded Mirrors 700
Excavation 700
The Far Side of the Lake **700**

Temple, Lou Jane
Bread on Arrival 207
The Cornbread Killer 207
Death by Rhubarb 207
The Heaven Lee Series 105, 138
Red Beans and Vice **207**
Revenge of the Barbecue Queens 207
A Stiff Risotto 207

Tenn, William
Here Comes Civilization **803**
The Human Angle 803
Immodest Proposals 803
Of All Possible Worlds 803
Of Men and Monsters 746, 791
The Seven Sexes 803
The Square Root of Man 803

Tennant, Emma
Sylvia and Ted 848, 852

Tennant, Peter
Death of a Valkyrie 635

Thackara, James
America's Children 1078, 1168

Thames, Susan
I'll Be Home Late Tonight 855

Tharoor, Shashi
The Great Indian Novel 1208
Riot 1152, **1208**
Show Business 1208

Thayer, James
Five Past Midnight 131

Thayer, Steve
Saint Mudd 119

Theroux, Paul
Hotel Honolulu 1092
Millroy the Magician 1095

Thoene, Bodie
All Rivers to the Sea 942, 1053
Ashes of Remembrance 1053
The Galway Chronicles 1026, 1060
Jerusalem Heart 942
The Jerusalem Scrolls 930, **942**, **1053**
Jerusalem Vigil 942, 1053
Jerusalem's Heart 1053
Thunder from Jerusalem 942, 1053
The Zion Covenant Series 942

Thoene, Brock
The Jerusalem Scrolls **942**, **1053**

Thoene, Jake
The Portraits of Destiny Series 1013

Thom, James Alexander
Sign-Talker 957

Thomas, Donald S.
Mad Hatter Summer 187, 927
Sherlock Holmes and the Voice from the Crypt 896

Thomas, Graham
Malice in Cornwall 54

Thomas, Jeffrey
Terror Incognita 639, 693, 697

Thomas, Jodi
The Texan's Dream **415**
The Texan's Touch 415
To Kiss a Texan 415
To Wed in Texas 415
Twilight in Texas 270, 415
Two Texas Hearts 415

Thomas, Ross
The Singapore Wink 185
Voodoo, Ltd. 107

Thomas, Scott
Cobwebs and Whispers **701**

Thompson, James M.
Night Blood **702**

Thompson, Paul B.
Brother of the Dragon **604**
Children of the Plains 604
The Dargonesti 604
The Qualinesti 604
Red Sands 565, 604
Riverwind the Plainsman 604

Thompson, Victoria
The Sarah Brandt Series 24, 200

Thomsen, Brian
The Mage in the Iron Mask 565

Thomson, June
The Inspector Finch Series 43

Thon, Melanie Rae
First, Body 1121, 1162

Thorne, Tamara
Candle Bay **703**
Eternity 703
Haunted 673, 703
Moonfall 703

Thornton, Betsy
The Chloe Newcombe Series 125

Thornton, Elizabeth
The Bride's Bodyguard 416
The Perfect Princess 293, **416**
Prince Charming 416
Princess Charming 309
Strangers at Dawn 416
Whisper His Name 416
You Only Love Twice 416

Thrasher, L.L.
The Lizbet Lange Series 52

Thrasher, Travis
The Promise Remains 1054
The Watermark 1030, **1054**

Thurlo, Aimee
Bad Medicine 506
Blackening Song **506**
Death Walker 506
The Ella Clah Series 35, 39, 61
Enemy Way 506
Red Mesa 506
Shooting Chant 428, 444, 506

Thurlo, David
Blackening Song **506**

Thurston, Carol
The Eye of Horus 101

Tigges, John
Monster 662

Tillis, Tracey
Deadly Masquerade 272
Flashpoint 312, 365
Night Watch 365

Tilton, Lois
Written in Venom 517

Tippette, Giles
Southwest of Heaven 509

Tishy, Cecelia
Fall to Pieces 189

Tobin, Betsy
Bone House 872, 1086, 1091, 1182

Todd, Caroline
Watchers of Time **208**, **943**

Todd, Charles
Legacy of the Dead 208, 943
Search the Dark 208, 943
A Test of Wills 208, 943
Watchers of Time **208**, **208**, **943**, **943**
Wings of Fire 208, 943

Todd, Marilyn
The Claudia Seferius Series 184

Toibin, Colm
Blackwater Lightship 1111

Toland, John
Gods of War 937

Tolkien, J.R.R.
The Hobbit 584

Torres, Ana Teresa
Dona Ines vs. Oblivion 948

Torrey, Joanna
He Goes, She Goes **1209**
Hungry 1209

Tourney, Leonard
The Matthew Stock Series 933, 934
The Players' Boy Is Dead 148

Townsend, Tom
The Dragon Trader 605
Never Trust a One-Eyed Wizard 605
Shadow Kiss **605**
The Trouble with an Elf 605

Tranter, Nigel
Macbeth the King 921

Traver, Robert
Anatomy of a Murder 1139
Travis, Elizabeth
The Ben and Carrie Porter Series 128
Tremain, Rose
Music & Silence 862, 1069
Tremayne, Peter
Act of Mercy **209**, 816, **944**
The Monk Who Vanished 209, 944
The Sister Fidelma Series 70, 180, 865
The Spider's Web 209, 944
The Subtle Serpent 209, 944
Suffer Little Children 209, 944
Valley of the Shadow 209, 944
Tremblay, William
The June Rise **507**, **945**
Trevor, William
Death in Summer 1138
Trobaugh, Augusta
Praise Jerusalem 1029
Trocheck, Kathy Hogan
The Callahan Garrity Series 18, 102
Tronstad, Janet
An Angel for Dry Creek 1035, 1052
A Bride for Dry Creek 1045
A Gentleman for Dry Creek 1022
Trow, M.J.
The Inspector Lestrade Series 958
Tsoutsouris, Linda
Beloved Protector **361**
Tsypkin, Leonid
Summer in Baden-Baden **946**
Tubb, E.C.
Pawn of the Omphalos 769
Turner, Jamie Langston
By the Light of a Thousand Stars 1055
A Garden to Keep **1055**
Some Wildflower in My Heart 1055
Suncatchers 1055
Turner, Nancy E.
These Is My Words 947
The Water and the Blood **947**
Turow, Scott
Presumed Innocent 1074, 1139
Turteltaub, H.N.
Over the Wine-Dark Sea 931
Turtledove, Harry
Aftershocks 606, 804
The American Front 606
The Best Alternate History Stories of the 20th Century **804**
Darkness Descending 606, 804
A Different Flesh 799
Down in the Bottomlands 804
Into the Darkness 606, 804
Marching through Peachtree **606**
Sentry Peak 606, 804
Two-Rivers, E. Donald
Survivor's Medicine 455, 500
Tyler, Anne
The Accidental Tourist 1169
Back When We Were Grownups 1115, 1130, 1136, 1188
Dinner at the Homesick Restaurant 1159, 1195
Saint Maybe 1085
Tyree, Omar
A Do Right Man 1210
For the Love of Money 1210
Just Say No! 1122, **1210**
Single Mom 1210
Sweet St. Louis 1210

U

Ulitskaya, Ludmila
The Funeral Party 1151
Unsworth, Barry
Losing Nelson 1069
Pascali's Island 893
Updike, John
Licks of Love 1072
The Witches of Eastwick 382, 1068
Urbancik, John
A Game of Colors **704**
Uris, Leon
Exodus 942

V

van Belkom, Edo
Death Drives a Semi 658, 693, 705
Lord Soth 705
Six-Inch Spikes 705
Teeth 565, **705**
Wyrm Wolf 705
Yours Truly, Jackie the Stripper 705
Van de Wetering, Janwillem
The Maine Massacre 42
Van Gieson, Judith
Hotshots 140
The Neil Hamel Series 7, 19, 28
North of the Border 39, 149
Raptor 25
Van Thal, Herbert
The Mammoth Book of Great Detective Stories 57
van Vogt, A.E.
Slan 794
Vance, Jack
The Killing Machine 743
Ports of Call 721
Showboat World 788
To Live Forever 794
Vande Velde, Vivian
The Conjurer Princess 605
Magic Can Be Murder 538
Spellbound 519, 594
Vandermeer, Jeff
The Book of Frog 607
The Book of Lost Places 607
City of Saints and Madmen **607**
The Hoegbotton Guide to the Early History of Ambergris 607
Vanneman, Alan
Sherlock Holmes and the Giant Rat of Sumatra 5, **210**
Vansittart, Peter
Hermes in Paris 900
Vardeman, Robert E.
Dark Legacy 564
Vargas Llosa, Mario
Aunt Julia and the Scriptwriter 948
Death in the Andes 1211
The Feast of the Goat **948**, **1211**
In Praise of the Stepmother 948, 1211
The Notebooks of Don Rigoberto 948, 1211
The Storyteller 1211
The War of the End of the World 948
Who Killed Palomino Molero? 948, 1211
Varley, John
Titan 726
Vaughan, Robert
Touch the Face of God 1000
Vaughan, Susan
Dangerous Attraction **417**
Vaughn, Ellen
The Strand 1023
Vazquez Montalban, Manuel
Galindez 948
Verge, Lisa Ann
The Fairy Bride 384
Verne, Jules
Paris in the 20th Century 787
Vernon, John
All for Love 508, 949
A Book of Reasons 949
La Salle 949
The Last Canyon **508**, 827, **949**
Lindbergh's Son 949
Peter Doyle 949
Verweerd, Johanna
The Winter Garden 967, 980
Veryan, Patricia
The Riddle of Alabaster Royal 258
Vidal, Gore
Burr 912
The Golden Age 897, 937, 1066, 1130, 1212
Hollywood 1202
Viehl, S.L.
Beyond Varallan 805
Endurance 805
Shockball **805**
Stardoc 805
Viets, Elaine
The Francesca Vierling Series 53
Vijayaraghavan, Vineeta
Motherland 1104, 1208
Villiers de L'Isle Adam, Auguste
Tomorrow's Eve **806**
Vine, Barbara
Grasshopper 127, 211
No Night Is Too Long 1145
Vinge, Joan D.
The Summer Queen 757, 789
Vinge, Vernor
Across Realtime 807
The Collected Stories of Vernor Vinge **807**
A Deepness in the Sky 734, 807
A Fire upon the Deep 721, 736, 789, 807
Marooned in Realtime 807
Tatja Grimm's World 807
Vitola, Denise
Quantum Moon 801
Vollmann, William T.
Argall **950**, 1091, 1167, 1183, **1212**
Butterfly Stories 950, 1212
Fathers and Crows 950
The Ice-Shirt 950, 1212
The Rifles 905, 950, 1212
The Royal Family 950, 1110, 1176, 1212
Second Dream, Fathers and Crows 1212
Volsky, Paula
Curse of the Witch-Queen 599
Illusion 532
The Wolf of Winter 595
Vonnegut, Kurt Jr.
Bagombo Snuff Box 1081
Vories, Eugene C.
Monte 509
Monte's Revenge **509**
Vreeland, Susan
Girl in Hyacinth Blue 951
The Passion of Artemisia **951**
What Love Sees 951
Vukcevich, Ray
Meet Me in the Moon Room 689

W

Wade, Susan
Walking Rain 9
Wadsworth, Ann
Light Coming Back **1213**
Wagner, Karl Edward
The Year's Best Horror Series 653
Waide, Peggy
Mightier than the Sword 229, 416
Wainscott, Tina
The Wrong Mr. Right 250, 255, 353
Wakefield, H. Russell
They Return at Evening 622
Waldo, Anna Lee
Circle of Stars **510**, 818, 871, **952**, 962
Circle of Stones 510, 952
Prairie 952
Sacajawea 510, 952
Wales, Ken
Sea of Glory **953**, **1056**
Walker, Alice
Meridian 1147
The Way Forward Is with a Broken Heart 1089, 1122, 1207
Walker, Blair S.
The Darryl Billups Series 143
Walker, Dale L.
Legends & Lies 500
Walker, Jim
The Ice Princess 1042
Murder at Gettysburg 133, 159, 169, 898
Murder at Pearl Harbor 1056
The Mysteries in Time Series 1062
The Wells Fargo Trail Series 972, 973
Walker, Margaret
Jubilee 918
Walker, Mary Willis
The Molly Cates Series 98
The Red Scream 167, 198
Wall, Anita
Ties of Love 421
Waller, Robert James
The Bridges of Madison County 1181

Walters, Minette
The Breaker 179, 211
The Dark Room 211
The Echo 211
The Scold's Bridle 211
The Sculptress 154, 211
The Shape of Snakes **211**

Walton, Jo
The King's Name **608**
The King's Peace 608

Wandrei, Donald
Don't Dream 671
Sonnets for Midnight 669

Ward, C.E.
Vengeful Ghosts 652

Ward, James
Pool of Twilight 525

Ward, Linda
A Devilish Husband **257**

Warner, Mignon
The Edwina Charles Series 79

Warren, Pat
The Way We Wed 327, 341

Warrington, Freda
The Amber Citadel 609
The Obsidian Tower **609**
The Sapphire Throne 609
Sorrow's Light 609

Waters, Sarah
Tipping the Velvet 1213

Watson, Colin
The Flaxborough Series 14

Watson, Peter
The Landscape of Lies 134

Watt-Evans, Lawrence
The Book of Silence 548
Crosstime Traffic 610, 727, 766
The Dragon Society **610**
Dragon Weather 523, 526, 550, 610
Night of Madness 572, 610, 611
Out of This World 516, 600, 610, 751
Split Heirs 524, 588
Touched by the Gods 549, 560, 561, 580, 585, 606, 610

Watts, Peter
Maelstrom **808**
Starfish 808

Waugh, Carolyn-Rossel
Thirteen Horrors of Halloween 628

Weatherford, Joyce
Heart of the Beast **511**

Weaver, Carrie
Promises, Promises 341

Webb, Betty
Desert Noir 28, 125

Webb, Debra
The Bodyguard's Baby 410

Webb, Don
A Spell for the Fulfillment of Desire 689

Webb, James H.
Lost Soldiers 1186

Webb, Wendy
Gothic Ghosts 633, 674
Phobias 651

Weber, David
The Apocalypse Troll 809
Ashes of Victory 809
In Enemy Hands 809
March to the Sea **809**
More than Honor 809
The War God's Own 809

Weil, Grete
The Bride Price 858

Weinberg, Robert
The Armageddon Box 706
The Black Lodge 706
Dead Man's Kiss 706
The Devil's Auction 706
Dial Your Dreams **706**
A Logical Magician 706
Rivals of Dracula 631

Weiner, Steve
The Museum of Love 954
The Yellow Sailor 857, **954**

Weinstein, Lewis
The Heretic 956

Weir, Charlene
A Cold Christmas 90, **212**
Consider the Crows 212
Family Practice 212
Murder Take Two 212
The Susan Wren Series 145
The Winter Widow 212

Weis, Margaret
The Dragonking 611
The Elven Star 612
The Ghost Legion 611, 612
Guardians of the Lost **611**
The King's Sacrifice 611
The Lost King 612
The Search for Magic **612**
The Soulforge 611, 612
Testament of the Dragon 612
Well of Darkness 611

Weiss, David
Sacred and Profane 929

Welch, James
Heart Song of Charging Elk 842
The Heartsong of Charging Elk 1176

Welch, Ronald
Knight Crusader 860

Weld, William F.
Big Ugly 955
Mackerel by Moonlight 955
Stillwater **955**

Weldon, Fay
The Cloning of Joanna May 1093

Wellen, Edward
Perps 85

Wellman, Manly Wade
The Devil Is Not Mocked and Other Warnings **707**
John the Balladeer 707
The Third Cry to Legba and Other Invocations 707
The Valley So Low 707
Who Fears the Devil 707
Worse Things Waiting 707

Wells, H.G.
The Best Stories of H.G. Wells 787

Wells, Ken
Junior's Leg **1214**
Meely LaBauve 1214

Welsh, Irvine
Glue 1126

Welsh, Kate
A Family for Christmas 1057
For the Sake of Her Child 968, 1057
The Girl Next Door **1057**
Never Lie to an Angel 1057
Small-Town Dreams 1057
Their Forever Love 1047, 1057, 1061

Wesley, Valerie Wilson
The Tamara Hayle Series 21, 220

Wessel, John
Kiss It Goodbye **213**
Pretty Ballerina 213
This Far, No Further 213

Wesson, Marianne
The Cinda Hayes Series 66
Render Up the Body 167, 198
A Suggestion of Death 121

West, Morris L.
Clowns of God 956
Devil's Advocate 956
Eminence 956
The Last Confession 844, **956**
Lazarus 956
The Shoes of the Fisherman 956
The Tower of Babel 942

West, Paul
The Women of Whitechapel 153

West, Roselyn
The Outcast 273

Westbrook, Robert
The Warrior Circle 80

Westin, Janet Eddy
Love and Glory 228

Westlake, Donald E.
Firebreak **202**
A Good Story and Other Stories 40, 85, 175
The Hook 107
Trust Me on This 115

Wetherell, W.D.
Morning 1084, 1102

Wharton, Ken
Divine Intervention **810**

Wharton, William
Birdy 1141

Wheeler, Joe L.
Christmas from the Heart 1033

Wheeler, Richard S.
Aftershocks 957
Buffalo Commons 957
Cheyenne Winter 426, 429
Dodging Red Cloud 957
Downriver **512, 957**
The Fate 482
Flint's Gift 439, 443, 512
Masterson 457, 488, 512, 957
Restitution 512
Second Lives 957
Sun Mountain 457, 470, 488, 512
Witness 512

White, Gloria
The Ronnie Ventana Series 217

White, James
The Galactic Gourmet 805

White, Karen
In the Shadow of the Moon 418
Whispers of Goodbye **418**

White, Randy Wayne
The Doc Ford Series 94, 115
North of Havana 75

White, Robin
Siberian Light 130

White, Stephen
The Alan Gregory Series 121
Critical Conditions 141
Higher Authority 76
The Program 123, 190

Whitefeather, Sheri
Skyler Hawk: Lone Brave 387

Whitehead, Colson
John Henry Days 1128, 1154

Whitlow, Robert
The List 976

Whitman, David
Scary Rednecks 679

Whitson, Stephanie Grace
Edge of the Wilderness 1058
Heart of the Sandhill **1058**
Karyn's Memory Box 1058
Nora's Ribbon of Memories 1058
Sarah's Patchwork 1058
Valley of the Shadow 1058

Whyte, Jack
The Camulod Chronicles 907
Uther 829

Wick, Lori
Bamboo and Lace 984, **1059**
Beyond the Picket Fence 1059
City Girl 1059
Every Little Thing about You 1059
The Hawk and the Jewel 1042
The Kensington Chronicles 1013, 1015
The Princess 1059
The Proposal 1020
A Texas Sky 1059

Wiggs, Susan
The Charm School 419
Halfway to Heaven 324, **419**
The Horsemaster's Daughter 419
The Hostage 419
The Mistress 342, 419
The You I Never Knew 330, 419

Wilbee, Brenda
Shipwreck 1042

Wilcox, Valerie
The Kellie Montgomery Series 63

Wilde, Oscar
The Picture of Dorian Gray 1126

Wilentz, Amy
Martyrs' Crossing 1109

Wilkins, Gina
A Perfect Stranger 242

Wilkinson, Cherry
Seducing Mr. Right **223**

Wilks, Eileen
The Pregnant Heiress 246

Willard, Fred
Down on Ponce 18

Willard, Tom
The Black Sabre Chronicles 864
Wings of Honor 509

Williams, Charles
Dead Calm 171

Williams, Cindy Harris
A Scandalous Wager **420**

Williams, Conrad
Head Injuries 708
Nearly People **708**

Williams, Gerard
Dr. Mortimer and the Aldgate Mystery 896, 899, 908, 915, **958**
Dr. Mortimer and the Barking Man Mystery 58, 958

Williams, Harper
The Thing in the Woods 646

Williams, Jeanne
Home Mountain 482

Williams, Joy
The Quick and the Dead 1148

Williams, Sean
A Dark Imbalance 743

Williams, Sheila
A Woman's Liberation **811**

Williams, Tad
Caliban's Hour 536
Otherland 554, 555, 560
The Sea of Silver Light 571
The Stone of Farewell 530, 580, 609

Williams, Walter Jon
Metropolitan 721, 789

Williamson, Chet
Lowland Rider 687

Williamson, J.N.
Affinity **709**
Blood Lines 709
The Book of Websters 709
Frights of Fancy 693
The Haunt 641, 709
The Monastery 709
The Night Seasons 709

Williamson, Penn
Mortal Sins 867

Willingham, Bess
Bedeviled Barrister 420
The Husband Hunt 420
The Lady's Mummy 420
The Minx of Mayfair 420
A Scandalous Wager **420**
The Smuggler's Bride 420

Willis, Connie
The Bellwether 811
The Doomsday Book 811
Impossible Things 811
Remake 811
To Say Nothing of the Dog 811
A Woman's Liberation **811**

Willman, Marianne
Once upon a Rose **384**

Wiloch, Thomas
Mr. Templeton's Toyshop 635, 700

Wilson, Charles
Embryo 783

Wilson, Cherry
Outcasts of Picture Rocks 470

Wilson, Colin
The Mind Parasites 670

Wilson, David Niall
The Fall of the House of Escher and Other Illusions 693
This Is My Blood 690

Wilson, F. Paul
All the Rage 710
The Barrens and Other Stories 696
Conspiracies 710
Freakshow 634, 638
Hosts **710**
Implant 677
The Keep 710
Legacies 710
Pelts 666
Reborn 637
Soft and Others 706
The Tomb 710

Wilson, Gayle
Anne's Perfect Husband 260
The Bride's Protector 414
My Lady's Dare 346, 416

Wilson, James
The Dark Clue **959**
The Earth Shall Weep 959

Wilson, John
North with Franklin 905, 949

Wilson, John Morgan
The Benjamin Justice Series 221

Wilson, Laura
Dying Voices 214
A Little Death 214
My Best Friend 82, 211, **214**

Wilson, Mary Ann
Valentine for an Angel 350

Wilson, Rachel
Heaven Sent **421**
Heaven's Promise 421
My Wild Irish Rose 386, 421
Restless Spirits 421
Spirit of Love 421
Sweet Charity 421

Wilson, Robert
The Big Killing 960
Blood Is Dirt 960
The Company of Strangers 131, **215**, 863, **960**
A Darkening Star 960
Instruments of Darkness 960
Second Fire 714
A Small Death in Lisbon 171, 215, 960

Wilson, Sloan
The Man in the Gray Flannel Suit 1141

Wimberley, Darryl
Dead Man's Bay 3, 216
A Rock and a Hard Place 216
Strawman's Hammock **216**

Wind, Ruth
Beautiful Stranger 330, 422
Born Brave **422**
For Christmas, Forever 422
In the Midnight Rain 330, 339, 422
The Last Chance Ranch 225
Meant to Be Married 422
Rainsinger 261
Rio Grande Wedding 422

Windle, Janice Woods
Hill Country 513, 961
True Women 513, 961
Will's War **513**, **961**

Windsor, Linda
Border Rose 1060
Hi Honey, I'm Home 1060
It Had to Be You 1049, 1060
Maire 1060
Not Exactly Eden 1060
Riona **1060**

Wingfield, R.D.
The Inspector Frost Series 44

Winkleman, Betty J.
A Place of Darkness **101**

Winn, Bonnie K.
A Family All Her Own **1061**
Family Found 1061
The Hijacked Wife 1061
The Mommy Makeover 1061
Substitute Father 1061
The Wrong Brother 1061

Winston, Anne Marie
Risque Business 246

Wise, Robert L.
Be Not Afraid 1019, 1039
The People of the Covenant Series 990, 994, 1053
The Tail of the Dragon 989, 991

Wise, Steven W.
Long Train Passing 992

Wiseman, Thomas
A Game of Secrets 928

Wishnia, K.J.A.
23 Shades of Black 217
The Glass Factory 217
Red House **217**
Soft Money 217

Wisler, G. Clifton
Ross's Gap 449, 450

Witherspoon, Mary Elizabeth
The Morning Cool 855

Witten, Matt
Breakfast at Madeleine's 218
Grand Delusion 218
The Killing Bee **218**
Strange Bedfellows 218

Wohl, Burton
Soldier in Paradise 950

Wojtasik, Ted
No Strange Fire 999

Wolf, Joan
The Gamble 348
The Horsemasters 940
Royal Bride 388

Wolfe, Gene
In Green's Jungles 726

Wolfe, Tom
The Bonfire of the Vanities 1190
A Man in Full 1119

Wolff, Isabel
The Trials of Tiffany Trott 252, 357, 359, 394, 1125

Wolverton, Cheryl
For Love of Hawk 968
For Love of Zach 1052
Healing Hearts 1022
This Side of Paradise 1036
What the Doctor Ordered 1046

Wolzien, Valerie
Deck the Halls with Murder 219
Murder in the Forecast **219**
Permit for Murder 219
Shore to Die 219
The Susan Henshaw Series 89
This Old Murder 219
Weddings Are Murder 157

Wood, Barbara
The Dreaming 962
Green City in the Sun 962
The Magdelene Scrolls 962
Perfect Harmony 962
The Prophetess 962
Sacred Ground 818, 871, 879, 913, **962**

Woodman, Richard
The Privateersman 854

Woodrell, Daniel
The Rene Shade Series 112

Woods, James
The General's Dog 183

Woods, Paula L.
The Charlotte Justice Series 21
Inner City Blues 220
Stormy Weather **220**

Woods, Sherryl
Marrying a Delacourt 364

Woodworth, Deborah
Dancing Dead **1062**
A Deadly Shaker Spring 1062
Death of a Winter Shaker 1062
Killing Gifts 851, 1062
A Simple Shaker Murder 1062
Sins of a Shaker Summer 1062
The Sister Rose Callahan Series 33

Woolley, Persia
The Guinevere Trilogy 907

Worcester, Wayne
The Jewel of Covent Garden 158, 210

Work, James C.
Ride South to Purgatory 514
Ride West to Dawn **514**
The Tobermory Manuscript 514

Wormser, G. Ranger
Abraham Goode 711
The Scarecrow and Other Stories **711**

Worster, Donald
A River Running West 949

Worth, Lenora
Ben's Bundle of Joy 995, 1063
His Brother's Wife 1063
Logan's Child 968
One Golden Christmas 1063
The Reluctant Hero 1063
Wedding at Wildwood 1063
When Love Came to Town 1045, **1063**

Wouk, Herman
The Hope 942
The Winds of War 1165

Wright, Sally S.
The Ben Reese Series 156, 996, 1009, 1062

Wright, Stephen
M31 661

Wright, T.M.
The Ascending 712
Boundaries 712
Goodlow's Ghosts 712
The Last Vampire **712**
Little Boy Lost 712
The School 712

Wright, Vinita Hampton
Velma Still Cooks in Leeway 1001, 1002, 1029

Wubbels, Lance
The Gentle Hills Series 1007, 1017
In the Shadow of a Secret 971
One Small Miracle 992, 1051

Wurts, Janny
The Fugitive Prince 585
The Grand Conspiracy 549, 555, 561
The Keeper of the Keys 534, 586
Master of the White Storm 530, 572
Shadowfane 545, 557
The Warhost of Vastmark 560

Wylie, Philip
When Worlds Collide 767

Wyndham, John
The Day of the Triffids 735
Re-Birth 730, 732
The Secret People 582

Stowaway to Mars 785
Tales of Gooseflesh and Laughter 727

Wynn, Patricia
The Birth of Blue Satan 881
The Christmas Spirit 275

Y

Yaffe, James
A Nice Murder for Mom 129

Yan, Gelling
The Lost Daughter of Happiness 817

Yanow, Morton Leonard
The Nolan 956

Yarbro, Chelsea Quinn
The Angry Angel 632, 963
Better in the Dark 621
Blood Games 685
Blood Roses 713, 963
Come Twilight 713, 963
Communion Blood 713, 963
Crusader's Torch 562
Darker Light 963
A Feast in Exile **713**, 922, **963**
Mansions of Darkness 713
Writ in Blood 713

Yates, Richard
Collected Stories of Richard Yates 1072
A Good School 1159

Y'Barbo, Kathleen
The English Garden **1020**

Yeager, Dorian
The Victoria Bowering Series 45

Yeovil, Jack
Beasts in Velvet 613
Drachenfels **613**
Genevieve Undead 613

Yermakov, Nicholas
The Slaying of the Shrew **880**

Yolen, Jane
Briar Rose 579
Child of Faerie 605
The Wild Hunt 538
The Wizard's Map 519, 594

Yorke, Margaret
Almost the Truth 1148
The Patrick Grant Series 97

Youmans, Marly
Catherwood 964
Little Jordan 964
The Wolf Pit 914, **964**

Z

Zahn, Timothy
Angelmass **812**
Conqueror's Legacy 812
Distant Friends 812
The Icarus Hunt 796, 812
The Last Command 812
Spinneret 812

Zakour, John
The Plutonium Blonde **813**

Zambreno, Mary Frances
A Plague of Sorcerers 538, 542, 594

Zaroulis, N.L.
Call the Darkness Light 894

Zelazny, Roger
The Doors of His Face, the Lamps of His Mouth 745
My Name Is Legion 748
A Night in the Lonesome October 623
Nine Princes in Amber 582

Zelitch, Simone
Louisa 1078, 1106, 1135, 1175

Zicree, Marc Scott
Magic Time **614**

Zigal, Thomas
The Kurt Muller Series 108

Zimlich, Jan
The Black Rose 310

Zimmer, Michael
Where the Buffalo Roam 460

Zimmerman, R.D.
The Todd Mills Series 221

Zindel, Paul
The Doom Stone 714
Loch 714
Night of the Bat **714**
Raptor 714
Rats 714
Reef of Death 714

Zollinger, Norman
Riders to Cibola 509

Zubrin, Robert
First Landing **814**

Zubro, Mark Richard
Another Dead Teenager 221
Drop Dead 221
Political Poison 221
Sex and Murder.com **221**
Sorry Now 221
The Truth Can Get You Killed 221

Zucker, Benjamin
Blue 1064
Green 978, **1064**

Title Index

This index alphabetically lists all titles featured in entries and those listed within entries under "Other books by the same author" and "Other books you might like." Each title is followed by the author's name and the number of the entry where the book is described or listed. Bold numbers indicate featured main entries; light-face numbers refer to books recommended for further reading.

A

1st to Die
Patterson, James 1181

4 X 4
Oliveri, Michael **679**

The 7th Guest
Costello, Matthew J. 663

12 Tales Told from Women's Perspective
Piekarski, Vicki 430

23 Shades of Black
Wishnia, K.J.A. 217

24 Hours
Iles, Greg 123

48
Herbert, James 730

50 Greatest Mysteries of All Time
Penzler, Otto 57

100 Wicked Little Witch Stories
Dziemianowicz, Stefan 704

101 Damnations
Harman, Andrew 518

411
Garton, Ray 638

613 West Jefferson
Lliteras, D.S. 988

999
Sarrantonio, Al 653

1812
Nevin, David 912

1945
Forstchen, William R. 864

1984
Orwell, George 782

2000 Kisses
Skye, Christina 399

The $10,000,000 Texas Wedding
Christenberry, Judy 344

The Aaron Gunner Series
Haywood, Gar Anthony 192

Abandon
Hunter, Jillian **303**

Abandon in Place
Oltion, Jerry 785

The Abbess Helewise Series
Clare, Alys 70, 209

The Abel Jones Series
Parry, Owen 1, 133, 159

Abide with Me
Harris, E. Lynn 1122

The Abigail Timberlake Series
Myers, Tamar 67

The Abomination
Golding, Paul 1159, 1198

The Abounding Love Series
Stoks, Peggy 1050

About a Boy
Hornby, Nick 1126

About Last Night
Bond, Stephanie 240

About the Author
Colapinto, John **1092**

Above the Rainbow
Mahon, Annette 343

Abraham Goode
Wormser, G. Ranger 711

Absences: Charlie Goode's Ghosts
Tem, Steve Rasnic 700

Absent Friends
Linscott, Gillian 153, 208

Absolute Power
Baldacci, David 1186

Absolute Power
Russell, Ray 672

Absolute Trouble
Jerott, Michelle 224

Absolutely, Positively
Krentz, Jayne Ann 383

The Accidental Bride
Feather, Jane 276

Accidental Roommates
Maclay, Charlotte 236

An Accidental Shroud
Eccles, Marjorie 64

The Accidental Tourist
Tyler, Anne 1169

According to Queeney
Bainbridge, Beryl **1069**

Accordion Crimes
Proulx, Annie 1170

Ace
Langan, Ruth 327, 328

Acorna
McCaffrey, Anne 755

Acorna's Search
McCaffrey, Anne **772**

Acorna's World
McCaffrey, Anne 725

Across a Moonlit Sea
Canham, Marsha 326

Across a Wine Dark Sea
Bryan, Jessica 401, 562

Across Realtime
Vinge, Vernor 807

Act of God
Healy, Jeremiah 111

Act of Mercy
Tremayne, Peter **209**, 816, **944**

Act of Passion
Miles, Rosalind 907

Acts of Honor
Hinze, Vicki 242

The Actual
Bellow, Saul 1072

Adam and Eve on a Raft
Goulart, Ron **85**, 142

The Adam Dalgliesh Series
James, P.D. 30, 44, 116, 211

Addie and the Laird
Castle, Linda Lea 253

Adventures in Time and Space with Max Merriwell
Murphy, Pat **781**

The Adventures of Allegra Fullerton
Begiebing, Robert J. 894

The Adventures of Dr. Esterhazy
Davidson, Avram 607

The Adventures of Elizabeth Fortune
Cheatham, K. Follis 458, 474

The Adventuress
Rabe, Sheila 376

The Advocate
Mesce, Bill Jr. 906

Affair
Quick, Amanda 375, 377

An Affair of Honor
Hern, Candice 298, 349, 362

An Affair of Honor
Marius, Richard 848

Affinity
Williamson, J.N. **709**

African Skies
Rispin, Karen 975

After All These Years
Isaacs, Susan 1131

After Anne
Henke, Roxanne 992

After Doomsday
Anderson, Poul 818

After Goliath
Cassill, R.V. 858

After I Dream
Lee, Rachel 283, 330, 331, 399

After Shocks
Finch, Paul 652

After the King
Greenberg, Martin H. 753

After the Kiss
Ranney, Karen 309

After the Night
Howard, Linda 411, 412

After the Plague
Boyle, T. Coraghessan **1081**, 1091, 1193

After the War
Adams, Alice 821, 870

After the War
Marius, Richard 855

After Things Fell Apart
Goulart, Ron 730, 738

Afterimage
Humphreys, Helen 877, 927, 1067, 1099, 1102, 1189, 1213

Aftermath
Robinson, Peter **186**

Aftershocks
Turtledove, Harry 606, 804

Aftershocks
Wheeler, Richard S. 957

Against a Dark Background
Banks, Iain 721

Against the Giants
Emerson, Ru 563

Agatha Raisin and the Fairies of Fryfam
Beaton, M.C. 14

Agatha Raisin and the Love from Hell
Beaton, M.C. **14**

Agatha Raisin and the Murderous Marriage
Beaton, M.C. 14

Agatha Raisin and the Terrible Tourist
Beaton, M.C. 14

Agatha Raisin and the Wellspring of Death
Beaton, M.C. 14

Agatha Raisin and the Wizard of Evesham
Beaton, M.C. 14

The Agatha Raisin Series
Beaton, M.C. 27, 96, 191

Agatite
Reynolds, Clay 498

The Age of Miracles
Gilchrist, Ellen 1080, 1162

Agent of Chaos
Etheridge, Rutledge 750

Agent of Destruction
Etheridge, Rutledge 750

Ahab's Wife
Naslund, Sena Jeter 894

Ahmed and the Oblivion Machines
Bradbury, Ray 1082

Airy Hall
D'Aguiar, Fred 846

The Alan Banks Series
Robinson, Peter 23, 97, 116, 155, 179

The Alan Gregory Series
White, Stephen 121

The Alan Markby/Meredith Mitchell Series
Granger, Ann 165

Alan Mendelsohn, Boy from Mars
Pinkwater, D. Manus 749

Aldair, Master of Ships
Barrett, Neal Jr. 524

The Alex Delaware Series
Kellerman, Jonathan 121

The Alex McKnight Series
Hamilton, Steve 90, 93

Alex, the Life of a Child
Deford, Frank 849

The Alexandra Cooper Series
Fairstein, Linda 20

Ali and Nino
Said, Kurban 1191

Alias Grace
Atwood, Margaret 1067, 1139

The Alibi
Brown, Sandra 245, 1086

Alice at 80
Slavitt, David R. 927

Alice at Heart
Smith, Deborah **401**

Alice's Tulips
Dallas, Sandra 877, 1153

Alicia's Song
Plunkett, Susan **371**, 372

Alien Abductions
Greenberg, Martin H. 754

Alien Pets
Little, Denise 574, 575

Alien Rites
Hightower, Lynn 744

Alien Sex
Datlow, Ellen 643

Alien Taste
Spencer, Wen **801**

The Alien Years
Silverberg, Robert 791, 797

The Alienist
Carr, Caleb 203, 932

Aliens Ate My Homework
Coville, Bruce 538

Alight in the Void
Anderson, Poul 807

All about Love
Laurens, Stephanie 329

All about Passion
Laurens, Stephanie 329

All-American Alien Boy
Steele, Allen 802

All Families Are Psychotic
Coupland, Douglas **1094**, 1126

All for Love
Vernon, John 508, 949

All I Desire
Devine, Thea 385

All I Desire
Rogers, Rosemary 385

All I Want for Christmas
Rabe, Sheila 265, 376

All of Us Are Dying and Other Stories
Johnson, George Clayton 678

All Rivers to the Sea
Thoene, Bodie 942, 1053

All Shook Up
Andersen, Susan 292

All Signs Point to Murder
Goldring, Kat **81**

All That Counts
Oswald, Georg M. **1177**

All That Glitters
Morris, Gilbert 1006

All the Dead Were Strangers
Black, Ethan **20**, **1076**

All the Finest Girls
Styron, Alexandra **1206**

All the Queen's Men
Howard, Linda 302

All the Rage
Wilson, F. Paul 710

All Things New
Crow, Donna Fletcher 966

All through the Night
Forster, Suzanne **282**, 285

All Together in One Place
Kirkpatrick, Jane 437, 1011

Alliance
Oltion, Jerry 785

Allies and Aliens
Allen, Roger MacBride 742

An Alluring Lady
Roberts, Meg-Lynn 393

Almost
Benedict, Elizabeth **1073**, 1112, 1163

Almost a Lady
Betts, Heidi 234

Almost Home
Freethy, Barbara 225, 386

Almost No Memory
Davis, Lydia 1099

Almost the Truth
Yorke, Margaret 1148

Alone with the Dead
Randisi, Robert J. 37, 497

The Alpine Icon
Daheim, Mary 51

The Alpine Journey
Daheim, Mary 51

The Alpine Kindred
Daheim, Mary 51

The Alpine Legacy
Daheim, Mary 51

The Alpine Menace
Daheim, Mary 51

The Alpine Nemesis
Daheim, Mary **51**

Altogether in One Place
Kirkpatrick, Jane 470

Always Coming Home
Le Guin, Ursula K. 571

Always Forever
Chadbourn, Mark **533**

Always Outnumbered, Always Outgunned
Mosley, Walter 1166

Always You
Gregory, Jill 294

The Amanda Pepper Series
Roberts, Gillian 6, 81, 106

Amanda's Wedding
Colgan, Jenny 394

The Amarantha Knight Reader
Kilpatrick, Nancy 658

Amateur's Guide to the Night
Robison, Mary 1188

The Amazing Adventures of Kavalier & Clay
Chabon, Michael 874, 1100, 1191

The Amazing Maurice and His Educated Rodents
Pratchett, Terry **587**, 588

The Amazon Quest
Morris, Gilbert 1027, 1028

Amber Beach
Lowell, Elizabeth 340

The Amber Citadel
Warrington, Freda 609

The Amber Room
Bunn, T. Davis 1056

Ambition and Love
Just, Ward S. 1134

Ambrose Bierce and the Death of Kings
Hall, Oakley **95**, **878**, 896

Ambrose Bierce and the Queen of Spades
Hall, Oakley 95, 878

The Ambrose Bierce Series
Hall, Oakley 135

The Ambush of My Name
Marks, Jeffrey **903**

The Amelia Peabody Series
Peters, Elizabeth 191

America, America
Kazan, Elia 1117, 1178

American by Blood
Huebner, Andrew 449, 450, 466, 514, 824, 945

The American Cowboy
James, Will 464

The American Family Portrait Series
Cavanaugh, Jack 1028

The American Front
Turtledove, Harry 606

American Gods
Gaiman, Neil 694

An American Killing
Smith, Mary-Ann Tirone 198

American Star
Collins, Jackie 1108

American Woman
Garcia y Robertson, R. 869, 911

The American Zone
Smith, L. Neil **799**

America's Children
Thackara, James 1078, 1168

The Amethyst Heart
Stokes, Penelope J. 967

The Amhearst Mysteries
Roper, Gayle G. 970

The Amhearst Series
Roper, Gayle G. 985, 1008, 1009, 1037

Among the Missing
Chaon, Dan 1160, 1205

Among the Missing
Laymon, Richard 663, 664

The Amos Walker Series
Estleman, Loren D. 174, 206

Ample Portions
Christner, Dianne 979

Amy, Number Seven
Kaye, Marilyn 776

Anatomy of a Murder
Traver, Robert 1139

Ancient Echoes
Holdstock, Robert 558

Ancient Images
Campbell, Ramsey 619

The Ancient Track
Lovecraft, H.P. **669**

Ancients of Days
McAuley, Paul J. 771

And All through the House
McBain, Ed 152

And One Wore Gray
Graham, Heather 273

. . .And the Angel with Television Eyes
Shirley, John **694**

And This Too Shall Pass
Harris, E. Lynn 1005, 1122

The Andi Pauling Series
Roberts, Lillian H. 45

The Andrew Broom Series
McInerny, Ralph 113

Angel at Troublesome Creek
Ballard, Mignon F. 522

Angel Christmas
Balogh, Mary 366

Angel Face
Forster, Suzanne **283**

Angel Fire East
Brooks, Terry 530

An Angel for Dry Creek
Tronstad, Janet 1035, 1052

Angel in Black
Collins, Max Allan 40, 41, 161, 841, 923

Angel in the Dark
Dain, Catherine 52

Angel in the Front Room, Devil out Back
Diehl, Stanford 1, **59**, 122

The Angel Maker
Pearson, Ridley 78

The Angel of Darkness
Carr, Caleb 936

Angel of Death
Krich, Rochelle 137

The Angel of the Opera
Siciliano, Sam 695

Angel Rogue
Putney, Mary Jo 400

Angel Souls and Devil Hearts
Golden, Christopher 642

An Angel to Die For
Ballard, Mignon F. **522**

Angel with a Sword
Cherryh, C.J. 725

The Angela Benbow/Caledonia Wingate Series
Sawyer, Corinne Holt 91

The Angelina Amalfi Series
Pence, Joanne 105, 120

Angelmass
Zahn, Timothy **812**

Angel's Head
Smolens, John 1199

An Angel's Touch
Pozzessere, Heather Graham 265

The Angry Angel
Yarbro, Chelsea Quinn 632, 963

Angry Young Spaceman
Munroe, Jim **780**

Animus
Kelleher, Ed 641

The Anna Lee Series
Cody, Liza 11

The Anna Papers
Gilchrist, Ellen 1103

The Anna Pigeon Series
Barr, Nevada 3, 7, 19, 102

Annals of the Heechee
Pohl, Frederik 785

Anne's Perfect Husband
Wilson, Gayle 260

Annie Get Your Groom
Gabriel, Kristin 289

Annie, Get Your Guy
Foster, Lori 286

The Annie Laurance/Max Darling Series
Hart, Carolyn 6, 177

The Annie MacPherson Series
Smith, Janet 63

The Annie McGrogan Series
Farrell, Gillian B. 45

Anno Dracula
Newman, Kim 62, 695

The Annotated H.P. Lovecraft
Lovecraft, H.P. 671

Anonymous Tip
Farris, Michael P. 991

Another Chance to Dream
Kurland, Lynn 323

Another Dead Teenager
Zubro, Mark Richard 221

The Another Homecoming Series
Oke, Janette 977

Another Summer
Bockoven, Georgia **239**

Answered Prayers
Capote, Truman 1145

The Anthony Ryan/Joe Gregory Series
Dee, Ed 152

Anti-Man
Koontz, Dean R. 797

Antibodies
Anderson, Kevin J. 715, 737, 773

Antietam
Reasoner, James 919

An Antique Vintage
Pelan, John 676

Antrax
Brooks, Terry **530**, 611

Any Small Thing Can Save You
Adam, Christina **1065**, 1128

Any Way the Wind Blows
Harris, E. Lynn **1122**, 1145, 1210

Anything Goes
Churchill, Jill 33, 839

Apache Fire
Lane, Elizabeth 326

Apacheria
Page, Jake 804

Apaches
Hall, Oakley 878

Aphrodite's Kiss
Kenner, Julie 299, 363

Apocalypse
King, J. Robert **564**

The Apocalypse Troll
Weber, David 809

Apollyon
LaHaye, Tim 1016

Apostrophes and Apocalypses
Barnes, John 722

Appetite for Murder
Lamalle, Cecile 138

Appleseed
Clute, John **736**

The Appointment
Muller, Herta **1168**

The April Fool's Day Murder
Harris, Lee 996

April Is Forever
Fell, Doris Elaine 1019

Aquaboogie
Straight, Susan 1205

Aquarius Descending
Lawrence, Martha C. 140

Arcadia
Crace, Jim 1095

Archangel
Harris, Robert 130

Archer's Goon
Jones, Diana Wynne 519

The Archer's Tale
Cornwell, Bernard 831, **843**, 901

Are You Loathsome Tonight?
Brite, Poppy Z. 658

Arena
Forstchen, William R. 564

Argall
Vollmann, William T. **950**, 1091, 1167, 1183, **1212**

Aria
Segal, Susan **1194**

The Arkady Renko Series
Smith, Martin Cruz 130

Arkansas
Leavitt, David 1145

The Armageddon Box
Weinberg, Robert 706

Arms and the Women
Hill, Reginald 116

Arranged Marriage
Divakaruni, Chitra Banerjee 1104

Arrogance
Scott, Joanna 833

The Arrow over the Door
Bruchac, Joseph 464

Arrows of the Sun
Tarr, Judith 603

The Art of Dying
Killian, Diana **1009**

Artemisia
Banti, Anna 951

Artemisia
Lapierre, Alexandra 951

Arthur
Lawhead, Stephen R. 901

The Arthurian Warlord Trilogy
Cornwell, Bernard 843

The Artist of the Missing
LaFarge, Paul 900

Artorius Rex
Gloag, John 829

As the Sun Goes Down
Lebbon, Tim 666, 698

Ascendance
Salvatore, R.A. 597

The Ascendant Sun
Asaro, Catherine 716

The Ascending
Wright, T.M. 712

The Ash Garden
Bock, Dennis **1078**, 1171

The Ash-Tree Press Annual Macabre 1997
Adrian, Jack 615

The Ash-Tree Press Annual Macabre 1998
Adrian, Jack 615

The Ash-Tree Press Annual Macabre 1999
Adrian, Jack 615

The Ash-Tree Press Annual Macabre 2000
Adrian, Jack 615

The Ash-Tree Press Annual Macabre 2001
Adrian, Jack **615**

Ashenden
Maugham, W. Somerset 118

Ashes and Ice
Peterson, Tracie 1042

Ashes of Aries
Lawrence, Martha C. **140**

Ashes of Elements
Clare, Alys 865

Ashes of Heaven
Johnston, Terry C. 890

Ashes of Remembrance
Thoene, Bodie 1053

Ashes of the Elements
Clare, Alys 875, 933, 934, 944

Ashes of Victory
Weber, David 809

Ashling
Carmody, Isobelle **732**

Ashton's Bride
O'Brien, Judith 323

Asking for the Moon
Hill, Reginald 116

The Asking Price
Stirling, Jessica 938

Asking Questions
Keating, H.R.F. 132

The Aspern Papers
James, Henry 1161

Assassin Fantastic
Greenberg, Martin H. **552**

Assassins
LaHaye, Tim 1016

Assassin's Apprentice
Hobb, Robin 552

Assassin's Blood
Shuman, Malcolm 195

Assassin's Quest
Hobb, Robin 554

The Assemblers of Infinity
Anderson, Kevin J. 798

The Association
Little, Bentley **668**

The Astonished Eye
Knight, Tracy **567**

At End of Day
Higgins, George V. 1076, 1096, 1118, 1123

At Play in the Promised Land
Noble, Diane 1033

At the Mountains of Madness and Other Novels
Lovecraft, H.P. 670

At Winter's End
Silverberg, Robert 724, 757

The Atheling
Chetwin, Grace 776

Athena's Conquest
Blair, Catherine 230, 238, 398

Atlanta Graves
Birmingham, Ruth 18

The Atlantic Abomination
Brunner, John 794

Atlantis Found
Cussler, Clive 1097

Atlantis Found
Garcia y Robertson, R. 546

Atom
Aylett, Steve 720

Atonement
McEwan, Ian 872

The Atonement Child
Rivers, Francine 966

The Atticus Kodiak Series
Rucka, Greg 111

The Aubrey-Maturin Series
O'Brian, Patrick 854

The Auctioneer
Samson, Joan 668

Audubon's Watch
Brown, John Gregory 817, **833**, 913, **1085**

Augur's Teacher
Smith, Sherwood **800**

The Augusta Goodnight Series
Ballard, Mignon F. 9

Aunt Dimity and the Duke
Atherton, Nancy 9

Aunt Dimity Beats the Devil
Atherton, Nancy 9

Aunt Dimity: Detective
Atherton, Nancy **9**

Aunt Dimity Digs In
Atherton, Nancy 9

Aunt Dimity's Christmas
Atherton, Nancy 9

Aunt Dimity's Good Deed
Atherton, Nancy 9

Aunt Julia and the Scriptwriter
Vargas Llosa, Mario 948

The Aurelio Zen Series
Dibdin, Michael 164

Aurian
Furey, Maggie 545

Austerlitz
Sebald, Winfried Georg 1171

Austin City Blue
Grape, Jan **88**

Autumn Flame
Hayworth, Lynne 297

Autumn Kittens
Bennett, Janice **232**

Autumn of the Gun
Compton, Ralph 482

The Autumn of the Patriarch
Garcia Marquez, Gabriel 948

Autumn's Awakening
Brand, Irene 974

Avalon
Lawhead, Stephen R. 570

Avatar
Beman, Donald 620

Avatar
Cadigan, Pat 731

The Avenging Angel
Burns, Rex 76

Avenue X
Collins, Nancy 629

Awakened by His Kiss
Lyons, Judith 341

The Awakening
Smith, Debra White 1048, 1049

Awakening Alex
Langan, Ruth **327**, 328, 347

Awakening Heart
Carlson, Melody 1049

An Awfully Big Adventure
Bainbridge, Beryl 1069

Axiomatic
Egan, Greg 766

Aztec
Jennings, Gary 889

Aztec Autumn
Jennings, Gary 889

Aztec Blood
Jennings, Gary **889**

B

Babe in Paradise
Silver, Marisa 1107

The Baby Bequest
Meier, Susan 341

The Baby Bond
Darcy, Lilian 268

The Baby Bonus
Hingle, Metsy 301

Baby, Don't Go
Andersen, Susan 333, 363

Baby, I'm Yours
Andersen, Susan 289

Baby Is Three
Sturgeon, Theodore 727, 803

Baby Love
Anderson, Catherine 225

Baby Mine
LaPierre, Janet 139

Baby on the Way
Richer, Lois 1043

Bachelor by Design
Gabriel, Kristin 289

Bachelor on the Prowl
Michaels, Kasey **353**

The Bachelor Prince
Macomber, Debbie 474

The Bachelor Tax
Davidson, Carolyn 409

The Bachelor Trap
Gabriel, Kristin 289

Back in Kansas
Salonen, Debra **387**

Back to Malachi
Conley, Robert J. 438

Back to School Murder
Meier, Leslie 157

Back When We Were Grownups
Tyler, Anne 1115, 1130, 1136, 1188

Backflash
Stark, Richard 202

Backstage Murder
Freydont, Shelley 71

Bad Boy
Goldsmith, Olivia 264, 274, 1126

A Bad Day for Ali Baba
Gardner, Craig Shaw 521

Bad Intentions
Partridge, Norman 629

The Bad Lands
Hall, Oakley 878

The Bad Luck Wedding Night
Dawson, Geralyn 319, 408

Bad Medicine
Thurlo, Aimee 506

The Bad Neighbor Murder
Russell, Charlotte Murray 191

Bad News
Laymon, Richard 651

Bad Seed
Shannon, Harry **693**

Bad Timing
Berne, Betsy 1210

Bad Timing and Other Stories
Brown, Molly **727**

Badger Boy
Kelton, Elmer 425, 468, 827, 895, 1137

Bag Limit
Havill, Steven F. **108**

Bag of Bones
King, Stephen 660

Bagombo Snuff Box
Vonnegut, Kurt Jr. 1081

Balak
Rainey, Stephen Mark 683

The Balcony
Morris, Lynn 1049

The Ballad of Pinewood Lake
Sherman, Jory 503

Ballymoon
Gunn, Alistair G. 701

Baltimore Blues
Lippman, Laura 143

Balzac and the Little Chinese Seamstress
Dai, Sijie **1098**

Bamboo and Lace
Wick, Lori 984, **1059**

Bang the Drum Slowly
Harris, Mark 1114, 1132

The Barbed Coil
Jones, J.V. 540

The Bargain
Coughlin, Patricia 261

Barjack
Conley, Robert J. 447

Barnacle Bill the Spacer
Shepard, Lucius 760

A Barnstormer in Oz
Farmer, Philip Jose 577

The Baron
Garnett, Juliana 295

The Baron Brand
Sherman, Jory 503

Baron of the Sacramentos
Blakely, Mike 476

The Baron Range
Sherman, Jory 462, 497, 503

The Baron War
Sherman, Jory **503**

Baroness of Blood
Bergstrom, Elaine 613

The Barons of Texas
Sherman, Jory 503

Baroque and Desperate
Myers, Tamar 163

Barrenlands
Durgin, Doranna 543

The Barrens and Other Stories
Wilson, F. Paul 696

The Bartholomew Hoare Series
Perkins, Wilder 12

Basket Case
Hiaasen, Carl 100, **115**

Bastion of Darkness
Salvatore, R.A. 597

Bats
Johnstone, William W. 714

Bats out of Hell
Hannah, Barry 1121

Bats out of Hell
Smith, Guy N. 714

Battle Lines
Reasoner, James 821

Battleaxe
Douglass, Sara 540

Battlemind
Keith, William H. Jr. 765

The Bavarian Gate
Dalmas, John 741, 742

The Bay of Angels
Brookner, Anita 1073, 1203

Be Cool
Leonard, Elmore 115, 1118

Be My Baby
Andersen, Susan 286

Be My Baby Tonight
Michaels, Kasey 353, 354

Be My Valentine
Rabe, Sheila 376

Be Not Afraid
Wise, Robert L. 1019, 1039

The Beach House
Bockoven, Georgia 239

The Bean Trees
Kingsolver, Barbara 1094

Bear Paw
Mullins, Gene **484**

The Bear Paw Horses
Henry, Will 461, 493

Bear v. Shark
Bachelder, Chris 1084

The Bearkeeper's Daughter
Bradshaw, Gillian 831, 920

The Beast God Forgot to Invent
Harrison, Jim 1199

The Beast House
Laymon, Richard 662

Beasts
Oates, Joyce Carol 1075, **1173**, 1185, 1187

Beasts in Velvet
Yeovil, Jack 613

The Beasts of Barakhai
Reichert, Mickey Zucker **590**

The Beasts of Brahm
Hansom, Mark **646**

The Beau Brummell Series
Stevens, Rosemary 10, 12, 182, 820

Beautiful Stranger
Wind, Ruth 330, 422

The Beauty
Delacroix, Claire 244, 266, 269, 368

Beauty and the Bachelor
Gabriel, Kristin 289

Because It Is Bitter, and Because It Is My Heart
Oates, Joyce Carol 1090

Because of You
Maxwell, Cathy 348

Because You're Mine
Kleypas, Lisa 319

Bedeviled Barrister
Willingham, Bess 420

Bee Season
Goldberg, Myla 978

The Beekeeper's Apprentice
King, Laurie R. 153

Before I Sleep
Lee, Rachel 330, 331

Before She Dies
Havill, Steven F. 108

The Beggar Maid
Munro, Alice 1169

The Beginner's Book of Dreams
Benedict, Elizabeth 1073

Beguiled
Borchardt, Alice 336, 337, 829

Beguiled
Paul, Susan Spencer 368

Behind Time
Abbey, Lynn **515**

Behold a Pale Horse
Musser, Joe 1031

Behold a Red Horse
Smith, Cotton **504**

Beholder's Eye
Czerneda, Julie E. 740

Being Dead
Crace, Jim 1095

Bel Canto
Patchett, Ann 1195

A Belated Bride
Hawkins, Karen 311

The Beleaguered Earl
Lane, Allison 325

Believe in Me
Litton, Josie **336**, 337, 338

Believe Them
Robison, Mary 1188

Bell, Book and Beyond
Cacek, P.D. 704

Bell, Cook, and Candle
Pence, Joanne **170**

The Bell in the Fog and Other Stories
Atherton, Gertrude 711

Bella Donna
Cherne, Barbara **836**

The Bellamy's Blossoms Series
Aiken, Ginny 1063

Bellocq's Women
Everett, Peter 837, 848, 867

Bellows Falls
Mayor, Archer 151

The Bellwether
Willis, Connie 811

The Belly of the Bow
Parker, K.J. 585

Beloved Protector
O'Brien, Linda 234, **361**, 409

Beloved Stranger
Pella, Judith 1040

The Ben Abbott Series
Scott, Justin 100, 106, 218

The Ben and Carrie Porter Series
Travis, Elizabeth 128

The Ben Cooper Series
Booth, Stephen 186

The Ben Kincaid Series
Bernhardt, William 113

The Ben Reese Series
Wright, Sally S. 156, 996, 1009, 1062

A Bend in the River
Naipaul, V.S. 1170

A Bend in the Road
Sparks, Nicholas **1200**

Beneath the Shattered Moons
Bishop, Michael 740

Beneath These Stones
Granger, Ann 87

The Benjamin Franklin Series
Hall, Robert Lee 815

The Benjamin January Series
Hambly, Barbara 2, 73, 196, 207, 867, 935

The Benjamin Justice Series
Wilson, John Morgan 221

The Benni Harper Series
Fowler, Earlene 4, 28, 51, 189

Ben's Bundle of Joy
Worth, Lenora 995, 1063

The Berlin Noir Series
Kerr, Philip 960

The Bernie Gunther Series
Kerr, Philip 126

The Bernie Rhodenbarr Series
Block, Lawrence 16, 72, 202

Bertie and the Crime of Passion
Lovesey, Peter 58

The Bertie, Prince of Wales Series
Lovesey, Peter 62, 851

The Best Alternate History Stories of the 20th Century
Turtledove, Harry **804**

The Best American Mystery Stories
Block, Lawrence 84

Best American Mystery Stories of the Century
Hillerman, Tony 57

The Best Cellar
Goodrum, Charles 128

The Best Intentions
Hern, Candice 298

The Best Kept Secret
Roberts, Les 185

The Best-Known Man in the World & Other Misfits
Pearlman, Daniel **786**

The Best Laid Plans
Sheldon, Sidney 1130

The Best of Cemetery Dance
Chizmar, Richard 653

The Best of D.F. Lewis
Lewis, D.F. 688

The Best of Ghosts and Scholars
Dalby, Richard 650

The Best of Jackson Payne
Fuller, Jack 1122, 1210

The Best of Lester Del Rey
Del Rey, Lester 715

The Best of Robert Bloch
Bloch, Robert 678

The Best Stories of H.G. Wells
Wells, H.G. 787

Best Western Stories of Lewis B. Patten
Patten, Lewis B. 494

Bet Against the House
Dain, Catherine 52

Bethany's Song
Plunkett, Susan **372**

Betrayal
Rabe, Jean **589**

Betrayal in Death
Robb, J.D. 1166

Betrayed
Dow, Rosey **989**, 1048

The Betsy Devonshire Series
Ferris, Monica 4

Better in the Dark
Yarbro, Chelsea Quinn 621

Better than Sex
Holtzer, Susan **120**

Between Earth and Sky
Osborn, Karen 447, 507

Between the Covers
Linz, Cathie 334, 335

Beulah Hill
Heffernan, William 196, 884

Bewitching
Barnett, Jill 821

Beyond Eden
Coulter, Catherine 1108

Beyond Ragnarok
Reichert, Mickey Zucker 590

Beyond the Blue Moon
Green, Simon R. 523, 535, 578, 609

Beyond the Galactic Lens
Kern, Gregory 769

Beyond the Gathering Storm
Oke, Janette 1034

Beyond the Great Snow Mountains
L'Amour, Louis 431

Beyond the Highland Mist
Moning, Karen Marie 358

Beyond the Hundredth Meridian
Stegner, Wallace 949

Beyond the Lamplight
Burleson, Donald R. 706

Beyond the Outposts
Brand, Max 432, 435

Beyond the Picket Fence
Wick, Lori 1059

Beyond the River
McGowan, Wynema 440, 482

Beyond the Shroud
Hautala, Rick 641

Beyond the Sunrise
Balogh, Mary 308, 389

Beyond the Vision
McDonald, Kay L. 466

Beyond the Void
Dalton, Sean 768

Beyond Varallan
Viehl, S.L. 805

Bianca
Elegant, Robert 836

A Bicycle Built for Murder
Kingsbury, Kate 136

Bid Time Return
Matheson, Richard 546

Big as Life
Howard, Maureen 1120

Big Bad City
McBain, Ed 152

Big Bad Love
Brown, Larry 1155

Big Bang
Goulart, Ron 813

Big Bend
Roorbach, Bill 1149

Big Easy Backroad
Hegwood, Martin 112

The Big Fix
Simon, Roger L. 72

Big Gurl
Metzger, Thom 705

The Big Killing
Wilson, Robert 960

The Big Mike Series
Allen, Garrison 26, 162

The Big Picture
Kennedy, Douglas 1177

The Big Thaw
Harstad, Donald 93

Big Thunder
Atkins, Peter 694

Big Ugly
Weld, William F. 955

Biggie and the Fricaseed Fat Man
Bell, Nancy 15

Biggie and the Mangled Mortician
Bell, Nancy 15

Biggie and the Meddlesome Mailman
Bell, Nancy 15

Biggie and the Poisoned Politician
Bell, Nancy 15

Biggie and the Quincy Ghost
Bell, Nancy **15**

The Biggie Weatherford Series
Bell, Nancy 114

The Bighead
Lee, Edward 638

Bikini Planet
Garnett, David **752**

The Bill Crane Series
Latimer, Jonathan 56

The Bill Gastner Series
Havill, Steven F. 93, 151

The Bill Slider Series
Harrod-Eagles, Cynthia 30

Billy Bathgate
Doctorow, E.L. 885

Billy Phelan's Greatest Game
Kennedy, William 897

The Binding Oath
Downing, Sybil 475, 477, 930

The Bingo Palace
Erdrich, Louise 1205

Biofire
Garton, Ray 638

The Biographer's Tale
Byatt, A.S. 1092, 1144, 1182, 1189

A Bird in Hand
Lane, Allison 325

The Bird Yard
Martin, J. Wallis 179

Birdman
Hayder, Mo 1123

Bird's-Eye View
Freedman, J.F. 1076

Birds of a Feather
Lane, Allison 325

Birds of Prey
Jance, J.A. 129

Birdsong
Faulks, Sebastian 857, 925

Birdy
Wharton, William 1141

The Birth of Blue Satan
Wynn, Patricia 881

The Birthday Boys
Bainbridge, Beryl 905, 1069

Birthright
Arnold, Judith 226

The Bishop and the Beggar Girl of St. Germain
Greeley, Andrew M. 1117

The Bishop's Tale
Frazer, Margaret 865

Bite
Laymon, Richard 663, 664

Bitten
Armstrong, Kelley **1068**, 1071, 1185, 1187

Bitter Blood
Taylor, Karen E. 625

Bitter Medicine
Paretsky, Sara 1131

Bitter Sugar
Garcia-Aguilera, Carolina **75**

Bitter Trumpet
Grove, Fred 459

Bitterroot
Burke, James Lee **1088**, 1146

Bittersweet Rain
Brown, Sandra 1086

The Black Album
Kureishi, Hanif 1143

Black Alley
Spillane, Mickey 201

Black and Blue
Rankin, Ian 178

Black and Secret Midnight
Schunk, Laurel 1051

The Black Angel
Samuel, Barbara 329

The Black Book
Pamuk, Orhan 1178

Black Butterflies
Shirley, John 616

The Black Castle
Daniels, Les 685

The Black Chalice
Jakober, Marie **562**, 603

The Black Coat
Little, Constance 144

Black Corridors
Little, Constance 144

Black Cross
Iles, Greg 123

The Black Dahlia
Ellroy, James 161

Black Diamond
Holtzer, Susan 120

Black Dog
Booth, Stephen 23, 179

Black Dust
Joyce, Graham **655**, 700

Black Eagle Rising
Jacoby, Kate 561

The Black Echo
Connelly, Michael 1088

The Black Eye
Little, Constance **144**

The Black Flame
Abbey, Lynn 608

The Black Grail
Broderick, Damien 570, 726

The Black Honeymoon
Little, Constance 144

Black Hornet
Sallis, James 166, 192

Black House
King, Stephen **659**, 1071, **1140**

The Black Knave
Potter, Patricia 373

Black Leather Required
Schow, David J. 624

Black Light
Hunter, Stephen 122, 887

Black Lightning
Saul, John 627, 687

The Black Lodge
Weinberg, Robert 706

Black Mountain
Standiford, Les 25

Black Narcissus
Hamilton, Laurell K. 625

Black Night
Strayhorn, S.J. 673

The Black Rider and Other Stories
Brand, Max 430, 461, 491

The Black Rood
Lawhead, Stephen R. 570, 901

The Black Rose
Due, Tananarive 1089, 1207

The Black Rose
Huebner, Fredrick 121

The Black Rose
Zimlich, Jan 310

The Black Sabre Chronicles
Willard, Tom 864

The Black Spaniel and Other Stories
Hichens, Robert 647

The Black Stocking
Little, Constance 144

Black Sun Rising
Friedman, C.S. 600

The Black Swan
Lackey, Mercedes 568, 569

Black Trillium
Bradley, Marion Zimmer 725

Black Water Transit
Stroud, Carsten **204**, 1076

Black Wine
Dorsey, Candas Jane 747

Black Wing
Kirchoff, Mary 525

Blackening Song
Thurlo, Aimee **506**

Blackfeet Season
Munn, Vella 911

Blackheart Highway
Barre, Richard 189

The Blacksheep Prince's Bride
Shields, Martha 334

The Blackstone Chronicles
Saul, John 687

Blackwater Lightship
Toibin, Colm 1111

Blackwater Sound
Hall, James W. **94**

Blackwater Spirits
Monfredo, Miriam Grace 2, 159, 909

Blade's Lady
Brand, Fiona 242

The Blanchard Secret
Cornick, Nicola 259, 260

Blast from the Past
Friedman, Kinky 72, 1150

The Blazing Tree
Adamson, Mary Jo 2

Bleeders
Pronzini, Bill 111, **174**

Bleeding Maize and Blue
Holtzer, Susan 120, 156

Blessed Assurance
Gurganus, Allan 1120

Blessed Baby
Richer, Lois 974, 995, 1041, **1043**

Blessed Child
Bright, Bill **975**

Blessing in Disguise
Mindel, Jenna **356**

Blessing in Disguise
Snelling, Lauraine 1050

The Blind Assassin
Atwood, Margaret 1073, 1156

Blind Faith
Pella, Judith 1040

A Blind Man Can See How Much I Love You
Bloom, Amy 1147

Blind Voices
Reamy, Tom 638

Blindfold
Anderson, Kevin J. 715

Blindsighted
Slaughter, Karin **197**

Blonde
Oates, Joyce Carol 1173, 1174

Blood
Moorcock, Michael 582

Blood and Burning
Budrys, Algis 803

Blood and Chocolate
Klause, Annette Curtis 322

Blood and Gold
Rice, Anne **685**, 713, **922**, 963, 1071, **1185**, 1187

Blood and Money
Easton, Robert 434

Blood and Rubles
Kaminsky, Stuart M. 130

Blood and Smoke
King, Stephen 1124

Blood and Thunder
Collins, Max Allan 41

Blood and Water and Others
McGrath, Patrick 786

Blood at the Root
Robinson, Peter 186

The Blood Countess
Codrescu, Andrei 922

Blood Country
Logue, Mary 145

Blood Crazy
Clark, Simon 735

Blood Farm
Siciliano, Sam 695

Blood Feud
Siciliano, Sam 695

Blood Games
Killough, Lee **657**

Blood Games
Yarbro, Chelsea Quinn 685

Blood Hostages
King, J. Robert 565

Blood Hunt
Killough, Lee 657

Blood Is Dirt
Wilson, Robert 960

Blood Is Not Enough
Datlow, Ellen 654

Blood Lines
Harrod-Eagles, Cynthia 104

Blood Lines
Williamson, J.N. 709

Blood Links
Killough, Lee 657

Blood Lure
Barr, Nevada 25

Blood Money
Krich, Rochelle 137

Blood Music
Bear, Greg 710, 798

Blood of Heaven
Myers, Bill 1016, 1032

Blood of Mugwump
Rice, Doug 712

Blood of Texas
Camp, Will 495

Blood of the Fold
Goodkind, Terry 549, 550

Blood of the Impaler
Sackett, Jeffrey 692

Blood on the Moon
Cohen, Barney 744

Blood on the Plains
Cole, Judd 484

Blood on the Wind
Bogue, Lucile **426**

Blood Roses
Yarbro, Chelsea Quinn 713, 963

Blood Secrets
Taylor, Karen E. 645, 699

Blood Sinister
Harrod-Eagles, Cynthia **104**

Blood Song
Johnston, Terry C. 466

Blood to Drink
Skinner, Robert 196, 935

Blood Trail
Huff, Tanya 657

Bloodhounds
Lovesey, Peter 146

The Blooding of the Guns
Fullerton, Alexander **866**, 954

Bloodlines
Coleman, Loren 564

Bloodlines
D'Aguiar, Fred **846**

Bloodroot
Albert, Susan Wittig **4**

Bloodroot
Even, Aaron Roy 910, 955

Bloodshed and Three Novellas
Ozick, Cynthia 1161

Bloodstream
Gerritsen, Tess 78

Bloodtide
Burgess, Melvin **730**

The Bloody Benders
Hodgson, Ken 463

Bloody Bones
Hamilton, Laurell K. 645

The Bloody Chamber
Carter, Angela 579

The Bloody Quarter
Savage, Les Jr. 500, 501

Bloody Season
Estleman, Loren D. 485

Bloody Secrets
Garcia-Aguilera, Carolina 75

Bloody Shame
Garcia-Aguilera, Carolina 75

Bloody Waters
Garcia-Aguilera, Carolina 75

The Blossom and the Nettle
Noble, Diane 1033

Blue
Zucker, Benjamin 1064

The Blue and the Gray Undercover
Gorman, Ed **456**

The Blue Bottle Club
Stokes, Penelope J. 1039, 1051

Blue Christmas and Other Holiday Homicides
Collins, Max Allan **40**, 175

The Blue Devil
Skinner, Melynda Beth **398**

Blue Diary
Hoffman, Alice 1086, 1139, 1163

The Blue Jay Shaman
McClendon, Lise 477

Blue Kansas Sky
Bishop, Michael 748

The Blue Last
Grimes, Martha **92**

Blue Light
Mosley, Walter 779, 1126, 1166

Blue Magic
Clayton, Jo 591, 592

Blue Mist on the Danube
Fell, Doris Elaine 992

Blue Moon
Hamilton, Laurell K. 645

Blue Moon
Landis, Jill Marie 297, 471

Blue Moon Rising
Green, Simon R. 548

Blue Nowhere
Deaver, Jeffery 57

Blue Plate Special
Birmingham, Ruth **18**

The Blue Room and Other Ghost Stories
Galbraith, Lettice 618

Blue Wolf
McClendon, Lise **477**

Blue World
McCammon, Robert R. 629, 707

Bluebottle
Sallis, James 192

The Blues Ain't Nothin'
Jens, Tina 684

The Bluestocking on His Knee
Scott, Regina 356, 392

Blush
Forster, Suzanne 283

The Blushing Bride
Stacy, Judith 284, 408, 409

The Bo Bradley Series
Padgett, Abigail 102, 140

Bobby's Girl
Austin, J.D. 719

Bodmin, 1349
Kalechofsky, Roberta 832, 843

Body Guard
Brockmann, Suzanne 222, 399

The Body in the Big Apple
Page, Katherine Hall 1037

The Body in the Bog
Page, Katherine Hall 1037

The Body in the Bonfire
Page, Katherine Hall **1037**

The Body in the Bookcase
Page, Katherine Hall 69, 1037

The Body in the Fjord
Page, Katherine Hall 1037

The Body in the Moonlight
Page, Katherine Hall 1037

Body Language
Craft, Michael 45

The Body on the Beach
Brett, Simon 14, 27

Body Rides
Laymon, Richard 627, 663, 664

The Body Snatchers
Finney, Jack 660, 710

The Body They May Kill
Stallsmith, Audrey 1037

The Bodyguard's Assignment
Stevens, Amanda 410

The Bodyguard's Baby
Webb, Debra 410

Bold as Love
Jones, Gwyneth **764**

Bolo Brigade
Keith, William H. Jr. 765

Bolo Rising
Keith, William H. Jr. 765

Bolo Strike
Keith, William H. Jr. **765**

Bombay Mail
Blochman, Lawrence G. 132

Bombingham
Grooms, Anthony **1119**, 1154

The Bone Doll's Twin
Flewelling, Lynn **544**

Bone House
Tobin, Betsy 872, 1086, 1091, 1182

Bone Hunter
Andrews, Sarah 7

A Bone of Contention
Gregory, Susanna 843

Bone Walker
Gear, Kathleen O'Neal 61, 424, **871**

The Bones of the Buried
Roberts, David **183**, 839, **923**, 943

The Bonesetter's Daughter
Tan, Amy 1104, 1113, 1129

The Boneyard
Nickaell, Robin 639

The Bonfire of the Vanities
Wolfe, Tom 1190

Bonnie Winter
Masterton, Graham **672**

Boobytrap
Pronzini, Bill 174

The Book of Books Series
Cavanaugh, Jack 979, 1003

The Book of Common Prayer
Monahan, Brent 703

The Book of Frog
Vandermeer, Jeff 607

The Book of Guys
Keillor, Garrison 1136

The Book of Hours
Bunn, T. Davis 976, 1010

The Book of Kills
McInerny, Ralph 156

The Book of Lost Places
Vandermeer, Jeff 607

A Book of Reasons
Vernon, John 949

The Book of Saladin
Saladin, Tariq 1105

The Book of Shadows
Grace, C.L. 86, 875

The Book of Silence
Watt-Evans, Lawrence 548

The Book of the Stone
Paxson, Diana L. 566

The Book of Websters
Williamson, J.N. 709

Booked for a Hanging
Crider, Bill 49

Booked for Murder
McDermid, Val 154

The Bookman's Wake
Dunning, John 128

Books of Blood
Barker, Clive 1071

Boomerang
Hannah, Barry 1121

Boone's Lick
McMurtry, Larry 895, 945, 957

Border Crossings
Bellacera, Carole 231

Border Crossings
Fleming, David L. 424

Border Fire
Scott, Amanda 390

The Border Hostage
Henley, Virginia **883**

Border Justice
Bean, Frederic 440

Border Lord
Smith, Haywood 241, 390

Border Rose
Windsor, Linda 1060

Border Storm
Scott, Amanda 390

The Borderland
Shrake, Edwin 895

Borderlands
Blake, James Carlos 825

Borderlands
Coleman, Jane Candia 446, 452

The Borders of Infinity
Bujold, Lois McMaster 728

Bordersnakes
Crumley, James 50

Borgel
Pinkwater, D. Manus 538

The Borgia Prince
Bennetts, Pamela 916

The Borgia Testament
Balchin, Nigel 916

Born a Hero
Riggs, Paula Detmer 422

Born Brave
Wind, Ruth **422**

Born in Ice
Roberts, Nora 1187

Born of Passion
Cassidy, Carla 422

Born to Be Wild
Berg, Patti 363

Born to Exile
Eisenstein, Phyllis 551

Born to Protect
Kantra, Virginia 422

Borrowed Bride
Coughlin, Patricia 261

The Bottoms
Lansdale, Joe R. 887

Bound for the Promise-Land
Smith, Troy D. 505

Boundaries
Wright, T.M. 712

Bow Down to Nul
Aldiss, Brian W. 791

The Bowman Test
Elias, Albert J. 783

A Boy and His Tank
Frankowski, Leo 765

The Boy-Bishop's Glovemaker
Jecks, Michael 875

Boy Toy
Craft, Michael 45

The Boy Who Never Grew Up
Handler, David 100

Boys' Life
McCammon, Robert R. 567

The Boy's Tale
Frazer, Margaret 865

The Brady Coyne Series
Tapply, William G. 111, 113, 168

Bragg's Fancy Woman
Frazee, Steve 453

The Brahmins
Lottman, Eileen 937

Brain World
Reynolds, Mack 719

The Brains of Rats
Blumlein, Michael 616, 624

Brainstorm
Krauzer, Steven M. 709, 775

Brandish
Hirt, Douglas 462

The Brass Command
Henry, Will 441

Brave the Betrayal
Applegate, K.A. 519, 520

Brazen Virtue
Roberts, Nora 245

Breach of Duty
Jance, J.A. 465

Breach of Promise
Fairchild, Elisabeth 275

A Breach of Promise
Perry, Anne 172, 915

Bread on Arrival
Temple, Lou Jane 207

Break It Down
Davis, Lydia 1099

The Breaker
Walters, Minette 179, 211

Breakfast at Madeleine's
Witten, Matt 218

Breakheart Hill
Cook, Thomas H. 59, 82

Breaking and Entering
Keating, H.R.F. **132**

Breath of Magic
Medeiros, Teresa 350

Breath of Scandal
Brown, Sandra 312

The Breeds of Man
Busby, F.M. 753

Brendan
Buechner, Frederick 886

The Brentwood Witches
Jordan, Brenda 543

Bretta Martyn
Smith, L. Neil 799

The Bretta Solomon Series
Harrison, Janis 4, 67

Briar Rose
Yolen, Jane 579

The Bridal Season
Brockway, Connie 321

The Bride
Garwood, Julie 269

Bride and Doom
Hager, Jean 157

The Bride Finder
Carroll, Susan 881

A Bride for Dry Creek
Tronstad, Janet 1045

A Bride for Lord Challmond
Raleigh, Debbie 258, 377, 378, 393

A Bride for McCain
Burton, Mary 247

The Bride-in-Law
Browning, Dixie 246

Bride of Frankenstein
Dreadstone, Carl 691

Bride of the Mist
Skye, Christina 399

The Bride of Willow Creek
Osborne, Maggie **364**

Bride on the Run
Lane, Elizabeth 247, 326

The Bride Price
Weil, Grete 858

The Bride Sale
Hern, Candice 227, **298**

The Bride Thief
Paul, Susan Spencer 368

The Bridegroom
Jin, Ha 1098

The Bride's Bodyguard
Thornton, Elizabeth 416

The Bride's Kimono
Massey, Sujata **150**

The Brides of Culdee Creek Series
Morgan, Kathleen 1014

The Brides of Montclair Series
Peart, Jane 1028, 1040

The Brides of Prairie Gold
Osborne, Maggie 364

The Brides of the West Series
Copeland, Lori 1014

The Bride's Protector
Wilson, Gayle 414

Bridesmaids Revisited
Cannell, Dorothy 31

The Bridge
Skipp, John 666

Bridge over Dark Gods
Morrish, Furze 644

The Bridges of Madison County
Waller, Robert James 1181

Bridget Jones: The Edge of Reason
Fielding, Helen 345

Bridget Jones's Diary
Fielding, Helen 252, 345, 357, 359, 1125

Brigands of the Moon
Cummings, Ray 794

Brigham's Day
Gates, John 76

The Bright Face of Danger
Brand, Max 430, 431, 432, 435, 473, 486, 489

A Bright Tragic Thing
Clark, L.D. 451, 456

Brightly Burning
Lackey, Mercedes 568, 569

A Brighton Flirtation
King, Valerie 230, 280, 305

Brighton Honeymoon
South, Sheri Cobb 404

Bring Me a Dream
Amos, Robyn **224**

Bring the Jubilee
Moore, Ward 804

Bringing out Betsy
Rabe, Sheila 376

The Britt Montero Series
Buchanan, Edna 75

Broke Heart Blues
Oates, Joyce Carol 1173, 1174

Broke Loose
Conley, Robert J. 447

The Broken Hearts Club
Black, Ethan 20, 1076

Broken Honor
Potter, Patricia 347, **373**

The Broken Lands
Edric, Robert 905

Broken Lines
Bannister, Jo 11

The Broken Promise Land
Muller, Marcia 189

Broken Promises
Oliver, Patricia 349, **362**

The Broken Sword
Anderson, Poul 517

Broken Vows
Daniells, Cory 267

Broken Wings
Blackstock, Terri 971, 1000, 1030

Bronte
Hughes, Glyn 904

The Bronze Horseman
Simons, Paullina 870, 876, 892

The Brother Athelstan Series
Harding, Paul 70

The Brother Cadfael Series
Peters, Ellis 865, 944

Brother Death
Perry, Steve 750

Brother John
Etheridge, Rutledge **750**

Brother of the Dragon
Thompson, Paul B. **604**

Brother to Shadows
Norton, Andre 725

Brother Wind
Harrison, Sue 879

Brothers and Sisters
Campbell, Bebe Moore 1089

A Brother's Honor
Ferguson, Jo Ann 278, 279

Brothers in Blood
Englade, Ken 454

The Brothers Majere
Stein, Kevin 556

Brothers of Cain
Monfredo, Miriam Grace 133, **159**, 169, 898, **909**

The Brothers of Glastonbury
Sedley, Kate 194, 933, 934

Brothers of the Head
Aldiss, Brian W. 764

Brown Girl in the Ring
Hopkinson, Nalo 760

The Brownstone
Eulo, Ken 667

A Brush with Death
Pim, Sheila 173

The Brutal Language of Love
Erian, Alicia 1149

Bubba Talks of Life, Love, Sex, Whiskey, Politics, Foreigners, Teenagers, Movies, Food, Football, and Other Matters
Jenkins, Dan 1132

Bubbles Unbound
Strohmeyer, Sarah 13, 38

The Buchanan Campaign
Shelley, Rick 795

Bucking the Tiger
Olds, Bruce **485**, **1176**

The Buckskin Line
Kelton, Elmer 425, 468, 895, 1137

The Buddha of Suburbia
Kureishi, Hanif 1150

Buffalo Commons
Wheeler, Richard S. 957

Buffalo Gordon
Lewis, J.P. Sinclair 864

Buffalo Palace
Johnston, Terry C. 890

Buffalo Valley
Macomber, Debbie **474**

Bug Park
Hogan, James P. 759

Bull God
Gellis, Roberta 547, 576

Buller's Victory
Hough, Richard 866

The Bulrush Murders
Rothenberg, Rebecca 189

A Bungalow for Two
Page, Carole Gift 982, **1035**

Burial
Masterton, Graham 672

Burial Ground
Shuman, Malcolm 195

Burning Desire
Bannister, Jo 11

Burning Down the House
Rafael, Lev **176**

The Burning Point
Putney, Mary Jo 301

The Burning Road
Benson, Ann 832, 844

The Burning Sky
Olsen, T.V. 487

Burning Tears of Sassurum
Baker, Sharon 718

The Burning Times
Kalogridis, Jeanne 844

Burnt
Olsen, Lance 720

Burnt Offerings
Hamilton, Laurell K. 645

Burnt Offerings
Marasco, Robert 640

Burnt Umber
Greene, Sheldon 852, 892, 913

Burr
Vidal, Gore 912

The Bushido Incident
Crawford, Betty Ann 793

Bushwhacked Bride
Riley, Eugenia 313, 371, 372, 380

But Why Shoot the Magistrate?
Sprinkle, Patricia Houck 1051

Butchers Hill
Lippman, Laura 143

Butcher's Moon
Stark, Richard 202

Buttercup Baby
Fox, Karen 249, **287**

Butterfly Lost
Cole, David 39

Butterfly Stories
Vollmann, William T. 950, 1212

Button Bright
Kurland, Michael 709

Buzz Cut
Hall, James W. 94

By Bizarre Hands
Lansdale, Joe R. 629

By Blood Alone
Dietz, William C. 746

By Blood Possessed
Santangelo, Elena 1

By Flare of Northern Lights
Champlin, Tim **439**

By Force of Arms
Dietz, William C. 746

By Force of Arms
Nelson, James L. 939

By Love Undone
Enoch, Suzanne 260

By Possession
Hunter, Madeline 407

By the Light of a Thousand Stars
Turner, Jamie Langston 1055

Byrne
Burgess, Anthony 846

Byzantium
Ennis, Michael 920

Byzantium
Lawhead, Stephen R. 570, 901

C

Cabal
Barker, Clive 694

The Cabal and Other Stories
Gilchrist, Ellen 1072, 1081, 1155, 1193, 1201

Caesar
McCullough, Colleen 1183

Cage of Bones and Other Deadly Obsessions
Everson, John 693, 698

Cages
Gorman, Ed 706

Cain
Huggins, James Byron 1003

Calder Pride
Dailey, Janet 265

Caleb's Price
Smith, Troy D. **505**

Caliban's Hour
Williams, Tad 536

The California Chronicles
Noble, Diane 998, 1028, 1050

California Ghost
Hill, William 703

Call Down the Stars
Harrison, Sue 871, **879**

Call Each River Jordan
Parry, Owen **169**, 864, 909, **914**, 964

Call Home the Heart
Stirling, Jessica 938

The Call of Cthulhu and Other Weird Stories
Lovecraft, H.P. 670, 671

Call of Duty
Lovelace, Merline 335

Call the Darkness Light
Zaroulis, N.L. 894

Call the Dead Again
Granger, Ann 87

The Callahan Garrity Series
Trocheck, Kathy Hogan 18, 102

Called by a Panther
Lewin, Michael Z. 142

The Calling of Emily Evans
Oke, Janette 1058

The Cambridge Chronicles
Crow, Donna Fletcher 1013, 1031

Camelot in Orbit
Landis, Arthur 600

Camels West
de la Garza, Phyllis 446, 448

Cameron's Crossing
McCutchan, Philip 953

The Campaign
Quayle, Marilyn Tucker 1004

The Camulod Chronicles
Whyte, Jack 907

Can This Be Christmas
Macomber, Debbie 474

Can You Feel Anything When I Do This?
Sheckley, Robert 727

Canby's Legion
Baldwin, Bill 742, 795

The Candi Covington Series
DeLoach, Nora 21

Candle Bay
Thorne, Tamara **703**

A Candle for a Corpse
Granger, Ann 87

Candlelight Ghost Stories
Morris, Anthony 636

The Candlelight Reader
Czichas, Casey 636, 697

Candles for Elizabeth
Kiernan, Caitlin R. 656

Candy
Southern, Terry 1150

Cane River
Tademy, Lalita 817, 855, 884, 961, 1089, 1164, **1207**

The Canon of Maverick Brands
Bonham, Frank 427

Can't Stop Loving You
Taylor, Janelle 413

Can't Take My Eyes Off of You
Michaels, Kasey 353, 354

A Canticle for Leibowitz
Miller, Walter N. Jr. 732

Canyon
McCourtney, Lorena 1023

Cape Refuge
Blackstock, Terri **970**, 985

Capili
Aleman Velasco, Miguel 889

A Capital Holiday
Dailey, Janet **265**

A Capital Offense
Parker, Gary E. 1039

Captain
Shelley, Rick 795

The Captain Bartholomew Hoare Series
Perkins, Wilder 853, 854

Captain Cupid Calls the Shots
Fairchild, Elisabeth 275, 315, 355, 378

Captain Cutthroat
Carr, John Dickson 12

Captain Jack's Woman
Laurens, Stephanie 309, 317

Captain, My Captain
Meroff, Deborah 894

Captain Nemo's Library
Enquist, Per Olov 862, 1110

The Captain's Bride
Jarrett, Miranda 328

The Captain's Courtship
Huntington, Kate 304, 397

Captains Outrageous
Lansdale, Joe R. **472**

Captain's Rangers
Kelton, Elmer 1137

The Captain's Wife
Kelley, Douglas **894**

Captive Angel
Porter, Cheryl Ann 415

The Captive Bride
Paul, Susan Spencer 368

Captive of Desire
Langan, Ruth 326

The Carl Houseman Series
Harstad, Donald 108, 151, 168

The Carl Wilcox Series
Adams, Harold 33, 110

Carley's Song
Sprinkle, Patricia Houck **1051**

The Carlotta Carlyle Series
Barnes, Linda 143, 217

Carnal Innocence
Roberts, Nora 395, 412

The Carol Ann Gibson Series
Mickelbury, Penny 220

Carol Christmas
Jensen, Muriel 306

Carolina Moon
McCorkle, Jill 1157

Carolina Moon
Roberts, Nora 331, 340, 383

Caroline and the Preacher
Schmidt, Anna 1045, 1046, 1061

Carousel
Janes, J. Robert 888

Carousel of Progress
Tanney, Katherine 1107

Carp Fishing on Valium and Other Tales of the Stranger Road Traveled
Parker, Graham 1158

Carpe Jugulum
Pratchett, Terry 587

Carried Away
Barnett, Jill 228, 821

Carried Away
Civil-Brown, Sue 256

Carry Me Across the Water
Canin, Ethan C. 1129, 1168

Carter Beats the Devil
Gold, Glen David 841, 847, **874**

The Case Has Altered
Grimes, Martha 92

The Case of Cabin 13
McCarver, Sam 5, 153

The Case of Compartment 7
McCarver, Sam 153

A Case of Curiosities
Kurzweil, Allen 1144

The Case of the 2nd Seance
McCarver, Sam 153

The Case of the Ripper's Revenge
McCarver, Sam **153**

Casefile: The Best of the "Nameless Detective"
Pronzini, Bill 175

Cases
Gores, Joe 83

The Casey Jones Series
Munger, Katy 18, 34, 143, 217

Casey on the Loose
Deford, Frank 849

Casey's Journey
McGinley, Marjorie M. 479

Cassandra's Song
Page, Carole Gift 1035, 1036, 1044, 1045, 1046

Cast a Road Before Me
Collins, Brandilyn 980, 981

Castle Crespin
Andrews, Allen 559

Castle for Rent
DeChancie, John 588

The Castle of the Silver Wheel
Edgerton, Teresa 591

The Castle of the Winds
Rohan, Michael Scott 595

The Castlemere Series
Bannister, Jo 64

The Cat Caliban Series
Borton, D.B. 124

Cat-Eyed Trouble
Skinner, Robert 196, 935

Cat in the Dark
Murphy, Shirley Rousseau 162

Cat Laughing Last
Murphy, Shirley Rousseau **162**

Cat Raise the Dead
Murphy, Shirley Rousseau 162

Cat Spitting Mad
Murphy, Shirley Rousseau 162

Cat to the Dogs
Murphy, Shirley Rousseau 162

Cat under Fire
Murphy, Shirley Rousseau 162

The Cat Who Robbed a Bank
Braun, Lilian Jackson 26

The Cat Who Sang for the Birds
Braun, Lilian Jackson 26

The Cat Who Saw Stars
Braun, Lilian Jackson 26

The Cat Who Series
Braun, Lilian Jackson 162

The Cat Who Smelled a Rat
Braun, Lilian Jackson 26

The Cat Who Tailed a Thief
Braun, Lilian Jackson 26

The Cat Who Went Up the Creek
Braun, Lilian Jackson **26**

Catacombs
McCusker, Paul 1024

Catamount
Peak, Michael 574

Catch a Fallen Angel
Kane, Kathleen 249, 313

Catch Me If You Can
Bruhns, Nina 417

Catch of the Season
Scott, Regina 291, 392, 393

Catch the Lightning
Asaro, Catherine 716

Catching Kelly
Civil-Brown, Sue 256, 354, 376

The Catherine le Vendeur Series
Newman, Sharan 834, 861

Catherwood
Youmans, Marly 964

The Catiline Conspiracy
Roberts, John Maddox 184, 924

Cat's Paw
Taylor, L.A. 574

Catseye
Forstchen, William R. 864

Catskill
Hayes, John R. **110**, 828, 839, **882**, 885, 955

Cattle Drive to Dodge
Conwell, Kent 492, 505

Caught
Green, Henry 876

Caught
Lee, Rachel 395

Caught in the Light
Goddard, Robert 82, 849

Caught under the Mistletoe
Hoffman, Kate 306

The Cavan Breed
Savage, Les Jr. 500, 501

Caveat
Kalpakian, Laura 478

A Cavern of Black Ice
Jones, J.V. 596

The Caverns of Socrates
McKiernan, Dennis L. 579, 580

The Cecil Younger Series
Straley, John 74

A Ceiling of Stars
Creel, Ann Howard 845

The Celestial Buffet
Dunlap, Susan 40

The Celia Grant Series
Sherwood, John 173, 181

The Cellar
Laymon, Richard 662

Cellars
Shirley, John 694

The Celtic Crusades Series
Lawhead, Stephen R. 1003, 1060

Celtika
Holdstock, Robert **558**

Centennial
Michener, James A. 1137

The Center of Things
McPhee, Jenny 1160

A Century of British Mystery and Suspense
Perry, Anne 84

A Century of Great Suspense Stories
Deaver, Jeffery **57**

A Century of Great Western Stories
Jakes, John 455, 460

A Certain Justice
Lescroart, John 141

Certain Prey
Sandford, John 908

Cetaganda
Bujold, Lois McMaster 734, 812

The Chairman
Kraus, Harry Lee 1012

Chalktown
Haynes, Melinda 1154

The Chance
Layton, Edith 348

A Chance on Lovin' You
Snoe, Eboni 403

Chancellorsville
Reasoner, James 919

A Change of Heart
Hern, Candice 298

The Changeling
Rusch, Kristine Kathryn 575

Changelings
Bannister, Jo 11

Changespell
Durgin, Doranna 592, 593

Changewar
Leiber, Fritz 767

The Changing Trail
Dunham, Tracy 454, 471

Changing Trains
Haseloff, Cynthia 423

Changing Vision
Czerneda, Julie E. 740

The Chantry Guild
Dickson, Gordon R. 716, 734

Chanur's Legacy
Cherryh, C.J. 743

Chapel Noir
Douglas, Carole Nelson **62**, **856**, 900, 915

Charles
Lincoln, Victoria 917

The Charles Dodgson/Arthur Conan Doyle Series
Rogow, Roberta 927, 959

Charlie and the Sir
Roderus, Frank **499**

The Charlie Greene Series
Millhiser, Marlys 34, 80

The Charlie Resnick Series
Harvey, John 104, 155, 178

Charlotte Gray
Faulks, Sebastian 863, 888, 960

The Charlotte Justice Series
Woods, Paula L. 21

The Charly Poisson Series
Lamalle, Cecile 207

Charm City
Lippman, Laura 143

The Charm School
Wiggs, Susan 419

Charmed and Dangerous
Ashford, Jane 400

Charming Billy
McDermott, Alice 1117

Charming the Prince
Medeiros, Teresa 396

The Chas Wheatley Series
Richman, Phyllis 105, 138, 170

Chase the Morning
Rohan, Michael Scott 595

Chase the Sun
Bittner, Rosanne 471

Chase Your Dreams
Mahon, Annette 343

Chasing Rainbow
Civil-Brown, Sue 256

Chasing the Devil's Tail
Fulmer, David **73**, 196, **867**

Chasm
Laws, Stephen 708

Chasm City
Reynolds, Alastair 721, 757, **789**

The Chatham School Affair
Cook, Thomas H. 82, 214

Cheating Death
Keating, H.R.F. 132

Chelsea Horror Hotel
Ramone, Dee Dee **684**

The Cheney Duvall Series
Morris, Lynn 1025

Cherish
Anderson, Catherine 225

Cherished Love
Bittner, Rosanne 280

The Cherokee Dragon
Conley, Robert J. 447, 466

Cherokee Dragon
Conley, Robert J. 842

Cherokee Nights
Dellin, Genell 270

Cherokee Rose
Alter, Judy 424, 498

The Cherry Blossom Corpse
Barnard, Robert 49

The Chessboard Queen
Newman, Sharan 528

Cheyenne Raiders
Jordan, Robert 895

Cheyenne Summer
Munn, Vella 826, **911**

Cheyenne Winter
Wheeler, Richard S. 426, 429

The Chicago Nordejoong Series
McKernan, Victoria 3

Chickadee
Bedford, Deborah 967

Child of Faerie
Yolen, Jane 605

Child of Grace
Copeland, Lori 983

Child of Promise
Morgan, Kathleen **1025**, 1026

The Child of the Holy Grail
Miles, Rosalind 829, 831, 901, **907**

Child of the River
McAuley, Paul J. 771

Child of Thunder
Reichert, Mickey Zucker 590

The Child Queen
McKenzie, Nancy 528

A Child Shall Lead Them
Page, Carole Gift 965, 1035, **1036**, 1041, 1043

The Children in the Woods
Busch, Frederick 1192

Children of the Atom
Shiras, Wilmar H. 753

Children of the Damned
Sellwood, A.V. 738

Children of the Lion
Roberson, Jennifer **591**

Children of the Plains
Thompson, Paul B. 604

The Children of the Pool and Other Stories
Machen, Arthur 680

Children of the Shaman
Rydill, Jessica **596**

The Children of the Sun
Hall, Oakley 878

Children's Games
LaPierre, Janet 139

A Child's Promise
Bedford, Deborah 967

Chile Death
Albert, Susan Wittig 4, 105

The China Bayles Series
Albert, Susan Wittig 32, 67, 89, 120

China Mountain Zhang
McHugh, Maureen 774

The Chinese Fire Drill
Roberts, Les **185**

The Chip Harrison Series
Block, Lawrence 56

The Chloe Newcombe Series
Thornton, Betsy 125

Chocolate Jesus and Other Weird Perversions
Staley, Shane Ryan 698

Chocolate Kisses
Brownley, Margaret 344

Choice Cuts
Boileau, Thomas 677

A Choice to Cherish
Maki, Alan 1019

Choke
Palahniuk, Chuck 1177

Chopper Ops
Maloney, Mack 769

The Chosen Child
Masterton, Graham 672

Christmas Angels
Dier, Debra 366

Christmas Belle
Balogh, Mary 304

Christmas Belles
Carroll, Susan 271

The Christmas Box
Evans, Richard Paul 983, 1033

A Christmas Bride
Balogh, Mary 227, 271, 367

A Christmas Bride
Ferguson, Jo Ann 271, 279

The Christmas Carrolls
Metzger, Barbara 275

The Christmas Charm
Collum, Lynn 258, 271

Christmas Cookie Murder
Meier, Leslie 157

A Christmas Courtship
Heath, Sandra 275

Christmas from the Heart
Wheeler, Joe L. 1033

The Christmas Gift
Savery, Jeanne 315, 389

Christmas Knight
Skye, Christina 277

The Christmas Quilt
Davis, Thomas J. 983

The Christmas Spirit
Wynn, Patricia 275

Christmas Spirits
Kurland, Lynn 277

Christmas Vows: $5.00 Extra
Copeland, Lori **983**, 1033

A Christmas Wedding
Greeley, Andrew M. 1117

The Christmas Wish
Raleigh, Debbie **377**, 378

Christmas Wishes
Metzger, Barbara 304

Christmas with a Stranger
Spencer, Catherine 306

Chromosome 6
Cook, Robin 1093

ChronoSpace
Steele, Allen **802**

Chumley's Gold
Overholser, Wayne D. **489**, 491

The Cider House Rules
Irving, John 1130

Cimarron Blood
Luckey, William A. 503

Cimarron Rose
Burke, James Lee 1088

Cincinnati Red Stalkings
Soos, Troy 119, 200

The Cinda Hayes Series
Wesson, Marianne 66

Cinderella After Midnight
Darcy, Lilian **268**

The Cinderella Deal
Crusie, Jennifer 236

Cinnabar Shadows
Abbey, Lynn 515

Cinnamon and Roses
Betts, Heidi 234

Circle at Center
Niles, Douglas 583

The Circle of Destiny Series
Kraus, Jim 1050, 1054

Circle of Friends
Binchy, Maeve 1111

The Circle of Reason
Ghosh, Amitav 1116

Circle of Seven
Jacobsen, Clay 976, 1004

Circle of Stars
Waldo, Anna Lee **510**, 818, 871, **952**, 962

Circle of Stones
Waldo, Anna Lee 510, 952

Circle of the Lily
Jones, Jill 382

Circles of Confusion
Henry, April 134

Circuit of Heaven
Danvers, Dennis 731

A Citizen of the Country
Smith, Sarah 921

The City and the Stars
Clarke, Arthur C. 790

City Fishing
Tem, Steve Rasnic 616, 656, 688, 700

City Girl
Wick, Lori 1059

City in Love
Shakar, Alex 1196

City Infernal
Lee, Edward **667**

City Jitters
Fowler, Christopher 648, 786

City Life
Barthelme, Donald 720

The City, Not Long After
Murphy, Pat 781

City of Assassins
Hammell, Ian 552

City of Dreams
Swerling, Beverly **939**

City of God
Holland, Cecelia 916

City of Light
Belfer, Lauren 24, 839

The City of Ravens
Baker, Richard 578

City of Saints and Madmen
Vandermeer, Jeff **607**

City of the Sorcerers
Herbert, Mary H. 556

City of Widows
Estleman, Loren D. 493

City Primeval
Leonard, Elmore 1123

The City Watch Trilogy
Pratchett, Terry 588

Civil Blood
McMillan, Ann 133, 159, 169, 898, 909, 914

A Civil Campaign
Bujold, Lois McMaster 728

A Civil Contract
Heyer, Georgette 257

The CJ Floyd Series
Greer, Robert 192, 216

Claiming of Deerfoot: A Western Duo
Dawson, Peter 489

The Claire Claiborne Series
Dunbar, Sophie 38, 177

The Claire Malloy Series
Hess, Joan 67

The Clairvoyant Countess
Gilman, Dorothy 79, 522

The Clandestine Circle
Herbert, Mary H. 556

A Clandestine Courtship
Lane, Allison 258

The Clara Gamadge Series
Boylan, Eleanor 91

Clarke County, Space
Steele, Allen 788, 802

A Clash of Kings
Martin, George R.R. 549

The Claudia Seferius Series
Todd, Marilyn 184

Clay Dancers
Dawkins, Cecil 61

The Clerk's Tale
Frazer, Margaret **70**, **865**

Cleveland Local
Roberts, Les 185

The Client
Grisham, John 1123

The Cliff Lansing Series
Hackler, Micah S. 108

Climb the Wind
Sargent, Pamela 799

Climbing Olympus
Anderson, Kevin J. 715, 771

The Clique
Mount, Ferdinand 1167

The Cloning of Joanna May
Weldon, Fay 1093

Close Range
Proulx, Annie 891, 1081, 1146

A Close Run Thing
Mallinson, Allan 854

Close to the Bone
Morris, Mark 706

Close to the Bone
Tapply, William G. 206

The Closed Worlds
Hamilton, Edmond 719

Closing Time
Fusilli, Jim **74**

Cloud Castles
Rohan, Michael Scott 595

The Cloud Sketcher
Rayner, Richard 877

Clouds
Gunn, Robin Jones 993

The Clouds Above
Greig, Andrew **876**

Cloudy in the West
Kelton, Elmer 468, 490, 499

Clowns of God
West, Morris L. 956

The Club Dumas
Perez-Reverte, Arturo 171, 1182

A Clue for the Puzzle Lady
Hall, Parnell 96

Clypsis
Carver, Jeffrey A. 769

Coast Road
Delinsky, Barbara 1101, 1103

Cobwebs and Whispers
Thomas, Scott **701**

Cocaine Nights
Ballard, J.G. 1070

The Cockatrice Boys
Aiken, Joan 533

Code of Honor
Pickens, Andrea 370

Code to Zero
Follett, Ken 863

Coffee to Die For
French, Linda 32

The Coffin Dancer
Deaver, Jeffery 57

The Coffin Ed Johnson/Grave Digger Jones Series
Himes, Chester 196

A Coffin for Charley
Butler, Gwendoline 30

Coffin Gap
Savage, Les Jr. 439, 443, 460

Coffin's Game
Butler, Gwendoline 30

Coffin's Ghost
Butler, Gwendoline **30**

Coffin's Got the Dead Guy on the Inside
Snyder, Keith 199

Cold
Smolens, John 1195, **1199**

Cold Blood
Chizmar, Richard 628, 651

The Cold Blue Blood
Handler, David **100**, 115

A Cold Christmas
Weir, Charlene 90, **212**

Cold Comfort
Kilpatrick, Nancy 630, **658**

A Cold Day in Hell
Johnston, Terry C. 466

Cold Fire
Koontz, Dean R. 675

The Cold Heart of Capricorn
Lawrence, Martha C. 140

Cold Hit
Fairstein, Linda 66

Cold Hunter's Moon
Greenlief, K.C. **90**, 145, 212

Cold Iron
Michaels, Melisa 522

Cold Is the Grave
Robinson, Peter 186

Cold Kiss
Longstreet, Roxanne 617, 702

Cold Medina
Hardwick, Gary 166, 216

Cold Mountain
Frazier, Charles 964

Cold Night, Warm Stranger
Gregory, Jill 294, 409

The Cold Six Thousand
Ellroy, James 1211

Cold Tea on a Hot Day
Matlock, Curtiss Ann 225

Cold Whisper
Hautala, Rick 641

Coldheart Canyon
Barker, Clive **619**, **1071**, 1140, 1185

Coldwater
McConnochie, Mardi 819, 887, **904**, 1148, **1156**

Colfax
Conley, Robert J. 842

The Colin Harpur Series
James, Bill 178

The Collected Ghost Stories of E.F. Benson
Benson, E.F. 622

The Collected Ghost Stories of Oliver Onions
Onions, Oliver 680

Collected Stories
Bellow, Saul **1072**

Collected Stories
Matheson, Richard 678

Collected Stories of Richard Yates
Yates, Richard 1072

The Collected Stories of Vernor Vinge
Vinge, Vernor **807**

The Colonel's Lady
Oliver, Patricia 362

The Color of Death
Alexander, Bruce 815

Color the Sidewalk for Me
Collins, Brandilyn **980**, 1038

The Colorado Bride
Burton, Mary 234, **247**, 391

Colorado Shadows
Pendergrass, Tess 495

Colorado Twilight
Pendergrass, Tess **495**

Colorado Wings
Peterson, Tracie 1042

The Colors of Chaos
Modesitt, L.E. Jr. 526

Colossus
Jones, D.F. 798

Colours in the Steel
Parker, K.J. 585

Colt Lighting
Champlin, Tim 492, 505

The Columbia River
Sherman, Jory 503

Columbus Slaughters Braves
Friedman, Mark **1114**

Coma
Cook, Robin 677

Comanche Dawn
Blakely, Mike 447, 507, 827, 1137

Comanche Flame
Dellin, Genell 270

Comanche Moon
McMurtry, Larry 468, 1137

Comanchero Blood
Andrews, Patrick E. 425, 469

Come Back Dead
Faherty, Terence 83

Come Back to Me
Litton, Josie 336, **337**, 338

Come Midnight
Forster, Suzanne 395

Come, My Little Angel
Noble, Diane 983, **1033**

Come out Tonight
Laymon, Richard 662

Come the Morning
Drake, Shannon 883

Come the Night
Skye, Christina 317

Come Twilight
Yarbro, Chelsea Quinn 713, 963

Come Up and See Me Sometime
Krouse, Erika 1149, 1193, 1209

Comeback
Stark, Richard 202

Comfort and Joy
Madden, Sandra **342**

The Comforter
Bryant, Dorothy 747

Commencement
James, Roby 755

A Commerical Enterprise
Heath, Sandra 318

A Common Life
Karon, Jan 1007

Common or Garden Crime
Pim, Sheila 136, 173, 181

Common Threads
Hoffman, Nina Kiriki 658

Communion Blood
Yarbro, Chelsea Quinn 713, 963

Company of Glass
Leith, Valery 572

The Company of Strangers
Wilson, Robert 131, **215**, 863, **960**

The Complete Ivory
Egan, Doris 728

The Complete Stories
Hurston, Zora Neale 1128

Complete Tales and Poems
Poe, Edgar Allan 669

Compromising Positions
Isaacs, Susan 1131

A Compromising Situation
Donnelly, Shannon 230

Conan the Rebel
Anderson, Poul 517, 818

Conard County: Boots and Badges
Lee, Rachel 330, 331

The Concise Cuddy
Healy, Jeremiah 147

Confessions of a Fallen Standard Bearer
Makine, Andrei 1151

Confessions of a Pagan Nun
Horsley, Kate **886**, 952

Conjure Wife
Leiber, Fritz 682

The Conjurer Princess
Vande Velde, Vivian 605

Conjuring Maud
Danze, Philip **847**

The Connor O'Neill/Fran Wilson Series
Green, Christine 64, 87, 165

Conor
Langan, Ruth 254

The Conqueror
Anton, Shari 269

The Conqueror's Child
Charnas, Suzy McKee 732

Conqueror's Legacy
Zahn, Timothy 812

The Conrad Voort Series
Black, Ethan 204

Consider the Crows
Weir, Charlene 212

Considering Kate
Roberts, Nora 343, 382

Conspiracies
Wilson, F. Paul 710

The Constable Evans Series
Bowen, Rhys 830

A Constellation of Cats
Little, Denise **574**, 575

Contact and Commune
Smith, L. Neil 799

Contagion
Cook, Robin 1093

Contemporary American Fiction
Hornby, Nick 1126

Continue Laughing
Reiner, Carl 1158

The Contract Surgeon
O'Brien, Dan 890

Controlling Interests
Peterson, Tracie 1006

The Convenient Marriage
Heyer, Georgette 257

The Convict and Other Stories
Burke, James Lee 1088

A Cook in Time
Pence, Joanne 170

Cook Up a Crime
Russell, Charlotte Murray 191

Cooking Most Deadly
Pence, Joanne 170

Cook's Night Out
Pence, Joanne 170

Cooks Overboard
Pence, Joanne 170

Cooper's Wife
Hart, Jillian 296, 997

The Copelands
Bowman, Doug 511

Coq au Vin
Carter, Charlotte 856

The Cork O'Connor Series
Krueger, William Kent 90, 93, 145, 151

The Cornbread Killer
Temple, Lou Jane 207

Corpse de Ballet
Pall, Ellen 71

Corpus Earthling
Charbonneau, Louis 773, 794

The Corrections
Franzen, Jonathan 1107, **1113**, 1163

Corsair
Bunch, Chris 729

Cortez on Jupiter
Hogan, Ernest 758

Cosette
Kalpakian, Laura 900

Cosmic Carousel
Garnett, David 752

The Cosmic Geoids
Taine, John 787

Cotton Comes to Harlem
Himes, Chester 166

Couching at the Door
Broster, D.K. 647

Could I Have This Dance?
Kraus, Harry Lee **1012**

The Council of Blades
Kidd, Paul 563

The Counterfeit Heinlein
Janiver, Laurence M. **763**

The Countess
Delacroix, Claire 269

Counting Coup
Gearino, G.D. 115

Courageous Bride
Peart, Jane 977, 1034

Courting an Angel
Grasso, Patricia 293

Courting Claire
O'Brien, Linda 361

Courting Katarina
Steward, Carol 251, 1043, 1052

The Courts of Love
Gilchrist, Ellen 1143, 1169

The Courtship Gift
Parsons, Julie 1180

The Cove
Coulter, Catherine 340

A Covenant of Love
Morris, Gilbert 1027

Cow Thief Trail
Foster, Bennett 480

The Cowboy and the Vampire
Hays, Clark 712

The Cowboy Finds a Bride
Linz, Cathie 334, 335

Cowboy in the Making
James, Will **464**

The Cowboy's Bride
Aarsen, Carolyne 965

Coyote Run
Bendell, Don 459

The Crab
Brown, Stan **531**

The Crack in Space
Dick, Philip K. 752, 779

Crack Shot
Browning, Sinclair **28**

Cradle and All
Patterson, James 1181

The Cradle Will Rock
Kearney, Susan 410

The Crane
Soesbee, Ree 531

Crash
Ballard, J.G. 1108

Crash Diet
McCorkle, Jill 1157

Crashing Down
O'Brien, Meg 387

The Crater
Slotkin, Richard 864

The Crawling Abbatoir
Mundt, Martin 697

Crawling at Night
Power, Nani 1077, 1164

Crazy for You
Crusie, Jennifer 286

Crazy Horse
Dugan, Bill 890

Crazy Horse in Stillness
Heyen, William 890

Crazybone
Pronzini, Bill 174

Creature Fantastic
Little, Denise 574, **575**

Creatures of Habit
McCorkle, Jill 1065, 1075, 1079, 1115, **1157**, 1192

Creekers
Lee, Edward 662

Creeping Venom
Pim, Sheila **173**

Creme de la Crime
Hutchings, Janet 84

Crescent in the Sky
Moffitt, Donald 774

Crewel World
Ferris, Monica 67

Crime of Olga Arbyelina
Makine, Andrei 1151

Crime on Her Mind
Hart, Carolyn 31

Crime Studio
Aylett, Steve 720

Crime through Time
Monfredo, Miriam Grace 8

Crime through Time II
Monfredo, Miriam Grace 8

Crime through Time III
Newman, Sharan 8

A Criminal Appeal
Schanker, D.R. 113

Criminal Justice
Parker, Barbara 1143

Criminals
Livesey, Margot 1148

Crimson Kiss
Baker, Trisha **617**

The Crimson Roses of Fountain Court
Darty, Peggy 418

Cripple Creek
Hirt, Douglas 462, 495

Critical Conditions
White, Stephen 141

Critical Space
Rucka, Greg 123, **190**

Cross and Crescent
Shwartz, Susan 796

The Crossroad
Lewis, Beverly 1018

Crossroad Blues
Atkins, Ace 112

Crossroads of Time
Norton, Andre 741

Crosstime Traffic
Watt-Evans, Lawrence 610, 727, 766

The Crossword Murder
Blanc, Nero 96

The Crow Maiden
Singleton, Sarah 568, **598**

The Crown of Silence
Constantine, Storm 536, 549

Crucifax Autumn
Garton, Ray 626

The Cruel Mother
LaPierre, Janet 139

The Cruel Sea
Monsarrat, Nicholas 953

Cruelty and Silence
Makiya, Kanan 902

Cruising for Murder
Sussman, Susan 816

Crusade
Lowder, James 562

Crusader
Douglass, Sara 540

The Crusader
Eisner, Michael A. 831, 843, **860**, 901, 941

The Crusader
Hurley, Frank X. 860

Crusader's Torch
Yarbro, Chelsea Quinn 562

Crusoe's Daughter
Gardam, Jane 870

A Cry for Self Help
Girdner, Jacqueline 80

Cry of the Tinamou
Babb, Sanora 454, 471

Cry of the Wind
Harrison, Sue 879

Crying Wolf
Abrahams, Peter 1

Crypt Orchids
Schow, David J. 696

Crystal Clear
Heller, Jane 1125

The Crystal Sorcerers
Forstchen, William R. 537

Cupid's Kiss
Harbaugh, Karen 287, 350

The Cure
Ferris, Paul 783

Curly Smoke
Holtzer, Susan 120

A Curse of Silence
Haney, Lauren 101

Curse of the Witch-Queen
Volsky, Paula 599

Cursed and Consulted
Cook, Rick 521, **537**

Curses!
Elkins, Aaron 195

Cut and Branded
Curtis, Jack 440

Cut 'n' Run
Deford, Frank 849

Cuts
Laymon, Richard 662

Cutter's Run
Tapply, William G. 206

The Cutting Edge
Etchison, Dennis 634

Cutting Loose
Lewin, Michael Z. 142

Cuttings
Grant, Anne Underwood 103

The Cybernetic Shogun
Milan, Victor 758

Cycle of the Werewolves
King, Stephen 1068

Cyteen
Cherryh, C.J. 716

D

Daddy by Accident
Riggs, Paula Detmer 344

Daddy in Dress Blues
Linz, Cathie 334, 335

Daddy on the Way
Richer, Lois 1043

Daddy's Gone A-Hunting
Skinner, Robert 196, 935

Daggers of Gold
Deauville, Katherine 276

Dagon and Other Macabre Tales
Lovecraft, H.P. 670

The Dain Curse
Hammett, Dashiell 99

The Daisy Dalrymple Series
Dunn, Carola 183

Dakota Home
Macomber, Debbie 474

Dale Loves Sophie to Death
Dew, Robb Forman 850, 1102

Dalva
Harrison, Jim 1137, 1157

The Dalziel and Pascoe Series
Hill, Reginald 23, 44, 97, 186

Damascus Gate
Stone, Robert 902

Damascus Journey
Lacy, Al 1014, 1015

The Dame Frevisse Series
Frazer, Margaret 86, 194, 209

Damned If You Do
Houghton, Gordon 667

Damned in Paradise
Collins, Max Allan 41

The Damsel
Delacroix, Claire 269

Dana's Valley
Oke, Janette 1032

Dance Down the Stars
Clayton, Jo 593

A Dance in Heather
Beard, Julie 229

Dance of Death
Elrod, P.N. 632

Dance on a Sinking Ship
Kilian, Michael 816

Dance to the Piper
Roberts, Nora 1187

Dance upon the Air
Roberts, Nora **382**, 383

Dancers on Horseback
Bogue, Lucile 426

Dances with Wolves
Blake, Michael 425, 826

Dancing Bear
Crumley, James 50

Dancing Dead
Woodworth, Deborah **1062**

Dancing with Clara
Balogh, Mary 388

Dancing with Death
Coggin, Joan 36

Dancing with the Virgins
Booth, Stephen **23**

The Dandelion Murders
Rothenberg, Rebecca 189

Danger in the Shadows
Henderson, Dee 999, 1023

Danger Ridge
McGuire, Tim 480

A Dangerous Arrangement
Gedney, Mona 291

Dangerous Attraction
Vaughan, Susan **417**

A Dangerous Dalliance
Scott, Regina 392, 393

Dangerous Dilemmas
Palfrey, Evelyn **365**

A Dangerous Friend
Just, Ward S. 1134

Dangerous Games
Randall, Marta 793

Dangerous Gifts
Smith, Haywood 288

Dangerous Lady
Scott, Amanda 390

Dangerous Liaisons
Price, Maggie 417

The Dangerous Lord
Jeffries, Sabrina 329

A Dangerous Magic
Little, Denise 574, 575

A Dangerous Man
Rogers, Rosemary 385

Dangerous Passions
Martin, Kat 346, 347

A Dangerous Road
Nelscott, Kris 122, 166

A Dangerous Silence
Palmer, Catherine 1038

Dangerously Irresistible
Gabriel, Kristin **289**, 333

The Dani Ross Series
Morris, Gilbert 970, 1008, 1009, 1037, 1048

The Daniel and Jennifer Kaine Series
Hoff, B.J. 1048

Daniel's Gift
Freethy, Barbara 239

The Dante Game
Langton, Jane 164

Daredevils, Ltd.
Goulart, Ron 756, 763

The Dargonesti
Thompson, Paul B. 604

Daring
Hunter, Jillian 303

Daring the Devil
LaFoy, Leslie 324

A Dark-Adapted Eye
Rendell, Ruth 154

The Dark between the Stars
Anderson, Poul 716

Dark Carnival
Bradbury, Ray 623, 1082

Dark Channel
Garton, Ray 638

The Dark Clue
Wilson, James **959**

A Dark Coffin
Butler, Gwendoline 30

Dark Coulee
Logue, Mary 145

Dark Dance
Lee, Tanith 623

Dark Detectives
Jones, Stephen 653, 654

Dark Dreams
Daniells, Cory **267**

Dark Father
Piccirilli, Tom 682

The Dark Half
King, Stephen 781

Dark Hollow
Connolly, John **42**

Dark Horse
Herbert, Mary H. 556

The Dark Horse
James, Will 464

A Dark Imbalance
Williams, Sean 743

Dark Inheritance
Gear, Kathleen O'Neal 871

Dark Is the Moon
Irvine, Ian 560

Dark Legacy
Vardeman, Robert E. 564

The Dark Moon
Gray, Julia 551

Dark of the Night
Jones, Stephen 653, 654

Dark Paradise
Hoag, Tami 412

Dark Road to Daylight
Parker, Gary E. 1039

The Dark Room
Walters, Minette 211

Dark Sanctuary
Gregory, H.B. **644**

Dark Shadows on the Moon
Ford, John B. **635**

Dark Thicket
Kelton, Elmer 895

The Dark Tide
McKiernan, Dennis L. 541

Dark Trail
Gorman, Ed 438, 456, 479

Dark Trail to Dodge
Smith, Cotton 504

Dark Waters
Stone, Robert S. 601

Dark Water's Embrace
Leigh, Stephen 805

The Dark Way
Conley, Robert J. 842

The Dark Wing
Hunt, Walter **761**

Darkenheight
Niles, Douglas 583

A Darkening Star
Wilson, Robert 960

Darker
Clark, Simon 735

A Darker Justice
Bissell, Sallie **19**

Darker Light
Yarbro, Chelsea Quinn 963

A Darker Place
King, Laurie R. 139

Darkest Hour
Chadbourn, Mark 533

Darkling I Listen
Sutcliffe, Katherine 411, **412**

Darkness
Siciliano, Sam 686, **695**

A Darkness at Sethanon
Feist, Raymond E. 541, 554, 555, 560

Darkness at the Door
Dain, Catherine **52**

Darkness Demands
Clark, Simon 626, 735

Darkness Descending
Turtledove, Harry 606, 804

Darkness Divided
Shirley, John 656

A Darkness More than Night
Connelly, Michael 1076, 1096

Darkness Take My Hand
Lehane, Dennis 1074

Darkside
Etchison, Dennis 642

Darktown Strutters
Brown, Wesley 846

Darling?
Schmidt, Heidi Jon **1193**

The Darryl Billups Series
Walker, Blair S. 143

Date with the Perfect Dead Man
Griffin, Annie 91

Daughter of Destiny
Fobes, Tracy 281

Daughter of Fortune
Allende, Isabel 817, 1067

Daughter of Ireland
Massey, Sonja 386

Daughter of Joy
Morgan, Kathleen 1025, 1026

Daughter of Lir
Tarr, Judith 818, 879, **940**, 941, 962

Daughter of Shadows
Seymour, Miranda 916

Daughter of the Bear King
Arnason, Eleanor 592

Daughter of the Blood
Bishop, Anne 527

Daughter of Twin Oaks
Snelling, Lauraine 1050

A Daughter's Destiny
Ferguson, Jo Ann 278, 279

The Daughters of Faith Series
Lemmons, Thom 990, 994, 1053

The Daughters of Fortune Series
Pella, Judith 977

Daughters of the House
Roberts, Michele 925

The Dave Brandstetter Series
Hansen, Joseph 221

The Dave Robicheaux Series
Burke, James Lee 22, 50, 59, 94, 112, 1088, 1127

David at Olivet
Hamilton, Wallace 858

The Dawn of Fury
Compton, Ralph 434

The Dawning
Cave, Hugh B. 666

The Dawning of a New Age
Rabe, Jean 589

Dawnthief
Barclay, James 523, 569, 589

The Day Before Midnight
Hunter, Stephen 887

Day Dreamer
Landis, Jill Marie 471

A Day Late and a Dollar Short
McMillan, Terry 1101, 1122, 1207

Day of Reckoning
Herman, Kathy **1001**

Day of the Bees
Sanchez, Thomas 888

The Day of the Drones
Lightner, A.M. 779

Day of the Tempest
Rabe, Jean 589

The Day of the Triffids
Wyndham, John 735

The Day of Their Return
Anderson, Poul 810

The Day the Cowboys Quit
Kelton, Elmer 1137

The Day the Music Died
Gorman, Ed 83

The Day to Remember Series
Chaikin, Linda 1040

The Daybreak Series
Hoff, B.J. 970, 996, 1008

Days
Robison, Mary 1188

Days of Cain
Dunn, J.R. 802

The Dazzle of Day
Gloss, Molly 1082

Dazzling Brightness
Gellis, Roberta 547

The de Burgh Bride
Simmons, Deborah 396

The Deacon's Daughter
Berger, Eileen 968

Dead Air
Krich, Rochelle 137

Dead Ball
Rosen, R.D. **188**

Dead Calm
Williams, Charles 171

Dead Cat Bounce
Graves, Sarah 89

Dead End
Myers, Helen R. 347, 373

Dead End
Olson, Paul F. 648

Dead in Hog Heaven
Caverly, Carol 472, 477

Dead in the Water
Holder, Nancy 681

Dead Love
Beman, Donald **620**

Dead Man's Bay
Wimberley, Darryl 3, 216

Dead Man's Cache
Arnold, A.J. 490, 499

Dead Man's Kiss
Weinberg, Robert 706

Dead Man's Walk
McMurtry, Larry 468, 503

Dead Meat
Kerr, Philip 130

Dead Meat
Tapply, William G. 42

Dead of Winter
Hall, Patricia 97

Dead on Arrival
Hall, Patricia 97

Dead on Demand
Engstrom, Elizabeth **633**

Dead Reckoning
Blakely, Mike 440

Dead Reckoning
Llewellyn, Sam 171

Dead Sleep
Iles, Greg **123**

Dead Solid Perfect
Jenkins, Dan 1132

Dead Souls
Rankin, Ian 178

Dead to Rights
Jance, J.A. 125, 465

Dead to Rites
Angus, Sylvia 195

Dead Weight
Havill, Steven F. 108

The Deadhouse
Fairstein, Linda **66**

Deadlines
Skipp, John 679

Deadly Dreams
Schiller, Gerald A. 677

Deadly Hunger and Other Stories
Hensley, Joe L. 40

Deadly Illumination
Stier, Serena **203**

Deadly Image
Cooper, Edmund 797, 806

Deadly Masquerade
Tillis, Tracey 272

Deadly Meeting
Bernard, Robert 176

Deadly Nightshade
Riggs, Cynthia 46

Deadly Pursuit
Olsen, T.V. 486

Deadly Season
Champlin, Tim 440

Deadly Secrets on the St. Johns
Sprinkle, Patricia Houck 1051

A Deadly Shaker Spring
Woodworth, Deborah 1062

A Deadly Vineyard Holiday
Craig, Philip R. 46

Deadwood
Hirt, Douglas 462

The Deadwood Beetle
Dressler, Mylene **1106**

The Dean's December
Bellow, Saul 1072

Dear Cupid
Ortolon, Julie 226, 354, **363**, 369

Dear Future
D'Aguiar, Fred 846

Dear Silver
McCourtney, Lorena 1023

Dearest Max
Miller, Barbara 355

Dearly Departed
Housewright, David 908

Death al Dente
King, Peter 135

Death Among the Dons
Neel, Janet 165

Death and the Chapman
Sedley, Kate 933, 934

Death at Bishop's Keep
Paige, Robin 187

Death at Daisy's Folly
Paige, Robin 58

Death at the Dog
Cannan, Joanna 136

Death by Accident
Crider, Bill 48, 49

Death by Darjeeling
Childs, Laura **32**, 67, 163

Death by Jury
Lutz, John 147

Death by Rhubarb
Temple, Lou Jane 207

Death Comes as Epiphany
Newman, Sharan 70, 209

Death Comes as the End
Christie, Agatha 101

Death Cruise
Block, Lawrence 816

Death Drives a Semi
van Belkom, Edo 658, 693, 705

Death Hits the Fan
Girdner, Jacqueline 80

Death in a Hot Flash
Isenberg, Jane 124

Death in Paradise
Parker, Robert B. **168**

Death in Summer
Trevor, William 1138

Death in the Andes
Vargas Llosa, Mario 1211

Death in the Fifth Position
Box, Edgar 71

Death Is a Cabaret
Morgan, Deborah **160**

Death Is in the Air
Kingsbury, Kate **136**

Death Marks Time in Trampas: A Western Quintet
Flynn, T.T. 434, 452, 491, 501

Death Masque
Elrod, P.N. 632

Death of a Colonial
Alexander, Bruce 815

The Death of a Constant Lover
Rafael, Lev 176

Death of a Darklord
Hamilton, Laurell K. 682

Death of a Dunwoody Matron
Sprinkle, Patricia Houck 1051

Death of a Garden Pest
Ripley, Ann 181

Death of a Healing Woman
Martin, Allana 149, 475

Death of a Myth Maker
Martin, Allana 149, 475

Death of a Partner
Neel, Janet 165

Death of a Political Plant
Ripley, Ann 181

Death of a Russian Priest
Kaminsky, Stuart M. 130

Death of a Saint Maker
Martin, Allana 149

Death of a Salesperson and Other Untimely Exits
Barnard, Robert 142, 146

Death of a Valkyrie
Tennant, Peter 635

Death of a Winter Shaker
Woodworth, Deborah 1062

Death of an Evangelista
Martin, Allana 149

Death of an Old Goat
Barnard, Robert 176

A Death of Distinction
Eccles, Marjorie 64

A Death of Honor
Faust, Joe Clifford 744

The Death of Kings
Danielson, Peter 858

The Death of Kings
Gooden, Philip 880

Death of the Dragon
Greenwood, Ed 553

Death of the Last Villista
Martin, Allana **149**, **475**

Death of the Party
Dain, Catherine 52

The Death of Vishnu
Suri, Manil 1104, 1170, 1208

Death on a Casual Friday
Duncan, Sharon **63**

The Death on Demand Series
Hart, Carolyn 32

Death on Site
Neel, Janet 165

Death on the Appian Way
Benton, Kenneth 924

Death on the Downs
Brett, Simon **27**

Death Rattle
Johnston, Terry C. 463, 512, 890, 957

Death Rides an Ill Wind
Grilley, Kate 219

Death Rides the Denver Stage
Patten, Lewis B. 480

The Death Ship
Russell, William Clark 681

Death Stalks a Holiday
Parker, Gary E. 1039

Death Walker
Thurlo, Aimee 506

Deathday
Dietz, William C. **746**

Deathport
Campbell, Ramsey 634

The Deb Ralston Series
Martin, Lee 76, 88

The Deborah Knott Series
Maron, Margaret 197

Debt of Bones
Goodkind, Terry **549**, 550

The Deceased
Piccirilli, Tom 682

The Deceiver
Forsyth, Frederick 1204

The Deception
Reed, Barry 1204

Deck the Halls with Murder
Wolzien, Valerie 219

Decked
Clark, Carol Higgins 34

Declare
Powers, Tim 781, 1151

Decoded Mirrors
Tem, Steve Rasnic 700

Decorations in a Ruined Cemetery
Brown, John Gregory 833, 1085

The Dee Laguerre Series
Mitchell, Kirk 125

The Deep
Benchley, Peter 1097

Deep Dixie
Jones, Annie 1063

Deep Fathom
Rollins, James **792**

Deep into That Darkness Peering
Piccirilli, Tom 688

Deep Water Death
Alam, Glynn Marsh **3**

Deep Wizardry
Duane, Diane 538, 542

Deepdrive
Jablokov, Alexander 793

A Deeper Magic
Hunter, Jillian 303

The Deepest Sea
Barnitz, Charles 559

A Deepness in the Sky
Vinge, Vernor 734, 807

Defender
Cherryh, C.J. **734**

The Defiant Governess
Pickens, Andrea 370

The Defiant Heart
Gordon, Anita 338

The Defiant Hero
Brockmann, Suzanne 242

Deirdre and Don Juan
Beverley, Jo 356

Delacey's Angel
Ellis, Monique 397

The Delicate Dependency
Talbot, Michael 685

Delicate Prey
Bowles, Paul 1080

Delight
Hunter, Jillian 303

The Delilah Doolittle Series
Guiver, Patricia 17

Demolition Angel
Crais, Robert 47, 123, 1096

Demon and Other Tales
Oates, Joyce Carol 700

The Demon Apostle
Salvatore, R.A. 597

The Demon Awakens
Salvatore, R.A. 535

The Demon King
Bunch, Chris 563, 729

Demon Knight
Hood, Ken 535

Demon Lovers and Strange Seductions
Carter, Margaret L. 643

The Demon of Undoing
Alton, Andrea 563

The Demon Prince
Morgan, Kathleen 267

Demonesque
Climer, Stephen Lee 641

Demonology
Moody, Rick 1095

Demons
Shirley, John 682, 694

Demons and Dinosaurs
de Camp, L. Sprague 669

Demons, Freaks and Other Abnormalities
Laimo, Michael 639

Depraved
Schechter, Harold 932

Depth of Glory
Stone, Irving 837

Deranged
Schechter, Harold 932

Derby Dugan's Depression Funnies
De Haven, Tom 1100

Dervish Is Digital
Cadigan, Pat **731**

Deryni Rising
Kurtz, Katherine 544

Descent into the Depths of the Earth
Kidd, Paul 563

Desecration
LaHaye, Tim **1016**

Desert Autumn
Craft, Michael **45**, 71

Desert Heat
Jance, J.A. 465

A Desert in Bohemia
Paton Walsh, Jill 1098, 1106, 1168, 1212

Desert Manhunt
Cole, Judd 484

Desert Noir
Webb, Betty 28, 125

Desire
Jordan, Nicole **309**, 385

Desire
Quick, Amanda 321

The Desiree Shapiro Series
Eichler, Selma 34

Desmodus
Tem, Melanie 712

Desperate
Criswell, Millie 332

Desperate Acts
Coleman, Jane Candia 446

A Desperate, Decaying Darkness
Castro, Adam-Troy 683

Desperate Highway
Roberts, John Maddox 924

Desperately Seeking Dad
Perry, Marta 987, 1021, 1041

Desperation
King, Stephen 660

Destiny
Haydon, Elizabeth 552, **554**

Destiny
Shayne, Maggie 382, 395

Destiny of the Sword
Duncan, Dave 585

Destiny Valley
Grove, Fred 459, **459**, 460

The Destruction of the Inn
Eickhoff, Randy Lee 886

The Detective and Mr. Dickens
Palmer, William J. 917

Deus lo Volt!
Connell, Evan S. 831, 860

Devall's Angel
Lane, Allison 257, 325, 362, 377, 379

Deviant
Schechter, Harold 932

The Devil and Ms. Moody
Forster, Suzanne 235

The Devil and the Deep Blue Sea
Sherman, Beth 81

Devil in a Blue Dress
Mosley, Walter 161, 935, 1131

The Devil in Harbour
Gavin, Catherine 866

Devil in the Dark
Rogers, Evelyn 360, 418

The Devil in Velvet
Carr, John Dickson 522

The Devil Inside
Coulter, Stephen 946

The Devil Is Dead
Lafferty, R.A. 567

The Devil Is Loose
Shelby, Graham 941

The Devil Is Not Mocked and Other Warnings
Wellman, Manly Wade **707**

The Devil Knows You're Dead
Block, Lawrence 22

The Devil on Horseback
Paine, Lauran 492, 493

The Devil-Tree of El Dorado
Aubrey, Frank **717**

The Devil Went Down to Austin
Riordan, Rick 88

A Devilish Husband
Clayton, Alana **257**

Devil's Advocate
West, Morris L. 956

The Devil's Apprentice
Marston, Edward **148**

The Devil's Auction
Weinberg, Robert 706

Devil's Cantina
Crais, Robert 1096

Devil's Claw
Jance, J.A. 125, 465

Devil's Island
Hagee, John **994**

Devil's Kisses
Lovecraft, Linda 643

The Devil's Larder
Crace, Jim **1095**

The Devil's Lode: A Western Trio
Flynn, T.T. 431, 432, 435, 452, 455, 489

The Devil's Own Luck
Donachie, David 822, **853**, 854

Devil's Rim
Brown, Sam 459

The Devil's Teardrop
Deaver, Jeffery 57

Devlin's Light
Stewart, Mariah 410

Devoted
Borchardt, Alice 338, 829

Dhammara
Furey, Maggie 523, 545, 609, 611

The Diabolical Baron
Putney, Mary Jo 325

Diagnosis Impossible
Hoch, Edward D. 117, 118

Dial M for Meat Loaf
Hart, Ellen **105**

Dial Your Dreams
Weinberg, Robert **706**

Dialogues of the Dead or Paronomania!
Hill, Reginald **116**

Diamond Dust
Desai, Anita 1104

Diamond Eyes
Lutz, John 147

A Diamond in the Rough
Pickens, Andrea **370**

Diamond in the Ruff
Carmichael, Emily **249**

Diamondback
Dearl, Elizabeth 502

Diamonds
MacDonald, Shari 1005

The Diana Tregarde Series
Lackey, Mercedes 140

Diary of a Vampire
Bowen, Gary 690

The Dido Hoare Series
Macdonald, Marianne 128

Die for Love
Peters, Elizabeth 49

Die Laughing
Allen, Steve 1158

Die Trying
Child, Lee 442

Die upon a Kiss
Hambly, Barbara 909, 914

Dierdre and Don Juan
Beverley, Jo 325

A Different Flesh
Turtledove, Harry 799

The Digital Effect
Perry, Steve 763

The Dime Museum Murders
Stashower, Daniel 203

Dingley Falls
Malone, Michael 1153

Dinner at the Homesick Restaurant
Tyler, Anne 1159, 1195

Dinosaurs
Greenberg, Martin H. 753

Dirk Gently's Holistic Detective Agency
Adams, Douglas 756

Dirty Havana Trilogy
Gutierrez, Pedro Juan 1092

Dirty Linen
Kilmer, Nicholas 134

Dirty White Boys
Hunter, Stephen 122, 887, 1127

Dirty Work
Brown, Larry 1088

Discover the Destroyer
Applegate, K.A. 519, 520

Disgrace
Coetzee, J.M. 1138

Disguised Blessing
Bockoven, Georgia 239

Disobedience
Hamilton, Jane 1113

The Disposable Man
Mayor, Archer 151

The Distance
Muller, Eddie **161**

A Distance of Ground
Grove, Fred 460, 506, 509

The Distance Travelled
Savory, Brett A. 667, **689**

Distant Bells
Noble, Diane 1033

A Distant Episode
Bowles, Paul 1080

Distant Friends
Zahn, Timothy 812

The Distant Land of My Father
Caldwell, Bo **835**

Distant Love
Bell, Ann 999

Distant Memory
Gansky, Alton 985, 999

Distant Stars
Delany, Samuel R. 748

The Distinguished Guest
Miller, Sue 1163

Dive Deep and Deadly
Alam, Glynn Marsh 3

Divine Endurance
Jones, Gwyneth 764

Divine Intervention
Wharton, Ken **810**

The Djinn in the Nightingale's Eye
Byatt, A.S. 1178

The DKA Series
Gores, Joe 174

Do Androids Dream of Electric Sheep?
Dick, Philip K. 797

Do Not Exceed the Stated Dose
Lovesey, Peter 146

A Do Right Man
Tyree, Omar 1210

Do You Hear What I Hear?
Jacobs, Holly **306**

The Doberman Wore Black
Moore, Barbara 17

The Doc Adams Series
Boyer, Rick 46, 206

The Doc Ford Series
White, Randy Wayne 94, 115

Doc Holliday
Braun, Matt 485

Doc Holliday's Gone
Coleman, Jane Candia 434, **445**, 446, 491

Doc Holliday's Woman
Coleman, Jane Candia 445, 485, 493

Doc Sidhe
Allston, Aaron 516

The Doctor and the Dead Man's Chest
Hathaway, Robin **106**

Doctor Brodie's Report
Borges, Jorge Luis 787

Dr. Dad
Arnold, Judith 226

The Doctor Digs a Grave
Hathaway, Robin 106

The Doctor Makes a Dollhouse Call
Hathaway, Robin 106

Doctor Mirabilis
Blish, James 956

Dr. Mortimer and the Aldgate Mystery
Williams, Gerard 896, 899, 908, 915, **958**

Dr. Mortimer and the Barking Man Mystery
Williams, Gerard 58, 958

The Doctor Next Door
Perry, Marta 1041, 1046

The Doctor's Miracle
Schmidt, Anna 1044, **1046**

The Document
Roper, Gayle G. 1018

Dodging Red Cloud
Wheeler, Richard S. 957

Dog Eat Dog
Berenson, Laurien 17

The Dog Who Bit a Policeman
Kaminsky, Stuart M. 130

The Dog Who Knew Too Much
Benjamin, Carol Lea 16

Dogged Persistence
Anderson, Kevin J. **715**

Dogland
Shetterly, Will 539

The Dogs
Brown, Rebecca 1065

Doing Wrong
Keating, H.R.F. 132

Dolley
Brown, Rita Mae 912

Dollmaker
Janes, J. Robert 126

Dolores Claiborne
King, Stephen 1073

The Domesday Book Series
Marston, Edward 865, 933, 934

Domination
Cecilione, Michael 625

The Don and Mr. Dickens
Palmer, William J. 187

Don Diablo: A Western Story
Brand, Max 431, 433

Dona Ines vs. Oblivion
Torres, Ana Teresa 948

Done Wrong
Bland, Eleanor Taylor 21

The Donovan Legacy
Roberts, Nora 1187

The Dons and Mr. Dickens
Palmer, William J. 822, 917, 959

Don't Cry for Me, Hot Pastrami
Kahn, Sharon **129**

Don't Dream
Wandrei, Donald 671

Don't Tell Anyone
Busch, Frederick 1081

Don't the Moon Look Lonesome
Crouch, Stanley 1122, 1194, 1210

Doom City
Grant, Charles L. 648

The Doom Stone
Zindel, Paul 714

Doomed to Repeat It
goldberg, d.g.k. **641**

The Doomsday Book
Willis, Connie 811

The Doomsday Conspiracy
Sheldon, Sidney 1082

The Doomsday Marshal and the Comancheros
Hogan, Ray 423

Doomspell
McNish, Cliff 581

DoOon Mode
Anthony, Piers 518, 600

The Door in the Hedge
McKinley, Robin 579

A Door into Ocean
Slonczewski, Joan 747

The Door into Summer
Heinlein, Robert A. 754

The Door of the Unreal
Biss, Gerald 646

The Door through Washington Square
Bergstrom, Elizabeth 515, 573

The Doors of His Face, the Lamps of His Mouth
Zelazny, Roger 745

The Doran Fairweather Series
Hardwick, Mollie 36

The Dorothy Martin Series
Dams, Jeanne M. 14, 27

A Double Coffin
Butler, Gwendoline 30

Double Honor
Horsfall, Melissa **1002**

The Double Man
Binder, Eando 759

Double Vengeance
Dunckle, John **449**

The Doublet Affair
Buckley, Fiona 29, 834

Dove Amongst the Hawks
Doherty, P.C. 86, 194

Down for the Count
Kaminsky, Stuart M. 161

Down in the Bottomlands
Turtledove, Harry 804

Down on Ponce
Willard, Fred 18

Down to Sleep
Gifune, Greg F. 639

Down to the Sea
Forstchen, William R. 864

Downbelow Station
Cherryh, C.J. 740, 770, 788

Downfall
Rabe, Jean 589, 612

Downriver
Wheeler, Richard S. **512**, **957**

A Dozen Black Roses
Collins, Nancy 629

Drachenfels
Yeovil, Jack **613**

Dracula
Stoker, Bram 631, 632, 686, 695

Dracula in London
Elrod, P.N. **631**

Dracula in Love
Shirley, John 692

Dracula, Prince of Darkness
Greenberg, Martin H. 631

The Dracula Tape
Saberhagen, Fred 632, 692

Dracula Unbound
Aldiss, Brian W. 692

The Dragon and the Gnarly King
Dickson, Gordon R. 524

The Dragon and the Unicorn
Attanasio, A.A. 566

The Dragon Queen
Borchardt, Alice **528**, **829**

The Dragon Sleeping
Gardner, Craig Shaw 605

The Dragon Society
Watt-Evans, Lawrence **610**

The Dragon Trader
Townsend, Tom 605

Dragon War
Acres, Mark 610

Dragon Weather
Watt-Evans, Lawrence 523, 526, 550, 610

Dragondoom
McKiernan, Dennis L. 610

Dragonfly in Amber
Gabaldon, Diana 288, 868

The Dragonking
Weis, Margaret 611

Dragon's Bluff
Herbert, Mary H. **556**

The Dragons of Magic
King, J. Robert **565**

The Dragons of the Cuyahoga
Swann, S. Andrew **602**

Dragon's Queen
Dennis, Carol 590

Dragonslayer
Drew, Wayland 610

The Dragonstone
McKiernan, Dennis L. 526

Dragstrip
Bartholomew, Nancy 13

The Dramaturges of Yan
Brunner, John 772

Drawing Blood
Brite, Poppy Z. 640

Drawing Dead
Hautman, Pete 107

Dreadful Sanctuary
Russell, Eric Frank 794

Dream a Little Dream
Phillips, Susan Elizabeth 369

Dream Lover
Henley, Virginia 883

Dream of Me
Litton, Josie 336, 337, **338**

The Dream Stalker
Coel, Margaret 35

Dream Thief
Lawhead, Stephen R. 569

A Dream to Follow
Snelling, Lauraine **1050**

The Dream Voyagers
Bunn, T. Davis 976

Dream West
Nevin, David 912, 949

Dreamcastle
Bowkett, Stephen 724

Dreamcatcher
Bowkett, Stephen 724

Dreamcatcher
King, Stephen **660**, 675, 1082, 1166, 1185

Dreamer
Harper, Steven **755**

Dreamer
Johnson, Charles Richard 1119

The Dreamer
McGoldrick, May 352

Dreaming
Barnett, Jill 821

The Dreaming
Wood, Barbara 962

Dreaming in Smoke
Sullivan, Tricia 758

Dreaming of Castles
Martin, Gail Gaymer 1021, 1022

Dreamland
Baker, Kevin 874

The Dreammaker
Stacy, Judith 408, 409

Dreams of My Russian Summers
Makine, Andrei 1151

Dreamseeker's Road
Deitz, Tom 527

The Dreamthief's Daughter
Moorcock, Michael 560, **582**

Dreamweaver
Kane, Kathleen 313

Dreamweaver's Dilemma
Bujold, Lois McMaster 728

The Dress Lodger
Holman, Sheri 838

Driftglider and Other Stories
Osier, Jeffrey 688

Drive Me Wild
Ortolon, Julie 292, 363

Driving Blind
Bradbury, Ray 1082

Driving Lessons
Matlock, Curtiss Ann 231

Drop Dead
Zubro, Mark Richard 221

The Drowning Room
Pye, Michael 939

Druids
Llywelyn, Morgan 886, 952

Drummer in the Dark
Bunn, T. Davis **976**

Drums of Autumn
Gabaldon, Diana 288, 868

Drums of Change
Oke, Janette 1058

Druss the Legend
Gemmell, David 557

The Duffy House Series
Evers, Crabbe 188

Dugan under Ground
De Haven, Tom **1100**

Duke of Egypt
Moor, Margriet de 1165

Dun Lady's Jess
Durgin, Doranna 590

The Duncan Kincaid/Gemma James Series
Crombie, Deborah 87, 165

Dune
Herbert, Frank 718, 757

Dune Messiah
Herbert, Frank 777

Dungeons and Dragons
Barrett, Neal Jr. 524

The Dunwich Horror and Others
Lovecraft, H.P. 670

A Durable Fire
Bernhard, Virginia 950

The Dutch
Roberts, Les 185

The Dutchman's Dilemma
Meyers, Maan 939

The Dwelling
Elliott, Tom 640

The Dying Animal
Roth, Philip 1173, 1177, 1184

Dying Fall
Hall, Patricia 97

Dying Inside
Silverberg, Robert 797

Dying on the Vine
King, Peter 135

The Dying Trade
Donachie, David 853, **854**

Dying Voices
Wilson, Laura 214

The Dylan St. John Series
Funderburk, Robert 981

E

The E.J. Pugh Series
Cooper, Susan Rogers 49

Eager to Please
Parsons, Julie **1180**

Eagle Pilot
Stengl, Jill 1000

Eagle's Cry
Nevin, David 912

The Eagle's Daughter
Tarr, Judith 940

Early Autumn
Parker, Robert B. 199

The Early Fears
Bloch, Robert 671

The Earth Abideth
Dickinson, David 851

Earth Made of Glass
Barnes, John 722

The Earth Shall Weep
Wilson, James 959

The Earth Strikes Back
Chizmar, Richard 628, 666

The Earth Wire and Other Stories
Lane, Joel 655

Earthbound
Matheson, Richard 620

Earthman, Go Home!
Anderson, Poul 719, 743

The Earthquake Bird
Jones, Susanna **127**, 150

Earthsong
Elgin, Suzette Haden 747, 811

East into Upper East
Prawer, Ruth 1190

East Is East
Boyle, T. Coraghessan 1081

East of the Sun, West of the Moon
Bellacera, Carole **231**

Easter in Calico
Curtis, Jack 457, 470, 488

Easy Money
Siler, Jenny 50, 199

Easy Pickin's
Harris, Fred 110

The Easy Rawlins Series
Mosley, Walter 166, 192, 196

Eat, Drink and Be Buried
King, Peter 135

Eaters of the Dead
Crichton, Michael 1097

The Ebon Mask
Byers, Richard Lee 532

Eccentric Circles
Lickiss, Rebecca 515, **573**

The Echo
Walters, Minette 211

Echo Burning
Child, Lee 149, **442**

Echo House
Just, Ward S. 1134

Echoes
Gunn, Robin Jones 993

Echoes in Time
Norton, Andre 784

Echoes of Darkness
Maynard, L.H. 674, 701

Echoes of Lies
Bannister, Jo **11**

Echoes of Mercy
Cote, Lyn 985

Eclipse Bay
Krentz, Jayne Ann 331

Eden
Bean, Frederic 481, 495

Eden Springs
Corey, G. Roger 1019, 1030

The Edge of Human
Jeter, K.W. 797

Edge of the Wilderness
Whitson, Stephanie Grace 1058

The Edge of Town
Garlock, Dorothy **290**, 882

The Edgecliffe Manor Series
Peart, Jane 1015, 1026

Edgewater Angels
Meallet, Sandro **1160**

The Edith Wharton Murders
Rafael, Lev 176

The Edward X. Delaney Series
Sanders, Lawrence 152

The Edwina Charles Series
Warner, Mignon 79

Eleanor
Lerman, Rhoda 928

Electric God
Hyde, Catherine Ryan 1175

The Electric Kid
Kilworth, Gary 776

Elementals
Byatt, A.S. 1169

Elementary, My Dear Groucho
Goulart, Ron 85

The Elementary Particles
Houellebecq, Michel 1085, 1173, 1198

The Elena Jarvis Series
Herndon, Nancy 81, 88, 149

The Elephant
Mrozek, Slawomir 720

Elfsong
Cunningham, Elaine 597

Eli
Myers, Bill 1032

Elidor
Garner, Alan 581

The Elizabeth I Series
Harper, Karen 29, 65, 834, 861, 880

Elizabeth and the Major
Collum, Lynn 420

The Elizabeth Chase Series
Lawrence, Martha C. 52, 79

The Elizabeth Elliot Series
Allen, Irene 1062

The Elizabeth MacPherson Series
McCrumb, Sharyn 6, 114

The Ella Clah Series
Thurlo, Aimee 35, 39, 61

The Ellie Haskell Series
Cannell, Dorothy 9

Ellipsis
Greenleaf, Stephen 190

Ellis Island
Stewart, Fred Mustard 937

Elminster in Hell
Greenwood, Ed **553**

Elminster in Myth Drannor
Greenwood, Ed 553, 584, 597

Elsewhere
Shetterly, Will 598, 602

Elusive Passion
Smith, Kathryn 293, 375, **402**, 416

The Elusive Voice
Adamson, Mary Jo **2**

The Elven Star
Weis, Margaret 612

Embers of Time
Riley, Eugenia 380

Embrace the Dawn
Morgan, Kathleen 1025, **1026**

Embryo
Klein, Daniel M. 783

Embryo
Wilson, Charles 783

Emerald Aisle
McInerny, Ralph **156**

Emerald City
Egan, Jennifer 1108

The Emerald Isle
Hunt, Angela Elwell 1004

Emerald Windows
Blackstock, Terri 970, **971**, 1035, 1045

Emerald's Fire
Snoe, Eboni 403

Emigre Journeys
Hussein, Abdullah **1129**

Eminence
West, Morris L. 956

The Emma Marsh Series
Dean, Elizabeth 144

Empire
Piper, H. Beam 777

Empire
Simak, Clifford D. 768

Empire & Ecolitan
Modesitt, L.E. Jr. **777**, 778

Empire Falls
Russo, Richard 1113, 1130, 1136

The Empire of Fear
Stableford, Brian 685, 713

Empire of Unreason
Keyes, J. Gregory 516, 751

The Empty Chair
Deaver, Jeffery 57

Empty Cradle
Harper, Karen 312, 381

The Empty House and Other Ghost Stories
Blackwood, Algernon 647

Enchanted by Your Kisses
Britton, Pamela 309

Enchanter
Douglass, Sara **540**

The Enchantment
Binder, Pam **237**

The Enchantress
McGoldrick, May 352

End of Act Three
Morris, Gilbert 1027, 1028

End of Days
Danvers, Dennis 722

The End of Eternity
Asimov, Isaac 802

The End-of-Everything Man
De Haven, Tom 1100

End of the Story
Davis, Lydia 1099

End over End
Kennedy, Kate 1086, **1139**

Endangered
Chaikin, Linda 1027

Endorphins
Kilpatrick, Nancy 658

The Ends of the Earth
Shepard, Lucius 582

Endurance
Viehl, S.L. 805

Endymion
Simmons, Dan 721, 736

Enemies of the System
Aldiss, Brian W. 779, 782

The Enemy Reborn
Stackpole, Michael A. 599

Enemy Way
Thurlo, Aimee 506

The Enemy Within
Hegan, Christine 312

The English Garden
Martin, Gail Gaymer **1020**

English Ivy
Palmer, Catherine 1020, 1038

The English Patient
Ondaatje, Michael 876

The Enigma of Arrival
Naipaul, V.S. 1170

Ensign Flandry
Anderson, Poul 768, 777, 812

Enslaved
Henley, Virginia 883

Entering Tenebrea
Dawson, Roxann 743

Entertain the End
Applegate, K.A. **519**

Entities
Russell, Eric Frank **794**

Envy
Brown, Sandra **245**, **1086**

The Ephesus Fragment
Parker, Gary E. 1039

Epiphany
McCusker, Paul 1024, 1032, 1033, 1038

Eric Brighteyes
Haggard, H. Rider 517

The Ernest Lehmann Series
Gerson, Jack 126

The Ernie Carpenter Series
James, Dean 163

Escapade
Satterthwait, Walter 187, 926

Escape
McCourtney, Lorena 1017, 1023

Escape from Castle Quarras
Niles, Douglas 556

Escardy Gap
Crowther, Peter 739

The Eskimo Invasion
Howard, Hayden 801

Estate of Mind
Myers, Tamar 163

Ester's Child
Sasson, Jean P. **930**

The Eternal
Chadbourn, Mark 665

Eternal Sunset
Giron, Sephera 640

Eternity
Shayne, Maggie 395

Eternity
Thorne, Tamara 703

The Eugenia Potter Series
Rich, Virginia 1037

Eva Luna
Allende, Isabel 817, 1067

Eva Moves the Furniture
Livesey, Margot 1079, **1148**, 1193

Evan and Elle
Bowen, Rhys 24

Evan Can Wait
Bowen, Rhys 24, 55

Evan Help Us
Bowen, Rhys 24

Evanly Choirs
Bowen, Rhys 24

Evans Above
Bowen, Rhys 24

The Eve Duncan Series
Johansen, Iris 78

The Eve Elliott Series
Lee, Barbara 205

Eve of St. Hyacinth
Sedley, Kate 194, 933, 934

Even the Wicked
Block, Lawrence 22

Evermeet
Cunningham, Elaine 583

Everville
Barker, Clive 619

Every Breath She Takes
Forster, Suzanne 283

Every Dead Thing
Connolly, John 42

Every Hidden Thing
Dickson, Athol 966

Every Little Thing about You
Wick, Lori 1059

Every Man for Himself
Bainbridge, Beryl 1069

Every Tongue Got to Confess
Hurston, Zora Neale **1128**

Everybody Dies
Block, Lawrence 22

Everything but the Squeal
Hallinan, Timothy 199

Everything in Its Time
Davis, Dee 237

Everything You Need
Kennedy, A.L. **1138**

Eve's Daughters
Austin, Lynn N. 967, 1038

The Evidence Against Her
Dew, Robb Forman 845, 848, **850**, 891, 925, 938, **1102**, 1163

The Evil Eye
Price, David 636

Evolution's Shore
McDonald, Ian 739

Ex-Libris
King, Ross 820, 853, 1182

Excavation
Rollins, James 792

Excavation
Tem, Steve Rasnic 700

An Excess of Enchantments
Gardner, Craig Shaw 537, 588

Excession
Banks, Iain 721

Excuse Me? Whose Baby?
Diamond, Jacqueline 380

The Executioners
MacDonald, John D. 665

The Executives
Fullerton, Alexander 866

The Executor and Other Ghost Stories
Rowlands, David G. 652

The Exile Kiss
Effinger, George Alec 774

The Exile of Ellendon
Marden, William 551

The Exiles
Long, William Stuart 904

The Exiles
Rawn, Melanie 551

Exile's Return
Greeno, Gayle 551

The Exile's Return
Jacoby, Kate 551

Exile's Return
Jacoby, Kate 561

Exile's Song
Bradley, Marion Zimmer 725

Exodus
Uris, Leon 942

Explorers in Hell
Drake, David 553

Exposed
Leto, Julie Elizabeth 240

The Extraordinary Adventures of Secret Agent Shipov
Okudzhava, Bulat S. 946

The Extraterrestrial
Shock, Julian 737

Eye
Schow, David J. 656

Eye Contact
Craft, Michael 45

An Eye for Gold
Andrews, Sarah 7

The Eye of God
Grace, C.L. 86, 875

The Eye of Horus
Thurston, Carol 101

Eye of the Cat
McWilliams, A.L. 482

Eye of the Cricket
Sallis, James 192

The Eye of the Needle
Follett, Ken 863

Eyes of Elisha
Collins, Brandilyn 980, **981**

The Eyre Affair
Fforde, Jasper 778

F

Fabulous Harbors
Moorcock, Michael 582, 607

Face
Lebbon, Tim **665**

Face Down Among the Winchester Geese
Emerson, Kathy Lynn 65, 861

Face Down Before Rebel Hooves
Emerson, Kathy Lynn **65**, **861**, 875

Face Down Beneath the Eleanor Cross
Emerson, Kathy Lynn 65, 861

Face Down in the Marrow-Bone Pie
Emerson, Kathy Lynn 65, 861

Face Down under the Wych Elm
Emerson, Kathy Lynn 65, 861

Face Down upon an Herbal
Emerson, Kathy Lynn 65, 861

A Face Turned Backwards
Haney, Lauren 101

The Facts in the Case of E.A. Poe
Sinclair, Andrew 193

Fadeaway
Rosen, R.D. 188

Faded Coat of Blue
Parry, Owen 169, 914

The Faded Flower
McCusker, Paul **1024**

Faerie Tale
Feist, Raymond E. 527, 642, 659

The Faery Convention
Davis, Brett 533, 602

Faery Magic
Putney, Mary Jo 281, 303, 384

Fahrenheit 451
Bradbury, Ray 668, 782, 1082

Fair Game
Krich, Rochelle 137

Fair Haven
Ross, JoAnn 386

Fair Laughs the Morn
Gray, Genevieve 476, 510

The Fair Maid of Bohemia
Marston, Edward 148

The Fair Rules of Evil
Smith, David C. 644

The Fairest Among Women
Horn, Shifra 1197

Fairness
Mount, Ferdinand **1167**, 1171, 1173

The Fairy Bride
Verge, Lisa Ann 384

Fairy Tale
Hunter, Jillian 303

Fairyland
McAuley, Paul J. 771

Fairytale
Shayne, Maggie 384, 395, 401

The Faith Fairchild Series
Page, Katherine Hall 36, 996

Faith in the Flesh
Lebbon, Tim 666

Faith of the Fallen
Goodkind, Terry 549, 550, 572, 609, 611

The Faith on the Homefront Series
Stokes, Penelope J. 977, 1034

The Faithful Narrative of a Pastor's Disappearance
Anastas, Benjamin 1133

Faithless
Oates, Joyce Carol 1173, 1174, 1199, 1203

Falcon and the Sword
Beard, Julie 229

The Falconer Series
Morson, Ian 934

Fall from Grace
Chance, Megan 294

A Fall in Denver
Andrews, Sarah 7

Fall of a Cosmonaut
Kaminsky, Stuart M. 130

The Fall of Neskaya
Bradley, Marion Zimmer **725**

The Fall of the House of Escher and Other Illusions
Wilson, David Niall 693

The Fall of the King
Jensen, Johannes Vilhelm 862

Fall to Pieces
Tishy, Cecelia 189

Fallen
Bradley, Celeste **241**

Fallen
Gram, Dewey 627

Falling Angels
Chevalier, Tracy 819, **838**, 848, 959, **1090**, 1205

The Falls
Rankin, Ian **178**

The False Inspector Dew
Lovesey, Peter 5

False Memory
Koontz, Dean R. 661

Family
McCarthy, Kevin 775

The Family
Puzo, Mario **916**, 1152, **1183**

Family Affairs
Kitt, Sandra 272

A Family All Her Own
Winn, Bonnie K. **1061**

Family and Friends
Brookner, Anita 1143

A Family at Last
Aarsen, Carolyne 965, 1047, 1061

Family Business
Lewin, Michael Z. 142

Family Dancing
Leavitt, David 1145

A Family for Andi
Berger, Eileen 968

A Family for Christmas
Welsh, Kate 1057

A Family for Gillian
Blair, Catherine **238**

A Family for Jana
Berger, Eileen **968**

Family Found
Winn, Bonnie K. 1061

A Family in the Making
Froemke, Marcy 997

The Family Jewels and Other Stories
Cannell, Dorothy **31**

Family Planning
Lewin, Michael Z. 142

Family Practice
Weir, Charlene 212

A Family-Style Christmas
Aarsen, Carolyne 965, 968

A Family to Call Her Own
Hannon, Irene 968

A Family to Cherish
Page, Carole Gift 995, 1035, 1036

Famous Blue Raincoat
Gorman, Ed 40, 117, 175

The Famous Heroine
Balogh, Mary 393

The Fan
Abrahams, Peter 1

The Fanny Zindel Series
Stevens, Serita 129

The Fantastic Adventures of Robin Hood
Greenberg, Martin H. 753

A Far and Deadly Cry
Holbrook, Teri 92

The Far Canyon
Kelton, Elmer 895

The Far Field
Meidav, Edie 1152

Far from Home
Bockoven, Georgia 239

Far Frontiers
Greenberg, Martin H. 552

Far Harbor
Ross, JoAnn 239

The Far Horizon
Killdeer, John 512

The Far Side of the Lake
Tem, Steve Rasnic **700**

Farewell to Lankhmar
Leiber, Fritz 767

Faro's Daughter
Heyer, Georgette 377, 379

The Farseekers
Carmody, Isobelle 732

The Fashionable Spy
Hendrickson, Emily 374

Fast Copy
Jenkins, Dan 1066, 1130

Fat Tuesday
Brown, Sandra 245

Fatal Cure
Cook, Robin 1070, 1093

The Fatal Frontier
Gorman, Ed 484, 511

Fatal Legacy
Corley, Elizabeth **43**

A Fatal Vineyard Season
Craig, Philip R. 46

The Fate
Wheeler, Richard S. 482

Fated Genes
Kraus, Harry Lee 1012

Father and Son
Brown, Larry 1180

The Father Grif Series
Delffs, Dudley J. 1018, 1062

The Father Mark Townsend Series
Reynolds, Brad 35

Father Most Blessed
Perry, Marta 1041, 1061

Father to Be
Pappano, Marilyn 366

Fathers and Crows
Vollmann, William T. 950

The Father's Day Murder
Harris, Lee 996

A Father's Place
Perry, Marta **1041**

A Father's Promise
Perry, Marta 1041

Fault Line
Andrews, Sarah **7**

The Favorite Uncle Remus
Chandler, Joel 1128

Fax Me a Bagel
Kahn, Sharon 129

The Fay Croaker Series
Bishop, Paul 47

Fear and Trembling
Nothomb, Amelie 1133

Fear Nothing
Koontz, Dean R. 661, 664

Fear of Blue Skies
Burgin, Richard 1087

Fearful Symmetries
Swann, S. Andrew 602

Fearless Jones
Mosley, Walter 122, 1088, 1089, 1118, 1127, 1166

A Feast in Exile
Yarbro, Chelsea Quinn **713**, 922, **963**

The Feast of the Goat
Vargas Llosa, Mario **948**, **1211**

A Feast Unknown
Farmer, Philip Jose 801

Feather Crowns
Mason, Bobbie Ann 1155

A Feather on the Breath of God
Nunez, Sigrid 1172

Feeding the Ghosts
D'Aguiar, Fred 846

The Feelies
Farren, Mick 793

Feersum Endjinn
Banks, Iain 721

Feet of Clay
Pratchett, Terry 588

The Feline Wizard
Stasheff, Christopher 587

Female Intelligence
Heller, Jane **1125**

The Female Man
Russ, Joanna 811

The Fencing Master
Perez-Reverte, Arturo 171, 1182

A Feral Darkness
Durgin, Doranna **543**

Ferney
Long, James 529, 598

Ferris Beach
McCorkle, Jill 1157

Fever
Sutcliffe, Katherine 412

Fever Rising
Ferguson, Maggie 272

A Few Minutes Past Midnight
Kaminsky, Stuart M. 828, 923

The Fey Croaker Series
Bishop, Paul 137

The Fey: Sacrifice
Rusch, Kristine Kathryn 527

Fiance Wanted!
Dale, Ruth Jean 250, 255, 353

Fiddler's Fair
Lackey, Mercedes 568

Fielder's Choice
Bowen, Michael 188

The Fiery Cross
Gabaldon, Diana **288**, **868**, 869

The Fifth Elephant
Pratchett, Terry 587

Fighting Gravity
Rambach, Peggy **1184**, 1197

Film Strip
Bartholomew, Nancy 13

Final Account
Robinson, Peter 186

The Final Addiction
Condon, Richard 1142

The Final Assault
Berry, Stephen Ames 795

The Final Battle
Dietz, William C. 742

The Final Bow
Justice, Alan David 1031

The Final Country
Crumley, James **50**

The Final Dream and Other Visions
Pearlman, Daniel 786

Final Edit
Carter, Robert A. 128

Final Impact
Navarro, Yvonne 767

Final Jeopardy
Fairstein, Linda 66

Final Vinyl Days
McCorkle, Jill 1157

Finally Found
Cote, Lyn 985

Finally Home
Cote, Lyn 974, 985

Finder
Rucka, Greg 190

Finding Her Prince
Darcy, Lilian 268

Finding Laura
Hooper, Kay 340

Finding Moon
Hillerman, Tony 1066

Finding Mr. Right
Carmichael, Emily 249

A Fine and Private Place
Davies, Freda **55**

Finity
Barnes, John 722

Finity's End
Cherryh, C.J. 734

Fire
Rodgers, Alan 708

Fire and Ice
Scott, DeLoras 391

Fire Angels
Routley, Jane 572

Fire-Hunter
Kjelgard, Jim 723

Fire in Beulah
Askew, Rilla 947

Fire in the Rock
Martin, Joe **1154**

Fire Lilies
Massey, Cynthia Leal **476**

Fire Music
Gray, Julia 551

Fire of Heaven
Myers, Bill 1032

Fire on the Waters
Poyer, David 898

A Fire upon the Deep
Vinge, Vernor 721, 736, 789, 807

Firebird
Graham, Janice 457

The Firebrand
McGoldrick, May 352

Firebrand Bride
Lynnford, Janet 348

Firebreak
Stark, Richard **202**

Firelord
Godwin, Parke 566

Firemask
Bunch, Chris 729, 809

Firestarter
King, Stephen 709, 775

Firestorm
Bergren, Lisa Tawn 999

Fireworks
Moore, James A. 660, **675**

The Firm
Grisham, John 1096

First, Body
Thon, Melanie Rae 1121, 1162

The First Century Diaries Series
Edwards, Gene 994, 1053

First Comes Love
Bevarly, Elizabeth 235, 236, 261, 264, 299, 369, 380

The First Duelist
Etheridge, Rutledge 750

First Evidence
Goddard, Ken 773

First Gray, Then White, Then Blue
Moor, Margriet de **1165**

First Horses
Gish, Robert Franklin 453

The First King of Shannara
Brooks, Terry 530

First Kiss
Pappano, Marilyn 366

First Lady
Malone, Michael **1153**

First Lady
Phillips, Susan Elizabeth 265, 344, 369

First Landing
Zubrin, Robert **814**

First Light
Craig, Philip R. **46**

The First North Americans Series
Gear, Kathleen O'Neal 871

First Prize
Cline, Edward 840

The First Time
Fielding, Joy 1101

First to Ride
Crowell, Pers 723

The First Waltz
Bell, Donna 230, 262

Fistful of Digits
Hodder-Williams, Christopher 808

Fitting Ends and Other Stories
Chaon, Dan 1147

Five Card Stud
Gunn, Elizabeth 93

The Five Jars
James, M.R. 650

Five Past Midnight
Thayer, James 131

Five Quarters of the Orange
Harris, Joanne 835, 930

Five Smooth Stones
Fairbairn, Ann 1119, 1206

Flame
McGoldrick, May 352

The Flaming Corsage
Kennedy, William 897

The Flanders Panel
Perez-Reverte, Arturo 171, 1182

Flashfire
Stark, Richard 202

Flashpoint
Tillis, Tracey 312, 365

The Flaxborough Series
Watson, Colin 14

Flee the Darkness
Jeffrey, Grant R. 989, 1016

The Flee the Darkness Series
Jeffrey, Grant R. 991

Fleeced
Clark, Carol Higgins **34**

Flesh and Silver
Burns, Stephen L. 805

The Flesh Artist
Taylor, Lucy 656

Flight Dreams
Craft, Michael 45

The Flight of the Maidens
Gardam, Jane 821, 845, **870**, 925, 938

Flight to Canada
Reed, Ishmael 846

Flights of Angels
Gilchrist, Ellen 1157

Flights of Love
Schlink, Bernhard 1124, **1192**

The Flint Knife
Benson, E.F. 622

Flint's Gift
Wheeler, Richard S. 439, 443, 512

The Flip Side of Sin
McMillan, Rosalyn 1179

The Floating Girl
Massey, Sujata 150

Floating in My Mother's Palm
Hegi, Ursula 1124

Floating Worlds
Holland, Cecelia 789

Flood Tide
Cussler, Clive 1097

The Florentine
Shulman, Sandra 836

The Flower Master
Massey, Sujata 150

Flowerdust
Jones, Gwyneth 764

Fluid Mosaic
Arnzen, Michael D. **616**

Fluke
Blinder, Martin 874

Flute Song
Burleson, Donald R. 661

Flutie
Glancy, Diane 467, 481, 513

Fly Me to the Moon
Adams, Kylie 274

Flying Blind
Collins, Max Allan 41, 841

Flying Eagle
Champlin, Tim **440**

Foggy Mountain Breakdown
McCrumb, Sharyn 31

The Folks
Garton, Ray **638**

Follow That Baby!
Sharpe, Isabel 380

Followin' a Dream
Snoe, Eboni **403**

The Folly of Eustace and Other Stories
Hichens, Robert 647

Fools
Cadigan, Pat 731

Fools Die
Puzo, Mario 1183

Fool's Paradise
Phillips, Tori 326

Foolscap
Malone, Michael 1153

Footfall
Niven, Larry 746

Footloose Convoy
McGinley, Marjorie M. 479

For Christmas, Forever
Wind, Ruth 422

For Every Evil
Hart, Ellen 105

For Fear of the Night
Grant, Charles L. 642

For Love
Miller, Sue 1163

For Love of Hawk
Wolverton, Cheryl 968

For Love of Zach
Wolverton, Cheryl 1052

For My Daughters
Delinsky, Barbara 1205

For My Lady's Kiss
Needham, Linda 321

For Rouenna
Nunez, Sigrid **1172**

For the Love of Money
Tyree, Omar 1210

For the Sake of Her Child
Welsh, Kate 968, 1057

For Your Eyes Only
Fleming, Ian 118

For Your Heart Only
Smith, Debra White **1048**

Forbid Them Not
Farris, Michael P. **991**

A Forbidden Embrace
Jacobs, Anna **305**

Forbidden Garden
Fobes, Tracy 281

Forbidden Lover
Stevens, Amanda 410

The Forbidden Zone
Strieber, Whitley 699

Foreigner
Cherryh, C.J. 728

The Forest of Forever
Swann, Thomas Burnett 547

Forests of the Heart
De Lint, Charles 539

Forever After
Anderson, Catherine 225, 364

Forever After
Ford, Bette 403

Forever Enchanted
Shayne, Maggie 395, 401

Forever Friends
Billerbeck, Kristin 986

The Forever Husband
Alexander, Kathryn 1035

Forever My Lady
Holling, Jen 390

Forever Peace
Haldeman, Joe 796

The Forever War
Haldeman, Joe 761

Forging the Runes
Sherman, Josepha 575

The Forgiving Heart
Kastner, Debra 1047

The Forgiving Hour
Hatcher, Robin Lee 993, 1023, 1055

Forgotten
McCourtney, Lorena 1023

The Forgotten Dimension
Garnett, David 752

Forgotten Lullaby
Herron, Rita 299

Forgotten Tales of Terror
Lamb, Hugh 615

The Forlorn
Freer, David 751

The Forlorn Hope
Drake, David 765

The Forsaken
Fulghum, Stephen Ray 687

Fortress Draconis
Stackpole, Michael A. **599**

Fortress of Dragons
Cherryh, C.J. 734

Fortunate Lives
Dew, Robb Forman 850, 1102

The Fortunate Pilgrim
Puzo, Mario 916

Fortune's Favorites
McCullough, Colleen 1211

Fortune's Lady
Richardson, Evelyn **379**

The Fortunes of the Black Hills Series
Bly, Stephen A. 1050

Foucault's Pendulum
Eco, Umberto 1164

Foundation
Asimov, Isaac 777

The Foundling
Heyer, Georgette 404

Four and Twenty Blackbirds
Lackey, Mercedes 523, 569

Four Blondes
Bushnell, Candace 1125

Four Corners of Night
Holden, Craig 119, 885

Four of a Kind
Morris, Gilbert 1027, 1028

Four to Score
Evanovich, Janet 274

The Fourth Hand
Irving, John 1084, 1111, **1130**, 1214

The Fourth Horseman
Eickhoff, Randy Lee 485, 493

Foxfire
Oates, Joyce Carol 1172

Fractal Paisleys
Di Filippo, Paul 720, 745

Frame of Reference
Oltion, Jerry 785

Framed in Cornwall
Bolitho, Janie 54

Framed in Lace
Ferris, Monica 67

The Fran Varaday Series
Granger, Ann 11

The Francesca Vierling Series
Viets, Elaine 53

Francesca's Rake
Kerstan, Lynn 241

The Frankenstein Papers
Saberhagen, Fred 691

Frankenstein: The Legacy
Schildt, Christopher **691**, 692

Frankenstein Unbound
Aldiss, Brian W. 691

Franklin's Crossing
Reynolds, Clay 498

Freakshow
Wilson, F. Paul 634, 638

Fred & Edie
Dawson, Jill 838, 847, **848**, 943

Free Fall
Crais, Robert 111, 1096

Freedom Express
Maloney, Mack 769

Freedom's Altar
Price, Charles F. 910

Freedom's Challenge
McCaffrey, Anne 772

Freehold
Dietz, William C. 729, 784

The Fremont Jones Series
Day, Dianne 24, 878

French Leave
South, Sheri Cobb **404**

The French Lieutenant's Woman
Fowles, John 1102

French Quarter
Cameron, Stella 245, 272

French Silk
Brown, Sandra 301

Frenchman's Creek
Du Maurier, Daphne 881

Frida
Mujica, Barbara 951

Friday Night in Beast House
Laymon, Richard **662**

Friday's Child
Chaikin, Linda **977**, 1020

Fried Green Tomatoes at the Whistle Stop Cafe
Flagg, Fannie 1094, 1136

A Friend from England
Brookner, Anita 1172

Friend of My Youth
Munro, Alice 1162

A Friend of the Earth
Boyle, T. Coraghessan 1081

Friends
Hackenberry, Charles 451

Friends and Enemies
Bly, Stephen A. **972**, 973

Friends Come in Boxes
Coney, Michael G. 722

The Friends of Eddie Coyle
Higgins, George V. 1134

The Friends of Pancho Villa
Blake, James Carlos 424, 513, 825

Fright Line
Byers, Richard Lee 532

Frights of Fancy
Williamson, J.N. 693

From a Sealed Room
Kadish, Rachel 978

From Fancy's Realm
Baldwin, Louisa 618

From the Corner of His Eye
Koontz, Dean R. 661, 1074

From the Dust Returned
Bradbury, Ray **623**, 1070, **1082**, 1171

From These Ashes
Brown, Fredric 715

From Weird and Distant Shores
Kiernan, Caitlin R. **656**

Frontiers
Reece, Colleen L. 969

Frontiersville High
Bowkett, Stephen 724

Frostwing
Knaak, Richard A. 541, 596

The Fugitive Prince
Wurts, Janny 585

Fugitive's Trail
Conley, Robert J. 447

Fugue Devil and Other Weird Horrors
Rainey, Stephen Mark 683

Fulton County Blues
Birmingham, Ruth 18

Funeral in Blue
Perry, Anne **172**, 898, **915**

The Funeral Party
Ulitskaya, Ludmila 1151

Funland
Laymon, Richard 687

The Funnies
Lennon, J. Robert 473, 1146

Funny Accent
Shulgasser-Parker, Barbara **1197**

The Furies
Roberts, Keith 762

Fury
Rushdie, Salman 1170, **1190**, 1193

The Fury and the Terror
Farris, John 709

Future Crimes
Greenberg, Martin H. 552, 754

Future Net
Greenberg, Martin H. 753

Futureland
Mosley, Walter **779**, 786, 1070, **1166**

Futures
Crowther, Peter **739**

G

Gabriella
Murray, Earl 449, 450, 957

Gabrielle
Sattler, Veronica 388

Gabriel's Gift
Kureishi, Hanif **1143**, 1202

Gabriel's Story
Durham, David Anthony 884, 961

The Gail Connor Series
Parker, Barbara 75

The Gaius Diary
Edwards, Gene **990**

The Galactic Gourmet
White, James 805

Galactic Patrol
Smith, Edward E. 768

Galatea in 2-D
Allston, Aaron 516

Galilee
Barker, Clive 619

Galindez
Vazquez Montalban, Manuel 948

The Gallant Guardian
Richardson, Evelyn 278, 379

Gallant Waif
Gracie, Anne 259

The Gallatin Convergence
Smith, L. Neil 799

Gallows Hill
Duncan, Lois 849

The Gallows Land
Pronzini, Bill 480

The Galway Chronicles
Thoene, Bodie 1026, 1060

The Gamble
Wolf, Joan 348

The Gambler's Fortune
McKenna, Juliet E. 578

Gambler's Row: A Western Trio
Savage, Les Jr. **500**

The Game
Joyce, Brenda 254

A Game of Chance
Howard, Linda 302

A Game of Colors
Urbancik, John **704**

A Game of Secrets
Wiseman, Thomas 928

A Game of Thrones
Martin, George R.R. 536, 541, 544, 545, 550

Game Without Rules
Gilbert, Michael 118

Gameplayers
Bowkett, Stephen 724

Games
Ellson, Hal 663

The Games Psyborgs Play
Barbet, Pierre 755

Gap Creek
Morgan, Robert 891, 910

The Garbage Chronicles
Herbert, Brian 757

A Garden Folly
Hern, Candice 278, 298, 356, 379

The Garden of Eden
Brand, Max 717

A Garden to Keep
Turner, Jamie Langston **1055**

The Garden Tour Affair
Ripley, Ann 181

Gargoyles
Nayes, Alan **677**, **783**

Garnethill
Mina, Denise 178

The Garr Reed Series
Dickson, Athol 981

Garters and Spurs
Scott, DeLoras 391

Gatekeeper
Craig, Terry L. 1016

Gates of Ivory, Gates of Horn
Holdstock, Robert 558

The Gates of Noon
Rohan, Michael Scott 595

Gateway House
Overholser, Wayne D. 490, 491

Gateway to the Gods
Applegate, K.A. 519, 520

The Gathering Dark
Grubb, Jeff 564

A Gathering of Finches
Kirkpatrick, Jane 1011

A Gathering of Spies
Altman, John 215, 863

The Gauntlet
Brand, Max **430**

Geek Love
Dunn, Katherine 638

Genellan: First Victory
Gier, Scott 795

General Murders
Estleman, Loren D. 147

The General's Daughter
DeMille, Nelson 1131

The General's Dog
Woods, James 183

The General's Notorious Widow
Bly, Stephen A. 972, 973

Generation X
Coupland, Douglas 1094

Genevieve of Tombstone
Duncklee, John 449

Genevieve Undead
Yeovil, Jack 613

The Gentle Hills Series
Wubbels, Lance 1007, 1017

Gentle Touch
Hunt, Angela Elwell 1032

Gentle Warrior
Garwood, Julie 405

A Gentleman for Dry Creek
Tronstad, Janet 1022

The Gentleman Thief
Simmons, Deborah 396

Geodesic Dreams
Dozois, Gardner 748

The George Sansi Series
Mann, Paul 132

The George Smiley Series
Le Carre, John 215

Gerald's Game
King, Stephen 664

A German Requiem
Kerr, Philip 131

The Germanicus Mosaic
Rowe, Rosemary 180

Geronimo, an American Legend
Conley, Robert J. 842

Get Lucky
Brockmann, Suzanne 242, 283

The Getaway Special
Oltion, Jerry **785**

Getaways
Darty, Peggy 1049

The Gettin' Place
Straight, Susan 1205

Getting Lucky
Pappano, Marilyn 366

Gettysburg
Reasoner, James **919**

The Ghost and Katie Coyle
Kelleher, Annie 351

Ghost Brand of the Wishbones
Dawson, Peter 430, 501

The Ghost Companion
Haining, Peter 615

Ghost Dancing
Linzer, Anna 453

A Ghost for Maggie
Carmichael, Emily 249, 351

Ghost Killer
Chandler, Scott **627**

The Ghost Legion
Weis, Margaret 611, 612

Ghost Mine
Frazee, Steve 439, 443, 453

Ghost Moon
Robards, Karen 381

A Ghost of a Chance
Crider, Bill 48, 49

Ghost of a Flea
Sallis, James **192**

Ghost of a Smile
Boehm, Deborah 1128

The Ghost of Gaston Revere
Hansom, Mark 646

The Ghost of Hannah Mendes
Ragen, Naomi 1064

The Ghost of John Wayne and Other Stories
Gonzalez, Ray 430, **455**

Ghost of My Dreams
Ray, Angie 351

Ghost of the White Nights
Modesitt, L.E. Jr. 741, 777, **778**

The Ghost Pirates
Hodgson, William Hope 681

Ghost Quartet
Burgin, Richard 1087

Ghost Stories of an Antiquary
James, M.R. 650

The Ghost Trail
Dunham, Tracy 426, 429, 471

The Ghost Wagon and Other Great Western Adventures
Brand, Max 491

The Ghost Walker
Coel, Margaret 35

The Ghost War
Maloney, Mack 769

Ghost with Blue Eyes
Randisi, Robert J. 497

Ghost Wolf of Thunder Mountain
Henry, Will 445, 461

A Ghostly Crew
Johnson, Roger **652**

The Ghosts' High Noon
Carr, John Dickson 73

Ghosts in Daylight
Onions, Oliver 680

Ghosttide
O'Keefe, Claudia 633, 674

Ghouls & Gore & Twisted Terrors
Ford, John B. 636

The Giant Rat of Sumatra
Boyer, Rick 210

The Giant's House
McCracken, Elizabeth 1158

The Gideon Oliver Series
Elkins, Aaron 100, 106

The Gideon Page Series
Stockley, Grif 113, 141

The Gift
Bunn, T. Davis 983

Gift of Joy
Henley, Virginia 265

The Gift of Stones
Crace, Jim 1095

The Gift of the Mestizo
McGinley, Marjorie M. **479**

Gifted Touch
Metz, Melinda **775**, 776

Gifts of Grace
Bulock, Lynn 1052

The Gil Mayo Series
Eccles, Marjorie 155

The Ginger Struve Barnes Series
Murray, Donna Huston 120

The Gingerbread Man
Shayne, Maggie **395**

The Girl at the End of the Line
Mathes, Charles 9

The Girl from the Golden Horn
Said, Kurban 1129, 1152, **1191**, 1208

Girl in Hyacinth Blue
Vreeland, Susan 951

The Girl Next Door
Welsh, Kate **1057**

The Girl Who Knew Tomorrow
Sherburne, Zoe 776

The Girl Who Ran Off with Daddy
Handler, David 100

Girl with a Pearl Earring
Chevalier, Tracy 837, 838, 1067, 1090

Girlfriend in a Coma
Coupland, Douglas 1094

The Girls' Guide to Hunting and Fishing
Bank, Melissa 345, 1087, 1125

The Girls in The High-Heeled Shoes
Kurland, Michael 33, 899

Girls' Night Out
Dziemianowicz, Stefan 654

Give and Take
Schmidt, Anna 1046

Giving Up America
Abraham, Pearl 1064

Glare Ice
Logue, Mary 90, **145**, 212

The Glass Factory
Wishnia, K.J.A. 217

The Glass Key
Hammett, Dashiell 99

The Glass Prison
Cook, Monte 737

The Glasswright's Apprentice
Klasky, Mindy 523

The Glenbrooke Series
Gunn, Robin Jones 984, 1006, 1007, 1018

Glenraven
Bradley, Marion Zimmer 725

The Gloria Damasco Series
Corpi, Lucha 52, 75, 140

Gloriana
Moorcock, Michael 778

Glory
Copeland, Lori 983

Glory
Coppel, Alfred 788

The Glory Game
Laumer, Keith 761

Glory's People
Coppel, Alfred 728

Glue
Welsh, Irvine 1126

Glutton for Punishment
Lamalle, Cecile 138

Gnome Man's Land
Friesner, Esther 521

Goat Dance
Clegg, Douglas 676

The Goblin Tower
de Camp, L. Sprague 590

Gob's Grief
Adrian, Chris 1187, 1195

The Godfather
Puzo, Mario 916, 1117, 1183

God's Country Club
Storey, Gail Donohue 1144

God's Dice
Swann, S. Andrew 602

Gods of War
Toland, John 937

Going Overboard
Skye, Christina **399**

Going Postal
Houarner, Gerard Daniel 651

The Gold Coast
DeMille, Nelson 1183

The Gold Coin
Kane, Andrea 312

Gold Dust
Carmichael, Emily 249

Gold Mountain
Kody, Bob 459, 504

Gold of Cortes
McGuire, Tim 439, 443, 480

The Golden
Shepard, Lucius 621

The Golden Age
Vidal, Gore 897, 937, 1066, 1130, 1212

The Golden Angel
Morris, Gilbert **1027**, 1028

The Golden Cat
King, Gabriel 574

The Golden Chance
Olsen, T.V. 487, 490, 499

Golden Fire
Fast, Jonathan 963

Golden Gate
Seth, Vikram 846

The Golden Goblet
McGraw, Eloise 577

The Golden Gong and Other Night-Pieces
Burke, Jonathan 680

The Golden Keel
Bagley, Desmond 171

The Golden Naginata
Salmonson, Jessica Amanda 531

The Golden Quill
Grun, Bernard 929

The Golden Sword
Patton, Fiona **586**

The Golden Trail of Murder
Paxon, John 465

The Goldsmith's Daughter
Sedley, Kate **933**

Goldtown
Cleary, Rita 443

The Goldy Bear Schulz Series
Davidson, Diane Mott 4, 89, 105, 120, 170, 207, 1037

Golf's Best Short Stories
Staudohar, Paul D. 1132

Gone Bamboo
Bourdain, Anthony 202

Gone Fishin'
Mosley, Walter 1166

Gone the Dreams and the Dancing
Jones, Douglas C. 826

Gone to Soldiers
Piercy, Marge 1165

Gone Wild
Hall, James W. 94

Gone with the Wind
Mitchell, Margaret 273, 918

The Good German
Kanon, Joseph **131**, 828, **892**, **1135**, 1171, 1186, 1191

Good Girls Do
Leto, Julie Elizabeth 333

Good Harbor
Diamant, Anita **1103**

A Good House
Burnard, Bonnie 1113

The Good Journey
Gilchrist, Micaela **454**, **873**

A Good Man to Have in Camp
Nesbitt, John D. 486

The Good Men
Craig, Charmaine **844**

Good Morning, Irene
Douglas, Carole Nelson 62, 856

The Good Mother
Miller, Sue 1163

Good Night, Mr. Holmes
Douglas, Carole Nelson 62, 856

A Good School
Yates, Richard 1159

The Good Soldier
Ford, Ford Madox 1135, 1142

A Good Story and Other Stories
Westlake, Donald E. 40, 85, 175

A Good Town
Hirt, Douglas **462**

Goodbye Chicago
Burnett, W.R. 119

Goodbye, Columbus and Five Short Stories
Roth, Philip 1072

Goodlow's Ghosts
Wright, T.M. 712

Goodnight, Little Sister
Kazan, Frances 893

Goodnight, Sweet Prince
Dickinson, David **58**, **851**

Goon
Lee, Edward 667, 705

The Gorgon Child
Barnes, Steven 750

The Gospel of Judas
Mawer, Simon 1092, 1175

The Goth Opera
Cornell, Paul 738

Gothic Ghosts
Webb, Wendy 633, 674

Gotta Get Next to You
Emery, Lynn **272**

The Gourmet Detective Series
King, Peter 138, 207

Grace in Autumn
Copeland, Lori 984

Graciela of the Border
Duncklee, John 449

Grail
Lawhead, Stephen R. 570, 901

The Grail of Hearts
Shwartz, Susan 566, 570, 796

The Grand Complication
Kurzweil, Allen 1085, **1144**, 1161, 1182

The Grand Conspiracy
Wurts, Janny 549, 555, 561

Grand Delusion
Witten, Matt 218

A Grand Design
Jensen, Emma 318, 370

Grand Design: The Hope Chest
Fox, Karen 287

The Grand Ones of San Ildefonso
Paine, Lauran 492, 493

Grandmother Spider
Doss, James D. 61

Grandmother's House
LaPierre, Janet 139

The Granite Shield
Patton, Fiona 586

Grant Speaks
Ehrlich, Ev 903

Grasshopper
Vine, Barbara 127, 211

A Grave Coffin
Butler, Gwendoline 30

Grave Markings
Arnzen, Michael D. 616

Grave Music
Harrod-Eagles, Cynthia 104

Graves' Retreat
Gorman, Ed 456

Graveyard Plots
Pronzini, Bill 175

Gravity
Gerritsen, Tess 78, 1094

Gravity Dreams
Modesitt, L.E. Jr. 777, 778

Gravity's Angels
Swanwick, Michael 760

Gray Warrior
Edwards, Hank 423

Great American Plain
Sernovitz, Gary **1195**

The Great and Secret Show
Barker, Clive 619

The Great Baby Caper
Riley, Eugenia **380**

Great Black Kanba
Little, Constance 144

Great Caesar's Ghost
Sterling, Cynthia 313

The Great Divide
Bunn, T. Davis 976

The Great Explosion
Russell, Eric Frank 794

The Great Game
Kurland, Michael 58, 856, 896, **899**, 908, 915, 926, 958

The Great Gatsby
Fitzgerald, F. Scott 1167

The Great Indian Novel
Tharoor, Shashi 1208

The Great Northwest Series
Chaikin, Linda 1011

The Great Trek
Grey, Zane 458

Great Untold Stories of Fantasy and Horror
Moskowitz, Sam 615

Green
Zucker, Benjamin 978, **1064**

Green City in the Sun
Wood, Barbara 962

A Green-Eyed Hurricane
Hegwood, Martin 112

Green Grow the Victims
Dams, Jeanne M. 830

The Green Millennium
Leiber, Fritz 767

Green Shadows, White Whale
Bradbury, Ray 1082

Greener than You Think
Moore, Ward 735

Grendel
Gardner, John 517

The Gresham Chronicles
Blackwell, Lawana 1013, 1027

Grimm Memorials
Gates, R. Patrick 626

A Groom to Come Home To
Brand, Irene 974

A Groom Worth Waiting For
Stovall, Crystal 1057

Groucho Marx and the Broadway Murders
Goulart, Ron 85, 882

Groucho Marx, Master Detective
Goulart, Ron 85

Groucho Marx, Private Eye
Goulart, Ron 85

The Groucho Marx Series
Goulart, Ron 72, 841

The Ground Beneath Her Feet
Rushdie, Salman 1143, 1189, 1190

The Ground She Walks Upon
McKinney, Meagan 313

Ground Zero
Anderson, Kevin J. 715

The Grover Bramlett Series
Armistead, John 59, 112

The Guardian
Henderson, Dee 999, 1000

The Guardian
Miller, Barbara **355**

Guardian Angel
Garwood, Julie 328

A Guardian's Angel
Ferguson, Jo Ann **278**

Guardians of the Lost
Weis, Margaret **611**

The Guardians of the North Series
Morris, Alan 1034, 1058

Guardians of Time
Anderson, Poul 818

Guardsmen of Tomorrow
Greenberg, Martin H. 552

Guenevere: Queen of the Summer Country
Miles, Rosalind 907

Guerrillas
Naipaul, V.S. 1170

Guests
Little, Bentley 668

The Guido Brunetti Series
Leon, Donna 164

Guilt
Lescroart, John 141

Guilt by Association
Farris, Michael P. 991

Guilty as Sin
Hoag, Tami 395

The Guinevere Trilogy
Newman, Sharan 907

The Guinevere Trilogy
Woolley, Persia 907

The Gully Dwarves
Parkinson, Dan 556

Gumshoe Gorilla
Hartman, Keith **756**, 813

The Gumshoe, the Witch, and the Virtual Corpse
Hartman, Keith 756

Gun Boss
Ballas, Jack 451

Gunman's Goal
Brand, Max 432, 435

Gunman's Rhapsody
Parker, Robert B. 1176

Guns of Billy Free
Bowman, Doug 479

Guns of Freedom: A Western Duo
Hogan, Ray 432, 435, 489

The Guns of Morgette
Boyer, G.G. 429

Gust Front
Ringo, John 729, 765

Gypsy
Janes, J. Robert 126

Gypsy Lord
Martin, Kat 881

H

Hail Hibbler
Goulart, Ron 752

Hair of the Dog
Berenson, Laurien 17

Hair Raiser
Cohen, Nancy J. 38

Half a Life
Bulychev, Kir 787

Half a Life
Naipaul, V.S. **1170**, 1190, 1208

Half Magic
Eager, Edward 581

Half the Day Is Night
McHugh, Maureen 774

The Halfling's Gem
Salvatore, R.A. 584

Halfway to Heaven
Wiggs, Susan 324, **419**

Halide's Gift
Kazan, Frances **893**, 902

Halloween Candy
Sipos, Thomas M. **696**

Hallowe'en Hauntings
Haining, Peter 628

Halloween Horrors
Ryan, Alan 628

The Halloween Husband
Heath, Sandra 291

Halloween Knight
Phillips, Tori 368

The Halloween Tree
Bradbury, Ray 623

The Hammer of Eden
Follett, Ken 863

The Hammer of God
Clarke, Arthur C. 767

Hammerfall
Cherryh, C.J. 734

Hammett: Crime Stories and Other Writings
Hammett, Dashiell 41, **99**, 201

Hand in Glove
Goddard, Robert 183

Hand Me a Crime
Russell, Charlotte Murray 191

The Hand of Ganz
Haiblum, Isidore 752

A Handful of Heaven
Hannah, Kristin 371, 372

Handling Sin
Malone, Michael 1153

The Handmaid's Tale
Atwood, Margaret 811

The Hands of Llyr
Norton, Andre 784

A Hanging at Sweetwater
Overholser, Stephen 488

Hanging Curve
Soos, Troy 200

The Hanging Garden
Rankin, Ian 178

Hannah and the Horseman
Black, Michelle 423

The Hannah Ives Series
Talley, Marcia 102

The Hannah Malloy/Kiki Goldstein Series
Griffin, Annie 77, 80

The Hannah Swenson Series
Fluke, Joanne 170

The Hannah Wolfe Series
Dunant, Sarah 11

Hannibal
Harris, Thomas 1180

Happy Birthday Murder
Harris, Lee **996**

Happy Endings
Cornell, Paul 738

The Happy Room
Palmer, Catherine 980, **1038**

Hard Bargain
D'Amato, Barbara 53

The Hard Blue Sky
Grau, Shirley Ann 1214

Hard Bounty
Hodgson, Ken **463**

Hard Case
D'Amato, Barbara 53

Hard Christmas
D'Amato, Barbara 53

Hard Evidence
D'Amato, Barbara 53

Hard Road
D'Amato, Barbara **53**

Hard Texas Winter
Lewis, Preston 463

Hard to Forget
Broadrick, Annette 246

Hard Women
D'Amato, Barbara 53

Harmful Intent
Cook, Robin 1093

Harmony in Flesh and Black
Kilmer, Nicholas 134

The Harmony Series
Gulley, Philip 984, 1007, 1018

Harold, Claudia, and Their Son Duncan
Gordimer, Nadine 1116

Harp of Winds
Furey, Maggie 545

The Harrison Raines Series
Kilian, Michael 1

The Harrowing of Gwynedd
Kurtz, Katherine 536

The Harry Bosch Series
Connelly, Michael 20, 47, 94, 204

Harry Gold
Dillon, Millicent 835, 892

The Harry Kline Series
Luber, Philip 121

Harry Potter and the Goblet of Fire
Rowling, J.K. 542

The Harry Starbranch Series
Bean, Gregory 25

Hart's War
Katzenbach, John 906

The Harvest
Brass, Perry 1093

Harvest
Gerritsen, Tess 78

Harvest Dance
Bedford, Deborah 967

Harvest of Murder
Ripley, Ann **181**

Harvest of Truth
Leon, Bonnie 1017

Harvest Tales and Midnight Revels
Mayhew, Michael 633

The Hatbox Baby
Brown, Carrie 874

Hateship, Friendship, Courtship, Loveship, Marriage
Munro, Alice 1075, 1099, 1124, **1169**, 1188

The Haunt
Williamson, J.N. 641, 709

Haunted
Metz, Melinda **776**

Haunted
Thorne, Tamara 673, 703

The Haunted Stars
Hamilton, Edmond 785

The Haunting
Jensen, Ruby Jean 673

Haunting Women
Ryan, Alan 654

Haussmann, or The Distinction
LaFarge, Paul 833, **900**

Havana Heat
Garcia-Aguilera, Carolina 75

Havana Twist
Matera, Lia 75

Have Baby, Need Beau
Herron, Rita 299

Have Gown, Need Groom
Herron, Rita 299

Hawaiian Sunrise
Snelling, Lauraine 1050, 1059

The Hawk and the Jewel
Wick, Lori 1042

Hawkmistress!
Bradley, Marion Zimmer 267, 732

Hayseed
Roderus, Frank 499

Hazard's Price
Stone, Robert S. **601**

He Could Be the One
Bevarly, Elizabeth 235, 236, 363

He Goes, She Goes
Torrey, Joanna **1209**

Head Injuries
Williams, Conrad 708

Header
Lee, Edward 667

Healing Hearts
Wolverton, Cheryl 1022

The Healing Touch Series
Alexander, Hannah 1012

A Healthy Place to Die
King, Peter 135

The Hearing
Lescroart, John 141

Hearn's Valley
Overholser, Wayne D. 489, 490

Heart and Soul
Funderburk, Robert 1051

The Heart Breaker
Jordan, Nicole 309, 332

The Heart of a Chief
Bruchac, Joseph 464

Heart of a Husband
Alexander, Kathryn 974

Heart of a Lawman
Rosemoor, Patricia 387, 413

Heart of Deception
Chase, Taylor 254

Heart of Midnight
King, J. Robert 613

The Heart of Myrial
Furey, Maggie 545

Heart of Night
Chase, Taylor **254**

Heart of Stone
DeMartino, Denny 744

Heart of the Beast
Weatherford, Joyce **511**

Heart of the Dove
Fobes, Tracy 281

Heart of the Sandhill
Whitson, Stephanie Grace **1058**

Heart of the Sea
Roberts, Nora 287, 383

Heart Song of Charging Elk
Welch, James 842

Heartbreaker
Robards, Karen 381

Heartless
Martin, Kat **346**, 347

The Heart's Haven
Barnett, Jill 821

Hearts in Atlantis
King, Stephen 660

The Heartsong of Charging Elk
Welch, James 1176

Heartwood
Burke, James Lee 1204

The Heat of the Day
Bowen, Elizabeth 876

The Heather Moon
King, Susan 316

The Heathersleigh Hall Series
Phillips, Michael 1028

Heaven and Earth
Roberts, Nora 256, 382, **383**

The Heaven Lee Series
Temple, Lou Jane 105, 138

Heaven on Earth
Pappano, Marilyn **366**

Heaven Sent
Hart, Jillian 974, 982, **997**

Heaven Sent
Madden, Sandra 342

Heaven Sent
Wilson, Rachel **421**

Heaven, Texas
Phillips, Susan Elizabeth 354, 376

Heaven to Touch
Sattler, Veronica 388

The Heavenly Daze Series
Copeland, Lori 1007

The Heavenly Fugitive
Morris, Gilbert **1028**

Heaven's Promise
Wilson, Rachel 421

Heaven's Road
Pella, Judith 1040

Heaven's Time
Plunkett, Susan 371, 372

Heaven's Wager
Dekker, Ted 988

The Heavenward Path
Dalkey, Kara 531

Heir to the Shadows
Bishop, Anne 527

The Heiress
Delacroix, Claire 269

The Heiress
Deveraux, Jude 883

The Heiress and the Bodyguard
Corey, Ryanne 236

The Heiress Bride
Paul, Susan Spencer 368

Heiress to Love
Bell, Donna 230, 348, 355

The Heirs of Cahira O'Connor Series
Hunt, Angela Elwell 1026, 1060

The Heirs of the Kingdom
Oldenbourg, Zoe 860, 902

The Helen Bradley Series
Rushford, Patricia H. 985, 996, 1009, 1062

The Helen Sorby/Miles Kachigan Series
Cercone, Karen Rose 24, 200

The Helen West Series
Fyfield, Frances 154

Hell-for-Leather Rider
Flynn, T.T. 452

A Hell of a Dog
Benjamin, Carol Lea 16

The Hellbound Heart
Barker, Clive 640

Helliconia Winter
Aldiss, Brian W. 757

Hellraiser
Barker, Clive 1071

Hellstrom's Hive
Herbert, Frank 762

Helltracks
Nolan, William F. 678

Hemlock Bay
Coulter, Catherine 1203

Henderson the Rain King
Bellow, Saul 1094

The Henrie O Series
Hart, Carolyn 15, 51, 91

The Henry Rios Series
Nava, Michael 221

Her Infinite Variety
Berkman, Pamela Rafael **823**

Her Kind of Hero
Steward, Carol 987, 1021, 1052

Her Man Friday
Bevarly, Elizabeth 292

Her Own Rules
Bradford, Barbara Taylor 1108

Her Secret Affair
Smith, Barbara Dawson 400

Her Secret Longing
Martin, Gail Gaymer 1021, 1022

Her Sister's Child
Darcy, Lilian 268

Here Be Dragons
Penman, Sharon Kay 952

Here Be Monsters
Stasheff, Christopher **600**

Here Comes Civilization
Tenn, William **803**

The Hereafter Gang
Barrett, Neal Jr. 524

Here's Your Hat What's Your Hurry
McCracken, Elizabeth 1158

Heresy
Audley, Anselm **718**

The Heretic
Weinstein, Lewis 956

Heretics
Gifune, Greg F. **639**

Hermes in Paris
Vansittart, Peter 900

A Hero for Kelsey
Aarsen, Carolyne 965

The Hero in the Shadows
Gemmell, David 548

The Hero Returns
Blair, Catherine 238, 397

A Heroine of the World
Lee, Tanith 532

Hexes
Piccirilli, Tom 682

Hey Jack!
Hannah, Barry 1121

Hi Honey, I'm Home
Windsor, Linda 1060

Hidden Agenda
Alers, Rochelle 222, 403

Hidden Gifts
Hamlin, Rick 1044

Hidden Gold
Frazee, Steve 453

Hidden Jewel
Andrews, V.C. 1214

The Hidden Land
Dean, Pamela 520, 581, 605

Hidden Places
Austin, Lynn N. 1017

The Hidden Side of the Moon
Russ, Joanna 726

Hidden Treasure
Bly, Stephen A. 973

Hide and Seek
Adair, Cherry **222**, 242

Hide and Seek
Palmer, Catherine 1038

Hideous Dreams
Maynard, L.H. **674**

A Hiding Place
Azzopardi, Trezza 1189

The High and the Mighty
Gann, Ernest Kellogg 1141

High Aztec
Hogan, Ernest 758

High Energy
Joy, Dara 310

High Fidelity
Hornby, Nick 1126

High Five
Evanovich, Janet 274

High Intensity
Joy, Dara 310

High Lonesome
Hannah, Barry 1121

The High Place
Cabell, James Branch 603

High Seas Murder
Freydont, Shelley 71

High Street
Jacobs, Anna 305

Higher Authority
White, Stephen 76

Highland Dream
Mallory, Tess 371

A Highland Folly
Ferguson, Jo Ann 279

Highland Hopes
Parker, Gary E. **1039**

Highland Princess
Smith, Haywood 316, 337

Highland Promise
Howell, Hannah 244

Highland Spirits
Scott, Amanda 390

Highland Treasure
Scott, Amanda 390

The Highlander
Langan, Ruth 244

The Highlander's Touch
Moning, Karen Marie 237, 358

A Highwayman Came Riding
Smith, Joan 317

Highwire Moon
Straight, Susan **1205**

The Hijacked Wife
Winn, Bonnie K. 1061

The Hilda Johansson Series
Dams, Jeanne M. 24, 200

The Hildegarde Withers Series
Palmer, Stuart 191

Hill Country
Windle, Janice Woods 513, 961

The Hillary Scarborough Series
Carter, Paula 60

The Hindenburg Murders
Collins, Max Allan 828, 841

A Hint of Heather
Lee, Rebecca Hagan 390

A Hint of Witchcraft
Gilbert, Anna 872

The Hinterlands
Morgan, Robert 910

The Hired Hero
Pickens, Andrea 279, 370, 374, 389

The Hireling's Tale
Bannister, Jo 11

His-and-Hers Twins
Herron, Rita 299

His Answered Prayer
Richer, Lois 1043, 1047

His Baby!
Child, Maureen 255

His Betrothed
Callen, Gayle 285, 326

His Brother's Wife
Worth, Lenora 1063

His Daddy's Eyes
Salonen, Debra 387

His Father's Son
Bennett, Nigel **621**

His Forbidden Touch
O'Brien, Linda 361

His Grace Endures
Jensen, Emma 362, 379

His Lady Midnight
Ferguson, Jo Ann **279**

His Lordship's Swan
Kirkland, Martha 318, 393

His Scandalous Duchess
Blayne, Sara 385

Historical Christmas Stories
Scott, DeLoras 391

A History of the World in 10 1/2 Chapters
Barnes, Julian 1095

The History of Tom Jones
Fielding, Henry 1095

Hit List
Block, Lawrence 190, 202

The Hitchhiker's Guide to the Galaxy
Adams, Douglas 1167

A Hive of Suspects
Pim, Sheila 173

Hoare and the Matter of Treason
Perkins, Wilder 822

The Hobbit
Tolkien, J.R.R. 584

The Hoegbotton Guide to the Early History of Ambergris
Vandermeer, Jeff 607

Hogfather
Pratchett, Terry 588

The Holding
Dain, Claudia 266, 316, 320

Holding the Line
Shelley, Rick **795**

Hole in the Wall
Coel, Margaret 444

The Hole of the Pit
Ross, Adrian 644

Holiday Cheer
Alers, Rochelle 300

A Holiday of Love
McNaught, Judith 366

The Hollis Ball/Sam Westcott Series
Chappell, Helen 205

The Hollow Land
Gardam, Jane 870

The Hollowing
Holdstock, Robert 558

The Holly and the Ivy
Fairchild, Elisabeth 275, 304

The Holly Winter Series
Conant, Susan 16, 17

Hollywood
Vidal, Gore 1202

Hollywood and LeVine
Bergman, Andrew 83, 161

Holy Clues
Kendrick, Stephen 896

The Holy Innocents
Sedley, Kate 194, 934

The Holy Road
Blake, Michael **425**, **826**, 827, 911

The Holy Terror
Sallee, Wayne Allen 687

Holy Terror in the Hebrides
Dams, Jeanne M. 54

Home Mountain
Williams, Jeanne 482

A Home of Her Own
Connors, Cathleen **982**

The Homecoming
Gouge, Louise M. 1005

Homefall
Bunch, Chris **729**

Homeland
Jakes, John 937

Homeland
Kingsolver, Barbara 1080

The Homer Kelly Series
Langton, Jane 106

Hometown Legend
Jenkins, Jerry B. 1001, **1005**

Hometown Wedding
Lane, Elizabeth 326

Homework
Livesey, Margot 1148

Honeymoon and Other Stories
Canty, Kevin 1149

Honky Tonk Kat
Kijewski, Karen 189

Honor
Coel, Margaret 444

Honor at Daybreak
Kelton, Elmer 436, 442, 469

Honor's Disguise
Heitzmann, Kristen 998

Honor's Quest
Heitzmann, Kristen 998

Honor's Reward
Heitzmann, Kristen 998

The Honourable Constance Ethel Morrison-Burke Series
Porter, Joyce 14, 191

The Hook
Westlake, Donald E. 107

Hope
Copeland, Lori 983

Hope
Deighton, Len 1191

The Hope
Wouk, Herman 942

Hope to Die
Block, Lawrence **22**

Hope's End
Chambers, Stephen **733**

Hope's Garden
Cote, Lyn 233, 985, 997, 1057, 1063

A Horde of Fools
Buchanan, James David **437**

Hornet's Nest
Cornwell, Patricia 1153

Horror at Halloween
Fletcher, Jo 628

Horror Show
Kihn, Greg 619

The Horse King
Knaak, Richard A. 612

The Horse Soldier
Lovelace, Merline 361

The Horse Whisperer
Evans, Nicholas 1174, 1181

The Horse You Came In On
Grimes, Martha 92

Horseman, Pass By
McMurtry, Larry 1146

The Horsemasters
Wolf, Joan 940

The Horsemaster's Daughter
Wiggs, Susan 419

Horses I Have Known
James, Will 464

Horses of Heaven
Bradshaw, Gillian 831

The Horus Killings
Doherty, P.C. 101

Hostage
Crais, Robert 20, **47**, 168, 204, **1096**

The Hostage
Wiggs, Susan 419

The Hostage Bride
Feather, Jane 276, 352

Hosts
Wilson, F. Paul **710**

Hot and Bothered
Foster, Lori **285**

Hot as Sin
Dixon, Debra 286

Hot Six
Evanovich, Janet 274

Hot Sky at Midnight
Silverberg, Robert 797

Hot Springs
Hunter, Stephen 122, 885, 887, 935, 1127

Hotel Honolulu
Theroux, Paul 1092

The Hotel New Hampshire
Irving, John 1130, 1197

Hotel of the Saints
Hegi, Ursula **1124**

Hotshots
Van Gieson, Judith 140

The Hounds of Tindalos
Long, Frank Belknap 671

The Hour of the Oxrun Dead
Grant, Charles L. 663, 668

House Atreides
Herbert, Brian 757

House Corrino
Herbert, Brian **757**

A House for Mr. Biswas
Naipaul, V.S. 1170

The House Gun
Gordimer, Nadine 1116

House Harkonnen
Herbert, Brian 757

The House of Death
Doherty, P.C. 859, 920, 924

The House of Gold
Brand, Max **431**

The House of Memory
Clifford, Nicholas 835

House of Pain
Giron, Sephera **640**

The House of the Spirits
Allende, Isabel 817, 1067

The House of Winslow Series
Morris, Gilbert 1015, 1040

The House on Hope Street
Steel, Danielle 1101

The House on Mulberry Street
Meyers, Maan 200, 203

The House on Nazareth Hill
Campbell, Ramsey 620, 626

The House on Olive Street
Carr, Robyn 250

The House on the Borderland
Hodgson, William Hope 670

The House Spider and Other Strange Visitors
Newton, Kurt 683, 697

The House That Jack Built
Masterton, Graham 672

The House with a Clock in Its Walls
Bellairs, John 623

Household Words
Silber, Joan 1198

Houses
Little, Bentley 668

How Do I Look?
Dawson, Jill 848

How Stella Got Her Groove Back
McMillan, Terry 403

How to Be Good
Hornby, Nick **1126**

How to Marry a Marquis
Quinn, Julia 229

How to Murder the Man of Your Dreams
Cannell, Dorothy 31, 49

How to Murder Your Mother-in-Law
Cannell, Dorothy 31

How to Trap a Tycoon
Bevarly, Elizabeth 236

Howl's Moving Castle
Jones, Diana Wynne 594

Hrolf Kraki's Saga
Anderson, Poul 517

The Hum Bug
Schechter, Harold **193**, **502**, **932**, 936

The Human Angle
Tenn, William 803

Human Nature
Cornell, Paul 738

Humboldt's Gift
Bellow, Saul 1072

The Hunger
Strieber, Whitley 617, 699, 702

A Hunger in the Soul
Resnick, Mike 788

Hungry
Torrey, Joanna 1209

The Hunt
Sizemore, Susan 575

The Hunt for Hawke's Daughter
Barrett, Jean 410

Hunt the Man Down
Patten, Lewis B. 494

Hunter
Huggins, James Byron 1003

The Hunters
Messud, Claire **1161**

Hunter's Moon
Stabenow, Dana 68

Hunting a Detroit Tiger
Soos, Troy 200

Hurricane Season
Bjorneby, Karen **1075**

A Husband by Law
Sterling, Cynthia 415

The Husband Hunt
Willingham, Bess 420

The Husband List
Alexander, Victoria 229, 257, 324

Husband, Lover, Stranger
Forster, Suzanne 283

Husband Material
Ireland, Liz 263

Husband Needed
Linz, Cathie 251

The Husband Test
Krahn, Betina **321**

Hush Puppy
Berenson, Laurien 17

Hyde Park Murder
Roosevelt, Elliott 33

I

I Am Dracula
Andersson, C. Dean 686, 692

I Am Frankenstein
Andersson, C. Dean 691

I Am of Irelaunde
Osborne-McKnight, Juliene 886

I Been in Sorrow's Kitchen and Licked out All the Pots
Straight, Susan 1119, 1205

I, Claudius
Graves, Robert 931

I Do, I Do, I Do
Osborne, Maggie 364

I Dream of You
McCoy, Judi 249, 287, **350**, 351

I, Elizabeth
Miles, Rosalind 907

I Gave at the Orifice
McLaughlin, Mark 635

I Like Being Killed
Fischer, Tibor 1099

I Love You and There Is Nothing You Can Do about It
Houarner, Gerard Daniel 639, 683

I Married a Communist
Roth, Philip 1191

I, Pearl Hart
Coleman, Jane Candia 445, 446

I Remember Love
Hardwick, Mollie 849

I, Strahd
Elrod, P.N. 613, 632

I Thee Wed
Quick, Amanda 375

I, Vampire
Romkey, Michael 621, 686

I Waxed My Legs for This?
Jacobs, Holly 306

Icarus Descending
Savile, Steve 688

The Icarus Hunt
Zahn, Timothy 796, 812

Ice
Bowkett, Stephen **724**

Ice
Kavan, Anna 724

The Ice Child
McGregor, Elizabeth **905**

Ice Mage
Gray, Julia 551

Ice Maiden
Brown, Debra Lee 244, 338

The Ice Princess
Walker, Jim 1042

The Ice Schooner
Moorcock, Michael 595, 724

The Ice-Shirt
Vollmann, William T. 950, 1212

Iceberg
Cussler, Clive 1097

Icebones
Baxter, Stephen **723**

Iced
Clark, Carol Higgins 34

The Iciest Sin
Keating, H.R.F. 132

Identity Unknown
Brockmann, Suzanne 242

The Idylls of the Queen
Karr, Phyllis Ann 528

If Beale Street Could Talk
Baldwin, James 1179

If I Had You
Kurland, Lynn 323

If This World Were Mine
Harris, E. Lynn 1122

The Ignored
Little, Bentley 668

I'll Be Damned
Staley, Shane Ryan **698**

I'll Be Home Late Tonight
Thames, Susan 855

Ill Met by Moonlight
Hoyt, Sarah A. **559**

Ill Met in Lankhmar
Leiber, Fritz 530

Ill Met in Mexico
Russell, Charlotte Murray 191

Illegal Alien
Sawyer, Robert 744

The Illegal Man
Dearen, Patrick 469, 478

Illusion
Ewing, Jean R. 385

Illusion
Volsky, Paula 532

Illusions
Pronzini, Bill 174

The Ilse Witch
Brooks, Terry 530

Imagine
Barnett, Jill 228, 287, 350, 821

Imagining Don Giovanni
Rudel, Anthony J. 852, **929**

Imajica
Barker, Clive 1071

The Immaculate Deception
Pears, Iain 164

Immodest Proposals
Tenn, William 803

The Immortal
Hunt, Angela Elwell 1004

The Immortality Option
Hogan, James P. 759

Impact-20
Nolan, William F. 678

Impact Parameter and Other Quantum Realities
Landis, Geoffrey A. **766**

Imperial Legions
Seddon, Andrew M. 979, 1003

Imperial Purple
Bradshaw, Gillian 831

Implant
Wilson, F. Paul 677

Impossible Saints
Roberts, Michele 925

The Impossible Texan
Shaw, Allie 234, 419

Impossible Things
Willis, Connie 811

Impressionist
King, Joan 837

An Improper Proposal
Cabot, Patricia 400

An Improper Pursuit
Bell, Donna 279, 398

Impulse
Coulter, Catherine 1199

In a Class by Itself
Brown, Sandra 1086

In a Dry Season
Robinson, Peter 186

In a Free State
Naipaul, V.S. 1170

In a Strange City
Lippman, Laura **143**

In and Out
Coward, Mat **44**

In Big Trouble
Lippman, Laura 143

In Country
Mason, Bobbie Ann 1172

In Cuba I Was a German Shepherd
Menendez, Ana 1120

In Darkness Waiting
Shirley, John 694

In Enemy Hands
Weber, David 809

In Fields of Freedom
Leon, Bonnie 1017

In God's Own Time
Scofield, Ruth 1047

In Green's Jungles
Wolfe, Gene 726

In Hollow Houses
Braunbeck, Gary A. 575, 737

In Kensington Gardens Once. . .
Keating, H.R.F. 146

In Mayan Splendor
Long, Frank Belknap 669

In My Other Life
Silber, Joan 1198

In Pale Battalions
Goddard, Robert 208

In Praise of the Stepmother
Vargas Llosa, Mario 948, 1211

In Praise of Younger Men
Ellis, Lyn 231

In Search of the Grand Canyon
Fraser, Mary Ann 949

In Space No One Can Hear You Laugh
Resnick, Mike 788

In Sunlight, in a Beautiful Garden
Cambor, Kathleen 850, 955, 961

In the Bleak Midwinter
Spencer-Fleming, Julia 90

In the City
Silber, Joan 1198

In the Company of Angels
Kelby, N.M. 847

In the Company of Others
Czerneda, Julie E. 716, **740**

In the Dark
Laymon, Richard **663**, 664

In the Dark and Other Ghost Stories
Penn, Mary E. 618

In the Electric Mist with Confederate Dead
Burke, James Lee 1, 1214

In the Flesh
Barker, Clive 1071

In the Forest of Harm
Bissell, Sallie 19, **1074**

In the Heat of the Night
Ball, John 59, 122

In the House of the Lord
Flynn, Robert 451

In the Land of Little Sticks
Savage, Les Jr. 500, 501

In the Land of Winter
Grant, Richard 539

In the Midnight Hour
Randall, Kimberly 282

In the Midnight Rain
Wind, Ruth 330, 339, 422

In the Mirror
Singleton, Sarah 636

In the Palm of Darkness
Montero, Mayra 1164

In the Rift
Bradley, Marion Zimmer 725

In the Rogue Blood
Blake, James Carlos 424, 825

In the Shadow of a Secret
Wubbels, Lance 971

In the Shadow of Love
John, Sally D. 1006, 1023

In the Shadow of Our House
Blackwood, Scott **1077**

In the Shadow of the Moon
White, Karen 418

In the Shape of a Boar
Norfolk, Lawrence **913**, 954, 1064, **1171**

In the Still of the Night
Churchill, Jill 33, 839

In the Time of the Butterflies
Alvarez, Julia 948

In the Time of the Poisoned Queen
Dukthas, Ann 29

In This Mountain
Karon, Jan **1007**

In Too Deep
Foster, Lori 240

In Too Deep
Taylor, Janelle 347, 373, 387, **413**

In Winter's Shadow
Bradshaw, Gillian 595

In Your Arms
Rogers, Rosemary 385

Incident at Buffalo Crossing
Conley, Robert J. 447

Incognito
Ray, Francis 224, 365

The Incomparable Miss Compton
Scott, Regina **392**, 393

Independence Day
Ford, Richard 1202

India
Garland, Sherry 871

The Indian Fighter's Return
Cummings, Jack 481

Indian Sign
Roberts, Les 185

The Indians Won
Smith, Martin Cruz 799

The Indifference of Heaven
Braunbeck, Gary A. 694

Indigo
Joyce, Graham 655

Indigo Slam
Crais, Robert 47, 1096

Indiscreet
Balogh, Mary 227

Indiscretion
Hunter, Jillian 303

The Indwelling
LaHaye, Tim 1016

An Infamous Army
Heyer, Georgette 389

Infernal Affairs
Heller, Jane 1125

The Infernal Device
Kurland, Michael 899

The Infidel
Musser, Joe **1031**

The Infinite Plan
Allende, Isabel 817, 1067, 1172

Infinity
Shayne, Maggie 395

Inheritor
Cherryh, C.J. 734

Inner City Blues
Woods, Paula L. 220

Innocence
Fitzgerald, Penelope 1201

Innocence
Forster, Suzanne 283

The Innocent
Stevens, Amanda **410**

Innocent Graves
Robinson, Peter 186

An Innocent Imposter
Rabe, Sheila 376

Innocents Within
Daley, Robert 863

Insatiable
Dvorkin, David 617, 702

Insatiable
Leto, Julie Elizabeth **333**

The Inscription
Binder, Pam 237

Inside the Illusion
Applegate, K.A. 520

The Inspector Barnaby Series
Graham, Caroline 55, 87, 104, 165

The Inspector Finch Series
Thomson, June 43

The Inspector Frost Series
Wingfield, R.D. 44

Inspector Ghote: His Life and Crimes
Keating, H.R.F. 132

The Inspector Lestrade Series
Trow, M.J. 958

The Inspector Lloyd/Judy Hill Series
McGown, Jill 64, 87, 104, 165

The Inspector Mayo Series
Eccles, Marjorie 55

The Inspector Morrisey Series
Mitchell, Kay 55

The Inspector Morse Series
Dexter, Colin 44, 97, 116

The Inspector Otani Series
Melville, James 150

The Inspector Sloan Series
Aird, Catherine 104

The Inspector Tom Barnaby Series
Graham, Caroline 43

The Inspector Wexford Series
Rendell, Ruth 23, 43, 116, 179, 186

Inspired Sleep
Cohen, Robert 1196

Instruments of Darkness
Wilson, Robert 960

Intended
McGoldrick, May 352

Interpreter of Maladies
Lahiri, Jhumpa 1104

Interview with the Vampire
Rice, Anne 690

Intimacy
Kureishi, Hanif 1143

Intimacy and Midnight All Day
Kureishi, Hanif 1107

An Intimate Arrangement
Lawrence, Nancy 230

Intimate Enemies
Abe, Shana 316

Into Battle
Gilbert, Michael 208

Into the Darkness
Turtledove, Harry 606, 804

Into the Far Mountains
Grove, Fred 459, 460

Into the Fire
McKiernan, Dennis L. 579, 580

Into the Forge
McKiernan, Dennis L. 555, 579, 580

Intrigued
Small, Bertrice 282

Intrigues
Green, Sharon 544

The Intruder
Metz, Melinda 775, 776

Intrusions
Hegi, Ursula 1124

Invader
Cherryh, C.J. 719, 733

Invaders from the Dark
La Spina, Greye 646

Invasion
King, J. Robert 564, 565, 566

Invasion of Privacy
Healy, Jeremiah 111

Inventing the Abbotts and Other Stories
Miller, Sue 1163

The Inventory
Lustiger, Gila 892

Inversions
Banks, Iain 721

The Invisible Circus
Egan, Jennifer 1108

The Invisible Country
McAuley, Paul J. 771

The Invisible Ring
Bishop, Anne 527

The Invitation
Moser, Nancy 1030

Involuntary Daddy
Lee, Rachel 330

Irene at Large
Douglas, Carole Nelson 62, 856

The Irene Kelly Series
Burke, Jan 53, 98

Irene's Last Waltz
Douglas, Carole Nelson 62, 856

The Irish Cottage Murder
Deere, Dicey 173

The Irish Devil
Fletcher, Donna 288

Irish Fire
Baker, Jeanette 386

Irish Gold
Greeley, Andrew M. 1111

Irish Hope
Fletcher, Donna 316

The Irish Rogue
Jensen, Emma 279, 392

Irish Tenure
McInerny, Ralph 156

Iron Dawn
Stover, Matthew Woodring 608

Iron Fist
Allston, Aaron 516

Iron Lace
Richards, Emilie 301

The Iron Lance
Lawhead, Stephen R. 570, 901

The Iron Lords
Offutt, Andrew J. 548

Iron Shoes
Giles, Molly 1159

The Iron Throne
Hawke, Simon 880

The Ironclad Alibi
Kilian, Michael **133**, **898**

Ironhand's Daughter
Gemmell, David 548

Ironweed
Kennedy, William 897

Iroshi
Osborne, Cary 750

The Irredeemable Miss Renfield
Scott, Regina **393**

Irregardless of Murder
Kennedy, Ellen Edwards 970, 985, **1008**

Irresistible
Balogh, Mary 227

Irresistible
Black, Ethan 20, 1076

Isaac Asimov's Father's Day
Dozois, Gardner 1166

The Ishbane Conspiracy
Alcorn, Angela 1054

Island Bride
Chaikin, Linda 977

Island Magic
Alers, Rochelle 403

The Island of Heavenly Daze
Copeland, Lori 984

Island of Tears
Soos, Troy **200**, 203, **936**

The Island Wife
Stirling, Jessica 938

Isle of Destiny
Flint, Kenneth 520

Isn't It Romantic
Korbel, Kathleen 261

It
King, Stephen 660

It Had to Be You
Windsor, Linda 1049, 1060

It Happened One Night
LaFoy, Leslie 324

It Must Be Love
Gibson, Rachel 292, 363

It Takes a Rebel
Bond, Stephanie 236, 240

Italian Fever
Martin, Valerie 1203

The Italian Garden
Lennox, Judith 836, 951

The Italian Girl
Hall, Patricia 97

It's in His Kiss
Shelley, Deborah 223

It's Murder Going Home
Millhiser, Marlys 205

J

The J.W. Jackson Series
Craig, Philip R. 100, 106, 206

Jacaranda Vines
McKinley, Tamara 1209

Jack, Knave and Fool
Alexander, Bruce 815

The Jack McMorrow Series
Boyle, Gerry 151

Jack of Diamonds
Spencer, Elizabeth 1201

Jack of Kinrowan
De Lint, Charles 539

The Jackal of Nar
Marco, John 585, 609

Jackdaws
Follett, Ken **863**, 888, 960, 1151

The Jackie Walsh Series
Cleary, Melissa 16

Jackson's Way
LaFoy, Leslie 234, **324**, 391

The Jacobia Tiptree Series
Graves, Sarah 100, 157, 219

Jacob's Ladder
McCaig, Donald 964

Jacob's Way
Morris, Gilbert 1027, 1028

Jade
Brooks, Betty 868

The Jade Cabinet
Ducornet, Rikki 927

The Jade Figurine
Foxx, Jack 185

Jade Island
Lowell, Elizabeth 340

Jade Woman
Gash, Jonathan 185

The Jagged Orbit
Brunner, John 779

Jago
Newman, Kim 694

Jaguar Princess
Bell, Clare 889

Jane and the Genius of the Place
Barron, Stephanie 12, 822

Jane and the Man of the Cloth
Barron, Stephanie 12, 822

Jane and the Prisoner of Wool House
Barron, Stephanie **12**, **822**

Jane and the Stillroom Maid
Barron, Stephanie 12, 822

Jane and the Unpleasantness at Scargrave Manor
Barron, Stephanie 12, 822

Jane and the Wandering Eye
Barron, Stephanie 12, 822

The Jane Austen Series
Barron, Stephanie 10, 815, 820, 959

The Jane Whitefield Series
Perry, Thomas 19, 190

The Janus Mask
Knaak, Richard A. 540

The Jasmine Trade
Hamilton, Denise 39, **98**, 137

Jason Evers: His Own Story
Roderus, Frank 499

The Jasper Forest
Gray, Julia **551**

The Jazz Bird
Holden, Craig **119**, **885**, 897

Jem (and Sam)
Mount, Ferdinand 1167

The Jenny Cain Series
Pickard, Nancy 120

Jenny's Mountain
Long, Elaine 469

The Jeremy Faro Series
Knight, Alanna 172

Jerlayne
Abbey, Lynn 515

Jerusalem
Holland, Cecelia 860, 902

Jerusalem Heart
Thoene, Bodie 942

The Jerusalem Scrolls
Thoene, Bodie 930, **942**, **1053**

Jerusalem Vigil
Thoene, Bodie 942, 1053

Jerusalem's Heart
Thoene, Bodie 1053

Jessamy Court
Maybury, Anne 314

Jesse
McCoy, Max 446, 448

The Jesse Stone Series
Parker, Robert B. 47

The Jesus Creek Series
Adams, Deborah 15, 114

The Jewel of Covent Garden
Worcester, Wayne 158, 210

The Jewel of the North
King, Peter 73, 95, **135**

The Jewel of the Pacific Series
Chaikin, Linda 1059

Jewelry Talks
Klein, Richard 1095, **1142**

Jewels
Perrin, Robert 851

Jewels of the Sun
Roberts, Nora 351, 384

Jezebel
Sutcliffe, Katherine 412

Jezebel's Sister
Carmichael, Emily 249

The Jill Smith Series
Dunlap, Susan 137

The Jimjams
Green, Michael 703

Jingo
Pratchett, Terry 587

The Jo Beth Siddon Series
Lanier, Virginia 3, 16, 17, 18

The Joan Spencer Series
Frommer, Sarah Hoskinson 124

The Joanna Brady Series
Jance, J.A. 145, 212

The Jocelyn O'Roarke Series
Dentinger, Jane 45, 71

Joe
Brown, Larry 1140

The Joe Dante Series
Newman, Christopher 152

The Joe Grey Series
Murphy, Shirley Rousseau 26

The Joe Gunther Series
Mayor, Archer 168

The Joe Leaphorn/Jim Chee Series
Hillerman, Tony 35

John Crust and Snuffling Pig
McGinley, Marjorie M. 479

The John Francis Cuddy Series
Healy, Jeremiah 74, 174, 206

John Henry Days
Whitehead, Colson 1128, 1154

The John J. Malone Series
Rice, Craig 56

The John Marshall Tanner Series
Greenleaf, Stephen 22, 111, 141, 174, 206, 213

The John McLeish/Francesca Wilson Series
Neel, Janet 87, 104

The John Rebus Series
Rankin, Ian 155

John Stone and the Choctaw Kid
Davis, Wayne 425

John the Balladeer
Wellman, Manly Wade 707

Joining
Lindsey, Johanna 295

The Jonah Watch
Cady, Jack 681

Jonah's Gourd Vine
Hurston, Zora Neale 1128

The Jonathan Argyll Series
Pears, Iain 134

Jormungard
Frith, Nigel 517

The Joshua Croft Series
Satterthwait, Walter 50

The Joshua Sequence
Huebner, Fredrick 121

Joshua the Homecoming
Girzone, Joseph F. 983

The Journal of Callie Wade
Miller, Dawn 483

The Journal of Mrs. Pepys
George, Sara 1069

A Journal of the Plague Year
Defoe, Daniel 832

A Journey by Chance
John, Sally D. **1006**

Journey of the Dead
Estleman, Loren D. 478

Journey to Fusang
Sanders, William 778

Journey to Otherwhere
Smith, Sherwood 800

Journey to Shiloh
Henry, Will 461

Journey to the Crimson Sea
Kraus, Jim 1013

The Journeyer
Jennings, Gary 889

Joyride
Coughlin, Patricia 261

Jubilee
Walker, Margaret 918

Judas Eyes
Hoffman, Barry 705

The Judas Tree
Clark, Simon 735

Judging Sara
Rutledge, Cynthia 987, **1044**

Judgment by Fire
Huebner, Fredrick 121

The Jules Clement Series
Harrison, Jamie 108

The Julian Kestrel Series
Ross, Kate 10, 12, 820

The Julie Hayes Series
Davis, Dorothy Salisbury 52, 79

Julius Knipl, Real Estate Photographer
Katchor, Ben 1100

July Thunder
Lee, Rachel **330**

Jump Pay
Shelley, Rick 795

June
Copeland, Lori 983

The June Rise
Tremblay, William **507**, **945**

Junior's Leg
Wells, Ken **1214**

Juniper Tree Burning
Long, Goldberry 1077

Juno & Juliet
Gough, Julian 1160

Just Another Pretty Face
Schuler, Candace 333

Just as I Am
Harris, E. Lynn 1122

Just Before Dawn
Alers, Rochelle 365

Just Friends
Mahon, Annette 343

Just in Time
Campbell, Marilyn 546

Just Once
Landis, Jill Marie 471

Just Say No!
Tyree, Omar 1122, **1210**

Just the Way You Are
Freethy, Barbara 231

Just This Once
Gregory, Jill 294

Just West of Heaven
Kane, Kathleen **313**

The Justice
Hunt, Angela Elwell 976, **1004**

K

K Falls
Moody, Skye Kathleen 444

Kaleidoscope
Gilman, Dorothy **79**

Kaleidoscope
Janes, J. Robert **126**, **888**

The Kali O'Brien Series
Jacobs, Jonnie 167

The Kalif's War
Dalmas, John 765

Kamikaze L'Amour
Kadrey, Richard 764

Kane
Borton, Douglas 665

Kane of Old Mars
Moorcock, Michael 582

The Karen Hightower Series
Edghill, Rosemary 81

The Karen Pelletier Series
Dobson, Joanne 156, 176

Karyn's Memory Box
Whitson, Stephanie Grace 1058

The Kate Cavanaugh Series
John, Cathie 205

The Kate Fansler Series
Cross, Amanda 156

The Kate Jasper Series
Girdner, Jacqueline 91

The Kate Martinelli Series
King, Laurie R. 137

The Kate Shugak Series
Stabenow, Dana 19

The Kathryn Swinbrooke Series
Grace, C.L. 194

Kavin's World
Mason, David 540

The Kay Scarpetta Series
Cornwell, Patricia 66, 78, 197

Kedrigern in Wanderland
Morressey, John 537

Keegan's Lady
Anderson, Catherine 290

The Keep
Wilson, F. Paul 710

Keep Still
Bland, Eleanor Taylor 21

Keep the Giraffe Burning
Sladek, John 798

Keeper
Rucka, Greg 190

Keeper of Hearts
Christner, Dianne **979**

Keeper of Swans
Butler, Nancy 318

The Keeper of the Keys
Wurts, Janny 534, 586

Keeper of the King
Bennett, Nigel 621

Keeper of the Stone
Allan, Margaret 510

Keepers
LaPierre, Janet **139**

The Kellie Montgomery Series
Wilcox, Valerie 63

Kelly and the Three-Toed Horse
Bowen, Peter 475, 827

Kelly Country
Chandler, A. Bertram 804

The Kensington Chronicles
Wick, Lori 1013, 1015

The Kevin Kerney Series
McGarrity, Michael 25, 151

The Key
Roper, Gayle G. 971, 992, 1035

Key to Forever
Skye, Christina 399

The Key to Rebecca
Follett, Ken 863

Key West
Cameron, Stella 340

The Keys to D'Esperance
Brenchley, Chaz 655

The Kif Strike Back
Cherryh, C.J. 812

Kill and Tell
Howard, Linda 245, 302, 381

The Killer Angels
Shaara, Michael 919

The Killer Gun
Paine, Lauran 492, 493

Killer Stuff
Fiffer, Sharon **69**, 160

Killer Wedding
Farmer, Jerrilyn 60

A Killing at Ball's Bluff
Kilian, Michael 133, 909

The Killing Bee
Witten, Matt **218**

Killing Cassidy
Dams, Jeanne M. 54

Killing Cynthia Ann
Brashear, Charles 454, 466

Killing Floor
Child, Lee 59, 442

Killing Gifts
Woodworth, Deborah 851, 1062

A Killing in Kiowa
Patten, Lewis B. 494

A Killing in New Town
Horsley, Kate 886

The Killing Machine
Vance, Jack 743

The Killing Man
Spillane, Mickey 201

The Killing Maze
Cole, David 39

Killing Me Softly
Eccles, Marjorie 64

The Killing of the Saints
Abella, Alex 672

Killing the Shadows
McDermid, Val **154**

Killing Time
Harrod-Eagles, Cynthia 104

Killobyte
Anthony, Piers 518

The Kindness of Women
Ballard, J.G. 1070

Kindred
Butler, Octavia 811

King and Goddess
Tarr, Judith 603, 940

The King David Report
Heym, Stefan 858

The King Edward Plot
Hall, Robert Lee 851

King Hereafter
Dunnett, Dorothy 921

The King Is Dead
Sammon, Paul M. 684

The King Is Dead
Shankman, Sarah 77

King of Morning, Queen of Day
McDonald, Ian 529, 559, 568, 598

The King of the Sun
McFedries, A.A. **773**

The King of Ys
Anderson, Poul 818

King Pinch
Cook, David 604

King Solomon's Mines
Haggard, H. Rider 717, 792

King Tut's Private Eye
Levin, Lee 101

Kingdom of Shadows
Furst, Alan 863, 906, 1168

Kingdom of the Grail
Attanasio, A.A. 570, 901

Kingdom of the Grail
Tarr, Judith 603, 829, 901, 941

The Kingless Land
Greenwood, Ed 553

The King's Dragon
Elliott, Kate 586

The King's Gambit
Roberts, John Maddox 184

Kings in Hell
Morris, Janet 553

The King's Name
Walton, Jo **608**

The King's Peace
Walton, Jo 608

The King's Sacrifice
Weis, Margaret 611

The Kingsley House
Ryan, Arliss 910

The Kinsey Millhone Series
Grafton, Sue 63

The Kinship and Courage Series
Kirkpatrick, Jane 973, 998

Kinship Theory
Kaplan, Hester 1093

Kirinyaga
Resnick, Mike 788

The Kiss
Steel, Danielle 1203

Kiss an Angel
Phillips, Susan Elizabeth 369

Kiss and Tell
Adair, Cherry 222, 223, 302, 414

A Kiss at Midnight
Abe, Shana 266, 368

A Kiss for Mama
Ferguson, Jo Ann **280**

Kiss in the Dark
Sawyer, Meryl 302

Kiss It Goodbye
Wessel, John **213**

A Kiss of Adventure
Palmer, Catherine 1038

A Kiss of Shadows
Hamilton, Laurell K. 527, 602

Kiss of the Bees
Jance, J.A. 28, 39, 465

Kiss of the Highlander
Moning, Karen Marie 237, **358**

Kiss of the Spider Woman
Puig, Manuel 1145

Kiss the Girls
Patterson, James 1096

Kissed a Sad Goodbye
Crombie, Deborah 92

Kisses of Death
Collins, Max Allan 40, **41**, 147, 201, **841**

Kissing a Stranger
Porter, Margaret Evans 259

Kissing the Beehive
Carroll, Jonathan 529

The Kit DeLeeuw Series
Katz, Jon 218

Knave and the Game
Janiver, Laurence M. 763

Knave in Hand
Janiver, Laurence M. 763

Knave of Hearts
Anton, Shari 295

The Knight
Garnett, Juliana 303, 406

The Knight and Knave of Swords
Leiber, Fritz 532

Knight Crusader
Welch, Ronald 860

Knight Errant
Garcia y Robertson, R. **546**, 868, **869**

A Knight in Shining Armor
Deveraux, Jude 323, 869

A Knight of Ghosts and Shadows
Anderson, Poul 728

The Knight of the Sacred Lake
Miles, Rosalind 907

A Knight to Remember
Dodd, Christina 406

Knights
Miller, Linda Lael 869

The Knights of Christmas
Barclay, Suzanne 367

The Knowing Crystal
Morgan, Kathleen 267

Knuckles and Tales
Collins, Nancy **629**

Komarr
Bujold, Lois McMaster 728

The Korine McFail Series
Herman, Julie Wray 103

Krondor, the Assassins
Feist, Raymond E. 552

Krondor the Betrayal
Feist, Raymond E. 545

The Kruton Interface
DeChancie, John 752

The Kurt Muller Series
Zigal, Thomas 108

L

L.A. Requiem
Crais, Robert 47, 1096

La Salle
Vernon, John 949

The Labor Day Murder
Harris, Lee 996

Lack of the Irish
McInerny, Ralph 156

The Ladies Auxiliary
Mirvis, Tova 978

The Lady and the Outlaw
Scott, DeLoras 391

Lady Be Good
Phillips, Susan Elizabeth 369

Lady Crymsyn
Elrod, P.N. 632, 657

Lady Delafont's Dilemma
Simpson, Donna 397

Lady Diana's Daring Deed
Gedney, Mona 291

Lady Diana's Darlings
Huntington, Kate 304

Lady Ferry and Other Uncanny People
Jewett, Sarah Orne 711

Lady Fortune
Stuart, Anne 411

Lady Hilary's Halloween
Gedney, Mona **291**

The Lady in Gray
Oliver, Patricia 291, 362

Lady in Waiting
Domning, Denise 254, 276, 326

Lady in Waiting
Sutcliff, Rosemary 883

Lady in White
Domning, Denise 254

Lady Jane's Nemesis
Oliver, Patricia 362

Lady May's Folly
Simpson, Donna 397

Lady Miracle
King, Susan 316

Lady Miranda's Masquerade
Collum, Lynn 258

Lady of Horses
Tarr, Judith 940, 941

A Lady of Letters
Pickens, Andrea 370

Lady of Light
Morgan, Kathleen 1025, 1026

Lady of Moray
Copeland, Bonnie 921

A Lady of Quality
Gedney, Mona 291

Lady of Valor
St. John, Tina 407

Lady Oracle
Atwood, Margaret 1108

Lady Pirate
Sands, Lynsay 320

Lady Polly
Cornick, Nicola **259**, 260

Lady Reckless
LaFoy, Leslie 324

Lady Serena's Surrender
Savery, Jeanne 389

Lady Vanishes
Benjamin, Carol Lea 16

The Lady's Companion
Kelly, Carla 315

The Lady's Mummy
Willingham, Bess 420

Laird of the Wind
King, Susan 316

Lake News
Delinsky, Barbara 1101, 1194

The Lake of Dead Languages
Goodman, Carol **82**

Lake Wobegon Days
Keillor, Garrison 1136

Lake Wobegon Summer 1956
Keillor, Garrison 1114, **1136**

Lakota Winds
Taylor, Janelle 413

Lambing out and Other Stories
Blue, Mary Clearman 468

Lament for a Dead Cowboy
Dain, Catherine 52

The Lamorna Wink
Grimes, Martha 54, 92

Lancelot Du Lethe
King, J. Robert **566**

Land Beyond the Map
Bulmer, Kenneth 520

The Land of Green Plums
Muller, Herta 1168

The Land of Laughs
Carroll, Jonathan 659, 781

The Landscape of Lies
Watson, Peter 134

Landslayer's Law
Deitz, Tom 583

The Language of Fear
James, Del 684

The Lani People
Bone, J.F. 774

Larimont
Cade, Will 484, 511

Larkspur
Garlock, Dorothy 290

The Larkswood Legacy
Cornick, Nicola 259, 260

The Larry Cole Series
Holton, Hugh 216

Last Act in Palmyra
Davis, Lindsey 180

The Last Bird
Coel, Margaret 444

The Last Bride in Texas
Stacy, Judith 408, 409

The Last Canyon
Vernon, John **508**, 827, **949**

Last Chance
Landis, Jill Marie 471

Last Chance Bride
Hart, Jillian 296, 997

The Last Chance Ranch
Wind, Ruth 225

The Last Command
Zahn, Timothy 812

The Last Confession
West, Morris L. 844, **956**

The Last Continent
Pratchett, Terry 518, 587

The Last Dance
McBain, Ed 152

The Last Days of Christ the Vampire
Eccarius, J.G. 690

The Last Don
Puzo, Mario 916, 1183

The Last Dragonlord
Bertin, Joanne 590, 610

The Last Enchantment
Stewart, Mary 566

The Last Frontier
Coughlin, Patricia 261

The Last Full Measure
Shaara, Jeff 903

The Last Gift
Parker, Gary E. 1039

The Last Good Kiss
Crumley, James 50

The Last Good Man
Eagle, Kathleen 450

The Last Hawk
Asaro, Catherine 716

The Last Hellion
Chase, Loretta 307

The Last Hero
Pratchett, Terry 587, **588**

The Last Highlander
Cross, Claire 323

The Last Human
De Haven, Tom 1100

The Last Klick
Flynn, Robert 451

The Last Legion
Bunch, Chris 729

The Last Life
Messud, Claire 1161

The Last Lovely City
Adams, Alice 1080, 1155

The Last Mammoth
Allan, Margaret 447, 487, 507, 723

The Last Man Standing
Baldacci, David 1127

The Last Manly Man
Hayter, Sparkle 80

The Last Mayan
Shuman, Malcolm **195**

The Last Mystery of Edgar Allan Poe
Meyers, Manny 193, 932

The Last Night I Spent with You
Montero, Mayra 1164

Last Night in Paradise
Roiphe, Katie 1189

Last of the Dixie Heroes
Abrahams, Peter **1**

Last Puzzle and Testament
Hall, Parnell 96

Last Refuge
Scarborough, Elizabeth Ann 1078

The Last Report on the Miracles at Little No Horse
Erdrich, Louise 826, 1133

The Last Samurai
Dewitt, Helen 1109, 1198

The Last Sanctuary
Holden, Craig 119, 885

The Last Santini Virgin
Child, Maureen 255

Last Seen in Massilia
Saylor, Steven 184

The Last Sin Eater
Rivers, Francine 1039

The Last Song Dogs
Browning, Sinclair 28

The Last Stand
Hoyt, Edwin P. 824

The Last Station
Parini, Jay 946

The Last Summer of Reason
Djaout, Tahar **1105**

The Last Thane
Niles, Douglas 583

The Last Thing He Wanted
Didion, Joan 1134, 1138, 1206, 1211

The Last Time They Met
Shreve, Anita 1174

The Last True Cowboy
Eagle, Kathleen 450

The Last Trumpet
Rainey, Stephen Mark 683

The Last Vampire
Strieber, Whitley 645, **699**

The Last Vampire
Wright, T.M. **712**

Last Virgin in California
Child, Maureen **255**

The Last Virginia Gentleman
Kilian, Michael 898

The Last Voice They Hear
Campbell, Ramsey 626

The Last Waltz
Balogh, Mary 362

The Last Wizard
Hawke, Simon 880

Last Year's River
Jones, Allen Morris **467**, 845, **891**, 947, 961

The Late Mr. Shakespeare
Nye, Robert 823

The Laughing Hangman
Marston, Edward 148

The Laura Fleming Series
Kelner, Toni L.P. 6, 77, 114

The Laura Principal Series
Spring, Michelle 11

The Laura Winslow Series
Cole, David 28

Lavender Lies
Albert, Susan Wittig 4, 157

Law Dog
Butts, J. Lee **438**

The Law of Averages
Barthelme, Frederick 1080, 1087, 1121

The Law of Love
Esquivel, Laura 1112

Law of the Gun
Bean, Frederic 458, 479

Lawless
Gorman, Ed 456

Lawman
Plumley, Lisa 361

The Lawman Gets Lucky
Linz, Cathie 334, 335

The Lawman Meets His Bride
McKinney, Meagan 373

The Lawman Takes a Wife
Avery, Anne 247

The Lawman's Last Stand
Taylor, Vickie 414

Lay the Mountains Low
Johnston, Terry C. 890

Lazarus
West, Morris L. 956

Lazarus, Arise
Kilmer, Nicholas **134**

Leap of Faith
Steel, Danielle **1203**

Learning by Heart
Livesey, Margot 1148

The Least Likely Bride
Feather, Jane 276

Leaving Disneyland
Parsons, Alexander **1179**

Leaving Missouri
Recknor, Ellen 483

Leaving Tabasco
Boullosa, Carmen 1091

Leavings
Cacek, P.D. 630, 683

The Lecturer's Tale
Hynes, James **649**

The Lee Squires Series
Andreae, Christine 7

Left Behind
LaHaye, Tim 637

The Left Hand of Darkness
Le Guin, Ursula K. 811

Left to Die
Roderus, Frank 499

Legacies
Wilson, F. Paul 710

The Legacies of Faith Series
Brand, Irene 979, 990, 994, 1053

The Legacy of Heorot
Niven, Larry 740

The Legacy of Lehr
Kurtz, Katherine 744

Legacy of Steel
Herbert, Mary H. 556

Legacy of the Dead
Todd, Charles 208, 943

Legacy of the Wolf
Roberson, Jennifer 591, **592**

Legend
Randisi, Robert J. 497

Legend of a Badman: A Western Quintet
Hogan, Ray 461, 494, 496

The Legend of Bagger Vance
Pressfield, Steven 1132

The Legend of Luke
Jacques, Brian 587

The Legend of Sotoju Mountain
Henry, Will **461**

Legend of the Duelist
Etheridge, Rutledge 750

The Legend of Thunder Moon
Brand, Max 1137

The Legend That Was Earth
Hogan, James P. 759

Legends & Lies
Walker, Dale L. 500

Legends Lake
Ross, JoAnn **386**

Legends of the Fall
Harrison, Jim 1195

Legends of the Night
Rainey, Stephen Mark **683**

Legion of Thunder
Nicholls, Stan 580, 606

The Legionnaires
Enquist, Per Olov 862, 1110

Legions of Hell
Cherryh, C.J. 553

Legs
Kennedy, William 885, 897

Lei of Love
Mahon, Annette 343

Lempriere's Dictionary
Norfolk, Lawrence 913, 1171

Leningrad Nights
Joyce, Graham 655, 708

The Leo Bloodworth/Serendipity Dahlquist Series
Lochte, Dick 56

The Leo Hagerty Series
Ford, G.M. 56

Leota's Garden
Rivers, Francine 967, 980, 1038

Lesser Kindred
Kerner, Elizabeth 610

Let Freedom Ring
Lacy, Al 1014, 1015

Let It Bleed
Rankin, Ian 178

Lethal Harvest
Cutrer, William 975

Lethal Mercy
Kraus, Harry Lee 1012

Let's Get Criminal
Rafael, Lev 176

Letters from an Age of Reason
Hague, Nora 838, **877**, 914, 964

Letters from Yellowstone
Smith, Diane 891

Letters of the Heart
Bergren, Lisa Tawn **233**, **969**

Letters to Callie
Miller, Dawn **483**

Letting Loose
Civil-Brown, Sue 256

Leviathan
Huggins, James Byron 1003

The Lew Griffin Series
Sallis, James 73, 216

Liar's Moon
Kimball, Philip 873

Libbie
Alter, Judy 824

Libby's Story
Baer, Judy 1024

Liberty Falling
Barr, Nevada 66

Lick Creek
Kessler, Brad 887, 955

Licks of Love
Updike, John 1072

The Lieutenant Tromp Kramer Series
McClure, James 132

The Lieutenant's Lady
Huntington, Kate 304

Life After God
Coupland, Douglas 1094

Life Before Man
Atwood, Margaret 1197

Life Support
Gerritsen, Tess 78

A Lifetime of Heaven
Ryan, Nan 241

Light Coming Back
Wadsworth, Ann **1213**

A Light in the Window
Karon, Jan 1007

The Light of Falling Stars
Lennon, J. Robert 473, 1146

Light the Night
Culea, John 991

The Lighthouse at the End of the World
Marlowe, Stephen 932

Lightning Field
Spiotta, Dana 1107, **1202**

Lightning in a Drought Year
Black, Michelle 423

Lights Out
Abrahams, Peter 1

Lightstorm
Hamilton, Peter 739

Like a Lamb to the Slaughter
Block, Lawrence 48, 99

Like Gold Refined
Oke, Janette 1034

Like No Other
George, Melanie 277

Like Water for Chocolate
Esquivel, Laura 1067, 1112

Likely to Die
Fairstein, Linda 66

A Likeness in Stone
Martin, J. Wallis 211

Lilies That Fester
Harrison, Janis **103**

Lily
Gaffney, Patricia 227

Lily Nevada
Holland, Cecelia 446, 448, 449, 450, 457, 470, 488

Lily White
Isaacs, Susan 1131

The Lincoln Rhyme Series
Deaver, Jeffery 20

Lincoln's Ransom
Champlin, Tim 439, 440, 456, 487, 498

Lindbergh's Son
Vernon, John 949

The Lineage of Grace Series
Rivers, Francine 994, 1053

The Lion at Sea
Hennessy, Max 866

The Lion of Farside
Dalmas, John 741, 742

Lion of Macedon
Gemmell, David 547

The Lion Returns
Dalmas, John 741, 742

The Lion Throne
Roberson, Jennifer **593**

Lionheart
Fullerton, Alexander 866

Lionheart!
Rofheart, Martha 941

The Liquidator
Mount, Ferdinand 1167

The List
Whitlow, Robert 976

The List of 7
Frost, Mark 926

Listen to the Shadows
Reah, Danuta **179**

Little Boy Lost
Wright, T.M. 712

The Little Country
De Lint, Charles 659

A Little Death
Wilson, Laura 214

Little Jordan
Youmans, Marly 964

A Little Local Murder
Barnard, Robert 27

Little Miss Evil
Rafael, Lev 176

Little Myth Marker
Asprin, Robert Lynn 521

Little Saigon
Parker, T. Jefferson 98

Little White Lies
Benrey, Ron 996, 1008, 1009

The Littlest Witness
Stevens, Amanda 410

Live Girls
Garton, Ray 625, 699

The Living One
Gannett, Lewis 623

Living with Aliens
DeChancie, John 749

Living with Saints
O'Connell, Mary **1175**

Living with the Hyenas
Flynn, Robert 451

Lizardskin
Stroud, Carsten 204

The Lizbet Lange Series
Thrasher, L.L. 52

Local Girls
Hoffman, Alice 1103, 1198

Loch
Zindel, Paul 714

A Locket for Maggie
Page, Carole Gift 1019, 1035, 1036

Lockwood
Paine, Lauran 492, **492**, 493

Lofty Ambitions
Christner, Dianne 979

Logan's Child
Worth, Lenora 968

A Logical Magician
Weinberg, Robert 706

Loitering with Intent
Spark, Muriel 1156

London Bridges
Stevenson, Jane **1204**

The London Vampire Panic
Romkey, Michael **686**

Lone Eagle
Steel, Danielle 1203

Lone Hand
Olsen, T.V. 486

The Lone Rider
Brand, Max **432**

Lone Star Christmas
Palmer, Diana 263

Lone Survivor
Hodgson, Ken 463

Lonesome Dove
McMurtry, Larry 1212

Lonesome Land
Bowers, B.M. 495

The Long Afternoon of Earth
Aldiss, Brian W. 790

The Long Awaited Child
Peterson, Tracie 1042

Long-Awaited Wedding
Fell, Doris Elaine 992

The Long Dark Tea-Time of the Soul
Adams, Douglas 813

The Long Good Boy
Benjamin, Carol Lea **16**

The Long Home
Gay, William 1157

The Long Journey Home
Coldsmith, Don 423, 842

Long Journey to Deep Canon
Flynn, T.T. **452**, 501

The Long-Legged Fly
Sallis, James 192

A Long Line of Dead Men
Block, Lawrence 22

The Long Lost
Campbell, Ramsey 626

The Long March
Fitzpatrick, Marie-Louise 464

The Long Ones
Lansdale, Joe R. 472

Long Remember
Kantor, MacKinlay 919

The Long Shadow
Gilbert, Anna 872

Long Time No See
Isaacs, Susan 198, **1131**, 1136

The Long Tomorrow
Brackett, Leigh 732

The Long Trail Home
Bly, Stephen A. 972, 973

The Long Trail Home
Dunham, Tracy 454

Long Train Passing
Wise, Steven W. 992

The Long Way Home
Snelling, Lauraine 1050

The Long Winter
Christopher, John 724

The Longest Memory
D'Aguiar, Fred 846

The Longest Single Note and Other Strange Compositions
Crowther, Peter 655

Longing
Landis, J.D. 833, 852, 929, 1085, 1156

Longtusk
Baxter, Stephen 879

Look at Me
Egan, Jennifer **1108**, 1188

Look to the Mountain
Cannon, LeGrand 868

Look to Windward
Banks, Iain **721**

Look What the Stork Brought
Browning, Dixie 246

Looker
Kilian, Michael 898

Looker
Saralegui, Jorge 705

Looking for Laura
Arnold, Judith **226**, 299

Looking for Rachel Wallace
Parker, Robert B. 190

Looking Glass
Cherne, Barbara 836

The Looking Glass
Roberts, Michele 870, **925**

The Loop
Coomer, Joe 1144

Loot
Elkins, Aaron 134

Lord Carew's Bride
Balogh, Mary 325, 349

Lord Carlton's Courtship
Raleigh, Debbie 377, 378, 420

Lord Glenraven's Return
Barbour, Anne 349

Lord Harry's Daughter
Richardson, Evelyn 379, 389

Lord Langdon's Kiss
Greene, Elena 305, 420

The Lord Meren Series
Robinson, Lynda S. 101

Lord Monteith's Gift
Butler, Nancy 370

Lord Mumford's Minx
Raleigh, Debbie 377, 378

Lord of Danger
Stuart, Anne 411

Lord of the Dead
Holland, Tom 922

Lord of the Isles
Drake, David 541

Lord of the Necropolis
DeWeese, Gene 613

Lord of the Storm
Davis, Justine 267, 310

Lord of the Two Lands
Tarr, Judith 603

Lord of the Vampires
Kalogridis, Jeanne 632

Lord of Thunder
Norton, Andre 772

Lord of Vengeance
St. John, Tina 405, 407

Lord Prestimion
Silverberg, Robert 593, 797

Lord St. Claire's Angel
Simpson, Donna 397

Lord Soth
van Belkom, Edo 705

Lord Stanhope's Proposal
Benson, Jessica 420

Lords of the Plain
Crawford, Max 827

Lords of the Psychon
Galouye, Daniel F. 746, 791

The Lords of Vaumartin
Holland, Cecelia 844

Los Alamos
Kanon, Joseph 131, 892, 1135

Losing Nelson
Unsworth, Barry 1069

Lost Angels
Schow, David J. 648

The Lost Band
Coldsmith, Don 447, 507

The Lost Bird
Coel, Margaret 35

The Lost Colony
Olsen, T.V. 486

The Lost Daughter of Happiness
Yan, Gelling 817

Lost Horizon
Hilton, James 717

Lost in His Love
Cote, Lyn 985

Lost in the Funhouse
Barth, John 720

Lost in Translation
Ball, Margaret 543

The Lost King
Weis, Margaret 612

The Lost Language of Cranes
Leavitt, David 1145

The Lost Library of Cormanthyr
Odom, Mel 584

The Lost Ones
Cameron, Ian 717, 792

Lost Pages
Di Filippo, Paul 745, 760, 786

The Lost Queen
Lofts, Norah 862, 1110

Lost Romance Ranch
Jones, Annie 1055

Lost Soldiers
Webb, James H. 1186

Lost Souls
Brite, Poppy Z. 625, 699

The Lost World
Crichton, Michael 1093

The Lost World
Doyle, Arthur Conan 717

Lot Lizards
Garton, Ray 638

Lottie and the Rustler
Castle, Linda Lea 253

Louisa
Zelitch, Simone 1078, 1106, 1135, 1175

The Louise Eldridge Series
Ripley, Ann 103, 173

Louisiana Hotshot
Smith, Julie 177

Louisiana Purchase
Hotchner, A.E. 912

Love: A User's Guide
Naylor, Clare 394

Love and Glory
Westin, Janet Eddy 228

Love and Infamy
Deford, Frank 849

Love and the Single Corpse
Griffin, Annie 91

The Love Artist
Alison, Jane 1091

A Love Beyond Time
Aitken, Judie 296, 372

Love Came Just in Time
Kurland, Lynn 358

Love Child
Hingle, Metsy 301

Love, etc.
Barnes, Julian 1099, 1102, 1142

A Love for Lydia
Savery, Jeanne 389

A Love for Safekeeping
Martin, Gail Gaymer 982, **1021**

Love Her Madly
Smith, Mary-Ann Tirone **198**

Love in a Blue Time
Kureishi, Hanif 1143

Love in a Mist
Grasso, Patricia 293

Love in Another Town
Bradford, Barbara Taylor 1199

Love in Bloom's
Arnold, Judith 226

Love in Vein
Brite, Poppy Z. 643, 654

Love Is a Gentle Stranger
Bacher, June Masters 1011

Love Just in Time
Speer, Flora 546

Love Lies Bleeding
Albert, Susan Wittig 4

Love Life
Mason, Bobbie Ann 1155

The Love of a Good Woman
Munro, Alice 1169, 1201

Love One Another
Hansen, Valerie 982, **995**

The Love Song of J. Edgar Hoover
Friedman, Kinky 72

Love Story
Segal, Eric 1181

Love to Love You Baby
Michaels, Kasey 353, **354**

Love to Water My Soul
Kirkpatrick, Jane 1058

The Lovejoy Series
Gash, Jonathan 69, 160

A Lovely Monster
DeMarinis, Rick 806

The Lover
Jordan, Nicole 309

The Lovers
Hawks, Kate 881

Lovers and Other Lunatics
Riley, Eugenia 380

Love's Reward
Ewing, Jean R. 374

Loving Chloe
Mapson, Jo-Ann 1165

Loving Lizbeth
Langan, Ruth 327

Loving Thy Neighbor
Scofield, Ruth 982, 995, 1036, 1041, 1043, **1047**

Loving You Was My Undoing
Gonzalez-Rubio, Javier 476

Low Country
Siddons, Anne Rivers 1073

Lowell Limpett: And Two Stories
Just, Ward S. **1134**

A Lower Deep
Piccirilli, Tom **682**

Lowland Rider
Williamson, Chet 687

Lt. Kent: Lone Wolf
Lyons, Judith **341**

The Luanne Fogarty Series
Alam, Glynn Marsh 216

The Lucas Davenport Series
Sandford, John 20, 204

Lucifer's Hammer
Niven, Larry 767

Luck in the Shadows
Flewelling, Lynn 544

The Luck of Huemac
Peters, Daniel 889

The Luck of the Draw
Dain, Catherine 52

The Luckless Elopement
Mack, Dorothy 356

Lucky Bucky in Oz
Neill, John R. 577

Lucky Us
Silber, Joan **1198**

Lucky You
Hiaasen, Carl 115

The Lucy Stone Series
Meier, Leslie 89

Lucy Sullivan Is Getting Married
Keyes, Marian 357, 359

Lucy's Christmas Angel
Heath, Sandra 366

Lud-in-the-Mist
Mirrlees, Hope 571

The Luis Balam Series
Alexander, Gary 195

The Luke Thanet Series
Simpson, Dorothy 43

The Lunatic Cafe
Hamilton, Laurell K. 645

The Lupe Solano Series
Garcia-Aguilera, Carolina 167, 217

Lurid Dreams
Harness, Charles L. 802

Lydia Cassatt Reading the Morning Paper
Chessman, Harriet Scott **837**, 951

Lying Awake
Salzman, Mark 1175

The Lying Days
Gordimer, Nadine 1116

Lying with the Enemy
Binding, Tim 888

Lynch: A Gothic Western
Collins, Nancy 629

M

The "M" Word
Isenberg, Jane 124

M31
Wright, Stephen 661

Ma Calhoun's Boys
Gibson, Robin 440

Macabre Delights and Twisted Tales
Ford, John B. 635, 636

Macbeth the King
Tranter, Nigel 921

Machine Sex
Dorsey, Candas Jane 747

The MacKenzies: David
Leigh, Ana 332

The MacKenzies: Flint
Leigh, Ana 332

The MacKenzies: Jared
Leigh, Ana 332

The MacKenzies: Josh
Leigh, Ana 332

The MacKenzies: Luke
Leigh, Ana 332

The MacKenzies: Zach
Leigh, Ana **332**

Mackerel by Moonlight
Weld, William F. 955

The Mackintosh Bride
Brown, Debra Lee **244**

Mad Elaine
Stevenson, Helen 1144

Mad Hatter Summer
Thomas, Donald S. 187, 927

The Mad Herringtons
Perrine, Jane Myers 378

Mad Merlin
King, J. Robert 558, 564, 565, 566

Madbond
Springer, Nancy 590, 592

Maddie's Justice
LaFoy, Leslie 294, 296, 324

Madigan's Wife
Jones, Linda Winstead 417

Madman
Hansom, Mark 646

Madoc, Prince of America
Knight, Bernard 952

Madonna of the Seven Hills
Plaidy, Jean 916

Madrigal
Janes, J. Robert 126

Maelstrom
Watts, Peter **808**

The Magdelene Scrolls
Wood, Barbara 962

The Mage in the Iron Mask
Thomsen, Brian 565

Maggody and the Moonbeams
Hess, Joan **114**

The Maggody Militia
Hess, Joan 114

The Maggody Series
Hess, Joan 15

A Maggot
Fowles, John 1085

Magic
Cates, Kimberly 303, 358

Magic Can Be Murder
Vande Velde, Vivian 538

The Magic Chest of Oz
Abbott, Donald 577

The Magic Dishpan of Oz
Freedman, Jeff 577

The Magic Goes Away
Niven, Larry 556

The Magic Mirror
Blackwood, Algernon 680

The Magic of Ordinary Days
Creel, Ann Howard 821, **845**, 850, 870, 891, 925, 938, 947, 955

Magic Slippers
Boswell, Barbara 243, 268

Magic Terror
Straub, Peter 1166

Magic Time
Kinsella, W.P. 1114

Magic Time
Zicree, Marc Scott **614**

A Magical Moment
Jackson, Monica 272, 383

The Magicians
Gunn, James 522

The Magician's Wife
Moore, Brian 900

The Magickers
Drake, Emily **542**

MagicNet
DeChancie, John 518

The Magnificent Marquess
Eastwood, Gail 379

The Magnificent Savages
Stewart, Fred Mustard 937

The Magus
Fowles, John 1073

The Maiden and the Unicorn
Martyn, Isolde 276

Maiden Voyage
Bass, Cynthia 816

The Maiden's Heart
Beard, Julie 229

The Maiden's Tale
Frazer, Margaret 70

The Mail Order Bride Series
Lacy, Al 973

Mail-Order Cinderella
Jensen, Kathryn 268

The Maine Massacre
Van de Wetering, Janwillem 42

Maire
Windsor, Linda 1060

Majestic
Strieber, Whitley 675

Majic Man
Collins, Max Allan 40, 41, 841

Major
Shelley, Rick 795

Major Ingredients
Russell, Eric Frank 715, 794, 803

Major Washington
Kilian, Michael 898

The Major's Mistake
Pickens, Andrea 370

The Maker of Universes
Farmer, Philip Jose 520, 583

The Making of a Monster
Peterson, Gail 684

Malcolm's Honor
Hart, Jillian 296, 997

Malice in Cornwall
Thomas, Graham 54

Malice in Miniature
Dams, Jeanne M. 54

Malinche and Cortes
Shedd, Margaret 889

Mall Purchase Night
Cook, Rick 537

The Maltese Falcon
Hammett, Dashiell 99

Mamaw
Dodd, Susan M. 852

Mamigon
Hashian, Jack 893

Mammoth
Baxter, Stephen 723

The Mammoth Book of Best New Horror 12
Jones, Stephen **653**

The Mammoth Book of Dracula
Jones, Stephen 631, 653, 654

The Mammoth Book of Frankenstein
Jones, Stephen 654

The Mammoth Book of Great Detective Stories
Van Thal, Herbert 57

The Mammoth Book of Historical Detectives
Ashley, Mike 8

The Mammoth Book of Historical Whodunnits
Ashley, Mike 8

The Mammoth Book of More Historical Whodunnits
Ashley, Mike **8**

The Mammoth Book of Vampire Stories by Women
Jones, Stephen 653, **654**

The Mammoth Hunters
Auel, Jean M. 723

A Man and a Woman and a Man
Liebrecht, Savyon 1197

The Man Behind the Badge
Taylor, Vickie 414

Man from Wyoming
Coolidge, Dane **448**

The Man in Flames
Filippini, Serge 956

A Man in Full
Wolfe, Tom 1119

The Man in the Gray Flannel Suit
Wilson, Sloan 1141

The Man in the Moon Must Die
Bredenberg, Jeff 759

Man on a Mission
Cassidy, Carla 417

Man on a Red Horse
Grove, Fred 460

The Man Responsible
Robinett, Stephen 763

The Man Who Cancelled Himself
Handler, David 100

The Man Who Folded Himself
Gerrold, David 754

The Man Who Hated Banks and Other Stories
Gilbert, Michael 146

The Man Who Loved Women to Death
Handler, David 100

The Man Who Rode Midnight
Kelton, Elmer 479

Man with a Squirrel
Kilmer, Nicholas 134

Man Without a Past
Olsen, T.V. **486**

Man Without Medicine
Haseloff, Cynthia 446, 448, 449, 450, 467, 480

Man Without Memory
Burgin, Richard 1087

Manassas
Reasoner, James 919

Manhattan Heat
Eulo, Ken 672

The Manhattan Hunt Club
Saul, John **687**

The Manhunters
Kelton, Elmer 1137

Manhunting in Mississippi
Bond, Stephanie 223, 235

Manifest Destiny
Garfield, Brian 508

Manifest Destiny
Longyear, Barry 734

Manifold: Space
Baxter, Stephen 723, 807

Manifold: Time
Baxter, Stephen 723

Man. . .Mercenary. . .Monarch
Pickart, Joan Elliot 268

Mansions of Darkness
Yarbro, Chelsea Quinn 713

The Many Aspects of Mobile Home Living
Clark, Martin 1153

The Map of Love
Soueif, Ahdaf 1116, 1129, 1178

The Marble Mask
Mayor, Archer 134, 151

The Marble Quilt
Leavitt, David 1120, **1145**

The March of the Musicians
Enquist, Per Olov 1110

March to the Sea
Weber, David **809**

Marching through Peachtree
Turtledove, Harry **606**

Marching to Valhalla
Blake, Michael 425, 438, 826

The Marcus Didius Falco Series
Davis, Lindsey 184, 924

The Margaret Binton Series
Barth, John 96

The Margaret Priam Series
Christmas, Joyce 34

Margaret's Peace
Hall, Linda 967, 993

The Margot Fortier Series
Fennelly, Tony 13

Mari
Barker, Jane Valentine 481, 498, 513

Mariana
Kearsley, Susanna 314

The Mariana Morgan Series
Dain, Catherine 79

Marian's Christmas Wish
Kelly, Carla 315

Marigolds for Mourning
Stallsmith, Audrey 1005

The Marine and the Princess
Linz, Cathie **334**

The Mark
LaHaye, Tim 1016

The Mark Manning Series
Craft, Michael 221

The Mark of the Lion Series
Rivers, Francine 979, 990, 994

The Mark Twain Series
Heck, Peter J. 95, 135

The Markham of the Marines Series
Connery, Tom 854

The Markowitz Family
Goodman, Allegra 1100

The Marla Shore Series
Cohen, Nancy J. 13

Marooned in Realtime
Vinge, Vernor 807

Marooned with a Marine
Child, Maureen 255

The Marquis' Kiss
Scott, Regina 392, 393

Marriage a la Mode
Fairchild, Elisabeth 275

The Marriage Bed
Dain, Claudia **266**, 320, 368, 396

The Marriage Bed
Mittman, Stephanie 364

The Marriage Contract
Maxwell, Cathy 348

The Marriage Knot
McBride, Mary 361

The Marriage of Sticks
Carroll, Jonathan 539

The Marriage Prize
Henley, Virginia 883

Married in Haste
Maxwell, Cathy 348

Married to the Boss
Foster, Lori 286

Marry in Haste
Kerstan, Lynn 258

Marry Me, Maddie?
Herron, Rita 226, 256, 264, **299**, 353

Marrying a Delacourt
Woods, Sherryl 364

The Marrying Kind
Rutledge, Cynthia 1044, 1045

The Marrying Man
Criswell, Millie 253, 264, 284, 408

Marrying Walker McKay
Copeland, Lori 983

Mars
Bova, Ben 814

Mars Crossing
Landis, Geoffrey A. 766, 771, 814

The Mars Monopoly
Sohl, Jerry 793

The Marshal and the Forgery
Nabb, Magdalen 164

The Marshal and the Heiress
Potter, Patricia 373

The Marshal and the Madwoman
Nabb, Magdalen 164

The Marshal at the Villa Torrini
Nabb, Magdalen 164

The Marshal Makes His Report
Nabb, Magdalen 164

The Marshal's Own Case
Nabb, Magdalen 164

Martha Peake
McGrath, Patrick 840, 939, 1098, 1110, 1212

The Marti McAlister Series
Bland, Eleanor Taylor 220

Martian Knightlife
Hogan, James P. **759**

Martian Rainbow
Forward, Robert 771

Martians in Maggody
Hess, Joan 114

Martin and Hannah
Clement, Catherine 852

Martin Bauman
Leavitt, David 1145, 1173

The Marty Hopkins Series
Carlson, P.M. 145, 212

Martyrs' Crossing
Wilentz, Amy 1109

Mary, Mary
Parsons, Julie 1180

The Mary Russell/Sherlock Holmes Series
King, Laurie R. 158, 899, 958

The Mask of the Sun
Saberhagen, Fred 802

The Masked Gun
Cord, Barry 480

Maskerade
Pratchett, Terry 524

The Masks of Auntie Laveau
Randisi, Robert J. **177**

Mason & Dixon
Pynchon, Thomas 950

Massacre Island
Hegwood, Martin **112**

Master Georgie
Bainbridge, Beryl 1069

Master of Lies
Masterton, Graham 682

The Master of Petersburg
Coetzee, J.M. 946

Master of the Crossroads
Bell, Madison Smartt 1134

Master of the Fearful Depths
Adkins, Patrick H. 547

Master of the Five Magics
Hardy, Lyndon 548

Master of the White Storm
Wurts, Janny 530, 572

The Master Sniper
Hunter, Stephen 1127

The Masterharper of Pern
McCaffrey, Anne 772

Masterpiece of Murder
Kruger, Mary 203

The Masters of Bow Street
Creasey, John 10, 182, 815

Masters of Darkness
Etchison, Dennis 634

Masters of Darkness II
Etchison, Dennis 634

Masters of Darkness III
Etchison, Dennis 634

The Masters of Rome Series
McCullough, Colleen 924

Masters of Souls
Hansom, Mark 646

Masterson
Wheeler, Richard S. 457, 488, 512, 957

A Match for Mother
Gedney, Mona 291

The Matchmaker
Becnel, Rexanne 311, 400

The Matchmakers
Oke, Janette 1024

The Matisse Stories
Byatt, A.S. 1120

Matricide at St. Martha's
Edwards, Ruth Dudley 176

Matrix
Mason, Douglas R. 808

The Matt Scudder Series
Block, Lawrence 42, 74, 213

A Matter of Scandal
Enoch, Suzanne 311

The Matthew Bartholomew Series
Gregory, Susanna 944

The Matthew Stock Series
Tourney, Leonard 933, 934

Mattie and the Blacksmith
Castle, Linda Lea **253**, 284, 408

Maui Rose
Mahon, Annette 343

The Maxey Burnell Series
Cail, Carol 51

Maxie's Demon
Rohan, Michael Scott 595

The Maze Maker
Ayrton, Michael 547

Maze of Moonlight
Baudino, Gael 603

McKendree
Hirt, Douglas 462

Me
Keillor, Garrison 1136

Me and the Boys
Recknor, Ellen 483

Mean High Tide
Hall, James W. 94

Meant to Be Married
Wind, Ruth 422

A Measure of Grace
Lacy, Al **1014**, 1015

The Med Series
Leinster, Murray 805

The Medusa Tree
Dressler, Mylene 1106

Meely LaBauve
Wells, Ken 1214

Meet Me at Midnight
Enoch, Suzanne 229, 319, 375, 402

Meet Me at Midnight
Navin, Jacqueline 360

Meet Me in the Moon Room
Vukcevich, Ray 689

Mefisto in Onyx
Ellison, Harlan 627

The Meg Langslow Series
Andrews, Donna 89, 144

The Melanie Travers Series
Berenson, Laurien 16

The Melissa Craig Series
Rowlands, Betty 27, 54

Memories
McQuay, Mike 802

The Memory of Fire
Foy, George 764

Men Beyond the Law
Brand, Max 430, 432, 435, 486

Men Like Rats
Chilson, Robert 746, 791

Men, Martians, and Machines
Russell, Eric Frank 794

The Mercenary
Adair, Cherry 222, 223

Mercenary
Pournelle, Jerry 729, 784

The Merchant of Death
Grace, C.L. 86, 875

The Merchant of Menace
Churchill, Jill 839

The Merchant of Venus
Hart, Ellen 60

Merchanter's Luck
Cherryh, C.J. 796

The Merchants of Souls
Barnes, John **722**

The Mercy Rule
Lescroart, John 141

Merely Married
Coughlin, Patricia 261

Meridian
Walker, Alice 1147

The Meriwether Journal
Shuman, Malcolm 195

Merlin
Greenberg, Martin H. 552, 754

Merlin
Nye, Robert 558

The Merlin of St. Gilles Well
Chamberlin, Ann 562, 603

The Merlin of the Oak Wood
Chamberlin, Ann 818

Merlin's Bones
Saberhagen, Fred 558

Merlin's Gift
McDowell, Ian 558

Merlin's Wood
Holdstock, Robert 558

The Mermaid
Krahn, Betina 321

The Mermaids Singing
McDermid, Val 154

The Merman's Children
Anderson, Poul 517

Merrick
Rice, Anne 685, 1185

The Merry Widows: Sarah
Michaels, Theresa 296

Merry's Christmas
Gedney, Mona 275, 291

Mesmer
Lebbon, Tim 665, 666

Message in a Bottle
Sparks, Nicholas 1181, 1200

The Message of the Mute Dog
Russell, Charlotte Murray **191**

The Messenger
Montero, Mayra 1164

The Messenger of Zhuvastou
Offutt, Andrew J. 585

Messing around with Max
Foster, Lori 286

MetaHorror
Etchison, Dennis 634

Metaplanetary
Daniel, Tony 736

Meteor in the Madhouse
Forrest, Leon 1133, 1154

Methods of Execution
Huebner, Fredrick 121

Metropolitan
Williams, Walter Jon 721, 789

The Mexican Tree Duck
Crumley, James 50

The Michael Stone Series
Salter, Anna 197

Michaelmas
Budrys, Algis 800

The Michelle Mitchell Series
Allyn, Doug 3

The Mickey Rawlings Series
Soos, Troy 188, 936

Middle Age
Oates, Joyce Carol 1112, 1163, 1173, **1174**

Midlife Can Be Murder
Isenberg, Jane **124**

Midnight
Koontz, Dean R. 710

Midnight All Day
Kureishi, Hanif 1143

Midnight Bayou
Roberts, Nora 382, **1187**

Midnight Blue
Collins, Nancy 629

A Midnight Clear
Hill, Donna 300

A Midnight Clear
Kerstan, Lynn 275

Midnight Falcon
Gemmell, David **548**

Midnight in Ruby Bayou
Lowell, Elizabeth 331, 340, 413

Midnight Jewels
Krentz, Jayne Ann 245

Midnight Lady
Rogers, Rosemary 385

The Midnight Louie Series
Douglas, Carole Nelson 26, 162, 856

Midnight Magic
Mason, Bobbie Ann 1155

Midnight Mass
Bowles, Paul 1080

Midnight Pleasures
James, Eloisa 329

The Midnight Raymond Chandler
Chandler, Raymond 41, 99, 201

Midnight Robber
Hopkinson, Nalo 760

Midnight Sun
Bergren, Lisa Tawn 1042

Midnight Tales
Harvey, William Fryer 622

The Midnight Tour
Laymon, Richard 662

Midnight's Children
Rushdie, Salman 1190

Midsummer
Costello, Matthew J. 660

Midsummer Murder
Freydont, Shelley 45, **71**

Midway Between
Norwood, Warren 761

A Midwinter's Tale
Greeley, Andrew M. 1117, 1135, 1174

Mightier than the Sword
Waide, Peggy 229, 416

The Mike Hammer Collection. Volume 1
Spillane, Mickey 201

The Mike Hammer Collection. Volume 2
Spillane, Mickey 201

The Mike Yeadings Series
Curzon, Claire 64, 97

The Mile High Club
Friedman, Kinky 72

Miles, Mystery & Mayhem
Bujold, Lois McMaster **728**

Milkrun
Mlynowski, Sarah 252, 345, **357**

Millennium Baby
Arnold, Judith 226

Millennium Macabre
Meikle, William 652, 701

A Million Open Doors
Barnes, John 722

The Millionaire's Pregnant Bride
Browning, Dixie 246

The Millionaire's Proposition
Patrick, Natalie 268

Millroy the Magician
Theroux, Paul 1095

The Milton Kovak Series
Cooper, Susan Rogers 93

Mimi's Ghost
Parks, Tim 1177, 1187

Mina
Kiraly, Mina 632

The Mind Parasites
Wilson, Colin 670

The Mind Spider and Other Strange Visitors
Newton, Kurt 639

Mind Switch
Knight, Damon 670

The Mind Thing
Brown, Fredric 801

The Mindwarpers
Russell, Eric Frank 794

Mine to Take
Joy, Dara 310

The Mineral Palace
Julavits, Heidi 1113

The Ming and I
Myers, Tamar 163

Minus Time
Bush, Catherine 1094

Minutes to Burn
Hurwitz, Gregg Andrew **762**

The Minx of Mayfair
Willingham, Bess 420

Mirabilis
Cokal, Susann 844, 913, 1083, **1091**

A Miracle in Paradise
Garcia-Aguilera, Carolina 75

Miracle of the Jacal
Randisi, Robert J. **497**

Miracle on a Mountain
Bogue, Lucile 426

The Miracle Strip
Bartholomew, Nancy 13

Miracles in Maggody
Hess, Joan 114

Mirage
Janes, J. Robert 888

The Miriam's Journal Series
Bender, Carrie 1018

Mirror Dance
Bujold, Lois McMaster 728

Mirror Image
Brown, Sandra 381

Mirror Image
Steel, Danielle 1203

The Mirror of Helen
Purtill, Richard 547

Mischief
Quick, Amanda 375

Misery Loves Maggody
Hess, Joan 77, 114

Miss Bianca
Sharp, Margery 587

Miss Chartley's Guided Tour
Kelly, Carla 318

Miss Cheney's Charade
Hendrickson, Emily 370

Miss Darby's Duenna
South, Sheri Cobb 404

Miss Davenport's Christmas
Chesney, Marion 304

Miss Dornton's Hero
Fairchild, Elisabeth 397

Miss Drayton's Downfall
Oliver, Patricia 362

Miss Grimsley's Oxford Career
Kelly, Carla 315, 370

Miss Lacey's Last Fling
Hern, Candice 298

Miss Lockhart's Letters
Metzger, Barbara 233

Miss Maitland's Letters
Kirkland, Martha 233, 318

Miss Match
Carroll, Leslie **252**

Miss Seeton's Finest Hour
Crane, Hamilton 136

Miss Truelove Beckons
Simpson, Donna **397**

Miss Verey's Proposal
Cornick, Nicola 259, 260

Miss Wyoming
Coupland, Douglas 1094

The Miss Zukas Series
Dereske, Jo 51

The Missing World
Livesey, Margot 1148, 1184

Mission Child
McHugh, Maureen 774

Mission to Universe
Dickson, Gordon R. 796

Mistletoe Kittens
Ferguson, Jo Ann 232

Mistletoe Man
Albert, Susan Wittig 4

Mistletoe Mayhem
Huntington, Kate 238, 304

The Mistress
Wiggs, Susan 342, 419

Mistress of Death
Anthony, Piers 750

Mistress of Mellyn
Holt, Victoria 411

Mistress of Mistresses
Eddison, E.R. 536

The Mistress of Rosecliffe
Becnel, Rexanne 266

The Mistress of Spices
Divakaruni, Chitra Banerjee 1104

Mistress of the Catacombs
Drake, David **541**

The Mists of Avalon
Bradley, Marion Zimmer 528, 940

Mistwalker
Heald, Denise Lopes 716

The Mitch Tobin Series
Coe, Tucker 22

The Mitford Years Series
Karon, Jan 984, 1117

Mitz: The Marmoset of Bloomsbury
Nunez, Sigrid 1172

The Moghul
Hoover, Thomas 963

Molly and the Confidence Man
Overholser, Stephen 488

The Molly Bearpaw Series
Hager, Jean 35, 212

The Molly Cates Series
Walker, Mary Willis 98

Molly Dear
Fine, Stephen 806

A Moment of Weakness
Kingsbury, Karen 971

The Mommy Club
Bird, Sarah 1093

The Mommy Makeover
Winn, Bonnie K. 1061

Monahan's Gamble
Bevarly, Elizabeth 235, 236

The Monastery
Williamson, J.N. 709

Monday Man
Gabriel, Kristin 235

Monday's Child
Chaikin, Linda 977

Money, Money, Money
McBain, Ed **152**

The Money-Whipped Steer-Job Three-Jack Give-Up Artist
Jenkins, Dan 1114, **1132**

The Monitor, the Miners, and the Shree
Killough, Lee 780

The Monk Who Vanished
Tremayne, Peter 209, 944

The Monsieur Pamplemousse Series
Bond, Michael 138

Monster
Tigges, John 662

The Monster from Earth's End
Leinster, Murray 735

The Monster of Minnesota
Sumner, Mark 737

Monsters in Our Midst
Bloch, Robert 651

The Monsters of Morley Manor
Coville, Bruce **538**

A Monstrous Regiment of Women
King, Laurie R. 208

Montana Man
Hart, Jillian 296, 997

A Montclair Homecoming
Peart, Jane 971, 1035

Monte
Vories, Eugene C. 509

Monte's Revenge
Vories, Eugene C. **509**

The Monument
Makiya, Kanan 902

Monument Rock
L'Amour, Louis 456, 461, 494

Monuments
Reynolds, Clay 498

Moo
Smiley, Jane 649

Mood Swings to Murder
Isenberg, Jane 124

The Moon Maid
Garcia y Robertson, R. 546

Moon Medicine
Blakely, Mike **827**

Moon Mirror
Norton, Andre 557, 784

Moon of Bitter Cold
Chiaventone, Frederick J. **441**

Moon of Ice
Linaweaver, Brad 804

Moon over Water
Macomber, Debbie 474

The Moon Pearl
McCunn, Ruthanne 835

Moonfall
Thorne, Tamara 703

Moonglow
Sutcliffe, Katherine 412

Moonglow, Texas
McBride, Mary 263

Moonlight and Vines
De Lint, Charles 539

The Moons of Jupiter
Munro, Alice 1149

Moonseed
Baxter, Stephen 723

Moonshadow
Neri, Penelope 418

The Moonstone Mass
Spofford, Harriet Prescott 711

Moontide
Patrick, Erin **681**

The Moorchild
McGraw, Eloise 577

The Moor's Last Sigh
Rushdie, Salman 1190

More Annotated Lovecraft
Lovecraft, H.P. 671

More Die of Heartbreak
Bellow, Saul 1141

More Ghost Stories of an Antiquary
James, M.R. 650

The More I See You
Kurland, Lynn 323

More Murder, They Wrote
Foxwell, Elizabeth 84

More Oddments
Pronzini, Bill 142, **175**

More Shapes than One
Chappell, Fred 700, 707

More than a Mistress
Balogh, Mary 227

More than Honor
Weber, David 809

More than Memory
Garlock, Dorothy 339

More to Love
Browning, Dixie 246

Morgan's Run
McCullough, Colleen 819, 904, 1212

Morgan's Woman
French, Judith E. 294

Morgette in the Yukon
Boyer, G.G. 429

Morgette on the Barbary Coast
Boyer, G.G. **429**

Morning
Wetherell, W.D. 1084, 1102

The Morning After
Forster, Suzanne 283

The Morning After
Roiphe, Katie 1189

Morning Comes Softly
Macomber, Debbie 421

The Morning Cool
Witherspoon, Mary Elizabeth 855

Morning Glory
Spencer, LaVyrle 290

A Morning in Eden
Gilbert, Anna **872**

Morningsong
Rushford, Patricia H. 1044, 1046

The Moroni Traveler Series
Irvine, Robert 76

Mortal Fear
Iles, Greg 123

The Mortal Nuts
Hautman, Pete 107

Mortal Sins
Williamson, Penn 867

Mortal Stakes
Parker, Robert B. 188

Mortalis
Salvatore, R.A. 597

The Most Important Little Boy in the World
Briggs, Dean 975

Most Likely to Die
Girdner, Jacqueline 80

Moth
Sallis, James 192

A Mother at Heart
Aarsen, Carolyne 965

Mother Earth, Father Sky
Harrison, Sue 879

A Mother for Amanda
Schmidt, Anna 995, 997, 1046

Mother Nature
Andrews, Sarah 7

Mother Ocean, Daughter Sea
Marcellas, Diana **576**

Mother of Kings
Anderson, Poul **517**, **818**

Motherland
Vijayaraghavan, Vineeta 1104, 1208

Motherless Brooklyn
Lethem, Jonathan 37, 199, 211

Mother's Day Miracle
Richer, Lois 1043

The Mother's Day Murder
Harris, Lee 996

A Mother's Heart
Caille, Julie 280

A Mother's Love
Bergren, Lisa Tawn 233

Moulin Rouge
La Mure, Pierre 837

The Mountain King
Hautala, Rick 662

Mountain Man's Vengeance
Lake, Robert 463, 512

Mountain Time
Coleman, Jane Candia **446**

Mountain Windsong
Conley, Robert J. 842

Mourn the Living
Collins, Max Allan 40

The Mourners' Bench
Dodd, Susan M. 852

The Mouse in the Mountain
Davis, Norbert **56**

Moving On
Coleman, Jane Candia 427, 433, 445, 458, 474, 483, 500

Moving Target
Lowell, Elizabeth 302, **340**

Moving to the Country
Cheska, Anna 872

Mozart and the Archbooby
Neider, Charles 929

Mr. Audubon's Lucy
Kennedy, Lucy 833

Mr. Calder and Mr. Behrens
Gilbert, Michael 118

Mr. Fox and Other Feral Tales
Partridge, Norman 689

Mr. Maybe
Green, Jane 394

Mr. Montgomery's Quest
Kirkland, Martha **318**

Mr. Perfect
Howard, Linda 302, 331

Mr. Sammler's Planet
Bellow, Saul 1072, 1138

Mr. Sandman
Howard, Lyle 709

Mr. Templeton's Toyshop
Wiloch, Thomas 635, 700

Mr. White's Confession
Clark, Robert 110

Mrs. Amworth
Benson, E.F. **622**

Mrs. Bridge
Connell, Evan S. 1161

Mrs. Drew Plays Her Hand
Kelly, Carla 238, 315, 404

The Mrs. Eugenia Potter Series
Pickard, Nancy 207

The Mrs. Malory Series
Holt, Hazel 14, 27, 54

Mrs. McVinnie's London Season
Kelly, Carla 262

Mrs. Million
Hautman, Pete 107

The Mrs. Murphy Series
Brown, Rita Mae 26, 162

The Mrs. Pargeter Series
Brett, Simon 96

Mrs. Pargeter's Pound of Flesh
Brett, Simon 38

Mrs. Shakespeare
Nye, Robert 823

Much Ado about Nothing
Churchill, Jill 839

Much Obliged
Benson, Jessica 370

Mudd in Your Eye
Oltion, Jerry 785

Muddle Earth
Brunner, John 752

Mulch
Ripley, Ann 181

Mules and Men
Hurston, Zora Neale 1128

The Muller Fokker Effect
Sladek, John 798

The Mummy
Rice, Anne 922

The Munch Mancini Series
Seranella, Barbara 102, 217

Murder at Ball's Bluff
Kilian, Michael 898

Murder at Bertram's Bower
Peale, Cynthia 830

Murder at Buckingham Palace
Clarke, T.E.B. 183

Murder at Ebbets Field
Soos, Troy 200

Murder at Gettysburg
Walker, Jim 133, 159, 169, 898

Murder at Manassas
Kilian, Michael 133, 159, 169, 898

Murder at Midnight
Roosevelt, Elliott 928

Murder at Pearl Harbor
Walker, Jim 1056

Murder at Spirit Cave
Bean, Frederic 428, 502

Murder at the Palace
Roosevelt, Elliott 136

Murder at the Panionic Games
Edwards, Michael B. **859**

Murder at the President's Door
Roosevelt, Elliott **928**

Murder at the Spirit Cave
Bean, Frederic 444, 465, 472, 475, 477, 482, 506, 511, 513

Murder at the Vicarage
Christie, Agatha 36

Murder at Witches' Bluff
Ravenwolf, Silver 522

Murder at Wrigley Field
Soos, Troy 200

Murder Boogies with Elvis
George, Anne **77**

Murder by Manicure
Cohen, Nancy J. **38**

Murder Carries a Torch
George, Anne 77

Murder for Halloween
Slung, Michele 628

Murder Gets a Life
George, Anne 77

Murder: His and Hers
Collins, Max Allan 40

Murder in a Hot Flash
Millhiser, Marlys 124

Murder in Georgetown
Roosevelt, Elliott 928

Murder in Grub Street
Alexander, Bruce 815

A Murder in Macedon
Apostolou, Anna 859

Murder in Mendocino
Kittredge, Mary 139

Murder in Scorpio
Lawrence, Martha C. 140

Murder in the Air
Hart, Ellen 105

Murder in the Chateau
Roosevelt, Elliott 928

Murder in the Forecast
Wolzien, Valerie **219**

Murder in the Lincoln Bedroom
Roosevelt, Elliott 928

Murder in the Map Room
Roosevelt, Elliott 928

Murder in the Marais
Black, Cara 126

Murder in the Spirit Cave
Bean, Frederic 474

A Murder in Thebes
Apostolou, Anna 859

Murder Is an Art
Crider, Bill 48, 124

Murder Is the Deal of the Day
Randisi, Robert J. 177

Murder Makes Waves
George, Anne 77

Murder Me Now
Meyers, Annette 839

Murder Most Fowl
Crider, Bill 49

Murder Most Medieval
Greenberg, Martin H. 8

Murder, My Deer
Girdner, Jacqueline 80

The Murder of Edgar Allan Poe
Hatvary, George Egon 193, 932

Murder on a Bad Hair Day
George, Anne 38

Murder on Martha's Vineyard
Osborne, David 46

Murder on Martha's Vineyard
Roos, Kelly 46

Murder on the Astral Plane
Girdner, Jacqueline 80

Murder on the Lusitania
Allen, Conrad 5, 816

Murder on the Mauretania
Allen, Conrad 5, 816

Murder on the Minnesota
Allen, Conrad **5**, **816**

Murder on the Trans-Siberian Express
Kaminsky, Stuart M. **130**

Murder on the Twelfth Night
Hays, Tony 109

Murder on the Yellow Brick Road
Kaminsky, Stuart M. 53

Murder Runs in the Family
George, Anne 77

Murder Sets Seed
Harrison, Janis 103

Murder Shoots the Bull
George, Anne 77

Murder Take Two
Weir, Charlene 212

Murder Takes a Break
Crider, Bill 48

Murder through the Ages
Jakubowski, Maxim 8

Murder with Peacocks
Andrews, Donna 6, 60, 157

Murder with Puffins
Andrews, Donna 6

The Murderer's Tale
Frazer, Margaret 70

Murder@Maggody.com
Hess, Joan 114

Murdock's Family
Riggs, Paula Detmer 335

Murphy's Law
Bowen, Rhys **24**, 200, **830**

Mus of Kerbridge
Kidd, Paul 563

Muscle Memory
Tapply, William G. 206

The Museum of Horrors
Etchison, Dennis **634**, 653

The Museum of Love
Weiner, Steve 954

Music & Silence
Tremain, Rose 862, 1069

The Music Box
Kane, Andrea 312

Must the Maiden Die
Monfredo, Miriam Grace 159, 909

The Mustard Seed Series
Moser, Nancy 981

Mutagenesis
Collins, Helen 740

Mutant
Kuttner, Henry 753

The Mutant Files
Greenberg, Martin H. **753**

Mutant Prime
Haber, Karen 753

The Mutants Are Coming
Haiblum, Isidore 753

Mutation
Cook, Robin 783

The Mutual Friend
Busch, Frederick 917

My Best Friend
Wilson, Laura 82, 211, **214**

My Brain Escapes Me
Rhine, Robert Steven 689

My Champion
Campbell, Glynnis 407

My Darling Valentine
Beck, Kathleen 378

My Dog Is More than Just a Dog to Me
Hekkanen, Ernest 1100

My Dream of You
O'Faolain, Nuala 1111

My Fair Lord
Beard, Julie 229

My Favorite Science Fiction Story
Greenberg, Martin H. 754

My First Horse
James, Will 464

My Happy Life
Millet, Lydia 1209

My Hard Bargain
Kirn, Walter 1141

My Heart Stood Still
Kurland, Lynn **323**, 358

My Heart's Desire
Grasso, Patricia 293

My Lady Beloved
St. James, Lael **405**, 406

My Lady de Burgh
Simmons, Deborah 368, **396**

My Lady Governess
Counts, Wilma 262

My Lady Innkeeper
Metzger, Barbara 398

My Lady Nightingale
Richardson, Evelyn 315, 379

My Lady Notorious
Beverley, Jo 307, 329, 352

My Lady Wayward
St. James, Lael 405, **406**

My Lady's Dare
Wilson, Gayle 346, 416

My Life, Starring Dara Falcon
Beattie, Ann 1198

My Little Blue Dress
Maddox, Bruno **1150**

My Lord de Burgh
Simmons, Deborah 396

My Lord Highwayman
King, Valerie 317

My Lord Protector
Hale, Deborah 352

My Lord Savage
Lane, Elizabeth **326**

My Name Is Legion
Zelazny, Roger 748

My Name Is Red
Pamuk, Orhan 1105, 1152, **1178**

My Outlaw
Miller, Linda Lael 372

My Phillipe
Miller, Barbara 355

My Scottish Summer
Brockway, Connie **243**

My Sweet Valentine
Donnelly, Shannon 378

My Wayward Lady
Richardson, Evelyn 260, 379

My Wild Irish Rose
Wilson, Rachel 386, 421

The Mysteries in Time Series
Walker, Jim 1062

A Mystery of Errors
Hawke, Simon 109, 148, 880

The Mystery of Orchard House
Coggin, Joan 36

Mystery Walk
McCammon, Robert R. 637

Mystic River
Lehane, Dennis 37, 74, 199, 1076, 1096, 1118, 1123

The Mystic Rose
Lawhead, Stephen R. **570**, **901**, 941

Mystic Sweet Communion
Kirkpatrick, Jane 1011

Mystic Warriors
Bittner, Rosanne 423, 911

Mystify the Magician
Applegate, K.A. 519, **520**

Myth-ing Persons
Asprin, Robert Lynn 521

Myth-ion Improbable
Asprin, Robert Lynn **521**

Myths, Legends, and True History
Landis, Geoffrey A. 766

N

Nadya
Murphy, Pat 781

The Nagasaki Vector
Smith, L. Neil 799

Nailed by the Heart
Clark, Simon 735

The Naked Savages
Stewart, Fred Mustard 937

Naked Sleeper
Nunez, Sigrid 1172

Naked to the Stars
Dickson, Gordon R. 784, 795

Name Dropping
Heller, Jane 1125

Name Games
Craft, Michael 45

The Name of the Rose
Eco, Umberto 1182

Named of the Dragon
Kearsley, Susanna 314

The Nameless Detective Series
Pronzini, Bill 22

Nameless Sins
Collins, Nancy 629

The Naming of Parts
Lebbon, Tim 665, 666

The Nanny
Stacy, Judith 253, **408**, 409

The Nanotech Chronicles
Flynn, Michael 798

Naomi's Room
Aycliffe, Jonathan 626, 673

The Napoleon Wager
Forstchen, William R. 516, 751

Narcissus in Chains
Hamilton, Laurell K. **645**

Nashborough
Donald, Elsie Burch 845, 850, **855**, 961

The Nate Heller Series
Collins, Max Allan 83, 928

Native Tongue
Hiaasen, Carl 94, 115

A Natural Attachment
Kingsley, Katherine 238, 404

Natural Causes
Palmer, Michael 78

The Nature of Balance
Lebbon, Tim 665, **666**

The Nautical Chart
Perez-Reverte, Arturo **171**, 1144, **1182**

Navajo's Woman
Barton, Beverly 417

Navy Seal Dad
Hingle, Metsy 301

The Neal Hockaday Series
Adcock, Thomas 22

Neanderthal
Darnton, John 792

Nearly People
Williams, Conrad **708**

Necklace of Skulls
Drummond, Ivor 132

Necrochip
Harrod-Eagles, Cynthia 104

Needful Things
King, Stephen 668

Needles and Sins
Arnzen, Michael D. 616

The Negotiator
Henderson, Dee 999, 1000

The Neil Hamel Series
Van Gieson, Judith 7, 19, 28

The Neil Hockaday Series
Adcock, Thomas 37

Nekropolis
McHugh, Maureen **774**

The Nell Bray Series
Linscott, Gillian 958

Nemesis
Asimov, Isaac 770

Netherworld
Byers, Richard Lee 532

Never a Lady
Smith, Barbara Dawson 400

Never Change
Berg, Elizabeth 1086

Never Come Down
Black, Michelle 423

Never Die
Hannah, Barry 1121

Never Lie to an Angel
Welsh, Kate 1057

Never Love a Cowboy
Gregory, Jill 294

Never Love a Cowboy
Heath, Lorraine 409

Never Nosh a Matzo Ball
Kahn, Sharon 129

Never Say Never Again
Carrington, Tori 251

Never Sound Retreat
Forstchen, William R. 864

Never Trust a One-Eyed Wizard
Townsend, Tom 605

Nevermore
Hjortsberg, William 187, 193

Nevermore
Schechter, Harold 95, 135, 193, 502, 932

NeverNever
Shetterly, Will 568, 614

The New Life
Pamuk, Orhan 1178

New Life for the Dead
Rodgers, Alan 683

New Mexico Sunset
Peterson, Tracie 1042

A New Song
Karon, Jan 1007

The New Year's Eve Murder
Harris, Lee 996

New York by Knight
Friesner, Esther 533, 602, 614

The New York Trilogy
Auster, Paul 192

The Newpointe 911 Series
Blackstock, Terri 999, 1012

The Next Santini Bride
Child, Maureen 255

Next Stop, Paradise
Civil-Brown, Sue 249, **256**, 351, 383

Next Week Will Be Better
Ruryk, Jean 69, 160

Niagara Falls All over Again
McCracken, Elizabeth **1158**, 1188

A Nice Murder for Mom
Yaffe, James 129

The Nicholas Bracewell Series
Marston, Edward 109, 834, 861, 880

The Nick & Julia Lambrose Series
Iakovou, Takis 177

The Nick Revill Series
Gooden, Philip 148

The Nick Stefanos Series
Pelecanos, George P. 50, 213

The Nicolette Scott Series
Davis, Val 7, 125

Nifft the Lean
Shea, Michael 601

Night and Day
Stuart, Anne 411

Night Blood
Thompson, James M. **702**

Night Butterfly
McFall, Patricia 127, 150

The Night Class
Piccirilli, Tom 682

The Night Comes On
Duffy, Steve 701

Night Fires
Dare, Justine 251

Night Hawk's Bride
Hart, Jillian **296**, 391, 997

Night in the Lonesome October
Laymon, Richard 663, **664**

A Night in the Lonesome October
Zelazny, Roger 623

The Night Inspector
Busch, Frederick 830, 936

The Night Listener
Maupin, Armistead 1213

The Night Men
Snyder, Keith **199**

Night Music
Mitchell, Sara 1044

The Night, My Friend
Hoch, Edward D. 117, 118

Night of Dracula
Schildt, Christopher 691, **692**

Night of Madness
Watt-Evans, Lawrence 572, 610, 611

Night of the Bat
Zindel, Paul **714**

Night of the Comanche Moon
Flynn, T.T. 460

The Night of the Hunter
Grubb, Davis 665

The Night of the Triffids
Clark, Simon **735**

Night of the Wolf
Borchardt, Alice 322, 528, 829

Night Passage
Parker, Robert B. 168

The Night People and Other Stories
Hoch, Edward D. 48, **117**

Night Players
Cacek, P.D. 617, **625**

Night Prayers
Cacek, P.D. 625, 645, 699

The Night Remembers
Eagle, Kathleen 387, 450

The Night Seasons
Williamson, J.N. 709

Night Secrets
Martin, Kat 346, 347

Night Shapes
Nolan, William F. 678, 696

Night Shield
Roberts, Nora 251, 383

The Night the Stars Fell
Kingston, Christina **317**

The Night Travellers
Spencer, Elizabeth 1201

The Night Visitor
Doss, James D. 61

Night Watch
Kendrick, Stephen **896**

Night Watch
Tillis, Tracey 365

Night Whispers
Cliford, Emmett 1153

A Night with Casanova
Mankowitz, Wolf 929

Nightchild
Barclay, James **523**

Nighthawk
Kyle, Kristen 310

The Nightingale
Dalkey, Kara 579

The Nightingale's Song
Eschenburg, Kathleen **273**

Nightmare Blue
Dozois, Gardner 748

The Nightmare Exhibition
Crisp, Quentin 636

Nightmare in Shining Armor
Myers, Tamar **163**

Nightmare's Disciple
Pulver, Joseph 682

Night's Black Agents
Leiber, Fritz 767

Nights of the Round Table
Lawrence, Margery 622

Night's Soft Pains
Maynard, L.H. 674

Nightscapes
Pendragon, Michael 635, 697

Nightshade
Saul, John 687

Nighttime Guardian
Stevens, Amanda 410

The Nighttime Is the Right Time
Crider, Bill **48**, 117

Nightwatch
Bailey, Robin W. 586

Nightwing
Smith, Martin Cruz 714

Nimbus
Jablokov, Alexander 807

Nimisha's Ship
McCaffrey, Anne 772

The Nine Gates
Brugalette, Philip 553

Nine Ghosts
Malden, R.H. 650

Nine Princes in Amber
Zelazny, Roger 582

No Birds Sang
Bannister, Jo 11

No Crystal Stair
Rutland, Eva 228

No Decent Gentleman
Grasso, Patricia 293

No Earthly Notion
Dodd, Susan M. 852

No Earthly Sunne
Ball, Margaret 583

No Eye Can See
Kirkpatrick, Jane 437, 470, 1011

No Future
Cornell, Paul 738

No Honeymoon for Death
Kruger, Mary 5

No Man's Mistress
Balogh, Mary **227**

No Man's World
Bulmer, Kenneth 769

No Mercy
Curtis, Jack 490, 499

No Night Is Too Long
Vine, Barbara 1145

No Other Love
Camp, Candace 317

No Place for a Lady
Piekarski, Vicki **496**

No Strange Fire
Wojtasik, Ted 999

No Time for Crime
Russell, Charlotte Murray 191

No Way Out
Kane, Andrea **312**

No World of Their Own
Anderson, Poul 755

Nobility
McGuire, Tim 480

Noble Outlaw
Braun, Matt 493

The Nobody
Farr, Diane 377

Nobody Does It Better
Kenner, Julie 240

Nobody Loves a Centurion
Roberts, John Maddox **184**, **924**, 931

Nobody's Baby but Mine
Phillips, Susan Elizabeth 369

Nobody's Princess
Greene, Jennifer 261

Nocturne
Chadbourn, Mark 533

Nocturne
McBain, Ed 152

The Nolan
Yanow, Morton Leonard 956

The Nomad
Hawke, Simon 880

Non-Stop
Aldiss, Brian W. 726

None but Man
Dickson, Gordon R. 719

None to Accompany Me
Gordimer, Nadine 1116

Noonshade
Barclay, James 523, 550, 572, 611

Nora's Ribbon of Memories
Whitson, Stephanie Grace 1058

Nordic Nights
McClendon, Lise 477

North by Night
Ayres, Katherine 464

North Dallas Forty
Gent, Peter 1132

North of Havana
White, Randy Wayne 75

North of the Border
Van Gieson, Judith 39, 149

North Wind
Jones, Gwyneth 764

North with Franklin
Wilson, John 905, 949

The Northern Lights Series
Bergren, Lisa Tawn 1011

Norwegian Wood
Murakami, Haruki 1110, 1192

Not a Day Goes By
Harris, E. Lynn 1122

Not Exactly Eden
Windsor, Linda 1060

Not for Glory
Rosenberg, Joel 784, 809

Not for the Night Time
Gift, Theo 618

Not in Solitude
Gantz, Kenneth F. 814

Not Safe After Dark and Other Stories
Robinson, Peter 142, 146

Not the Only Planet
Broderick, Damien **726**

Not Without Solitude
Gantz, Kenneth F. 771

Not Without You
Taylor, Janelle 413

The Note
Hunt, Angela Elwell 1004

The Notebook
Sparks, Nicholas 1200

The Notebooks of Don Rigoberto
Vargas Llosa, Mario 948, 1211

Nothing but the Truth
Lescroart, John 141

Nothing Like the Sun
Burgess, Anthony 823

Nothing to Declare
Coles, Manning 118

Notorious
Sutcliffe, Katherine 412

Now He Thinks He's Dead
Goulart, Ron 85

Now That You're Back
Kennedy, A.L. 1138

Now You See Her
Howard, Linda 302

Nowhere Else on Earth
Humphreys, Josephine 884, 910, 1167, 1183

Nowhere, Now Here
Creel, Ann Howard 845

The Nudger Dilemmas
Lutz, John **147**

Nugget City
Overholser, Wayne D. 489, 490, 491

Number 90 and Other Ghost Stories
Croker, B.M. 618

The Nun's Tale
Robb, Candace M. 70

O

O Careless Love
Dodd, Susan M. 852

O Gentle Death
Neel, Janet **165**

O Pioneer
Pohl, Frederik 780

O Sacred Head
Kilmer, Nicholas 134

The Oath
Lescroart, John **141**

An Obedient Father
Sharma, Akhil 1129

Obernewtyn
Carmody, Isobelle 732

Obsession
Mills-Macias, Kathi 1048

Obsidian Butterfly
Hamilton, Laurell K. 645, 657

The Orc Wars
Dalmas, John 741, 742

The Orchid Hunter
Landis, Jill Marie 319

Ordeal at Litchfield
Clarke, Anthony 209

An Ordinary Woman
Holland, Cecelia 437

Original Bliss
Kennedy, A.L. 1138

The Other Adonis
Deford, Frank **849**, 868, 869

The Other Wind
Le Guin, Ursula K. **571**

Otherland
Williams, Tad 554, 555, 560

Otherwise Engaged
Summers, Cara 289

Our Arcadia
Lippincott, Robin 847

Our Game
Le Carre, John 130

Our Husband
Bond, Stephanie 240

Our Lady of the Harbor
De Lint, Charles 529

Our Lady of the Lost and Found
Schoemperlen, Diane 1175

Out for Blood
Cooke, John Peyton 690

Out of Phaze
Anthony, Piers 516, 751

Out of Season
Havill, Steven F. 108

Out of Space and Time
Smith, Clark Ashton 671

Out of the Blackout
Barnard, Robert 92, 136

Out of the Mouths of Graves
Bloch, Robert 48, 117

Out of Their Minds
Simak, Clifford D. 567

Out of This World
Watt-Evans, Lawrence 516, 600, 610, 751

Out of Time
Abbey, Lynn 515, 543, 573

Out of Time
Hogan, James P. 759

Out There
Rose, Gerald **793**

Out to Canaan
Karon, Jan 1007

The Outcast
Hawke, Simon 880

The Outcast
West, Roselyn 273

Outcasts
McGuire, Tim **480**

Outcasts of Picture Rocks
Wilson, Cherry 470

Outcry
Schechter, Harold 932

Outlander
Gabaldon, Diana 237, 288, 358, 868

Outlandish Companion
Gabaldon, Diana 288

The Outlaw
Bean, Frederic 436, 442

The Outlaw
Jordan, Nicole 309

The Outlaw
McDaniel, Sylvia 409

The Outlaw Bride
Chastain, Sandra 361

Outlaw Mountain
Jance, J.A. 125

The Outlaw Redeemer
Brand, Max 433, 434, 455, 460, 489

Outlaw School
Ore, Rebecca 779, 782

The Outlaws
Overholser, Wayne D. 489, 490, **490**, 491

Outlaw's Bride
McKade, Maureen 247

The Outlaw's Twin Sister
Bly, Stephen A. 972, **973**

Outpost
Resnick, Mike 788

Outrageous
Dodd, Christina 276

The Outsider
Metz, Melinda 749, 775, 776

Outward Bound
Hogan, James P. 759

Over Sea, Under Stone
Cooper, Susan 570

Over the Edge
Brockmann, Suzanne 222, 242, 399

Over the Wine-Dark Sea
Turteltaub, H.N. 931

The Overland Kid: A Western Trio
Brand, Max 427, 431, 434, 445, 494, 496

The Overland Trail
Lee, W.W. 478

The Owl Service
Garner, Alan 519

Owlsight
Lackey, Mercedes 568, 569

The Owner
Deford, Frank 849

The Oxford Book of American Detective Stories
Hillerman, Tony 57

The Oxford Book of English Detective Stories
Craig, Patricia 57

P

Pacific Street
Holland, Cecelia 878

Pact of the Fathers
Campbell, Ramsey **626**

Pagan Babies
Leonard, Elmore 107

The Page Turner
Leavitt, David 1145

Pages for You
Brownrigg, Sylvia 1121, 1213

Painted Desert
Barthelme, Frederick 1150

The Painted Face
Onions, Oliver 680

A Painted House
Grisham, John 1077

Painted in Blood
Taylor, Lucy 624

Painted True
McClendon, Lise 477

The Painter Knight
Patton, Fiona 586

The Painter of Birds
Jorge, Lidia 1120

The Painting
Boeshaar, Andrea 969

Painting the Roses Red
Malone, Michael 1153

Palais-Royal
Sennett, Richard 900

Pale Horse Coming
Hunter, Stephen **122**, 825, **887**, 897, **1127**, 1179, 1186

Pale Shadow
Skinner, Robert **196**, 841, 867, 885, **935**

Pallas
Smith, L. Neil 799

Pancho and Black Jack
Bean, Frederic 476

Pandora
Rice, Anne 685, 922, 1185

Pandora
Rodgers, Alan 661

Pandora's Children
Lance, Kathryn 810

The Panther's Hoard
Berberick, Nancy Varian 612

The Paper Grail
Blaylock, James P. 781

Par Four
Gunn, Elizabeth 93

A Paradigm of Earth
Dorsey, Candas Jane **747**

Paradise
Morrison, Toni 1089

Paradise County
Robards, Karen 381

Paradise Island
Hale, Gena 399

Paradise Lost
Jance, J.A. **125**, **465**

The Paradox Planet
Spruill, Steven G. 763

The Parched Sea
Denning, Troy 597

Paris in the 20th Century
Verne, Jules 787

Park City
Beattie, Ann 1192

The Parliament of Blood
Ciencin, Scott 702

Partisan
Swann, S. Andrew 602

Partners
Sizemore, Susan 645

Partners in Wonder
Ellison, Harlan 679

Pascali's Island
Unsworth, Barry 893

Pashazade
Grimwood, Jon Courtenay 774

Passages of Gold
Kraus, Jim 1013

The Passenger
Benson, E.F. 622

Passing
Jones, Patricia 1133

Passing
Larsen, Nella 1207

The Passion
Jordan, Nicole 309

The Passion of Artemisia
Vreeland, Susan **951**

The Passion Ruby
Snoe, Eboni 403

Past Dying
Shuman, Malcolm 195

Past Imperfect
Greenberg, Martin H. **754**

Past Tense
Tapply, William G. **206**

The Path of Daggers
Jordan, Robert 545

Paths to Otherwhere
Hogan, James P. 741, 778

Pathways
Bergren, Lisa Tawn 971, 1000, 1030

The Patricia Conley Series
Coleman, Evelyn 220

The Patrick Grant Series
Yorke, Margaret 97

The Patrick Kenzie/Angela Gennaro Series
Lehane, Dennis 50, 94, 213

A Patriot's Heart
Piel, Stobie 297

Patterns
Cadigan, Pat 731

The Paul Devlin Series
Heffernan, William 152

The Paul Madriani Series
Martini, Steve 141

Paula
Allende, Isabel 817

Pawn of the Omphalos
Tubb, E.C. 769

The Peace Chief
Conley, Robert J. 441

Peace Like a River
Enger, Leif **1109**

The Peacemakers
Cavanaugh, Jack 1019

The Peaches Dann Series
Squire, Elizabeth Daniels 15, 77, 129

Pearl Cove
Lowell, Elizabeth 340

The Pecos Kid: A Western Duo
Cushman, Dan 431, 432, 435, 494, 500

A Peculiar Thing
King, Mary 469

The Pedlar's Pack
Baldwin, Louisa 618

Pegasus in Space
McCaffrey, Anne 772

The Peggy O'Neill Series
Lake, M.D. 156

The Pelican Brief
Grisham, John 1097

Pelts
Wilson, F. Paul 666

Pendulum
Christopher, John 738

Penny Town Justice
McWilliams, A.L. 482

A Penny Urned
Myers, Tamar 163

Pentacle
Piccirilli, Tom 682

The People of the Covenant Series
Wise, Robert L. 990, 994, 1053

People of the Masks
Gear, Kathleen O'Neal 510

People of the Mist
Gear, Kathleen O'Neal 510

The People of the Peacock
Hoch, Edward D. 118

The People of the Promise Series
Shott, James R. 990, 994

People of the Silence
Gear, Kathleen O'Neal 441

Perchance
Kurland, Michael 899

Perchance to Dream
Little, Denise 574, 575

Perdido Street Station
Mieville, China 607

The Perennial Killer
Ripley, Ann 181

A Perfect Arrangement
Berne, Suzanne 1070

The Perfect Couple
Hansen, Valerie 995, 1022

A Perfect Crime
Abrahams, Peter 1

The Perfect Daughter
Linscott, Gillian 838, 856, 923, 943

The Perfect Gift
Skye, Christina 399

The Perfect Groom
Scofield, Ruth 1047

Perfect Harmony
Wood, Barbara 962

The Perfect Host
Sturgeon, Theodore 745

A Perfect Match
Savery, Jeanne 280, **389**

The Perfect Mistress
Krahn, Betina 321

A Perfect Persecution
Lucas, James R. 966, 991

The Perfect Princess
Thornton, Elizabeth 293, **416**

Perfect Recall
Beattie, Ann 1072, 1077, 1155, 1162, 1196, 1201

Perfect Sin
Martin, Kat 293, 346, 347

A Perfect Stranger
Wilkins, Gina 242

Perhaps She'll Die
Preston, M.K. 465

The Peril Trek: A Western Trio
Brand, Max 433

Perils of the Night
Hall, Patricia 97

Permed to Death
Cohen, Nancy J. 38

Permit for Murder
Wolzien, Valerie 219

Permutation City
Egan, Greg 731

Perpetuity Blues
Barrett, Neal Jr. 524

Perps
Wellen, Edward 85

The Persian Pickle Club
Dallas, Sandra 33

Person or Persons Unknown
Alexander, Bruce 815

A Personal Devil
Gellis, Roberta 875

Personal Velocity
Miller, Rebecca **1162**

Petals in the Storm
Putney, Mary Jo 308

The Peter Bartholomew Series
Gunning, Sally 46, 219

The Peter Diamond Series
Lovesey, Peter 23, 44, 186

Peter Doyle
Vernon, John 949

The Peter McGarr Series
Gill, Bartholomew 173

Peter Straub's Ghosts
Straub, Peter 633, 634, 674

Phantom Perfumes and Other Shades
Ashley, Mike 615

The Phantom Tollbooth
Juster, Norton 581

Phantom Universe
Garnett, David 752

Phantom Waltz
Anderson, Catherine 225

Phantoms in the Night
Savage, Les Jr. 501

Phase IV
Malzberg, Barry 762

Phobias
Webb, Wendy 651

The Phoebe Mullins Series
Sturges, Karen 71

The Phoenix
Boetius, Henning **828**

Phoenix Cafe
Jones, Gwyneth 764

A Phule and His Money
Asprin, Robert Lynn 521

Phule's Company
Asprin, Robert Lynn 521

The Pickup
Gordimer, Nadine 1101, 1112, **1116**, 1170, 1190

The Picture of Dorian Gray
Wilde, Oscar 1126

Picture Postcard
Huebner, Fredrick 121

Picture Rock
Bly, Stephen A. 972, 973

Pictures of Perfection
Hill, Reginald 116

A Piece of the Night
Roberts, Michele 925

The Pigs Are Flying
Rodda, Emily 594

Pigs Don't Fly
Brown, Mary 587

The Pillars of Creation
Goodkind, Terry **550**

Pillars of Salt
Faqir, Fadia 1116

The Pillars of the World
Bishop, Anne **527**

Pink Marble and Never Say Die
Dunn, Dawn **630**

The Pinkerton Eye
Bristow, Allen P. **436**

The Pinkerton Lady Series
Roddy, Lee 972

A Pirate of Her Own
MacGregor, Kinley 328

Pisces Rising
Lawrence, Martha C. 140

The Pistoleer
Blake, James Carlos 424, 825

The Pixilated Peeress
de Camp, L. Sprague 600

A Place Called Freedom
Follett, Ken 840, 863

A Place Called Wiregrass
Morris, Michael 1002, **1029**

A Place of Darkness
Haney, Lauren **101**

A Place of Execution
McDermid, Val 23, 154, 186, 214

A Place on Earth
Berry, Wendell 872

A Place to Call Home
Smith, Deborah 401

Places in the Dark
Cook, Thomas H. 110

A Plague of Sorcerers
Zambreno, Mary Frances 538, 542, 594

A Plague of Spies
Kurland, Michael 899

The Plainswoman
Brown, Irene Bennett 495

Planar Powers
King, J. Robert 564, 565, 566

Planeswalker
Abbey, Lynn 515

Planet America
Maloney, Mack **768**

Planet of Whispers
Kelly, James Patrick 718

The Planets of Death
Collins, Michael 809

The Plants
McKenney, Kenneth 735

Platte River
Bass, Rick 1146

The Platypus of Doom and Other Nihilists
Cover, Arthur Byron 524

The Players
Cowell, Stephanie 823

Players
Reynolds, Clay 498

The Players' Boy Is Dead
Tourney, Leonard 148

The Playmaker
Keneally, Thomas 819, 904

Plays Well with Others
Gurganus, Allan 1120

A Pleasing Terror
James, M.R. **650**

Plum Island
DeMille, Nelson 1097, 1123

Plunder Squad
Stark, Richard 202

The Plutonium Blonde
Zakour, John **813**

Pobby and Dingan
Rice, Ben 1148

Pocahontas
Donnell, Susan 950

The Poet and the Paragon
Boucher, Rita 262, 392

Point Deception
Muller, Marcia 139

Point of Impact
Hunter, Stephen 122, 204, 1127

Points in Time
Bowles, Paul 1080

Poison for the Prince
Eyre, Elizabeth 836

The Poisonwood Bible
Kingsolver, Barbara 1134, 1211

Political Poison
Zubro, Mark Richard 221

Pool of Radiance
Bebris, Carrie **525**

Pool of Twilight
Ward, James 525

Pop Goes the Weasel
Patterson, James 1181

The Pope's Rhinoceros
Norfolk, Lawrence 913, 1171

Porch Swings & Picket Fences
Bergren, Lisa Tawn 233, 986

The Portia McTeague Series
Sultan, Faye 66

Portrait in Sepia
Allende, Isabel **817**, **1067**, 1112, 1124, 1205

The Portraits of Destiny Series
Thoene, Jake 1013

Ports of Call
Vance, Jack 721

Post Mortem
Olson, Paul F. 633, 674

The Postcard
Lewis, Beverly 1018

Postcards
Proulx, Annie 1147

Powder Smoke & Other Stories
Haycox, Ernest 433

The Power
Robinson, Frank M. 775

The Power of Love
Daley, Margaret **987**

The Practical Heart
Gurganus, Allan 1079, **1120**

Prairie
Waldo, Anna Lee 952

Prairie Brides
Ford, Linda 969

The Prairie Chicken Kill
Crider, Bill 48

The Prairieton Raid
Paine, Lauran 492, 493

Praise Jerusalem
Trobaugh, Augusta 1029

Pray for Texas
Smith, Cotton 504

A Prayer for Owen Meany
Irving, John 1136

A Prayer for the Dying
O'Nan, Stewart 832, 1083

The Prayer of the Bone
Bryers, Paul 42

Prayers to Broken Stones
Simmons, Dan 630

Precious Blood
Graversen, Pat 703

Precursor
Cherryh, C.J. 734

The Pregnant Heiress
Wilks, Eileen 246

Prepared for Murder
Lamalle, Cecile **138**

The Presence
Saul, John 687

The President
Hudson, Parker 976, 1004

Presumed Innocent
Turow, Scott 1074, 1139

Pretender
Miller, Barbara 355

The Pretender
Reding, Jaclyn 241

Pretty Ballerina
Wessel, John 213

Pretty Boy Floyd
McMurtry, Larry 825

The Price
Kraus, Jim 1013

Pride and Prejudice
Austen, Jane 359

Pride of Kings
Tarr, Judith **603**, **941**

Pride, Prejudice and Jasmin Field
Nathan, Melissa **359**, 394

Priestess of Avalon
Bradley, Marion Zimmer 831, 907

Primary Colors
Anonymous 1211

The Prime of Miss Jean Brodie
Spark, Muriel 1161

Primitive People
Prose, Francine 1116

A Prince Among Them
Lacy, Al **1015**

Prince Charming
Thornton, Elizabeth 416

Prince Charming in Dress Blues
Child, Maureen 255, 335

The Prince in Waiting
Christopher, John 730

Prince Joe
Brockmann, Suzanne 422

A Prince of a Guy
Rabe, Sheila 226, 264, 274, 299, 343, 354, 369, **376**

Prince of Charming
Fox, Karen 287

Prince of Demons
Reichert, Mickey Zucker 590

Prince of Dogs
Elliott, Kate 526

Prince of Dreams
Krinard, Susan 322

Prince of Havoc
Stackpole, Michael A. 599

The Prince of Shadow
Benjamin, Curt **526**

Prince of Shadows
Krinard, Susan 322

Prince of Swords
Stuart, Anne 411

The Prince of Tides
Conroy, Pat 1075, 1173, 1203

Prince of Wolves
Krinard, Susan 322, 1068

The Prince's Bride-to-Be
Parv, Valerie 334

The Princess
Delacroix, Claire 269

The Princess
Wick, Lori 1059

Princess Charming
Heller, Jane 1125

Princess Charming
Thornton, Elizabeth 309

Princess of Fire
Drake, Shannon 336, 337

Princess of the Veil
Mittermeyer, Helen 336, 338

The Prioress' Tale
Frazer, Margaret 70, 865

The Priscilla Diary
Edwards, Gene 990

The Prisoner Bride
Paul, Susan Spencer **368**, 396

The Prisoners of Arionn
Herbert, Brian 757

Prisoners of the Sky
MacApp, C.C. 733

A Private Affair
Hill, Donna 884

Private Fame
Burgin, Richard 1087

Private Investigations
Carrington, Tori 251

Private Justice
Blackstock, Terri 971

Private Lessons
Leto, Julie Elizabeth 333

Private Passions
Alers, Rochelle 224

A Private View
Brookner, Anita 1184

The Privateersman
Woodman, Richard 854

Privileged to Kill
Havill, Steven F. 108

Prized Possessions
Stirling, Jessica **938**

The Probability Man
Ball, Brian 772

Probability Sun
Kress, Nancy 743, 772

The Problem of the Evil Editor
Rogow, Roberta 187, 926

The Problem of the Missing Miss
Rogow, Roberta 187, 926

The Problem of the Spiteful Spiritualist
Rogow, Roberta 187, 926

The Problem of the Surly Servant
Rogow, Roberta **187**, 915, **926**

The Prodigal Daughter
Gray, Ginna 301

The Prodigal Sorcerer
Sumner, Mark 564

The Prodigal Spy
Kanon, Joseph 131, 215, 892, 1135

Prodigal Summer
Kingsolver, Barbara 1065

The Prodigal's Return
Bulock, Lynn 1046, 1057

The Prodigy
Gansky, Alton **637**, 975

Profundis
Cowper, Richard 806

The Program
White, Stephen 123, 190

The Progress of Love
Munro, Alice 1169

Prolonged Exposure
Havill, Steven F. 108

Prometheus
Forstchen, William R. 864

The Promise
Boyd, Donna 1068

The Promise
Kraus, Jim 1013, 1025

The Promise
McGoldrick, May **352**

The Promise in a Kiss
Laurens, Stephanie **329**

Promise Me Forever
Macomber, Debbie 474

Promise Me Spring
Hatcher, Robin Lee 421

A Promise of Fire
Sattler, Veronica 388

Promise of Glory
Moreau, C.X. 919

The Promise of Jenny Jones
Osborne, Maggie 294, 332, 364, 391

A Promise of Love
Ranney, Karen 390

A Promise of Roses
Betts, Heidi 234

The Promise Remains
Thrasher, Travis 1054

Promised to a Stranger
O'Brien, Linda 361

Promises, Promises
Weaver, Carrie 341

The Proof House
Parker, K.J. 585

A Proper Companion
Hern, Candice 278

Proper Intentions
Christner, Dianne 979

The Proper Wife
Justiss, Julia **311**

Property of Blood
Nabb, Magdalen **164**

Prophecy
Haydon, Elizabeth 554, 1140

The Prophecy Machine
Barrett, Neal Jr. 518, 524

Prophet Motive
Jones, Cleo 76

The Prophetess
Wood, Barbara 962

The Proposal
Wick, Lori 1020

Protect and Defend
Patterson, Richard North 1134

The Protector
Henderson, Dee **999**, 1000

Provinces of Night
Gay, William 1121

A Prudent Match
Matthews, Laura 238

The Psychotechnic League
Anderson, Poul 734

Public Secrets
Roberts, Nora 412

Publish and Perish
Hynes, James 649

The Publisher
Fullerton, Alexander 866

The Pumpkin Rollers
Kelton, Elmer 468, 504

The Puppet King
Niles, Douglas 583

The Puppet Master
Dalmas, John **741**

The Puppet Masters
Heinlein, Robert A. 660, 710

Pure Chance
Leto, Julie Elizabeth 333

Pure Justice
Ledbetter, Suzann 451

The Purification Ceremony
Sullivan, Mark T. 19

The Purloined Letters
Lane, Allison 325

Purple Cane Road
Burke, James Lee 1088

Pursuing Amy
Kaye, Marilyn 775

Puzzled to Death
Hall, Parnell **96**

Pyramid Scheme
Freer, David **751**

Q

Quakertown
Martin, Lee 887, 947

The Qualinesti
Thompson, Paul B. 604

The Quality of Mercy
Kellerman, Faye 109, 880

Quantum Moon
Vitola, Denise 801

Quantum Rose
Asaro, Catherine 716

Quarantine
Crace, Jim 1095

The Quarry Series
Collins, Max Allan 202

Quatermass and the Pit
Kneale, Nigel 675

Queen of Ambition
Buckley, Fiona **29**, **834**

Queen of Angels
Bear, Greg 758

Queen of Demons
Drake, David 541, 563, 599

Queen of Swords
Tarr, Judith 941

Queen of the Darkness
Bishop, Anne 527

Queen of the Demonweb Pits
Kidd, Paul **563**

The Queen of the Tambourine
Gardam, Jane 870

Queen Victoria's Bomb
Clark, Ronald 778

Queenie
Munro, Alice 1169

Queenmaker
Edghill, India **858**

The Queen's Head
Marston, Edward 29

The Queen's Man
Penman, Sharon Kay 941

The Queen's Physician
Maas, Edgar 862

Queen's Ransom
Buckley, Fiona 29, 834

The Queen's Squadron
Meluch, R.M. 761

The Quest
Binder, Pam 237, 323

The Quest
Kraus, Jim **1013**

The Quest
Moser, Nancy 1030

Quest of the Dawn Man
Rosny, J.H. 723

The Questing of Kedrigern
Morressey, John 521

The Quick and the Dead
Williams, Joy 1148

Quicksilver's Knight
Stasheff, Christopher 600

The Quiet Game
Iles, Greg 123

A Quiet Strength
Oke, Janette 1034

Quincey Morris, Vampire
Elrod, P.N. **632**, 686

Quincie Bolliver
King, Mary **469**

R

The Rabbi David Small Series
Kemelman, Harry 129

The Race for Autumn's Glory
Fell, Doris Elaine 992

The Race for God
Herbert, Brian 757

The Rachel Alexander Series
Benjamin, Carol Lea 17

Rachel in Love
Murphy, Pat 781

The Rachel O'Connor Series
Freeman, Mary 103, 181, 219

Rachel's Choice
French, Judith E. 418

Rachel's Hope
Page, Carole Gift 1036

The Radiant Seas
Asaro, Catherine 716

Raffling Ryan
Michaels, Kasey 250, 255, 354, 380

The Rag & Bone Shop
Rackham, Jeff 833, **917**

Rag Man
Hautman, Pete **107**

Rage of a Demon King
Feist, Raymond E. 530, 535

The Ragman's Memory
Mayor, Archer 151

Ragtime
Doctorow, E.L. 874

The Railway Children
Nesbit, Edith 581

The Rain Tree
Cook, Will 487, 498

Rainbow Man
Engh, M.J. 747

Rainbow Rider: A Western Trio
Overholser, Wayne D. 430, 489, **491**

Rainbow's End
Grimes, Martha 92

The Rainmaker
Grisham, John 141

Rainsinger
Wind, Ruth 261

The Rainy Season
Blaylock, James P. 515, 567, 573

Raise the Titanic
Cussler, Clive 1097

Raising Baby Jane
Darcy, Lilian 268

Raising Holy Hell
Olds, Bruce 485, 1176

Rajan
Lukeman, Tim 531

The Rake
Putney, Mary Jo 227

The Rake and the Wallflower
Lane, Allison **325**

The Rakehell's Reform
Fairchild, Elisabeth 275

The Rake's Fiancee
Kirkland, Martha 291, 318

A Rake's Reform
Barbour, Anne 279, 392

The Rake's Retreat
Butler, Nancy 374, 377

The Rake's Revenge
Hendrickson, Emily 305

The Ranch
Steel, Danielle 1203

The Rancher Gets Hitched
Linz, Cathie 335

Randall's Round
Scott, Eleanor 650

Rangers of the Lone Star
Grey, Zane 458

Rangle River
Grey, Zane 445, 458, 486, 494

Ransom
Garwood, Julie 244

Ransom of Love
Lacy, Al 1014

Ransomed Heart
Mitchell, Sara 972

Raptor
Jennings, Gary 889

Raptor
Van Gieson, Judith 25

Raptor
Zindel, Paul 714

Ratha's Creature
Bell, Clare 574

Rats
Zindel, Paul 714

Rats, Bats, and Vats
Freer, David 751

Rattlesnake Crossing
Jance, J.A. 125

Rattlesnake Gulch
McGinley, Marjorie M. 479

Rattlesnake Mesa
Dawson, Peter 461, 473

Ravelstein
Bellow, Saul 1072, 1145, 1158

Raven Mocker
Coldsmith, Don 962

Ravenheart
Gemmell, David 548

Ravished
Quick, Amanda 309, 400

Rawhide
Flynn, T.T. 452

The Rayford Goodman Series
Cutler, Stan 72

Re-Animator
Rovin, Jeff 691

Re-Birth
Wyndham, John 730, 732

The Reader
Schlink, Bernhard 1192

Reality Check
Anthony, Piers 518

Really, Really, Really, Really Weird Stories
Shirley, John 624

Realm of the Reaper
Applegate, K.A. 520

The Realms of Gold
Drabble, Margaret 1204

Reap the Whirlwind
Johnston, Terry C. 466

The Reaper
Lovesey, Peter 146

Rebecca
Du Maurier, Daphne 314

Rebel
Moore, Arthur 473

Rebel Agent
Dietz, William C. 746

Rebel Dreams
Rice, Patricia 352

The Rebellious Twin
Kennedy, Shirley 305

Rebel's Cage
Jacoby, Kate **561**, 578

Reborn
Wilson, F. Paul 637

Reckless
Kenner, Julie 223

The Reckless Barrister
Kihlstrom, April 279, 392

A Reckless Encounter
Rogers, Rosemary **385**

Reckless Sleep
Levy, Roger 731

The Reckoning
Huggins, James Byron 1003

The Reckoning
Lewis, Beverly 1018

The Reckoning
McLain, John **481**

Red Beans and Vice
Temple, Lou Jane **207**

Red Death
Elrod, P.N. 632

Red Dragon
Harris, Thomas 154

Red Dust
McAuley, Paul J. 814

The Red Eagle
Hogan, Ray 452

Red Earth and Pouring Rain
Chandra, Vikram 849

Red Gold
Furst, Alan 126, 888, 960

Red Grass River
Blake, James Carlos 424, 481, 513

Red Hart Magic
Norton, Andre 519, 543, 573

The Red Harvest
Hammett, Dashiell 99

Red Hook
Cohen, Gabriel **37**

Red House
Wishnia, K.J.A. **217**

Red Is the River
Olsen, T.V. 486, 487

Red Magic
Rabe, Jean 589

Red Mesa
Thurlo, Aimee 506

The Red of His Shadow
Montero, Mayra **1164**

Red on Rose
Jones, Patricia **1133**

The Red Pony
Steinbeck, John 1146

Red, Red Robin
Gallagher, Stephen 664

Red, Red Rose
Farrell, Marjorie 315

The Red River
Bean, Frederic 441, 508

Red River Stage
Grove, Fred 459, 460

Red Sands
Thompson, Paul B. 565, 604

The Red Scream
Walker, Mary Willis 167, 198

Red Sky at Night
Hall, James W. 94

The Red Tent
Diamant, Anita 1103

Red, White and Blue
Isaacs, Susan 1131

Redcoat
Cornwell, Bernard 843

Redeeming Claire
Rutledge, Cynthia 997, 1044, **1045**, 1052

Redeeming Love
Rivers, Francine 988

The Redemption of Sarah Cain
Lewis, Beverly 965, 1018, 1036

Rediscovery
Bradley, Marion Zimmer 725

Redworld
Harness, Charles L. 810

Reef of Death
Zindel, Paul 714

Reel
Janiver, Laurence M. 763

Reese's Wild Wager
McCauley, Barbara 235

The Reeve's Tale
Frazer, Margaret 70, 865

Refiner's Fire
Bambola, Sylvia 966

Reflecting the Sky
Rozan, S.K. 185

Reforming a Rake
Enoch, Suzanne 408

Reforming Lord Ragsdale
Kelly, Carla 392

The Reforming of Matthew Dunn
Kantra, Virginia 335

The Regan O'Reilly Series
Clark, Carol Higgins 80

Regards from the Dead Princess
Mourad, Kenize 893

A Regency Christmas Carol
Layton, Edith 248

A Regency Christmas Eve
Butler, Nancy 248, 367

A Regency Christmas Feast
Balogh, Mary 248

A Regency Christmas Present
Fairchild, Elisabeth 232, 248

Regency Christmas Spirits
Butler, Nancy **248**

Regeneration
Barker, Pat 857

The Regeneration Trilogy
Barker, Pat 943

The Regiment
Dalmas, John 729

The Rei Shimura Series
Massey, Sujata 127

Reinventing Romeo
Lane, Connie 422

Rejar
Joy, Dara 310

Relic
Child, Lincoln 662

The Religion
Conde, Nicholas 672

The Reluctant Detective and Other Stories
Lewin, Michael Z. **142**

The Reluctant Heiress
Richardson, Evelyn 379

The Reluctant Hero
Worth, Lenora 1063

The Reluctant Sorcerer
Hawke, Simon 524

Remake
Willis, Connie 811

Remaking History
Robinson, Kim Stanley 760

The Remember Box
Sprinkle, Patricia Houck 1051

Remember the Morning
Fleming, Thomas 840

Remember Your Lies
Jones, Jill 327

Remembering the Roses
Duckworth, Marion 1055

Render Up the Body
Wesson, Marianne 167, 198

The Rendezvous with Destiny Series
Bunn, T. Davis 1034, 1040

The Rene Shade Series
Woodrell, Daniel 112

Renegade
Bean, Frederic 426, 429, 895

The Renegade Dragon
Radford, Irene 557

Renegade River
Cheshire, Giff 426, 429, 430, 501

The Renegade Steals a Lady
Taylor, Vickie **414**

The Renegades: Cole
Dellin, Genell 270

The Renegades: Nick
Dellin, Genell 270

The Renegades: Rafe
Dellin, Genell **270**

The Reno Saga
Morris, Gilbert 972, 973

Repair to Her Grave
Graves, Sarah 89

Replica
Bowker, Richard 806

The Reproductive System
Sladek, John **798**

Republic of Fear
Makiya, Kanan 902

Requiem
Heinlein, Robert A. 1082

Requiem
Joyce, Graham 655

Requiem for a Lost Empire
Makine, Andrei **1151**

Rescue
Healy, Jeremiah 111

The Rescue
Sparks, Nicholas 1200

Resistance
Shreve, Anita 1165

Resolutions
Cox, Carol 969

Restitution
Wheeler, Richard S. 512

Restless Spirits
Wilson, Rachel 421

Restoration and Romance
Curtis, Barbara **986**

Retribution
Fulton, John **1115**

The Return
Edwards, Gene 990

The Return
McCall, Dinah 339

The Return of Henry Starr
Slotkin, Richard 842

The Return of Jericho Pike
Armstrong, John D. 503

The Return of Kavin
Mason, David 589

The Return of Merlin
Chopra, Deepak 558

The Return of the Soul and Other Stories
Hichens, Robert **647**

The Return of the Spanish Lady
Davis, Val 68

Return to Harmony
Oke, Janette 1054

Return to Mars
Bova, Ben 771

Return to Otherness
Kuttner, Henry 715

Reunions
Berger, Eileen 968

Revelation
Haydon, Elizabeth **555**

Revelation Space
Reynolds, Alastair 736, 739, 789, 807, 812

The Revenant
Odom, Mel 584

Revenge of the Barbecue Queens
Temple, Lou Jane 207

Revenge of the Wrought-Iron Flamingos
Andrews, Donna **6**

Revolution #9
Abrahams, Peter 1

Revolutionary
Swann, S. Andrew 602

Rhapsody
Haydon, Elizabeth 554

Rhythms
Hill, Donna **884**, 947

Ribbon of Years
Hatcher, Robin Lee 1039

The Ribbons of Steel Series
Pella, Judith 972

Ribofunk
Di Filippo, Paul 745

Richard Dare
Baldwin, Louisa 618

The Richard Jury Series
Grimes, Martha 30

The Richard Sharpe Series
Cornwell, Bernard 843

The Riddle and Other Stories
de la Mare, Walter 680

The Riddle of Alabaster Royal
Veryan, Patricia 258

The Riddled Night
Leith, Valery 561, 572, 578

The Riddlemaster of Hed
McKillip, Patricia 591

Ride East! Ride West!
Powers, Anne 843

Ride for Rimfire
Edwards, Hank 504

Ride for the Roses
Kingston, Christina 317, 348, 355

Ride South to Purgatory
Work, James C. 514

Ride to Glory
Flynn, T.T. 452

Ride West to Dawn
Work, James C. **514**

Riders of the Sundown
Overholser, Wayne D. 491

Riders to Cibola
Zollinger, Norman 509

Rides of the Midway
Durkee, Lee 1109

The Ridgeline Mystery Series
Gansky, Alton 1012

Riding through Shadows
Foster, Sharon Ewell 1051

Riding with Hannah and the Horseman
Boggs, Johnny D. 474

The Rifles
Vollmann, William T. 905, 950, 1212

Right as Rain
Pelecanos, George P. 37

The Right Hand of Amon
Haney, Lauren 101

The Right Hand of Evil
Saul, John 687

Rim of the Desert
Haycox, Ernest 490, 499

Rime Isle
Leiber, Fritz 596

The Rina Lazarus/Peter Decker Series
Kellerman, Faye 137

The Rincewind Trilogy
Pratchett, Terry 588

Ring Game
Hautman, Pete 107

Ring of Truth
Pickard, Nancy 167

Ringstones
Sarban 529, 559, 598

Rio Grande Wedding
Wind, Ruth 422

Riona
Windsor, Linda **1060**

Riot
Tharoor, Shashi 1152, **1208**

Ripper
Clark, Mark 153

The Ripper of Storyville
Hoch, Edward D. 117, 118

Rise of a Merchant Prince
Feist, Raymond E. 532

The Rise of Endymion
Simmons, Dan 777, 789, 812

Rise the Euphrates
Edgarian, Carol 893

Rise to Rebellion
Shaara, Jeff 840, 939

The Rising Tide
Odom, Mel 584

The Risk Pool
Russo, Richard 1106

Risque Business
Winston, Anne Marie 246

Ritual of Proof
Joy, Dara **310**

Ritual Sins
Stuart, Anne 283

The Rival
Rusch, Kristine Kathryn 591

Rivals of Dracula
Parry, Michel 631

Rivals of Dracula
Weinberg, Robert 631

The River and the Horseman
Skimin, Robert 824

River Come Down
Black, Michelle 824

The River Midnight
Nattel, Lilian 1064

River of Darkness
Airth, Rennie 208

The River of Time
Brin, David 766

A River out of Eden
Hockenberry, John 436, 442

A River Running West
Worster, Donald 949

The River Sorrow
Holden, Craig 119, 885

River Walk
Cleary, Rita 441, **443**, 508

River's End
Roberts, Nora 1169, 1174, 1187

Rivers of Gold
Peterson, Tracie **1042**

Riverwatch
Nassise, Joseph M. **676**

Riverwind the Plainsman
Thompson, Paul B. 604

Road Kill
Friedman, Kinky 72

The Road to Wellville
Boyle, T. Coraghessan 1081

A Road We Do Not Know
Chiaventone, Frederick J. 441

The Roaring Boy
Marston, Edward 148

Robak in Black
Hensley, Joe L. **113**

Robak's Cross
Hensley, Joe L. 113

Robak's Fire
Hensley, Joe L. 113

Robak's Firm
Hensley, Joe L. 113

Robak's Run
Hensley, Joe L. 113

Robak's Witch
Hensley, Joe L. 113

Robber Bride
Simmons, Deborah 396

Robbers
Cook, Christopher 825

The Robe
Douglas, Lloyd C. 942

Robert Bloch's Psychos
Bloch, Robert 634

The Robert Bone Series
Stacey, Susannah 43

The Robert Skinner Series
Jardine, Quintin 178

The Robin Hudson Series
Hayter, Sparkle 144

The Robot Who Looked Like Me
Sheckley, Robert 715, 803

Robots and Changelings
Del Rey, Lester 727

The Rock
Makiya, Kanan **902**, 930, 942, **1152**

A Rock and a Hard Place
Wimberley, Darryl 216

The Rock of Kiever
Brand, Max 434

Rock Solid
Greene, Jennifer 250

Rocky and the Senator's Daughter
Browning, Dixie **246**, 335

The Rocky Mountain Legacy Series
Heitzmann, Kristen 1050

Rode Hard, Put Away Dead
Browning, Sinclair 28, 428, 436, 442, 444, 472, 477, 502, 506

Roderick
Sladek, John 798

The Roger the Chapman Series
Sedley, Kate 86

Rogue Bolo
Laumer, Keith 765

A Rogue for Christmas
Huntington, Kate **304**

Rogue Reynard
Norton, Andre 587

A Rogue's Proposal
Laurens, Stephanie 329

Rogues to Riches
King, J. Robert 566

The Roma Sub Rosa Series
Saylor, Steven 920, 924

Roman Nights
Burns, Ron 180

Roman Shadows
Burns, Ron 184

Romance
McBain, Ed 152

The Romance of Charles Dickens
Bloom, Ursula 917

Romance of the Rose
Beard, Julie 229

The Romance Reader
Abraham, Pearl 978

Romancing the Rogue
Smith, Barbara Dawson 400

A Romantic Way to Die
Crider, Bill **49**

Romeo and Julia
Kimberlin, Annie 232

The Ronnie Ventana Series
White, Gloria 217

Roofworld
Fowler, Christopher 687

Rookie
Jenkins, Jerry B. 1005

The Room in the Tower and Other Stories
Benson, E.F. 622

A Room of My Own
Tatlock, Ann 1017

Rooms of the Heart
Hill, Donna 884

The Root Worker
Burton, Rainelle 1133, 1164

Roots of Murder
Harrison, Janis 103, 181

Rora
Huggins, James Byron **1003**

Roscoe
Kennedy, William 825, **897**

The Rose and the Skull
Crook, Jeff 612

The Rose and the Warrior
Monk, Karyn 405

A Rose at Midnight
Navin, Jacqueline 360

A Rose by the Door
Bedford, Deborah **967**

Rose Cottage
Stewart, Mary 9

The Rose Demon
Doherty, P.C. 86, 194

A Rose for Jenny
Page, Carole Gift 1035, 1036

The Rose Garden
Brennan, Maeve 872

The Rose in the Wheel
Rizzolo, S.K. **182**

The Rose Legacy
Heitzmann, Kristen 998

The Rose of Death and Other Mysterious Delusions
Hawthorne, Julian 647

The Rose Thieves
Schmidt, Heidi Jon 1193

Roses Are Red
Patterson, James 1127, 1181

Ross Henry
Brown, Sam 459

Ross Mcdonald's Lew Archer, Private Investigator
Macdonald, Ross 41, 99, 201

Ross's Gap
Wisler, G. Clifton 449, 450

Rough Cider
Lovesey, Peter 55, 92, 214

Rough Wrangler, Tender Kisses
Gregory, Jill 294, 324

The Route 66 Series
Jones, Annie 1006

The Rover
Odom, Mel **584**

Rowan of Rin
Rodda, Emily **594**

The Royal Assassin
Hobb, Robin 540

Royal Bride
Wolf, Joan 388

The Royal Family
Vollmann, William T. 950, 1110, 1176, 1212

A Royal Marriage
Colter, Cara 334

The Royal Physician's Visit
Enquist, Per Olov **862**, **1110**

Royal Whodunnits
Ashley, Mike 8

The Ruby Rothman Series
Kahn, Sharon 124

Rubyfruit Jungle
Brown, Rita Mae 1213

Rude Behavior
Jenkins, Dan 1132

Rueful Death
Albert, Susan Wittig 4

Ruin
Stackpole, Michael A. 599

Ruins
Anderson, Kevin J. 715

Rulers of Darkness
Spruill, Steven G. 617, 702

Rules of Surrender
Dodd, Christina 319, 408

Rumble Tumble
Lansdale, Joe R. 472

Rumors of Angels
Coniglio, John Vincent 1010

Run Catch Kiss
Sohn, Amy 1100

Run for Your Life
Kane, Andrea 312

The Runaway Princess
Forsythe, Patricia 334, 343

The Rundlestone of Oz
McGraw, Eloise **577**

Runestone
Coldsmith, Don 952

The Runner
Reich, Christopher 131, 906

Running Blind
Child, Lee 442

Running Wild
Ballard, J.G. 1070

Running with the Demon
Brooks, Terry 530

Rushing to Paradise
Ballard, J.G. 1070

The Russia House
Le Carre, John 1151

The Russians Series
Phillips, Michael 1003, 1028

Rustlers
Rispin, Karen 1012

Rustler's Venom
Lee, W.W. 503

S

Sacajawea
Waldo, Anna Lee 510, 952

Sacrament
Barker, Clive 619

Sacred and Profane
Weiss, David 929

Sacred Ground
Wood, Barbara 818, 871, 879, 913, **962**

A Sacred Place
Leon, Bonnie 1017, 1042

The Sacrilege
Roberts, John Maddox 184, 924

Saddled
Fossen, Delores 253, **284**

Sadie's Song
Hall, Linda 1001, 1002, 1029

Safe Conduct
Benedict, Elizabeth 1073

The Sage
Stasheff, Christopher 600

Sahara
Cussler, Clive 1097

Sailing to Byzantium
Kay, Guy Gavriel 570

Sailing to Utopia
Moorcock, Michael 582

Sailor
Jessup, Richard 953

St. Burl's Obituary
Akst, Daniel 1066

Saint Maybe
Tyler, Anne 1085

Saint Mudd
Thayer, Steve 119

Saintly Murders
Grace, C.L. **86**, **875**

The Saint's Day Deaths
Noyer, Albert 180, 184, 209

Saint's Rest
Miles, Keith 119

Salamander
Janes, J. Robert 888

The Salaryman's Wife
Massey, Sujata 150

Salem Street
Jacobs, Anna 305

Sally Hemmings
Chase-Riboud, Barbara 918

Sally's in the Alley
Davis, Norbert 56

Salt
Roberts, Adam 790

Salt Dancers
Hegi, Ursula 1124

The Salt Letters
Balint, Christine **819**

Salt Line
Spencer, Elizabeth 1201

Salt Snake and Other Bloody Cuts
Clark, Simon 655

The Samantha Turner Series
Landreth, Marsha 197

Samuel Johnson Is Indignant
Davis, Lydia **1099**

Samurai Boogie
Tasker, Peter 127

Sanctuary
Lewis, Beverly 1018

The Sand-Reckoner
Bradshaw, Gillian 831, 859

The Sandalwood Princess
Chase, Loretta 398

Sandman
Janes, J. Robert 126, 888, 960

The Sands of Mars
Clarke, Arthur C. 814

The Sands of Sakkara
Meade, Glenn 215, 906

The Sano Ichiro Series
Rowland, Laura Joh 150

Santa and Pete
Moore, Christopher 1179

Santa Paws
Alexander, Victoria 232

Sap Rising
Lincoln, Christine 1112, **1147**

The Sapphire Throne
Warrington, Freda 609

The Sarah and Meg Quilliam Series
Bishop, Claudia 32, 138

Sarah and the Rogue
Scott, DeLoras **391**

The Sarah Booth Delaney Series
Haines, Carolyn 4, 163

The Sarah Brandt Series
Thompson, Victoria 24, 200

The Sarah Kelling/Max Bittersohn Series
MacLeod, Charlotte 6, 177

Sarah's Patchwork
Whitson, Stephanie Grace 1058

Sarah's Window
Graham, Janice **457**

The Sarsen Witch
Kernaghan, Eileen 534

The Satanic Verses
Rushdie, Salman 1105, 1152, 1178, 1190

Saturday Night Dead
Rosen, R.D. 188

Saturnalia
Roberts, John Maddox 184, 924

Savage Desire
Rogers, Rosemary 385

The Savage Girl
Shakar, Alex 1177, **1196**

Savage Season
Lansdale, Joe R. 472

The Savages in Love and War
Stewart, Fred Mustard **937**

Save the Last Dance for Me
Gorman, Ed **83**

Saving Cinderella
Darcy, Lilian 268

Saving Grace
Garwood, Julie 295

Saving His Son
Herron, Rita 299

Say You Love Me
Lindsey, Johanna 346

Scandal in Venice
McCabe, Amanda 349

Scandalized
Foster, Lori 286

Scandalmonger
Safire, William 912

Scandalous
Hill, Donna 884

Scandalous
Robards, Karen 293, 346, 375, 381, 402, 416

A Scandalous Affair
Hill, Donna 884

A Scandalous Bequest
Kihlstrom, April 356

A Scandalous Marriage
Maxwell, Cathy 348

The Scandalous Miss Delaney
Blair, Catherine 238

A Scandalous Proposal
Justiss, Julia 311

Scandalous Secrets
Oliver, Patricia 362

A Scandalous Virtue
Hiatt, Brenda 311

A Scandalous Wager
Willingham, Bess **420**

Scandal's Bride
Laurens, Stephanie 329

Scandal's Daughter
Dunn, Carola 374

Scar Tissue
Tapply, William G. 206

The Scarecrow and Other Stories
Wormser, G. Ranger **711**

Scarlet Music
Ohanneson, Joan 1031

The Scarlet Pimpernel
Orczy, Emmuska 307

Scarlett
Ripley, Alexandra 918

The Scarletti Curse
Feehan, Christine 277, 360

Scary Rednecks
Whitman, David 679

Scent of Lilacs
Bonander, Jane 270

The Scent of Magic
McNish, Cliff **581**

The Scent of Magic
Norton, Andre 784

Scenting Hallowed Blood
Constantine, Storm 536, 607

Scholar of Decay
Huff, Tanya 613

The School
Wright, T.M. 712

The School Board Murders
O'Kane, Leslie 218

Schooling
McGowan, Heather **1159**

Scion of Cyador
Modesitt, L.E. Jr. 777, 778

Scissorman
Chadbourn, Mark 533

The Scold's Bridle
Walters, Minette 211

Scorch
Nauman, A.D. **782**

The Scotswoman
Fletcher, Inglis 868

Scottish Brides
Dodd, Christina 243

Scottish Magic
Howell, Hannah 243

The Scottish Rose
Jones, Jill 323

The Scottish Shores Series
Johnson, Grace 1026

Scream in Silence
Bland, Eleanor Taylor 21

Screamplays
Chizmar, Richard 696

The Sculptress
Walters, Minette 154, 211

The Scumble River Series
Swanson, Denise 81

The Sea Devil's Eye
Odom, Mel 584

Sea Dragon Heir
Constantine, Storm 536, 540

The Sea Hag
Drake, David 541

The Sea Lepers
Lieberman, Gerald F. 953

The Sea Nymph
Langan, Ruth 297, 327, 328

Sea of Glory
Wales, Ken **953**, **1056**

The Sea of Silver Light
Williams, Tad 571

Sea of Swords
Salvatore, R.A. **597**

The Sea Sprite
Langan, Ruth 327, **328**

The Sea Witch
Langan, Ruth 328

Seance for a Vampire
Saberhagen, Fred 695

Search for Last Chance
McWilliams, A.L. **482**

The Search for Magic
Weis, Margaret **612**

Search for the Fox
Overholser, Stephen 488

Search the Dark
Todd, Charles 208, 943

Searching for Stardust
McCourtney, Lorena 1023

A Searching Heart
Oke, Janette 1034

The Sea's Furthest End
Broderick, Damien 726

Seaside
Blackstock, Terri 970, 971

Season for Miracles
Pappano, Marilyn 366, 382

A Season in the Highlands
Deveraux, Jude 243, 277

Season of Storms
Kearsley, Susanna **314**

Season of Wishes
Skye, Christina 399

Season of Yellow Leaf
Jones, Douglas C. 826

Seasonal Rain and Other Stories
Flynn, Robert 451

Seasons
Martin, Gail Gaymer 1021, 1022

The Seasons under Heaven Series
LaHaye, Beverly 1010

The Seat Beside Me
Moser, Nancy **1030**

Second Chance Groom
Riley, Eugenia 380

Second Chances
Hansen, Valerie 995, 997, 1052, 1057

Second Chances
Shwartz, Susan **796**

Second Chances
Smith, Debra White 1023, 1048, 1049, 1055

The Second Chances Series
Blackstock, Terri 993, 1006

Second Contact
Austin, J.D. **719**

Second Dream, Fathers and Crows
Vollmann, William T. 1212

Second Fire
Wilson, Robert 714

Second Lives
Wheeler, Richard S. 957

Second Star to the Right
Kruesi, Mary Alice 287

Second Time Around
Steward, Carol 1052

The Secret
Martin, Kat 346, **347**

The Secret Admirer
Mahon, Annette **343**, 353

Secret Admirer
Stevens, Amanda 410

Secret Bodyguard
Daniels, B.J. 414

The Secret Clan: Abducted Heiress
Scott, Amanda **390**

The Secret Diary of Dr. Watson
Janda, Anita 899, 908, 926

Secret Fantasy
Phillips, Carly 240

The Secret History
Tartt, Donna 82

The Secret Life of Colours
Savile, Steve 688

The Secret Life of Connor Monahan
Bevarly, Elizabeth **235**

Secret Love
Jackson, Brenda 224

A Secret Love
Laurens, Stephanie 329

Secret Love
Schneider, Bart 1119, 1154

The Secret of Life
McAuley, Paul J. 739, **771**

The Secret of the Rose Series
Phillips, Michael 1040

Secret of the Wolf
Krinard, Susan **322**

The Secret People
Wyndham, John 582

The Secret Place
Lacy, Al 1014, 1015

Secret Sins
Ross, JoAnn 386

Secret Star
Roberts, Nora 382

Secret Vows
McCall, Mary Reed 295, 407

The Secrets of Catie Hazard
Jarrett, Miranda 307, 308

The Secrets of Heathersleigh Hall Series
Phillips, Michael 1020, 1027

Secrets of the Heart
Martin, Gail Gaymer 1021, **1022**, 1063

Secrets of the Stone
Taylor, Harriet Peck 871

The Sedgemoor Strangler and Other Stories of Crime
Lovesey, Peter 142, **146**

Seducing Celeste
Langan, Ruth 327, 328

Seducing Lord Sinclair
Solomon, Hayley Ann 420

Seducing Mr. Right
Adair, Cherry 222, **223**

Seducing Sullivan
Leto, Julie Elizabeth 333

Seducing Summer
Blake, Toni 223

The Seduction
Jordan, Nicole 309, 329

The Seduction of Ellen
Ryan, Nan 296

The Seduction of Roxanne
Jones, Linda Winstead 247

Seductive
Devine, Thea 282

See Jane Date
Senate, Melissa 252, 345, 357, **394**

See No Evil
Bland, Eleanor Taylor 21

The Seeds of Doom
Hinchcliffe, Philip 735

The Seeds of Time
Cail, Carol 465

The Seeker
Hawke, Simon 604

The Seeker
Metz, Melinda 775, 776

The Seekers
Hawkins, Paul A. 426, 429

The Seekers Series
Herr, Ethel L. 979, 1003

Seeking Single Male
Bond, Stephanie 240, 261, 299

Seeking the Dream Brother
Bennett, M.J. 593

Seer's Blood
Durgin, Doranna 543

Seize the Night
Koontz, Dean R. 661

Selected Poems
Smith, Clark Ashton 669

Selected Stories
Beaumont, Charles 678

Selected Stories
Munro, Alice 1115

Semi-Tough
Jenkins, Dan 1132

Seminole Song
Munn, Vella 911

The Senator's Agenda
Larson, Bob 976, 1004

The Senator's Other Daughter
Bly, Stephen A. 972

The Senator's Wife
Robards, Karen 312, 381

Send Me No Flowers
Gabriel, Kristin 289

Send No Flowers
Brown, Sandra 1086

A Sensitive Kind of Murder
Girdner, Jacqueline **80**

Sent to His Account
Dillon, Eilis 173

Sentimental, Heartbroken Rednecks
Bottoms, Greg **1079**

Sentimental Journey
Barnett, Jill **228**, **821**, 845, 870, 876, 925

Sentinels
Pronzini, Bill 174

Sentry Peak
Turtledove, Harry 606, 804

September Song
Greeley, Andrew M. **1117**

Serenity Bay
Nordberg, Bette 1001, 1002, 1029

The Serenity Inn Series
Rizzo, Kay D. 1014

The Sergeant Bragg/Constable Morton Series
Harrison, Ray 172

The Sergeant Cribb/Constable Thackeray Series
Lovesey, Peter 172

Sergeant Verity and the Blood Royal
Selwyn, Francis 851

The Sergeant Verity Series
Selwyn, Francis 172

The Serpent's Shadow
Lackey, Mercedes 568

Servant of the Shard
Salvatore, R.A. 597

Servants of the Dragon
Drake, David 541

Servants of Twilight
Koontz, Dean R. 1185

A Servant's Tale
Fox, Paula 1206

Set in Darkness
Rankin, Ian 178

The Seven Sexes
Tenn, William 803

Seven Up
Evanovich, Janet **274**, 376

The Seventh Enemy
Tapply, William G. 206

Seventh Heaven
Anderson, Catherine 225

The Seventh Sentinel
Kirchoff, Mary 604

The Seventh Telling
Chefitz, Mitchell 978

Several Deceptions
Stevenson, Jane 1204

The Seville Communion
Perez-Reverte, Arturo 171, 1182

Sex and Murder.com
Zubro, Mark Richard **221**

Sex and the Single Vampire
Kilpatrick, Nancy 658

Sex and Violence in Zero G
Steele, Allen 802

Sex Appeal
Foster, Lori 286

Shackled
Garton, Ray 638

Shades of a Desperado
Sala, Sharon 313

Shades of Justice
Huebner, Fredrick **121**

Shades of Murder
Granger, Ann **87**

Shades of Twilight
Howard, Linda 283

Shadow
Parker, K.J. **585**

Shadow Climber
Reichert, Mickey Zucker 552

Shadow Dreams
Massie, Elizabeth 629, 630

The Shadow in Renegade Basin
Savage, Les Jr. 431, 455, 500, **501**

Shadow Kiss
Townsend, Tom **605**

Shadow Lover
Stuart, Anne 245, 411

Shadow Man
Etchison, Dennis 619, 626, 664

Shadow of a Dark Queen
Feist, Raymond E. 536, 599

Shadow of Doubt
Blackstock, Terri 970

Shadow of Earth
Eisenstein, Phyllis 799

Shadow of the Seer
Rohan, Michael Scott **595**

The Shadow on the Blind
Baldwin, Louisa **618**

A Shadow on the Glass
Irvine, Ian 560

A Shadow on the Wall
Aycliffe, Jonathan 644

The Shadow out of Time
Lovecraft, H.P. **670**

The Shadow over Innsmouth
Lovecraft, H.P. 671

The Shadow Sorceress
Modesitt, L.E. Jr. 549, 777, 778

Shadow Valley Rising
Overholser, Stephen **488**

The Shadow Within
Cavelos, Jeanne 770

Shadowfane
Wurts, Janny 545, 557

Shadowkings
Cobley, Michael **535**

Shadowland
Straub, Peter 644

Shadows and Silence
Roden, Barbara 674

Shadows at Midnight
Maynard, L.H. 652

Shadows at Sunset
Stuart, Anne 360

The Shadows Beneath
Finch, Paul 701

Shadows of Glory
Parry, Owen 2, 169, 914

Shadows of Sin
Krich, Rochelle **137**

Shadows out of Hell
Offutt, Andrew J. 535

Shadow's Witness
Kemp, Paul 578

Shadowspawn
Offutt, Andrew J. 599

The Shadowy Horses
Kearsley, Susanna 314

The Shadowy Third
Glasgow, Ellen 711

The Shakespeare & Smythe Series
Hawke, Simon 29

The Shakespeare and Smythe Series
Hawke, Simon 834

Shakespearean Detectives
Ashley, Mike 8

Shakespearean Whodunnits
Ashley, Mike 8

Shakespeare's Champion
Harris, Charlaine 102

Shakespeare's Christmas
Harris, Charlaine 102

Shakespeare's Counselor
Harris, Charlaine **102**

Shakespeare's Landlord
Harris, Charlaine 102

Shakespeare's Trollop
Harris, Charlaine 102

Shallow Grave
Harrod-Eagles, Cynthia 104

The Shaman Laughs
Doss, James D. 61

The Shaman Series
Doss, James D. 35

Shaman Woods
Fields, Morgan 704

The Shaman's Bones
Doss, James D. 61

The Shaman's Game
Doss, James D. 61

Shame
Rushdie, Salman 1190

Shampoo Planet
Coupland, Douglas 1094

The Shape of Snakes
Walters, Minette **211**

Shapechanger's Song
Roberson, Jennifer 576, 591, 592, 593

The Sharon McCone Series
Muller, Marcia 7, 63, 143

Sharp Edges
Krentz, Jayne Ann 302

The Shattered Mask
Byers, Richard Lee **532**

Shawnee Bride
Lane, Elizabeth 326

She Is the Darkness
Cook, Glen 608

She Needed Me
Kirn, Walter 1141

She Who Hears the Sun
Jekel, Pamela 911

Sheep
Maginn, Simon 673

A Shelter in the Storm
Smith, Debra White 1048, 1049

The Shepherd Kings
Tarr, Judith 940, 941

The Shepherd's Voice
Hatcher, Robin Lee 1017

The Sheriff Dan Rhodes Series
Crider, Bill 108

Sherlock Holmes and the Giant Rat of Sumatra
Vanneman, Alan 5, **210**

Sherlock Holmes and the Ice Palace Murders
Millett, Larry 158, 908

Sherlock Holmes and the Red Demon
Millett, Larry 158, 908

Sherlock Holmes and the Rune Stone Mystery
Millett, Larry 158, 908

Sherlock Holmes and the Secret Alliance
Millett, Larry **158**, 210, 830, 896, 899, **908**, 958

Sherlock Holmes and the Voice from the Crypt
Thomas, Donald S. 896

The Sherlock Holmes Series
Doyle, Arthur Conan 158, 210

Sherlock Holmes: The Missing Years
Jamyang Norbu 158, 210, 856, 899

Sherlock Holmes vs. Jack the Ripper
Queen, Ellery 62

The Sherwood Game
Friesner, Esther 758

The Shield of Time
Anderson, Poul 818

Shifter
Reeves-Stevens, Garfield 568, 801

Shifting Stars
Lambert, Page 438, 467

Shiloh
Reasoner, James 919

Shiloh and Other Stories
Mason, Bobbie Ann 1155

Shimmering Splendor
Gellis, Roberta 547

The Shining
King, Stephen 620

Shining Through
Isaacs, Susan 1131

The Shining Trail
Fuller, Iola 873

A Ship Possessed
Gansky, Alton 637, 1056

The Shipping News
Proulx, Annie 1066

Shipwreck
Wilbee, Brenda 1042

Shipwreck Season
Hill, Donna 884

Shirley, Goodness, and Mercy
Macomber, Debbie 249, 265, 366

Shiva Descending
Benford, Gregory 767

Shock
Cook, Robin **1093**

Shock Rock
Gelb, Jeff 684

Shockball
Viehl, S.L. **805**

Shockwave Rider
Brunner, John 782, 808

The Shoes of the Fisherman
West, Morris L. 956

A Shoot in Cleveland
Roberts, Les 185

A Shoot on Martha's Vineyard
Craig, Philip R. 46

Shooting at Midnight
Rucka, Greg 190

Shooting Chant
Thurlo, Aimee 428, 444, 506

Shooting Dr. Jack
Green, Norman **1118**

The Shore of Women
Sargent, Pamela 747

Shore to Die
Wolzien, Valerie 219

Short Money
Hautman, Pete 107

Shortgrass Song
Blakely, Mike 508, 827

Shoveling Smoke
Maron, Margaret 31

Show Business
Tharoor, Shashi 1208

Show Control
Snyder, Keith 199

Showboat World
Vance, Jack 788

Showers in Season
LaHaye, Beverly 966

A Shrine of Murders
Grace, C.L. 86, 875

Shrine of Stars
McAuley, Paul J. 771

Shroud of Shadow
Baudino, Gael 527

Shroud of Silence
Slama, Carol D. 1059

The Shy Tulip Murders
Rothenberg, Rebecca 189

Siberian Light
White, Robin 130

The Sicilian
Puzo, Mario 916, 1183

Sick Days
Staley, Shane Ryan 698

Sick Puppy
Hiaasen, Carl 115

Sidhe-Devil
Allston, Aaron **516**

The Sidmouth Letters
Gardam, Jane 870

Siege at Fort Defiance
Legg, John 468

The Siege of Arrandin
Herniman, Marcus 557

Siege of Darkness
Salvatore, R.A. 525

The Sierra Lavatoni Series
Bartholomew, Nancy 38

The Sigma Protocol
Ludlum, Robert 1127

Sign-Talker
Thom, James Alexander 957

Signals of Distress
Crace, Jim 1095

The Sigrid Harald Series
Maron, Margaret 88

The Silas Diary
Edwards, Gene 990

Silence Is Deadly
Biggle, Lloyd 763, 813

The Silence of the Lambs
Harris, Thomas 123

Silent Children
Campbell, Ramsey 626

The Silent Cry
Perry, Anne 172, 915

The Silent Gun
Hirt, Douglas 473

Silent Honor
Steel, Danielle 1106

Silent Joe
Parker, T. Jefferson 47

Silent Knight
Phillips, Tori 266, 396

Silent Moon
Relling, William 672

Silent Sea
Homewood, Harry 953

The Silent Strength of Stones
Hoffman, Nina Kiriki 539

The Silent Suitor
Fairchild, Elisabeth 388

The Silent Woman
Dodd, Susan M. **852**, 938, 954

The Silent Woman
Marston, Edward 148

The Silicon Man
Platt, Charles 722

Silk
Kiernan, Caitlin R. 656

Silk and Steel
Martin, Kat 324

Silk and Stone
Smith, Deborah 401

Silkroads and Shadows
Shwartz, Susan 796

The Silly Season
Holtzer, Susan 120

Silver Bells
Forster, Gwynne 300

The Silver Call
McKiernan, Dennis L. **580**

The Silver Coin
Kane, Andrea 312

The Silver Eggheads
Leiber, Fritz 722, 767

Silver Lining
Osborne, Maggie 332, 364, 415

The Silver Mirror
Gellis, Roberta 276

Silver Moon Song
Dellin, Genell 270

The Silver Skull
Daniels, Les 713

The Silver Stair
Rabe, Jean 589

Silver Wings, Santiago Blue
Dailey, Janet 228

The Silver Wolf
Borchardt, Alice 322, 528, 685, 829

Silver Wolf, Black Falcon
McKiernan, Dennis L. 554, 579, 580

Silver Zephyr
Seger, Maura 401

Silverfall
Greenwood, Ed 553

Silverthorn
Feist, Raymond E. 557

The Simbul's Gift
Abbey, Lynn 515, 597

Similar Monsters
Savile, Steve **688**

Simmer All Night
Dawson, Geralyn 284, 402, 419

The Simon Forman Series
Cook, Judith 65

The Simona Griffo Series
Crespi, Camilla 170

Simple Prayers
Golding, Michael 832

A Simple Shaker Murder
Woodworth, Deborah 1062

Simply Irresistible
Gibson, Rachel 292

Simply Love
Anderson, Catherine 364

Simply Magic
Kane, Kathleen 313

Simulacron-3
Galouye, Daniel F. 731

Since You've Been Gone
Madden, Sandra 342

Since You've Been Gone
Perry, Marta 1041

Sincerely Yours
Lacy, Al 1014

Sing It to Her Bones
Talley, Marcia 205

The Singapore Wink
Thomas, Ross 185

Singing Boy
McFarland, Dennis 1196

Singing in the Comeback Choir
Campbell, Bebe Moore 1089, 1194

Single & Single
Le Carre, John 1191

Single Mom
Tyree, Omar 1210

Single White Vampire Seeks Same
Greenberg, Martin H. **643**

Sins of a Shaker Summer
Woodworth, Deborah 1062

Sir Apropos of Nothing
David, Peter 601

The Sir John Fielding Series
Alexander, Bruce 10, 12, 182, 820

The Sir Robert Carey Series
Chisholm, P.F. 148

Sis Boom Bah
Heller, Jane 1125

Sister Crazy
Richler, Emma 1206

The Sister Fidelma Series
Tremayne, Peter 70, 180, 865

The Sister Frevisse Series
Frazer, Margaret 944

Sister India
Payne, Peggy 1208

Sister Noon
Fowler, Karen Joy 437, 817, 938, 1090

Sister of My Heart
Divakaruni, Chitra Banerjee 1104

The Sister Rose Callahan Series
Woodworth, Deborah 33

The Sister Season
Girard, Paula Tanner 262

Sister Wife
Gates, John **76**

Sisters of Cain
Monfredo, Miriam Grace 159, 909

Sisters of the Confederacy
Snelling, Lauraine 1050

A Sister's Quest
Ferguson, Jo Ann 278, 279

The Sistrum and Other Ghost Stories
Perrin, Alice 618

Six Ghost Stories
Jackson, T.G. 650

Six-Inch Spikes
van Belkom, Edo 705

A Six-Letter Word for Death
Moyes, Patricia 96

Six-Pound Walleye
Gunn, Elizabeth **93**

Skating on the Edge
goldberg, d.g.k. 641

Skeleton at the Feast
Hall, Patricia **97**

Skeleton Canyon
Jance, J.A. 125

Skeleton in the Grass
Barnard, Robert 183

Sketches with Wolves
Fiedler, Jacqueline **68**

Skin
Mezrich, Ben 773

Skin Deep, Blood Red
Skinner, Robert 196, 935

Skin Folk
Hopkinson, Nalo **760**

Skin Tight
Hiaasen, Carl 107

The Skip Langdon Series
Smith, Julie 88

Skirmish
Michaels, Melisa 796

The Skull of Truth
Coville, Bruce 538, 605

Skull Session
Hecht, Daniel 705

The Sky Ghost
Maloney, Mack 769

The Sky, the Stars, the Wilderness
Bass, Rick 427, 452, 456, 492, 505

Skyfire
Maloney, Mack 768

The Skylark of Space
Smith, Edward E. 785

Skyler Hawk: Lone Brave
Whitefeather, Sheri 387

The Skypirate
Davis, Justine 267

Slammerkin
Donoghue, Emma 877, 913

Slan
van Vogt, A.E. 794

Slaughter
Kelton, Elmer 895

Slaughtermatic
Aylett, Steve 720

Slaves of Obsession
Perry, Anne 133, 159, 169, 172, 909, 915

The Slaying of the Shrew
Hawke, Simon **109**, **880**

Sleep No More
Rolt, L.T.C. 650

The Sleep of Death
Gooden, Philip 109

The Sleep of Stone
Cooper, Louise 591

Sleep with Me
Kureishi, Hanif 1143

The Sleeping Beauty
Ivory, Judith 360

The Sleeping Beauty
Navin, Jacqueline **360**

Sleeping with the Buffalo
Adam, Christina 1065

A Slender Thread
Peterson, Tracie 1039

Sleuth
Shaffer, Anthony 663

Sleuths of the Century
Breen, Jon L. 84

Slice and Dice
Hart, Ellen 105

The Slicing Edge of Death
Cook, Judith 109, 148

Slightly Shady
Quick, Amanda 293, **375**, 402, 416

Slightly Single
Markham, Wendy 252, **345**, 357, 359

Slippin' into Darkness
Partridge, Norman 664

Slow Dancing
Benedict, Elizabeth 1073

Slow Dancing through Time
Dozois, Gardner 748

A Small Colonial War
Frezza, Robert 784

A Small Death in Lisbon
Wilson, Robert 171, 215, 960

Small Felonies
Pronzini, Bill 175

Small-Town Dreams
Welsh, Kate 1057

Small Town in Germany
Le Carre, John 1135

Small World
Lodge, David 1150

The Smell of Telescopes
Hughes, Rhys 635

The Smiling Country
Kelton, Elmer 462, 468, 497

Smilla's Sense of Snow
Hoeg, Peter 127

Smoke-Filled Rooms
Nelscott, Kris **166**

Smoke Signals
Ramos, Octavio Jr. 698

Smoker
Rucka, Greg 190

The Smokey Dalton Series
Nelscott, Kris 83

Smoking Mirror Blues
Hogan, Ernest **758**

Smoking Poppy
Joyce, Graham 655

The Smuggler's Bride
Willingham, Bess 420

Smuggler's Moon
Alexander, Bruce **815**, 853, 881

Snagged
Clark, Carol Higgins 34

Snake-Bite and Other Stories
Hichens, Robert 647

Snake Mountain
Craven, Jerry 462, 497

Snapshot
Barnes, Linda 168

The Snare
Spencer, Elizabeth 1201

Sniper's Moon
Stroud, Carsten 204

Snow
Miller, Calvin 1032

Snow Falling on Cedars
Guterson, David 845

Snow in September
Lee, Rachel 327, 330, 331, 413

Snow Mountain Passage
Houston, James D. 894, 957, 1083

Snow White and the Seven Samurai
Holt, Tom 518

Snowfall
Sala, Sharon 395

The Snows of Jaspre
Caraker, Mary 810

So Faux, So Good
Myers, Tamar 163

So I Am Glad
Kennedy, A.L. 1138

So Little Time
Lacy, Al 1015

So Wild a Heart
Camp, Candace 241, 346

Soft and Others
Wilson, F. Paul 706

Soft Metal
Brand, Max 434

Soft Money
Wishnia, K.J.A. 217

A Soft Place to Fall
Bretton, Barbara 225

Soft Rain
Cornelissen, Cornelia 464

The Soft Touch
Krahn, Betina 321

Sojourn
Salvatore, R.A. 556

Soldier in Paradise
Wohl, Burton 950

A Soldier of the Great War
Helprin, Mark 857

Soldiers
Dalmas, John **742**

A Soldier's Duty
Ricks, Thomas E. **1186**

Soldiers Live
Cook, Glen 606

Sole Survivor
Koontz, Dean R. 661

Solis
Attanasio, A.A. 736

Solo Command
Allston, Aaron 516

Some Days You Get the Bear
Block, Lawrence 85, 175

Some Enchanted Season
Pappano, Marilyn 366

Some Wildflower in My Heart
Turner, Jamie Langston 1055

Someday Soon
Taylor, Janelle 413

Someone in the Dark
Derleth, August 671

Someone Like You
Dahl, Roald 48

Someone to Love
Michaels, Kasey 229, 319, 353, 354, 375

Someone to Watch over Me
Bausch, Richard 1147, 1155

Someone to Watch over Me
Churchill, Jill **33**, **839**, 928

Someone to Watch over Me
Kleypas, Lisa 319, 342, 346, 375, 402

Someplace to Be Flying
De Lint, Charles 539

Something about Eve
Salonen, Debra 387

Something More
Cornell, Paul 533, **738**

Something to Celebrate
Mason, Felicia 300

Something to Kill For
Holtzer, Susan 69, 160

Something Wicked
Beverley, Jo 260

Something Wicked This Way Comes
Bradbury, Ray 623

Sometimes They Bite
Block, Lawrence 117

Sometimes You Get the Bear
Block, Lawrence 147

Somewhere I'll Find You
Kleypas, Lisa 319

Somewhere in France
Gardiner, John Rolfe 857

Somewhere My Love
Fox, Karen 287

A Son Comes Home
Bentz, Joseph 988, 1024, 1038

A Song for Arbonne
Kay, Guy Gavriel 532

The Song of Erin Series
Hoff, B.J. 1013, 1015, 1026, 1027, 1060

The Song of Phaid the Gambler
Farren, Mick 790

Song of the Axe
Dann, John R. 879, 962

Song of the Exile
Davenport, Kiana 1059

Song of the River
Harrison, Sue 879

Song of the Wolf
Bittner, Rosanne 467

Songs of a Dead Dreamer
Ligotti, Thomas 700

Sonnets for Midnight
Wandrei, Donald 669

The Sons of Noah and Other Stories
Cady, Jack 707

Sophie's Choice
Styron, William 1106

The Sorcerer's Chessman
Hansom, Mark 646

The Sorcerers of Majipoor
Silverberg, Robert 592

The Sorcerers of Sodom
Elwood, Roger 637

Sorcerer's World
Broderick, Damien 726

The Sorceress in Stained Glass
Dalby, Richard 615

Sorceress of the Witch World
Norton, Andre 554

The Sorcerous Sea
Severance, Carol 571

Sorrel
Cleary, Rita 443

Sorrow's Light
Warrington, Freda 609

Sorry Now
Zubro, Mark Richard 221

The Sot-Weed Factor
Barth, John 950

Soul Harvest
LaHaye, Tim 1016

Soul Mountain
Gao, Xingjian 1098, 1170

Soul of the Fire
Goodkind, Terry 549, 550

Soul of the Robot
Bayley, Barrington J. 780

Soul of the Sacred Earth
Munn, Vella 911

The Soul Slayer
Doherty, P.C. 65

Soul Survivor
Plunkett, Susan 371, 372

The Soulforge
Weis, Margaret 611, 612

Soulsmith
Deitz, Tom 539, 568

The Sounds of Rescue, the Signs of Hope
Flynn, Robert 451

South of Sanity
Ledbetter, Suzann 369

Southern Comforts
Ross, JoAnn 386

The Southern Sisters Series
George, Anne 15, 91, 114, 163

The Southern Woman
Spencer, Elizabeth 1079, 1115, 1157, **1201**

Southwest of Heaven
Tippette, Giles 509

The Sowers Trilogy
Leon, Bonnie 1040

Space for Hire
Nolan, William F. 756, 813

Space Wasters
Garnett, David 752

Spadework
Pronzini, Bill 99, 147, 174, 175

Spandau Phoenix
Iles, Greg 123

Spangle
Jennings, Gary 889

The Spanish Bit Saga
Coldsmith, Don 911

Spanish Blood
Blakely, Mike 492, 505

The Spanish Bride
McCabe, Amanda **349**

Spanish Jack
Conley, Robert J. **447**, **842**

Spanking Watson
Friedman, Kinky 72

Spares
Smith, Michael Marshall 677

Sparrowhawk—Jack Frake
Cline, Edward **840**

Speak of the Devil
Gores, Joe 40, 85, 175

Speaking Dreams
Park, Severna 774

Speaking in Tongues
Deaver, Jeffery 57

A Special Kind of Family
Berger, Eileen 968, 974

The Specialty of the House
Ellin, Stanley 48, 117

A Species of Revenge
Eccles, Marjorie 64

A Spell for the Fulfillment of Desire
Webb, Don 689

Spell of the Witch World
Norton, Andre 576

A Spell of Winter
Dunmore, Helen 850

The Spell Sword
Bradley, Marion Zimmer 576

Spellbinder
Bowkett, Stephen 724

Spellbound
Vande Velde, Vivian 519, 594

Spence + Lila
Mason, Bobbie Ann 1155

Spherical Harmonic
Asaro, Catherine **716**

Sphynxes Wild
Friesner, Esther 537

Spiced to Death
King, Peter 135

Spider Woman's Granddaughters
Allen, Paula Gunn 467

The Spider's Web
Tremayne, Peter 209, 944

Spies, Lies, and Lovers
Hayes, Sally Tyler 414

Spikes
Griffith, Michael 1114, 1132

Spinneret
Zahn, Timothy 812

Spiral
Healy, Jeremiah 111

The Spiral Dance
Garcia y Robertson, R. 546, 869

Spirit
Masterton, Graham 672

The Spirit of Dorsai
Dickson, Gordon R. 750

Spirit of Love
Wilson, Rachel 421

Spirit of the Eagle
Munn, Vella 911

Spirit of the Stone
Furey, Maggie **545**

The Spirit Returns
Burgin, Richard **1087**

The Spirit Woman
Coel, Margaret 35, 444

Spirits White as Lightning
Lackey, Mercedes **568**

The Spitfire
Birmingham, Sonya 332

Split Heirs
Watt-Evans, Lawrence 524, 588

The Sporting Club
Browning, Sinclair 28

Spotlight
Bellacera, Carole 231

SPQR
Roberts, John Maddox 924

The SPQR Series
Roberts, John Maddox 920

The Spring Cleaning Murders
Cannell, Dorothy 31

The Sputnik Sweetheart
Murakami, Haruki 1199

The Spy's Bride
Collum, Lynn 258

The Square Root of Man
Tenn, William 803

Squeezeplay
Nighbert, David F. 188

Squelch
Halkin, John 762

The Squire's Tale
Frazer, Margaret 70, 865, 933, 934

Stage Trails West
Bonham, Frank **427**

The Stain
Kraus, Harry Lee 1012

Stainless Steel Hearts
Kraus, Harry Lee 1012

Stakeout on Page Street
Gores, Joe 41, 99, 201

Stalker
Kellerman, Faye 1074

Stalking Darkness
Flewelling, Lynn 544

The Stalking Horse
Monfredo, Miriam Grace 159, 909

Stalking Moon
Cole, David **39**

Stalking Tender Prey
Constantine, Storm 536

Stalking the Angel
Crais, Robert 98

Stalking the Unicorn
Resnick, Mike 756

Stallion Gate
Smith, Martin Cruz 1078

The Stan Kraychik Series
Michaels, Grant 176

Stand-In Groom
Brockmann, Suzanne 236

Stand on Zanzibar
Brunner, John 758

Standoff
Brown, Sandra 245, 1086

The Stanley Hastings Series
Hall, Parnell 72

Star Bones Weep the Blood of Angels
Storm, Sue 689

Star Brat
Morressey, John 749

The Star Colony
Laumer, Keith 733

Star-Crossed
Krinard, Susan 310

Star Fox
Anderson, Poul 761

Star Hawk
Maloney, Mack 768

The Star King
Grant, Susan 310

The Star Kings
Hamilton, Edmond 769

Star of Cursrah
Emery, Clayton 597, 601

Star Prey
Ehly, Ehren M. 619

The Star Scroll
Rawn, Melanie 544

A Star Shines over Mt. Morris Park
Roth, Henry 1160

Star Soldiers
Norton, Andre 729, **784**, 809

The Star Stone
Stasheff, Christopher 600

Star Struck
McDermid, Val 154

Starborne
Silverberg, Robert 726, 797

The Starbuck Chronicles
Cornwell, Bernard 843

Starcarbon
Gilchrist, Ellen 1200

Starcatcher
Potter, Patricia 373

Stardoc
Viehl, S.L. 805

Starfall
Greenberg, Martin H. 552, 754

Starfighters of Adumar
Allston, Aaron 516

Starfinder
Potter, Patricia 373

Starfish
Watts, Peter 808

The Stargazey
Grimes, Martha 92

Starhawk
Maloney, Mack **769**

Starkeeper
Potter, Patricia 373

Stark's War
Hemry, John G. 742

The Starletta Duvall Series
Smith-Levin, Judith 21, 220

Starlight
Jarrett, Miranda 307, 308

Starship
Anderson, Poul 788

Starswarm
Pournelle, Jerry 780

Starwolf
Hamilton, Edmond 768

Stealing Shadows
Hooper, Kay 410

The Steam Driven Boy
Sladek, John 798

The Steampunk Trilogy
Di Filippo, Paul 607, 745

Steelheart
Dietz, William C. 746

The Stepford Wives
Levin, Ira 668

The Stephanie Plum Series
Evanovich, Janet 13, 144, 198

Steppin' on a Rainbow
Friedman, Kinky **72**

The Stewart Hoag Series
Handler, David 218

The Stickmen
Lee, Edward 661, 667

Stickrock
Crum, Laura 439, 443, 506

A Stiff Risotto
Temple, Lou Jane 207

The Still
Feintuch, David 544, 550, 606

Still She Haunts Me
Roiphe, Katie 847, 926, **927**, **1189**

Stillwater
Weld, William F. **955**

Stillwater Smith
Roderus, Frank 499

The Sting of Senorita Scorpion: A Western Trio
Savage, Les Jr. 500, 501

Stinger
McCammon, Robert R. 661

Stinker from Space
Service, Pamela 749

A Stitch in Time
Ferris, Monica 67

Stocking Stuffers
Lansdowne, Judith A. 232, 248

A Stockingful of Joy
Howell, Hannah 263

Stolen Away
Collins, Max Allan 841

The Stolen Bride
Paul, Susan Spencer 368

Stolen Faces
Bishop, Michael 733, 810

The Stolen Gods
Page, Jake 61

Stolen Gold
Brand, Max **433**

A Stolen Tongue
Holman, Sheri 86, 194

Stone Angels
Jefferies, Mike 676

The Stone Circle
Goshgarian, Gary 676

The Stone Flower Garden
Smith, Deborah 401

The Stone Maiden
King, Susan 266, 316

The Stone of Farewell
Williams, Tad 530, 580, 609

Stone of Tears
Goodkind, Terry 549

The Stone Prince
Patton, Fiona 586

Stone Song
Blevins, Winfred 890

The Stone War
Robins, Madeleine 614

The Stone Woman
Ali, Tariq 893

Stonehenge
Cornwell, Bernard 843, 879

Stonekiller
Janes, J. Robert 126, 888

Stones from the River
Hegi, Ursula 1124

Stopping at Slowyear
Pohl, Frederik 728

The Store
Little, Bentley 668

Stories from Mesa Country
Coleman, Jane Candia 433, 445

Stories of Darkness and Dread
Brennan, Joseph Payne 707

The Stories of Elizabeth Spencer
Spencer, Elizabeth 1201

The Stories of Eva Luna
Allende, Isabel 1067

Stories of Exile and Alienation
Hussein, Abdullah 1129

The Stories of Paul Bowles
Bowles, Paul **1080**, 1115

The Stories of Ray Bradbury
Bradbury, Ray 623, 678

Storm
Christner, Dianne 979

Storm
Grant, Reg 1031

Storm Breaking
Lackey, Mercedes 569

Storm Caller
Severance, Carol 608

Storm Force
Bunch, Chris 729

The Storm of Heaven
Harlan, Thomas 562

A Storm of Swords
Martin, George R.R. 526, 596

Storm of Time
Dark, Eleanor 819, 904

A Storm of Wings
Harrison, M. John 586

Storm over the Lightening L
Blair, Clifford 458

Storm Riders
Gorman, Ed 446, 448, 456

Storm Track
Maron, Margaret 219

Stormblade
Berberick, Nancy Varian 525

Stormy Weather
Hiaasen, Carl 115, 1214

Stormy Weather
Woods, Paula L. **220**

Story and Other Stories
Davis, Lydia 1099

The Story of a Marriage
Baldwin, Louisa 618

The Story Teller
Coel, Margaret 35, 444

The Storyteller
Vargas Llosa, Mario 1211

Stowaway to Mars
Wyndham, John 785

Straight from the Heart
Delinsky, Barbara 1101

Straight on 'Til Morning
Golden, Christopher **642**, 659

The Strand
Vaughn, Ellen 1023

Stranded with the Sergeant
Linz, Cathie 334, **335**

Strange Bedfellows
Witten, Matt 218

Strange Days
Dozois, Gardner **748**, 786

Strange Eons
Bloch, Robert 670

Strange Highways
Koontz, Dean R. 706

Strange Seas and Shores
Davidson, Avram 745

Strange Tales from the Strand
Adrian, Jack 615

Strange Things and Stranger Places
Campbell, Ramsey 688

Strange Trades
Di Filippo, Paul **745**, 748

The Stranger
DeWitt, Jean 327

Stranger in My Arms
Kleypas, Lisa 319

A Stranger in the Mirror
Sheldon, Sidney 1158

Strangers
Dozois, Gardner 748

Strangers at Dawn
Thornton, Elizabeth 416

Strangers in the Night
Riley, Eugenia 380

Stranger's Touch
Carrington, Tori 251

A Stranger's Wife
Osborne, Maggie 364

Strangewood
Golden, Christopher 642

Strathmere's Bride
Navin, Jacqueline 360

The Strawberry Season
Stirling, Jessica 938

Strawman's Hammock
Wimberley, Darryl **216**

The Strayed Sheep of Charun
Roberts, John Maddox 718

Street of Knives
Harris, Cyril 912

The Streeter Series
Stone, Michael 213

Streets of Fire
Cook, Thomas H. 122, 166

Streets of Laredo
McMurtry, Larry 479

Strike Three, You're Dead
Rosen, R.D. 188

Strip Poker
Bartholomew, Nancy **13**

Strip Tease
Hiaasen, Carl 115

Striped Holes
Broderick, Damien 726

Strong Motion
Franzen, Jonathan 1113

Stryker's Wife
Browning, Dixie 341

A Student of Weather
Hay, Elizabeth 1156

Studs Lonigan
Farrell, James 1117

A Study in Death
McDowell, Iain **155**

A Study in Sorcery
Kurland, Michael 756

The Sub
Disch, Thomas M. 649

Substitute Father
Winn, Bonnie K. 1061

Subterranean
Rollins, James 792

The Subtle Serpent
Tremayne, Peter 209, 944

Subtraction
Robison, Mary 1188

Succumb
Dee, Ron 620

A Sudden Change of Heart
Bradford, Barbara Taylor 1103, 1174

The Sudden Star
Sargent, Pamela 805

A Sudden Wild Magic
Jones, Diana Wynne 542

Suddenly Home
Lough, Loree 1063

Suddenly You
Kleypas, Lisa **319**, 320, 419

Suffer Little Children
Tremayne, Peter 209, 944

The Sugar House
Lippman, Laura 143, 205

Sugarplum Surprises
Fairchild, Elisabeth **275**

A Suggestion of Death
Wesson, Marianne 121

A Suitable Boy
Seth, Vikram 1178

Suite Seduction
Kelly, Leslie 333

Sula
Morrison, Toni 918, 1207

Summer Dreams
Jones, Veda Boyd 969, 986

Summer in Baden-Baden
Tsypkin, Leonid **946**

Summer Island
Hannah, Kristin 231

Summer Moon
Landis, Jill Marie 415, **471**

Summer of Pearls
Blakely, Mike 463, 512, 827

Summer of the Drums
Olsen, T.V. 873

Summer of the Soldiers
Chastain, Sandra 228

The Summer Queen
Vinge, Joan D. 757, 789

Summer's End
Hayworth, Lynne 288, **297**

Summer's End
Seidel, Kathleen Gilles 239

Summer's Promise
Brand, Irene 965, **974**, 1036, 1041, 1043, 1057

The Summoning God
Gear, Kathleen O'Neal 424, 871, 962

The Sun Coast Chronicles
Blackstock, Terri 1048

The Sun, He Dies
Highwater, Jamake 889

The Sun Is God
Noonan, Michael 959

Sun Mountain
Wheeler, Richard S. 457, 470, 488, 512

The Sunbird
Smith, Wilbur 792

Sunburn
Shames, Laurence 107

Sunburn Lake
De Haven, Tom 1100

Suncatchers
Turner, Jamie Langston 1055

Sunderlies Seeking
Greeno, Gayle 571, 596

The Sundial
Jackson, Shirley 781

The Sunny Childs Series
Birmingham, Ruth 143

Sunrise
Jarrett, Miranda 297, 307, 308, 342

Sunrise on Stradbury Square
Fell, Doris Elaine **992**

Sunrise Song
Eagle, Kathleen 450

The Sunroom
Lewis, Beverly 980, 1032

Sunset Express
Crais, Robert 47

A Sunset Touch
Eccles, Marjorie **64**

Sunsets
Gunn, Robin Jones 993

The Super Barbarians
Brunner, John 746

Super-Cannes
Ballard, J.G. **1070**

The Superintendent's Daughter
Eccles, Marjorie 64

Surfacing
Atwood, Margaret 1138

The Surgeon
Gerritsen, Tess **78**

Surrender
Hingle, Metsy 301

Surrender My Love
Lindsey, Johanna 337

Surrender of the Heart
John, Sally D. 1006

The Surrogate Assassin
Leppek, Christopher 158

The Survival of Juan Oro
Brand, Max **434**

Survivor
Janiver, Laurence M. 763

Survivor
King, Tabitha 1184

Survivor's Medicine
Two-Rivers, E. Donald 455, 500

The Susan Henshaw Series
Wolzien, Valerie 89

The Susan Wren Series
Weir, Charlene 145

The Susanna, Lady Appleton Series
Emerson, Kathy Lynn 29, 834

Suspension
Crabbe, Richard E. 936

Suspicion of Betrayal
Parker, Barbara 167

Suspicion of Deceit
Parker, Barbara 167

Suspicion of Guilt
Parker, Barbara 167

Suspicion of Innocence
Parker, Barbara 167

Suspicion of Malice
Parker, Barbara 167

Suspicion of Vengeance
Parker, Barbara **167**

Suzanne's Diary for Nicholas
Patterson, James **1181**

Swamp Foetus
Brite, Poppy Z. 629, 656

The Swan Maiden
King, Susan 244, 316

Swarm
Herzog, Arthur 762

Sweet Boundless
Heitzmann, Kristen 998

Sweet Charity
Wilson, Rachel 421

Sweet Georgia
Birmingham, Ruth 18

Sweet Light
Arnold, Judith 306

Sweet Myth-tery of Life
Asprin, Robert Lynn 521

Sweet Nothings
Anderson, Catherine **225**

Sweet Poison
Roberts, David 183, 923

Sweet St. Louis
Tyree, Omar 1210

Sweet, Savage Death
Papazoglou, Orania 49

Sweet Success
Mallery, Susan **344**

Sweet Talking Man
Krahn, Betina 253, 284, 321, 342, 419

Sweet Tranquility
Bell, Donna 230

Sweeter than Sin
Garland, Kit 270

The Sweetest Thing
Freethy, Barbara 344

Sweetheart, Sweetheart
Taylor, Bernard 620

A Sweetness to the Soul
Kirkpatrick, Jane 1011

Sweetwater
Garlock, Dorothy 290

Swell Foop
Anthony, Piers **518**, 521

Swift as Desire
Esquivel, Laura **1112**

Swim the Moon
Brandon, Paul **529**

The Switch
Brown, Sandra 245

Sword-Born
Roberson, Jennifer 580, 591, 592, 593

Sword-Breaker
Roberson, Jennifer 592, 593

The Sword in the Storm
Gemmell, David 548

The Sword Maiden
King, Susan **316**

Sword-Maker
Roberson, Jennifer 593

The Sword of Bedwyr
Salvatore, R.A. 548

The Sword of Flame
Furey, Maggie 545

Sword of MacLeod
Fox, Karen 287

The Sword of Maiden's Tears
Edghill, Rosemary 575

The Sword of Shannara
Brooks, Terry 584

Sword of the Demon
Lupoff, Richard A. 531

The Sword of Winter
Randall, Marta 595

Sword-Singer
Roberson, Jennifer 593

Swordmaker
Roberson, Jennifer 592

Swords Across the Thames
Garwood, Haley E. 883

Swords Against Death
Leiber, Fritz 589, 599

Swordsinger
Roberson, Jennifer 591, 592

The Swordsman's Oath
McKenna, Juliet E. 578

Swordsmistress of Chaos
Kirk, Richard 608

Sylvia and Ted
Tennant, Emma 848, 852

The Sylvia Strange Series
Lovett, Sarah 121

Synners
Cadigan, Pat 731

T

The Tail of the Dragon
Wise, Robert L. 989, 991

Tails You Lose
Smedman, Lisa 614

The Tainted Snuff Box
Stevens, Rosemary 815, 822, 853

Take a Thief
Lackey, Mercedes **569**

Take Back Plenty
Greenland, Colin 770

Take by Storm
Madden, Sandra 328, 342

The Taking
Beman, Donald 620

A Talent for Trouble
Barbour, Anne 291

Tales from Earthsea
Le Guin, Ursula K. 571, 582

Tales from the Texas Woods
Moorcock, Michael 433

Tales of Devilry and Doom
Ford, John B. 635, **636**

Tales of Gooseflesh and Laughter
Wyndham, John 727

Tales of H.P. Lovecraft
Lovecraft, H.P. 671

The Tales of London Series
Blackwell, Lawana 1020

Tales of Love and Death
Congdon, Don 643

Tales of Mithgar
McKiernan, Dennis L. 579

Tales of Pain and Wonder
Kiernan, Caitlin R. 656

Tales of the Galactic Midway
Resnick, Mike 788

Tales of the Grotesque
Lewis, L.A. 622

Tales of the Velvet Comet
Resnick, Mike **788**

Tales of the Wild West
Brand, Max 430, 452

Tales of Uncle Trapspringer
McKeone, Dixie Lee 584

Tales of Yesteryear
Auchincloss, Louis 1209

Talion Revenant
Stackpole, Michael A. 599

The Talisman
King, Stephen 642, 659, 1140

Talk about Love
Shelley, Deborah 343

Talk Before Sleep
Berg, Elizabeth 1103

Talking in the Dark
Louis, Laura Glen **1149**

Talking to Strange Men
Rendell, Ruth 214

Tall, Dark, and Difficult
Coughlin, Patricia **261**

Tall, Dark, and Wanted
Hayes, Morgan 414

Tall, Dead, and Handsome
Griffin, Annie **91**

Tallchief
McCall, Dinah 330

Talonspotting
Harman, Andrew 588

Tam Lin
Dean, Pamela 579

The Tamara Hayle Series
Wesley, Valerie Wilson 21, 220

Tame the Wild Wind
Bittner, Rosanne 471

The Taming
Deveraux, Jude 269

Taming Lord Renwick
Savery, Jeanne 389

The Taming of Jackson Cade
James, B.J. 246

Taming the Duke
Manning, Jackie 259

Taming the Wolf
Simmons, Deborah 396

Tangents
Bear, Greg 766

Tangle Box
Brooks, Terry 530

A Tangled Web
Bell, Donna **230**

Taos
Blacker, Irwin R. 476, 510

A Tapestry of Lions
Roberson, Jennifer 591

The Tar Aiym Krang
Foster, Alan Dean 772

Tara Road
Binchy, Maeve 1169

Target: Point Zero
Maloney, Mack 768, 769

Targett
Randisi, Robert J. 497

Tarnished Icons
Kaminsky, Stuart M. 130

Tatja Grimm's World
Vinge, Vernor 807

Taylor's Temptation
Brockmann, Suzanne **242**

Tea from an Empty Cup
Cadigan, Pat 731

Tears in a Bottle
Bambola, Sylvia **966**

Tears of Ice
Livingston, Gary 954

Tears of the Heart
Paine, Lauran **493**

The Tears of the Madonna
Herman, George 836

Tears of the Moon
Roberts, Nora 383

Tears of the Night Sky
Baker, Linda P. 612

The Teddy Morelli Series
French, Linda 51

Teeth
van Belkom, Edo 565, **705**

Tehanu
Le Guin, Ursula K. 571

Tell Me I'm Dreamin'
Snoe, Eboni 403

Tell Me Lies
Crusie, Jennifer 286, 292

Tell Me Lies
Dain, Claudia 266

Tell My Horse
Hurston, Zora Neale 1128

Tell No One
Coben, Harlan 47, 123

Tell No Tales
Bland, Eleanor Taylor 21

The Telling
Le Guin, Ursula K. 571, 780

The Telling of Lies
Findley, Timothy 42

The Tempe Brennan Series
Reichs, Kathy 66, 197

Temple
Reilly, Matt 1070

The Temple of Elemental Evil
Reid, Thomas M. 563

The Temple of Optimism
Fleming, James 838

Temple of the Muses
Roberts, John Maddox 184

Temple of the Winds
Goodkind, Terry 549, 550

Temple's Prize
Castle, Linda Lea 253

Tempt Me Twice
Smith, Barbara Dawson **400**

Temptation
Deveraux, Jude 1148

The Temptation
Moser, Nancy 1030

The Temptation of Rory Monahan
Bevarly, Elizabeth 235, 236

Tempting
Johnson, Susan 282, 285

Tempting Fate
Sawyer, Meryl 222, 283

Tempting Fortune
Beverley, Jo 307, 308

Tempting Harriet
Balogh, Mary 262

Tempting Mr. Wright
Civil-Brown, Sue 250, 256

Tempting Tess
Jarrett, Liz 223

The Temptress
Delacroix, Claire **269**

Ten and Me
Boggs, Johnny D. 509

Ten North Frederick
O'Hara, John 1090

The Ten Thousand
Ford, Michael Curtis 859, 931

Tender Escape
Poarch, Candice 365

Tender Love
Brand, Irene 974

The Tender Vine
Heitzmann, Kristen **998**

The Tender Years
Oke, Janette 1034

Tenderness and Fire
Funderburk, Robert 1005

Tending to Virginia
McCorkle, Jill 1157

Tenebrea's Hope
Dawson, Roxann **743**

Tennant's Rock
McGiffen, Steve **478**, 855, 877, 910

Terminal
Cook, Robin 78

Terminal Justice
Gansky, Alton 975

Terminal Logic
Scott, Jefferson 989

The Terminal Man
Crichton, Michael 808

Terminal Mercy
Stewart, Ed 1012

Terminal Weird
Remick, Jack 616

Terms of Endearment
McMurtry, Larry 1181

The Terracotta Palace
Maybury, Anne 314

The Terror
Machen, Arthur 666

Terror by Night
Benson, E.F. 622

Terror Incognita
Thomas, Jeffrey 639, 693, 697

Tess
Smith, Bobbi 361

The Tess Darcy Series
Hager, Jean 32

The Tess Monaghan Series
Lippman, Laura 18

The Test of Love
Brand, Irene 974, 1022

A Test of Wills
Todd, Charles 208, 943

Testament of the Dragon
Weis, Margaret 612

Tested by Fire
Herman, Kathy 1001

Testimony
Chadbourn, Mark 533

The Texan's Dream
Thomas, Jodi **415**

The Texan's Touch
Thomas, Jodi 415

Texas
Smith, Debra White 1048, 1049

Texas Angel
Pella, Judith 1040

Texas Destiny
Heath, Lorraine 415

Texas Empire
Braun, Matt 425, 462, 469, 497

Texas Rose
Smith, Debra White 1049

A Texas Sky
Wick, Lori 1059

Texas Splendor
Heath, Lorraine 270

Texican Blood Fight
Andrews, Patrick E. 438

The Texts of Festival
Farren, Mick 764

That Fateful Lightning
Parry, Richard 903

That Scandalous Heiress
Kirkland, Martha 230, 318

The Theft
Kane, Andrea 312

Their Eyes Were Watching God
Hurston, Zora Neale 1128

Their Forever Love
Welsh, Kate 1047, 1057, 1061

Them
Oates, Joyce Carol 1174

Then and Now
Hix, Willa 372

The Theo Bloomer Series
Hadley, Joan 103

A Theory of Relativity
Mitchard, Jacquelyn 1086, 1200

Theory of War
Brady, Joan 846

There and Back Again
Murphy, Pat 781

There Are No Ghosts in the Soviet Union and Other Stories
Hill, Reginald 146

There Comes a Season
Steward, Carol 1052

There Was a Season
Olsen, T.V. 487, 873

There Will Be Time
Anderson, Poul 754

The Theresa Fortunato Series
Green, Kate 52, 79, 140

The Theresa Galloway Series
Grimes, Terris McMahon 21

These Granite Islands
Stonich, Sarah 850, 1077, 1101, 1109

These High Green Hills
Karon, Jan 1007

These Is My Words
Turner, Nancy E. 947

These Old Shades
Heyer, Georgette 404

They Called Her Mrs. Doc
Oke, Janette 1025

They Return at Evening
Wakefield, H. Russell 622

Thicker than Blood
Lutz, John 147

Thief of Always
Barker, Clive 1071

Thief of Dreams
Balogh, Mary 298

The Thief of Dreams
Cole, Adrian 569

A Thief of Time
Hillerman, Tony 61

The Thief-Taker
Banks, T.F. 10, 182, 815, **820**, 822, 853, 915

Thief Taker
Jeffreys, J.G. 182

The Thief's Gamble
McKenna, Juliet E. 569, 578, 589, 601

Thieves' House
Leiber, Fritz 569

A Thin Ghost and Others
James, M.R. 650

The Thin Man
Hammett, Dashiell 99

Thin Moon and Cold Mist
Gear, Kathleen O'Neal 871

The Thin Woman
Cannell, Dorothy 36

The Thing
Foster, Alan Dean 660

The Thing in the Woods
Williams, Harper 646

The Thing on the Doorstep and Other Weird Stories
Lovecraft, H.P. 670, **671**

Things Beyond Midnight
Nolan, William F. 678

Things Remembered
Bockoven, Georgia 239

Thinks—
Lodge, David 1069

The Third Cry to Legba and Other Invocations
Wellman, Manly Wade 707

Third Man Out
Stevenson, Richard 897

The Third Witch
Reisert, Rebecca **921**

Thirdspace
David, Peter 770

Thirteen Horrors of Halloween
Waugh, Carolyn-Rossel 628

Thirteenth Woman and Other Stories
Davis, Lydia 1099

The Thirty-Third Hour
Chefitz, Mitchell **978**, 1064

This Body
Doud, Laurel 849

This Club Frowns on Murder
Borowitz, Albert 34

This Dog for Hire
Benjamin, Carol Lea 16

This Far, No Further
Wessel, John 213

This Flesh Unknown
Braunbeck, Gary A. 1071

This Heart of Mine
Phillips, Susan Elizabeth 226, 256, 264, **369**

This Is All I Ask
Kurland, Lynn 323

This Is My Blood
Wilson, David Niall 690

This Little Piggy Went to Murder
Hart, Ellen 105

This Man Colter
Black, Michelle 423

This Mortal Coil
Asquith, Cynthia 680

This Ol' Drought Ain't Broke Us Yet
Garry, Jim 433

This Old Murder
Wolzien, Valerie 219

This Perfect Family
Potter, Patricia 339

This Rock
Morgan, Robert **910**

This Rough Magic
Stewart, Mary 314

This Side of Heaven
Robards, Karen 297, 352

This Side of Paradise
Wolverton, Cheryl 1036

This Symbiotic Fascination
Jacob, Charlee 658

This Time for Keeps
Kane, Kathleen 313

This Time Forever
Steward, Carol **1052**

The Thomas and Charlotte Pitt Series
Perry, Anne 915

The Thomas Black Series
Emerson, Earl 174

The Thomas Lynley/Barbara Havers Series
George, Elizabeth 30, 92

The Thomas Street Horror
Paul, Raymond 2

Thornhold
Cunningham, Elaine 525

Those Other People
King, Mary 469

Those Who Hunt the Night
Hambly, Barbara 686, 695, 922, 963

Though None Go with Me
Jenkins, Jerry B. 1005, 1010

A Thousand Words for Stranger
Czerneda, Julie E. 740

The Thran
King, J. Robert 564, 565

Three Apples Fell from Heaven
Marcom, Micheline Aharonian 1105

The Three Cornered War
Dalmas, John 741, 742

The Three Dirty Women Series
Herman, Julie Wray 181

Three for a Letter
Reed, Mary **180**, **920**

Three Hainish Novels
Le Guin, Ursula K. 571

The Three Lives of Littleton Blue
Bowman, Doug 504, 514

Three to Get Deadly
Evanovich, Janet 274

Three Weddings and a Giggle
Higgs, Liz Curtis 986

Three Wishes
Delinsky, Barbara 1135, 1200

Threshold
Kiernan, Caitlin R. 656

Threshold
Myers, Bill 981, 1032

Thrice Bound
Gellis, Roberta **547**

Thrice upon a Time
Hogan, James P. 754

Thrillers
Chizmar, Richard 628

Throne of Isis
Tarr, Judith 603

Through a Gold Eagle
Monfredo, Miriam Grace 159, 909

Through the Dolls' House Door
Gardam, Jane 870

Thumbsucker
Kirn, Walter 1109, 1141

Thunder and Roses
Putney, Mary Jo 227, 298

Thunder from Jerusalem
Thoene, Bodie 942, 1053

Thunder Horse
Bowen, Peter 465, 472, 475, 477, 511

Thunder in the East
Maloney, Mack 768

The Thunder Keeper
Coel, Margaret **35**, **444**

Thunder Road
Curry, Chris 675

Thunderhead
Preston, Douglas 792

Thursday's Child
Chaikin, Linda 977

Thus Was Adonis Murdered
Caudwell, Sarah 36

The Thyme Will Tell Series
Stallsmith, Audrey 970, 981, 1008

Tideland
Cullin, Mitch 1121

Tides of War
Pressfield, Steven 931

Tie-Fast Country
Flynn, Robert **451**

Ties of Love
Wall, Anita 421

Ties of Power
Czerneda, Julie E. 740

Tiger Skin
Hunt, Violet 646

Tiger's Palette
Fiedler, Jacqueline 68

Tight as a Tick
Kelner, Toni L.P. 69, 160

Tight Little Stitches in a Dead Man's Back
Lansdale, Joe R. 708

Tik Tok
Sladek, John 798

Timberline
Bedford, Deborah 967

Time and Again
Finney, Jack 546

Time Exposure
Lutz, John 147

Time for the Death of a King
Dukthas, Ann 65

Time Future
McArthur, Maxine **770**

Time in Eclipse
Garnett, David 752

The Time of Feasting
Farren, Mick 699

The Time of Her Life
Dew, Robb Forman 850, 1102

Time of the Rabies
Laxalt, Robert 1083

Time of the Vampires
Elrod, P.N. 631

A Time of War
Morris, Gilbert 1056

Time Safari
Drake, David 754

The Time Streams
King, J. Robert 515, 566

A Time to Dance
Kingsbury, Karen 993, 1010

Time to Hunt
Hunter, Stephen 122, 887, 1127

A Time to Kill
Grisham, John 1088, 1139

Timeless
Scott, DeLoras 391

Timeline
Crichton, Michael 869, 1071, 1204

A Timely Death
Neel, Janet 165

Timepool
Plunkett, Susan 371, 372

Times and Seasons
LaHaye, Beverly 988

Time's Arrow
Amis, Martin 1078

Time's Witness
Malone, Michael 1153

The Timothy Diary
Edwards, Gene 990

Tin Cup in the Storm Country
Patten, Lewis B. 494

Tin Star
Randisi, Robert J. 497

Tipping the Velvet
Waters, Sarah 1213

'Tis the Season
Arnold, Judith 226

'Tis the Season
Hill, Donna **300**

'Tis the Season
Paul, Susan Spencer **367**

The Tish Series
Rinehart, Mary Roberts 191

The Titan
Stewart, Fred Mustard 937

Titan
Varley, John 726

The Titanic Murders
Collins, Max Allan 5

The Titas Diary
Edwards, Gene 990

To Catch a Cook
Pence, Joanne 170

To Davy Jones Below
Dunn, Carola 923

To Die For
Neel, Janet 165

To Dream Again
John, Sally D. 988, 1006

To Each His Own
Eagle, Kathleen 450

To Find a Place
Easton, Robert 431, 432, 435, 445

To Galilee with Love
Berger, Eileen 968

To Kiss a Spy
Feather, Jane **276**

To Kiss a Texan
Thomas, Jodi 415

To Live Forever
Vance, Jack 794

To Love and Honor
Brand, Irene 974, 987, 1021

To Perish in Penzance
Dams, Jeanne M. **54**

To Reign in Hell
Brust, Steven A. 553

To Rome with Love
Smith, Debra White 1048, **1049**

To Ruin a Queen
Buckley, Fiona 29, 834

To Say Nothing of the Dog
Willis, Connie 811

To Shield the Queen
Buckley, Fiona 29, 834

To Tame a Duke
Grasso, Patricia **293**

To Tame a Highland Warrior
Moning, Karen Marie 358

To Tame a Rogue
Kay, Linda 371

To Tame a Wild Heart
Fobes, Tracy **281**

To the End
Marshall, William 185

To the Hermitage
Bradbury, Malcolm 946, 1069

To the Honor of the Fleet
Pilpel, Robert H. 866

To Trust a Stranger
Robards, Karen **381**

To Visit the Queen
Duane, Diane 574

To Wed in Texas
Thomas, Jodi 415

The Tobermory Manuscript
Work, James C. 514

The Toby Peters Series
Kaminsky, Stuart M. 841, 928

The Todd Mills Series
Zimmerman, R.D. 221

Together We Kill
Spillane, Mickey **201**

The Tom Barnaby Series
Graham, Caroline 64, 116

The Tom Pollard Series
Lemarchand, Elizabeth 30

The Tom Ripley Series
Highsmith, Patricia 202

Tomahawk Canyon
Ballas, Jack 459, 492, 504, 505, 514

The Tomb
Wilson, F. Paul 710

Tombstone Conspiracy
Champlin, Tim 439, 440, 456, 514

The Tommyknockers
King, Stephen 660

Tomorrow I Die
Spillane, Mickey 41, 201

Tomorrow's Eve
Villiers de L'Isle Adam, Auguste **806**

Tongues of Conscience
Hichens, Robert 647

Tonight or Never
Joy, Dara 310

The Tonto Woman and other Western Stories
Leonard, Elmore 434, 461, 491

The Tony Hill/Carol Jordan Series
McDermid, Val 178

Too Far Afield
Grass, Gunter 1151

Too Good to Be True
Michaels, Kasey 226, 274, 353, 354

Too Hot to Sleep
Bond, Stephanie 240

Too Long at the Dance
Blakely, Mike 827

Too Many Tomcats and Other Feline Tales of Suspense
Collins, Barbara 26, 162

Too Much Temptation
Foster, Lori 285, **286**

Too Soon Dead
Kurland, Michael 899

Too Wicked to Love
Smith, Barbara Dawson 400

The Tooth Fairy
Joyce, Graham 655

Torments
Cantrell, Lisa 640

The Tortilla Curtain
Boyle, T. Coraghessan 1081, 1116, 1202

The Torturer's Apprentice
Biguenet, John 1087, 1142

The Tory Bauer Series
Taylor, Kathleen 13

Total Control
Baldacci, David 1141

Touch Not the Cat
Fobes, Tracy 281

Touch Not the Cat
Stewart, Mary 314, 776

A Touch of Betrayal
Palmer, Catherine 1027

A Touch of Black Velvet
Alexander, Carrie 333

Touch of Enchantment
Medeiros, Teresa 358

A Touch of Mortality
Granger, Ann 87

Touch of the Wolf
Krinard, Susan 322, 401

Touch the Face of God
Vaughan, Robert 1000

Touched by Magic
Durgin, Doranna 543

Touched by the Gods
Watt-Evans, Lawrence 549, 560, 561, 580, 585, 606, 610

Tough, Tough Toys for Tough, Tough Boys
Self, Will 1081

The Tower and the Hive
McCaffrey, Anne 772

The Tower of Babel
West, Morris L. 942

The Tower of Doom
Anthony, Mark 604

The Tower of Fear
Cook, Glen 586

Tower of Glass
Silverberg, Robert **797**

The Tower on the Rift
Irvine, Ian 560

The Town Called Hope Series
Palmer, Catherine 1014

Toxicology
Aylett, Steve **720**

The Toyotomi Blades
Furutani, Dale 150

Track of a Killer
Overholser, Stephen 488

The Trade Ellis Series
Browning, Sinclair 39, 125

Trader
De Lint, Charles 539

Tragic Casements
Onions, Oliver **680**

Trail of the Apache Kid
Patten, Lewis B. 494

Trail of the Rogues
Grove, Fred 459

A Trail to Wounded Knee
Champlin, Tim 439, 945

Trails in Darkness
Howard, Robert E. 589

Trails West
Cunningham, Eugene 445, 496

The Traitor's Daughter
Powell, Elizabeth **374**

Traitor's Moon
Flewelling, Lynn 544

The Tranquility Alternative
Steele, Allen 802

Transformation
Haydon, Elizabeth 555

The Translator
Just, Ward S. 1134

The Transvection Machine
Hoch, Edward D. 759

Trauma
Masterton, Graham 672

Traveling on One Leg
Muller, Herta 1168

Traveller
Adams, Richard 1065

The Treachery of Kings
Barrett, Neal Jr. **524**

The Treachery of Time
Gilbert, Anna 872

Treason
Nevin, David **912**

The Treason of Dortrean
Herniman, Marcus **557**

The Treasure
Kraus, Jim 1013

Treasure of the Templars
Champlin, Tim 439, 440, 487, 498

The Treasure of Timbuktu
Palmer, Catherine 1031

Treasures of the North
Peterson, Tracie 1042

Treasures of the Sun
Olsen, T.V. 486, **487**

The Treatment
Hayder, Mo **1123**

The Trees of Zharka
Mackenroth, Nancy 718

The Tres Navarre Series
Riordan, Rick 149

Triage
Johnson, Matt **651**

Trial by Fire
Blackstock, Terri 970, 971

The Trial of Soren Qvist
Lewis, Janet 956

The Trials of Angela
Criswell, Millie 264

The Trials of Tiffany Trott
Wolff, Isabel 252, 357, 359, 394, 1125

Trick or Treat
Chizmar, Richard **628**

Trick or Treat Murder
Meier, Leslie 157

Triple Play
Gunn, Elizabeth 93

Triple Witch
Graves, Sarah 89

Tripwire
Child, Lee 442

The Triumph of Katie Byrne
Bradford, Barbara Taylor 1074

The Triune Man
Lupoff, Richard A. 759

The Troll's Grindstone
Boyer, Elizabeth 583

Trooper Donovan
Roderus, Frank 499

Tropical Freeze
Hall, James W. 94

Trouble Comes Back
Snyder, Keith 199

Trouble in Paradise
Parker, Robert B. 168

Trouble in the Town Hall
Dams, Jeanne M. 54

Trouble Man
Gorman, Ed 456, 473

Trouble No More
Grooms, Anthony 1119

The Trouble with an Elf
Townsend, Tom 605

The Trouble with Harriet
Cannell, Dorothy 31

The Trouble with Harriet
Counts, Wilma **262**

The Trouble with Mary
Criswell, Millie 264, 274, 354, 369, 376, 380

The Troublesome Angel
Hansen, Valerie 965, 995

Trudging to Eden
Antieau, Kim 658

True Colours
Cornick, Nicola 259, 260

True Confessions
Gibson, Rachel **292**

True Devotion
Henderson, Dee 999, 1000

True History of the Kelly Gang
Carey, Peter 825, 842, 1176, 1183

True Love
Criswell, Millie 264

A True Prince
Sattler, Veronica 388

True Valor
Henderson, Dee **1000**, 1030

True Women
Windle, Janice Woods 513, 961

The Truelove Bride
Abe, Shana 281, 405

The Truest Heart
James, Samantha 406

The Truest Pleasure
Morgan, Robert 910

Truly Madly Yours
Gibson, Rachel 235, 256, 292, 376

The Truman Smith Series
Crider, Bill 112

The Trumpet Is Blown
Lamb, David 1105

Trumpet on the Land
Johnston, Terry C. 466

Trust Me on This
Westlake, Donald E. 115

Trust No One
Sawyer, Meryl 381

The Truth Can Get You Killed
Zubro, Mark Richard 221

The Truth Seeker
Henderson, Dee 999, 1000

The Truth Teller
Hunt, Angela Elwell 975, 1004

Trying to Save Piggy Sneed
Irving, John 1130

Tryst of Fate
Sharpe, Isabel 255

Tucker Peak
Mayor, Archer **151**

Tuesday's Child
Chaikin, Linda 977

Tularosa
McGarrity, Michael 149

Tumbled Wall
Browning, Dixie 246

The Tumbleweed Murders
Rothenberg, Rebecca **189**

Tumbleweeds
Henry, Will 452, 461, 468, 496, 503

A Tupolev Too Far
Aldiss, Brian W. 745

Turkey Day Murder
Meier, Leslie 157

Turn the Stars Upside Down
Johnston, Terry C. **466**, 824, 826, 842, **890**, 945

Turnabout
Healy, Jeremiah **111**

Turning on the Girls
Benard, Cheryl 1142, 1209

TV
Brown, Brian **1084**

Twanged
Clark, Carol Higgins 34, 1194

Twas the Night Before
Jenkins, Jerry B. 1005, 1033

Twenty-One
Just, Ward S. 1134

The Twenty-Seventh City
Franzen, Jonathan 1113

Twice Dead
Dearl, Elizabeth 428, 436, 442, 444, 472, 475, 502

Twice upon a Time
Little, Denise 574, 575

Twilight in Texas
Thomas, Jodi 270, 415

Twilight's End
Oltion, Jerry 785

Twin Blessings
Aarsen, Carolyne **965**, 1036, 1041, 1043

A Twist at the End
Saylor, Steven 95, 135

The Twisted Root
Perry, Anne 172, 915

The Two-Bear Mambo
Lansdale, Joe R. 472

Two for Joy
Reed, Mary 180, 920

Two for Texas
Burke, James Lee 1088

Two for the Dough
Evanovich, Janet 274

The Two-Headed Eagle
Biggin, John 954

Two Murders in My Double Life
Skvorecky, Josef 1092, 1168

Two O'Clock, Eastern Wartime
Dunning, John 882, 906

The Two of Minds
Keith, William H. Jr. 765

Two Sexy
Bond, Stephanie **240**

Two Texas Hearts
Thomas, Jodi 415

The Two-Timers
Shaw, Bob 759

Tycoon
Robbins, Harold 1084

The Tycoon and the Townie
Lane, Elizabeth 326

The Tyrant
Brand, Max 431, 432, 433, 434, 435

U

The Ugly Duckling
Johansen, Iris 222, 302, 340, 381, 411, 413

The Ultimatum
Bunn, T. Davis 976, 1004

Ulysses
Skimin, Robert 903

Umbrella
Mount, Ferdinand 1167

Unashamed
Rivers, Francine 1110

Unbound
Kaewert, Julie 128

Unbreathed Memories
Talley, Marcia 205

Uncatalogued
Kaewert, Julie **128**

Uncommon Courtship
Kirkland, Martha 318

An Uncommon Enemy
Black, Michelle **423**, **824**

An Uncommon Governess
Ellis, Monique 238

An Uncommon Hero
Ferrarella, Marie 373

Under Suspicion
Lee, Rachel **331**, 347, 383

Under the Burning Sun
DeRosso, H.A. 427, 453

Under the Color of Law
McGarrity, Michael 428

Under the Eagle
Scarrow, Simon **931**

Under the Eye of God
Gerrold, David 797

Under the Fang
McCammon, Robert R. 634

Under the Gun
Olsen, T.V. 487

Under the Kissing Bough
Donnelly, Shannon **271**, 304

Under the Overtree
Moore, James A. 675

Under the Unknown
Applegate, K.A. 519

Undercover Angel
Rutledge, Cynthia 1044, 1045

Underdog
Lewin, Michael Z. 142

Underworld
DeLillo, Don 1180, 1202

The Undying Monster
Kerruish, J.D. 646

An Unexpected Husband
Ferguson, Jo Ann 278, 280

The Unflappable Miss Fairchild
Scott, Regina 392

Unforgettable Faith
Rutledge, Cynthia 1044, 1045

The Unfortunate Queen Matilda
Beamish, Noel de Vic 862

Unholy Fire
Strieber, Whitley 699

The Unicorn
Lassieur, A.J. 565

Unicorn and Dragon
Abbey, Lynn 559, 603

Unicorn U
Friesner, Esther 588

University
Little, Bentley 649

The Unknown Ajax
Heyer, Georgette 404

The Unknown Errors of Our Lives
Divakaruni, Chitra Banerjee 1075, **1104**, 1128, 1188

Unknown Regions
Holdstock, Robert 558

The Unknown Soldier
Reichert, Mickey Zucker 590

Unleashed
Berenson, Laurien 17

The Unlikely Angel
Krahn, Betina 321

Unlikely Angels
Noble, Diane 1033

An Unlikely Father
Collum, Lynn 258

The Unnatural
Prill, David 649

The Unpleasant Profession of Jonathan Hoag
Heinlein, Robert A. 670

Unprintable
Kaewert, Julie 128

Unraveled Sleeve
Ferris, Monica **67**

Unsigned
Kaewert, Julie 128

Unsolicited
Kaewert, Julie 128

Unspeakable
Brown, Sandra 245

An Unspoken Promise
Bockoven, Georgia 239

An Unsuitable Job for a Woman
James, P.D. 11, 154

An Unsuitable Match
Oliver, Patricia 305

The Unsuitable Miss Martingale
Hazard, Barbara 278

The Unsung Hero
Brockmann, Suzanne 242

Untamed Time
Plunkett, Susan 371, 372

Until Relieved
Shelley, Rick 795

Until Shadows Fall
Cook, Will 466

Until She Sleeps
Lebbon, Tim 665

Until the End
Coyle, Harold 458, 474

Until There Was You
Ray, Francis 403

Until Tomorrow
Gunn, Robin Jones 1054

Until Tomorrow
Landis, Jill Marie 364, 471

Untitled
Kaewert, Julie 128

Unwelcome Words
Bowles, Paul 1080

Unwrapped
Dain, Claudia 266

The Unwritten Order
Ames, John Edwards 484

Up and Down
Coward, Mat 44

Up Country
DeMille, Nelson 1172

Up in the Air
Kirn, Walter **1141**, 1196

Up, out of Cities That Blow Hot and Cold
Jacob, Charlee 624, 698

Upon a Dark Night
Lovesey, Peter 146

Upon a Midnight Clear
Martin, Gail Gaymer 1021, 1022

The Uprising
Monahan, Brent 676

Urban Gothic
Howe, David J. **648**

Urban Horrors
Nolan, William F. 648

The Urbino McIntyre Series
Sklepowich, Edward 164

The Ursula Blanchard Series
Buckley, Fiona 65, 861, 880

Use of Weapons
Banks, Iain 721

The Ushers
Lee, Edward 667, 698

Uther
Whyte, Jack 829

V

V
Crispin, A.C. 800

The V.I. Warshawski Series
Paretsky, Sara 53

The Vacant Throne
Greenwood, Ed 553

Vacation Stories
Ramon y Cajal, Santiago **787**

Vacuum Diagrams
Baxter, Stephen 766

The Valentine Charm
Collum, Lynn 258

Valentine for an Angel
Wilson, Mary Ann 350

A Valentine for Vanessa
Kirkwood, Kathryn 378

Valentine Kisses
Bell, Donna 230

Valentine Murder
Meier, Leslie 157

Valentine Wedding
Feather, Jane 276

The Valentine Wish
Raleigh, Debbie **378**

The Valhalla Exchange
Patterson, Harry 126

Valhalla Rising
Cussler, Clive **1097**

The Valiant Heart
Gordon, Anita 336

The Valley of Horses
Auel, Jean M. 940

Valley of Lights
Gallagher, Stephen 710

Valley of Promises
Leon, Bonnie 1017

Valley of the Shadow
Tremayne, Peter 209, 944

Valley of the Shadow
Whitson, Stephanie Grace 1058

The Valley So Low
Wellman, Manly Wade 707

The Vampire Armand
Rice, Anne 685, 922, 1185

Vampire Beat
Courtney, Vincent 657

The Vampire Chronicles
Rice, Anne 922

Vampire Hunter
Romkey, Michael 686

The Vampire Journals
Briery, Tracy 621

The Vampire Lestat
Rice, Anne 621, 685

Vampire Nation
Sipos, Thomas M. 696

The Vampire Odyssey
Ciencin, Scott 703

The Vampire Papers
Romkey, Michael 686

The Vampire Princess
Romkey, Michael 686

The Vampire Stories of Nancy Kilpatrick
Kilpatrick, Nancy 658

The Vampire Virus
Romkey, Michael 686

The Vampire Viscount
Harbaugh, Karen 922, 963

Vampire Vow
Schiefelbein, Michael **690**

The Vampire's Apprentice
Byers, Richard Lee 532, 712

The Vampires of Alfama
Kast, Pierre 713

Vampyre Bites
Grant, Linda 170

Vang: The Military Form
Rowley, Christopher 740

Vanished
Gansky, Alton 637, 1000

Vargr Moon
King, Bernard 517

Varney the Vampyre
Rymer, James Malcolm 695

The Vault
Lovesey, Peter 146

Vazkor, Son of Vazkor
Lee, Tanith 534

Vector
Cook, Robin 1093

The Veejay Haskell Series
Dunlap, Susan 139

Veiled Threats
Donnelly, Deborah **60**

The Veiled Web
Asaro, Catherine 808

Velma Still Cooks in Leeway
Wright, Vinita Hampton 1001, 1002, 1029

Velvet
Feather, Jane 308

The Velvet Shadow
Hunt, Angela Elwell 1004, 1025

The Velvet Touch
Hoch, Edward D. 85, 117, 118

Vendetta
Collins, Jackie 1194

Vendetta Gold
Blakely, Mike 827

Vengeful Ghosts
Ward, C.E. 652

The Venus Diamond Series
Moody, Skye Kathleen 63

Venus with Pistol
Lyall, Gavin 171

The Veritas Conflict
Feldhahn, Shaunti 1054

The Very Comely Countess
Jarrett, Miranda **307**, 308

The Very Daring Duchess
Jarrett, Miranda 307, **308**

A Very Eligible Corpse
Griffin, Annie 91

The Very Gothic Christmas
Feehan, Christine **277**

Very Old Bones
Kennedy, William 897

The Very Thought of You
Kurland, Lynn 323

Very Truly Yours
Beard, Julie **229**

Vespers
Rovin, Jeff 714

Vicksburg
Reasoner, James 919

The Victim in Victoria Station
Dams, Jeanne M. 54

The Victoria Bowering Series
Yeager, Dorian 45

The Victorian Serenade Series
Blackwell, Lawana 1015

The Victors
Cavanaugh, Jack 1056

Vietnam and Other Alien Worlds
Haldeman, Joe 807

The View from Hell
Shirley, John 667, 694

The Vigil
Reynolds, Clay **498**

The Vikings
Edison, Michael 1097

The Viking's Heart
Navin, Jacqueline 360

Viking's Prize
Crosby, Tanya Anne 337

The Viking's Woman
Graham, Heather 336

Vikram and the Vampire
Burton, Richard 713

A Vile Justice
Haney, Lauren 101

The Villa
Roberts, Nora 301, 382, 1187

Vinas Solamnus
King, J. Robert 564

The Vineyard
Delinsky, Barbara 1101

Vineyard Blues
Craig, Philip R. 46

Vineyard Shadows
Craig, Philip R. 46

The Violent Land
Overholser, Wayne D. 490

Violet
Feather, Jane 308

The Violet Land
Overholser, Wayne D. 489

Violets Are Blue
Patterson, James 1153, 1181

Violets in the Snow
Grasso, Patricia 293

Violin
Rice, Anne 1185

The Virgin and the Dinosaur
Garcia y Robertson, R. 546

Virgin Planet
Anderson, Poul 733

The Virgin Spring
Brown, Debra Lee 244, 288

Virgin Without a Memory
Taylor, Vickie 414

Virgintooth
Ivanhoe, Mark 712

Virtuosity
Bisson, Terry 731

The Virtuoso
Moor, Margriet de 1165

The Virtuous Cyprian
Cornick, Nicola 259, **260**

Visible Amazement
Garnett, Gale Zoe 1159, 1206

The Visible Man
Dozois, Gardner 748

The Vision of Emma Blau
Hegi, Ursula 930, 1124

A Vision of Light
Riley, Judith Merkle 288

The Visitant
Gear, Kathleen O'Neal 424, 506, 871

Visiting Hours
Rembo, Kent 663

The Visitors
Simak, Clifford D. 800

Vittorio, the Vampire
Rice, Anne 685, 922, 1185

The Vivero Letter
Bagley, Desmond 195

The Voice of Allah
Hoyt, Edwin P. 902

The Voice of Our Shadow
Carroll, Jonathan 515

Voice of the Demon
Jacoby, Kate 561

Voices in the Hill: Western Stories
Frazee, Steve **453**

Voodoo Dreams
Rhodes, Jewell Parker 1164

Voodoo, Ltd.
Thomas, Ross 107

Voodoo River
Crais, Robert 47

Vote of Intolerance
McDowell, Josh 991

A Vow to Cherish
Raney, Deborah 1024

Voyage
Baxter, Stephen 723, 739

Voyage
Schulte, Elaine 1049

Voyage of the Fox Rider
McKiernan, Dennis L. 530, 571

The Voyage of the Narwhal
Barrett, Andrea 905

Voyager
Gabaldon, Diana 288, 546, 868

Vulcan's Forge
Shwartz, Susan 796

Vulcan's Hammer
Dick, Philip K. 798

Vulcan's Heart
Shwartz, Susan 796

W

The Wager
Hingle, Metsy **301**

The Wagered Wife
Counts, Wilma 262, 349

The Wailing Asteroid
Leinster, Murray 785

Waiting
Jin, Ha 1102

Waiting for Morning
Kingsbury, Karen 1010

Waiting for the Moon
Hannah, Kristin 382

The Waiting Game
Fullerton, Alexander 866

Wake Not the Dragon
Ferguson, Jo Ann 278

Wake Up, Little Susie
Gorman, Ed 83

A Walk Among the Tombstones
Block, Lawrence 22

A Walk in the Woods
Gilbert, Anna 872

A Walk on the Dark Side
Dunn, Dawn 630

A Walk to Remember
Sparks, Nicholas 1200

Walker of Worlds
De Haven, Tom 1100

Walker's Widow
Betts, Heidi **234**, 294, 391

Walkin' the Dog
Mosley, Walter 1166, 1180

The Walking
Little, Bentley 668

Walking Rain
Wade, Susan 9

The Wall Around Eden
Slonczewski, Joan 725

The Wall Around the World
Cogswell, Theodore 790

The Wall at the Edge of the World
Aikin, Jim 790

Waltzing in Ragtime
Charbonneau, Ellen 878

The Wanderer
Leiber, Fritz **767**

Wanting You
Ryan, Nan 324, 342

The Wanton Angel
Marston, Edward 148

War Amongst the Angels
Moorcock, Michael 582

The War between the Tates
Lurie, Alison 1143

War Brides
Battle, Lois 228

War Fever
Ballard, J.G. 1070

War for the Oaks
Bull, Emma 598, 602, 614

The War God's Own
Weber, David 809

The War of the End of the World
Vargas Llosa, Mario 948

War of the Gods
Anderson, Poul 517

The War of the Lord's Veil
Nichols, Adam 606

The War of the Rats
Robbins, David L. 131, 215

War of the Three Waters
Niles, Douglas 583

War of Two Worlds
Anderson, Poul 800

War Story
Edelman, Gwen **1107**

The Warding of Witch World
Norton, Andre 784

Warhorse
Barton, Wayne 478

The Warhost of Vastmark
Wurts, Janny 560

Warlock
Hall, Oakley 878

Warlock
Harrison, Jim 1084

Warlock Games
Byers, Richard Lee 532

The Warlord Chronicles
Cornwell, Bernard 829, 907

A Warmth in Winter
Copeland, Lori **984**

The Warning
Bunn, T. Davis 976, 1016

A Warning to the Curious and Other Ghost Stories
James, M.R. 650

Warning Whispers
Burrage, A.M. 622

The Warrior and the Witch
Miller, Carl 534

The Warrior Circle
Westbrook, Robert 80

Warrior Heart
Bonander, Jane 270

The Warrior's Apprentice
Bujold, Lois McMaster 809

The Warrior's Bond
McKenna, Juliet E. 561, **578**

The Warrior's Damsel
Hampton, Denise **295**, 407

Warrior's Honor
Kasser, Michael 463, 512

A Warrior's Honor
Moore, Margaret 407

Warrior's Song
Pella, Judith 1040, 1058

Warstrider
Keith, William H. Jr. 765

The Wary Widow
Hazard, Barbara 325, 389

Was It Something I Said
Block, Valerie 1125

Washington's Dirigible
Barnes, John 722

Watch by Moonlight
Hawks, Kate 840, **881**

Watchdog
Berenson, Laurien 17

The Watcher
Metz, Melinda 775, 776

Watchers of Time
Todd, Charles **208**, **943**

Watching Trees Grow
Hamilton, Peter 741

The Water and the Blood
Turner, Nancy E. **947**

Water at the Blue Earth
Creel, Ann Howard 845

The Water Nymph
Jaffe, Michele 883

The Water of Death
Johnston, Paul 738

Water Sleeps
Cook, Glen 580

The Waterfall
Neggers, Carla 327, 331, 373, 413

Waterfalls
Gunn, Robin Jones 993

The Watermark
Thrasher, Travis 1030, **1054**

The Waters Between
Bruchac, Joseph 447, 507

The Way between the Worlds
Irvine, Ian **560**

The Way Forward Is with a Broken Heart
Walker, Alice 1089, 1122, 1207

The Way Home
Chance, Megan 290

The Way Home
Hannon, Irene 1047, 1061

The Way Home
Schulze, Dallas 239

The Way of Light
Constantine, Storm **536**

The Way of the Coyote
Kelton, Elmer **468**, **895**, **1137**, 1176

The Way of the Rose
Leith, Valery **572**

The Way through the Mountains
Frazee, Steve 453

The Way We Wed
Warren, Pat 327, 341

A Way with Women
McBride, Jule 289

Wayfaring Strangers
Champlin, Tim 439, 440, 487

Wayward Moon
DeMartino, Denny **744**

We Have Always Lived in the Castle
Jackson, Shirley 623

We Look Like Men of War
Forstchen, William R. **864**

We Need to Dream All This Again
Pomerance, Bernard 890

We Were the Mulvaneys
Oates, Joyce Carol 1174

The Weary Generations
Hussein, Abdullah 1129

The Weathermonger
Dickinson, Peter 533, 730, 738

The Weaver Takes a Wife
South, Sheri Cobb 404

The Weaver's Inheritance
Sedley, Kate **194**, 875, 933, **934**

The Weaver's Tale
Sedley, Kate 194

Weaveworld
Barker, Clive 619, 642, 659

Web of the Witch World
Norton, Andre 534, 555

The Webster Chronicle
Akst, Daniel **1066**

The Wedding
Garwood, Julie 269

The Wedding
Steel, Danielle 1203

Wedding Arbor
Hansen, Valerie 987

The Wedding Arbor
Hansen, Valerie 995, 1021

Wedding at Waverly Creek
Hart, Jessica 343

Wedding at Wildwood
Worth, Lenora 1063

The Wedding Charm
Collum, Lynn **258**

Wedding Day Murder
Meier, Leslie 60, **157**

The Wedding Dress
Parker, Gary E. 980, 1024

The Wedding Gamble
Justiss, Julia 259, 311

The Wedding Game
Holtzer, Susan 120

The Wedding Guest
Gilbert, Anna 872

The Wedding Jewel
Fell, Doris Elaine 992

Wedding on the Way
Richer, Lois 1043

The Wedding Party
Carr, Robyn **250**

The Wedding Planner
Criswell, Millie 264

The Wedding Raffle
Dawson, Geralyn 253

The Wedding Wager
Hale, Deborah 259, 311

The Wedding Wager
Maxwell, Cathy 321, **348**, 355

The Wedding Wish
Raleigh, Debbie 378

Weddings Are Murder
Wolzien, Valerie 157

Wednesday's Child
Chaikin, Linda 977

Weighed in the Balance
Perry, Anne 172

The Weirdstone of Brisingamen
Garner, Alan 520, 542

Welcome to Temptation
Crusie, Jennifer 282, 285, 286

The Welding Quirt: A Western Trio
Brand, Max 431, 433

We'll Meet Again
Clark, Mary Higgins 1180

Well of Darkness
Weis, Margaret 611

A Well-Pleasured Lady
Dodd, Christina 307

The Wells Fargo Trail Series
Walker, Jim 972, 973

The Werewolf's Kiss
Scotch, Cheri 322

The Werewolf's Tale
Jacocoma, Richard 657

The Wesley Farrell Series
Skinner, Robert 73, 192

A Western Family Christmas
Criswell, Millie **263**

The Western Wizard
Reichert, Mickey Zucker 590

The Westerners: Stories of the West
Grey, Zane 432, 435, 458, 496

The Westward Chronicles
Peterson, Tracie 973, 998

The Westward Dreams Series
Peart, Jane 998

Wetbones
Shirley, John 694

What Are You Like?
Enright, Anne 1111

What Did Miss Darrington See?
Salmonson, Jessica Amanda 654

What I Lived For
Oates, Joyce Carol 1131

What Love Sees
Vreeland, Susan 951

What Once We Loved
Kirkpatrick, Jane **470**, **1011**

What Strange Stars and Skies
Davidson, Avram 760

What the Doctor Ordered
Wolverton, Cheryl 1046

What the Heart Knows
Eagle, Kathleen 339

What the Lady Wants
Crusie, Jennifer 289

What to Do about Annie?
Criswell, Millie 263, **264**

What You Owe Me
Campbell, Bebe Moore **1089**, 1166, 1210

Whatever Doesn't Kill You
Roberts, Gillian 139

When Cowboys Die
Dearen, Patrick 508

When Did We Lose Harriet?
Sprinkle, Patricia Houck 1051

When Dreams Come True
Maxwell, Cathy 281, 303, 348

When Freedom Grows
Leon, Bonnie 1017

When Heaven Weeps
Dekker, Ted **988**

When I Wake
Lee, Rachel 331

When Jayne Met Erik
Bevarly, Elizabeth 235, **236**, 246

When Joy Came to Stay
Kingsbury, Karen 1010

When Lightning Strikes
Hannah, Kristin 313

When Love Came to Town
Worth, Lenora 1045, **1063**

When the Far Hills Bloom
Noble, Diane 1033

When the Last Leaf Falls
Myers, Bill **1032**

When the Sun Goes Down
Lebbon, Tim 655

When the World Was Steady
Messud, Claire 1161

When They Come from Space
Clifton, Mark 800

When This Cruel War Is Over
Fleming, Thomas 903, 914, 919

When Tomorrow Comes
Oke, Janette **1034**

When Venus Fell
Smith, Deborah 401

When We Were Orphans
Ishiguro, Kazuo 835, 1131

When Worlds Collide
Wylie, Philip 767

The Whenabouts of Burr
Kurland, Michael 799

Where Dreams Begin
Kleypas, Lisa 319

Where I'm Bound
Ballard, Allen B. 864, 919

Where I'm Calling From
Carver, Raymond 1087

Where I've Been and Where I'm Going
Oates, Joyce Carol 1173

Where the Buffalo Roam
Zimmer, Michael 460

Where the Heart Is
Hatcher, Robin Lee 290, 421

Where the Ni-Lach
Bennett, M.J. 725

Where the Ships Die
Dietz, William C. 746

Where Town and Country Meet
Baldwin, Louisa 618

Where We Lived
Fitzpatrick, Christina 1160

Where Yesterday Lives
Kingsbury, Karen 1010

While England Sleeps
Leavitt, David 1090

While He Was Sleeping
Summers, Cara 240

While I Was Gone
Miller, Sue 1163

Whipping Boy
Byrne, John 637

Whirlpool
McCourtney, Lorena **1023**, 1055

Whirlwind
Grant, Charles L. 737, 773

Whiskey River
Estleman, Loren D. 119

Whisper His Name
Thornton, Elizabeth 416

A Whisper of Danger
Palmer, Catherine 1038

A Whisper of Roses
Medeiros, Teresa 390

Whisper the Guns
Cline, Edward 840

The Whispering Pines Series
Carlson, Mary 984, 993, 1007

Whispers
Gunn, Robin Jones 1059

Whispers
Koontz, Dean R. 627

Whispers from Yesterday
Hatcher, Robin Lee 1010

Whispers in the Dark
Bland, Eleanor Taylor **21**

Whispers of Goodbye
White, Karen **418**

Whispers of the Heart
Scofield, Ruth 1047

White
Lebbon, Tim 665, 666, 708

The White Abacus
Broderick, Damien 726

The White Bird
Paine, Lauran 514

White Boys and River Girls
Grove, Paula K. 1201

The White Castle
Pamuk, Orhan 1178

The White Company
Doyle, Arthur Conan 843

White Desert
Estleman, Loren D. 502

The White Gold Wielder
Donaldson, Stephen R. 545

The White Guns
Reeman, Douglas 866

The White Horses
Bauer, C.A. 453, 457, 470, 483, 488, 500

White Lion's Lady
St. John, Tina **407**

The White Man in a Tree and Other Stories
Kurlansky, Mark 1190

White Mare's Daughter
Tarr, Judith 940

White Moon Tree
Hawkins, Paul A. 451

White of the Moon
Jones, Stephen 653, 654

White People
Gurganus, Allan 1120

White Plume Mountain
Kidd, Paul 563

White Queen
Jones, Gwyneth 764

The White Room
Matthews, A.J. **673**

White Shell Woman
Doss, James D. **61**

White Teeth
Smith, Zadie 1082, 1090

The Whitechapel Conspiracy
Perry, Anne 58, 62, 856

The Whitechapel Horror
Hanna, Edward 62, 153

Whitehorse
Sutcliffe, Katherine 412

Who Fears the Devil
Wellman, Manly Wade 707

Who Killed Father Christmas?
Moyes, Patricia 31

Who Killed Palomino Molero?
Vargas Llosa, Mario 948, 1211

Who Killed the Curate?
Coggin, Joan **36**

Who Rides with Wyatt?
Henry, Will 485

The Whole Truth
Pickard, Nancy 198

Why Did I Ever?
Robison, Mary **1188**

Why Did She Die?
Coggin, Joan 36

Wicked
Barnett, Jill 228, 269, 316, 321, 396

Wicked
Johnson, Susan 385

Wicked Fix
Graves, Sarah 89

Wicked Promise
Martin, Kat 298, 346, 347

Wicked Widow
Quick, Amanda 375

The Wicked Winter
Sedley, Kate 194, 933, 934

Widdershins
Onions, Oliver 647, 680

The Widow
Stuart, Anne **411**

A Widow for One Year
Irving, John 1130, 1156

The Widowed Bride
Kihlstrom, April 325

The Widowed Miss Mordaunt
Savery, Jeanne 389

The Widow's Kiss
Feather, Jane 276

The Widow's Little Secret
Stacy, Judith 234, 247, 408, **409**

Wife for a Day
Berg, Patti 289, 292

Wife with Amnesia
Hingle, Metsy 301

The Wig My Father Wore
Enright, Anne **1111**

The Wil Hardesty Series
Barre, Richard 74

Wild
Barnett, Jill 228, 281

The Wild
Strieber, Whitley 699

Wild Angel
Murphy, Pat 781

The Wild Blue and Gray
Sanders, William 804

The Wild Boy
Rochelle, Warren **791**

The Wild Colonial Boy
Hynes, James 649

Wild Flower
Porter, Cheryl Ann 296

The Wild Girl
Roberts, Michele 925

Wild Honey
Sattler, Veronica 388

The Wild Hunt
Yolen, Jane 538

Wild Life
Gloss, Molly 1083, 1140, 1165

Wild Magic
Pierce, Tamora 594

The Wild One
Metz, Melinda 775

The Wild Swans
Holmes, Kate 384

Wild Winds
Taylor, Janelle 413

Wilde West
Satterthwait, Walter 95, 135

The Wildest Shore
Cach, Lisa 320

Wildflowers
Gunn, Robin Jones **993**

The Wildrose Series
Glover, Ruth 998, 1011

Wildwood Boys
Blake, James Carlos 424, 825

The Wiley Wastrel
Kihlstrom, April 318

The Wilkie Collins/Charles Dickens Series
Palmer, William J. 172

Will James Book of Cowboy Stories
James, Will 464

Will Shakespeare
Mortimer, John 823

Will You Still Love Me Tomorrow?
Gorman, Ed 83

Willed to Wed
Counts, Wilma 262

The Willful Miss Winthrop
Counts, Wilma 262

The Willful Widow
Richardson, Evelyn 257

William F. Nolan's Dark Universe
Nolan, William F. **678**

The William Falconer Series
Morson, Ian 861, 865, 933, 944

Willows on the Windrush
Fell, Doris Elaine 992

Will's War
Windle, Janice Woods **513**, **961**

Winchester Affidavit
Boyer, G.G. 429

The Winchester Horror
Nolan, William F. 678

The Wind at Midnight
Pangborn, Georgia Wood 711

The Wind Done Gone
Randall, Alice **918**, 964

The Wind from the Hills
Stirling, Jessica 938

Wind over Wisconsin
Derleth, August 873

Wind Walker
Johnston, Terry C. 890

Wind Warrior
Munn, Vella 911

Windfall
Carmichael, Emily 249

The Winds of Freedom Series
Schalesky, Marlo M. 1058

The Winds of War
Wouk, Herman 1165

Winged Magic
Herbert, Mary H. 556

The Wingman
Maloney, Mack 768

Wings of a Dove
Bush, Beverly 1002, 1029

Wings of Dawn
Brouwer, Sigmund 1060

Wings of Fire
Todd, Charles 208, 943

Wings of Honor
Willard, Tom 509

The Wings of the Dove
James, Henry 1167

Winning Can Be Murder
Crider, Bill 49

Winter by Degrees
Smolens, John 1199

Winter Fire
Hayworth, Lynne 297

Winter Fire
Lowell, Elizabeth 340

The Winter Garden
Verweerd, Johanna 967, 980

Winter Journey
Colegate, Isabel 1189

Winter Nights
Ray, Francis 300

Winter Rain
Johnston, Terry C. 895

Winter Solstice
Pilcher, Rosamunde 1200

The Winter Widow
Weir, Charlene 212

Winter's Children
Coney, Michael G. 724

Winter's Heart
Jordan, Robert 550

Winter's Secret
Cote, Lyn **985**, 1021

Winter's Warriors
Gemmell, David 548

The Wire in the Blood
McDermid, Val 154

Wish List
Dain, Claudia 266

Wish List
Kleypas, Lisa **320**

Wish upon a Cowboy
Kane, Kathleen 313, 350

Wish You Well
Baldacci, David 1157, 1184, 1200

Wish You Were Here
Ridgway, Christie 341

Wishes
Deveraux, Jude 268

Wishin' on a Star
Snoe, Eboni 403

Wishing
Jarrett, Miranda 307, 308

The Wishing Season
Friesner, Esther 543

The Wishmaster
Atkins, Peter 696

The Witch and the Warrior
Monk, Karyn 405

Wit'ch Fire
Clemens, James 534

Wit'ch Gate
Clemens, James **534**

Witch-Light
Holder, Nancy 704

Wit'ch Storm
Clemens, James 534

Wit'ch War
Clemens, James 534, 561

Witches
Griffith, Kathryn Meyer 704

The Witches of Eastwick
Updike, John 382, 1068

With All Josie's Heart
Stovall, Crystal 1022

With Baby in Mind
James, Arlene 965

With Heart
Garlock, Dorothy 290

With Hope
Garlock, Dorothy 290

With Song
Garlock, Dorothy 290

With This Ring
Kelly, Carla 315, 397

With This Ring
Quick, Amanda 375

With Wounds Still Wet
Sallee, Wayne Allen 616

The Withdrawing Room
MacLeod, Charlotte 144

Within the Sea of the Dead
Ford, John B. 635

Without a Hero
Boyle, T. Coraghessan 1081

Witness
Wheeler, Richard S. 512

Wives and Mistresses
Morris, Suzanne 937

The Wiz Biz
Cook, Rick 537

A Wizard in Peace
Stasheff, Christopher 600

A Wizard in War
Stasheff, Christopher 600

The Wizard of Berner's Abbey
Hansom, Mark 646

The Wizard of Death
Forrest, Richard 53

The Wizard of Oz
Baum, L. Frank 577

The Wizardry Compiled
Cook, Rick 537

The Wizardry Quested
Cook, Rick 537

Wizard's Bane
Cook, Rick 537

Wizard's First Rule
Goodkind, Terry 541, 601

The Wizard's Map
Yolen, Jane 519, 594

The Wizard's Shadow
Dexter, Susan 537

WLT: A Radio Romance
Keillor, Garrison 1136

Wobegon Boy
Keillor, Garrison 1136

The Wolf Hunt
Bradshaw, Gillian 818, **831**, 921

A Wolf in Death's Clothing
Quinn, Elizabeth 68

Wolf in Sheep's Clothing
Campbell, Ann 163

Wolf Justice
Durgin, Doranna 543

The Wolf King
Borchardt, Alice 528, 829

Wolf Mountain Moon
Johnston, Terry C. 466

Wolf, No Wolf
Bowen, Peter 68

The Wolf of Haskell Hall
Shannon, Colleen 322, 360, 418

The Wolf of Winter
Volsky, Paula 595

The Wolf Pit
Youmans, Marly 914, **964**

The Wolf Story
Huggins, James Byron 1003

The Wolf Strain
Brand, Max 430, **435**

The Wolf Whispered Death
Moore, Barbara 68

The Wolfen
Strieber, Whitley 699, 1068

Wolfwinter
Swann, Thomas Burnett 595

Wolverine's Daughter
Durgin, Doranna 543

The Woman at Ox-Yoke
Patten, Lewis B. **494**

A Woman Betrayed
Delinsky, Barbara 1101

The Woman for Dusty Conrad
Carrington, Tori **251**

The Woman in the Cloak
Hill, Pamela 886

Woman Lit by Fireflies
Harrison, Jim 1088

The Woman Next Door
Delinsky, Barbara **1101**

Woman of Grace
Morgan, Kathleen 1025, 1026

A Woman of Passion
Henley, Virginia 883

Woman of the Frontier
Grey, Zane 458, 462, 483, 497

A Woman of the Iron People
Arnason, Eleanor 593

A Woman of Virtue
Carlyle, Liz 260

The Woman Who Fell from Grace
Handler, David 100

A Woman's Liberation
Willis, Connie **811**

The Women of the West Series
Oke, Janette 1014

The Women of Valor Series
Larson, Elyse 977, 1034

The Women of Whitechapel
West, Paul 153

Wonderful
Barnett, Jill 228, 303

Wonders Never Cease
Salonen, Debra 387

Wonders of the Heart
Scofield, Ruth 1047

Wondrous Strange
Spriggs, Robin **697**

The Wood Beyond
Hill, Reginald 116

The Wooden Sea
Carroll, Jonathan 567, 573

Woodlands
Gunn, Robin Jones 993

A Word After Dying
Granger, Ann 87

Word of Honor
Blackstock, Terri 970, 971

Word of Honor
DeMille, Nelson 1186

Words of Love
Bell, Donna 230

The World According to Garp
Irving, John 1130

The World Below
Miller, Sue **1163**

World Fall
Niles, Douglas **583**

The World Next Door
Ferguson, Brad 741

World of Hurt
Rosen, R.D. 188

A World of Thieves
Blake, James Carlos **424**, **825**, 841, 887

The World Weaver
Etchison, Craig **749**

World's End
Chadbourn, Mark 533

The World's Finest Mystery & Crime Stories: First Annual Collection
Gorman, Ed 84

The World's Finest Mystery & Crime Stories: Second Annual Collection
Gorman, Ed **84**

The Worm Ouroboros
Eddison, E.R. 582

Worse than Death
Gottlieb, Sherry 645

Worse Things Waiting
Wellman, Manly Wade 707

Worthy of Riches
Leon, Bonnie 1001, **1017**

Worthy's Town
Rolens, Sharon 882, 1066

Wrack and Roll
Denton, Bradley 764

The Wrath of Squat
Coville, Bruce 538

Wreck the Halls
Graves, Sarah **89**

The Wrecked, Blessed Body of Shelton Lafleur
Brown, John Gregory 833, 1085

Wren's War
Smith, Sherwood 800

Writ in Blood
Yarbro, Chelsea Quinn 713

Writer of the Purple Rage
Lansdale, Joe R. 472

Written in the Heart
Stacy, Judith 408, 409, 419

Written in Venom
Tilton, Lois 517

Written on Her Heart
Maki, Alan 992, **1019**

Written on the Wind
Pella, Judith **1040**

The Wrong Brother
Winn, Bonnie K. 1061

The Wrong Case
Crumley, James 50

The Wrong Child
Kay, Patricia 225

The Wrong Dog
Benjamin, Carol Lea 16

The Wrong Man
Hirt, Douglas 462

The Wrong Mr. Right
Wainscott, Tina 250, 255, 353

The Wrong Reflection
Bradshaw, Gillian 831

Wrong Things
Brite, Poppy Z. **624**, 679

The Wyn Lewis Series
Kaufelt, David A. 218

Wyrm Wolf
van Belkom, Edo 705

X

The Xibalba Murders
Hamilton, Lyn 195

Xone of Contention
Anthony, Piers 518

Y

Y2K
Hyatt, Michael 989

The Y2K Bug
Simon, Frank 989

A Yank at Valhalla
Hamilton, Edmond 751

Yaril's Children
Bennett, M.J. 576

A Year and a Day
Henley, Virginia 883

The Year of the Horsetails
Tapsell, R.F. 940

Year of Wonders
Brooks, Geraldine **832**, **1083**

The Year the Horses Came
Mackey, Mary 940

The Year's Best Fantasy and Horror: Fourteenth Annual Collection
Datlow, Ellen 653

The Year's Best Horror Series
Wagner, Karl Edward 653

The Years of Fear
Grove, Fred **460**

The Years with Laura Diaz
Fuentes, Carlos 817, 948, 1067

Yellow
Lynch, Daniel 878

Yellow Jack
Russell, Josh 867, 935

The Yellow Room Conspiracy
Dickinson, Peter 214

The Yellow Sailor
Weiner, Steve 857, **954**

Yellowstone Kelly
Henry, Will 461

The Yellowthread Series
Marshall, William 132

Yesterday Will Make You Cry
Himes, Chester 1179

Yon Ill Wind
Anthony, Piers 518

Yonder Stands Your Orphan
Hannah, Barry **1121**

The Yorkshire Lady
Miller, Nadine 398

You Are My Sunshine
Saxton, Judith 821

You Can Hear the Echo
King, Mary 469

You Gotta Play Hurt
Jenkins, Dan 1132

The You I Never Knew
Wiggs, Susan 330, 419

You Never Can Tell
Eagle, Kathleen **450**

You Only Love Once
Carrington, Tori 251

You Only Love Twice
Thornton, Elizabeth 416

You Sane Men
Janiver, Laurence M. 763

You Sexy Thing
Carrington, Tori 251

Young Adolf
Bainbridge, Beryl 1069

The Young Savages
Stewart, Fred Mustard 937

Younger than Springtime
Greeley, Andrew M. 1117

Your Blues Ain't Like Mine
Campbell, Bebe Moore 1089

Your Wish Is My Command
Kauffman, Donna 237

You're the One
McCoy, Judi **351**

Yours Truly, Jackie the Stripper
van Belkom, Edo 705

Z

Zen Attitude
Massey, Sujata 150

Zigzagging Down a Wild Trail
Mason, Bobbie Ann 1079, 1080, 1099, 1124, **1155**, 1162

Zimmerman's Algorithm
Swann, S. Andrew 602

The Zion Covenant Series
Thoene, Bodie 942